California

Cities, Towns & Counties

2009

California

Cities, Towns & Counties

2009

State & Municipal Profiles Series

Woodside, California

Titles from Information Publications

State & Municipal Profiles Series

Almanac of the 50 States

California Cities, Towns & Counties
Florida Cities, Towns & Counties
The New Jersey Municipal Data Book
Connecticut Municipal Profiles
Massachusetts Municipal Profiles
North Carolina Cities, Towns & Counties

American Profiles Series

Asian Americans: A Statistical Sourcebook and Guide to Government Data
Black Americans: A Statistical Sourcebook and Guide to Government Data
Hispanic Americans: A Statistical Sourcebook and Guide to Government Data

Essential Topics Series

Energy, Transportation & the Environment:
A Statistical Sourcebook and Guide to Government Data

ISBN 978-0-911273-48-9 Paper
ISBN 978-0-911273-49-6 CD
California Cities, Towns & Counties 2009

Printed in the United States of America

Information Publications, Inc.
2995 Woodside Rd., Suite 400-182
Woodside, CA 94062-2446

www.informationpublications.com
info@informationpublications.com

Toll Free Phone 877.544.INFO (4636)
Toll Free Fax 877.544.4635

Direct Dial Phone 650.568.6170
Direct Dial Fax 650.568.6150

Table of Contents

Detailed Table of Contents . . . . . vi-ix

Map of California Counties x

Introduction & Explanation of the Categories . . . . . xiii-xvii

Disclaimer xvii

Municipal Profiles 3-482

County Profiles 485-542

Appendices

- **Appendix A** State of California Overview 545-552
- **Appendix B** List of Municipalities by County 553-555
- **Appendix C** Census 2000 Data for Selected Counties 557-570
- **Appendix D** Census 2000 Data for Selected Municipalities 571-610
- **Appendix E** Additional Public School District Information 611-680
- **Appendix F** Comparative Tables for California Counties 681-683
- **Appendix G** Comparative Tables for California Municipalities 685-696
- **Appendix H** State and Federal Representatives for California 697-699

Order Form

Municipal Profiles

Adelanto 3
Agoura Hills. 4
Alameda 5
Albany 6
Alhambra 7
Aliso Viejo 8
Alturas. 9
Amador City 10
American Canyon 11
Anaheim 12
Anderson. 13
Angels Camp. 14
Angels City . . . . . see Angels Camp
Antioch 15
Apple Valley 16
Arcadia 17
Arcata 18
Arroyo Grande. 19
Artesia. 20
Arvin 21
Atascadero 22
Atherton 23
Atwater 24
Auburn 25
Avalon 26
Avenal 27
Azusa. 28
Bakersfield 29
Baldwin Park. 30
Banning. 31
Barstow. 32
Beaumont. 33
Bell 34
Bell Gardens. 35
Bellflower 36
Belmont 37
Belvedere 38
Benicia 39
Berkeley 40
Beverly Hills 41
Big Bear Lake 42
Biggs 43
Bishop. 44
Blue Lake 45
Blythe 46
Bradbury. 47
Brawley 48
Brea. 49
Brentwood 50
Brisbane 51
Buellton. 52
Buena Park. 53
Burbank 54
Burlingame. 55
Calabasas. 56
Calexico. 57
California City 58
Calimesa. 59
Calipatria 60
Calistoga. 61
Camarillo. 62
Campbell. 63
Canyon Lake. 64
Capitola. 65
Carlsbad 66
Carmel-by-the-Sea 67
Carpinteria 68
Carson. 69
Cathedral City. 70
Ceres. 71
Cerritos 72
Chico 73
Chino. 74
Chino Hills. 75
Chowchilla. 76
Chula Vista 77
Citrus Heights. 78
Claremont. 79
Clayton 80
Clearlake. 81
Cloverdale. 82
Clovis. 83
Coachella 84
Coalinga 85
Colfax 86
Colma 87
Colton 88
Colusa. 89
Commerce 90
Compton 91
Concord. 92
Corcoran 93
Corning 94
Corona. 95
Coronado 96
Corte Madera 97
Costa Mesa. 98
Cotati. 99
Covina 100
Crescent City 101
Cudahy 102
Culver City. 103
Cupertino 104
Cypress 105
Daly City 106
Dana Point 107
Danville. 108
Davis 109
Del Mar 110
Del Rey Oaks 111
Delano. 112
Desert Hot Springs. 113
Diamond Bar 114
Dinuba 115
Dixon 116
Dorris 117
Dos Palos 118
Downey 119
Duarte. 120
Dublin 121
Dunsmuir 122
East Palo Alto 123
El Cajon. 124
El Centro 125
El Cerrito 126
El Monte 127
El Paso de Robles. . . see Paso Robles
El Segundo 128
Elk Grove. 129
Emeryville 130
Encinitas. 131
Escalon 132
Escondido 133
Etna. 134
Eureka. 135
Exeter 136
Fairfax. 137
Fairfield 138
Farmersville 139
Ferndale 140
Fillmore 141
Firebaugh 142
Folsom 143
Fontana. 144
Fort Bragg. 145
Fort Jones 146
Fortuna 147
Foster City. 148
Fountain Valley 149
Fowler 150
Fremont. 151
Fresno 152
Fullerton 153
Galt 154
Garden Grove 155
Gardena 156
Gilroy 157
Glendale 158
Glendora 159
Goleta 160
Gonzales. 161
Grand Terrace. 162
Grass Valley 163
Greenfield 164
Gridley. 165

Municipal Profiles (con't)

Grover Beach ... 166
Guadalupe ... 167
Gustine ... 168
Half Moon Bay ... 169
Hanford ... 170
Hawaiian Gardens ... 171
Hawthorne ... 172
Hayward ... 173
Healdsburg ... 174
Hemet ... 175
Hercules ... 176
Hermosa Beach ... 177
Hesperia ... 178
Hidden Hills ... 179
Highland ... 180
Hillsborough ... 181
Hollister ... 182
Holtville ... 183
Hughson ... 184
Huntington Beach ... 185
Huntington Park ... 186
Huron ... 187
Imperial ... 188
Imperial Beach ... 189
Indian Wells ... 190
Indio ... 191
Industry ... 192
Inglewood ... 193
Ione ... 194
Irvine ... 195
Irwindale ... 196
Isleton ... 197
Jackson ... 198
Kerman ... 199
King City ... 200
Kingsburg ... 201
La Canada Flintridge ... 202
La Habra ... 203
La Habra Heights ... 204
La Mesa ... 205
La Mirada ... 206
La Palma ... 207
La Puente ... 208
La Quinta ... 209
La Verne ... 210
Lafayette ... 211
Laguna Beach ... 212
Laguna Hills ... 213
Laguna Niguel ... 214
Laguna Woods ... 215
Lake Elsinore ... 216
Lake Forest ... 217
Lakeport ... 218
Lakewood ... 219
Lancaster ... 220
Larkspur ... 221
Lathrop ... 222
Lawndale ... 223
Lemon Grove ... 224
Lemoore ... 225
Lincoln ... 226
Lindsay ... 227
Live Oak ... 228
Livermore ... 229
Livingston ... 230
Lodi ... 231
Loma Linda ... 232
Lomita ... 233
Lompoc ... 234
Long Beach ... 235
Loomis ... 236
Los Alamitos ... 237
Los Altos ... 238
Los Altos Hills ... 239
Los Angeles ... 240
Los Banos ... 241
Los Gatos ... 242
Loyalton ... 243
Lynwood ... 244
Madera ... 245
Malibu ... 246
Mammoth Lakes ... 247
Manhattan Beach ... 248
Manteca ... 249
Maricopa ... 250
Marina ... 251
Martinez ... 252
Marysville ... 253
Maywood ... 254
McFarland ... 255
Mendota ... 256
Menifee ... 257
Menlo Park ... 258
Merced ... 259
Mill Valley ... 260
Millbrae ... 261
Milpitas ... 262
Mission Viejo ... 263
Modesto ... 264
Monrovia ... 265
Montague ... 266
Montclair ... 267
Monte Sereno ... 268
Montebello ... 269
Monterey ... 270
Monterey Park ... 271
Moorpark ... 272
Moraga ... 273
Moreno Valley ... 274
Morgan Hill ... 275
Morro Bay ... 276
Mount Shasta ... 277
Mountain View ... 278
Murrieta ... 279
Napa ... 280
National City ... 281
Needles ... 282
Nevada City ... 283
Newark ... 284
Newman ... 285
Newport Beach ... 286
Norco ... 287
Norwalk ... 288
Novato ... 289
Oakdale ... 290
Oakland ... 291
Oakley ... 292
Oceanside ... 293
Ojai ... 294
Ontario ... 295
Orange ... 296
Orange Cove ... 297
Orinda ... 298
Orland ... 299
Oroville ... 300
Oxnard ... 301
Pacific Grove ... 302
Pacifica ... 303
Palm Desert ... 304
Palm Springs ... 305
Palmdale ... 306
Palo Alto ... 307
Palos Verdes Estates ... 308
Paradise ... 309
Paramount ... 310
Parlier ... 311
Pasadena ... 312
Paso Robles ... 313
Patterson ... 314
Perris ... 315
Petaluma ... 316
Pico Rivera ... 317
Piedmont ... 318
Pinole ... 319
Pismo Beach ... 320
Pittsburg ... 321
Placentia ... 322
Placerville ... 323
Pleasant Hill ... 324
Pleasanton ... 325
Plymouth ... 326
Point Arena ... 327
Pomona ... 328
Port Hueneme ... 329
Porterville ... 330

Municipal Profiles (con't)

Portola 331
Portola Valley 332
Poway 333
Rancho Cordova 334
Rancho Cucamonga 335
Rancho Mirage 336
Rancho Palos Verdes 337
Rancho Santa Margarita 338
Red Bluff 339
Redding 340
Redlands 341
Redondo Beach 342
Redwood City 343
Reedley 344
Rialto 345
Richmond 346
Ridgecrest 347
Rio Dell 348
Rio Vista 349
Ripon 350
Riverbank 351
Riverside 352
Rocklin 353
Rohnert Park 354
Rolling Hills 355
Rolling Hills Estates 356
Rosemead 357
Roseville 358
Ross 359
Sacramento 360
St. Helena 361
Salinas 362
San Anselmo 363
San Bernardino 364
San Bruno 365
San Buenaventura . . . . . see Ventura
San Carlos 366
San Clemente 367
San Diego 368
San Dimas 369
San Fernando 370
San Francisco 371
San Gabriel 372
San Jacinto 373
San Joaquin 374
San Jose 375
San Juan Bautista 376
San Juan Capistrano 377
San Leandro 378
San Luis Obispo 379
San Marcos 380
San Marino 381
San Mateo 382
San Pablo 383
San Rafael 384
San Ramon 385
Sand City 386
Sanger 387
Santa Ana 388
Santa Barbara 389
Santa Clara 390
Santa Clarita 391
Santa Cruz 392
Santa Fe Springs 393
Santa Maria 394
Santa Monica 395
Santa Paula 396
Santa Rosa 397
Santee 398
Saratoga 399
Sausalito 400
Scotts Valley 401
Seal Beach 402
Seaside 403
Sebastopol 404
Selma 405
Shafter 406
Shasta Lake 407
Sierra Madre 408
Signal Hill 409
Simi Valley 410
Solana Beach 411
Soledad 412
Solvang 413
Sonoma 414
Sonora 415
South El Monte 416
South Gate 417
South Lake Tahoe 418
South Pasadena 419
South San Francisco 420
Stanton 421
Stockton 422
Suisun City 423
Sunnyvale 424
Susanville 425
Sutter Creek 426
Taft 427
Tehachapi 428
Tehama 429
Temecula 430
Temple City 431
Thousand Oaks 432
Tiburon 433
Torrance 434
Tracy 435
Trinidad 436
Truckee 437
Tulare 438
Tulelake 439
Turlock 440
Tustin 441
Twentynine Palms 442
Ukiah 443
Union City 444
Upland 445
Vacaville 446
Vallejo 447
Ventura 448
Vernon 449
Victorville 450
Villa Park 451
Visalia 452
Vista 453
Walnut 454
Walnut Creek 455
Wasco 456
Waterford 457
Watsonville 458
Weed 459
West Covina 460
West Hollywood 461
West Sacramento 462
Westlake Village 463
Westminster 464
Westmorland 465
Wheatland 466
Whittier 467
Wildomar 468
Williams 469
Willits 470
Willows 471
Windsor 472
Winters 473
Woodlake 474
Woodland 475
Woodside 476
Yorba Linda 477
Yountville 478
Yreka 479
Yuba City 480
Yucaipa 481
Yucca Valley 482

County Profiles

Alameda County 485
Alpine County 486
Amador County 487
Butte County 488
Calaveras County 489
Colusa County 490
Contra Costa County 491
Del Norte County 492
El Dorado County 493
Fresno County 494
Glenn County 495
Humboldt County 496
Imperial County 497
Inyo County 498
Kern County 499
Kings County 500
Lake County 501
Lassen County 502
Los Angeles County 503
Madera County 504
Marin County 505
Mariposa County 506
Mendocino County 507
Merced County 508
Modoc County 509
Mono County 510
Monterey County 511
Napa County 512
Nevada County 513
Orange County 514
Placer County 515
Plumas County 516
Riverside County 517
Sacramento County 518
San Benito County 519
San Bernardino County 520
San Diego County 521
San Francisco County 522
San Joaquin County 523
San Luis Obispo County 524
San Mateo County 525
Santa Barbara County 526
Santa Clara County 527
Santa Cruz County 528
Shasta County 529
Sierra County 530
Siskiyou County 531
Solano County 532
Sonoma County 533
Stanislaus County 534
Sutter County 535
Tehama County 536
Trinity County 537
Tulare County 538
Tuolumne County 539
Ventura County 540
Yolo County 541
Yuba County 542

(Map appears courtesy of the California Department of Finance, from the 2005 California State Abstract)

California

Cities, Towns & Counties

2009

California Cities, Towns & Counties is an annual reference book published by Information Publications since 1987. It is part of the **State & Municipal Profiles Series**, which also includes the ***Almanac of the 50 States***, as well as municipal and county profile books on Connecticut, Florida, Massachusetts, New Jersey, and North Carolina. Drawing from a variety of established sources, ***California Cities, Towns & Counties*** provides concise, comprehensive one-page profiles for all 480 incorporated places (cities and towns) and 58 counties in California. When new cities incorporate, new profiles will be added as information becomes available.

This book contains one page for every incorporated city and county in the state. Pages in the **Municipal Profiles** and **County Profiles** sections are arranged alphabetically. Each page organizes the data into nine categories to allow rapid access to data and easy comparisons: ***Demographics & Socioeconomic Characteristics***, ***General Information***, ***Voters & Officials***, ***Public Safety***, ***Public Library***, ***Housing & Construction***, ***Municipal Finance*** and ***County Finance***, and ***School System***. Following the municipal and county profiles, there are eight **Appendices**, listed at the end of the introduction.

Please note that a few of the municipalities in this volume are known by several names. The city of Angels Camp is also known as Angels City, Paso Robles is also known as El Paso del Robles, and Ventura is also known as San Buenaventura.

Of the 58 counties, three (Alpine, Mariposa, and Trinity Counties) have no incorporated places at all, and the number of incorporated places in the remaining counties ranges from 1 (in Calaveras, Del Norte, Inyo, Lassen, Modoc, Mono, and Plumas Counties), to 88 in Los Angeles County.

Introduction to the Data

The information in this volume has been obtained from a variety of sources. To aid researchers with questions about the methodology behind the data or the terms used, we have identified the source for each piece of data. These questions can best be answered by the original collectors of the data, who are cited in the **Explanation of the Categories**.

With the exception of the names of local and county officials, almost all of the information was originally collected by an agency of the state or federal government. Using such information assures a high level of accuracy, reliability, and comprehensiveness. However, not all the information collected by government agencies has been published, nor is it necessarily readily available. Many government agencies collect information largely for their own internal use, and the data remains stored in the original materials used for collection. We have selected the most appropriate items from the available information.

Our goal is to provide accurate, reliable, and useful information, based on the most recent sources available, for all 480 municipalities and 58 counties in California. Data in the profiles is the latest available for all local governing bodies as of March 15, 2009. The dates of the information are indicated in the headings themselves. Where no date is shown for a given category, one is provided below.

Information Publications conducted a series of mail, phone, email, and online surveys from January to March 2009 to obtain the current names of **government officials**, **police chiefs**, **fire chiefs**, **librarians**, and **school superintendents**. Information gathered from the surveys is used to supplement other sources to provide complete and up-to-date information.

The notation "NA" stands for "not available." Although we strive to obtain all available data, there are several reasons that data may not be available. Many agencies only provide data for places of a certain size or population, so data is not available from many of the smaller municipalities. Other times, "NA" indicates that the information was never sent to the data collecting agency, or was not available at the data collecting agency at press time. Reporting is often voluntary, and some towns have chosen not to report. Finally, sometimes the category or descriptor simply does not apply to the town (for example, in the case of towns without police or fire chiefs).

Readers should also note that the numbers for subcategories do not always add up to the total shown. In some cases, this is due to rounding error in the original data collection; other times, only certain subgroups of a larger category are presented.

Explanation of the Categories

Demographics & Socioeconomic Characteristics

All information in this category, with a few exceptions, comes from the US Bureau of the Census, from one of two sources: the 2000 Decennial Census or the 2007 American Community Survey.

The American Community Survey (ACS), which surveys a monthly sample of the population, is beginning to track much of the information previously only measured by the Decennial Census. Currently, the ACS provides data on a nationwide and statewide level, as well as for cities and counties with populations over 65,000. The 2007 American Community Survey provided data for 40 of California's 58 counties and 118 of its 480 municipalities. For those places currently tracked by the ACS, we have provided that data in the profiles. Most of the demographic and housing data in these profiles comes from the ACS, except where indicated. For the remainder of the profiles, the demographic and housing data shown comes from the 2000 Decennial Census, with a few exceptions (see below). However, to ensure consistency and allow comparisons, for those counties and cities with ACS data, we have provided the appropriate information from the 2000 Decennial Census in **Appendices C** and **D** for counties and cities, respectively. Data categories are the same as those provided in the Decennial Census, as discussed below.

Starting with the 2007 edition of the ACS, coverage has expanded to all communities with populations greater than 20,000 (with 3-year averages not included in this book). By 2010, the Bureau of the Census hopes to use the ACS to track all the information currently collected in the long form of the Decennial Census. Keep in mind when using using ACS data that, owing to the margin of error inherent in any sampling process, the ACS provides different figures for the total population than the Census Bureau's Population Division statistics. All demographic information is based on the total computed by the ACS, *not* the Census Population Estimates figure for that year. In order to avoid confusion, information obtained from the two sources should never be presented together. You can find out more information about the ACS at http://www.census.gov/acs/www.

For counties and municipalities that are are not currently tracked by the ACS, most demographic data comes from the 2000 Decennial Census, with a few exceptions. The **2020 population** projections on the county pages and the **2008 population** estimates for both the city and county pages are prepared by the California Department of Finance's Demographic Research Unit. **Civilian labor force** and **unemployment rate** data is prepared by the California Employment Development Department, and presents the annual average data for 2008.

Race, as used by the Bureau of the Census, is not meant to denote any scientific or biological concept of race. The subgroups displayed here represent the self-categorization of respondents. It should also be noted that **Hispanic origin** is not a racial category. Persons may be of any race, and be of Hispanic origin as well.

Educational Attainment applies to persons who are 25 years or older. College graduates are persons with at least a four-year degree.

Income and Poverty as reported in the 2000 US Census is from the previous calendar year, 1999.

A **household** includes all the persons occupying a housing unit. A **family household** includes a householder and one or more other persons living in the same household who are related to the householder by birth, marriage, or adoption. The number of family households always equals the number of families; however, a family household may also include nonrelatives living with the family. A **nonfamily household** includes a householder living alone or with nonrelatives only. Not all persons live in households. Some, for example, are members of the armed forces or inmates of institutions, or live in group quarters. As a result, the total number of persons in a city or town can be greater than the number of persons living in all households of that town. The subgroups displayed here under households were selected for potential interest and by no means represent a full breakdown of all types of households. Readers should also note that there is overlap among types of households. For example, the same household may have members both under 18 years of age and over 65 years of age.

Total civilian labor force includes all persons at least 16 years of age who are not members of the armed forces, and are either employed or unemployed. **Self-employed workers** refers to workers who own non-incorporated businesses.

General Information

All **local officials'** names were obtained through Information Publications' own survey process.

The **address** and **telephone number** shown are for the central location of municipal or county business (i.e., the city hall or county administrative offices), and were obtained from surveys. Other information such as **website**, **elevation**, **incorporation date**, and **government type** was also obtained from the surveys. **Persons per square mile** is calculated by Information Publications based on the 2008 population estimates and land area as reported by the 2000 US Census. **Land area** and **water area** are from the 2000 US Census. (The Census reported the measurement in square meters. This figure has been converted into square miles in the profiles using a conversion factor of 2,589,988 square meters per square mile.)

Incorporation date and **government type** for municipalities are further verified against the California Roster, prepared by the Office of the California Secretary of State, and with web research. General law cities derive their power from acts of the state legislature. Their powers are enumerated and structured as specified by the state Government Code. Charter cities are formed by citizens adopting a charter and establishing the organization of the basic laws of the city. The state legislature has less control over charter cities' local affairs.

General law counties elect members of their Board of Supervisors by district, and charter counties have the option of electing their Board members by district or at large.

The **sales tax rate** has been obtained from the California State Board of Equalization.

Voters & Government Officials

Registered voter data is compiled from information provided by the Office of the Secretary of State, Board of Elections, in their Report of Registration, dated October 20, 2008. Numbers do not add up to the total because not all party affiliations are shown, only Democratic, Republican, and those who decline to state a party.

US Congressional Districts and State Senate Districts come from the California State Senate's official website. State Assembly Districts are from the Assembly's site. US Congressional District information is also verified with our surveys and 2000 Census information.

Local and **county officials**' names, and names of the members of the county Boards of Supervisors were gathered from our surveys and from web research. Each county's Board of Supervisors consists of five members who represent specific districts within the county. However, San Francisco is a consolidated city and county and has a Board of Supervisors with eleven members who represent specific districts.

Public Library

All information on libraries, both city and county, was taken from two main sources: the 2008 California Library Directory (available online at http://www.library.ca.gov), and "California Library Statistics, 2006-2007 fiscal year," published by the Library Development Services Bureau of the California State Library in Sacramento. Municipal profile pages include information on city public libraries. If there is no city library but there is a county library branch located in the community, the name and address of the county library branch is listed. For municipalities that are supported by branch(es) of county libraries, corresponding county library statistics are shown.

Public Safety

The names of the **police** and **fire chiefs** (municipal pages) and **sheriffs** (county pages) come from our surveys. **Number of officers, violent crimes, property crimes**, and cases of **arson** come from the 2007 "Crime in the United States" report by the Federal Bureau of Investigation's Uniform Crime Reports division. **Violent crime** is defined as murder, forcible sex, robbery, and aggravated assault. **Property crime** is defined as larceny, burglary, and motor vehicle theft. Statistics in the county profiles are not county totals. They report data for the county sheriff's departments serving the municipalities without their own police departments, and the unincorporated areas of each county. They do not include crime data for cities with their own police departments.

Cities showing "NA" in either the Police or Fire sections have no municipal police or fire department, and have usually contracted with the county sheriff's department, county fire marshal, or another municipal police or fire district for these services. "(County)" denotes that police services or fire services are provided by the county. The town of Corte Madera and the city of Larkspur are both served by the Twin Cities Police Authority. Crime figures in those profiles are combined across the two places.

Housing and Construction

Housing unit data for 2000 comes from the 2000 Census. **Housing unit** data for 2008 comes from the California Department of Finance, Demographic Research Unit. Data in the county profiles is for the unincorporated areas of the county only, and does not represent the total for the entire county.

A **housing unit** is a house, apartment, mobile home or trailer, group of rooms, or single room occupied as a separate living quarter or, if vacant, intended as a separate living quarter. Separate living quarters are those in which the occupants live and eat separately from any other persons in the building, and which have direct access from the outside of the building or through a common hall.

For this publication, a **single-family unit** is defined as a housing unit which does not share the building with any other housing units, nor is its building attached to any other structure. In Census terminology, it is defined a single, detached unit. **Single-family home** as listed is equivalent to the Census term "specified owner-occupied unit" refers to single-family houses on less than 10 acres without a business or medical office on the property.

Value is the Census respondent's estimate of how much the house would sell for if it were on the market. **Median value** represents the middle value of the distribution of these estimates, such that half the houses have higher values than the median and half have lower values. The 2000 Decennial Census only measured **Median home value** up to $1 million. All municipalities with a higher value are marked "$1,000,000+." **Median rent** is defined in a similar fashion.

Statistics for **new privately-owned housing units authorized by building permit** come from the US Bureau of the Census' Manufacturing, Mining, and Construction Statistics for 2007. Places that issue building permits are asked to report monthly to the Bureau.

Municipal Finance/County Finance

Municipal finance information comes from the "Financial Transactions Concerning Cities of California for fiscal year 2005-06," annual report from the State Controller. The information published by the State Controller was extracted from reports prepared by city fiscal officers and submitted to the state. Six cities (Beaumont, Gustine, Loyalton, San Diego, Taft, and Tulelake) failed to submit reports. In addition, Menifee and Wildomar were incorporated in 2008, and so do not have finance data for FY2005-06. All line items in the ***Municipal Finance*** section come from the Total Revenues and Total Expenditures columns of the report.

County Finance information comes from "Counties of California, Financial Transactions Annual Report for 2006-07," also published by the State Controller. Again, the State Controller extracts the data from reports filed by county Auditors. **Property taxation** data comes from the same report, but is applicable for the 2007-08 fiscal year.

School System

Name, **address**, **telephone number**, **superintendent**, and **grade plan** of public school districts were obtained from the California Public School Directory, prepared by the California State Department of Education in Sacramento. It can be found online at http://www.cde.ca.gov/re/sd/index.asp. The above information is supplemented with our surveys. Many cities are served by more than one public school district. If the Public School Directory showed a district had at least one school located in the city on the profile page, we show that district as serving that city.

Due to space limitations, detailed information about only one school district can be shown on each profile page. The district shown on the profile page will be either the only district for that city, or the district with the highest grade level. If there are other districts serving the municipality, they are listed at the bottom of the page. Information about the other districts can be found in **Appendix E**.

The following will help clarify the terminology used in the school district names: A **unified school district** includes both elementary and high school educational levels. **Elementary school districts** include a grade range of kindergarten through eight (although not necessarily all grades). **High school districts** include grade nine and above but may also include grades seven and eight. The word **union** in the name of a school district indicates that it was formed from two or more districts. A **joint district** includes territory from more than one county.

All other information displayed under headings for this section comes from data provided by the California State Department of Education, Data & Statistics Division, and is for the school year 2007-08 except where indicated. The information can be accessed through DataQuest, a Web-based program at www.cde.ca.gov/ds/.

Eight municipalities (Capitola, Goleta, Modesto, Petaluma, Point Arena, Santa Barbara, Santa Cruz, and Santa Rosa) have **Common Administration Districts** for their elementary and high schools. These districts report some data separately for each school system, and pool some data across systems. For these municipalities, districts are listed separately in the profile pages and **Appendix E**. Information in these sections is separate for each district, except where marked. In cases of several districts merging into a single district during the past year, the address and superintentendent given are for the new district, but the data is for the old (separate) districts.

Enrollment includes all regular day school students enrolled for all grades in the district.

High school graduates shows graduates for the 2006-07 school year in districts that have high schools. **Dropout rate** shows the percent of dropouts during a single year.

Pupil/teacher ratio shows the number of pupils per teacher. **Students per Computer** shows the number of K-12 public school students divided by the number of computers used for instructionally-related purposes that are owned or leased by schools.

Average daily cost is computed by the California Department of Education, and is based on the amount of current expense divided by the average daily attendance (ADA).

Average teacher salary comes from the report "Selected Certificated Salaries and Related Statistics, 2007-08," and refer to employees on the teacher salary schedule. Teacher salaries for the county profiles are calculated by dividing the total amount paid for salaries by the number of full-time equivalent (FTE) teachers.

California Achievement Test (CAT/6) is one of the standardized tests of the California Standardized Testing and Reporting (STAR). For more information on STAR and STAR-related test results, please refer to http://star.cde.ca.gov/. The **CAT/6** scores for 2008 are reported for the subjects tested at each grade level: reading, language, mathematics, and spelling for grades 2 through 8 and reading, language, mathematics, and science for grades 9 through 11. We have included reading and mathematics scores for grades 3 and 7. **50th National Percentile Rank** refers to the percent of students in the group scoring in the top half nationally.

Academic Performance Index (API) is part of the California's Public Schools Accountability Act of 1999, and a key part of California's participation in the No Child Left Behind program. The **API** compares the academic performance and growth of schools on a variety of academic measures to a set of statewide standards. The school profiles list the number of program criteria that each district meets, as well as whether or not the district passed on several key measures, such as the **total performance index**, participation and performance goals in **English Language Arts (ELA)** and **math**, and **graduation rate** (if applicable).

The 2006-07 **SAT test** scores for Grade 12 were also provided by the California Department of Education's Program Evaluation Division, and are weighted averages for all high schools in the district. Scores in the **critical reading**, **math**, and **writing** sections range from 200 to 800 each. On the county profile pages, scores shown are the weighted averages of all the high schools in the county and were computed by the Program Evaluation Division.

The goals of education are complex, and standardized tests measure the degree of attainment of only a few of those goals. Standardized test scores should not be the only criterion used to evaluate an educational program. The reader must realize that only a small amount of the information that is required for a total evaluation is provided in district profiles, and for a more in-depth look, the reader should talk with the districts directly and do extensive research of all data available from the schools, the districts, and the California Department of Education.

Appendices

The appendices supplement the information that appears on the individual profile pages. Information in the appendices comes from the same source as the corresponding item on the profile page unless otherwise noted below.

Appendix A is the profile for the state of California, taken from the 2009 edition of the ***Almanac of the 50 States***, also published by Information Publications. Please refer to that volume for similar information on each of the 50 States, the District of Columbia, and the United States in general.

Appendix B lists California's municipalities by county.

Appendix C provides demographic and housing data from the 2000 Decennial Census for the 40 counties tracked by the 2007 American Community Survey.

Appendix D provides demographic and housing data from the 2000 Decennial Census for the 118 cities tracked by the 2007 American Community Survey.

Appendix E lists additional information on public school districts.

Appendix F presents comparative tables for counties in California.

Appendix G presents comparative tables for cities and towns in California.

Appendix H lists US Senators, US Congressional Representatives, California State Senators, and State Assembly members.

Abbreviations

Actg	Acting
ADA	Average Daily Attendance
Admin	Administrator
Atty	Attorney
Avg	Average
CalFire	California Department of Forestry & Fire Protection
(County)	Services provided by County
Chr	Chairperson
Comm	Community
Dep	Deputy
Dev	Development
Dir	Director
ELA	English Language Arts
est	Estimate
Fin	Finance
FY	Fiscal year ending June 30
H'holds	Households
Int	Interim
Mgr	Manager
NA	Not available or not applicable
NCFPD	North County Fire Protection District
Pct	Percent
SF	Single-family
Svcs	Services
Vol	Volunteer position

Disclaimer

California Cities, Towns & Counties contains thousands of pieces of information. Reasonable precautions, along with a good deal of care, were taken in its preparation. Despite our efforts, it is possible that some of the information contained in this book may not be accurate. Some errors may be due to errors in the original source materials; others may have been made by the compilers of this volume. An incorrect spelling may occur, a figure may be inverted, and similar mistakes may exist. The compilers, editors, typist, printers, and others working on this volume are all human, and in a work of this magnitude the possibility of error can never be fully eliminated. If any piece of information is believed to be inaccurate, please contact the publisher. We are eager to eliminate any errors from coming editions and we will be pleased to check a piece of information. The publisher is also aware that some users may apply the data in this book in various remunerative projects. Although we have taken reasonable, responsible measures to insure total accuracy, we cannot take responsibility for liability or losses suffered by users of the data. The information provided here is believed to be correct at the time of publication. No other guarantees are made or implied.

The publisher assumes no liability for losses incurred by users, and warrants only that diligence and due care were used in the production of this volume.

A Final Word

California Cities, Towns & Counties is revised and updated on an annual basis in order to provide the most recent and accurate data available. The best suggestions for improvement in a ready-reference source such as this come from the regular users of the work. Therefore, we actively solicit your comments and ideas. If you know how this book could become more useful to you, please contact us.

The Editors
California Cities, Towns & Counties
Information Publications, Inc.
2995 Woodside Road, Suite 400-182
Woodside, CA 94062

www.informationpublications.com
info@informationpublications.com

Toll-free Phone: 877-544-4636
Toll-free Fax: 877-544-4635

Publisher: Eric Weiner
Editors: Beth Ann Allen, Stephen Rauch
Assistant Editor: Jeff Brenion

California

Cities, Towns & Counties

2009

Demographics & Socio-Economic Characteristics

(2000 Decennial Census, except as noted)

Population

1990* 8,517
2000 18,130
Male 9,698
Female 8,432
Jan. 2008 (estimate)§ 28,181
Persons per sq. mi. of land 526.7

Race & Hispanic Origin, 2000

Race
White 9,147
Black/African American 2,377
North American Native 292
Asian 290
Pacific Islander 32
Other Race 4,819
Two or more races 1,173
Hispanic origin, total 8,299
Mexican 6,415
Puerto Rican 150
Cuban 41
Other Hispanic 1,693

Age & Nativity, 2000

Under 5 years 1,938
18 years and over 11,244
65 years and over 931
85 years and over 62
Median Age 26.9
Native-born 14,799
Foreign-born 3,308

Educational Attainment, 2000

Population 25 years and over 9,750
Less than 9th grade 11.5%
High school grad or higher 67.1%
Bachelor's degree or higher 5.9%
Graduate degree 2.0%

Income & Poverty, 1999

Per capita income $10,053
Median household income $31,594
Median family income $35,254
Persons in poverty 22.2%
H'holds receiving public assistance 616
H'holds receiving social security 933

Households, 2000

Total households 4,714
With persons under 18 2,938
With persons over 65 700
Family households 3,843
Single person households 676
Persons per household 3.53
Persons per family 3.89

Household Population, 2008§§

Persons living in households 26,937
Persons living in group quarters 1,244
Persons per household 3.7

Labor & Employment

Total civilian labor force, 2008§§ 6,800
Unemployment rate, 2008 . . . . . 12.1%
Total civilian labor force, 2000 5,568

Employed persons 16 years and over by occupation, 2000

Managers & professionals 826
Service occupations 821
Sales & office occupations 1,189
Farming, fishing & forestry 35
Construction & maintenance 633
Production & transportation 1,362
Self-employed persons 180

* US Census Bureau
** 2000 Decennial Census
§ California Department of Finance
§§ California Employment Development Dept

General Information

City of Adelanto
11600 Air Expressway
PO Box 10
Adelanto, CA 92301
760-246-2300

Website . . . . . www.ci.adelanto.ca.us
Elevation . . . . . 2,900 ft.
Land Area (sq. miles) 53.5
Water Area (sq. miles) 0
Year of Incorporation 1970
Government type . . . . . Chartered
Sales tax rate 8.75%

Voters & Officials

Registered Voters, October 2008

Total 7,956
Democrats 3,853
Republicans 2,087
Declined to state 1,638

Legislative Districts

US Congressional 25
State Senatorial 17, 18
State Assembly 36

Local Officials, 2009

Mayor . . . . . Charley Glasper
Manager . . . . . Jim Hart
City Clerk . . . . . Cindy Herrera
Attorney . . . . . Todd Litfin
Finance Dir . . . . . Bill Aylward
Public Works . . . . . Rick Gomez
Planning/Dev Dir . . . . . Rick Gomez
Building . . . . . Chuck Classen
Police Chief . . . . . Lee Watkins
Fire Battalion Chief . . . . . Rick McClintock

Public Safety

Number of officers, 2007 . . . . . NA
Violent crimes, 2007 153
Property crimes, 2007 758
Arson, 2007 11

Public Library

Adelanto Branch Library
San Bernardino County Library System
11497 Bartlett
Adelanto, CA 92301
760-246-5661

Branch Librarian . . . . . Carollee Stater

Library system statistics, FY 2007

Population served 1,177,092
Internet terminals 12
Annual users 45,343

Per capita:

Operating income $14.27
percent from local government 73.3%
Operating expenditure $13.86
Total materials 0.86
Print holdings 0.79
Visits per capita 5.83

Housing & Construction

Housing Units

Total, 2008§ 8,546
Single family units, attached 148
Single family units, detached 6,687
Multiple family units 1,203
Mobile home units 508
Occupied 7,259
Vacancy rate 15.1%
Median rent, 2000** $474
Median SF home value, 2000** $81,700

New Privately Owned Housing Units Authorized by Building Permit, 2007*

	Units	Construction Cost
Single	307	$46,194,654
Total	307	$46,194,654

Municipal Finance

(For local fiscal year ended in 2006)

Revenues

Total $26,349,626
Taxes 6,269,290
Special benefits assessment 0
Licenses & permits 1,970,317
Fines & forfeitures 94,403
Revenues from use of money & property 188,368
Intergovernmental 2,987,919
Service charges 11,758,950
Other revenues 3,080,379
Other financing sources 0

Expenditures

Total $23,692,945
General government 2,317,015
Public safety 13,146,286
Transportation 3,144,364
Community development 2,504,145
Health 2,296,623
Culture & leisure 284,512
Other 0

Local School District

(Data from School year 2007-08 except as noted)

Victor Valley Union High
16350 Mojave Dr
Victorville, CA 92395
(760) 955-3201

Superintendent . . . . . Julian Weaver
Grade plan 7-12
Number of schools 12
Enrollment 13,671
High school graduates, 2006-07 1,459
Dropout rate 16.3%
Pupil/teacher ratio 24.1
Average class size 30.2
Students per computer 5.0
Classrooms with internet 566
Avg. Daily Attendance (ADA) 10,395
Cost per ADA $7,840
Avg. Teacher Salary $60,749

California Achievement Tests 6th ed., 2008

(Pct scoring at or above 50th National Percentile Rank)

	Math	Reading	Language
Grade 3	NA	NA	NA
Grade 7	42%	40%	37%

Academic Performance Index, 2008

Number of students tested 8,599
Number of valid scores 7,799
2007 API (base) 669
2008 API (growth) 669

SAT Testing, 2006-07

Enrollment, Grade 12 1,663
Number taking test 386
percent taking test 23.2%
percent with total score 1,500+ 6.50%

Average Scores:

Math	Verbal	Writing	Total
452	450	450	1,352

Federal No Child Left Behind, 2008

(Adequate Yearly Progress standards met)

	Participation Rate	Pct Proficient
ELA	Yes	No
Math	No	No

API criteria . . . . . Yes
Graduation rate . . . . . No
\# criteria met/possible 30/21

Other school districts for this city

(see Appendix E for information on these districts)

Adelanto Elem

See Introduction for an explanation of all data sources.

Demographics & Socio-Economic Characteristics

(2000 Decennial Census, except as noted)

Population

1990* . . . 20,390
2000 . . . 20,537
Male . . . 10,224
Female . . . 10,313
Jan. 2008 (estimate)§ . . . 23,337
Persons per sq. mi. of land . . . 2,846.0

Race & Hispanic Origin, 2000

Race
White . . . 17,858
Black/African American . . . 272
North American Native . . . 51
Asian . . . 1,335
Pacific Islander . . . 21
Other Race . . . 429
Two or more races . . . 571
Hispanic origin, total . . . 1,407
Mexican . . . 793
Puerto Rican . . . 49
Cuban . . . 53
Other Hispanic . . . 512

Age & Nativity, 2000

Under 5 years . . . 1,241
18 years and over . . . 14,282
65 years and over . . . 1,273
85 years and over . . . 113
Median Age . . . 37.6
Native-born . . . 17,573
Foreign-born . . . 2,751

Educational Attainment, 2000

Population 25 years and over . . . 12,860
Less than 9th grade . . . 1.5%
High school grad or higher . . . 94.8%
Bachelor's degree or higher . . . 48.4%
Graduate degree . . . 17.9%

Income & Poverty, 1999

Per capita income . . . $39,700
Median household income . . . $87,008
Median family income . . . $95,765
Persons in poverty . . . 3.4%
H'holds receiving public assistance . . . 38
H'holds receiving social security . . . 953

Households, 2000

Total households . . . 6,874
With persons under 18 . . . 3,369
With persons over 65 . . . 951
Family households . . . 5,591
Single person households . . . 948
Persons per household . . . 2.98
Persons per family . . . 3.30

Household Population, 2008§§

Persons living in households . . . 23,314
Persons living in group quarters . . . 23
Persons per household . . . 3.1

Labor & Employment

Total civilian labor force, 2008§§ . . . 12,500
Unemployment rate, 2008 . . . 3.3%
Total civilian labor force, 2000 . . . 10,645

Employed persons 16 years and over by occupation, 2000

Managers & professionals . . . 5,679
Service occupations . . . 814
Sales & office occupations . . . 2,968
Farming, fishing & forestry . . . 0
Construction & maintenance . . . 451
Production & transportation . . . 373
Self-employed persons . . . 1,211

* US Census Bureau
** 2000 Decennial Census
§ California Department of Finance
§§ California Employment Development Dept

General Information

City of Agoura Hills
30001 Ladyface Court
Agoura Hills, CA 91301
818-597-7300

Website . . . www.ci.agoura-hills.ca.us
Elevation . . . 936 ft.
Land Area (sq. miles) . . . 8.2
Water Area (sq. miles) . . . 0
Year of Incorporation . . . 1982
Government type . . . General law
Sales tax rate . . . 9.25%

Voters & Officials

Registered Voters, October 2008

Total . . . 13,108
Democrats . . . 5,419
Republicans . . . 4,600
Declined to state . . . 2,553

Legislative Districts

US Congressional . . . 30
State Senatorial . . . 23
State Assembly . . . 41

Local Officials, 2009

Mayor . . . Denis Weber
Manager . . . Greg Ramirez
City Clerk . . . Kimberly M. Rodrigues
Attorney . . . Craig Steele
Finance Dir . . . Christy Pinuelas
Public Works . . . NA
Planning/Dev Dir . . . Mike Kamino
Building . . . Amir Hamidzadeh
Police Chief . . . Tim Martin
Emergency/Fire Dir . . . Joseph Graham

Public Safety

Number of officers, 2007 . . . NA
Violent crimes, 2007 . . . 49
Property crimes, 2007 . . . 348
Arson, 2007 . . . 6

Public Library

Agoura Hills Library
Los Angeles County Public Library System
29901 Ladyface Court
Agoura Hills, CA 91301
818-889-2278

Branch Librarian . . . Raya Sagi

Library system statistics, FY 2007

Population served . . . 3,673,313
Internet terminals . . . 749
Annual users . . . 3,748,771

Per capita:

Operating income . . . $30.06
percent from local government . . . 93.6%
Operating expenditure . . . $28.36
Total materials . . . 2.22
Print holdings . . . 1.97
Visits per capita . . . 3.25

Housing & Construction

Housing Units

Total, 2008§ . . . 7,584
Single family units, attached . . . 979
Single family units, detached . . . 5,292
Multiple family units . . . 1,313
Mobile home units . . . 0
Occupied . . . 7,456
Vacancy rate . . . 1.7%
Median rent, 2000** . . . $1,215
Median SF home value, 2000** . . . $366,600

New Privately Owned Housing Units Authorized by Building Permit, 2007*

	Units	Construction Cost
Single	7	$4,149,564
Total	7	$4,149,564

Municipal Finance

(For local fiscal year ended in 2006)

Revenues

Total . . . $18,605,145
Taxes . . . 13,672,553
Special benefits assessment . . . 0
Licenses & permits . . . 309,927
Fines & forfeitures . . . 315,266
Revenues from use of money & property . . . 668,310
Intergovernmental . . . 1,337,931
Service charges . . . 2,108,946
Other revenues . . . 192,212
Other financing sources . . . 0

Expenditures

Total . . . $12,030,491
General government . . . 3,165,343
Public safety . . . 2,784,192
Transportation . . . 3,226,413
Community development . . . 1,712,922
Health . . . 93,419
Culture & leisure . . . 1,048,202
Other . . . 0

Local School District

(Data from School year 2007-08 except as noted)

Las Virgenes Unified
4111 North Las Virgenes Rd
Calabasas, CA 91302
(818) 880-4000

Superintendent . . . Donald Zimring
Grade plan . . . K-12
Number of schools . . . 15
Enrollment . . . 11,803
High school graduates, 2006-07 . . . 1,004
Dropout rate . . . 1.4%
Pupil/teacher ratio . . . 25.0
Average class size . . . 28.8
Students per computer . . . 6.1
Classrooms with internet . . . 515
Avg. Daily Attendance (ADA) . . . 11,596
Cost per ADA . . . $8,255
Avg. Teacher Salary . . . $66,468

California Achievement Tests 6th ed., 2008

(Pct scoring at or above 50th National Percentile Rank)

	Math	Reading	Language
Grade 3	82%	67%	75%
Grade 7	80%	75%	75%

Academic Performance Index, 2008

Number of students tested . . . 9,240
Number of valid scores . . . 9,058
2007 API (base) . . . 872
2008 API (growth) . . . 876

SAT Testing, 2006-07

Enrollment, Grade 12 . . . 1,069
Number taking test . . . 746
percent taking test . . . 69.8%
percent with total score 1,500+ . . . 54.20%

Average Scores:

Math	Verbal	Writing	Total
578	549	570	1,697

Federal No Child Left Behind, 2008

(Adequate Yearly Progress standards met)

	Participation Rate	Pct Proficient
ELA	Yes	Yes
Math	Yes	Yes

API criteria . . . Yes
Graduation rate . . . Yes
\# criteria met/possible . . . 34/34

Other school districts for this city

(see Appendix E for information on these districts)

None

See Introduction for an explanation of all data sources.

Demographics & Socio-Economic Characteristics†

(2007 American Community Survey, except as noted)

Population

1990* 76,459
2007 75,642
Male 36,870
Female 38,772
Jan. 2008 (estimate)§ 75,823
Persons per sq. mi. of land 7,020.6

Race & Hispanic Origin, 2007

Race
White 38,241
Black/African American 3,897
North American Native 320
Asian 26,836
Pacific Islander 0
Other Race 1,786
Two or more races 4,562
Hispanic origin, total 7,993
Mexican 4,437
Puerto Rican 1,014
Cuban 170
Other Hispanic 2,372

Age & Nativity, 2007

Under 5 years 5,233
18 years and over 58,825
65 years and over 9,165
85 years and over 904
Median Age 39.1
Native-born 51,842
Foreign-born 23,800

Educational Attainment, 2007

Population 25 years and over 53,482
Less than 9th grade 6.2%
High school grad or higher 90.1%
Bachelor's degree or higher 47.9%
Graduate degree 15.9%

Income & Poverty, 2007

Per capita income $35,470
Median household income $71,262
Median family income $88,458
Persons in poverty 10.6%
H'holds receiving public assistance 842
H'holds receiving social security 6,758

Households, 2007

Total households 29,091
With persons under 18 9,191
With persons over 65 6,474
Family households 18,073
Single person households 8,504
Persons per household 2.58
Persons per family 3.21

Household Population, 2008§§

Persons living in households 75,097
Persons living in group quarters 726
Persons per household 2.4

Labor & Employment

Total civilian labor force, 2008§§ 40,600
Unemployment rate, 2008 .... 4.2%
Total civilian labor force, 2000* 38,998

Employed persons 16 years and over by occupation, 2007

Managers & professionals 17,779
Service occupations 4,945
Sales & office occupations 9,639
Farming, fishing & forestry 73
Construction & maintenance 2,075
Production & transportation 2,861
Self-employed persons 2,807

† see Appendix D for 2000 Decennial Census Data
* US Census Bureau
** 2007 American Community Survey
§ California Department of Finance
§§ California Employment Development Dept

General Information

City of Alameda
2263 Santa Clara Ave
Alameda, CA 94501
510-747-7400

Website .... www.ci.alameda.ca.us
Elevation .... 30 ft.
Land Area (sq. miles) 10.8
Water Area (sq. miles) 12.2
Year of Incorporation 1854
Government type .... Chartered
Sales tax rate 9.75%

Voters & Officials

Registered Voters, October 2008

Total 44,049
Democrats 24,411
Republicans 7,152
Declined to state 10,350

Legislative Districts

US Congressional 13
State Senatorial 9
State Assembly 16

Local Officials, 2009

Mayor .... Beverly Johnson
Manager .... Debra Kurita
City Clerk .... Lara Weisiger
Attorney .... Teresa Highsmith
Finance Dir .... Juelle Ann Buyer
Public Works .... Matthew Naclerio
Planning/Dev Dir .... Leslie Little
Building .... Cathy Woodbury
Police Chief .... Walter Tibbet
Emergency/Fire Dir .... David Kapler

Public Safety

Number of officers, 2007 99
Violent crimes, 2007 205
Property crimes, 2007 1,976
Arson, 2007 17

Public Library

Alameda Free Library
Alameda Free Library System
1550 Oak St
Alameda, CA 94501
510-747-7777

Director .... Jane Chisaki

Library system statistics, FY 2007

Population served 75,254
Internet terminals 80
Annual users 81,625

Per capita:

Operating income $34.15
percent from local government 94.3%
Operating expenditure $33.89
Total materials 3.07
Print holdings 2.88
Visits per capita 6.07

Housing & Construction

Housing Units

Total, 2008§ 32,527
Single family units, attached 4,011
Single family units, detached 13,379
Multiple family units 14,837
Mobile home units 300
Occupied 31,602
Vacancy rate 2.8%
Median rent, 2007** $1,189
Median SF home value, 2007** $691,300

New Privately Owned Housing Units Authorized by Building Permit, 2007*

	Units	Construction Cost
Single	104	$38,310,568
Total	106	$38,690,843

Municipal Finance

(For local fiscal year ended in 2006)

Revenues

Total $162,447,358
Taxes 57,375,427
Special benefits assessment 2,917,990
Licenses & permits 2,153,028
Fines & forfeitures 941,793
Revenues from use of money & property 6,584,937
Intergovernmental 15,815,555
Service charges 71,166,479
Other revenues 5,155,276
Other financing sources 336,873

Expenditures

Total $153,433,508
General government 12,450,812
Public safety 49,141,975
Transportation 9,184,978
Community development 7,670,033
Health 3,883,997
Culture & leisure 28,998,070
Other 0

Local School District

(Data from School year 2007-08 except as noted)

Alameda City Unified
2200 Central Ave
Alameda, CA 94501
(510) 337-7060

Superintendent .... Kirsten Vital
Grade plan K-12
Number of schools 19
Enrollment 10,315
High school graduates, 2006-07 711
Dropout rate 2.8%
Pupil/teacher ratio 20.6
Average class size 24.6
Students per computer 4.6
Classrooms with internet 539
Avg. Daily Attendance (ADA) 9,686
Cost per ADA $8,008
Avg. Teacher Salary $62,223

California Achievement Tests 6th ed., 2008

(Pct scoring at or above 50th National Percentile Rank)

	Math	Reading	Language
Grade 3	71%	53%	63%
Grade 7	63%	59%	60%

Academic Performance Index, 2008

Number of students tested 7,737
Number of valid scores 7,386
2007 API (base) 805
2008 API (growth) 812

SAT Testing, 2006-07

Enrollment, Grade 12 872
Number taking test 469
percent taking test 53.8%
percent with total score 1,500+ 28.00%

Average Scores:

Math	Verbal	Writing	Total
533	494	493	1,520

Federal No Child Left Behind, 2008

(Adequate Yearly Progress standards met)

	Participation Rate	Pct Proficient
ELA	Yes	No
Math	Yes	No

API criteria .... Yes
Graduation rate .... Yes
\# criteria met/possible 38/35

Other school districts for this city

(see Appendix E for information on these districts)

None

See Introduction for an explanation of all data sources.

Demographics & Socio-Economic Characteristics

(2000 Decennial Census, except as noted)

Population

1990* . . . 16,327
2000 . . . 16,444
Male . . . 7,669
Female . . . 8,775
Jan. 2008 (estimate)§ . . . 16,877
Persons per sq. mi. of land . . . 9,927.6

Race & Hispanic Origin, 2000

Race
White . . . 10,078
Black/African American . . . 675
North American Native . . . 64
Asian . . . 4,126
Pacific Islander . . . 22
Other Race . . . 521
Two or more races . . . 958
Hispanic origin, total . . . 1,312
Mexican . . . 684
Puerto Rican . . . 59
Cuban . . . 25
Other Hispanic . . . 544

Age & Nativity, 2000

Under 5 years . . . 988
18 years and over . . . 12,686
65 years and over . . . 1,819
85 years and over . . . 291
Median Age . . . 36.3
Native-born . . . 11,685
Foreign-born . . . 4,759

Educational Attainment, 2000

Population 25 years and over . . . 11,574
Less than 9th grade . . . 2.0%
High school grad or higher . . . 93.8%
Bachelor's degree or higher . . . 64.0%
Graduate degree . . . 34.0%

Income & Poverty, 1999

Per capita income . . . $28,494
Median household income . . . $54,919
Median family income . . . $64,269
Persons in poverty . . . 7.9%
H'holds receiving public assistance . . . 94
H'holds receiving social security . . . 1,341

Households, 2000

Total households . . . 7,011
With persons under 18 . . . 2,419
With persons over 65 . . . 1,394
Family households . . . 4,272
Single person households . . . 2,049
Persons per household . . . 2.34
Persons per family . . . 2.92

Household Population, 2008§§

Persons living in households . . . 16,844
Persons living in group quarters . . . 33
Persons per household . . . 2.4

Labor & Employment

Total civilian labor force, 2008§§ . . . 9,200
Unemployment rate, 2008 . . . 2.4%
Total civilian labor force, 2000 . . . 8,859

Employed persons 16 years and over by occupation, 2000

Managers & professionals . . . 5,560
Service occupations . . . 592
Sales & office occupations . . . 1,835
Farming, fishing & forestry . . . 0
Construction & maintenance . . . 319
Production & transportation . . . 368
Self-employed persons . . . 982

* US Census Bureau
** 2000 Decennial Census
§ California Department of Finance
§§ California Employment Development Dept

General Information

City of Albany
1000 San Pablo Ave
Albany, CA 94706
510-528-5710

Website . . . www.albanyca.org
Elevation . . . NA
Land Area (sq. miles) . . . 1.7
Water Area (sq. miles) . . . 3.8
Year of Incorporation . . . 1908
Government type . . . Chartered
Sales tax rate . . . 9.75%

Voters & Officials

Registered Voters, October 2008

Total . . . 10,672
Democrats . . . 6,850
Republicans . . . 822
Declined to state . . . 2,422

Legislative Districts

US Congressional . . . 9
State Senatorial . . . 9
State Assembly . . . 14

Local Officials, 2009

Mayor . . . Marge Atkinson
Manager . . . Beth Pollard
City Clerk . . . Jacqueline Bucholz
Attorney . . . Robert Zweben
Finance Dir . . . Charles Adams
Public Works . . . NA
Community Dev Dir . . . Ann Chaney
Building . . . NA
Police Chief . . . Michael McQuiston
Fire Chief . . . Marc McGinn

Public Safety

Number of officers, 2007 . . . 26
Violent crimes, 2007 . . . 45
Property crimes, 2007 . . . 776
Arson, 2007 . . . 3

Public Library

Albany Library
Alameda County Library System
1247 Marin Ave
Albany, CA 94706
510-526-3720

Branch Librarian . . . Ronnie Davis

Library system statistics, FY 2007

Population served . . . 527,926
Internet terminals . . . 193
Annual users . . . 358,689

Per capita:

Operating income . . . $41.07
percent from local government . . . 94.7%
Operating expenditure . . . $36.47
Total materials . . . 2.21
Print holdings . . . 1.91
Visits per capita . . . 4.32

Housing & Construction

Housing Units

Total, 2008§ . . . 7,351
Single family units, attached . . . 198
Single family units, detached . . . 3,784
Multiple family units . . . 3,363
Mobile home units . . . 6
Occupied . . . 7,110
Vacancy rate . . . 3.3%
Median rent, 2000** . . . $947
Median SF home value, 2000** . . . $334,800

New Privately Owned Housing Units Authorized by Building Permit, 2007*

	Units	Construction Cost
Single	4	$962,892
Total	7	$1,562,618

Municipal Finance

(For local fiscal year ended in 2006)

Revenues

Total . . . $21,189,973
Taxes . . . 12,996,274
Special benefits assessment . . . 1,909,224
Licenses & permits . . . 241,926
Fines & forfeitures . . . 153,709
Revenues from use of money & property . . . 1,079,193
Intergovernmental . . . 1,084,326
Service charges . . . 3,625,853
Other revenues . . . 99,468
Other financing sources . . . 0

Expenditures

Total . . . $20,385,760
General government . . . 2,430,272
Public safety . . . 10,031,629
Transportation . . . 3,636,152
Community development . . . 935,836
Health . . . 771,312
Culture & leisure . . . 2,580,559
Other . . . 0

Local School District

(Data from School year 2007-08 except as noted)

Albany Unified
904 Talbot Ave
Albany, CA 94706
(510) 558-3750

Superintendent . . . Marla Stephenson
Grade plan . . . K-12
Number of schools . . . 6
Enrollment . . . 3,810
High school graduates, 2006-07 . . . 274
Dropout rate . . . 2.1%
Pupil/teacher ratio . . . 20.5
Average class size . . . 26.0
Students per computer . . . 4.6
Classrooms with internet . . . 130
Avg. Daily Attendance (ADA) . . . 3,696
Cost per ADA . . . $8,733
Avg. Teacher Salary . . . $64,086

California Achievement Tests 6th ed., 2008

(Pct scoring at or above 50th National Percentile Rank)

	Math	Reading	Language
Grade 3	76%	76%	75%
Grade 7	80%	72%	73%

Academic Performance Index, 2008

Number of students tested . . . 2,863
Number of valid scores . . . 2,721
2007 API (base) . . . 860
2008 API (growth) . . . 854

SAT Testing, 2006-07

Enrollment, Grade 12 . . . 286
Number taking test . . . 192
percent taking test . . . 67.1%
percent with total score 1,500+ . . . 50.70%

Average Scores:

Math	Verbal	Writing	Total
605	568	552	1,725

Federal No Child Left Behind, 2008

(Adequate Yearly Progress standards met)

	Participation Rate	Pct Proficient
ELA	No	Yes
Math	No	Yes

API criteria . . . Yes
Graduation rate . . . Yes
\# criteria met/possible . . . 34/32

Other school districts for this city

(see Appendix E for information on these districts)

None

See Introduction for an explanation of all data sources.

Demographics & Socio-Economic Characteristics†

(2007 American Community Survey, except as noted)

Population

1990* ... 82,106
2007 ... 88,393
Male ... 44,644
Female ... 43,749
Jan. 2008 (estimate)§ ... 89,259
Persons per sq. mi. of land ... 11,744.6

Race & Hispanic Origin, 2007

Race
White ... 18,714
Black/African American ... 1,026
North American Native ... 321
Asian ... 47,413
Pacific Islander ... 260
Other Race ... 19,610
Two or more races ... 1,049
Hispanic origin, total ... 31,714
Mexican ... 25,377
Puerto Rican ... 147
Cuban ... 370
Other Hispanic ... 5,820

Age & Nativity, 2007

Under 5 years ... 4,724
18 years and over ... 71,652
65 years and over ... 10,696
85 years and over ... 1,115
Median Age ... 37.8
Native-born ... 36,415
Foreign-born ... 51,978

Educational Attainment, 2007

Population 25 years and over ... 60,944
Less than 9th grade ... 11.0%
High school grad or higher ... 80.4%
Bachelor's degree or higher ... 34.0%
Graduate degree ... 10.1%

Income & Poverty, 2007

Per capita income ... $23,592
Median household income ... $52,029
Median family income ... $57,024
Persons in poverty ... 11.6%
H'holds receiving public assistance ... 732
H'holds receiving social security ... 6,005

Households, 2007

Total households ... 29,715
With persons under 18 ... 10,010
With persons over 65 ... 7,350
Family households ... 20,961
Single person households ... 5,976
Persons per household ... 2.93
Persons per family ... 3.37

Household Population, 2008§§

Persons living in households ... 87,336
Persons living in group quarters ... 1,923
Persons per household ... 3.0

Labor & Employment

Total civilian labor force, 2008§§ ... 46,400
Unemployment rate, 2008 ... 6.4%
Total civilian labor force, 2000* ... 40,163

Employed persons 16 years and over by occupation, 2007

Managers & professionals ... 16,177
Service occupations ... 9,034
Sales & office occupations ... 12,638
Farming, fishing & forestry ... 309
Construction & maintenance ... 3,280
Production & transportation ... 5,562
Self-employed persons ... 2,847

† see Appendix D for 2000 Decennial Census Data
* US Census Bureau
** 2007 American Community Survey
§ California Department of Finance
§§ California Employment Development Dept

General Information

City of Alhambra
111 S First St
Alhambra, CA 91801
626-570-5007

Website ... www.cityofalhambra.org
Elevation ... 483 ft.
Land Area (sq. miles) ... 7.6
Water Area (sq. miles) ... 0
Year of Incorporation ... 1903
Government type ... Chartered
Sales tax rate ... 9.25%

Voters & Officials

Registered Voters, October 2008

Total ... 35,234
Democrats ... 16,876
Republicans ... 7,565
Declined to state ... 9,475

Legislative Districts

US Congressional ... 29
State Senatorial ... 22
State Assembly ... 49

Local Officials, 2009

Mayor ... Barbara A Messina
Manager ... Julio Fuentes
City Clerk ... Frances Moore
Attorney ... Joseph Montes
Finance Dir ... Howard Longballa
Public Works ... Mary Chavez
Planning/Dev Dir ... Michael Martin
Building ... Ali Cayir
Police Chief ... James Hudson
Emergency/Fire Dir ... Bruce A Stedman

Public Safety

Number of officers, 2007 ... 85
Violent crimes, 2007 ... 285
Property crimes, 2007 ... 2,120
Arson, 2007 ... 16

Public Library

Alhambra Public Library
410 W Main St
Alhambra, CA 91801
626-570-5079

Director ... Carmen Hernandez

Library statistics, FY 2007

Population served ... 89,488
Internet terminals ... 19
Annual users ... 44,525

Per capita:

Operating income ... $25.36
percent from local government ... 93.8%
Operating expenditure ... $23.41
Total materials ... 1.76
Print holdings ... 1.61
Visits per capita ... 5.36

Housing & Construction

Housing Units

Total, 2008§ ... 30,216
Single family units, attached ... 3,286
Single family units, detached ... 12,747
Multiple family units ... 14,166
Mobile home units ... 17
Occupied ... 29,252
Vacancy rate ... 3.2%
Median rent, 2007** ... $1,047
Median SF home value, 2007** ... $557,500

New Privately Owned Housing Units Authorized by Building Permit, 2007*

	Units	Construction Cost
Single	19	$3,882,564
Total	78	$10,602,912

Municipal Finance

(For local fiscal year ended in 2006)

Revenues

Total ... $89,951,247
Taxes ... 35,597,461
Special benefits assessment ... 6,624,545
Licenses & permits ... 932,326
Fines & forfeitures ... 1,951,910
Revenues from use of money & property ... 2,179,175
Intergovernmental ... 9,018,967
Service charges ... 21,706,004
Other revenues ... 2,562,627
Other financing sources ... 9,378,232

Expenditures

Total ... $81,236,907
General government ... 6,291,426
Public safety ... 34,536,765
Transportation ... 8,949,354
Community development ... 3,581,580
Health ... 8,195,592
Culture & leisure ... 9,418,938
Other ... 0

Local School District

(Data from School year 2007-08 except as noted)

Alhambra Unified
1515 West Mission Rd
Alhambra, CA 91803
(626) 943-3000

Superintendent ... Donna Perez
Grade plan ... K-12
Number of schools ... 18
Enrollment ... 18,976
High school graduates, 2006-07 ... 1,869
Dropout rate ... 1.6%
Pupil/teacher ratio ... 23.7
Average class size ... 29.2
Students per computer ... 4.2
Classrooms with internet ... 762
Avg. Daily Attendance (ADA) ... 19,060
Cost per ADA ... $8,203
Avg. Teacher Salary ... $68,117

California Achievement Tests 6th ed., 2008

(Pct scoring at or above 50th National Percentile Rank)

	Math	Reading	Language
Grade 3	64%	41%	54%
Grade 7	66%	55%	55%

Academic Performance Index, 2008

Number of students tested ... 14,756
Number of valid scores ... 14,057
2007 API (base) ... 768
2008 API (growth) ... 782

SAT Testing, 2006-07

Enrollment, Grade 12 ... 2,260
Number taking test ... 1,020
percent taking test ... 45.1%
percent with total score 1,500+ ... 22.70%

Average Scores:

Math	Verbal	Writing	Total
548	478	478	1,504

Federal No Child Left Behind, 2008

(Adequate Yearly Progress standards met)

	Participation Rate	Pct Proficient
ELA	Yes	No
Math	Yes	No

API criteria ... Yes
Graduation rate ... Yes
\# criteria met/possible ... 34/32

Other school districts for this city

(see Appendix E for information on these districts)

None

See Introduction for an explanation of all data sources.

Demographics & Socio-Economic Characteristics

(2000 Decennial Census, except as noted)

Population

1990* ... NA
2000 ... 40,166
  Male ... 19,394
  Female ... 20,772
Jan. 2008 (estimate)§ ... 45,249
  Persons per sq. mi. of land ... 4,436.2

Race & Hispanic Origin, 2000

Race
  White ... 31,395
  Black/African American ... 828
  North American Native ... 158
  Asian ... 4,413
  Pacific Islander ... 88
  Other Race ... 1,411
  Two or more races ... 1,873
Hispanic origin, total ... 4,680
  Mexican ... 2,857
  Puerto Rican ... 232
  Cuban ... 141
  Other Hispanic ... 1,450

Age & Nativity, 2000

Under 5 years ... 4,043
18 years and over ... 29,699
65 years and over ... 1,350
85 years and over ... 80
  Median Age ... 32.7
Native-born ... 32,320
Foreign-born ... 7,905

Educational Attainment, 2000

Population 25 years and over ... 27,893
Less than 9th grade ... 1.4%
High school grad or higher ... 96.1%
Bachelor's degree or higher ... 48.6%
Graduate degree ... 14.0%

Income & Poverty, 1999

Per capita income ... $35,244
Median household income ... $76,409
Median family income ... $84,592
Persons in poverty ... 2.8%
H'holds receiving public assistance ... 204
H'holds receiving social security ... 1,032

Households, 2000

Total households ... 16,147
  With persons under 18 ... 6,280
  With persons over 65 ... 1,061
  Family households ... 10,683
  Single person households ... 3,846
Persons per household ... 2.49
Persons per family ... 3.01

Household Population, 2008§§

Persons living in households ... 45,089
Persons living in group quarters ... 160
Persons per household ... 2.6

Labor & Employment

Total civilian labor force, 2008§§ ... 28,700
  Unemployment rate, 2008 ... 2.7%
Total civilian labor force, 2000 ... NA

Employed persons 16 years and over by occupation, 2000

  Managers & professionals ... 13,018
  Service occupations ... 1,945
  Sales & office occupations ... 7,117
  Farming, fishing & forestry ... 0
  Construction & maintenance ... 756
  Production & transportation ... 1,134
  Self-employed persons ... 1,909

* US Census Bureau
** 2000 Decennial Census
§ California Department of Finance
§§ California Employment Development Dept

General Information

City of Aliso Viejo
12 Journey
Suite 100
Aliso Viejo, CA 92656
949-425-2500

Website ... www.cityofalisoviejo.com
Elevation ... NA
Land Area (sq. miles) ... 10.2
Water Area (sq. miles) ... 0
Year of Incorporation ... 2001
Government type ... General law
Sales tax rate ... 8.75%

Voters & Officials

Registered Voters, October 2008

Total ... 27,596
  Democrats ... 8,068
  Republicans ... 11,921
  Declined to state ... 6,464

Legislative Districts

US Congressional ... 48
State Senatorial ... 38
State Assembly ... 70, 73

Local Officials, 2009

Mayor ... Donald A. Garcia
City Manager ... Mark A. Pulone
City Clerk ... Susan A. Ramos (Int)
Attorney ... Scott C. Smith
Finance Dir ... Gina M. Tharani
Public Works ... John Whitman
Planning Dir ... Eugenia Garcia
Building ... John Van Steinburg
Police Chief ... Rich Paddock
Fire Chief ... Ed Fleming

Public Safety

Number of officers, 2007 ... NA
Violent crimes, 2007 ... 31
Property crimes, 2007 ... 526
Arson, 2007 ... 2

Public Library

Aliso Viejo Branch Library
Orange County Public Library System
1 Journey
Aliso Viejo, CA 92656
949-360-1730

Branch Librarian ... Timothy Scott

Library system statistics, FY 2007

Population served ... 1,532,758
Internet terminals ... 505
  Annual users ... 680,874

Per capita:

Operating income ... $24.71
  percent from local government ... 90.0%
Operating expenditure ... $24.18
Total materials ... 1.93
Print holdings ... 1.84
Visits per capita ... 4.02

Housing & Construction

Housing Units

Total, 2008§ ... 18,047
  Single family units, attached ... 4,947
  Single family units, detached ... 6,463
  Multiple family units ... 6,622
  Mobile home units ... 15
  Occupied ... 17,548
  Vacancy rate ... 2.8%
Median rent, 2000** ... $1,268
Median SF home value, 2000** ... $260,200

New Privately Owned Housing Units Authorized by Building Permit, 2007*

	Units	Construction Cost
Single	66	$23,005,813
Total	78	$25,933,319

Municipal Finance

(For local fiscal year ended in 2006)

Revenues

Total ... $18,113,210
Taxes ... 10,860,541
Special benefits assessment ... 0
Licenses & permits ... 559,012
Fines & forfeitures ... 301,715
Revenues from use of money & property ... 471,472
Intergovernmental ... 3,858,876
Service charges ... 2,041,336
Other revenues ... 20,258
Other financing sources ... 0

Expenditures

Total ... $12,506,901
General government ... 3,164,880
Public safety ... 5,197,410
Transportation ... 1,678,940
Community development ... 2,418,090
Health ... 0
Culture & leisure ... 47,581
Other ... 0

Local School District

(Data from School year 2007-08 except as noted)

Capistrano Unified
33122 Valle Rd
San Juan Capistrano, CA 92675
(949) 234-9200

Superintendent ... A. Carter
Grade plan ... K-12
Number of schools ... 61
Enrollment ... 52,390
High school graduates, 2006-07 ... 3,205
Dropout rate ... 0.5%
Pupil/teacher ratio ... 23.4
Average class size ... 28.7
Students per computer ... 4.8
Classrooms with internet ... 2,308
Avg. Daily Attendance (ADA) ... 50,036
  Cost per ADA ... $7,694
Avg. Teacher Salary ... $75,390

California Achievement Tests 6th ed., 2008

(Pct scoring at or above 50th National Percentile Rank)

	Math	Reading	Language
Grade 3	71%	56%	63%
Grade 7	73%	71%	68%

Academic Performance Index, 2008

Number of students tested ... 39,589
Number of valid scores ... 38,275
2007 API (base) ... 826
2008 API (growth) ... 837

SAT Testing, 2006-07

Enrollment, Grade 12 ... 3,414
Number taking test ... 1,770
  percent taking test ... 51.9%
  percent with total score 1,500+ ... 34.90%

Average Scores:

Math	Verbal	Writing	Total
552	541	537	1,630

Federal No Child Left Behind, 2008

(Adequate Yearly Progress standards met)

	Participation Rate	Pct Proficient
ELA	Yes	No
Math	Yes	Yes

API criteria ... Yes
Graduation rate ... Yes
criteria met/possible ... 42/41

Other school districts for this city

(see Appendix E for information on these districts)

Saddleback Unified

See Introduction for an explanation of all data sources.

Demographics & Socio-Economic Characteristics

(2000 Decennial Census, except as noted)

Population

1990* . . . 3,231
2000 . . . 2,892
Male . . . 1,374
Female . . . 1,518
Jan. 2008 (estimate)§ . . . 2,804
Persons per sq. mi. of land . . . 1,274.5

Race & Hispanic Origin, 2000

Race
White . . . 2,484
Black/African American . . . 9
North American Native . . . 127
Asian . . . 21
Pacific Islander . . . 3
Other Race . . . 140
Two or more races . . . 108
Hispanic origin, total . . . 344
Mexican . . . 262
Puerto Rican . . . 3
Cuban . . . 0
Other Hispanic . . . 79

Age & Nativity, 2000

Under 5 years . . . 203
18 years and over . . . 2,061
65 years and over . . . 488
85 years and over . . . 67
Median Age . . . 38.1
Native-born . . . 2,755
Foreign-born . . . 223

Educational Attainment, 2000

Population 25 years and over . . . 1,921
Less than 9th grade . . . 5.7%
High school grad or higher . . . 77.1%
Bachelor's degree or higher . . . 10.8%
Graduate degree . . . 3.8%

Income & Poverty, 1999

Per capita income . . . $19,281
Median household income . . . $24,351
Median family income . . . $31,385
Persons in poverty . . . 27.0%
H'holds receiving public assistance . . . 146
H'holds receiving social security . . . 390

Households, 2000

Total households . . . 1,181
With persons under 18 . . . 448
With persons over 65 . . . 326
Family households . . . 753
Single person households . . . 384
Persons per household . . . 2.38
Persons per family . . . 3.00

Household Population, 2008§§

Persons living in households . . . 2,724
Persons living in group quarters . . . 80
Persons per household . . . 2.3

Labor & Employment

Total civilian labor force, 2008§§ . . . 1,180
Unemployment rate, 2008 . . . 13.6%
Total civilian labor force, 2000 . . . 1,231

Employed persons 16 years and over by occupation, 2000

Managers & professionals . . . 257
Service occupations . . . 329
Sales & office occupations . . . 228
Farming, fishing & forestry . . . 23
Construction & maintenance . . . 75
Production & transportation . . . 116
Self-employed persons . . . 115

* US Census Bureau
** 2000 Decennial Census
§ California Department of Finance
§§ California Employment Development Dept

General Information

City of Alturas
200 North St
Alturas, CA 96101
530-233-2512

Email . . . cary@cityofalturas.org
Elevation . . . 4,366 ft.
Land Area (sq. miles) . . . 2.2
Water Area (sq. miles) . . . 0
Year of Incorporation . . . 1901
Government type . . . General law
Sales tax rate . . . 8.25%

Voters & Officials

Registered Voters, October 2008

Total . . . 1,636
Democrats . . . 573
Republicans . . . 701
Declined to state . . . 279

Legislative Districts

US Congressional . . . 4
State Senatorial . . . 1
State Assembly . . . 2

Local Officials, 2009

Mayor . . . John E. Dederick
Manager/Admin . . . NA
City Clerk . . . Cary L. Baker
Attorney . . . Albert M. Monaco Jr
Finance Dir . . . Kathie Alves
Public Works . . . Chester Robertson
Planning/Dev Dir . . . Chester Robertson
Building . . . Sue Traugott
Police Chief . . . Ken Barnes
Emergency/Fire Dir . . . Steve Jacques

Public Safety

Number of officers, 2007 . . . 6
Violent crimes, 2007 . . . 5
Property crimes, 2007 . . . 90
Arson, 2007 . . . 2

Public Library

Main Branch
Modoc County Library System
212 W Third St
Alturas, CA 96101
530-233-6326

County Librarian . . . Cheryl Baker

Library system statistics, FY 2007

Population served . . . 9,721
Internet terminals . . . 15
Annual users . . . 7,191

Per capita:

Operating income . . . $35.81
percent from local government . . . 92.8%
Operating expenditure . . . $39.34
Total materials . . . 7.28
Print holdings . . . 6.89
Visits per capita . . . NA

Housing & Construction

Housing Units

Total, 2008§ . . . 1,381
Single family units, attached . . . 57
Single family units, detached . . . 1,021
Multiple family units . . . 191
Mobile home units . . . 112
Occupied . . . 1,193
Vacancy rate . . . 13.6%
Median rent, 2000** . . . $395
Median SF home value, 2000** . . . $64,600

New Privately Owned Housing Units Authorized by Building Permit, 2007*

	Units	Construction Cost
Single	0	$0
Total	0	$0

Municipal Finance

(For local fiscal year ended in 2006)

Revenues

Total . . . $3,166,458
Taxes . . . 1,096,182
Special benefits assessment . . . 16,777
Licenses & permits . . . 25,407
Fines & forfeitures . . . 11,934
Revenues from use of money & property . . . 86,007
Intergovernmental . . . 480,166
Service charges . . . 1,077,057
Other revenues . . . 372,928
Other financing sources . . . 0

Expenditures

Total . . . $3,422,701
General government . . . 246,992
Public safety . . . 1,158,561
Transportation . . . 397,149
Community development . . . 87,819
Health . . . 741,566
Culture & leisure . . . 87,892
Other . . . 0

Local School District

(Data from School year 2007-08 except as noted)

Modoc Joint Unified
906 West Fourth St
Alturas, CA 96101
(530) 233-7201

Superintendent . . . Lane Bates
Grade plan . . . K-12
Number of schools . . . 10
Enrollment . . . 1,417
High school graduates, 2006-07 . . . 136
Dropout rate . . . 4.1%
Pupil/teacher ratio . . . 18.7
Average class size . . . 14.8
Students per computer . . . 4.5
Classrooms with internet . . . 62
Avg. Daily Attendance (ADA) . . . 881
Cost per ADA . . . $9,387
Avg. Teacher Salary . . . $50,398

California Achievement Tests 6th ed., 2008

(Pct scoring at or above 50th National Percentile Rank)

	Math	Reading	Language
Grade 3	67%	54%	63%
Grade 7	55%	65%	56%

Academic Performance Index, 2008

Number of students tested . . . 742
Number of valid scores . . . 701
2007 API (base) . . . 737
2008 API (growth) . . . 746

SAT Testing, 2006-07

Enrollment, Grade 12 . . . 149
Number taking test . . . 29
percent taking test . . . 19.5%
percent with total score 1,500+ . . . 13.40%

Average Scores:

Math	Verbal	Writing	Total
503	518	491	1,512

Federal No Child Left Behind, 2008

(Adequate Yearly Progress standards met)

	Participation Rate	Pct Proficient
ELA	Yes	Yes
Math	Yes	Yes

API criteria . . . Yes
Graduation rate . . . Yes
criteria met/possible . . . 18/18

Other school districts for this city

(see Appendix E for information on these districts)

None

See Introduction for an explanation of all data sources.

Demographics & Socio-Economic Characteristics

(2000 Decennial Census, except as noted)

Population

1990* . . . 196
2000 . . . 196
Male . . . 94
Female . . . 102
Jan. 2008 (estimate)$^{\$}$ . . . 208
Persons per sq. mi. of land . . . 693.3

Race & Hispanic Origin, 2000

Race
White . . . 178
Black/African American . . . 0
North American Native . . . 2
Asian . . . 0
Pacific Islander . . . 0
Other Race . . . 8
Two or more races . . . 8
Hispanic origin, total . . . 18
Mexican . . . 14
Puerto Rican . . . 1
Cuban . . . 0
Other Hispanic . . . 3

Age & Nativity, 2000

Under 5 years . . . 10
18 years and over . . . 158
65 years and over . . . 26
85 years and over . . . 5
Median Age . . . 41.5
Native-born . . . 201
Foreign-born . . . 0

Educational Attainment, 2000

Population 25 years and over . . . 142
Less than 9th grade . . . 0.0%
High school grad or higher . . . 95.8%
Bachelor's degree or higher . . . 28.9%
Graduate degree . . . 12.7%

Income & Poverty, 1999

Per capita income . . . $17,963
Median household income . . . $45,625
Median family income . . . $39,861
Persons in poverty . . . 23.5%
H'holds receiving public assistance . . . 4
H'holds receiving social security . . . 23

Households, 2000

Total households . . . 85
With persons under 18 . . . 23
With persons over 65 . . . 23
Family households . . . 55
Single person households . . . 23
Persons per household . . . 2.31
Persons per family . . . 2.76

Household Population, 2008$^{\$\$}$

Persons living in households . . . 208
Persons living in group quarters . . . 0
Persons per household . . . 2.1

Labor & Employment

Total civilian labor force, 2008$^{\$\$}$ . . . 160
Unemployment rate, 2008 . . . 4.4%
Total civilian labor force, 2000 . . . 128

Employed persons 16 years and over by occupation, 2000

Managers & professionals . . . 37
Service occupations . . . 35
Sales & office occupations . . . 38
Farming, fishing & forestry . . . 2
Construction & maintenance . . . 4
Production & transportation . . . 9
Self-employed persons . . . 26

* US Census Bureau
** 2000 Decennial Census
§ California Department of Finance
§§ California Employment Development Dept

General Information

City of Amador City
PO Box 200
Amador, CA 95601
209-267-0682

Website . . . www.amadorcity.net
Elevation . . . NA
Land Area (sq. miles) . . . 0.3
Water Area (sq. miles) . . . 0
Year of Incorporation . . . 1915
Government type . . . General law
Sales tax rate . . . 8.75%

Voters & Officials

Registered Voters, October 2008

Total . . . 132
Democrats . . . 44
Republicans . . . 54
Declined to state . . . 26

Legislative Districts

US Congressional . . . 3
State Senatorial . . . 1
State Assembly . . . 10

Local Officials, 2009

Mayor . . . Richard Lynch
Manager/Admin . . . NA
City Clerk . . . Joyce Davidson
Attorney . . . Lawrence Lacey
Finance Dir . . . Janet Spencer
Public Works . . . NA
Planning/Dev Dir . . . NA
Building . . . NA
Police Chief . . . (County)
Emergency/Fire Dir . . . NA

Public Safety

Number of officers, 2007 . . . NA
Violent crimes, 2007 . . . NA
Property crimes, 2007 . . . NA
Arson, 2007 . . . NA

Public Library

Amador City Branch
Amador County Library System
14203 Highway 49
Amador City, CA 95601
209-223-6400

County Librarian . . . Laura Einstadter

Library system statistics, FY 2007

Population served . . . 38,435
Internet terminals . . . 18
Annual users . . . 74,880

Per capita:

Operating income . . . $24.71
percent from local government . . . 94.0%
Operating expenditure . . . $20.44
Total materials . . . 2.18
Print holdings . . . 1.97
Visits per capita . . . 2.04

Housing & Construction

Housing Units

Total, 2008$^{\$}$ . . . 103
Single family units, attached . . . 12
Single family units, detached . . . 84
Multiple family units . . . 7
Mobile home units . . . 0
Occupied . . . 97
Vacancy rate . . . 5.8%
Median rent, 2000** . . . $729
Median SF home value, 2000** . . . $160,700

New Privately Owned Housing Units Authorized by Building Permit, 2007*

	Units	Construction Cost
Single	0	$0
Total	0	$0

Municipal Finance

(For local fiscal year ended in 2006)

Revenues

Total . . . $304,938
Taxes . . . 57,433
Special benefits assessment . . . 0
Licenses & permits . . . 5,172
Fines & forfeitures . . . 168
Revenues from use of money & property . . . 34,472
Intergovernmental . . . 128,269
Service charges . . . 77,783
Other revenues . . . 1,641
Other financing sources . . . 0

Expenditures

Total . . . $269,665
General government . . . 1,197
Public safety . . . 128,883
Transportation . . . 72,124
Community development . . . 7,692
Health . . . 57,595
Culture & leisure . . . 2,174
Other . . . 0

Local School District

(Data from School year 2007-08 except as noted)

Amador County Unified
217 Rex Ave
Jackson, CA 95642
(209) 223-1750

Superintendent . . . Dick Glock
Grade plan . . . K-12
Number of schools . . . 12
Enrollment . . . 4,362
High school graduates, 2006-07 . . . 373
Dropout rate . . . 3.8%
Pupil/teacher ratio . . . 22.8
Average class size . . . 23.3
Students per computer . . . 3.9
Classrooms with internet . . . 308
Avg. Daily Attendance (ADA) . . . 4,219
Cost per ADA . . . $6,964
Avg. Teacher Salary . . . $60,591

California Achievement Tests 6th ed., 2008

(Pct scoring at or above 50th National Percentile Rank)

	Math	Reading	Language
Grade 3	59%	52%	54%
Grade 7	54%	60%	55%

Academic Performance Index, 2008

Number of students tested . . . 3,491
Number of valid scores . . . 3,322
2007 API (base) . . . 751
2008 API (growth) . . . 769

SAT Testing, 2006-07

Enrollment, Grade 12 . . . 442
Number taking test . . . 103
percent taking test . . . 23.3%
percent with total score 1,500+ . . . 13.60%

Average Scores:

Math	Verbal	Writing	Total
519	520	516	1,555

Federal No Child Left Behind, 2008

(Adequate Yearly Progress standards met)

	Participation Rate	Pct Proficient
ELA	Yes	No
Math	Yes	No

API criteria . . . Yes
Graduation rate . . . Yes
criteria met/possible . . . 26/22

Other school districts for this city

(see Appendix E for information on these districts)

None

See Introduction for an explanation of all data sources.

Demographics & Socio-Economic Characteristics

(2000 Decennial Census, except as noted)

Population

1990*	NA
2000	9,774
Male	4,814
Female	4,960
Jan. 2008 (estimate)§	16,293
Persons per sq. mi. of land	3,973.9

Race & Hispanic Origin, 2000

Race	
White	5,786
Black/African American	717
North American Native	80
Asian	1,579
Pacific Islander	126
Other Race	845
Two or more races	641
Hispanic origin, total	1,731
Mexican	1,280
Puerto Rican	50
Cuban	15
Other Hispanic	386

Age & Nativity, 2000

Under 5 years	603
18 years and over	6,998
65 years and over	1,306
85 years and over	125
Median Age	36.9
Native-born	7,764
Foreign-born	2,049

Educational Attainment, 2000

Population 25 years and over	6,207
Less than 9th grade	7.2%
High school grad or higher	79.0%
Bachelor's degree or higher	16.7%
Graduate degree	4.0%

Income & Poverty, 1999

Per capita income	$18,440
Median household income	$52,105
Median family income	$61,536
Persons in poverty	8.7%
H'holds receiving public assistance	110
H'holds receiving social security	889

Households, 2000

Total households	3,209
With persons under 18	1,397
With persons over 65	918
Family households	2,452
Single person households	600
Persons per household	3.00
Persons per family	3.40

Household Population, 2008§§

Persons living in households	16,159
Persons living in group quarters	134
Persons per household	2.9

Labor & Employment

Total civilian labor force, 2008§§	5,700
Unemployment rate, 2008	8.5%
Total civilian labor force, 2000	4,525

Employed persons 16 years and over by occupation, 2000

Managers & professionals	1,089
Service occupations	704
Sales & office occupations	1,192
Farming, fishing & forestry	31
Construction & maintenance	604
Production & transportation	579
Self-employed persons	257

* US Census Bureau
** 2000 Decennial Census
§ California Department of Finance
§§ California Employment Development Dept

General Information

City of American Canyon
300 Crawford Way
American Canyon, CA 94503
707-647-4360

Website	www.ci.american-canyon.ca.us
Elevation	NA
Land Area (sq. miles)	4.1
Water Area (sq. miles)	0
Year of Incorporation	1992
Government type	General law
Sales tax rate	8.75%

Voters & Officials

Registered Voters, October 2008

Total	8,251
Democrats	4,390
Republicans	1,638
Declined to state	1,883

Legislative Districts

US Congressional	1
State Senatorial	2
State Assembly	7

Local Officials, 2009

Mayor	Leon Garcia
Manager	Richard Ramirez
City Clerk	Dorothy Roadman
Attorney	William Ross
Finance Dir	Barry Whitley
Public Works	Charlie Beck (Int)
Planning/Dev Dir	Brent Cooper
Building	NA
Police Chief	Brian Banducci
Emergency/Fire Dir	Glen Weeks

Public Safety

Number of officers, 2007	NA
Violent crimes, 2007	51
Property crimes, 2007	433
Arson, 2007	2

Public Library

American Canyon Library
Napa City/County Library
3421 Broadway/Hwy 29, librAddr2
American Canyon, CA 94503
707-644-1136

County Library Dir	Danis Kreimeier

Library system statistics, FY 2007

Population served	129,976
Internet terminals	58
Annual users	NA

Per capita:

Operating income	$50.32
percent from local government	88.9%
Operating expenditure	$45.25
Total materials	1.58
Print holdings	1.37
Visits per capita	3.16

Housing & Construction

Housing Units

Total, 2008§	5,591
Single family units, attached	23
Single family units, detached	4,444
Multiple family units	345
Mobile home units	779
Occupied	5,481
Vacancy rate	2.0%
Median rent, 2000**	$924
Median SF home value, 2000**	$177,600

New Privately Owned Housing Units Authorized by Building Permit, 2007*

	Units	Construction Cost
Single	40	$15,039,438
Total	40	$15,039,438

Municipal Finance

(For local fiscal year ended in 2006)

Revenues

Total	$29,363,917
Taxes	11,679,453
Special benefits assessment	0
Licenses & permits	814,930
Fines & forfeitures	86,040
Revenues from use of money & property	1,528,624
Intergovernmental	1,573,516
Service charges	11,822,615
Other revenues	1,858,739
Other financing sources	0

Expenditures

Total	$21,725,137
General government	3,222,349
Public safety	3,454,704
Transportation	2,869,693
Community development	3,474,417
Health	2,856,570
Culture & leisure	2,622,298
Other	0

Local School District

(Data from School year 2007-08 except as noted)

Napa Valley Unified
2425 Jefferson St
Napa, CA 94558
(707) 253-3715

Superintendent	John Glaser
Grade plan	K-12
Number of schools	37
Enrollment	17,552
High school graduates, 2006-07	1,092
Dropout rate	3.6%
Pupil/teacher ratio	19.1
Average class size	24.6
Students per computer	4.2
Classrooms with internet	844
Avg. Daily Attendance (ADA)	14,837
Cost per ADA	$8,130
Avg. Teacher Salary	$66,178

California Achievement Tests 6th ed., 2008

(Pct scoring at or above 50th National Percentile Rank)

	Math	Reading	Language
Grade 3	56%	41%	50%
Grade 7	56%	50%	51%

Academic Performance Index, 2008

Number of students tested	13,136
Number of valid scores	12,469
2007 API (base)	755
2008 API (growth)	765

SAT Testing, 2006-07

Enrollment, Grade 12	1,328
Number taking test	406
percent taking test	30.6%
percent with total score 1,500+	18.70%

Average Scores:

Math	Verbal	Writing	Total
538	521	515	1,574

Federal No Child Left Behind, 2008

(Adequate Yearly Progress standards met)

	Participation Rate	Pct Proficient
ELA	Yes	No
Math	Yes	No

API criteria	Yes
Graduation rate	Yes
# criteria met/possible	42/39

Other school districts for this city

(see Appendix E for information on these districts)

None

See Introduction for an explanation of all data sources.

Demographics & Socio-Economic Characteristics†

(2007 American Community Survey, except as noted)

Population
1990* 266,406
2007 342,856
  Male 166,742
  Female 176,114
Jan. 2008 (estimate)§ 346,823
  Persons per sq. mi. of land 7,092.5

Race & Hispanic Origin, 2007
Race
  White 222,471
  Black/African American 6,847
  North American Native 1,213
  Asian 42,511
  Pacific Islander 1,166
  Other Race 59,760
  Two or more races 8,888
Hispanic origin, total 186,794
  Mexican 161,888
  Puerto Rican 1,183
  Cuban 2,244
  Other Hispanic 21,479

Age & Nativity, 2007
Under 5 years 26,850
18 years and over 242,566
65 years and over 32,229
85 years and over 3,419
  Median Age 32.5
Native-born 209,214
Foreign-born 133,642

Educational Attainment, 2007
Population 25 years and over 209,645
Less than 9th grade 16.9%
High school grad or higher 71.7%
Bachelor's degree or higher 21.8%
Graduate degree 6.8%

Income & Poverty, 2007
Per capita income $22,490
Median household income $57,059
Median family income $60,552
Persons in poverty 12.5%
H'holds receiving public assistance 2,616
H'holds receiving social security 20,938

Households, 2007
Total households 99,382
  With persons under 18 45,139
  With persons over 65 21,988
  Family households 75,169
  Single person households 18,376
Persons per household 3.42
Persons per family 3.86

Household Population, 2008§§
Persons living in households 343,027
Persons living in group quarters 3,796
Persons per household 3.5

Labor & Employment
Total civilian labor force, 2008§§ 178,100
  Unemployment rate, 2008 .... 6.8%
Total civilian labor force, 2000* 152,255

Employed persons 16 years and over by occupation, 2007
  Managers & professionals 40,215
  Service occupations 30,934
  Sales & office occupations 45,836
  Farming, fishing & forestry 132
  Construction & maintenance 17,287
  Production & transportation 26,973
  Self-employed persons 9,650

† see Appendix D for 2000 Decennial Census Data
* US Census Bureau
** 2007 American Community Survey
§ California Department of Finance
§§ California Employment Development Dept

General Information

City of Anaheim
200 S Anaheim Blvd
Anaheim, CA 92805
714-765-5166

Website .... www.anaheim.net
Elevation .... 160 ft.
Land Area (sq. miles) 48.9
Water Area (sq. miles) 1.5
Year of Incorporation 1876
Government type .... Chartered
Sales tax rate 8.75%

Voters & Officials

Registered Voters, October 2008
Total 143,169
  Democrats 52,855
  Republicans 58,298
  Declined to state 26,621

Legislative Districts
US Congressional 40, 42, 47
State Senatorial 29, 33, 34
State Assembly 60, 67-69, 71

Local Officials, 2009
Mayor .... Curt Pringle
Manager .... David Morgan
City Clerk .... Linda Andal
Attorney .... Jack White
Finance Dir .... William Sweeney
Public Works .... Natalie Meeks
Planning/Dev Dir .... Sheri Vander Dussen
Building .... NA
Police Chief .... John Welter
Emergency/Fire Dir .... Roger Smith

Public Safety

Number of officers, 2007 412
Violent crimes, 2007 1,423
Property crimes, 2007 8,798
Arson, 2007 41

Public Library

Central Library
Anaheim Public Library System
500 W Broadway
Anaheim, CA 92805
714-765-1810

City Librarian .... Carol Stone

Library system statistics, FY 2007
Population served 345,556
Internet terminals 36
  Annual users 257,089

Per capita:
Operating income $32.30
  percent from local government 92.8%
Operating expenditure $30.45
Total materials 1.79
Print holdings 1.65
Visits per capita 4.00

Housing & Construction

Housing Units
Total, 2008§ 101,791
  Single family units, attached 9,064
  Single family units, detached 43,712
  Multiple family units 44,630
  Mobile home units 4,385
  Occupied 98,985
  Vacancy rate 2.8%
Median rent, 2007** $1,188
Median SF home value, 2007** $591,100

New Privately Owned Housing Units Authorized by Building Permit, 2007*

	Units	Construction Cost
Single	35	$9,886,431
Total	875	$142,645,443

Municipal Finance

(For local fiscal year ended in 2006)

Revenues
Total $912,446,740
Taxes 266,599,671
Special benefits assessment 5,782,760
Licenses & permits 4,645,862
Fines & forfeitures 4,594,558
Revenues from use of money & property 22,342,323
Intergovernmental 100,034,380
Service charges 487,959,985
Other revenues 20,487,201
Other financing sources 0

Expenditures
Total $923,150,553
General government 47,129,188
Public safety 161,825,316
Transportation 36,371,447
Community development 103,193,378
Health 46,913,734
Culture & leisure 86,898,238
Other 0

Local School District

(Data from School year 2007-08 except as noted)

Anaheim Union High
PO Box 3520
Anaheim, CA 92803
(714) 999-3511

Superintendent .... Joseph Farley
Grade plan 7-12
Number of schools 22
Enrollment 33,343
High school graduates, 2006-07 3,668
Dropout rate 1.7%
Pupil/teacher ratio 23.7
Average class size 20.2
Students per computer 3.4
Classrooms with internet 1,839
Avg. Daily Attendance (ADA) 33,034
  Cost per ADA $8,336
Avg. Teacher Salary $79,030

California Achievement Tests 6th ed., 2008
(Pct scoring at or above 50th National Percentile Rank)

	Math	Reading	Language
Grade 3	NA	NA	NA
Grade 7	49%	43%	43%

Academic Performance Index, 2008
Number of students tested 27,739
Number of valid scores 26,586
2007 API (base) 715
2008 API (growth) 729

SAT Testing, 2006-07
Enrollment, Grade 12 4,777
Number taking test 1,591
  percent taking test 33.3%
  percent with total score 1,500+ 15.00%

Average Scores:

Math	Verbal	Writing	Total
519	485	489	1,493

Federal No Child Left Behind, 2008
(Adequate Yearly Progress standards met)

	Participation Rate	Pct Proficient
ELA	Yes	No
Math	Yes	No

API criteria .... Yes
Graduation rate .... Yes
criteria met/possible 42/35

Other school districts for this city
(see Appendix E for information on these districts)
Complete list in Appendix E

See Introduction for an explanation of all data sources.

Demographics & Socio-Economic Characteristics

(2000 Decennial Census, except as noted)

Population

1990* . . . 8,299
2000 . . . 9,022
Male . . . 4,207
Female . . . 4,815
Jan. 2008 (estimate)§ . . . 10,579
Persons per sq. mi. of land . . . 1,653.0

Race & Hispanic Origin, 2000

Race
White . . . 7,805
Black/African American . . . 56
North American Native . . . 373
Asian . . . 160
Pacific Islander . . . 11
Other Race . . . 210
Two or more races . . . 407
Hispanic origin, total . . . 659
Mexican . . . 537
Puerto Rican . . . 17
Cuban . . . 2
Other Hispanic . . . 103

Age & Nativity, 2000

Under 5 years . . . 743
18 years and over . . . 6,175
65 years and over . . . 1,251
85 years and over . . . 201
Median Age . . . 32.2
Native-born . . . 8,637
Foreign-born . . . 423

Educational Attainment, 2000

Population 25 years and over . . . 5,339
Less than 9th grade . . . 6.4%
High school grad or higher . . . 76.0%
Bachelor's degree or higher . . . 7.0%
Graduate degree . . . 1.7%

Income & Poverty, 1999

Per capita income . . . $11,744
Median household income . . . $24,558
Median family income . . . $29,259
Persons in poverty . . . 27.9%
H'holds receiving public assistance . . . 413
H'holds receiving social security . . . 891

Households, 2000

Total households . . . 3,372
With persons under 18 . . . 1,467
With persons over 65 . . . 873
Family households . . . 2,320
Single person households . . . 895
Persons per household . . . 2.64
Persons per family . . . 3.14

Household Population, 2008§§

Persons living in households . . . 10,461
Persons living in group quarters . . . 118
Persons per household . . . 2.6

Labor & Employment

Total civilian labor force, 2008§§ . . . 4,400
Unemployment rate, 2008 . . . 12.2%
Total civilian labor force, 2000 . . . 3,813

Employed persons 16 years and over by occupation, 2000

Managers & professionals . . . 702
Service occupations . . . 837
Sales & office occupations . . . 971
Farming, fishing & forestry . . . 20
Construction & maintenance . . . 314
Production & transportation . . . 567
Self-employed persons . . . 236

* US Census Bureau
** 2000 Decennial Census
§ California Department of Finance
§§ California Employment Development Dept

General Information

City of Anderson
1887 Howard St
Anderson, CA 96007
530-378-6626

Website . . . www.ci.anderson.ca.us
Elevation . . . 430 ft.
Land Area (sq. miles) . . . 6.4
Water Area (sq. miles) . . . 0.2
Year of Incorporation . . . 1956
Government type . . . General law
Sales tax rate . . . 8.25%

Voters & Officials

Registered Voters, October 2008

Total . . . 4,170
Democrats . . . 1,500
Republicans . . . 1,606
Declined to state . . . 848

Legislative Districts

US Congressional . . . 2
State Senatorial . . . 4
State Assembly . . . 2

Local Officials, 2009

Mayor . . . Butch Schaefer
Manager . . . Scott Morgan
City Clerk . . . Scott Morgan
Attorney . . . Michael C. Fitzpatrick
Finance Dir . . . Dana Shigley
Public Works . . . Richard Barchus
Planning/Dev Dir . . . John Stokes
Building . . . NA
Police Chief . . . Dale Webb
Emergency/Fire Dir . . . Joe Piccinini

Public Safety

Number of officers, 2007 . . . 20
Violent crimes, 2007 . . . 45
Property crimes, 2007 . . . 438
Arson, 2007 . . . 3

Public Library

Anderson Library
Shasta County Library System
3200 W Center St
Anderson, CA 96007
530-365-7685

Branch Librarian . . . Martee Boban

Library system statistics, FY 2007

Population served . . . 181,401
Internet terminals . . . 8
Annual users . . . 15,226

Per capita:

Operating income . . . $9.89
percent from local government . . . 96.3%
Operating expenditure . . . $12.63
Total materials . . . 1.23
Print holdings . . . 1.12
Visits per capita . . . NA

Housing & Construction

Housing Units

Total, 2008§ . . . 4,203
Single family units, attached . . . 213
Single family units, detached . . . 2,700
Multiple family units . . . 1,111
Mobile home units . . . 179
Occupied . . . 3,960
Vacancy rate . . . 5.8%
Median rent, 2000** . . . $478
Median SF home value, 2000** . . . $86,900

New Privately Owned Housing Units Authorized by Building Permit, 2007*

	Units	Construction Cost
Single	20	$3,415,297
Total	20	$3,415,297

Municipal Finance

(For local fiscal year ended in 2006)

Revenues

Total . . . $10,826,514
Taxes . . . 4,161,213
Special benefits assessment . . . 164,562
Licenses & permits . . . 217,070
Fines & forfeitures . . . 130,787
Revenues from use of money & property . . . 370,289
Intergovernmental . . . 2,835,439
Service charges . . . 2,604,648
Other revenues . . . 270,450
Other financing sources . . . 72,056

Expenditures

Total . . . $10,284,898
General government . . . 841,934
Public safety . . . 3,006,557
Transportation . . . 1,361,319
Community development . . . 1,453,760
Health . . . 1,066,913
Culture & leisure . . . 1,341,303
Other . . . 42,273

Local School District

(Data from School year 2007-08 except as noted)

Anderson Union High
1469 Ferry St
Anderson, CA 96007
(530) 378-0568

Superintendent . . . Tim Azevedo
Grade plan . . . 9-12
Number of schools . . . 7
Enrollment . . . 2,195
High school graduates, 2006-07 . . . 465
Dropout rate . . . 4.3%
Pupil/teacher ratio . . . 22.5
Average class size . . . 19.5
Students per computer . . . 1.3
Classrooms with internet . . . 132
Avg. Daily Attendance (ADA) . . . 1,795
Cost per ADA . . . $9,500
Avg. Teacher Salary . . . $60,935

California Achievement Tests 6th ed., 2008

(Pct scoring at or above 50th National Percentile Rank)

	Math	Reading	Language
Grade 3	NA	NA	NA
Grade 7	NA	NA	NA

Academic Performance Index, 2008

Number of students tested . . . 1,592
Number of valid scores . . . 1,456
2007 API (base) . . . 717
2008 API (growth) . . . 730

SAT Testing, 2006-07

Enrollment, Grade 12 . . . 587
Number taking test . . . 101
percent taking test . . . 17.2%
percent with total score 1,500+ . . . 8.20%

Average Scores:

Math	Verbal	Writing	Total
514	499	490	1,503

Federal No Child Left Behind, 2008

(Adequate Yearly Progress standards met)

	Participation Rate	Pct Proficient
ELA	Yes	Yes
Math	Yes	Yes

API criteria . . . Yes
Graduation rate . . . Yes
\# criteria met/possible . . . 14/14

Other school districts for this city

(see Appendix E for information on these districts)

Cascade Union Elem, Happy Valley Union Elem, Pacheco Union Elem

See Introduction for an explanation of all data sources.

Demographics & Socio-Economic Characteristics

(2000 Decennial Census, except as noted)

Population

1990* . . . 2,409
2000 . . . 3,004
Male . . . 1,443
Female . . . 1,561
Jan. 2008 (estimate)§ . . . 3,593
Persons per sq. mi. of land . . . 1,197.7

Race & Hispanic Origin, 2000

Race
White . . . 2,798
Black/African American . . . 6
North American Native . . . 55
Asian . . . 14
Pacific Islander . . . 1
Other Race . . . 43
Two or more races . . . 87
Hispanic origin, total . . . 243
Mexican . . . 197
Puerto Rican . . . 5
Cuban . . . 0
Other Hispanic . . . 41

Age & Nativity, 2000

Under 5 years . . . 156
18 years and over . . . 2,275
65 years and over . . . 547
85 years and over . . . 62
Median Age . . . 41.4
Native-born . . . 2,869
Foreign-born . . . 131

Educational Attainment, 2000

Population 25 years and over . . . 2,094
Less than 9th grade . . . 4.8%
High school grad or higher . . . 85.3%
Bachelor's degree or higher . . . 16.3%
Graduate degree . . . 5.7%

Income & Poverty, 1999

Per capita income . . . $19,599
Median household income . . . $33,371
Median family income . . . $48,125
Persons in poverty . . . 12.9%
H'holds receiving public assistance . . . 27
H'holds receiving social security . . . 427

Households, 2000

Total households . . . 1,286
With persons under 18 . . . 392
With persons over 65 . . . 407
Family households . . . 856
Single person households . . . 373
Persons per household . . . 2.34
Persons per family . . . 2.82

Household Population, 2008§§

Persons living in households . . . 3,593
Persons living in group quarters . . . 0
Persons per household . . . 2.2

Labor & Employment

Total civilian labor force, 2008§§ . . . 1,650
Unemployment rate, 2008 . . . 9.9%
Total civilian labor force, 2000 . . . 1,383

Employed persons 16 years and over by occupation, 2000

Managers & professionals . . . 395
Service occupations . . . 239
Sales & office occupations . . . 342
Farming, fishing & forestry . . . 4
Construction & maintenance . . . 160
Production & transportation . . . 121
Self-employed persons . . . 160

* US Census Bureau
** 2000 Decennial Census
§ California Department of Finance
§§ California Employment Development Dept

General Information

City of Angels Camp
PO Box 667
Angels Camp, CA 95222
209-736-2181

Website . . . www.angelscamp.gov
Elevation . . . NA
Land Area (sq. miles) . . . 3.0
Water Area (sq. miles) . . . 0
Year of Incorporation . . . 1912
Government type . . . General law
Sales tax rate . . . 8.25%

Voters & Officials

Registered Voters, October 2008

Total . . . 2,324
Democrats . . . 800
Republicans . . . 1,012
Declined to state . . . 367

Legislative Districts

US Congressional . . . 3
State Senatorial . . . 1
State Assembly . . . 25

Local Officials, 2009

Mayor . . . Jack Lynch
City Administrator . . . Timothy Shearer
City Clerk . . . Mary Kelly
Attorney . . . Richard Matranga
Finance Dir . . . Melisa Ralston
Public Works . . . Rick Soracco
Planning Dir . . . David Hanham
Building . . . Bruce Silva
Police Chief . . . Dale Mendenhall
Fire Chief . . . Scott Kenley

Public Safety

Number of officers, 2007 . . . 9
Violent crimes, 2007 . . . 20
Property crimes, 2007 . . . 74
Arson, 2007 . . . 3

Public Library

Angels Camp Branch
Calaveras County Library System
426 N Main St
Angels Camp, CA 95222
209-736-2198

Branch Librarian . . . Diana Lewis

Library system statistics, FY 2007

Population served . . . 46,028
Internet terminals . . . 20
Annual users . . . 25,550

Per capita:

Operating income . . . $13.72
percent from local government . . . 87.3%
Operating expenditure . . . $13.72
Total materials . . . 2.28
Print holdings . . . 2.02
Visits per capita . . . 1.61

Housing & Construction

Housing Units

Total, 2008§ . . . 1,812
Single family units, attached . . . 67
Single family units, detached . . . 1,294
Multiple family units . . . 235
Mobile home units . . . 216
Occupied . . . 1,638
Vacancy rate . . . 9.6%
Median rent, 2000** . . . $565
Median SF home value, 2000** . . . $146,400

New Privately Owned Housing Units Authorized by Building Permit, 2007*

	Units	Construction Cost
Single	16	$4,254,015
Total	16	$4,254,015

Municipal Finance

(For local fiscal year ended in 2006)

Revenues

Total . . . $8,648,709
Taxes . . . 2,291,712
Special benefits assessment . . . 176,790
Licenses & permits . . . 251,508
Fines & forfeitures . . . 25,732
Revenues from use of money & property . . . 335,071
Intergovernmental . . . 2,317,575
Service charges . . . 3,236,076
Other revenues . . . 14,245
Other financing sources . . . 0

Expenditures

Total . . . $8,294,423
General government . . . 352,599
Public safety . . . 1,894,064
Transportation . . . 853,357
Community development . . . 541,956
Health . . . 3,493,496
Culture & leisure . . . 198,278
Other . . . 0

Local School District

(Data from School year 2007-08 except as noted)

Bret Harte Union High
PO Box 7000
Angels Camp, CA 95221
(209) 736-8340

Superintendent . . . Michael Chimente
Grade plan . . . 9-12
Number of schools . . . 3
Enrollment . . . 915
High school graduates, 2006-07 . . . 229
Dropout rate . . . 0.6%
Pupil/teacher ratio . . . 18.0
Average class size . . . 20.9
Students per computer . . . 2.7
Classrooms with internet . . . 51
Avg. Daily Attendance (ADA) . . . 867
Cost per ADA . . . $11,719
Avg. Teacher Salary . . . $65,975

California Achievement Tests 6th ed., 2008

(Pct scoring at or above 50th National Percentile Rank)

	Math	Reading	Language
Grade 3	NA	NA	NA
Grade 7	NA	NA	NA

Academic Performance Index, 2008

Number of students tested . . . 645
Number of valid scores . . . 613
2007 API (base) . . . 755
2008 API (growth) . . . 762

SAT Testing, 2006-07

Enrollment, Grade 12 . . . 235
Number taking test . . . 87
percent taking test . . . 37.0%
percent with total score 1,500+ . . . 20.90%

Average Scores:

Math	Verbal	Writing	Total
519	519	516	1,554

Federal No Child Left Behind, 2008

(Adequate Yearly Progress standards met)

	Participation Rate	Pct Proficient
ELA	No	Yes
Math	Yes	Yes

API criteria . . . Yes
Graduation rate . . . Yes
criteria met/possible . . . 14/13

Other school districts for this city

(see Appendix E for information on these districts)

Mark Twain Union Elem

See Introduction for an explanation of all data sources.

Demographics & Socio-Economic Characteristics†

(2007 American Community Survey, except as noted)

Population

1990* 62,195
2007 104,426
Male 50,158
Female 54,268
Jan. 2008 (estimate)§ 100,361
Persons per sq. mi. of land 3,730.9

Race & Hispanic Origin, 2007

Race
White 49,180
Black/African American 20,332
North American Native 863
Asian 7,501
Pacific Islander 711
Other Race 19,647
Two or more races 6,192
Hispanic origin, total 27,456
Mexican 19,378
Puerto Rican 2,003
Cuban 41
Other Hispanic 6,034

Age & Nativity, 2007

Under 5 years 8,218
18 years and over 72,120
65 years and over 7,794
85 years and over 951
Median Age 32.7
Native-born 83,907
Foreign-born 20,519

Educational Attainment, 2007

Population 25 years and over 60,411
Less than 9th grade 5.0%
High school grad or higher 85.7%
Bachelor's degree or higher 20.3%
Graduate degree 5.8%

Income & Poverty, 2007

Per capita income $26,091
Median household income $70,285
Median family income $70,903
Persons in poverty 12.4%
H'holds receiving public assistance 1,141
H'holds receiving social security 7,269

Households, 2007

Total households 32,067
With persons under 18 15,804
With persons over 65 5,310
Family households 26,338
Single person households 4,429
Persons per household 3.26
Persons per family 3.55

Household Population, 2008§§

Persons living in households 99,945
Persons living in group quarters 416
Persons per household 3.0

Labor & Employment

Total civilian labor force, 2008§§ 49,400
Unemployment rate, 2008 .... 7.0%
Total civilian labor force, 2000* 43,893

Employed persons 16 years and over by occupation, 2007

Managers & professionals 13,279
Service occupations 6,669
Sales & office occupations 15,249
Farming, fishing & forestry 0
Construction & maintenance 5,839
Production & transportation 4,338
Self-employed persons 2,775

† see Appendix D for 2000 Decennial Census Data
* US Census Bureau
** 2007 American Community Survey
§ California Department of Finance
§§ California Employment Development Dept

General Information

City of Antioch
3rd and H Streets
Antioch, CA 94509
925-779-7000

Website .... www.ci.antioch.ca.us
Elevation .... 25 ft.
Land Area (sq. miles) 26.9
Water Area (sq. miles) 0.6
Year of Incorporation 1872
Government type .... General law
Sales tax rate 9.25%

Voters & Officials

Registered Voters, October 2008

Total 43,459
Democrats 24,062
Republicans 9,384
Declined to state 8,293

Legislative Districts

US Congressional 10
State Senatorial 7
State Assembly 11

Local Officials, 2009

Mayor .... James D. Davis
Manager .... Jim Jakel
City Clerk .... Jolene Martin
Attorney .... Lynn Tracy Nerland
Finance Dir .... Dawn Merchant
Public Works .... Ron Bernal
Planning/Dev Dir .... Joseph Brandt
Building .... NA
Police Chief .... Jim Hyde
Fire/Emergency Mgmt .... NA

Public Safety

Number of officers, 2007 118
Violent crimes, 2007 860
Property crimes, 2007 3,122
Arson, 2007 50

Public Library

Antioch Library
Contra Costa County Library System
501 W 18th St
Antioch, CA 94509
925-757-9224

Branch Librarian .... P. Chan

Library system statistics, FY 2007

Population served 938,513
Internet terminals 324
Annual users 670,618

Per capita:

Operating income $27.05
percent from local government 82.0%
Operating expenditure $27.82
Total materials 1.57
Print holdings 1.41
Visits per capita 3.65

Housing & Construction

Housing Units

Total, 2008§ 33,936
Single family units, attached 2,205
Single family units, detached 25,601
Multiple family units 5,861
Mobile home units 269
Occupied 33,059
Vacancy rate 2.6%
Median rent, 2007** $1,319
Median SF home value, 2007** $494,500

New Privately Owned Housing Units Authorized by Building Permit, 2007*

	Units	Construction Cost
Single	158	$44,654,893
Total	158	$44,654,893

Municipal Finance

(For local fiscal year ended in 2006)

Revenues

Total $85,533,798
Taxes 32,446,750
Special benefits assessment 2,698,717
Licenses & permits 1,851,583
Fines & forfeitures 375,963
Revenues from use of money & property 2,726,607
Intergovernmental 8,288,387
Service charges 30,772,085
Other revenues 6,373,706
Other financing sources 0

Expenditures

Total $76,479,426
General government 6,861,790
Public safety 23,784,897
Transportation 8,983,804
Community development 9,187,626
Health 2,118,726
Culture & leisure 7,816,170
Other 0

Local School District

(Data from School year 2007-08 except as noted)

Antioch Unified
510 G St
Antioch, CA 94509
(925) 706-4100

Superintendent .... Deborah Sims
Grade plan K-12
Number of schools 26
Enrollment 20,086
High school graduates, 2006-07 1,279
Dropout rate 8.1%
Pupil/teacher ratio 20.7
Average class size 27.5
Students per computer 5.0
Classrooms with internet 927
Avg. Daily Attendance (ADA) 18,934
Cost per ADA $7,448
Avg. Teacher Salary $61,953

California Achievement Tests 6th ed., 2008

(Pct scoring at or above 50th National Percentile Rank)

	Math	Reading	Language
Grade 3	47%	30%	39%
Grade 7	44%	41%	40%

Academic Performance Index, 2008

Number of students tested 14,984
Number of valid scores 13,987
2007 API (base) 716
2008 API (growth) 712

SAT Testing, 2006-07

Enrollment, Grade 12 1,813
Number taking test 431
percent taking test 23.8%
percent with total score 1,500+ 9.60%

Average Scores:

Math	Verbal	Writing	Total
492	482	472	1,446

Federal No Child Left Behind, 2008

(Adequate Yearly Progress standards met)

	Participation Rate	Pct Proficient
ELA	Yes	No
Math	Yes	No

API criteria .... Yes
Graduation rate .... No
\# criteria met/possible 46/39

Other school districts for this city

(see Appendix E for information on these districts)

None

See Introduction for an explanation of all data sources.

Demographics & Socio-Economic Characteristics†

(2007 American Community Survey, except as noted)

Population

1990* ... 46,079
2007 ... 69,835
Male ... 33,119
Female ... 36,716
Jan. 2008 (estimate)§ ... 70,092
Persons per sq. mi. of land ... 956.2

Race & Hispanic Origin, 2007

Race
White ... 42,373
Black/African American ... 6,823
North American Native ... 1,418
Asian ... 1,099
Pacific Islander ... 101
Other Race ... 15,177
Two or more races ... 2,844
Hispanic origin, total ... 23,455
Mexican ... NA
Puerto Rican ... NA
Cuban ... NA
Other Hispanic ... NA

Age & Nativity, 2007

Under 5 years ... 4,861
18 years and over ... 48,235
65 years and over ... 9,759
85 years and over ... 572
Median Age ... 32.6
Native-born ... 61,194
Foreign-born ... 8,641

Educational Attainment, 2007

Population 25 years and over ... 42,179
Less than 9th grade ... 7.8%
High school grad or higher ... 77.8%
Bachelor's degree or higher ... 15.3%
Graduate degree ... 5.5%

Income & Poverty, 2007

Per capita income ... $21,763
Median household income ... $48,446
Median family income ... $50,720
Persons in poverty ... 18.8%
H'holds receiving public assistance ... 779
H'holds receiving social security ... 7,981

Households, 2007

Total households ... 23,784
With persons under 18 ... 9,638
With persons over 65 ... 6,620
Family households ... 17,855
Single person households ... 4,930
Persons per household ... 2.94
Persons per family ... 3.36

Household Population, 2008§§

Persons living in households ... 69,729
Persons living in group quarters ... 363
Persons per household ... 3.1

Labor & Employment

Total civilian labor force, 2008§§ ... 26,500
Unemployment rate, 2008 ... 8.8%
Total civilian labor force, 2000* ... 21,690

Employed persons 16 years and over by occupation, 2007

Managers & professionals ... NA
Service occupations ... NA
Sales & office occupations ... NA
Farming, fishing & forestry ... NA
Construction & maintenance ... NA
Production & transportation ... NA
Self-employed persons ... 2,001

† see Appendix D for 2000 Decennial Census Data
* US Census Bureau
** 2007 American Community Survey
§ California Department of Finance
§§ California Employment Development Dept

General Information

Town of Apple Valley
14955 Dale Evans Pkwy
Apple Valley, CA 92307
760-240-7000

Website ... www.applevalley.org
Elevation ... NA
Land Area (sq. miles) ... 73.3
Water Area (sq. miles) ... 0.3
Year of Incorporation ... 1988
Government type ... General law
Sales tax rate ... 8.75%

Voters & Officials

Registered Voters, October 2008

Total ... 33,920
Democrats ... 10,594
Republicans ... 16,449
Declined to state ... 5,318

Legislative Districts

US Congressional ... 41
State Senatorial ... 17
State Assembly ... 59

Local Officials, 2009

Mayor ... Rick Roelle
Manager ... Frank Robinson
City Clerk ... LaVonda Pearson
Attorney ... John Brown
Finance Dir ... William Pattison
Public Works ... Dennis Cron
Community Dev Dir ... Kenneth Henderson
Building ... Clause Stewart
Police Chief ... Bart Belknap
Fire Chief ... Doug Qualls

Public Safety

Number of officers, 2007 ... NA
Violent crimes, 2007 ... 269
Property crimes, 2007 ... 1,902
Arson, 2007 ... 16

Public Library

Apple Valley Branch Library
San Bernardino County Library System
14901 Dale Evans Pkwy
Apple Valley, CA 92307
760-247-2022

Branch Librarian ... Natalie Griffith

Library system statistics, FY 2007

Population served ... 1,177,092
Internet terminals ... 12
Annual users ... 45,343

Per capita:

Operating income ... $14.27
percent from local government ... 73.3%
Operating expenditure ... $13.86
Total materials ... 0.86
Print holdings ... 0.79
Visits per capita ... 5.83

Housing & Construction

Housing Units

Total, 2008§ ... 24,925
Single family units, attached ... 727
Single family units, detached ... 19,380
Multiple family units ... 3,775
Mobile home units ... 1,043
Occupied ... 22,841
Vacancy rate ... 8.4%
Median rent, 2007** ... $1,064
Median SF home value, 2007** ... $318,700

New Privately Owned Housing Units Authorized by Building Permit, 2007*

	Units	Construction Cost
Single	149	$23,307,984
Total	165	$24,152,342

Municipal Finance

(For local fiscal year ended in 2006)

Revenues

Total ... $55,232,774
Taxes ... 20,523,382
Special benefits assessment ... 0
Licenses & permits ... 2,897,225
Fines & forfeitures ... 197,175
Revenues from use of money & property ... 2,392,461
Intergovernmental ... 11,089,321
Service charges ... 15,118,870
Other revenues ... 3,014,340
Other financing sources ... 0

Expenditures

Total ... $49,147,611
General government ... 7,009,482
Public safety ... 8,261,042
Transportation ... 14,456,888
Community development ... 8,405,475
Health ... 8,325,271
Culture & leisure ... 2,394,709
Other ... 294,744

Local School District

(Data from School year 2007-08 except as noted)

Apple Valley Unified
22974 Bear Valley Rd
Apple Valley, CA 92308
(760) 247-8001

Superintendent ... Robert Seevers
Grade plan ... K-12
Number of schools ... 18
Enrollment ... 15,789
High school graduates, 2006-07 ... 943
Dropout rate ... 6.1%
Pupil/teacher ratio ... 24.0
Average class size ... 27.4
Students per computer ... 5.2
Classrooms with internet ... 623
Avg. Daily Attendance (ADA) ... 14,196
Cost per ADA ... $7,392
Avg. Teacher Salary ... $64,028

California Achievement Tests 6th ed., 2008

(Pct scoring at or above 50th National Percentile Rank)

	Math	Reading	Language
Grade 3	57%	40%	48%
Grade 7	45%	46%	43%

Academic Performance Index, 2008

Number of students tested ... 11,340
Number of valid scores ... 10,200
2007 API (base) ... 727
2008 API (growth) ... 744

SAT Testing, 2006-07

Enrollment, Grade 12 ... 1,175
Number taking test ... 314
percent taking test ... 26.7%
percent with total score 1,500+ ... 13.00%

Average Scores:

Math	Verbal	Writing	Total
494	499	490	1,483

Federal No Child Left Behind, 2008

(Adequate Yearly Progress standards met)

	Participation Rate	Pct Proficient
ELA	Yes	No
Math	Yes	No

API criteria ... Yes
Graduation rate ... No
\# criteria met/possible ... 34/29

Other school districts for this city

(see Appendix E for information on these districts)

None

See Introduction for an explanation of all data sources.

Demographics & Socio-Economic Characteristics

(2000 Decennial Census, except as noted)

Population

1990* . . . 48,290
2000 . . . 53,054
Male . . . 24,941
Female . . . 28,113
Jan. 2008 (estimate)§ . . . 56,491
Persons per sq. mi. of land . . . 5,135.5

Race & Hispanic Origin, 2000

Race
White . . . 24,180
Black/African American . . . 601
North American Native . . . 132
Asian . . . 24,091
Pacific Islander . . . 42
Other Race . . . 2,209
Two or more races . . . 1,799
Hispanic origin, total . . . 5,629
Mexican . . . 3,847
Puerto Rican . . . 104
Cuban . . . 182
Other Hispanic . . . 1,496

Age & Nativity, 2000

Under 5 years . . . 2,447
18 years and over . . . 40,700
65 years and over . . . 8,213
85 years and over . . . 1,176
Median Age . . . 40.5
Native-born . . . 29,877
Foreign-born . . . 23,074

Educational Attainment, 2000

Population 25 years and over . . . 36,799
Less than 9th grade . . . 4.3%
High school grad or higher . . . 89.7%
Bachelor's degree or higher . . . 44.4%
Graduate degree . . . 17.3%

Income & Poverty, 1999

Per capita income . . . $28,400
Median household income . . . $56,100
Median family income . . . $66,657
Persons in poverty . . . 7.8%
H'holds receiving public assistance . . . 405
H'holds receiving social security . . . 4,793

Households, 2000

Total households . . . 19,149
With persons under 18 . . . 7,221
With persons over 65 . . . 5,649
Family households . . . 14,143
Single person households . . . 4,274
Persons per household . . . 2.74
Persons per family . . . 3.23

Household Population, 2008§§

Persons living in households . . . 55,910
Persons living in group quarters . . . 581
Persons per household . . . 2.9

Labor & Employment

Total civilian labor force, 2008§§ . . . 28,600
Unemployment rate, 2008 . . . 4.2%
Total civilian labor force, 2000 . . . 24,501

Employed persons 16 years and over by occupation, 2000

Managers & professionals . . . 11,818
Service occupations . . . 2,052
Sales & office occupations . . . 7,449
Farming, fishing & forestry . . . 0
Construction & maintenance . . . 868
Production & transportation . . . 1,225
Self-employed persons . . . 2,515

* US Census Bureau
** 2000 Decennial Census
§ California Department of Finance
§§ California Employment Development Dept

General Information

City of Arcadia
240 W Huntington Dr
Arcadia, CA 91007
626-574-5455

Website . . . www.ci.arcadia.ca.us
Elevation . . . 485 ft.
Land Area (sq. miles) . . . 11.0
Water Area (sq. miles) . . . 0.1
Year of Incorporation . . . 1903
Government type . . . Chartered
Sales tax rate . . . 9.25%

Voters & Officials

Registered Voters, October 2008

Total . . . 29,144
Democrats . . . 8,258
Republicans . . . 11,206
Declined to state . . . 8,816

Legislative Districts

US Congressional . . . 26
State Senatorial . . . 29
State Assembly . . . 44, 59

Local Officials, 2009

Mayor . . . Robert Harbicht
City Manager . . . Donald Penman
City Clerk . . . James Barrows
Attorney . . . Stephen P. Deitsch
Admin Svcs Dir . . . Hue Quach
Public Works . . . Patrick Malloy
Development Svcs Dir . . . Jason Kruckeberg
Building . . . Don Stockham
Police Chief . . . Robert Sanderson
Fire Chief . . . Tony Trabbie

Public Safety

Number of officers, 2007 . . . 63
Violent crimes, 2007 . . . 156
Property crimes, 2007 . . . 1,704
Arson, 2007 . . . 1

Public Library

Arcadia Public Library
20 W Duarte Rd
Arcadia, CA 91006
626-821-5567

Director . . . Janet Sporleder

Library statistics, FY 2007

Population served . . . 56,556
Internet terminals . . . 207
Annual users . . . 112,939

Per capita:

Operating income . . . $50.42
percent from local government . . . 94.2%
Operating expenditure . . . $48.96
Total materials . . . 3.60
Print holdings . . . 3.41
Visits per capita . . . 10.77

Housing & Construction

Housing Units

Total, 2008§ . . . 20,304
Single family units, attached . . . 1,730
Single family units, detached . . . 11,857
Multiple family units . . . 6,691
Mobile home units . . . 26
Occupied . . . 19,469
Vacancy rate . . . 4.1%
Median rent, 2000** . . . $830
Median SF home value, 2000** . . . $393,700

New Privately Owned Housing Units Authorized by Building Permit, 2007*

	Units	Construction Cost
Single	93	$28,456,968
Total	163	$34,603,415

Municipal Finance

(For local fiscal year ended in 2006)

Revenues

Total . . . $67,146,170
Taxes . . . 34,449,848
Special benefits assessment . . . 424,193
Licenses & permits . . . 1,231,990
Fines & forfeitures . . . 475,738
Revenues from use of money & property . . . 2,219,587
Intergovernmental . . . 6,443,109
Service charges . . . 15,042,092
Other revenues . . . 6,859,613
Other financing sources . . . 0

Expenditures

Total . . . $55,955,930
General government . . . 8,298,273
Public safety . . . 25,017,410
Transportation . . . 5,043,573
Community development . . . 4,708,804
Health . . . 948,404
Culture & leisure . . . 5,108,160
Other . . . 0

Local School District

(Data from School year 2007-08 except as noted)

Arcadia Unified
234 Campus Dr
Arcadia, CA 91007
(626) 821-8300

Superintendent . . . Joel Shawn
Grade plan . . . K-12
Number of schools . . . 11
Enrollment . . . 9,900
High school graduates, 2006-07 . . . 939
Dropout rate . . . 0.3%
Pupil/teacher ratio . . . 23.0
Average class size . . . 27.0
Students per computer . . . 2.4
Classrooms with internet . . . 390
Avg. Daily Attendance (ADA) . . . 9,840
Cost per ADA . . . $7,367
Avg. Teacher Salary . . . $76,787

California Achievement Tests 6th ed., 2008

(Pct scoring at or above 50th National Percentile Rank)

	Math	Reading	Language
Grade 3	88%	71%	79%
Grade 7	90%	80%	80%

Academic Performance Index, 2008

Number of students tested . . . 7,954
Number of valid scores . . . 7,633
2007 API (base) . . . 894
2008 API (growth) . . . 904

SAT Testing, 2006-07

Enrollment, Grade 12 . . . 1,000
Number taking test . . . 622
percent taking test . . . 62.2%
percent with total score 1,500+ . . . 46.10%

Average Scores:

Math	Verbal	Writing	Total
612	544	554	1,710

Federal No Child Left Behind, 2008

(Adequate Yearly Progress standards met)

	Participation Rate	Pct Proficient
ELA	Yes	Yes
Math	Yes	Yes

API criteria . . . Yes
Graduation rate . . . Yes
criteria met/possible . . . 34/34

Other school districts for this city

(see Appendix E for information on these districts)

El Monte Elem

See Introduction for an explanation of all data sources.

Demographics & Socio-Economic Characteristics

(2000 Decennial Census, except as noted)

Population

1990* 15,197
2000 16,651
Male 8,285
Female 8,366
Jan. 2008 (estimate)§ 17,558
Persons per sq. mi. of land 1,908.5

Race & Hispanic Origin, 2000

Race
White 14,072
Black/African American 259
North American Native 442
Asian 378
Pacific Islander 34
Other Race 581
Two or more races 885
Hispanic origin, total 1,202
Mexican 784
Puerto Rican 54
Cuban 28
Other Hispanic 336

Age & Nativity, 2000

Under 5 years 665
18 years and over 14,100
65 years and over 1,444
85 years and over 188
Median Age 25.8
Native-born 15,604
Foreign-born 1,110

Educational Attainment, 2000

Population 25 years and over 8,813
Less than 9th grade 4.9%
High school grad or higher 87.6%
Bachelor's degree or higher 41.6%
Graduate degree 13.6%

Income & Poverty, 1999

Per capita income $15,531
Median household income $22,315
Median family income $36,716
Persons in poverty 29.7%
H'holds receiving public assistance 348
H'holds receiving social security 1,240

Households, 2000

Total households 7,051
With persons under 18 1,522
With persons over 65 1,096
Family households 2,815
Single person households 2,451
Persons per household 2.16
Persons per family 2.81

Household Population, 2008§§

Persons living in households 15,805
Persons living in group quarters 1,753
Persons per household 2.1

Labor & Employment

Total civilian labor force, 2008§§ 9,300
Unemployment rate, 2008 .... 7.5%
Total civilian labor force, 2000 9,235

Employed persons 16 years and over by occupation, 2000

Managers & professionals 3,209
Service occupations 1,828
Sales & office occupations 1,956
Farming, fishing & forestry 204
Construction & maintenance 391
Production & transportation 821
Self-employed persons 725

* US Census Bureau
** 2000 Decennial Census
§ California Department of Finance
§§ California Employment Development Dept

General Information

City of Arcata
736 F St
Arcata, CA 95521
707-822-5951

Website .... www.cityofarcata.org
Elevation .... 33 ft.
Land Area (sq. miles) 9.2
Water Area (sq. miles) 1.9
Year of Incorporation 1858
Government type .... General law
Sales tax rate 9.00%

Voters & Officials

Registered Voters, October 2008

Total 11,448
Democrats 5,461
Republicans 1,342
Declined to state 3,332

Legislative Districts

US Congressional 1
State Senatorial 2
State Assembly 1

Local Officials, 2009

Mayor .... Mark Wheetley
Manager/Clerk .... Michael M. Hackett
Clerk .... Bridget Dory (Dep)
Attorney .... Nancy Diamond
Finance Dir .... Janet Luzzi
Public Works .... R. Charles Class
Planning/Dev Dir .... Larry Oetker
Building .... Dean Renfer
Police Chief .... Randy Mendosa
Emergency/Fire Dir .... John McFarland

Public Safety

Number of officers, 2007 23
Violent crimes, 2007 51
Property crimes, 2007 524
Arson, 2007 .... NA

Public Library

Arcata Library
Humboldt County Library System
500 Seventh St
Arcata, CA 95521
707-822-5954

Branch Librarian .... Maggie Nystrom

Library system statistics, FY 2007

Population served 131,959
Internet terminals 46
Annual users 20,083

Per capita:

Operating income $22.91
percent from local government 90.6%
Operating expenditure $18.80
Total materials 2.54
Print holdings 2.38
Visits per capita 4.15

Housing & Construction

Housing Units

Total, 2008§ 7,650
Single family units, attached 309
Single family units, detached 3,533
Multiple family units 3,124
Mobile home units 684
Occupied 7,417
Vacancy rate 3.1%
Median rent, 2000** $546
Median SF home value, 2000** $149,000

New Privately Owned Housing Units Authorized by Building Permit, 2007*

	Units	Construction Cost
Single	37	$4,545,629
Total	52	$5,744,519

Municipal Finance

(For local fiscal year ended in 2006)

Revenues

Total $16,713,640
Taxes 6,152,110
Special benefits assessment 34,106
Licenses & permits 201,999
Fines & forfeitures 306,997
Revenues from use of money & property 561,924
Intergovernmental 1,837,801
Service charges 6,414,284
Other revenues 1,204,419
Other financing sources 0

Expenditures

Total $14,920,139
General government 1,189,984
Public safety 3,625,757
Transportation 1,955,821
Community development 1,439,219
Health 3,068,257
Culture & leisure 1,211,053
Other 0

Local School District

(Data from School year 2007-08 except as noted)

Northern Humboldt Union High
2755 McKinleyville Ave
McKinleyville, CA 95519
(707) 839-6470

Superintendent .... Kenny Richards
Grade plan 9-12
Number of schools 7
Enrollment 1,775
High school graduates, 2006-07 402
Dropout rate 2.7%
Pupil/teacher ratio 20.1
Average class size 23.9
Students per computer 2.7
Classrooms with internet 115
Avg. Daily Attendance (ADA) 1,613
Cost per ADA $9,767
Avg. Teacher Salary $59,111

California Achievement Tests 6th ed., 2008

(Pct scoring at or above 50th National Percentile Rank)

	Math	Reading	Language
Grade 3	NA	NA	NA
Grade 7	NA	NA	NA

Academic Performance Index, 2008

Number of students tested 1,265
Number of valid scores 1,211
2007 API (base) 735
2008 API (growth) 765

SAT Testing, 2006-07

Enrollment, Grade 12 480
Number taking test 162
percent taking test 33.8%
percent with total score 1,500+ 24.60%

Average Scores:

Math	Verbal	Writing	Total
553	560	546	1,659

Federal No Child Left Behind, 2008

(Adequate Yearly Progress standards met)

	Participation Rate	Pct Proficient
ELA	Yes	Yes
Math	Yes	Yes

API criteria .... Yes
Graduation rate .... Yes
criteria met/possible 14/14

Other school districts for this city

(see Appendix E for information on these districts)

Arcata Elem, Jacoby Creek Elem, Pacific Union Elem, Peninsula Union Elem

See Introduction for an explanation of all data sources.

Demographics & Socio-Economic Characteristics

(2000 Decennial Census, except as noted)

Population

1990* 14,378
2000 15,851
Male 7,459
Female 8,392
Jan. 2008 (estimate)§ 17,036
Persons per sq. mi. of land 2,988.8

Race & Hispanic Origin, 2000

Race
White 14,020
Black/African American 99
North American Native 71
Asian 489
Pacific Islander 28
Other Race 597
Two or more races 547
Hispanic origin, total 1,770
Mexican 1,365
Puerto Rican 22
Cuban 5
Other Hispanic 378

Age & Nativity, 2000

Under 5 years 896
18 years and over 12,154
65 years and over 3,222
85 years and over 471
Median Age 41.9
Native-born 15,128
Foreign-born 922

Educational Attainment, 2000

Population 25 years and over 11,120
Less than 9th grade 3.6%
High school grad or higher 87.2%
Bachelor's degree or higher 28.2%
Graduate degree 7.9%

Income & Poverty, 1999

Per capita income $24,311
Median household income $48,236
Median family income $55,494
Persons in poverty 6.9%
H'holds receiving public assistance 175
H'holds receiving social security 2,377

Households, 2000

Total households 6,478
With persons under 18 2,025
With persons over 65 2,219
Family households 4,350
Single person households 1,766
Persons per household 2.41
Persons per family 2.94

Household Population, 2008§§

Persons living in households 16,826
Persons living in group quarters 210
Persons per household 2.3

Labor & Employment

Total civilian labor force, 2008§§ 9,000
Unemployment rate, 2008 .... 5.0%
Total civilian labor force, 2000 7,573

Employed persons 16 years and over by occupation, 2000

Managers & professionals 2,691
Service occupations 1,115
Sales & office occupations 2,130
Farming, fishing & forestry 34
Construction & maintenance 612
Production & transportation 599
Self-employed persons 863

* US Census Bureau
** 2000 Decennial Census
§ California Department of Finance
§§ California Employment Development Dept

General Information

City of Arroyo Grande
PO Box 550
Arroyo Grande, CA 93421
805-473-5400

Website .... www.arroyogrande.org
Elevation .... 120 ft.
Land Area (sq. miles) 5.7
Water Area (sq. miles) 0
Year of Incorporation 1911
Government type .... General law
Sales tax rate 8.75%

Voters & Officials

Registered Voters, October 2008

Total 11,346
Democrats 4,081
Republicans 4,916
Declined to state 1,843

Legislative Districts

US Congressional 22
State Senatorial 15
State Assembly 33

Local Officials, 2009

Mayor .... Tony Ferrara
Manager .... Steven Adams
City Clerk .... Kelly Wetmore
Attorney .... Timothy Carmel
Finance Dir .... Angela Kraetsch
Public Works .... Don Spagnolo
Planning/Dev Dir .... Rob Strong
Building .... Johnathan Hurst
Police Chief .... Steven Annibali
Fire Chief .... Michael Hubert

Public Safety

Number of officers, 2007 27
Violent crimes, 2007 26
Property crimes, 2007 366
Arson, 2007 1

Public Library

Arroyo Grande Branch Library
San Luis Obispo City-County Library System
800 W Branch St
Arroyo Grande, CA 93420
805-473-7161

Branch Librarian .... Deborah Schlanser

Library system statistics, FY 2007

Population served 235,386
Internet terminals 3
Annual users 10,554

Per capita:

Operating income $33.17
percent from local government 90.2%
Operating expenditure $30.54
Total materials 1.72
Print holdings 1.46
Visits per capita 5.51

Housing & Construction

Housing Units

Total, 2008§ 7,565
Single family units, attached 669
Single family units, detached 5,064
Multiple family units 1,284
Mobile home units 548
Occupied 7,259
Vacancy rate 4.0%
Median rent, 2000** $725
Median SF home value, 2000** $233,200

New Privately Owned Housing Units Authorized by Building Permit, 2007*

	Units	Construction Cost
Single	44	$8,197,988
Total	123	$16,866,073

Municipal Finance

(For local fiscal year ended in 2006)

Revenues

Total $19,589,460
Taxes 10,231,159
Special benefits assessment 97,655
Licenses & permits 321,112
Fines & forfeitures 119,993
Revenues from use of money & property 591,455
Intergovernmental 1,250,483
Service charges 6,316,916
Other revenues 660,687
Other financing sources 0

Expenditures

Total $19,040,375
General government 2,697,652
Public safety 7,122,949
Transportation 2,964,130
Community development 1,401,997
Health 243,232
Culture & leisure 1,883,645
Other 0

Local School District

(Data from School year 2007-08 except as noted)

Lucia Mar Unified
602 Orchard St
Arroyo Grande, CA 93420
(805) 474-3000

Superintendent .... James Hogeboom
Grade plan K-12
Number of schools 17
Enrollment 10,820
High school graduates, 2006-07 791
Dropout rate 2.1%
Pupil/teacher ratio 20.6
Average class size 24.9
Students per computer 3.1
Classrooms with internet 582
Avg. Daily Attendance (ADA) 10,496
Cost per ADA $7,542
Avg. Teacher Salary $59,928

California Achievement Tests 6th ed., 2008

(Pct scoring at or above 50th National Percentile Rank)

	Math	Reading	Language
Grade 3	68%	52%	54%
Grade 7	63%	58%	55%

Academic Performance Index, 2008

Number of students tested 8,356
Number of valid scores 7,964
2007 API (base) 782
2008 API (growth) 790

SAT Testing, 2006-07

Enrollment, Grade 12 876
Number taking test 317
percent taking test 36.2%
percent with total score 1,500+ 22.40%

Average Scores:

Math	Verbal	Writing	Total
534	523	518	1,575

Federal No Child Left Behind, 2008

(Adequate Yearly Progress standards met)

	Participation Rate	Pct Proficient
ELA	Yes	No
Math	Yes	Yes

API criteria .... Yes
Graduation rate .... Yes
criteria met/possible 36/34

Other school districts for this city

(see Appendix E for information on these districts)

None

See Introduction for an explanation of all data sources.

Demographics & Socio-Economic Characteristics

(2000 Decennial Census, except as noted)

Population

1990*	15,464
2000	16,380
Male	8,212
Female	8,168
Jan. 2008 (estimate)§	17,552
Persons per sq. mi. of land	10,970.0

Race & Hispanic Origin, 2000

Race	
White	7,236
Black/African American	582
North American Native	127
Asian	4,490
Pacific Islander	89
Other Race	3,025
Two or more races	831
Hispanic origin, total	6,272
Mexican	5,307
Puerto Rican	34
Cuban	34
Other Hispanic	897

Age & Nativity, 2000

Under 5 years	1,203
18 years and over	11,929
65 years and over	2,025
85 years and over	285
Median Age	33.9
Native-born	8,872
Foreign-born	7,508

Educational Attainment, 2000

Population 25 years and over	10,301
Less than 9th grade	18.8%
High school grad or higher	66.0%
Bachelor's degree or higher	18.8%
Graduate degree	5.2%

Income & Poverty, 1999

Per capita income	$15,763
Median household income	$44,500
Median family income	$47,017
Persons in poverty	11.1%
H'holds receiving public assistance	195
H'holds receiving social security	1,003

Households, 2000

Total households	4,470
With persons under 18	2,114
With persons over 65	1,272
Family households	3,625
Single person households	682
Persons per household	3.54
Persons per family	3.87

Household Population, 2008§§

Persons living in households	16,980
Persons living in group quarters	572
Persons per household	3.7

Labor & Employment

Total civilian labor force, 2008§§	8,300
Unemployment rate, 2008	5.1%
Total civilian labor force, 2000	7,236

Employed persons 16 years and over by occupation, 2000

Managers & professionals	1,596
Service occupations	1,054
Sales & office occupations	2,202
Farming, fishing & forestry	7
Construction & maintenance	554
Production & transportation	1,376
Self-employed persons	563

* US Census Bureau
** 2000 Decennial Census
§ California Department of Finance
§§ California Employment Development Dept

General Information

City of Artesia
18747 Clarkdale Ave
Artesia, CA 90701
562-865-6262

Website	www.cityofartesia.us
Elevation	50 ft.
Land Area (sq. miles)	1.6
Water Area (sq. miles)	0
Year of Incorporation	1959
Government type	General law
Sales tax rate	9.25%

Voters & Officials

Registered Voters, October 2008

Total	6,444
Democrats	3,154
Republicans	1,715
Declined to state	1,376

Legislative Districts

US Congressional	39
State Senatorial	27
State Assembly	56

Local Officials, 2009

Mayor	Sally Flowers
Manager	Maria Dadian
City Clerk	Gloria Considine
Attorney	Kevin Ennis
Finance Dir	Justine Menzel
Public Works	Chuck Burckardt
Planning/Dev Dir	NA
Building	NA
Police Chief	(County)
Fire/Emergency Mgmt	(County)

Public Safety

Number of officers, 2007	NA
Violent crimes, 2007	86
Property crimes, 2007	345
Arson, 2007	5

Public Library

Artesia Library
Los Angeles County Public Library System
18722 S Clarkdale Ave
Artesia, CA 90701
562-865-6614

Branch Librarian ..... Christine Candelaria

Library system statistics, FY 2007

Population served	3,673,313
Internet terminals	749
Annual users	3,748,771

Per capita:

Operating income	$30.06
percent from local government	93.6%
Operating expenditure	$28.36
Total materials	2.22
Print holdings	1.97
Visits per capita	3.25

Housing & Construction

Housing Units

Total, 2008§	4,713
Single family units, attached	327
Single family units, detached	3,224
Multiple family units	1,066
Mobile home units	96
Occupied	4,583
Vacancy rate	2.8%
Median rent, 2000**	$795
Median SF home value, 2000**	$192,300

New Privately Owned Housing Units Authorized by Building Permit, 2007*

	Units	Construction Cost
Single	1	$150,100
Total	1	$150,100

Municipal Finance

(For local fiscal year ended in 2006)

Revenues

Total	$9,449,392
Taxes	5,032,875
Special benefits assessment	125,936
Licenses & permits	587,822
Fines & forfeitures	308,336
Revenues from use of money & property	307,392
Intergovernmental	1,490,566
Service charges	919,140
Other revenues	677,325
Other financing sources	0

Expenditures

Total	$9,109,288
General government	2,122,287
Public safety	2,227,359
Transportation	2,725,673
Community development	798,175
Health	661,892
Culture & leisure	573,902
Other	0

Local School District

(Data from School year 2007-08 except as noted)

ABC Unified
16700 Norwalk Blvd
Cerritos, CA 90703
(562) 926-5566

Superintendent	Gary Smuts
Grade plan	K-12
Number of schools	30
Enrollment	20,860
High school graduates, 2006-07	1,621
Dropout rate	2.0%
Pupil/teacher ratio	22.6
Average class size	26.8
Students per computer	3.9
Classrooms with internet	1,014
Avg. Daily Attendance (ADA)	20,919
Cost per ADA	$8,129
Avg. Teacher Salary	$72,259

California Achievement Tests 6th ed., 2008

(Pct scoring at or above 50th National Percentile Rank)

	Math	Reading	Language
Grade 3	62%	42%	54%
Grade 7	60%	55%	55%

Academic Performance Index, 2008

Number of students tested	16,210
Number of valid scores	15,478
2007 API (base)	784
2008 API (growth)	795

SAT Testing, 2006-07

Enrollment, Grade 12	1,827
Number taking test	860
percent taking test	47.1%
percent with total score 1,500+	31.30%

Average Scores:

Math	Verbal	Writing	Total
589	530	538	1,657

Federal No Child Left Behind, 2008

(Adequate Yearly Progress standards met)

	Participation Rate	Pct Proficient
ELA	Yes	No
Math	Yes	No

API criteria	Yes
Graduation rate	Yes
# criteria met/possible	42/40

Other school districts for this city

(see Appendix E for information on these districts)

None

See Introduction for an explanation of all data sources.

Demographics & Socio-Economic Characteristics

(2000 Decennial Census, except as noted)

Population

1990* 9,286
2000 12,956
Male 6,816
Female 6,140
Jan. 2008 (estimate)§ 16,517
Persons per sq. mi. of land 3,441.0

Race & Hispanic Origin, 2000

Race
White 5,836
Black/African American 140
North American Native 189
Asian 143
Pacific Islander 15
Other Race 6,031
Two or more races 602
Hispanic origin, total 11,341
Mexican 9,826
Puerto Rican 66
Cuban 6
Other Hispanic 1,443

Age & Nativity, 2000

Under 5 years 1,470
18 years and over 7,769
65 years and over 753
85 years and over 80
Median Age 23.3
Native-born 6,416
Foreign-born 6,528

Educational Attainment, 2000

Population 25 years and over 6,047
Less than 9th grade 58.4%
High school grad or higher 22.6%
Bachelor's degree or higher 2.2%
Graduate degree 0.8%

Income & Poverty, 1999

Per capita income $7,408
Median household income $23,674
Median family income $24,816
Persons in poverty 32.4%
H'holds receiving public assistance 160
H'holds receiving social security 570

Households, 2000

Total households 3,010
With persons under 18 2,112
With persons over 65 552
Family households 2,645
Single person households 286
Persons per household 4.28
Persons per family 4.51

Household Population, 2008§§

Persons living in households 16,446
Persons living in group quarters 71
Persons per household 4.4

Labor & Employment

Total civilian labor force, 2008§§ 6,300
Unemployment rate, 2008 . . . . 26.6%
Total civilian labor force, 2000 4,732

Employed persons 16 years and over by occupation, 2000

Managers & professionals 293
Service occupations 293
Sales & office occupations 401
Farming, fishing & forestry 1,513
Construction & maintenance 195
Production & transportation 561
Self-employed persons 104

* US Census Bureau
** 2000 Decennial Census
§ California Department of Finance
§§ California Employment Development Dept

General Information

City of Arvin
200 Campus Dr
Arvin, CA 93203
661-854-3134

Website . . . . www.arvin.org
Elevation . . . . 445 ft.
Land Area (sq. miles) 4.8
Water Area (sq. miles) 0
Year of Incorporation 1960
Government type . . . . General law
Sales tax rate 9.25%

Voters & Officials

Registered Voters, October 2008

Total 3,355
Democrats 2,139
Republicans 582
Declined to state 548

Legislative Districts

US Congressional 20
State Senatorial 16
State Assembly 30

Local Officials, 2009

Mayor . . . . Tim Tarver
City Manager . . . . Alan Christensen
City Clerk . . . . Cecilia Vela
Attorney . . . . Rachel Richman
Finance Dir . . . . David Powell
Public Works . . . . Travis Nighbert
Planning/Dev Dir . . . . Issac George
Building . . . . Russ Johnson
Police Chief . . . . Tommy Tunson
Emergency/Fire Dir . . . . Dennis Thompson

Public Safety

Number of officers, 2007 16
Violent crimes, 2007 105
Property crimes, 2007 643
Arson, 2007 30

Public Library

Arvin Branch Library
Kern County Library System
201 Campus Dr
Arvin, CA 93203
661-854-5934

Branch Librarian . . . . Marcus Clough

Library system statistics, FY 2007

Population served 801,648
Internet terminals 237
Annual users 337,030

Per capita:

Operating income $12.11
percent from local government 90.4%
Operating expenditure $12.11
Total materials 1.37
Print holdings 1.29
Visits per capita 2.09

Housing & Construction

Housing Units

Total, 2008§ 3,887
Single family units, attached 218
Single family units, detached 2,654
Multiple family units 758
Mobile home units 257
Occupied 3,721
Vacancy rate 4.3%
Median rent, 2000** $403
Median SF home value, 2000** $77,000

New Privately Owned Housing Units Authorized by Building Permit, 2007*

	Units	Construction Cost
Single	38	$3,245,706
Total	38	$3,245,706

Municipal Finance

(For local fiscal year ended in 2006)

Revenues

Total $6,914,459
Taxes 2,195,394
Special benefits assessment 1,407,819
Licenses & permits 444,865
Fines & forfeitures 121,215
Revenues from use of money & property 207,196
Intergovernmental 888,399
Service charges 1,583,854
Other revenues 65,717
Other financing sources 0

Expenditures

Total $6,308,282
General government 2,886,775
Public safety 1,672,787
Transportation 1,268,135
Community development 269,792
Health 0
Culture & leisure 210,793
Other 0

Local School District

(Data from School year 2007-08 except as noted)

Kern Union High
5801 Sundale Ave
Bakersfield, CA 93309
(661) 827-3100

Superintendent . . . . Donald Carter
Grade plan 9-12
Number of schools 22
Enrollment 37,341
High school graduates, 2006-07 6,321
Dropout rate 5.3%
Pupil/teacher ratio 23.3
Average class size 26.2
Students per computer 4.2
Classrooms with internet 1,524
Avg. Daily Attendance (ADA) 37,540
Cost per ADA $8,547
Avg. Teacher Salary $63,074

California Achievement Tests 6th ed., 2008

(Pct scoring at or above 50th National Percentile Rank)

	Math	Reading	Language
Grade 3	NA	NA	NA
Grade 7	NA	NA	NA

Academic Performance Index, 2008

Number of students tested 26,804
Number of valid scores 24,540
2007 API (base) 654
2008 API (growth) 661

SAT Testing, 2006-07

Enrollment, Grade 12 8,277
Number taking test 2,144
percent taking test 25.9%
percent with total score 1,500+ 9.90%

Average Scores:

Math	Verbal	Writing	Total
488	471	464	1,423

Federal No Child Left Behind, 2008

(Adequate Yearly Progress standards met)

	Participation Rate	Pct Proficient
ELA	Yes	No
Math	Yes	No

API criteria . . . . Yes
Graduation rate . . . . No
criteria met/possible 34/29

Other school districts for this city

(see Appendix E for information on these districts)

Arvin Union Elem, Di Giorgio Elem

See Introduction for an explanation of all data sources.

Demographics & Socio-Economic Characteristics

(2000 Decennial Census, except as noted)

Population

1990* ... 23,138
2000 ... 26,411
Male ... 13,605
Female ... 12,806
Jan. 2008 (estimate)§ ... 28,590
Persons per sq. mi. of land ... 1,070.8

Race & Hispanic Origin, 2000

Race
White ... 23,451
Black/African American ... 623
North American Native ... 247
Asian ... 336
Pacific Islander ... 30
Other Race ... 842
Two or more races ... 882
Hispanic origin, total ... 2,783
Mexican ... 2,067
Puerto Rican ... 79
Cuban ... 19
Other Hispanic ... 618

Age & Nativity, 2000

Under 5 years ... 1,423
18 years and over ... 19,639
65 years and over ... 3,044
85 years and over ... 349
Median Age ... 38.2
Native-born ... 25,257
Foreign-born ... 1,174

Educational Attainment, 2000

Population 25 years and over ... 17,412
Less than 9th grade ... 2.7%
High school grad or higher ... 88.4%
Bachelor's degree or higher ... 20.3%
Graduate degree ... 5.5%

Income & Poverty, 1999

Per capita income ... $20,029
Median household income ... $48,725
Median family income ... $55,009
Persons in poverty ... 8.6%
H'holds receiving public assistance ... 233
H'holds receiving social security ... 2,395

Households, 2000

Total households ... 9,531
With persons under 18 ... 3,680
With persons over 65 ... 2,114
Family households ... 6,812
Single person households ... 2,094
Persons per household ... 2.62
Persons per family ... 3.05

Household Population, 2008§§

Persons living in households ... 26,947
Persons living in group quarters ... 1,643
Persons per household ... 2.5

Labor & Employment

Total civilian labor force, 2008§§ ... 15,500
Unemployment rate, 2008 ... 4.6%
Total civilian labor force, 2000 ... 12,835

Employed persons 16 years and over by occupation, 2000

Managers & professionals ... 4,015
Service occupations ... 2,428
Sales & office occupations ... 3,064
Farming, fishing & forestry ... 72
Construction & maintenance ... 1,468
Production & transportation ... 1,237
Self-employed persons ... 1,665

* US Census Bureau
** 2000 Decennial Census
§ California Department of Finance
§§ California Employment Development Dept

General Information

City of Atascadero
6907 El Camino Real
Atascadero, CA 93422
805-461-5000

Website ... www.atascadero.org
Elevation ... 855 ft.
Land Area (sq. miles) ... 26.7
Water Area (sq. miles) ... 0
Year of Incorporation ... 1979
Government type ... General law
Sales tax rate ... 8.25%

Voters & Officials

Registered Voters, October 2008

Total ... 16,815
Democrats ... 5,361
Republicans ... 7,587
Declined to state ... 2,987

Legislative Districts

US Congressional ... 22
State Senatorial ... 15
State Assembly ... 33

Local Officials, 2009

Mayor ... Ellen Beraud
City Manager ... Wade McKinney
City Clerk ... Marcia Torgerson
Attorney ... Brian Pierik
Admin Svcs Dir ... Rachelle Rickard
Public Works ... Russ Thompson
Community Dev Dir ... Warren Frace
Building ... NA
Police Chief ... Jim Mulhall
Fire Chief ... Kurt Stone

Public Safety

Number of officers, 2007 ... 29
Violent crimes, 2007 ... 106
Property crimes, 2007 ... 565
Arson, 2007 ... 18

Public Library

Atascadero Library
San Luis Obispo City-County Library System
6850 Morro Rd
Atascadero, CA 93422
805-461-6161

Branch Librarian ... Deborah Schlanser

Library system statistics, FY 2007

Population served ... 235,386
Internet terminals ... 3
Annual users ... 10,554

Per capita:

Operating income ... $33.17
percent from local government ... 90.2%
Operating expenditure ... $30.54
Total materials ... 1.72
Print holdings ... 1.46
Visits per capita ... 5.51

Housing & Construction

Housing Units

Total, 2008§ ... 11,102
Single family units, attached ... 459
Single family units, detached ... 7,896
Multiple family units ... 2,190
Mobile home units ... 557
Occupied ... 10,747
Vacancy rate ... 3.2%
Median rent, 2000** ... $701
Median SF home value, 2000** ... $201,600

New Privately Owned Housing Units Authorized by Building Permit, 2007*

	Units	Construction Cost
Single	154	$26,035,275
Total	154	$26,035,275

Municipal Finance

(For local fiscal year ended in 2006)

Revenues

Total ... $27,609,875
Taxes ... 17,078,021
Special benefits assessment ... 278,821
Licenses & permits ... 984,249
Fines & forfeitures ... 103,029
Revenues from use of money & property ... 901,271
Intergovernmental ... 2,888,153
Service charges ... 4,052,579
Other revenues ... 1,323,752
Other financing sources ... 0

Expenditures

Total ... $22,200,869
General government ... 2,177,357
Public safety ... 7,792,525
Transportation ... 3,319,273
Community development ... 2,214,555
Health ... 3,753,823
Culture & leisure ... 2,670,157
Other ... 273,179

Local School District

(Data from School year 2007-08 except as noted)

Atascadero Unified
5601 West Mall
Atascadero, CA 93422
(805) 462-4200

Superintendent ... John Rogers
Grade plan ... K-12
Number of schools ... 12
Enrollment ... 5,037
High school graduates, 2006-07 ... 415
Dropout rate ... 2.8%
Pupil/teacher ratio ... 20.1
Average class size ... 23.0
Students per computer ... 4.3
Classrooms with internet ... 284
Avg. Daily Attendance (ADA) ... 4,865
Cost per ADA ... $7,733
Avg. Teacher Salary ... $62,344

California Achievement Tests 6th ed., 2008

(Pct scoring at or above 50th National Percentile Rank)

	Math	Reading	Language
Grade 3	65%	53%	54%
Grade 7	65%	67%	60%

Academic Performance Index, 2008

Number of students tested ... 3,877
Number of valid scores ... 3,682
2007 API (base) ... 789
2008 API (growth) ... 791

SAT Testing, 2006-07

Enrollment, Grade 12 ... 472
Number taking test ... 138
percent taking test ... 29.2%
percent with total score 1,500+ ... 20.30%

Average Scores:

Math	Verbal	Writing	Total
562	547	540	1,649

Federal No Child Left Behind, 2008

(Adequate Yearly Progress standards met)

	Participation Rate	Pct Proficient
ELA	Yes	No
Math	Yes	No

API criteria ... Yes
Graduation rate ... Yes
criteria met/possible ... 26/22

Other school districts for this city

(see Appendix E for information on these districts)

None

See Introduction for an explanation of all data sources.

Demographics & Socio-Economic Characteristics

(2000 Decennial Census, except as noted)

Population

1990* 7,163
2000 7,194
Male 3,479
Female 3,715
Jan. 2008 (estimate)§ 7,475
Persons per sq. mi. of land 1,525.5

Race & Hispanic Origin, 2000

Race
White 6,141
Black/African American 50
North American Native 12
Asian 704
Pacific Islander 30
Other Race 72
Two or more races 185
Hispanic origin, total 200
Mexican 107
Puerto Rican 5
Cuban 4
Other Hispanic 84

Age & Nativity, 2000

Under 5 years 371
18 years and over 5,491
65 years and over 1,451
85 years and over 183
Median Age 45.3
Native-born 6,178
Foreign-born 1,032

Educational Attainment, 2000

Population 25 years and over 4,961
Less than 9th grade 1.4%
High school grad or higher 96.7%
Bachelor's degree or higher 76.2%
Graduate degree 40.2%

Income & Poverty, 1999

Per capita income $112,408
Median household income $200,001
Median family income $200,001
Persons in poverty 1.7%
H'holds receiving public assistance 15
H'holds receiving social security 786

Households, 2000

Total households 2,413
With persons under 18 838
With persons over 65 923
Family households 1,984
Single person households 308
Persons per household 2.85
Persons per family 3.06

Household Population, 2008§§

Persons living in households 7,157
Persons living in group quarters 318
Persons per household 2.9

Labor & Employment

Total civilian labor force, 2008§§ 3,300
Unemployment rate, 2008 .... 2.9%
Total civilian labor force, 2000 3,230

Employed persons 16 years and over by occupation, 2000

Managers & professionals 2,220
Service occupations 194
Sales & office occupations 599
Farming, fishing & forestry 0
Construction & maintenance 57
Production & transportation 96
Self-employed persons 454

* US Census Bureau
** 2000 Decennial Census
§ California Department of Finance
§§ California Employment Development Dept

General Information

Town of Atherton
91 Ashfield Rd
Atherton, CA 94027
650-752-0500

Website .... www.ci.atherton.ca.us
Elevation .... 50 ft.
Land Area (sq. miles) 4.9
Water Area (sq. miles) 0
Year of Incorporation 1923
Government type .... General law
Sales tax rate 9.25%

Voters & Officials

Registered Voters, October 2008

Total 5,481
Democrats 1,756
Republicans 2,495
Declined to state 1,078

Legislative Districts

US Congressional 14
State Senatorial 11
State Assembly 21

Local Officials, 2009

Mayor .... Jerry Carlson
Manager .... Jerry Gruber
City Clerk .... Kathi Hamilton (Actg)
Attorney .... Marc Hynes
Finance Dir .... Louise Ho
Public Works .... Duncan Jones
Planning/Dev Dir .... Lisa Costa-Sanders
Building .... Mike Wasmann
Police Chief .... Glenn Nielsen
Fire Dir .... Harold Schapelhouman

Public Safety

Number of officers, 2007 21
Violent crimes, 2007 12
Property crimes, 2007 205
Arson, 2007 2

Public Library

Atherton Library
San Mateo County Library System
2 Dinkelspiel Station Ln
Atherton, CA 94027
650-328-2422

Branch Librarian .... Susan Goetz

Library system statistics, FY 2007

Population served 278,388
Internet terminals 26
Annual users 49,920

Per capita:

Operating income $90.21
percent from local government 63.5%
Operating expenditure $60.41
Total materials 2.65
Print holdings 2.16
Visits per capita 5.44

Housing & Construction

Housing Units

Total, 2008§ 2,560
Single family units, attached 32
Single family units, detached 2,521
Multiple family units 7
Mobile home units 0
Occupied 2,483
Vacancy rate 3.0%
Median rent, 2000** $2,001
Median SF home value, 2000** .. $1,000,001

New Privately Owned Housing Units Authorized by Building Permit, 2007*

	Units	Construction Cost
Single	14	$30,429,125
Total	14	$30,429,125

Municipal Finance

(For local fiscal year ended in 2006)

Revenues

Total $12,799,361
Taxes 6,849,078
Special benefits assessment 1,839,347
Licenses & permits 1,332,403
Fines & forfeitures 57,453
Revenues from use of money & property 409,811
Intergovernmental 1,846,968
Service charges 288,037
Other revenues 176,264
Other financing sources 0

Expenditures

Total $10,146,574
General government 1,637,382
Public safety 4,234,065
Transportation 2,826,608
Community development 991,943
Health 0
Culture & leisure 456,576
Other 0

Local School District

(Data from School year 2007-08 except as noted)

Sequoia Union High
480 James Ave
Redwood City, CA 94062
(650) 369-1411

Superintendent .... Patrick Gemma
Grade plan 9-12
Number of schools 6
Enrollment 8,510
High school graduates, 2006-07 1,546
Dropout rate 3.2%
Pupil/teacher ratio 19.7
Average class size 26.4
Students per computer 3.0
Classrooms with internet 402
Avg. Daily Attendance (ADA) 7,811
Cost per ADA $11,470
Avg. Teacher Salary $76,194

California Achievement Tests 6th ed., 2008

(Pct scoring at or above 50th National Percentile Rank)

	Math	Reading	Language
Grade 3	NA	NA	NA
Grade 7	NA	NA	NA

Academic Performance Index, 2008

Number of students tested 5,874
Number of valid scores 5,525
2007 API (base) 753
2008 API (growth) 753

SAT Testing, 2006-07

Enrollment, Grade 12 2,000
Number taking test 945
percent taking test 47.3%
percent with total score 1,500+ 29.10%

Average Scores:

Math	Verbal	Writing	Total
546	530	530	1,606

Federal No Child Left Behind, 2008

(Adequate Yearly Progress standards met)

	Participation Rate	Pct Proficient
ELA	Yes	No
Math	Yes	No

API criteria .... Yes
Graduation rate .... Yes
criteria met/possible 28/25

Other school districts for this city

(see Appendix E for information on these districts)

Las Lomitas Elem

See Introduction for an explanation of all data sources.

Demographics & Socio-Economic Characteristics

(2000 Decennial Census, except as noted)

Population

1990* 22,282
2000 23,113
Male 11,236
Female 11,877
Jan. 2008 (estimate)§ 27,571
Persons per sq. mi. of land 5,105.7

Race & Hispanic Origin, 2000

Race
White 13,252
Black/African American 1,153
North American Native 293
Asian 1,254
Pacific Islander 83
Other Race 5,659
Two or more races 1,419
Hispanic origin, total 9,594
Mexican 8,333
Puerto Rican 96
Cuban 21
Other Hispanic 1,144

Age & Nativity, 2000

Under 5 years 2,169
18 years and over 15,041
65 years and over 2,104
85 years and over 167
Median Age 28.5
Native-born 18,079
Foreign-born 4,817

Educational Attainment, 2000

Population 25 years and over 12,440
Less than 9th grade 16.9%
High school grad or higher 70.3%
Bachelor's degree or higher 12.3%
Graduate degree 4.0%

Income & Poverty, 1999

Per capita income $15,162
Median household income $37,344
Median family income $39,789
Persons in poverty 18.4%
H'holds receiving public assistance 543
H'holds receiving social security 1,704

Households, 2000

Total households 7,247
With persons under 18 3,640
With persons over 65 1,526
Family households 5,670
Single person households 1,274
Persons per household 3.15
Persons per family 3.55

Household Population, 2008§§

Persons living in households 26,112
Persons living in group quarters 1,459
Persons per household 3.1

Labor & Employment

Total civilian labor force, 2008§§ 12,100
Unemployment rate, 2008 . . . . 12.9%
Total civilian labor force, 2000 10,176

Employed persons 16 years and over by occupation, 2000

Managers & professionals 2,362
Service occupations 1,421
Sales & office occupations 1,933
Farming, fishing & forestry 567
Construction & maintenance 917
Production & transportation 1,658
Self-employed persons 430

* US Census Bureau
** 2000 Decennial Census
§ California Department of Finance
§§ California Employment Development Dept

General Information

City of Atwater
750 Bellevue Rd
Atwater, CA 95301
209-357-6310

Website . . . . www.atwater.org
Elevation . . . . 150 ft.
Land Area (sq. miles) 5.4
Water Area (sq. miles) 0
Year of Incorporation 1922
Government type . . . . General law
Sales tax rate 8.25%

Voters & Officials

Registered Voters, October 2008

Total 11,256
Democrats 4,594
Republicans 4,690
Declined to state 1,616

Legislative Districts

US Congressional 18
State Senatorial 12
State Assembly 17

Local Officials, 2009

Mayor . . . . Carol Joan Faul
Manager . . . . Gregory B. Wellman
City Clerk . . . . Jeanna Del Real
Attorney . . . . Dennis Meyers
Finance Dir . . . . Staley E. Feathers
Public Works . . . . Dave Church
Planning/Dev Dir . . . . Charlie Woods
Building . . . . NA
Police Chief . . . . Richard Hawthorne
Emergency/Fire Dir . . . . Ed Banks

Public Safety

Number of officers, 2007 34
Violent crimes, 2007 103
Property crimes, 2007 1,021
Arson, 2007 8

Public Library

Atwater Branch Library
Merced County Library System
1600 Third St
Atwater, CA 95301
209-358-6651

Branch Librarian . . . . Amanda Kelly

Library system statistics, FY 2007

Population served 251,510
Internet terminals 91
Annual users 124,530

Per capita:

Operating income $8.99
percent from local government 91.3%
Operating expenditure $8.99
Total materials 1.61
Print holdings 1.60
Visits per capita 1.75

Housing & Construction

Housing Units

Total, 2008§ 9,529
Single family units, attached 584
Single family units, detached 6,616
Multiple family units 1,822
Mobile home units 507
Occupied 8,511
Vacancy rate 10.7%
Median rent, 2000** $521
Median SF home value, 2000** $103,100

New Privately Owned Housing Units Authorized by Building Permit, 2007*

	Units	Construction Cost
Single	52	$9,798,949
Total	52	$9,798,949

Municipal Finance

(For local fiscal year ended in 2006)

Revenues

Total $27,273,965
Taxes 8,498,641
Special benefits assessment 363,002
Licenses & permits 846,142
Fines & forfeitures 102,689
Revenues from use of money & property 965,778
Intergovernmental 3,960,637
Service charges 10,725,000
Other revenues 1,812,076
Other financing sources 0

Expenditures

Total $20,275,233
General government 3,235,816
Public safety 5,608,569
Transportation 1,372,238
Community development 2,060,113
Health 4,801,893
Culture & leisure 1,148,531
Other 0

Local School District

(Data from School year 2007-08 except as noted)

Merced Union High
PO Box 2147
Merced, CA 95344
(209) 385-6412

Superintendent . . . . Scott Scambray
Grade plan 9-12
Number of schools 8
Enrollment 10,680
High school graduates, 2006-07 1,890
Dropout rate 3.6%
Pupil/teacher ratio 21.9
Average class size 26.0
Students per computer 3.7
Classrooms with internet 514
Avg. Daily Attendance (ADA) 10,568
Cost per ADA $8,153
Avg. Teacher Salary $63,476

California Achievement Tests 6th ed., 2008

(Pct scoring at or above 50th National Percentile Rank)

	Math	Reading	Language
Grade 3	NA	NA	NA
Grade 7	NA	NA	NA

Academic Performance Index, 2008

Number of students tested 7,904
Number of valid scores 7,415
2007 API (base) 678
2008 API (growth) 700

SAT Testing, 2006-07

Enrollment, Grade 12 2,234
Number taking test 639
percent taking test 28.6%
percent with total score 1,500+ 9.90%

Average Scores:

Math	Verbal	Writing	Total
481	461	466	1,408

Federal No Child Left Behind, 2008

(Adequate Yearly Progress standards met)

	Participation Rate	Pct Proficient
ELA	Yes	No
Math	Yes	No

API criteria . . . . Yes
Graduation rate . . . . Yes
\# criteria met/possible 34/31

Other school districts for this city

(see Appendix E for information on these districts)

Atwater Elem

See Introduction for an explanation of all data sources.

Demographics & Socio-Economic Characteristics

(2000 Decennial Census, except as noted)

Population

1990* . . . 10,592
2000 . . . 12,462
Male . . . 5,793
Female . . . 6,669
Jan. 2008 (estimate)§ . . . 13,273
Persons per sq. mi. of land . . . 1,793.6

Race & Hispanic Origin, 2000

Race
White . . . 11,641
Black/African American . . . 57
North American Native . . . 104
Asian . . . 165
Pacific Islander . . . 12
Other Race . . . 189
Two or more races . . . 294
Hispanic origin, total . . . 744
Mexican . . . 453
Puerto Rican . . . 22
Cuban . . . 13
Other Hispanic . . . 256

Age & Nativity, 2000

Under 5 years . . . 663
18 years and over . . . 9,560
65 years and over . . . 2,261
85 years and over . . . 392
Median Age . . . 41.2
Native-born . . . 11,706
Foreign-born . . . 761

Educational Attainment, 2000

Population 25 years and over . . . 8,758
Less than 9th grade . . . 3.2%
High school grad or higher . . . 91.0%
Bachelor's degree or higher . . . 27.7%
Graduate degree . . . 8.6%

Income & Poverty, 1999

Per capita income . . . $26,258
Median household income . . . $48,999
Median family income . . . $62,250
Persons in poverty . . . 6.7%
H'holds receiving public assistance . . . 118
H'holds receiving social security . . . 1,628

Households, 2000

Total households . . . 5,302
With persons under 18 . . . 1,605
With persons over 65 . . . 1,578
Family households . . . 3,284
Single person households . . . 1,681
Persons per household . . . 2.31
Persons per family . . . 2.91

Household Population, 2008§§

Persons living in households . . . 13,067
Persons living in group quarters . . . 206
Persons per household . . . 2.2

Labor & Employment

Total civilian labor force, 2008§§ . . . 8,900
Unemployment rate, 2008 . . . 5.4%
Total civilian labor force, 2000 . . . 6,274

Employed persons 16 years and over by occupation, 2000

Managers & professionals . . . 2,174
Service occupations . . . 1,018
Sales & office occupations . . . 1,700
Farming, fishing & forestry . . . 39
Construction & maintenance . . . 638
Production & transportation . . . 498
Self-employed persons . . . 814

* US Census Bureau
** 2000 Decennial Census
§ California Department of Finance
§§ California Employment Development Dept

General Information

City of Auburn
1225 Lincoln Way
Auburn, CA 95603
530-823-4211

Website . . . www.auburn.ca.gov
Elevation . . . 1,297 ft.
Land Area (sq. miles) . . . 7.4
Water Area (sq. miles) . . . 0
Year of Incorporation . . . 1888
Government type . . . General law
Sales tax rate . . . 8.25%

Voters & Officials

Registered Voters, October 2008

Total . . . 8,565
Democrats . . . 2,780
Republicans . . . 3,733
Declined to state . . . 1,692

Legislative Districts

US Congressional . . . 4
State Senatorial . . . 1
State Assembly . . . 3, 4

Local Officials, 2009

Mayor . . . J. M. "Mike" Holmes
Manager . . . Robert Richardson
City Clerk . . . Joseph Labrie
Attorney . . . Michael Colantuono
Finance Dir . . . Andy Heath
Public Works . . . Jack Warren
Planning/Dev Dir . . . Will Wong
Building . . . NA
Police Chief . . . Valerie Harris
Emergency/Fire Dir . . . Mark D'Ambrogi

Public Safety

Number of officers, 2007 . . . 21
Violent crimes, 2007 . . . 49
Property crimes, 2007 . . . 373
Arson, 2007 . . . 2

Public Library

Auburn Library
Placer County Library System
350 Nevada St
Auburn, CA 95603
530-886-4500

Branch Librarian . . . NA

Library system statistics, FY 2007

Population served . . . 180,819
Internet terminals . . . 56
Annual users . . . 48,341

Per capita:

Operating income . . . $24.99
percent from local government . . . 85.7%
Operating expenditure . . . $24.01
Total materials . . . 1.96
Print holdings . . . 1.74
Visits per capita . . . 3.30

Housing & Construction

Housing Units

Total, 2008§ . . . 6,004
Single family units, attached . . . 211
Single family units, detached . . . 4,113
Multiple family units . . . 1,680
Mobile home units . . . 0
Occupied . . . 5,852
Vacancy rate . . . 2.5%
Median rent, 2000** . . . $674
Median SF home value, 2000** . . . $214,900

New Privately Owned Housing Units Authorized by Building Permit, 2007*

	Units	Construction Cost
Single	26	$8,193,402
Total	35	$9,013,965

Municipal Finance

(For local fiscal year ended in 2006)

Revenues

Total . . . $21,687,305
Taxes . . . 9,166,725
Special benefits assessment . . . 0
Licenses & permits . . . 354,500
Fines & forfeitures . . . 115,833
Revenues from use of money & property . . . 590,365
Intergovernmental . . . 1,705,461
Service charges . . . 3,972,472
Other revenues . . . 816,949
Other financing sources . . . 4,965,000

Expenditures

Total . . . $21,884,244
General government . . . 2,666,547
Public safety . . . 5,342,901
Transportation . . . 3,683,843
Community development . . . 1,353,570
Health . . . 3,588,854
Culture & leisure . . . 283,529
Other . . . 4,965,000

Local School District

(Data from School year 2007-08 except as noted)

Placer Union High
PO Box 5048
Auburn, CA 95604
(530) 886-4400

Superintendent . . . Bart O'Brien
Grade plan . . . 9-12
Number of schools . . . 6
Enrollment . . . 4,588
High school graduates, 2006-07 . . . 1,091
Dropout rate . . . 1.4%
Pupil/teacher ratio . . . 22.5
Average class size . . . 25.4
Students per computer . . . 3.6
Classrooms with internet . . . 242
Avg. Daily Attendance (ADA) . . . 4,382
Cost per ADA . . . $8,031
Avg. Teacher Salary . . . $63,368

California Achievement Tests 6th ed., 2008

(Pct scoring at or above 50th National Percentile Rank)

	Math	Reading	Language
Grade 3	NA	NA	NA
Grade 7	NA	NA	NA

Academic Performance Index, 2008

Number of students tested . . . 3,384
Number of valid scores . . . 3,277
2007 API (base) . . . 769
2008 API (growth) . . . 768

SAT Testing, 2006-07

Enrollment, Grade 12 . . . 1,210
Number taking test . . . 418
percent taking test . . . 34.6%
percent with total score 1,500+ . . . 23.60%

Average Scores:

Math	Verbal	Writing	Total
550	536	526	1,612

Federal No Child Left Behind, 2008

(Adequate Yearly Progress standards met)

	Participation Rate	Pct Proficient
ELA	No	No
Math	Yes	No

API criteria . . . Yes
Graduation rate . . . Yes
\# criteria met/possible . . . 18/15

Other school districts for this city

(see Appendix E for information on these districts)

Ackerman Elem, Auburn Union Elem

See Introduction for an explanation of all data sources.

Demographics & Socio-Economic Characteristics

(2000 Decennial Census, except as noted)

Population

1990* 2,918
2000 3,127
Male 1,559
Female 1,568
Jan. 2008 (estimate)§ 3,532
Persons per sq. mi. of land 1,261.4

Race & Hispanic Origin, 2000

Race
White 2,240
Black/African American 23
North American Native 32
Asian 19
Pacific Islander 7
Other Race 637
Two or more races 169
Hispanic origin, total 1,437
Mexican 1,378
Puerto Rican 3
Cuban 5
Other Hispanic 51

Age & Nativity, 2000

Under 5 years 246
18 years and over 2,178
65 years and over 315
85 years and over 38
Median Age 33.7
Native-born 2,399
Foreign-born 782

Educational Attainment, 2000

Population 25 years and over 1,957
Less than 9th grade 12.9%
High school grad or higher 75.6%
Bachelor's degree or higher 20.2%
Graduate degree 6.3%

Income & Poverty, 1999

Per capita income $21,032
Median household income $39,327
Median family income $46,406
Persons in poverty 10.5%
H'holds receiving public assistance 24
H'holds receiving social security 258

Households, 2000

Total households 1,158
With persons under 18 470
With persons over 65 241
Family households 719
Single person households 362
Persons per household 2.65
Persons per family 3.38

Household Population, 2008§§

Persons living in households 3,470
Persons living in group quarters 62
Persons per household 2.8

Labor & Employment

Total civilian labor force, 2008§§ 2,000
Unemployment rate, 2008 .... 3.2%
Total civilian labor force, 2000 1,711

Employed persons 16 years and over by occupation, 2000

Managers & professionals 341
Service occupations 544
Sales & office occupations 432
Farming, fishing & forestry 1
Construction & maintenance 162
Production & transportation 170
Self-employed persons 103

* US Census Bureau
** 2000 Decennial Census
§ California Department of Finance
§§ California Employment Development Dept

General Information

City of Avalon
410 Avalon Canyon Rd
PO Box 707
Avalon, CA 90704
310-510-0220

Website .... www.cityofavalon.com
Elevation .... 36 ft.
Land Area (sq. miles) 2.8
Water Area (sq. miles) 0.3
Year of Incorporation 1913
Government type .... General law
Sales tax rate 9.75%

Voters & Officials

Registered Voters, October 2008

Total 1,577
Democrats 595
Republicans 629
Declined to state 259

Legislative Districts

US Congressional 46
State Senatorial 27
State Assembly 54

Local Officials, 2009

Mayor .... Robert Kennedy
Manager .... Pete Woolson
City Clerk .... Denise Radde
Attorney .... Pamela Albers
Finance Dir .... Betty Jo Garcia
Public Works .... Pastor Lopez
Planning/Dev Dir .... Amanda Cook
Building .... Keith LeFever
Police Chief .... Edison Cook
Emergency/Fire Dir .... Steve Hoefs

Public Safety

Number of officers, 2007 .... NA
Violent crimes, 2007 39
Property crimes, 2007 162
Arson, 2007 1

Public Library

Avalon Library
Los Angeles County Public Library System
215 Summer Ave
Avalon, CA 90704
310-510-1050

Branch Librarian .... Linda Hoffman (Actg)

Library system statistics, FY 2007

Population served 3,673,313
Internet terminals 749
Annual users 3,748,771

Per capita:

Operating income $30.06
percent from local government 93.6%
Operating expenditure $28.36
Total materials 2.22
Print holdings 1.97
Visits per capita 3.25

Housing & Construction

Housing Units

Total, 2008§ 1,937
Single family units, attached 490
Single family units, detached 502
Multiple family units 936
Mobile home units 9
Occupied 1,237
Vacancy rate 36.1%
Median rent, 2000** $814
Median SF home value, 2000** $388,100

New Privately Owned Housing Units Authorized by Building Permit, 2007*

	Units	Construction Cost
Single	1	$988,980
Total	1	$988,980

Municipal Finance

(For local fiscal year ended in 2006)

Revenues

Total $16,199,958
Taxes 6,410,845
Special benefits assessment 0
Licenses & permits 302,100
Fines & forfeitures 81,401
Revenues from use of money & property 333,492
Intergovernmental 452,300
Service charges 8,443,339
Other revenues 176,481
Other financing sources 0

Expenditures

Total $15,195,911
General government 1,992,118
Public safety 3,189,776
Transportation 5,688,501
Community development 1,126,775
Health 2,979,427
Culture & leisure 219,314
Other 0

Local School District

(Data from School year 2007-08 except as noted)

Long Beach Unified
1515 Hughes Way
Long Beach, CA 90810
(562) 997-8000

Superintendent .... Christopher Steinhauser
Grade plan K-12
Number of schools 93
Enrollment 88,186
High school graduates, 2006-07 4,706
Dropout rate 5.1%
Pupil/teacher ratio 20.9
Average class size 27.3
Students per computer 4.9
Classrooms with internet 4,149
Avg. Daily Attendance (ADA) 87,009
Cost per ADA $8,964
Avg. Teacher Salary $70,071

California Achievement Tests 6th ed., 2008

(Pct scoring at or above 50th National Percentile Rank)

	Math	Reading	Language
Grade 3	60%	34%	41%
Grade 7	47%	43%	41%

Academic Performance Index, 2008

Number of students tested 67,372
Number of valid scores 64,269
2007 API (base) 729
2008 API (growth) 744

SAT Testing, 2006-07

Enrollment, Grade 12 6,154
Number taking test 2,120
percent taking test 34.5%
percent with total score 1,500+ 14.30%

Average Scores:

Math	Verbal	Writing	Total
496	478	476	1,450

Federal No Child Left Behind, 2008

(Adequate Yearly Progress standards met)

	Participation Rate	Pct Proficient
ELA	Yes	No
Math	Yes	No

API criteria .... Yes
Graduation rate .... Yes
criteria met/possible 46/43

Other school districts for this city

(see Appendix E for information on these districts)

None

See Introduction for an explanation of all data sources.

Demographics & Socio-Economic Characteristics

(2000 Decennial Census, except as noted)

Population

1990* 9,770
2000 14,674
Male 10,909
Female 3,765
Jan. 2008 (estimate)§ 16,609
Persons per sq. mi. of land 869.6

Race & Hispanic Origin, 2000

Race
White 5,259
Black/African American 1,850
North American Native 139
Asian 57
Pacific Islander 8
Other Race 6,952
Two or more races 409
Hispanic origin, total 9,667
Mexican 8,780
Puerto Rican 15
Cuban 3
Other Hispanic 869

Age & Nativity, 2000

Under 5 years 924
18 years and over 11,464
65 years and over 477
85 years and over 51
Median Age 31.0
Native-born 11,001
Foreign-born 3,710

Educational Attainment, 2000

Population 25 years and over 9,415
Less than 9th grade 24.2%
High school grad or higher 56.1%
Bachelor's degree or higher 4.1%
Graduate degree 1.0%

Income & Poverty, 1999

Per capita income $14,090
Median household income $29,710
Median family income $28,019
Persons in poverty 16.9%
H'holds receiving public assistance 182
H'holds receiving social security 349

Households, 2000

Total households 1,928
With persons under 18 1,294
With persons over 65 286
Family households 1,641
Single person households 218
Persons per household 4.14
Persons per family 4.30

Household Population, 2008§§

Persons living in households 9,039
Persons living in group quarters 7,570
Persons per household 4.3

Labor & Employment

Total civilian labor force, 2008§§ 4,200
Unemployment rate, 2008 .... 19.3%
Total civilian labor force, 2000 3,368

Employed persons 16 years and over by occupation, 2000

Managers & professionals 350
Service occupations 376
Sales & office occupations 418
Farming, fishing & forestry 838
Construction & maintenance 220
Production & transportation 362
Self-employed persons 89

* US Census Bureau
** 2000 Decennial Census
§ California Department of Finance
§§ California Employment Development Dept

General Information

City of Avenal
919 Skyline Blvd
City Hall
Avenal, CA 93204
559-386-5766

Website .... NA
Elevation .... NA
Land Area (sq. miles) 19.1
Water Area (sq. miles) 0
Year of Incorporation 1979
Government type .... General law
Sales tax rate 8.25%

Voters & Officials

Registered Voters, October 2008

Total 1,672
Democrats 808
Republicans 530
Declined to state 261

Legislative Districts

US Congressional 20
State Senatorial 16
State Assembly 30

Local Officials, 2009

Mayor .... Harlin Casida
Manager .... Melissa G. Whitten
City Clerk .... Pamela Johanne Bonilla
Attorney .... Mike Farley
Finance Dir .... Esther O. Strong
Public Works .... Jerry Watson
Planning/Dev Dir .... Steve Sopp
Building .... NA
Police Chief .... Don Deeds
Emergency/Fire Dir .... Mark Hahn

Public Safety

Number of officers, 2007 .... NA
Violent crimes, 2007 44
Property crimes, 2007 133
Arson, 2007 .... NA

Public Library

Avenal Library
Kings County Library System
501 E Kings St
Avenal, CA 93204
559-386-5741

Branch Librarian .... Sheryl Tune

Library system statistics, FY 2007

Population served 151,381
Internet terminals 59
Annual users 42,581

Per capita:

Operating income $11.91
percent from local government 86.5%
Operating expenditure $11.91
Total materials 1.20
Print holdings 1.17
Visits per capita .... NA

Housing & Construction

Housing Units

Total, 2008§ 2,258
Single family units, attached 147
Single family units, detached 1,401
Multiple family units 614
Mobile home units 96
Occupied 2,113
Vacancy rate 6.4%
Median rent, 2000** $488
Median SF home value, 2000** $69,700

New Privately Owned Housing Units Authorized by Building Permit, 2007*

	Units	Construction Cost
Single	21	$2,328,434
Total	21	$2,328,434

Municipal Finance

(For local fiscal year ended in 2006)

Revenues

Total $9,172,398
Taxes 2,128,658
Special benefits assessment 0
Licenses & permits 70,503
Fines & forfeitures 59,675
Revenues from use of money & property 717,607
Intergovernmental 1,711,985
Service charges 4,037,789
Other revenues 446,181
Other financing sources 0

Expenditures

Total $9,283,399
General government 517,189
Public safety 1,365,048
Transportation 491,598
Community development 2,016,882
Health 1,485,373
Culture & leisure 447,283
Other 0

Local School District

(Data from School year 2007-08 except as noted)

Reef-Sunset Unified
205 North Park Ave
Avenal, CA 93204
(559) 386-9083

Superintendent .... Suzanne Monroe
Grade plan K-12
Number of schools 9
Enrollment 2,590
High school graduates, 2006-07 96
Dropout rate 1.0%
Pupil/teacher ratio 20.0
Average class size 22.7
Students per computer 3.4
Classrooms with internet 400
Avg. Daily Attendance (ADA) 2,354
Cost per ADA $9,305
Avg. Teacher Salary $56,811

California Achievement Tests 6th ed., 2008

(Pct scoring at or above 50th National Percentile Rank)

	Math	Reading	Language
Grade 3	31%	12%	17%
Grade 7	26%	21%	17%

Academic Performance Index, 2008

Number of students tested 1,906
Number of valid scores 1,689
2007 API (base) 607
2008 API (growth) 604

SAT Testing, 2006-07

Enrollment, Grade 12 121
Number taking test 28
percent taking test 23.1%
percent with total score 1,500+ 3.30%

Average Scores:

Math	Verbal	Writing	Total
422	425	415	1,262

Federal No Child Left Behind, 2008

(Adequate Yearly Progress standards met)

	Participation Rate	Pct Proficient
ELA	Yes	No
Math	Yes	No

API criteria .... No
Graduation rate .... Yes
\# criteria met/possible 22/11

Other school districts for this city

(see Appendix E for information on these districts)

None

See Introduction for an explanation of all data sources.

Demographics & Socio-Economic Characteristics

(2000 Decennial Census, except as noted)

Population

1990* 41,333
2000 44,712
Male 22,075
Female 22,637
Jan. 2008 (estimate)§ 48,743
Persons per sq. mi. of land 5,476.7

Race & Hispanic Origin, 2000

Race
White 23,406
Black/African American 1,688
North American Native 585
Asian 2,747
Pacific Islander 77
Other Race 13,646
Two or more races 2,563
Hispanic origin, total 28,522
Mexican 23,836
Puerto Rican 208
Cuban 129
Other Hispanic 4,349

Age & Nativity, 2000

Under 5 years 4,138
18 years and over 30,932
65 years and over 3,098
85 years and over 315
Median Age 27.1
Native-born 29,278
Foreign-born 15,093

Educational Attainment, 2000

Population 25 years and over 23,725
Less than 9th grade 22.1%
High school grad or higher 60.7%
Bachelor's degree or higher 14.2%
Graduate degree 4.3%

Income & Poverty, 1999

Per capita income $13,412
Median household income $39,191
Median family income $40,918
Persons in poverty 17.7%
H'holds receiving public assistance 775
H'holds receiving social security 2,246

Households, 2000

Total households 12,549
With persons under 18 6,222
With persons over 65 2,382
Family households 9,294
Single person households 2,347
Persons per household 3.41
Persons per family 3.90

Household Population, 2008§§

Persons living in households 46,794
Persons living in group quarters 1,949
Persons per household 3.6

Labor & Employment

Total civilian labor force, 2008§§ 21,700
Unemployment rate, 2008 .... 8.2%
Total civilian labor force, 2000 19,633

Employed persons 16 years and over by occupation, 2000

Managers & professionals 4,205
Service occupations 3,165
Sales & office occupations 4,996
Farming, fishing & forestry 97
Construction & maintenance 1,771
Production & transportation 3,617
Self-employed persons 922

* US Census Bureau
** 2000 Decennial Census
§ California Department of Finance
§§ California Employment Development Dept

General Information

City of Azusa
213 E Foothill Blvd
Azusa, CA 91702
626-812-5200

Website .... www.ci.azusa.ca.us
Elevation .... 612 ft.
Land Area (sq. miles) 8.9
Water Area (sq. miles) 0
Year of Incorporation 1898
Government type .... General law
Sales tax rate 9.25%

Voters & Officials

Registered Voters, October 2008

Total 16,368
Democrats 7,868
Republicans 4,581
Declined to state 3,211

Legislative Districts

US Congressional 25, 30, 42
State Senatorial 24
State Assembly 57

Local Officials, 2009

Mayor .... Joseph Rocha
Manager .... Francis Delach
City Clerk .... Vera Mendoza
Attorney .... Best, Best & Kreiger
Finance Dir .... Alan Kreimeier
Public Works .... James Makshanoff
Comm/Econ Dev Dir .... Bruce Coleman
Building .... NA
Police Chief .... Bob Garcia
Fire/Emergency Mgmt .... (County)

Public Safety

Number of officers, 2007 62
Violent crimes, 2007 206
Property crimes, 2007 1,273
Arson, 2007 8

Public Library

Azusa City Library
729 N Dalton Ave
Azusa, CA 91702
626-812-5232

Director .... Albert Tovar

Library statistics, FY 2007

Population served 48,640
Internet terminals 45
Annual users 17,255

Per capita:

Operating income $26.42
percent from local government 92.9%
Operating expenditure $22.68
Total materials 2.79
Print holdings 2.65
Visits per capita 2.09

Housing & Construction

Housing Units

Total, 2008§ 13,588
Single family units, attached 1,769
Single family units, detached 6,293
Multiple family units 4,937
Mobile home units 589
Occupied 13,103
Vacancy rate 3.6%
Median rent, 2000** $743
Median SF home value, 2000** $149,300

New Privately Owned Housing Units Authorized by Building Permit, 2007*

	Units	Construction Cost
Single	159	$43,585,124
Total	170	$45,320,691

Municipal Finance

(For local fiscal year ended in 2006)

Revenues

Total $93,192,301
Taxes 21,826,832
Special benefits assessment 0
Licenses & permits 411,425
Fines & forfeitures 549,718
Revenues from use of money & property 2,590,832
Intergovernmental 4,248,925
Service charges 60,541,554
Other revenues 3,023,015
Other financing sources 0

Expenditures

Total $80,900,638
General government 4,514,981
Public safety 15,451,005
Transportation 4,456,447
Community development 2,364,352
Health 3,856,444
Culture & leisure 3,838,173
Other 1,153,433

Local School District

(Data from School year 2007-08 except as noted)

Azusa Unified
PO Box 500
Azusa, CA 91702
(626) 967-6211

Superintendent .... Cynthia McGuire
Grade plan K-12
Number of schools 18
Enrollment 11,219
High school graduates, 2006-07 562
Dropout rate 3.1%
Pupil/teacher ratio 21.0
Average class size 26.9
Students per computer 4.1
Classrooms with internet 550
Avg. Daily Attendance (ADA) 11,019
Cost per ADA $8,264
Avg. Teacher Salary .... NA

California Achievement Tests 6th ed., 2008

(Pct scoring at or above 50th National Percentile Rank)

	Math	Reading	Language
Grade 3	45%	23%	34%
Grade 7	36%	33%	31%

Academic Performance Index, 2008

Number of students tested 8,805
Number of valid scores 8,229
2007 API (base) 660
2008 API (growth) 672

SAT Testing, 2006-07

Enrollment, Grade 12 591
Number taking test 179
percent taking test 30.3%
percent with total score 1,500+ 7.30%

Average Scores:

Math	Verbal	Writing	Total
463	436	441	1,340

Federal No Child Left Behind, 2008

(Adequate Yearly Progress standards met)

	Participation Rate	Pct Proficient
ELA	Yes	No
Math	Yes	No

API criteria .... Yes
Graduation rate .... Yes
criteria met/possible 34/26

Other school districts for this city

(see Appendix E for information on these districts)

None

See Introduction for an explanation of all data sources.

Demographics & Socio-Economic Characteristics†

(2007 American Community Survey, except as noted)

Population

1990*	174,820
2007	324,540
Male	158,400
Female	166,140
Jan. 2008 (estimate)§	328,692
Persons per sq. mi. of land	2,906.2

Race & Hispanic Origin, 2007

Race	
White	184,720
Black/African American	26,710
North American Native	2,215
Asian	17,646
Pacific Islander	317
Other Race	80,472
Two or more races	12,460
Hispanic origin, total	135,819
Mexican	121,859
Puerto Rican	857
Cuban	0
Other Hispanic	13,103

Age & Nativity, 2007

Under 5 years	29,992
18 years and over	227,440
65 years and over	27,932
85 years and over	3,786
Median Age	29.4
Native-born	261,995
Foreign-born	62,545

Educational Attainment, 2007

Population 25 years and over	191,005
Less than 9th grade	13.1%
High school grad or higher	74.5%
Bachelor's degree or higher	18.6%
Graduate degree	7.2%

Income & Poverty, 2007

Per capita income	$22,278
Median household income	$51,664
Median family income	$56,782
Persons in poverty	15.5%
H'holds receiving public assistance	4,677
H'holds receiving social security	23,125

Households, 2007

Total households	102,185
With persons under 18	50,557
With persons over 65	19,789
Family households	77,953
Single person households	20,443
Persons per household	3.10
Persons per family	3.54

Household Population, 2008§§

Persons living in households	324,905
Persons living in group quarters	3,787
Persons per household	3.0

Labor & Employment

Total civilian labor force, 2008§§	154,300
Unemployment rate, 2008	6.8%
Total civilian labor force, 2000*	111,452

Employed persons 16 years and over by occupation, 2007

Managers & professionals	41,809
Service occupations	26,737
Sales & office occupations	33,927
Farming, fishing & forestry	4,017
Construction & maintenance	15,030
Production & transportation	16,399
Self-employed persons	9,513

† see Appendix D for 2000 Decennial Census Data
* US Census Bureau
** 2007 American Community Survey
§ California Department of Finance
§§ California Employment Development Dept

General Information

City of Bakersfield
1501 Truxtun Ave
Bakersfield, CA 93301
661-326-3767

Website	www.bakersfieldcity.us
Elevation	408 ft.
Land Area (sq. miles)	113.1
Water Area (sq. miles)	1.3
Year of Incorporation	1898
Government type	Chartered
Sales tax rate	8.25%

Voters & Officials

Registered Voters, October 2008

Total	138,812
Democrats	50,289
Republicans	63,065
Declined to state	21,049

Legislative Districts

US Congressional	20, 22
State Senatorial	16, 18
State Assembly	30, 32

Local Officials, 2009

Mayor	Harvey L. Hall
Manager	Alan Tandy
City Clerk	Pamela A. McCarthy
Attorney	Virginia Gennaro
Finance Dir	Nelson Smith
Public Works	Raul Rojas
Comm/Econ Dev Dir	Donna Kunz
Building	Phil Burns
Police Chief	William Rector
Emergency/Fire Dir	Ron Fraze

Public Safety

Number of officers, 2007	340
Violent crimes, 2007	1,961
Property crimes, 2007	16,058
Arson, 2007	91

Public Library

Beale Memorial Library
Kern County Library System
701 Truxtun Ave
Bakersfield, CA 93301
661-868-0701

Director	Diane Duquette

Library system statistics, FY 2007

Population served	801,648
Internet terminals	237
Annual users	337,030

Per capita:

Operating income	$12.11
percent from local government	90.4%
Operating expenditure	$12.11
Total materials	1.37
Print holdings	1.29
Visits per capita	2.09

Housing & Construction

Housing Units

Total, 2008§	114,187
Single family units, attached	3,224
Single family units, detached	81,193
Multiple family units	27,051
Mobile home units	2,719
Occupied	107,948
Vacancy rate	5.5%
Median rent, 2007**	$868
Median SF home value, 2007**	$300,500

New Privately Owned Housing Units Authorized by Building Permit, 2007*

	Units	Construction Cost
Single	1,820	$272,107,393
Total	2,133	$295,518,263

Municipal Finance

(For local fiscal year ended in 2006)

Revenues

Total	$324,073,564
Taxes	140,416,439
Special benefits assessment	2,289,376
Licenses & permits	4,262,899
Fines & forfeitures	2,174,364
Revenues from use of money & property	11,352,206
Intergovernmental	25,672,982
Service charges	135,417,748
Other revenues	2,487,550
Other financing sources	0

Expenditures

Total	$265,109,531
General government	14,864,054
Public safety	92,315,109
Transportation	21,534,746
Community development	31,857,311
Health	56,404,890
Culture & leisure	30,252,803
Other	0

Local School District

(Data from School year 2007-08 except as noted)

Kern Union High
5801 Sundale Ave
Bakersfield, CA 93309
(661) 827-3100

Superintendent	Donald Carter
Grade plan	9-12
Number of schools	22
Enrollment	37,341
High school graduates, 2006-07	6,321
Dropout rate	5.3%
Pupil/teacher ratio	23.3
Average class size	26.2
Students per computer	4.2
Classrooms with internet	1,524
Avg. Daily Attendance (ADA)	37,540
Cost per ADA	$8,547
Avg. Teacher Salary	$63,074

California Achievement Tests 6th ed., 2008

(Pct scoring at or above 50th National Percentile Rank)

	Math	Reading	Language
Grade 3	NA	NA	NA
Grade 7	NA	NA	NA

Academic Performance Index, 2008

Number of students tested	26,804
Number of valid scores	24,540
2007 API (base)	654
2008 API (growth)	661

SAT Testing, 2006-07

Enrollment, Grade 12	8,277
Number taking test	2,144
percent taking test	25.9%
percent with total score 1,500+	9.90%

Average Scores:

Math	Verbal	Writing	Total
488	471	464	1,423

Federal No Child Left Behind, 2008

(Adequate Yearly Progress standards met)

	Participation Rate	Pct Proficient
ELA	Yes	No
Math	Yes	No

API criteria	Yes
Graduation rate	No
# criteria met/possible	34/29

Other school districts for this city

(see Appendix E for information on these districts)

Complete list in Appendix E

Demographics & Socio-Economic Characteristics†

(2007 American Community Survey, except as noted)

Population

1990*	69,330
2007	76,945
Male	38,908
Female	38,037
Jan. 2008 (estimate)§	81,281
Persons per sq. mi. of land	12,131.5

Race & Hispanic Origin, 2007

Race	
White	20,348
Black/African American	806
North American Native	329
Asian	9,875
Pacific Islander	0
Other Race	43,810
Two or more races	1,777
Hispanic origin, total	NA
Mexican	54,755
Puerto Rican	0
Cuban	44
Other Hispanic	7,364

Age & Nativity, 2007

Under 5 years	7,046
18 years and over	52,605
65 years and over	7,211
85 years and over	837
Median Age	29.6
Native-born	40,820
Foreign-born	36,125

Educational Attainment, 2007

Population 25 years and over	43,551
Less than 9th grade	24.7%
High school grad or higher	58.9%
Bachelor's degree or higher	9.3%
Graduate degree	2.6%

Income & Poverty, 2007

Per capita income	$14,237
Median household income	$52,491
Median family income	$55,545
Persons in poverty	11.1%
H'holds receiving public assistance	458
H'holds receiving social security	4,174

Households, 2007

Total households	16,631
With persons under 18	9,901
With persons over 65	4,435
Family households	14,285
Single person households	1,368
Persons per household	4.58
Persons per family	4.79

Household Population, 2008§§

Persons living in households	80,675
Persons living in group quarters	606
Persons per household	4.6

Labor & Employment

Total civilian labor force, 2008§§	33,800
Unemployment rate, 2008	9.5%
Total civilian labor force, 2000*	29,024

Employed persons 16 years and over by occupation, 2007

Managers & professionals	4,975
Service occupations	6,861
Sales & office occupations	7,297
Farming, fishing & forestry	0
Construction & maintenance	4,193
Production & transportation	8,429
Self-employed persons	1,509

† see Appendix D for 2000 Decennial Census Data
* US Census Bureau
** 2007 American Community Survey
§ California Department of Finance
§§ California Employment Development Dept

General Information

City of Baldwin Park
14403 E Pacific Ave
Baldwin Park, CA 91706
626-960-4011

Website	www.baldwinpark.com
Elevation	374 ft.
Land Area (sq. miles)	6.7
Water Area (sq. miles)	0.1
Year of Incorporation	1956
Government type	General law
Sales tax rate	9.25%

Voters & Officials

Registered Voters, October 2008

Total	25,345
Democrats	14,488
Republicans	4,595
Declined to state	5,301

Legislative Districts

US Congressional	32
State Senatorial	24
State Assembly	57

Local Officials, 2009

Mayor	Manuel Lozano
Manager	Vijay Singhal
City Clerk	Susan Rubio
Attorney	Joseph W. Pannone
Finance Dir	NA
Public Works	William Galvez
Community Dev Mgr	Marc Castagnola
Building	Gene Logan
Police Chief	Lili Hadsell
Fire/Emergency Mgmt	NA

Public Safety

Number of officers, 2007	77
Violent crimes, 2007	281
Property crimes, 2007	1,914
Arson, 2007	16

Public Library

Baldwin Park Library
Los Angeles County Public Library System
4181 Baldwin Park Blvd
Baldwin Park, CA 91706
626-962-6947

Branch Librarian	Rafael Gonzalez

Library system statistics, FY 2007

Population served	3,673,313
Internet terminals	749
Annual users	3,748,771

Per capita:

Operating income	$30.06
percent from local government	93.6%
Operating expenditure	$28.36
Total materials	2.22
Print holdings	1.97
Visits per capita	3.25

Housing & Construction

Housing Units

Total, 2008§	17,867
Single family units, attached	1,878
Single family units, detached	12,081
Multiple family units	3,565
Mobile home units	343
Occupied	17,386
Vacancy rate	2.7%
Median rent, 2007**	$1,075
Median SF home value, 2007**	$438,400

New Privately Owned Housing Units Authorized by Building Permit, 2007*

	Units	Construction Cost
Single	28	$4,926,911
Total	28	$4,926,911

Municipal Finance

(For local fiscal year ended in 2006)

Revenues

Total	$33,361,431
Taxes	18,751,265
Special benefits assessment	1,467,135
Licenses & permits	1,232,262
Fines & forfeitures	1,350,965
Revenues from use of money & property	384,920
Intergovernmental	5,753,099
Service charges	2,423,056
Other revenues	1,657,440
Other financing sources	341,289

Expenditures

Total	$35,449,313
General government	7,909,036
Public safety	15,510,816
Transportation	4,484,669
Community development	4,736,965
Health	320,633
Culture & leisure	2,487,194
Other	0

Local School District

(Data from School year 2007-08 except as noted)

Baldwin Park Unified
3699 North Holly Ave
Baldwin Park, CA 91706
(626) 962-3311

Superintendent	Mark Skvarna
Grade plan	K-12
Number of schools	23
Enrollment	19,696
High school graduates, 2006-07	1,179
Dropout rate	19.9%
Pupil/teacher ratio	24.0
Average class size	27.8
Students per computer	5.6
Classrooms with internet	634
Avg. Daily Attendance (ADA)	16,401
Cost per ADA	$8,084
Avg. Teacher Salary	$71,617

California Achievement Tests 6th ed., 2008

(Pct scoring at or above 50th National Percentile Rank)

	Math	Reading	Language
Grade 3	47%	21%	30%
Grade 7	47%	38%	37%

Academic Performance Index, 2008

Number of students tested	12,846
Number of valid scores	12,317
2007 API (base)	675
2008 API (growth)	686

SAT Testing, 2006-07

Enrollment, Grade 12	1,525
Number taking test	282
percent taking test	18.5%
percent with total score 1,500+	4.70%

Average Scores:

Math	Verbal	Writing	Total
457	434	433	1,324

Federal No Child Left Behind, 2008

(Adequate Yearly Progress standards met)

	Participation Rate	Pct Proficient
ELA	Yes	No
Math	Yes	No

API criteria	Yes
Graduation rate	Yes
# criteria met/possible	34/28

Other school districts for this city

(see Appendix E for information on these districts)

None

See Introduction for an explanation of all data sources.

Demographics & Socio-Economic Characteristics

(2000 Decennial Census, except as noted)

Population

1990* . . . 20,570
2000 . . . 23,562
Male . . . 11,220
Female . . . 12,342
Jan. 2008 (estimate)§ . . . 28,348
Persons per sq. mi. of land . . . 1,227.2

Race & Hispanic Origin, 2000

Race
White . . . 15,124
Black/African American . . . 2,014
North American Native . . . 593
Asian . . . 1,268
Pacific Islander . . . 30
Other Race . . . 3,505
Two or more races . . . 1,028
Hispanic origin, total . . . 7,119
Mexican . . . 6,061
Puerto Rican . . . 50
Cuban . . . 27
Other Hispanic . . . 981

Age & Nativity, 2000

Under 5 years . . . 1,599
18 years and over . . . 17,332
65 years and over . . . 6,316
85 years and over . . . 547
Median Age . . . 40.7
Native-born . . . 20,100
Foreign-born . . . 3,343

Educational Attainment, 2000

Population 25 years and over . . . 15,386
Less than 9th grade . . . 8.5%
High school grad or higher . . . 76.0%
Bachelor's degree or higher . . . 12.6%
Graduate degree . . . 5.6%

Income & Poverty, 1999

Per capita income . . . $16,231
Median household income . . . $32,076
Median family income . . . $38,995
Persons in poverty . . . 19.6%
H'holds receiving public assistance . . . 647
H'holds receiving social security . . . 4,248

Households, 2000

Total households . . . 8,923
With persons under 18 . . . 2,721
With persons over 65 . . . 4,187
Family households . . . 6,239
Single person households . . . 2,298
Persons per household . . . 2.60
Persons per family . . . 3.11

Household Population, 2008§§

Persons living in households . . . 28,010
Persons living in group quarters . . . 338
Persons per household . . . 2.6

Labor & Employment

Total civilian labor force, 2008§§ . . . 11,600
Unemployment rate, 2008 . . . 9.9%
Total civilian labor force, 2000 . . . 8,248

Employed persons 16 years and over by occupation, 2000

Managers & professionals . . . 1,551
Service occupations . . . 1,518
Sales & office occupations . . . 2,465
Farming, fishing & forestry . . . 32
Construction & maintenance . . . 818
Production & transportation . . . 1,123
Self-employed persons . . . 624

* US Census Bureau
** 2000 Decennial Census
§ California Department of Finance
§§ California Employment Development Dept

General Information

City of Banning
99 E Ramsey St
PO Box 998
Banning, CA 92220
951-922-3105

Website . . . www.ci.banning.ca.us
Elevation . . . 2,349 ft.
Land Area (sq. miles) . . . 23.1
Water Area (sq. miles) . . . 0
Year of Incorporation . . . 1913
Government type . . . General law
Sales tax rate . . . 8.75%

Voters & Officials

Registered Voters, October 2008

Total . . . 13,189
Democrats . . . 5,322
Republicans . . . 5,513
Declined to state . . . 1,824

Legislative Districts

US Congressional . . . 41
State Senatorial . . . 37
State Assembly . . . 65

Local Officials, 2009

Mayor . . . Bob E. Botts
Manager . . . Brian Nakamura
City Clerk . . . Marie Calderon
Attorney . . . David Aleshire
Finance Dir . . . Bonnie Johnson
Public Works . . . Duane Burk
Planning/Dev Dir . . . Matthew Bassi (Int)
Building . . . Tim Steenson
Police Chief . . . Leonard Purvis
Fire/Emergency Mgmt . . . NA

Public Safety

Number of officers, 2007 . . . 40
Violent crimes, 2007 . . . 209
Property crimes, 2007 . . . 769
Arson, 2007 . . . 0

Public Library

Banning Library District
Banning Unified School Dist Lib Sys
21 W Nicolet St
Banning, CA 92220
951-849-3192

Director . . . Patti Hanley

Library system statistics, FY 2007

Population served . . . 30,816
Internet terminals . . . 10
Annual users . . . 21,964

Per capita:

Operating income . . . $22.45
percent from local government . . . 94.4%
Operating expenditure . . . $22.46
Total materials . . . 2.01
Print holdings . . . 1.83
Visits per capita . . . 3.07

Housing & Construction

Housing Units

Total, 2008§ . . . 11,631
Single family units, attached . . . 728
Single family units, detached . . . 8,728
Multiple family units . . . 1,019
Mobile home units . . . 1,156
Occupied . . . 10,655
Vacancy rate . . . 8.4%
Median rent, 2000** . . . $564
Median SF home value, 2000** . . . $110,000

New Privately Owned Housing Units Authorized by Building Permit, 2007*

	Units	Construction Cost
Single	14	$2,693,480
Total	14	$2,693,480

Municipal Finance

(For local fiscal year ended in 2006)

Revenues

Total . . . $74,224,758
Taxes . . . 10,074,551
Special benefits assessment . . . 62,467
Licenses & permits . . . 436,660
Fines & forfeitures . . . 388,573
Revenues from use of money & property . . . 19,995,737
Intergovernmental . . . 3,717,802
Service charges . . . 38,772,785
Other revenues . . . 776,183
Other financing sources . . . 0

Expenditures

Total . . . $72,889,582
General government . . . 3,453,080
Public safety . . . 10,351,778
Transportation . . . 6,424,285
Community development . . . 1,009,881
Health . . . 4,788,340
Culture & leisure . . . 1,249,720
Other . . . 0

Local School District

(Data from School year 2007-08 except as noted)

Banning Unified
161 West Williams St
Banning, CA 92220
(951) 922-0200

Superintendent . . . Lynne Kennedy
Grade plan . . . K-12
Number of schools . . . 9
Enrollment . . . 4,983
High school graduates, 2006-07 . . . 262
Dropout rate . . . 7.7%
Pupil/teacher ratio . . . 20.5
Average class size . . . 26.0
Students per computer . . . 3.5
Classrooms with internet . . . 227
Avg. Daily Attendance (ADA) . . . 4,738
Cost per ADA . . . $8,828
Avg. Teacher Salary . . . $64,096

California Achievement Tests 6th ed., 2008

(Pct scoring at or above 50th National Percentile Rank)

	Math	Reading	Language
Grade 3	46%	27%	34%
Grade 7	39%	33%	34%

Academic Performance Index, 2008

Number of students tested . . . 3,831
Number of valid scores . . . 3,428
2007 API (base) . . . 654
2008 API (growth) . . . 674

SAT Testing, 2006-07

Enrollment, Grade 12 . . . 304
Number taking test . . . 88
percent taking test . . . 29.0%
percent with total score 1,500+ . . . 5.90%

Average Scores:

Math	Verbal	Writing	Total
446	422	429	1,297

Federal No Child Left Behind, 2008

(Adequate Yearly Progress standards met)

	Participation Rate	Pct Proficient
ELA	Yes	No
Math	Yes	No

API criteria . . . Yes
Graduation rate . . . Yes
\# criteria met/possible . . . 38/27

Other school districts for this city

(see Appendix E for information on these districts)

None

Demographics & Socio-Economic Characteristics
(2000 Decennial Census, except as noted)

Population
1990* . . . 21,472
2000 . . . 21,119
Male . . . 10,536
Female . . . 10,583
Jan. 2008 (estimate)§ . . . 23,952
Persons per sq. mi. of land . . . 712.9

Race & Hispanic Origin, 2000
Race
White . . . 12,059
Black/African American . . . 2,450
North American Native . . . 510
Asian . . . 650
Pacific Islander . . . 200
Other Race . . . 3,886
Two or more races . . . 1,364
Hispanic origin, total . . . 7,708
Mexican . . . 5,301
Puerto Rican . . . 186
Cuban . . . 30
Other Hispanic . . . 2,191

Age & Nativity, 2000
Under 5 years . . . 1,755
18 years and over . . . 14,615
65 years and over . . . 2,549
85 years and over . . . 237
Median Age . . . 32.1
Native-born . . . 18,473
Foreign-born . . . 2,515

Educational Attainment, 2000
Population 25 years and over . . . 12,407
Less than 9th grade . . . 8.8%
High school grad or higher . . . 77.6%
Bachelor's degree or higher . . . 9.1%
Graduate degree . . . 3.3%

Income & Poverty, 1999
Per capita income . . . $16,132
Median household income . . . $35,069
Median family income . . . $40,160
Persons in poverty . . . 19.7%
H'holds receiving public assistance . . . 634
H'holds receiving social security . . . 1,907

Households, 2000
Total households . . . 7,647
With persons under 18 . . . 3,178
With persons over 65 . . . 1,728
Family households . . . 5,252
Single person households . . . 1,981
Persons per household . . . 2.71
Persons per family . . . 3.27

Household Population, 2008§§
Persons living in households . . . 23,641
Persons living in group quarters . . . 311
Persons per household . . . 2.9

Labor & Employment
Total civilian labor force, 2008§§ . . . 10,600
Unemployment rate, 2008 . . . 9.9%
Total civilian labor force, 2000 . . . 8,769

Employed persons 16 years and over by occupation, 2000
Managers & professionals . . . 1,795
Service occupations . . . 1,440
Sales & office occupations . . . 2,419
Farming, fishing & forestry . . . 37
Construction & maintenance . . . 919
Production & transportation . . . 1,251
Self-employed persons . . . 340

* US Census Bureau
** 2000 Decennial Census
§ California Department of Finance
§§ California Employment Development Dept

General Information
City of Barstow
220 E Mtn View St
Suite A
Barstow, CA 92311
760-256-3531

Website . . . www.barstowca.org
Elevation . . . 2,106 ft.
Land Area (sq. miles) . . . 33.6
Water Area (sq. miles) . . . 0
Year of Incorporation . . . 1947
Government type . . . General law
Sales tax rate . . . 8.75%

Voters & Officials
Registered Voters, October 2008
Total . . . 9,302
Democrats . . . 3,870
Republicans . . . 2,973
Declined to state . . . 2,005

Legislative Districts
US Congressional . . . 25
State Senatorial . . . 18
State Assembly . . . 34

Local Officials, 2009
Mayor . . . Lawrence Dale
Manager . . . Richard Rowe (Int)
City Clerk . . . JoAnne Cousino
Attorney . . . Yvette Abich
Finance Dir . . . Gil Olivarez
Public Works . . . Todd Edwards
Planning/Dev Dir . . . Brent Morrow
Building . . . Bob Cooper
Police Chief . . . Diane Burns
Fire Chief . . . Darrell Jauss

Public Safety
Number of officers, 2007 . . . 32
Violent crimes, 2007 . . . 337
Property crimes, 2007 . . . 1,209
Arson, 2007 . . . 15

Public Library
Barstow Branch Library
San Bernardino County Library System
304 E Buena Vista
Barstow, CA 92311
760-256-4850

Branch Librarian . . . Joyce Burk

Library system statistics, FY 2007
Population served . . . 1,177,092
Internet terminals . . . 12
Annual users . . . 45,343

Per capita:
Operating income . . . $14.27
percent from local government . . . 73.3%
Operating expenditure . . . $13.86
Total materials . . . 0.86
Print holdings . . . 0.79
Visits per capita . . . 5.83

Housing & Construction
Housing Units
Total, 2008§ . . . 9,990
Single family units, attached . . . 356
Single family units, detached . . . 5,549
Multiple family units . . . 2,970
Mobile home units . . . 1,115
Occupied . . . 8,284
Vacancy rate . . . 17.1%
Median rent, 2000** . . . $504
Median SF home value, 2000** . . . $75,700

New Privately Owned Housing Units Authorized by Building Permit, 2007*

	Units	Construction Cost
Single	71	$8,640,108
Total	71	$8,640,108

Municipal Finance
(For local fiscal year ended in 2006)

Revenues
Total . . . $29,945,301
Taxes . . . 16,560,296
Special benefits assessment . . . 0
Licenses & permits . . . 293,766
Fines & forfeitures . . . 226,652
Revenues from use of money & property . . . 689,491
Intergovernmental . . . 1,969,609
Service charges . . . 8,002,363
Other revenues . . . 2,203,124
Other financing sources . . . 0

Expenditures
Total . . . $25,097,819
General government . . . 2,394,162
Public safety . . . 6,209,705
Transportation . . . 3,753,031
Community development . . . 5,712,940
Health . . . 5,908,903
Culture & leisure . . . 1,119,078
Other . . . 0

Local School District
(Data from School year 2007-08 except as noted)
Barstow Unified
551 South Avenue H
Barstow, CA 92311
(760) 255-6000

Superintendent . . . Susan Levine
Grade plan . . . K-12
Number of schools . . . 13
Enrollment . . . 6,949
High school graduates, 2006-07 . . . 323
Dropout rate . . . 6.9%
Pupil/teacher ratio . . . 20.3
Average class size . . . 25.9
Students per computer . . . 4.1
Classrooms with internet . . . 624
Avg. Daily Attendance (ADA) . . . 6,492
Cost per ADA . . . $8,121
Avg. Teacher Salary . . . $56,288

California Achievement Tests 6th ed., 2008
(Pct scoring at or above 50th National Percentile Rank)

	Math	Reading	Language
Grade 3	43%	30%	38%
Grade 7	30%	30%	26%

Academic Performance Index, 2008
Number of students tested . . . 5,136
Number of valid scores . . . 4,636
2007 API (base) . . . 664
2008 API (growth) . . . 682

SAT Testing, 2006-07
Enrollment, Grade 12 . . . 414
Number taking test . . . 126
percent taking test . . . 30.4%
percent with total score 1,500+ . . . 6.80%

Average Scores:

Math	Verbal	Writing	Total
446	441	440	1,327

Federal No Child Left Behind, 2008
(Adequate Yearly Progress standards met)

	Participation Rate	Pct Proficient
ELA	Yes	No
Math	Yes	No

API criteria . . . Yes
Graduation rate . . . No
\# criteria met/possible . . . 30/23

Other school districts for this city
(see Appendix E for information on these districts)
None

See Introduction for an explanation of all data sources.

Demographics & Socio-Economic Characteristics

(2000 Decennial Census, except as noted)

Population

1990* . . . 9,685
2000 . . . 11,384
Male . . . 5,443
Female . . . 5,941
Jan. 2008 (estimate)§ . . . 31,477
Persons per sq. mi. of land . . . 1,157.2

Race & Hispanic Origin, 2000

Race
White . . . 7,751
Black/African American . . . 331
North American Native . . . 265
Asian . . . 189
Pacific Islander . . . 8
Other Race . . . 2,314
Two or more races . . . 526
Hispanic origin, total . . . 4,122
Mexican . . . 3,504
Puerto Rican . . . 22
Cuban . . . 16
Other Hispanic . . . 580

Age & Nativity, 2000

Under 5 years . . . 1,049
18 years and over . . . 7,632
65 years and over . . . 1,216
85 years and over . . . 166
Median Age . . . 30.3
Native-born . . . 9,465
Foreign-born . . . 1,850

Educational Attainment, 2000

Population 25 years and over . . . 6,468
Less than 9th grade . . . 11.8%
High school grad or higher . . . 69.4%
Bachelor's degree or higher . . . 8.8%
Graduate degree . . . 3.4%

Income & Poverty, 1999

Per capita income . . . $14,141
Median household income . . . $29,721
Median family income . . . $37,403
Persons in poverty . . . 19.8%
H'holds receiving public assistance . . . 275
H'holds receiving social security . . . 1,128

Households, 2000

Total households . . . 3,881
With persons under 18 . . . 1,832
With persons over 65 . . . 870
Family households . . . 2,784
Single person households . . . 867
Persons per household . . . 2.89
Persons per family . . . 3.39

Household Population, 2008§§

Persons living in households . . . 31,322
Persons living in group quarters . . . 155
Persons per household . . . 2.9

Labor & Employment

Total civilian labor force, 2008§§ . . . 6,800
Unemployment rate, 2008 . . . 10.5%
Total civilian labor force, 2000 . . . 4,843

Employed persons 16 years and over by occupation, 2000

Managers & professionals . . . 825
Service occupations . . . 1,014
Sales & office occupations . . . 1,169
Farming, fishing & forestry . . . 22
Construction & maintenance . . . 590
Production & transportation . . . 774
Self-employed persons . . . 223

* US Census Bureau
** 2000 Decennial Census
§ California Department of Finance
§§ California Employment Development Dept

General Information

City of Beaumont
550 E 6th St
Beaumont, CA 92223
951-769-8520

Website . . . www.ci.beaumont.ca.us
Elevation . . . 2,573 ft.
Land Area (sq. miles) . . . 27.2
Water Area (sq. miles) . . . 0
Year of Incorporation . . . 1912
Government type . . . General law
Sales tax rate . . . 8.75%

Voters & Officials

Registered Voters, October 2008

Total . . . 12,570
Democrats . . . 4,603
Republicans . . . 5,060
Declined to state . . . 2,302

Legislative Districts

US Congressional . . . 41
State Senatorial . . . 37
State Assembly . . . 65

Local Officials, 2009

Mayor . . . Brian BeForge
City Manager . . . Alan Kapanicas
City Clerk . . . Karen Thompson
Attorney . . . Joseph Aklufi
Finance Dir . . . William Aylward
Public Works . . . NA
Planning Dir . . . Ernest Egger
Building . . . NA
Police Chief . . . Frank Coe
Fire/Emergency Mgmt . . . NA

Public Safety

Number of officers, 2007 . . . 45
Violent crimes, 2007 . . . 46
Property crimes, 2007 . . . 660
Arson, 2007 . . . 0

Public Library

Beaumont Library District
125 E Eighth St
Beaumont, CA 92223
951-845-1357

Director . . . Clara DiFelice

Library statistics, FY 2007

Population served . . . 52,893
Internet terminals . . . 9
Annual users . . . 12,909

Per capita:

Operating income . . . $22.80
percent from local government . . . 92.5%
Operating expenditure . . . $15.08
Total materials . . . 1.23
Print holdings . . . 1.13
Visits per capita . . . 1.81

Housing & Construction

Housing Units

Total, 2008§ . . . 11,800
Single family units, attached . . . 172
Single family units, detached . . . 10,190
Multiple family units . . . 1,091
Mobile home units . . . 347
Occupied . . . 10,658
Vacancy rate . . . 9.7%
Median rent, 2000** . . . $489
Median SF home value, 2000** . . . $98,600

New Privately Owned Housing Units Authorized by Building Permit, 2007*

	Units	Construction Cost
Single	1,033	$186,813,587
Total	1,033	$186,813,587

Municipal Finance

(For local fiscal year ended in 2006)

Revenues

Total . . . NA
Taxes . . . NA
Special benefits assessment . . . NA
Licenses & permits . . . NA
Fines & forfeitures . . . NA
Revenues from use of money & property . . . NA
Intergovernmental . . . NA
Service charges . . . NA
Other revenues . . . NA
Other financing sources . . . NA

Expenditures

Total . . . NA
General government . . . NA
Public safety . . . NA
Transportation . . . NA
Community development . . . NA
Health . . . NA
Culture & leisure . . . NA
Other . . . NA

Local School District

(Data from School year 2007-08 except as noted)

Beaumont Unified
PO Box 187
Beaumont, CA 92223
(951) 845-1631

Superintendent . . . Barry Kayrell
Grade plan . . . K-12
Number of schools . . . 12
Enrollment . . . 7,757
High school graduates, 2006-07 . . . 329
Dropout rate . . . 3.7%
Pupil/teacher ratio . . . 23.9
Average class size . . . 26.3
Students per computer . . . 4.0
Classrooms with internet . . . 396
Avg. Daily Attendance (ADA) . . . 7,447
Cost per ADA . . . $7,520
Avg. Teacher Salary . . . $61,544

California Achievement Tests 6th ed., 2008

(Pct scoring at or above 50th National Percentile Rank)

	Math	Reading	Language
Grade 3	63%	41%	49%
Grade 7	52%	45%	45%

Academic Performance Index, 2008

Number of students tested . . . 6,091
Number of valid scores . . . 5,536
2007 API (base) . . . 729
2008 API (growth) . . . 752

SAT Testing, 2006-07

Enrollment, Grade 12 . . . 347
Number taking test . . . 82
percent taking test . . . 23.6%
percent with total score 1,500+ . . . 11.00%

Average Scores:

Math	Verbal	Writing	Total
497	491	475	1,463

Federal No Child Left Behind, 2008

(Adequate Yearly Progress standards met)

	Participation Rate	Pct Proficient
ELA	Yes	No
Math	Yes	No

API criteria . . . Yes
Graduation rate . . . Yes
\# criteria met/possible . . . 38/35

Other school districts for this city

(see Appendix E for information on these districts)

None

See Introduction for an explanation of all data sources.

Demographics & Socio-Economic Characteristics

(2000 Decennial Census, except as noted)

Population

1990* . . . 34,365
2000 . . . 36,664
Male . . . 18,516
Female . . . 18,148
Jan. 2008 (estimate)§ . . . 38,762
Persons per sq. mi. of land . . . 15,504.8

Race & Hispanic Origin, 2000

Race
White . . . 17,764
Black/African American . . . 468
North American Native . . . 470
Asian . . . 391
Pacific Islander . . . 22
Other Race . . . 15,798
Two or more races . . . 1,751
Hispanic origin, total . . . 33,328
Mexican . . . 24,558
Puerto Rican . . . 180
Cuban . . . 939
Other Hispanic . . . 7,651

Age & Nativity, 2000

Under 5 years . . . 3,957
18 years and over . . . 23,712
65 years and over . . . 1,964
85 years and over . . . 250
Median Age . . . 25.9
Native-born . . . 17,137
Foreign-born . . . 19,530

Educational Attainment, 2000

Population 25 years and over . . . 19,045
Less than 9th grade . . . 38.6%
High school grad or higher . . . 35.1%
Bachelor's degree or higher . . . 4.0%
Graduate degree . . . 1.3%

Income & Poverty, 1999

Per capita income . . . $9,905
Median household income . . . $29,946
Median family income . . . $30,504
Persons in poverty . . . 23.9%
H'holds receiving public assistance . . . 748
H'holds receiving social security . . . 1,250

Households, 2000

Total households . . . 8,918
With persons under 18 . . . 5,774
With persons over 65 . . . 1,498
Family households . . . 7,616
Single person households . . . 981
Persons per household . . . 4.05
Persons per family . . . 4.27

Household Population, 2008§§

Persons living in households . . . 38,224
Persons living in group quarters . . . 538
Persons per household . . . 4.2

Labor & Employment

Total civilian labor force, 2008§§ . . . 16,000
Unemployment rate, 2008 . . . 10.1%
Total civilian labor force, 2000 . . . 13,912

Employed persons 16 years and over by occupation, 2000

Managers & professionals . . . 1,552
Service occupations . . . 1,917
Sales & office occupations . . . 3,039
Farming, fishing & forestry . . . 71
Construction & maintenance . . . 1,401
Production & transportation . . . 4,426
Self-employed persons . . . 795

* US Census Bureau
** 2000 Decennial Census
§ California Department of Finance
§§ California Employment Development Dept

General Information

City of Bell
6330 Pine Ave
Bell, CA 90201
323-588-6211

Website . . . NA
Elevation . . . 145 ft.
Land Area (sq. miles) . . . 2.5
Water Area (sq. miles) . . . 0.2
Year of Incorporation . . . 1927
Government type . . . General law
Sales tax rate . . . 9.25%

Voters & Officials

Registered Voters, October 2008

Total . . . 9,364
Democrats . . . 6,023
Republicans . . . 1,296
Declined to state . . . 1,703

Legislative Districts

US Congressional . . . 34
State Senatorial . . . 30
State Assembly . . . 50

Local Officials, 2009

Mayor . . . Oscar Hernandez
Manager . . . Robert Rizzo
City Clerk . . . Rebecca Valdez
Attorney . . . Edward Lee
Finance Dir . . . Lourdes Garcia
Public Works . . . Carlos Alvarado
Planning Dir . . . Dennis Tarango
Building . . . NA
Police Chief . . . Andreas Probst
Fire/Emergency Mgmt . . . NA

Public Safety

Number of officers, 2007 . . . 36
Violent crimes, 2007 . . . 175
Property crimes, 2007 . . . 581
Arson, 2007 . . . NA

Public Library

Bell Library
Los Angeles County Public Library System
4411 E Gage Ave
Bell, CA 90201
323-560-2149

Branch Librarian . . . Martin Delgado

Library system statistics, FY 2007

Population served . . . 3,673,313
Internet terminals . . . 749
Annual users . . . 3,748,771

Per capita:

Operating income . . . $30.06
percent from local government . . . 93.6%
Operating expenditure . . . $28.36
Total materials . . . 2.22
Print holdings . . . 1.97
Visits per capita . . . 3.25

Housing & Construction

Housing Units

Total, 2008§ . . . 9,304
Single family units, attached . . . 1,517
Single family units, detached . . . 3,596
Multiple family units . . . 3,730
Mobile home units . . . 461
Occupied . . . 9,005
Vacancy rate . . . 3.2%
Median rent, 2000** . . . $642
Median SF home value, 2000** . . . $167,100

New Privately Owned Housing Units Authorized by Building Permit, 2007*

	Units	Construction Cost
Single	18	$2,601,000
Total	18	$2,601,000

Municipal Finance

(For local fiscal year ended in 2006)

Revenues

Total . . . $31,862,785
Taxes . . . 12,537,087
Special benefits assessment . . . 236,127
Licenses & permits . . . 387,019
Fines & forfeitures . . . 1,342,673
Revenues from use of money & property . . . 1,049,542
Intergovernmental . . . 3,952,713
Service charges . . . 3,073,244
Other revenues . . . 59,380
Other financing sources . . . 9,225,000

Expenditures

Total . . . $37,010,024
General government . . . 6,416,410
Public safety . . . 17,354,246
Transportation . . . 2,048,760
Community development . . . 6,599,551
Health . . . 2,069,095
Culture & leisure . . . 2,521,962
Other . . . 0

Local School District

(Data from School year 2007-08 except as noted)

Los Angeles Unified
333 South Beaudry Ave
Los Angeles, CA 90017
(213) 241-1000

Superintendent . . . Ramon Cortines
Grade plan . . . PK-12
Number of schools . . . 827
Enrollment . . . 693,680
High school graduates, 2006-07 . . . 28,545
Dropout rate . . . 7.8%
Pupil/teacher ratio . . . 19.8
Average class size . . . 24.9
Students per computer . . . 3.7
Classrooms with internet . . . 31,112
Avg. Daily Attendance (ADA) . . . 653,672
Cost per ADA . . . $10,053
Avg. Teacher Salary . . . $63,391

California Achievement Tests 6th ed., 2008

(Pct scoring at or above 50th National Percentile Rank)

	Math	Reading	Language
Grade 3	49%	27%	39%
Grade 7	37%	33%	33%

Academic Performance Index, 2008

Number of students tested . . . 495,046
Number of valid scores . . . 471,641
2007 API (base) . . . 662
2008 API (growth) . . . 683

SAT Testing, 2006-07

Enrollment, Grade 12 . . . 32,370
Number taking test . . . 15,447
percent taking test . . . 47.7%
percent with total score 1,500+ . . . 12.50%

Average Scores:

Math	Verbal	Writing	Total
443	438	441	1,322

Federal No Child Left Behind, 2008

(Adequate Yearly Progress standards met)

	Participation Rate	Pct Proficient
ELA	Yes	No
Math	Yes	No

API criteria . . . Yes
Graduation rate . . . Yes
\# criteria met/possible . . . 46/38

Other school districts for this city

(see Appendix E for information on these districts)

None

See Introduction for an explanation of all data sources.

Demographics & Socio-Economic Characteristics

(2000 Decennial Census, except as noted)

Population

1990*	42,355
2000	44,054
Male	22,301
Female	21,753
Jan. 2008 (estimate)§	46,766
Persons per sq. mi. of land	18,706.4

Race & Hispanic Origin, 2000

Race	
White	21,180
Black/African American	429
North American Native	730
Asian	270
Pacific Islander	45
Other Race	19,329
Two or more races	2,071
Hispanic origin, total	41,132
Mexican	32,875
Puerto Rican	110
Cuban	147
Other Hispanic	8,000

Age & Nativity, 2000

Under 5 years	5,043
18 years and over	26,659
65 years and over	1,736
85 years and over	179
Median Age	23.8
Native-born	21,838
Foreign-born	22,216

Educational Attainment, 2000

Population 25 years and over	20,942
Less than 9th grade	42.7%
High school grad or higher	31.3%
Bachelor's degree or higher	4.0%
Graduate degree	1.8%

Income & Poverty, 1999

Per capita income	$8,415
Median household income	$30,597
Median family income	$30,419
Persons in poverty	27.0%
H'holds receiving public assistance	1,330
H'holds receiving social security	958

Households, 2000

Total households	9,466
With persons under 18	7,025
With persons over 65	1,229
Family households	8,511
Single person households	684
Persons per household	4.61
Persons per family	4.69

Household Population, 2008§§

Persons living in households	46,310
Persons living in group quarters	456
Persons per household	4.8

Labor & Employment

Total civilian labor force, 2008§§	17,400
Unemployment rate, 2008	12.2%
Total civilian labor force, 2000	14,933

Employed persons 16 years and over by occupation, 2000

Managers & professionals	1,167
Service occupations	2,177
Sales & office occupations	3,248
Farming, fishing & forestry	151
Construction & maintenance	1,285
Production & transportation	5,020
Self-employed persons	676

* US Census Bureau
** 2000 Decennial Census
§ California Department of Finance
§§ California Employment Development Dept

General Information

City of Bell Gardens
7100 S Garfield Ave
Bell Gardens, CA 90201
562-806-7700

Website	www.bellgardens.org
Elevation	125 ft.
Land Area (sq. miles)	2.5
Water Area (sq. miles)	0
Year of Incorporation	1961
Government type	General law
Sales tax rate	9.25%

Voters & Officials

Registered Voters, October 2008

Total	11,112
Democrats	7,090
Republicans	1,324
Declined to state	2,212

Legislative Districts

US Congressional	34
State Senatorial	30
State Assembly	50

Local Officials, 2009

Mayor	Priscilla Flores
Manager	G.Steve Simonian
City Clerk	Vida Barone (Int)
Attorney	Arnold Alvarez-Glasman
Finance Dir	Rafaela King (Int)
Public Works	John Oropeza
Planning/Dev Dir	Carmen Morales
Building	George Suarez
Police Chief	Keith Kilmer
Emergency/Fire Dir	Phil Schneider

Public Safety

Number of officers, 2007	52
Violent crimes, 2007	218
Property crimes, 2007	862
Arson, 2007	4

Public Library

Bell Gardens Library
Los Angeles County Public Library System
7110 S Garfield Ave
Bell Gardens, CA 90201
562-927-1309

Branch Librarian	Susan Schlaeger

Library system statistics, FY 2007

Population served	3,673,313
Internet terminals	749
Annual users	3,748,771

Per capita:

Operating income	$30.06
percent from local government	93.6%
Operating expenditure	$28.36
Total materials	2.22
Print holdings	1.97
Visits per capita	3.25

Housing & Construction

Housing Units

Total, 2008§	9,921
Single family units, attached	2,470
Single family units, detached	4,001
Multiple family units	3,054
Mobile home units	396
Occupied	9,594
Vacancy rate	3.3%
Median rent, 2000**	$665
Median SF home value, 2000**	$175,000

New Privately Owned Housing Units Authorized by Building Permit, 2007*

	Units	Construction Cost
Single	28	$4,266,840
Total	37	$5,474,100

Municipal Finance

(For local fiscal year ended in 2006)

Revenues

Total	$33,520,422
Taxes	17,809,591
Special benefits assessment	0
Licenses & permits	490,883
Fines & forfeitures	443,550
Revenues from use of money & property	1,223,775
Intergovernmental	2,759,797
Service charges	2,491,406
Other revenues	1,106,453
Other financing sources	7,194,967

Expenditures

Total	$35,070,940
General government	4,880,592
Public safety	10,124,773
Transportation	4,747,457
Community development	643,947
Health	1,303,904
Culture & leisure	11,964,203
Other	0

Local School District

(Data from School year 2007-08 except as noted)

Montebello Unified
123 South Montebello Blvd
Montebello, CA 90640
(323) 887-7900

Superintendent	Edward Velasquez
Grade plan	K-12
Number of schools	29
Enrollment	33,493
High school graduates, 2006-07	1,721
Dropout rate	3.2%
Pupil/teacher ratio	23.7
Average class size	29.7
Students per computer	6.6
Classrooms with internet	2,124
Avg. Daily Attendance (ADA)	32,764
Cost per ADA	$8,211
Avg. Teacher Salary	$70,515

California Achievement Tests 6th ed., 2008

(Pct scoring at or above 50th National Percentile Rank)

	Math	Reading	Language
Grade 3	47%	24%	38%
Grade 7	39%	31%	32%

Academic Performance Index, 2008

Number of students tested	26,036
Number of valid scores	24,510
2007 API (base)	668
2008 API (growth)	679

SAT Testing, 2006-07

Enrollment, Grade 12	2,168
Number taking test	580
percent taking test	26.8%
percent with total score 1,500+	6.60%

Average Scores:

Math	Verbal	Writing	Total
461	443	440	1,344

Federal No Child Left Behind, 2008

(Adequate Yearly Progress standards met)

	Participation Rate	Pct Proficient
ELA	Yes	No
Math	Yes	No

API criteria	Yes
Graduation rate	Yes
# criteria met/possible	30/25

Other school districts for this city

(see Appendix E for information on these districts)

None

See Introduction for an explanation of all data sources.

Demographics & Socio-Economic Characteristics†
(2007 American Community Survey, except as noted)

Population
1990* 61,815
2007 69,477
Male 34,693
Female 34,784
Jan. 2008 (estimate)§ 77,110
Persons per sq. mi. of land 12,641.0

Race & Hispanic Origin, 2007
Race
White 27,191
Black/African American 7,254
North American Native 312
Asian 12,701
Pacific Islander 358
Other Race 19,878
Two or more races 1,783
Hispanic origin, total 25,784
Mexican 21,463
Puerto Rican 512
Cuban 0
Other Hispanic 3,809

Age & Nativity, 2007
Under 5 years 4,593
18 years and over 50,302
65 years and over 7,876
85 years and over 1,047
Median Age 33.7
Native-born 49,002
Foreign-born 20,475

Educational Attainment, 2007
Population 25 years and over 43,467
Less than 9th grade 10.8%
High school grad or higher 81.1%
Bachelor's degree or higher 22.2%
Graduate degree 4.9%

Income & Poverty, 2007
Per capita income $22,610
Median household income $48,264
Median family income $60,041
Persons in poverty 7.5%
H'holds receiving public assistance 537
H'holds receiving social security 5,548

Households, 2007
Total households 23,502
With persons under 18 9,864
With persons over 65 5,452
Family households 16,738
Single person households 5,318
Persons per household 2.94
Persons per family 3.50

Household Population, 2008§§
Persons living in households 76,487
Persons living in group quarters 623
Persons per household 3.2

Labor & Employment
Total civilian labor force, 2008§§ 37,100
Unemployment rate, 2008 .... 7.6%
Total civilian labor force, 2000* 31,863

Employed persons 16 years and over by occupation, 2007
Managers & professionals .... NA
Service occupations .... NA
Sales & office occupations .... NA
Farming, fishing & forestry .... NA
Construction & maintenance .... NA
Production & transportation .... NA
Self-employed persons 1,088

† see Appendix D for 2000 Decennial Census Data
* US Census Bureau
** 2007 American Community Survey
§ California Department of Finance
§§ California Employment Development Dept

General Information
City of Bellflower
16600 Civic Center Dr
Bellflower, CA 90706
562-804-1424

Website .... www.bellflower.org
Elevation .... 71 ft.
Land Area (sq. miles) 6.1
Water Area (sq. miles) 0.1
Year of Incorporation 1957
Government type .... General law
Sales tax rate 9.25%

Voters & Officials
Registered Voters, October 2008
Total 29,215
Democrats 15,077
Republicans 7,536
Declined to state 5,391

Legislative Districts
US Congressional 34
State Senatorial 27
State Assembly 50

Local Officials, 2009
Mayor .... Randy Bomgaars
City Manager .... Michael J. Egan
City Clerk .... Debra D. Bauchop
Attorney .... Joseph W. Pannone
Finance Dir .... Tae Rhee
Public Works .... Deborah Chankin
Community Dev Dir .... Brian K. Lee
Building .... NA
Public Safety Dir .... Joel Hockman
Emergency/Fire Dir .... (County)

Public Safety
Number of officers, 2007 .... NA
Violent crimes, 2007 507
Property crimes, 2007 2,524
Arson, 2007 13

Public Library
Clifton M. Brakensiek Library
Los Angeles County Public Library System
9945 E Flower St
Bellflower, CA 90706
562-925-5543

Branch Librarian .... Susan Kane

Library system statistics, FY 2007
Population served 3,673,313
Internet terminals 749
Annual users 3,748,771

Per capita:
Operating income $30.06
percent from local government 93.6%
Operating expenditure $28.36
Total materials 2.22
Print holdings 1.97
Visits per capita 3.25

Housing & Construction
Housing Units
Total, 2008§ 24,506
Single family units, attached 2,085
Single family units, detached 11,249
Multiple family units 9,570
Mobile home units 1,602
Occupied 23,616
Vacancy rate 3.6%
Median rent, 2007** $996
Median SF home value, 2007** $517,300

New Privately Owned Housing Units Authorized by Building Permit, 2007*

	Units	Construction Cost
Single	21	$3,221,337
Total	46	$4,042,747

Municipal Finance
(For local fiscal year ended in 2006)

Revenues
Total $31,768,412
Taxes 21,663,095
Special benefits assessment 0
Licenses & permits 750,458
Fines & forfeitures 1,627,310
Revenues from use of money & property 979,070
Intergovernmental 5,644,074
Service charges 787,206
Other revenues 317,199
Other financing sources 0

Expenditures
Total $30,708,102
General government 3,243,691
Public safety 9,703,976
Transportation 7,119,501
Community development 5,672,022
Health 0
Culture & leisure 4,968,912
Other 0

Local School District
(Data from School year 2007-08 except as noted)
Bellflower Unified
16703 South Clark Ave
Bellflower, CA 90706
(562) 866-9011

Superintendent .... Rick Kemppainen
Grade plan K-12
Number of schools 15
Enrollment 14,672
High school graduates, 2006-07 953
Dropout rate 3.9%
Pupil/teacher ratio 22.1
Average class size 26.1
Students per computer 4.7
Classrooms with internet 668
Avg. Daily Attendance (ADA) 14,472
Cost per ADA $7,782
Avg. Teacher Salary $65,560

California Achievement Tests 6th ed., 2008
(Pct scoring at or above 50th National Percentile Rank)

	Math	Reading	Language
Grade 3	63%	38%	48%
Grade 7	49%	42%	45%

Academic Performance Index, 2008
Number of students tested 11,317
Number of valid scores 10,546
2007 API (base) 739
2008 API (growth) 751

SAT Testing, 2006-07
Enrollment, Grade 12 1,187
Number taking test 329
percent taking test 27.7%
percent with total score 1,500+ 8.90%

Average Scores:

Math	Verbal	Writing	Total
472	458	454	1,384

Federal No Child Left Behind, 2008
(Adequate Yearly Progress standards met)

	Participation Rate	Pct Proficient
ELA	Yes	No
Math	Yes	No

API criteria .... Yes
Graduation rate .... Yes
\# criteria met/possible 42/40

Other school districts for this city
(see Appendix E for information on these districts)
None

See Introduction for an explanation of all data sources.

Demographics & Socio-Economic Characteristics

(2000 Decennial Census, except as noted)

Population

1990* 24,127
2000 25,123
Male 12,350
Female 12,773
Jan. 2008 (estimate)§ 26,078
Persons per sq. mi. of land 5,795.1

Race & Hispanic Origin, 2000

Race
White 18,889
Black/African American 422
North American Native 72
Asian 3,878
Pacific Islander 136
Other Race 659
Two or more races 1,067
Hispanic origin, total 2,090
Mexican 936
Puerto Rican 95
Cuban 38
Other Hispanic 1,021

Age & Nativity, 2000

Under 5 years 1,512
18 years and over 20,278
65 years and over 3,327
85 years and over 375
Median Age 38.8
Native-born 19,465
Foreign-born 5,673

Educational Attainment, 2000

Population 25 years and over 18,793
Less than 9th grade 1.8%
High school grad or higher 94.2%
Bachelor's degree or higher 51.7%
Graduate degree 21.2%

Income & Poverty, 1999

Per capita income $42,812
Median household income $80,905
Median family income $95,722
Persons in poverty 3.9%
H'holds receiving public assistance 76
H'holds receiving social security 2,223

Households, 2000

Total households 10,418
With persons under 18 2,916
With persons over 65 2,266
Family households 6,547
Single person households 2,838
Persons per household 2.35
Persons per family 2.89

Household Population, 2008§§

Persons living in households 25,451
Persons living in group quarters 627
Persons per household 2.4

Labor & Employment

Total civilian labor force, 2008§§ 14,900
Unemployment rate, 2008 .... 4.1%
Total civilian labor force, 2000 14,677

Employed persons 16 years and over by occupation, 2000

Managers & professionals 7,745
Service occupations 998
Sales & office occupations 3,786
Farming, fishing & forestry 0
Construction & maintenance 874
Production & transportation 835
Self-employed persons 1,101

* US Census Bureau
** 2000 Decennial Census
§ California Department of Finance
§§ California Employment Development Dept

General Information

City of Belmont
One Twin Pines Ln
Belmont, CA 94002
650-595-7413

Website .... www.belmont.gov
Elevation .... 35 ft.
Land Area (sq. miles) 4.5
Water Area (sq. miles) 0
Year of Incorporation 1926
Government type .... General law
Sales tax rate 9.25%

Voters & Officials

Registered Voters, October 2008

Total 16,032
Democrats 7,934
Republicans 3,650
Declined to state 3,821

Legislative Districts

US Congressional 14
State Senatorial 8
State Assembly 19

Local Officials, 2009

Mayor .... David Braunstein
Manager .... Jack Crist
City Clerk .... Terri Cook
Attorney .... Marc Zafferano
Finance Dir .... Thomas Fil
Public Works .... Ray Davis
Planning/Dev Dir .... Carlos de Melo
Building .... Carlos de Melo
Police Chief .... Don Mattei
Fire Chief .... Doug Fry

Public Safety

Number of officers, 2007 29
Violent crimes, 2007 24
Property crimes, 2007 357
Arson, 2007 9

Public Library

Belmont Library
San Mateo County Library System
1110 Alameda de las Pulgas
Belmont, CA 94002
650-591-8286

Branch Librarian .... Linda Chiochios

Library system statistics, FY 2007

Population served 278,388
Internet terminals 26
Annual users 49,920

Per capita:

Operating income $90.21
percent from local government 63.5%
Operating expenditure $60.41
Total materials 2.65
Print holdings 2.16
Visits per capita 5.44

Housing & Construction

Housing Units

Total, 2008§ 10,822
Single family units, attached 649
Single family units, detached 6,302
Multiple family units 3,871
Mobile home units 0
Occupied 10,701
Vacancy rate 1.1%
Median rent, 2000** $1,116
Median SF home value, 2000** $593,200

New Privately Owned Housing Units Authorized by Building Permit, 2007*

	Units	Construction Cost
Single	2	$800,000
Total	2	$800,000

Municipal Finance

(For local fiscal year ended in 2006)

Revenues

Total $32,790,261
Taxes 11,004,440
Special benefits assessment 0
Licenses & permits 517,868
Fines & forfeitures 192,995
Revenues from use of money & property 822,709
Intergovernmental 2,276,100
Service charges 9,781,481
Other revenues 694,668
Other financing sources 7,500,000

Expenditures

Total $31,474,844
General government 5,051,302
Public safety 7,465,559
Transportation 1,799,012
Community development 1,630,238
Health 6,857,329
Culture & leisure 8,671,404
Other 0

Local School District

(Data from School year 2007-08 except as noted)

Sequoia Union High
480 James Ave
Redwood City, CA 94062
(650) 369-1411

Superintendent .... Patrick Gemma
Grade plan 9-12
Number of schools 6
Enrollment 8,510
High school graduates, 2006-07 1,546
Dropout rate 3.2%
Pupil/teacher ratio 19.7
Average class size 26.4
Students per computer 3.0
Classrooms with internet 402
Avg. Daily Attendance (ADA) 7,811
Cost per ADA $11,470
Avg. Teacher Salary $76,194

California Achievement Tests 6th ed., 2008

(Pct scoring at or above 50th National Percentile Rank)

	Math	Reading	Language
Grade 3	NA	NA	NA
Grade 7	NA	NA	NA

Academic Performance Index, 2008

Number of students tested 5,874
Number of valid scores 5,525
2007 API (base) 753
2008 API (growth) 753

SAT Testing, 2006-07

Enrollment, Grade 12 2,000
Number taking test 945
percent taking test 47.3%
percent with total score 1,500+ 29.10%

Average Scores:

Math	Verbal	Writing	Total
546	530	530	1,606

Federal No Child Left Behind, 2008

(Adequate Yearly Progress standards met)

	Participation Rate	Pct Proficient
ELA	Yes	No
Math	Yes	No

API criteria .... Yes
Graduation rate .... Yes
\# criteria met/possible 28/25

Other school districts for this city

(see Appendix E for information on these districts)

Belmont-Redwood Shores Elem

See Introduction for an explanation of all data sources.

Demographics & Socio-Economic Characteristics

(2000 Decennial Census, except as noted)

Population

1990* 2,147
2000 2,125
Male 983
Female 1,142
Jan. 2008 (estimate)§ 2,161
Persons per sq. mi. of land 4,322.0

Race & Hispanic Origin, 2000

Race
White 2,060
Black/African American 2
North American Native 1
Asian 38
Pacific Islander 1
Other Race 11
Two or more races 12
Hispanic origin, total 46
Mexican 17
Puerto Rican 2
Cuban 0
Other Hispanic 27

Age & Nativity, 2000

Under 5 years 96
18 years and over 1,701
65 years and over 576
85 years and over 54
Median Age 52.7
Native-born 1,901
Foreign-born 220

Educational Attainment, 2000

Population 25 years and over 1,642
Less than 9th grade 0.0%
High school grad or higher 98.8%
Bachelor's degree or higher 75.4%
Graduate degree 34.7%

Income & Poverty, 1999

Per capita income $113,595
Median household income $130,796
Median family income $185,590
Persons in poverty 5.7%
H'holds receiving public assistance 0
H'holds receiving social security 354

Households, 2000

Total households 956
With persons under 18 231
With persons over 65 409
Family households 657
Single person households 258
Persons per household 2.22
Persons per family 2.68

Household Population, 2008§§

Persons living in households 2,161
Persons living in group quarters 0
Persons per household 2.2

Labor & Employment

Total civilian labor force, 2008§§ .... NA
Unemployment rate, 2008 .... NA
Total civilian labor force, 2000 899

Employed persons 16 years and over by occupation, 2000

Managers & professionals 603
Service occupations 59
Sales & office occupations 209
Farming, fishing & forestry 0
Construction & maintenance 6
Production & transportation 0
Self-employed persons 189

* US Census Bureau
** 2000 Decennial Census
§ California Department of Finance
§§ California Employment Development Dept

General Information

City of Belvedere
450 San Rafael Ave
Belvedere, CA 94920
415-435-3838

Website .... www.cityofbelvedere.org
Elevation .... NA
Land Area (sq. miles) 0.5
Water Area (sq. miles) 1.9
Year of Incorporation 1896
Government type .... General law
Sales tax rate 9.00%

Voters & Officials

Registered Voters, October 2008

Total 1,592
Democrats 613
Republicans 581
Declined to state 350

Legislative Districts

US Congressional 6
State Senatorial 3
State Assembly 6

Local Officials, 2009

Mayor .... Thomas Cromwell
City Manager .... George J. Rodericks
City Clerk .... Leslie Carpentiers (Dep)
Attorney .... Robert Epstein
Finance Dir .... Rebecca Eastman
Public Works .... George J. Rodericks
Planning Dir .... Pierce Macdonald
Building .... Lee Braun
Police Chief .... Mark Campbell
Fire Chief .... Richard Pearce

Public Safety

Number of officers, 2007 7
Violent crimes, 2007 1
Property crimes, 2007 22
Arson, 2007 0

Public Library

Belvedere-Tiburon Library
1501 Tiburon Blvd
Tiburon, CA 94920
415-789-2665

Director .... Deborah Mazzolini

Library statistics, FY 2007

Population served 11,031
Internet terminals 20
Annual users 34,682

Per capita:

Operating income $143.66
percent from local government 81.0%
Operating expenditure $136.94
Total materials 7.15
Print holdings 5.65
Visits per capita .... NA

Housing & Construction

Housing Units

Total, 2008§ 1,065
Single family units, attached 54
Single family units, detached 874
Multiple family units 137
Mobile home units 0
Occupied 962
Vacancy rate 9.7%
Median rent, 2000** $2,001
Median SF home value, 2000** .. $1,000,001

New Privately Owned Housing Units Authorized by Building Permit, 2007*

	Units	Construction Cost
Single	2	$190,000
Total	2	$190,000

Municipal Finance

(For local fiscal year ended in 2006)

Revenues

Total $5,564,274
Taxes 3,400,270
Special benefits assessment 548,816
Licenses & permits 412,175
Fines & forfeitures 189,740
Revenues from use of money & property 202,112
Intergovernmental 375,624
Service charges 330,737
Other revenues 104,800
Other financing sources 0

Expenditures

Total $6,271,660
General government 677,156
Public safety 2,117,235
Transportation 1,060,139
Community development 1,293,917
Health 974,259
Culture & leisure 148,954
Other 0

Local School District

(Data from School year 2007-08 except as noted)

Tamalpais Union High
PO Box 605
Larkspur, CA 94977
(415) 945-3720

Superintendent .... Laurie Kimbrel
Grade plan 9-12
Number of schools 5
Enrollment 3,889
High school graduates, 2006-07 959
Dropout rate 0.8%
Pupil/teacher ratio 17.4
Average class size 24.4
Students per computer 2.6
Classrooms with internet 232
Avg. Daily Attendance (ADA) 3,715
Cost per ADA $13,492
Avg. Teacher Salary $81,923

California Achievement Tests 6th ed., 2008

(Pct scoring at or above 50th National Percentile Rank)

	Math	Reading	Language
Grade 3	NA	NA	NA
Grade 7	NA	NA	NA

Academic Performance Index, 2008

Number of students tested 2,800
Number of valid scores 2,766
2007 API (base) 848
2008 API (growth) 855

SAT Testing, 2006-07

Enrollment, Grade 12 997
Number taking test 730
percent taking test 73.2%
percent with total score 1,500+ 58.30%

Average Scores:

Math	Verbal	Writing	Total
574	574	574	1,722

Federal No Child Left Behind, 2008

(Adequate Yearly Progress standards met)

	Participation Rate	Pct Proficient
ELA	Yes	Yes
Math	Yes	Yes

API criteria .... Yes
Graduation rate .... Yes
\# criteria met/possible 10/10

Other school districts for this city

(see Appendix E for information on these districts)

Reed Union Elem

See Introduction for an explanation of all data sources.

Demographics & Socio-Economic Characteristics

(2000 Decennial Census, except as noted)

Population

1990*	24,437
2000	26,865
Male	13,066
Female	13,799
Jan. 2008 (estimate)§	27,978
Persons per sq. mi. of land	2,168.8

Race & Hispanic Origin, 2000

Race	
White	21,195
Black/African American	1,295
North American Native	162
Asian	2,031
Pacific Islander	78
Other Race	712
Two or more races	1,392
Hispanic origin, total	2,424
Mexican	1,482
Puerto Rican	113
Cuban	36
Other Hispanic	793

Age & Nativity, 2000

Under 5 years	1,510
18 years and over	19,582
65 years and over	2,498
85 years and over	239
Median Age	38.9
Native-born	24,437
Foreign-born	2,530

Educational Attainment, 2000

Population 25 years and over	17,930
Less than 9th grade	2.6%
High school grad or higher	91.7%
Bachelor's degree or higher	37.3%
Graduate degree	13.0%

Income & Poverty, 1999

Per capita income	$31,226
Median household income	$67,617
Median family income	$77,974
Persons in poverty	4.3%
H'holds receiving public assistance	147
H'holds receiving social security	2,138

Households, 2000

Total households	10,328
With persons under 18	4,060
With persons over 65	1,870
Family households	7,244
Single person households	2,440
Persons per household	2.60
Persons per family	3.10

Household Population, 2008§§

Persons living in households	27,924
Persons living in group quarters	54
Persons per household	2.5

Labor & Employment

Total civilian labor force, 2008§§	17,000
Unemployment rate, 2008	4.3%
Total civilian labor force, 2000	14,681

Employed persons 16 years and over by occupation, 2000

Managers & professionals	6,455
Service occupations	1,785
Sales & office occupations	3,677
Farming, fishing & forestry	42
Construction & maintenance	1,005
Production & transportation	1,175
Self-employed persons	1,313

* US Census Bureau
** 2000 Decennial Census
§ California Department of Finance
§§ California Employment Development Dept

General Information

City of Benicia
250 East L St
Benicia, CA 94510
707-746-4200

Website	www.ci.benicia.ca.us
Elevation	33 ft.
Land Area (sq. miles)	12.9
Water Area (sq. miles)	2.7
Year of Incorporation	1850
Government type	General law
Sales tax rate	8.38%

Voters & Officials

Registered Voters, October 2008

Total	17,027
Democrats	8,351
Republicans	4,560
Declined to state	3,335

Legislative Districts

US Congressional	7
State Senatorial	2
State Assembly	8

Local Officials, 2009

Mayor	Elizabeth Patterson
Manager	Jim Erickson
City Clerk	Lisa Wolfe
Attorney	Heather McLaughlin
Finance Dir	Rob Sousa
Public Works	Dan Schiada
Community Dev Dir	Charlie Knox
Building	NA
Police Chief	Sandra Spagnoli
Fire Chief	Steven Vucurevich

Public Safety

Number of officers, 2007	33
Violent crimes, 2007	57
Property crimes, 2007	475
Arson, 2007	13

Public Library

Benicia Public Library
150 East L St
Benicia, CA 94510
707-746-4343

Director	Diane Smikahl

Library statistics, FY 2007

Population served	27,916
Internet terminals	20
Annual users	63,554

Per capita:

Operating income	$77.98
percent from local government	87.5%
Operating expenditure	$77.98
Total materials	4.32
Print holdings	3.55
Visits per capita	8.34

Housing & Construction

Housing Units

Total, 2008§	11,307
Single family units, attached	1,049
Single family units, detached	7,428
Multiple family units	2,504
Mobile home units	326
Occupied	11,072
Vacancy rate	2.1%
Median rent, 2000**	$892
Median SF home value, 2000**	$274,600

New Privately Owned Housing Units Authorized by Building Permit, 2007*

	Units	Construction Cost
Single	39	$7,690,222
Total	39	$7,690,222

Municipal Finance

(For local fiscal year ended in 2006)

Revenues

Total	$70,382,871
Taxes	24,846,802
Special benefits assessment	442,713
Licenses & permits	917,532
Fines & forfeitures	66,718
Revenues from use of money & property	1,659,276
Intergovernmental	3,452,587
Service charges	21,069,455
Other revenues	711,662
Other financing sources	17,216,126

Expenditures

Total	$59,704,657
General government	5,866,336
Public safety	13,269,209
Transportation	4,732,320
Community development	2,868,238
Health	11,716,610
Culture & leisure	7,847,527
Other	0

Local School District

(Data from School year 2007-08 except as noted)

Benicia Unified
350 East K St
Benicia, CA 94510
(707) 747-8300

Superintendent	Janice Adams
Grade plan	K-12
Number of schools	7
Enrollment	5,015
High school graduates, 2006-07	435
Dropout rate	4.4%
Pupil/teacher ratio	20.6
Average class size	25.6
Students per computer	4.3
Classrooms with internet	280
Avg. Daily Attendance (ADA)	4,888
Cost per ADA	$7,576
Avg. Teacher Salary	$64,540

California Achievement Tests 6th ed., 2008

(Pct scoring at or above 50th National Percentile Rank)

	Math	Reading	Language
Grade 3	72%	58%	70%
Grade 7	69%	70%	66%

Academic Performance Index, 2008

Number of students tested	3,885
Number of valid scores	3,728
2007 API (base)	826
2008 API (growth)	818

SAT Testing, 2006-07

Enrollment, Grade 12	486
Number taking test	228
percent taking test	46.9%
percent with total score 1,500+	32.10%

Average Scores:

Math	Verbal	Writing	Total
555	531	526	1,612

Federal No Child Left Behind, 2008

(Adequate Yearly Progress standards met)

	Participation Rate	Pct Proficient
ELA	Yes	Yes
Math	Yes	Yes

API criteria	Yes
Graduation rate	Yes
# criteria met/possible	38/38

Other school districts for this city

(see Appendix E for information on these districts)

None

See Introduction for an explanation of all data sources.

Demographics & Socio-Economic Characteristics†

(2007 American Community Survey, except as noted)

Population

1990* 102,724
2007 111,680
Male 55,338
Female 56,342
Jan. 2008 (estimate)§ 106,697
Persons per sq. mi. of land 10,161.6

Race & Hispanic Origin, 2007

Race
White 70,830
Black/African American 11,662
North American Native 207
Asian 19,574
Pacific Islander 68
Other Race 4,127
Two or more races 5,212
Hispanic origin, total 11,032
Mexican 8,658
Puerto Rican 535
Cuban 102
Other Hispanic 1,737

Age & Nativity, 2007

Under 5 years 6,060
18 years and over 93,524
65 years and over 11,849
85 years and over 1,864
Median Age 34.1
Native-born 91,105
Foreign-born 20,575

Educational Attainment, 2007

Population 25 years and over 68,204
Less than 9th grade 5.3%
High school grad or higher 91.0%
Bachelor's degree or higher 65.7%
Graduate degree 36.5%

Income & Poverty, 2007

Per capita income $34,598
Median household income $57,189
Median family income $93,297
Persons in poverty 21.0%
H'holds receiving public assistance 642
H'holds receiving social security 8,178

Households, 2007

Total households 41,224
With persons under 18 9,582
With persons over 65 7,830
Family households 18,854
Single person households 15,344
Persons per household 2.32
Persons per family 3.07

Household Population, 2008§§

Persons living in households 100,031
Persons living in group quarters 6,666
Persons per household 2.2

Labor & Employment

Total civilian labor force, 2008§§ 59,300
Unemployment rate, 2008 ..... 5.9%
Total civilian labor force, 2000* 59,097

Employed persons 16 years and over by occupation, 2007

Managers & professionals 31,549
Service occupations 5,555
Sales & office occupations 10,754
Farming, fishing & forestry 209
Construction & maintenance 3,183
Production & transportation 1,878
Self-employed persons 7,924

† see Appendix D for 2000 Decennial Census Data
* US Census Bureau
** 2007 American Community Survey
§ California Department of Finance
§§ California Employment Development Dept

General Information

City of Berkeley
2180 Milvia St
Berkeley, CA 94704
510-981-2489

Website ..... www.ci.berkeley.ca.us
Elevation ..... 152 ft.
Land Area (sq. miles) 10.5
Water Area (sq. miles) 7.2
Year of Incorporation 1878
Government type ..... Chartered
Sales tax rate 9.75%

Voters & Officials

Registered Voters, October 2008

Total 86,020
Democrats 55,918
Republicans 4,017
Declined to state 20,785

Legislative Districts

US Congressional 9
State Senatorial 9
State Assembly 14

Local Officials, 2009

Mayor ..... Tom Bates
Manager ..... Phil Kamlarz
City Clerk ..... Deanna Despain (Actg)
Attorney ..... Zach Cowan (Actg)
Finance Dir ..... Robert Hicks
Public Works ..... Claudette Ford
Planning/Dev Dir ..... Dan Marks
Building ..... NA
Police Chief ..... Doug Hambleton
Emergency/Fire Dir ..... Debra Pryor

Public Safety

Number of officers, 2007 168
Violent crimes, 2007 639
Property crimes, 2007 7,116
Arson, 2007 29

Public Library

Central Library
Berkeley Public Library System
2090 Kittredge St
Berkeley, CA 94704
510-981-6100

Director ..... Donna Corbeil

Library system statistics, FY 2007

Population served 106,347
Internet terminals 9
Annual users 164,104

Per capita:

Operating income $126.58
percent from local government 92.2%
Operating expenditure $126.60
Total materials 3.93
Print holdings 3.19
Visits per capita 12.59

Housing & Construction

Housing Units

Total, 2008§ 48,036
Single family units, attached 1,760
Single family units, detached 20,162
Multiple family units 26,055
Mobile home units 59
Occupied 46,013
Vacancy rate 4.2%
Median rent, 2007** $1,083
Median SF home value, 2007** $755,300

New Privately Owned Housing Units Authorized by Building Permit, 2007*

	Units	Construction Cost
Single	14	$4,267,410
Total	74	$10,917,321

Municipal Finance

(For local fiscal year ended in 2006)

Revenues

Total $289,129,278
Taxes 119,900,064
Special benefits assessment 12,791,296
Licenses & permits 545,681
Fines & forfeitures 9,828,587
Revenues from use of money & property 6,444,134
Intergovernmental 35,385,708
Service charges 103,320,129
Other revenues 913,679
Other financing sources 0

Expenditures

Total $278,530,509
General government 25,100,046
Public safety 77,793,287
Transportation 31,072,105
Community development 49,363,152
Health 61,387,914
Culture & leisure 30,031,381
Other 3,782,624

Local School District

(Data from School year 2007-08 except as noted)

Berkeley Unified
2134 Martin Luther King Jr Way
Berkeley, CA 94704
(510) 644-6206

Superintendent ..... William Huyett
Grade plan PK-12
Number of schools 16
Enrollment 8,954
High school graduates, 2006-07 704
Dropout rate 3.7%
Pupil/teacher ratio 17.7
Average class size 25.4
Students per computer 5.4
Classrooms with internet 440
Avg. Daily Attendance (ADA) 8,554
Cost per ADA $11,884
Avg. Teacher Salary $62,596

California Achievement Tests 6th ed., 2008

(Pct scoring at or above 50th National Percentile Rank)

	Math	Reading	Language
Grade 3	60%	50%	55%
Grade 7	52%	54%	53%

Academic Performance Index, 2008

Number of students tested 6,195
Number of valid scores 5,945
2007 API (base) 746
2008 API (growth) 760

SAT Testing, 2006-07

Enrollment, Grade 12 819
Number taking test 480
percent taking test 58.6%
percent with total score 1,500+ 39.40%

Average Scores:

Math	Verbal	Writing	Total
559	552	548	1,659

Federal No Child Left Behind, 2008

(Adequate Yearly Progress standards met)

	Participation Rate	Pct Proficient
ELA	Yes	No
Math	Yes	No

API criteria ..... Yes
Graduation rate ..... Yes
criteria met/possible 34/27

Other school districts for this city

(see Appendix E for information on these districts)

None

See Introduction for an explanation of all data sources.

Demographics & Socio-Economic Characteristics

(2000 Decennial Census, except as noted)

Population

1990* . . . 31,971
2000 . . . 33,784
Male . . . 15,371
Female . . . 18,413
Jan. 2008 (estimate)§ . . . 35,983
Persons per sq. mi. of land . . . 6,312.8

Race & Hispanic Origin, 2000

Race
White . . . 28,736
Black/African American . . . 597
North American Native . . . 43
Asian . . . 2,383
Pacific Islander . . . 10
Other Race . . . 508
Two or more races . . . 1,507
Hispanic origin, total . . . 1,565
Mexican . . . 607
Puerto Rican . . . 57
Cuban . . . 54
Other Hispanic . . . 847

Age & Nativity, 2000

Under 5 years . . . 1,266
18 years and over . . . 27,033
65 years and over . . . 5,949
85 years and over . . . 927
Median Age . . . 41.3
Native-born . . . 20,892
Foreign-born . . . 12,937

Educational Attainment, 2000

Population 25 years and over . . . 25,078
Less than 9th grade . . . 3.1%
High school grad or higher . . . 90.8%
Bachelor's degree or higher . . . 54.5%
Graduate degree . . . 24.8%

Income & Poverty, 1999

Per capita income . . . $65,507
Median household income . . . $70,945
Median family income . . . $102,611
Persons in poverty . . . 9.1%
H'holds receiving public assistance . . . 273
H'holds receiving social security . . . 3,944

Households, 2000

Total households . . . 15,035
With persons under 18 . . . 3,856
With persons over 65 . . . 4,436
Family households . . . 8,263
Single person households . . . 5,737
Persons per household . . . 2.24
Persons per family . . . 3.02

Household Population, 2008§§

Persons living in households . . . 35,944
Persons living in group quarters . . . 39
Persons per household . . . 2.4

Labor & Employment

Total civilian labor force, 2008§§ . . . 19,600
Unemployment rate, 2008 . . . 5.2%
Total civilian labor force, 2000 . . . 16,818

Employed persons 16 years and over by occupation, 2000

Managers & professionals . . . 9,552
Service occupations . . . 1,208
Sales & office occupations . . . 4,439
Farming, fishing & forestry . . . 14
Construction & maintenance . . . 250
Production & transportation . . . 453
Self-employed persons . . . 2,725

* US Census Bureau
** 2000 Decennial Census
§ California Department of Finance
§§ California Employment Development Dept

General Information

City of Beverly Hills
455 N Rexford Dr
Beverly Hills, CA 90210
310-285-1000

Website . . . www.beverlyhills.org
Elevation . . . 225 ft.
Land Area (sq. miles) . . . 5.7
Water Area (sq. miles) . . . 0
Year of Incorporation . . . 1914
Government type . . . General law
Sales tax rate . . . 9.25%

Voters & Officials

Registered Voters, October 2008

Total . . . 21,934
Democrats . . . 10,600
Republicans . . . 5,475
Declined to state . . . 5,123

Legislative Districts

US Congressional . . . 30
State Senatorial . . . 23
State Assembly . . . 42

Local Officials, 2009

Mayor . . . Barry Brucker
Manager . . . Roderick J. Wood
City Clerk . . . Byron Pope
Attorney . . . Laurence Wiener
Finance Dir . . . Scott G. Miller
Public Works . . . David Gustavson
Dev Dir . . . Anne Browning-McIntosh (Int)
Building . . . George Chavez
Police Chief . . . David Snowden
Emergency/Fire Dir . . . Timothy Scranton

Public Safety

Number of officers, 2007 . . . 130
Violent crimes, 2007 . . . 157
Property crimes, 2007 . . . 1,169
Arson, 2007 . . . 4

Public Library

Beverly Hills Public Library
Beverly Hills Public Library System
444 N Rexford Dr
Beverly Hills, CA 90210
310-288-2220

Director . . . Nancy Hunt-Coffey

Library system statistics, FY 2007

Population served . . . 36,084
Internet terminals . . . 60
Annual users . . . 180,639

Per capita:

Operating income . . . $289.27
percent from local government . . . 94.1%
Operating expenditure . . . $262.38
Total materials . . . 11.61
Print holdings . . . 10.74
Visits per capita . . . 13.79

Housing & Construction

Housing Units

Total, 2008§ . . . 16,125
Single family units, attached . . . 236
Single family units, detached . . . 5,751
Multiple family units . . . 10,110
Mobile home units . . . 28
Occupied . . . 15,290
Vacancy rate . . . 5.2%
Median rent, 2000** . . . $1,171
Median SF home value, 2000** . . $1,000,001

New Privately Owned Housing Units Authorized by Building Permit, 2007*

	Units	Construction Cost
Single	29	$35,910,810
Total	51	$45,110,810

Municipal Finance

(For local fiscal year ended in 2006)

Revenues

Total . . . $205,734,891
Taxes . . . 112,788,582
Special benefits assessment . . . 0
Licenses & permits . . . 7,035,275
Fines & forfeitures . . . 6,211,273
Revenues from use of money & property . . . 7,059,260
Intergovernmental . . . 8,121,629
Service charges . . . 62,872,911
Other revenues . . . 1,645,961
Other financing sources . . . 0

Expenditures

Total . . . $176,145,016
General government . . . 32,402,279
Public safety . . . 57,584,877
Transportation . . . 17,424,681
Community development . . . 11,059,738
Health . . . 20,490,421
Culture & leisure . . . 20,473,329
Other . . . 0

Local School District

(Data from School year 2007-08 except as noted)

Beverly Hills Unified
255 South Lasky Dr
Beverly Hills, CA 90212
(310) 551-5100

Superintendent . . . Jerry Gross
Grade plan . . . K-12
Number of schools . . . 6
Enrollment . . . 5,305
High school graduates, 2006-07 . . . 481
Dropout rate . . . 1.7%
Pupil/teacher ratio . . . 17.8
Average class size . . . 24.1
Students per computer . . . 4.3
Classrooms with internet . . . 306
Avg. Daily Attendance (ADA) . . . 5,156
Cost per ADA . . . $10,218
Avg. Teacher Salary . . . $69,076

California Achievement Tests 6th ed., 2008

(Pct scoring at or above 50th National Percentile Rank)

	Math	Reading	Language
Grade 3	79%	51%	70%
Grade 7	80%	73%	77%

Academic Performance Index, 2008

Number of students tested . . . 4,190
Number of valid scores . . . 4,022
2007 API (base) . . . 857
2008 API (growth) . . . 852

SAT Testing, 2006-07

Enrollment, Grade 12 . . . 501
Number taking test . . . 363
percent taking test . . . 72.5%
percent with total score 1,500+ . . . 56.90%

Average Scores:

Math	Verbal	Writing	Total
594	570	582	1,746

Federal No Child Left Behind, 2008

(Adequate Yearly Progress standards met)

	Participation Rate	Pct Proficient
ELA	Yes	Yes
Math	Yes	Yes

API criteria . . . Yes
Graduation rate . . . Yes
criteria met/possible . . . 34/34

Other school districts for this city

(see Appendix E for information on these districts)

None

See Introduction for an explanation of all data sources.

Demographics & Socio-Economic Characteristics

(2000 Decennial Census, except as noted)

Population

1990*	5,351
2000	5,438
Male	2,812
Female	2,626
Jan. 2008 (estimate)§	6,256
Persons per sq. mi. of land	993.0

Race & Hispanic Origin, 2000

Race	
White	4,958
Black/African American	37
North American Native	53
Asian	41
Pacific Islander	2
Other Race	194
Two or more races	153
Hispanic origin, total	745
Mexican	622
Puerto Rican	12
Cuban	5
Other Hispanic	106

Age & Nativity, 2000

Under 5 years	290
18 years and over	4,211
65 years and over	945
85 years and over	79
Median Age	42.9
Native-born	4,873
Foreign-born	566

Educational Attainment, 2000

Population 25 years and over	3,979
Less than 9th grade	3.7%
High school grad or higher	85.3%
Bachelor's degree or higher	23.0%
Graduate degree	7.6%

Income & Poverty, 1999

Per capita income	$21,517
Median household income	$34,447
Median family income	$41,848
Persons in poverty	13.4%
H'holds receiving public assistance	101
H'holds receiving social security	823

Households, 2000

Total households	2,343
With persons under 18	651
With persons over 65	684
Family households	1,495
Single person households	690
Persons per household	2.31
Persons per family	2.83

Household Population, 2008§§

Persons living in households	6,231
Persons living in group quarters	25
Persons per household	2.4

Labor & Employment

Total civilian labor force, 2008§§	3,100
Unemployment rate, 2008	5.7%
Total civilian labor force, 2000	2,586

Employed persons 16 years and over by occupation, 2000

Managers & professionals	816
Service occupations	527
Sales & office occupations	657
Farming, fishing & forestry	0
Construction & maintenance	304
Production & transportation	128
Self-employed persons	428

* US Census Bureau
** 2000 Decennial Census
§ California Department of Finance
§§ California Employment Development Dept

General Information

City of Big Bear Lake
39707 Big Bear Blvd
PO Box 10000
Big Bear Lake, CA 92315
909-866-5831

Website	www.citybigbearlake.com
Elevation	6,754 ft.
Land Area (sq. miles)	6.3
Water Area (sq. miles)	0.2
Year of Incorporation	1980
Government type	Chartered
Sales tax rate	8.75%

Voters & Officials

Registered Voters, October 2008

Total	3,294
Democrats	840
Republicans	1,791
Declined to state	500

Legislative Districts

US Congressional	41
State Senatorial	31
State Assembly	65

Local Officials, 2009

Mayor	Rick Herrick
Manager	Jeff Mathieu
City Clerk	Katherine Jefferies
Attorney	Best, Best & Kreiger
Finance Dir	Kathleen Smith
Public Works	David Lawrence
Planning/Dev Dir	Jim Miller
Building	NA
Police Chief	Greg Garland
Emergency/Fire Dir	(vacant)

Public Safety

Number of officers, 2007	NA
Violent crimes, 2007	42
Property crimes, 2007	286
Arson, 2007	1

Public Library

Big Bear Lake Branch Library
San Bernardino County Library System
41930 Garstin Dr
Big Bear Lake, CA 92315
909-866-5571

Branch Librarian	Pamela Heiman

Library system statistics, FY 2007

Population served	1,177,092
Internet terminals	12
Annual users	45,343

Per capita:

Operating income	$14.27
percent from local government	73.3%
Operating expenditure	$13.86
Total materials	0.86
Print holdings	0.79
Visits per capita	5.83

Housing & Construction

Housing Units

Total, 2008§	9,528
Single family units, attached	330
Single family units, detached	8,023
Multiple family units	781
Mobile home units	394
Occupied	2,565
Vacancy rate	73.1%
Median rent, 2000**	$581
Median SF home value, 2000**	$193,300

New Privately Owned Housing Units Authorized by Building Permit, 2007*

	Units	Construction Cost
Single	78	$21,934,209
Total	78	$21,934,209

Municipal Finance

(For local fiscal year ended in 2006)

Revenues

Total	$29,051,599
Taxes	8,472,549
Special benefits assessment	145,984
Licenses & permits	737,550
Fines & forfeitures	155,040
Revenues from use of money & property	1,694,687
Intergovernmental	1,035,962
Service charges	16,616,538
Other revenues	193,289
Other financing sources	0

Expenditures

Total	$28,313,403
General government	3,277,819
Public safety	2,136,857
Transportation	4,804,311
Community development	1,861,078
Health	5,242,749
Culture & leisure	438,919
Other	0

Local School District

(Data from School year 2007-08 except as noted)

Bear Valley Unified
Box 1529
Big Bear Lake, CA 92315
(909) 866-4631

Superintendent	Carole Ferraud
Grade plan	K-12
Number of schools	7
Enrollment	3,128
High school graduates, 2006-07	231
Dropout rate	1.9%
Pupil/teacher ratio	22.5
Average class size	24.6
Students per computer	4.2
Classrooms with internet	144
Avg. Daily Attendance (ADA)	2,996
Cost per ADA	$7,643
Avg. Teacher Salary	$66,876

California Achievement Tests 6th ed., 2008

(Pct scoring at or above 50th National Percentile Rank)

	Math	Reading	Language
Grade 3	48%	41%	50%
Grade 7	57%	57%	58%

Academic Performance Index, 2008

Number of students tested	2,454
Number of valid scores	2,214
2007 API (base)	759
2008 API (growth)	769

SAT Testing, 2006-07

Enrollment, Grade 12	241
Number taking test	106
percent taking test	44.0%
percent with total score 1,500+	24.90%

Average Scores:

Math	Verbal	Writing	Total
531	516	508	1,555

Federal No Child Left Behind, 2008

(Adequate Yearly Progress standards met)

	Participation Rate	Pct Proficient
ELA	Yes	Yes
Math	Yes	Yes

API criteria	Yes
Graduation rate	Yes
# criteria met/possible	26/26

Other school districts for this city

(see Appendix E for information on these districts)

None

See Introduction for an explanation of all data sources.

Demographics & Socio-Economic Characteristics

(2000 Decennial Census, except as noted)

Population

1990* 1,581
2000 1,793
Male 852
Female 941
Jan. 2008 (estimate)§ 1,776
Persons per sq. mi. of land 3,552.0

Race & Hispanic Origin, 2000

Race
White 1,336
Black/African American 8
North American Native 33
Asian 15
Pacific Islander 0
Other Race 332
Two or more races 69
Hispanic origin, total 494
Mexican 449
Puerto Rican 4
Cuban 0
Other Hispanic 41

Age & Nativity, 2000

Under 5 years 139
18 years and over 1,180
65 years and over 188
85 years and over 12
Median Age 30.1
Native-born 1,548
Foreign-born 251

Educational Attainment, 2000

Population 25 years and over 1,028
Less than 9th grade 16.6%
High school grad or higher 65.6%
Bachelor's degree or higher 6.9%
Graduate degree 2.4%

Income & Poverty, 1999

Per capita income $12,386
Median household income $33,250
Median family income $39,063
Persons in poverty 17.5%
H'holds receiving public assistance 61
H'holds receiving social security 137

Households, 2000

Total households 571
With persons under 18 285
With persons over 65 141
Family households 450
Single person households 98
Persons per household 3.14
Persons per family 3.55

Household Population, 2008§§

Persons living in households 1,776
Persons living in group quarters 0
Persons per household 3.0

Labor & Employment

Total civilian labor force, 2008§§ 900
Unemployment rate, 2008 .... 10.5%
Total civilian labor force, 2000 754

Employed persons 16 years and over by occupation, 2000

Managers & professionals 142
Service occupations 102
Sales & office occupations 169
Farming, fishing & forestry 41
Construction & maintenance 88
Production & transportation 124
Self-employed persons 61

* US Census Bureau
** 2000 Decennial Census
§ California Department of Finance
§§ California Employment Development Dept

General Information

City of Biggs
PO Box 307
Biggs, CA 95917
530-868-5493

Website .... www.biggs-ca.gov
Elevation .... 94 ft.
Land Area (sq. miles) 0.5
Water Area (sq. miles) 0
Year of Incorporation 1903
Government type .... General law
Sales tax rate 8.25%

Voters & Officials

Registered Voters, October 2008

Total 779
Democrats 302
Republicans 308
Declined to state 135

Legislative Districts

US Congressional 2
State Senatorial 4
State Assembly 2

Local Officials, 2009

Mayor .... Roger L. Frith
City Administrator .... Peter R. Carr
City Clerk .... Deanna Carbajal
Attorney .... Gregory Einhorn
Finance Dir .... Deanna Carbajal
Public Works .... Paul Pratt
Planning/Dev Dir .... Scott Friend
Building .... NA
Police Chief .... Gary D. Keeler
Emergency/Fire Dir .... Michael Brown

Public Safety

Number of officers, 2007 .... NA
Violent crimes, 2007 22
Property crimes, 2007 41
Arson, 2007 0

Public Library

Biggs Branch Library
Butte County Library System
464A B St
Biggs, CA 95917
530-868-5724

Branch Supervisor .... Derek Wolfgram

Library system statistics, FY 2007

Population served 218,069
Internet terminals 47
Annual users 90,296

Per capita:

Operating income $12.21
percent from local government 84.5%
Operating expenditure $12.71
Total materials 1.41
Print holdings 1.33
Visits per capita 3.01

Housing & Construction

Housing Units

Total, 2008§ 627
Single family units, attached 28
Single family units, detached 523
Multiple family units 35
Mobile home units 41
Occupied 585
Vacancy rate 6.7%
Median rent, 2000** $488
Median SF home value, 2000** $81,000

New Privately Owned Housing Units Authorized by Building Permit, 2007*

	Units	Construction Cost
Single	NA	NA
Total	NA	NA

Municipal Finance

(For local fiscal year ended in 2006)

Revenues

Total $3,752,287
Taxes 319,049
Special benefits assessment 0
Licenses & permits 632
Fines & forfeitures 132
Revenues from use of money & property 138,798
Intergovernmental 643,921
Service charges 2,590,824
Other revenues 58,931
Other financing sources 0

Expenditures

Total $5,418,020
General government 296,341
Public safety 613,741
Transportation 224,401
Community development 991,282
Health 368,764
Culture & leisure 473,775
Other 0

Local School District

(Data from School year 2007-08 except as noted)

Biggs Unified
300 B St
Biggs, CA 95917
(530) 868-1281

Superintendent .... Bill Cornelius
Grade plan K-12
Number of schools 7
Enrollment 623
High school graduates, 2006-07 41
Dropout rate 4.5%
Pupil/teacher ratio 13.1
Average class size 18.2
Students per computer 2.8
Classrooms with internet 131
Avg. Daily Attendance (ADA) 622
Cost per ADA $8,833
Avg. Teacher Salary $54,643

California Achievement Tests 6th ed., 2008

(Pct scoring at or above 50th National Percentile Rank)

	Math	Reading	Language
Grade 3	53%	37%	47%
Grade 7	43%	50%	38%

Academic Performance Index, 2008

Number of students tested 481
Number of valid scores 426
2007 API (base) 665
2008 API (growth) 685

SAT Testing, 2006-07

Enrollment, Grade 12 58
Number taking test 15
percent taking test 25.9%
percent with total score 1,500+ 6.90%

Average Scores:

Math	Verbal	Writing	Total
457	455	433	1,345

Federal No Child Left Behind, 2008

(Adequate Yearly Progress standards met)

	Participation Rate	Pct Proficient
ELA	Yes	No
Math	Yes	No

API criteria .... Yes
Graduation rate .... Yes
\# criteria met/possible 22/17

Other school districts for this city

(see Appendix E for information on these districts)

None

See Introduction for an explanation of all data sources.

Demographics & Socio-Economic Characteristics

(2000 Decennial Census, except as noted)

Population

1990* . . . 3,475
2000 . . . 3,575
Male . . . 1,711
Female . . . 1,864
Jan. 2008 (estimate)§ . . . 3,551
Persons per sq. mi. of land . . . 1,972.8

Race & Hispanic Origin, 2000

Race
White . . . 3,025
Black/African American . . . 7
North American Native . . . 73
Asian . . . 45
Pacific Islander . . . 1
Other Race . . . 232
Two or more races . . . 192
Hispanic origin, total . . . 621
Mexican . . . 540
Puerto Rican . . . 4
Cuban . . . 0
Other Hispanic . . . 77

Age & Nativity, 2000

Under 5 years . . . 217
18 years and over . . . 2,711
65 years and over . . . 688
85 years and over . . . 128
Median Age . . . 39.9
Native-born . . . 3,164
Foreign-born . . . 365

Educational Attainment, 2000

Population 25 years and over . . . 2,434
Less than 9th grade . . . 5.6%
High school grad or higher . . . 77.7%
Bachelor's degree or higher . . . 12.4%
Graduate degree . . . 5.2%

Income & Poverty, 1999

Per capita income . . . $17,660
Median household income . . . $27,338
Median family income . . . $34,423
Persons in poverty . . . 15.8%
H'holds receiving public assistance . . . 63
H'holds receiving social security . . . 557

Households, 2000

Total households . . . 1,684
With persons under 18 . . . 469
With persons over 65 . . . 506
Family households . . . 832
Single person households . . . 744
Persons per household . . . 2.08
Persons per family . . . 2.93

Household Population, 2008§§

Persons living in households . . . 3,474
Persons living in group quarters . . . 77
Persons per household . . . 2.0

Labor & Employment

Total civilian labor force, 2008§§ . . . 1,860
Unemployment rate, 2008 . . . 6.0%
Total civilian labor force, 2000 . . . 1,726

Employed persons 16 years and over by occupation, 2000

Managers & professionals . . . 387
Service occupations . . . 421
Sales & office occupations . . . 457
Farming, fishing & forestry . . . 44
Construction & maintenance . . . 145
Production & transportation . . . 181
Self-employed persons . . . 119

* US Census Bureau
** 2000 Decennial Census
§ California Department of Finance
§§ California Employment Development Dept

General Information

City of Bishop
377 W Line St
PO Box 1236
Bishop, CA 93515
760-873-5863

Website . . . ca-bishop.us
Elevation . . . 4,147 ft.
Land Area (sq. miles) . . . 1.8
Water Area (sq. miles) . . . 0
Year of Incorporation . . . 1903
Government type . . . General law
Sales tax rate . . . 8.75%

Voters & Officials

Registered Voters, October 2008

Total . . . 1,688
Democrats . . . 589
Republicans . . . 686
Declined to state . . . 339

Legislative Districts

US Congressional . . . 25
State Senatorial . . . 18
State Assembly . . . 34

Local Officials, 2009

Mayor . . . Susan Cullen
Administrator . . . Richard F. Pucci
City Clerk . . . Richard F. Pucci
Attorney . . . Peter Tracy
Finance Dir . . . Richard E. Pucci
Public Works . . . David Grah
Planning/Dev Dir . . . Richard F. Pucci
Building . . . Dave Grah
Police Chief . . . Kathleen Sheehan
Emergency/Fire Dir . . . Ray Seguine

Public Safety

Number of officers, 2007 . . . 14
Violent crimes, 2007 . . . 30
Property crimes, 2007 . . . 178
Arson, 2007 . . . 0

Public Library

Bishop Branch Library
Inyo County Free Library System
210 Academy Ave
Bishop, CA 93514
760-873-5115

Branch Librarian . . . Sue Franz

Library system statistics, FY 2007

Population served . . . 18,383
Internet terminals . . . 10
Annual users . . . 20,730

Per capita:

Operating income . . . $36.81
percent from local government . . . 97.1%
Operating expenditure . . . $36.81
Total materials . . . 5.76
Print holdings . . . 5.43
Visits per capita . . . NA

Housing & Construction

Housing Units

Total, 2008§ . . . 1,894
Single family units, attached . . . 78
Single family units, detached . . . 847
Multiple family units . . . 597
Mobile home units . . . 372
Occupied . . . 1,710
Vacancy rate . . . 9.7%
Median rent, 2000** . . . $540
Median SF home value, 2000** . . . $145,200

New Privately Owned Housing Units Authorized by Building Permit, 2007*

	Units	Construction Cost
Single	0	$0
Total	12	$398,395

Municipal Finance

(For local fiscal year ended in 2006)

Revenues

Total . . . $7,766,655
Taxes . . . 4,839,276
Special benefits assessment . . . 0
Licenses & permits . . . 29,581
Fines & forfeitures . . . 22,142
Revenues from use of money & property . . . 253,847
Intergovernmental . . . 347,879
Service charges . . . 1,646,953
Other revenues . . . 626,977
Other financing sources . . . 0

Expenditures

Total . . . $6,834,622
General government . . . 1,634,803
Public safety . . . 2,624,826
Transportation . . . 429,294
Community development . . . 475,325
Health . . . 539,695
Culture & leisure . . . 298,152
Other . . . 0

Local School District

(Data from School year 2007-08 except as noted)

Bishop Joint Union High
301 North Fowler St
Bishop, CA 93514
(760) 872-3680

Superintendent . . . Maggie Kingsbury
Grade plan . . . 9-12
Number of schools . . . 2
Enrollment . . . 764
High school graduates, 2006-07 . . . 185
Dropout rate . . . 4.7%
Pupil/teacher ratio . . . 24.0
Average class size . . . 23.7
Students per computer . . . 2.2
Classrooms with internet . . . 58
Avg. Daily Attendance (ADA) . . . 718
Cost per ADA . . . $8,820
Avg. Teacher Salary . . . $65,642

California Achievement Tests 6th ed., 2008

(Pct scoring at or above 50th National Percentile Rank)

	Math	Reading	Language
Grade 3	NA	NA	NA
Grade 7	NA	NA	NA

Academic Performance Index, 2008

Number of students tested . . . 524
Number of valid scores . . . 504
2007 API (base) . . . 707
2008 API (growth) . . . 709

SAT Testing, 2006-07

Enrollment, Grade 12 . . . 192
Number taking test . . . 86
percent taking test . . . 44.8%
percent with total score 1,500+ . . . 25.50%

Average Scores:

Math	Verbal	Writing	Total
522	522	499	1,543

Federal No Child Left Behind, 2008

(Adequate Yearly Progress standards met)

	Participation Rate	Pct Proficient
ELA	No	Yes
Math	Yes	Yes

API criteria . . . Yes
Graduation rate . . . Yes
\# criteria met/possible . . . 12/11

Other school districts for this city

(see Appendix E for information on these districts)

Bishop Union Elem

See Introduction for an explanation of all data sources.

Demographics & Socio-Economic Characteristics

(2000 Decennial Census, except as noted)

Population

1990* . . . 1,235
2000 . . . 1,135
Male . . . 547
Female . . . 588
Jan. 2008 (estimate)§ . . . 1,166
Persons per sq. mi. of land . . . 1,943.3

Race & Hispanic Origin, 2000

Race
White . . . 1,007
Black/African American . . . 6
North American Native . . . 61
Asian . . . 15
Pacific Islander . . . 1
Other Race . . . 13
Two or more races . . . 32
Hispanic origin, total . . . 28
Mexican . . . 11
Puerto Rican . . . 1
Cuban . . . 4
Other Hispanic . . . 12

Age & Nativity, 2000

Under 5 years . . . 58
18 years and over . . . 886
65 years and over . . . 141
85 years and over . . . 20
Median Age . . . 38.8
Native-born . . . 1,063
Foreign-born . . . 30

Educational Attainment, 2000

Population 25 years and over . . . 792
Less than 9th grade . . . 6.2%
High school grad or higher . . . 85.6%
Bachelor's degree or higher . . . 28.3%
Graduate degree . . . 7.7%

Income & Poverty, 1999

Per capita income . . . $17,603
Median household income . . . $32,500
Median family income . . . $37,500
Persons in poverty . . . 10.7%
H'holds receiving public assistance . . . 15
H'holds receiving social security . . . 124

Households, 2000

Total households . . . 504
With persons under 18 . . . 149
With persons over 65 . . . 111
Family households . . . 298
Single person households . . . 159
Persons per household . . . 2.25
Persons per family . . . 2.84

Household Population, 2008§§

Persons living in households . . . 1,166
Persons living in group quarters . . . 0
Persons per household . . . 2.2

Labor & Employment

Total civilian labor force, 2008§§ . . . 600
Unemployment rate, 2008 . . . 6.2%
Total civilian labor force, 2000 . . . 621

Employed persons 16 years and over by occupation, 2000

Managers & professionals . . . 175
Service occupations . . . 89
Sales & office occupations . . . 166
Farming, fishing & forestry . . . 6
Construction & maintenance . . . 44
Production & transportation . . . 95
Self-employed persons . . . 70

* US Census Bureau
** 2000 Decennial Census
§ California Department of Finance
§§ California Employment Development Dept

General Information

City of Blue Lake
111 Greenwood Ave
PO Box 458
Blue Lake, CA 95525
707-668-5655

Website . . . NA
Elevation . . . NA
Land Area (sq. miles) . . . 0.6
Water Area (sq. miles) . . . 0
Year of Incorporation . . . 1910
Government type . . . General law
Sales tax rate . . . 8.25%

Voters & Officials

Registered Voters, October 2008

Total . . . 810
Democrats . . . 355
Republicans . . . 189
Declined to state . . . 171

Legislative Districts

US Congressional . . . 1
State Senatorial . . . 2
State Assembly . . . 1

Local Officials, 2009

Mayor . . . Sherman Schapiro
Manager . . . Wiley Buck
City Clerk . . . Karen Nessler
Attorney . . . Richard Platz
Finance Dir . . . Wiley Buck
Public Works . . . NA
Planning/Dev Dir . . . NA
Building . . . NA
Police Chief . . . David Gundersen
Emergency/Fire Dir. . Raymond Stonebarger

Public Safety

Number of officers, 2007 . . . 5
Violent crimes, 2007 . . . 4
Property crimes, 2007 . . . 61
Arson, 2007 . . . 1

Public Library

Blue Lake Library
Humboldt County Library System
111 Greenwood Ave
Blue Lake, CA 95525
707-668-4207

Branch Librarian . . . (vacant)

Library system statistics, FY 2007

Population served . . . 131,959
Internet terminals . . . 46
Annual users . . . 20,083

Per capita:

Operating income . . . $22.91
percent from local government . . . 90.6%
Operating expenditure . . . $18.80
Total materials . . . 2.54
Print holdings . . . 2.38
Visits per capita . . . 4.15

Housing & Construction

Housing Units

Total, 2008§ . . . 579
Single family units, attached . . . 21
Single family units, detached . . . 383
Multiple family units . . . 104
Mobile home units . . . 71
Occupied . . . 526
Vacancy rate . . . 9.2%
Median rent, 2000** . . . $583
Median SF home value, 2000** . . . $119,000

New Privately Owned Housing Units Authorized by Building Permit, 2007*

	Units	Construction Cost
Single	3	$614,487
Total	3	$614,487

Municipal Finance

(For local fiscal year ended in 2006)

Revenues

Total . . . $1,693,457
Taxes . . . 274,935
Special benefits assessment . . . 0
Licenses & permits . . . 10,134
Fines & forfeitures . . . 8,852
Revenues from use of money & property . . . 223,780
Intergovernmental . . . 458,368
Service charges . . . 680,352
Other revenues . . . 37,036
Other financing sources . . . 0

Expenditures

Total . . . $1,395,684
General government . . . 143,295
Public safety . . . 289,572
Transportation . . . 105,780
Community development . . . 133,334
Health . . . 251,665
Culture & leisure . . . 188,247
Other . . . 0

Local School District

(Data from School year 2007-08 except as noted)

Northern Humboldt Union High
2755 McKinleyville Ave
McKinleyville, CA 95519
(707) 839-6470

Superintendent . . . Kenny Richards
Grade plan . . . 9-12
Number of schools . . . 7
Enrollment . . . 1,775
High school graduates, 2006-07 . . . 402
Dropout rate . . . 2.7%
Pupil/teacher ratio . . . 20.1
Average class size . . . 23.9
Students per computer . . . 2.7
Classrooms with internet . . . 115
Avg. Daily Attendance (ADA) . . . 1,613
Cost per ADA . . . $9,767
Avg. Teacher Salary . . . $59,111

California Achievement Tests 6th ed., 2008

(Pct scoring at or above 50th National Percentile Rank)

	Math	Reading	Language
Grade 3	NA	NA	NA
Grade 7	NA	NA	NA

Academic Performance Index, 2008

Number of students tested . . . 1,265
Number of valid scores . . . 1,211
2007 API (base) . . . 735
2008 API (growth) . . . 765

SAT Testing, 2006-07

Enrollment, Grade 12 . . . 480
Number taking test . . . 162
percent taking test . . . 33.8%
percent with total score 1,500+ . . . 24.60%

Average Scores:

Math	Verbal	Writing	Total
553	560	546	1,659

Federal No Child Left Behind, 2008

(Adequate Yearly Progress standards met)

	Participation Rate	Pct Proficient
ELA	Yes	Yes
Math	Yes	Yes

API criteria . . . Yes
Graduation rate . . . Yes
criteria met/possible . . . 14/14

Other school districts for this city

(see Appendix E for information on these districts)

Blue Lake Union Elem, Green Point Elem

Demographics & Socio-Economic Characteristics

(2000 Decennial Census, except as noted)

Population

1990* 8,428
2000 12,155
Male 6,054
Female 6,101
Jan. 2008 (estimate)§ 21,695
Persons per sq. mi. of land 896.5

Race & Hispanic Origin, 2000

Race
White 6,735
Black/African American 1,014
North American Native 174
Asian 168
Pacific Islander 24
Other Race 3,499
Two or more races 541
Hispanic origin, total 5,571
Mexican 4,800
Puerto Rican 25
Cuban 4
Other Hispanic 742

Age & Nativity, 2000

Under 5 years 1,186
18 years and over 8,029
65 years and over 1,207
85 years and over 128
Median Age 30.7
Native-born 10,479
Foreign-born 1,346

Educational Attainment, 2000

Population 25 years and over 6,761
Less than 9th grade 15.6%
High school grad or higher 68.1%
Bachelor's degree or higher 9.0%
Graduate degree 3.3%

Income & Poverty, 1999

Per capita income $14,424
Median household income $35,324
Median family income $40,783
Persons in poverty 19.9%
H'holds receiving public assistance 223
H'holds receiving social security 1,066

Households, 2000

Total households 4,103
With persons under 18 1,915
With persons over 65 866
Family households 2,976
Single person households 940
Persons per household 2.91
Persons per family 3.45

Household Population, 2008§§

Persons living in households 13,541
Persons living in group quarters 8,154
Persons per household 3.0

Labor & Employment

Total civilian labor force, 2008§§ 7,100
Unemployment rate, 2008 .... 10.3%
Total civilian labor force, 2000 4,992

Employed persons 16 years and over by occupation, 2000

Managers & professionals 993
Service occupations 1,265
Sales & office occupations 1,017
Farming, fishing & forestry 188
Construction & maintenance 439
Production & transportation 638
Self-employed persons 173

* US Census Bureau
** 2000 Decennial Census
§ California Department of Finance
§§ California Employment Development Dept

General Information

City of Blythe
235 N Broadway
Blythe, CA 92225
760-922-6161

Website .... www.cityofblythe.ca.gov
Elevation .... 270 ft.
Land Area (sq. miles) 24.2
Water Area (sq. miles) 0.8
Year of Incorporation 1916
Government type .... General law
Sales tax rate 8.75%

Voters & Officials

Registered Voters, October 2008

Total 5,067
Democrats 2,220
Republicans 1,986
Declined to state 675

Legislative Districts

US Congressional 45
State Senatorial 40
State Assembly 80

Local Officials, 2009

Mayor .... Robert Crain
Manager .... David Lane
City Clerk .... Patti Whitney
Attorney .... J. Scott Zundel
Finance Dir .... Helen Colbert
Public Works .... Jim Rodkey
Planning/Dev Dir .... Jennifer Wellman
Building .... Darrell Covel
Police Chief .... Steve Smith
Emergency/Fire Dir .... Billy Kem

Public Safety

Number of officers, 2007 25
Violent crimes, 2007 99
Property crimes, 2007 593
Arson, 2007 24

Public Library

Palo Verde Valley District Library
125 W Chanslorway
Blythe, CA 92225
760-922-5371

Director .... Brenda Lugo

Library statistics, FY 2007

Population served 44,186
Internet terminals 5
Annual users 6,866

Per capita:

Operating income $7.00
percent from local government 63.4%
Operating expenditure $6.72
Total materials 1.08
Print holdings 1.04
Visits per capita 1.86

Housing & Construction

Housing Units

Total, 2008§ 5,444
Single family units, attached 152
Single family units, detached 3,020
Multiple family units 1,381
Mobile home units 891
Occupied 4,567
Vacancy rate 16.1%
Median rent, 2000** $501
Median SF home value, 2000** $90,800

New Privately Owned Housing Units Authorized by Building Permit, 2007*

	Units	Construction Cost
Single	62	$7,170,626
Total	64	$7,302,355

Municipal Finance

(For local fiscal year ended in 2006)

Revenues

Total $29,722,320
Taxes 6,714,649
Special benefits assessment 152,733
Licenses & permits 201,039
Fines & forfeitures 43,397
Revenues from use of money & property 546,959
Intergovernmental 9,336,743
Service charges 10,139,395
Other revenues 2,587,405
Other financing sources 0

Expenditures

Total $21,238,498
General government 1,967,481
Public safety 5,252,555
Transportation 2,572,878
Community development 2,556,311
Health 4,289,098
Culture & leisure 2,141,512
Other 0

Local School District

(Data from School year 2007-08 except as noted)

Palo Verde Unified
295 North First St
Blythe, CA 92225
(760) 922-4164

Superintendent .... Alan Jensen
Grade plan K-12
Number of schools 7
Enrollment 3,674
High school graduates, 2006-07 166
Dropout rate 7.4%
Pupil/teacher ratio 22.3
Average class size 23.8
Students per computer 5.5
Classrooms with internet 375
Avg. Daily Attendance (ADA) 3,494
Cost per ADA $8,306
Avg. Teacher Salary $59,152

California Achievement Tests 6th ed., 2008

(Pct scoring at or above 50th National Percentile Rank)

	Math	Reading	Language
Grade 3	40%	26%	37%
Grade 7	40%	35%	31%

Academic Performance Index, 2008

Number of students tested 2,758
Number of valid scores 2,541
2007 API (base) 666
2008 API (growth) 672

SAT Testing, 2006-07

Enrollment, Grade 12 237
Number taking test 64
percent taking test 27.0%
percent with total score 1,500+ 9.70%

Average Scores:

Math	Verbal	Writing	Total
472	461	461	1,394

Federal No Child Left Behind, 2008

(Adequate Yearly Progress standards met)

	Participation Rate	Pct Proficient
ELA	No	No
Math	Yes	No

API criteria .... Yes
Graduation rate .... No
\# criteria met/possible 30/17

Other school districts for this city

(see Appendix E for information on these districts)

None

See Introduction for an explanation of all data sources.

Demographics & Socio-Economic Characteristics

(2000 Decennial Census, except as noted)

Population

1990* 829
2000 855
Male 406
Female 449
Jan. 2008 (estimate)§ 948
Persons per sq. mi. of land 498.9

Race & Hispanic Origin, 2000

Race
White 603
Black/African American 15
North American Native 2
Asian 167
Pacific Islander 0
Other Race 48
Two or more races 20
Hispanic origin, total 119
Mexican 88
Puerto Rican 6
Cuban 10
Other Hispanic 15

Age & Nativity, 2000

Under 5 years 39
18 years and over 644
65 years and over 131
85 years and over 15
Median Age 41.8
Native-born 645
Foreign-born 217

Educational Attainment, 2000

Population 25 years and over 605
Less than 9th grade 3.8%
High school grad or higher 91.2%
Bachelor's degree or higher 48.9%
Graduate degree 22.0%

Income & Poverty, 1999

Per capita income $57,717
Median household income $100,454
Median family income $106,736
Persons in poverty 2.0%
H'holds receiving public assistance 2
H'holds receiving social security 96

Households, 2000

Total households 284
With persons under 18 109
With persons over 65 90
Family households 240
Single person households 34
Persons per household 3.01
Persons per family 3.21

Household Population, 2008§§

Persons living in households 948
Persons living in group quarters 0
Persons per household 3.1

Labor & Employment

Total civilian labor force, 2008§§ 500
Unemployment rate, 2008 .... 3.4%
Total civilian labor force, 2000 431

Employed persons 16 years and over by occupation, 2000

Managers & professionals 232
Service occupations 43
Sales & office occupations 108
Farming, fishing & forestry 2
Construction & maintenance 9
Production & transportation 21
Self-employed persons 64

* US Census Bureau
** 2000 Decennial Census
§ California Department of Finance
§§ California Employment Development Dept

General Information

City of Bradbury
600 Winston Ave
Bradbury, CA 91008
626-358-3218

Website .... www.cityofbradbury.org
Elevation .... NA
Land Area (sq. miles) 1.9
Water Area (sq. miles) 0
Year of Incorporation 1957
Government type .... General law
Sales tax rate 9.25%

Voters & Officials

Registered Voters, October 2008

Total 606
Democrats 143
Republicans 305
Declined to state 134

Legislative Districts

US Congressional 26
State Senatorial 29
State Assembly 59

Local Officials, 2009

Mayor .... Richard G. Barakat
City Manager .... Michelle Keith
City Clerk .... Claudia Saldana
Attorney .... Cary S. Reisman
Finance Dir .... Michelle Keith
Public Works .... (County)
Planning/Dev Dir .... David D. Meyer
Building .... Dan Van Dorpe
Police Chief .... (County)
Fire/Emergency Mgmt .... (County)

Public Safety

Number of officers, 2007 .... NA
Violent crimes, 2007 0
Property crimes, 2007 13
Arson, 2007 0

Public Library

Served by Duarte City Library

Library system statistics, FY 2007

Population served .... NA
Internet terminals .... NA
Annual users .... NA

Per capita:

Operating income .... NA
percent from local government .... NA
Operating expenditure .... NA
Total materials .... NA
Print holdings .... NA
Visits per capita .... NA

Housing & Construction

Housing Units

Total, 2008§ 333
Single family units, attached 0
Single family units, detached 331
Multiple family units 2
Mobile home units 0
Occupied 304
Vacancy rate 8.7%
Median rent, 2000** $1,469
Median SF home value, 2000** $644,900

New Privately Owned Housing Units Authorized by Building Permit, 2007*

	Units	Construction Cost
Single	11	$6,781,363
Total	11	$6,781,363

Municipal Finance

(For local fiscal year ended in 2006)

Revenues

Total $787,132
Taxes 473,751
Special benefits assessment 0
Licenses & permits 0
Fines & forfeitures 0
Revenues from use of money & property 81,524
Intergovernmental 146,392
Service charges 85,465
Other revenues 0
Other financing sources 0

Expenditures

Total $681,428
General government 325,911
Public safety 78,909
Transportation 44,700
Community development 202,772
Health 0
Culture & leisure 29,136
Other 0

Local School District

(Data from School year 2007-08 except as noted)

Duarte Unified
1620 Huntington Dr
Duarte, CA 91010
(626) 599-5000

Superintendent .... Dean Conklin
Grade plan K-12
Number of schools 8
Enrollment 4,296
High school graduates, 2006-07 257
Dropout rate 1.5%
Pupil/teacher ratio 21.4
Average class size 27.3
Students per computer 3.7
Classrooms with internet 204
Avg. Daily Attendance (ADA) 4,279
Cost per ADA $7,907
Avg. Teacher Salary $64,310

California Achievement Tests 6th ed., 2008

(Pct scoring at or above 50th National Percentile Rank)

	Math	Reading	Language
Grade 3	53%	33%	44%
Grade 7	45%	38%	37%

Academic Performance Index, 2008

Number of students tested 3,344
Number of valid scores 3,132
2007 API (base) 708
2008 API (growth) 725

SAT Testing, 2006-07

Enrollment, Grade 12 303
Number taking test 108
percent taking test 35.6%
percent with total score 1,500+ 10.90%

Average Scores:

Math	Verbal	Writing	Total
475	454	450	1,379

Federal No Child Left Behind, 2008

(Adequate Yearly Progress standards met)

	Participation Rate	Pct Proficient
ELA	Yes	Yes
Math	Yes	Yes

API criteria .... Yes
Graduation rate .... Yes
criteria met/possible 36/36

Other school districts for this city

(see Appendix E for information on these districts)

None

See Introduction for an explanation of all data sources.

Demographics & Socio-Economic Characteristics

(2000 Decennial Census, except as noted)

Population

1990*	18,923
2000	22,052
Male	10,855
Female	11,197
Jan. 2008 (estimate)§	26,513
Persons per sq. mi. of land	4,571.2

Race & Hispanic Origin, 2000

Race	
White	11,638
Black/African American	540
North American Native	244
Asian	288
Pacific Islander	41
Other Race	8,349
Two or more races	952
Hispanic origin, total	16,280
Mexican	14,606
Puerto Rican	55
Cuban	9
Other Hispanic	1,610

Age & Nativity, 2000

Under 5 years	1,941
18 years and over	14,454
65 years and over	2,120
85 years and over	227
Median Age	29.7
Native-born	16,142
Foreign-born	5,954

Educational Attainment, 2000

Population 25 years and over	12,217
Less than 9th grade	25.5%
High school grad or higher	56.6%
Bachelor's degree or higher	10.4%
Graduate degree	3.1%

Income & Poverty, 1999

Per capita income	$12,881
Median household income	$31,277
Median family income	$35,514
Persons in poverty	26.3%
H'holds receiving public assistance	704
H'holds receiving social security	1,736

Households, 2000

Total households	6,631
With persons under 18	3,598
With persons over 65	1,505
Family households	5,264
Single person households	1,133
Persons per household	3.28
Persons per family	3.71

Household Population, 2008§§

Persons living in households	26,201
Persons living in group quarters	312
Persons per household	3.2

Labor & Employment

Total civilian labor force, 2008§§	12,600
Unemployment rate, 2008	25.1%
Total civilian labor force, 2000	8,554

Employed persons 16 years and over by occupation, 2000

Managers & professionals	1,696
Service occupations	1,509
Sales & office occupations	1,718
Farming, fishing & forestry	764
Construction & maintenance	772
Production & transportation	892
Self-employed persons	427

* US Census Bureau
** 2000 Decennial Census
§ California Department of Finance
§§ California Employment Development Dept

General Information

City of Brawley
383 Main St
Brawley, CA 92227
760-351-3080

Email	alma.benavides@cityofbrawley.com
Elevation	-113 ft.
Land Area (sq. miles)	5.8
Water Area (sq. miles)	0
Year of Incorporation	1908
Government type	General law
Sales tax rate	8.75%

Voters & Officials

Registered Voters, October 2008

Total	8,899
Democrats	4,619
Republicans	2,774
Declined to state	1,237

Legislative Districts

US Congressional	51
State Senatorial	40
State Assembly	80

Local Officials, 2009

Mayor	Steve Vasquez
City Manager	Gary Burroughs
City Clerk	Alma Benson
Attorney	Dennis Morita
Finance Dir	Fred Selk
Public Works	Yazmin Arellano
Planning/Dev Dir	Gordon Gaste
Building	Franciso Soto
Police Chief	Mark Gillmore
Emergency/Fire Dir.	Frank Contreras

Public Safety

Number of officers, 2007	28
Violent crimes, 2007	64
Property crimes, 2007	1,162
Arson, 2007	11

Public Library

Brawley Public Library
400 Main St
Brawley, CA 92227
760-344-1891

Director	Marjo Mello

Library statistics, FY 2007

Population served	25,694
Internet terminals	26
Annual users	9,000

Per capita:

Operating income	$19.99
percent from local government	96.1%
Operating expenditure	$19.21
Total materials	2.05
Print holdings	1.97
Visits per capita	2.20

Housing & Construction

Housing Units

Total, 2008§	8,577
Single family units, attached	368
Single family units, detached	5,550
Multiple family units	2,204
Mobile home units	455
Occupied	8,082
Vacancy rate	5.8%
Median rent, 2000**	$481
Median SF home value, 2000**	$97,800

New Privately Owned Housing Units Authorized by Building Permit, 2007*

	Units	Construction Cost
Single	84	$17,004,572
Total	84	$17,004,572

Municipal Finance

(For local fiscal year ended in 2006)

Revenues

Total	$30,934,576
Taxes	8,481,537
Special benefits assessment	0
Licenses & permits	326,889
Fines & forfeitures	48,768
Revenues from use of money & property	499,092
Intergovernmental	6,811,347
Service charges	13,362,291
Other revenues	664,876
Other financing sources	739,776

Expenditures

Total	$27,829,635
General government	1,464,464
Public safety	5,444,467
Transportation	5,128,447
Community development	5,074,884
Health	3,815,393
Culture & leisure	2,219,823
Other	0

Local School District

(Data from School year 2007-08 except as noted)

Brawley Union High
480 North Imperial Ave
Brawley, CA 92227
(760) 312-5819

Superintendent	Antonio Munguia
Grade plan	9-12
Number of schools	3
Enrollment	1,981
High school graduates, 2006-07	352
Dropout rate	2.9%
Pupil/teacher ratio	23.9
Average class size	27.1
Students per computer	4.0
Classrooms with internet	101
Avg. Daily Attendance (ADA)	1,817
Cost per ADA	$8,779
Avg. Teacher Salary	$73,148

California Achievement Tests 6th ed., 2008

(Pct scoring at or above 50th National Percentile Rank)

	Math	Reading	Language
Grade 3	NA	NA	NA
Grade 7	NA	NA	NA

Academic Performance Index, 2008

Number of students tested	1,430
Number of valid scores	1,369
2007 API (base)	661
2008 API (growth)	682

SAT Testing, 2006-07

Enrollment, Grade 12	466
Number taking test	135
percent taking test	29.0%
percent with total score 1,500+	8.40%

Average Scores:

Math	Verbal	Writing	Total
460	453	449	1,362

Federal No Child Left Behind, 2008

(Adequate Yearly Progress standards met)

	Participation Rate	Pct Proficient
ELA	Yes	Yes
Math	Yes	Yes

API criteria	Yes
Graduation rate	Yes
# criteria met/possible	18/18

Other school districts for this city

(see Appendix E for information on these districts)

Brawley Elem, Magnolia Union Elem, Mulberry Elem

See Introduction for an explanation of all data sources.

Demographics & Socio-Economic Characteristics

(2000 Decennial Census, except as noted)

Population

1990* 32,873
2000 35,410
Male 17,278
Female 18,132
Jan. 2008 (estimate)§ 40,081
Persons per sq. mi. of land 3,817.2

Race & Hispanic Origin, 2000

Race
White 27,384
Black/African American 447
North American Native 184
Asian 3,218
Pacific Islander 77
Other Race 2,748
Two or more races 1,352
Hispanic origin, total 7,205
Mexican 5,752
Puerto Rican 138
Cuban 71
Other Hispanic 1,244

Age & Nativity, 2000

Under 5 years 2,145
18 years and over 26,328
65 years and over 4,023
85 years and over 397
Median Age 36.4
Native-born 29,070
Foreign-born 6,052

Educational Attainment, 2000

Population 25 years and over 23,098
Less than 9th grade 4.6%
High school grad or higher 88.4%
Bachelor's degree or higher 33.5%
Graduate degree 11.6%

Income & Poverty, 1999

Per capita income $26,307
Median household income $59,759
Median family income $68,423
Persons in poverty 5.3%
H'holds receiving public assistance 213
H'holds receiving social security 2,878

Households, 2000

Total households 13,067
With persons under 18 4,890
With persons over 65 2,951
Family households 9,301
Single person households 3,011
Persons per household 2.70
Persons per family 3.21

Household Population, 2008§§

Persons living in households 39,953
Persons living in group quarters 128
Persons per household 2.8

Labor & Employment

Total civilian labor force, 2008§§ 22,000
Unemployment rate, 2008 .... 3.6%
Total civilian labor force, 2000 18,900

Employed persons 16 years and over by occupation, 2000

Managers & professionals 8,051
Service occupations 1,948
Sales & office occupations 5,651
Farming, fishing & forestry 0
Construction & maintenance 894
Production & transportation 1,663
Self-employed persons 1,211

* US Census Bureau
** 2000 Decennial Census
§ California Department of Finance
§§ California Employment Development Dept

General Information

City of Brea
1 Civic Center Circle
Brea, CA 92821
714-990-7600

Website .... www.cityofbrea.net
Elevation .... 349 ft.
Land Area (sq. miles) 10.5
Water Area (sq. miles) 0
Year of Incorporation 1917
Government type .... General law
Sales tax rate 8.75%

Voters & Officials

Registered Voters, October 2008

Total 23,938
Democrats 6,893
Republicans 12,075
Declined to state 4,107

Legislative Districts

US Congressional 42
State Senatorial 29
State Assembly 72

Local Officials, 2009

Mayor .... John Beauman
Manager .... Tim O'Donnell
City Clerk .... Lucinda Williams
Attorney .... James Markman
Finance Dir .... Bill Gallardo
Public Works .... Bill Higgins
Development Svcs Dir .... Charlie View
Building .... Gabriel Linares
Police Chief .... Bill Hutchinson
Emergency/Fire Dir .... Alford Nero

Public Safety

Number of officers, 2007 106
Violent crimes, 2007 77
Property crimes, 2007 1,513
Arson, 2007 7

Public Library

Brea Branch Library
Orange County Public Library System
1 Civic Center Circle
Brea, CA 92821
714-671-1722

Branch Librarian .... Cheryl Nakaji

Library system statistics, FY 2007

Population served 1,532,758
Internet terminals 505
Annual users 680,874

Per capita:

Operating income $24.71
percent from local government 90.0%
Operating expenditure $24.18
Total materials 1.93
Print holdings 1.84
Visits per capita 4.02

Housing & Construction

Housing Units

Total, 2008§ 14,581
Single family units, attached 1,095
Single family units, detached 8,499
Multiple family units 4,117
Mobile home units 870
Occupied 14,299
Vacancy rate 1.9%
Median rent, 2000** $935
Median SF home value, 2000** $261,700

New Privately Owned Housing Units Authorized by Building Permit, 2007*

	Units	Construction Cost
Single	5	$1,131,989
Total	5	$1,131,989

Municipal Finance

(For local fiscal year ended in 2006)

Revenues

Total $68,115,421
Taxes 31,634,166
Special benefits assessment 440,930
Licenses & permits 463,024
Fines & forfeitures 1,551,306
Revenues from use of money & property 1,487,132
Intergovernmental 2,905,809
Service charges 25,763,010
Other revenues 3,870,044
Other financing sources 0

Expenditures

Total $67,316,319
General government 7,982,573
Public safety 30,201,471
Transportation 6,809,193
Community development 2,811,421
Health 2,851,694
Culture & leisure 6,149,824
Other 0

Local School District

(Data from School year 2007-08 except as noted)

Brea-Olinda Unified
PO Box 300
Brea, CA 92822
(714) 990-7800

Superintendent .... Arthur Roland
Grade plan K-12
Number of schools 9
Enrollment 6,033
High school graduates, 2006-07 488
Dropout rate 0.9%
Pupil/teacher ratio 24.3
Average class size 27.8
Students per computer 5.2
Classrooms with internet 286
Avg. Daily Attendance (ADA) 5,909
Cost per ADA $7,617
Avg. Teacher Salary $69,094

California Achievement Tests 6th ed., 2008

(Pct scoring at or above 50th National Percentile Rank)

	Math	Reading	Language
Grade 3	77%	59%	68%
Grade 7	76%	72%	70%

Academic Performance Index, 2008

Number of students tested 4,682
Number of valid scores 4,517
2007 API (base) 832
2008 API (growth) 840

SAT Testing, 2006-07

Enrollment, Grade 12 507
Number taking test 295
percent taking test 58.2%
percent with total score 1,500+ ... 35.90%

Average Scores:

Math	Verbal	Writing	Total
563	520	530	1,613

Federal No Child Left Behind, 2008

(Adequate Yearly Progress standards met)

	Participation Rate	Pct Proficient
ELA	Yes	Yes
Math	Yes	Yes

API criteria .... Yes
Graduation rate .... Yes
criteria met/possible 30/30

Other school districts for this city

(see Appendix E for information on these districts)

None

Demographics & Socio-Economic Characteristics

(2000 Decennial Census, except as noted)

Population

1990* . . . 7,563
2000 . . . 23,302
Male . . . 11,487
Female . . . 11,815
Jan. 2008 (estimate)§ . . . 50,614
Persons per sq. mi. of land . . . 4,363.3

Race & Hispanic Origin, 2000

Race
White . . . 17,201
Black/African American . . . 579
North American Native . . . 143
Asian . . . 666
Pacific Islander . . . 73
Other Race . . . 3,387
Two or more races . . . 1,253
Hispanic origin, total . . . 6,565
Mexican . . . 5,266
Puerto Rican . . . 204
Cuban . . . 22
Other Hispanic . . . 1,073

Age & Nativity, 2000

Under 5 years . . . 2,263
18 years and over . . . 15,659
65 years and over . . . 2,233
85 years and over . . . 173
Median Age . . . 32.7
Native-born . . . 19,993
Foreign-born . . . 3,291

Educational Attainment, 2000

Population 25 years and over . . . 14,125
Less than 9th grade . . . 7.6%
High school grad or higher . . . 82.9%
Bachelor's degree or higher . . . 20.9%
Graduate degree . . . 5.8%

Income & Poverty, 1999

Per capita income . . . $24,909
Median household income . . . $69,198
Median family income . . . $75,753
Persons in poverty . . . 5.8%
H'holds receiving public assistance . . . 146
H'holds receiving social security . . . 1,764

Households, 2000

Total households . . . 7,497
With persons under 18 . . . 3,816
With persons over 65 . . . 1,577
Family households . . . 6,127
Single person households . . . 1,079
Persons per household . . . 3.10
Persons per family . . . 3.43

Household Population, 2008§§

Persons living in households . . . 50,487
Persons living in group quarters . . . 127
Persons per household . . . 3.0

Labor & Employment

Total civilian labor force, 2008§§ . . . 11,000
Unemployment rate, 2008 . . . 5.5%
Total civilian labor force, 2000 . . . 9,856

Employed persons 16 years and over by occupation, 2000

Managers & professionals . . . 3,397
Service occupations . . . 1,419
Sales & office occupations . . . 2,422
Farming, fishing & forestry . . . 116
Construction & maintenance . . . 1,336
Production & transportation . . . 769
Self-employed persons . . . 750

* US Census Bureau
** 2000 Decennial Census
§ California Department of Finance
§§ California Employment Development Dept

General Information

City of Brentwood
708 Third St
Brentwood, CA 94513
925-516-5400

Website . . . www.ci.brentwood.ca.us
Elevation . . . 79 ft.
Land Area (sq. miles) . . . 11.6
Water Area (sq. miles) . . . 0
Year of Incorporation . . . 1948
Government type . . . General law
Sales tax rate . . . 9.25%

Voters & Officials

Registered Voters, October 2008

Total . . . 23,722
Democrats . . . 10,233
Republicans . . . 8,335
Declined to state . . . 4,342

Legislative Districts

US Congressional . . . 11
State Senatorial . . . 7
State Assembly . . . 15

Local Officials, 2009

Mayor . . . Robert Taylor
Manager . . . Donna Landeros
City Clerk . . . Margaret Wimberly
Attorney . . . Damien Brower
Finance Dir . . . Pam Ehler
Public Works . . . Bailey Grewal
Planning/Dev Dir . . . Casey McCann
Building . . . NA
Police Chief . . . Mark Evenson
Fire/Emergency Mgmt . . . NA

Public Safety

Number of officers, 2007 . . . 61
Violent crimes, 2007 . . . 124
Property crimes, 2007 . . . 1,271
Arson, 2007 . . . 27

Public Library

Brentwood Library
Contra Costa County Library System
751 Third St
Brentwood, CA 94513
925-634-4101

Branch Librarian . . . Leonard Roudman

Library system statistics, FY 2007

Population served . . . 938,513
Internet terminals . . . 324
Annual users . . . 670,618

Per capita:

Operating income . . . $27.05
percent from local government . . . 82.0%
Operating expenditure . . . $27.82
Total materials . . . 1.57
Print holdings . . . 1.41
Visits per capita . . . 3.65

Housing & Construction

Housing Units

Total, 2008§ . . . 17,309
Single family units, attached . . . 527
Single family units, detached . . . 15,405
Multiple family units . . . 1,026
Mobile home units . . . 351
Occupied . . . 16,673
Vacancy rate . . . 3.7%
Median rent, 2000** . . . $830
Median SF home value, 2000** . . . $252,500

New Privately Owned Housing Units Authorized by Building Permit, 2007*

	Units	Construction Cost
Single	357	$77,461,321
Total	357	$77,461,321

Municipal Finance

(For local fiscal year ended in 2006)

Revenues

Total . . . $114,176,196
Taxes . . . 33,615,475
Special benefits assessment . . . 4,906,681
Licenses & permits . . . 3,420,199
Fines & forfeitures . . . 192,181
Revenues from use of money & property . . . 4,246,342
Intergovernmental . . . 3,477,900
Service charges . . . 51,532,100
Other revenues . . . 12,785,318
Other financing sources . . . 0

Expenditures

Total . . . $90,357,385
General government . . . 13,731,214
Public safety . . . 18,622,613
Transportation . . . 8,768,230
Community development . . . 9,188,713
Health . . . 13,905,647
Culture & leisure . . . 9,491,178
Other . . . 0

Local School District

(Data from School year 2007-08 except as noted)

Liberty Union High
20 Oak St
Brentwood, CA 94513
(925) 634-2166

Superintendent . . . Daniel Smith
Grade plan . . . 9-12
Number of schools . . . 5
Enrollment . . . 6,795
High school graduates, 2006-07 . . . 1,114
Dropout rate . . . 2.3%
Pupil/teacher ratio . . . 23.2
Average class size . . . 27.5
Students per computer . . . 4.1
Classrooms with internet . . . 295
Avg. Daily Attendance (ADA) . . . 6,323
Cost per ADA . . . $8,026
Avg. Teacher Salary . . . $64,026

California Achievement Tests 6th ed., 2008

(Pct scoring at or above 50th National Percentile Rank)

	Math	Reading	Language
Grade 3	NA	NA	NA
Grade 7	NA	NA	NA

Academic Performance Index, 2008

Number of students tested . . . 4,929
Number of valid scores . . . 4,710
2007 API (base) . . . 690
2008 API (growth) . . . 723

SAT Testing, 2006-07

Enrollment, Grade 12 . . . 1,519
Number taking test . . . 457
percent taking test . . . 30.1%
percent with total score 1,500+ . . . 12.20%

Average Scores:

Math	Verbal	Writing	Total
491	482	475	1,448

Federal No Child Left Behind, 2008

(Adequate Yearly Progress standards met)

	Participation Rate	Pct Proficient
ELA	Yes	No
Math	Yes	No

API criteria . . . Yes
Graduation rate . . . Yes
\# criteria met/possible . . . 30/24

Other school districts for this city

(see Appendix E for information on these districts)

Brentwood Union Elem

See Introduction for an explanation of all data sources.

Demographics & Socio-Economic Characteristics

(2000 Decennial Census, except as noted)

Population

1990* . . . 2,952
2000 . . . 3,597
Male . . . 1,806
Female . . . 1,791
Jan. 2008 (estimate)§ . . . 3,861
Persons per sq. mi. of land . . . 1,170.0

Race & Hispanic Origin, 2000

Race
White . . . 2,624
Black/African American . . . 38
North American Native . . . 24
Asian . . . 524
Pacific Islander . . . 22
Other Race . . . 180
Two or more races . . . 185
Hispanic origin, total . . . 550
Mexican . . . 267
Puerto Rican . . . 31
Cuban . . . 9
Other Hispanic . . . 243

Age & Nativity, 2000

Under 5 years . . . 161
18 years and over . . . 2,959
65 years and over . . . 292
85 years and over . . . 24
Median Age . . . 40.3
Native-born . . . 2,788
Foreign-born . . . 735

Educational Attainment, 2000

Population 25 years and over . . . 2,708
Less than 9th grade . . . 2.6%
High school grad or higher . . . 90.4%
Bachelor's degree or higher . . . 40.3%
Graduate degree . . . 16.9%

Income & Poverty, 1999

Per capita income . . . $37,162
Median household income . . . $63,684
Median family income . . . $81,484
Persons in poverty . . . 5.6%
H'holds receiving public assistance . . . 39
H'holds receiving social security . . . 328

Households, 2000

Total households . . . 1,620
With persons under 18 . . . 401
With persons over 65 . . . 244
Family households . . . 850
Single person households . . . 564
Persons per household . . . 2.20
Persons per family . . . 2.89

Household Population, 2008§§

Persons living in households . . . 3,821
Persons living in group quarters . . . 40
Persons per household . . . 2.2

Labor & Employment

Total civilian labor force, 2008§§ . . . 2,300
Unemployment rate, 2008 . . . 7.7%
Total civilian labor force, 2000 . . . 2,216

Employed persons 16 years and over by occupation, 2000

Managers & professionals . . . 980
Service occupations . . . 249
Sales & office occupations . . . 486
Farming, fishing & forestry . . . 0
Construction & maintenance . . . 194
Production & transportation . . . 188
Self-employed persons . . . 291

* US Census Bureau
** 2000 Decennial Census
§ California Department of Finance
§§ California Employment Development Dept

General Information

City of Brisbane
50 Park Place
Brisbane, CA 94005
415-508-2110

Website . . . www.ci.brisbane.ca.us
Elevation . . . NA
Land Area (sq. miles) . . . 3.3
Water Area (sq. miles) . . . 17.2
Year of Incorporation . . . 1961
Government type . . . General law
Sales tax rate . . . 9.25%

Voters & Officials

Registered Voters, October 2008

Total . . . 2,628
Democrats . . . 1,445
Republicans . . . 347
Declined to state . . . 713

Legislative Districts

US Congressional . . . 12
State Senatorial . . . 8
State Assembly . . . 19

Local Officials, 2009

Mayor . . . Sepi Richardson
Manager . . . Clay Holstine
City Clerk . . . Sheri Spediacci
Attorney . . . Hal Toppel
Finance Dir . . . Stuart Schillinger
Public Works . . . Randy Breault
Planning/Dev Dir . . . Bill Prince
Building . . . NA
Police Chief . . . Tom Hitchcock
Emergency/Fire Dir . . . Ron Myers

Public Safety

Number of officers, 2007 . . . 18
Violent crimes, 2007 . . . 10
Property crimes, 2007 . . . 129
Arson, 2007 . . . 0

Public Library

Brisbane Library
San Mateo County Library System
250 Visitacion Ave
Brisbane, CA 94005
415-467-2060

Branch Librarian . . . Chet Mulawka

Library system statistics, FY 2007

Population served . . . 278,388
Internet terminals . . . 26
Annual users . . . 49,920

Per capita:

Operating income . . . $90.21
percent from local government . . . 63.5%
Operating expenditure . . . $60.41
Total materials . . . 2.65
Print holdings . . . 2.16
Visits per capita . . . 5.44

Housing & Construction

Housing Units

Total, 2008§ . . . 1,933
Single family units, attached . . . 262
Single family units, detached . . . 1,086
Multiple family units . . . 542
Mobile home units . . . 43
Occupied . . . 1,720
Vacancy rate . . . 11.0%
Median rent, 2000** . . . $975
Median SF home value, 2000** . . . $382,300

New Privately Owned Housing Units Authorized by Building Permit, 2007*

	Units	Construction Cost
Single	9	$4,581,200
Total	12	$5,331,200

Municipal Finance

(For local fiscal year ended in 2006)

Revenues

Total . . . $23,491,111
Taxes . . . 8,096,430
Special benefits assessment . . . 2,036,011
Licenses & permits . . . 440,477
Fines & forfeitures . . . 115,574
Revenues from use of money & property . . . 800,838
Intergovernmental . . . 2,469,084
Service charges . . . 4,385,090
Other revenues . . . 5,147,607
Other financing sources . . . 0

Expenditures

Total . . . $22,742,686
General government . . . 3,635,528
Public safety . . . 6,540,695
Transportation . . . 2,518,371
Community development . . . 5,155,368
Health . . . 941,121
Culture & leisure . . . 2,796,104
Other . . . 0

Local School District

(Data from School year 2007-08 except as noted)

Jefferson Union High
699 Serramonte Blvd, Suite 100
Daly City, CA 94015
(650) 550-7900

Superintendent . . . Michael Crilly
Grade plan . . . 9-12
Number of schools . . . 5
Enrollment . . . 5,330
High school graduates, 2006-07 . . . 1,105
Dropout rate . . . 3.0%
Pupil/teacher ratio . . . 30.8
Average class size . . . 25.9
Students per computer . . . 4.3
Classrooms with internet . . . 276
Avg. Daily Attendance (ADA) . . . 5,128
Cost per ADA . . . $8,239
Avg. Teacher Salary . . . $58,641

California Achievement Tests 6th ed., 2008

(Pct scoring at or above 50th National Percentile Rank)

	Math	Reading	Language
Grade 3	NA	NA	NA
Grade 7	NA	NA	NA

Academic Performance Index, 2008

Number of students tested . . . 3,846
Number of valid scores . . . 3,651
2007 API (base) . . . 730
2008 API (growth) . . . 732

SAT Testing, 2006-07

Enrollment, Grade 12 . . . 1,255
Number taking test . . . 532
percent taking test . . . 42.4%
percent with total score 1,500+ . . . 17.90%

Average Scores:

Math	Verbal	Writing	Total
510	471	474	1,455

Federal No Child Left Behind, 2008

(Adequate Yearly Progress standards met)

	Participation Rate	Pct Proficient
ELA	No	No
Math	Yes	Yes

API criteria . . . Yes
Graduation rate . . . Yes
\# criteria met/possible . . . 34/31

Other school districts for this city

(see Appendix E for information on these districts)

Brisbane Elem

See Introduction for an explanation of all data sources.

Demographics & Socio-Economic Characteristics

(2000 Decennial Census, except as noted)

Population

1990* ... NA
2000 ... 3,828
Male ... 1,900
Female ... 1,928
Jan. 2008 (estimate)§ ... 4,700
Persons per sq. mi. of land ... 2,937.5

Race & Hispanic Origin, 2000

Race
White ... 3,120
Black/African American ... 21
North American Native ... 44
Asian ... 42
Pacific Islander ... 8
Other Race ... 468
Two or more races ... 125
Hispanic origin, total ... 985
Mexican ... 873
Puerto Rican ... 6
Cuban ... 2
Other Hispanic ... 104

Age & Nativity, 2000

Under 5 years ... 256
18 years and over ... 2,792
65 years and over ... 521
85 years and over ... 64
Median Age ... 37.8
Native-born ... 3,237
Foreign-born ... 595

Educational Attainment, 2000

Population 25 years and over ... 2,527
Less than 9th grade ... 7.8%
High school grad or higher ... 80.6%
Bachelor's degree or higher ... 19.8%
Graduate degree ... 6.0%

Income & Poverty, 1999

Per capita income ... $20,907
Median household income ... $48,490
Median family income ... $54,839
Persons in poverty ... 8.8%
H'holds receiving public assistance ... 43
H'holds receiving social security ... 431

Households, 2000

Total households ... 1,433
With persons under 18 ... 535
With persons over 65 ... 386
Family households ... 1,000
Single person households ... 342
Persons per household ... 2.67
Persons per family ... 3.17

Household Population, 2008§§

Persons living in households ... 4,694
Persons living in group quarters ... 6
Persons per household ... 2.6

Labor & Employment

Total civilian labor force, 2008§§ ... 2,200
Unemployment rate, 2008 ... 2.8%
Total civilian labor force, 2000 ... 1,939

Employed persons 16 years and over by occupation, 2000

Managers & professionals ... 550
Service occupations ... 376
Sales & office occupations ... 499
Farming, fishing & forestry ... 69
Construction & maintenance ... 140
Production & transportation ... 238
Self-employed persons ... 236

* US Census Bureau
** 2000 Decennial Census
§ California Department of Finance
§§ California Employment Development Dept

General Information

City of Buellton
PO Box 1819
Buellton, CA 93427
805-686-0137

Website ... www.cityofbuellton.com
Elevation ... NA
Land Area (sq. miles) ... 1.6
Water Area (sq. miles) ... 0
Year of Incorporation ... 1992
Government type ... General law
Sales tax rate ... 8.75%

Voters & Officials

Registered Voters, October 2008

Total ... 2,556
Democrats ... 880
Republicans ... 1,091
Declined to state ... 457

Legislative Districts

US Congressional ... 24
State Senatorial ... 19
State Assembly ... 35

Local Officials, 2009

Mayor ... Russ Hicks
Manager ... Steven Thompson
City Clerk ... Steven Thompson
Attorney ... Don Kircher
Finance Dir ... Kathy Wollin
Public Works ... Bill Albrecht
Planning/Dev Dir ... Marc Bierdzinski
Building ... NA
Police Chief ... Bill Brown
Emergency/Fire Dir ... John Scherrei

Public Safety

Number of officers, 2007 ... NA
Violent crimes, 2007 ... 11
Property crimes, 2007 ... 100
Arson, 2007 ... 1

Public Library

Buellton Branch Library
Lompoc Public Library System
140 W Hwy 246
Buellton, CA 93427
805-688-3115

Branch Librarian ... Liz Chapman

Library system statistics, FY 2007

Population served ... 72,152
Internet terminals ... 20
Annual users ... 87,394

Per capita:

Operating income ... $17.87
percent from local government ... 78.0%
Operating expenditure ... $16.38
Total materials ... 1.79
Print holdings ... 1.57
Visits per capita ... 3.37

Housing & Construction

Housing Units

Total, 2008§ ... 1,840
Single family units, attached ... 120
Single family units, detached ... 1,149
Multiple family units ... 152
Mobile home units ... 419
Occupied ... 1,778
Vacancy rate ... 3.4%
Median rent, 2000** ... $725
Median SF home value, 2000** ... $269,500

New Privately Owned Housing Units Authorized by Building Permit, 2007*

	Units	Construction Cost
Single	NA	NA
Total	NA	NA

Municipal Finance

(For local fiscal year ended in 2006)

Revenues

Total ... $7,459,744
Taxes ... 4,240,760
Special benefits assessment ... 0
Licenses & permits ... 0
Fines & forfeitures ... 17,485
Revenues from use of money & property ... 565,974
Intergovernmental ... 394,155
Service charges ... 2,086,589
Other revenues ... 154,781
Other financing sources ... 0

Expenditures

Total ... $9,321,579
General government ... 1,712,031
Public safety ... 1,287,564
Transportation ... 869,341
Community development ... 572,663
Health ... 528,724
Culture & leisure ... 2,969,686
Other ... 0

Local School District

(Data from School year 2007-08 except as noted)

Santa Ynez Valley Union High
PO Box 398
Santa Ynez, CA 93460
(805) 688-6487

Superintendent ... Paul Turnbull
Grade plan ... 9-12
Number of schools ... 2
Enrollment ... 1,130
High school graduates, 2006-07 ... 257
Dropout rate ... 1.3%
Pupil/teacher ratio ... 23.1
Average class size ... 24.3
Students per computer ... 2.4
Classrooms with internet ... 73
Avg. Daily Attendance (ADA) ... 1,069
Cost per ADA ... $10,952
Avg. Teacher Salary ... $69,469

California Achievement Tests 6th ed., 2008

(Pct scoring at or above 50th National Percentile Rank)

	Math	Reading	Language
Grade 3	NA	NA	NA
Grade 7	NA	NA	NA

Academic Performance Index, 2008

Number of students tested ... 819
Number of valid scores ... 793
2007 API (base) ... 795
2008 API (growth) ... 787

SAT Testing, 2006-07

Enrollment, Grade 12 ... 279
Number taking test ... 136
percent taking test ... 48.8%
percent with total score 1,500+ ... 32.30%

Average Scores:

Math	Verbal	Writing	Total
537	539	526	1,602

Federal No Child Left Behind, 2008

(Adequate Yearly Progress standards met)

	Participation Rate	Pct Proficient
ELA	No	Yes
Math	Yes	Yes

API criteria ... Yes
Graduation rate ... Yes
\# criteria met/possible ... 20/19

Other school districts for this city

(see Appendix E for information on these districts)

Buellton Union Elem

See Introduction for an explanation of all data sources.

Demographics & Socio-Economic Characteristics†

(2007 American Community Survey, except as noted)

Population

1990* ... 68,784
2007 ... 85,992
Male ... 42,823
Female ... 43,169
Jan. 2008 (estimate)§ ... 82,768
Persons per sq. mi. of land ... 7,808.3

Race & Hispanic Origin, 2007

Race
White ... 33,153
Black/African American ... 5,356
North American Native ... 1,010
Asian ... 17,950
Pacific Islander ... 61
Other Race ... 26,012
Two or more races ... 2,450
Hispanic origin, total ... 36,123
Mexican ... 32,170
Puerto Rican ... 64
Cuban ... 259
Other Hispanic ... 3,630

Age & Nativity, 2007

Under 5 years ... 6,868
18 years and over ... 61,391
65 years and over ... 7,394
85 years and over ... 951
Median Age ... 31.5
Native-born ... 55,793
Foreign-born ... 30,199

Educational Attainment, 2007

Population 25 years and over ... 51,728
Less than 9th grade ... 12.2%
High school grad or higher ... 77.7%
Bachelor's degree or higher ... 22.7%
Graduate degree ... 6.9%

Income & Poverty, 2007

Per capita income ... $21,914
Median household income ... $62,901
Median family income ... $63,641
Persons in poverty ... 10.0%
H'holds receiving public assistance ... 1,456
H'holds receiving social security ... 4,581

Households, 2007

Total households ... 23,710
With persons under 18 ... 11,931
With persons over 65 ... 5,090
Family households ... 20,427
Single person households ... 1,983
Persons per household ... 3.61
Persons per family ... 3.72

Household Population, 2008§§

Persons living in households ... 81,834
Persons living in group quarters ... 934
Persons per household ... 3.4

Labor & Employment

Total civilian labor force, 2008§§ ... 43,000
Unemployment rate, 2008 ... 6.6%
Total civilian labor force, 2000* ... 36,763

Employed persons 16 years and over by occupation, 2007

Managers & professionals ... 11,765
Service occupations ... 6,805
Sales & office occupations ... 13,195
Farming, fishing & forestry ... 0
Construction & maintenance ... 4,089
Production & transportation ... 5,379
Self-employed persons ... 2,518

† see Appendix D for 2000 Decennial Census Data
* US Census Bureau
** 2007 American Community Survey
§ California Department of Finance
§§ California Employment Development Dept

General Information

City of Buena Park
6650 Beach Blvd
Buena Park, CA 90621
714-562-3500

Website ... www.buenapark.com
Elevation ... 74 ft.
Land Area (sq. miles) ... 10.6
Water Area (sq. miles) ... 0.1
Year of Incorporation ... 1953
Government type ... General law
Sales tax rate ... 8.75%

Voters & Officials

Registered Voters, October 2008

Total ... 37,883
Democrats ... 15,087
Republicans ... 13,710
Declined to state ... 7,563

Legislative Districts

US Congressional ... 40
State Senatorial ... 33-35
State Assembly ... 56

Local Officials, 2009

Mayor ... Jim Dow
Manager ... Rick Warsinksi
City Clerk ... Shalice Reynoso
Attorney ... Steven Dorsey
Finance Dir ... Sung Hyun
Public Works ... Jim Biery
Planning/Dev Dir ... Joel Rosen
Building ... NA
Police Chief ... Tom Monson
Fire/Emergency Mgmt ... NA

Public Safety

Number of officers, 2007 ... 93
Violent crimes, 2007 ... 317
Property crimes, 2007 ... 2,058
Arson, 2007 ... 29

Public Library

Buena Park Library District
7150 La Palma Ave
Buena Park, CA 90620
714-826-4100

Director ... Louise Mazerov

Library statistics, FY 2007

Population served ... 82,452
Internet terminals ... 9
Annual users ... 65,202

Per capita:

Operating income ... $26.54
percent from local government ... 79.8%
Operating expenditure ... $26.55
Total materials ... 1.34
Print holdings ... 1.21
Visits per capita ... 3.54

Housing & Construction

Housing Units

Total, 2008§ ... 24,280
Single family units, attached ... 1,958
Single family units, detached ... 14,191
Multiple family units ... 7,840
Mobile home units ... 291
Occupied ... 23,777
Vacancy rate ... 2.1%
Median rent, 2007** ... $1,281
Median SF home value, 2007** ... $595,200

New Privately Owned Housing Units Authorized by Building Permit, 2007*

	Units	Construction Cost
Single	88	$17,882,162
Total	88	$17,882,162

Municipal Finance

(For local fiscal year ended in 2006)

Revenues

Total ... $69,316,729
Taxes ... 39,895,980
Special benefits assessment ... 0
Licenses & permits ... 558,366
Fines & forfeitures ... 1,010,864
Revenues from use of money & property ... 1,680,010
Intergovernmental ... 7,145,216
Service charges ... 17,482,909
Other revenues ... 1,543,384
Other financing sources ... 0

Expenditures

Total ... $69,581,046
General government ... 5,098,805
Public safety ... 27,744,974
Transportation ... 14,802,528
Community development ... 4,776,171
Health ... 3,111,066
Culture & leisure ... 3,913,274
Other ... 0

Local School District

(Data from School year 2007-08 except as noted)

Fullerton Joint Union High
1051 West Bastanchury Rd
Fullerton, CA 92833
(714) 870-2800

Superintendent ... George Giokaris
Grade plan ... 9-12
Number of schools ... 8
Enrollment ... 16,321
High school graduates, 2006-07 ... 2,914
Dropout rate ... 2.3%
Pupil/teacher ratio ... 27.7
Average class size ... 29.9
Students per computer ... 3.7
Classrooms with internet ... 724
Avg. Daily Attendance (ADA) ... 15,436
Cost per ADA ... $7,977
Avg. Teacher Salary ... $82,860

California Achievement Tests 6th ed., 2008

(Pct scoring at or above 50th National Percentile Rank)

	Math	Reading	Language
Grade 3	NA	NA	NA
Grade 7	NA	NA	NA

Academic Performance Index, 2008

Number of students tested ... 10,832
Number of valid scores ... 10,168
2007 API (base) ... 775
2008 API (growth) ... 794

SAT Testing, 2006-07

Enrollment, Grade 12 ... 2,962
Number taking test ... 1,527
percent taking test ... 51.6%
percent with total score 1,500+ ... 32.20%

Average Scores:

Math	Verbal	Writing	Total
568	529	536	1,633

Federal No Child Left Behind, 2008

(Adequate Yearly Progress standards met)

	Participation Rate	Pct Proficient
ELA	Yes	No
Math	Yes	No

API criteria ... Yes
Graduation rate ... Yes
\# criteria met/possible ... 34/32

Other school districts for this city

(see Appendix E for information on these districts)

Complete list in Appendix E

See Introduction for an explanation of all data sources.

Demographics & Socio-Economic Characteristics†

(2007 American Community Survey, except as noted)

Population

1990* . . . 93,643
2007 . . . 96,972
Male . . . 47,111
Female . . . 49,861
Jan. 2008 (estimate)§ . . . 108,029
Persons per sq. mi. of land . . . 6,244.5

Race & Hispanic Origin, 2007

Race
White . . . 69,126
Black/African American . . . 3,386
North American Native . . . 199
Asian . . . 9,953
Pacific Islander . . . 338
Other Race . . . 11,328
Two or more races . . . 2,642
Hispanic origin, total . . . 20,141
Mexican . . . 14,546
Puerto Rican . . . 73
Cuban . . . 344
Other Hispanic . . . 5,178

Age & Nativity, 2007

Under 5 years . . . 5,945
18 years and over . . . 78,313
65 years and over . . . 12,697
85 years and over . . . 2,106
Median Age . . . 40.3
Native-born . . . 68,519
Foreign-born . . . 28,453

Educational Attainment, 2007

Population 25 years and over . . . 71,702
Less than 9th grade . . . 7.1%
High school grad or higher . . . 86.7%
Bachelor's degree or higher . . . 34.0%
Graduate degree . . . 9.3%

Income & Poverty, 2007

Per capita income . . . $32,770
Median household income . . . $60,440
Median family income . . . $72,491
Persons in poverty . . . 7.7%
H'holds receiving public assistance . . . 502
H'holds receiving social security . . . 8,309

Households, 2007

Total households . . . 40,474
With persons under 18 . . . 11,301
With persons over 65 . . . 9,084
Family households . . . 23,839
Single person households . . . 13,380
Persons per household . . . 2.39
Persons per family . . . 3.09

Household Population, 2008§§

Persons living in households . . . 107,203
Persons living in group quarters . . . 826
Persons per household . . . 2.5

Labor & Employment

Total civilian labor force, 2008§§ . . . 61,500
Unemployment rate, 2008 . . . 6.1%
Total civilian labor force, 2000* . . . 52,720

Employed persons 16 years and over by occupation, 2007

Managers & professionals . . . 22,936
Service occupations . . . 5,902
Sales & office occupations . . . 12,979
Farming, fishing & forestry . . . 0
Construction & maintenance . . . 4,512
Production & transportation . . . 4,508
Self-employed persons . . . 7,825

† see Appendix D for 2000 Decennial Census Data
* US Census Bureau
** 2007 American Community Survey
§ California Department of Finance
§§ California Employment Development Dept

General Information

City of Burbank
275 E Olive Ave
Burbank, CA 91502
818-238-5850

Website . . . www.ci.burbank.ca.us
Elevation . . . 122 ft.
Land Area (sq. miles) . . . 17.3
Water Area (sq. miles) . . . 0
Year of Incorporation . . . 1911
Government type . . . Chartered
Sales tax rate . . . 9.25%

Voters & Officials

Registered Voters, October 2008

Total . . . 54,758
Democrats . . . 24,468
Republicans . . . 16,294
Declined to state . . . 11,514

Legislative Districts

US Congressional . . . 27, 29
State Senatorial . . . 21
State Assembly . . . 43

Local Officials, 2009

Mayor . . . Dave Golonski
Manager . . . Michael Flad
City Clerk . . . Margarita Campos
Attorney . . . Dennis Barlow
Finance Dir . . . Donna Anderson
Public Works . . . Bonnie Teaford
Planning/Dev Dir . . . Gregg Hermann
Building . . . John Cheng
Police Chief . . . Tim Stehr
Emergency/Fire Dir . . . Tracy Pansini

Public Safety

Number of officers, 2007 . . . 154
Violent crimes, 2007 . . . 274
Property crimes, 2007 . . . 2,767
Arson, 2007 . . . 18

Public Library

Burbank Public Library
Burbank Public Library System
110 N Glenoaks Blvd
Burbank, CA 91502
818-238-5551

Director . . . Sharon Cohen

Library system statistics, FY 2007

Population served . . . 107,921
Internet terminals . . . 16
Annual users . . . 198,307

Per capita:

Operating income . . . $58.49
percent from local government . . . 87.2%
Operating expenditure . . . $50.99
Total materials . . . 4.18
Print holdings . . . 3.72
Visits per capita . . . 10.14

Housing & Construction

Housing Units

Total, 2008§ . . . 44,055
Single family units, attached . . . 1,752
Single family units, detached . . . 19,940
Multiple family units . . . 22,251
Mobile home units . . . 112
Occupied . . . 42,781
Vacancy rate . . . 2.9%
Median rent, 2007** . . . $1,167
Median SF home value, 2007** . . . $665,200

New Privately Owned Housing Units Authorized by Building Permit, 2007*

	Units	Construction Cost
Single	31	$10,804,443
Total	185	$46,722,259

Municipal Finance

(For local fiscal year ended in 2006)

Revenues

Total . . . $587,041,592
Taxes . . . 92,118,397
Special benefits assessment . . . 0
Licenses & permits . . . 3,617,331
Fines & forfeitures . . . 3,473,577
Revenues from use of money & property . . . 12,910,577
Intergovernmental . . . 33,611,565
Service charges . . . 427,901,142
Other revenues . . . 13,409,003
Other financing sources . . . 0

Expenditures

Total . . . $571,381,428
General government . . . 27,320,340
Public safety . . . 71,183,714
Transportation . . . 26,333,944
Community development . . . 23,280,523
Health . . . 26,492,119
Culture & leisure . . . 14,835,981
Other . . . 6,478,864

Local School District

(Data from School year 2007-08 except as noted)

Burbank Unified
1900 West Olive Ave
Burbank, CA 91506
(818) 729-4400

Superintendent . . . Gregory Bowman
Grade plan . . . K-12
Number of schools . . . 21
Enrollment . . . 16,640
High school graduates, 2006-07 . . . 1,334
Dropout rate . . . 11.3%
Pupil/teacher ratio . . . 20.8
Average class size . . . 26.6
Students per computer . . . 5.4
Classrooms with internet . . . 701
Avg. Daily Attendance (ADA) . . . 14,957
Cost per ADA . . . $7,955
Avg. Teacher Salary . . . $65,822

California Achievement Tests 6th ed., 2008

(Pct scoring at or above 50th National Percentile Rank)

	Math	Reading	Language
Grade 3	67%	45%	58%
Grade 7	61%	56%	57%

Academic Performance Index, 2008

Number of students tested . . . 12,012
Number of valid scores . . . 11,471
2007 API (base) . . . 788
2008 API (growth) . . . 797

SAT Testing, 2006-07

Enrollment, Grade 12 . . . 1,599
Number taking test . . . 571
percent taking test . . . 35.7%
percent with total score 1,500+ . . . 18.30%

Average Scores:

Math	Verbal	Writing	Total
511	502	503	1,516

Federal No Child Left Behind, 2008

(Adequate Yearly Progress standards met)

	Participation Rate	Pct Proficient
ELA	Yes	No
Math	Yes	No

API criteria . . . Yes
Graduation rate . . . Yes
\# criteria met/possible . . . 38/36

Other school districts for this city

(see Appendix E for information on these districts)

None

See Introduction for an explanation of all data sources.

Demographics & Socio-Economic Characteristics

(2000 Decennial Census, except as noted)

Population

1990* ... 26,801
2000 ... 28,158
  Male ... 13,454
  Female ... 14,704
Jan. 2008 (estimate)§ ... 28,867
  Persons per sq. mi. of land ... 6,713.3

Race & Hispanic Origin, 2000

Race
  White ... 21,648
  Black/African American ... 296
  North American Native ... 65
  Asian ... 3,881
  Pacific Islander ... 135
  Other Race ... 1,019
  Two or more races ... 1,114
Hispanic origin, total ... 2,995
  Mexican ... 1,265
  Puerto Rican ... 91
  Cuban ... 40
  Other Hispanic ... 1,599

Age & Nativity, 2000

Under 5 years ... 1,574
18 years and over ... 22,756
65 years and over ... 4,287
85 years and over ... 771
  Median Age ... 38.4
Native-born ... 21,100
Foreign-born ... 6,875

Educational Attainment, 2000

Population 25 years and over ... 21,111
Less than 9th grade ... 3.1%
High school grad or higher ... 92.9%
Bachelor's degree or higher ... 47.9%
Graduate degree ... 17.7%

Income & Poverty, 1999

Per capita income ... $43,565
Median household income ... $68,526
Median family income ... $91,309
Persons in poverty ... 5.6%
H'holds receiving public assistance ... 147
H'holds receiving social security ... 2,916

Households, 2000

Total households ... 12,511
  With persons under 18 ... 3,185
  With persons over 65 ... 2,905
  Family households ... 6,954
  Single person households ... 4,448
Persons per household ... 2.21
Persons per family ... 2.93

Household Population, 2008§§

Persons living in households ... 28,381
Persons living in group quarters ... 486
Persons per household ... 2.2

Labor & Employment

Total civilian labor force, 2008§§ ... 16,200
  Unemployment rate, 2008 ... 3.4%
Total civilian labor force, 2000 ... 15,729

Employed persons 16 years and over by occupation, 2000

  Managers & professionals ... 8,064
  Service occupations ... 1,648
  Sales & office occupations ... 4,085
  Farming, fishing & forestry ... 0
  Construction & maintenance ... 847
  Production & transportation ... 741
  Self-employed persons ... 1,537

* US Census Bureau
** 2000 Decennial Census
§ California Department of Finance
§§ California Employment Development Dept

General Information

City of Burlingame
501 Primrose Rd
Burlingame, CA 94010
650-558-7200

Website ... www.burlingame.org
Elevation ... 34 ft.
Land Area (sq. miles) ... 4.3
Water Area (sq. miles) ... 1.7
Year of Incorporation ... 1908
Government type ... General law
Sales tax rate ... 9.25%

Voters & Officials

Registered Voters, October 2008

Total ... 16,978
  Democrats ... 8,289
  Republicans ... 4,178
  Declined to state ... 3,878

Legislative Districts

US Congressional ... 12
State Senatorial ... 8
State Assembly ... 19

Local Officials, 2009

Mayor ... Ann Keighra
Manager ... Jim Nantell
City Clerk ... Mary Ellen Kearney
Attorney ... Clark Guinan
Finance Dir ... Jesus Nava
Public Works ... Syed Murtuza
Planning/Dev Dir ... NA
Building ... NA
Police Chief ... Jack Vanetten
Emergency/Fire Dir ... Don Dornell

Public Safety

Number of officers, 2007 ... 42
Violent crimes, 2007 ... 57
Property crimes, 2007 ... 848
Arson, 2007 ... 6

Public Library

Burlingame Main Library
Burlingame Public Library System
480 Primrose Rd
Burlingame, CA 94010
650-558-7474

Director ... Alfred Escoffier

Library system statistics, FY 2007

Population served ... 36,801
Internet terminals ... 65
  Annual users ... 120,486

Per capita:

Operating income ... $104.31
  percent from local government ... 92.7%
Operating expenditure ... $101.29
Total materials ... 6.97
Print holdings ... 6.29
Visits per capita ... 11.77

Housing & Construction

Housing Units

Total, 2008§ ... 12,971
  Single family units, attached ... 423
  Single family units, detached ... 6,164
  Multiple family units ... 6,384
  Mobile home units ... 0
  Occupied ... 12,686
  Vacancy rate ... 2.2%
Median rent, 2000** ... $1,108
Median SF home value, 2000** ... $685,900

New Privately Owned Housing Units Authorized by Building Permit, 2007*

	Units	Construction Cost
Single	9	$6,969,241
Total	12	$7,619,241

Municipal Finance

(For local fiscal year ended in 2006)

Revenues

Total ... $67,716,611
Taxes ... 30,608,663
Special benefits assessment ... 0
Licenses & permits ... 858,515
Fines & forfeitures ... 984,001
Revenues from use of
  money & property ... 1,560,014
Intergovernmental ... 4,923,916
Service charges ... 25,870,727
Other revenues ... 2,910,775
Other financing sources ... 0

Expenditures

Total ... $69,290,593
General government ... 5,798,360
Public safety ... 18,947,375
Transportation ... 9,501,022
Community development ... 2,631,708
Health ... 8,740,719
Culture & leisure ... 9,871,225
Other ... 0

Local School District

(Data from School year 2007-08 except as noted)

San Mateo Union High
650 North Delaware St
San Mateo, CA 94401
(650) 558-2299

Superintendent ... David Miller
Grade plan ... 9-12
Number of schools ... 7
Enrollment ... 8,626
High school graduates, 2006-07 ... 1,833
Dropout rate ... 1.3%
Pupil/teacher ratio ... 21.3
Average class size ... 26.9
Students per computer ... 4.0
Classrooms with internet ... 425
Avg. Daily Attendance (ADA) ... 8,291
  Cost per ADA ... $9,930
Avg. Teacher Salary ... $74,785

California Achievement Tests 6th ed., 2008

(Pct scoring at or above 50th National Percentile Rank)

	Math	Reading	Language
Grade 3	NA	NA	NA
Grade 7	NA	NA	NA

Academic Performance Index, 2008

Number of students tested ... 6,229
Number of valid scores ... 6,003
2007 API (base) ... 774
2008 API (growth) ... 781

SAT Testing, 2006-07

Enrollment, Grade 12 ... 2,145
Number taking test ... 1,188
  percent taking test ... 55.4%
  percent with total score 1,500+ ... 37.60%

Average Scores:

Math	Verbal	Writing	Total
572	534	536	1,642

Federal No Child Left Behind, 2008

(Adequate Yearly Progress standards met)

	Participation Rate	Pct Proficient
ELA	Yes	No
Math	Yes	No

API criteria ... Yes
Graduation rate ... Yes
criteria met/possible ... 32/30

Other school districts for this city

(see Appendix E for information on these districts)

Burlingame Elem

See Introduction for an explanation of all data sources.

Demographics & Socio-Economic Characteristics

(2000 Decennial Census, except as noted)

Population

1990* . . . NA
2000 . . . 20,033
Male . . . 9,737
Female . . . 10,296
Jan. 2008 (estimate)§ . . . 23,725
Persons per sq. mi. of land . . . 1,811.1

Race & Hispanic Origin, 2000

Race
White . . . 17,412
Black/African American . . . 236
North American Native . . . 27
Asian . . . 1,544
Pacific Islander . . . 9
Other Race . . . 262
Two or more races . . . 543
Hispanic origin, total . . . 949
Mexican . . . 466
Puerto Rican . . . 40
Cuban . . . 39
Other Hispanic . . . 404

Age & Nativity, 2000

Under 5 years . . . 1,223
18 years and over . . . 14,296
65 years and over . . . 1,716
85 years and over . . . 118
Median Age . . . 38.5
Native-born . . . 16,256
Foreign-born . . . 3,844

Educational Attainment, 2000

Population 25 years and over . . . 13,263
Less than 9th grade . . . 0.8%
High school grad or higher . . . 97.2%
Bachelor's degree or higher . . . 57.9%
Graduate degree . . . 24.4%

Income & Poverty, 1999

Per capita income . . . $48,189
Median household income . . . $93,860
Median family income . . . $107,330
Persons in poverty . . . 3.3%
H'holds receiving public assistance . . . 49
H'holds receiving social security . . . 1,185

Households, 2000

Total households . . . 7,229
With persons under 18 . . . 3,209
With persons over 65 . . . 1,215
Family households . . . 5,543
Single person households . . . 1,228
Persons per household . . . 2.76
Persons per family . . . 3.14

Household Population, 2008§§

Persons living in households . . . 23,665
Persons living in group quarters . . . 60
Persons per household . . . 2.8

Labor & Employment

Total civilian labor force, 2008§§ . . . 12,300
Unemployment rate, 2008 . . . 3.2%
Total civilian labor force, 2000 . . . 10,625

Employed persons 16 years and over by occupation, 2000

Managers & professionals . . . 6,229
Service occupations . . . 752
Sales & office occupations . . . 2,698
Farming, fishing & forestry . . . 0
Construction & maintenance . . . 304
Production & transportation . . . 269
Self-employed persons . . . 1,584

* US Census Bureau
** 2000 Decennial Census
§ California Department of Finance
§§ California Employment Development Dept

General Information

City of Calabasas
26135 Mureau Rd
Calabasas, CA 91302
818-878-4225

Website . . . www.cityofcalabasas.com
Elevation . . . NA
Land Area (sq. miles) . . . 13.1
Water Area (sq. miles) . . . 0.1
Year of Incorporation . . . 1991
Government type . . . General law
Sales tax rate . . . 9.25%

Voters & Officials

Registered Voters, October 2008

Total . . . 13,874
Democrats . . . 6,357
Republicans . . . 4,347
Declined to state . . . 2,627

Legislative Districts

US Congressional . . . 30
State Senatorial . . . 23
State Assembly . . . 41

Local Officials, 2009

Mayor . . . Mary Sue Maurer
Manager . . . Anthony Coroalles
City Clerk . . . Gwen Peirce
Attorney . . . Michael Colantuono
Finance Dir . . . Gary Lysik
Public Works . . . Robert Yalda
Community Dev Dir . . . Maureen Tamuri
Building . . . Sparky Cohen
Police Chief . . . NA
Fire/Emergency Mgmt . . . NA

Public Safety

Number of officers, 2007 . . . NA
Violent crimes, 2007 . . . 16
Property crimes, 2007 . . . 393
Arson, 2007 . . . 2

Public Library

Calabasas City Library
23975 Park Sorrento, librAddr2
Calabasas, CA 91302
818-225-7616

Director . . . Barbara Lockwood

Library statistics, FY 2007

Population served . . . 23,652
Internet terminals . . . 14
Annual users . . . 15,104

Per capita:

Operating income . . . $56.27
percent from local government . . . 96.3%
Operating expenditure . . . $46.36
Total materials . . . 1.63
Print holdings . . . 1.35
Visits per capita . . . 2.28

Housing & Construction

Housing Units

Total, 2008§ . . . 8,605
Single family units, attached . . . 804
Single family units, detached . . . 6,010
Multiple family units . . . 1,538
Mobile home units . . . 253
Occupied . . . 8,328
Vacancy rate . . . 3.2%
Median rent, 2000** . . . $1,233
Median SF home value, 2000** . . . $497,900

New Privately Owned Housing Units Authorized by Building Permit, 2007*

	Units	Construction Cost
Single	8	$8,978,522
Total	8	$8,978,522

Municipal Finance

(For local fiscal year ended in 2006)

Revenues

Total . . . $31,915,605
Taxes . . . 18,271,782
Special benefits assessment . . . 2,447,516
Licenses & permits . . . 1,896,112
Fines & forfeitures . . . 249,677
Revenues from use of money & property . . . 1,490,291
Intergovernmental . . . 3,063,521
Service charges . . . 1,905,776
Other revenues . . . 2,590,930
Other financing sources . . . 0

Expenditures

Total . . . $26,834,718
General government . . . 6,452,156
Public safety . . . 3,555,040
Transportation . . . 7,031,080
Community development . . . 6,287,406
Health . . . 468,646
Culture & leisure . . . 3,040,390
Other . . . 0

Local School District

(Data from School year 2007-08 except as noted)

Las Virgenes Unified
4111 North Las Virgenes Rd
Calabasas, CA 91302
(818) 880-4000

Superintendent . . . Donald Zimring
Grade plan . . . K-12
Number of schools . . . 15
Enrollment . . . 11,803
High school graduates, 2006-07 . . . 1,004
Dropout rate . . . 1.4%
Pupil/teacher ratio . . . 25.0
Average class size . . . 28.8
Students per computer . . . 6.1
Classrooms with internet . . . 515
Avg. Daily Attendance (ADA) . . . 11,596
Cost per ADA . . . $8,255
Avg. Teacher Salary . . . $66,468

California Achievement Tests 6th ed., 2008

(Pct scoring at or above 50th National Percentile Rank)

	Math	Reading	Language
Grade 3	82%	67%	75%
Grade 7	80%	75%	75%

Academic Performance Index, 2008

Number of students tested . . . 9,240
Number of valid scores . . . 9,058
2007 API (base) . . . 872
2008 API (growth) . . . 876

SAT Testing, 2006-07

Enrollment, Grade 12 . . . 1,069
Number taking test . . . 746
percent taking test . . . 69.8%
percent with total score 1,500+ . . . 54.20%

Average Scores:

Math	Verbal	Writing	Total
578	549	570	1,697

Federal No Child Left Behind, 2008

(Adequate Yearly Progress standards met)

	Participation Rate	Pct Proficient
ELA	Yes	Yes
Math	Yes	Yes

API criteria . . . Yes
Graduation rate . . . Yes
criteria met/possible . . . 34/34

Other school districts for this city

(see Appendix E for information on these districts)

None

See Introduction for an explanation of all data sources.

Demographics & Socio-Economic Characteristics

(2000 Decennial Census, except as noted)

Population

1990* 18,633
2000 27,109
Male 12,629
Female 14,480
Jan. 2008 (estimate)§ 38,733
Persons per sq. mi. of land 6,247.3

Race & Hispanic Origin, 2000

Race
White 12,621
Black/African American 134
North American Native 181
Asian 492
Pacific Islander 6
Other Race 12,739
Two or more races 936
Hispanic origin, total 25,832
Mexican 23,781
Puerto Rican 35
Cuban 3
Other Hispanic 2,013

Age & Nativity, 2000

Under 5 years 2,109
18 years and over 17,645
65 years and over 2,815
85 years and over 211
Median Age 29.2
Native-born 13,185
Foreign-born 13,857

Educational Attainment, 2000

Population 25 years and over 14,961
Less than 9th grade 36.2%
High school grad or higher 47.4%
Bachelor's degree or higher 9.1%
Graduate degree 3.1%

Income & Poverty, 1999

Per capita income $9,981
Median household income $28,929
Median family income $30,277
Persons in poverty 25.5%
H'holds receiving public assistance 1,009
H'holds receiving social security 2,198

Households, 2000

Total households 6,814
With persons under 18 4,341
With persons over 65 2,124
Family households 5,983
Single person households 710
Persons per household 3.96
Persons per family 4.21

Household Population, 2008§§

Persons living in households 38,630
Persons living in group quarters 103
Persons per household 3.9

Labor & Employment

Total civilian labor force, 2008§§ 14,700
Unemployment rate, 2008 .... 25.5%
Total civilian labor force, 2000 9,903

Employed persons 16 years and over by occupation, 2000

Managers & professionals 1,610
Service occupations 1,591
Sales & office occupations 2,753
Farming, fishing & forestry 990
Construction & maintenance 585
Production & transportation 954
Self-employed persons 602

* US Census Bureau
** 2000 Decennial Census
§ California Department of Finance
§§ California Employment Development Dept

General Information

City of Calexico
608 Heber Ave
Calexico, CA 92231
760-768-2110

Website .... www.calexico.ca.gov
Elevation .... 2 ft.
Land Area (sq. miles) 6.2
Water Area (sq. miles) 0
Year of Incorporation 1908
Government type .... General law
Sales tax rate 8.75%

Voters & Officials

Registered Voters, October 2008

Total 13,237
Democrats 8,767
Republicans 1,662
Declined to state 2,488

Legislative Districts

US Congressional 51
State Senatorial 40
State Assembly 80

Local Officials, 2009

Mayor .... Louis Fuentes
Manager .... Ralph Velez
City Clerk .... Lourdes Cordova
Attorney .... Jennifer Lyon
Finance Dir .... Judy Hashem
Public Works .... Luis Estrada
Planning Dir .... Loiver Alvaraso
Building .... Armando Villas
Police Chief .... James Lee Neujahr
Fire Chief .... Peter Mercado

Public Safety

Number of officers, 2007 47
Violent crimes, 2007 94
Property crimes, 2007 1,278
Arson, 2007 7

Public Library

Camarena Memorial Public Library
Camarena Memorial Public Library System
850 Encinas Ave
Calexico, CA 92231
760-768-2170

Director .... Sandra Tauler

Library system statistics, FY 2007

Population served 37,552
Internet terminals 19
Annual users 65,377

Per capita:

Operating income $21.45
percent from local government 88.4%
Operating expenditure $19.77
Total materials 2.04
Print holdings 1.97
Visits per capita 2.66

Housing & Construction

Housing Units

Total, 2008§ 10,101
Single family units, attached 523
Single family units, detached 6,926
Multiple family units 2,447
Mobile home units 205
Occupied 9,858
Vacancy rate 2.4%
Median rent, 2000** $517
Median SF home value, 2000** $108,200

New Privately Owned Housing Units Authorized by Building Permit, 2007*

	Units	Construction Cost
Single	127	$17,199,546
Total	230	$26,268,593

Municipal Finance

(For local fiscal year ended in 2006)

Revenues

Total $35,735,999
Taxes 12,897,056
Special benefits assessment 0
Licenses & permits 940,374
Fines & forfeitures 604,673
Revenues from use of money & property 1,330,208
Intergovernmental 5,059,833
Service charges 12,351,319
Other revenues 2,552,536
Other financing sources 0

Expenditures

Total $31,641,906
General government 1,645,950
Public safety 9,877,202
Transportation 4,393,094
Community development 4,818,750
Health 4,563,916
Culture & leisure 1,784,595
Other 0

Local School District

(Data from School year 2007-08 except as noted)

Calexico Unified
PO Box 792
Calexico, CA 92232
(760) 768-3888

Superintendent .... David Groesbeck
Grade plan K-12
Number of schools 12
Enrollment 9,283
High school graduates, 2006-07 506
Dropout rate 3.3%
Pupil/teacher ratio 20.8
Average class size 24.1
Students per computer 6.2
Classrooms with internet 463
Avg. Daily Attendance (ADA) 9,395
Cost per ADA $8,279
Avg. Teacher Salary $61,552

California Achievement Tests 6th ed., 2008

(Pct scoring at or above 50th National Percentile Rank)

	Math	Reading	Language
Grade 3	40%	19%	30%
Grade 7	37%	32%	34%

Academic Performance Index, 2008

Number of students tested 7,346
Number of valid scores 6,873
2007 API (base) 657
2008 API (growth) 680

SAT Testing, 2006-07

Enrollment, Grade 12 684
Number taking test 119
percent taking test 17.4%
percent with total score 1,500+ 5.30%

Average Scores:

Math	Verbal	Writing	Total
472	451	442	1,365

Federal No Child Left Behind, 2008

(Adequate Yearly Progress standards met)

	Participation Rate	Pct Proficient
ELA	Yes	No
Math	Yes	No

API criteria .... Yes
Graduation rate .... Yes
\# criteria met/possible 22/16

Other school districts for this city

(see Appendix E for information on these districts)

None

See Introduction for an explanation of all data sources.

Demographics & Socio-Economic Characteristics

(2000 Decennial Census, except as noted)

Population

1990* . . . 5,955
2000 . . . 8,385
Male . . . 4,182
Female . . . 4,203
Jan. 2008 (estimate)§ . . . 14,365
Persons per sq. mi. of land . . . 70.6

Race & Hispanic Origin, 2000

Race
White . . . 5,718
Black/African American . . . 1,075
North American Native . . . 131
Asian . . . 313
Pacific Islander . . . 27
Other Race . . . 623
Two or more races . . . 498
Hispanic origin, total . . . 1,422
Mexican . . . 977
Puerto Rican . . . 79
Cuban . . . 7
Other Hispanic . . . 359

Age & Nativity, 2000

Under 5 years . . . 561
18 years and over . . . 5,807
65 years and over . . . 899
85 years and over . . . 63
Median Age . . . 36.1
Native-born . . . 7,714
Foreign-born . . . 607

Educational Attainment, 2000

Population 25 years and over . . . 5,227
Less than 9th grade . . . 5.4%
High school grad or higher . . . 82.8%
Bachelor's degree or higher . . . 12.1%
Graduate degree . . . 4.6%

Income & Poverty, 1999

Per capita income . . . $19,902
Median household income . . . $45,735
Median family income . . . $51,402
Persons in poverty . . . 17.1%
H'holds receiving public assistance . . . 250
H'holds receiving social security . . . 836

Households, 2000

Total households . . . 3,067
With persons under 18 . . . 1,312
With persons over 65 . . . 668
Family households . . . 2,257
Single person households . . . 649
Persons per household . . . 2.72
Persons per family . . . 3.15

Household Population, 2008§§

Persons living in households . . . 11,783
Persons living in group quarters . . . 2,582
Persons per household . . . 2.8

Labor & Employment

Total civilian labor force, 2008§§ . . . 4,900
Unemployment rate, 2008 . . . 7.6%
Total civilian labor force, 2000 . . . 3,560

Employed persons 16 years and over by occupation, 2000

Managers & professionals . . . 966
Service occupations . . . 701
Sales & office occupations . . . 813
Farming, fishing & forestry . . . 5
Construction & maintenance . . . 431
Production & transportation . . . 311
Self-employed persons . . . 179

* US Census Bureau
** 2000 Decennial Census
§ California Department of Finance
§§ California Employment Development Dept

General Information

City of California City
21000 Hacienda Blvd
California City, CA 93505
760-373-8661

Website . . . californiacity-ca.us
Elevation . . . 2,445
Land Area (sq. miles) . . . 203.6
Water Area (sq. miles) . . . 0.1
Year of Incorporation . . . 1965
Government type . . . General law
Sales tax rate . . . 8.25%

Voters & Officials

Registered Voters, October 2008

Total . . . 4,856
Democrats . . . 1,590
Republicans . . . 1,971
Declined to state . . . 1,039

Legislative Districts

US Congressional . . . 22
State Senatorial . . . 18
State Assembly . . . 34

Local Officials, 2009

Mayor . . . David Evans
Manager . . . Linda Lunsford II
City Clerk . . . Denise Hilliker
Attorney . . . Wayne K. Lemieux
Finance Dir . . . Kathy Bailey
Public Works . . . Michael Bevins
Planning Dir . . . Linda Lunsford
Building . . . Dalton Oliver
Police Chief . . . Steve Colerick
Fire Chief . . . Kenneth Mylander

Public Safety

Number of officers, 2007 . . . 16
Violent crimes, 2007 . . . 61
Property crimes, 2007 . . . 301
Arson, 2007 . . . 6

Public Library

California City Branch Library
Kern County Library System
9507 California City Blvd
California City, CA 93505
760-373-4757

Branch Librarian . . . Iva Nunez-Martinez

Library system statistics, FY 2007

Population served . . . 801,648
Internet terminals . . . 237
Annual users . . . 337,030

Per capita:

Operating income . . . $12.11
percent from local government . . . 90.4%
Operating expenditure . . . $12.11
Total materials . . . 1.37
Print holdings . . . 1.29
Visits per capita . . . 2.09

Housing & Construction

Housing Units

Total, 2008§ . . . 4,883
Single family units, attached . . . 68
Single family units, detached . . . 3,803
Multiple family units . . . 670
Mobile home units . . . 342
Occupied . . . 4,204
Vacancy rate . . . 13.9%
Median rent, 2000** . . . $535
Median SF home value, 2000** . . . $81,900

New Privately Owned Housing Units Authorized by Building Permit, 2007*

	Units	Construction Cost
Single	241	$29,291,638
Total	374	$37,861,023

Municipal Finance

(For local fiscal year ended in 2006)

Revenues

Total . . . $15,386,093
Taxes . . . 2,942,517
Special benefits assessment . . . 3,945,059
Licenses & permits . . . 797,941
Fines & forfeitures . . . 34,677
Revenues from use of money & property . . . 429,519
Intergovernmental . . . 1,110,525
Service charges . . . 5,523,670
Other revenues . . . 602,185
Other financing sources . . . 0

Expenditures

Total . . . $13,331,062
General government . . . 2,553,792
Public safety . . . 3,959,613
Transportation . . . 1,704,633
Community development . . . 737,249
Health . . . 1,110,098
Culture & leisure . . . 514,575
Other . . . 0

Local School District

(Data from School year 2007-08 except as noted)

Mojave Unified
3500 Douglas Ave
Mojave, CA 93501
(661) 824-4001

Superintendent . . . Larry Phelps
Grade plan . . . K-12
Number of schools . . . 10
Enrollment . . . 3,041
High school graduates, 2006-07 . . . 151
Dropout rate . . . 6.7%
Pupil/teacher ratio . . . 24.1
Average class size . . . 24.4
Students per computer . . . 5.0
Classrooms with internet . . . 128
Avg. Daily Attendance (ADA) . . . 2,821
Cost per ADA . . . $8,080
Avg. Teacher Salary . . . $58,614

California Achievement Tests 6th ed., 2008

(Pct scoring at or above 50th National Percentile Rank)

	Math	Reading	Language
Grade 3	44%	34%	45%
Grade 7	29%	31%	28%

Academic Performance Index, 2008

Number of students tested . . . 2,255
Number of valid scores . . . 1,846
2007 API (base) . . . 631
2008 API (growth) . . . 659

SAT Testing, 2006-07

Enrollment, Grade 12 . . . 194
Number taking test . . . 31
percent taking test . . . 16.0%
percent with total score 1,500+ . . . 6.20%

Average Scores:

Math	Verbal	Writing	Total
468	470	464	1,402

Federal No Child Left Behind, 2008

(Adequate Yearly Progress standards met)

	Participation Rate	Pct Proficient
ELA	No	No
Math	Yes	No

API criteria . . . Yes
Graduation rate . . . No
\# criteria met/possible . . . 30/15

Other school districts for this city

(see Appendix E for information on these districts)

Muroc Joint Unified

See Introduction for an explanation of all data sources.

Demographics & Socio-Economic Characteristics

(2000 Decennial Census, except as noted)

Population

1990* . . . 4,647
2000 . . . 7,139
Male . . . 3,354
Female . . . 3,785
Jan. 2008 (estimate)§ . . . 7,536
Persons per sq. mi. of land . . . 483.1

Race & Hispanic Origin, 2000

Race
White . . . 6,363
Black/African American . . . 42
North American Native . . . 47
Asian . . . 76
Pacific Islander . . . 7
Other Race . . . 385
Two or more races . . . 219
Hispanic origin, total . . . 1,008
Mexican . . . 822
Puerto Rican . . . 10
Cuban . . . 3
Other Hispanic . . . 173

Age & Nativity, 2000

Under 5 years . . . 324
18 years and over . . . 5,584
65 years and over . . . 1,858
85 years and over . . . 260
Median Age . . . 44.4
Native-born . . . 6,745
Foreign-born . . . 626

Educational Attainment, 2000

Population 25 years and over . . . 5,107
Less than 9th grade . . . 4.0%
High school grad or higher . . . 81.8%
Bachelor's degree or higher . . . 14.5%
Graduate degree . . . 6.3%

Income & Poverty, 1999

Per capita income . . . $20,242
Median household income . . . $37,849
Median family income . . . $43,220
Persons in poverty . . . 12.5%
H'holds receiving public assistance . . . 115
H'holds receiving social security . . . 1,342

Households, 2000

Total households . . . 2,982
With persons under 18 . . . 800
With persons over 65 . . . 1,275
Family households . . . 2,006
Single person households . . . 839
Persons per household . . . 2.36
Persons per family . . . 2.87

Household Population, 2008§§

Persons living in households . . . 7,440
Persons living in group quarters . . . 96
Persons per household . . . 2.4

Labor & Employment

Total civilian labor force, 2008§§ . . . 4,300
Unemployment rate, 2008 . . . 9.1%
Total civilian labor force, 2000 . . . 3,071

Employed persons 16 years and over by occupation, 2000

Managers & professionals . . . 884
Service occupations . . . 439
Sales & office occupations . . . 907
Farming, fishing & forestry . . . 0
Construction & maintenance . . . 217
Production & transportation . . . 378
Self-employed persons . . . 233

* US Census Bureau
** 2000 Decennial Census
§ California Department of Finance
§§ California Employment Development Dept

General Information

City of Calimesa
908 Park Ave
Calimesa, CA 92320
909-795-9801

Website . . . www.cityofcalimesa.net
Elevation . . . NA
Land Area (sq. miles) . . . 15.6
Water Area (sq. miles) . . . 0
Year of Incorporation . . . 1990
Government type . . . General Law
Sales tax rate . . . 8.75%

Voters & Officials

Registered Voters, October 2008

Total . . . 4,300
Democrats . . . 1,372
Republicans . . . 2,132
Declined to state . . . 615

Legislative Districts

US Congressional . . . 41
State Senatorial . . . 37
State Assembly . . . 65

Local Officials, 2009

Mayor . . . Jim Hyatt
Manager . . . Randy Anstine
City Clerk . . . Darlene Gerdes
Attorney . . . Kevin Ennis
Finance Dir . . . Vacant
Public Works . . . Bob French
Planning/Dev Dir . . . Gus Romo
Building . . . NA
Police Chief . . . Ed Harvey
Emergency/Fire Dir . . . Andrew Bennett

Public Safety

Number of officers, 2007 . . . NA
Violent crimes, 2007 . . . 8
Property crimes, 2007 . . . 204
Arson, 2007 . . . 0

Public Library

Calimesa Library
Riverside County Library Service
974 Calimesa Blvd
Calimesa, CA 92320
909-795-9807

Branch Librarian . . . Yelena Antonov

Library system statistics, FY 2007

Population served . . . 1,047,996
Internet terminals . . . 37
Annual users . . . 69,346

Per capita:

Operating income . . . $19.38
percent from local government . . . 49.8%
Operating expenditure . . . $20.45
Total materials . . . 1.43
Print holdings . . . 1.30
Visits per capita . . . 4.06

Housing & Construction

Housing Units

Total, 2008§ . . . 3,372
Single family units, attached . . . 113
Single family units, detached . . . 1,883
Multiple family units . . . 121
Mobile home units . . . 1,255
Occupied . . . 3,097
Vacancy rate . . . 8.2%
Median rent, 2000** . . . $644
Median SF home value, 2000** . . . $131,900

New Privately Owned Housing Units Authorized by Building Permit, 2007*

	Units	Construction Cost
Single	44	$9,789,049
Total	44	$9,789,049

Municipal Finance

(For local fiscal year ended in 2006)

Revenues

Total . . . $4,927,097
Taxes . . . 3,194,064
Special benefits assessment . . . 37,357
Licenses & permits . . . 176,157
Fines & forfeitures . . . 45,893
Revenues from use of money & property . . . 101,203
Intergovernmental . . . 857,162
Service charges . . . 378,955
Other revenues . . . 136,306
Other financing sources . . . 0

Expenditures

Total . . . $5,513,718
General government . . . 1,005,533
Public safety . . . 2,155,033
Transportation . . . 594,817
Community development . . . 1,642,209
Health . . . 0
Culture & leisure . . . 36,938
Other . . . 79,188

Local School District

(Data from School year 2007-08 except as noted)

Yucaipa-Calimesa Joint Unified
12797 Third St
Yucaipa, CA 92399
(909) 797-0174

Superintendent . . . Sherry Kendrick
Grade plan . . . K-12
Number of schools . . . 15
Enrollment . . . 10,023
High school graduates, 2006-07 . . . 615
Dropout rate . . . 5.6%
Pupil/teacher ratio . . . 23.7
Average class size . . . 28.7
Students per computer . . . 5.0
Classrooms with internet . . . 439
Avg. Daily Attendance (ADA) . . . 9,545
Cost per ADA . . . $7,594
Avg. Teacher Salary . . . $70,909

California Achievement Tests 6th ed., 2008

(Pct scoring at or above 50th National Percentile Rank)

	Math	Reading	Language
Grade 3	61%	42%	47%
Grade 7	56%	54%	48%

Academic Performance Index, 2008

Number of students tested . . . 7,633
Number of valid scores . . . 7,117
2007 API (base) . . . 750
2008 API (growth) . . . 763

SAT Testing, 2006-07

Enrollment, Grade 12 . . . 749
Number taking test . . . 263
percent taking test . . . 35.1%
percent with total score 1,500+ . . . 14.20%

Average Scores:

Math	Verbal	Writing	Total
475	480	479	1,434

Federal No Child Left Behind, 2008

(Adequate Yearly Progress standards met)

	Participation Rate	Pct Proficient
ELA	Yes	No
Math	Yes	No

API criteria . . . Yes
Graduation rate . . . Yes
criteria met/possible . . . 28/25

Other school districts for this city

(see Appendix E for information on these districts)

None

See Introduction for an explanation of all data sources.

Demographics & Socio-Economic Characteristics

(2000 Decennial Census, except as noted)

Population

1990* 2,690
2000 7,289
Male 5,716
Female 1,573
Jan. 2008 (estimate)§ 7,774
Persons per sq. mi. of land 2,101.1

Race & Hispanic Origin, 2000

Race
White 2,361
Black/African American 1,554
North American Native 53
Asian 46
Pacific Islander 2
Other Race 3,109
Two or more races 164
Hispanic origin, total 4,180
Mexican 3,929
Puerto Rican 8
Cuban 0
Other Hispanic 243

Age & Nativity, 2000

Under 5 years 290
18 years and over 6,100
65 years and over 274
85 years and over 17
Median Age 32.6
Native-born 6,092
Foreign-born 1,155

Educational Attainment, 2000

Population 25 years and over 5,146
Less than 9th grade 17.5%
High school grad or higher 61.7%
Bachelor's degree or higher 2.2%
Graduate degree 0.4%

Income & Poverty, 1999

Per capita income $13,970
Median household income $30,962
Median family income $31,302
Persons in poverty 10.6%
H'holds receiving public assistance 82
H'holds receiving social security 184

Households, 2000

Total households 899
With persons under 18 525
With persons over 65 194
Family households 757
Single person households 127
Persons per household 3.55
Persons per family 3.90

Household Population, 2008§§

Persons living in households 3,600
Persons living in group quarters 4,174
Persons per household 3.6

Labor & Employment

Total civilian labor force, 2008§§ 1,600
Unemployment rate, 2008 .... 23.5%
Total civilian labor force, 2000 1,118

Employed persons 16 years and over by occupation, 2000

Managers & professionals 148
Service occupations 249
Sales & office occupations 214
Farming, fishing & forestry 122
Construction & maintenance 75
Production & transportation 164
Self-employed persons 75

* US Census Bureau
** 2000 Decennial Census
§ California Department of Finance
§§ California Employment Development Dept

General Information

City of Calipatria
125 N Park Ave
Calipatria, CA 92233
760-348-4141

Website .... NA
Elevation .... -184 ft.
Land Area (sq. miles) 3.7
Water Area (sq. miles) 0
Year of Incorporation 1919
Government type .... General law
Sales tax rate 8.75%

Voters & Officials

Registered Voters, October 2008

Total 1,190
Democrats 661
Republicans 278
Declined to state 218

Legislative Districts

US Congressional 51
State Senatorial 40
State Assembly 80

Local Officials, 2009

Mayor .... Fred R. Beltran
Manager .... Romualdo Medina
City Clerk .... Catherine Hoff
Attorney .... William Smerdon
Finance Dir .... Katy Lopez
Public Works .... (vacant)
Planning/Dev Dir .... (vacant)
Building .... NA
Police Chief .... Reggie Gomez
Emergency/Fire Dir .... Chris Hall

Public Safety

Number of officers, 2007 6
Violent crimes, 2007 0
Property crimes, 2007 16
Arson, 2007 0

Public Library

Calipatria Branch Library
Imperial County Library System
105 S Lake
Calipatria, CA 92233
760-348-2630

Branch Librarian .... Teresa Woelke

Library system statistics, FY 2007

Population served 55,503
Internet terminals 27
Annual users 21,222

Per capita:

Operating income $14.19
percent from local government 83.9%
Operating expenditure $12.85
Total materials 1.05
Print holdings 0.96
Visits per capita 0.80

Housing & Construction

Housing Units

Total, 2008§ 1,084
Single family units, attached 38
Single family units, detached 750
Multiple family units 233
Mobile home units 63
Occupied 1,013
Vacancy rate 6.6%
Median rent, 2000** $481
Median SF home value, 2000** $76,200

New Privately Owned Housing Units Authorized by Building Permit, 2007*

	Units	Construction Cost
Single	NA	NA
Total	NA	NA

Municipal Finance

(For local fiscal year ended in 2006)

Revenues

Total $3,191,495
Taxes 789,966
Special benefits assessment 571
Licenses & permits 22,495
Fines & forfeitures 4,001
Revenues from use of money & property 82,552
Intergovernmental 793,430
Service charges 1,012,665
Other revenues 485,815
Other financing sources 0

Expenditures

Total $4,062,948
General government 315,135
Public safety 841,324
Transportation 1,779,196
Community development 175,423
Health 861,793
Culture & leisure 80,288
Other 9,789

Local School District

(Data from School year 2007-08 except as noted)

Calipatria Unified
501 West Main St
Calipatria, CA 92233
(760) 348-2892

Superintendent .... Douglas Kline
Grade plan K-12
Number of schools 4
Enrollment 1,156
High school graduates, 2006-07 91
Dropout rate 3.3%
Pupil/teacher ratio 18.6
Average class size 22.1
Students per computer 3.8
Classrooms with internet 80
Avg. Daily Attendance (ADA) 1,173
Cost per ADA $8,582
Avg. Teacher Salary $54,658

California Achievement Tests 6th ed., 2008

(Pct scoring at or above 50th National Percentile Rank)

	Math	Reading	Language
Grade 3	58%	32%	43%
Grade 7	55%	40%	45%

Academic Performance Index, 2008

Number of students tested 908
Number of valid scores 832
2007 API (base) 733
2008 API (growth) 752

SAT Testing, 2006-07

Enrollment, Grade 12 94
Number taking test 32
percent taking test 34.0%
percent with total score 1,500+ 5.30%

Average Scores:

Math	Verbal	Writing	Total
425	424	428	1,277

Federal No Child Left Behind, 2008

(Adequate Yearly Progress standards met)

	Participation Rate	Pct Proficient
ELA	Yes	Yes
Math	Yes	Yes

API criteria .... Yes
Graduation rate .... Yes
\# criteria met/possible 18/18

Other school districts for this city

(see Appendix E for information on these districts)

None

See Introduction for an explanation of all data sources.

Demographics & Socio-Economic Characteristics
(2000 Decennial Census, except as noted)

Population
1990* 4,468
2000 5,190
Male 2,590
Female 2,600
Jan. 2008 (estimate)§ 5,302
Persons per sq. mi. of land 2,039.2

Race & Hispanic Origin, 2000
Race
White 3,978
Black/African American 17
North American Native 51
Asian 51
Pacific Islander 1
Other Race 914
Two or more races 178
Hispanic origin, total 1,978
Mexican 1,770
Puerto Rican 10
Cuban 6
Other Hispanic 192

Age & Nativity, 2000
Under 5 years 368
18 years and over 3,982
65 years and over 1,015
85 years and over 188
Median Age 38.1
Native-born 3,679
Foreign-born 1,511

Educational Attainment, 2000
Population 25 years and over 3,518
Less than 9th grade 18.6%
High school grad or higher 70.8%
Bachelor's degree or higher 21.2%
Graduate degree 5.9%

Income & Poverty, 1999
Per capita income $21,134
Median household income $38,454
Median family income $44,375
Persons in poverty 7.9%
H'holds receiving public assistance 55
H'holds receiving social security 751

Households, 2000
Total households 2,042
With persons under 18 636
With persons over 65 727
Family households 1,243
Single person households 641
Persons per household 2.51
Persons per family 3.20

Household Population, 2008§§
Persons living in households 5,235
Persons living in group quarters 67
Persons per household 2.5

Labor & Employment
Total civilian labor force, 2008§§ 3,100
Unemployment rate, 2008 .... 3.9%
Total civilian labor force, 2000 2,455

Employed persons 16 years and over by occupation, 2000
Managers & professionals 555
Service occupations 651
Sales & office occupations 538
Farming, fishing & forestry 185
Construction & maintenance 202
Production & transportation 243
Self-employed persons 305

* US Census Bureau
** 2000 Decennial Census
§ California Department of Finance
§§ California Employment Development Dept

General Information
City of Calistoga
1232 Washington St
Calistoga, CA 94515
707-942-2800

Website .... www.ci.calistoga.ca.us
Elevation .... 362 ft.
Land Area (sq. miles) 2.6
Water Area (sq. miles) 0
Year of Incorporation 1886
Government type .... General law
Sales tax rate 8.75%

Voters & Officials
Registered Voters, October 2008
Total 2,291
Democrats 1,199
Republicans 548
Declined to state 426

Legislative Districts
US Congressional 1
State Senatorial 2
State Assembly 7

Local Officials, 2009
Mayor .... Jack Gingles
Manager .... James McCann
City Clerk .... Susan Sneddon
Attorney .... Michelle Kenyon
Finance Dir .... David Spilman (Int)
Public Works .... Dan Takasugi
Planning/Dev Dir .... Charlene Gallina
Building .... Charlene Gallina
Police Chief .... Jonathan Mills
Emergency/Fire Dir .... Steve Campbell

Public Safety
Number of officers, 2007 11
Violent crimes, 2007 23
Property crimes, 2007 128
Arson, 2007 0

Public Library
Calistoga Public Library
Napa City/County Library
1108 Myrtle St
Calistoga, CA 94515
707-942-4833
County Library Dir .... Danis Kreimeier

Library system statistics, FY 2007
Population served 129,976
Internet terminals 58
Annual users .... NA

Per capita:
Operating income $50.32
percent from local government 88.9%
Operating expenditure $45.25
Total materials 1.58
Print holdings 1.37
Visits per capita 3.16

Housing & Construction
Housing Units
Total, 2008§ 2,341
Single family units, attached 99
Single family units, detached 1,086
Multiple family units 551
Mobile home units 605
Occupied 2,127
Vacancy rate 9.1%
Median rent, 2000** $719
Median SF home value, 2000** $273,100

New Privately Owned Housing Units Authorized by Building Permit, 2007*

	Units	Construction Cost
Single	14	$3,763,911
Total	14	$3,763,911

Municipal Finance
(For local fiscal year ended in 2006)

Revenues
Total $14,418,686
Taxes 4,502,773
Special benefits assessment 420,259
Licenses & permits 293,463
Fines & forfeitures 76,656
Revenues from use of money & property 187,336
Intergovernmental 1,376,875
Service charges 4,154,846
Other revenues 1,035,059
Other financing sources 2,371,419

Expenditures
Total $12,031,926
General government 2,749,343
Public safety 2,551,645
Transportation 666,386
Community development 1,242,079
Health 2,375,485
Culture & leisure 488,834
Other 140,600

Local School District
(Data from School year 2007-08 except as noted)
Calistoga Joint Unified
1520 Lake St
Calistoga, CA 94515
(707) 942-4703

Superintendent .... Jeff Johnson
Grade plan K-12
Number of schools 3
Enrollment 826
High school graduates, 2006-07 47
Dropout rate 3.3%
Pupil/teacher ratio 16.5
Average class size 20.3
Students per computer 2.4
Classrooms with internet 65
Avg. Daily Attendance (ADA) 846
Cost per ADA $11,454
Avg. Teacher Salary $78,970

California Achievement Tests 6th ed., 2008
(Pct scoring at or above 50th National Percentile Rank)

	Math	Reading	Language
Grade 3	47%	31%	50%
Grade 7	37%	38%	40%

Academic Performance Index, 2008
Number of students tested 651
Number of valid scores 616
2007 API (base) 695
2008 API (growth) 725

SAT Testing, 2006-07
Enrollment, Grade 12 130
Number taking test 21
percent taking test 16.2%
percent with total score 1,500+ 6.20%

Average Scores:

Math	Verbal	Writing	Total
533	477	471	1,481

Federal No Child Left Behind, 2008
(Adequate Yearly Progress standards met)

	Participation Rate	Pct Proficient
ELA	Yes	Yes
Math	Yes	No

API criteria .... Yes
Graduation rate .... Yes
\# criteria met/possible 22/20

Other school districts for this city
(see Appendix E for information on these districts)
None

See Introduction for an explanation of all data sources.

Demographics & Socio-Economic Characteristics

(2000 Decennial Census, except as noted)

Population

1990* . . . 52,303
2000 . . . 57,077
Male . . . 27,641
Female . . . 29,436
Jan. 2008 (estimate)§ . . . 65,453
Persons per sq. mi. of land . . . 3,463.1

Race & Hispanic Origin, 2000

Race
White . . . 46,036
Black/African American . . . 856
North American Native . . . 299
Asian . . . 4,129
Pacific Islander . . . 114
Other Race . . . 3,605
Two or more races . . . 2,038
Hispanic origin, total . . . 8,869
Mexican . . . 7,049
Puerto Rican . . . 188
Cuban . . . 75
Other Hispanic . . . 1,557

Age & Nativity, 2000

Under 5 years . . . 3,739
18 years and over . . . 42,658
65 years and over . . . 9,680
85 years and over . . . 1,447
Median Age . . . 38.9
Native-born . . . 49,498
Foreign-born . . . 7,624

Educational Attainment, 2000

Population 25 years and over . . . 38,973
Less than 9th grade . . . 3.6%
High school grad or higher . . . 90.6%
Bachelor's degree or higher . . . 32.9%
Graduate degree . . . 11.2%

Income & Poverty, 1999

Per capita income . . . $28,635
Median household income . . . $62,457
Median family income . . . $72,676
Persons in poverty . . . 5.3%
H'holds receiving public assistance . . . 317
H'holds receiving social security . . . 6,803

Households, 2000

Total households . . . 21,438
With persons under 18 . . . 7,625
With persons over 65 . . . 6,809
Family households . . . 15,240
Single person households . . . 5,165
Persons per household . . . 2.62
Persons per family . . . 3.12

Household Population, 2008§§

Persons living in households . . . 63,717
Persons living in group quarters . . . 1,736
Persons per household . . . 2.6

Labor & Employment

Total civilian labor force, 2008§§ . . . 32,200
Unemployment rate, 2008 . . . 4.5%
Total civilian labor force, 2000 . . . 27,471

Employed persons 16 years and over by occupation, 2000

Managers & professionals . . . 11,316
Service occupations . . . 3,343
Sales & office occupations . . . 7,308
Farming, fishing & forestry . . . 154
Construction & maintenance . . . 2,133
Production & transportation . . . 2,230
Self-employed persons . . . 2,362

* US Census Bureau
** 2000 Decennial Census
§ California Department of Finance
§§ California Employment Development Dept

General Information

City of Camarillo
601 Carmen Dr
Camarillo, CA 93010
805-388-5353

Website . . . www.ci.camarillo.ca.us
Elevation . . . 160 ft.
Land Area (sq. miles) . . . 18.9
Water Area (sq. miles) . . . 0
Year of Incorporation . . . 1964
Government type . . . General law
Sales tax rate . . . 8.25%

Voters & Officials

Registered Voters, October 2008

Total . . . 40,432
Democrats . . . 13,881
Republicans . . . 18,130
Declined to state . . . 6,784

Legislative Districts

US Congressional . . . 24
State Senatorial . . . 19
State Assembly . . . 37

Local Officials, 2009

Mayor . . . Don Waunch
Manager . . . Jerry Bankston
City Clerk . . . Jeffrie Madland
Attorney . . . Brian Pierik
Finance Dir . . . Ronnie Campbell
Public Works . . . Tom Fox
Planning/Dev Dir . . . Bob Burrow
Building . . . NA
Police Chief . . . Steve Decesari
Emergency/Fire Dir . . . Bob Roper

Public Safety

Number of officers, 2007 . . . NA
Violent crimes, 2007 . . . 94
Property crimes, 2007 . . . 1,062
Arson, 2007 . . . 9

Public Library

Camarillo Library
Ventura County Library System
4101 Las Posas Rd
Camarillo, CA 93010
805-388-5222

Branch Librarian . . . Sandi Banks

Library system statistics, FY 2007

Population served . . . 439,444
Internet terminals . . . 188
Annual users . . . 216,575

Per capita:

Operating income . . . $25.05
percent from local government . . . 86.2%
Operating expenditure . . . $25.02
Total materials . . . 1.81
Print holdings . . . 1.70
Visits per capita . . . NA

Housing & Construction

Housing Units

Total, 2008§ . . . 24,975
Single family units, attached . . . 4,495
Single family units, detached . . . 14,861
Multiple family units . . . 4,561
Mobile home units . . . 1,058
Occupied . . . 24,257
Vacancy rate . . . 2.9%
Median rent, 2000** . . . $975
Median SF home value, 2000** . . . $252,100

New Privately Owned Housing Units Authorized by Building Permit, 2007*

	Units	Construction Cost
Single	8	$1,216,931
Total	110	$10,601,817

Municipal Finance

(For local fiscal year ended in 2006)

Revenues

Total . . . $72,354,924
Taxes . . . 27,871,573
Special benefits assessment . . . 265,876
Licenses & permits . . . 1,923,752
Fines & forfeitures . . . 488,436
Revenues from use of money & property . . . 3,337,085
Intergovernmental . . . 17,017,525
Service charges . . . 20,209,920
Other revenues . . . 1,240,757
Other financing sources . . . 0

Expenditures

Total . . . $69,221,075
General government . . . 3,423,552
Public safety . . . 11,806,935
Transportation . . . 31,894,106
Community development . . . 7,947,874
Health . . . 5,432,432
Culture & leisure . . . 547,060
Other . . . 0

Local School District

(Data from School year 2007-08 except as noted)

Oxnard Union High
309 South K St
Oxnard, CA 93030
(805) 385-2500

Superintendent . . . Jody Dunlap
Grade plan . . . 9-12
Number of schools . . . 10
Enrollment . . . 16,868
High school graduates, 2006-07 . . . 2,756
Dropout rate . . . 4.4%
Pupil/teacher ratio . . . 25.2
Average class size . . . 28.2
Students per computer . . . 4.7
Classrooms with internet . . . 635
Avg. Daily Attendance (ADA) . . . 15,420
Cost per ADA . . . $8,186
Avg. Teacher Salary . . . $72,428

California Achievement Tests 6th ed., 2008

(Pct scoring at or above 50th National Percentile Rank)

	Math	Reading	Language
Grade 3	74%	54%	56%
Grade 7	89%	81%	70%

Academic Performance Index, 2008

Number of students tested . . . 11,929
Number of valid scores . . . 11,323
2007 API (base) . . . 673
2008 API (growth) . . . 693

SAT Testing, 2006-07

Enrollment, Grade 12 . . . 3,865
Number taking test . . . 916
percent taking test . . . 23.7%
percent with total score 1,500+ . . . 11.20%

Average Scores:

Math	Verbal	Writing	Total
509	489	485	1,483

Federal No Child Left Behind, 2008

(Adequate Yearly Progress standards met)

	Participation Rate	Pct Proficient
ELA	Yes	No
Math	Yes	No

API criteria . . . Yes
Graduation rate . . . No
\# criteria met/possible . . . 38/35

Other school districts for this city

(see Appendix E for information on these districts)

Pleasant Valley Elem

See Introduction for an explanation of all data sources.

Demographics & Socio-Economic Characteristics

(2000 Decennial Census, except as noted)

Population

1990* 36,048
2000 38,138
Male 18,933
Female 19,205
Jan. 2008 (estimate)§ 40,161
Persons per sq. mi. of land 7,171.6

Race & Hispanic Origin, 2000

Race
White 27,758
Black/African American 964
North American Native 248
Asian 5,402
Pacific Islander 88
Other Race 1,859
Two or more races 1,819
Hispanic origin, total 5,083
Mexican 3,601
Puerto Rican 122
Cuban 48
Other Hispanic 1,312

Age & Nativity, 2000

Under 5 years 2,491
18 years and over 29,919
65 years and over 3,703
85 years and over 493
Median Age 35.2
Native-born 29,906
Foreign-born 8,281

Educational Attainment, 2000

Population 25 years and over 27,211
Less than 9th grade 3.4%
High school grad or higher 89.7%
Bachelor's degree or higher 39.7%
Graduate degree 13.4%

Income & Poverty, 1999

Per capita income $34,441
Median household income $67,214
Median family income $78,663
Persons in poverty 4.8%
H'holds receiving public assistance 255
H'holds receiving social security 2,822

Households, 2000

Total households 15,920
With persons under 18 4,798
With persons over 65 2,696
Family households 9,121
Single person households 4,846
Persons per household 2.38
Persons per family 3.02

Household Population, 2008§§

Persons living in households 39,871
Persons living in group quarters 290
Persons per household 2.4

Labor & Employment

Total civilian labor force, 2008§§ 22,600
Unemployment rate, 2008 .... 5.1%
Total civilian labor force, 2000 22,520

Employed persons 16 years and over by occupation, 2000

Managers & professionals 10,951
Service occupations 2,243
Sales & office occupations 5,417
Farming, fishing & forestry 8
Construction & maintenance 1,400
Production & transportation 1,740
Self-employed persons 1,688

* US Census Bureau
** 2000 Decennial Census
§ California Department of Finance
§§ California Employment Development Dept

General Information

City of Campbell
70 N First St
Campbell, CA 95008
408-866-2100

Website .... www.cityofcampbell.com
Elevation .... 195 ft.
Land Area (sq. miles) 5.6
Water Area (sq. miles) 0.1
Year of Incorporation 1952
Government type .... General law
Sales tax rate 9.50%

Voters & Officials

Registered Voters, October 2008

Total 19,857
Democrats 9,111
Republicans 5,073
Declined to state 4,763

Legislative Districts

US Congressional 15
State Senatorial 11
State Assembly 24

Local Officials, 2009

Mayor .... Jane P. Kennedy
Manager .... Daniel Rich
City Clerk .... Anne Bybee
Attorney .... William Seligmann
Finance Dir .... Jesse Takahashi
Public Works .... Bob Kass
Community Dev Dir .... (vacant)
Building .... Bill Bruckart
Police Chief .... Greg Finch
Fire/Emergency Mgmt .... NA

Public Safety

Number of officers, 2007 43
Violent crimes, 2007 101
Property crimes, 2007 1,514
Arson, 2007 23

Public Library

Campbell Library
Santa Clara County Library System
77 Harrison Ave
Campbell, CA 95008
408-866-1991

Branch Librarian .... Terri Lehan

Library system statistics, FY 2007

Population served 419,141
Internet terminals 133
Annual users 650,000

Per capita:

Operating income $77.89
percent from local government 85.7%
Operating expenditure $66.37
Total materials 4.01
Print holdings 3.27
Visits per capita 6.16

Housing & Construction

Housing Units

Total, 2008§ 16,932
Single family units, attached 2,095
Single family units, detached 7,341
Multiple family units 7,239
Mobile home units 257
Occupied 16,554
Vacancy rate 2.2%
Median rent, 2000** $1,154
Median SF home value, 2000** $436,800

New Privately Owned Housing Units Authorized by Building Permit, 2007*

	Units	Construction Cost
Single	33	$7,786,851
Total	35	$8,197,654

Municipal Finance

(For local fiscal year ended in 2006)

Revenues

Total $35,231,171
Taxes 19,822,390
Special benefits assessment 1,101,438
Licenses & permits 1,764,719
Fines & forfeitures 297,357
Revenues from use of money & property 3,543,975
Intergovernmental 3,148,642
Service charges 4,420,758
Other revenues 1,131,892
Other financing sources 0

Expenditures

Total $37,026,604
General government 3,659,397
Public safety 19,451,890
Transportation 2,896,224
Community development 4,139,740
Health 0
Culture & leisure 6,879,353
Other 0

Local School District

(Data from School year 2007-08 except as noted)

Campbell Union High
3235 Union Ave
San Jose, CA 95124
(408) 371-0960

Superintendent .... Rhonda Farber
Grade plan 9-12
Number of schools 7
Enrollment 7,838
High school graduates, 2006-07 1,447
Dropout rate 4.5%
Pupil/teacher ratio 22.5
Average class size 25.4
Students per computer 3.8
Classrooms with internet 368
Avg. Daily Attendance (ADA) 7,486
Cost per ADA $8,580
Avg. Teacher Salary $64,628

California Achievement Tests 6th ed., 2008

(Pct scoring at or above 50th National Percentile Rank)

	Math	Reading	Language
Grade 3	NA	NA	NA
Grade 7	NA	NA	NA

Academic Performance Index, 2008

Number of students tested 5,602
Number of valid scores 5,320
2007 API (base) 752
2008 API (growth) 749

SAT Testing, 2006-07

Enrollment, Grade 12 1,842
Number taking test 792
percent taking test 43.0%
percent with total score 1,500+ 27.70%

Average Scores:

Math	Verbal	Writing	Total
551	530	526	1,607

Federal No Child Left Behind, 2008

(Adequate Yearly Progress standards met)

	Participation Rate	Pct Proficient
ELA	Yes	No
Math	Yes	No

API criteria .... Yes
Graduation rate .... No
\# criteria met/possible 30/27

Other school districts for this city

(see Appendix E for information on these districts)

Campbell Union Elem, Moreland Elem

See Introduction for an explanation of all data sources.

Demographics & Socio-Economic Characteristics

(2000 Decennial Census, except as noted)

Population

1990* . . . 7,938
2000 . . . 9,952
Male . . . 4,886
Female . . . 5,066
Jan. 2008 (estimate)§ . . . 11,051
Persons per sq. mi. of land . . . 2,762.8

Race & Hispanic Origin, 2000

Race
White . . . 9,248
Black/African American . . . 81
North American Native . . . 35
Asian . . . 153
Pacific Islander . . . 11
Other Race . . . 181
Two or more races . . . 243
Hispanic origin, total . . . 848
Mexican . . . 594
Puerto Rican . . . 34
Cuban . . . 19
Other Hispanic . . . 201

Age & Nativity, 2000

Under 5 years . . . 551
18 years and over . . . 7,374
65 years and over . . . 1,683
85 years and over . . . 80
Median Age . . . 40.8
Native-born . . . 9,779
Foreign-born . . . 438

Educational Attainment, 2000

Population 25 years and over . . . 6,948
Less than 9th grade . . . 0.6%
High school grad or higher . . . 92.3%
Bachelor's degree or higher . . . 23.5%
Graduate degree . . . 6.2%

Income & Poverty, 1999

Per capita income . . . $29,646
Median household income . . . $70,106
Median family income . . . $72,317
Persons in poverty . . . 5.0%
H'holds receiving public assistance . . . 107
H'holds receiving social security . . . 1,158

Households, 2000

Total households . . . 3,643
With persons under 18 . . . 1,370
With persons over 65 . . . 1,123
Family households . . . 2,940
Single person households . . . 522
Persons per household . . . 2.73
Persons per family . . . 3.00

Household Population, 2008§§

Persons living in households . . . 11,035
Persons living in group quarters . . . 16
Persons per household . . . 2.8

Labor & Employment

Total civilian labor force, 2008§§ . . . 6,600
Unemployment rate, 2008 . . . 4.8%
Total civilian labor force, 2000 . . . 4,692

Employed persons 16 years and over by occupation, 2000

Managers & professionals . . . 1,745
Service occupations . . . 544
Sales & office occupations . . . 1,436
Farming, fishing & forestry . . . 0
Construction & maintenance . . . 409
Production & transportation . . . 360
Self-employed persons . . . 512

* US Census Bureau
** 2000 Decennial Census
§ California Department of Finance
§§ California Employment Development Dept

General Information

City of Canyon Lake
31516 Railroad Canyon Rd
Canyon Lake, CA 92587
951-244-2955

Website . . . www.cityofcanyonlake.com
Elevation . . . NA
Land Area (sq. miles) . . . 4.0
Water Area (sq. miles) . . . 0.7
Year of Incorporation . . . 1990
Government type . . . General law
Sales tax rate . . . 8.75%

Voters & Officials

Registered Voters, October 2008

Total . . . 6,168
Democrats . . . 1,311
Republicans . . . 3,666
Declined to state . . . 915

Legislative Districts

US Congressional . . . 49
State Senatorial . . . 37
State Assembly . . . 64

Local Officials, 2009

Mayor . . . Mary Craton
Manager/Admin . . . Lori A. Moss
City Clerk . . . Sarah Manwaring (Actg)
Attorney . . . Elizabeth Martyn
Finance Dir . . . NA
Public Works . . . NA
Planning/Dev Dir . . . NA
Building . . . NA
Police Chief . . . James McElvain
Fire Chief . . . John Hawkins

Public Safety

Number of officers, 2007 . . . NA
Violent crimes, 2007 . . . 23
Property crimes, 2007 . . . 170
Arson, 2007 . . . 0

Public Library

Canyon Lake Branch Library
Riverside County Library Service
31516 Railroad Canyon Rd
Canyon Lake, CA 92587
951-244-9181

Branch Librarian . . . Cynthia Thompson

Library system statistics, FY 2007

Population served . . . 1,047,996
Internet terminals . . . 37
Annual users . . . 69,346

Per capita:

Operating income . . . $19.38
percent from local government . . . 49.8%
Operating expenditure . . . $20.45
Total materials . . . 1.43
Print holdings . . . 1.30
Visits per capita . . . 4.06

Housing & Construction

Housing Units

Total, 2008§ . . . 4,416
Single family units, attached . . . 164
Single family units, detached . . . 4,020
Multiple family units . . . 90
Mobile home units . . . 142
Occupied . . . 3,977
Vacancy rate . . . 9.9%
Median rent, 2000** . . . $1,171
Median SF home value, 2000** . . . $227,800

New Privately Owned Housing Units Authorized by Building Permit, 2007*

	Units	Construction Cost
Single	19	$12,232,729
Total	19	$12,232,729

Municipal Finance

(For local fiscal year ended in 2006)

Revenues

Total . . . $3,887,199
Taxes . . . 2,190,671
Special benefits assessment . . . 0
Licenses & permits . . . 346,320
Fines & forfeitures . . . 28,885
Revenues from use of money & property . . . 227,664
Intergovernmental . . . 868,247
Service charges . . . 47,259
Other revenues . . . 178,153
Other financing sources . . . 0

Expenditures

Total . . . $3,112,606
General government . . . 455,303
Public safety . . . 1,465,875
Transportation . . . 866,012
Community development . . . 325,416
Health . . . 0
Culture & leisure . . . 0
Other . . . 0

Local School District

(Data from School year 2007-08 except as noted)

Lake Elsinore Unified
545 Chaney St
Lake Elsinore, CA 92530
(951) 253-7000

Superintendent . . . Frank Passarella
Grade plan . . . K-12
Number of schools . . . 26
Enrollment . . . 22,109
High school graduates, 2006-07 . . . 1,211
Dropout rate . . . 2.1%
Pupil/teacher ratio . . . 22.2
Average class size . . . 27.7
Students per computer . . . 5.2
Classrooms with internet . . . 1,221
Avg. Daily Attendance (ADA) . . . 21,229
Cost per ADA . . . $8,008
Avg. Teacher Salary . . . $68,317

California Achievement Tests 6th ed., 2008

(Pct scoring at or above 50th National Percentile Rank)

	Math	Reading	Language
Grade 3	61%	39%	50%
Grade 7	50%	47%	43%

Academic Performance Index, 2008

Number of students tested . . . 16,937
Number of valid scores . . . 14,554
2007 API (base) . . . 729
2008 API (growth) . . . 775

SAT Testing, 2006-07

Enrollment, Grade 12 . . . 1,425
Number taking test . . . 360
percent taking test . . . 25.3%
percent with total score 1,500+ . . . 9.80%

Average Scores:

Math	Verbal	Writing	Total
485	480	471	1,436

Federal No Child Left Behind, 2008

(Adequate Yearly Progress standards met)

	Participation Rate	Pct Proficient
ELA	Yes	Yes
Math	Yes	Yes

API criteria . . . Yes
Graduation rate . . . Yes
\# criteria met/possible . . . 38/38

Other school districts for this city

(see Appendix E for information on these districts)

None

See Introduction for an explanation of all data sources.

Demographics & Socio-Economic Characteristics

(2000 Decennial Census, except as noted)

Population

1990* 10,171
2000 10,033
Male 4,766
Female 5,267
Jan. 2008 (estimate)§ 10,015
Persons per sq. mi. of land 6,259.4

Race & Hispanic Origin, 2000

Race
White 8,412
Black/African American 117
North American Native 57
Asian 401
Pacific Islander 20
Other Race 555
Two or more races 471
Hispanic origin, total 1,267
Mexican 949
Puerto Rican 35
Cuban 16
Other Hispanic 267

Age & Nativity, 2000

Under 5 years 488
18 years and over 8,187
65 years and over 1,420
85 years and over 222
Median Age 38.4
Native-born 8,985
Foreign-born 1,219

Educational Attainment, 2000

Population 25 years and over 7,468
Less than 9th grade 2.6%
High school grad or higher 91.3%
Bachelor's degree or higher 34.6%
Graduate degree 12.3%

Income & Poverty, 1999

Per capita income $27,609
Median household income $46,048
Median family income $59,473
Persons in poverty 7.0%
H'holds receiving public assistance 103
H'holds receiving social security 1,117

Households, 2000

Total households 4,692
With persons under 18 1,138
With persons over 65 1,067
Family households 2,279
Single person households 1,738
Persons per household 2.11
Persons per family 2.79

Household Population, 2008§§

Persons living in households 9,859
Persons living in group quarters 156
Persons per household 2.1

Labor & Employment

Total civilian labor force, 2008§§ 6,500
Unemployment rate, 2008 .... 3.6%
Total civilian labor force, 2000 6,048

Employed persons 16 years and over by occupation, 2000

Managers & professionals 2,450
Service occupations 1,033
Sales & office occupations 1,366
Farming, fishing & forestry 22
Construction & maintenance 538
Production & transportation 462
Self-employed persons 659

* US Census Bureau
** 2000 Decennial Census
§ California Department of Finance
§§ California Employment Development Dept

General Information

City of Capitola
420 Capitola Ave
Capitola, CA 95010
831-475-7300

Website .... www.ci.capitola.ca.us
Elevation .... NA
Land Area (sq. miles) 1.6
Water Area (sq. miles) 0.1
Year of Incorporation 1949
Government type .... General law
Sales tax rate 9.25%

Voters & Officials

Registered Voters, October 2008

Total 6,235
Democrats 3,393
Republicans 1,196
Declined to state 1,094

Legislative Districts

US Congressional 17
State Senatorial 11
State Assembly 27

Local Officials, 2009

Mayor .... Robert "Bob" Begun
Manager .... Richard Hill
City Clerk .... Pamela Greeninger
Attorney .... John Barisone
Finance Dir .... Charles Comstock (Int)
Public Works .... Steven Jesberg
Planning/Dev Dir .... Jamie Goldstein
Building .... Daniel Kostelec
Police Chief .... Richard Ehle
Emergency/Fire Dir .... Bruce Clark

Public Safety

Number of officers, 2007 22
Violent crimes, 2007 85
Property crimes, 2007 811
Arson, 2007 5

Public Library

Capitola Branch Library
Santa Cruz Libraries
2005 Wharf Rd
Capitola, CA 95010
831-420-5329

Branch Librarian .... Wendy Smith

Library system statistics, FY 2007

Population served 205,669
Internet terminals 24
Annual users 23,239

Per capita:

Operating income $59.06
percent from local government 95.9%
Operating expenditure $58.55
Total materials 2.52
Print holdings 2.13
Visits per capita .... NA

Housing & Construction

Housing Units

Total, 2008§ 5,412
Single family units, attached 516
Single family units, detached 1,997
Multiple family units 2,249
Mobile home units 650
Occupied 4,782
Vacancy rate 11.6%
Median rent, 2000** $973
Median SF home value, 2000** $397,600

New Privately Owned Housing Units Authorized by Building Permit, 2007*

	Units	Construction Cost
Single	17	$6,087,139
Total	72	$14,127,774

Municipal Finance

(For local fiscal year ended in 2006)

Revenues

Total $13,851,842
Taxes 9,414,862
Special benefits assessment 61,530
Licenses & permits 332,170
Fines & forfeitures 511,705
Revenues from use of money & property 504,341
Intergovernmental 885,607
Service charges 1,927,400
Other revenues 180,013
Other financing sources 34,214

Expenditures

Total $11,750,865
General government 2,077,452
Public safety 5,254,590
Transportation 1,402,518
Community development 1,348,656
Health 0
Culture & leisure 1,667,649
Other 0

Local School District

(Data from School year 2007-08 except as noted)
‡combined elementary and high school data

Santa Cruz City High
405 Old San Jose Rd
Soquel, CA 95073
(831) 429-3410

Superintendent .... Alan Pagano
Grade plan K-12
Number of schools 9
Enrollment 4,847
High school graduates, 2006-07 905
Dropout rate 1.2%
Pupil/teacher ratio 22.9
Average class size 24.4
Students per computer 3.7
Classrooms with internet 244
Avg. Daily Attendance (ADA)‡ 6,438
Cost per ADA‡ $9,723
Avg. Teacher Salary‡ $60,324

California Achievement Tests 6th ed., 2008

(Pct scoring at or above 50th National Percentile Rank)

	Math	Reading	Language
Grade 3	NA	NA	NA
Grade 7	65%	68%	64%

Academic Performance Index, 2008

Number of students tested 3,635
Number of valid scores 3,485
2007 API (base) 745
2008 API (growth) 753

SAT Testing, 2006-07

Enrollment, Grade 12 997
Number taking test 404
percent taking test 40.5%
percent with total score 1,500+ 29.30%

Average Scores:

Math	Verbal	Writing	Total
557	547	540	1,644

Federal No Child Left Behind, 2008

(Adequate Yearly Progress standards met)

	Participation Rate	Pct Proficient
ELA	No	No
Math	No	No

API criteria .... Yes
Graduation rate .... Yes
criteria met/possible 26/16

Other school districts for this city

(see Appendix E for information on these districts)

Santa Cruz City Elem, Soquel Union Elem

See Introduction for an explanation of all data sources.

Demographics & Socio-Economic Characteristics†

(2007 American Community Survey, except as noted)

Population

1990* ... 63,126
2007 ... 95,796
Male ... 46,867
Female ... 48,929
Jan. 2008 (estimate)§ ... 103,811
Persons per sq. mi. of land ... 2,775.7

Race & Hispanic Origin, 2007

Race
White ... 81,296
Black/African American ... 630
North American Native ... 190
Asian ... 7,146
Pacific Islander ... 0
Other Race ... 3,908
Two or more races ... 2,626
Hispanic origin, total ... NA
Mexican ... NA
Puerto Rican ... NA
Cuban ... NA
Other Hispanic ... NA

Age & Nativity, 2007

Under 5 years ... 7,013
18 years and over ... 71,346
65 years and over ... 13,424
85 years and over ... 1,521
Median Age ... 39.7
Native-born ... 82,067
Foreign-born ... 13,729

Educational Attainment, 2007

Population 25 years and over ... 66,096
Less than 9th grade ... 2.1%
High school grad or higher ... 96.4%
Bachelor's degree or higher ... 49.3%
Graduate degree ... 18.5%

Income & Poverty, 2007

Per capita income ... $41,638
Median household income ... $79,444
Median family income ... $100,932
Persons in poverty ... 5.9%
H'holds receiving public assistance ... 490
H'holds receiving social security ... 9,421

Households, 2007

Total households ... 39,101
With persons under 18 ... 13,047
With persons over 65 ... 8,995
Family households ... 25,205
Single person households ... 11,043
Persons per household ... 2.45
Persons per family ... 3.07

Household Population, 2008§§

Persons living in households ... 103,146
Persons living in group quarters ... 665
Persons per household ... 2.5

Labor & Employment

Total civilian labor force, 2008§§ ... 48,200
Unemployment rate, 2008 ... 3.9%
Total civilian labor force, 2000* ... 40,328

Employed persons 16 years and over by occupation, 2007

Managers & professionals ... 23,145
Service occupations ... 5,001
Sales & office occupations ... 13,139
Farming, fishing & forestry ... 0
Construction & maintenance ... 2,476
Production & transportation ... 1,841
Self-employed persons ... 5,351

† see Appendix D for 2000 Decennial Census Data
* US Census Bureau
** 2007 American Community Survey
§ California Department of Finance
§§ California Employment Development Dept

General Information

City of Carlsbad
1200 Carlsbad Village Dr
Carlsbad, CA 92008
760-434-2820

Website ... www.ci.carlsbad.ca.us
Elevation ... 39 ft.
Land Area (sq. miles) ... 37.4
Water Area (sq. miles) ... 3.4
Year of Incorporation ... 1952
Government type ... General law
Sales tax rate ... 8.75%

Voters & Officials

Registered Voters, October 2008

Total ... 60,321
Democrats ... 17,608
Republicans ... 26,541
Declined to state ... 13,713

Legislative Districts

US Congressional ... 50
State Senatorial ... 38
State Assembly ... 74

Local Officials, 2009

Mayor ... Claude Lewis
Manager ... Lisa Hildabrand (Int)
City Clerk ... Lorraine Wood
Attorney ... Ronald Ball
Finance Dir ... Lisa Irvine
Public Works ... Glen Pruim
Planning/Dev Dir ... Sandra Holder
Building ... Will Foss
Police Chief ... Tom Zoll
Fire Chief ... Kevin Crawford

Public Safety

Number of officers, 2007 ... 112
Violent crimes, 2007 ... 318
Property crimes, 2007 ... 2,448
Arson, 2007 ... 10

Public Library

Dove Library
Carlsbad City Library System
1775 Dove Lane
Carlsbad, CA 92011
760-602-2038

Director ... Heather Pizzuto

Library system statistics, FY 2007

Population served ... 101,337
Internet terminals ... 63
Annual users ... 157,790

Per capita:

Operating income ... $97.18
percent from local government ... 95.4%
Operating expenditure ... $95.82
Total materials ... 3.46
Print holdings ... 2.99
Visits per capita ... 6.77

Housing & Construction

Housing Units

Total, 2008§ ... 44,027
Single family units, attached ... 5,772
Single family units, detached ... 23,882
Multiple family units ... 13,081
Mobile home units ... 1,292
Occupied ... 41,063
Vacancy rate ... 6.7%
Median rent, 2007** ... $1,386
Median SF home value, 2007** ... $690,600

New Privately Owned Housing Units Authorized by Building Permit, 2007*

	Units	Construction Cost
Single	242	$88,416,814
Total	350	$103,834,400

Municipal Finance

(For local fiscal year ended in 2006)

Revenues

Total ... $236,631,341
Taxes ... 104,834,058
Special benefits assessment ... 2,023,367
Licenses & permits ... 2,504,019
Fines & forfeitures ... 985,451
Revenues from use of money & property ... 12,493,232
Intergovernmental ... 15,887,428
Service charges ... 43,108,877
Other revenues ... 12,543,956
Other financing sources ... 42,250,953

Expenditures

Total ... $215,112,987
General government ... 16,092,722
Public safety ... 46,712,985
Transportation ... 27,217,921
Community development ... 18,269,008
Health ... 15,069,549
Culture & leisure ... 52,179,190
Other ... 869,264

Local School District

(Data from School year 2007-08 except as noted)

Carlsbad Unified
6225 El Camino Real
Carlsbad, CA 92009
(760) 331-5000

Superintendent ... John Roach
Grade plan ... K-12
Number of schools ... 15
Enrollment ... 10,741
High school graduates, 2006-07 ... 693
Dropout rate ... 1.9%
Pupil/teacher ratio ... 22.6
Average class size ... 27.8
Students per computer ... 3.5
Classrooms with internet ... 1,515
Avg. Daily Attendance (ADA) ... 10,479
Cost per ADA ... $7,575
Avg. Teacher Salary ... $66,530

California Achievement Tests 6th ed., 2008

(Pct scoring at or above 50th National Percentile Rank)

	Math	Reading	Language
Grade 3	78%	64%	72%
Grade 7	73%	69%	66%

Academic Performance Index, 2008

Number of students tested ... 8,209
Number of valid scores ... 7,875
2007 API (base) ... 829
2008 API (growth) ... 846

SAT Testing, 2006-07

Enrollment, Grade 12 ... 794
Number taking test ... 338
percent taking test ... 42.6%
percent with total score 1,500+ ... 25.10%

Average Scores:

Math	Verbal	Writing	Total
538	520	520	1,578

Federal No Child Left Behind, 2008

(Adequate Yearly Progress standards met)

	Participation Rate	Pct Proficient
ELA	Yes	No
Math	Yes	Yes

API criteria ... Yes
Graduation rate ... Yes
criteria met/possible ... 36/35

Other school districts for this city

(see Appendix E for information on these districts)

None

See Introduction for an explanation of all data sources.

Demographics & Socio-Economic Characteristics

(2000 Decennial Census, except as noted)

Population

1990* . . . 4,239
2000 . . . 4,081
Male . . . 1,777
Female . . . 2,304
Jan. 2008 (estimate)§ . . . 4,049
Persons per sq. mi. of land . . . 3,680.9

Race & Hispanic Origin, 2000

Race
White . . . 3,860
Black/African American . . . 18
North American Native . . . 13
Asian . . . 92
Pacific Islander . . . 6
Other Race . . . 37
Two or more races . . . 55
Hispanic origin, total . . . 120
Mexican . . . 61
Puerto Rican . . . 5
Cuban . . . 3
Other Hispanic . . . 51

Age & Nativity, 2000

Under 5 years . . . 73
18 years and over . . . 3,678
65 years and over . . . 1,258
85 years and over . . . 181
Median Age . . . 54.3
Native-born . . . 3,641
Foreign-born . . . 434

Educational Attainment, 2000

Population 25 years and over . . . 3,542
Less than 9th grade . . . 0.0%
High school grad or higher . . . 97.3%
Bachelor's degree or higher . . . 54.7%
Graduate degree . . . 24.2%

Income & Poverty, 1999

Per capita income . . . $48,739
Median household income . . . $58,163
Median family income . . . $81,259
Persons in poverty . . . 6.6%
H'holds receiving public assistance . . . 4
H'holds receiving social security . . . 960

Households, 2000

Total households . . . 2,285
With persons under 18 . . . 283
With persons over 65 . . . 947
Family households . . . 1,109
Single person households . . . 1,007
Persons per household . . . 1.79
Persons per family . . . 2.39

Household Population, 2008§§

Persons living in households . . . 4,049
Persons living in group quarters . . . 0
Persons per household . . . 1.8

Labor & Employment

Total civilian labor force, 2008§§ . . . 2,400
Unemployment rate, 2008 . . . 1.5%
Total civilian labor force, 2000 . . . 2,034

Employed persons 16 years and over by occupation, 2000

Managers & professionals . . . 975
Service occupations . . . 263
Sales & office occupations . . . 520
Farming, fishing & forestry . . . 8
Construction & maintenance . . . 118
Production & transportation . . . 118
Self-employed persons . . . 423

* US Census Bureau
** 2000 Decennial Census
§ California Department of Finance
§§ California Employment Development Dept

General Information

City of Carmel-by-the-Sea
PO Box CC
Carmel-by-the-Sea, CA 93921
831-620-2000

Website . . . ci.carmel.ca.us
Elevation . . . NA
Land Area (sq. miles) . . . 1.1
Water Area (sq. miles) . . . 0
Year of Incorporation . . . 1916
Government type . . . General law
Sales tax rate . . . 8.25%

Voters & Officials

Registered Voters, October 2008

Total . . . 2,896
Democrats . . . 1,170
Republicans . . . 1,057
Declined to state . . . 538

Legislative Districts

US Congressional . . . 17
State Senatorial . . . 15
State Assembly . . . 27

Local Officials, 2009

Mayor . . . Sue McCloud
Manager . . . Rich Guillen
City Clerk . . . Heidi Burch
Attorney . . . Donald Freeman
Finance Dir . . . Joyce Giuffre
Public Works . . . Stu Ross
Planning/Dev Dir . . . NA
Building . . . NA
Public Safety Dir . . . George Rawson
(combined police and fire position)

Public Safety

Number of officers, 2007 . . . 13
Violent crimes, 2007 . . . 9
Property crimes, 2007 . . . 158
Arson, 2007 . . . 0

Public Library

Main Branch
Harrison Memorial Library System
Ocean & Lincoln Ave
Carmel-by-the-Sea, CA 93921
831-624-4629

Director . . . Janet Cubbage

Library system statistics, FY 2007

Population served . . . 4,053
Internet terminals . . . 12
Annual users . . . 11,858

Per capita:

Operating income . . . $290.25
percent from local government . . . 75.6%
Operating expenditure . . . $325.87
Total materials . . . 21.06
Print holdings . . . 19.84
Visits per capita . . . 20.80

Housing & Construction

Housing Units

Total, 2008§ . . . 3,363
Single family units, attached . . . 114
Single family units, detached . . . 2,756
Multiple family units . . . 493
Mobile home units . . . 0
Occupied . . . 2,306
Vacancy rate . . . 31.4%
Median rent, 2000** . . . $1,120
Median SF home value, 2000** . . . $675,300

New Privately Owned Housing Units Authorized by Building Permit, 2007*

	Units	Construction Cost
Single	8	$4,724,550
Total	12	$5,524,550

Municipal Finance

(For local fiscal year ended in 2006)

Revenues

Total . . . $12,462,258
Taxes . . . 10,591,577
Special benefits assessment . . . 45,760
Licenses & permits . . . 544,059
Fines & forfeitures . . . 237,545
Revenues from use of money & property . . . 502,715
Intergovernmental . . . 399,197
Service charges . . . 35,751
Other revenues . . . 105,654
Other financing sources . . . 0

Expenditures

Total . . . $11,482,357
General government . . . 3,243,706
Public safety . . . 4,383,582
Transportation . . . 900,867
Community development . . . 541,913
Health . . . 0
Culture & leisure . . . 2,412,289
Other . . . 0

Local School District

(Data from School year 2007-08 except as noted)

Carmel Unified
PO Box 222700
Carmel, CA 93923
(831) 624-1546

Superintendent . . . Marvin Biasotti
Grade plan . . . K-12
Number of schools . . . 6
Enrollment . . . 2,090
High school graduates, 2006-07 . . . 177
Dropout rate . . . 0.6%
Pupil/teacher ratio . . . 15.0
Average class size . . . 19.3
Students per computer . . . 2.2
Classrooms with internet . . . 148
Avg. Daily Attendance (ADA) . . . 2,022
Cost per ADA . . . $16,638
Avg. Teacher Salary . . . $76,401

California Achievement Tests 6th ed., 2008

(Pct scoring at or above 50th National Percentile Rank)

	Math	Reading	Language
Grade 3	87%	75%	77%
Grade 7	84%	82%	78%

Academic Performance Index, 2008

Number of students tested . . . 1,632
Number of valid scores . . . 1,562
2007 API (base) . . . 869
2008 API (growth) . . . 881

SAT Testing, 2006-07

Enrollment, Grade 12 . . . 184
Number taking test . . . 110
percent taking test . . . 59.8%
percent with total score 1,500+ . . . 35.30%

Average Scores:

Math	Verbal	Writing	Total
534	517	523	1,574

Federal No Child Left Behind, 2008

(Adequate Yearly Progress standards met)

	Participation Rate	Pct Proficient
ELA	Yes	Yes
Math	Yes	Yes

API criteria . . . Yes
Graduation rate . . . Yes
\# criteria met/possible . . . 26/26

Other school districts for this city

(see Appendix E for information on these districts)

None

See Introduction for an explanation of all data sources.

Demographics & Socio-Economic Characteristics

(2000 Decennial Census, except as noted)

Population

1990* . . . 13,747
2000 . . . 14,194
Male . . . 7,125
Female . . . 7,069
Jan. 2008 (estimate)§ . . . 14,271
Persons per sq. mi. of land . . . 5,285.6

Race & Hispanic Origin, 2000

Race
White . . . 10,418
Black/African American . . . 84
North American Native . . . 140
Asian . . . 338
Pacific Islander . . . 26
Other Race . . . 2,568
Two or more races . . . 620
Hispanic origin, total . . . 6,175
Mexican . . . 5,476
Puerto Rican . . . 21
Cuban . . . 7
Other Hispanic . . . 671

Age & Nativity, 2000

Under 5 years . . . 890
18 years and over . . . 10,559
65 years and over . . . 1,766
85 years and over . . . 231
Median Age . . . 35.9
Native-born . . . 10,691
Foreign-born . . . 3,686

Educational Attainment, 2000

Population 25 years and over . . . 9,525
Less than 9th grade . . . 13.6%
High school grad or higher . . . 76.3%
Bachelor's degree or higher . . . 26.5%
Graduate degree . . . 8.1%

Income & Poverty, 1999

Per capita income . . . $21,563
Median household income . . . $47,729
Median family income . . . $54,849
Persons in poverty . . . 10.4%
H'holds receiving public assistance . . . 49
H'holds receiving social security . . . 1,313

Households, 2000

Total households . . . 4,989
With persons under 18 . . . 1,838
With persons over 65 . . . 1,305
Family households . . . 3,334
Single person households . . . 1,273
Persons per household . . . 2.82
Persons per family . . . 3.38

Household Population, 2008§§

Persons living in households . . . 14,146
Persons living in group quarters . . . 125
Persons per household . . . 2.8

Labor & Employment

Total civilian labor force, 2008§§ . . . 8,500
Unemployment rate, 2008 . . . 2.4%
Total civilian labor force, 2000 . . . 7,417

Employed persons 16 years and over by occupation, 2000

Managers & professionals . . . 2,431
Service occupations . . . 1,332
Sales & office occupations . . . 1,767
Farming, fishing & forestry . . . 225
Construction & maintenance . . . 798
Production & transportation . . . 639
Self-employed persons . . . 888

* US Census Bureau
** 2000 Decennial Census
§ California Department of Finance
§§ California Employment Development Dept

General Information

City of Carpinteria
5775 Carpinteria Ave
Carpinteria, CA 93013
805-684-5405

Website . . . www.ci.carpinteria.ca.us
Elevation . . . 14 ft.
Land Area (sq. miles) . . . 2.7
Water Area (sq. miles) . . . 4.6
Year of Incorporation . . . 1965
Government type . . . General law
Sales tax rate . . . 8.75%

Voters & Officials

Registered Voters, October 2008

Total . . . 6,806
Democrats . . . 3,273
Republicans . . . 1,918
Declined to state . . . 1,242

Legislative Districts

US Congressional . . . 23
State Senatorial . . . 19
State Assembly . . . 35

Local Officials, 2009

Mayor . . . Gregg Carty
Manager . . . Dave Durflinger
City Clerk . . . Jayne Diaz
Attorney . . . Peter Brown
Finance Dir . . . John Thornberry
Public Works . . . (vacant)
Planning/Dev Dir . . . Jackie Campbell
Building . . . NA
Police Chief . . . NA
Emergency/Fire Dir . . . Mike Mingge

Public Safety

Number of officers, 2007 . . . NA
Violent crimes, 2007 . . . 28
Property crimes, 2007 . . . 227
Arson, 2007 . . . 2

Public Library

Carpinteria Library
Santa Barbara Public Library
5141 Carpinteria Ave
Carpinteria, CA 93013
805-684-4314

Director . . . Tara O'Reilly

Library system statistics, FY 2007

Population served . . . 233,434
Internet terminals . . . 86
Annual users . . . 66,000

Per capita:

Operating income . . . $25.05
percent from local government . . . 84.4%
Operating expenditure . . . $27.43
Total materials . . . 1.73
Print holdings . . . 1.48
Visits per capita . . . 12.44

Housing & Construction

Housing Units

Total, 2008§ . . . 5,551
Single family units, attached . . . 428
Single family units, detached . . . 2,165
Multiple family units . . . 2,018
Mobile home units . . . 940
Occupied . . . 5,069
Vacancy rate . . . 8.7%
Median rent, 2000** . . . $938
Median SF home value, 2000** . . . $382,400

New Privately Owned Housing Units Authorized by Building Permit, 2007*

	Units	Construction Cost
Single	6	$2,300,000
Total	6	$2,300,000

Municipal Finance

(For local fiscal year ended in 2006)

Revenues

Total . . . $9,833,071
Taxes . . . 6,082,865
Special benefits assessment . . . 244,225
Licenses & permits . . . 191,172
Fines & forfeitures . . . 127,193
Revenues from use of money & property . . . 311,318
Intergovernmental . . . 972,172
Service charges . . . 1,862,896
Other revenues . . . 41,230
Other financing sources . . . 0

Expenditures

Total . . . $9,264,512
General government . . . 1,979,565
Public safety . . . 2,872,970
Transportation . . . 1,836,410
Community development . . . 926,236
Health . . . 66,590
Culture & leisure . . . 1,582,741
Other . . . 0

Local School District

(Data from School year 2007-08 except as noted)

Carpinteria Unified
1400 Linden Ave
Carpinteria, CA 93013
(805) 684-4511

Superintendent . . . Paul Cordeiro
Grade plan . . . K-12
Number of schools . . . 8
Enrollment . . . 2,553
High school graduates, 2006-07 . . . 169
Dropout rate . . . 3.4%
Pupil/teacher ratio . . . 19.9
Average class size . . . 24.4
Students per computer . . . 3.0
Classrooms with internet . . . 142
Avg. Daily Attendance (ADA) . . . 2,527
Cost per ADA . . . $8,595
Avg. Teacher Salary . . . NA

California Achievement Tests 6th ed., 2008

(Pct scoring at or above 50th National Percentile Rank)

	Math	Reading	Language
Grade 3	57%	38%	48%
Grade 7	50%	53%	53%

Academic Performance Index, 2008

Number of students tested . . . 1,950
Number of valid scores . . . 1,827
2007 API (base) . . . 748
2008 API (growth) . . . 751

SAT Testing, 2006-07

Enrollment, Grade 12 . . . 216
Number taking test . . . 64
percent taking test . . . 29.6%
percent with total score 1,500+ . . . 15.30%

Average Scores:

Math	Verbal	Writing	Total
502	485	479	1,466

Federal No Child Left Behind, 2008

(Adequate Yearly Progress standards met)

	Participation Rate	Pct Proficient
ELA	Yes	No
Math	Yes	Yes

API criteria . . . Yes
Graduation rate . . . Yes
criteria met/possible . . . 26/24

Other school districts for this city

(see Appendix E for information on these districts)

None

See Introduction for an explanation of all data sources.

Demographics & Socio-Economic Characteristics†

(2007 American Community Survey, except as noted)

Population

1990* . . . 83,995
2007 . . . 98,731
Male . . . 47,298
Female . . . 51,433
Jan. 2008 (estimate)§ . . . 97,960
Persons per sq. mi. of land . . . 5,210.6

Race & Hispanic Origin, 2007

Race
White . . . 27,323
Black/African American . . . 31,414
North American Native . . . 866
Asian . . . 23,589
Pacific Islander . . . 4,165
Other Race . . . 8,122
Two or more races . . . 3,252
Hispanic origin, total . . . 31,489
Mexican . . . 24,935
Puerto Rican . . . 319
Cuban . . . 465
Other Hispanic . . . 5,770

Age & Nativity, 2007

Under 5 years . . . 6,707
18 years and over . . . 75,964
65 years and over . . . 15,037
85 years and over . . . 1,417
Median Age . . . 37.1
Native-born . . . 67,452
Foreign-born . . . 31,279

Educational Attainment, 2007

Population 25 years and over . . . 65,309
Less than 9th grade . . . 9.0%
High school grad or higher . . . 80.2%
Bachelor's degree or higher . . . 26.6%
Graduate degree . . . 8.6%

Income & Poverty, 2007

Per capita income . . . $23,929
Median household income . . . $62,094
Median family income . . . $66,749
Persons in poverty . . . 7.7%
H'holds receiving public assistance . . . 820
H'holds receiving social security . . . 8,070

Households, 2007

Total households . . . 26,413
With persons under 18 . . . 10,848
With persons over 65 . . . 9,583
Family households . . . 21,347
Single person households . . . 4,153
Persons per household . . . 3.67
Persons per family . . . 3.98

Household Population, 2008§§

Persons living in households . . . 96,620
Persons living in group quarters . . . 1,340
Persons per household . . . 3.8

Labor & Employment

Total civilian labor force, 2008§§ . . . 46,800
Unemployment rate, 2008 . . . 7.6%
Total civilian labor force, 2000* . . . 40,514

Employed persons 16 years and over by occupation, 2007

Managers & professionals . . . 14,446
Service occupations . . . 8,215
Sales & office occupations . . . 11,909
Farming, fishing & forestry . . . 0
Construction & maintenance . . . 2,712
Production & transportation . . . 7,257
Self-employed persons . . . 2,487

† see Appendix D for 2000 Decennial Census Data
* US Census Bureau
** 2007 American Community Survey
§ California Department of Finance
§§ California Employment Development Dept

General Information

City of Carson
701 E Carson St
Carson, CA 90745
310-830-7600

Website . . . www.ci.carson.ca.us
Elevation . . . 40 ft.
Land Area (sq. miles) . . . 18.8
Water Area (sq. miles) . . . 0.1
Year of Incorporation . . . 1968
Government type . . . General law
Sales tax rate . . . 9.25%

Voters & Officials

Registered Voters, October 2008

Total . . . 48,177
Democrats . . . 29,505
Republicans . . . 7,891
Declined to state . . . 9,145

Legislative Districts

US Congressional . . . 37
State Senatorial . . . 28
State Assembly . . . 55

Local Officials, 2009

Mayor . . . Jim Dear
City Manager . . . Jerome Groomes
City Clerk . . . Helen S. Kawagoe
Attorney . . . William B. Wynder
Admin Svcs Dir . . . Jackie Acosta
Public Works . . . Uli Fe'esago
Dev Svcs Mgr . . . M. Victor Rollinger
Building . . . NA
Police Captain . . . Todd Rogers
Fire/Emergency Mgmt . . . Robert Valdez

Public Safety

Number of officers, 2007 . . . NA
Violent crimes, 2007 . . . 684
Property crimes, 2007 . . . 2,605
Arson, 2007 . . . 37

Public Library

Carson Regional Library
Los Angeles County Public Library System
151 E Carson St
Carson, CA 90745
310-830-0901

Branch Manager . . . Leticia B. Tan

Library system statistics, FY 2007

Population served . . . 3,673,313
Internet terminals . . . 749
Annual users . . . 3,748,771

Per capita:

Operating income . . . $30.06
percent from local government . . . 93.6%
Operating expenditure . . . $28.36
Total materials . . . 2.22
Print holdings . . . 1.97
Visits per capita . . . 3.25

Housing & Construction

Housing Units

Total, 2008§ . . . 26,442
Single family units, attached . . . 2,280
Single family units, detached . . . 18,654
Multiple family units . . . 3,003
Mobile home units . . . 2,505
Occupied . . . 25,722
Vacancy rate . . . 2.7%
Median rent, 2007** . . . $1,148
Median SF home value, 2007** . . . $516,900

New Privately Owned Housing Units Authorized by Building Permit, 2007*

	Units	Construction Cost
Single	NA	NA
Total	NA	NA

Municipal Finance

(For local fiscal year ended in 2006)

Revenues

Total . . . $70,013,802
Taxes . . . 48,939,876
Special benefits assessment . . . 0
Licenses & permits . . . 3,077,289
Fines & forfeitures . . . 1,754,645
Revenues from use of money & property . . . 2,089,461
Intergovernmental . . . 6,642,073
Service charges . . . 3,365,159
Other revenues . . . 4,145,299
Other financing sources . . . 0

Expenditures

Total . . . $66,051,234
General government . . . 12,887,966
Public safety . . . 20,227,012
Transportation . . . 12,643,566
Community development . . . 4,656,355
Health . . . 171,090
Culture & leisure . . . 15,465,245
Other . . . 0

Local School District

(Data from School year 2007-08 except as noted)

Los Angeles Unified
333 South Beaudry Ave
Los Angeles, CA 90017
(213) 241-1000

Superintendent . . . Ramon Cortines
Grade plan . . . PK-12
Number of schools . . . 827
Enrollment . . . 693,680
High school graduates, 2006-07 . . . 28,545
Dropout rate . . . 7.8%
Pupil/teacher ratio . . . 19.8
Average class size . . . 24.9
Students per computer . . . 3.7
Classrooms with internet . . . 31,112
Avg. Daily Attendance (ADA) . . . 653,672
Cost per ADA . . . $10,053
Avg. Teacher Salary . . . $63,391

California Achievement Tests 6th ed., 2008

(Pct scoring at or above 50th National Percentile Rank)

	Math	Reading	Language
Grade 3	49%	27%	39%
Grade 7	37%	33%	33%

Academic Performance Index, 2008

Number of students tested . . . 495,046
Number of valid scores . . . 471,641
2007 API (base) . . . 662
2008 API (growth) . . . 683

SAT Testing, 2006-07

Enrollment, Grade 12 . . . 32,370
Number taking test . . . 15,447
percent taking test . . . 47.7%
percent with total score 1,500+ . . . 12.50%

Average Scores:

Math	Verbal	Writing	Total
443	438	441	1,322

Federal No Child Left Behind, 2008

(Adequate Yearly Progress standards met)

	Participation Rate	Pct Proficient
ELA	Yes	No
Math	Yes	No

API criteria . . . Yes
Graduation rate . . . Yes
criteria met/possible . . . 46/38

Other school districts for this city

(see Appendix E for information on these districts)

Compton Unified

See Introduction for an explanation of all data sources.

Demographics & Socio-Economic Characteristics

(2000 Decennial Census, except as noted)

Population

1990* ... 30,085
2000 ... 42,647
Male ... 21,608
Female ... 21,039
Jan. 2008 (estimate)§ ... 52,465
Persons per sq. mi. of land ... 2,732.6

Race & Hispanic Origin, 2000

Race
White ... 27,845
Black/African American ... 1,169
North American Native ... 440
Asian ... 1,575
Pacific Islander ... 32
Other Race ... 9,834
Two or more races ... 1,752
Hispanic origin, total ... 21,312
Mexican ... 17,791
Puerto Rican ... 177
Cuban ... 82
Other Hispanic ... 3,262

Age & Nativity, 2000

Under 5 years ... 3,763
18 years and over ... 29,380
65 years and over ... 5,203
85 years and over ... 487
Median Age ... 32.0
Native-born ... 30,248
Foreign-born ... 12,671

Educational Attainment, 2000

Population 25 years and over ... 25,700
Less than 9th grade ... 14.6%
High school grad or higher ... 69.0%
Bachelor's degree or higher ... 14.7%
Graduate degree ... 5.6%

Income & Poverty, 1999

Per capita income ... $16,215
Median household income ... $38,887
Median family income ... $42,461
Persons in poverty ... 13.6%
H'holds receiving public assistance ... 519
H'holds receiving social security ... 4,013

Households, 2000

Total households ... 14,027
With persons under 18 ... 6,093
With persons over 65 ... 3,874
Family households ... 9,628
Single person households ... 3,252
Persons per household ... 3.03
Persons per family ... 3.63

Household Population, 2008§§

Persons living in households ... 52,270
Persons living in group quarters ... 195
Persons per household ... 3.1

Labor & Employment

Total civilian labor force, 2008§§ ... 26,400
Unemployment rate, 2008 ... 8.4%
Total civilian labor force, 2000 ... 18,626

Employed persons 16 years and over by occupation, 2000

Managers & professionals ... 3,800
Service occupations ... 5,278
Sales & office occupations ... 4,391
Farming, fishing & forestry ... 57
Construction & maintenance ... 2,264
Production & transportation ... 1,510
Self-employed persons ... 1,985

* US Census Bureau
** 2000 Decennial Census
§ California Department of Finance
§§ California Employment Development Dept

General Information

City of Cathedral City
68700 Avenida Lalo Guerrero
Cathedral City, CA 92234
760-770-0340

Website ... www.cathedralcity.gov
Elevation ... NA
Land Area (sq. miles) ... 19.2
Water Area (sq. miles) ... 0.3
Year of Incorporation ... 1981
Government type ... General law
Sales tax rate ... 8.75%

Voters & Officials

Registered Voters, October 2008

Total ... 19,297
Democrats ... 7,701
Republicans ... 8,264
Declined to state ... 2,758

Legislative Districts

US Congressional ... 45
State Senatorial ... 40
State Assembly ... 80

Local Officials, 2009

Mayor ... Kathleen J. DeRosa
Manager ... Donald Bradley
City Clerk ... Pat Hammers
Attorney ... Charles Green
Finance Dir ... T. Scott
Public Works ... Pat Milos
Planning Dir ... Leisa Lukes
Building ... Gilbert Estrada
Police Chief ... Stanley Henry
Emergency/Fire Dir ... Bill Soqui

Public Safety

Number of officers, 2007 ... 56
Violent crimes, 2007 ... 204
Property crimes, 2007 ... 1,787
Arson, 2007 ... 1

Public Library

Cathedral City Branch Library
Riverside County Library Service
33-520 Date Palm Dr
Cathedral City, CA 92234
760-328-4262

Branch Librarian ... Amy Dodson

Library system statistics, FY 2007

Population served ... 1,047,996
Internet terminals ... 37
Annual users ... 69,346

Per capita:

Operating income ... $19.38
percent from local government ... 49.8%
Operating expenditure ... $20.45
Total materials ... 1.43
Print holdings ... 1.30
Visits per capita ... 4.06

Housing & Construction

Housing Units

Total, 2008§ ... 21,561
Single family units, attached ... 2,659
Single family units, detached ... 11,557
Multiple family units ... 4,497
Mobile home units ... 2,848
Occupied ... 17,008
Vacancy rate ... 21.1%
Median rent, 2000** ... $695
Median SF home value, 2000** ... $125,500

New Privately Owned Housing Units Authorized by Building Permit, 2007*

	Units	Construction Cost
Single	40	$8,432,977
Total	50	$10,063,880

Municipal Finance

(For local fiscal year ended in 2006)

Revenues

Total ... $66,768,801
Taxes ... 21,238,650
Special benefits assessment ... 1,320,467
Licenses & permits ... 1,156,679
Fines & forfeitures ... 402,432
Revenues from use of money & property ... 1,840,218
Intergovernmental ... 5,785,793
Service charges ... 1,970,517
Other revenues ... 2,196,301
Other financing sources ... 30,857,744

Expenditures

Total ... $45,191,477
General government ... 4,692,986
Public safety ... 17,301,269
Transportation ... 14,938,058
Community development ... 6,916,169
Health ... 834,842
Culture & leisure ... 508,153
Other ... 0

Local School District

(Data from School year 2007-08 except as noted)

Palm Springs Unified
980 East Tahquitz Canyon Way
Palm Springs, CA 92262
(760) 416-6000

Superintendent ... Lorri McCune
Grade plan ... K-12
Number of schools ... 25
Enrollment ... 24,400
High school graduates, 2006-07 ... 1,146
Dropout rate ... 5.8%
Pupil/teacher ratio ... 21.9
Average class size ... 28.3
Students per computer ... 5.9
Classrooms with internet ... 1,311
Avg. Daily Attendance (ADA) ... 22,873
Cost per ADA ... $8,379
Avg. Teacher Salary ... $66,086

California Achievement Tests 6th ed., 2008

(Pct scoring at or above 50th National Percentile Rank)

	Math	Reading	Language
Grade 3	44%	28%	36%
Grade 7	37%	35%	32%

Academic Performance Index, 2008

Number of students tested ... 18,458
Number of valid scores ... 17,207
2007 API (base) ... 673
2008 API (growth) ... 700

SAT Testing, 2006-07

Enrollment, Grade 12 ... 1,704
Number taking test ... 438
percent taking test ... 25.7%
percent with total score 1,500+ ... 8.90%

Average Scores:

Math	Verbal	Writing	Total
469	468	454	1,391

Federal No Child Left Behind, 2008

(Adequate Yearly Progress standards met)

	Participation Rate	Pct Proficient
ELA	Yes	No
Math	Yes	No

API criteria ... Yes
Graduation rate ... No
\# criteria met/possible ... 38/31

Other school districts for this city

(see Appendix E for information on these districts)

None

See Introduction for an explanation of all data sources.

Demographics & Socio-Economic Characteristics

(2000 Decennial Census, except as noted)

Population

1990* . . . 26,314
2000 . . . 34,609
Male . . . 17,039
Female . . . 17,570
Jan. 2008 (estimate)§ . . . 42,813
Persons per sq. mi. of land . . . 6,204.8

Race & Hispanic Origin, 2000

Race
White . . . 22,324
Black/African American . . . 951
North American Native . . . 485
Asian . . . 1,743
Pacific Islander . . . 130
Other Race . . . 7,061
Two or more races . . . 1,915
Hispanic origin, total . . . 13,115
Mexican . . . 11,185
Puerto Rican . . . 168
Cuban . . . 27
Other Hispanic . . . 1,735

Age & Nativity, 2000

Under 5 years . . . 2,993
18 years and over . . . 22,718
65 years and over . . . 2,812
85 years and over . . . 244
Median Age . . . 29.4
Native-born . . . 27,974
Foreign-born . . . 6,560

Educational Attainment, 2000

Population 25 years and over . . . 19,149
Less than 9th grade . . . 14.2%
High school grad or higher . . . 67.0%
Bachelor's degree or higher . . . 8.3%
Graduate degree . . . 2.5%

Income & Poverty, 1999

Per capita income . . . $14,420
Median household income . . . $40,736
Median family income . . . $43,587
Persons in poverty . . . 12.8%
H'holds receiving public assistance . . . 743
H'holds receiving social security . . . 2,369

Households, 2000

Total households . . . 10,435
With persons under 18 . . . 5,627
With persons over 65 . . . 2,089
Family households . . . 8,532
Single person households . . . 1,467
Persons per household . . . 3.31
Persons per family . . . 3.62

Household Population, 2008§§

Persons living in households . . . 42,714
Persons living in group quarters . . . 99
Persons per household . . . 3.3

Labor & Employment

Total civilian labor force, 2008§§ . . . 18,300
Unemployment rate, 2008 . . . 14.0%
Total civilian labor force, 2000 . . . 15,209

Employed persons 16 years and over by occupation, 2000

Managers & professionals . . . 2,497
Service occupations . . . 2,314
Sales & office occupations . . . 3,423
Farming, fishing & forestry . . . 284
Construction & maintenance . . . 1,613
Production & transportation . . . 2,967
Self-employed persons . . . 1,001

* US Census Bureau
** 2000 Decennial Census
§ California Department of Finance
§§ California Employment Development Dept

General Information

City of Ceres
2720 Second St
Ceres, CA 95307
209-538-5700

Website . . . www.ci.ceres.ca.us
Elevation . . . 90 ft.
Land Area (sq. miles) . . . 6.9
Water Area (sq. miles) . . . 0
Year of Incorporation . . . 1918
Government type . . . General law
Sales tax rate . . . 8.88%

Voters & Officials

Registered Voters, October 2008

Total . . . 17,962
Democrats . . . 8,611
Republicans . . . 5,899
Declined to state . . . 2,729

Legislative Districts

US Congressional . . . 18
State Senatorial . . . 12
State Assembly . . . 26

Local Officials, 2009

Mayor . . . Anthony Cannella
Manager . . . Brad Kilger
City Clerk . . . Cindy Heidorn
Attorney . . . Michael Lyions
Finance Dir . . . Sarah Ragsdale
Public Works . . . Phil Scott
Planning/Dev Dir . . . Kenneth Craig
Building . . . Kenneth Craig
Police Chief . . . Art de Werk
Emergency/Fire Dir . . . Art de Werk

Public Safety

Number of officers, 2007 . . . 46
Violent crimes, 2007 . . . 192
Property crimes, 2007 . . . 2,055
Arson, 2007 . . . NA

Public Library

Ceres Library
Stanislaus County Free Library
2250 Magnolia
Ceres, CA 95307
209-537-8938

Branch Librarian . . . Christopher Dear

Library system statistics, FY 2007

Population served . . . 521,497
Internet terminals . . . 128
Annual users . . . 256,298

Per capita:

Operating income . . . $20.76
percent from local government . . . 91.0%
Operating expenditure . . . $20.19
Total materials . . . 1.66
Print holdings . . . 1.56
Visits per capita . . . NA

Housing & Construction

Housing Units

Total, 2008§ . . . 13,279
Single family units, attached . . . 347
Single family units, detached . . . 10,406
Multiple family units . . . 1,814
Mobile home units . . . 712
Occupied . . . 12,864
Vacancy rate . . . 3.1%
Median rent, 2000** . . . $607
Median SF home value, 2000** . . . $119,900

New Privately Owned Housing Units Authorized by Building Permit, 2007*

	Units	Construction Cost
Single	119	$22,362,708
Total	147	$25,318,941

Municipal Finance

(For local fiscal year ended in 2006)

Revenues

Total . . . $34,861,454
Taxes . . . 16,463,032
Special benefits assessment . . . 1,501,779
Licenses & permits . . . 1,028,155
Fines & forfeitures . . . 517,146
Revenues from use of money & property . . . 1,474,835
Intergovernmental . . . 2,268,393
Service charges . . . 11,258,815
Other revenues . . . 349,299
Other financing sources . . . 0

Expenditures

Total . . . $30,491,001
General government . . . 2,231,573
Public safety . . . 11,780,448
Transportation . . . 6,204,687
Community development . . . 1,157,778
Health . . . 3,658,135
Culture & leisure . . . 2,033,835
Other . . . 0

Local School District

(Data from School year 2007-08 except as noted)

Ceres Unified
PO Box 307
Modesto, CA 95358
(209) 556-1500

Superintendent . . . Walt Hanline
Grade plan . . . K-12
Number of schools . . . 21
Enrollment . . . 12,476
High school graduates, 2006-07 . . . 541
Dropout rate . . . 4.6%
Pupil/teacher ratio . . . 21.8
Average class size . . . 26.9
Students per computer . . . 5.2
Classrooms with internet . . . 650
Avg. Daily Attendance (ADA) . . . 11,687
Cost per ADA . . . $7,408
Avg. Teacher Salary . . . $68,121

California Achievement Tests 6th ed., 2008

(Pct scoring at or above 50th National Percentile Rank)

	Math	Reading	Language
Grade 3	53%	30%	37%
Grade 7	48%	46%	41%

Academic Performance Index, 2008

Number of students tested . . . 9,160
Number of valid scores . . . 8,609
2007 API (base) . . . 721
2008 API (growth) . . . 737

SAT Testing, 2006-07

Enrollment, Grade 12 . . . 689
Number taking test . . . 97
percent taking test . . . 14.1%
percent with total score 1,500+ . . . 6.00%

Average Scores:

Math	Verbal	Writing	Total
486	475	474	1,435

Federal No Child Left Behind, 2008

(Adequate Yearly Progress standards met)

	Participation Rate	Pct Proficient
ELA	Yes	No
Math	Yes	No

API criteria . . . Yes
Graduation rate . . . No
criteria met/possible . . . 34/28

Other school districts for this city

(see Appendix E for information on these districts)

None

See Introduction for an explanation of all data sources.

Demographics & Socio-Economic Characteristics

(2000 Decennial Census, except as noted)

Population

1990* 53,240
2000 51,488
Male 25,056
Female 26,432
Jan. 2008 (estimate)§ 54,870
Persons per sq. mi. of land 6,380.2

Race & Hispanic Origin, 2000

Race
White 13,851
Black/African American 3,432
North American Native 142
Asian 30,091
Pacific Islander 96
Other Race 1,930
Two or more races 1,946
Hispanic origin, total 5,349
Mexican 3,565
Puerto Rican 130
Cuban 169
Other Hispanic 1,485

Age & Nativity, 2000

Under 5 years 2,395
18 years and over 38,878
65 years and over 4,969
85 years and over 334
Median Age 39.3
Native-born 28,052
Foreign-born 23,455

Educational Attainment, 2000

Population 25 years and over 34,351
Less than 9th grade 4.0%
High school grad or higher 90.7%
Bachelor's degree or higher 43.7%
Graduate degree 14.3%

Income & Poverty, 1999

Per capita income $25,249
Median household income $73,030
Median family income $76,944
Persons in poverty 5.0%
H'holds receiving public assistance 397
H'holds receiving social security 2,836

Households, 2000

Total households 15,390
With persons under 18 7,086
With persons over 65 3,649
Family households 13,657
Single person households 1,363
Persons per household 3.34
Persons per family 3.54

Household Population, 2008§§

Persons living in households 54,777
Persons living in group quarters 93
Persons per household 3.5

Labor & Employment

Total civilian labor force, 2008§§ 29,700
Unemployment rate, 2008 .... 4.0%
Total civilian labor force, 2000 25,424

Employed persons 16 years and over by occupation, 2000

Managers & professionals 11,721
Service occupations 2,012
Sales & office occupations 7,638
Farming, fishing & forestry 8
Construction & maintenance 1,100
Production & transportation 1,887
Self-employed persons 2,391

* US Census Bureau
** 2000 Decennial Census
§ California Department of Finance
§§ California Employment Development Dept

General Information

City of Cerritos
PO Box 3130
Cerritos, CA 90703
562-860-0311

Website .... www.ci.cerritos.ca.us
Elevation .... 45 ft.
Land Area (sq. miles) 8.6
Water Area (sq. miles) 0.3
Year of Incorporation 1956
Government type .... Chartered
Sales tax rate 9.25%

Voters & Officials

Registered Voters, October 2008

Total 30,174
Democrats 12,163
Republicans 9,353
Declined to state 7,804

Legislative Districts

US Congressional 39
State Senatorial 27
State Assembly 56

Local Officials, 2009

Mayor .... Jim Edwards
Manager .... Art Gallucci
City Clerk .... Josephine Triggs
Attorney .... Mark Steres
Finance Dir .... Becky Lingad
Public Works .... Hal Arbogast
Planning/Dev Dir .... Torrey Contreras
Building .... Torrey Contreras
Police Chief .... Greg Berg
Fire/Emergency Mgmt .... Greg Berg

Public Safety

Number of officers, 2007 .... NA
Violent crimes, 2007 138
Property crimes, 2007 1,880
Arson, 2007 13

Public Library

Cerritos Public Library
Cerritos Public Library System
18025 Bloomfield Ave
Cerritos, CA 90703
562-916-1350

City Librarian .... Don Buckley

Library system statistics, FY 2007

Population served 54,943
Internet terminals 155
Annual users 312,644

Per capita:

Operating income $101.11
percent from local government 98.8%
Operating expenditure $92.04
Total materials 4.38
Print holdings 4.06
Visits per capita 19.86

Housing & Construction

Housing Units

Total, 2008§ 15,900
Single family units, attached 1,220
Single family units, detached 13,389
Multiple family units 1,259
Mobile home units 32
Occupied 15,680
Vacancy rate 1.4%
Median rent, 2000** $1,260
Median SF home value, 2000** $281,000

New Privately Owned Housing Units Authorized by Building Permit, 2007*

	Units	Construction Cost
Single	8	$3,100,904
Total	8	$3,100,904

Municipal Finance

(For local fiscal year ended in 2006)

Revenues

Total $96,950,096
Taxes 36,683,898
Special benefits assessment 786,884
Licenses & permits 1,005,957
Fines & forfeitures 1,305,866
Revenues from use of money & property 14,541,933
Intergovernmental 2,037,049
Service charges 28,099,885
Other revenues 12,488,624
Other financing sources 0

Expenditures

Total $90,751,883
General government 16,946,172
Public safety 13,543,809
Transportation 12,946,959
Community development 4,490,279
Health 4,792,939
Culture & leisure 22,828,808
Other 0

Local School District

(Data from School year 2007-08 except as noted)

ABC Unified
16700 Norwalk Blvd
Cerritos, CA 90703
(562) 926-5566

Superintendent .... Gary Smuts
Grade plan K-12
Number of schools 30
Enrollment 20,860
High school graduates, 2006-07 1,621
Dropout rate 2.0%
Pupil/teacher ratio 22.6
Average class size 26.8
Students per computer 3.9
Classrooms with internet 1,014
Avg. Daily Attendance (ADA) 20,919
Cost per ADA $8,129
Avg. Teacher Salary $72,259

California Achievement Tests 6th ed., 2008

(Pct scoring at or above 50th National Percentile Rank)

	Math	Reading	Language
Grade 3	62%	42%	54%
Grade 7	60%	55%	55%

Academic Performance Index, 2008

Number of students tested 16,210
Number of valid scores 15,478
2007 API (base) 784
2008 API (growth) 795

SAT Testing, 2006-07

Enrollment, Grade 12 1,827
Number taking test 860
percent taking test 47.1%
percent with total score 1,500+ 31.30%

Average Scores:

Math	Verbal	Writing	Total
589	530	538	1,657

Federal No Child Left Behind, 2008

(Adequate Yearly Progress standards met)

	Participation Rate	Pct Proficient
ELA	Yes	No
Math	Yes	No

API criteria .... Yes
Graduation rate .... Yes
criteria met/possible 42/40

Other school districts for this city

(see Appendix E for information on these districts)

None

See Introduction for an explanation of all data sources.

Demographics & Socio-Economic Characteristics†

(2007 American Community Survey, except as noted)

Population

1990* 40,079
2007 83,460
Male 38,968
Female 44,492
Jan. 2008 (estimate)§ 86,949
Persons per sq. mi. of land 3,139.0

Race & Hispanic Origin, 2007

Race
White 69,389
Black/African American 1,265
North American Native 668
Asian 3,002
Pacific Islander 73
Other Race 3,904
Two or more races 5,159
Hispanic origin, total 10,600
Mexican . . . . . NA
Puerto Rican . . . . . NA
Cuban . . . . . NA
Other Hispanic . . . . . NA

Age & Nativity, 2007

Under 5 years 5,106
18 years and over 68,271
65 years and over 6,870
85 years and over 1,886
Median Age 25.8
Native-born 76,260
Foreign-born 7,200

Educational Attainment, 2007

Population 25 years and over 43,061
Less than 9th grade 3.3%
High school grad or higher 88.4%
Bachelor's degree or higher 35.1%
Graduate degree 11.1%

Income & Poverty, 2007

Per capita income $21,291
Median household income $36,205
Median family income $53,290
Persons in poverty 19.7%
H'holds receiving public assistance . . . 1,590
H'holds receiving social security 6,385

Households, 2007

Total households 32,846
With persons under 18 9,408
With persons over 65 5,298
Family households 16,363
Single person households 10,191
Persons per household 2.46
Persons per family 3.00

Household Population, 2008§§

Persons living in households 82,730
Persons living in group quarters 4,219
Persons per household 2.3

Labor & Employment

Total civilian labor force, 2008§§ 34,200
Unemployment rate, 2008 . . . . . 7.8%
Total civilian labor force, 2000* 30,344

Employed persons 16 years and over by occupation, 2007

Managers & professionals 14,012
Service occupations 8,773
Sales & office occupations 10,865
Farming, fishing & forestry 941
Construction & maintenance 2,488
Production & transportation 3,420
Self-employed persons 2,529

† see Appendix D for 2000 Decennial Census Data
* US Census Bureau
** 2007 American Community Survey
§ California Department of Finance
§§ California Employment Development Dept

General Information

City of Chico
411 Main St
PO Box 3420
Chico, CA 95927
530-896-7200

Website . . . . . www.ci.chico.ca.us
Elevation . . . . . 200 ft.
Land Area (sq. miles) 27.7
Water Area (sq. miles) 0
Year of Incorporation 1872
Government type . . . . . Chartered
Sales tax rate 8.25%

Voters & Officials

Registered Voters, October 2008

Total 47,618
Democrats 19,819
Republicans 15,064
Declined to state 9,702

Legislative Districts

US Congressional 2
State Senatorial 4
State Assembly 3

Local Officials, 2009

Mayor . . . . . Ann Schwab
Manager . . . . . Dave Burkland
City Clerk . . . . . Deborah Presson
Attorney . . . . . Lori Barker
Finance Dir . . . . . Jennifer Hennessy
Public Works . . . . . NA
Planning/Dev Dir . . . . . NA
Building . . . . . NA
Police Chief . . . . . Bruce Hagerty
Emergency/Fire Dir . . . . . Steve Brown

Public Safety

Number of officers, 2007 97
Violent crimes, 2007 385
Property crimes, 2007 2,454
Arson, 2007 58

Public Library

Chico Branch
Butte County Library System
1108 Sherman Ave
Chico, CA 95926
530-891-2723

Branch Librarian . . . . . Susan Rauen

Library system statistics, FY 2007

Population served 218,069
Internet terminals 47
Annual users 90,296

Per capita:

Operating income $12.21
percent from local government 84.5%
Operating expenditure $12.71
Total materials 1.41
Print holdings 1.33
Visits per capita 3.01

Housing & Construction

Housing Units

Total, 2008§ 36,484
Single family units, attached 993
Single family units, detached 19,167
Multiple family units 14,470
Mobile home units 1,854
Occupied 35,265
Vacancy rate 3.3%
Median rent, 2007** $887
Median SF home value, 2007** $330,600

New Privately Owned Housing Units Authorized by Building Permit, 2007*

	Units	Construction Cost
Single	261	$48,986,466
Total	368	$59,245,966

Municipal Finance

(For local fiscal year ended in 2006)

Revenues

Total $74,289,960
Taxes 37,621,980
Special benefits assessment 554,885
Licenses & permits 5,284,550
Fines & forfeitures 915,349
Revenues from use of money & property 1,650,683
Intergovernmental 8,159,870
Service charges 19,011,107
Other revenues 1,091,536
Other financing sources 0

Expenditures

Total $72,197,871
General government 4,161,120
Public safety 31,024,407
Transportation 10,996,793
Community development 10,574,444
Health 11,288,614
Culture & leisure 4,152,493
Other 0

Local School District

(Data from School year 2007-08 except as noted)

Chico Unified
1163 East Seventh St
Chico, CA 95928
(530) 891-3000

Superintendent . . . . . Kelly Staley
Grade plan K-12
Number of schools 26
Enrollment 13,486
High school graduates, 2006-07 921
Dropout rate 3.1%
Pupil/teacher ratio 20.1
Average class size 25.6
Students per computer 3.1
Classrooms with internet 694
Avg. Daily Attendance (ADA) 12,441
Cost per ADA $8,278
Avg. Teacher Salary $61,998

California Achievement Tests 6th ed., 2008

(Pct scoring at or above 50th National Percentile Rank)

	Math	Reading	Language
Grade 3	57%	47%	53%
Grade 7	60%	62%	60%

Academic Performance Index, 2008

Number of students tested 9,843
Number of valid scores 9,489
2007 API (base) 758
2008 API (growth) 770

SAT Testing, 2006-07

Enrollment, Grade 12 1,080
Number taking test 361
percent taking test 33.4%
percent with total score 1,500+ . . . 20.70%

Average Scores:

Math	Verbal	Writing	Total
547	519	505	1,571

Federal No Child Left Behind, 2008

(Adequate Yearly Progress standards met)

	Participation Rate	Pct Proficient
ELA	Yes	No
Math	Yes	No

API criteria . . . . . Yes
Graduation rate . . . . . Yes
\# criteria met/possible 38/32

Other school districts for this city

(see Appendix E for information on these districts)

None

See Introduction for an explanation of all data sources.

Demographics & Socio-Economic Characteristics†

(2007 American Community Survey, except as noted)

Population

1990* 59,682
2007 83,914
Male 43,560
Female 40,354
Jan. 2008 (estimate)§ 82,670
Persons per sq. mi. of land 3,918.0

Race & Hispanic Origin, 2007

Race
White 43,244
Black/African American 6,246
North American Native 512
Asian 2,900
Pacific Islander 35
Other Race 28,736
Two or more races 2,241
Hispanic origin, total 48,735
Mexican 41,059
Puerto Rican 819
Cuban 251
Other Hispanic 6,606

Age & Nativity, 2007

Under 5 years 5,990
18 years and over 64,037
65 years and over 5,176
85 years and over 567
Median Age 29.8
Native-born 66,165
Foreign-born 17,749

Educational Attainment, 2007

Population 25 years and over 52,382
Less than 9th grade 10.9%
High school grad or higher 71.7%
Bachelor's degree or higher 13.2%
Graduate degree 3.4%

Income & Poverty, 2007

Per capita income $21,147
Median household income $70,394
Median family income $73,366
Persons in poverty 1.7%
H'holds receiving public assistance 444
H'holds receiving social security 4,282

Households, 2007

Total households 20,534
With persons under 18 10,612
With persons over 65 3,789
Family households 16,600
Single person households 3,243
Persons per household 3.67
Persons per family 4.09

Household Population, 2008§§

Persons living in households 71,751
Persons living in group quarters 10,919
Persons per household 3.6

Labor & Employment

Total civilian labor force, 2008§§ 35,500
Unemployment rate, 2008 .... 7.1%
Total civilian labor force, 2000* 29,142

Employed persons 16 years and over by occupation, 2007

Managers & professionals 8,167
Service occupations 5,538
Sales & office occupations 11,747
Farming, fishing & forestry 346
Construction & maintenance 5,235
Production & transportation 5,477
Self-employed persons 1,829

† see Appendix D for 2000 Decennial Census Data
* US Census Bureau
** 2007 American Community Survey
§ California Department of Finance
§§ California Employment Development Dept

General Information

City of Chino
PO Box 667
Chino, CA 91708
909-627-7577

Website .... www.cityofchino.org
Elevation .... 720 ft.
Land Area (sq. miles) 21.1
Water Area (sq. miles) 0
Year of Incorporation 1910
Government type .... General law
Sales tax rate 8.75%

Voters & Officials

Registered Voters, October 2008

Total 30,574
Democrats 12,191
Republicans 12,444
Declined to state 4,860

Legislative Districts

US Congressional 42
State Senatorial 29, 32
State Assembly 61

Local Officials, 2009

Mayor .... Dennis Yates
Manager .... Patrick J. Glover
City Clerk .... Lenna J. Tanner
Attorney .... Jimmy Gutierrez
Finance Dir .... David Cain
Public Works .... Jose Alire
Planning/Dev Dir .... Chuck Coe
Building .... Michael Heroux
Police Chief .... Stan Stewart
Emergency/Fire Dir .... Paul Benson

Public Safety

Number of officers, 2007 99
Violent crimes, 2007 232
Property crimes, 2007 2,500
Arson, 2007 14

Public Library

Chino Branch Library
San Bernardino County Library System
13180 Central Ave
Chino, CA 91710
909-465-5280

Branch Librarian .... Jennifer Fukunaga

Library system statistics, FY 2007

Population served 1,177,092
Internet terminals 12
Annual users 45,343

Per capita:

Operating income $14.27
percent from local government 73.3%
Operating expenditure $13.86
Total materials 0.86
Print holdings 0.79
Visits per capita 5.83

Housing & Construction

Housing Units

Total, 2008§ 20,577
Single family units, attached 952
Single family units, detached 14,664
Multiple family units 4,433
Mobile home units 528
Occupied 19,894
Vacancy rate 3.3%
Median rent, 2007** $1,159
Median SF home value, 2007** $521,900

New Privately Owned Housing Units Authorized by Building Permit, 2007*

	Units	Construction Cost
Single	395	$89,005,692
Total	410	$91,718,427

Municipal Finance

(For local fiscal year ended in 2006)

Revenues

Total $101,308,351
Taxes 29,648,456
Special benefits assessment 503,335
Licenses & permits 86,562
Fines & forfeitures 503,942
Revenues from use of money & property 5,791,721
Intergovernmental 6,019,359
Service charges 52,502,623
Other revenues 6,252,353
Other financing sources 0

Expenditures

Total $100,273,320
General government 10,156,049
Public safety 31,769,357
Transportation 9,332,370
Community development 7,274,087
Health 16,790,036
Culture & leisure 8,371,294
Other 0

Local School District

(Data from School year 2007-08 except as noted)

Chino Valley Unified
5130 Riverside Dr
Chino, CA 91710
(909) 628-1201

Superintendent .... Edmond Heatley
Grade plan K-12
Number of schools 36
Enrollment 33,047
High school graduates, 2006-07 2,318
Dropout rate 2.4%
Pupil/teacher ratio 23.3
Average class size 27.6
Students per computer 5.4
Classrooms with internet 1,461
Avg. Daily Attendance (ADA) 32,268
Cost per ADA $7,400
Avg. Teacher Salary $73,141

California Achievement Tests 6th ed., 2008

(Pct scoring at or above 50th National Percentile Rank)

	Math	Reading	Language
Grade 3	68%	43%	56%
Grade 7	65%	59%	58%

Academic Performance Index, 2008

Number of students tested 25,850
Number of valid scores 25,049
2007 API (base) 782
2008 API (growth) 784

SAT Testing, 2006-07

Enrollment, Grade 12 2,589
Number taking test 1,060
percent taking test 40.9%
percent with total score 1,500+ 18.00%

Average Scores:

Math	Verbal	Writing	Total
505	482	479	1,466

Federal No Child Left Behind, 2008

(Adequate Yearly Progress standards met)

	Participation Rate	Pct Proficient
ELA	Yes	No
Math	Yes	No

API criteria .... Yes
Graduation rate .... Yes
criteria met/possible 38/35

Other school districts for this city

(see Appendix E for information on these districts)

None

See Introduction for an explanation of all data sources.

Demographics & Socio-Economic Characteristics†

(2007 American Community Survey, except as noted)

Population

1990*	NA
2007	78,212
Male	37,547
Female	40,665
Jan. 2008 (estimate)§	78,957
Persons per sq. mi. of land	1,762.4

Race & Hispanic Origin, 2007

Race	
White	44,624
Black/African American	2,728
North American Native	187
Asian	18,251
Pacific Islander	92
Other Race	10,370
Two or more races	1,960
Hispanic origin, total	NA
Mexican	NA
Puerto Rican	NA
Cuban	NA
Other Hispanic	NA

Age & Nativity, 2007

Under 5 years	5,237
18 years and over	56,473
65 years and over	4,724
85 years and over	270
Median Age	34.1
Native-born	58,603
Foreign-born	19,609

Educational Attainment, 2007

Population 25 years and over	48,318
Less than 9th grade	3.1%
High school grad or higher	91.1%
Bachelor's degree or higher	42.1%
Graduate degree	11.7%

Income & Poverty, 2007

Per capita income	$32,901
Median household income	$96,733
Median family income	$102,745
Persons in poverty	3.5%
H'holds receiving public assistance	58
H'holds receiving social security	3,395

Households, 2007

Total households	23,957
With persons under 18	10,593
With persons over 65	3,417
Family households	19,729
Single person households	3,597
Persons per household	3.26
Persons per family	3.64

Household Population, 2008§§

Persons living in households	78,806
Persons living in group quarters	151
Persons per household	3.5

Labor & Employment

Total civilian labor force, 2008§§	41,200
Unemployment rate, 2008	3.9%
Total civilian labor force, 2000*	33,661

Employed persons 16 years and over by occupation, 2007

Managers & professionals	19,537
Service occupations	4,645
Sales & office occupations	11,862
Farming, fishing & forestry	0
Construction & maintenance	1,835
Production & transportation	2,294
Self-employed persons	3,162

† see Appendix D for 2000 Decennial Census Data
* US Census Bureau
** 2007 American Community Survey
§ California Department of Finance
§§ California Employment Development Dept

General Information

City of Chino Hills
2001 Grand Ave
Chino Hills, CA 91709
909-364-2600

Website	www.chinohills.org
Elevation	NA
Land Area (sq. miles)	44.8
Water Area (sq. miles)	0.1
Year of Incorporation	1991
Government type	General Law
Sales tax rate	8.75%

Voters & Officials

Registered Voters, October 2008

Total	38,081
Democrats	12,443
Republicans	16,517
Declined to state	7,752

Legislative Districts

US Congressional	42
State Senatorial	29
State Assembly	60

Local Officials, 2009

Mayor	Peter J. Rogers
Manager	Michael S. Fleager
City Clerk	Mary M. McDuffee
Attorney	Mark Hensley
Finance Dir	Judy R. Lancaster
Public Works	John Mura
Planning/Dev Dir	Christine Kelly
Building	Ward Winston
Police Chief	Tom Neeley
Emergency/Fire Dir	Paul Benson

Public Safety

Number of officers, 2007	NA
Violent crimes, 2007	74
Property crimes, 2007	1,111
Arson, 2007	8

Public Library

Chino Hills Library
San Bernardino County Library System
2003 Grand Ave
Chino Hills, CA 91709
909-590-5380

Branch Librarian	Patti Diaz

Library system statistics, FY 2007

Population served	1,177,092
Internet terminals	12
Annual users	45,343

Per capita:

Operating income	$14.27
percent from local government	73.3%
Operating expenditure	$13.86
Total materials	0.86
Print holdings	0.79
Visits per capita	5.83

Housing & Construction

Housing Units

Total, 2008§	22,960
Single family units, attached	1,378
Single family units, detached	18,477
Multiple family units	2,419
Mobile home units	686
Occupied	22,538
Vacancy rate	1.8%
Median rent, 2007**	$1,699
Median SF home value, 2007**	$612,400

New Privately Owned Housing Units Authorized by Building Permit, 2007*

	Units	Construction Cost
Single	26	$5,265,597
Total	26	$5,265,597

Municipal Finance

(For local fiscal year ended in 2006)

Revenues

Total	$85,356,354
Taxes	14,976,127
Special benefits assessment	5,373,288
Licenses & permits	4,119,206
Fines & forfeitures	585,743
Revenues from use of money & property	4,499,869
Intergovernmental	6,841,816
Service charges	33,449,106
Other revenues	15,511,199
Other financing sources	0

Expenditures

Total	$78,795,967
General government	18,139,551
Public safety	7,830,314
Transportation	17,562,112
Community development	6,684,548
Health	7,043,334
Culture & leisure	8,136,062
Other	0

Local School District

(Data from School year 2007-08 except as noted)

Chino Valley Unified
5130 Riverside Dr
Chino, CA 91710
(909) 628-1201

Superintendent	Edmond Heatley
Grade plan	K-12
Number of schools	36
Enrollment	33,047
High school graduates, 2006-07	2,318
Dropout rate	2.4%
Pupil/teacher ratio	23.3
Average class size	27.6
Students per computer	5.4
Classrooms with internet	1,461
Avg. Daily Attendance (ADA)	32,268
Cost per ADA	$7,400
Avg. Teacher Salary	$73,141

California Achievement Tests 6th ed., 2008

(Pct scoring at or above 50th National Percentile Rank)

	Math	Reading	Language
Grade 3	68%	43%	56%
Grade 7	65%	59%	58%

Academic Performance Index, 2008

Number of students tested	25,850
Number of valid scores	25,049
2007 API (base)	782
2008 API (growth)	784

SAT Testing, 2006-07

Enrollment, Grade 12	2,589
Number taking test	1,060
percent taking test	40.9%
percent with total score 1,500+	18.00%

Average Scores:

Math	Verbal	Writing	Total
505	482	479	1,466

Federal No Child Left Behind, 2008

(Adequate Yearly Progress standards met)

	Participation Rate	Pct Proficient
ELA	Yes	No
Math	Yes	No

API criteria	Yes
Graduation rate	Yes
# criteria met/possible	38/35

Other school districts for this city

(see Appendix E for information on these districts)

None

See Introduction for an explanation of all data sources.

Demographics & Socio-Economic Characteristics

(2000 Decennial Census, except as noted)

Population

1990* 5,930
2000 11,127
Male 3,763
Female 7,364
Jan. 2008 (estimate)§ 18,780
Persons per sq. mi. of land 2,645.1

Race & Hispanic Origin, 2000

Race
White 7,061
Black/African American 1,142
North American Native 289
Asian 147
Pacific Islander 29
Other Race 1,798
Two or more races 661
Hispanic origin, total 3,138
Mexican 2,558
Puerto Rican 80
Cuban 14
Other Hispanic 486

Age & Nativity, 2000

Under 5 years 692
18 years and over 8,653
65 years and over 1,039
85 years and over 138
Median Age 34.1
Native-born 9,927
Foreign-born 1,240

Educational Attainment, 2000

Population 25 years and over 7,602
Less than 9th grade 12.5%
High school grad or higher 60.8%
Bachelor's degree or higher 6.3%
Graduate degree 2.0%

Income & Poverty, 1999

Per capita income $11,927
Median household income $30,729
Median family income $35,741
Persons in poverty 13.0%
H'holds receiving public assistance 230
H'holds receiving social security 873

Households, 2000

Total households 2,562
With persons under 18 1,156
With persons over 65 719
Family households 1,909
Single person households 562
Persons per household 2.94
Persons per family 3.42

Household Population, 2008§§

Persons living in households 10,776
Persons living in group quarters 8,004
Persons per household 2.9

Labor & Employment

Total civilian labor force, 2008§§ 4,200
Unemployment rate, 2008 . . . . . 10.6%
Total civilian labor force, 2000 3,072

Employed persons 16 years and over by occupation, 2000

Managers & professionals 544
Service occupations 434
Sales & office occupations 671
Farming, fishing & forestry 208
Construction & maintenance 273
Production & transportation 484
Self-employed persons 240

* US Census Bureau
** 2000 Decennial Census
§ California Department of Finance
§§ California Employment Development Dept

General Information

City of Chowchilla
130 S Second St
Chowchilla, CA 93610
559-665-8615

Website . . . . . www.ci.chowchilla.ca.us
Elevation . . . . . 240 ft.
Land Area (sq. miles) 7.1
Water Area (sq. miles) 0
Year of Incorporation 1923
Government type . . . . . General law
Sales tax rate 8.75%

Voters & Officials

Registered Voters, October 2008

Total 3,817
Democrats 1,316
Republicans 1,769
Declined to state 563

Legislative Districts

US Congressional 19
State Senatorial 14
State Assembly 25

Local Officials, 2009

Mayor . . . . . Justin White
Manager . . . . . Nancy Red
City Clerk . . . . . Nancy Red
Attorney . . . . . Neal Costanzo
Finance Dir . . . . . Connie Wright
Public Works . . . . . (vacant)
Community Dir . . . . . Angel Johnstone
Building . . . . . NA
Police Chief . . . . . Jay Varney
Fire Chief . . . . . Harry Turner

Public Safety

Number of officers, 2007 19
Violent crimes, 2007 21
Property crimes, 2007 324
Arson, 2007 3

Public Library

Chowchilla Branch Library
Madera County Library System
300 Kings Ave
Chowchilla, CA 93610
559-665-2630

Branch Librarian . . . . . Karen Esteves

Library system statistics, FY 2007

Population served 148,721
Internet terminals 26
Annual users 43,295

Per capita:

Operating income $10.35
percent from local government 95.5%
Operating expenditure $9.22
Total materials 1.88
Print holdings 1.79
Visits per capita 1.97

Housing & Construction

Housing Units

Total, 2008§ 3,884
Single family units, attached 31
Single family units, detached 3,144
Multiple family units 673
Mobile home units 36
Occupied 3,669
Vacancy rate 5.5%
Median rent, 2000** $545
Median SF home value, 2000** $83,800

New Privately Owned Housing Units Authorized by Building Permit, 2007*

	Units	Construction Cost
Single	58	$11,559,044
Total	58	$11,559,044

Municipal Finance

(For local fiscal year ended in 2006)

Revenues

Total $16,243,297
Taxes 6,771,856
Special benefits assessment 175,861
Licenses & permits 8,049
Fines & forfeitures 102,836
Revenues from use of money & property 455,729
Intergovernmental 3,437,718
Service charges 5,092,832
Other revenues 198,416
Other financing sources 0

Expenditures

Total $17,590,364
General government 890,066
Public safety 2,586,718
Transportation 2,632,889
Community development 6,306,298
Health 2,535,491
Culture & leisure 1,135,211
Other 0

Local School District

(Data from School year 2007-08 except as noted)

Chowchilla Union High
805 Humboldt Ave
Chowchilla, CA 93610
(559) 665-3662

Superintendent . . . . . Ronald Seals
Grade plan 9-12
Number of schools 2
Enrollment 996
High school graduates, 2006-07 169
Dropout rate 3.3%
Pupil/teacher ratio 21.2
Average class size 25.8
Students per computer 4.0
Classrooms with internet 47
Avg. Daily Attendance (ADA) 960
Cost per ADA $8,086
Avg. Teacher Salary $54,226

California Achievement Tests 6th ed., 2008

(Pct scoring at or above 50th National Percentile Rank)

	Math	Reading	Language
Grade 3	NA	NA	NA
Grade 7	NA	NA	NA

Academic Performance Index, 2008

Number of students tested 734
Number of valid scores 669
2007 API (base) 684
2008 API (growth) 671

SAT Testing, 2006-07

Enrollment, Grade 12 197
Number taking test 56
percent taking test 28.4%
percent with total score 1,500+ 10.20%

Average Scores:

Math	Verbal	Writing	Total
485	450	452	1,387

Federal No Child Left Behind, 2008

(Adequate Yearly Progress standards met)

	Participation Rate	Pct Proficient
ELA	Yes	No
Math	Yes	No

API criteria . . . . . Yes
Graduation rate . . . . . Yes
\# criteria met/possible 22/17

Other school districts for this city

(see Appendix E for information on these districts)

Alview-Dairyland Union Elem, Chowchilla Elem

See Introduction for an explanation of all data sources.

Demographics & Socio-Economic Characteristics†

(2007 American Community Survey, except as noted)

Population

1990* . . . 135,163
2007 . . . 227,336
Male . . . 110,467
Female . . . 116,869
Jan. 2008 (estimate)§ . . . 231,305
Persons per sq. mi. of land . . . 4,730.2

Race & Hispanic Origin, 2007

Race
White . . . 118,802
Black/African American . . . 7,731
North American Native . . . 1,148
Asian . . . 37,534
Pacific Islander . . . 2,294
Other Race . . . 48,187
Two or more races . . . 11,640
Hispanic origin, total . . . 124,396
Mexican . . . 113,619
Puerto Rican . . . 1,905
Cuban . . . 647
Other Hispanic . . . 8,225

Age & Nativity, 2007

Under 5 years . . . 16,983
18 years and over . . . 162,812
65 years and over . . . 25,660
85 years and over . . . 3,386
Median Age . . . 34.3
Native-born . . . 152,746
Foreign-born . . . 74,590

Educational Attainment, 2007

Population 25 years and over . . . 141,234
Less than 9th grade . . . 9.8%
High school grad or higher . . . 79.6%
Bachelor's degree or higher . . . 25.4%
Graduate degree . . . 7.0%

Income & Poverty, 2007

Per capita income . . . $23,916
Median household income . . . $60,986
Median family income . . . $67,766
Persons in poverty . . . 9.1%
H'holds receiving public assistance . . . 1,511
H'holds receiving social security . . . 16,385

Households, 2007

Total households . . . 72,294
With persons under 18 . . . 32,667
With persons over 65 . . . 16,883
Family households . . . 56,268
Single person households . . . 12,598
Persons per household . . . 3.10
Persons per family . . . 3.53

Household Population, 2008§§

Persons living in households . . . 229,866
Persons living in group quarters . . . 1,439
Persons per household . . . 3.1

Labor & Employment

Total civilian labor force, 2008§§ . . . 91,500
Unemployment rate, 2008 . . . 7.0%
Total civilian labor force, 2000* . . . 76,065

Employed persons 16 years and over by occupation, 2007

Managers & professionals . . . 32,666
Service occupations . . . 13,440
Sales & office occupations . . . 31,963
Farming, fishing & forestry . . . 587
Construction & maintenance . . . 9,606
Production & transportation . . . 11,879
Self-employed persons . . . 8,508

† see Appendix D for 2000 Decennial Census Data
* US Census Bureau
** 2007 American Community Survey
§ California Department of Finance
§§ California Employment Development Dept

General Information

City of Chula Vista
276 Fourth Ave
Chula Vista, CA 91910
619-691-5031

Website . . . www.chulavistaca.gov
Elevation . . . 75 ft.
Land Area (sq. miles) . . . 48.9
Water Area (sq. miles) . . . 2.4
Year of Incorporation . . . 1911
Government type . . . Chartered
Sales tax rate . . . 8.75%

Voters & Officials

Registered Voters, October 2008

Total . . . 106,079
Democrats . . . 45,111
Republicans . . . 33,377
Declined to state . . . 23,919

Legislative Districts

US Congressional . . . 51
State Senatorial . . . 40
State Assembly . . . 78, 79

Local Officials, 2009

Mayor . . . Cheryl Cox
Manager . . . James D. Sandoval
City Clerk . . . Donna Norris
Attorney . . . Bart Miesfeld
Finance Dir . . . Maria Kachadoorian
Public Works . . . Richard Hopkins
Planning/Dev Dir . . . NA
Building . . . NA
Police Chief . . . Richard Emerson
Emergency/Fire Dir . . . David Hanneman

Public Safety

Number of officers, 2007 . . . 255
Violent crimes, 2007 . . . 921
Property crimes, 2007 . . . 7,279
Arson, 2007 . . . 28

Public Library

Chula Vista Civic Center Library
Chula Vista Public Library System
365 F Street
Chula Vista, CA 91910
619-691-5069

Director . . . Leah Browder (Int)

Library system statistics, FY 2007

Population served . . . 227,723
Internet terminals . . . 108
Annual users . . . 50,139

Per capita:

Operating income . . . $35.93
percent from local government . . . 86.5%
Operating expenditure . . . $31.96
Total materials . . . 2.03
Print holdings . . . 1.87
Visits per capita . . . 5.04

Housing & Construction

Housing Units

Total, 2008§ . . . 77,593
Single family units, attached . . . 5,494
Single family units, detached . . . 42,120
Multiple family units . . . 26,417
Mobile home units . . . 3,562
Occupied . . . 75,259
Vacancy rate . . . 3.0%
Median rent, 2007** . . . $1,092
Median SF home value, 2007** . . . $569,000

New Privately Owned Housing Units Authorized by Building Permit, 2007*

	Units	Construction Cost
Single	312	$72,151,182
Total	576	$109,294,407

Municipal Finance

(For local fiscal year ended in 2006)

Revenues

Total . . . $261,771,004
Taxes . . . 135,806,164
Special benefits assessment . . . 6,239,544
Licenses & permits . . . 3,407,530
Fines & forfeitures . . . 1,515,968
Revenues from use of money & property . . . 5,718,693
Intergovernmental . . . 23,754,911
Service charges . . . 57,204,369
Other revenues . . . 10,939,861
Other financing sources . . . 17,183,964

Expenditures

Total . . . $266,617,990
General government . . . 39,742,721
Public safety . . . 75,281,728
Transportation . . . 33,083,997
Community development . . . 32,042,776
Health . . . 24,852,570
Culture & leisure . . . 61,614,198
Other . . . 0

Local School District

(Data from School year 2007-08 except as noted)

Sweetwater Union High
1130 Fifth Ave
Chula Vista, CA 91911
(619) 691-5500

Superintendent . . . Jesus Gandara
Grade plan . . . 7-12
Number of schools . . . 31
Enrollment . . . 42,591
High school graduates, 2006-07 . . . 5,510
Dropout rate . . . 2.9%
Pupil/teacher ratio . . . 22.5
Average class size . . . 26.7
Students per computer . . . 4.9
Classrooms with internet . . . 2,349
Avg. Daily Attendance (ADA) . . . 41,210
Cost per ADA . . . $8,570
Avg. Teacher Salary . . . $71,623

California Achievement Tests 6th ed., 2008

(Pct scoring at or above 50th National Percentile Rank)

	Math	Reading	Language
Grade 3	NA	NA	NA
Grade 7	52%	47%	44%

Academic Performance Index, 2008

Number of students tested . . . 33,960
Number of valid scores . . . 30,640
2007 API (base) . . . 698
2008 API (growth) . . . 715

SAT Testing, 2006-07

Enrollment, Grade 12 . . . 7,523
Number taking test . . . 2,357
percent taking test . . . 31.3%
percent with total score 1,500+ . . . 9.50%

Average Scores:

Math	Verbal	Writing	Total
469	458	450	1,377

Federal No Child Left Behind, 2008

(Adequate Yearly Progress standards met)

	Participation Rate	Pct Proficient
ELA	Yes	No
Math	Yes	No

API criteria . . . Yes
Graduation rate . . . Yes
\# criteria met/possible . . . 42/39

Other school districts for this city

(see Appendix E for information on these districts)

Chula Vista Elem

See Introduction for an explanation of all data sources.

Demographics & Socio-Economic Characteristics†

(2007 American Community Survey, except as noted)

Population

1990*	NA
2007	88,576
Male	43,564
Female	45,012
Jan. 2008 (estimate)§	87,321
Persons per sq. mi. of land	6,106.4

Race & Hispanic Origin, 2007

Race	
White	74,049
Black/African American	3,166
North American Native	225
Asian	3,371
Pacific Islander	116
Other Race	6,043
Two or more races	1,606
Hispanic origin, total	11,004
Mexican	6,426
Puerto Rican	473
Cuban	0
Other Hispanic	4,105

Age & Nativity, 2007

Under 5 years	4,669
18 years and over	68,192
65 years and over	13,293
85 years and over	2,288
Median Age	36.8
Native-born	75,073
Foreign-born	13,503

Educational Attainment, 2007

Population 25 years and over	59,020
Less than 9th grade	5.3%
High school grad or higher	89.0%
Bachelor's degree or higher	15.7%
Graduate degree	3.4%

Income & Poverty, 2007

Per capita income	$24,180
Median household income	$51,200
Median family income	$56,101
Persons in poverty	10.5%
H'holds receiving public assistance	1,111
H'holds receiving social security	9,365

Households, 2007

Total households	35,199
With persons under 18	11,512
With persons over 65	8,708
Family households	23,166
Single person households	9,339
Persons per household	2.51
Persons per family	2.95

Household Population, 2008§§

Persons living in households	86,444
Persons living in group quarters	877
Persons per household	2.5

Labor & Employment

Total civilian labor force, 2008§§	51,800
Unemployment rate, 2008	5.0%
Total civilian labor force, 2000*	43,843

Employed persons 16 years and over by occupation, 2007

Managers & professionals	12,502
Service occupations	7,764
Sales & office occupations	13,621
Farming, fishing & forestry	210
Construction & maintenance	6,043
Production & transportation	3,409
Self-employed persons	2,434

† see Appendix D for 2000 Decennial Census Data
* US Census Bureau
** 2007 American Community Survey
§ California Department of Finance
§§ California Employment Development Dept

General Information

City of Citrus Heights
6237 Fountain Square Dr
Citrus Heights, CA 95621
916-725-2448

Website	www.citrusheights.net
Elevation	NA
Land Area (sq. miles)	14.3
Water Area (sq. miles)	0
Year of Incorporation	1997
Government type	General law
Sales tax rate	8.75%

Voters & Officials

Registered Voters, October 2008

Total	43,300
Democrats	15,522
Republicans	17,661
Declined to state	8,021

Legislative Districts

US Congressional	3
State Senatorial	6
State Assembly	5

Local Officials, 2009

Mayor	James Shelby
Manager	Henry Tingle
City Clerk	Amy Van
Attorney	Ruthann Ziegler
Finance Dir	Stefani Daniell
Public Works	David Wheaton
Planning/Dev Dir	Rhonda Sherman
Building	Jim Green
Police Chief	Chris Boyd
Fire/Emergency Mgmt	NA

Public Safety

Number of officers, 2007	NA
Violent crimes, 2007	NA
Property crimes, 2007	NA
Arson, 2007	NA

Public Library

Sylvan Oaks Library
Sacramento Public Library System
6700 Auburn Blvd
Citrus Heights, CA 95621
916-264-2770

Branch Manager	Rosemary Lovely

Library system statistics, FY 2007

Population served	1,335,969
Internet terminals	49
Annual users	27,435

Per capita:

Operating income	$25.83
percent from local government	91.0%
Operating expenditure	$23.08
Total materials	1.57
Print holdings	1.45
Visits per capita	1.18

Housing & Construction

Housing Units

Total, 2008§	35,675
Single family units, attached	3,531
Single family units, detached	19,880
Multiple family units	10,384
Mobile home units	1,880
Occupied	34,226
Vacancy rate	4.1%
Median rent, 2007**	$959
Median SF home value, 2007**	$332,300

New Privately Owned Housing Units Authorized by Building Permit, 2007*

	Units	Construction Cost
Single	42	$9,684,155
Total	46	$9,979,341

Municipal Finance

(For local fiscal year ended in 2006)

Revenues

Total	$54,117,331
Taxes	32,690,672
Special benefits assessment	186,806
Licenses & permits	763,030
Fines & forfeitures	392,443
Revenues from use of money & property	2,702,911
Intergovernmental	15,548,361
Service charges	1,652,158
Other revenues	180,950
Other financing sources	0

Expenditures

Total	$58,969,441
General government	3,913,739
Public safety	23,425,745
Transportation	21,453,316
Community development	9,438,319
Health	286,750
Culture & leisure	334,557
Other	0

Local School District

(Data from School year 2007-08 except as noted)

San Juan Unified
PO Box 477
Carmichael, CA 95609
(916) 971-7700

Superintendent	Pat Jaurequi
Grade plan	K-12
Number of schools	77
Enrollment	47,400
High school graduates, 2006-07	3,761
Dropout rate	8.0%
Pupil/teacher ratio	21.2
Average class size	22.6
Students per computer	3.1
Classrooms with internet	2,091
Avg. Daily Attendance (ADA)	42,550
Cost per ADA	$8,163
Avg. Teacher Salary	$69,097

California Achievement Tests 6th ed., 2008

(Pct scoring at or above 50th National Percentile Rank)

	Math	Reading	Language
Grade 3	63%	49%	55%
Grade 7	61%	58%	55%

Academic Performance Index, 2008

Number of students tested	34,531
Number of valid scores	31,698
2007 API (base)	767
2008 API (growth)	777

SAT Testing, 2006-07

Enrollment, Grade 12	4,509
Number taking test	1,443
percent taking test	32.0%
percent with total score 1,500+	20.10%

Average Scores:

Math	Verbal	Writing	Total
545	531	526	1,602

Federal No Child Left Behind, 2008

(Adequate Yearly Progress standards met)

	Participation Rate	Pct Proficient
ELA	Yes	No
Math	Yes	No

API criteria	Yes
Graduation rate	No
# criteria met/possible	46/42

Other school districts for this city

(see Appendix E for information on these districts)

None

See Introduction for an explanation of all data sources.

Demographics & Socio-Economic Characteristics

(2000 Decennial Census, except as noted)

Population

1990* ... 32,503
2000 ... 33,998
Male ... 15,969
Female ... 18,029
Jan. 2008 (estimate)§ ... 37,242
Persons per sq. mi. of land ... 2,842.9

Race & Hispanic Origin, 2000

Race
White ... 24,983
Black/African American ... 1,692
North American Native ... 189
Asian ... 3,912
Pacific Islander ... 45
Other Race ... 1,769
Two or more races ... 1,408
Hispanic origin, total ... 5,221
Mexican ... 3,624
Puerto Rican ... 140
Cuban ... 149
Other Hispanic ... 1,308

Age & Nativity, 2000

Under 5 years ... 1,474
18 years and over ... 26,967
65 years and over ... 4,966
85 years and over ... 690
Median Age ... 35.8
Native-born ... 28,600
Foreign-born ... 5,378

Educational Attainment, 2000

Population 25 years and over ... 20,829
Less than 9th grade ... 2.7%
High school grad or higher ... 92.4%
Bachelor's degree or higher ... 52.4%
Graduate degree ... 28.3%

Income & Poverty, 1999

Per capita income ... $28,843
Median household income ... $65,910
Median family income ... $78,389
Persons in poverty ... 6.8%
H'holds receiving public assistance ... 261
H'holds receiving social security ... 3,194

Households, 2000

Total households ... 11,281
With persons under 18 ... 3,824
With persons over 65 ... 3,278
Family households ... 7,810
Single person households ... 2,810
Persons per household ... 2.56
Persons per family ... 3.08

Household Population, 2008§§

Persons living in households ... 31,800
Persons living in group quarters ... 5,442
Persons per household ... 2.7

Labor & Employment

Total civilian labor force, 2008§§ ... 16,900
Unemployment rate, 2008 ... 3.9%
Total civilian labor force, 2000 ... 17,564

Employed persons 16 years and over by occupation, 2000

Managers & professionals ... 9,207
Service occupations ... 1,668
Sales & office occupations ... 3,542
Farming, fishing & forestry ... 11
Construction & maintenance ... 776
Production & transportation ... 842
Self-employed persons ... 1,338

* US Census Bureau
** 2000 Decennial Census
§ California Department of Finance
§§ California Employment Development Dept

General Information

City of Claremont
PO Box 880
Claremont, CA 91711
909-399-5460

Website ... www.ci.claremont.ca.us
Elevation ... 1,169 ft.
Land Area (sq. miles) ... 13.1
Water Area (sq. miles) ... 0.3
Year of Incorporation ... 1907
Government type ... General law
Sales tax rate ... 9.25%

Voters & Officials

Registered Voters, October 2008

Total ... 21,669
Democrats ... 9,674
Republicans ... 7,113
Declined to state ... 3,963

Legislative Districts

US Congressional ... 26
State Senatorial ... 29
State Assembly ... 59

Local Officials, 2009

Mayor ... Corey Calaycay
Manager ... Jeffrey Parker
City Clerk ... Lynne Fryman
Attorney ... Sonia Carvalho
Finance Dir ... Adam Pirrie (Int)
Public Works ... Craig Bradshaw
Community Dev Dir ... Tony Witt
Building ... Jeff Baughman
Police Chief ... Paul Cooper
Fire/Emergency Mgmt ... NA

Public Safety

Number of officers, 2007 ... 42
Violent crimes, 2007 ... 87
Property crimes, 2007 ... 975
Arson, 2007 ... 9

Public Library

Claremont Library
Los Angeles County Public Library System
208 N Harvard Ave
Claremont, CA 91711
909-621-4902

Branch Librarian ... Don Slaven

Library system statistics, FY 2007

Population served ... 3,673,313
Internet terminals ... 749
Annual users ... 3,748,771

Per capita:

Operating income ... $30.06
percent from local government ... 93.6%
Operating expenditure ... $28.36
Total materials ... 2.22
Print holdings ... 1.97
Visits per capita ... 3.25

Housing & Construction

Housing Units

Total, 2008§ ... 12,139
Single family units, attached ... 919
Single family units, detached ... 8,463
Multiple family units ... 2,744
Mobile home units ... 13
Occupied ... 11,847
Vacancy rate ... 2.4%
Median rent, 2000** ... $771
Median SF home value, 2000** ... $251,000

New Privately Owned Housing Units Authorized by Building Permit, 2007*

	Units	Construction Cost
Single	43	$16,265,181
Total	273	$28,074,563

Municipal Finance

(For local fiscal year ended in 2006)

Revenues

Total ... $44,643,791
Taxes ... 17,143,916
Special benefits assessment ... 1,826,665
Licenses & permits ... 940,867
Fines & forfeitures ... 596,138
Revenues from use of money & property ... 639,115
Intergovernmental ... 3,434,865
Service charges ... 9,587,984
Other revenues ... 4,414,241
Other financing sources ... 6,060,000

Expenditures

Total ... $46,683,733
General government ... 3,349,112
Public safety ... 15,436,989
Transportation ... 4,855,202
Community development ... 2,881,825
Health ... 5,386,349
Culture & leisure ... 3,817,124
Other ... 10,957,132

Local School District

(Data from School year 2007-08 except as noted)

Claremont Unified
170 West San Jose Ave
Claremont, CA 91711
(909) 398-0609

Superintendent ... David Cash
Grade plan ... K-12
Number of schools ... 12
Enrollment ... 6,968
High school graduates, 2006-07 ... 540
Dropout rate ... 1.7%
Pupil/teacher ratio ... 16.7
Average class size ... 28.5
Students per computer ... 4.4
Classrooms with internet ... 297
Avg. Daily Attendance (ADA) ... 6,851
Cost per ADA ... $7,865
Avg. Teacher Salary ... $67,923

California Achievement Tests 6th ed., 2008

(Pct scoring at or above 50th National Percentile Rank)

	Math	Reading	Language
Grade 3	69%	58%	65%
Grade 7	68%	73%	64%

Academic Performance Index, 2008

Number of students tested ... 5,364
Number of valid scores ... 5,098
2007 API (base) ... 809
2008 API (growth) ... 818

SAT Testing, 2006-07

Enrollment, Grade 12 ... 544
Number taking test ... 385
percent taking test ... 70.8%
percent with total score 1,500+ ... 42.80%

Average Scores:

Math	Verbal	Writing	Total
536	523	524	1,583

Federal No Child Left Behind, 2008

(Adequate Yearly Progress standards met)

	Participation Rate	Pct Proficient
ELA	Yes	Yes
Math	Yes	Yes

API criteria ... Yes
Graduation rate ... Yes
\# criteria met/possible ... 34/34

Other school districts for this city

(see Appendix E for information on these districts)

None

See Introduction for an explanation of all data sources.

Demographics & Socio-Economic Characteristics

(2000 Decennial Census, except as noted)

Population

1990* 7,317
2000 10,762
Male 5,270
Female 5,492
Jan. 2008 (estimate)§ 10,784
Persons per sq. mi. of land 2,765.1

Race & Hispanic Origin, 2000

Race
White 9,465
Black/African American 120
North American Native 20
Asian 579
Pacific Islander 11
Other Race 166
Two or more races 401
Hispanic origin, total 681
Mexican 381
Puerto Rican 23
Cuban 15
Other Hispanic 262

Age & Nativity, 2000

Under 5 years 749
18 years and over 7,911
65 years and over 974
85 years and over 66
Median Age 40.2
Native-born 9,905
Foreign-born 887

Educational Attainment, 2000

Population 25 years and over 7,440
Less than 9th grade 0.8%
High school grad or higher 97.5%
Bachelor's degree or higher 51.8%
Graduate degree 15.5%

Income & Poverty, 1999

Per capita income $42,048
Median household income $101,651
Median family income $107,448
Persons in poverty 2.6%
H'holds receiving public assistance 47
H'holds receiving social security 721

Households, 2000

Total households 3,883
With persons under 18 1,577
With persons over 65 686
Family households 3,208
Single person households 506
Persons per household 2.76
Persons per family 3.04

Household Population, 2008§§

Persons living in households 10,758
Persons living in group quarters 26
Persons per household 2.7

Labor & Employment

Total civilian labor force, 2008§§ 6,500
Unemployment rate, 2008 .... 1.3%
Total civilian labor force, 2000 5,871

Employed persons 16 years and over by occupation, 2000

Managers & professionals 3,169
Service occupations 539
Sales & office occupations 1,571
Farming, fishing & forestry 0
Construction & maintenance 267
Production & transportation 269
Self-employed persons 574

* US Census Bureau
** 2000 Decennial Census
§ California Department of Finance
§§ California Employment Development Dept

General Information

City of Clayton
6000 Heritage Trail
Clayton, CA 94517
925-673-7300

Website .... www.ci.clayton.ca.us
Elevation .... 394 ft.
Land Area (sq. miles) 3.9
Water Area (sq. miles) 0
Year of Incorporation 1964
Government type .... General law
Sales tax rate 9.25%

Voters & Officials

Registered Voters, October 2008

Total 7,358
Democrats 2,825
Republicans 3,023
Declined to state 1,245

Legislative Districts

US Congressional 7
State Senatorial 7
State Assembly 11

Local Officials, 2009

Mayor .... Julie K Pierce
Manager .... Gary Napper
City Clerk .... Laci Jackson
Attorney .... J. Daniel Adams
Finance Dir .... Merry Pelletier
Public Works .... NA
Planning/Dev Dir .... David Woltering
Building .... NA
Police Chief .... Dan Lawrence
Fire/Emergency Mgmt .... NA

Public Safety

Number of officers, 2007 10
Violent crimes, 2007 9
Property crimes, 2007 165
Arson, 2007 0

Public Library

Clayton Community Library
Contra Costa County Library System
6125 Clayton Rd
Clayton, CA 94517
925-673-0659

Branch Librarian .... Karen Hansen-Smith

Library system statistics, FY 2007

Population served 938,513
Internet terminals 324
Annual users 670,618

Per capita:

Operating income $27.05
percent from local government 82.0%
Operating expenditure $27.82
Total materials 1.57
Print holdings 1.41
Visits per capita 3.65

Housing & Construction

Housing Units

Total, 2008§ 3,995
Single family units, attached 681
Single family units, detached 3,263
Multiple family units 46
Mobile home units 5
Occupied 3,954
Vacancy rate 1.0%
Median rent, 2000** $1,516
Median SF home value, 2000** $358,700

New Privately Owned Housing Units Authorized by Building Permit, 2007*

	Units	Construction Cost
Single	NA	NA
Total	NA	NA

Municipal Finance

(For local fiscal year ended in 2006)

Revenues

Total $7,606,791
Taxes 2,264,636
Special benefits assessment 850,183
Licenses & permits 71,280
Fines & forfeitures 54,103
Revenues from use of money & property 383,456
Intergovernmental 1,302,889
Service charges 239,708
Other revenues 2,440,536
Other financing sources 0

Expenditures

Total $5,067,105
General government 1,359,700
Public safety 1,768,152
Transportation 1,411,119
Community development 352,962
Health 0
Culture & leisure 175,172
Other 0

Local School District

(Data from School year 2007-08 except as noted)

Mt. Diablo Unified
1936 Carlotta Dr
Concord, CA 94519
(925) 682-8000

Superintendent .... Richard Nicholl
Grade plan K-12
Number of schools 55
Enrollment 35,355
High school graduates, 2006-07 2,153
Dropout rate 6.0%
Pupil/teacher ratio 20.4
Average class size 26.4
Students per computer 5.2
Classrooms with internet 1,777
Avg. Daily Attendance (ADA) 33,956
Cost per ADA $8,368
Avg. Teacher Salary $60,714

California Achievement Tests 6th ed., 2008

(Pct scoring at or above 50th National Percentile Rank)

	Math	Reading	Language
Grade 3	60%	45%	55%
Grade 7	53%	53%	51%

Academic Performance Index, 2008

Number of students tested 26,357
Number of valid scores 25,920
2007 API (base) 747
2008 API (growth) 755

SAT Testing, 2006-07

Enrollment, Grade 12 2,734
Number taking test 1,063
percent taking test 38.9%
percent with total score 1,500+ 22.80%

Average Scores:

Math	Verbal	Writing	Total
543	521	518	1,582

Federal No Child Left Behind, 2008

(Adequate Yearly Progress standards met)

	Participation Rate	Pct Proficient
ELA	Yes	No
Math	Yes	No

API criteria .... Yes
Graduation rate .... Yes
criteria met/possible 46/36

Other school districts for this city

(see Appendix E for information on these districts)

None

See Introduction for an explanation of all data sources.

Demographics & Socio-Economic Characteristics

(2000 Decennial Census, except as noted)

Population

1990* . . . 11,804
2000 . . . 13,142
Male . . . 6,293
Female . . . 6,849
Jan. 2008 (estimate)§ . . . 14,247
Persons per sq. mi. of land . . . 1,396.8

Race & Hispanic Origin, 2000

Race
White . . . 10,823
Black/African American . . . 684
North American Native . . . 354
Asian . . . 149
Pacific Islander . . . 21
Other Race . . . 480
Two or more races . . . 631
Hispanic origin, total . . . 1,449
Mexican . . . 1,080
Puerto Rican . . . 32
Cuban . . . 10
Other Hispanic . . . 327

Age & Nativity, 2000

Under 5 years . . . 817
18 years and over . . . 9,755
65 years and over . . . 2,674
85 years and over . . . 314
Median Age . . . 41.1
Native-born . . . 12,244
Foreign-born . . . 929

Educational Attainment, 2000

Population 25 years and over . . . 8,885
Less than 9th grade . . . 8.0%
High school grad or higher . . . 67.8%
Bachelor's degree or higher . . . 5.1%
Graduate degree . . . 2.0%

Income & Poverty, 1999

Per capita income . . . $12,538
Median household income . . . $19,863
Median family income . . . $25,504
Persons in poverty . . . 28.2%
H'holds receiving public assistance . . . 860
H'holds receiving social security . . . 2,504

Households, 2000

Total households . . . 5,532
With persons under 18 . . . 1,706
With persons over 65 . . . 1,971
Family households . . . 3,312
Single person households . . . 1,822
Persons per household . . . 2.35
Persons per family . . . 2.96

Household Population, 2008§§

Persons living in households . . . 14,128
Persons living in group quarters . . . 119
Persons per household . . . 2.4

Labor & Employment

Total civilian labor force, 2008§§ . . . 4,300
Unemployment rate, 2008 . . . 15.2%
Total civilian labor force, 2000 . . . 4,020

Employed persons 16 years and over by occupation, 2000

Managers & professionals . . . 670
Service occupations . . . 1,027
Sales & office occupations . . . 793
Farming, fishing & forestry . . . 61
Construction & maintenance . . . 385
Production & transportation . . . 463
Self-employed persons . . . 548

* US Census Bureau
** 2000 Decennial Census
§ California Department of Finance
§§ California Employment Development Dept

General Information

City of Clearlake
14050 Olympic Dr
Clearlake, CA 95422
707-994-8201

Website . . . www.clearlake.ca.us
Elevation . . . 1,378 ft.
Land Area (sq. miles) . . . 10.2
Water Area (sq. miles) . . . 0.4
Year of Incorporation . . . 1980
Government type . . . General law
Sales tax rate . . . 8.75%

Voters & Officials

Registered Voters, October 2008

Total . . . 6,479
Democrats . . . 3,304
Republicans . . . 1,339
Declined to state . . . 1,440

Legislative Districts

US Congressional . . . 1
State Senatorial . . . 2
State Assembly . . . 1

Local Officials, 2009

Mayor . . . Chuck Leonard
Administrator . . . Dale Neiman
City Clerk . . . Melissa Swanson
Attorney . . . Mala Subramanian
Finance Dir . . . Michael Vivrette
Public Works . . . NA
Planning/Dev Dir . . . NA
Building . . . NA
Police Chief . . . Allan McClain
Emergency/Fire Dir . . . Jim McMurray

Public Safety

Number of officers, 2007 . . . 22
Violent crimes, 2007 . . . 67
Property crimes, 2007 . . . 654
Arson, 2007 . . . 7

Public Library

Redbud Library
Lake County Library System
14785 Burns Valley Rd
Clearlake, CA 95422
707-994-5115

Branch Librarian . . . Irwin Feldman

Library system statistics, FY 2007

Population served . . . 64,276
Internet terminals . . . 24
Annual users . . . 20,128

Per capita:

Operating income . . . $20.31
percent from local government . . . 53.0%
Operating expenditure . . . $18.27
Total materials . . . 2.08
Print holdings . . . 1.98
Visits per capita . . . 3.73

Housing & Construction

Housing Units

Total, 2008§ . . . 8,166
Single family units, attached . . . 429
Single family units, detached . . . 3,683
Multiple family units . . . 743
Mobile home units . . . 3,311
Occupied . . . 5,941
Vacancy rate . . . 27.3%
Median rent, 2000** . . . $498
Median SF home value, 2000** . . . $81,800

New Privately Owned Housing Units Authorized by Building Permit, 2007*

	Units	Construction Cost
Single	115	$15,645,479
Total	171	$20,272,802

Municipal Finance

(For local fiscal year ended in 2006)

Revenues

Total . . . $7,873,348
Taxes . . . 4,560,050
Special benefits assessment . . . 0
Licenses & permits . . . 557,653
Fines & forfeitures . . . 659,489
Revenues from use of money & property . . . 202,101
Intergovernmental . . . 1,322,918
Service charges . . . 463,646
Other revenues . . . 33,182
Other financing sources . . . 74,309

Expenditures

Total . . . $6,711,358
General government . . . 1,248,566
Public safety . . . 3,203,171
Transportation . . . 608,036
Community development . . . 1,505,109
Health . . . 0
Culture & leisure . . . 146,476
Other . . . 0

Local School District

(Data from School year 2007-08 except as noted)

Konocti Unified
PO Box 5000
Lower Lake, CA 95457
(707) 994-6475

Superintendent . . . William MacDougall
Grade plan . . . K-12
Number of schools . . . 10
Enrollment . . . 3,069
High school graduates, 2006-07 . . . 168
Dropout rate . . . 5.8%
Pupil/teacher ratio . . . 17.7
Average class size . . . 21.4
Students per computer . . . 4.6
Classrooms with internet . . . 189
Avg. Daily Attendance (ADA) . . . 2,912
Cost per ADA . . . $9,402
Avg. Teacher Salary . . . $49,066

California Achievement Tests 6th ed., 2008

(Pct scoring at or above 50th National Percentile Rank)

	Math	Reading	Language
Grade 3	53%	33%	43%
Grade 7	46%	48%	40%

Academic Performance Index, 2008

Number of students tested . . . 2,336
Number of valid scores . . . 2,049
2007 API (base) . . . 662
2008 API (growth) . . . 675

SAT Testing, 2006-07

Enrollment, Grade 12 . . . 220
Number taking test . . . 24
percent taking test . . . 10.9%
percent with total score 1,500+ . . . 5.50%

Average Scores:

Math	Verbal	Writing	Total
486	495	504	1,485

Federal No Child Left Behind, 2008

(Adequate Yearly Progress standards met)

	Participation Rate	Pct Proficient
ELA	Yes	No
Math	Yes	No

API criteria . . . Yes
Graduation rate . . . Yes
\# criteria met/possible . . . 32/25

Other school districts for this city

(see Appendix E for information on these districts)

None

See Introduction for an explanation of all data sources.

Demographics & Socio-Economic Characteristics
(2000 Decennial Census, except as noted)

Population
1990* . . . 4,924
2000 . . . 6,831
Male . . . 3,402
Female . . . 3,429
Jan. 2008 (estimate)§ . . . 8,577
Persons per sq. mi. of land . . . 3,430.8

Race & Hispanic Origin, 2000
Race
White . . . 5,323
Black/African American . . . 12
North American Native . . . 106
Asian . . . 71
Pacific Islander . . . 5
Other Race . . . 1,045
Two or more races . . . 269
Hispanic origin, total . . . 1,823
Mexican . . . 1,559
Puerto Rican . . . 13
Cuban . . . 5
Other Hispanic . . . 246

Age & Nativity, 2000
Under 5 years . . . 478
18 years and over . . . 4,968
65 years and over . . . 974
85 years and over . . . 121
Median Age . . . 36.0
Native-born . . . 5,836
Foreign-born . . . 1,251

Educational Attainment, 2000
Population 25 years and over . . . 4,555
Less than 9th grade . . . 11.4%
High school grad or higher . . . 72.8%
Bachelor's degree or higher . . . 15.2%
Graduate degree . . . 4.0%

Income & Poverty, 1999
Per capita income . . . $19,750
Median household income . . . $42,309
Median family income . . . $50,000
Persons in poverty . . . 10.6%
H'holds receiving public assistance . . . 97
H'holds receiving social security . . . 773

Households, 2000
Total households . . . 2,495
With persons under 18 . . . 980
With persons over 65 . . . 702
Family households . . . 1,742
Single person households . . . 621
Persons per household . . . 2.71
Persons per family . . . 3.24

Household Population, 2008§§
Persons living in households . . . 8,500
Persons living in group quarters . . . 77
Persons per household . . . 2.6

Labor & Employment
Total civilian labor force, 2008§§ . . . 3,600
Unemployment rate, 2008 . . . 8.0%
Total civilian labor force, 2000 . . . 3,294

Employed persons 16 years and over by occupation, 2000
Managers & professionals . . . 731
Service occupations . . . 492
Sales & office occupations . . . 720
Farming, fishing & forestry . . . 194
Construction & maintenance . . . 363
Production & transportation . . . 597
Self-employed persons . . . 304

* US Census Bureau
** 2000 Decennial Census
§ California Department of Finance
§§ California Employment Development Dept

General Information
City of Cloverdale
124 N Cloverdale Blvd
PO Box 217
Cloverdale, CA 95425
707-894-2521

Website . . . www.cloverdale.net
Elevation . . . 316 ft.
Land Area (sq. miles) . . . 2.5
Water Area (sq. miles) . . . 0
Year of Incorporation . . . 1872
Government type . . . General law
Sales tax rate . . . 9.00%

Voters & Officials
Registered Voters, October 2008
Total . . . 3,994
Democrats . . . 2,021
Republicans . . . 1,105
Declined to state . . . 720

Legislative Districts
US Congressional . . . 1
State Senatorial . . . 2
State Assembly . . . 1

Local Officials, 2009
Mayor . . . Joseph Palla
Manager . . . Nina D. Regor
City Clerk . . . Michele P. Winterbottom
Attorney . . . Eric Danly
Finance Dir . . . Diana G. Edwards
Public Works . . . Bob Crabb
Planning/Dev Dir . . . Bruce Kibby
Building . . . Clif Castle
Police Chief . . . Mark Tuma
Emergency/Fire Dir . . . Brian Elliot

Public Safety
Number of officers, 2007 . . . 13
Violent crimes, 2007 . . . 28
Property crimes, 2007 . . . 179
Arson, 2007 . . . 1

Public Library
Cloverdale Regional Library
Sonoma County Library System
401 N Cloverdale Blvd
Cloverdale, CA 95425
707-894-5271

Branch Librarian . . . Deborah Hand

Library system statistics, FY 2007
Population served . . . 481,785
Internet terminals . . . 140
Annual users . . . 299,464

Per capita:
Operating income . . . $32.97
percent from local government . . . 87.7%
Operating expenditure . . . $30.18
Total materials . . . 1.60
Print holdings . . . 1.49
Visits per capita . . . 5.11

Housing & Construction
Housing Units
Total, 2008§ . . . 3,382
Single family units, attached . . . 204
Single family units, detached . . . 2,526
Multiple family units . . . 443
Mobile home units . . . 209
Occupied . . . 3,222
Vacancy rate . . . 4.7%
Median rent, 2000** . . . $760
Median SF home value, 2000** . . . $214,600

New Privately Owned Housing Units Authorized by Building Permit, 2007*

	Units	Construction Cost
Single	6	$1,096,267
Total	6	$1,096,267

Municipal Finance
(For local fiscal year ended in 2006)

Revenues
Total . . . $9,885,224
Taxes . . . 3,984,955
Special benefits assessment . . . 277,613
Licenses & permits . . . 170,738
Fines & forfeitures . . . 32,338
Revenues from use of money & property . . . 445,304
Intergovernmental . . . 1,068,114
Service charges . . . 3,879,652
Other revenues . . . 26,510
Other financing sources . . . 0

Expenditures
Total . . . $9,425,522
General government . . . 1,184,601
Public safety . . . 2,248,205
Transportation . . . 1,232,970
Community development . . . 1,058,289
Health . . . 1,664,865
Culture & leisure . . . 336,198
Other . . . 0

Local School District
(Data from School year 2007-08 except as noted)
Cloverdale Unified
97 School St
Cloverdale, CA 95425
(707) 894-1920

Superintendent . . . Claudia Rosatti
Grade plan . . . K-12
Number of schools . . . 5
Enrollment . . . 1,520
High school graduates, 2006-07 . . . 82
Dropout rate . . . 5.7%
Pupil/teacher ratio . . . 18.3
Average class size . . . 23.3
Students per computer . . . 5.4
Classrooms with internet . . . 84
Avg. Daily Attendance (ADA) . . . 1,481
Cost per ADA . . . $8,478
Avg. Teacher Salary . . . $57,575

California Achievement Tests 6th ed., 2008
(Pct scoring at or above 50th National Percentile Rank)

	Math	Reading	Language
Grade 3	41%	32%	35%
Grade 7	41%	33%	28%

Academic Performance Index, 2008
Number of students tested . . . 1,167
Number of valid scores . . . 1,102
2007 API (base) . . . 721
2008 API (growth) . . . 724

SAT Testing, 2006-07
Enrollment, Grade 12 . . . 104
Number taking test . . . 29
percent taking test . . . 27.9%
percent with total score 1,500+ . . . 13.50%

Average Scores:

Math	Verbal	Writing	Total
510	468	473	1,451

Federal No Child Left Behind, 2008
(Adequate Yearly Progress standards met)

	Participation Rate	Pct Proficient
ELA	No	No
Math	Yes	No

API criteria . . . Yes
Graduation rate . . . No
\# criteria met/possible . . . 26/16

Other school districts for this city
(see Appendix E for information on these districts)
None

See Introduction for an explanation of all data sources.

Demographics & Socio-Economic Characteristics†

(2007 American Community Survey, except as noted)

Population

1990* . . . 50,323
2007 . . . 92,987
Male . . . 45,655
Female . . . 47,332
Jan. 2008 (estimate)§ . . . 94,289
Persons per sq. mi. of land . . . 5,514.0

Race & Hispanic Origin, 2007

Race
White . . . 64,152
Black/African American . . . 2,342
North American Native . . . 701
Asian . . . 6,008
Pacific Islander . . . 302
Other Race . . . 14,960
Two or more races . . . 4,522
Hispanic origin, total . . . 24,127
Mexican . . . 20,251
Puerto Rican . . . 372
Cuban . . . 39
Other Hispanic . . . 3,465

Age & Nativity, 2007

Under 5 years . . . 6,323
18 years and over . . . 66,944
65 years and over . . . 9,099
85 years and over . . . 1,065
Median Age . . . 32.7
Native-born . . . 83,075
Foreign-born . . . 9,912

Educational Attainment, 2007

Population 25 years and over . . . 57,430
Less than 9th grade . . . 4.0%
High school grad or higher . . . 91.0%
Bachelor's degree or higher . . . 26.1%
Graduate degree . . . 7.2%

Income & Poverty, 2007

Per capita income . . . $26,143
Median household income . . . $59,825
Median family income . . . $75,869
Persons in poverty . . . 10.0%
H'holds receiving public assistance . . . 335
H'holds receiving social security . . . 6,744

Households, 2007

Total households . . . 32,085
With persons under 18 . . . 13,532
With persons over 65 . . . 6,221
Family households . . . 22,436
Single person households . . . 7,558
Persons per household . . . 2.88
Persons per family . . . 3.47

Household Population, 2008§§

Persons living in households . . . 93,809
Persons living in group quarters . . . 480
Persons per household . . . 2.9

Labor & Employment

Total civilian labor force, 2008§§ . . . 43,400
Unemployment rate, 2008 . . . 5.6%
Total civilian labor force, 2000* . . . 33,552

Employed persons 16 years and over by occupation, 2007

Managers & professionals . . . 15,760
Service occupations . . . 7,235
Sales & office occupations . . . 12,493
Farming, fishing & forestry . . . 309
Construction & maintenance . . . 3,551
Production & transportation . . . 3,061
Self-employed persons . . . 3,375

† see Appendix D for 2000 Decennial Census Data
* US Census Bureau
** 2007 American Community Survey
§ California Department of Finance
§§ California Employment Development Dept

General Information

City of Clovis
1033 Fifth St
Clovis, CA 93612
559-324-2060

Website . . . www.cityofclovis.com
Elevation . . . 361 ft.
Land Area (sq. miles) . . . 17.1
Water Area (sq. miles) . . . 0
Year of Incorporation . . . 1912
Government type . . . General law
Sales tax rate . . . 8.98%

Voters & Officials

Registered Voters, October 2008

Total . . . 49,363
Democrats . . . 14,867
Republicans . . . 25,745
Declined to state . . . 5,825

Legislative Districts

US Congressional . . . 21
State Senatorial . . . 14
State Assembly . . . 29

Local Officials, 2009

Mayor . . . Bob Whalen
Manager . . . Kathleen Millison
City Clerk . . . John Holt
Attorney . . . David Wolfe
Finance Dir . . . Robert Woolley
Public Works . . . Mike Leonardo
Planning/Dev Dir . . . Dwight Kroll
Building . . . Mark Meyers
Police Chief . . . Janet Davis
Fire Chief . . . Rich Bennett

Public Safety

Number of officers, 2007 . . . 108
Violent crimes, 2007 . . . 133
Property crimes, 2007 . . . 2,843
Arson, 2007 . . . 16

Public Library

Clovis Regional Library
Fresno County Public Library System
1155 Fifth St
Clovis, CA 93612
559-299-9531

Branch Librarian . . . Joseph Augustino

Library system statistics, FY 2007

Population served . . . 889,019
Internet terminals . . . 277
Annual users . . . 861,240

Per capita:

Operating income . . . $23.69
percent from local government . . . 89.3%
Operating expenditure . . . $23.37
Total materials . . . 2.89
Print holdings . . . 2.69
Visits per capita . . . NA

Housing & Construction

Housing Units

Total, 2008§ . . . 34,118
Single family units, attached . . . 550
Single family units, detached . . . 24,378
Multiple family units . . . 8,273
Mobile home units . . . 917
Occupied . . . 32,902
Vacancy rate . . . 3.6%
Median rent, 2007** . . . $902
Median SF home value, 2007** . . . $354,500

New Privately Owned Housing Units Authorized by Building Permit, 2007*

	Units	Construction Cost
Single	570	$135,544,819
Total	721	$152,824,200

Municipal Finance

(For local fiscal year ended in 2006)

Revenues

Total . . . $117,738,915
Taxes . . . 36,558,508
Special benefits assessment . . . 0
Licenses & permits . . . 2,984,255
Fines & forfeitures . . . 298,141
Revenues from use of money & property . . . 4,213,121
Intergovernmental . . . 7,957,615
Service charges . . . 63,585,430
Other revenues . . . 141,845
Other financing sources . . . 2,000,000

Expenditures

Total . . . $134,352,174
General government . . . 8,649,970
Public safety . . . 32,214,153
Transportation . . . 15,305,811
Community development . . . 7,697,643
Health . . . 47,630,152
Culture & leisure . . . 6,669,345
Other . . . 0

Local School District

(Data from School year 2007-08 except as noted)

Clovis Unified
1450 Herndon Ave
Clovis, CA 93611
(559) 327-9100

Superintendent . . . Terry Bradley
Grade plan . . . K-12
Number of schools . . . 45
Enrollment . . . 36,810
High school graduates, 2006-07 . . . 2,323
Dropout rate . . . 2.1%
Pupil/teacher ratio . . . 20.9
Average class size . . . 25.7
Students per computer . . . 6.6
Classrooms with internet . . . 1,717
Avg. Daily Attendance (ADA) . . . 35,797
Cost per ADA . . . $8,009
Avg. Teacher Salary . . . $60,424

California Achievement Tests 6th ed., 2008

(Pct scoring at or above 50th National Percentile Rank)

	Math	Reading	Language
Grade 3	72%	54%	62%
Grade 7	70%	65%	61%

Academic Performance Index, 2008

Number of students tested . . . 28,254
Number of valid scores . . . 27,033
2007 API (base) . . . 827
2008 API (growth) . . . 841

SAT Testing, 2006-07

Enrollment, Grade 12 . . . 2,810
Number taking test . . . 1,302
percent taking test . . . 46.3%
percent with total score 1,500+ . . . 21.80%

Average Scores:

Math	Verbal	Writing	Total
514	489	485	1,488

Federal No Child Left Behind, 2008

(Adequate Yearly Progress standards met)

	Participation Rate	Pct Proficient
ELA	Yes	Yes
Math	Yes	Yes

API criteria . . . Yes
Graduation rate . . . Yes
\# criteria met/possible . . . 42/42

Other school districts for this city

(see Appendix E for information on these districts)

Fresno Unified

Demographics & Socio-Economic Characteristics

(2000 Decennial Census, except as noted)

Population

1990* 16,896
2000 22,724
Male 11,365
Female 11,359
Jan. 2008 (estimate)§ 40,517
Persons per sq. mi. of land 1,947.9

Race & Hispanic Origin, 2000

Race
White 8,810
Black/African American 103
North American Native 191
Asian 71
Pacific Islander 7
Other Race 12,854
Two or more races 688
Hispanic origin, total 22,132
Mexican 19,824
Puerto Rican 13
Cuban 2
Other Hispanic 2,293

Age & Nativity, 2000

Under 5 years 2,535
18 years and over 13,454
65 years and over 1,128
85 years and over 67
Median Age 22.8
Native-born 11,825
Foreign-born 10,665

Educational Attainment, 2000

Population 25 years and over 10,540
Less than 9th grade 43.8%
High school grad or higher 31.9%
Bachelor's degree or higher 1.9%
Graduate degree 0.9%

Income & Poverty, 1999

Per capita income $7,416
Median household income $28,590
Median family income $28,320
Persons in poverty 28.5%
H'holds receiving public assistance 470
H'holds receiving social security 940

Households, 2000

Total households 4,807
With persons under 18 3,658
With persons over 65 848
Family households 4,482
Single person households 254
Persons per household 4.72
Persons per family 4.80

Household Population, 2008§§

Persons living in households 40,473
Persons living in group quarters 44
Persons per household 4.8

Labor & Employment

Total civilian labor force, 2008§§ 12,000
Unemployment rate, 2008 .... 13.9%
Total civilian labor force, 2000 8,391

Employed persons 16 years and over by occupation, 2000

Managers & professionals 669
Service occupations 2,292
Sales & office occupations 1,252
Farming, fishing & forestry 1,425
Construction & maintenance 1,010
Production & transportation 764
Self-employed persons 202

* US Census Bureau
** 2000 Decennial Census
§ California Department of Finance
§§ California Employment Development Dept

General Information

City of Coachella
1515 Sixth St
Coachella, CA 92236
760-398-3502

Website .... www.coachella.org
Elevation .... 71 ft.
Land Area (sq. miles) 20.8
Water Area (sq. miles) 0
Year of Incorporation 1946
Government type .... General law
Sales tax rate 8.75%

Voters & Officials

Registered Voters, October 2008

Total 8,664
Democrats 5,422
Republicans 2,223
Declined to state 863

Legislative Districts

US Congressional 45
State Senatorial 40
State Assembly 80

Local Officials, 2009

Mayor .... Eduardo Garcia
Manager .... Tim Brown
City Clerk .... Isabel Castillon
Attorney .... Carlos Campos
Finance Dir .... John Gerardi
Public Works .... Paul Toor
Planning/Dev Dir .... Carmen L. Manriquez
Building .... Paul Toor
Police Chief .... Rodney Vigue
Fire Chief .... Alex Gregg

Public Safety

Number of officers, 2007 .... NA
Violent crimes, 2007 302
Property crimes, 2007 1,560
Arson, 2007 8

Public Library

Coachella Branch Library
Riverside County Library Service
1538 Seventh St
Coachella, CA 92236
760-398-5148
Branch LibrarianMiguel Guitron-Rodriguez

Library system statistics, FY 2007

Population served 1,047,996
Internet terminals 37
Annual users 69,346

Per capita:

Operating income $19.38
percent from local government 49.8%
Operating expenditure $20.45
Total materials 1.43
Print holdings 1.30
Visits per capita 4.06

Housing & Construction

Housing Units

Total, 2008§ 8,814
Single family units, attached 319
Single family units, detached 6,276
Multiple family units 1,762
Mobile home units 457
Occupied 8,428
Vacancy rate 4.4%
Median rent, 2000** $470
Median SF home value, 2000** $83,700

New Privately Owned Housing Units Authorized by Building Permit, 2007*

	Units	Construction Cost
Single	196	$32,336,575
Total	196	$32,336,575

Municipal Finance

(For local fiscal year ended in 2006)

Revenues

Total $28,018,321
Taxes 9,344,301
Special benefits assessment 575,747
Licenses & permits 2,216,124
Fines & forfeitures 252,887
Revenues from use of money & property 681,462
Intergovernmental 4,458,181
Service charges 9,242,716
Other revenues 1,246,903
Other financing sources 0

Expenditures

Total $25,264,133
General government 4,937,605
Public safety 6,147,705
Transportation 10,161,618
Community development 1,841,578
Health 918,236
Culture & leisure 1,257,391
Other 0

Local School District

(Data from School year 2007-08 except as noted)

Coachella Valley Unified
PO Box 847
Thermal, CA 92274
(760) 399-5137

Superintendent .... Carey Carlson
Grade plan K-12
Number of schools 22
Enrollment 18,203
High school graduates, 2006-07 754
Dropout rate 4.5%
Pupil/teacher ratio 21.0
Average class size 25.6
Students per computer 4.5
Classrooms with internet 932
Avg. Daily Attendance (ADA) 18,519
Cost per ADA $8,586
Avg. Teacher Salary $61,982

California Achievement Tests 6th ed., 2008

(Pct scoring at or above 50th National Percentile Rank)

	Math	Reading	Language
Grade 3	32%	15%	23%
Grade 7	27%	25%	25%

Academic Performance Index, 2008

Number of students tested 14,005
Number of valid scores 12,912
2007 API (base) 596
2008 API (growth) 632

SAT Testing, 2006-07

Enrollment, Grade 12 855
Number taking test 240
percent taking test 28.1%
percent with total score 1,500+ 2.70%

Average Scores:

Math	Verbal	Writing	Total
418	402	411	1,231

Federal No Child Left Behind, 2008

(Adequate Yearly Progress standards met)

	Participation Rate	Pct Proficient
ELA	Yes	No
Math	Yes	No

API criteria .... Yes
Graduation rate .... Yes
\# criteria met/possible 26/19

Other school districts for this city

(see Appendix E for information on these districts)

None

See Introduction for an explanation of all data sources.

Demographics & Socio-Economic Characteristics

(2000 Decennial Census, except as noted)

Population

1990* 8,212
2000 11,668
Male 6,067
Female 5,601
Jan. 2008 (estimate)§ 19,064
Persons per sq. mi. of land 3,231.2

Race & Hispanic Origin, 2000

Race
White 6,687
Black/African American 276
North American Native 177
Asian 193
Pacific Islander 28
Other Race 3,769
Two or more races 538
Hispanic origin, total 5,811
Mexican 5,015
Puerto Rican 23
Cuban 3
Other Hispanic 770

Age & Nativity, 2000

Under 5 years 1,068
18 years and over 7,793
65 years and over 988
85 years and over 124
Median Age 28.6
Native-born 9,426
Foreign-born 2,316

Educational Attainment, 2000

Population 25 years and over 6,500
Less than 9th grade 19.4%
High school grad or higher 65.0%
Bachelor's degree or higher 11.8%
Graduate degree 4.9%

Income & Poverty, 1999

Per capita income $14,425
Median household income $38,133
Median family income $41,208
Persons in poverty 19.2%
H'holds receiving public assistance 206
H'holds receiving social security 766

Households, 2000

Total households 3,515
With persons under 18 1,770
With persons over 65 690
Family households 2,631
Single person households 724
Persons per household 3.09
Persons per family 3.59

Household Population, 2008§§

Persons living in households 12,186
Persons living in group quarters 6,878
Persons per household 3.2

Labor & Employment

Total civilian labor force, 2008§§ 6,100
Unemployment rate, 2008 .... 12.2%
Total civilian labor force, 2000 4,829

Employed persons 16 years and over by occupation, 2000

Managers & professionals 896
Service occupations 1,209
Sales & office occupations 821
Farming, fishing & forestry 425
Construction & maintenance 436
Production & transportation 384
Self-employed persons 218

* US Census Bureau
** 2000 Decennial Census
§ California Department of Finance
§§ California Employment Development Dept

General Information

City of Coalinga
155 W Durian
Coalinga, CA 93210
559-935-1533

Website .... www.coalinga.com
Elevation .... 667 ft.
Land Area (sq. miles) 5.9
Water Area (sq. miles) 0
Year of Incorporation 1906
Government type .... General law
Sales tax rate 8.98%

Voters & Officials

Registered Voters, October 2008

Total 4,271
Democrats 1,638
Republicans 1,658
Declined to state 640

Legislative Districts

US Congressional 20
State Senatorial 16
State Assembly 30

Local Officials, 2009

Mayor .... Ron Lander
Manager .... Bill Skinner
City Clerk .... Cindy Johnson
Attorney .... Dale Bacigalupi
Finance Dir .... Robert Barron
Public Works .... (vacant)
Community Dev Dir .... Bill Skinner
Building .... John Self
Police Chief .... Cal Minor
Fire Chief .... Daniel Hernandez

Public Safety

Number of officers, 2007 18
Violent crimes, 2007 93
Property crimes, 2007 498
Arson, 2007 .... NA

Public Library

Coalinga District Library
Coalinga-Huron Unified School Dist Lib Sys
305 N Fourth St
Coalinga, CA 93210
559-935-1058

Director .... Carol Kreamer

Library system statistics, FY 2007

Population served 28,496
Internet terminals 9
Annual users 19,220

Per capita:

Operating income $36.70
percent from local government 85.8%
Operating expenditure $31.07
Total materials 3.11
Print holdings 2.95
Visits per capita 2.03

Housing & Construction

Housing Units

Total, 2008§ 4,238
Single family units, attached 213
Single family units, detached 2,763
Multiple family units 943
Mobile home units 319
Occupied 3,858
Vacancy rate 9.0%
Median rent, 2000** $468
Median SF home value, 2000** $86,900

New Privately Owned Housing Units Authorized by Building Permit, 2007*

	Units	Construction Cost
Single	72	$15,117,993
Total	72	$15,117,993

Municipal Finance

(For local fiscal year ended in 2006)

Revenues

Total $26,189,090
Taxes 3,983,054
Special benefits assessment 0
Licenses & permits 274,114
Fines & forfeitures 20,796
Revenues from use of money & property 1,201,589
Intergovernmental 809,255
Service charges 19,770,464
Other revenues 129,818
Other financing sources 0

Expenditures

Total $24,879,011
General government 2,369,119
Public safety 11,712,567
Transportation 1,961,694
Community development 499,865
Health 1,873,111
Culture & leisure 1,034,958
Other 0

Local School District

(Data from School year 2007-08 except as noted)

Coalinga-Huron Joint Unified
657 Sunset St
Coalinga, CA 93210
(559) 935-7500

Superintendent .... Cecelia Greenberg-English
Grade plan K-12
Number of schools 11
Enrollment 4,416
High school graduates, 2006-07 215
Dropout rate 6.2%
Pupil/teacher ratio 22.4
Average class size 26.6
Students per computer 5.3
Classrooms with internet 246
Avg. Daily Attendance (ADA) 4,194
Cost per ADA $8,377
Avg. Teacher Salary $60,598

California Achievement Tests 6th ed., 2008

(Pct scoring at or above 50th National Percentile Rank)

	Math	Reading	Language
Grade 3	40%	21%	29%
Grade 7	38%	31%	36%

Academic Performance Index, 2008

Number of students tested 3,293
Number of valid scores 3,038
2007 API (base) 651
2008 API (growth) 655

SAT Testing, 2006-07

Enrollment, Grade 12 284
Number taking test 63
percent taking test 22.2%
percent with total score 1,500+ 6.70%

Average Scores:

Math	Verbal	Writing	Total
463	448	442	1,353

Federal No Child Left Behind, 2008

(Adequate Yearly Progress standards met)

	Participation Rate	Pct Proficient
ELA	No	No
Math	Yes	No

API criteria .... Yes
Graduation rate .... No
\# criteria met/possible 26/15

Other school districts for this city

(see Appendix E for information on these districts)

None

See Introduction for an explanation of all data sources.

Demographics & Socio-Economic Characteristics

(2000 Decennial Census, except as noted)

Population

1990* 1,306
2000 1,496
Male 724
Female 772
Jan. 2008 (estimate)§ 1,855
Persons per sq. mi. of land 1,426.9

Race & Hispanic Origin, 2000

Race
White 1,394
Black/African American 9
North American Native 9
Asian 2
Pacific Islander 0
Other Race 35
Two or more races 47
Hispanic origin, total 124
Mexican 99
Puerto Rican 3
Cuban 0
Other Hispanic 22

Age & Nativity, 2000

Under 5 years 94
18 years and over 1,069
65 years and over 208
85 years and over 28
Median Age 36.4
Native-born 1,556
Foreign-born 40

Educational Attainment, 2000

Population 25 years and over 1,000
Less than 9th grade 3.6%
High school grad or higher 79.3%
Bachelor's degree or higher 18.5%
Graduate degree 5.2%

Income & Poverty, 1999

Per capita income $16,440
Median household income $37,391
Median family income $43,125
Persons in poverty 12.7%
H'holds receiving public assistance 52
H'holds receiving social security 213

Households, 2000

Total households 614
With persons under 18 238
With persons over 65 163
Family households 395
Single person households 175
Persons per household 2.43
Persons per family 2.97

Household Population, 2008§§

Persons living in households 1,854
Persons living in group quarters 1
Persons per household 2.4

Labor & Employment

Total civilian labor force, 2008§§ 1,000
Unemployment rate, 2008 .... 8.9%
Total civilian labor force, 2000 724

Employed persons 16 years and over by occupation, 2000

Managers & professionals 195
Service occupations 135
Sales & office occupations 192
Farming, fishing & forestry 0
Construction & maintenance 78
Production & transportation 84
Self-employed persons 70

* US Census Bureau
** 2000 Decennial Census
§ California Department of Finance
§§ California Employment Development Dept

General Information

City of Colfax
33 South Main
PO Box 702
Colfax, CA 95713
530-346-2313

Website .... www.ci.colfax.ca.us
Elevation .... NA
Land Area (sq. miles) 1.3
Water Area (sq. miles) 0
Year of Incorporation 1910
Government type .... General law
Sales tax rate 8.25%

Voters & Officials

Registered Voters, October 2008

Total 949
Democrats 308
Republicans 364
Declined to state 208

Legislative Districts

US Congressional 4
State Senatorial 1
State Assembly 3

Local Officials, 2009

Mayor .... Suzanne Roberts
Manager .... Joan L. Phillipe
City Clerk .... Karen Pierce
Attorney .... Scott Browne
Finance Dir .... Dau Luc
Public Works .... David Woodford
Planning/Dev Dir .... Gary Price
Building .... Gabe Armstrong
Police Chief .... NA
Emergency/Fire Dir .... Chris Paulus

Public Safety

Number of officers, 2007 .... NA
Violent crimes, 2007 .... NA
Property crimes, 2007 .... NA
Arson, 2007 .... NA

Public Library

Colfax Library
Placer County Library System
2 W Church St
Colfax, CA 95713
530-346-8211

Branch Librarian .... Gunda Pramuk

Library system statistics, FY 2007

Population served 180,819
Internet terminals 56
Annual users 48,341

Per capita:

Operating income $24.99
percent from local government 85.7%
Operating expenditure $24.01
Total materials 1.96
Print holdings 1.74
Visits per capita 3.30

Housing & Construction

Housing Units

Total, 2008§ 816
Single family units, attached 22
Single family units, detached 525
Multiple family units 235
Mobile home units 34
Occupied 789
Vacancy rate 3.3%
Median rent, 2000** $652
Median SF home value, 2000** $149,400

New Privately Owned Housing Units Authorized by Building Permit, 2007*

	Units	Construction Cost
Single	1	$114,838
Total	1	$114,838

Municipal Finance

(For local fiscal year ended in 2006)

Revenues

Total $3,556,245
Taxes 1,297,455
Special benefits assessment 27,700
Licenses & permits 55,521
Fines & forfeitures 8,691
Revenues from use of money & property 116,727
Intergovernmental 660,353
Service charges 1,326,037
Other revenues 63,761
Other financing sources 0

Expenditures

Total $3,119,411
General government 380,440
Public safety 1,024,699
Transportation 305,576
Community development 348,858
Health 936,189
Culture & leisure 123,649
Other 0

Local School District

(Data from School year 2007-08 except as noted)

Placer Union High
PO Box 5048
Auburn, CA 95604
(530) 886-4400

Superintendent .... Bart O'Brien
Grade plan 9-12
Number of schools 6
Enrollment 4,588
High school graduates, 2006-07 1,091
Dropout rate 1.4%
Pupil/teacher ratio 22.5
Average class size 25.4
Students per computer 3.6
Classrooms with internet 242
Avg. Daily Attendance (ADA) 4,382
Cost per ADA $8,031
Avg. Teacher Salary $63,368

California Achievement Tests 6th ed., 2008

(Pct scoring at or above 50th National Percentile Rank)

	Math	Reading	Language
Grade 3	NA	NA	NA
Grade 7	NA	NA	NA

Academic Performance Index, 2008

Number of students tested 3,384
Number of valid scores 3,277
2007 API (base) 769
2008 API (growth) 768

SAT Testing, 2006-07

Enrollment, Grade 12 1,210
Number taking test 418
percent taking test 34.6%
percent with total score 1,500+ 23.60%

Average Scores:

Math	Verbal	Writing	Total
550	536	526	1,612

Federal No Child Left Behind, 2008

(Adequate Yearly Progress standards met)

	Participation Rate	Pct Proficient
ELA	No	No
Math	Yes	No

API criteria .... Yes
Graduation rate .... Yes
\# criteria met/possible 18/15

Other school districts for this city

(see Appendix E for information on these districts)

Colfax Elem

See Introduction for an explanation of all data sources.

Demographics & Socio-Economic Characteristics

(2000 Decennial Census, except as noted)

Population

1990* . . . 1,103
2000 . . . 1,191
Male . . . 556
Female . . . 635
Jan. 2008 (estimate)§ . . . 1,613
Persons per sq. mi. of land . . . 848.9

Race & Hispanic Origin, 2000

Race
White . . . 576
Black/African American . . . 17
North American Native . . . 0
Asian . . . 282
Pacific Islander . . . 3
Other Race . . . 232
Two or more races . . . 81
Hispanic origin, total . . . 523
Mexican . . . 265
Puerto Rican . . . 12
Cuban . . . 0
Other Hispanic . . . 246

Age & Nativity, 2000

Under 5 years . . . 62
18 years and over . . . 897
65 years and over . . . 185
85 years and over . . . 47
Median Age . . . 36.9
Native-born . . . 644
Foreign-born . . . 521

Educational Attainment, 2000

Population 25 years and over . . . 770
Less than 9th grade . . . 16.6%
High school grad or higher . . . 74.0%
Bachelor's degree or higher . . . 13.4%
Graduate degree . . . 3.2%

Income & Poverty, 1999

Per capita income . . . $20,241
Median household income . . . $58,750
Median family income . . . $60,556
Persons in poverty . . . 4.9%
H'holds receiving public assistance . . . 8
H'holds receiving social security . . . 102

Households, 2000

Total households . . . 329
With persons under 18 . . . 146
With persons over 65 . . . 106
Family households . . . 245
Single person households . . . 57
Persons per household . . . 3.47
Persons per family . . . 3.92

Household Population, 2008§§

Persons living in households . . . 1,564
Persons living in group quarters . . . 49
Persons per household . . . 3.5

Labor & Employment

Total civilian labor force, 2008§§ . . . NA
Unemployment rate, 2008 . . . NA
Total civilian labor force, 2000 . . . 534

Employed persons 16 years and over by occupation, 2000

Managers & professionals . . . 97
Service occupations . . . 96
Sales & office occupations . . . 179
Farming, fishing & forestry . . . 3
Construction & maintenance . . . 54
Production & transportation . . . 88
Self-employed persons . . . 25

* US Census Bureau
** 2000 Decennial Census
§ California Department of Finance
§§ California Employment Development Dept

General Information

Town of Colma
1198 El Camino Real
Colma, CA 94014
650-997-8300

Website . . . www.colma.ca.gov
Elevation . . . NA
Land Area (sq. miles) . . . 1.9
Water Area (sq. miles) . . . 0
Year of Incorporation . . . 1924
Government type . . . General law
Sales tax rate . . . 9.25%

Voters & Officials

Registered Voters, October 2008

Total . . . 718
Democrats . . . 428
Republicans . . . 74
Declined to state . . . 188

Legislative Districts

US Congressional . . . 12
State Senatorial . . . 8
State Assembly . . . 12

Local Officials, 2009

Mayor . . . Joanne F del Rosario
City Manager . . . Laura Allen (Int)
City Clerk . . . Laura Allen (Int)
Attorney . . . Roger Peters
Finance Dir . . . (vacant)
Public Works . . . Rick Mao
City Planner . . . Andrea Ouse
Building . . . Mike Cully
Police Chief . . . Robert Lotti
Fire Chief . . . Geoff Balton

Public Safety

Number of officers, 2007 . . . 19
Violent crimes, 2007 . . . 14
Property crimes, 2007 . . . 373
Arson, 2007 . . . 1

Public Library

Served by County Library

Library system statistics, FY 2007

Population served . . . NA
Internet terminals . . . NA
Annual users . . . NA

Per capita:

Operating income . . . NA
percent from local government . . . NA
Operating expenditure . . . NA
Total materials . . . NA
Print holdings . . . NA
Visits per capita . . . NA

Housing & Construction

Housing Units

Total, 2008§ . . . 460
Single family units, attached . . . 66
Single family units, detached . . . 220
Multiple family units . . . 168
Mobile home units . . . 6
Occupied . . . 445
Vacancy rate . . . 3.3%
Median rent, 2000** . . . $1,003
Median SF home value, 2000** . . . $312,000

New Privately Owned Housing Units Authorized by Building Permit, 2007*

	Units	Construction Cost
Single	2	$500,000
Total	2	$500,000

Municipal Finance

(For local fiscal year ended in 2006)

Revenues

Total . . . $14,878,837
Taxes . . . 12,249,212
Special benefits assessment . . . 0
Licenses & permits . . . 46,385
Fines & forfeitures . . . 126,642
Revenues from use of money & property . . . 1,346,577
Intergovernmental . . . 262,071
Service charges . . . 161,059
Other revenues . . . 686,891
Other financing sources . . . 0

Expenditures

Total . . . $19,905,183
General government . . . 4,092,558
Public safety . . . 4,612,647
Transportation . . . 1,105,503
Community development . . . 9,409,455
Health . . . 0
Culture & leisure . . . 685,020
Other . . . 0

Local School District

(Data from School year 2007-08 except as noted)

Jefferson Union High
699 Serramonte Blvd, Suite 100
Daly City, CA 94015
(650) 550-7900

Superintendent . . . Michael Crilly
Grade plan . . . 9-12
Number of schools . . . 5
Enrollment . . . 5,330
High school graduates, 2006-07 . . . 1,105
Dropout rate . . . 3.0%
Pupil/teacher ratio . . . 30.8
Average class size . . . 25.9
Students per computer . . . 4.3
Classrooms with internet . . . 276
Avg. Daily Attendance (ADA) . . . 5,128
Cost per ADA . . . $8,239
Avg. Teacher Salary . . . $58,641

California Achievement Tests 6th ed., 2008

(Pct scoring at or above 50th National Percentile Rank)

	Math	Reading	Language
Grade 3	NA	NA	NA
Grade 7	NA	NA	NA

Academic Performance Index, 2008

Number of students tested . . . 3,846
Number of valid scores . . . 3,651
2007 API (base) . . . 730
2008 API (growth) . . . 732

SAT Testing, 2006-07

Enrollment, Grade 12 . . . 1,255
Number taking test . . . 532
percent taking test . . . 42.4%
percent with total score 1,500+ . . . 17.90%

Average Scores:

Math	Verbal	Writing	Total
510	471	474	1,455

Federal No Child Left Behind, 2008

(Adequate Yearly Progress standards met)

	Participation Rate	Pct Proficient
ELA	No	No
Math	Yes	Yes

API criteria . . . Yes
Graduation rate . . . Yes
criteria met/possible . . . 34/31

Other school districts for this city

(see Appendix E for information on these districts)

Jefferson Elem

See Introduction for an explanation of all data sources.

Demographics & Socio-Economic Characteristics

(2000 Decennial Census, except as noted)

Population

1990*	40,213
2000	47,662
Male	23,492
Female	24,170
Jan. 2008 (estimate)§	51,918
Persons per sq. mi. of land	3,438.3

Race & Hispanic Origin, 2000

Race	
White	20,343
Black/African American	5,246
North American Native	600
Asian	2,521
Pacific Islander	108
Other Race	16,425
Two or more races	2,419
Hispanic origin, total	28,934
Mexican	23,813
Puerto Rican	318
Cuban	100
Other Hispanic	4,703

Age & Nativity, 2000

Under 5 years	4,773
18 years and over	31,007
65 years and over	3,053
85 years and over	286
Median Age	26.8
Native-born	36,496
Foreign-born	11,515

Educational Attainment, 2000

Population 25 years and over	25,738
Less than 9th grade	15.0%
High school grad or higher	68.8%
Bachelor's degree or higher	12.2%
Graduate degree	3.8%

Income & Poverty, 1999

Per capita income	$13,460
Median household income	$35,777
Median family income	$37,911
Persons in poverty	19.6%
H'holds receiving public assistance	1,053
H'holds receiving social security	2,514

Households, 2000

Total households	14,520
With persons under 18	7,690
With persons over 65	2,295
Family households	10,904
Single person households	2,810
Persons per household	3.26
Persons per family	3.76

Household Population, 2008§§

Persons living in households	51,654
Persons living in group quarters	264
Persons per household	3.4

Labor & Employment

Total civilian labor force, 2008§§	25,300
Unemployment rate, 2008	8.7%
Total civilian labor force, 2000	20,758

Employed persons 16 years and over by occupation, 2000

Managers & professionals	4,194
Service occupations	3,239
Sales & office occupations	5,098
Farming, fishing & forestry	71
Construction & maintenance	2,159
Production & transportation	4,166
Self-employed persons	987

* US Census Bureau
** 2000 Decennial Census
§ California Department of Finance
§§ California Employment Development Dept

General Information

City of Colton
650 N La Cadena Dr
Colton, CA 92324
909-370-5099

Website	www.ci.colton.ca.us
Elevation	1,000 ft.
Land Area (sq. miles)	15.1
Water Area (sq. miles)	0.6
Year of Incorporation	1887
Government type	General law
Sales tax rate	8.75%

Voters & Officials

Registered Voters, October 2008

Total	19,443
Democrats	10,188
Republicans	5,163
Declined to state	3,341

Legislative Districts

US Congressional	41, 43
State Senatorial	31, 32
State Assembly	62

Local Officials, 2009

Mayor	Kelly J. Chastain
Manager	Daryl Parrish
City Clerk	Eileen C. Gomez
Attorney	Dean Derleth
Finance Dir	Dilu DeAlwis
Public Works	Maritza Tapia (Int)
Planning/Dev Dir	David R. Zamora
Building	Andres Soto
Police Chief	Bob Miller
Emergency/Fire Dir	Tom Hendrix

Public Safety

Number of officers, 2007	71
Violent crimes, 2007	245
Property crimes, 2007	1,929
Arson, 2007	5

Public Library

Main Library
Colton Public Library System
656 N Ninth St
Colton, CA 92324
909-370-5084

Director	Ruth Ann Martinez

Library system statistics, FY 2007

Population served	51,797
Internet terminals	14
Annual users	NA

Per capita:

Operating income	$27.79
percent from local government	93.3%
Operating expenditure	$17.52
Total materials	1.89
Print holdings	1.70
Visits per capita	2.14

Housing & Construction

Housing Units

Total, 2008§	16,251
Single family units, attached	602
Single family units, detached	9,654
Multiple family units	5,180
Mobile home units	815
Occupied	15,049
Vacancy rate	7.4%
Median rent, 2000**	$618
Median SF home value, 2000**	$105,200

New Privately Owned Housing Units Authorized by Building Permit, 2007*

	Units	Construction Cost
Single	43	$7,114,303
Total	43	$7,114,303

Municipal Finance

(For local fiscal year ended in 2006)

Revenues

Total	$101,845,827
Taxes	24,441,378
Special benefits assessment	322,395
Licenses & permits	528,270
Fines & forfeitures	1,046,842
Revenues from use of money & property	1,777,420
Intergovernmental	4,717,238
Service charges	60,696,123
Other revenues	8,316,161
Other financing sources	0

Expenditures

Total	$96,857,619
General government	5,933,130
Public safety	21,914,237
Transportation	6,479,757
Community development	2,119,244
Health	5,175,672
Culture & leisure	5,076,048
Other	0

Local School District

(Data from School year 2007-08 except as noted)

Colton Joint Unified
1212 Valencia Dr
Colton, CA 92324
(909) 580-5000

Superintendent	James Downs
Grade plan	K-12
Number of schools	28
Enrollment	24,528
High school graduates, 2006-07	1,053
Dropout rate	9.6%
Pupil/teacher ratio	21.6
Average class size	27.4
Students per computer	5.7
Classrooms with internet	1,230
Avg. Daily Attendance (ADA)	23,370
Cost per ADA	$8,107
Avg. Teacher Salary	$66,484

California Achievement Tests 6th ed., 2008

(Pct scoring at or above 50th National Percentile Rank)

	Math	Reading	Language
Grade 3	40%	25%	33%
Grade 7	35%	34%	33%

Academic Performance Index, 2008

Number of students tested	18,558
Number of valid scores	17,077
2007 API (base)	659
2008 API (growth)	673

SAT Testing, 2006-07

Enrollment, Grade 12	1,681
Number taking test	401
percent taking test	23.9%
percent with total score 1,500+	4.60%

Average Scores:

Math	Verbal	Writing	Total
439	436	430	1,305

Federal No Child Left Behind, 2008

(Adequate Yearly Progress standards met)

	Participation Rate	Pct Proficient
ELA	No	No
Math	Yes	No

API criteria	Yes
Graduation rate	No
# criteria met/possible	38/25

Other school districts for this city

(see Appendix E for information on these districts)

None

See Introduction for an explanation of all data sources.

Demographics & Socio-Economic Characteristics

(2000 Decennial Census, except as noted)

Population

1990*	4,934
2000	5,402
Male	2,697
Female	2,705
Jan. 2008 (estimate)§	5,727
Persons per sq. mi. of land	3,368.8

Race & Hispanic Origin, 2000

Race	
White	3,709
Black/African American	16
North American Native	95
Asian	79
Pacific Islander	42
Other Race	1,258
Two or more races	203
Hispanic origin, total	2,253
Mexican	2,011
Puerto Rican	5
Cuban	0
Other Hispanic	237

Age & Nativity, 2000

Under 5 years	450
18 years and over	3,773
65 years and over	618
85 years and over	58
Median Age	32.0
Native-born	4,242
Foreign-born	1,116

Educational Attainment, 2000

Population 25 years and over	3,209
Less than 9th grade	17.8%
High school grad or higher	69.6%
Bachelor's degree or higher	13.6%
Graduate degree	4.0%

Income & Poverty, 1999

Per capita income	$15,251
Median household income	$35,250
Median family income	$41,833
Persons in poverty	16.7%
H'holds receiving public assistance	91
H'holds receiving social security	523

Households, 2000

Total households	1,897
With persons under 18	846
With persons over 65	468
Family households	1,366
Single person households	450
Persons per household	2.81
Persons per family	3.33

Household Population, 2008§§

Persons living in households	5,654
Persons living in group quarters	73
Persons per household	2.8

Labor & Employment

Total civilian labor force, 2008§§	3,180
Unemployment rate, 2008	9.4%
Total civilian labor force, 2000	2,469

Employed persons 16 years and over by occupation, 2000

Managers & professionals	545
Service occupations	368
Sales & office occupations	643
Farming, fishing & forestry	245
Construction & maintenance	230
Production & transportation	263
Self-employed persons	200

* US Census Bureau
** 2000 Decennial Census
§ California Department of Finance
§§ California Employment Development Dept

General Information

City of Colusa
425 Webster St
PO Box 1063
Colusa, CA 95932
530-458-4740

Website	www.colusa-ca.gov
Elevation	61 ft.
Land Area (sq. miles)	1.7
Water Area (sq. miles)	0
Year of Incorporation	1868
Government type	General law
Sales tax rate	8.25%

Voters & Officials

Registered Voters, October 2008

Total	2,299
Democrats	858
Republicans	1,051
Declined to state	326

Legislative Districts

US Congressional	2
State Senatorial	4
State Assembly	2

Local Officials, 2009

Mayor	Robert Mackaben
City Manager	Jan McClintock
City Clerk	Lori Reische
Attorney	Jacob Knapp
Finance Dir	Susan Price
Public Works	Patty Hickel
Planning/Dev Dir	John Linhart
Building	Mike Barrett
Police Chief	Lyle Montgomery
Emergency/Fire Dir	Randall Dunn

Public Safety

Number of officers, 2007	8
Violent crimes, 2007	14
Property crimes, 2007	164
Arson, 2007	0

Public Library

Main Branch
Colusa County Free Library
738 Market St
Colusa, CA 95932
530-458-7671

Director	Ellen Brow

Library system statistics, FY 2007

Population served	21,951
Internet terminals	28
Annual users	11,172

Per capita:

Operating income	$29.05
percent from local government	76.6%
Operating expenditure	$29.05
Total materials	4.60
Print holdings	4.18
Visits per capita	1.32

Housing & Construction

Housing Units

Total, 2008§	2,123
Single family units, attached	84
Single family units, detached	1,607
Multiple family units	380
Mobile home units	52
Occupied	2,000
Vacancy rate	5.8%
Median rent, 2000**	$505
Median SF home value, 2000**	$113,500

New Privately Owned Housing Units Authorized by Building Permit, 2007*

	Units	Construction Cost
Single	0	$0
Total	80	$6,789,516

Municipal Finance

(For local fiscal year ended in 2006)

Revenues

Total	$8,226,820
Taxes	2,262,185
Special benefits assessment	78,491
Licenses & permits	63,539
Fines & forfeitures	40,310
Revenues from use of money & property	201,781
Intergovernmental	2,302,601
Service charges	3,248,622
Other revenues	29,291
Other financing sources	0

Expenditures

Total	$7,415,098
General government	489,051
Public safety	1,704,021
Transportation	424,989
Community development	1,381,296
Health	2,525,562
Culture & leisure	353,061
Other	0

Local School District

(Data from School year 2007-08 except as noted)

Colusa Unified
745 10th St
Colusa, CA 95932
(530) 458-7791

Superintendent	Larry Yeghoian
Grade plan	K-12
Number of schools	5
Enrollment	1,354
High school graduates, 2006-07	84
Dropout rate	1.8%
Pupil/teacher ratio	19.4
Average class size	21.2
Students per computer	3.7
Classrooms with internet	71
Avg. Daily Attendance (ADA)	1,343
Cost per ADA	$8,409
Avg. Teacher Salary	$58,676

California Achievement Tests 6th ed., 2008

(Pct scoring at or above 50th National Percentile Rank)

	Math	Reading	Language
Grade 3	52%	43%	51%
Grade 7	46%	43%	43%

Academic Performance Index, 2008

Number of students tested	1,005
Number of valid scores	949
2007 API (base)	696
2008 API (growth)	703

SAT Testing, 2006-07

Enrollment, Grade 12	99
Number taking test	39
percent taking test	39.4%
percent with total score 1,500+	15.20%

Average Scores:

Math	Verbal	Writing	Total
486	477	476	1,439

Federal No Child Left Behind, 2008

(Adequate Yearly Progress standards met)

	Participation Rate	Pct Proficient
ELA	Yes	No
Math	Yes	No

API criteria	Yes
Graduation rate	Yes
# criteria met/possible	22/16

Other school districts for this city

(see Appendix E for information on these districts)

None

Demographics & Socio-Economic Characteristics

(2000 Decennial Census, except as noted)

Population

1990* . . . 12,135
2000 . . . 12,568
Male . . . 6,172
Female . . . 6,396
Jan. 2008 (estimate)§ . . . 13,536
Persons per sq. mi. of land . . . 2,050.9

Race & Hispanic Origin, 2000

Race
White . . . 5,625
Black/African American . . . 98
North American Native . . . 199
Asian . . . 136
Pacific Islander . . . 10
Other Race . . . 5,900
Two or more races . . . 600
Hispanic origin, total . . . 11,765
Mexican . . . 9,941
Puerto Rican . . . 37
Cuban . . . 64
Other Hispanic . . . 1,723

Age & Nativity, 2000

Under 5 years . . . 1,113
18 years and over . . . 8,316
65 years and over . . . 1,281
85 years and over . . . 106
Median Age . . . 28.2
Native-born . . . 7,697
Foreign-born . . . 4,886

Educational Attainment, 2000

Population 25 years and over . . . 6,876
Less than 9th grade . . . 30.3%
High school grad or higher . . . 45.8%
Bachelor's degree or higher . . . 4.6%
Graduate degree . . . 1.6%

Income & Poverty, 1999

Per capita income . . . $11,117
Median household income . . . $34,040
Median family income . . . $36,572
Persons in poverty . . . 17.7%
H'holds receiving public assistance . . . 192
H'holds receiving social security . . . 997

Households, 2000

Total households . . . 3,284
With persons under 18 . . . 1,823
With persons over 65 . . . 981
Family households . . . 2,685
Single person households . . . 508
Persons per household . . . 3.80
Persons per family . . . 4.17

Household Population, 2008§§

Persons living in households . . . 13,333
Persons living in group quarters . . . 203
Persons per household . . . 4.0

Labor & Employment

Total civilian labor force, 2008§§ . . . 5,400
Unemployment rate, 2008 . . . 13.7%
Total civilian labor force, 2000 . . . 4,718

Employed persons 16 years and over by occupation, 2000

Managers & professionals . . . 632
Service occupations . . . 521
Sales & office occupations . . . 1,177
Farming, fishing & forestry . . . 7
Construction & maintenance . . . 523
Production & transportation . . . 1,153
Self-employed persons . . . 274

* US Census Bureau
** 2000 Decennial Census
§ California Department of Finance
§§ California Employment Development Dept

General Information

City of Commerce
2535 Commerce Way
Commerce, CA 90040
323-722-4805

Website . . . www.ci.commerce.ca.us
Elevation . . . 140 ft.
Land Area (sq. miles) . . . 6.6
Water Area (sq. miles) . . . 0
Year of Incorporation . . . 1960
Government type . . . General law
Sales tax rate . . . 9.25%

Voters & Officials

Registered Voters, October 2008

Total . . . 5,670
Democrats . . . 4,006
Republicans . . . 619
Declined to state . . . 838

Legislative Districts

US Congressional . . . 34
State Senatorial . . . 30
State Assembly . . . 50

Local Officials, 2009

Mayor . . . Hugo Argumendo
City Administrator . . . Jorge J. Rifa
City Clerk . . . Linda Kay Olivieri
Attorney . . . W. Anthony Willoughby (Int)
Finance Dir . . . Vilko Domic
Public Works . . . Robert Zarrilli
Community Dev Dir . . . Robert Zarrilli
Building . . . (County)
Police Chief . . . (County)
Fire/Emergency Mgmt . . . (County)

Public Safety

Number of officers, 2007 . . . NA
Violent crimes, 2007 . . . 149
Property crimes, 2007 . . . 1,137
Arson, 2007 . . . 9

Public Library

Central Library
City of Commerce Public Library System
5655 Jillson St
Commerce, CA 90040
323-722-6660

Director . . . Evelyn Fullmore

Library system statistics, FY 2007

Population served . . . 13,494
Internet terminals . . . 44
Annual users . . . 30,433

Per capita:

Operating income . . . $216.35
percent from local government . . . 94.8%
Operating expenditure . . . $207.59
Total materials . . . 9.30
Print holdings . . . 7.90
Visits per capita . . . 22.73

Housing & Construction

Housing Units

Total, 2008§ . . . 3,447
Single family units, attached . . . 615
Single family units, detached . . . 1,945
Multiple family units . . . 883
Mobile home units . . . 4
Occupied . . . 3,353
Vacancy rate . . . 2.7%
Median rent, 2000** . . . $623
Median SF home value, 2000** . . . $156,000

New Privately Owned Housing Units Authorized by Building Permit, 2007*

	Units	Construction Cost
Single	21	$2,588,577
Total	21	$2,588,577

Municipal Finance

(For local fiscal year ended in 2006)

Revenues

Total . . . $52,432,324
Taxes . . . 23,090,796
Special benefits assessment . . . 0
Licenses & permits . . . 20,900,394
Fines & forfeitures . . . 487,983
Revenues from use of money & property . . . 3,715,124
Intergovernmental . . . 1,554,718
Service charges . . . 2,290,035
Other revenues . . . 393,274
Other financing sources . . . 0

Expenditures

Total . . . $45,961,238
General government . . . 10,171,024
Public safety . . . 12,753,276
Transportation . . . 4,708,986
Community development . . . 3,737,235
Health . . . 0
Culture & leisure . . . 13,283,142
Other . . . 666,240

Local School District

(Data from School year 2007-08 except as noted)

Montebello Unified
123 South Montebello Blvd
Montebello, CA 90640
(323) 887-7900

Superintendent . . . Edward Velasquez
Grade plan . . . K-12
Number of schools . . . 29
Enrollment . . . 33,493
High school graduates, 2006-07 . . . 1,721
Dropout rate . . . 3.2%
Pupil/teacher ratio . . . 23.7
Average class size . . . 29.7
Students per computer . . . 6.6
Classrooms with internet . . . 2,124
Avg. Daily Attendance (ADA) . . . 32,764
Cost per ADA . . . $8,211
Avg. Teacher Salary . . . $70,515

California Achievement Tests 6th ed., 2008

(Pct scoring at or above 50th National Percentile Rank)

	Math	Reading	Language
Grade 3	47%	24%	38%
Grade 7	39%	31%	32%

Academic Performance Index, 2008

Number of students tested . . . 26,036
Number of valid scores . . . 24,510
2007 API (base) . . . 668
2008 API (growth) . . . 679

SAT Testing, 2006-07

Enrollment, Grade 12 . . . 2,168
Number taking test . . . 580
percent taking test . . . 26.8%
percent with total score 1,500+ . . . 6.60%

Average Scores:

Math	Verbal	Writing	Total
461	443	440	1,344

Federal No Child Left Behind, 2008

(Adequate Yearly Progress standards met)

	Participation Rate	Pct Proficient
ELA	Yes	No
Math	Yes	No

API criteria . . . Yes
Graduation rate . . . Yes
\# criteria met/possible . . . 30/25

Other school districts for this city

(see Appendix E for information on these districts)

Los Angeles Unified

See Introduction for an explanation of all data sources.

Demographics & Socio-Economic Characteristics†

(2007 American Community Survey, except as noted)

Population

1990* . . . 90,454
2007 . . . 100,037
Male . . . 49,934
Female . . . 50,103
Jan. 2008 (estimate)§ . . . 99,242
Persons per sq. mi. of land . . . 9,825.9

Race & Hispanic Origin, 2007

Race
White . . . 35,791
Black/African American . . . 31,054
North American Native . . . 447
Asian . . . 143
Pacific Islander . . . 560
Other Race . . . 29,577
Two or more races . . . 2,465
Hispanic origin, total . . . NA
Mexican . . . 57,363
Puerto Rican . . . 182
Cuban . . . 0
Other Hispanic . . . 10,171

Age & Nativity, 2007

Under 5 years . . . 10,186
18 years and over . . . 63,908
65 years and over . . . 6,103
85 years and over . . . 716
Median Age . . . 25.7
Native-born . . . 66,957
Foreign-born . . . 33,080

Educational Attainment, 2007

Population 25 years and over . . . 51,645
Less than 9th grade . . . 27.6%
High school grad or higher . . . 57.2%
Bachelor's degree or higher . . . 6.2%
Graduate degree . . . 2.4%

Income & Poverty, 2007

Per capita income . . . $13,025
Median household income . . . $44,467
Median family income . . . $44,795
Persons in poverty . . . 24.3%
H'holds receiving public assistance . . . 2,299
H'holds receiving social security . . . 5,329

Households, 2007

Total households . . . 23,392
With persons under 18 . . . 14,067
With persons over 65 . . . 4,832
Family households . . . 19,208
Single person households . . . 3,465
Persons per household . . . 4.28
Persons per family . . . 4.65

Household Population, 2008§§

Persons living in households . . . 98,592
Persons living in group quarters . . . 650
Persons per household . . . 4.4

Labor & Employment

Total civilian labor force, 2008§§ . . . 36,400
Unemployment rate, 2008 . . . 13.1%
Total civilian labor force, 2000* . . . 31,421

Employed persons 16 years and over by occupation, 2007

Managers & professionals . . . 5,354
Service occupations . . . 5,397
Sales & office occupations . . . 11,828
Farming, fishing & forestry . . . 100
Construction & maintenance . . . 4,843
Production & transportation . . . 11,111
Self-employed persons . . . 1,974

† see Appendix D for 2000 Decennial Census Data
* US Census Bureau
** 2007 American Community Survey
§ California Department of Finance
§§ California Employment Development Dept

General Information

City of Compton
205 S Willowbrook Ave
Compton, CA 90220
310-605-5500

Website . . . www.comptoncity.org
Elevation . . . 66 ft.
Land Area (sq. miles) . . . 10.1
Water Area (sq. miles) . . . 0.1
Year of Incorporation . . . 1888
Government type . . . Chartered
Sales tax rate . . . 9.25%

Voters & Officials

Registered Voters, October 2008

Total . . . 37,850
Democrats . . . 28,100
Republicans . . . 3,299
Declined to state . . . 4,962

Legislative Districts

US Congressional . . . 37
State Senatorial . . . 25
State Assembly . . . 52

Local Officials, 2009

Mayor . . . Eric Perrodin
Manager . . . Charles Evans
City Clerk . . . Alita Godwin
Attorney . . . Craig Cornwell
Finance Dir . . . Willie Norfleet
Public Works . . . L. Alan Pyeatt
Planning/Dev Dir . . . Gay Morris
Building . . . Patrick Steward
Police Chief . . . NA
Emergency/Fire Dir . . . Jon Thompson

Public Safety

Number of officers, 2007 . . . NA
Violent crimes, 2007 . . . 1,623
Property crimes, 2007 . . . 2,805
Arson, 2007 . . . 82

Public Library

Compton Library
Los Angeles County Public Library System
240 W Compton Blvd
Compton, CA 90220
310-637-0202

Branch Librarian . . . Sharon Johnson

Library system statistics, FY 2007

Population served . . . 3,673,313
Internet terminals . . . 749
Annual users . . . 3,748,771

Per capita:

Operating income . . . $30.06
percent from local government . . . 93.6%
Operating expenditure . . . $28.36
Total materials . . . 2.22
Print holdings . . . 1.97
Visits per capita . . . 3.25

Housing & Construction

Housing Units

Total, 2008§ . . . 24,112
Single family units, attached . . . 2,150
Single family units, detached . . . 16,086
Multiple family units . . . 5,228
Mobile home units . . . 648
Occupied . . . 22,625
Vacancy rate . . . 6.2%
Median rent, 2007** . . . $797
Median SF home value, 2007** . . . $428,900

New Privately Owned Housing Units Authorized by Building Permit, 2007*

	Units	Construction Cost
Single	24	$2,738,053
Total	32	$3,381,595

Municipal Finance

(For local fiscal year ended in 2006)

Revenues

Total . . . $103,755,795
Taxes . . . 48,668,210
Special benefits assessment . . . 4,601,012
Licenses & permits . . . 976,963
Fines & forfeitures . . . 1,847,630
Revenues from use of money & property . . . 1,819,140
Intergovernmental . . . 18,913,991
Service charges . . . 25,613,953
Other revenues . . . 1,314,896
Other financing sources . . . 0

Expenditures

Total . . . $95,777,644
General government . . . 24,108,949
Public safety . . . 32,078,275
Transportation . . . 6,839,447
Community development . . . 14,964,999
Health . . . 9,952,052
Culture & leisure . . . 1,419,945
Other . . . 0

Local School District

(Data from School year 2007-08 except as noted)

Compton Unified
501 South Santa Fe Ave
Compton, CA 90221
(310) 639-4321

Superintendent . . . Kaye Burnside
Grade plan . . . K-12
Number of schools . . . 40
Enrollment . . . 28,081
High school graduates, 2006-07 . . . 722
Dropout rate . . . 10.2%
Pupil/teacher ratio . . . 22.9
Average class size . . . 27.2
Students per computer . . . 6.3
Classrooms with internet . . . 1,137
Avg. Daily Attendance (ADA) . . . 26,704
Cost per ADA . . . $9,053
Avg. Teacher Salary . . . $61,789

California Achievement Tests 6th ed., 2008

(Pct scoring at or above 50th National Percentile Rank)

	Math	Reading	Language
Grade 3	39%	20%	31%
Grade 7	25%	19%	19%

Academic Performance Index, 2008

Number of students tested . . . 21,505
Number of valid scores . . . 19,873
2007 API (base) . . . 608
2008 API (growth) . . . 627

SAT Testing, 2006-07

Enrollment, Grade 12 . . . 1,287
Number taking test . . . 322
percent taking test . . . 25.0%
percent with total score 1,500+ . . . 1.90%

Average Scores:

Math	Verbal	Writing	Total
389	388	391	1,168

Federal No Child Left Behind, 2008

(Adequate Yearly Progress standards met)

	Participation Rate	Pct Proficient
ELA	No	No
Math	Yes	No

API criteria . . . Yes
Graduation rate . . . No
\# criteria met/possible . . . 30/16

Other school districts for this city

(see Appendix E for information on these districts)

None

See Introduction for an explanation of all data sources.

Demographics & Socio-Economic Characteristics†

(2007 American Community Survey, except as noted)

Population

1990* . . . 111,348
2007 . . . 124,300
Male . . . 62,709
Female . . . 61,591
Jan. 2008 (estimate)§ . . . 123,776
Persons per sq. mi. of land . . . 4,112.2

Race & Hispanic Origin, 2007

Race
White . . . 81,098
Black/African American . . . 3,778
North American Native . . . 244
Asian . . . 11,992
Pacific Islander . . . 707
Other Race . . . 19,004
Two or more races . . . 7,477
Hispanic origin, total . . . 35,385
Mexican . . . 23,735
Puerto Rican . . . 617
Cuban . . . 360
Other Hispanic . . . 10,673

Age & Nativity, 2007

Under 5 years . . . 7,919
18 years and over . . . 92,614
65 years and over . . . 12,950
85 years and over . . . 1,433
Median Age . . . 35.5
Native-born . . . 90,187
Foreign-born . . . 34,113

Educational Attainment, 2007

Population 25 years and over . . . 79,318
Less than 9th grade . . . 7.6%
High school grad or higher . . . 87.0%
Bachelor's degree or higher . . . 33.0%
Graduate degree . . . 10.4%

Income & Poverty, 2007

Per capita income . . . $30,102
Median household income . . . $63,376
Median family income . . . $71,322
Persons in poverty . . . 10.5%
H'holds receiving public assistance . . . 958
H'holds receiving social security . . . 9,480

Households, 2007

Total households . . . 45,238
With persons under 18 . . . 17,021
With persons over 65 . . . 8,576
Family households . . . 31,117
Single person households . . . 10,294
Persons per household . . . 2.72
Persons per family . . . 3.25

Household Population, 2008§§

Persons living in households . . . 122,354
Persons living in group quarters . . . 1,422
Persons per household . . . 2.7

Labor & Employment

Total civilian labor force, 2008§§ . . . 70,400
Unemployment rate, 2008 . . . 6.7%
Total civilian labor force, 2000* . . . 62,926

Employed persons 16 years and over by occupation, 2007

Managers & professionals . . . 20,221
Service occupations . . . 14,150
Sales & office occupations . . . 17,931
Farming, fishing & forestry . . . 184
Construction & maintenance . . . 6,481
Production & transportation . . . 4,515
Self-employed persons . . . 6,423

† see Appendix D for 2000 Decennial Census Data
* US Census Bureau
** 2007 American Community Survey
§ California Department of Finance
§§ California Employment Development Dept

General Information

City of Concord
1950 Parkside Dr
Concord, CA 94519
925-671-3158

Website . . . www.cityofconcord.org
Elevation . . . 70 ft.
Land Area (sq. miles) . . . 30.1
Water Area (sq. miles) . . . 0
Year of Incorporation . . . 1905
Government type . . . General law
Sales tax rate . . . 9.25%

Voters & Officials

Registered Voters, October 2008

Total . . . 57,387
Democrats . . . 27,934
Republicans . . . 15,543
Declined to state . . . 11,274

Legislative Districts

US Congressional . . . 7, 10
State Senatorial . . . 7
State Assembly . . . 11

Local Officials, 2009

Mayor . . . Laura M. Hoffmeister
City Manager . . . Daniel E. Keen
City Clerk . . . Mary Rae Lehman
Attorney . . . Craig Labadie
Finance Dir . . . Margaret Lefebvre
Public Works . . . Qamar Khan
Planning/Dev Dir . . . Jim Forsberg
Building . . . Vance Phillips
Police Chief . . . David Livingston
Emergency/Fire Dir . . . Keith Richter

Public Safety

Number of officers, 2007 . . . 154
Violent crimes, 2007 . . . 492
Property crimes, 2007 . . . 4,998
Arson, 2007 . . . 23

Public Library

Concord Library
Contra Costa County Library System
2900 Salvio St
Concord, CA 94519
925-646-5455

Branch Librarian . . . Maureen Kilmurray

Library system statistics, FY 2007

Population served . . . 938,513
Internet terminals . . . 324
Annual users . . . 670,618

Per capita:

Operating income . . . $27.05
percent from local government . . . 82.0%
Operating expenditure . . . $27.82
Total materials . . . 1.57
Print holdings . . . 1.41
Visits per capita . . . 3.65

Housing & Construction

Housing Units

Total, 2008§ . . . 46,539
Single family units, attached . . . 2,911
Single family units, detached . . . 27,789
Multiple family units . . . 14,462
Mobile home units . . . 1,377
Occupied . . . 45,443
Vacancy rate . . . 2.4%
Median rent, 2007** . . . $1,137
Median SF home value, 2007** . . . $580,300

New Privately Owned Housing Units Authorized by Building Permit, 2007*

	Units	Construction Cost
Single	101	$30,219,193
Total	101	$30,219,193

Municipal Finance

(For local fiscal year ended in 2006)

Revenues

Total . . . $110,177,183
Taxes . . . 60,414,028
Special benefits assessment . . . 3,382,101
Licenses & permits . . . 2,657,988
Fines & forfeitures . . . 488,368
Revenues from use of money & property . . . 4,636,895
Intergovernmental . . . 9,734,437
Service charges . . . 27,633,691
Other revenues . . . 1,229,675
Other financing sources . . . 0

Expenditures

Total . . . $115,799,433
General government . . . 12,233,706
Public safety . . . 38,017,580
Transportation . . . 27,226,336
Community development . . . 6,952,036
Health . . . 15,144,747
Culture & leisure . . . 16,225,028
Other . . . 0

Local School District

(Data from School year 2007-08 except as noted)

Mt. Diablo Unified
1936 Carlotta Dr
Concord, CA 94519
(925) 682-8000

Superintendent . . . Richard Nicholl
Grade plan . . . K-12
Number of schools . . . 55
Enrollment . . . 35,355
High school graduates, 2006-07 . . . 2,153
Dropout rate . . . 6.0%
Pupil/teacher ratio . . . 20.4
Average class size . . . 26.4
Students per computer . . . 5.2
Classrooms with internet . . . 1,777
Avg. Daily Attendance (ADA) . . . 33,956
Cost per ADA . . . $8,368
Avg. Teacher Salary . . . $60,714

California Achievement Tests 6th ed., 2008

(Pct scoring at or above 50th National Percentile Rank)

	Math	Reading	Language
Grade 3	60%	45%	55%
Grade 7	53%	53%	51%

Academic Performance Index, 2008

Number of students tested . . . 26,357
Number of valid scores . . . 25,920
2007 API (base) . . . 747
2008 API (growth) . . . 755

SAT Testing, 2006-07

Enrollment, Grade 12 . . . 2,734
Number taking test . . . 1,063
percent taking test . . . 38.9%
percent with total score 1,500+ . . . 22.80%

Average Scores:

Math	Verbal	Writing	Total
543	521	518	1,582

Federal No Child Left Behind, 2008

(Adequate Yearly Progress standards met)

	Participation Rate	Pct Proficient
ELA	Yes	No
Math	Yes	No

API criteria . . . Yes
Graduation rate . . . Yes
\# criteria met/possible . . . 46/36

Other school districts for this city

(see Appendix E for information on these districts)

None

See Introduction for an explanation of all data sources.

Demographics & Socio-Economic Characteristics

(2000 Decennial Census, except as noted)

Population

1990* . . . 13,364
2000 . . . 14,458
Male . . . 9,761
Female . . . 4,697
Jan. 2008 (estimate)§ . . . 26,047
Persons per sq. mi. of land . . . 4,069.8

Race & Hispanic Origin, 2000

Race
White . . . 4,927
Black/African American . . . 2,054
North American Native . . . 206
Asian . . . 103
Pacific Islander . . . 12
Other Race . . . 6,711
Two or more races . . . 445
Hispanic origin, total . . . 8,618
Mexican . . . 7,866
Puerto Rican . . . 15
Cuban . . . 10
Other Hispanic . . . 727

Age & Nativity, 2000

Under 5 years . . . 962
18 years and over . . . 10,931
65 years and over . . . 774
85 years and over . . . 86
Median Age . . . 30.7
Native-born . . . 12,151
Foreign-born . . . 2,088

Educational Attainment, 2000

Population 25 years and over . . . 9,238
Less than 9th grade . . . 16.7%
High school grad or higher . . . 62.4%
Bachelor's degree or higher . . . 5.6%
Graduate degree . . . 1.2%

Income & Poverty, 1999

Per capita income . . . $13,458
Median household income . . . $30,783
Median family income . . . $32,852
Persons in poverty . . . 17.3%
H'holds receiving public assistance . . . 298
H'holds receiving social security . . . 649

Households, 2000

Total households . . . 2,769
With persons under 18 . . . 1,549
With persons over 65 . . . 575
Family households . . . 2,229
Single person households . . . 442
Persons per household . . . 3.44
Persons per family . . . 3.83

Household Population, 2008§§

Persons living in households . . . 12,914
Persons living in group quarters . . . 13,133
Persons per household . . . 3.6

Labor & Employment

Total civilian labor force, 2008§§ . . . 4,400
Unemployment rate, 2008 . . . 10.7%
Total civilian labor force, 2000 . . . 3,434

Employed persons 16 years and over by occupation, 2000

Managers & professionals . . . 559
Service occupations . . . 537
Sales & office occupations . . . 540
Farming, fishing & forestry . . . 396
Construction & maintenance . . . 276
Production & transportation . . . 659
Self-employed persons . . . 96

* US Census Bureau
** 2000 Decennial Census
§ California Department of Finance
§§ California Employment Development Dept

General Information

City of Corcoran
1033 Chittenden Ave
Corcoran, CA 93212
559-992-2151

Website . . . cityofcorcoran.com
Elevation . . . 207 ft.
Land Area (sq. miles) . . . 6.4
Water Area (sq. miles) . . . 0
Year of Incorporation . . . 1914
Government type . . . General law
Sales tax rate . . . 8.25%

Voters & Officials

Registered Voters, October 2008

Total . . . 4,204
Democrats . . . 2,327
Republicans . . . 1,229
Declined to state . . . 495

Legislative Districts

US Congressional . . . 20
State Senatorial . . . 16
State Assembly . . . 30

Local Officials, 2009

Mayor . . . Dick Haile
Manager . . . Ronald L. Hoggard
City Clerk . . . Lorraine P. Lopez
Attorney . . . Michael Farley
Finance Dir . . . Joyce Venegas
Public Works . . . Steve Kroeker
Planning/Dev Dir . . . Jeri Grant
Building . . . NA
Police Chief . . . Reuben Shortnacy
Fire/Emergency Mgmt . . . NA

Public Safety

Number of officers, 2007 . . . 17
Violent crimes, 2007 . . . 45
Property crimes, 2007 . . . 216
Arson, 2007 . . . 4

Public Library

Corcoran Branch
Kings County Library System
1001A Chittenden
Corcoran, CA 93212
559-992-3314

Branch Librarian . . . NA

Library system statistics, FY 2007

Population served . . . 151,381
Internet terminals . . . 59
Annual users . . . 42,581

Per capita:

Operating income . . . $11.91
percent from local government . . . 86.5%
Operating expenditure . . . $11.91
Total materials . . . 1.20
Print holdings . . . 1.17
Visits per capita . . . NA

Housing & Construction

Housing Units

Total, 2008§ . . . 3,951
Single family units, attached . . . 180
Single family units, detached . . . 2,899
Multiple family units . . . 707
Mobile home units . . . 165
Occupied . . . 3,626
Vacancy rate . . . 8.2%
Median rent, 2000** . . . $491
Median SF home value, 2000** . . . $74,900

New Privately Owned Housing Units Authorized by Building Permit, 2007*

	Units	Construction Cost
Single	35	$4,851,088
Total	35	$4,851,088

Municipal Finance

(For local fiscal year ended in 2006)

Revenues

Total . . . $29,762,712
Taxes . . . 3,261,360
Special benefits assessment . . . 0
Licenses & permits . . . 178,587
Fines & forfeitures . . . 32,212
Revenues from use of money & property . . . 639,639
Intergovernmental . . . 2,770,063
Service charges . . . 5,606,555
Other revenues . . . 1,850,296
Other financing sources . . . 15,424,000

Expenditures

Total . . . $28,343,733
General government . . . 168,262
Public safety . . . 2,752,862
Transportation . . . 1,960,042
Community development . . . 2,336,539
Health . . . 2,505,464
Culture & leisure . . . 635,033
Other . . . 0

Local School District

(Data from School year 2007-08 except as noted)

Corcoran Joint Unified
1520 Patterson Ave
Corcoran, CA 93212
(559) 992-8888

Superintendent . . . Richard Merlo
Grade plan . . . K-12
Number of schools . . . 7
Enrollment . . . 3,211
High school graduates, 2006-07 . . . 125
Dropout rate . . . 5.4%
Pupil/teacher ratio . . . 18.7
Average class size . . . 24.1
Students per computer . . . 2.9
Classrooms with internet . . . 163
Avg. Daily Attendance (ADA) . . . 3,095
Cost per ADA . . . $9,021
Avg. Teacher Salary . . . $60,162

California Achievement Tests 6th ed., 2008

(Pct scoring at or above 50th National Percentile Rank)

	Math	Reading	Language
Grade 3	48%	30%	40%
Grade 7	35%	29%	29%

Academic Performance Index, 2008

Number of students tested . . . 2,491
Number of valid scores . . . 2,279
2007 API (base) . . . 689
2008 API (growth) . . . 714

SAT Testing, 2006-07

Enrollment, Grade 12 . . . 196
Number taking test . . . 54
percent taking test . . . 27.6%
percent with total score 1,500+ . . . 6.60%

Average Scores:

Math	Verbal	Writing	Total
441	435	427	1,303

Federal No Child Left Behind, 2008

(Adequate Yearly Progress standards met)

	Participation Rate	Pct Proficient
ELA	No	No
Math	Yes	No

API criteria . . . Yes
Graduation rate . . . Yes
criteria met/possible . . . 26/23

Other school districts for this city

(see Appendix E for information on these districts)

None

See Introduction for an explanation of all data sources.

Demographics & Socio-Economic Characteristics

(2000 Decennial Census, except as noted)

Population

1990* . . . 5,870
2000 . . . 6,741
Male . . . 3,247
Female . . . 3,494
Jan. 2008 (estimate)§ . . . 7,226
Persons per sq. mi. of land . . . 2,491.7

Race & Hispanic Origin, 2000

Race
White . . . 5,021
Black/African American . . . 35
North American Native . . . 147
Asian . . . 36
Pacific Islander . . . 6
Other Race . . . 1,174
Two or more races . . . 322
Hispanic origin, total . . . 1,943
Mexican . . . 1,670
Puerto Rican . . . 11
Cuban . . . 1
Other Hispanic . . . 261

Age & Nativity, 2000

Under 5 years . . . 614
18 years and over . . . 4,548
65 years and over . . . 794
85 years and over . . . 119
Median Age . . . 30.9
Native-born . . . 5,729
Foreign-born . . . 1,049

Educational Attainment, 2000

Population 25 years and over . . . 4,010
Less than 9th grade . . . 15.7%
High school grad or higher . . . 69.7%
Bachelor's degree or higher . . . 7.3%
Graduate degree . . . 1.3%

Income & Poverty, 1999

Per capita income . . . $12,357
Median household income . . . $25,357
Median family income . . . $32,151
Persons in poverty . . . 26.3%
H'holds receiving public assistance . . . 257
H'holds receiving social security . . . 830

Households, 2000

Total households . . . 2,422
With persons under 18 . . . 1,079
With persons over 65 . . . 631
Family households . . . 1,643
Single person households . . . 652
Persons per household . . . 2.76
Persons per family . . . 3.33

Household Population, 2008§§

Persons living in households . . . 7,169
Persons living in group quarters . . . 57
Persons per household . . . 2.7

Labor & Employment

Total civilian labor force, 2008§§ . . . 2,960
Unemployment rate, 2008 . . . 10.6%
Total civilian labor force, 2000 . . . 2,688

Employed persons 16 years and over by occupation, 2000

Managers & professionals . . . 351
Service occupations . . . 534
Sales & office occupations . . . 576
Farming, fishing & forestry . . . 121
Construction & maintenance . . . 178
Production & transportation . . . 625
Self-employed persons . . . 268

* US Census Bureau
** 2000 Decennial Census
§ California Department of Finance
§§ California Employment Development Dept

General Information

City of Corning
794 3rd St
Corning, CA 96021
530-824-7033

Website . . . www.corning.org
Elevation . . . 272 ft.
Land Area (sq. miles) . . . 2.9
Water Area (sq. miles) . . . 0
Year of Incorporation . . . 1907
Government type . . . General law
Sales tax rate . . . 8.25%

Voters & Officials

Registered Voters, October 2008

Total . . . 2,573
Democrats . . . 981
Republicans . . . 950
Declined to state . . . 479

Legislative Districts

US Congressional . . . 2
State Senatorial . . . 4
State Assembly . . . 2

Local Officials, 2009

Mayor . . . Gary Strack
Manager . . . Stephen Kimbrough
City Clerk . . . Lisa M. Linnet
Attorney . . . Michael Fitzpatrick
Finance Dir . . . Stephen Kimbrough
Public Works . . . John Brewer
Planning/Dev Dir . . . John Stoufer
Building . . . Terry Hoofard
Police Chief . . . Anthony Cardenas
Emergency/Fire Dir . . . Martin Spannaus

Public Safety

Number of officers, 2007 . . . 13
Violent crimes, 2007 . . . 45
Property crimes, 2007 . . . 265
Arson, 2007 . . . 6

Public Library

Corning Branch Library
Tehama County Library System
740 Third St
Corning, CA 96021
530-824-7050

Branch Librarian . . . Caryn Brown

Library system statistics, FY 2007

Population served . . . 61,774
Internet terminals . . . 21
Annual users . . . 15,734

Per capita:

Operating income . . . $9.05
percent from local government . . . 89.6%
Operating expenditure . . . $8.17
Total materials . . . 1.93
Print holdings . . . 1.86
Visits per capita . . . 1.33

Housing & Construction

Housing Units

Total, 2008§ . . . 2,843
Single family units, attached . . . 70
Single family units, detached . . . 1,737
Multiple family units . . . 797
Mobile home units . . . 239
Occupied . . . 2,634
Vacancy rate . . . 7.4%
Median rent, 2000** . . . $426
Median SF home value, 2000** . . . $79,600

New Privately Owned Housing Units Authorized by Building Permit, 2007*

	Units	Construction Cost
Single	23	$3,469,068
Total	31	$4,119,178

Municipal Finance

(For local fiscal year ended in 2006)

Revenues

Total . . . $7,657,567
Taxes . . . 3,609,652
Special benefits assessment . . . 74,987
Licenses & permits . . . 138,797
Fines & forfeitures . . . 52,845
Revenues from use of money & property . . . 205,791
Intergovernmental . . . 779,483
Service charges . . . 2,685,763
Other revenues . . . 110,249
Other financing sources . . . 0

Expenditures

Total . . . $7,205,123
General government . . . 643,244
Public safety . . . 2,776,572
Transportation . . . 560,393
Community development . . . 354,954
Health . . . 1,452,710
Culture & leisure . . . 179,948
Other . . . 0

Local School District

(Data from School year 2007-08 except as noted)

Corning Union High
643 Blackburn Ave
Corning, CA 96021
(530) 824-8000

Superintendent . . . Bruce Cole
Grade plan . . . 9-12
Number of schools . . . 3
Enrollment . . . 1,056
High school graduates, 2006-07 . . . 209
Dropout rate . . . 3.3%
Pupil/teacher ratio . . . 18.0
Average class size . . . 22.2
Students per computer . . . 4.8
Classrooms with internet . . . 58
Avg. Daily Attendance (ADA) . . . 993
Cost per ADA . . . $9,292
Avg. Teacher Salary . . . $53,000

California Achievement Tests 6th ed., 2008

(Pct scoring at or above 50th National Percentile Rank)

	Math	Reading	Language
Grade 3	NA	NA	NA
Grade 7	NA	NA	NA

Academic Performance Index, 2008

Number of students tested . . . 804
Number of valid scores . . . 759
2007 API (base) . . . 666
2008 API (growth) . . . 688

SAT Testing, 2006-07

Enrollment, Grade 12 . . . 272
Number taking test . . . 53
percent taking test . . . 19.5%
percent with total score 1,500+ . . . 7.40%

Average Scores:

Math	Verbal	Writing	Total
480	475	464	1,419

Federal No Child Left Behind, 2008

(Adequate Yearly Progress standards met)

	Participation Rate	Pct Proficient
ELA	Yes	No
Math	Yes	No

API criteria . . . Yes
Graduation rate . . . Yes
criteria met/possible . . . 22/19

Other school districts for this city

(see Appendix E for information on these districts)

Corning Union Elem, Kirkwood Elem, Richfield Elem

See Introduction for an explanation of all data sources.

Demographics & Socio-Economic Characteristics†

(2007 American Community Survey, except as noted)

Population

1990* . . . 76,095
2007 . . . 156,394
Male . . . 76,668
Female . . . 79,726
Jan. 2008 (estimate)§ . . . 147,428
Persons per sq. mi. of land . . . 4,200.2

Race & Hispanic Origin, 2007

Race
White . . . 97,065
Black/African American . . . 10,549
North American Native . . . 1,197
Asian . . . 11,651
Pacific Islander . . . 616
Other Race . . . 27,698
Two or more races . . . 7,618
Hispanic origin, total . . . 62,627
Mexican . . . 49,391
Puerto Rican . . . 173
Cuban . . . 476
Other Hispanic . . . 12,587

Age & Nativity, 2007

Under 5 years . . . 11,007
18 years and over . . . 111,167
65 years and over . . . 7,665
85 years and over . . . 296
Median Age . . . 29.3
Native-born . . . 118,015
Foreign-born . . . 38,379

Educational Attainment, 2007

Population 25 years and over . . . 93,866
Less than 9th grade . . . 8.1%
High school grad or higher . . . 85.1%
Bachelor's degree or higher . . . 24.0%
Graduate degree . . . 7.7%

Income & Poverty, 2007

Per capita income . . . $28,963
Median household income . . . $78,620
Median family income . . . $85,450
Persons in poverty . . . 5.4%
H'holds receiving public assistance . . . 489
H'holds receiving social security . . . 6,693

Households, 2007

Total households . . . 45,542
With persons under 18 . . . 23,916
With persons over 65 . . . 6,210
Family households . . . 36,853
Single person households . . . 6,654
Persons per household . . . 3.43
Persons per family . . . 3.79

Household Population, 2008§§

Persons living in households . . . 146,796
Persons living in group quarters . . . 632
Persons per household . . . 3.3

Labor & Employment

Total civilian labor force, 2008§§ . . . 85,500
Unemployment rate, 2008 . . . 6.3%
Total civilian labor force, 2000* . . . 60,557

Employed persons 16 years and over by occupation, 2007

Managers & professionals . . . 26,525
Service occupations . . . 12,335
Sales & office occupations . . . 26,613
Farming, fishing & forestry . . . 539
Construction & maintenance . . . 7,716
Production & transportation . . . 8,840
Self-employed persons . . . 5,872

† see Appendix D for 2000 Decennial Census Data
* US Census Bureau
** 2007 American Community Survey
§ California Department of Finance
§§ California Employment Development Dept

General Information

City of Corona
400 S Vicentia Ave
PO Box 940
Corona, CA 92882
951-736-2400

Website . . . www.discovercorona.org
Elevation . . . 678 ft.
Land Area (sq. miles) . . . 35.1
Water Area (sq. miles) . . . 0
Year of Incorporation . . . 1896
Government type . . . General law
Sales tax rate . . . 8.75%

Voters & Officials

Registered Voters, October 2008

Total . . . 59,194
Democrats . . . 19,950
Republicans . . . 26,032
Declined to state . . . 10,838

Legislative Districts

US Congressional . . . 44
State Senatorial . . . 37
State Assembly . . . 71

Local Officials, 2009

Mayor . . . Jeff Miller
Manager . . . Beth Groves
City Clerk . . . Victoria Wasko
Attorney . . . Best, Best & Krieger
Finance Dir . . . Debra Foster
Public Works . . . Amad Qattan
Planning/Dev Dir . . . Brad Robbins
Building . . . Keith Clarke
Police Chief . . . Richard Gonzales
Fire Chief . . . Michael Warren

Public Safety

Number of officers, 2007 . . . 181
Violent crimes, 2007 . . . 340
Property crimes, 2007 . . . 4,022
Arson, 2007 . . . 21

Public Library

Corona Public Library
650 S Main St
Corona, CA 92882
951-736-2384

Director . . . Julie Frederickson

Library statistics, FY 2007

Population served . . . 146,164
Internet terminals . . . 7
Annual users . . . 43,416

Per capita:

Operating income . . . $23.57
percent from local government . . . 92.9%
Operating expenditure . . . $19.08
Total materials . . . 1.03
Print holdings . . . 0.96
Visits per capita . . . 3.62

Housing & Construction

Housing Units

Total, 2008§ . . . 45,485
Single family units, attached . . . 2,186
Single family units, detached . . . 31,623
Multiple family units . . . 10,063
Mobile home units . . . 1,613
Occupied . . . 43,827
Vacancy rate . . . 3.7%
Median rent, 2007** . . . $1,216
Median SF home value, 2007** . . . $535,600

New Privately Owned Housing Units Authorized by Building Permit, 2007*

	Units	Construction Cost
Single	76	$24,622,639
Total	116	$30,296,391

Municipal Finance

(For local fiscal year ended in 2006)

Revenues

Total . . . $184,696,783
Taxes . . . 95,390,037
Special benefits assessment . . . 380,669
Licenses & permits . . . 4,195,701
Fines & forfeitures . . . 1,619,755
Revenues from use of money & property . . . 3,880,329
Intergovernmental . . . 17,718,776
Service charges . . . 37,234,805
Other revenues . . . 24,276,711
Other financing sources . . . 0

Expenditures

Total . . . $153,311,124
General government . . . 21,345,285
Public safety . . . 56,407,802
Transportation . . . 16,397,982
Community development . . . 13,844,570
Health . . . 6,360,705
Culture & leisure . . . 13,421,272
Other . . . 0

Local School District

(Data from School year 2007-08 except as noted)

Corona-Norco Unified
2820 Clark Ave
Norco, CA 92860
(951) 736-5000

Superintendent . . . Kent Bechler
Grade plan . . . K-12
Number of schools . . . 50
Enrollment . . . 51,322
High school graduates, 2006-07 . . . 2,991
Dropout rate . . . 2.8%
Pupil/teacher ratio . . . 21.5
Average class size . . . 26.9
Students per computer . . . 5.3
Classrooms with internet . . . 2,277
Avg. Daily Attendance (ADA) . . . 49,812
Cost per ADA . . . $7,597
Avg. Teacher Salary . . . $74,860

California Achievement Tests 6th ed., 2008

(Pct scoring at or above 50th National Percentile Rank)

	Math	Reading	Language
Grade 3	61%	42%	50%
Grade 7	57%	52%	50%

Academic Performance Index, 2008

Number of students tested . . . 39,882
Number of valid scores . . . 37,055
2007 API (base) . . . 762
2008 API (growth) . . . 773

SAT Testing, 2006-07

Enrollment, Grade 12 . . . 3,657
Number taking test . . . 1,268
percent taking test . . . 34.7%
percent with total score 1,500+ . . . 13.60%

Average Scores:

Math	Verbal	Writing	Total
486	472	471	1,429

Federal No Child Left Behind, 2008

(Adequate Yearly Progress standards met)

	Participation Rate	Pct Proficient
ELA	Yes	Yes
Math	Yes	No

API criteria . . . Yes
Graduation rate . . . Yes
\# criteria met/possible . . . 42/41

Other school districts for this city

(see Appendix E for information on these districts)

Alvord Unified

See Introduction for an explanation of all data sources.

Demographics & Socio-Economic Characteristics

(2000 Decennial Census, except as noted)

Population

1990*	26,540
2000	24,100
Male	14,049
Female	10,051
Jan. 2008 (estimate)§	23,101
Persons per sq. mi. of land	3,000.1

Race & Hispanic Origin, 2000

Race	
White	20,341
Black/African American	1,241
North American Native	159
Asian	896
Pacific Islander	72
Other Race	757
Two or more races	634
Hispanic origin, total	2,369
Mexican	1,629
Puerto Rican	155
Cuban	29
Other Hispanic	556

Age & Nativity, 2000

Under 5 years	957
18 years and over	20,251
65 years and over	3,817
85 years and over	523
Median Age	34.2
Native-born	22,043
Foreign-born	2,183

Educational Attainment, 2000

Population 25 years and over	15,256
Less than 9th grade	0.6%
High school grad or higher	96.1%
Bachelor's degree or higher	48.2%
Graduate degree	22.9%

Income & Poverty, 1999

Per capita income	$34,656
Median household income	$66,544
Median family income	$82,959
Persons in poverty	3.7%
H'holds receiving public assistance	118
H'holds receiving social security	2,433

Households, 2000

Total households	7,734
With persons under 18	2,166
With persons over 65	2,522
Family households	4,935
Single person households	2,388
Persons per household	2.27
Persons per family	2.84

Household Population, 2008§§

Persons living in households	18,179
Persons living in group quarters	4,922
Persons per household	2.3

Labor & Employment

Total civilian labor force, 2008§§	8,800
Unemployment rate, 2008	3.8%
Total civilian labor force, 2000	7,694

Employed persons 16 years and over by occupation, 2000

Managers & professionals	4,198
Service occupations	1,005
Sales & office occupations	1,581
Farming, fishing & forestry	0
Construction & maintenance	322
Production & transportation	333
Self-employed persons	964

* US Census Bureau
** 2000 Decennial Census
§ California Department of Finance
§§ California Employment Development Dept

General Information

City of Coronado
1825 Strand Way
Coronado, CA 92118
619-522-7300

Website	www.coronado.ca.us
Elevation	25 ft.
Land Area (sq. miles)	7.7
Water Area (sq. miles)	24.9
Year of Incorporation	1890
Government type	General law
Sales tax rate	8.75%

Voters & Officials

Registered Voters, October 2008

Total	10,647
Democrats	2,641
Republicans	5,289
Declined to state	2,331

Legislative Districts

US Congressional	53
State Senatorial	40
State Assembly	79

Local Officials, 2009

Mayor	Tom Smisek
Manager	Mark Ochenduszko
City Clerk	Linda Hascup
Attorney	Morgan Foley
Finance Dir	Leslie Suelter
Public Works	Scott Huth
Community Dev Dir	Tony Pena
Building	NA
Police Chief	Lou Scanlon
Fire Chief	Kim Raddatz

Public Safety

Number of officers, 2007	41
Violent crimes, 2007	26
Property crimes, 2007	535
Arson, 2007	4

Public Library

Coronado Public Library
640 Orange Ave
Coronado, CA 92118
619-522-7390

Director	Christian Esquevin

Library statistics, FY 2007

Population served	22,957
Internet terminals	17
Annual users	NA

Per capita:

Operating income	$90.87
percent from local government	95.5%
Operating expenditure	$91.25
Total materials	7.85
Print holdings	6.75
Visits per capita	14.70

Housing & Construction

Housing Units

Total, 2008§	9,611
Single family units, attached	868
Single family units, detached	4,506
Multiple family units	4,214
Mobile home units	23
Occupied	7,825
Vacancy rate	18.6%
Median rent, 2000**	$1,024
Median SF home value, 2000**	$683,400

New Privately Owned Housing Units Authorized by Building Permit, 2007*

	Units	Construction Cost
Single	57	$23,580,307
Total	61	$24,808,258

Municipal Finance

(For local fiscal year ended in 2006)

Revenues

Total	$62,414,747
Taxes	28,468,950
Special benefits assessment	0
Licenses & permits	595,140
Fines & forfeitures	225,061
Revenues from use of money & property	1,947,776
Intergovernmental	5,204,465
Service charges	10,748,107
Other revenues	15,225,248
Other financing sources	0

Expenditures

Total	$44,218,936
General government	2,617,624
Public safety	14,056,096
Transportation	7,815,771
Community development	2,231,824
Health	5,274,028
Culture & leisure	12,223,593
Other	0

Local School District

(Data from School year 2007-08 except as noted)

Coronado Unified
201 Sixth St
Coronado, CA 92118
(619) 522-8900

Superintendent	Jeffrey Felix
Grade plan	K-12
Number of schools	5
Enrollment	3,007
High school graduates, 2006-07	252
Dropout rate	1.8%
Pupil/teacher ratio	21.9
Average class size	26.6
Students per computer	2.6
Classrooms with internet	847
Avg. Daily Attendance (ADA)	2,931
Cost per ADA	$8,217
Avg. Teacher Salary	$64,096

California Achievement Tests 6th ed., 2008

(Pct scoring at or above 50th National Percentile Rank)

	Math	Reading	Language
Grade 3	82%	67%	77%
Grade 7	84%	83%	82%

Academic Performance Index, 2008

Number of students tested	2,330
Number of valid scores	2,227
2007 API (base)	876
2008 API (growth)	878

SAT Testing, 2006-07

Enrollment, Grade 12	257
Number taking test	196
percent taking test	76.3%
percent with total score 1,500+	56.40%

Average Scores:

Math	Verbal	Writing	Total
557	555	550	1,662

Federal No Child Left Behind, 2008

(Adequate Yearly Progress standards met)

	Participation Rate	Pct Proficient
ELA	No	Yes
Math	Yes	Yes

API criteria	Yes
Graduation rate	Yes
# criteria met/possible	22/21

Other school districts for this city

(see Appendix E for information on these districts)

None

See Introduction for an explanation of all data sources.

Demographics & Socio-Economic Characteristics

(2000 Decennial Census, except as noted)

Population

1990* . . . 8,272
2000 . . . 9,100
Male . . . 4,259
Female . . . 4,841
Jan. 2008 (estimate)§ . . . 9,512
Persons per sq. mi. of land . . . 2,972.5

Race & Hispanic Origin, 2000

Race
White . . . 7,977
Black/African American . . . 80
North American Native . . . 29
Asian . . . 553
Pacific Islander . . . 17
Other Race . . . 118
Two or more races . . . 326
Hispanic origin, total . . . 436
Mexican . . . 184
Puerto Rican . . . 31
Cuban . . . 7
Other Hispanic . . . 214

Age & Nativity, 2000

Under 5 years . . . 636
18 years and over . . . 6,974
65 years and over . . . 1,206
85 years and over . . . 114
Median Age . . . 40.7
Native-born . . . 7,756
Foreign-born . . . 1,388

Educational Attainment, 2000

Population 25 years and over . . . 6,738
Less than 9th grade . . . 1.6%
High school grad or higher . . . 95.4%
Bachelor's degree or higher . . . 63.3%
Graduate degree . . . 23.3%

Income & Poverty, 1999

Per capita income . . . $46,326
Median household income . . . $79,839
Median family income . . . $95,471
Persons in poverty . . . 4.5%
H'holds receiving public assistance . . . 13
H'holds receiving social security . . . 862

Households, 2000

Total households . . . 3,776
With persons under 18 . . . 1,264
With persons over 65 . . . 892
Family households . . . 2,472
Single person households . . . 937
Persons per household . . . 2.41
Persons per family . . . 2.89

Household Population, 2008§§

Persons living in households . . . 9,504
Persons living in group quarters . . . 8
Persons per household . . . 2.4

Labor & Employment

Total civilian labor force, 2008§§ . . . 5,300
Unemployment rate, 2008 . . . 2.9%
Total civilian labor force, 2000 . . . 5,121

Employed persons 16 years and over by occupation, 2000

Managers & professionals . . . 3,052
Service occupations . . . 549
Sales & office occupations . . . 1,010
Farming, fishing & forestry . . . 0
Construction & maintenance . . . 258
Production & transportation . . . 156
Self-employed persons . . . 976

* US Census Bureau
** 2000 Decennial Census
§ California Department of Finance
§§ California Employment Development Dept

General Information

Town of Corte Madera
300 Tamalpais Dr
Corte Madera, CA 94925
415-927-5050

Website . . . www.ci.corte-madera.ca.us
Elevation . . . 27 ft.
Land Area (sq. miles) . . . 3.2
Water Area (sq. miles) . . . 1.2
Year of Incorporation . . . 1916
Government type . . . General law
Sales tax rate . . . 9.00%

Voters & Officials

Registered Voters, October 2008

Total . . . 6,094
Democrats . . . 3,353
Republicans . . . 1,135
Declined to state . . . 1,377

Legislative Districts

US Congressional . . . 6
State Senatorial . . . 3
State Assembly . . . 6

Local Officials, 2009

Mayor . . . John Dupar
Manager . . . David Bracken
City Clerk . . . Christine Green
Attorney . . . Jeff Walter
Finance Dir . . . George T. Warman Jr
Public Works . . . Debra Sue Johnson
Planning/Dev Dir . . . Robert Pendoley
Building . . . NA
Police Chief . . . Phillip Green
Emergency/Fire Dir . . . Roger Sprehn

Public Safety

(Twin Cities Police Authority for Corte Madera & Larkspur)

Number of officers, 2007 . . . 34
Violent crimes, 2007 . . . 19
Property crimes, 2007 . . . 555
Arson, 2007 . . . 2

Public Library

Corte Madera Regional Library
Marin County Free Library System
707 Meadowsweet Dr
Corte Madera, CA 94925
415-924-3515

Branch Librarian . . . Nancy Davis

Library system statistics, FY 2007

Population served . . . 140,989
Internet terminals . . . 95
Annual users . . . 198,739

Per capita:

Operating income . . . $77.23
percent from local government . . . 90.0%
Operating expenditure . . . $77.23
Total materials . . . 3.56
Print holdings . . . 3.12
Visits per capita . . . 7.73

Housing & Construction

Housing Units

Total, 2008§ . . . 3,980
Single family units, attached . . . 416
Single family units, detached . . . 2,624
Multiple family units . . . 930
Mobile home units . . . 10
Occupied . . . 3,904
Vacancy rate . . . 1.9%
Median rent, 2000** . . . $1,347
Median SF home value, 2000** . . . $561,300

New Privately Owned Housing Units Authorized by Building Permit, 2007*

	Units	Construction Cost
Single	0	$0
Total	0	$0

Municipal Finance

(For local fiscal year ended in 2006)

Revenues

Total . . . $19,690,205
Taxes . . . 14,373,665
Special benefits assessment . . . 0
Licenses & permits . . . 154,189
Fines & forfeitures . . . 76,277
Revenues from use of money & property . . . 101,772
Intergovernmental . . . 783,348
Service charges . . . 3,132,426
Other revenues . . . 68,528
Other financing sources . . . 1,000,000

Expenditures

Total . . . $23,760,231
General government . . . 2,886,450
Public safety . . . 7,191,017
Transportation . . . 1,825,251
Community development . . . 1,594,212
Health . . . 7,158,427
Culture & leisure . . . 3,104,874
Other . . . 0

Local School District

(Data from School year 2007-08 except as noted)

Tamalpais Union High
PO Box 605
Larkspur, CA 94977
(415) 945-3720

Superintendent . . . Laurie Kimbrel
Grade plan . . . 9-12
Number of schools . . . 5
Enrollment . . . 3,889
High school graduates, 2006-07 . . . 959
Dropout rate . . . 0.8%
Pupil/teacher ratio . . . 17.4
Average class size . . . 24.4
Students per computer . . . 2.6
Classrooms with internet . . . 232
Avg. Daily Attendance (ADA) . . . 3,715
Cost per ADA . . . $13,492
Avg. Teacher Salary . . . $81,923

California Achievement Tests 6th ed., 2008

(Pct scoring at or above 50th National Percentile Rank)

	Math	Reading	Language
Grade 3	NA	NA	NA
Grade 7	NA	NA	NA

Academic Performance Index, 2008

Number of students tested . . . 2,800
Number of valid scores . . . 2,766
2007 API (base) . . . 848
2008 API (growth) . . . 855

SAT Testing, 2006-07

Enrollment, Grade 12 . . . 997
Number taking test . . . 730
percent taking test . . . 73.2%
percent with total score 1,500+ . . . 58.30%

Average Scores:

Math	Verbal	Writing	Total
574	574	574	1,722

Federal No Child Left Behind, 2008

(Adequate Yearly Progress standards met)

	Participation Rate	Pct Proficient
ELA	Yes	Yes
Math	Yes	Yes

API criteria . . . Yes
Graduation rate . . . Yes
criteria met/possible . . . 10/10

Other school districts for this city

(see Appendix E for information on these districts)

Larkspur Elem

See Introduction for an explanation of all data sources.

Demographics & Socio-Economic Characteristics†

(2007 American Community Survey, except as noted)

Population

1990* ... 96,357
2007 ... 114,057
Male ... 61,607
Female ... 52,450
Jan. 2008 (estimate)§ ... 113,955
Persons per sq. mi. of land ... 7,304.8

Race & Hispanic Origin, 2007

Race
White ... 82,443
Black/African American ... 1,732
North American Native ... 412
Asian ... 9,557
Pacific Islander ... 126
Other Race ... 17,414
Two or more races ... 2,373
Hispanic origin, total ... 38,991
Mexican ... 33,121
Puerto Rican ... 303
Cuban ... 599
Other Hispanic ... 4,968

Age & Nativity, 2007

Under 5 years ... 8,895
18 years and over ... 86,923
65 years and over ... 8,396
85 years and over ... 1,212
Median Age ... 32.7
Native-born ... 79,159
Foreign-born ... 34,898

Educational Attainment, 2007

Population 25 years and over ... 75,437
Less than 9th grade ... 9.3%
High school grad or higher ... 83.8%
Bachelor's degree or higher ... 31.1%
Graduate degree ... 10.4%

Income & Poverty, 2007

Per capita income ... $31,218
Median household income ... $63,619
Median family income ... $70,717
Persons in poverty ... 11.0%
H'holds receiving public assistance ... 903
H'holds receiving social security ... 5,429

Households, 2007

Total households ... 40,816
With persons under 18 ... 13,874
With persons over 65 ... 6,057
Family households ... 23,044
Single person households ... 12,978
Persons per household ... 2.72
Persons per family ... 3.51

Household Population, 2008§§

Persons living in households ... 110,970
Persons living in group quarters ... 2,985
Persons per household ... 2.8

Labor & Employment

Total civilian labor force, 2008§§ ... 68,200
Unemployment rate, 2008 ... 4.7%
Total civilian labor force, 2000* ... 59,456

Employed persons 16 years and over by occupation, 2007

Managers & professionals ... 23,745
Service occupations ... 13,791
Sales & office occupations ... 14,705
Farming, fishing & forestry ... 321
Construction & maintenance ... 5,353
Production & transportation ... 4,278
Self-employed persons ... 6,572

† see Appendix D for 2000 Decennial Census Data
* US Census Bureau
** 2007 American Community Survey
§ California Department of Finance
§§ California Employment Development Dept

General Information

City of Costa Mesa
PO Box 1200
Costa Mesa, CA 92628
714-754-5000

Website ... www.ci.costa-mesa.ca.us
Elevation ... 101 ft.
Land Area (sq. miles) ... 15.6
Water Area (sq. miles) ... 0.1
Year of Incorporation ... 1953
Government type ... General law
Sales tax rate ... 8.75%

Voters & Officials

Registered Voters, October 2008

Total ... 56,673
Democrats ... 17,553
Republicans ... 23,502
Declined to state ... 12,518

Legislative Districts

US Congressional ... 46
State Senatorial ... 35
State Assembly ... 68

Local Officials, 2009

Mayor ... Allan R. Mansoor
Manager ... Allan Roeder
City Clerk ... Julie Folcik
Attorney ... Kimberly Hall Barlow
Finance Dir ... Marc Puckett
Public Works ... Peter Naghavi
Planning/Dev Dir ... Donald Lamm
Building ... Khanh Nguyen
Police Chief ... Chris Shawkey
Fire Chief ... Mike Morgan

Public Safety

Number of officers, 2007 ... 163
Violent crimes, 2007 ... 258
Property crimes, 2007 ... 3,336
Arson, 2007 ... 9

Public Library

Costa Mesa/Donald Dungan Branch Library
Orange County Public Library System
1855 Park Ave
Costa Mesa, CA 92627
949-646-8845
Branch Librarian ... Dolores Madrigal

Library system statistics, FY 2007

Population served ... 1,532,758
Internet terminals ... 505
Annual users ... 680,874

Per capita:

Operating income ... $24.71
percent from local government ... 90.0%
Operating expenditure ... $24.18
Total materials ... 1.93
Print holdings ... 1.84
Visits per capita ... 4.02

Housing & Construction

Housing Units

Total, 2008§ ... 41,020
Single family units, attached ... 4,177
Single family units, detached ... 15,775
Multiple family units ... 19,987
Mobile home units ... 1,081
Occupied ... 39,801
Vacancy rate ... 3.0%
Median rent, 2007** ... $1,387
Median SF home value, 2007** ... $704,200

New Privately Owned Housing Units Authorized by Building Permit, 2007*

	Units	Construction Cost
Single	38	$8,866,355
Total	590	$71,327,067

Municipal Finance

(For local fiscal year ended in 2006)

Revenues

Total ... $115,482,265
Taxes ... 82,694,495
Special benefits assessment ... 0
Licenses & permits ... 1,608,840
Fines & forfeitures ... 3,038,052
Revenues from use of money & property ... 4,778,140
Intergovernmental ... 11,652,757
Service charges ... 6,054,958
Other revenues ... 746,298
Other financing sources ... 4,908,725

Expenditures

Total ... $109,807,283
General government ... 31,361,825
Public safety ... 56,226,909
Transportation ... 8,177,464
Community development ... 10,121,799
Health ... 400,377
Culture & leisure ... 3,518,909
Other ... 0

Local School District

(Data from School year 2007-08 except as noted)

Newport-Mesa Unified
PO Box 1368
Newport Beach, CA 92663
(714) 424-5000

Superintendent ... Jeffery Hubbard
Grade plan ... PK-12
Number of schools ... 32
Enrollment ... 21,338
High school graduates, 2006-07 ... 1,366
Dropout rate ... 2.0%
Pupil/teacher ratio ... 22.2
Average class size ... 26.7
Students per computer ... 3.9
Classrooms with internet ... 1,049
Avg. Daily Attendance (ADA) ... 20,930
Cost per ADA ... $10,187
Avg. Teacher Salary ... $70,130

California Achievement Tests 6th ed., 2008

(Pct scoring at or above 50th National Percentile Rank)

	Math	Reading	Language
Grade 3	64%	49%	58%
Grade 7	63%	58%	57%

Academic Performance Index, 2008

Number of students tested ... 16,274
Number of valid scores ... 15,705
2007 API (base) ... 793
2008 API (growth) ... 797

SAT Testing, 2006-07

Enrollment, Grade 12 ... 1,534
Number taking test ... 871
percent taking test ... 56.8%
percent with total score 1,500+ ... 35.80%

Average Scores:

Math	Verbal	Writing	Total
542	524	528	1,594

Federal No Child Left Behind, 2008

(Adequate Yearly Progress standards met)

	Participation Rate	Pct Proficient
ELA	Yes	No
Math	Yes	Yes

API criteria ... Yes
Graduation rate ... Yes
\# criteria met/possible ... 40/38

Other school districts for this city

(see Appendix E for information on these districts)

None

See Introduction for an explanation of all data sources.

Demographics & Socio-Economic Characteristics
(2000 Decennial Census, except as noted)

Population

1990* 5,714
2000 6,471
Male 3,152
Female 3,319
Jan. 2008 (estimate)§ 7,532
Persons per sq. mi. of land 3,964.2

Race & Hispanic Origin, 2000

Race
White 5,407
Black/African American 151
North American Native 58
Asian 233
Pacific Islander 15
Other Race 285
Two or more races 322
Hispanic origin, total 810
Mexican 581
Puerto Rican 33
Cuban 4
Other Hispanic 192

Age & Nativity, 2000

Under 5 years 416
18 years and over 4,807
65 years and over 458
85 years and over 43
Median Age 33.9
Native-born 5,804
Foreign-born 678

Educational Attainment, 2000

Population 25 years and over 4,241
Less than 9th grade 5.0%
High school grad or higher 86.0%
Bachelor's degree or higher 23.4%
Graduate degree 7.0%

Income & Poverty, 1999

Per capita income $24,206
Median household income $52,808
Median family income $62,419
Persons in poverty 8.3%
H'holds receiving public assistance 56
H'holds receiving social security 412

Households, 2000

Total households 2,532
With persons under 18 963
With persons over 65 351
Family households 1,609
Single person households 604
Persons per household 2.55
Persons per family 3.05

Household Population, 2008§§

Persons living in households 7,514
Persons living in group quarters 18
Persons per household 2.5

Labor & Employment

Total civilian labor force, 2008§§ 4,000
Unemployment rate, 2008 .... 5.7%
Total civilian labor force, 2000 3,645

Employed persons 16 years and over by occupation, 2000

Managers & professionals 1,112
Service occupations 498
Sales & office occupations 1,022
Farming, fishing & forestry 0
Construction & maintenance 460
Production & transportation 399
Self-employed persons 329

* US Census Bureau
** 2000 Decennial Census
§ California Department of Finance
§§ California Employment Development Dept

General Information

City of Cotati
201 W Sierra Ave
Cotati, CA 94931
707-792-4600

Website .... www.ci.cotati.ca.us
Elevation .... NA
Land Area (sq. miles) 1.9
Water Area (sq. miles) 0
Year of Incorporation 1963
Government type .... General law
Sales tax rate 9.00%

Voters & Officials

Registered Voters, October 2008

Total 4,005
Democrats 2,162
Republicans 765
Declined to state 849

Legislative Districts

US Congressional 6
State Senatorial 3
State Assembly 6

Local Officials, 2009

Mayor .... John Guardino
City Manager .... Dianne Thompson
City Clerk .... Tamara Taylor
Attorney .... Rich Rudnansky
Admin Svcs Dir .... Jone Hayes
Public Works .... Damien O'Bid
Dev Dir .... Marsha Sue Lustig (Actg)
Building .... NA
Police Chief .... Robert Stewart
Fire Chief .... Frank Treanor (Int)

Public Safety

Number of officers, 2007 13
Violent crimes, 2007 34
Property crimes, 2007 154
Arson, 2007 2

Public Library

Rohnert Park-Cotati Regional Library
Sonoma County Library System
6250 Lynne Conde Way
Rohnert Park, CA 95428
707-584-9121

Branch Librarian .... Kathy Dennison

Library system statistics, FY 2007

Population served 481,785
Internet terminals 140
Annual users 299,464

Per capita:

Operating income $32.97
percent from local government 87.7%
Operating expenditure $30.18
Total materials 1.60
Print holdings 1.49
Visits per capita 5.11

Housing & Construction

Housing Units

Total, 2008§ 3,087
Single family units, attached 550
Single family units, detached 1,680
Multiple family units 736
Mobile home units 121
Occupied 3,023
Vacancy rate 2.1%
Median rent, 2000** $885
Median SF home value, 2000** $231,500

New Privately Owned Housing Units Authorized by Building Permit, 2007*

	Units	Construction Cost
Single	3	$540,580
Total	3	$540,580

Municipal Finance
(For local fiscal year ended in 2006)

Revenues

Total $11,008,500
Taxes 4,075,446
Special benefits assessment 39,712
Licenses & permits 190,968
Fines & forfeitures 69,198
Revenues from use of money & property 468,511
Intergovernmental 679,984
Service charges 5,245,744
Other revenues 238,937
Other financing sources 0

Expenditures

Total $8,808,444
General government 899,042
Public safety 2,794,776
Transportation 645,573
Community development 556,143
Health 1,871,774
Culture & leisure 312,712
Other 471,073

Local School District
(Data from School year 2007-08 except as noted)

Cotati-Rohnert Park Unified
5860 Labath Ave
Rohnert Park, CA 94928
(707) 792-4722

Superintendent .... Barbara Vrankovich
Grade plan K-12
Number of schools 15
Enrollment 6,655
High school graduates, 2006-07 477
Dropout rate 3.7%
Pupil/teacher ratio 21.9
Average class size 26.1
Students per computer 4.9
Classrooms with internet 319
Avg. Daily Attendance (ADA) 6,439
Cost per ADA $8,498
Avg. Teacher Salary $60,779

California Achievement Tests 6th ed., 2008
(Pct scoring at or above 50th National Percentile Rank)

	Math	Reading	Language
Grade 3	58%	43%	55%
Grade 7	50%	53%	52%

Academic Performance Index, 2008

Number of students tested 5,067
Number of valid scores 4,875
2007 API (base) 743
2008 API (growth) 750

SAT Testing, 2006-07

Enrollment, Grade 12 562
Number taking test 141
percent taking test 25.1%
percent with total score 1,500+ 14.40%

Average Scores:

Math	Verbal	Writing	Total
529	504	505	1,538

Federal No Child Left Behind, 2008
(Adequate Yearly Progress standards met)

	Participation Rate	Pct Proficient
ELA	Yes	No
Math	Yes	Yes

API criteria .... Yes
Graduation rate .... Yes
criteria met/possible 34/31

Other school districts for this city
(see Appendix E for information on these districts)

None

See Introduction for an explanation of all data sources.

Demographics & Socio-Economic Characteristics

(2000 Decennial Census, except as noted)

Population

1990* ... 43,207
2000 ... 46,837
  Male ... 22,441
  Female ... 24,396
Jan. 2008 (estimate)§ ... 49,552
  Persons per sq. mi. of land ... 7,078.9

Race & Hispanic Origin, 2000

Race
  White ... 29,084
  Black/African American ... 2,354
  North American Native ... 420
  Asian ... 4,598
  Pacific Islander ... 97
  Other Race ... 8,047
  Two or more races ... 2,237
Hispanic origin, total ... 18,871
  Mexican ... 14,373
  Puerto Rican ... 323
  Cuban ... 236
  Other Hispanic ... 3,939

Age & Nativity, 2000

Under 5 years ... 3,470
18 years and over ... 33,691
65 years and over ... 5,105
85 years and over ... 535
  Median Age ... 33.5
Native-born ... 37,693
Foreign-born ... 9,451

Educational Attainment, 2000

Population 25 years and over ... 29,422
Less than 9th grade ... 5.6%
High school grad or higher ... 81.9%
Bachelor's degree or higher ... 18.8%
Graduate degree ... 5.5%

Income & Poverty, 1999

Per capita income ... $20,231
Median household income ... $48,474
Median family income ... $55,111
Persons in poverty ... 11.5%
H'holds receiving public assistance ... 638
H'holds receiving social security ... 3,663

Households, 2000

Total households ... 15,971
  With persons under 18 ... 6,859
  With persons over 65 ... 3,622
  Family households ... 11,762
  Single person households ... 3,321
Persons per household ... 2.89
Persons per family ... 3.36

Household Population, 2008§§

Persons living in households ... 48,950
Persons living in group quarters ... 602
Persons per household ... 3.0

Labor & Employment

Total civilian labor force, 2008§§ ... 26,500
  Unemployment rate, 2008 ... 5.2%
Total civilian labor force, 2000 ... 22,756

Employed persons 16 years and over by occupation, 2000

  Managers & professionals ... 6,553
  Service occupations ... 3,075
  Sales & office occupations ... 6,827
  Farming, fishing & forestry ... 0
  Construction & maintenance ... 2,011
  Production & transportation ... 2,993
  Self-employed persons ... 1,228

* US Census Bureau
** 2000 Decennial Census
§ California Department of Finance
§§ California Employment Development Dept

General Information

City of Covina
125 E College St
Covina, CA 91723
626-858-7212

Website ... www.ci.covina.ca.us
Elevation ... 546 ft.
Land Area (sq. miles) ... 7.0
Water Area (sq. miles) ... 0
Year of Incorporation ... 1901
Government type ... General law
Sales tax rate ... 9.25%

Voters & Officials

Registered Voters, October 2008

Total ... 23,127
  Democrats ... 9,890
  Republicans ... 8,305
  Declined to state ... 3,992

Legislative Districts

US Congressional ... 32
State Senatorial ... 24
State Assembly ... 57

Local Officials, 2009

Mayor ... Kevin Stapleton
City Manager ... Cynthia Kurtz (Int)
City Clerk ... Rosie Fabian
Attorney ... Edward W. Lee
Finance Dir ... Victoria Gallo (Int)
Public Works ... Steve Henley
Community Dev Dir ... Robert Neiuber
Building ... Kyle Randall
Police Chief ... Kim Raney
Emergency/Fire Dir ... (County)

Public Safety

Number of officers, 2007 ... 59
Violent crimes, 2007 ... 216
Property crimes, 2007 ... 1,845
Arson, 2007 ... 18

Public Library

Covina Public Library
234 N Second Ave
Covina, CA 91723
626-967-3935

Director ... Roger Possner

Library statistics, FY 2007

Population served ... 49,720
Internet terminals ... 38
  Annual users ... 23,687

Per capita:

Operating income ... $28.47
  percent from local government ... 89.8%
Operating expenditure ... $27.11
Total materials ... 1.98
Print holdings ... 1.88
Visits per capita ... 5.58

Housing & Construction

Housing Units

Total, 2008§ ... 16,533
  Single family units, attached ... 1,321
  Single family units, detached ... 9,450
  Multiple family units ... 5,174
  Mobile home units ... 588
  Occupied ... 16,136
  Vacancy rate ... 2.4%
Median rent, 2000** ... $742
Median SF home value, 2000** ... $189,500

New Privately Owned Housing Units Authorized by Building Permit, 2007*

	Units	Construction Cost
Single	0	$0
Total	10	$958,908

Municipal Finance

(For local fiscal year ended in 2006)

Revenues

Total ... $44,941,110
Taxes ... 24,325,406
Special benefits assessment ... 227,723
Licenses & permits ... 714,957
Fines & forfeitures ... 801,161
Revenues from use of
  money & property ... 607,385
Intergovernmental ... 3,937,165
Service charges ... 12,538,175
Other revenues ... 1,789,138
Other financing sources ... 0

Expenditures

Total ... $39,589,751
General government ... 4,100,884
Public safety ... 17,671,782
Transportation ... 3,467,545
Community development ... 1,926,609
Health ... 3,419,682
Culture & leisure ... 3,253,520
Other ... 0

Local School District

(Data from School year 2007-08 except as noted)

Covina-Valley Unified
PO Box 269
Covina, CA 91723
(626) 974-7000

Superintendent ... Louis Pappas
Grade plan ... K-12
Number of schools ... 19
Enrollment ... 14,646
High school graduates, 2006-07 ... 1,178
Dropout rate ... 1.7%
Pupil/teacher ratio ... 23.3
Average class size ... 25.5
Students per computer ... 4.3
Classrooms with internet ... 720
Avg. Daily Attendance (ADA) ... 14,219
  Cost per ADA ... $7,978
Avg. Teacher Salary ... $65,572

California Achievement Tests 6th ed., 2008

(Pct scoring at or above 50th National Percentile Rank)

	Math	Reading	Language
Grade 3	55%	34%	45%
Grade 7	52%	47%	45%

Academic Performance Index, 2008

Number of students tested ... 11,633
Number of valid scores ... 10,871
2007 API (base) ... 731
2008 API (growth) ... 747

SAT Testing, 2006-07

Enrollment, Grade 12 ... 1,306
Number taking test ... 508
  percent taking test ... 38.9%
  percent with total score 1,500+ ... 14.10%

Average Scores:

Math	Verbal	Writing	Total
487	476	472	1,435

Federal No Child Left Behind, 2008

(Adequate Yearly Progress standards met)

	Participation Rate	Pct Proficient
ELA	Yes	No
Math	Yes	No

API criteria ... Yes
Graduation rate ... Yes
criteria met/possible ... 38/35

Other school districts for this city

(see Appendix E for information on these districts)

Azusa Unified, Charter Oak Unified

See Introduction for an explanation of all data sources.

Demographics & Socio-Economic Characteristics

(2000 Decennial Census, except as noted)

Population

1990* 4,380
2000 4,006
Male 1,851
Female 2,155
Jan. 2008 (estimate)§ 7,683
Persons per sq. mi. of land 4,268.3

Race & Hispanic Origin, 2000

Race
White 3,138
Black/African American 21
North American Native 244
Asian 185
Pacific Islander 5
Other Race 171
Two or more races 242
Hispanic origin, total 441
Mexican 336
Puerto Rican 18
Cuban 1
Other Hispanic 86

Age & Nativity, 2000

Under 5 years 365
18 years and over 2,800
65 years and over 555
85 years and over 74
Median Age 32.1
Native-born 3,571
Foreign-born 317

Educational Attainment, 2000

Population 25 years and over 2,346
Less than 9th grade 7.7%
High school grad or higher 71.3%
Bachelor's degree or higher 13.3%
Graduate degree 3.5%

Income & Poverty, 1999

Per capita income $12,833
Median household income $20,133
Median family income $22,058
Persons in poverty 31.6%
H'holds receiving public assistance 250
H'holds receiving social security 472

Households, 2000

Total households 1,578
With persons under 18 614
With persons over 65 381
Family households 920
Single person households 565
Persons per household 2.40
Persons per family 3.12

Household Population, 2008§§

Persons living in households 4,039
Persons living in group quarters 3,644
Persons per household 2.4

Labor & Employment

Total civilian labor force, 2008§§ 1,600
Unemployment rate, 2008 . . . . 10.9%
Total civilian labor force, 2000 1,398

Employed persons 16 years and over by occupation, 2000

Managers & professionals 310
Service occupations 461
Sales & office occupations 245
Farming, fishing & forestry 43
Construction & maintenance 73
Production & transportation 82
Self-employed persons 127

* US Census Bureau
** 2000 Decennial Census
§ California Department of Finance
§§ California Employment Development Dept

General Information

City of Crescent City
377 J Street
Crescent City, CA 95531
707-464-7483

Website . . . . www.crescentcity.org
Elevation . . . . 44 ft.
Land Area (sq. miles) 1.8
Water Area (sq. miles) 0.3
Year of Incorporation 1854
Government type . . . . General law
Sales tax rate 8.25%

Voters & Officials

Registered Voters, October 2008

Total 1,697
Democrats 703
Republicans 505
Declined to state 375

Legislative Districts

US Congressional 1
State Senatorial 4
State Assembly 1

Local Officials, 2009

Mayor . . . . Irene R. Tynes
Manager . . . . Eli Naffah
City Clerk . . . . L. Dianne Nickerson
Attorney . . . . Robert N. Black
Finance Dir . . . . Stan Arend (Int)
Public Works . . . . James Barnts
Planning/Dev Dir . . . . William Caplinger
Building . . . . Leslie Orr
Police Chief . . . . Doug Plack
Fire Chief . . . . Steve Wakefield

Public Safety

Number of officers, 2007 13
Violent crimes, 2007 29
Property crimes, 2007 233
Arson, 2007 1

Public Library

Main Branch
Del Norte County Library District
190 Price Mall
Crescent City, CA 95531
707-464-9793

Director . . . . Russell Long

Library system statistics, FY 2007

Population served 29,341
Internet terminals 4
Annual users 19,968

Per capita:

Operating income $7.33
percent from local government 71.3%
Operating expenditure $7.82
Total materials 1.62
Print holdings 1.53
Visits per capita 3.79

Housing & Construction

Housing Units

Total, 2008§ 1,845
Single family units, attached 56
Single family units, detached 938
Multiple family units 817
Mobile home units 34
Occupied 1,659
Vacancy rate 10.1%
Median rent, 2000** $434
Median SF home value, 2000** $87,600

New Privately Owned Housing Units Authorized by Building Permit, 2007*

	Units	Construction Cost
Single	1	$200,000
Total	1	$200,000

Municipal Finance

(For local fiscal year ended in 2006)

Revenues

Total $13,054,641
Taxes 2,619,309
Special benefits assessment 0
Licenses & permits 79,883
Fines & forfeitures 10,483
Revenues from use of money & property 180,709
Intergovernmental 3,425,891
Service charges 5,380,896
Other revenues 57,470
Other financing sources 1,300,000

Expenditures

Total $10,903,360
General government 909,710
Public safety 1,572,002
Transportation 419,932
Community development 3,339,420
Health 1,733,454
Culture & leisure 1,110,358
Other 0

Local School District

(Data from School year 2007-08 except as noted)

Del Norte County Unified
301 West Washington Blvd
Crescent City, CA 95531
(707) 464-0200

Superintendent . . . . Janice Moorehouse
Grade plan K-12
Number of schools 11
Enrollment 3,904
High school graduates, 2006-07 218
Dropout rate 3.8%
Pupil/teacher ratio 20.0
Average class size 25.0
Students per computer 3.2
Classrooms with internet 248
Avg. Daily Attendance (ADA) 3,611
Cost per ADA $9,640
Avg. Teacher Salary $60,042

California Achievement Tests 6th ed., 2008

(Pct scoring at or above 50th National Percentile Rank)

	Math	Reading	Language
Grade 3	54%	43%	46%
Grade 7	47%	47%	41%

Academic Performance Index, 2008

Number of students tested 2,856
Number of valid scores 2,602
2007 API (base) 725
2008 API (growth) 720

SAT Testing, 2006-07

Enrollment, Grade 12 317
Number taking test 89
percent taking test 28.1%
percent with total score 1,500+ 10.70%

Average Scores:

Math	Verbal	Writing	Total
510	472	464	1,446

Federal No Child Left Behind, 2008

(Adequate Yearly Progress standards met)

	Participation Rate	Pct Proficient
ELA	Yes	No
Math	Yes	No

API criteria . . . . Yes
Graduation rate . . . . Yes
\# criteria met/possible 34/27

Other school districts for this city

(see Appendix E for information on these districts)

None

See Introduction for an explanation of all data sources.

Demographics & Socio-Economic Characteristics

(2000 Decennial Census, except as noted)

Population

1990* . . . 22,817
2000 . . . 24,208
Male . . . 11,963
Female . . . 12,245
Jan. 2008 (estimate)§ . . . 25,879
Persons per sq. mi. of land . . . 23,526.4

Race & Hispanic Origin, 2000

Race
White . . . 10,443
Black/African American . . . 300
North American Native . . . 310
Asian . . . 178
Pacific Islander . . . 42
Other Race . . . 11,634
Two or more races . . . 1,301
Hispanic origin, total . . . 22,790
Mexican . . . 16,520
Puerto Rican . . . 146
Cuban . . . 235
Other Hispanic . . . 5,889

Age & Nativity, 2000

Under 5 years . . . 2,908
18 years and over . . . 14,543
65 years and over . . . 884
85 years and over . . . 81
Median Age . . . 23.8
Native-born . . . 11,346
Foreign-born . . . 12,862

Educational Attainment, 2000

Population 25 years and over . . . 11,453
Less than 9th grade . . . 39.6%
High school grad or higher . . . 32.6%
Bachelor's degree or higher . . . 3.0%
Graduate degree . . . 1.1%

Income & Poverty, 1999

Per capita income . . . $8,688
Median household income . . . $29,040
Median family income . . . $28,833
Persons in poverty . . . 28.2%
H'holds receiving public assistance . . . 701
H'holds receiving social security . . . 760

Households, 2000

Total households . . . 5,419
With persons under 18 . . . 3,986
With persons over 65 . . . 718
Family households . . . 4,809
Single person households . . . 439
Persons per household . . . 4.47
Persons per family . . . 4.58

Household Population, 2008§§

Persons living in households . . . 25,867
Persons living in group quarters . . . 12
Persons per household . . . 4.7

Labor & Employment

Total civilian labor force, 2008§§ . . . 9,900
Unemployment rate, 2008 . . . 10.6%
Total civilian labor force, 2000 . . . 8,485

Employed persons 16 years and over by occupation, 2000

Managers & professionals . . . 815
Service occupations . . . 1,132
Sales & office occupations . . . 1,812
Farming, fishing & forestry . . . 26
Construction & maintenance . . . 921
Production & transportation . . . 2,851
Self-employed persons . . . 375

* US Census Bureau
** 2000 Decennial Census
§ California Department of Finance
§§ California Employment Development Dept

General Information

City of Cudahy
5220 Santa Ana St
Cudahy, CA 90201
323-773-5143

Email . . . clerklarry101@aol.com
Elevation . . . 121 ft
Land Area (sq. miles) . . . 1.1
Water Area (sq. miles) . . . 0
Year of Incorporation . . . 1960
Government type . . . General law
Sales tax rate . . . 9.25%

Voters & Officials

Registered Voters, October 2008

Total . . . 5,803
Democrats . . . 3,728
Republicans . . . 735
Declined to state . . . 1,102

Legislative Districts

US Congressional . . . 34
State Senatorial . . . 30
State Assembly . . . 50

Local Officials, 2009

Mayor . . . David M Silva
City Manager . . . George A Perez
City Clerk . . . Larry Galvan
Attorney . . . David Olivas
Finance Dir . . . Mellie Deano
Public Works . . . Carlos Alvarado
Planning/Dev Dir . . . Saul Bouvar
Building . . . George
Police Chief . . . Frank Hauptmann
Fire/Emergency Mgmt . . . NA

Public Safety

Number of officers, 2007 . . . NA
Violent crimes, 2007 . . . 143
Property crimes, 2007 . . . 558
Arson, 2007 . . . 1

Public Library

Cudahy Library
Los Angeles County Public Library System
5218 Santa Ana St
Cudahy, CA 90201
323-771-1345

Branch Librarian . . . Meera Prasad

Library system statistics, FY 2007

Population served . . . 3,673,313
Internet terminals . . . 749
Annual users . . . 3,748,771

Per capita:

Operating income . . . $30.06
percent from local government . . . 93.6%
Operating expenditure . . . $28.36
Total materials . . . 2.22
Print holdings . . . 1.97
Visits per capita . . . 3.25

Housing & Construction

Housing Units

Total, 2008§ . . . 5,653
Single family units, attached . . . 1,293
Single family units, detached . . . 1,709
Multiple family units . . . 2,237
Mobile home units . . . 414
Occupied . . . 5,528
Vacancy rate . . . 2.2%
Median rent, 2000** . . . $677
Median SF home value, 2000** . . . $151,600

New Privately Owned Housing Units Authorized by Building Permit, 2007*

	Units	Construction Cost
Single	0	$0
Total	0	$0

Municipal Finance

(For local fiscal year ended in 2006)

Revenues

Total . . . $8,972,870
Taxes . . . 5,938,755
Special benefits assessment . . . 76,625
Licenses & permits . . . 333,460
Fines & forfeitures . . . 721,139
Revenues from use of money & property . . . 222,036
Intergovernmental . . . 1,368,479
Service charges . . . 132,124
Other revenues . . . 180,252
Other financing sources . . . 0

Expenditures

Total . . . $6,795,156
General government . . . 989,089
Public safety . . . 2,884,084
Transportation . . . 1,247,450
Community development . . . 668,858
Health . . . 18,277
Culture & leisure . . . 987,398
Other . . . 0

Local School District

(Data from School year 2007-08 except as noted)

Los Angeles Unified
333 South Beaudry Ave
Los Angeles, CA 90017
(213) 241-1000

Superintendent . . . Ramon Cortines
Grade plan . . . PK-12
Number of schools . . . 827
Enrollment . . . 693,680
High school graduates, 2006-07 . . . 28,545
Dropout rate . . . 7.8%
Pupil/teacher ratio . . . 19.8
Average class size . . . 24.9
Students per computer . . . 3.7
Classrooms with internet . . . 31,112
Avg. Daily Attendance (ADA) . . . 653,672
Cost per ADA . . . $10,053
Avg. Teacher Salary . . . $63,391

California Achievement Tests 6th ed., 2008

(Pct scoring at or above 50th National Percentile Rank)

	Math	Reading	Language
Grade 3	49%	27%	39%
Grade 7	37%	33%	33%

Academic Performance Index, 2008

Number of students tested . . . 495,046
Number of valid scores . . . 471,641
2007 API (base) . . . 662
2008 API (growth) . . . 683

SAT Testing, 2006-07

Enrollment, Grade 12 . . . 32,370
Number taking test . . . 15,447
percent taking test . . . 47.7%
percent with total score 1,500+ . . . 12.50%

Average Scores:

Math	Verbal	Writing	Total
443	438	441	1,322

Federal No Child Left Behind, 2008

(Adequate Yearly Progress standards met)

	Participation Rate	Pct Proficient
ELA	Yes	No
Math	Yes	No

API criteria . . . Yes
Graduation rate . . . Yes
\# criteria met/possible . . . 46/38

Other school districts for this city

(see Appendix E for information on these districts)

None

See Introduction for an explanation of all data sources.

Demographics & Socio-Economic Characteristics

(2000 Decennial Census, except as noted)

Population

1990* 38,793
2000 38,816
Male 18,117
Female 20,699
Jan. 2008 (estimate)§ 40,694
Persons per sq. mi. of land 7,979.2

Race & Hispanic Origin, 2000

Race
White 22,996
Black/African American 4,644
North American Native 277
Asian 4,667
Pacific Islander 80
Other Race 3,945
Two or more races 2,207
Hispanic origin, total 9,199
Mexican 5,738
Puerto Rican 133
Cuban 444
Other Hispanic 2,884

Age & Nativity, 2000

Under 5 years 2,129
18 years and over 30,720
65 years and over 5,390
85 years and over 674
Median Age 39.1
Native-born 28,487
Foreign-born 10,329

Educational Attainment, 2000

Population 25 years and over 28,340
Less than 9th grade 6.0%
High school grad or higher 87.2%
Bachelor's degree or higher 41.2%
Graduate degree 17.3%

Income & Poverty, 1999

Per capita income $29,025
Median household income $51,792
Median family income $61,451
Persons in poverty 8.5%
H'holds receiving public assistance 385
H'holds receiving social security 3,737

Households, 2000

Total households 16,611
With persons under 18 4,716
With persons over 65 3,822
Family households 9,513
Single person households 5,727
Persons per household 2.31
Persons per family 3.02

Household Population, 2008§§

Persons living in households 40,170
Persons living in group quarters 524
Persons per household 2.4

Labor & Employment

Total civilian labor force, 2008§§ 25,000
Unemployment rate, 2008 . . . . . 5.1%
Total civilian labor force, 2000 21,438

Employed persons 16 years and over by occupation, 2000

Managers & professionals 10,107
Service occupations 2,331
Sales & office occupations 5,540
Farming, fishing & forestry 0
Construction & maintenance 1,099
Production & transportation 1,208
Self-employed persons 2,322

* US Census Bureau
** 2000 Decennial Census
§ California Department of Finance
§§ California Employment Development Dept

General Information

City of Culver City
9770 Culver Blvd
Culver City, CA 90232
310-253-5851

Website . . . . . www.culvercity.org
Elevation . . . . . 94 ft.
Land Area (sq. miles) 5.1
Water Area (sq. miles) 0
Year of Incorporation 1917
Government type . . . . . Chartered
Sales tax rate 9.25%

Voters & Officials

Registered Voters, October 2008

Total 24,724
Democrats 14,342
Republicans 4,301
Declined to state 5,001

Legislative Districts

US Congressional 33
State Senatorial 26
State Assembly 47

Local Officials, 2009

Mayor . . . . . D. Scott Malsin
City Manager . . . . . Jerry Fulwood
City Clerk . . . . . Martin Cole
Attorney . . . . . Carol Schwab
Finance Dir . . . . . Jeff Muir
Public Works . . . . . Charles Herbertson
Planning/Dev Dir . . . . . Sol Blumenfeld
Building . . . . . Craig Johnson
Police Chief . . . . . Donald Pedersen
Fire Chief . . . . . Jeffrey Eastman

Public Safety

Number of officers, 2007 116
Violent crimes, 2007 181
Property crimes, 2007 1,459
Arson, 2007 1

Public Library

Culver City Library
Los Angeles County Public Library System
4975 Overland Ave
Culver City, CA 90230
310-559-1676

Branch Librarian . . . . . Laura Frakes

Library system statistics, FY 2007

Population served 3,673,313
Internet terminals 749
Annual users 3,748,771

Per capita:

Operating income $30.06
percent from local government 93.6%
Operating expenditure $28.36
Total materials 2.22
Print holdings 1.97
Visits per capita 3.25

Housing & Construction

Housing Units

Total, 2008§ 17,148
Single family units, attached 1,912
Single family units, detached 6,623
Multiple family units 8,432
Mobile home units 181
Occupied 16,629
Vacancy rate 3.0%
Median rent, 2000** $887
Median SF home value, 2000** $311,100

New Privately Owned Housing Units Authorized by Building Permit, 2007*

	Units	Construction Cost
Single	5	$1,184,704
Total	5	$1,184,704

Municipal Finance

(For local fiscal year ended in 2006)

Revenues

Total $118,839,142
Taxes 61,215,727
Special benefits assessment 45,173
Licenses & permits 2,067,737
Fines & forfeitures 4,242,406
Revenues from use of money & property 3,457,431
Intergovernmental 9,229,148
Service charges 35,014,426
Other revenues 3,567,094
Other financing sources 0

Expenditures

Total $115,549,187
General government 15,683,164
Public safety 42,646,267
Transportation 19,943,438
Community development 14,462,599
Health 15,925,948
Culture & leisure 6,887,771
Other 0

Local School District

(Data from School year 2007-08 except as noted)

Culver City Unified
4034 Irving Pl
Culver City, CA 90232
(310) 842-4220

Superintendent . . . . . Myrna Rivera Cote
Grade plan K-12
Number of schools 9
Enrollment 6,656
High school graduates, 2006-07 495
Dropout rate 2.5%
Pupil/teacher ratio 20.8
Average class size 26.3
Students per computer 7.3
Classrooms with internet 334
Avg. Daily Attendance (ADA) 6,433
Cost per ADA $8,372
Avg. Teacher Salary $62,041

California Achievement Tests 6th ed., 2008

(Pct scoring at or above 50th National Percentile Rank)

	Math	Reading	Language
Grade 3	69%	49%	59%
Grade 7	58%	60%	57%

Academic Performance Index, 2008

Number of students tested 5,193
Number of valid scores 5,028
2007 API (base) 780
2008 API (growth) 790

SAT Testing, 2006-07

Enrollment, Grade 12 600
Number taking test 302
percent taking test 50.3%
percent with total score 1,500+ . . . 24.30%

Average Scores:

Math	Verbal	Writing	Total
495	498	497	1,490

Federal No Child Left Behind, 2008

(Adequate Yearly Progress standards met)

	Participation Rate	Pct Proficient
ELA	Yes	Yes
Math	Yes	Yes

API criteria . . . . . Yes
Graduation rate . . . . . Yes
criteria met/possible 34/34

Other school districts for this city

(see Appendix E for information on these districts)

Los Angeles Unified

See Introduction for an explanation of all data sources.

Demographics & Socio-Economic Characteristics

(2000 Decennial Census, except as noted)

Population

1990* 40,263
2000 50,546
Male 25,207
Female 25,339
Jan. 2008 (estimate)§ 55,551
Persons per sq. mi. of land 5,096.4

Race & Hispanic Origin, 2000

Race
White 25,342
Black/African American 347
North American Native 101
Asian 22,462
Pacific Islander 67
Other Race 639
Two or more races 1,588
Hispanic origin, total 2,010
Mexican 1,145
Puerto Rican 66
Cuban 35
Other Hispanic 764

Age & Nativity, 2000

Under 5 years 3,060
18 years and over 37,083
65 years and over 5,560
85 years and over 697
Median Age 38.0
Native-born 28,998
Foreign-born 21,659

Educational Attainment, 2000

Population 25 years and over 34,521
Less than 9th grade 1.7%
High school grad or higher 95.5%
Bachelor's degree or higher 65.4%
Graduate degree 33.4%

Income & Poverty, 1999

Per capita income $44,749
Median household income $100,411
Median family income $109,455
Persons in poverty 4.8%
H'holds receiving public assistance 179
H'holds receiving social security 3,373

Households, 2000

Total households 18,204
With persons under 18 7,871
With persons over 65 3,800
Family households 13,613
Single person households 3,567
Persons per household 2.75
Persons per family 3.19

Household Population, 2008§§

Persons living in households 55,070
Persons living in group quarters 481
Persons per household 2.8

Labor & Employment

Total civilian labor force, 2008§§ 24,600
Unemployment rate, 2008 . . . . 3.8%
Total civilian labor force, 2000 24,520

Employed persons 16 years and over by occupation, 2000

Managers & professionals 17,021
Service occupations 1,013
Sales & office occupations 4,266
Farming, fishing & forestry 42
Construction & maintenance 586
Production & transportation 1,031
Self-employed persons 1,656

* US Census Bureau
** 2000 Decennial Census
§ California Department of Finance
§§ California Employment Development Dept

General Information

City of Cupertino
10300 Torre Ave
Cupertino, CA 95014
408-777-3200

Website . . . . www.cupertino.org
Elevation . . . . 236 ft.
Land Area (sq. miles) 10.9
Water Area (sq. miles) 0
Year of Incorporation 1955
Government type . . . . General law
Sales tax rate 9.25%

Voters & Officials

Registered Voters, October 2008

Total 27,443
Democrats 10,334
Republicans 6,367
Declined to state 10,034

Legislative Districts

US Congressional 15
State Senatorial 11
State Assembly 22

Local Officials, 2009

Mayor . . . . Orrin Mahoney
Manager . . . . Dave Knapp
City Clerk . . . . Kim Smith
Attorney . . . . (vacant)
Finance Dir . . . . Carol Atwood
Public Works . . . . Ralph Qualls
Planning/Dev Dir . . . . (vacant)
Building . . . . Greg Casteel
Police Chief . . . . Terrence Calderone
Fire/Emergency Mgmt . . . . Ken Vogel

Public Safety

Number of officers, 2007 . . . . NA
Violent crimes, 2007 53
Property crimes, 2007 837
Arson, 2007 22

Public Library

Cupertino Library
Santa Clara County Library System
10800 Torre Ave
Cupertino, CA 95014
408-446-1677

Branch Librarian . . . . Ja-Lih Lee

Library system statistics, FY 2007

Population served 419,141
Internet terminals 133
Annual users 650,000

Per capita:

Operating income $77.89
percent from local government 85.7%
Operating expenditure $66.37
Total materials 4.01
Print holdings 3.27
Visits per capita 6.16

Housing & Construction

Housing Units

Total, 2008§ 20,172
Single family units, attached 2,145
Single family units, detached 12,235
Multiple family units 5,783
Mobile home units 9
Occupied 19,660
Vacancy rate 2.5%
Median rent, 2000** $1,693
Median SF home value, 2000** $649,000

New Privately Owned Housing Units Authorized by Building Permit, 2007*

	Units	Construction Cost
Single	83	$57,906,912
Total	83	$57,906,912

Municipal Finance

(For local fiscal year ended in 2006)

Revenues

Total $50,178,811
Taxes 28,101,585
Special benefits assessment 0
Licenses & permits 2,130,376
Fines & forfeitures 639,332
Revenues from use of money & property 1,473,642
Intergovernmental 3,284,896
Service charges 11,564,606
Other revenues 2,984,374
Other financing sources 0

Expenditures

Total $43,769,902
General government 10,237,361
Public safety 7,587,614
Transportation 4,437,869
Community development 6,794,558
Health 2,103,515
Culture & leisure 12,608,985
Other 0

Local School District

(Data from School year 2007-08 except as noted)

Fremont Union High
PO Box F
Sunnyvale, CA 94087
(408) 522-2200

Superintendent . . . . Polly Bove
Grade plan 9-12
Number of schools 6
Enrollment 10,333
High school graduates, 2006-07 2,224
Dropout rate 1.0%
Pupil/teacher ratio 23.9
Average class size 28.7
Students per computer 3.6
Classrooms with internet 416
Avg. Daily Attendance (ADA) 10,314
Cost per ADA $8,843
Avg. Teacher Salary $72,288

California Achievement Tests 6th ed., 2008

(Pct scoring at or above 50th National Percentile Rank)

	Math	Reading	Language
Grade 3	NA	NA	NA
Grade 7	NA	NA	NA

Academic Performance Index, 2008

Number of students tested 7,579
Number of valid scores 7,305
2007 API (base) 840
2008 API (growth) 857

SAT Testing, 2006-07

Enrollment, Grade 12 2,423
Number taking test 1,756
percent taking test 72.5%
percent with total score 1,500+ 59.10%

Average Scores:

Math	Verbal	Writing	Total
638	574	578	1,790

Federal No Child Left Behind, 2008

(Adequate Yearly Progress standards met)

	Participation Rate	Pct Proficient
ELA	No	Yes
Math	Yes	Yes

API criteria . . . . Yes
Graduation rate . . . . Yes
\# criteria met/possible 30/29

Other school districts for this city

(see Appendix E for information on these districts)

Cupertino Union Elem, Montebello Elem

See Introduction for an explanation of all data sources.

Demographics & Socio-Economic Characteristics

(2000 Decennial Census, except as noted)

Population

1990* . . . 42,655
2000 . . . 46,229
Male . . . 22,513
Female . . . 23,716
Jan. 2008 (estimate)§ . . . 49,541
Persons per sq. mi. of land . . . 7,506.2

Race & Hispanic Origin, 2000

Race
White . . . 30,332
Black/African American . . . 1,280
North American Native . . . 274
Asian . . . 9,618
Pacific Islander . . . 184
Other Race . . . 2,515
Two or more races . . . 2,026
Hispanic origin, total . . . 7,235
Mexican . . . 5,321
Puerto Rican . . . 163
Cuban . . . 152
Other Hispanic . . . 1,599

Age & Nativity, 2000

Under 5 years . . . 2,770
18 years and over . . . 33,735
65 years and over . . . 4,879
85 years and over . . . 350
Median Age . . . 36.7
Native-born . . . 36,640
Foreign-born . . . 9,894

Educational Attainment, 2000

Population 25 years and over . . . 30,168
Less than 9th grade . . . 3.1%
High school grad or higher . . . 89.7%
Bachelor's degree or higher . . . 31.2%
Graduate degree . . . 10.7%

Income & Poverty, 1999

Per capita income . . . $25,798
Median household income . . . $64,377
Median family income . . . $70,060
Persons in poverty . . . 6.1%
H'holds receiving public assistance . . . 423
H'holds receiving social security . . . 3,489

Households, 2000

Total households . . . 15,654
With persons under 18 . . . 6,732
With persons over 65 . . . 3,639
Family households . . . 12,243
Single person households . . . 2,750
Persons per household . . . 2.93
Persons per family . . . 3.31

Household Population, 2008§§

Persons living in households . . . 49,220
Persons living in group quarters . . . 321
Persons per household . . . 3.0

Labor & Employment

Total civilian labor force, 2008§§ . . . 27,800
Unemployment rate, 2008 . . . 5.6%
Total civilian labor force, 2000 . . . 23,879

Employed persons 16 years and over by occupation, 2000

Managers & professionals . . . 9,550
Service occupations . . . 2,493
Sales & office occupations . . . 6,558
Farming, fishing & forestry . . . 12
Construction & maintenance . . . 1,835
Production & transportation . . . 2,202
Self-employed persons . . . 1,589

* US Census Bureau
** 2000 Decennial Census
§ California Department of Finance
§§ California Employment Development Dept

General Information

City of Cypress
5275 Orange Ave
Cypress, CA 90630
714-229-6700

Website . . . www.ci.cypress.ca.us
Elevation . . . 36 ft.
Land Area (sq. miles) . . . 6.6
Water Area (sq. miles) . . . 0
Year of Incorporation . . . 1956
Government type . . . Chartered
Sales tax rate . . . 8.75%

Voters & Officials

Registered Voters, October 2008

Total . . . 28,404
Democrats . . . 9,706
Republicans . . . 11,986
Declined to state . . . 5,635

Legislative Districts

US Congressional . . . 40
State Senatorial . . . 35
State Assembly . . . 67

Local Officials, 2009

Mayor . . . Douglas A. Bailey
City Manager . . . John B. Bahorski
City Clerk . . . Denise Basham
Attorney . . . William Wynder
Finance Dir . . . Richard Storey
Public Works . . . Douglas Dancs
Community Dev Dir . . . Ted Commerdinger
Building . . . NA
Police Chief . . . Mark Yokoyama
Emergency/Fire Dir . . . Chip Prather

Public Safety

Number of officers, 2007 . . . 57
Violent crimes, 2007 . . . 96
Property crimes, 2007 . . . 919
Arson, 2007 . . . 8

Public Library

Cypress Branch Library
Orange County Public Library System
5331 Orange Ave
Cypress, CA 90630
714-826-0350

Branch Librarian . . . Helen Richardson

Library system statistics, FY 2007

Population served . . . 1,532,758
Internet terminals . . . 505
Annual users . . . 680,874

Per capita:

Operating income . . . $24.71
percent from local government . . . 90.0%
Operating expenditure . . . $24.18
Total materials . . . 1.93
Print holdings . . . 1.84
Visits per capita . . . 4.02

Housing & Construction

Housing Units

Total, 2008§ . . . 16,611
Single family units, attached . . . 2,692
Single family units, detached . . . 10,184
Multiple family units . . . 3,371
Mobile home units . . . 364
Occupied . . . 16,223
Vacancy rate . . . 2.3%
Median rent, 2000** . . . $922
Median SF home value, 2000** . . . $252,800

New Privately Owned Housing Units Authorized by Building Permit, 2007*

	Units	Construction Cost
Single	22	$5,759,475
Total	26	$6,372,971

Municipal Finance

(For local fiscal year ended in 2006)

Revenues

Total . . . $36,083,277
Taxes . . . 23,855,536
Special benefits assessment . . . 933,466
Licenses & permits . . . 300,533
Fines & forfeitures . . . 480,357
Revenues from use of money & property . . . 3,147,317
Intergovernmental . . . 3,922,745
Service charges . . . 3,245,319
Other revenues . . . 198,004
Other financing sources . . . 0

Expenditures

Total . . . $27,956,120
General government . . . 4,992,994
Public safety . . . 12,282,576
Transportation . . . 6,371,782
Community development . . . 2,417,473
Health . . . 273,983
Culture & leisure . . . 1,617,312
Other . . . 0

Local School District

(Data from School year 2007-08 except as noted)

Anaheim Union High
PO Box 3520
Anaheim, CA 92803
(714) 999-3511

Superintendent . . . Joseph Farley
Grade plan . . . 7-12
Number of schools . . . 22
Enrollment . . . 33,343
High school graduates, 2006-07 . . . 3,668
Dropout rate . . . 1.7%
Pupil/teacher ratio . . . 23.7
Average class size . . . 20.2
Students per computer . . . 3.4
Classrooms with internet . . . 1,839
Avg. Daily Attendance (ADA) . . . 33,034
Cost per ADA . . . $8,336
Avg. Teacher Salary . . . $79,030

California Achievement Tests 6th ed., 2008

(Pct scoring at or above 50th National Percentile Rank)

	Math	Reading	Language
Grade 3	NA	NA	NA
Grade 7	49%	43%	43%

Academic Performance Index, 2008

Number of students tested . . . 27,739
Number of valid scores . . . 26,586
2007 API (base) . . . 715
2008 API (growth) . . . 729

SAT Testing, 2006-07

Enrollment, Grade 12 . . . 4,777
Number taking test . . . 1,591
percent taking test . . . 33.3%
percent with total score 1,500+ . . . 15.00%

Average Scores:

Math	Verbal	Writing	Total
519	485	489	1,493

Federal No Child Left Behind, 2008

(Adequate Yearly Progress standards met)

	Participation Rate	Pct Proficient
ELA	Yes	No
Math	Yes	No

API criteria . . . Yes
Graduation rate . . . Yes
\# criteria met/possible . . . 42/35

Other school districts for this city

(see Appendix E for information on these districts)

Cypress Elem

See Introduction for an explanation of all data sources.

Demographics & Socio-Economic Characteristics†

(2007 American Community Survey, except as noted)

Population

1990* . . . 92,311
2007 . . . 104,752
Male . . . 53,358
Female . . . 51,394
Jan. 2008 (estimate)§ . . . 106,361
Persons per sq. mi. of land . . . 13,994.9

Race & Hispanic Origin, 2007

Race
White . . . 33,705
Black/African American . . . 3,517
North American Native . . . 171
Asian . . . 52,451
Pacific Islander . . . 2,036
Other Race . . . 8,515
Two or more races . . . 4,357
Hispanic origin, total . . . 25,502
Mexican . . . 12,330
Puerto Rican . . . 903
Cuban . . . 466
Other Hispanic . . . 11,803

Age & Nativity, 2007

Under 5 years . . . 5,867
18 years and over . . . 85,066
65 years and over . . . 12,389
85 years and over . . . 999
Median Age . . . 38.5
Native-born . . . 49,112
Foreign-born . . . 55,640

Educational Attainment, 2007

Population 25 years and over . . . 71,250
Less than 9th grade . . . 8.7%
High school grad or higher . . . 85.7%
Bachelor's degree or higher . . . 35.3%
Graduate degree . . . 7.9%

Income & Poverty, 2007

Per capita income . . . $27,656
Median household income . . . $74,987
Median family income . . . $82,896
Persons in poverty . . . 3.3%
H'holds receiving public assistance . . . 465
H'holds receiving social security . . . 7,764

Households, 2007

Total households . . . 30,236
With persons under 18 . . . 11,054
With persons over 65 . . . 8,315
Family households . . . 22,025
Single person households . . . 5,670
Persons per household . . . 3.43
Persons per family . . . 3.93

Household Population, 2008§§

Persons living in households . . . 105,571
Persons living in group quarters . . . 790
Persons per household . . . 3.4

Labor & Employment

Total civilian labor force, 2008§§ . . . 54,900
Unemployment rate, 2008 . . . 5.9%
Total civilian labor force, 2000* . . . 52,893

Employed persons 16 years and over by occupation, 2007

Managers & professionals . . . 13,452
Service occupations . . . 13,276
Sales & office occupations . . . 19,265
Farming, fishing & forestry . . . 54
Construction & maintenance . . . 5,374
Production & transportation . . . 5,731
Self-employed persons . . . 3,231

† see Appendix D for 2000 Decennial Census Data
* US Census Bureau
** 2007 American Community Survey
§ California Department of Finance
§§ California Employment Development Dept

General Information

City of Daly City
333 90th St
Daly City, CA 94015
650-991-8000

Website . . . www.ci.daly-city.ca.us
Elevation . . . 400 ft.
Land Area (sq. miles) . . . 7.6
Water Area (sq. miles) . . . 0
Year of Incorporation . . . 1911
Government type . . . General law
Sales tax rate . . . 9.25%

Voters & Officials

Registered Voters, October 2008

Total . . . 45,301
Democrats . . . 25,010
Republicans . . . 6,070
Declined to state . . . 12,730

Legislative Districts

US Congressional . . . 12
State Senatorial . . . 8
State Assembly . . . 12, 19

Local Officials, 2009

Mayor . . . Sal Torres
Manager . . . Patricia E. Martel
City Clerk . . . Annette Harpona
Attorney . . . Rose L. Zimmerman
Finance Dir . . . Don McVey
Public Works . . . Patrick Sweetland
Planning/Dev Dir . . . Richard Berger
Building . . . Val Mandapat
Police Chief . . . Gary McLane
Emergency/Fire Dir . . . Ron D. Myers

Public Safety

Number of officers, 2007 . . . 110
Violent crimes, 2007 . . . 293
Property crimes, 2007 . . . 2,111
Arson, 2007 . . . 44

Public Library

Serramonte Library
Daly City Public Library System
40 Wembley Dr
Daly City, CA 94015
650-991-8023

Director . . . Carol Simmons

Library system statistics, FY 2007

Population served . . . 106,160
Internet terminals . . . 53
Annual users . . . 185,086

Per capita:

Operating income . . . $31.16
percent from local government . . . 89.5%
Operating expenditure . . . $29.20
Total materials . . . 2.04
Print holdings . . . 1.72
Visits per capita . . . 4.96

Housing & Construction

Housing Units

Total, 2008§ . . . 31,778
Single family units, attached . . . 4,517
Single family units, detached . . . 16,136
Multiple family units . . . 10,455
Mobile home units . . . 670
Occupied . . . 31,401
Vacancy rate . . . 1.2%
Median rent, 2007** . . . $1,446
Median SF home value, 2007** . . . $661,300

New Privately Owned Housing Units Authorized by Building Permit, 2007*

	Units	Construction Cost
Single	22	$8,980,162
Total	36	$11,588,964

Municipal Finance

(For local fiscal year ended in 2006)

Revenues

Total . . . $93,973,284
Taxes . . . 42,078,907
Special benefits assessment . . . 451,561
Licenses & permits . . . 1,566,687
Fines & forfeitures . . . 2,529,254
Revenues from use of money & property . . . 3,531,274
Intergovernmental . . . 16,239,769
Service charges . . . 20,756,578
Other revenues . . . 6,819,254
Other financing sources . . . 0

Expenditures

Total . . . $95,179,150
General government . . . 7,617,275
Public safety . . . 34,356,927
Transportation . . . 9,940,297
Community development . . . 8,948,003
Health . . . 2,497,102
Culture & leisure . . . 20,725,199
Other . . . 0

Local School District

(Data from School year 2007-08 except as noted)

Jefferson Union High
699 Serramonte Blvd, Suite 100
Daly City, CA 94015
(650) 550-7900

Superintendent . . . Michael Crilly
Grade plan . . . 9-12
Number of schools . . . 5
Enrollment . . . 5,330
High school graduates, 2006-07 . . . 1,105
Dropout rate . . . 3.0%
Pupil/teacher ratio . . . 30.8
Average class size . . . 25.9
Students per computer . . . 4.3
Classrooms with internet . . . 276
Avg. Daily Attendance (ADA) . . . 5,128
Cost per ADA . . . $8,239
Avg. Teacher Salary . . . $58,641

California Achievement Tests 6th ed., 2008

(Pct scoring at or above 50th National Percentile Rank)

	Math	Reading	Language
Grade 3	NA	NA	NA
Grade 7	NA	NA	NA

Academic Performance Index, 2008

Number of students tested . . . 3,846
Number of valid scores . . . 3,651
2007 API (base) . . . 730
2008 API (growth) . . . 732

SAT Testing, 2006-07

Enrollment, Grade 12 . . . 1,255
Number taking test . . . 532
percent taking test . . . 42.4%
percent with total score 1,500+ . . . 17.90%

Average Scores:

Math	Verbal	Writing	Total
510	471	474	1,455

Federal No Child Left Behind, 2008

(Adequate Yearly Progress standards met)

	Participation Rate	Pct Proficient
ELA	No	No
Math	Yes	Yes

API criteria . . . Yes
Graduation rate . . . Yes
\# criteria met/possible . . . 34/31

Other school districts for this city

(see Appendix E for information on these districts)

Bayshore Elem, Brisbane Elem, Jefferson Elem, South San Francisco Unified

See Introduction for an explanation of all data sources.

Demographics & Socio-Economic Characteristics

(2000 Decennial Census, except as noted)

Population

1990* ... 31,896
2000 ... 35,110
Male ... 17,566
Female ... 17,544
Jan. 2008 (estimate)§ ... 36,982
Persons per sq. mi. of land ... 5,603.3

Race & Hispanic Origin, 2000

Race
White ... 30,633
Black/African American ... 288
North American Native ... 201
Asian ... 884
Pacific Islander ... 36
Other Race ... 2,080
Two or more races ... 988
Hispanic origin, total ... 5,440
Mexican ... 4,316
Puerto Rican ... 70
Cuban ... 61
Other Hispanic ... 993

Age & Nativity, 2000

Under 5 years ... 1,958
18 years and over ... 27,878
65 years and over ... 4,568
85 years and over ... 403
Median Age ... 39.8
Native-born ... 29,394
Foreign-born ... 5,457

Educational Attainment, 2000

Population 25 years and over ... 25,264
Less than 9th grade ... 3.6%
High school grad or higher ... 90.7%
Bachelor's degree or higher ... 41.0%
Graduate degree ... 15.8%

Income & Poverty, 1999

Per capita income ... $37,938
Median household income ... $63,043
Median family income ... $73,373
Persons in poverty ... 6.6%
H'holds receiving public assistance ... 140
H'holds receiving social security ... 3,141

Households, 2000

Total households ... 14,456
With persons under 18 ... 4,081
With persons over 65 ... 3,194
Family households ... 9,286
Single person households ... 3,755
Persons per household ... 2.41
Persons per family ... 2.90

Household Population, 2008§§

Persons living in households ... 36,740
Persons living in group quarters ... 242
Persons per household ... 2.5

Labor & Employment

Total civilian labor force, 2008§§ ... 22,900
Unemployment rate, 2008 ... 3.8%
Total civilian labor force, 2000 ... 19,648

Employed persons 16 years and over by occupation, 2000

Managers & professionals ... 8,029
Service occupations ... 2,737
Sales & office occupations ... 5,458
Farming, fishing & forestry ... 28
Construction & maintenance ... 1,478
Production & transportation ... 1,170
Self-employed persons ... 2,592

* US Census Bureau
** 2000 Decennial Census
§ California Department of Finance
§§ California Employment Development Dept

General Information

City of Dana Point
33282 Golden Lantern
Dana Point, CA 92629
949-248-3500

Website ... www.danapoint.org
Elevation ... 350 ft.
Land Area (sq. miles) ... 6.6
Water Area (sq. miles) ... 22.8
Year of Incorporation ... 1989
Government type ... General law
Sales tax rate ... 8.75%

Voters & Officials

Registered Voters, October 2008

Total ... 24,123
Democrats ... 6,446
Republicans ... 11,601
Declined to state ... 4,863

Legislative Districts

US Congressional ... 48
State Senatorial ... 35
State Assembly ... 73

Local Officials, 2009

Mayor ... Joel Bishop
Manager ... Doug Chotkevys
City Clerk ... Kathy Ward
Attorney ... Patrick Munoz
Finance Dir ... Mike Killebrew
Public Works ... Brad Fowler
Planning/Dev Dir ... Kyle Butterwick
Building ... Mark Sutton
Police Chief ... Mark Levy
Emergency/Fire Dir ... Rick Robinson

Public Safety

Number of officers, 2007 ... NA
Violent crimes, 2007 ... 47
Property crimes, 2007 ... 552
Arson, 2007 ... 5

Public Library

Dana Point Branch Library
Orange County Public Library System
33841 Niguel Rd
Dana Point, CA 92629
949-496-5517

Branch Librarian ... John Dunham

Library system statistics, FY 2007

Population served ... 1,532,758
Internet terminals ... 505
Annual users ... 680,874

Per capita:

Operating income ... $24.71
percent from local government ... 90.0%
Operating expenditure ... $24.18
Total materials ... 1.93
Print holdings ... 1.84
Visits per capita ... 4.02

Housing & Construction

Housing Units

Total, 2008§ ... 15,942
Single family units, attached ... 2,271
Single family units, detached ... 7,933
Multiple family units ... 5,445
Mobile home units ... 293
Occupied ... 14,698
Vacancy rate ... 7.8%
Median rent, 2000** ... $1,139
Median SF home value, 2000** ... $381,400

New Privately Owned Housing Units Authorized by Building Permit, 2007*

	Units	Construction Cost
Single	37	$20,398,286
Total	37	$20,398,286

Municipal Finance

(For local fiscal year ended in 2006)

Revenues

Total ... $36,185,474
Taxes ... 23,253,525
Special benefits assessment ... 0
Licenses & permits ... 690,828
Fines & forfeitures ... 468,382
Revenues from use of money & property ... 1,740,370
Intergovernmental ... 7,887,854
Service charges ... 1,845,478
Other revenues ... 299,037
Other financing sources ... 0

Expenditures

Total ... $37,026,249
General government ... 5,312,108
Public safety ... 8,162,663
Transportation ... 12,693,806
Community development ... 6,643,933
Health ... 0
Culture & leisure ... 4,213,739
Other ... 0

Local School District

(Data from School year 2007-08 except as noted)

Capistrano Unified
33122 Valle Rd
San Juan Capistrano, CA 92675
(949) 234-9200

Superintendent ... A. Carter
Grade plan ... K-12
Number of schools ... 61
Enrollment ... 52,390
High school graduates, 2006-07 ... 3,205
Dropout rate ... 0.5%
Pupil/teacher ratio ... 23.4
Average class size ... 28.7
Students per computer ... 4.8
Classrooms with internet ... 2,308
Avg. Daily Attendance (ADA) ... 50,036
Cost per ADA ... $7,694
Avg. Teacher Salary ... $75,390

California Achievement Tests 6th ed., 2008

(Pct scoring at or above 50th National Percentile Rank)

	Math	Reading	Language
Grade 3	71%	56%	63%
Grade 7	73%	71%	68%

Academic Performance Index, 2008

Number of students tested ... 39,589
Number of valid scores ... 38,275
2007 API (base) ... 826
2008 API (growth) ... 837

SAT Testing, 2006-07

Enrollment, Grade 12 ... 3,414
Number taking test ... 1,770
percent taking test ... 51.9%
percent with total score 1,500+ ... 34.90%

Average Scores:

Math	Verbal	Writing	Total
552	541	537	1,630

Federal No Child Left Behind, 2008

(Adequate Yearly Progress standards met)

	Participation Rate	Pct Proficient
ELA	Yes	No
Math	Yes	Yes

API criteria ... Yes
Graduation rate ... Yes
\# criteria met/possible ... 42/41

Other school districts for this city

(see Appendix E for information on these districts)

None

See Introduction for an explanation of all data sources.

Demographics & Socio-Economic Characteristics

(2000 Decennial Census, except as noted)

Population

1990* ... 31,306
2000 ... 41,715
Male ... 20,228
Female ... 21,487
Jan. 2008 (estimate)§ ... 42,629
Persons per sq. mi. of land ... 2,355.2

Race & Hispanic Origin, 2000

Race
White ... 36,000
Black/African American ... 382
North American Native ... 86
Asian ... 3,756
Pacific Islander ... 48
Other Race ... 381
Two or more races ... 1,062
Hispanic origin, total ... 1,945
Mexican ... 946
Puerto Rican ... 126
Cuban ... 52
Other Hispanic ... 821

Age & Nativity, 2000

Under 5 years ... 2,961
18 years and over ... 29,798
65 years and over ... 4,300
85 years and over ... 583
Median Age ... 39.9
Native-born ... 37,472
Foreign-born ... 4,655

Educational Attainment, 2000

Population 25 years and over ... 28,443
Less than 9th grade ... 0.7%
High school grad or higher ... 96.6%
Bachelor's degree or higher ... 59.4%
Graduate degree ... 21.1%

Income & Poverty, 1999

Per capita income ... $50,773
Median household income ... $114,064
Median family income ... $125,867
Persons in poverty ... 2.2%
H'holds receiving public assistance ... 81
H'holds receiving social security ... 2,863

Households, 2000

Total households ... 14,816
With persons under 18 ... 6,432
With persons over 65 ... 2,779
Family households ... 11,865
Single person households ... 2,295
Persons per household ... 2.78
Persons per family ... 3.13

Household Population, 2008§§

Persons living in households ... 42,165
Persons living in group quarters ... 464
Persons per household ... 2.7

Labor & Employment

Total civilian labor force, 2008§§ ... 23,800
Unemployment rate, 2008 ... 3.2%
Total civilian labor force, 2000 ... 21,605

Employed persons 16 years and over by occupation, 2000

Managers & professionals ... 12,151
Service occupations ... 1,189
Sales & office occupations ... 5,957
Farming, fishing & forestry ... 16
Construction & maintenance ... 844
Production & transportation ... 750
Self-employed persons ... 2,165

* US Census Bureau
** 2000 Decennial Census
§ California Department of Finance
§§ California Employment Development Dept

General Information

Town of Danville
510 LaGonda Way
Danville, CA 94526
925-314-3300

Website ... www.ci.danville.ca.us
Elevation ... 368 ft.
Land Area (sq. miles) ... 18.1
Water Area (sq. miles) ... 0
Year of Incorporation ... 1982
Government type ... General law
Sales tax rate ... 9.25%

Voters & Officials

Registered Voters, October 2008

Total ... 27,827
Democrats ... 9,533
Republicans ... 12,375
Declined to state ... 5,036

Legislative Districts

US Congressional ... 11
State Senatorial ... 7
State Assembly ... 15

Local Officials, 2009

Mayor ... Newell Arnerich
Manager ... Joe Calabrigo
City Clerk ... Marie Sunseri
Attorney ... Rob Ewing
Finance Dir ... Elizabeth Hudson
Public Works ... Steve Lake
Development Svcs ... Steve Lake
Building ... Mike Leontiades
Police Chief ... Chris Wenzel
Fire/Emergency Mgmt ... NA

Public Safety

Number of officers, 2007 ... NA
Violent crimes, 2007 ... 22
Property crimes, 2007 ... 643
Arson, 2007 ... 1

Public Library

Danville Library
Contra Costa County Library System
400 Front St
Danville, CA 94526
925-837-4889

Branch Librarian ... Seng Lovan

Library system statistics, FY 2007

Population served ... 938,513
Internet terminals ... 324
Annual users ... 670,618

Per capita:

Operating income ... $27.05
percent from local government ... 82.0%
Operating expenditure ... $27.82
Total materials ... 1.57
Print holdings ... 1.41
Visits per capita ... 3.65

Housing & Construction

Housing Units

Total, 2008§ ... 15,713
Single family units, attached ... 2,570
Single family units, detached ... 12,077
Multiple family units ... 1,066
Mobile home units ... 0
Occupied ... 15,387
Vacancy rate ... 2.1%
Median rent, 2000** ... $1,604
Median SF home value, 2000** ... $541,400

New Privately Owned Housing Units Authorized by Building Permit, 2007*

	Units	Construction Cost
Single	20	$14,260,919
Total	75	$21,648,836

Municipal Finance

(For local fiscal year ended in 2006)

Revenues

Total ... $30,557,935
Taxes ... 17,949,838
Special benefits assessment ... 3,569,983
Licenses & permits ... 972,368
Fines & forfeitures ... 361,221
Revenues from use of money & property ... 1,944,406
Intergovernmental ... 2,987,895
Service charges ... 2,633,853
Other revenues ... 138,371
Other financing sources ... 0

Expenditures

Total ... $28,323,817
General government ... 5,120,409
Public safety ... 7,018,736
Transportation ... 8,324,106
Community development ... 2,721,533
Health ... 0
Culture & leisure ... 5,139,033
Other ... 0

Local School District

(Data from School year 2007-08 except as noted)

San Ramon Valley Unified
699 Old Orchard Dr
Danville, CA 94526
(925) 552-5500

Superintendent ... Steven Enoch
Grade plan ... K-12
Number of schools ... 34
Enrollment ... 25,959
High school graduates, 2006-07 ... 1,818
Dropout rate ... 0.6%
Pupil/teacher ratio ... 21.3
Average class size ... 26.5
Students per computer ... 4.3
Classrooms with internet ... 1,361
Avg. Daily Attendance (ADA) ... 25,488
Cost per ADA ... $7,914
Avg. Teacher Salary ... $64,878

California Achievement Tests 6th ed., 2008

(Pct scoring at or above 50th National Percentile Rank)

	Math	Reading	Language
Grade 3	87%	72%	78%
Grade 7	85%	81%	80%

Academic Performance Index, 2008

Number of students tested ... 20,092
Number of valid scores ... 19,436
2007 API (base) ... 893
2008 API (growth) ... 904

SAT Testing, 2006-07

Enrollment, Grade 12 ... 1,905
Number taking test ... 1,273
percent taking test ... 66.8%
percent with total score 1,500+ ... 50.80%

Average Scores:

Math	Verbal	Writing	Total
582	556	555	1,693

Federal No Child Left Behind, 2008

(Adequate Yearly Progress standards met)

	Participation Rate	Pct Proficient
ELA	Yes	Yes
Math	Yes	Yes

API criteria ... Yes
Graduation rate ... Yes
\# criteria met/possible ... 38/38

Other school districts for this city

(see Appendix E for information on these districts)

None

See Introduction for an explanation of all data sources.

Demographics & Socio-Economic Characteristics

(2000 Decennial Census, except as noted)

Population

1990*	46,209
2000	60,308
Male	28,763
Female	31,545
Jan. 2008 (estimate)§	65,814
Persons per sq. mi. of land	6,268.0

Race & Hispanic Origin, 2000

Race	
White	42,256
Black/African American	1,417
North American Native	407
Asian	10,576
Pacific Islander	144
Other Race	2,572
Two or more races	2,936
Hispanic origin, total	5,793
Mexican	3,966
Puerto Rican	170
Cuban	58
Other Hispanic	1,599

Age & Nativity, 2000

Under 5 years	2,772
18 years and over	49,072
65 years and over	4,004
85 years and over	517
Median Age	25.2
Native-born	49,976
Foreign-born	10,365

Educational Attainment, 2000

Population 25 years and over	30,375
Less than 9th grade	1.3%
High school grad or higher	96.4%
Bachelor's degree or higher	68.6%
Graduate degree	36.1%

Income & Poverty, 1999

Per capita income	$22,937
Median household income	$42,454
Median family income	$74,051
Persons in poverty	23.4%
H'holds receiving public assistance	243
H'holds receiving social security	2,824

Households, 2000

Total households	22,948
With persons under 18	6,302
With persons over 65	2,822
Family households	11,291
Single person households	5,727
Persons per household	2.50
Persons per family	3.00

Household Population, 2008§§

Persons living in households	62,733
Persons living in group quarters	3,081
Persons per household	2.5

Labor & Employment

Total civilian labor force, 2008§§	39,600
Unemployment rate, 2008	4.7%
Total civilian labor force, 2000	33,017

Employed persons 16 years and over by occupation, 2000

Managers & professionals	19,105
Service occupations	3,538
Sales & office occupations	6,465
Farming, fishing & forestry	114
Construction & maintenance	852
Production & transportation	1,497
Self-employed persons	1,756

* US Census Bureau
** 2000 Decennial Census
§ California Department of Finance
§§ California Employment Development Dept

General Information

City of Davis
23 Russell Blvd
Davis, CA 95616
530-757-5602

Website	www.cityofdavis.org
Elevation	50 ft.
Land Area (sq. miles)	10.5
Water Area (sq. miles)	0
Year of Incorporation	1917
Government type	General law
Sales tax rate	8.75%

Voters & Officials

Registered Voters, October 2008

Total	40,996
Democrats	22,198
Republicans	6,563
Declined to state	10,131

Legislative Districts

US Congressional	1
State Senatorial	5
State Assembly	8

Local Officials, 2009

Mayor	Ruth Asmundson
Manager	Bill Emlen
City Clerk	Zoe Mirabile
Attorney	Harriet Steiner
Finance Dir	Paul Navazio
Public Works	Bob Weir
Community Dev Dir	Katherine Hess
Building	NA
Police Chief	Landy Black
Fire Chief	Rose Conroy

Public Safety

Number of officers, 2007	57
Violent crimes, 2007	169
Property crimes, 2007	2,121
Arson, 2007	26

Public Library

Davis Branch Library
Yolo County Library System
315 E 14th St
Davis, CA 95616
530-757-5593

Branch Librarian	James Johnstone

Library system statistics, FY 2007

Population served	139,923
Internet terminals	43
Annual users	276,902

Per capita:

Operating income	$33.44
percent from local government	89.8%
Operating expenditure	$27.76
Total materials	2.68
Print holdings	2.44
Visits per capita	4.51

Housing & Construction

Housing Units

Total, 2008§	25,876
Single family units, attached	2,417
Single family units, detached	11,551
Multiple family units	11,523
Mobile home units	385
Occupied	25,313
Vacancy rate	2.2%
Median rent, 2000**	$775
Median SF home value, 2000**	$238,500

New Privately Owned Housing Units Authorized by Building Permit, 2007*

	Units	Construction Cost
Single	28	$6,234,811
Total	44	$9,119,492

Municipal Finance

(For local fiscal year ended in 2006)

Revenues

Total	$91,599,520
Taxes	36,717,831
Special benefits assessment	1,245
Licenses & permits	880,470
Fines & forfeitures	891,257
Revenues from use of money & property	2,654,420
Intergovernmental	16,533,032
Service charges	32,760,702
Other revenues	1,160,563
Other financing sources	0

Expenditures

Total	$88,842,036
General government	4,073,280
Public safety	20,368,354
Transportation	12,499,925
Community development	6,482,005
Health	14,771,662
Culture & leisure	22,422,040
Other	0

Local School District

(Data from School year 2007-08 except as noted)

Davis Joint Unified
526 B St
Davis, CA 95616
(530) 757-5300

Superintendent	James Quezon-Hammond
Grade plan	K-12
Number of schools	17
Enrollment	8,484
High school graduates, 2006-07	685
Dropout rate	0.9%
Pupil/teacher ratio	20.1
Average class size	25.3
Students per computer	3.0
Classrooms with internet	2,824
Avg. Daily Attendance (ADA)	8,284
Cost per ADA	$8,305
Avg. Teacher Salary	$63,810

California Achievement Tests 6th ed., 2008

(Pct scoring at or above 50th National Percentile Rank)

	Math	Reading	Language
Grade 3	79%	70%	72%
Grade 7	81%	79%	78%

Academic Performance Index, 2008

Number of students tested	6,436
Number of valid scores	6,155
2007 API (base)	868
2008 API (growth)	872

SAT Testing, 2006-07

Enrollment, Grade 12	748
Number taking test	519
percent taking test	69.4%
percent with total score 1,500+	57.90%

Average Scores:

Math	Verbal	Writing	Total
606	592	584	1,782

Federal No Child Left Behind, 2008

(Adequate Yearly Progress standards met)

	Participation Rate	Pct Proficient
ELA	Yes	Yes
Math	No	Yes

API criteria	Yes
Graduation rate	Yes
# criteria met/possible	34/33

Other school districts for this city

(see Appendix E for information on these districts)

None

Demographics & Socio-Economic Characteristics

(2000 Decennial Census, except as noted)

Population

1990*	4,860
2000	4,389
Male	2,248
Female	2,141
Jan. 2008 (estimate)§	4,580
Persons per sq. mi. of land	2,694.1

Race & Hispanic Origin, 2000

Race	
White	4,132
Black/African American	11
North American Native	15
Asian	126
Pacific Islander	5
Other Race	25
Two or more races	75
Hispanic origin, total	170
Mexican	109
Puerto Rican	7
Cuban	2
Other Hispanic	52

Age & Nativity, 2000

Under 5 years	164
18 years and over	3,791
65 years and over	620
85 years and over	51
Median Age	43.5
Native-born	3,797
Foreign-born	592

Educational Attainment, 2000

Population 25 years and over	3,587
Less than 9th grade	0.2%
High school grad or higher	97.7%
Bachelor's degree or higher	72.4%
Graduate degree	36.7%

Income & Poverty, 1999

Per capita income	$62,425
Median household income	$81,001
Median family income	$92,270
Persons in poverty	8.7%
H'holds receiving public assistance	8
H'holds receiving social security	489

Households, 2000

Total households	2,178
With persons under 18	355
With persons over 65	446
Family households	1,083
Single person households	797
Persons per household	2.01
Persons per family	2.61

Household Population, 2008§§

Persons living in households	4,578
Persons living in group quarters	2
Persons per household	2.1

Labor & Employment

Total civilian labor force, 2008§§	3,000
Unemployment rate, 2008	2.9%
Total civilian labor force, 2000	2,548

Employed persons 16 years and over by occupation, 2000

Managers & professionals	1,665
Service occupations	114
Sales & office occupations	543
Farming, fishing & forestry	18
Construction & maintenance	37
Production & transportation	98
Self-employed persons	367

* US Census Bureau
** 2000 Decennial Census
§ California Department of Finance
§§ California Employment Development Dept

General Information

City of Del Mar
1050 Camino Del Mar
Del Mar, CA 92014
858-755-9313

Website	www.delmar.ca.us
Elevation	NA
Land Area (sq. miles)	1.7
Water Area (sq. miles)	0.1
Year of Incorporation	1959
Government type	Chartered
Sales tax rate	8.75%

Voters & Officials

Registered Voters, October 2008

Total	3,113
Democrats	1,156
Republicans	1,055
Declined to state	781

Legislative Districts

US Congressional	50
State Senatorial	39
State Assembly	74

Local Officials, 2009

Mayor	Crystal Crawford
City Manager	Karen Brust
City Clerk	Mercedes Martin
Attorney	Kimberly Johnson (Int)
Finance Dir	Teresa McBroome
Public Works	David Scherer
Planning/Dev Dir	Brian Mooney (Int)
Building	Brian Mooney
Police Captain	Donald Fowler
Fire Chief	David Ott

Public Safety

Number of officers, 2007	NA
Violent crimes, 2007	18
Property crimes, 2007	217
Arson, 2007	1

Public Library

Del Mar Library
San Diego County Library System
1309 Camino del Mar
Del Mar, CA 92014
858-755-8869

Branch Librarian	Gretchen Schmidt

Library system statistics, FY 2007

Population served	1,049,868
Internet terminals	394
Annual users	NA

Per capita:

Operating income	$33.43
percent from local government	80.6%
Operating expenditure	$31.30
Total materials	1.54
Print holdings	1.32
Visits per capita	6.31

Housing & Construction

Housing Units

Total, 2008§	2,611
Single family units, attached	366
Single family units, detached	1,369
Multiple family units	876
Mobile home units	0
Occupied	2,225
Vacancy rate	14.8%
Median rent, 2000**	$1,246
Median SF home value, 2000**	$923,400

New Privately Owned Housing Units Authorized by Building Permit, 2007*

	Units	Construction Cost
Single	NA	NA
Total	NA	NA

Municipal Finance

(For local fiscal year ended in 2006)

Revenues

Total	$16,772,922
Taxes	6,997,698
Special benefits assessment	0
Licenses & permits	406,246
Fines & forfeitures	956,378
Revenues from use of money & property	990,058
Intergovernmental	1,081,998
Service charges	5,674,448
Other revenues	666,096
Other financing sources	0

Expenditures

Total	$15,924,601
General government	2,115,278
Public safety	4,136,717
Transportation	1,782,660
Community development	1,184,913
Health	2,169,425
Culture & leisure	2,091,173
Other	0

Local School District

(Data from School year 2007-08 except as noted)

San Dieguito Union High
710 Encinitas Blvd
Encinitas, CA 92024
(760) 753-6491

Superintendent	Ken Noah
Grade plan	7-12
Number of schools	10
Enrollment	12,482
High school graduates, 2006-07	1,874
Dropout rate	1.4%
Pupil/teacher ratio	25.4
Average class size	30.5
Students per computer	3.5
Classrooms with internet	613
Avg. Daily Attendance (ADA)	12,349
Cost per ADA	$8,092
Avg. Teacher Salary	$75,620

California Achievement Tests 6th ed., 2008

(Pct scoring at or above 50th National Percentile Rank)

	Math	Reading	Language
Grade 3	NA	NA	NA
Grade 7	83%	79%	78%

Academic Performance Index, 2008

Number of students tested	10,153
Number of valid scores	9,873
2007 API (base)	853
2008 API (growth)	855

SAT Testing, 2006-07

Enrollment, Grade 12	2,038
Number taking test	1,532
percent taking test	75.2%
percent with total score 1,500+	57.90%

Average Scores:

Math	Verbal	Writing	Total
590	555	560	1,705

Federal No Child Left Behind, 2008

(Adequate Yearly Progress standards met)

	Participation Rate	Pct Proficient
ELA	Yes	Yes
Math	Yes	Yes

API criteria	Yes
Graduation rate	Yes
# criteria met/possible	30/30

Other school districts for this city

(see Appendix E for information on these districts)

Del Mar Union Elem

See Introduction for an explanation of all data sources.

Demographics & Socio-Economic Characteristics

(2000 Decennial Census, except as noted)

Population

1990* . . . 1,661
2000 . . . 1,650
Male . . . 784
Female . . . 866
Jan. 2008 (estimate)§ . . . 1,627
Persons per sq. mi. of land . . . 3,254.0

Race & Hispanic Origin, 2000

Race
White . . . 1,425
Black/African American . . . 26
North American Native . . . 14
Asian . . . 85
Pacific Islander . . . 0
Other Race . . . 42
Two or more races . . . 58
Hispanic origin, total . . . 109
Mexican . . . 58
Puerto Rican . . . 4
Cuban . . . 6
Other Hispanic . . . 41

Age & Nativity, 2000

Under 5 years . . . 80
18 years and over . . . 1,334
65 years and over . . . 262
85 years and over . . . 22
Median Age . . . 43.8
Native-born . . . 1,449
Foreign-born . . . 201

Educational Attainment, 2000

Population 25 years and over . . . 1,248
Less than 9th grade . . . 1.0%
High school grad or higher . . . 91.4%
Bachelor's degree or higher . . . 34.3%
Graduate degree . . . 14.8%

Income & Poverty, 1999

Per capita income . . . $30,035
Median household income . . . $59,423
Median family income . . . $70,119
Persons in poverty . . . 5.0%
H'holds receiving public assistance . . . 4
H'holds receiving social security . . . 194

Households, 2000

Total households . . . 704
With persons under 18 . . . 186
With persons over 65 . . . 190
Family households . . . 450
Single person households . . . 191
Persons per household . . . 2.34
Persons per family . . . 2.86

Household Population, 2008§§

Persons living in households . . . 1,627
Persons living in group quarters . . . 0
Persons per household . . . 2.3

Labor & Employment

Total civilian labor force, 2008§§ . . . 1,200
Unemployment rate, 2008 . . . 2.0%
Total civilian labor force, 2000 . . . 973

Employed persons 16 years and over by occupation, 2000

Managers & professionals . . . 419
Service occupations . . . 148
Sales & office occupations . . . 253
Farming, fishing & forestry . . . 0
Construction & maintenance . . . 83
Production & transportation . . . 50
Self-employed persons . . . 162

* US Census Bureau
** 2000 Decennial Census
§ California Department of Finance
§§ California Employment Development Dept

General Information

City of Del Rey Oaks
650 Canyon Del Rey Rd
Del Rey Oaks, CA 93940
831-394-8511

Website . . . www.delreyoaks.org
Elevation . . . NA
Land Area (sq. miles) . . . 0.5
Water Area (sq. miles) . . . 0
Year of Incorporation . . . 1953
Government type . . . General law
Sales tax rate . . . 9.25%

Voters & Officials

Registered Voters, October 2008

Total . . . 1,054
Democrats . . . 528
Republicans . . . 290
Declined to state . . . 194

Legislative Districts

US Congressional . . . 17
State Senatorial . . . 15
State Assembly . . . 27

Local Officials, 2009

Mayor . . . Joseph P. Russell
Manager . . . Dewey D. Evans (Int)
City Clerk . . . Kim Carvalho
Attorney . . . Robert Wellington
Finance Dir . . . Dewey D. Evans (Int)
Public Works . . . NA
Planning/Dev Dir . . . NA
Building . . . NA
Police Chief . . . Ronald Langford
Fire/Emergency Mgmt . . . NA

Public Safety

Number of officers, 2007 . . . 6
Violent crimes, 2007 . . . 0
Property crimes, 2007 . . . 29
Arson, 2007 . . . 0

Public Library

Served by County Library

Library system statistics, FY 2007

Population served . . . NA
Internet terminals . . . NA
Annual users . . . NA

Per capita:

Operating income . . . NA
percent from local government . . . NA
Operating expenditure . . . NA
Total materials . . . NA
Print holdings . . . NA
Visits per capita . . . NA

Housing & Construction

Housing Units

Total, 2008§ . . . 727
Single family units, attached . . . 25
Single family units, detached . . . 567
Multiple family units . . . 132
Mobile home units . . . 3
Occupied . . . 704
Vacancy rate . . . 3.2%
Median rent, 2000** . . . $1,284
Median SF home value, 2000** . . . $312,500

New Privately Owned Housing Units Authorized by Building Permit, 2007*

	Units	Construction Cost
Single	0	$0
Total	0	$0

Municipal Finance

(For local fiscal year ended in 2006)

Revenues

Total . . . $1,810,959
Taxes . . . 942,231
Special benefits assessment . . . 323,534
Licenses & permits . . . 24,914
Fines & forfeitures . . . 13,759
Revenues from use of money & property . . . 14,374
Intergovernmental . . . 317,501
Service charges . . . 168,531
Other revenues . . . 6,115
Other financing sources . . . 0

Expenditures

Total . . . $1,713,501
General government . . . 267,627
Public safety . . . 1,155,977
Transportation . . . 97,064
Community development . . . 66,390
Health . . . 0
Culture & leisure . . . 126,443
Other . . . 0

Local School District

(Data from School year 2007-08 except as noted)

Monterey Peninsula Unified
PO Box 1031
Monterey, CA 93942
(831) 645-1200

Superintendent . . . Marilyn Shepherd
Grade plan . . . K-12
Number of schools . . . 22
Enrollment . . . 11,613
High school graduates, 2006-07 . . . 590
Dropout rate . . . 2.0%
Pupil/teacher ratio . . . 20.5
Average class size . . . 24.3
Students per computer . . . 8.5
Classrooms with internet . . . 518
Avg. Daily Attendance (ADA) . . . 10,537
Cost per ADA . . . $8,271
Avg. Teacher Salary . . . $57,857

California Achievement Tests 6th ed., 2008

(Pct scoring at or above 50th National Percentile Rank)

	Math	Reading	Language
Grade 3	56%	35%	43%
Grade 7	49%	44%	43%

Academic Performance Index, 2008

Number of students tested . . . 8,210
Number of valid scores . . . 7,687
2007 API (base) . . . 716
2008 API (growth) . . . 728

SAT Testing, 2006-07

Enrollment, Grade 12 . . . 682
Number taking test . . . 262
percent taking test . . . 38.4%
percent with total score 1,500+ . . . 15.10%

Average Scores:

Math	Verbal	Writing	Total
504	487	481	1,472

Federal No Child Left Behind, 2008

(Adequate Yearly Progress standards met)

	Participation Rate	Pct Proficient
ELA	Yes	No
Math	Yes	No

API criteria . . . Yes
Graduation rate . . . Yes
\# criteria met/possible . . . 42/36

Other school districts for this city

(see Appendix E for information on these districts)

None

See Introduction for an explanation of all data sources.

Demographics & Socio-Economic Characteristics

(2000 Decennial Census, except as noted)

Population

1990* . . . 22,762
2000 . . . 38,824
Male . . . 21,935
Female . . . 16,889
Jan. 2008 (estimate)§ . . . 53,855
Persons per sq. mi. of land . . . 5,332.2

Race & Hispanic Origin, 2000

Race
White . . . 10,157
Black/African American . . . 2,115
North American Native . . . 352
Asian . . . 6,165
Pacific Islander . . . 22
Other Race . . . 18,276
Two or more races . . . 1,737
Hispanic origin, total . . . 26,584
Mexican . . . 23,428
Puerto Rican . . . 166
Cuban . . . 3
Other Hispanic . . . 2,987

Age & Nativity, 2000

Under 5 years . . . 3,537
18 years and over . . . 26,206
65 years and over . . . 2,899
85 years and over . . . 324
Median Age . . . 27.9
Native-born . . . 24,088
Foreign-born . . . 14,893

Educational Attainment, 2000

Population 25 years and over . . . 21,789
Less than 9th grade . . . 32.4%
High school grad or higher . . . 48.7%
Bachelor's degree or higher . . . 5.5%
Graduate degree . . . 1.3%

Income & Poverty, 1999

Per capita income . . . $11,068
Median household income . . . $28,143
Median family income . . . $29,026
Persons in poverty . . . 24.6%
H'holds receiving public assistance . . . 859
H'holds receiving social security . . . 1,897

Households, 2000

Total households . . . 8,409
With persons under 18 . . . 5,352
With persons over 65 . . . 1,982
Family households . . . 7,245
Single person households . . . 912
Persons per household . . . 4.02
Persons per family . . . 4.27

Household Population, 2008§§

Persons living in households . . . 42,549
Persons living in group quarters . . . 11,306
Persons per household . . . 4.1

Labor & Employment

Total civilian labor force, 2008§§ . . . 17,800
Unemployment rate, 2008 . . . 25.9%
Total civilian labor force, 2000 . . . 13,361

Employed persons 16 years and over by occupation, 2000

Managers & professionals . . . 1,461
Service occupations . . . 1,413
Sales & office occupations . . . 1,852
Farming, fishing & forestry . . . 2,407
Construction & maintenance . . . 452
Production & transportation . . . 1,734
Self-employed persons . . . 450

* US Census Bureau
** 2000 Decennial Census
§ California Department of Finance
§§ California Employment Development Dept

General Information

City of Delano
1015 11th Ave
PO Box 3010
Delano, CA 93215
661-721-3300

Website . . . www.delano-ca.org
Elevation . . . 316 ft.
Land Area (sq. miles) . . . 10.1
Water Area (sq. miles) . . . 0.1
Year of Incorporation . . . 1915
Government type . . . General law
Sales tax rate . . . 9.25%

Voters & Officials

Registered Voters, October 2008

Total . . . 10,603
Democrats . . . 6,434
Republicans . . . 2,475
Declined to state . . . 1,484

Legislative Districts

US Congressional . . . 20
State Senatorial . . . 16
State Assembly . . . 30

Local Officials, 2009

Mayor . . . Sam Ramirez
Manager . . . Abdel Salem
City Clerk . . . Phyllis Kraft
Attorney . . . Alan Peake
Finance Dir . . . (vacant)
Public Works . . . John Alderson
Planning/Dev Dir . . . Keith Woodcock
Building . . . Leonard Brown
Police Chief . . . Mark DeRosia
Fire/Emergency Mgmt . . . NA

Public Safety

Number of officers, 2007 . . . 48
Violent crimes, 2007 . . . 282
Property crimes, 2007 . . . 1,863
Arson, 2007 . . . NA

Public Library

Delano Branch Library
Kern County Library System
925 10th Ave
Delano, CA 93215
661-725-1078

Branch Librarian . . . Bill Westerhart

Library system statistics, FY 2007

Population served . . . 801,648
Internet terminals . . . 237
Annual users . . . 337,030

Per capita:

Operating income . . . $12.11
percent from local government . . . 90.4%
Operating expenditure . . . $12.11
Total materials . . . 1.37
Print holdings . . . 1.29
Visits per capita . . . 2.09

Housing & Construction

Housing Units

Total, 2008§ . . . 10,772
Single family units, attached . . . 549
Single family units, detached . . . 7,699
Multiple family units . . . 2,074
Mobile home units . . . 450
Occupied . . . 10,258
Vacancy rate . . . 4.8%
Median rent, 2000** . . . $467
Median SF home value, 2000** . . . $86,700

New Privately Owned Housing Units Authorized by Building Permit, 2007*

	Units	Construction Cost
Single	130	$18,285,300
Total	153	$19,740,700

Municipal Finance

(For local fiscal year ended in 2006)

Revenues

Total . . . $36,133,097
Taxes . . . 12,567,090
Special benefits assessment . . . 188,446
Licenses & permits . . . 439,703
Fines & forfeitures . . . 177,545
Revenues from use of money & property . . . 1,075,866
Intergovernmental . . . 11,651,700
Service charges . . . 8,487,952
Other revenues . . . 1,544,795
Other financing sources . . . 0

Expenditures

Total . . . $30,095,737
General government . . . 1,991,756
Public safety . . . 14,289,849
Transportation . . . 3,129,436
Community development . . . 4,193,935
Health . . . 3,039,430
Culture & leisure . . . 1,220,378
Other . . . 0

Local School District

(Data from School year 2007-08 except as noted)

Delano Joint Union High
1747 Princeton St
Delano, CA 93215
(661) 725-4000

Superintendent . . . Rosalina Rivera
Grade plan . . . 9-12
Number of schools . . . 4
Enrollment . . . 4,561
High school graduates, 2006-07 . . . 755
Dropout rate . . . 4.4%
Pupil/teacher ratio . . . 22.3
Average class size . . . 26.0
Students per computer . . . 2.8
Classrooms with internet . . . 195
Avg. Daily Attendance (ADA) . . . 4,447
Cost per ADA . . . $8,519
Avg. Teacher Salary . . . $55,698

California Achievement Tests 6th ed., 2008

(Pct scoring at or above 50th National Percentile Rank)

	Math	Reading	Language
Grade 3	NA	NA	NA
Grade 7	NA	NA	NA

Academic Performance Index, 2008

Number of students tested . . . 3,292
Number of valid scores . . . 3,245
2007 API (base) . . . 658
2008 API (growth) . . . 674

SAT Testing, 2006-07

Enrollment, Grade 12 . . . 858
Number taking test . . . 191
percent taking test . . . 22.3%
percent with total score 1,500+ . . . 5.40%

Average Scores:

Math	Verbal	Writing	Total
473	429	427	1,329

Federal No Child Left Behind, 2008

(Adequate Yearly Progress standards met)

	Participation Rate	Pct Proficient
ELA	Yes	Yes
Math	Yes	Yes

API criteria . . . Yes
Graduation rate . . . No
criteria met/possible . . . 22/21

Other school districts for this city

(see Appendix E for information on these districts)

Delano Union Elem

See Introduction for an explanation of all data sources.

Demographics & Socio-Economic Characteristics

(2000 Decennial Census, except as noted)

Population

1990* . . . 11,668
2000 . . . 16,582
Male . . . 8,155
Female . . . 8,427
Jan. 2008 (estimate)§ . . . 26,068
Persons per sq. mi. of land . . . 1,118.8

Race & Hispanic Origin, 2000

Race
White . . . 11,306
Black/African American . . . 1,014
North American Native . . . 238
Asian . . . 326
Pacific Islander . . . 14
Other Race . . . 2,717
Two or more races . . . 967
Hispanic origin, total . . . 6,699
Mexican . . . 5,536
Puerto Rican . . . 58
Cuban . . . 30
Other Hispanic . . . 1,075

Age & Nativity, 2000

Under 5 years . . . 1,564
18 years and over . . . 11,063
65 years and over . . . 1,846
85 years and over . . . 200
Median Age . . . 30.1
Native-born . . . 13,048
Foreign-born . . . 3,411

Educational Attainment, 2000

Population 25 years and over . . . 9,537
Less than 9th grade . . . 11.0%
High school grad or higher . . . 70.9%
Bachelor's degree or higher . . . 8.9%
Graduate degree . . . 2.4%

Income & Poverty, 1999

Per capita income . . . $11,954
Median household income . . . $25,987
Median family income . . . $29,126
Persons in poverty . . . 26.8%
H'holds receiving public assistance . . . 384
H'holds receiving social security . . . 1,669

Households, 2000

Total households . . . 5,859
With persons under 18 . . . 2,533
With persons over 65 . . . 1,381
Family households . . . 3,757
Single person households . . . 1,620
Persons per household . . . 2.80
Persons per family . . . 3.45

Household Population, 2008§§

Persons living in households . . . 25,894
Persons living in group quarters . . . 174
Persons per household . . . 2.9

Labor & Employment

Total civilian labor force, 2008§§ . . . 9,300
Unemployment rate, 2008 . . . 11.7%
Total civilian labor force, 2000 . . . 6,571

Employed persons 16 years and over by occupation, 2000

Managers & professionals . . . 983
Service occupations . . . 1,719
Sales & office occupations . . . 1,550
Farming, fishing & forestry . . . 7
Construction & maintenance . . . 906
Production & transportation . . . 732
Self-employed persons . . . 411

* US Census Bureau
** 2000 Decennial Census
§ California Department of Finance
§§ California Employment Development Dept

General Information

City of Desert Hot Springs
65950 Pierson Blvd
Desert Hot Springs, CA 92240
760-329-6411

Website . . . www.cityofdhs.org
Elevation . . . 1,000 ft.
Land Area (sq. miles) . . . 23.3
Water Area (sq. miles) . . . 0
Year of Incorporation . . . 1963
Government type . . . Chartered
Sales tax rate . . . 8.75%

Voters & Officials

Registered Voters, October 2008

Total . . . 8,230
Democrats . . . 2,785
Republicans . . . 3,881
Declined to state . . . 1,205

Legislative Districts

US Congressional . . . 41
State Senatorial . . . 37
State Assembly . . . 80

Local Officials, 2009

Mayor . . . Yvonne Parks
Manager . . . Rick Daniels
City Clerk . . . Cynthia Lugo
Attorney . . . Ruben Duran
Finance Dir . . . Jason Simpson
Public Works . . . Jonathan Hoy
Planning/Dev Dir . . . Rudy Acosta
Building . . . Don Gleeson
Police Chief . . . Patrick Williams
Emergency/Fire Dir . . . David Avila

Public Safety

Number of officers, 2007 . . . 25
Violent crimes, 2007 . . . 276
Property crimes, 2007 . . . 1,718
Arson, 2007 . . . 0

Public Library

Desert Hot Springs Branch Library
Riverside County Library Service
11691 West Dr
Desert Hot Springs, CA 92240
760-329-5926

Branch Librarian . . . Helen Kerrigan

Library system statistics, FY 2007

Population served . . . 1,047,996
Internet terminals . . . 37
Annual users . . . 69,346

Per capita:

Operating income . . . $19.38
percent from local government . . . 49.8%
Operating expenditure . . . $20.45
Total materials . . . 1.43
Print holdings . . . 1.30
Visits per capita . . . 4.06

Housing & Construction

Housing Units

Total, 2008§ . . . 10,907
Single family units, attached . . . 180
Single family units, detached . . . 7,358
Multiple family units . . . 2,690
Mobile home units . . . 679
Occupied . . . 9,085
Vacancy rate . . . 16.7%
Median rent, 2000** . . . $509
Median SF home value, 2000** . . . $81,400

New Privately Owned Housing Units Authorized by Building Permit, 2007*

	Units	Construction Cost
Single	113	$18,437,347
Total	148	$22,300,326

Municipal Finance

(For local fiscal year ended in 2006)

Revenues

Total . . . $23,390,419
Taxes . . . 12,161,177
Special benefits assessment . . . 1,702,409
Licenses & permits . . . 2,359,929
Fines & forfeitures . . . 115,650
Revenues from use of money & property . . . 810,099
Intergovernmental . . . 3,083,938
Service charges . . . 3,070,884
Other revenues . . . 86,333
Other financing sources . . . 0

Expenditures

Total . . . $22,227,410
General government . . . 3,784,136
Public safety . . . 8,222,937
Transportation . . . 4,788,286
Community development . . . 4,389,631
Health . . . 79,852
Culture & leisure . . . 962,568
Other . . . 0

Local School District

(Data from School year 2007-08 except as noted)

Palm Springs Unified
980 East Tahquitz Canyon Way
Palm Springs, CA 92262
(760) 416-6000

Superintendent . . . Lorri McCune
Grade plan . . . K-12
Number of schools . . . 25
Enrollment . . . 24,400
High school graduates, 2006-07 . . . 1,146
Dropout rate . . . 5.8%
Pupil/teacher ratio . . . 21.9
Average class size . . . 28.3
Students per computer . . . 5.9
Classrooms with internet . . . 1,311
Avg. Daily Attendance (ADA) . . . 22,873
Cost per ADA . . . $8,379
Avg. Teacher Salary . . . $66,086

California Achievement Tests 6th ed., 2008

(Pct scoring at or above 50th National Percentile Rank)

	Math	Reading	Language
Grade 3	44%	28%	36%
Grade 7	37%	35%	32%

Academic Performance Index, 2008

Number of students tested . . . 18,458
Number of valid scores . . . 17,207
2007 API (base) . . . 673
2008 API (growth) . . . 700

SAT Testing, 2006-07

Enrollment, Grade 12 . . . 1,704
Number taking test . . . 438
percent taking test . . . 25.7%
percent with total score 1,500+ . . . 8.90%

Average Scores:

Math	Verbal	Writing	Total
469	468	454	1,391

Federal No Child Left Behind, 2008

(Adequate Yearly Progress standards met)

	Participation Rate	Pct Proficient
ELA	Yes	No
Math	Yes	No

API criteria . . . Yes
Graduation rate . . . No
\# criteria met/possible . . . 38/31

Other school districts for this city

(see Appendix E for information on these districts)

None

See Introduction for an explanation of all data sources.

Demographics & Socio-Economic Characteristics

(2000 Decennial Census, except as noted)

Population

1990* 53,672
2000 56,287
Male 27,566
Female 28,721
Jan. 2008 (estimate)§ 60,360
Persons per sq. mi. of land 4,078.4

Race & Hispanic Origin, 2000

Race
White 23,103
Black/African American 2,680
North American Native 185
Asian 24,066
Pacific Islander 67
Other Race 3,818
Two or more races 2,368
Hispanic origin, total 10,393
Mexican 7,580
Puerto Rican 197
Cuban 228
Other Hispanic 2,388

Age & Nativity, 2000

Under 5 years 3,216
18 years and over 41,104
65 years and over 4,213
85 years and over 291
Median Age 36.5
Native-born 34,762
Foreign-born 21,587

Educational Attainment, 2000

Population 25 years and over 36,322
Less than 9th grade 2.9%
High school grad or higher 90.7%
Bachelor's degree or higher 42.3%
Graduate degree 13.4%

Income & Poverty, 1999

Per capita income $25,472
Median household income $68,871
Median family income $71,911
Persons in poverty 6.0%
H'holds receiving public assistance 359
H'holds receiving social security 2,498

Households, 2000

Total households 17,651
With persons under 18 8,489
With persons over 65 3,124
Family households 14,801
Single person households 2,201
Persons per household 3.18
Persons per family 3.47

Household Population, 2008§§

Persons living in households 60,242
Persons living in group quarters 118
Persons per household 3.3

Labor & Employment

Total civilian labor force, 2008§§ 33,100
Unemployment rate, 2008 . . . . . 5.3%
Total civilian labor force, 2000 28,395

Employed persons 16 years and over by occupation, 2000

Managers & professionals 12,709
Service occupations 2,073
Sales & office occupations 8,601
Farming, fishing & forestry 26
Construction & maintenance 1,364
Production & transportation 2,015
Self-employed persons 2,283

* US Census Bureau
** 2000 Decennial Census
§ California Department of Finance
§§ California Employment Development Dept

General Information

City of Diamond Bar
21825 Copley Dr
Diamond Bar, CA 91765
909-839-7000

Website . . . . . www.ci.diamond-bar.ca.us
Elevation . . . . . 550 ft.
Land Area (sq. miles) 14.8
Water Area (sq. miles) 0
Year of Incorporation 1989
Government type . . . . . General law
Sales tax rate 9.25%

Voters & Officials

Registered Voters, October 2008

Total 29,380
Democrats 10,187
Republicans 10,172
Declined to state 7,970

Legislative Districts

US Congressional 42
State Senatorial 29
State Assembly 60

Local Officials, 2009

Mayor . . . . . Ron Everett
Manager . . . . . James DeStefano
City Clerk . . . . . Tommye Cribbins
Attorney . . . . . Michael Jenkins
Finance Dir . . . . . Linda Magnuson
Public Works . . . . . David Liu
Planning/Dev Dir . . . . . Greg Gubman (Actg)
Building . . . . . Dennis Tarango
Police Chief . . . . . (County)
Fire/Emergency Mgmt . . . . . (County)

Public Safety

Number of officers, 2007 . . . . . NA
Violent crimes, 2007 133
Property crimes, 2007 1,058
Arson, 2007 6

Public Library

Diamond Bar Library
Los Angeles County Public Library System
1061 S Grand Ave
Diamond Bar, CA 91765
909-861-4978

Branch Librarian . . . . . Irene Wang

Library system statistics, FY 2007

Population served 3,673,313
Internet terminals 749
Annual users 3,748,771

Per capita:

Operating income $30.06
percent from local government 93.6%
Operating expenditure $28.36
Total materials 2.22
Print holdings 1.97
Visits per capita 3.25

Housing & Construction

Housing Units

Total, 2008§ 18,380
Single family units, attached 2,531
Single family units, detached 12,937
Multiple family units 2,579
Mobile home units 333
Occupied 18,066
Vacancy rate 1.7%
Median rent, 2000** $1,012
Median SF home value, 2000** $245,800

New Privately Owned Housing Units Authorized by Building Permit, 2007*

	Units	Construction Cost
Single	70	$14,804,978
Total	70	$14,804,978

Municipal Finance

(For local fiscal year ended in 2006)

Revenues

Total $25,339,532
Taxes 11,361,029
Special benefits assessment 504,909
Licenses & permits 687,457
Fines & forfeitures 589,922
Revenues from use of money & property 2,286,451
Intergovernmental 7,111,016
Service charges 2,727,783
Other revenues 70,965
Other financing sources 0

Expenditures

Total $25,845,268
General government 3,800,649
Public safety 4,755,974
Transportation 8,796,871
Community development 3,442,696
Health 349,491
Culture & leisure 4,699,587
Other 0

Local School District

(Data from School year 2007-08 except as noted)

Walnut Valley Unified
880 South Lemon Ave
Walnut, CA 91789
(909) 595-1261

Superintendent . . . . . Cynthia Simms
Grade plan K-12
Number of schools 15
Enrollment 15,316
High school graduates, 2006-07 1,527
Dropout rate 1.8%
Pupil/teacher ratio 23.2
Average class size 28.5
Students per computer 5.1
Classrooms with internet 738
Avg. Daily Attendance (ADA) 15,162
Cost per ADA $7,443
Avg. Teacher Salary $71,372

California Achievement Tests 6th ed., 2008

(Pct scoring at or above 50th National Percentile Rank)

	Math	Reading	Language
Grade 3	82%	60%	71%
Grade 7	81%	74%	75%

Academic Performance Index, 2008

Number of students tested 12,371
Number of valid scores 12,061
2007 API (base) 869
2008 API (growth) 876

SAT Testing, 2006-07

Enrollment, Grade 12 1,552
Number taking test 1,192
percent taking test 76.8%
percent with total score 1,500+ 52.20%

Average Scores:

Math	Verbal	Writing	Total
593	528	529	1,650

Federal No Child Left Behind, 2008

(Adequate Yearly Progress standards met)

	Participation Rate	Pct Proficient
ELA	Yes	No
Math	Yes	Yes

API criteria . . . . . Yes
Graduation rate . . . . . Yes
\# criteria met/possible 38/37

Other school districts for this city

(see Appendix E for information on these districts)

Pomona Unified

See Introduction for an explanation of all data sources.

Demographics & Socio-Economic Characteristics

(2000 Decennial Census, except as noted)

Population

1990* 12,743
2000 16,844
Male 8,554
Female 8,290
Jan. 2008 (estimate)§ 20,993
Persons per sq. mi. of land 6,174.4

Race & Hispanic Origin, 2000

Race
White 8,816
Black/African American 60
North American Native 215
Asian 442
Pacific Islander 23
Other Race 6,398
Two or more races 890
Hispanic origin, total 12,647
Mexican 11,052
Puerto Rican 21
Cuban 7
Other Hispanic 1,567

Age & Nativity, 2000

Under 5 years 1,645
18 years and over 10,821
65 years and over 1,527
85 years and over 196
Median Age 25.9
Native-born 11,598
Foreign-born 5,280

Educational Attainment, 2000

Population 25 years and over 8,736
Less than 9th grade 31.9%
High school grad or higher 51.1%
Bachelor's degree or higher 6.8%
Graduate degree 2.8%

Income & Poverty, 1999

Per capita income $11,566
Median household income $33,345
Median family income $33,769
Persons in poverty 26.1%
H'holds receiving public assistance 420
H'holds receiving social security 1,146

Households, 2000

Total households 4,493
With persons under 18 2,618
With persons over 65 1,068
Family households 3,724
Single person households 647
Persons per household 3.72
Persons per family 4.02

Household Population, 2008§§

Persons living in households 20,879
Persons living in group quarters 114
Persons per household 3.8

Labor & Employment

Total civilian labor force, 2008§§ 9,300
Unemployment rate, 2008 .... 15.8%
Total civilian labor force, 2000 7,183

Employed persons 16 years and over by occupation, 2000

Managers & professionals 1,066
Service occupations 922
Sales & office occupations 1,223
Farming, fishing & forestry 1,072
Construction & maintenance 507
Production & transportation 1,069
Self-employed persons 415

* US Census Bureau
** 2000 Decennial Census
§ California Department of Finance
§§ California Employment Development Dept

General Information

City of Dinuba
405 E El Monte
Dinuba, CA 93618
559-591-5900

Website .... www.dinuba.org
Elevation .... 328 ft.
Land Area (sq. miles) 3.4
Water Area (sq. miles) 0
Year of Incorporation 1906
Government type .... Chartered
Sales tax rate 9.50%

Voters & Officials

Registered Voters, October 2008

Total 6,032
Democrats 2,774
Republicans 2,318
Declined to state 771

Legislative Districts

US Congressional 21
State Senatorial 16
State Assembly 31

Local Officials, 2009

Mayor .... Mark Wallace
Manager .... J. Edward Todd
City Clerk .... Linda Barkley
Attorney .... Dan McCloskey
Finance Dir .... Beth Nunes
Public Works .... Blanca Beltran
Planning/Dev Dir .... Jayne Anderson
Building .... Jayne Anderson
Police Chief .... James Olvera
Fire Chief .... Myles Chute

Public Safety

Number of officers, 2007 37
Violent crimes, 2007 132
Property crimes, 2007 949
Arson, 2007 9

Public Library

Dinuba Branch Library
Tulare County Free Library System
150 S I St
Dinuba, CA 93618
559-591-5828

Branch Librarian .... Deanna Warkentin

Library system statistics, FY 2007

Population served 321,604
Internet terminals 83
Annual users 86,301

Per capita:

Operating income $10.97
percent from local government 86.0%
Operating expenditure $8.74
Total materials 1.08
Print holdings 1.05
Visits per capita 0.96

Housing & Construction

Housing Units

Total, 2008§ 5,698
Single family units, attached 282
Single family units, detached 4,245
Multiple family units 912
Mobile home units 259
Occupied 5,484
Vacancy rate 3.8%
Median rent, 2000** $488
Median SF home value, 2000** $97,000

New Privately Owned Housing Units Authorized by Building Permit, 2007*

	Units	Construction Cost
Single	125	$15,991,615
Total	129	$16,203,901

Municipal Finance

(For local fiscal year ended in 2006)

Revenues

Total $24,267,189
Taxes 7,372,017
Special benefits assessment 108,854
Licenses & permits 367,637
Fines & forfeitures 96,100
Revenues from use of money & property 390,460
Intergovernmental 3,350,699
Service charges 9,082,700
Other revenues 2,092,768
Other financing sources 1,405,954

Expenditures

Total $21,830,742
General government 3,419,164
Public safety 5,035,826
Transportation 1,556,820
Community development 4,250,041
Health 4,154,130
Culture & leisure 1,506,977
Other 0

Local School District

(Data from School year 2007-08 except as noted)

Dinuba Unified
1327 East El Monte Way
Dinuba, CA 93618
(559) 595-7200

Superintendent .... Jerry Sessions
Grade plan K-12
Number of schools 10
Enrollment 5,804
High school graduates, 2006-07 361
Dropout rate 3.3%
Pupil/teacher ratio 20.0
Average class size 23.7
Students per computer 3.3
Classrooms with internet 279
Avg. Daily Attendance (ADA) 5,595
Cost per ADA $8,184
Avg. Teacher Salary $61,163

California Achievement Tests 6th ed., 2008

(Pct scoring at or above 50th National Percentile Rank)

	Math	Reading	Language
Grade 3	49%	28%	42%
Grade 7	32%	31%	29%

Academic Performance Index, 2008

Number of students tested 4,475
Number of valid scores 4,196
2007 API (base) 669
2008 API (growth) 690

SAT Testing, 2006-07

Enrollment, Grade 12 449
Number taking test 86
percent taking test 19.2%
percent with total score 1,500+ 6.20%

Average Scores:

Math	Verbal	Writing	Total
478	450	467	1,395

Federal No Child Left Behind, 2008

(Adequate Yearly Progress standards met)

	Participation Rate	Pct Proficient
ELA	Yes	No
Math	Yes	No

API criteria .... Yes
Graduation rate .... Yes
\# criteria met/possible 26/20

Other school districts for this city

(see Appendix E for information on these districts)

None

See Introduction for an explanation of all data sources.

Demographics & Socio-Economic Characteristics

(2000 Decennial Census, except as noted)

Population

1990*	10,401
2000	16,103
Male	8,062
Female	8,041
Jan. 2008 (estimate)§	17,577
Persons per sq. mi. of land	2,663.2

Race & Hispanic Origin, 2000

Race	
White	11,354
Black/African American	311
North American Native	160
Asian	501
Pacific Islander	48
Other Race	2,877
Two or more races	852
Hispanic origin, total	5,414
Mexican	4,606
Puerto Rican	62
Cuban	10
Other Hispanic	736

Age & Nativity, 2000

Under 5 years	1,393
18 years and over	10,947
65 years and over	1,163
85 years and over	113
Median Age	31.5
Native-born	13,116
Foreign-born	2,973

Educational Attainment, 2000

Population 25 years and over	9,609
Less than 9th grade	11.4%
High school grad or higher	77.5%
Bachelor's degree or higher	18.7%
Graduate degree	6.3%

Income & Poverty, 1999

Per capita income	$20,139
Median household income	$54,472
Median family income	$58,849
Persons in poverty	8.0%
H'holds receiving public assistance	164
H'holds receiving social security	953

Households, 2000

Total households	5,073
With persons under 18	2,589
With persons over 65	824
Family households	4,167
Single person households	658
Persons per household	3.17
Persons per family	3.45

Household Population, 2008§§

Persons living in households	17,536
Persons living in group quarters	41
Persons per household	3.1

Labor & Employment

Total civilian labor force, 2008§§	9,000
Unemployment rate, 2008	5.4%
Total civilian labor force, 2000	7,743

Employed persons 16 years and over by occupation, 2000

Managers & professionals	2,084
Service occupations	1,211
Sales & office occupations	2,028
Farming, fishing & forestry	146
Construction & maintenance	806
Production & transportation	1,095
Self-employed persons	596

* US Census Bureau
** 2000 Decennial Census
§ California Department of Finance
§§ California Employment Development Dept

General Information

City of Dixon
600 East A St
Dixon, CA 95620
707-678-7000

Website	www.ci.dixon.ca.us
Elevation	NA
Land Area (sq. miles)	6.6
Water Area (sq. miles)	0.1
Year of Incorporation	1878
Government type	General law
Sales tax rate	8.38%

Voters & Officials

Registered Voters, October 2008

Total	8,354
Democrats	3,428
Republicans	3,002
Declined to state	1,613

Legislative Districts

US Congressional	10
State Senatorial	5
State Assembly	8

Local Officials, 2009

Mayor	Jack Batchelor
Manager	Nancy Huston (Int)
City Clerk	Janice Beaman
Attorney	Michael Dean
Finance Dir	Sandra Sato (Int)
Public Works	Jeff Matheson (Int)
Community Dev Dir	Dave Dowswell
Building	NA
Police Chief	Donald Mort
Fire Chief	Frank Moore (Int)

Public Safety

Number of officers, 2007	24
Violent crimes, 2007	73
Property crimes, 2007	820
Arson, 2007	4

Public Library

Dixon Public Library District
230 N First St
Dixon, CA 95620
707-678-5447

Director	Gregg Atkins

Library statistics, FY 2007

Population served	25,907
Internet terminals	14
Annual users	17,628

Per capita:

Operating income	$42.00
percent from local government	84.1%
Operating expenditure	$39.76
Total materials	1.81
Print holdings	1.75
Visits per capita	3.23

Housing & Construction

Housing Units

Total, 2008§	5,813
Single family units, attached	216
Single family units, detached	4,687
Multiple family units	824
Mobile home units	86
Occupied	5,702
Vacancy rate	1.9%
Median rent, 2000**	$723
Median SF home value, 2000**	$170,900

New Privately Owned Housing Units Authorized by Building Permit, 2007*

	Units	Construction Cost
Single	2	$70,417
Total	13	$742,412

Municipal Finance

(For local fiscal year ended in 2006)

Revenues

Total	$21,944,803
Taxes	11,042,257
Special benefits assessment	277,148
Licenses & permits	206,988
Fines & forfeitures	72,236
Revenues from use of money & property	328,120
Intergovernmental	2,230,822
Service charges	5,845,901
Other revenues	1,941,331
Other financing sources	0

Expenditures

Total	$26,240,598
General government	6,991,549
Public safety	6,681,882
Transportation	5,039,419
Community development	2,393,732
Health	1,717,067
Culture & leisure	2,983,249
Other	0

Local School District

(Data from School year 2007-08 except as noted)

Dixon Unified
180 South First St, Ste 6
Dixon, CA 95620
(707) 678-5582

Superintendent	Roger Halberg
Grade plan	K-12
Number of schools	9
Enrollment	4,127
High school graduates, 2006-07	257
Dropout rate	5.4%
Pupil/teacher ratio	20.9
Average class size	26.1
Students per computer	4.9
Classrooms with internet	240
Avg. Daily Attendance (ADA)	3,874
Cost per ADA	$7,427
Avg. Teacher Salary	NA

California Achievement Tests 6th ed., 2008

(Pct scoring at or above 50th National Percentile Rank)

	Math	Reading	Language
Grade 3	50%	36%	41%
Grade 7	57%	60%	55%

Academic Performance Index, 2008

Number of students tested	3,128
Number of valid scores	2,922
2007 API (base)	744
2008 API (growth)	746

SAT Testing, 2006-07

Enrollment, Grade 12	324
Number taking test	99
percent taking test	30.6%
percent with total score 1,500+	13.30%

Average Scores:

Math	Verbal	Writing	Total
511	495	476	1,482

Federal No Child Left Behind, 2008

(Adequate Yearly Progress standards met)

	Participation Rate	Pct Proficient
ELA	Yes	No
Math	Yes	No

API criteria	Yes
Graduation rate	No
# criteria met/possible	28/22

Other school districts for this city

(see Appendix E for information on these districts)

None

See Introduction for an explanation of all data sources.

Demographics & Socio-Economic Characteristics

(2000 Decennial Census, except as noted)

Population

1990* .892
2000 .886
Male .427
Female .459
Jan. 2008 (estimate)§ .864
Persons per sq. mi. of land 1,234.3

Race & Hispanic Origin, 2000

Race
White .732
Black/African American .0
North American Native .49
Asian .1
Pacific Islander .1
Other Race .72
Two or more races .31
Hispanic origin, total .145
Mexican .134
Puerto Rican .0
Cuban .0
Other Hispanic .11

Age & Nativity, 2000

Under 5 years .52
18 years and over .615
65 years and over .140
85 years and over .22
Median Age 35.3
Native-born .819
Foreign-born .83

Educational Attainment, 2000

Population 25 years and over .566
Less than 9th grade 10.6%
High school grad or higher 70.1%
Bachelor's degree or higher 4.2%
Graduate degree 1.1%

Income & Poverty, 1999

Per capita income $11,447
Median household income $21,801
Median family income $24,265
Persons in poverty 19.4%
H'holds receiving public assistance .19
H'holds receiving social security .137

Households, 2000

Total households .342
With persons under 18 .125
With persons over 65 .102
Family households .240
Single person households .93
Persons per household 2.59
Persons per family 3.13

Household Population, 2008§§

Persons living in households .864
Persons living in group quarters .0
Persons per household 2.4

Labor & Employment

Total civilian labor force, 2008§§ NA
Unemployment rate, 2008 NA
Total civilian labor force, 2000 .341

Employed persons 16 years and over by occupation, 2000

Managers & professionals .53
Service occupations .61
Sales & office occupations .84
Farming, fishing & forestry .34
Construction & maintenance .38
Production & transportation .44
Self-employed persons .29

* US Census Bureau
** 2000 Decennial Census
§ California Department of Finance
§§ California Employment Development Dept

General Information

City of Dorris
PO Box 768
City Hall
Dorris, CA 96023
530-397-3511

Website NA
Elevation 4,240 ft.
Land Area (sq. miles) 0.7
Water Area (sq. miles) .0
Year of Incorporation 1908
Government type General law
Sales tax rate 8.25%

Voters & Officials

Registered Voters, October 2008

Total .375
Democrats .128
Republicans .166
Declined to state .64

Legislative Districts

US Congressional .2
State Senatorial .4
State Assembly .2

Local Officials, 2009

Mayor Liz Clontz
Manager Carol McKay
City Clerk Shelly Ferr
Attorney John Kenny
Finance Dir NA
Public Works Bill Stevenson
Planning/Dev Dir NA
Building NA
Police Chief NA
Emergency/Fire Dir. Wayne Frost

Public Safety

Number of officers, 2007 NA
Violent crimes, 2007 .5
Property crimes, 2007 .11
Arson, 2007 .0

Public Library

Dorris Branch Library
Siskiyou County Free Library System
800 W 3rd St
Dorris, CA 96023
530-397-4932

Branch Librarian Gail Emmons

Library system statistics, FY 2007

Population served 45,953
Internet terminals .31
Annual users 48,766

Per capita:

Operating income $20.36
percent from local government 90.2%
Operating expenditure $20.12
Total materials 4.06
Print holdings 3.88
Visits per capita NA

Housing & Construction

Housing Units

Total, 2008§ .408
Single family units, attached .2
Single family units, detached .318
Multiple family units .16
Mobile home units .72
Occupied .354
Vacancy rate 13.2%
Median rent, 2000** $456
Median SF home value, 2000** $53,100

New Privately Owned Housing Units Authorized by Building Permit, 2007*

	Units	Construction Cost
Single	2	$90,000
Total	2	$90,000

Municipal Finance

(For local fiscal year ended in 2006)

Revenues

Total $2,159,429
Taxes 130,180
Special benefits assessment 101,226
Licenses & permits 38,822
Fines & forfeitures 8,539
Revenues from use of money & property 10,078
Intergovernmental 1,253,584
Service charges 245,640
Other revenues 371,360
Other financing sources .0

Expenditures

Total $1,845,756
General government 68,740
Public safety 295,674
Transportation 71,195
Community development 434,968
Health 61,993
Culture & leisure 694,337
Other 5,000

Local School District

(Data from School year 2007-08 except as noted)

Butte Valley Unified
PO Box 709
Dorris, CA 96023
(530) 397-4000

Superintendent Ed Traverso
Grade plan K-12
Number of schools .6
Enrollment .323
High school graduates, 2006-07 .31
Dropout rate 11.2%
Pupil/teacher ratio 13.8
Average class size 14.7
Students per computer 1.8
Classrooms with internet .23
Avg. Daily Attendance (ADA) .299
Cost per ADA $14,163
Avg. Teacher Salary NA

California Achievement Tests 6th ed., 2008

(Pct scoring at or above 50th National Percentile Rank)

	Math	Reading	Language
Grade 3	55%	30%	40%
Grade 7	54%	54%	62%

Academic Performance Index, 2008

Number of students tested .244
Number of valid scores .219
2007 API (base) .687
2008 API (growth) .734

SAT Testing, 2006-07

Enrollment, Grade 12 .36
Number taking test .6
percent taking test 16.7%
percent with total score 1,500+ NA

Average Scores:

Math	Verbal	Writing	Total
NA	NA	NA	NA

Federal No Child Left Behind, 2008

(Adequate Yearly Progress standards met)

	Participation Rate	Pct Proficient
ELA	Yes	No
Math	Yes	Yes

API criteria Yes
Graduation rate Yes
criteria met/possible 22/20

Other school districts for this city

(see Appendix E for information on these districts)

None

See Introduction for an explanation of all data sources.

Demographics & Socio-Economic Characteristics

(2000 Decennial Census, except as noted)

Population

1990* . . . 4,196
2000 . . . 4,581
Male . . . 2,261
Female . . . 2,320
Jan. 2008 (estimate)§ . . . 5,024
Persons per sq. mi. of land . . . 3,349.3

Race & Hispanic Origin, 2000

Race
White . . . 2,985
Black/African American . . . 190
North American Native . . . 63
Asian . . . 28
Pacific Islander . . . 0
Other Race . . . 1,155
Two or more races . . . 160
Hispanic origin, total . . . 2,482
Mexican . . . 2,208
Puerto Rican . . . 1
Cuban . . . 3
Other Hispanic . . . 270

Age & Nativity, 2000

Under 5 years . . . 390
18 years and over . . . 2,980
65 years and over . . . 477
85 years and over . . . 58
Median Age . . . 30.3
Native-born . . . 3,793
Foreign-born . . . 854

Educational Attainment, 2000

Population 25 years and over . . . 2,636
Less than 9th grade . . . 19.8%
High school grad or higher . . . 56.8%
Bachelor's degree or higher . . . 4.3%
Graduate degree . . . 1.9%

Income & Poverty, 1999

Per capita income . . . $13,163
Median household income . . . $29,147
Median family income . . . $35,906
Persons in poverty . . . 22.9%
H'holds receiving public assistance . . . 130
H'holds receiving social security . . . 453

Households, 2000

Total households . . . 1,424
With persons under 18 . . . 722
With persons over 65 . . . 347
Family households . . . 1,116
Single person households . . . 266
Persons per household . . . 3.20
Persons per family . . . 3.63

Household Population, 2008§§

Persons living in households . . . 5,000
Persons living in group quarters . . . 24
Persons per household . . . 3.1

Labor & Employment

Total civilian labor force, 2008§§ . . . 2,000
Unemployment rate, 2008 . . . 16.9%
Total civilian labor force, 2000 . . . 1,660

Employed persons 16 years and over by occupation, 2000

Managers & professionals . . . 264
Service occupations . . . 193
Sales & office occupations . . . 381
Farming, fishing & forestry . . . 148
Construction & maintenance . . . 188
Production & transportation . . . 196
Self-employed persons . . . 90

* US Census Bureau
** 2000 Decennial Census
§ California Department of Finance
§§ California Employment Development Dept

General Information

City of Dos Palos
1546 Golden Gate Ave
Dos Palos, CA 93620
209-392-2174

Website . . . NA
Elevation . . . 115 ft.
Land Area (sq. miles) . . . 1.5
Water Area (sq. miles) . . . 0
Year of Incorporation . . . 1935
Government type . . . General law
Sales tax rate . . . 8.25%

Voters & Officials

Registered Voters, October 2008

Total . . . 1,990
Democrats . . . 925
Republicans . . . 741
Declined to state . . . 241

Legislative Districts

US Congressional . . . 18
State Senatorial . . . 12
State Assembly . . . 17

Local Officials, 2009

Mayor . . . Michael Burns
Manager . . . Darrell Fonseca
City Clerk . . . Josey rodriguez
Attorney . . . Ed Amaral
Treasurer . . . Lori Lima
Public Works . . . Michael Smith
Planning/Dev Dir . . . Dewayne Jones
Building . . . Dewayne Jones
Police Chief . . . Barry Mann
Fire Chief . . . Dewayne Jones

Public Safety

Number of officers, 2007 . . . 7
Violent crimes, 2007 . . . 35
Property crimes, 2007 . . . 156
Arson, 2007 . . . 0

Public Library

Dos Palos Branch Library
Merced County Library System
2002 Almond
Dos Palos, CA 93620
209-392-2155

Branch Librarian . . . Pat Leisman

Library system statistics, FY 2007

Population served . . . 251,510
Internet terminals . . . 91
Annual users . . . 124,530

Per capita:

Operating income . . . $8.99
percent from local government . . . 91.3%
Operating expenditure . . . $8.99
Total materials . . . 1.61
Print holdings . . . 1.60
Visits per capita . . . 1.75

Housing & Construction

Housing Units

Total, 2008§ . . . 1,693
Single family units, attached . . . 55
Single family units, detached . . . 1,472
Multiple family units . . . 126
Mobile home units . . . 40
Occupied . . . 1,615
Vacancy rate . . . 4.6%
Median rent, 2000** . . . $510
Median SF home value, 2000** . . . $89,100

New Privately Owned Housing Units Authorized by Building Permit, 2007*

	Units	Construction Cost
Single	22	$2,625,966
Total	22	$2,625,966

Municipal Finance

(For local fiscal year ended in 2006)

Revenues

Total . . . $4,269,655
Taxes . . . 1,171,627
Special benefits assessment . . . 0
Licenses & permits . . . 81,727
Fines & forfeitures . . . 17,703
Revenues from use of money & property . . . 81,727
Intergovernmental . . . 817,183
Service charges . . . 1,773,827
Other revenues . . . 325,861
Other financing sources . . . 0

Expenditures

Total . . . $3,283,146
General government . . . 159,481
Public safety . . . 726,860
Transportation . . . 473,342
Community development . . . 349,820
Health . . . 800,255
Culture & leisure . . . 107,896
Other . . . 0

Local School District

(Data from School year 2007-08 except as noted)

Dos Palos-Oro Loma Joint Unified
2041 Almond St
Dos Palos, CA 93620
(209) 392-0200

Superintendent . . . Brian Walker
Grade plan . . . K-12
Number of schools . . . 6
Enrollment . . . 2,693
High school graduates, 2006-07 . . . 157
Dropout rate . . . 2.1%
Pupil/teacher ratio . . . 19.7
Average class size . . . 22.6
Students per computer . . . 4.1
Classrooms with internet . . . 174
Avg. Daily Attendance (ADA) . . . 2,597
Cost per ADA . . . $9,094
Avg. Teacher Salary . . . $56,648

California Achievement Tests 6th ed., 2008

(Pct scoring at or above 50th National Percentile Rank)

	Math	Reading	Language
Grade 3	41%	23%	40%
Grade 7	39%	37%	35%

Academic Performance Index, 2008

Number of students tested . . . 2,049
Number of valid scores . . . 1,908
2007 API (base) . . . 683
2008 API (growth) . . . 684

SAT Testing, 2006-07

Enrollment, Grade 12 . . . 176
Number taking test . . . 36
percent taking test . . . 20.5%
percent with total score 1,500+ . . . 3.40%

Average Scores:

Math	Verbal	Writing	Total
468	428	435	1,331

Federal No Child Left Behind, 2008

(Adequate Yearly Progress standards met)

	Participation Rate	Pct Proficient
ELA	No	No
Math	Yes	No

API criteria . . . Yes
Graduation rate . . . Yes
criteria met/possible . . . 26/20

Other school districts for this city

(see Appendix E for information on these districts)

None

See Introduction for an explanation of all data sources.

Demographics & Socio-Economic Characteristics†

(2007 American Community Survey, except as noted)

Population

1990* . . . 91,444
2007 . . . 109,920
Male . . . 54,742
Female . . . 55,178
Jan. 2008 (estimate)§ . . . 113,379
Persons per sq. mi. of land . . . 9,143.5

Race & Hispanic Origin, 2007

Race
White . . . 71,545
Black/African American . . . 2,066
North American Native . . . 321
Asian . . . 4,916
Pacific Islander . . . 113
Other Race . . . 29,034
Two or more races . . . 1,925
Hispanic origin, total . . . NA
Mexican . . . 65,004
Puerto Rican . . . 552
Cuban . . . 1,715
Other Hispanic . . . 15,419

Age & Nativity, 2007

Under 5 years . . . 7,996
18 years and over . . . 75,971
65 years and over . . . 9,798
85 years and over . . . 1,866
Median Age . . . 31.6
Native-born . . . 71,579
Foreign-born . . . 38,341

Educational Attainment, 2007

Population 25 years and over . . . 66,824
Less than 9th grade . . . 11.0%
High school grad or higher . . . 71.5%
Bachelor's degree or higher . . . 16.9%
Graduate degree . . . 5.3%

Income & Poverty, 2007

Per capita income . . . $22,104
Median household income . . . $59,376
Median family income . . . $63,419
Persons in poverty . . . 11.1%
H'holds receiving public assistance . . . 497
H'holds receiving social security . . . 7,888

Households, 2007

Total households . . . 32,736
With persons under 18 . . . 15,599
With persons over 65 . . . 7,067
Family households . . . 25,016
Single person households . . . 6,825
Persons per household . . . 3.34
Persons per family . . . 3.88

Household Population, 2008§§

Persons living in households . . . 111,614
Persons living in group quarters . . . 1,765
Persons per household . . . 3.3

Labor & Employment

Total civilian labor force, 2008§§ . . . 54,900
Unemployment rate, 2008 . . . 6.0%
Total civilian labor force, 2000* . . . 47,182

Employed persons 16 years and over by occupation, 2007

Managers & professionals . . . 11,857
Service occupations . . . 6,467
Sales & office occupations . . . 15,098
Farming, fishing & forestry . . . 0
Construction & maintenance . . . 4,016
Production & transportation . . . 8,811
Self-employed persons . . . 2,898

† see Appendix D for 2000 Decennial Census Data
* US Census Bureau
** 2007 American Community Survey
§ California Department of Finance
§§ California Employment Development Dept

General Information

City of Downey
11111 Brookshire Ave
PO Box 7016
Downey, CA 90241
562-869-7331

Website . . . www.downeyca.org
Elevation . . . 119 ft.
Land Area (sq. miles) . . . 12.4
Water Area (sq. miles) . . . 0.2
Year of Incorporation . . . 1956
Government type . . . Chartered
Sales tax rate . . . 9.25%

Voters & Officials

Registered Voters, October 2008

Total . . . 47,404
Democrats . . . 23,874
Republicans . . . 13,778
Declined to state . . . 8,058

Legislative Districts

US Congressional . . . 34
State Senatorial . . . 27
State Assembly . . . 50, 58

Local Officials, 2009

Mayor . . . Mario A. Guerra
City Manager . . . Gerald M. Caton
City Clerk . . . Kathleen L. Midstokke
Attorney . . . Edward W. Lee
Finance Dir . . . John Michicoff
Public Works . . . Brian Ragland
Planning/Dev Dir . . . Gilbert Livas
Building . . . Linda Haines
Police Chief . . . Roy Campos
Emergency/Fire Dir . . . Mark Sauter

Public Safety

Number of officers, 2007 . . . 106
Violent crimes, 2007 . . . 516
Property crimes, 2007 . . . 3,896
Arson, 2007 . . . 13

Public Library

Downey City Library
11121 Brookshire Ave
Downey, CA 90241
562-904-7360

City Librarian . . . Nancy Messineo

Library statistics, FY 2007

Population served . . . 113,587
Internet terminals . . . 18
Annual users . . . 46,880

Per capita:

Operating income . . . $22.49
percent from local government . . . 92.2%
Operating expenditure . . . $21.00
Total materials . . . 1.16
Print holdings . . . 1.09
Visits per capita . . . 3.17

Housing & Construction

Housing Units

Total, 2008§ . . . 35,071
Single family units, attached . . . 1,696
Single family units, detached . . . 20,493
Multiple family units . . . 12,689
Mobile home units . . . 193
Occupied . . . 34,294
Vacancy rate . . . 2.2%
Median rent, 2007** . . . $1,073
Median SF home value, 2007** . . . $613,100

New Privately Owned Housing Units Authorized by Building Permit, 2007*

	Units	Construction Cost
Single	79	$34,621,796
Total	79	$34,621,796

Municipal Finance

(For local fiscal year ended in 2006)

Revenues

Total . . . $119,366,476
Taxes . . . 46,468,940
Special benefits assessment . . . 1,087,677
Licenses & permits . . . 1,857,957
Fines & forfeitures . . . 1,750,581
Revenues from use of money & property . . . 4,505,228
Intergovernmental . . . 10,404,977
Service charges . . . 23,670,380
Other revenues . . . 8,985,736
Other financing sources . . . 20,635,000

Expenditures

Total . . . $77,507,605
General government . . . 4,371,129
Public safety . . . 40,389,363
Transportation . . . 7,987,090
Community development . . . 5,652,762
Health . . . 1,434,287
Culture & leisure . . . 10,498,058
Other . . . 0

Local School District

(Data from School year 2007-08 except as noted)

Downey Unified
PO Box 7017
Downey, CA 90241
(562) 469-6500

Superintendent . . . Wendy Doty
Grade plan . . . K-12
Number of schools . . . 20
Enrollment . . . 22,358
High school graduates, 2006-07 . . . 1,449
Dropout rate . . . 0.7%
Pupil/teacher ratio . . . 22.4
Average class size . . . 28.6
Students per computer . . . 5.5
Classrooms with internet . . . 932
Avg. Daily Attendance (ADA) . . . 22,084
Cost per ADA . . . $7,710
Avg. Teacher Salary . . . $75,246

California Achievement Tests 6th ed., 2008

(Pct scoring at or above 50th National Percentile Rank)

	Math	Reading	Language
Grade 3	57%	36%	44%
Grade 7	47%	46%	42%

Academic Performance Index, 2008

Number of students tested . . . 17,594
Number of valid scores . . . 16,432
2007 API (base) . . . 730
2008 API (growth) . . . 746

SAT Testing, 2006-07

Enrollment, Grade 12 . . . 1,863
Number taking test . . . 475
percent taking test . . . 25.5%
percent with total score 1,500+ . . . 10.80%

Average Scores:

Math	Verbal	Writing	Total
495	479	476	1,450

Federal No Child Left Behind, 2008

(Adequate Yearly Progress standards met)

	Participation Rate	Pct Proficient
ELA	Yes	No
Math	Yes	No

API criteria . . . Yes
Graduation rate . . . Yes
\# criteria met/possible . . . 38/34

Other school districts for this city

(see Appendix E for information on these districts)

None

See Introduction for an explanation of all data sources.

Demographics & Socio-Economic Characteristics

(2000 Decennial Census, except as noted)

Population

1990*	20,688
2000	21,486
Male	10,232
Female	11,254
Jan. 2008 (estimate)§	22,953
Persons per sq. mi. of land	3,425.8

Race & Hispanic Origin, 2000

Race	
White	11,178
Black/African American	1,952
North American Native	201
Asian	2,711
Pacific Islander	24
Other Race	4,296
Two or more races	1,124
Hispanic origin, total	9,326
Mexican	7,321
Puerto Rican	80
Cuban	97
Other Hispanic	1,828

Age & Nativity, 2000

Under 5 years	1,613
18 years and over	15,429
65 years and over	2,556
85 years and over	419
Median Age	34.5
Native-born	14,427
Foreign-born	7,059

Educational Attainment, 2000

Population 25 years and over	13,617
Less than 9th grade	12.9%
High school grad or higher	74.4%
Bachelor's degree or higher	23.6%
Graduate degree	7.3%

Income & Poverty, 1999

Per capita income	$19,648
Median household income	$50,744
Median family income	$56,556
Persons in poverty	11.0%
H'holds receiving public assistance	268
H'holds receiving social security	1,631

Households, 2000

Total households	6,635
With persons under 18	2,958
With persons over 65	1,660
Family households	4,892
Single person households	1,427
Persons per household	3.16
Persons per family	3.70

Household Population, 2008§§

Persons living in households	22,463
Persons living in group quarters	490
Persons per household	3.3

Labor & Employment

Total civilian labor force, 2008§§	11,600
Unemployment rate, 2008	4.9%
Total civilian labor force, 2000	10,032

Employed persons 16 years and over by occupation, 2000

Managers & professionals	3,142
Service occupations	1,461
Sales & office occupations	2,803
Farming, fishing & forestry	19
Construction & maintenance	764
Production & transportation	1,298
Self-employed persons	702

* US Census Bureau
** 2000 Decennial Census
§ California Department of Finance
§§ California Employment Development Dept

General Information

City of Duarte
1600 Huntington Dr
Duarte, CA 91010
626-357-7931

Website	www.accessduarte.com
Elevation	510 ft.
Land Area (sq. miles)	6.7
Water Area (sq. miles)	0
Year of Incorporation	1957
Government type	General law
Sales tax rate	9.25%

Voters & Officials

Registered Voters, October 2008

Total	10,776
Democrats	5,269
Republicans	3,153
Declined to state	1,964

Legislative Districts

US Congressional	32
State Senatorial	24
State Assembly	44, 59

Local Officials, 2009

Mayor	Phil Reyes
Manager	Darrell George
City Clerk	Marla Akana
Attorney	Rutan & Tucker
Finance Dir	Kristen Petersen
Public Works	NA
Planning/Dev Dir	Ed Cox
Building	(County)
Police Chief	(County)
Fire/Emergency Mgmt	NA

Public Safety

Number of officers, 2007	NA
Violent crimes, 2007	84
Property crimes, 2007	523
Arson, 2007	4

Public Library

Duarte Library
Los Angeles County Public Library System
1301 Buena Vista St
Duarte, CA 91010
626-358-1865

Branch Librarian	Pui-Ching Ho

Library system statistics, FY 2007

Population served	3,673,313
Internet terminals	749
Annual users	3,748,771

Per capita:

Operating income	$30.06
percent from local government	93.6%
Operating expenditure	$28.36
Total materials	2.22
Print holdings	1.97
Visits per capita	3.25

Housing & Construction

Housing Units

Total, 2008§	6,948
Single family units, attached	874
Single family units, detached	4,343
Multiple family units	1,502
Mobile home units	229
Occupied	6,775
Vacancy rate	2.5%
Median rent, 2000**	$791
Median SF home value, 2000**	$173,500

New Privately Owned Housing Units Authorized by Building Permit, 2007*

	Units	Construction Cost
Single	1	$138,170
Total	21	$1,051,830

Municipal Finance

(For local fiscal year ended in 2006)

Revenues

Total	$15,350,702
Taxes	8,322,249
Special benefits assessment	1,007,965
Licenses & permits	489,309
Fines & forfeitures	232,244
Revenues from use of money & property	441,819
Intergovernmental	3,201,509
Service charges	617,007
Other revenues	1,038,600
Other financing sources	0

Expenditures

Total	$13,972,998
General government	508,336
Public safety	4,894,282
Transportation	3,381,332
Community development	3,216,473
Health	245,758
Culture & leisure	1,726,817
Other	0

Local School District

(Data from School year 2007-08 except as noted)

Duarte Unified
1620 Huntington Dr
Duarte, CA 91010
(626) 599-5000

Superintendent	Dean Conklin
Grade plan	K-12
Number of schools	8
Enrollment	4,296
High school graduates, 2006-07	257
Dropout rate	1.5%
Pupil/teacher ratio	21.4
Average class size	27.3
Students per computer	3.7
Classrooms with internet	204
Avg. Daily Attendance (ADA)	4,279
Cost per ADA	$7,907
Avg. Teacher Salary	$64,310

California Achievement Tests 6th ed., 2008

(Pct scoring at or above 50th National Percentile Rank)

	Math	Reading	Language
Grade 3	53%	33%	44%
Grade 7	45%	38%	37%

Academic Performance Index, 2008

Number of students tested	3,344
Number of valid scores	3,132
2007 API (base)	708
2008 API (growth)	725

SAT Testing, 2006-07

Enrollment, Grade 12	303
Number taking test	108
percent taking test	35.6%
percent with total score 1,500+	10.90%

Average Scores:

Math	Verbal	Writing	Total
475	454	450	1,379

Federal No Child Left Behind, 2008

(Adequate Yearly Progress standards met)

	Participation Rate	Pct Proficient
ELA	Yes	Yes
Math	Yes	Yes

API criteria	Yes
Graduation rate	Yes
# criteria met/possible	36/36

Other school districts for this city

(see Appendix E for information on these districts)

None

See Introduction for an explanation of all data sources.

Demographics & Socio-Economic Characteristics

(2000 Decennial Census, except as noted)

Population

1990* 23,229
2000 29,973
Male 15,782
Female 14,191
Jan. 2008 (estimate)§ 46,934
Persons per sq. mi. of land 3,724.9

Race & Hispanic Origin, 2000

Race
White 20,793
Black/African American 3,024
North American Native 220
Asian 3,101
Pacific Islander 95
Other Race 1,576
Two or more races 1,164
Hispanic origin, total 4,059
Mexican 1,878
Puerto Rican 89
Cuban 47
Other Hispanic 2,045

Age & Nativity, 2000

Under 5 years 1,758
18 years and over 23,691
65 years and over 1,381
85 years and over 90
Median Age 34.3
Native-born 25,966
Foreign-born 4,070

Educational Attainment, 2000

Population 25 years and over 20,995
Less than 9th grade 2.9%
High school grad or higher 86.3%
Bachelor's degree or higher 32.9%
Graduate degree 9.1%

Income & Poverty, 1999

Per capita income $29,451
Median household income $77,283
Median family income $83,123
Persons in poverty 2.4%
H'holds receiving public assistance 155
H'holds receiving social security 1,160

Households, 2000

Total households 9,325
With persons under 18 3,519
With persons over 65 1,041
Family households 6,505
Single person households 1,987
Persons per household 2.65
Persons per family 3.13

Household Population, 2008§§

Persons living in households 41,594
Persons living in group quarters 5,340
Persons per household 2.7

Labor & Employment

Total civilian labor force, 2008§§ 15,700
Unemployment rate, 2008 . . . . . 3.7%
Total civilian labor force, 2000 14,946

Employed persons 16 years and over by occupation, 2000

Managers & professionals 6,759
Service occupations 1,521
Sales & office occupations 4,156
Farming, fishing & forestry 8
Construction & maintenance 1,044
Production & transportation 988
Self-employed persons 943

* US Census Bureau
** 2000 Decennial Census
§ California Department of Finance
§§ California Employment Development Dept

General Information

City of Dublin
100 Civic Plaza
Dublin, CA 94568
925-833-6650

Website . . . . . www.ci.dublin.ca.us
Elevation . . . . . 360 ft.
Land Area (sq. miles) 12.6
Water Area (sq. miles) 0
Year of Incorporation 1982
Government type . . . . . General law
Sales tax rate 9.75%

Voters & Officials

Registered Voters, October 2008

Total 21,143
Democrats 9,149
Republicans 5,920
Declined to state 5,229

Legislative Districts

US Congressional 11
State Senatorial 9
State Assembly 18

Local Officials, 2009

Mayor . . . . . Tim Sbranti
City Manager . . . . . Joni Pattillo
City Clerk . . . . . Caroline Soto
Attorney . . . . . John Bakker
Finance Dir . . . . . Paul S. Rankin
Public Works . . . . . Melissa Morton
Planning/Dev Dir . . . . . Jeri Ram
Building . . . . . Gregory Shreeve
Police Chief . . . . . Casey Nice
Emergency/Fire Dir . . . . . Sheldon Gilbert

Public Safety

Number of officers, 2007 . . . . . NA
Violent crimes, 2007 76
Property crimes, 2007 756
Arson, 2007 7

Public Library

Dublin Library
Alameda County Library System
200 Civic Plaza
Dublin, CA 94568
925-828-1315

Branch Librarian . . . . . Lee Jouthas

Library system statistics, FY 2007

Population served 527,926
Internet terminals 193
Annual users 358,689

Per capita:

Operating income $41.07
percent from local government 94.7%
Operating expenditure $36.47
Total materials 2.21
Print holdings 1.91
Visits per capita 4.32

Housing & Construction

Housing Units

Total, 2008§ 16,029
Single family units, attached 1,304
Single family units, detached 8,138
Multiple family units 6,559
Mobile home units 28
Occupied 15,463
Vacancy rate 3.5%
Median rent, 2000** $1,356
Median SF home value, 2000** $330,700

New Privately Owned Housing Units Authorized by Building Permit, 2007*

	Units	Construction Cost
Single	38	$14,202,577
Total	118	$42,342,155

Municipal Finance

(For local fiscal year ended in 2006)

Revenues

Total $69,671,761
Taxes 52,102,409
Special benefits assessment 760,994
Licenses & permits 3,005,652
Fines & forfeitures 340,336
Revenues from use of money & property 2,980,930
Intergovernmental 2,595,337
Service charges 7,605,254
Other revenues 280,849
Other financing sources 0

Expenditures

Total $64,126,691
General government 5,100,629
Public safety 21,091,378
Transportation 10,833,614
Community development 9,024,760
Health 1,914,190
Culture & leisure 16,162,120
Other 0

Local School District

(Data from School year 2007-08 except as noted)

Dublin Unified
7471 Larkdale Ave
Dublin, CA 94568
(925) 828-2551

Superintendent . . . . . Stephen Hanke
Grade plan K-12
Number of schools 10
Enrollment 5,556
High school graduates, 2006-07 329
Dropout rate 1.5%
Pupil/teacher ratio 20.5
Average class size 24.6
Students per computer 3.9
Classrooms with internet 1,278
Avg. Daily Attendance (ADA) 5,394
Cost per ADA $8,468
Avg. Teacher Salary $73,982

California Achievement Tests 6th ed., 2008

(Pct scoring at or above 50th National Percentile Rank)

	Math	Reading	Language
Grade 3	80%	60%	75%
Grade 7	70%	67%	66%

Academic Performance Index, 2008

Number of students tested 4,088
Number of valid scores 3,901
2007 API (base) 833
2008 API (growth) 841

SAT Testing, 2006-07

Enrollment, Grade 12 360
Number taking test 149
percent taking test 41.4%
percent with total score 1,500+ 25.00%

Average Scores:

Math	Verbal	Writing	Total
564	511	513	1,588

Federal No Child Left Behind, 2008

(Adequate Yearly Progress standards met)

	Participation Rate	Pct Proficient
ELA	Yes	Yes
Math	Yes	Yes

API criteria . . . . . Yes
Graduation rate . . . . . Yes
\# criteria met/possible 38/38

Other school districts for this city

(see Appendix E for information on these districts)

None

See Introduction for an explanation of all data sources.

Demographics & Socio-Economic Characteristics

(2000 Decennial Census, except as noted)

Population

1990* ... 2,129
2000 ... 1,923
Male ... 950
Female ... 973
Jan. 2008 (estimate)§ ... 1,831
Persons per sq. mi. of land ... 1,017.2

Race & Hispanic Origin, 2000

Race
White ... 1,743
Black/African American ... 36
North American Native ... 38
Asian ... 10
Pacific Islander ... 1
Other Race ... 45
Two or more races ... 50
Hispanic origin, total ... 191
Mexican ... 171
Puerto Rican ... 6
Cuban ... 0
Other Hispanic ... 14

Age & Nativity, 2000

Under 5 years ... 83
18 years and over ... 1,493
65 years and over ... 362
85 years and over ... 43
Median Age ... 43.5
Native-born ... 1,840
Foreign-born ... 75

Educational Attainment, 2000

Population 25 years and over ... 1,380
Less than 9th grade ... 4.0%
High school grad or higher ... 86.6%
Bachelor's degree or higher ... 11.4%
Graduate degree ... 3.4%

Income & Poverty, 1999

Per capita income ... $15,982
Median household income ... $23,191
Median family income ... $27,420
Persons in poverty ... 19.1%
H'holds receiving public assistance ... 43
H'holds receiving social security ... 329

Households, 2000

Total households ... 867
With persons under 18 ... 227
With persons over 65 ... 273
Family households ... 492
Single person households ... 307
Persons per household ... 2.22
Persons per family ... 2.84

Household Population, 2008§§

Persons living in households ... 1,831
Persons living in group quarters ... 0
Persons per household ... 2.1

Labor & Employment

Total civilian labor force, 2008§§ ... 700
Unemployment rate, 2008 ... 12.3%
Total civilian labor force, 2000 ... 684

Employed persons 16 years and over by occupation, 2000

Managers & professionals ... 124
Service occupations ... 155
Sales & office occupations ... 155
Farming, fishing & forestry ... 6
Construction & maintenance ... 66
Production & transportation ... 99
Self-employed persons ... 81

* US Census Bureau
** 2000 Decennial Census
§ California Department of Finance
§§ California Employment Development Dept

General Information

City of Dunsmuir
5915 Dunsmuir Ave
Dunsmuir, CA 96025
530-235-4822

Website ... www.ci.dunsmuir.ca.us
Elevation ... 2,289 ft.
Land Area (sq. miles) ... 1.8
Water Area (sq. miles) ... 0
Year of Incorporation ... 1909
Government type ... General law
Sales tax rate ... 8.25%

Voters & Officials

Registered Voters, October 2008

Total ... 992
Democrats ... 468
Republicans ... 249
Declined to state ... 206

Legislative Districts

US Congressional ... 2
State Senatorial ... 4
State Assembly ... 2

Local Officials, 2009

Mayor ... Kathay Edmondson
Manager ... J Keith Anderson
City Clerk ... Kathy Wilson
Attorney ... John Kenny
Finance Dir ... Tony Banke
Public Works ... Carl Morzenti
Planning/Dev Dir ... NA
Building ... Dave Smith
Police Chief ... NA
Emergency/Fire Dir ... Dan Padilla

Public Safety

Number of officers, 2007 ... NA
Violent crimes, 2007 ... 9
Property crimes, 2007 ... 26
Arson, 2007 ... 0

Public Library

Dunsmuir Branch Library
Siskiyou County Free Library System
5714 Dunsmuir Ave
Dunsmuir, CA 96025
530-235-2035

Branch Librarian ... Donna Huber

Library system statistics, FY 2007

Population served ... 45,953
Internet terminals ... 31
Annual users ... 48,766

Per capita:

Operating income ... $20.36
percent from local government ... 90.2%
Operating expenditure ... $20.12
Total materials ... 4.06
Print holdings ... 3.88
Visits per capita ... NA

Housing & Construction

Housing Units

Total, 2008§ ... 1,177
Single family units, attached ... 23
Single family units, detached ... 798
Multiple family units ... 310
Mobile home units ... 46
Occupied ... 872
Vacancy rate ... 25.9%
Median rent, 2000** ... $476
Median SF home value, 2000** ... $89,100

New Privately Owned Housing Units Authorized by Building Permit, 2007*

	Units	Construction Cost
Single	5	$974,250
Total	5	$974,250

Municipal Finance

(For local fiscal year ended in 2006)

Revenues

Total ... $3,683,863
Taxes ... 586,164
Special benefits assessment ... 24,737
Licenses & permits ... 43,365
Fines & forfeitures ... 16,168
Revenues from use of money & property ... 58,493
Intergovernmental ... 947,007
Service charges ... 1,967,412
Other revenues ... 40,517
Other financing sources ... 0

Expenditures

Total ... $4,186,880
General government ... 461,706
Public safety ... 692,389
Transportation ... 556,797
Community development ... 1,024,249
Health ... 878,414
Culture & leisure ... 3,938
Other ... 148,451

Local School District

(Data from School year 2007-08 except as noted)

Dunsmuir Joint Union High
5805 High School Way
Dunsmuir, CA 96025
(530) 235-4835

Superintendent ... Leonard Foreman
Grade plan ... 9-12
Number of schools ... 2
Enrollment ... 100
High school graduates, 2006-07 ... 21
Dropout rate ... 6.5%
Pupil/teacher ratio ... 12.2
Average class size ... 15.5
Students per computer ... 1.7
Classrooms with internet ... 11
Avg. Daily Attendance (ADA) ... 98
Cost per ADA ... $13,210
Avg. Teacher Salary ... $43,607

California Achievement Tests 6th ed., 2008

(Pct scoring at or above 50th National Percentile Rank)

	Math	Reading	Language
Grade 3	NA	NA	NA
Grade 7	NA	NA	NA

Academic Performance Index, 2008

Number of students tested ... 83
Number of valid scores ... 68
2007 API (base) ... 673
2008 API (growth) ... 674

SAT Testing, 2006-07

Enrollment, Grade 12 ... 28
Number taking test ... 6
percent taking test ... 21.4%
percent with total score 1,500+ ... NA

Average Scores:

Math	Verbal	Writing	Total
NA	NA	NA	NA

Federal No Child Left Behind, 2008

(Adequate Yearly Progress standards met)

	Participation Rate	Pct Proficient
ELA	Yes	Yes
Math	Yes	Yes

API criteria ... Yes
Graduation rate ... Yes
\# criteria met/possible ... 6/6

Other school districts for this city

(see Appendix E for information on these districts)

Dunsmuir Elem

See Introduction for an explanation of all data sources.

Demographics & Socio-Economic Characteristics

(2000 Decennial Census, except as noted)

Population

1990*	23,451
2000	29,506
Male	15,198
Female	14,308
Jan. 2008 (estimate)§	32,897
Persons per sq. mi. of land	13,158.8

Race & Hispanic Origin, 2000

Race	
White	7,962
Black/African American	6,796
North American Native	246
Asian	657
Pacific Islander	2,252
Other Race	10,248
Two or more races	1,345
Hispanic origin, total	17,346
Mexican	14,550
Puerto Rican	70
Cuban	12
Other Hispanic	2,714

Age & Nativity, 2000

Under 5 years	2,943
18 years and over	19,187
65 years and over	1,519
85 years and over	111
Median Age	25.8
Native-born	16,546
Foreign-born	12,904

Educational Attainment, 2000

Population 25 years and over	15,170
Less than 9th grade	30.7%
High school grad or higher	48.2%
Bachelor's degree or higher	10.6%
Graduate degree	3.6%

Income & Poverty, 1999

Per capita income	$13,774
Median household income	$45,006
Median family income	$44,342
Persons in poverty	15.8%
H'holds receiving public assistance	346
H'holds receiving social security	1,368

Households, 2000

Total households	6,976
With persons under 18	3,962
With persons over 65	1,194
Family households	5,275
Single person households	1,272
Persons per household	4.20
Persons per family	4.64

Household Population, 2008§§

Persons living in households	32,708
Persons living in group quarters	189
Persons per household	4.3

Labor & Employment

Total civilian labor force, 2008§§	13,000
Unemployment rate, 2008	11.6%
Total civilian labor force, 2000	12,309

Employed persons 16 years and over by occupation, 2000

Managers & professionals	2,062
Service occupations	3,626
Sales & office occupations	2,632
Farming, fishing & forestry	29
Construction & maintenance	1,350
Production & transportation	1,650
Self-employed persons	866

* US Census Bureau
** 2000 Decennial Census
§ California Department of Finance
§§ California Employment Development Dept

General Information

City of East Palo Alto
2415 University Ave
East Palo Alto, CA 94303
650-853-3100

Website	www.ci.east-palo-alto.ca.us
Elevation	21 ft.
Land Area (sq. miles)	2.5
Water Area (sq. miles)	0
Year of Incorporation	1983
Government type	General law
Sales tax rate	9.25%

Voters & Officials

Registered Voters, October 2008

Total	10,034
Democrats	6,295
Republicans	1,285
Declined to state	2,098

Legislative Districts

US Congressional	14
State Senatorial	11
State Assembly	21

Local Officials, 2009

Mayor	Patricia Foster
Manager	Alvin James
City Clerk	Alvin James
Attorney	(vacant)
Finance Dir	Stephanie Osaze
Public Works	Anthony Docto Jr
Planning/Dev Dir	(vacant)
Building	NA
Police Chief	Ronald Davis
Fire/Emergency Mgmt	NA

Public Safety

Number of officers, 2007	31
Violent crimes, 2007	261
Property crimes, 2007	688
Arson, 2007	1

Public Library

East Palo Alto Library
San Mateo County Library System
2415 University Ave
East Palo Alto, CA 94303
650-321-7712

Branch Librarian	Sereptha Strong

Library system statistics, FY 2007

Population served	278,388
Internet terminals	26
Annual users	49,920

Per capita:

Operating income	$90.21
percent from local government	63.5%
Operating expenditure	$60.41
Total materials	2.65
Print holdings	2.16
Visits per capita	5.44

Housing & Construction

Housing Units

Total, 2008§	7,775
Single family units, attached	342
Single family units, detached	3,977
Multiple family units	3,297
Mobile home units	159
Occupied	7,694
Vacancy rate	1.0%
Median rent, 2000**	$854
Median SF home value, 2000**	$302,100

New Privately Owned Housing Units Authorized by Building Permit, 2007*

	Units	Construction Cost
Single	70	$15,773,101
Total	79	$17,481,113

Municipal Finance

(For local fiscal year ended in 2006)

Revenues

Total	$18,577,593
Taxes	11,718,533
Special benefits assessment	0
Licenses & permits	489,289
Fines & forfeitures	255,930
Revenues from use of money & property	630,500
Intergovernmental	2,004,690
Service charges	2,858,273
Other revenues	620,378
Other financing sources	0

Expenditures

Total	$18,173,574
General government	3,096,262
Public safety	9,568,429
Transportation	1,987,561
Community development	958,630
Health	1,732,951
Culture & leisure	317,881
Other	0

Local School District

(Data from School year 2007-08 except as noted)

Sequoia Union High
480 James Ave
Redwood City, CA 94062
(650) 369-1411

Superintendent	Patrick Gemma
Grade plan	9-12
Number of schools	6
Enrollment	8,510
High school graduates, 2006-07	1,546
Dropout rate	3.2%
Pupil/teacher ratio	19.7
Average class size	26.4
Students per computer	3.0
Classrooms with internet	402
Avg. Daily Attendance (ADA)	7,811
Cost per ADA	$11,470
Avg. Teacher Salary	$76,194

California Achievement Tests 6th ed., 2008

(Pct scoring at or above 50th National Percentile Rank)

	Math	Reading	Language
Grade 3	NA	NA	NA
Grade 7	NA	NA	NA

Academic Performance Index, 2008

Number of students tested	5,874
Number of valid scores	5,525
2007 API (base)	753
2008 API (growth)	753

SAT Testing, 2006-07

Enrollment, Grade 12	2,000
Number taking test	945
percent taking test	47.3%
percent with total score 1,500+	29.10%

Average Scores:

Math	Verbal	Writing	Total
546	530	530	1,606

Federal No Child Left Behind, 2008

(Adequate Yearly Progress standards met)

	Participation Rate	Pct Proficient
ELA	Yes	No
Math	Yes	No

API criteria	Yes
Graduation rate	Yes
# criteria met/possible	28/25

Other school districts for this city

(see Appendix E for information on these districts)

Ravenswood City Elem

Demographics & Socio-Economic Characteristics†

(2007 American Community Survey, except as noted)

Population

1990* 88,693
2007 97,964
  Male 46,374
  Female 51,590
Jan. 2008 (estimate)§ 97,934
  Persons per sq. mi. of land 6,707.8

Race & Hispanic Origin, 2007

Race
  White 69,928
  Black/African American 5,930
  North American Native 836
  Asian 3,584
  Pacific Islander 2,185
  Other Race 11,873
  Two or more races 3,628
Hispanic origin, total 29,854
  Mexican .... NA
  Puerto Rican .... NA
  Cuban .... NA
  Other Hispanic .... NA

Age & Nativity, 2007

Under 5 years 8,469
18 years and over 70,944
65 years and over 9,358
85 years and over 1,995
  Median Age 32.7
Native-born 77,164
Foreign-born 20,800

Educational Attainment, 2007

Population 25 years and over 59,403
Less than 9th grade 8.7%
High school grad or higher 81.4%
Bachelor's degree or higher 17.1%
Graduate degree 4.7%

Income & Poverty, 2007

Per capita income $20,614
Median household income $49,183
Median family income $56,060
Persons in poverty 20.6%
H'holds receiving public assistance 1,885
H'holds receiving social security 7,346

Households, 2007

Total households 32,652
  With persons under 18 12,918
  With persons over 65 5,787
  Family households 21,934
  Single person households 7,783
Persons per household 2.92
Persons per family 3.53

Household Population, 2008§§

Persons living in households 95,361
Persons living in group quarters 2,573
Persons per household 2.8

Labor & Employment

Total civilian labor force, 2008§§ 52,400
  Unemployment rate, 2008 .... 8.3%
Total civilian labor force, 2000* 43,745

Employed persons 16 years and over by occupation, 2007

  Managers & professionals 10,952
  Service occupations 11,050
  Sales & office occupations 11,899
  Farming, fishing & forestry 0
  Construction & maintenance 4,335
  Production & transportation 4,473
  Self-employed persons 3,866

† see Appendix D for 2000 Decennial Census Data
* US Census Bureau
** 2007 American Community Survey
§ California Department of Finance
§§ California Employment Development Dept

General Information

City of El Cajon
200 E Main St
El Cajon, CA 92020
619-441-1776

Website .... www.ci.el-cajon.ca.us
Elevation .... 435 ft.
Land Area (sq. miles) 14.6
Water Area (sq. miles) 0
Year of Incorporation 1912
Government type .... General law
Sales tax rate 9.75%

Voters & Officials

Registered Voters, October 2008

Total 39,663
  Democrats 13,687
  Republicans 15,960
  Declined to state 8,162

Legislative Districts

US Congressional 52
State Senatorial 36
State Assembly 77

Local Officials, 2009

Mayor .... Mark Lewis
Manager .... Kathi Henry
City Clerk .... Kathie J. Rutledge
Attorney .... Morgan Foley
Finance Dir .... Michael Shelton
Public Works .... Rob Turner
Planning/Dev Dir .... Melissa Ayres
Building .... Dan Pavao
Police Chief .... Pat Sprecco
Emergency/Fire Dir .... Mike Scott

Public Safety

Number of officers, 2007 139
Violent crimes, 2007 494
Property crimes, 2007 3,952
Arson, 2007 14

Public Library

El Cajon Library
San Diego County Library System
201 E Douglas Ave
El Cajon, CA 92020
619-588-3726

Branch Librarian .... Cheryl Doty

Library system statistics, FY 2007

Population served 1,049,868
Internet terminals 394
  Annual users .... NA

Per capita:

Operating income $33.43
  percent from local government 80.6%
Operating expenditure $31.30
Total materials 1.54
Print holdings 1.32
Visits per capita 6.31

Housing & Construction

Housing Units

Total, 2008§ 35,545
  Single family units, attached 1,566
  Single family units, detached 13,744
  Multiple family units 18,201
  Mobile home units 2,034
  Occupied 34,544
  Vacancy rate 2.8%
Median rent, 2007** $958
Median SF home value, 2007** $457,500

New Privately Owned Housing Units Authorized by Building Permit, 2007*

	Units	Construction Cost
Single	31	$17,484,642
Total	31	$17,484,642

Municipal Finance

(For local fiscal year ended in 2006)

Revenues

Total $86,609,542
Taxes 51,594,397
Special benefits assessment 369,001
Licenses & permits 1,418,791
Fines & forfeitures 1,875,443
Revenues from use of
  money & property 3,276,516
Intergovernmental 8,713,094
Service charges 16,250,689
Other revenues 3,111,611
Other financing sources 0

Expenditures

Total $78,640,261
General government 6,803,486
Public safety 42,962,536
Transportation 7,960,776
Community development 3,964,347
Health 11,480,116
Culture & leisure 5,469,000
Other 0

Local School District

(Data from School year 2007-08 except as noted)

Grossmont Union High
PO Box 1043
La Mesa, CA 91944
(619) 644-8000

Superintendent .... Robert Collins
Grade plan PK-12
Number of schools 19
Enrollment 24,195
High school graduates, 2006-07 4,597
Dropout rate 3.3%
Pupil/teacher ratio 24.2
Average class size 25.8
Students per computer 3.3
Classrooms with internet 1,450
Avg. Daily Attendance (ADA) 19,436
  Cost per ADA $8,940
Avg. Teacher Salary $68,475

California Achievement Tests 6th ed., 2008

(Pct scoring at or above 50th National Percentile Rank)

	Math	Reading	Language
Grade 3	NA	NA	NA
Grade 7	NA	NA	NA

Academic Performance Index, 2008

Number of students tested 14,311
Number of valid scores 13,392
2007 API (base) 704
2008 API (growth) 713

SAT Testing, 2006-07

Enrollment, Grade 12 5,999
Number taking test 1,875
  percent taking test 31.3%
  percent with total score 1,500+ 15.30%

Average Scores:

Math	Verbal	Writing	Total
513	495	494	1,502

Federal No Child Left Behind, 2008

(Adequate Yearly Progress standards met)

	Participation Rate	Pct Proficient
ELA	Yes	No
Math	Yes	No

API criteria .... Yes
Graduation rate .... Yes
\# criteria met/possible 34/31

Other school districts for this city

(see Appendix E for information on these districts)

Dehesa Elem, La Mesa-Spring Valley Elem

See Introduction for an explanation of all data sources.

Demographics & Socio-Economic Characteristics

(2000 Decennial Census, except as noted)

Population

1990* . . . 31,384
2000 . . . 37,835
Male . . . 18,594
Female . . . 19,241
Jan. 2008 (estimate)§ . . . 43,316
Persons per sq. mi. of land . . . 4,512.1

Race & Hispanic Origin, 2000

Race
White . . . 17,728
Black/African American . . . 1,195
North American Native . . . 369
Asian . . . 1,324
Pacific Islander . . . 37
Other Race . . . 15,771
Two or more races . . . 1,411
Hispanic origin, total . . . 28,219
Mexican . . . 25,251
Puerto Rican . . . 79
Cuban . . . 41
Other Hispanic . . . 2,848

Age & Nativity, 2000

Under 5 years . . . 3,161
18 years and over . . . 25,119
65 years and over . . . 3,529
85 years and over . . . 299
Median Age . . . 30.0
Native-born . . . 24,784
Foreign-born . . . 13,017

Educational Attainment, 2000

Population 25 years and over . . . 21,582
Less than 9th grade . . . 22.4%
High school grad or higher . . . 62.9%
Bachelor's degree or higher . . . 14.0%
Graduate degree . . . 5.6%

Income & Poverty, 1999

Per capita income . . . $13,874
Median household income . . . $33,161
Median family income . . . $36,910
Persons in poverty . . . 22.2%
H'holds receiving public assistance . . . 1,287
H'holds receiving social security . . . 2,915

Households, 2000

Total households . . . 11,439
With persons under 18 . . . 6,075
With persons over 65 . . . 2,627
Family households . . . 8,908
Single person households . . . 2,156
Persons per household . . . 3.23
Persons per family . . . 3.71

Household Population, 2008§§

Persons living in households . . . 42,429
Persons living in group quarters . . . 887
Persons per household . . . 3.2

Labor & Employment

Total civilian labor force, 2008§§ . . . 21,400
Unemployment rate, 2008 . . . 21.6%
Total civilian labor force, 2000 . . . 14,788

Employed persons 16 years and over by occupation, 2000

Managers & professionals . . . 3,723
Service occupations . . . 2,736
Sales & office occupations . . . 3,294
Farming, fishing & forestry . . . 869
Construction & maintenance . . . 1,065
Production & transportation . . . 1,356
Self-employed persons . . . 937

* US Census Bureau
** 2000 Decennial Census
§ California Department of Finance
§§ California Employment Development Dept

General Information

City of El Centro
1275 Main St
El Centro, CA 92243
760-337-4540

Website . . . www.cityofelcentro.org
Elevation . . . -40 ft.
Land Area (sq. miles) . . . 9.6
Water Area (sq. miles) . . . 0
Year of Incorporation . . . 1908
Government type . . . General law
Sales tax rate . . . 8.75%

Voters & Officials

Registered Voters, October 2008

Total . . . 15,975
Democrats . . . 8,144
Republicans . . . 4,900
Declined to state . . . 2,453

Legislative Districts

US Congressional . . . 51
State Senatorial . . . 40
State Assembly . . . 80

Local Officials, 2009

Mayor . . . Benjamin Solomon
Manager . . . Ruben Duran
City Clerk . . . L. Diane Caldwell
Attorney . . . Luis F. Hernandez
Finance Dir . . . Leticia Salcido
Public Works . . . Terry Hagen
Planning Dir . . . Norma Villicana
Building . . . Bob Williams
Police Chief . . . Harold Carter (Int)
Emergency/Fire Dir . . . Chris Petree

Public Safety

Number of officers, 2007 . . . 48
Violent crimes, 2007 . . . 266
Property crimes, 2007 . . . 2,072
Arson, 2007 . . . NA

Public Library

El Centro Public Main Library
El Centro Public Library System
539 State St
El Centro, CA 92243
760-337-4565

Director . . . Roland Banks

Library system statistics, FY 2007

Population served . . . 42,071
Internet terminals . . . 12
Annual users . . . 26,081

Per capita:

Operating income . . . $12.13
percent from local government . . . 91.2%
Operating expenditure . . . $10.88
Total materials . . . 2.86
Print holdings . . . 2.70
Visits per capita . . . 2.49

Housing & Construction

Housing Units

Total, 2008§ . . . 14,138
Single family units, attached . . . 563
Single family units, detached . . . 7,733
Multiple family units . . . 4,524
Mobile home units . . . 1,318
Occupied . . . 13,192
Vacancy rate . . . 6.7%
Median rent, 2000** . . . $527
Median SF home value, 2000** . . . $104,300

New Privately Owned Housing Units Authorized by Building Permit, 2007*

	Units	Construction Cost
Single	64	$12,561,045
Total	194	$19,848,629

Municipal Finance

(For local fiscal year ended in 2006)

Revenues

Total . . . $123,301,679
Taxes . . . 21,543,370
Special benefits assessment . . . 57,353
Licenses & permits . . . 627,032
Fines & forfeitures . . . 364,230
Revenues from use of money & property . . . 1,753,502
Intergovernmental . . . 3,498,429
Service charges . . . 91,768,088
Other revenues . . . 2,040,691
Other financing sources . . . 1,648,984

Expenditures

Total . . . $120,955,416
General government . . . 3,980,503
Public safety . . . 12,546,528
Transportation . . . 5,082,102
Community development . . . 5,379,964
Health . . . 85,068,650
Culture & leisure . . . 2,199,850
Other . . . 0

Local School District

(Data from School year 2007-08 except as noted)

Central Union High
351 West Ross Ave
El Centro, CA 92243
(760) 336-4500

Superintendent . . . C. Budde
Grade plan . . . 9-12
Number of schools . . . 3
Enrollment . . . 4,221
High school graduates, 2006-07 . . . 746
Dropout rate . . . 2.2%
Pupil/teacher ratio . . . 23.1
Average class size . . . 27.0
Students per computer . . . 3.5
Classrooms with internet . . . 183
Avg. Daily Attendance (ADA) . . . 4,074
Cost per ADA . . . $7,716
Avg. Teacher Salary . . . $68,127

California Achievement Tests 6th ed., 2008

(Pct scoring at or above 50th National Percentile Rank)

	Math	Reading	Language
Grade 3	NA	NA	NA
Grade 7	NA	NA	NA

Academic Performance Index, 2008

Number of students tested . . . 3,132
Number of valid scores . . . 2,911
2007 API (base) . . . 676
2008 API (growth) . . . 685

SAT Testing, 2006-07

Enrollment, Grade 12 . . . 817
Number taking test . . . 303
percent taking test . . . 37.1%
percent with total score 1,500+ . . . 10.40%

Average Scores:

Math	Verbal	Writing	Total
468	459	450	1,377

Federal No Child Left Behind, 2008

(Adequate Yearly Progress standards met)

	Participation Rate	Pct Proficient
ELA	Yes	Yes
Math	Yes	Yes

API criteria . . . Yes
Graduation rate . . . Yes
\# criteria met/possible . . . 18/18

Other school districts for this city

(see Appendix E for information on these districts)

El Centro Elem, McCabe Union Elem, Meadows Union Elem

Demographics & Socio-Economic Characteristics

(2000 Decennial Census, except as noted)

Population

1990* 22,869
2000 23,171
Male 10,956
Female 12,215
Jan. 2008 (estimate)§ 23,320
Persons per sq. mi. of land....6,477.8

Race & Hispanic Origin, 2000

Race
White 13,391
Black/African American 1,978
North American Native 116
Asian 5,649
Pacific Islander....59
Other Race 708
Two or more races 1,270
Hispanic origin, total 1,838
Mexican....953
Puerto Rican....59
Cuban 27
Other Hispanic 799

Age & Nativity, 2000

Under 5 years 1,079
18 years and over 19,479
65 years and over 4,733
85 years and over 668
Median Age 42.7
Native-born 17,275
Foreign-born 5,904

Educational Attainment, 2000

Population 25 years and over....17,999
Less than 9th grade....3.0%
High school grad or higher 92.6%
Bachelor's degree or higher 56.0%
Graduate degree....25.7%

Income & Poverty, 1999

Per capita income....$32,593
Median household income....$57,253
Median family income $69,397
Persons in poverty....6.7%
H'holds receiving public assistance 136
H'holds receiving social security 3,152

Households, 2000

Total households 10,208
With persons under 18....2,333
With persons over 65 3,361
Family households....5,970
Single person households....3,106
Persons per household 2.25
Persons per family....2.81

Household Population, 2008§§

Persons living in households....23,144
Persons living in group quarters....176
Persons per household 2.2

Labor & Employment

Total civilian labor force, 2008§§ 14,100
Unemployment rate, 2008 ....5.5%
Total civilian labor force, 2000 12,653

Employed persons 16 years and over by occupation, 2000

Managers & professionals 7,052
Service occupations....1,048
Sales & office occupations 2,931
Farming, fishing & forestry....7
Construction & maintenance 490
Production & transportation 592
Self-employed persons....1,418

* US Census Bureau
** 2000 Decennial Census
§ California Department of Finance
§§ California Employment Development Dept

General Information

City of El Cerrito
10940 San Pablo Ave
El Cerrito, CA 94530
510-215-4300

Website ....www.el-cerrito.org
Elevation ....66 ft.
Land Area (sq. miles) 3.6
Water Area (sq. miles)....0
Year of Incorporation 1917
Government type....General law
Sales tax rate....9.75%

Voters & Officials

Registered Voters, October 2008

Total....14,498
Democrats....9,147
Republicans 1,575
Declined to state 3,135

Legislative Districts

US Congressional 10
State Senatorial....7
State Assembly....14

Local Officials, 2009

Mayor....Sandia M. Potter
City Manager ....Scott Hanin
City Clerk ....Cheryl Morse
Attorney ....Sky Woodruff
Finance Dir....Mary Dodge
Public Works ....Jerry Bradshaw
Community Dev Dir ....Mitch Oshinsky
Building....Brian Fenty
Police Chief....Scott Kirkland
Fire Chief....Lance Maples

Public Safety

Number of officers, 2007 41
Violent crimes, 2007....177
Property crimes, 2007....1,145
Arson, 2007....NA

Public Library

El Cerrito Library
Contra Costa County Library System
6510 Stockton Ave
El Cerrito, CA 94530
510-526-7512

Branch Librarian ....Laura Martinengo

Library system statistics, FY 2007

Population served 938,513
Internet terminals 324
Annual users 670,618

Per capita:

Operating income $27.05
percent from local government....82.0%
Operating expenditure....$27.82
Total materials 1.57
Print holdings....1.41
Visits per capita 3.65

Housing & Construction

Housing Units

Total, 2008§....10,699
Single family units, attached....355
Single family units, detached 7,347
Multiple family units 2,965
Mobile home units 32
Occupied....10,440
Vacancy rate....2.4%
Median rent, 2000** $907
Median SF home value, 2000**....$291,300

New Privately Owned Housing Units Authorized by Building Permit, 2007*

	Units	Construction Cost
Single	0	$0
Total	0	$0

Municipal Finance

(For local fiscal year ended in 2006)

Revenues

Total....$25,832,486
Taxes 14,264,916
Special benefits assessment 1,846,917
Licenses & permits 349,546
Fines & forfeitures....349,227
Revenues from use of money & property....476,259
Intergovernmental....2,991,622
Service charges....5,028,278
Other revenues....525,721
Other financing sources....0

Expenditures

Total....$28,421,377
General government....6,127,231
Public safety....12,933,627
Transportation....3,014,272
Community development 1,564,169
Health 1,335,651
Culture & leisure....3,446,427
Other....0

Local School District

(Data from School year 2007-08 except as noted)

West Contra Costa Unified
1108 Bissell Ave
Richmond, CA 94801
(510) 231-1101

Superintendent....Bruce Harter
Grade plan....K-12
Number of schools....65
Enrollment 30,830
High school graduates, 2006-07....1,622
Dropout rate....9.3%
Pupil/teacher ratio....19.7
Average class size....24.8
Students per computer 6.4
Classrooms with internet....1,508
Avg. Daily Attendance (ADA)....28,599
Cost per ADA....$9,365
Avg. Teacher Salary....$56,030

California Achievement Tests 6th ed., 2008

(Pct scoring at or above 50th National Percentile Rank)

	Math	Reading	Language
Grade 3	47%	27%	38%
Grade 7	36%	33%	31%

Academic Performance Index, 2008

Number of students tested....22,407
Number of valid scores....20,863
2007 API (base) 674
2008 API (growth)....682

SAT Testing, 2006-07

Enrollment, Grade 12 1,839
Number taking test....853
percent taking test....46.4%
percent with total score 1,500+....13.90%

Average Scores:

Math	Verbal	Writing	Total
462	455	456	1,373

Federal No Child Left Behind, 2008

(Adequate Yearly Progress standards met)

	Participation Rate	Pct Proficient
ELA	Yes	No
Math	Yes	No

API criteria....Yes
Graduation rate ....No
\# criteria met/possible....42/34

Other school districts for this city

(see Appendix E for information on these districts)

None

See Introduction for an explanation of all data sources.

Demographics & Socio-Economic Characteristics[†]

(2007 American Community Survey, except as noted)

Population

1990* ... 106,209
2007 ... 113,308
Male ... 51,545
Female ... 61,763
Jan. 2008 (estimate)[§] ... 126,053
Persons per sq. mi. of land ... 13,130.5

Race & Hispanic Origin, 2007

Race
White ... 38,070
Black/African American ... 1,282
North American Native ... 272
Asian ... 28,651
Pacific Islander ... 27
Other Race ... 43,569
Two or more races ... 1,437
Hispanic origin, total ... 78,835
Mexican ... 71,681
Puerto Rican ... 0
Cuban ... 126
Other Hispanic ... 7,028

Age & Nativity, 2007

Under 5 years ... 9,884
18 years and over ... 81,113
65 years and over ... 10,299
85 years and over ... 1,846
Median Age ... 31.7
Native-born ... 51,788
Foreign-born ... 61,520

Educational Attainment, 2007

Population 25 years and over ... 68,134
Less than 9th grade ... 34.5%
High school grad or higher ... 51.2%
Bachelor's degree or higher ... 10.8%
Graduate degree ... 1.7%

Income & Poverty, 2007

Per capita income ... $13,098
Median household income ... $41,376
Median family income ... $43,235
Persons in poverty ... 19.5%
H'holds receiving public assistance ... 1,712
H'holds receiving social security ... 5,702

Households, 2007

Total households ... 26,757
With persons under 18 ... 14,843
With persons over 65 ... 6,516
Family households ... 22,859
Single person households ... 3,014
Persons per household ... 4.18
Persons per family ... 4.51

Household Population, 2008[§§]

Persons living in households ... 124,783
Persons living in group quarters ... 1,270
Persons per household ... 4.4

Labor & Employment

Total civilian labor force, 2008[§§] ... 52,400
Unemployment rate, 2008 ... 9.4%
Total civilian labor force, 2000* ... NA

Employed persons 16 years and over by occupation, 2007

Managers & professionals ... 8,257
Service occupations ... 9,595
Sales & office occupations ... 10,995
Farming, fishing & forestry ... 0
Construction & maintenance ... 6,290
Production & transportation ... 12,670
Self-employed persons ... 3,718

† see Appendix D for 2000 Decennial Census Data
* US Census Bureau
** 2007 American Community Survey
§ California Department of Finance
§§ California Employment Development Dept

General Information

City of El Monte
11333 Valley Blvd
El Monte, CA 91731
626-580-2016

Website ... www.ci.el-monte.ca.us
Elevation ... 283 ft.
Land Area (sq. miles) ... 9.6
Water Area (sq. miles) ... 0.1
Year of Incorporation ... 1912
Government type ... General law
Sales tax rate ... 9.75%

Voters & Officials

Registered Voters, October 2008

Total ... 31,270
Democrats ... 16,500
Republicans ... 6,017
Declined to state ... 7,451

Legislative Districts

US Congressional ... 32
State Senatorial ... 24
State Assembly ... 49

Local Officials, 2009

Mayor ... Ernest Gutierrez
City Manager ... James Mussenden
City Clerk ... Lorene Gutierrez
Attorney ... E. Clarke Moseley
Admin Svcs Dir ... Marcie Medina
Public Works ... (vacant)
Comm Dev Dir ... Kev Tcharkhoutian (Int)
Building ... NA
Police Chief ... Thomas Armstrong
Fire/Emergency Mgmt ... NA

Public Safety

Number of officers, 2007 ... 152
Violent crimes, 2007 ... 686
Property crimes, 2007 ... 2,810
Arson, 2007 ... 22

Public Library

El Monte Library
Los Angeles County Public Library System
3224 Tyler Ave
El Monte, CA 91731
626-444-9506

Branch Librarian ... Tony Ramirez

Library system statistics, FY 2007

Population served ... 3,673,313
Internet terminals ... 749
Annual users ... 3,748,771

Per capita:

Operating income ... $30.06
percent from local government ... 93.6%
Operating expenditure ... $28.36
Total materials ... 2.22
Print holdings ... 1.97
Visits per capita ... 3.25

Housing & Construction

Housing Units

Total, 2008[§] ... 28,817
Single family units, attached ... 3,391
Single family units, detached ... 15,499
Multiple family units ... 8,521
Mobile home units ... 1,406
Occupied ... 28,065
Vacancy rate ... 2.6%
Median rent, 2007** ... $992
Median SF home value, 2007** ... $445,500

New Privately Owned Housing Units Authorized by Building Permit, 2007*

	Units	Construction Cost
Single	99	$8,920,046
Total	99	$8,920,046

Municipal Finance

(For local fiscal year ended in 2006)

Revenues

Total ... $84,755,206
Taxes ... 55,632,511
Special benefits assessment ... 29,833
Licenses & permits ... 1,076,350
Fines & forfeitures ... 1,891,839
Revenues from use of money & property ... 1,382,315
Intergovernmental ... 18,741,151
Service charges ... 5,499,946
Other revenues ... 501,261
Other financing sources ... 0

Expenditures

Total ... $83,441,404
General government ... 19,584,131
Public safety ... 37,309,993
Transportation ... 9,573,718
Community development ... 8,515,179
Health ... 73,282
Culture & leisure ... 5,478,130
Other ... 0

Local School District

(Data from School year 2007-08 except as noted)

El Monte Union High
3537 Johnson Ave
El Monte, CA 91731
(626) 444-9005

Superintendent ... Kathy Furnald
Grade plan ... 9-12
Number of schools ... 7
Enrollment ... 10,614
High school graduates, 2006-07 ... 1,665
Dropout rate ... 1.8%
Pupil/teacher ratio ... 23.4
Average class size ... 27.3
Students per computer ... 2.8
Classrooms with internet ... 529
Avg. Daily Attendance (ADA) ... 10,804
Cost per ADA ... $8,087
Avg. Teacher Salary ... $68,066

California Achievement Tests 6th ed., 2008

(Pct scoring at or above 50th National Percentile Rank)

	Math	Reading	Language
Grade 3	NA	NA	NA
Grade 7	NA	NA	NA

Academic Performance Index, 2008

Number of students tested ... 7,727
Number of valid scores ... 7,301
2007 API (base) ... 648
2008 API (growth) ... 670

SAT Testing, 2006-07

Enrollment, Grade 12 ... 2,388
Number taking test ... 700
percent taking test ... 29.3%
percent with total score 1,500+ ... 9.70%

Average Scores:

Math	Verbal	Writing	Total
492	450	447	1,389

Federal No Child Left Behind, 2008

(Adequate Yearly Progress standards met)

	Participation Rate	Pct Proficient
ELA	Yes	No
Math	Yes	No

API criteria ... Yes
Graduation rate ... Yes
\# criteria met/possible ... 27/24

Other school districts for this city

(see Appendix E for information on these districts)

El Monte Elem, Mountain View Elem

Demographics & Socio-Economic Characteristics

(2000 Decennial Census, except as noted)

Population

1990* . . . 15,223
2000 . . . 16,033
Male . . . 7,966
Female . . . 8,067
Jan. 2008 (estimate)§ . . . 17,002
Persons per sq. mi. of land . . . 3,091.3

Race & Hispanic Origin, 2000

Race
White . . . 13,405
Black/African American . . . 187
North American Native . . . 75
Asian . . . 1,028
Pacific Islander . . . 47
Other Race . . . 562
Two or more races . . . 729
Hispanic origin, total . . . 1,765
Mexican . . . 1,058
Puerto Rican . . . 62
Cuban . . . 50
Other Hispanic . . . 595

Age & Nativity, 2000

Under 5 years . . . 956
18 years and over . . . 12,394
65 years and over . . . 1,529
85 years and over . . . 157
Median Age . . . 36.4
Native-born . . . 13,997
Foreign-born . . . 1,973

Educational Attainment, 2000

Population 25 years and over . . . 11,420
Less than 9th grade . . . 1.1%
High school grad or higher . . . 92.8%
Bachelor's degree or higher . . . 40.8%
Graduate degree . . . 13.0%

Income & Poverty, 1999

Per capita income . . . $33,996
Median household income . . . $61,341
Median family income . . . $74,007
Persons in poverty . . . 4.5%
H'holds receiving public assistance . . . 74
H'holds receiving social security . . . 1,141

Households, 2000

Total households . . . 7,060
With persons under 18 . . . 2,103
With persons over 65 . . . 1,204
Family households . . . 3,908
Single person households . . . 2,420
Persons per household . . . 2.27
Persons per family . . . 3.00

Household Population, 2008§§

Persons living in households . . . 16,979
Persons living in group quarters . . . 23
Persons per household . . . 2.4

Labor & Employment

Total civilian labor force, 2008§§ . . . 11,100
Unemployment rate, 2008 . . . 3.4%
Total civilian labor force, 2000 . . . 9,598

Employed persons 16 years and over by occupation, 2000

Managers & professionals . . . 4,291
Service occupations . . . 1,134
Sales & office occupations . . . 2,468
Farming, fishing & forestry . . . 13
Construction & maintenance . . . 649
Production & transportation . . . 659
Self-employed persons . . . 607

* US Census Bureau
** 2000 Decennial Census
§ California Department of Finance
§§ California Employment Development Dept

General Information

City of El Segundo
350 Main St
El Segundo, CA 90245
310-524-2300

Website . . . www.elsegundo.org
Elevation . . . 90 ft.
Land Area (sq. miles) . . . 5.5
Water Area (sq. miles) . . . 5.3
Year of Incorporation . . . 1917
Government type . . . General law
Sales tax rate . . . 9.25%

Voters & Officials

Registered Voters, October 2008

Total . . . 10,421
Democrats . . . 3,501
Republicans . . . 4,217
Declined to state . . . 2,199

Legislative Districts

US Congressional . . . 36
State Senatorial . . . 28
State Assembly . . . 53

Local Officials, 2009

Mayor . . . Kelly McDowell
Manager . . . Jack Wayt
City Clerk . . . Cindy Mortesen
Attorney . . . Mark Hensley
Finance Dir . . . Deborah Cullen
Public Works . . . Dana Greenwood
Planning/Dev Dir . . . Greg Carpenter
Building . . . Sam Lee
Police Chief . . . David Cummings
Emergency/Fire Dir . . . Kevin Smith

Public Safety

Number of officers, 2007 . . . 65
Violent crimes, 2007 . . . 36
Property crimes, 2007 . . . 776
Arson, 2007 . . . 5

Public Library

El Segundo Public Library
El Segundo Public Library System
111 W Mariposa Ave
El Segundo, CA 90245
310-524-2722

Director . . . Debra Brighton

Library system statistics, FY 2007

Population served . . . 17,076
Internet terminals . . . 65
Annual users . . . 5,546

Per capita:

Operating income . . . $114.31
percent from local government . . . 97.6%
Operating expenditure . . . $113.90
Total materials . . . 10.62
Print holdings . . . 9.74
Visits per capita . . . 19.17

Housing & Construction

Housing Units

Total, 2008§ . . . 7,357
Single family units, attached . . . 426
Single family units, detached . . . 3,145
Multiple family units . . . 3,775
Mobile home units . . . 11
Occupied . . . 7,154
Vacancy rate . . . 2.8%
Median rent, 2000** . . . $882
Median SF home value, 2000** . . . $371,900

New Privately Owned Housing Units Authorized by Building Permit, 2007*

	Units	Construction Cost
Single	23	$7,274,369
Total	23	$7,274,369

Municipal Finance

(For local fiscal year ended in 2006)

Revenues

Total . . . $86,855,155
Taxes . . . 41,079,909
Special benefits assessment . . . 0
Licenses & permits . . . 1,235,450
Fines & forfeitures . . . 635,652
Revenues from use of money & property . . . 2,116,650
Intergovernmental . . . 21,394,065
Service charges . . . 19,521,887
Other revenues . . . 871,542
Other financing sources . . . 0

Expenditures

Total . . . $86,834,799
General government . . . 8,510,915
Public safety . . . 28,159,422
Transportation . . . 24,086,592
Community development . . . 2,430,085
Health . . . 2,334,204
Culture & leisure . . . 11,651,539
Other . . . 0

Local School District

(Data from School year 2007-08 except as noted)

El Segundo Unified
641 Sheldon St
El Segundo, CA 90245
(310) 615-2650

Superintendent . . . Geoff Yantz
Grade plan . . . K-12
Number of schools . . . 5
Enrollment . . . 3,319
High school graduates, 2006-07 . . . 301
Dropout rate . . . 1.5%
Pupil/teacher ratio . . . 22.6
Average class size . . . 27.4
Students per computer . . . 5.8
Classrooms with internet . . . 144
Avg. Daily Attendance (ADA) . . . 3,242
Cost per ADA . . . $7,999
Avg. Teacher Salary . . . $69,420

California Achievement Tests 6th ed., 2008

(Pct scoring at or above 50th National Percentile Rank)

	Math	Reading	Language
Grade 3	82%	67%	74%
Grade 7	85%	75%	74%

Academic Performance Index, 2008

Number of students tested . . . 2,538
Number of valid scores . . . 2,450
2007 API (base) . . . 849
2008 API (growth) . . . 865

SAT Testing, 2006-07

Enrollment, Grade 12 . . . 299
Number taking test . . . 178
percent taking test . . . 59.5%
percent with total score 1,500+ . . . 32.40%

Average Scores:

Math	Verbal	Writing	Total
517	512	516	1,545

Federal No Child Left Behind, 2008

(Adequate Yearly Progress standards met)

	Participation Rate	Pct Proficient
ELA	No	No
Math	Yes	Yes

API criteria . . . Yes
Graduation rate . . . Yes
criteria met/possible . . . 26/24

Other school districts for this city

(see Appendix E for information on these districts)

None

See Introduction for an explanation of all data sources.

Demographics & Socio-Economic Characteristics†

(2007 American Community Survey, except as noted)

Population

1990* ....NA
2007 138,072
Male 65,418
Female 72,654
Jan. 2008 (estimate)§ 139,542
Persons per sq. mi. of land 9,180.4

Race & Hispanic Origin, 2007

Race
White 65,157
Black/African American 14,699
North American Native 192
Asian 32,699
Pacific Islander 1,166
Other Race 18,811
Two or more races 5,348
Hispanic origin, total 25,614
Mexican 17,754
Puerto Rican 1,087
Cuban 0
Other Hispanic 6,773

Age & Nativity, 2007

Under 5 years 12,371
18 years and over 94,687
65 years and over 9,475
85 years and over 492
Median Age 32.0
Native-born 108,581
Foreign-born 29,491

Educational Attainment, 2007

Population 25 years and over 84,079
Less than 9th grade 4.6%
High school grad or higher 90.5%
Bachelor's degree or higher 32.0%
Graduate degree 9.0%

Income & Poverty, 2007

Per capita income $29,761
Median household income $79,622
Median family income $83,969
Persons in poverty 8.0%
H'holds receiving public assistance 624
H'holds receiving social security 6,594

Households, 2007

Total households 43,902
With persons under 18 22,809
With persons over 65 6,535
Family households 35,400
Single person households 7,094
Persons per household 3.13
Persons per family 3.52

Household Population, 2008§§

Persons living in households 138,862
Persons living in group quarters 680
Persons per household 3.0

Labor & Employment

Total civilian labor force, 2008§§ 36,000
Unemployment rate, 2008 ....5.8%
Total civilian labor force, 2000* 45,053

Employed persons 16 years and over by occupation, 2007

Managers & professionals 27,378
Service occupations 10,804
Sales & office occupations 18,713
Farming, fishing & forestry 0
Construction & maintenance 6,084
Production & transportation 4,768
Self-employed persons 5,228

† see Appendix D for 2000 Decennial Census Data
* US Census Bureau
** 2007 American Community Survey
§ California Department of Finance
§§ California Employment Development Dept

General Information

City of Elk Grove
8380 Laguna Palms Way
Elk Grove, CA 95758
916-683-7111

Website ....www.elkgrovecity.org
Elevation ....NA
Land Area (sq. miles) 15.2
Water Area (sq. miles) 0
Year of Incorporation 2000
Government type ....General law
Sales tax rate 8.75%

Voters & Officials

Registered Voters, October 2008

Total 72,512
Democrats 31,798
Republicans 23,938
Declined to state 14,109

Legislative Districts

US Congressional 3, 5
State Senatorial 1, 6
State Assembly 15

Local Officials, 2009

Mayor ....Patrick Hume
City Manager ....Laura S. Gill
City Clerk ....Susan J. Blackston
Attorney ....Susan Burns Cochran
Finance Dir ....Rebecca L. Craig
Public Works ....Richard Shepard
Planning Dir ....Don Hazen
Building ....Richard Renfro
Police Chief ....Robert Lehner
Fire Chief ....Steve Foster

Public Safety

Number of officers, 2007 123
Violent crimes, 2007 505
Property crimes, 2007 3,683
Arson, 2007 6

Public Library

Elk Grove Branch Library
Sacramento Public Library System
8962 Elk Grove Blvd
Elk Grove, CA 95624
916-264-2700

Branch Supervisor ....Pat Sandefur

Library system statistics, FY 2007

Population served 1,335,969
Internet terminals 49
Annual users 27,435

Per capita:

Operating income $25.83
percent from local government 91.0%
Operating expenditure $23.08
Total materials 1.57
Print holdings 1.45
Visits per capita 1.18

Housing & Construction

Housing Units

Total, 2008§ 47,423
Single family units, attached 1,327
Single family units, detached 42,979
Multiple family units 2,844
Mobile home units 273
Occupied 46,323
Vacancy rate 2.3%
Median rent, 2007** $1,371
Median SF home value, 2007** $425,500

New Privately Owned Housing Units Authorized by Building Permit, 2007*

	Units	Construction Cost
Single	693	$135,094,031
Total	693	$135,094,031

Municipal Finance

(For local fiscal year ended in 2006)

Revenues

Total $168,926,068
Taxes 117,815,381
Special benefits assessment 1,671,205
Licenses & permits 3,574,108
Fines & forfeitures 511,633
Revenues from use of money & property 8,801,990
Intergovernmental 21,049,413
Service charges 13,695,767
Other revenues 1,723,117
Other financing sources 83,454

Expenditures

Total $177,663,894
General government 25,652,767
Public safety 30,153,912
Transportation 72,124,707
Community development 41,164,728
Health 8,342,912
Culture & leisure 224,868
Other 0

Local School District

(Data from School year 2007-08 except as noted)

Elk Grove Unified
9510 Elk Grove-Florin Rd
Elk Grove, CA 95624
(916) 686-5085

Superintendent ....Steven Ladd
Grade plan K-12
Number of schools 65
Enrollment 62,294
High school graduates, 2006-07 3,684
Dropout rate 3.4%
Pupil/teacher ratio 20.9
Average class size 26.1
Students per computer 6.2
Classrooms with internet 2,844
Avg. Daily Attendance (ADA) 59,792
Cost per ADA $7,926
Avg. Teacher Salary $63,945

California Achievement Tests 6th ed., 2008

(Pct scoring at or above 50th National Percentile Rank)

	Math	Reading	Language
Grade 3	61%	42%	51%
Grade 7	60%	55%	54%

Academic Performance Index, 2008

Number of students tested 47,449
Number of valid scores 44,718
2007 API (base) 764
2008 API (growth) 775

SAT Testing, 2006-07

Enrollment, Grade 12 4,535
Number taking test 1,820
percent taking test 40.1%
percent with total score 1,500+ 16.10%

Average Scores:

Math	Verbal	Writing	Total
492	475	470	1,437

Federal No Child Left Behind, 2008

(Adequate Yearly Progress standards met)

	Participation Rate	Pct Proficient
ELA	Yes	No
Math	Yes	No

API criteria ....Yes
Graduation rate ....Yes
\# criteria met/possible 46/44

Other school districts for this city

(see Appendix E for information on these districts)

None

See Introduction for an explanation of all data sources.

Demographics & Socio-Economic Characteristics

(2000 Decennial Census, except as noted)

Population

1990* 5,740
2000 6,882
Male 3,444
Female 3,438
Jan. 2008 (estimate)§ 9,727
Persons per sq. mi. of land 8,105.8

Race & Hispanic Origin, 2000

Race
White 3,096
Black/African American 1,339
North American Native 34
Asian 1,760
Pacific Islander 17
Other Race 288
Two or more races 348
Hispanic origin, total 616
Mexican 354
Puerto Rican 33
Cuban 12
Other Hispanic 217

Age & Nativity, 2000

Under 5 years 257
18 years and over 6,099
65 years and over 671
85 years and over 69
Median Age 35.2
Native-born 4,957
Foreign-born 1,925

Educational Attainment, 2000

Population 25 years and over 5,115
Less than 9th grade 2.6%
High school grad or higher 89.7%
Bachelor's degree or higher 53.5%
Graduate degree 25.4%

Income & Poverty, 1999

Per capita income $33,260
Median household income $45,359
Median family income $57,063
Persons in poverty 13.2%
H'holds receiving public assistance 113
H'holds receiving social security 620

Households, 2000

Total households 3,975
With persons under 18 487
With persons over 65 576
Family households 1,166
Single person households 2,205
Persons per household 1.71
Persons per family 2.69

Household Population, 2008§§

Persons living in households 9,660
Persons living in group quarters 67
Persons per household 1.7

Labor & Employment

Total civilian labor force, 2008§§ 4,600
Unemployment rate, 2008 .... 4.5%
Total civilian labor force, 2000 4,401

Employed persons 16 years and over by occupation, 2000

Managers & professionals 2,360
Service occupations 437
Sales & office occupations 912
Farming, fishing & forestry 0
Construction & maintenance 108
Production & transportation 407
Self-employed persons 355

* US Census Bureau
** 2000 Decennial Census
§ California Department of Finance
§§ California Employment Development Dept

General Information

City of Emeryville
1333 Park Ave
Emeryville, CA 94608
510-596-4300

Website .... www.ci.emeryville.ca.us
Elevation .... NA
Land Area (sq. miles) 1.2
Water Area (sq. miles) 0.7
Year of Incorporation 1896
Government type .... General law
Sales tax rate 9.75%

Voters & Officials

Registered Voters, October 2008

Total 5,921
Democrats 3,572
Republicans 424
Declined to state 1,589

Legislative Districts

US Congressional 9
State Senatorial 9
State Assembly 14

Local Officials, 2009

Mayor .... Richard Kassis
City Manager .... Patrick O'Keeffe
City Clerk .... Karen Hemphill
Attorney .... Michael Biddle
Finance Dir .... Edmund Suen
Public Works .... Maurice Kaufman
Planning Dir .... Charles Bryant
Building .... Victor Gonzales
Police Chief .... Ken James
Fire Chief .... Stephen Cutright

Public Safety

Number of officers, 2007 39
Violent crimes, 2007 112
Property crimes, 2007 1,156
Arson, 2007 0

Public Library

Served by Oakland Public Library

Library system statistics, FY 2007

Population served .... NA
Internet terminals .... NA
Annual users .... NA

Per capita:

Operating income .... NA
percent from local government .... NA
Operating expenditure .... NA
Total materials .... NA
Print holdings .... NA
Visits per capita .... NA

Housing & Construction

Housing Units

Total, 2008§ 5,988
Single family units, attached 397
Single family units, detached 270
Multiple family units 5,284
Mobile home units 37
Occupied 5,570
Vacancy rate 7.0%
Median rent, 2000** $985
Median SF home value, 2000** $161,600

New Privately Owned Housing Units Authorized by Building Permit, 2007*

	Units	Construction Cost
Single	3	$875,000
Total	139	$34,938,622

Municipal Finance

(For local fiscal year ended in 2006)

Revenues

Total $38,181,850
Taxes 21,283,921
Special benefits assessment 1,680,644
Licenses & permits 1,706,608
Fines & forfeitures 462,126
Revenues from use of money & property 2,722,088
Intergovernmental 1,837,837
Service charges 7,332,080
Other revenues 1,156,546
Other financing sources 0

Expenditures

Total $33,926,820
General government 8,194,290
Public safety 12,877,521
Transportation 544,799
Community development 8,888,284
Health 348,104
Culture & leisure 3,073,822
Other 0

Local School District

(Data from School year 2007-08 except as noted)

Emery Unified
4727 San Pablo Ave
Emeryville, CA 94608
(510) 601-4000

Superintendent .... John Sugiyama
Grade plan K-12
Number of schools 2
Enrollment 815
High school graduates, 2006-07 33
Dropout rate 5.1%
Pupil/teacher ratio 18.0
Average class size 20.9
Students per computer 4.5
Classrooms with internet 180
Avg. Daily Attendance (ADA) 775
Cost per ADA $13,653
Avg. Teacher Salary $61,822

California Achievement Tests 6th ed., 2008

(Pct scoring at or above 50th National Percentile Rank)

	Math	Reading	Language
Grade 3	39%	25%	33%
Grade 7	22%	32%	20%

Academic Performance Index, 2008

Number of students tested 600
Number of valid scores 516
2007 API (base) 656
2008 API (growth) 671

SAT Testing, 2006-07

Enrollment, Grade 12 36
Number taking test 16
percent taking test 44.4%
percent with total score 1,500+ 5.60%

Average Scores:

Math	Verbal	Writing	Total
415	412	398	1,225

Federal No Child Left Behind, 2008

(Adequate Yearly Progress standards met)

	Participation Rate	Pct Proficient
ELA	Yes	No
Math	Yes	No

API criteria .... Yes
Graduation rate .... No
\# criteria met/possible 22/19

Other school districts for this city

(see Appendix E for information on these districts)

None

See Introduction for an explanation of all data sources.

Demographics & Socio-Economic Characteristics

(2000 Decennial Census, except as noted)

Population

1990*	55,386
2000	58,014
Male	28,890
Female	29,124
Jan. 2008 (estimate)§	63,864
Persons per sq. mi. of land	3,343.7

Race & Hispanic Origin, 2000

Race	
White	50,241
Black/African American	340
North American Native	267
Asian	1,798
Pacific Islander	69
Other Race	3,645
Two or more races	1,654
Hispanic origin, total	8,584
Mexican	6,919
Puerto Rican	130
Cuban	86
Other Hispanic	1,449

Age & Nativity, 2000

Under 5 years	3,411
18 years and over	44,637
65 years and over	6,055
85 years and over	958
Median Age	37.9
Native-born	50,080
Foreign-born	8,115

Educational Attainment, 2000

Population 25 years and over	40,674
Less than 9th grade	4.9%
High school grad or higher	91.1%
Bachelor's degree or higher	50.0%
Graduate degree	19.7%

Income & Poverty, 1999

Per capita income	$34,336
Median household income	$63,954
Median family income	$78,104
Persons in poverty	7.3%
H'holds receiving public assistance	248
H'holds receiving social security	4,159

Households, 2000

Total households	22,830
With persons under 18	7,481
With persons over 65	4,130
Family households	14,283
Single person households	5,864
Persons per household	2.52
Persons per family	3.06

Household Population, 2008§§

Persons living in households	63,305
Persons living in group quarters	559
Persons per household	2.6

Labor & Employment

Total civilian labor force, 2008§§	39,200
Unemployment rate, 2008	4.2%
Total civilian labor force, 2000	32,681

Employed persons 16 years and over by occupation, 2000

Managers & professionals	15,932
Service occupations	4,228
Sales & office occupations	7,680
Farming, fishing & forestry	103
Construction & maintenance	1,983
Production & transportation	1,473
Self-employed persons	4,498

* US Census Bureau
** 2000 Decennial Census
§ California Department of Finance
§§ California Employment Development Dept

General Information

City of Encinitas
505 S Vulcan Ave
Encinitas, CA 92024
760-633-2600

Website	www.ci.encinitas.ca.us
Elevation	NA
Land Area (sq. miles)	19.1
Water Area (sq. miles)	1.0
Year of Incorporation	1986
Government type	General Law
Sales tax rate	8.75%

Voters & Officials

Registered Voters, October 2008

Total	38,219
Democrats	13,734
Republicans	13,132
Declined to state	9,399

Legislative Districts

US Congressional	50
State Senatorial	38
State Assembly	74

Local Officials, 2009

Mayor	Maggie Houlihan
Manager	Phil Cotton
City Clerk	Deborah Cervone
Attorney	Glenn Sabine
Finance Dir	Jennifer Smith
Public Works	Larry Watt
Planning/Dev Dir	Patrick Murphy
Building	Mark Beauchamp
Police Chief	Don Fowler
Fire Chief	Mark Muir

Public Safety

Number of officers, 2007	NA
Violent crimes, 2007	159
Property crimes, 2007	1,144
Arson, 2007	7

Public Library

Enicinitas Branch
San Diego County Library System
540 Cornish Dr
Encinitas, CA 92024
760-753-7376

Branch Librarian	Sandy Housley

Library system statistics, FY 2007

Population served	1,049,868
Internet terminals	394
Annual users	NA

Per capita:

Operating income	$33.43
percent from local government	80.6%
Operating expenditure	$31.30
Total materials	1.54
Print holdings	1.32
Visits per capita	6.31

Housing & Construction

Housing Units

Total, 2008§	25,719
Single family units, attached	4,589
Single family units, detached	14,594
Multiple family units	5,767
Mobile home units	769
Occupied	24,627
Vacancy rate	4.3%
Median rent, 2000**	$977
Median SF home value, 2000**	$353,300

New Privately Owned Housing Units Authorized by Building Permit, 2007*

	Units	Construction Cost
Single	109	$32,533,916
Total	129	$34,648,471

Municipal Finance

(For local fiscal year ended in 2006)

Revenues

Total	$70,796,145
Taxes	43,192,282
Special benefits assessment	536,420
Licenses & permits	202,792
Fines & forfeitures	832,874
Revenues from use of money & property	3,153,534
Intergovernmental	5,813,052
Service charges	15,505,609
Other revenues	1,559,582
Other financing sources	0

Expenditures

Total	$65,760,313
General government	13,749,668
Public safety	21,570,823
Transportation	11,726,726
Community development	7,563,814
Health	4,639,942
Culture & leisure	6,509,340
Other	0

Local School District

(Data from School year 2007-08 except as noted)

San Dieguito Union High
710 Encinitas Blvd
Encinitas, CA 92024
(760) 753-6491

Superintendent	Ken Noah
Grade plan	7-12
Number of schools	10
Enrollment	12,482
High school graduates, 2006-07	1,874
Dropout rate	1.4%
Pupil/teacher ratio	25.4
Average class size	30.5
Students per computer	3.5
Classrooms with internet	613
Avg. Daily Attendance (ADA)	12,349
Cost per ADA	$8,092
Avg. Teacher Salary	$75,620

California Achievement Tests 6th ed., 2008

(Pct scoring at or above 50th National Percentile Rank)

	Math	Reading	Language
Grade 3	NA	NA	NA
Grade 7	83%	79%	78%

Academic Performance Index, 2008

Number of students tested	10,153
Number of valid scores	9,873
2007 API (base)	853
2008 API (growth)	855

SAT Testing, 2006-07

Enrollment, Grade 12	2,038
Number taking test	1,532
percent taking test	75.2%
percent with total score 1,500+	57.90%

Average Scores:

Math	Verbal	Writing	Total
590	555	560	1,705

Federal No Child Left Behind, 2008

(Adequate Yearly Progress standards met)

	Participation Rate	Pct Proficient
ELA	Yes	Yes
Math	Yes	Yes

API criteria	Yes
Graduation rate	Yes
# criteria met/possible	30/30

Other school districts for this city

(see Appendix E for information on these districts)

Cardiff Elem, Encinitas Union Elem

See Introduction for an explanation of all data sources.

Demographics & Socio-Economic Characteristics

(2000 Decennial Census, except as noted)

Population

1990* . . . 4,437
2000 . . . 5,963
Male . . . 2,937
Female . . . 3,026
Jan. 2008 (estimate)§ . . . 7,131
Persons per sq. mi. of land . . . 3,565.5

Race & Hispanic Origin, 2000

Race
White . . . 5,082
Black/African American . . . 34
North American Native . . . 57
Asian . . . 65
Pacific Islander . . . 11
Other Race . . . 520
Two or more races . . . 194
Hispanic origin, total . . . 1,125
Mexican . . . 923
Puerto Rican . . . 16
Cuban . . . 0
Other Hispanic . . . 186

Age & Nativity, 2000

Under 5 years . . . 375
18 years and over . . . 4,120
65 years and over . . . 756
85 years and over . . . 91
Median Age . . . 35.5
Native-born . . . 5,328
Foreign-born . . . 583

Educational Attainment, 2000

Population 25 years and over . . . 3,564
Less than 9th grade . . . 8.4%
High school grad or higher . . . 79.0%
Bachelor's degree or higher . . . 12.7%
Graduate degree . . . 3.1%

Income & Poverty, 1999

Per capita income . . . $19,016
Median household income . . . $49,797
Median family income . . . $55,488
Persons in poverty . . . 8.5%
H'holds receiving public assistance . . . 32
H'holds receiving social security . . . 647

Households, 2000

Total households . . . 2,056
With persons under 18 . . . 924
With persons over 65 . . . 543
Family households . . . 1,597
Single person households . . . 402
Persons per household . . . 2.89
Persons per family . . . 3.31

Household Population, 2008§§

Persons living in households . . . 7,105
Persons living in group quarters . . . 26
Persons per household . . . 2.9

Labor & Employment

Total civilian labor force, 2008§§ . . . 3,500
Unemployment rate, 2008 . . . 9.2%
Total civilian labor force, 2000 . . . 2,838

Employed persons 16 years and over by occupation, 2000

Managers & professionals . . . 620
Service occupations . . . 344
Sales & office occupations . . . 825
Farming, fishing & forestry . . . 97
Construction & maintenance . . . 254
Production & transportation . . . 439
Self-employed persons . . . 187

* US Census Bureau
** 2000 Decennial Census
§ California Department of Finance
§§ California Employment Development Dept

General Information

City of Escalon
PO Box 248
Escalon, CA 95320
209-838-4100

Website . . . cityofescalon.org
Elevation . . . NA
Land Area (sq. miles) . . . 2.0
Water Area (sq. miles) . . . 0
Year of Incorporation . . . 1957
Government type . . . General law
Sales tax rate . . . 8.75%

Voters & Officials

Registered Voters, October 2008

Total . . . 3,493
Democrats . . . 1,183
Republicans . . . 1,623
Declined to state . . . 521

Legislative Districts

US Congressional . . . 11
State Senatorial . . . 14
State Assembly . . . 26

Local Officials, 2009

Mayor . . . Walt Murken
City Manager . . . Greg Greeson
City Clerk . . . Lisa Nebe
Attorney . . . Ann Siprelle
Finance Dir . . . Tammy Alcantor
Public Works . . . Patrick Riggs
Planning/Dev Dir . . . Duane Peterson
Building . . . NA
Police Chief . . . Douglas Dunford
Emergency/Fire Dir . . . Rick Mello

Public Safety

Number of officers, 2007 . . . 11
Violent crimes, 2007 . . . 21
Property crimes, 2007 . . . 270
Arson, 2007 . . . 0

Public Library

Escalon Library
Stockton-San Joaquin County Public Library
1540 Second St
Escalon, CA 95320
209-805-7323

Branch Librarian . . . Anne Stevens

Library system statistics, FY 2007

Population served . . . 619,292
Internet terminals . . . 125
Annual users . . . 255,083

Per capita:

Operating income . . . $21.59
percent from local government . . . 96.0%
Operating expenditure . . . $19.98
Total materials . . . 1.65
Print holdings . . . 1.52
Visits per capita . . . 2.20

Housing & Construction

Housing Units

Total, 2008§ . . . 2,504
Single family units, attached . . . 20
Single family units, detached . . . 2,098
Multiple family units . . . 251
Mobile home units . . . 135
Occupied . . . 2,415
Vacancy rate . . . 3.6%
Median rent, 2000** . . . $541
Median SF home value, 2000** . . . $144,000

New Privately Owned Housing Units Authorized by Building Permit, 2007*

	Units	Construction Cost
Single	19	$4,718,238
Total	19	$4,718,238

Municipal Finance

(For local fiscal year ended in 2006)

Revenues

Total . . . $8,748,332
Taxes . . . 3,063,389
Special benefits assessment . . . 102,742
Licenses & permits . . . 307,691
Fines & forfeitures . . . 51,797
Revenues from use of money & property . . . 629,536
Intergovernmental . . . 563,725
Service charges . . . 3,627,954
Other revenues . . . 401,498
Other financing sources . . . 0

Expenditures

Total . . . $6,279,469
General government . . . 195,588
Public safety . . . 2,274,178
Transportation . . . 174,046
Community development . . . 601,572
Health . . . 1,310,267
Culture & leisure . . . 705,931
Other . . . 0

Local School District

(Data from School year 2007-08 except as noted)

Escalon Unified
1520 Yosemite Ave
Escalon, CA 95320
(209) 838-3591

Superintendent . . . Dave Mantooth
Grade plan . . . K-12
Number of schools . . . 7
Enrollment . . . 3,104
High school graduates, 2006-07 . . . 251
Dropout rate . . . 3.1%
Pupil/teacher ratio . . . 21.5
Average class size . . . 26.1
Students per computer . . . 3.6
Classrooms with internet . . . 146
Avg. Daily Attendance (ADA) . . . 3,045
Cost per ADA . . . $7,634
Avg. Teacher Salary . . . $61,449

California Achievement Tests 6th ed., 2008

(Pct scoring at or above 50th National Percentile Rank)

	Math	Reading	Language
Grade 3	54%	39%	38%
Grade 7	57%	55%	51%

Academic Performance Index, 2008

Number of students tested . . . 2,459
Number of valid scores . . . 2,313
2007 API (base) . . . 739
2008 API (growth) . . . 754

SAT Testing, 2006-07

Enrollment, Grade 12 . . . 280
Number taking test . . . 73
percent taking test . . . 26.1%
percent with total score 1,500+ . . . 10.70%

Average Scores:

Math	Verbal	Writing	Total
488	475	474	1,437

Federal No Child Left Behind, 2008

(Adequate Yearly Progress standards met)

	Participation Rate	Pct Proficient
ELA	Yes	No
Math	Yes	No

API criteria . . . Yes
Graduation rate . . . Yes
criteria met/possible . . . 26/20

Other school districts for this city

(see Appendix E for information on these districts)

None

See Introduction for an explanation of all data sources.

Demographics & Socio-Economic Characteristics†

(2007 American Community Survey, except as noted)

Population

1990* . . . 108,635
2007 . . . 128,819
Male . . . 62,803
Female . . . 66,016
Jan. 2008 (estimate)§ . . . 143,389
Persons per sq. mi. of land . . . 3,950.1

Race & Hispanic Origin, 2007

Race
White . . . 93,544
Black/African American . . . 3,286
North American Native . . . 1,295
Asian . . . 6,437
Pacific Islander . . . 531
Other Race . . . 20,536
Two or more races . . . 3,190
Hispanic origin, total . . . 53,542
Mexican . . . 49,965
Puerto Rican . . . 909
Cuban . . . 0
Other Hispanic . . . 2,668

Age & Nativity, 2007

Under 5 years . . . 10,572
18 years and over . . . 92,598
65 years and over . . . 15,982
85 years and over . . . 2,355
Median Age . . . 34.6
Native-born . . . 94,735
Foreign-born . . . 34,084

Educational Attainment, 2007

Population 25 years and over . . . 80,339
Less than 9th grade . . . 11.4%
High school grad or higher . . . 77.8%
Bachelor's degree or higher . . . 22.2%
Graduate degree . . . 7.6%

Income & Poverty, 2007

Per capita income . . . $23,988
Median household income . . . $49,424
Median family income . . . $54,179
Persons in poverty . . . 12.5%
H'holds receiving public assistance . . . 1,587
H'holds receiving social security . . . 11,339

Households, 2007

Total households . . . 43,151
With persons under 18 . . . 18,560
With persons over 65 . . . 11,019
Family households . . . 29,885
Single person households . . . 10,319
Persons per household . . . 2.93
Persons per family . . . 3.53

Household Population, 2008§§

Persons living in households . . . 141,624
Persons living in group quarters . . . 1,765
Persons per household . . . 3.1

Labor & Employment

Total civilian labor force, 2008§§ . . . 72,900
Unemployment rate, 2008 . . . 6.2%
Total civilian labor force, 2000* . . . 61,197

Employed persons 16 years and over by occupation, 2007

Managers & professionals . . . 19,399
Service occupations . . . 14,023
Sales & office occupations . . . 13,437
Farming, fishing & forestry . . . 339
Construction & maintenance . . . 6,751
Production & transportation . . . 7,692
Self-employed persons . . . 7,420

† see Appendix D for 2000 Decennial Census Data
* US Census Bureau
** 2007 American Community Survey
§ California Department of Finance
§§ California Employment Development Dept

General Information

City of Escondido
201 N Broadway
Escondido, CA 92025
760-839-4880

Website . . . www.ci.escondido.ca.us
Elevation . . . 684 ft.
Land Area (sq. miles) . . . 36.3
Water Area (sq. miles) . . . 0.2
Year of Incorporation . . . 1888
Government type . . . General law
Sales tax rate . . . 8.75%

Voters & Officials

Registered Voters, October 2008

Total . . . 52,811
Democrats . . . 15,780
Republicans . . . 22,958
Declined to state . . . 11,511

Legislative Districts

US Congressional . . . 50
State Senatorial . . . 38
State Assembly . . . 74, 75

Local Officials, 2009

Mayor . . . Lori Holt-Pfeiler
Manager . . . Clay Phillips
City Clerk . . . Marsha Whalen
Attorney . . . Jeffrey Epp
Finance Dir . . . Gilbert Rojas
Public Works . . . Ed Domingue
Planning/Dev Dir . . . Jonathan Brindle
Building . . . Joe Russo
Police Chief . . . Jim Maher
Emergency/Fire Dir . . . Mike Lowry

Public Safety

Number of officers, 2007 . . . 164
Violent crimes, 2007 . . . 657
Property crimes, 2007 . . . 4,329
Arson, 2007 . . . 23

Public Library

Escondido Public Library
Escondido Public Library System
239 S Kalmia St
Escondido, CA 92025
760-839-4683

City Librarian . . . Laura Mitchell

Library system statistics, FY 2007

Population served . . . 141,788
Internet terminals . . . 58
Annual users . . . 242,698

Per capita:

Operating income . . . $30.29
percent from local government . . . 89.5%
Operating expenditure . . . $30.29
Total materials . . . 2.56
Print holdings . . . 2.25
Visits per capita . . . 6.12

Housing & Construction

Housing Units

Total, 2008§ . . . 47,379
Single family units, attached . . . 2,939
Single family units, detached . . . 23,547
Multiple family units . . . 17,016
Mobile home units . . . 3,877
Occupied . . . 46,083
Vacancy rate . . . 2.7%
Median rent, 2007** . . . $1,029
Median SF home value, 2007** . . . $469,600

New Privately Owned Housing Units Authorized by Building Permit, 2007*

	Units	Construction Cost
Single	131	$35,253,450
Total	236	$51,091,674

Municipal Finance

(For local fiscal year ended in 2006)

Revenues

Total . . . $184,985,002
Taxes . . . 59,078,143
Special benefits assessment . . . 534,503
Licenses & permits . . . 1,466,492
Fines & forfeitures . . . 1,601,859
Revenues from use of money & property . . . 6,230,662
Intergovernmental . . . 20,028,921
Service charges . . . 79,178,011
Other revenues . . . 15,294,105
Other financing sources . . . 1,572,306

Expenditures

Total . . . $171,510,675
General government . . . 11,358,976
Public safety . . . 54,512,324
Transportation . . . 19,233,344
Community development . . . 12,327,376
Health . . . 27,493,331
Culture & leisure . . . 12,572,737
Other . . . 0

Local School District

(Data from School year 2007-08 except as noted)

Escondido Union High
302 North Midway Dr
Escondido, CA 92027
(760) 291-3200

Superintendent . . . Edward Nelson
Grade plan . . . 9-12
Number of schools . . . 7
Enrollment . . . 9,300
High school graduates, 2006-07 . . . 1,665
Dropout rate . . . 3.8%
Pupil/teacher ratio . . . 23.9
Average class size . . . 27.1
Students per computer . . . 3.9
Classrooms with internet . . . 403
Avg. Daily Attendance (ADA) . . . 8,177
Cost per ADA . . . $7,825
Avg. Teacher Salary . . . $63,842

California Achievement Tests 6th ed., 2008

(Pct scoring at or above 50th National Percentile Rank)

	Math	Reading	Language
Grade 3	NA	NA	NA
Grade 7	NA	NA	NA

Academic Performance Index, 2008

Number of students tested . . . 6,092
Number of valid scores . . . 5,762
2007 API (base) . . . 701
2008 API (growth) . . . 716

SAT Testing, 2006-07

Enrollment, Grade 12 . . . 2,101
Number taking test . . . 703
percent taking test . . . 33.5%
percent with total score 1,500+ . . . 16.30%

Average Scores:

Math	Verbal	Writing	Total
508	497	486	1,491

Federal No Child Left Behind, 2008

(Adequate Yearly Progress standards met)

	Participation Rate	Pct Proficient
ELA	Yes	Yes
Math	Yes	Yes

API criteria . . . Yes
Graduation rate . . . Met on Appeal
\# criteria met/possible . . . 26/26

Other school districts for this city

(see Appendix E for information on these districts)

Escondido Union Elem, San Pasqual Union Elem

See Introduction for an explanation of all data sources.

Demographics & Socio-Economic Characteristics

(2000 Decennial Census, except as noted)

Population

1990* 835
2000 781
  Male 381
  Female 400
Jan. 2008 (estimate)[§] 751
  Persons per sq. mi. of land 938.8

Race & Hispanic Origin, 2000

Race
  White 691
  Black/African American 1
  North American Native 47
  Asian 5
  Pacific Islander 0
  Other Race 8
  Two or more races 29
Hispanic origin, total 27
  Mexican 21
  Puerto Rican 4
  Cuban 0
  Other Hispanic 2

Age & Nativity, 2000

Under 5 years 27
18 years and over 577
65 years and over 177
85 years and over 21
  Median Age 44.1
Native-born 778
Foreign-born 22

Educational Attainment, 2000

Population 25 years and over 537
Less than 9th grade 6.0%
High school grad or higher 85.8%
Bachelor's degree or higher 14.7%
Graduate degree 3.5%

Income & Poverty, 1999

Per capita income $13,737
Median household income $25,179
Median family income $30,461
Persons in poverty 20.0%
H'holds receiving public assistance 11
H'holds receiving social security 148

Households, 2000

Total households 329
  With persons under 18 103
  With persons over 65 130
  Family households 211
  Single person households 102
Persons per household 2.37
Persons per family 2.98

Household Population, 2008[§§]

Persons living in households 751
Persons living in group quarters 0
Persons per household 2.2

Labor & Employment

Total civilian labor force, 2008[§§] ....NA
  Unemployment rate, 2008 ....NA
Total civilian labor force, 2000 357

Employed persons 16 years and over by occupation, 2000

  Managers & professionals 97
  Service occupations 48
  Sales & office occupations 91
  Farming, fishing & forestry 22
  Construction & maintenance 24
  Production & transportation 40
  Self-employed persons 55

* US Census Bureau
** 2000 Decennial Census
§ California Department of Finance
§§ California Employment Development Dept

General Information

City of Etna
442 Main St (physical)
PO Box 460 (mail)
Etna, CA 96027
530-467-5256

Email ....etnacity@sisqtel.net
Elevation ....2,929 ft.
Land Area (sq. miles) 0.8
Water Area (sq. miles) 0
Year of Incorporation 1878
Government type ....General law
Sales tax rate 8.25%

Voters & Officials

Registered Voters, October 2008

Total 461
  Democrats 147
  Republicans 218
  Declined to state 72

Legislative Districts

US Congressional 2
State Senatorial 4
State Assembly 2

Local Officials, 2009

Mayor ....Christopher Liles
Manager/Admin ....NA
City Clerk ....Pamela Russell
Attorney ....John Kenney
Finance Dir ....NA
Public Works ....Francis Murphy
Planning/Dev Dir ....NA
Building ....NA
Police Chief ....Josh Short
Emergency/Fire Dir ....Larry Hicks

Public Safety

Number of officers, 2007 2
Violent crimes, 2007 0
Property crimes, 2007 7
Arson, 2007 0

Public Library

Etna Branch Library
Siskiyou County Free Library System
Main Street
Etna, CA 96027
530-467-3400

Branch Librarian ....NA

Library system statistics, FY 2007

Population served 45,953
Internet terminals 31
  Annual users 48,766

Per capita:

Operating income $20.36
  percent from local government 90.2%
Operating expenditure $20.12
Total materials 4.06
Print holdings 3.88
Visits per capita ....NA

Housing & Construction

Housing Units

Total, 2008[§] 368
  Single family units, attached 10
  Single family units, detached 271
  Multiple family units 32
  Mobile home units 55
  Occupied 335
  Vacancy rate 9.0%
Median rent, 2000** $455
Median SF home value, 2000** $92,400

New Privately Owned Housing Units Authorized by Building Permit, 2007*

	Units	Construction Cost
Single	NA	NA
Total	NA	NA

Municipal Finance

(For local fiscal year ended in 2006)

Revenues

Total $1,371,548
Taxes 154,061
Special benefits assessment 0
Licenses & permits 749
Fines & forfeitures 3,555
Revenues from use of
  money & property 24,127
Intergovernmental 522,010
Service charges 630,678
Other revenues 36,368
Other financing sources 0

Expenditures

Total $1,235,518
General government 108,852
Public safety 376,037
Transportation 59,294
Community development 125,967
Health 117,614
Culture & leisure 317,117
Other 2,709

Local School District

(Data from School year 2007-08 except as noted)

Scotts Valley Unified Unified
PO Box 687
Fort Jones, CA 96032
(530) 468-2727

Superintendent ....Emily Houck
Grade plan K-12
Number of schools 11
Enrollment 699
High school graduates, 2006-07 0
Dropout rate ....NA
Pupil/teacher ratio 13.5
Average class size 16.2
Students per computer 2.4
Classrooms with internet 58
Avg. Daily Attendance (ADA) 651
  Cost per ADA $12,062
Avg. Teacher Salary ....NA

California Achievement Tests 6th ed., 2008

(Pct scoring at or above 50th National Percentile Rank)

	Math	Reading	Language
Grade 3	71%	49%	58%
Grade 7	60%	69%	58%

Academic Performance Index, 2008

Number of students tested 533
Number of valid scores 510
2007 API (base) ....B
2008 API (growth) 799

SAT Testing, 2006-07

Enrollment, Grade 12 48
Number taking test 3
  percent taking test 6.3%
  percent with total score 1,500+ ....NA

Average Scores:

Math	Verbal	Writing	Total
NA	NA	NA	NA

Federal No Child Left Behind, 2008

(Adequate Yearly Progress standards met)

	Participation Rate	Pct Proficient
ELA	Yes	Yes
Math	Yes	Yes

API criteria ....Yes
Graduation rate ....NA
\# criteria met/possible 13/13

Other school districts for this city

(see Appendix E for information on these districts)

None

See Introduction for an explanation of all data sources.

Demographics & Socio-Economic Characteristics

(2000 Decennial Census, except as noted)

Population

1990* . . . 27,025
2000 . . . 26,128
Male . . . 12,937
Female . . . 13,191
Jan. 2008 (estimate)§ . . . 26,157
Persons per sq. mi. of land . . . 2,753.4

Race & Hispanic Origin, 2000

Race
White . . . 21,544
Black/African American . . . 427
North American Native . . . 1,101
Asian . . . 928
Pacific Islander . . . 86
Other Race . . . 709
Two or more races . . . 1,333
Hispanic origin, total . . . 2,031
Mexican . . . 1,510
Puerto Rican . . . 45
Cuban . . . 22
Other Hispanic . . . 454

Age & Nativity, 2000

Under 5 years . . . 1,500
18 years and over . . . 20,287
65 years and over . . . 3,567
85 years and over . . . 541
Median Age . . . 36.6
Native-born . . . 24,499
Foreign-born . . . 1,430

Educational Attainment, 2000

Population 25 years and over . . . 17,033
Less than 9th grade . . . 5.4%
High school grad or higher . . . 81.7%
Bachelor's degree or higher . . . 16.9%
Graduate degree . . . 5.5%

Income & Poverty, 1999

Per capita income . . . $16,174
Median household income . . . $25,849
Median family income . . . $33,438
Persons in poverty . . . 22.9%
H'holds receiving public assistance . . . 1,041
H'holds receiving social security . . . 3,140

Households, 2000

Total households . . . 10,957
With persons under 18 . . . 3,134
With persons over 65 . . . 2,629
Family households . . . 5,886
Single person households . . . 3,871
Persons per household . . . 2.26
Persons per family . . . 2.93

Household Population, 2008§§

Persons living in households . . . 24,805
Persons living in group quarters . . . 1,352
Persons per household . . . 2.2

Labor & Employment

Total civilian labor force, 2008§§ . . . 11,900
Unemployment rate, 2008 . . . 7.7%
Total civilian labor force, 2000 . . . 11,838

Employed persons 16 years and over by occupation, 2000

Managers & professionals . . . 2,596
Service occupations . . . 2,577
Sales & office occupations . . . 2,998
Farming, fishing & forestry . . . 183
Construction & maintenance . . . 987
Production & transportation . . . 1,353
Self-employed persons . . . 1,196

* US Census Bureau
** 2000 Decennial Census
§ California Department of Finance
§§ California Employment Development Dept

General Information

City of Eureka
531 K St
Eureka, CA 95501
707-441-4172

Website . . . www.ci.eureka.ca.gov
Elevation . . . 44 ft.
Land Area (sq. miles) . . . 9.5
Water Area (sq. miles) . . . 5.0
Year of Incorporation . . . 1856
Government type . . . Chartered
Sales tax rate . . . 8.50%

Voters & Officials

Registered Voters, October 2008

Total . . . 14,578
Democrats . . . 6,423
Republicans . . . 4,031
Declined to state . . . 3,006

Legislative Districts

US Congressional . . . 1
State Senatorial . . . 2
State Assembly . . . 1

Local Officials, 2009

Mayor . . . Virginia Bass
Manager . . . David Tyson
City Clerk . . . Kathleen Franco
Attorney . . . Scheryl Schaffner
Finance Dir . . . Valerie Warner
Public Works . . . Mike Knight
Planning/Dev Dir . . . Kevin Hamblin
Building . . . Mike Knight
Police Chief . . . Garr Nielsen
Fire Chief . . . Eric Smith

Public Safety

Number of officers, 2007 . . . 44
Violent crimes, 2007 . . . NA
Property crimes, 2007 . . . 1,517
Arson, 2007 . . . 20

Public Library

Eureka Main Library
Humboldt County Library System
1313 Third St
Eureka, CA 95501
707-269-1900

Director . . . NA

Library system statistics, FY 2007

Population served . . . 131,959
Internet terminals . . . 46
Annual users . . . 20,083

Per capita:

Operating income . . . $22.91
percent from local government . . . 90.6%
Operating expenditure . . . $18.80
Total materials . . . 2.54
Print holdings . . . 2.38
Visits per capita . . . 4.15

Housing & Construction

Housing Units

Total, 2008§ . . . 11,804
Single family units, attached . . . 381
Single family units, detached . . . 7,282
Multiple family units . . . 3,967
Mobile home units . . . 174
Occupied . . . 11,115
Vacancy rate . . . 5.8%
Median rent, 2000** . . . $495
Median SF home value, 2000** . . . $114,000

New Privately Owned Housing Units Authorized by Building Permit, 2007*

	Units	Construction Cost
Single	14	$2,194,382
Total	18	$2,494,382

Municipal Finance

(For local fiscal year ended in 2006)

Revenues

Total . . . $41,957,219
Taxes . . . 17,156,282
Special benefits assessment . . . 0
Licenses & permits . . . 22,454
Fines & forfeitures . . . 210,893
Revenues from use of money & property . . . 971,521
Intergovernmental . . . 3,576,638
Service charges . . . 14,175,334
Other revenues . . . 3,559,097
Other financing sources . . . 2,285,000

Expenditures

Total . . . $34,909,956
General government . . . 3,637,055
Public safety . . . 12,051,492
Transportation . . . 5,699,725
Community development . . . 3,966,038
Health . . . 3,751,967
Culture & leisure . . . 1,969,966
Other . . . 0

Local School District

(Data from School year 2007-08 except as noted)

Eureka City Unified
3200 Walford Ave
Eureka, CA 95503
(707) 441-2400

Superintendent . . . Gregg Haulk
Grade plan . . . K-12
Number of schools . . . 12
Enrollment . . . 4,414
High school graduates, 2006-07 . . . 384
Dropout rate . . . 6.0%
Pupil/teacher ratio . . . 18.5
Average class size . . . 22.4
Students per computer . . . 3.8
Classrooms with internet . . . 266
Avg. Daily Attendance (ADA) . . . 4,166
Cost per ADA . . . $8,369
Avg. Teacher Salary . . . NA

California Achievement Tests 6th ed., 2008

(Pct scoring at or above 50th National Percentile Rank)

	Math	Reading	Language
Grade 3	57%	40%	44%
Grade 7	60%	57%	52%

Academic Performance Index, 2008

Number of students tested . . . 3,262
Number of valid scores . . . 3,068
2007 API (base) . . . 747
2008 API (growth) . . . 755

SAT Testing, 2006-07

Enrollment, Grade 12 . . . 475
Number taking test . . . 104
percent taking test . . . 21.9%
percent with total score 1,500+ . . . 15.00%

Average Scores:

Math	Verbal	Writing	Total
557	541	524	1,622

Federal No Child Left Behind, 2008

(Adequate Yearly Progress standards met)

	Participation Rate	Pct Proficient
ELA	Yes	No
Math	Yes	No

API criteria . . . Yes
Graduation rate . . . No
criteria met/possible . . . 34/29

Other school districts for this city

(see Appendix E for information on these districts)

Freshwater Elem, Garfield Elem, South Bay Union Elem

See Introduction for an explanation of all data sources.

Demographics & Socio-Economic Characteristics
(2000 Decennial Census, except as noted)

Population
1990* . . . 7,276
2000 . . . 9,168
Male . . . 4,416
Female . . . 4,752
Jan. 2008 (estimate)§ . . . 10,656
Persons per sq. mi. of land . . . 4,843.6

Race & Hispanic Origin, 2000
Race
White . . . 6,393
Black/African American . . . 63
North American Native . . . 135
Asian . . . 119
Pacific Islander . . . 4
Other Race . . . 2,127
Two or more races . . . 327
Hispanic origin, total . . . 3,507
Mexican . . . 3,076
Puerto Rican . . . 25
Cuban . . . 6
Other Hispanic . . . 400

Age & Nativity, 2000
Under 5 years . . . 814
18 years and over . . . 6,075
65 years and over . . . 1,019
85 years and over . . . 146
Median Age . . . 30.1
Native-born . . . 7,787
Foreign-born . . . 1,335

Educational Attainment, 2000
Population 25 years and over . . . 5,168
Less than 9th grade . . . 14.9%
High school grad or higher . . . 68.5%
Bachelor's degree or higher . . . 12.4%
Graduate degree . . . 3.3%

Income & Poverty, 1999
Per capita income . . . $13,795
Median household income . . . $33,738
Median family income . . . $37,033
Persons in poverty . . . 19.1%
H'holds receiving public assistance . . . 216
H'holds receiving social security . . . 835

Households, 2000
Total households . . . 3,001
With persons under 18 . . . 1,464
With persons over 65 . . . 712
Family households . . . 2,327
Single person households . . . 563
Persons per household . . . 3.02
Persons per family . . . 3.43

Household Population, 2008§§
Persons living in households . . . 10,564
Persons living in group quarters . . . 92
Persons per household . . . 3.1

Labor & Employment
Total civilian labor force, 2008§§ . . . 5,100
Unemployment rate, 2008 . . . 6.8%
Total civilian labor force, 2000 . . . 3,876

Employed persons 16 years and over by occupation, 2000
Managers & professionals . . . 920
Service occupations . . . 558
Sales & office occupations . . . 866
Farming, fishing & forestry . . . 237
Construction & maintenance . . . 355
Production & transportation . . . 627
Self-employed persons . . . 214

* US Census Bureau
** 2000 Decennial Census
§ California Department of Finance
§§ California Employment Development Dept

General Information
City of Exeter
PO Box 237
Exeter, CA 93221
559-592-9244

Email . . . sguillen@exetercityhall.com
Elevation . . . 386 ft.
Land Area (sq. miles) . . . 2.2
Water Area (sq. miles) . . . 0
Year of Incorporation . . . 1911
Government type . . . Chartered
Sales tax rate . . . 8.75%

Voters & Officials

Registered Voters, October 2008
Total . . . 4,246
Democrats . . . 1,202
Republicans . . . 2,268
Declined to state . . . 606

Legislative Districts
US Congressional . . . 21
State Senatorial . . . 18
State Assembly . . . 34

Local Officials, 2009
Mayor . . . Leon Ooley
Manager . . . John H. Kunkel Jr
City Clerk . . . John H. Kunkel Jr
Attorney . . . Steve Kabot
Finance Dir . . . Sheri Emerson
Public Works . . . Felix Ortiz
Planning/Dev Dir . . . Greg Collins
Building . . . NA
Police Chief . . . Clifton Bush
Emergency/Fire Dir . . . Pete Gonzales

Public Safety
Number of officers, 2007 . . . 16
Violent crimes, 2007 . . . 21
Property crimes, 2007 . . . 319
Arson, 2007 . . . NA

Public Library
Exeter Library
Tulare County Free Library System
230 E Chestnut
Exeter, CA 93221
559-592-5361

Branch Librarian . . . Kathryn Ramsey

Library system statistics, FY 2007
Population served . . . 321,604
Internet terminals . . . 83
Annual users . . . 86,301

Per capita:
Operating income . . . $10.97
percent from local government . . . 86.0%
Operating expenditure . . . $8.74
Total materials . . . 1.08
Print holdings . . . 1.05
Visits per capita . . . 0.96

Housing & Construction

Housing Units
Total, 2008§ . . . 3,606
Single family units, attached . . . 107
Single family units, detached . . . 2,914
Multiple family units . . . 397
Mobile home units . . . 188
Occupied . . . 3,416
Vacancy rate . . . 5.3%
Median rent, 2000** . . . $522
Median SF home value, 2000** . . . $96,800

New Privately Owned Housing Units Authorized by Building Permit, 2007*

	Units	Construction Cost
Single	11	$1,759,100
Total	13	$2,034,690

Municipal Finance
(For local fiscal year ended in 2006)

Revenues
Total . . . $8,406,808
Taxes . . . 2,979,429
Special benefits assessment . . . 0
Licenses & permits . . . 226,923
Fines & forfeitures . . . 88,121
Revenues from use of money & property . . . 264,733
Intergovernmental . . . 2,028,355
Service charges . . . 2,757,192
Other revenues . . . 62,055
Other financing sources . . . 0

Expenditures
Total . . . $8,582,180
General government . . . 479,811
Public safety . . . 2,068,547
Transportation . . . 793,446
Community development . . . 1,795,771
Health . . . 1,816,833
Culture & leisure . . . 418,831
Other . . . 0

Local School District
(Data from School year 2007-08 except as noted)
Exeter Union High
134 South E St
Exeter, CA 93221
(559) 592-9421

Superintendent . . . Renee Whitson
Grade plan . . . 9-12
Number of schools . . . 4
Enrollment . . . 1,152
High school graduates, 2006-07 . . . 199
Dropout rate . . . 2.7%
Pupil/teacher ratio . . . 21.9
Average class size . . . 27.5
Students per computer . . . 3.3
Classrooms with internet . . . 55
Avg. Daily Attendance (ADA) . . . 1,104
Cost per ADA . . . $8,778
Avg. Teacher Salary . . . $65,638

California Achievement Tests 6th ed., 2008
(Pct scoring at or above 50th National Percentile Rank)

	Math	Reading	Language
Grade 3	NA	NA	NA
Grade 7	NA	NA	NA

Academic Performance Index, 2008
Number of students tested . . . 849
Number of valid scores . . . 798
2007 API (base) . . . 701
2008 API (growth) . . . 722

SAT Testing, 2006-07
Enrollment, Grade 12 . . . 253
Number taking test . . . 57
percent taking test . . . 22.5%
percent with total score 1,500+ . . . 14.20%

Average Scores:

Math	Verbal	Writing	Total
516	534	520	1,570

Federal No Child Left Behind, 2008
(Adequate Yearly Progress standards met)

	Participation Rate	Pct Proficient
ELA	Yes	Yes
Math	Yes	Yes

API criteria . . . Yes
Graduation rate . . . Yes
criteria met/possible . . . 18/18

Other school districts for this city
(see Appendix E for information on these districts)
Exeter Union Elem

See Introduction for an explanation of all data sources.

Demographics & Socio-Economic Characteristics

(2000 Decennial Census, except as noted)

Population

1990* . . . 6,931
2000 . . . 7,319
Male . . . 3,505
Female . . . 3,814
Jan. 2008 (estimate)§ . . . 7,412
Persons per sq. mi. of land . . . 3,529.5

Race & Hispanic Origin, 2000

Race
White . . . 6,689
Black/African American . . . 85
North American Native . . . 35
Asian . . . 144
Pacific Islander . . . 12
Other Race . . . 112
Two or more races . . . 242
Hispanic origin, total . . . 418
Mexican . . . 156
Puerto Rican . . . 30
Cuban . . . 12
Other Hispanic . . . 220

Age & Nativity, 2000

Under 5 years . . . 377
18 years and over . . . 5,914
65 years and over . . . 693
85 years and over . . . 70
Median Age . . . 41.6
Native-born . . . 6,455
Foreign-born . . . 702

Educational Attainment, 2000

Population 25 years and over . . . 5,446
Less than 9th grade . . . 1.1%
High school grad or higher . . . 96.0%
Bachelor's degree or higher . . . 48.8%
Graduate degree . . . 18.7%

Income & Poverty, 1999

Per capita income . . . $34,080
Median household income . . . $58,465
Median family income . . . $68,308
Persons in poverty . . . 6.3%
H'holds receiving public assistance . . . 24
H'holds receiving social security . . . 570

Households, 2000

Total households . . . 3,306
With persons under 18 . . . 946
With persons over 65 . . . 540
Family households . . . 1,813
Single person households . . . 1,029
Persons per household . . . 2.20
Persons per family . . . 2.76

Household Population, 2008§§

Persons living in households . . . 7,382
Persons living in group quarters . . . 30
Persons per household . . . 2.2

Labor & Employment

Total civilian labor force, 2008§§ . . . 4,700
Unemployment rate, 2008 . . . 7.2%
Total civilian labor force, 2000 . . . 4,553

Employed persons 16 years and over by occupation, 2000

Managers & professionals . . . 2,094
Service occupations . . . 507
Sales & office occupations . . . 1,213
Farming, fishing & forestry . . . 6
Construction & maintenance . . . 339
Production & transportation . . . 178
Self-employed persons . . . 789

* US Census Bureau
** 2000 Decennial Census
§ California Department of Finance
§§ California Employment Development Dept

General Information

Town of Fairfax
142 Bolinas Rd
Fairfax, CA 94930
415-453-1584

Website . . . townoffairfax.org
Elevation . . . 120 ft.
Land Area (sq. miles) . . . 2.1
Water Area (sq. miles) . . . 0
Year of Incorporation . . . 1931
Government type . . . General law
Sales tax rate . . . 9.00%

Voters & Officials

Registered Voters, October 2008

Total . . . 5,439
Democrats . . . 3,492
Republicans . . . 450
Declined to state . . . 1,092

Legislative Districts

US Congressional . . . 6
State Senatorial . . . 3
State Assembly . . . 6

Local Officials, 2009

Mayor . . . David Weinsoff
Manager . . . Michael Rock
City Clerk . . . Judy Anderson
Attorney . . . Jim Karpiak
Finance Dir . . . Laurie Ireland-Ashley
Public Works . . . Kathy Wilkie
Planning/Dev Dir . . . (vacant)
Building . . . Mark Lockaby
Police Chief . . . Ken Hughes
Emergency/Fire Dir . . . Roger Meagor

Public Safety

Number of officers, 2007 . . . 11
Violent crimes, 2007 . . . 18
Property crimes, 2007 . . . 110
Arson, 2007 . . . 4

Public Library

Fairfax Regional Library
Marin County Free Library System
2097 Sir Francis Drake Blvd
Fairfax, CA 94930
415-453-8151

Branch Librarian . . . Gail Wiemann

Library system statistics, FY 2007

Population served . . . 140,989
Internet terminals . . . 95
Annual users . . . 198,739

Per capita:

Operating income . . . $77.23
percent from local government . . . 90.0%
Operating expenditure . . . $77.23
Total materials . . . 3.56
Print holdings . . . 3.12
Visits per capita . . . 7.73

Housing & Construction

Housing Units

Total, 2008§ . . . 3,424
Single family units, attached . . . 193
Single family units, detached . . . 2,337
Multiple family units . . . 883
Mobile home units . . . 11
Occupied . . . 3,312
Vacancy rate . . . 3.3%
Median rent, 2000** . . . $1,108
Median SF home value, 2000** . . . $418,300

New Privately Owned Housing Units Authorized by Building Permit, 2007*

	Units	Construction Cost
Single	3	$2,100,000
Total	3	$2,100,000

Municipal Finance

(For local fiscal year ended in 2006)

Revenues

Total . . . $7,339,057
Taxes . . . 5,683,949
Special benefits assessment . . . 0
Licenses & permits . . . 283,367
Fines & forfeitures . . . 75,751
Revenues from use of money & property . . . 150,512
Intergovernmental . . . 869,232
Service charges . . . 259,738
Other revenues . . . 16,508
Other financing sources . . . 0

Expenditures

Total . . . $7,293,264
General government . . . 1,488,249
Public safety . . . 3,648,264
Transportation . . . 1,332,992
Community development . . . 493,970
Health . . . 0
Culture & leisure . . . 329,789
Other . . . 0

Local School District

(Data from School year 2007-08 except as noted)

Tamalpais Union High
PO Box 605
Larkspur, CA 94977
(415) 945-3720

Superintendent . . . Laurie Kimbrel
Grade plan . . . 9-12
Number of schools . . . 5
Enrollment . . . 3,889
High school graduates, 2006-07 . . . 959
Dropout rate . . . 0.8%
Pupil/teacher ratio . . . 17.4
Average class size . . . 24.4
Students per computer . . . 2.6
Classrooms with internet . . . 232
Avg. Daily Attendance (ADA) . . . 3,715
Cost per ADA . . . $13,492
Avg. Teacher Salary . . . $81,923

California Achievement Tests 6th ed., 2008

(Pct scoring at or above 50th National Percentile Rank)

	Math	Reading	Language
Grade 3	NA	NA	NA
Grade 7	NA	NA	NA

Academic Performance Index, 2008

Number of students tested . . . 2,800
Number of valid scores . . . 2,766
2007 API (base) . . . 848
2008 API (growth) . . . 855

SAT Testing, 2006-07

Enrollment, Grade 12 . . . 997
Number taking test . . . 730
percent taking test . . . 73.2%
percent with total score 1,500+ . . . 58.30%

Average Scores:

Math	Verbal	Writing	Total
574	574	574	1,722

Federal No Child Left Behind, 2008

(Adequate Yearly Progress standards met)

	Participation Rate	Pct Proficient
ELA	Yes	Yes
Math	Yes	Yes

API criteria . . . Yes
Graduation rate . . . Yes
\# criteria met/possible . . . 10/10

Other school districts for this city

(see Appendix E for information on these districts)

Ross Valley Elem

See Introduction for an explanation of all data sources.

Demographics & Socio-Economic Characteristics†

(2007 American Community Survey, except as noted)

Population

1990* . . . 77,211
2007 . . . 111,007
Male . . . 56,370
Female . . . 54,637
Jan. 2008 (estimate)§ . . . 106,753
Persons per sq. mi. of land . . . 2,831.6

Race & Hispanic Origin, 2007

Race
White . . . 49,625
Black/African American . . . 22,373
North American Native . . . 621
Asian . . . 15,890
Pacific Islander . . . 581
Other Race . . . 15,627
Two or more races . . . 6,290
Hispanic origin, total . . . 28,836
Mexican . . . 20,766
Puerto Rican . . . 1,095
Cuban . . . 89
Other Hispanic . . . 6,886

Age & Nativity, 2007

Under 5 years . . . 9,882
18 years and over . . . 80,541
65 years and over . . . 10,793
85 years and over . . . 1,321
Median Age . . . 32.4
Native-born . . . 83,543
Foreign-born . . . 27,464

Educational Attainment, 2007

Population 25 years and over . . . 68,825
Less than 9th grade . . . 8.1%
High school grad or higher . . . 81.8%
Bachelor's degree or higher . . . 18.6%
Graduate degree . . . 4.7%

Income & Poverty, 2007

Per capita income . . . $25,014
Median household income . . . $65,481
Median family income . . . $71,247
Persons in poverty . . . 10.4%
H'holds receiving public assistance . . . 1,591
H'holds receiving social security . . . 7,345

Households, 2007

Total households . . . 34,750
With persons under 18 . . . 15,094
With persons over 65 . . . 7,224
Family households . . . 26,243
Single person households . . . 6,315
Persons per household . . . 3.15
Persons per family . . . 3.52

Household Population, 2008§§

Persons living in households . . . 103,593
Persons living in group quarters . . . 3,160
Persons per household . . . 2.9

Labor & Employment

Total civilian labor force, 2008§§ . . . 49,000
Unemployment rate, 2008 . . . 7.6%
Total civilian labor force, 2000* . . . 41,962

Employed persons 16 years and over by occupation, 2007

Managers & professionals . . . 16,150
Service occupations . . . 8,321
Sales & office occupations . . . 13,599
Farming, fishing & forestry . . . 933
Construction & maintenance . . . 5,999
Production & transportation . . . 5,843
Self-employed persons . . . 2,375

† see Appendix D for 2000 Decennial Census Data
* US Census Bureau
** 2007 American Community Survey
§ California Department of Finance
§§ California Employment Development Dept

General Information

City of Fairfield
1000 Webster St
Civic Center
Fairfield, CA 94533
707-428-7400

Website . . . www.ci.fairfield.ca.us
Elevation . . . 15 ft.
Land Area (sq. miles) . . . 37.7
Water Area (sq. miles) . . . 0
Year of Incorporation . . . 1903
Government type . . . General law
Sales tax rate . . . 8.38%

Voters & Officials

Registered Voters, October 2008

Total . . . 43,391
Democrats . . . 21,835
Republicans . . . 11,329
Declined to state . . . 8,744

Legislative Districts

US Congressional . . . 10
State Senatorial . . . 5
State Assembly . . . 8

Local Officials, 2009

Mayor . . . Harry T. Price
Manager . . . Sean P. Quinn
City Clerk . . . Arletta K. Cortright
Attorney . . . Greg Stepanicich
Finance Dir . . . Robert Leland Jr
Public Works . . . Gene S. Cortright
Planning/Dev Dir . . . Eve Somjen
Building . . . Tom Garcia
Police Chief . . . Kenton Rainey
Emergency/Fire Dir . . . Vince Webster

Public Safety

Number of officers, 2007 . . . 127
Violent crimes, 2007 . . . 632
Property crimes, 2007 . . . 4,352
Arson, 2007 . . . 30

Public Library

Fairfield Civic Center Library
Solano County Library System
1150 Kentucky St
Fairfield, CA 94533
707-421-6500

Branch Librarian . . . Cara Swartz

Library system statistics, FY 2007

Population served . . . 371,000
Internet terminals . . . 248
Annual users . . . 562,512

Per capita:

Operating income . . . $54.42
percent from local government . . . 94.0%
Operating expenditure . . . $47.19
Total materials . . . 1.88
Print holdings . . . 1.57
Visits per capita . . . 5.20

Housing & Construction

Housing Units

Total, 2008§ . . . 38,317
Single family units, attached . . . 2,519
Single family units, detached . . . 26,183
Multiple family units . . . 8,723
Mobile home units . . . 892
Occupied . . . 35,995
Vacancy rate . . . 6.1%
Median rent, 2007** . . . $1,068
Median SF home value, 2007** . . . $493,500

New Privately Owned Housing Units Authorized by Building Permit, 2007*

	Units	Construction Cost
Single	180	$31,686,232
Total	206	$33,919,892

Municipal Finance

(For local fiscal year ended in 2006)

Revenues

Total . . . $151,153,061
Taxes . . . 63,589,671
Special benefits assessment . . . 5,632,160
Licenses & permits . . . 2,052,396
Fines & forfeitures . . . 635,551
Revenues from use of money & property . . . 6,598,337
Intergovernmental . . . 25,568,102
Service charges . . . 43,301,480
Other revenues . . . 3,775,364
Other financing sources . . . 0

Expenditures

Total . . . $143,186,782
General government . . . 6,791,709
Public safety . . . 38,349,381
Transportation . . . 35,991,654
Community development . . . 14,600,397
Health . . . 107,401
Culture & leisure . . . 14,120,813
Other . . . 0

Local School District

(Data from School year 2007-08 except as noted)

Fairfield-Suisun Unified
2490 Hilborn Rd
Fairfield, CA 94534
(707) 399-5000

Superintendent . . . Jacki Cottingim
Grade plan . . . K-12
Number of schools . . . 31
Enrollment . . . 22,774
High school graduates, 2006-07 . . . 1,306
Dropout rate . . . 5.0%
Pupil/teacher ratio . . . 20.8
Average class size . . . 26.8
Students per computer . . . 4.5
Classrooms with internet . . . 1,128
Avg. Daily Attendance (ADA) . . . 21,946
Cost per ADA . . . $7,610
Avg. Teacher Salary . . . $61,992

California Achievement Tests 6th ed., 2008

(Pct scoring at or above 50th National Percentile Rank)

	Math	Reading	Language
Grade 3	53%	35%	45%
Grade 7	52%	48%	48%

Academic Performance Index, 2008

Number of students tested . . . 17,275
Number of valid scores . . . 16,630
2007 API (base) . . . 714
2008 API (growth) . . . 724

SAT Testing, 2006-07

Enrollment, Grade 12 . . . 1,755
Number taking test . . . 603
percent taking test . . . 34.4%
percent with total score 1,500+ . . . 14.80%

Average Scores:

Math	Verbal	Writing	Total
491	474	469	1,434

Federal No Child Left Behind, 2008

(Adequate Yearly Progress standards met)

	Participation Rate	Pct Proficient
ELA	Yes	No
Math	Yes	No

API criteria . . . Yes
Graduation rate . . . Yes
criteria met/possible . . . 46/38

Other school districts for this city

(see Appendix E for information on these districts)

Travis Unified

See Introduction for an explanation of all data sources.

Demographics & Socio-Economic Characteristics

(2000 Decennial Census, except as noted)

Population

1990* . . . 6,235
2000 . . . 8,737
Male . . . 4,428
Female . . . 4,309
Jan. 2008 (estimate)§ . . . 10,524
Persons per sq. mi. of land . . . 5,538.9

Race & Hispanic Origin, 2000

Race
White . . . 3,701
Black/African American . . . 35
North American Native . . . 154
Asian . . . 100
Pacific Islander . . . 3
Other Race . . . 4,224
Two or more races . . . 520
Hispanic origin, total . . . 6,292
Mexican . . . 5,522
Puerto Rican . . . 26
Cuban . . . 0
Other Hispanic . . . 744

Age & Nativity, 2000

Under 5 years . . . 890
18 years and over . . . 5,383
65 years and over . . . 553
85 years and over . . . 51
Median Age . . . 24.3
Native-born . . . 5,887
Foreign-born . . . 2,811

Educational Attainment, 2000

Population 25 years and over . . . 4,426
Less than 9th grade . . . 38.2%
High school grad or higher . . . 39.8%
Bachelor's degree or higher . . . 2.0%
Graduate degree . . . 0.0%

Income & Poverty, 1999

Per capita income . . . $8,624
Median household income . . . $27,682
Median family income . . . $29,629
Persons in poverty . . . 30.4%
H'holds receiving public assistance . . . 255
H'holds receiving social security . . . 556

Households, 2000

Total households . . . 2,151
With persons under 18 . . . 1,363
With persons over 65 . . . 439
Family households . . . 1,855
Single person households . . . 228
Persons per household . . . 4.05
Persons per family . . . 4.32

Household Population, 2008§§

Persons living in households . . . 10,505
Persons living in group quarters . . . 19
Persons per household . . . 4.1

Labor & Employment

Total civilian labor force, 2008§§ . . . 4,400
Unemployment rate, 2008 . . . 13.7%
Total civilian labor force, 2000 . . . 3,361

Employed persons 16 years and over by occupation, 2000

Managers & professionals . . . 260
Service occupations . . . 671
Sales & office occupations . . . 698
Farming, fishing & forestry . . . 534
Construction & maintenance . . . 255
Production & transportation . . . 406
Self-employed persons . . . 154

* US Census Bureau
** 2000 Decennial Census
§ California Department of Finance
§§ California Employment Development Dept

General Information

City of Farmersville
909 W Visalia Rd
Farmersville, CA 93223
559-747-0458

Website . . . NA
Elevation . . . 360 ft.
Land Area (sq. miles) . . . 1.9
Water Area (sq. miles) . . . 0
Year of Incorporation . . . 1960
Government type . . . General law
Sales tax rate . . . 9.25%

Voters & Officials

Registered Voters, October 2008

Total . . . 2,588
Democrats . . . 1,250
Republicans . . . 674
Declined to state . . . 543

Legislative Districts

US Congressional . . . 21
State Senatorial . . . 18
State Assembly . . . 34

Local Officials, 2009

Mayor . . . Leonel Benavides
Manager . . . Rene Miller
City Clerk . . . NA
Attorney . . . Michael Farley
Finance Dir . . . Patricia Miller
Public Works . . . Eliseo Martinez
Planning/Dev Dir . . . Karl Schoettler
Building . . . Jose Lopez
Police Chief . . . Mario Krstic
Emergency/Fire Dir . . . Brian Kyle

Public Safety

Number of officers, 2007 . . . 15
Violent crimes, 2007 . . . 55
Property crimes, 2007 . . . 243
Arson, 2007 . . . 6

Public Library

Farmersville Library
147 E Front St
Farmersville, CA 93223
559-747-1783

Branch Librarian . . . NA

Library statistics, FY 2007

Population served . . . NA
Internet terminals . . . NA
Annual users . . . NA

Per capita:

Operating income . . . NA
percent from local government . . . NA
Operating expenditure . . . NA
Total materials . . . NA
Print holdings . . . NA
Visits per capita . . . NA

Housing & Construction

Housing Units

Total, 2008§ . . . 2,673
Single family units, attached . . . 90
Single family units, detached . . . 2,166
Multiple family units . . . 312
Mobile home units . . . 105
Occupied . . . 2,535
Vacancy rate . . . 5.2%
Median rent, 2000** . . . $472
Median SF home value, 2000** . . . $78,800

New Privately Owned Housing Units Authorized by Building Permit, 2007*

	Units	Construction Cost
Single	33	$5,168,922
Total	33	$5,168,922

Municipal Finance

(For local fiscal year ended in 2006)

Revenues

Total . . . $8,351,417
Taxes . . . 2,010,177
Special benefits assessment . . . 43,095
Licenses & permits . . . 259,243
Fines & forfeitures . . . 227,667
Revenues from use of money & property . . . 80,780
Intergovernmental . . . 3,050,290
Service charges . . . 1,942,535
Other revenues . . . 737,630
Other financing sources . . . 0

Expenditures

Total . . . $7,043,209
General government . . . 639,207
Public safety . . . 1,697,167
Transportation . . . 776,437
Community development . . . 1,540,233
Health . . . 1,048,252
Culture & leisure . . . 123,187
Other . . . 859,719

Local School District

(Data from School year 2007-08 except as noted)

Farmersville Unified
571 East Citrus
Farmersville, CA 93223
(559) 592-2010

Superintendent . . . Janet Jones
Grade plan . . . K-12
Number of schools . . . 6
Enrollment . . . 2,407
High school graduates, 2006-07 . . . 156
Dropout rate . . . 4.1%
Pupil/teacher ratio . . . 17.3
Average class size . . . 22.3
Students per computer . . . 2.7
Classrooms with internet . . . 156
Avg. Daily Attendance (ADA) . . . 2,395
Cost per ADA . . . $9,014
Avg. Teacher Salary . . . $61,991

California Achievement Tests 6th ed., 2008

(Pct scoring at or above 50th National Percentile Rank)

	Math	Reading	Language
Grade 3	30%	19%	21%
Grade 7	36%	31%	24%

Academic Performance Index, 2008

Number of students tested . . . 1,876
Number of valid scores . . . 1,691
2007 API (base) . . . 640
2008 API (growth) . . . 648

SAT Testing, 2006-07

Enrollment, Grade 12 . . . 169
Number taking test . . . 49
percent taking test . . . 29.0%
percent with total score 1,500+ . . . 3.60%

Average Scores:

Math	Verbal	Writing	Total
418	387	392	1,197

Federal No Child Left Behind, 2008

(Adequate Yearly Progress standards met)

	Participation Rate	Pct Proficient
ELA	Yes	No
Math	Yes	Yes

API criteria . . . Yes
Graduation rate . . . Yes
\# criteria met/possible . . . 20/16

Other school districts for this city

(see Appendix E for information on these districts)

None

See Introduction for an explanation of all data sources.

Demographics & Socio-Economic Characteristics

(2000 Decennial Census, except as noted)

Population

1990* 1,331
2000 1,382
Male 641
Female 741
Jan. 2008 (estimate)§ 1,428
Persons per sq. mi. of land 1,428.0

Race & Hispanic Origin, 2000

Race
White 1,290
Black/African American 4
North American Native 7
Asian 8
Pacific Islander 1
Other Race 18
Two or more races 54
Hispanic origin, total 59
Mexican 37
Puerto Rican 3
Cuban 0
Other Hispanic 19

Age & Nativity, 2000

Under 5 years 79
18 years and over 1,067
65 years and over 230
85 years and over 21
Median Age 42.9
Native-born 1,397
Foreign-born 24

Educational Attainment, 2000

Population 25 years and over 991
Less than 9th grade 1.8%
High school grad or higher 92.9%
Bachelor's degree or higher 25.6%
Graduate degree 6.4%

Income & Poverty, 1999

Per capita income $21,727
Median household income $37,955
Median family income $49,706
Persons in poverty 7.2%
H'holds receiving public assistance 20
H'holds receiving social security 226

Households, 2000

Total households 611
With persons under 18 168
With persons over 65 184
Family households 392
Single person households 184
Persons per household 2.26
Persons per family 2.83

Household Population, 2008§§

Persons living in households 1,428
Persons living in group quarters 0
Persons per household 2.2

Labor & Employment

Total civilian labor force, 2008§§ 700
Unemployment rate, 2008 .... 1.6%
Total civilian labor force, 2000 672

Employed persons 16 years and over by occupation, 2000

Managers & professionals 233
Service occupations 103
Sales & office occupations 173
Farming, fishing & forestry 18
Construction & maintenance 71
Production & transportation 61
Self-employed persons 125

* US Census Bureau
** 2000 Decennial Census
§ California Department of Finance
§§ California Employment Development Dept

General Information

City of Ferndale
834 Main St
PO Box 1095
Ferndale, CA 95536
707-786-4224

Website .... http://ci.ferndale.ca.us
Elevation .... 50 ft.
Land Area (sq. miles) 1.0
Water Area (sq. miles) 0
Year of Incorporation 1893
Government type .... General law
Sales tax rate 8.25%

Voters & Officials

Registered Voters, October 2008

Total 945
Democrats 373
Republicans 376
Declined to state 154

Legislative Districts

US Congressional 1
State Senatorial 2
State Assembly 1

Local Officials, 2009

Mayor .... Jeff Farley
Manager .... Jay Parrish
City Clerk .... Nancy Kaytis-Slocum
Attorney .... David Martinek
Finance Dir .... Debbi Austrus
Public Works .... Tim Miranda
City Planner .... George Williamson
Building .... Arnie Kemp
Police Chief .... Karl Poppelreiter
Emergency/Fire Dir .... Tom Grinsell

Public Safety

Number of officers, 2007 4
Violent crimes, 2007 1
Property crimes, 2007 18
Arson, 2007 0

Public Library

Ferndale Library
Humboldt County Library System
807 Main St
Ferndale, CA 95536
707-786-9559

Branch Librarian .... Bonnie von Braun

Library system statistics, FY 2007

Population served 131,959
Internet terminals 46
Annual users 20,083

Per capita:

Operating income $22.91
percent from local government 90.6%
Operating expenditure $18.80
Total materials 2.54
Print holdings 2.38
Visits per capita 4.15

Housing & Construction

Housing Units

Total, 2008§ 694
Single family units, attached 27
Single family units, detached 565
Multiple family units 93
Mobile home units 9
Occupied 641
Vacancy rate 7.6%
Median rent, 2000** $559
Median SF home value, 2000** $162,100

New Privately Owned Housing Units Authorized by Building Permit, 2007*

	Units	Construction Cost
Single	1	$139,056
Total	1	$139,056

Municipal Finance

(For local fiscal year ended in 2006)

Revenues

Total $1,408,665
Taxes 499,744
Special benefits assessment 0
Licenses & permits 45,177
Fines & forfeitures 6,223
Revenues from use of money & property 23,140
Intergovernmental 304,385
Service charges 476,833
Other revenues 53,163
Other financing sources 0

Expenditures

Total $1,399,229
General government 252,433
Public safety 628,843
Transportation 115,098
Community development 128,156
Health 255,013
Culture & leisure 19,686
Other 0

Local School District

(Data from School year 2007-08 except as noted)

Ferndale Unified
1231 Main St
Ferndale, CA 95536
(707) 786-5900

Superintendent .... Sam Garamendi
Grade plan K-12
Number of schools 2
Enrollment 473
High school graduates, 2006-07 44
Dropout rate 1.1%
Pupil/teacher ratio 15.9
Average class size 16.6
Students per computer 3.3
Classrooms with internet 31
Avg. Daily Attendance (ADA) 466
Cost per ADA $8,561
Avg. Teacher Salary $54,132

California Achievement Tests 6th ed., 2008

(Pct scoring at or above 50th National Percentile Rank)

	Math	Reading	Language
Grade 3	44%	46%	46%
Grade 7	59%	70%	73%

Academic Performance Index, 2008

Number of students tested 373
Number of valid scores 352
2007 API (base) 801
2008 API (growth) 781

SAT Testing, 2006-07

Enrollment, Grade 12 46
Number taking test 26
percent taking test 56.5%
percent with total score 1,500+ 28.30%

Average Scores:

Math	Verbal	Writing	Total
529	490	486	1,505

Federal No Child Left Behind, 2008

(Adequate Yearly Progress standards met)

	Participation Rate	Pct Proficient
ELA	Yes	Yes
Math	Yes	Yes

API criteria .... Yes
Graduation rate .... Yes
\# criteria met/possible 14/14

Other school districts for this city

(see Appendix E for information on these districts)

None

See Introduction for an explanation of all data sources.

Demographics & Socio-Economic Characteristics

(2000 Decennial Census, except as noted)

Population

- 1990* ... 11,992
- 2000 ... 13,643
  - Male ... 6,880
  - Female ... 6,763
- Jan. 2008 (estimate)§ ... 15,641
  - Persons per sq. mi. of land ... 5,586.1

Race & Hispanic Origin, 2000

- Race
  - White ... 7,304
  - Black/African American ... 44
  - North American Native ... 192
  - Asian ... 132
  - Pacific Islander ... 18
  - Other Race ... 5,394
  - Two or more races ... 559
- Hispanic origin, total ... 9,090
  - Mexican ... 8,134
  - Puerto Rican ... 20
  - Cuban ... 11
  - Other Hispanic ... 925

Age & Nativity, 2000

- Under 5 years ... 1,142
- 18 years and over ... 9,230
- 65 years and over ... 1,416
- 85 years and over ... 239
  - Median Age ... 29.8
- Native-born ... 9,684
- Foreign-born ... 3,795

Educational Attainment, 2000

- Population 25 years and over ... 7,557
- Less than 9th grade ... 25.6%
- High school grad or higher ... 63.1%
- Bachelor's degree or higher ... 11.9%
- Graduate degree ... 4.5%

Income & Poverty, 1999

- Per capita income ... $15,010
- Median household income ... $45,510
- Median family income ... $47,449
- Persons in poverty ... 12.8%
- H'holds receiving public assistance ... 173
- H'holds receiving social security ... 956

Households, 2000

- Total households ... 3,762
  - With persons under 18 ... 1,956
  - With persons over 65 ... 969
  - Family households ... 3,034
  - Single person households ... 605
- Persons per household ... 3.56
- Persons per family ... 3.94

Household Population, 2008§§

- Persons living in households ... 15,395
- Persons living in group quarters ... 246
- Persons per household ... 3.6

Labor & Employment

- Total civilian labor force, 2008§§ ... 6,700
  - Unemployment rate, 2008 ... 9.1%
- Total civilian labor force, 2000 ... 5,687

Employed persons 16 years and over by occupation, 2000

- Managers & professionals ... 1,211
- Service occupations ... 807
- Sales & office occupations ... 1,246
- Farming, fishing & forestry ... 190
- Construction & maintenance ... 688
- Production & transportation ... 1,117
- Self-employed persons ... 413

* US Census Bureau
** 2000 Decennial Census
§ California Department of Finance
§§ California Employment Development Dept

General Information

City of Fillmore
250 Central
Fillmore, CA 93015
805-524-3701

- Website ... www.fillmoreca.com
- Elevation ... 469 ft.
- Land Area (sq. miles) ... 2.8
- Water Area (sq. miles) ... 0
- Year of Incorporation ... 1914
- Government type ... General law
- Sales tax rate ... 8.25%

Voters & Officials

Registered Voters, October 2008

- Total ... 6,117
  - Democrats ... 2,939
  - Republicans ... 1,843
  - Declined to state ... 1,059

Legislative Districts

- US Congressional ... 24
- State Senatorial ... 17
- State Assembly ... 37

Local Officials, 2009

- Mayor ... Patti Walker
- Manager ... NA
- City Clerk ... Clay Westling
- Attorney ... Ted Schneider
- Finance Dir ... Barbara Smith
- Public Works ... Bert Rapp
- Planning/Dev Dir ... Kevin McSweeney
- Building ... Michael McGivney
- Police Chief ... Tim Hagel
- Emergency/Fire Dir ... Bill Herrera

Public Safety

- Number of officers, 2007 ... NA
- Violent crimes, 2007 ... 52
- Property crimes, 2007 ... 306
- Arson, 2007 ... 3

Public Library

Fillmore Library
Ventura County Library System
502 Second St
Fillmore, CA 93015
805-524-3355

- Branch Librarian ... Cathy Thomason

Library system statistics, FY 2007

- Population served ... 439,444
- Internet terminals ... 188
  - Annual users ... 216,575

Per capita:

- Operating income ... $25.05
  - percent from local government ... 86.2%
- Operating expenditure ... $25.02
- Total materials ... 1.81
- Print holdings ... 1.70
- Visits per capita ... NA

Housing & Construction

Housing Units

- Total, 2008§ ... 4,405
  - Single family units, attached ... 281
  - Single family units, detached ... 3,182
  - Multiple family units ... 616
  - Mobile home units ... 326
  - Occupied ... 4,302
  - Vacancy rate ... 2.3%
- Median rent, 2000** ... $777
- Median SF home value, 2000** ... $169,800

New Privately Owned Housing Units Authorized by Building Permit, 2007*

	Units	Construction Cost
Single	29	$6,871,574
Total	29	$6,871,574

Municipal Finance

(For local fiscal year ended in 2006)

Revenues

- Total ... $15,722,144
- Taxes ... 4,687,486
- Special benefits assessment ... 249,672
- Licenses & permits ... 268,024
- Fines & forfeitures ... 75,925
- Revenues from use of money & property ... 288,682
- Intergovernmental ... 1,911,851
- Service charges ... 4,112,663
- Other revenues ... 4,127,841
- Other financing sources ... 0

Expenditures

- Total ... $14,339,551
- General government ... 842,227
- Public safety ... 3,673,175
- Transportation ... 1,568,062
- Community development ... 743,165
- Health ... 4,987,091
- Culture & leisure ... 331,636
- Other ... 0

Local School District

(Data from School year 2007-08 except as noted)

Fillmore Unified
PO Box 697
Fillmore, CA 93016
(805) 524-6000

- Superintendent ... Jeff Sweeney
- Grade plan ... K-12
- Number of schools ... 7
- Enrollment ... 3,812
- High school graduates, 2006-07 ... 232
- Dropout rate ... 2.2%
- Pupil/teacher ratio ... 21.6
- Average class size ... 26.0
- Students per computer ... 5.2
- Classrooms with internet ... 194
- Avg. Daily Attendance (ADA) ... 3,688
  - Cost per ADA ... $8,291
- Avg. Teacher Salary ... $61,326

California Achievement Tests 6th ed., 2008

(Pct scoring at or above 50th National Percentile Rank)

	Math	Reading	Language
Grade 3	42%	31%	38%
Grade 7	37%	43%	38%

Academic Performance Index, 2008

- Number of students tested ... 2,925
- Number of valid scores ... 2,747
- 2007 API (base) ... 699
- 2008 API (growth) ... 697

SAT Testing, 2006-07

- Enrollment, Grade 12 ... 243
- Number taking test ... 78
  - percent taking test ... 32.1%
  - percent with total score 1,500+ ... 11.10%

Average Scores:

Math	Verbal	Writing	Total
480	466	463	1,409

Federal No Child Left Behind, 2008

(Adequate Yearly Progress standards met)

	Participation Rate	Pct Proficient
ELA	Yes	No
Math	Yes	No

- API criteria ... Yes
- Graduation rate ... Yes
- # criteria met/possible ... 26/19

Other school districts for this city

(see Appendix E for information on these districts)

None

See Introduction for an explanation of all data sources.

Demographics & Socio-Economic Characteristics

(2000 Decennial Census, except as noted)

Population

1990* 4,429
2000 5,743
Male 2,986
Female 2,757
Jan. 2008 (estimate)§ 6,812
Persons per sq. mi. of land 2,432.9

Race & Hispanic Origin, 2000

Race
White 2,504
Black/African American 66
North American Native 78
Asian 50
Pacific Islander 1
Other Race 2,786
Two or more races 258
Hispanic origin, total 5,026
Mexican 4,477
Puerto Rican 4
Cuban 2
Other Hispanic 543

Age & Nativity, 2000

Under 5 years 562
18 years and over 3,486
65 years and over 367
85 years and over 31
Median Age 24.9
Native-born 3,441
Foreign-born 2,331

Educational Attainment, 2000

Population 25 years and over 2,909
Less than 9th grade 44.8%
High school grad or higher 36.4%
Bachelor's degree or higher 3.5%
Graduate degree 1.0%

Income & Poverty, 1999

Per capita income $9,290
Median household income $31,533
Median family income $33,018
Persons in poverty 22.7%
H'holds receiving public assistance 127
H'holds receiving social security 295

Households, 2000

Total households 1,418
With persons under 18 929
With persons over 65 281
Family households 1,247
Single person households 133
Persons per household 4.01
Persons per family 4.28

Household Population, 2008§§

Persons living in households 6,751
Persons living in group quarters 61
Persons per household 4.1

Labor & Employment

Total civilian labor force, 2008§§ 2,800
Unemployment rate, 2008 . . . . 18.7%
Total civilian labor force, 2000 2,210

Employed persons 16 years and over by occupation, 2000

Managers & professionals 241
Service occupations 293
Sales & office occupations 258
Farming, fishing & forestry 454
Construction & maintenance 118
Production & transportation 390
Self-employed persons 92

* US Census Bureau
** 2000 Decennial Census
§ California Department of Finance
§§ California Employment Development Dept

General Information

City of Firebaugh
1575 11th St
Firebaugh, CA 93622
559-659-2043

Website . . . . www.ci.firebaugh.ca.us
Elevation . . . . 151 ft.
Land Area (sq. miles) 2.8
Water Area (sq. miles) 0.1
Year of Incorporation 1914
Government type . . . . General law
Sales tax rate 8.98%

Voters & Officials

Registered Voters, October 2008

Total 1,799
Democrats 995
Republicans 492
Declined to state 196

Legislative Districts

US Congressional 20
State Senatorial 16
State Assembly 31

Local Officials, 2009

Mayor . . . . Marcia Sablan
Manager . . . . Jose Antonio Ramirez
City Clerk . . . . Priscilla Meza
Attorney . . . . Meggin Boranian
Finance Dir . . . . Odi Ortiz
Public Works . . . . Ben Gallegos
Planning/Dev Dir . . . . Collins & Schoettler
Building . . . . William Van Ryn
Police Chief . . . . Elsa Lopez
Emergency/Fire Dir . . . . John Borboa

Public Safety

Number of officers, 2007 13
Violent crimes, 2007 13
Property crimes, 2007 213
Arson, 2007 0

Public Library

Firebaugh Branch Library
Fresno County Public Library System
1315 O St
Firebaugh, CA 93622
559-659-2820

Branch Librarian . . . . Pat Pondepxer

Library system statistics, FY 2007

Population served 889,019
Internet terminals 277
Annual users 861,240

Per capita:

Operating income $23.69
percent from local government 89.3%
Operating expenditure $23.37
Total materials 2.89
Print holdings 2.69
Visits per capita . . . . NA

Housing & Construction

Housing Units

Total, 2008§ 1,838
Single family units, attached 155
Single family units, detached 1,236
Multiple family units 335
Mobile home units 112
Occupied 1,648
Vacancy rate 10.3%
Median rent, 2000** $517
Median SF home value, 2000** $80,900

New Privately Owned Housing Units Authorized by Building Permit, 2007*

	Units	Construction Cost
Single	33	$6,115,571
Total	33	$6,115,571

Municipal Finance

(For local fiscal year ended in 2006)

Revenues

Total $7,942,461
Taxes 2,017,066
Special benefits assessment 19,696
Licenses & permits 72,710
Fines & forfeitures 20,096
Revenues from use of money & property 78,697
Intergovernmental 1,692,888
Service charges 2,050,502
Other revenues 20,806
Other financing sources 1,970,000

Expenditures

Total $8,300,271
General government 461,901
Public safety 1,537,999
Transportation 1,059,513
Community development 257,497
Health 718,440
Culture & leisure 509,920
Other 0

Local School District

(Data from School year 2007-08 except as noted)

Firebaugh-Las Deltas Unified
1976 Morris Kyle Dr
Firebaugh, CA 93622
(559) 659-1476

Superintendent . . . . Violet Chuck
Grade plan K-12
Number of schools 6
Enrollment 2,223
High school graduates, 2006-07 126
Dropout rate 7.0%
Pupil/teacher ratio 20.3
Average class size 25.2
Students per computer 3.4
Classrooms with internet 139
Avg. Daily Attendance (ADA) 2,197
Cost per ADA $8,307
Avg. Teacher Salary $56,059

California Achievement Tests 6th ed., 2008

(Pct scoring at or above 50th National Percentile Rank)

	Math	Reading	Language
Grade 3	41%	20%	28%
Grade 7	38%	28%	26%

Academic Performance Index, 2008

Number of students tested 1,700
Number of valid scores 1,552
2007 API (base) 692
2008 API (growth) 704

SAT Testing, 2006-07

Enrollment, Grade 12 175
Number taking test 46
percent taking test 26.3%
percent with total score 1,500+ 3.40%

Average Scores:

Math	Verbal	Writing	Total
430	409	440	1,279

Federal No Child Left Behind, 2008

(Adequate Yearly Progress standards met)

	Participation Rate	Pct Proficient
ELA	Yes	No
Math	Yes	No

API criteria . . . . Yes
Graduation rate . . . . No
\# criteria met/possible 22/18

Other school districts for this city

(see Appendix E for information on these districts)

None

See Introduction for an explanation of all data sources.

Demographics & Socio-Economic Characteristics†

(2007 American Community Survey, except as noted)

Population

1990* 29,802
2007 74,795
Male 42,920
Female 31,875
Jan. 2008 (estimate)§ 72,590
Persons per sq. mi. of land 3,345.2

Race & Hispanic Origin, 2007

Race
White 53,739
Black/African American 5,248
North American Native 354
Asian 9,667
Pacific Islander 0
Other Race 4,719
Two or more races 1,068
Hispanic origin, total 6,577
Mexican .... NA
Puerto Rican .... NA
Cuban .... NA
Other Hispanic .... NA

Age & Nativity, 2007

Under 5 years 4,708
18 years and over 57,221
65 years and over 6,238
85 years and over 1,039
Median Age 36.5
Native-born 65,463
Foreign-born 9,332

Educational Attainment, 2007

Population 25 years and over 51,450
Less than 9th grade 3.6%
High school grad or higher 89.0%
Bachelor's degree or higher 38.9%
Graduate degree 11.9%

Income & Poverty, 2007

Per capita income $35,482
Median household income $87,542
Median family income $109,032
Persons in poverty 1.8%
H'holds receiving public assistance 192
H'holds receiving social security 4,995

Households, 2007

Total households 24,928
With persons under 18 9,174
With persons over 65 4,748
Family households 16,723
Single person households 6,572
Persons per household 2.54
Persons per family 3.17

Household Population, 2008§§

Persons living in households 65,745
Persons living in group quarters 6,845
Persons per household 2.6

Labor & Employment

Total civilian labor force, 2008§§ 28,100
Unemployment rate, 2008 .... 3.2%
Total civilian labor force, 2000* 25,276

Employed persons 16 years and over by occupation, 2007

Managers & professionals 17,546
Service occupations 3,916
Sales & office occupations 8,721
Farming, fishing & forestry 0
Construction & maintenance 1,940
Production & transportation 1,278
Self-employed persons 2,817

† see Appendix D for 2000 Decennial Census Data
* US Census Bureau
** 2007 American Community Survey
§ California Department of Finance
§§ California Employment Development Dept

General Information

City of Folsom
50 Natoma St
Folsom, CA 95630
916-355-7200

Website .... www.folsom.ca.us
Elevation .... 218 ft.
Land Area (sq. miles) 21.7
Water Area (sq. miles) 2.4
Year of Incorporation 1946
Government type .... Charter
Sales tax rate 8.75%

Voters & Officials

Registered Voters, October 2008

Total 36,530
Democrats 11,136
Republicans 16,924
Declined to state 7,200

Legislative Districts

US Congressional 3
State Senatorial 1
State Assembly 5

Local Officials, 2009

Mayor .... Stephen E. Miklos
Manager .... Kerry Miller
City Clerk .... Christa Schmidt
Attorney .... Bruce C. Cline
Finance Dir .... Jim Francis
Public Works .... Rich Lorenz
Planning/Dev Dir .... David Miller
Building .... NA
Police Chief .... Sam Spiegel
Emergency/Fire Dir .... Dan Haverty

Public Safety

Number of officers, 2007 78
Violent crimes, 2007 98
Property crimes, 2007 1,594
Arson, 2007 13

Public Library

Folsom Public Library
411 Stafford St
Folsom, CA 95630
916-355-7374

Director .... Katy Curl

Library statistics, FY 2007

Population served 70,835
Internet terminals 26
Annual users 40,871

Per capita:

Operating income $26.91
percent from local government 89.4%
Operating expenditure $26.58
Total materials 1.05
Print holdings 0.93
Visits per capita 3.70

Housing & Construction

Housing Units

Total, 2008§ 26,245
Single family units, attached 653
Single family units, detached 18,245
Multiple family units 6,457
Mobile home units 890
Occupied 25,118
Vacancy rate 4.3%
Median rent, 2007** $1,251
Median SF home value, 2007** $492,500

New Privately Owned Housing Units Authorized by Building Permit, 2007*

	Units	Construction Cost
Single	176	$44,187,629
Total	197	$47,141,603

Municipal Finance

(For local fiscal year ended in 2006)

Revenues

Total $134,955,985
Taxes 56,738,213
Special benefits assessment 434,739
Licenses & permits 1,778,002
Fines & forfeitures 297,115
Revenues from use of money & property 3,959,595
Intergovernmental 4,769,771
Service charges 31,332,002
Other revenues 32,146,548
Other financing sources 3,500,000

Expenditures

Total $127,322,629
General government 6,836,879
Public safety 34,271,217
Transportation 15,509,046
Community development 16,370,523
Health 13,599,379
Culture & leisure 20,738,707
Other 0

Local School District

(Data from School year 2007-08 except as noted)

Folsom-Cordova Unified
125 East Bidwell St
Folsom, CA 95630
(916) 355-1100

Superintendent .... Patrick Godwin
Grade plan K-12
Number of schools 34
Enrollment 19,029
High school graduates, 2006-07 1,033
Dropout rate 3.1%
Pupil/teacher ratio 21.4
Average class size 26.5
Students per computer 4.7
Classrooms with internet 926
Avg. Daily Attendance (ADA) 18,524
Cost per ADA $7,778
Avg. Teacher Salary $65,021

California Achievement Tests 6th ed., 2008

(Pct scoring at or above 50th National Percentile Rank)

	Math	Reading	Language
Grade 3	68%	54%	61%
Grade 7	64%	63%	63%

Academic Performance Index, 2008

Number of students tested 14,486
Number of valid scores 13,534
2007 API (base) 805
2008 API (growth) 812

SAT Testing, 2006-07

Enrollment, Grade 12 1,123
Number taking test 435
percent taking test 38.7%
percent with total score 1,500+ 24.70%

Average Scores:

Math	Verbal	Writing	Total
546	525	522	1,593

Federal No Child Left Behind, 2008

(Adequate Yearly Progress standards met)

	Participation Rate	Pct Proficient
ELA	Yes	No
Math	Yes	Yes

API criteria .... Yes
Graduation rate .... Yes
\# criteria met/possible 38/37

Other school districts for this city

(see Appendix E for information on these districts)

None

See Introduction for an explanation of all data sources.

Demographics & Socio-Economic Characteristics†

(2007 American Community Survey, except as noted)

Population

1990* 87,535
2007 193,716
Male 97,172
Female 96,544
Jan. 2008 (estimate)§ 188,498
Persons per sq. mi. of land 5,221.6

Race & Hispanic Origin, 2007

Race
White 102,206
Black/African American 20,877
North American Native 1,154
Asian 13,925
Pacific Islander 1,545
Other Race 45,952
Two or more races 8,057
Hispanic origin, total 117,802
Mexican 104,051
Puerto Rican 755
Cuban 923
Other Hispanic 12,073

Age & Nativity, 2007

Under 5 years 17,605
18 years and over 129,557
65 years and over 10,516
85 years and over 1,401
Median Age 28.2
Native-born 132,011
Foreign-born 61,705

Educational Attainment, 2007

Population 25 years and over 107,864
Less than 9th grade 13.3%
High school grad or higher 72.7%
Bachelor's degree or higher 15.4%
Graduate degree 4.7%

Income & Poverty, 2007

Per capita income $19,321
Median household income $61,198
Median family income $61,740
Persons in poverty 10.1%
H'holds receiving public assistance . . . 1,379
H'holds receiving social security 8,277

Households, 2007

Total households 47,904
With persons under 18 28,555
With persons over 65 7,175
Family households 41,995
Single person households 4,525
Persons per household 4.03
Persons per family 4.20

Household Population, 2008§§

Persons living in households 187,939
Persons living in group quarters 559
Persons per household 4.0

Labor & Employment

Total civilian labor force, 2008§§ 63,300
Unemployment rate, 2008 . . . . . 8.3%
Total civilian labor force, 2000* 51,968

Employed persons 16 years and over by occupation, 2007

Managers & professionals 21,104
Service occupations 13,439
Sales & office occupations 23,195
Farming, fishing & forestry 0
Construction & maintenance 10,649
Production & transportation 18,712
Self-employed persons 5,174

† see Appendix D for 2000 Decennial Census Data
* US Census Bureau
** 2007 American Community Survey
§ California Department of Finance
§§ California Employment Development Dept

General Information

City of Fontana
8353 Sierra Ave
Fontana, CA 92335
909-350-7600

Website . . . . . www.fontana.org
Elevation . . . . . 1,232 ft.
Land Area (sq. miles) 36.1
Water Area (sq. miles) 0
Year of Incorporation 1952
Government type . . . . . General law
Sales tax rate 8.75%

Voters & Officials

Registered Voters, October 2008

Total 64,678
Democrats 31,855
Republicans 18,532
Declined to state 11,990

Legislative Districts

US Congressional 43
State Senatorial 32
State Assembly 62, 63

Local Officials, 2009

Mayor . . . . . Mark Nuaimi
City Manager . . . . . Kenneth Hunt
City Clerk . . . . . Tonia Lewis
Attorney . . . . . Clark Alsop
Finance Dir . . . . . Lisa Strong
Public Works . . . . . Chuck Hays
Community Dev Dir . . . . . Don Williams
Building . . . . . Andy Shipper
Police Chief . . . . . Rod Jones
Fire Chief . . . . . Terry Welsh

Public Safety

Number of officers, 2007 189
Violent crimes, 2007 896
Property crimes, 2007 4,152
Arson, 2007 13

Public Library

Fontana Branch Library
San Bernardino County Library System
16860 Valencia Ave
Fontana, CA 92335
909-822-2321

Branch Librarian . . . . . Renee Lavoto

Library system statistics, FY 2007

Population served 205,010
Internet terminals 459
Annual users 574,764

Per capita:

Operating income $15.41
percent from local government 85.0%
Operating expenditure $13.99
Total materials 1.21
Print holdings 1.14
Visits per capita 2.87

Housing & Construction

Housing Units

Total, 2008§ 49,945
Single family units, attached 1,307
Single family units, detached 39,668
Multiple family units 7,684
Mobile home units 1,286
Occupied 47,316
Vacancy rate 5.3%
Median rent, 2007** $974
Median SF home value, 2007** $454,700

New Privately Owned Housing Units Authorized by Building Permit, 2007*

	Units	Construction Cost
Single	794	$182,410,089
Total	820	$184,535,083

Municipal Finance

(For local fiscal year ended in 2006)

Revenues

Total $150,338,616
Taxes 50,655,603
Special benefits assessment 12,585,246
Licenses & permits 22,018,598
Fines & forfeitures 1,526,710
Revenues from use of money & property 8,479,063
Intergovernmental 12,499,468
Service charges 31,092,353
Other revenues 11,481,575
Other financing sources 0

Expenditures

Total $171,266,611
General government 30,224,596
Public safety 38,377,187
Transportation 34,260,319
Community development 30,796,854
Health 13,669,686
Culture & leisure 23,561,331
Other 0

Local School District

(Data from School year 2007-08 except as noted)

Fontana Unified
PO Box 5090
Fontana, CA 92335
(909) 357-5000

Superintendent . . . . . Cali Olsen-Binks
Grade plan K-12
Number of schools 44
Enrollment 41,959
High school graduates, 2006-07 2,044
Dropout rate 5.9%
Pupil/teacher ratio 22.9
Average class size 26.3
Students per computer 5.2
Classrooms with internet 2,005
Avg. Daily Attendance (ADA) 40,421
Cost per ADA $8,246
Avg. Teacher Salary $66,501

California Achievement Tests 6th ed., 2008

(Pct scoring at or above 50th National Percentile Rank)

	Math	Reading	Language
Grade 3	42%	24%	33%
Grade 7	40%	37%	33%

Academic Performance Index, 2008

Number of students tested 31,880
Number of valid scores 30,205
2007 API (base) 681
2008 API (growth) 694

SAT Testing, 2006-07

Enrollment, Grade 12 2,791
Number taking test 629
percent taking test 22.5%
percent with total score 1,500+ 4.90%

Average Scores:

Math	Verbal	Writing	Total
448	431	437	1,316

Federal No Child Left Behind, 2008

(Adequate Yearly Progress standards met)

	Participation Rate	Pct Proficient
ELA	Yes	No
Math	Yes	No

API criteria . . . . . Yes
Graduation rate . . . . . No
\# criteria met/possible 44/38

Other school districts for this city

(see Appendix E for information on these districts)

Etiwanda Elem

See Introduction for an explanation of all data sources.

Demographics & Socio-Economic Characteristics

(2000 Decennial Census, except as noted)

Population

1990* ... 6,078
2000 ... 7,026
Male ... 3,523
Female ... 3,503
Jan. 2008 (estimate)§ ... 6,890
Persons per sq. mi. of land ... 2,551.9

Race & Hispanic Origin, 2000

Race
White ... 5,583
Black/African American ... 73
North American Native ... 130
Asian ... 62
Pacific Islander ... 10
Other Race ... 847
Two or more races ... 321
Hispanic origin, total ... 1,596
Mexican ... 1,377
Puerto Rican ... 10
Cuban ... 3
Other Hispanic ... 206

Age & Nativity, 2000

Under 5 years ... 475
18 years and over ... 5,295
65 years and over ... 977
85 years and over ... 157
Median Age ... 36.2
Native-born ... 6,077
Foreign-born ... 951

Educational Attainment, 2000

Population 25 years and over ... 4,585
Less than 9th grade ... 5.7%
High school grad or higher ... 81.1%
Bachelor's degree or higher ... 13.6%
Graduate degree ... 5.2%

Income & Poverty, 1999

Per capita income ... $15,832
Median household income ... $28,539
Median family income ... $36,000
Persons in poverty ... 20.0%
H'holds receiving public assistance ... 247
H'holds receiving social security ... 928

Households, 2000

Total households ... 2,840
With persons under 18 ... 939
With persons over 65 ... 737
Family households ... 1,645
Single person households ... 1,009
Persons per household ... 2.35
Persons per family ... 3.04

Household Population, 2008§§

Persons living in households ... 6,764
Persons living in group quarters ... 126
Persons per household ... 2.3

Labor & Employment

Total civilian labor force, 2008§§ ... 3,600
Unemployment rate, 2008 ... 8.1%
Total civilian labor force, 2000 ... 3,410

Employed persons 16 years and over by occupation, 2000

Managers & professionals ... 621
Service occupations ... 993
Sales & office occupations ... 519
Farming, fishing & forestry ... 162
Construction & maintenance ... 359
Production & transportation ... 466
Self-employed persons ... 284

* US Census Bureau
** 2000 Decennial Census
§ California Department of Finance
§§ California Employment Development Dept

General Information

City of Fort Bragg
416 N Franklin St
Fort Bragg, CA 95437
707-961-2825

Website ... www.city.fortbragg.com
Elevation ... NA
Land Area (sq. miles) ... 2.7
Water Area (sq. miles) ... 0
Year of Incorporation ... 1889
Government type ... General law
Sales tax rate ... 8.75%

Voters & Officials

Registered Voters, October 2008

Total ... 3,503
Democrats ... 1,856
Republicans ... 643
Declined to state ... 721

Legislative Districts

US Congressional ... 1
State Senatorial ... 2
State Assembly ... 1

Local Officials, 2009

Mayor ... Doug Hammerstrom
Manager ... Linda Ruffing
City Clerk ... Cynthia VanWormer
Attorney ... Mike Gogna
Finance Dir ... Patricia Frost
Public Works ... David Goble
Community Dev Dir ... Marie Jones
Building ... (County)
Police Chief ... Mark Puthoff
Emergency/Fire Dir ... Steve Orsi

Public Safety

Number of officers, 2007 ... 14
Violent crimes, 2007 ... 42
Property crimes, 2007 ... 297
Arson, 2007 ... 4

Public Library

Fort Bragg Branch Library
Marin County Free Library System
499 Laurel St
Fort Bragg, CA 95437
707-964-2020

Branch Librarian ... Robin Watters

Library system statistics, FY 2007

Population served ... 90,291
Internet terminals ... 20
Annual users ... 37,258

Per capita:

Operating income ... $18.48
percent from local government ... 58.6%
Operating expenditure ... $19.03
Total materials ... 2.07
Print holdings ... 1.94
Visits per capita ... NA

Housing & Construction

Housing Units

Total, 2008§ ... 3,161
Single family units, attached ... 158
Single family units, detached ... 2,053
Multiple family units ... 787
Mobile home units ... 163
Occupied ... 2,942
Vacancy rate ... 6.9%
Median rent, 2000** ... $623
Median SF home value, 2000** ... $160,200

New Privately Owned Housing Units Authorized by Building Permit, 2007*

	Units	Construction Cost
Single	NA	NA
Total	NA	NA

Municipal Finance

(For local fiscal year ended in 2006)

Revenues

Total ... $12,415,066
Taxes ... 5,055,547
Special benefits assessment ... 46,611
Licenses & permits ... 91,075
Fines & forfeitures ... 51,201
Revenues from use of money & property ... 440,145
Intergovernmental ... 1,901,265
Service charges ... 2,589,867
Other revenues ... 326,900
Other financing sources ... 1,912,455

Expenditures

Total ... $13,307,100
General government ... 1,018,243
Public safety ... 3,440,229
Transportation ... 2,548,895
Community development ... 1,372,310
Health ... 2,434,014
Culture & leisure ... 992,439
Other ... 0

Local School District

(Data from School year 2007-08 except as noted)

Fort Bragg Unified
312 South Lincoln St
Fort Bragg, CA 95437
(707) 961-2850

Superintendent ... Donald Armstrong
Grade plan ... K-12
Number of schools ... 8
Enrollment ... 1,926
High school graduates, 2006-07 ... 113
Dropout rate ... 2.9%
Pupil/teacher ratio ... 16.1
Average class size ... 19.4
Students per computer ... 3.0
Classrooms with internet ... 220
Avg. Daily Attendance (ADA) ... 1,852
Cost per ADA ... $9,122
Avg. Teacher Salary ... $51,508

California Achievement Tests 6th ed., 2008

(Pct scoring at or above 50th National Percentile Rank)

	Math	Reading	Language
Grade 3	57%	48%	50%
Grade 7	45%	43%	38%

Academic Performance Index, 2008

Number of students tested ... 1,432
Number of valid scores ... 1,360
2007 API (base) ... 742
2008 API (growth) ... 766

SAT Testing, 2006-07

Enrollment, Grade 12 ... 140
Number taking test ... 61
percent taking test ... 43.6%
percent with total score 1,500+ ... 21.40%

Average Scores:

Math	Verbal	Writing	Total
508	517	531	1,556

Federal No Child Left Behind, 2008

(Adequate Yearly Progress standards met)

	Participation Rate	Pct Proficient
ELA	Yes	No
Math	Yes	No

API criteria ... Yes
Graduation rate ... Yes
criteria met/possible ... 22/20

Other school districts for this city

(see Appendix E for information on these districts)

None

Demographics & Socio-Economic Characteristics

(2000 Decennial Census, except as noted)

Population

1990* 639
2000 660
Male 312
Female 348
Jan. 2008 (estimate)§ 657
Persons per sq. mi. of land 1,095.0

Race & Hispanic Origin, 2000

Race
White 585
Black/African American 1
North American Native 21
Asian 0
Pacific Islander 3
Other Race 10
Two or more races 40
Hispanic origin, total 53
Mexican 43
Puerto Rican 0
Cuban 0
Other Hispanic 10

Age & Nativity, 2000

Under 5 years 44
18 years and over 504
65 years and over 146
85 years and over 21
Median Age 42.9
Native-born 693
Foreign-born 12

Educational Attainment, 2000

Population 25 years and over 483
Less than 9th grade 6.2%
High school grad or higher 82.0%
Bachelor's degree or higher 5.6%
Graduate degree 2.9%

Income & Poverty, 1999

Per capita income $15,301
Median household income $21,563
Median family income $25,625
Persons in poverty 27.7%
H'holds receiving public assistance 30
H'holds receiving social security 141

Households, 2000

Total households 298
With persons under 18 94
With persons over 65 110
Family households 186
Single person households 100
Persons per household 2.21
Persons per family 2.81

Household Population, 2008§§

Persons living in households 657
Persons living in group quarters 0
Persons per household 2.1

Labor & Employment

Total civilian labor force, 2008§§ .... NA
Unemployment rate, 2008 .... NA
Total civilian labor force, 2000 277

Employed persons 16 years and over by occupation, 2000

Managers & professionals 50
Service occupations 45
Sales & office occupations 75
Farming, fishing & forestry 16
Construction & maintenance 33
Production & transportation 20
Self-employed persons 35

* US Census Bureau
** 2000 Decennial Census
§ California Department of Finance
§§ California Employment Development Dept

General Information

Town of Fort Jones
11960 East St
PO Box 40
Fort Jones, CA 96032
530-468-2281

Email .... ftjones@sisqtel.net
Elevation .... 2,747 ft.
Land Area (sq. miles) 0.6
Water Area (sq. miles) 0
Year of Incorporation 1872
Government type .... General law
Sales tax rate 8.25%

Voters & Officials

Registered Voters, October 2008

Total 372
Democrats 115
Republicans 171
Declined to state 66

Legislative Districts

US Congressional 2
State Senatorial 4
State Assembly 2

Local Officials, 2009

Mayor .... Tom McCulley
Manager/Admin .... Linda Romaine
City Clerk .... Linda Romaine
Attorney .... Robert Winston
Treasurer .... Dianne Wilson
Public Works .... Ken Smith
Planning/Comm Dev .... NA
Building .... NA
Police Chief .... (County)
Fire Chief .... Terry Hayes

Public Safety

Number of officers, 2007 .... NA
Violent crimes, 2007 1
Property crimes, 2007 11
Arson, 2007 0

Public Library

Fort Jones Branch Library
Siskiyou County Free Library System
11960 East St
Fort Jones, CA 96032
530-468-2383

Branch Librarian .... Theresa Johnson

Library system statistics, FY 2007

Population served 45,953
Internet terminals 31
Annual users 48,766

Per capita:

Operating income $20.36
percent from local government 90.2%
Operating expenditure $20.12
Total materials 4.06
Print holdings 3.88
Visits per capita .... NA

Housing & Construction

Housing Units

Total, 2008§ 345
Single family units, attached 11
Single family units, detached 243
Multiple family units 36
Mobile home units 55
Occupied 315
Vacancy rate 8.7%
Median rent, 2000** $505
Median SF home value, 2000** $80,800

New Privately Owned Housing Units Authorized by Building Permit, 2007*

	Units	Construction Cost
Single	NA	NA
Total	NA	NA

Municipal Finance

(For local fiscal year ended in 2006)

Revenues

Total $652,260
Taxes 214,645
Special benefits assessment 900
Licenses & permits 140
Fines & forfeitures 2,491
Revenues from use of money & property 34,072
Intergovernmental 161,929
Service charges 226,040
Other revenues 12,043
Other financing sources 0

Expenditures

Total $771,190
General government 81,101
Public safety 204,857
Transportation 70,258
Community development 220,322
Health 23,387
Culture & leisure 72,126
Other 0

Local School District

(Data from School year 2007-08 except as noted)

Scotts Valley Unified Unified
PO Box 687
Fort Jones, CA 96032
(530) 468-2727

Superintendent .... Emily Houck
Grade plan K-12
Number of schools 11
Enrollment 699
High school graduates, 2006-07 0
Dropout rate .... NA
Pupil/teacher ratio 13.5
Average class size 16.2
Students per computer 2.4
Classrooms with internet 58
Avg. Daily Attendance (ADA) 651
Cost per ADA $12,062
Avg. Teacher Salary .... NA

California Achievement Tests 6th ed., 2008

(Pct scoring at or above 50th National Percentile Rank)

	Math	Reading	Language
Grade 3	71%	49%	58%
Grade 7	60%	69%	58%

Academic Performance Index, 2008

Number of students tested 533
Number of valid scores 510
2007 API (base) .... B
2008 API (growth) 799

SAT Testing, 2006-07

Enrollment, Grade 12 48
Number taking test 3
percent taking test 6.3%
percent with total score 1,500+ .... NA

Average Scores:

Math	Verbal	Writing	Total
NA	NA	NA	NA

Federal No Child Left Behind, 2008

(Adequate Yearly Progress standards met)

	Participation Rate	Pct Proficient
ELA	Yes	Yes
Math	Yes	Yes

API criteria .... Yes
Graduation rate .... NA
criteria met/possible 13/13

Other school districts for this city

(see Appendix E for information on these districts)

None

See Introduction for an explanation of all data sources.

Demographics & Socio-Economic Characteristics

(2000 Decennial Census, except as noted)

Population

1990*	8,788
2000	10,497
Male	5,013
Female	5,484
Jan. 2008 (estimate)§	11,374
Persons per sq. mi. of land	2,369.6

Race & Hispanic Origin, 2000

Race	
White	9,278
Black/African American	47
North American Native	305
Asian	102
Pacific Islander	18
Other Race	415
Two or more races	332
Hispanic origin, total	1,097
Mexican	931
Puerto Rican	14
Cuban	13
Other Hispanic	139

Age & Nativity, 2000

Under 5 years	723
18 years and over	7,763
65 years and over	1,814
85 years and over	275
Median Age	37.9
Native-born	9,680
Foreign-born	683

Educational Attainment, 2000

Population 25 years and over	6,800
Less than 9th grade	5.6%
High school grad or higher	81.3%
Bachelor's degree or higher	14.1%
Graduate degree	3.5%

Income & Poverty, 1999

Per capita income	$16,574
Median household income	$31,129
Median family income	$38,867
Persons in poverty	17.0%
H'holds receiving public assistance	209
H'holds receiving social security	1,516

Households, 2000

Total households	4,185
With persons under 18	1,449
With persons over 65	1,258
Family households	2,777
Single person households	1,175
Persons per household	2.45
Persons per family	2.98

Household Population, 2008§§

Persons living in households	11,108
Persons living in group quarters	266
Persons per household	2.4

Labor & Employment

Total civilian labor force, 2008§§	4,700
Unemployment rate, 2008	5.8%
Total civilian labor force, 2000	4,661

Employed persons 16 years and over by occupation, 2000

Managers & professionals	1,153
Service occupations	864
Sales & office occupations	989
Farming, fishing & forestry	196
Construction & maintenance	387
Production & transportation	753
Self-employed persons	473

* US Census Bureau
** 2000 Decennial Census
§ California Department of Finance
§§ California Employment Development Dept

General Information

City of Fortuna
621 11th St
Fortuna, CA 95540
707-725-7600

Website	www.sunnyfortuna.com
Elevation	61 ft.
Land Area (sq. miles)	4.8
Water Area (sq. miles)	0
Year of Incorporation	1906
Government type	Charter City
Sales tax rate	8.25%

Voters & Officials

Registered Voters, October 2008

Total	6,336
Democrats	2,276
Republicans	2,573
Declined to state	1,156

Legislative Districts

US Congressional	1
State Senatorial	2
State Assembly	1

Local Officials, 2009

Mayor	Patrick Whitchurch
City Manager	Duane Rigge
Senior Admin Asst	Linda Jensen
Attorney	Dave Tranberg
Finance Dir	Paul Rodriguez
Public Works	Dennis Ryan
Community Dev Dir	Liz Shorey (Dep)
Building	Gary Goade
Police Chief	Kris Kitna
Emergency/Fire Dir	Lon Winburn

Public Safety

Number of officers, 2007	14
Violent crimes, 2007	24
Property crimes, 2007	377
Arson, 2007	4

Public Library

Fortuna Library
Humboldt County Library System
775 14th St
Fortuna, CA 95540
707-725-3460

Branch Librarian	Chris Cooper

Library system statistics, FY 2007

Population served	131,959
Internet terminals	46
Annual users	20,083

Per capita:

Operating income	$22.91
percent from local government	90.6%
Operating expenditure	$18.80
Total materials	2.54
Print holdings	2.38
Visits per capita	4.15

Housing & Construction

Housing Units

Total, 2008§	4,839
Single family units, attached	235
Single family units, detached	3,229
Multiple family units	930
Mobile home units	445
Occupied	4,587
Vacancy rate	5.2%
Median rent, 2000**	$526
Median SF home value, 2000**	$130,700

New Privately Owned Housing Units Authorized by Building Permit, 2007*

	Units	Construction Cost
Single	19	$3,768,893
Total	47	$6,349,760

Municipal Finance

(For local fiscal year ended in 2006)

Revenues

Total	$9,084,026
Taxes	3,540,910
Special benefits assessment	49,843
Licenses & permits	155,133
Fines & forfeitures	92,982
Revenues from use of money & property	548,990
Intergovernmental	743,879
Service charges	3,832,864
Other revenues	119,425
Other financing sources	0

Expenditures

Total	$16,762,785
General government	506,801
Public safety	1,976,271
Transportation	1,179,212
Community development	1,170,041
Health	10,055,198
Culture & leisure	913,543
Other	0

Local School District

(Data from School year 2007-08 except as noted)

Fortuna Union High
379 12th St
Fortuna, CA 95540
(707) 725-4461

Superintendent	Gordon Dexter
Grade plan	9-12
Number of schools	4
Enrollment	1,232
High school graduates, 2006-07	218
Dropout rate	2.6%
Pupil/teacher ratio	21.4
Average class size	23.8
Students per computer	2.8
Classrooms with internet	81
Avg. Daily Attendance (ADA)	1,119
Cost per ADA	$8,720
Avg. Teacher Salary	$57,839

California Achievement Tests 6th ed., 2008

(Pct scoring at or above 50th National Percentile Rank)

	Math	Reading	Language
Grade 3	NA	NA	NA
Grade 7	NA	NA	NA

Academic Performance Index, 2008

Number of students tested	871
Number of valid scores	837
2007 API (base)	674
2008 API (growth)	699

SAT Testing, 2006-07

Enrollment, Grade 12	264
Number taking test	67
percent taking test	25.4%
percent with total score 1,500+	13.60%

Average Scores:

Math	Verbal	Writing	Total
528	513	506	1,547

Federal No Child Left Behind, 2008

(Adequate Yearly Progress standards met)

	Participation Rate	Pct Proficient
ELA	Yes	Yes
Math	No	Yes

API criteria	Yes
Graduation rate	Yes
# criteria met/possible	14/13

Other school districts for this city

(see Appendix E for information on these districts)

Fortuna Union Elem, Rohnerville Elem

See Introduction for an explanation of all data sources.

Demographics & Socio-Economic Characteristics

(2000 Decennial Census, except as noted)

Population

1990* 28,176
2000 28,803
Male 14,165
Female 14,638
Jan. 2008 (estimate)§ 30,308
Persons per sq. mi. of land 7,975.8

Race & Hispanic Origin, 2000

Race
White 17,087
Black/African American 602
North American Native 34
Asian 9,368
Pacific Islander 167
Other Race 355
Two or more races 1,190
Hispanic origin, total 1,531
Mexican 626
Puerto Rican 61
Cuban 37
Other Hispanic 807

Age & Nativity, 2000

Under 5 years 1,685
18 years and over 22,705
65 years and over 2,902
85 years and over 250
Median Age 38.1
Native-born 18,662
Foreign-born 10,141

Educational Attainment, 2000

Population 25 years and over 21,232
Less than 9th grade 1.5%
High school grad or higher 95.6%
Bachelor's degree or higher 59.8%
Graduate degree 24.2%

Income & Poverty, 1999

Per capita income $45,754
Median household income $95,279
Median family income $106,099
Persons in poverty 2.8%
H'holds receiving public assistance 107
H'holds receiving social security 1,919

Households, 2000

Total households 11,613
With persons under 18 3,715
With persons over 65 2,092
Family households 7,928
Single person households 2,739
Persons per household 2.47
Persons per family 2.97

Household Population, 2008§§

Persons living in households 30,221
Persons living in group quarters 87
Persons per household 2.5

Labor & Employment

Total civilian labor force, 2008§§ 16,900
Unemployment rate, 2008 .... 3.5%
Total civilian labor force, 2000 16,420

Employed persons 16 years and over by occupation, 2000

Managers & professionals 9,942
Service occupations 982
Sales & office occupations 3,967
Farming, fishing & forestry 7
Construction & maintenance 578
Production & transportation 575
Self-employed persons 1,152

* US Census Bureau
** 2000 Decennial Census
§ California Department of Finance
§§ California Employment Development Dept

General Information

City of Foster City
610 Foster City Blvd
Foster City, CA 94404
650-286-3200

Website .... www.fostercity.org
Elevation .... NA
Land Area (sq. miles) 3.8
Water Area (sq. miles) 16.2
Year of Incorporation 1971
Government type .... General law
Sales tax rate 9.25%

Voters & Officials

Registered Voters, October 2008

Total 17,100
Democrats 7,733
Republicans 3,976
Declined to state 4,910

Legislative Districts

US Congressional 12
State Senatorial 8
State Assembly 19

Local Officials, 2009

Mayor .... John Kiramis
City Manager .... James C. Hardy
City Clerk .... Therese L Calic
Attorney .... Jean Savaree
Finance Dir .... Ricardo Santiago
Public Works .... Ramon Towne
Community Dev Dir .... Richard Marks
Building .... Chuck Haney
Police Chief .... Craig Courtin
Fire Chief .... Tom Reaves

Public Safety

Number of officers, 2007 38
Violent crimes, 2007 22
Property crimes, 2007 481
Arson, 2007 4

Public Library

Foster City Library
San Mateo County Library System
1000 E Hillsdale Blvd
Foster City, CA 94404
650-574-4842

Branch Librarian .... Barbara Escoffier

Library system statistics, FY 2007

Population served 278,388
Internet terminals 26
Annual users 49,920

Per capita:

Operating income $90.21
percent from local government 63.5%
Operating expenditure $60.41
Total materials 2.65
Print holdings 2.16
Visits per capita 5.44

Housing & Construction

Housing Units

Total, 2008§ 12,477
Single family units, attached 2,464
Single family units, detached 4,808
Multiple family units 5,198
Mobile home units 7
Occupied 12,145
Vacancy rate 2.7%
Median rent, 2000** $1,620
Median SF home value, 2000** $566,500

New Privately Owned Housing Units Authorized by Building Permit, 2007*

	Units	Construction Cost
Single	0	$0
Total	0	$0

Municipal Finance

(For local fiscal year ended in 2006)

Revenues

Total $27,967,158
Taxes 9,612,570
Special benefits assessment 0
Licenses & permits 556,083
Fines & forfeitures 190,439
Revenues from use of money & property 2,196,247
Intergovernmental 1,816,337
Service charges 12,654,443
Other revenues 941,039
Other financing sources 0

Expenditures

Total $27,831,308
General government 2,568,888
Public safety 15,683,122
Transportation 577,527
Community development 3,744,332
Health 0
Culture & leisure 5,257,439
Other 0

Local School District

(Data from School year 2007-08 except as noted)

San Mateo Union High
650 North Delaware St
San Mateo, CA 94401
(650) 558-2299

Superintendent .... David Miller
Grade plan 9-12
Number of schools 7
Enrollment 8,626
High school graduates, 2006-07 1,833
Dropout rate 1.3%
Pupil/teacher ratio 21.3
Average class size 26.9
Students per computer 4.0
Classrooms with internet 425
Avg. Daily Attendance (ADA) 8,291
Cost per ADA $9,930
Avg. Teacher Salary $74,785

California Achievement Tests 6th ed., 2008

(Pct scoring at or above 50th National Percentile Rank)

	Math	Reading	Language
Grade 3	NA	NA	NA
Grade 7	NA	NA	NA

Academic Performance Index, 2008

Number of students tested 6,229
Number of valid scores 6,003
2007 API (base) 774
2008 API (growth) 781

SAT Testing, 2006-07

Enrollment, Grade 12 2,145
Number taking test 1,188
percent taking test 55.4%
percent with total score 1,500+ 37.60%

Average Scores:

Math	Verbal	Writing	Total
572	534	536	1,642

Federal No Child Left Behind, 2008

(Adequate Yearly Progress standards met)

	Participation Rate	Pct Proficient
ELA	Yes	No
Math	Yes	No

API criteria .... Yes
Graduation rate .... Yes
\# criteria met/possible 32/30

Other school districts for this city

(see Appendix E for information on these districts)

San Mateo-Foster City Elem

See Introduction for an explanation of all data sources.

Demographics & Socio-Economic Characteristics

(2000 Decennial Census, except as noted)

Population

1990* ... 53,691
2000 ... 54,978
Male ... 26,872
Female ... 28,106
Jan. 2008 (estimate)§ ... 57,925
Persons per sq. mi. of land ... 6,508.4

Race & Hispanic Origin, 2000

Race
White ... 35,196
Black/African American ... 611
North American Native ... 252
Asian ... 14,165
Pacific Islander ... 220
Other Race ... 2,172
Two or more races ... 2,362
Hispanic origin, total ... 5,870
Mexican ... 4,176
Puerto Rican ... 140
Cuban ... 128
Other Hispanic ... 1,426

Age & Nativity, 2000

Under 5 years ... 3,278
18 years and over ... 42,073
65 years and over ... 6,236
85 years and over ... 756
Median Age ... 38.1
Native-born ... 39,822
Foreign-born ... 15,173

Educational Attainment, 2000

Population 25 years and over ... 37,554
Less than 9th grade ... 4.0%
High school grad or higher ... 88.6%
Bachelor's degree or higher ... 34.4%
Graduate degree ... 11.3%

Income & Poverty, 1999

Per capita income ... $26,521
Median household income ... $69,734
Median family income ... $74,502
Persons in poverty ... 4.3%
H'holds receiving public assistance ... 469
H'holds receiving social security ... 4,146

Households, 2000

Total households ... 18,162
With persons under 18 ... 7,003
With persons over 65 ... 4,278
Family households ... 14,227
Single person households ... 2,912
Persons per household ... 3.00
Persons per family ... 3.35

Household Population, 2008§§

Persons living in households ... 57,413
Persons living in group quarters ... 512
Persons per household ... 3.1

Labor & Employment

Total civilian labor force, 2008§§ ... 33,700
Unemployment rate, 2008 ... 4.4%
Total civilian labor force, 2000 ... 28,802

Employed persons 16 years and over by occupation, 2000

Managers & professionals ... 12,047
Service occupations ... 2,808
Sales & office occupations ... 8,514
Farming, fishing & forestry ... 4
Construction & maintenance ... 1,779
Production & transportation ... 2,469
Self-employed persons ... 2,518

* US Census Bureau
** 2000 Decennial Census
§ California Department of Finance
§§ California Employment Development Dept

General Information

City of Fountain Valley
10200 Slater Ave
Fountain Valley, CA 92708
714-593-4400

Website ... www.fountainvalley.org
Elevation ... 28 ft.
Land Area (sq. miles) ... 8.9
Water Area (sq. miles) ... 0
Year of Incorporation ... 1957
Government type ... General law
Sales tax rate ... 8.75%

Voters & Officials

Registered Voters, October 2008

Total ... 36,107
Democrats ... 10,421
Republicans ... 17,214
Declined to state ... 7,056

Legislative Districts

US Congressional ... 46
State Senatorial ... 35
State Assembly ... 68

Local Officials, 2009

Council Member ... John J. Collins
City Manager ... Raymond Kromer
City Clerk ... Robin Roberts
Attorney ... Alan Burns
Finance Dir ... Elizabeth Fox
Public Works ... Mark Lewis
Planning/Dev Dir ... Andy Perea
Building ... Bill Walker
Police Chief ... Paul Sorrell
Emergency/Fire Dir ... Bill Walker

Public Safety

Number of officers, 2007 ... 62
Violent crimes, 2007 ... 111
Property crimes, 2007 ... 1,443
Arson, 2007 ... 5

Public Library

Fountain Valley Branch Library
Orange County Public Library System
17635 Los Alamos St
Fountain Valley, CA 92708
714-962-1324

Branch Librarian ... Jane Deely

Library system statistics, FY 2007

Population served ... 1,532,758
Internet terminals ... 505
Annual users ... 680,874

Per capita:

Operating income ... $24.71
percent from local government ... 90.0%
Operating expenditure ... $24.18
Total materials ... 1.93
Print holdings ... 1.84
Visits per capita ... 4.02

Housing & Construction

Housing Units

Total, 2008§ ... 18,785
Single family units, attached ... 2,200
Single family units, detached ... 12,393
Multiple family units ... 3,794
Mobile home units ... 398
Occupied ... 18,469
Vacancy rate ... 1.7%
Median rent, 2000** ... $1,058
Median SF home value, 2000** ... $289,500

New Privately Owned Housing Units Authorized by Building Permit, 2007*

	Units	Construction Cost
Single	5	$1,640,107
Total	52	$7,318,059

Municipal Finance

(For local fiscal year ended in 2006)

Revenues

Total ... $50,301,770
Taxes ... 26,272,996
Special benefits assessment ... 41,981
Licenses & permits ... 1,420,744
Fines & forfeitures ... 843,989
Revenues from use of money & property ... 2,466,188
Intergovernmental ... 3,508,493
Service charges ... 13,763,840
Other revenues ... 1,983,539
Other financing sources ... 0

Expenditures

Total ... $49,379,521
General government ... 3,359,629
Public safety ... 21,045,388
Transportation ... 7,830,782
Community development ... 1,700,077
Health ... 3,333,723
Culture & leisure ... 3,715,766
Other ... 0

Local School District

(Data from School year 2007-08 except as noted)

Huntington Beach Union High
5832 Bolsa Ave
Huntington Beach, CA 92649
(714) 903-7000

Superintendent ... Van Riley
Grade plan ... 9-12
Number of schools ... 9
Enrollment ... 16,052
High school graduates, 2006-07 ... 3,154
Dropout rate ... 1.3%
Pupil/teacher ratio ... 25.4
Average class size ... 23.4
Students per computer ... 3.8
Classrooms with internet ... 611
Avg. Daily Attendance (ADA) ... 15,841
Cost per ADA ... $8,287
Avg. Teacher Salary ... $76,735

California Achievement Tests 6th ed., 2008

(Pct scoring at or above 50th National Percentile Rank)

	Math	Reading	Language
Grade 3	NA	NA	NA
Grade 7	NA	NA	NA

Academic Performance Index, 2008

Number of students tested ... 11,830
Number of valid scores ... 11,519
2007 API (base) ... 763
2008 API (growth) ... 795

SAT Testing, 2006-07

Enrollment, Grade 12 ... 3,647
Number taking test ... 1,435
percent taking test ... 39.4%
percent with total score 1,500+ ... 25.50%

Average Scores:

Math	Verbal	Writing	Total
561	527	525	1,613

Federal No Child Left Behind, 2008

(Adequate Yearly Progress standards met)

	Participation Rate	Pct Proficient
ELA	No	No
Math	Yes	No

API criteria ... Yes
Graduation rate ... Yes
\# criteria met/possible ... 34/31

Other school districts for this city

(see Appendix E for information on these districts)

Fountain Valley Elem, Garden Grove Unified, Ocean View Elem

See Introduction for an explanation of all data sources.

Demographics & Socio-Economic Characteristics

(2000 Decennial Census, except as noted)

Population

1990*	3,208
2000	3,979
Male	1,944
Female	2,035
Jan. 2008 (estimate)§	5,573
Persons per sq. mi. of land	2,786.5

Race & Hispanic Origin, 2000

Race	
White	1,953
Black/African American	82
North American Native	64
Asian	222
Pacific Islander	3
Other Race	1,500
Two or more races	155
Hispanic origin, total	2,677
Mexican	2,361
Puerto Rican	6
Cuban	0
Other Hispanic	310

Age & Nativity, 2000

Under 5 years	317
18 years and over	2,669
65 years and over	475
85 years and over	78
Median Age	31.5
Native-born	3,225
Foreign-born	767

Educational Attainment, 2000

Population 25 years and over	2,124
Less than 9th grade	17.0%
High school grad or higher	64.3%
Bachelor's degree or higher	10.5%
Graduate degree	2.1%

Income & Poverty, 1999

Per capita income	$12,446
Median household income	$35,280
Median family income	$37,979
Persons in poverty	21.2%
H'holds receiving public assistance	86
H'holds receiving social security	337

Households, 2000

Total households	1,242
With persons under 18	620
With persons over 65	342
Family households	962
Single person households	243
Persons per household	3.16
Persons per family	3.65

Household Population, 2008§§

Persons living in households	5,480
Persons living in group quarters	93
Persons per household	3.2

Labor & Employment

Total civilian labor force, 2008§§	2,100
Unemployment rate, 2008	11.8%
Total civilian labor force, 2000	1,630

Employed persons 16 years and over by occupation, 2000

Managers & professionals	287
Service occupations	299
Sales & office occupations	338
Farming, fishing & forestry	87
Construction & maintenance	80
Production & transportation	325
Self-employed persons	73

* US Census Bureau
** 2000 Decennial Census
§ California Department of Finance
§§ California Employment Development Dept

General Information

City of Fowler
128 S Fifth St
Fowler, CA 93625
559-834-3113

Website	www.fowlercity.org
Elevation	NA
Land Area (sq. miles)	2.0
Water Area (sq. miles)	0
Year of Incorporation	1908
Government type	General law
Sales tax rate	8.98%

Voters & Officials

Registered Voters, October 2008

Total	2,134
Democrats	987
Republicans	815
Declined to state	229

Legislative Districts

US Congressional	20
State Senatorial	16
State Assembly	31

Local Officials, 2009

Mayor	Jim Simonian
City Manager	David Elias
City Clerk	Jeannie Davis
Attorney	David Wolfe
Finance Dir	Ronney Wong
Public Works	David Weisser
Planning/Dev Dir	Randy Deaver
Building	David Navarrette
Police Chief	Darrell Jamgochian
Emergency/Fire Dir.	Darrell Jamgochian

Public Safety

Number of officers, 2007	10
Violent crimes, 2007	9
Property crimes, 2007	219
Arson, 2007	1

Public Library

Fowler Branch Library
Fresno County Public Library System
119 E Merced St
Fowler, CA 93625
559-834-3114

Branch Librarian	NA

Library system statistics, FY 2007

Population served	889,019
Internet terminals	277
Annual users	861,240

Per capita:

Operating income	$23.69
percent from local government	89.3%
Operating expenditure	$23.37
Total materials	2.89
Print holdings	2.69
Visits per capita	NA

Housing & Construction

Housing Units

Total, 2008§	1,751
Single family units, attached	72
Single family units, detached	1,301
Multiple family units	333
Mobile home units	45
Occupied	1,703
Vacancy rate	2.7%
Median rent, 2000**	$416
Median SF home value, 2000**	$93,300

New Privately Owned Housing Units Authorized by Building Permit, 2007*

	Units	Construction Cost
Single	101	$13,640,930
Total	103	$13,824,445

Municipal Finance

(For local fiscal year ended in 2006)

Revenues

Total	$6,423,311
Taxes	2,896,968
Special benefits assessment	0
Licenses & permits	462,447
Fines & forfeitures	12,926
Revenues from use of money & property	45,920
Intergovernmental	1,105,467
Service charges	1,519,758
Other revenues	379,825
Other financing sources	0

Expenditures

Total	$5,628,725
General government	753,686
Public safety	1,120,447
Transportation	809,920
Community development	494,070
Health	362,333
Culture & leisure	51,796
Other	343,000

Local School District

(Data from School year 2007-08 except as noted)

Fowler Unified
658 East Adams Ave
Fowler, CA 93625
(559) 834-6080

Superintendent	John Cruz
Grade plan	K-12
Number of schools	7
Enrollment	2,293
High school graduates, 2006-07	142
Dropout rate	1.4%
Pupil/teacher ratio	20.3
Average class size	25.0
Students per computer	4.1
Classrooms with internet	222
Avg. Daily Attendance (ADA)	2,187
Cost per ADA	$8,187
Avg. Teacher Salary	$56,643

California Achievement Tests 6th ed., 2008

(Pct scoring at or above 50th National Percentile Rank)

	Math	Reading	Language
Grade 3	42%	33%	45%
Grade 7	53%	43%	41%

Academic Performance Index, 2008

Number of students tested	1,686
Number of valid scores	1,562
2007 API (base)	722
2008 API (growth)	731

SAT Testing, 2006-07

Enrollment, Grade 12	165
Number taking test	58
percent taking test	35.2%
percent with total score 1,500+	5.50%

Average Scores:

Math	Verbal	Writing	Total
431	421	428	1,280

Federal No Child Left Behind, 2008

(Adequate Yearly Progress standards met)

	Participation Rate	Pct Proficient
ELA	Yes	No
Math	Yes	No

API criteria	Yes
Graduation rate	Yes
# criteria met/possible	30/27

Other school districts for this city

(see Appendix E for information on these districts)

None

See Introduction for an explanation of all data sources.

Demographics & Socio-Economic Characteristics†

(2007 American Community Survey, except as noted)

Population

1990* . . . 173,339
2007 . . . 214,957
Male . . . 107,939
Female . . . 107,018
Jan. 2008 (estimate)§ . . . 213,512
Persons per sq. mi. of land . . . 2,783.7

Race & Hispanic Origin, 2007

Race
White . . . 80,730
Black/African American . . . 5,779
North American Native . . . 855
Asian . . . 103,476
Pacific Islander . . . 2,605
Other Race . . . 13,110
Two or more races . . . 8,402
Hispanic origin, total . . . 33,005
Mexican . . . 27,329
Puerto Rican . . . 835
Cuban . . . 257
Other Hispanic . . . 4,584

Age & Nativity, 2007

Under 5 years . . . 14,837
18 years and over . . . 158,348
65 years and over . . . 21,757
85 years and over . . . 3,358
Median Age . . . 37.0
Native-born . . . 122,351
Foreign-born . . . 92,606

Educational Attainment, 2007

Population 25 years and over . . . 143,363
Less than 9th grade . . . 4.7%
High school grad or higher . . . 91.0%
Bachelor's degree or higher . . . 51.2%
Graduate degree . . . 21.3%

Income & Poverty, 2007

Per capita income . . . $37,259
Median household income . . . $93,342
Median family income . . . $103,846
Persons in poverty . . . 4.5%
H'holds receiving public assistance . . . 990
H'holds receiving social security . . . 10,675

Households, 2007

Total households . . . 68,752
With persons under 18 . . . 32,662
With persons over 65 . . . 12,282
Family households . . . 53,758
Single person households . . . 11,146
Persons per household . . . 3.07
Persons per family . . . 3.49

Household Population, 2008§§

Persons living in households . . . 211,753
Persons living in group quarters . . . 1,759
Persons per household . . . 3.0

Labor & Employment

Total civilian labor force, 2008§§ . . . 111,500
Unemployment rate, 2008 . . . 4.4%
Total civilian labor force, 2000* . . . 106,368

Employed persons 16 years and over by occupation, 2007

Managers & professionals . . . 57,307
Service occupations . . . 11,976
Sales & office occupations . . . 23,730
Farming, fishing & forestry . . . 215
Construction & maintenance . . . 5,630
Production & transportation . . . 7,297
Self-employed persons . . . 6,495

† see Appendix D for 2000 Decennial Census Data
* US Census Bureau
** 2007 American Community Survey
§ California Department of Finance
§§ California Employment Development Dept

General Information

City of Fremont
3300 Capitol Avenue
PO Box 5006
Fremont, CA 94537-5006
510-284-4000

Website . . . www.fremont.gov
Elevation . . . 53 ft.
Land Area (sq. miles) . . . 76.7
Water Area (sq. miles) . . . 10.4
Year of Incorporation . . . 1956
Government type . . . General law
Sales tax rate . . . 9.75%

Voters & Officials

Registered Voters, October 2008

Total . . . 97,523
Democrats . . . 45,901
Republicans . . . 19,314
Declined to state . . . 28,640

Legislative Districts

US Congressional . . . 13
State Senatorial . . . 10
State Assembly . . . 20

Local Officials, 2009

Mayor . . . Robert Wasserman
Manager . . . Fred Diaz
City Clerk . . . Dawn Abrahamson
Attorney . . . Harvey Levine
Finance Dir . . . Harriet Commons
Public Works . . . Jim Pierson
Community Dev Dir . . . Jill Keimach
Building . . . NA
Police Chief . . . Craig Steckler
Fire Chief . . . Bruce Martin

Public Safety

Number of officers, 2007 . . . 190
Violent crimes, 2007 . . . 606
Property crimes, 2007 . . . 5,173
Arson, 2007 . . . 18

Public Library

Fremont Main Library
Alameda County Library System
2400 Stevenson Blvd
Fremont, CA 94538
510-745-1401

County Librarian . . . Jean Hofacket

Library system statistics, FY 2007

Population served . . . 527,926
Internet terminals . . . 193
Annual users . . . 358,689

Per capita:

Operating income . . . $41.07
percent from local government . . . 94.7%
Operating expenditure . . . $36.47
Total materials . . . 2.21
Print holdings . . . 1.91
Visits per capita . . . 4.32

Housing & Construction

Housing Units

Total, 2008§ . . . 72,059
Single family units, attached . . . 7,221
Single family units, detached . . . 42,466
Multiple family units . . . 21,616
Mobile home units . . . 756
Occupied . . . 70,799
Vacancy rate . . . 1.8%
Median rent, 2007** . . . $1,451
Median SF home value, 2007** . . . $688,700

New Privately Owned Housing Units Authorized by Building Permit, 2007*

	Units	Construction Cost
Single	192	$47,372,383
Total	402	$81,528,809

Municipal Finance

(For local fiscal year ended in 2006)

Revenues

Total . . . $169,921,022
Taxes . . . 112,782,365
Special benefits assessment . . . 2,976,949
Licenses & permits . . . 6,497,858
Fines & forfeitures . . . 2,815,070
Revenues from use of money & property . . . 8,830,721
Intergovernmental . . . 15,404,552
Service charges . . . 16,235,453
Other revenues . . . 4,378,054
Other financing sources . . . 0

Expenditures

Total . . . $164,877,965
General government . . . 14,769,450
Public safety . . . 91,607,682
Transportation . . . 15,489,318
Community development . . . 16,858,711
Health . . . 9,789,451
Culture & leisure . . . 16,363,353
Other . . . 0

Local School District

(Data from School year 2007-08 except as noted)

Fremont Unified
PO Box 5008
Fremont, CA 94537
(510) 657-2350

Superintendent . . . Milt Werner
Grade plan . . . K-12
Number of schools . . . 41
Enrollment . . . 31,948
High school graduates, 2006-07 . . . 2,161
Dropout rate . . . 1.6%
Pupil/teacher ratio . . . 21.1
Average class size . . . 26.5
Students per computer . . . 4.9
Classrooms with internet . . . 1,857
Avg. Daily Attendance (ADA) . . . 31,080
Cost per ADA . . . $8,031
Avg. Teacher Salary . . . $75,621

California Achievement Tests 6th ed., 2008

(Pct scoring at or above 50th National Percentile Rank)

	Math	Reading	Language
Grade 3	77%	58%	69%
Grade 7	76%	70%	69%

Academic Performance Index, 2008

Number of students tested . . . 24,532
Number of valid scores . . . 23,405
2007 API (base) . . . 836
2008 API (growth) . . . 850

SAT Testing, 2006-07

Enrollment, Grade 12 . . . 2,374
Number taking test . . . 1,384
percent taking test . . . 58.3%
percent with total score 1,500+ . . . 43.20%

Average Scores:

Math	Verbal	Writing	Total
603	557	564	1,724

Federal No Child Left Behind, 2008

(Adequate Yearly Progress standards met)

	Participation Rate	Pct Proficient
ELA	Yes	Yes
Math	Yes	Yes

API criteria . . . Yes
Graduation rate . . . Yes
criteria met/possible . . . 42/42

Other school districts for this city

(see Appendix E for information on these districts)

None

See Introduction for an explanation of all data sources.

Demographics & Socio-Economic Characteristics†

(2007 American Community Survey, except as noted)

Population

1990* 354,202
2007 476,460
Male 235,585
Female 240,875
Jan. 2008 (estimate)§ 486,171
Persons per sq. mi. of land 4,656.8

Race & Hispanic Origin, 2007

Race
White 255,936
Black/African American 37,716
North American Native 5,443
Asian 56,377
Pacific Islander 569
Other Race 102,279
Two or more races 18,140
Hispanic origin, total 207,432
Mexican 192,797
Puerto Rican 780
Cuban 278
Other Hispanic 13,577

Age & Nativity, 2007

Under 5 years 43,509
18 years and over 331,651
65 years and over 42,230
85 years and over 8,078
Median Age 29.1
Native-born 380,345
Foreign-born 96,115

Educational Attainment, 2007

Population 25 years and over 272,383
Less than 9th grade 12.9%
High school grad or higher 74.9%
Bachelor's degree or higher 19.8%
Graduate degree 6.4%

Income & Poverty, 2007

Per capita income $19,771
Median household income $44,513
Median family income $50,194
Persons in poverty 21.9%
H'holds receiving public assistance 13,826
H'holds receiving social security 32,430

Households, 2007

Total households 155,026
With persons under 18 67,491
With persons over 65 30,140
Family households 106,986
Single person households 37,415
Persons per household 3.02
Persons per family 3.64

Household Population, 2008§§

Persons living in households 477,402
Persons living in group quarters 8,769
Persons per household 3.1

Labor & Employment

Total civilian labor force, 2008§§ 229,200
Unemployment rate, 2008 ....9.9%
Total civilian labor force, 2000* 179,876

Employed persons 16 years and over by occupation, 2007

Managers & professionals 58,578
Service occupations 38,820
Sales & office occupations 55,470
Farming, fishing & forestry 4,047
Construction & maintenance 18,805
Production & transportation 26,001
Self-employed persons 13,293

† see Appendix D for 2000 Decennial Census Data
* US Census Bureau
** 2007 American Community Survey
§ California Department of Finance
§§ California Employment Development Dept

General Information

City of Fresno
2600 Fresno St
Fresno, CA 93721
559-621-7650

Website ....www.fresno.gov
Elevation ....296 ft.
Land Area (sq. miles) 104.4
Water Area (sq. miles) 0.4
Year of Incorporation 1885
Government type ....Chartered
Sales tax rate 8.98%

Voters & Officials

Registered Voters, October 2008

Total 202,648
Democrats 87,235
Republicans 79,183
Declined to state 23,540

Legislative Districts

US Congressional 19-21
State Senatorial 14, 16
State Assembly 29, 31

Local Officials, 2009

Mayor ....Ashley Swearingen
Manager ....Andy Souza
City Clerk ....Rebecca Klisch
Attorney ....James C. Sanchez
Finance Dir ....(vacant)
Public Works ....Patrick Weimiller
Planning/Dev Dir ....NA
Building ....NA
Police Chief ....Jerry Dyer
Emergency/Fire Dir ....Randy Bruegman

Public Safety

Number of officers, 2007 817
Violent crimes, 2007 3,043
Property crimes, 2007 20,969
Arson, 2007 222

Public Library

Central Library
Fresno County Public Library System
2420 Mariposa St
Fresno, CA 93721
559-488-3195

Director ....Karen Cobb

Library system statistics, FY 2007

Population served 889,019
Internet terminals 277
Annual users 861,240

Per capita:

Operating income $23.69
percent from local government 89.3%
Operating expenditure $23.37
Total materials 2.89
Print holdings 2.69
Visits per capita ....NA

Housing & Construction

Housing Units

Total, 2008§ 166,206
Single family units, attached 6,028
Single family units, detached 100,466
Multiple family units 55,789
Mobile home units 3,923
Occupied 156,225
Vacancy rate 6.0%
Median rent, 2007** $806
Median SF home value, 2007** $282,100

New Privately Owned Housing Units Authorized by Building Permit, 2007*

	Units	Construction Cost
Single	2,016	$314,839,970
Total	2,887	$379,301,492

Municipal Finance

(For local fiscal year ended in 2006)

Revenues

Total $584,047,003
Taxes 206,562,307
Special benefits assessment 0
Licenses & permits 10,350,977
Fines & forfeitures 1,868,313
Revenues from use of money & property 8,483,445
Intergovernmental 82,487,907
Service charges 230,395,865
Other revenues 19,847,162
Other financing sources 24,051,027

Expenditures

Total $521,351,095
General government 21,089,497
Public safety 182,727,252
Transportation 123,292,086
Community development 25,350,859
Health 80,013,763
Culture & leisure 38,341,587
Other 0

Local School District

(Data from School year 2007-08 except as noted)

Fresno Unified
2309 Tulare St
Fresno, CA 93721
(559) 457-3000

Superintendent ....Michael Hanson
Grade plan K-12
Number of schools 108
Enrollment 76,460
High school graduates, 2006-07 3,480
Dropout rate 7.9%
Pupil/teacher ratio 19.5
Average class size 25.1
Students per computer 3.9
Classrooms with internet 3,676
Avg. Daily Attendance (ADA) 69,774
Cost per ADA $9,413
Avg. Teacher Salary $64,816

California Achievement Tests 6th ed., 2008

(Pct scoring at or above 50th National Percentile Rank)

	Math	Reading	Language
Grade 3	42%	25%	34%
Grade 7	39%	33%	34%

Academic Performance Index, 2008

Number of students tested 54,887
Number of valid scores 49,980
2007 API (base) 670
2008 API (growth) 684

SAT Testing, 2006-07

Enrollment, Grade 12 4,029
Number taking test 1,220
percent taking test 30.3%
percent with total score 1,500+ 8.00%

Average Scores:

Math	Verbal	Writing	Total
457	440	436	1,333

Federal No Child Left Behind, 2008

(Adequate Yearly Progress standards met)

	Participation Rate	Pct Proficient
ELA	Yes	No
Math	Yes	No

API criteria ....Yes
Graduation rate ....Yes
\# criteria met/possible 46/39

Other school districts for this city

(see Appendix E for information on these districts)

Complete list in Appendix E

See Introduction for an explanation of all data sources.

Demographics & Socio-Economic Characteristics†

(2007 American Community Survey, except as noted)

Population

1990* . . . 114,144
2007 . . . 126,955
Male . . . 61,651
Female . . . 65,304
Jan. 2008 (estimate)§ . . . 137,437
Persons per sq. mi. of land . . . 6,190.9

Race & Hispanic Origin, 2007

Race
White . . . 64,285
Black/African American . . . 4,332
North American Native . . . 608
Asian . . . 26,862
Pacific Islander . . . 321
Other Race . . . 28,392
Two or more races . . . 2,155
Hispanic origin, total . . . 37,710
Mexican . . . 34,197
Puerto Rican . . . 170
Cuban . . . 222
Other Hispanic . . . 3,121

Age & Nativity, 2007

Under 5 years . . . 8,975
18 years and over . . . 95,846
65 years and over . . . 16,174
85 years and over . . . 2,505
Median Age . . . 36.7
Native-born . . . 89,873
Foreign-born . . . 37,082

Educational Attainment, 2007

Population 25 years and over . . . 81,293
Less than 9th grade . . . 4.9%
High school grad or higher . . . 90.0%
Bachelor's degree or higher . . . 41.0%
Graduate degree . . . 13.5%

Income & Poverty, 2007

Per capita income . . . $31,839
Median household income . . . $65,875
Median family income . . . $75,648
Persons in poverty . . . 8.2%
H'holds receiving public assistance . . . 668
H'holds receiving social security . . . 11,246

Households, 2007

Total households . . . 44,005
With persons under 18 . . . 15,697
With persons over 65 . . . 10,919
Family households . . . 30,740
Single person households . . . 9,998
Persons per household . . . 2.83
Persons per family . . . 3.39

Household Population, 2008§§

Persons living in households . . . 134,222
Persons living in group quarters . . . 3,215
Persons per household . . . 2.9

Labor & Employment

Total civilian labor force, 2008§§ . . . 72,600
Unemployment rate, 2008 . . . 5.9%
Total civilian labor force, 2000* . . . 62,938

Employed persons 16 years and over by occupation, 2007

Managers & professionals . . . 26,168
Service occupations . . . 6,195
Sales & office occupations . . . 18,206
Farming, fishing & forestry . . . 0
Construction & maintenance . . . 3,639
Production & transportation . . . 5,991
Self-employed persons . . . 4,826

† see Appendix D for 2000 Decennial Census Data
* US Census Bureau
** 2007 American Community Survey
§ California Department of Finance
§§ California Employment Development Dept

General Information

City of Fullerton
303 W Commonwealth Ave
Fullerton, CA 92832
714-738-6300

Website . . . www.ci.fullerton.ca.us
Elevation . . . 155 ft.
Land Area (sq. miles) . . . 22.2
Water Area (sq. miles) . . . 0
Year of Incorporation . . . 1904
Government type . . . General law
Sales tax rate . . . 8.75%

Voters & Officials

Registered Voters, October 2008

Total . . . 70,242
Democrats . . . 23,330
Republicans . . . 30,055
Declined to state . . . 13,951

Legislative Districts

US Congressional . . . 40, 47
State Senatorial . . . 33, 34
State Assembly . . . 72

Local Officials, 2009

Mayor . . . Don Bankhead
Manager . . . Chris Meyer
City Clerk . . . Beverley White
Attorney . . . Richard Jones
Finance Dir . . . Glenn Steinbrink
Public Works . . . NA
Planning/Dev Dir . . . John Godlewski
Building . . . NA
Police Chief . . . Patrick McKinley
Emergency/Fire Dir . . . Wolfgang Knabe

Public Safety

Number of officers, 2007 . . . 159
Violent crimes, 2007 . . . 467
Property crimes, 2007 . . . 4,128
Arson, 2007 . . . 21

Public Library

Fullerton Main Library
Fullerton Public Library System
353 W Commonwealth Ave
Fullerton, CA 92832
714-738-6380

Director . . . Maureen Gebelein

Library system statistics, FY 2007

Population served . . . 137,367
Internet terminals . . . 37
Annual users . . . 114,285

Per capita:

Operating income . . . $26.55
percent from local government . . . 91.0%
Operating expenditure . . . $26.03
Total materials . . . 2.42
Print holdings . . . 2.22
Visits per capita . . . 3.72

Housing & Construction

Housing Units

Total, 2008§ . . . 47,044
Single family units, attached . . . 3,862
Single family units, detached . . . 23,954
Multiple family units . . . 18,307
Mobile home units . . . 921
Occupied . . . 45,823
Vacancy rate . . . 2.6%
Median rent, 2007** . . . $1,218
Median SF home value, 2007** . . . $659,800

New Privately Owned Housing Units Authorized by Building Permit, 2007*

	Units	Construction Cost
Single	35	$6,524,779
Total	37	$6,672,224

Municipal Finance

(For local fiscal year ended in 2006)

Revenues

Total . . . $125,578,137
Taxes . . . 57,507,267
Special benefits assessment . . . 0
Licenses & permits . . . 1,793,201
Fines & forfeitures . . . 2,958,391
Revenues from use of money & property . . . 3,682,980
Intergovernmental . . . 10,793,191
Service charges . . . 46,721,491
Other revenues . . . 2,121,616
Other financing sources . . . 0

Expenditures

Total . . . $120,804,813
General government . . . 5,466,243
Public safety . . . 48,397,810
Transportation . . . 10,400,327
Community development . . . 7,159,347
Health . . . 11,653,737
Culture & leisure . . . 13,011,252
Other . . . 0

Local School District

(Data from School year 2007-08 except as noted)

Fullerton Joint Union High
1051 West Bastanchury Rd
Fullerton, CA 92833
(714) 870-2800

Superintendent . . . George Giokaris
Grade plan . . . 9-12
Number of schools . . . 8
Enrollment . . . 16,321
High school graduates, 2006-07 . . . 2,914
Dropout rate . . . 2.3%
Pupil/teacher ratio . . . 27.7
Average class size . . . 29.9
Students per computer . . . 3.7
Classrooms with internet . . . 724
Avg. Daily Attendance (ADA) . . . 15,436
Cost per ADA . . . $7,977
Avg. Teacher Salary . . . $82,860

California Achievement Tests 6th ed., 2008

(Pct scoring at or above 50th National Percentile Rank)

	Math	Reading	Language
Grade 3	NA	NA	NA
Grade 7	NA	NA	NA

Academic Performance Index, 2008

Number of students tested . . . 10,832
Number of valid scores . . . 10,168
2007 API (base) . . . 775
2008 API (growth) . . . 794

SAT Testing, 2006-07

Enrollment, Grade 12 . . . 2,962
Number taking test . . . 1,527
percent taking test . . . 51.6%
percent with total score 1,500+ . . . 32.20%

Average Scores:

Math	Verbal	Writing	Total
568	529	536	1,633

Federal No Child Left Behind, 2008

(Adequate Yearly Progress standards met)

	Participation Rate	Pct Proficient
ELA	Yes	No
Math	Yes	No

API criteria . . . Yes
Graduation rate . . . Yes
criteria met/possible . . . 34/32

Other school districts for this city

(see Appendix E for information on these districts)

Fullerton Elem, Placentia-Yorba Linda Unified

See Introduction for an explanation of all data sources.

Demographics & Socio-Economic Characteristics

(2000 Decennial Census, except as noted)

Population

1990* . . . 8,889
2000 . . . 19,472
Male . . . 9,636
Female . . . 9,836
Jan. 2008 (estimate)§ . . . 23,913
Persons per sq. mi. of land . . . 4,053.1

Race & Hispanic Origin, 2000

Race
White . . . 13,726
Black/African American . . . 225
North American Native . . . 204
Asian . . . 553
Pacific Islander . . . 31
Other Race . . . 3,616
Two or more races . . . 1,117
Hispanic origin, total . . . 6,465
Mexican . . . 5,649
Puerto Rican . . . 60
Cuban . . . 11
Other Hispanic . . . 745

Age & Nativity, 2000

Under 5 years . . . 1,737
18 years and over . . . 12,762
65 years and over . . . 1,653
85 years and over . . . 150
Median Age . . . 30.6
Native-born . . . 16,214
Foreign-born . . . 3,311

Educational Attainment, 2000

Population 25 years and over . . . 11,413
Less than 9th grade . . . 12.5%
High school grad or higher . . . 75.2%
Bachelor's degree or higher . . . 14.0%
Graduate degree . . . 2.7%

Income & Poverty, 1999

Per capita income . . . $16,620
Median household income . . . $45,052
Median family income . . . $47,845
Persons in poverty . . . 10.5%
H'holds receiving public assistance . . . 340
H'holds receiving social security . . . 1,342

Households, 2000

Total households . . . 5,974
With persons under 18 . . . 3,213
With persons over 65 . . . 1,167
Family households . . . 4,885
Single person households . . . 869
Persons per household . . . 3.23
Persons per family . . . 3.57

Household Population, 2008§§

Persons living in households . . . 23,725
Persons living in group quarters . . . 188
Persons per household . . . 3.2

Labor & Employment

Total civilian labor force, 2008§§ . . . 10,600
Unemployment rate, 2008 . . . 11.1%
Total civilian labor force, 2000 . . . 8,986

Employed persons 16 years and over by occupation, 2000

Managers & professionals . . . 1,963
Service occupations . . . 1,265
Sales & office occupations . . . 2,186
Farming, fishing & forestry . . . 283
Construction & maintenance . . . 1,067
Production & transportation . . . 1,293
Self-employed persons . . . 507

* US Census Bureau
** 2000 Decennial Census
§ California Department of Finance
§§ California Employment Development Dept

General Information

City of Galt
380 Civic Dr
Galt, CA 95632
209-366-7130

Website . . . www.ci.galt.ca.us
Elevation . . . 47 ft.
Land Area (sq. miles) . . . 5.9
Water Area (sq. miles) . . . 0
Year of Incorporation . . . 1946
Government type . . . General law
Sales tax rate . . . 9.25%

Voters & Officials

Registered Voters, October 2008

Total . . . 9,902
Democrats . . . 3,763
Republicans . . . 3,954
Declined to state . . . 1,759

Legislative Districts

US Congressional . . . 3
State Senatorial . . . 1
State Assembly . . . 15

Local Officials, 2009

Mayor . . . Randy Shelton
Manager . . . Ted Anderson
City Clerk . . . Elizabeth Aguire
Attorney . . . Steve Rudolph
Finance Dir . . . Inez Kiriu
Public Works . . . Gregg Halladay
Community Dev Dir . . . Curt Campion
Building . . . NA
Police Chief . . . Loren Cattolico
Fire Services . . . Steve Foster

Public Safety

Number of officers, 2007 . . . 32
Violent crimes, 2007 . . . 94
Property crimes, 2007 . . . 888
Arson, 2007 . . . 7

Public Library

Marian Lawrence Library
Sacramento Public Library System
1000 Caroline Ave
Galt, CA 95632
916-264-2770

Branch Librarian . . . Diane Christensen

Library system statistics, FY 2007

Population served . . . 1,335,969
Internet terminals . . . 49
Annual users . . . 27,435

Per capita:

Operating income . . . $25.83
percent from local government . . . 91.0%
Operating expenditure . . . $23.08
Total materials . . . 1.57
Print holdings . . . 1.45
Visits per capita . . . 1.18

Housing & Construction

Housing Units

Total, 2008§ . . . 7,630
Single family units, attached . . . 226
Single family units, detached . . . 6,210
Multiple family units . . . 822
Mobile home units . . . 372
Occupied . . . 7,339
Vacancy rate . . . 3.8%
Median rent, 2000** . . . $604
Median SF home value, 2000** . . . $135,300

New Privately Owned Housing Units Authorized by Building Permit, 2007*

	Units	Construction Cost
Single	46	$7,062,184
Total	46	$7,062,184

Municipal Finance

(For local fiscal year ended in 2006)

Revenues

Total . . . $36,433,893
Taxes . . . 15,415,440
Special benefits assessment . . . 788,999
Licenses & permits . . . 489,435
Fines & forfeitures . . . 91,687
Revenues from use of money & property . . . 4,578,843
Intergovernmental . . . 3,423,598
Service charges . . . 11,510,285
Other revenues . . . 135,606
Other financing sources . . . 0

Expenditures

Total . . . $27,900,477
General government . . . 3,404,485
Public safety . . . 5,225,299
Transportation . . . 3,974,675
Community development . . . 2,251,485
Health . . . 5,704,177
Culture & leisure . . . 5,696,088
Other . . . 86,674

Local School District

(Data from School year 2007-08 except as noted)

Galt Joint Union High
417 C St, Suite B
Galt, CA 95632
(209) 745-0249

Superintendent . . . Thomas Gemma
Grade plan . . . 9-12
Number of schools . . . 2
Enrollment . . . 2,475
High school graduates, 2006-07 . . . 435
Dropout rate . . . 2.3%
Pupil/teacher ratio . . . 22.5
Average class size . . . 26.2
Students per computer . . . 3.7
Classrooms with internet . . . 107
Avg. Daily Attendance (ADA) . . . 2,365
Cost per ADA . . . $7,765
Avg. Teacher Salary . . . $62,399

California Achievement Tests 6th ed., 2008

(Pct scoring at or above 50th National Percentile Rank)

	Math	Reading	Language
Grade 3	NA	NA	NA
Grade 7	NA	NA	NA

Academic Performance Index, 2008

Number of students tested . . . 1,784
Number of valid scores . . . 1,707
2007 API (base) . . . 731
2008 API (growth) . . . 726

SAT Testing, 2006-07

Enrollment, Grade 12 . . . 501
Number taking test . . . 136
percent taking test . . . 27.2%
percent with total score 1,500+ . . . 11.80%

Average Scores:

Math	Verbal	Writing	Total
494	478	471	1,443

Federal No Child Left Behind, 2008

(Adequate Yearly Progress standards met)

	Participation Rate	Pct Proficient
ELA	Yes	Yes
Math	Yes	Yes

API criteria . . . Yes
Graduation rate . . . Yes
\# criteria met/possible . . . 22/22

Other school districts for this city

(see Appendix E for information on these districts)

Galt Joint Union Elem

See Introduction for an explanation of all data sources.

Demographics & Socio-Economic Characteristics†

(2007 American Community Survey, except as noted)

Population

1990* . . . 143,050
2007 . . . 145,923
Male . . . 75,751
Female . . . 70,172
Jan. 2008 (estimate)§ . . . 173,067
Persons per sq. mi. of land . . . 9,614.8

Race & Hispanic Origin, 2007

Race
White . . . 57,814
Black/African American . . . 667
North American Native . . . 1,977
Asian . . . 45,598
Pacific Islander . . . 651
Other Race . . . 36,687
Two or more races . . . 2,529
Hispanic origin, total . . . 57,029
Mexican . . . 50,550
Puerto Rican . . . 856
Cuban . . . 342
Other Hispanic . . . 5,281

Age & Nativity, 2007

Under 5 years . . . 10,845
18 years and over . . . 107,326
65 years and over . . . 16,055
85 years and over . . . 2,108
Median Age . . . 35.3
Native-born . . . 86,685
Foreign-born . . . 59,238

Educational Attainment, 2007

Population 25 years and over . . . 93,134
Less than 9th grade . . . 13.2%
High school grad or higher . . . 71.7%
Bachelor's degree or higher . . . 19.9%
Graduate degree . . . 5.0%

Income & Poverty, 2007

Per capita income . . . $21,022
Median household income . . . $59,981
Median family income . . . $62,354
Persons in poverty . . . 9.4%
H'holds receiving public assistance . . . 1,045
H'holds receiving social security . . . 9,740

Households, 2007

Total households . . . 38,920
With persons under 18 . . . 17,016
With persons over 65 . . . 10,320
Family households . . . 30,639
Single person households . . . 6,797
Persons per household . . . 3.68
Persons per family . . . 4.09

Household Population, 2008§§

Persons living in households . . . 170,833
Persons living in group quarters . . . 2,234
Persons per household . . . 3.7

Labor & Employment

Total civilian labor force, 2008§§ . . . 86,400
Unemployment rate, 2008 . . . 6.6%
Total civilian labor force, 2000* . . . 74,424

Employed persons 16 years and over by occupation, 2007

Managers & professionals . . . 18,925
Service occupations . . . 11,754
Sales & office occupations . . . 16,968
Farming, fishing & forestry . . . 132
Construction & maintenance . . . 6,710
Production & transportation . . . 11,156
Self-employed persons . . . 4,680

† see Appendix D for 2000 Decennial Census Data
* US Census Bureau
** 2007 American Community Survey
§ California Department of Finance
§§ California Employment Development Dept

General Information

City of Garden Grove
PO Box 3070
Garden Grove, CA 92842
714-741-5000

Website . . . www.ci.garden-grove.ca.us
Elevation . . . 90 ft.
Land Area (sq. miles) . . . 18.0
Water Area (sq. miles) . . . 0
Year of Incorporation . . . 1956
Government type . . . General law
Sales tax rate . . . 8.75%

Voters & Officials

Registered Voters, October 2008

Total . . . 79,341
Democrats . . . 28,017
Republicans . . . 32,346
Declined to state . . . 16,005

Legislative Districts

US Congressional . . . 40, 46-47
State Senatorial . . . 34, 35
State Assembly . . . 67, 68, 69

Local Officials, 2009

Mayor . . . William J. Dalton
Manager . . . Matthew Fertal
City Clerk . . . Kathy Bailor
Attorney . . . Tom Nixon
Finance Dir . . . Kingsley Okereke
Public Works . . . Keith Jones
Planning/Dev Dir . . . Susan Emery
Building . . . NA
Police Chief . . . Joe Polisar
Fire Chief . . . David Bertka

Public Safety

Number of officers, 2007 . . . 165
Violent crimes, 2007 . . . 645
Property crimes, 2007 . . . 4,152
Arson, 2007 . . . 34

Public Library

Garden Grove Regional Library
Orange County Public Library System
11200 Stanford Ave
Garden Grove, CA 92840
714-530-0711

Branch Librarian . . . Su Chae

Library system statistics, FY 2007

Population served . . . 1,532,758
Internet terminals . . . 505
Annual users . . . 680,874

Per capita:

Operating income . . . $24.71
percent from local government . . . 90.0%
Operating expenditure . . . $24.18
Total materials . . . 1.93
Print holdings . . . 1.84
Visits per capita . . . 4.02

Housing & Construction

Housing Units

Total, 2008§ . . . 47,232
Single family units, attached . . . 4,492
Single family units, detached . . . 26,807
Multiple family units . . . 14,105
Mobile home units . . . 1,828
Occupied . . . 46,310
Vacancy rate . . . 2.0%
Median rent, 2007** . . . $1,206
Median SF home value, 2007** . . . $568,700

New Privately Owned Housing Units Authorized by Building Permit, 2007*

	Units	Construction Cost
Single	41	$8,733,189
Total	175	$24,982,643

Municipal Finance

(For local fiscal year ended in 2006)

Revenues

Total . . . $146,241,161
Taxes . . . 63,241,079
Special benefits assessment . . . 2,010,212
Licenses & permits . . . 1,545,260
Fines & forfeitures . . . 2,937,965
Revenues from use of money & property . . . 2,318,925
Intergovernmental . . . 18,646,485
Service charges . . . 54,322,006
Other revenues . . . 1,219,229
Other financing sources . . . 0

Expenditures

Total . . . $137,912,131
General government . . . 6,296,123
Public safety . . . 56,236,976
Transportation . . . 12,877,774
Community development . . . 33,888,027
Health . . . 637,235
Culture & leisure . . . 7,547,639
Other . . . 0

Local School District

(Data from School year 2007-08 except as noted)

Garden Grove Unified
10331 Stanford Ave
Garden Grove, CA 92840
(714) 663-6000

Superintendent . . . Laura Schwalm
Grade plan . . . K-12
Number of schools . . . 67
Enrollment . . . 48,669
High school graduates, 2006-07 . . . 2,803
Dropout rate . . . 1.2%
Pupil/teacher ratio . . . 23.1
Average class size . . . 26.9
Students per computer . . . 5.2
Classrooms with internet . . . 2,130
Avg. Daily Attendance (ADA) . . . 47,531
Cost per ADA . . . $8,420
Avg. Teacher Salary . . . $77,535

California Achievement Tests 6th ed., 2008

(Pct scoring at or above 50th National Percentile Rank)

	Math	Reading	Language
Grade 3	59%	31%	44%
Grade 7	58%	52%	52%

Academic Performance Index, 2008

Number of students tested . . . 37,558
Number of valid scores . . . 35,426
2007 API (base) . . . 767
2008 API (growth) . . . 778

SAT Testing, 2006-07

Enrollment, Grade 12 . . . 3,163
Number taking test . . . 1,156
percent taking test . . . 36.6%
percent with total score 1,500+ . . . 16.50%

Average Scores:

Math	Verbal	Writing	Total
521	480	480	1,481

Federal No Child Left Behind, 2008

(Adequate Yearly Progress standards met)

	Participation Rate	Pct Proficient
ELA	Yes	No
Math	Yes	No

API criteria . . . Yes
Graduation rate . . . Yes
\# criteria met/possible . . . 42/40

Other school districts for this city

(see Appendix E for information on these districts)

Orange Unified, Westminster Elem

See Introduction for an explanation of all data sources.

Demographics & Socio-Economic Characteristics

(2000 Decennial Census, except as noted)

Population

1990* . . . 49,847
2000 . . . 57,746
Male . . . 28,143
Female . . . 29,603
Jan. 2008 (estimate)§ . . . 61,781
Persons per sq. mi. of land . . . 10,651.9

Race & Hispanic Origin, 2000

Race
White . . . 13,755
Black/African American . . . 15,010
North American Native . . . 367
Asian . . . 15,489
Pacific Islander . . . 424
Other Race . . . 9,784
Two or more races . . . 2,917
Hispanic origin, total . . . 18,372
Mexican . . . 13,133
Puerto Rican . . . 401
Cuban . . . 196
Other Hispanic . . . 4,642

Age & Nativity, 2000

Under 5 years . . . 4,348
18 years and over . . . 42,832
65 years and over . . . 7,146
85 years and over . . . 687
Median Age . . . 34.4
Native-born . . . 38,832
Foreign-born . . . 18,986

Educational Attainment, 2000

Population 25 years and over . . . 38,196
Less than 9th grade . . . 11.1%
High school grad or higher . . . 74.0%
Bachelor's degree or higher . . . 16.6%
Graduate degree . . . 3.8%

Income & Poverty, 1999

Per capita income . . . $17,263
Median household income . . . $38,988
Median family income . . . $44,906
Persons in poverty . . . 15.5%
H'holds receiving public assistance . . . 1,347
H'holds receiving social security . . . 4,588

Households, 2000

Total households . . . 20,324
With persons under 18 . . . 7,777
With persons over 65 . . . 5,042
Family households . . . 14,031
Single person households . . . 5,191
Persons per household . . . 2.80
Persons per family . . . 3.38

Household Population, 2008§§

Persons living in households . . . 60,977
Persons living in group quarters . . . 804
Persons per household . . . 2.9

Labor & Employment

Total civilian labor force, 2008§§ . . . 30,000
Unemployment rate, 2008 . . . 7.0%
Total civilian labor force, 2000 . . . 25,823

Employed persons 16 years and over by occupation, 2000

Managers & professionals . . . 6,665
Service occupations . . . 3,795
Sales & office occupations . . . 7,132
Farming, fishing & forestry . . . 58
Construction & maintenance . . . 1,755
Production & transportation . . . 4,494
Self-employed persons . . . 1,407

* US Census Bureau
** 2000 Decennial Census
§ California Department of Finance
§§ California Employment Development Dept

General Information

City of Gardena
1700 W 162 S
PO Box 47003
Gardena, CA 90247
310-217-9500

Website . . . www.ci.gardena.ca.us
Elevation . . . 40 ft.
Land Area (sq. miles) . . . 5.8
Water Area (sq. miles) . . . 0
Year of Incorporation . . . 1930
Government type . . . General law
Sales tax rate . . . 9.25%

Voters & Officials

Registered Voters, October 2008

Total . . . 25,622
Democrats . . . 15,303
Republicans . . . 4,513
Declined to state . . . 4,837

Legislative Districts

US Congressional . . . 35
State Senatorial . . . 25
State Assembly . . . 51

Local Officials, 2009

Mayor . . . Paul K. Tanaka
City Manager . . . Mitchell Lansdell
City Clerk . . . Maria E. Marquez
Attorney . . . Peter Wallin
Finance Dir . . . D. Christine Hach
Public Works . . . Bruce Pollack
Planning/Dev Dir . . . (vacant)
Building . . . Ed Jafari
Police Chief . . . Edward Medrano
Fire Chief . . . Robert Valdillez

Public Safety

Number of officers, 2007 . . . 85
Violent crimes, 2007 . . . 448
Property crimes, 2007 . . . 1,428
Arson, 2007 . . . 9

Public Library

Gardena Mayme Dear Library
Los Angeles County Public Library System
1731 W Gardena Blvd
Gardena, CA 90247
310-323-6363

Comm Library Mgr . . . Ruth Morse

Library system statistics, FY 2007

Population served . . . 3,673,313
Internet terminals . . . 749
Annual users . . . 3,748,771

Per capita:

Operating income . . . $30.06
percent from local government . . . 93.6%
Operating expenditure . . . $28.36
Total materials . . . 2.22
Print holdings . . . 1.97
Visits per capita . . . 3.25

Housing & Construction

Housing Units

Total, 2008§ . . . 21,501
Single family units, attached . . . 1,714
Single family units, detached . . . 9,316
Multiple family units . . . 9,368
Mobile home units . . . 1,103
Occupied . . . 20,768
Vacancy rate . . . 3.4%
Median rent, 2000** . . . $710
Median SF home value, 2000** . . . $179,500

New Privately Owned Housing Units Authorized by Building Permit, 2007*

	Units	Construction Cost
Single	80	$16,673,000
Total	98	$19,716,000

Municipal Finance

(For local fiscal year ended in 2006)

Revenues

Total . . . $67,208,727
Taxes . . . 42,821,204
Special benefits assessment . . . 860,961
Licenses & permits . . . 666,724
Fines & forfeitures . . . 1,773,704
Revenues from use of money & property . . . 509,643
Intergovernmental . . . 8,228,178
Service charges . . . 6,682,229
Other revenues . . . 4,506,084
Other financing sources . . . 1,160,000

Expenditures

Total . . . $61,068,356
General government . . . 5,957,345
Public safety . . . 28,092,595
Transportation . . . 17,036,133
Community development . . . 5,662,128
Health . . . 342,133
Culture & leisure . . . 2,063,808
Other . . . 1,895,047

Local School District

(Data from School year 2007-08 except as noted)

Los Angeles Unified
333 South Beaudry Ave
Los Angeles, CA 90017
(213) 241-1000

Superintendent . . . Ramon Cortines
Grade plan . . . PK-12
Number of schools . . . 827
Enrollment . . . 693,680
High school graduates, 2006-07 . . . 28,545
Dropout rate . . . 7.8%
Pupil/teacher ratio . . . 19.8
Average class size . . . 24.9
Students per computer . . . 3.7
Classrooms with internet . . . 31,112
Avg. Daily Attendance (ADA) . . . 653,672
Cost per ADA . . . $10,053
Avg. Teacher Salary . . . $63,391

California Achievement Tests 6th ed., 2008

(Pct scoring at or above 50th National Percentile Rank)

	Math	Reading	Language
Grade 3	49%	27%	39%
Grade 7	37%	33%	33%

Academic Performance Index, 2008

Number of students tested . . . 495,046
Number of valid scores . . . 471,641
2007 API (base) . . . 662
2008 API (growth) . . . 683

SAT Testing, 2006-07

Enrollment, Grade 12 . . . 32,370
Number taking test . . . 15,447
percent taking test . . . 47.7%
percent with total score 1,500+ . . . 12.50%

Average Scores:

Math	Verbal	Writing	Total
443	438	441	1,322

Federal No Child Left Behind, 2008

(Adequate Yearly Progress standards met)

	Participation Rate	Pct Proficient
ELA	Yes	No
Math	Yes	No

API criteria . . . Yes
Graduation rate . . . Yes
\# criteria met/possible . . . 46/38

Other school districts for this city

(see Appendix E for information on these districts)

None

See Introduction for an explanation of all data sources.

Demographics & Socio-Economic Characteristics

(2000 Decennial Census, except as noted)

Population

1990* . . . 31,487
2000 . . . 41,464
Male . . . 20,656
Female . . . 20,808
Jan. 2008 (estimate)§ . . . 51,173
Persons per sq. mi. of land . . . 3,218.4

Race & Hispanic Origin, 2000

Race
White . . . 24,426
Black/African American . . . 745
North American Native . . . 661
Asian . . . 1,810
Pacific Islander . . . 105
Other Race . . . 11,499
Two or more races . . . 2,218
Hispanic origin, total . . . 22,298
Mexican . . . 19,226
Puerto Rican . . . 175
Cuban . . . 32
Other Hispanic . . . 2,865

Age & Nativity, 2000

Under 5 years . . . 3,903
18 years and over . . . 27,963
65 years and over . . . 2,815
85 years and over . . . 335
Median Age . . . 29.9
Native-born . . . 31,545
Foreign-born . . . 10,042

Educational Attainment, 2000

Population 25 years and over . . . 24,105
Less than 9th grade . . . 16.7%
High school grad or higher . . . 70.1%
Bachelor's degree or higher . . . 19.1%
Graduate degree . . . 5.8%

Income & Poverty, 1999

Per capita income . . . $22,071
Median household income . . . $62,135
Median family income . . . $65,330
Persons in poverty . . . 10.2%
H'holds receiving public assistance . . . 501
H'holds receiving social security . . . 2,093

Households, 2000

Total households . . . 11,869
With persons under 18 . . . 6,338
With persons over 65 . . . 2,038
Family households . . . 9,590
Single person households . . . 1,702
Persons per household . . . 3.46
Persons per family . . . 3.74

Household Population, 2008§§

Persons living in households . . . 50,743
Persons living in group quarters . . . 430
Persons per household . . . 3.5

Labor & Employment

Total civilian labor force, 2008§§ . . . 20,800
Unemployment rate, 2008 . . . 9.1%
Total civilian labor force, 2000 . . . 20,404

Employed persons 16 years and over by occupation, 2000

Managers & professionals . . . 5,511
Service occupations . . . 2,741
Sales & office occupations . . . 5,405
Farming, fishing & forestry . . . 622
Construction & maintenance . . . 2,095
Production & transportation . . . 2,885
Self-employed persons . . . 1,146

* US Census Bureau
** 2000 Decennial Census
§ California Department of Finance
§§ California Employment Development Dept

General Information

City of Gilroy
7351 Rosanna St
Gilroy, CA 95020
408-846-0400

Website . . . www.ci.gilroy.ca.us
Elevation . . . 200 ft.
Land Area (sq. miles) . . . 15.9
Water Area (sq. miles) . . . 0
Year of Incorporation . . . 1870
Government type . . . Chartered
Sales tax rate . . . 9.25%

Voters & Officials

Registered Voters, October 2008

Total . . . 18,234
Democrats . . . 9,127
Republicans . . . 4,923
Declined to state . . . 3,569

Legislative Districts

US Congressional . . . 15
State Senatorial . . . 13
State Assembly . . . 28

Local Officials, 2009

Mayor . . . Al Pinheiro
City Administrator . . . Thomas Haglund
City Clerk . . . Shawna Freels
Attorney . . . Linda Callon
Finance Dir . . . Christina Turner
Public Works . . . Carla Ruigh
Planning/Dev Dir . . . Wendie Rooney
Building . . . Kristi Abrams
Police Chief . . . Denise Turner
Emergency/Fire Dir . . . Dale Foster

Public Safety

Number of officers, 2007 . . . 60
Violent crimes, 2007 . . . 251
Property crimes, 2007 . . . 2,016
Arson, 2007 . . . NA

Public Library

Gilroy Library
Santa Clara County Library System
7387 Rosanna St
Gilroy, CA 95020
408-842-8208

Branch Librarian . . . Lani Yoshimura

Library system statistics, FY 2007

Population served . . . 419,141
Internet terminals . . . 133
Annual users . . . 650,000

Per capita:

Operating income . . . $77.89
percent from local government . . . 85.7%
Operating expenditure . . . $66.37
Total materials . . . 4.01
Print holdings . . . 3.27
Visits per capita . . . 6.16

Housing & Construction

Housing Units

Total, 2008§ . . . 14,853
Single family units, attached . . . 925
Single family units, detached . . . 9,991
Multiple family units . . . 3,506
Mobile home units . . . 431
Occupied . . . 14,509
Vacancy rate . . . 2.3%
Median rent, 2000** . . . $936
Median SF home value, 2000** . . . $344,100

New Privately Owned Housing Units Authorized by Building Permit, 2007*

	Units	Construction Cost
Single	175	$51,210,046
Total	216	$55,744,316

Municipal Finance

(For local fiscal year ended in 2006)

Revenues

Total . . . $72,167,530
Taxes . . . 36,494,966
Special benefits assessment . . . 0
Licenses & permits . . . 13,417
Fines & forfeitures . . . 0
Revenues from use of money & property . . . 3,872,165
Intergovernmental . . . 5,008,214
Service charges . . . 25,093,561
Other revenues . . . 1,685,207
Other financing sources . . . 0

Expenditures

Total . . . $81,462,557
General government . . . 5,518,988
Public safety . . . 24,641,801
Transportation . . . 10,012,323
Community development . . . 26,673,043
Health . . . 3,557,652
Culture & leisure . . . 5,819,610
Other . . . 0

Local School District

(Data from School year 2007-08 except as noted)

Gilroy Unified
7810 Arroyo Cir
Gilroy, CA 95020
(408) 847-2700

Superintendent . . . Deborah Flores
Grade plan . . . K-12
Number of schools . . . 16
Enrollment . . . 10,435
High school graduates, 2006-07 . . . 547
Dropout rate . . . 5.2%
Pupil/teacher ratio . . . 20.4
Average class size . . . 27.3
Students per computer . . . 4.5
Classrooms with internet . . . 491
Avg. Daily Attendance (ADA) . . . 10,033
Cost per ADA . . . $8,028
Avg. Teacher Salary . . . $63,661

California Achievement Tests 6th ed., 2008

(Pct scoring at or above 50th National Percentile Rank)

	Math	Reading	Language
Grade 3	58%	39%	45%
Grade 7	50%	43%	43%

Academic Performance Index, 2008

Number of students tested . . . 7,684
Number of valid scores . . . 7,134
2007 API (base) . . . 734
2008 API (growth) . . . 751

SAT Testing, 2006-07

Enrollment, Grade 12 . . . 688
Number taking test . . . 189
percent taking test . . . 27.5%
percent with total score 1,500+ . . . 11.60%

Average Scores:

Math	Verbal	Writing	Total
487	482	479	1,448

Federal No Child Left Behind, 2008

(Adequate Yearly Progress standards met)

	Participation Rate	Pct Proficient
ELA	Yes	No
Math	Yes	Yes

API criteria . . . Yes
Graduation rate . . . Yes
\# criteria met/possible . . . 34/33

Other school districts for this city

(see Appendix E for information on these districts)

None

See Introduction for an explanation of all data sources.

Demographics & Socio-Economic Characteristics†

(2007 American Community Survey, except as noted)

Population

1990* . . . 180,038
2007 . . . 200,859
Male . . . 95,449
Female . . . 105,410
Jan. 2008 (estimate)§ . . . 207,157
Persons per sq. mi. of land . . . 6,769.8

Race & Hispanic Origin, 2007

Race
White . . . 141,772
Black/African American . . . 4,819
North American Native . . . 1,309
Asian . . . 33,332
Pacific Islander . . . 237
Other Race . . . 17,220
Two or more races . . . 2,170
Hispanic origin, total . . . 33,093
Mexican . . . 20,525
Puerto Rican . . . 151
Cuban . . . 1,421
Other Hispanic . . . 10,996

Age & Nativity, 2007

Under 5 years . . . 9,259
18 years and over . . . 162,907
65 years and over . . . 29,267
85 years and over . . . 3,899
Median Age . . . 41.4
Native-born . . . 88,510
Foreign-born . . . 112,349

Educational Attainment, 2007

Population 25 years and over . . . 143,431
Less than 9th grade . . . 7.6%
High school grad or higher . . . 86.6%
Bachelor's degree or higher . . . 39.5%
Graduate degree . . . 12.4%

Income & Poverty, 2007

Per capita income . . . $28,716
Median household income . . . $51,719
Median family income . . . $62,914
Persons in poverty . . . 13.9%
H'holds receiving public assistance . . . 2,313
H'holds receiving social security . . . 14,127

Households, 2007

Total households . . . 72,951
With persons under 18 . . . 22,123
With persons over 65 . . . 20,294
Family households . . . 48,687
Single person households . . . 20,985
Persons per household . . . 2.72
Persons per family . . . 3.41

Household Population, 2008§§

Persons living in households . . . 204,293
Persons living in group quarters . . . 2,864
Persons per household . . . 2.8

Labor & Employment

Total civilian labor force, 2008§§ . . . 106,400
Unemployment rate, 2008 . . . 6.5%
Total civilian labor force, 2000* . . . 91,672

Employed persons 16 years and over by occupation, 2007

Managers & professionals . . . 39,496
Service occupations . . . 11,873
Sales & office occupations . . . 26,002
Farming, fishing & forestry . . . 57
Construction & maintenance . . . 7,585
Production & transportation . . . 10,380
Self-employed persons . . . 12,037

† see Appendix D for 2000 Decennial Census Data
* US Census Bureau
** 2007 American Community Survey
§ California Department of Finance
§§ California Employment Development Dept

General Information

City of Glendale
613 E Broadway
Glendale, CA 91206
818-548-4000

Website . . . www.ci.glendale.ca.us
Elevation . . . 571 ft.
Land Area (sq. miles) . . . 30.6
Water Area (sq. miles) . . . 0
Year of Incorporation . . . 1906
Government type . . . Chartered
Sales tax rate . . . 9.25%

Voters & Officials

Registered Voters, October 2008

Total . . . 89,218
Democrats . . . 35,621
Republicans . . . 28,201
Declined to state . . . 21,443

Legislative Districts

US Congressional . . . 29
State Senatorial . . . 21
State Assembly . . . 38, 43

Local Officials, 2009

Mayor . . . John Drayman
Manager . . . James Starbird
City Clerk . . . Ardashes Kassakhian
Attorney . . . Scott H. Howard
Finance Dir . . . Bob Elliot
Public Works . . . Steve Zurn
Planning/Dev Dir . . . Hassan Haghani
Building . . . Stuart Tom
Police Chief . . . Randy Adams
Fire/Emergency Mgmt . . . Harold Scoggins

Public Safety

Number of officers, 2007 . . . 261
Violent crimes, 2007 . . . 375
Property crimes, 2007 . . . 3,667
Arson, 2007 . . . 12

Public Library

Glendale Public Library
Glendale Public Library System
222 E Harvard St
Glendale, CA 91205
818-548-2021

Director . . . Cindy Cleary (Int)

Library system statistics, FY 2007

Population served . . . 207,157
Internet terminals . . . 83
Annual users . . . 223,176

Per capita:

Operating income . . . $38.79
percent from local government . . . 94.8%
Operating expenditure . . . $36.76
Total materials . . . 3.68
Print holdings . . . 3.38
Visits per capita . . . 5.49

Housing & Construction

Housing Units

Total, 2008§ . . . 74,799
Single family units, attached . . . 3,814
Single family units, detached . . . 26,114
Multiple family units . . . 44,774
Mobile home units . . . 97
Occupied . . . 72,863
Vacancy rate . . . 2.6%
Median rent, 2007** . . . $1,146
Median SF home value, 2007** . . . $720,300

New Privately Owned Housing Units Authorized by Building Permit, 2007*

	Units	Construction Cost
Single	23	$7,483,000
Total	610	$61,244,803

Municipal Finance

(For local fiscal year ended in 2006)

Revenues

Total . . . $465,056,207
Taxes . . . 98,949,450
Special benefits assessment . . . 11,351,529
Licenses & permits . . . 6,042,356
Fines & forfeitures . . . 2,998,395
Revenues from use of money & property . . . 14,861,701
Intergovernmental . . . 31,413,842
Service charges . . . 291,796,676
Other revenues . . . 7,642,258
Other financing sources . . . 0

Expenditures

Total . . . $524,754,754
General government . . . 15,665,404
Public safety . . . 105,216,711
Transportation . . . 49,034,769
Community development . . . 41,596,490
Health . . . 29,124,599
Culture & leisure . . . 31,464,369
Other . . . 0

Local School District

(Data from School year 2007-08 except as noted)

Glendale Unified
223 North Jackson St
Glendale, CA 91206
(818) 241-3111

Superintendent . . . Michael Escalante
Grade plan . . . K-12
Number of schools . . . 32
Enrollment . . . 27,035
High school graduates, 2006-07 . . . 2,090
Dropout rate . . . 1.5%
Pupil/teacher ratio . . . 21.0
Average class size . . . 27.6
Students per computer . . . 4.7
Classrooms with internet . . . 1,228
Avg. Daily Attendance (ADA) . . . 27,295
Cost per ADA . . . $8,270
Avg. Teacher Salary . . . $68,293

California Achievement Tests 6th ed., 2008

(Pct scoring at or above 50th National Percentile Rank)

	Math	Reading	Language
Grade 3	69%	46%	60%
Grade 7	67%	60%	62%

Academic Performance Index, 2008

Number of students tested . . . 21,324
Number of valid scores . . . 20,305
2007 API (base) . . . 807
2008 API (growth) . . . 818

SAT Testing, 2006-07

Enrollment, Grade 12 . . . 2,544
Number taking test . . . 1,102
percent taking test . . . 43.3%
percent with total score 1,500+ . . . 26.50%

Average Scores:

Math	Verbal	Writing	Total
557	507	516	1,580

Federal No Child Left Behind, 2008

(Adequate Yearly Progress standards met)

	Participation Rate	Pct Proficient
ELA	Yes	No
Math	Yes	No

API criteria . . . Yes
Graduation rate . . . Yes
\# criteria met/possible . . . 38/36

Other school districts for this city

(see Appendix E for information on these districts)

None

See Introduction for an explanation of all data sources.

Demographics & Socio-Economic Characteristics

(2000 Decennial Census, except as noted)

Population

1990* ... 47,828
2000 ... 49,415
Male ... 23,844
Female ... 25,571
Jan. 2008 (estimate)§ ... 52,362
Persons per sq. mi. of land ... 2,741.5

Race & Hispanic Origin, 2000

Race
White ... 39,681
Black/African American ... 740
North American Native ... 321
Asian ... 3,064
Pacific Islander ... 38
Other Race ... 3,579
Two or more races ... 1,992
Hispanic origin, total ... 10,740
Mexican ... 7,871
Puerto Rican ... 173
Cuban ... 199
Other Hispanic ... 2,497

Age & Nativity, 2000

Under 5 years ... 3,103
18 years and over ... 35,766
65 years and over ... 6,183
85 years and over ... 736
Median Age ... 36.9
Native-born ... 42,685
Foreign-born ... 7,034

Educational Attainment, 2000

Population 25 years and over ... 32,253
Less than 9th grade ... 4.1%
High school grad or higher ... 87.1%
Bachelor's degree or higher ... 25.7%
Graduate degree ... 9.1%

Income & Poverty, 1999

Per capita income ... $25,993
Median household income ... $60,013
Median family income ... $66,674
Persons in poverty ... 5.8%
H'holds receiving public assistance ... 372
H'holds receiving social security ... 4,123

Households, 2000

Total households ... 16,819
With persons under 18 ... 7,101
With persons over 65 ... 4,146
Family households ... 12,861
Single person households ... 3,206
Persons per household ... 2.88
Persons per family ... 3.30

Household Population, 2008§§

Persons living in households ... 51,349
Persons living in group quarters ... 1,013
Persons per household ... 3.0

Labor & Employment

Total civilian labor force, 2008§§ ... 28,800
Unemployment rate, 2008 ... 3.8%
Total civilian labor force, 2000 ... 24,756

Employed persons 16 years and over by occupation, 2000

Managers & professionals ... 9,470
Service occupations ... 2,921
Sales & office occupations ... 6,810
Farming, fishing & forestry ... 58
Construction & maintenance ... 2,104
Production & transportation ... 2,348
Self-employed persons ... 1,917

* US Census Bureau
** 2000 Decennial Census
§ California Department of Finance
§§ California Employment Development Dept

General Information

City of Glendora
116 E Foothill Blvd
Glendora, CA 91741
626-914-8200

Website ... www.ci.glendora.ca.us
Elevation ... 776 ft.
Land Area (sq. miles) ... 19.1
Water Area (sq. miles) ... 0.1
Year of Incorporation ... 1911
Government type ... General law
Sales tax rate ... 9.25%

Voters & Officials

Registered Voters, October 2008

Total ... 29,658
Democrats ... 8,917
Republicans ... 14,604
Declined to state ... 4,856

Legislative Districts

US Congressional ... 26
State Senatorial ... 29
State Assembly ... 59

Local Officials, 2009

Mayor ... Karen K. Davies
Manager ... Chris Jeffers
City Clerk ... Kathleen R. Sessman
Attorney ... D. Wayne Leech
Finance Dir ... Josh Betta
Public Works ... Dave Davies (Actg)
Planning/Dev Dir ... Jeff Kugel
Building ... Dave Davies
Police Chief ... Charles Montoya
Fire/Emergency Mgmt ... NA

Public Safety

Number of officers, 2007 ... 59
Violent crimes, 2007 ... 83
Property crimes, 2007 ... 1,494
Arson, 2007 ... 16

Public Library

Glendora Library & Cultural Center
140 S Glendora Ave
Glendora, CA 91741
626-852-4891

Director ... Robin Weed-Brown

Library statistics, FY 2007

Population served ... 52,557
Internet terminals ... 15
Annual users ... 40,545

Per capita:

Operating income ... $42.91
percent from local government ... 92.2%
Operating expenditure ... $39.68
Total materials ... 2.78
Print holdings ... 2.28
Visits per capita ... 5.06

Housing & Construction

Housing Units

Total, 2008§ ... 17,354
Single family units, attached ... 1,094
Single family units, detached ... 12,639
Multiple family units ... 2,778
Mobile home units ... 843
Occupied ... 17,024
Vacancy rate ... 1.9%
Median rent, 2000** ... $822
Median SF home value, 2000** ... $225,000

New Privately Owned Housing Units Authorized by Building Permit, 2007*

	Units	Construction Cost
Single	15	$3,135,847
Total	18	$3,630,994

Municipal Finance

(For local fiscal year ended in 2006)

Revenues

Total ... $50,614,337
Taxes ... 17,840,307
Special benefits assessment ... 365,484
Licenses & permits ... 851,973
Fines & forfeitures ... 550,289
Revenues from use of money & property ... 2,561,423
Intergovernmental ... 3,227,905
Service charges ... 12,793,236
Other revenues ... 3,720
Other financing sources ... 12,420,000

Expenditures

Total ... $42,320,127
General government ... 2,050,217
Public safety ... 11,860,939
Transportation ... 5,408,449
Community development ... 2,612,782
Health ... 3,658
Culture & leisure ... 5,842,171
Other ... 0

Local School District

(Data from School year 2007-08 except as noted)

Glendora Unified
500 North Loraine Ave
Glendora, CA 91741
(626) 963-1611

Superintendent ... Catherine Nichols
Grade plan ... K-12
Number of schools ... 10
Enrollment ... 7,328
High school graduates, 2006-07 ... 688
Dropout rate ... 1.1%
Pupil/teacher ratio ... 23.2
Average class size ... 27.4
Students per computer ... 4.5
Classrooms with internet ... 346
Avg. Daily Attendance (ADA) ... 7,296
Cost per ADA ... $7,688
Avg. Teacher Salary ... $70,409

California Achievement Tests 6th ed., 2008

(Pct scoring at or above 50th National Percentile Rank)

	Math	Reading	Language
Grade 3	78%	60%	72%
Grade 7	81%	71%	70%

Academic Performance Index, 2008

Number of students tested ... 5,680
Number of valid scores ... 5,506
2007 API (base) ... 828
2008 API (growth) ... 839

SAT Testing, 2006-07

Enrollment, Grade 12 ... 692
Number taking test ... 350
percent taking test ... 50.6%
percent with total score 1,500+ ... 26.50%

Average Scores:

Math	Verbal	Writing	Total
528	511	505	1,544

Federal No Child Left Behind, 2008

(Adequate Yearly Progress standards met)

	Participation Rate	Pct Proficient
ELA	Yes	Yes
Math	Yes	Yes

API criteria ... Yes
Graduation rate ... Yes
\# criteria met/possible ... 34/34

Other school districts for this city

(see Appendix E for information on these districts)

Azusa Unified, Charter Oak Unified

See Introduction for an explanation of all data sources.

Demographics & Socio-Economic Characteristics

(2000 Decennial Census, except as noted)

Population

1990* .... NA
2000 55,204
Male 27,380
Female 27,824
Jan. 2008 (estimate)§ 30,400
Persons per sq. mi. of land 1,155.9

Race & Hispanic Origin, 2000

Race
White 43,397
Black/African American 703
North American Native 451
Asian 3,548
Pacific Islander 60
Other Race 5,098
Two or more races 1,947
Hispanic origin, total 12,326
Mexican 10,351
Puerto Rican 118
Cuban 54
Other Hispanic 1,803

Age & Nativity, 2000

Under 5 years 3,121
18 years and over 42,454
65 years and over 8,042
85 years and over 870
Median Age 38.2
Native-born 45,513
Foreign-born 9,854

Educational Attainment, 2000

Population 25 years and over 37,454
Less than 9th grade 4.9%
High school grad or higher 87.8%
Bachelor's degree or higher 39.0%
Graduate degree 15.7%

Income & Poverty, 1999

Per capita income $28,890
Median household income $60,314
Median family income $67,956
Persons in poverty 6.7%
H'holds receiving public assistance 283
H'holds receiving social security 5,811

Households, 2000

Total households 19,954
With persons under 18 6,701
With persons over 65 5,574
Family households 13,467
Single person households 4,489
Persons per household 2.72
Persons per family 3.18

Household Population, 2008§§

Persons living in households 30,058
Persons living in group quarters 342
Persons per household 2.7

Labor & Employment

Total civilian labor force, 2008§§ 17,600
Unemployment rate, 2008 .... 2.6%
Total civilian labor force, 2000 .... NA

Employed persons 16 years and over by occupation, 2000

Managers & professionals 12,645
Service occupations 3,772
Sales & office occupations 6,766
Farming, fishing & forestry 328
Construction & maintenance 2,082
Production & transportation 2,512
Self-employed persons 3,229

* US Census Bureau
** 2000 Decennial Census
§ California Department of Finance
§§ California Employment Development Dept

General Information

City of Goleta
130 Cremona Dr
Suite B
Goleta, CA 93117
805-961-7500

Website .... www.cityofgoleta.org
Elevation .... NA
Land Area (sq. miles) 26.3
Water Area (sq. miles) 0.1
Year of Incorporation 2002
Government type .... General law
Sales tax rate 8.75%

Voters & Officials

Registered Voters, October 2008

Total 16,715
Democrats 7,529
Republicans 4,910
Declined to state 3,510

Legislative Districts

US Congressional 23
State Senatorial 18
State Assembly 35

Local Officials, 2009

Mayor .... Roger S. Aceves
Manager .... Daniel Singer
City Clerk .... Deborah S. Constantino
Attorney .... Tim W. Giles
Finance Dir .... Tina Rivera
Public Works .... Steve Wagner
Planning/Dev Dir .... Steve Chase
Building .... Steve Chase
Police Chief .... Phil Willis
Emergency/Fire Dir .... Randy Coleman

Public Safety

Number of officers, 2007 .... NA
Violent crimes, 2007 53
Property crimes, 2007 377
Arson, 2007 0

Public Library

Goleta Library
Santa Barbara Public Library
500 N Fairview Ave
Goleta, CA 93117
805-964-7878

Supervisor .... Pamela Bury

Library system statistics, FY 2007

Population served 233,434
Internet terminals 86
Annual users 66,000

Per capita:

Operating income $25.05
percent from local government 84.4%
Operating expenditure $27.43
Total materials 1.73
Print holdings 1.48
Visits per capita 12.44

Housing & Construction

Housing Units

Total, 2008§ 11,516
Single family units, attached 1,588
Single family units, detached 5,870
Multiple family units 3,437
Mobile home units 621
Occupied 11,231
Vacancy rate 2.5%
Median rent, 2000** $989
Median SF home value, 2000** $425,700

New Privately Owned Housing Units Authorized by Building Permit, 2007*

	Units	Construction Cost
Single	14	$3,150,000
Total	14	$3,150,000

Municipal Finance

(For local fiscal year ended in 2006)

Revenues

Total $23,173,284
Taxes 15,709,635
Special benefits assessment 295,690
Licenses & permits 410,223
Fines & forfeitures 201,787
Revenues from use of money & property 539,838
Intergovernmental 4,886,236
Service charges 966,280
Other revenues 163,595
Other financing sources 0

Expenditures

Total $19,409,057
General government 3,880,259
Public safety 5,518,619
Transportation 4,810,988
Community development 3,688,991
Health 326,563
Culture & leisure 1,183,637
Other 0

Local School District

(Data from School year 2007-08 except as noted)
‡combined elementary and high school data

Santa Barbara High
720 Santa Barbara St
Santa Barbara, CA 93101
(805) 963-4331

Superintendent .... J. Sarvis
Grade plan 6-12
Number of schools 13
Enrollment 10,196
High school graduates, 2006-07 1,468
Dropout rate 2.8%
Pupil/teacher ratio 26.0
Average class size 26.7
Students per computer 4.9
Classrooms with internet 453
Avg. Daily Attendance (ADA)‡ 14,151
Cost per ADA‡ $8,313
Avg. Teacher Salary‡ $64,731

California Achievement Tests 6th ed., 2008

(Pct scoring at or above 50th National Percentile Rank)

	Math	Reading	Language
Grade 3	NA	NA	NA
Grade 7	62%	60%	60%

Academic Performance Index, 2008

Number of students tested 8,121
Number of valid scores 7,830
2007 API (base) 753
2008 API (growth) 771

SAT Testing, 2006-07

Enrollment, Grade 12 1,738
Number taking test 836
percent taking test 48.1%
percent with total score 1,500+ 32.40%

Average Scores:

Math	Verbal	Writing	Total
560	547	537	1,644

Federal No Child Left Behind, 2008

(Adequate Yearly Progress standards met)

	Participation Rate	Pct Proficient
ELA	Yes	No
Math	Yes	No

API criteria .... Yes
Graduation rate .... Yes
\# criteria met/possible 34/28

Other school districts for this city

(see Appendix E for information on these districts)

Goleta Union Elem

See Introduction for an explanation of all data sources.

Demographics & Socio-Economic Characteristics

(2000 Decennial Census, except as noted)

Population

1990* . . . 4,660
2000 . . . 7,525
Male . . . 3,913
Female . . . 3,612
Jan. 2008 (estimate)§ . . . 8,803
Persons per sq. mi. of land . . . 6,287.9

Race & Hispanic Origin, 2000

Race
White . . . 2,617
Black/African American . . . 60
North American Native . . . 106
Asian . . . 154
Pacific Islander . . . 13
Other Race . . . 4,213
Two or more races . . . 362
Hispanic origin, total . . . 6,474
Mexican . . . 5,623
Puerto Rican . . . 47
Cuban . . . 6
Other Hispanic . . . 798

Age & Nativity, 2000

Under 5 years . . . 775
18 years and over . . . 4,683
65 years and over . . . 431
85 years and over . . . 46
Median Age . . . 24.5
Native-born . . . 4,618
Foreign-born . . . 3,108

Educational Attainment, 2000

Population 25 years and over . . . 3,696
Less than 9th grade . . . 36.7%
High school grad or higher . . . 46.1%
Bachelor's degree or higher . . . 7.2%
Graduate degree . . . 1.7%

Income & Poverty, 1999

Per capita income . . . $12,438
Median household income . . . $41,582
Median family income . . . $41,773
Persons in poverty . . . 20.7%
H'holds receiving public assistance . . . 145
H'holds receiving social security . . . 325

Households, 2000

Total households . . . 1,695
With persons under 18 . . . 1,163
With persons over 65 . . . 322
Family households . . . 1,502
Single person households . . . 157
Persons per household . . . 4.42
Persons per family . . . 4.61

Household Population, 2008§§

Persons living in households . . . 8,730
Persons living in group quarters . . . 73
Persons per household . . . 4.4

Labor & Employment

Total civilian labor force, 2008§§ . . . 4,000
Unemployment rate, 2008 . . . 16.0%
Total civilian labor force, 2000 . . . 3,367

Employed persons 16 years and over by occupation, 2000

Managers & professionals . . . 373
Service occupations . . . 449
Sales & office occupations . . . 558
Farming, fishing & forestry . . . 664
Construction & maintenance . . . 194
Production & transportation . . . 575
Self-employed persons . . . 114

* US Census Bureau
** 2000 Decennial Census
§ California Department of Finance
§§ California Employment Development Dept

General Information

City of Gonzales
147 Fourth St
PO Box 647
Gonzales, CA 93926
831-675-5000

Website . . . www.ci.gonzales.ca.us
Elevation . . . NA
Land Area (sq. miles) . . . 1.4
Water Area (sq. miles) . . . 0
Year of Incorporation . . . 1947
Government type . . . General law
Sales tax rate . . . 8.25%

Voters & Officials

Registered Voters, October 2008

Total . . . 2,517
Democrats . . . 1,517
Republicans . . . 466
Declined to state . . . 451

Legislative Districts

US Congressional . . . 17
State Senatorial . . . 12
State Assembly . . . 28

Local Officials, 2009

Mayor . . . Maria Orozco
Manager . . . Rene L. Mendez
City Clerk . . . Rene L. Mendez
Attorney . . . Michael Rodriquez
Finance Dir . . . NA
Public Works . . . Carlos Lopez
Planning/Dev Dir . . . Bill Farrel
Building . . . Michael Lechman
Police Chief . . . Paul Miller
Fire Chief . . . Rick Rubbo

Public Safety

Number of officers, 2007 . . . 14
Violent crimes, 2007 . . . 38
Property crimes, 2007 . . . 289
Arson, 2007 . . . 0

Public Library

Gonzales Branch Library
Monterey County Free Libraries
851 V 5th St
Gonzales, CA 93926
831-675-2209

Branch Librarian . . . Elizabeth Lopez

Library system statistics, FY 2007

Population served . . . 226,803
Internet terminals . . . 160
Annual users . . . 229,676

Per capita:

Operating income . . . $29.19
percent from local government . . . 91.7%
Operating expenditure . . . $27.42
Total materials . . . 1.92
Print holdings . . . 1.81
Visits per capita . . . 3.65

Housing & Construction

Housing Units

Total, 2008§ . . . 2,023
Single family units, attached . . . 133
Single family units, detached . . . 1,474
Multiple family units . . . 374
Mobile home units . . . 42
Occupied . . . 1,989
Vacancy rate . . . 1.7%
Median rent, 2000** . . . $676
Median SF home value, 2000** . . . $163,400

New Privately Owned Housing Units Authorized by Building Permit, 2007*

	Units	Construction Cost
Single	1	$341,583
Total	1	$341,583

Municipal Finance

(For local fiscal year ended in 2006)

Revenues

Total . . . $12,396,548
Taxes . . . 2,598,521
Special benefits assessment . . . 716,658
Licenses & permits . . . 220,057
Fines & forfeitures . . . 39,058
Revenues from use of money & property . . . 518,743
Intergovernmental . . . 1,287,420
Service charges . . . 2,970,153
Other revenues . . . 914,438
Other financing sources . . . 3,131,500

Expenditures

Total . . . $6,504,928
General government . . . 363,021
Public safety . . . 2,084,151
Transportation . . . 687,917
Community development . . . 528,538
Health . . . 1,351,183
Culture & leisure . . . 509,588
Other . . . 5,519

Local School District

(Data from School year 2007-08 except as noted)

Gonzales Unified
PO Drawer G
Gonzales, CA 93926
(831) 675-0100

Superintendent . . . Elizabeth Modena
Grade plan . . . K-12
Number of schools . . . 4
Enrollment . . . 2,251
High school graduates, 2006-07 . . . 113
Dropout rate . . . 6.0%
Pupil/teacher ratio . . . 19.2
Average class size . . . 26.5
Students per computer . . . 2.9
Classrooms with internet . . . 201
Avg. Daily Attendance (ADA) . . . 2,179
Cost per ADA . . . $8,740
Avg. Teacher Salary . . . $62,618

California Achievement Tests 6th ed., 2008

(Pct scoring at or above 50th National Percentile Rank)

	Math	Reading	Language
Grade 3	40%	13%	30%
Grade 7	27%	26%	27%

Academic Performance Index, 2008

Number of students tested . . . 1,721
Number of valid scores . . . 1,597
2007 API (base) . . . 669
2008 API (growth) . . . 656

SAT Testing, 2006-07

Enrollment, Grade 12 . . . 166
Number taking test . . . 19
percent taking test . . . 11.5%
percent with total score 1,500+ . . . 2.40%

Average Scores:

Math	Verbal	Writing	Total
434	436	447	1,317

Federal No Child Left Behind, 2008

(Adequate Yearly Progress standards met)

	Participation Rate	Pct Proficient
ELA	Yes	No
Math	Yes	No

API criteria . . . Yes
Graduation rate . . . No
\# criteria met/possible . . . 22/11

Other school districts for this city

(see Appendix E for information on these districts)

None

See Introduction for an explanation of all data sources.

Demographics & Socio-Economic Characteristics

(2000 Decennial Census, except as noted)

Population

1990* ... 10,946
2000 ... 11,626
Male ... 5,479
Female ... 6,147
Jan. 2008 (estimate)§ ... 12,543
Persons per sq. mi. of land ... 3,583.7

Race & Hispanic Origin, 2000

Race
White ... 8,575
Black/African American ... 537
North American Native ... 84
Asian ... 653
Pacific Islander ... 36
Other Race ... 1,133
Two or more races ... 608
Hispanic origin, total ... 2,954
Mexican ... 2,318
Puerto Rican ... 58
Cuban ... 18
Other Hispanic ... 560

Age & Nativity, 2000

Under 5 years ... 765
18 years and over ... 8,566
65 years and over ... 1,245
85 years and over ... 174
Median Age ... 35.3
Native-born ... 10,501
Foreign-born ... 1,292

Educational Attainment, 2000

Population 25 years and over ... 7,597
Less than 9th grade ... 3.4%
High school grad or higher ... 87.9%
Bachelor's degree or higher ... 24.3%
Graduate degree ... 11.6%

Income & Poverty, 1999

Per capita income ... $21,787
Median household income ... $53,649
Median family income ... $61,068
Persons in poverty ... 7.4%
H'holds receiving public assistance ... 54
H'holds receiving social security ... 881

Households, 2000

Total households ... 4,221
With persons under 18 ... 1,659
With persons over 65 ... 815
Family households ... 3,052
Single person households ... 915
Persons per household ... 2.70
Persons per family ... 3.15

Household Population, 2008§§

Persons living in households ... 12,334
Persons living in group quarters ... 209
Persons per household ... 2.8

Labor & Employment

Total civilian labor force, 2008§§ ... 7,500
Unemployment rate, 2008 ... 4.3%
Total civilian labor force, 2000 ... 6,192

Employed persons 16 years and over by occupation, 2000

Managers & professionals ... 2,261
Service occupations ... 683
Sales & office occupations ... 1,764
Farming, fishing & forestry ... 13
Construction & maintenance ... 545
Production & transportation ... 651
Self-employed persons ... 395

* US Census Bureau
** 2000 Decennial Census
§ California Department of Finance
§§ California Employment Development Dept

General Information

City of Grand Terrace
22795 Barton Rd
Grand Terrace, CA 92313
909-824-6621

Website ... www.cityofgrandterrace.org
Elevation ... NA
Land Area (sq. miles) ... 3.5
Water Area (sq. miles) ... 0
Year of Incorporation ... 1978
Government type ... General law
Sales tax rate ... 8.75%

Voters & Officials

Registered Voters, October 2008

Total ... 6,439
Democrats ... 2,450
Republicans ... 2,677
Declined to state ... 1,042

Legislative Districts

US Congressional ... 41
State Senatorial ... 31
State Assembly ... 63

Local Officials, 2009

Mayor ... Maryetta Ferre
Manager ... Steve Berry (Actg)
City Clerk ... Brenda Mesa
Attorney ... John Harper
Finance Dir ... Bernie Simon
Public Works ... NA
Community Dev Dir ... Joyce Powers
Building ... Richard Shields
Police Chief ... Dave Williams
Emergency/Fire Dir ... Dan Wooters

Public Safety

Number of officers, 2007 ... NA
Violent crimes, 2007 ... 22
Property crimes, 2007 ... 242
Arson, 2007 ... 5

Public Library

Grand Terrace Branch Library
San Bernardino County Library System
22795 Barton Rd
Grand Terrace, CA 92313
909-783-0147

Branch Librarian ... Erin Christmas

Library system statistics, FY 2007

Population served ... 1,177,092
Internet terminals ... 12
Annual users ... 45,343

Per capita:

Operating income ... $14.27
percent from local government ... 73.3%
Operating expenditure ... $13.86
Total materials ... 0.86
Print holdings ... 0.79
Visits per capita ... 5.83

Housing & Construction

Housing Units

Total, 2008§ ... 4,580
Single family units, attached ... 191
Single family units, detached ... 2,923
Multiple family units ... 1,216
Mobile home units ... 250
Occupied ... 4,337
Vacancy rate ... 5.3%
Median rent, 2000** ... $777
Median SF home value, 2000** ... $142,600

New Privately Owned Housing Units Authorized by Building Permit, 2007*

	Units	Construction Cost
Single	3	$1,538,379
Total	17	$3,916,911

Municipal Finance

(For local fiscal year ended in 2006)

Revenues

Total ... $8,958,878
Taxes ... 3,247,076
Special benefits assessment ... 2,376
Licenses & permits ... 271,143
Fines & forfeitures ... 95,369
Revenues from use of money & property ... 303,018
Intergovernmental ... 687,916
Service charges ... 2,834,628
Other revenues ... 1,517,352
Other financing sources ... 0

Expenditures

Total ... $7,291,063
General government ... 1,089,864
Public safety ... 1,732,255
Transportation ... 723,472
Community development ... 396,020
Health ... 1,609,368
Culture & leisure ... 1,740,084
Other ... 0

Local School District

(Data from School year 2007-08 except as noted)

Colton Joint Unified
1212 Valencia Dr
Colton, CA 92324
(909) 580-5000

Superintendent ... James Downs
Grade plan ... K-12
Number of schools ... 28
Enrollment ... 24,528
High school graduates, 2006-07 ... 1,053
Dropout rate ... 9.6%
Pupil/teacher ratio ... 21.6
Average class size ... 27.4
Students per computer ... 5.7
Classrooms with internet ... 1,230
Avg. Daily Attendance (ADA) ... 23,370
Cost per ADA ... $8,107
Avg. Teacher Salary ... $66,484

California Achievement Tests 6th ed., 2008

(Pct scoring at or above 50th National Percentile Rank)

	Math	Reading	Language
Grade 3	40%	25%	33%
Grade 7	35%	34%	33%

Academic Performance Index, 2008

Number of students tested ... 18,558
Number of valid scores ... 17,077
2007 API (base) ... 659
2008 API (growth) ... 673

SAT Testing, 2006-07

Enrollment, Grade 12 ... 1,681
Number taking test ... 401
percent taking test ... 23.9%
percent with total score 1,500+ ... 4.60%

Average Scores:

Math	Verbal	Writing	Total
439	436	430	1,305

Federal No Child Left Behind, 2008

(Adequate Yearly Progress standards met)

	Participation Rate	Pct Proficient
ELA	No	No
Math	Yes	No

API criteria ... Yes
Graduation rate ... No
\# criteria met/possible ... 38/25

Other school districts for this city

(see Appendix E for information on these districts)

None

See Introduction for an explanation of all data sources.

Demographics & Socio-Economic Characteristics

(2000 Decennial Census, except as noted)

Population

1990* . . . 9,048
2000 . . . 10,922
Male . . . 4,915
Female . . . 6,007
Jan. 2008 (estimate)§ . . . 12,929
Persons per sq. mi. of land . . . 3,153.4

Race & Hispanic Origin, 2000

Race
White . . . 10,038
Black/African American . . . 29
North American Native . . . 146
Asian . . . 115
Pacific Islander . . . 8
Other Race . . . 181
Two or more races . . . 405
Hispanic origin, total . . . 717
Mexican . . . 506
Puerto Rican . . . 38
Cuban . . . 10
Other Hispanic . . . 163

Age & Nativity, 2000

Under 5 years . . . 700
18 years and over . . . 8,375
65 years and over . . . 2,403
85 years and over . . . 526
Median Age . . . 39.3
Native-born . . . 10,803
Foreign-born . . . 358

Educational Attainment, 2000

Population 25 years and over . . . 7,303
Less than 9th grade . . . 3.1%
High school grad or higher . . . 86.6%
Bachelor's degree or higher . . . 17.4%
Graduate degree . . . 5.2%

Income & Poverty, 1999

Per capita income . . . $16,877
Median household income . . . $28,182
Median family income . . . $33,220
Persons in poverty . . . 14.8%
H'holds receiving public assistance . . . 200
H'holds receiving social security . . . 1,749

Households, 2000

Total households . . . 5,016
With persons under 18 . . . 1,460
With persons over 65 . . . 1,716
Family households . . . 2,677
Single person households . . . 1,961
Persons per household . . . 2.13
Persons per family . . . 2.80

Household Population, 2008§§

Persons living in households . . . 12,579
Persons living in group quarters . . . 350
Persons per household . . . 2.0

Labor & Employment

Total civilian labor force, 2008§§ . . . 5,820
Unemployment rate, 2008 . . . 5.9%
Total civilian labor force, 2000 . . . 4,980

Employed persons 16 years and over by occupation, 2000

Managers & professionals . . . 1,309
Service occupations . . . 1,032
Sales & office occupations . . . 1,329
Farming, fishing & forestry . . . 52
Construction & maintenance . . . 423
Production & transportation . . . 623
Self-employed persons . . . 552

* US Census Bureau
** 2000 Decennial Census
§ California Department of Finance
§§ California Employment Development Dept

General Information

City of Grass Valley
125 E Main St
Grass Valley, CA 95945
530-274-4310

Website . . . www.cityofgrassvalley.com
Elevation . . . 2,411 ft.
Land Area (sq. miles) . . . 4.1
Water Area (sq. miles) . . . 0
Year of Incorporation . . . 1893
Government type . . . Chartered
Sales tax rate . . . 8.38%

Voters & Officials

Registered Voters, October 2008

Total . . . 6,880
Democrats . . . 2,612
Republicans . . . 2,486
Declined to state . . . 1,384

Legislative Districts

US Congressional . . . 4
State Senatorial . . . 4
State Assembly . . . 3

Local Officials, 2009

Mayor . . . Lisa Swarthout
Manager . . . Daniel C. Holler
City Clerk . . . Kristi K. Bashor
Attorney . . . Ruthann G. Ziegler
Finance Dir . . . (vacant)
Public Works . . . Tim Kiser
Planning/Dev Dir . . . Joe Heckel
Building . . . NA
Police Chief . . . John Foster
Emergency/Fire Dir . . . Tony Clarabut

Public Safety

Number of officers, 2007 . . . 28
Violent crimes, 2007 . . . 66
Property crimes, 2007 . . . 368
Arson, 2007 . . . 0

Public Library

Grass Valley Library
Nevada County Library System
207 Mill St
Grass Valley, CA 95945
530-273-4117

Branch Librarian . . . Judith Mariuz

Library system statistics, FY 2007

Population served . . . 99,766
Internet terminals . . . 41
Annual users . . . 46,411

Per capita:

Operating income . . . $24.65
percent from local government . . . 89.7%
Operating expenditure . . . $24.33
Total materials . . . 2.13
Print holdings . . . 1.85
Visits per capita . . . 4.86

Housing & Construction

Housing Units

Total, 2008§ . . . 6,469
Single family units, attached . . . 259
Single family units, detached . . . 3,099
Multiple family units . . . 2,415
Mobile home units . . . 696
Occupied . . . 6,161
Vacancy rate . . . 4.8%
Median rent, 2000** . . . $650
Median SF home value, 2000** . . . $151,300

New Privately Owned Housing Units Authorized by Building Permit, 2007*

	Units	Construction Cost
Single	14	$4,000,000
Total	18	$4,663,922

Municipal Finance

(For local fiscal year ended in 2006)

Revenues

Total . . . $17,919,341
Taxes . . . 9,440,889
Special benefits assessment . . . 296,249
Licenses & permits . . . 28,257
Fines & forfeitures . . . 169,262
Revenues from use of money & property . . . 376,863
Intergovernmental . . . 1,943,444
Service charges . . . 5,469,593
Other revenues . . . 194,784
Other financing sources . . . 0

Expenditures

Total . . . $16,704,163
General government . . . 2,173,639
Public safety . . . 6,725,781
Transportation . . . 707,524
Community development . . . 1,698,327
Health . . . 3,434,505
Culture & leisure . . . 780,260
Other . . . 0

Local School District

(Data from School year 2007-08 except as noted)

Nevada Joint Union High
11645 Ridge Rd
Grass Valley, CA 95945
(530) 273-3351

Superintendent . . . Ralf Swenson
Grade plan . . . 9-12
Number of schools . . . 9
Enrollment . . . 3,942
High school graduates, 2006-07 . . . 819
Dropout rate . . . 2.2%
Pupil/teacher ratio . . . 26.6
Average class size . . . 27.0
Students per computer . . . 3.5
Classrooms with internet . . . 192
Avg. Daily Attendance (ADA) . . . 3,728
Cost per ADA . . . $8,660
Avg. Teacher Salary . . . $65,021

California Achievement Tests 6th ed., 2008

(Pct scoring at or above 50th National Percentile Rank)

	Math	Reading	Language
Grade 3	NA	NA	NA
Grade 7	NA	NA	NA

Academic Performance Index, 2008

Number of students tested . . . 2,879
Number of valid scores . . . 2,795
2007 API (base) . . . 765
2008 API (growth) . . . 789

SAT Testing, 2006-07

Enrollment, Grade 12 . . . 954
Number taking test . . . 343
percent taking test . . . 36.0%
percent with total score 1,500+ . . . 23.70%

Average Scores:

Math	Verbal	Writing	Total
554	539	530	1,623

Federal No Child Left Behind, 2008

(Adequate Yearly Progress standards met)

	Participation Rate	Pct Proficient
ELA	Yes	Yes
Math	Yes	Yes

API criteria . . . Yes
Graduation rate . . . Yes
\# criteria met/possible . . . 14/14

Other school districts for this city

(see Appendix E for information on these districts)
Complete list in Appendix E

See Introduction for an explanation of all data sources.

Demographics & Socio-Economic Characteristics

(2000 Decennial Census, except as noted)

Population

1990* 7,464
2000 12,583
Male 6,551
Female 6,032
Jan. 2008 (estimate)§ 17,316
Persons per sq. mi. of land 10,185.9

Race & Hispanic Origin, 2000

Race
White 4,989
Black/African American 148
North American Native 150
Asian 97
Pacific Islander 19
Other Race 6,537
Two or more races 643
Hispanic origin, total 11,055
Mexican 9,814
Puerto Rican 16
Cuban 2
Other Hispanic 1,223

Age & Nativity, 2000

Under 5 years 1,316
18 years and over 7,760
65 years and over 629
85 years and over 54
Median Age 24.1
Native-born 6,758
Foreign-born 5,870

Educational Attainment, 2000

Population 25 years and over 6,141
Less than 9th grade 50.8%
High school grad or higher 31.0%
Bachelor's degree or higher 3.7%
Graduate degree 1.6%

Income & Poverty, 1999

Per capita income $9,226
Median household income $37,602
Median family income $35,520
Persons in poverty 21.5%
H'holds receiving public assistance 164
H'holds receiving social security 613

Households, 2000

Total households 2,643
With persons under 18 1,893
With persons over 65 465
Family households 2,361
Single person households 207
Persons per household 4.75
Persons per family 4.83

Household Population, 2008§§

Persons living in households 17,220
Persons living in group quarters 96
Persons per household 4.7

Labor & Employment

Total civilian labor force, 2008§§ 6,300
Unemployment rate, 2008 .... 13.0%
Total civilian labor force, 2000 5,309

Employed persons 16 years and over by occupation, 2000

Managers & professionals 531
Service occupations 554
Sales & office occupations 557
Farming, fishing & forestry 1,914
Construction & maintenance 314
Production & transportation 730
Self-employed persons 152

* US Census Bureau
** 2000 Decennial Census
§ California Department of Finance
§§ California Employment Development Dept

General Information

City of Greenfield
PO Box 127
Greenfield, CA 93927
831-674-5591

Website .... www.ci.greenfield.ca.us
Elevation .... NA
Land Area (sq. miles) 1.7
Water Area (sq. miles) 0
Year of Incorporation 1947
Government type .... General law
Sales tax rate 8.25%

Voters & Officials

Registered Voters, October 2008

Total 3,240
Democrats 2,076
Republicans 545
Declined to state 534

Legislative Districts

US Congressional 17
State Senatorial 12
State Assembly 28

Local Officials, 2009

Mayor .... John Huerta Jr
Manager .... Roger L. Wong
City Clerk .... Ann Rathbun
Attorney .... John Bakker
Finance Dir .... Ann Rathbun
Public Works .... Glen Rudy
Community Dev Dir .... (vacant)
Building .... NA
Police Chief .... Joseph Grebmeier
Fire Chief .... John Sims

Public Safety

Number of officers, 2007 16
Violent crimes, 2007 .... NA
Property crimes, 2007 540
Arson, 2007 .... NA

Public Library

Greenfield Branch Library
Monterey County Free Libraries
315 El Camino Real
Greenfield, CA 93927
831-674-2614

Branch Librarian .... Barbara Brown

Library system statistics, FY 2007

Population served 226,803
Internet terminals 160
Annual users 229,676

Per capita:

Operating income $29.19
percent from local government 91.7%
Operating expenditure $27.42
Total materials 1.92
Print holdings 1.81
Visits per capita 3.65

Housing & Construction

Housing Units

Total, 2008§ 3,764
Single family units, attached 282
Single family units, detached 2,830
Multiple family units 566
Mobile home units 86
Occupied 3,649
Vacancy rate 3.1%
Median rent, 2000** $673
Median SF home value, 2000** $125,300

New Privately Owned Housing Units Authorized by Building Permit, 2007*

	Units	Construction Cost
Single	73	$11,077,381
Total	98	$12,837,283

Municipal Finance

(For local fiscal year ended in 2006)

Revenues

Total $16,199,937
Taxes 4,882,537
Special benefits assessment 98,487
Licenses & permits 625,123
Fines & forfeitures 69,387
Revenues from use of money & property 405,985
Intergovernmental 1,939,226
Service charges 3,095,203
Other revenues 2,583,989
Other financing sources 2,500,000

Expenditures

Total $10,204,950
General government 805,275
Public safety 2,941,877
Transportation 545,876
Community development 1,066,215
Health 2,113,680
Culture & leisure 1,654,124
Other 0

Local School District

(Data from School year 2007-08 except as noted)

King City Joint Union High
800 Broadway
King City, CA 93930
(831) 385-0606

Superintendent .... Tom Michaelson
Grade plan 9-12
Number of schools 4
Enrollment 2,184
High school graduates, 2006-07 344
Dropout rate 2.4%
Pupil/teacher ratio 25.1
Average class size 27.4
Students per computer 3.0
Classrooms with internet 92
Avg. Daily Attendance (ADA) 2,068
Cost per ADA $9,008
Avg. Teacher Salary $81,391

California Achievement Tests 6th ed., 2008

(Pct scoring at or above 50th National Percentile Rank)

	Math	Reading	Language
Grade 3	NA	NA	NA
Grade 7	NA	NA	NA

Academic Performance Index, 2008

Number of students tested 1,654
Number of valid scores 1,573
2007 API (base) 599
2008 API (growth) 635

SAT Testing, 2006-07

Enrollment, Grade 12 436
Number taking test 110
percent taking test 25.2%
percent with total score 1,500+ 4.60%

Average Scores:

Math	Verbal	Writing	Total
428	418	426	1,272

Federal No Child Left Behind, 2008

(Adequate Yearly Progress standards met)

	Participation Rate	Pct Proficient
ELA	Yes	Yes
Math	Yes	No

API criteria .... Yes
Graduation rate .... Yes
criteria met/possible 18/14

Other school districts for this city

(see Appendix E for information on these districts)

Greenfield Union

See Introduction for an explanation of all data sources.

Demographics & Socio-Economic Characteristics

(2000 Decennial Census, except as noted)

Population

1990* . . . 4,631
2000 . . . 5,382
Male . . . 2,568
Female . . . 2,814
Jan. 2008 (estimate)§ . . . 6,403
Persons per sq. mi. of land . . . 4,001.9

Race & Hispanic Origin, 2000

Race
White . . . 3,583
Black/African American . . . 17
North American Native . . . 83
Asian . . . 187
Pacific Islander . . . 1
Other Race . . . 1,295
Two or more races . . . 216
Hispanic origin, total . . . 2,079
Mexican . . . 1,800
Puerto Rican . . . 5
Cuban . . . 0
Other Hispanic . . . 274

Age & Nativity, 2000

Under 5 years . . . 389
18 years and over . . . 3,764
65 years and over . . . 857
85 years and over . . . 134
Median Age . . . 32.9
Native-born . . . 4,250
Foreign-born . . . 1,200

Educational Attainment, 2000

Population 25 years and over . . . 3,385
Less than 9th grade . . . 23.1%
High school grad or higher . . . 59.2%
Bachelor's degree or higher . . . 7.6%
Graduate degree . . . 2.8%

Income & Poverty, 1999

Per capita income . . . $12,267
Median household income . . . $24,368
Median family income . . . $29,957
Persons in poverty . . . 23.1%
H'holds receiving public assistance . . . 167
H'holds receiving social security . . . 631

Households, 2000

Total households . . . 1,841
With persons under 18 . . . 772
With persons over 65 . . . 591
Family households . . . 1,266
Single person households . . . 488
Persons per household . . . 2.86
Persons per family . . . 3.48

Household Population, 2008§§

Persons living in households . . . 6,281
Persons living in group quarters . . . 122
Persons per household . . . 2.8

Labor & Employment

Total civilian labor force, 2008§§ . . . 2,600
Unemployment rate, 2008 . . . 18.6%
Total civilian labor force, 2000 . . . 2,324

Employed persons 16 years and over by occupation, 2000

Managers & professionals . . . 330
Service occupations . . . 317
Sales & office occupations . . . 401
Farming, fishing & forestry . . . 234
Construction & maintenance . . . 280
Production & transportation . . . 287
Self-employed persons . . . 126

* US Census Bureau
** 2000 Decennial Census
§ California Department of Finance
§§ California Employment Development Dept

General Information

City of Gridley
685 Kentucky St
Gridley, CA 95948
530-846-5695

Website . . . www.gridley.ca.us
Elevation . . . 91 ft.
Land Area (sq. miles) . . . 1.6
Water Area (sq. miles) . . . 0
Year of Incorporation . . . 1905
Government type . . . General law
Sales tax rate . . . 8.25%

Voters & Officials

Registered Voters, October 2008

Total . . . 2,627
Democrats . . . 1,022
Republicans . . . 969
Declined to state . . . 499

Legislative Districts

US Congressional . . . 2
State Senatorial . . . 4
State Assembly . . . 3

Local Officials, 2009

Mayor . . . Jerry Ann Fichter
Manager/Admin . . . (vacant)
City Clerk . . . Rob Hickey
Attorney . . . Brant Bordsen
Finance Dir . . . Brad Wilkie
Public Works . . . Alvie Davis
Planning/Dev Dir . . . Andrea Redamonti
Building . . . Keith Gebhardt
Police Chief . . . Gary Keeler
Fire Chief . . . Mike Brown

Public Safety

Number of officers, 2007 . . . 17
Violent crimes, 2007 . . . 76
Property crimes, 2007 . . . 191
Arson, 2007 . . . 0

Public Library

Gridley Branch
Butte County Library System
299 Spruce St
Gridley, CA 95948
530-846-3323

Branch Librarian . . . Lori Lute

Library system statistics, FY 2007

Population served . . . 218,069
Internet terminals . . . 47
Annual users . . . 90,296

Per capita:

Operating income . . . $12.21
percent from local government . . . 84.5%
Operating expenditure . . . $12.71
Total materials . . . 1.41
Print holdings . . . 1.33
Visits per capita . . . 3.01

Housing & Construction

Housing Units

Total, 2008§ . . . 2,420
Single family units, attached . . . 52
Single family units, detached . . . 2,005
Multiple family units . . . 285
Mobile home units . . . 78
Occupied . . . 2,271
Vacancy rate . . . 6.2%
Median rent, 2000** . . . $467
Median SF home value, 2000** . . . $86,000

New Privately Owned Housing Units Authorized by Building Permit, 2007*

	Units	Construction Cost
Single	76	$16,348,062
Total	76	$16,348,062

Municipal Finance

(For local fiscal year ended in 2006)

Revenues

Total . . . $14,811,844
Taxes . . . 4,160,693
Special benefits assessment . . . 80,972
Licenses & permits . . . 458,121
Fines & forfeitures . . . -13,500
Revenues from use of money & property . . . 225,528
Intergovernmental . . . 823,630
Service charges . . . 8,464,145
Other revenues . . . 484,857
Other financing sources . . . 127,398

Expenditures

Total . . . $12,473,775
General government . . . 1,066,844
Public safety . . . 3,193,291
Transportation . . . 621,510
Community development . . . 985,761
Health . . . 1,442,534
Culture & leisure . . . 244,799
Other . . . 0

Local School District

(Data from School year 2007-08 except as noted)

Gridley Unified
429 Magnolia St
Gridley, CA 95948
(530) 846-4721

Superintendent . . . Clark Redfield
Grade plan . . . K-12
Number of schools . . . 7
Enrollment . . . 1,969
High school graduates, 2006-07 . . . 173
Dropout rate . . . 2.3%
Pupil/teacher ratio . . . 18.7
Average class size . . . 22.6
Students per computer . . . 5.2
Classrooms with internet . . . 107
Avg. Daily Attendance (ADA) . . . 2,004
Cost per ADA . . . $7,850
Avg. Teacher Salary . . . $57,479

California Achievement Tests 6th ed., 2008

(Pct scoring at or above 50th National Percentile Rank)

	Math	Reading	Language
Grade 3	55%	33%	51%
Grade 7	42%	46%	41%

Academic Performance Index, 2008

Number of students tested . . . 1,528
Number of valid scores . . . 1,439
2007 API (base) . . . 720
2008 API (growth) . . . 744

SAT Testing, 2006-07

Enrollment, Grade 12 . . . 187
Number taking test . . . 41
percent taking test . . . 21.9%
percent with total score 1,500+ . . . 7.50%

Average Scores:

Math	Verbal	Writing	Total
487	468	475	1,430

Federal No Child Left Behind, 2008

(Adequate Yearly Progress standards met)

	Participation Rate	Pct Proficient
ELA	Yes	No
Math	Yes	Yes

API criteria . . . Yes
Graduation rate . . . Yes
\# criteria met/possible . . . 22/20

Other school districts for this city

(see Appendix E for information on these districts)

Manzanita Elem

See Introduction for an explanation of all data sources.

Demographics & Socio-Economic Characteristics
(2000 Decennial Census, except as noted)

Population
1990* 11,656
2000 13,067
Male 6,334
Female 6,733
Jan. 2008 (estimate)§ 13,213
Persons per sq. mi. of land 5,744.8

Race & Hispanic Origin, 2000
Race
White 10,421
Black/African American 135
North American Native 221
Asian 490
Pacific Islander 39
Other Race 1,206
Two or more races 555
Hispanic origin, total 2,941
Mexican 2,432
Puerto Rican 35
Cuban 14
Other Hispanic 460

Age & Nativity, 2000
Under 5 years 910
18 years and over 9,721
65 years and over 1,505
85 years and over 166
Median Age 35.2
Native-born 11,492
Foreign-born 1,514

Educational Attainment, 2000
Population 25 years and over 8,522
Less than 9th grade 4.6%
High school grad or higher 82.8%
Bachelor's degree or higher 19.5%
Graduate degree 6.5%

Income & Poverty, 1999
Per capita income $18,812
Median household income $38,087
Median family income $41,859
Persons in poverty 11.2%
H'holds receiving public assistance 266
H'holds receiving social security 1,272

Households, 2000
Total households 5,023
With persons under 18 1,829
With persons over 65 1,110
Family households 3,306
Single person households 1,236
Persons per household 2.58
Persons per family 3.07

Household Population, 2008§§
Persons living in households 13,087
Persons living in group quarters 126
Persons per household 2.5

Labor & Employment
Total civilian labor force, 2008§§ 8,000
Unemployment rate, 2008 . . . . 5.4%
Total civilian labor force, 2000 6,713

Employed persons 16 years and over by occupation, 2000
Managers & professionals 1,862
Service occupations 1,377
Sales & office occupations 1,544
Farming, fishing & forestry 107
Construction & maintenance 770
Production & transportation 674
Self-employed persons 685

* US Census Bureau
** 2000 Decennial Census
§ California Department of Finance
§§ California Employment Development Dept

General Information
City of Grover Beach
154 S Eighth Street
Grover Beach, CA 93433
805-473-4567

Website . . . . www.grover.org
Elevation . . . . 50 ft.
Land Area (sq. miles) 2.3
Water Area (sq. miles) 0
Year of Incorporation 1959
Government type . . . . General law
Sales tax rate 8.75%

Voters & Officials
Registered Voters, October 2008
Total 7,072
Democrats 2,790
Republicans 2,406
Declined to state 1,453

Legislative Districts
US Congressional 23
State Senatorial 15
State Assembly 33

Local Officials, 2009
Mayor . . . . John P. Shoals
Manager . . . . Robert Perrault
City Clerk . . . . Donna L. McMahon
Attorney . . . . Martin D. Koczanowicz
Finance Dir . . . . Gayla R. Chapman
Public Works . . . . J. Michael Ford
Community Dev Dir . . . . Patricia Beck (Int)
Building . . . . NA
Police Chief . . . . Jim Copsey
Fire Chief . . . . Mike Hubert

Public Safety
Number of officers, 2007 19
Violent crimes, 2007 . . . . NA
Property crimes, 2007 276
Arson, 2007 3

Public Library
Served by County Library

Library system statistics, FY 2007
Population served . . . . NA
Internet terminals . . . . NA
Annual users . . . . NA

Per capita:
Operating income . . . . NA
percent from local government . . . . NA
Operating expenditure . . . . NA
Total materials . . . . NA
Print holdings . . . . NA
Visits per capita . . . . NA

Housing & Construction
Housing Units
Total, 2008§ 5,670
Single family units, attached 792
Single family units, detached 3,291
Multiple family units 1,340
Mobile home units 247
Occupied 5,292
Vacancy rate 6.7%
Median rent, 2000** $747
Median SF home value, 2000** $184,800

New Privately Owned Housing Units Authorized by Building Permit, 2007*

	Units	Construction Cost
Single	36	$5,704,384
Total	42	$6,333,731

Municipal Finance
(For local fiscal year ended in 2006)

Revenues
Total $10,829,640
Taxes 4,840,561
Special benefits assessment 423,366
Licenses & permits 92,493
Fines & forfeitures 119,568
Revenues from use of money & property 353,155
Intergovernmental 992,794
Service charges 4,004,915
Other revenues 2,788
Other financing sources 0

Expenditures
Total $10,240,525
General government 1,646,298
Public safety 3,690,954
Transportation 629,061
Community development 540,122
Health 1,091,700
Culture & leisure 636,561
Other 0

Local School District
(Data from School year 2007-08 except as noted)
Lucia Mar Unified
602 Orchard St
Arroyo Grande, CA 93420
(805) 474-3000

Superintendent . . . . James Hogeboom
Grade plan K-12
Number of schools 17
Enrollment 10,820
High school graduates, 2006-07 791
Dropout rate 2.1%
Pupil/teacher ratio 20.6
Average class size 24.9
Students per computer 3.1
Classrooms with internet 582
Avg. Daily Attendance (ADA) 10,496
Cost per ADA $7,542
Avg. Teacher Salary $59,928

California Achievement Tests 6th ed., 2008
(Pct scoring at or above 50th National Percentile Rank)

	Math	Reading	Language
Grade 3	68%	52%	54%
Grade 7	63%	58%	55%

Academic Performance Index, 2008
Number of students tested 8,356
Number of valid scores 7,964
2007 API (base) 782
2008 API (growth) 790

SAT Testing, 2006-07
Enrollment, Grade 12 876
Number taking test 317
percent taking test 36.2%
percent with total score 1,500+ 22.40%

Average Scores:

Math	Verbal	Writing	Total
534	523	518	1,575

Federal No Child Left Behind, 2008
(Adequate Yearly Progress standards met)

	Participation Rate	Pct Proficient
ELA	Yes	No
Math	Yes	Yes

API criteria . . . . Yes
Graduation rate . . . . Yes
criteria met/possible 36/34

Other school districts for this city
(see Appendix E for information on these districts)
None

See Introduction for an explanation of all data sources.

Demographics & Socio-Economic Characteristics

(2000 Decennial Census, except as noted)

Population

1990* 5,479
2000 5,659
Male 2,886
Female 2,773
Jan. 2008 (estimate)§ 6,541
Persons per sq. mi. of land 4,672.1

Race & Hispanic Origin, 2000

Race
White 2,577
Black/African American 40
North American Native 105
Asian 333
Pacific Islander 9
Other Race 2,190
Two or more races 405
Hispanic origin, total 4,781
Mexican 4,307
Puerto Rican 6
Cuban 7
Other Hispanic 461

Age & Nativity, 2000

Under 5 years 522
18 years and over 3,642
65 years and over 482
85 years and over 46
Median Age 26.7
Native-born 3,359
Foreign-born 2,294

Educational Attainment, 2000

Population 25 years and over 2,966
Less than 9th grade 41.5%
High school grad or higher 43.6%
Bachelor's degree or higher 4.3%
Graduate degree 1.4%

Income & Poverty, 1999

Per capita income $11,608
Median household income $31,205
Median family income $31,042
Persons in poverty 24.8%
H'holds receiving public assistance 176
H'holds receiving social security 423

Households, 2000

Total households 1,414
With persons under 18 871
With persons over 65 368
Family households 1,217
Single person households 159
Persons per household 4.00
Persons per family 4.24

Household Population, 2008§§

Persons living in households 6,541
Persons living in group quarters 0
Persons per household 4.0

Labor & Employment

Total civilian labor force, 2008§§ 2,600
Unemployment rate, 2008 . . . . . 7.0%
Total civilian labor force, 2000 2,271

Employed persons 16 years and over by occupation, 2000

Managers & professionals 177
Service occupations 402
Sales & office occupations 442
Farming, fishing & forestry 531
Construction & maintenance 160
Production & transportation 363
Self-employed persons 99

* US Census Bureau
** 2000 Decennial Census
§ California Department of Finance
§§ California Employment Development Dept

General Information

City of Guadalupe
918 Obispo Street
Guadalupe, CA 93434
805-343-1340

Website . . . . . www.ci.guadalupe.ca.us
Elevation . . . . . 85 ft.
Land Area (sq. miles) 1.4
Water Area (sq. miles) 0
Year of Incorporation 1946
Government type . . . . . General law
Sales tax rate 8.75%

Voters & Officials

Registered Voters, October 2008

Total 1,982
Democrats 1,179
Republicans 342
Declined to state 381

Legislative Districts

US Congressional 23
State Senatorial 15
State Assembly 33

Local Officials, 2009

Mayor . . . . . Lupe Alvarez
Manager . . . . . Carolyn Galloway-Cooper
City Clerk . . . . . Brenda Hoff
Attorney . . . . . David Fleishman
Finance Dir . . . . . Al Hernandez
Public Works . . . . . Mike Pena
Community Dev Dir . . . . . John Rickenbach
Building . . . . . NA
Police Chief . . . . . George Mitchell
Fire Chief . . . . . Jack Owen

Public Safety

Number of officers, 2007 12
Violent crimes, 2007 9
Property crimes, 2007 90
Arson, 2007 1

Public Library

Guadalupe Library
Santa Maria Public Library
4719 W Main St, librAddr2
Guadalupe, CA 93434
805-925-0994

Branch Librarian . . . . . Lea Cryor

Library system statistics, FY 2007

Population served 118,839
Internet terminals 141
Annual users 273,093

Per capita:

Operating income $21.45
percent from local government 82.1%
Operating expenditure $17.72
Total materials 2.35
Print holdings 2.06
Visits per capita 14.96

Housing & Construction

Housing Units

Total, 2008§ 1,693
Single family units, attached 168
Single family units, detached 1,157
Multiple family units 360
Mobile home units 8
Occupied 1,652
Vacancy rate 2.4%
Median rent, 2000** $601
Median SF home value, 2000** $112,800

New Privately Owned Housing Units Authorized by Building Permit, 2007*

	Units	Construction Cost
Single	0	$0
Total	0	$0

Municipal Finance

(For local fiscal year ended in 2006)

Revenues

Total $7,015,888
Taxes 1,216,529
Special benefits assessment 106,286
Licenses & permits 242,766
Fines & forfeitures 24,130
Revenues from use of money & property 23,654
Intergovernmental 2,694,275
Service charges 2,690,748
Other revenues 17,500
Other financing sources 0

Expenditures

Total $10,519,954
General government 829,672
Public safety 1,739,433
Transportation 647,106
Community development 406,115
Health 944,889
Culture & leisure 333,254
Other 0

Local School District

(Data from School year 2007-08 except as noted)

Santa Maria Joint Union High
2560 Skyway Dr
Santa Maria, CA 93455
(805) 922-4573

Superintendent . . . . . Jeffery Hearn
Grade plan 9-12
Number of schools 4
Enrollment 7,746
High school graduates, 2006-07 1,248
Dropout rate 3.2%
Pupil/teacher ratio 24.8
Average class size 26.5
Students per computer 1.9
Classrooms with internet 317
Avg. Daily Attendance (ADA) 7,514
Cost per ADA $7,864
Avg. Teacher Salary $70,761

California Achievement Tests 6th ed., 2008

(Pct scoring at or above 50th National Percentile Rank)

	Math	Reading	Language
Grade 3	NA	NA	NA
Grade 7	NA	NA	NA

Academic Performance Index, 2008

Number of students tested 5,688
Number of valid scores 5,378
2007 API (base) 680
2008 API (growth) 692

SAT Testing, 2006-07

Enrollment, Grade 12 1,657
Number taking test 366
percent taking test 22.1%
percent with total score 1,500+ 8.60%

Average Scores:

Math	Verbal	Writing	Total
495	465	464	1,424

Federal No Child Left Behind, 2008

(Adequate Yearly Progress standards met)

	Participation Rate	Pct Proficient
ELA	Yes	No
Math	No	No

API criteria . . . . . Yes
Graduation rate . . . . . Yes
criteria met/possible 26/21

Other school districts for this city

(see Appendix E for information on these districts)

Guadalupe Union Elem

See Introduction for an explanation of all data sources.

Demographics & Socio-Economic Characteristics

(2000 Decennial Census, except as noted)

Population

1990* . . . 3,931
2000 . . . 4,698
Male . . . 2,287
Female . . . 2,411
Jan. 2008 (estimate)§ . . . 5,199
Persons per sq. mi. of land . . . 3,249.4

Race & Hispanic Origin, 2000

Race
White . . . 3,395
Black/African American . . . 34
North American Native . . . 46
Asian . . . 71
Pacific Islander . . . 3
Other Race . . . 891
Two or more races . . . 258
Hispanic origin, total . . . 1,648
Mexican . . . 1,436
Puerto Rican . . . 11
Cuban . . . 3
Other Hispanic . . . 198

Age & Nativity, 2000

Under 5 years . . . 350
18 years and over . . . 3,277
65 years and over . . . 748
85 years and over . . . 87
Median Age . . . 34.8
Native-born . . . 3,529
Foreign-born . . . 1,313

Educational Attainment, 2000

Population 25 years and over . . . 2,945
Less than 9th grade . . . 22.0%
High school grad or higher . . . 61.3%
Bachelor's degree or higher . . . 9.4%
Graduate degree . . . 2.0%

Income & Poverty, 1999

Per capita income . . . $16,821
Median household income . . . $38,824
Median family income . . . $45,583
Persons in poverty . . . 17.4%
H'holds receiving public assistance . . . 120
H'holds receiving social security . . . 627

Households, 2000

Total households . . . 1,683
With persons under 18 . . . 659
With persons over 65 . . . 560
Family households . . . 1,217
Single person households . . . 415
Persons per household . . . 2.79
Persons per family . . . 3.34

Household Population, 2008§§

Persons living in households . . . 5,199
Persons living in group quarters . . . 0
Persons per household . . . 2.7

Labor & Employment

Total civilian labor force, 2008§§ . . . 2,500
Unemployment rate, 2008 . . . 7.0%
Total civilian labor force, 2000 . . . 2,054

Employed persons 16 years and over by occupation, 2000

Managers & professionals . . . 280
Service occupations . . . 399
Sales & office occupations . . . 532
Farming, fishing & forestry . . . 123
Construction & maintenance . . . 165
Production & transportation . . . 406
Self-employed persons . . . 164

* US Census Bureau
** 2000 Decennial Census
§ California Department of Finance
§§ California Employment Development Dept

General Information

City of Gustine
682 Third Ave
PO Box 16
Gustine, CA 95322
209-854-6471

Website . . . www.ci.gustine.ca.us
Elevation . . . NA
Land Area (sq. miles) . . . 1.6
Water Area (sq. miles) . . . 0
Year of Incorporation . . . 1915
Government type . . . General law
Sales tax rate . . . 8.25%

Voters & Officials

Registered Voters, October 2008

Total . . . 2,262
Democrats . . . 1,155
Republicans . . . 739
Declined to state . . . 287

Legislative Districts

US Congressional . . . 18
State Senatorial . . . 12
State Assembly . . . 17

Local Officials, 2009

Mayor . . . Rich Ford
Manager . . . Margaret Silveira
City Clerk . . . Kelly Buendia
Attorney . . . Thomas Ebersole
Finance Dir . . . Roberta Casteel
Public Works . . . Ernie Garza
Planning/Comm Dev . . . NA
Building . . . Precision Inspection
Police Chief . . . Richard Calderon
Fire Chief . . . Pat Borrelli

Public Safety

Number of officers, 2007 . . . 8
Violent crimes, 2007 . . . 22
Property crimes, 2007 . . . 109
Arson, 2007 . . . 1

Public Library

Gustine Branch Library
Merced County Library System
205 Sixth St
Gustine, CA 95322
209-854-3013

Branch Librarian . . . Nola Ramirez

Library system statistics, FY 2007

Population served . . . 251,510
Internet terminals . . . 91
Annual users . . . 124,530

Per capita:

Operating income . . . $8.99
percent from local government . . . 91.3%
Operating expenditure . . . $8.99
Total materials . . . 1.61
Print holdings . . . 1.60
Visits per capita . . . 1.75

Housing & Construction

Housing Units

Total, 2008§ . . . 2,005
Single family units, attached . . . 31
Single family units, detached . . . 1,643
Multiple family units . . . 203
Mobile home units . . . 128
Occupied . . . 1,914
Vacancy rate . . . 4.5%
Median rent, 2000** . . . $510
Median SF home value, 2000** . . . $114,100

New Privately Owned Housing Units Authorized by Building Permit, 2007*

	Units	Construction Cost
Single	22	$2,752,622
Total	22	$2,752,622

Municipal Finance

(For local fiscal year ended in 2006)

Revenues

Total . . . NA
Taxes . . . NA
Special benefits assessment . . . NA
Licenses & permits . . . NA
Fines & forfeitures . . . NA
Revenues from use of money & property . . . NA
Intergovernmental . . . NA
Service charges . . . NA
Other revenues . . . NA
Other financing sources . . . NA

Expenditures

Total . . . NA
General government . . . NA
Public safety . . . NA
Transportation . . . NA
Community development . . . NA
Health . . . NA
Culture & leisure . . . NA
Other . . . NA

Local School District

(Data from School year 2007-08 except as noted)

Gustine Unified
1500 Meredith Ave
Gustine, CA 95322
(209) 854-3784

Superintendent . . . Gail McWilliams
Grade plan . . . K-12
Number of schools . . . 6
Enrollment . . . 1,943
High school graduates, 2006-07 . . . 107
Dropout rate . . . 3.2%
Pupil/teacher ratio . . . 19.3
Average class size . . . 24.0
Students per computer . . . 6.1
Classrooms with internet . . . 101
Avg. Daily Attendance (ADA) . . . 1,877
Cost per ADA . . . $7,834
Avg. Teacher Salary . . . $56,547

California Achievement Tests 6th ed., 2008

(Pct scoring at or above 50th National Percentile Rank)

	Math	Reading	Language
Grade 3	42%	32%	39%
Grade 7	45%	45%	40%

Academic Performance Index, 2008

Number of students tested . . . 1,457
Number of valid scores . . . 1,335
2007 API (base) . . . 692
2008 API (growth) . . . 708

SAT Testing, 2006-07

Enrollment, Grade 12 . . . 134
Number taking test . . . 24
percent taking test . . . 17.9%
percent with total score 1,500+ . . . 8.20%

Average Scores:

Math	Verbal	Writing	Total
474	455	478	1,407

Federal No Child Left Behind, 2008

(Adequate Yearly Progress standards met)

	Participation Rate	Pct Proficient
ELA	Yes	No
Math	Yes	No

API criteria . . . Yes
Graduation rate . . . No
\# criteria met/possible . . . 22/17

Other school districts for this city

(see Appendix E for information on these districts)

None

See Introduction for an explanation of all data sources.

Demographics & Socio-Economic Characteristics

(2000 Decennial Census, except as noted)

Population

1990* 8,886
2000 11,842
  Male 6,277
  Female 5,565
Jan. 2008 (estimate)§ 13,046
  Persons per sq. mi. of land 2,007.1

Race & Hispanic Origin, 2000

Race
  White 9,150
  Black/African American 463
  North American Native 52
  Asian 402
  Pacific Islander 14
  Other Race 1,307
  Two or more races 454
Hispanic origin, total 2,751
  Mexican 2,359
  Puerto Rican 39
  Cuban 18
  Other Hispanic 335

Age & Nativity, 2000

Under 5 years 699
18 years and over 9,215
65 years and over 1,137
85 years and over 80
  Median Age 38.7
Native-born 9,085
Foreign-born 2,890

Educational Attainment, 2000

Population 25 years and over 8,397
Less than 9th grade 12.6%
High school grad or higher 77.2%
Bachelor's degree or higher 35.5%
Graduate degree 13.4%

Income & Poverty, 1999

Per capita income $37,963
Median household income $78,473
Median family income $92,204
Persons in poverty 5.8%
H'holds receiving public assistance 63
H'holds receiving social security 956

Households, 2000

Total households 4,004
  With persons under 18 1,347
  With persons over 65 890
  Family households 2,773
  Single person households 923
Persons per household 2.75
Persons per family 3.20

Household Population, 2008§§

Persons living in households 12,198
Persons living in group quarters 848
Persons per household 2.8

Labor & Employment

Total civilian labor force, 2008§§ 6,500
  Unemployment rate, 2008 .... 5.8%
Total civilian labor force, 2000 6,255

Employed persons 16 years and over by occupation, 2000

  Managers & professionals 2,596
  Service occupations 885
  Sales & office occupations 1,396
  Farming, fishing & forestry 230
  Construction & maintenance 488
  Production & transportation 410
  Self-employed persons 619

* US Census Bureau
** 2000 Decennial Census
§ California Department of Finance
§§ California Employment Development Dept

General Information

City of Half Moon Bay
501 Main St
Half Moon Bay, CA 94019
650-726-8270

Website .... www.half-moon-bay.ca.us
Elevation .... 69 ft.
Land Area (sq. miles) 6.5
Water Area (sq. miles) 0
Year of Incorporation 1959
Government type .... General law
Sales tax rate 9.25%

Voters & Officials

Registered Voters, October 2008

Total 7,101
  Democrats 3,324
  Republicans 1,789
  Declined to state 1,614

Legislative Districts

US Congressional 14
State Senatorial 8
State Assembly 19

Local Officials, 2009

Mayor .... John Muller
Manager .... Michael Dolder
City Clerk .... Siobhan Smith
Attorney .... Anthony Condotti
Finance Dir .... Hector Lwin
Public Works .... Rick Mao
Planning Dir .... Steve Flint
Building .... NA
Police Chief .... Don O'Keefe
Fire Chief .... Paul Cole

Public Safety

Number of officers, 2007 18
Violent crimes, 2007 21
Property crimes, 2007 256
Arson, 2007 2

Public Library

Half Moon Bay Library
San Mateo County Library System
620 Correas St
Half Moon Bay, CA 94019
650-726-2316

Branch Librarian .... Maya Kennedy

Library system statistics, FY 2007

Population served 278,388
Internet terminals 26
  Annual users 49,920

Per capita:

Operating income $90.21
  percent from local government 63.5%
Operating expenditure $60.41
Total materials 2.65
Print holdings 2.16
Visits per capita 5.44

Housing & Construction

Housing Units

Total, 2008§ 4,483
  Single family units, attached 536
  Single family units, detached 2,827
  Multiple family units 693
  Mobile home units 427
  Occupied 4,392
  Vacancy rate 2.0%
Median rent, 2000** $1,269
Median SF home value, 2000** $499,500

New Privately Owned Housing Units Authorized by Building Permit, 2007*

	Units	Construction Cost
Single	19	$4,895,769
Total	21	$5,134,569

Municipal Finance

(For local fiscal year ended in 2006)

Revenues

Total $13,307,925
Taxes 8,066,768
Special benefits assessment 0
Licenses & permits 287,012
Fines & forfeitures 73,766
Revenues from use of
  money & property 558,963
Intergovernmental 826,224
Service charges 3,405,419
Other revenues 89,773
Other financing sources 0

Expenditures

Total $13,823,834
General government 1,589,806
Public safety 3,805,913
Transportation 1,740,351
Community development 1,922,041
Health 3,172,400
Culture & leisure 1,593,323
Other 0

Local School District

(Data from School year 2007-08 except as noted)

Cabrillo Unified
498 Kelly Ave
Half Moon Bay, CA 94019
(650) 712-7100

Superintendent .... Robert Gaskill
Grade plan K-12
Number of schools 7
Enrollment 3,363
High school graduates, 2006-07 239
Dropout rate 3.8%
Pupil/teacher ratio 21.7
Average class size 24.7
Students per computer 4.8
Classrooms with internet 168
Avg. Daily Attendance (ADA) 3,427
  Cost per ADA $7,639
Avg. Teacher Salary $63,222

California Achievement Tests 6th ed., 2008

(Pct scoring at or above 50th National Percentile Rank)

	Math	Reading	Language
Grade 3	58%	46%	51%
Grade 7	59%	63%	57%

Academic Performance Index, 2008

Number of students tested 2,540
Number of valid scores 2,462
2007 API (base) 772
2008 API (growth) 777

SAT Testing, 2006-07

Enrollment, Grade 12 313
Number taking test 134
  percent taking test 42.8%
  percent with total score 1,500+ 31.00%

Average Scores:

Math	Verbal	Writing	Total
564	548	550	1,662

Federal No Child Left Behind, 2008

(Adequate Yearly Progress standards met)

	Participation Rate	Pct Proficient
ELA	Yes	No
Math	Yes	No

API criteria .... Yes
Graduation rate .... Yes
criteria met/possible 26/19

Other school districts for this city

(see Appendix E for information on these districts)

None

See Introduction for an explanation of all data sources.

Demographics & Socio-Economic Characteristics

(2000 Decennial Census, except as noted)

Population

1990* 30,897
2000 41,686
Male 20,411
Female 21,275
Jan. 2008 (estimate)§ 51,965
Persons per sq. mi. of land 3,966.8

Race & Hispanic Origin, 2000

Race
White 26,704
Black/African American 2,090
North American Native 569
Asian 1,190
Pacific Islander 74
Other Race 8,669
Two or more races 2,390
Hispanic origin, total 16,116
Mexican 13,921
Puerto Rican 109
Cuban 22
Other Hispanic 2,064

Age & Nativity, 2000

Under 5 years 3,636
18 years and over 28,505
65 years and over 4,301
85 years and over 607
Median Age 30.9
Native-born 36,053
Foreign-born 5,676

Educational Attainment, 2000

Population 25 years and over 24,658
Less than 9th grade 12.3%
High school grad or higher 74.5%
Bachelor's degree or higher 14.4%
Graduate degree 3.9%

Income & Poverty, 1999

Per capita income $17,504
Median household income $37,582
Median family income $41,395
Persons in poverty 16.9%
H'holds receiving public assistance 1,114
H'holds receiving social security 3,462

Households, 2000

Total households 13,931
With persons under 18 6,444
With persons over 65 2,980
Family households 10,383
Single person households 2,864
Persons per household 2.93
Persons per family 3.39

Household Population, 2008§§

Persons living in households 51,117
Persons living in group quarters 848
Persons per household 3.0

Labor & Employment

Total civilian labor force, 2008§§ 23,400
Unemployment rate, 2008 .... 9.3%
Total civilian labor force, 2000 17,970

Employed persons 16 years and over by occupation, 2000

Managers & professionals 4,769
Service occupations 3,511
Sales & office occupations 3,673
Farming, fishing & forestry 618
Construction & maintenance 1,252
Production & transportation 2,068
Self-employed persons 982

* US Census Bureau
** 2000 Decennial Census
§ California Department of Finance
§§ California Employment Development Dept

General Information

City of Hanford
319 N Douty
Hanford, CA 93230
559-585-2500

Website .... www.ci.hanford.ca.us
Elevation .... 246 ft.
Land Area (sq. miles) 13.1
Water Area (sq. miles) 0
Year of Incorporation 1891
Government type .... General law
Sales tax rate 8.25%

Voters & Officials

Registered Voters, October 2008

Total 22,252
Democrats 8,265
Republicans 10,391
Declined to state 2,836

Legislative Districts

US Congressional 20
State Senatorial 16
State Assembly 30

Local Officials, 2009

Mayor .... David G. Ayers
Manager .... Gary W. Misenhimer
City Clerk .... Karen Madruga
Attorney .... Robert Dowd
Finance Dir .... Tom Dibble
Public Works .... Lou Camara
Comm Dev Dir .... NA
Building .... Jim Kochar
Police Chief .... Carlos Mestas
Emergency/Fire Dir .... Tim Ieronimo

Public Safety

Number of officers, 2007 46
Violent crimes, 2007 151
Property crimes, 2007 1,674
Arson, 2007 33

Public Library

Hanford Library
Kings County Library System
401 N Douty St
Hanford, CA 93230
559-582-0261

Director .... Eleanor Louise Hodges

Library system statistics, FY 2007

Population served 151,381
Internet terminals 59
Annual users 42,581

Per capita:

Operating income $11.91
percent from local government 86.5%
Operating expenditure $11.91
Total materials 1.20
Print holdings 1.17
Visits per capita .... NA

Housing & Construction

Housing Units

Total, 2008§ 17,806
Single family units, attached 864
Single family units, detached 12,994
Multiple family units 3,605
Mobile home units 343
Occupied 16,850
Vacancy rate 5.4%
Median rent, 2000** $569
Median SF home value, 2000** $102,900

New Privately Owned Housing Units Authorized by Building Permit, 2007*

	Units	Construction Cost
Single	266	$41,716,700
Total	279	$42,567,161

Municipal Finance

(For local fiscal year ended in 2006)

Revenues

Total $49,882,231
Taxes 17,465,996
Special benefits assessment 712,025
Licenses & permits 1,145,468
Fines & forfeitures 239,785
Revenues from use of money & property 2,658,841
Intergovernmental 6,079,147
Service charges 19,466,397
Other revenues 2,114,572
Other financing sources 0

Expenditures

Total $37,657,375
General government 777,555
Public safety 10,064,223
Transportation 4,256,310
Community development 3,457,453
Health 10,964,907
Culture & leisure 3,192,310
Other 0

Local School District

(Data from School year 2007-08 except as noted)

Hanford Joint Union High
823 West Lacey Blvd
Hanford, CA 93230
(559) 583-5901

Superintendent .... William Fishbough
Grade plan 9-12
Number of schools 5
Enrollment 3,873
High school graduates, 2006-07 609
Dropout rate 4.2%
Pupil/teacher ratio 23.1
Average class size 26.0
Students per computer 3.2
Classrooms with internet 182
Avg. Daily Attendance (ADA) 3,663
Cost per ADA $7,718
Avg. Teacher Salary $61,814

California Achievement Tests 6th ed., 2008

(Pct scoring at or above 50th National Percentile Rank)

	Math	Reading	Language
Grade 3	NA	NA	NA
Grade 7	NA	NA	NA

Academic Performance Index, 2008

Number of students tested 2,894
Number of valid scores 2,710
2007 API (base) 676
2008 API (growth) 668

SAT Testing, 2006-07

Enrollment, Grade 12 839
Number taking test 217
percent taking test 25.9%
percent with total score 1,500+ 8.30%

Average Scores:

Math	Verbal	Writing	Total
466	459	447	1,372

Federal No Child Left Behind, 2008

(Adequate Yearly Progress standards met)

	Participation Rate	Pct Proficient
ELA	Yes	No
Math	Yes	Yes

API criteria .... Yes
Graduation rate .... No
\# criteria met/possible 22/20

Other school districts for this city

(see Appendix E for information on these districts)

Complete list in Appendix E

See Introduction for an explanation of all data sources.

Demographics & Socio-Economic Characteristics

(2000 Decennial Census, except as noted)

Population

1990* . . . 13,639
2000 . . . 14,779
Male . . . 7,566
Female . . . 7,213
Jan. 2008 (estimate)§ . . . 15,900
Persons per sq. mi. of land . . . 15,900.0

Race & Hispanic Origin, 2000

Race
White . . . 5,651
Black/African American . . . 657
North American Native . . . 189
Asian . . . 1,300
Pacific Islander . . . 109
Other Race . . . 6,156
Two or more races . . . 717
Hispanic origin, total . . . 10,869
Mexican . . . 9,577
Puerto Rican . . . 39
Cuban . . . 27
Other Hispanic . . . 1,226

Age & Nativity, 2000

Under 5 years . . . 1,521
18 years and over . . . 9,343
65 years and over . . . 914
85 years and over . . . 84
Median Age . . . 25.4
Native-born . . . 8,110
Foreign-born . . . 6,805

Educational Attainment, 2000

Population 25 years and over . . . 7,631
Less than 9th grade . . . 32.1%
High school grad or higher . . . 45.6%
Bachelor's degree or higher . . . 6.7%
Graduate degree . . . 2.1%

Income & Poverty, 1999

Per capita income . . . $10,728
Median household income . . . $34,500
Median family income . . . $31,840
Persons in poverty . . . 22.0%
H'holds receiving public assistance . . . 344
H'holds receiving social security . . . 734

Households, 2000

Total households . . . 3,507
With persons under 18 . . . 2,110
With persons over 65 . . . 713
Family households . . . 2,867
Single person households . . . 498
Persons per household . . . 4.21
Persons per family . . . 4.52

Household Population, 2008§§

Persons living in households . . . 15,896
Persons living in group quarters . . . 4
Persons per household . . . 4.4

Labor & Employment

Total civilian labor force, 2008§§ . . . 6,400
Unemployment rate, 2008 . . . 8.0%
Total civilian labor force, 2000 . . . 5,579

Employed persons 16 years and over by occupation, 2000

Managers & professionals . . . 707
Service occupations . . . 1,241
Sales & office occupations . . . 1,303
Farming, fishing & forestry . . . 26
Construction & maintenance . . . 536
Production & transportation . . . 1,276
Self-employed persons . . . 246

* US Census Bureau
** 2000 Decennial Census
§ California Department of Finance
§§ California Employment Development Dept

General Information

City of Hawaiian Gardens
21815 Pioneer Blvd
Hawaiian Gardens, CA 90716
562-420-2641

Website . . . www.hgcity.org
Elevation . . . 29 ft.
Land Area (sq. miles) . . . 1.0
Water Area (sq. miles) . . . 0
Year of Incorporation . . . 1964
Government type . . . General law
Sales tax rate . . . 9.25%

Voters & Officials

Registered Voters, October 2008

Total . . . 3,946
Democrats . . . 2,150
Republicans . . . 787
Declined to state . . . 815

Legislative Districts

US Congressional . . . 39
State Senatorial . . . 27
State Assembly . . . 56

Local Officials, 2009

Mayor . . . Michiko A. Oyama-Canada
Manager . . . Ernesto Marquez
City Clerk . . . Suzanne Underwood
Attorney . . . John Cavanaugh
Finance Dir . . . David Sung
Public Works . . . Joe Vasquez
Community Dev Dir . . . Joseph Colombo
Building . . . NA
Police Chief . . . David Fender
Fire Chief . . . Albert Bennett

Public Safety

Number of officers, 2007 . . . NA
Violent crimes, 2007 . . . 149
Property crimes, 2007 . . . 407
Arson, 2007 . . . NA

Public Library

Hawaiian Gardens Library
Los Angeles County Public Library System
12100 E Carson St #E
Hawaiian Gardens, CA 90716
562-496-1212

Branch Librarian . . . Marie Ortiz

Library system statistics, FY 2007

Population served . . . 3,673,313
Internet terminals . . . 749
Annual users . . . 3,748,771

Per capita:

Operating income . . . $30.06
percent from local government . . . 93.6%
Operating expenditure . . . $28.36
Total materials . . . 2.22
Print holdings . . . 1.97
Visits per capita . . . 3.25

Housing & Construction

Housing Units

Total, 2008§ . . . 3,721
Single family units, attached . . . 504
Single family units, detached . . . 1,525
Multiple family units . . . 1,417
Mobile home units . . . 275
Occupied . . . 3,602
Vacancy rate . . . 3.2%
Median rent, 2000** . . . $718
Median SF home value, 2000** . . . $139,500

New Privately Owned Housing Units Authorized by Building Permit, 2007*

	Units	Construction Cost
Single	15	$1,795,180
Total	15	$1,795,180

Municipal Finance

(For local fiscal year ended in 2006)

Revenues

Total . . . $17,700,926
Taxes . . . 2,341,592
Special benefits assessment . . . 245,816
Licenses & permits . . . 266,478
Fines & forfeitures . . . 176,780
Revenues from use of money & property . . . 261,082
Intergovernmental . . . 1,803,364
Service charges . . . 241,879
Other revenues . . . 12,363,935
Other financing sources . . . 0

Expenditures

Total . . . $16,072,454
General government . . . 4,353,154
Public safety . . . 2,851,466
Transportation . . . 2,979,880
Community development . . . 1,534,205
Health . . . 0
Culture & leisure . . . 4,353,749
Other . . . 0

Local School District

(Data from School year 2007-08 except as noted)

ABC Unified
16700 Norwalk Blvd
Cerritos, CA 90703
(562) 926-5566

Superintendent . . . Gary Smuts
Grade plan . . . K-12
Number of schools . . . 30
Enrollment . . . 20,860
High school graduates, 2006-07 . . . 1,621
Dropout rate . . . 2.0%
Pupil/teacher ratio . . . 22.6
Average class size . . . 26.8
Students per computer . . . 3.9
Classrooms with internet . . . 1,014
Avg. Daily Attendance (ADA) . . . 20,919
Cost per ADA . . . $8,129
Avg. Teacher Salary . . . $72,259

California Achievement Tests 6th ed., 2008

(Pct scoring at or above 50th National Percentile Rank)

	Math	Reading	Language
Grade 3	62%	42%	54%
Grade 7	60%	55%	55%

Academic Performance Index, 2008

Number of students tested . . . 16,210
Number of valid scores . . . 15,478
2007 API (base) . . . 784
2008 API (growth) . . . 795

SAT Testing, 2006-07

Enrollment, Grade 12 . . . 1,827
Number taking test . . . 860
percent taking test . . . 47.1%
percent with total score 1,500+ . . . 31.30%

Average Scores:

Math	Verbal	Writing	Total
589	530	538	1,657

Federal No Child Left Behind, 2008

(Adequate Yearly Progress standards met)

	Participation Rate	Pct Proficient
ELA	Yes	No
Math	Yes	No

API criteria . . . Yes
Graduation rate . . . Yes
criteria met/possible . . . 42/40

Other school districts for this city

(see Appendix E for information on these districts)

None

Demographics & Socio-Economic Characteristics†

(2007 American Community Survey, except as noted)

Population

1990* ... 71,349
2007 ... 92,321
Male ... 43,491
Female ... 48,830
Jan. 2008 (estimate)§ ... 90,014
Persons per sq. mi. of land ... 14,756.4

Race & Hispanic Origin, 2007

Race
White ... 39,496
Black/African American ... 26,784
North American Native ... 86
Asian ... 5,286
Pacific Islander ... 0
Other Race ... 19,021
Two or more races ... 1,648
Hispanic origin, total ... 47,539
Mexican ... 31,438
Puerto Rican ... 396
Cuban ... 553
Other Hispanic ... 15,152

Age & Nativity, 2007

Under 5 years ... 9,106
18 years and over ... 63,776
65 years and over ... 5,530
85 years and over ... 671
Median Age ... 30.7
Native-born ... 59,090
Foreign-born ... 33,231

Educational Attainment, 2007

Population 25 years and over ... 54,349
Less than 9th grade ... 15.3%
High school grad or higher ... 72.1%
Bachelor's degree or higher ... 14.5%
Graduate degree ... 4.2%

Income & Poverty, 2007

Per capita income ... $17,698
Median household income ... $41,798
Median family income ... $45,501
Persons in poverty ... 16.6%
H'holds receiving public assistance ... 1,383
H'holds receiving social security ... 3,731

Households, 2007

Total households ... 29,128
With persons under 18 ... 13,188
With persons over 65 ... 3,884
Family households ... 20,481
Single person households ... 7,255
Persons per household ... 3.12
Persons per family ... 3.79

Household Population, 2008§§

Persons living in households ... 89,514
Persons living in group quarters ... 500
Persons per household ... 3.1

Labor & Employment

Total civilian labor force, 2008§§ ... 42,600
Unemployment rate, 2008 ... 9.9%
Total civilian labor force, 2000* ... 36,633

Employed persons 16 years and over by occupation, 2007

Managers & professionals ... 7,619
Service occupations ... 9,501
Sales & office occupations ... 11,716
Farming, fishing & forestry ... 165
Construction & maintenance ... 3,830
Production & transportation ... 7,068
Self-employed persons ... 2,965

† see Appendix D for 2000 Decennial Census Data
* US Census Bureau
** 2007 American Community Survey
§ California Department of Finance
§§ California Employment Development Dept

General Information

City of Hawthorne
4455 W 126th St
Hawthorne, CA 90250
310-349-2901

Website ... www.cityofhawthorne.com
Elevation ... 69 ft.
Land Area (sq. miles) ... 6.1
Water Area (sq. miles) ... 0
Year of Incorporation ... 1922
Government type ... General law
Sales tax rate ... 9.25%

Voters & Officials

Registered Voters, October 2008

Total ... 30,656
Democrats ... 19,089
Republicans ... 4,786
Declined to state ... 5,542

Legislative Districts

US Congressional ... 35
State Senatorial ... 25
State Assembly ... 51

Local Officials, 2009

Mayor ... Larry Guidi
Manager ... Jag Pathirana
City Clerk ... Angie Reyes English
Attorney ... Russel Miyahira
Finance Dir ... Jag Pathirana
Public Works ... Arnie Shadbehr
Planning/Dev Dir ... Harold Roth
Building ... Ray Shun
Police Chief ... Mike Heffner
Emergency/Fire Dir. ... P. Michael Freeman

Public Safety

Number of officers, 2007 ... 96
Violent crimes, 2007 ... 765
Property crimes, 2007 ... 1,992
Arson, 2007 ... 5

Public Library

Hawthorne Library
Los Angeles County Public Library System
12700 S Grevillea Ave
Hawthorne, CA 90250
310-679-8193

Branch Librarian ... Sharon Johnson (Actg)

Library system statistics, FY 2007

Population served ... 3,673,313
Internet terminals ... 749
Annual users ... 3,748,771

Per capita:

Operating income ... $30.06
percent from local government ... 93.6%
Operating expenditure ... $28.36
Total materials ... 2.22
Print holdings ... 1.97
Visits per capita ... 3.25

Housing & Construction

Housing Units

Total, 2008§ ... 30,268
Single family units, attached ... 2,471
Single family units, detached ... 8,362
Multiple family units ... 19,262
Mobile home units ... 173
Occupied ... 29,152
Vacancy rate ... 3.7%
Median rent, 2007** ... $904
Median SF home value, 2007** ... $591,400

New Privately Owned Housing Units Authorized by Building Permit, 2007*

	Units	Construction Cost
Single	18	$3,584,678
Total	161	$29,579,890

Municipal Finance

(For local fiscal year ended in 2006)

Revenues

Total ... $126,764,143
Taxes ... 38,375,506
Special benefits assessment ... 719,168
Licenses & permits ... 1,447,999
Fines & forfeitures ... 2,557,398
Revenues from use of money & property ... 2,376,912
Intergovernmental ... 42,691,136
Service charges ... 3,911,315
Other revenues ... 4,204,709
Other financing sources ... 30,480,000

Expenditures

Total ... $93,856,481
General government ... 11,882,557
Public safety ... 38,055,509
Transportation ... 7,072,087
Community development ... 32,122,956
Health ... 523,076
Culture & leisure ... 4,200,296
Other ... 0

Local School District

(Data from School year 2007-08 except as noted)

Centinela Valley Union High
14901 South Inglewood Ave
Lawndale, CA 90260
(310) 263-3200

Superintendent ... Jose Fernandez
Grade plan ... 9-12
Number of schools ... 5
Enrollment ... 7,648
High school graduates, 2006-07 ... 1,005
Dropout rate ... 5.6%
Pupil/teacher ratio ... 21.7
Average class size ... 27.9
Students per computer ... 3.0
Classrooms with internet ... 353
Avg. Daily Attendance (ADA) ... 7,096
Cost per ADA ... $8,357
Avg. Teacher Salary ... $61,333

California Achievement Tests 6th ed., 2008

(Pct scoring at or above 50th National Percentile Rank)

	Math	Reading	Language
Grade 3	NA	NA	NA
Grade 7	NA	NA	NA

Academic Performance Index, 2008

Number of students tested ... 5,550
Number of valid scores ... 5,104
2007 API (base) ... 598
2008 API (growth) ... 618

SAT Testing, 2006-07

Enrollment, Grade 12 ... 1,581
Number taking test ... 561
percent taking test ... 35.5%
percent with total score 1,500+ ... 5.90%

Average Scores:

Math	Verbal	Writing	Total
424	415	414	1,253

Federal No Child Left Behind, 2008

(Adequate Yearly Progress standards met)

	Participation Rate	Pct Proficient
ELA	Yes	No
Math	Yes	No

API criteria ... Yes
Graduation rate ... Yes
\# criteria met/possible ... 26/23

Other school districts for this city

(see Appendix E for information on these districts)

Hawthorne Elem, Wiseburn Elem

See Introduction for an explanation of all data sources.

Demographics & Socio-Economic Characteristics†

(2007 American Community Survey, except as noted)

Population

1990* . . . 111,498
2007 . . . 129,885
Male . . . 65,809
Female . . . 64,076
Jan. 2008 (estimate)§ . . . 149,205
Persons per sq. mi. of land . . . 3,368.1

Race & Hispanic Origin, 2007

Race
White . . . 44,728
Black/African American . . . 17,586
North American Native . . . 1,375
Asian . . . 29,246
Pacific Islander . . . 3,839
Other Race . . . 28,079
Two or more races . . . 5,032
Hispanic origin, total . . . 46,828
Mexican . . . 36,985
Puerto Rican . . . 2,438
Cuban . . . 69
Other Hispanic . . . 7,336

Age & Nativity, 2007

Under 5 years . . . 8,009
18 years and over . . . 97,865
65 years and over . . . 10,852
85 years and over . . . 2,066
Median Age . . . 34.5
Native-born . . . 84,487
Foreign-born . . . 45,398

Educational Attainment, 2007

Population 25 years and over . . . 83,573
Less than 9th grade . . . 9.6%
High school grad or higher . . . 83.1%
Bachelor's degree or higher . . . 25.2%
Graduate degree . . . 6.2%

Income & Poverty, 2007

Per capita income . . . $25,487
Median household income . . . $60,771
Median family income . . . $66,689
Persons in poverty . . . 10.8%
H'holds receiving public assistance . . . 1,941
H'holds receiving social security . . . 8,707

Households, 2007

Total households . . . 40,836
With persons under 18 . . . 17,058
With persons over 65 . . . 7,189
Family households . . . 28,549
Single person households . . . 9,309
Persons per household . . . 3.13
Persons per family . . . 3.68

Household Population, 2008§§

Persons living in households . . . 146,706
Persons living in group quarters . . . 2,499
Persons per household . . . 3.1

Labor & Employment

Total civilian labor force, 2008§§ . . . 70,600
Unemployment rate, 2008 . . . 6.9%
Total civilian labor force, 2000* . . . 67,535

Employed persons 16 years and over by occupation, 2007

Managers & professionals . . . 17,053
Service occupations . . . 11,638
Sales & office occupations . . . 19,008
Farming, fishing & forestry . . . 0
Construction & maintenance . . . 8,105
Production & transportation . . . 9,268
Self-employed persons . . . 3,722

† see Appendix D for 2000 Decennial Census Data
* US Census Bureau
** 2007 American Community Survey
§ California Department of Finance
§§ California Employment Development Dept

General Information

City of Hayward
777 B St
Hayward, CA 94541
510-583-4000

Website . . . www.hayward-ca.gov
Elevation . . . 111 ft.
Land Area (sq. miles) . . . 44.3
Water Area (sq. miles) . . . 18.7
Year of Incorporation . . . 1876
Government type . . . Chartered
Sales tax rate . . . 9.75%

Voters & Officials

Registered Voters, October 2008

Total . . . 57,133
Democrats . . . 34,879
Republicans . . . 7,913
Declined to state . . . 11,958

Legislative Districts

US Congressional . . . 13
State Senatorial . . . 10
State Assembly . . . 18, 20

Local Officials, 2009

Mayor . . . Michael Sweeney
Manager . . . Gregory T. Jones
City Clerk . . . (vacant)
Attorney . . . Michael Lawson
Finance Dir . . . Debra Auker
Public Works . . . Robert Bauman
Planning/Dev Dir . . . NA
Building . . . Glen Martinez
Police Chief . . . Ron Ace
Fire Chief . . . Craig Bueno

Public Safety

Number of officers, 2007 . . . 194
Violent crimes, 2007 . . . 881
Property crimes, 2007 . . . 4,667
Arson, 2007 . . . 60

Public Library

Hayward Public Library
Hayward Public Library System
835 C St
Hayward, CA 94541
510-293-8685

Director . . . Lisa Rosenblum

Library system statistics, FY 2007

Population served . . . 147,845
Internet terminals . . . 53
Annual users . . . 123,943

Per capita:

Operating income . . . $27.22
percent from local government . . . 92.7%
Operating expenditure . . . $27.22
Total materials . . . 1.11
Print holdings . . . 0.87
Visits per capita . . . 4.01

Housing & Construction

Housing Units

Total, 2008§ . . . 48,273
Single family units, attached . . . 3,578
Single family units, detached . . . 24,223
Multiple family units . . . 18,171
Mobile home units . . . 2,301
Occupied . . . 47,098
Vacancy rate . . . 2.4%
Median rent, 2007** . . . $1,194
Median SF home value, 2007** . . . $562,300

New Privately Owned Housing Units Authorized by Building Permit, 2007*

	Units	Construction Cost
Single	255	$85,175,508
Total	255	$85,175,508

Municipal Finance

(For local fiscal year ended in 2006)

Revenues

Total . . . $197,299,984
Taxes . . . 80,578,788
Special benefits assessment . . . 999,802
Licenses & permits . . . 3,016,001
Fines & forfeitures . . . 1,266,615
Revenues from use of money & property . . . 4,908,674
Intergovernmental . . . 20,294,267
Service charges . . . 59,939,233
Other revenues . . . 13,133,254
Other financing sources . . . 13,163,350

Expenditures

Total . . . $193,817,671
General government . . . 13,752,245
Public safety . . . 68,600,163
Transportation . . . 29,476,977
Community development . . . 14,709,140
Health . . . 30,476,563
Culture & leisure . . . 4,716,711
Other . . . 0

Local School District

(Data from School year 2007-08 except as noted)

Hayward Unified
PO Box 5000
Hayward, CA 94540
(510) 784-2600

Superintendent . . . Dale Vigil
Grade plan . . . K-12
Number of schools . . . 33
Enrollment . . . 21,612
High school graduates, 2006-07 . . . 1,198
Dropout rate . . . 4.9%
Pupil/teacher ratio . . . 19.9
Average class size . . . 26.8
Students per computer . . . 5.9
Classrooms with internet . . . 1,074
Avg. Daily Attendance (ADA) . . . 20,751
Cost per ADA . . . $8,856
Avg. Teacher Salary . . . $73,033

California Achievement Tests 6th ed., 2008

(Pct scoring at or above 50th National Percentile Rank)

	Math	Reading	Language
Grade 3	40%	22%	33%
Grade 7	37%	36%	35%

Academic Performance Index, 2008

Number of students tested . . . 16,069
Number of valid scores . . . 14,454
2007 API (base) . . . 674
2008 API (growth) . . . 688

SAT Testing, 2006-07

Enrollment, Grade 12 . . . 1,531
Number taking test . . . 519
percent taking test . . . 33.9%
percent with total score 1,500+ . . . 9.10%

Average Scores:

Math	Verbal	Writing	Total
460	447	445	1,352

Federal No Child Left Behind, 2008

(Adequate Yearly Progress standards met)

	Participation Rate	Pct Proficient
ELA	Yes	No
Math	Yes	No

API criteria . . . Yes
Graduation rate . . . Yes
criteria met/possible . . . 42/33

Other school districts for this city

(see Appendix E for information on these districts)

None

See Introduction for an explanation of all data sources.

Demographics & Socio-Economic Characteristics

(2000 Decennial Census, except as noted)

Population

1990* . . . 9,469
2000 . . . 10,722
Male . . . 5,223
Female . . . 5,499
Jan. 2008 (estimate)§ . . . 11,706
Persons per sq. mi. of land . . . 3,080.5

Race & Hispanic Origin, 2000

Race
White . . . 8,566
Black/African American . . . 54
North American Native . . . 193
Asian . . . 80
Pacific Islander . . . 6
Other Race . . . 1,441
Two or more races . . . 382
Hispanic origin, total . . . 3,090
Mexican . . . 2,753
Puerto Rican . . . 15
Cuban . . . 26
Other Hispanic . . . 296

Age & Nativity, 2000

Under 5 years . . . 632
18 years and over . . . 7,934
65 years and over . . . 1,507
85 years and over . . . 230
Median Age . . . 37.4
Native-born . . . 8,628
Foreign-born . . . 2,021

Educational Attainment, 2000

Population 25 years and over . . . 7,032
Less than 9th grade . . . 11.2%
High school grad or higher . . . 81.0%
Bachelor's degree or higher . . . 29.2%
Graduate degree . . . 9.0%

Income & Poverty, 1999

Per capita income . . . $22,245
Median household income . . . $48,995
Median family income . . . $55,386
Persons in poverty . . . 9.3%
H'holds receiving public assistance . . . 71
H'holds receiving social security . . . 1,203

Households, 2000

Total households . . . 3,968
With persons under 18 . . . 1,422
With persons over 65 . . . 1,102
Family households . . . 2,701
Single person households . . . 1,026
Persons per household . . . 2.69
Persons per family . . . 3.23

Household Population, 2008§§

Persons living in households . . . 11,583
Persons living in group quarters . . . 123
Persons per household . . . 2.6

Labor & Employment

Total civilian labor force, 2008§§ . . . 5,900
Unemployment rate, 2008 . . . 6.4%
Total civilian labor force, 2000 . . . 5,376

Employed persons 16 years and over by occupation, 2000

Managers & professionals . . . 1,851
Service occupations . . . 726
Sales & office occupations . . . 1,204
Farming, fishing & forestry . . . 213
Construction & maintenance . . . 524
Production & transportation . . . 603
Self-employed persons . . . 443

* US Census Bureau
** 2000 Decennial Census
§ California Department of Finance
§§ California Employment Development Dept

General Information

City of Healdsburg
401 Grove St
Healdsburg, CA 95448
707-431-3317

Website . . . www.ci.healdsburg.ca.us
Elevation . . . 106 ft.
Land Area (sq. miles) . . . 3.8
Water Area (sq. miles) . . . 0
Year of Incorporation . . . 1867
Government type . . . General law
Sales tax rate . . . 9.00%

Voters & Officials

Registered Voters, October 2008

Total . . . 6,000
Democrats . . . 3,185
Republicans . . . 1,452
Declined to state . . . 1,105

Legislative Districts

US Congressional . . . 1
State Senatorial . . . 2
State Assembly . . . 1

Local Officials, 2009

Mayor . . . Eric Ziedrich
Manager . . . Marjie Pettus
City Clerk . . . Maria Curiel
Attorney . . . Michael Gogna
Finance Dir . . . Vacant
Public Works . . . Mike Kirn
Planning/Dev Dir . . . Rick Tooker
Building . . . NA
Police Chief . . . Susan Jones
Emergency/Fire Dir . . . Randy Collins

Public Safety

Number of officers, 2007 . . . 18
Violent crimes, 2007 . . . 19
Property crimes, 2007 . . . 279
Arson, 2007 . . . 4

Public Library

Healdsburg Regional Library
Sonoma County Library System
139 Piper St
Healdsburg, CA 95448
707-433-3772

Branch Librarian . . . Catherine Bassett

Library system statistics, FY 2007

Population served . . . 481,785
Internet terminals . . . 140
Annual users . . . 299,464

Per capita:

Operating income . . . $32.97
percent from local government . . . 87.7%
Operating expenditure . . . $30.18
Total materials . . . 1.60
Print holdings . . . 1.49
Visits per capita . . . 5.11

Housing & Construction

Housing Units

Total, 2008§ . . . 4,615
Single family units, attached . . . 280
Single family units, detached . . . 3,298
Multiple family units . . . 938
Mobile home units . . . 99
Occupied . . . 4,427
Vacancy rate . . . 4.1%
Median rent, 2000** . . . $868
Median SF home value, 2000** . . . $263,800

New Privately Owned Housing Units Authorized by Building Permit, 2007*

	Units	Construction Cost
Single	32	$9,146,600
Total	32	$9,146,600

Municipal Finance

(For local fiscal year ended in 2006)

Revenues

Total . . . $41,962,063
Taxes . . . 7,641,662
Special benefits assessment . . . 0
Licenses & permits . . . 109,161
Fines & forfeitures . . . 65,030
Revenues from use of money & property . . . 1,557,132
Intergovernmental . . . 1,407,684
Service charges . . . 21,775,263
Other revenues . . . -23,248,869
Other financing sources . . . 32,655,000

Expenditures

Total . . . $40,972,183
General government . . . 1,157,490
Public safety . . . 6,594,516
Transportation . . . 1,754,380
Community development . . . 3,779,847
Health . . . 9,062,651
Culture & leisure . . . 343,959
Other . . . 0

Local School District

(Data from School year 2007-08 except as noted)

Healdsburg Unified
1028 Prince St
Healdsburg, CA 95448
(707) 431-3488

Superintendent . . . Jeff Harding
Grade plan . . . K-12
Number of schools . . . 4
Enrollment . . . 2,266
High school graduates, 2006-07 . . . 187
Dropout rate . . . 4.7%
Pupil/teacher ratio . . . 20.4
Average class size . . . 25.6
Students per computer . . . 4.7
Classrooms with internet . . . 122
Avg. Daily Attendance (ADA) . . . 2,172
Cost per ADA . . . $9,053
Avg. Teacher Salary . . . $58,946

California Achievement Tests 6th ed., 2008

(Pct scoring at or above 50th National Percentile Rank)

	Math	Reading	Language
Grade 3	41%	23%	31%
Grade 7	47%	43%	41%

Academic Performance Index, 2008

Number of students tested . . . 1,724
Number of valid scores . . . 1,660
2007 API (base) . . . 715
2008 API (growth) . . . 730

SAT Testing, 2006-07

Enrollment, Grade 12 . . . 260
Number taking test . . . 94
percent taking test . . . 36.2%
percent with total score 1,500+ . . . 23.10%

Average Scores:

Math	Verbal	Writing	Total
539	514	515	1,568

Federal No Child Left Behind, 2008

(Adequate Yearly Progress standards met)

	Participation Rate	Pct Proficient
ELA	Yes	No
Math	Yes	No

API criteria . . . Yes
Graduation rate . . . Yes
criteria met/possible . . . 26/18

Other school districts for this city

(see Appendix E for information on these districts)

Alexander Valley Union Elem, West Side Union Elem

See Introduction for an explanation of all data sources.

Demographics & Socio-Economic Characteristics†

(2007 American Community Survey, except as noted)

Population

1990* . . . 36,094
2007 . . . 77,001
Male . . . 35,092
Female . . . 41,909
Jan. 2008 (estimate)§ . . . 74,185
Persons per sq. mi. of land . . . 2,897.9

Race & Hispanic Origin, 2007

Race
White . . . 54,241
Black/African American . . . 1,854
North American Native . . . 1,514
Asian . . . 3,000
Pacific Islander . . . 778
Other Race . . . 12,158
Two or more races . . . 3,456
Hispanic origin, total . . . 21,677
Mexican . . . NA
Puerto Rican . . . NA
Cuban . . . NA
Other Hispanic . . . NA

Age & Nativity, 2007

Under 5 years . . . 7,220
18 years and over . . . 55,836
65 years and over . . . 19,857
85 years and over . . . 3,630
Median Age . . . 38.0
Native-born . . . 63,864
Foreign-born . . . 13,137

Educational Attainment, 2007

Population 25 years and over . . . 49,913
Less than 9th grade . . . 8.2%
High school grad or higher . . . 77.4%
Bachelor's degree or higher . . . 14.8%
Graduate degree . . . 4.5%

Income & Poverty, 2007

Per capita income . . . $17,820
Median household income . . . $34,847
Median family income . . . $37,725
Persons in poverty . . . 19.2%
H'holds receiving public assistance . . . 1,149
H'holds receiving social security . . . 14,733

Households, 2007

Total households . . . 29,721
With persons under 18 . . . 9,836
With persons over 65 . . . 13,379
Family households . . . 18,571
Single person households . . . 9,956
Persons per household . . . 2.56
Persons per family . . . 3.25

Household Population, 2008§§

Persons living in households . . . 72,506
Persons living in group quarters . . . 1,679
Persons per household . . . 2.3

Labor & Employment

Total civilian labor force, 2008§§ . . . 26,500
Unemployment rate, 2008 . . . 10.9%
Total civilian labor force, 2000* . . . 18,864

Employed persons 16 years and over by occupation, 2007

Managers & professionals . . . NA
Service occupations . . . NA
Sales & office occupations . . . NA
Farming, fishing & forestry . . . NA
Construction & maintenance . . . NA
Production & transportation . . . NA
Self-employed persons . . . 1,064

† see Appendix D for 2000 Decennial Census Data
* US Census Bureau
** 2007 American Community Survey
§ California Department of Finance
§§ California Employment Development Dept

General Information

City of Hemet
445 E Florida Ave
Hemet, CA 92543
951-765-2301

Website . . . www.cityofhemet.org
Elevation . . . 1,596 ft.
Land Area (sq. miles) . . . 25.6
Water Area (sq. miles) . . . 0
Year of Incorporation . . . 1910
Government type . . . General law
Sales tax rate . . . 8.75%

Voters & Officials

Registered Voters, October 2008

Total . . . 33,403
Democrats . . . 12,168
Republicans . . . 14,467
Declined to state . . . 5,246

Legislative Districts

US Congressional . . . 45
State Senatorial . . . 37
State Assembly . . . 65

Local Officials, 2009

Mayor . . . Eric McBride
City Manager . . . Len Wood
City Clerk . . . Sarah McComas (Actg)
Attorney . . . Eric Vail
Finance Dir . . . Tom Kanarr
Public Works . . . Mike Gow
Planning Dir . . . Richard Masyczek
Building . . . Colin McNie
Police Chief . . . Richard Dana
Fire Chief . . . Matt Shobert (Int)

Public Safety

Number of officers, 2007 . . . 84
Violent crimes, 2007 . . . 479
Property crimes, 2007 . . . 3,117
Arson, 2007 . . . 18

Public Library

Hemet Public Library
300 E Latham
Hemet, CA 92543
951-765-2440

Director . . . Wayne Disher

Library statistics, FY 2007

Population served . . . 71,705
Internet terminals . . . 34
Annual users . . . 63,833

Per capita:

Operating income . . . $33.98
percent from local government . . . 86.4%
Operating expenditure . . . $33.19
Total materials . . . 1.33
Print holdings . . . 1.14
Visits per capita . . . 5.24

Housing & Construction

Housing Units

Total, 2008§ . . . 35,748
Single family units, attached . . . 2,178
Single family units, detached . . . 17,059
Multiple family units . . . 6,732
Mobile home units . . . 9,779
Occupied . . . 31,290
Vacancy rate . . . 12.5%
Median rent, 2007** . . . $847
Median SF home value, 2007** . . . $208,200

New Privately Owned Housing Units Authorized by Building Permit, 2007*

	Units	Construction Cost
Single	395	$136,360,613
Total	613	$151,806,249

Municipal Finance

(For local fiscal year ended in 2006)

Revenues

Total . . . $77,030,311
Taxes . . . 21,843,205
Special benefits assessment . . . 3,012,294
Licenses & permits . . . 2,877,161
Fines & forfeitures . . . 384,871
Revenues from use of money & property . . . 1,136,996
Intergovernmental . . . 14,534,223
Service charges . . . 24,496,171
Other revenues . . . 8,745,390
Other financing sources . . . 0

Expenditures

Total . . . $77,329,383
General government . . . 612,039
Public safety . . . 31,162,500
Transportation . . . 15,666,351
Community development . . . 5,707,827
Health . . . 13,319,784
Culture & leisure . . . 3,173,035
Other . . . 0

Local School District

(Data from School year 2007-08 except as noted)

Hemet Unified
1791 West Acacia Ave
Hemet, CA 92545
(951) 765-5100

Superintendent . . . Philip Pendley
Grade plan . . . K-12
Number of schools . . . 28
Enrollment . . . 23,567
High school graduates, 2006-07 . . . 1,266
Dropout rate . . . 5.7%
Pupil/teacher ratio . . . 21.2
Average class size . . . 27.7
Students per computer . . . 5.9
Classrooms with internet . . . 1,069
Avg. Daily Attendance (ADA) . . . 23,546
Cost per ADA . . . $7,940
Avg. Teacher Salary . . . $66,015

California Achievement Tests 6th ed., 2008

(Pct scoring at or above 50th National Percentile Rank)

	Math	Reading	Language
Grade 3	51%	34%	40%
Grade 7	48%	44%	42%

Academic Performance Index, 2008

Number of students tested . . . 17,977
Number of valid scores . . . 16,481
2007 API (base) . . . 719
2008 API (growth) . . . 729

SAT Testing, 2006-07

Enrollment, Grade 12 . . . 1,800
Number taking test . . . 358
percent taking test . . . 19.9%
percent with total score 1,500+ . . . 8.60%

Average Scores:

Math	Verbal	Writing	Total
493	487	481	1,461

Federal No Child Left Behind, 2008

(Adequate Yearly Progress standards met)

	Participation Rate	Pct Proficient
ELA	Yes	No
Math	Yes	No

API criteria . . . Yes
Graduation rate . . . Yes
criteria met/possible . . . 42/38

Other school districts for this city

(see Appendix E for information on these districts)

None

See Introduction for an explanation of all data sources.

Demographics & Socio-Economic Characteristics

(2000 Decennial Census, except as noted)

Population

1990* 16,829
2000 19,488
Male 9,247
Female 10,241
Jan. 2008 (estimate)§ 24,324
Persons per sq. mi. of land 3,742.2

Race & Hispanic Origin, 2000

Race
White 5,453
Black/African American 3,659
North American Native 49
Asian 8,327
Pacific Islander 90
Other Race 872
Two or more races 1,038
Hispanic origin, total 2,106
Mexican 1,154
Puerto Rican 92
Cuban 28
Other Hispanic 832

Age & Nativity, 2000

Under 5 years 1,145
18 years and over 14,302
65 years and over 1,433
85 years and over 101
Median Age 36.7
Native-born 13,046
Foreign-born 6,253

Educational Attainment, 2000

Population 25 years and over 12,383
Less than 9th grade 3.6%
High school grad or higher 90.5%
Bachelor's degree or higher 35.9%
Graduate degree 8.6%

Income & Poverty, 1999

Per capita income $27,699
Median household income $75,196
Median family income $82,214
Persons in poverty 3.1%
H'holds receiving public assistance 68
H'holds receiving social security 802

Households, 2000

Total households 6,423
With persons under 18 2,972
With persons over 65 1,092
Family households 5,000
Single person households 1,144
Persons per household 3.03
Persons per family 3.46

Household Population, 2008§§

Persons living in households 24,285
Persons living in group quarters 39
Persons per household 3.0

Labor & Employment

Total civilian labor force, 2008§§ 11,500
Unemployment rate, 2008 .... 4.1%
Total civilian labor force, 2000 10,380

Employed persons 16 years and over by occupation, 2000

Managers & professionals 3,978
Service occupations 970
Sales & office occupations 3,526
Farming, fishing & forestry 5
Construction & maintenance 602
Production & transportation 972
Self-employed persons 572

* US Census Bureau
** 2000 Decennial Census
§ California Department of Finance
§§ California Employment Development Dept

General Information

City of Hercules
111 Civic Dr
Hercules, CA 94547
510-799-8200

Website .... www.ci.hercules.ca.us
Elevation .... NA
Land Area (sq. miles) 6.5
Water Area (sq. miles) 11.8
Year of Incorporation 1900
Government type .... General law
Sales tax rate 9.25%

Voters & Officials

Registered Voters, October 2008

Total 12,353
Democrats 7,349
Republicans 1,837
Declined to state 2,809

Legislative Districts

US Congressional 7
State Senatorial 7
State Assembly 11

Local Officials, 2009

Mayor .... Joe Eddy McDonald
City Manager .... Nelson Oliva
City Clerk .... Doreen Mathews
Attorney .... Alfred Cabral
Finance Dir .... Gloria Leon
Public Works .... Erwin Blancaflor
Economic Dev Dir .... Steve Lawton
Building .... NA
Police Chief .... Fred Deltorchio
Emergency/Fire Dir .... Gary Boyles

Public Safety

Number of officers, 2007 26
Violent crimes, 2007 51
Property crimes, 2007 490
Arson, 2007 4

Public Library

Hercules Public Library
Contra Costa County Library System
109 Civic Dr
Hercules, CA 94547
510-245-2420

Branch Director .... Elliot Warren

Library system statistics, FY 2007

Population served 938,513
Internet terminals 324
Annual users 670,618

Per capita:

Operating income $27.05
percent from local government 82.0%
Operating expenditure $27.82
Total materials 1.57
Print holdings 1.41
Visits per capita 3.65

Housing & Construction

Housing Units

Total, 2008§ 8,304
Single family units, attached 1,631
Single family units, detached 5,508
Multiple family units 1,165
Mobile home units 0
Occupied 8,148
Vacancy rate 1.9%
Median rent, 2000** $1,111
Median SF home value, 2000** $241,500

New Privately Owned Housing Units Authorized by Building Permit, 2007*

	Units	Construction Cost
Single	4	$420,245
Total	4	$420,245

Municipal Finance

(For local fiscal year ended in 2006)

Revenues

Total $26,291,133
Taxes 8,957,444
Special benefits assessment 3,231,593
Licenses & permits 0
Fines & forfeitures 63,565
Revenues from use of money & property 2,002,173
Intergovernmental 2,572,706
Service charges 7,807,898
Other revenues 1,655,754
Other financing sources 0

Expenditures

Total $31,887,803
General government 4,972,290
Public safety 5,074,641
Transportation 2,239,165
Community development 1,727,297
Health 5,668,269
Culture & leisure 10,097,187
Other 0

Local School District

(Data from School year 2007-08 except as noted)

West Contra Costa Unified
1108 Bissell Ave
Richmond, CA 94801
(510) 231-1101

Superintendent .... Bruce Harter
Grade plan K-12
Number of schools 65
Enrollment 30,830
High school graduates, 2006-07 1,622
Dropout rate 9.3%
Pupil/teacher ratio 19.7
Average class size 24.8
Students per computer 6.4
Classrooms with internet 1,508
Avg. Daily Attendance (ADA) 28,599
Cost per ADA $9,365
Avg. Teacher Salary $56,030

California Achievement Tests 6th ed., 2008

(Pct scoring at or above 50th National Percentile Rank)

	Math	Reading	Language
Grade 3	47%	27%	38%
Grade 7	36%	33%	31%

Academic Performance Index, 2008

Number of students tested 22,407
Number of valid scores 20,863
2007 API (base) 674
2008 API (growth) 682

SAT Testing, 2006-07

Enrollment, Grade 12 1,839
Number taking test 853
percent taking test 46.4%
percent with total score 1,500+ 13.90%

Average Scores:

Math	Verbal	Writing	Total
462	455	456	1,373

Federal No Child Left Behind, 2008

(Adequate Yearly Progress standards met)

	Participation Rate	Pct Proficient
ELA	Yes	No
Math	Yes	No

API criteria .... Yes
Graduation rate .... No
\# criteria met/possible 42/34

Other school districts for this city

(see Appendix E for information on these districts)

John Swett Unified

See Introduction for an explanation of all data sources.

Demographics & Socio-Economic Characteristics

(2000 Decennial Census, except as noted)

Population

1990* . . . 18,219
2000 . . . 18,566
Male . . . 9,846
Female . . . 8,720
Jan. 2008 (estimate)§ . . . 19,527
Persons per sq. mi. of land . . . 13,947.9

Race & Hispanic Origin, 2000

Race
White . . . 16,632
Black/African American . . . 150
North American Native . . . 74
Asian . . . 817
Pacific Islander . . . 41
Other Race . . . 312
Two or more races . . . 540
Hispanic origin, total . . . 1,253
Mexican . . . 714
Puerto Rican . . . 74
Cuban . . . 47
Other Hispanic . . . 418

Age & Nativity, 2000

Under 5 years . . . 768
18 years and over . . . 16,339
65 years and over . . . 1,268
85 years and over . . . 152
Median Age . . . 34.2
Native-born . . . 16,952
Foreign-born . . . 1,490

Educational Attainment, 2000

Population 25 years and over . . . 15,207
Less than 9th grade . . . 0.4%
High school grad or higher . . . 97.5%
Bachelor's degree or higher . . . 67.6%
Graduate degree . . . 23.3%

Income & Poverty, 1999

Per capita income . . . $54,244
Median household income . . . $81,153
Median family income . . . $104,645
Persons in poverty . . . 4.5%
H'holds receiving public assistance . . . 93
H'holds receiving social security . . . 991

Households, 2000

Total households . . . 9,476
With persons under 18 . . . 1,408
With persons over 65 . . . 943
Family households . . . 3,558
Single person households . . . 3,736
Persons per household . . . 1.95
Persons per family . . . 2.65

Household Population, 2008§§

Persons living in households . . . 19,414
Persons living in group quarters . . . 113
Persons per household . . . 2.0

Labor & Employment

Total civilian labor force, 2008§§ . . . 15,400
Unemployment rate, 2008 . . . 3.1%
Total civilian labor force, 2000 . . . 13,320

Employed persons 16 years and over by occupation, 2000

Managers & professionals . . . 7,870
Service occupations . . . 894
Sales & office occupations . . . 3,273
Farming, fishing & forestry . . . 0
Construction & maintenance . . . 413
Production & transportation . . . 419
Self-employed persons . . . 1,313

* US Census Bureau
** 2000 Decennial Census
§ California Department of Finance
§§ California Employment Development Dept

General Information

City of Hermosa Beach
1315 Valley Dr
Hermosa Beach, CA 90254
310-318-0239

Website . . . www.hermosabch.org
Elevation . . . 15 ft.
Land Area (sq. miles) . . . 1.4
Water Area (sq. miles) . . . 4.5
Year of Incorporation . . . 1907
Government type . . . General law
Sales tax rate . . . 9.25%

Voters & Officials

Registered Voters, October 2008

Total . . . 13,169
Democrats . . . 4,808
Republicans . . . 4,506
Declined to state . . . 3,172

Legislative Districts

US Congressional . . . 36
State Senatorial . . . 28
State Assembly . . . 53

Local Officials, 2009

Mayor . . . Patrick "Kit" Bobko
Manager . . . Stephen Burrell
City Clerk . . . Elaine Doerfling
Attorney . . . Michael Jenkins
Finance Dir . . . Viki Copeland
Public Works . . . Richard Morgan
Planning/Dev Dir . . . Ken Robertson
Building . . . Ken Robertson
Police Chief . . . Greg Savelli
Emergency/Fire Dir . . . David Lantzer (Int)

Public Safety

Number of officers, 2007 . . . 39
Violent crimes, 2007 . . . 67
Property crimes, 2007 . . . 552
Arson, 2007 . . . 2

Public Library

Hermosa Beach Library
Los Angeles County Public Library System
550 Pier Ave
Hermosa Beach, CA 90254
310-379-8475

Branch Librarian . . . Elmita Brown

Library system statistics, FY 2007

Population served . . . 3,673,313
Internet terminals . . . 749
Annual users . . . 3,748,771

Per capita:

Operating income . . . $30.06
percent from local government . . . 93.6%
Operating expenditure . . . $28.36
Total materials . . . 2.22
Print holdings . . . 1.97
Visits per capita . . . 3.25

Housing & Construction

Housing Units

Total, 2008§ . . . 9,884
Single family units, attached . . . 1,053
Single family units, detached . . . 4,198
Multiple family units . . . 4,551
Mobile home units . . . 82
Occupied . . . 9,516
Vacancy rate . . . 3.7%
Median rent, 2000** . . . $1,146
Median SF home value, 2000** . . . $519,200

New Privately Owned Housing Units Authorized by Building Permit, 2007*

	Units	Construction Cost
Single	39	$13,447,733
Total	39	$13,447,733

Municipal Finance

(For local fiscal year ended in 2006)

Revenues

Total . . . $29,293,725
Taxes . . . 17,538,763
Special benefits assessment . . . 0
Licenses & permits . . . 1,055,421
Fines & forfeitures . . . 1,627,272
Revenues from use of money & property . . . 1,399,104
Intergovernmental . . . 2,369,124
Service charges . . . 4,905,766
Other revenues . . . 398,275
Other financing sources . . . 0

Expenditures

Total . . . $28,150,961
General government . . . 5,795,278
Public safety . . . 13,671,617
Transportation . . . 3,179,612
Community development . . . 3,509,654
Health . . . 0
Culture & leisure . . . 1,994,800
Other . . . 0

Local School District

(Data from School year 2007-08 except as noted)

Redondo Beach Unified
1401 Inglewood Ave
Redondo Beach, CA 90278
(310) 379-5449

Superintendent . . . Steven Keller
Grade plan . . . K-12
Number of schools . . . 12
Enrollment . . . 8,215
High school graduates, 2006-07 . . . 603
Dropout rate . . . 2.9%
Pupil/teacher ratio . . . 21.5
Average class size . . . 25.6
Students per computer . . . 5.1
Classrooms with internet . . . 391
Avg. Daily Attendance (ADA) . . . 7,969
Cost per ADA . . . $8,352
Avg. Teacher Salary . . . $68,773

California Achievement Tests 6th ed., 2008

(Pct scoring at or above 50th National Percentile Rank)

	Math	Reading	Language
Grade 3	74%	60%	68%
Grade 7	73%	71%	67%

Academic Performance Index, 2008

Number of students tested . . . 6,180
Number of valid scores . . . 5,950
2007 API (base) . . . 834
2008 API (growth) . . . 844

SAT Testing, 2006-07

Enrollment, Grade 12 . . . 748
Number taking test . . . 319
percent taking test . . . 42.7%
percent with total score 1,500+ . . . 28.10%

Average Scores:

Math	Verbal	Writing	Total
554	529	530	1,613

Federal No Child Left Behind, 2008

(Adequate Yearly Progress standards met)

	Participation Rate	Pct Proficient
ELA	Yes	Yes
Math	Yes	Yes

API criteria . . . Yes
Graduation rate . . . Yes
criteria met/possible . . . 38/38

Other school districts for this city

(see Appendix E for information on these districts)

Hermosa Beach City Elem, Manhattan Beach Unified

See Introduction for an explanation of all data sources.

Demographics & Socio-Economic Characteristics†

(2007 American Community Survey, except as noted)

Population

1990* 50,418
2007 90,312
Male 46,624
Female 43,688
Jan. 2008 (estimate)§ 87,820
Persons per sq. mi. of land 1,304.9

Race & Hispanic Origin, 2007

Race
White 64,290
Black/African American 4,838
North American Native 1,764
Asian 1,556
Pacific Islander 0
Other Race 15,429
Two or more races 2,435
Hispanic origin, total 48,505
Mexican 41,388
Puerto Rican 768
Cuban 0
Other Hispanic 6,349

Age & Nativity, 2007

Under 5 years 8,668
18 years and over 60,893
65 years and over 8,237
85 years and over 933
Median Age 28.0
Native-born 73,227
Foreign-born 17,085

Educational Attainment, 2007

Population 25 years and over 50,481
Less than 9th grade 11.2%
High school grad or higher 74.6%
Bachelor's degree or higher 7.3%
Graduate degree 2.4%

Income & Poverty, 2007

Per capita income $17,427
Median household income $48,197
Median family income $49,166
Persons in poverty 15.8%
H'holds receiving public assistance . . . 1,190
H'holds receiving social security 6,740

Households, 2007

Total households 24,806
With persons under 18 13,475
With persons over 65 5,666
Family households 20,397
Single person households 3,675
Persons per household 3.60
Persons per family 3.93

Household Population, 2008§§

Persons living in households 87,489
Persons living in group quarters 331
Persons per household 3.3

Labor & Employment

Total civilian labor force, 2008§§ 30,700
Unemployment rate, 2008 . . . . 10.4%
Total civilian labor force, 2000* 25,193

Employed persons 16 years and over by occupation, 2007

Managers & professionals 6,395
Service occupations 5,654
Sales & office occupations 7,590
Farming, fishing & forestry 48
Construction & maintenance 7,231
Production & transportation 7,507
Self-employed persons 2,598

† see Appendix D for 2000 Decennial Census Data
* US Census Bureau
** 2007 American Community Survey
§ California Department of Finance
§§ California Employment Development Dept

General Information

City of Hesperia
9700 Seventh Ave
Hesperia, CA 92345
760-947-1000

Website . . . . www.cityofhesperia.us
Elevation . . . . 3,500 ft.
Land Area (sq. miles) 67.3
Water Area (sq. miles) 0.1
Year of Incorporation 1988
Government type . . . . General Law
Sales tax rate 8.75%

Voters & Officials

Registered Voters, October 2008

Total 33,867
Democrats 12,109
Republicans 14,096
Declined to state 5,982

Legislative Districts

US Congressional 41
State Senatorial 17
State Assembly 59

Local Officials, 2009

Mayor . . . . Thurston Smith
Manager . . . . Mike Podegracz
City Clerk . . . . Vicki Soderquist
Attorney . . . . Eric Dunn
Finance Dir . . . . Brian Johnson
Public Works . . . . Dale Burke
Planning/Dev Dir . . . . Scott Priester
Building . . . . Tom Harp
Police Chief . . . . Lance Clark
Emergency/Fire Dir . . . . Tim Wessel

Public Safety

Number of officers, 2007 . . . . NA
Violent crimes, 2007 322
Property crimes, 2007 2,018
Arson, 2007 25

Public Library

Hesperia Branch Library
San Bernardino County Library System
9565 Seventh Ave
Hesperia, CA 92345
760-244-4898

Branch Librarian . . . Ann Marie Wentworth

Library system statistics, FY 2007

Population served 1,177,092
Internet terminals 12
Annual users 45,343

Per capita:

Operating income $14.27
percent from local government 73.3%
Operating expenditure $13.86
Total materials 0.86
Print holdings 0.79
Visits per capita 5.83

Housing & Construction

Housing Units

Total, 2008§ 28,535
Single family units, attached 893
Single family units, detached 23,192
Multiple family units 3,146
Mobile home units 1,304
Occupied 26,689
Vacancy rate 6.5%
Median rent, 2007** $1,069
Median SF home value, 2007** $335,300

New Privately Owned Housing Units Authorized by Building Permit, 2007*

	Units	Construction Cost
Single	326	$75,576,320
Total	360	$79,590,730

Municipal Finance

(For local fiscal year ended in 2006)

Revenues

Total $48,849,214
Taxes 30,208,804
Special benefits assessment 0
Licenses & permits 5,586,585
Fines & forfeitures 633,281
Revenues from use of money & property 1,986,764
Intergovernmental 6,724,118
Service charges 1,094,047
Other revenues 2,615,615
Other financing sources 0

Expenditures

Total $48,039,530
General government 3,900,392
Public safety 9,751,119
Transportation 10,022,314
Community development 24,365,705
Health 0
Culture & leisure 0
Other 0

Local School District

(Data from School year 2007-08 except as noted)

Hesperia Unified
15576 Main St
Hesperia, CA 92345
(760) 244-4411

Superintendent . . . . Mark McKinney
Grade plan K-12
Number of schools 29
Enrollment 22,481
High school graduates, 2006-07 1,208
Dropout rate 4.9%
Pupil/teacher ratio 22.7
Average class size 27.0
Students per computer 5.2
Classrooms with internet 979
Avg. Daily Attendance (ADA) 20,763
Cost per ADA $7,578
Avg. Teacher Salary $59,696

California Achievement Tests 6th ed., 2008

(Pct scoring at or above 50th National Percentile Rank)

	Math	Reading	Language
Grade 3	47%	30%	39%
Grade 7	43%	42%	40%

Academic Performance Index, 2008

Number of students tested 17,216
Number of valid scores 15,965
2007 API (base) 700
2008 API (growth) 715

SAT Testing, 2006-07

Enrollment, Grade 12 1,345
Number taking test 315
percent taking test 23.4%
percent with total score 1,500+ 9.10%

Average Scores:

Math	Verbal	Writing	Total
482	473	471	1,426

Federal No Child Left Behind, 2008

(Adequate Yearly Progress standards met)

	Participation Rate	Pct Proficient
ELA	Yes	No
Math	Yes	No

API criteria . . . . Yes
Graduation rate . . . . No
\# criteria met/possible 34/28

Other school districts for this city

(see Appendix E for information on these districts)

None

See Introduction for an explanation of all data sources.

Demographics & Socio-Economic Characteristics

(2000 Decennial Census, except as noted)

Population

1990* . . . 1,729
2000 . . . 1,875
Male . . . 902
Female . . . 973
Jan. 2008 (estimate)§ . . . 2,016
Persons per sq. mi. of land . . . 1,185.9

Race & Hispanic Origin, 2000

Race
White . . . 1,762
Black/African American . . . 12
North American Native . . . 6
Asian . . . 40
Pacific Islander . . . 0
Other Race . . . 29
Two or more races . . . 26
Hispanic origin, total . . . 125
Mexican . . . 67
Puerto Rican . . . 2
Cuban . . . 2
Other Hispanic . . . 54

Age & Nativity, 2000

Under 5 years . . . 127
18 years and over . . . 1,256
65 years and over . . . 189
85 years and over . . . 12
Median Age . . . 40.4
Native-born . . . 1,637
Foreign-born . . . 238

Educational Attainment, 2000

Population 25 years and over . . . 1,184
Less than 9th grade . . . 1.9%
High school grad or higher . . . 92.3%
Bachelor's degree or higher . . . 57.9%
Graduate degree . . . 28.0%

Income & Poverty, 1999

Per capita income . . . $94,096
Median household income . . . $200,001
Median family income . . . $200,001
Persons in poverty . . . 3.5%
H'holds receiving public assistance . . . 3
H'holds receiving social security . . . 127

Households, 2000

Total households . . . 568
With persons under 18 . . . 298
With persons over 65 . . . 129
Family households . . . 506
Single person households . . . 43
Persons per household . . . 3.30
Persons per family . . . 3.39

Household Population, 2008§§

Persons living in households . . . 2,016
Persons living in group quarters . . . 0
Persons per household . . . 3.5

Labor & Employment

Total civilian labor force, 2008§§ . . . 900
Unemployment rate, 2008 . . . 1.8%
Total civilian labor force, 2000 . . . 799

Employed persons 16 years and over by occupation, 2000

Managers & professionals . . . 505
Service occupations . . . 80
Sales & office occupations . . . 178
Farming, fishing & forestry . . . 0
Construction & maintenance . . . 7
Production & transportation . . . 13
Self-employed persons . . . 116

* US Census Bureau
** 2000 Decennial Census
§ California Department of Finance
§§ California Employment Development Dept

General Information

City of Hidden Hills
6165 Spring Valley Rd
Hidden Hills, CA 91302
818-888-9281

Website . . . www.hiddenhillscity.org
Elevation . . . NA
Land Area (sq. miles) . . . 1.7
Water Area (sq. miles) . . . 0
Year of Incorporation . . . 1961
Government type . . . General law
Sales tax rate . . . 9.25%

Voters & Officials

Registered Voters, October 2008

Total . . . 1,316
Democrats . . . 525
Republicans . . . 544
Declined to state . . . 201

Legislative Districts

US Congressional . . . 30
State Senatorial . . . 23
State Assembly . . . 41

Local Officials, 2009

Mayor . . . Steve Freedland
City Manager . . . Cherie Paglia
City Clerk . . . Deana Graybill (Dep)
Attorney . . . Roxanne Diaz
Finance Dir . . . Randee Weinberger
Public Works . . . Dirk Lovett
Planning/Dev Dir . . . Dirk Lovett
Building . . . Greg Robinson
Police Chief . . . (County)
Emergency/Fire Dir . . . James Doran

Public Safety

Number of officers, 2007 . . . NA
Violent crimes, 2007 . . . 0
Property crimes, 2007 . . . 29
Arson, 2007 . . . 0

Public Library

Served by County Library

Library system statistics, FY 2007

Population served . . . NA
Internet terminals . . . NA
Annual users . . . NA

Per capita:

Operating income . . . NA
percent from local government . . . NA
Operating expenditure . . . NA
Total materials . . . NA
Print holdings . . . NA
Visits per capita . . . NA

Housing & Construction

Housing Units

Total, 2008§ . . . 607
Single family units, attached . . . 2
Single family units, detached . . . 605
Multiple family units . . . 0
Mobile home units . . . 0
Occupied . . . 583
Vacancy rate . . . 4.0%
Median rent, 2000** . . . $1,208
Median SF home value, 2000** . . $1,000,001

New Privately Owned Housing Units Authorized by Building Permit, 2007*

	Units	Construction Cost
Single	5	$3,749,364
Total	5	$3,749,364

Municipal Finance

(For local fiscal year ended in 2006)

Revenues

Total . . . $1,929,000
Taxes . . . 939,972
Special benefits assessment . . . 0
Licenses & permits . . . 400,239
Fines & forfeitures . . . 18,995
Revenues from use of money & property . . . 180,383
Intergovernmental . . . 157,660
Service charges . . . 101,736
Other revenues . . . 130,015
Other financing sources . . . 0

Expenditures

Total . . . $1,397,088
General government . . . 444,434
Public safety . . . 318,389
Transportation . . . 108,599
Community development . . . 340,665
Health . . . 102,047
Culture & leisure . . . 82,954
Other . . . 0

Local School District

(Data from School year 2007-08 except as noted)

Las Virgenes Unified
4111 North Las Virgenes Rd
Calabasas, CA 91302
(818) 880-4000

Superintendent . . . Donald Zimring
Grade plan . . . K-12
Number of schools . . . 15
Enrollment . . . 11,803
High school graduates, 2006-07 . . . 1,004
Dropout rate . . . 1.4%
Pupil/teacher ratio . . . 25.0
Average class size . . . 28.8
Students per computer . . . 6.1
Classrooms with internet . . . 515
Avg. Daily Attendance (ADA) . . . 11,596
Cost per ADA . . . $8,255
Avg. Teacher Salary . . . $66,468

California Achievement Tests 6th ed., 2008

(Pct scoring at or above 50th National Percentile Rank)

	Math	Reading	Language
Grade 3	82%	67%	75%
Grade 7	80%	75%	75%

Academic Performance Index, 2008

Number of students tested . . . 9,240
Number of valid scores . . . 9,058
2007 API (base) . . . 872
2008 API (growth) . . . 876

SAT Testing, 2006-07

Enrollment, Grade 12 . . . 1,069
Number taking test . . . 746
percent taking test . . . 69.8%
percent with total score 1,500+ . . . 54.20%

Average Scores:

Math	Verbal	Writing	Total
578	549	570	1,697

Federal No Child Left Behind, 2008

(Adequate Yearly Progress standards met)

	Participation Rate	Pct Proficient
ELA	Yes	Yes
Math	Yes	Yes

API criteria . . . Yes
Graduation rate . . . Yes
criteria met/possible . . . 34/34

Other school districts for this city

(see Appendix E for information on these districts)

None

See Introduction for an explanation of all data sources.

Demographics & Socio-Economic Characteristics

(2000 Decennial Census, except as noted)

Population

1990* . . . 34,439
2000 . . . 44,605
Male . . . 21,775
Female . . . 22,830
Jan. 2008 (estimate)§ . . . 52,503
Persons per sq. mi. of land . . . 3,860.5

Race & Hispanic Origin, 2000

Race
White . . . 25,089
Black/African American . . . 5,403
North American Native . . . 581
Asian . . . 2,740
Pacific Islander . . . 152
Other Race . . . 8,307
Two or more races . . . 2,333
Hispanic origin, total . . . 16,342
Mexican . . . 13,397
Puerto Rican . . . 245
Cuban . . . 68
Other Hispanic . . . 2,632

Age & Nativity, 2000

Under 5 years . . . 4,225
18 years and over . . . 28,730
65 years and over . . . 2,887
85 years and over . . . 222
Median Age . . . 29.3
Native-born . . . 36,099
Foreign-born . . . 8,530

Educational Attainment, 2000

Population 25 years and over . . . 24,657
Less than 9th grade . . . 11.4%
High school grad or higher . . . 72.0%
Bachelor's degree or higher . . . 16.1%
Graduate degree . . . 5.8%

Income & Poverty, 1999

Per capita income . . . $16,039
Median household income . . . $41,230
Median family income . . . $43,649
Persons in poverty . . . 21.3%
H'holds receiving public assistance . . . 1,330
H'holds receiving social security . . . 2,656

Households, 2000

Total households . . . 13,478
With persons under 18 . . . 7,207
With persons over 65 . . . 2,208
Family households . . . 10,780
Single person households . . . 2,074
Persons per household . . . 3.29
Persons per family . . . 3.64

Household Population, 2008§§

Persons living in households . . . 52,263
Persons living in group quarters . . . 240
Persons per household . . . 3.5

Labor & Employment

Total civilian labor force, 2008§§ . . . 23,200
Unemployment rate, 2008 . . . 10.2%
Total civilian labor force, 2000 . . . 19,036

Employed persons 16 years and over by occupation, 2000

Managers & professionals . . . 4,924
Service occupations . . . 3,307
Sales & office occupations . . . 4,302
Farming, fishing & forestry . . . 78
Construction & maintenance . . . 1,936
Production & transportation . . . 2,511
Self-employed persons . . . 1,059

* US Census Bureau
** 2000 Decennial Census
§ California Department of Finance
§§ California Employment Development Dept

General Information

City of Highland
27215 Base Line
Highland, CA 92346
909-864-6861

Website . . . www.ci.highland.ca.us
Elevation . . . NA
Land Area (sq. miles) . . . 13.6
Water Area (sq. miles) . . . 0.2
Year of Incorporation . . . 1987
Government type . . . General Law
Sales tax rate . . . 8.75%

Voters & Officials

Registered Voters, October 2008

Total . . . 22,985
Democrats . . . 9,190
Republicans . . . 9,077
Declined to state . . . 3,736

Legislative Districts

US Congressional . . . 41
State Senatorial . . . 31
State Assembly . . . 59, 63

Local Officials, 2009

Mayor . . . Penny Lilburn
Manager . . . Joe Hughes
City Clerk . . . Betty Hughes
Attorney . . . Craig Steele
Finance Dir . . . Chuck Dantuono
Public Works . . . Ernie Wong
Community Dev Dir . . . John Jaquess
Building . . . NA
Police Chief . . . Bobby Phillips
Fire Chief . . . Mary Stock

Public Safety

Number of officers, 2007 . . . NA
Violent crimes, 2007 . . . 325
Property crimes, 2007 . . . 1,336
Arson, 2007 . . . 13

Public Library

Highland Branch Library
San Bernardino County Library System
27167 Base Line
Highland, CA 92346
909-862-8549

Branch Librarian . . . Harriet Foucher

Library system statistics, FY 2007

Population served . . . 1,177,092
Internet terminals . . . 12
Annual users . . . 45,343

Per capita:

Operating income . . . $14.27
percent from local government . . . 73.3%
Operating expenditure . . . $13.86
Total materials . . . 0.86
Print holdings . . . 0.79
Visits per capita . . . 5.83

Housing & Construction

Housing Units

Total, 2008§ . . . 16,643
Single family units, attached . . . 555
Single family units, detached . . . 12,500
Multiple family units . . . 2,727
Mobile home units . . . 861
Occupied . . . 15,098
Vacancy rate . . . 9.3%
Median rent, 2000** . . . $574
Median SF home value, 2000** . . . $128,500

New Privately Owned Housing Units Authorized by Building Permit, 2007*

	Units	Construction Cost
Single	75	$20,731,402
Total	75	$20,731,402

Municipal Finance

(For local fiscal year ended in 2006)

Revenues

Total . . . $24,771,531
Taxes . . . 11,212,290
Special benefits assessment . . . 2,881,138
Licenses & permits . . . 830,172
Fines & forfeitures . . . 175,894
Revenues from use of money & property . . . 1,666,566
Intergovernmental . . . 6,723,614
Service charges . . . 985,513
Other revenues . . . 296,344
Other financing sources . . . 0

Expenditures

Total . . . $25,394,323
General government . . . 1,410,417
Public safety . . . 11,020,052
Transportation . . . 6,784,236
Community development . . . 3,027,678
Health . . . 0
Culture & leisure . . . 3,151,940
Other . . . 0

Local School District

(Data from School year 2007-08 except as noted)

San Bernardino City Unified
777 North F St
San Bernardino, CA 92410
(909) 381-1100

Superintendent . . . Arturo Delgado
Grade plan . . . K-12
Number of schools . . . 70
Enrollment . . . 56,727
High school graduates, 2006-07 . . . 2,198
Dropout rate . . . 8.3%
Pupil/teacher ratio . . . 21.9
Average class size . . . 26.8
Students per computer . . . 4.0
Classrooms with internet . . . 2,351
Avg. Daily Attendance (ADA) . . . 51,623
Cost per ADA . . . $9,872
Avg. Teacher Salary . . . $67,331

California Achievement Tests 6th ed., 2008

(Pct scoring at or above 50th National Percentile Rank)

	Math	Reading	Language
Grade 3	40%	21%	29%
Grade 7	34%	30%	28%

Academic Performance Index, 2008

Number of students tested . . . 41,283
Number of valid scores . . . 37,234
2007 API (base) . . . 643
2008 API (growth) . . . 656

SAT Testing, 2006-07

Enrollment, Grade 12 . . . 2,200
Number taking test . . . 946
percent taking test . . . 43.0%
percent with total score 1,500+ . . . 9.60%

Average Scores:

Math	Verbal	Writing	Total
441	432	431	1,304

Federal No Child Left Behind, 2008

(Adequate Yearly Progress standards met)

	Participation Rate	Pct Proficient
ELA	Yes	No
Math	Yes	No

API criteria . . . Yes
Graduation rate . . . Yes
criteria met/possible . . . 44/32

Other school districts for this city

(see Appendix E for information on these districts)

Redlands Unified

See Introduction for an explanation of all data sources.

Demographics & Socio-Economic Characteristics

(2000 Decennial Census, except as noted)

Population

1990* 10,667
2000 10,825
Male 5,262
Female 5,563
Jan. 2008 (estimate)§ 11,272
Persons per sq. mi. of land 1,818.1

Race & Hispanic Origin, 2000

Race
White 7,772
Black/African American 54
North American Native 7
Asian 2,602
Pacific Islander 25
Other Race 76
Two or more races 289
Hispanic origin, total 304
Mexican 120
Puerto Rican 9
Cuban 17
Other Hispanic 158

Age & Nativity, 2000

Under 5 years 551
18 years and over 8,110
65 years and over 2,014
85 years and over 162
Median Age 45.5
Native-born 8,251
Foreign-born 2,572

Educational Attainment, 2000

Population 25 years and over 7,593
Less than 9th grade 0.4%
High school grad or higher 96.4%
Bachelor's degree or higher 70.0%
Graduate degree 35.8%

Income & Poverty, 1999

Per capita income $98,643
Median household income $193,157
Median family income $200,001
Persons in poverty 2.8%
H'holds receiving public assistance 22
H'holds receiving social security 1,149

Households, 2000

Total households 3,689
With persons under 18 1,417
With persons over 65 1,337
Family households 3,163
Single person households 409
Persons per household 2.93
Persons per family 3.14

Household Population, 2008§§

Persons living in households 11,270
Persons living in group quarters 2
Persons per household 3.0

Labor & Employment

Total civilian labor force, 2008§§ 4,800
Unemployment rate, 2008 . . . . 1.8%
Total civilian labor force, 2000 4,699

Employed persons 16 years and over by occupation, 2000

Managers & professionals 3,349
Service occupations 176
Sales & office occupations 967
Farming, fishing & forestry 0
Construction & maintenance 66
Production & transportation 82
Self-employed persons 758

* US Census Bureau
** 2000 Decennial Census
§ California Department of Finance
§§ California Employment Development Dept

General Information

Town of Hillsborough
1600 Floribunda Ave
Hillsborough, CA 94010
650-375-7400

Website . . . . www.hillsborough.net
Elevation . . . . 32 ft.
Land Area (sq. miles) 6.2
Water Area (sq. miles) 0
Year of Incorporation 1910
Government type . . . . General law
Sales tax rate 9.25%

Voters & Officials

Registered Voters, October 2008

Total 7,486
Democrats 2,415
Republicans 3,205
Declined to state 1,670

Legislative Districts

US Congressional 12
State Senatorial 8
State Assembly 19

Local Officials, 2009

Mayor . . . . Christine M. Krolik
Manager . . . . Anthony Constantouros
City Clerk . . . . Miyuki Yokoyama
Attorney . . . . Norman Book
Finance Dir . . . . Edna Masbad
Public Works . . . . Martha DeBry
Planning & Bldg Dir. . . . . Elizabeth Cullinan
Building . . . . John Mullins
Police Chief . . . . Matthew O'Connor
Fire Chief . . . . Don Dornell

Public Safety

Number of officers, 2007 23
Violent crimes, 2007 2
Property crimes, 2007 95
Arson, 2007 0

Public Library

Served by Burlingame & San Mateo City Libraries

Library system statistics, FY 2007

Population served . . . . NA
Internet terminals . . . . NA
Annual users . . . . NA

Per capita:

Operating income . . . . NA
percent from local government . . . . NA
Operating expenditure . . . . NA
Total materials . . . . NA
Print holdings . . . . NA
Visits per capita . . . . NA

Housing & Construction

Housing Units

Total, 2008§ 3,889
Single family units, attached 12
Single family units, detached 3,868
Multiple family units 9
Mobile home units 0
Occupied 3,797
Vacancy rate 2.4%
Median rent, 2000** $2,001
Median SF home value, 2000** . . $1,000,001

New Privately Owned Housing Units Authorized by Building Permit, 2007*

	Units	Construction Cost
Single	20	$32,065,976
Total	20	$32,065,976

Municipal Finance

(For local fiscal year ended in 2006)

Revenues

Total $29,963,352
Taxes 10,955,033
Special benefits assessment 2,378,560
Licenses & permits 1,017,788
Fines & forfeitures 33,123
Revenues from use of money & property 1,340,155
Intergovernmental 1,504,224
Service charges 12,590,717
Other revenues 143,752
Other financing sources 0

Expenditures

Total $34,040,204
General government 808,960
Public safety 11,696,409
Transportation 2,758,816
Community development 1,270,993
Health 7,776,216
Culture & leisure 730,311
Other 0

Local School District

(Data from School year 2007-08 except as noted)

San Mateo Union High
650 North Delaware St
San Mateo, CA 94401
(650) 558-2299

Superintendent . . . . David Miller
Grade plan 9-12
Number of schools 7
Enrollment 8,626
High school graduates, 2006-07 1,833
Dropout rate 1.3%
Pupil/teacher ratio 21.3
Average class size 26.9
Students per computer 4.0
Classrooms with internet 425
Avg. Daily Attendance (ADA) 8,291
Cost per ADA $9,930
Avg. Teacher Salary $74,785

California Achievement Tests 6th ed., 2008

(Pct scoring at or above 50th National Percentile Rank)

	Math	Reading	Language
Grade 3	NA	NA	NA
Grade 7	NA	NA	NA

Academic Performance Index, 2008

Number of students tested 6,229
Number of valid scores 6,003
2007 API (base) 774
2008 API (growth) 781

SAT Testing, 2006-07

Enrollment, Grade 12 2,145
Number taking test 1,188
percent taking test 55.4%
percent with total score 1,500+ 37.60%

Average Scores:

Math	Verbal	Writing	Total
572	534	536	1,642

Federal No Child Left Behind, 2008

(Adequate Yearly Progress standards met)

	Participation Rate	Pct Proficient
ELA	Yes	No
Math	Yes	No

API criteria . . . . Yes
Graduation rate . . . . Yes
\# criteria met/possible 32/30

Other school districts for this city

(see Appendix E for information on these districts)

Hillsborough City Elem

See Introduction for an explanation of all data sources.

Demographics & Socio-Economic Characteristics

(2000 Decennial Census, except as noted)

Population

1990*	19,212
2000	34,413
Male	17,366
Female	17,047
Jan. 2008 (estimate)§	37,051
Persons per sq. mi. of land	5,613.8

Race & Hispanic Origin, 2000

Race	
White	20,341
Black/African American	469
North American Native	390
Asian	965
Pacific Islander	63
Other Race	10,312
Two or more races	1,873
Hispanic origin, total	18,949
Mexican	16,381
Puerto Rican	121
Cuban	21
Other Hispanic	2,426

Age & Nativity, 2000

Under 5 years	3,442
18 years and over	22,499
65 years and over	2,151
85 years and over	231
Median Age	29.0
Native-born	27,410
Foreign-born	7,204

Educational Attainment, 2000

Population 25 years and over	19,303
Less than 9th grade	15.0%
High school grad or higher	72.3%
Bachelor's degree or higher	15.0%
Graduate degree	4.2%

Income & Poverty, 1999

Per capita income	$18,857
Median household income	$56,104
Median family income	$57,494
Persons in poverty	9.4%
H'holds receiving public assistance	461
H'holds receiving social security	1,681

Households, 2000

Total households	9,716
With persons under 18	5,584
With persons over 65	1,578
Family households	8,045
Single person households	1,235
Persons per household	3.52
Persons per family	3.82

Household Population, 2008§§

Persons living in households	36,880
Persons living in group quarters	171
Persons per household	3.6

Labor & Employment

Total civilian labor force, 2008§§	16,500
Unemployment rate, 2008	10.8%
Total civilian labor force, 2000	16,331

Employed persons 16 years and over by occupation, 2000

Managers & professionals	4,436
Service occupations	2,368
Sales & office occupations	3,768
Farming, fishing & forestry	561
Construction & maintenance	1,843
Production & transportation	2,146
Self-employed persons	906

* US Census Bureau
** 2000 Decennial Census
§ California Department of Finance
§§ California Employment Development Dept

General Information

City of Hollister
375 Fifth St
Hollister, CA 95023
831-636-4301

Website	www.hollister.ca.gov
Elevation	291 ft.
Land Area (sq. miles)	6.6
Water Area (sq. miles)	0
Year of Incorporation	1872
Government type	General law
Sales tax rate	9.25%

Voters & Officials

Registered Voters, October 2008

Total	14,266
Democrats	7,379
Republicans	3,580
Declined to state	2,748

Legislative Districts

US Congressional	17
State Senatorial	12
State Assembly	28

Local Officials, 2009

Mayor	Eugenia Sanchez
Manager	Clint G. Quilter
City Clerk	Geri Johnson, MMC
Attorney	Stephanie Atigh
Finance Dir	Robert Galvan
Public Works	Steve Wittry
Development Svcs Dir	Bill Avera
Building	NA
Police Chief	Jeff Miller
Fire Chief	Fred Cheshire

Public Safety

Number of officers, 2007	28
Violent crimes, 2007	194
Property crimes, 2007	883
Arson, 2007	13

Public Library

Main Branch
San Benito County Free Library
470 Fifth St
Hollister, CA 95023
831-636-4107

County Librarian	Nora Conte

Library system statistics, FY 2007

Population served	55,978
Internet terminals	49
Annual users	105,480

Per capita:

Operating income	$10.82
percent from local government	83.3%
Operating expenditure	$10.77
Total materials	1.61
Print holdings	1.52
Visits per capita	11.07

Housing & Construction

Housing Units

Total, 2008§	10,584
Single family units, attached	525
Single family units, detached	7,980
Multiple family units	1,773
Mobile home units	306
Occupied	10,362
Vacancy rate	2.1%
Median rent, 2000**	$769
Median SF home value, 2000**	$266,300

New Privately Owned Housing Units Authorized by Building Permit, 2007*

	Units	Construction Cost
Single	1	$400,000
Total	1	$400,000

Municipal Finance

(For local fiscal year ended in 2006)

Revenues

Total	$17,222,545
Taxes	8,152,361
Special benefits assessment	810,437
Licenses & permits	211,289
Fines & forfeitures	210,791
Revenues from use of money & property	300,960
Intergovernmental	737,030
Service charges	6,799,677
Other revenues	0
Other financing sources	0

Expenditures

Total	$24,655,247
General government	4,714,611
Public safety	9,032,184
Transportation	4,197,805
Community development	967,989
Health	3,244,680
Culture & leisure	174,065
Other	0

Local School District

(Data from School year 2007-08 except as noted)

San Benito High
1220 Monterey St
Hollister, CA 95023
(831) 637-5831

Superintendent	Stan Rose
Grade plan	9-12
Number of schools	2
Enrollment	3,159
High school graduates, 2006-07	558
Dropout rate	3.1%
Pupil/teacher ratio	26.3
Average class size	27.0
Students per computer	6.1
Classrooms with internet	134
Avg. Daily Attendance (ADA)	3,010
Cost per ADA	$8,180
Avg. Teacher Salary	$65,091

California Achievement Tests 6th ed., 2008

(Pct scoring at or above 50th National Percentile Rank)

	Math	Reading	Language
Grade 3	NA	NA	NA
Grade 7	NA	NA	NA

Academic Performance Index, 2008

Number of students tested	2,334
Number of valid scores	2,196
2007 API (base)	689
2008 API (growth)	722

SAT Testing, 2006-07

Enrollment, Grade 12	679
Number taking test	208
percent taking test	30.6%
percent with total score 1,500+	14.10%

Average Scores:

Math	Verbal	Writing	Total
500	483	474	1,457

Federal No Child Left Behind, 2008

(Adequate Yearly Progress standards met)

	Participation Rate	Pct Proficient
ELA	Yes	Yes
Math	Yes	No

API criteria	Yes
Graduation rate	Yes
# criteria met/possible	22/21

Other school districts for this city

(see Appendix E for information on these districts)

Cienega Union Elem, Hollister Elem, North County Joint Union Elem, Southside Elem

See Introduction for an explanation of all data sources.

Demographics & Socio-Economic Characteristics

(2000 Decennial Census, except as noted)

Population

1990* . . . 4,820
2000 . . . 5,612
Male . . . 2,720
Female . . . 2,892
Jan. 2008 (estimate)§ . . . 6,467
Persons per sq. mi. of land . . . 5,879.1

Race & Hispanic Origin, 2000

Race
White . . . 3,051
Black/African American . . . 35
North American Native . . . 47
Asian . . . 47
Pacific Islander . . . 4
Other Race . . . 2,197
Two or more races . . . 231
Hispanic origin, total . . . 4,144
Mexican . . . 3,805
Puerto Rican . . . 4
Cuban . . . 6
Other Hispanic . . . 329

Age & Nativity, 2000

Under 5 years . . . 490
18 years and over . . . 3,639
65 years and over . . . 623
85 years and over . . . 101
Median Age . . . 30.0
Native-born . . . 3,657
Foreign-born . . . 1,975

Educational Attainment, 2000

Population 25 years and over . . . 3,113
Less than 9th grade . . . 27.0%
High school grad or higher . . . 56.9%
Bachelor's degree or higher . . . 9.4%
Graduate degree . . . 2.3%

Income & Poverty, 1999

Per capita income . . . $12,505
Median household income . . . $36,318
Median family income . . . $39,347
Persons in poverty . . . 17.9%
H'holds receiving public assistance . . . 119
H'holds receiving social security . . . 391

Households, 2000

Total households . . . 1,564
With persons under 18 . . . 913
With persons over 65 . . . 385
Family households . . . 1,340
Single person households . . . 193
Persons per household . . . 3.51
Persons per family . . . 3.80

Household Population, 2008§§

Persons living in households . . . 6,337
Persons living in group quarters . . . 130
Persons per household . . . 3.5

Labor & Employment

Total civilian labor force, 2008§§ . . . 3,100
Unemployment rate, 2008 . . . 20.6%
Total civilian labor force, 2000 . . . 2,179

Employed persons 16 years and over by occupation, 2000

Managers & professionals . . . 407
Service occupations . . . 349
Sales & office occupations . . . 506
Farming, fishing & forestry . . . 208
Construction & maintenance . . . 197
Production & transportation . . . 267
Self-employed persons . . . 117

* US Census Bureau
** 2000 Decennial Census
§ California Department of Finance
§§ California Employment Development Dept

General Information

City of Holtville
121 W 5th St
Holtville, CA 92250
760-356-4170

Website . . . www.holtville.ca.gov
Elevation . . . -10 ft.
Land Area (sq. miles) . . . 1.1
Water Area (sq. miles) . . . 0
Year of Incorporation . . . 1908
Government type . . . General law
Sales tax rate . . . 8.75%

Voters & Officials

Registered Voters, October 2008

Total . . . 2,114
Democrats . . . 1,015
Republicans . . . 676
Declined to state . . . 335

Legislative Districts

US Congressional . . . 51
State Senatorial . . . 40
State Assembly . . . 80

Local Officials, 2009

Mayor . . . Bianca Padilla
Manager . . . Laura Fischer
City Clerk . . . Glyn Snyder
Attorney . . . Steve Walker
Finance Dir . . . Rosa Ramirez
Public Works . . . Gerald Peacher
Planning/Dev Dir . . . NA
Building . . . NA
Police Chief . . . Rick Watson
Fire Chief . . . Alex Silva

Public Safety

Number of officers, 2007 . . . 7
Violent crimes, 2007 . . . 6
Property crimes, 2007 . . . 114
Arson, 2007 . . . 1

Public Library

Holtville Branch Library
Imperial County Library System
101 E Sixth
Holtville, CA 92250
760-356-2385

Branch Librarian . . . Julio Manriquez

Library system statistics, FY 2007

Population served . . . 55,503
Internet terminals . . . 27
Annual users . . . 21,222

Per capita:

Operating income . . . $14.19
percent from local government . . . 83.9%
Operating expenditure . . . $12.85
Total materials . . . 1.05
Print holdings . . . 0.96
Visits per capita . . . 0.80

Housing & Construction

Housing Units

Total, 2008§ . . . 1,891
Single family units, attached . . . 111
Single family units, detached . . . 1,144
Multiple family units . . . 441
Mobile home units . . . 195
Occupied . . . 1,828
Vacancy rate . . . 3.3%
Median rent, 2000** . . . $493
Median SF home value, 2000** . . . $93,500

New Privately Owned Housing Units Authorized by Building Permit, 2007*

	Units	Construction Cost
Single	NA	NA
Total	NA	NA

Municipal Finance

(For local fiscal year ended in 2006)

Revenues

Total . . . $4,768,055
Taxes . . . 1,157,670
Special benefits assessment . . . 16,273
Licenses & permits . . . 1,685
Fines & forfeitures . . . 48,197
Revenues from use of money & property . . . 19,629
Intergovernmental . . . 766,606
Service charges . . . 2,733,285
Other revenues . . . 24,710
Other financing sources . . . 0

Expenditures

Total . . . $5,500,590
General government . . . 644,490
Public safety . . . 1,162,171
Transportation . . . 152,913
Community development . . . 395,408
Health . . . 1,854,295
Culture & leisure . . . 139,749
Other . . . 0

Local School District

(Data from School year 2007-08 except as noted)

Holtville Unified
621 East Sixth St
Holtville, CA 92250
(760) 356-2974

Superintendent . . . Jon LeDoux
Grade plan . . . K-12
Number of schools . . . 5
Enrollment . . . 1,781
High school graduates, 2006-07 . . . 155
Dropout rate . . . 1.4%
Pupil/teacher ratio . . . 20.8
Average class size . . . 24.5
Students per computer . . . 3.0
Classrooms with internet . . . 123
Avg. Daily Attendance (ADA) . . . 1,788
Cost per ADA . . . $8,355
Avg. Teacher Salary . . . $55,816

California Achievement Tests 6th ed., 2008

(Pct scoring at or above 50th National Percentile Rank)

	Math	Reading	Language
Grade 3	46%	32%	44%
Grade 7	42%	32%	39%

Academic Performance Index, 2008

Number of students tested . . . 1,372
Number of valid scores . . . 1,284
2007 API (base) . . . 715
2008 API (growth) . . . 729

SAT Testing, 2006-07

Enrollment, Grade 12 . . . 172
Number taking test . . . 72
percent taking test . . . 41.9%
percent with total score 1,500+ . . . 5.80%

Average Scores:

Math	Verbal	Writing	Total
416	432	415	1,263

Federal No Child Left Behind, 2008

(Adequate Yearly Progress standards met)

	Participation Rate	Pct Proficient
ELA	Yes	No
Math	Yes	Yes

API criteria . . . Yes
Graduation rate . . . Yes
\# criteria met/possible . . . 22/21

Other school districts for this city

(see Appendix E for information on these districts)

None

See Introduction for an explanation of all data sources.

Demographics & Socio-Economic Characteristics

(2000 Decennial Census, except as noted)

Population

1990* ... 3,259
2000 ... 3,980
Male ... 1,957
Female ... 2,023
Jan. 2008 (estimate)§ ... 6,187
Persons per sq. mi. of land ... 5,624.5

Race & Hispanic Origin, 2000

Race
White ... 2,738
Black/African American ... 24
North American Native ... 57
Asian ... 44
Pacific Islander ... 5
Other Race ... 967
Two or more races ... 145
Hispanic origin, total ... 1,545
Mexican ... 1,380
Puerto Rican ... 18
Cuban ... 0
Other Hispanic ... 147

Age & Nativity, 2000

Under 5 years ... 291
18 years and over ... 2,647
65 years and over ... 383
85 years and over ... 44
Median Age ... 30.6
Native-born ... 3,161
Foreign-born ... 853

Educational Attainment, 2000

Population 25 years and over ... 2,254
Less than 9th grade ... 20.9%
High school grad or higher ... 60.9%
Bachelor's degree or higher ... 6.8%
Graduate degree ... 1.7%

Income & Poverty, 1999

Per capita income ... $13,636
Median household income ... $40,385
Median family income ... $46,325
Persons in poverty ... 19.1%
H'holds receiving public assistance ... 104
H'holds receiving social security ... 331

Households, 2000

Total households ... 1,223
With persons under 18 ... 636
With persons over 65 ... 286
Family households ... 993
Single person households ... 197
Persons per household ... 3.25
Persons per family ... 3.63

Household Population, 2008§§

Persons living in households ... 6,181
Persons living in group quarters ... 6
Persons per household ... 3.3

Labor & Employment

Total civilian labor force, 2008§§ ... 2,100
Unemployment rate, 2008 ... 13.5%
Total civilian labor force, 2000 ... 1,739

Employed persons 16 years and over by occupation, 2000

Managers & professionals ... 300
Service occupations ... 248
Sales & office occupations ... 374
Farming, fishing & forestry ... 74
Construction & maintenance ... 201
Production & transportation ... 297
Self-employed persons ... 142

* US Census Bureau
** 2000 Decennial Census
§ California Department of Finance
§§ California Employment Development Dept

General Information

City of Hughson
7018 Pine St
PO Box 9
Hughson, CA 95326
209-883-4055

Website ... www.hughson.org
Elevation ... NA
Land Area (sq. miles) ... 1.1
Water Area (sq. miles) ... 0
Year of Incorporation ... 1972
Government type ... General law
Sales tax rate ... 8.38%

Voters & Officials

Registered Voters, October 2008

Total ... 3,137
Democrats ... 1,141
Republicans ... 1,377
Declined to state ... 489

Legislative Districts

US Congressional ... 19
State Senatorial ... 14
State Assembly ... 25

Local Officials, 2009

Mayor ... Ramon Bawanan
Manager ... Joe Donabed
City Clerk ... Mary Hemminger
Attorney ... John W. Stovall
Finance Dir ... Deborah Paul
Public Works ... David Chase
Planning/Dev Dir ... Thom Clark
Building ... Thom Clark
Police Chief ... Janet Rasmussen
Emergency/Fire Dir ... Scott Berner

Public Safety

Number of officers, 2007 ... 6
Violent crimes, 2007 ... 1
Property crimes, 2007 ... 172
Arson, 2007 ... 0

Public Library

Hughson Library
Stanislaus County Free Library
2412 Third St
Hughson, CA 95326
209-883-2293

Branch Librarian ... Isabel Figueroa

Library system statistics, FY 2007

Population served ... 521,497
Internet terminals ... 128
Annual users ... 256,298

Per capita:

Operating income ... $20.76
percent from local government ... 91.0%
Operating expenditure ... $20.19
Total materials ... 1.66
Print holdings ... 1.56
Visits per capita ... NA

Housing & Construction

Housing Units

Total, 2008§ ... 1,937
Single family units, attached ... 65
Single family units, detached ... 1,576
Multiple family units ... 207
Mobile home units ... 89
Occupied ... 1,891
Vacancy rate ... 2.4%
Median rent, 2000** ... $503
Median SF home value, 2000** ... $117,900

New Privately Owned Housing Units Authorized by Building Permit, 2007*

	Units	Construction Cost
Single	31	$7,008,325
Total	31	$7,008,325

Municipal Finance

(For local fiscal year ended in 2006)

Revenues

Total ... $6,942,287
Taxes ... 1,929,485
Special benefits assessment ... 63,915
Licenses & permits ... 29,414
Fines & forfeitures ... 59,573
Revenues from use of money & property ... 206,932
Intergovernmental ... 640,637
Service charges ... 3,980,091
Other revenues ... 32,240
Other financing sources ... 0

Expenditures

Total ... $9,385,206
General government ... 553,827
Public safety ... 1,258,742
Transportation ... 1,558,076
Community development ... 406,599
Health ... 3,757,717
Culture & leisure ... 66,530
Other ... 0

Local School District

(Data from School year 2007-08 except as noted)

Hughson Unified
PO Box 189
Hughson, CA 95326
(209) 883-4428

Superintendent ... Brian Beck
Grade plan ... K-12
Number of schools ... 5
Enrollment ... 2,165
High school graduates, 2006-07 ... 156
Dropout rate ... 2.1%
Pupil/teacher ratio ... 19.8
Average class size ... 22.4
Students per computer ... 3.2
Classrooms with internet ... 113
Avg. Daily Attendance (ADA) ... 2,109
Cost per ADA ... $8,673
Avg. Teacher Salary ... $61,344

California Achievement Tests 6th ed., 2008

(Pct scoring at or above 50th National Percentile Rank)

	Math	Reading	Language
Grade 3	63%	48%	49%
Grade 7	48%	48%	50%

Academic Performance Index, 2008

Number of students tested ... 1,651
Number of valid scores ... 1,589
2007 API (base) ... 754
2008 API (growth) ... 766

SAT Testing, 2006-07

Enrollment, Grade 12 ... 171
Number taking test ... 41
percent taking test ... 24.0%
percent with total score 1,500+ ... 12.90%

Average Scores:

Math	Verbal	Writing	Total
518	522	493	1,533

Federal No Child Left Behind, 2008

(Adequate Yearly Progress standards met)

	Participation Rate	Pct Proficient
ELA	Yes	No
Math	Yes	Yes

API criteria ... Yes
Graduation rate ... Yes
\# criteria met/possible ... 22/21

Other school districts for this city

(see Appendix E for information on these districts)

None

See Introduction for an explanation of all data sources.

Demographics & Socio-Economic Characteristics†

(2007 American Community Survey, except as noted)

Population

1990* . . . 181,519
2007 . . . 188,056
Male . . . 94,926
Female . . . 93,130
Jan. 2008 (estimate)§ . . . 201,993
Persons per sq. mi. of land . . . 7,651.3

Race & Hispanic Origin, 2007

Race
White . . . 145,579
Black/African American . . . 1,693
North American Native . . . 673
Asian . . . 19,651
Pacific Islander . . . 1,407
Other Race . . . 13,432
Two or more races . . . 5,621
Hispanic origin, total . . . 28,977
Mexican . . . 22,491
Puerto Rican . . . 969
Cuban . . . 700
Other Hispanic . . . 4,817

Age & Nativity, 2007

Under 5 years . . . 9,741
18 years and over . . . 149,180
65 years and over . . . 25,118
85 years and over . . . 3,256
Median Age . . . 39.4
Native-born . . . 157,503
Foreign-born . . . 30,553

Educational Attainment, 2007

Population 25 years and over . . . 131,226
Less than 9th grade . . . 2.4%
High school grad or higher . . . 93.3%
Bachelor's degree or higher . . . 40.8%
Graduate degree . . . 14.4%

Income & Poverty, 2007

Per capita income . . . $40,630
Median household income . . . $81,112
Median family income . . . $101,023
Persons in poverty . . . 5.5%
H'holds receiving public assistance . . . 489
H'holds receiving social security . . . 19,392

Households, 2007

Total households . . . 72,756
With persons under 18 . . . 21,497
With persons over 65 . . . 18,278
Family households . . . 46,137
Single person households . . . 19,896
Persons per household . . . 2.58
Persons per family . . . 3.19

Household Population, 2008§§

Persons living in households . . . 201,201
Persons living in group quarters . . . 792
Persons per household . . . 2.6

Labor & Employment

Total civilian labor force, 2008§§ . . . 125,300
Unemployment rate, 2008 . . . 4.3%
Total civilian labor force, 2000* . . . 106,999

Employed persons 16 years and over by occupation, 2007

Managers & professionals . . . 45,935
Service occupations . . . 11,016
Sales & office occupations . . . 28,187
Farming, fishing & forestry . . . 57
Construction & maintenance . . . 7,467
Production & transportation . . . 7,004
Self-employed persons . . . 9,591

† see Appendix D for 2000 Decennial Census Data
* US Census Bureau
** 2007 American Community Survey
§ California Department of Finance
§§ California Employment Development Dept

General Information

City of Huntington Beach
2000 Main St
Huntington Beach, CA 92648
714-536-5511

Website . . . www.surfcity-hb.org
Elevation . . . 28 ft.
Land Area (sq. miles) . . . 26.4
Water Area (sq. miles) . . . 5.2
Year of Incorporation . . . 1909
Government type . . . Chartered
Sales tax rate . . . 8.75%

Voters & Officials

Registered Voters, October 2008

Total . . . 129,193
Democrats . . . 37,076
Republicans . . . 59,938
Declined to state . . . 26,226

Legislative Districts

US Congressional . . . 46
State Senatorial . . . 35
State Assembly . . . 67

Local Officials, 2009

Mayor . . . Keith Bohr
Administrator . . . Fred Wilson
City Clerk . . . Joan Flynn
Attorney . . . Jennifer McGrath
Finance Dir . . . Dan Villella
Public Works . . . Travis Hopkins
Planning/Dev Dir . . . Scott Hess
Building . . . Ross Cranmer
Police Chief . . . Kenneth Small
Emergency/Fire Dir . . . Duane Olson

Public Safety

Number of officers, 2007 . . . 219
Violent crimes, 2007 . . . 376
Property crimes, 2007 . . . 4,035
Arson, 2007 . . . 42

Public Library

Central Library
Huntington Beach Library System
7111 Talbert Ave
Huntington Beach, CA 92648
714-960-8836

Director . . . Ronald Hayden

Library system statistics, FY 2007

Population served . . . 202,250
Internet terminals . . . 73
Annual users . . . 80,564

Per capita:

Operating income . . . $28.23
percent from local government . . . 65.1%
Operating expenditure . . . $24.27
Total materials . . . 2.13
Print holdings . . . 2.04
Visits per capita . . . 4.34

Housing & Construction

Housing Units

Total, 2008§ . . . 78,007
Single family units, attached . . . 9,467
Single family units, detached . . . 38,581
Multiple family units . . . 26,818
Mobile home units . . . 3,141
Occupied . . . 75,940
Vacancy rate . . . 2.7%
Median rent, 2007** . . . $1,410
Median SF home value, 2007** . . . $763,100

New Privately Owned Housing Units Authorized by Building Permit, 2007*

	Units	Construction Cost
Single	53	$18,373,505
Total	55	$18,577,417

Municipal Finance

(For local fiscal year ended in 2006)

Revenues

Total . . . $247,062,871
Taxes . . . 114,840,754
Special benefits assessment . . . 1,326,446
Licenses & permits . . . 4,338,657
Fines & forfeitures . . . 4,171,469
Revenues from use of money & property . . . 9,708,428
Intergovernmental . . . 28,369,570
Service charges . . . 80,034,119
Other revenues . . . 4,273,428
Other financing sources . . . 0

Expenditures

Total . . . $240,227,817
General government . . . 26,634,303
Public safety . . . 92,834,666
Transportation . . . 31,701,222
Community development . . . 7,631,144
Health . . . 19,728,055
Culture & leisure . . . 26,564,712
Other . . . 0

Local School District

(Data from School year 2007-08 except as noted)

Huntington Beach Union High
5832 Bolsa Ave
Huntington Beach, CA 92649
(714) 903-7000

Superintendent . . . Van Riley
Grade plan . . . 9-12
Number of schools . . . 9
Enrollment . . . 16,052
High school graduates, 2006-07 . . . 3,154
Dropout rate . . . 1.3%
Pupil/teacher ratio . . . 25.4
Average class size . . . 23.4
Students per computer . . . 3.8
Classrooms with internet . . . 611
Avg. Daily Attendance (ADA) . . . 15,841
Cost per ADA . . . $8,287
Avg. Teacher Salary . . . $76,735

California Achievement Tests 6th ed., 2008

(Pct scoring at or above 50th National Percentile Rank)

	Math	Reading	Language
Grade 3	NA	NA	NA
Grade 7	NA	NA	NA

Academic Performance Index, 2008

Number of students tested . . . 11,830
Number of valid scores . . . 11,519
2007 API (base) . . . 763
2008 API (growth) . . . 795

SAT Testing, 2006-07

Enrollment, Grade 12 . . . 3,647
Number taking test . . . 1,435
percent taking test . . . 39.4%
percent with total score 1,500+ . . . 25.50%

Average Scores:

Math	Verbal	Writing	Total
561	527	525	1,613

Federal No Child Left Behind, 2008

(Adequate Yearly Progress standards met)

	Participation Rate	Pct Proficient
ELA	No	No
Math	Yes	No

API criteria . . . Yes
Graduation rate . . . Yes
criteria met/possible . . . 34/31

Other school districts for this city

(see Appendix E for information on these districts)
Complete list in Appendix E

See Introduction for an explanation of all data sources.

Demographics & Socio-Economic Characteristics

(2000 Decennial Census, except as noted)

Population

1990* ... 56,065
2000 ... 61,348
Male ... 30,716
Female ... 30,632
Jan. 2008 (estimate)§ ... 64,747
Persons per sq. mi. of land ... 21,582.3

Race & Hispanic Origin, 2000

Race
White ... 25,412
Black/African American ... 478
North American Native ... 620
Asian ... 489
Pacific Islander ... 38
Other Race ... 31,328
Two or more races ... 2,983
Hispanic origin, total ... 58,636
Mexican ... 44,948
Puerto Rican ... 234
Cuban ... 689
Other Hispanic ... 12,765

Age & Nativity, 2000

Under 5 years ... 6,406
18 years and over ... 39,379
65 years and over ... 3,136
85 years and over ... 299
Median Age ... 25.6
Native-born ... 27,042
Foreign-born ... 34,328

Educational Attainment, 2000

Population 25 years and over ... 31,390
Less than 9th grade ... 43.1%
High school grad or higher ... 32.2%
Bachelor's degree or higher ... 4.7%
Graduate degree ... 1.8%

Income & Poverty, 1999

Per capita income ... $9,340
Median household income ... $28,941
Median family income ... $29,844
Persons in poverty ... 25.1%
H'holds receiving public assistance ... 1,481
H'holds receiving social security ... 2,381

Households, 2000

Total households ... 14,860
With persons under 18 ... 9,695
With persons over 65 ... 2,477
Family households ... 12,663
Single person households ... 1,623
Persons per household ... 4.12
Persons per family ... 4.34

Household Population, 2008§§

Persons living in households ... 64,566
Persons living in group quarters ... 181
Persons per household ... 4.3

Labor & Employment

Total civilian labor force, 2008§§ ... 26,800
Unemployment rate, 2008 ... 11.4%
Total civilian labor force, 2000 ... 23,016

Employed persons 16 years and over by occupation, 2000

Managers & professionals ... 2,406
Service occupations ... 3,178
Sales & office occupations ... 4,965
Farming, fishing & forestry ... 99
Construction & maintenance ... 1,875
Production & transportation ... 7,784
Self-employed persons ... 841

* US Census Bureau
** 2000 Decennial Census
§ California Department of Finance
§§ California Employment Development Dept

General Information

City of Huntington Park
6550 Miles Ave
Huntington Park, CA 90255
323-582-6161

Website ... www.huntingtonpark.org
Elevation ... 160 ft.
Land Area (sq. miles) ... 3.0
Water Area (sq. miles) ... 0
Year of Incorporation ... 1906
Government type ... General law
Sales tax rate ... 9.25%

Voters & Officials

Registered Voters, October 2008

Total ... 14,603
Democrats ... 9,722
Republicans ... 1,766
Declined to state ... 2,528

Legislative Districts

US Congressional ... 34
State Senatorial ... 30
State Assembly ... 46

Local Officials, 2009

Mayor ... Elba Guerrero
Manager ... Gregory Korduner
City Clerk ... Rosanna Ramirez
Attorney ... Francisco Leal
Finance Dir ... Elba Padilla (Actg)
Public Works ... Gene Viramontes
Community Dev Dir ... Henry Gray
Building ... NA
Police Chief ... Paul Wadley
Fire/Emergency Mgmt ... (County)

Public Safety

Number of officers, 2007 ... 63
Violent crimes, 2007 ... 603
Property crimes, 2007 ... 2,777
Arson, 2007 ... 19

Public Library

Huntington Park Library
Los Angeles County Public Library System
6518 Miles Ave
Huntington Park, CA 90255
323-583-1461

Branch Librarian ... Norma Montero

Library system statistics, FY 2007

Population served ... 3,673,313
Internet terminals ... 749
Annual users ... 3,748,771

Per capita:

Operating income ... $30.06
percent from local government ... 93.6%
Operating expenditure ... $28.36
Total materials ... 2.22
Print holdings ... 1.97
Visits per capita ... 3.25

Housing & Construction

Housing Units

Total, 2008§ ... 15,446
Single family units, attached ... 2,381
Single family units, detached ... 5,276
Multiple family units ... 7,774
Mobile home units ... 15
Occupied ... 14,968
Vacancy rate ... 3.1%
Median rent, 2000** ... $590
Median SF home value, 2000** ... $164,700

New Privately Owned Housing Units Authorized by Building Permit, 2007*

	Units	Construction Cost
Single	1	$99,551
Total	3	$289,683

Municipal Finance

(For local fiscal year ended in 2006)

Revenues

Total ... $81,805,397
Taxes ... 22,867,654
Special benefits assessment ... 1,543,203
Licenses & permits ... 372,136
Fines & forfeitures ... 2,821,557
Revenues from use of money & property ... 1,317,902
Intergovernmental ... 6,313,585
Service charges ... 8,983,394
Other revenues ... 4,535,966
Other financing sources ... 33,050,000

Expenditures

Total ... $43,123,151
General government ... 12,181,328
Public safety ... 14,272,165
Transportation ... 7,136,988
Community development ... 2,670,815
Health ... 1,703,039
Culture & leisure ... 1,626,843
Other ... 0

Local School District

(Data from School year 2007-08 except as noted)

Los Angeles Unified
333 South Beaudry Ave
Los Angeles, CA 90017
(213) 241-1000

Superintendent ... Ramon Cortines
Grade plan ... PK-12
Number of schools ... 827
Enrollment ... 693,680
High school graduates, 2006-07 ... 28,545
Dropout rate ... 7.8%
Pupil/teacher ratio ... 19.8
Average class size ... 24.9
Students per computer ... 3.7
Classrooms with internet ... 31,112
Avg. Daily Attendance (ADA) ... 653,672
Cost per ADA ... $10,053
Avg. Teacher Salary ... $63,391

California Achievement Tests 6th ed., 2008

(Pct scoring at or above 50th National Percentile Rank)

	Math	Reading	Language
Grade 3	49%	27%	39%
Grade 7	37%	33%	33%

Academic Performance Index, 2008

Number of students tested ... 495,046
Number of valid scores ... 471,641
2007 API (base) ... 662
2008 API (growth) ... 683

SAT Testing, 2006-07

Enrollment, Grade 12 ... 32,370
Number taking test ... 15,447
percent taking test ... 47.7%
percent with total score 1,500+ ... 12.50%

Average Scores:

Math	Verbal	Writing	Total
443	438	441	1,322

Federal No Child Left Behind, 2008

(Adequate Yearly Progress standards met)

	Participation Rate	Pct Proficient
ELA	Yes	No
Math	Yes	No

API criteria ... Yes
Graduation rate ... Yes
\# criteria met/possible ... 46/38

Other school districts for this city

(see Appendix E for information on these districts)

None

See Introduction for an explanation of all data sources.

Demographics & Socio-Economic Characteristics

(2000 Decennial Census, except as noted)

Population

1990* . . . 4,766
2000 . . . 6,306
Male . . . 3,513
Female . . . 2,793
Jan. 2008 (estimate)§ . . . 7,554
Persons per sq. mi. of land . . . 5,810.8

Race & Hispanic Origin, 2000

Race
White . . . 1,284
Black/African American . . . 20
North American Native . . . 62
Asian . . . 25
Pacific Islander . . . 8
Other Race . . . 4,715
Two or more races . . . 192
Hispanic origin, total . . . 6,197
Mexican . . . 5,481
Puerto Rican . . . 5
Cuban . . . 0
Other Hispanic . . . 711

Age & Nativity, 2000

Under 5 years . . . 699
18 years and over . . . 3,840
65 years and over . . . 266
85 years and over . . . 19
Median Age . . . 23.5
Native-born . . . 2,915
Foreign-born . . . 3,387

Educational Attainment, 2000

Population 25 years and over . . . 3,062
Less than 9th grade . . . 62.2%
High school grad or higher . . . 21.6%
Bachelor's degree or higher . . . 0.0%
Graduate degree . . . 0.0%

Income & Poverty, 1999

Per capita income . . . $9,425
Median household income . . . $24,609
Median family income . . . $23,939
Persons in poverty . . . 39.2%
H'holds receiving public assistance . . . 194
H'holds receiving social security . . . 202

Households, 2000

Total households . . . 1,378
With persons under 18 . . . 966
With persons over 65 . . . 205
Family households . . . 1,209
Single person households . . . 102
Persons per household . . . 4.45
Persons per family . . . 4.44

Household Population, 2008§§

Persons living in households . . . 7,382
Persons living in group quarters . . . 172
Persons per household . . . 4.5

Labor & Employment

Total civilian labor force, 2008§§ . . . 3,400
Unemployment rate, 2008 . . . 26.4%
Total civilian labor force, 2000 . . . 2,697

Employed persons 16 years and over by occupation, 2000

Managers & professionals . . . 166
Service occupations . . . 276
Sales & office occupations . . . 284
Farming, fishing & forestry . . . 808
Construction & maintenance . . . 107
Production & transportation . . . 278
Self-employed persons . . . 72

* US Census Bureau
** 2000 Decennial Census
§ California Department of Finance
§§ California Employment Development Dept

General Information

City of Huron
36311 Lassen
PO Box 339
Huron, CA 93234
559-945-2241

Website . . . www.cityofhuron.com
Elevation . . . 368 ft.
Land Area (sq. miles) . . . 1.3
Water Area (sq. miles) . . . 0
Year of Incorporation . . . 1951
Government type . . . General law
Sales tax rate . . . 8.98%

Voters & Officials

Registered Voters, October 2008

Total . . . 931
Democrats . . . 643
Republicans . . . 132
Declined to state . . . 89

Legislative Districts

US Congressional . . . 20
State Senatorial . . . 16
State Assembly . . . 30

Local Officials, 2009

Mayor . . . Ramon Dominguez
Manager . . . (vacant)
City Clerk . . . Juanita Veliz
Attorney . . . Daniel T. McCloskey
Finance Dir . . . (vacant)
Public Works . . . (vacant)
Planning/Dev Dir . . . (vacant)
Building . . . NA
Police Chief . . . Frank L. Steenport
Fire/Emergency Mgmt . . . NA

Public Safety

Number of officers, 2007 . . . 12
Violent crimes, 2007 . . . 44
Property crimes, 2007 . . . 194
Arson, 2007 . . . 10

Public Library

Huron Branch Library
Coalinga-Huron Unified School Dist Lib Sys
36050 O St
Huron, CA 93234
559-945-2284

Branch Librarian . . . Judy Ramirez

Library system statistics, FY 2007

Population served . . . 28,496
Internet terminals . . . 9
Annual users . . . 19,220

Per capita:

Operating income . . . $36.70
percent from local government . . . 85.8%
Operating expenditure . . . $31.07
Total materials . . . 3.11
Print holdings . . . 2.95
Visits per capita . . . 2.03

Housing & Construction

Housing Units

Total, 2008§ . . . 1,665
Single family units, attached . . . 204
Single family units, detached . . . 530
Multiple family units . . . 817
Mobile home units . . . 114
Occupied . . . 1,624
Vacancy rate . . . 2.5%
Median rent, 2000** . . . $363
Median SF home value, 2000** . . . $75,800

New Privately Owned Housing Units Authorized by Building Permit, 2007*

	Units	Construction Cost
Single	9	$791,528
Total	110	$9,738,900

Municipal Finance

(For local fiscal year ended in 2006)

Revenues

Total . . . $8,286,295
Taxes . . . 1,197,671
Special benefits assessment . . . 0
Licenses & permits . . . 54,156
Fines & forfeitures . . . 47,948
Revenues from use of money & property . . . 107,495
Intergovernmental . . . 4,485,941
Service charges . . . 1,855,231
Other revenues . . . 23,853
Other financing sources . . . 514,000

Expenditures

Total . . . $8,260,027
General government . . . 193,657
Public safety . . . 1,133,512
Transportation . . . 303,023
Community development . . . 773,859
Health . . . 4,903,468
Culture & leisure . . . 15,367
Other . . . 0

Local School District

(Data from School year 2007-08 except as noted)

Coalinga-Huron Joint Unified
657 Sunset St
Coalinga, CA 93210
(559) 935-7500

Superintendent . . Cecelia Greenberg-English
Grade plan . . . K-12
Number of schools . . . 11
Enrollment . . . 4,416
High school graduates, 2006-07 . . . 215
Dropout rate . . . 6.2%
Pupil/teacher ratio . . . 22.4
Average class size . . . 26.6
Students per computer . . . 5.3
Classrooms with internet . . . 246
Avg. Daily Attendance (ADA) . . . 4,194
Cost per ADA . . . $8,377
Avg. Teacher Salary . . . $60,598

California Achievement Tests 6th ed., 2008

(Pct scoring at or above 50th National Percentile Rank)

	Math	Reading	Language
Grade 3	40%	21%	29%
Grade 7	38%	31%	36%

Academic Performance Index, 2008

Number of students tested . . . 3,293
Number of valid scores . . . 3,038
2007 API (base) . . . 651
2008 API (growth) . . . 655

SAT Testing, 2006-07

Enrollment, Grade 12 . . . 284
Number taking test . . . 63
percent taking test . . . 22.2%
percent with total score 1,500+ . . . 6.70%

Average Scores:

Math	Verbal	Writing	Total
463	448	442	1,353

Federal No Child Left Behind, 2008

(Adequate Yearly Progress standards met)

	Participation Rate	Pct Proficient
ELA	No	No
Math	Yes	No

API criteria . . . Yes
Graduation rate . . . No
\# criteria met/possible . . . 26/15

Other school districts for this city

(see Appendix E for information on these districts)

None

See Introduction for an explanation of all data sources.

Demographics & Socio-Economic Characteristics

(2000 Decennial Census, except as noted)

Population

1990* ... 4,113
2000 ... 7,560
Male ... 3,718
Female ... 3,842
Jan. 2008 (estimate)§ ... 12,752
Persons per sq. mi. of land ... 3,269.7

Race & Hispanic Origin, 2000

Race
White ... 4,425
Black/African American ... 201
North American Native ... 57
Asian ... 205
Pacific Islander ... 13
Other Race ... 2,336
Two or more races ... 323
Hispanic origin, total ... 4,619
Mexican ... 4,124
Puerto Rican ... 30
Cuban ... 0
Other Hispanic ... 465

Age & Nativity, 2000

Under 5 years ... 728
18 years and over ... 4,890
65 years and over ... 474
85 years and over ... 41
Median Age ... 29.9
Native-born ... 5,846
Foreign-born ... 1,572

Educational Attainment, 2000

Population 25 years and over ... 4,172
Less than 9th grade ... 10.5%
High school grad or higher ... 78.6%
Bachelor's degree or higher ... 16.9%
Graduate degree ... 7.2%

Income & Poverty, 1999

Per capita income ... $16,538
Median household income ... $49,451
Median family income ... $53,053
Persons in poverty ... 11.3%
H'holds receiving public assistance ... 120
H'holds receiving social security ... 404

Households, 2000

Total households ... 2,308
With persons under 18 ... 1,361
With persons over 65 ... 358
Family households ... 1,910
Single person households ... 324
Persons per household ... 3.26
Persons per family ... 3.60

Household Population, 2008§§

Persons living in households ... 12,720
Persons living in group quarters ... 32
Persons per household ... 3.2

Labor & Employment

Total civilian labor force, 2008§§ ... 13,700
Unemployment rate, 2008 ... 9.8%
Total civilian labor force, 2000 ... 3,290

Employed persons 16 years and over by occupation, 2000

Managers & professionals ... 1,092
Service occupations ... 631
Sales & office occupations ... 664
Farming, fishing & forestry ... 40
Construction & maintenance ... 256
Production & transportation ... 333
Self-employed persons ... 147

* US Census Bureau
** 2000 Decennial Census
§ California Department of Finance
§§ California Employment Development Dept

General Information

City of Imperial
420 S Imperial Ave
Imperial, CA 92251
760-355-4371

Website ... www.imperial.ca.gov
Elevation ... -60 ft.
Land Area (sq. miles) ... 3.9
Water Area (sq. miles) ... 0
Year of Incorporation ... 1904
Government type ... General law
Sales tax rate ... 8.75%

Voters & Officials

Registered Voters, October 2008

Total ... 5,006
Democrats ... 2,097
Republicans ... 1,838
Declined to state ... 909

Legislative Districts

US Congressional ... 51
State Senatorial ... 40
State Assembly ... 80

Local Officials, 2009

Mayor ... Doug Cox
Manager ... Marlene Best
City Clerk ... Debra Jackson
Attorney ... Dennis Morita
Finance Dir ... Laura Gutierrez
Public Works ... Jackie Loper
Planning Dir ... Jorge Galvan
Building ... NA
Police Chief ... Miguel Colon
Emergency/Fire Dir ... Tony Rouhotas

Public Safety

Number of officers, 2007 ... 18
Violent crimes, 2007 ... 5
Property crimes, 2007 ... 208
Arson, 2007 ... 1

Public Library

City of Imperial Public Library
200 W Ninth St
Imperial, CA 92251
760-355-1332

Director ... Christina Carter

Library statistics, FY 2007

Population served ... 11,852
Internet terminals ... 11
Annual users ... 18,505

Per capita:

Operating income ... $13.16
percent from local government ... 92.9%
Operating expenditure ... $12.04
Total materials ... 2.62
Print holdings ... 2.52
Visits per capita ... 2.79

Housing & Construction

Housing Units

Total, 2008§ ... 4,082
Single family units, attached ... 117
Single family units, detached ... 3,481
Multiple family units ... 450
Mobile home units ... 34
Occupied ... 3,944
Vacancy rate ... 3.4%
Median rent, 2000** ... $597
Median SF home value, 2000** ... $101,600

New Privately Owned Housing Units Authorized by Building Permit, 2007*

	Units	Construction Cost
Single	253	$31,159,221
Total	301	$34,393,317

Municipal Finance

(For local fiscal year ended in 2006)

Revenues

Total ... $16,531,011
Taxes ... 4,211,971
Special benefits assessment ... 14,373
Licenses & permits ... 1,374,224
Fines & forfeitures ... 32,457
Revenues from use of money & property ... 99,087
Intergovernmental ... 1,087,041
Service charges ... 5,190,960
Other revenues ... 4,520,898
Other financing sources ... 0

Expenditures

Total ... $12,519,298
General government ... 1,408,637
Public safety ... 2,177,155
Transportation ... 753,172
Community development ... 1,351,333
Health ... 2,110,986
Culture & leisure ... 852,397
Other ... 0

Local School District

(Data from School year 2007-08 except as noted)

Imperial Unified
219 North E St
Imperial, CA 92251
(760) 355-3200

Superintendent ... Madeline Willis
Grade plan ... K-12
Number of schools ... 6
Enrollment ... 3,464
High school graduates, 2006-07 ... 188
Dropout rate ... 0.4%
Pupil/teacher ratio ... 22.0
Average class size ... 25.7
Students per computer ... 3.7
Classrooms with internet ... 172
Avg. Daily Attendance (ADA) ... 3,485
Cost per ADA ... $6,998
Avg. Teacher Salary ... $67,293

California Achievement Tests 6th ed., 2008

(Pct scoring at or above 50th National Percentile Rank)

	Math	Reading	Language
Grade 3	64%	45%	59%
Grade 7	58%	48%	49%

Academic Performance Index, 2008

Number of students tested ... 2,699
Number of valid scores ... 2,566
2007 API (base) ... 790
2008 API (growth) ... 803

SAT Testing, 2006-07

Enrollment, Grade 12 ... 190
Number taking test ... 63
percent taking test ... 33.2%
percent with total score 1,500+ ... 6.80%

Average Scores:

Math	Verbal	Writing	Total
468	443	439	1,350

Federal No Child Left Behind, 2008

(Adequate Yearly Progress standards met)

	Participation Rate	Pct Proficient
ELA	Yes	No
Math	Yes	Yes

API criteria ... Yes
Graduation rate ... Yes
criteria met/possible ... 26/25

Other school districts for this city

(see Appendix E for information on these districts)

None

See Introduction for an explanation of all data sources.

Demographics & Socio-Economic Characteristics

(2000 Decennial Census, except as noted)

Population

1990*	26,512
2000	26,992
Male	13,475
Female	13,517
Jan. 2008 (estimate)§	28,200
Persons per sq. mi. of land	6,558.1

Race & Hispanic Origin, 2000

Race	
White	16,805
Black/African American	1,421
North American Native	298
Asian	1,767
Pacific Islander	163
Other Race	4,796
Two or more races	1,742
Hispanic origin, total	10,818
Mexican	9,081
Puerto Rican	245
Cuban	41
Other Hispanic	1,451

Age & Nativity, 2000

Under 5 years	2,264
18 years and over	19,044
65 years and over	2,029
85 years and over	148
Median Age	28.6
Native-born	21,482
Foreign-born	5,498

Educational Attainment, 2000

Population 25 years and over	15,320
Less than 9th grade	9.3%
High school grad or higher	77.0%
Bachelor's degree or higher	11.7%
Graduate degree	3.0%

Income & Poverty, 1999

Per capita income	$16,003
Median household income	$35,882
Median family income	$37,352
Persons in poverty	18.7%
H'holds receiving public assistance	607
H'holds receiving social security	1,653

Households, 2000

Total households	9,272
With persons under 18	4,138
With persons over 65	1,554
Family households	6,449
Single person households	1,983
Persons per household	2.84
Persons per family	3.30

Household Population, 2008§§

Persons living in households	27,534
Persons living in group quarters	666
Persons per household	2.9

Labor & Employment

Total civilian labor force, 2008§§	4,600
Unemployment rate, 2008	15.7%
Total civilian labor force, 2000	11,897

Employed persons 16 years and over by occupation, 2000

Managers & professionals	2,385
Service occupations	2,307
Sales & office occupations	3,007
Farming, fishing & forestry	90
Construction & maintenance	1,356
Production & transportation	1,314
Self-employed persons	713

* US Census Bureau
** 2000 Decennial Census
§ California Department of Finance
§§ California Employment Development Dept

General Information

City of Imperial Beach
825 Imperial Beach Blvd
Imperial Beach, CA 91932
619-423-8300

Website	www.cityofib.com
Elevation	25 ft.
Land Area (sq. miles)	4.3
Water Area (sq. miles)	0.3
Year of Incorporation	1956
Government type	General law
Sales tax rate	8.75%

Voters & Officials

Registered Voters, October 2008

Total	10,818
Democrats	4,165
Republicans	3,184
Declined to state	2,837

Legislative Districts

US Congressional	53
State Senatorial	40
State Assembly	79

Local Officials, 2009

Mayor	James C. Janney
City Manager	Gary Brown
City Clerk	Jacqueline Hald
Attorney	James P. Lough
Finance Dir	Mike McGrane
Public Works	Hank Levien
Community Dev Dir	Greg Wade
Building	Ed Wilczak
Police Chief	Lisa Miller
Public Safety Dir	Frank Sotelo

Public Safety

Number of officers, 2007	NA
Violent crimes, 2007	157
Property crimes, 2007	696
Arson, 2007	10

Public Library

Imperial Beach Library
San Diego County Library System
810 Imperial Beach Blvd
Imperial Beach, CA 91932
619-424-6981

Branch Librarian	(vacant)

Library system statistics, FY 2007

Population served	1,049,868
Internet terminals	394
Annual users	NA

Per capita:

Operating income	$33.43
percent from local government	80.6%
Operating expenditure	$31.30
Total materials	1.54
Print holdings	1.32
Visits per capita	6.31

Housing & Construction

Housing Units

Total, 2008§	9,968
Single family units, attached	687
Single family units, detached	4,098
Multiple family units	4,843
Mobile home units	340
Occupied	9,489
Vacancy rate	4.8%
Median rent, 2000**	$690
Median SF home value, 2000**	$171,700

New Privately Owned Housing Units Authorized by Building Permit, 2007*

	Units	Construction Cost
Single	19	$4,814,226
Total	24	$5,514,226

Municipal Finance

(For local fiscal year ended in 2006)

Revenues

Total	$19,330,387
Taxes	6,648,128
Special benefits assessment	11,351
Licenses & permits	242,503
Fines & forfeitures	386,684
Revenues from use of money & property	146,458
Intergovernmental	1,145,920
Service charges	9,365,889
Other revenues	1,383,454
Other financing sources	0

Expenditures

Total	$19,746,136
General government	2,629,730
Public safety	8,247,209
Transportation	3,415,310
Community development	223,067
Health	3,545,319
Culture & leisure	1,685,501
Other	0

Local School District

(Data from School year 2007-08 except as noted)

Sweetwater Union High
1130 Fifth Ave
Chula Vista, CA 91911
(619) 691-5500

Superintendent	Jesus Gandara
Grade plan	7-12
Number of schools	31
Enrollment	42,591
High school graduates, 2006-07	5,510
Dropout rate	2.9%
Pupil/teacher ratio	22.5
Average class size	26.7
Students per computer	4.9
Classrooms with internet	2,349
Avg. Daily Attendance (ADA)	41,210
Cost per ADA	$8,570
Avg. Teacher Salary	$71,623

California Achievement Tests 6th ed., 2008

(Pct scoring at or above 50th National Percentile Rank)

	Math	Reading	Language
Grade 3	NA	NA	NA
Grade 7	52%	47%	44%

Academic Performance Index, 2008

Number of students tested	33,960
Number of valid scores	30,640
2007 API (base)	698
2008 API (growth)	715

SAT Testing, 2006-07

Enrollment, Grade 12	7,523
Number taking test	2,357
percent taking test	31.3%
percent with total score 1,500+	9.50%

Average Scores:

Math	Verbal	Writing	Total
469	458	450	1,377

Federal No Child Left Behind, 2008

(Adequate Yearly Progress standards met)

	Participation Rate	Pct Proficient
ELA	Yes	No
Math	Yes	No

API criteria	Yes
Graduation rate	Yes
# criteria met/possible	42/39

Other school districts for this city

(see Appendix E for information on these districts)

South Bay Union Elem

See Introduction for an explanation of all data sources.

Demographics & Socio-Economic Characteristics

(2000 Decennial Census, except as noted)

Population

1990* 2,647
2000 3,816
Male 1,802
Female 2,014
Jan. 2008 (estimate)§ 5,025
Persons per sq. mi. of land 380.7

Race & Hispanic Origin, 2000

Race
White 3,676
Black/African American 15
North American Native 8
Asian 57
Pacific Islander 3
Other Race 18
Two or more races 39
Hispanic origin, total 113
Mexican 72
Puerto Rican 2
Cuban 1
Other Hispanic 38

Age & Nativity, 2000

Under 5 years 49
18 years and over 3,526
65 years and over 1,763
85 years and over 128
Median Age 63.4
Native-born 3,477
Foreign-born 315

Educational Attainment, 2000

Population 25 years and over 3,431
Less than 9th grade 1.5%
High school grad or higher 94.0%
Bachelor's degree or higher 39.4%
Graduate degree 14.7%

Income & Poverty, 1999

Per capita income $76,187
Median household income $93,986
Median family income $119,110
Persons in poverty 3.4%
H'holds receiving public assistance 19
H'holds receiving social security 1,224

Households, 2000

Total households 1,982
With persons under 18 179
With persons over 65 1,188
Family households 1,324
Single person households 562
Persons per household 1.93
Persons per family 2.28

Household Population, 2008§§

Persons living in households 5,025
Persons living in group quarters 0
Persons per household 2.0

Labor & Employment

Total civilian labor force, 2008§§ 1,800
Unemployment rate, 2008 . . . . . 2.9%
Total civilian labor force, 2000 1,254

Employed persons 16 years and over by occupation, 2000

Managers & professionals 501
Service occupations 134
Sales & office occupations 491
Farming, fishing & forestry 0
Construction & maintenance 47
Production & transportation 49
Self-employed persons 247

* US Census Bureau
** 2000 Decennial Census
§ California Department of Finance
§§ California Employment Development Dept

General Information

City of Indian Wells
44-950 Eldorado Dr
Indian Wells, CA 92210
760-346-2489

Website . . . . . www.cityofindianwells.org
Elevation . . . . . NA
Land Area (sq. miles) 13.2
Water Area (sq. miles) 0.2
Year of Incorporation 1967
Government type . . . . . Chartered
Sales tax rate 8.75%

Voters & Officials

Registered Voters, October 2008

Total 3,078
Democrats 601
Republicans 2,010
Declined to state 375

Legislative Districts

US Congressional 45
State Senatorial 37
State Assembly 64

Local Officials, 2009

Mayor . . . . . Larry Spicer
Manager . . . . . Greg Johnson
City Clerk . . . . . Greg Johnson
Attorney . . . . . Stephen P. Deitsch
Finance Dir . . . . . Kevin McCarthy
Public Works . . . . . Tim Wassil
Planning/Dev Dir . . . . . Corrie Kates
Building . . . . . NA
Police Chief . . . . . Matthew Jimenez
Emergency/Fire Dir . . . . . Ignacio Otero

Public Safety

Number of officers, 2007 . . . . . NA
Violent crimes, 2007 3
Property crimes, 2007 272
Arson, 2007 1

Public Library

Served by County Library

Library system statistics, FY 2007

Population served . . . . . NA
Internet terminals . . . . . NA
Annual users . . . . . NA

Per capita:

Operating income . . . . . NA
percent from local government . . . . . NA
Operating expenditure . . . . . NA
Total materials . . . . . NA
Print holdings . . . . . NA
Visits per capita . . . . . NA

Housing & Construction

Housing Units

Total, 2008§ 4,973
Single family units, attached 884
Single family units, detached 3,373
Multiple family units 708
Mobile home units 8
Occupied 2,566
Vacancy rate 48.4%
Median rent, 2000** $670
Median SF home value, 2000** $400,700

New Privately Owned Housing Units Authorized by Building Permit, 2007*

	Units	Construction Cost
Single	85	$29,620,383
Total	85	$29,620,383

Municipal Finance

(For local fiscal year ended in 2006)

Revenues

Total $26,220,832
Taxes 10,818,492
Special benefits assessment 3,334,843
Licenses & permits 615,834
Fines & forfeitures 96,056
Revenues from use of money & property 3,639,519
Intergovernmental 322,433
Service charges 6,496,322
Other revenues 897,333
Other financing sources 0

Expenditures

Total $23,070,038
General government 1,467,445
Public safety 4,581,126
Transportation 2,433,960
Community development 5,288,545
Health 710,836
Culture & leisure 8,588,126
Other 0

Local School District

(Data from School year 2007-08 except as noted)

Desert Sands Unified
47-950 Dune Palms Rd
La Quinta, CA 92253
(760) 777-4200

Superintendent . . . . . Sharon McGehee
Grade plan K-12
Number of schools 33
Enrollment 28,775
High school graduates, 2006-07 1,630
Dropout rate 4.0%
Pupil/teacher ratio 22.2
Average class size 28.2
Students per computer 5.6
Classrooms with internet 1,229
Avg. Daily Attendance (ADA) 27,315
Cost per ADA $8,140
Avg. Teacher Salary $70,970

California Achievement Tests 6th ed., 2008

(Pct scoring at or above 50th National Percentile Rank)

	Math	Reading	Language
Grade 3	56%	35%	46%
Grade 7	44%	44%	43%

Academic Performance Index, 2008

Number of students tested 21,857
Number of valid scores 20,761
2007 API (base) 734
2008 API (growth) 752

SAT Testing, 2006-07

Enrollment, Grade 12 2,045
Number taking test 660
percent taking test 32.3%
percent with total score 1,500+ 13.40%

Average Scores:

Math	Verbal	Writing	Total
489	480	480	1,449

Federal No Child Left Behind, 2008

(Adequate Yearly Progress standards met)

	Participation Rate	Pct Proficient
ELA	Yes	No
Math	Yes	Yes

API criteria . . . . . Yes
Graduation rate . . . . . Yes
\# criteria met/possible 38/36

Other school districts for this city

(see Appendix E for information on these districts)

Palm Springs Unified

See Introduction for an explanation of all data sources.

Demographics & Socio-Economic Characteristics†

(2007 American Community Survey, except as noted)

Population

1990* 36,793
2007 70,791
Male 33,795
Female 36,996
Jan. 2008 (estimate)§ 81,512
Persons per sq. mi. of land 3,052.9

Race & Hispanic Origin, 2007

Race
White 52,077
Black/African American 2,227
North American Native 184
Asian 356
Pacific Islander 0
Other Race 14,290
Two or more races 1,657
Hispanic origin, total .... NA
Mexican .... NA
Puerto Rican .... NA
Cuban .... NA
Other Hispanic .... NA

Age & Nativity, 2007

Under 5 years 6,277
18 years and over 51,360
65 years and over 7,067
85 years and over 725
Median Age 29.6
Native-born 47,864
Foreign-born 22,927

Educational Attainment, 2007

Population 25 years and over 41,817
Less than 9th grade 19.0%
High school grad or higher 69.8%
Bachelor's degree or higher 16.6%
Graduate degree 5.5%

Income & Poverty, 2007

Per capita income $22,209
Median household income $56,039
Median family income $57,488
Persons in poverty 16.8%
H'holds receiving public assistance 849
H'holds receiving social security 5,263

Households, 2007

Total households 22,234
With persons under 18 9,225
With persons over 65 5,021
Family households 16,431
Single person households 3,891
Persons per household 3.16
Persons per family 3.67

Household Population, 2008§§

Persons living in households 80,656
Persons living in group quarters 856
Persons per household 3.5

Labor & Employment

Total civilian labor force, 2008§§ 27,400
Unemployment rate, 2008 .... 9.3%
Total civilian labor force, 2000* 19,382

Employed persons 16 years and over by occupation, 2007

Managers & professionals 6,441
Service occupations 9,280
Sales & office occupations 9,404
Farming, fishing & forestry 881
Construction & maintenance 4,802
Production & transportation 2,958
Self-employed persons 2,427

† see Appendix D for 2000 Decennial Census Data
* US Census Bureau
** 2007 American Community Survey
§ California Department of Finance
§§ California Employment Development Dept

General Information

City of Indio
100 Civic Center Mall
PO Drawer 1788
Indio, CA 92202
760-391-4000

Website .... www.indio.org
Elevation .... 14 ft.
Land Area (sq. miles) 26.7
Water Area (sq. miles) 0
Year of Incorporation 1930
Government type .... General law
Sales tax rate 8.75%

Voters & Officials

Registered Voters, October 2008

Total 25,945
Democrats 11,125
Republicans 10,599
Declined to state 3,474

Legislative Districts

US Congressional 45
State Senatorial 40
State Assembly 80

Local Officials, 2009

Mayor .... Melanie Fesmire
Manager .... Glenn D. Southard
City Clerk .... Cynthia Hernandez
Attorney .... Edward Kotkin
Finance Dir .... Susan Mahoney
Public Works .... Jim Smith
Planning/Dev Dir .... Steve Copenhaver
Building .... Tom Hosey
Police Chief .... Brad Ramos
Emergency/Fire Dir .... Ray Paiz

Public Safety

Number of officers, 2007 85
Violent crimes, 2007 350
Property crimes, 2007 2,830
Arson, 2007 2

Public Library

Max McCandless Branch Library
Riverside County Library Service
200 Civic Center Mall
Indio, CA 92201
760-347-2383

Branch Librarian .... Donna McCune

Library system statistics, FY 2007

Population served 1,047,996
Internet terminals 37
Annual users 69,346

Per capita:

Operating income $19.38
percent from local government 49.8%
Operating expenditure $20.45
Total materials 1.43
Print holdings 1.30
Visits per capita 4.06

Housing & Construction

Housing Units

Total, 2008§ 27,794
Single family units, attached 878
Single family units, detached 18,312
Multiple family units 5,344
Mobile home units 3,260
Occupied 22,799
Vacancy rate 18.0%
Median rent, 2007** $907
Median SF home value, 2007** $360,400

New Privately Owned Housing Units Authorized by Building Permit, 2007*

	Units	Construction Cost
Single	293	$51,504,653
Total	373	$55,188,896

Municipal Finance

(For local fiscal year ended in 2006)

Revenues

Total $126,876,558
Taxes 29,797,498
Special benefits assessment 37,947,324
Licenses & permits 7,393,177
Fines & forfeitures 547,938
Revenues from use of money & property 4,530,305
Intergovernmental 6,361,561
Service charges 6,054,230
Other revenues 27,244,525
Other financing sources 7,000,000

Expenditures

Total $91,763,316
General government 8,613,425
Public safety 22,002,500
Transportation 49,271,163
Community development 9,076,483
Health 0
Culture & leisure 2,799,745
Other 0

Local School District

(Data from School year 2007-08 except as noted)

Desert Sands Unified
47-950 Dune Palms Rd
La Quinta, CA 92253
(760) 777-4200

Superintendent .... Sharon McGehee
Grade plan K-12
Number of schools 33
Enrollment 28,775
High school graduates, 2006-07 1,630
Dropout rate 4.0%
Pupil/teacher ratio 22.2
Average class size 28.2
Students per computer 5.6
Classrooms with internet 1,229
Avg. Daily Attendance (ADA) 27,315
Cost per ADA $8,140
Avg. Teacher Salary $70,970

California Achievement Tests 6th ed., 2008

(Pct scoring at or above 50th National Percentile Rank)

	Math	Reading	Language
Grade 3	56%	35%	46%
Grade 7	44%	44%	43%

Academic Performance Index, 2008

Number of students tested 21,857
Number of valid scores 20,761
2007 API (base) 734
2008 API (growth) 752

SAT Testing, 2006-07

Enrollment, Grade 12 2,045
Number taking test 660
percent taking test 32.3%
percent with total score 1,500+ 13.40%

Average Scores:

Math	Verbal	Writing	Total
489	480	480	1,449

Federal No Child Left Behind, 2008

(Adequate Yearly Progress standards met)

	Participation Rate	Pct Proficient
ELA	Yes	No
Math	Yes	Yes

API criteria .... Yes
Graduation rate .... Yes
\# criteria met/possible 38/36

Other school districts for this city

(see Appendix E for information on these districts)

None

See Introduction for an explanation of all data sources.

Demographics & Socio-Economic Characteristics

(2000 Decennial Census, except as noted)

Population

1990* 631
2000 777
Male 432
Female 345
Jan. 2008 (estimate)§ 798
Persons per sq. mi. of land.......68.2

Race & Hispanic Origin, 2000

Race
White 426
Black/African American 33
North American Native 21
Asian 30
Pacific Islander.......0
Other Race 229
Two or more races 38
Hispanic origin, total 468
Mexican.......379
Puerto Rican.......1
Cuban 2
Other Hispanic 86

Age & Nativity, 2000

Under 5 years 55
18 years and over 591
65 years and over 149
85 years and over 41
Median Age 37.1
Native-born 730
Foreign-born 274

Educational Attainment, 2000

Population 25 years and over.......619
Less than 9th grade.......10.5%
High school grad or higher 66.6%
Bachelor's degree or higher 12.0%
Graduate degree.......4.2%

Income & Poverty, 1999

Per capita income.......$9,877
Median household income.......$49,423
Median family income $47,321
Persons in poverty.......14.4%
H'holds receiving public assistance 18
H'holds receiving social security 38

Households, 2000

Total households 121
With persons under 18.......65
With persons over 65 31
Family households.......93
Single person households.......24
Persons per household 4.24
Persons per family.......4.60

Household Population, 2008§§

Persons living in households.......534
Persons living in group quarters.......264
Persons per household 4.5

Labor & Employment

Total civilian labor force, 2008§§ 400
Unemployment rate, 2008 ....12.6%
Total civilian labor force, 2000 324

Employed persons 16 years and over by occupation, 2000

Managers & professionals 52
Service occupations.......65
Sales & office occupations 72
Farming, fishing & forestry.......0
Construction & maintenance 24
Production & transportation 66
Self-employed persons.......22

* US Census Bureau
** 2000 Decennial Census
§ California Department of Finance
§§ California Employment Development Dept

General Information

City of Industry
15625 E. Stafford St, Suite 100
Industry, CA 91744
626-333-2211

Website ....www.cityofindustry.org
Elevation ....NA
Land Area (sq. miles) 11.7
Water Area (sq. miles).......0.2
Year of Incorporation 1957
Government type.......Chartered
Sales tax rate.......9.25%

Voters & Officials

Registered Voters, October 2008

Total.......82
Democrats.......22
Republicans 48
Declined to state 10

Legislative Districts

US Congressional 32, 38
State Senatorial.......24, 29
State Assembly 49, 57, 58, 60

Local Officials, 2009

Mayor.......David Perez
Manager ....Kevin Radecki
City Clerk ....Jodi Scrivens
Attorney ....Michele Vadon
Finance Dir.......Dudley Lang
Public Works ....John Ballas
Planning/Dev Dir.......Mike Kissell
Building.......(County)
Police Chief.......(County)
Fire/Emergency Mgmt ....(County)

Public Safety

Number of officers, 2007 ....NA
Violent crimes, 2007 112
Property crimes, 2007.......1,708
Arson, 2007.......4

Public Library

Served by County Library

Library system statistics, FY 2007

Population served ....NA
Internet terminals ....NA
Annual users ....NA

Per capita:

Operating income ....NA
percent from local government.......NA
Operating expenditure.......NA
Total materials ....NA
Print holdings.......NA
Visits per capita ....NA

Housing & Construction

Housing Units

Total, 2008§.......123
Single family units, attached.......23
Single family units, detached 100
Multiple family units 0
Mobile home units 0
Occupied.......120
Vacancy rate.......2.4%
Median rent, 2000** $663
Median SF home value, 2000** $179,500

New Privately Owned Housing Units Authorized by Building Permit, 2007*

	Units	Construction Cost
Single	NA	NA
Total	NA	NA

Municipal Finance

(For local fiscal year ended in 2006)

Revenues

Total.......$73,331,710
Taxes 44,832,130
Special benefits assessment 0
Licenses & permits 1,170,579
Fines & forfeitures.......508,901
Revenues from use of money & property.......7,844,595
Intergovernmental.......312,655
Service charges.......18,261,258
Other revenues.......401,592
Other financing sources.......0

Expenditures

Total.......$91,453,237
General government 11,590,016
Public safety 7,105,255
Transportation.......3,486,858
Community development 48,451,230
Health 14,887,175
Culture & leisure 2,151,096
Other 907,214

Local School District

(Data from School year 2007-08 except as noted)

Hacienda La Puente Unified
PO Box 60002
City of Industry, CA 91716
(626) 933-1000

Superintendent.......Barbara Nakaoka
Grade plan.......K-12
Number of schools.......38
Enrollment 21,997
High school graduates, 2006-07.......1,366
Dropout rate.......3.8%
Pupil/teacher ratio.......21.1
Average class size.......22.7
Students per computer 3.4
Classrooms with internet.......1,139
Avg. Daily Attendance (ADA).......21,871
Cost per ADA.......$8,228
Avg. Teacher Salary.......$63,465

California Achievement Tests 6th ed., 2008

(Pct scoring at or above 50th National Percentile Rank)

	Math	Reading	Language
Grade 3	55%	31%	45%
Grade 7	51%	46%	45%

Academic Performance Index, 2008

Number of students tested.......17,075
Number of valid scores.......16,098
2007 API (base) 738
2008 API (growth).......748

SAT Testing, 2006-07

Enrollment, Grade 12 1,819
Number taking test 686
percent taking test.......37.7%
percent with total score 1,500+.......17.00%

Average Scores:

Math	Verbal	Writing	Total
523	475	476	1,474

Federal No Child Left Behind, 2008

(Adequate Yearly Progress standards met)

	Participation Rate	Pct Proficient
ELA	Yes	No
Math	Yes	No

API criteria ....Yes
Graduation rate ....No
\# criteria met/possible.......38/34

Other school districts for this city

(see Appendix E for information on these districts)

Bassett Unified

See Introduction for an explanation of all data sources.

Demographics & Socio-Economic Characteristics†

(2007 American Community Survey, except as noted)

Population

1990* 109,602
2007 106,581
Male 50,024
Female 56,557
Jan. 2008 (estimate)§ 118,878
Persons per sq. mi. of land 13,063.5

Race & Hispanic Origin, 2007

Race
White 15,590
Black/African American 44,631
North American Native 823
Asian 2,751
Pacific Islander 0
Other Race 40,348
Two or more races 2,438
Hispanic origin, total 54,690
Mexican 45,522
Puerto Rican 916
Cuban 315
Other Hispanic 7,937

Age & Nativity, 2007

Under 5 years 8,987
18 years and over 75,079
65 years and over 9,677
85 years and over 731
Median Age 33.3
Native-born 73,652
Foreign-born 32,929

Educational Attainment, 2007

Population 25 years and over 65,767
Less than 9th grade 17.1%
High school grad or higher 72.2%
Bachelor's degree or higher 16.3%
Graduate degree 4.6%

Income & Poverty, 2007

Per capita income $18,336
Median household income $40,525
Median family income $41,203
Persons in poverty 20.7%
H'holds receiving public assistance . . . 1,593
H'holds receiving social security 7,201

Households, 2007

Total households 37,080
With persons under 18 16,154
With persons over 65 7,295
Family households 23,815
Single person households 11,605
Persons per household 2.84
Persons per family 3.63

Household Population, 2008§§

Persons living in households 117,508
Persons living in group quarters 1,370
Persons per household 3.2

Labor & Employment

Total civilian labor force, 2008§§ 54,600
Unemployment rate, 2008 . . . . . 9.5%
Total civilian labor force, 2000* 47,184

Employed persons 16 years and over by occupation, 2007

Managers & professionals 11,118
Service occupations 12,948
Sales & office occupations 11,631
Farming, fishing & forestry 0
Construction & maintenance 5,248
Production & transportation 6,453
Self-employed persons 4,056

† see Appendix D for 2000 Decennial Census Data
* US Census Bureau
** 2007 American Community Survey
§ California Department of Finance
§§ California Employment Development Dept

General Information

City of Inglewood
1 Manchester Blvd
Inglewood, CA 90301
310-412-5111

Website . . . . . www.cityofinglewood.org
Elevation . . . . . 118 ft.
Land Area (sq. miles) 9.1
Water Area (sq. miles) 0
Year of Incorporation 1908
Government type . . . . . Chartered
Sales tax rate 9.75%

Voters & Officials

Registered Voters, October 2008

Total 49,221
Democrats 37,014
Republicans 3,608
Declined to state 6,986

Legislative Districts

US Congressional 35
State Senatorial 25
State Assembly 51

Local Officials, 2009

Mayor . . . . . Roosevelt Dorn
City Admin . . Timothy Wannamaker (Actg)
City Clerk . . . . . Yvonne Horton
Attorney . . . . . Cal Saunders
Finance Dir . . . . . Wanda Brown
Public Works . . . . . Glen Kau
Planning/Dev Dir . . . . . NA
Building . . . . . NA
Police Chief . . . . . Jacqueline Seabrooks
Fire/Emergency Mgmt . . . . . NA

Public Safety

Number of officers, 2007 190
Violent crimes, 2007 1,036
Property crimes, 2007 2,987
Arson, 2007 16

Public Library

Inglewood Public Library
Inglewood Public Library System
101 W Manchester Blvd
Inglewood, CA 90301
310-412-5380

Director . . . . . Richard Siminski

Library system statistics, FY 2007

Population served 119,212
Internet terminals 38
Annual users 29,210

Per capita:

Operating income $23.69
percent from local government 96.5%
Operating expenditure $23.69
Total materials 3.73
Print holdings 3.63
Visits per capita 2.04

Housing & Construction

Housing Units

Total, 2008§ 38,967
Single family units, attached 3,234
Single family units, detached 14,347
Multiple family units 21,148
Mobile home units 238
Occupied 37,108
Vacancy rate 4.8%
Median rent, 2007** $928
Median SF home value, 2007** $530,800

New Privately Owned Housing Units Authorized by Building Permit, 2007*

	Units	Construction Cost
Single	35	$5,893,904
Total	49	$7,723,904

Municipal Finance

(For local fiscal year ended in 2006)

Revenues

Total $154,671,902
Taxes 70,254,656
Special benefits assessment 4,632,002
Licenses & permits 1,673,703
Fines & forfeitures 4,430,365
Revenues from use of money & property 3,216,701
Intergovernmental 10,543,108
Service charges 49,400,701
Other revenues 4,385,666
Other financing sources 6,135,000

Expenditures

Total $144,895,562
General government 26,732,324
Public safety 46,815,464
Transportation 8,676,643
Community development 23,467,885
Health 12,371,856
Culture & leisure 10,820,949
Other 2,558,689

Local School District

(Data from School year 2007-08 except as noted)

Inglewood Unified
401 South Inglewood Ave
Inglewood, CA 90301
(310) 419-2700

Superintendent . . . . . Pamela Short-Powell
Grade plan K-12
Number of schools 20
Enrollment 15,234
High school graduates, 2006-07 703
Dropout rate 4.2%
Pupil/teacher ratio 23.3
Average class size 26.7
Students per computer 5.8
Classrooms with internet 732
Avg. Daily Attendance (ADA) 14,270
Cost per ADA $8,544
Avg. Teacher Salary $57,794

California Achievement Tests 6th ed., 2008

(Pct scoring at or above 50th National Percentile Rank)

	Math	Reading	Language
Grade 3	54%	29%	40%
Grade 7	33%	30%	30%

Academic Performance Index, 2008

Number of students tested 11,481
Number of valid scores 10,500
2007 API (base) 673
2008 API (growth) 688

SAT Testing, 2006-07

Enrollment, Grade 12 877
Number taking test 289
percent taking test 33.0%
percent with total score 1,500+ 2.70%

Average Scores:

Math	Verbal	Writing	Total
387	396	401	1,184

Federal No Child Left Behind, 2008

(Adequate Yearly Progress standards met)

	Participation Rate	Pct Proficient
ELA	Yes	No
Math	Yes	No

API criteria . . . . . Yes
Graduation rate . . . . . Yes
criteria met/possible 26/23

Other school districts for this city

(see Appendix E for information on these districts)

Los Angeles Unified

See Introduction for an explanation of all data sources.

Demographics & Socio-Economic Characteristics

(2000 Decennial Census, except as noted)

Population

1990* . . . 6,516
2000 . . . 7,129
Male . . . 5,645
Female . . . 1,484
Jan. 2008 (estimate)§ . . . 7,416
Persons per sq. mi. of land . . . 1,577.9

Race & Hispanic Origin, 2000

Race
White . . . 4,128
Black/African American . . . 1,271
North American Native . . . 164
Asian . . . 120
Pacific Islander . . . 12
Other Race . . . 1,292
Two or more races . . . 142
Hispanic origin, total . . . 1,437
Mexican . . . 1,182
Puerto Rican . . . 10
Cuban . . . 2
Other Hispanic . . . 243

Age & Nativity, 2000

Under 5 years . . . 223
18 years and over . . . 5,859
65 years and over . . . 398
85 years and over . . . 32
Median Age . . . 34.3
Native-born . . . 7,004
Foreign-born . . . 210

Educational Attainment, 2000

Population 25 years and over . . . 5,011
Less than 9th grade . . . 8.3%
High school grad or higher . . . 67.3%
Bachelor's degree or higher . . . 8.5%
Graduate degree . . . 4.1%

Income & Poverty, 1999

Per capita income . . . $20,340
Median household income . . . $40,625
Median family income . . . $48,911
Persons in poverty . . . 4.6%
H'holds receiving public assistance . . . 58
H'holds receiving social security . . . 325

Households, 2000

Total households . . . 1,081
With persons under 18 . . . 445
With persons over 65 . . . 277
Family households . . . 780
Single person households . . . 248
Persons per household . . . 2.68
Persons per family . . . 3.14

Household Population, 2008§§

Persons living in households . . . 3,526
Persons living in group quarters . . . 3,890
Persons per household . . . 2.5

Labor & Employment

Total civilian labor force, 2008§§ . . . 1,780
Unemployment rate, 2008 . . . 5.7%
Total civilian labor force, 2000 . . . 1,415

Employed persons 16 years and over by occupation, 2000

Managers & professionals . . . 340
Service occupations . . . 394
Sales & office occupations . . . 310
Farming, fishing & forestry . . . 16
Construction & maintenance . . . 126
Production & transportation . . . 184
Self-employed persons . . . 107

* US Census Bureau
** 2000 Decennial Census
§ California Department of Finance
§§ California Employment Development Dept

General Information

City of Ione
1 E Main St (physical)
PO Box 398 (mail)
Ione, CA 95640
209-274-2412

Website . . . www.ione-ca.com
Elevation . . . NA
Land Area (sq. miles) . . . 4.7
Water Area (sq. miles) . . . 0
Year of Incorporation . . . 1953
Government type . . . General law
Sales tax rate . . . 8.75%

Voters & Officials

Registered Voters, October 2008

Total . . . 2,044
Democrats . . . 655
Republicans . . . 993
Declined to state . . . 284

Legislative Districts

US Congressional . . . 3
State Senatorial . . . 1
State Assembly . . . 10

Local Officials, 2009

Mayor . . . Andrea Bonham
Manager . . . Kimberly Kerr
City Clerk . . . Janice Traverso
Attorney . . . Kristen Castanos
Treasurer . . . Sharon Long
Public Works . . . Don Myshrall
Planning Dir . . . David Young
Building . . . Don Myshrall
Police Chief . . . Michael Johnson
Fire Chief . . . Ken Mackey

Public Safety

Number of officers, 2007 . . . 5
Violent crimes, 2007 . . . 10
Property crimes, 2007 . . . 77
Arson, 2007 . . . 1

Public Library

Ione Branch
Amador County Library System
25 E Main St, librAddr2
Ione, CA 95640
209-274-2560

Branch Librarian . . . Donnell Junes

Library system statistics, FY 2007

Population served . . . 38,435
Internet terminals . . . 18
Annual users . . . 74,880

Per capita:

Operating income . . . $24.71
percent from local government . . . 94.0%
Operating expenditure . . . $20.44
Total materials . . . 2.18
Print holdings . . . 1.97
Visits per capita . . . 2.04

Housing & Construction

Housing Units

Total, 2008§ . . . 1,495
Single family units, attached . . . 54
Single family units, detached . . . 1,203
Multiple family units . . . 153
Mobile home units . . . 85
Occupied . . . 1,399
Vacancy rate . . . 6.4%
Median rent, 2000** . . . $642
Median SF home value, 2000** . . . $132,400

New Privately Owned Housing Units Authorized by Building Permit, 2007*

	Units	Construction Cost
Single	48	$7,899,284
Total	48	$7,899,284

Municipal Finance

(For local fiscal year ended in 2006)

Revenues

Total . . . $4,997,590
Taxes . . . 2,315,858
Special benefits assessment . . . 12,521
Licenses & permits . . . 248,532
Fines & forfeitures . . . 3,289
Revenues from use of money & property . . . 177,179
Intergovernmental . . . 483,507
Service charges . . . 1,754,470
Other revenues . . . 2,234
Other financing sources . . . 0

Expenditures

Total . . . $2,895,025
General government . . . 318,749
Public safety . . . 994,884
Transportation . . . 142,682
Community development . . . 126,309
Health . . . 747,599
Culture & leisure . . . 564,802
Other . . . 0

Local School District

(Data from School year 2007-08 except as noted)

Amador County Unified
217 Rex Ave
Jackson, CA 95642
(209) 223-1750

Superintendent . . . Dick Glock
Grade plan . . . K-12
Number of schools . . . 12
Enrollment . . . 4,362
High school graduates, 2006-07 . . . 373
Dropout rate . . . 3.8%
Pupil/teacher ratio . . . 22.8
Average class size . . . 23.3
Students per computer . . . 3.9
Classrooms with internet . . . 308
Avg. Daily Attendance (ADA) . . . 4,219
Cost per ADA . . . $6,964
Avg. Teacher Salary . . . $60,591

California Achievement Tests 6th ed., 2008

(Pct scoring at or above 50th National Percentile Rank)

	Math	Reading	Language
Grade 3	59%	52%	54%
Grade 7	54%	60%	55%

Academic Performance Index, 2008

Number of students tested . . . 3,491
Number of valid scores . . . 3,322
2007 API (base) . . . 751
2008 API (growth) . . . 769

SAT Testing, 2006-07

Enrollment, Grade 12 . . . 442
Number taking test . . . 103
percent taking test . . . 23.3%
percent with total score 1,500+ . . . 13.60%

Average Scores:

Math	Verbal	Writing	Total
519	520	516	1,555

Federal No Child Left Behind, 2008

(Adequate Yearly Progress standards met)

	Participation Rate	Pct Proficient
ELA	Yes	No
Math	Yes	No

API criteria . . . Yes
Graduation rate . . . Yes
\# criteria met/possible . . . 26/22

Other school districts for this city

(see Appendix E for information on these districts)

None

See Introduction for an explanation of all data sources.

Demographics & Socio-Economic Characteristics†

(2007 American Community Survey, except as noted)

Population

1990*	110,330
2007	205,813
Male	102,908
Female	102,905
Jan. 2008 (estimate)§	209,806
Persons per sq. mi. of land	4,541.3

Race & Hispanic Origin, 2007

Race	
White	110,963
Black/African American	4,970
North American Native	203
Asian	76,882
Pacific Islander	1,149
Other Race	6,297
Two or more races	5,349
Hispanic origin, total	20,614
Mexican	13,270
Puerto Rican	814
Cuban	543
Other Hispanic	5,987

Age & Nativity, 2007

Under 5 years	11,533
18 years and over	160,403
65 years and over	12,062
85 years and over	2,082
Median Age	32.9
Native-born	134,641
Foreign-born	71,172

Educational Attainment, 2007

Population 25 years and over	125,032
Less than 9th grade	1.2%
High school grad or higher	96.3%
Bachelor's degree or higher	63.5%
Graduate degree	25.9%

Income & Poverty, 2007

Per capita income	$41,425
Median household income	$98,923
Median family income	$111,455
Persons in poverty	8.7%
H'holds receiving public assistance	300
H'holds receiving social security	7,919

Households, 2007

Total households	69,990
With persons under 18	25,760
With persons over 65	8,357
Family households	46,950
Single person households	15,796
Persons per household	2.77
Persons per family	3.27

Household Population, 2008§§

Persons living in households	201,529
Persons living in group quarters	8,277
Persons per household	2.7

Labor & Employment

Total civilian labor force, 2008§§	85,900
Unemployment rate, 2008	3.9%
Total civilian labor force, 2000*	77,665

Employed persons 16 years and over by occupation, 2007

Managers & professionals	61,675
Service occupations	9,502
Sales & office occupations	27,190
Farming, fishing & forestry	102
Construction & maintenance	3,484
Production & transportation	3,194
Self-employed persons	9,042

† see Appendix D for 2000 Decennial Census Data
* US Census Bureau
** 2007 American Community Survey
§ California Department of Finance
§§ California Employment Development Dept

General Information

City of Irvine
One Civic Center Plaza
PO Box 19575
Irvine, CA 92623
949-724-6001

Website	www.ci.irvine.ca.us
Elevation	NA
Land Area (sq. miles)	46.2
Water Area (sq. miles)	0.3
Year of Incorporation	1971
Government type	Chartered
Sales tax rate	8.75%

Voters & Officials

Registered Voters, October 2008

Total	110,525
Democrats	35,660
Republicans	41,138
Declined to state	29,901

Legislative Districts

US Congressional	48
State Senatorial	33, 35
State Assembly	70

Local Officials, 2009

Mayor	Sukhee Kang
Manager	Sean Joyce
City Clerk	Sharie Apodaca
Attorney	Phil Kohn
Finance Dir	Rick Paikoff
Public Works	Manual Gomez
Planning/Dev Dir	Douglas Williford
Building	Eric Tolles
Police Chief	Dave Maggard
Fire/Emergency Mgmt	Brian Stephens

Public Safety

Number of officers, 2007	173
Violent crimes, 2007	143
Property crimes, 2007	3,256
Arson, 2007	53

Public Library

Heritage Park Branch Library
Orange County Public Library System
14361 Yale Ave
Irvine, CA 92604
949-936-4040

Branch Librarian	Trish Noa

Library system statistics, FY 2007

Population served	1,532,758
Internet terminals	505
Annual users	680,874

Per capita:

Operating income	$24.71
percent from local government	90.0%
Operating expenditure	$24.18
Total materials	1.93
Print holdings	1.84
Visits per capita	4.02

Housing & Construction

Housing Units

Total, 2008§	77,680
Single family units, attached	14,591
Single family units, detached	27,880
Multiple family units	34,187
Mobile home units	1,022
Occupied	74,151
Vacancy rate	4.5%
Median rent, 2007**	$1,829
Median SF home value, 2007**	$738,200

New Privately Owned Housing Units Authorized by Building Permit, 2007*

	Units	Construction Cost
Single	229	$65,498,257
Total	2,689	$384,528,970

Municipal Finance

(For local fiscal year ended in 2006)

Revenues

Total	$275,428,482
Taxes	134,685,518
Special benefits assessment	3,821,668
Licenses & permits	2,162,723
Fines & forfeitures	2,169,041
Revenues from use of money & property	13,124,601
Intergovernmental	16,081,909
Service charges	29,876,411
Other revenues	73,506,611
Other financing sources	0

Expenditures

Total	$189,699,191
General government	23,763,746
Public safety	53,444,461
Transportation	54,656,464
Community development	26,866,472
Health	136,787
Culture & leisure	30,831,261
Other	0

Local School District

(Data from School year 2007-08 except as noted)

Irvine Unified
5050 Barranca Pkwy
Irvine, CA 92604
(949) 936-5000

Superintendent	Gwen Gross
Grade plan	K-12
Number of schools	35
Enrollment	26,128
High school graduates, 2006-07	2,038
Dropout rate	0.9%
Pupil/teacher ratio	23.3
Average class size	27.0
Students per computer	5.0
Classrooms with internet	1,123
Avg. Daily Attendance (ADA)	25,996
Cost per ADA	$7,906
Avg. Teacher Salary	$72,720

California Achievement Tests 6th ed., 2008

(Pct scoring at or above 50th National Percentile Rank)

	Math	Reading	Language
Grade 3	83%	68%	78%
Grade 7	86%	81%	80%

Academic Performance Index, 2008

Number of students tested	20,509
Number of valid scores	19,620
2007 API (base)	888
2008 API (growth)	898

SAT Testing, 2006-07

Enrollment, Grade 12	2,114
Number taking test	1,388
percent taking test	65.7%
percent with total score 1,500+	54.00%

Average Scores:

Math	Verbal	Writing	Total
626	572	575	1,773

Federal No Child Left Behind, 2008

(Adequate Yearly Progress standards met)

	Participation Rate	Pct Proficient
ELA	Yes	Yes
Math	Yes	Yes

API criteria	Yes
Graduation rate	Yes
# criteria met/possible	42/42

Other school districts for this city

(see Appendix E for information on these districts)

None

See Introduction for an explanation of all data sources.

Demographics & Socio-Economic Characteristics

(2000 Decennial Census, except as noted)

Population

1990*	1,050
2000	1,446
Male	691
Female	755
Jan. 2008 (estimate)§	1,724
Persons per sq. mi. of land	185.4

Race & Hispanic Origin, 2000

Race	
White	680
Black/African American	6
North American Native	27
Asian	24
Pacific Islander	2
Other Race	644
Two or more races	63
Hispanic origin, total	1,277
Mexican	1,074
Puerto Rican	4
Cuban	2
Other Hispanic	197

Age & Nativity, 2000

Under 5 years	124
18 years and over	963
65 years and over	117
85 years and over	10
Median Age	28.5
Native-born	1,072
Foreign-born	400

Educational Attainment, 2000

Population 25 years and over	806
Less than 9th grade	21.0%
High school grad or higher	60.0%
Bachelor's degree or higher	7.3%
Graduate degree	2.4%

Income & Poverty, 1999

Per capita income	$13,144
Median household income	$45,000
Median family income	$46,827
Persons in poverty	16.6%
H'holds receiving public assistance	36
H'holds receiving social security	131

Households, 2000

Total households	365
With persons under 18	214
With persons over 65	94
Family households	293
Single person households	57
Persons per household	3.96
Persons per family	4.35

Household Population, 2008§§

Persons living in households	1,722
Persons living in group quarters	2
Persons per household	4.2

Labor & Employment

Total civilian labor force, 2008§§	700
Unemployment rate, 2008	7.5%
Total civilian labor force, 2000	626

Employed persons 16 years and over by occupation, 2000

Managers & professionals	154
Service occupations	120
Sales & office occupations	168
Farming, fishing & forestry	8
Construction & maintenance	38
Production & transportation	87
Self-employed persons	30

* US Census Bureau
** 2000 Decennial Census
§ California Department of Finance
§§ California Employment Development Dept

General Information

City of Irwindale
5050 N Irwindale Ave
Irwindale, CA 91706
626-430-2200

Website	www.ci.irwindale.ca.us
Elevation	467 ft.
Land Area (sq. miles)	9.3
Water Area (sq. miles)	0.2
Year of Incorporation	1957
Government type	Chartered
Sales tax rate	9.25%

Voters & Officials

Registered Voters, October 2008

Total	836
Democrats	542
Republicans	145
Declined to state	120

Legislative Districts

US Congressional	32
State Senatorial	24
State Assembly	57

Local Officials, 2009

Mayor	Larry G. Burrola
Manager	Robert Griego
City Clerk	Linda J. Kimbro
Attorney	Fred Galante
Finance Dir	Laura Nomura
Public Works	Kwok Tam
Planning/Dev Dir	Ray Hamada
Building	Kwok Tam
Police Chief	Solomon Benudiz
Emergency/Fire Dir	Ron Watson

Public Safety

Number of officers, 2007	28
Violent crimes, 2007	28
Property crimes, 2007	243
Arson, 2007	NA

Public Library

Irwindale Public Library
5050 N Irwindale Ave
Irwindale, CA 91706
626-430-2229

City Librarian: Patricia Sullivan

Library statistics, FY 2007

Population served	1,655
Internet terminals	8
Annual users	7,459

Per capita:

Operating income	$222.43
percent from local government	98.9%
Operating expenditure	$222.43
Total materials	12.56
Print holdings	9.79
Visits per capita	23.83

Housing & Construction

Housing Units

Total, 2008§	430
Single family units, attached	16
Single family units, detached	369
Multiple family units	37
Mobile home units	8
Occupied	414
Vacancy rate	3.7%
Median rent, 2000**	$584
Median SF home value, 2000**	$176,700

New Privately Owned Housing Units Authorized by Building Permit, 2007*

	Units	Construction Cost
Single	0	$0
Total	0	$0

Municipal Finance

(For local fiscal year ended in 2006)

Revenues

Total	$24,245,539
Taxes	18,652,578
Special benefits assessment	0
Licenses & permits	570,367
Fines & forfeitures	376,452
Revenues from use of money & property	1,628,237
Intergovernmental	1,092,671
Service charges	1,648,621
Other revenues	276,613
Other financing sources	0

Expenditures

Total	$19,517,531
General government	7,065,279
Public safety	5,766,859
Transportation	1,235,556
Community development	3,473,536
Health	0
Culture & leisure	1,976,301
Other	0

Local School District

(Data from School year 2007-08 except as noted)

Covina-Valley Unified
PO Box 269
Covina, CA 91723
(626) 974-7000

Superintendent	Louis Pappas
Grade plan	K-12
Number of schools	19
Enrollment	14,646
High school graduates, 2006-07	1,178
Dropout rate	1.7%
Pupil/teacher ratio	23.3
Average class size	25.5
Students per computer	4.3
Classrooms with internet	720
Avg. Daily Attendance (ADA)	14,219
Cost per ADA	$7,978
Avg. Teacher Salary	$65,572

California Achievement Tests 6th ed., 2008

(Pct scoring at or above 50th National Percentile Rank)

	Math	Reading	Language
Grade 3	55%	34%	45%
Grade 7	52%	47%	45%

Academic Performance Index, 2008

Number of students tested	11,633
Number of valid scores	10,871
2007 API (base)	731
2008 API (growth)	747

SAT Testing, 2006-07

Enrollment, Grade 12	1,306
Number taking test	508
percent taking test	38.9%
percent with total score 1,500+	14.10%

Average Scores:

Math	Verbal	Writing	Total
487	476	472	1,435

Federal No Child Left Behind, 2008

(Adequate Yearly Progress standards met)

	Participation Rate	Pct Proficient
ELA	Yes	No
Math	Yes	No

API criteria	Yes
Graduation rate	Yes
# criteria met/possible	38/35

Other school districts for this city

(see Appendix E for information on these districts)

None

See Introduction for an explanation of all data sources.

Demographics & Socio-Economic Characteristics

(2000 Decennial Census, except as noted)

Population

1990* 833
2000 828
Male 419
Female 409
Jan. 2008 (estimate)§ 817
Persons per sq. mi. of land 2,042.5

Race & Hispanic Origin, 2000

Race
White 576
Black/African American 12
North American Native 12
Asian 81
Pacific Islander 2
Other Race 83
Two or more races 62
Hispanic origin, total 223
Mexican 203
Puerto Rican 5
Cuban 2
Other Hispanic 13

Age & Nativity, 2000

Under 5 years 53
18 years and over 617
65 years and over 136
85 years and over 20
Median Age 38.5
Native-born 640
Foreign-born 163

Educational Attainment, 2000

Population 25 years and over 553
Less than 9th grade 15.0%
High school grad or higher 70.0%
Bachelor's degree or higher 11.6%
Graduate degree 3.1%

Income & Poverty, 1999

Per capita income $19,767
Median household income $33,958
Median family income $40,833
Persons in poverty 14.5%
H'holds receiving public assistance 18
H'holds receiving social security 124

Households, 2000

Total households 343
With persons under 18 119
With persons over 65 106
Family households 210
Single person households 112
Persons per household 2.41
Persons per family 3.08

Household Population, 2008§§

Persons living in households 817
Persons living in group quarters 0
Persons per household 2.4

Labor & Employment

Total civilian labor force, 2008§§ 400
Unemployment rate, 2008 .... 7.7%
Total civilian labor force, 2000 351

Employed persons 16 years and over by occupation, 2000

Managers & professionals 47
Service occupations 95
Sales & office occupations 66
Farming, fishing & forestry 8
Construction & maintenance 75
Production & transportation 35
Self-employed persons 30

* US Census Bureau
** 2000 Decennial Census
§ California Department of Finance
§§ California Employment Development Dept

General Information

City of Isleton
101 Second St
PO Box 716
Isleton, CA 95641
916-777-7770

Website .... NA
Elevation .... 5 ft.
Land Area (sq. miles) 0.4
Water Area (sq. miles) 0.1
Year of Incorporation 1923
Government type .... General law
Sales tax rate 8.75%

Voters & Officials

Registered Voters, October 2008

Total 452
Democrats 235
Republicans 105
Declined to state 89

Legislative Districts

US Congressional 10
State Senatorial 5
State Assembly 15

Local Officials, 2009

Mayor .... Gene Resler
Manager .... Bruce Pope
City Clerk .... Linda Garcia (Int)
Attorney .... David Larsen
Finance Dir .... Bruce Pope
Public Works .... NA
Planning/Dev Dir .... John Hieser
Building .... Esequiel Mota
Police Chief .... Ron Jole
Emergency/Fire Dir .... Bob Bartley

Public Safety

Number of officers, 2007 6
Violent crimes, 2007 14
Property crimes, 2007 42
Arson, 2007 0

Public Library

Isleton Branch Library
Sacramento Public Library System
412 Union St
Isleton, CA 95641
916-264-2700

Branch Librarian .... Natalie Beaver

Library system statistics, FY 2007

Population served 1,335,969
Internet terminals 49
Annual users 27,435

Per capita:

Operating income $25.83
percent from local government 91.0%
Operating expenditure $23.08
Total materials 1.57
Print holdings 1.45
Visits per capita 1.18

Housing & Construction

Housing Units

Total, 2008§ 378
Single family units, attached 0
Single family units, detached 223
Multiple family units 108
Mobile home units 47
Occupied 338
Vacancy rate 10.6%
Median rent, 2000** $522
Median SF home value, 2000** $123,900

New Privately Owned Housing Units Authorized by Building Permit, 2007*

	Units	Construction Cost
Single	18	$4,202,835
Total	18	$4,202,835

Municipal Finance

(For local fiscal year ended in 2006)

Revenues

Total $3,377,376
Taxes 554,741
Special benefits assessment 1,766
Licenses & permits 19,884
Fines & forfeitures 15,446
Revenues from use of money & property 1,175
Intergovernmental 1,319,865
Service charges 342,538
Other revenues 8,461
Other financing sources 1,113,500

Expenditures

Total $3,273,761
General government 444,613
Public safety 727,283
Transportation 309,613
Community development 132,003
Health 1,353,547
Culture & leisure 306,702
Other 0

Local School District

(Data from School year 2007-08 except as noted)

River Delta Joint Unified
445 Montezuma St
Rio Vista, CA 94571
(707) 374-1700

Superintendent .... Richard Hennes
Grade plan K-12
Number of schools 12
Enrollment 2,213
High school graduates, 2006-07 138
Dropout rate 3.5%
Pupil/teacher ratio 17.9
Average class size 22.1
Students per computer 3.5
Classrooms with internet 274
Avg. Daily Attendance (ADA) 2,053
Cost per ADA $9,801
Avg. Teacher Salary $52,353

California Achievement Tests 6th ed., 2008

(Pct scoring at or above 50th National Percentile Rank)

	Math	Reading	Language
Grade 3	46%	37%	44%
Grade 7	56%	49%	43%

Academic Performance Index, 2008

Number of students tested 1,601
Number of valid scores 1,474
2007 API (base) 698
2008 API (growth) 718

SAT Testing, 2006-07

Enrollment, Grade 12 144
Number taking test 58
percent taking test 40.3%
percent with total score 1,500+ 21.50%

Average Scores:

Math	Verbal	Writing	Total
506	498	506	1,510

Federal No Child Left Behind, 2008

(Adequate Yearly Progress standards met)

	Participation Rate	Pct Proficient
ELA	Yes	No
Math	Yes	Yes

API criteria .... Yes
Graduation rate .... Yes
\# criteria met/possible 26/23

Other school districts for this city

(see Appendix E for information on these districts)

None

See Introduction for an explanation of all data sources.

Demographics & Socio-Economic Characteristics

(2000 Decennial Census, except as noted)

Population

1990* . . . 3,545
2000 . . . 3,989
Male . . . 1,777
Female . . . 2,212
Jan. 2008 (estimate)§ . . . 4,319
Persons per sq. mi. of land . . . 1,234.0

Race & Hispanic Origin, 2000

Race
White . . . 3,731
Black/African American . . . 20
North American Native . . . 55
Asian . . . 23
Pacific Islander . . . 3
Other Race . . . 74
Two or more races . . . 83
Hispanic origin, total . . . 258
Mexican . . . 190
Puerto Rican . . . 9
Cuban . . . 1
Other Hispanic . . . 58

Age & Nativity, 2000

Under 5 years . . . 229
18 years and over . . . 3,193
65 years and over . . . 1,149
85 years and over . . . 257
Median Age . . . 46.6
Native-born . . . 4,291
Foreign-born . . . 176

Educational Attainment, 2000

Population 25 years and over . . . 3,241
Less than 9th grade . . . 3.1%
High school grad or higher . . . 88.7%
Bachelor's degree or higher . . . 20.2%
Graduate degree . . . 6.7%

Income & Poverty, 1999

Per capita income . . . $21,399
Median household income . . . $35,944
Median family income . . . $45,887
Persons in poverty . . . 8.8%
H'holds receiving public assistance . . . 52
H'holds receiving social security . . . 750

Households, 2000

Total households . . . 1,746
With persons under 18 . . . 453
With persons over 65 . . . 698
Family households . . . 1,024
Single person households . . . 630
Persons per household . . . 2.13
Persons per family . . . 2.74

Household Population, 2008§§

Persons living in households . . . 4,051
Persons living in group quarters . . . 268
Persons per household . . . 2.0

Labor & Employment

Total civilian labor force, 2008§§ . . . 2,470
Unemployment rate, 2008 . . . 6.8%
Total civilian labor force, 2000 . . . 1,954

Employed persons 16 years and over by occupation, 2000

Managers & professionals . . . 737
Service occupations . . . 403
Sales & office occupations . . . 415
Farming, fishing & forestry . . . 9
Construction & maintenance . . . 190
Production & transportation . . . 126
Self-employed persons . . . 338

* US Census Bureau
** 2000 Decennial Census
§ California Department of Finance
§§ California Employment Development Dept

General Information

City of Jackson
33 Broadway
Jackson, CA 95642
209-223-1646

Website . . . www.ci.jackson.ca.us
Elevation . . . 1,235 ft.
Land Area (sq. miles) . . . 3.5
Water Area (sq. miles) . . . 0
Year of Incorporation . . . 1905
Government type . . . General law
Sales tax rate . . . 8.75%

Voters & Officials

Registered Voters, October 2008

Total . . . 2,568
Democrats . . . 927
Republicans . . . 1,157
Declined to state . . . 360

Legislative Districts

US Congressional . . . 3
State Senatorial . . . 1
State Assembly . . . 10

Local Officials, 2009

Mayor . . . Connie Gonsalves
City Manager . . . Michael Daly
City Clerk . . . Gisele L. Cangelosi
Attorney . . . Andrew Morris
Finance Dir . . . Carla Soracco
Public Works . . . Jeffery McCrory
City Planner . . . Susan Peters
Building . . . Larry White
Police Chief . . . Scott Morrison
Fire Chief . . . Mark Morton

Public Safety

Number of officers, 2007 . . . 11
Violent crimes, 2007 . . . 24
Property crimes, 2007 . . . 157
Arson, 2007 . . . 2

Public Library

Main Branch
Amador County Library System
530 Sutter St
Jackson, CA 95642
209-223-6400

Director . . . Judy Ramm

Library system statistics, FY 2007

Population served . . . 38,435
Internet terminals . . . 18
Annual users . . . 74,880

Per capita:

Operating income . . . $24.71
percent from local government . . . 94.0%
Operating expenditure . . . $20.44
Total materials . . . 2.18
Print holdings . . . 1.97
Visits per capita . . . 2.04

Housing & Construction

Housing Units

Total, 2008§ . . . 2,152
Single family units, attached . . . 112
Single family units, detached . . . 1,383
Multiple family units . . . 421
Mobile home units . . . 236
Occupied . . . 2,022
Vacancy rate . . . 6.0%
Median rent, 2000** . . . $675
Median SF home value, 2000** . . . $149,200

New Privately Owned Housing Units Authorized by Building Permit, 2007*

	Units	Construction Cost
Single	7	$1,280,262
Total	7	$1,280,262

Municipal Finance

(For local fiscal year ended in 2006)

Revenues

Total . . . $10,435,057
Taxes . . . 2,751,386
Special benefits assessment . . . 32,071
Licenses & permits . . . 218,080
Fines & forfeitures . . . 39,897
Revenues from use of money & property . . . 365,411
Intergovernmental . . . 2,088,151
Service charges . . . 3,608,922
Other revenues . . . 1,331,139
Other financing sources . . . 0

Expenditures

Total . . . $10,192,688
General government . . . 966,355
Public safety . . . 1,831,890
Transportation . . . 1,110,299
Community development . . . 1,724,261
Health . . . 1,450,249
Culture & leisure . . . 313,475
Other . . . 0

Local School District

(Data from School year 2007-08 except as noted)

Amador County Unified
217 Rex Ave
Jackson, CA 95642
(209) 223-1750

Superintendent . . . Dick Glock
Grade plan . . . K-12
Number of schools . . . 12
Enrollment . . . 4,362
High school graduates, 2006-07 . . . 373
Dropout rate . . . 3.8%
Pupil/teacher ratio . . . 22.8
Average class size . . . 23.3
Students per computer . . . 3.9
Classrooms with internet . . . 308
Avg. Daily Attendance (ADA) . . . 4,219
Cost per ADA . . . $6,964
Avg. Teacher Salary . . . $60,591

California Achievement Tests 6th ed., 2008

(Pct scoring at or above 50th National Percentile Rank)

	Math	Reading	Language
Grade 3	59%	52%	54%
Grade 7	54%	60%	55%

Academic Performance Index, 2008

Number of students tested . . . 3,491
Number of valid scores . . . 3,322
2007 API (base) . . . 751
2008 API (growth) . . . 769

SAT Testing, 2006-07

Enrollment, Grade 12 . . . 442
Number taking test . . . 103
percent taking test . . . 23.3%
percent with total score 1,500+ . . . 13.60%

Average Scores:

Math	Verbal	Writing	Total
519	520	516	1,555

Federal No Child Left Behind, 2008

(Adequate Yearly Progress standards met)

	Participation Rate	Pct Proficient
ELA	Yes	No
Math	Yes	No

API criteria . . . Yes
Graduation rate . . . Yes
\# criteria met/possible . . . 26/22

Other school districts for this city

(see Appendix E for information on these districts)

None

See Introduction for an explanation of all data sources.

Demographics & Socio-Economic Characteristics

(2000 Decennial Census, except as noted)

Population
1990* 5,448
2000 8,551
Male 4,231
Female 4,320
Jan. 2008 (estimate)§ 13,880
Persons per sq. mi. of land 6,309.1

Race & Hispanic Origin, 2000
Race
White 3,634
Black/African American 31
North American Native 167
Asian 709
Pacific Islander 2
Other Race 3,624
Two or more races 384
Hispanic origin, total 5,552
Mexican 4,922
Puerto Rican 5
Cuban 0
Other Hispanic 625

Age & Nativity, 2000
Under 5 years 783
18 years and over 5,532
65 years and over 695
85 years and over 75
Median Age 27.1
Native-born 6,077
Foreign-born 2,214

Educational Attainment, 2000
Population 25 years and over 4,427
Less than 9th grade 30.5%
High school grad or higher 50.5%
Bachelor's degree or higher 8.8%
Graduate degree 4.2%

Income & Poverty, 1999
Per capita income $11,495
Median household income $31,188
Median family income $34,120
Persons in poverty 19.6%
H'holds receiving public assistance 129
H'holds receiving social security 624

Households, 2000
Total households 2,389
With persons under 18 1,393
With persons over 65 529
Family households 1,994
Single person households 330
Persons per household 3.57
Persons per family 3.91

Household Population, 2008§§
Persons living in households 13,849
Persons living in group quarters 31
Persons per household 3.6

Labor & Employment
Total civilian labor force, 2008§§ 4,200
Unemployment rate, 2008 .... 13.5%
Total civilian labor force, 2000 3,316

Employed persons 16 years and over by occupation, 2000
Managers & professionals 572
Service occupations 474
Sales & office occupations 663
Farming, fishing & forestry 449
Construction & maintenance 186
Production & transportation 473
Self-employed persons 115

* US Census Bureau
** 2000 Decennial Census
§ California Department of Finance
§§ California Employment Development Dept

General Information

City of Kerman
850 S Madera Ave
Kerman, CA 93630
559-846-9384

Website .... www.cityofkerman.net
Elevation .... NA
Land Area (sq. miles) 2.2
Water Area (sq. miles) 0
Year of Incorporation 1946
Government type .... General law
Sales tax rate 8.98%

Voters & Officials

Registered Voters, October 2008
Total 4,196
Democrats 1,979
Republicans 1,460
Declined to state 482

Legislative Districts
US Congressional 19
State Senatorial 16
State Assembly 31

Local Officials, 2009
Mayor .... Trinidad M. Rodriguez
Manager .... Ron Manfredi
City Clerk .... Renee Holdcroft
Attorney .... Mark Blum
Finance Dir .... Tim Przybyla
Public Works .... Ken Moore
Planning/Dev Dir .... Luis Patlan
Building .... NA
Police Chief .... William Newton
Fire Chief .... Randy Breugman

Public Safety

Number of officers, 2007 18
Violent crimes, 2007 28
Property crimes, 2007 351
Arson, 2007 4

Public Library

Kerman Branch Library
Fresno County Public Library System
15081 W Kearney Plaza
Kerman, CA 93630
559-846-8804

Branch Librarian .... Rita Del Testa

Library system statistics, FY 2007
Population served 889,019
Internet terminals 277
Annual users 861,240

Per capita:
Operating income $23.69
percent from local government 89.3%
Operating expenditure $23.37
Total materials 2.89
Print holdings 2.69
Visits per capita .... NA

Housing & Construction

Housing Units
Total, 2008§ 3,915
Single family units, attached 153
Single family units, detached 2,879
Multiple family units 767
Mobile home units 116
Occupied 3,799
Vacancy rate 3.0%
Median rent, 2000** $481
Median SF home value, 2000** $97,900

New Privately Owned Housing Units Authorized by Building Permit, 2007*

	Units	Construction Cost
Single	84	$17,119,532
Total	84	$17,119,532

Municipal Finance

(For local fiscal year ended in 2006)

Revenues
Total $10,685,471
Taxes 3,360,651
Special benefits assessment 92,782
Licenses & permits 362,120
Fines & forfeitures 66,542
Revenues from use of money & property 321,147
Intergovernmental 772,420
Service charges 3,928,494
Other revenues 1,781,315
Other financing sources 0

Expenditures
Total $9,558,557
General government 502,685
Public safety 2,026,009
Transportation 1,256,940
Community development 445,733
Health 2,315,427
Culture & leisure 706,256
Other 0

Local School District

(Data from School year 2007-08 except as noted)

Kerman Unified
151 South First St
Kerman, CA 93630
(559) 846-5383

Superintendent .... Robert Frausto
Grade plan K-12
Number of schools 7
Enrollment 4,220
High school graduates, 2006-07 178
Dropout rate 3.5%
Pupil/teacher ratio 21.3
Average class size 25.0
Students per computer 4.6
Classrooms with internet 189
Avg. Daily Attendance (ADA) 4,167
Cost per ADA $7,197
Avg. Teacher Salary $59,230

California Achievement Tests 6th ed., 2008
(Pct scoring at or above 50th National Percentile Rank)

	Math	Reading	Language
Grade 3	44%	27%	35%
Grade 7	52%	40%	37%

Academic Performance Index, 2008
Number of students tested 3,302
Number of valid scores 2,969
2007 API (base) 733
2008 API (growth) 742

SAT Testing, 2006-07
Enrollment, Grade 12 204
Number taking test 67
percent taking test 32.8%
percent with total score 1,500+ 7.80%

Average Scores:

Math	Verbal	Writing	Total
433	427	420	1,280

Federal No Child Left Behind, 2008
(Adequate Yearly Progress standards met)

	Participation Rate	Pct Proficient
ELA	Yes	No
Math	Yes	Yes

API criteria .... Yes
Graduation rate .... Yes
criteria met/possible 30/29

Other school districts for this city
(see Appendix E for information on these districts)
None

See Introduction for an explanation of all data sources.

Demographics & Socio-Economic Characteristics

(2000 Decennial Census, except as noted)

Population

1990* 7,634
2000 11,094
Male 5,952
Female 5,142
Jan. 2008 (estimate)$ 11,852
Persons per sq. mi. of land 3,203.2

Race & Hispanic Origin, 2000

Race
White 4,669
Black/African American 65
North American Native 116
Asian 136
Pacific Islander 15
Other Race 5,598
Two or more races 495
Hispanic origin, total 8,922
Mexican 7,828
Puerto Rican 20
Cuban 3
Other Hispanic 1,071

Age & Nativity, 2000

Under 5 years 1,090
18 years and over 7,138
65 years and over 686
85 years and over 70
Median Age 25.3
Native-born 5,943
Foreign-born 5,292

Educational Attainment, 2000

Population 25 years and over 5,784
Less than 9th grade 42.4%
High school grad or higher 41.2%
Bachelor's degree or higher 8.0%
Graduate degree 1.9%

Income & Poverty, 1999

Per capita income $11,685
Median household income $34,398
Median family income $33,750
Persons in poverty 20.9%
H'holds receiving public assistance 264
H'holds receiving social security 489

Households, 2000

Total households 2,736
With persons under 18 1,657
With persons over 65 505
Family households 2,252
Single person households 368
Persons per household 4.03
Persons per family 4.28

Household Population, 2008$$

Persons living in households 11,668
Persons living in group quarters 184
Persons per household 4.0

Labor & Employment

Total civilian labor force, 2008$$ 5,700
Unemployment rate, 2008 .... 14.4%
Total civilian labor force, 2000 4,763

Employed persons 16 years and over by occupation, 2000

Managers & professionals 642
Service occupations 626
Sales & office occupations 500
Farming, fishing & forestry 1,338
Construction & maintenance 278
Production & transportation 673
Self-employed persons 235

* US Census Bureau
** 2000 Decennial Census
$ California Department of Finance
$$ California Employment Development Dept

General Information

City of King City
212 S Vanderhurst Ave
King City, CA 93930
831-385-3281

Website .... www.kingcity.com
Elevation .... 330 ft.
Land Area (sq. miles) 3.7
Water Area (sq. miles) 0.1
Year of Incorporation 1911
Government type .... General law
Sales tax rate 8.25%

Voters & Officials

Registered Voters, October 2008

Total 2,480
Democrats 1,358
Republicans 688
Declined to state 363

Legislative Districts

US Congressional 17
State Senatorial 12
State Assembly 28

Local Officials, 2009

Mayor .... Jeff Pereira
Manager .... Michael Powers
City Clerk .... Erica Sonne
Attorney .... Roy Hanley
Finance Dir .... James Larson
Public Works .... NA
Planning/Dev Dir .... NA
Building .... Jose Martinez (Int)
Police Chief .... Nick Baldiviez
Emergency/Fire Dir .... Danny Conaster

Public Safety

Number of officers, 2007 19
Violent crimes, 2007 76
Property crimes, 2007 348
Arson, 2007 4

Public Library

King City Branch Library
Monterey County Free Libraries
402 Broadway
King City, CA 93930
831-385-3677

Branch Librarian .... NA

Library system statistics, FY 2007

Population served 226,803
Internet terminals 160
Annual users 229,676

Per capita:

Operating income $29.19
percent from local government 91.7%
Operating expenditure $27.42
Total materials 1.92
Print holdings 1.81
Visits per capita 3.65

Housing & Construction

Housing Units

Total, 2008$ 3,009
Single family units, attached 282
Single family units, detached 1,712
Multiple family units 725
Mobile home units 290
Occupied 2,916
Vacancy rate 3.1%
Median rent, 2000** $644
Median SF home value, 2000** $138,700

New Privately Owned Housing Units Authorized by Building Permit, 2007*

	Units	Construction Cost
Single	26	$5,049,461
Total	46	$8,040,969

Municipal Finance

(For local fiscal year ended in 2006)

Revenues

Total $8,923,310
Taxes 4,460,100
Special benefits assessment 5,045
Licenses & permits 444,654
Fines & forfeitures 79,169
Revenues from use of money & property 171,853
Intergovernmental 1,034,232
Service charges 1,821,275
Other revenues 906,982
Other financing sources 0

Expenditures

Total $7,855,914
General government 1,723,940
Public safety 2,379,150
Transportation 1,147,844
Community development 1,610,958
Health 530,438
Culture & leisure 463,584
Other 0

Local School District

(Data from School year 2007-08 except as noted)

King City Joint Union High
800 Broadway
King City, CA 93930
(831) 385-0606

Superintendent .... Tom Michaelson
Grade plan 9-12
Number of schools 4
Enrollment 2,184
High school graduates, 2006-07 344
Dropout rate 2.4%
Pupil/teacher ratio 25.1
Average class size 27.4
Students per computer 3.0
Classrooms with internet 92
Avg. Daily Attendance (ADA) 2,068
Cost per ADA $9,008
Avg. Teacher Salary $81,391

California Achievement Tests 6th ed., 2008

(Pct scoring at or above 50th National Percentile Rank)

	Math	Reading	Language
Grade 3	NA	NA	NA
Grade 7	NA	NA	NA

Academic Performance Index, 2008

Number of students tested 1,654
Number of valid scores 1,573
2007 API (base) 599
2008 API (growth) 635

SAT Testing, 2006-07

Enrollment, Grade 12 436
Number taking test 110
percent taking test 25.2%
percent with total score 1,500+ 4.60%

Average Scores:

Math	Verbal	Writing	Total
428	418	426	1,272

Federal No Child Left Behind, 2008

(Adequate Yearly Progress standards met)

	Participation Rate	Pct Proficient
ELA	Yes	Yes
Math	Yes	No

API criteria .... Yes
Graduation rate .... Yes
\# criteria met/possible 18/14

Other school districts for this city

(see Appendix E for information on these districts)

Bitterwater-Tully Union Elem, King City Union

See Introduction for an explanation of all data sources.

Demographics & Socio-Economic Characteristics

(2000 Decennial Census, except as noted)

Population

1990* . . . 7,205
2000 . . . 9,199
Male . . . 4,397
Female . . . 4,802
Jan. 2008 (estimate)§ . . . 11,259
Persons per sq. mi. of land . . . 4,895.2

Race & Hispanic Origin, 2000

Race
White . . . 6,617
Black/African American . . . 41
North American Native . . . 62
Asian . . . 252
Pacific Islander . . . 13
Other Race . . . 1,804
Two or more races . . . 410
Hispanic origin, total . . . 3,166
Mexican . . . 2,822
Puerto Rican . . . 3
Cuban . . . 5
Other Hispanic . . . 336

Age & Nativity, 2000

Under 5 years . . . 712
18 years and over . . . 6,435
65 years and over . . . 1,216
85 years and over . . . 184
Median Age . . . 33.8
Native-born . . . 8,367
Foreign-born . . . 819

Educational Attainment, 2000

Population 25 years and over . . . 5,772
Less than 9th grade . . . 10.0%
High school grad or higher . . . 76.5%
Bachelor's degree or higher . . . 20.9%
Graduate degree . . . 4.8%

Income & Poverty, 1999

Per capita income . . . $16,137
Median household income . . . $40,490
Median family income . . . $44,737
Persons in poverty . . . 11.3%
H'holds receiving public assistance . . . 139
H'holds receiving social security . . . 904

Households, 2000

Total households . . . 3,226
With persons under 18 . . . 1,410
With persons over 65 . . . 839
Family households . . . 2,458
Single person households . . . 688
Persons per household . . . 2.82
Persons per family . . . 3.29

Household Population, 2008§§

Persons living in households . . . 11,168
Persons living in group quarters . . . 91
Persons per household . . . 2.9

Labor & Employment

Total civilian labor force, 2008§§ . . . 5,500
Unemployment rate, 2008 . . . 7.8%
Total civilian labor force, 2000 . . . 4,280

Employed persons 16 years and over by occupation, 2000

Managers & professionals . . . 1,178
Service occupations . . . 599
Sales & office occupations . . . 1,046
Farming, fishing & forestry . . . 160
Construction & maintenance . . . 368
Production & transportation . . . 553
Self-employed persons . . . 337

* US Census Bureau
** 2000 Decennial Census
§ California Department of Finance
§§ California Employment Development Dept

General Information

City of Kingsburg
1401 Draper St
Kingsburg, CA 93631
559-897-5821

Website . . . www.cityofkingsburg-ca.gov
Elevation . . . 297 ft.
Land Area (sq. miles) . . . 2.3
Water Area (sq. miles) . . . 0
Year of Incorporation . . . 1908
Government type . . . Chartered
Sales tax rate . . . 8.98%

Voters & Officials

Registered Voters, October 2008

Total . . . 5,753
Democrats . . . 1,490
Republicans . . . 3,375
Declined to state . . . 616

Legislative Districts

US Congressional . . . 21
State Senatorial . . . 14
State Assembly . . . 30

Local Officials, 2009

Mayor . . . Bruce Blayney
Manager . . . Donald Pauley
City Clerk . . . Susan Bauch
Attorney . . . Michael Noland
Finance Dir . . . Don Jensen
Public Works . . . NA
Planning/Dev Dir . . . Terry Schmal
Building . . . Daryl Sonksen
Police Chief . . . Jeff Dunn
Emergency/Fire Dir . . . Gary Rocha

Public Safety

Number of officers, 2007 . . . 16
Violent crimes, 2007 . . . 14
Property crimes, 2007 . . . 442
Arson, 2007 . . . 4

Public Library

Kingsburg Branch Library
Fresno County Public Library System
1399 Draper
Kingsburg, CA 93631
559-897-3710

Branch Librarian . . . Marjorie Hall

Library system statistics, FY 2007

Population served . . . 889,019
Internet terminals . . . 277
Annual users . . . 861,240

Per capita:

Operating income . . . $23.69
percent from local government . . . 89.3%
Operating expenditure . . . $23.37
Total materials . . . 2.89
Print holdings . . . 2.69
Visits per capita . . . NA

Housing & Construction

Housing Units

Total, 2008§ . . . 4,036
Single family units, attached . . . 102
Single family units, detached . . . 3,065
Multiple family units . . . 705
Mobile home units . . . 164
Occupied . . . 3,879
Vacancy rate . . . 3.9%
Median rent, 2000** . . . $541
Median SF home value, 2000** . . . $117,300

New Privately Owned Housing Units Authorized by Building Permit, 2007*

	Units	Construction Cost
Single	9	$1,957,833
Total	9	$1,957,833

Municipal Finance

(For local fiscal year ended in 2006)

Revenues

Total . . . $10,432,526
Taxes . . . 3,305,514
Special benefits assessment . . . 36,029
Licenses & permits . . . 300,895
Fines & forfeitures . . . 78,237
Revenues from use of money & property . . . 218,318
Intergovernmental . . . 864,942
Service charges . . . 4,579,149
Other revenues . . . 483,718
Other financing sources . . . 565,724

Expenditures

Total . . . $13,364,839
General government . . . 1,043,336
Public safety . . . 6,307,598
Transportation . . . 551,050
Community development . . . 1,802,514
Health . . . 1,064,021
Culture & leisure . . . 935,247
Other . . . 933

Local School District

(Data from School year 2007-08 except as noted)

Kingsburg Joint Union High
1900 18th Ave
Kingsburg, CA 93631
(559) 897-7721

Superintendent . . . Linda Clark
Grade plan . . . 9-12
Number of schools . . . 2
Enrollment . . . 1,227
High school graduates, 2006-07 . . . 208
Dropout rate . . . 1.5%
Pupil/teacher ratio . . . 22.3
Average class size . . . 22.6
Students per computer . . . 4.6
Classrooms with internet . . . 70
Avg. Daily Attendance (ADA) . . . 1,214
Cost per ADA . . . $7,419
Avg. Teacher Salary . . . $63,943

California Achievement Tests 6th ed., 2008

(Pct scoring at or above 50th National Percentile Rank)

	Math	Reading	Language
Grade 3	NA	NA	NA
Grade 7	NA	NA	NA

Academic Performance Index, 2008

Number of students tested . . . 884
Number of valid scores . . . 834
2007 API (base) . . . 735
2008 API (growth) . . . 741

SAT Testing, 2006-07

Enrollment, Grade 12 . . . 258
Number taking test . . . 86
percent taking test . . . 33.3%
percent with total score 1,500+ . . . 16.70%

Average Scores:

Math	Verbal	Writing	Total
499	477	487	1,463

Federal No Child Left Behind, 2008

(Adequate Yearly Progress standards met)

	Participation Rate	Pct Proficient
ELA	Yes	Yes
Math	Yes	Yes

API criteria . . . Yes
Graduation rate . . . Yes
\# criteria met/possible . . . 18/18

Other school districts for this city

(see Appendix E for information on these districts)

Clay Joint Elem, Kingsburg Joint Union Elem

See Introduction for an explanation of all data sources.

Demographics & Socio-Economic Characteristics

(2000 Decennial Census, except as noted)

Population

1990*	19,378
2000	20,318
Male	9,796
Female	10,522
Jan. 2008 (estimate)§	21,276
Persons per sq. mi. of land	2,445.5

Race & Hispanic Origin, 2000

Race	
White	15,142
Black/African American	73
North American Native	36
Asian	4,180
Pacific Islander	9
Other Race	206
Two or more races	672
Hispanic origin, total	976
Mexican	502
Puerto Rican	20
Cuban	106
Other Hispanic	348

Age & Nativity, 2000

Under 5 years	1,048
18 years and over	14,269
65 years and over	2,842
85 years and over	328
Median Age	42.1
Native-born	16,408
Foreign-born	3,973

Educational Attainment, 2000

Population 25 years and over	13,303
Less than 9th grade	1.3%
High school grad or higher	95.9%
Bachelor's degree or higher	63.5%
Graduate degree	29.6%

Income & Poverty, 1999

Per capita income	$52,838
Median household income	$109,989
Median family income	$122,779
Persons in poverty	4.2%
H'holds receiving public assistance	59
H'holds receiving social security	1,850

Households, 2000

Total households	6,823
With persons under 18	3,100
With persons over 65	1,945
Family households	5,693
Single person households	985
Persons per household	2.95
Persons per family	3.27

Household Population, 2008§§

Persons living in households	21,086
Persons living in group quarters	190
Persons per household	3.1

Labor & Employment

Total civilian labor force, 2008§§	10,600
Unemployment rate, 2008	2.7%
Total civilian labor force, 2000	9,325

Employed persons 16 years and over by occupation, 2000

Managers & professionals	5,951
Service occupations	465
Sales & office occupations	2,009
Farming, fishing & forestry	7
Construction & maintenance	335
Production & transportation	230
Self-employed persons	1,341

* US Census Bureau
** 2000 Decennial Census
§ California Department of Finance
§§ California Employment Development Dept

General Information

City of La Canada Flintridge
1327 Foothill Blvd
La Canada Flintridge, CA 91011
818-790-8880

Website	www.lcf.ca.gov
Elevation	NA
Land Area (sq. miles)	8.7
Water Area (sq. miles)	0
Year of Incorporation	1976
Government type	General law
Sales tax rate	9.25%

Voters & Officials

Registered Voters, October 2008

Total	14,084
Democrats	4,231
Republicans	6,939
Declined to state	2,486

Legislative Districts

US Congressional	26
State Senatorial	21
State Assembly	44

Local Officials, 2009

Mayor	Stephen A. Del Guercio
City Manager	Mark R. Alexander
City Clerk	Sylvia Baca
Attorney	Mark Steres
Finance Dir	Jeffrey Wang
Public Works	Edward Hitti
Community Dev Dir	Robert Stanley
Building	NA
Police Chief	NA
Fire/Emergency Mgmt	NA

Public Safety

Number of officers, 2007	NA
Violent crimes, 2007	25
Property crimes, 2007	431
Arson, 2007	NA

Public Library

La Canada Flintridge Library
Los Angeles County Public Library System
4545 N Oakwood Ave
La Canada Flintridge, CA 91011
818-790-3330

Branch Librarian	Sue Renyer

Library system statistics, FY 2007

Population served	3,673,313
Internet terminals	749
Annual users	3,748,771

Per capita:

Operating income	$30.06
percent from local government	93.6%
Operating expenditure	$28.36
Total materials	2.22
Print holdings	1.97
Visits per capita	3.25

Housing & Construction

Housing Units

Total, 2008§	7,069
Single family units, attached	200
Single family units, detached	6,562
Multiple family units	307
Mobile home units	0
Occupied	6,902
Vacancy rate	2.4%
Median rent, 2000**	$1,148
Median SF home value, 2000**	$587,800

New Privately Owned Housing Units Authorized by Building Permit, 2007*

	Units	Construction Cost
Single	20	$10,193,666
Total	20	$10,193,666

Municipal Finance

(For local fiscal year ended in 2006)

Revenues

Total	$16,375,173
Taxes	7,694,448
Special benefits assessment	27,124
Licenses & permits	1,512,565
Fines & forfeitures	190,693
Revenues from use of money & property	954,385
Intergovernmental	3,316,306
Service charges	2,409,256
Other revenues	270,396
Other financing sources	0

Expenditures

Total	$14,427,305
General government	2,338,771
Public safety	2,388,941
Transportation	2,681,009
Community development	3,161,145
Health	1,768,951
Culture & leisure	2,088,488
Other	0

Local School District

(Data from School year 2007-08 except as noted)

La Canada Unified
4490 Cornishon Ave
La Canada, CA 91011
(818) 952-8300

Superintendent	James Stratton
Grade plan	K-12
Number of schools	5
Enrollment	4,109
High school graduates, 2006-07	399
Dropout rate	0.1%
Pupil/teacher ratio	23.4
Average class size	26.1
Students per computer	4.3
Classrooms with internet	189
Avg. Daily Attendance (ADA)	4,071
Cost per ADA	$7,969
Avg. Teacher Salary	$67,318

California Achievement Tests 6th ed., 2008

(Pct scoring at or above 50th National Percentile Rank)

	Math	Reading	Language
Grade 3	88%	75%	80%
Grade 7	92%	88%	86%

Academic Performance Index, 2008

Number of students tested	3,260
Number of valid scores	3,204
2007 API (base)	914
2008 API (growth)	917

SAT Testing, 2006-07

Enrollment, Grade 12	399
Number taking test	357
percent taking test	89.5%
percent with total score 1,500+	72.90%

Average Scores:

Math	Verbal	Writing	Total
606	581	584	1,771

Federal No Child Left Behind, 2008

(Adequate Yearly Progress standards met)

	Participation Rate	Pct Proficient
ELA	Yes	Yes
Math	Yes	Yes

API criteria	Yes
Graduation rate	Yes
# criteria met/possible	26/26

Other school districts for this city

(see Appendix E for information on these districts)

None

See Introduction for an explanation of all data sources.

Demographics & Socio-Economic Characteristics

(2000 Decennial Census, except as noted)

Population

1990* ... 51,266
2000 ... 58,974
Male ... 29,059
Female ... 29,915
Jan. 2008 (estimate)§ ... 62,635
Persons per sq. mi. of land ... 8,580.1

Race & Hispanic Origin, 2000

Race
White ... 37,153
Black/African American ... 926
North American Native ... 564
Asian ... 3,498
Pacific Islander ... 127
Other Race ... 13,953
Two or more races ... 2,753
Hispanic origin, total ... 28,922
Mexican ... 24,195
Puerto Rican ... 281
Cuban ... 181
Other Hispanic ... 4,265

Age & Nativity, 2000

Under 5 years ... 4,950
18 years and over ... 41,822
65 years and over ... 6,366
85 years and over ... 804
Median Age ... 31.5
Native-born ... 43,236
Foreign-born ... 15,955

Educational Attainment, 2000

Population 25 years and over ... 36,104
Less than 9th grade ... 13.3%
High school grad or higher ... 73.4%
Bachelor's degree or higher ... 18.2%
Graduate degree ... 5.6%

Income & Poverty, 1999

Per capita income ... $18,923
Median household income ... $47,652
Median family income ... $51,971
Persons in poverty ... 12.8%
H'holds receiving public assistance ... 597
H'holds receiving social security ... 4,572

Households, 2000

Total households ... 18,947
With persons under 18 ... 8,262
With persons over 65 ... 4,365
Family households ... 14,013
Single person households ... 3,970
Persons per household ... 3.08
Persons per family ... 3.56

Household Population, 2008§§

Persons living in households ... 62,040
Persons living in group quarters ... 595
Persons per household ... 3.2

Labor & Employment

Total civilian labor force, 2008§§ ... 32,300
Unemployment rate, 2008 ... 6.0%
Total civilian labor force, 2000 ... 27,846

Employed persons 16 years and over by occupation, 2000

Managers & professionals ... 7,457
Service occupations ... 4,253
Sales & office occupations ... 7,713
Farming, fishing & forestry ... 99
Construction & maintenance ... 2,414
Production & transportation ... 4,108
Self-employed persons ... 1,639

* US Census Bureau
** 2000 Decennial Census
§ California Department of Finance
§§ California Employment Development Dept

General Information

City of La Habra
Civic Center
PO Box 337
La Habra, CA 90633
562-905-9700

Website ... www.lahabracity.com
Elevation ... 298 ft.
Land Area (sq. miles) ... 7.3
Water Area (sq. miles) ... 0
Year of Incorporation ... 1925
Government type ... General law
Sales tax rate ... 9.25%

Voters & Officials

Registered Voters, October 2008

Total ... 27,777
Democrats ... 10,490
Republicans ... 11,296
Declined to state ... 4,901

Legislative Districts

US Congressional ... 42
State Senatorial ... 29
State Assembly ... 60, 72

Local Officials, 2009

Mayor ... Tom Beamish
City Manager ... Don Hannah
City Clerk ... Tamara D. Mason
Attorney ... Richard Jones
Finance Dir ... James Sadro
Public Works ... Steve Castellanos
Planning/Dev Dir ... Michael Haack
Building ... Roy Fewell
Police Chief ... Dave Hinnig (Int)
Fire/Emergency Mgmt ... NA

Public Safety

Number of officers, 2007 ... 68
Violent crimes, 2007 ... 209
Property crimes, 2007 ... 1,451
Arson, 2007 ... 5

Public Library

La Habra Branch Library
Orange County Public Library System
221 E La Habra Blvd
La Habra, CA 90631
562-694-0078

Branch Librarian ... Jill Patterson

Library system statistics, FY 2007

Population served ... 1,532,758
Internet terminals ... 505
Annual users ... 680,874

Per capita:

Operating income ... $24.71
percent from local government ... 90.0%
Operating expenditure ... $24.18
Total materials ... 1.93
Print holdings ... 1.84
Visits per capita ... 4.02

Housing & Construction

Housing Units

Total, 2008§ ... 19,932
Single family units, attached ... 1,750
Single family units, detached ... 10,581
Multiple family units ... 6,868
Mobile home units ... 733
Occupied ... 19,425
Vacancy rate ... 2.5%
Median rent, 2000** ... $787
Median SF home value, 2000** ... $199,500

New Privately Owned Housing Units Authorized by Building Permit, 2007*

	Units	Construction Cost
Single	23	$4,784,845
Total	23	$4,784,845

Municipal Finance

(For local fiscal year ended in 2006)

Revenues

Total ... $62,418,887
Taxes ... 29,297,981
Special benefits assessment ... 0
Licenses & permits ... 796,546
Fines & forfeitures ... 698,402
Revenues from use of money & property ... 3,521,617
Intergovernmental ... 5,125,709
Service charges ... 22,971,002
Other revenues ... 7,630
Other financing sources ... 0

Expenditures

Total ... $52,000,419
General government ... 2,619,052
Public safety ... 19,682,991
Transportation ... 7,900,943
Community development ... 4,632,123
Health ... 3,066,684
Culture & leisure ... 7,176,778
Other ... 0

Local School District

(Data from School year 2007-08 except as noted)

Fullerton Joint Union High
1051 West Bastanchury Rd
Fullerton, CA 92833
(714) 870-2800

Superintendent ... George Giokaris
Grade plan ... 9-12
Number of schools ... 8
Enrollment ... 16,321
High school graduates, 2006-07 ... 2,914
Dropout rate ... 2.3%
Pupil/teacher ratio ... 27.7
Average class size ... 29.9
Students per computer ... 3.7
Classrooms with internet ... 724
Avg. Daily Attendance (ADA) ... 15,436
Cost per ADA ... $7,977
Avg. Teacher Salary ... $82,860

California Achievement Tests 6th ed., 2008

(Pct scoring at or above 50th National Percentile Rank)

	Math	Reading	Language
Grade 3	NA	NA	NA
Grade 7	NA	NA	NA

Academic Performance Index, 2008

Number of students tested ... 10,832
Number of valid scores ... 10,168
2007 API (base) ... 775
2008 API (growth) ... 794

SAT Testing, 2006-07

Enrollment, Grade 12 ... 2,962
Number taking test ... 1,527
percent taking test ... 51.6%
percent with total score 1,500+ ... 32.20%

Average Scores:

Math	Verbal	Writing	Total
568	529	536	1,633

Federal No Child Left Behind, 2008

(Adequate Yearly Progress standards met)

	Participation Rate	Pct Proficient
ELA	Yes	No
Math	Yes	No

API criteria ... Yes
Graduation rate ... Yes
\# criteria met/possible ... 34/32

Other school districts for this city

(see Appendix E for information on these districts)

La Habra City Elem

See Introduction for an explanation of all data sources.

Demographics & Socio-Economic Characteristics

(2000 Decennial Census, except as noted)

Population

1990* . . . 6,226
2000 . . . 5,712
Male . . . 2,843
Female . . . 2,869
Jan. 2008 (estimate)§ . . . 6,140
Persons per sq. mi. of land . . . 990.3

Race & Hispanic Origin, 2000

Race
White . . . 4,136
Black/African American . . . 69
North American Native . . . 19
Asian . . . 1,051
Pacific Islander . . . 6
Other Race . . . 221
Two or more races . . . 210
Hispanic origin, total . . . 779
Mexican . . . 581
Puerto Rican . . . 28
Cuban . . . 18
Other Hispanic . . . 152

Age & Nativity, 2000

Under 5 years . . . 277
18 years and over . . . 4,312
65 years and over . . . 850
85 years and over . . . 72
Median Age . . . 42.4
Native-born . . . 4,209
Foreign-born . . . 1,193

Educational Attainment, 2000

Population 25 years and over . . . 3,850
Less than 9th grade . . . 1.4%
High school grad or higher . . . 92.8%
Bachelor's degree or higher . . . 49.2%
Graduate degree . . . 22.5%

Income & Poverty, 1999

Per capita income . . . $47,258
Median household income . . . $101,080
Median family income . . . $103,647
Persons in poverty . . . 3.2%
H'holds receiving public assistance . . . 22
H'holds receiving social security . . . 587

Households, 2000

Total households . . . 1,887
With persons under 18 . . . 727
With persons over 65 . . . 591
Family households . . . 1,591
Single person households . . . 222
Persons per household . . . 3.03
Persons per family . . . 3.29

Household Population, 2008§§

Persons living in households . . . 6,140
Persons living in group quarters . . . 0
Persons per household . . . 3.1

Labor & Employment

Total civilian labor force, 2008§§ . . . 3,000
Unemployment rate, 2008 . . . 2.7%
Total civilian labor force, 2000 . . . 2,562

Employed persons 16 years and over by occupation, 2000

Managers & professionals . . . 1,435
Service occupations . . . 221
Sales & office occupations . . . 555
Farming, fishing & forestry . . . 16
Construction & maintenance . . . 185
Production & transportation . . . 75
Self-employed persons . . . 401

* US Census Bureau
** 2000 Decennial Census
§ California Department of Finance
§§ California Employment Development Dept

General Information

City of La Habra Heights
1245 N Hacienda Rd
La Habra Heights, CA 90631
562-694-6302

Website . . . www.la-habra-heights.org
Elevation . . . NA
Land Area (sq. miles) . . . 6.2
Water Area (sq. miles) . . . 0
Year of Incorporation . . . 1978
Government type . . . General law
Sales tax rate . . . 9.25%

Voters & Officials

Registered Voters, October 2008

Total . . . 3,590
Democrats . . . 849
Republicans . . . 2,006
Declined to state . . . 615

Legislative Districts

US Congressional . . . 42
State Senatorial . . . 29
State Assembly . . . 60

Local Officials, 2009

Mayor . . . Stan Carroll
City Manager . . . Shauna Clark
City Clerk . . . Shauna Clark
Attorney . . . Sandra Levin
Finance Dir . . . Arlene Mosley
Public Works . . . Bruce Barrette
Planning/Dev Dir . . . Shauna Clark
Building . . . David VanDusen
Police Chief . . . NA
Fire/Emergency Mgmt . . . Gary Turner (Int)

Public Safety

Number of officers, 2007 . . . NA
Violent crimes, 2007 . . . 8
Property crimes, 2007 . . . 90
Arson, 2007 . . . 2

Public Library

Served by County Library

Library system statistics, FY 2007

Population served . . . NA
Internet terminals . . . NA
Annual users . . . NA

Per capita:

Operating income . . . NA
percent from local government . . . NA
Operating expenditure . . . NA
Total materials . . . NA
Print holdings . . . NA
Visits per capita . . . NA

Housing & Construction

Housing Units

Total, 2008§ . . . 2,024
Single family units, attached . . . 24
Single family units, detached . . . 1,992
Multiple family units . . . 8
Mobile home units . . . 0
Occupied . . . 1,958
Vacancy rate . . . 3.3%
Median rent, 2000** . . . $746
Median SF home value, 2000** . . . $464,300

New Privately Owned Housing Units Authorized by Building Permit, 2007*

	Units	Construction Cost
Single	5	$4,867,765
Total	5	$4,867,765

Municipal Finance

(For local fiscal year ended in 2006)

Revenues

Total . . . $5,115,750
Taxes . . . 1,912,243
Special benefits assessment . . . 1,026,672
Licenses & permits . . . 375,678
Fines & forfeitures . . . 59,277
Revenues from use of money & property . . . 323,230
Intergovernmental . . . 450,687
Service charges . . . 424,817
Other revenues . . . 303,146
Other financing sources . . . 240,000

Expenditures

Total . . . $4,077,389
General government . . . 818,415
Public safety . . . 1,759,228
Transportation . . . 436,438
Community development . . . 829,294
Health . . . 0
Culture & leisure . . . 234,014
Other . . . 0

Local School District

(Data from School year 2007-08 except as noted)

Fullerton Joint Union High
1051 West Bastanchury Rd
Fullerton, CA 92833
(714) 870-2800

Superintendent . . . George Giokaris
Grade plan . . . 9-12
Number of schools . . . 8
Enrollment . . . 16,321
High school graduates, 2006-07 . . . 2,914
Dropout rate . . . 2.3%
Pupil/teacher ratio . . . 27.7
Average class size . . . 29.9
Students per computer . . . 3.7
Classrooms with internet . . . 724
Avg. Daily Attendance (ADA) . . . 15,436
Cost per ADA . . . $7,977
Avg. Teacher Salary . . . $82,860

California Achievement Tests 6th ed., 2008

(Pct scoring at or above 50th National Percentile Rank)

	Math	Reading	Language
Grade 3	NA	NA	NA
Grade 7	NA	NA	NA

Academic Performance Index, 2008

Number of students tested . . . 10,832
Number of valid scores . . . 10,168
2007 API (base) . . . 775
2008 API (growth) . . . 794

SAT Testing, 2006-07

Enrollment, Grade 12 . . . 2,962
Number taking test . . . 1,527
percent taking test . . . 51.6%
percent with total score 1,500+ . . . 32.20%

Average Scores:

Math	Verbal	Writing	Total
568	529	536	1,633

Federal No Child Left Behind, 2008

(Adequate Yearly Progress standards met)

	Participation Rate	Pct Proficient
ELA	Yes	No
Math	Yes	No

API criteria . . . Yes
Graduation rate . . . Yes
\# criteria met/possible . . . 34/32

Other school districts for this city

(see Appendix E for information on these districts)

East Whittier City Elem, Lowell Joint Elem

See Introduction for an explanation of all data sources.

Demographics & Socio-Economic Characteristics

(2000 Decennial Census, except as noted)

Population

1990* . . . 52,931
2000 . . . 54,749
Male . . . 25,826
Female . . . 28,923
Jan. 2008 (estimate)§ . . . 56,666
Persons per sq. mi. of land . . . 6,093.1

Race & Hispanic Origin, 2000

Race
White . . . 44,148
Black/African American . . . 2,660
North American Native . . . 364
Asian . . . 2,238
Pacific Islander . . . 217
Other Race . . . 2,782
Two or more races . . . 2,340
Hispanic origin, total . . . 7,402
Mexican . . . 5,636
Puerto Rican . . . 266
Cuban . . . 69
Other Hispanic . . . 1,431

Age & Nativity, 2000

Under 5 years . . . 3,109
18 years and over . . . 43,897
65 years and over . . . 9,318
85 years and over . . . 1,749
Median Age . . . 37.3
Native-born . . . 48,378
Foreign-born . . . 6,373

Educational Attainment, 2000

Population 25 years and over . . . 38,412
Less than 9th grade . . . 2.5%
High school grad or higher . . . 89.6%
Bachelor's degree or higher . . . 27.6%
Graduate degree . . . 9.4%

Income & Poverty, 1999

Per capita income . . . $22,372
Median household income . . . $41,693
Median family income . . . $50,398
Persons in poverty . . . 9.2%
H'holds receiving public assistance . . . 513
H'holds receiving social security . . . 6,337

Households, 2000

Total households . . . 24,186
With persons under 18 . . . 6,468
With persons over 65 . . . 6,466
Family households . . . 13,386
Single person households . . . 8,275
Persons per household . . . 2.22
Persons per family . . . 2.86

Household Population, 2008§§

Persons living in households . . . 55,620
Persons living in group quarters . . . 1,046
Persons per household . . . 2.3

Labor & Employment

Total civilian labor force, 2008§§ . . . 34,200
Unemployment rate, 2008 . . . 5.0%
Total civilian labor force, 2000 . . . 28,614

Employed persons 16 years and over by occupation, 2000

Managers & professionals . . . 10,075
Service occupations . . . 4,123
Sales & office occupations . . . 8,406
Farming, fishing & forestry . . . 38
Construction & maintenance . . . 2,352
Production & transportation . . . 2,218
Self-employed persons . . . 2,082

* US Census Bureau
** 2000 Decennial Census
§ California Department of Finance
§§ California Employment Development Dept

General Information

City of La Mesa
8130 Allison Ave
La Mesa, CA 91941
619-463-6611

Website . . . www.cityoflamesa.com
Elevation . . . 540 ft.
Land Area (sq. miles) . . . 9.3
Water Area (sq. miles) . . . 0
Year of Incorporation . . . 1912
Government type . . . General law
Sales tax rate . . . 9.50%

Voters & Officials

Registered Voters, October 2008

Total . . . 31,697
Democrats . . . 12,383
Republicans . . . 11,273
Declined to state . . . 6,617

Legislative Districts

US Congressional . . . 52
State Senatorial . . . 36
State Assembly . . . 77

Local Officials, 2009

Mayor . . . Art Madrid
Manager . . . Sandra Kerl
City Clerk . . . Mary Kennedy
Attorney . . . Glenn Sabine
Finance Dir . . . Gary Ameling
Public Works . . . Greg Humora
Planning/Dev Dir . . . Dave Witt
Building . . . Jessie Wu
Police Chief . . . Al Lanning
Emergency/Fire Dir . . . Dave Burk

Public Safety

Number of officers, 2007 . . . 62
Violent crimes, 2007 . . . 238
Property crimes, 2007 . . . 2,234
Arson, 2007 . . . 8

Public Library

La Mesa Library
San Diego County Library System
8055 University Ave
La Mesa, CA 91941
619-469-2093

Branch Librarian . . . Judy Chatterjee

Library system statistics, FY 2007

Population served . . . 1,049,868
Internet terminals . . . 394
Annual users . . . NA

Per capita:

Operating income . . . $33.43
percent from local government . . . 80.6%
Operating expenditure . . . $31.30
Total materials . . . 1.54
Print holdings . . . 1.32
Visits per capita . . . 6.31

Housing & Construction

Housing Units

Total, 2008§ . . . 25,279
Single family units, attached . . . 1,955
Single family units, detached . . . 11,395
Multiple family units . . . 11,595
Mobile home units . . . 334
Occupied . . . 24,513
Vacancy rate . . . 3.0%
Median rent, 2000** . . . $759
Median SF home value, 2000** . . . $198,700

New Privately Owned Housing Units Authorized by Building Permit, 2007*

	Units	Construction Cost
Single	5	$1,187,686
Total	302	$27,084,795

Municipal Finance

(For local fiscal year ended in 2006)

Revenues

Total . . . $45,310,106
Taxes . . . 24,988,353
Special benefits assessment . . . 0
Licenses & permits . . . 703,005
Fines & forfeitures . . . 669,413
Revenues from use of money & property . . . 1,642,679
Intergovernmental . . . 5,026,813
Service charges . . . 12,168,857
Other revenues . . . 110,986
Other financing sources . . . 0

Expenditures

Total . . . $51,079,981
General government . . . 4,536,763
Public safety . . . 25,820,290
Transportation . . . 4,078,227
Community development . . . 1,875,653
Health . . . 8,801,821
Culture & leisure . . . 5,967,227
Other . . . 0

Local School District

(Data from School year 2007-08 except as noted)

Grossmont Union High
PO Box 1043
La Mesa, CA 91944
(619) 644-8000

Superintendent . . . Robert Collins
Grade plan . . . PK-12
Number of schools . . . 19
Enrollment . . . 24,195
High school graduates, 2006-07 . . . 4,597
Dropout rate . . . 3.3%
Pupil/teacher ratio . . . 24.2
Average class size . . . 25.8
Students per computer . . . 3.3
Classrooms with internet . . . 1,450
Avg. Daily Attendance (ADA) . . . 19,436
Cost per ADA . . . $8,940
Avg. Teacher Salary . . . $68,475

California Achievement Tests 6th ed., 2008

(Pct scoring at or above 50th National Percentile Rank)

	Math	Reading	Language
Grade 3	NA	NA	NA
Grade 7	NA	NA	NA

Academic Performance Index, 2008

Number of students tested . . . 14,311
Number of valid scores . . . 13,392
2007 API (base) . . . 704
2008 API (growth) . . . 713

SAT Testing, 2006-07

Enrollment, Grade 12 . . . 5,999
Number taking test . . . 1,875
percent taking test . . . 31.3%
percent with total score 1,500+ . . . 15.30%

Average Scores:

Math	Verbal	Writing	Total
513	495	494	1,502

Federal No Child Left Behind, 2008

(Adequate Yearly Progress standards met)

	Participation Rate	Pct Proficient
ELA	Yes	No
Math	Yes	No

API criteria . . . Yes
Graduation rate . . . Yes
\# criteria met/possible . . . 34/31

Other school districts for this city

(see Appendix E for information on these districts)

La Mesa-Spring Valley Elem

See Introduction for an explanation of all data sources.

Demographics & Socio-Economic Characteristics

(2000 Decennial Census, except as noted)

Population

1990* 40,452
2000 46,783
Male 22,582
Female 24,201
Jan. 2008 (estimate)§ 50,092
Persons per sq. mi. of land 6,422.1

Race & Hispanic Origin, 2000

Race
White 30,155
Black/African American 903
North American Native 350
Asian 6,963
Pacific Islander 125
Other Race 6,379
Two or more races 1,908
Hispanic origin, total 15,657
Mexican 11,950
Puerto Rican 223
Cuban 277
Other Hispanic 3,207

Age & Nativity, 2000

Under 5 years 2,948
18 years and over 34,528
65 years and over 6,463
85 years and over 585
Median Age 35.4
Native-born 36,156
Foreign-born 10,626

Educational Attainment, 2000

Population 25 years and over 29,489
Less than 9th grade 5.9%
High school grad or higher 84.5%
Bachelor's degree or higher 25.2%
Graduate degree 8.3%

Income & Poverty, 1999

Per capita income $22,404
Median household income $61,632
Median family income $66,598
Persons in poverty 5.4%
H'holds receiving public assistance 384
H'holds receiving social security 4,558

Households, 2000

Total households 14,580
With persons under 18 6,190
With persons over 65 4,594
Family households 11,523
Single person households 2,525
Persons per household 3.10
Persons per family 3.49

Household Population, 2008§§

Persons living in households 47,591
Persons living in group quarters 2,501
Persons per household 3.2

Labor & Employment

Total civilian labor force, 2008§§ 25,000
Unemployment rate, 2008 .... 4.5%
Total civilian labor force, 2000 22,390

Employed persons 16 years and over by occupation, 2000

Managers & professionals 7,634
Service occupations 2,543
Sales & office occupations 6,864
Farming, fishing & forestry 4
Construction & maintenance 1,521
Production & transportation 2,596
Self-employed persons 1,345

* US Census Bureau
** 2000 Decennial Census
§ California Department of Finance
§§ California Employment Development Dept

General Information

City of La Mirada
13700 La Mirada Blvd
La Mirada, CA 90638
562-943-0131

Website .... www.cityoflamirada.org
Elevation .... 181 ft.
Land Area (sq. miles) 7.8
Water Area (sq. miles) 0
Year of Incorporation 1960
Government type .... General law
Sales tax rate 9.25%

Voters & Officials

Registered Voters, October 2008

Total 25,942
Democrats 10,062
Republicans 10,502
Declined to state 4,374

Legislative Districts

US Congressional 39
State Senatorial 30
State Assembly 60

Local Officials, 2009

Mayor .... Hal Malkin
City Manager .... Thomas E. Robinson
City Clerk .... Anne Haraksin
Attorney .... James Markman
Admin Svcs Dir .... Kevin Prelgovisk
Public Works .... Steve Forster
Planning/Dev Dir .... Reuben Arceo
Building .... NA
Police Chief .... NA
Fire/Emergency Mgmt .... NA

Public Safety

Number of officers, 2007 .... NA
Violent crimes, 2007 115
Property crimes, 2007 1,080
Arson, 2007 14

Public Library

La Mirada Library
Los Angeles County Public Library System
13800 La Mirada Blvd
La Mirada, CA 90638
562-943-0277

Branch Librarian .... Jenny McCarty

Library system statistics, FY 2007

Population served 3,673,313
Internet terminals 749
Annual users 3,748,771

Per capita:

Operating income $30.06
percent from local government 93.6%
Operating expenditure $28.36
Total materials 2.22
Print holdings 1.97
Visits per capita 3.25

Housing & Construction

Housing Units

Total, 2008§ 15,075
Single family units, attached 800
Single family units, detached 11,892
Multiple family units 2,217
Mobile home units 166
Occupied 14,840
Vacancy rate 1.6%
Median rent, 2000** $870
Median SF home value, 2000** $210,700

New Privately Owned Housing Units Authorized by Building Permit, 2007*

	Units	Construction Cost
Single	1	$188,067
Total	113	$4,260,275

Municipal Finance

(For local fiscal year ended in 2006)

Revenues

Total $48,773,885
Taxes 21,323,930
Special benefits assessment 89,918
Licenses & permits 735,435
Fines & forfeitures 588,411
Revenues from use of money & property 2,122,279
Intergovernmental 2,461,863
Service charges 6,048,495
Other revenues 202,564
Other financing sources 15,200,990

Expenditures

Total $31,668,185
General government 2,848,329
Public safety 7,586,004
Transportation 5,615,710
Community development 1,660,568
Health 69,549
Culture & leisure 13,888,025
Other 0

Local School District

(Data from School year 2007-08 except as noted)

Norwalk-La Mirada Unified
12820 Pioneer Blvd
Norwalk, CA 90650
(562) 868-0431

Superintendent .... Ginger Shattuck
Grade plan K-12
Number of schools 29
Enrollment 22,092
High school graduates, 2006-07 1,386
Dropout rate 3.7%
Pupil/teacher ratio 23.8
Average class size 28.7
Students per computer 2.6
Classrooms with internet 939
Avg. Daily Attendance (ADA) 21,245
Cost per ADA $8,086
Avg. Teacher Salary $68,396

California Achievement Tests 6th ed., 2008

(Pct scoring at or above 50th National Percentile Rank)

	Math	Reading	Language
Grade 3	53%	34%	46%
Grade 7	46%	44%	44%

Academic Performance Index, 2008

Number of students tested 16,844
Number of valid scores 16,023
2007 API (base) 695
2008 API (growth) 715

SAT Testing, 2006-07

Enrollment, Grade 12 1,622
Number taking test 524
percent taking test 32.3%
percent with total score 1,500+ 9.00%

Average Scores:

Math	Verbal	Writing	Total
461	449	448	1,358

Federal No Child Left Behind, 2008

(Adequate Yearly Progress standards met)

	Participation Rate	Pct Proficient
ELA	Yes	No
Math	Yes	No

API criteria .... Yes
Graduation rate .... Yes
\# criteria met/possible 38/34

Other school districts for this city

(see Appendix E for information on these districts)

Whittier City Elem

See Introduction for an explanation of all data sources.

Demographics & Socio-Economic Characteristics

(2000 Decennial Census, except as noted)

Population

1990* . . . 15,392
2000 . . . 15,408
Male . . . 7,527
Female . . . 7,881
Jan. 2008 (estimate)§ . . . 16,176
Persons per sq. mi. of land . . . 8,986.7

Race & Hispanic Origin, 2000

Race
White . . . 6,632
Black/African American . . . 710
North American Native . . . 48
Asian . . . 6,900
Pacific Islander . . . 45
Other Race . . . 534
Two or more races . . . 539
Hispanic origin, total . . . 1,736
Mexican . . . 1,113
Puerto Rican . . . 62
Cuban . . . 52
Other Hispanic . . . 509

Age & Nativity, 2000

Under 5 years . . . 867
18 years and over . . . 11,743
65 years and over . . . 1,575
85 years and over . . . 83
Median Age . . . 38.1
Native-born . . . 9,641
Foreign-born . . . 5,490

Educational Attainment, 2000

Population 25 years and over . . . 10,335
Less than 9th grade . . . 2.7%
High school grad or higher . . . 90.4%
Bachelor's degree or higher . . . 38.1%
Graduate degree . . . 11.1%

Income & Poverty, 1999

Per capita income . . . $26,598
Median household income . . . $68,438
Median family income . . . $74,524
Persons in poverty . . . 4.8%
H'holds receiving public assistance . . . 65
H'holds receiving social security . . . 1,089

Households, 2000

Total households . . . 4,979
With persons under 18 . . . 2,065
With persons over 65 . . . 1,145
Family households . . . 4,225
Single person households . . . 576
Persons per household . . . 3.09
Persons per family . . . 3.35

Household Population, 2008§§

Persons living in households . . . 16,145
Persons living in group quarters . . . 31
Persons per household . . . 3.2

Labor & Employment

Total civilian labor force, 2008§§ . . . 9,100
Unemployment rate, 2008 . . . 5.4%
Total civilian labor force, 2000 . . . 7,811

Employed persons 16 years and over by occupation, 2000

Managers & professionals . . . 3,286
Service occupations . . . 742
Sales & office occupations . . . 2,319
Farming, fishing & forestry . . . 0
Construction & maintenance . . . 432
Production & transportation . . . 626
Self-employed persons . . . 802

* US Census Bureau
** 2000 Decennial Census
§ California Department of Finance
§§ California Employment Development Dept

General Information

City of La Palma
7822 Walker St
La Palma, CA 90623
714-690-3300

Website . . . www.cityoflapalma.org
Elevation . . . 44 ft.
Land Area (sq. miles) . . . 1.8
Water Area (sq. miles) . . . 0
Year of Incorporation . . . 1955
Government type . . . General law
Sales tax rate . . . 8.75%

Voters & Officials

Registered Voters, October 2008

Total . . . 8,846
Democrats . . . 3,200
Republicans . . . 3,473
Declined to state . . . 1,903

Legislative Districts

US Congressional . . . 40
State Senatorial . . . 35
State Assembly . . . 67

Local Officials, 2009

Mayor . . . Mark Waldman
City Manager . . . Dominic Lazzaretto
Admin Services . . . Laurie Murray
Attorney . . . Joel Kuperberg
Finance Dir . . . Keith Neves
Public Works . . . Jeff Moneda
Community Dev Dir . . . John Di Mario
Building . . . NA
Police Chief . . . Ed Ethell
Emergency/Fire Dir . . . Chip Prather (Int)

Public Safety

Number of officers, 2007 . . . 24
Violent crimes, 2007 . . . 45
Property crimes, 2007 . . . 296
Arson, 2007 . . . NA

Public Library

La Palma Branch Library
Orange County Public Library System
7842 Walker St
La Palma, CA 90623
714-523-8585

Branch Librarian . . . Susan Sassone

Library system statistics, FY 2007

Population served . . . 1,532,758
Internet terminals . . . 505
Annual users . . . 680,874

Per capita:

Operating income . . . $24.71
percent from local government . . . 90.0%
Operating expenditure . . . $24.18
Total materials . . . 1.93
Print holdings . . . 1.84
Visits per capita . . . 4.02

Housing & Construction

Housing Units

Total, 2008§ . . . 5,131
Single family units, attached . . . 376
Single family units, detached . . . 3,637
Multiple family units . . . 1,091
Mobile home units . . . 27
Occupied . . . 5,043
Vacancy rate . . . 1.7%
Median rent, 2000** . . . $955
Median SF home value, 2000** . . . $286,900

New Privately Owned Housing Units Authorized by Building Permit, 2007*

	Units	Construction Cost
Single	0	$0
Total	0	$0

Municipal Finance

(For local fiscal year ended in 2006)

Revenues

Total . . . $11,714,029
Taxes . . . 5,202,461
Special benefits assessment . . . 0
Licenses & permits . . . 62,388
Fines & forfeitures . . . 139,338
Revenues from use of money & property . . . 1,585,122
Intergovernmental . . . 1,136,645
Service charges . . . 3,548,282
Other revenues . . . 39,793
Other financing sources . . . 0

Expenditures

Total . . . $11,728,891
General government . . . 1,164,357
Public safety . . . 5,261,222
Transportation . . . 760,365
Community development . . . 703,975
Health . . . 195,422
Culture & leisure . . . 1,503,521
Other . . . 0

Local School District

(Data from School year 2007-08 except as noted)

Anaheim Union High
PO Box 3520
Anaheim, CA 92803
(714) 999-3511

Superintendent . . . Joseph Farley
Grade plan . . . 7-12
Number of schools . . . 22
Enrollment . . . 33,343
High school graduates, 2006-07 . . . 3,668
Dropout rate . . . 1.7%
Pupil/teacher ratio . . . 23.7
Average class size . . . 20.2
Students per computer . . . 3.4
Classrooms with internet . . . 1,839
Avg. Daily Attendance (ADA) . . . 33,034
Cost per ADA . . . $8,336
Avg. Teacher Salary . . . $79,030

California Achievement Tests 6th ed., 2008

(Pct scoring at or above 50th National Percentile Rank)

	Math	Reading	Language
Grade 3	NA	NA	NA
Grade 7	49%	43%	43%

Academic Performance Index, 2008

Number of students tested . . . 27,739
Number of valid scores . . . 26,586
2007 API (base) . . . 715
2008 API (growth) . . . 729

SAT Testing, 2006-07

Enrollment, Grade 12 . . . 4,777
Number taking test . . . 1,591
percent taking test . . . 33.3%
percent with total score 1,500+ . . . 15.00%

Average Scores:

Math	Verbal	Writing	Total
519	485	489	1,493

Federal No Child Left Behind, 2008

(Adequate Yearly Progress standards met)

	Participation Rate	Pct Proficient
ELA	Yes	No
Math	Yes	No

API criteria . . . Yes
Graduation rate . . . Yes
criteria met/possible . . . 42/35

Other school districts for this city

(see Appendix E for information on these districts)

Buena Park Elem, Centralia Elem, Cypress Elem, Fullerton Joint Union High

See Introduction for an explanation of all data sources.

Demographics & Socio-Economic Characteristics

(2000 Decennial Census, except as noted)

Population

1990* . . . 36,955
2000 . . . 41,063
Male . . . 20,543
Female . . . 20,520
Jan. 2008 (estimate)§ . . . 43,256
Persons per sq. mi. of land . . . 12,358.9

Race & Hispanic Origin, 2000

Race
White . . . 16,060
Black/African American . . . 804
North American Native . . . 524
Asian . . . 2,940
Pacific Islander . . . 68
Other Race . . . 18,535
Two or more races . . . 2,132
Hispanic origin, total . . . 34,122
Mexican . . . 28,108
Puerto Rican . . . 217
Cuban . . . 81
Other Hispanic . . . 5,716

Age & Nativity, 2000

Under 5 years . . . 3,711
18 years and over . . . 27,178
65 years and over . . . 3,148
85 years and over . . . 231
Median Age . . . 27.7
Native-born . . . 23,159
Foreign-born . . . 17,850

Educational Attainment, 2000

Population 25 years and over . . . 22,423
Less than 9th grade . . . 29.1%
High school grad or higher . . . 49.7%
Bachelor's degree or higher . . . 7.8%
Graduate degree . . . 2.1%

Income & Poverty, 1999

Per capita income . . . $11,336
Median household income . . . $41,222
Median family income . . . $41,079
Persons in poverty . . . 18.6%
H'holds receiving public assistance . . . 681
H'holds receiving social security . . . 2,079

Households, 2000

Total households . . . 9,461
With persons under 18 . . . 5,777
With persons over 65 . . . 2,364
Family households . . . 8,182
Single person households . . . 955
Persons per household . . . 4.34
Persons per family . . . 4.48

Household Population, 2008§§

Persons living in households . . . 43,224
Persons living in group quarters . . . 32
Persons per household . . . 4.5

Labor & Employment

Total civilian labor force, 2008§§ . . . 19,300
Unemployment rate, 2008 . . . 8.9%
Total civilian labor force, 2000 . . . 16,555

Employed persons 16 years and over by occupation, 2000

Managers & professionals . . . 2,311
Service occupations . . . 2,473
Sales & office occupations . . . 3,611
Farming, fishing & forestry . . . 17
Construction & maintenance . . . 1,686
Production & transportation . . . 4,934
Self-employed persons . . . 930

* US Census Bureau
** 2000 Decennial Census
§ California Department of Finance
§§ California Employment Development Dept

General Information

City of La Puente
15900 E Main St
La Puente, CA 91744
626-855-1500

Website . . . www.lapuente.org
Elevation . . . 330 ft.
Land Area (sq. miles) . . . 3.5
Water Area (sq. miles) . . . 0
Year of Incorporation . . . 1956
Government type . . . General law
Sales tax rate . . . 9.25%

Voters & Officials

Registered Voters, October 2008

Total . . . 13,836
Democrats . . . 8,444
Republicans . . . 2,378
Declined to state . . . 2,520

Legislative Districts

US Congressional . . . 38
State Senatorial . . . 24
State Assembly . . . 57

Local Officials, 2009

Mayor . . . Louie A. Lujan
Manager . . . Frank Tripepi (Int)
City Clerk . . . Amy M. Turner
Attorney . . . James Casso
Finance Dir . . . Young Kim
Public Works . . . Rene Salas
Redevelopment Dir . . . Gregg Yamachika
Building . . . NA
Police Chief . . . (County)
Fire/Emergency Mgmt . . . (County)

Public Safety

Number of officers, 2007 . . . NA
Violent crimes, 2007 . . . 222
Property crimes, 2007 . . . 751
Arson, 2007 . . . NA

Public Library

La Puente Library
Los Angeles County Public Library System
15920 E Central Ave
La Puente, CA 91744
626-968-4613

Branch Manager . . . Jeannette Freels

Library system statistics, FY 2007

Population served . . . 3,673,313
Internet terminals . . . 749
Annual users . . . 3,748,771

Per capita:

Operating income . . . $30.06
percent from local government . . . 93.6%
Operating expenditure . . . $28.36
Total materials . . . 2.22
Print holdings . . . 1.97
Visits per capita . . . 3.25

Housing & Construction

Housing Units

Total, 2008§ . . . 9,711
Single family units, attached . . . 642
Single family units, detached . . . 6,370
Multiple family units . . . 2,590
Mobile home units . . . 109
Occupied . . . 9,512
Vacancy rate . . . 2.1%
Median rent, 2000** . . . $678
Median SF home value, 2000** . . . $146,500

New Privately Owned Housing Units Authorized by Building Permit, 2007*

	Units	Construction Cost
Single	1	$127,050
Total	1	$127,050

Municipal Finance

(For local fiscal year ended in 2006)

Revenues

Total . . . $15,782,347
Taxes . . . 9,381,892
Special benefits assessment . . . 0
Licenses & permits . . . 432,731
Fines & forfeitures . . . 579,267
Revenues from use of money & property . . . 183,710
Intergovernmental . . . 2,517,731
Service charges . . . 692,547
Other revenues . . . 1,994,469
Other financing sources . . . 0

Expenditures

Total . . . $12,788,005
General government . . . 2,772,262
Public safety . . . 4,721,749
Transportation . . . 2,134,943
Community development . . . 1,521,702
Health . . . 242,709
Culture & leisure . . . 1,394,640
Other . . . 0

Local School District

(Data from School year 2007-08 except as noted)

Hacienda La Puente Unified
PO Box 60002
City of Industry, CA 91716
(626) 933-1000

Superintendent . . . Barbara Nakaoka
Grade plan . . . K-12
Number of schools . . . 38
Enrollment . . . 21,997
High school graduates, 2006-07 . . . 1,366
Dropout rate . . . 3.8%
Pupil/teacher ratio . . . 21.1
Average class size . . . 22.7
Students per computer . . . 3.4
Classrooms with internet . . . 1,139
Avg. Daily Attendance (ADA) . . . 21,871
Cost per ADA . . . $8,228
Avg. Teacher Salary . . . $63,465

California Achievement Tests 6th ed., 2008

(Pct scoring at or above 50th National Percentile Rank)

	Math	Reading	Language
Grade 3	55%	31%	45%
Grade 7	51%	46%	45%

Academic Performance Index, 2008

Number of students tested . . . 17,075
Number of valid scores . . . 16,098
2007 API (base) . . . 738
2008 API (growth) . . . 748

SAT Testing, 2006-07

Enrollment, Grade 12 . . . 1,819
Number taking test . . . 686
percent taking test . . . 37.7%
percent with total score 1,500+ . . . 17.00%

Average Scores:

Math	Verbal	Writing	Total
523	475	476	1,474

Federal No Child Left Behind, 2008

(Adequate Yearly Progress standards met)

	Participation Rate	Pct Proficient
ELA	Yes	No
Math	Yes	No

API criteria . . . Yes
Graduation rate . . . No
\# criteria met/possible . . . 38/34

Other school districts for this city

(see Appendix E for information on these districts)

Bassett Unified, Rowland Unified

See Introduction for an explanation of all data sources.

Demographics & Socio-Economic Characteristics

(2000 Decennial Census, except as noted)

Population

1990* . . . 11,215
2000 . . . 23,694
Male . . . 11,619
Female . . . 12,075
Jan. 2008 (estimate)§ . . . 42,958
Persons per sq. mi. of land . . . 1,350.9

Race & Hispanic Origin, 2000

Race
White . . . 18,602
Black/African American . . . 336
North American Native . . . 171
Asian . . . 446
Pacific Islander . . . 21
Other Race . . . 3,282
Two or more races . . . 836
Hispanic origin, total . . . 7,584
Mexican . . . 6,474
Puerto Rican . . . 57
Cuban . . . 37
Other Hispanic . . . 1,016

Age & Nativity, 2000

Under 5 years . . . 1,847
18 years and over . . . 16,789
65 years and over . . . 3,173
85 years and over . . . 155
Median Age . . . 36.4
Native-born . . . 20,289
Foreign-born . . . 3,365

Educational Attainment, 2000

Population 25 years and over . . . 15,514
Less than 9th grade . . . 5.6%
High school grad or higher . . . 84.9%
Bachelor's degree or higher . . . 26.7%
Graduate degree . . . 9.3%

Income & Poverty, 1999

Per capita income . . . $27,284
Median household income . . . $54,552
Median family income . . . $56,848
Persons in poverty . . . 7.8%
H'holds receiving public assistance . . . 193
H'holds receiving social security . . . 2,669

Households, 2000

Total households . . . 8,445
With persons under 18 . . . 3,428
With persons over 65 . . . 2,219
Family households . . . 6,556
Single person households . . . 1,434
Persons per household . . . 2.80
Persons per family . . . 3.16

Household Population, 2008§§

Persons living in households . . . 42,918
Persons living in group quarters . . . 40
Persons per household . . . 2.9

Labor & Employment

Total civilian labor force, 2008§§ . . . 15,100
Unemployment rate, 2008 . . . 4.4%
Total civilian labor force, 2000 . . . 10,747

Employed persons 16 years and over by occupation, 2000

Managers & professionals . . . 3,791
Service occupations . . . 2,402
Sales & office occupations . . . 2,673
Farming, fishing & forestry . . . 27
Construction & maintenance . . . 896
Production & transportation . . . 558
Self-employed persons . . . 1,293

* US Census Bureau
** 2000 Decennial Census
§ California Department of Finance
§§ California Employment Development Dept

General Information

City of La Quinta
78-495 Calle Tampico
La Quinta, CA 92253
760-777-7000

Website . . . www.la-quinta.org
Elevation . . . NA
Land Area (sq. miles) . . . 31.8
Water Area (sq. miles) . . . 0.4
Year of Incorporation . . . 1982
Government type . . . Chartered
Sales tax rate . . . 8.75%

Voters & Officials

Registered Voters, October 2008

Total . . . 18,701
Democrats . . . 5,428
Republicans . . . 9,908
Declined to state . . . 2,721

Legislative Districts

US Congressional . . . 45
State Senatorial . . . 37
State Assembly . . . 80

Local Officials, 2009

Mayor . . . Don Adolph
Manager . . . Thomas Genovese
City Clerk . . . Veronica Montecino
Attorney . . . M. Katherine Jenson
Finance Dir . . . John Falconer
Public Works . . . Timothy R. Jonasson
Planning Dir . . . Les Johnson
Building . . . Tom Hartung
Police Chief . . . Rodney Vigue
Emergency/Fire Dir . . . Dorian Cooley

Public Safety

Number of officers, 2007 . . . NA
Violent crimes, 2007 . . . 209
Property crimes, 2007 . . . 1,620
Arson, 2007 . . . 6

Public Library

La Quinta Branch Library
Riverside County Library Service
78-225 Calle Tampico
La Quinta, CA 92253
760-564-4767

Branch Librarian . . . Irene Wickstrom

Library system statistics, FY 2007

Population served . . . 1,047,996
Internet terminals . . . 37
Annual users . . . 69,346

Per capita:

Operating income . . . $19.38
percent from local government . . . 49.8%
Operating expenditure . . . $20.45
Total materials . . . 1.43
Print holdings . . . 1.30
Visits per capita . . . 4.06

Housing & Construction

Housing Units

Total, 2008§ . . . 21,058
Single family units, attached . . . 1,841
Single family units, detached . . . 17,035
Multiple family units . . . 1,925
Mobile home units . . . 257
Occupied . . . 15,056
Vacancy rate . . . 28.5%
Median rent, 2000** . . . $817
Median SF home value, 2000** . . . $174,200

New Privately Owned Housing Units Authorized by Building Permit, 2007*

	Units	Construction Cost
Single	448	$108,101,943
Total	456	$109,054,793

Municipal Finance

(For local fiscal year ended in 2006)

Revenues

Total . . . $68,955,524
Taxes . . . 29,509,158
Special benefits assessment . . . 818,526
Licenses & permits . . . 4,403,840
Fines & forfeitures . . . 342,420
Revenues from use of money & property . . . 4,763,313
Intergovernmental . . . 7,352,688
Service charges . . . 5,552,454
Other revenues . . . 16,213,125
Other financing sources . . . 0

Expenditures

Total . . . $47,307,669
General government . . . 5,974,974
Public safety . . . 10,901,947
Transportation . . . 17,305,117
Community development . . . 4,239,724
Health . . . 0
Culture & leisure . . . 8,385,907
Other . . . 500,000

Local School District

(Data from School year 2007-08 except as noted)

Desert Sands Unified
47-950 Dune Palms Rd
La Quinta, CA 92253
(760) 777-4200

Superintendent . . . Sharon McGehee
Grade plan . . . K-12
Number of schools . . . 33
Enrollment . . . 28,775
High school graduates, 2006-07 . . . 1,630
Dropout rate . . . 4.0%
Pupil/teacher ratio . . . 22.2
Average class size . . . 28.2
Students per computer . . . 5.6
Classrooms with internet . . . 1,229
Avg. Daily Attendance (ADA) . . . 27,315
Cost per ADA . . . $8,140
Avg. Teacher Salary . . . $70,970

California Achievement Tests 6th ed., 2008

(Pct scoring at or above 50th National Percentile Rank)

	Math	Reading	Language
Grade 3	56%	35%	46%
Grade 7	44%	44%	43%

Academic Performance Index, 2008

Number of students tested . . . 21,857
Number of valid scores . . . 20,761
2007 API (base) . . . 734
2008 API (growth) . . . 752

SAT Testing, 2006-07

Enrollment, Grade 12 . . . 2,045
Number taking test . . . 660
percent taking test . . . 32.3%
percent with total score 1,500+ . . . 13.40%

Average Scores:

Math	Verbal	Writing	Total
489	480	480	1,449

Federal No Child Left Behind, 2008

(Adequate Yearly Progress standards met)

	Participation Rate	Pct Proficient
ELA	Yes	No
Math	Yes	Yes

API criteria . . . Yes
Graduation rate . . . Yes
\# criteria met/possible . . . 38/36

Other school districts for this city

(see Appendix E for information on these districts)

None

See Introduction for an explanation of all data sources.

Demographics & Socio-Economic Characteristics

(2000 Decennial Census, except as noted)

Population

1990* 30,897
2000 31,638
Male 15,218
Female 16,420
Jan. 2008 (estimate)§ 34,046
Persons per sq. mi. of land 4,101.9

Race & Hispanic Origin, 2000

Race
White 24,379
Black/African American 1,016
North American Native 203
Asian 2,278
Pacific Islander 55
Other Race 2,348
Two or more races 1,359
Hispanic origin, total 7,315
Mexican 5,553
Puerto Rican 118
Cuban 145
Other Hispanic 1,499

Age & Nativity, 2000

Under 5 years 1,830
18 years and over 23,663
65 years and over 4,160
85 years and over 564
Median Age 37.7
Native-born 27,243
Foreign-born 4,602

Educational Attainment, 2000

Population 25 years and over 20,448
Less than 9th grade 3.6%
High school grad or higher 88.7%
Bachelor's degree or higher 31.6%
Graduate degree 12.2%

Income & Poverty, 1999

Per capita income $26,689
Median household income $61,326
Median family income $70,344
Persons in poverty 4.6%
H'holds receiving public assistance 140
H'holds receiving social security 2,782

Households, 2000

Total households 11,070
With persons under 18 4,291
With persons over 65 2,974
Family households 8,344
Single person households 2,170
Persons per household 2.79
Persons per family 3.23

Household Population, 2008§§

Persons living in households 32,821
Persons living in group quarters 1,225
Persons per household 2.9

Labor & Employment

Total civilian labor force, 2008§§ 18,800
Unemployment rate, 2008 .... 4.3%
Total civilian labor force, 2000 16,446

Employed persons 16 years and over by occupation, 2000

Managers & professionals 6,755
Service occupations 1,965
Sales & office occupations 4,338
Farming, fishing & forestry 0
Construction & maintenance 1,100
Production & transportation 1,449
Self-employed persons 1,179

* US Census Bureau
** 2000 Decennial Census
§ California Department of Finance
§§ California Employment Development Dept

General Information

City of La Verne
3660 D St
La Verne, CA 91750
909-596-8726

Website .... www.ci.la-verne.ca.us
Elevation .... 1,050 ft.
Land Area (sq. miles) 8.3
Water Area (sq. miles) 0.1
Year of Incorporation 1906
Government type .... General law
Sales tax rate 9.25%

Voters & Officials

Registered Voters, October 2008

Total 19,422
Democrats 6,733
Republicans 8,825
Declined to state 3,069

Legislative Districts

US Congressional 26
State Senatorial 29
State Assembly 59

Local Officials, 2009

Mayor .... Dom Kenrick
Manager .... Martin Lomeli
City Clerk .... Evelyn Clark
Attorney .... Robert L. Kress
Finance Dir .... Ron Clark
Public Works .... Dan Keesey
Community Dev Dir .... Hal Fredericksen
Building .... NA
Police Chief .... Scott Pickwith
Fire Chief .... John Breaux

Public Safety

Number of officers, 2007 50
Violent crimes, 2007 82
Property crimes, 2007 821
Arson, 2007 5

Public Library

La Verne Library
Los Angeles County Public Library System
3640 D St
La Verne, CA 91750
909-596-1934

Branch Librarian .... George May

Library system statistics, FY 2007

Population served 3,673,313
Internet terminals 749
Annual users 3,748,771

Per capita:

Operating income $30.06
percent from local government 93.6%
Operating expenditure $28.36
Total materials 2.22
Print holdings 1.97
Visits per capita 3.25

Housing & Construction

Housing Units

Total, 2008§ 11,428
Single family units, attached 597
Single family units, detached 7,604
Multiple family units 1,464
Mobile home units 1,763
Occupied 11,211
Vacancy rate 1.9%
Median rent, 2000** $856
Median SF home value, 2000** $242,100

New Privately Owned Housing Units Authorized by Building Permit, 2007*

	Units	Construction Cost
Single	30	$6,523,526
Total	87	$7,928,245

Municipal Finance

(For local fiscal year ended in 2006)

Revenues

Total $43,829,814
Taxes 14,834,577
Special benefits assessment 1,609,534
Licenses & permits 1,069,553
Fines & forfeitures 704,672
Revenues from use of money & property 721,344
Intergovernmental 3,527,803
Service charges 11,423,571
Other revenues 1,558,760
Other financing sources 8,380,000

Expenditures

Total $43,021,967
General government 10,346,710
Public safety 16,487,054
Transportation 2,891,872
Community development 933,171
Health 615,716
Culture & leisure 2,720,099
Other 0

Local School District

(Data from School year 2007-08 except as noted)

Bonita Unified
115 West Allen Ave
San Dimas, CA 91773
(909) 971-8200

Superintendent .... Gary Rapkin
Grade plan K-12
Number of schools 14
Enrollment 10,100
High school graduates, 2006-07 806
Dropout rate 1.2%
Pupil/teacher ratio 23.8
Average class size 27.4
Students per computer 4.8
Classrooms with internet 485
Avg. Daily Attendance (ADA) 9,920
Cost per ADA $7,796
Avg. Teacher Salary $69,444

California Achievement Tests 6th ed., 2008

(Pct scoring at or above 50th National Percentile Rank)

	Math	Reading	Language
Grade 3	68%	53%	59%
Grade 7	63%	61%	60%

Academic Performance Index, 2008

Number of students tested 7,820
Number of valid scores 7,483
2007 API (base) 799
2008 API (growth) 818

SAT Testing, 2006-07

Enrollment, Grade 12 914
Number taking test 388
percent taking test 42.5%
percent with total score 1,500+ 20.80%

Average Scores:

Math	Verbal	Writing	Total
504	502	501	1,507

Federal No Child Left Behind, 2008

(Adequate Yearly Progress standards met)

	Participation Rate	Pct Proficient
ELA	Yes	No
Math	Yes	No

API criteria .... Yes
Graduation rate .... Yes
\# criteria met/possible 38/36

Other school districts for this city

(see Appendix E for information on these districts)

None

See Introduction for an explanation of all data sources.

Demographics & Socio-Economic Characteristics

(2000 Decennial Census, except as noted)

Population

1990* 23,501
2000 23,908
Male 11,671
Female 12,237
Jan. 2008 (estimate)§ 23,962
Persons per sq. mi. of land 1,576.4

Race & Hispanic Origin, 2000

Race
White 20,754
Black/African American 131
North American Native 53
Asian 1,967
Pacific Islander 21
Other Race 194
Two or more races 788
Hispanic origin, total 945
Mexican 474
Puerto Rican 34
Cuban 14
Other Hispanic 423

Age & Nativity, 2000

Under 5 years 1,308
18 years and over 17,722
65 years and over 3,447
85 years and over 385
Median Age 42.3
Native-born 20,921
Foreign-born 2,542

Educational Attainment, 2000

Population 25 years and over 16,627
Less than 9th grade 0.7%
High school grad or higher 97.7%
Bachelor's degree or higher 68.0%
Graduate degree 29.8%

Income & Poverty, 1999

Per capita income $54,319
Median household income $102,107
Median family income $120,364
Persons in poverty 2.8%
H'holds receiving public assistance 70
H'holds receiving social security 2,037

Households, 2000

Total households 9,152
With persons under 18 3,417
With persons over 65 2,277
Family households 6,755
Single person households 1,841
Persons per household 2.60
Persons per family 3.02

Household Population, 2008§§

Persons living in households 23,826
Persons living in group quarters 136
Persons per household 2.6

Labor & Employment

Total civilian labor force, 2008§§ 13,000
Unemployment rate, 2008 .... 2.2%
Total civilian labor force, 2000 11,776

Employed persons 16 years and over by occupation, 2000

Managers & professionals 7,449
Service occupations 899
Sales & office occupations 2,332
Farming, fishing & forestry 15
Construction & maintenance 483
Production & transportation 414
Self-employed persons 1,795

* US Census Bureau
** 2000 Decennial Census
§ California Department of Finance
§§ California Employment Development Dept

General Information

City of Lafayette
3675 Mt Diablo Blvd
210
Lafayette, CA 94549
925-284-1968

Website .... www.ci.lafayette.ca.us
Elevation .... 302 ft.
Land Area (sq. miles) 15.2
Water Area (sq. miles) 0.2
Year of Incorporation 1968
Government type .... General law
Sales tax rate 9.25%

Voters & Officials

Registered Voters, October 2008

Total 16,631
Democrats 7,381
Republicans 5,569
Declined to state 3,018

Legislative Districts

US Congressional 10
State Senatorial 7
State Assembly 14

Local Officials, 2009

Mayor .... Mike Anderson
Manager .... Steven Falk
City Clerk .... Joanne Robbins
Attorney .... Malathy Subramanian
Finance Dir .... Tracy Robinson
Public Works .... Ron Lefler
Planning/Dev Dir .... Ann Merideth
Building .... NA
Police Chief .... Mike Hubbard
Fire/Emergency Mgmt .... NA

Public Safety

Number of officers, 2007 .... NA
Violent crimes, 2007 25
Property crimes, 2007 433
Arson, 2007 0

Public Library

Lafayette Library
Contra Costa County Library System
952 Moraga Rd
Lafayette, CA 94549
925-283-3872

Branch Librarian .... Susan Weaver

Library system statistics, FY 2007

Population served 938,513
Internet terminals 324
Annual users 670,618

Per capita:

Operating income $27.05
percent from local government 82.0%
Operating expenditure $27.82
Total materials 1.57
Print holdings 1.41
Visits per capita 3.65

Housing & Construction

Housing Units

Total, 2008§ 9,505
Single family units, attached 294
Single family units, detached 7,554
Multiple family units 1,657
Mobile home units 0
Occupied 9,320
Vacancy rate 2.0%
Median rent, 2000** $1,076
Median SF home value, 2000** $583,000

New Privately Owned Housing Units Authorized by Building Permit, 2007*

	Units	Construction Cost
Single	NA	NA
Total	NA	NA

Municipal Finance

(For local fiscal year ended in 2006)

Revenues

Total $19,715,636
Taxes 8,196,737
Special benefits assessment 682,607
Licenses & permits 336,574
Fines & forfeitures 395,683
Revenues from use of money & property 1,188,533
Intergovernmental 2,826,741
Service charges 2,103,198
Other revenues 3,985,563
Other financing sources 0

Expenditures

Total $22,506,471
General government 2,191,440
Public safety 3,308,749
Transportation 14,724,761
Community development 1,137,104
Health 0
Culture & leisure 1,144,417
Other 0

Local School District

(Data from School year 2007-08 except as noted)

Acalanes Union High
1212 Pleasant Hill Rd
Lafayette, CA 94549
(925) 280-3900

Superintendent .... Jim Negri
Grade plan 9-12
Number of schools 6
Enrollment 5,905
High school graduates, 2006-07 1,343
Dropout rate 0.5%
Pupil/teacher ratio 19.8
Average class size 22.7
Students per computer 3.6
Classrooms with internet 267
Avg. Daily Attendance (ADA) 5,781
Cost per ADA $9,251
Avg. Teacher Salary $73,421

California Achievement Tests 6th ed., 2008

(Pct scoring at or above 50th National Percentile Rank)

	Math	Reading	Language
Grade 3	NA	NA	NA
Grade 7	NA	NA	NA

Academic Performance Index, 2008

Number of students tested 4,273
Number of valid scores 4,195
2007 API (base) 882
2008 API (growth) 886

SAT Testing, 2006-07

Enrollment, Grade 12 1,385
Number taking test 1,148
percent taking test 82.9%
percent with total score 1,500+ 69.30%

Average Scores:

Math	Verbal	Writing	Total
596	580	585	1,761

Federal No Child Left Behind, 2008

(Adequate Yearly Progress standards met)

	Participation Rate	Pct Proficient
ELA	Yes	Yes
Math	Yes	Yes

API criteria .... Yes
Graduation rate .... Yes
criteria met/possible 14/14

Other school districts for this city

(see Appendix E for information on these districts)

Lafayette Elem

See Introduction for an explanation of all data sources.

Demographics & Socio-Economic Characteristics

(2000 Decennial Census, except as noted)

Population

1990*	23,170
2000	23,727
Male	12,081
Female	11,646
Jan. 2008 (estimate)§	25,131
Persons per sq. mi. of land	2,855.8

Race & Hispanic Origin, 2000

Race	
White	21,826
Black/African American	190
North American Native	86
Asian	494
Pacific Islander	20
Other Race	524
Two or more races	587
Hispanic origin, total	1,570
Mexican	1,100
Puerto Rican	38
Cuban	37
Other Hispanic	395

Age & Nativity, 2000

Under 5 years	992
18 years and over	19,976
65 years and over	3,146
85 years and over	364
Median Age	43.4
Native-born	20,691
Foreign-born	2,626

Educational Attainment, 2000

Population 25 years and over	18,941
Less than 9th grade	1.1%
High school grad or higher	96.2%
Bachelor's degree or higher	56.1%
Graduate degree	22.8%

Income & Poverty, 1999

Per capita income	$58,732
Median household income	$75,808
Median family income	$100,778
Persons in poverty	5.0%
H'holds receiving public assistance	101
H'holds receiving social security	2,350

Households, 2000

Total households	11,511
With persons under 18	2,283
With persons over 65	2,382
Family households	5,776
Single person households	4,227
Persons per household	2.05
Persons per family	2.69

Household Population, 2008§§

Persons living in households	25,009
Persons living in group quarters	122
Persons per household	2.1

Labor & Employment

Total civilian labor force, 2008§§	16,800
Unemployment rate, 2008	3.8%
Total civilian labor force, 2000	14,384

Employed persons 16 years and over by occupation, 2000

Managers & professionals	7,990
Service occupations	1,236
Sales & office occupations	3,723
Farming, fishing & forestry	28
Construction & maintenance	511
Production & transportation	371
Self-employed persons	2,388

* US Census Bureau
** 2000 Decennial Census
§ California Department of Finance
§§ California Employment Development Dept

General Information

City of Laguna Beach
505 Forest Ave
Laguna Beach, CA 92651
949-497-3311

Website	www.lagunabeachcity.net
Elevation	40 ft.
Land Area (sq. miles)	8.8
Water Area (sq. miles)	0.9
Year of Incorporation	1927
Government type	General law
Sales tax rate	9.25%

Voters & Officials

Registered Voters, October 2008

Total	18,964
Democrats	7,326
Republicans	6,890
Declined to state	3,847

Legislative Districts

US Congressional	48
State Senatorial	35
State Assembly	70

Local Officials, 2009

Mayor	Kelly Boyd
Manager	Kenneth Frank
City Clerk	Martha Anderson
Attorney	Phil Kohn
Finance Dir	Gavin Curran
Public Works	Steve May
Planning/Dev Dir	John Montgomery
Building	John Gustafson
Police Chief	Michael Sellers
Emergency/Fire Dir	Mike Macey

Public Safety

Number of officers, 2007	47
Violent crimes, 2007	49
Property crimes, 2007	495
Arson, 2007	12

Public Library

Laguna Beach Branch Library
Orange County Public Library System
363 Glenneyre St
Laguna Beach, CA 92651
949-497-1733

Branch Librarian	Marianna Hof

Library system statistics, FY 2007

Population served	1,532,758
Internet terminals	505
Annual users	680,874

Per capita:

Operating income	$24.71
percent from local government	90.0%
Operating expenditure	$24.18
Total materials	1.93
Print holdings	1.84
Visits per capita	4.02

Housing & Construction

Housing Units

Total, 2008§	13,253
Single family units, attached	759
Single family units, detached	8,308
Multiple family units	3,862
Mobile home units	324
Occupied	11,765
Vacancy rate	11.2%
Median rent, 2000**	$1,096
Median SF home value, 2000**	$653,900

New Privately Owned Housing Units Authorized by Building Permit, 2007*

	Units	Construction Cost
Single	28	$14,246,902
Total	30	$14,600,269

Municipal Finance

(For local fiscal year ended in 2006)

Revenues

Total	$77,287,296
Taxes	38,818,829
Special benefits assessment	869,390
Licenses & permits	1,264,362
Fines & forfeitures	1,598,358
Revenues from use of money & property	1,617,412
Intergovernmental	17,273,730
Service charges	13,769,168
Other revenues	2,076,047
Other financing sources	0

Expenditures

Total	$68,246,919
General government	3,224,408
Public safety	34,002,104
Transportation	10,907,429
Community development	2,720,537
Health	8,788,708
Culture & leisure	8,603,733
Other	0

Local School District

(Data from School year 2007-08 except as noted)

Laguna Beach Unified
550 Blumont St
Laguna Beach, CA 92651
(949) 497-7700

Superintendent	Robert Fraisse
Grade plan	K-12
Number of schools	4
Enrollment	2,900
High school graduates, 2006-07	225
Dropout rate	0.2%
Pupil/teacher ratio	21.3
Average class size	25.2
Students per computer	4.3
Classrooms with internet	150
Avg. Daily Attendance (ADA)	2,777
Cost per ADA	$12,246
Avg. Teacher Salary	$84,932

California Achievement Tests 6th ed., 2008

(Pct scoring at or above 50th National Percentile Rank)

	Math	Reading	Language
Grade 3	78%	66%	74%
Grade 7	76%	69%	62%

Academic Performance Index, 2008

Number of students tested	2,224
Number of valid scores	2,168
2007 API (base)	846
2008 API (growth)	858

SAT Testing, 2006-07

Enrollment, Grade 12	234
Number taking test	177
percent taking test	75.6%
percent with total score 1,500+	55.60%

Average Scores:

Math	Verbal	Writing	Total
564	552	552	1,668

Federal No Child Left Behind, 2008

(Adequate Yearly Progress standards met)

	Participation Rate	Pct Proficient
ELA	Yes	Yes
Math	No	Yes

API criteria	Yes
Graduation rate	Yes
# criteria met/possible	22/21

Other school districts for this city

(see Appendix E for information on these districts)

None

See Introduction for an explanation of all data sources.

Demographics & Socio-Economic Characteristics
(2000 Decennial Census, except as noted)

Population
1990* . . . NA
2000 . . . 31,178
Male . . . 14,992
Female . . . 16,186
Jan. 2008 (estimate)§ . . . 33,421
Persons per sq. mi. of land . . . 5,304.9

Race & Hispanic Origin, 2000
Race
White . . . 23,954
Black/African American . . . 429
North American Native . . . 138
Asian . . . 3,181
Pacific Islander . . . 47
Other Race . . . 2,241
Two or more races . . . 1,188
Hispanic origin, total . . . 5,113
Mexican . . . 3,693
Puerto Rican . . . 95
Cuban . . . 65
Other Hispanic . . . 1,260

Age & Nativity, 2000
Under 5 years . . . 1,915
18 years and over . . . 23,004
65 years and over . . . 3,788
85 years and over . . . 946
Median Age . . . 37.7
Native-born . . . 24,292
Foreign-born . . . 6,985

Educational Attainment, 2000
Population 25 years and over . . . 21,025
Less than 9th grade . . . 3.5%
High school grad or higher . . . 91.0%
Bachelor's degree or higher . . . 39.3%
Graduate degree . . . 13.8%

Income & Poverty, 1999
Per capita income . . . $36,133
Median household income . . . $70,234
Median family income . . . $81,334
Persons in poverty . . . 4.9%
H'holds receiving public assistance . . . 165
H'holds receiving social security . . . 2,511

Households, 2000
Total households . . . 10,895
With persons under 18 . . . 4,320
With persons over 65 . . . 2,622
Family households . . . 7,947
Single person households . . . 2,356
Persons per household . . . 2.82
Persons per family . . . 3.29

Household Population, 2008§§
Persons living in households . . . 32,997
Persons living in group quarters . . . 424
Persons per household . . . 3.1

Labor & Employment
Total civilian labor force, 2008§§ . . . 18,300
Unemployment rate, 2008 . . . 4.4%
Total civilian labor force, 2000 . . . 15,772

Employed persons 16 years and over by occupation, 2000
Managers & professionals . . . 6,814
Service occupations . . . 2,026
Sales & office occupations . . . 4,619
Farming, fishing & forestry . . . 6
Construction & maintenance . . . 760
Production & transportation . . . 832
Self-employed persons . . . 1,669

* US Census Bureau
** 2000 Decennial Census
§ California Department of Finance
§§ California Employment Development Dept

General Information
City of Laguna Hills
24035 El Toro Rd
Laguna Hills, CA 92653
949-707-2600

Website . . . www.ci.laguna-hills.ca.us
Elevation . . . NA
Land Area (sq. miles) . . . 6.3
Water Area (sq. miles) . . . 0
Year of Incorporation . . . 1991
Government type . . . General law
Sales tax rate . . . 8.75%

Voters & Officials

Registered Voters, October 2008
Total . . . 19,752
Democrats . . . 5,310
Republicans . . . 9,561
Declined to state . . . 4,065

Legislative Districts
US Congressional . . . 48
State Senatorial . . . 33
State Assembly . . . 73

Local Officials, 2009
Mayor . . . Joel Lautenschleger
Manager . . . Bruce E. Channing
City Clerk . . . Peggy Johns
Attorney . . . Gregory E. Simonian
Finance Dir . . . Don White
Public Works . . . Ken Rosenfield
Planning/Dev Dir . . . Vern Jones
Building . . . NA
Police Chief . . . Steve Doan
Fire/Emergency Mgmt . . . NA

Public Safety
Number of officers, 2007 . . . NA
Violent crimes, 2007 . . . 55
Property crimes, 2007 . . . 643
Arson, 2007 . . . 7

Public Library
Served by County Library

Library system statistics, FY 2007
Population served . . . NA
Internet terminals . . . NA
Annual users . . . NA

Per capita:
Operating income . . . NA
percent from local government . . . NA
Operating expenditure . . . NA
Total materials . . . NA
Print holdings . . . NA
Visits per capita . . . NA

Housing & Construction

Housing Units
Total, 2008§ . . . 11,153
Single family units, attached . . . 2,183
Single family units, detached . . . 5,873
Multiple family units . . . 2,880
Mobile home units . . . 217
Occupied . . . 10,807
Vacancy rate . . . 3.1%
Median rent, 2000** . . . $1,184
Median SF home value, 2000** . . . $330,500

New Privately Owned Housing Units Authorized by Building Permit, 2007*

	Units	Construction Cost
Single	1	$1,683,693
Total	1	$1,683,693

Municipal Finance
(For local fiscal year ended in 2006)

Revenues
Total . . . $24,666,237
Taxes . . . 17,207,532
Special benefits assessment . . . 0
Licenses & permits . . . 330,992
Fines & forfeitures . . . 485,977
Revenues from use of money & property . . . 428,822
Intergovernmental . . . 3,450,386
Service charges . . . 766,256
Other revenues . . . 1,996,272
Other financing sources . . . 0

Expenditures
Total . . . $23,284,731
General government . . . 3,872,041
Public safety . . . 5,670,483
Transportation . . . 5,597,702
Community development . . . 1,632,305
Health . . . 0
Culture & leisure . . . 6,263,114
Other . . . 249,086

Local School District
(Data from School year 2007-08 except as noted)
Saddleback Valley Unified
25631 Peter A Hartman Way
Mission Viejo, CA 92691
(949) 586-1234

Superintendent . . . Steven Fish
Grade plan . . . K-12
Number of schools . . . 37
Enrollment . . . 33,558
High school graduates, 2006-07 . . . 2,390
Dropout rate . . . 1.2%
Pupil/teacher ratio . . . 23.6
Average class size . . . 28.6
Students per computer . . . 4.3
Classrooms with internet . . . 1,478
Avg. Daily Attendance (ADA) . . . 33,062
Cost per ADA . . . $7,562
Avg. Teacher Salary . . . $77,293

California Achievement Tests 6th ed., 2008
(Pct scoring at or above 50th National Percentile Rank)

	Math	Reading	Language
Grade 3	73%	58%	66%
Grade 7	72%	71%	68%

Academic Performance Index, 2008
Number of students tested . . . 26,076
Number of valid scores . . . 22,315
2007 API (base) . . . 837
2008 API (growth) . . . 847

SAT Testing, 2006-07
Enrollment, Grade 12 . . . 2,741
Number taking test . . . 1,312
percent taking test . . . 47.9%
percent with total score 1,500+ . . . 32.70%

Average Scores:

Math	Verbal	Writing	Total
565	537	535	1,637

Federal No Child Left Behind, 2008
(Adequate Yearly Progress standards met)

	Participation Rate	Pct Proficient
ELA	Yes	No
Math	Yes	Yes

API criteria . . . Yes
Graduation rate . . . Yes
\# criteria met/possible . . . 38/37

Other school districts for this city
(see Appendix E for information on these districts)
None

See Introduction for an explanation of all data sources.

Demographics & Socio-Economic Characteristics

(2000 Decennial Census, except as noted)

Population

1990* 44,400
2000 61,891
Male 30,137
Female 31,754
Jan. 2008 (estimate)§ 66,877
Persons per sq. mi. of land 4,549.5

Race & Hispanic Origin, 2000

Race
White 51,682
Black/African American 776
North American Native 180
Asian 4,784
Pacific Islander 73
Other Race 2,155
Two or more races 2,241
Hispanic origin, total 6,425
Mexican 4,346
Puerto Rican 180
Cuban 167
Other Hispanic 1,732

Age & Nativity, 2000

Under 5 years 4,346
18 years and over 45,433
65 years and over 5,495
85 years and over 520
Median Age 37.5
Native-born 51,094
Foreign-born 10,869

Educational Attainment, 2000

Population 25 years and over 41,898
Less than 9th grade 1.4%
High school grad or higher 95.2%
Bachelor's degree or higher 47.8%
Graduate degree 16.4%

Income & Poverty, 1999

Per capita income $39,167
Median household income $80,733
Median family income $93,613
Persons in poverty 4.0%
H'holds receiving public assistance 306
H'holds receiving social security 3,818

Households, 2000

Total households 23,217
With persons under 18 9,197
With persons over 65 3,871
Family households 16,793
Single person households 4,774
Persons per household 2.65
Persons per family 3.10

Household Population, 2008§§

Persons living in households 66,574
Persons living in group quarters 303
Persons per household 2.8

Labor & Employment

Total civilian labor force, 2008§§ 38,600
Unemployment rate, 2008 .... 4.1%
Total civilian labor force, 2000 33,023

Employed persons 16 years and over by occupation, 2000

Managers & professionals 16,015
Service occupations 2,889
Sales & office occupations 10,153
Farming, fishing & forestry 0
Construction & maintenance 1,124
Production & transportation 1,633
Self-employed persons 3,474

* US Census Bureau
** 2000 Decennial Census
§ California Department of Finance
§§ California Employment Development Dept

General Information

City of Laguna Niguel
27801 La Paz Rd
Laguna Niguel, CA 92677
949-362-4300

Website .... www.ci.laguna-niguel.ca.us
Elevation .... NA
Land Area (sq. miles) 14.7
Water Area (sq. miles) 0.1
Year of Incorporation 1989
Government type .... General law
Sales tax rate 8.75%

Voters & Officials

Registered Voters, October 2008

Total 42,625
Democrats 11,496
Republicans 20,742
Declined to state 8,708

Legislative Districts

US Congressional 48
State Senatorial 33
State Assembly 73

Local Officials, 2009

Mayor .... Robert Ming
Manager .... Tim Casey
City Clerk .... Pamela Lawrence (Actg)
Attorney .... Terry Dixon
Finance Dir .... Cheryl Dyas
Public Works .... Ken Montgomery
Community Dev Dir .... Robert Lenard
Building .... Robert Lenard
Police Chief .... Linda Solorza
Fire/Emergency Mgmt .... NA

Public Safety

Number of officers, 2007 .... NA
Violent crimes, 2007 47
Property crimes, 2007 665
Arson, 2007 4

Public Library

Laguna Niguel Branch Library
Orange County Public Library System
30341 Crown Valley Pkwy
Laguna Niguel, CA 92677
949-249-5252

Branch Librarian .... Loretta Farley

Library system statistics, FY 2007

Population served 1,532,758
Internet terminals 505
Annual users 680,874

Per capita:

Operating income $24.71
percent from local government 90.0%
Operating expenditure $24.18
Total materials 1.93
Print holdings 1.84
Visits per capita 4.02

Housing & Construction

Housing Units

Total, 2008§ 24,908
Single family units, attached 5,007
Single family units, detached 13,834
Multiple family units 6,051
Mobile home units 16
Occupied 24,211
Vacancy rate 2.8%
Median rent, 2000** $1,205
Median SF home value, 2000** $374,800

New Privately Owned Housing Units Authorized by Building Permit, 2007*

	Units	Construction Cost
Single	66	$26,502,399
Total	66	$26,502,399

Municipal Finance

(For local fiscal year ended in 2006)

Revenues

Total $40,159,425
Taxes 29,631,954
Special benefits assessment 0
Licenses & permits 1,210,486
Fines & forfeitures 398,168
Revenues from use of money & property 1,734,366
Intergovernmental 4,131,111
Service charges 1,384,567
Other revenues 1,668,773
Other financing sources 0

Expenditures

Total $29,516,386
General government 3,925,963
Public safety 8,025,389
Transportation 6,014,068
Community development 5,443,739
Health 0
Culture & leisure 6,107,227
Other 0

Local School District

(Data from School year 2007-08 except as noted)

Capistrano Unified
33122 Valle Rd
San Juan Capistrano, CA 92675
(949) 234-9200

Superintendent .... A. Carter
Grade plan K-12
Number of schools 61
Enrollment 52,390
High school graduates, 2006-07 3,205
Dropout rate 0.5%
Pupil/teacher ratio 23.4
Average class size 28.7
Students per computer 4.8
Classrooms with internet 2,308
Avg. Daily Attendance (ADA) 50,036
Cost per ADA $7,694
Avg. Teacher Salary $75,390

California Achievement Tests 6th ed., 2008

(Pct scoring at or above 50th National Percentile Rank)

	Math	Reading	Language
Grade 3	71%	56%	63%
Grade 7	73%	71%	68%

Academic Performance Index, 2008

Number of students tested 39,589
Number of valid scores 38,275
2007 API (base) 826
2008 API (growth) 837

SAT Testing, 2006-07

Enrollment, Grade 12 3,414
Number taking test 1,770
percent taking test 51.9%
percent with total score 1,500+ ... 34.90%

Average Scores:

Math	Verbal	Writing	Total
552	541	537	1,630

Federal No Child Left Behind, 2008

(Adequate Yearly Progress standards met)

	Participation Rate	Pct Proficient
ELA	Yes	No
Math	Yes	Yes

API criteria .... Yes
Graduation rate .... Yes
criteria met/possible 42/41

Other school districts for this city

(see Appendix E for information on these districts)

None

See Introduction for an explanation of all data sources.

Demographics & Socio-Economic Characteristics

(2000 Decennial Census, except as noted)

Population

1990* .... NA
2000 16,507
Male 5,635
Female 10,872
Jan. 2008 (estimate)§ 18,442
Persons per sq. mi. of land 5,763.1

Race & Hispanic Origin, 2000

Race
White 15,866
Black/African American 41
North American Native 20
Asian 412
Pacific Islander 9
Other Race 31
Two or more races 128
Hispanic origin, total 340
Mexican 181
Puerto Rican 19
Cuban 16
Other Hispanic 124

Age & Nativity, 2000

Under 5 years 39
18 years and over 16,414
65 years and over 14,268
85 years and over 3,500
Median Age 78.0
Native-born 13,651
Foreign-born 2,601

Educational Attainment, 2000

Population 25 years and over 16,175
Less than 9th grade 2.7%
High school grad or higher 89.1%
Bachelor's degree or higher 28.5%
Graduate degree 12.3%

Income & Poverty, 1999

Per capita income $32,071
Median household income $30,493
Median family income $46,889
Persons in poverty 5.9%
H'holds receiving public assistance 75
H'holds receiving social security 10,084

Households, 2000

Total households 11,699
With persons under 18 62
With persons over 65 10,785
Family households 3,984
Single person households 7,273
Persons per household 1.40
Persons per family 2.06

Household Population, 2008§§

Persons living in households 18,368
Persons living in group quarters 74
Persons per household 1.5

Labor & Employment

Total civilian labor force, 2008§§ 2,700
Unemployment rate, 2008 .... 6.7%
Total civilian labor force, 2000 2,297

Employed persons 16 years and over by occupation, 2000

Managers & professionals 833
Service occupations 304
Sales & office occupations 832
Farming, fishing & forestry 0
Construction & maintenance 66
Production & transportation 115
Self-employed persons 327

* US Census Bureau
** 2000 Decennial Census
§ California Department of Finance
§§ California Employment Development Dept

General Information

City of Laguna Woods
24264 El Toro Rd
Laguna Woods, CA 92637
949-639-0500

Website .... www.lagunawoodscity.org
Elevation .... NA
Land Area (sq. miles) 3.2
Water Area (sq. miles) 0
Year of Incorporation 1999
Government type .... General Law
Sales tax rate 8.75%

Voters & Officials

Registered Voters, October 2008

Total 15,949
Democrats 6,582
Republicans 6,629
Declined to state 2,310

Legislative Districts

US Congressional 48
State Senatorial 33
State Assembly 70

Local Officials, 2009

Mayor .... Bert Hack
Manager .... Leslie Keane
Deputy Clerk .... Yolie Trippy
Attorney .... Stephen McEwen
Finance Dir .... Douglas Reilly
Public Works .... Douglas Reilly
Planning/Dev Dir .... NA
Building .... NA
Police Chief .... Bill Griffin
Fire Chief .... (County)

Public Safety

Number of officers, 2007 .... NA
Violent crimes, 2007 3
Property crimes, 2007 92
Arson, 2007 0

Public Library

Served by County Library

Library system statistics, FY 2007

Population served .... NA
Internet terminals .... NA
Annual users .... NA

Per capita:

Operating income .... NA
percent from local government .... NA
Operating expenditure .... NA
Total materials .... NA
Print holdings .... NA
Visits per capita .... NA

Housing & Construction

Housing Units

Total, 2008§ 13,629
Single family units, attached 4,012
Single family units, detached 727
Multiple family units 8,864
Mobile home units 26
Occupied 12,591
Vacancy rate 7.6%
Median rent, 2000** $1,036
Median SF home value, 2000** $124,300

New Privately Owned Housing Units Authorized by Building Permit, 2007*

	Units	Construction Cost
Single	0	$0
Total	0	$0

Municipal Finance

(For local fiscal year ended in 2006)

Revenues

Total $9,440,485
Taxes 3,965,205
Special benefits assessment 0
Licenses & permits 253,610
Fines & forfeitures 302,202
Revenues from use of money & property 151,128
Intergovernmental 4,203,698
Service charges 564,642
Other revenues 0
Other financing sources 0

Expenditures

Total $8,677,813
General government 4,388,547
Public safety 1,411,694
Transportation 2,000,362
Community development 452,736
Health 84,056
Culture & leisure 193,778
Other 146,640

Local School District

(Data from School year 2007-08 except as noted)

Saddleback Valley Unified
25631 Peter A Hartman Way
Mission Viejo, CA 92691
(949) 586-1234

Superintendent .... Steven Fish
Grade plan K-12
Number of schools 37
Enrollment 33,558
High school graduates, 2006-07 2,390
Dropout rate 1.2%
Pupil/teacher ratio 23.6
Average class size 28.6
Students per computer 4.3
Classrooms with internet 1,478
Avg. Daily Attendance (ADA) 33,062
Cost per ADA $7,562
Avg. Teacher Salary $77,293

California Achievement Tests 6th ed., 2008

(Pct scoring at or above 50th National Percentile Rank)

	Math	Reading	Language
Grade 3	73%	58%	66%
Grade 7	72%	71%	68%

Academic Performance Index, 2008

Number of students tested 26,076
Number of valid scores 22,315
2007 API (base) 837
2008 API (growth) 847

SAT Testing, 2006-07

Enrollment, Grade 12 2,741
Number taking test 1,312
percent taking test 47.9%
percent with total score 1,500+ 32.70%

Average Scores:

Math	Verbal	Writing	Total
565	537	535	1,637

Federal No Child Left Behind, 2008

(Adequate Yearly Progress standards met)

	Participation Rate	Pct Proficient
ELA	Yes	No
Math	Yes	Yes

API criteria .... Yes
Graduation rate .... Yes
criteria met/possible 38/37

Other school districts for this city

(see Appendix E for information on these districts)

None

See Introduction for an explanation of all data sources.

Demographics & Socio-Economic Characteristics

(2000 Decennial Census, except as noted)

Population

1990* 18,285
2000 28,928
Male 14,431
Female 14,497
Jan. 2008 (estimate)§ 49,807
Persons per sq. mi. of land 1,473.6

Race & Hispanic Origin, 2000

Race
White 18,981
Black/African American 1,501
North American Native 374
Asian 592
Pacific Islander 87
Other Race 5,880
Two or more races 1,513
Hispanic origin, total 11,007
Mexican 8,585
Puerto Rican 184
Cuban 69
Other Hispanic 2,169

Age & Nativity, 2000

Under 5 years 2,834
18 years and over 18,509
65 years and over 1,933
85 years and over 161
Median Age 28.7
Native-born 24,260
Foreign-born 5,030

Educational Attainment, 2000

Population 25 years and over 16,067
Less than 9th grade 11.8%
High school grad or higher 71.3%
Bachelor's degree or higher 8.6%
Graduate degree 2.1%

Income & Poverty, 1999

Per capita income $15,413
Median household income $41,884
Median family income $47,563
Persons in poverty 17.0%
H'holds receiving public assistance 537
H'holds receiving social security 1,859

Households, 2000

Total households 8,817
With persons under 18 4,757
With persons over 65 1,470
Family households 6,874
Single person households 1,426
Persons per household 3.27
Persons per family 3.66

Household Population, 2008§§

Persons living in households 49,734
Persons living in group quarters 73
Persons per household 3.3

Labor & Employment

Total civilian labor force, 2008§§ 17,300
Unemployment rate, 2008 .... 8.3%
Total civilian labor force, 2000 12,218

Employed persons 16 years and over by occupation, 2000

Managers & professionals 2,488
Service occupations 1,806
Sales & office occupations 3,300
Farming, fishing & forestry 67
Construction & maintenance 1,698
Production & transportation 1,993
Self-employed persons 803

* US Census Bureau
** 2000 Decennial Census
§ California Department of Finance
§§ California Employment Development Dept

General Information

City of Lake Elsinore
130 S Main St
Lake Elsinore, CA 92530
951-674-3124

Website .... www.lake-elsinore.org
Elevation .... NA
Land Area (sq. miles) 33.8
Water Area (sq. miles) 5.0
Year of Incorporation 1888
Government type .... General law
Sales tax rate 8.75%

Voters & Officials

Registered Voters, October 2008

Total 15,516
Democrats 5,392
Republicans 6,150
Declined to state 3,186

Legislative Districts

US Congressional 49
State Senatorial 37
State Assembly 64, 66

Local Officials, 2009

Mayor .... Daryl Hickman
Manager .... Robert Brady
City Clerk .... Vivian M. Munson
Attorney .... Barbara Leibold
Finance Dir .... Matt Pressey
Public Works .... Ken Seumalo
Planning/Dev Dir .... Rolfe Preisendanz
Building .... Robin Chipman
Police Chief .... Louis Fetherolf
Emergency/Fire Dir .... Steve Gallegos

Public Safety

Number of officers, 2007 .... NA
Violent crimes, 2007 184
Property crimes, 2007 1,657
Arson, 2007 2

Public Library

Lake Elsinore Branch Library
Riverside County Library Service
600 W Graham
Lake Elsinore, CA 92530
951-674-4517

Branch Librarian .... Thomas Vose

Library system statistics, FY 2007

Population served 1,047,996
Internet terminals 37
Annual users 69,346

Per capita:

Operating income $19.38
percent from local government 49.8%
Operating expenditure $20.45
Total materials 1.43
Print holdings 1.30
Visits per capita 4.06

Housing & Construction

Housing Units

Total, 2008§ 16,140
Single family units, attached 2,928
Single family units, detached 9,910
Multiple family units 2,516
Mobile home units 786
Occupied 14,952
Vacancy rate 7.4%
Median rent, 2000** $633
Median SF home value, 2000** $144,800

New Privately Owned Housing Units Authorized by Building Permit, 2007*

	Units	Construction Cost
Single	490	$98,568,931
Total	771	$120,159,933

Municipal Finance

(For local fiscal year ended in 2006)

Revenues

Total $95,335,539
Taxes 20,925,915
Special benefits assessment 1,569,396
Licenses & permits 6,090,429
Fines & forfeitures 480,524
Revenues from use of money & property 3,504,397
Intergovernmental 1,668,488
Service charges 8,655,913
Other revenues 52,440,477
Other financing sources 0

Expenditures

Total $43,758,225
General government 2,956,772
Public safety 10,218,748
Transportation 6,057,113
Community development 19,323,117
Health 0
Culture & leisure 3,767,235
Other 1,435,240

Local School District

(Data from School year 2007-08 except as noted)

Lake Elsinore Unified
545 Chaney St
Lake Elsinore, CA 92530
(951) 253-7000

Superintendent .... Frank Passarella
Grade plan K-12
Number of schools 26
Enrollment 22,109
High school graduates, 2006-07 1,211
Dropout rate 2.1%
Pupil/teacher ratio 22.2
Average class size 27.7
Students per computer 5.2
Classrooms with internet 1,221
Avg. Daily Attendance (ADA) 21,229
Cost per ADA $8,008
Avg. Teacher Salary $68,317

California Achievement Tests 6th ed., 2008

(Pct scoring at or above 50th National Percentile Rank)

	Math	Reading	Language
Grade 3	61%	39%	50%
Grade 7	50%	47%	43%

Academic Performance Index, 2008

Number of students tested 16,937
Number of valid scores 14,554
2007 API (base) 729
2008 API (growth) 775

SAT Testing, 2006-07

Enrollment, Grade 12 1,425
Number taking test 360
percent taking test 25.3%
percent with total score 1,500+ 9.80%

Average Scores:

Math	Verbal	Writing	Total
485	480	471	1,436

Federal No Child Left Behind, 2008

(Adequate Yearly Progress standards met)

	Participation Rate	Pct Proficient
ELA	Yes	Yes
Math	Yes	Yes

API criteria .... Yes
Graduation rate .... Yes
criteria met/possible 38/38

Other school districts for this city

(see Appendix E for information on these districts)

None

See Introduction for an explanation of all data sources.

Demographics & Socio-Economic Characteristics†

(2007 American Community Survey, except as noted)

Population

1990* .... NA
2007 78,130
Male 40,709
Female 37,421
Jan. 2008 (estimate)§ 78,317
Persons per sq. mi. of land 6,265.4

Race & Hispanic Origin, 2007

Race
White 47,120
Black/African American 2,077
North American Native 181
Asian 9,214
Pacific Islander 68
Other Race 17,108
Two or more races 2,362
Hispanic origin, total 21,238
Mexican 16,463
Puerto Rican 169
Cuban 148
Other Hispanic 4,458

Age & Nativity, 2007

Under 5 years 6,752
18 years and over 57,667
65 years and over 7,114
85 years and over 829
Median Age 37.2
Native-born 56,993
Foreign-born 21,137

Educational Attainment, 2007

Population 25 years and over 51,299
Less than 9th grade 7.1%
High school grad or higher 89.6%
Bachelor's degree or higher 38.8%
Graduate degree 12.1%

Income & Poverty, 2007

Per capita income $34,440
Median household income $86,285
Median family income $96,133
Persons in poverty 7.5%
H'holds receiving public assistance 307
H'holds receiving social security 5,191

Households, 2007

Total households 25,701
With persons under 18 10,282
With persons over 65 5,094
Family households 18,981
Single person households 5,235
Persons per household 3.04
Persons per family 3.39

Household Population, 2008§§

Persons living in households 77,473
Persons living in group quarters 844
Persons per household 3.0

Labor & Employment

Total civilian labor force, 2008§§ 37,800
Unemployment rate, 2008 .... 3.6%
Total civilian labor force, 2000* 32,354

Employed persons 16 years and over by occupation, 2007

Managers & professionals 17,734
Service occupations 4,881
Sales & office occupations 11,763
Farming, fishing & forestry 577
Construction & maintenance 3,820
Production & transportation 2,743
Self-employed persons 3,682

† see Appendix D for 2000 Decennial Census Data
* US Census Bureau
** 2007 American Community Survey
§ California Department of Finance
§§ California Employment Development Dept

General Information

City of Lake Forest
25550 Commercentre Dr
Suite 100
Lake Forest, CA 92630
949-461-3400

Website .... www.ci.lake-forest.ca.us
Elevation .... NA
Land Area (sq. miles) 12.5
Water Area (sq. miles) 0.1
Year of Incorporation 1991
Government type .... General Law
Sales tax rate 8.75%

Voters & Officials

Registered Voters, October 2008

Total 45,087
Democrats 12,284
Republicans 21,950
Declined to state 9,056

Legislative Districts

US Congressional 48
State Senatorial 33
State Assembly 70

Local Officials, 2009

Mayor .... Mark Tettemer
City Manager .... Robert C. Dunek
City Clerk .... Debra Rose (Actg)
Attorney .... Scott C. Smith
Finance Dir .... Elizabeth Andrew
Public Works .... Robert Woodings
Planning/Dev Dir .... Gayle Ackerman
Building .... Gayle Ackerman
Police Chief .... Don Barnes
Fire Battalion Chief .... Ed Fleming

Public Safety

Number of officers, 2007 .... NA
Violent crimes, 2007 93
Property crimes, 2007 1,052
Arson, 2007 25

Public Library

El Toro Branch Library
Orange County Public Library System
24672 Raymond Way
Lake Forest, CA 92630
949-855-8173

Branch Librarian .... Roxanne Burg

Library system statistics, FY 2007

Population served 1,532,758
Internet terminals 505
Annual users 680,874

Per capita:

Operating income $24.71
percent from local government 90.0%
Operating expenditure $24.18
Total materials 1.93
Print holdings 1.84
Visits per capita 4.02

Housing & Construction

Housing Units

Total, 2008§ 26,384
Single family units, attached 3,923
Single family units, detached 14,165
Multiple family units 7,010
Mobile home units 1,286
Occupied 25,711
Vacancy rate 2.6%
Median rent, 2007** $1,649
Median SF home value, 2007** $630,700

New Privately Owned Housing Units Authorized by Building Permit, 2007*

	Units	Construction Cost
Single	0	$0
Total	0	$0

Municipal Finance

(For local fiscal year ended in 2006)

Revenues

Total $42,099,183
Taxes 31,031,522
Special benefits assessment 0
Licenses & permits 616,067
Fines & forfeitures 476,953
Revenues from use of money & property 2,743,369
Intergovernmental 5,321,862
Service charges 735,162
Other revenues 1,174,248
Other financing sources 0

Expenditures

Total $39,856,057
General government 4,079,427
Public safety 11,781,758
Transportation 17,300,201
Community development 3,363,489
Health 61,989
Culture & leisure 3,269,193
Other 0

Local School District

(Data from School year 2007-08 except as noted)

Saddleback Valley Unified
25631 Peter A Hartman Way
Mission Viejo, CA 92691
(949) 586-1234

Superintendent .... Steven Fish
Grade plan K-12
Number of schools 37
Enrollment 33,558
High school graduates, 2006-07 2,390
Dropout rate 1.2%
Pupil/teacher ratio 23.6
Average class size 28.6
Students per computer 4.3
Classrooms with internet 1,478
Avg. Daily Attendance (ADA) 33,062
Cost per ADA $7,562
Avg. Teacher Salary $77,293

California Achievement Tests 6th ed., 2008

(Pct scoring at or above 50th National Percentile Rank)

	Math	Reading	Language
Grade 3	73%	58%	66%
Grade 7	72%	71%	68%

Academic Performance Index, 2008

Number of students tested 26,076
Number of valid scores 22,315
2007 API (base) 837
2008 API (growth) 847

SAT Testing, 2006-07

Enrollment, Grade 12 2,741
Number taking test 1,312
percent taking test 47.9%
percent with total score 1,500+ 32.70%

Average Scores:

Math	Verbal	Writing	Total
565	537	535	1,637

Federal No Child Left Behind, 2008

(Adequate Yearly Progress standards met)

	Participation Rate	Pct Proficient
ELA	Yes	No
Math	Yes	Yes

API criteria .... Yes
Graduation rate .... Yes
\# criteria met/possible 38/37

Other school districts for this city

(see Appendix E for information on these districts)

None

Demographics & Socio-Economic Characteristics

(2000 Decennial Census, except as noted)

Population

1990* 4,390
2000 4,820
Male 2,241
Female 2,579
Jan. 2008 (estimate)§ 5,045
Persons per sq. mi. of land 1,868.5

Race & Hispanic Origin, 2000

Race
White 4,276
Black/African American 36
North American Native 96
Asian 72
Pacific Islander 8
Other Race 168
Two or more races 164
Hispanic origin, total 552
Mexican 431
Puerto Rican 12
Cuban 6
Other Hispanic 103

Age & Nativity, 2000

Under 5 years 274
18 years and over 3,639
65 years and over 1,013
85 years and over 191
Median Age 40.8
Native-born 4,387
Foreign-born 269

Educational Attainment, 2000

Population 25 years and over 3,131
Less than 9th grade 7.3%
High school grad or higher 80.3%
Bachelor's degree or higher 14.8%
Graduate degree 5.7%

Income & Poverty, 1999

Per capita income $17,215
Median household income $32,226
Median family income $37,900
Persons in poverty 14.9%
H'holds receiving public assistance 141
H'holds receiving social security 736

Households, 2000

Total households 1,967
With persons under 18 642
With persons over 65 651
Family households 1,234
Single person households 610
Persons per household 2.36
Persons per family 2.93

Household Population, 2008§§

Persons living in households 4,871
Persons living in group quarters 174
Persons per household 2.4

Labor & Employment

Total civilian labor force, 2008§§ 2,230
Unemployment rate, 2008 .... 9.7%
Total civilian labor force, 2000 2,088

Employed persons 16 years and over by occupation, 2000

Managers & professionals 541
Service occupations 378
Sales & office occupations 528
Farming, fishing & forestry 20
Construction & maintenance 208
Production & transportation 208
Self-employed persons 174

* US Census Bureau
** 2000 Decennial Census
§ California Department of Finance
§§ California Employment Development Dept

General Information

City of Lakeport
225 Park St
Lakeport, CA 95453
707-263-5615

Website .... cityoflakeport.com
Elevation .... 1,343 ft.
Land Area (sq. miles) 2.7
Water Area (sq. miles) 0.1
Year of Incorporation 1888
Government type .... General law
Sales tax rate 8.75%

Voters & Officials

Registered Voters, October 2008

Total 2,782
Democrats 1,136
Republicans 977
Declined to state 539

Legislative Districts

US Congressional 1
State Senatorial 2
State Assembly 1

Local Officials, 2009

Mayor .... Ronald Bertsch
City Manager .... Jerry Gillham
City Clerk .... Janel Chapman
Attorney .... Steve Brookes
Finance Dir .... Janet Tavernier
Public Works .... Doug Grider
Planning/Dev Dir .... Mark Brannigan
Building .... Tom Carlton
Police Chief .... Kevin Burke
Emergency/Fire Dir .... Ken Wells

Public Safety

Number of officers, 2007 13
Violent crimes, 2007 14
Property crimes, 2007 130
Arson, 2007 4

Public Library

Main Branch
Lake County Library System
1425 N High St
Lakeport, CA 95453
707-263-8816

County Librarian .... Kathleen Jansen

Library system statistics, FY 2007

Population served 64,276
Internet terminals 24
Annual users 20,128

Per capita:

Operating income $20.31
percent from local government 53.0%
Operating expenditure $18.27
Total materials 2.08
Print holdings 1.98
Visits per capita 3.73

Housing & Construction

Housing Units

Total, 2008§ 2,449
Single family units, attached 119
Single family units, detached 1,479
Multiple family units 395
Mobile home units 456
Occupied 2,013
Vacancy rate 17.8%
Median rent, 2000** $608
Median SF home value, 2000** $125,900

New Privately Owned Housing Units Authorized by Building Permit, 2007*

	Units	Construction Cost
Single	22	$4,648,386
Total	22	$4,648,386

Municipal Finance

(For local fiscal year ended in 2006)

Revenues

Total $8,107,620
Taxes 3,029,315
Special benefits assessment 0
Licenses & permits 108,771
Fines & forfeitures 40,346
Revenues from use of money & property 166,720
Intergovernmental 852,799
Service charges 3,840,684
Other revenues 68,985
Other financing sources 0

Expenditures

Total $6,616,781
General government 1,187,977
Public safety 1,389,051
Transportation 644,124
Community development 455,189
Health 1,653,488
Culture & leisure 260,777
Other 0

Local School District

(Data from School year 2007-08 except as noted)

Lakeport Unified
2508 Howard Ave
Lakeport, CA 95453
(707) 262-3000

Superintendent .... Erin Smith-Hagberg
Grade plan K-12
Number of schools 6
Enrollment 1,709
High school graduates, 2006-07 122
Dropout rate 5.9%
Pupil/teacher ratio 20.6
Average class size 22.7
Students per computer 4.0
Classrooms with internet 85
Avg. Daily Attendance (ADA) 1,624
Cost per ADA $8,506
Avg. Teacher Salary $51,463

California Achievement Tests 6th ed., 2008

(Pct scoring at or above 50th National Percentile Rank)

	Math	Reading	Language
Grade 3	65%	40%	55%
Grade 7	53%	53%	50%

Academic Performance Index, 2008

Number of students tested 1,332
Number of valid scores 1,256
2007 API (base) 740
2008 API (growth) 749

SAT Testing, 2006-07

Enrollment, Grade 12 126
Number taking test 46
percent taking test 36.5%
percent with total score 1,500+ 19.80%

Average Scores:

Math	Verbal	Writing	Total
507	505	486	1,498

Federal No Child Left Behind, 2008

(Adequate Yearly Progress standards met)

	Participation Rate	Pct Proficient
ELA	Yes	No
Math	Yes	No

API criteria .... Yes
Graduation rate .... Yes
\# criteria met/possible 26/19

Other school districts for this city

(see Appendix E for information on these districts)

None

See Introduction for an explanation of all data sources.

Demographics & Socio-Economic Characteristics†

(2007 American Community Survey, except as noted)

Population

1990*	73,557
2007	89,289
Male	45,059
Female	44,230
Jan. 2008 (estimate)§	83,486
Persons per sq. mi. of land	8,881.5

Race & Hispanic Origin, 2007

Race	
White	45,383
Black/African American	6,719
North American Native	1,701
Asian	14,314
Pacific Islander	1,002
Other Race	16,676
Two or more races	3,494
Hispanic origin, total	25,580
Mexican	21,702
Puerto Rican	616
Cuban	142
Other Hispanic	3,120

Age & Nativity, 2007

Under 5 years	5,753
18 years and over	65,317
65 years and over	9,639
85 years and over	1,366
Median Age	35.7
Native-born	68,699
Foreign-born	20,590

Educational Attainment, 2007

Population 25 years and over	56,260
Less than 9th grade	5.5%
High school grad or higher	90.5%
Bachelor's degree or higher	27.3%
Graduate degree	7.7%

Income & Poverty, 2007

Per capita income	$27,274
Median household income	$71,505
Median family income	$75,776
Persons in poverty	3.0%
H'holds receiving public assistance	288
H'holds receiving social security	6,939

Households, 2007

Total households	28,122
With persons under 18	12,460
With persons over 65	6,639
Family households	21,585
Single person households	4,943
Persons per household	3.18
Persons per family	3.64

Household Population, 2008§§

Persons living in households	83,292
Persons living in group quarters	194
Persons per household	3.1

Labor & Employment

Total civilian labor force, 2008§§	45,900
Unemployment rate, 2008	4.8%
Total civilian labor force, 2000*	39,306

Employed persons 16 years and over by occupation, 2007

Managers & professionals	15,076
Service occupations	6,267
Sales & office occupations	15,191
Farming, fishing & forestry	0
Construction & maintenance	3,907
Production & transportation	4,855
Self-employed persons	1,924

† see Appendix D for 2000 Decennial Census Data
* US Census Bureau
** 2007 American Community Survey
§ California Department of Finance
§§ California Employment Development Dept

General Information

City of Lakewood
5050 Clark Ave
Lakewood, CA 90712
562-866-9771

Website	www.lakewoodcity.org
Elevation	50 ft.
Land Area (sq. miles)	9.4
Water Area (sq. miles)	0.1
Year of Incorporation	1954
Government type	General law
Sales tax rate	9.25%

Voters & Officials

Registered Voters, October 2008

Total	43,882
Democrats	19,734
Republicans	14,821
Declined to state	7,474

Legislative Districts

US Congressional	39
State Senatorial	27
State Assembly	55, 56

Local Officials, 2009

Mayor	Steve Croft
Manager	Howard Chambers
City Clerk	Denise Hayward
Attorney	Steven Skolnik
Admin Svcs Dir	Diane Perkin
Public Works	Lisa Rapp
Planning/Dev Dir	Jack Gonsalves
Building	NA
Police Chief	NA
Fire/Emergency Mgmt	NA

Public Safety

Number of officers, 2007	NA
Violent crimes, 2007	457
Property crimes, 2007	2,478
Arson, 2007	8

Public Library

Angelo M. Iacoboni Library
Los Angeles County Public Library System
4990 Clark Ave
Lakewood, CA 90712
562-866-1777

Branch Librarian	Donna Walters

Library system statistics, FY 2007

Population served	3,673,313
Internet terminals	749
Annual users	3,748,771

Per capita:

Operating income	$30.06
percent from local government	93.6%
Operating expenditure	$28.36
Total materials	2.22
Print holdings	1.97
Visits per capita	3.25

Housing & Construction

Housing Units

Total, 2008§	27,423
Single family units, attached	741
Single family units, detached	22,243
Multiple family units	4,341
Mobile home units	98
Occupied	26,964
Vacancy rate	1.7%
Median rent, 2007**	$1,208
Median SF home value, 2007**	$579,900

New Privately Owned Housing Units Authorized by Building Permit, 2007*

	Units	Construction Cost
Single	1	$249,260
Total	22	$1,836,510

Municipal Finance

(For local fiscal year ended in 2006)

Revenues

Total	$55,791,261
Taxes	28,569,986
Special benefits assessment	0
Licenses & permits	824,688
Fines & forfeitures	632,950
Revenues from use of money & property	2,574,373
Intergovernmental	6,485,326
Service charges	15,691,440
Other revenues	1,012,498
Other financing sources	0

Expenditures

Total	$53,273,923
General government	4,555,521
Public safety	12,279,540
Transportation	8,262,797
Community development	6,119,420
Health	4,085,645
Culture & leisure	9,924,557
Other	3,654

Local School District

(Data from School year 2007-08 except as noted)

Long Beach Unified
1515 Hughes Way
Long Beach, CA 90810
(562) 997-8000

Superintendent	Christopher Steinhauser
Grade plan	K-12
Number of schools	93
Enrollment	88,186
High school graduates, 2006-07	4,706
Dropout rate	5.1%
Pupil/teacher ratio	20.9
Average class size	27.3
Students per computer	4.9
Classrooms with internet	4,149
Avg. Daily Attendance (ADA)	87,009
Cost per ADA	$8,964
Avg. Teacher Salary	$70,071

California Achievement Tests 6th ed., 2008

(Pct scoring at or above 50th National Percentile Rank)

	Math	Reading	Language
Grade 3	60%	34%	41%
Grade 7	47%	43%	41%

Academic Performance Index, 2008

Number of students tested	67,372
Number of valid scores	64,269
2007 API (base)	729
2008 API (growth)	744

SAT Testing, 2006-07

Enrollment, Grade 12	6,154
Number taking test	2,120
percent taking test	34.5%
percent with total score 1,500+	14.30%

Average Scores:

Math	Verbal	Writing	Total
496	478	476	1,450

Federal No Child Left Behind, 2008

(Adequate Yearly Progress standards met)

	Participation Rate	Pct Proficient
ELA	Yes	No
Math	Yes	No

API criteria	Yes
Graduation rate	Yes
# criteria met/possible	46/43

Other school districts for this city

(see Appendix E for information on these districts)

ABC Unified, Bellflower Unified, Paramount Unified

Demographics & Socio-Economic Characteristics†

(2007 American Community Survey, except as noted)

Population

1990* 97,291
2007 155,902
Male 81,274
Female 74,628
Jan. 2008 (estimate)§ 145,243
Persons per sq. mi. of land 1,545.1

Race & Hispanic Origin, 2007

Race
White 83,027
Black/African American 28,255
North American Native 864
Asian 7,341
Pacific Islander 509
Other Race 29,697
Two or more races 6,209
Hispanic origin, total 62,080
Mexican 45,412
Puerto Rican 1,107
Cuban 1,172
Other Hispanic 14,389

Age & Nativity, 2007

Under 5 years 14,521
18 years and over 105,034
65 years and over 10,949
85 years and over 686
Median Age 28.6
Native-born 135,894
Foreign-born 20,008

Educational Attainment, 2007

Population 25 years and over 86,481
Less than 9th grade 6.5%
High school grad or higher 81.7%
Bachelor's degree or higher 15.3%
Graduate degree 4.5%

Income & Poverty, 2007

Per capita income $19,410
Median household income $49,641
Median family income $54,226
Persons in poverty 18.2%
H'holds receiving public assistance 1,727
H'holds receiving social security 8,972

Households, 2007

Total households 45,131
With persons under 18 22,734
With persons over 65 7,875
Family households 34,015
Single person households 8,934
Persons per household 3.34
Persons per family 3.88

Household Population, 2008§§

Persons living in households 137,332
Persons living in group quarters 7,911
Persons per household 3.1

Labor & Employment

Total civilian labor force, 2008§§ 56,300
Unemployment rate, 2008 .... 10.7%
Total civilian labor force, 2000* 48,623

Employed persons 16 years and over by occupation, 2007

Managers & professionals 16,577
Service occupations 11,208
Sales & office occupations 15,823
Farming, fishing & forestry 0
Construction & maintenance 8,841
Production & transportation 6,845
Self-employed persons 4,387

† see Appendix D for 2000 Decennial Census Data
* US Census Bureau
** 2007 American Community Survey
§ California Department of Finance
§§ California Employment Development Dept

General Information

City of Lancaster
44933 N Fern Ave
Lancaster, CA 93534
661-723-6000

Website .... www.cityoflancasterca.org
Elevation .... 2,355 ft.
Land Area (sq. miles) 94.0
Water Area (sq. miles) 0.2
Year of Incorporation 1977
Government type .... General law
Sales tax rate 9.25%

Voters & Officials

Registered Voters, October 2008

Total 59,174
Democrats 23,540
Republicans 23,537
Declined to state 9,351

Legislative Districts

US Congressional 22, 25
State Senatorial 17
State Assembly 36

Local Officials, 2009

Mayor .... R. Rex Parris
City Manager .... Mark V. Bozigian
City Clerk .... Geri K. Bryan
Attorney .... David R. McEwen
Finance Dir .... Barbara Boswell
Public Works .... Randy Williams
Planning/Dev Dir .... Brian Ludicke
Building .... Robert Neal
Police Chief .... Axel Anderson
Emergency/Fire Dir .... Mike Metro

Public Safety

Number of officers, 2007 .... NA
Violent crimes, 2007 1,311
Property crimes, 2007 5,056
Arson, 2007 89

Public Library

Lancaster Library
Los Angeles County Public Library System
601 W Lancaster Blvd
Lancaster, CA 93534
661-948-5029

Branch Librarian .... Charles Billodeaux

Library system statistics, FY 2007

Population served 3,673,313
Internet terminals 749
Annual users 3,748,771

Per capita:

Operating income $30.06
percent from local government 93.6%
Operating expenditure $28.36
Total materials 2.22
Print holdings 1.97
Visits per capita 3.25

Housing & Construction

Housing Units

Total, 2008§ 48,973
Single family units, attached 1,188
Single family units, detached 33,718
Multiple family units 10,569
Mobile home units 3,498
Occupied 44,843
Vacancy rate 8.4%
Median rent, 2007** $1,122
Median SF home value, 2007** $329,500

New Privately Owned Housing Units Authorized by Building Permit, 2007*

	Units	Construction Cost
Single	806	$138,290,298
Total	808	$138,599,933

Municipal Finance

(For local fiscal year ended in 2006)

Revenues

Total $116,097,123
Taxes 70,007,368
Special benefits assessment 4,950,311
Licenses & permits 5,997,877
Fines & forfeitures 1,681,703
Revenues from use of money & property 3,952,577
Intergovernmental 11,530,961
Service charges 14,322,290
Other revenues 3,654,036
Other financing sources 0

Expenditures

Total $86,701,125
General government 6,084,187
Public safety 21,000,626
Transportation 22,106,270
Community development 18,753,770
Health 1,573,911
Culture & leisure 15,489,938
Other 0

Local School District

(Data from School year 2007-08 except as noted)

Antelope Valley Union High
44811 North Sierra Hwy
Lancaster, CA 93534
(661) 948-7655

Superintendent .... David Vierra
Grade plan 9-12
Number of schools 14
Enrollment 26,453
High school graduates, 2006-07 3,778
Dropout rate 4.4%
Pupil/teacher ratio 23.0
Average class size 26.0
Students per computer 4.0
Classrooms with internet 1,530
Avg. Daily Attendance (ADA) 23,462
Cost per ADA $8,393
Avg. Teacher Salary $62,133

California Achievement Tests 6th ed., 2008

(Pct scoring at or above 50th National Percentile Rank)

	Math	Reading	Language
Grade 3	NA	NA	NA
Grade 7	NA	NA	NA

Academic Performance Index, 2008

Number of students tested 17,439
Number of valid scores 16,491
2007 API (base) 657
2008 API (growth) 660

SAT Testing, 2006-07

Enrollment, Grade 12 5,784
Number taking test 1,303
percent taking test 22.5%
percent with total score 1,500+ 8.00%

Average Scores:

Math	Verbal	Writing	Total
467	473	468	1,408

Federal No Child Left Behind, 2008

(Adequate Yearly Progress standards met)

	Participation Rate	Pct Proficient
ELA	Yes	No
Math	Yes	No

API criteria .... Yes
Graduation rate .... No
\# criteria met/possible 36/32

Other school districts for this city

(see Appendix E for information on these districts)

Eastside Union Elem, Lancaster Elem, Westside Union Elem, Wilsona Elem

See Introduction for an explanation of all data sources.

Demographics & Socio-Economic Characteristics

(2000 Decennial Census, except as noted)

Population

1990* . . . 11,070
2000 . . . 12,014
Male . . . 5,439
Female . . . 6,575
Jan. 2008 (estimate)§ . . . 12,204
Persons per sq. mi. of land . . . 3,936.8

Race & Hispanic Origin, 2000

Race
White . . . 10,963
Black/African American . . . 96
North American Native . . . 26
Asian . . . 466
Pacific Islander . . . 15
Other Race . . . 131
Two or more races . . . 317
Hispanic origin, total . . . 515
Mexican . . . 229
Puerto Rican . . . 28
Cuban . . . 18
Other Hispanic . . . 240

Age & Nativity, 2000

Under 5 years . . . 560
18 years and over . . . 10,048
65 years and over . . . 2,370
85 years and over . . . 401
Median Age . . . 45.9
Native-born . . . 10,414
Foreign-born . . . 1,588

Educational Attainment, 2000

Population 25 years and over . . . 9,743
Less than 9th grade . . . 1.3%
High school grad or higher . . . 97.2%
Bachelor's degree or higher . . . 62.6%
Graduate degree . . . 26.3%

Income & Poverty, 1999

Per capita income . . . $56,983
Median household income . . . $66,710
Median family income . . . $104,028
Persons in poverty . . . 3.6%
H'holds receiving public assistance . . . 18
H'holds receiving social security . . . 1,751

Households, 2000

Total households . . . 6,142
With persons under 18 . . . 1,227
With persons over 65 . . . 1,732
Family households . . . 2,901
Single person households . . . 2,650
Persons per household . . . 1.93
Persons per family . . . 2.69

Household Population, 2008§§

Persons living in households . . . 12,049
Persons living in group quarters . . . 155
Persons per household . . . 2.0

Labor & Employment

Total civilian labor force, 2008§§ . . . 7,100
Unemployment rate, 2008 . . . 3.2%
Total civilian labor force, 2000 . . . 6,918

Employed persons 16 years and over by occupation, 2000

Managers & professionals . . . 3,852
Service occupations . . . 615
Sales & office occupations . . . 1,990
Farming, fishing & forestry . . . 0
Construction & maintenance . . . 224
Production & transportation . . . 94
Self-employed persons . . . 1,188

* US Census Bureau
** 2000 Decennial Census
§ California Department of Finance
§§ California Employment Development Dept

General Information

City of Larkspur
400 Magnolia Ave
Larkspur, CA 94939
415-927-5110

Website . . . www.ci.larkspur.ca.us
Elevation . . . 43 ft.
Land Area (sq. miles) . . . 3.1
Water Area (sq. miles) . . . 0.1
Year of Incorporation . . . 1908
Government type . . . General law
Sales tax rate . . . 9.00%

Voters & Officials

Registered Voters, October 2008

Total . . . 8,264
Democrats . . . 4,563
Republicans . . . 1,679
Declined to state . . . 1,744

Legislative Districts

US Congressional . . . 6
State Senatorial . . . 3
State Assembly . . . 6

Local Officials, 2009

Mayor . . . Dan Hillmer
Manager . . . Jean Bonander
City Clerk . . . Cynthia Huisman
Attorney . . . Sky Woodruff
Finance Dir . . . Amy Koenig
Public Works . . . Hamid Shamsapour
Planning Dir . . . Nancy Kaufman
Building . . . NA
Police Chief . . . Philip Green
Fire Chief . . . Robert Sinnott

Public Safety

(Twin Cities Police Authority for Corte Madera & Larkspur)

Number of officers, 2007 . . . 34
Violent crimes, 2007 . . . 19
Property crimes, 2007 . . . 555
Arson, 2007 . . . 2

Public Library

Larkspur Public Library
400 Magnolia Ave
Larkspur, CA 94939
415-927-5005

Director . . . Frances Gordon

Library statistics, FY 2007

Population served . . . 12,121
Internet terminals . . . 0
Annual users . . . NA

Per capita:

Operating income . . . $50.18
percent from local government . . . 88.5%
Operating expenditure . . . $50.19
Total materials . . . 4.20
Print holdings . . . 3.20
Visits per capita . . . NA

Housing & Construction

Housing Units

Total, 2008§ . . . 6,444
Single family units, attached . . . 371
Single family units, detached . . . 2,457
Multiple family units . . . 3,377
Mobile home units . . . 239
Occupied . . . 6,172
Vacancy rate . . . 4.2%
Median rent, 2000** . . . $1,321
Median SF home value, 2000** . . . $663,000

New Privately Owned Housing Units Authorized by Building Permit, 2007*

	Units	Construction Cost
Single	8	$3,929,411
Total	8	$3,929,411

Municipal Finance

(For local fiscal year ended in 2006)

Revenues

Total . . . $13,469,342
Taxes . . . 9,617,888
Special benefits assessment . . . 105,654
Licenses & permits . . . 166,318
Fines & forfeitures . . . 105,523
Revenues from use of money & property . . . 311,710
Intergovernmental . . . 1,229,039
Service charges . . . 1,753,505
Other revenues . . . 179,705
Other financing sources . . . 0

Expenditures

Total . . . $14,359,222
General government . . . 1,437,541
Public safety . . . 6,665,993
Transportation . . . 2,420,276
Community development . . . 1,245,502
Health . . . 0
Culture & leisure . . . 2,589,910
Other . . . 0

Local School District

(Data from School year 2007-08 except as noted)

Tamalpais Union High
PO Box 605
Larkspur, CA 94977
(415) 945-3720

Superintendent . . . Laurie Kimbrel
Grade plan . . . 9-12
Number of schools . . . 5
Enrollment . . . 3,889
High school graduates, 2006-07 . . . 959
Dropout rate . . . 0.8%
Pupil/teacher ratio . . . 17.4
Average class size . . . 24.4
Students per computer . . . 2.6
Classrooms with internet . . . 232
Avg. Daily Attendance (ADA) . . . 3,715
Cost per ADA . . . $13,492
Avg. Teacher Salary . . . $81,923

California Achievement Tests 6th ed., 2008

(Pct scoring at or above 50th National Percentile Rank)

	Math	Reading	Language
Grade 3	NA	NA	NA
Grade 7	NA	NA	NA

Academic Performance Index, 2008

Number of students tested . . . 2,800
Number of valid scores . . . 2,766
2007 API (base) . . . 848
2008 API (growth) . . . 855

SAT Testing, 2006-07

Enrollment, Grade 12 . . . 997
Number taking test . . . 730
percent taking test . . . 73.2%
percent with total score 1,500+ . . . 58.30%

Average Scores:

Math	Verbal	Writing	Total
574	574	574	1,722

Federal No Child Left Behind, 2008

(Adequate Yearly Progress standards met)

	Participation Rate	Pct Proficient
ELA	Yes	Yes
Math	Yes	Yes

API criteria . . . Yes
Graduation rate . . . Yes
\# criteria met/possible . . . 10/10

Other school districts for this city

(see Appendix E for information on these districts)

Larkspur Elem

See Introduction for an explanation of all data sources.

Demographics & Socio-Economic Characteristics

(2000 Decennial Census, except as noted)

Population

1990* 6,841
2000 10,445
Male 5,300
Female 5,145
Jan. 2008 (estimate)§ 17,429
Persons per sq. mi. of land 1,062.7

Race & Hispanic Origin, 2000

Race
White 5,319
Black/African American 469
North American Native 126
Asian 1,395
Pacific Islander 56
Other Race 2,205
Two or more races 875
Hispanic origin, total 4,031
Mexican 3,307
Puerto Rican 109
Cuban 5
Other Hispanic 610

Age & Nativity, 2000

Under 5 years 919
18 years and over 6,806
65 years and over 631
85 years and over 48
Median Age 30.0
Native-born 8,082
Foreign-born 2,252

Educational Attainment, 2000

Population 25 years and over 5,822
Less than 9th grade 9.9%
High school grad or higher 74.0%
Bachelor's degree or higher 10.9%
Graduate degree 2.4%

Income & Poverty, 1999

Per capita income $16,032
Median household income $55,037
Median family income $57,319
Persons in poverty 9.2%
H'holds receiving public assistance 115
H'holds receiving social security 546

Households, 2000

Total households 2,908
With persons under 18 1,713
With persons over 65 475
Family households 2,483
Single person households 301
Persons per household 3.59
Persons per family 3.82

Household Population, 2008§§

Persons living in households 17,419
Persons living in group quarters 10
Persons per household 3.7

Labor & Employment

Total civilian labor force, 2008§§ 5,600
Unemployment rate, 2008 .... 7.2%
Total civilian labor force, 2000 4,622

Employed persons 16 years and over by occupation, 2000

Managers & professionals 929
Service occupations 665
Sales & office occupations 1,084
Farming, fishing & forestry 86
Construction & maintenance 628
Production & transportation 899
Self-employed persons 212

* US Census Bureau
** 2000 Decennial Census
§ California Department of Finance
§§ California Employment Development Dept

General Information

City of Lathrop
390 Towne Centre Dr
Lathrop, CA 95330
209-941-7200

Website .... www.ci.lathrop.ca.us
Elevation .... NA
Land Area (sq. miles) 16.4
Water Area (sq. miles) 0.3
Year of Incorporation 1989
Government type .... General Law
Sales tax rate 8.75%

Voters & Officials

Registered Voters, October 2008

Total 5,280
Democrats 2,699
Republicans 1,522
Declined to state 861

Legislative Districts

US Congressional 18
State Senatorial 5
State Assembly 17

Local Officials, 2009

Mayor .... Kristy Sayles
Interim City Manager .... Cary Keaten
City Clerk .... Rick Caldeira
Attorney .... Salvador V. Navarrete
Finance Dir .... Terri Vigna
Public Works .... Steve Salvatore
Community Dev Dir .... Marilyn Ponton
Building .... NA
Police Chief .... Dolores Delgado
Fire/Emerg Mgmt ..... Fred Manding (Int)

Public Safety

Number of officers, 2007 .... NA
Violent crimes, 2007 .... NA
Property crimes, 2007 .... NA
Arson, 2007 .... NA

Public Library

Lathrop Library
Stockton-San Joaquin County Public Library
15461 7th St
Lathrop, CA 95330
209-937-8221

Branch Librarian .... Kathleen Buffleben

Library system statistics, FY 2007

Population served 619,292
Internet terminals 125
Annual users 255,083

Per capita:

Operating income $21.59
percent from local government 96.0%
Operating expenditure $19.98
Total materials 1.65
Print holdings 1.52
Visits per capita 2.20

Housing & Construction

Housing Units

Total, 2008§ 4,917
Single family units, attached 328
Single family units, detached 4,132
Multiple family units 106
Mobile home units 351
Occupied 4,763
Vacancy rate 3.1%
Median rent, 2000** $742
Median SF home value, 2000** $150,600

New Privately Owned Housing Units Authorized by Building Permit, 2007*

	Units	Construction Cost
Single	198	$45,528,120
Total	198	$45,528,120

Municipal Finance

(For local fiscal year ended in 2006)

Revenues

Total $57,089,980
Taxes 16,992,620
Special benefits assessment 998,464
Licenses & permits 2,756,101
Fines & forfeitures 134,898
Revenues from use of money & property 2,147,840
Intergovernmental 2,788,751
Service charges 14,151,042
Other revenues 17,120,264
Other financing sources 0

Expenditures

Total $30,242,503
General government 3,450,263
Public safety 3,619,829
Transportation 8,336,845
Community development 6,135,973
Health 2,639,705
Culture & leisure 923,578
Other 0

Local School District

(Data from School year 2007-08 except as noted)

Manteca Unified
PO Box 32
Manteca, CA 95336
(209) 825-3200

Superintendent .... Jason Messer
Grade plan K-12
Number of schools 28
Enrollment 23,654
High school graduates, 2006-07 1,290
Dropout rate 3.3%
Pupil/teacher ratio 21.7
Average class size 26.2
Students per computer 5.0
Classrooms with internet 1,280
Avg. Daily Attendance (ADA) 22,902
Cost per ADA $7,460
Avg. Teacher Salary $59,600

California Achievement Tests 6th ed., 2008

(Pct scoring at or above 50th National Percentile Rank)

	Math	Reading	Language
Grade 3	55%	37%	46%
Grade 7	47%	47%	44%

Academic Performance Index, 2008

Number of students tested 17,956
Number of valid scores 16,762
2007 API (base) 724
2008 API (growth) 731

SAT Testing, 2006-07

Enrollment, Grade 12 1,597
Number taking test 493
percent taking test 30.9%
percent with total score 1,500+ ... 10.30%

Average Scores:

Math	Verbal	Writing	Total
471	468	454	1,393

Federal No Child Left Behind, 2008

(Adequate Yearly Progress standards met)

	Participation Rate	Pct Proficient
ELA	Yes	No
Math	Yes	No

API criteria .... Yes
Graduation rate .... Yes
criteria met/possible 46/41

Other school districts for this city

(see Appendix E for information on these districts)

None

See Introduction for an explanation of all data sources.

Demographics & Socio-Economic Characteristics

(2000 Decennial Census, except as noted)

Population

1990*	27,331
2000	31,711
Male	16,036
Female	15,675
Jan. 2008 (estimate)§	33,540
Persons per sq. mi. of land	16,770.0

Race & Hispanic Origin, 2000

Race	
White	13,394
Black/African American	3,998
North American Native	313
Asian	3,055
Pacific Islander	289
Other Race	8,584
Two or more races	2,078
Hispanic origin, total	16,515
Mexican	10,423
Puerto Rican	341
Cuban	352
Other Hispanic	5,399

Age & Nativity, 2000

Under 5 years	2,950
18 years and over	21,609
65 years and over	1,788
85 years and over	126
Median Age	29.3
Native-born	19,440
Foreign-born	12,289

Educational Attainment, 2000

Population 25 years and over	18,353
Less than 9th grade	17.5%
High school grad or higher	63.4%
Bachelor's degree or higher	12.5%
Graduate degree	4.0%

Income & Poverty, 1999

Per capita income	$13,702
Median household income	$39,012
Median family income	$37,909
Persons in poverty	17.2%
H'holds receiving public assistance	796
H'holds receiving social security	1,449

Households, 2000

Total households	9,555
With persons under 18	4,886
With persons over 65	1,454
Family households	7,025
Single person households	1,801
Persons per household	3.31
Persons per family	3.80

Household Population, 2008§§

Persons living in households	33,454
Persons living in group quarters	86
Persons per household	3.5

Labor & Employment

Total civilian labor force, 2008§§	16,700
Unemployment rate, 2008	7.5%
Total civilian labor force, 2000	14,306

Employed persons 16 years and over by occupation, 2000

Managers & professionals	2,718
Service occupations	2,765
Sales & office occupations	4,030
Farming, fishing & forestry	0
Construction & maintenance	1,421
Production & transportation	2,264
Self-employed persons	791

* US Census Bureau
** 2000 Decennial Census
§ California Department of Finance
§§ California Employment Development Dept

General Information

City of Lawndale
14717 Burin Ave
Lawndale, CA 90260
310-973-3200

Website	www.lawndalecity.org
Elevation	55 ft.
Land Area (sq. miles)	2.0
Water Area (sq. miles)	0
Year of Incorporation	1959
Government type	General law
Sales tax rate	9.25%

Voters & Officials

Registered Voters, October 2008

Total	11,475
Democrats	6,237
Republicans	2,339
Declined to state	2,404

Legislative Districts

US Congressional	35
State Senatorial	25
State Assembly	51

Local Officials, 2009

Mayor	Harold Hofmann
Manager	Keith Breskin
City Clerk	Paula Hartwill
Attorney	Tiffany Israel
Finance Dir	Ken Louie
Public Works	Marlene Miyoshi
Planning/Dev Dir	NA
Building	Otis Ginoza
Police Chief	NA
Fire/Emergency Mgmt	NA

Public Safety

Number of officers, 2007	NA
Violent crimes, 2007	247
Property crimes, 2007	498
Arson, 2007	5

Public Library

Lawndale Library
Los Angeles County Public Library System
14615 Burin Ave
Lawndale, CA 90260
310-676-0177

Branch Librarian	Melissa McCollum

Library system statistics, FY 2007

Population served	3,673,313
Internet terminals	749
Annual users	3,748,771

Per capita:

Operating income	$30.06
percent from local government	93.6%
Operating expenditure	$28.36
Total materials	2.22
Print holdings	1.97
Visits per capita	3.25

Housing & Construction

Housing Units

Total, 2008§	9,962
Single family units, attached	1,606
Single family units, detached	4,986
Multiple family units	3,242
Mobile home units	128
Occupied	9,645
Vacancy rate	3.2%
Median rent, 2000**	$783
Median SF home value, 2000**	$178,700

New Privately Owned Housing Units Authorized by Building Permit, 2007*

	Units	Construction Cost
Single	0	$0
Total	0	$0

Municipal Finance

(For local fiscal year ended in 2006)

Revenues

Total	$17,496,247
Taxes	10,713,883
Special benefits assessment	0
Licenses & permits	535,451
Fines & forfeitures	681,629
Revenues from use of money & property	839,813
Intergovernmental	3,284,636
Service charges	1,189,362
Other revenues	251,473
Other financing sources	0

Expenditures

Total	$13,990,170
General government	2,759,652
Public safety	4,201,463
Transportation	3,441,244
Community development	1,682,429
Health	97,561
Culture & leisure	1,807,821
Other	0

Local School District

(Data from School year 2007-08 except as noted)

Centinela Valley Union High
14901 South Inglewood Ave
Lawndale, CA 90260
(310) 263-3200

Superintendent	Jose Fernandez
Grade plan	9-12
Number of schools	5
Enrollment	7,648
High school graduates, 2006-07	1,005
Dropout rate	5.6%
Pupil/teacher ratio	21.7
Average class size	27.9
Students per computer	3.0
Classrooms with internet	353
Avg. Daily Attendance (ADA)	7,096
Cost per ADA	$8,357
Avg. Teacher Salary	$61,333

California Achievement Tests 6th ed., 2008

(Pct scoring at or above 50th National Percentile Rank)

	Math	Reading	Language
Grade 3	NA	NA	NA
Grade 7	NA	NA	NA

Academic Performance Index, 2008

Number of students tested	5,550
Number of valid scores	5,104
2007 API (base)	598
2008 API (growth)	618

SAT Testing, 2006-07

Enrollment, Grade 12	1,581
Number taking test	561
percent taking test	35.5%
percent with total score 1,500+	5.90%

Average Scores:

Math	Verbal	Writing	Total
424	415	414	1,253

Federal No Child Left Behind, 2008

(Adequate Yearly Progress standards met)

	Participation Rate	Pct Proficient
ELA	Yes	No
Math	Yes	No

API criteria	Yes
Graduation rate	Yes
# criteria met/possible	26/23

Other school districts for this city

(see Appendix E for information on these districts)

Lawndale Elem

See Introduction for an explanation of all data sources.

Demographics & Socio-Economic Characteristics

(2000 Decennial Census, except as noted)

Population

1990* 23,984
2000 24,918
Male 12,070
Female 12,848
Jan. 2008 (estimate)§ 25,611
Persons per sq. mi. of land 6,739.7

Race & Hispanic Origin, 2000

Race
White 14,859
Black/African American 3,010
North American Native 273
Asian 1,433
Pacific Islander 209
Other Race 3,364
Two or more races 1,770
Hispanic origin, total 7,107
Mexican 5,733
Puerto Rican 187
Cuban 42
Other Hispanic 1,145

Age & Nativity, 2000

Under 5 years 1,714
18 years and over 18,032
65 years and over 2,997
85 years and over 429
Median Age 34.7
Native-born 21,341
Foreign-born 3,613

Educational Attainment, 2000

Population 25 years and over 15,693
Less than 9th grade 6.4%
High school grad or higher 80.0%
Bachelor's degree or higher 15.3%
Graduate degree 5.2%

Income & Poverty, 1999

Per capita income $17,002
Median household income $39,823
Median family income $45,844
Persons in poverty 13.5%
H'holds receiving public assistance 476
H'holds receiving social security 2,087

Households, 2000

Total households 8,488
With persons under 18 3,526
With persons over 65 2,046
Family households 5,960
Single person households 1,898
Persons per household 2.87
Persons per family 3.36

Household Population, 2008§§

Persons living in households 25,020
Persons living in group quarters 591
Persons per household 2.9

Labor & Employment

Total civilian labor force, 2008§§ 13,700
Unemployment rate, 2008 .... 7.5%
Total civilian labor force, 2000 11,595

Employed persons 16 years and over by occupation, 2000

Managers & professionals 2,981
Service occupations 1,988
Sales & office occupations 3,202
Farming, fishing & forestry 20
Construction & maintenance 1,152
Production & transportation 1,322
Self-employed persons 693

* US Census Bureau
** 2000 Decennial Census
§ California Department of Finance
§§ California Employment Development Dept

General Information

City of Lemon Grove
3232 Main St
Lemon Grove, CA 91945
619-825-3800

Website .... www.ci.lemon-grove.ca.us
Elevation .... 450 ft.
Land Area (sq. miles) 3.8
Water Area (sq. miles) 0
Year of Incorporation 1977
Government type .... General law
Sales tax rate 8.75%

Voters & Officials

Registered Voters, October 2008

Total 12,686
Democrats 5,539
Republicans 4,073
Declined to state 2,477

Legislative Districts

US Congressional 53
State Senatorial 39
State Assembly 78

Local Officials, 2009

Mayor .... Mary Teresa Sessom
Manager .... Graham Mitchell
City Clerk .... Susan Garcia
Attorney .... James Lough
Finance Dir .... Betty Hofman
Public Works .... NA
Planning/Dev Dir .... Robert Larkins
Building .... NA
Police Chief .... Guy Chambers
Fire Chief .... Jon Torchia

Public Safety

Number of officers, 2007 .... NA
Violent crimes, 2007 159
Property crimes, 2007 591
Arson, 2007 4

Public Library

Lemon Grove Library
San Diego County Library System
8073 Broadway
Lemon Grove, CA 91945
619-463-9810

Branch Librarian .... Jenne Bregstrom

Library system statistics, FY 2007

Population served 1,049,868
Internet terminals 394
Annual users .... NA

Per capita:

Operating income $33.43
percent from local government 80.6%
Operating expenditure $31.30
Total materials 1.54
Print holdings 1.32
Visits per capita 6.31

Housing & Construction

Housing Units

Total, 2008§ 8,778
Single family units, attached 716
Single family units, detached 5,801
Multiple family units 2,164
Mobile home units 97
Occupied 8,544
Vacancy rate 2.7%
Median rent, 2000** $710
Median SF home value, 2000** $164,900

New Privately Owned Housing Units Authorized by Building Permit, 2007*

	Units	Construction Cost
Single	6	$834,077
Total	6	$834,077

Municipal Finance

(For local fiscal year ended in 2006)

Revenues

Total $12,505,730
Taxes 9,421,637
Special benefits assessment 91,852
Licenses & permits 257,974
Fines & forfeitures 281,073
Revenues from use of money & property 505,832
Intergovernmental 1,391,027
Service charges 491,640
Other revenues 64,695
Other financing sources 0

Expenditures

Total $13,116,620
General government 1,270,778
Public safety 7,578,925
Transportation 1,682,115
Community development 1,178,509
Health 0
Culture & leisure 1,406,293
Other 0

Local School District

(Data from School year 2007-08 except as noted)

Grossmont Union High
PO Box 1043
La Mesa, CA 91944
(619) 644-8000

Superintendent .... Robert Collins
Grade plan PK-12
Number of schools 19
Enrollment 24,195
High school graduates, 2006-07 4,597
Dropout rate 3.3%
Pupil/teacher ratio 24.2
Average class size 25.8
Students per computer 3.3
Classrooms with internet 1,450
Avg. Daily Attendance (ADA) 19,436
Cost per ADA $8,940
Avg. Teacher Salary $68,475

California Achievement Tests 6th ed., 2008

(Pct scoring at or above 50th National Percentile Rank)

	Math	Reading	Language
Grade 3	NA	NA	NA
Grade 7	NA	NA	NA

Academic Performance Index, 2008

Number of students tested 14,311
Number of valid scores 13,392
2007 API (base) 704
2008 API (growth) 713

SAT Testing, 2006-07

Enrollment, Grade 12 5,999
Number taking test 1,875
percent taking test 31.3%
percent with total score 1,500+ 15.30%

Average Scores:

Math	Verbal	Writing	Total
513	495	494	1,502

Federal No Child Left Behind, 2008

(Adequate Yearly Progress standards met)

	Participation Rate	Pct Proficient
ELA	Yes	No
Math	Yes	No

API criteria .... Yes
Graduation rate .... Yes
\# criteria met/possible 34/31

Other school districts for this city

(see Appendix E for information on these districts)

Lemon Grove

See Introduction for an explanation of all data sources.

Demographics & Socio-Economic Characteristics

(2000 Decennial Census, except as noted)

Population

1990* . . . 13,622
2000 . . . 19,712
Male . . . 9,768
Female . . . 9,944
Jan. 2008 (estimate)§ . . . 24,502
Persons per sq. mi. of land . . . 2,882.6

Race & Hispanic Origin, 2000

Race
White . . . 11,687
Black/African American . . . 1,435
North American Native . . . 313
Asian . . . 1,649
Pacific Islander . . . 65
Other Race . . . 3,420
Two or more races . . . 1,143
Hispanic origin, total . . . 6,013
Mexican . . . 5,068
Puerto Rican . . . 91
Cuban . . . 12
Other Hispanic . . . 842

Age & Nativity, 2000

Under 5 years . . . 1,895
18 years and over . . . 12,884
65 years and over . . . 1,249
85 years and over . . . 83
Median Age . . . 27.8
Native-born . . . 16,694
Foreign-born . . . 2,830

Educational Attainment, 2000

Population 25 years and over . . . 10,509
Less than 9th grade . . . 10.1%
High school grad or higher . . . 79.0%
Bachelor's degree or higher . . . 16.5%
Graduate degree . . . 4.5%

Income & Poverty, 1999

Per capita income . . . $15,876
Median household income . . . $40,314
Median family income . . . $44,006
Persons in poverty . . . 13.1%
H'holds receiving public assistance . . . 412
H'holds receiving social security . . . 1,000

Households, 2000

Total households . . . 6,450
With persons under 18 . . . 3,361
With persons over 65 . . . 953
Family households . . . 4,926
Single person households . . . 1,121
Persons per household . . . 3.06
Persons per family . . . 3.46

Household Population, 2008§§

Persons living in households . . . 24,500
Persons living in group quarters . . . 2
Persons per household . . . 3.2

Labor & Employment

Total civilian labor force, 2008§§ . . . 11,000
Unemployment rate, 2008 . . . 8.9%
Total civilian labor force, 2000 . . . 8,448

Employed persons 16 years and over by occupation, 2000

Managers & professionals . . . 2,018
Service occupations . . . 1,671
Sales & office occupations . . . 1,978
Farming, fishing & forestry . . . 332
Construction & maintenance . . . 596
Production & transportation . . . 887
Self-employed persons . . . 392

* US Census Bureau
** 2000 Decennial Census
§ California Department of Finance
§§ California Employment Development Dept

General Information

City of Lemoore
119 Fox St
Lemoore, CA 93245
559-924-6700

Website . . . www.lemoore.com
Elevation . . . NA
Land Area (sq. miles) . . . 8.5
Water Area (sq. miles) . . . 0
Year of Incorporation . . . 1900
Government type . . . Charter
Sales tax rate . . . 8.25%

Voters & Officials

Registered Voters, October 2008

Total . . . 9,611
Democrats . . . 3,105
Republicans . . . 4,614
Declined to state . . . 1,526

Legislative Districts

US Congressional . . . 20
State Senatorial . . . 16
State Assembly . . . 30

Local Officials, 2009

Mayor . . . John Murray
Manager . . . Jeff Briltz
City Clerk . . . Nanci Lima
Attorney . . . Don Neufeld
Finance Dir . . . Nancy Cota
Public Works . . . David Wlaschin
Planning/Dev Dir . . . Holly Smyth
Building . . . NA
Police Chief . . . Kim Morrell
Emergency/Fire Dir . . . John Gibson

Public Safety

Number of officers, 2007 . . . 31
Violent crimes, 2007 . . . 79
Property crimes, 2007 . . . 733
Arson, 2007 . . . NA

Public Library

Lemoore Library
Kings County Library System
457 C St
Lemoore, CA 93245
559-924-2188

Branch Librarian . . . Christine Baize

Library system statistics, FY 2007

Population served . . . 151,381
Internet terminals . . . 59
Annual users . . . 42,581

Per capita:

Operating income . . . $11.91
percent from local government . . . 86.5%
Operating expenditure . . . $11.91
Total materials . . . 1.20
Print holdings . . . 1.17
Visits per capita . . . NA

Housing & Construction

Housing Units

Total, 2008§ . . . 8,196
Single family units, attached . . . 154
Single family units, detached . . . 5,490
Multiple family units . . . 2,223
Mobile home units . . . 329
Occupied . . . 7,748
Vacancy rate . . . 5.5%
Median rent, 2000** . . . $541
Median SF home value, 2000** . . . $110,900

New Privately Owned Housing Units Authorized by Building Permit, 2007*

	Units	Construction Cost
Single	96	$15,547,258
Total	108	$16,501,472

Municipal Finance

(For local fiscal year ended in 2006)

Revenues

Total . . . $23,127,434
Taxes . . . 7,147,829
Special benefits assessment . . . 224,311
Licenses & permits . . . 480,915
Fines & forfeitures . . . 84,331
Revenues from use of money & property . . . 866,610
Intergovernmental . . . 1,447,491
Service charges . . . 9,203,572
Other revenues . . . 3,672,375
Other financing sources . . . 0

Expenditures

Total . . . $18,547,568
General government . . . 1,495,932
Public safety . . . 3,732,605
Transportation . . . 1,939,974
Community development . . . 2,991,636
Health . . . 3,791,672
Culture & leisure . . . 2,237,050
Other . . . 0

Local School District

(Data from School year 2007-08 except as noted)

Lemoore Union High
5 Powell Ave
Lemoore, CA 93245
(559) 924-6610

Superintendent . . . Dwight Miller
Grade plan . . . 9-12
Number of schools . . . 5
Enrollment . . . 2,264
High school graduates, 2006-07 . . . 379
Dropout rate . . . 3.4%
Pupil/teacher ratio . . . 21.0
Average class size . . . 24.2
Students per computer . . . 2.5
Classrooms with internet . . . 115
Avg. Daily Attendance (ADA) . . . 2,134
Cost per ADA . . . $8,166
Avg. Teacher Salary . . . $61,329

California Achievement Tests 6th ed., 2008

(Pct scoring at or above 50th National Percentile Rank)

	Math	Reading	Language
Grade 3	NA	NA	NA
Grade 7	NA	NA	NA

Academic Performance Index, 2008

Number of students tested . . . 1,645
Number of valid scores . . . 1,533
2007 API (base) . . . 695
2008 API (growth) . . . 704

SAT Testing, 2006-07

Enrollment, Grade 12 . . . 475
Number taking test . . . 125
percent taking test . . . 26.3%
percent with total score 1,500+ . . . 9.90%

Average Scores:

Math	Verbal	Writing	Total
488	468	458	1,414

Federal No Child Left Behind, 2008

(Adequate Yearly Progress standards met)

	Participation Rate	Pct Proficient
ELA	Yes	Yes
Math	Yes	No

API criteria . . . Yes
Graduation rate . . . Yes
\# criteria met/possible . . . 18/16

Other school districts for this city

(see Appendix E for information on these districts)

Island Union Elem, Lemoore Union Elem, Central Union Elem

See Introduction for an explanation of all data sources.

Demographics & Socio-Economic Characteristics
(2000 Decennial Census, except as noted)

Population
1990* . . . 7,248
2000 . . . 11,205
Male . . . 5,485
Female . . . 5,720
Jan. 2008 (estimate)§ . . . 39,758
Persons per sq. mi. of land . . . 2,172.6

Race & Hispanic Origin, 2000
Race
White . . . 8,924
Black/African American . . . 49
North American Native . . . 141
Asian . . . 121
Pacific Islander . . . 16
Other Race . . . 1,509
Two or more races . . . 445
Hispanic origin, total . . . 2,911
Mexican . . . 2,507
Puerto Rican . . . 45
Cuban . . . 7
Other Hispanic . . . 352

Age & Nativity, 2000
Under 5 years . . . 921
18 years and over . . . 7,843
65 years and over . . . 1,262
85 years and over . . . 149
Median Age . . . 32.4
Native-born . . . 9,609
Foreign-born . . . 1,330

Educational Attainment, 2000
Population 25 years and over . . . 6,675
Less than 9th grade . . . 8.7%
High school grad or higher . . . 80.6%
Bachelor's degree or higher . . . 11.1%
Graduate degree . . . 3.5%

Income & Poverty, 1999
Per capita income . . . $19,447
Median household income . . . $45,547
Median family income . . . $51,166
Persons in poverty . . . 11.9%
H'holds receiving public assistance . . . 209
H'holds receiving social security . . . 969

Households, 2000
Total households . . . 3,874
With persons under 18 . . . 1,700
With persons over 65 . . . 847
Family households . . . 3,033
Single person households . . . 666
Persons per household . . . 2.86
Persons per family . . . 3.20

Household Population, 2008§§
Persons living in households . . . 39,644
Persons living in group quarters . . . 114
Persons per household . . . 2.3

Labor & Employment
Total civilian labor force, 2008§§ . . . 7,600
Unemployment rate, 2008 . . . 12.0%
Total civilian labor force, 2000 . . . 5,164

Employed persons 16 years and over by occupation, 2000
Managers & professionals . . . 1,121
Service occupations . . . 687
Sales & office occupations . . . 1,310
Farming, fishing & forestry . . . 60
Construction & maintenance . . . 714
Production & transportation . . . 902
Self-employed persons . . . 336

* US Census Bureau
** 2000 Decennial Census
§ California Department of Finance
§§ California Employment Development Dept

General Information
City of Lincoln
600 Sixth St
Lincoln, CA 95648
916-434-2400

Website . . . www.ci.lincoln.ca.us
Elevation . . . 164 ft.
Land Area (sq. miles) . . . 18.3
Water Area (sq. miles) . . . 0
Year of Incorporation . . . 1890
Government type . . . General law
Sales tax rate . . . 8.25%

Voters & Officials

Registered Voters, October 2008
Total . . . 23,187
Democrats . . . 7,226
Republicans . . . 11,642
Declined to state . . . 3,755

Legislative Districts
US Congressional . . . 4
State Senatorial . . . 4
State Assembly . . . 4

Local Officials, 2009
Mayor . . . Spencer Short
Manager . . . Jim Estep
City Clerk . . . Patricia Avila
Attorney . . . Tim Hayes
Admin Svcs Dir . . . Steven Ambrose
Public Works . . . John Pedri
Planning/Dev Dir . . . Rodney Campbell
Building . . . NA
Police Chief . . . Brian Vizzusi
Fire Chief . . . Dave Whitt

Public Safety
Number of officers, 2007 . . . 36
Violent crimes, 2007 . . . 54
Property crimes, 2007 . . . 456
Arson, 2007 . . . 6

Public Library
Lincoln Public Library
590 Fifth St
Lincoln, CA 95648
916-645-3607

Director . . . Darla Wegener

Library statistics, FY 2007
Population served . . . 37,410
Internet terminals . . . 7
Annual users . . . 5,608

Per capita:
Operating income . . . $15.22
percent from local government . . . 98.1%
Operating expenditure . . . $15.22
Total materials . . . 0.79
Print holdings . . . 0.76
Visits per capita . . . 0.68

Housing & Construction

Housing Units
Total, 2008§ . . . 17,514
Single family units, attached . . . 236
Single family units, detached . . . 15,967
Multiple family units . . . 1,215
Mobile home units . . . 96
Occupied . . . 16,900
Vacancy rate . . . 3.5%
Median rent, 2000** . . . $646
Median SF home value, 2000** . . . $142,800

New Privately Owned Housing Units Authorized by Building Permit, 2007*

	Units	Construction Cost
Single	379	$92,831,456
Total	403	$96,008,105

Municipal Finance
(For local fiscal year ended in 2006)

Revenues
Total . . . $82,014,516
Taxes . . . 11,386,804
Special benefits assessment . . . 2,251,429
Licenses & permits . . . 13,944,693
Fines & forfeitures . . . 108,477
Revenues from use of money & property . . . 2,511,140
Intergovernmental . . . 5,180,304
Service charges . . . 43,923,365
Other revenues . . . 2,708,304
Other financing sources . . . 0

Expenditures
Total . . . $96,511,748
General government . . . 6,762,630
Public safety . . . 9,526,984
Transportation . . . 29,370,179
Community development . . . 24,758,888
Health . . . 13,955,913
Culture & leisure . . . 1,714,014
Other . . . 0

Local School District
(Data from School year 2007-08 except as noted)
Western Placer Unified
600 Sixth St, Fourth Floor
Lincoln, CA 95648
(916) 645-6350

Superintendent . . . Scott Leaman
Grade plan . . . K-12
Number of schools . . . 12
Enrollment . . . 9,182
High school graduates, 2006-07 . . . 648
Dropout rate . . . 7.1%
Pupil/teacher ratio . . . 21.5
Average class size . . . 16.4
Students per computer . . . 5.9
Classrooms with internet . . . 414
Avg. Daily Attendance (ADA) . . . 5,884
Cost per ADA . . . $7,482
Avg. Teacher Salary . . . $61,629

California Achievement Tests 6th ed., 2008
(Pct scoring at or above 50th National Percentile Rank)

	Math	Reading	Language
Grade 3	67%	47%	50%
Grade 7	61%	56%	50%

Academic Performance Index, 2008
Number of students tested . . . 4,652
Number of valid scores . . . 4,316
2007 API (base) . . . 768
2008 API (growth) . . . 787

SAT Testing, 2006-07
Enrollment, Grade 12 . . . 629
Number taking test . . . 80
percent taking test . . . 12.7%
percent with total score 1,500+ . . . 7.20%

Average Scores:

Math	Verbal	Writing	Total
524	537	521	1,582

Federal No Child Left Behind, 2008
(Adequate Yearly Progress standards met)

	Participation Rate	Pct Proficient
ELA	Yes	No
Math	Yes	Yes

API criteria . . . Yes
Graduation rate . . . Yes
\# criteria met/possible . . . 32/29

Other school districts for this city
(see Appendix E for information on these districts)
None

See Introduction for an explanation of all data sources.

Demographics & Socio-Economic Characteristics
(2000 Decennial Census, except as noted)

Population
1990* . . . 8,338
2000 . . . 10,297
Male . . . 5,215
Female . . . 5,082
Jan. 2008 (estimate)§ . . . 11,546
Persons per sq. mi. of land . . . 4,810.8

Race & Hispanic Origin, 2000
Race
White . . . 4,616
Black/African American . . . 59
North American Native . . . 155
Asian . . . 109
Pacific Islander . . . 15
Other Race . . . 4,970
Two or more races . . . 373
Hispanic origin, total . . . 8,029
Mexican . . . 7,140
Puerto Rican . . . 40
Cuban . . . 0
Other Hispanic . . . 849

Age & Nativity, 2000
Under 5 years . . . 1,141
18 years and over . . . 6,385
65 years and over . . . 936
85 years and over . . . 149
Median Age . . . 25.4
Native-born . . . 6,739
Foreign-born . . . 3,559

Educational Attainment, 2000
Population 25 years and over . . . 5,055
Less than 9th grade . . . 44.0%
High school grad or higher . . . 38.4%
Bachelor's degree or higher . . . 5.2%
Graduate degree . . . 1.1%

Income & Poverty, 1999
Per capita income . . . $8,230
Median household income . . . $24,305
Median family income . . . $24,934
Persons in poverty . . . 39.3%
H'holds receiving public assistance . . . 339
H'holds receiving social security . . . 672

Households, 2000
Total households . . . 2,717
With persons under 18 . . . 1,599
With persons over 65 . . . 638
Family households . . . 2,209
Single person households . . . 432
Persons per household . . . 3.74
Persons per family . . . 4.16

Household Population, 2008§§
Persons living in households . . . 11,397
Persons living in group quarters . . . 149
Persons per household . . . 3.8

Labor & Employment
Total civilian labor force, 2008§§ . . . 5,100
Unemployment rate, 2008 . . . 13.0%
Total civilian labor force, 2000 . . . 3,911

Employed persons 16 years and over by occupation, 2000
Managers & professionals . . . 426
Service occupations . . . 497
Sales & office occupations . . . 522
Farming, fishing & forestry . . . 1,112
Construction & maintenance . . . 191
Production & transportation . . . 569
Self-employed persons . . . 188

* US Census Bureau
** 2000 Decennial Census
§ California Department of Finance
§§ California Employment Development Dept

General Information
City of Lindsay
251 E Honolulu St
PO Box 369
Lindsay, CA 93247
559-562-7103

Website . . . www.lindsay.ca.us
Elevation . . . 383 ft.
Land Area (sq. miles) . . . 2.4
Water Area (sq. miles) . . . 0
Year of Incorporation . . . 1910
Government type . . . Chartered
Sales tax rate . . . 8.75%

Voters & Officials
Registered Voters, October 2008
Total . . . 2,306
Democrats . . . 1,138
Republicans . . . 657
Declined to state . . . 414

Legislative Districts
US Congressional . . . 21
State Senatorial . . . 16
State Assembly . . . 34

Local Officials, 2009
Mayor . . . Ed Murray
Manager . . . Scot B. Townsend
City Clerk . . . Kenny D. Walker
Attorney . . . Julia Lew
Finance Dir . . . Kenny C. Walker
Public Works . . . Michael Camarena
Community Dev Dir . . . Diane Bucaroff
Building . . . George Lowery
Police Chief . . . Richard Wilkinson
Emergency/Fire Dir. . . . Richard Wilkinson

Public Safety
Number of officers, 2007 . . . 14
Violent crimes, 2007 . . . 75
Property crimes, 2007 . . . 406
Arson, 2007 . . . 1

Public Library
Lindsay Library
Tulare County Free Library System
165 N Gale Hill St
Lindsay, CA 93247
559-562-3021

Branch Librarian . . . Brenda Biesterfeld

Library system statistics, FY 2007
Population served . . . 321,604
Internet terminals . . . 83
Annual users . . . 86,301

Per capita:
Operating income . . . $10.97
percent from local government . . . 86.0%
Operating expenditure . . . $8.74
Total materials . . . 1.08
Print holdings . . . 1.05
Visits per capita . . . 0.96

Housing & Construction
Housing Units
Total, 2008§ . . . 3,146
Single family units, attached . . . 204
Single family units, detached . . . 2,033
Multiple family units . . . 724
Mobile home units . . . 185
Occupied . . . 2,984
Vacancy rate . . . 5.2%
Median rent, 2000** . . . $466
Median SF home value, 2000** . . . $79,600

New Privately Owned Housing Units Authorized by Building Permit, 2007*

	Units	Construction Cost
Single	1	$71,670
Total	1	$71,670

Municipal Finance
(For local fiscal year ended in 2006)

Revenues
Total . . . $12,566,315
Taxes . . . 2,720,730
Special benefits assessment . . . 27,500
Licenses & permits . . . 175,085
Fines & forfeitures . . . 43,262
Revenues from use of money & property . . . 124,246
Intergovernmental . . . 5,395,886
Service charges . . . 3,845,108
Other revenues . . . 234,498
Other financing sources . . . 0

Expenditures
Total . . . $12,376,205
General government . . . 873,839
Public safety . . . 2,337,614
Transportation . . . 2,384,164
Community development . . . 3,055,649
Health . . . 2,040,297
Culture & leisure . . . 411,316
Other . . . 0

Local School District
(Data from School year 2007-08 except as noted)
Lindsay Unified
371 East Hermosa St
Lindsay, CA 93247
(559) 562-5111

Superintendent . . . Janet Kliegl
Grade plan . . . K-12
Number of schools . . . 7
Enrollment . . . 4,041
High school graduates, 2006-07 . . . 179
Dropout rate . . . 7.1%
Pupil/teacher ratio . . . 20.1
Average class size . . . 23.6
Students per computer . . . 2.4
Classrooms with internet . . . 1,681
Avg. Daily Attendance (ADA) . . . 4,253
Cost per ADA . . . $7,844
Avg. Teacher Salary . . . $58,450

California Achievement Tests 6th ed., 2008
(Pct scoring at or above 50th National Percentile Rank)

	Math	Reading	Language
Grade 3	34%	10%	17%
Grade 7	30%	32%	26%

Academic Performance Index, 2008
Number of students tested . . . 3,073
Number of valid scores . . . 2,828
2007 API (base) . . . 645
2008 API (growth) . . . 635

SAT Testing, 2006-07
Enrollment, Grade 12 . . . 224
Number taking test . . . 52
percent taking test . . . 23.2%
percent with total score 1,500+ . . . 4.50%

Average Scores:

Math	Verbal	Writing	Total
448	424	436	1,308

Federal No Child Left Behind, 2008
(Adequate Yearly Progress standards met)

	Participation Rate	Pct Proficient
ELA	Yes	No
Math	Yes	No

API criteria . . . Yes
Graduation rate . . . No
\# criteria met/possible . . . 22/16

Other school districts for this city
(see Appendix E for information on these districts)
None

See Introduction for an explanation of all data sources.

Demographics & Socio-Economic Characteristics

(2000 Decennial Census, except as noted)

Population

1990* . . . 4,320
2000 . . . 6,229
Male . . . 2,974
Female . . . 3,255
Jan. 2008 (estimate)§ . . . 8,539
Persons per sq. mi. of land . . . 4,494.2

Race & Hispanic Origin, 2000

Race
White . . . 3,094
Black/African American . . . 98
North American Native . . . 118
Asian . . . 600
Pacific Islander . . . 4
Other Race . . . 2,032
Two or more races . . . 283
Hispanic origin, total . . . 3,028
Mexican . . . 2,722
Puerto Rican . . . 10
Cuban . . . 1
Other Hispanic . . . 295

Age & Nativity, 2000

Under 5 years . . . 479
18 years and over . . . 4,172
65 years and over . . . 665
85 years and over . . . 103
Median Age . . . 30.5
Native-born . . . 4,356
Foreign-born . . . 2,086

Educational Attainment, 2000

Population 25 years and over . . . 3,710
Less than 9th grade . . . 26.3%
High school grad or higher . . . 50.3%
Bachelor's degree or higher . . . 4.6%
Graduate degree . . . 0.9%

Income & Poverty, 1999

Per capita income . . . $9,571
Median household income . . . $25,754
Median family income . . . $31,075
Persons in poverty . . . 29.5%
H'holds receiving public assistance . . . 177
H'holds receiving social security . . . 570

Households, 2000

Total households . . . 1,729
With persons under 18 . . . 931
With persons over 65 . . . 433
Family households . . . 1,393
Single person households . . . 294
Persons per household . . . 3.43
Persons per family . . . 3.85

Household Population, 2008§§

Persons living in households . . . 8,147
Persons living in group quarters . . . 392
Persons per household . . . 3.6

Labor & Employment

Total civilian labor force, 2008§§ . . . 2,700
Unemployment rate, 2008 . . . 22.6%
Total civilian labor force, 2000 . . . 2,216

Employed persons 16 years and over by occupation, 2000

Managers & professionals . . . 256
Service occupations . . . 268
Sales & office occupations . . . 260
Farming, fishing & forestry . . . 338
Construction & maintenance . . . 206
Production & transportation . . . 406
Self-employed persons . . . 62

* US Census Bureau
** 2000 Decennial Census
§ California Department of Finance
§§ California Employment Development Dept

General Information

City of Live Oak
9955 Live Oak Blvd
Live Oak, CA 95953
530-695-2112

Website . . . www.liveoakcity.org
Elevation . . . 75 ft.
Land Area (sq. miles) . . . 1.9
Water Area (sq. miles) . . . 0
Year of Incorporation . . . 1947
Government type . . . General law
Sales tax rate . . . 8.25%

Voters & Officials

Registered Voters, October 2008

Total . . . 2,808
Democrats . . . 1,283
Republicans . . . 923
Declined to state . . . 476

Legislative Districts

US Congressional . . . 17
State Senatorial . . . 4
State Assembly . . . 2

Local Officials, 2009

Mayor . . . Diane Hodges
City Manager . . . Jim Goodwin
City Clerk . . . Melissa Dempsey
Attorney . . . Brant Bordsen
Finance Dir . . . Satwant Singh Takhar
Public Works . . . NA
Planning Dir . . . (vacant)
Building . . . James Little
Police Chief . . . James Casner
Fire Captain . . . Dan Root

Public Safety

Number of officers, 2007 . . . NA
Violent crimes, 2007 . . . NA
Property crimes, 2007 . . . NA
Arson, 2007 . . . NA

Public Library

Live Oak Library
Sutter County Library System
10321 Live Oak Blvd
Live Oak, CA 95953
530-695-2021

Branch Librarian . . . Arlene Wheeler

Library system statistics, FY 2007

Population served . . . 93,919
Internet terminals . . . 53
Annual users . . . 112,000

Per capita:

Operating income . . . $13.36
percent from local government . . . 64.0%
Operating expenditure . . . $13.36
Total materials . . . 1.51
Print holdings . . . 1.47
Visits per capita . . . 10.49

Housing & Construction

Housing Units

Total, 2008§ . . . 2,412
Single family units, attached . . . 92
Single family units, detached . . . 1,936
Multiple family units . . . 242
Mobile home units . . . 142
Occupied . . . 2,292
Vacancy rate . . . 5.0%
Median rent, 2000** . . . $385
Median SF home value, 2000** . . . $85,700

New Privately Owned Housing Units Authorized by Building Permit, 2007*

	Units	Construction Cost
Single	53	$9,860,270
Total	53	$9,860,270

Municipal Finance

(For local fiscal year ended in 2006)

Revenues

Total . . . $18,217,866
Taxes . . . 3,020,281
Special benefits assessment . . . 169,237
Licenses & permits . . . 1,255,178
Fines & forfeitures . . . 12,070
Revenues from use of money & property . . . 615,942
Intergovernmental . . . 1,774,360
Service charges . . . 6,833,506
Other revenues . . . 3,176,057
Other financing sources . . . 1,361,235

Expenditures

Total . . . $10,275,847
General government . . . 764,528
Public safety . . . 897,892
Transportation . . . 563,673
Community development . . . 1,837,980
Health . . . 2,406,554
Culture & leisure . . . 650,853
Other . . . 0

Local School District

(Data from School year 2007-08 except as noted)

Live Oak Unified
2201 Pennington Rd
Live Oak, CA 95953
(530) 695-5400

Superintendent . . . Tom Pritchard
Grade plan . . . K-12
Number of schools . . . 6
Enrollment . . . 1,906
High school graduates, 2006-07 . . . 101
Dropout rate . . . 5.9%
Pupil/teacher ratio . . . 21.6
Average class size . . . 25.2
Students per computer . . . 3.7
Classrooms with internet . . . 99
Avg. Daily Attendance (ADA) . . . 1,874
Cost per ADA . . . $7,758
Avg. Teacher Salary . . . $59,008

California Achievement Tests 6th ed., 2008

(Pct scoring at or above 50th National Percentile Rank)

	Math	Reading	Language
Grade 3	48%	22%	34%
Grade 7	51%	44%	43%

Academic Performance Index, 2008

Number of students tested . . . 1,472
Number of valid scores . . . 1,376
2007 API (base) . . . 697
2008 API (growth) . . . 705

SAT Testing, 2006-07

Enrollment, Grade 12 . . . 119
Number taking test . . . 40
percent taking test . . . 33.6%
percent with total score 1,500+ . . . 11.80%

Average Scores:

Math	Verbal	Writing	Total
481	452	451	1,384

Federal No Child Left Behind, 2008

(Adequate Yearly Progress standards met)

	Participation Rate	Pct Proficient
ELA	Yes	No
Math	Yes	No

API criteria . . . Yes
Graduation rate . . . Yes
\# criteria met/possible . . . 30/25

Other school districts for this city

(see Appendix E for information on these districts)

Nuestro Elem

See Introduction for an explanation of all data sources.

Demographics & Socio-Economic Characteristics†

(2007 American Community Survey, except as noted)

Population

1990* 56,741
2007 79,213
Male 36,957
Female 42,256
Jan. 2008 (estimate)§ 83,604
Persons per sq. mi. of land 3,498.1

Race & Hispanic Origin, 2007

Race
White 59,145
Black/African American 1,595
North American Native 347
Asian 6,447
Pacific Islander 168
Other Race 7,327
Two or more races 4,184
Hispanic origin, total 13,922
Mexican .... NA
Puerto Rican .... NA
Cuban .... NA
Other Hispanic .... NA

Age & Nativity, 2007

Under 5 years 3,641
18 years and over 57,866
65 years and over 6,498
85 years and over 1,332
Median Age 37.5
Native-born 66,737
Foreign-born 12,476

Educational Attainment, 2007

Population 25 years and over 51,138
Less than 9th grade 4.9%
High school grad or higher 91.7%
Bachelor's degree or higher 39.0%
Graduate degree 12.9%

Income & Poverty, 2007

Per capita income $40,254
Median household income $92,300
Median family income $102,606
Persons in poverty 8.4%
H'holds receiving public assistance 769
H'holds receiving social security 4,510

Households, 2007

Total households 28,092
With persons under 18 10,597
With persons over 65 4,316
Family households 19,475
Single person households 7,098
Persons per household 2.80
Persons per family 3.33

Household Population, 2008§§

Persons living in households 83,315
Persons living in group quarters 289
Persons per household 2.8

Labor & Employment

Total civilian labor force, 2008§§ 41,900
Unemployment rate, 2008 .... 4.0%
Total civilian labor force, 2000* 39,874

Employed persons 16 years and over by occupation, 2007

Managers & professionals 18,742
Service occupations 5,423
Sales & office occupations 10,712
Farming, fishing & forestry 0
Construction & maintenance 3,434
Production & transportation 3,248
Self-employed persons 2,014

† see Appendix D for 2000 Decennial Census Data
* US Census Bureau
** 2007 American Community Survey
§ California Department of Finance
§§ California Employment Development Dept

General Information

City of Livermore
1052 S Livermore Ave
Livermore, CA 94550
925-960-4000

Website .... www.ci.livermore.ca.us
Elevation .... 486 ft.
Land Area (sq. miles) 23.9
Water Area (sq. miles) 0
Year of Incorporation 1876
Government type .... General law
Sales tax rate 9.75%

Voters & Officials

Registered Voters, October 2008

Total 47,483
Democrats 18,779
Republicans 16,776
Declined to state 9,867

Legislative Districts

US Congressional 10
State Senatorial 9
State Assembly 15

Local Officials, 2009

Mayor .... Marshall Kamena
Manager .... Linda Barton
City Clerk .... Susan Gibbs
Attorney .... John Pomidor
Finance Dir .... Monica Potter
Public Works .... Dan McIntyre
Comm Dev Dir .... Marc Roberts
Building .... Marc Roberts
Police Chief .... Steve Sweeney
Fire Chief .... Bill Cody

Public Safety

Number of officers, 2007 89
Violent crimes, 2007 169
Property crimes, 2007 2,069
Arson, 2007 31

Public Library

Livermore Public Library
Livermore Public Library System
1188 S Livermore Ave
Livermore, CA 94550
925-373-5500

Director .... Susan Gallinger

Library system statistics, FY 2007

Population served 82,845
Internet terminals 87
Annual users 169,109

Per capita:

Operating income $67.26
percent from local government 91.1%
Operating expenditure $60.74
Total materials 3.22
Print holdings 2.93
Visits per capita 8.11

Housing & Construction

Housing Units

Total, 2008§ 29,955
Single family units, attached 2,621
Single family units, detached 21,624
Multiple family units 5,279
Mobile home units 431
Occupied 29,406
Vacancy rate 1.8%
Median rent, 2007** $1,261
Median SF home value, 2007** $666,000

New Privately Owned Housing Units Authorized by Building Permit, 2007*

	Units	Construction Cost
Single	142	$43,816,304
Total	191	$53,486,466

Municipal Finance

(For local fiscal year ended in 2006)

Revenues

Total $144,901,748
Taxes 53,791,315
Special benefits assessment 1,760,299
Licenses & permits 2,155,478
Fines & forfeitures 699,407
Revenues from use of money & property 7,005,866
Intergovernmental 8,261,898
Service charges 58,266,685
Other revenues 12,960,800
Other financing sources 0

Expenditures

Total $140,798,238
General government 15,539,296
Public safety 36,117,966
Transportation 39,428,770
Community development 17,042,235
Health 14,585,815
Culture & leisure 8,877,781
Other 0

Local School District

(Data from School year 2007-08 except as noted)

Livermore Valley Joint Unified
685 East Jack London Blvd
Livermore, CA 94551
(925) 606-3200

Superintendent .... Brenda Miller
Grade plan K-12
Number of schools 19
Enrollment 13,201
High school graduates, 2006-07 1,004
Dropout rate 2.4%
Pupil/teacher ratio 21.2
Average class size 24.7
Students per computer 4.0
Classrooms with internet 664
Avg. Daily Attendance (ADA) 13,052
Cost per ADA $7,850
Avg. Teacher Salary $63,827

California Achievement Tests 6th ed., 2008

(Pct scoring at or above 50th National Percentile Rank)

	Math	Reading	Language
Grade 3	74%	53%	62%
Grade 7	60%	60%	57%

Academic Performance Index, 2008

Number of students tested 10,083
Number of valid scores 9,622
2007 API (base) 790
2008 API (growth) 793

SAT Testing, 2006-07

Enrollment, Grade 12 1,108
Number taking test 458
percent taking test 41.3%
percent with total score 1,500+ 29.00%

Average Scores:

Math	Verbal	Writing	Total
555	540	534	1,629

Federal No Child Left Behind, 2008

(Adequate Yearly Progress standards met)

	Participation Rate	Pct Proficient
ELA	Yes	No
Math	Yes	No

API criteria .... Yes
Graduation rate .... Yes
\# criteria met/possible 38/35

Other school districts for this city

(see Appendix E for information on these districts)

None

See Introduction for an explanation of all data sources.

Demographics & Socio-Economic Characteristics

(2000 Decennial Census, except as noted)

Population

1990* ... 7,317
2000 ... 10,473
Male ... 5,263
Female ... 5,210
Jan. 2008 (estimate)§ ... 13,795
Persons per sq. mi. of land ... 3,941.4

Race & Hispanic Origin, 2000

Race
White ... 3,825
Black/African American ... 77
North American Native ... 97
Asian ... 1,513
Pacific Islander ... 8
Other Race ... 4,350
Two or more races ... 603
Hispanic origin, total ... 7,521
Mexican ... 6,852
Puerto Rican ... 10
Cuban ... 0
Other Hispanic ... 659

Age & Nativity, 2000

Under 5 years ... 1,000
18 years and over ... 6,526
65 years and over ... 669
85 years and over ... 69
Median Age ... 24.9
Native-born ... 5,240
Foreign-born ... 5,110

Educational Attainment, 2000

Population 25 years and over ... 5,223
Less than 9th grade ... 46.9%
High school grad or higher ... 37.1%
Bachelor's degree or higher ... 6.2%
Graduate degree ... 1.2%

Income & Poverty, 1999

Per capita income ... $9,231
Median household income ... $32,500
Median family income ... $33,939
Persons in poverty ... 24.8%
H'holds receiving public assistance ... 221
H'holds receiving social security ... 384

Households, 2000

Total households ... 2,390
With persons under 18 ... 1,629
With persons over 65 ... 488
Family households ... 2,143
Single person households ... 208
Persons per household ... 4.37
Persons per family ... 4.57

Household Population, 2008§§

Persons living in households ... 13,758
Persons living in group quarters ... 37
Persons per household ... 4.3

Labor & Employment

Total civilian labor force, 2008§§ ... 5,100
Unemployment rate, 2008 ... 14.4%
Total civilian labor force, 2000 ... 4,249

Employed persons 16 years and over by occupation, 2000

Managers & professionals ... 417
Service occupations ... 537
Sales & office occupations ... 653
Farming, fishing & forestry ... 644
Construction & maintenance ... 272
Production & transportation ... 1,094
Self-employed persons ... 232

* US Census Bureau
** 2000 Decennial Census
§ California Department of Finance
§§ California Employment Development Dept

General Information

City of Livingston
1416 C St
Livingston, CA 95334
209-394-8041

Website ... www.livingstoncity.com
Elevation ... NA
Land Area (sq. miles) ... 3.5
Water Area (sq. miles) ... 0
Year of Incorporation ... 1922
Government type ... General law
Sales tax rate ... 8.25%

Voters & Officials

Registered Voters, October 2008

Total ... 4,043
Democrats ... 2,546
Republicans ... 811
Declined to state ... 579

Legislative Districts

US Congressional ... 18
State Senatorial ... 12
State Assembly ... 17

Local Officials, 2009

Mayor ... Gurpal Samra
Manager ... Richard Warne
City Clerk ... Martha Nateras
Attorney ... Malathy Subramanian
Finance Dir ... Antonio Silva
Public Works ... Paul Creighton
Planning/Dev Dir ... Donna Kenney
Building ... NA
Police Chief ... William Eldridge
Emergency/Fire Dir. ... Mikkel Martin

Public Safety

Number of officers, 2007 ... 19
Violent crimes, 2007 ... 97
Property crimes, 2007 ... 399
Arson, 2007 ... 3

Public Library

Livingston Branch Library
Merced County Library System
1212 Main St
Livingston, CA 95334
209-394-7330

Branch Librarian ... Yvette Enos

Library system statistics, FY 2007

Population served ... 251,510
Internet terminals ... 91
Annual users ... 124,530

Per capita:

Operating income ... $8.99
percent from local government ... 91.3%
Operating expenditure ... $8.99
Total materials ... 1.61
Print holdings ... 1.60
Visits per capita ... 1.75

Housing & Construction

Housing Units

Total, 2008§ ... 3,318
Single family units, attached ... 80
Single family units, detached ... 2,686
Multiple family units ... 511
Mobile home units ... 41
Occupied ... 3,237
Vacancy rate ... 2.4%
Median rent, 2000** ... $538
Median SF home value, 2000** ... $92,700

New Privately Owned Housing Units Authorized by Building Permit, 2007*

	Units	Construction Cost
Single	79	$15,081,984
Total	79	$15,081,984

Municipal Finance

(For local fiscal year ended in 2006)

Revenues

Total ... $17,659,601
Taxes ... 6,715,291
Special benefits assessment ... 528,628
Licenses & permits ... 872,030
Fines & forfeitures ... 85,047
Revenues from use of money & property ... 415,278
Intergovernmental ... 933,153
Service charges ... 7,810,134
Other revenues ... 300,040
Other financing sources ... 0

Expenditures

Total ... $14,329,680
General government ... 929,324
Public safety ... 3,096,833
Transportation ... 873,836
Community development ... 2,355,135
Health ... 4,604,725
Culture & leisure ... 1,028,995
Other ... 0

Local School District

(Data from School year 2007-08 except as noted)

Merced Union High
PO Box 2147
Merced, CA 95344
(209) 385-6412

Superintendent ... Scott Scambray
Grade plan ... 9-12
Number of schools ... 8
Enrollment ... 10,680
High school graduates, 2006-07 ... 1,890
Dropout rate ... 3.6%
Pupil/teacher ratio ... 21.9
Average class size ... 26.0
Students per computer ... 3.7
Classrooms with internet ... 514
Avg. Daily Attendance (ADA) ... 10,568
Cost per ADA ... $8,153
Avg. Teacher Salary ... $63,476

California Achievement Tests 6th ed., 2008

(Pct scoring at or above 50th National Percentile Rank)

	Math	Reading	Language
Grade 3	NA	NA	NA
Grade 7	NA	NA	NA

Academic Performance Index, 2008

Number of students tested ... 7,904
Number of valid scores ... 7,415
2007 API (base) ... 678
2008 API (growth) ... 700

SAT Testing, 2006-07

Enrollment, Grade 12 ... 2,234
Number taking test ... 639
percent taking test ... 28.6%
percent with total score 1,500+ ... 9.90%

Average Scores:

Math	Verbal	Writing	Total
481	461	466	1,408

Federal No Child Left Behind, 2008

(Adequate Yearly Progress standards met)

	Participation Rate	Pct Proficient
ELA	Yes	No
Math	Yes	No

API criteria ... Yes
Graduation rate ... Yes
\# criteria met/possible ... 34/31

Other school districts for this city

(see Appendix E for information on these districts)

Livingston Union Elem

See Introduction for an explanation of all data sources.

Demographics & Socio-Economic Characteristics

(2000 Decennial Census, except as noted)

Population

1990* . . . 51,874
2000 . . . 56,999
Male . . . 27,819
Female . . . 29,180
Jan. 2008 (estimate)§ . . . 63,362
Persons per sq. mi. of land . . . 5,193.6

Race & Hispanic Origin, 2000

Race
White . . . 42,421
Black/African American . . . 344
North American Native . . . 494
Asian . . . 2,881
Pacific Islander . . . 68
Other Race . . . 7,972
Two or more races . . . 2,819
Hispanic origin, total . . . 15,464
Mexican . . . 13,215
Puerto Rican . . . 176
Cuban . . . 30
Other Hispanic . . . 2,043

Age & Nativity, 2000

Under 5 years . . . 4,495
18 years and over . . . 40,908
65 years and over . . . 8,141
85 years and over . . . 1,301
Median Age . . . 34.1
Native-born . . . 46,296
Foreign-born . . . 10,741

Educational Attainment, 2000

Population 25 years and over . . . 35,047
Less than 9th grade . . . 12.4%
High school grad or higher . . . 72.9%
Bachelor's degree or higher . . . 15.6%
Graduate degree . . . 4.8%

Income & Poverty, 1999

Per capita income . . . $18,719
Median household income . . . $39,570
Median family income . . . $47,020
Persons in poverty . . . 16.4%
H'holds receiving public assistance . . . 957
H'holds receiving social security . . . 5,869

Households, 2000

Total households . . . 20,692
With persons under 18 . . . 8,068
With persons over 65 . . . 5,440
Family households . . . 14,349
Single person households . . . 5,259
Persons per household . . . 2.71
Persons per family . . . 3.25

Household Population, 2008§§

Persons living in households . . . 62,298
Persons living in group quarters . . . 1,064
Persons per household . . . 2.8

Labor & Employment

Total civilian labor force, 2008§§ . . . 32,000
Unemployment rate, 2008 . . . 7.8%
Total civilian labor force, 2000 . . . 26,111

Employed persons 16 years and over by occupation, 2000

Managers & professionals . . . 6,673
Service occupations . . . 3,583
Sales & office occupations . . . 6,245
Farming, fishing & forestry . . . 1,019
Construction & maintenance . . . 2,547
Production & transportation . . . 4,110
Self-employed persons . . . 1,750

* US Census Bureau
** 2000 Decennial Census
§ California Department of Finance
§§ California Employment Development Dept

General Information

City of Lodi
PO Box 3006
Lodi, CA 95241
209-333-6702

Website . . . www.lodi.gov
Elevation . . . 51 ft.
Land Area (sq. miles) . . . 12.2
Water Area (sq. miles) . . . 0.1
Year of Incorporation . . . 1906
Government type . . . General law
Sales tax rate . . . 8.75%

Voters & Officials

Registered Voters, October 2008

Total . . . 27,532
Democrats . . . 8,765
Republicans . . . 14,092
Declined to state . . . 3,603

Legislative Districts

US Congressional . . . 11
State Senatorial . . . 14
State Assembly . . . 10, 26

Local Officials, 2009

Mayor . . . Larry D. Hansen
City Manager . . . Blair King
City Clerk . . . Randi Johl
Attorney . . . Stephen Schwabauer
Budget Manager . . . Jordan Ayers
Public Works . . . F. Wally Sandelin
Planning/Dev Dir . . . Konradt Bartlam (Int)
Building . . . Randy Hatch
Police Chief . . . David Main
Fire Chief . . . Mike Pretz

Public Safety

Number of officers, 2007 . . . 76
Violent crimes, 2007 . . . 230
Property crimes, 2007 . . . 2,762
Arson, 2007 . . . 3

Public Library

Lodi Public Library
201 W Locust St
Lodi, CA 95240
209-333-5566

Director . . . Nancy Martinez

Library statistics, FY 2007

Population served . . . 63,395
Internet terminals . . . 20
Annual users . . . 35,260

Per capita:

Operating income . . . $26.26
percent from local government . . . 89.5%
Operating expenditure . . . $26.07
Total materials . . . 2.24
Print holdings . . . 2.14
Visits per capita . . . 4.54

Housing & Construction

Housing Units

Total, 2008§ . . . 23,353
Single family units, attached . . . 1,487
Single family units, detached . . . 15,127
Multiple family units . . . 6,274
Mobile home units . . . 465
Occupied . . . 22,604
Vacancy rate . . . 3.2%
Median rent, 2000** . . . $621
Median SF home value, 2000** . . . $141,500

New Privately Owned Housing Units Authorized by Building Permit, 2007*

	Units	Construction Cost
Single	20	$3,944,066
Total	20	$3,944,066

Municipal Finance

(For local fiscal year ended in 2006)

Revenues

Total . . . $182,074,456
Taxes . . . 41,486,970
Special benefits assessment . . . 0
Licenses & permits . . . 85,460
Fines & forfeitures . . . 1,112,525
Revenues from use of money & property . . . 2,314,283
Intergovernmental . . . 7,019,572
Service charges . . . 80,197,863
Other revenues . . . 49,857,783
Other financing sources . . . 0

Expenditures

Total . . . $127,262,062
General government . . . 8,760,332
Public safety . . . 22,091,631
Transportation . . . 9,567,422
Community development . . . 3,662,142
Health . . . 6,825,799
Culture & leisure . . . 6,304,376
Other . . . 0

Local School District

(Data from School year 2007-08 except as noted)

Lodi Unified
1305 East Vine St
Lodi, CA 95240
(209) 331-7000

Superintendent . . . Cathy Washer
Grade plan . . . K-12
Number of schools . . . 54
Enrollment . . . 31,609
High school graduates, 2006-07 . . . 1,655
Dropout rate . . . 3.9%
Pupil/teacher ratio . . . 19.7
Average class size . . . 24.9
Students per computer . . . 4.4
Classrooms with internet . . . 1,521
Avg. Daily Attendance (ADA) . . . 29,005
Cost per ADA . . . $8,333
Avg. Teacher Salary . . . $63,130

California Achievement Tests 6th ed., 2008

(Pct scoring at or above 50th National Percentile Rank)

	Math	Reading	Language
Grade 3	51%	31%	38%
Grade 7	46%	44%	41%

Academic Performance Index, 2008

Number of students tested . . . 22,778
Number of valid scores . . . 21,545
2007 API (base) . . . 708
2008 API (growth) . . . 720

SAT Testing, 2006-07

Enrollment, Grade 12 . . . 2,299
Number taking test . . . 588
percent taking test . . . 25.6%
percent with total score 1,500+ . . . 11.70%

Average Scores:

Math	Verbal	Writing	Total
515	484	481	1,480

Federal No Child Left Behind, 2008

(Adequate Yearly Progress standards met)

	Participation Rate	Pct Proficient
ELA	Yes	No
Math	Yes	No

API criteria . . . Yes
Graduation rate . . . Yes
\# criteria met/possible . . . 46/39

Other school districts for this city

(see Appendix E for information on these districts)

None

See Introduction for an explanation of all data sources.

Demographics & Socio-Economic Characteristics

(2000 Decennial Census, except as noted)

Population

1990* . . . 17,400
2000 . . . 18,681
Male . . . 8,659
Female . . . 10,022
Jan. 2008 (estimate)§ . . . 22,632
Persons per sq. mi. of land . . . 3,100.3

Race & Hispanic Origin, 2000

Race
White . . . 10,121
Black/African American . . . 1,347
North American Native . . . 92
Asian . . . 4,555
Pacific Islander . . . 33
Other Race . . . 1,403
Two or more races . . . 1,130
Hispanic origin, total . . . 3,050
Mexican . . . 1,959
Puerto Rican . . . 162
Cuban . . . 50
Other Hispanic . . . 879

Age & Nativity, 2000

Under 5 years . . . 1,152
18 years and over . . . 14,581
65 years and over . . . 2,885
85 years and over . . . 625
Median Age . . . 34.0
Native-born . . . 13,054
Foreign-born . . . 5,528

Educational Attainment, 2000

Population 25 years and over . . . 12,544
Less than 9th grade . . . 5.5%
High school grad or higher . . . 88.1%
Bachelor's degree or higher . . . 44.7%
Graduate degree . . . 21.2%

Income & Poverty, 1999

Per capita income . . . $20,189
Median household income . . . $38,204
Median family income . . . $45,774
Persons in poverty . . . 14.6%
H'holds receiving public assistance . . . 280
H'holds receiving social security . . . 1,812

Households, 2000

Total households . . . 7,536
With persons under 18 . . . 2,230
With persons over 65 . . . 1,858
Family households . . . 4,499
Single person households . . . 2,351
Persons per household . . . 2.41
Persons per family . . . 3.09

Household Population, 2008§§

Persons living in households . . . 21,681
Persons living in group quarters . . . 951
Persons per household . . . 2.5

Labor & Employment

Total civilian labor force, 2008§§ . . . 10,500
Unemployment rate, 2008 . . . 4.8%
Total civilian labor force, 2000 . . . 8,644

Employed persons 16 years and over by occupation, 2000

Managers & professionals . . . 4,512
Service occupations . . . 1,258
Sales & office occupations . . . 1,662
Farming, fishing & forestry . . . 9
Construction & maintenance . . . 264
Production & transportation . . . 503
Self-employed persons . . . 628

* US Census Bureau
** 2000 Decennial Census
§ California Department of Finance
§§ California Employment Development Dept

General Information

City of Loma Linda
25541 Barton Rd
Loma Linda, CA 92354
909-799-2800

Website . . . www.lomalinda-ca.gov
Elevation . . . 1,081 ft.
Land Area (sq. miles) . . . 7.3
Water Area (sq. miles) . . . 0
Year of Incorporation . . . 1970
Government type . . . Chartered
Sales tax rate . . . 8.75%

Voters & Officials

Registered Voters, October 2008

Total . . . 10,618
Democrats . . . 3,442
Republicans . . . 4,270
Declined to state . . . 2,437

Legislative Districts

US Congressional . . . 41
State Senatorial . . . 31
State Assembly . . . 63

Local Officials, 2009

Mayor . . . Stan Brauer
Manager . . . Dennis Halloway
City Clerk . . . Pamela Byrnes-O'Camb
Attorney . . . Richard Holdaway
Finance Dir . . . Diana DeAnda
Public Works . . . Jarb Thaipeir
Planning/Dev Dir . . . Deborah Woldruff
Building . . . NA
Police Chief . . . (County)
Fire Chief . . . Jeff Sander

Public Safety

Number of officers, 2007 . . . NA
Violent crimes, 2007 . . . 28
Property crimes, 2007 . . . 613
Arson, 2007 . . . 4

Public Library

Loma Linda Branch Library
San Bernardino County Library System
25581 Barton Rd
Loma Linda, CA 92354
909-796-8621

Branch Librarian . . . Stan Sewell

Library system statistics, FY 2007

Population served . . . 1,177,092
Internet terminals . . . 12
Annual users . . . 45,343

Per capita:

Operating income . . . $14.27
percent from local government . . . 73.3%
Operating expenditure . . . $13.86
Total materials . . . 0.86
Print holdings . . . 0.79
Visits per capita . . . 5.83

Housing & Construction

Housing Units

Total, 2008§ . . . 9,163
Single family units, attached . . . 939
Single family units, detached . . . 3,925
Multiple family units . . . 3,737
Mobile home units . . . 562
Occupied . . . 8,541
Vacancy rate . . . 6.8%
Median rent, 2000** . . . $660
Median SF home value, 2000** . . . $165,200

New Privately Owned Housing Units Authorized by Building Permit, 2007*

	Units	Construction Cost
Single	40	$8,688,929
Total	42	$8,891,651

Municipal Finance

(For local fiscal year ended in 2006)

Revenues

Total . . . $28,168,356
Taxes . . . 9,663,630
Special benefits assessment . . . 700,473
Licenses & permits . . . 966,538
Fines & forfeitures . . . 505,137
Revenues from use of money & property . . . 1,703,643
Intergovernmental . . . 1,680,605
Service charges . . . 9,053,269
Other revenues . . . 3,895,061
Other financing sources . . . 0

Expenditures

Total . . . $23,054,872
General government . . . 3,134,017
Public safety . . . 5,868,322
Transportation . . . 1,634,185
Community development . . . 1,422,865
Health . . . 4,828,032
Culture & leisure . . . 646,357
Other . . . 0

Local School District

(Data from School year 2007-08 except as noted)

Redlands Unified
PO Box 3008
Redlands, CA 92374
(909) 307-5300

Superintendent . . . Lori Rhodes
Grade plan . . . K-12
Number of schools . . . 23
Enrollment . . . 21,482
High school graduates, 2006-07 . . . 1,528
Dropout rate . . . 3.4%
Pupil/teacher ratio . . . 21.9
Average class size . . . 26.4
Students per computer . . . 4.7
Classrooms with internet . . . 1,387
Avg. Daily Attendance (ADA) . . . 20,556
Cost per ADA . . . $7,835
Avg. Teacher Salary . . . $71,787

California Achievement Tests 6th ed., 2008

(Pct scoring at or above 50th National Percentile Rank)

	Math	Reading	Language
Grade 3	63%	47%	53%
Grade 7	58%	53%	52%

Academic Performance Index, 2008

Number of students tested . . . 16,436
Number of valid scores . . . 15,340
2007 API (base) . . . 774
2008 API (growth) . . . 779

SAT Testing, 2006-07

Enrollment, Grade 12 . . . 1,794
Number taking test . . . 649
percent taking test . . . 36.2%
percent with total score 1,500+ . . . 19.30%

Average Scores:

Math	Verbal	Writing	Total
520	501	506	1,527

Federal No Child Left Behind, 2008

(Adequate Yearly Progress standards met)

	Participation Rate	Pct Proficient
ELA	Yes	No
Math	Yes	Yes

API criteria . . . Yes
Graduation rate . . . Yes
\# criteria met/possible . . . 42/40

Other school districts for this city

(see Appendix E for information on these districts)

None

See Introduction for an explanation of all data sources.

Demographics & Socio-Economic Characteristics

(2000 Decennial Census, except as noted)

Population

1990* . . . 19,382
2000 . . . 20,046
Male . . . 9,616
Female . . . 10,430
Jan. 2008 (estimate)§ . . . 21,056
Persons per sq. mi. of land . . . 11,082.1

Race & Hispanic Origin, 2000

Race
White . . . 13,263
Black/African American . . . 838
North American Native . . . 141
Asian . . . 2,287
Pacific Islander . . . 105
Other Race . . . 2,163
Two or more races . . . 1,249
Hispanic origin, total . . . 5,252
Mexican . . . 3,665
Puerto Rican . . . 120
Cuban . . . 146
Other Hispanic . . . 1,321

Age & Nativity, 2000

Under 5 years . . . 1,577
18 years and over . . . 14,933
65 years and over . . . 2,180
85 years and over . . . 256
Median Age . . . 35.5
Native-born . . . 16,048
Foreign-born . . . 3,936

Educational Attainment, 2000

Population 25 years and over . . . 13,424
Less than 9th grade . . . 7.0%
High school grad or higher . . . 80.2%
Bachelor's degree or higher . . . 22.9%
Graduate degree . . . 7.2%

Income & Poverty, 1999

Per capita income . . . $22,127
Median household income . . . $43,303
Median family income . . . $53,003
Persons in poverty . . . 11.0%
H'holds receiving public assistance . . . 323
H'holds receiving social security . . . 1,643

Households, 2000

Total households . . . 8,015
With persons under 18 . . . 2,897
With persons over 65 . . . 1,665
Family households . . . 5,035
Single person households . . . 2,452
Persons per household . . . 2.48
Persons per family . . . 3.13

Household Population, 2008§§

Persons living in households . . . 20,923
Persons living in group quarters . . . 133
Persons per household . . . 2.6

Labor & Employment

Total civilian labor force, 2008§§ . . . 11,600
Unemployment rate, 2008 . . . 5.1%
Total civilian labor force, 2000 . . . 10,024

Employed persons 16 years and over by occupation, 2000

Managers & professionals . . . 3,352
Service occupations . . . 1,243
Sales & office occupations . . . 2,907
Farming, fishing & forestry . . . 14
Construction & maintenance . . . 788
Production & transportation . . . 1,159
Self-employed persons . . . 978

* US Census Bureau
** 2000 Decennial Census
§ California Department of Finance
§§ California Employment Development Dept

General Information

City of Lomita
PO Box 339
Lomita, CA 90717
310-325-7110

Website . . . www.lomita.com/cityhall
Elevation . . . 100 ft.
Land Area (sq. miles) . . . 1.9
Water Area (sq. miles) . . . 0
Year of Incorporation . . . 1964
Government type . . . General law
Sales tax rate . . . 9.25%

Voters & Officials

Registered Voters, October 2008

Total . . . 10,112
Democrats . . . 4,035
Republicans . . . 3,585
Declined to state . . . 2,008

Legislative Districts

US Congressional . . . 36
State Senatorial . . . 28
State Assembly . . . 53

Local Officials, 2009

Mayor . . . Susan Dever
Manager . . . Tom Odom V
City Clerk . . . Dawn Tomita
Attorney . . . Christi Hogin
Finance Dir . . . Patsy Chavez
Public Works . . . Wendell Johnson
Planning/Dev Dir . . . Gary Sugano
Building . . . NA
Police Chief . . . Rowina Anda
Fire Chief . . . NA

Public Safety

Number of officers, 2007 . . . NA
Violent crimes, 2007 . . . 124
Property crimes, 2007 . . . 429
Arson, 2007 . . . 4

Public Library

Lomita Library
Los Angeles County Public Library System
24200 Narbonne Ave
Lomita, CA 90717
310-539-4515

Branch Librarian . . . Linda Shimane

Library system statistics, FY 2007

Population served . . . 3,673,313
Internet terminals . . . 749
Annual users . . . 3,748,771

Per capita:

Operating income . . . $30.06
percent from local government . . . 93.6%
Operating expenditure . . . $28.36
Total materials . . . 2.22
Print holdings . . . 1.97
Visits per capita . . . 3.25

Housing & Construction

Housing Units

Total, 2008§ . . . 8,317
Single family units, attached . . . 774
Single family units, detached . . . 4,017
Multiple family units . . . 3,028
Mobile home units . . . 498
Occupied . . . 8,036
Vacancy rate . . . 3.4%
Median rent, 2000** . . . $784
Median SF home value, 2000** . . . $262,100

New Privately Owned Housing Units Authorized by Building Permit, 2007*

	Units	Construction Cost
Single	NA	NA
Total	NA	NA

Municipal Finance

(For local fiscal year ended in 2006)

Revenues

Total . . . $13,265,285
Taxes . . . 5,580,970
Special benefits assessment . . . 0
Licenses & permits . . . 492,315
Fines & forfeitures . . . 715,817
Revenues from use of money & property . . . 677,126
Intergovernmental . . . 1,706,283
Service charges . . . 3,915,194
Other revenues . . . 177,580
Other financing sources . . . 0

Expenditures

Total . . . $12,267,638
General government . . . 2,337,030
Public safety . . . 2,367,165
Transportation . . . 1,860,192
Community development . . . 1,419,586
Health . . . 0
Culture & leisure . . . 1,036,981
Other . . . 0

Local School District

(Data from School year 2007-08 except as noted)

Los Angeles Unified
333 South Beaudry Ave
Los Angeles, CA 90017
(213) 241-1000

Superintendent . . . Ramon Cortines
Grade plan . . . PK-12
Number of schools . . . 827
Enrollment . . . 693,680
High school graduates, 2006-07 . . . 28,545
Dropout rate . . . 7.8%
Pupil/teacher ratio . . . 19.8
Average class size . . . 24.9
Students per computer . . . 3.7
Classrooms with internet . . . 31,112
Avg. Daily Attendance (ADA) . . . 653,672
Cost per ADA . . . $10,053
Avg. Teacher Salary . . . $63,391

California Achievement Tests 6th ed., 2008

(Pct scoring at or above 50th National Percentile Rank)

	Math	Reading	Language
Grade 3	49%	27%	39%
Grade 7	37%	33%	33%

Academic Performance Index, 2008

Number of students tested . . . 495,046
Number of valid scores . . . 471,641
2007 API (base) . . . 662
2008 API (growth) . . . 683

SAT Testing, 2006-07

Enrollment, Grade 12 . . . 32,370
Number taking test . . . 15,447
percent taking test . . . 47.7%
percent with total score 1,500+ . . . 12.50%

Average Scores:

Math	Verbal	Writing	Total
443	438	441	1,322

Federal No Child Left Behind, 2008

(Adequate Yearly Progress standards met)

	Participation Rate	Pct Proficient
ELA	Yes	No
Math	Yes	No

API criteria . . . Yes
Graduation rate . . . Yes
criteria met/possible . . . 46/38

Other school districts for this city

(see Appendix E for information on these districts)

None

See Introduction for an explanation of all data sources.

Demographics & Socio-Economic Characteristics

(2000 Decennial Census, except as noted)

Population

1990* . . . 37,649
2000 . . . 41,103
Male . . . 21,806
Female . . . 19,297
Jan. 2008 (estimate)§ . . . 42,957
Persons per sq. mi. of land . . . 3,703.2

Race & Hispanic Origin, 2000

Race
White . . . 27,050
Black/African American . . . 3,017
North American Native . . . 651
Asian . . . 1,605
Pacific Islander . . . 133
Other Race . . . 6,446
Two or more races . . . 2,201
Hispanic origin, total . . . 15,337
Mexican . . . 12,978
Puerto Rican . . . 174
Cuban . . . 69
Other Hispanic . . . 2,116

Age & Nativity, 2000

Under 5 years . . . 3,273
18 years and over . . . 28,793
65 years and over . . . 3,856
85 years and over . . . 377
Median Age . . . 32.2
Native-born . . . 33,743
Foreign-born . . . 7,335

Educational Attainment, 2000

Population 25 years and over . . . 24,975
Less than 9th grade . . . 12.2%
High school grad or higher . . . 74.4%
Bachelor's degree or higher . . . 13.8%
Graduate degree . . . 4.4%

Income & Poverty, 1999

Per capita income . . . $15,509
Median household income . . . $37,587
Median family income . . . $42,199
Persons in poverty . . . 14.1%
H'holds receiving public assistance . . . 843
H'holds receiving social security . . . 3,153

Households, 2000

Total households . . . 13,059
With persons under 18 . . . 5,888
With persons over 65 . . . 2,790
Family households . . . 9,310
Single person households . . . 3,066
Persons per household . . . 2.88
Persons per family . . . 3.42

Household Population, 2008§§

Persons living in households . . . 38,701
Persons living in group quarters . . . 4,256
Persons per household . . . 2.9

Labor & Employment

Total civilian labor force, 2008§§ . . . 19,900
Unemployment rate, 2008 . . . 9.8%
Total civilian labor force, 2000 . . . 16,830

Employed persons 16 years and over by occupation, 2000

Managers & professionals . . . 3,981
Service occupations . . . 3,115
Sales & office occupations . . . 3,988
Farming, fishing & forestry . . . 668
Construction & maintenance . . . 1,585
Production & transportation . . . 1,928
Self-employed persons . . . 1,006

* US Census Bureau
** 2000 Decennial Census
§ California Department of Finance
§§ California Employment Development Dept

General Information

City of Lompoc
100 Civic Center Plaza
PO Box 8001
Lompoc, CA 93438
805-736-1261

Website . . . www.cityoflompoc.com
Elevation . . . 104 ft.
Land Area (sq. miles) . . . 11.6
Water Area (sq. miles) . . . 0
Year of Incorporation . . . 1888
Government type . . . General law
Sales tax rate . . . 8.75%

Voters & Officials

Registered Voters, October 2008

Total . . . 15,310
Democrats . . . 5,729
Republicans . . . 6,221
Declined to state . . . 2,659

Legislative Districts

US Congressional . . . 24
State Senatorial . . . 19
State Assembly . . . 33

Local Officials, 2009

Mayor . . . Dick DeWees
Manager . . . Laurel Barclona
City Clerk . . . Donna N. Terrones
Attorney . . . Matthew Granger
Finance Dir . . . John Walk
Public Works . . . Larry Bean
Planning/Dev Dir . . . Arlene Pelster
Building . . . NA
Police Chief . . . Timothy Dabney
Emergency/Fire Dir . . . Linual White

Public Safety

Number of officers, 2007 . . . 49
Violent crimes, 2007 . . . 272
Property crimes, 2007 . . . 871
Arson, 2007 . . . 4

Public Library

Lompoc Public Library
Lompoc Public Library System
501 E North Ave
Lompoc, CA 93436
805-736-3477

Director . . . Molly Blaschke

Library system statistics, FY 2007

Population served . . . 72,152
Internet terminals . . . 20
Annual users . . . 87,394

Per capita:

Operating income . . . $17.87
percent from local government . . . 78.0%
Operating expenditure . . . $16.38
Total materials . . . 1.79
Print holdings . . . 1.57
Visits per capita . . . 3.37

Housing & Construction

Housing Units

Total, 2008§ . . . 14,140
Single family units, attached . . . 1,045
Single family units, detached . . . 7,499
Multiple family units . . . 4,656
Mobile home units . . . 940
Occupied . . . 13,558
Vacancy rate . . . 4.1%
Median rent, 2000** . . . $639
Median SF home value, 2000** . . . $148,300

New Privately Owned Housing Units Authorized by Building Permit, 2007*

	Units	Construction Cost
Single	83	$19,586,027
Total	91	$20,446,227

Municipal Finance

(For local fiscal year ended in 2006)

Revenues

Total . . . $61,424,109
Taxes . . . 16,507,093
Special benefits assessment . . . 223,531
Licenses & permits . . . 207,559
Fines & forfeitures . . . 170,856
Revenues from use of money & property . . . 1,698,578
Intergovernmental . . . 5,171,355
Service charges . . . 36,456,307
Other revenues . . . 895,080
Other financing sources . . . 93,750

Expenditures

Total . . . $74,239,887
General government . . . 1,541,371
Public safety . . . 12,331,207
Transportation . . . 8,081,255
Community development . . . 3,096,395
Health . . . 13,701,257
Culture & leisure . . . 10,044,821
Other . . . 0

Local School District

(Data from School year 2007-08 except as noted)

Lompoc Unified
PO Box 8000
Lompoc, CA 93438
(805) 742-3300

Superintendent . . . Frank Lynch
Grade plan . . . K-12
Number of schools . . . 17
Enrollment . . . 10,551
High school graduates, 2006-07 . . . 570
Dropout rate . . . 3.0%
Pupil/teacher ratio . . . 21.3
Average class size . . . 24.7
Students per computer . . . 3.6
Classrooms with internet . . . 614
Avg. Daily Attendance (ADA) . . . 10,089
Cost per ADA . . . $8,324
Avg. Teacher Salary . . . $64,912

California Achievement Tests 6th ed., 2008

(Pct scoring at or above 50th National Percentile Rank)

	Math	Reading	Language
Grade 3	50%	37%	44%
Grade 7	45%	47%	47%

Academic Performance Index, 2008

Number of students tested . . . 7,973
Number of valid scores . . . 7,589
2007 API (base) . . . 727
2008 API (growth) . . . 727

SAT Testing, 2006-07

Enrollment, Grade 12 . . . 670
Number taking test . . . 216
percent taking test . . . 32.2%
percent with total score 1,500+ . . . 13.40%

Average Scores:

Math	Verbal	Writing	Total
493	485	477	1,455

Federal No Child Left Behind, 2008

(Adequate Yearly Progress standards met)

	Participation Rate	Pct Proficient
ELA	Yes	No
Math	Yes	No

API criteria . . . Yes
Graduation rate . . . Yes
\# criteria met/possible . . . 34/26

Other school districts for this city

(see Appendix E for information on these districts)

None

See Introduction for an explanation of all data sources.

Demographics & Socio-Economic Characteristics†

(2007 American Community Survey, except as noted)

Population

1990* . . . 429,433
2007 . . . 458,302
Male . . . 221,695
Female . . . 236,607
Jan. 2008 (estimate)§ . . . 492,642
Persons per sq. mi. of land . . . 9,774.6

Race & Hispanic Origin, 2007

Race
White . . . 193,486
Black/African American . . . 63,496
North American Native . . . 3,078
Asian . . . 64,667
Pacific Islander . . . 3,032
Other Race . . . 113,214
Two or more races . . . 17,329
Hispanic origin, total . . . 177,638
Mexican . . . 148,211
Puerto Rican . . . 1,922
Cuban . . . 1,202
Other Hispanic . . . 26,303

Age & Nativity, 2007

Under 5 years . . . 35,630
18 years and over . . . 334,847
65 years and over . . . 40,213
85 years and over . . . 6,585
Median Age . . . 33.0
Native-born . . . 324,894
Foreign-born . . . 133,408

Educational Attainment, 2007

Population 25 years and over . . . 281,600
Less than 9th grade . . . 12.6%
High school grad or higher . . . 77.6%
Bachelor's degree or higher . . . 28.2%
Graduate degree . . . 9.8%

Income & Poverty, 2007

Per capita income . . . $24,323
Median household income . . . $48,290
Median family income . . . $54,331
Persons in poverty . . . 18.2%
H'holds receiving public assistance . . . 7,547
H'holds receiving social security . . . 28,810

Households, 2007

Total households . . . 158,561
With persons under 18 . . . 57,814
With persons over 65 . . . 27,671
Family households . . . 97,368
Single person households . . . 49,738
Persons per household . . . 2.83
Persons per family . . . 3.65

Household Population, 2008§§

Persons living in households . . . 482,257
Persons living in group quarters . . . 10,385
Persons per household . . . 2.9

Labor & Employment

Total civilian labor force, 2008§§ . . . 240,200
Unemployment rate, 2008 . . . 8.3%
Total civilian labor force, 2000* . . . 209,167

Employed persons 16 years and over by occupation, 2007

Managers & professionals . . . 69,883
Service occupations . . . 41,991
Sales & office occupations . . . 52,411
Farming, fishing & forestry . . . 262
Construction & maintenance . . . 17,834
Production & transportation . . . 30,013
Self-employed persons . . . 13,338

† see Appendix D for 2000 Decennial Census Data
* US Census Bureau
** 2007 American Community Survey
§ California Department of Finance
§§ California Employment Development Dept

General Information

City of Long Beach
333 W Ocean Blvd
Long Beach, CA 90802
562-570-6555

Website . . . www.longbeach.gov
Elevation . . . 29 ft.
Land Area (sq. miles) . . . 50.4
Water Area (sq. miles) . . . 15.4
Year of Incorporation . . . 1897
Government type . . . Chartered
Sales tax rate . . . 9.25%

Voters & Officials

Registered Voters, October 2008

Total . . . 214,244
Democrats . . . 108,148
Republicans . . . 54,623
Declined to state . . . 41,573

Legislative Districts

US Congressional . . . 37, 39, 46
State Senatorial . . . 25, 27, 28
State Assembly . . . 52, 54, 55

Local Officials, 2009

Mayor . . . Bob Foster
Manager . . . Patrick H. West
City Clerk . . . Larry G. Herrera
Attorney . . . Robert E. Shannon
Finance Dir . . . David Nakamota
Public Works . . . Michael P. Conway
Development Services . . . (vacant)
Building . . . NA
Police Chief . . . Anthony W. Batts
Emergency/Fire Dir . . . David W. Ellis

Public Safety

Number of officers, 2007 . . . 970
Violent crimes, 2007 . . . 3,426
Property crimes, 2007 . . . 12,979
Arson, 2007 . . . 123

Public Library

Main Library
Long Beach Public Library System
101 Pacific Ave
Long Beach, CA 90822
562-570-7500

Director . . . Eleanore Schmidt

Library system statistics, FY 2007

Population served . . . 492,912
Internet terminals . . . 129
Annual users . . . 349,614

Per capita:

Operating income . . . $29.89
percent from local government . . . 90.1%
Operating expenditure . . . $29.67
Total materials . . . 1.97
Print holdings . . . 1.85
Visits per capita . . . 2.62

Housing & Construction

Housing Units

Total, 2008§ . . . 174,993
Single family units, attached . . . 10,115
Single family units, detached . . . 69,316
Multiple family units . . . 93,033
Mobile home units . . . 2,529
Occupied . . . 166,282
Vacancy rate . . . 5.0%
Median rent, 2007** . . . $957
Median SF home value, 2007** . . . $580,200

New Privately Owned Housing Units Authorized by Building Permit, 2007*

	Units	Construction Cost
Single	60	$15,894,367
Total	238	$40,170,442

Municipal Finance

(For local fiscal year ended in 2006)

Revenues

Total . . . $1,670,672,698
Taxes . . . 257,672,865
Special benefits assessment . . . 0
Licenses & permits . . . 15,447,485
Fines & forfeitures . . . 16,387,429
Revenues from use of money & property . . . 65,516,820
Intergovernmental . . . 184,550,669
Service charges . . . 1,064,392,055
Other revenues . . . 45,218,761
Other financing sources . . . 21,486,614

Expenditures

Total . . . $1,514,250,200
General government . . . 38,589,713
Public safety . . . 273,866,697
Transportation . . . 341,850,966
Community development . . . 121,198,622
Health . . . 129,889,383
Culture & leisure . . . 153,760,616
Other . . . 275,634,878

Local School District

(Data from School year 2007-08 except as noted)

Long Beach Unified
1515 Hughes Way
Long Beach, CA 90810
(562) 997-8000

Superintendent . . . Christopher Steinhauser
Grade plan . . . K-12
Number of schools . . . 93
Enrollment . . . 88,186
High school graduates, 2006-07 . . . 4,706
Dropout rate . . . 5.1%
Pupil/teacher ratio . . . 20.9
Average class size . . . 27.3
Students per computer . . . 4.9
Classrooms with internet . . . 4,149
Avg. Daily Attendance (ADA) . . . 87,009
Cost per ADA . . . $8,964
Avg. Teacher Salary . . . $70,071

California Achievement Tests 6th ed., 2008

(Pct scoring at or above 50th National Percentile Rank)

	Math	Reading	Language
Grade 3	60%	34%	41%
Grade 7	47%	43%	41%

Academic Performance Index, 2008

Number of students tested . . . 67,372
Number of valid scores . . . 64,269
2007 API (base) . . . 729
2008 API (growth) . . . 744

SAT Testing, 2006-07

Enrollment, Grade 12 . . . 6,154
Number taking test . . . 2,120
percent taking test . . . 34.5%
percent with total score 1,500+ . . . 14.30%

Average Scores:

Math	Verbal	Writing	Total
496	478	476	1,450

Federal No Child Left Behind, 2008

(Adequate Yearly Progress standards met)

	Participation Rate	Pct Proficient
ELA	Yes	No
Math	Yes	No

API criteria . . . Yes
Graduation rate . . . Yes
\# criteria met/possible . . . 46/43

Other school districts for this city

(see Appendix E for information on these districts)

Los Angeles Unified, Paramount Unified

See Introduction for an explanation of all data sources.

Demographics & Socio-Economic Characteristics

(2000 Decennial Census, except as noted)

Population

1990* 5,705
2000 6,260
Male 3,110
Female 3,150
Jan. 2008 (estimate)§ 6,624
Persons per sq. mi. of land 907.4

Race & Hispanic Origin, 2000

Race
White 5,575
Black/African American 12
North American Native 60
Asian 202
Pacific Islander 11
Other Race 126
Two or more races 274
Hispanic origin, total 430
Mexican 301
Puerto Rican 13
Cuban 8
Other Hispanic 108

Age & Nativity, 2000

Under 5 years 356
18 years and over 4,459
65 years and over 733
85 years and over 69
Median Age 38.4
Native-born 6,268
Foreign-born 159

Educational Attainment, 2000

Population 25 years and over 4,150
Less than 9th grade 2.4%
High school grad or higher 89.6%
Bachelor's degree or higher 19.2%
Graduate degree 5.7%

Income & Poverty, 1999

Per capita income $30,384
Median household income $60,444
Median family income $64,837
Persons in poverty 3.5%
H'holds receiving public assistance 4
H'holds receiving social security 613

Households, 2000

Total households 2,206
With persons under 18 950
With persons over 65 504
Family households 1,729
Single person households 371
Persons per household 2.82
Persons per family 3.17

Household Population, 2008§§

Persons living in households 6,590
Persons living in group quarters 34
Persons per household 2.7

Labor & Employment

Total civilian labor force, 2008§§ 4,500
Unemployment rate, 2008 .... 4.1%
Total civilian labor force, 2000 3,200

Employed persons 16 years and over by occupation, 2000

Managers & professionals 1,101
Service occupations 437
Sales & office occupations 920
Farming, fishing & forestry 5
Construction & maintenance 338
Production & transportation 320
Self-employed persons 448

* US Census Bureau
** 2000 Decennial Census
§ California Department of Finance
§§ California Employment Development Dept

General Information

Town of Loomis
6140 Horseshoe Bar Rd
Suite K
Loomis, CA 95650
916-652-1840

Website .... www.loomis.ca.gov
Elevation .... 399 ft.
Land Area (sq. miles) 7.3
Water Area (sq. miles) 0
Year of Incorporation 1984
Government type .... General law
Sales tax rate 8.25%

Voters & Officials

Registered Voters, October 2008

Total 4,145
Democrats 1,112
Republicans 2,146
Declined to state 756

Legislative Districts

US Congressional 4
State Senatorial 4
State Assembly 4

Local Officials, 2009

Mayor .... Walt Scherer
Manager .... Perry Beck
City Clerk .... Crickett Strock
Attorney .... Dave Larsen
Finance Dir .... Roger Carroll
Public Works .... Brian Fragiao
Planning/Dev Dir .... Kathy Kerdus
Building .... NA
Police Chief .... NA
Fire Chief .... Dave Wheeler

Public Safety

Number of officers, 2007 .... NA
Violent crimes, 2007 .... NA
Property crimes, 2007 .... NA
Arson, 2007 .... NA

Public Library

Loomis Library
Placer County Library System
6050 Library Dr
Loomis, CA 95650
916-652-7061

Branch Librarian .... Elizabeth Enright

Library system statistics, FY 2007

Population served 180,819
Internet terminals 56
Annual users 48,341

Per capita:

Operating income $24.99
percent from local government 85.7%
Operating expenditure $24.01
Total materials 1.96
Print holdings 1.74
Visits per capita 3.30

Housing & Construction

Housing Units

Total, 2008§ 2,460
Single family units, attached 217
Single family units, detached 2,069
Multiple family units 60
Mobile home units 114
Occupied 2,407
Vacancy rate 2.2%
Median rent, 2000** $793
Median SF home value, 2000** $170,800

New Privately Owned Housing Units Authorized by Building Permit, 2007*

	Units	Construction Cost
Single	11	$3,816,152
Total	11	$3,816,152

Municipal Finance

(For local fiscal year ended in 2006)

Revenues

Total $4,898,290
Taxes 3,780,812
Special benefits assessment 102,090
Licenses & permits 130,011
Fines & forfeitures 11,409
Revenues from use of money & property 271,614
Intergovernmental 418,764
Service charges 116,900
Other revenues 66,690
Other financing sources 0

Expenditures

Total $4,348,837
General government 741,302
Public safety 1,170,428
Transportation 2,012,832
Community development 373,440
Health 2,450
Culture & leisure 48,385
Other 0

Local School District

(Data from School year 2007-08 except as noted)

Placer Union High
PO Box 5048
Auburn, CA 95604
(530) 886-4400

Superintendent .... Bart O'Brien
Grade plan 9-12
Number of schools 6
Enrollment 4,588
High school graduates, 2006-07 1,091
Dropout rate 1.4%
Pupil/teacher ratio 22.5
Average class size 25.4
Students per computer 3.6
Classrooms with internet 242
Avg. Daily Attendance (ADA) 4,382
Cost per ADA $8,031
Avg. Teacher Salary $63,368

California Achievement Tests 6th ed., 2008

(Pct scoring at or above 50th National Percentile Rank)

	Math	Reading	Language
Grade 3	NA	NA	NA
Grade 7	NA	NA	NA

Academic Performance Index, 2008

Number of students tested 3,384
Number of valid scores 3,277
2007 API (base) 769
2008 API (growth) 768

SAT Testing, 2006-07

Enrollment, Grade 12 1,210
Number taking test 418
percent taking test 34.6%
percent with total score 1,500+ 23.60%

Average Scores:

Math	Verbal	Writing	Total
550	536	526	1,612

Federal No Child Left Behind, 2008

(Adequate Yearly Progress standards met)

	Participation Rate	Pct Proficient
ELA	No	No
Math	Yes	No

API criteria .... Yes
Graduation rate .... Yes
criteria met/possible 18/15

Other school districts for this city

(see Appendix E for information on these districts)

Loomis Union Elem

See Introduction for an explanation of all data sources.

Demographics & Socio-Economic Characteristics

(2000 Decennial Census, except as noted)

Population

1990* ... 11,676
2000 ... 11,536
  Male ... 5,466
  Female ... 6,070
Jan. 2008 (estimate)[§] ... 12,191
  Persons per sq. mi. of land ... 3,047.8

Race & Hispanic Origin, 2000

Race
  White ... 8,879
  Black/African American ... 369
  North American Native ... 67
  Asian ... 1,095
  Pacific Islander ... 38
  Other Race ... 619
  Two or more races ... 469
Hispanic origin, total ... 1,848
  Mexican ... 1,314
  Puerto Rican ... 50
  Cuban ... 35
  Other Hispanic ... 449

Age & Nativity, 2000

Under 5 years ... 573
18 years and over ... 8,624
65 years and over ... 1,704
85 years and over ... 309
  Median Age ... 37.3
Native-born ... 9,642
Foreign-born ... 1,618

Educational Attainment, 2000

Population 25 years and over ... 7,674
Less than 9th grade ... 5.0%
High school grad or higher ... 87.3%
Bachelor's degree or higher ... 29.8%
Graduate degree ... 9.0%

Income & Poverty, 1999

Per capita income ... $26,014
Median household income ... $55,286
Median family income ... $60,767
Persons in poverty ... 4.9%
H'holds receiving public assistance ... 123
H'holds receiving social security ... 913

Households, 2000

Total households ... 4,246
  With persons under 18 ... 1,686
  With persons over 65 ... 980
  Family households ... 3,037
  Single person households ... 925
Persons per household ... 2.62
Persons per family ... 3.06

Household Population, 2008[§§]

Persons living in households ... 11,785
Persons living in group quarters ... 406
Persons per household ... 2.7

Labor & Employment

Total civilian labor force, 2008[§§] ... 6,800
  Unemployment rate, 2008 ... 2.7%
Total civilian labor force, 2000 ... 5,870

Employed persons 16 years and over by occupation, 2000

  Managers & professionals ... 2,310
  Service occupations ... 828
  Sales & office occupations ... 1,777
  Farming, fishing & forestry ... 18
  Construction & maintenance ... 289
  Production & transportation ... 499
  Self-employed persons ... 452

* US Census Bureau
** 2000 Decennial Census
§ California Department of Finance
§§ California Employment Development Dept

General Information

City of Los Alamitos
3191 Katella
Los Alamitos, CA 90720
562-431-3538

Website ... www.ci.los-alamitos.ca.us
Elevation ... 22 ft.
Land Area (sq. miles) ... 4.0
Water Area (sq. miles) ... 0.1
Year of Incorporation ... 1960
Government type ... Chartered
Sales tax rate ... 8.75%

Voters & Officials

Registered Voters, October 2008

Total ... 6,989
  Democrats ... 2,440
  Republicans ... 2,993
  Declined to state ... 1,266

Legislative Districts

US Congressional ... 40
State Senatorial ... 35
State Assembly ... 67

Local Officials, 2009

Mayor ... (vacant)
Manager ... Nita McKay (Int)
City Clerk ... Susan C. Vanderpool
Attorney ... Dean Derleth
Finance Dir ... Nita McKay
Public Works ... Steven Mendoza (Int)
Planning/Dev Dir ... Steven Mendoza
Building ... NA
Police Chief ... Todd Mattern
Fire/Emergency Mgmt ... NA

Public Safety

Number of officers, 2007 ... 22
Violent crimes, 2007 ... 34
Property crimes, 2007 ... 340
Arson, 2007 ... 5

Public Library

Los Alamitos-Rossmoor Branch Library
Orange County Public Library System
12700 Montecito Rd.
Seal Beach, CA 90740
562-430-1048

County Librarian ... Helen Fried

Library system statistics, FY 2007

Population served ... 1,532,758
Internet terminals ... 505
  Annual users ... 680,874

Per capita:

Operating income ... $24.71
  percent from local government ... 90.0%
Operating expenditure ... $24.18
Total materials ... 1.93
Print holdings ... 1.84
Visits per capita ... 4.02

Housing & Construction

Housing Units

Total, 2008[§] ... 4,422
  Single family units, attached ... 269
  Single family units, detached ... 1,945
  Multiple family units ... 2,079
  Mobile home units ... 129
  Occupied ... 4,338
  Vacancy rate ... 1.9%
Median rent, 2000** ... $883
Median SF home value, 2000** ... $307,100

New Privately Owned Housing Units Authorized by Building Permit, 2007*

	Units	Construction Cost
Single	4	$700,000
Total	4	$700,000

Municipal Finance

(For local fiscal year ended in 2006)

Revenues

Total ... $15,798,108
Taxes ... 8,571,437
Special benefits assessment ... 233,885
Licenses & permits ... 233,723
Fines & forfeitures ... 463,236
Revenues from use of
  money & property ... 447,830
Intergovernmental ... 1,274,681
Service charges ... 1,018,092
Other revenues ... 190,224
Other financing sources ... 3,365,000

Expenditures

Total ... $17,308,638
General government ... 2,481,687
Public safety ... 4,461,303
Transportation ... 2,382,968
Community development ... 1,004,955
Health ... 0
Culture & leisure ... 6,977,725
Other ... 0

Local School District

(Data from School year 2007-08 except as noted)

Los Alamitos Unified
10293 Bloomfield St
Los Alamitos, CA 90720
(562) 799-4700

Superintendent ... Gregory Franklin
Grade plan ... PK-12
Number of schools ... 10
Enrollment ... 9,372
High school graduates, 2006-07 ... 734
Dropout rate ... 0.6%
Pupil/teacher ratio ... 23.3
Average class size ... 27.9
Students per computer ... 5.3
Classrooms with internet ... 407
Avg. Daily Attendance (ADA) ... 9,283
  Cost per ADA ... $7,266
Avg. Teacher Salary ... $76,063

California Achievement Tests 6th ed., 2008

(Pct scoring at or above 50th National Percentile Rank)

	Math	Reading	Language
Grade 3	82%	61%	72%
Grade 7	74%	80%	79%

Academic Performance Index, 2008

Number of students tested ... 7,384
Number of valid scores ... 7,153
2007 API (base) ... 871
2008 API (growth) ... 881

SAT Testing, 2006-07

Enrollment, Grade 12 ... 794
Number taking test ... 509
  percent taking test ... 64.1%
  percent with total score 1,500+ ... 40.40%

Average Scores:

Math	Verbal	Writing	Total
544	524	529	1,597

Federal No Child Left Behind, 2008

(Adequate Yearly Progress standards met)

	Participation Rate	Pct Proficient
ELA	Yes	Yes
Math	Yes	Yes

API criteria ... Yes
Graduation rate ... Yes
\# criteria met/possible ... 38/38

Other school districts for this city

(see Appendix E for information on these districts)

None

See Introduction for an explanation of all data sources.

Demographics & Socio-Economic Characteristics

(2000 Decennial Census, except as noted)

Population

1990* 26,303
2000 27,693
Male 13,352
Female 14,341
Jan. 2008 (estimate)§ 28,291
Persons per sq. mi. of land 4,420.5

Race & Hispanic Origin, 2000

Race
White 22,250
Black/African American 130
North American Native 48
Asian 4,271
Pacific Islander 45
Other Race 183
Two or more races 766
Hispanic origin, total 822
Mexican 439
Puerto Rican 37
Cuban 20
Other Hispanic 326

Age & Nativity, 2000

Under 5 years 1,629
18 years and over 21,132
65 years and over 5,346
85 years and over 708
Median Age 44.2
Native-born 22,728
Foreign-born 4,857

Educational Attainment, 2000

Population 25 years and over 20,128
Less than 9th grade 0.7%
High school grad or higher 97.2%
Bachelor's degree or higher 71.3%
Graduate degree 35.8%

Income & Poverty, 1999

Per capita income $66,776
Median household income $126,740
Median family income $148,201
Persons in poverty 2.3%
H'holds receiving public assistance 70
H'holds receiving social security 3,149

Households, 2000

Total households 10,462
With persons under 18 3,653
With persons over 65 3,423
Family households 8,026
Single person households 1,955
Persons per household 2.61
Persons per family 2.98

Household Population, 2008§§

Persons living in households 27,872
Persons living in group quarters 419
Persons per household 2.6

Labor & Employment

Total civilian labor force, 2008§§ 12,900
Unemployment rate, 2008 ....3.0%
Total civilian labor force, 2000 12,941

Employed persons 16 years and over by occupation, 2000

Managers & professionals 9,499
Service occupations 510
Sales & office occupations 2,031
Farming, fishing & forestry 12
Construction & maintenance 295
Production & transportation 364
Self-employed persons 1,519

* US Census Bureau
** 2000 Decennial Census
§ California Department of Finance
§§ California Employment Development Dept

General Information

City of Los Altos
1 N San Antonio Rd
Los Altos, CA 94022
650-947-2700

Website ....www.ci.los-altos.ca.us
Elevation ....170 ft.
Land Area (sq. miles) 6.4
Water Area (sq. miles) 0
Year of Incorporation 1952
Government type ....General law
Sales tax rate 9.25%

Voters & Officials

Registered Voters, October 2008

Total 19,364
Democrats 8,080
Republicans 6,508
Declined to state 4,278

Legislative Districts

US Congressional 14
State Senatorial 11
State Assembly 21

Local Officials, 2009

Mayor ....Megan Satterlee
Manager ....Douglas J. Schmitz
City Clerk ....Susan Kitchens
Attorney ....Jolie Houston
Finance Dir ....Russell Morreale
Public Works ....Jim Gustafson
Planning/Dev Dir ....James Walgren
Building ....Kirk Ballard
Police Chief ....Tuck Younis
Fire/Emergency Mgmt ....(County)

Public Safety

Number of officers, 2007 30
Violent crimes, 2007 18
Property crimes, 2007 293
Arson, 2007 1

Public Library

Los Altos Library
Santa Clara County Library System
13 S San Antonio Rd
Los Altos, CA 94022
650-948-7683

Branch Librarian ....Cheryl Houts

Library system statistics, FY 2007

Population served 419,141
Internet terminals 133
Annual users 650,000

Per capita:

Operating income $77.89
percent from local government 85.7%
Operating expenditure $66.37
Total materials 4.01
Print holdings 3.27
Visits per capita 6.16

Housing & Construction

Housing Units

Total, 2008§ 10,820
Single family units, attached 383
Single family units, detached 9,219
Multiple family units 1,202
Mobile home units 16
Occupied 10,552
Vacancy rate 2.5%
Median rent, 2000** $1,727
Median SF home value, 2000** $983,000

New Privately Owned Housing Units Authorized by Building Permit, 2007*

	Units	Construction Cost
Single	41	$31,355,949
Total	123	$52,755,949

Municipal Finance

(For local fiscal year ended in 2006)

Revenues

Total $32,292,935
Taxes 17,616,734
Special benefits assessment 0
Licenses & permits 1,434,954
Fines & forfeitures 158,192
Revenues from use of money & property 1,331,291
Intergovernmental 2,386,952
Service charges 9,226,875
Other revenues 137,937
Other financing sources 0

Expenditures

Total $25,769,444
General government 3,252,308
Public safety 10,127,171
Transportation 2,215,544
Community development 2,819,082
Health 4,447,837
Culture & leisure 2,767,405
Other 140,097

Local School District

(Data from School year 2007-08 except as noted)

Mountain View-Los Altos Union High
1299 Bryant Ave
Mountain View, CA 94040
(650) 940-4650

Superintendent ....Barry Groves
Grade plan 9-12
Number of schools 3
Enrollment 3,620
High school graduates, 2006-07 868
Dropout rate 1.2%
Pupil/teacher ratio 20.3
Average class size 23.9
Students per computer 4.9
Classrooms with internet 229
Avg. Daily Attendance (ADA) 3,563
Cost per ADA $12,454
Avg. Teacher Salary $93,283

California Achievement Tests 6th ed., 2008

(Pct scoring at or above 50th National Percentile Rank)

	Math	Reading	Language
Grade 3	NA	NA	NA
Grade 7	NA	NA	NA

Academic Performance Index, 2008

Number of students tested 2,682
Number of valid scores 2,581
2007 API (base) 812
2008 API (growth) 820

SAT Testing, 2006-07

Enrollment, Grade 12 967
Number taking test 693
percent taking test 71.7%
percent with total score 1,500+ 55.30%

Average Scores:

Math	Verbal	Writing	Total
599	575	573	1,747

Federal No Child Left Behind, 2008

(Adequate Yearly Progress standards met)

	Participation Rate	Pct Proficient
ELA	Yes	No
Math	Yes	Yes

API criteria ....Yes
Graduation rate ....Yes
\# criteria met/possible 24/23

Other school districts for this city

(see Appendix E for information on these districts)

Cupertino Union Elem, Los Altos Elem

See Introduction for an explanation of all data sources.

Demographics & Socio-Economic Characteristics

(2000 Decennial Census, except as noted)

Population

1990* . . . 7,514
2000 . . . 7,902
Male . . . 3,898
Female . . . 4,004
Jan. 2008 (estimate)§ . . . 8,837
Persons per sq. mi. of land . . . 1,027.6

Race & Hispanic Origin, 2000

Race
White . . . 5,922
Black/African American . . . 47
North American Native . . . 7
Asian . . . 1,667
Pacific Islander . . . 7
Other Race . . . 36
Two or more races . . . 216
Hispanic origin, total . . . 170
Mexican . . . 58
Puerto Rican . . . 5
Cuban . . . 11
Other Hispanic . . . 96

Age & Nativity, 2000

Under 5 years . . . 355
18 years and over . . . 6,041
65 years and over . . . 1,342
85 years and over . . . 94
Median Age . . . 46.7
Native-born . . . 6,118
Foreign-born . . . 1,882

Educational Attainment, 2000

Population 25 years and over . . . 5,729
Less than 9th grade . . . 1.6%
High school grad or higher . . . 96.9%
Bachelor's degree or higher . . . 78.1%
Graduate degree . . . 41.4%

Income & Poverty, 1999

Per capita income . . . $92,840
Median household income . . . $173,570
Median family income . . . $181,865
Persons in poverty . . . 3.9%
H'holds receiving public assistance . . . 21
H'holds receiving social security . . . 794

Households, 2000

Total households . . . 2,740
With persons under 18 . . . 994
With persons over 65 . . . 862
Family households . . . 2,340
Single person households . . . 287
Persons per household . . . 2.86
Persons per family . . . 3.02

Household Population, 2008§§

Persons living in households . . . 8,772
Persons living in group quarters . . . 65
Persons per household . . . 2.9

Labor & Employment

Total civilian labor force, 2008§§ . . . NA
Unemployment rate, 2008 . . . NA
Total civilian labor force, 2000 . . . 3,711

Employed persons 16 years and over by occupation, 2000

Managers & professionals . . . 2,710
Service occupations . . . 193
Sales & office occupations . . . 592
Farming, fishing & forestry . . . 14
Construction & maintenance . . . 36
Production & transportation . . . 99
Self-employed persons . . . 398

* US Census Bureau
** 2000 Decennial Census
§ California Department of Finance
§§ California Employment Development Dept

General Information

Town of Los Altos Hills
26379 Fremont Rd
Los Altos Hills, CA 94022
650-941-7222

Website . . . www.losaltoshills.ca.gov
Elevation . . . 215 ft.
Land Area (sq. miles) . . . 8.6
Water Area (sq. miles) . . . 0
Year of Incorporation . . . 1956
Government type . . . General law
Sales tax rate . . . 9.25%

Voters & Officials

Registered Voters, October 2008

Total . . . 5,848
Democrats . . . 2,078
Republicans . . . 2,158
Declined to state . . . 1,477

Legislative Districts

US Congressional . . . 14
State Senatorial . . . 11
State Assembly . . . 21

Local Officials, 2009

Mayor . . . Jean H. Mordo
Manager . . . Carl Cahill
Town Clerk . . . Karen Jost
Attorney . . . Steve Mattas
Finance Dir . . . Nick Pegueros
Public Works . . . Richard Chiu
Planning/Dev Dir . . . Debbie Pedro
Building . . . William Carino
Police Chief . . . (County)
Fire/Emergency Mgmt . . . (County)

Public Safety

Number of officers, 2007 . . . NA
Violent crimes, 2007 . . . 2
Property crimes, 2007 . . . 69
Arson, 2007 . . . 2

Public Library

Served by County Library

Library system statistics, FY 2007

Population served . . . NA
Internet terminals . . . NA
Annual users . . . NA

Per capita:

Operating income . . . NA
percent from local government . . . NA
Operating expenditure . . . NA
Total materials . . . NA
Print holdings . . . NA
Visits per capita . . . NA

Housing & Construction

Housing Units

Total, 2008§ . . . 3,124
Single family units, attached . . . 32
Single family units, detached . . . 3,060
Multiple family units . . . 26
Mobile home units . . . 6
Occupied . . . 3,041
Vacancy rate . . . 2.7%
Median rent, 2000** . . . $1,810
Median SF home value, 2000** . . $1,000,001

New Privately Owned Housing Units Authorized by Building Permit, 2007*

	Units	Construction Cost
Single	22	$16,297,600
Total	22	$16,297,600

Municipal Finance

(For local fiscal year ended in 2006)

Revenues

Total . . . $8,647,038
Taxes . . . 3,524,382
Special benefits assessment . . . 0
Licenses & permits . . . 442,541
Fines & forfeitures . . . 40,706
Revenues from use of money & property . . . 580,324
Intergovernmental . . . 448,067
Service charges . . . 3,362,759
Other revenues . . . 248,259
Other financing sources . . . 0

Expenditures

Total . . . $8,324,594
General government . . . 1,397,615
Public safety . . . 892,790
Transportation . . . 1,530,088
Community development . . . 1,956,069
Health . . . 2,314,578
Culture & leisure . . . 233,454
Other . . . 0

Local School District

(Data from School year 2007-08 except as noted)

Mountain View-Los Altos Union High
1299 Bryant Ave
Mountain View, CA 94040
(650) 940-4650

Superintendent . . . Barry Groves
Grade plan . . . 9-12
Number of schools . . . 3
Enrollment . . . 3,620
High school graduates, 2006-07 . . . 868
Dropout rate . . . 1.2%
Pupil/teacher ratio . . . 20.3
Average class size . . . 23.9
Students per computer . . . 4.9
Classrooms with internet . . . 229
Avg. Daily Attendance (ADA) . . . 3,563
Cost per ADA . . . $12,454
Avg. Teacher Salary . . . $93,283

California Achievement Tests 6th ed., 2008

(Pct scoring at or above 50th National Percentile Rank)

	Math	Reading	Language
Grade 3	NA	NA	NA
Grade 7	NA	NA	NA

Academic Performance Index, 2008

Number of students tested . . . 2,682
Number of valid scores . . . 2,581
2007 API (base) . . . 812
2008 API (growth) . . . 820

SAT Testing, 2006-07

Enrollment, Grade 12 . . . 967
Number taking test . . . 693
percent taking test . . . 71.7%
percent with total score 1,500+ . . . 55.30%

Average Scores:

Math	Verbal	Writing	Total
599	575	573	1,747

Federal No Child Left Behind, 2008

(Adequate Yearly Progress standards met)

	Participation Rate	Pct Proficient
ELA	Yes	No
Math	Yes	Yes

API criteria . . . Yes
Graduation rate . . . Yes
\# criteria met/possible . . . 24/23

Other school districts for this city

(see Appendix E for information on these districts)

Los Altos Elem

See Introduction for an explanation of all data sources.

Demographics & Socio-Economic Characteristics†

(2007 American Community Survey, except as noted)

Population

1990* 3,485,398
2007 3,806,003
Male 1,912,140
Female 1,893,863
Jan. 2008 (estimate)§ 4,045,873
Persons per sq. mi. of land 8,624.8

Race & Hispanic Origin, 2007

Race
White 1,886,443
Black/African American 382,009
North American Native 17,852
Asian 396,319
Pacific Islander 6,024
Other Race 999,812
Two or more races 117,544
Hispanic origin, total 1,841,881
Mexican 1,270,660
Puerto Rican 16,440
Cuban 13,316
Other Hispanic 541,465

Age & Nativity, 2007

Under 5 years 274,737
18 years and over 2,854,808
65 years and over 390,689
85 years and over 53,201
Median Age 33.9
Native-born 2,288,824
Foreign-born 1,517,179

Educational Attainment, 2007

Population 25 years and over 2,437,461
Less than 9th grade 15.7%
High school grad or higher 72.9%
Bachelor's degree or higher 29.5%
Graduate degree 9.8%

Income & Poverty, 2007

Per capita income $26,896
Median household income $47,781
Median family income $51,371
Persons in poverty 18.5%
H'holds receiving public assistance 47,688
H'holds receiving social security 256,374

Households, 2007

Total households 1,284,430
With persons under 18 451,355
With persons over 65 271,462
Family households 790,840
Single person households 385,363
Persons per household 2.90
Persons per family 3.68

Household Population, 2008§§

Persons living in households 3,959,760
Persons living in group quarters 86,113
Persons per household 3.0

Labor & Employment

Total civilian labor force, 2008§§ 1,939,400
Unemployment rate, 2008 .... 8.3%
Total civilian labor force, 2000* 1,688,652

Employed persons 16 years and over by occupation, 2007

Managers & professionals 611,154
Service occupations 346,057
Sales & office occupations 444,499
Farming, fishing & forestry 2,614
Construction & maintenance 161,688
Production & transportation 233,551
Self-employed persons 218,103

† see Appendix D for 2000 Decennial Census Data
* US Census Bureau
** 2007 American Community Survey
§ California Department of Finance
§§ California Employment Development Dept

General Information

City of Los Angeles
200 N Spring St
Los Angeles, CA 90012
213-978-0600

Website .... www.lacity.org
Elevation .... 330 ft.
Land Area (sq. miles) 469.1
Water Area (sq. miles) 29.2
Year of Incorporation 1850
Government type .... Chartered
Sales tax rate 9.25%

Voters & Officials

Registered Voters, October 2008

Total 1,574,589
Democrats 901,736
Republicans 282,438
Declined to state 321,974

Legislative Districts

US Congressional 25-37, 39, 46
State Senatorial 17, 20-30
State Assembly 37-48, 51-55

Local Officials, 2009

Mayor .... Antonio R. Villaraigosa
City Administrative Officer .... Ray Ciranna
City Clerk .... Karen E. Kalfayan (Int)
Attorney .... Rockard Delgadillo
Finance Dir .... Laura Chick
Public Works .... John L. Reamer Jr
Planning/Dev Dir .... Richard Benbow
Building .... Andrew Adelman
Police Chief .... William Bratton
Fire/Emergency Mgmt .... Douglas Barry

Public Safety

Number of officers, 2007 9,538
Violent crimes, 2007 27,806
Property crimes, 2007 101,457
Arson, 2007 2,207

Public Library

Central Library
Los Angeles Public Library System
630 W Fifth St
Los Angeles, CA 90071
213-228-7571

Director .... Fontayne Holmes

Library system statistics, FY 2007

Population served 4,018,080
Internet terminals 2,269
Annual users 4,995,278

Per capita:

Operating income $30.36
percent from local government 91.9%
Operating expenditure $30.36
Total materials 1.68
Print holdings 1.56
Visits per capita 3.98

Housing & Construction

Housing Units

Total, 2008§ 1,399,309
Single family units, attached 88,450
Single family units, detached 530,708
Multiple family units 771,063
Mobile home units 9,088
Occupied 1,334,539
Vacancy rate 4.6%
Median rent, 2007** $986
Median SF home value, 2007** $633,800

New Privately Owned Housing Units Authorized by Building Permit, 2007*

	Units	Construction Cost
Single	1,551	$510,748,890
Total	9,762	$1,918,505,590

Municipal Finance

(For local fiscal year ended in 2006)

Revenues

Total $12,322,309,719
Taxes 3,267,366,023
Special benefits assessment 143,045,951
Licenses & permits 53,572,513
Fines & forfeitures 137,524,922
Revenues from use of money & property 372,892,960
Intergovernmental 616,688,179
Service charges 5,481,543,319
Other revenues 705,356,852
Other financing sources 1,544,319,000

Expenditures

Total $11,047,964,404
General government 903,624,383
Public safety 2,694,749,041
Transportation 1,718,096,248
Community development 630,913,879
Health 914,210,449
Culture & leisure 508,439,404
Other 0

Local School District

(Data from School year 2007-08 except as noted)

Los Angeles Unified
333 South Beaudry Ave
Los Angeles, CA 90017
(213) 241-1000

Superintendent .... Ramon Cortines
Grade plan PK-12
Number of schools 827
Enrollment 693,680
High school graduates, 2006-07 28,545
Dropout rate 7.8%
Pupil/teacher ratio 19.8
Average class size 24.9
Students per computer 3.7
Classrooms with internet 31,112
Avg. Daily Attendance (ADA) 653,672
Cost per ADA $10,053
Avg. Teacher Salary $63,391

California Achievement Tests 6th ed., 2008

(Pct scoring at or above 50th National Percentile Rank)

	Math	Reading	Language
Grade 3	49%	27%	39%
Grade 7	37%	33%	33%

Academic Performance Index, 2008

Number of students tested 495,046
Number of valid scores 471,641
2007 API (base) 662
2008 API (growth) 683

SAT Testing, 2006-07

Enrollment, Grade 12 32,370
Number taking test 15,447
percent taking test 47.7%
percent with total score 1,500+ 12.50%

Average Scores:

Math	Verbal	Writing	Total
443	438	441	1,322

Federal No Child Left Behind, 2008

(Adequate Yearly Progress standards met)

	Participation Rate	Pct Proficient
ELA	Yes	No
Math	Yes	No

API criteria .... Yes
Graduation rate .... Yes
\# criteria met/possible 46/38

Other school districts for this city

(see Appendix E for information on these districts)

Compton Unified, Montebello Unified

See Introduction for an explanation of all data sources.

Demographics & Socio-Economic Characteristics

(2000 Decennial Census, except as noted)

Population

1990* . . . 14,519
2000 . . . 25,869
Male . . . 12,871
Female . . . 12,998
Jan. 2008 (estimate)§ . . . 36,052
Persons per sq. mi. of land . . . 4,506.5

Race & Hispanic Origin, 2000

Race
White . . . 15,161
Black/African American . . . 1,100
North American Native . . . 350
Asian . . . 606
Pacific Islander . . . 85
Other Race . . . 6,960
Two or more races . . . 1,607
Hispanic origin, total . . . 13,048
Mexican . . . 10,753
Puerto Rican . . . 142
Cuban . . . 15
Other Hispanic . . . 2,138

Age & Nativity, 2000

Under 5 years . . . 2,422
18 years and over . . . 16,780
65 years and over . . . 2,395
85 years and over . . . 271
Median Age . . . 29.7
Native-born . . . 20,994
Foreign-born . . . 4,884

Educational Attainment, 2000

Population 25 years and over . . . 14,681
Less than 9th grade . . . 15.8%
High school grad or higher . . . 69.6%
Bachelor's degree or higher . . . 9.9%
Graduate degree . . . 2.5%

Income & Poverty, 1999

Per capita income . . . $15,582
Median household income . . . $43,690
Median family income . . . $45,304
Persons in poverty . . . 12.0%
H'holds receiving public assistance . . . 411
H'holds receiving social security . . . 1,807

Households, 2000

Total households . . . 7,721
With persons under 18 . . . 4,145
With persons over 65 . . . 1,663
Family households . . . 6,225
Single person households . . . 1,220
Persons per household . . . 3.33
Persons per family . . . 3.69

Household Population, 2008§§

Persons living in households . . . 35,877
Persons living in group quarters . . . 175
Persons per household . . . 3.2

Labor & Employment

Total civilian labor force, 2008§§ . . . 12,900
Unemployment rate, 2008 . . . 13.3%
Total civilian labor force, 2000 . . . 10,745

Employed persons 16 years and over by occupation, 2000

Managers & professionals . . . 2,510
Service occupations . . . 1,597
Sales & office occupations . . . 2,007
Farming, fishing & forestry . . . 504
Construction & maintenance . . . 1,202
Production & transportation . . . 1,470
Self-employed persons . . . 632

* US Census Bureau
** 2000 Decennial Census
§ California Department of Finance
§§ California Employment Development Dept

General Information

City of Los Banos
520 J St
Los Banos, CA 93635
209-827-7000

Website . . . www.losbanos.org
Elevation . . . 120 ft.
Land Area (sq. miles) . . . 8.0
Water Area (sq. miles) . . . 0.1
Year of Incorporation . . . 1907
Government type . . . General law
Sales tax rate . . . 8.75%

Voters & Officials

Registered Voters, October 2008

Total . . . 12,695
Democrats . . . 6,307
Republicans . . . 4,018
Declined to state . . . 1,969

Legislative Districts

US Congressional . . . 18
State Senatorial . . . 12
State Assembly . . . 17

Local Officials, 2009

Mayor . . . Tommy Jones
Manager . . . Steve Rath
City Clerk . . . Lucy Mallonee
Attorney . . . William A. Vaughn
Finance Dir . . . Melinda J. Wall
Public Works . . . Mark Fachin (Int)
Planning Dir . . . Paula Fitzgerald
Building . . . Chet Guintini
Police Chief . . . Dan Fitchie (Int)
Fire Chief . . . Chet Guintini

Public Safety

Number of officers, 2007 . . . 47
Violent crimes, 2007 . . . 142
Property crimes, 2007 . . . 946
Arson, 2007 . . . 0

Public Library

Los Banos Branch Library
Merced County Library System
1312 Seventh St
Los Banos, CA 93635
209-826-5254

Branch Librarian . . . Lenny Costa

Library system statistics, FY 2007

Population served . . . 251,510
Internet terminals . . . 91
Annual users . . . 124,530

Per capita:

Operating income . . . $8.99
percent from local government . . . 91.3%
Operating expenditure . . . $8.99
Total materials . . . 1.61
Print holdings . . . 1.60
Visits per capita . . . 1.75

Housing & Construction

Housing Units

Total, 2008§ . . . 11,596
Single family units, attached . . . 275
Single family units, detached . . . 9,813
Multiple family units . . . 1,231
Mobile home units . . . 277
Occupied . . . 11,092
Vacancy rate . . . 4.4%
Median rent, 2000** . . . $562
Median SF home value, 2000** . . . $140,200

New Privately Owned Housing Units Authorized by Building Permit, 2007*

	Units	Construction Cost
Single	119	$27,603,530
Total	119	$27,603,530

Municipal Finance

(For local fiscal year ended in 2006)

Revenues

Total . . . $58,827,056
Taxes . . . 17,054,318
Special benefits assessment . . . 665,575
Licenses & permits . . . 1,421,327
Fines & forfeitures . . . 197,504
Revenues from use of money & property . . . 1,760,682
Intergovernmental . . . 3,879,169
Service charges . . . 18,255,670
Other revenues . . . 15,592,811
Other financing sources . . . 0

Expenditures

Total . . . $49,507,661
General government . . . 1,565,614
Public safety . . . 8,271,288
Transportation . . . 4,341,542
Community development . . . 3,766,670
Health . . . 16,453,937
Culture & leisure . . . 4,706,510
Other . . . 0

Local School District

(Data from School year 2007-08 except as noted)

Los Banos Unified
1717 South 11th St
Los Banos, CA 93635
(209) 826-3801

Superintendent . . . Steve Tietjen
Grade plan . . . K-12
Number of schools . . . 11
Enrollment . . . 8,948
High school graduates, 2006-07 . . . 473
Dropout rate . . . 3.6%
Pupil/teacher ratio . . . 20.6
Average class size . . . 25.2
Students per computer . . . 3.7
Classrooms with internet . . . 387
Avg. Daily Attendance (ADA) . . . 8,480
Cost per ADA . . . $7,772
Avg. Teacher Salary . . . $60,795

California Achievement Tests 6th ed., 2008

(Pct scoring at or above 50th National Percentile Rank)

	Math	Reading	Language
Grade 3	44%	26%	35%
Grade 7	45%	41%	41%

Academic Performance Index, 2008

Number of students tested . . . 6,712
Number of valid scores . . . 6,248
2007 API (base) . . . 712
2008 API (growth) . . . 723

SAT Testing, 2006-07

Enrollment, Grade 12 . . . 534
Number taking test . . . 124
percent taking test . . . 23.2%
percent with total score 1,500+ . . . 7.10%

Average Scores:

Math	Verbal	Writing	Total
471	468	470	1,409

Federal No Child Left Behind, 2008

(Adequate Yearly Progress standards met)

	Participation Rate	Pct Proficient
ELA	Yes	No
Math	Yes	No

API criteria . . . Yes
Graduation rate . . . Yes
criteria met/possible . . . 30/26

Other school districts for this city

(see Appendix E for information on these districts)

None

See Introduction for an explanation of all data sources.

Demographics & Socio-Economic Characteristics

(2000 Decennial Census, except as noted)

Population

1990* . . . 27,357
2000 . . . 28,592
Male . . . 13,576
Female . . . 15,016
Jan. 2008 (estimate)§ . . . 30,296
Persons per sq. mi. of land . . . 2,831.4

Race & Hispanic Origin, 2000

Race
White . . . 24,784
Black/African American . . . 226
North American Native . . . 87
Asian . . . 2,173
Pacific Islander . . . 21
Other Race . . . 366
Two or more races . . . 935
Hispanic origin, total . . . 1,491
Mexican . . . 873
Puerto Rican . . . 60
Cuban . . . 22
Other Hispanic . . . 536

Age & Nativity, 2000

Under 5 years . . . 1,419
18 years and over . . . 22,540
65 years and over . . . 4,384
85 years and over . . . 748
Median Age . . . 41.2
Native-born . . . 24,423
Foreign-born . . . 4,260

Educational Attainment, 2000

Population 25 years and over . . . 21,403
Less than 9th grade . . . 1.4%
High school grad or higher . . . 96.0%
Bachelor's degree or higher . . . 58.9%
Graduate degree . . . 25.3%

Income & Poverty, 1999

Per capita income . . . $56,094
Median household income . . . $94,319
Median family income . . . $119,194
Persons in poverty . . . 4.3%
H'holds receiving public assistance . . . 85
H'holds receiving social security . . . 2,750

Households, 2000

Total households . . . 11,988
With persons under 18 . . . 3,430
With persons over 65 . . . 2,840
Family households . . . 7,303
Single person households . . . 3,565
Persons per household . . . 2.33
Persons per family . . . 2.93

Household Population, 2008§§

Persons living in households . . . 29,594
Persons living in group quarters . . . 702
Persons per household . . . 2.4

Labor & Employment

Total civilian labor force, 2008§§ . . . 15,600
Unemployment rate, 2008 . . . 3.9%
Total civilian labor force, 2000 . . . 15,595

Employed persons 16 years and over by occupation, 2000

Managers & professionals . . . 9,762
Service occupations . . . 772
Sales & office occupations . . . 3,548
Farming, fishing & forestry . . . 31
Construction & maintenance . . . 522
Production & transportation . . . 513
Self-employed persons . . . 1,531

* US Census Bureau
** 2000 Decennial Census
§ California Department of Finance
§§ California Employment Development Dept

General Information

Town of Los Gatos
110 E Main St
Los Gatos, CA 95030
408-354-6834

Website . . . www.losgatosca.gov
Elevation . . . 385 ft.
Land Area (sq. miles) . . . 10.7
Water Area (sq. miles) . . . 0.1
Year of Incorporation . . . 1887
Government type . . . General law
Sales tax rate . . . 9.25%

Voters & Officials

Registered Voters, October 2008

Total . . . 18,707
Democrats . . . 7,917
Republicans . . . 6,340
Declined to state . . . 3,814

Legislative Districts

US Congressional . . . 15
State Senatorial . . . 15
State Assembly . . . 21

Local Officials, 2009

Mayor . . . Mike Wasserman
Manager . . . Greg Larson
City Clerk . . . Jackie Rose
Attorney . . . Orry Korb
Finance Dir . . . Steve Conway
Public Works . . . Todd Capurso
Planning/Dev Dir . . . Bud Lortz
Building . . . Anthony Ghiossi
Police Chief . . . Scott Seaman
Fire/Emergency Mgmt . . . (County)

Public Safety

Number of officers, 2007 . . . 42
Violent crimes, 2007 . . . 35
Property crimes, 2007 . . . 625
Arson, 2007 . . . 29

Public Library

Los Gatos Public Library
110 E Main St
Los Gatos, CA 95030
408-354-6898

Director . . . Peggy Conaway

Library statistics, FY 2007

Population served . . . 29,407
Internet terminals . . . 13
Annual users . . . 22,768

Per capita:

Operating income . . . $67.66
percent from local government . . . 91.3%
Operating expenditure . . . $51.03
Total materials . . . 5.06
Print holdings . . . 4.16
Visits per capita . . . 6.70

Housing & Construction

Housing Units

Total, 2008§ . . . 12,952
Single family units, attached . . . 1,841
Single family units, detached . . . 7,172
Multiple family units . . . 3,816
Mobile home units . . . 123
Occupied . . . 12,556
Vacancy rate . . . 3.1%
Median rent, 2000** . . . $1,331
Median SF home value, 2000** . . . $784,600

New Privately Owned Housing Units Authorized by Building Permit, 2007*

	Units	Construction Cost
Single	34	$27,716,417
Total	34	$27,716,417

Municipal Finance

(For local fiscal year ended in 2006)

Revenues

Total . . . $33,827,846
Taxes . . . 20,150,232
Special benefits assessment . . . 37,110
Licenses & permits . . . 1,561,722
Fines & forfeitures . . . 569,015
Revenues from use of money & property . . . 1,593,597
Intergovernmental . . . 2,392,144
Service charges . . . 4,071,674
Other revenues . . . 3,452,352
Other financing sources . . . 0

Expenditures

Total . . . $28,621,082
General government . . . 2,752,117
Public safety . . . 11,811,378
Transportation . . . 3,736,861
Community development . . . 5,270,297
Health . . . 551,164
Culture & leisure . . . 4,481,227
Other . . . 18,038

Local School District

(Data from School year 2007-08 except as noted)

Los Gatos-Saratoga Joint Union High
17421 Farley Road West
Los Gatos, CA 95030
(408) 354-2520

Superintendent . . . Cary Matsuoka
Grade plan . . . 9-12
Number of schools . . . 2
Enrollment . . . 3,164
High school graduates, 2006-07 . . . 729
Dropout rate . . . 0.3%
Pupil/teacher ratio . . . 21.5
Average class size . . . 25.5
Students per computer . . . 2.5
Classrooms with internet . . . 168
Avg. Daily Attendance (ADA) . . . 3,100
Cost per ADA . . . $10,706
Avg. Teacher Salary . . . $88,151

California Achievement Tests 6th ed., 2008

(Pct scoring at or above 50th National Percentile Rank)

	Math	Reading	Language
Grade 3	NA	NA	NA
Grade 7	NA	NA	NA

Academic Performance Index, 2008

Number of students tested . . . 2,298
Number of valid scores . . . 2,269
2007 API (base) . . . 872
2008 API (growth) . . . 879

SAT Testing, 2006-07

Enrollment, Grade 12 . . . 753
Number taking test . . . 578
percent taking test . . . 76.8%
percent with total score 1,500+ . . . 70.50%

Average Scores:

Math	Verbal	Writing	Total
641	607	614	1,862

Federal No Child Left Behind, 2008

(Adequate Yearly Progress standards met)

	Participation Rate	Pct Proficient
ELA	No	Yes
Math	Yes	Yes

API criteria . . . Yes
Graduation rate . . . Yes
\# criteria met/possible . . . 14/13

Other school districts for this city

(see Appendix E for information on these districts)
Complete list in Appendix E

See Introduction for an explanation of all data sources.

Demographics & Socio-Economic Characteristics

(2000 Decennial Census, except as noted)

Population

1990* 931
2000 862
Male 419
Female 443
Jan. 2008 (estimate)§ 851
Persons per sq. mi. of land 2,836.7

Race & Hispanic Origin, 2000

Race
White 818
Black/African American 2
North American Native 23
Asian 1
Pacific Islander 0
Other Race 5
Two or more races 13
Hispanic origin, total 62
Mexican 48
Puerto Rican 0
Cuban 3
Other Hispanic 11

Age & Nativity, 2000

Under 5 years 51
18 years and over 611
65 years and over 135
85 years and over 28
Median Age 38.6
Native-born 840
Foreign-born 34

Educational Attainment, 2000

Population 25 years and over 562
Less than 9th grade 6.4%
High school grad or higher 78.1%
Bachelor's degree or higher 7.5%
Graduate degree 2.5%

Income & Poverty, 1999

Per capita income $15,732
Median household income $34,063
Median family income $39,750
Persons in poverty 17.5%
H'holds receiving public assistance 28
H'holds receiving social security 91

Households, 2000

Total households 323
With persons under 18 135
With persons over 65 82
Family households 235
Single person households 77
Persons per household 2.58
Persons per family 3.00

Household Population, 2008§§

Persons living in households 821
Persons living in group quarters 30
Persons per household 2.3

Labor & Employment

Total civilian labor force, 2008§§ 370
Unemployment rate, 2008 .... 13.2%
Total civilian labor force, 2000 370

Employed persons 16 years and over by occupation, 2000

Managers & professionals 74
Service occupations 70
Sales & office occupations 57
Farming, fishing & forestry 10
Construction & maintenance 49
Production & transportation 66
Self-employed persons 20

* US Census Bureau
** 2000 Decennial Census
§ California Department of Finance
§§ California Employment Development Dept

General Information

City of Loyalton
210 Front St
City Hall
Loyalton, CA 96118
530-993-6750

Email .... cityofloyalton@gotsky.com
Elevation .... 4,936 ft.
Land Area (sq. miles) 0.3
Water Area (sq. miles) 0
Year of Incorporation 1901
Government type .... General law
Sales tax rate 8.25%

Voters & Officials

Registered Voters, October 2008

Total 466
Democrats 169
Republicans 181
Declined to state 83

Legislative Districts

US Congressional 4
State Senatorial 1
State Assembly 3

Local Officials, 2009

Mayor .... Mike Hudson
Manager/Admin .... NA
City Clerk .... Kathy LeBlanc
Attorney .... Steve Gross
Finance Dir .... Jennifer Hood
Public Works .... John Cussins
Planning Dir .... Tim Beals
Building .... Tim Beals
Police Chief .... (County)
Fire Chief .... Joe Marin

Public Safety

Number of officers, 2007 .... NA
Violent crimes, 2007 .... NA
Property crimes, 2007 .... NA
Arson, 2007 .... NA

Public Library

Loyalton Station Library
Plumas County Library System
511 Main St
Loyalton, CA 96118
530-993-1105

Branch Librarian .... Carolynne Foreman

Library system statistics, FY 2007

Population served 24,613
Internet terminals 18
Annual users 19,223

Per capita:

Operating income $27.64
percent from local government 81.9%
Operating expenditure $27.64
Total materials 3.15
Print holdings 3.07
Visits per capita .... NA

Housing & Construction

Housing Units

Total, 2008§ 377
Single family units, attached 13
Single family units, detached 328
Multiple family units 3
Mobile home units 33
Occupied 352
Vacancy rate 6.6%
Median rent, 2000** $504
Median SF home value, 2000** $84,000

New Privately Owned Housing Units Authorized by Building Permit, 2007*

	Units	Construction Cost
Single	NA	NA
Total	NA	NA

Municipal Finance

(For local fiscal year ended in 2006)

Revenues

Total .... NA
Taxes .... NA
Special benefits assessment .... NA
Licenses & permits .... NA
Fines & forfeitures .... NA
Revenues from use of money & property .... NA
Intergovernmental .... NA
Service charges .... NA
Other revenues .... NA
Other financing sources .... NA

Expenditures

Total .... NA
General government .... NA
Public safety .... NA
Transportation .... NA
Community development .... NA
Health .... NA
Culture & leisure .... NA
Other .... NA

Local School District

(Data from School year 2007-08 except as noted)

Sierra-Plumas Joint Unified
PO Box 157
Sierraville, CA 96126
(530) 994-1044

Superintendent .... Stan Hardeman
Grade plan K-12
Number of schools 7
Enrollment 493
High school graduates, 2006-07 47
Dropout rate 7.0%
Pupil/teacher ratio 14.1
Average class size 12.3
Students per computer 3.4
Classrooms with internet 36
Avg. Daily Attendance (ADA) 450
Cost per ADA $13,272
Avg. Teacher Salary $49,608

California Achievement Tests 6th ed., 2008

(Pct scoring at or above 50th National Percentile Rank)

	Math	Reading	Language
Grade 3	67%	70%	78%
Grade 7	52%	63%	48%

Academic Performance Index, 2008

Number of students tested 362
Number of valid scores 339
2007 API (base) 760
2008 API (growth) 770

SAT Testing, 2006-07

Enrollment, Grade 12 55
Number taking test 30
percent taking test 54.6%
percent with total score 1,500+ 18.20%

Average Scores:

Math	Verbal	Writing	Total
494	482	480	1,456

Federal No Child Left Behind, 2008

(Adequate Yearly Progress standards met)

	Participation Rate	Pct Proficient
ELA	Yes	Yes
Math	Yes	Yes

API criteria .... Yes
Graduation rate .... Yes
\# criteria met/possible 14/14

Other school districts for this city

(see Appendix E for information on these districts)

None

See Introduction for an explanation of all data sources.

Demographics & Socio-Economic Characteristics†

(2007 American Community Survey, except as noted)

Population

1990* 61,945
2007 69,537
Male 32,658
Female 36,879
Jan. 2008 (estimate)§ 73,147
Persons per sq. mi. of land 14,928.0

Race & Hispanic Origin, 2007

Race
White 23,910
Black/African American 6,876
North American Native 378
Asian 39
Pacific Islander 222
Other Race 36,489
Two or more races 1,623
Hispanic origin, total .... NA
Mexican 50,955
Puerto Rican 259
Cuban 0
Other Hispanic 8,633

Age & Nativity, 2007

Under 5 years 5,036
18 years and over 46,344
65 years and over 2,630
85 years and over 443
Median Age 27.8
Native-born 39,984
Foreign-born 29,553

Educational Attainment, 2007

Population 25 years and over 37,798
Less than 9th grade 27.0%
High school grad or higher 45.7%
Bachelor's degree or higher 2.9%
Graduate degree 0.8%

Income & Poverty, 2007

Per capita income $12,909
Median household income $43,044
Median family income $43,694
Persons in poverty 15.3%
H'holds receiving public assistance 661
H'holds receiving social security 2,476

Households, 2007

Total households 14,745
With persons under 18 9,331
With persons over 65 1,567
Family households 12,825
Single person households 1,565
Persons per household 4.39
Persons per family 4.71

Household Population, 2008§§

Persons living in households 70,947
Persons living in group quarters 2,200
Persons per household 4.9

Labor & Employment

Total civilian labor force, 2008§§ 27,900
Unemployment rate, 2008 .... 12.1%
Total civilian labor force, 2000* 24,121

Employed persons 16 years and over by occupation, 2007

Managers & professionals .... NA
Service occupations .... NA
Sales & office occupations .... NA
Farming, fishing & forestry .... NA
Construction & maintenance .... NA
Production & transportation .... NA
Self-employed persons 2,154

† see Appendix D for 2000 Decennial Census Data
* US Census Bureau
** 2007 American Community Survey
§ California Department of Finance
§§ California Employment Development Dept

General Information

City of Lynwood
11330 Bullis Rd
Lynwood, CA 90262
310-603-0220

Website .... www.lynwood.ca.us
Elevation .... 85 ft.
Land Area (sq. miles) 4.9
Water Area (sq. miles) 0
Year of Incorporation 1921
Government type .... General law
Sales tax rate 9.25%

Voters & Officials

Registered Voters, October 2008

Total 20,546
Democrats 14,190
Republicans 2,077
Declined to state 3,487

Legislative Districts

US Congressional 39
State Senatorial 27
State Assembly 50

Local Officials, 2009

Mayor .... Maria Teresa Santillian
Manager .... Roger Haley
City Clerk .... Maria Quinonez
Attorney .... Fran Gallewte
Finance Dir .... Robert Torrez (Dep)
Public Works .... Daniel Ojada
Planning/Dev Dir .... Johsn Collin
Building .... NA
Police Chief .... (County)
Emergency/Fire Dir .... James W. Powers

Public Safety

Number of officers, 2007 .... NA
Violent crimes, 2007 721
Property crimes, 2007 1,847
Arson, 2007 35

Public Library

Lynwood Library
Los Angeles County Public Library System
11320 Bullis Rd
Lynwood, CA 90262
310-635-7121

Branch Librarian .... Glorieta Navo

Library system statistics, FY 2007

Population served 3,673,313
Internet terminals 749
Annual users 3,748,771

Per capita:

Operating income $30.06
percent from local government 93.6%
Operating expenditure $28.36
Total materials 2.22
Print holdings 1.97
Visits per capita 3.25

Housing & Construction

Housing Units

Total, 2008§ 14,999
Single family units, attached 1,691
Single family units, detached 8,169
Multiple family units 5,027
Mobile home units 112
Occupied 14,405
Vacancy rate 4.0%
Median rent, 2007** $931
Median SF home value, 2007** $467,500

New Privately Owned Housing Units Authorized by Building Permit, 2007*

	Units	Construction Cost
Single	42	$7,050,217
Total	42	$7,050,217

Municipal Finance

(For local fiscal year ended in 2006)

Revenues

Total $40,228,585
Taxes 19,526,581
Special benefits assessment 2,120,370
Licenses & permits 565,733
Fines & forfeitures 907,119
Revenues from use of money & property 2,028,134
Intergovernmental 6,301,897
Service charges 8,620,213
Other revenues 158,538
Other financing sources 0

Expenditures

Total $72,884,483
General government 10,366,917
Public safety 11,936,798
Transportation 9,115,242
Community development 8,424,937
Health 2,513,549
Culture & leisure 24,950,316
Other 0

Local School District

(Data from School year 2007-08 except as noted)

Lynwood Unified
11321 Bullis Rd
Lynwood, CA 90262
(310) 886-1600

Superintendent .... Dhyan Lal
Grade plan K-12
Number of schools 20
Enrollment 17,619
High school graduates, 2006-07 787
Dropout rate 13.1%
Pupil/teacher ratio 21.5
Average class size 25.5
Students per computer 3.2
Classrooms with internet 776
Avg. Daily Attendance (ADA) 16,915
Cost per ADA $8,526
Avg. Teacher Salary $62,718

California Achievement Tests 6th ed., 2008

(Pct scoring at or above 50th National Percentile Rank)

	Math	Reading	Language
Grade 3	43%	21%	36%
Grade 7	29%	25%	24%

Academic Performance Index, 2008

Number of students tested 13,077
Number of valid scores 12,283
2007 API (base) 644
2008 API (growth) 668

SAT Testing, 2006-07

Enrollment, Grade 12 1,024
Number taking test 308
percent taking test 30.1%
percent with total score 1,500+ 2.70%

Average Scores:

Math	Verbal	Writing	Total
395	405	406	1,206

Federal No Child Left Behind, 2008

(Adequate Yearly Progress standards met)

	Participation Rate	Pct Proficient
ELA	Yes	No
Math	Yes	No

API criteria .... Yes
Graduation rate .... No
\# criteria met/possible 26/16

Other school districts for this city

(see Appendix E for information on these districts)

None

See Introduction for an explanation of all data sources.

Demographics & Socio-Economic Characteristics

(2000 Decennial Census, except as noted)

Population

1990* 29,281
2000 43,207
Male 21,904
Female 21,303
Jan. 2008 (estimate)§ 56,710
Persons per sq. mi. of land 4,610.6

Race & Hispanic Origin, 2000

Race
White 20,804
Black/African American 1,665
North American Native 1,207
Asian 618
Pacific Islander 44
Other Race 16,425
Two or more races 2,444
Hispanic origin, total 29,274
Mexican 25,562
Puerto Rican 107
Cuban 21
Other Hispanic 3,584

Age & Nativity, 2000

Under 5 years 4,634
18 years and over 27,902
65 years and over 3,813
85 years and over 495
Median Age 26.2
Native-born 29,610
Foreign-born 13,760

Educational Attainment, 2000

Population 25 years and over 22,755
Less than 9th grade 31.1%
High school grad or higher 52.8%
Bachelor's degree or higher 9.3%
Graduate degree 2.6%

Income & Poverty, 1999

Per capita income $11,674
Median household income $31,033
Median family income $31,927
Persons in poverty 32.2%
H'holds receiving public assistance . . . 1,497
H'holds receiving social security 2,888

Households, 2000

Total households 11,978
With persons under 18 6,472
With persons over 65 2,712
Family households 9,435
Single person households 2,013
Persons per household 3.57
Persons per family 3.90

Household Population, 2008§§

Persons living in households 56,182
Persons living in group quarters 528
Persons per household 3.6

Labor & Employment

Total civilian labor force, 2008§§ 23,300
Unemployment rate, 2008 . . . . . 13.4%
Total civilian labor force, 2000 17,447

Employed persons 16 years and over by occupation, 2000

Managers & professionals 2,820
Service occupations 2,564
Sales & office occupations 3,002
Farming, fishing & forestry 1,972
Construction & maintenance 1,231
Production & transportation 2,598
Self-employed persons 882

* US Census Bureau
** 2000 Decennial Census
§ California Department of Finance
§§ California Employment Development Dept

General Information

City of Madera
205 W 4th St
Madera, CA 93637
559-661-5400

Website . . . . . www.cityofmadera.org
Elevation . . . . . 270 ft.
Land Area (sq. miles) 12.3
Water Area (sq. miles) 0
Year of Incorporation 1907
Government type . . . . . General law
Sales tax rate 8.75%

Voters & Officials

Registered Voters, October 2008

Total 15,441
Democrats 6,965
Republicans 5,600
Declined to state 2,425

Legislative Districts

US Congressional 19
State Senatorial 12
State Assembly 25, 29

Local Officials, 2009

Mayor . . . . . Sam Armentrout
City Administrator . . . . . David Tooley
City Clerk . . . . . Sonia Alvarez
Attorney . . . . . Richard K. Denhalter
Finance Dir . . . . . David B. Croff
Public Works . . . . . Matt Bullis
Community Dev Dir . . . . . David Merchen
Building . . . . . Steve Woodworth
Police Chief . . . . . Mike Kime
Division Fire Chief . . . . . David Irion

Public Safety

Number of officers, 2007 58
Violent crimes, 2007 415
Property crimes, 2007 1,272
Arson, 2007 0

Public Library

Madera Library
Madera County Library System
121 North G St
Madera, CA 93637
559-675-7871

County Librarian . . . . . Linda Sitterding

Library system statistics, FY 2007

Population served 148,721
Internet terminals 26
Annual users 43,295

Per capita:

Operating income $10.35
percent from local government 95.5%
Operating expenditure $9.22
Total materials 1.88
Print holdings 1.79
Visits per capita 1.97

Housing & Construction

Housing Units

Total, 2008§ 16,418
Single family units, attached 748
Single family units, detached 11,540
Multiple family units 3,828
Mobile home units 302
Occupied 15,705
Vacancy rate 4.3%
Median rent, 2000** $527
Median SF home value, 2000** $93,600

New Privately Owned Housing Units Authorized by Building Permit, 2007*

	Units	Construction Cost
Single	218	$26,970,971
Total	241	$28,793,038

Municipal Finance

(For local fiscal year ended in 2006)

Revenues

Total $62,354,947
Taxes 22,845,101
Special benefits assessment 1,079,786
Licenses & permits 1,358,734
Fines & forfeitures 244,501
Revenues from use of money & property 2,016,840
Intergovernmental 8,158,109
Service charges 20,615,201
Other revenues 4,270,175
Other financing sources 1,766,500

Expenditures

Total $51,805,039
General government 3,217,218
Public safety 10,220,730
Transportation 10,672,865
Community development 3,924,924
Health 14,412,639
Culture & leisure 2,863,601
Other 4,155,331

Local School District

(Data from School year 2007-08 except as noted)

Madera Unified
1902 Howard Rd
Madera, CA 93637
(559) 675-4500

Superintendent . . . . . John Stafford
Grade plan K-12
Number of schools 26
Enrollment 18,941
High school graduates, 2006-07 859
Dropout rate 7.7%
Pupil/teacher ratio 21.0
Average class size 24.0
Students per computer 2.7
Classrooms with internet 914
Avg. Daily Attendance (ADA) 17,917
Cost per ADA $7,924
Avg. Teacher Salary $60,225

California Achievement Tests 6th ed., 2008

(Pct scoring at or above 50th National Percentile Rank)

	Math	Reading	Language
Grade 3	51%	25%	36%
Grade 7	42%	38%	37%

Academic Performance Index, 2008

Number of students tested 14,100
Number of valid scores 13,390
2007 API (base) 704
2008 API (growth) 717

SAT Testing, 2006-07

Enrollment, Grade 12 1,172
Number taking test 147
percent taking test 12.5%
percent with total score 1,500+ 3.80%

Average Scores:

Math	Verbal	Writing	Total
476	469	456	1,401

Federal No Child Left Behind, 2008

(Adequate Yearly Progress standards met)

	Participation Rate	Pct Proficient
ELA	Yes	No
Math	Yes	Yes

API criteria . . . . . Yes
Graduation rate . . . . . Yes
criteria met/possible 34/33

Other school districts for this city

(see Appendix E for information on these districts)

Golden Valley Unified

See Introduction for an explanation of all data sources.

Demographics & Socio-Economic Characteristics

(2000 Decennial Census, except as noted)

Population

1990* . . . NA
2000 . . . 12,575
Male . . . 6,216
Female . . . 6,359
Jan. 2008 (estimate)§ . . . 13,700
Persons per sq. mi. of land . . . 688.4

Race & Hispanic Origin, 2000

Race
White . . . 11,558
Black/African American . . . 113
North American Native . . . 27
Asian . . . 313
Pacific Islander . . . 12
Other Race . . . 210
Two or more races . . . 342
Hispanic origin, total . . . 689
Mexican . . . 375
Puerto Rican . . . 29
Cuban . . . 16
Other Hispanic . . . 269

Age & Nativity, 2000

Under 5 years . . . 568
18 years and over . . . 10,108
65 years and over . . . 1,762
85 years and over . . . 131
Median Age . . . 42.9
Native-born . . . 10,707
Foreign-born . . . 1,807

Educational Attainment, 2000

Population 25 years and over . . . 9,149
Less than 9th grade . . . 0.6%
High school grad or higher . . . 95.9%
Bachelor's degree or higher . . . 59.4%
Graduate degree . . . 26.7%

Income & Poverty, 1999

Per capita income . . . $74,336
Median household income . . . $102,031
Median family income . . . $123,293
Persons in poverty . . . 7.5%
H'holds receiving public assistance . . . 21
H'holds receiving social security . . . 1,235

Households, 2000

Total households . . . 5,137
With persons under 18 . . . 1,392
With persons over 65 . . . 1,263
Family households . . . 3,165
Single person households . . . 1,404
Persons per household . . . 2.39
Persons per family . . . 2.86

Household Population, 2008§§

Persons living in households . . . 13,400
Persons living in group quarters . . . 300
Persons per household . . . 2.5

Labor & Employment

Total civilian labor force, 2008§§ . . . 7,700
Unemployment rate, 2008 . . . 2.6%
Total civilian labor force, 2000 . . . 6,597

Employed persons 16 years and over by occupation, 2000

Managers & professionals . . . 3,694
Service occupations . . . 806
Sales & office occupations . . . 1,431
Farming, fishing & forestry . . . 0
Construction & maintenance . . . 245
Production & transportation . . . 235
Self-employed persons . . . 1,374

* US Census Bureau
** 2000 Decennial Census
§ California Department of Finance
§§ California Employment Development Dept

General Information

City of Malibu
23815 Stuart Ranch Rd
Malibu, CA 90265
310-456-2489

Website . . . www.ci.malibu.ca.us
Elevation . . . NA
Land Area (sq. miles) . . . 19.9
Water Area (sq. miles) . . . 81.1
Year of Incorporation . . . 1991
Government type . . . General law
Sales tax rate . . . 9.25%

Voters & Officials

Registered Voters, October 2008

Total . . . 8,701
Democrats . . . 3,829
Republicans . . . 2,698
Declined to state . . . 1,750

Legislative Districts

US Congressional . . . 30
State Senatorial . . . 23
State Assembly . . . 41

Local Officials, 2009

Mayor . . . Andy Stern
Manager . . . Jim Thorsen
City Clerk . . . Lisa Pope
Attorney . . . Christi Hogin
Finance Dir . . . Reva Feldman
Public Works . . . Bob Brager
Planning/Dev Dir . . . Stacey Lundin
Building . . . Craig George
Police Chief . . . NA
Fire/Emergency Mgmt . . . NA

Public Safety

Number of officers, 2007 . . . NA
Violent crimes, 2007 . . . 29
Property crimes, 2007 . . . 323
Arson, 2007 . . . 6

Public Library

Malibu Library
Los Angeles County Public Library System
23519 W Civic Center Way
Malibu, CA 90265
310-456-6438

Branch Librarian . . . Winona Phillabaum

Library system statistics, FY 2007

Population served . . . 3,673,313
Internet terminals . . . 749
Annual users . . . 3,748,771

Per capita:

Operating income . . . $30.06
percent from local government . . . 93.6%
Operating expenditure . . . $28.36
Total materials . . . 2.22
Print holdings . . . 1.97
Visits per capita . . . 3.25

Housing & Construction

Housing Units

Total, 2008§ . . . 6,382
Single family units, attached . . . 491
Single family units, detached . . . 4,039
Multiple family units . . . 1,242
Mobile home units . . . 610
Occupied . . . 5,351
Vacancy rate . . . 16.2%
Median rent, 2000** . . . $1,652
Median SF home value, 2000** . . $1,000,001

New Privately Owned Housing Units Authorized by Building Permit, 2007*

	Units	Construction Cost
Single	31	$20,136,877
Total	31	$20,136,877

Municipal Finance

(For local fiscal year ended in 2006)

Revenues

Total . . . $48,740,433
Taxes . . . 13,601,944
Special benefits assessment . . . 358,427
Licenses & permits . . . 2,862,908
Fines & forfeitures . . . 701,503
Revenues from use of money & property . . . 725,662
Intergovernmental . . . 6,217,354
Service charges . . . 1,655,606
Other revenues . . . 5,037,029
Other financing sources . . . 17,580,000

Expenditures

Total . . . $44,651,531
General government . . . 3,993,576
Public safety . . . 4,796,921
Transportation . . . 4,447,035
Community development . . . 29,875,021
Health . . . 55,197
Culture & leisure . . . 1,483,781
Other . . . 0

Local School District

(Data from School year 2007-08 except as noted)

Santa Monica-Malibu Unified
1651 16th St
Santa Monica, CA 90404
(310) 450-8338

Superintendent . . . Tim Cuneo
Grade plan . . . K-12
Number of schools . . . 17
Enrollment . . . 11,688
High school graduates, 2006-07 . . . 848
Dropout rate . . . 2.9%
Pupil/teacher ratio . . . 20.1
Average class size . . . 25.4
Students per computer . . . 3.5
Classrooms with internet . . . 596
Avg. Daily Attendance (ADA) . . . 11,424
Cost per ADA . . . $9,835
Avg. Teacher Salary . . . $67,843

California Achievement Tests 6th ed., 2008

(Pct scoring at or above 50th National Percentile Rank)

	Math	Reading	Language
Grade 3	76%	59%	69%
Grade 7	69%	69%	68%

Academic Performance Index, 2008

Number of students tested . . . 8,897
Number of valid scores . . . 8,505
2007 API (base) . . . 819
2008 API (growth) . . . 832

SAT Testing, 2006-07

Enrollment, Grade 12 . . . 954
Number taking test . . . 632
percent taking test . . . 66.3%
percent with total score 1,500+ . . . 44.00%

Average Scores:

Math	Verbal	Writing	Total
556	542	544	1,642

Federal No Child Left Behind, 2008

(Adequate Yearly Progress standards met)

	Participation Rate	Pct Proficient
ELA	No	Yes
Math	Yes	Yes

API criteria . . . Yes
Graduation rate . . . Yes
\# criteria met/possible . . . 34/33

Other school districts for this city

(see Appendix E for information on these districts)

None

See Introduction for an explanation of all data sources.

Demographics & Socio-Economic Characteristics

(2000 Decennial Census, except as noted)

Population

1990* 4,785
2000 7,093
Male 4,034
Female 3,059
Jan. 2008 (estimate)§ 7,413
Persons per sq. mi. of land 298.9

Race & Hispanic Origin, 2000

Race
White 5,902
Black/African American 29
North American Native 35
Asian 90
Pacific Islander 9
Other Race 876
Two or more races 152
Hispanic origin, total 1,575
Mexican 1,305
Puerto Rican 66
Cuban 4
Other Hispanic 200

Age & Nativity, 2000

Under 5 years 402
18 years and over 5,499
65 years and over 307
85 years and over 8
Median Age 32.2
Native-born 5,939
Foreign-born 1,155

Educational Attainment, 2000

Population 25 years and over 4,664
Less than 9th grade 6.4%
High school grad or higher 87.0%
Bachelor's degree or higher 34.0%
Graduate degree 10.6%

Income & Poverty, 1999

Per capita income $24,526
Median household income $44,570
Median family income $52,561
Persons in poverty 14.4%
H'holds receiving public assistance 85
H'holds receiving social security 245

Households, 2000

Total households 2,814
With persons under 18 856
With persons over 65 229
Family households 1,516
Single person households 796
Persons per household 2.44
Persons per family 3.09

Household Population, 2008§§

Persons living in households 7,195
Persons living in group quarters 218
Persons per household 2.2

Labor & Employment

Total civilian labor force, 2008§§ 5,210
Unemployment rate, 2008 . . . . 5.6%
Total civilian labor force, 2000 4,561

Employed persons 16 years and over by occupation, 2000

Managers & professionals 1,473
Service occupations 1,125
Sales & office occupations 941
Farming, fishing & forestry 5
Construction & maintenance 486
Production & transportation 283
Self-employed persons 498

* US Census Bureau
** 2000 Decennial Census
§ California Department of Finance
§§ California Employment Development Dept

General Information

Town of Mammoth Lakes
PO Box 1609
Mammoth Lakes, CA 93546
760-934-8989

Website . . . . www.ci.mammoth-lakes.ca.us
Elevation . . . . 7,890 ft
Land Area (sq. miles) 24.8
Water Area (sq. miles) 0.4
Year of Incorporation 1984
Government type . . . . General law
Sales tax rate 8.75%

Voters & Officials

Registered Voters, October 2008

Total 3,407
Democrats 1,161
Republicans 1,056
Declined to state 974

Legislative Districts

US Congressional 25
State Senatorial 1
State Assembly 25

Local Officials, 2009

Mayor . . . . Skip Harvey
Manager . . . . Robert F. Clark
City Clerk . . . . Anita Hatter
Attorney . . . . Peter Tracy
Finance Dir . . . . Brad Koehn
Public Works . . . . Ray Jarvis
Planning/Dev Dir . . . . Mark Wardlaw
Building . . . . Byron Pohlman
Police Chief . . . . Randy Schienle
Emergency/Fire Dir . . . . Brent Harper

Public Safety

Number of officers, 2007 22
Violent crimes, 2007 37
Property crimes, 2007 241
Arson, 2007 1

Public Library

Mammoth Lakes Library
Mono County Library System
400 Sierra Park Rd
Mammoth Lakes, CA 93546
760-934-4777

Branch Librarian . . . . Doug Oldham

Library system statistics, FY 2007

Population served 13,985
Internet terminals 51
Annual users 46,068

Per capita:

Operating income $52.81
percent from local government 88.8%
Operating expenditure $52.81
Total materials 8.54
Print holdings 7.73
Visits per capita 9.11

Housing & Construction

Housing Units

Total, 2008§ 9,235
Single family units, attached 1,003
Single family units, detached 2,318
Multiple family units 5,721
Mobile home units 193
Occupied 3,264
Vacancy rate 64.7%
Median rent, 2000** $715
Median SF home value, 2000** $298,600

New Privately Owned Housing Units Authorized by Building Permit, 2007*

	Units	Construction Cost
Single	31	$19,603,826
Total	42	$21,876,824

Municipal Finance

(For local fiscal year ended in 2006)

Revenues

Total $35,764,933
Taxes 17,756,157
Special benefits assessment 337,110
Licenses & permits 2,553,495
Fines & forfeitures 172,453
Revenues from use of money & property 450,037
Intergovernmental 8,717,682
Service charges 4,212,373
Other revenues 1,565,626
Other financing sources 0

Expenditures

Total $30,163,207
General government 4,512,753
Public safety 4,403,269
Transportation 9,494,628
Community development 8,685,356
Health 0
Culture & leisure 3,067,201
Other 0

Local School District

(Data from School year 2007-08 except as noted)

Mammoth Unified
PO Box 3509
Mammoth Lakes, CA 93546
(760) 934-6802

Superintendent . . . . Frank Romero
Grade plan K-12
Number of schools 5
Enrollment 1,197
High school graduates, 2006-07 69
Dropout rate 11.7%
Pupil/teacher ratio 17.8
Average class size 19.9
Students per computer 5.8
Classrooms with internet 71
Avg. Daily Attendance (ADA) 1,099
Cost per ADA $9,960
Avg. Teacher Salary $62,024

California Achievement Tests 6th ed., 2008

(Pct scoring at or above 50th National Percentile Rank)

	Math	Reading	Language
Grade 3	44%	33%	33%
Grade 7	56%	58%	53%

Academic Performance Index, 2008

Number of students tested 847
Number of valid scores 798
2007 API (base) 729
2008 API (growth) 748

SAT Testing, 2006-07

Enrollment, Grade 12 73
Number taking test 33
percent taking test 45.2%
percent with total score 1,500+ 26.00%

Average Scores:

Math	Verbal	Writing	Total
521	527	544	1,592

Federal No Child Left Behind, 2008

(Adequate Yearly Progress standards met)

	Participation Rate	Pct Proficient
ELA	Yes	No
Math	Yes	Yes

API criteria . . . . Yes
Graduation rate . . . . No
\# criteria met/possible 22/18

Other school districts for this city

(see Appendix E for information on these districts)

None

See Introduction for an explanation of all data sources.

Demographics & Socio-Economic Characteristics

(2000 Decennial Census, except as noted)

Population

1990* . . . 32,063
2000 . . . 33,852
Male . . . 17,052
Female . . . 16,800
Jan. 2008 (estimate)§ . . . 36,505
Persons per sq. mi. of land . . . 9,360.3

Race & Hispanic Origin, 2000

Race
White . . . 30,124
Black/African American . . . 208
North American Native . . . 70
Asian . . . 2,043
Pacific Islander . . . 41
Other Race . . . 415
Two or more races . . . 951
Hispanic origin, total . . . 1,756
Mexican . . . 955
Puerto Rican . . . 75
Cuban . . . 91
Other Hispanic . . . 635

Age & Nativity, 2000

Under 5 years . . . 2,197
18 years and over . . . 26,316
65 years and over . . . 3,526
85 years and over . . . 291
Median Age . . . 37.7
Native-born . . . 30,932
Foreign-born . . . 3,107

Educational Attainment, 2000

Population 25 years and over . . . 25,067
Less than 9th grade . . . 0.7%
High school grad or higher . . . 96.8%
Bachelor's degree or higher . . . 67.6%
Graduate degree . . . 28.6%

Income & Poverty, 1999

Per capita income . . . $61,136
Median household income . . . $100,750
Median family income . . . $122,686
Persons in poverty . . . 3.3%
H'holds receiving public assistance . . . 93
H'holds receiving social security . . . 2,472

Households, 2000

Total households . . . 14,474
With persons under 18 . . . 4,225
With persons over 65 . . . 2,618
Family households . . . 8,392
Single person households . . . 4,246
Persons per household . . . 2.34
Persons per family . . . 2.98

Household Population, 2008§§

Persons living in households . . . 36,491
Persons living in group quarters . . . 14
Persons per household . . . 2.4

Labor & Employment

Total civilian labor force, 2008§§ . . . 23,100
Unemployment rate, 2008 . . . 2.6%
Total civilian labor force, 2000 . . . 19,752

Employed persons 16 years and over by occupation, 2000

Managers & professionals . . . 12,370
Service occupations . . . 1,210
Sales & office occupations . . . 4,687
Farming, fishing & forestry . . . 0
Construction & maintenance . . . 553
Production & transportation . . . 405
Self-employed persons . . . 2,171

* US Census Bureau
** 2000 Decennial Census
§ California Department of Finance
§§ California Employment Development Dept

General Information

City of Manhattan Beach
1400 Highland Ave
Manhattan Beach, CA 90266
310-802-5000

Website . . . www.citymb.info
Elevation . . . 120 ft.
Land Area (sq. miles) . . . 3.9
Water Area (sq. miles) . . . 6.4
Year of Incorporation . . . 1912
Government type . . . General law
Sales tax rate . . . 9.25%

Voters & Officials

Registered Voters, October 2008

Total . . . 24,143
Democrats . . . 8,933
Republicans . . . 9,611
Declined to state . . . 4,671

Legislative Districts

US Congressional . . . 36
State Senatorial . . . 28
State Assembly . . . 53

Local Officials, 2009

Mayor . . . Richard Montgomery
Manager . . . Geoff Dolan
City Clerk . . . Liza Tamura
Attorney . . . Robert Wadden Jr
Finance Dir . . . Bruce Moe
Public Works . . . Jim Arndt
Planning/Dev Dir . . . Richard Thompson
Building . . . Richard Thompson
Police Chief . . . Rod Uyeda
Emergency/Fire Dir . . . Scott Ferguson

Public Safety

Number of officers, 2007 . . . 58
Violent crimes, 2007 . . . 54
Property crimes, 2007 . . . 1,027
Arson, 2007 . . . 2

Public Library

Manhattan Beach Library
Los Angeles County Public Library System
1320 Highland Ave
Manhattan Beach, CA 90266
310-545-8595

Branch Librarian . . . Don Gould

Library system statistics, FY 2007

Population served . . . 3,673,313
Internet terminals . . . 749
Annual users . . . 3,748,771

Per capita:

Operating income . . . $30.06
percent from local government . . . 93.6%
Operating expenditure . . . $28.36
Total materials . . . 2.22
Print holdings . . . 1.97
Visits per capita . . . 3.25

Housing & Construction

Housing Units

Total, 2008§ . . . 15,486
Single family units, attached . . . 1,417
Single family units, detached . . . 10,600
Multiple family units . . . 3,436
Mobile home units . . . 33
Occupied . . . 14,911
Vacancy rate . . . 3.7%
Median rent, 2000** . . . $1,358
Median SF home value, 2000** . . . $672,600

New Privately Owned Housing Units Authorized by Building Permit, 2007*

	Units	Construction Cost
Single	146	$54,252,176
Total	146	$54,252,176

Municipal Finance

(For local fiscal year ended in 2006)

Revenues

Total . . . $70,378,022
Taxes . . . 32,438,039
Special benefits assessment . . . 422,171
Licenses & permits . . . 1,816,850
Fines & forfeitures . . . 2,007,378
Revenues from use of money & property . . . 3,708,213
Intergovernmental . . . 3,307,660
Service charges . . . 21,922,524
Other revenues . . . 4,755,187
Other financing sources . . . 0

Expenditures

Total . . . $81,291,108
General government . . . 4,847,509
Public safety . . . 38,907,890
Transportation . . . 13,287,249
Community development . . . 2,873,069
Health . . . 5,461,582
Culture & leisure . . . 8,922,307
Other . . . 0

Local School District

(Data from School year 2007-08 except as noted)

Manhattan Beach Unified
325 South Peck Ave
Manhattan Beach, CA 90266
(310) 318-7345

Superintendent . . . Beverly Rohrer
Grade plan . . . K-12
Number of schools . . . 7
Enrollment . . . 6,332
High school graduates, 2006-07 . . . 546
Dropout rate . . . 2.2%
Pupil/teacher ratio . . . 21.2
Average class size . . . 28.2
Students per computer . . . 5.8
Classrooms with internet . . . 304
Avg. Daily Attendance (ADA) . . . 6,214
Cost per ADA . . . $8,020
Avg. Teacher Salary . . . $65,918

California Achievement Tests 6th ed., 2008

(Pct scoring at or above 50th National Percentile Rank)

	Math	Reading	Language
Grade 3	91%	81%	84%
Grade 7	91%	86%	85%

Academic Performance Index, 2008

Number of students tested . . . 4,669
Number of valid scores . . . 4,587
2007 API (base) . . . 900
2008 API (growth) . . . 909

SAT Testing, 2006-07

Enrollment, Grade 12 . . . 557
Number taking test . . . 441
percent taking test . . . 79.2%
percent with total score 1,500+ . . . 60.70%

Average Scores:

Math	Verbal	Writing	Total
584	560	571	1,715

Federal No Child Left Behind, 2008

(Adequate Yearly Progress standards met)

	Participation Rate	Pct Proficient
ELA	Yes	Yes
Math	Yes	Yes

API criteria . . . Yes
Graduation rate . . . Yes
\# criteria met/possible . . . 22/22

Other school districts for this city

(see Appendix E for information on these districts)

None

See Introduction for an explanation of all data sources.

Demographics & Socio-Economic Characteristics

(2000 Decennial Census, except as noted)

Population

1990* 40,773
2000 49,258
Male 24,161
Female 25,097
Jan. 2008 (estimate)§ 66,451
Persons per sq. mi. of land 4,179.3

Race & Hispanic Origin, 2000

Race
White 36,534
Black/African American 1,406
North American Native 643
Asian 1,733
Pacific Islander 179
Other Race 5,693
Two or more races 3,070
Hispanic origin, total 12,363
Mexican 9,732
Puerto Rican 451
Cuban 55
Other Hispanic 2,125

Age & Nativity, 2000

Under 5 years 3,716
18 years and over 33,691
65 years and over 4,576
85 years and over 558
Median Age 32.5
Native-born 43,924
Foreign-born 5,277

Educational Attainment, 2000

Population 25 years and over 29,506
Less than 9th grade 7.1%
High school grad or higher 78.3%
Bachelor's degree or higher 11.0%
Graduate degree 3.1%

Income & Poverty, 1999

Per capita income $18,241
Median household income $46,677
Median family income $51,587
Persons in poverty 9.5%
H'holds receiving public assistance 780
H'holds receiving social security 3,667

Households, 2000

Total households 16,368
With persons under 18 7,860
With persons over 65 3,227
Family households 12,485
Single person households 3,051
Persons per household 2.98
Persons per family 3.39

Household Population, 2008§§

Persons living in households 65,974
Persons living in group quarters 477
Persons per household 3.0

Labor & Employment

Total civilian labor force, 2008§§ 27,600
Unemployment rate, 2008 .... 9.0%
Total civilian labor force, 2000 22,386

Employed persons 16 years and over by occupation, 2000

Managers & professionals 5,093
Service occupations 2,911
Sales & office occupations 5,909
Farming, fishing & forestry 308
Construction & maintenance 2,686
Production & transportation 3,654
Self-employed persons 1,046

* US Census Bureau
** 2000 Decennial Census
§ California Department of Finance
§§ California Employment Development Dept

General Information

City of Manteca
1001 W Center St
Manteca, CA 95337
209-239-8400

Website .... www.ci.manteca.ca.us
Elevation .... 35 ft.
Land Area (sq. miles) 15.9
Water Area (sq. miles) 0
Year of Incorporation 1918
Government type .... General law
Sales tax rate 9.25%

Voters & Officials

Registered Voters, October 2008

Total 26,770
Democrats 10,900
Republicans 10,390
Declined to state 4,272

Legislative Districts

US Congressional 11
State Senatorial 5
State Assembly 26

Local Officials, 2009

Mayor .... Willie W. Weatherford
City Manager .... Steven J. Pinkerton
City Clerk .... Joann L. Tilton
Attorney .... John Brinton
Finance Dir .... Suzanne Mallory
Public Works .... Mark Houghton
Community Dev Dir .... Mark Nelson
Building .... Michael Hosier
Police Chief .... David Bricker
Fire Chief .... Krik Waters (Int)

Public Safety

Number of officers, 2007 77
Violent crimes, 2007 242
Property crimes, 2007 2,647
Arson, 2007 28

Public Library

Manteca Library
Stockton-San Joaquin County Public Library
320 W Center St
Manteca, CA 95336
209-937-8221

Branch Librarian .... Diane Bills

Library system statistics, FY 2007

Population served 619,292
Internet terminals 125
Annual users 255,083

Per capita:

Operating income $21.59
percent from local government 96.0%
Operating expenditure $19.98
Total materials 1.65
Print holdings 1.52
Visits per capita 2.20

Housing & Construction

Housing Units

Total, 2008§ 22,485
Single family units, attached 739
Single family units, detached 17,198
Multiple family units 3,697
Mobile home units 851
Occupied 21,730
Vacancy rate 3.4%
Median rent, 2000** $724
Median SF home value, 2000** $156,100

New Privately Owned Housing Units Authorized by Building Permit, 2007*

	Units	Construction Cost
Single	496	$79,725,144
Total	536	$83,225,144

Municipal Finance

(For local fiscal year ended in 2006)

Revenues

Total $102,073,315
Taxes 19,979,378
Special benefits assessment 0
Licenses & permits 819,636
Fines & forfeitures 265,458
Revenues from use of money & property 3,449,837
Intergovernmental 11,674,115
Service charges 63,531,199
Other revenues 2,353,692
Other financing sources 0

Expenditures

Total $95,898,877
General government 3,183,425
Public safety 18,678,824
Transportation 20,498,515
Community development 3,544,410
Health 31,350,707
Culture & leisure 7,967,078
Other 0

Local School District

(Data from School year 2007-08 except as noted)

Manteca Unified
PO Box 32
Manteca, CA 95336
(209) 825-3200

Superintendent .... Jason Messer
Grade plan K-12
Number of schools 28
Enrollment 23,654
High school graduates, 2006-07 1,290
Dropout rate 3.3%
Pupil/teacher ratio 21.7
Average class size 26.2
Students per computer 5.0
Classrooms with internet 1,280
Avg. Daily Attendance (ADA) 22,902
Cost per ADA $7,460
Avg. Teacher Salary $59,600

California Achievement Tests 6th ed., 2008

(Pct scoring at or above 50th National Percentile Rank)

	Math	Reading	Language
Grade 3	55%	37%	46%
Grade 7	47%	47%	44%

Academic Performance Index, 2008

Number of students tested 17,956
Number of valid scores 16,762
2007 API (base) 724
2008 API (growth) 731

SAT Testing, 2006-07

Enrollment, Grade 12 1,597
Number taking test 493
percent taking test 30.9%
percent with total score 1,500+ 10.30%

Average Scores:

Math	Verbal	Writing	Total
471	468	454	1,393

Federal No Child Left Behind, 2008

(Adequate Yearly Progress standards met)

	Participation Rate	Pct Proficient
ELA	Yes	No
Math	Yes	No

API criteria .... Yes
Graduation rate .... Yes
\# criteria met/possible 46/41

Other school districts for this city

(see Appendix E for information on these districts)

None

See Introduction for an explanation of all data sources.

Demographics & Socio-Economic Characteristics

(2000 Decennial Census, except as noted)

Population

1990* ... 1,193
2000 ... 1,111
Male ... 586
Female ... 525
Jan. 2008 (estimate)§ ... 1,132
Persons per sq. mi. of land ... 754.7

Race & Hispanic Origin, 2000

Race
White ... 954
Black/African American ... 0
North American Native ... 22
Asian ... 5
Pacific Islander ... 0
Other Race ... 99
Two or more races ... 31
Hispanic origin, total ... 150
Mexican ... 135
Puerto Rican ... 0
Cuban ... 4
Other Hispanic ... 11

Age & Nativity, 2000

Under 5 years ... 71
18 years and over ... 780
65 years and over ... 125
85 years and over ... 6
Median Age ... 36.4
Native-born ... 1,036
Foreign-born ... 62

Educational Attainment, 2000

Population 25 years and over ... 705
Less than 9th grade ... 10.6%
High school grad or higher ... 67.4%
Bachelor's degree or higher ... 3.3%
Graduate degree ... 1.3%

Income & Poverty, 1999

Per capita income ... $15,692
Median household income ... $27,917
Median family income ... $31,761
Persons in poverty ... 20.9%
H'holds receiving public assistance ... 27
H'holds receiving social security ... 143

Households, 2000

Total households ... 404
With persons under 18 ... 154
With persons over 65 ... 98
Family households ... 302
Single person households ... 95
Persons per household ... 2.75
Persons per family ... 3.22

Household Population, 2008§§

Persons living in households ... 1,132
Persons living in group quarters ... 0
Persons per household ... 2.8

Labor & Employment

Total civilian labor force, 2008§§ ... 600
Unemployment rate, 2008 ... 10.9%
Total civilian labor force, 2000 ... 408

Employed persons 16 years and over by occupation, 2000

Managers & professionals ... 43
Service occupations ... 60
Sales & office occupations ... 74
Farming, fishing & forestry ... 18
Construction & maintenance ... 74
Production & transportation ... 85
Self-employed persons ... 10

* US Census Bureau
** 2000 Decennial Census
§ California Department of Finance
§§ California Employment Development Dept

General Information

City of Maricopa
PO Box 548
Maricopa, CA 93252
661-769-8279

Website ... NA
Elevation ... 854 ft.
Land Area (sq. miles) ... 1.5
Water Area (sq. miles) ... 0
Year of Incorporation ... 1911
Government type ... General law
Sales tax rate ... 8.25%

Voters & Officials

Registered Voters, October 2008

Total ... 456
Democrats ... 124
Republicans ... 216
Declined to state ... 79

Legislative Districts

US Congressional ... 22
State Senatorial ... 18
State Assembly ... 32

Local Officials, 2009

Mayor ... Gary L. Mock
Manager ... Robert E. Wilburn
City Clerk ... Gail Bullard
Attorney ... Alan Peake
Finance Dir ... NA
Public Works ... NA
Planning/Dev Dir ... NA
Building ... NA
Police Chief ... Paul Stotesbury
Fire/Emergency Mgmt ... NA

Public Safety

Number of officers, 2007 ... NA
Violent crimes, 2007 ... NA
Property crimes, 2007 ... NA
Arson, 2007 ... NA

Public Library

Served by County Library

Library system statistics, FY 2007

Population served ... NA
Internet terminals ... NA
Annual users ... NA

Per capita:

Operating income ... NA
percent from local government ... NA
Operating expenditure ... NA
Total materials ... NA
Print holdings ... NA
Visits per capita ... NA

Housing & Construction

Housing Units

Total, 2008§ ... 458
Single family units, attached ... 7
Single family units, detached ... 244
Multiple family units ... 14
Mobile home units ... 193
Occupied ... 402
Vacancy rate ... 12.2%
Median rent, 2000** ... $485
Median SF home value, 2000** ... $50,200

New Privately Owned Housing Units Authorized by Building Permit, 2007*

	Units	Construction Cost
Single	0	$0
Total	0	$0

Municipal Finance

(For local fiscal year ended in 2006)

Revenues

Total ... $640,782
Taxes ... 233,819
Special benefits assessment ... 0
Licenses & permits ... 8,906
Fines & forfeitures ... 3,246
Revenues from use of money & property ... 9,325
Intergovernmental ... 136,997
Service charges ... 212,032
Other revenues ... 36,457
Other financing sources ... 0

Expenditures

Total ... $566,134
General government ... 40,773
Public safety ... 256,580
Transportation ... 50,852
Community development ... 0
Health ... 188,248
Culture & leisure ... 29,681
Other ... 0

Local School District

(Data from School year 2007-08 except as noted)

Maricopa Unified
955 Stanislaus St
Maricopa, CA 93252
(661) 769-8231

Superintendent ... Terry Wolfe
Grade plan ... K-12
Number of schools ... 3
Enrollment ... 716
High school graduates, 2006-07 ... 18
Dropout rate ... 3.0%
Pupil/teacher ratio ... 19.1
Average class size ... 20.7
Students per computer ... 1.4
Classrooms with internet ... 402
Avg. Daily Attendance (ADA) ... 302
Cost per ADA ... $11,132
Avg. Teacher Salary ... NA

California Achievement Tests 6th ed., 2008

(Pct scoring at or above 50th National Percentile Rank)

	Math	Reading	Language
Grade 3	29%	24%	43%
Grade 7	13%	22%	17%

Academic Performance Index, 2008

Number of students tested ... 246
Number of valid scores ... 215
2007 API (base) ... 650
2008 API (growth) ... 649

SAT Testing, 2006-07

Enrollment, Grade 12 ... 26
Number taking test ... 9
percent taking test ... 34.6%
percent with total score 1,500+ ... NA

Average Scores:

Math	Verbal	Writing	Total
NA	NA	NA	NA

Federal No Child Left Behind, 2008

(Adequate Yearly Progress standards met)

	Participation Rate	Pct Proficient
ELA	Yes	No
Math	Yes	No

API criteria ... Yes
Graduation rate ... Yes
criteria met/possible ... 16/10

Other school districts for this city

(see Appendix E for information on these districts)

None

See Introduction for an explanation of all data sources.

Demographics & Socio-Economic Characteristics

(2000 Decennial Census, except as noted)

Population

1990* 26,436
2000 25,101
Male 14,367
Female 10,734
Jan. 2008 (estimate)§ 19,171
Persons per sq. mi. of land 2,203.6

Race & Hispanic Origin, 2000

Race
White 10,979
Black/African American 3,600
North American Native 186
Asian 4,084
Pacific Islander 528
Other Race 3,718
Two or more races 2,006
Hispanic origin, total 5,822
Mexican 4,752
Puerto Rican 284
Cuban 20
Other Hispanic 766

Age & Nativity, 2000

Under 5 years 1,435
18 years and over 19,745
65 years and over 1,978
85 years and over 96
Median Age 32.3
Native-born 19,344
Foreign-born 5,708

Educational Attainment, 2000

Population 25 years and over 16,307
Less than 9th grade 8.8%
High school grad or higher 71.8%
Bachelor's degree or higher 14.3%
Graduate degree 4.8%

Income & Poverty, 1999

Per capita income $18,860
Median household income $43,000
Median family income $46,139
Persons in poverty 10.0%
H'holds receiving public assistance 429
H'holds receiving social security 1,411

Households, 2000

Total households 6,745
With persons under 18 2,709
With persons over 65 1,447
Family households 4,812
Single person households 1,442
Persons per household 2.79
Persons per family 3.25

Household Population, 2008§§

Persons living in households 19,040
Persons living in group quarters 131
Persons per household 2.8

Labor & Employment

Total civilian labor force, 2008§§ 11,000
Unemployment rate, 2008 .... 5.0%
Total civilian labor force, 2000 10,298

Employed persons 16 years and over by occupation, 2000

Managers & professionals 2,486
Service occupations 2,202
Sales & office occupations 2,724
Farming, fishing & forestry 345
Construction & maintenance 815
Production & transportation 874
Self-employed persons 695

* US Census Bureau
** 2000 Decennial Census
§ California Department of Finance
§§ California Employment Development Dept

General Information

City of Marina
211 Hillcrest Ave
Marina, CA 93933
831-884-1278

Website .... www.ci.marina.ca.us
Elevation .... 40 ft.
Land Area (sq. miles) 8.7
Water Area (sq. miles) 0.9
Year of Incorporation 1975
Government type .... Chartered
Sales tax rate 8.25%

Voters & Officials

Registered Voters, October 2008

Total 8,602
Democrats 4,207
Republicans 2,099
Declined to state 1,949

Legislative Districts

US Congressional 17
State Senatorial 15
State Assembly 27, 28

Local Officials, 2009

Mayor .... Bruce C. Delgado
Manager .... Anthony Altfeld
City Clerk .... Joy P. Junsay
Attorney .... Robert Wellington
Finance Dir .... Lauren Lai
Public Works .... Christine di Iorio
Planning/Dev Dir .... Christine di Lorio
Building .... Christine di Iorio
Police Chief .... Edmundo Rodriguez
Emergency/Fire Dir .... Harald Kelley

Public Safety

Number of officers, 2007 31
Violent crimes, 2007 50
Property crimes, 2007 586
Arson, 2007 .... NA

Public Library

Marina Branch Library
Monterey County Free Libraries
190 Seaside Circle
Marina, CA 93933
831-883-7507

Branch Librarian .... Kurt Ellison

Library system statistics, FY 2007

Population served 226,803
Internet terminals 160
Annual users 229,676

Per capita:

Operating income $29.19
percent from local government 91.7%
Operating expenditure $27.42
Total materials 1.92
Print holdings 1.81
Visits per capita 3.65

Housing & Construction

Housing Units

Total, 2008§ 8,709
Single family units, attached 1,537
Single family units, detached 3,510
Multiple family units 3,205
Mobile home units 457
Occupied 6,880
Vacancy rate 21.0%
Median rent, 2000** $778
Median SF home value, 2000** $247,100

New Privately Owned Housing Units Authorized by Building Permit, 2007*

	Units	Construction Cost
Single	23	$5,186,186
Total	23	$5,186,186

Municipal Finance

(For local fiscal year ended in 2006)

Revenues

Total $15,869,365
Taxes 8,160,431
Special benefits assessment 0
Licenses & permits 235,195
Fines & forfeitures 120,612
Revenues from use of money & property 988,133
Intergovernmental 2,937,242
Service charges 2,703,469
Other revenues 574,264
Other financing sources 150,019

Expenditures

Total $17,964,077
General government 2,545,792
Public safety 5,735,222
Transportation 3,196,070
Community development 5,063,288
Health 0
Culture & leisure 1,423,705
Other 0

Local School District

(Data from School year 2007-08 except as noted)

Monterey Peninsula Unified
PO Box 1031
Monterey, CA 93942
(831) 645-1200

Superintendent .... Marilyn Shepherd
Grade plan K-12
Number of schools 22
Enrollment 11,613
High school graduates, 2006-07 590
Dropout rate 2.0%
Pupil/teacher ratio 20.5
Average class size 24.3
Students per computer 8.5
Classrooms with internet 518
Avg. Daily Attendance (ADA) 10,537
Cost per ADA $8,271
Avg. Teacher Salary $57,857

California Achievement Tests 6th ed., 2008

(Pct scoring at or above 50th National Percentile Rank)

	Math	Reading	Language
Grade 3	56%	35%	43%
Grade 7	49%	44%	43%

Academic Performance Index, 2008

Number of students tested 8,210
Number of valid scores 7,687
2007 API (base) 716
2008 API (growth) 728

SAT Testing, 2006-07

Enrollment, Grade 12 682
Number taking test 262
percent taking test 38.4%
percent with total score 1,500+ 15.10%

Average Scores:

Math	Verbal	Writing	Total
504	487	481	1,472

Federal No Child Left Behind, 2008

(Adequate Yearly Progress standards met)

	Participation Rate	Pct Proficient
ELA	Yes	No
Math	Yes	No

API criteria .... Yes
Graduation rate .... Yes
\# criteria met/possible 42/36

Other school districts for this city

(see Appendix E for information on these districts)

None

See Introduction for an explanation of all data sources.

Demographics & Socio-Economic Characteristics

(2000 Decennial Census, except as noted)

Population

1990* . . . 31,808
2000 . . . 35,866
Male . . . 17,794
Female . . . 18,072
Jan. 2008 (estimate)§ . . . 36,144
Persons per sq. mi. of land . . . 2,938.5

Race & Hispanic Origin, 2000

Race
White . . . 29,064
Black/African American . . . 1,201
North American Native . . . 264
Asian . . . 2,378
Pacific Islander . . . 84
Other Race . . . 1,181
Two or more races . . . 1,694
Hispanic origin, total . . . 3,660
Mexican . . . 2,096
Puerto Rican . . . 135
Cuban . . . 37
Other Hispanic . . . 1,392

Age & Nativity, 2000

Under 5 years . . . 2,000
18 years and over . . . 27,738
65 years and over . . . 3,628
85 years and over . . . 380
Median Age . . . 38.6
Native-born . . . 32,714
Foreign-born . . . 3,453

Educational Attainment, 2000

Population 25 years and over . . . 25,201
Less than 9th grade . . . 1.8%
High school grad or higher . . . 91.1%
Bachelor's degree or higher . . . 32.1%
Graduate degree . . . 9.6%

Income & Poverty, 1999

Per capita income . . . $29,701
Median household income . . . $63,010
Median family income . . . $77,411
Persons in poverty . . . 5.1%
H'holds receiving public assistance . . . 304
H'holds receiving social security . . . 2,890

Households, 2000

Total households . . . 14,300
With persons under 18 . . . 4,648
With persons over 65 . . . 2,562
Family households . . . 9,204
Single person households . . . 3,922
Persons per household . . . 2.41
Persons per family . . . 2.96

Household Population, 2008§§

Persons living in households . . . 34,800
Persons living in group quarters . . . 1,344
Persons per household . . . 2.4

Labor & Employment

Total civilian labor force, 2008§§ . . . 22,200
Unemployment rate, 2008 . . . 4.9%
Total civilian labor force, 2000 . . . 19,919

Employed persons 16 years and over by occupation, 2000

Managers & professionals . . . 7,914
Service occupations . . . 1,931
Sales & office occupations . . . 5,946
Farming, fishing & forestry . . . 10
Construction & maintenance . . . 2,033
Production & transportation . . . 1,335
Self-employed persons . . . 1,440

* US Census Bureau
** 2000 Decennial Census
§ California Department of Finance
§§ California Employment Development Dept

General Information

City of Martinez
525 Henrietta St
Martinez, CA 94553
925-372-3500

Website . . . www.cityofmartinez.org
Elevation . . . 23 ft.
Land Area (sq. miles) . . . 12.3
Water Area (sq. miles) . . . 1.2
Year of Incorporation . . . 1876
Government type . . . General law
Sales tax rate . . . 9.25%

Voters & Officials

Registered Voters, October 2008

Total . . . 21,716
Democrats . . . 10,886
Republicans . . . 5,591
Declined to state . . . 4,108

Legislative Districts

US Congressional . . . 7
State Senatorial . . . 7
State Assembly . . . 11

Local Officials, 2009

Mayor . . . Rob Schroder
City Manager . . . Philip Vince
City Clerk . . . Richard Hernandez
Attorney . . . Jeffrey Walter
Finance Dir . . . Lianne Marshall
Public Works . . . Dave Scola
Comm Dev Dir . . . Karen Majors
Building . . . Dave Scola
Police Chief . . . Tom Simonetti
Fire/Emergency Mgmt . . . (County)

Public Safety

Number of officers, 2007 . . . 39
Violent crimes, 2007 . . . 122
Property crimes, 2007 . . . 1,182
Arson, 2007 . . . 0

Public Library

Martinez Library
Contra Costa County Library System
740 Court St
Martinez, CA 94553
925-646-2898

Branch Librarian . . . Jan Aaronian

Library system statistics, FY 2007

Population served . . . 938,513
Internet terminals . . . 324
Annual users . . . 670,618

Per capita:

Operating income . . . $27.05
percent from local government . . . 82.0%
Operating expenditure . . . $27.82
Total materials . . . 1.57
Print holdings . . . 1.41
Visits per capita . . . 3.65

Housing & Construction

Housing Units

Total, 2008§ . . . 14,953
Single family units, attached . . . 2,245
Single family units, detached . . . 9,589
Multiple family units . . . 3,095
Mobile home units . . . 24
Occupied . . . 14,649
Vacancy rate . . . 2.0%
Median rent, 2000** . . . $870
Median SF home value, 2000** . . . $254,300

New Privately Owned Housing Units Authorized by Building Permit, 2007*

	Units	Construction Cost
Single	31	$6,560,713
Total	31	$6,560,713

Municipal Finance

(For local fiscal year ended in 2006)

Revenues

Total . . . $34,905,028
Taxes . . . 15,581,508
Special benefits assessment . . . 648,224
Licenses & permits . . . 610,279
Fines & forfeitures . . . 258,913
Revenues from use of money & property . . . 938,750
Intergovernmental . . . 3,846,564
Service charges . . . 11,258,832
Other revenues . . . 1,761,958
Other financing sources . . . 0

Expenditures

Total . . . $29,992,783
General government . . . 2,923,923
Public safety . . . 8,876,213
Transportation . . . 4,657,363
Community development . . . 1,819,266
Health . . . 34,838
Culture & leisure . . . 3,021,774
Other . . . 0

Local School District

(Data from School year 2007-08 except as noted)

Martinez Unified
921 Susana St
Martinez, CA 94553
(925) 313-0480

Superintendent . . . Dan White
Grade plan . . . K-12
Number of schools . . . 8
Enrollment . . . 4,077
High school graduates, 2006-07 . . . 320
Dropout rate . . . 3.8%
Pupil/teacher ratio . . . 20.8
Average class size . . . 27.5
Students per computer . . . 3.8
Classrooms with internet . . . 211
Avg. Daily Attendance (ADA) . . . 3,962
Cost per ADA . . . $7,589
Avg. Teacher Salary . . . $61,851

California Achievement Tests 6th ed., 2008

(Pct scoring at or above 50th National Percentile Rank)

	Math	Reading	Language
Grade 3	76%	52%	63%
Grade 7	61%	63%	59%

Academic Performance Index, 2008

Number of students tested . . . 3,093
Number of valid scores . . . 2,945
2007 API (base) . . . 777
2008 API (growth) . . . 798

SAT Testing, 2006-07

Enrollment, Grade 12 . . . 367
Number taking test . . . 127
percent taking test . . . 34.6%
percent with total score 1,500+ . . . 21.30%

Average Scores:

Math	Verbal	Writing	Total
553	518	504	1,575

Federal No Child Left Behind, 2008

(Adequate Yearly Progress standards met)

	Participation Rate	Pct Proficient
ELA	Yes	No
Math	Yes	Yes

API criteria . . . Yes
Graduation rate . . . Yes
\# criteria met/possible . . . 28/27

Other school districts for this city

(see Appendix E for information on these districts)

None

See Introduction for an explanation of all data sources.

Demographics & Socio-Economic Characteristics
(2000 Decennial Census, except as noted)

Population

1990* . . . 12,324
2000 . . . 12,268
Male . . . 6,122
Female . . . 6,146
Jan. 2008 (estimate)§ . . . 12,719
Persons per sq. mi. of land . . . 3,634.0

Race & Hispanic Origin, 2000

Race
White . . . 8,704
Black/African American . . . 589
North American Native . . . 282
Asian . . . 735
Pacific Islander . . . 23
Other Race . . . 1,239
Two or more races . . . 696
Hispanic origin, total . . . 2,152
Mexican . . . 1,745
Puerto Rican . . . 56
Cuban . . . 11
Other Hispanic . . . 340

Age & Nativity, 2000

Under 5 years . . . 896
18 years and over . . . 8,893
65 years and over . . . 1,602
85 years and over . . . 213
Median Age . . . 32.4
Native-born . . . 10,847
Foreign-born . . . 1,451

Educational Attainment, 2000

Population 25 years and over . . . 7,478
Less than 9th grade . . . 9.6%
High school grad or higher . . . 73.8%
Bachelor's degree or higher . . . 10.9%
Graduate degree . . . 3.1%

Income & Poverty, 1999

Per capita income . . . $15,315
Median household income . . . $28,494
Median family income . . . $33,474
Persons in poverty . . . 18.2%
H'holds receiving public assistance . . . 391
H'holds receiving social security . . . 1,272

Households, 2000

Total households . . . 4,687
With persons under 18 . . . 1,694
With persons over 65 . . . 1,141
Family households . . . 2,828
Single person households . . . 1,478
Persons per household . . . 2.49
Persons per family . . . 3.14

Household Population, 2008§§

Persons living in households . . . 12,112
Persons living in group quarters . . . 607
Persons per household . . . 2.6

Labor & Employment

Total civilian labor force, 2008§§ . . . 6,500
Unemployment rate, 2008 . . . 10.4%
Total civilian labor force, 2000 . . . 5,306

Employed persons 16 years and over by occupation, 2000

Managers & professionals . . . 1,182
Service occupations . . . 864
Sales & office occupations . . . 1,359
Farming, fishing & forestry . . . 110
Construction & maintenance . . . 546
Production & transportation . . . 723
Self-employed persons . . . 362

* US Census Bureau
** 2000 Decennial Census
§ California Department of Finance
§§ California Employment Development Dept

General Information

City of Marysville
526 C St
Marysville, CA 95901
530-749-3901

Website . . . www.marysville.ca.us
Elevation . . . 63 ft.
Land Area (sq. miles) . . . 3.5
Water Area (sq. miles) . . . 0.1
Year of Incorporation . . . 1851
Government type . . . Chartered
Sales tax rate . . . 8.25%

Voters & Officials

Registered Voters, October 2008

Total . . . 5,160
Democrats . . . 2,009
Republicans . . . 2,001
Declined to state . . . 907

Legislative Districts

US Congressional . . . 2
State Senatorial . . . 4
State Assembly . . . 3

Local Officials, 2009

Mayor . . . Bill Harris
Manager . . . Stephen Casey
City Clerk . . . Billie Fangman
Attorney . . . Seth Merewitz
Finance Dir . . . W. Dixon Coulter
Public Works . . . Dave Lamon
Comm Svcs Coord . . . Gary Price
Building . . . NA
Police Chief . . . Wallace Fullerton
Emergency/Fire Dir . . . Curtis Williges

Public Safety

Number of officers, 2007 . . . 22
Violent crimes, 2007 . . . 167
Property crimes, 2007 . . . 579
Arson, 2007 . . . 1

Public Library

Yuba County Library
303 Second St
Marysville, CA 95901
530-749-7380

Director . . . Loren McCrory

Library statistics, FY 2007

Population served . . . 70,745
Internet terminals . . . 27
Annual users . . . 25,000

Per capita:

Operating income . . . $13.04
percent from local government . . . 96.2%
Operating expenditure . . . $13.04
Total materials . . . 2.09
Print holdings . . . 1.94
Visits per capita . . . 2.90

Housing & Construction

Housing Units

Total, 2008§ . . . 5,023
Single family units, attached . . . 339
Single family units, detached . . . 2,791
Multiple family units . . . 1,885
Mobile home units . . . 8
Occupied . . . 4,710
Vacancy rate . . . 6.2%
Median rent, 2000** . . . $480
Median SF home value, 2000** . . . $89,000

New Privately Owned Housing Units Authorized by Building Permit, 2007*

	Units	Construction Cost
Single	2	$510,400
Total	6	$860,400

Municipal Finance
(For local fiscal year ended in 2006)

Revenues

Total . . . $11,177,383
Taxes . . . 4,592,719
Special benefits assessment . . . 0
Licenses & permits . . . 288,781
Fines & forfeitures . . . 1,172,567
Revenues from use of money & property . . . 261,452
Intergovernmental . . . 2,386,366
Service charges . . . 1,435,030
Other revenues . . . 1,040,468
Other financing sources . . . 0

Expenditures

Total . . . $12,864,908
General government . . . 1,324,265
Public safety . . . 5,557,214
Transportation . . . 2,863,719
Community development . . . 813,798
Health . . . 1,438,386
Culture & leisure . . . 867,526
Other . . . 0

Local School District
(Data from School year 2007-08 except as noted)

Marysville Joint Unified
1919 B St
Marysville, CA 95901
(530) 741-6000

Superintendent . . . Gay Todd
Grade plan . . . K-12
Number of schools . . . 24
Enrollment . . . 9,948
High school graduates, 2006-07 . . . 536
Dropout rate . . . 4.5%
Pupil/teacher ratio . . . 21.5
Average class size . . . 23.9
Students per computer . . . 3.8
Classrooms with internet . . . 486
Avg. Daily Attendance (ADA) . . . 9,706
Cost per ADA . . . $8,302
Avg. Teacher Salary . . . $61,202

California Achievement Tests 6th ed., 2008
(Pct scoring at or above 50th National Percentile Rank)

	Math	Reading	Language
Grade 3	49%	31%	40%
Grade 7	45%	42%	38%

Academic Performance Index, 2008

Number of students tested . . . 7,420
Number of valid scores . . . 6,714
2007 API (base) . . . 703
2008 API (growth) . . . 721

SAT Testing, 2006-07

Enrollment, Grade 12 . . . 662
Number taking test . . . 150
percent taking test . . . 22.7%
percent with total score 1,500+ . . . 6.70%

Average Scores:

Math	Verbal	Writing	Total
484	451	438	1,373

Federal No Child Left Behind, 2008
(Adequate Yearly Progress standards met)

	Participation Rate	Pct Proficient
ELA	Yes	No
Math	Yes	No

API criteria . . . Yes
Graduation rate . . . Yes
\# criteria met/possible . . . 38/35

Other school districts for this city
(see Appendix E for information on these districts)

Plumas Elem

See Introduction for an explanation of all data sources.

Demographics & Socio-Economic Characteristics

(2000 Decennial Census, except as noted)

Population

1990* . . . 27,850
2000 . . . 28,083
Male . . . 14,324
Female . . . 13,759
Jan. 2008 (estimate)§ . . . 29,971
Persons per sq. mi. of land . . . 24,975.8

Race & Hispanic Origin, 2000

Race
White . . . 12,073
Black/African American . . . 102
North American Native . . . 320
Asian . . . 101
Pacific Islander . . . 37
Other Race . . . 14,177
Two or more races . . . 1,273
Hispanic origin, total . . . 27,051
Mexican . . . 21,556
Puerto Rican . . . 51
Cuban . . . 209
Other Hispanic . . . 5,235

Age & Nativity, 2000

Under 5 years . . . 3,192
18 years and over . . . 17,691
65 years and over . . . 1,185
85 years and over . . . 133
Median Age . . . 24.9
Native-born . . . 12,593
Foreign-born . . . 15,490

Educational Attainment, 2000

Population 25 years and over . . . 13,756
Less than 9th grade . . . 47.1%
High school grad or higher . . . 29.6%
Bachelor's degree or higher . . . 2.3%
Graduate degree . . . 0.8%

Income & Poverty, 1999

Per capita income . . . $8,926
Median household income . . . $30,480
Median family income . . . $30,361
Persons in poverty . . . 24.3%
H'holds receiving public assistance . . . 554
H'holds receiving social security . . . 813

Households, 2000

Total households . . . 6,469
With persons under 18 . . . 4,526
With persons over 65 . . . 908
Family households . . . 5,698
Single person households . . . 542
Persons per household . . . 4.33
Persons per family . . . 4.47

Household Population, 2008§§

Persons living in households . . . 29,877
Persons living in group quarters . . . 94
Persons per household . . . 4.5

Labor & Employment

Total civilian labor force, 2008§§ . . . 12,300
Unemployment rate, 2008 . . . 11.1%
Total civilian labor force, 2000 . . . 10,545

Employed persons 16 years and over by occupation, 2000

Managers & professionals . . . 951
Service occupations . . . 1,348
Sales & office occupations . . . 1,948
Farming, fishing & forestry . . . 47
Construction & maintenance . . . 1,052
Production & transportation . . . 3,993
Self-employed persons . . . 450

* US Census Bureau
** 2000 Decennial Census
§ California Department of Finance
§§ California Employment Development Dept

General Information

City of Maywood
4319 E Slauson Ave
Maywood, CA 90270
323-562-5700

Website . . . www.cityofmaywood.com
Elevation . . . 150 ft
Land Area (sq. miles) . . . 1.2
Water Area (sq. miles) . . . 0
Year of Incorporation . . . 1924
Government type . . . General law
Sales tax rate . . . 9.25%

Voters & Officials

Registered Voters, October 2008

Total . . . 7,422
Democrats . . . 4,873
Republicans . . . 760
Declined to state . . . 1,495

Legislative Districts

US Congressional . . . 34
State Senatorial . . . 22
State Assembly . . . 46

Local Officials, 2009

Mayor . . . Veronica Guardado
Manager . . . Paul Phillips
City Clerk . . . Patricia Bravo
Attorney . . . Marco Martinez
Finance Dir . . . Hilda Flores
Public Works . . . NA
Planning/Dev Dir . . . Paul Phillips
Building . . . David Margo
Police Chief . . . Frank Hauptmann (Int)
Fire/Emergency Mgmt . . . NA

Public Safety

Number of officers, 2007 . . . 38
Violent crimes, 2007 . . . 175
Property crimes, 2007 . . . 446
Arson, 2007 . . . 1

Public Library

Maywood Cesar Chavez Library
Los Angeles County Public Library System
4323 E Slauson Ave
Maywood, CA 90270
323-771-8600

Branch Librarian . . . Norman Dilley

Library system statistics, FY 2007

Population served . . . 3,673,313
Internet terminals . . . 749
Annual users . . . 3,748,771

Per capita:

Operating income . . . $30.06
percent from local government . . . 93.6%
Operating expenditure . . . $28.36
Total materials . . . 2.22
Print holdings . . . 1.97
Visits per capita . . . 3.25

Housing & Construction

Housing Units

Total, 2008§ . . . 6,826
Single family units, attached . . . 1,120
Single family units, detached . . . 2,822
Multiple family units . . . 2,876
Mobile home units . . . 8
Occupied . . . 6,590
Vacancy rate . . . 3.5%
Median rent, 2000** . . . $602
Median SF home value, 2000** . . . $156,100

New Privately Owned Housing Units Authorized by Building Permit, 2007*

	Units	Construction Cost
Single	8	$1,718,909
Total	12	$2,354,263

Municipal Finance

(For local fiscal year ended in 2006)

Revenues

Total . . . $11,272,826
Taxes . . . 6,161,323
Special benefits assessment . . . 171,695
Licenses & permits . . . 376,971
Fines & forfeitures . . . 631,976
Revenues from use of money & property . . . 82,704
Intergovernmental . . . 979,189
Service charges . . . 2,852,662
Other revenues . . . 16,306
Other financing sources . . . 0

Expenditures

Total . . . $12,388,504
General government . . . 1,324,129
Public safety . . . 7,449,149
Transportation . . . 1,519,507
Community development . . . 1,196,185
Health . . . 60,146
Culture & leisure . . . 839,388
Other . . . 0

Local School District

(Data from School year 2007-08 except as noted)

Los Angeles Unified
333 South Beaudry Ave
Los Angeles, CA 90017
(213) 241-1000

Superintendent . . . Ramon Cortines
Grade plan . . . PK-12
Number of schools . . . 827
Enrollment . . . 693,680
High school graduates, 2006-07 . . . 28,545
Dropout rate . . . 7.8%
Pupil/teacher ratio . . . 19.8
Average class size . . . 24.9
Students per computer . . . 3.7
Classrooms with internet . . . 31,112
Avg. Daily Attendance (ADA) . . . 653,672
Cost per ADA . . . $10,053
Avg. Teacher Salary . . . $63,391

California Achievement Tests 6th ed., 2008

(Pct scoring at or above 50th National Percentile Rank)

	Math	Reading	Language
Grade 3	49%	27%	39%
Grade 7	37%	33%	33%

Academic Performance Index, 2008

Number of students tested . . . 495,046
Number of valid scores . . . 471,641
2007 API (base) . . . 662
2008 API (growth) . . . 683

SAT Testing, 2006-07

Enrollment, Grade 12 . . . 32,370
Number taking test . . . 15,447
percent taking test . . . 47.7%
percent with total score 1,500+ . . . 12.50%

Average Scores:

Math	Verbal	Writing	Total
443	438	441	1,322

Federal No Child Left Behind, 2008

(Adequate Yearly Progress standards met)

	Participation Rate	Pct Proficient
ELA	Yes	No
Math	Yes	No

API criteria . . . Yes
Graduation rate . . . Yes
\# criteria met/possible . . . 46/38

Other school districts for this city

(see Appendix E for information on these districts)

None

See Introduction for an explanation of all data sources.

Demographics & Socio-Economic Characteristics

(2000 Decennial Census, except as noted)

Population

1990* 7,005
2000 9,618
Male 5,476
Female 4,142
Jan. 2008 (estimate)§ 13,390
Persons per sq. mi. of land 6,376.2

Race & Hispanic Origin, 2000

Race
White 2,740
Black/African American 307
North American Native 157
Asian 66
Pacific Islander 8
Other Race 5,889
Two or more races 451
Hispanic origin, total 8,239
Mexican 7,180
Puerto Rican 21
Cuban 8
Other Hispanic 1,030

Age & Nativity, 2000

Under 5 years 920
18 years and over 6,241
65 years and over 466
85 years and over 42
Median Age 25.4
Native-born 5,807
Foreign-born 3,710

Educational Attainment, 2000

Population 25 years and over 4,879
Less than 9th grade 41.7%
High school grad or higher 40.2%
Bachelor's degree or higher 3.2%
Graduate degree 0.5%

Income & Poverty, 1999

Per capita income $9,524
Median household income $24,821
Median family income $24,190
Persons in poverty 31.0%
H'holds receiving public assistance 230
H'holds receiving social security 412

Households, 2000

Total households 1,990
With persons under 18 1,364
With persons over 65 361
Family households 1,789
Single person households 154
Persons per household 4.30
Persons per family 4.45

Household Population, 2008§§

Persons living in households 12,043
Persons living in group quarters 1,347
Persons per household 4.4

Labor & Employment

Total civilian labor force, 2008§§ 4,300
Unemployment rate, 2008 .... 20.7%
Total civilian labor force, 2000 3,241

Employed persons 16 years and over by occupation, 2000

Managers & professionals 284
Service occupations 371
Sales & office occupations 415
Farming, fishing & forestry 763
Construction & maintenance 175
Production & transportation 434
Self-employed persons 67

* US Census Bureau
** 2000 Decennial Census
§ California Department of Finance
§§ California Employment Development Dept

General Information

City of McFarland
401 W Kern
Mc Farland, CA 93250
661-792-3091

Website .... mcfarlandcity.org
Elevation .... 350 ft.
Land Area (sq. miles) 2.1
Water Area (sq. miles) 0
Year of Incorporation 1957
Government type .... General law
Sales tax rate 8.25%

Voters & Officials

Registered Voters, October 2008

Total 2,725
Democrats 1,684
Republicans 553
Declined to state 421

Legislative Districts

US Congressional 20
State Senatorial 16
State Assembly 30

Local Officials, 2009

Mayor .... Kenneth Rosson
City Administrator .... Gerald Forde
City Clerk .... Blanca Reyes-Garza
Attorney .... Thomas Schroeter
Finance Dir .... (vacant)
Public Works .... Rey De Leon
Planning/Dev Dir .... Gerald Ford
Building .... Roger Stahl
Police Chief .... Shaun Beasley
Fire/Emergency Mgmt .... NA

Public Safety

Number of officers, 2007 .... NA
Violent crimes, 2007 .... NA
Property crimes, 2007 .... NA
Arson, 2007 .... NA

Public Library

McFarland Branch Library
Kern County Library System
500 W Kern Ave
McFarland, CA 93250
661-792-2318

Branch Librarian .... Tina Garcia

Library system statistics, FY 2007

Population served 801,648
Internet terminals 237
Annual users 337,030

Per capita:

Operating income $12.11
percent from local government 90.4%
Operating expenditure $12.11
Total materials 1.37
Print holdings 1.29
Visits per capita 2.09

Housing & Construction

Housing Units

Total, 2008§ 2,770
Single family units, attached 246
Single family units, detached 2,099
Multiple family units 396
Mobile home units 29
Occupied 2,714
Vacancy rate 2.0%
Median rent, 2000** $463
Median SF home value, 2000** $76,000

New Privately Owned Housing Units Authorized by Building Permit, 2007*

	Units	Construction Cost
Single	NA	NA
Total	NA	NA

Municipal Finance

(For local fiscal year ended in 2006)

Revenues

Total $5,013,347
Taxes 1,290,030
Special benefits assessment 36,372
Licenses & permits 1,515
Fines & forfeitures 36,714
Revenues from use of money & property 85,096
Intergovernmental 428,603
Service charges 3,046,236
Other revenues 88,781
Other financing sources 0

Expenditures

Total $6,346,634
General government 851,470
Public safety 1,105,902
Transportation 759,517
Community development 407,031
Health 2,285,426
Culture & leisure 0
Other 207,381

Local School District

(Data from School year 2007-08 except as noted)

McFarland Unified
601 Second St
McFarland, CA 93250
(661) 792-3081

Superintendent .... Gabriel McCurtis
Grade plan K-12
Number of schools 6
Enrollment 3,249
High school graduates, 2006-07 158
Dropout rate 10.7%
Pupil/teacher ratio 18.8
Average class size 22.5
Students per computer 2.9
Classrooms with internet 173
Avg. Daily Attendance (ADA) 3,064
Cost per ADA $9,521
Avg. Teacher Salary $59,359

California Achievement Tests 6th ed., 2008

(Pct scoring at or above 50th National Percentile Rank)

	Math	Reading	Language
Grade 3	41%	16%	23%
Grade 7	30%	28%	30%

Academic Performance Index, 2008

Number of students tested 2,377
Number of valid scores 2,168
2007 API (base) 636
2008 API (growth) 651

SAT Testing, 2006-07

Enrollment, Grade 12 202
Number taking test 55
percent taking test 27.2%
percent with total score 1,500+ 3.00%

Average Scores:

Math	Verbal	Writing	Total
402	385	405	1,192

Federal No Child Left Behind, 2008

(Adequate Yearly Progress standards met)

	Participation Rate	Pct Proficient
ELA	Yes	No
Math	Yes	No

API criteria .... Yes
Graduation rate .... No
\# criteria met/possible 22/11

Other school districts for this city

(see Appendix E for information on these districts)

None

Demographics & Socio-Economic Characteristics

(2000 Decennial Census, except as noted)

Population

1990* . . . 6,821
2000 . . . 7,890
Male . . . 4,462
Female . . . 3,428
Jan. 2008 (estimate)§ . . . 9,788
Persons per sq. mi. of land . . . 5,151.6

Race & Hispanic Origin, 2000

Race
White . . . 2,156
Black/African American . . . 52
North American Native . . . 103
Asian . . . 57
Pacific Islander . . . 13
Other Race . . . 4,980
Two or more races . . . 529
Hispanic origin, total . . . 7,468
Mexican . . . 5,575
Puerto Rican . . . 9
Cuban . . . 2
Other Hispanic . . . 1,882

Age & Nativity, 2000

Under 5 years . . . 725
18 years and over . . . 5,217
65 years and over . . . 413
85 years and over . . . 19
Median Age . . . 25.4
Native-born . . . 3,876
Foreign-born . . . 4,015

Educational Attainment, 2000

Population 25 years and over . . . 3,990
Less than 9th grade . . . 57.8%
High school grad or higher . . . 23.2%
Bachelor's degree or higher . . . 0.5%
Graduate degree . . . 0.0%

Income & Poverty, 1999

Per capita income . . . $6,967
Median household income . . . $23,705
Median family income . . . $22,984
Persons in poverty . . . 41.5%
H'holds receiving public assistance . . . 128
H'holds receiving social security . . . 283

Households, 2000

Total households . . . 1,825
With persons under 18 . . . 1,135
With persons over 65 . . . 322
Family households . . . 1,545
Single person households . . . 166
Persons per household . . . 4.32
Persons per family . . . 4.38

Household Population, 2008§§

Persons living in households . . . 9,780
Persons living in group quarters . . . 8
Persons per household . . . 4.4

Labor & Employment

Total civilian labor force, 2008§§ . . . 4,200
Unemployment rate, 2008 . . . 29.1%
Total civilian labor force, 2000 . . . 3,343

Employed persons 16 years and over by occupation, 2000

Managers & professionals . . . 122
Service occupations . . . 224
Sales & office occupations . . . 309
Farming, fishing & forestry . . . 1,019
Construction & maintenance . . . 79
Production & transportation . . . 528
Self-employed persons . . . 53

* US Census Bureau
** 2000 Decennial Census
§ California Department of Finance
§§ California Employment Development Dept

General Information

City of Mendota
643 Quince St
Mendota, CA 93640
559-655-3291

Website . . . www.ci.mendota.ca.us
Elevation . . . NA
Land Area (sq. miles) . . . 1.9
Water Area (sq. miles) . . . 0
Year of Incorporation . . . 1942
Government type . . . General law
Sales tax rate . . . 8.98%

Voters & Officials

Registered Voters, October 2008

Total . . . 1,803
Democrats . . . 1,249
Republicans . . . 318
Declined to state . . . 140

Legislative Districts

US Congressional . . . 20
State Senatorial . . . 16
State Assembly . . . 31

Local Officials, 2009

Mayor . . . Robert Silva
Manager . . . Gabriel A. Gonzalez
City Clerk . . . Krystal Chojnacki
Attorney . . . Thomas T. Watson
Finance Dir . . . Gabriel A. Gonzalez
Public Works . . . Domingo Morales
Planning/Dev Dir . . . Jeff O'Neal
Building . . . NA
Police Chief . . . Margaret Mims
Emergency/Fire Dir . . . Keith Larkin

Public Safety

Number of officers, 2007 . . . NA
Violent crimes, 2007 . . . NA
Property crimes, 2007 . . . NA
Arson, 2007 . . . NA

Public Library

Mendota Branch Library
Fresno County Public Library System
667 Quince St
Mendota, CA 93640
559-655-3391

Branch Librarian . . . Sonia Bautista

Library system statistics, FY 2007

Population served . . . 889,019
Internet terminals . . . 277
Annual users . . . 861,240

Per capita:

Operating income . . . $23.69
percent from local government . . . 89.3%
Operating expenditure . . . $23.37
Total materials . . . 2.89
Print holdings . . . 2.69
Visits per capita . . . NA

Housing & Construction

Housing Units

Total, 2008§ . . . 2,279
Single family units, attached . . . 139
Single family units, detached . . . 1,340
Multiple family units . . . 727
Mobile home units . . . 73
Occupied . . . 2,217
Vacancy rate . . . 2.7%
Median rent, 2000** . . . $447
Median SF home value, 2000** . . . $82,700

New Privately Owned Housing Units Authorized by Building Permit, 2007*

	Units	Construction Cost
Single	97	$13,277,595
Total	97	$13,277,595

Municipal Finance

(For local fiscal year ended in 2006)

Revenues

Total . . . $7,420,156
Taxes . . . 2,199,251
Special benefits assessment . . . 0
Licenses & permits . . . 144,185
Fines & forfeitures . . . 18,990
Revenues from use of money & property . . . 376,125
Intergovernmental . . . 1,804,310
Service charges . . . 2,624,914
Other revenues . . . 252,381
Other financing sources . . . 0

Expenditures

Total . . . $6,329,644
General government . . . 574,158
Public safety . . . 518,754
Transportation . . . 1,264,824
Community development . . . 518,490
Health . . . 2,130,635
Culture & leisure . . . 193,134
Other . . . 0

Local School District

(Data from School year 2007-08 except as noted)

Mendota Unified
115 McCabe Ave
Mendota, CA 93640
(559) 655-4942

Superintendent . . . Gilbert Rossette
Grade plan . . . K-12
Number of schools . . . 7
Enrollment . . . 3,075
High school graduates, 2006-07 . . . 138
Dropout rate . . . 26.3%
Pupil/teacher ratio . . . 22.7
Average class size . . . 24.2
Students per computer . . . 5.9
Classrooms with internet . . . 491
Avg. Daily Attendance (ADA) . . . 2,406
Cost per ADA . . . $8,861
Avg. Teacher Salary . . . $54,398

California Achievement Tests 6th ed., 2008

(Pct scoring at or above 50th National Percentile Rank)

	Math	Reading	Language
Grade 3	43%	18%	35%
Grade 7	26%	23%	26%

Academic Performance Index, 2008

Number of students tested . . . 1,925
Number of valid scores . . . 1,671
2007 API (base) . . . 657
2008 API (growth) . . . 695

SAT Testing, 2006-07

Enrollment, Grade 12 . . . 242
Number taking test . . . 34
percent taking test . . . 14.1%
percent with total score 1,500+ . . . 0.40%

Average Scores:

Math	Verbal	Writing	Total
406	386	387	1,179

Federal No Child Left Behind, 2008

(Adequate Yearly Progress standards met)

	Participation Rate	Pct Proficient
ELA	Yes	Yes
Math	Yes	Yes

API criteria . . . Yes
Graduation rate . . . Yes
\# criteria met/possible . . . 18/18

Other school districts for this city

(see Appendix E for information on these districts)

None

See Introduction for an explanation of all data sources.

Demographics & Socio-Economic Characteristics†

(2007 American Community Survey, except as noted)

Population

1990* ....NA
2007 ....NA
Male ....NA
Female ....NA
Jan. 2008 (estimate)§ ....NA
Persons per sq. mi. of land ....NA

Race & Hispanic Origin, 2007

Race
White ....NA
Black/African American ....NA
North American Native ....NA
Asian ....NA
Pacific Islander ....NA
Other Race ....NA
Two or more races ....NA
Hispanic origin, total ....NA
Mexican ....NA
Puerto Rican ....NA
Cuban ....NA
Other Hispanic ....NA

Age & Nativity, 2007

Under 5 years ....NA
18 years and over ....NA
65 years and over ....NA
85 years and over ....NA
Median Age ....NA
Native-born ....NA
Foreign-born ....NA

Educational Attainment, 2007

Population 25 years and over ....NA
Less than 9th grade ....NA
High school grad or higher ....NA
Bachelor's degree or higher ....NA
Graduate degree ....NA

Income & Poverty, 2007

Per capita income ....NA
Median household income ....NA
Median family income ....NA
Persons in poverty ....NA
H'holds receiving public assistance ....NA
H'holds receiving social security ....NA

Households, 2007

Total households ....NA
With persons under 18 ....NA
With persons over 65 ....NA
Family households ....NA
Single person households ....NA
Persons per household ....NA
Persons per family ....NA

Household Population, 2008§§

Persons living in households ....NA
Persons living in group quarters ....NA
Persons per household ....NA

Labor & Employment

Total civilian labor force, 2008§§ ....NA
Unemployment rate, 2008 ....NA
Total civilian labor force, 2000* ....NA

Employed persons 16 years and over by occupation, 2007

Managers & professionals ....NA
Service occupations ....NA
Sales & office occupations ....NA
Farming, fishing & forestry ....NA
Construction & maintenance ....NA
Production & transportation ....NA
Self-employed persons ....NA

† see Appendix D for 2000 Decennial Census Data
* US Census Bureau
** 2007 American Community Survey
§ California Department of Finance
§§ California Employment Development Dept

General Information

City of Menifee
29714 Haun Rd
Menifee, CA 92586
951-672-6777

Website ....www.cityofmenifee.us
Elevation ....NA
Land Area (sq. miles) ....NA
Water Area (sq. miles) ....NA
Year of Incorporation 2008
Government type ....NA
Sales tax rate 8.75%

Voters & Officials

Registered Voters, October 2008

Total ....NA
Democrats ....NA
Republicans ....NA
Declined to state ....NA

Legislative Districts

US Congressional ....NA
State Senatorial ....NA
State Assembly ....NA

Local Officials, 2009

Mayor ....Wallace Edgerton
Manager ....George Wentz
City Clerk ....Kathy Bennett
Attorney ....Elizabeth Martyn
Finance Dir ....Misty Cheng
Public Works ....Bob Cartwright
Planning Dir ....Carmen Cave
Building ....Addison Smith
Police Chief ....(County)
Fire Chief ....(County)

Public Safety

Number of officers, 2007 ....NA
Violent crimes, 2007 ....NA
Property crimes, 2007 ....NA
Arson, 2007 ....NA

Public Library

Paloma Valley Library
Riverside County Library Service
31375 Bradley Road
Menifee, CA 92584
951-301-3682

Library Manager ....Cara Larson

Library system statistics, FY 2007

Population served 1,047,996
Internet terminals 37
Annual users 69,346

Per capita:

Operating income $19.38
percent from local government 49.8%
Operating expenditure $20.45
Total materials 1.43
Print holdings 1.30
Visits per capita 4.06

Housing & Construction

Housing Units

Total, 2008§ ....NA
Single family units, attached ....NA
Single family units, detached ....NA
Multiple family units ....NA
Mobile home units ....NA
Occupied ....NA
Vacancy rate ....NA
Median rent, 2007** ....NA
Median SF home value, 2007** ....NA

New Privately Owned Housing Units Authorized by Building Permit, 2007*

	Units	Construction Cost
Single	NA	NA
Total	NA	NA

Municipal Finance

(For local fiscal year ended in 2006)

Revenues

Total ....NA
Taxes ....NA
Special benefits assessment ....NA
Licenses & permits ....NA
Fines & forfeitures ....NA
Revenues from use of money & property ....NA
Intergovernmental ....NA
Service charges ....NA
Other revenues ....NA
Other financing sources ....NA

Expenditures

Total ....NA
General government ....NA
Public safety ....NA
Transportation ....NA
Community development ....NA
Health ....NA
Culture & leisure ....NA
Other ....NA

Local School District

(Data from School year 2007-08 except as noted)

Perris Union High
155 East Fourth St
Perris, CA 92570
(951) 943-6369

Superintendent ....Jonathan Greenberg
Grade plan 7-12
Number of schools 8
Enrollment 9,764
High school graduates, 2006-07 1,323
Dropout rate 4.8%
Pupil/teacher ratio 24.5
Average class size 28.4
Students per computer 6.9
Classrooms with internet 419
Avg. Daily Attendance (ADA) 8,911
Cost per ADA $8,412
Avg. Teacher Salary $67,839

California Achievement Tests 6th ed., 2008

(Pct scoring at or above 50th National Percentile Rank)

	Math	Reading	Language
Grade 3	NA	NA	NA
Grade 7	31%	27%	26%

Academic Performance Index, 2008

Number of students tested 7,751
Number of valid scores 7,119
2007 API (base) 657
2008 API (growth) 675

SAT Testing, 2006-07

Enrollment, Grade 12 1,619
Number taking test 381
percent taking test 23.5%
percent with total score 1,500+ 8.00%

Average Scores:

Math	Verbal	Writing	Total
474	460	455	1,389

Federal No Child Left Behind, 2008

(Adequate Yearly Progress standards met)

	Participation Rate	Pct Proficient
ELA	Yes	No
Math	Yes	No

API criteria ....Yes
Graduation rate ....No
criteria met/possible 30/18

Other school districts for this city

(see Appendix E for information on these districts)

Menifee Union Elem

See Introduction for an explanation of all data sources.

Demographics & Socio-Economic Characteristics

(2000 Decennial Census, except as noted)

Population

1990* 28,040
2000 30,785
Male 14,920
Female 15,865
Jan. 2008 (estimate)§ 31,490
Persons per sq. mi. of land 3,117.8

Race & Hispanic Origin, 2000

Race
White 22,274
Black/African American 2,163
North American Native 136
Asian 2,201
Pacific Islander 389
Other Race 2,635
Two or more races 987
Hispanic origin, total 4,803
Mexican 3,502
Puerto Rican 46
Cuban 31
Other Hispanic 1,224

Age & Nativity, 2000

Under 5 years 2,030
18 years and over 24,048
65 years and over 4,889
85 years and over 884
Median Age 37.4
Native-born 23,780
Foreign-born 7,006

Educational Attainment, 2000

Population 25 years and over 22,454
Less than 9th grade 4.9%
High school grad or higher 89.0%
Bachelor's degree or higher 61.7%
Graduate degree 30.7%

Income & Poverty, 1999

Per capita income $53,341
Median household income $84,609
Median family income $105,550
Persons in poverty 6.7%
H'holds receiving public assistance 224
H'holds receiving social security 2,989

Households, 2000

Total households 12,387
With persons under 18 3,515
With persons over 65 3,231
Family households 7,120
Single person households 3,979
Persons per household 2.41
Persons per family 3.12

Household Population, 2008§§

Persons living in households 30,546
Persons living in group quarters 944
Persons per household 2.4

Labor & Employment

Total civilian labor force, 2008§§ 16,200
Unemployment rate, 2008 ....3.8%
Total civilian labor force, 2000 15,849

Employed persons 16 years and over by occupation, 2000

Managers & professionals 9,695
Service occupations 1,415
Sales & office occupations 2,927
Farming, fishing & forestry 14
Construction & maintenance 557
Production & transportation 821
Self-employed persons 1,671

* US Census Bureau
** 2000 Decennial Census
§ California Department of Finance
§§ California Employment Development Dept

General Information

City of Menlo Park
701 Laurel St
Menlo Park, CA 94025
650-330-6600

Website ....www.menlopark.org
Elevation ....70 ft.
Land Area (sq. miles) 10.1
Water Area (sq. miles) 7.3
Year of Incorporation 1927
Government type ....General law
Sales tax rate 9.25%

Voters & Officials

Registered Voters, October 2008

Total 20,580
Democrats 10,282
Republicans 5,112
Declined to state 4,486

Legislative Districts

US Congressional 14
State Senatorial 11
State Assembly 21

Local Officials, 2009

Mayor ....Heyward Robinson
Manager ....Glen Rojas
City Clerk ....Margaret S. Roberts
Attorney ....William McClure
Finance Dir ....Carol Augustine
Public Works ....Kent Steffens
Planning/Dev Dir ....Arlinda Heineck
Building ....NA
Police Chief ....Bruce Goitia
Fire Chief ....Harold Schapelhouman

Public Safety

Number of officers, 2007 51
Violent crimes, 2007 74
Property crimes, 2007 560
Arson, 2007 1

Public Library

Menlo Park Main Library
Menlo Park Public Library System
800 Alma St
Menlo Park, CA 94025
650-330-2500

Director ....Susan Holmer

Library system statistics, FY 2007

Population served 31,146
Internet terminals 26
Annual users 99,884

Per capita:

Operating income $66.74
percent from local government 75.3%
Operating expenditure $66.44
Total materials 5.79
Print holdings 4.60
Visits per capita ....NA

Housing & Construction

Housing Units

Total, 2008§ 12,790
Single family units, attached 930
Single family units, detached 6,915
Multiple family units 4,940
Mobile home units 5
Occupied 12,539
Vacancy rate 2.0%
Median rent, 2000** $1,319
Median SF home value, 2000** $778,500

New Privately Owned Housing Units Authorized by Building Permit, 2007*

	Units	Construction Cost
Single	10	$7,199,241
Total	10	$7,199,241

Municipal Finance

(For local fiscal year ended in 2006)

Revenues

Total $43,798,104
Taxes 22,471,268
Special benefits assessment 947,613
Licenses & permits 1,659,857
Fines & forfeitures 811,157
Revenues from use of money & property 3,021,081
Intergovernmental 3,213,595
Service charges 11,449,953
Other revenues 223,580
Other financing sources 0

Expenditures

Total $47,527,962
General government 4,355,083
Public safety 9,620,620
Transportation 7,398,107
Community development 3,437,659
Health 1,606,318
Culture & leisure 17,783,144
Other 0

Local School District

(Data from School year 2007-08 except as noted)

Sequoia Union High
480 James Ave
Redwood City, CA 94062
(650) 369-1411

Superintendent ....Patrick Gemma
Grade plan 9-12
Number of schools 6
Enrollment 8,510
High school graduates, 2006-07 1,546
Dropout rate 3.2%
Pupil/teacher ratio 19.7
Average class size 26.4
Students per computer 3.0
Classrooms with internet 402
Avg. Daily Attendance (ADA) 7,811
Cost per ADA $11,470
Avg. Teacher Salary $76,194

California Achievement Tests 6th ed., 2008

(Pct scoring at or above 50th National Percentile Rank)

	Math	Reading	Language
Grade 3	NA	NA	NA
Grade 7	NA	NA	NA

Academic Performance Index, 2008

Number of students tested 5,874
Number of valid scores 5,525
2007 API (base) 753
2008 API (growth) 753

SAT Testing, 2006-07

Enrollment, Grade 12 2,000
Number taking test 945
percent taking test 47.3%
percent with total score 1,500+ 29.10%

Average Scores:

Math	Verbal	Writing	Total
546	530	530	1,606

Federal No Child Left Behind, 2008

(Adequate Yearly Progress standards met)

	Participation Rate	Pct Proficient
ELA	Yes	No
Math	Yes	No

API criteria ....Yes
Graduation rate ....Yes
\# criteria met/possible 28/25

Other school districts for this city

(see Appendix E for information on these districts)

Las Lomitas Elem, Menlo Park City Elem

See Introduction for an explanation of all data sources.

Demographics & Socio-Economic Characteristics†

(2007 American Community Survey, except as noted)

Population

1990* . . . 56,216
2007 . . . 73,224
Male . . . 36,673
Female . . . 36,551
Jan. 2008 (estimate)§ . . . 80,608
Persons per sq. mi. of land . . . 4,050.7

Race & Hispanic Origin, 2007

Race
White . . . 29,464
Black/African American . . . 5,590
North American Native . . . 531
Asian . . . 8,061
Pacific Islander . . . 350
Other Race . . . 26,473
Two or more races . . . 2,755
Hispanic origin, total . . . 36,097
Mexican . . . NA
Puerto Rican . . . NA
Cuban . . . NA
Other Hispanic . . . NA

Age & Nativity, 2007

Under 5 years . . . 8,128
18 years and over . . . 49,798
65 years and over . . . 6,787
85 years and over . . . 481
Median Age . . . 25.8
Native-born . . . 55,769
Foreign-born . . . 17,455

Educational Attainment, 2007

Population 25 years and over . . . 37,887
Less than 9th grade . . . 19.8%
High school grad or higher . . . 66.2%
Bachelor's degree or higher . . . 16.7%
Graduate degree . . . 6.4%

Income & Poverty, 2007

Per capita income . . . $16,392
Median household income . . . $31,726
Median family income . . . $32,840
Persons in poverty . . . 28.9%
H'holds receiving public assistance . . . 2,813
H'holds receiving social security . . . 6,019

Households, 2007

Total households . . . 23,644
With persons under 18 . . . 11,859
With persons over 65 . . . 4,383
Family households . . . 17,116
Single person households . . . 5,066
Persons per household . . . 3.08
Persons per family . . . 3.44

Household Population, 2008§§

Persons living in households . . . 79,238
Persons living in group quarters . . . 1,370
Persons per household . . . 3.0

Labor & Employment

Total civilian labor force, 2008§§ . . . 30,600
Unemployment rate, 2008 . . . 12.5%
Total civilian labor force, 2000* . . . 25,629

Employed persons 16 years and over by occupation, 2007

Managers & professionals . . . 7,789
Service occupations . . . 4,385
Sales & office occupations . . . 6,653
Farming, fishing & forestry . . . 1,931
Construction & maintenance . . . 2,233
Production & transportation . . . 5,096
Self-employed persons . . . 1,538

† see Appendix D for 2000 Decennial Census Data
* US Census Bureau
** 2007 American Community Survey
§ California Department of Finance
§§ California Employment Development Dept

General Information

City of Merced
678 W 18th St
Merced, CA 95340
209-385-6834

Website . . . www.cityofmerced.org
Elevation . . . 172 ft.
Land Area (sq. miles) . . . 19.9
Water Area (sq. miles) . . . 0
Year of Incorporation . . . 1889
Government type . . . Chartered
Sales tax rate . . . 8.75%

Voters & Officials

Registered Voters, October 2008

Total . . . 31,006
Democrats . . . 14,945
Republicans . . . 10,841
Declined to state . . . 4,217

Legislative Districts

US Congressional . . . 18
State Senatorial . . . 12
State Assembly . . . 17

Local Officials, 2009

Mayor . . . Ellie Wooten
Manager . . . John M. Bramble
City Clerk . . . John M. Bramble
Attorney . . . Gregory Diaz
Finance Dir . . . Bradley Grant
Public Works . . . (vacant)
Planning/Dev Dir . . . (vacant)
Building . . . Don Spiva
Police Chief . . . Russell Thomas
Emergency/Fire Dir . . . Ken Mitten

Public Safety

Number of officers, 2007 . . . 107
Violent crimes, 2007 . . . 611
Property crimes, 2007 . . . 3,821
Arson, 2007 . . . 63

Public Library

Main Branch
Merced County Library System
2100 O St
Merced, CA 95340
209-385-7484

County Librarian . . . Jacque Meriam

Library system statistics, FY 2007

Population served . . . 251,510
Internet terminals . . . 91
Annual users . . . 124,530

Per capita:

Operating income . . . $8.99
percent from local government . . . 91.3%
Operating expenditure . . . $8.99
Total materials . . . 1.61
Print holdings . . . 1.60
Visits per capita . . . 1.75

Housing & Construction

Housing Units

Total, 2008§ . . . 28,066
Single family units, attached . . . 944
Single family units, detached . . . 18,130
Multiple family units . . . 8,284
Mobile home units . . . 708
Occupied . . . 26,497
Vacancy rate . . . 5.6%
Median rent, 2007** . . . $673
Median SF home value, 2007** . . . $290,700

New Privately Owned Housing Units Authorized by Building Permit, 2007*

	Units	Construction Cost
Single	208	$27,162,491
Total	216	$27,870,043

Municipal Finance

(For local fiscal year ended in 2006)

Revenues

Total . . . $135,650,980
Taxes . . . 30,592,102
Special benefits assessment . . . 938,121
Licenses & permits . . . 3,097,562
Fines & forfeitures . . . 650,294
Revenues from use of money & property . . . 5,556,083
Intergovernmental . . . 10,715,925
Service charges . . . 65,369,879
Other revenues . . . 10,468,805
Other financing sources . . . 8,262,209

Expenditures

Total . . . $95,460,162
General government . . . 6,927,461
Public safety . . . 35,783,210
Transportation . . . 3,736,656
Community development . . . 18,625,253
Health . . . 17,245,935
Culture & leisure . . . 6,870,091
Other . . . 0

Local School District

(Data from School year 2007-08 except as noted)

Merced Union High
PO Box 2147
Merced, CA 95344
(209) 385-6412

Superintendent . . . Scott Scambray
Grade plan . . . 9-12
Number of schools . . . 8
Enrollment . . . 10,680
High school graduates, 2006-07 . . . 1,890
Dropout rate . . . 3.6%
Pupil/teacher ratio . . . 21.9
Average class size . . . 26.0
Students per computer . . . 3.7
Classrooms with internet . . . 514
Avg. Daily Attendance (ADA) . . . 10,568
Cost per ADA . . . $8,153
Avg. Teacher Salary . . . $63,476

California Achievement Tests 6th ed., 2008

(Pct scoring at or above 50th National Percentile Rank)

	Math	Reading	Language
Grade 3	NA	NA	NA
Grade 7	NA	NA	NA

Academic Performance Index, 2008

Number of students tested . . . 7,904
Number of valid scores . . . 7,415
2007 API (base) . . . 678
2008 API (growth) . . . 700

SAT Testing, 2006-07

Enrollment, Grade 12 . . . 2,234
Number taking test . . . 639
percent taking test . . . 28.6%
percent with total score 1,500+ . . . 9.90%

Average Scores:

Math	Verbal	Writing	Total
481	461	466	1,408

Federal No Child Left Behind, 2008

(Adequate Yearly Progress standards met)

	Participation Rate	Pct Proficient
ELA	Yes	No
Math	Yes	No

API criteria . . . Yes
Graduation rate . . . Yes
\# criteria met/possible . . . 34/31

Other school districts for this city

(see Appendix E for information on these districts)

McSwain Union Elem, Merced City Elem, Plainsburg Union Elem, Weaver Union Elem

Demographics & Socio-Economic Characteristics

(2000 Decennial Census, except as noted)

Population

1990* 13,038
2000 13,600
Male 6,306
Female 7,294
Jan. 2008 (estimate)§ 13,925
Persons per sq. mi. of land 2,962.8

Race & Hispanic Origin, 2000

Race
White 12,435
Black/African American 135
North American Native 34
Asian 563
Pacific Islander 29
Other Race 89
Two or more races 315
Hispanic origin, total 472
Mexican 206
Puerto Rican 29
Cuban 17
Other Hispanic 220

Age & Nativity, 2000

Under 5 years 749
18 years and over 10,718
65 years and over 2,090
85 years and over 396
Median Age 43.9
Native-born 12,218
Foreign-born 1,342

Educational Attainment, 2000

Population 25 years and over 10,235
Less than 9th grade 0.7%
High school grad or higher 98.0%
Bachelor's degree or higher 71.0%
Graduate degree 32.9%

Income & Poverty, 1999

Per capita income $64,179
Median household income $90,794
Median family income $119,669
Persons in poverty 4.4%
H'holds receiving public assistance 48
H'holds receiving social security 1,576

Households, 2000

Total households 6,147
With persons under 18 1,714
With persons over 65 1,559
Family households 3,420
Single person households 2,098
Persons per household 2.20
Persons per family 2.85

Household Population, 2008§§

Persons living in households 13,834
Persons living in group quarters 91
Persons per household 2.2

Labor & Employment

Total civilian labor force, 2008§§ 7,400
Unemployment rate, 2008 .... 3.1%
Total civilian labor force, 2000 7,251

Employed persons 16 years and over by occupation, 2000

Managers & professionals 4,693
Service occupations 383
Sales & office occupations 1,621
Farming, fishing & forestry 11
Construction & maintenance 268
Production & transportation 128
Self-employed persons 1,643

* US Census Bureau
** 2000 Decennial Census
§ California Department of Finance
§§ California Employment Development Dept

General Information

City of Mill Valley
26 Corte Madera Ave
Mill Valley, CA 94941
415-388-4033

Website .... www.cityofmillvalley.org
Elevation .... 80 ft.
Land Area (sq. miles) 4.7
Water Area (sq. miles) 0.1
Year of Incorporation 1900
Government type .... General law
Sales tax rate 9.00%

Voters & Officials

Registered Voters, October 2008

Total 9,877
Democrats 6,066
Republicans 1,397
Declined to state 2,068

Legislative Districts

US Congressional 6
State Senatorial 3
State Assembly 6

Local Officials, 2009

Mayor .... Andrew Berman
Manager .... Anne Montgomery
City Clerk .... Kimberly Wilson
Attorney .... Greg Stepanicich
Finance Dir .... Eric Erickson
Public Works .... Wayne Bush
Community Dev Dir .... (vacant)
Building .... Dan Martin
Public Safety Dir .... Robert Ritter
(combined police and fire position)

Public Safety

Number of officers, 2007 23
Violent crimes, 2007 16
Property crimes, 2007 184
Arson, 2007 1

Public Library

Mill Valley Public Library
375 Throckmorton Ave
Mill Valley, CA 94941
415-389-4292

City Librarian .... Anji Brenner

Library statistics, FY 2007

Population served 13,822
Internet terminals 13
Annual users 34,964

Per capita:

Operating income $122.98
percent from local government 81.6%
Operating expenditure $114.40
Total materials 10.19
Print holdings 8.77
Visits per capita 15.51

Housing & Construction

Housing Units

Total, 2008§ 6,367
Single family units, attached 552
Single family units, detached 4,153
Multiple family units 1,662
Mobile home units 0
Occupied 6,227
Vacancy rate 2.2%
Median rent, 2000** $1,233
Median SF home value, 2000** $746,200

New Privately Owned Housing Units Authorized by Building Permit, 2007*

	Units	Construction Cost
Single	17	$12,158,500
Total	17	$12,158,500

Municipal Finance

(For local fiscal year ended in 2006)

Revenues

Total $25,480,634
Taxes 14,817,952
Special benefits assessment 1,197,937
Licenses & permits 510,549
Fines & forfeitures 326,105
Revenues from use of money & property 1,097,667
Intergovernmental 1,228,477
Service charges 5,978,954
Other revenues 322,993
Other financing sources 0

Expenditures

Total $25,230,399
General government 2,475,657
Public safety 8,206,936
Transportation 2,839,152
Community development 1,935,096
Health 2,078,041
Culture & leisure 7,695,517
Other 0

Local School District

(Data from School year 2007-08 except as noted)

Tamalpais Union High
PO Box 605
Larkspur, CA 94977
(415) 945-3720

Superintendent .... Laurie Kimbrel
Grade plan 9-12
Number of schools 5
Enrollment 3,889
High school graduates, 2006-07 959
Dropout rate 0.8%
Pupil/teacher ratio 17.4
Average class size 24.4
Students per computer 2.6
Classrooms with internet 232
Avg. Daily Attendance (ADA) 3,715
Cost per ADA $13,492
Avg. Teacher Salary $81,923

California Achievement Tests 6th ed., 2008

(Pct scoring at or above 50th National Percentile Rank)

	Math	Reading	Language
Grade 3	NA	NA	NA
Grade 7	NA	NA	NA

Academic Performance Index, 2008

Number of students tested 2,800
Number of valid scores 2,766
2007 API (base) 848
2008 API (growth) 855

SAT Testing, 2006-07

Enrollment, Grade 12 997
Number taking test 730
percent taking test 73.2%
percent with total score 1,500+ 58.30%

Average Scores:

Math	Verbal	Writing	Total
574	574	574	1,722

Federal No Child Left Behind, 2008

(Adequate Yearly Progress standards met)

	Participation Rate	Pct Proficient
ELA	Yes	Yes
Math	Yes	Yes

API criteria .... Yes
Graduation rate .... Yes
criteria met/possible 10/10

Other school districts for this city

(see Appendix E for information on these districts)

Mill Valley Elem

See Introduction for an explanation of all data sources.

Demographics & Socio-Economic Characteristics

(2000 Decennial Census, except as noted)

Population

1990* . . . 20,412
2000 . . . 20,718
Male . . . 9,801
Female . . . 10,917
Jan. 2008 (estimate)§ . . . 21,387
Persons per sq. mi. of land . . . 6,683.4

Race & Hispanic Origin, 2000

Race
White . . . 13,061
Black/African American . . . 165
North American Native . . . 47
Asian . . . 5,651
Pacific Islander . . . 238
Other Race . . . 745
Two or more races . . . 811
Hispanic origin, total . . . 2,376
Mexican . . . 1,090
Puerto Rican . . . 117
Cuban . . . 11
Other Hispanic . . . 1,158

Age & Nativity, 2000

Under 5 years . . . 955
18 years and over . . . 16,456
65 years and over . . . 4,313
85 years and over . . . 725
Median Age . . . 42.3
Native-born . . . 13,639
Foreign-born . . . 7,088

Educational Attainment, 2000

Population 25 years and over . . . 15,273
Less than 9th grade . . . 5.4%
High school grad or higher . . . 87.1%
Bachelor's degree or higher . . . 33.8%
Graduate degree . . . 10.9%

Income & Poverty, 1999

Per capita income . . . $33,193
Median household income . . . $68,404
Median family income . . . $82,061
Persons in poverty . . . 3.3%
H'holds receiving public assistance . . . 53
H'holds receiving social security . . . 2,657

Households, 2000

Total households . . . 7,956
With persons under 18 . . . 2,440
With persons over 65 . . . 2,916
Family households . . . 5,511
Single person households . . . 1,994
Persons per household . . . 2.56
Persons per family . . . 3.08

Household Population, 2008§§

Persons living in households . . . 21,055
Persons living in group quarters . . . 332
Persons per household . . . 2.6

Labor & Employment

Total civilian labor force, 2008§§ . . . 10,000
Unemployment rate, 2008 . . . 2.6%
Total civilian labor force, 2000 . . . 9,827

Employed persons 16 years and over by occupation, 2000

Managers & professionals . . . 3,991
Service occupations . . . 1,126
Sales & office occupations . . . 2,969
Farming, fishing & forestry . . . 8
Construction & maintenance . . . 779
Production & transportation . . . 778
Self-employed persons . . . 956

* US Census Bureau
** 2000 Decennial Census
§ California Department of Finance
§§ California Employment Development Dept

General Information

City of Millbrae
621 Magnolia Ave
Millbrae, CA 94030
650-259-2334

Website . . . www.ci.millbrae.ca.us
Elevation . . . 25 ft.
Land Area (sq. miles) . . . 3.2
Water Area (sq. miles) . . . 0
Year of Incorporation . . . 1948
Government type . . . General law
Sales tax rate . . . 9.25%

Voters & Officials

Registered Voters, October 2008

Total . . . 12,004
Democrats . . . 5,910
Republicans . . . 2,728
Declined to state . . . 2,975

Legislative Districts

US Congressional . . . 12
State Senatorial . . . 8
State Assembly . . . 19

Local Officials, 2009

Mayor . . . Robert Gottschalk
Manager . . . Marcia Raines
City Clerk . . . Deborah Konkol
Attorney . . . Joan Cassman
Finance Dir . . . LaRae Brown
Public Works . . . Ron Popp
Planning/Dev Dir . . . Ralph Petty
Building . . . Mark Matthews
Police Chief . . . Tom Hitchcock
Fire Chief . . . Dennis Haag

Public Safety

Number of officers, 2007 . . . 20
Violent crimes, 2007 . . . 39
Property crimes, 2007 . . . 344
Arson, 2007 . . . 4

Public Library

Millbrae Library
San Mateo County Library System
1 Library Ave
Millbrae, CA 94030
650-697-7607

Branch Librarian . . . Ruth Stout

Library system statistics, FY 2007

Population served . . . 278,388
Internet terminals . . . 26
Annual users . . . 49,920

Per capita:

Operating income . . . $90.21
percent from local government . . . 63.5%
Operating expenditure . . . $60.41
Total materials . . . 2.65
Print holdings . . . 2.16
Visits per capita . . . 5.44

Housing & Construction

Housing Units

Total, 2008§ . . . 8,230
Single family units, attached . . . 269
Single family units, detached . . . 5,327
Multiple family units . . . 2,623
Mobile home units . . . 11
Occupied . . . 8,124
Vacancy rate . . . 1.3%
Median rent, 2000** . . . $1,161
Median SF home value, 2000** . . . $552,500

New Privately Owned Housing Units Authorized by Building Permit, 2007*

	Units	Construction Cost
Single	6	$3,387,900
Total	6	$3,387,900

Municipal Finance

(For local fiscal year ended in 2006)

Revenues

Total . . . $26,442,471
Taxes . . . 11,242,827
Special benefits assessment . . . 1,103,918
Licenses & permits . . . 494,523
Fines & forfeitures . . . 209,764
Revenues from use of money & property . . . 853,610
Intergovernmental . . . 1,560,824
Service charges . . . 10,757,505
Other revenues . . . 219,500
Other financing sources . . . 0

Expenditures

Total . . . $33,505,147
General government . . . 2,450,417
Public safety . . . 8,673,011
Transportation . . . 1,159,601
Community development . . . 1,495,065
Health . . . 13,072,375
Culture & leisure . . . 3,233,092
Other . . . 0

Local School District

(Data from School year 2007-08 except as noted)

San Mateo Union High
650 North Delaware St
San Mateo, CA 94401
(650) 558-2299

Superintendent . . . David Miller
Grade plan . . . 9-12
Number of schools . . . 7
Enrollment . . . 8,626
High school graduates, 2006-07 . . . 1,833
Dropout rate . . . 1.3%
Pupil/teacher ratio . . . 21.3
Average class size . . . 26.9
Students per computer . . . 4.0
Classrooms with internet . . . 425
Avg. Daily Attendance (ADA) . . . 8,291
Cost per ADA . . . $9,930
Avg. Teacher Salary . . . $74,785

California Achievement Tests 6th ed., 2008

(Pct scoring at or above 50th National Percentile Rank)

	Math	Reading	Language
Grade 3	NA	NA	NA
Grade 7	NA	NA	NA

Academic Performance Index, 2008

Number of students tested . . . 6,229
Number of valid scores . . . 6,003
2007 API (base) . . . 774
2008 API (growth) . . . 781

SAT Testing, 2006-07

Enrollment, Grade 12 . . . 2,145
Number taking test . . . 1,188
percent taking test . . . 55.4%
percent with total score 1,500+ . . . 37.60%

Average Scores:

Math	Verbal	Writing	Total
572	534	536	1,642

Federal No Child Left Behind, 2008

(Adequate Yearly Progress standards met)

	Participation Rate	Pct Proficient
ELA	Yes	No
Math	Yes	No

API criteria . . . Yes
Graduation rate . . . Yes
criteria met/possible . . . 32/30

Other school districts for this city

(see Appendix E for information on these districts)

Millbrae Elem

Demographics & Socio-Economic Characteristics†

(2007 American Community Survey, except as noted)

Population

1990* 50,686
2007 66,494
Male 35,644
Female 30,850
Jan. 2008 (estimate)§ 69,419
Persons per sq. mi. of land 5,104.3

Race & Hispanic Origin, 2007

Race
White 15,890
Black/African American 2,626
North American Native 378
Asian 40,309
Pacific Islander 233
Other Race 4,892
Two or more races 2,166
Hispanic origin, total 9,833
Mexican .... NA
Puerto Rican .... NA
Cuban .... NA
Other Hispanic .... NA

Age & Nativity, 2007

Under 5 years 3,934
18 years and over 52,370
65 years and over 5,146
85 years and over 489
Median Age 36.8
Native-born 32,380
Foreign-born 34,114

Educational Attainment, 2007

Population 25 years and over 46,095
Less than 9th grade 7.1%
High school grad or higher 86.0%
Bachelor's degree or higher 38.5%
Graduate degree 12.9%

Income & Poverty, 2007

Per capita income $30,780
Median household income $85,186
Median family income $91,232
Persons in poverty 9.0%
H'holds receiving public assistance 445
H'holds receiving social security 2,988

Households, 2007

Total households 18,395
With persons under 18 7,839
With persons over 65 3,317
Family households 13,971
Single person households 3,703
Persons per household 3.37
Persons per family 3.85

Household Population, 2008§§

Persons living in households 66,245
Persons living in group quarters 3,174
Persons per household 3.5

Labor & Employment

Total civilian labor force, 2008§§ 31,800
Unemployment rate, 2008 .... 6.2%
Total civilian labor force, 2000* 31,480

Employed persons 16 years and over by occupation, 2007

Managers & professionals 15,383
Service occupations 4,083
Sales & office occupations 6,827
Farming, fishing & forestry 59
Construction & maintenance 1,747
Production & transportation 3,971
Self-employed persons 553

† see Appendix D for 2000 Decennial Census Data
* US Census Bureau
** 2007 American Community Survey
§ California Department of Finance
§§ California Employment Development Dept

General Information

City of Milpitas
455 E Calaveras Blvd
Milpitas, CA 95035
408-586-3000

Website .... www.ci.milpitas.ca.gov
Elevation .... 15 ft.
Land Area (sq. miles) 13.6
Water Area (sq. miles) 0.1
Year of Incorporation 1954
Government type .... General law
Sales tax rate 9.25%

Voters & Officials

Registered Voters, October 2008

Total 25,813
Democrats 11,004
Republicans 5,584
Declined to state 8,448

Legislative Districts

US Congressional 15
State Senatorial 10
State Assembly 20

Local Officials, 2009

Mayor .... Bob Livengood
Manager .... Tom Williams
City Clerk .... Mary Lavelle
Attorney .... Michael Ogaz
Finance Dir .... Emma Karlen
Public Works .... Greg Armendariz
Planning Dir .... James Lindsay
Building .... Keyvan Irannejad
Police Chief .... Dennis Graham
Fire Chief .... vacant

Public Safety

Number of officers, 2007 88
Violent crimes, 2007 179
Property crimes, 2007 2,104
Arson, 2007 11

Public Library

Milpitas Community Library
Santa Clara County Library System
40 N Milpitas Blvd
Milpitas, CA 95035
408-262-1171

Branch Librarian .... Linda Arbaugh

Library system statistics, FY 2007

Population served 419,141
Internet terminals 133
Annual users 650,000

Per capita:

Operating income $77.89
percent from local government 85.7%
Operating expenditure $66.37
Total materials 4.01
Print holdings 3.27
Visits per capita 6.16

Housing & Construction

Housing Units

Total, 2008§ 19,073
Single family units, attached 2,225
Single family units, detached 11,061
Multiple family units 5,198
Mobile home units 589
Occupied 18,818
Vacancy rate 1.3%
Median rent, 2007** $1,437
Median SF home value, 2007** $664,000

New Privately Owned Housing Units Authorized by Building Permit, 2007*

	Units	Construction Cost
Single	79	$21,285,310
Total	174	$39,501,427

Municipal Finance

(For local fiscal year ended in 2006)

Revenues

Total $93,973,446
Taxes 40,240,821
Special benefits assessment 287,078
Licenses & permits 6,504,085
Fines & forfeitures 852,094
Revenues from use of money & property 3,987,645
Intergovernmental 5,952,903
Service charges 31,033,182
Other revenues 5,115,638
Other financing sources 0

Expenditures

Total $91,881,547
General government 13,886,434
Public safety 34,722,341
Transportation 10,923,647
Community development 9,511,315
Health 7,493,876
Culture & leisure 5,178,790
Other 0

Local School District

(Data from School year 2007-08 except as noted)

Milpitas Unified
1331 East Calaveras Blvd
Milpitas, CA 95035
(408) 635-2600

Superintendent .... Karl Black
Grade plan K-12
Number of schools 14
Enrollment 9,585
High school graduates, 2006-07 723
Dropout rate 1.7%
Pupil/teacher ratio 22.1
Average class size 26.6
Students per computer 5.3
Classrooms with internet 455
Avg. Daily Attendance (ADA) 9,625
Cost per ADA $7,491
Avg. Teacher Salary $70,932

California Achievement Tests 6th ed., 2008

(Pct scoring at or above 50th National Percentile Rank)

	Math	Reading	Language
Grade 3	69%	43%	55%
Grade 7	69%	63%	60%

Academic Performance Index, 2008

Number of students tested 7,399
Number of valid scores 7,046
2007 API (base) 798
2008 API (growth) 810

SAT Testing, 2006-07

Enrollment, Grade 12 797
Number taking test 407
percent taking test 51.1%
percent with total score 1,500+ 26.40%

Average Scores:

Math	Verbal	Writing	Total
534	496	494	1,524

Federal No Child Left Behind, 2008

(Adequate Yearly Progress standards met)

	Participation Rate	Pct Proficient
ELA	Yes	No
Math	Yes	No

API criteria .... Yes
Graduation rate .... Yes
\# criteria met/possible 38/35

Other school districts for this city

(see Appendix E for information on these districts)

None

See Introduction for an explanation of all data sources.

Demographics & Socio-Economic Characteristics†

(2007 American Community Survey, except as noted)

Population

1990* 72,820
2007 92,673
Male 46,466
Female 46,207
Jan. 2008 (estimate)§ 98,572
Persons per sq. mi. of land 5,271.2

Race & Hispanic Origin, 2007

Race
White 73,082
Black/African American 1,020
North American Native 845
Asian 9,240
Pacific Islander 186
Other Race 5,731
Two or more races 2,569
Hispanic origin, total 12,539
Mexican 10,486
Puerto Rican 187
Cuban 119
Other Hispanic 1,747

Age & Nativity, 2007

Under 5 years 6,981
18 years and over 69,726
65 years and over 13,214
85 years and over 2,226
Median Age 40.0
Native-born 76,417
Foreign-born 16,256

Educational Attainment, 2007

Population 25 years and over 62,348
Less than 9th grade 3.2%
High school grad or higher 93.1%
Bachelor's degree or higher 44.6%
Graduate degree 16.6%

Income & Poverty, 2007

Per capita income $39,513
Median household income $92,614
Median family income $105,716
Persons in poverty 4.7%
H'holds receiving public assistance 281
H'holds receiving social security 8,547

Households, 2007

Total households 32,820
With persons under 18 11,886
With persons over 65 9,113
Family households 23,405
Single person households 7,664
Persons per household 2.80
Persons per family 3.37

Household Population, 2008§§

Persons living in households 97,507
Persons living in group quarters 1,065
Persons per household 2.9

Labor & Employment

Total civilian labor force, 2008§§ 56,500
Unemployment rate, 2008 .... 3.8%
Total civilian labor force, 2000* 48,579

Employed persons 16 years and over by occupation, 2007

Managers & professionals 23,217
Service occupations 4,689
Sales & office occupations 13,640
Farming, fishing & forestry 125
Construction & maintenance 2,909
Production & transportation 2,148
Self-employed persons 3,777

† see Appendix D for 2000 Decennial Census Data
* US Census Bureau
** 2007 American Community Survey
§ California Department of Finance
§§ California Employment Development Dept

General Information

City of Mission Viejo
200 Civic Center
Mission Viejo, CA 92691
949-470-3000

Website .... cityofmissionviejo.org
Elevation .... NA
Land Area (sq. miles) 18.7
Water Area (sq. miles) 0.4
Year of Incorporation 1988
Government type .... General law
Sales tax rate 8.75%

Voters & Officials

Registered Voters, October 2008

Total 62,298
Democrats 16,711
Republicans 31,472
Declined to state 11,824

Legislative Districts

US Congressional 42
State Senatorial 33
State Assembly 71

Local Officials, 2009

Mayor .... Frank Ury
Manager .... Dennis Wilberg
City Clerk .... Karen Hamman
Attorney .... William Curley III
Finance Dir .... Irwin Bornstein
Public Works .... Mark Chagnon
Planning/Dev Dir .... Chuck Wilson
Building .... Dennis Bogle
Police Chief .... (County)
Emergency/Fire Dir .... (County)

Public Safety

Number of officers, 2007 .... NA
Violent crimes, 2007 82
Property crimes, 2007 1,313
Arson, 2007 14

Public Library

Mission Viejo City Library
100 Civic Center
Mission Viejo, CA 92691
949-830-7100

Director .... Valerie Maginnis

Library statistics, FY 2007

Population served 98,483
Internet terminals 31
Annual users 231,590

Per capita:

Operating income $28.02
percent from local government 75.0%
Operating expenditure $29.52
Total materials 1.64
Print holdings 1.51
Visits per capita 6.00

Housing & Construction

Housing Units

Total, 2008§ 33,713
Single family units, attached 4,021
Single family units, detached 24,474
Multiple family units 5,129
Mobile home units 89
Occupied 33,165
Vacancy rate 1.6%
Median rent, 2007** $1,657
Median SF home value, 2007** $680,400

New Privately Owned Housing Units Authorized by Building Permit, 2007*

	Units	Construction Cost
Single	0	$0
Total	0	$0

Municipal Finance

(For local fiscal year ended in 2006)

Revenues

Total $67,504,228
Taxes 47,964,154
Special benefits assessment 0
Licenses & permits 1,627,614
Fines & forfeitures 834,282
Revenues from use of money & property 1,904,030
Intergovernmental 9,517,854
Service charges 3,987,325
Other revenues 1,668,969
Other financing sources 0

Expenditures

Total $61,085,481
General government 9,728,753
Public safety 14,215,741
Transportation 13,347,694
Community development 5,238,270
Health 0
Culture & leisure 18,555,023
Other 0

Local School District

(Data from School year 2007-08 except as noted)

Capistrano Unified
33122 Valle Rd
San Juan Capistrano, CA 92675
(949) 234-9200

Superintendent .... A. Carter
Grade plan K-12
Number of schools 61
Enrollment 52,390
High school graduates, 2006-07 3,205
Dropout rate 0.5%
Pupil/teacher ratio 23.4
Average class size 28.7
Students per computer 4.8
Classrooms with internet 2,308
Avg. Daily Attendance (ADA) 50,036
Cost per ADA $7,694
Avg. Teacher Salary $75,390

California Achievement Tests 6th ed., 2008

(Pct scoring at or above 50th National Percentile Rank)

	Math	Reading	Language
Grade 3	71%	56%	63%
Grade 7	73%	71%	68%

Academic Performance Index, 2008

Number of students tested 39,589
Number of valid scores 38,275
2007 API (base) 826
2008 API (growth) 837

SAT Testing, 2006-07

Enrollment, Grade 12 3,414
Number taking test 1,770
percent taking test 51.9%
percent with total score 1,500+ 34.90%

Average Scores:

Math	Verbal	Writing	Total
552	541	537	1,630

Federal No Child Left Behind, 2008

(Adequate Yearly Progress standards met)

	Participation Rate	Pct Proficient
ELA	Yes	No
Math	Yes	Yes

API criteria .... Yes
Graduation rate .... Yes
\# criteria met/possible 42/41

Other school districts for this city

(see Appendix E for information on these districts)

None

See Introduction for an explanation of all data sources.

Demographics & Socio-Economic Characteristics†

(2007 American Community Survey, except as noted)

Population

1990*	164,730
2007	198,456
Male	95,754
Female	102,702
Jan. 2008 (estimate)§	209,936
Persons per sq. mi. of land	5,864.1

Race & Hispanic Origin, 2007

Race	
White	149,913
Black/African American	5,915
North American Native	1,915
Asian	11,833
Pacific Islander	740
Other Race	20,072
Two or more races	8,068
Hispanic origin, total	71,819
Mexican	66,218
Puerto Rican	813
Cuban	297
Other Hispanic	4,491

Age & Nativity, 2007

Under 5 years	17,208
18 years and over	140,086
65 years and over	23,514
85 years and over	3,260
Median Age	33.0
Native-born	164,491
Foreign-born	33,965

Educational Attainment, 2007

Population 25 years and over	121,976
Less than 9th grade	10.0%
High school grad or higher	79.1%
Bachelor's degree or higher	20.1%
Graduate degree	6.1%

Income & Poverty, 2007

Per capita income	$22,906
Median household income	$47,470
Median family income	$57,229
Persons in poverty	15.5%
H'holds receiving public assistance	2,719
H'holds receiving social security	18,408

Households, 2007

Total households	65,526
With persons under 18	25,918
With persons over 65	15,944
Family households	45,259
Single person households	16,492
Persons per household	3.00
Persons per family	3.65

Household Population, 2008§§

Persons living in households	206,705
Persons living in group quarters	3,231
Persons per household	2.9

Labor & Employment

Total civilian labor force, 2008§§	101,600
Unemployment rate, 2008	9.6%
Total civilian labor force, 2000*	85,177

Employed persons 16 years and over by occupation, 2007

Managers & professionals	24,158
Service occupations	12,667
Sales & office occupations	22,022
Farming, fishing & forestry	1,227
Construction & maintenance	7,521
Production & transportation	11,548
Self-employed persons	6,134

† see Appendix D for 2000 Decennial Census Data
* US Census Bureau
** 2007 American Community Survey
§ California Department of Finance
§§ California Employment Development Dept

General Information

City of Modesto
1010 Tenth St
PO Box 642
Modesto, CA 95353
209-577-5200

Website	www.modestogov.com
Elevation	87 ft.
Land Area (sq. miles)	35.8
Water Area (sq. miles)	0.2
Year of Incorporation	1884
Government type	Chartered
Sales tax rate	8.38%

Voters & Officials

Registered Voters, October 2008

Total	98,245
Democrats	42,261
Republicans	36,382
Declined to state	15,390

Legislative Districts

US Congressional	18-19
State Senatorial	12, 14
State Assembly	25, 26

Local Officials, 2009

Mayor	Jim Ridenour
City Manager	Greg Nyhoff
City Clerk	Stephanie Lopez
Attorney	Susana Alcala-Wood
Finance Dir	Wayne Padilla
Public Works	Nick Pinhey
Community Dev Dir	Brent Sinclair
Building	(vacant)
Police Chief	Roy Wasden
Fire Chief	James Miguel

Public Safety

Number of officers, 2007	271
Violent crimes, 2007	1,490
Property crimes, 2007	12,030
Arson, 2007	129

Public Library

Modesto Library
Stanislaus County Free Library
1500 I St
Modesto, CA 95354
209-558-7800

Director . . . Vanessa Czopek

Library system statistics, FY 2007

Population served	521,497
Internet terminals	128
Annual users	256,298

Per capita:

Operating income	$20.76
percent from local government	91.0%
Operating expenditure	$20.19
Total materials	1.66
Print holdings	1.56
Visits per capita	NA

Housing & Construction

Housing Units

Total, 2008§	74,700
Single family units, attached	4,010
Single family units, detached	52,785
Multiple family units	15,854
Mobile home units	2,051
Occupied	72,232
Vacancy rate	3.3%
Median rent, 2007**	$951
Median SF home value, 2007**	$349,700

New Privately Owned Housing Units Authorized by Building Permit, 2007*

	Units	Construction Cost
Single	285	$55,124,326
Total	555	$81,240,201

Municipal Finance

(For local fiscal year ended in 2006)

Revenues

Total	$301,507,982
Taxes	105,267,307
Special benefits assessment	38,996,651
Licenses & permits	835,766
Fines & forfeitures	1,590,006
Revenues from use of money & property	4,942,365
Intergovernmental	20,844,728
Service charges	123,774,925
Other revenues	5,256,234
Other financing sources	0

Expenditures

Total	$243,579,365
General government	13,893,507
Public safety	75,764,491
Transportation	49,315,634
Community development	23,338,972
Health	21,143,699
Culture & leisure	20,989,763
Other	0

Local School District

(Data from School year 2007-08 except as noted)
‡combined elementary and high school data

Modesto City High
426 Locust St
Modesto, CA 95351
(209) 576-4011

Superintendent	Arturo Flores
Grade plan	9-12
Number of schools	7
Enrollment	15,742
High school graduates, 2006-07	2,825
Dropout rate	4.7%
Pupil/teacher ratio	25.6
Average class size	27.5
Students per computer	4.5
Classrooms with internet	596
Avg. Daily Attendance (ADA)‡	30,234
Cost per ADA‡	$8,630
Avg. Teacher Salary‡	$80,360

California Achievement Tests 6th ed., 2008

(Pct scoring at or above 50th National Percentile Rank)

	Math	Reading	Language
Grade 3	NA	NA	NA
Grade 7	NA	NA	NA

Academic Performance Index, 2008

Number of students tested	11,213
Number of valid scores	10,732
2007 API (base)	711
2008 API (growth)	720

SAT Testing, 2006-07

Enrollment, Grade 12	3,607
Number taking test	754
percent taking test	20.9%
percent with total score 1,500+	11.50%

Average Scores:

Math	Verbal	Writing	Total
521	509	505	1,535

Federal No Child Left Behind, 2008

(Adequate Yearly Progress standards met)

	Participation Rate	Pct Proficient
ELA	No	No
Math	No	No

API criteria	Yes
Graduation rate	No
# criteria met/possible	34/27

Other school districts for this city

(see Appendix E for information on these districts)

Complete list in Appendix E

See Introduction for an explanation of all data sources.

Demographics & Socio-Economic Characteristics

(2000 Decennial Census, except as noted)

Population

1990* ... 35,761
2000 ... 36,929
Male ... 17,717
Female ... 19,212
Jan. 2008 (estimate)§ ... 39,327
Persons per sq. mi. of land ... 2,870.6

Race & Hispanic Origin, 2000

Race
White ... 23,237
Black/African American ... 3,202
North American Native ... 323
Asian ... 2,594
Pacific Islander ... 48
Other Race ... 5,765
Two or more races ... 1,760
Hispanic origin, total ... 13,012
Mexican ... 9,854
Puerto Rican ... 233
Cuban ... 205
Other Hispanic ... 2,720

Age & Nativity, 2000

Under 5 years ... 2,967
18 years and over ... 26,822
65 years and over ... 3,837
85 years and over ... 540
Median Age ... 33.7
Native-born ... 28,901
Foreign-born ... 7,916

Educational Attainment, 2000

Population 25 years and over ... 23,634
Less than 9th grade ... 9.5%
High school grad or higher ... 78.0%
Bachelor's degree or higher ... 25.1%
Graduate degree ... 8.2%

Income & Poverty, 1999

Per capita income ... $21,686
Median household income ... $45,375
Median family income ... $49,703
Persons in poverty ... 13.0%
H'holds receiving public assistance ... 759
H'holds receiving social security ... 2,941

Households, 2000

Total households ... 13,502
With persons under 18 ... 5,308
With persons over 65 ... 2,863
Family households ... 9,091
Single person households ... 3,517
Persons per household ... 2.71
Persons per family ... 3.29

Household Population, 2008§§

Persons living in households ... 39,034
Persons living in group quarters ... 293
Persons per household ... 2.8

Labor & Employment

Total civilian labor force, 2008§§ ... 21,100
Unemployment rate, 2008 ... 6.6%
Total civilian labor force, 2000 ... 18,104

Employed persons 16 years and over by occupation, 2000

Managers & professionals ... 6,282
Service occupations ... 2,606
Sales & office occupations ... 4,938
Farming, fishing & forestry ... 46
Construction & maintenance ... 1,175
Production & transportation ... 1,804
Self-employed persons ... 1,475

* US Census Bureau
** 2000 Decennial Census
§ California Department of Finance
§§ California Employment Development Dept

General Information

City of Monrovia
415 S Ivy Ave
Monrovia, CA 91016
626-932-5550

Website ... www.cityofmonrovia.org
Elevation ... 560 ft.
Land Area (sq. miles) ... 13.7
Water Area (sq. miles) ... 0.1
Year of Incorporation ... 1887
Government type ... General law
Sales tax rate ... 9.25%

Voters & Officials

Registered Voters, October 2008

Total ... 18,871
Democrats ... 7,911
Republicans ... 6,637
Declined to state ... 3,553

Legislative Districts

US Congressional ... 26
State Senatorial ... 29
State Assembly ... 44, 59

Local Officials, 2009

Mayor ... Rob Hammond
Manager ... Scott Ochoa
City Clerk ... Linda B. Proctor
Attorney ... Craig Steele
Finance Dir ... Mark D. Alvarado
Public Works ... Ron Bow
Planning/Dev Dir ... Alice Griselle
Building ... NA
Police Chief ... Roger Johnson
Fire Chief ... Chris Donovan

Public Safety

Number of officers, 2007 ... 54
Violent crimes, 2007 ... 135
Property crimes, 2007 ... 1,126
Arson, 2007 ... 4

Public Library

Monrovia Public Library
843 E Olive Ave
Monrovia, CA 91016
626-256-8274

Division Manager ... Monica Greening

Library statistics, FY 2007

Population served ... 39,309
Internet terminals ... 14
Annual users ... 24,639

Per capita:

Operating income ... $38.05
percent from local government ... 95.0%
Operating expenditure ... $34.96
Total materials ... 3.04
Print holdings ... 2.96
Visits per capita ... NA

Housing & Construction

Housing Units

Total, 2008§ ... 14,190
Single family units, attached ... 1,563
Single family units, detached ... 7,878
Multiple family units ... 4,634
Mobile home units ... 115
Occupied ... 13,727
Vacancy rate ... 3.3%
Median rent, 2000** ... $746
Median SF home value, 2000** ... $229,600

New Privately Owned Housing Units Authorized by Building Permit, 2007*

	Units	Construction Cost
Single	55	$11,167,000
Total	123	$28,459,678

Municipal Finance

(For local fiscal year ended in 2006)

Revenues

Total ... $40,208,240
Taxes ... 22,874,935
Special benefits assessment ... 1,318,524
Licenses & permits ... 734,941
Fines & forfeitures ... 716,885
Revenues from use of money & property ... 1,064,905
Intergovernmental ... 4,167,966
Service charges ... 8,820,507
Other revenues ... 509,577
Other financing sources ... 0

Expenditures

Total ... $40,548,564
General government ... 3,470,580
Public safety ... 19,866,467
Transportation ... 3,546,366
Community development ... 3,477,466
Health ... 1,329,017
Culture & leisure ... 4,351,092
Other ... 0

Local School District

(Data from School year 2007-08 except as noted)

Monrovia Unified
325 East Huntington Dr
Monrovia, CA 91016
(626) 471-2000

Superintendent ... Louise Taylor
Grade plan ... PK-12
Number of schools ... 10
Enrollment ... 6,192
High school graduates, 2006-07 ... 369
Dropout rate ... 2.4%
Pupil/teacher ratio ... 22.4
Average class size ... 26.0
Students per computer ... 4.0
Classrooms with internet ... 358
Avg. Daily Attendance (ADA) ... 6,048
Cost per ADA ... $8,304
Avg. Teacher Salary ... $69,631

California Achievement Tests 6th ed., 2008

(Pct scoring at or above 50th National Percentile Rank)

	Math	Reading	Language
Grade 3	55%	37%	47%
Grade 7	56%	54%	51%

Academic Performance Index, 2008

Number of students tested ... 4,655
Number of valid scores ... 4,455
2007 API (base) ... 754
2008 API (growth) ... 774

SAT Testing, 2006-07

Enrollment, Grade 12 ... 470
Number taking test ... 155
percent taking test ... 33.0%
percent with total score 1,500+ ... 12.10%

Average Scores:

Math	Verbal	Writing	Total
481	476	472	1,429

Federal No Child Left Behind, 2008

(Adequate Yearly Progress standards met)

	Participation Rate	Pct Proficient
ELA	Yes	No
Math	Yes	No

API criteria ... Yes
Graduation rate ... Yes
\# criteria met/possible ... 34/32

Other school districts for this city

(see Appendix E for information on these districts)

None

Demographics & Socio-Economic Characteristics

(2000 Decennial Census, except as noted)

Population

1990*	1,415
2000	1,456
Male	717
Female	739
Jan. 2008 (estimate)§	1,496
Persons per sq. mi. of land	831.1

Race & Hispanic Origin, 2000

Race	
White	1,296
Black/African American	1
North American Native	74
Asian	2
Pacific Islander	1
Other Race	32
Two or more races	50
Hispanic origin, total	79
Mexican	51
Puerto Rican	4
Cuban	0
Other Hispanic	24

Age & Nativity, 2000

Under 5 years	89
18 years and over	1,038
65 years and over	177
85 years and over	19
Median Age	36.2
Native-born	1,498
Foreign-born	27

Educational Attainment, 2000

Population 25 years and over	959
Less than 9th grade	3.3%
High school grad or higher	79.4%
Bachelor's degree or higher	6.9%
Graduate degree	1.7%

Income & Poverty, 1999

Per capita income	$12,661
Median household income	$22,991
Median family income	$28,672
Persons in poverty	25.3%
H'holds receiving public assistance	60
H'holds receiving social security	178

Households, 2000

Total households	560
With persons under 18	221
With persons over 65	143
Family households	391
Single person households	142
Persons per household	2.57
Persons per family	3.07

Household Population, 2008§§

Persons living in households	1,477
Persons living in group quarters	19
Persons per household	2.4

Labor & Employment

Total civilian labor force, 2008§§	NA
Unemployment rate, 2008	NA
Total civilian labor force, 2000	629

Employed persons 16 years and over by occupation, 2000

Managers & professionals	105
Service occupations	153
Sales & office occupations	128
Farming, fishing & forestry	21
Construction & maintenance	84
Production & transportation	89
Self-employed persons	100

* US Census Bureau
** 2000 Decennial Census
§ California Department of Finance
§§ California Employment Development Dept

General Information

City of Montague
PO Box 428
Montague, CA 96064
530-459-3030

Website	NA
Elevation	2,538 ft.
Land Area (sq. miles)	1.8
Water Area (sq. miles)	0
Year of Incorporation	1909
Government type	General law
Sales tax rate	8.25%

Voters & Officials

Registered Voters, October 2008

Total	715
Democrats	203
Republicans	325
Declined to state	137

Legislative Districts

US Congressional	2
State Senatorial	4
State Assembly	2

Local Officials, 2009

Mayor	John Hammond
Manager/Admin	NA
City Clerk	Janie Sprague
Attorney	John Kenny
Finance Commissioner	Jayne Keller
Public Works	Frank Hoag
Planning Dir	Stan Eisner
Building	NA
Police Chief	(County)
Fire Chief	Jasen Vela

Public Safety

Number of officers, 2007	NA
Violent crimes, 2007	3
Property crimes, 2007	25
Arson, 2007	1

Public Library

Montague Branch Library
Siskiyou County Free Library System
1030 13th St
Montague, CA 96064
530-459-5473

Branch Librarian	Essie Biggs

Library system statistics, FY 2007

Population served	45,953
Internet terminals	31
Annual users	48,766

Per capita:

Operating income	$20.36
percent from local government	90.2%
Operating expenditure	$20.12
Total materials	4.06
Print holdings	3.88
Visits per capita	NA

Housing & Construction

Housing Units

Total, 2008§	661
Single family units, attached	15
Single family units, detached	488
Multiple family units	53
Mobile home units	105
Occupied	608
Vacancy rate	8.0%
Median rent, 2000**	$471
Median SF home value, 2000**	$73,300

New Privately Owned Housing Units Authorized by Building Permit, 2007*

	Units	Construction Cost
Single	NA	NA
Total	NA	NA

Municipal Finance

(For local fiscal year ended in 2006)

Revenues

Total	$2,027,764
Taxes	373,280
Special benefits assessment	113,153
Licenses & permits	3,006
Fines & forfeitures	3,782
Revenues from use of money & property	69,543
Intergovernmental	1,019,244
Service charges	391,001
Other revenues	54,755
Other financing sources	0

Expenditures

Total	$1,617,077
General government	104,625
Public safety	816,967
Transportation	151,215
Community development	140,188
Health	104,877
Culture & leisure	72,883
Other	0

Local School District

(Data from School year 2007-08 except as noted)

Yreka Union High
431 Knapp St
Yreka, CA 96097
(530) 842-2521

Superintendent	Mark Greenfield
Grade plan	9-12
Number of schools	3
Enrollment	796
High school graduates, 2006-07	148
Dropout rate	2.3%
Pupil/teacher ratio	19.6
Average class size	23.0
Students per computer	1.8
Classrooms with internet	74
Avg. Daily Attendance (ADA)	772
Cost per ADA	$9,573
Avg. Teacher Salary	$58,927

California Achievement Tests 6th ed., 2008

(Pct scoring at or above 50th National Percentile Rank)

	Math	Reading	Language
Grade 3	NA	NA	NA
Grade 7	NA	NA	NA

Academic Performance Index, 2008

Number of students tested	584
Number of valid scores	562
2007 API (base)	719
2008 API (growth)	748

SAT Testing, 2006-07

Enrollment, Grade 12	176
Number taking test	47
percent taking test	26.7%
percent with total score 1,500+	17.10%

Average Scores:

Math	Verbal	Writing	Total
541	512	498	1,551

Federal No Child Left Behind, 2008

(Adequate Yearly Progress standards met)

	Participation Rate	Pct Proficient
ELA	No	Yes
Math	Yes	Yes

API criteria	Yes
Graduation rate	Yes
# criteria met/possible	14/13

Other school districts for this city

(see Appendix E for information on these districts)

Complete list in Appendix E

See Introduction for an explanation of all data sources.

Demographics & Socio-Economic Characteristics

(2000 Decennial Census, except as noted)

Population

1990* 28,434
2000 33,049
Male 16,492
Female 16,557
Jan. 2008 (estimate)§ 37,017
Persons per sq. mi. of land 7,258.2

Race & Hispanic Origin, 2000

Race
White 14,796
Black/African American 2,112
North American Native 319
Asian 2,688
Pacific Islander 101
Other Race 11,442
Two or more races 1,591
Hispanic origin, total 19,823
Mexican 15,851
Puerto Rican 145
Cuban 153
Other Hispanic 3,674

Age & Nativity, 2000

Under 5 years 2,930
18 years and over 22,101
65 years and over 2,756
85 years and over 348
Median Age 29.0
Native-born 21,824
Foreign-born 11,295

Educational Attainment, 2000

Population 25 years and over 18,765
Less than 9th grade 18.2%
High school grad or higher 60.4%
Bachelor's degree or higher 9.6%
Graduate degree 2.5%

Income & Poverty, 1999

Per capita income $13,556
Median household income $40,797
Median family income $42,815
Persons in poverty 17.2%
H'holds receiving public assistance 565
H'holds receiving social security 2,029

Households, 2000

Total households 8,800
With persons under 18 4,822
With persons over 65 1,841
Family households 7,053
Single person households 1,323
Persons per household 3.69
Persons per family 4.04

Household Population, 2008§§

Persons living in households 36,405
Persons living in group quarters 612
Persons per household 3.9

Labor & Employment

Total civilian labor force, 2008§§ 16,500
Unemployment rate, 2008 .... 7.6%
Total civilian labor force, 2000 13,746

Employed persons 16 years and over by occupation, 2000

Managers & professionals 2,417
Service occupations 2,077
Sales & office occupations 3,491
Farming, fishing & forestry 102
Construction & maintenance 1,463
Production & transportation 2,952
Self-employed persons 709

* US Census Bureau
** 2000 Decennial Census
§ California Department of Finance
§§ California Employment Development Dept

General Information

City of Montclair
5111 Benito Street
P.O. Box 2308
Montclair, CA 91763
909-626-8571

Website .... www.ci.montclair.ca.us
Elevation .... 977 ft.
Land Area (sq. miles) 5.1
Water Area (sq. miles) 0
Year of Incorporation 1956
Government type .... General law
Sales tax rate 9.00%

Voters & Officials

Registered Voters, October 2008

Total 12,321
Democrats 6,238
Republicans 3,437
Declined to state 2,180

Legislative Districts

US Congressional 26
State Senatorial 32
State Assembly 61

Local Officials, 2009

Mayor .... Paul M. Eaton
City Manager .... Lee C. McDougal
City Clerk .... Donna M. Jackson
Attorney .... Diane E. Robbins
Finance Dir .... Richard Beltran (Int)
Public Works .... Marilyn J. Staats
Community Dev Dir .... Steve Lustro
Building .... Merry Westerlin
Police Chief .... Keith Jones (Actg)
Fire Chief .... Troy Ament

Public Safety

Number of officers, 2007 57
Violent crimes, 2007 235
Property crimes, 2007 2,346
Arson, 2007 4

Public Library

Montclair Branch Library
San Bernardino County Library System
9955 Fremont Ave
Montclair, CA 91763
909-624-4671

Branch Manager .... Clint Reese

Library system statistics, FY 2007

Population served 1,177,092
Internet terminals 12
Annual users 45,343

Per capita:

Operating income $14.27
percent from local government 73.3%
Operating expenditure $13.86
Total materials 0.86
Print holdings 0.79
Visits per capita 5.83

Housing & Construction

Housing Units

Total, 2008§ 9,677
Single family units, attached 758
Single family units, detached 5,655
Multiple family units 2,403
Mobile home units 861
Occupied 9,394
Vacancy rate 2.9%
Median rent, 2000** $671
Median SF home value, 2000** $135,700

New Privately Owned Housing Units Authorized by Building Permit, 2007*

	Units	Construction Cost
Single	58	$12,472,447
Total	143	$19,408,913

Municipal Finance

(For local fiscal year ended in 2006)

Revenues

Total $68,677,312
Taxes 24,688,701
Special benefits assessment 0
Licenses & permits 1,307,958
Fines & forfeitures 1,007,241
Revenues from use of money & property 1,719,209
Intergovernmental 3,393,031
Service charges 4,120,126
Other revenues 1,141,046
Other financing sources 31,300,000

Expenditures

Total $34,061,346
General government 4,838,408
Public safety 16,702,962
Transportation 3,952,037
Community development 3,010,372
Health 4,063,823
Culture & leisure 1,493,744
Other 0

Local School District

(Data from School year 2007-08 except as noted)

Chaffey Joint Union High
211 West Fifth St
Ontario, CA 91762
(909) 988-8511

Superintendent .... Mathew Holton
Grade plan 9-12
Number of schools 11
Enrollment 25,108
High school graduates, 2006-07 4,562
Dropout rate 2.6%
Pupil/teacher ratio 25.2
Average class size 29.3
Students per computer 4.6
Classrooms with internet 1,703
Avg. Daily Attendance (ADA) 24,014
Cost per ADA $7,815
Avg. Teacher Salary $77,140

California Achievement Tests 6th ed., 2008

(Pct scoring at or above 50th National Percentile Rank)

	Math	Reading	Language
Grade 3	NA	NA	NA
Grade 7	NA	NA	NA

Academic Performance Index, 2008

Number of students tested 18,219
Number of valid scores 17,278
2007 API (base) 720
2008 API (growth) 734

SAT Testing, 2006-07

Enrollment, Grade 12 5,840
Number taking test 1,782
percent taking test 30.5%
percent with total score 1,500+ 12.30%

Average Scores:

Math	Verbal	Writing	Total
492	475	471	1,438

Federal No Child Left Behind, 2008

(Adequate Yearly Progress standards met)

	Participation Rate	Pct Proficient
ELA	No	Yes
Math	Yes	No

API criteria .... Yes
Graduation rate .... Yes
\# criteria met/possible 38/36

Other school districts for this city

(see Appendix E for information on these districts)

Ontario-Montclair Elem

See Introduction for an explanation of all data sources.

Demographics & Socio-Economic Characteristics
(2000 Decennial Census, except as noted)

Population
1990* . . . 3,287
2000 . . . 3,483
Male . . . 1,741
Female . . . 1,742
Jan. 2008 (estimate)§ . . . 3,579
Persons per sq. mi. of land . . . 2,236.9

Race & Hispanic Origin, 2000
Race
White . . . 2,912
Black/African American . . . 6
North American Native . . . 2
Asian . . . 428
Pacific Islander . . . 1
Other Race . . . 37
Two or more races . . . 97
Hispanic origin, total . . . 125
Mexican . . . 70
Puerto Rican . . . 5
Cuban . . . 5
Other Hispanic . . . 45

Age & Nativity, 2000
Under 5 years . . . 206
18 years and over . . . 2,513
65 years and over . . . 505
85 years and over . . . 38
Median Age . . . 43.0
Native-born . . . 3,040
Foreign-born . . . 519

Educational Attainment, 2000
Population 25 years and over . . . 2,425
Less than 9th grade . . . 1.1%
High school grad or higher . . . 97.2%
Bachelor's degree or higher . . . 71.3%
Graduate degree . . . 33.5%

Income & Poverty, 1999
Per capita income . . . $76,577
Median household income . . . $154,268
Median family income . . . $156,706
Persons in poverty . . . 4.2%
H'holds receiving public assistance . . . 30
H'holds receiving social security . . . 274

Households, 2000
Total households . . . 1,211
With persons under 18 . . . 500
With persons over 65 . . . 340
Family households . . . 1,024
Single person households . . . 152
Persons per household . . . 2.88
Persons per family . . . 3.13

Household Population, 2008§§
Persons living in households . . . 3,579
Persons living in group quarters . . . 0
Persons per household . . . 2.9

Labor & Employment
Total civilian labor force, 2008§§ . . . NA
Unemployment rate, 2008 . . . NA
Total civilian labor force, 2000 . . . 1,538

Employed persons 16 years and over by occupation, 2000
Managers & professionals . . . 1,057
Service occupations . . . 79
Sales & office occupations . . . 304
Farming, fishing & forestry . . . 0
Construction & maintenance . . . 5
Production & transportation . . . 56
Self-employed persons . . . 229

* US Census Bureau
** 2000 Decennial Census
§ California Department of Finance
§§ California Employment Development Dept

General Information
City of Monte Sereno
18041 Saratoga-Los Gatos Rd
Monte Sereno, CA 95030
408-354-7635

Website . . . www.montesereno.org
Elevation . . . 503 ft.
Land Area (sq. miles) . . . 1.6
Water Area (sq. miles) . . . 0
Year of Incorporation . . . 1957
Government type . . . General law
Sales tax rate . . . 9.25%

Voters & Officials
Registered Voters, October 2008
Total . . . 2,442
Democrats . . . 939
Republicans . . . 971
Declined to state . . . 458

Legislative Districts
US Congressional . . . 14
State Senatorial . . . 15
State Assembly . . . 21

Local Officials, 2009
Mayor . . . A. Curtis Wright
City Manager . . . Brian Loventhal
City Clerk . . . Andrea Chelemengos
Attorney . . . Kirsten Powell
Finance Dir . . . Sue L'Heureux
Public Works . . . Mo Sharma
Planning Dir . . . Brian Loventhal
Building . . . Howard Bell
Police Chief . . . NA
Fire/Emergency Mgmt . . . (County)

Public Safety
Number of officers, 2007 . . . NA
Violent crimes, 2007 . . . 2
Property crimes, 2007 . . . 48
Arson, 2007 . . . 1

Public Library
Served by County Library

Library system statistics, FY 2007
Population served . . . NA
Internet terminals . . . NA
Annual users . . . NA

Per capita:
Operating income . . . NA
percent from local government . . . NA
Operating expenditure . . . NA
Total materials . . . NA
Print holdings . . . NA
Visits per capita . . . NA

Housing & Construction
Housing Units
Total, 2008§ . . . 1,255
Single family units, attached . . . 13
Single family units, detached . . . 1,151
Multiple family units . . . 91
Mobile home units . . . 0
Occupied . . . 1,229
Vacancy rate . . . 2.1%
Median rent, 2000** . . . $1,711
Median SF home value, 2000** . . . $1,000,001

New Privately Owned Housing Units Authorized by Building Permit, 2007*

	Units	Construction Cost
Single	14	$9,910,831
Total	14	$9,910,831

Municipal Finance
(For local fiscal year ended in 2006)

Revenues
Total . . . $2,319,136
Taxes . . . 1,040,822
Special benefits assessment . . . 184,233
Licenses & permits . . . 430,043
Fines & forfeitures . . . 12,632
Revenues from use of money & property . . . 188,572
Intergovernmental . . . 282,338
Service charges . . . 163,317
Other revenues . . . 17,179
Other financing sources . . . 0

Expenditures
Total . . . $1,905,222
General government . . . 1,272,247
Public safety . . . 406,393
Transportation . . . 98,050
Community development . . . 128,532
Health . . . 0
Culture & leisure . . . 0
Other . . . 0

Local School District
(Data from School year 2007-08 except as noted)
Los Gatos-Saratoga Joint Union High
17421 Farley Road West
Los Gatos, CA 95030
(408) 354-2520

Superintendent . . . Cary Matsuoka
Grade plan . . . 9-12
Number of schools . . . 2
Enrollment . . . 3,164
High school graduates, 2006-07 . . . 729
Dropout rate . . . 0.3%
Pupil/teacher ratio . . . 21.5
Average class size . . . 25.5
Students per computer . . . 2.5
Classrooms with internet . . . 168
Avg. Daily Attendance (ADA) . . . 3,100
Cost per ADA . . . $10,706
Avg. Teacher Salary . . . $88,151

California Achievement Tests 6th ed., 2008
(Pct scoring at or above 50th National Percentile Rank)

	Math	Reading	Language
Grade 3	NA	NA	NA
Grade 7	NA	NA	NA

Academic Performance Index, 2008
Number of students tested . . . 2,298
Number of valid scores . . . 2,269
2007 API (base) . . . 872
2008 API (growth) . . . 879

SAT Testing, 2006-07
Enrollment, Grade 12 . . . 753
Number taking test . . . 578
percent taking test . . . 76.8%
percent with total score 1,500+ . . . 70.50%

Average Scores:

Math	Verbal	Writing	Total
641	607	614	1,862

Federal No Child Left Behind, 2008
(Adequate Yearly Progress standards met)

	Participation Rate	Pct Proficient
ELA	No	Yes
Math	Yes	Yes

API criteria . . . Yes
Graduation rate . . . Yes
\# criteria met/possible . . . 14/13

Other school districts for this city
(see Appendix E for information on these districts)
Los Gatos Union Elem

See Introduction for an explanation of all data sources.

Demographics & Socio-Economic Characteristics

(2000 Decennial Census, except as noted)

Population

1990* ... 59,564
2000 ... 62,150
Male ... 29,850
Female ... 32,300
Jan. 2008 (estimate)§ ... 65,668
Persons per sq. mi. of land ... 8,008.3

Race & Hispanic Origin, 2000

Race
White ... 29,098
Black/African American ... 559
North American Native ... 767
Asian ... 7,232
Pacific Islander ... 51
Other Race ... 21,040
Two or more races ... 3,403
Hispanic origin, total ... 46,347
Mexican ... 38,881
Puerto Rican ... 230
Cuban ... 136
Other Hispanic ... 7,100

Age & Nativity, 2000

Under 5 years ... 5,059
18 years and over ... 44,374
65 years and over ... 7,735
85 years and over ... 835
Median Age ... 31.4
Native-born ... 38,440
Foreign-born ... 23,520

Educational Attainment, 2000

Population 25 years and over ... 37,862
Less than 9th grade ... 19.1%
High school grad or higher ... 62.1%
Bachelor's degree or higher ... 14.3%
Graduate degree ... 4.2%

Income & Poverty, 1999

Per capita income ... $15,125
Median household income ... $38,805
Median family income ... $41,257
Persons in poverty ... 16.8%
H'holds receiving public assistance ... 1,479
H'holds receiving social security ... 5,293

Households, 2000

Total households ... 18,844
With persons under 18 ... 8,754
With persons over 65 ... 5,583
Family households ... 14,865
Single person households ... 3,216
Persons per household ... 3.28
Persons per family ... 3.67

Household Population, 2008§§

Persons living in households ... 65,359
Persons living in group quarters ... 309
Persons per household ... 3.4

Labor & Employment

Total civilian labor force, 2008§§ ... 29,200
Unemployment rate, 2008 ... 8.4%
Total civilian labor force, 2000 ... 25,042

Employed persons 16 years and over by occupation, 2000

Managers & professionals ... 5,897
Service occupations ... 3,304
Sales & office occupations ... 7,444
Farming, fishing & forestry ... 16
Construction & maintenance ... 1,728
Production & transportation ... 4,478
Self-employed persons ... 1,393

* US Census Bureau
** 2000 Decennial Census
§ California Department of Finance
§§ California Employment Development Dept

General Information

City of Montebello
1600 W Beverly Blvd
Montebello, CA 90640
323-887-1200

Website ... www.cityofmontebello.com
Elevation ... 260 ft.
Land Area (sq. miles) ... 8.2
Water Area (sq. miles) ... 0.1
Year of Incorporation ... 1920
Government type ... General law
Sales tax rate ... 9.25%

Voters & Officials

Registered Voters, October 2008

Total ... 26,419
Democrats ... 16,241
Republicans ... 4,736
Declined to state ... 4,470

Legislative Districts

US Congressional ... 38
State Senatorial ... 30
State Assembly ... 58

Local Officials, 2009

Mayor ... Rosemarie Vasquez
City Administrator ... Richard Torres
City Clerk ... Robert J. King
Attorney ... Arnold M. Alvarez-Glasman
Finance Dir ... Chickwan Tam
Public Works ... NA
Planning Dir ... Michael Huntley
Building ... Tom Castillo
Police Chief ... Daniel Weast (Int)
Fire Chief ... James Duncan (Int)

Public Safety

Number of officers, 2007 ... 78
Violent crimes, 2007 ... 242
Property crimes, 2007 ... 1,948
Arson, 2007 ... 43

Public Library

Montebello Library
Los Angeles County Public Library System
1550 W Beverly Blvd
Montebello, CA 90640
323-722-6551

Branch Librarian ... Lisa Castaneda

Library system statistics, FY 2007

Population served ... 3,673,313
Internet terminals ... 749
Annual users ... 3,748,771

Per capita:

Operating income ... $30.06
percent from local government ... 93.6%
Operating expenditure ... $28.36
Total materials ... 2.22
Print holdings ... 1.97
Visits per capita ... 3.25

Housing & Construction

Housing Units

Total, 2008§ ... 19,581
Single family units, attached ... 1,581
Single family units, detached ... 9,382
Multiple family units ... 8,385
Mobile home units ... 233
Occupied ... 19,004
Vacancy rate ... 3.0%
Median rent, 2000** ... $698
Median SF home value, 2000** ... $199,000

New Privately Owned Housing Units Authorized by Building Permit, 2007*

	Units	Construction Cost
Single	11	$2,520,987
Total	11	$2,520,987

Municipal Finance

(For local fiscal year ended in 2006)

Revenues

Total ... $83,398,370
Taxes ... 35,204,466
Special benefits assessment ... 0
Licenses & permits ... 1,351,225
Fines & forfeitures ... 866,109
Revenues from use of money & property ... 2,061,375
Intergovernmental ... 19,759,735
Service charges ... 23,146,453
Other revenues ... 1,009,007
Other financing sources ... 0

Expenditures

Total ... $91,268,608
General government ... 10,882,417
Public safety ... 28,144,052
Transportation ... 35,273,521
Community development ... 3,376,188
Health ... 2,761,752
Culture & leisure ... 9,605,530
Other ... 0

Local School District

(Data from School year 2007-08 except as noted)

Montebello Unified
123 South Montebello Blvd
Montebello, CA 90640
(323) 887-7900

Superintendent ... Edward Velasquez
Grade plan ... K-12
Number of schools ... 29
Enrollment ... 33,493
High school graduates, 2006-07 ... 1,721
Dropout rate ... 3.2%
Pupil/teacher ratio ... 23.7
Average class size ... 29.7
Students per computer ... 6.6
Classrooms with internet ... 2,124
Avg. Daily Attendance (ADA) ... 32,764
Cost per ADA ... $8,211
Avg. Teacher Salary ... $70,515

California Achievement Tests 6th ed., 2008

(Pct scoring at or above 50th National Percentile Rank)

	Math	Reading	Language
Grade 3	47%	24%	38%
Grade 7	39%	31%	32%

Academic Performance Index, 2008

Number of students tested ... 26,036
Number of valid scores ... 24,510
2007 API (base) ... 668
2008 API (growth) ... 679

SAT Testing, 2006-07

Enrollment, Grade 12 ... 2,168
Number taking test ... 580
percent taking test ... 26.8%
percent with total score 1,500+ ... 6.60%

Average Scores:

Math	Verbal	Writing	Total
461	443	440	1,344

Federal No Child Left Behind, 2008

(Adequate Yearly Progress standards met)

	Participation Rate	Pct Proficient
ELA	Yes	No
Math	Yes	No

API criteria ... Yes
Graduation rate ... Yes
\# criteria met/possible ... 30/25

Other school districts for this city

(see Appendix E for information on these districts)

None

See Introduction for an explanation of all data sources.

Demographics & Socio-Economic Characteristics

(2000 Decennial Census, except as noted)

Population

1990* ... 31,954
2000 ... 29,674
  Male ... 14,596
  Female ... 15,078
Jan. 2008 (estimate)§ ... 29,322
  Persons per sq. mi. of land ... 3,490.7

Race & Hispanic Origin, 2000

Race
  White ... 23,985
  Black/African American ... 749
  North American Native ... 170
  Asian ... 2,205
  Pacific Islander ... 86
  Other Race ... 1,159
  Two or more races ... 1,320
Hispanic origin, total ... 3,222
  Mexican ... 1,960
  Puerto Rican ... 163
  Cuban ... 43
  Other Hispanic ... 1,056

Age & Nativity, 2000

Under 5 years ... 1,477
18 years and over ... 24,747
65 years and over ... 4,410
85 years and over ... 737
  Median Age ... 36.1
Native-born ... 24,466
Foreign-born ... 5,307

Educational Attainment, 2000

Population 25 years and over ... 20,809
Less than 9th grade ... 2.9%
High school grad or higher ... 91.6%
Bachelor's degree or higher ... 46.2%
Graduate degree ... 18.7%

Income & Poverty, 1999

Per capita income ... $27,133
Median household income ... $49,109
Median family income ... $58,757
Persons in poverty ... 7.1%
H'holds receiving public assistance ... 134
H'holds receiving social security ... 3,174

Households, 2000

Total households ... 12,600
  With persons under 18 ... 2,959
  With persons over 65 ... 3,131
  Family households ... 6,478
  Single person households ... 4,668
Persons per household ... 2.13
Persons per family ... 2.82

Household Population, 2008§§

Persons living in households ... 26,839
Persons living in group quarters ... 2,483
Persons per household ... 2.1

Labor & Employment

Total civilian labor force, 2008§§ ... 17,600
  Unemployment rate, 2008 ... 3.8%
Total civilian labor force, 2000 ... 14,482

Employed persons 16 years and over by occupation, 2000

  Managers & professionals ... 6,451
  Service occupations ... 2,112
  Sales & office occupations ... 3,443
  Farming, fishing & forestry ... 185
  Construction & maintenance ... 1,000
  Production & transportation ... 742
  Self-employed persons ... 1,542

* US Census Bureau
** 2000 Decennial Census
§ California Department of Finance
§§ California Employment Development Dept

General Information

City of Monterey
City Hall
Monterey, CA 93940
831-646-3935

Website ... www.monterey.org
Elevation ... 40 ft.
Land Area (sq. miles) ... 8.4
Water Area (sq. miles) ... 3.3
Year of Incorporation ... 1890
Government type ... Chartered
Sales tax rate ... 8.25%

Voters & Officials

Registered Voters, October 2008

Total ... 14,079
  Democrats ... 6,904
  Republicans ... 3,595
  Declined to state ... 2,991

Legislative Districts

US Congressional ... 17
State Senatorial ... 15
State Assembly ... 27

Local Officials, 2009

Mayor ... Chuck DellaSala
Manager ... Fred Meurer
City Clerk ... Bonnie Gawf
Attorney ... Deborah Mall
Finance Dir ... Don Rhoads
Public Works ... Bill Reichmuth
Planning/Dev Dir ... Bill Reichmuth
Building ... John Kuehl
Police Chief ... Tim Shelby
Emergency/Fire Dir ... Sam Mazza

Public Safety

Number of officers, 2007 ... 51
Violent crimes, 2007 ... 166
Property crimes, 2007 ... 1,277
Arson, 2007 ... NA

Public Library

Monterey Public Library
625 Pacific St
Monterey, CA 93940
831-646-3932

Director ... Kim Bui-Burton

Library statistics, FY 2007

Population served ... 30,121
Internet terminals ... 12
  Annual users ... NA

Per capita:

Operating income ... $90.23
  percent from local government ... 93.1%
Operating expenditure ... $91.87
Total materials ... 4.06
Print holdings ... 3.64
Visits per capita ... 11.77

Housing & Construction

Housing Units

Total, 2008§ ... 13,549
  Single family units, attached ... 914
  Single family units, detached ... 5,934
  Multiple family units ... 6,680
  Mobile home units ... 21
  Occupied ... 12,783
  Vacancy rate ... 5.7%
Median rent, 2000** ... $888
Median SF home value, 2000** ... $399,800

New Privately Owned Housing Units Authorized by Building Permit, 2007*

	Units	Construction Cost
Single	7	$4,477,556
Total	7	$4,477,556

Municipal Finance

(For local fiscal year ended in 2006)

Revenues

Total ... $77,524,138
Taxes ... 35,576,180
Special benefits assessment ... 1,116,356
Licenses & permits ... 487,881
Fines & forfeitures ... 414,828
Revenues from use of
  money & property ... 6,698,345
Intergovernmental ... 2,730,061
Service charges ... 29,250,210
Other revenues ... 1,250,277
Other financing sources ... 0

Expenditures

Total ... $78,842,713
General government ... 7,498,380
Public safety ... 18,951,607
Transportation ... 18,715,754
Community development ... 2,914,391
Health ... 2,193,788
Culture & leisure ... 16,118,488
Other ... 12,450,305

Local School District

(Data from School year 2007-08 except as noted)

Monterey Peninsula Unified
PO Box 1031
Monterey, CA 93942
(831) 645-1200

Superintendent ... Marilyn Shepherd
Grade plan ... K-12
Number of schools ... 22
Enrollment ... 11,613
High school graduates, 2006-07 ... 590
Dropout rate ... 2.0%
Pupil/teacher ratio ... 20.5
Average class size ... 24.3
Students per computer ... 8.5
Classrooms with internet ... 518
Avg. Daily Attendance (ADA) ... 10,537
  Cost per ADA ... $8,271
Avg. Teacher Salary ... $57,857

California Achievement Tests 6th ed., 2008

(Pct scoring at or above 50th National Percentile Rank)

	Math	Reading	Language
Grade 3	56%	35%	43%
Grade 7	49%	44%	43%

Academic Performance Index, 2008

Number of students tested ... 8,210
Number of valid scores ... 7,687
2007 API (base) ... 716
2008 API (growth) ... 728

SAT Testing, 2006-07

Enrollment, Grade 12 ... 682
Number taking test ... 262
  percent taking test ... 38.4%
  percent with total score 1,500+ ... 15.10%

Average Scores:

Math	Verbal	Writing	Total
504	487	481	1,472

Federal No Child Left Behind, 2008

(Adequate Yearly Progress standards met)

	Participation Rate	Pct Proficient
ELA	Yes	No
Math	Yes	No

API criteria ... Yes
Graduation rate ... Yes
\# criteria met/possible ... 42/36

Other school districts for this city

(see Appendix E for information on these districts)

None

See Introduction for an explanation of all data sources.

Demographics & Socio-Economic Characteristics

(2000 Decennial Census, except as noted)

Population

1990* . . . 60,738
2000 . . . 60,051
Male . . . 28,845
Female . . . 31,206
Jan. 2008 (estimate)§ . . . 64,434
Persons per sq. mi. of land . . . 8,478.2

Race & Hispanic Origin, 2000

Race
White . . . 12,786
Black/African American . . . 226
North American Native . . . 391
Asian . . . 37,125
Pacific Islander . . . 37
Other Race . . . 7,474
Two or more races . . . 2,012
Hispanic origin, total . . . 17,359
Mexican . . . 14,123
Puerto Rican . . . 152
Cuban . . . 122
Other Hispanic . . . 2,962

Age & Nativity, 2000

Under 5 years . . . 3,343
18 years and over . . . 47,283
65 years and over . . . 10,747
85 years and over . . . 1,043
Median Age . . . 38.4
Native-born . . . 27,822
Foreign-born . . . 32,111

Educational Attainment, 2000

Population 25 years and over . . . 42,271
Less than 9th grade . . . 15.6%
High school grad or higher . . . 71.6%
Bachelor's degree or higher . . . 25.1%
Graduate degree . . . 7.4%

Income & Poverty, 1999

Per capita income . . . $17,661
Median household income . . . $40,724
Median family income . . . $43,507
Persons in poverty . . . 15.5%
H'holds receiving public assistance . . . 1,523
H'holds receiving social security . . . 5,489

Households, 2000

Total households . . . 19,564
With persons under 18 . . . 7,049
With persons over 65 . . . 7,623
Family households . . . 15,246
Single person households . . . 3,393
Persons per household . . . 3.06
Persons per family . . . 3.43

Household Population, 2008§§

Persons living in households . . . 64,157
Persons living in group quarters . . . 277
Persons per household . . . 3.2

Labor & Employment

Total civilian labor force, 2008§§ . . . 30,100
Unemployment rate, 2008 . . . 5.6%
Total civilian labor force, 2000 . . . 25,767

Employed persons 16 years and over by occupation, 2000

Managers & professionals . . . 8,332
Service occupations . . . 3,654
Sales & office occupations . . . 7,671
Farming, fishing & forestry . . . 12
Construction & maintenance . . . 1,199
Production & transportation . . . 3,402
Self-employed persons . . . 1,835

* US Census Bureau
** 2000 Decennial Census
§ California Department of Finance
§§ California Employment Development Dept

General Information

City of Monterey Park
320 W Newmark Ave
Monterey Park, CA 91754
626-307-1359

Website . . . www.ci.monterey-park.ca.us
Elevation . . . 381 ft.
Land Area (sq. miles) . . . 7.6
Water Area (sq. miles) . . . 0
Year of Incorporation . . . 1916
Government type . . . General law
Sales tax rate . . . 9.25%

Voters & Officials

Registered Voters, October 2008

Total . . . 26,456
Democrats . . . 12,085
Republicans . . . 5,536
Declined to state . . . 7,952

Legislative Districts

US Congressional . . . 29, 32
State Senatorial . . . 24
State Assembly . . . 49

Local Officials, 2009

Mayor . . . Benjamin "Frank" Venti
City Manager . . . June Yotsua (Int)
City Clerk . . . David Barron
Attorney . . . Anthony Canzoneri
Finance Dir . . . David Dong
Public Works . . . Elias Saykali
Development Svcs Dir . . . Adolfo Reta
Building . . . NA
Police Chief . . . Jones Moy
Emergency/Fire Dir . . . Cathy Orchard

Public Safety

Number of officers, 2007 . . . 76
Violent crimes, 2007 . . . 196
Property crimes, 2007 . . . 1,290
Arson, 2007 . . . 0

Public Library

Monterey Park Bruggemeyer Library
318 S Ramona Ave
Monterey Park, CA 91754
626-307-1418

City Librarian . . . Linda Wilson

Library statistics, FY 2007

Population served . . . 64,508
Internet terminals . . . 58
Annual users . . . 78,148

Per capita:

Operating income . . . $27.81
percent from local government . . . 93.1%
Operating expenditure . . . $26.52
Total materials . . . 2.73
Print holdings . . . 2.57
Visits per capita . . . 5.65

Housing & Construction

Housing Units

Total, 2008§ . . . 20,734
Single family units, attached . . . 2,204
Single family units, detached . . . 11,782
Multiple family units . . . 6,668
Mobile home units . . . 80
Occupied . . . 20,073
Vacancy rate . . . 3.2%
Median rent, 2000** . . . $722
Median SF home value, 2000** . . . $216,500

New Privately Owned Housing Units Authorized by Building Permit, 2007*

	Units	Construction Cost
Single	56	$15,066,726
Total	56	$15,066,726

Municipal Finance

(For local fiscal year ended in 2006)

Revenues

Total . . . $60,441,734
Taxes . . . 26,119,438
Special benefits assessment . . . 1,421,461
Licenses & permits . . . 1,271,467
Fines & forfeitures . . . 1,224,489
Revenues from use of money & property . . . 1,723,770
Intergovernmental . . . 7,652,598
Service charges . . . 20,513,435
Other revenues . . . 515,076
Other financing sources . . . 0

Expenditures

Total . . . $62,006,059
General government . . . 5,184,560
Public safety . . . 22,127,886
Transportation . . . 3,680,135
Community development . . . 11,779,353
Health . . . 5,311,983
Culture & leisure . . . 5,497,784
Other . . . 0

Local School District

(Data from School year 2007-08 except as noted)

Alhambra Unified
1515 West Mission Rd
Alhambra, CA 91803
(626) 943-3000

Superintendent . . . Donna Perez
Grade plan . . . K-12
Number of schools . . . 18
Enrollment . . . 18,976
High school graduates, 2006-07 . . . 1,869
Dropout rate . . . 1.6%
Pupil/teacher ratio . . . 23.7
Average class size . . . 29.2
Students per computer . . . 4.2
Classrooms with internet . . . 762
Avg. Daily Attendance (ADA) . . . 19,060
Cost per ADA . . . $8,203
Avg. Teacher Salary . . . $68,117

California Achievement Tests 6th ed., 2008

(Pct scoring at or above 50th National Percentile Rank)

	Math	Reading	Language
Grade 3	64%	41%	54%
Grade 7	66%	55%	55%

Academic Performance Index, 2008

Number of students tested . . . 14,756
Number of valid scores . . . 14,057
2007 API (base) . . . 768
2008 API (growth) . . . 782

SAT Testing, 2006-07

Enrollment, Grade 12 . . . 2,260
Number taking test . . . 1,020
percent taking test . . . 45.1%
percent with total score 1,500+ . . . 22.70%

Average Scores:

Math	Verbal	Writing	Total
548	478	478	1,504

Federal No Child Left Behind, 2008

(Adequate Yearly Progress standards met)

	Participation Rate	Pct Proficient
ELA	Yes	No
Math	Yes	No

API criteria . . . Yes
Graduation rate . . . Yes
\# criteria met/possible . . . 34/32

Other school districts for this city

(see Appendix E for information on these districts)

Garvey Elem, Los Angeles Unified, Montebello Unified

See Introduction for an explanation of all data sources.

Demographics & Socio-Economic Characteristics

(2000 Decennial Census, except as noted)

Population

1990*	25,494
2000	31,415
Male	15,678
Female	15,737
Jan. 2008 (estimate)§	36,814
Persons per sq. mi. of land	1,937.6

Race & Hispanic Origin, 2000

Race	
White	23,378
Black/African American	476
North American Native	149
Asian	1,770
Pacific Islander	46
Other Race	4,381
Two or more races	1,215
Hispanic origin, total	8,735
Mexican	7,255
Puerto Rican	107
Cuban	70
Other Hispanic	1,303

Age & Nativity, 2000

Under 5 years	2,546
18 years and over	20,674
65 years and over	1,429
85 years and over	119
Median Age	31.5
Native-born	25,281
Foreign-born	5,993

Educational Attainment, 2000

Population 25 years and over	17,947
Less than 9th grade	9.0%
High school grad or higher	84.7%
Bachelor's degree or higher	34.2%
Graduate degree	11.4%

Income & Poverty, 1999

Per capita income	$25,383
Median household income	$76,642
Median family income	$78,909
Persons in poverty	6.9%
H'holds receiving public assistance	178
H'holds receiving social security	1,240

Households, 2000

Total households	8,994
With persons under 18	5,212
With persons over 65	1,078
Family households	7,703
Single person households	888
Persons per household	3.49
Persons per family	3.71

Household Population, 2008§§

Persons living in households	36,802
Persons living in group quarters	12
Persons per household	3.5

Labor & Employment

Total civilian labor force, 2008§§	18,800
Unemployment rate, 2008	5.9%
Total civilian labor force, 2000	15,784

Employed persons 16 years and over by occupation, 2000

Managers & professionals	6,142
Service occupations	2,222
Sales & office occupations	4,183
Farming, fishing & forestry	165
Construction & maintenance	901
Production & transportation	1,478
Self-employed persons	1,236

* US Census Bureau
** 2000 Decennial Census
§ California Department of Finance
§§ California Employment Development Dept

General Information

City of Moorpark
799 Moorpark Ave
Moorpark, CA 93021
805-517-6200

Website	www.ci.moorpark.ca.us
Elevation	513 ft.
Land Area (sq. miles)	19.0
Water Area (sq. miles)	0.3
Year of Incorporation	1983
Government type	General law
Sales tax rate	8.25%

Voters & Officials

Registered Voters, October 2008

Total	19,405
Democrats	6,727
Republicans	8,235
Declined to state	3,597

Legislative Districts

US Congressional	24
State Senatorial	19
State Assembly	37

Local Officials, 2009

Mayor	Janice Parvin
Manager	Steven Kueny
City Clerk	Deborah Traffenstedt
Attorney	Joseph Montes
Finance Dir	Ronald Ahlers
Public Works	Yugal Lall
Planning/Dev Dir	Barry Hogan
Building	NA
Police Chief	Ronald Nelson
Emergency/Fire Dir.	Bob Roper

Public Safety

Number of officers, 2007	NA
Violent crimes, 2007	41
Property crimes, 2007	579
Arson, 2007	2

Public Library

Moorpark Public Library
(Previously a branch of County Library)
699 Moorpark Ave
Moorpark, CA 93021
805-517-6370

City Librarian: Barbara Wolfe

Library system statistics, FY 2007

Population served	36,150
Internet terminals	12
Annual users	14,893
Per capita:	
Operating income	$11.07
percent from local government	96.1%
Operating expenditure	$8.16
Total materials	1.11
Print holdings	1.00
Visits per capita	1.82

Housing & Construction

Housing Units

Total, 2008§	10,605
Single family units, attached	1,253
Single family units, detached	7,630
Multiple family units	1,424
Mobile home units	298
Occupied	10,488
Vacancy rate	1.1%
Median rent, 2000**	$1,172
Median SF home value, 2000**	$281,300

New Privately Owned Housing Units Authorized by Building Permit, 2007*

	Units	Construction Cost
Single	92	$17,799,111
Total	92	$17,799,111

Municipal Finance

(For local fiscal year ended in 2006)

Revenues

Total	$40,620,938
Taxes	18,031,545
Special benefits assessment	7,948,797
Licenses & permits	1,118,814
Fines & forfeitures	340,445
Revenues from use of money & property	2,258,905
Intergovernmental	3,310,480
Service charges	7,084,579
Other revenues	527,373
Other financing sources	0

Expenditures

Total	$27,156,955
General government	2,738,112
Public safety	6,380,602
Transportation	9,888,165
Community development	4,478,754
Health	335,194
Culture & leisure	3,336,128
Other	0

Local School District

(Data from School year 2007-08 except as noted)

Moorpark Unified
5297 Maureen Lane
Moorpark, CA 93021
(805) 378-6300

Superintendent	Ellen Smith
Grade plan	K-12
Number of schools	11
Enrollment	7,418
High school graduates, 2006-07	606
Dropout rate	2.7%
Pupil/teacher ratio	22.1
Average class size	25.9
Students per computer	0.0
Classrooms with internet	0
Avg. Daily Attendance (ADA)	7,360
Cost per ADA	$7,918
Avg. Teacher Salary	$62,414

California Achievement Tests 6th ed., 2008

(Pct scoring at or above 50th National Percentile Rank)

	Math	Reading	Language
Grade 3	70%	58%	64%
Grade 7	68%	70%	66%

Academic Performance Index, 2008

Number of students tested	5,711
Number of valid scores	5,517
2007 API (base)	819
2008 API (growth)	821

SAT Testing, 2006-07

Enrollment, Grade 12	711
Number taking test	281
percent taking test	39.5%
percent with total score 1,500+	24.60%

Average Scores:

Math	Verbal	Writing	Total
547	527	536	1,610

Federal No Child Left Behind, 2008

(Adequate Yearly Progress standards met)

	Participation Rate	Pct Proficient
ELA	Yes	No
Math	Yes	Yes

API criteria	Yes
Graduation rate	Yes
# criteria met/possible	30/28

Other school districts for this city

(see Appendix E for information on these districts)

None

See Introduction for an explanation of all data sources.

Demographics & Socio-Economic Characteristics

(2000 Decennial Census, except as noted)

Population

1990* . . . 15,852
2000 . . . 16,290
Male . . . 7,679
Female . . . 8,611
Jan. 2008 (estimate)§ . . . 16,138
Persons per sq. mi. of land . . . 1,735.3

Race & Hispanic Origin, 2000

Race
White . . . 13,212
Black/African American . . . 165
North American Native . . . 25
Asian . . . 2,026
Pacific Islander . . . 14
Other Race . . . 237
Two or more races . . . 611
Hispanic origin, total . . . 775
Mexican . . . 404
Puerto Rican . . . 27
Cuban . . . 13
Other Hispanic . . . 331

Age & Nativity, 2000

Under 5 years . . . 650
18 years and over . . . 12,595
65 years and over . . . 2,577
85 years and over . . . 213
Median Age . . . 42.0
Native-born . . . 14,079
Foreign-born . . . 2,563

Educational Attainment, 2000

Population 25 years and over . . . 10,601
Less than 9th grade . . . 0.5%
High school grad or higher . . . 97.1%
Bachelor's degree or higher . . . 67.5%
Graduate degree . . . 30.5%

Income & Poverty, 1999

Per capita income . . . $45,437
Median household income . . . $98,080
Median family income . . . $116,113
Persons in poverty . . . 2.7%
H'holds receiving public assistance . . . 46
H'holds receiving social security . . . 1,564

Households, 2000

Total households . . . 5,662
With persons under 18 . . . 2,033
With persons over 65 . . . 1,644
Family households . . . 4,325
Single person households . . . 1,089
Persons per household . . . 2.59
Persons per family . . . 2.99

Household Population, 2008§§

Persons living in households . . . 14,507
Persons living in group quarters . . . 1,631
Persons per household . . . 2.5

Labor & Employment

Total civilian labor force, 2008§§ . . . 9,200
Unemployment rate, 2008 . . . 9.5%
Total civilian labor force, 2000 . . . 8,153

Employed persons 16 years and over by occupation, 2000

Managers & professionals . . . 4,621
Service occupations . . . 588
Sales & office occupations . . . 1,867
Farming, fishing & forestry . . . 7
Construction & maintenance . . . 172
Production & transportation . . . 292
Self-employed persons . . . 892

* US Census Bureau
** 2000 Decennial Census
§ California Department of Finance
§§ California Employment Development Dept

General Information

Town of Moraga
2100 Donald Dr
PO Box 188
Moraga, CA 94556
925-376-2590

Website . . . www.moraga.ca.us
Elevation . . . NA
Land Area (sq. miles) . . . 9.3
Water Area (sq. miles) . . . 0
Year of Incorporation . . . 1974
Government type . . . General law
Sales tax rate . . . 9.25%

Voters & Officials

Registered Voters, October 2008

Total . . . 10,616
Democrats . . . 4,230
Republicans . . . 3,887
Declined to state . . . 2,154

Legislative Districts

US Congressional . . . 10
State Senatorial . . . 7
State Assembly . . . 14

Local Officials, 2009

Mayor . . . Lynda Deschambault
Manager . . . Philip Vince
City Clerk . . . Darlene Colaso
Attorney . . . Michelle Kenyon
Finance Dir . . . Emily Boyd
Public Works . . . Jill Mercurio
Planning/Dev Dir . . . Lori Salamack
Building . . . NA
Police Chief . . . Mark Ruppenthal
Emergency/Fire Dir . . . Pete Nowicki

Public Safety

Number of officers, 2007 . . . 13
Violent crimes, 2007 . . . 15
Property crimes, 2007 . . . 255
Arson, 2007 . . . 3

Public Library

Moraga Library
Contra Costa County Library System
1500 St Mary's Rd
Moraga, CA 94556
925-376-6852

Branch Librarian . . . Linda Waldroup

Library system statistics, FY 2007

Population served . . . 938,513
Internet terminals . . . 324
Annual users . . . 670,618

Per capita:

Operating income . . . $27.05
percent from local government . . . 82.0%
Operating expenditure . . . $27.82
Total materials . . . 1.57
Print holdings . . . 1.41
Visits per capita . . . 3.65

Housing & Construction

Housing Units

Total, 2008§ . . . 5,791
Single family units, attached . . . 968
Single family units, detached . . . 4,028
Multiple family units . . . 788
Mobile home units . . . 7
Occupied . . . 5,693
Vacancy rate . . . 1.7%
Median rent, 2000** . . . $1,112
Median SF home value, 2000** . . . $538,500

New Privately Owned Housing Units Authorized by Building Permit, 2007*

	Units	Construction Cost
Single	NA	NA
Total	NA	NA

Municipal Finance

(For local fiscal year ended in 2006)

Revenues

Total . . . $6,666,135
Taxes . . . 4,416,539
Special benefits assessment . . . 245,382
Licenses & permits . . . 60
Fines & forfeitures . . . 57,776
Revenues from use of money & property . . . 264,063
Intergovernmental . . . 706,474
Service charges . . . 588,080
Other revenues . . . 64,461
Other financing sources . . . 323,300

Expenditures

Total . . . $8,390,792
General government . . . 844,502
Public safety . . . 2,384,164
Transportation . . . 1,619,160
Community development . . . 2,181,757
Health . . . 0
Culture & leisure . . . 1,361,209
Other . . . 0

Local School District

(Data from School year 2007-08 except as noted)

Acalanes Union High
1212 Pleasant Hill Rd
Lafayette, CA 94549
(925) 280-3900

Superintendent . . . Jim Negri
Grade plan . . . 9-12
Number of schools . . . 6
Enrollment . . . 5,905
High school graduates, 2006-07 . . . 1,343
Dropout rate . . . 0.5%
Pupil/teacher ratio . . . 19.8
Average class size . . . 22.7
Students per computer . . . 3.6
Classrooms with internet . . . 267
Avg. Daily Attendance (ADA) . . . 5,781
Cost per ADA . . . $9,251
Avg. Teacher Salary . . . $73,421

California Achievement Tests 6th ed., 2008

(Pct scoring at or above 50th National Percentile Rank)

	Math	Reading	Language
Grade 3	NA	NA	NA
Grade 7	NA	NA	NA

Academic Performance Index, 2008

Number of students tested . . . 4,273
Number of valid scores . . . 4,195
2007 API (base) . . . 882
2008 API (growth) . . . 886

SAT Testing, 2006-07

Enrollment, Grade 12 . . . 1,385
Number taking test . . . 1,148
percent taking test . . . 82.9%
percent with total score 1,500+ . . . 69.30%

Average Scores:

Math	Verbal	Writing	Total
596	580	585	1,761

Federal No Child Left Behind, 2008

(Adequate Yearly Progress standards met)

	Participation Rate	Pct Proficient
ELA	Yes	Yes
Math	Yes	Yes

API criteria . . . Yes
Graduation rate . . . Yes
\# criteria met/possible . . . 14/14

Other school districts for this city

(see Appendix E for information on these districts)

Moraga Elem

See Introduction for an explanation of all data sources.

Demographics & Socio-Economic Characteristics†

(2007 American Community Survey, except as noted)

Population

1990* . . . 118,779
2007 . . . 190,990
Male . . . 94,005
Female . . . 96,985
Jan. 2008 (estimate)§ . . . 183,860
Persons per sq. mi. of land . . . 3,591.0

Race & Hispanic Origin, 2007

Race
White . . . 66,923
Black/African American . . . 32,522
North American Native . . . 522
Asian . . . 7,388
Pacific Islander . . . 1,324
Other Race . . . 77,256
Two or more races . . . 5,055
Hispanic origin, total . . . 105,719
Mexican . . . 93,621
Puerto Rican . . . 1,338
Cuban . . . 451
Other Hispanic . . . 10,309

Age & Nativity, 2007

Under 5 years . . . 16,562
18 years and over . . . 129,519
65 years and over . . . 10,228
85 years and over . . . 1,412
Median Age . . . 26.7
Native-born . . . 143,394
Foreign-born . . . 47,596

Educational Attainment, 2007

Population 25 years and over . . . 103,903
Less than 9th grade . . . 13.5%
High school grad or higher . . . 69.9%
Bachelor's degree or higher . . . 14.7%
Graduate degree . . . 4.4%

Income & Poverty, 2007

Per capita income . . . $17,540
Median household income . . . $55,613
Median family income . . . $56,701
Persons in poverty . . . 15.0%
H'holds receiving public assistance . . . 1,193
H'holds receiving social security . . . 7,849

Households, 2007

Total households . . . 49,016
With persons under 18 . . . 28,254
With persons over 65 . . . 7,078
Family households . . . 41,606
Single person households . . . 5,746
Persons per household . . . 3.89
Persons per family . . . 4.18

Household Population, 2008§§

Persons living in households . . . 183,163
Persons living in group quarters . . . 697
Persons per household . . . 3.7

Labor & Employment

Total civilian labor force, 2008§§ . . . 87,600
Unemployment rate, 2008 . . . 10.0%
Total civilian labor force, 2000* . . . 61,663

Employed persons 16 years and over by occupation, 2007

Managers & professionals . . . 18,975
Service occupations . . . 14,046
Sales & office occupations . . . 20,710
Farming, fishing & forestry . . . 114
Construction & maintenance . . . 12,367
Production & transportation . . . 14,901
Self-employed persons . . . 6,413

† see Appendix D for 2000 Decennial Census Data
* US Census Bureau
** 2007 American Community Survey
§ California Department of Finance
§§ California Employment Development Dept

General Information

City of Moreno Valley
PO Box 88005
Moreno Valley, CA 92552
951-413-3000

Website . . . www.moreno-valley.ca.us
Elevation . . . 1,597 ft.
Land Area (sq. miles) . . . 51.2
Water Area (sq. miles) . . . 0.4
Year of Incorporation . . . 1984
Government type . . . General law
Sales tax rate . . . 8.75%

Voters & Officials

Registered Voters, October 2008

Total . . . 65,997
Democrats . . . 32,264
Republicans . . . 19,274
Declined to state . . . 11,726

Legislative Districts

US Congressional . . . 45
State Senatorial . . . 37
State Assembly . . . 63, 64, 65

Local Officials, 2009

Mayor . . . Richard A. Stewart
Manager . . . Robert Gutierrez
City Clerk . . . Jane Halstead
Attorney . . . Robert Herrick
Finance Dir . . . Steve Elam
Public Works . . . Chris Vogt
Planning/Dev Dir . . . Kyle Kollar
Building . . . Gary Kyle
Police Chief . . . John Anderson
Emergency/Fire Dir . . . John Clark

Public Safety

Number of officers, 2007 . . . NA
Violent crimes, 2007 . . . 1,024
Property crimes, 2007 . . . 6,371
Arson, 2007 . . . 16

Public Library

Moreno Valley Public Library
25480 Alessandro Blvd
Moreno Valley, CA 92553
951-413-3880

Director . . . Cynthia Pirtle

Library statistics, FY 2007

Population served . . . 180,466
Internet terminals . . . 12
Annual users . . . 37,978

Per capita:

Operating income . . . $15.02
percent from local government . . . 93.9%
Operating expenditure . . . $15.74
Total materials . . . 0.74
Print holdings . . . 0.69
Visits per capita . . . 0.93

Housing & Construction

Housing Units

Total, 2008§ . . . 53,127
Single family units, attached . . . 1,031
Single family units, detached . . . 42,595
Multiple family units . . . 8,458
Mobile home units . . . 1,043
Occupied . . . 49,927
Vacancy rate . . . 6.0%
Median rent, 2007** . . . $1,216
Median SF home value, 2007** . . . $379,300

New Privately Owned Housing Units Authorized by Building Permit, 2007*

	Units	Construction Cost
Single	392	$92,532,683
Total	824	$123,742,278

Municipal Finance

(For local fiscal year ended in 2006)

Revenues

Total . . . $113,446,132
Taxes . . . 50,483,482
Special benefits assessment . . . 8,746,806
Licenses & permits . . . 4,427,603
Fines & forfeitures . . . 1,618,996
Revenues from use of money & property . . . 3,724,939
Intergovernmental . . . 13,630,804
Service charges . . . 26,043,883
Other revenues . . . 4,769,619
Other financing sources . . . 0

Expenditures

Total . . . $89,723,369
General government . . . 8,096,906
Public safety . . . 38,705,924
Transportation . . . 14,008,295
Community development . . . 18,706,467
Health . . . 211,532
Culture & leisure . . . 9,326,584
Other . . . 0

Local School District

(Data from School year 2007-08 except as noted)

Moreno Valley Unified
25634 Alessandro Blvd
Moreno Valley, CA 92553
(951) 571-7500

Superintendent . . . Rowena Lagrosa
Grade plan . . . K-12
Number of schools . . . 39
Enrollment . . . 37,126
High school graduates, 2006-07 . . . 1,833
Dropout rate . . . 7.7%
Pupil/teacher ratio . . . 22.3
Average class size . . . 27.9
Students per computer . . . 4.4
Classrooms with internet . . . 1,542
Avg. Daily Attendance (ADA) . . . 35,485
Cost per ADA . . . $7,946
Avg. Teacher Salary . . . $68,655

California Achievement Tests 6th ed., 2008

(Pct scoring at or above 50th National Percentile Rank)

	Math	Reading	Language
Grade 3	47%	28%	38%
Grade 7	40%	37%	35%

Academic Performance Index, 2008

Number of students tested . . . 28,285
Number of valid scores . . . 26,065
2007 API (base) . . . 669
2008 API (growth) . . . 686

SAT Testing, 2006-07

Enrollment, Grade 12 . . . 2,739
Number taking test . . . 627
percent taking test . . . 22.9%
percent with total score 1,500+ . . . 6.10%

Average Scores:

Math	Verbal	Writing	Total
455	444	444	1,343

Federal No Child Left Behind, 2008

(Adequate Yearly Progress standards met)

	Participation Rate	Pct Proficient
ELA	Yes	No
Math	Yes	No

API criteria . . . Yes
Graduation rate . . . No
\# criteria met/possible . . . 44/35

Other school districts for this city

(see Appendix E for information on these districts)

Val Verde Unified

See Introduction for an explanation of all data sources.

Demographics & Socio-Economic Characteristics

(2000 Decennial Census, except as noted)

Population

1990* 23,928
2000 33,556
Male 16,655
Female 16,901
Jan. 2008 (estimate)§ 39,218
Persons per sq. mi. of land 3,352.0

Race & Hispanic Origin, 2000

Race
White 24,296
Black/African American 573
North American Native 362
Asian 2,020
Pacific Islander 77
Other Race 4,505
Two or more races 1,723
Hispanic origin, total 9,229
Mexican 7,501
Puerto Rican 108
Cuban 36
Other Hispanic 1,584

Age & Nativity, 2000

Under 5 years 2,729
18 years and over 23,310
65 years and over 2,508
85 years and over 279
Median Age 34.0
Native-born 28,531
Foreign-born 5,104

Educational Attainment, 2000

Population 25 years and over 20,658
Less than 9th grade 6.1%
High school grad or higher 86.8%
Bachelor's degree or higher 33.5%
Graduate degree 11.1%

Income & Poverty, 1999

Per capita income $33,047
Median household income $81,958
Median family income $90,134
Persons in poverty 4.6%
H'holds receiving public assistance 252
H'holds receiving social security 1,736

Households, 2000

Total households 10,846
With persons under 18 5,152
With persons over 65 1,779
Family households 8,628
Single person households 1,643
Persons per household 3.05
Persons per family 3.38

Household Population, 2008§§

Persons living in households 38,705
Persons living in group quarters 513
Persons per household 3.1

Labor & Employment

Total civilian labor force, 2008§§ 17,500
Unemployment rate, 2008 . . . . . 7.8%
Total civilian labor force, 2000 17,192

Employed persons 16 years and over by occupation, 2000

Managers & professionals 7,245
Service occupations 1,799
Sales & office occupations 4,129
Farming, fishing & forestry 231
Construction & maintenance 1,601
Production & transportation 1,290
Self-employed persons 1,236

* US Census Bureau
** 2000 Decennial Census
§ California Department of Finance
§§ California Employment Development Dept

General Information

City of Morgan Hill
17555 Peak Ave
Morgan Hill, CA 95037
408-779-7271

Website . . . . . www.morganhill.ca.gov
Elevation . . . . . 345 ft.
Land Area (sq. miles) 11.7
Water Area (sq. miles) 0
Year of Incorporation 1906
Government type . . . . . General law
Sales tax rate 9.25%

Voters & Officials

Registered Voters, October 2008

Total 18,415
Democrats 7,676
Republicans 6,235
Declined to state 3,845

Legislative Districts

US Congressional 11
State Senatorial 15
State Assembly 27

Local Officials, 2009

Mayor . . . . . Steve Tate
Manager . . . . . J. Edward Tewes
City Clerk . . . . . Irma Torrez
Attorney . . . . . Tawny Wan
Finance Dir . . . . . M. Roorda
Public Works . . . . . Jim Ashcraft
Planning/Dev Dir . . . . . Kathy M. Previsich
Building . . . . . Jim Fruit
Police Chief . . . . . Bruce Cumming
Fire/Emergency Mgmt . . . . . NA

Public Safety

Number of officers, 2007 35
Violent crimes, 2007 84
Property crimes, 2007 887
Arson, 2007 . . . . . NA

Public Library

Morgan Hill Library
Santa Clara County Library System
660 W Main Ave
Morgan Hill, CA 95037
408-779-3196

Branch Librarian . . . . . Roseann Macek

Library system statistics, FY 2007

Population served 419,141
Internet terminals 133
Annual users 650,000

Per capita:

Operating income $77.89
percent from local government 85.7%
Operating expenditure $66.37
Total materials 4.01
Print holdings 3.27
Visits per capita 6.16

Housing & Construction

Housing Units

Total, 2008§ 12,821
Single family units, attached 1,892
Single family units, detached 7,967
Multiple family units 2,050
Mobile home units 912
Occupied 12,537
Vacancy rate 2.2%
Median rent, 2000** $1,112
Median SF home value, 2000** $435,200

New Privately Owned Housing Units Authorized by Building Permit, 2007*

	Units	Construction Cost
Single	147	$41,792,080
Total	147	$41,792,080

Municipal Finance

(For local fiscal year ended in 2006)

Revenues

Total $50,729,862
Taxes 18,790,231
Special benefits assessment 150,161
Licenses & permits 1,009,115
Fines & forfeitures 144,125
Revenues from use of money & property 1,960,708
Intergovernmental 2,184,701
Service charges 24,367,859
Other revenues 2,097,205
Other financing sources 25,757

Expenditures

Total $51,981,167
General government 3,336,813
Public safety 13,856,155
Transportation 5,108,909
Community development 3,748,693
Health 10,375,496
Culture & leisure 3,898,242
Other 0

Local School District

(Data from School year 2007-08 except as noted)

Morgan Hill Unified
15600 Concord Cir
Morgan Hill, CA 95037
(408) 201-6023

Superintendent . . . . . Alan Nishino
Grade plan K-12
Number of schools 15
Enrollment 9,521
High school graduates, 2006-07 529
Dropout rate 3.2%
Pupil/teacher ratio 22.5
Average class size 28.0
Students per computer 5.9
Classrooms with internet 558
Avg. Daily Attendance (ADA) 8,716
Cost per ADA $7,587
Avg. Teacher Salary $64,577

California Achievement Tests 6th ed., 2008

(Pct scoring at or above 50th National Percentile Rank)

	Math	Reading	Language
Grade 3	58%	39%	48%
Grade 7	52%	57%	54%

Academic Performance Index, 2008

Number of students tested 6,985
Number of valid scores 6,607
2007 API (base) 756
2008 API (growth) 768

SAT Testing, 2006-07

Enrollment, Grade 12 615
Number taking test 281
percent taking test 45.7%
percent with total score 1,500+ 24.10%

Average Scores:

Math	Verbal	Writing	Total
532	506	498	1,536

Federal No Child Left Behind, 2008

(Adequate Yearly Progress standards met)

	Participation Rate	Pct Proficient
ELA	Yes	No
Math	Yes	No

API criteria . . . . . Yes
Graduation rate . . . . . Yes
\# criteria met/possible 38/32

Other school districts for this city

(see Appendix E for information on these districts)

None

Demographics & Socio-Economic Characteristics

(2000 Decennial Census, except as noted)

Population

1990* 9,664
2000 10,350
Male 4,941
Female 5,409
Jan. 2008 (estimate)§ 10,548
Persons per sq. mi. of land 2,028.5

Race & Hispanic Origin, 2000

Race
White 9,257
Black/African American 70
North American Native 98
Asian 187
Pacific Islander 9
Other Race 424
Two or more races 305
Hispanic origin, total 1,183
Mexican 949
Puerto Rican 18
Cuban 2
Other Hispanic 214

Age & Nativity, 2000

Under 5 years 378
18 years and over 8,784
65 years and over 2,506
85 years and over 353
Median Age 45.7
Native-born 9,568
Foreign-born 740

Educational Attainment, 2000

Population 25 years and over 7,911
Less than 9th grade 2.6%
High school grad or higher 90.5%
Bachelor's degree or higher 27.8%
Graduate degree 10.6%

Income & Poverty, 1999

Per capita income $21,687
Median household income $34,379
Median family income $43,508
Persons in poverty 12.7%
H'holds receiving public assistance 133
H'holds receiving social security 1,847

Households, 2000

Total households 4,986
With persons under 18 915
With persons over 65 1,742
Family households 2,611
Single person households 1,893
Persons per household 2.04
Persons per family 2.65

Household Population, 2008§§

Persons living in households 10,350
Persons living in group quarters 198
Persons per household 2.0

Labor & Employment

Total civilian labor force, 2008§§ 5,500
Unemployment rate, 2008 .... 3.7%
Total civilian labor force, 2000 4,664

Employed persons 16 years and over by occupation, 2000

Managers & professionals 1,501
Service occupations 982
Sales & office occupations 1,086
Farming, fishing & forestry 113
Construction & maintenance 426
Production & transportation 377
Self-employed persons 670

* US Census Bureau
** 2000 Decennial Census
§ California Department of Finance
§§ California Employment Development Dept

General Information

City of Morro Bay
595 Harbor
Morro Bay, CA 93442
805-772-6200

Website .... www.morro-bay.ca.us
Elevation .... 200 ft.
Land Area (sq. miles) 5.2
Water Area (sq. miles) 5.0
Year of Incorporation 1964
Government type .... General law
Sales tax rate 8.75%

Voters & Officials

Registered Voters, October 2008

Total 2,196
Democrats 1,029
Republicans 552
Declined to state 488

Legislative Districts

US Congressional 23
State Senatorial 15
State Assembly 33

Local Officials, 2009

Mayor .... Janice Peters
Manager .... Andrea Lucker (Int)
City Clerk .... Bridgett Bauer
Attorney .... Robert Schultz
Finance Dir .... Susan Slayton
Public Works .... Bruce Ambo
Planning/Dev Dir .... Bruce Ambo
Building .... Dan Doris
Police Chief .... John DeRohan
Fire Chief .... Mike Pond

Public Safety

Number of officers, 2007 16
Violent crimes, 2007 21
Property crimes, 2007 153
Arson, 2007 9

Public Library

Morro Bay Library
San Luis Obispo City-County Library System
625 Harbor St
Morro Bay, CA 93442
805-772-6394

Branch Librarian .... Jude Long

Library system statistics, FY 2007

Population served 235,386
Internet terminals 3
Annual users 10,554

Per capita:

Operating income $33.17
percent from local government 90.2%
Operating expenditure $30.54
Total materials 1.72
Print holdings 1.46
Visits per capita 5.51

Housing & Construction

Housing Units

Total, 2008§ 6,640
Single family units, attached 405
Single family units, detached 4,345
Multiple family units 1,131
Mobile home units 759
Occupied 5,297
Vacancy rate 20.2%
Median rent, 2000** $697
Median SF home value, 2000** $245,500

New Privately Owned Housing Units Authorized by Building Permit, 2007*

	Units	Construction Cost
Single	46	$8,910,801
Total	46	$8,910,801

Municipal Finance

(For local fiscal year ended in 2006)

Revenues

Total $19,250,745
Taxes 7,411,495
Special benefits assessment 15,020
Licenses & permits 118,539
Fines & forfeitures 80,600
Revenues from use of money & property 343,039
Intergovernmental 1,621,787
Service charges 8,563,800
Other revenues 1,096,465
Other financing sources 0

Expenditures

Total $16,513,235
General government 1,974,500
Public safety 4,653,297
Transportation 2,575,548
Community development 1,725,706
Health 1,034,201
Culture & leisure 1,711,692
Other 0

Local School District

(Data from School year 2007-08 except as noted)

San Luis Coastal Unified
1500 Lizzie St
San Luis Obispo, CA 93401
(805) 549-1200

Superintendent .... Edward Valentine
Grade plan K-12
Number of schools 16
Enrollment 7,145
High school graduates, 2006-07 570
Dropout rate 1.1%
Pupil/teacher ratio 23.8
Average class size 23.6
Students per computer 3.2
Classrooms with internet 452
Avg. Daily Attendance (ADA) 6,805
Cost per ADA $9,535
Avg. Teacher Salary $69,299

California Achievement Tests 6th ed., 2008

(Pct scoring at or above 50th National Percentile Rank)

	Math	Reading	Language
Grade 3	70%	64%	66%
Grade 7	71%	64%	64%

Academic Performance Index, 2008

Number of students tested 5,349
Number of valid scores 5,111
2007 API (base) 820
2008 API (growth) 824

SAT Testing, 2006-07

Enrollment, Grade 12 593
Number taking test 253
percent taking test 42.7%
percent with total score 1,500+ 30.70%

Average Scores:

Math	Verbal	Writing	Total
556	554	542	1,652

Federal No Child Left Behind, 2008

(Adequate Yearly Progress standards met)

	Participation Rate	Pct Proficient
ELA	Yes	No
Math	Yes	No

API criteria .... Yes
Graduation rate .... Yes
criteria met/possible 30/27

Other school districts for this city

(see Appendix E for information on these districts)

None

See Introduction for an explanation of all data sources.

Demographics & Socio-Economic Characteristics

(2000 Decennial Census, except as noted)

Population

1990* 3,460
2000 3,621
Male 1,694
Female 1,927
Jan. 2008 (estimate)§ 3,602
Persons per sq. mi. of land 973.5

Race & Hispanic Origin, 2000

Race
White 3,323
Black/African American 55
North American Native 16
Asian 59
Pacific Islander 5
Other Race 77
Two or more races 86
Hispanic origin, total 211
Mexican 138
Puerto Rican 16
Cuban 1
Other Hispanic 56

Age & Nativity, 2000

Under 5 years 187
18 years and over 2,753
65 years and over 632
85 years and over 103
Median Age 41.9
Native-born 3,289
Foreign-born 277

Educational Attainment, 2000

Population 25 years and over 2,431
Less than 9th grade 2.3%
High school grad or higher 89.2%
Bachelor's degree or higher 25.8%
Graduate degree 10.1%

Income & Poverty, 1999

Per capita income $20,629
Median household income $26,500
Median family income $37,313
Persons in poverty 18.8%
H'holds receiving public assistance 68
H'holds receiving social security 521

Households, 2000

Total households 1,669
With persons under 18 500
With persons over 65 462
Family households 926
Single person households 634
Persons per household 2.14
Persons per family 2.83

Household Population, 2008§§

Persons living in households 3,554
Persons living in group quarters 48
Persons per household 2.0

Labor & Employment

Total civilian labor force, 2008§§ 1,900
Unemployment rate, 2008 . . . . 5.9%
Total civilian labor force, 2000 1,865

Employed persons 16 years and over by occupation, 2000

Managers & professionals 580
Service occupations 357
Sales & office occupations 527
Farming, fishing & forestry 35
Construction & maintenance 99
Production & transportation 165
Self-employed persons 342

* US Census Bureau
** 2000 Decennial Census
§ California Department of Finance
§§ California Employment Development Dept

General Information

City of Mount Shasta
305 N Mt Shasta Blvd
Mount Shasta, CA 96067
530-926-7510

Website . . . . www.ci.mt-shasta.ca.us
Elevation . . . . 3,554 ft.
Land Area (sq. miles) 3.7
Water Area (sq. miles) 0
Year of Incorporation 1905
Government type . . . . General law
Sales tax rate 8.25%

Voters & Officials

Registered Voters, October 2008

Total 7,290
Democrats 2,999
Republicans 2,418
Declined to state 1,414

Legislative Districts

US Congressional 2
State Senatorial 4
State Assembly 2

Local Officials, 2009

Mayor . . . . Tim Stearns
Manager/Admin . . . . Kevin R. Plett
City Clerk . . . . Prudence Kennedy
Attorney . . . . John Kenny
Finance Dir . . . . Ted Marcon
Public Works . . . . Rod Bryan
City Planner . . . . Keith McKinley
Building . . . . Dave Smith
Police Chief . . . . Parish Cross
Emergency/Fire Dir . . . . Matt Melo

Public Safety

Number of officers, 2007 9
Violent crimes, 2007 8
Property crimes, 2007 103
Arson, 2007 0

Public Library

Mt. Shasta Branch Library
Siskiyou County Free Library System
515 Alma St
Mount Shasta, CA 96067
530-926-2031

Branch Librarian . . . . Terry Thompson

Library system statistics, FY 2007

Population served 45,953
Internet terminals 31
Annual users 48,766

Per capita:

Operating income $20.36
percent from local government 90.2%
Operating expenditure $20.12
Total materials 4.06
Print holdings 3.88
Visits per capita . . . . NA

Housing & Construction

Housing Units

Total, 2008§ 1,888
Single family units, attached 89
Single family units, detached 1,203
Multiple family units 522
Mobile home units 74
Occupied 1,752
Vacancy rate 7.2%
Median rent, 2000** $537
Median SF home value, 2000** $124,800

New Privately Owned Housing Units Authorized by Building Permit, 2007*

	Units	Construction Cost
Single	6	$1,219,514
Total	10	$1,656,014

Municipal Finance

(For local fiscal year ended in 2006)

Revenues

Total $5,203,310
Taxes 2,296,312
Special benefits assessment 47,727
Licenses & permits 34,050
Fines & forfeitures 61,394
Revenues from use of money & property 123,386
Intergovernmental 945,637
Service charges 1,582,472
Other revenues 112,332
Other financing sources 0

Expenditures

Total $5,393,970
General government 436,720
Public safety 1,479,294
Transportation 500,223
Community development 911,800
Health 1,234,320
Culture & leisure 7,695
Other 0

Local School District

(Data from School year 2007-08 except as noted)

Siskiyou Union High
624 Everitt Memorial Hwy
Mt. Shasta, CA 96067
(530) 926-3006

Superintendent . . . . Michael Matheson
Grade plan 7-12
Number of schools 8
Enrollment 1,029
High school graduates, 2006-07 170
Dropout rate 5.8%
Pupil/teacher ratio 17.1
Average class size 17.7
Students per computer 2.4
Classrooms with internet 72
Avg. Daily Attendance (ADA) 679
Cost per ADA $11,519
Avg. Teacher Salary $52,824

California Achievement Tests 6th ed., 2008

(Pct scoring at or above 50th National Percentile Rank)

	Math	Reading	Language
Grade 3	NA	NA	NA
Grade 7	NA	NA	NA

Academic Performance Index, 2008

Number of students tested 564
Number of valid scores 542
2007 API (base) 758
2008 API (growth) 753

SAT Testing, 2006-07

Enrollment, Grade 12 203
Number taking test 69
percent taking test 34.0%
percent with total score 1,500+ 15.80%

Average Scores:

Math	Verbal	Writing	Total
496	486	497	1,479

Federal No Child Left Behind, 2008

(Adequate Yearly Progress standards met)

	Participation Rate	Pct Proficient
ELA	Yes	Yes
Math	Yes	Yes

API criteria . . . . Yes
Graduation rate . . . . Yes
\# criteria met/possible 14/14

Other school districts for this city

(see Appendix E for information on these districts)

Mt. Shasta Union Elem

See Introduction for an explanation of all data sources.

Demographics & Socio-Economic Characteristics†

(2007 American Community Survey, except as noted)

Population

1990* 67,460
2007 70,000
Male 36,573
Female 33,427
Jan. 2008 (estimate)§ 73,932
Persons per sq. mi. of land 6,110.1

Race & Hispanic Origin, 2007

Race
White 43,317
Black/African American 825
North American Native 47
Asian 17,416
Pacific Islander 86
Other Race 6,236
Two or more races 2,073
Hispanic origin, total 14,840
Mexican 12,099
Puerto Rican 0
Cuban 139
Other Hispanic 2,602

Age & Nativity, 2007

Under 5 years 4,839
18 years and over 57,499
65 years and over 9,600
85 years and over 1,278
Median Age 38.5
Native-born 43,217
Foreign-born 26,783

Educational Attainment, 2007

Population 25 years and over 52,151
Less than 9th grade 6.5%
High school grad or higher 91.1%
Bachelor's degree or higher 57.6%
Graduate degree 30.3%

Income & Poverty, 2007

Per capita income $49,527
Median household income $82,648
Median family income $105,079
Persons in poverty 6.0%
H'holds receiving public assistance 711
H'holds receiving social security 5,408

Households, 2007

Total households 30,225
With persons under 18 7,022
With persons over 65 6,762
Family households 15,954
Single person households 11,648
Persons per household 2.30
Persons per family 3.12

Household Population, 2008§§

Persons living in households 73,416
Persons living in group quarters 516
Persons per household 2.3

Labor & Employment

Total civilian labor force, 2008§§ 42,100
Unemployment rate, 2008 .... 4.3%
Total civilian labor force, 2000* 42,310

Employed persons 16 years and over by occupation, 2007

Managers & professionals 24,730
Service occupations 4,161
Sales & office occupations 6,394
Farming, fishing & forestry 0
Construction & maintenance 1,647
Production & transportation 1,491
Self-employed persons 2,389

† see Appendix D for 2000 Decennial Census Data
* US Census Bureau
** 2007 American Community Survey
§ California Department of Finance
§§ California Employment Development Dept

General Information

City of Mountain View
500 Castro St
Mountain View, CA 94041
650-903-6300

Website .... www.mountainview.gov
Elevation .... 97 ft.
Land Area (sq. miles) 12.1
Water Area (sq. miles) 0.2
Year of Incorporation 1902
Government type .... Chartered
Sales tax rate 9.25%

Voters & Officials

Registered Voters, October 2008

Total 33,935
Democrats 16,963
Republicans 6,292
Declined to state 9,467

Legislative Districts

US Congressional 14
State Senatorial 13
State Assembly 22

Local Officials, 2009

Mayor .... Margaret Abe-Koga
Manager .... Kevin C. Duggan
City Clerk .... Angelita M. Salvador
Attorney .... Michael Martello
Finance Dir .... Patty Kong (Int)
Public Works .... Cathy Lazarus
Planning/Dev Dir .... Randal Tsuda
Building .... David Basinger (Int)
Police Chief .... Scott Vermeer
Fire Chief .... Scott Vermeer (Int)

Public Safety

Number of officers, 2007 98
Violent crimes, 2007 238
Property crimes, 2007 1,519
Arson, 2007 12

Public Library

Mountain View Public Library
585 Franklin St
Mountain View, CA 94041
650-903-6335

Director .... Karen Burnett

Library statistics, FY 2007

Population served 73,262
Internet terminals 47
Annual users 131,078

Per capita:

Operating income $63.88
percent from local government 94.0%
Operating expenditure $58.84
Total materials 3.91
Print holdings 3.34
Visits per capita 11.15

Housing & Construction

Housing Units

Total, 2008§ 33,475
Single family units, attached 4,038
Single family units, detached 9,318
Multiple family units 18,888
Mobile home units 1,231
Occupied 32,247
Vacancy rate 3.7%
Median rent, 2007** $1,384
Median SF home value, 2007** $804,400

New Privately Owned Housing Units Authorized by Building Permit, 2007*

	Units	Construction Cost
Single	267	$70,705,402
Total	371	$92,205,402

Municipal Finance

(For local fiscal year ended in 2006)

Revenues

Total $156,915,714
Taxes 58,829,881
Special benefits assessment 0
Licenses & permits 2,684,611
Fines & forfeitures 579,532
Revenues from use of money & property 10,008,464
Intergovernmental 5,481,694
Service charges 66,407,240
Other revenues 12,924,292
Other financing sources 0

Expenditures

Total $152,026,134
General government 24,790,101
Public safety 34,514,478
Transportation 16,855,542
Community development 6,531,504
Health 21,213,570
Culture & leisure 29,446,064
Other 0

Local School District

(Data from School year 2007-08 except as noted)

Mountain View-Los Altos Union High
1299 Bryant Ave
Mountain View, CA 94040
(650) 940-4650

Superintendent .... Barry Groves
Grade plan 9-12
Number of schools 3
Enrollment 3,620
High school graduates, 2006-07 868
Dropout rate 1.2%
Pupil/teacher ratio 20.3
Average class size 23.9
Students per computer 4.9
Classrooms with internet 229
Avg. Daily Attendance (ADA) 3,563
Cost per ADA $12,454
Avg. Teacher Salary $93,283

California Achievement Tests 6th ed., 2008

(Pct scoring at or above 50th National Percentile Rank)

	Math	Reading	Language
Grade 3	NA	NA	NA
Grade 7	NA	NA	NA

Academic Performance Index, 2008

Number of students tested 2,682
Number of valid scores 2,581
2007 API (base) 812
2008 API (growth) 820

SAT Testing, 2006-07

Enrollment, Grade 12 967
Number taking test 693
percent taking test 71.7%
percent with total score 1,500+ 55.30%

Average Scores:

Math	Verbal	Writing	Total
599	575	573	1,747

Federal No Child Left Behind, 2008

(Adequate Yearly Progress standards met)

	Participation Rate	Pct Proficient
ELA	Yes	No
Math	Yes	Yes

API criteria .... Yes
Graduation rate .... Yes
\# criteria met/possible 24/23

Other school districts for this city

(see Appendix E for information on these districts)

Mountain View-Whisman Elem

See Introduction for an explanation of all data sources.

Demographics & Socio-Economic Characteristics†

(2007 American Community Survey, except as noted)

Population

1990* .....NA
2007 89,885
Male 46,395
Female 43,490
Jan. 2008 (estimate)§ 100,173
Persons per sq. mi. of land 3,527.2

Race & Hispanic Origin, 2007

Race
White 66,085
Black/African American 6,419
North American Native 597
Asian 7,024
Pacific Islander 112
Other Race 5,721
Two or more races 3,927
Hispanic origin, total 18,512
Mexican 14,613
Puerto Rican 742
Cuban 0
Other Hispanic 3,157

Age & Nativity, 2007

Under 5 years 7,019
18 years and over 62,980
65 years and over 8,665
85 years and over 530
Median Age 31.3
Native-born 77,253
Foreign-born 12,632

Educational Attainment, 2007

Population 25 years and over 53,852
Less than 9th grade 1.7%
High school grad or higher 93.1%
Bachelor's degree or higher 29.1%
Graduate degree 9.1%

Income & Poverty, 2007

Per capita income $30,132
Median household income $78,883
Median family income $90,930
Persons in poverty 4.4%
H'holds receiving public assistance 339
H'holds receiving social security 6,117

Households, 2007

Total households 28,196
With persons under 18 13,802
With persons over 65 5,759
Family households 21,479
Single person households 5,471
Persons per household 3.17
Persons per family 3.69

Household Population, 2008§§

Persons living in households 99,513
Persons living in group quarters 660
Persons per household 3.0

Labor & Employment

Total civilian labor force, 2008§§ 27,900
Unemployment rate, 2008 .....5.6%
Total civilian labor force, 2000* 19,763

Employed persons 16 years and over by occupation, 2007

Managers & professionals 14,131
Service occupations 5,380
Sales & office occupations 14,086
Farming, fishing & forestry 0
Construction & maintenance 4,687
Production & transportation 4,041
Self-employed persons 4,640

† see Appendix D for 2000 Decennial Census Data
* US Census Bureau
** 2007 American Community Survey
§ California Department of Finance
§§ California Employment Development Dept

General Information

City of Murrieta
24601 Jefferson Avenue
One Town Square
Murrieta, CA 92562
951-304-2489

Website .....www.murrieta.org
Elevation .....NA
Land Area (sq. miles) 28.4
Water Area (sq. miles) 0
Year of Incorporation 1991
Government type .....General Law
Sales tax rate 8.75%

Voters & Officials

Registered Voters, October 2008

Total 44,279
Democrats 11,635
Republicans 22,429
Declined to state 8,414

Legislative Districts

US Congressional 45
State Senatorial 36
State Assembly 64, 66

Local Officials, 2009

Mayor .....Gary Thomasian
Manager .....Rick Dudley
City Clerk .....A. Kay Vinson
Attorney .....Leslie Devaney
Finance Dir .....Suzanne Wellcome
Public Works .....Patrick Thomas
Planning/Dev Dir .....Mary Lanier
Building .....Allen Brock
Police Chief .....Mark Wright
Fire Chief .....Paul Christman

Public Safety

Number of officers, 2007 82
Violent crimes, 2007 118
Property crimes, 2007 1,955
Arson, 2007 3

Public Library

Murrieta Public Library
Eight Town Square
Murrieta, CA 92563
951-304-2665

City Librarian .....Loretta McKinney

Library statistics, FY 2007

Population served 97,257
Internet terminals 40
Annual users 26,812

Per capita:

Operating income $22.10
percent from local government 89.6%
Operating expenditure $22.10
Total materials 0.85
Print holdings 0.78
Visits per capita 1.62

Housing & Construction

Housing Units

Total, 2008§ 34,248
Single family units, attached 559
Single family units, detached 24,487
Multiple family units 7,489
Mobile home units 1,713
Occupied 32,664
Vacancy rate 4.6%
Median rent, 2007** $1,320
Median SF home value, 2007** $459,300

New Privately Owned Housing Units Authorized by Building Permit, 2007*

	Units	Construction Cost
Single	93	$30,502,324
Total	183	$39,622,324

Municipal Finance

(For local fiscal year ended in 2006)

Revenues

Total $66,877,345
Taxes 42,964,417
Special benefits assessment 247,640
Licenses & permits 2,423,583
Fines & forfeitures 598,461
Revenues from use of money & property 6,288,793
Intergovernmental 5,314,336
Service charges 3,954,550
Other revenues 5,085,565
Other financing sources 0

Expenditures

Total $83,534,451
General government 7,144,901
Public safety 15,663,210
Transportation 10,858,070
Community development 39,717,618
Health 0
Culture & leisure 10,150,652
Other 0

Local School District

(Data from School year 2007-08 except as noted)

Murrieta Valley Unified
41870 McAlby Ct
Murrieta, CA 92562
(951) 696-1600

Superintendent .....Stan Scheer
Grade plan K-12
Number of schools 18
Enrollment 21,226
High school graduates, 2006-07 1,313
Dropout rate 2.4%
Pupil/teacher ratio 23.1
Average class size 26.7
Students per computer 6.2
Classrooms with internet 933
Avg. Daily Attendance (ADA) 20,300
Cost per ADA $7,520
Avg. Teacher Salary $71,085

California Achievement Tests 6th ed., 2008

(Pct scoring at or above 50th National Percentile Rank)

	Math	Reading	Language
Grade 3	69%	51%	59%
Grade 7	63%	61%	57%

Academic Performance Index, 2008

Number of students tested 16,687
Number of valid scores 15,686
2007 API (base) 799
2008 API (growth) 812

SAT Testing, 2006-07

Enrollment, Grade 12 1,536
Number taking test 678
percent taking test 44.1%
percent with total score 1,500+ 21.00%

Average Scores:

Math	Verbal	Writing	Total
506	491	486	1,483

Federal No Child Left Behind, 2008

(Adequate Yearly Progress standards met)

	Participation Rate	Pct Proficient
ELA	Yes	No
Math	Yes	Yes

API criteria .....Yes
Graduation rate .....Yes
criteria met/possible 40/39

Other school districts for this city

(see Appendix E for information on these districts)

Menifee Elem, Perris High

See Introduction for an explanation of all data sources.

Demographics & Socio-Economic Characteristics†

(2007 American Community Survey, except as noted)

Population

1990* 61,842
2007 71,664
Male 36,730
Female 34,934
Jan. 2008 (estimate)§ 77,106
Persons per sq. mi. of land 4,356.3

Race & Hispanic Origin, 2007

Race
White 65,054
Black/African American 187
North American Native 729
Asian 548
Pacific Islander 177
Other Race 3,948
Two or more races 1,021
Hispanic origin, total 26,452
Mexican . . . . . NA
Puerto Rican . . . . . NA
Cuban . . . . . NA
Other Hispanic . . . . . NA

Age & Nativity, 2007

Under 5 years 5,012
18 years and over 54,636
65 years and over 10,595
85 years and over 2,250
Median Age 37.9
Native-born 52,552
Foreign-born 19,112

Educational Attainment, 2007

Population 25 years and over 48,850
Less than 9th grade 18.1%
High school grad or higher 74.0%
Bachelor's degree or higher 20.5%
Graduate degree 5.7%

Income & Poverty, 2007

Per capita income $28,264
Median household income $58,472
Median family income $68,904
Persons in poverty 12.6%
H'holds receiving public assistance 251
H'holds receiving social security 8,139

Households, 2007

Total households 27,387
With persons under 18 8,161
With persons over 65 7,602
Family households 16,753
Single person households 8,537
Persons per household 2.59
Persons per family 3.30

Household Population, 2008§§

Persons living in households 75,647
Persons living in group quarters 1,459
Persons per household 2.6

Labor & Employment

Total civilian labor force, 2008§§ 45,500
Unemployment rate, 2008 . . . . . 5.3%
Total civilian labor force, 2000* 35,996

Employed persons 16 years and over by occupation, 2007

Managers & professionals 9,303
Service occupations 7,680
Sales & office occupations 8,018
Farming, fishing & forestry 2,775
Construction & maintenance 4,225
Production & transportation 4,134
Self-employed persons 3,075

† see Appendix D for 2000 Decennial Census Data
* US Census Bureau
** 2007 American Community Survey
§ California Department of Finance
§§ California Employment Development Dept

General Information

City of Napa
955 School St
PO Box 660
Napa, CA 94559
707-257-9503

Website . . . . . www.cityofnapa.org
Elevation . . . . . 17 ft.
Land Area (sq. miles) 17.7
Water Area (sq. miles) 0.1
Year of Incorporation 1872
Government type . . . . . Chartered
Sales tax rate 8.75%

Voters & Officials

Registered Voters, October 2008

Total 38,733
Democrats 19,076
Republicans 10,788
Declined to state 6,962

Legislative Districts

US Congressional 1
State Senatorial 2
State Assembly 7

Local Officials, 2009

Mayor . . . . . Jill Techel
Manager . . . . . Michael Parness
City Clerk . . . . . Sara Cox
Attorney . . . . . Michael Barrett
Finance Dir . . . . . Carole Wilson
Public Works . . . . . Mike O'Bryon
Planning/Dev Dir . . . . . Tambri Heyden
Building . . . . . Steve Jensen
Police Chief . . . . . Rich Melton
Emergency/Fire Dir . . . . . Tim Borman

Public Safety

Number of officers, 2007 69
Violent crimes, 2007 288
Property crimes, 2007 2,351
Arson, 2007 10

Public Library

Napa Main Library
Napa City/County Library
580 Coombs St
Napa, CA 94559
707-253-4241

County Library Dir . . . . . Danis Kreimeier

Library system statistics, FY 2007

Population served 129,976
Internet terminals 58
Annual users . . . . . NA

Per capita:

Operating income $50.32
percent from local government 88.9%
Operating expenditure $45.25
Total materials 1.58
Print holdings 1.37
Visits per capita 3.16

Housing & Construction

Housing Units

Total, 2008§ 30,094
Single family units, attached 2,426
Single family units, detached 18,172
Multiple family units 8,107
Mobile home units 1,389
Occupied 29,230
Vacancy rate 2.9%
Median rent, 2007** $1,068
Median SF home value, 2007** $608,500

New Privately Owned Housing Units Authorized by Building Permit, 2007*

	Units	Construction Cost
Single	129	$35,107,235
Total	187	$43,088,823

Municipal Finance

(For local fiscal year ended in 2006)

Revenues

Total $113,489,206
Taxes 44,289,098
Special benefits assessment 0
Licenses & permits 1,062,533
Fines & forfeitures 296,050
Revenues from use of money & property 1,823,401
Intergovernmental 17,476,569
Service charges 43,397,251
Other revenues 1,385,643
Other financing sources 3,758,661

Expenditures

Total $116,185,730
General government 8,639,421
Public safety 31,092,507
Transportation 12,993,624
Community development 19,776,683
Health 13,143,446
Culture & leisure 8,524,456
Other 0

Local School District

(Data from School year 2007-08 except as noted)

Napa Valley Unified
2425 Jefferson St
Napa, CA 94558
(707) 253-3715

Superintendent . . . . . John Glaser
Grade plan K-12
Number of schools 37
Enrollment 17,552
High school graduates, 2006-07 1,092
Dropout rate 3.6%
Pupil/teacher ratio 19.1
Average class size 24.6
Students per computer 4.2
Classrooms with internet 844
Avg. Daily Attendance (ADA) 14,837
Cost per ADA $8,130
Avg. Teacher Salary $66,178

California Achievement Tests 6th ed., 2008

(Pct scoring at or above 50th National Percentile Rank)

	Math	Reading	Language
Grade 3	56%	41%	50%
Grade 7	56%	50%	51%

Academic Performance Index, 2008

Number of students tested 13,136
Number of valid scores 12,469
2007 API (base) 755
2008 API (growth) 765

SAT Testing, 2006-07

Enrollment, Grade 12 1,328
Number taking test 406
percent taking test 30.6%
percent with total score 1,500+ 18.70%

Average Scores:

Math	Verbal	Writing	Total
538	521	515	1,574

Federal No Child Left Behind, 2008

(Adequate Yearly Progress standards met)

	Participation Rate	Pct Proficient
ELA	Yes	No
Math	Yes	No

API criteria . . . . . Yes
Graduation rate . . . . . Yes
\# criteria met/possible 42/39

Other school districts for this city

(see Appendix E for information on these districts)

None

See Introduction for an explanation of all data sources.

Demographics & Socio-Economic Characteristics

(2000 Decennial Census, except as noted)

Population

1990* . . . 54,249
2000 . . . 54,260
Male . . . 27,452
Female . . . 26,808
Jan. 2008 (estimate)§ . . . 61,194
Persons per sq. mi. of land . . . 8,269.5

Race & Hispanic Origin, 2000

Race
White . . . 19,070
Black/African American . . . 3,026
North American Native . . . 513
Asian . . . 10,077
Pacific Islander . . . 478
Other Race . . . 18,181
Two or more races . . . 2,915
Hispanic origin, total . . . 32,053
Mexican . . . 28,544
Puerto Rican . . . 358
Cuban . . . 52
Other Hispanic . . . 3,099

Age & Nativity, 2000

Under 5 years . . . 4,410
18 years and over . . . 37,918
65 years and over . . . 5,989
85 years and over . . . 638
Median Age . . . 28.7
Native-born . . . 31,918
Foreign-born . . . 22,487

Educational Attainment, 2000

Population 25 years and over . . . 30,325
Less than 9th grade . . . 22.6%
High school grad or higher . . . 57.2%
Bachelor's degree or higher . . . 9.0%
Graduate degree . . . 2.1%

Income & Poverty, 1999

Per capita income . . . $11,582
Median household income . . . $29,826
Median family income . . . $31,497
Persons in poverty . . . 20.7%
H'holds receiving public assistance . . . 1,394
H'holds receiving social security . . . 3,592

Households, 2000

Total households . . . 15,018
With persons under 18 . . . 7,758
With persons over 65 . . . 4,094
Family households . . . 11,802
Single person households . . . 2,513
Persons per household . . . 3.39
Persons per family . . . 3.79

Household Population, 2008§§

Persons living in households . . . 53,040
Persons living in group quarters . . . 8,154
Persons per household . . . 3.5

Labor & Employment

Total civilian labor force, 2008§§ . . . 23,800
Unemployment rate, 2008 . . . 11.9%
Total civilian labor force, 2000 . . . 19,891

Employed persons 16 years and over by occupation, 2000

Managers & professionals . . . 2,735
Service occupations . . . 4,649
Sales & office occupations . . . 4,518
Farming, fishing & forestry . . . 165
Construction & maintenance . . . 2,253
Production & transportation . . . 3,444
Self-employed persons . . . 942

* US Census Bureau
** 2000 Decennial Census
§ California Department of Finance
§§ California Employment Development Dept

General Information

City of National City
1243 National City Blvd
National City, CA 91950
619-336-4200

Website . . . www.ci.national-city.ca.us
Elevation . . . 25 ft.
Land Area (sq. miles) . . . 7.4
Water Area (sq. miles) . . . 1.9
Year of Incorporation . . . 1887
Government type . . . General law
Sales tax rate . . . 9.75%

Voters & Officials

Registered Voters, October 2008

Total . . . 17,232
Democrats . . . 8,897
Republicans . . . 3,771
Declined to state . . . 3,877

Legislative Districts

US Congressional . . . 51
State Senatorial . . . 40
State Assembly . . . 79

Local Officials, 2009

Mayor . . . Ron Morrison
Manager . . . Chris Zapata
City Clerk . . . Michael Dalla
Attorney . . . George Eiser
Finance Dir . . . Jeanette Ladrido
Public Works . . . Joe Smith
Planning/Dev Dir . . . Roger Post
Building . . . NA
Police Chief . . . Adolfo Gonzales
Emergency/Fire Dir . . . Roderick Juniel

Public Safety

Number of officers, 2007 . . . 91
Violent crimes, 2007 . . . 424
Property crimes, 2007 . . . 2,169
Arson, 2007 . . . 8

Public Library

National City Public Library
1401 National City Blvd
National City, CA 91950
619-470-5800

Director . . . Minh Duong

Library statistics, FY 2007

Population served . . . 61,115
Internet terminals . . . 119
Annual users . . . 136,209

Per capita:

Operating income . . . $47.48
percent from local government . . . 83.2%
Operating expenditure . . . $46.08
Total materials . . . 3.36
Print holdings . . . 3.04
Visits per capita . . . 5.26

Housing & Construction

Housing Units

Total, 2008§ . . . 15,721
Single family units, attached . . . 1,405
Single family units, detached . . . 6,829
Multiple family units . . . 7,050
Mobile home units . . . 437
Occupied . . . 15,310
Vacancy rate . . . 2.6%
Median rent, 2000** . . . $573
Median SF home value, 2000** . . . $141,500

New Privately Owned Housing Units Authorized by Building Permit, 2007*

	Units	Construction Cost
Single	71	$15,801,846
Total	76	$16,580,064

Municipal Finance

(For local fiscal year ended in 2006)

Revenues

Total . . . $57,057,224
Taxes . . . 32,689,583
Special benefits assessment . . . 0
Licenses & permits . . . 672,530
Fines & forfeitures . . . 844,943
Revenues from use of money & property . . . 1,606,628
Intergovernmental . . . 8,777,779
Service charges . . . 12,118,143
Other revenues . . . 347,618
Other financing sources . . . 0

Expenditures

Total . . . $64,032,372
General government . . . 5,135,205
Public safety . . . 28,561,174
Transportation . . . 8,752,502
Community development . . . 4,266,483
Health . . . 6,169,705
Culture & leisure . . . 11,147,303
Other . . . 0

Local School District

(Data from School year 2007-08 except as noted)

Sweetwater Union High
1130 Fifth Ave
Chula Vista, CA 91911
(619) 691-5500

Superintendent . . . Jesus Gandara
Grade plan . . . 7-12
Number of schools . . . 31
Enrollment . . . 42,591
High school graduates, 2006-07 . . . 5,510
Dropout rate . . . 2.9%
Pupil/teacher ratio . . . 22.5
Average class size . . . 26.7
Students per computer . . . 4.9
Classrooms with internet . . . 2,349
Avg. Daily Attendance (ADA) . . . 41,210
Cost per ADA . . . $8,570
Avg. Teacher Salary . . . $71,623

California Achievement Tests 6th ed., 2008

(Pct scoring at or above 50th National Percentile Rank)

	Math	Reading	Language
Grade 3	NA	NA	NA
Grade 7	52%	47%	44%

Academic Performance Index, 2008

Number of students tested . . . 33,960
Number of valid scores . . . 30,640
2007 API (base) . . . 698
2008 API (growth) . . . 715

SAT Testing, 2006-07

Enrollment, Grade 12 . . . 7,523
Number taking test . . . 2,357
percent taking test . . . 31.3%
percent with total score 1,500+ . . . 9.50%

Average Scores:

Math	Verbal	Writing	Total
469	458	450	1,377

Federal No Child Left Behind, 2008

(Adequate Yearly Progress standards met)

	Participation Rate	Pct Proficient
ELA	Yes	No
Math	Yes	No

API criteria . . . Yes
Graduation rate . . . Yes
\# criteria met/possible . . . 42/39

Other school districts for this city

(see Appendix E for information on these districts)

National Elem

See Introduction for an explanation of all data sources.

Demographics & Socio-Economic Characteristics

(2000 Decennial Census, except as noted)

Population

1990* . . . 5,191
2000 . . . 4,830
Male . . . 2,375
Female . . . 2,455
Jan. 2008 (estimate)§ . . . 5,807
Persons per sq. mi. of land . . . 194.9

Race & Hispanic Origin, 2000

Race
White . . . 3,761
Black/African American . . . 78
North American Native . . . 338
Asian . . . 69
Pacific Islander . . . 6
Other Race . . . 308
Two or more races . . . 270
Hispanic origin, total . . . 887
Mexican . . . 676
Puerto Rican . . . 6
Cuban . . . 2
Other Hispanic . . . 203

Age & Nativity, 2000

Under 5 years . . . 336
18 years and over . . . 3,498
65 years and over . . . 758
85 years and over . . . 85
Median Age . . . 39.0
Native-born . . . 4,665
Foreign-born . . . 187

Educational Attainment, 2000

Population 25 years and over . . . 3,152
Less than 9th grade . . . 7.8%
High school grad or higher . . . 72.6%
Bachelor's degree or higher . . . 9.3%
Graduate degree . . . 4.5%

Income & Poverty, 1999

Per capita income . . . $15,156
Median household income . . . $26,108
Median family income . . . $33,264
Persons in poverty . . . 26.1%
H'holds receiving public assistance . . . 176
H'holds receiving social security . . . 780

Households, 2000

Total households . . . 1,940
With persons under 18 . . . 684
With persons over 65 . . . 588
Family households . . . 1,269
Single person households . . . 562
Persons per household . . . 2.48
Persons per family . . . 3.03

Household Population, 2008§§

Persons living in households . . . 5,796
Persons living in group quarters . . . 11
Persons per household . . . 2.6

Labor & Employment

Total civilian labor force, 2008§§ . . . 2,200
Unemployment rate, 2008 . . . 5.7%
Total civilian labor force, 2000 . . . 1,837

Employed persons 16 years and over by occupation, 2000

Managers & professionals . . . 385
Service occupations . . . 539
Sales & office occupations . . . 283
Farming, fishing & forestry . . . 0
Construction & maintenance . . . 214
Production & transportation . . . 307
Self-employed persons . . . 82

* US Census Bureau
** 2000 Decennial Census
§ California Department of Finance
§§ California Employment Development Dept

General Information

City of Needles
817 Third St
City Hall
Needles, CA 92363
760-326-2113

Website . . . www.cityofneedles.com
Elevation . . . 488 ft.
Land Area (sq. miles) . . . 29.8
Water Area (sq. miles) . . . 0.4
Year of Incorporation . . . 1913
Government type . . . Chartered
Sales tax rate . . . 8.75%

Voters & Officials

Registered Voters, October 2008

Total . . . 2,052
Democrats . . . 902
Republicans . . . 620
Declined to state . . . 408

Legislative Districts

US Congressional . . . 41
State Senatorial . . . 18
State Assembly . . . 34

Local Officials, 2009

Mayor . . . Jeff Williams
Manager . . . William W. Way Jr
City Clerk . . . Dale Jones
Attorney . . . Best, Best & Krieger
Finance Dir . . . Bonnie Luttrell
Public Works . . . NA
Planning/Dev Dir . . . Laura Zingg
Building . . . NA
Police Chief . . . Robert Wickum
Emergency/Fire Dir . . . Robert Lyons

Public Safety

Number of officers, 2007 . . . NA
Violent crimes, 2007 . . . 29
Property crimes, 2007 . . . 192
Arson, 2007 . . . 14

Public Library

Needles Branch Library
San Bernardino County Library System
1111 Bailey
Needles, CA 92363
760-326-9255

Branch Librarian . . . Kirsten Mouton

Library system statistics, FY 2007

Population served . . . 1,177,092
Internet terminals . . . 12
Annual users . . . 45,343

Per capita:

Operating income . . . $14.27
percent from local government . . . 73.3%
Operating expenditure . . . $13.86
Total materials . . . 0.86
Print holdings . . . 0.79
Visits per capita . . . 5.83

Housing & Construction

Housing Units

Total, 2008§ . . . 2,917
Single family units, attached . . . 110
Single family units, detached . . . 1,531
Multiple family units . . . 621
Mobile home units . . . 655
Occupied . . . 2,218
Vacancy rate . . . 24.0%
Median rent, 2000** . . . $463
Median SF home value, 2000** . . . $71,800

New Privately Owned Housing Units Authorized by Building Permit, 2007*

	Units	Construction Cost
Single	5	$1,495,909
Total	5	$1,495,909

Municipal Finance

(For local fiscal year ended in 2006)

Revenues

Total . . . $7,170,288
Taxes . . . 3,212,835
Special benefits assessment . . . 0
Licenses & permits . . . 190,477
Fines & forfeitures . . . 53,356
Revenues from use of money & property . . . 476,377
Intergovernmental . . . 925,108
Service charges . . . 2,312,135
Other revenues . . . 0
Other financing sources . . . 0

Expenditures

Total . . . $7,329,276
General government . . . 899,974
Public safety . . . 2,348,110
Transportation . . . 808,261
Community development . . . 370,571
Health . . . 1,056,748
Culture & leisure . . . 1,845,612
Other . . . 0

Local School District

(Data from School year 2007-08 except as noted)

Needles Unified
1900 Erin Dr
Needles, CA 92363
(760) 326-3891

Superintendent . . . Dave Renquest
Grade plan . . . K-12
Number of schools . . . 7
Enrollment . . . 1,076
High school graduates, 2006-07 . . . 68
Dropout rate . . . 10.2%
Pupil/teacher ratio . . . 19.5
Average class size . . . 21.1
Students per computer . . . 3.0
Classrooms with internet . . . 68
Avg. Daily Attendance (ADA) . . . 968
Cost per ADA . . . $11,982
Avg. Teacher Salary . . . $60,146

California Achievement Tests 6th ed., 2008

(Pct scoring at or above 50th National Percentile Rank)

	Math	Reading	Language
Grade 3	49%	41%	49%
Grade 7	58%	50%	46%

Academic Performance Index, 2008

Number of students tested . . . 771
Number of valid scores . . . 698
2007 API (base) . . . 656
2008 API (growth) . . . 699

SAT Testing, 2006-07

Enrollment, Grade 12 . . . 74
Number taking test . . . 21
percent taking test . . . 28.4%
percent with total score 1,500+ . . . 8.10%

Average Scores:

Math	Verbal	Writing	Total
489	476	462	1,427

Federal No Child Left Behind, 2008

(Adequate Yearly Progress standards met)

	Participation Rate	Pct Proficient
ELA	Yes	Yes
Math	Yes	Yes

API criteria . . . Yes
Graduation rate . . . Yes
criteria met/possible . . . 18/18

Other school districts for this city

(see Appendix E for information on these districts)

None

See Introduction for an explanation of all data sources.

Demographics & Socio-Economic Characteristics

(2000 Decennial Census, except as noted)

Population

1990* . . . 2,855
2000 . . . 3,001
Male . . . 1,479
Female . . . 1,522
Jan. 2008 (estimate)§ . . . 3,074
Persons per sq. mi. of land . . . 1,463.8

Race & Hispanic Origin, 2000

Race
White . . . 2,829
Black/African American . . . 13
North American Native . . . 41
Asian . . . 22
Pacific Islander . . . 1
Other Race . . . 22
Two or more races . . . 73
Hispanic origin, total . . . 104
Mexican . . . 53
Puerto Rican . . . 3
Cuban . . . 5
Other Hispanic . . . 43

Age & Nativity, 2000

Under 5 years . . . 99
18 years and over . . . 2,411
65 years and over . . . 447
85 years and over . . . 73
Median Age . . . 43.5
Native-born . . . 2,789
Foreign-born . . . 80

Educational Attainment, 2000

Population 25 years and over . . . 2,051
Less than 9th grade . . . 0.8%
High school grad or higher . . . 92.2%
Bachelor's degree or higher . . . 35.7%
Graduate degree . . . 16.0%

Income & Poverty, 1999

Per capita income . . . $22,399
Median household income . . . $36,667
Median family income . . . $46,149
Persons in poverty . . . 7.1%
H'holds receiving public assistance . . . 38
H'holds receiving social security . . . 387

Households, 2000

Total households . . . 1,313
With persons under 18 . . . 367
With persons over 65 . . . 328
Family households . . . 740
Single person households . . . 459
Persons per household . . . 2.14
Persons per family . . . 2.71

Household Population, 2008§§

Persons living in households . . . 2,887
Persons living in group quarters . . . 187
Persons per household . . . 2.0

Labor & Employment

Total civilian labor force, 2008§§ . . . 1,730
Unemployment rate, 2008 . . . 10.2%
Total civilian labor force, 2000 . . . 1,462

Employed persons 16 years and over by occupation, 2000

Managers & professionals . . . 566
Service occupations . . . 189
Sales & office occupations . . . 370
Farming, fishing & forestry . . . 0
Construction & maintenance . . . 124
Production & transportation . . . 104
Self-employed persons . . . 263

* US Census Bureau
** 2000 Decennial Census
§ California Department of Finance
§§ California Employment Development Dept

General Information

City of Nevada City
317 Broad St
Nevada City, CA 95959
530-265-2496

Email cathy.wilcox-barnes@co.nevada.ca.us
Elevation . . . 2,525 ft.
Land Area (sq. miles) . . . 2.1
Water Area (sq. miles) . . . 0
Year of Incorporation . . . 1856
Government type . . . General law
Sales tax rate . . . 8.88%

Voters & Officials

Registered Voters, October 2008

Total . . . 2,095
Democrats . . . 942
Republicans . . . 535
Declined to state . . . 438

Legislative Districts

US Congressional . . . 4
State Senatorial . . . 4
State Assembly . . . 3

Local Officials, 2009

Mayor . . . Barbara Coffman
Manager . . . Gene Albaugh
City Clerk . . . Neil Locke
Attorney . . . Jeff Massey
Finance Dir . . . Catrina Andes
Public Works . . . Verne Taylor
City Planner . . . Cindy Siegfried
Building . . . (County)
Police Chief . . . Louis Trovato
Emergency/Fire Dir . . . Sam Goodspeed

Public Safety

Number of officers, 2007 . . . 11
Violent crimes, 2007 . . . 10
Property crimes, 2007 . . . 61
Arson, 2007 . . . 0

Public Library

Madelyn Helling Branch Library
Nevada County Library System
980 Helling Way
Nevada City, CA 95959
530-265-7050

County Librarian . . . Mary Ann Trygg

Library system statistics, FY 2007

Population served . . . 99,766
Internet terminals . . . 41
Annual users . . . 46,411

Per capita:

Operating income . . . $24.65
percent from local government . . . 89.7%
Operating expenditure . . . $24.33
Total materials . . . 2.13
Print holdings . . . 1.85
Visits per capita . . . 4.86

Housing & Construction

Housing Units

Total, 2008§ . . . 1,523
Single family units, attached . . . 53
Single family units, detached . . . 1,161
Multiple family units . . . 234
Mobile home units . . . 75
Occupied . . . 1,413
Vacancy rate . . . 7.2%
Median rent, 2000** . . . $707
Median SF home value, 2000** . . . $229,600

New Privately Owned Housing Units Authorized by Building Permit, 2007*

	Units	Construction Cost
Single	NA	NA
Total	NA	NA

Municipal Finance

(For local fiscal year ended in 2006)

Revenues

Total . . . $7,635,639
Taxes . . . 2,661,705
Special benefits assessment . . . 232,717
Licenses & permits . . . 298
Fines & forfeitures . . . 34,548
Revenues from use of money & property . . . 92,470
Intergovernmental . . . 481,265
Service charges . . . 1,852,744
Other revenues . . . 91,892
Other financing sources . . . 2,188,000

Expenditures

Total . . . $7,027,180
General government . . . 860,621
Public safety . . . 1,708,503
Transportation . . . 608,137
Community development . . . 106,168
Health . . . 2,989,768
Culture & leisure . . . 363,825
Other . . . 0

Local School District

(Data from School year 2007-08 except as noted)

Nevada Joint Union High
11645 Ridge Rd
Grass Valley, CA 95945
(530) 273-3351

Superintendent . . . Ralf Swenson
Grade plan . . . 9-12
Number of schools . . . 9
Enrollment . . . 3,942
High school graduates, 2006-07 . . . 819
Dropout rate . . . 2.2%
Pupil/teacher ratio . . . 26.6
Average class size . . . 27.0
Students per computer . . . 3.5
Classrooms with internet . . . 192
Avg. Daily Attendance (ADA) . . . 3,728
Cost per ADA . . . $8,660
Avg. Teacher Salary . . . $65,021

California Achievement Tests 6th ed., 2008

(Pct scoring at or above 50th National Percentile Rank)

	Math	Reading	Language
Grade 3	NA	NA	NA
Grade 7	NA	NA	NA

Academic Performance Index, 2008

Number of students tested . . . 2,879
Number of valid scores . . . 2,795
2007 API (base) . . . 765
2008 API (growth) . . . 789

SAT Testing, 2006-07

Enrollment, Grade 12 . . . 954
Number taking test . . . 343
percent taking test . . . 36.0%
percent with total score 1,500+ . . . 23.70%

Average Scores:

Math	Verbal	Writing	Total
554	539	530	1,623

Federal No Child Left Behind, 2008

(Adequate Yearly Progress standards met)

	Participation Rate	Pct Proficient
ELA	Yes	Yes
Math	Yes	Yes

API criteria . . . Yes
Graduation rate . . . Yes
\# criteria met/possible . . . 14/14

Other school districts for this city

(see Appendix E for information on these districts)

Nevada City Elem, Twin Ridges Elem

See Introduction for an explanation of all data sources.

Demographics & Socio-Economic Characteristics

(2000 Decennial Census, except as noted)

Population

1990* . . . 37,861
2000 . . . 42,471
Male . . . 21,386
Female . . . 21,085
Jan. 2008 (estimate)§ . . . 43,872
Persons per sq. mi. of land . . . 3,133.7

Race & Hispanic Origin, 2000

Race
White . . . 22,179
Black/African American . . . 1,705
North American Native . . . 273
Asian . . . 9,047
Pacific Islander . . . 426
Other Race . . . 5,839
Two or more races . . . 3,002
Hispanic origin, total . . . 12,145
Mexican . . . 9,240
Puerto Rican . . . 373
Cuban . . . 71
Other Hispanic . . . 2,461

Age & Nativity, 2000

Under 5 years . . . 3,062
18 years and over . . . 30,896
65 years and over . . . 3,324
85 years and over . . . 240
Median Age . . . 33.1
Native-born . . . 29,049
Foreign-born . . . 13,422

Educational Attainment, 2000

Population 25 years and over . . . 26,582
Less than 9th grade . . . 9.8%
High school grad or higher . . . 79.2%
Bachelor's degree or higher . . . 24.2%
Graduate degree . . . 7.1%

Income & Poverty, 1999

Per capita income . . . $23,641
Median household income . . . $69,350
Median family income . . . $71,351
Persons in poverty . . . 5.5%
H'holds receiving public assistance . . . 323
H'holds receiving social security . . . 2,363

Households, 2000

Total households . . . 12,992
With persons under 18 . . . 5,955
With persons over 65 . . . 2,466
Family households . . . 10,345
Single person households . . . 1,837
Persons per household . . . 3.26
Persons per family . . . 3.59

Household Population, 2008§§

Persons living in households . . . 43,783
Persons living in group quarters . . . 89
Persons per household . . . 3.3

Labor & Employment

Total civilian labor force, 2008§§ . . . 22,700
Unemployment rate, 2008 . . . 5.7%
Total civilian labor force, 2000 . . . 21,524

Employed persons 16 years and over by occupation, 2000

Managers & professionals . . . 6,588
Service occupations . . . 2,418
Sales & office occupations . . . 5,904
Farming, fishing & forestry . . . 17
Construction & maintenance . . . 1,922
Production & transportation . . . 3,603
Self-employed persons . . . 948

* US Census Bureau
** 2000 Decennial Census
§ California Department of Finance
§§ California Employment Development Dept

General Information

City of Newark
37101 Newark Blvd
Newark, CA 94560
510-578-4000

Website . . . www.newark.org
Elevation . . . 16 ft.
Land Area (sq. miles) . . . 14.0
Water Area (sq. miles) . . . 0
Year of Incorporation . . . 1955
Government type . . . General law
Sales tax rate . . . 9.75%

Voters & Officials

Registered Voters, October 2008

Total . . . 19,424
Democrats . . . 10,630
Republicans . . . 3,582
Declined to state . . . 4,477

Legislative Districts

US Congressional . . . 13
State Senatorial . . . 10
State Assembly . . . 20

Local Officials, 2009

Mayor . . . David W. Smith
Manager . . . John Becker
City Clerk . . . Sheila Harrington
Attorney . . . Gary Galliano
Finance Dir . . . Dennis Jones
Public Works . . . Peggy Claassen
Planning/Dev Dir . . . Terrence Grindall
Building . . . NA
Police Chief . . . James Leal
Emergency/Fire Dir. . . Demetrious Schaffer

Public Safety

Number of officers, 2007 . . . 55
Violent crimes, 2007 . . . 224
Property crimes, 2007 . . . 1,721
Arson, 2007 . . . NA

Public Library

Newark Library
Alameda County Library System
6300 Civic Terrace Ave
Newark, CA 94560
510-795-2627

Branch Librarian . . . Kathy Steel-Sabo

Library system statistics, FY 2007

Population served . . . 527,926
Internet terminals . . . 193
Annual users . . . 358,689

Per capita:

Operating income . . . $41.07
percent from local government . . . 94.7%
Operating expenditure . . . $36.47
Total materials . . . 2.21
Print holdings . . . 1.91
Visits per capita . . . 4.32

Housing & Construction

Housing Units

Total, 2008§ . . . 13,423
Single family units, attached . . . 1,240
Single family units, detached . . . 9,212
Multiple family units . . . 2,912
Mobile home units . . . 59
Occupied . . . 13,262
Vacancy rate . . . 1.2%
Median rent, 2000** . . . $1,093
Median SF home value, 2000** . . . $303,700

New Privately Owned Housing Units Authorized by Building Permit, 2007*

	Units	Construction Cost
Single	6	$2,603,462
Total	6	$2,603,462

Municipal Finance

(For local fiscal year ended in 2006)

Revenues

Total . . . $40,928,654
Taxes . . . 28,431,545
Special benefits assessment . . . 878,658
Licenses & permits . . . 994,998
Fines & forfeitures . . . 194,677
Revenues from use of money & property . . . 1,247,813
Intergovernmental . . . 3,419,173
Service charges . . . 4,275,739
Other revenues . . . 1,486,051
Other financing sources . . . 0

Expenditures

Total . . . $40,219,095
General government . . . 4,093,655
Public safety . . . 21,710,096
Transportation . . . 5,760,183
Community development . . . 1,831,912
Health . . . 271,516
Culture & leisure . . . 6,551,733
Other . . . 0

Local School District

(Data from School year 2007-08 except as noted)

Newark Unified
5715 Musick Ave
Newark, CA 94560
(510) 818-4112

Superintendent . . . Kevin Harrigan
Grade plan . . . K-12
Number of schools . . . 15
Enrollment . . . 7,142
High school graduates, 2006-07 . . . 454
Dropout rate . . . 4.1%
Pupil/teacher ratio . . . 19.6
Average class size . . . 25.9
Students per computer . . . 3.8
Classrooms with internet . . . 408
Avg. Daily Attendance (ADA) . . . 6,949
Cost per ADA . . . $8,450
Avg. Teacher Salary . . . $72,153

California Achievement Tests 6th ed., 2008

(Pct scoring at or above 50th National Percentile Rank)

	Math	Reading	Language
Grade 3	55%	32%	42%
Grade 7	46%	41%	43%

Academic Performance Index, 2008

Number of students tested . . . 5,425
Number of valid scores . . . 5,037
2007 API (base) . . . 739
2008 API (growth) . . . 752

SAT Testing, 2006-07

Enrollment, Grade 12 . . . 550
Number taking test . . . 256
percent taking test . . . 46.6%
percent with total score 1,500+ . . . 16.70%

Average Scores:

Math	Verbal	Writing	Total
501	470	470	1,441

Federal No Child Left Behind, 2008

(Adequate Yearly Progress standards met)

	Participation Rate	Pct Proficient
ELA	Yes	No
Math	Yes	No

API criteria . . . Yes
Graduation rate . . . Yes
criteria met/possible . . . 42/36

Other school districts for this city

(see Appendix E for information on these districts)

None

See Introduction for an explanation of all data sources.

Demographics & Socio-Economic Characteristics

(2000 Decennial Census, except as noted)

Population

1990* 4,151
2000 7,093
Male 3,562
Female 3,531
Jan. 2008 (estimate)§ 10,586
Persons per sq. mi. of land 7,561.4

Race & Hispanic Origin, 2000

Race
White 4,310
Black/African American 89
North American Native 94
Asian 131
Pacific Islander 5
Other Race 2,051
Two or more races 413
Hispanic origin, total 3,648
Mexican 3,209
Puerto Rican 29
Cuban 1
Other Hispanic 409

Age & Nativity, 2000

Under 5 years 627
18 years and over 4,591
65 years and over 623
85 years and over 80
Median Age 29.3
Native-born 5,234
Foreign-born 1,843

Educational Attainment, 2000

Population 25 years and over 3,855
Less than 9th grade 20.3%
High school grad or higher 65.2%
Bachelor's degree or higher 9.4%
Graduate degree 3.5%

Income & Poverty, 1999

Per capita income $14,781
Median household income $39,460
Median family income $42,523
Persons in poverty 12.8%
H'holds receiving public assistance 36
H'holds receiving social security 545

Households, 2000

Total households 2,079
With persons under 18 1,149
With persons over 65 426
Family households 1,701
Single person households 304
Persons per household 3.38
Persons per family 3.74

Household Population, 2008§§

Persons living in households 10,520
Persons living in group quarters 66
Persons per household 3.4

Labor & Employment

Total civilian labor force, 2008§§ 3,300
Unemployment rate, 2008 .... 15.9%
Total civilian labor force, 2000 2,768

Employed persons 16 years and over by occupation, 2000

Managers & professionals 548
Service occupations 306
Sales & office occupations 486
Farming, fishing & forestry 237
Construction & maintenance 280
Production & transportation 451
Self-employed persons 166

* US Census Bureau
** 2000 Decennial Census
§ California Department of Finance
§§ California Employment Development Dept

General Information

City of Newman
1162 Main St
Newman, CA 95360
209-862-3725

Website .... www.cityofnewman.com
Elevation .... 91 ft.
Land Area (sq. miles) 1.4
Water Area (sq. miles) 0
Year of Incorporation 1908
Government type .... General law
Sales tax rate 8.38%

Voters & Officials

Registered Voters, October 2008

Total 3,580
Democrats 1,632
Republicans 1,133
Declined to state 646

Legislative Districts

US Congressional 18
State Senatorial 12
State Assembly 17

Local Officials, 2009

Mayor .... Ed Katen
Manager .... Michael E. Holland
City Clerk .... Michael E. Holland
Attorney .... Thomas Hallinan
Finance Dir .... Sonya Silva
Public Works .... Garner Reynolds
Planning/Dev Dir .... Michael E. Holland
Building .... Precision Inspection
Police Chief .... Adam McGill
Emergency/Fire Dir .... Melvin Souza

Public Safety

Number of officers, 2007 13
Violent crimes, 2007 36
Property crimes, 2007 330
Arson, 2007 0

Public Library

Newman Library
Stanislaus County Free Library
1305 Kern St
Newman, CA 95360
209-862-2010

Branch Librarian .... Barbara Pearson

Library system statistics, FY 2007

Population served 521,497
Internet terminals 128
Annual users 256,298

Per capita:

Operating income $20.76
percent from local government 91.0%
Operating expenditure $20.19
Total materials 1.66
Print holdings 1.56
Visits per capita .... NA

Housing & Construction

Housing Units

Total, 2008§ 3,243
Single family units, attached 76
Single family units, detached 2,777
Multiple family units 364
Mobile home units 26
Occupied 3,099
Vacancy rate 4.4%
Median rent, 2000** $518
Median SF home value, 2000** $108,500

New Privately Owned Housing Units Authorized by Building Permit, 2007*

	Units	Construction Cost
Single	113	$25,097,732
Total	113	$25,097,732

Municipal Finance

(For local fiscal year ended in 2006)

Revenues

Total $10,427,589
Taxes 2,319,077
Special benefits assessment 17,331
Licenses & permits 248,760
Fines & forfeitures 39,846
Revenues from use of money & property 380,065
Intergovernmental 2,192,940
Service charges 5,051,821
Other revenues 177,749
Other financing sources 0

Expenditures

Total $6,225,757
General government 541,077
Public safety 1,735,054
Transportation 435,574
Community development 645,979
Health 2,041,943
Culture & leisure 197,664
Other 0

Local School District

(Data from School year 2007-08 except as noted)

Newman-Crows Landing Unified
890 Main St
Newman, CA 95360
(209) 862-2933

Superintendent .... Rick Fauss
Grade plan K-12
Number of schools 9
Enrollment 2,676
High school graduates, 2006-07 131
Dropout rate 2.2%
Pupil/teacher ratio 21.1
Average class size 24.1
Students per computer 6.2
Classrooms with internet 245
Avg. Daily Attendance (ADA) 2,527
Cost per ADA $7,915
Avg. Teacher Salary $61,947

California Achievement Tests 6th ed., 2008

(Pct scoring at or above 50th National Percentile Rank)

	Math	Reading	Language
Grade 3	51%	29%	39%
Grade 7	47%	48%	44%

Academic Performance Index, 2008

Number of students tested 2,034
Number of valid scores 1,889
2007 API (base) 720
2008 API (growth) 722

SAT Testing, 2006-07

Enrollment, Grade 12 363
Number taking test 38
percent taking test 10.5%
percent with total score 1,500+ 3.60%

Average Scores:

Math	Verbal	Writing	Total
459	454	474	1,387

Federal No Child Left Behind, 2008

(Adequate Yearly Progress standards met)

	Participation Rate	Pct Proficient
ELA	Yes	No
Math	Yes	No

API criteria .... Yes
Graduation rate .... Yes
criteria met/possible 26/21

Other school districts for this city

(see Appendix E for information on these districts)

None

See Introduction for an explanation of all data sources.

Demographics & Socio-Economic Characteristics†

(2007 American Community Survey, except as noted)

Population

1990* 66,643
2007 89,125
Male 42,162
Female 46,963
Jan. 2008 (estimate)§ 84,554
Persons per sq. mi. of land 5,713.1

Race & Hispanic Origin, 2007

Race
White 79,202
Black/African American 1,375
North American Native 185
Asian 6,177
Pacific Islander 80
Other Race 946
Two or more races 1,160
Hispanic origin, total 4,757
Mexican 2,791
Puerto Rican 474
Cuban 45
Other Hispanic 1,447

Age & Nativity, 2007

Under 5 years 4,102
18 years and over 71,334
65 years and over 16,685
85 years and over 1,805
Median Age 43.7
Native-born 79,888
Foreign-born 9,237

Educational Attainment, 2007

Population 25 years and over 63,214
Less than 9th grade 0.2%
High school grad or higher 98.3%
Bachelor's degree or higher 63.5%
Graduate degree 28.2%

Income & Poverty, 2007

Per capita income $83,494
Median household income $110,511
Median family income $162,976
Persons in poverty 3.7%
H'holds receiving public assistance 118
H'holds receiving social security 10,858

Households, 2007

Total households 37,815
With persons under 18 8,851
With persons over 65 11,180
Family households 21,961
Single person households 12,232
Persons per household 2.33
Persons per family 3.01

Household Population, 2008§§

Persons living in households 83,614
Persons living in group quarters 940
Persons per household 2.2

Labor & Employment

Total civilian labor force, 2008§§ 45,900
Unemployment rate, 2008 .... 3.3%
Total civilian labor force, 2000* 39,508

Employed persons 16 years and over by occupation, 2007

Managers & professionals 28,190
Service occupations 3,719
Sales & office occupations 11,588
Farming, fishing & forestry 44
Construction & maintenance 1,034
Production & transportation 632
Self-employed persons 5,933

† see Appendix D for 2000 Decennial Census Data
* US Census Bureau
** 2007 American Community Survey
§ California Department of Finance
§§ California Employment Development Dept

General Information

City of Newport Beach
3300 Newport Blvd
Newport Beach, CA 92663
949-644-3309

Website .... www.city.newport-beach.ca.us
Elevation .... NA
Land Area (sq. miles) 14.8
Water Area (sq. miles) 25.1
Year of Incorporation 1906
Government type .... Chartered
Sales tax rate 8.75%

Voters & Officials

Registered Voters, October 2008

Total 63,554
Democrats 13,850
Republicans 35,870
Declined to state 11,492

Legislative Districts

US Congressional 48
State Senatorial 35
State Assembly 68, 70

Local Officials, 2009

Mayor .... Edward D. Selich
Manager .... Homer Bludau
City Clerk .... Leilani Brown
Attorney .... David Hunt
Finance Dir .... Dennis Danner
Public Works .... Steve Badum
Planning/Dev Dir .... David Lepo
Building .... Jay Elbettar
Police Chief .... John Klein
Emergency/Fire Dir .... Steve Lewis

Public Safety

Number of officers, 2007 145
Violent crimes, 2007 172
Property crimes, 2007 2,228
Arson, 2007 9

Public Library

Central Library
Newport Beach Public Library System
1000 Avocado Ave
Newport Beach, CA 92660
949-717-3800

City Librarian .... Linda Katsouleas

Library system statistics, FY 2007

Population served 84,218
Internet terminals 97
Annual users 177,244

Per capita:

Operating income $76.27
percent from local government 85.1%
Operating expenditure $76.27
Total materials 4.06
Print holdings 3.60
Visits per capita 11.60

Housing & Construction

Housing Units

Total, 2008§ 42,711
Single family units, attached 7,166
Single family units, detached 19,267
Multiple family units 15,415
Mobile home units 863
Occupied 38,051
Vacancy rate 10.9%
Median rent, 2007** $1,927
Median SF home value, 2007** $1,000,001

New Privately Owned Housing Units Authorized by Building Permit, 2007*

	Units	Construction Cost
Single	102	$67,663,930
Total	148	$80,608,490

Municipal Finance

(For local fiscal year ended in 2006)

Revenues

Total $177,303,224
Taxes 105,265,464
Special benefits assessment 45,093
Licenses & permits 4,422,114
Fines & forfeitures 4,042,036
Revenues from use of money & property 13,632,372
Intergovernmental 15,208,556
Service charges 32,259,745
Other revenues 2,427,844
Other financing sources 0

Expenditures

Total $180,043,851
General government 12,061,369
Public safety 57,625,359
Transportation 10,643,244
Community development 11,028,781
Health 25,060,950
Culture & leisure 42,544,295
Other 0

Local School District

(Data from School year 2007-08 except as noted)

Newport-Mesa Unified
PO Box 1368
Newport Beach, CA 92663
(714) 424-5000

Superintendent .... Jeffery Hubbard
Grade plan PK-12
Number of schools 32
Enrollment 21,338
High school graduates, 2006-07 1,366
Dropout rate 2.0%
Pupil/teacher ratio 22.2
Average class size 26.7
Students per computer 3.9
Classrooms with internet 1,049
Avg. Daily Attendance (ADA) 20,930
Cost per ADA $10,187
Avg. Teacher Salary $70,130

California Achievement Tests 6th ed., 2008

(Pct scoring at or above 50th National Percentile Rank)

	Math	Reading	Language
Grade 3	64%	49%	58%
Grade 7	63%	58%	57%

Academic Performance Index, 2008

Number of students tested 16,274
Number of valid scores 15,705
2007 API (base) 793
2008 API (growth) 797

SAT Testing, 2006-07

Enrollment, Grade 12 1,534
Number taking test 871
percent taking test 56.8%
percent with total score 1,500+ 35.80%

Average Scores:

Math	Verbal	Writing	Total
542	524	528	1,594

Federal No Child Left Behind, 2008

(Adequate Yearly Progress standards met)

	Participation Rate	Pct Proficient
ELA	Yes	No
Math	Yes	Yes

API criteria .... Yes
Graduation rate .... Yes
\# criteria met/possible 40/38

Other school districts for this city

(see Appendix E for information on these districts)

None

See Introduction for an explanation of all data sources.

Demographics & Socio-Economic Characteristics

(2000 Decennial Census, except as noted)

Population

1990* . . . 23,302
2000 . . . 24,157
Male . . . 13,582
Female . . . 10,575
Jan. 2008 (estimate)§ . . . 27,255
Persons per sq. mi. of land . . . 1,933.0

Race & Hispanic Origin, 2000

Race
White . . . 19,915
Black/African American . . . 1,481
North American Native . . . 182
Asian . . . 280
Pacific Islander . . . 33
Other Race . . . 1,538
Two or more races . . . 728
Hispanic origin, total . . . 5,504
Mexican . . . 4,829
Puerto Rican . . . 60
Cuban . . . 59
Other Hispanic . . . 556

Age & Nativity, 2000

Under 5 years . . . 1,152
18 years and over . . . 18,744
65 years and over . . . 1,604
85 years and over . . . 124
Median Age . . . 36.3
Native-born . . . 22,127
Foreign-born . . . 1,670

Educational Attainment, 2000

Population 25 years and over . . . 16,509
Less than 9th grade . . . 5.4%
High school grad or higher . . . 75.4%
Bachelor's degree or higher . . . 11.9%
Graduate degree . . . 4.6%

Income & Poverty, 1999

Per capita income . . . $20,710
Median household income . . . $62,652
Median family income . . . $66,204
Persons in poverty . . . 4.1%
H'holds receiving public assistance . . . 192
H'holds receiving social security . . . 1,363

Households, 2000

Total households . . . 6,136
With persons under 18 . . . 2,729
With persons over 65 . . . 1,157
Family households . . . 4,944
Single person households . . . 841
Persons per household . . . 3.15
Persons per family . . . 3.43

Household Population, 2008§§

Persons living in households . . . 22,632
Persons living in group quarters . . . 4,623
Persons per household . . . 3.2

Labor & Employment

Total civilian labor force, 2008§§ . . . 13,800
Unemployment rate, 2008 . . . 6.9%
Total civilian labor force, 2000 . . . 9,805

Employed persons 16 years and over by occupation, 2000

Managers & professionals . . . 2,796
Service occupations . . . 1,268
Sales & office occupations . . . 2,435
Farming, fishing & forestry . . . 97
Construction & maintenance . . . 1,310
Production & transportation . . . 1,296
Self-employed persons . . . 998

* US Census Bureau
** 2000 Decennial Census
§ California Department of Finance
§§ California Employment Development Dept

General Information

City of Norco
2870 Clark Ave
Norco, CA 92860
951-735-3900

Website . . . www.ci.norco.ca.us
Elevation . . . 680 ft.
Land Area (sq. miles) . . . 14.1
Water Area (sq. miles) . . . 0.3
Year of Incorporation . . . 1964
Government type . . . Chartered
Sales tax rate . . . 8.75%

Voters & Officials

Registered Voters, October 2008

Total . . . 11,778
Democrats . . . 3,265
Republicans . . . 6,096
Declined to state . . . 1,897

Legislative Districts

US Congressional . . . 44
State Senatorial . . . 37
State Assembly . . . 71

Local Officials, 2009

Mayor . . . Kathy Azevedo
City Manager . . . Jeff Allred
City Clerk . . . Brenda Jacobs
Attorney . . . John Harper
Finance Dir . . . Andy Okoro
Public Works . . . Bill Thompson
Planning Dir . . . Steve King
Building . . . NA
Police Chief . . . Ross Cooper
Emergency/Fire Dir . . . Jack Frye

Public Safety

Number of officers, 2007 . . . NA
Violent crimes, 2007 . . . 95
Property crimes, 2007 . . . 942
Arson, 2007 . . . 3

Public Library

Norco Branch Library
Riverside County Library Service
3954 Old Hammer Rd
Norco, CA 91760
951-735-5329

Branch Librarian . . . Debra Langguth

Library system statistics, FY 2007

Population served . . . 1,047,996
Internet terminals . . . 37
Annual users . . . 69,346

Per capita:

Operating income . . . $19.38
percent from local government . . . 49.8%
Operating expenditure . . . $20.45
Total materials . . . 1.43
Print holdings . . . 1.30
Visits per capita . . . 4.06

Housing & Construction

Housing Units

Total, 2008§ . . . 7,222
Single family units, attached . . . 137
Single family units, detached . . . 6,807
Multiple family units . . . 186
Mobile home units . . . 92
Occupied . . . 7,059
Vacancy rate . . . 2.3%
Median rent, 2000** . . . $867
Median SF home value, 2000** . . . $207,400

New Privately Owned Housing Units Authorized by Building Permit, 2007*

	Units	Construction Cost
Single	4	$1,131,525
Total	4	$1,131,525

Municipal Finance

(For local fiscal year ended in 2006)

Revenues

Total . . . $39,308,336
Taxes . . . 11,449,047
Special benefits assessment . . . 648,033
Licenses & permits . . . 578,036
Fines & forfeitures . . . 340,650
Revenues from use of money & property . . . 1,653,507
Intergovernmental . . . 2,620,519
Service charges . . . 14,973,297
Other revenues . . . 7,045,247
Other financing sources . . . 0

Expenditures

Total . . . $40,490,094
General government . . . 941,388
Public safety . . . 10,901,784
Transportation . . . 3,680,647
Community development . . . 2,527,154
Health . . . 9,035,896
Culture & leisure . . . 3,396,932
Other . . . 0

Local School District

(Data from School year 2007-08 except as noted)

Corona-Norco Unified
2820 Clark Ave
Norco, CA 92860
(951) 736-5000

Superintendent . . . Kent Bechler
Grade plan . . . K-12
Number of schools . . . 50
Enrollment . . . 51,322
High school graduates, 2006-07 . . . 2,991
Dropout rate . . . 2.8%
Pupil/teacher ratio . . . 21.5
Average class size . . . 26.9
Students per computer . . . 5.3
Classrooms with internet . . . 2,277
Avg. Daily Attendance (ADA) . . . 49,812
Cost per ADA . . . $7,597
Avg. Teacher Salary . . . $74,860

California Achievement Tests 6th ed., 2008

(Pct scoring at or above 50th National Percentile Rank)

	Math	Reading	Language
Grade 3	61%	42%	50%
Grade 7	57%	52%	50%

Academic Performance Index, 2008

Number of students tested . . . 39,882
Number of valid scores . . . 37,055
2007 API (base) . . . 762
2008 API (growth) . . . 773

SAT Testing, 2006-07

Enrollment, Grade 12 . . . 3,657
Number taking test . . . 1,268
percent taking test . . . 34.7%
percent with total score 1,500+ . . . 13.60%

Average Scores:

Math	Verbal	Writing	Total
486	472	471	1,429

Federal No Child Left Behind, 2008

(Adequate Yearly Progress standards met)

	Participation Rate	Pct Proficient
ELA	Yes	Yes
Math	Yes	No

API criteria . . . Yes
Graduation rate . . . Yes
\# criteria met/possible . . . 42/41

Other school districts for this city

(see Appendix E for information on these districts)

None

See Introduction for an explanation of all data sources.

Demographics & Socio-Economic Characteristics†

(2007 American Community Survey, except as noted)

Population

1990* 94,279
2007 112,001
  Male 56,563
  Female 55,438
Jan. 2008 (estimate)§ 109,695
  Persons per sq. mi. of land 11,308.8

Race & Hispanic Origin, 2007

Race
  White 66,791
  Black/African American 5,935
  North American Native 1,060
  Asian 17,045
  Pacific Islander 0
  Other Race 18,429
  Two or more races 2,741
Hispanic origin, total 75,377
  Mexican 60,247
  Puerto Rican 401
  Cuban 971
  Other Hispanic 13,758

Age & Nativity, 2007

Under 5 years 6,742
18 years and over 82,582
65 years and over 10,009
85 years and over 1,123
  Median Age 34.7
Native-born 68,595
Foreign-born 43,406

Educational Attainment, 2007

Population 25 years and over 69,341
Less than 9th grade 14.8%
High school grad or higher 69.3%
Bachelor's degree or higher 14.9%
Graduate degree 3.9%

Income & Poverty, 2007

Per capita income $17,007
Median household income $55,209
Median family income $59,688
Persons in poverty 9.1%
H'holds receiving public assistance 1,164
H'holds receiving social security 6,984

Households, 2007

Total households 28,265
  With persons under 18 14,476
  With persons over 65 6,478
  Family households 23,191
  Single person households 4,424
Persons per household 3.82
Persons per family 4.29

Household Population, 2008§§

Persons living in households 107,848
Persons living in group quarters 1,847
Persons per household 4.0

Labor & Employment

Total civilian labor force, 2008§§ 49,800
  Unemployment rate, 2008 .... 8.0%
Total civilian labor force, 2000* 42,782

Employed persons 16 years and over by occupation, 2007

  Managers & professionals 11,320
  Service occupations 8,595
  Sales & office occupations 16,044
  Farming, fishing & forestry 0
  Construction & maintenance 5,414
  Production & transportation 6,583
  Self-employed persons 2,073

† see Appendix D for 2000 Decennial Census Data
* US Census Bureau
** 2007 American Community Survey
§ California Department of Finance
§§ California Employment Development Dept

General Information

City of Norwalk
12700 Norwalk Blvd
Norwalk, CA 90650
562-929-5700

Website .... www.ci.norwalk.ca.us
Elevation .... 93 ft.
Land Area (sq. miles) 9.7
Water Area (sq. miles) 0.1
Year of Incorporation 1957
Government type .... General law
Sales tax rate 9.25%

Voters & Officials

Registered Voters, October 2008

Total 41,457
  Democrats 23,373
  Republicans 8,863
  Declined to state 7,655

Legislative Districts

US Congressional 38
State Senatorial 30
State Assembly 56

Local Officials, 2009

Mayor .... Mike Mendez
Manager .... Ernie Garcia
City Clerk .... Theresa Devoy
Attorney .... Steven Dorsey
Finance Dir .... (vacant)
Public Works .... Gary DiCorpo
Planning/Dev Dir .... Kurt Anderson
Building .... Anthony Weimholt
Police Chief .... Pat Maxwell
Fire/Emergency Mgmt .... NA

Public Safety

Number of officers, 2007 .... NA
Violent crimes, 2007 607
Property crimes, 2007 2,631
Arson, 2007 26

Public Library

Norwalk Library
Los Angeles County Public Library System
12350 Imperial Hwy
Norwalk, CA 90650
562-868-0775

Branch Librarian .... Joseph Zagami

Library system statistics, FY 2007

Population served 3,673,313
Internet terminals 749
  Annual users 3,748,771

Per capita:

Operating income $30.06
  percent from local government 93.6%
Operating expenditure $28.36
Total materials 2.22
Print holdings 1.97
Visits per capita 3.25

Housing & Construction

Housing Units

Total, 2008§ 27,814
  Single family units, attached 1,430
  Single family units, detached 20,173
  Multiple family units 5,738
  Mobile home units 473
  Occupied 27,142
  Vacancy rate 2.4%
Median rent, 2007** $1,121
Median SF home value, 2007** $486,900

New Privately Owned Housing Units Authorized by Building Permit, 2007*

	Units	Construction Cost
Single	1	$296,409
Total	1	$296,409

Municipal Finance

(For local fiscal year ended in 2006)

Revenues

Total $77,918,762
Taxes 35,848,469
Special benefits assessment 0
Licenses & permits 922,393
Fines & forfeitures 1,914,983
Revenues from use of
  money & property 1,397,036
Intergovernmental 19,376,551
Service charges 10,716,792
Other revenues 7,742,538
Other financing sources 0

Expenditures

Total $73,009,055
General government 12,756,241
Public safety 12,825,674
Transportation 20,907,277
Community development 10,765,734
Health 4,582,092
Culture & leisure 7,174,315
Other 0

Local School District

(Data from School year 2007-08 except as noted)

Norwalk-La Mirada Unified
12820 Pioneer Blvd
Norwalk, CA 90650
(562) 868-0431

Superintendent .... Ginger Shattuck
Grade plan K-12
Number of schools 29
Enrollment 22,092
High school graduates, 2006-07 1,386
Dropout rate 3.7%
Pupil/teacher ratio 23.8
Average class size 28.7
Students per computer 2.6
Classrooms with internet 939
Avg. Daily Attendance (ADA) 21,245
  Cost per ADA $8,086
Avg. Teacher Salary $68,396

California Achievement Tests 6th ed., 2008

(Pct scoring at or above 50th National Percentile Rank)

	Math	Reading	Language
Grade 3	53%	34%	46%
Grade 7	46%	44%	44%

Academic Performance Index, 2008

Number of students tested 16,844
Number of valid scores 16,023
2007 API (base) 695
2008 API (growth) 715

SAT Testing, 2006-07

Enrollment, Grade 12 1,622
Number taking test 524
  percent taking test 32.3%
  percent with total score 1,500+ 9.00%

Average Scores:

Math	Verbal	Writing	Total
461	449	448	1,358

Federal No Child Left Behind, 2008

(Adequate Yearly Progress standards met)

	Participation Rate	Pct Proficient
ELA	Yes	No
Math	Yes	No

API criteria .... Yes
Graduation rate .... Yes
criteria met/possible 38/34

Other school districts for this city

(see Appendix E for information on these districts)

Little Lake City Elem

See Introduction for an explanation of all data sources.

Demographics & Socio-Economic Characteristics

(2000 Decennial Census, except as noted)

Population

1990* . . . 47,585
2000 . . . 47,630
Male . . . 23,033
Female . . . 24,597
Jan. 2008 (estimate)§ . . . 52,737
Persons per sq. mi. of land . . . 1,903.9

Race & Hispanic Origin, 2000

Race
White . . . 39,414
Black/African American . . . 948
North American Native . . . 246
Asian . . . 2,479
Pacific Islander . . . 82
Other Race . . . 2,587
Two or more races . . . 1,874
Hispanic origin, total . . . 6,229
Mexican . . . 3,620
Puerto Rican . . . 112
Cuban . . . 43
Other Hispanic . . . 2,454

Age & Nativity, 2000

Under 5 years . . . 2,802
18 years and over . . . 36,633
65 years and over . . . 6,194
85 years and over . . . 860
Median Age . . . 39.6
Native-born . . . 39,597
Foreign-born . . . 8,198

Educational Attainment, 2000

Population 25 years and over . . . 33,603
Less than 9th grade . . . 3.8%
High school grad or higher . . . 90.5%
Bachelor's degree or higher . . . 37.0%
Graduate degree . . . 12.2%

Income & Poverty, 1999

Per capita income . . . $32,402
Median household income . . . $63,453
Median family income . . . $74,434
Persons in poverty . . . 5.5%
H'holds receiving public assistance . . . 382
H'holds receiving social security . . . 4,364

Households, 2000

Total households . . . 18,524
With persons under 18 . . . 6,285
With persons over 65 . . . 4,251
Family households . . . 12,419
Single person households . . . 4,661
Persons per household . . . 2.52
Persons per family . . . 3.01

Household Population, 2008§§

Persons living in households . . . 51,867
Persons living in group quarters . . . 870
Persons per household . . . 2.5

Labor & Employment

Total civilian labor force, 2008§§ . . . 26,900
Unemployment rate, 2008 . . . 5.4%
Total civilian labor force, 2000 . . . 25,800

Employed persons 16 years and over by occupation, 2000

Managers & professionals . . . 10,800
Service occupations . . . 3,553
Sales & office occupations . . . 6,985
Farming, fishing & forestry . . . 14
Construction & maintenance . . . 1,919
Production & transportation . . . 1,602
Self-employed persons . . . 2,783

* US Census Bureau
** 2000 Decennial Census
§ California Department of Finance
§§ California Employment Development Dept

General Information

City of Novato
75 Rowland Way
#200
Novato, CA 94945
415-899-8900

Website . . . www.ci.novato.ca.us
Elevation . . . 18 ft.
Land Area (sq. miles) . . . 27.7
Water Area (sq. miles) . . . 0.6
Year of Incorporation . . . 1960
Government type . . . General law
Sales tax rate . . . 9.00%

Voters & Officials

Registered Voters, October 2008

Total . . . 29,439
Democrats . . . 14,565
Republicans . . . 7,487
Declined to state . . . 6,223

Legislative Districts

US Congressional . . . 6
State Senatorial . . . 3
State Assembly . . . 6

Local Officials, 2009

Mayor . . . Jim Leland
Manager . . . Patricia E. Thompson (Int)
City Clerk . . . Shirley Gremmels
Attorney . . . Jeffrey Walter
Finance Dir . . . Mary Neilan
Public Works . . . Glenn Young
Planning/Dev Dir . . . Dave Wallace
Building . . . Ron Averiette
Police Chief . . . Joseph Kreins
Emergency/Fire Dir . . . Marc Revere

Public Safety

Number of officers, 2007 . . . 57
Violent crimes, 2007 . . . 157
Property crimes, 2007 . . . 1,192
Arson, 2007 . . . NA

Public Library

Novato Regional Library
Marin County Free Library System
1720 Novato Blvd
Novato, CA 94947
415-897-1141

Branch Librarian . . . Donna Mettier

Library system statistics, FY 2007

Population served . . . 140,989
Internet terminals . . . 95
Annual users . . . 198,739

Per capita:

Operating income . . . $77.23
percent from local government . . . 90.0%
Operating expenditure . . . $77.23
Total materials . . . 3.56
Print holdings . . . 3.12
Visits per capita . . . 7.73

Housing & Construction

Housing Units

Total, 2008§ . . . 20,905
Single family units, attached . . . 2,673
Single family units, detached . . . 12,196
Multiple family units . . . 5,318
Mobile home units . . . 718
Occupied . . . 20,389
Vacancy rate . . . 2.5%
Median rent, 2000** . . . $1,146
Median SF home value, 2000** . . . $381,400

New Privately Owned Housing Units Authorized by Building Permit, 2007*

	Units	Construction Cost
Single	159	$48,932,553
Total	311	$64,158,777

Municipal Finance

(For local fiscal year ended in 2006)

Revenues

Total . . . $62,664,318
Taxes . . . 23,028,009
Special benefits assessment . . . 5,416,656
Licenses & permits . . . 1,131,392
Fines & forfeitures . . . 596,565
Revenues from use of money & property . . . 1,576,152
Intergovernmental . . . 3,211,787
Service charges . . . 8,882,785
Other revenues . . . 524,906
Other financing sources . . . 18,296,066

Expenditures

Total . . . $39,994,566
General government . . . 5,831,423
Public safety . . . 11,793,295
Transportation . . . 9,475,427
Community development . . . 6,495,082
Health . . . 0
Culture & leisure . . . 6,399,339
Other . . . 0

Local School District

(Data from School year 2007-08 except as noted)

Novato Unified
1015 Seventh St
Novato, CA 94945
(415) 897-4201

Superintendent . . . Jan La Torre-Derby
Grade plan . . . K-12
Number of schools . . . 18
Enrollment . . . 7,891
High school graduates, 2006-07 . . . 592
Dropout rate . . . 1.8%
Pupil/teacher ratio . . . 19.6
Average class size . . . 23.2
Students per computer . . . 5.0
Classrooms with internet . . . 404
Avg. Daily Attendance (ADA) . . . 7,468
Cost per ADA . . . $8,003
Avg. Teacher Salary . . . $57,695

California Achievement Tests 6th ed., 2008

(Pct scoring at or above 50th National Percentile Rank)

	Math	Reading	Language
Grade 3	68%	56%	63%
Grade 7	71%	69%	66%

Academic Performance Index, 2008

Number of students tested . . . 5,805
Number of valid scores . . . 5,579
2007 API (base) . . . 815
2008 API (growth) . . . 817

SAT Testing, 2006-07

Enrollment, Grade 12 . . . 629
Number taking test . . . 349
percent taking test . . . 55.5%
percent with total score 1,500+ . . . 35.10%

Average Scores:

Math	Verbal	Writing	Total
539	532	530	1,601

Federal No Child Left Behind, 2008

(Adequate Yearly Progress standards met)

	Participation Rate	Pct Proficient
ELA	Yes	No
Math	Yes	Yes

API criteria . . . Yes
Graduation rate . . . Yes
criteria met/possible . . . 34/33

Other school districts for this city

(see Appendix E for information on these districts)

None

See Introduction for an explanation of all data sources.

Demographics & Socio-Economic Characteristics

(2000 Decennial Census, except as noted)

Population

1990* 11,961
2000 15,503
Male 7,431
Female 8,072
Jan. 2008 (estimate)§ 19,337
Persons per sq. mi. of land 3,867.4

Race & Hispanic Origin, 2000

Race
White 12,995
Black/African American 74
North American Native 169
Asian 183
Pacific Islander 18
Other Race 1,437
Two or more races 627
Hispanic origin, total 3,109
Mexican 2,521
Puerto Rican 47
Cuban 5
Other Hispanic 536

Age & Nativity, 2000

Under 5 years 1,159
18 years and over 11,015
65 years and over 1,982
85 years and over 299
Median Age 34.5
Native-born 14,095
Foreign-born 1,555

Educational Attainment, 2000

Population 25 years and over 9,875
Less than 9th grade 8.7%
High school grad or higher 74.9%
Bachelor's degree or higher 10.2%
Graduate degree 3.2%

Income & Poverty, 1999

Per capita income $17,019
Median household income $39,338
Median family income $44,024
Persons in poverty 11.3%
H'holds receiving public assistance 300
H'holds receiving social security 1,663

Households, 2000

Total households 5,610
With persons under 18 2,367
With persons over 65 1,380
Family households 4,052
Single person households 1,283
Persons per household 2.73
Persons per family 3.20

Household Population, 2008§§

Persons living in households 19,158
Persons living in group quarters 179
Persons per household 2.7

Labor & Employment

Total civilian labor force, 2008§§ 8,700
Unemployment rate, 2008 . . . . . 9.8%
Total civilian labor force, 2000 7,330

Employed persons 16 years and over by occupation, 2000

Managers & professionals 1,647
Service occupations 1,134
Sales & office occupations 1,611
Farming, fishing & forestry 140
Construction & maintenance 831
Production & transportation 1,214
Self-employed persons 416

* US Census Bureau
** 2000 Decennial Census
§ California Department of Finance
§§ California Employment Development Dept

General Information

City of Oakdale
280 N Third Ave
Oakdale, CA 95361
209-845-3571

Website . . . . . www.ci.oakdale.ca.us
Elevation . . . . . 155 ft.
Land Area (sq. miles) 5.0
Water Area (sq. miles) 0
Year of Incorporation 1906
Government type . . . . . General law
Sales tax rate 8.38%

Voters & Officials

Registered Voters, October 2008

Total 9,114
Democrats 3,158
Republicans 4,009
Declined to state 1,467

Legislative Districts

US Congressional 19
State Senatorial 14
State Assembly 25

Local Officials, 2009

Mayor . . . . . Farrell Jackson
Manager . . . . . Steven Hallam
City Clerk . . . . . Nancy Lilly
Attorney . . . . . Tom Hallinan
Finance Dir . . . . . Albert Avila
Public Works . . . . . David Meyers
Planning/Dev Dir . . . . . Danelle Stylos
Building . . . . . NA
Police Chief . . . . . Marten West
Fire Chief . . . . . Michael Botto

Public Safety

Number of officers, 2007 27
Violent crimes, 2007 49
Property crimes, 2007 1,041
Arson, 2007 8

Public Library

Oakdale Library
Stanislaus County Free Library
151 S First Ave
Oakdale, CA 95361
209-847-4204

Branch Librarian . . . . . Jim Griffin

Library system statistics, FY 2007

Population served 521,497
Internet terminals 128
Annual users 256,298

Per capita:

Operating income $20.76
percent from local government 91.0%
Operating expenditure $20.19
Total materials 1.66
Print holdings 1.56
Visits per capita . . . . . NA

Housing & Construction

Housing Units

Total, 2008§ 7,227
Single family units, attached 256
Single family units, detached 5,520
Multiple family units 1,208
Mobile home units 243
Occupied 6,985
Vacancy rate 3.4%
Median rent, 2000** $579
Median SF home value, 2000** $125,300

New Privately Owned Housing Units Authorized by Building Permit, 2007*

	Units	Construction Cost
Single	211	$20,803,540
Total	213	$20,959,413

Municipal Finance

(For local fiscal year ended in 2006)

Revenues

Total $19,998,808
Taxes 10,708,690
Special benefits assessment 580,672
Licenses & permits 842,712
Fines & forfeitures 177,310
Revenues from use of money & property 1,233,282
Intergovernmental 1,192,181
Service charges 5,026,067
Other revenues 237,894
Other financing sources 0

Expenditures

Total $22,377,556
General government 941,644
Public safety 9,999,676
Transportation 4,570,221
Community development 1,183,700
Health 1,956,302
Culture & leisure 1,606,498
Other 0

Local School District

(Data from School year 2007-08 except as noted)

Oakdale Joint Unified
168 South Third Ave
Oakdale, CA 95361
(209) 848-4884

Superintendent . . . . . Fred Rich
Grade plan K-12
Number of schools 9
Enrollment 5,234
High school graduates, 2006-07 370
Dropout rate 3.5%
Pupil/teacher ratio 21.8
Average class size 25.7
Students per computer 3.8
Classrooms with internet 0
Avg. Daily Attendance (ADA) 4,942
Cost per ADA $8,078
Avg. Teacher Salary $65,423

California Achievement Tests 6th ed., 2008

(Pct scoring at or above 50th National Percentile Rank)

	Math	Reading	Language
Grade 3	59%	41%	49%
Grade 7	58%	66%	57%

Academic Performance Index, 2008

Number of students tested 4,086
Number of valid scores 3,798
2007 API (base) 757
2008 API (growth) 777

SAT Testing, 2006-07

Enrollment, Grade 12 443
Number taking test 131
percent taking test 29.6%
percent with total score 1,500+ 15.10%

Average Scores:

Math	Verbal	Writing	Total
520	504	496	1,520

Federal No Child Left Behind, 2008

(Adequate Yearly Progress standards met)

	Participation Rate	Pct Proficient
ELA	Yes	Yes
Math	Yes	Yes

API criteria . . . . . Yes
Graduation rate . . . . . Yes
\# criteria met/possible 26/26

Other school districts for this city

(see Appendix E for information on these districts)

None

See Introduction for an explanation of all data sources.

Demographics & Socio-Economic Characteristics†

(2007 American Community Survey, except as noted)

Population

1990* 372,242
2007 358,829
Male 174,113
Female 184,716
Jan. 2008 (estimate)§ 420,183
Persons per sq. mi. of land 7,489.9

Race & Hispanic Origin, 2007

Race
White 142,540
Black/African American 113,292
North American Native 1,288
Asian 49,908
Pacific Islander 1,326
Other Race 38,591
Two or more races 11,884
Hispanic origin, total 87,199
Mexican 62,789
Puerto Rican 2,138
Cuban 623
Other Hispanic 21,649

Age & Nativity, 2007

Under 5 years 25,812
18 years and over 278,866
65 years and over 40,711
85 years and over 5,406
Median Age 37.1
Native-born 260,604
Foreign-born 98,225

Educational Attainment, 2007

Population 25 years and over 248,622
Less than 9th grade 11.4%
High school grad or higher 79.0%
Bachelor's degree or higher 35.0%
Graduate degree 15.5%

Income & Poverty, 2007

Per capita income $30,123
Median household income $46,475
Median family income $52,020
Persons in poverty 17.6%
H'holds receiving public assistance 6,368
H'holds receiving social security 30,634

Households, 2007

Total households 147,683
With persons under 18 40,425
With persons over 65 30,460
Family households 76,325
Single person households 57,147
Persons per household 2.40
Persons per family 3.30

Household Population, 2008§§

Persons living in households 412,926
Persons living in group quarters 7,257
Persons per household 2.6

Labor & Employment

Total civilian labor force, 2008§§ 200,300
Unemployment rate, 2008 .... 9.5%
Total civilian labor force, 2000* 190,666

Employed persons 16 years and over by occupation, 2007

Managers & professionals 66,015
Service occupations 29,733
Sales & office occupations 39,178
Farming, fishing & forestry 147
Construction & maintenance 15,107
Production & transportation 17,835
Self-employed persons 18,047

† see Appendix D for 2000 Decennial Census Data
* US Census Bureau
** 2007 American Community Survey
§ California Department of Finance
§§ California Employment Development Dept

General Information

City of Oakland
1 Frank Ogawa Plaza
Oakland, CA 94612
510-238-3301

Website .... www.oaklandnet.com
Elevation .... 42 ft.
Land Area (sq. miles) 56.1
Water Area (sq. miles) 22.1
Year of Incorporation 1852
Government type .... Chartered
Sales tax rate 9.75%

Voters & Officials

Registered Voters, October 2008

Total 219,102
Democrats 149,703
Republicans 13,302
Declined to state 44,692

Legislative Districts

US Congressional 9, 13
State Senatorial 9
State Assembly 14, 16, 18

Local Officials, 2009

Mayor .... Ronald V. Dellums
Manager .... Dan Lindheim
City Clerk .... LaTonda Simmons
Attorney .... John Russo
Finance Dir .... William Noland
Public Works .... Raul Godinez
Planning/Dev Dir .... NA
Building .... NA
Police Chief .... Wayne Tucker
Fire Chief .... Gerald A. Simon (Int)

Public Safety

Number of officers, 2007 722
Violent crimes, 2007 7,605
Property crimes, 2007 23,664
Arson, 2007 287

Public Library

Main Library
Oakland Public Library System
125 14th St
Oakland, CA 94612
510-238-6611

Director .... Carmen Martinez

Library system statistics, FY 2007

Population served 435,710
Internet terminals 160
Annual users 370,694

Per capita:

Operating income $56.66
percent from local government 95.9%
Operating expenditure $56.66
Total materials 4.50
Print holdings 4.27
Visits per capita 7.10

Housing & Construction

Housing Units

Total, 2008§ 164,053
Single family units, attached 6,775
Single family units, detached 72,659
Multiple family units 84,163
Mobile home units 456
Occupied 157,055
Vacancy rate 4.3%
Median rent, 2007** $926
Median SF home value, 2007** $595,000

New Privately Owned Housing Units Authorized by Building Permit, 2007*

	Units	Construction Cost
Single	265	$79,637,401
Total	981	$204,694,648

Municipal Finance

(For local fiscal year ended in 2006)

Revenues

Total $1,101,262,247
Taxes 438,061,561
Special benefits assessment 18,092,572
Licenses & permits 17,191,014
Fines & forfeitures 24,039,814
Revenues from use of money & property 31,174,122
Intergovernmental 160,258,131
Service charges 370,637,727
Other revenues 20,603,753
Other financing sources 21,203,553

Expenditures

Total $1,207,568,943
General government 212,866,096
Public safety 297,498,300
Transportation 462,422,857
Community development 78,524,506
Health 66,172,748
Culture & leisure 70,510,656
Other 0

Local School District

(Data from School year 2007-08 except as noted)

Oakland Unified
1025 Second Ave
Oakland, CA 94606
(510) 879-8582

Superintendent .... Vincent Matthews
Grade plan K-12
Number of schools 153
Enrollment 46,431
High school graduates, 2006-07 2,185
Dropout rate 10.5%
Pupil/teacher ratio 17.7
Average class size 21.6
Students per computer 5.8
Classrooms with internet 2,090
Avg. Daily Attendance (ADA) 36,750
Cost per ADA $11,466
Avg. Teacher Salary $54,158

California Achievement Tests 6th ed., 2008

(Pct scoring at or above 50th National Percentile Rank)

	Math	Reading	Language
Grade 3	45%	27%	38%
Grade 7	32%	29%	30%

Academic Performance Index, 2008

Number of students tested 29,083
Number of valid scores 26,249
2007 API (base) 658
2008 API (growth) 674

SAT Testing, 2006-07

Enrollment, Grade 12 2,664
Number taking test 1,232
percent taking test 46.3%
percent with total score 1,500+ 9.70%

Average Scores:

Math	Verbal	Writing	Total
438	414	413	1,265

Federal No Child Left Behind, 2008

(Adequate Yearly Progress standards met)

	Participation Rate	Pct Proficient
ELA	No	No
Math	No	No

API criteria .... Yes
Graduation rate .... Yes
\# criteria met/possible 44/33

Other school districts for this city

(see Appendix E for information on these districts)

None

See Introduction for an explanation of all data sources.

Demographics & Socio-Economic Characteristics

(2000 Decennial Census, except as noted)

Population

1990* .... NA
2000 25,619
Male 12,943
Female 12,676
Jan. 2008 (estimate)§ 33,210
Persons per sq. mi. of land 2,678.2

Race & Hispanic Origin, 2000

Race
White 19,342
Black/African American 876
North American Native 227
Asian 733
Pacific Islander 75
Other Race 2,711
Two or more races 1,655
Hispanic origin, total 6,399
Mexican 4,753
Puerto Rican 226
Cuban 27
Other Hispanic 1,393

Age & Nativity, 2000

Under 5 years 2,177
18 years and over 16,780
65 years and over 1,378
85 years and over 107
Median Age 31.5
Native-born 23,008
Foreign-born 2,457

Educational Attainment, 2000

Population 25 years and over 14,827
Less than 9th grade 4.7%
High school grad or higher 84.8%
Bachelor's degree or higher 13.7%
Graduate degree 3.1%

Income & Poverty, 1999

Per capita income $21,895
Median household income $65,589
Median family income $68,888
Persons in poverty 4.9%
H'holds receiving public assistance 150
H'holds receiving social security 1,289

Households, 2000

Total households 7,832
With persons under 18 4,415
With persons over 65 1,035
Family households 6,464
Single person households 1,017
Persons per household 3.26
Persons per family 3.56

Household Population, 2008§§

Persons living in households 33,143
Persons living in group quarters 67
Persons per household 3.2

Labor & Employment

Total civilian labor force, 2008§§ 14,000
Unemployment rate, 2008 .... 4.4%
Total civilian labor force, 2000 .... NA

Employed persons 16 years and over by occupation, 2000

Managers & professionals 3,060
Service occupations 1,928
Sales & office occupations 3,623
Farming, fishing & forestry 51
Construction & maintenance 1,902
Production & transportation 1,562
Self-employed persons 767

* US Census Bureau
** 2000 Decennial Census
§ California Department of Finance
§§ California Employment Development Dept

General Information

City of Oakley
3231 Main St
Oakley, CA 94561
925-625-7000

Website .... www.ci.oakley.ca.us
Elevation .... NA
Land Area (sq. miles) 12.4
Water Area (sq. miles) 0.1
Year of Incorporation 1999
Government type .... General Law
Sales tax rate 9.25%

Voters & Officials

Registered Voters, October 2008

Total 13,821
Democrats 6,938
Republicans 3,709
Declined to state 2,582

Legislative Districts

US Congressional 10
State Senatorial 7
State Assembly 11, 15

Local Officials, 2009

Mayor .... Carol Rios
Manager .... Bryan Montgomery
City Clerk .... Nancy Ortenblad
Attorney .... Alison Barratt-Green
Finance Dir .... Paul Abelson
Public Works .... Jason Vogan
Planning/Dev Dir .... Rebecca Willis
Building .... Brent Smith
Police Chief .... Chris Thorsen
Emergency/Fire Dir .... NA

Public Safety

Number of officers, 2007 .... NA
Violent crimes, 2007 117
Property crimes, 2007 738
Arson, 2007 10

Public Library

Oakley Library
Contra Costa County Library System
1050 Neroly Rd
Oakley, CA 94561
925-625-2400

Branch Librarian .... Jenny Wu

Library system statistics, FY 2007

Population served 938,513
Internet terminals 324
Annual users 670,618

Per capita:

Operating income $27.05
percent from local government 82.0%
Operating expenditure $27.82
Total materials 1.57
Print holdings 1.41
Visits per capita 3.65

Housing & Construction

Housing Units

Total, 2008§ 10,476
Single family units, attached 84
Single family units, detached 9,727
Multiple family units 244
Mobile home units 421
Occupied 10,322
Vacancy rate 1.5%
Median rent, 2000** $944
Median SF home value, 2000** $187,400

New Privately Owned Housing Units Authorized by Building Permit, 2007*

	Units	Construction Cost
Single	277	$94,421,082
Total	539	$119,883,304

Municipal Finance

(For local fiscal year ended in 2006)

Revenues

Total $30,584,442
Taxes 14,562,583
Special benefits assessment 2,396,545
Licenses & permits 3,000,421
Fines & forfeitures 64,981
Revenues from use of money & property 1,327,432
Intergovernmental 2,131,399
Service charges 6,945,525
Other revenues 155,556
Other financing sources 0

Expenditures

Total $24,448,615
General government 1,592,048
Public safety 5,443,705
Transportation 2,746,724
Community development 13,802,736
Health 0
Culture & leisure 863,402
Other 0

Local School District

(Data from School year 2007-08 except as noted)

Liberty Union High
20 Oak St
Brentwood, CA 94513
(925) 634-2166

Superintendent .... Daniel Smith
Grade plan 9-12
Number of schools 5
Enrollment 6,795
High school graduates, 2006-07 1,114
Dropout rate 2.3%
Pupil/teacher ratio 23.2
Average class size 27.5
Students per computer 4.1
Classrooms with internet 295
Avg. Daily Attendance (ADA) 6,323
Cost per ADA $8,026
Avg. Teacher Salary $64,026

California Achievement Tests 6th ed., 2008

(Pct scoring at or above 50th National Percentile Rank)

	Math	Reading	Language
Grade 3	NA	NA	NA
Grade 7	NA	NA	NA

Academic Performance Index, 2008

Number of students tested 4,929
Number of valid scores 4,710
2007 API (base) 690
2008 API (growth) 723

SAT Testing, 2006-07

Enrollment, Grade 12 1,519
Number taking test 457
percent taking test 30.1%
percent with total score 1,500+ 12.20%

Average Scores:

Math	Verbal	Writing	Total
491	482	475	1,448

Federal No Child Left Behind, 2008

(Adequate Yearly Progress standards met)

	Participation Rate	Pct Proficient
ELA	Yes	No
Math	Yes	No

API criteria .... Yes
Graduation rate .... Yes
\# criteria met/possible 30/24

Other school districts for this city

(see Appendix E for information on these districts)

Oakley Union Elem

See Introduction for an explanation of all data sources.

Demographics & Socio-Economic Characteristics†

(2007 American Community Survey, except as noted)

Population

1990* . . . 128,398
2007 . . . 168,814
Male . . . 81,438
Female . . . 87,376
Jan. 2008 (estimate)§ . . . 178,806
Persons per sq. mi. of land . . . 4,404.1

Race & Hispanic Origin, 2007

Race
White . . . 108,078
Black/African American . . . 9,121
North American Native . . . 1,031
Asian . . . 13,730
Pacific Islander . . . 678
Other Race . . . 28,291
Two or more races . . . 7,885
Hispanic origin, total . . . 57,439
Mexican . . . 50,401
Puerto Rican . . . 1,117
Cuban . . . 783
Other Hispanic . . . 5,138

Age & Nativity, 2007

Under 5 years . . . 13,799
18 years and over . . . 128,151
65 years and over . . . 23,448
85 years and over . . . 2,918
Median Age . . . 36.0
Native-born . . . 131,233
Foreign-born . . . 37,581

Educational Attainment, 2007

Population 25 years and over . . . 109,886
Less than 9th grade . . . 9.5%
High school grad or higher . . . 82.1%
Bachelor's degree or higher . . . 26.6%
Graduate degree . . . 8.7%

Income & Poverty, 2007

Per capita income . . . $27,759
Median household income . . . $64,992
Median family income . . . $74,304
Persons in poverty . . . 7.8%
H'holds receiving public assistance . . . 2,104
H'holds receiving social security . . . 18,119

Households, 2007

Total households . . . 59,452
With persons under 18 . . . 19,713
With persons over 65 . . . 16,781
Family households . . . 40,673
Single person households . . . 13,873
Persons per household . . . 2.82
Persons per family . . . 3.36

Household Population, 2008§§

Persons living in households . . . 177,526
Persons living in group quarters . . . 1,280
Persons per household . . . 2.9

Labor & Employment

Total civilian labor force, 2008§§ . . . 86,000
Unemployment rate, 2008 . . . 5.7%
Total civilian labor force, 2000* . . . 72,201

Employed persons 16 years and over by occupation, 2007

Managers & professionals . . . 23,574
Service occupations . . . 15,482
Sales & office occupations . . . 22,140
Farming, fishing & forestry . . . 269
Construction & maintenance . . . 7,529
Production & transportation . . . 9,642
Self-employed persons . . . 6,526

† see Appendix D for 2000 Decennial Census Data
* US Census Bureau
** 2007 American Community Survey
§ California Department of Finance
§§ California Employment Development Dept

General Information

City of Oceanside
300 N Coast Hwy
Oceanside, CA 92054
760-435-3000

Website . . . www.ci.oceanside.ca.us
Elevation . . . 47 ft.
Land Area (sq. miles) . . . 40.6
Water Area (sq. miles) . . . 1.0
Year of Incorporation . . . 1888
Government type . . . General law
Sales tax rate . . . 8.75%

Voters & Officials

Registered Voters, October 2008

Total . . . 73,934
Democrats . . . 24,458
Republicans . . . 29,443
Declined to state . . . 16,555

Legislative Districts

US Congressional . . . 49
State Senatorial . . . 38
State Assembly . . . 73, 74

Local Officials, 2009

Mayor . . . Jim Wood
City Manager . . . Peter Weiss
City Clerk . . . Barbara Riegel Wayne
Attorney . . . John Mullen
Finance Dir . . . Teri Ferro
Public Works . . . Don Hadley
Development Services Dir . . . George Buell
Building . . . Jim Zicaro
Police Chief . . . Frank McCoy
Emergency/Fire Dir . . . Terry Garrison

Public Safety

Number of officers, 2007 . . . 200
Violent crimes, 2007 . . . 910
Property crimes, 2007 . . . 4,588
Arson, 2007 . . . 31

Public Library

Oceanside Public Library
Oceanside Public Library System
330 N Coast Hwy
Oceanside, CA 92054
760-435-5600

Director . . . Deborah Polich

Library system statistics, FY 2007

Population served . . . 176,644
Internet terminals . . . 104
Annual users . . . 150,679

Per capita:

Operating income . . . $27.15
percent from local government . . . 91.9%
Operating expenditure . . . $27.07
Total materials . . . 1.91
Print holdings . . . 1.73
Visits per capita . . . 3.45

Housing & Construction

Housing Units

Total, 2008§ . . . 64,789
Single family units, attached . . . 8,364
Single family units, detached . . . 33,880
Multiple family units . . . 18,978
Mobile home units . . . 3,567
Occupied . . . 61,425
Vacancy rate . . . 5.2%
Median rent, 2007** . . . $1,224
Median SF home value, 2007** . . . $488,500

New Privately Owned Housing Units Authorized by Building Permit, 2007*

	Units	Construction Cost
Single	149	$44,252,310
Total	209	$53,614,179

Municipal Finance

(For local fiscal year ended in 2006)

Revenues

Total . . . $285,155,944
Taxes . . . 74,650,288
Special benefits assessment . . . 2,358,395
Licenses & permits . . . 0
Fines & forfeitures . . . 2,159,185
Revenues from use of money & property . . . 8,343,612
Intergovernmental . . . 28,692,757
Service charges . . . 94,939,605
Other revenues . . . 11,062,102
Other financing sources . . . 62,950,000

Expenditures

Total . . . $214,345,810
General government . . . 11,698,145
Public safety . . . 63,394,394
Transportation . . . 18,941,583
Community development . . . 26,638,644
Health . . . 42,836,718
Culture & leisure . . . 13,314,856
Other . . . 0

Local School District

(Data from School year 2007-08 except as noted)

Oceanside Unified
2111 Mission Ave
Oceanside, CA 92058
(760) 966-4000

Superintendent . . . Larry Perondi
Grade plan . . . K-12
Number of schools . . . 29
Enrollment . . . 21,222
High school graduates, 2006-07 . . . 1,034
Dropout rate . . . 4.8%
Pupil/teacher ratio . . . 19.9
Average class size . . . 24.8
Students per computer . . . 3.9
Classrooms with internet . . . 1,097
Avg. Daily Attendance (ADA) . . . 19,419
Cost per ADA . . . $8,763
Avg. Teacher Salary . . . $70,190

California Achievement Tests 6th ed., 2008

(Pct scoring at or above 50th National Percentile Rank)

	Math	Reading	Language
Grade 3	55%	37%	46%
Grade 7	55%	45%	45%

Academic Performance Index, 2008

Number of students tested . . . 15,198
Number of valid scores . . . 14,026
2007 API (base) . . . 748
2008 API (growth) . . . 758

SAT Testing, 2006-07

Enrollment, Grade 12 . . . 1,412
Number taking test . . . 365
percent taking test . . . 25.9%
percent with total score 1,500+ . . . 13.20%

Average Scores:

Math	Verbal	Writing	Total
522	499	493	1,514

Federal No Child Left Behind, 2008

(Adequate Yearly Progress standards met)

	Participation Rate	Pct Proficient
ELA	Yes	No
Math	Yes	No

API criteria . . . Yes
Graduation rate . . . Yes
\# criteria met/possible . . . 42/39

Other school districts for this city

(see Appendix E for information on these districts)

Fallbrook Union Elem, Vista Unified, Carlsbad Unified, Bonsall Union Elem

See Introduction for an explanation of all data sources.

Demographics & Socio-Economic Characteristics

(2000 Decennial Census, except as noted)

Population

1990*	7,613
2000	7,862
Male	3,692
Female	4,170
Jan. 2008 (estimate)[§]	8,156
Persons per sq. mi. of land	1,853.6

Race & Hispanic Origin, 2000

Race	
White	6,919
Black/African American	47
North American Native	39
Asian	124
Pacific Islander	13
Other Race	492
Two or more races	228
Hispanic origin, total	1,245
Mexican	981
Puerto Rican	10
Cuban	12
Other Hispanic	242

Age & Nativity, 2000

Under 5 years	386
18 years and over	5,901
65 years and over	1,405
85 years and over	309
Median Age	42.0
Native-born	6,742
Foreign-born	745

Educational Attainment, 2000

Population 25 years and over	5,145
Less than 9th grade	5.1%
High school grad or higher	88.0%
Bachelor's degree or higher	31.6%
Graduate degree	13.5%

Income & Poverty, 1999

Per capita income	$25,670
Median household income	$44,593
Median family income	$52,917
Persons in poverty	10.0%
H'holds receiving public assistance	104
H'holds receiving social security	1,076

Households, 2000

Total households	3,088
With persons under 18	1,054
With persons over 65	950
Family households	1,987
Single person households	897
Persons per household	2.48
Persons per family	3.06

Household Population, 2008[§§]

Persons living in households	7,966
Persons living in group quarters	190
Persons per household	2.5

Labor & Employment

Total civilian labor force, 2008[§§]	4,200
Unemployment rate, 2008	8.4%
Total civilian labor force, 2000	3,585

Employed persons 16 years and over by occupation, 2000

Managers & professionals	1,382
Service occupations	460
Sales & office occupations	1,001
Farming, fishing & forestry	16
Construction & maintenance	281
Production & transportation	197
Self-employed persons	540

* US Census Bureau
** 2000 Decennial Census
§ California Department of Finance
§§ California Employment Development Dept

General Information

City of Ojai
401 S Ventura
Ojai, CA 93023
805-646-5581

Website	www.ci.ojai.ca.us
Elevation	746 ft.
Land Area (sq. miles)	4.4
Water Area (sq. miles)	0
Year of Incorporation	1921
Government type	General law
Sales tax rate	8.25%

Voters & Officials

Registered Voters, October 2008

Total	5,089
Democrats	2,366
Republicans	1,512
Declined to state	909

Legislative Districts

US Congressional	24
State Senatorial	19
State Assembly	37

Local Officials, 2009

Mayor	Joe DeVito
Manager	Jere Kersnar
City Clerk	Carlon Strobel
Attorney	Monte Widders
Finance Dir	Susan Mears
Public Works	Mike Culver
Planning/Dev Dir	Jere Kersnar
Building	NA
Police Chief	Chris Dunn
Fire Chief	Bryan Vanden Bossche

Public Safety

Number of officers, 2007	NA
Violent crimes, 2007	10
Property crimes, 2007	253
Arson, 2007	0

Public Library

Ojai Library
Ventura County Library System
111 E Ojai Ave
Ojai, CA 93023
805-646-1639

Branch Librarian	Kit Willis

Library system statistics, FY 2007

Population served	439,444
Internet terminals	188
Annual users	216,575

Per capita:

Operating income	$25.05
percent from local government	86.2%
Operating expenditure	$25.02
Total materials	1.81
Print holdings	1.70
Visits per capita	NA

Housing & Construction

Housing Units

Total, 2008[§]	3,337
Single family units, attached	292
Single family units, detached	2,281
Multiple family units	756
Mobile home units	8
Occupied	3,193
Vacancy rate	4.3%
Median rent, 2000**	$814
Median SF home value, 2000**	$272,100

New Privately Owned Housing Units Authorized by Building Permit, 2007*

	Units	Construction Cost
Single	8	$2,386,670
Total	8	$2,386,670

Municipal Finance

(For local fiscal year ended in 2006)

Revenues

Total	$9,100,004
Taxes	5,406,675
Special benefits assessment	329,052
Licenses & permits	200,459
Fines & forfeitures	114,123
Revenues from use of money & property	191,024
Intergovernmental	1,438,977
Service charges	1,060,797
Other revenues	358,897
Other financing sources	0

Expenditures

Total	$8,418,668
General government	1,637,134
Public safety	2,701,454
Transportation	2,361,847
Community development	624,774
Health	38,155
Culture & leisure	1,055,304
Other	0

Local School District

(Data from School year 2007-08 except as noted)

Ojai Unified
PO Box 878
Ojai, CA 93024
(805) 640-4300

Superintendent	Tim Baird
Grade plan	K-12
Number of schools	9
Enrollment	3,225
High school graduates, 2006-07	258
Dropout rate	1.8%
Pupil/teacher ratio	21.5
Average class size	25.6
Students per computer	3.5
Classrooms with internet	173
Avg. Daily Attendance (ADA)	3,048
Cost per ADA	$8,261
Avg. Teacher Salary	$63,230

California Achievement Tests 6th ed., 2008

(Pct scoring at or above 50th National Percentile Rank)

	Math	Reading	Language
Grade 3	63%	54%	58%
Grade 7	66%	65%	60%

Academic Performance Index, 2008

Number of students tested	2,410
Number of valid scores	2,319
2007 API (base)	794
2008 API (growth)	796

SAT Testing, 2006-07

Enrollment, Grade 12	296
Number taking test	133
percent taking test	44.9%
percent with total score 1,500+	28.00%

Average Scores:

Math	Verbal	Writing	Total
554	520	523	1,597

Federal No Child Left Behind, 2008

(Adequate Yearly Progress standards met)

	Participation Rate	Pct Proficient
ELA	Yes	No
Math	Yes	No

API criteria	Yes
Graduation rate	Yes
# criteria met/possible	26/24

Other school districts for this city

(see Appendix E for information on these districts)

None

See Introduction for an explanation of all data sources.

Demographics & Socio-Economic Characteristics†

(2007 American Community Survey, except as noted)

Population

1990* ... 133,179
2007 ... 156,027
Male ... 76,527
Female ... 79,500
Jan. 2008 (estimate)§ ... 173,690
Persons per sq. mi. of land ... 3,487.8

Race & Hispanic Origin, 2007

Race
White ... 61,071
Black/African American ... 13,271
North American Native ... 541
Asian ... 6,403
Pacific Islander ... 52
Other Race ... 66,863
Two or more races ... 7,826
Hispanic origin, total ... 99,157
Mexican ... 89,333
Puerto Rican ... 744
Cuban ... 647
Other Hispanic ... 8,433

Age & Nativity, 2007

Under 5 years ... 11,138
18 years and over ... 112,080
65 years and over ... 11,247
85 years and over ... 1,300
Median Age ... 30.4
Native-born ... 109,676
Foreign-born ... 46,351

Educational Attainment, 2007

Population 25 years and over ... 91,704
Less than 9th grade ... 18.3%
High school grad or higher ... 69.0%
Bachelor's degree or higher ... 15.6%
Graduate degree ... 3.6%

Income & Poverty, 2007

Per capita income ... $19,693
Median household income ... $57,104
Median family income ... $59,721
Persons in poverty ... 9.5%
H'holds receiving public assistance ... 967
H'holds receiving social security ... 9,085

Households, 2007

Total households ... 44,119
With persons under 18 ... 20,372
With persons over 65 ... 7,890
Family households ... 34,919
Single person households ... 7,628
Persons per household ... 3.54
Persons per family ... 3.94

Household Population, 2008§§

Persons living in households ... 172,592
Persons living in group quarters ... 1,098
Persons per household ... 3.8

Labor & Employment

Total civilian labor force, 2008§§ ... 83,300
Unemployment rate, 2008 ... 8.5%
Total civilian labor force, 2000* ... 68,521

Employed persons 16 years and over by occupation, 2007

Managers & professionals ... 13,703
Service occupations ... 11,372
Sales & office occupations ... 22,939
Farming, fishing & forestry ... 186
Construction & maintenance ... 9,613
Production & transportation ... 17,418
Self-employed persons ... 5,242

† see Appendix D for 2000 Decennial Census Data
* US Census Bureau
** 2007 American Community Survey
§ California Department of Finance
§§ California Employment Development Dept

General Information

City of Ontario
303 East B St
Ontario, CA 91764
909-395-2010

Website ... www.ci.ontario.ca.us
Elevation ... 988 ft.
Land Area (sq. miles) ... 49.8
Water Area (sq. miles) ... 0.1
Year of Incorporation ... 1891
Government type ... General law
Sales tax rate ... 8.75%

Voters & Officials

Registered Voters, October 2008

Total ... 57,251
Democrats ... 27,226
Republicans ... 18,659
Declined to state ... 9,341

Legislative Districts

US Congressional ... 43
State Senatorial ... 32
State Assembly ... 61

Local Officials, 2009

Mayor ... Paul S. Leon
Manager ... Gregory Devereaux
City Clerk ... Mary Wirtes
Attorney ... John Brown
Finance Dir ... Grant Yee
Public Works ... Ken Jeske
Planning/Dev Dir ... Otto Kroutil
Building ... Kevin Shear
Police Chief ... Jim Doyle
Fire Chief ... Chris Hughes

Public Safety

Number of officers, 2007 ... 231
Violent crimes, 2007 ... 854
Property crimes, 2007 ... 5,850
Arson, 2007 ... 52

Public Library

Ontario Main Library
Ontario City Library System
215 East C Street
Ontario, CA 91764
909-395-2004

Director ... Judy Evans

Library system statistics, FY 2007

Population served ... 172,701
Internet terminals ... 50
Annual users ... 129,111

Per capita:

Operating income ... $19.35
percent from local government ... 90.9%
Operating expenditure ... $17.97
Total materials ... 1.46
Print holdings ... 1.28
Visits per capita ... 3.53

Housing & Construction

Housing Units

Total, 2008§ ... 47,276
Single family units, attached ... 3,649
Single family units, detached ... 27,569
Multiple family units ... 13,895
Mobile home units ... 2,163
Occupied ... 45,543
Vacancy rate ... 3.7%
Median rent, 2007** ... $1,140
Median SF home value, 2007** ... $433,200

New Privately Owned Housing Units Authorized by Building Permit, 2007*

	Units	Construction Cost
Single	307	$45,692,775
Total	630	$72,775,733

Municipal Finance

(For local fiscal year ended in 2006)

Revenues

Total ... $291,977,716
Taxes ... 136,376,038
Special benefits assessment ... 796,287
Licenses & permits ... 2,594,463
Fines & forfeitures ... 1,621,327
Revenues from use of money & property ... 7,753,771
Intergovernmental ... 23,760,124
Service charges ... 104,343,506
Other revenues ... 14,732,200
Other financing sources ... 0

Expenditures

Total ... $248,066,662
General government ... 16,174,961
Public safety ... 79,759,336
Transportation ... 17,060,931
Community development ... 37,262,858
Health ... 36,483,840
Culture & leisure ... 23,984,212
Other ... 0

Local School District

(Data from School year 2007-08 except as noted)

Chaffey Joint Union High
211 West Fifth St
Ontario, CA 91762
(909) 988-8511

Superintendent ... Mathew Holton
Grade plan ... 9-12
Number of schools ... 11
Enrollment ... 25,108
High school graduates, 2006-07 ... 4,562
Dropout rate ... 2.6%
Pupil/teacher ratio ... 25.2
Average class size ... 29.3
Students per computer ... 4.6
Classrooms with internet ... 1,703
Avg. Daily Attendance (ADA) ... 24,014
Cost per ADA ... $7,815
Avg. Teacher Salary ... $77,140

California Achievement Tests 6th ed., 2008

(Pct scoring at or above 50th National Percentile Rank)

	Math	Reading	Language
Grade 3	NA	NA	NA
Grade 7	NA	NA	NA

Academic Performance Index, 2008

Number of students tested ... 18,219
Number of valid scores ... 17,278
2007 API (base) ... 720
2008 API (growth) ... 734

SAT Testing, 2006-07

Enrollment, Grade 12 ... 5,840
Number taking test ... 1,782
percent taking test ... 30.5%
percent with total score 1,500+ ... 12.30%

Average Scores:

Math	Verbal	Writing	Total
492	475	471	1,438

Federal No Child Left Behind, 2008

(Adequate Yearly Progress standards met)

	Participation Rate	Pct Proficient
ELA	No	Yes
Math	Yes	No

API criteria ... Yes
Graduation rate ... Yes
criteria met/possible ... 38/36

Other school districts for this city

(see Appendix E for information on these districts)

Chino Valley Unified, Mountain View Elem, Ontario-Montclair Elem

See Introduction for an explanation of all data sources.

Demographics & Socio-Economic Characteristics†

(2007 American Community Survey, except as noted)

Population

1990*	110,658
2007	142,097
Male	71,632
Female	70,465
Jan. 2008 (estimate)§	140,849
Persons per sq. mi. of land	6,019.2

Race & Hispanic Origin, 2007

Race	
White	88,497
Black/African American	3,038
North American Native	1,310
Asian	14,549
Pacific Islander	40
Other Race	31,934
Two or more races	2,729
Hispanic origin, total	55,238
Mexican	50,182
Puerto Rican	314
Cuban	405
Other Hispanic	4,337

Age & Nativity, 2007

Under 5 years	9,961
18 years and over	103,457
65 years and over	14,159
85 years and over	1,153
Median Age	35.2
Native-born	103,915
Foreign-born	38,182

Educational Attainment, 2007

Population 25 years and over	87,437
Less than 9th grade	7.6%
High school grad or higher	84.0%
Bachelor's degree or higher	31.2%
Graduate degree	10.3%

Income & Poverty, 2007

Per capita income	$30,890
Median household income	$75,024
Median family income	$85,730
Persons in poverty	7.7%
H'holds receiving public assistance	563
H'holds receiving social security	9,631

Households, 2007

Total households	42,800
With persons under 18	18,869
With persons over 65	9,651
Family households	30,949
Single person households	9,253
Persons per household	3.20
Persons per family	3.71

Household Population, 2008§§

Persons living in households	135,381
Persons living in group quarters	5,468
Persons per household	3.1

Labor & Employment

Total civilian labor force, 2008§§	74,800
Unemployment rate, 2008	4.8%
Total civilian labor force, 2000*	64,812

Employed persons 16 years and over by occupation, 2007

Managers & professionals	26,494
Service occupations	11,789
Sales & office occupations	18,065
Farming, fishing & forestry	418
Construction & maintenance	6,923
Production & transportation	5,274
Self-employed persons	4,942

† see Appendix D for 2000 Decennial Census Data
* US Census Bureau
** 2007 American Community Survey
§ California Department of Finance
§§ California Employment Development Dept

General Information

City of Orange
300 E Chapman Ave
Orange, CA 92866
714-744-5500

Website	www.cityoforange.org
Elevation	187 ft.
Land Area (sq. miles)	23.4
Water Area (sq. miles)	0.5
Year of Incorporation	1888
Government type	General law
Sales tax rate	8.75%

Voters & Officials

Registered Voters, October 2008

Total	70,026
Democrats	21,096
Republicans	33,212
Declined to state	12,864

Legislative Districts

US Congressional	40
State Senatorial	33
State Assembly	60, 71, 72

Local Officials, 2009

Mayor	Carolyn Cavecche
Manager	John Sibley
City Clerk	Mary E. Murphy
Attorney	David DeBerry
Finance Dir.	Rich Jacobs
Public Works	Joe DeFrancesco
Planning/Dev Dir.	Alice Angus
Building	NA
Police Chief	Bob Gustafson
Emergency/Fire Dir.	Bart Lewis

Public Safety

Number of officers, 2007	162
Violent crimes, 2007	266
Property crimes, 2007	3,049
Arson, 2007	46

Public Library

Main Library
Orange Public Library System
407 E Chapman Ave
Orange, CA 92866
714-288-2410

Director	Nora Jacob

Library system statistics, FY 2007

Population served	138,640
Internet terminals	113
Annual users	81,515

Per capita:

Operating income	$32.46
percent from local government	97.6%
Operating expenditure	$26.37
Total materials	1.92
Print holdings	1.72
Visits per capita	1.78

Housing & Construction

Housing Units

Total, 2008§	44,319
Single family units, attached	5,218
Single family units, detached	25,129
Multiple family units	12,633
Mobile home units	1,339
Occupied	43,290
Vacancy rate	2.3%
Median rent, 2007**	$1,315
Median SF home value, 2007**	$660,600

New Privately Owned Housing Units Authorized by Building Permit, 2007*

	Units	Construction Cost
Single	262	$33,871,236
Total	826	$89,858,164

Municipal Finance

(For local fiscal year ended in 2006)

Revenues

Total	$137,058,766
Taxes	72,925,394
Special benefits assessment	1,522,939
Licenses & permits	1,132,434
Fines & forfeitures	2,083,736
Revenues from use of money & property	4,015,773
Intergovernmental	15,119,756
Service charges	36,625,305
Other revenues	3,633,429
Other financing sources	0

Expenditures

Total	$139,327,580
General government	11,375,970
Public safety	59,576,799
Transportation	12,632,059
Community development	6,097,454
Health	9,080,353
Culture & leisure	20,913,771
Other	0

Local School District

(Data from School year 2007-08 except as noted)

Orange Unified
PO Box 11022
Orange, CA 92867
(714) 628-4000

Superintendent	Renae Dreier
Grade plan	K-12
Number of schools	43
Enrollment	30,127
High school graduates, 2006-07	1,959
Dropout rate	1.5%
Pupil/teacher ratio	22.1
Average class size	27.2
Students per computer	5.1
Classrooms with internet	1,383
Avg. Daily Attendance (ADA)	28,411
Cost per ADA	$7,954
Avg. Teacher Salary	$70,298

California Achievement Tests 6th ed., 2008

(Pct scoring at or above 50th National Percentile Rank)

	Math	Reading	Language
Grade 3	61%	43%	52%
Grade 7	57%	58%	55%

Academic Performance Index, 2008

Number of students tested	22,272
Number of valid scores	21,079
2007 API (base)	783
2008 API (growth)	787

SAT Testing, 2006-07

Enrollment, Grade 12	2,286
Number taking test	971
percent taking test	42.5%
percent with total score 1,500+	24.60%

Average Scores:

Math	Verbal	Writing	Total
535	515	519	1,569

Federal No Child Left Behind, 2008

(Adequate Yearly Progress standards met)

	Participation Rate	Pct Proficient
ELA	Yes	No
Math	Yes	No

API criteria	Yes
Graduation rate	Yes
# criteria met/possible	42/38

Other school districts for this city

(see Appendix E for information on these districts)

None

See Introduction for an explanation of all data sources.

Demographics & Socio-Economic Characteristics

(2000 Decennial Census, except as noted)

Population

1990* 5,604
2000 7,722
Male 4,005
Female 3,717
Jan. 2008 (estimate)§ 10,775
Persons per sq. mi. of land 7,183.3

Race & Hispanic Origin, 2000

Race
White 2,591
Black/African American 24
North American Native 187
Asian 115
Pacific Islander 0
Other Race 4,544
Two or more races 261
Hispanic origin, total 6,996
Mexican 5,828
Puerto Rican 6
Cuban 0
Other Hispanic 1,162

Age & Nativity, 2000

Under 5 years 876
18 years and over 4,603
65 years and over 384
85 years and over 30
Median Age 22.8
Native-born 3,854
Foreign-born 3,905

Educational Attainment, 2000

Population 25 years and over 3,562
Less than 9th grade 58.6%
High school grad or higher 24.8%
Bachelor's degree or higher 1.7%
Graduate degree 0.3%

Income & Poverty, 1999

Per capita income $7,126
Median household income $22,357
Median family income $22,525
Persons in poverty 44.4%
H'holds receiving public assistance 205
H'holds receiving social security 286

Households, 2000

Total households 1,694
With persons under 18 1,179
With persons over 65 296
Family households 1,512
Single person households 121
Persons per household 4.56
Persons per family 4.66

Household Population, 2008§§

Persons living in households 10,775
Persons living in group quarters 0
Persons per household 4.7

Labor & Employment

Total civilian labor force, 2008§§ 3,700
Unemployment rate, 2008 . . . . . 22.7%
Total civilian labor force, 2000 2,943

Employed persons 16 years and over by occupation, 2000

Managers & professionals 191
Service occupations 401
Sales & office occupations 244
Farming, fishing & forestry 953
Construction & maintenance 122
Production & transportation 298
Self-employed persons 80

* US Census Bureau
** 2000 Decennial Census
§ California Department of Finance
§§ California Employment Development Dept

General Information

City of Orange Cove
633 Sixth St
Orange Cove, CA 93646
559-626-4488

Website . . . . . NA
Elevation . . . . . 425 ft.
Land Area (sq. miles) 1.5
Water Area (sq. miles) 0
Year of Incorporation 1948
Government type . . . . . General law
Sales tax rate 8.98%

Voters & Officials

Registered Voters, October 2008

Total 2,113
Democrats 1,358
Republicans 410
Declined to state 226

Legislative Districts

US Congressional 21
State Senatorial 16
State Assembly 29

Local Officials, 2009

Mayor . . . . . Victor Lopez
Manager . . . . . Alan J. Bengyal
City Clerk . . . . . June Bracamonte
Attorney . . . . . Tuttle & McCloskey
Finance Dir . . . . . Manuel Sandoval
Public Works . . . . . Sylvester Perez
Planning/Dev Dir . . . . . Julian Chapa
Building . . . . . Ray Hoak
Police Chief . . . . . (County)
Emergency/Fire Dir . . . . . Richard Hicks

Public Safety

Number of officers, 2007 . . . . . NA
Violent crimes, 2007 . . . . . NA
Property crimes, 2007 . . . . . NA
Arson, 2007 . . . . . NA

Public Library

Orange Cove Branch Library
Fresno County Public Library System
523 Park Blvd
Orange Cove, CA 93646
559-626-7942

Branch Librarian . . . . . Sandra Kuykendall

Library system statistics, FY 2007

Population served 889,019
Internet terminals 277
Annual users 861,240

Per capita:

Operating income $23.69
percent from local government 89.3%
Operating expenditure $23.37
Total materials 2.89
Print holdings 2.69
Visits per capita . . . . . NA

Housing & Construction

Housing Units

Total, 2008§ 2,413
Single family units, attached 206
Single family units, detached 1,285
Multiple family units 896
Mobile home units 26
Occupied 2,312
Vacancy rate 4.2%
Median rent, 2000** $486
Median SF home value, 2000** $80,200

New Privately Owned Housing Units Authorized by Building Permit, 2007*

	Units	Construction Cost
Single	54	$7,733,509
Total	62	$8,528,395

Municipal Finance

(For local fiscal year ended in 2006)

Revenues

Total $9,575,420
Taxes 1,611,538
Special benefits assessment 0
Licenses & permits 258,642
Fines & forfeitures 1,058
Revenues from use of money & property 256,180
Intergovernmental 3,542,776
Service charges 2,709,379
Other revenues 770,847
Other financing sources 425,000

Expenditures

Total $8,025,322
General government 358,582
Public safety 483,469
Transportation 896,276
Community development 75,730
Health 1,614,911
Culture & leisure 2,327,508
Other 0

Local School District

(Data from School year 2007-08 except as noted)

Kings Canyon Joint Unified
675 West Manning Ave
Reedley, CA 93654
(559) 637-1200

Superintendent . . . . . Juan Garza
Grade plan K-12
Number of schools 18
Enrollment 9,701
High school graduates, 2006-07 459
Dropout rate 8.4%
Pupil/teacher ratio 21.7
Average class size 26.8
Students per computer 3.1
Classrooms with internet 758
Avg. Daily Attendance (ADA) 9,407
Cost per ADA $8,504
Avg. Teacher Salary $62,017

California Achievement Tests 6th ed., 2008

(Pct scoring at or above 50th National Percentile Rank)

	Math	Reading	Language
Grade 3	44%	26%	32%
Grade 7	48%	40%	38%

Academic Performance Index, 2008

Number of students tested 7,025
Number of valid scores 6,437
2007 API (base) 679
2008 API (growth) 698

SAT Testing, 2006-07

Enrollment, Grade 12 658
Number taking test 103
percent taking test 15.7%
percent with total score 1,500+ 6.20%

Average Scores:

Math	Verbal	Writing	Total
480	462	460	1,402

Federal No Child Left Behind, 2008

(Adequate Yearly Progress standards met)

	Participation Rate	Pct Proficient
ELA	Yes	No
Math	Yes	No

API criteria . . . . . Yes
Graduation rate . . . . . No
\# criteria met/possible 26/20

Other school districts for this city

(see Appendix E for information on these districts)

None

Demographics & Socio-Economic Characteristics

(2000 Decennial Census, except as noted)

Population

1990* . . . 16,642
2000 . . . 17,599
Male . . . 8,521
Female . . . 9,078
Jan. 2008 (estimate)§ . . . 17,542
Persons per sq. mi. of land . . . 1,392.2

Race & Hispanic Origin, 2000

Race
White . . . 15,246
Black/African American . . . 82
North American Native . . . 26
Asian . . . 1,626
Pacific Islander . . . 7
Other Race . . . 112
Two or more races . . . 500
Hispanic origin, total . . . 560
Mexican . . . 256
Puerto Rican . . . 28
Cuban . . . 8
Other Hispanic . . . 268

Age & Nativity, 2000

Under 5 years . . . 959
18 years and over . . . 13,035
65 years and over . . . 3,212
85 years and over . . . 275
Median Age . . . 45.2
Native-born . . . 15,326
Foreign-born . . . 2,120

Educational Attainment, 2000

Population 25 years and over . . . 12,359
Less than 9th grade . . . 0.3%
High school grad or higher . . . 97.8%
Bachelor's degree or higher . . . 73.9%
Graduate degree . . . 34.3%

Income & Poverty, 1999

Per capita income . . . $65,428
Median household income . . . $117,637
Median family income . . . $132,531
Persons in poverty . . . 1.9%
H'holds receiving public assistance . . . 23
H'holds receiving social security . . . 2,163

Households, 2000

Total households . . . 6,596
With persons under 18 . . . 2,490
With persons over 65 . . . 2,138
Family households . . . 5,241
Single person households . . . 1,096
Persons per household . . . 2.66
Persons per family . . . 2.98

Household Population, 2008§§

Persons living in households . . . 17,475
Persons living in group quarters . . . 67
Persons per household . . . 2.6

Labor & Employment

Total civilian labor force, 2008§§ . . . 8,900
Unemployment rate, 2008 . . . 2.1%
Total civilian labor force, 2000 . . . 8,078

Employed persons 16 years and over by occupation, 2000

Managers & professionals . . . 5,275
Service occupations . . . 504
Sales & office occupations . . . 1,763
Farming, fishing & forestry . . . 27
Construction & maintenance . . . 158
Production & transportation . . . 219
Self-employed persons . . . 1,450

* US Census Bureau
** 2000 Decennial Census
§ California Department of Finance
§§ California Employment Development Dept

General Information

City of Orinda
PO Box 2000
Orinda, CA 94563
925-253-4200

Website . . . www.ci.orinda.ca.us
Elevation . . . 500 ft.
Land Area (sq. miles) . . . 12.6
Water Area (sq. miles) . . . 0
Year of Incorporation . . . 1985
Government type . . . General Law
Sales tax rate . . . 9.25%

Voters & Officials

Registered Voters, October 2008

Total . . . 13,054
Democrats . . . 5,855
Republicans . . . 4,373
Declined to state . . . 2,383

Legislative Districts

US Congressional . . . 10
State Senatorial . . . 7
State Assembly . . . 14

Local Officials, 2009

Mayor . . . Sue Severson
Manager . . . Janet Keeter
City Clerk . . . Michele Olsen
Attorney . . . Osa Wolff
Finance Dir . . . Beverli Marshall
Public Works . . . Chuck Swanson
Planning/Dev Dir . . . Emmanuel Ursu
Building . . . NA
Police Chief . . . William French
Fire Chief . . . Pete Nowicki

Public Safety

Number of officers, 2007 . . . NA
Violent crimes, 2007 . . . 13
Property crimes, 2007 . . . 308
Arson, 2007 . . . 3

Public Library

Orinda Library
Contra Costa County Library System
26 Orinda Way
Orinda, CA 94563
925-254-2184

Branch Librarian . . . Debbie Tyler

Library system statistics, FY 2007

Population served . . . 938,513
Internet terminals . . . 324
Annual users . . . 670,618

Per capita:

Operating income . . . $27.05
percent from local government . . . 82.0%
Operating expenditure . . . $27.82
Total materials . . . 1.57
Print holdings . . . 1.41
Visits per capita . . . 3.65

Housing & Construction

Housing Units

Total, 2008§ . . . 6,830
Single family units, attached . . . 188
Single family units, detached . . . 6,329
Multiple family units . . . 306
Mobile home units . . . 7
Occupied . . . 6,681
Vacancy rate . . . 2.2%
Median rent, 2000** . . . $1,239
Median SF home value, 2000** . . . $631,800

New Privately Owned Housing Units Authorized by Building Permit, 2007*

	Units	Construction Cost
Single	NA	NA
Total	NA	NA

Municipal Finance

(For local fiscal year ended in 2006)

Revenues

Total . . . $22,650,306
Taxes . . . 6,894,390
Special benefits assessment . . . 627,415
Licenses & permits . . . 0
Fines & forfeitures . . . 179,507
Revenues from use of money & property . . . 319,398
Intergovernmental . . . 1,052,279
Service charges . . . 2,281,709
Other revenues . . . 1,495,608
Other financing sources . . . 9,800,000

Expenditures

Total . . . $14,647,664
General government . . . 1,595,964
Public safety . . . 2,858,316
Transportation . . . 3,249,720
Community development . . . 4,605,107
Health . . . 0
Culture & leisure . . . 2,338,557
Other . . . 0

Local School District

(Data from School year 2007-08 except as noted)

Acalanes Union High
1212 Pleasant Hill Rd
Lafayette, CA 94549
(925) 280-3900

Superintendent . . . Jim Negri
Grade plan . . . 9-12
Number of schools . . . 6
Enrollment . . . 5,905
High school graduates, 2006-07 . . . 1,343
Dropout rate . . . 0.5%
Pupil/teacher ratio . . . 19.8
Average class size . . . 22.7
Students per computer . . . 3.6
Classrooms with internet . . . 267
Avg. Daily Attendance (ADA) . . . 5,781
Cost per ADA . . . $9,251
Avg. Teacher Salary . . . $73,421

California Achievement Tests 6th ed., 2008

(Pct scoring at or above 50th National Percentile Rank)

	Math	Reading	Language
Grade 3	NA	NA	NA
Grade 7	NA	NA	NA

Academic Performance Index, 2008

Number of students tested . . . 4,273
Number of valid scores . . . 4,195
2007 API (base) . . . 882
2008 API (growth) . . . 886

SAT Testing, 2006-07

Enrollment, Grade 12 . . . 1,385
Number taking test . . . 1,148
percent taking test . . . 82.9%
percent with total score 1,500+ . . . 69.30%

Average Scores:

Math	Verbal	Writing	Total
596	580	585	1,761

Federal No Child Left Behind, 2008

(Adequate Yearly Progress standards met)

	Participation Rate	Pct Proficient
ELA	Yes	Yes
Math	Yes	Yes

API criteria . . . Yes
Graduation rate . . . Yes
\# criteria met/possible . . . 14/14

Other school districts for this city

(see Appendix E for information on these districts)

Orinda Union Elem

See Introduction for an explanation of all data sources.

Demographics & Socio-Economic Characteristics

(2000 Decennial Census, except as noted)

Population

1990* 5,052
2000 6,281
Male 3,087
Female 3,194
Jan. 2008 (estimate)§ 7,353
Persons per sq. mi. of land 2,941.2

Race & Hispanic Origin, 2000

Race
White 4,263
Black/African American 37
North American Native 98
Asian 119
Pacific Islander 11
Other Race 1,514
Two or more races 239
Hispanic origin, total 2,340
Mexican 2,051
Puerto Rican 11
Cuban 0
Other Hispanic 278

Age & Nativity, 2000

Under 5 years 572
18 years and over 4,236
65 years and over 828
85 years and over 109
Median Age 31.0
Native-born 5,048
Foreign-born 1,348

Educational Attainment, 2000

Population 25 years and over 3,747
Less than 9th grade 19.1%
High school grad or higher 61.9%
Bachelor's degree or higher 7.9%
Graduate degree 2.3%

Income & Poverty, 1999

Per capita income $12,486
Median household income $27,973
Median family income $32,792
Persons in poverty 19.2%
H'holds receiving public assistance 150
H'holds receiving social security 686

Households, 2000

Total households 2,190
With persons under 18 980
With persons over 65 607
Family households 1,569
Single person households 511
Persons per household 2.86
Persons per family 3.36

Household Population, 2008§§

Persons living in households 7,315
Persons living in group quarters 38
Persons per household 2.9

Labor & Employment

Total civilian labor force, 2008§§ 2,810
Unemployment rate, 2008 .... 10.1%
Total civilian labor force, 2000 2,637

Employed persons 16 years and over by occupation, 2000

Managers & professionals 465
Service occupations 319
Sales & office occupations 613
Farming, fishing & forestry 343
Construction & maintenance 174
Production & transportation 494
Self-employed persons 225

* US Census Bureau
** 2000 Decennial Census
§ California Department of Finance
§§ California Employment Development Dept

General Information

City of Orland
815 Fourth St
Orland, CA 95963
530-865-1600

Website .... NA
Elevation .... 260 ft.
Land Area (sq. miles) 2.5
Water Area (sq. miles) 0
Year of Incorporation 1909
Government type .... General law
Sales tax rate 8.25%

Voters & Officials

Registered Voters, October 2008

Total 2,848
Democrats 962
Republicans 1,214
Declined to state 552

Legislative Districts

US Congressional 2
State Senatorial 4
State Assembly 2

Local Officials, 2009

Mayor .... Bruce T. Roundy
Manager .... Paul H. Poczobut Jr
City Clerk .... Angela Crook
Attorney .... Thomas N. Andrews
Finance Dir .... Daryl Brock
Public Works .... Jere Schmitke
Planning/Dev Dir .... Nancy Sailsbery
Building .... NA
Police Chief .... Robert Pasero
Fire Chief .... Jerry Kramer

Public Safety

Number of officers, 2007 11
Violent crimes, 2007 30
Property crimes, 2007 198
Arson, 2007 1

Public Library

Orland Free Library
333 Mill St
Orland, CA 95963
530-865-1640

City Librarian .... Marilyn Cochran

Library statistics, FY 2007

Population served 14,817
Internet terminals 5
Annual users 11,270

Per capita:

Operating income $22.53
percent from local government 97.5%
Operating expenditure $22.53
Total materials 4.22
Print holdings 4.21
Visits per capita .... NA

Housing & Construction

Housing Units

Total, 2008§ 2,643
Single family units, attached 59
Single family units, detached 1,932
Multiple family units 581
Mobile home units 71
Occupied 2,507
Vacancy rate 5.2%
Median rent, 2000** $484
Median SF home value, 2000** $88,000

New Privately Owned Housing Units Authorized by Building Permit, 2007*

	Units	Construction Cost
Single	39	$6,520,000
Total	39	$6,520,000

Municipal Finance

(For local fiscal year ended in 2006)

Revenues

Total $5,685,736
Taxes 2,913,956
Special benefits assessment 44,348
Licenses & permits 0
Fines & forfeitures 38,478
Revenues from use of money & property 128,427
Intergovernmental 612,524
Service charges 1,929,135
Other revenues 18,868
Other financing sources 0

Expenditures

Total $4,498,128
General government 304,549
Public safety 1,470,549
Transportation 285,745
Community development 620,762
Health 525,992
Culture & leisure 595,980
Other 0

Local School District

(Data from School year 2007-08 except as noted)

Orland Joint Unified
1320 Sixth St
Orland, CA 95963
(530) 865-1200

Superintendent .... Chris Von Kleist
Grade plan K-12
Number of schools 7
Enrollment 2,277
High school graduates, 2006-07 145
Dropout rate 2.5%
Pupil/teacher ratio 18.7
Average class size 21.9
Students per computer 6.2
Classrooms with internet 128
Avg. Daily Attendance (ADA) 2,209
Cost per ADA $8,491
Avg. Teacher Salary $56,610

California Achievement Tests 6th ed., 2008

(Pct scoring at or above 50th National Percentile Rank)

	Math	Reading	Language
Grade 3	51%	36%	44%
Grade 7	49%	41%	36%

Academic Performance Index, 2008

Number of students tested 1,749
Number of valid scores 1,648
2007 API (base) 696
2008 API (growth) 711

SAT Testing, 2006-07

Enrollment, Grade 12 167
Number taking test 33
percent taking test 19.8%
percent with total score 1,500+ 8.40%

Average Scores:

Math	Verbal	Writing	Total
505	468	461	1,434

Federal No Child Left Behind, 2008

(Adequate Yearly Progress standards met)

	Participation Rate	Pct Proficient
ELA	Yes	No
Math	Yes	No

API criteria .... Yes
Graduation rate .... Yes
\# criteria met/possible 26/22

Other school districts for this city

(see Appendix E for information on these districts)

Lake Elem, Plaza Elem, Capay Joint Union Elem

See Introduction for an explanation of all data sources.

Demographics & Socio-Economic Characteristics

(2000 Decennial Census, except as noted)

Population

1990* . . . 11,960
2000 . . . 13,004
Male . . . 6,364
Female . . . 6,640
Jan. 2008 (estimate)§ . . . 14,490
Persons per sq. mi. of land . . . 1,178.0

Race & Hispanic Origin, 2000

Race
White . . . 10,043
Black/African American . . . 524
North American Native . . . 511
Asian . . . 825
Pacific Islander . . . 34
Other Race . . . 362
Two or more races . . . 705
Hispanic origin, total . . . 1,073
Mexican . . . 763
Puerto Rican . . . 49
Cuban . . . 25
Other Hispanic . . . 236

Age & Nativity, 2000

Under 5 years . . . 1,093
18 years and over . . . 9,096
65 years and over . . . 1,908
85 years and over . . . 318
Median Age . . . 32.6
Native-born . . . 12,079
Foreign-born . . . 890

Educational Attainment, 2000

Population 25 years and over . . . 7,763
Less than 9th grade . . . 7.8%
High school grad or higher . . . 73.6%
Bachelor's degree or higher . . . 10.8%
Graduate degree . . . 3.5%

Income & Poverty, 1999

Per capita income . . . $12,345
Median household income . . . $21,911
Median family income . . . $27,666
Persons in poverty . . . 31.0%
H'holds receiving public assistance . . . 687
H'holds receiving social security . . . 1,606

Households, 2000

Total households . . . 4,881
With persons under 18 . . . 1,812
With persons over 65 . . . 1,355
Family households . . . 2,946
Single person households . . . 1,622
Persons per household . . . 2.50
Persons per family . . . 3.19

Household Population, 2008§§

Persons living in households . . . 13,658
Persons living in group quarters . . . 832
Persons per household . . . 2.4

Labor & Employment

Total civilian labor force, 2008§§ . . . 5,400
Unemployment rate, 2008 . . . 11.6%
Total civilian labor force, 2000 . . . 4,726

Employed persons 16 years and over by occupation, 2000

Managers & professionals . . . 1,010
Service occupations . . . 906
Sales & office occupations . . . 1,186
Farming, fishing & forestry . . . 84
Construction & maintenance . . . 386
Production & transportation . . . 547
Self-employed persons . . . 315

* US Census Bureau
** 2000 Decennial Census
§ California Department of Finance
§§ California Employment Development Dept

General Information

City of Oroville
1735 Montgomery St
Oroville, CA 95965
530-538-2401

Website . . . www.cityoforoville.org
Elevation . . . 174 ft.
Land Area (sq. miles) . . . 12.3
Water Area (sq. miles) . . . 0
Year of Incorporation . . . 1906
Government type . . . Chartered
Sales tax rate . . . 8.25%

Voters & Officials

Registered Voters, October 2008

Total . . . 6,120
Democrats . . . 2,165
Republicans . . . 2,288
Declined to state . . . 1,256

Legislative Districts

US Congressional . . . 4
State Senatorial . . . 4
State Assembly . . . 3

Local Officials, 2009

Mayor . . . Steve Jernigan
City Administrator . . . Sharon L. Atteberry
City Clerk . . . Sharon L. Atteberry
Attorney . . . Dwight L. Moore
Finance Dir . . . Diane MacMillan
Public Works . . . Eric Teitelman
Community Dev Dir . . . Eric Teitelman
Building . . . NA
Police Chief . . . Kirk Trostle
Fire Chief . . . Les Bowers (Int)

Public Safety

Number of officers, 2007 . . . 21
Violent crimes, 2007 . . . 198
Property crimes, 2007 . . . 1,028
Arson, 2007 . . . 3

Public Library

Main Branch
Butte County Library System
1820 Mitchell Ave
Oroville, CA 95966
530-538-7242

Director . . . Brenda Crotts

Library system statistics, FY 2007

Population served . . . 218,069
Internet terminals . . . 47
Annual users . . . 90,296

Per capita:

Operating income . . . $12.21
percent from local government . . . 84.5%
Operating expenditure . . . $12.71
Total materials . . . 1.41
Print holdings . . . 1.33
Visits per capita . . . 3.01

Housing & Construction

Housing Units

Total, 2008§ . . . 6,278
Single family units, attached . . . 206
Single family units, detached . . . 3,530
Multiple family units . . . 2,144
Mobile home units . . . 398
Occupied . . . 5,654
Vacancy rate . . . 9.9%
Median rent, 2000** . . . $445
Median SF home value, 2000** . . . $88,900

New Privately Owned Housing Units Authorized by Building Permit, 2007*

	Units	Construction Cost
Single	30	$4,393,636
Total	104	$9,927,679

Municipal Finance

(For local fiscal year ended in 2006)

Revenues

Total . . . $18,520,114
Taxes . . . 7,702,146
Special benefits assessment . . . 0
Licenses & permits . . . 247,621
Fines & forfeitures . . . 84,020
Revenues from use of money & property . . . 1,763,204
Intergovernmental . . . 3,438,810
Service charges . . . 5,144,112
Other revenues . . . 140,201
Other financing sources . . . 0

Expenditures

Total . . . $17,892,243
General government . . . 1,126,090
Public safety . . . 6,231,346
Transportation . . . 3,309,633
Community development . . . 5,063,574
Health . . . 1,294,068
Culture & leisure . . . 867,532
Other . . . 0

Local School District

(Data from School year 2007-08 except as noted)

Oroville Union High
2211 Washington Ave
Oroville, CA 95966
(530) 538-2300

Superintendent . . . Oran Roberts
Grade plan . . . 9-12
Number of schools . . . 5
Enrollment . . . 2,944
High school graduates, 2006-07 . . . 573
Dropout rate . . . 3.7%
Pupil/teacher ratio . . . 22.2
Average class size . . . 25.5
Students per computer . . . 4.1
Classrooms with internet . . . 159
Avg. Daily Attendance (ADA) . . . 2,538
Cost per ADA . . . $8,337
Avg. Teacher Salary . . . $57,118

California Achievement Tests 6th ed., 2008

(Pct scoring at or above 50th National Percentile Rank)

	Math	Reading	Language
Grade 3	NA	NA	NA
Grade 7	NA	NA	NA

Academic Performance Index, 2008

Number of students tested . . . 2,091
Number of valid scores . . . 1,991
2007 API (base) . . . 686
2008 API (growth) . . . 693

SAT Testing, 2006-07

Enrollment, Grade 12 . . . 700
Number taking test . . . 138
percent taking test . . . 19.7%
percent with total score 1,500+ . . . 8.30%

Average Scores:

Math	Verbal	Writing	Total
491	479	466	1,436

Federal No Child Left Behind, 2008

(Adequate Yearly Progress standards met)

	Participation Rate	Pct Proficient
ELA	Yes	Yes
Math	Yes	Yes

API criteria . . . Yes
Graduation rate . . . No
\# criteria met/possible . . . 22/21

Other school districts for this city

(see Appendix E for information on these districts)

Oroville Elem, Thermalito Union Elem, Golden Feather Union Elem

See Introduction for an explanation of all data sources.

Demographics & Socio-Economic Characteristics†

(2007 American Community Survey, except as noted)

Population

1990* . . . 142,216
2007 . . . 167,412
Male . . . 87,500
Female . . . 79,912
Jan. 2008 (estimate)§ . . . 194,905
Persons per sq. mi. of land . . . 7,703.8

Race & Hispanic Origin, 2007

Race
White . . . 86,616
Black/African American . . . 5,407
North American Native . . . 2,833
Asian . . . 18,802
Pacific Islander . . . 504
Other Race . . . 49,066
Two or more races . . . 4,184
Hispanic origin, total . . . 114,758
Mexican . . . 109,977
Puerto Rican . . . 815
Cuban . . . 125
Other Hispanic . . . 3,841

Age & Nativity, 2007

Under 5 years . . . 13,811
18 years and over . . . 122,123
65 years and over . . . 18,511
85 years and over . . . 2,293
Median Age . . . 31.6
Native-born . . . 99,601
Foreign-born . . . 67,811

Educational Attainment, 2007

Population 25 years and over . . . 102,782
Less than 9th grade . . . 24.5%
High school grad or higher . . . 61.2%
Bachelor's degree or higher . . . 17.0%
Graduate degree . . . 5.8%

Income & Poverty, 2007

Per capita income . . . $20,446
Median household income . . . $53,298
Median family income . . . $55,303
Persons in poverty . . . 13.9%
H'holds receiving public assistance . . . 1,590
H'holds receiving social security . . . 12,180

Households, 2007

Total households . . . 46,086
With persons under 18 . . . 20,613
With persons over 65 . . . 12,215
Family households . . . 35,682
Single person households . . . 8,435
Persons per household . . . 3.59
Persons per family . . . 4.07

Household Population, 2008§§

Persons living in households . . . 192,308
Persons living in group quarters . . . 2,597
Persons per household . . . 3.9

Labor & Employment

Total civilian labor force, 2008§§ . . . 89,600
Unemployment rate, 2008 . . . 8.7%
Total civilian labor force, 2000* . . . 76,109

Employed persons 16 years and over by occupation, 2007

Managers & professionals . . . 15,973
Service occupations . . . 13,334
Sales & office occupations . . . 17,541
Farming, fishing & forestry . . . 6,661
Construction & maintenance . . . 8,836
Production & transportation . . . 13,495
Self-employed persons . . . 4,806

† see Appendix D for 2000 Decennial Census Data
* US Census Bureau
** 2007 American Community Survey
§ California Department of Finance
§§ California Employment Development Dept

General Information

City of Oxnard
305 W Third St
Oxnard, CA 93030
805-385-7430

Website . . . www.ci.oxnard.ca.us
Elevation . . . 52 ft.
Land Area (sq. miles) . . . 25.3
Water Area (sq. miles) . . . 11.3
Year of Incorporation . . . 1903
Government type . . . General law
Sales tax rate . . . 8.75%

Voters & Officials

Registered Voters, October 2008

Total . . . 66,798
Democrats . . . 35,895
Republicans . . . 15,930
Declined to state . . . 12,422

Legislative Districts

US Congressional . . . 23
State Senatorial . . . 23
State Assembly . . . 35, 41

Local Officials, 2009

Mayor . . . Thomas E. Holden
Manager . . . Edmund Sotelo
City Clerk . . . Daniel Martinez
Attorney . . . Alan Holmberg
Finance Dir . . . James Cameron
Public Works . . . Ken Ortega
Community Dev Dir . . . Curtis Cannon
Building . . . Matthew Winegar
Police Chief . . . John Crombach
Emergency/Fire Dir . . . Joe Milligan

Public Safety

Number of officers, 2007 . . . 229
Violent crimes, 2007 . . . 845
Property crimes, 2007 . . . 4,275
Arson, 2007 . . . 72

Public Library

Oxnard Public Library
Oxnard Public Library System
251 South A St
Oxnard, CA 93030
805-385-7500

Director . . . Barbara Jean Murray

Library system statistics, FY 2007

Population served . . . 192,997
Internet terminals . . . 93
Annual users . . . 88,736

Per capita:

Operating income . . . $26.93
percent from local government . . . 90.6%
Operating expenditure . . . $24.24
Total materials . . . 2.15
Print holdings . . . 1.96
Visits per capita . . . 2.72

Housing & Construction

Housing Units

Total, 2008§ . . . 51,521
Single family units, attached . . . 4,633
Single family units, detached . . . 29,383
Multiple family units . . . 14,559
Mobile home units . . . 2,946
Occupied . . . 49,708
Vacancy rate . . . 3.5%
Median rent, 2007** . . . $1,093
Median SF home value, 2007** . . . $584,200

New Privately Owned Housing Units Authorized by Building Permit, 2007*

	Units	Construction Cost
Single	205	$46,877,535
Total	509	$76,062,730

Municipal Finance

(For local fiscal year ended in 2006)

Revenues

Total . . . $323,175,789
Taxes . . . 88,016,720
Special benefits assessment . . . 2,346,083
Licenses & permits . . . 5,937,173
Fines & forfeitures . . . 2,428,265
Revenues from use of money & property . . . 8,737,083
Intergovernmental . . . 27,396,455
Service charges . . . 115,795,454
Other revenues . . . 17,006,557
Other financing sources . . . 55,511,999

Expenditures

Total . . . $348,009,904
General government . . . 15,913,894
Public safety . . . 72,976,931
Transportation . . . 33,775,410
Community development . . . 15,667,261
Health . . . 121,555,745
Culture & leisure . . . 40,594,313
Other . . . 0

Local School District

(Data from School year 2007-08 except as noted)

Oxnard Union High
309 South K St
Oxnard, CA 93030
(805) 385-2500

Superintendent . . . Jody Dunlap
Grade plan . . . 9-12
Number of schools . . . 10
Enrollment . . . 16,868
High school graduates, 2006-07 . . . 2,756
Dropout rate . . . 4.4%
Pupil/teacher ratio . . . 25.2
Average class size . . . 28.2
Students per computer . . . 4.7
Classrooms with internet . . . 635
Avg. Daily Attendance (ADA) . . . 15,420
Cost per ADA . . . $8,186
Avg. Teacher Salary . . . $72,428

California Achievement Tests 6th ed., 2008

(Pct scoring at or above 50th National Percentile Rank)

	Math	Reading	Language
Grade 3	74%	54%	56%
Grade 7	89%	81%	70%

Academic Performance Index, 2008

Number of students tested . . . 11,929
Number of valid scores . . . 11,323
2007 API (base) . . . 673
2008 API (growth) . . . 693

SAT Testing, 2006-07

Enrollment, Grade 12 . . . 3,865
Number taking test . . . 916
percent taking test . . . 23.7%
percent with total score 1,500+ . . . 11.20%

Average Scores:

Math	Verbal	Writing	Total
509	489	485	1,483

Federal No Child Left Behind, 2008

(Adequate Yearly Progress standards met)

	Participation Rate	Pct Proficient
ELA	Yes	No
Math	Yes	No

API criteria . . . Yes
Graduation rate . . . No
\# criteria met/possible . . . 38/35

Other school districts for this city

(see Appendix E for information on these districts)

Hueneme Elem, Ocean View Elem, Oxnard Elem, Rio Elem

See Introduction for an explanation of all data sources.

Demographics & Socio-Economic Characteristics

(2000 Decennial Census, except as noted)

Population

1990* 16,117
2000 15,522
Male 7,167
Female 8,355
Jan. 2008 (estimate)§ 15,472
Persons per sq. mi. of land 5,335.2

Race & Hispanic Origin, 2000

Race
White 13,665
Black/African American 177
North American Native 86
Asian 698
Pacific Islander 41
Other Race 276
Two or more races 579
Hispanic origin, total 1,108
Mexican 656
Puerto Rican 34
Cuban 16
Other Hispanic 402

Age & Nativity, 2000

Under 5 years 558
18 years and over 12,756
65 years and over 3,037
85 years and over 427
Median Age 44.7
Native-born 13,550
Foreign-born 1,909

Educational Attainment, 2000

Population 25 years and over 11,884
Less than 9th grade 3.0%
High school grad or higher 92.2%
Bachelor's degree or higher 44.1%
Graduate degree 18.4%

Income & Poverty, 1999

Per capita income $31,277
Median household income $50,254
Median family income $59,569
Persons in poverty 5.3%
H'holds receiving public assistance 144
H'holds receiving social security 2,279

Households, 2000

Total households 7,316
With persons under 18 1,707
With persons over 65 2,219
Family households 3,973
Single person households 2,691
Persons per household 2.10
Persons per family 2.75

Household Population, 2008§§

Persons living in households 15,297
Persons living in group quarters 175
Persons per household 2.1

Labor & Employment

Total civilian labor force, 2008§§ 10,300
Unemployment rate, 2008 .... 3.0%
Total civilian labor force, 2000 8,650

Employed persons 16 years and over by occupation, 2000

Managers & professionals 4,076
Service occupations 1,261
Sales & office occupations 2,086
Farming, fishing & forestry 48
Construction & maintenance 521
Production & transportation 390
Self-employed persons 1,371

* US Census Bureau
** 2000 Decennial Census
§ California Department of Finance
§§ California Employment Development Dept

General Information

City of Pacific Grove
300 Forest Ave
Pacific Grove, CA 93950
831-648-3100

Website .... www.ci.pg.ca.us
Elevation .... 120 ft.
Land Area (sq. miles) 2.9
Water Area (sq. miles) 1.1
Year of Incorporation 1889
Government type .... Chartered
Sales tax rate 9.25%

Voters & Officials

Registered Voters, October 2008

Total 9,757
Democrats 5,001
Republicans 2,359
Declined to state 1,983

Legislative Districts

US Congressional 17
State Senatorial 15
State Assembly 27

Local Officials, 2009

Mayor .... Daniel E. Cort
Manager .... Charlene Wiseman
City Clerk .... Ann O'Rourke
Attorney .... David C. Laredo
Finance Dir .... Jim Becklenberg
Public Works .... Celia Martinez
Chief Planner .... Lynne Burgess
Building .... Dave Cushman
Police Chief .... Darius Engles
Fire Chief .... Andrew Miller

Public Safety

Number of officers, 2007 22
Violent crimes, 2007 23
Property crimes, 2007 388
Arson, 2007 0

Public Library

Pacific Grove Public Library
550 Central Ave
Pacific Grove, CA 93950
831-648-5760

Senior Librarian .... Mary Housel

Library statistics, FY 2007

Population served 15,444
Internet terminals 5
Annual users 7,112

Per capita:

Operating income $70.01
percent from local government 84.2%
Operating expenditure $60.25
Total materials 7.32
Print holdings 6.55
Visits per capita 9.12

Housing & Construction

Housing Units

Total, 2008§ 8,108
Single family units, attached 451
Single family units, detached 5,017
Multiple family units 2,549
Mobile home units 91
Occupied 7,343
Vacancy rate 9.4%
Median rent, 2000** $962
Median SF home value, 2000** $417,400

New Privately Owned Housing Units Authorized by Building Permit, 2007*

	Units	Construction Cost
Single	6	$2,293,268
Total	6	$2,293,268

Municipal Finance

(For local fiscal year ended in 2006)

Revenues

Total $19,025,935
Taxes 11,429,125
Special benefits assessment 0
Licenses & permits 501,448
Fines & forfeitures 143,858
Revenues from use of money & property 389,860
Intergovernmental 1,000,963
Service charges 5,297,087
Other revenues 263,594
Other financing sources 0

Expenditures

Total $21,861,481
General government 2,900,878
Public safety 7,694,788
Transportation 2,506,191
Community development 1,193,524
Health 1,363,232
Culture & leisure 6,202,868
Other 0

Local School District

(Data from School year 2007-08 except as noted)

Pacific Grove Unified
555 Sinex Ave
Pacific Grove, CA 93950
(831) 646-6520

Superintendent .... Ralph Porras
Grade plan K-12
Number of schools 5
Enrollment 1,676
High school graduates, 2006-07 145
Dropout rate 0.8%
Pupil/teacher ratio 16.8
Average class size 21.8
Students per computer 4.2
Classrooms with internet 124
Avg. Daily Attendance (ADA) 1,599
Cost per ADA $12,593
Avg. Teacher Salary $74,364

California Achievement Tests 6th ed., 2008

(Pct scoring at or above 50th National Percentile Rank)

	Math	Reading	Language
Grade 3	70%	64%	69%
Grade 7	68%	69%	70%

Academic Performance Index, 2008

Number of students tested 1,293
Number of valid scores 1,214
2007 API (base) 853
2008 API (growth) 857

SAT Testing, 2006-07

Enrollment, Grade 12 147
Number taking test 91
percent taking test 61.9%
percent with total score 1,500+ 39.50%

Average Scores:

Math	Verbal	Writing	Total
546	531	530	1,607

Federal No Child Left Behind, 2008

(Adequate Yearly Progress standards met)

	Participation Rate	Pct Proficient
ELA	Yes	No
Math	Yes	No

API criteria .... Yes
Graduation rate .... Yes
criteria met/possible 20/18

Other school districts for this city

(see Appendix E for information on these districts)

None

See Introduction for an explanation of all data sources.

Demographics & Socio-Economic Characteristics

(2000 Decennial Census, except as noted)

Population

1990* 37,670
2000 38,390
Male 18,926
Female 19,464
Jan. 2008 (estimate)§ 39,616
Persons per sq. mi. of land 3,144.1

Race & Hispanic Origin, 2000

Race
White 26,684
Black/African American 1,254
North American Native 190
Asian 5,868
Pacific Islander 263
Other Race 1,605
Two or more races 2,526
Hispanic origin, total 5,609
Mexican 2,483
Puerto Rican 298
Cuban 70
Other Hispanic 2,758

Age & Nativity, 2000

Under 5 years 2,170
18 years and over 29,500
65 years and over 3,742
85 years and over 305
Median Age 37.6
Native-born 31,244
Foreign-born 7,169

Educational Attainment, 2000

Population 25 years and over 26,438
Less than 9th grade 3.2%
High school grad or higher 91.5%
Bachelor's degree or higher 33.8%
Graduate degree 10.3%

Income & Poverty, 1999

Per capita income $30,183
Median household income $71,737
Median family income $78,361
Persons in poverty 2.9%
H'holds receiving public assistance 165
H'holds receiving social security 2,826

Households, 2000

Total households 13,994
With persons under 18 5,022
With persons over 65 2,791
Family households 9,654
Single person households 2,971
Persons per household 2.73
Persons per family 3.21

Household Population, 2008§§

Persons living in households 39,435
Persons living in group quarters 181
Persons per household 2.8

Labor & Employment

Total civilian labor force, 2008§§ 22,900
Unemployment rate, 2008 .... 5.5%
Total civilian labor force, 2000 22,074

Employed persons 16 years and over by occupation, 2000

Managers & professionals 8,333
Service occupations 2,719
Sales & office occupations 6,143
Farming, fishing & forestry 23
Construction & maintenance 2,102
Production & transportation 1,982
Self-employed persons 1,438

* US Census Bureau
** 2000 Decennial Census
§ California Department of Finance
§§ California Employment Development Dept

General Information

City of Pacifica
170 Santa Maria Ave
Pacifica, CA 94044
650-738-7300

Website .... www.cityofpacifica.org
Elevation .... 60 ft.
Land Area (sq. miles) 12.6
Water Area (sq. miles) 0
Year of Incorporation 1957
Government type .... General law
Sales tax rate 9.25%

Voters & Officials

Registered Voters, October 2008

Total 24,039
Democrats 13,320
Republicans 3,980
Declined to state 5,545

Legislative Districts

US Congressional 12
State Senatorial 8
State Assembly 19

Local Officials, 2009

Mayor .... Julie Lancelle Jr
Manager .... Stephen A. Rhodes
City Clerk .... Kathy O'Connell
Attorney .... Cecilia Quick
Finance Dir .... Ann Ritzma
Public Works .... Van Ocampo (Dep)
Planning/Dev Dir .... Michael Crabtree
Building .... Doug Rider
Police Chief .... Jim Saunders
Emergency/Fire Dir .... Ron Myers

Public Safety

Number of officers, 2007 39
Violent crimes, 2007 74
Property crimes, 2007 626
Arson, 2007 7

Public Library

Pacifica Library
San Mateo County Library System
104 Hilton Way
Pacifica, CA 94044
650-355-5196

Branch Librarian .... Thom Ball

Library system statistics, FY 2007

Population served 278,388
Internet terminals 26
Annual users 49,920

Per capita:

Operating income $90.21
percent from local government 63.5%
Operating expenditure $60.41
Total materials 2.65
Print holdings 2.16
Visits per capita 5.44

Housing & Construction

Housing Units

Total, 2008§ 14,439
Single family units, attached 791
Single family units, detached 10,410
Multiple family units 3,140
Mobile home units 98
Occupied 14,281
Vacancy rate 1.1%
Median rent, 2000** $1,261
Median SF home value, 2000** $367,700

New Privately Owned Housing Units Authorized by Building Permit, 2007*

	Units	Construction Cost
Single	101	$42,197,430
Total	101	$42,197,430

Municipal Finance

(For local fiscal year ended in 2006)

Revenues

Total $39,032,314
Taxes 17,436,070
Special benefits assessment 1,302,305
Licenses & permits 492,155
Fines & forfeitures 140,389
Revenues from use of money & property 489,530
Intergovernmental 5,883,085
Service charges 11,999,891
Other revenues 1,288,889
Other financing sources 0

Expenditures

Total $39,974,103
General government 4,739,643
Public safety 15,849,729
Transportation 3,965,944
Community development 2,165,905
Health 9,045,568
Culture & leisure 4,207,314
Other 0

Local School District

(Data from School year 2007-08 except as noted)

Jefferson Union High
699 Serramonte Blvd, Ste100
Daly City, CA 94015
(650) 550-7900

Superintendent .... Michael Crilly
Grade plan 9-12
Number of schools 5
Enrollment 5,330
High school graduates, 2006-07 1,105
Dropout rate 3.0%
Pupil/teacher ratio 30.8
Average class size 25.9
Students per computer 4.3
Classrooms with internet 276
Avg. Daily Attendance (ADA) 5,128
Cost per ADA $8,239
Avg. Teacher Salary $58,641

California Achievement Tests 6th ed., 2008

(Pct scoring at or above 50th National Percentile Rank)

	Math	Reading	Language
Grade 3	NA	NA	NA
Grade 7	NA	NA	NA

Academic Performance Index, 2008

Number of students tested 3,846
Number of valid scores 3,651
2007 API (base) 730
2008 API (growth) 732

SAT Testing, 2006-07

Enrollment, Grade 12 1,255
Number taking test 532
percent taking test 42.4%
percent with total score 1,500+ 17.90%

Average Scores:

Math	Verbal	Writing	Total
510	471	474	1,455

Federal No Child Left Behind, 2008

(Adequate Yearly Progress standards met)

	Participation Rate	Pct Proficient
ELA	No	No
Math	Yes	Yes

API criteria .... Yes
Graduation rate .... Yes
criteria met/possible 34/31

Other school districts for this city

(see Appendix E for information on these districts)

Pacifica Elem

See Introduction for an explanation of all data sources.

Demographics & Socio-Economic Characteristics

(2000 Decennial Census, except as noted)

Population

1990* . . . 23,252
2000 . . . 41,155
Male . . . 19,783
Female . . . 21,372
Jan. 2008 (estimate)§ . . . 50,907
Persons per sq. mi. of land . . . 2,086.4

Race & Hispanic Origin, 2000

Race
White . . . 35,739
Black/African American . . . 495
North American Native . . . 187
Asian . . . 1,056
Pacific Islander . . . 40
Other Race . . . 2,666
Two or more races . . . 972
Hispanic origin, total . . . 7,031
Mexican . . . 5,532
Puerto Rican . . . 104
Cuban . . . 65
Other Hispanic . . . 1,330

Age & Nativity, 2000

Under 5 years . . . 1,849
18 years and over . . . 34,025
65 years and over . . . 11,339
85 years and over . . . 1,148
Median Age . . . 48.0
Native-born . . . 34,663
Foreign-born . . . 6,621

Educational Attainment, 2000

Population 25 years and over . . . 31,802
Less than 9th grade . . . 3.0%
High school grad or higher . . . 88.9%
Bachelor's degree or higher . . . 31.4%
Graduate degree . . . 11.3%

Income & Poverty, 1999

Per capita income . . . $33,463
Median household income . . . $48,316
Median family income . . . $58,183
Persons in poverty . . . 9.2%
H'holds receiving public assistance . . . 236
H'holds receiving social security . . . 7,950

Households, 2000

Total households . . . 19,184
With persons under 18 . . . 3,932
With persons over 65 . . . 7,853
Family households . . . 11,405
Single person households . . . 6,221
Persons per household . . . 2.13
Persons per family . . . 2.67

Household Population, 2008§§

Persons living in households . . . 50,523
Persons living in group quarters . . . 384
Persons per household . . . 2.1

Labor & Employment

Total civilian labor force, 2008§§ . . . 25,600
Unemployment rate, 2008 . . . 5.0%
Total civilian labor force, 2000 . . . 18,161

Employed persons 16 years and over by occupation, 2000

Managers & professionals . . . 6,479
Service occupations . . . 3,663
Sales & office occupations . . . 5,103
Farming, fishing & forestry . . . 27
Construction & maintenance . . . 1,275
Production & transportation . . . 837
Self-employed persons . . . 2,288

* US Census Bureau
** 2000 Decennial Census
§ California Department of Finance
§§ California Employment Development Dept

General Information

City of Palm Desert
73-510 Fred Waring Dr
Palm Desert, CA 92260
760-346-0611

Website . . . www.cityofpalmdesert.org
Elevation . . . 243 ft.
Land Area (sq. miles) . . . 24.4
Water Area (sq. miles) . . . 0.2
Year of Incorporation . . . 1973
Government type . . . Chartered
Sales tax rate . . . 8.75%

Voters & Officials

Registered Voters, October 2008

Total . . . 24,650
Democrats . . . 7,730
Republicans . . . 12,410
Declined to state . . . 3,664

Legislative Districts

US Congressional . . . 45
State Senatorial . . . 37
State Assembly . . . 64

Local Officials, 2009

Mayor . . . Robert A. Spiegel
City Manager . . . John Wohlmuth
City Clerk . . . Rachelle Klassen
Attorney . . . David Erwin
Finance Dir . . . Paul Gibson
Public Works . . . Mark Greenwood
Planning/Dev Dir . . . Lauri Aylaian
Building . . . Russel Granke
Police Chief . . . Andrew Shouse
Emergency/Fire Dir . . . Dennis Dawson

Public Safety

Number of officers, 2007 . . . NA
Violent crimes, 2007 . . . 92
Property crimes, 2007 . . . 2,914
Arson, 2007 . . . 11

Public Library

Palm Desert Branch Library
Riverside County Library Service
73-300 Fred Waring Dr
Palm Desert, CA 92260
760-346-6552

Branch Librarian . . . Jeannie Kays

Library system statistics, FY 2007

Population served . . . 1,047,996
Internet terminals . . . 37
Annual users . . . 69,346

Per capita:

Operating income . . . $19.38
percent from local government . . . 49.8%
Operating expenditure . . . $20.45
Total materials . . . 1.43
Print holdings . . . 1.30
Visits per capita . . . 4.06

Housing & Construction

Housing Units

Total, 2008§ . . . 34,120
Single family units, attached . . . 9,697
Single family units, detached . . . 13,453
Multiple family units . . . 7,661
Mobile home units . . . 3,309
Occupied . . . 23,549
Vacancy rate . . . 31.0%
Median rent, 2000** . . . $744
Median SF home value, 2000** . . . $189,100

New Privately Owned Housing Units Authorized by Building Permit, 2007*

	Units	Construction Cost
Single	224	$124,512,390
Total	294	$140,812,390

Municipal Finance

(For local fiscal year ended in 2006)

Revenues

Total . . . $88,455,760
Taxes . . . 47,903,293
Special benefits assessment . . . 6,681,687
Licenses & permits . . . 2,265,497
Fines & forfeitures . . . 385,821
Revenues from use of money & property . . . 6,361,233
Intergovernmental . . . 2,231,615
Service charges . . . 14,104,111
Other revenues . . . 8,522,503
Other financing sources . . . 0

Expenditures

Total . . . $71,669,670
General government . . . 8,321,765
Public safety . . . 20,528,149
Transportation . . . 21,237,439
Community development . . . 7,686,401
Health . . . 576,810
Culture & leisure . . . 13,319,106
Other . . . 0

Local School District

(Data from School year 2007-08 except as noted)

Desert Sands Unified
47-950 Dune Palms Rd
La Quinta, CA 92253
(760) 777-4200

Superintendent . . . Sharon McGehee
Grade plan . . . K-12
Number of schools . . . 33
Enrollment . . . 28,775
High school graduates, 2006-07 . . . 1,630
Dropout rate . . . 4.0%
Pupil/teacher ratio . . . 22.2
Average class size . . . 28.2
Students per computer . . . 5.6
Classrooms with internet . . . 1,229
Avg. Daily Attendance (ADA) . . . 27,315
Cost per ADA . . . $8,140
Avg. Teacher Salary . . . $70,970

California Achievement Tests 6th ed., 2008

(Pct scoring at or above 50th National Percentile Rank)

	Math	Reading	Language
Grade 3	56%	35%	46%
Grade 7	44%	44%	43%

Academic Performance Index, 2008

Number of students tested . . . 21,857
Number of valid scores . . . 20,761
2007 API (base) . . . 734
2008 API (growth) . . . 752

SAT Testing, 2006-07

Enrollment, Grade 12 . . . 2,045
Number taking test . . . 660
percent taking test . . . 32.3%
percent with total score 1,500+ . . . 13.40%

Average Scores:

Math	Verbal	Writing	Total
489	480	480	1,449

Federal No Child Left Behind, 2008

(Adequate Yearly Progress standards met)

	Participation Rate	Pct Proficient
ELA	Yes	No
Math	Yes	Yes

API criteria . . . Yes
Graduation rate . . . Yes
criteria met/possible . . . 38/36

Other school districts for this city

(see Appendix E for information on these districts)

Palm Springs Unified

See Introduction for an explanation of all data sources.

Demographics & Socio-Economic Characteristics

(2000 Decennial Census, except as noted)

Population

1990* . . . 40,181
2000 . . . 42,807
Male . . . 22,208
Female . . . 20,599
Jan. 2008 (estimate)§ . . . 47,251
Persons per sq. mi. of land . . . 501.6

Race & Hispanic Origin, 2000

Race
White . . . 33,531
Black/African American . . . 1,681
North American Native . . . 401
Asian . . . 1,639
Pacific Islander . . . 59
Other Race . . . 4,188
Two or more races . . . 1,308
Hispanic origin, total . . . 10,155
Mexican . . . 7,910
Puerto Rican . . . 105
Cuban . . . 85
Other Hispanic . . . 2,055

Age & Nativity, 2000

Under 5 years . . . 2,028
18 years and over . . . 35,532
65 years and over . . . 11,229
85 years and over . . . 1,573
Median Age . . . 46.9
Native-born . . . 33,682
Foreign-born . . . 9,166

Educational Attainment, 2000

Population 25 years and over . . . 32,777
Less than 9th grade . . . 7.1%
High school grad or higher . . . 81.7%
Bachelor's degree or higher . . . 26.6%
Graduate degree . . . 10.6%

Income & Poverty, 1999

Per capita income . . . $25,957
Median household income . . . $35,973
Median family income . . . $45,318
Persons in poverty . . . 15.0%
H'holds receiving public assistance . . . 435
H'holds receiving social security . . . 8,583

Households, 2000

Total households . . . 20,516
With persons under 18 . . . 3,758
With persons over 65 . . . 8,061
Family households . . . 9,464
Single person households . . . 8,537
Persons per household . . . 2.05
Persons per family . . . 2.88

Household Population, 2008§§

Persons living in households . . . 46,555
Persons living in group quarters . . . 696
Persons per household . . . 2.1

Labor & Employment

Total civilian labor force, 2008§§ . . . 26,700
Unemployment rate, 2008 . . . 6.6%
Total civilian labor force, 2000 . . . 19,017

Employed persons 16 years and over by occupation, 2000

Managers & professionals . . . 5,625
Service occupations . . . 4,459
Sales & office occupations . . . 5,210
Farming, fishing & forestry . . . 32
Construction & maintenance . . . 1,432
Production & transportation . . . 1,083
Self-employed persons . . . 2,540

* US Census Bureau
** 2000 Decennial Census
§ California Department of Finance
§§ California Employment Development Dept

General Information

City of Palm Springs
PO Box 2743
Palm Springs, CA 92263
760-323-8299

Website . . . www.palmsprings-ca.gov
Elevation . . . 466 ft.
Land Area (sq. miles) . . . 94.2
Water Area (sq. miles) . . . 0.8
Year of Incorporation . . . 1938
Government type . . . Chartered
Sales tax rate . . . 8.75%

Voters & Officials

Registered Voters, October 2008

Total . . . 24,600
Democrats . . . 11,620
Republicans . . . 8,239
Declined to state . . . 3,866

Legislative Districts

US Congressional . . . 45
State Senatorial . . . 37
State Assembly . . . 80

Local Officials, 2009

Mayor . . . Steve Pougnet
Manager . . . David Ready
City Clerk . . . James Thompson
Attorney . . . Douglas Holland
Finance Dir . . . Geoffrey Kiehl
Public Works . . . David Barakian
Planning/Dev Dir . . . Craig Ewing
Building . . . Don Duckworth
Police Chief . . . David Dominguez
Fire Chief . . . Blake Goetz

Public Safety

Number of officers, 2007 . . . 89
Violent crimes, 2007 . . . 307
Property crimes, 2007 . . . 3,519
Arson, 2007 . . . NA

Public Library

Palm Springs Public Library
300 S Sunrise Way
Palm Springs, CA 92262
760-322-7323

Director . . . Barbara Roberts

Library statistics, FY 2007

Population served . . . 46,858
Internet terminals . . . 30
Annual users . . . 135,600

Per capita:

Operating income . . . $57.75
percent from local government . . . 97.8%
Operating expenditure . . . $49.05
Total materials . . . 3.25
Print holdings . . . 2.80
Visits per capita . . . 5.48

Housing & Construction

Housing Units

Total, 2008§ . . . 33,479
Single family units, attached . . . 6,679
Single family units, detached . . . 12,099
Multiple family units . . . 12,473
Mobile home units . . . 2,228
Occupied . . . 22,287
Vacancy rate . . . 33.4%
Median rent, 2000** . . . $631
Median SF home value, 2000** . . . $157,000

New Privately Owned Housing Units Authorized by Building Permit, 2007*

	Units	Construction Cost
Single	218	$54,654,693
Total	229	$55,812,693

Municipal Finance

(For local fiscal year ended in 2006)

Revenues

Total . . . $113,909,520
Taxes . . . 58,769,462
Special benefits assessment . . . 147,070
Licenses & permits . . . 2,028,770
Fines & forfeitures . . . 723,116
Revenues from use of money & property . . . 4,675,132
Intergovernmental . . . 12,017,469
Service charges . . . 33,204,597
Other revenues . . . 2,343,904
Other financing sources . . . 0

Expenditures

Total . . . $112,933,865
General government . . . 9,171,706
Public safety . . . 31,024,151
Transportation . . . 28,808,104
Community development . . . 12,222,853
Health . . . 3,192,567
Culture & leisure . . . 28,514,484
Other . . . 0

Local School District

(Data from School year 2007-08 except as noted)

Palm Springs Unified
980 East Tahquitz Canyon Way
Palm Springs, CA 92262
(760) 416-6000

Superintendent . . . Lorri McCune
Grade plan . . . K-12
Number of schools . . . 25
Enrollment . . . 24,400
High school graduates, 2006-07 . . . 1,146
Dropout rate . . . 5.8%
Pupil/teacher ratio . . . 21.9
Average class size . . . 28.3
Students per computer . . . 5.9
Classrooms with internet . . . 1,311
Avg. Daily Attendance (ADA) . . . 22,873
Cost per ADA . . . $8,379
Avg. Teacher Salary . . . $66,086

California Achievement Tests 6th ed., 2008

(Pct scoring at or above 50th National Percentile Rank)

	Math	Reading	Language
Grade 3	44%	28%	36%
Grade 7	37%	35%	32%

Academic Performance Index, 2008

Number of students tested . . . 18,458
Number of valid scores . . . 17,207
2007 API (base) . . . 673
2008 API (growth) . . . 700

SAT Testing, 2006-07

Enrollment, Grade 12 . . . 1,704
Number taking test . . . 438
percent taking test . . . 25.7%
percent with total score 1,500+ . . . 8.90%

Average Scores:

Math	Verbal	Writing	Total
469	468	454	1,391

Federal No Child Left Behind, 2008

(Adequate Yearly Progress standards met)

	Participation Rate	Pct Proficient
ELA	Yes	No
Math	Yes	No

API criteria . . . Yes
Graduation rate . . . No
\# criteria met/possible . . . 38/31

Other school districts for this city

(see Appendix E for information on these districts)

None

See Introduction for an explanation of all data sources.

Demographics & Socio-Economic Characteristics†

(2007 American Community Survey, except as noted)

Population
1990* . . . 68,842
2007 . . . 132,266
Male . . . 66,028
Female . . . 66,238
Jan. 2008 (estimate)§ . . . 147,897
Persons per sq. mi. of land . . . 1,408.5

Race & Hispanic Origin, 2007
Race
White . . . 51,115
Black/African American . . . 19,409
North American Native . . . 864
Asian . . . 5,921
Pacific Islander . . . 0
Other Race . . . 48,546
Two or more races . . . 6,411
Hispanic origin, total . . . 69,705
Mexican . . . 49,491
Puerto Rican . . . 1,088
Cuban . . . 578
Other Hispanic . . . 18,548

Age & Nativity, 2007
Under 5 years . . . 10,704
18 years and over . . . 86,900
65 years and over . . . 10,333
85 years and over . . . 1,055
Median Age . . . 30.5
Native-born . . . 96,092
Foreign-born . . . 36,174

Educational Attainment, 2007
Population 25 years and over . . . 74,614
Less than 9th grade . . . 10.6%
High school grad or higher . . . 76.0%
Bachelor's degree or higher . . . 16.0%
Graduate degree . . . 5.1%

Income & Poverty, 2007
Per capita income . . . $19,998
Median household income . . . $55,499
Median family income . . . $56,112
Persons in poverty . . . 18.1%
H'holds receiving public assistance . . . 1,274
H'holds receiving social security . . . 8,358

Households, 2007
Total households . . . 36,425
With persons under 18 . . . 19,390
With persons over 65 . . . 7,071
Family households . . . 30,199
Single person households . . . 4,927
Persons per household . . . 3.63
Persons per family . . . 3.94

Household Population, 2008§§
Persons living in households . . . 147,803
Persons living in group quarters . . . 94
Persons per household . . . 3.6

Labor & Employment
Total civilian labor force, 2008§§ . . . 56,200
Unemployment rate, 2008 . . . 9.4%
Total civilian labor force, 2000* . . . 48,183

Employed persons 16 years and over by occupation, 2007
Managers & professionals . . . 13,755
Service occupations . . . 9,466
Sales & office occupations . . . 14,224
Farming, fishing & forestry . . . 213
Construction & maintenance . . . 8,509
Production & transportation . . . 7,225
Self-employed persons . . . 3,834

† see Appendix D for 2000 Decennial Census Data
* US Census Bureau
** 2007 American Community Survey
§ California Department of Finance
§§ California Employment Development Dept

General Information

City of Palmdale
38300 Sierra Hwy
Suite A
Palmdale, CA 93550
661-267-5100

Website . . . www.cityofpalmdale.org
Elevation . . . 2,659 ft.
Land Area (sq. miles) . . . 105.0
Water Area (sq. miles) . . . 0.1
Year of Incorporation . . . 1962
Government type . . . General law
Sales tax rate . . . 9.25%

Voters & Officials

Registered Voters, October 2008
Total . . . 55,743
Democrats . . . 25,045
Republicans . . . 18,664
Declined to state . . . 9,554

Legislative Districts
US Congressional . . . 25
State Senatorial . . . 17
State Assembly . . . 36

Local Officials, 2009
Mayor . . . James Ledford Jr
Manager . . . Stephen H. Williams
City Clerk . . . Victoria Hancock
Attorney . . . W. Matthew Ditzhazy
Finance Dir . . . Betsy St. John
Public Works . . . Mike Mischel
Planning/Dev Dir . . . Asoka Herath
Building . . . Shane Walters
Police Chief . . . (County)
Fire/Emergency Mgmt . . . (County)

Public Safety

Number of officers, 2007 . . . NA
Violent crimes, 2007 . . . 1,043
Property crimes, 2007 . . . 4,302
Arson, 2007 . . . 46

Public Library

Palmdale City Library
Palmdale City Library System
700 E Palmdale Blvd
Palmdale, CA 93550
661-267-5600

City Librarian . . . Paul Miller

Library system statistics, FY 2007
Population served . . . 145,468
Internet terminals . . . 14
Annual users . . . 41,440

Per capita:
Operating income . . . $18.29
percent from local government . . . 94.3%
Operating expenditure . . . $18.29
Total materials . . . 1.03
Print holdings . . . 0.96
Visits per capita . . . 2.30

Housing & Construction

Housing Units
Total, 2008§ . . . 44,907
Single family units, attached . . . 905
Single family units, detached . . . 35,880
Multiple family units . . . 6,340
Mobile home units . . . 1,782
Occupied . . . 41,509
Vacancy rate . . . 7.6%
Median rent, 2007** . . . $995
Median SF home value, 2007** . . . $370,100

New Privately Owned Housing Units Authorized by Building Permit, 2007*

	Units	Construction Cost
Single	839	$186,302,604
Total	1,035	$197,785,292

Municipal Finance

(For local fiscal year ended in 2006)

Revenues
Total . . . $108,267,589
Taxes . . . 31,863,089
Special benefits assessment . . . 3,937,481
Licenses & permits . . . 8,385,952
Fines & forfeitures . . . 1,100,840
Revenues from use of money & property . . . 2,115,209
Intergovernmental . . . 23,685,649
Service charges . . . 30,356,972
Other revenues . . . 4,338,033
Other financing sources . . . 2,484,364

Expenditures
Total . . . $91,328,614
General government . . . 31,926,785
Public safety . . . 16,773,916
Transportation . . . 20,277,129
Community development . . . 8,211,461
Health . . . 0
Culture & leisure . . . 14,139,323
Other . . . 0

Local School District

(Data from School year 2007-08 except as noted)

Antelope Valley Union High
44811 North Sierra Hwy
Lancaster, CA 93534
(661) 948-7655

Superintendent . . . David Vierra
Grade plan . . . 9-12
Number of schools . . . 14
Enrollment . . . 26,453
High school graduates, 2006-07 . . . 3,778
Dropout rate . . . 4.4%
Pupil/teacher ratio . . . 23.0
Average class size . . . 26.0
Students per computer . . . 4.0
Classrooms with internet . . . 1,530
Avg. Daily Attendance (ADA) . . . 23,462
Cost per ADA . . . $8,393
Avg. Teacher Salary . . . $62,133

California Achievement Tests 6th ed., 2008
(Pct scoring at or above 50th National Percentile Rank)

	Math	Reading	Language
Grade 3	NA	NA	NA
Grade 7	NA	NA	NA

Academic Performance Index, 2008
Number of students tested . . . 17,439
Number of valid scores . . . 16,491
2007 API (base) . . . 657
2008 API (growth) . . . 660

SAT Testing, 2006-07
Enrollment, Grade 12 . . . 5,784
Number taking test . . . 1,303
percent taking test . . . 22.5%
percent with total score 1,500+ . . . 8.00%

Average Scores:

Math	Verbal	Writing	Total
467	473	468	1,408

Federal No Child Left Behind, 2008
(Adequate Yearly Progress standards met)

	Participation Rate	Pct Proficient
ELA	Yes	No
Math	Yes	No

API criteria . . . Yes
Graduation rate . . . No
\# criteria met/possible . . . 36/32

Other school districts for this city
(see Appendix E for information on these districts)
Keppel Union Elem, Palmdale Elem

See Introduction for an explanation of all data sources.

Demographics & Socio-Economic Characteristics

(2000 Decennial Census, except as noted)

Population

1990* 55,900
2000 58,598
Male 28,671
Female 29,927
Jan. 2008 (estimate)§ 63,367
Persons per sq. mi. of land 2,673.7

Race & Hispanic Origin, 2000

Race
White 44,391
Black/African American 1,184
North American Native 122
Asian 10,090
Pacific Islander 84
Other Race 827
Two or more races 1,900
Hispanic origin, total 2,722
Mexican 1,543
Puerto Rican 72
Cuban 75
Other Hispanic 1,032

Age & Nativity, 2000

Under 5 years 2,970
18 years and over 46,192
65 years and over 9,140
85 years and over 1,374
Median Age 40.2
Native-born 43,210
Foreign-born 15,573

Educational Attainment, 2000

Population 25 years and over 43,566
Less than 9th grade 1.7%
High school grad or higher 96.2%
Bachelor's degree or higher 74.4%
Graduate degree 43.0%

Income & Poverty, 1999

Per capita income $56,257
Median household income $90,377
Median family income $117,574
Persons in poverty 4.8%
H'holds receiving public assistance 245
H'holds receiving social security 5,851

Households, 2000

Total households 25,216
With persons under 18 7,137
With persons over 65 6,439
Family households 14,593
Single person households 8,209
Persons per household 2.30
Persons per family 2.95

Household Population, 2008§§

Persons living in households 62,618
Persons living in group quarters 749
Persons per household 2.3

Labor & Employment

Total civilian labor force, 2008§§ 32,000
Unemployment rate, 2008 .... 3.2%
Total civilian labor force, 2000 31,982

Employed persons 16 years and over by occupation, 2000

Managers & professionals 23,839
Service occupations 1,493
Sales & office occupations 4,638
Farming, fishing & forestry 9
Construction & maintenance 624
Production & transportation 766
Self-employed persons 3,126

* US Census Bureau
** 2000 Decennial Census
§ California Department of Finance
§§ California Employment Development Dept

General Information

City of Palo Alto
250 Hamilton Ave
PO Box 10250
Palo Alto, CA 94303
650-329-2100

Website .... www.cityofpaloalto.org
Elevation .... 23 ft.
Land Area (sq. miles) 23.7
Water Area (sq. miles) 2.0
Year of Incorporation 1894
Government type .... Chartered
Sales tax rate 9.25%

Voters & Officials

Registered Voters, October 2008

Total 38,558
Democrats 20,608
Republicans 6,825
Declined to state 10,062

Legislative Districts

US Congressional 14
State Senatorial 11
State Assembly 21

Local Officials, 2009

Mayor .... Peter Drekmeier
Manager .... James Keene
City Clerk .... Donna Grider
Attorney .... Gary Baum
Finance Dir .... Lalo Perez
Public Works .... Glenn Roberts
Planning/Dev Dir .... Steve Emslie
Building .... NA
Police Chief .... Dennis Burns
Emergency/Fire Dir .... Nick Marinaro

Public Safety

Number of officers, 2007 82
Violent crimes, 2007 64
Property crimes, 2007 1,440
Arson, 2007 15

Public Library

Palo Alto Main Library
Palo Alto City Library System
1213 Newell Rd
Palo Alto, CA 94303
650-329-2436

Director .... Diane Jennings

Library system statistics, FY 2007

Population served 62,615
Internet terminals 75
Annual users 161,005

Per capita:

Operating income $98.74
percent from local government 95.8%
Operating expenditure $96.28
Total materials 4.39
Print holdings 3.83
Visits per capita 13.77

Housing & Construction

Housing Units

Total, 2008§ 27,938
Single family units, attached 980
Single family units, detached 15,636
Multiple family units 11,158
Mobile home units 164
Occupied 27,045
Vacancy rate 3.2%
Median rent, 2000** $1,349
Median SF home value, 2000** $811,800

New Privately Owned Housing Units Authorized by Building Permit, 2007*

	Units	Construction Cost
Single	195	$83,921,263
Total	486	$209,649,078

Municipal Finance

(For local fiscal year ended in 2006)

Revenues

Total $356,168,000
Taxes 60,086,000
Special benefits assessment 0
Licenses & permits 5,162,000
Fines & forfeitures 1,789,000
Revenues from use of
money & property 17,558,000
Intergovernmental 6,911,000
Service charges 260,048,000
Other revenues 4,614,000
Other financing sources 0

Expenditures

Total $331,673,000
General government 34,240,000
Public safety 40,642,000
Transportation 10,493,000
Community development 13,260,000
Health 57,005,000
Culture & leisure 26,467,000
Other 0

Local School District

(Data from School year 2007-08 except as noted)

Palo Alto Unified
25 Churchill Ave
Palo Alto, CA 94306
(650) 329-3700

Superintendent .... Kevin Skelly
Grade plan K-12
Number of schools 19
Enrollment 11,204
High school graduates, 2006-07 783
Dropout rate 0.6%
Pupil/teacher ratio 14.9
Average class size 23.3
Students per computer 2.8
Classrooms with internet 3,973
Avg. Daily Attendance (ADA) 10,919
Cost per ADA $13,162
Avg. Teacher Salary $81,193

California Achievement Tests 6th ed., 2008

(Pct scoring at or above 50th National Percentile Rank)

	Math	Reading	Language
Grade 3	85%	78%	83%
Grade 7	89%	87%	85%

Academic Performance Index, 2008

Number of students tested 8,428
Number of valid scores 8,070
2007 API (base) 910
2008 API (growth) 918

SAT Testing, 2006-07

Enrollment, Grade 12 823
Number taking test 695
percent taking test 84.5%
percent with total score 1,500+ ... 76.20%

Average Scores:

Math	Verbal	Writing	Total
655	624	615	1,894

Federal No Child Left Behind, 2008

(Adequate Yearly Progress standards met)

	Participation Rate	Pct Proficient
ELA	No	Yes
Math	No	Yes

API criteria .... Yes
Graduation rate .... Yes
criteria met/possible 34/32

Other school districts for this city

(see Appendix E for information on these districts)

None

See Introduction for an explanation of all data sources.

Demographics & Socio-Economic Characteristics

(2000 Decennial Census, except as noted)

Population

1990* . . . 13,512
2000 . . . 13,340
Male . . . 6,538
Female . . . 6,802
Jan. 2008 (estimate)§ . . . 14,046
Persons per sq. mi. of land . . . 2,926.3

Race & Hispanic Origin, 2000

Race
White . . . 10,448
Black/African American . . . 132
North American Native . . . 18
Asian . . . 2,286
Pacific Islander . . . 16
Other Race . . . 80
Two or more races . . . 360
Hispanic origin, total . . . 378
Mexican . . . 190
Puerto Rican . . . 18
Cuban . . . 11
Other Hispanic . . . 159

Age & Nativity, 2000

Under 5 years . . . 697
18 years and over . . . 10,246
65 years and over . . . 2,660
85 years and over . . . 193
Median Age . . . 46.7
Native-born . . . 10,802
Foreign-born . . . 2,538

Educational Attainment, 2000

Population 25 years and over . . . 9,716
Less than 9th grade . . . 0.8%
High school grad or higher . . . 98.4%
Bachelor's degree or higher . . . 70.9%
Graduate degree . . . 31.0%

Income & Poverty, 1999

Per capita income . . . $69,040
Median household income . . . $123,534
Median family income . . . $133,563
Persons in poverty . . . 2.2%
H'holds receiving public assistance . . . 16
H'holds receiving social security . . . 1,706

Households, 2000

Total households . . . 4,993
With persons under 18 . . . 1,707
With persons over 65 . . . 1,759
Family households . . . 4,117
Single person households . . . 749
Persons per household . . . 2.67
Persons per family . . . 2.96

Household Population, 2008§§

Persons living in households . . . 14,041
Persons living in group quarters . . . 5
Persons per household . . . 2.8

Labor & Employment

Total civilian labor force, 2008§§ . . . 6,800
Unemployment rate, 2008 . . . 1.5%
Total civilian labor force, 2000 . . . 5,835

Employed persons 16 years and over by occupation, 2000

Managers & professionals . . . 3,955
Service occupations . . . 338
Sales & office occupations . . . 1,203
Farming, fishing & forestry . . . 0
Construction & maintenance . . . 110
Production & transportation . . . 134
Self-employed persons . . . 1,003

* US Census Bureau
** 2000 Decennial Census
§ California Department of Finance
§§ California Employment Development Dept

General Information

City of Palos Verdes Estates
340 Palos Verdes Dr W
Palos Verdes Estates, CA 90274
310-378-0383

Website . . . www.palosverdes.com/pve
Elevation . . . 217 ft.
Land Area (sq. miles) . . . 4.8
Water Area (sq. miles) . . . 0
Year of Incorporation . . . 1939
Government type . . . General law
Sales tax rate . . . 9.25%

Voters & Officials

Registered Voters, October 2008

Total . . . 9,859
Democrats . . . 2,553
Republicans . . . 5,388
Declined to state . . . 1,606

Legislative Districts

US Congressional . . . 46
State Senatorial . . . 25
State Assembly . . . 54

Local Officials, 2009

Mayor . . . Joseph Sherwood Jr
Manager . . . Joseph M. Hoefgen
City Clerk . . . Judy Smith
Attorney . . . Joseph W. Pannone
Finance Dir . . . Judy Smith
Public Works . . . Allan Rigg
Planning/Dev Dir . . . Allan Rigg
Building . . . NA
Police Chief . . . Daniel W. Dreiling
Fire/Emergency Mgmt . . . (County)

Public Safety

Number of officers, 2007 . . . 24
Violent crimes, 2007 . . . 4
Property crimes, 2007 . . . 163
Arson, 2007 . . . 6

Public Library

Malaga Cove Library
Palos Verdes Library District
2400 Via Campesina
Palos Verdes Estates, CA 90274
310-377-9584

Library Manager . . . Jennifer Addington

Library system statistics, FY 2007

Population served . . . 67,286
Internet terminals . . . 34
Annual users . . . 53,850

Per capita:

Operating income . . . $92.15
percent from local government . . . 84.1%
Operating expenditure . . . $85.75
Total materials . . . 3.52
Print holdings . . . 3.09
Visits per capita . . . 9.36

Housing & Construction

Housing Units

Total, 2008§ . . . 5,289
Single family units, attached . . . 40
Single family units, detached . . . 4,867
Multiple family units . . . 382
Mobile home units . . . 0
Occupied . . . 5,078
Vacancy rate . . . 4.0%
Median rent, 2000** . . . $1,351
Median SF home value, 2000** . . . $795,600

New Privately Owned Housing Units Authorized by Building Permit, 2007*

	Units	Construction Cost
Single	16	$11,879,168
Total	19	$12,181,308

Municipal Finance

(For local fiscal year ended in 2006)

Revenues

Total . . . $16,182,866
Taxes . . . 7,151,911
Special benefits assessment . . . 4,624,226
Licenses & permits . . . 740,292
Fines & forfeitures . . . 180,828
Revenues from use of money & property . . . 1,588,411
Intergovernmental . . . 872,681
Service charges . . . 561,341
Other revenues . . . 463,176
Other financing sources . . . 0

Expenditures

Total . . . $15,937,108
General government . . . 1,286,239
Public safety . . . 8,386,383
Transportation . . . 4,398,945
Community development . . . 1,046,662
Health . . . 0
Culture & leisure . . . 818,879
Other . . . 0

Local School District

(Data from School year 2007-08 except as noted)

Palos Verdes Peninsula Unified
3801 Via la Selva
Palos Verdes Estates, CA 90274
(310) 378-9966

Superintendent . . . Walker Williams
Grade plan . . . K-12
Number of schools . . . 17
Enrollment . . . 12,000
High school graduates, 2006-07 . . . 1,034
Dropout rate . . . 0.1%
Pupil/teacher ratio . . . 22.4
Average class size . . . 25.9
Students per computer . . . 4.5
Classrooms with internet . . . 602
Avg. Daily Attendance (ADA) . . . 11,751
Cost per ADA . . . $8,162
Avg. Teacher Salary . . . $67,734

California Achievement Tests 6th ed., 2008

(Pct scoring at or above 50th National Percentile Rank)

	Math	Reading	Language
Grade 3	89%	75%	81%
Grade 7	85%	80%	79%

Academic Performance Index, 2008

Number of students tested . . . 9,415
Number of valid scores . . . 9,216
2007 API (base) . . . 899
2008 API (growth) . . . 904

SAT Testing, 2006-07

Enrollment, Grade 12 . . . 1,046
Number taking test . . . 905
percent taking test . . . 86.5%
percent with total score 1,500+ . . . 66.40%

Average Scores:

Math	Verbal	Writing	Total
600	556	568	1,724

Federal No Child Left Behind, 2008

(Adequate Yearly Progress standards met)

	Participation Rate	Pct Proficient
ELA	Yes	Yes
Math	Yes	Yes

API criteria . . . Yes
Graduation rate . . . Yes
\# criteria met/possible . . . 38/38

Other school districts for this city

(see Appendix E for information on these districts)

None

See Introduction for an explanation of all data sources.

Demographics & Socio-Economic Characteristics

(2000 Decennial Census, except as noted)

Population

1990* 25,408
2000 26,408
Male 12,307
Female 14,101
Jan. 2008 (estimate)§ 26,368
Persons per sq. mi. of land 1,448.8

Race & Hispanic Origin, 2000

Race
White 24,751
Black/African American 51
North American Native 283
Asian 275
Pacific Islander 31
Other Race 320
Two or more races 697
Hispanic origin, total 1,127
Mexican 786
Puerto Rican 42
Cuban 9
Other Hispanic 290

Age & Nativity, 2000

Under 5 years 1,139
18 years and over 21,022
65 years and over 7,175
85 years and over 1,158
Median Age 46.6
Native-born 25,460
Foreign-born 991

Educational Attainment, 2000

Population 25 years and over 19,368
Less than 9th grade 2.8%
High school grad or higher 85.7%
Bachelor's degree or higher 19.4%
Graduate degree 6.6%

Income & Poverty, 1999

Per capita income $19,267
Median household income $31,863
Median family income $41,228
Persons in poverty 12.2%
H'holds receiving public assistance 552
H'holds receiving social security 5,327

Households, 2000

Total households 11,591
With persons under 18 2,933
With persons over 65 4,880
Family households 7,244
Single person households 3,709
Persons per household 2.22
Persons per family 2.77

Household Population, 2008§§

Persons living in households 25,748
Persons living in group quarters 620
Persons per household 2.2

Labor & Employment

Total civilian labor force, 2008§§ 12,200
Unemployment rate, 2008 . . . . . 6.5%
Total civilian labor force, 2000 10,471

Employed persons 16 years and over by occupation, 2000

Managers & professionals 2,964
Service occupations 1,995
Sales & office occupations 2,506
Farming, fishing & forestry 22
Construction & maintenance 1,079
Production & transportation 1,197
Self-employed persons 1,533

* US Census Bureau
** 2000 Decennial Census
§ California Department of Finance
§§ California Employment Development Dept

General Information

Town of Paradise
5555 Skyway
Paradise, CA 95969
530-872-6291

Website . . . . . www.townofparadise.com
Elevation . . . . . 1,708 ft.
Land Area (sq. miles) 18.2
Water Area (sq. miles) 0
Year of Incorporation 1979
Government type . . . . . General law
Sales tax rate 8.25%

Voters & Officials

Registered Voters, October 2008

Total 16,820
Democrats 5,524
Republicans 7,237
Declined to state 2,907

Legislative Districts

US Congressional 2
State Senatorial 4
State Assembly 3

Local Officials, 2009

Mayor . . . . . Frankie Rutledge
Manager . . . . . Charles L. Rough Jr
City Clerk . . . . . Joanna Gutierrez
Attorney . . . . . Dwight Moore
Finance Dir . . . . . Gina Will
Public Works . . . . . Dennis J Schmidt
Planning/Dev Dir . . . . . Albert J. McGreehan
Building . . . . . (vacant)
Police Chief . . . . . Gerald Carrigan
Fire Chief . . . . . Mark Haunschild

Public Safety

Number of officers, 2007 26
Violent crimes, 2007 55
Property crimes, 2007 755
Arson, 2007 9

Public Library

Paradise Branch
Butte County Library System
5922 Clark Rd
Paradise, CA 95969
530-872-6320

Branch Librarian . . . . . Elizabeth Stewart

Library system statistics, FY 2007

Population served 218,069
Internet terminals 47
Annual users 90,296

Per capita:

Operating income $12.21
percent from local government 84.5%
Operating expenditure $12.71
Total materials 1.41
Print holdings 1.33
Visits per capita 3.01

Housing & Construction

Housing Units

Total, 2008§ 12,768
Single family units, attached 338
Single family units, detached 8,857
Multiple family units 1,102
Mobile home units 2,471
Occupied 11,961
Vacancy rate 6.3%
Median rent, 2000** $573
Median SF home value, 2000** $129,100

New Privately Owned Housing Units Authorized by Building Permit, 2007*

	Units	Construction Cost
Single	47	$7,742,582
Total	47	$7,742,582

Municipal Finance

(For local fiscal year ended in 2006)

Revenues

Total $11,337,191
Taxes 5,734,593
Special benefits assessment 0
Licenses & permits 142,017
Fines & forfeitures 151,452
Revenues from use of money & property 104,107
Intergovernmental 4,229,170
Service charges 342,001
Other revenues 633,851
Other financing sources 0

Expenditures

Total $12,650,002
General government 1,820,054
Public safety 6,778,233
Transportation 3,389,127
Community development 332,055
Health 330,533
Culture & leisure 0
Other 0

Local School District

(Data from School year 2007-08 except as noted)

Paradise Unified
6696 Clark Rd
Paradise, CA 95969
(530) 872-6400

Superintendent . . . . . David Tooker
Grade plan K-12
Number of schools 14
Enrollment 4,882
High school graduates, 2006-07 383
Dropout rate 2.4%
Pupil/teacher ratio 21.0
Average class size 25.3
Students per computer 4.2
Classrooms with internet 266
Avg. Daily Attendance (ADA) 4,454
Cost per ADA $8,275
Avg. Teacher Salary $58,806

California Achievement Tests 6th ed., 2008

(Pct scoring at or above 50th National Percentile Rank)

	Math	Reading	Language
Grade 3	53%	45%	49%
Grade 7	53%	57%	50%

Academic Performance Index, 2008

Number of students tested 3,545
Number of valid scores 3,330
2007 API (base) 739
2008 API (growth) 743

SAT Testing, 2006-07

Enrollment, Grade 12 470
Number taking test 74
percent taking test 15.7%
percent with total score 1,500+ 8.90%

Average Scores:

Math	Verbal	Writing	Total
510	522	502	1,534

Federal No Child Left Behind, 2008

(Adequate Yearly Progress standards met)

	Participation Rate	Pct Proficient
ELA	No	Yes
Math	Yes	Yes

API criteria . . . . . Yes
Graduation rate . . . . . Yes
\# criteria met/possible 22/21

Other school districts for this city

(see Appendix E for information on these districts)

None

See Introduction for an explanation of all data sources.

Demographics & Socio-Economic Characteristics

(2000 Decennial Census, except as noted)

Population

1990* . . . 47,669
2000 . . . 55,266
Male . . . 27,113
Female . . . 28,153
Jan. 2008 (estimate)§ . . . 57,969
Persons per sq. mi. of land . . . 12,333.8

Race & Hispanic Origin, 2000

Race
White . . . 19,177
Black/African American . . . 7,508
North American Native . . . 586
Asian . . . 1,851
Pacific Islander . . . 464
Other Race . . . 23,040
Two or more races . . . 2,640
Hispanic origin, total . . . 39,945
Mexican . . . 33,129
Puerto Rican . . . 212
Cuban . . . 125
Other Hispanic . . . 6,479

Age & Nativity, 2000

Under 5 years . . . 6,054
18 years and over . . . 34,893
65 years and over . . . 2,849
85 years and over . . . 259
Median Age . . . 25.6
Native-born . . . 32,858
Foreign-born . . . 22,461

Educational Attainment, 2000

Population 25 years and over . . . 28,128
Less than 9th grade . . . 29.6%
High school grad or higher . . . 50.0%
Bachelor's degree or higher . . . 7.0%
Graduate degree . . . 2.7%

Income & Poverty, 1999

Per capita income . . . $11,487
Median household income . . . $36,749
Median family income . . . $37,276
Persons in poverty . . . 21.7%
H'holds receiving public assistance . . . 1,299
H'holds receiving social security . . . 2,246

Households, 2000

Total households . . . 13,972
With persons under 18 . . . 8,744
With persons over 65 . . . 2,156
Family households . . . 11,334
Single person households . . . 2,039
Persons per household . . . 3.93
Persons per family . . . 4.31

Household Population, 2008§§

Persons living in households . . . 57,649
Persons living in group quarters . . . 320
Persons per household . . . 4.1

Labor & Employment

Total civilian labor force, 2008§§ . . . 24,800
Unemployment rate, 2008 . . . 11.1%
Total civilian labor force, 2000 . . . 21,305

Employed persons 16 years and over by occupation, 2000

Managers & professionals . . . 3,399
Service occupations . . . 2,958
Sales & office occupations . . . 4,950
Farming, fishing & forestry . . . 34
Construction & maintenance . . . 1,988
Production & transportation . . . 5,529
Self-employed persons . . . 1,102

* US Census Bureau
** 2000 Decennial Census
§ California Department of Finance
§§ California Employment Development Dept

General Information

City of Paramount
16400 Colorado Ave
Paramount, CA 90723
562-220-2000

Website . . . www.paramountcity.com
Elevation . . . 67 ft.
Land Area (sq. miles) . . . 4.7
Water Area (sq. miles) . . . 0.1
Year of Incorporation . . . 1957
Government type . . . General law
Sales tax rate . . . 9.25%

Voters & Officials

Registered Voters, October 2008

Total . . . 16,730
Democrats . . . 10,504
Republicans . . . 2,627
Declined to state . . . 2,945

Legislative Districts

US Congressional . . . 39
State Senatorial . . . 27
State Assembly . . . 52

Local Officials, 2009

Mayor . . . Gene Daniels
Manager . . . Linda Benedetti-Leal
City Clerk . . . Lana Chikami
Attorney . . . John E. Cavanaugh
Finance Dir . . . Karina Lam
Public Works . . . Chris Cash
Community Dev Dir . . . Joe Perez
Building . . . NA
Police Chief . . . Christine Guyovich
Emergency/Fire Dir. . . . P. Michael Freeman

Public Safety

Number of officers, 2007 . . . NA
Violent crimes, 2007 . . . 483
Property crimes, 2007 . . . 1,936
Arson, 2007 . . . 16

Public Library

Paramount Library
Los Angeles County Public Library System
16254 Colorado Ave
Paramount, CA 90723
562-630-3171

Branch Librarian . . . Cherie Shih

Library system statistics, FY 2007

Population served . . . 3,673,313
Internet terminals . . . 749
Annual users . . . 3,748,771

Per capita:

Operating income . . . $30.06
percent from local government . . . 93.6%
Operating expenditure . . . $28.36
Total materials . . . 2.22
Print holdings . . . 1.97
Visits per capita . . . 3.25

Housing & Construction

Housing Units

Total, 2008§ . . . 14,608
Single family units, attached . . . 2,166
Single family units, detached . . . 6,064
Multiple family units . . . 5,006
Mobile home units . . . 1,372
Occupied . . . 13,987
Vacancy rate . . . 4.3%
Median rent, 2000** . . . $720
Median SF home value, 2000** . . . $154,300

New Privately Owned Housing Units Authorized by Building Permit, 2007*

	Units	Construction Cost
Single	5	$1,115,773
Total	9	$1,861,440

Municipal Finance

(For local fiscal year ended in 2006)

Revenues

Total . . . $35,490,006
Taxes . . . 19,143,911
Special benefits assessment . . . 0
Licenses & permits . . . 746,451
Fines & forfeitures . . . 775,684
Revenues from use of money & property . . . 601,797
Intergovernmental . . . 5,365,990
Service charges . . . 8,546,878
Other revenues . . . 309,295
Other financing sources . . . 0

Expenditures

Total . . . $30,363,569
General government . . . 4,388,173
Public safety . . . 7,348,893
Transportation . . . 6,829,127
Community development . . . 2,022,799
Health . . . 0
Culture & leisure . . . 3,595,941
Other . . . 0

Local School District

(Data from School year 2007-08 except as noted)

Paramount Unified
15110 California Ave
Paramount, CA 90723
(562) 602-6000

Superintendent . . . David Verdugo
Grade plan . . . K-12
Number of schools . . . 20
Enrollment . . . 15,952
High school graduates, 2006-07 . . . 654
Dropout rate . . . 7.3%
Pupil/teacher ratio . . . 21.4
Average class size . . . 26.7
Students per computer . . . 3.3
Classrooms with internet . . . 800
Avg. Daily Attendance (ADA) . . . 15,974
Cost per ADA . . . $8,338
Avg. Teacher Salary . . . $67,411

California Achievement Tests 6th ed., 2008

(Pct scoring at or above 50th National Percentile Rank)

	Math	Reading	Language
Grade 3	45%	22%	38%
Grade 7	35%	37%	35%

Academic Performance Index, 2008

Number of students tested . . . 12,511
Number of valid scores . . . 11,584
2007 API (base) . . . 686
2008 API (growth) . . . 705

SAT Testing, 2006-07

Enrollment, Grade 12 . . . 1,019
Number taking test . . . 238
percent taking test . . . 23.4%
percent with total score 1,500+ . . . 3.70%

Average Scores:

Math	Verbal	Writing	Total
445	413	414	1,272

Federal No Child Left Behind, 2008

(Adequate Yearly Progress standards met)

	Participation Rate	Pct Proficient
ELA	Yes	No
Math	Yes	No

API criteria . . . Yes
Graduation rate . . . No
\# criteria met/possible . . . 30/24

Other school districts for this city

(see Appendix E for information on these districts)

None

See Introduction for an explanation of all data sources.

Demographics & Socio-Economic Characteristics

(2000 Decennial Census, except as noted)

Population

1990* . . . 7,938
2000 . . . 11,145
Male . . . 5,802
Female . . . 5,343
Jan. 2008 (estimate)§ . . . 13,326
Persons per sq. mi. of land . . . 8,328.8

Race & Hispanic Origin, 2000

Race
White . . . 3,748
Black/African American . . . 65
North American Native . . . 216
Asian . . . 91
Pacific Islander . . . 5
Other Race . . . 6,623
Two or more races . . . 397
Hispanic origin, total . . . 10,807
Mexican . . . 9,631
Puerto Rican . . . 6
Cuban . . . 2
Other Hispanic . . . 1,168

Age & Nativity, 2000

Under 5 years . . . 1,172
18 years and over . . . 6,916
65 years and over . . . 544
85 years and over . . . 43
Median Age . . . 23.9
Native-born . . . 6,226
Foreign-born . . . 4,862

Educational Attainment, 2000

Population 25 years and over . . . 5,248
Less than 9th grade . . . 52.1%
High school grad or higher . . . 33.2%
Bachelor's degree or higher . . . 2.7%
Graduate degree . . . 0.2%

Income & Poverty, 1999

Per capita income . . . $7,078
Median household income . . . $24,539
Median family income . . . $24,275
Persons in poverty . . . 35.5%
H'holds receiving public assistance . . . 361
H'holds receiving social security . . . 556

Households, 2000

Total households . . . 2,446
With persons under 18 . . . 1,741
With persons over 65 . . . 427
Family households . . . 2,180
Single person households . . . 167
Persons per household . . . 4.51
Persons per family . . . 4.59

Household Population, 2008§§

Persons living in households . . . 13,224
Persons living in group quarters . . . 102
Persons per household . . . 4.6

Labor & Employment

Total civilian labor force, 2008§§ . . . 5,600
Unemployment rate, 2008 . . . 24.6%
Total civilian labor force, 2000 . . . 4,492

Employed persons 16 years and over by occupation, 2000

Managers & professionals . . . 380
Service occupations . . . 490
Sales & office occupations . . . 556
Farming, fishing & forestry . . . 917
Construction & maintenance . . . 155
Production & transportation . . . 782
Self-employed persons . . . 76

* US Census Bureau
** 2000 Decennial Census
§ California Department of Finance
§§ California Employment Development Dept

General Information

City of Parlier
1100 E Parlier Ave
Parlier, CA 93648
559-646-3545

Website . . . www.parlier.ca.us
Elevation . . . NA
Land Area (sq. miles) . . . 1.6
Water Area (sq. miles) . . . 0
Year of Incorporation . . . 1921
Government type . . . General law
Sales tax rate . . . 8.98%

Voters & Officials

Registered Voters, October 2008

Total . . . 3,169
Democrats . . . 1,974
Republicans . . . 671
Declined to state . . . 308

Legislative Districts

US Congressional . . . 20
State Senatorial . . . 16
State Assembly . . . 31

Local Officials, 2009

Mayor . . . Armando Lopez
Manager . . . Lou Martinez
City Clerk . . . Dorothy Garza
Attorney . . . Dale Bacigalupi
Finance Dir . . . Patricia Barboza
Public Works . . . Gilbert Gutierrez
Community Dev Dir . . . E. Shun Patlan
Building . . . NA
Police Chief . . . Ishmael Solis
Fire/Emergency Mgmt . . . (County)

Public Safety

Number of officers, 2007 . . . 15
Violent crimes, 2007 . . . 124
Property crimes, 2007 . . . 439
Arson, 2007 . . . 19

Public Library

Parlier Branch Library
Fresno County Public Library System
1130 E Parlier Ave
Parlier, CA 93648
559-646-3835

Branch Librarian . . . Consuelo Martin

Library system statistics, FY 2007

Population served . . . 889,019
Internet terminals . . . 277
Annual users . . . 861,240

Per capita:

Operating income . . . $23.69
percent from local government . . . 89.3%
Operating expenditure . . . $23.37
Total materials . . . 2.89
Print holdings . . . 2.69
Visits per capita . . . NA

Housing & Construction

Housing Units

Total, 2008§ . . . 3,098
Single family units, attached . . . 234
Single family units, detached . . . 2,181
Multiple family units . . . 669
Mobile home units . . . 14
Occupied . . . 2,866
Vacancy rate . . . 7.5%
Median rent, 2000** . . . $434
Median SF home value, 2000** . . . $81,400

New Privately Owned Housing Units Authorized by Building Permit, 2007*

	Units	Construction Cost
Single	33	$3,905,385
Total	33	$3,905,385

Municipal Finance

(For local fiscal year ended in 2006)

Revenues

Total . . . $8,366,805
Taxes . . . 2,056,623
Special benefits assessment . . . 30,795
Licenses & permits . . . 325,701
Fines & forfeitures . . . 64,032
Revenues from use of money & property . . . 205,288
Intergovernmental . . . 1,995,619
Service charges . . . 3,647,130
Other revenues . . . 41,617
Other financing sources . . . 0

Expenditures

Total . . . $6,702,680
General government . . . 263,297
Public safety . . . 1,706,655
Transportation . . . 1,057,199
Community development . . . 169,120
Health . . . 2,238,685
Culture & leisure . . . 316,247
Other . . . 0

Local School District

(Data from School year 2007-08 except as noted)

Parlier Unified
900 Newmark Ave
Parlier, CA 93648
(559) 646-2731

Superintendent . . . Henry Rodriguez
Grade plan . . . K-12
Number of schools . . . 8
Enrollment . . . 3,957
High school graduates, 2006-07 . . . 140
Dropout rate . . . 12.6%
Pupil/teacher ratio . . . 21.9
Average class size . . . 24.6
Students per computer . . . 5.0
Classrooms with internet . . . 242
Avg. Daily Attendance (ADA) . . . 3,263
Cost per ADA . . . $7,938
Avg. Teacher Salary . . . $49,870

California Achievement Tests 6th ed., 2008

(Pct scoring at or above 50th National Percentile Rank)

	Math	Reading	Language
Grade 3	36%	15%	25%
Grade 7	22%	22%	21%

Academic Performance Index, 2008

Number of students tested . . . 2,518
Number of valid scores . . . 2,251
2007 API (base) . . . 581
2008 API (growth) . . . 598

SAT Testing, 2006-07

Enrollment, Grade 12 . . . 206
Number taking test . . . 34
percent taking test . . . 16.5%
percent with total score 1,500+ . . . 1.00%

Average Scores:

Math	Verbal	Writing	Total
386	384	386	1,156

Federal No Child Left Behind, 2008

(Adequate Yearly Progress standards met)

	Participation Rate	Pct Proficient
ELA	Yes	No
Math	Yes	No

API criteria . . . Yes
Graduation rate . . . Yes
\# criteria met/possible . . . 22/13

Other school districts for this city

(see Appendix E for information on these districts)

None

See Introduction for an explanation of all data sources.

Demographics & Socio-Economic Characteristics†

(2007 American Community Survey, except as noted)

Population

1990* . . . 131,591
2007 . . . 136,936
Male . . . 65,791
Female . . . 71,145
Jan. 2008 (estimate)§ . . . 148,126
Persons per sq. mi. of land . . . 6,412.4

Race & Hispanic Origin, 2007

Race
White . . . 74,124
Black/African American . . . 15,317
North American Native . . . 380
Asian . . . 14,250
Pacific Islander . . . 0
Other Race . . . 28,963
Two or more races . . . 3,902
Hispanic origin, total . . . 49,831
Mexican . . . 40,345
Puerto Rican . . . 402
Cuban . . . 368
Other Hispanic . . . 8,716

Age & Nativity, 2007

Under 5 years . . . 9,467
18 years and over . . . 108,540
65 years and over . . . 16,420
85 years and over . . . 3,090
Median Age . . . 37.1
Native-born . . . 92,575
Foreign-born . . . 44,361

Educational Attainment, 2007

Population 25 years and over . . . 95,076
Less than 9th grade . . . 9.8%
High school grad or higher . . . 84.1%
Bachelor's degree or higher . . . 43.2%
Graduate degree . . . 20.0%

Income & Poverty, 2007

Per capita income . . . $36,300
Median household income . . . $66,465
Median family income . . . $80,540
Persons in poverty . . . 11.9%
H'holds receiving public assistance . . . 1,204
H'holds receiving social security . . . 11,498

Households, 2007

Total households . . . 51,133
With persons under 18 . . . 14,012
With persons over 65 . . . 11,045
Family households . . . 29,126
Single person households . . . 18,093
Persons per household . . . 2.55
Persons per family . . . 3.42

Household Population, 2008§§

Persons living in households . . . 144,608
Persons living in group quarters . . . 3,518
Persons per household . . . 2.6

Labor & Employment

Total civilian labor force, 2008§§ . . . 77,800
Unemployment rate, 2008 . . . 5.7%
Total civilian labor force, 2000* . . . 67,612

Employed persons 16 years and over by occupation, 2007

Managers & professionals . . . 33,767
Service occupations . . . 13,513
Sales & office occupations . . . 15,093
Farming, fishing & forestry . . . 0
Construction & maintenance . . . 3,612
Production & transportation . . . 4,425
Self-employed persons . . . 8,017

† see Appendix D for 2000 Decennial Census Data
* US Census Bureau
** 2007 American Community Survey
§ California Department of Finance
§§ California Employment Development Dept

General Information

City of Pasadena
100 N. Garfield Ave
Room S228
Pasadena, CA 91109
626-744-4000

Website . . . www.cityofpasadena.net
Elevation . . . 865 ft.
Land Area (sq. miles) . . . 23.1
Water Area (sq. miles) . . . 0.1
Year of Incorporation . . . 1886
Government type . . . Chartered
Sales tax rate . . . 9.25%

Voters & Officials

Registered Voters, October 2008

Total . . . 72,797
Democrats . . . 36,150
Republicans . . . 19,210
Declined to state . . . 14,467

Legislative Districts

US Congressional . . . 29
State Senatorial . . . 21
State Assembly . . . 44

Local Officials, 2009

Mayor . . . Bill Bogaard
Manager . . . Michael Beck
City Clerk . . . Mark Jomsky
Attorney . . . Michele Bagneris
Finance Dir . . . Steve Stark
Public Works . . . Martin Pastucha
Planning/Dev Dir . . . Richard Bruckner
Building . . . Sarkis Nazerian
Police Chief . . . Bernard Melekian
Emergency/Fire Dir . . . Dennis Downs

Public Safety

Number of officers, 2007 . . . 246
Violent crimes, 2007 . . . 744
Property crimes, 2007 . . . 4,304
Arson, 2007 . . . 23

Public Library

Pasadena Central Library
Pasadena Public Library System
285 E Walnut St
Pasadena, CA 91101
626-744-4066

Director . . . Jan Sanders

Library system statistics, FY 2007

Population served . . . 147,262
Internet terminals . . . 121
Annual users . . . 201,219

Per capita:

Operating income . . . $77.87
percent from local government . . . 95.2%
Operating expenditure . . . $77.73
Total materials . . . 7.45
Print holdings . . . 7.29
Visits per capita . . . 8.39

Housing & Construction

Housing Units

Total, 2008§ . . . 57,274
Single family units, attached . . . 5,282
Single family units, detached . . . 24,875
Multiple family units . . . 27,044
Mobile home units . . . 73
Occupied . . . 54,853
Vacancy rate . . . 4.2%
Median rent, 2007** . . . $1,146
Median SF home value, 2007** . . . $705,100

New Privately Owned Housing Units Authorized by Building Permit, 2007*

	Units	Construction Cost
Single	133	$25,269,158
Total	303	$64,154,841

Municipal Finance

(For local fiscal year ended in 2006)

Revenues

Total . . . $499,635,082
Taxes . . . 134,217,449
Special benefits assessment . . . 0
Licenses & permits . . . 4,807,798
Fines & forfeitures . . . 7,381,161
Revenues from use of money & property . . . 31,284,897
Intergovernmental . . . 36,324,064
Service charges . . . 256,915,124
Other revenues . . . 18,349,589
Other financing sources . . . 10,355,000

Expenditures

Total . . . $553,275,397
General government . . . 90,947,911
Public safety . . . 83,379,935
Transportation . . . 51,773,484
Community development . . . 44,719,129
Health . . . 25,244,941
Culture & leisure . . . 59,666,545
Other . . . 0

Local School District

(Data from School year 2007-08 except as noted)

Pasadena Unified
351 South Hudson Ave
Pasadena, CA 91101
(626) 795-6981

Superintendent . . . Edwin Diaz
Grade plan . . . K-12
Number of schools . . . 33
Enrollment . . . 20,905
High school graduates, 2006-07 . . . 1,058
Dropout rate . . . 4.1%
Pupil/teacher ratio . . . 20.7
Average class size . . . 25.6
Students per computer . . . 5.3
Classrooms with internet . . . 1,219
Avg. Daily Attendance (ADA) . . . 20,132
Cost per ADA . . . $9,704
Avg. Teacher Salary . . . $61,180

California Achievement Tests 6th ed., 2008

(Pct scoring at or above 50th National Percentile Rank)

	Math	Reading	Language
Grade 3	54%	33%	45%
Grade 7	44%	40%	39%

Academic Performance Index, 2008

Number of students tested . . . 15,095
Number of valid scores . . . 14,162
2007 API (base) . . . 707
2008 API (growth) . . . 720

SAT Testing, 2006-07

Enrollment, Grade 12 . . . 1,315
Number taking test . . . 553
percent taking test . . . 42.1%
percent with total score 1,500+ . . . 11.20%

Average Scores:

Math	Verbal	Writing	Total
451	442	440	1,333

Federal No Child Left Behind, 2008

(Adequate Yearly Progress standards met)

	Participation Rate	Pct Proficient
ELA	Yes	No
Math	Yes	No

API criteria . . . Yes
Graduation rate . . . Yes
criteria met/possible . . . 38/35

Other school districts for this city

(see Appendix E for information on these districts)

None

See Introduction for an explanation of all data sources.

Demographics & Socio-Economic Characteristics

(2000 Decennial Census, except as noted)

Population

1990* . . . 18,583
2000 . . . 24,297
Male . . . 12,316
Female . . . 11,981
Jan. 2008 (estimate)§ . . . 29,934
Persons per sq. mi. of land . . . 1,730.3

Race & Hispanic Origin, 2000

Race
White . . . 18,393
Black/African American . . . 806
North American Native . . . 316
Asian . . . 458
Pacific Islander . . . 34
Other Race . . . 3,325
Two or more races . . . 965
Hispanic origin, total . . . 6,735
Mexican . . . 5,712
Puerto Rican . . . 87
Cuban . . . 24
Other Hispanic . . . 912

Age & Nativity, 2000

Under 5 years . . . 1,749
18 years and over . . . 17,057
65 years and over . . . 3,262
85 years and over . . . 354
Median Age . . . 33.0
Native-born . . . 20,495
Foreign-born . . . 3,716

Educational Attainment, 2000

Population 25 years and over . . . 14,160
Less than 9th grade . . . 10.3%
High school grad or higher . . . 78.6%
Bachelor's degree or higher . . . 17.4%
Graduate degree . . . 5.5%

Income & Poverty, 1999

Per capita income . . . $17,974
Median household income . . . $39,217
Median family income . . . $44,322
Persons in poverty . . . 13.0%
H'holds receiving public assistance . . . 367
H'holds receiving social security . . . 2,594

Households, 2000

Total households . . . 8,556
With persons under 18 . . . 3,463
With persons over 65 . . . 2,344
Family households . . . 6,042
Single person households . . . 2,028
Persons per household . . . 2.73
Persons per family . . . 3.23

Household Population, 2008§§

Persons living in households . . . 29,682
Persons living in group quarters . . . 252
Persons per household . . . 2.6

Labor & Employment

Total civilian labor force, 2008§§ . . . 13,000
Unemployment rate, 2008 . . . 6.8%
Total civilian labor force, 2000 . . . 10,751

Employed persons 16 years and over by occupation, 2000

Managers & professionals . . . 2,632
Service occupations . . . 2,065
Sales & office occupations . . . 2,269
Farming, fishing & forestry . . . 347
Construction & maintenance . . . 1,169
Production & transportation . . . 1,617
Self-employed persons . . . 981

* US Census Bureau
** 2000 Decennial Census
§ California Department of Finance
§§ California Employment Development Dept

General Information

City of Paso Robles
1000 Spring Street
Paso Robles, CA 93446
805-237-3888

Website . . . www.prcity.com
Elevation . . . 721 ft.
Land Area (sq. miles) . . . 17.3
Water Area (sq. miles) . . . 0
Year of Incorporation . . . 1889
Government type . . . General law
Sales tax rate . . . 8.25%

Voters & Officials

Registered Voters, October 2008

Total . . . 15,304
Democrats . . . 4,845
Republicans . . . 7,044
Declined to state . . . 2,674

Legislative Districts

US Congressional . . . 22
State Senatorial . . . 15
State Assembly . . . 33

Local Officials, 2009

Mayor . . . Duane Picanco
Manager . . . James App
City Clerk . . . Dennis Fansler
Attorney . . . Iris Yang
Finance Dir . . . Jennifer Sorenson
Public Works . . . Doug Monn
Planning/Dev Dir . . . Ron Whisenand
Building . . . Doug Monn
Police Chief . . . Lisa Solomon
Emergency/Fire Dir . . . Ken Johnson

Public Safety

Number of officers, 2007 . . . 41
Violent crimes, 2007 . . . 106
Property crimes, 2007 . . . 931
Arson, 2007 . . . 3

Public Library

Paso Robles Public Library
Paso Robles Public Library System
1000 Spring St
Paso Robles, CA 93446
805-237-3870

Director . . . Julie Dahlen

Library system statistics, FY 2007

Population served . . . 29,514
Internet terminals . . . 19
Annual users . . . 26,066

Per capita:

Operating income . . . $56.90
percent from local government . . . 88.6%
Operating expenditure . . . $54.78
Total materials . . . 2.37
Print holdings . . . 2.05
Visits per capita . . . NA

Housing & Construction

Housing Units

Total, 2008§ . . . 11,636
Single family units, attached . . . 920
Single family units, detached . . . 7,860
Multiple family units . . . 2,439
Mobile home units . . . 417
Occupied . . . 11,325
Vacancy rate . . . 2.7%
Median rent, 2000** . . . $640
Median SF home value, 2000** . . . $166,000

New Privately Owned Housing Units Authorized by Building Permit, 2007*

	Units	Construction Cost
Single	43	$10,949,189
Total	45	$11,135,179

Municipal Finance

(For local fiscal year ended in 2006)

Revenues

Total . . . $53,984,005
Taxes . . . 27,095,469
Special benefits assessment . . . 973,633
Licenses & permits . . . 1,190,377
Fines & forfeitures . . . 307,138
Revenues from use of money & property . . . 2,325,409
Intergovernmental . . . 3,966,692
Service charges . . . 16,611,696
Other revenues . . . 1,513,591
Other financing sources . . . 0

Expenditures

Total . . . $57,202,980
General government . . . 2,188,273
Public safety . . . 13,039,165
Transportation . . . 19,144,416
Community development . . . 2,573,895
Health . . . 4,201,798
Culture & leisure . . . 6,007,779
Other . . . 0

Local School District

(Data from School year 2007-08 except as noted)

Paso Robles Joint Unified
PO Box 7010
Paso Robles, CA 93447
(805) 238-2222

Superintendent . . . Kathleen McNamara
Grade plan . . . K-12
Number of schools . . . 12
Enrollment . . . 6,910
High school graduates, 2006-07 . . . 469
Dropout rate . . . 3.5%
Pupil/teacher ratio . . . 19.2
Average class size . . . 23.1
Students per computer . . . 4.0
Classrooms with internet . . . 321
Avg. Daily Attendance (ADA) . . . 6,650
Cost per ADA . . . $8,053
Avg. Teacher Salary . . . $61,721

California Achievement Tests 6th ed., 2008

(Pct scoring at or above 50th National Percentile Rank)

	Math	Reading	Language
Grade 3	66%	44%	51%
Grade 7	47%	52%	46%

Academic Performance Index, 2008

Number of students tested . . . 5,181
Number of valid scores . . . 4,895
2007 API (base) . . . 743
2008 API (growth) . . . 752

SAT Testing, 2006-07

Enrollment, Grade 12 . . . 584
Number taking test . . . 130
percent taking test . . . 22.3%
percent with total score 1,500+ . . . 14.40%

Average Scores:

Math	Verbal	Writing	Total
518	527	509	1,554

Federal No Child Left Behind, 2008

(Adequate Yearly Progress standards met)

	Participation Rate	Pct Proficient
ELA	No	No
Math	Yes	No

API criteria . . . Yes
Graduation rate . . . Yes
\# criteria met/possible . . . 30/25

Other school districts for this city

(see Appendix E for information on these districts)

None

See Introduction for an explanation of all data sources.

Demographics & Socio-Economic Characteristics

(2000 Decennial Census, except as noted)

Population

1990* ... 8,626
2000 ... 11,606
Male ... 5,814
Female ... 5,792
Jan. 2008 (estimate)§ ... 21,229
Persons per sq. mi. of land ... 7,320.3

Race & Hispanic Origin, 2000

Race
White ... 6,459
Black/African American ... 219
North American Native ... 171
Asian ... 244
Pacific Islander ... 49
Other Race ... 3,661
Two or more races ... 803
Hispanic origin, total ... 6,611
Mexican ... 5,577
Puerto Rican ... 95
Cuban ... 5
Other Hispanic ... 934

Age & Nativity, 2000

Under 5 years ... 1,061
18 years and over ... 7,381
65 years and over ... 840
85 years and over ... 105
Median Age ... 27.5
Native-born ... 8,519
Foreign-born ... 2,886

Educational Attainment, 2000

Population 25 years and over ... 6,217
Less than 9th grade ... 24.0%
High school grad or higher ... 62.3%
Bachelor's degree or higher ... 11.0%
Graduate degree ... 3.2%

Income & Poverty, 1999

Per capita income ... $14,746
Median household income ... $47,780
Median family income ... $51,422
Persons in poverty ... 11.6%
H'holds receiving public assistance ... 142
H'holds receiving social security ... 672

Households, 2000

Total households ... 3,146
With persons under 18 ... 1,865
With persons over 65 ... 607
Family households ... 2,608
Single person households ... 422
Persons per household ... 3.62
Persons per family ... 3.94

Household Population, 2008§§

Persons living in households ... 21,000
Persons living in group quarters ... 229
Persons per household ... 3.6

Labor & Employment

Total civilian labor force, 2008§§ ... 6,000
Unemployment rate, 2008 ... 15.3%
Total civilian labor force, 2000 ... 5,090

Employed persons 16 years and over by occupation, 2000

Managers & professionals ... 1,087
Service occupations ... 565
Sales & office occupations ... 905
Farming, fishing & forestry ... 374
Construction & maintenance ... 676
Production & transportation ... 670
Self-employed persons ... 205

* US Census Bureau
** 2000 Decennial Census
§ California Department of Finance
§§ California Employment Development Dept

General Information

City of Patterson
1 Plaza
PO Box 667
Patterson, CA 95363
209-895-8000

Website ... www.ci.patterson.ca.us
Elevation ... 97 ft.
Land Area (sq. miles) ... 2.9
Water Area (sq. miles) ... 0
Year of Incorporation ... 1919
Government type ... General law
Sales tax rate ... 8.38%

Voters & Officials

Registered Voters, October 2008

Total ... 7,058
Democrats ... 3,603
Republicans ... 1,928
Declined to state ... 1,227

Legislative Districts

US Congressional ... 18
State Senatorial ... 12
State Assembly ... 26

Local Officials, 2009

Mayor ... Becky Campo
City Manager ... Cleve Morris
City Clerk ... Maricela Vela
Attorney ... George Logan
Finance Dir ... Margaret Souza
Public Works ... Michael Willett
Planning/Dev Dir ... Rod Simpson
Building ... NA
Police Chief ... Tyrone Spencer
Emergency/Fire Dir. ... James Kinnear

Public Safety

Number of officers, 2007 ... 19
Violent crimes, 2007 ... 52
Property crimes, 2007 ... 610
Arson, 2007 ... 6

Public Library

Patterson Library
Stanislaus County Free Library
46 N Salado
Patterson, CA 95363
209-892-6473

Branch Librarian ... Kelly Thompson

Library system statistics, FY 2007

Population served ... 521,497
Internet terminals ... 128
Annual users ... 256,298

Per capita:

Operating income ... $20.76
percent from local government ... 91.0%
Operating expenditure ... $20.19
Total materials ... 1.66
Print holdings ... 1.56
Visits per capita ... NA

Housing & Construction

Housing Units

Total, 2008§ ... 5,999
Single family units, attached ... 190
Single family units, detached ... 5,466
Multiple family units ... 214
Mobile home units ... 129
Occupied ... 5,783
Vacancy rate ... 3.6%
Median rent, 2000** ... $528
Median SF home value, 2000** ... $130,900

New Privately Owned Housing Units Authorized by Building Permit, 2007*

	Units	Construction Cost
Single	33	$8,380,443
Total	33	$8,380,443

Municipal Finance

(For local fiscal year ended in 2006)

Revenues

Total ... $31,497,296
Taxes ... 8,114,518
Special benefits assessment ... 5,697,107
Licenses & permits ... 2,175,695
Fines & forfeitures ... 127,719
Revenues from use of money & property ... 1,716,817
Intergovernmental ... 1,355,101
Service charges ... 10,522,326
Other revenues ... 1,788,013
Other financing sources ... 0

Expenditures

Total ... $14,545,812
General government ... 1,319,246
Public safety ... 2,537,611
Transportation ... 2,484,425
Community development ... 2,706,748
Health ... 2,671,942
Culture & leisure ... 891,660
Other ... 0

Local School District

(Data from School year 2007-08 except as noted)

Patterson Joint Unified
510 Keystone Blvd
Patterson, CA 95363
(209) 895-7700

Superintendent ... Patrick Sweeney
Grade plan ... K-12
Number of schools ... 8
Enrollment ... 5,669
High school graduates, 2006-07 ... 288
Dropout rate ... 4.6%
Pupil/teacher ratio ... 20.8
Average class size ... 26.6
Students per computer ... 6.0
Classrooms with internet ... 259
Avg. Daily Attendance (ADA) ... 5,101
Cost per ADA ... $7,599
Avg. Teacher Salary ... $56,598

California Achievement Tests 6th ed., 2008

(Pct scoring at or above 50th National Percentile Rank)

	Math	Reading	Language
Grade 3	51%	28%	41%
Grade 7	46%	37%	32%

Academic Performance Index, 2008

Number of students tested ... 4,322
Number of valid scores ... 3,981
2007 API (base) ... 677
2008 API (growth) ... 695

SAT Testing, 2006-07

Enrollment, Grade 12 ... 349
Number taking test ... 83
percent taking test ... 23.8%
percent with total score 1,500+ ... 6.90%

Average Scores:

Math	Verbal	Writing	Total
461	464	462	1,387

Federal No Child Left Behind, 2008

(Adequate Yearly Progress standards met)

	Participation Rate	Pct Proficient
ELA	Yes	No
Math	Yes	No

API criteria ... Yes
Graduation rate ... No
criteria met/possible ... 30/20

Other school districts for this city

(see Appendix E for information on these districts)

None

See Introduction for an explanation of all data sources.

Demographics & Socio-Economic Characteristics

(2000 Decennial Census, except as noted)

Population

1990*	21,460
2000	36,189
Male	17,739
Female	18,450
Jan. 2008 (estimate)§	53,605
Persons per sq. mi. of land	1,707.2

Race & Hispanic Origin, 2000

Race	
White	14,909
Black/African American	5,748
North American Native	529
Asian	995
Pacific Islander	121
Other Race	11,781
Two or more races	2,106
Hispanic origin, total	20,322
Mexican	16,783
Puerto Rican	251
Cuban	109
Other Hispanic	3,179

Age & Nativity, 2000

Under 5 years	3,923
18 years and over	21,857
65 years and over	2,259
85 years and over	219
Median Age	25.4
Native-born	26,413
Foreign-born	9,790

Educational Attainment, 2000

Population 25 years and over	18,332
Less than 9th grade	18.5%
High school grad or higher	61.0%
Bachelor's degree or higher	6.6%
Graduate degree	1.8%

Income & Poverty, 1999

Per capita income	$11,425
Median household income	$35,522
Median family income	$36,063
Persons in poverty	20.1%
H'holds receiving public assistance	898
H'holds receiving social security	1,800

Households, 2000

Total households	9,652
With persons under 18	6,144
With persons over 65	1,632
Family households	8,114
Single person households	1,179
Persons per household	3.73
Persons per family	4.00

Household Population, 2008§§

Persons living in households	53,373
Persons living in group quarters	232
Persons per household	3.8

Labor & Employment

Total civilian labor force, 2008§§	19,300
Unemployment rate, 2008	13.6%
Total civilian labor force, 2000	13,504

Employed persons 16 years and over by occupation, 2000

Managers & professionals	2,110
Service occupations	2,071
Sales & office occupations	2,967
Farming, fishing & forestry	52
Construction & maintenance	1,733
Production & transportation	3,001
Self-employed persons	617

* US Census Bureau
** 2000 Decennial Census
§ California Department of Finance
§§ California Employment Development Dept

General Information

City of Perris
101 N D Street
Perris, CA 92570
951-943-6100

Website	www.cityofperris.org
Elevation	1,457 ft.
Land Area (sq. miles)	31.4
Water Area (sq. miles)	0.1
Year of Incorporation	1911
Government type	General law
Sales tax rate	8.75%

Voters & Officials

Registered Voters, October 2008

Total	16,753
Democrats	8,577
Republicans	3,975
Declined to state	3,457

Legislative Districts

US Congressional	49
State Senatorial	37
State Assembly	65

Local Officials, 2009

Mayor	Daryl Busch
Manager	Richard Belmudez
City Clerk	Judy L. Haughney
Attorney	Eric Dunn
Finance Dir	Ron Carr
Public Works	Ron Carr
Planning/Dev Dir	Richard Belmudez
Building	Rene Avila
Police Chief	James McElvain
Emergency/Fire Dir	Don Cockrum

Public Safety

Number of officers, 2007	NA
Violent crimes, 2007	338
Property crimes, 2007	2,270
Arson, 2007	10

Public Library

Perris Branch Library
Riverside County Library Service
163 E San Jacinto
Perris, CA 92570
951-657-2358

Library Manager	Ron Stump

Library system statistics, FY 2007

Population served	1,047,996
Internet terminals	37
Annual users	69,346

Per capita:

Operating income	$19.38
percent from local government	49.8%
Operating expenditure	$20.45
Total materials	1.43
Print holdings	1.30
Visits per capita	4.06

Housing & Construction

Housing Units

Total, 2008§	15,392
Single family units, attached	323
Single family units, detached	11,603
Multiple family units	1,635
Mobile home units	1,831
Occupied	14,078
Vacancy rate	8.5%
Median rent, 2000**	$630
Median SF home value, 2000**	$91,300

New Privately Owned Housing Units Authorized by Building Permit, 2007*

	Units	Construction Cost
Single	599	$97,568,942
Total	695	$102,979,282

Municipal Finance

(For local fiscal year ended in 2006)

Revenues

Total	$75,817,360
Taxes	25,888,076
Special benefits assessment	1,691,226
Licenses & permits	4,931,885
Fines & forfeitures	648,970
Revenues from use of money & property	2,546,974
Intergovernmental	3,352,431
Service charges	6,257,313
Other revenues	30,500,485
Other financing sources	0

Expenditures

Total	$83,007,330
General government	4,199,850
Public safety	36,916,004
Transportation	22,013,592
Community development	9,167,465
Health	1,787,735
Culture & leisure	6,839,645
Other	96,356

Local School District

(Data from School year 2007-08 except as noted)

Perris Union High
155 East Fourth St
Perris, CA 92570
(951) 943-6369

Superintendent	Jonathan Greenberg
Grade plan	7-12
Number of schools	8
Enrollment	9,764
High school graduates, 2006-07	1,323
Dropout rate	4.8%
Pupil/teacher ratio	24.5
Average class size	28.4
Students per computer	6.9
Classrooms with internet	419
Avg. Daily Attendance (ADA)	8,911
Cost per ADA	$8,412
Avg. Teacher Salary	$67,839

California Achievement Tests 6th ed., 2008

(Pct scoring at or above 50th National Percentile Rank)

	Math	Reading	Language
Grade 3	NA	NA	NA
Grade 7	31%	27%	26%

Academic Performance Index, 2008

Number of students tested	7,751
Number of valid scores	7,119
2007 API (base)	657
2008 API (growth)	675

SAT Testing, 2006-07

Enrollment, Grade 12	1,619
Number taking test	381
percent taking test	23.5%
percent with total score 1,500+	8.00%

Average Scores:

Math	Verbal	Writing	Total
474	460	455	1,389

Federal No Child Left Behind, 2008

(Adequate Yearly Progress standards met)

	Participation Rate	Pct Proficient
ELA	Yes	No
Math	Yes	No

API criteria	Yes
Graduation rate	No
# criteria met/possible	30/18

Other school districts for this city

(see Appendix E for information on these districts)

Perris Elem, Val Verde Unified

See Introduction for an explanation of all data sources.

Demographics & Socio-Economic Characteristics

(2000 Decennial Census, except as noted)

Population

1990* 43,184
2000 54,548
Male 26,661
Female 27,887
Jan. 2008 (estimate)§ 57,418
Persons per sq. mi. of land 4,160.7

Race & Hispanic Origin, 2000

Race
White 45,906
Black/African American 632
North American Native 294
Asian 2,135
Pacific Islander 93
Other Race 3,317
Two or more races 2,171
Hispanic origin, total 7,985
Mexican 5,546
Puerto Rican 152
Cuban 45
Other Hispanic 2,242

Age & Nativity, 2000

Under 5 years 3,612
18 years and over 40,270
65 years and over 6,027
85 years and over 851
Median Age 37.1
Native-born 46,679
Foreign-born 7,859

Educational Attainment, 2000

Population 25 years and over 36,376
Less than 9th grade 5.6%
High school grad or higher 85.9%
Bachelor's degree or higher 30.1%
Graduate degree 9.3%

Income & Poverty, 1999

Per capita income $27,087
Median household income $61,679
Median family income $71,158
Persons in poverty 5.9%
H'holds receiving public assistance 212
H'holds receiving social security 4,601

Households, 2000

Total households 19,932
With persons under 18 7,788
With persons over 65 4,230
Family households 14,014
Single person households 4,500
Persons per household 2.70
Persons per family 3.16

Household Population, 2008§§

Persons living in households 56,678
Persons living in group quarters 740
Persons per household 2.6

Labor & Employment

Total civilian labor force, 2008§§ 32,400
Unemployment rate, 2008 .... 5.2%
Total civilian labor force, 2000 29,419

Employed persons 16 years and over by occupation, 2000

Managers & professionals 10,287
Service occupations 4,116
Sales & office occupations 7,880
Farming, fishing & forestry 175
Construction & maintenance 2,773
Production & transportation 2,931
Self-employed persons 2,749

* US Census Bureau
** 2000 Decennial Census
§ California Department of Finance
§§ California Employment Development Dept

General Information

City of Petaluma
City Hall
PO Box 61
Petaluma, CA 94953
707-778-4345

Website .... cityofpetaluma.net
Elevation .... 12 ft.
Land Area (sq. miles) 13.8
Water Area (sq. miles) 0.1
Year of Incorporation 1858
Government type .... Chartered
Sales tax rate 9.00%

Voters & Officials

Registered Voters, October 2008

Total 30,515
Democrats 16,275
Republicans 6,793
Declined to state 5,995

Legislative Districts

US Congressional 6
State Senatorial 3
State Assembly 6

Local Officials, 2009

Mayor .... Pamela Torliatt
Manager .... John C. Brown
City Clerk .... Claire Cooper
Attorney .... Eric Danly
Admin Svcs Dir .... NA
Public Works .... Vincent Marengo
Community Dev Dir .... Mike Moore
Building .... Mike Moore
Police Chief .... Steve Hood
Fire Chief .... Larry Anderson (Actg)

Public Safety

Number of officers, 2007 68
Violent crimes, 2007 226
Property crimes, 2007 1,034
Arson, 2007 11

Public Library

Petaluma Regional Library
Sonoma County Library System
100 Fairgrounds Dr
Petaluma, CA 95452
707-763-9801

Branch Librarian .... Doug Cisney

Library system statistics, FY 2007

Population served 481,785
Internet terminals 140
Annual users 299,464

Per capita:

Operating income $32.97
percent from local government 87.7%
Operating expenditure $30.18
Total materials 1.60
Print holdings 1.49
Visits per capita 5.11

Housing & Construction

Housing Units

Total, 2008§ 21,943
Single family units, attached 1,696
Single family units, detached 15,664
Multiple family units 3,652
Mobile home units 931
Occupied 21,541
Vacancy rate 1.8%
Median rent, 2000** $946
Median SF home value, 2000** $289,500

New Privately Owned Housing Units Authorized by Building Permit, 2007*

	Units	Construction Cost
Single	112	$25,397,958
Total	126	$28,010,377

Municipal Finance

(For local fiscal year ended in 2006)

Revenues

Total $102,918,891
Taxes 27,180,161
Special benefits assessment 292,145
Licenses & permits 3,099,691
Fines & forfeitures 638,844
Revenues from use of money & property 1,791,482
Intergovernmental 6,387,509
Service charges 35,101,151
Other revenues 7,930,867
Other financing sources 20,497,041

Expenditures

Total $110,143,898
General government 3,500,760
Public safety 27,670,686
Transportation 13,455,786
Community development 10,192,075
Health 38,720,557
Culture & leisure 5,467,175
Other 0

Local School District

(Data from School year 2007-08 except as noted)
‡combined elementary and high school data

Petaluma Joint Union High
200 Douglas St
Petaluma, CA 94952
(707) 778-4795

Superintendent .... Greta Viguie
Grade plan 7-12
Number of schools 10
Enrollment 5,726
High school graduates, 2006-07 788
Dropout rate 3.6%
Pupil/teacher ratio 21.1
Average class size 25.2
Students per computer 4.4
Classrooms with internet 259
Avg. Daily Attendance (ADA)‡ 7,594
Cost per ADA‡ $8,755
Avg. Teacher Salary‡ $62,191

California Achievement Tests 6th ed., 2008

(Pct scoring at or above 50th National Percentile Rank)

	Math	Reading	Language
Grade 3	45%	50%	53%
Grade 7	66%	63%	58%

Academic Performance Index, 2008

Number of students tested .... NA
Number of valid scores .... NA
2007 API (base) .... NA
2008 API (growth) .... NA

SAT Testing, 2006-07

Enrollment, Grade 12 805
Number taking test 374
percent taking test 46.5%
percent with total score 1,500+ 29.30%

Average Scores:

Math	Verbal	Writing	Total
533	523	529	1,585

Federal No Child Left Behind, 2008

(Adequate Yearly Progress standards met)

	Participation Rate	Pct Proficient
ELA	NA	NA
Math	NA	NA

API criteria .... NA
Graduation rate .... NA
\# criteria met/possible .... NA/NA

Other school districts for this city

(see Appendix E for information on these districts)

Complete list in Appendix E

See Introduction for an explanation of all data sources.

Demographics & Socio-Economic Characteristics

(2000 Decennial Census, except as noted)

Population

1990* ... 59,177
2000 ... 63,428
Male ... 31,132
Female ... 32,296
Jan. 2008 (estimate)§ ... 66,867
Persons per sq. mi. of land ... 8,056.3

Race & Hispanic Origin, 2000

Race
White ... 31,360
Black/African American ... 450
North American Native ... 859
Asian ... 1,681
Pacific Islander ... 78
Other Race ... 25,551
Two or more races ... 3,449
Hispanic origin, total ... 56,000
Mexican ... 48,033
Puerto Rican ... 236
Cuban ... 134
Other Hispanic ... 7,597

Age & Nativity, 2000

Under 5 years ... 5,228
18 years and over ... 43,784
65 years and over ... 6,958
85 years and over ... 611
Median Age ... 30.6
Native-born ... 41,768
Foreign-born ... 21,383

Educational Attainment, 2000

Population 25 years and over ... 37,044
Less than 9th grade ... 22.6%
High school grad or higher ... 55.1%
Bachelor's degree or higher ... 7.1%
Graduate degree ... 2.0%

Income & Poverty, 1999

Per capita income ... $13,011
Median household income ... $41,564
Median family income ... $45,422
Persons in poverty ... 12.4%
H'holds receiving public assistance ... 940
H'holds receiving social security ... 5,078

Households, 2000

Total households ... 16,468
With persons under 18 ... 8,915
With persons over 65 ... 4,924
Family households ... 13,872
Single person households ... 2,109
Persons per household ... 3.83
Persons per family ... 4.12

Household Population, 2008§§

Persons living in households ... 66,517
Persons living in group quarters ... 350
Persons per household ... 4.0

Labor & Employment

Total civilian labor force, 2008§§ ... 29,600
Unemployment rate, 2008 ... 7.0%
Total civilian labor force, 2000 ... 25,317

Employed persons 16 years and over by occupation, 2000

Managers & professionals ... 4,556
Service occupations ... 3,458
Sales & office occupations ... 6,775
Farming, fishing & forestry ... 76
Construction & maintenance ... 2,156
Production & transportation ... 6,468
Self-employed persons ... 1,295

* US Census Bureau
** 2000 Decennial Census
§ California Department of Finance
§§ California Employment Development Dept

General Information

City of Pico Rivera
PO Box 1016
Pico Rivera, CA 90660
562-942-2000

Website ... www.pico-rivera.org
Elevation ... 161 ft.
Land Area (sq. miles) ... 8.3
Water Area (sq. miles) ... 0.5
Year of Incorporation ... 1958
Government type ... General law
Sales tax rate ... 10.25%

Voters & Officials

Registered Voters, October 2008

Total ... 29,043
Democrats ... 18,984
Republicans ... 4,597
Declined to state ... 4,479

Legislative Districts

US Congressional ... 38
State Senatorial ... 30
State Assembly ... 58

Local Officials, 2009

Mayor ... Gracie Gallegos
Manager ... Charles P. Fuentes
City Clerk ... Daryl A. Betancur
Attorney ... Arnold Alvarez-Glasman
Finance Dir ... John Herrera (Int)
Public Works ... Al Cablay
Planning/Dev Dir ... Jeff Brauckmann
Building ... NA
Police Chief ... NA
Fire/Emergency Mgmt ... NA

Public Safety

Number of officers, 2007 ... NA
Violent crimes, 2007 ... 256
Property crimes, 2007 ... 1,559
Arson, 2007 ... 19

Public Library

Pico Rivera Library
Los Angeles County Public Library System
9001 Mines Ave
Pico Rivera, CA 90660
562-942-7394

Branch Librarian ... Rosemary Gurrola

Library system statistics, FY 2007

Population served ... 3,673,313
Internet terminals ... 749
Annual users ... 3,748,771

Per capita:

Operating income ... $30.06
percent from local government ... 93.6%
Operating expenditure ... $28.36
Total materials ... 2.22
Print holdings ... 1.97
Visits per capita ... 3.25

Housing & Construction

Housing Units

Total, 2008§ ... 16,952
Single family units, attached ... 945
Single family units, detached ... 12,698
Multiple family units ... 2,719
Mobile home units ... 590
Occupied ... 16,610
Vacancy rate ... 2.0%
Median rent, 2000** ... $700
Median SF home value, 2000** ... $166,800

New Privately Owned Housing Units Authorized by Building Permit, 2007*

	Units	Construction Cost
Single	48	$8,250,702
Total	54	$9,203,259

Municipal Finance

(For local fiscal year ended in 2006)

Revenues

Total ... $41,886,789
Taxes ... 21,420,250
Special benefits assessment ... 599,485
Licenses & permits ... 730,652
Fines & forfeitures ... 1,225,146
Revenues from use of money & property ... 756,140
Intergovernmental ... 13,349,474
Service charges ... 2,435,498
Other revenues ... 1,370,144
Other financing sources ... 0

Expenditures

Total ... $38,026,677
General government ... 9,034,843
Public safety ... 8,615,361
Transportation ... 7,918,722
Community development ... 7,175,892
Health ... 0
Culture & leisure ... 5,281,859
Other ... 0

Local School District

(Data from School year 2007-08 except as noted)

El Rancho Unified
9333 Loch Lomond Dr
Pico Rivera, CA 90660
(562) 942-1500

Superintendent ... Norbert Genis
Grade plan ... K-12
Number of schools ... 17
Enrollment ... 11,243
High school graduates, 2006-07 ... 721
Dropout rate ... 3.0%
Pupil/teacher ratio ... 22.2
Average class size ... 27.1
Students per computer ... 5.3
Classrooms with internet ... 513
Avg. Daily Attendance (ADA) ... 11,139
Cost per ADA ... $7,911
Avg. Teacher Salary ... $65,808

California Achievement Tests 6th ed., 2008

(Pct scoring at or above 50th National Percentile Rank)

	Math	Reading	Language
Grade 3	55%	33%	45%
Grade 7	50%	42%	47%

Academic Performance Index, 2008

Number of students tested ... 8,681
Number of valid scores ... 8,144
2007 API (base) ... 713
2008 API (growth) ... 722

SAT Testing, 2006-07

Enrollment, Grade 12 ... 877
Number taking test ... 353
percent taking test ... 40.3%
percent with total score 1,500+ ... 7.00%

Average Scores:

Math	Verbal	Writing	Total
441	418	428	1,287

Federal No Child Left Behind, 2008

(Adequate Yearly Progress standards met)

	Participation Rate	Pct Proficient
ELA	Yes	No
Math	Yes	No

API criteria ... Yes
Graduation rate ... Yes
criteria met/possible ... 26/23

Other school districts for this city

(see Appendix E for information on these districts)

None

Demographics & Socio-Economic Characteristics

(2000 Decennial Census, except as noted)

Population

1990* 10,602
2000 10,952
Male 5,270
Female 5,682
Jan. 2008 (estimate)§ 11,100
Persons per sq. mi. of land 6,529.4

Race & Hispanic Origin, 2000

Race
White 8,607
Black/African American 136
North American Native 12
Asian 1,754
Pacific Islander 4
Other Race 69
Two or more races 370
Hispanic origin, total 325
Mexican 153
Puerto Rican 5
Cuban 7
Other Hispanic 160

Age & Nativity, 2000

Under 5 years 582
18 years and over 7,639
65 years and over 1,481
85 years and over 196
Median Age 43.7
Native-born 9,713
Foreign-born 1,239

Educational Attainment, 2000

Population 25 years and over 7,258
Less than 9th grade 0.8%
High school grad or higher 98.1%
Bachelor's degree or higher 77.8%
Graduate degree 41.1%

Income & Poverty, 1999

Per capita income $70,539
Median household income $134,270
Median family income $149,857
Persons in poverty 2.0%
H'holds receiving public assistance 29
H'holds receiving social security 956

Households, 2000

Total households 3,804
With persons under 18 1,845
With persons over 65 1,054
Family households 3,105
Single person households 551
Persons per household 2.88
Persons per family 3.18

Household Population, 2008§§

Persons living in households 11,098
Persons living in group quarters 2
Persons per household 2.9

Labor & Employment

Total civilian labor force, 2008§§ 5,500
Unemployment rate, 2008 . . . . . 3.0%
Total civilian labor force, 2000 5,310

Employed persons 16 years and over by occupation, 2000

Managers & professionals 3,654
Service occupations 238
Sales & office occupations 1,039
Farming, fishing & forestry 0
Construction & maintenance 130
Production & transportation 108
Self-employed persons 950

* US Census Bureau
** 2000 Decennial Census
§ California Department of Finance
§§ California Employment Development Dept

General Information

City of Piedmont
120 Vista Ave
Piedmont, CA 94611
510-420-3040

Website . . . . . www.ci.piedmont.ca.us
Elevation . . . . . 300 ft.
Land Area (sq. miles) 1.7
Water Area (sq. miles) 0
Year of Incorporation 1907
Government type . . . . . Chartered
Sales tax rate 9.75%

Voters & Officials

Registered Voters, October 2008

Total 8,458
Democrats 4,680
Republicans 1,913
Declined to state 1,605

Legislative Districts

US Congressional 9
State Senatorial 9
State Assembly 16

Local Officials, 2009

Mayor . . . . . Abe Friedman
Manager . . . . . Geoffrey Grote
City Clerk . . . . . Ann Swift
Attorney . . . . . George S. Peyton Jr
Finance Dir . . . . . Mark Bichsel
Public Works . . . . . Larry Rosenberg
Planning/Dev Dir . . . . . NA
Building . . . . . Chester Nakahara
Police Chief . . . . . John Hunt (Int)
Emergency/Fire Dir . . . . . John Speakman

Public Safety

Number of officers, 2007 20
Violent crimes, 2007 10
Property crimes, 2007 207
Arson, 2007 2

Public Library

Served by Oakland Public Library

Library system statistics, FY 2007

Population served . . . . . NA
Internet terminals . . . . . NA
Annual users . . . . . NA

Per capita:

Operating income . . . . . NA
percent from local government . . . . . NA
Operating expenditure . . . . . NA
Total materials . . . . . NA
Print holdings . . . . . NA
Visits per capita . . . . . NA

Housing & Construction

Housing Units

Total, 2008§ 3,864
Single family units, attached 0
Single family units, detached 3,787
Multiple family units 69
Mobile home units 8
Occupied 3,809
Vacancy rate 1.4%
Median rent, 2000** $1,814
Median SF home value, 2000** $760,000

New Privately Owned Housing Units Authorized by Building Permit, 2007*

	Units	Construction Cost
Single	0	$0
Total	0	$0

Municipal Finance

(For local fiscal year ended in 2006)

Revenues

Total $22,109,074
Taxes 15,035,931
Special benefits assessment 84,286
Licenses & permits 382,067
Fines & forfeitures 100,308
Revenues from use of money & property 833,628
Intergovernmental 730,271
Service charges 4,527,375
Other revenues 105,005
Other financing sources 310,203

Expenditures

Total $20,316,158
General government 1,265,599
Public safety 9,101,160
Transportation 2,119,853
Community development 696,505
Health 2,260,150
Culture & leisure 4,872,891
Other 0

Local School District

(Data from School year 2007-08 except as noted)

Piedmont Unified
760 Magnolia Ave
Piedmont, CA 94611
(510) 594-2600

Superintendent . . . . . Constance Hubbard
Grade plan K-12
Number of schools 6
Enrollment 2,552
High school graduates, 2006-07 252
Dropout rate 0.0%
Pupil/teacher ratio 16.3
Average class size 23.9
Students per computer 3.8
Classrooms with internet 184
Avg. Daily Attendance (ADA) 2,491
Cost per ADA $11,387
Avg. Teacher Salary $69,703

California Achievement Tests 6th ed., 2008

(Pct scoring at or above 50th National Percentile Rank)

	Math	Reading	Language
Grade 3	89%	88%	87%
Grade 7	89%	89%	91%

Academic Performance Index, 2008

Number of students tested 1,931
Number of valid scores 1,914
2007 API (base) 915
2008 API (growth) 919

SAT Testing, 2006-07

Enrollment, Grade 12 252
Number taking test 212
percent taking test 84.1%
percent with total score 1,500+ . . . 75.80%

Average Scores:

Math	Verbal	Writing	Total
619	606	618	1,843

Federal No Child Left Behind, 2008

(Adequate Yearly Progress standards met)

	Participation Rate	Pct Proficient
ELA	No	Yes
Math	Yes	Yes

API criteria . . . . . Yes
Graduation rate . . . . . Yes
criteria met/possible 18/17

Other school districts for this city

(see Appendix E for information on these districts)

None

See Introduction for an explanation of all data sources.

Demographics & Socio-Economic Characteristics

(2000 Decennial Census, except as noted)

Population

1990* 17,460
2000 19,039
Male 9,145
Female 9,894
Jan. 2008 (estimate)§ 19,193
Persons per sq. mi. of land 3,691.0

Race & Hispanic Origin, 2000

Race
White 10,356
Black/African American 2,115
North American Native 108
Asian 4,134
Pacific Islander 70
Other Race 1,107
Two or more races 1,149
Hispanic origin, total 2,618
Mexican 1,505
Puerto Rican 90
Cuban 26
Other Hispanic 997

Age & Nativity, 2000

Under 5 years 1,083
18 years and over 14,272
65 years and over 2,456
85 years and over 302
Median Age 38.7
Native-born 15,193
Foreign-born 4,201

Educational Attainment, 2000

Population 25 years and over 13,045
Less than 9th grade 4.6%
High school grad or higher 88.3%
Bachelor's degree or higher 27.6%
Graduate degree 8.2%

Income & Poverty, 1999

Per capita income $25,170
Median household income $62,256
Median family income $70,172
Persons in poverty 5.0%
H'holds receiving public assistance 216
H'holds receiving social security 1,908

Households, 2000

Total households 6,743
With persons under 18 2,659
With persons over 65 1,698
Family households 5,059
Single person households 1,359
Persons per household 2.79
Persons per family 3.23

Household Population, 2008§§

Persons living in households 18,975
Persons living in group quarters 218
Persons per household 2.7

Labor & Employment

Total civilian labor force, 2008§§ 10,800
Unemployment rate, 2008 .... 3.9%
Total civilian labor force, 2000 9,696

Employed persons 16 years and over by occupation, 2000

Managers & professionals 3,227
Service occupations 1,510
Sales & office occupations 2,784
Farming, fishing & forestry 4
Construction & maintenance 916
Production & transportation 962
Self-employed persons 589

* US Census Bureau
** 2000 Decennial Census
§ California Department of Finance
§§ California Employment Development Dept

General Information

City of Pinole
2131 Pear Street
Pinole, CA 94564
510-724-9000

Website .... www.ci.pinole.ca.us
Elevation .... 21 ft.
Land Area (sq. miles) 5.2
Water Area (sq. miles) 8.1
Year of Incorporation 1903
Government type .... General law
Sales tax rate 9.75%

Voters & Officials

Registered Voters, October 2008

Total 9,942
Democrats 5,820
Republicans 1,856
Declined to state 1,876

Legislative Districts

US Congressional 7
State Senatorial 10
State Assembly 11

Local Officials, 2009

Mayor .... Mary Horton
Manager .... Belinda Espinosa
City Clerk .... Patricia Athenour
Attorney .... Benjamin Reyes
Finance Dir .... Richard Loomis
Public Works .... Dean Allison
Planning/Dev Dir .... Elizabeth Dunn
Building .... Winston Rhodes
Police Chief .... Paul Clancey (Int)
Emergency/Fire Dir .... Jim Parrott

Public Safety

Number of officers, 2007 32
Violent crimes, 2007 112
Property crimes, 2007 792
Arson, 2007 2

Public Library

Pinole Library
Contra Costa County Library System
2935 Pinole Valley Rd
Pinole, CA 94564
510-758-2741

Branch Librarian .... (vacant)

Library system statistics, FY 2007

Population served 938,513
Internet terminals 324
Annual users 670,618

Per capita:

Operating income $27.05
percent from local government 82.0%
Operating expenditure $27.82
Total materials 1.57
Print holdings 1.41
Visits per capita 3.65

Housing & Construction

Housing Units

Total, 2008§ 6,995
Single family units, attached 498
Single family units, detached 5,135
Multiple family units 1,347
Mobile home units 15
Occupied 6,909
Vacancy rate 1.2%
Median rent, 2000** $855
Median SF home value, 2000** $223,900

New Privately Owned Housing Units Authorized by Building Permit, 2007*

	Units	Construction Cost
Single	3	$969,056
Total	3	$969,056

Municipal Finance

(For local fiscal year ended in 2006)

Revenues

Total $24,423,759
Taxes 9,549,690
Special benefits assessment 0
Licenses & permits 315,496
Fines & forfeitures 109,539
Revenues from use of money & property 279,567
Intergovernmental 1,978,711
Service charges 5,398,036
Other revenues 298,921
Other financing sources 6,493,799

Expenditures

Total $26,438,597
General government 1,985,207
Public safety 15,497,074
Transportation 1,675,665
Community development 635,950
Health 4,359,842
Culture & leisure 2,284,859
Other 0

Local School District

(Data from School year 2007-08 except as noted)

West Contra Costa Unified
1108 Bissell Ave
Richmond, CA 94801
(510) 231-1101

Superintendent .... Bruce Harter
Grade plan K-12
Number of schools 65
Enrollment 30,830
High school graduates, 2006-07 1,622
Dropout rate 9.3%
Pupil/teacher ratio 19.7
Average class size 24.8
Students per computer 6.4
Classrooms with internet 1,508
Avg. Daily Attendance (ADA) 28,599
Cost per ADA $9,365
Avg. Teacher Salary $56,030

California Achievement Tests 6th ed., 2008

(Pct scoring at or above 50th National Percentile Rank)

	Math	Reading	Language
Grade 3	47%	27%	38%
Grade 7	36%	33%	31%

Academic Performance Index, 2008

Number of students tested 22,407
Number of valid scores 20,863
2007 API (base) 674
2008 API (growth) 682

SAT Testing, 2006-07

Enrollment, Grade 12 1,839
Number taking test 853
percent taking test 46.4%
percent with total score 1,500+ 13.90%

Average Scores:

Math	Verbal	Writing	Total
462	455	456	1,373

Federal No Child Left Behind, 2008

(Adequate Yearly Progress standards met)

	Participation Rate	Pct Proficient
ELA	Yes	No
Math	Yes	No

API criteria .... Yes
Graduation rate .... No
\# criteria met/possible 42/34

Other school districts for this city

(see Appendix E for information on these districts)

None

Demographics & Socio-Economic Characteristics

(2000 Decennial Census, except as noted)

Population

1990* . . . 7,669
2000 . . . 8,551
Male . . . 4,122
Female . . . 4,429
Jan. 2008 (estimate)§ . . . 8,603
Persons per sq. mi. of land . . . 2,389.7

Race & Hispanic Origin, 2000

Race
White . . . 7,811
Black/African American . . . 51
North American Native . . . 61
Asian . . . 250
Pacific Islander . . . 5
Other Race . . . 141
Two or more races . . . 232
Hispanic origin, total . . . 589
Mexican . . . 412
Puerto Rican . . . 39
Cuban . . . 6
Other Hispanic . . . 132

Age & Nativity, 2000

Under 5 years . . . 338
18 years and over . . . 7,244
65 years and over . . . 2,098
85 years and over . . . 228
Median Age . . . 46.8
Native-born . . . 7,859
Foreign-born . . . 678

Educational Attainment, 2000

Population 25 years and over . . . 6,651
Less than 9th grade . . . 2.5%
High school grad or higher . . . 91.9%
Bachelor's degree or higher . . . 37.1%
Graduate degree . . . 13.9%

Income & Poverty, 1999

Per capita income . . . $30,835
Median household income . . . $46,396
Median family income . . . $61,036
Persons in poverty . . . 9.0%
H'holds receiving public assistance . . . 62
H'holds receiving social security . . . 1,658

Households, 2000

Total households . . . 4,230
With persons under 18 . . . 786
With persons over 65 . . . 1,529
Family households . . . 2,323
Single person households . . . 1,499
Persons per household . . . 2.02
Persons per family . . . 2.58

Household Population, 2008§§

Persons living in households . . . 8,576
Persons living in group quarters . . . 27
Persons per household . . . 1.9

Labor & Employment

Total civilian labor force, 2008§§ . . . 5,000
Unemployment rate, 2008 . . . 4.9%
Total civilian labor force, 2000 . . . 4,181

Employed persons 16 years and over by occupation, 2000

Managers & professionals . . . 1,877
Service occupations . . . 656
Sales & office occupations . . . 947
Farming, fishing & forestry . . . 11
Construction & maintenance . . . 234
Production & transportation . . . 242
Self-employed persons . . . 560

* US Census Bureau
** 2000 Decennial Census
§ California Department of Finance
§§ California Employment Development Dept

General Information

City of Pismo Beach
760 Mattie Rd
Pismo Beach, CA 93449
805-773-4657

Website . . . www.pismobeach.org
Elevation . . . 33 ft.
Land Area (sq. miles) . . . 3.6
Water Area (sq. miles) . . . 9.8
Year of Incorporation . . . 1946
Government type . . . General law
Sales tax rate . . . 8.75%

Voters & Officials

Registered Voters, October 2008

Total . . . 5,857
Democrats . . . 1,996
Republicans . . . 2,485
Declined to state . . . 1,056

Legislative Districts

US Congressional . . . 23
State Senatorial . . . 15
State Assembly . . . 33

Local Officials, 2009

Mayor . . . Mary Ann Reiss
Manager . . . Kevin Rice
City Clerk . . . Lori Grigsby
Attorney . . . Dave Fleishman
Finance Dir . . . George Edes
Public Works . . . Dwayne Chisam
Planning/Dev Dir . . . Randy Bloom
Building . . . Don Moore
Police Chief . . . Jeff Norton
Emergency/Fire Dir . . . NA

Public Safety

Number of officers, 2007 . . . 21
Violent crimes, 2007 . . . 22
Property crimes, 2007 . . . 355
Arson, 2007 . . . 0

Public Library

Served by County Library

Library system statistics, FY 2007

Population served . . . NA
Internet terminals . . . NA
Annual users . . . NA

Per capita:

Operating income . . . NA
percent from local government . . . NA
Operating expenditure . . . NA
Total materials . . . NA
Print holdings . . . NA
Visits per capita . . . NA

Housing & Construction

Housing Units

Total, 2008§ . . . 5,761
Single family units, attached . . . 576
Single family units, detached . . . 3,128
Multiple family units . . . 970
Mobile home units . . . 1,087
Occupied . . . 4,434
Vacancy rate . . . 23.0%
Median rent, 2000** . . . $845
Median SF home value, 2000** . . . $313,100

New Privately Owned Housing Units Authorized by Building Permit, 2007*

	Units	Construction Cost
Single	38	$8,542,343
Total	47	$10,267,405

Municipal Finance

(For local fiscal year ended in 2006)

Revenues

Total . . . $24,463,759
Taxes . . . 11,090,967
Special benefits assessment . . . 16,938
Licenses & permits . . . 287,092
Fines & forfeitures . . . 142,390
Revenues from use of money & property . . . 1,011,127
Intergovernmental . . . 788,811
Service charges . . . 5,352,795
Other revenues . . . 1,704,488
Other financing sources . . . 4,069,151

Expenditures

Total . . . $24,863,948
General government . . . 2,365,586
Public safety . . . 6,139,583
Transportation . . . 2,405,469
Community development . . . 1,924,482
Health . . . 7,252,639
Culture & leisure . . . 1,091,708
Other . . . 0

Local School District

(Data from School year 2007-08 except as noted)

Lucia Mar Unified
602 Orchard St
Arroyo Grande, CA 93420
(805) 474-3000

Superintendent . . . James Hogeboom
Grade plan . . . K-12
Number of schools . . . 17
Enrollment . . . 10,820
High school graduates, 2006-07 . . . 791
Dropout rate . . . 2.1%
Pupil/teacher ratio . . . 20.6
Average class size . . . 24.9
Students per computer . . . 3.1
Classrooms with internet . . . 582
Avg. Daily Attendance (ADA) . . . 10,496
Cost per ADA . . . $7,542
Avg. Teacher Salary . . . $59,928

California Achievement Tests 6th ed., 2008

(Pct scoring at or above 50th National Percentile Rank)

	Math	Reading	Language
Grade 3	68%	52%	54%
Grade 7	63%	58%	55%

Academic Performance Index, 2008

Number of students tested . . . 8,356
Number of valid scores . . . 7,964
2007 API (base) . . . 782
2008 API (growth) . . . 790

SAT Testing, 2006-07

Enrollment, Grade 12 . . . 876
Number taking test . . . 317
percent taking test . . . 36.2%
percent with total score 1,500+ . . . 22.40%

Average Scores:

Math	Verbal	Writing	Total
534	523	518	1,575

Federal No Child Left Behind, 2008

(Adequate Yearly Progress standards met)

	Participation Rate	Pct Proficient
ELA	Yes	No
Math	Yes	Yes

API criteria . . . Yes
Graduation rate . . . Yes
\# criteria met/possible . . . 36/34

Other school districts for this city

(see Appendix E for information on these districts)

None

See Introduction for an explanation of all data sources.

Demographics & Socio-Economic Characteristics

(2000 Decennial Census, except as noted)

Population

1990* 47,564
2000 56,769
Male 27,887
Female 28,882
Jan. 2008 (estimate)§ 63,652
Persons per sq. mi. of land 4,080.3

Race & Hispanic Origin, 2000

Race
White 24,712
Black/African American 10,724
North American Native 423
Asian 7,179
Pacific Islander 491
Other Race 9,144
Two or more races 4,096
Hispanic origin, total 18,287
Mexican 13,087
Puerto Rican 703
Cuban 78
Other Hispanic 4,419

Age & Nativity, 2000

Under 5 years 4,739
18 years and over 39,270
65 years and over 4,660
85 years and over 564
Median Age 30.9
Native-born 42,715
Foreign-born 14,105

Educational Attainment, 2000

Population 25 years and over 33,388
Less than 9th grade 10.5%
High school grad or higher 75.7%
Bachelor's degree or higher 14.7%
Graduate degree 3.3%

Income & Poverty, 1999

Per capita income $18,241
Median household income $50,557
Median family income $54,472
Persons in poverty 11.4%
H'holds receiving public assistance 884
H'holds receiving social security 3,670

Households, 2000

Total households 17,741
With persons under 18 8,589
With persons over 65 3,368
Family households 13,479
Single person households 3,189
Persons per household 3.17
Persons per family 3.59

Household Population, 2008§§

Persons living in households 63,146
Persons living in group quarters 506
Persons per household 3.1

Labor & Employment

Total civilian labor force, 2008§§ 30,200
Unemployment rate, 2008 .... 10.0%
Total civilian labor force, 2000 26,620

Employed persons 16 years and over by occupation, 2000

Managers & professionals 5,923
Service occupations 4,720
Sales & office occupations 7,358
Farming, fishing & forestry 23
Construction & maintenance 3,267
Production & transportation 3,380
Self-employed persons 1,463

* US Census Bureau
** 2000 Decennial Census
§ California Department of Finance
§§ California Employment Development Dept

General Information

City of Pittsburg
65 Civic Ave
Pittsburg, CA 94565
925-252-6900

Website .... www.ci.pittsburg.ca.us
Elevation .... 28 ft.
Land Area (sq. miles) 15.6
Water Area (sq. miles) 1.2
Year of Incorporation 1903
Government type .... General law
Sales tax rate 9.25%

Voters & Officials

Registered Voters, October 2008

Total 23,972
Democrats 14,937
Republicans 3,575
Declined to state 4,570

Legislative Districts

US Congressional 7
State Senatorial 7
State Assembly 11

Local Officials, 2009

Mayor .... Nancy L. Parent
Manager .... Marc S. Grisham
City Clerk .... Alice E. Evenson
Attorney .... Ruthann Ziegler
Finance Dir .... Marie Simons
Public Works .... Matt Rodriguez
Comm Dev Dir .... Joe Sbranti
Building .... Curtis Smith
Police Chief .... Aaron Baker
Fire/Emergency Mgmt .... (County)

Public Safety

Number of officers, 2007 70
Violent crimes, 2007 250
Property crimes, 2007 2,402
Arson, 2007 4

Public Library

Pittsburg Library
Contra Costa County Library System
80 Power Ave
Pittsburg, CA 94565
925-427-8390

Branch Librarian .... Marian Partridge

Library system statistics, FY 2007

Population served 938,513
Internet terminals 324
Annual users 670,618

Per capita:

Operating income $27.05
percent from local government 82.0%
Operating expenditure $27.82
Total materials 1.57
Print holdings 1.41
Visits per capita 3.65

Housing & Construction

Housing Units

Total, 2008§ 20,818
Single family units, attached 1,298
Single family units, detached 14,269
Multiple family units 4,570
Mobile home units 681
Occupied 20,268
Vacancy rate 2.6%
Median rent, 2000** $880
Median SF home value, 2000** $165,100

New Privately Owned Housing Units Authorized by Building Permit, 2007*

	Units	Construction Cost
Single	229	$42,630,965
Total	559	$70,195,502

Municipal Finance

(For local fiscal year ended in 2006)

Revenues

Total $117,146,832
Taxes 19,029,511
Special benefits assessment 3,107,166
Licenses & permits 1,052,070
Fines & forfeitures 143,651
Revenues from use of money & property 2,205,919
Intergovernmental 16,131,734
Service charges 26,541,782
Other revenues 9,368,943
Other financing sources 39,566,056

Expenditures

Total $86,732,046
General government 4,758,496
Public safety 18,053,205
Transportation 8,543,497
Community development 15,068,795
Health 3,905,075
Culture & leisure 5,164,685
Other 0

Local School District

(Data from School year 2007-08 except as noted)

Pittsburg Unified
2000 Railroad Ave
Pittsburg, CA 94565
(925) 473-2300

Superintendent .... Barbara Wilson
Grade plan K-12
Number of schools 12
Enrollment 9,451
High school graduates, 2006-07 447
Dropout rate 7.0%
Pupil/teacher ratio 20.7
Average class size 26.1
Students per computer 5.1
Classrooms with internet 836
Avg. Daily Attendance (ADA) 9,142
Cost per ADA $8,092
Avg. Teacher Salary $58,097

California Achievement Tests 6th ed., 2008

(Pct scoring at or above 50th National Percentile Rank)

	Math	Reading	Language
Grade 3	39%	22%	31%
Grade 7	34%	32%	30%

Academic Performance Index, 2008

Number of students tested 6,922
Number of valid scores 6,485
2007 API (base) 674
2008 API (growth) 681

SAT Testing, 2006-07

Enrollment, Grade 12 652
Number taking test 133
percent taking test 20.4%
percent with total score 1,500+ 5.20%

Average Scores:

Math	Verbal	Writing	Total
452	441	440	1,333

Federal No Child Left Behind, 2008

(Adequate Yearly Progress standards met)

	Participation Rate	Pct Proficient
ELA	Yes	No
Math	Yes	No

API criteria .... Yes
Graduation rate .... No
\# criteria met/possible 38/29

Other school districts for this city

(see Appendix E for information on these districts)

Antioch Unified, Mt. Diablo Unified

See Introduction for an explanation of all data sources.

Demographics & Socio-Economic Characteristics

(2000 Decennial Census, except as noted)

Population

1990* . . . 41,259
2000 . . . 46,488
Male . . . 23,038
Female . . . 23,450
Jan. 2008 (estimate)§ . . . 51,727
Persons per sq. mi. of land . . . 7,837.4

Race & Hispanic Origin, 2000

Race
White . . . 31,500
Black/African American . . . 821
North American Native . . . 386
Asian . . . 5,190
Pacific Islander . . . 82
Other Race . . . 6,843
Two or more races . . . 1,666
Hispanic origin, total . . . 14,460
Mexican . . . 12,024
Puerto Rican . . . 92
Cuban . . . 135
Other Hispanic . . . 2,209

Age & Nativity, 2000

Under 5 years . . . 3,460
18 years and over . . . 33,920
65 years and over . . . 4,213
85 years and over . . . 375
Median Age . . . 33.3
Native-born . . . 35,545
Foreign-born . . . 11,554

Educational Attainment, 2000

Population 25 years and over . . . 29,970
Less than 9th grade . . . 9.2%
High school grad or higher . . . 81.5%
Bachelor's degree or higher . . . 31.3%
Graduate degree . . . 10.6%

Income & Poverty, 1999

Per capita income . . . $23,843
Median household income . . . $62,803
Median family income . . . $68,976
Persons in poverty . . . 8.7%
H'holds receiving public assistance . . . 331
H'holds receiving social security . . . 3,068

Households, 2000

Total households . . . 15,037
With persons under 18 . . . 6,288
With persons over 65 . . . 2,979
Family households . . . 11,691
Single person households . . . 2,410
Persons per household . . . 3.07
Persons per family . . . 3.42

Household Population, 2008§§

Persons living in households . . . 51,424
Persons living in group quarters . . . 303
Persons per household . . . 3.2

Labor & Employment

Total civilian labor force, 2008§§ . . . 28,700
Unemployment rate, 2008 . . . 4.7%
Total civilian labor force, 2000 . . . 24,548

Employed persons 16 years and over by occupation, 2000

Managers & professionals . . . 9,232
Service occupations . . . 2,956
Sales & office occupations . . . 6,698
Farming, fishing & forestry . . . 95
Construction & maintenance . . . 1,689
Production & transportation . . . 2,827
Self-employed persons . . . 1,668

* US Census Bureau
** 2000 Decennial Census
§ California Department of Finance
§§ California Employment Development Dept

General Information

City of Placentia
401 E Chapman Ave
Placentia, CA 92870
714-993-8117

Website . . . www.placentia.org
Elevation . . . 250 ft.
Land Area (sq. miles) . . . 6.6
Water Area (sq. miles) . . . 0
Year of Incorporation . . . 1926
Government type . . . Chartered
Sales tax rate . . . 8.75%

Voters & Officials

Registered Voters, October 2008

Total . . . 28,068
Democrats . . . 8,548
Republicans . . . 13,307
Declined to state . . . 5,173

Legislative Districts

US Congressional . . . 40, 42
State Senatorial . . . 29
State Assembly . . . 72

Local Officials, 2009

Mayor . . . Greg Sowards
City Admin . . . Troy L. Butzlaff
City Clerk . . . Patrick J. Melia
Attorney . . . Bradley R. Hogin
Finance Dir . . . Karen Ogawa
Public Works . . . Steve Drinovsky
Community Dev Dir . . . Raynald F. Pascua
Building . . . Robert Chang
Police Chief . . . James L. Anderson
Emergency/Fire Dir . . . Chip Prather

Public Safety

Number of officers, 2007 . . . 55
Violent crimes, 2007 . . . 90
Property crimes, 2007 . . . 710
Arson, 2007 . . . 14

Public Library

Placentia Library
411 E Chapman Ave
Placentia, CA 92870
714-528-1906

Director . . . Elizabeth Minter

Library statistics, FY 2007

Population served . . . 55,065
Internet terminals . . . 19
Annual users . . . 38,109

Per capita:

Operating income . . . $42.66
percent from local government . . . 78.7%
Operating expenditure . . . $42.66
Total materials . . . 1.95
Print holdings . . . 1.77
Visits per capita . . . 11.13

Housing & Construction

Housing Units

Total, 2008§ . . . 16,463
Single family units, attached . . . 2,065
Single family units, detached . . . 9,746
Multiple family units . . . 4,065
Mobile home units . . . 587
Occupied . . . 16,152
Vacancy rate . . . 1.9%
Median rent, 2000** . . . $890
Median SF home value, 2000** . . . $264,500

New Privately Owned Housing Units Authorized by Building Permit, 2007*

	Units	Construction Cost
Single	25	$6,230,984
Total	45	$8,520,305

Municipal Finance

(For local fiscal year ended in 2006)

Revenues

Total . . . $39,495,816
Taxes . . . 21,094,275
Special benefits assessment . . . 467,846
Licenses & permits . . . 534,907
Fines & forfeitures . . . 477,355
Revenues from use of money & property . . . 547,402
Intergovernmental . . . 6,239,270
Service charges . . . 4,472,472
Other revenues . . . 5,662,289
Other financing sources . . . 0

Expenditures

Total . . . $34,489,126
General government . . . 3,329,088
Public safety . . . 14,991,531
Transportation . . . 6,993,823
Community development . . . 2,924,367
Health . . . 2,566,330
Culture & leisure . . . 3,415,652
Other . . . 0

Local School District

(Data from School year 2007-08 except as noted)

Placentia-Yorba Linda Unified
1301 East Orangethorpe Ave
Placentia, CA 92870
(714) 996-2550

Superintendent . . . Dennis Smith
Grade plan . . . K-12
Number of schools . . . 32
Enrollment . . . 26,243
High school graduates, 2006-07 . . . 1,865
Dropout rate . . . 1.1%
Pupil/teacher ratio . . . 23.9
Average class size . . . 26.6
Students per computer . . . 4.4
Classrooms with internet . . . 1,176
Avg. Daily Attendance (ADA) . . . 25,745
Cost per ADA . . . $7,949
Avg. Teacher Salary . . . $75,643

California Achievement Tests 6th ed., 2008

(Pct scoring at or above 50th National Percentile Rank)

	Math	Reading	Language
Grade 3	68%	47%	57%
Grade 7	69%	64%	63%

Academic Performance Index, 2008

Number of students tested . . . 20,317
Number of valid scores . . . 19,531
2007 API (base) . . . 816
2008 API (growth) . . . 822

SAT Testing, 2006-07

Enrollment, Grade 12 . . . 1,939
Number taking test . . . 999
percent taking test . . . 51.5%
percent with total score 1,500+ . . . 33.40%

Average Scores:

Math	Verbal	Writing	Total
561	526	525	1,612

Federal No Child Left Behind, 2008

(Adequate Yearly Progress standards met)

	Participation Rate	Pct Proficient
ELA	Yes	No
Math	Yes	No

API criteria . . . Yes
Graduation rate . . . Yes
criteria met/possible . . . 38/36

Other school districts for this city

(see Appendix E for information on these districts)

None

See Introduction for an explanation of all data sources.

Demographics & Socio-Economic Characteristics

(2000 Decennial Census, except as noted)

Population

1990* . . . 8,355
2000 . . . 9,610
Male . . . 4,423
Female . . . 5,187
Jan. 2008 (estimate)§ . . . 10,271
Persons per sq. mi. of land . . . 1,770.9

Race & Hispanic Origin, 2000

Race
White . . . 8,511
Black/African American . . . 22
North American Native . . . 122
Asian . . . 85
Pacific Islander . . . 12
Other Race . . . 556
Two or more races . . . 302
Hispanic origin, total . . . 1,212
Mexican . . . 948
Puerto Rican . . . 15
Cuban . . . 3
Other Hispanic . . . 246

Age & Nativity, 2000

Under 5 years . . . 628
18 years and over . . . 7,150
65 years and over . . . 1,670
85 years and over . . . 278
Median Age . . . 38.3
Native-born . . . 8,713
Foreign-born . . . 867

Educational Attainment, 2000

Population 25 years and over . . . 6,307
Less than 9th grade . . . 4.4%
High school grad or higher . . . 83.3%
Bachelor's degree or higher . . . 19.6%
Graduate degree . . . 7.8%

Income & Poverty, 1999

Per capita income . . . $19,151
Median household income . . . $36,454
Median family income . . . $46,875
Persons in poverty . . . 11.8%
H'holds receiving public assistance . . . 210
H'holds receiving social security . . . 1,240

Households, 2000

Total households . . . 4,001
With persons under 18 . . . 1,340
With persons over 65 . . . 1,141
Family households . . . 2,486
Single person households . . . 1,250
Persons per household . . . 2.34
Persons per family . . . 2.90

Household Population, 2008§§

Persons living in households . . . 10,009
Persons living in group quarters . . . 262
Persons per household . . . 2.3

Labor & Employment

Total civilian labor force, 2008§§ . . . 5,400
Unemployment rate, 2008 . . . 10.4%
Total civilian labor force, 2000 . . . 4,542

Employed persons 16 years and over by occupation, 2000

Managers & professionals . . . 1,250
Service occupations . . . 737
Sales & office occupations . . . 1,228
Farming, fishing & forestry . . . 9
Construction & maintenance . . . 531
Production & transportation . . . 416
Self-employed persons . . . 467

* US Census Bureau
** 2000 Decennial Census
§ California Department of Finance
§§ California Employment Development Dept

General Information

City of Placerville
3101 Center St
Placerville, CA 95667
530-642-5200

Website . . . www.cityofplacerville.org
Elevation . . . 1,866 ft.
Land Area (sq. miles) . . . 5.8
Water Area (sq. miles) . . . 0
Year of Incorporation . . . 1854
Government type . . . General law
Sales tax rate . . . 8.50%

Voters & Officials

Registered Voters, October 2008

Total . . . 5,463
Democrats . . . 1,987
Republicans . . . 2,075
Declined to state . . . 1,063

Legislative Districts

US Congressional . . . 4
State Senatorial . . . 1
State Assembly . . . 4

Local Officials, 2009

Mayor . . . Patty Borelli
Manager . . . John Driscoll
City Clerk . . . Susan Zito
Attorney . . . John Driscoll
Finance Dir . . . Dave Warren
Public Works . . . Randy Pesses
Planning/Dev Dir . . . Steve Calfee
Building . . . NA
Police Chief . . . George Nielsen
Fire/Emergency Mgmt . . . NA

Public Safety

Number of officers, 2007 . . . 17
Violent crimes, 2007 . . . 71
Property crimes, 2007 . . . 235
Arson, 2007 . . . 2

Public Library

Main Branch
El Dorado County Library
345 Fair Lane
Placerville, CA 95667
530-621-5540

Director . . . Jeanne Amos

Library system statistics, FY 2007

Population served . . . 178,674
Internet terminals . . . 39
Annual users . . . 71,838

Per capita:

Operating income . . . $16.42
percent from local government . . . 85.4%
Operating expenditure . . . $16.31
Total materials . . . 2.07
Print holdings . . . 1.94
Visits per capita . . . 1.38

Housing & Construction

Housing Units

Total, 2008§ . . . 4,632
Single family units, attached . . . 260
Single family units, detached . . . 2,861
Multiple family units . . . 1,348
Mobile home units . . . 163
Occupied . . . 4,370
Vacancy rate . . . 5.7%
Median rent, 2000** . . . $652
Median SF home value, 2000** . . . $156,500

New Privately Owned Housing Units Authorized by Building Permit, 2007*

	Units	Construction Cost
Single	70	$11,100,000
Total	70	$11,100,000

Municipal Finance

(For local fiscal year ended in 2006)

Revenues

Total . . . $35,117,521
Taxes . . . 6,405,214
Special benefits assessment . . . 30,299
Licenses & permits . . . 96,102
Fines & forfeitures . . . 502,144
Revenues from use of money & property . . . 694,375
Intergovernmental . . . 1,958,483
Service charges . . . 3,930,978
Other revenues . . . 4,284,926
Other financing sources . . . 17,215,000

Expenditures

Total . . . $17,879,313
General government . . . 2,281,891
Public safety . . . 3,752,910
Transportation . . . 1,715,577
Community development . . . 1,176,624
Health . . . 5,656,546
Culture & leisure . . . 2,232,450
Other . . . 0

Local School District

(Data from School year 2007-08 except as noted)

El Dorado Union High
4675 Missouri Flat Rd
Placerville, CA 95667
(530) 622-5081

Superintendent . . . Sherry Smith
Grade plan . . . 9-12
Number of schools . . . 10
Enrollment . . . 7,280
High school graduates, 2006-07 . . . 1,540
Dropout rate . . . 2.1%
Pupil/teacher ratio . . . 22.7
Average class size . . . 27.4
Students per computer . . . 3.4
Classrooms with internet . . . 387
Avg. Daily Attendance (ADA) . . . 6,785
Cost per ADA . . . $8,116
Avg. Teacher Salary . . . $67,220

California Achievement Tests 6th ed., 2008

(Pct scoring at or above 50th National Percentile Rank)

	Math	Reading	Language
Grade 3	NA	NA	NA
Grade 7	NA	NA	NA

Academic Performance Index, 2008

Number of students tested . . . 5,316
Number of valid scores . . . 5,152
2007 API (base) . . . 804
2008 API (growth) . . . 821

SAT Testing, 2006-07

Enrollment, Grade 12 . . . 1,760
Number taking test . . . 681
percent taking test . . . 38.7%
percent with total score 1,500+ . . . 26.10%

Average Scores:

Math	Verbal	Writing	Total
557	531	520	1,608

Federal No Child Left Behind, 2008

(Adequate Yearly Progress standards met)

	Participation Rate	Pct Proficient
ELA	Yes	No
Math	Yes	No

API criteria . . . Yes
Graduation rate . . . Yes
\# criteria met/possible . . . 22/20

Other school districts for this city

(see Appendix E for information on these districts)

Complete list in Appendix E

Demographics & Socio-Economic Characteristics

(2000 Decennial Census, except as noted)

Population

1990* . . . 31,585
2000 . . . 32,837
Male . . . 15,931
Female . . . 16,906
Jan. 2008 (estimate)§ . . . 33,377
Persons per sq. mi. of land . . . 4,701.0

Race & Hispanic Origin, 2000

Race
White . . . 26,852
Black/African American . . . 504
North American Native . . . 155
Asian . . . 3,096
Pacific Islander . . . 90
Other Race . . . 763
Two or more races . . . 1,377
Hispanic origin, total . . . 2,767
Mexican . . . 1,471
Puerto Rican . . . 150
Cuban . . . 47
Other Hispanic . . . 1,099

Age & Nativity, 2000

Under 5 years . . . 1,993
18 years and over . . . 25,828
65 years and over . . . 4,332
85 years and over . . . 641
Median Age . . . 39.0
Native-born . . . 28,239
Foreign-born . . . 4,608

Educational Attainment, 2000

Population 25 years and over . . . 23,555
Less than 9th grade . . . 2.0%
High school grad or higher . . . 93.1%
Bachelor's degree or higher . . . 42.5%
Graduate degree . . . 13.1%

Income & Poverty, 1999

Per capita income . . . $33,076
Median household income . . . $67,489
Median family income . . . $79,001
Persons in poverty . . . 5.0%
H'holds receiving public assistance . . . 176
H'holds receiving social security . . . 3,039

Households, 2000

Total households . . . 13,753
With persons under 18 . . . 4,104
With persons over 65 . . . 3,024
Family households . . . 8,398
Single person households . . . 4,004
Persons per household . . . 2.35
Persons per family . . . 2.95

Household Population, 2008§§

Persons living in households . . . 32,917
Persons living in group quarters . . . 460
Persons per household . . . 2.3

Labor & Employment

Total civilian labor force, 2008§§ . . . 20,600
Unemployment rate, 2008 . . . 5.0%
Total civilian labor force, 2000 . . . 18,471

Employed persons 16 years and over by occupation, 2000

Managers & professionals . . . 8,693
Service occupations . . . 1,912
Sales & office occupations . . . 4,786
Farming, fishing & forestry . . . 12
Construction & maintenance . . . 1,462
Production & transportation . . . 923
Self-employed persons . . . 1,663

* US Census Bureau
** 2000 Decennial Census
§ California Department of Finance
§§ California Employment Development Dept

General Information

City of Pleasant Hill
100 Gregory Ln
Pleasant Hill, CA 94523
925-671-5270

Website . . . www.ci.pleasant-hill.ca.us
Elevation . . . 50 ft.
Land Area (sq. miles) . . . 7.1
Water Area (sq. miles) . . . 0
Year of Incorporation . . . 1961
Government type . . . General law
Sales tax rate . . . 9.25%

Voters & Officials

Registered Voters, October 2008

Total . . . 19,548
Democrats . . . 9,407
Republicans . . . 5,214
Declined to state . . . 3,990

Legislative Districts

US Congressional . . . 10
State Senatorial . . . 7
State Assembly . . . 14

Local Officials, 2009

Mayor . . . Michael Harris
Manager . . . June Catalano
City Clerk . . . Marty McInturf
Attorney . . . Debra Margolis
Finance Dir . . . Mark Celio
Public Works . . . Steve Wallace
Community Dev Dir . . . Steve Wallace
Building . . . Mike Nielsen
Police Chief . . . Peter Dunbar
Fire/Emergency Mgmt . . . NA

Public Safety

Number of officers, 2007 . . . 46
Violent crimes, 2007 . . . 125
Property crimes, 2007 . . . 1,607
Arson, 2007 . . . 12

Public Library

Contra Costa County Pleasant Hill Library
Contra Costa County Library System
1750 Oak Park Blvd
Pleasant Hill, CA 94523
925-646-6434

County Librarian . . . Anne Cain

Library system statistics, FY 2007

Population served . . . 938,513
Internet terminals . . . 324
Annual users . . . 670,618

Per capita:

Operating income . . . $27.05
percent from local government . . . 82.0%
Operating expenditure . . . $27.82
Total materials . . . 1.57
Print holdings . . . 1.41
Visits per capita . . . 3.65

Housing & Construction

Housing Units

Total, 2008§ . . . 14,497
Single family units, attached . . . 1,631
Single family units, detached . . . 8,435
Multiple family units . . . 4,379
Mobile home units . . . 52
Occupied . . . 14,206
Vacancy rate . . . 2.0%
Median rent, 2000** . . . $984
Median SF home value, 2000** . . . $294,000

New Privately Owned Housing Units Authorized by Building Permit, 2007*

	Units	Construction Cost
Single	6	$2,226,833
Total	6	$2,226,833

Municipal Finance

(For local fiscal year ended in 2006)

Revenues

Total . . . $22,535,598
Taxes . . . 16,806,119
Special benefits assessment . . . 408,361
Licenses & permits . . . 590,764
Fines & forfeitures . . . 194,731
Revenues from use of money & property . . . 776,802
Intergovernmental . . . 2,868,926
Service charges . . . 790,773
Other revenues . . . 99,122
Other financing sources . . . 0

Expenditures

Total . . . $22,832,068
General government . . . 3,493,962
Public safety . . . 9,819,082
Transportation . . . 7,397,654
Community development . . . 2,036,045
Health . . . 85,325
Culture & leisure . . . 0
Other . . . 0

Local School District

(Data from School year 2007-08 except as noted)

Mt. Diablo Unified
1936 Carlotta Dr
Concord, CA 94519
(925) 682-8000

Superintendent . . . Richard Nicholl
Grade plan . . . K-12
Number of schools . . . 55
Enrollment . . . 35,355
High school graduates, 2006-07 . . . 2,153
Dropout rate . . . 6.0%
Pupil/teacher ratio . . . 20.4
Average class size . . . 26.4
Students per computer . . . 5.2
Classrooms with internet . . . 1,777
Avg. Daily Attendance (ADA) . . . 33,956
Cost per ADA . . . $8,368
Avg. Teacher Salary . . . $60,714

California Achievement Tests 6th ed., 2008

(Pct scoring at or above 50th National Percentile Rank)

	Math	Reading	Language
Grade 3	60%	45%	55%
Grade 7	53%	53%	51%

Academic Performance Index, 2008

Number of students tested . . . 26,357
Number of valid scores . . . 25,920
2007 API (base) . . . 747
2008 API (growth) . . . 755

SAT Testing, 2006-07

Enrollment, Grade 12 . . . 2,734
Number taking test . . . 1,063
percent taking test . . . 38.9%
percent with total score 1,500+ . . . 22.80%

Average Scores:

Math	Verbal	Writing	Total
543	521	518	1,582

Federal No Child Left Behind, 2008

(Adequate Yearly Progress standards met)

	Participation Rate	Pct Proficient
ELA	Yes	No
Math	Yes	No

API criteria . . . Yes
Graduation rate . . . Yes
\# criteria met/possible . . . 46/36

Other school districts for this city

(see Appendix E for information on these districts)

None

See Introduction for an explanation of all data sources.

Demographics & Socio-Economic Characteristics†

(2007 American Community Survey, except as noted)

Population

1990* . . . 50,553
2007 . . . 69,348
Male . . . 35,646
Female . . . 33,702
Jan. 2008 (estimate)§ . . . 69,388
Persons per sq. mi. of land . . . 3,197.6

Race & Hispanic Origin, 2007

Race
White . . . 44,783
Black/African American . . . 2,317
North American Native . . . 424
Asian . . . 17,241
Pacific Islander . . . 0
Other Race . . . 2,011
Two or more races . . . 2,572
Hispanic origin, total . . . 5,370
Mexican . . . NA
Puerto Rican . . . NA
Cuban . . . NA
Other Hispanic . . . NA

Age & Nativity, 2007

Under 5 years . . . 5,126
18 years and over . . . 50,864
65 years and over . . . 7,902
85 years and over . . . 1,228
Median Age . . . 39.8
Native-born . . . 52,383
Foreign-born . . . 16,965

Educational Attainment, 2007

Population 25 years and over . . . 45,982
Less than 9th grade . . . 1.6%
High school grad or higher . . . 94.7%
Bachelor's degree or higher . . . 58.4%
Graduate degree . . . 23.1%

Income & Poverty, 2007

Per capita income . . . $48,728
Median household income . . . $113,345
Median family income . . . $131,048
Persons in poverty . . . 2.1%
H'holds receiving public assistance . . . 164
H'holds receiving social security . . . 4,478

Households, 2007

Total households . . . 24,939
With persons under 18 . . . 10,039
With persons over 65 . . . 4,797
Family households . . . 18,660
Single person households . . . 5,491
Persons per household . . . 2.76
Persons per family . . . 3.23

Household Population, 2008§§

Persons living in households . . . 69,153
Persons living in group quarters . . . 235
Persons per household . . . 2.8

Labor & Employment

Total civilian labor force, 2008§§ . . . 36,200
Unemployment rate, 2008 . . . 3.1%
Total civilian labor force, 2000* . . . 34,508

Employed persons 16 years and over by occupation, 2007

Managers & professionals . . . 20,351
Service occupations . . . 3,375
Sales & office occupations . . . 7,567
Farming, fishing & forestry . . . 0
Construction & maintenance . . . 1,187
Production & transportation . . . 1,123
Self-employed persons . . . 2,330

† see Appendix D for 2000 Decennial Census Data
* US Census Bureau
** 2007 American Community Survey
§ California Department of Finance
§§ California Employment Development Dept

General Information

City of Pleasanton
123 Main Street
PO Box 520
Pleasanton, CA 94566
925-931-5002

Website . . . www.ci.pleasanton.ca.us
Elevation . . . 352 ft.
Land Area (sq. miles) . . . 21.7
Water Area (sq. miles) . . . 0.2
Year of Incorporation . . . 1894
Government type . . . General law
Sales tax rate . . . 9.75%

Voters & Officials

Registered Voters, October 2008

Total . . . 41,762
Democrats . . . 16,299
Republicans . . . 14,594
Declined to state . . . 9,288

Legislative Districts

US Congressional . . . 11, 13
State Senatorial . . . 10
State Assembly . . . 15, 18, 20

Local Officials, 2009

Mayor . . . Jennifer Hosterman
City Manager . . . Nelson Fialho
City Clerk . . . Karen Diaz
Attorney . . . Michael H. Roush
Treasurer . . . David P. Culver
Public Works . . . Daniel Smith
Community Dev Dir . . . Brian Dolan
Building . . . George Thomas
Police Chief . . . Michael Fraser
Fire Chief . . . William Cody

Public Safety

Number of officers, 2007 . . . 84
Violent crimes, 2007 . . . 63
Property crimes, 2007 . . . 1,294
Arson, 2007 . . . 4

Public Library

Pleasanton Public Library
400 Old Bernal Ave
Pleasanton, CA 94566
925-931-3400

Director . . . Julie Farnsworth

Library statistics, FY 2007

Population served . . . 68,755
Internet terminals . . . 24
Annual users . . . 275,000

Per capita:

Operating income . . . $60.00
percent from local government . . . 95.3%
Operating expenditure . . . $57.20
Total materials . . . 2.87
Print holdings . . . 2.43
Visits per capita . . . 6.87

Housing & Construction

Housing Units

Total, 2008§ . . . 25,822
Single family units, attached . . . 2,754
Single family units, detached . . . 17,017
Multiple family units . . . 5,595
Mobile home units . . . 456
Occupied . . . 25,123
Vacancy rate . . . 2.7%
Median rent, 2007** . . . $1,524
Median SF home value, 2007** . . . $807,500

New Privately Owned Housing Units Authorized by Building Permit, 2007*

	Units	Construction Cost
Single	47	$28,731,817
Total	52	$29,679,216

Municipal Finance

(For local fiscal year ended in 2006)

Revenues

Total . . . $158,828,052
Taxes . . . 72,226,850
Special benefits assessment . . . 0
Licenses & permits . . . 2,047,269
Fines & forfeitures . . . 607,148
Revenues from use of money & property . . . 3,666,191
Intergovernmental . . . 8,631,066
Service charges . . . 50,550,498
Other revenues . . . 19,504,030
Other financing sources . . . 1,595,000

Expenditures

Total . . . $135,730,304
General government . . . 6,498,994
Public safety . . . 47,585,159
Transportation . . . 12,188,334
Community development . . . 15,874,758
Health . . . 11,747,791
Culture & leisure . . . 26,886,851
Other . . . 0

Local School District

(Data from School year 2007-08 except as noted)

Pleasanton Unified
4665 Bernal Ave
Pleasanton, CA 94566
(925) 462-5500

Superintendent . . . John Casey
Grade plan . . . K-12
Number of schools . . . 16
Enrollment . . . 14,864
High school graduates, 2006-07 . . . 1,189
Dropout rate . . . 0.5%
Pupil/teacher ratio . . . 20.5
Average class size . . . 26.4
Students per computer . . . 4.5
Classrooms with internet . . . 597
Avg. Daily Attendance (ADA) . . . 14,666
Cost per ADA . . . $8,531
Avg. Teacher Salary . . . $81,446

California Achievement Tests 6th ed., 2008

(Pct scoring at or above 50th National Percentile Rank)

	Math	Reading	Language
Grade 3	84%	70%	75%
Grade 7	85%	80%	81%

Academic Performance Index, 2008

Number of students tested . . . 11,517
Number of valid scores . . . 11,173
2007 API (base) . . . 893
2008 API (growth) . . . 897

SAT Testing, 2006-07

Enrollment, Grade 12 . . . 1,257
Number taking test . . . 850
percent taking test . . . 67.6%
percent with total score 1,500+ . . . 48.70%

Average Scores:

Math	Verbal	Writing	Total
579	549	548	1,676

Federal No Child Left Behind, 2008

(Adequate Yearly Progress standards met)

	Participation Rate	Pct Proficient
ELA	Yes	Yes
Math	Yes	Yes

API criteria . . . Yes
Graduation rate . . . Yes
\# criteria met/possible . . . 38/38

Other school districts for this city

(see Appendix E for information on these districts)

None

See Introduction for an explanation of all data sources.

Demographics & Socio-Economic Characteristics

(2000 Decennial Census, except as noted)

Population

1990* 811
2000 980
Male 448
Female 532
Jan. 2008 (estimate)§ 1,033
Persons per sq. mi. of land 1,147.8

Race & Hispanic Origin, 2000

Race
White 887
Black/African American 2
North American Native 22
Asian 11
Pacific Islander 0
Other Race 14
Two or more races 44
Hispanic origin, total 50
Mexican 22
Puerto Rican 0
Cuban 0
Other Hispanic 28

Age & Nativity, 2000

Under 5 years 74
18 years and over 693
65 years and over 165
85 years and over 18
Median Age 39.1
Native-born 935
Foreign-born 22

Educational Attainment, 2000

Population 25 years and over 578
Less than 9th grade 3.3%
High school grad or higher 84.6%
Bachelor's degree or higher 7.4%
Graduate degree 3.5%

Income & Poverty, 1999

Per capita income $16,197
Median household income $37,262
Median family income $43,611
Persons in poverty 10.1%
H'holds receiving public assistance 10
H'holds receiving social security 110

Households, 2000

Total households 392
With persons under 18 158
With persons over 65 128
Family households 272
Single person households 101
Persons per household 2.50
Persons per family 2.99

Household Population, 2008§§

Persons living in households 1,033
Persons living in group quarters 0
Persons per household 2.4

Labor & Employment

Total civilian labor force, 2008§§ 540
Unemployment rate, 2008 ....2.6%
Total civilian labor force, 2000 431

Employed persons 16 years and over by occupation, 2000

Managers & professionals 105
Service occupations 95
Sales & office occupations 114
Farming, fishing & forestry 4
Construction & maintenance 56
Production & transportation 51
Self-employed persons 37

* US Census Bureau
** 2000 Decennial Census
§ California Department of Finance
§§ California Employment Development Dept

General Information

City of Plymouth
PO Box 429
9426 Main St, CA 95669
209-245-6941

Website ....www.ci.plymouth.ca.us
Elevation ....1,086 ft.
Land Area (sq. miles) 0.9
Water Area (sq. miles) 0
Year of Incorporation 1917
Government type ....General law
Sales tax rate 8.75%

Voters & Officials

Registered Voters, October 2008

Total 580
Democrats 212
Republicans 241
Declined to state 95

Legislative Districts

US Congressional 3
State Senatorial 1
State Assembly 10

Local Officials, 2009

Mayor ....Jon Colburn
Manager ....Dixon Flynn
City Clerk ....Gloria Stoddard
Attorney ....Steven Rudolph
Finance Dir ....Jeff Gardner
Public Works ....Selby Beck
Planning/Dev Dir ....Paula Daneluk
Building ....Jeff Kelley
Police Chief ....NA
Fire/Emergency Mgmt ....(County)

Public Safety

Number of officers, 2007 ....NA
Violent crimes, 2007 ....NA
Property crimes, 2007 ....NA
Arson, 2007 ....NA

Public Library

Plymouth Branch
Amador County Library System
9375 Main St
Plymouth, CA 95669
209-245-6476

Branch Librarian ....Rae LeGrande

Library system statistics, FY 2007

Population served 38,435
Internet terminals 18
Annual users 74,880

Per capita:

Operating income $24.71
percent from local government 94.0%
Operating expenditure $20.44
Total materials 2.18
Print holdings 1.97
Visits per capita 2.04

Housing & Construction

Housing Units

Total, 2008§ 506
Single family units, attached 31
Single family units, detached 281
Multiple family units 50
Mobile home units 144
Occupied 434
Vacancy rate 14.2%
Median rent, 2000** $701
Median SF home value, 2000** $119,900

New Privately Owned Housing Units Authorized by Building Permit, 2007*

	Units	Construction Cost
Single	1	$86,371
Total	1	$86,371

Municipal Finance

(For local fiscal year ended in 2006)

Revenues

Total $1,630,529
Taxes 468,383
Special benefits assessment 0
Licenses & permits 24,810
Fines & forfeitures 527
Revenues from use of money & property 18,604
Intergovernmental 453,084
Service charges 584,850
Other revenues 80,271
Other financing sources 0

Expenditures

Total $2,410,106
General government 287,085
Public safety 125,013
Transportation 513,923
Community development 90,997
Health 487,611
Culture & leisure 82,429
Other 0

Local School District

(Data from School year 2007-08 except as noted)

Amador County Unified
217 Rex Ave
Jackson, CA 95642
(209) 223-1750

Superintendent ....Dick Glock
Grade plan K-12
Number of schools 12
Enrollment 4,362
High school graduates, 2006-07 373
Dropout rate 3.8%
Pupil/teacher ratio 22.8
Average class size 23.3
Students per computer 3.9
Classrooms with internet 308
Avg. Daily Attendance (ADA) 4,219
Cost per ADA $6,964
Avg. Teacher Salary $60,591

California Achievement Tests 6th ed., 2008

(Pct scoring at or above 50th National Percentile Rank)

	Math	Reading	Language
Grade 3	59%	52%	54%
Grade 7	54%	60%	55%

Academic Performance Index, 2008

Number of students tested 3,491
Number of valid scores 3,322
2007 API (base) 751
2008 API (growth) 769

SAT Testing, 2006-07

Enrollment, Grade 12 442
Number taking test 103
percent taking test 23.3%
percent with total score 1,500+ 13.60%

Average Scores:

Math	Verbal	Writing	Total
519	520	516	1,555

Federal No Child Left Behind, 2008

(Adequate Yearly Progress standards met)

	Participation Rate	Pct Proficient
ELA	Yes	No
Math	Yes	No

API criteria ....Yes
Graduation rate ....Yes
\# criteria met/possible 26/22

Other school districts for this city

(see Appendix E for information on these districts)

None

See Introduction for an explanation of all data sources.

Demographics & Socio-Economic Characteristics

(2000 Decennial Census, except as noted)

Population

1990* 407
2000 474
Male 249
Female 225
Jan. 2008 (estimate)§ 493
Persons per sq. mi. of land 352.1

Race & Hispanic Origin, 2000

Race
White 349
Black/African American 5
North American Native 18
Asian 1
Pacific Islander 0
Other Race 89
Two or more races 12
Hispanic origin, total 135
Mexican 133
Puerto Rican 0
Cuban 0
Other Hispanic 2

Age & Nativity, 2000

Under 5 years 40
18 years and over 318
65 years and over 43
85 years and over 3
Median Age 33.3
Native-born 375
Foreign-born 111

Educational Attainment, 2000

Population 25 years and over 268
Less than 9th grade 13.8%
High school grad or higher 77.2%
Bachelor's degree or higher 20.5%
Graduate degree 4.1%

Income & Poverty, 1999

Per capita income $12,591
Median household income $27,083
Median family income $32,885
Persons in poverty 26.6%
H'holds receiving public assistance 0
H'holds receiving social security 41

Households, 2000

Total households 191
With persons under 18 70
With persons over 65 35
Family households 109
Single person households 62
Persons per household 2.48
Persons per family 3.30

Household Population, 2008§§

Persons living in households 493
Persons living in group quarters 0
Persons per household 2.4

Labor & Employment

Total civilian labor force, 2008§§ 290
Unemployment rate, 2008 .... 2.4%
Total civilian labor force, 2000 270

Employed persons 16 years and over by occupation, 2000

Managers & professionals 68
Service occupations 73
Sales & office occupations 44
Farming, fishing & forestry 17
Construction & maintenance 39
Production & transportation 22
Self-employed persons 51

* US Census Bureau
** 2000 Decennial Census
§ California Department of Finance
§§ California Employment Development Dept

General Information

City of Point Arena
PO Box 67
Point Arena, CA 95468
707-882-2122

Website .... www.cityofpointarena.com
Elevation .... NA
Land Area (sq. miles) 1.4
Water Area (sq. miles) 0
Year of Incorporation 1908
Government type .... General law
Sales tax rate 8.75%

Voters & Officials

Registered Voters, October 2008

Total 249
Democrats 119
Republicans 31
Declined to state 68

Legislative Districts

US Congressional 1
State Senatorial 2
State Assembly 1

Local Officials, 2009

Mayor .... Lauren Sinnott
Manager .... Claudia Hillary
City Clerk .... Claudia Hillary
Attorney .... Joseph Brecher
Finance Dir .... NA
Public Works .... NA
Planning/Dev Dir .... Claudia Hillary
Building .... NA
Police Chief .... NA
Emergency/Fire Dir .... Michael Suddith

Public Safety

Number of officers, 2007 .... NA
Violent crimes, 2007 .... NA
Property crimes, 2007 .... NA
Arson, 2007 .... NA

Public Library

Coast Community Library
Marin County Free Library System
225 Main St
Point Arena, CA 95468
707-882-3114

Branch Librarian .... Tara Black

Library system statistics, FY 2007

Population served 90,291
Internet terminals 20
Annual users 37,258

Per capita:

Operating income $18.48
percent from local government 58.6%
Operating expenditure $19.03
Total materials 2.07
Print holdings 1.94
Visits per capita .... NA

Housing & Construction

Housing Units

Total, 2008§ 233
Single family units, attached 7
Single family units, detached 149
Multiple family units 58
Mobile home units 19
Occupied 205
Vacancy rate 12.0%
Median rent, 2000** $584
Median SF home value, 2000** $133,300

New Privately Owned Housing Units Authorized by Building Permit, 2007*

	Units	Construction Cost
Single	NA	NA
Total	NA	NA

Municipal Finance

(For local fiscal year ended in 2006)

Revenues

Total $729,198
Taxes 227,150
Special benefits assessment 0
Licenses & permits 2,435
Fines & forfeitures 280
Revenues from use of money & property 32,012
Intergovernmental 262,913
Service charges 193,481
Other revenues 10,927
Other financing sources 0

Expenditures

Total $645,299
General government 149,137
Public safety 103,180
Transportation 163,367
Community development 16,083
Health 139,206
Culture & leisure 74,326
Other 0

Local School District

(Data from School year 2007-08 except as noted)
‡combined elementary and high school data

Point Arena Joint Union High
PO Box 87
Point Arena, CA 95468
(707) 882-2803

Superintendent .... Mark Iacuaniello
Grade plan 9-12
Number of schools 2
Enrollment 176
High school graduates, 2006-07 38
Dropout rate 3.4%
Pupil/teacher ratio 10.6
Average class size 12.0
Students per computer 1.5
Classrooms with internet 24
Avg. Daily Attendance (ADA)‡ 364
Cost per ADA‡ $16,419
Avg. Teacher Salary‡ $48,273

California Achievement Tests 6th ed., 2008

(Pct scoring at or above 50th National Percentile Rank)

	Math	Reading	Language
Grade 3	NA	NA	NA
Grade 7	NA	NA	NA

Academic Performance Index, 2008

Number of students tested 121
Number of valid scores 111
2007 API (base) 659
2008 API (growth) 643

SAT Testing, 2006-07

Enrollment, Grade 12 45
Number taking test 15
percent taking test 33.3%
percent with total score 1,500+ 13.30%

Average Scores:

Math	Verbal	Writing	Total
499	481	491	1,471

Federal No Child Left Behind, 2008

(Adequate Yearly Progress standards met)

	Participation Rate	Pct Proficient
ELA	No	Yes
Math	Yes	Yes

API criteria .... Yes
Graduation rate .... Yes
\# criteria met/possible 6/5

Other school districts for this city

(see Appendix E for information on these districts)

Arena Union Elem

See Introduction for an explanation of all data sources.

Demographics & Socio-Economic Characteristics†

(2007 American Community Survey, except as noted)

Population

1990* . . . 131,723
2007 . . . 142,111
Male . . . 69,624
Female . . . 72,487
Jan. 2008 (estimate)§ . . . 163,405
Persons per sq. mi. of land . . . 7,166.9

Race & Hispanic Origin, 2007

Race
White . . . 40,423
Black/African American . . . 12,833
North American Native . . . 974
Asian . . . 9,472
Pacific Islander . . . 252
Other Race . . . 71,572
Two or more races . . . 6,585
Hispanic origin, total . . . 101,785
Mexican . . . 88,195
Puerto Rican . . . 1,038
Cuban . . . 518
Other Hispanic . . . 12,034

Age & Nativity, 2007

Under 5 years . . . 13,953
18 years and over . . . 97,174
65 years and over . . . 9,703
85 years and over . . . 1,265
Median Age . . . 28.3
Native-born . . . 93,748
Foreign-born . . . 48,363

Educational Attainment, 2007

Population 25 years and over . . . 79,399
Less than 9th grade . . . 19.2%
High school grad or higher . . . 65.4%
Bachelor's degree or higher . . . 13.5%
Graduate degree . . . 3.7%

Income & Poverty, 2007

Per capita income . . . $16,798
Median household income . . . $50,678
Median family income . . . $53,342
Persons in poverty . . . 15.4%
H'holds receiving public assistance . . . 1,834
H'holds receiving social security . . . 6,759

Households, 2007

Total households . . . 35,861
With persons under 18 . . . 18,855
With persons over 65 . . . 6,614
Family households . . . 28,561
Single person households . . . 5,465
Persons per household . . . 3.90
Persons per family . . . 4.29

Household Population, 2008§§

Persons living in households . . . 157,546
Persons living in group quarters . . . 5,859
Persons per household . . . 4.0

Labor & Employment

Total civilian labor force, 2008§§ . . . 67,400
Unemployment rate, 2008 . . . 8.4%
Total civilian labor force, 2000* . . . 59,371

Employed persons 16 years and over by occupation, 2007

Managers & professionals . . . 11,215
Service occupations . . . 11,204
Sales & office occupations . . . 17,051
Farming, fishing & forestry . . . 168
Construction & maintenance . . . 6,850
Production & transportation . . . 14,582
Self-employed persons . . . 3,591

† see Appendix D for 2000 Decennial Census Data
* US Census Bureau
** 2007 American Community Survey
§ California Department of Finance
§§ California Employment Development Dept

General Information

City of Pomona
505 S Garey Ave
Pomona, CA 91766
909-620-2311

Website . . . www.ci.pomona.ca.us
Elevation . . . 850 ft.
Land Area (sq. miles) . . . 22.8
Water Area (sq. miles) . . . 0
Year of Incorporation . . . 1888
Government type . . . Chartered
Sales tax rate . . . 9.25%

Voters & Officials

Registered Voters, October 2008

Total . . . 49,089
Democrats . . . 26,538
Republicans . . . 11,375
Declined to state . . . 9,196

Legislative Districts

US Congressional . . . 38
State Senatorial . . . 32
State Assembly . . . 61

Local Officials, 2009

Mayor . . . Elliott Rothman
City Manager . . . Linda Lowry
City Clerk . . . Marie Michel Macias
Attorney . . . Arnold Alvarez-Glasman
Finance Dir . . . Paula Chamberlain
Public Works . . . Tim D'Zmura
Planning/Dev Dir . . . Mark Lazzaretto
Building . . . Tim D'Zmura
Police Chief . . . Dave Keetle (Actg)
Fire/Emergency Mgmt . . . Greg Jones

Public Safety

Number of officers, 2007 . . . 194
Violent crimes, 2007 . . . 1,235
Property crimes, 2007 . . . 5,211
Arson, 2007 . . . 22

Public Library

Pomona Public Library
625 S Garey Ave
Pomona, CA 91766
909-620-2043

Director . . . Greg Shapton

Library statistics, FY 2007

Population served . . . 162,140
Internet terminals . . . 42
Annual users . . . 58,058

Per capita:

Operating income . . . $19.43
percent from local government . . . 90.7%
Operating expenditure . . . $18.91
Total materials . . . 2.67
Print holdings . . . 2.60
Visits per capita . . . 1.55

Housing & Construction

Housing Units

Total, 2008§ . . . 41,264
Single family units, attached . . . 3,343
Single family units, detached . . . 24,713
Multiple family units . . . 11,503
Mobile home units . . . 1,705
Occupied . . . 39,447
Vacancy rate . . . 4.4%
Median rent, 2007** . . . $997
Median SF home value, 2007** . . . $421,900

New Privately Owned Housing Units Authorized by Building Permit, 2007*

	Units	Construction Cost
Single	183	$28,814,771
Total	345	$43,256,373

Municipal Finance

(For local fiscal year ended in 2006)

Revenues

Total . . . $197,467,356
Taxes . . . 74,619,834
Special benefits assessment . . . 1,180,820
Licenses & permits . . . 2,733,486
Fines & forfeitures . . . 1,798,576
Revenues from use of money & property . . . 7,046,591
Intergovernmental . . . 22,781,034
Service charges . . . 38,948,067
Other revenues . . . 6,070,314
Other financing sources . . . 42,288,634

Expenditures

Total . . . $209,592,209
General government . . . 59,702,667
Public safety . . . 65,761,169
Transportation . . . 22,390,343
Community development . . . 15,421,698
Health . . . 11,257,900
Culture & leisure . . . 8,803,715
Other . . . 0

Local School District

(Data from School year 2007-08 except as noted)

Pomona Unified
PO Box 2900
Pomona, CA 91769
(909) 397-4800

Superintendent . . Thelma Melendez de Santa Ana
Grade plan . . . K-12
Number of schools . . . 44
Enrollment . . . 30,779
High school graduates, 2006-07 . . . 1,443
Dropout rate . . . 6.2%
Pupil/teacher ratio . . . 20.8
Average class size . . . 25.5
Students per computer . . . 2.4
Classrooms with internet . . . 1,546
Avg. Daily Attendance (ADA) . . . 29,821
Cost per ADA . . . $9,168
Avg. Teacher Salary . . . $68,768

California Achievement Tests 6th ed., 2008

(Pct scoring at or above 50th National Percentile Rank)

	Math	Reading	Language
Grade 3	43%	24%	37%
Grade 7	39%	34%	34%

Academic Performance Index, 2008

Number of students tested . . . 23,727
Number of valid scores . . . 22,089
2007 API (base) . . . 694
2008 API (growth) . . . 705

SAT Testing, 2006-07

Enrollment, Grade 12 . . . 1,607
Number taking test . . . 676
percent taking test . . . 42.1%
percent with total score 1,500+ . . . 12.90%

Average Scores:

Math	Verbal	Writing	Total
465	450	448	1,363

Federal No Child Left Behind, 2008

(Adequate Yearly Progress standards met)

	Participation Rate	Pct Proficient
ELA	Yes	No
Math	Yes	No

API criteria . . . Yes
Graduation rate . . . No
criteria met/possible . . . 38/32

Other school districts for this city

(see Appendix E for information on these districts)

None

See Introduction for an explanation of all data sources.

Demographics & Socio-Economic Characteristics
(2000 Decennial Census, except as noted)

Population
1990* . . . 20,319
2000 . . . 21,845
Male . . . 10,987
Female . . . 10,858
Jan. 2008 (estimate)§ . . . 22,202
Persons per sq. mi. of land . . . 5,045.9

Race & Hispanic Origin, 2000
Race
White . . . 12,510
Black/African American . . . 1,324
North American Native . . . 369
Asian . . . 1,383
Pacific Islander . . . 110
Other Race . . . 4,772
Two or more races . . . 1,377
Hispanic origin, total . . . 8,960
Mexican . . . 7,520
Puerto Rican . . . 129
Cuban . . . 23
Other Hispanic . . . 1,288

Age & Nativity, 2000
Under 5 years . . . 1,917
18 years and over . . . 15,814
65 years and over . . . 2,339
85 years and over . . . 241
Median Age . . . 30.3
Native-born . . . 17,285
Foreign-born . . . 4,561

Educational Attainment, 2000
Population 25 years and over . . . 12,904
Less than 9th grade . . . 11.4%
High school grad or higher . . . 75.4%
Bachelor's degree or higher . . . 15.4%
Graduate degree . . . 5.1%

Income & Poverty, 1999
Per capita income . . . $17,311
Median household income . . . $42,246
Median family income . . . $46,056
Persons in poverty . . . 11.6%
H'holds receiving public assistance . . . 403
H'holds receiving social security . . . 1,899

Households, 2000
Total households . . . 7,268
With persons under 18 . . . 3,043
With persons over 65 . . . 1,772
Family households . . . 4,999
Single person households . . . 1,749
Persons per household . . . 2.86
Persons per family . . . 3.42

Household Population, 2008§§
Persons living in households . . . 21,214
Persons living in group quarters . . . 988
Persons per household . . . 2.9

Labor & Employment
Total civilian labor force, 2008§§ . . . 10,900
Unemployment rate, 2008 . . . 6.9%
Total civilian labor force, 2000 . . . 9,233

Employed persons 16 years and over by occupation, 2000
Managers & professionals . . . 2,232
Service occupations . . . 1,179
Sales & office occupations . . . 2,714
Farming, fishing & forestry . . . 255
Construction & maintenance . . . 963
Production & transportation . . . 1,362
Self-employed persons . . . 538

* US Census Bureau
** 2000 Decennial Census
§ California Department of Finance
§§ California Employment Development Dept

General Information
City of Port Hueneme
250 N Ventura Rd
Port Hueneme, CA 93041
805-986-6500

Website . . . www.ci.port-hueneme.ca.us
Elevation . . . 12 ft.
Land Area (sq. miles) . . . 4.4
Water Area (sq. miles) . . . 0.2
Year of Incorporation . . . 1948
Government type . . . Chartered
Sales tax rate . . . 8.75%

Voters & Officials
Registered Voters, October 2008
Total . . . 8,964
Democrats . . . 4,306
Republicans . . . 2,587
Declined to state . . . 1,677

Legislative Districts
US Congressional . . . 23
State Senatorial . . . 23
State Assembly . . . 41

Local Officials, 2009
Mayor . . . Jonathan Sharkey
City Manager . . . David J. Norman
City Clerk . . . Michelle Ascencion (Dep)
Attorney . . . Mark Hensley
Finance Dir . . . Robert Bravo
Public Works . . . Andres Santamaria
Planning/Dev Dir . . . Greg Brown
Building . . . Steve Sutton
Police Chief . . . Fernando Estrella
Fire/Emergency Mgmt . . . NA

Public Safety
Number of officers, 2007 . . . 24
Violent crimes, 2007 . . . 93
Property crimes, 2007 . . . 398
Arson, 2007 . . . 4

Public Library
Ray D. Preuter Port Hueneme Library
Ventura County Library System
510 Park Ave
Port Hueneme, CA 93041
805-486-5460

Branch Librarian . . . Cathy Thomason

Library system statistics, FY 2007
Population served . . . 439,444
Internet terminals . . . 188
Annual users . . . 216,575

Per capita:
Operating income . . . $25.05
percent from local government . . . 86.2%
Operating expenditure . . . $25.02
Total materials . . . 1.81
Print holdings . . . 1.70
Visits per capita . . . NA

Housing & Construction
Housing Units
Total, 2008§ . . . 8,108
Single family units, attached . . . 2,202
Single family units, detached . . . 2,493
Multiple family units . . . 3,372
Mobile home units . . . 41
Occupied . . . 7,429
Vacancy rate . . . 8.4%
Median rent, 2000** . . . $803
Median SF home value, 2000** . . . $165,200

New Privately Owned Housing Units Authorized by Building Permit, 2007*

	Units	Construction Cost
Single	13	$2,915,878
Total	13	$2,915,878

Municipal Finance
(For local fiscal year ended in 2006)

Revenues
Total . . . $26,131,443
Taxes . . . 6,397,326
Special benefits assessment . . . 819,681
Licenses & permits . . . 249,073
Fines & forfeitures . . . 293,451
Revenues from use of money & property . . . 3,600,017
Intergovernmental . . . 2,633,026
Service charges . . . 10,936,772
Other revenues . . . 1,202,097
Other financing sources . . . 0

Expenditures
Total . . . $29,690,076
General government . . . 8,203,973
Public safety . . . 5,967,345
Transportation . . . 2,320,188
Community development . . . 2,565,634
Health . . . 6,579,199
Culture & leisure . . . 725,502
Other . . . 0

Local School District
(Data from School year 2007-08 except as noted)
Oxnard Union High
309 South K St
Oxnard, CA 93030
(805) 385-2500

Superintendent . . . Jody Dunlap
Grade plan . . . 9-12
Number of schools . . . 10
Enrollment . . . 16,868
High school graduates, 2006-07 . . . 2,756
Dropout rate . . . 4.4%
Pupil/teacher ratio . . . 25.2
Average class size . . . 28.2
Students per computer . . . 4.7
Classrooms with internet . . . 635
Avg. Daily Attendance (ADA) . . . 15,420
Cost per ADA . . . $8,186
Avg. Teacher Salary . . . $72,428

California Achievement Tests 6th ed., 2008
(Pct scoring at or above 50th National Percentile Rank)

	Math	Reading	Language
Grade 3	74%	54%	56%
Grade 7	89%	81%	70%

Academic Performance Index, 2008
Number of students tested . . . 11,929
Number of valid scores . . . 11,323
2007 API (base) . . . 673
2008 API (growth) . . . 693

SAT Testing, 2006-07
Enrollment, Grade 12 . . . 3,865
Number taking test . . . 916
percent taking test . . . 23.7%
percent with total score 1,500+ . . . 11.20%

Average Scores:

Math	Verbal	Writing	Total
509	489	485	1,483

Federal No Child Left Behind, 2008
(Adequate Yearly Progress standards met)

	Participation Rate	Pct Proficient
ELA	Yes	No
Math	Yes	No

API criteria . . . Yes
Graduation rate . . . No
criteria met/possible . . . 38/35

Other school districts for this city
(see Appendix E for information on these districts)
Hueneme Elem

See Introduction for an explanation of all data sources.

Demographics & Socio-Economic Characteristics

(2000 Decennial Census, except as noted)

Population

1990*	29,563
2000	39,615
Male	19,444
Female	20,171
Jan. 2008 (estimate)§	51,638
Persons per sq. mi. of land	3,688.4

Race & Hispanic Origin, 2000

Race	
White	21,690
Black/African American	506
North American Native	684
Asian	1,835
Pacific Islander	61
Other Race	12,959
Two or more races	1,880
Hispanic origin, total	19,589
Mexican	17,148
Puerto Rican	78
Cuban	6
Other Hispanic	2,357

Age & Nativity, 2000

Under 5 years	3,759
18 years and over	26,045
65 years and over	3,738
85 years and over	598
Median Age	28.6
Native-born	30,984
Foreign-born	9,041

Educational Attainment, 2000

Population 25 years and over	21,791
Less than 9th grade	22.3%
High school grad or higher	61.7%
Bachelor's degree or higher	11.0%
Graduate degree	3.6%

Income & Poverty, 1999

Per capita income	$12,745
Median household income	$32,046
Median family income	$35,136
Persons in poverty	25.0%
H'holds receiving public assistance	1,318
H'holds receiving social security	2,949

Households, 2000

Total households	11,884
With persons under 18	6,194
With persons over 65	2,530
Family households	9,170
Single person households	2,266
Persons per household	3.20
Persons per family	3.62

Household Population, 2008§§

Persons living in households	50,161
Persons living in group quarters	1,477
Persons per household	3.3

Labor & Employment

Total civilian labor force, 2008§§	21,000
Unemployment rate, 2008	9.9%
Total civilian labor force, 2000	16,135

Employed persons 16 years and over by occupation, 2000

Managers & professionals	3,744
Service occupations	2,491
Sales & office occupations	3,344
Farming, fishing & forestry	1,505
Construction & maintenance	1,148
Production & transportation	1,920
Self-employed persons	943

* US Census Bureau
** 2000 Decennial Census
§ California Department of Finance
§§ California Employment Development Dept

General Information

City of Porterville
291 N Main St
Porterville, CA 93257
559-782-7466

Website	www.ci.porterville.ca.us
Elevation	459 ft.
Land Area (sq. miles)	14.0
Water Area (sq. miles)	0.1
Year of Incorporation	1902
Government type	Chartered
Sales tax rate	9.25%

Voters & Officials

Registered Voters, October 2008

Total	16,041
Democrats	6,042
Republicans	6,537
Declined to state	2,732

Legislative Districts

US Congressional	21
State Senatorial	18
State Assembly	34

Local Officials, 2009

Mayor	Cameron Hamilton
Manager	John Lollis
City Clerk	John Lollis
Attorney	Julia Lew
Finance Dir	Maria Bemis
Public Works	Baldomero Rodriguez
Planning/Dev Dir	Brad Dunlap
Building	Gary Banks
Police Chief	Chuck McMillan
Emergency/Fire Dir	Mario Garcia

Public Safety

Number of officers, 2007	58
Violent crimes, 2007	289
Property crimes, 2007	2,349
Arson, 2007	5

Public Library

Porterville Public Library
41 W Thurman Ave
Porterville, CA 93257
559-784-0177

Director	Vikki Cervantes

Library statistics, FY 2007

Population served	51,467
Internet terminals	46
Annual users	46,326

Per capita:

Operating income	$11.73
percent from local government	87.4%
Operating expenditure	$10.86
Total materials	1.63
Print holdings	1.47
Visits per capita	3.40

Housing & Construction

Housing Units

Total, 2008§	16,219
Single family units, attached	483
Single family units, detached	11,772
Multiple family units	3,247
Mobile home units	717
Occupied	15,239
Vacancy rate	6.0%
Median rent, 2000**	$504
Median SF home value, 2000**	$93,500

New Privately Owned Housing Units Authorized by Building Permit, 2007*

	Units	Construction Cost
Single	176	$33,311,951
Total	229	$38,086,041

Municipal Finance

(For local fiscal year ended in 2006)

Revenues

Total	$49,150,102
Taxes	16,622,774
Special benefits assessment	171,699
Licenses & permits	427,283
Fines & forfeitures	190,382
Revenues from use of money & property	1,159,676
Intergovernmental	5,565,964
Service charges	22,385,085
Other revenues	1,668,930
Other financing sources	958,309

Expenditures

Total	$47,892,869
General government	2,364,766
Public safety	10,118,082
Transportation	8,582,711
Community development	2,159,219
Health	12,924,817
Culture & leisure	5,129,135
Other	0

Local School District

(Data from School year 2007-08 except as noted)

Porterville Unified
600 West Grand Ave
Porterville, CA 93257
(559) 793-2455

Superintendent	John Snavely
Grade plan	K-12
Number of schools	22
Enrollment	13,550
High school graduates, 2006-07	976
Dropout rate	5.4%
Pupil/teacher ratio	20.3
Average class size	25.9
Students per computer	3.7
Classrooms with internet	719
Avg. Daily Attendance (ADA)	12,970
Cost per ADA	$8,364
Avg. Teacher Salary	$68,039

California Achievement Tests 6th ed., 2008

(Pct scoring at or above 50th National Percentile Rank)

	Math	Reading	Language
Grade 3	52%	28%	41%
Grade 7	51%	39%	32%

Academic Performance Index, 2008

Number of students tested	10,187
Number of valid scores	9,249
2007 API (base)	692
2008 API (growth)	720

SAT Testing, 2006-07

Enrollment, Grade 12	1,326
Number taking test	281
percent taking test	21.2%
percent with total score 1,500+	8.10%

Average Scores:

Math	Verbal	Writing	Total
500	478	473	1,451

Federal No Child Left Behind, 2008

(Adequate Yearly Progress standards met)

	Participation Rate	Pct Proficient
ELA	Yes	No
Math	No	No

API criteria	Yes
Graduation rate	No
# criteria met/possible	34/28

Other school districts for this city

(see Appendix E for information on these districts)

Complete list in Appendix E

See Introduction for an explanation of all data sources.

Demographics & Socio-Economic Characteristics

(2000 Decennial Census, except as noted)

Population

1990* . . . 2,193
2000 . . . 2,227
Male . . . 1,097
Female . . . 1,130
Jan. 2008 (estimate)§ . . . 2,051
Persons per sq. mi. of land . . . 932.3

Race & Hispanic Origin, 2000

Race
White . . . 1,920
Black/African American . . . 10
North American Native . . . 59
Asian . . . 24
Pacific Islander . . . 2
Other Race . . . 130
Two or more races . . . 82
Hispanic origin, total . . . 263
Mexican . . . 224
Puerto Rican . . . 3
Cuban . . . 1
Other Hispanic . . . 35

Age & Nativity, 2000

Under 5 years . . . 138
18 years and over . . . 1,571
65 years and over . . . 301
85 years and over . . . 41
Median Age . . . 37.2
Native-born . . . 2,143
Foreign-born . . . 108

Educational Attainment, 2000

Population 25 years and over . . . 1,401
Less than 9th grade . . . 3.1%
High school grad or higher . . . 86.4%
Bachelor's degree or higher . . . 13.0%
Graduate degree . . . 5.1%

Income & Poverty, 1999

Per capita income . . . $14,734
Median household income . . . $28,103
Median family income . . . $35,156
Persons in poverty . . . 20.3%
H'holds receiving public assistance . . . 79
H'holds receiving social security . . . 211

Households, 2000

Total households . . . 899
With persons under 18 . . . 345
With persons over 65 . . . 219
Family households . . . 595
Single person households . . . 261
Persons per household . . . 2.45
Persons per family . . . 3.02

Household Population, 2008§§

Persons living in households . . . 2,030
Persons living in group quarters . . . 21
Persons per household . . . 2.1

Labor & Employment

Total civilian labor force, 2008§§ . . . 1,120
Unemployment rate, 2008 . . . 9.7%
Total civilian labor force, 2000 . . . 1,056

Employed persons 16 years and over by occupation, 2000

Managers & professionals . . . 201
Service occupations . . . 187
Sales & office occupations . . . 197
Farming, fishing & forestry . . . 22
Construction & maintenance . . . 178
Production & transportation . . . 179
Self-employed persons . . . 116

* US Census Bureau
** 2000 Decennial Census
§ California Department of Finance
§§ California Employment Development Dept

General Information

City of Portola
P.O. Box 1225
35 Third Ave
Portola, CA 96122
530-832-4216

Website . . . www.ci.portola.ca.us
Elevation . . . 4,834 ft.
Land Area (sq. miles) . . . 2.2
Water Area (sq. miles) . . . 0
Year of Incorporation . . . 1946
Government type . . . General law
Sales tax rate . . . 8.25%

Voters & Officials

Registered Voters, October 2008

Total . . . 1,219
Democrats . . . 457
Republicans . . . 378
Declined to state . . . 302

Legislative Districts

US Congressional . . . 4
State Senatorial . . . 1
State Assembly . . . 3

Local Officials, 2009

Mayor . . . Curt McBride
Manager . . . Jim Murphy
City Clerk . . . Leslie Tigan
Attorney . . . Steve Gross
Finance Dir . . . Susan Scarlett
Public Works . . . Todd Roberts
Planning Dir . . . Karen Downs
Building . . . Todd Roberts
Police Chief . . . NA
Fire Chief . . . Bob Stone

Public Safety

Number of officers, 2007 . . . NA
Violent crimes, 2007 . . . NA
Property crimes, 2007 . . . NA
Arson, 2007 . . . NA

Public Library

Portola Branch Library
Plumas County Library System
34 3rd Ave
Portola, CA 96122
530-832-4241

Branch Librarian . . . DeAnna Standley

Library system statistics, FY 2007

Population served . . . 24,613
Internet terminals . . . 18
Annual users . . . 19,223

Per capita:

Operating income . . . $27.64
percent from local government . . . 81.9%
Operating expenditure . . . $27.64
Total materials . . . 3.15
Print holdings . . . 3.07
Visits per capita . . . NA

Housing & Construction

Housing Units

Total, 2008§ . . . 1,063
Single family units, attached . . . 14
Single family units, detached . . . 798
Multiple family units . . . 182
Mobile home units . . . 69
Occupied . . . 948
Vacancy rate . . . 10.8%
Median rent, 2000** . . . $494
Median SF home value, 2000** . . . $95,500

New Privately Owned Housing Units Authorized by Building Permit, 2007*

	Units	Construction Cost
Single	6	$3,108,000
Total	6	$3,108,000

Municipal Finance

(For local fiscal year ended in 2006)

Revenues

Total . . . $3,436,060
Taxes . . . 709,758
Special benefits assessment . . . 0
Licenses & permits . . . 37,602
Fines & forfeitures . . . 2,114
Revenues from use of money & property . . . 285,580
Intergovernmental . . . 681,597
Service charges . . . 1,262,709
Other revenues . . . 456,700
Other financing sources . . . 0

Expenditures

Total . . . $2,617,509
General government . . . 347,819
Public safety . . . 278,238
Transportation . . . 266,621
Community development . . . 196,134
Health . . . 496,824
Culture & leisure . . . 430,019
Other . . . 70,198

Local School District

(Data from School year 2007-08 except as noted)

Plumas Unified
50 Church St
Quincy, CA 95971
(530) 283-6500

Superintendent . . . Glenn Harris
Grade plan . . . K-12
Number of schools . . . 12
Enrollment . . . 2,610
High school graduates, 2006-07 . . . 223
Dropout rate . . . 4.9%
Pupil/teacher ratio . . . 20.2
Average class size . . . 18.5
Students per computer . . . 4.3
Classrooms with internet . . . 184
Avg. Daily Attendance (ADA) . . . 2,205
Cost per ADA . . . $10,173
Avg. Teacher Salary . . . $58,155

California Achievement Tests 6th ed., 2008

(Pct scoring at or above 50th National Percentile Rank)

	Math	Reading	Language
Grade 3	62%	63%	67%
Grade 7	61%	66%	58%

Academic Performance Index, 2008

Number of students tested . . . 1,743
Number of valid scores . . . 1,421
2007 API (base) . . . 863
2008 API (growth) . . . 802

SAT Testing, 2006-07

Enrollment, Grade 12 . . . 233
Number taking test . . . 73
percent taking test . . . 31.3%
percent with total score 1,500+ . . . 13.70%

Average Scores:

Math	Verbal	Writing	Total
488	500	484	1,472

Federal No Child Left Behind, 2008

(Adequate Yearly Progress standards met)

	Participation Rate	Pct Proficient
ELA	Yes	Yes
Math	Yes	No

API criteria . . . Yes
Graduation rate . . . Yes
\# criteria met/possible . . . 20/19

Other school districts for this city

(see Appendix E for information on these districts)

None

See Introduction for an explanation of all data sources.

Demographics & Socio-Economic Characteristics

(2000 Decennial Census, except as noted)

Population

1990* . . . 4,194
2000 . . . 4,462
Male . . . 2,195
Female . . . 2,267
Jan. 2008 (estimate)§ . . . 4,639
Persons per sq. mi. of land . . . 504.2

Race & Hispanic Origin, 2000

Race
White . . . 4,146
Black/African American . . . 18
North American Native . . . 11
Asian . . . 178
Pacific Islander . . . 2
Other Race . . . 43
Two or more races . . . 64
Hispanic origin, total . . . 149
Mexican . . . 76
Puerto Rican . . . 7
Cuban . . . 4
Other Hispanic . . . 62

Age & Nativity, 2000

Under 5 years . . . 223
18 years and over . . . 3,441
65 years and over . . . 938
85 years and over . . . 164
Median Age . . . 47.5
Native-born . . . 4,047
Foreign-born . . . 575

Educational Attainment, 2000

Population 25 years and over . . . 3,319
Less than 9th grade . . . 0.5%
High school grad or higher . . . 98.7%
Bachelor's degree or higher . . . 77.4%
Graduate degree . . . 41.0%

Income & Poverty, 1999

Per capita income . . . $99,621
Median household income . . . $158,217
Median family income . . . $180,893
Persons in poverty . . . 2.3%
H'holds receiving public assistance . . . 0
H'holds receiving social security . . . 552

Households, 2000

Total households . . . 1,700
With persons under 18 . . . 532
With persons over 65 . . . 639
Family households . . . 1,269
Single person households . . . 339
Persons per household . . . 2.58
Persons per family . . . 2.93

Household Population, 2008§§

Persons living in households . . . 4,569
Persons living in group quarters . . . 70
Persons per household . . . 2.6

Labor & Employment

Total civilian labor force, 2008§§ . . . NA
Unemployment rate, 2008 . . . NA
Total civilian labor force, 2000 . . . 2,037

Employed persons 16 years and over by occupation, 2000

Managers & professionals . . . 1,442
Service occupations . . . 108
Sales & office occupations . . . 387
Farming, fishing & forestry . . . 7
Construction & maintenance . . . 32
Production & transportation . . . 32
Self-employed persons . . . 264

* US Census Bureau
** 2000 Decennial Census
§ California Department of Finance
§§ California Employment Development Dept

General Information

Town of Portola Valley
765 Portola Rd
Portola Valley, CA 94028
650-851-1700

Website . . . www.portolavalley.net
Elevation . . . NA
Land Area (sq. miles) . . . 9.2
Water Area (sq. miles) . . . 0
Year of Incorporation . . . 1964
Government type . . . General law
Sales tax rate . . . 9.25%

Voters & Officials

Registered Voters, October 2008

Total . . . 3,385
Democrats . . . 1,481
Republicans . . . 1,113
Declined to state . . . 671

Legislative Districts

US Congressional . . . 14
State Senatorial . . . 8
State Assembly . . . 21

Local Officials, 2009

Mayor . . . Ann Wengert
Manager . . . Angela Howard
City Clerk . . . Sharon Hanlon
Attorney . . . Sandy Sloan
Finance Dir . . . Angela Howard
Public Works . . . Howard Young
Planning Dir . . . Leslie Lambert
Building . . . NA
Police Chief . . . Greg Munks
Emergency/Fire Dir . . . Armando Muela

Public Safety

Number of officers, 2007 . . . NA
Violent crimes, 2007 . . . NA
Property crimes, 2007 . . . NA
Arson, 2007 . . . NA

Public Library

Portola Valley Library
San Mateo County Library System
4575 Alpine Rd
Portola Valley, CA 94028
650-851-0560

Branch Librarian . . . Susan Goetz

Library system statistics, FY 2007

Population served . . . 278,388
Internet terminals . . . 26
Annual users . . . 49,920

Per capita:

Operating income . . . $90.21
percent from local government . . . 63.5%
Operating expenditure . . . $60.41
Total materials . . . 2.65
Print holdings . . . 2.16
Visits per capita . . . 5.44

Housing & Construction

Housing Units

Total, 2008§ . . . 1,810
Single family units, attached . . . 33
Single family units, detached . . . 1,502
Multiple family units . . . 275
Mobile home units . . . 0
Occupied . . . 1,748
Vacancy rate . . . 3.4%
Median rent, 2000** . . . $2,001
Median SF home value, 2000** . . $1,000,001

New Privately Owned Housing Units Authorized by Building Permit, 2007*

	Units	Construction Cost
Single	10	$13,585,550
Total	10	$13,585,550

Municipal Finance

(For local fiscal year ended in 2006)

Revenues

Total . . . $5,745,549
Taxes . . . 3,817,099
Special benefits assessment . . . 0
Licenses & permits . . . 383,485
Fines & forfeitures . . . 20,593
Revenues from use of money & property . . . 381,337
Intergovernmental . . . 336,913
Service charges . . . 683,738
Other revenues . . . 122,384
Other financing sources . . . 0

Expenditures

Total . . . $4,196,230
General government . . . 1,513,006
Public safety . . . 553,074
Transportation . . . 668,371
Community development . . . 468,483
Health . . . 0
Culture & leisure . . . 993,296
Other . . . 0

Local School District

(Data from School year 2007-08 except as noted)

Sequoia Union High
480 James Ave
Redwood City, CA 94062
(650) 369-1411

Superintendent . . . Patrick Gemma
Grade plan . . . 9-12
Number of schools . . . 6
Enrollment . . . 8,510
High school graduates, 2006-07 . . . 1,546
Dropout rate . . . 3.2%
Pupil/teacher ratio . . . 19.7
Average class size . . . 26.4
Students per computer . . . 3.0
Classrooms with internet . . . 402
Avg. Daily Attendance (ADA) . . . 7,811
Cost per ADA . . . $11,470
Avg. Teacher Salary . . . $76,194

California Achievement Tests 6th ed., 2008

(Pct scoring at or above 50th National Percentile Rank)

	Math	Reading	Language
Grade 3	NA	NA	NA
Grade 7	NA	NA	NA

Academic Performance Index, 2008

Number of students tested . . . 5,874
Number of valid scores . . . 5,525
2007 API (base) . . . 753
2008 API (growth) . . . 753

SAT Testing, 2006-07

Enrollment, Grade 12 . . . 2,000
Number taking test . . . 945
percent taking test . . . 47.3%
percent with total score 1,500+ . . . 29.10%

Average Scores:

Math	Verbal	Writing	Total
546	530	530	1,606

Federal No Child Left Behind, 2008

(Adequate Yearly Progress standards met)

	Participation Rate	Pct Proficient
ELA	Yes	No
Math	Yes	No

API criteria . . . Yes
Graduation rate . . . Yes
\# criteria met/possible . . . 28/25

Other school districts for this city

(see Appendix E for information on these districts)

Portola Valley Elem

See Introduction for an explanation of all data sources.

Demographics & Socio-Economic Characteristics

(2000 Decennial Census, except as noted)

Population

1990* 43,516
2000 48,044
Male 23,661
Female 24,383
Jan. 2008 (estimate)§ 51,103
Persons per sq. mi. of land 1,303.6

Race & Hispanic Origin, 2000

Race
White 39,807
Black/African American 800
North American Native 231
Asian 3,584
Pacific Islander 133
Other Race 1,571
Two or more races 1,918
Hispanic origin, total 4,974
Mexican 3,655
Puerto Rican 228
Cuban 48
Other Hispanic 1,043

Age & Nativity, 2000

Under 5 years 2,895
18 years and over 33,303
65 years and over 4,138
85 years and over 516
Median Age 36.9
Native-born 43,159
Foreign-born 5,136

Educational Attainment, 2000

Population 25 years and over 29,788
Less than 9th grade 1.9%
High school grad or higher 93.1%
Bachelor's degree or higher 39.3%
Graduate degree 14.2%

Income & Poverty, 1999

Per capita income $29,788
Median household income $71,708
Median family income $77,875
Persons in poverty 4.3%
H'holds receiving public assistance 315
H'holds receiving social security 2,980

Households, 2000

Total households 15,467
With persons under 18 7,734
With persons over 65 2,743
Family households 12,874
Single person households 1,951
Persons per household 3.08
Persons per family 3.35

Household Population, 2008§§

Persons living in households 50,677
Persons living in group quarters 426
Persons per household 3.1

Labor & Employment

Total civilian labor force, 2008§§ 28,500
Unemployment rate, 2008 .... 3.5%
Total civilian labor force, 2000 23,785

Employed persons 16 years and over by occupation, 2000

Managers & professionals 10,215
Service occupations 3,241
Sales & office occupations 6,112
Farming, fishing & forestry 29
Construction & maintenance 1,723
Production & transportation 1,674
Self-employed persons 2,076

* US Census Bureau
** 2000 Decennial Census
§ California Department of Finance
§§ California Employment Development Dept

General Information

City of Poway
13325 Civic Center Dr
PO Box 789
Poway, CA 92074
858-668-4400

Website .... www.poway.org
Elevation .... 508 ft.
Land Area (sq. miles) 39.2
Water Area (sq. miles) 0.1
Year of Incorporation 1980
Government type .... General law
Sales tax rate 8.75%

Voters & Officials

Registered Voters, October 2008

Total 28,551
Democrats 7,298
Republicans 13,701
Declined to state 6,446

Legislative Districts

US Congressional 52
State Senatorial 36
State Assembly 75

Local Officials, 2009

Mayor .... Mickey Cafagna
Manager .... Rod Gould
City Clerk .... Linda A. Troyan
Attorney .... Lisa Foster
Finance Dir .... Tina White
Public Works .... (vacant)
Planning/Dev Dir .... Robert Manis
Building .... Robert Manis
Police Chief .... NA
Emergency/Fire Dir .... Mark Sanchez

Public Safety

Number of officers, 2007 .... NA
Violent crimes, 2007 102
Property crimes, 2007 751
Arson, 2007 3

Public Library

Poway Library
San Diego County Library System
13137 Poway Rd
Poway, CA 92064
858-513-2919

Branch Librarian .... Judy Chattergee

Library system statistics, FY 2007

Population served 1,049,868
Internet terminals 394
Annual users .... NA

Per capita:

Operating income $33.43
percent from local government 80.6%
Operating expenditure $31.30
Total materials 1.54
Print holdings 1.32
Visits per capita 6.31

Housing & Construction

Housing Units

Total, 2008§ 16,365
Single family units, attached 877
Single family units, detached 12,186
Multiple family units 2,610
Mobile home units 692
Occupied 16,108
Vacancy rate 1.6%
Median rent, 2000** $910
Median SF home value, 2000** $284,200

New Privately Owned Housing Units Authorized by Building Permit, 2007*

	Units	Construction Cost
Single	24	$7,869,631
Total	24	$7,869,631

Municipal Finance

(For local fiscal year ended in 2006)

Revenues

Total $81,676,997
Taxes 29,580,197
Special benefits assessment 2;856,036
Licenses & permits 945,737
Fines & forfeitures 789,123
Revenues from use of money & property 8,229,591
Intergovernmental 4,328,136
Service charges 32,710,405
Other revenues 2,237,772
Other financing sources 0

Expenditures

Total $78,188,099
General government 11,912,162
Public safety 18,328,373
Transportation 8,028,612
Community development 5,745,206
Health 7,631,556
Culture & leisure 8,307,998
Other 4,137,514

Local School District

(Data from School year 2007-08 except as noted)

Poway Unified
13626 Twin Peaks Rd
Poway, CA 92064
(858) 748-0010

Superintendent .... Donald Phillips
Grade plan K-12
Number of schools 34
Enrollment 33,283
High school graduates, 2006-07 2,522
Dropout rate 0.9%
Pupil/teacher ratio 22.8
Average class size 27.2
Students per computer 5.1
Classrooms with internet 1,548
Avg. Daily Attendance (ADA) 32,638
Cost per ADA $7,954
Avg. Teacher Salary $69,827

California Achievement Tests 6th ed., 2008

(Pct scoring at or above 50th National Percentile Rank)

	Math	Reading	Language
Grade 3	83%	67%	74%
Grade 7	82%	77%	76%

Academic Performance Index, 2008

Number of students tested 25,390
Number of valid scores 24,648
2007 API (base) 864
2008 API (growth) 872

SAT Testing, 2006-07

Enrollment, Grade 12 2,845
Number taking test 1,775
percent taking test 62.4%
percent with total score 1,500+ 43.00%

Average Scores:

Math	Verbal	Writing	Total
569	541	538	1,648

Federal No Child Left Behind, 2008

(Adequate Yearly Progress standards met)

	Participation Rate	Pct Proficient
ELA	Yes	Yes
Math	Yes	Yes

API criteria .... Yes
Graduation rate .... Yes
\# criteria met/possible 42/42

Other school districts for this city

(see Appendix E for information on these districts)

None

See Introduction for an explanation of all data sources.

Demographics & Socio-Economic Characteristics

(2000 Decennial Census, except as noted)

Population

1990* . . . NA
2000 . . . 55,060
Male . . . 26,897
Female . . . 28,163
Jan. 2008 (estimate)§ . . . 60,975
Persons per sq. mi. of land . . . 2,710.0

Race & Hispanic Origin, 2000

Race
White . . . 36,704
Black/African American . . . 6,245
North American Native . . . 521
Asian . . . 4,537
Pacific Islander . . . 300
Other Race . . . 3,151
Two or more races . . . 3,602
Hispanic origin, total . . . 7,100
Mexican . . . 4,969
Puerto Rican . . . 359
Cuban . . . 51
Other Hispanic . . . 1,721

Age & Nativity, 2000

Under 5 years . . . 4,468
18 years and over . . . 39,440
65 years and over . . . 5,568
85 years and over . . . 407
Median Age . . . 31.9
Native-born . . . 43,283
Foreign-born . . . 11,303

Educational Attainment, 2000

Population 25 years and over . . . 33,652
Less than 9th grade . . . 6.0%
High school grad or higher . . . 83.9%
Bachelor's degree or higher . . . 18.1%
Graduate degree . . . 5.0%

Income & Poverty, 1999

Per capita income . . . $18,121
Median household income . . . $40,095
Median family income . . . $43,211
Persons in poverty . . . 15.7%
H'holds receiving public assistance . . . 1,987
H'holds receiving social security . . . 4,444

Households, 2000

Total households . . . 20,407
With persons under 18 . . . 7,802
With persons over 65 . . . 4,039
Family households . . . 13,546
Single person households . . . 5,196
Persons per household . . . 2.68
Persons per family . . . 3.22

Household Population, 2008§§

Persons living in households . . . 60,625
Persons living in group quarters . . . 350
Persons per household . . . 2.6

Labor & Employment

Total civilian labor force, 2008§§ . . . 31,200
Unemployment rate, 2008 . . . 8.3%
Total civilian labor force, 2000 . . . NA

Employed persons 16 years and over by occupation, 2000

Managers & professionals . . . 7,628
Service occupations . . . 3,888
Sales & office occupations . . . 7,851
Farming, fishing & forestry . . . 36
Construction & maintenance . . . 2,222
Production & transportation . . . 2,694
Self-employed persons . . . 1,468

* US Census Bureau
** 2000 Decennial Census
§ California Department of Finance
§§ California Employment Development Dept

General Information

City of Rancho Cordova
2729 Prospect Park Dr
Rancho Cordova, CA 95670
916-851-8700

Website . . . www.cityofranchocordova.org
Elevation . . . NA
Land Area (sq. miles) . . . 22.5
Water Area (sq. miles) . . . 0.3
Year of Incorporation . . . 2003
Government type . . . General law
Sales tax rate . . . 8.75%

Voters & Officials

Registered Voters, October 2008

Total . . . 28,437
Democrats . . . 11,967
Republicans . . . 8,907
Declined to state . . . 6,076

Legislative Districts

US Congressional . . . 3, 5
State Senatorial . . . 6
State Assembly . . . 10

Local Officials, 2009

Mayor . . . Dan Skoglund
Manager . . . Ted Gaebler
City Clerk . . . Mindy Cuppy
Attorney . . . Adam Lindgren
Finance Dir . . . Donna Silva
Public Works . . . Cyrus Abhar
Planning/Dev Dir . . . Paul Junker
Building . . . Thomas Trimberger
Police Chief . . . Reuben Meeks
Fire/Emergency Mgmt . . . NA

Public Safety

Number of officers, 2007 . . . NA
Violent crimes, 2007 . . . NA
Property crimes, 2007 . . . NA
Arson, 2007 . . . NA

Public Library

Rancho Cordova Library
Sacramento Public Library System
9845 Folsom Blvd
Sacramento, CA 95827
916-264-2770

Branch Librarian . . . Ken Cooley

Library system statistics, FY 2007

Population served . . . 1,335,969
Internet terminals . . . 49
Annual users . . . 27,435

Per capita:

Operating income . . . $25.83
percent from local government . . . 91.0%
Operating expenditure . . . $23.08
Total materials . . . 1.57
Print holdings . . . 1.45
Visits per capita . . . 1.18

Housing & Construction

Housing Units

Total, 2008§ . . . 24,133
Single family units, attached . . . 2,064
Single family units, detached . . . 12,993
Multiple family units . . . 7,687
Mobile home units . . . 1,389
Occupied . . . 23,054
Vacancy rate . . . 4.5%
Median rent, 2000** . . . $659
Median SF home value, 2000** . . . $116,500

New Privately Owned Housing Units Authorized by Building Permit, 2007*

	Units	Construction Cost
Single	573	$144,682,990
Total	575	$145,023,990

Municipal Finance

(For local fiscal year ended in 2006)

Revenues

Total . . . $87,271,422
Taxes . . . 61,209,390
Special benefits assessment . . . 0
Licenses & permits . . . 4,100,583
Fines & forfeitures . . . 464,745
Revenues from use of money & property . . . 1,965,870
Intergovernmental . . . 3,314,109
Service charges . . . 6,306,657
Other revenues . . . 3,205,068
Other financing sources . . . 6,705,000

Expenditures

Total . . . $69,454,447
General government . . . 46,565,267
Public safety . . . 13,446,239
Transportation . . . 0
Community development . . . 9,442,941
Health . . . 0
Culture & leisure . . . 0
Other . . . 0

Local School District

(Data from School year 2007-08 except as noted)

Folsom-Cordova Unified
125 East Bidwell St
Folsom, CA 95630
(916) 355-1100

Superintendent . . . Patrick Godwin
Grade plan . . . K-12
Number of schools . . . 34
Enrollment . . . 19,029
High school graduates, 2006-07 . . . 1,033
Dropout rate . . . 3.1%
Pupil/teacher ratio . . . 21.4
Average class size . . . 26.5
Students per computer . . . 4.7
Classrooms with internet . . . 926
Avg. Daily Attendance (ADA) . . . 18,524
Cost per ADA . . . $7,778
Avg. Teacher Salary . . . $65,021

California Achievement Tests 6th ed., 2008

(Pct scoring at or above 50th National Percentile Rank)

	Math	Reading	Language
Grade 3	68%	54%	61%
Grade 7	64%	63%	63%

Academic Performance Index, 2008

Number of students tested . . . 14,486
Number of valid scores . . . 13,534
2007 API (base) . . . 805
2008 API (growth) . . . 812

SAT Testing, 2006-07

Enrollment, Grade 12 . . . 1,123
Number taking test . . . 435
percent taking test . . . 38.7%
percent with total score 1,500+ . . . 24.70%

Average Scores:

Math	Verbal	Writing	Total
546	525	522	1,593

Federal No Child Left Behind, 2008

(Adequate Yearly Progress standards met)

	Participation Rate	Pct Proficient
ELA	Yes	No
Math	Yes	Yes

API criteria . . . Yes
Graduation rate . . . Yes
criteria met/possible . . . 38/37

Other school districts for this city

(see Appendix E for information on these districts)

None

See Introduction for an explanation of all data sources.

Demographics & Socio-Economic Characteristics†

(2007 American Community Survey, except as noted)

Population

1990* ... 101,409
2007 ... 157,777
Male ... 78,564
Female ... 79,213
Jan. 2008 (estimate)§ ... 174,308
Persons per sq. mi. of land ... 4,660.6

Race & Hispanic Origin, 2007

Race
White ... 94,972
Black/African American ... 12,965
North American Native ... 1,768
Asian ... 15,242
Pacific Islander ... 1,019
Other Race ... 22,027
Two or more races ... 9,784
Hispanic origin, total ... 52,962
Mexican ... 42,369
Puerto Rican ... 899
Cuban ... 838
Other Hispanic ... 8,856

Age & Nativity, 2007

Under 5 years ... 10,402
18 years and over ... 115,307
65 years and over ... 11,106
85 years and over ... 1,135
Median Age ... 31.0
Native-born ... 129,911
Foreign-born ... 27,866

Educational Attainment, 2007

Population 25 years and over ... 97,040
Less than 9th grade ... 3.2%
High school grad or higher ... 91.8%
Bachelor's degree or higher ... 31.2%
Graduate degree ... 11.6%

Income & Poverty, 2007

Per capita income ... $31,518
Median household income ... $80,538
Median family income ... $88,059
Persons in poverty ... 5.3%
H'holds receiving public assistance ... 912
H'holds receiving social security ... 9,001

Households, 2007

Total households ... 50,630
With persons under 18 ... 21,034
With persons over 65 ... 8,407
Family households ... 37,362
Single person households ... 10,805
Persons per household ... 3.05
Persons per family ... 3.61

Household Population, 2008§§

Persons living in households ... 170,682
Persons living in group quarters ... 3,626
Persons per household ... 3.2

Labor & Employment

Total civilian labor force, 2008§§ ... 79,600
Unemployment rate, 2008 ... 5.1%
Total civilian labor force, 2000* ... 65,482

Employed persons 16 years and over by occupation, 2007

Managers & professionals ... 31,960
Service occupations ... 10,084
Sales & office occupations ... 27,838
Farming, fishing & forestry ... 184
Construction & maintenance ... 5,345
Production & transportation ... 6,931
Self-employed persons ... 5,840

† see Appendix D for 2000 Decennial Census Data
* US Census Bureau
** 2007 American Community Survey
§ California Department of Finance
§§ California Employment Development Dept

General Information

City of Rancho Cucamonga
10500 Civic Center Dr
PO Box 807
Rancho Cucamonga, CA 91729
909-477-2700

Website .. www.ci.rancho-cucamonga.ca.us
Elevation ... 1,110 ft.
Land Area (sq. miles) ... 37.4
Water Area (sq. miles) ... 0
Year of Incorporation ... 1977
Government type ... General law
Sales tax rate ... 8.75%

Voters & Officials

Registered Voters, October 2008

Total ... 81,176
Democrats ... 29,325
Republicans ... 34,084
Declined to state ... 14,640

Legislative Districts

US Congressional ... 26
State Senatorial ... 31
State Assembly ... 63

Local Officials, 2009

Mayor ... Donald J. Kurth
Manager ... Jack Lam
City Clerk ... Janice Reynolds
Attorney ... James Markman
Finance Dir ... Tamara Layne
Public Works ... Dave Blevins
Planning/Dev Dir ... James Troyer
Building ... Tran G. Huynh
Police Captain ... Joe Cusimano
Fire Chief ... Peter Bryan

Public Safety

Number of officers, 2007 ... NA
Violent crimes, 2007 ... 376
Property crimes, 2007 ... 3,930
Arson, 2007 ... 22

Public Library

Rancho Cucamonga Public Library
7368 Archibald Ave
Rancho Cucamonga, CA 91730
909-477-2720

Director ... Deborah Clark

Library statistics, FY 2007

Population served ... 172,331
Internet terminals ... 33
Annual users ... 7,418

Per capita:

Operating income ... $29.61
percent from local government ... 85.7%
Operating expenditure ... $28.87
Total materials ... 1.61
Print holdings ... 1.51
Visits per capita ... 14.66

Housing & Construction

Housing Units

Total, 2008§ ... 55,103
Single family units, attached ... 3,161
Single family units, detached ... 35,575
Multiple family units ... 14,987
Mobile home units ... 1,380
Occupied ... 53,441
Vacancy rate ... 3.0%
Median rent, 2007** ... $1,363
Median SF home value, 2007** ... $540,400

New Privately Owned Housing Units Authorized by Building Permit, 2007*

	Units	Construction Cost
Single	583	$114,319,315
Total	750	$131,601,643

Municipal Finance

(For local fiscal year ended in 2006)

Revenues

Total ... $146,849,549
Taxes ... 72,907,859
Special benefits assessment ... 10,313,756
Licenses & permits ... 1,792,524
Fines & forfeitures ... 870,104
Revenues from use of money & property ... 4,850,078
Intergovernmental ... 20,875,792
Service charges ... 23,941,350
Other revenues ... 11,298,086
Other financing sources ... 0

Expenditures

Total ... $122,092,130
General government ... 12,670,569
Public safety ... 28,149,094
Transportation ... 35,670,455
Community development ... 22,547,570
Health ... 1,088,609
Culture & leisure ... 16,407,740
Other ... 0

Local School District

(Data from School year 2007-08 except as noted)

Chaffey Joint Union High
211 West Fifth St
Ontario, CA 91762
(909) 988-8511

Superintendent ... Mathew Holton
Grade plan ... 9-12
Number of schools ... 11
Enrollment ... 25,108
High school graduates, 2006-07 ... 4,562
Dropout rate ... 2.6%
Pupil/teacher ratio ... 25.2
Average class size ... 29.3
Students per computer ... 4.6
Classrooms with internet ... 1,703
Avg. Daily Attendance (ADA) ... 24,014
Cost per ADA ... $7,815
Avg. Teacher Salary ... $77,140

California Achievement Tests 6th ed., 2008

(Pct scoring at or above 50th National Percentile Rank)

	Math	Reading	Language
Grade 3	NA	NA	NA
Grade 7	NA	NA	NA

Academic Performance Index, 2008

Number of students tested ... 18,219
Number of valid scores ... 17,278
2007 API (base) ... 720
2008 API (growth) ... 734

SAT Testing, 2006-07

Enrollment, Grade 12 ... 5,840
Number taking test ... 1,782
percent taking test ... 30.5%
percent with total score 1,500+ ... 12.30%

Average Scores:

Math	Verbal	Writing	Total
492	475	471	1,438

Federal No Child Left Behind, 2008

(Adequate Yearly Progress standards met)

	Participation Rate	Pct Proficient
ELA	No	Yes
Math	Yes	No

API criteria ... Yes
Graduation rate ... Yes
\# criteria met/possible ... 38/36

Other school districts for this city

(see Appendix E for information on these districts)

None

See Introduction for an explanation of all data sources.

Demographics & Socio-Economic Characteristics

(2000 Decennial Census, except as noted)

Population

1990* 9,778
2000 13,249
Male 6,341
Female 6,908
Jan. 2008 (estimate)§ 17,057
Persons per sq. mi. of land 701.9

Race & Hispanic Origin, 2000

Race
White 12,280
Black/African American 118
North American Native 26
Asian 165
Pacific Islander 15
Other Race 479
Two or more races 166
Hispanic origin, total 1,251
Mexican 959
Puerto Rican 25
Cuban 16
Other Hispanic 251

Age & Nativity, 2000

Under 5 years 369
18 years and over 11,887
65 years and over 5,699
85 years and over 599
Median Age 61.3
Native-born 11,085
Foreign-born 1,888

Educational Attainment, 2000

Population 25 years and over 11,337
Less than 9th grade 1.9%
High school grad or higher 91.9%
Bachelor's degree or higher 35.7%
Graduate degree 15.0%

Income & Poverty, 1999

Per capita income $58,603
Median household income $59,826
Median family income $78,384
Persons in poverty 5.8%
H'holds receiving public assistance 70
H'holds receiving social security 4,012

Households, 2000

Total households 6,813
With persons under 18 783
With persons over 65 3,869
Family households 4,077
Single person households 2,199
Persons per household 1.92
Persons per family 2.36

Household Population, 2008§§

Persons living in households 16,527
Persons living in group quarters 530
Persons per household 2.0

Labor & Employment

Total civilian labor force, 2008§§ 6,500
Unemployment rate, 2008 ..... 7.5%
Total civilian labor force, 2000 4,622

Employed persons 16 years and over by occupation, 2000

Managers & professionals 1,823
Service occupations 701
Sales & office occupations 1,278
Farming, fishing & forestry 12
Construction & maintenance 312
Production & transportation 192
Self-employed persons 747

* US Census Bureau
** 2000 Decennial Census
§ California Department of Finance
§§ California Employment Development Dept

General Information

City of Rancho Mirage
69825 Hwy 111
Rancho Mirage, CA 92270
760-324-4511

Website ..... www.ci.rancho-mirage.ca.us
Elevation ..... NA
Land Area (sq. miles) 24.3
Water Area (sq. miles) 0.4
Year of Incorporation 1973
Government type ..... Chartered
Sales tax rate 8.75%

Voters & Officials

Registered Voters, October 2008

Total 10,347
Democrats 3,352
Republicans 5,081
Declined to state 1,632

Legislative Districts

US Congressional 45
State Senatorial 37
State Assembly 64

Local Officials, 2009

Mayor ..... Ron Meepos
Manager ..... Patrick Pratt
City Clerk ..... Elena Keeran
Attorney ..... Steven B. Quintanilla
Finance Dir ..... Scott Morgan
Public Works ..... Bruce B. Harry
Planning/Dev Dir ..... Randy Bynder
Building ..... Steve Buchanan
Police Chief ..... Dan Wilham
Emergency/Fire Dir. ..... Jorge Rodriguez

Public Safety

Number of officers, 2007 ..... NA
Violent crimes, 2007 27
Property crimes, 2007 1,067
Arson, 2007 0

Public Library

Rancho Mirage Public Library
71-100 Highway 111
Rancho Mirage, CA 92270
760-341-7323

Director ..... Susan Cook (Int)

Library statistics, FY 2007

Population served 21,886
Internet terminals 16
Annual users 53,905

Per capita:

Operating income $140.72
percent from local government 86.4%
Operating expenditure $123.71
Total materials 4.88
Print holdings 3.88
Visits per capita 3.38

Housing & Construction

Housing Units

Total, 2008§ 14,634
Single family units, attached 3,680
Single family units, detached 7,147
Multiple family units 1,811
Mobile home units 1,996
Occupied 8,438
Vacancy rate 42.3%
Median rent, 2000** $658
Median SF home value, 2000** $288,100

New Privately Owned Housing Units Authorized by Building Permit, 2007*

	Units	Construction Cost
Single	62	$27,090,052
Total	62	$27,090,052

Municipal Finance

(For local fiscal year ended in 2006)

Revenues

Total $52,857,400
Taxes 17,930,507
Special benefits assessment 5,060,796
Licenses & permits 768,219
Fines & forfeitures 134,048
Revenues from use of money & property 2,328,717
Intergovernmental 1,179,179
Service charges 21,129,496
Other revenues 4,326,438
Other financing sources 0

Expenditures

Total $50,352,823
General government 6,583,965
Public safety 8,649,437
Transportation 17,286,188
Community development 13,863,837
Health 26,477
Culture & leisure 3,942,919
Other 0

Local School District

(Data from School year 2007-08 except as noted)

Palm Springs Unified
980 East Tahquitz Canyon Way
Palm Springs, CA 92262
(760) 416-6000

Superintendent ..... Lorri McCune
Grade plan K-12
Number of schools 25
Enrollment 24,400
High school graduates, 2006-07 1,146
Dropout rate 5.8%
Pupil/teacher ratio 21.9
Average class size 28.3
Students per computer 5.9
Classrooms with internet 1,311
Avg. Daily Attendance (ADA) 22,873
Cost per ADA $8,379
Avg. Teacher Salary $66,086

California Achievement Tests 6th ed., 2008

(Pct scoring at or above 50th National Percentile Rank)

	Math	Reading	Language
Grade 3	44%	28%	36%
Grade 7	37%	35%	32%

Academic Performance Index, 2008

Number of students tested 18,458
Number of valid scores 17,207
2007 API (base) 673
2008 API (growth) 700

SAT Testing, 2006-07

Enrollment, Grade 12 1,704
Number taking test 438
percent taking test 25.7%
percent with total score 1,500+ 8.90%

Average Scores:

Math	Verbal	Writing	Total
469	468	454	1,391

Federal No Child Left Behind, 2008

(Adequate Yearly Progress standards met)

	Participation Rate	Pct Proficient
ELA	Yes	No
Math	Yes	No

API criteria ..... Yes
Graduation rate ..... No
\# criteria met/possible 38/31

Other school districts for this city

(see Appendix E for information on these districts)

Central Elem, Cucamonga Elem

See Introduction for an explanation of all data sources.

Demographics & Socio-Economic Characteristics
(2000 Decennial Census, except as noted)

Population
1990* ... 41,659
2000 ... 41,145
Male ... 19,903
Female ... 21,242
Jan. 2008 (estimate)§ ... 42,964
Persons per sq. mi. of land ... 3,136.1

Race & Hispanic Origin, 2000
Race
White ... 27,660
Black/African American ... 815
North American Native ... 62
Asian ... 10,676
Pacific Islander ... 41
Other Race ... 497
Two or more races ... 1,394
Hispanic origin, total ... 2,339
Mexican ... 1,340
Puerto Rican ... 86
Cuban ... 74
Other Hispanic ... 839

Age & Nativity, 2000
Under 5 years ... 2,010
18 years and over ... 31,688
65 years and over ... 7,700
85 years and over ... 640
Median Age ... 44.7
Native-born ... 30,214
Foreign-born ... 11,087

Educational Attainment, 2000
Population 25 years and over ... 30,023
Less than 9th grade ... 1.1%
High school grad or higher ... 95.8%
Bachelor's degree or higher ... 58.0%
Graduate degree ... 26.2%

Income & Poverty, 1999
Per capita income ... $46,250
Median household income ... $95,503
Median family income ... $105,586
Persons in poverty ... 2.9%
H'holds receiving public assistance ... 132
H'holds receiving social security ... 4,690

Households, 2000
Total households ... 15,256
With persons under 18 ... 5,231
With persons over 65 ... 4,984
Family households ... 12,223
Single person households ... 2,569
Persons per household ... 2.66
Persons per family ... 3.00

Household Population, 2008§§
Persons living in households ... 42,455
Persons living in group quarters ... 509
Persons per household ... 2.8

Labor & Employment
Total civilian labor force, 2008§§ ... 22,100
Unemployment rate, 2008 ... 2.5%
Total civilian labor force, 2000 ... 18,890

Employed persons 16 years and over by occupation, 2000
Managers & professionals ... 11,572
Service occupations ... 925
Sales & office occupations ... 4,407
Farming, fishing & forestry ... 29
Construction & maintenance ... 584
Production & transportation ... 882
Self-employed persons ... 2,423

* US Census Bureau
** 2000 Decennial Census
§ California Department of Finance
§§ California Employment Development Dept

General Information
City of Rancho Palos Verdes
30940 Hawthorne Blvd
City Hall
Rancho Palos Verdes, CA 90275
310-377-0360

Website ... www.palosverdes.com/rpv
Elevation ... NA
Land Area (sq. miles) ... 13.7
Water Area (sq. miles) ... 0
Year of Incorporation ... 1973
Government type ... General law
Sales tax rate ... 9.25%

Voters & Officials

Registered Voters, October 2008
Total ... 27,226
Democrats ... 8,754
Republicans ... 12,475
Declined to state ... 5,086

Legislative Districts
US Congressional ... 46
State Senatorial ... 25
State Assembly ... 54

Local Officials, 2009
Mayor ... Larry Clark
City Manager ... Carolyn Lehr
City Clerk ... Carla Morreale
Attorney ... Carol Lynch
Finance Dir ... Dennis McLean
Public Works ... James Bell
Planning Dir ... Joel Rojas
Building ... Paul Christman
Police Chief ... (County)
Fire/Emergency Mgmt ... (County)

Public Safety
Number of officers, 2007 ... NA
Violent crimes, 2007 ... 41
Property crimes, 2007 ... 537
Arson, 2007 ... 7

Public Library
Miraleste Library
Palos Verdes Library District
29089 Palos Verdes Drive E
Rancho Palos Verdes, CA 90275
310-377-9584

Branch Librarian ... Jennifer Addington

Library system statistics, FY 2007
Population served ... 67,286
Internet terminals ... 34
Annual users ... 53,850

Per capita:
Operating income ... $92.15
percent from local government ... 84.1%
Operating expenditure ... $85.75
Total materials ... 3.52
Print holdings ... 3.09
Visits per capita ... 9.36

Housing & Construction

Housing Units
Total, 2008§ ... 15,845
Single family units, attached ... 1,287
Single family units, detached ... 12,258
Multiple family units ... 2,300
Mobile home units ... 0
Occupied ... 15,389
Vacancy rate ... 2.9%
Median rent, 2000** ... $1,496
Median SF home value, 2000** ... $560,500

New Privately Owned Housing Units Authorized by Building Permit, 2007*

	Units	Construction Cost
Single	19	$8,844,944
Total	19	$8,844,944

Municipal Finance
(For local fiscal year ended in 2006)

Revenues
Total ... $37,653,707
Taxes ... 15,678,169
Special benefits assessment ... 0
Licenses & permits ... 791,531
Fines & forfeitures ... 141,715
Revenues from use of money & property ... 1,034,271
Intergovernmental ... 13,828,686
Service charges ... 1,038,885
Other revenues ... 5,140,450
Other financing sources ... 0

Expenditures
Total ... $38,804,814
General government ... 5,410,007
Public safety ... 3,496,413
Transportation ... 3,260,519
Community development ... 4,872,522
Health ... 285,450
Culture & leisure ... 21,479,903
Other ... 0

Local School District
(Data from School year 2007-08 except as noted)
Palos Verdes Peninsula Unified
3801 Via la Selva
Palos Verdes Estates, CA 90274
(310) 378-9966

Superintendent ... Walker Williams
Grade plan ... K-12
Number of schools ... 17
Enrollment ... 12,000
High school graduates, 2006-07 ... 1,034
Dropout rate ... 0.1%
Pupil/teacher ratio ... 22.4
Average class size ... 25.9
Students per computer ... 4.5
Classrooms with internet ... 602
Avg. Daily Attendance (ADA) ... 11,751
Cost per ADA ... $8,162
Avg. Teacher Salary ... $67,734

California Achievement Tests 6th ed., 2008
(Pct scoring at or above 50th National Percentile Rank)

	Math	Reading	Language
Grade 3	89%	75%	81%
Grade 7	85%	80%	79%

Academic Performance Index, 2008
Number of students tested ... 9,415
Number of valid scores ... 9,216
2007 API (base) ... 899
2008 API (growth) ... 904

SAT Testing, 2006-07
Enrollment, Grade 12 ... 1,046
Number taking test ... 905
percent taking test ... 86.5%
percent with total score 1,500+ ... 66.40%

Average Scores:

Math	Verbal	Writing	Total
600	556	568	1,724

Federal No Child Left Behind, 2008
(Adequate Yearly Progress standards met)

	Participation Rate	Pct Proficient
ELA	Yes	Yes
Math	Yes	Yes

API criteria ... Yes
Graduation rate ... Yes
criteria met/possible ... 38/38

Other school districts for this city
(see Appendix E for information on these districts)
Desert Sands Unified

See Introduction for an explanation of all data sources.

Demographics & Socio-Economic Characteristics

(2000 Decennial Census, except as noted)

Population

1990* ... NA
2000 ... 47,214
Male ... 23,219
Female ... 23,995
Jan. 2008 (estimate)§ ... 49,764
Persons per sq. mi. of land ... 4,045.9

Race & Hispanic Origin, 2000

Race
White ... 38,523
Black/African American ... 826
North American Native ... 199
Asian ... 3,492
Pacific Islander ... 97
Other Race ... 2,119
Two or more races ... 1,958
Hispanic origin, total ... 6,139
Mexican ... 4,127
Puerto Rican ... 180
Cuban ... 160
Other Hispanic ... 1,672

Age & Nativity, 2000

Under 5 years ... 4,832
18 years and over ... 31,359
65 years and over ... 1,591
85 years and over ... 97
Median Age ... 31.9
Native-born ... 41,424
Foreign-born ... 6,294

Educational Attainment, 2000

Population 25 years and over ... 28,949
Less than 9th grade ... 1.4%
High school grad or higher ... 95.1%
Bachelor's degree or higher ... 43.8%
Graduate degree ... 11.9%

Income & Poverty, 1999

Per capita income ... $31,531
Median household income ... $78,475
Median family income ... $88,216
Persons in poverty ... 2.9%
H'holds receiving public assistance ... 190
H'holds receiving social security ... 1,137

Households, 2000

Total households ... 16,253
With persons under 18 ... 8,566
With persons over 65 ... 1,225
Family households ... 12,411
Single person households ... 2,883
Persons per household ... 2.90
Persons per family ... 3.35

Household Population, 2008§§

Persons living in households ... 49,750
Persons living in group quarters ... 14
Persons per household ... 3.0

Labor & Employment

Total civilian labor force, 2008§§ ... 29,900
Unemployment rate, 2008 ... 3.3%
Total civilian labor force, 2000 ... NA

Employed persons 16 years and over by occupation, 2000

Managers & professionals ... 12,477
Service occupations ... 2,423
Sales & office occupations ... 7,657
Farming, fishing & forestry ... 43
Construction & maintenance ... 1,159
Production & transportation ... 1,053
Self-employed persons ... 1,525

* US Census Bureau
** 2000 Decennial Census
§ California Department of Finance
§§ California Employment Development Dept

General Information

City of Rancho Santa Margarita
22112 El Paseo
Suite 101
Ranch Santa Margarita, CA 92688
949-635-1800

Website ... www.cityofrsm.org
Elevation ... NA
Land Area (sq. miles) ... 12.3
Water Area (sq. miles) ... 0
Year of Incorporation ... 2000
Government type ... General Law
Sales tax rate ... 8.75%

Voters & Officials

Registered Voters, October 2008

Total ... 28,506
Democrats ... 7,050
Republicans ... 14,724
Declined to state ... 5,700

Legislative Districts

US Congressional ... 42, 50
State Senatorial ... 33
State Assembly ... 71

Local Officials, 2009

Mayor ... Gary Thompson
Manager ... Steven E. Hayman
City Clerk ... Molly McLaughlin
Attorney ... Greg Simonian
Admin Svcs Dir ... Paul Boyer
Public Works ... Derek Wieske
Dev/Svcs Dir. ... Kathleen Haton
Building ... Kathleen Haton
Police Chief ... Chuck Wilmot
Emergency/Fire Dir. ... Chip Prather

Public Safety

Number of officers, 2007 ... NA
Violent crimes, 2007 ... 30
Property crimes, 2007 ... 538
Arson, 2007 ... 1

Public Library

Rancho Santa Margarita Branch Library
Orange County Public Library System
30902 La Promesa
Rancho Santa Margarita, CA 92688
949-459-6094

Sr. Branch Librar ... Santa Murphy

Library system statistics, FY 2007

Population served ... 1,532,758
Internet terminals ... 505
Annual users ... 680,874

Per capita:

Operating income ... $24.71
percent from local government ... 90.0%
Operating expenditure ... $24.18
Total materials ... 1.93
Print holdings ... 1.84
Visits per capita ... 4.02

Housing & Construction

Housing Units

Total, 2008§ ... 16,793
Single family units, attached ... 3,883
Single family units, detached ... 9,118
Multiple family units ... 3,792
Mobile home units ... 0
Occupied ... 16,526
Vacancy rate ... 1.6%
Median rent, 2000** ... $1,110
Median SF home value, 2000** ... $280,700

New Privately Owned Housing Units Authorized by Building Permit, 2007*

	Units	Construction Cost
Single	0	$0
Total	0	$0

Municipal Finance

(For local fiscal year ended in 2006)

Revenues

Total ... $18,419,635
Taxes ... 13,876,813
Special benefits assessment ... 0
Licenses & permits ... 465,362
Fines & forfeitures ... 321,302
Revenues from use of money & property ... 308,500
Intergovernmental ... 3,241,881
Service charges ... 129,442
Other revenues ... 76,335
Other financing sources ... 0

Expenditures

Total ... $16,029,536
General government ... 4,429,873
Public safety ... 6,340,171
Transportation ... 3,310,204
Community development ... 1,026,724
Health ... 0
Culture & leisure ... 922,564
Other ... 0

Local School District

(Data from School year 2007-08 except as noted)

Saddleback Valley Unified
25631 Peter A Hartman Way
Mission Viejo, CA 92691
(949) 586-1234

Superintendent ... Steven Fish
Grade plan ... K-12
Number of schools ... 37
Enrollment ... 33,558
High school graduates, 2006-07 ... 2,390
Dropout rate ... 1.2%
Pupil/teacher ratio ... 23.6
Average class size ... 28.6
Students per computer ... 4.3
Classrooms with internet ... 1,478
Avg. Daily Attendance (ADA) ... 33,062
Cost per ADA ... $7,562
Avg. Teacher Salary ... $77,293

California Achievement Tests 6th ed., 2008

(Pct scoring at or above 50th National Percentile Rank)

	Math	Reading	Language
Grade 3	73%	58%	66%
Grade 7	72%	71%	68%

Academic Performance Index, 2008

Number of students tested ... 26,076
Number of valid scores ... 22,315
2007 API (base) ... 837
2008 API (growth) ... 847

SAT Testing, 2006-07

Enrollment, Grade 12 ... 2,741
Number taking test ... 1,312
percent taking test ... 47.9%
percent with total score 1,500+ ... 32.70%

Average Scores:

Math	Verbal	Writing	Total
565	537	535	1,637

Federal No Child Left Behind, 2008

(Adequate Yearly Progress standards met)

	Participation Rate	Pct Proficient
ELA	Yes	No
Math	Yes	Yes

API criteria ... Yes
Graduation rate ... Yes
\# criteria met/possible ... 38/37

Other school districts for this city

(see Appendix E for information on these districts)

Capistrano Unified

See Introduction for an explanation of all data sources.

Demographics & Socio-Economic Characteristics

(2000 Decennial Census, except as noted)

Population

1990* 12,363
2000 13,147
Male 6,230
Female 6,917
Jan. 2008 (estimate)§ 13,828
Persons per sq. mi. of land 1,868.6

Race & Hispanic Origin, 2000

Race
White 11,397
Black/African American 81
North American Native 294
Asian 211
Pacific Islander 9
Other Race 759
Two or more races 396
Hispanic origin, total 1,799
Mexican 1,458
Puerto Rican 35
Cuban 10
Other Hispanic 296

Age & Nativity, 2000

Under 5 years 1,010
18 years and over 9,370
65 years and over 1,933
85 years and over 347
Median Age 33.7
Native-born 12,403
Foreign-born 796

Educational Attainment, 2000

Population 25 years and over 8,032
Less than 9th grade 7.3%
High school grad or higher 75.9%
Bachelor's degree or higher 8.7%
Graduate degree 1.9%

Income & Poverty, 1999

Per capita income $14,060
Median household income $27,029
Median family income $32,799
Persons in poverty 20.3%
H'holds receiving public assistance 482
H'holds receiving social security 1,581

Households, 2000

Total households 5,109
With persons under 18 2,005
With persons over 65 1,336
Family households 3,238
Single person households 1,567
Persons per household 2.47
Persons per family 3.07

Household Population, 2008§§

Persons living in households 13,293
Persons living in group quarters 535
Persons per household 2.4

Labor & Employment

Total civilian labor force, 2008§§ 6,220
Unemployment rate, 2008 .... 10.5%
Total civilian labor force, 2000 5,640

Employed persons 16 years and over by occupation, 2000

Managers & professionals 1,073
Service occupations 1,236
Sales & office occupations 1,243
Farming, fishing & forestry 97
Construction & maintenance 408
Production & transportation 952
Self-employed persons 477

* US Census Bureau
** 2000 Decennial Census
§ California Department of Finance
§§ California Employment Development Dept

General Information

City of Red Bluff
555 Washington St
Red Bluff, CA 96080
530-527-2605

Website .... www.ci.red-bluff.ca.us
Elevation .... 309 ft.
Land Area (sq. miles) 7.4
Water Area (sq. miles) 0.1
Year of Incorporation 1876
Government type .... General law
Sales tax rate 8.25%

Voters & Officials

Registered Voters, October 2008

Total 6,024
Democrats 2,242
Republicans 2,278
Declined to state 1,089

Legislative Districts

US Congressional 2
State Senatorial 4
State Assembly 2

Local Officials, 2009

Mayor .... Wayne Brown
Manager .... Martin J. Nichols
City Clerk .... Jo Anna Lopez
Attorney .... Richard Crabtree
Finance Dir .... Margaret VanWarmerdam
Public Works .... Mark Barthel
Planning Dir .... Scot Timboe
Building .... J.D. Ellison
Police Chief .... Scott Capilla
Emergency/Fire Dir. .... Michael Bachmeyer

Public Safety

Number of officers, 2007 24
Violent crimes, 2007 137
Property crimes, 2007 676
Arson, 2007 4

Public Library

Main Branch
Tehama County Library System
645 Madison St
Red Bluff, CA 96080
530-527-0604

Director .... Caryn Brown

Library system statistics, FY 2007

Population served 61,774
Internet terminals 21
Annual users 15,734

Per capita:

Operating income $9.05
percent from local government 89.6%
Operating expenditure $8.17
Total materials 1.93
Print holdings 1.86
Visits per capita 1.33

Housing & Construction

Housing Units

Total, 2008§ 6,117
Single family units, attached 234
Single family units, detached 3,566
Multiple family units 1,951
Mobile home units 366
Occupied 5,613
Vacancy rate 8.2%
Median rent, 2000** $483
Median SF home value, 2000** $87,000

New Privately Owned Housing Units Authorized by Building Permit, 2007*

	Units	Construction Cost
Single	27	$4,354,879
Total	39	$5,359,729

Municipal Finance

(For local fiscal year ended in 2006)

Revenues

Total $15,077,979
Taxes 6,700,155
Special benefits assessment 0
Licenses & permits 34,362
Fines & forfeitures 118,362
Revenues from use of money & property 486,501
Intergovernmental 2,019,418
Service charges 5,546,733
Other revenues 172,448
Other financing sources 0

Expenditures

Total $13,188,720
General government 2,099,210
Public safety 5,740,966
Transportation 1,311,769
Community development 681,236
Health 1,235,189
Culture & leisure 1,199,369
Other 0

Local School District

(Data from School year 2007-08 except as noted)

Red Bluff Joint Union High
PO Box 1507
Red Bluff, CA 96080
(530) 529-8700

Superintendent .... Daniel Curry
Grade plan 9-12
Number of schools 4
Enrollment 2,008
High school graduates, 2006-07 416
Dropout rate 3.7%
Pupil/teacher ratio 22.2
Average class size 24.9
Students per computer 3.0
Classrooms with internet 92
Avg. Daily Attendance (ADA) 1,897
Cost per ADA $9,778
Avg. Teacher Salary .... NA

California Achievement Tests 6th ed., 2008

(Pct scoring at or above 50th National Percentile Rank)

	Math	Reading	Language
Grade 3	NA	NA	NA
Grade 7	NA	NA	NA

Academic Performance Index, 2008

Number of students tested 1,393
Number of valid scores 1,306
2007 API (base) 677
2008 API (growth) 681

SAT Testing, 2006-07

Enrollment, Grade 12 480
Number taking test 77
percent taking test 16.0%
percent with total score 1,500+ 9.60%

Average Scores:

Math	Verbal	Writing	Total
551	518	510	1,579

Federal No Child Left Behind, 2008

(Adequate Yearly Progress standards met)

	Participation Rate	Pct Proficient
ELA	Yes	No
Math	Yes	No

API criteria .... Yes
Graduation rate .... Yes
\# criteria met/possible 20/17

Other school districts for this city

(see Appendix E for information on these districts)

Antelope Elem, Bend Elem, Red Bluff Union Elem, Reeds Creek Elem

See Introduction for an explanation of all data sources.

Demographics & Socio-Economic Characteristics†

(2007 American Community Survey, except as noted)

Population

1990* 66,462
2007 87,130
Male 40,878
Female 46,252
Jan. 2008 (estimate)§ 90,491
Persons per sq. mi. of land 1,549.5

Race & Hispanic Origin, 2007

Race
White 77,256
Black/African American 683
North American Native 2,710
Asian 2,333
Pacific Islander 0
Other Race 1,939
Two or more races 2,209
Hispanic origin, total 6,344
Mexican .... NA
Puerto Rican .... NA
Cuban .... NA
Other Hispanic .... NA

Age & Nativity, 2007

Under 5 years 4,209
18 years and over 70,166
65 years and over 14,490
85 years and over 2,528
Median Age 37.7
Native-born 83,417
Foreign-born 3,713

Educational Attainment, 2007

Population 25 years and over 59,524
Less than 9th grade 1.4%
High school grad or higher 89.7%
Bachelor's degree or higher 22.9%
Graduate degree 8.1%

Income & Poverty, 2007

Per capita income $24,829
Median household income $39,055
Median family income $51,252
Persons in poverty 15.0%
H'holds receiving public assistance 838
H'holds receiving social security 12,092

Households, 2007

Total households 36,132
With persons under 18 10,547
With persons over 65 9,666
Family households 22,052
Single person households 12,299
Persons per household 2.38
Persons per family 2.98

Household Population, 2008§§

Persons living in households 88,034
Persons living in group quarters 2,457
Persons per household 2.4

Labor & Employment

Total civilian labor force, 2008§§ 42,100
Unemployment rate, 2008 .... 8.8%
Total civilian labor force, 2000* 36,581

Employed persons 16 years and over by occupation, 2007

Managers & professionals 13,129
Service occupations 7,468
Sales & office occupations 12,862
Farming, fishing & forestry 36
Construction & maintenance 3,167
Production & transportation 3,747
Self-employed persons 4,426

† see Appendix D for 2000 Decennial Census Data
* US Census Bureau
** 2007 American Community Survey
§ California Department of Finance
§§ California Employment Development Dept

General Information

City of Redding
777 Cypress Ave
Redding, CA 96001
530-225-4002

Website .... www.ci.redding.ca.us
Elevation .... 557 ft.
Land Area (sq. miles) 58.4
Water Area (sq. miles) 1.2
Year of Incorporation 1887
Government type .... General law
Sales tax rate 8.25%

Voters & Officials

Registered Voters, October 2008

Total 47,184
Democrats 13,913
Republicans 22,687
Declined to state 8,654

Legislative Districts

US Congressional 2
State Senatorial 4
State Assembly 2

Local Officials, 2009

Mayor .... Rick Bosetti
Manager .... Kurt Starman
City Clerk .... Connie Strohmayer
Attorney .... Rick Duvernay
Finance Dir .... Steve Strong
Public Works .... Brian Crane
Development Svcs Dir .... Jim Hamilton
Building .... Wayne Gungl
Police Chief .... Peter Hansen
Emergency/Fire Dir .... Kevin Kreitman

Public Safety

Number of officers, 2007 117
Violent crimes, 2007 455
Property crimes, 2007 2,645
Arson, 2007 20

Public Library

Redding Library
Shasta County Library System
1100 Parkview Ave
Redding, CA 96001
530-245-7250

Director .... Linda Meilke (Actg)

Library system statistics, FY 2007

Population served 181,401
Internet terminals 8
Annual users 15,226

Per capita:

Operating income $9.89
percent from local government 96.3%
Operating expenditure $12.63
Total materials 1.23
Print holdings 1.12
Visits per capita .... NA

Housing & Construction

Housing Units

Total, 2008§ 38,018
Single family units, attached 1,010
Single family units, detached 24,923
Multiple family units 9,468
Mobile home units 2,617
Occupied 36,107
Vacancy rate 5.0%
Median rent, 2007** $797
Median SF home value, 2007** $274,400

New Privately Owned Housing Units Authorized by Building Permit, 2007*

	Units	Construction Cost
Single	233	$47,557,983
Total	379	$57,421,942

Municipal Finance

(For local fiscal year ended in 2006)

Revenues

Total $332,621,695
Taxes 51,318,997
Special benefits assessment 160,406
Licenses & permits 2,367,967
Fines & forfeitures 677,217
Revenues from use of money & property 10,400,384
Intergovernmental 30,927,370
Service charges 188,694,522
Other revenues 17,374,832
Other financing sources 30,700,000

Expenditures

Total $262,802,746
General government 6,334,109
Public safety 38,062,693
Transportation 9,526,006
Community development 27,541,154
Health 26,814,412
Culture & leisure 19,428,841
Other 0

Local School District

(Data from School year 2007-08 except as noted)

Shasta Union High
2200 Eureka Way, Suite B
Redding, CA 96001
(530) 241-3261

Superintendent .... Jim Cloney
Grade plan K-12
Number of schools 12
Enrollment 6,302
High school graduates, 2006-07 1,106
Dropout rate 2.7%
Pupil/teacher ratio 22.9
Average class size 24.9
Students per computer 4.1
Classrooms with internet 705
Avg. Daily Attendance (ADA) 5,548
Cost per ADA $8,670
Avg. Teacher Salary $63,137

California Achievement Tests 6th ed., 2008

(Pct scoring at or above 50th National Percentile Rank)

	Math	Reading	Language
Grade 3	NA	NA	NA
Grade 7	72%	79%	73%

Academic Performance Index, 2008

Number of students tested 4,192
Number of valid scores 3,964
2007 API (base) 774
2008 API (growth) 784

SAT Testing, 2006-07

Enrollment, Grade 12 1,357
Number taking test 310
percent taking test 22.8%
percent with total score 1,500+ 16.80%

Average Scores:

Math	Verbal	Writing	Total
557	548	540	1,645

Federal No Child Left Behind, 2008

(Adequate Yearly Progress standards met)

	Participation Rate	Pct Proficient
ELA	Yes	Yes
Math	Yes	Yes

API criteria .... Yes
Graduation rate .... Yes
\# criteria met/possible 16/16

Other school districts for this city

(see Appendix E for information on these districts)

Complete list in Appendix E

See Introduction for an explanation of all data sources.

Demographics & Socio-Economic Characteristics†

(2007 American Community Survey, except as noted)

Population

1990* 60,394
2007 73,539
Male 36,705
Female 36,834
Jan. 2008 (estimate)§ 71,807
Persons per sq. mi. of land 2,022.7

Race & Hispanic Origin, 2007

Race
White 50,304
Black/African American 4,285
North American Native 1,035
Asian 4,632
Pacific Islander 117
Other Race 9,741
Two or more races 3,425
Hispanic origin, total 20,679
Mexican . . . . NA
Puerto Rican . . . . NA
Cuban . . . . NA
Other Hispanic . . . . NA

Age & Nativity, 2007

Under 5 years 5,028
18 years and over 52,096
65 years and over 8,742
85 years and over 1,032
Median Age 33.1
Native-born 63,039
Foreign-born 10,500

Educational Attainment, 2007

Population 25 years and over 45,144
Less than 9th grade 4.1%
High school grad or higher 88.8%
Bachelor's degree or higher 34.7%
Graduate degree 19.2%

Income & Poverty, 2007

Per capita income $29,494
Median household income $65,782
Median family income $80,040
Persons in poverty 7.4%
H'holds receiving public assistance 456
H'holds receiving social security 5,977

Households, 2007

Total households 24,386
With persons under 18 9,808
With persons over 65 5,649
Family households 16,694
Single person households 6,506
Persons per household 2.93
Persons per family 3.61

Household Population, 2008§§

Persons living in households 69,841
Persons living in group quarters 1,966
Persons per household 2.7

Labor & Employment

Total civilian labor force, 2008§§ 37,900
Unemployment rate, 2008 . . . . 5.8%
Total civilian labor force, 2000* 31,985

Employed persons 16 years and over by occupation, 2007

Managers & professionals 15,085
Service occupations 5,257
Sales & office occupations 8,934
Farming, fishing & forestry 0
Construction & maintenance 1,826
Production & transportation 2,609
Self-employed persons 2,223

† see Appendix D for 2000 Decennial Census Data
* US Census Bureau
** 2007 American Community Survey
§ California Department of Finance
§§ California Employment Development Dept

General Information

City of Redlands
PO Box 3005
Redlands, CA 92373
909-798-7500

Website . . . . www.ci.redlands.ca.us
Elevation . . . . 1,302 ft.
Land Area (sq. miles) 35.5
Water Area (sq. miles) 0.3
Year of Incorporation 1888
Government type . . . . General law
Sales tax rate 8.75%

Voters & Officials

Registered Voters, October 2008

Total 38,450
Democrats 13,302
Republicans 17,316
Declined to state 6,188

Legislative Districts

US Congressional 41
State Senatorial 31
State Assembly 59, 62, 63

Local Officials, 2009

Mayor . . . . Jon Harrison
Manager . . . . N. Enrique Martinez
City Clerk . . . . Lorrie Poyzer
Attorney . . . . Daniel J. McHugh
Finance Dir . . . . Tina Kundig
Public Works . . . . Rosemary Hoerning (Int)
Planning/Dev Dir . . . . Oscar Orci (Int)
Building . . . . Richard Pepper
Police Chief . . . . James Bueermann
Fire Chief . . . . Jeff L. Frazier

Public Safety

Number of officers, 2007 92
Violent crimes, 2007 303
Property crimes, 2007 2,505
Arson, 2007 25

Public Library

A.K. Smiley Public Library
125 W Vine St
Redlands, CA 92373
909-798-7565

Director . . . . Larry Burgess

Library statistics, FY 2007

Population served 71,375
Internet terminals 17
Annual users 48,535

Per capita:

Operating income $30.22
percent from local government 83.5%
Operating expenditure $28.69
Total materials 2.50
Print holdings 2.42
Visits per capita 6.59

Housing & Construction

Housing Units

Total, 2008§ 26,719
Single family units, attached 900
Single family units, detached 17,254
Multiple family units 7,646
Mobile home units 919
Occupied 25,429
Vacancy rate 4.8%
Median rent, 2007** $985
Median SF home value, 2007** $419,900

New Privately Owned Housing Units Authorized by Building Permit, 2007*

	Units	Construction Cost
Single	133	$35,157,075
Total	133	$35,157,075

Municipal Finance

(For local fiscal year ended in 2006)

Revenues

Total $109,598,273
Taxes 41,090,013
Special benefits assessment 1,131,963
Licenses & permits 1,918,433
Fines & forfeitures 337,983
Revenues from use of money & property 3,063,018
Intergovernmental 12,235,319
Service charges 46,485,907
Other revenues 1,634,219
Other financing sources 1,701,418

Expenditures

Total $109,482,720
General government 7,687,403
Public safety 36,807,420
Transportation 12,895,496
Community development 2,553,897
Health 18,175,071
Culture & leisure 11,728,346
Other 754,173

Local School District

(Data from School year 2007-08 except as noted)
Redlands Unified
PO Box 3008
Redlands, CA 92374
(909) 307-5300

Superintendent . . . . Lori Rhodes
Grade plan K-12
Number of schools 23
Enrollment 21,482
High school graduates, 2006-07 1,528
Dropout rate 3.4%
Pupil/teacher ratio 21.9
Average class size 26.4
Students per computer 4.7
Classrooms with internet 1,387
Avg. Daily Attendance (ADA) 20,556
Cost per ADA $7,835
Avg. Teacher Salary $71,787

California Achievement Tests 6th ed., 2008

(Pct scoring at or above 50th National Percentile Rank)

	Math	Reading	Language
Grade 3	63%	47%	53%
Grade 7	58%	53%	52%

Academic Performance Index, 2008

Number of students tested 16,436
Number of valid scores 15,340
2007 API (base) 774
2008 API (growth) 779

SAT Testing, 2006-07

Enrollment, Grade 12 1,794
Number taking test 649
percent taking test 36.2%
percent with total score 1,500+ 19.30%

Average Scores:

Math	Verbal	Writing	Total
520	501	506	1,527

Federal No Child Left Behind, 2008

(Adequate Yearly Progress standards met)

	Participation Rate	Pct Proficient
ELA	Yes	No
Math	Yes	Yes

API criteria . . . . Yes
Graduation rate . . . . Yes
\# criteria met/possible 42/40

Other school districts for this city

(see Appendix E for information on these districts)

None

See Introduction for an explanation of all data sources.

Demographics & Socio-Economic Characteristics†

(2007 American Community Survey, except as noted)

Population

1990* . . . 60,167
2007 . . . 70,948
Male . . . 33,891
Female . . . 37,057
Jan. 2008 (estimate)§ . . . 67,488
Persons per sq. mi. of land . . . 10,712.4

Race & Hispanic Origin, 2007

Race
White . . . 57,808
Black/African American . . . 774
North American Native . . . 211
Asian . . . 7,863
Pacific Islander . . . 99
Other Race . . . 1,594
Two or more races . . . 2,599
Hispanic origin, total . . . 11,130
Mexican . . . 7,097
Puerto Rican . . . 267
Cuban . . . 595
Other Hispanic . . . 3,171

Age & Nativity, 2007

Under 5 years . . . 7,014
18 years and over . . . 54,563
65 years and over . . . 6,644
85 years and over . . . 510
Median Age . . . 38.5
Native-born . . . 59,234
Foreign-born . . . 11,714

Educational Attainment, 2007

Population 25 years and over . . . 50,345
Less than 9th grade . . . 0.6%
High school grad or higher . . . 96.1%
Bachelor's degree or higher . . . 56.0%
Graduate degree . . . 19.6%

Income & Poverty, 2007

Per capita income . . . $47,809
Median household income . . . $93,274
Median family income . . . $108,753
Persons in poverty . . . 4.0%
H'holds receiving public assistance . . . 63
H'holds receiving social security . . . 5,480

Households, 2007

Total households . . . 28,840
With persons under 18 . . . 8,896
With persons over 65 . . . 4,824
Family households . . . 16,972
Single person households . . . 9,654
Persons per household . . . 2.46
Persons per family . . . 3.24

Household Population, 2008§§

Persons living in households . . . 67,301
Persons living in group quarters . . . 187
Persons per household . . . 2.3

Labor & Employment

Total civilian labor force, 2008§§ . . . 46,400
Unemployment rate, 2008 . . . 3.9%
Total civilian labor force, 2000* . . . 39,746

Employed persons 16 years and over by occupation, 2007

Managers & professionals . . . 23,683
Service occupations . . . 1,945
Sales & office occupations . . . 8,885
Farming, fishing & forestry . . . 0
Construction & maintenance . . . 1,856
Production & transportation . . . 2,071
Self-employed persons . . . 4,446

† see Appendix D for 2000 Decennial Census Data
* US Census Bureau
** 2007 American Community Survey
§ California Department of Finance
§§ California Employment Development Dept

General Information

City of Redondo Beach
415 Diamond St
PO Box 270
Redondo Beach, CA 90277
310-372-1171

Website . . . www.redondo.org
Elevation . . . 59 ft.
Land Area (sq. miles) . . . 6.3
Water Area (sq. miles) . . . 0.1
Year of Incorporation . . . 1892
Government type . . . Chartered
Sales tax rate . . . 9.25%

Voters & Officials

Registered Voters, October 2008

Total . . . 40,852
Democrats . . . 15,656
Republicans . . . 13,813
Declined to state . . . 9,411

Legislative Districts

US Congressional . . . 36
State Senatorial . . . 28
State Assembly . . . 53

Local Officials, 2009

Mayor . . . Mike Gin
Manager . . . William Workman
City Clerk . . . Eleanor Manzano
Attorney . . . Michael W. Webb
Treasurer . . . Ernie O'Dell
Public Works . . . Sylvia Glazer
Planning Dir . . . Aaron Jones (Actg)
Building . . . Steve Huang
Police Chief . . . Joe Leonardi
Fire Chief . . . Dan Madrigal

Public Safety

Number of officers, 2007 . . . 99
Violent crimes, 2007 . . . 205
Property crimes, 2007 . . . 1,634
Arson, 2007 . . . 4

Public Library

Redondo Beach Public Library
Redondo Beach Public Library System
303 N Pacific Coast Hwy
Redondo Beach, CA 90277
310-318-0676

Director . . . Jean Scully

Library system statistics, FY 2007

Population served . . . 67,495
Internet terminals . . . 67
Annual users . . . 267,089

Per capita:

Operating income . . . $56.13
percent from local government . . . 90.8%
Operating expenditure . . . $56.15
Total materials . . . 3.47
Print holdings . . . 2.97
Visits per capita . . . 7.44

Housing & Construction

Housing Units

Total, 2008§ . . . 30,080
Single family units, attached . . . 4,426
Single family units, detached . . . 11,836
Multiple family units . . . 13,438
Mobile home units . . . 380
Occupied . . . 29,084
Vacancy rate . . . 3.3%
Median rent, 2007** . . . $1,498
Median SF home value, 2007** . . . $816,800

New Privately Owned Housing Units Authorized by Building Permit, 2007*

	Units	Construction Cost
Single	149	$41,557,401
Total	149	$41,557,401

Municipal Finance

(For local fiscal year ended in 2006)

Revenues

Total . . . $89,187,076
Taxes . . . 49,638,107
Special benefits assessment . . . 1,546,478
Licenses & permits . . . 2,203,041
Fines & forfeitures . . . 963,007
Revenues from use of money & property . . . 3,046,879
Intergovernmental . . . 4,985,728
Service charges . . . 26,003,853
Other revenues . . . 799,983
Other financing sources . . . 0

Expenditures

Total . . . $86,610,666
General government . . . 9,824,101
Public safety . . . 35,480,771
Transportation . . . 16,127,670
Community development . . . 10,187,058
Health . . . 6,613,845
Culture & leisure . . . 8,377,221
Other . . . 0

Local School District

(Data from School year 2007-08 except as noted)

Redondo Beach Unified
1401 Inglewood Ave
Redondo Beach, CA 90278
(310) 379-5449

Superintendent . . . Steven Keller
Grade plan . . . K-12
Number of schools . . . 12
Enrollment . . . 8,215
High school graduates, 2006-07 . . . 603
Dropout rate . . . 2.9%
Pupil/teacher ratio . . . 21.5
Average class size . . . 25.6
Students per computer . . . 5.1
Classrooms with internet . . . 391
Avg. Daily Attendance (ADA) . . . 7,969
Cost per ADA . . . $8,352
Avg. Teacher Salary . . . $68,773

California Achievement Tests 6th ed., 2008

(Pct scoring at or above 50th National Percentile Rank)

	Math	Reading	Language
Grade 3	74%	60%	68%
Grade 7	73%	71%	67%

Academic Performance Index, 2008

Number of students tested . . . 6,180
Number of valid scores . . . 5,950
2007 API (base) . . . 834
2008 API (growth) . . . 844

SAT Testing, 2006-07

Enrollment, Grade 12 . . . 748
Number taking test . . . 319
percent taking test . . . 42.7%
percent with total score 1,500+ . . . 28.10%

Average Scores:

Math	Verbal	Writing	Total
554	529	530	1,613

Federal No Child Left Behind, 2008

(Adequate Yearly Progress standards met)

	Participation Rate	Pct Proficient
ELA	Yes	Yes
Math	Yes	Yes

API criteria . . . Yes
Graduation rate . . . Yes
\# criteria met/possible . . . 38/38

Other school districts for this city

(see Appendix E for information on these districts)

None

See Introduction for an explanation of all data sources.

Demographics & Socio-Economic Characteristics†

(2007 American Community Survey, except as noted)

Population

1990* ... 66,072
2007 ... 69,559
Male ... 34,297
Female ... 35,262
Jan. 2008 (estimate)§ ... 77,269
Persons per sq. mi. of land ... 3,962.5

Race & Hispanic Origin, 2007

Race
White ... 54,023
Black/African American ... 2,731
North American Native ... 68
Asian ... 6,897
Pacific Islander ... 709
Other Race ... 3,396
Two or more races ... 1,735
Hispanic origin, total ... 23,438
Mexican ... 19,033
Puerto Rican ... 59
Cuban ... 0
Other Hispanic ... 4,346

Age & Nativity, 2007

Under 5 years ... 6,206
18 years and over ... 53,576
65 years and over ... 9,734
85 years and over ... 1,560
Median Age ... 41.9
Native-born ... 48,561
Foreign-born ... 20,998

Educational Attainment, 2007

Population 25 years and over ... 50,008
Less than 9th grade ... 6.1%
High school grad or higher ... 86.5%
Bachelor's degree or higher ... 37.9%
Graduate degree ... 14.3%

Income & Poverty, 2007

Per capita income ... $38,694
Median household income ... $66,182
Median family income ... $75,139
Persons in poverty ... 10.3%
H'holds receiving public assistance ... 61
H'holds receiving social security ... 6,192

Households, 2007

Total households ... 27,276
With persons under 18 ... 9,355
With persons over 65 ... 6,687
Family households ... 18,113
Single person households ... 7,121
Persons per household ... 2.50
Persons per family ... 3.06

Household Population, 2008§§

Persons living in households ... 75,342
Persons living in group quarters ... 1,927
Persons per household ... 2.6

Labor & Employment

Total civilian labor force, 2008§§ ... 42,600
Unemployment rate, 2008 ... 4.7%
Total civilian labor force, 2000* ... 41,470

Employed persons 16 years and over by occupation, 2007

Managers & professionals ... 13,787
Service occupations ... 8,398
Sales & office occupations ... 7,605
Farming, fishing & forestry ... 0
Construction & maintenance ... 2,426
Production & transportation ... 2,001
Self-employed persons ... 5,697

† see Appendix D for 2000 Decennial Census Data
* US Census Bureau
** 2007 American Community Survey
§ California Department of Finance
§§ California Employment Development Dept

General Information

City of Redwood City
1017 Middlefield Rd
Redwood City, CA 94063
650-780-7000

Website ... www.redwoodcity.org
Elevation ... 15 ft.
Land Area (sq. miles) ... 19.5
Water Area (sq. miles) ... 15.1
Year of Incorporation ... 1867
Government type ... Chartered
Sales tax rate ... 9.25%

Voters & Officials

Registered Voters, October 2008

Total ... 38,441
Democrats ... 19,157
Republicans ... 9,286
Declined to state ... 8,524

Legislative Districts

US Congressional ... 12, 14
State Senatorial ... 11
State Assembly ... 21

Local Officials, 2009

Mayor ... Rosanne S. Foust
City Manager ... Peter Ingram
City Clerk ... Silvia Vonderlinden
Attorney ... Stan Yamamoto
Finance Dir ... Brian Ponty
Public Works ... Larry Barwacz
Comm Dev Dir ... Chu Chang (Actg)
Building ... John LaTorra
Police Chief ... Louis Cobarruviaz
Fire Chief ... Jim Skinner

Public Safety

Number of officers, 2007 ... 96
Violent crimes, 2007 ... 336
Property crimes, 2007 ... 1,689
Arson, 2007 ... 4

Public Library

Redwood City Main Library
Redwood City Public Library System
1044 Middlefield Rd
Redwood City, CA 94063
650-780-7043

Director ... Dave Genesy

Library system statistics, FY 2007

Population served ... 77,025
Internet terminals ... 16
Annual users ... 50,000

Per capita:

Operating income ... $78.40
percent from local government ... 84.6%
Operating expenditure ... $81.09
Total materials ... 3.55
Print holdings ... 3.04
Visits per capita ... 1.75

Housing & Construction

Housing Units

Total, 2008§ ... 29,276
Single family units, attached ... 3,656
Single family units, detached ... 13,554
Multiple family units ... 11,233
Mobile home units ... 833
Occupied ... 28,595
Vacancy rate ... 2.3%
Median rent, 2007** ... $1,241
Median SF home value, 2007** ... $863,000

New Privately Owned Housing Units Authorized by Building Permit, 2007*

	Units	Construction Cost
Single	30	$9,845,496
Total	35	$10,415,145

Municipal Finance

(For local fiscal year ended in 2006)

Revenues

Total ... $136,341,834
Taxes ... 64,916,715
Special benefits assessment ... 1,160,716
Licenses & permits ... 1,167,751
Fines & forfeitures ... 1,027,476
Revenues from use of money & property ... 5,375,690
Intergovernmental ... 12,905,696
Service charges ... 44,025,833
Other revenues ... 5,761,957
Other financing sources ... 0

Expenditures

Total ... $139,782,480
General government ... 5,273,225
Public safety ... 44,423,826
Transportation ... 24,819,365
Community development ... 12,209,347
Health ... 12,700,504
Culture & leisure ... 15,424,131
Other ... 0

Local School District

(Data from School year 2007-08 except as noted)

Sequoia Union High
480 James Ave
Redwood City, CA 94062
(650) 369-1411

Superintendent ... Patrick Gemma
Grade plan ... 9-12
Number of schools ... 6
Enrollment ... 8,510
High school graduates, 2006-07 ... 1,546
Dropout rate ... 3.2%
Pupil/teacher ratio ... 19.7
Average class size ... 26.4
Students per computer ... 3.0
Classrooms with internet ... 402
Avg. Daily Attendance (ADA) ... 7,811
Cost per ADA ... $11,470
Avg. Teacher Salary ... $76,194

California Achievement Tests 6th ed., 2008

(Pct scoring at or above 50th National Percentile Rank)

	Math	Reading	Language
Grade 3	NA	NA	NA
Grade 7	NA	NA	NA

Academic Performance Index, 2008

Number of students tested ... 5,874
Number of valid scores ... 5,525
2007 API (base) ... 753
2008 API (growth) ... 753

SAT Testing, 2006-07

Enrollment, Grade 12 ... 2,000
Number taking test ... 945
percent taking test ... 47.3%
percent with total score 1,500+ ... 29.10%

Average Scores:

Math	Verbal	Writing	Total
546	530	530	1,606

Federal No Child Left Behind, 2008

(Adequate Yearly Progress standards met)

	Participation Rate	Pct Proficient
ELA	Yes	No
Math	Yes	No

API criteria ... Yes
Graduation rate ... Yes
criteria met/possible ... 28/25

Other school districts for this city

(see Appendix E for information on these districts)

Cabrillo Unified, Redwood City Elem

See Introduction for an explanation of all data sources.

Demographics & Socio-Economic Characteristics

(2000 Decennial Census, except as noted)

Population

1990* . . . 15,791
2000 . . . 20,756
Male . . . 10,670
Female . . . 10,086
Jan. 2008 (estimate)§ . . . 25,587
Persons per sq. mi. of land . . . 5,815.2

Race & Hispanic Origin, 2000

Race
White . . . 10,743
Black/African American . . . 89
North American Native . . . 251
Asian . . . 906
Pacific Islander . . . 15
Other Race . . . 7,830
Two or more races . . . 922
Hispanic origin, total . . . 14,028
Mexican . . . 12,379
Puerto Rican . . . 38
Cuban . . . 3
Other Hispanic . . . 1,608

Age & Nativity, 2000

Under 5 years . . . 1,912
18 years and over . . . 14,083
65 years and over . . . 2,344
85 years and over . . . 449
Median Age . . . 28.7
Native-born . . . 14,126
Foreign-born . . . 6,650

Educational Attainment, 2000

Population 25 years and over . . . 11,637
Less than 9th grade . . . 29.1%
High school grad or higher . . . 59.2%
Bachelor's degree or higher . . . 14.4%
Graduate degree . . . 4.1%

Income & Poverty, 1999

Per capita income . . . $12,096
Median household income . . . $34,682
Median family income . . . $37,027
Persons in poverty . . . 23.3%
H'holds receiving public assistance . . . 451
H'holds receiving social security . . . 1,559

Households, 2000

Total households . . . 5,761
With persons under 18 . . . 2,991
With persons over 65 . . . 1,457
Family households . . . 4,643
Single person households . . . 911
Persons per household . . . 3.53
Persons per family . . . 3.87

Household Population, 2008§§

Persons living in households . . . 25,192
Persons living in group quarters . . . 395
Persons per household . . . 3.6

Labor & Employment

Total civilian labor force, 2008§§ . . . 11,300
Unemployment rate, 2008 . . . 21.0%
Total civilian labor force, 2000 . . . 9,026

Employed persons 16 years and over by occupation, 2000

Managers & professionals . . . 1,654
Service occupations . . . 1,070
Sales & office occupations . . . 1,357
Farming, fishing & forestry . . . 1,200
Construction & maintenance . . . 523
Production & transportation . . . 1,137
Self-employed persons . . . 376

* US Census Bureau
** 2000 Decennial Census
§ California Department of Finance
§§ California Employment Development Dept

General Information

City of Reedley
845 G St
Reedley, CA 93654
559-637-4200

Website . . . www.reedley.com
Elevation . . . 348 ft.
Land Area (sq. miles) . . . 4.4
Water Area (sq. miles) . . . 0.1
Year of Incorporation . . . 1913
Government type . . . General law
Sales tax rate . . . 9.48%

Voters & Officials

Registered Voters, October 2008

Total . . . 7,950
Democrats . . . 3,117
Republicans . . . 3,509
Declined to state . . . 909

Legislative Districts

US Congressional . . . 21
State Senatorial . . . 14
State Assembly . . . 31

Local Officials, 2009

Mayor . . . Mary L. Fast
Manager . . . Rocky D. Rogers
City Clerk . . . Kay L. Pierce
Attorney . . . Dale Bacigalupi
Finance Dir . . . Lori Oken
Public Works . . . Russ Robertson
Planning/Dev Dir . . . David Brletic
Building . . . (vacant)
Police Chief . . . Steven H. Wright
Emergency/Fire Dir . . . Jerald Isaak

Public Safety

Number of officers, 2007 . . . 28
Violent crimes, 2007 . . . 136
Property crimes, 2007 . . . 699
Arson, 2007 . . . 20

Public Library

Reedley Branch Library
Fresno County Public Library System
1027 E St
Reedley, CA 93654
559-638-2818

Branch Librarian . . . Ernest Vitovec

Library system statistics, FY 2007

Population served . . . 889,019
Internet terminals . . . 277
Annual users . . . 861,240

Per capita:

Operating income . . . $23.69
percent from local government . . . 89.3%
Operating expenditure . . . $23.37
Total materials . . . 2.89
Print holdings . . . 2.69
Visits per capita . . . NA

Housing & Construction

Housing Units

Total, 2008§ . . . 7,229
Single family units, attached . . . 216
Single family units, detached . . . 5,346
Multiple family units . . . 1,476
Mobile home units . . . 191
Occupied . . . 6,974
Vacancy rate . . . 3.5%
Median rent, 2000** . . . $526
Median SF home value, 2000** . . . $104,200

New Privately Owned Housing Units Authorized by Building Permit, 2007*

	Units	Construction Cost
Single	157	$26,299,585
Total	157	$26,299,585

Municipal Finance

(For local fiscal year ended in 2006)

Revenues

Total . . . $21,373,700
Taxes . . . 5,827,986
Special benefits assessment . . . 112,817
Licenses & permits . . . 483,665
Fines & forfeitures . . . 129,861
Revenues from use of money & property . . . 328,551
Intergovernmental . . . 2,486,075
Service charges . . . 6,443,307
Other revenues . . . 2,322,076
Other financing sources . . . 3,239,362

Expenditures

Total . . . $17,568,349
General government . . . 349,978
Public safety . . . 4,664,533
Transportation . . . 2,602,610
Community development . . . 553,208
Health . . . 6,249,413
Culture & leisure . . . 1,591,102
Other . . . 0

Local School District

(Data from School year 2007-08 except as noted)

Kings Canyon Joint Unified
675 West Manning Ave
Reedley, CA 93654
(559) 637-1200

Superintendent . . . Juan Garza
Grade plan . . . K-12
Number of schools . . . 18
Enrollment . . . 9,701
High school graduates, 2006-07 . . . 459
Dropout rate . . . 8.4%
Pupil/teacher ratio . . . 21.7
Average class size . . . 26.8
Students per computer . . . 3.1
Classrooms with internet . . . 758
Avg. Daily Attendance (ADA) . . . 9,407
Cost per ADA . . . $8,504
Avg. Teacher Salary . . . $62,017

California Achievement Tests 6th ed., 2008

(Pct scoring at or above 50th National Percentile Rank)

	Math	Reading	Language
Grade 3	44%	26%	32%
Grade 7	48%	40%	38%

Academic Performance Index, 2008

Number of students tested . . . 7,025
Number of valid scores . . . 6,437
2007 API (base) . . . 679
2008 API (growth) . . . 698

SAT Testing, 2006-07

Enrollment, Grade 12 . . . 658
Number taking test . . . 103
percent taking test . . . 15.7%
percent with total score 1,500+ . . . 6.20%

Average Scores:

Math	Verbal	Writing	Total
480	462	460	1,402

Federal No Child Left Behind, 2008

(Adequate Yearly Progress standards met)

	Participation Rate	Pct Proficient
ELA	Yes	No
Math	Yes	No

API criteria . . . Yes
Graduation rate . . . No
\# criteria met/possible . . . 26/20

Other school districts for this city

(see Appendix E for information on these districts)

None

See Introduction for an explanation of all data sources.

Demographics & Socio-Economic Characteristics†

(2007 American Community Survey, except as noted)

Population

1990* 72,388
2007 108,969
Male 55,016
Female 53,953
Jan. 2008 (estimate)§ 99,767
Persons per sq. mi. of land 4,555.6

Race & Hispanic Origin, 2007

Race
White 63,623
Black/African American 15,239
North American Native 1,466
Asian 3,752
Pacific Islander 108
Other Race 19,416
Two or more races 5,365
Hispanic origin, total 69,827
Mexican 60,645
Puerto Rican 745
Cuban 554
Other Hispanic 7,883

Age & Nativity, 2007

Under 5 years 11,683
18 years and over 72,413
65 years and over 8,075
85 years and over 967
Median Age 29.1
Native-born 77,610
Foreign-born 31,359

Educational Attainment, 2007

Population 25 years and over 60,978
Less than 9th grade 17.9%
High school grad or higher 62.4%
Bachelor's degree or higher 7.6%
Graduate degree 2.2%

Income & Poverty, 2007

Per capita income $16,312
Median household income $51,819
Median family income $55,576
Persons in poverty 9.6%
H'holds receiving public assistance 1,575
H'holds receiving social security 6,027

Households, 2007

Total households 25,744
With persons under 18 15,163
With persons over 65 6,232
Family households 22,006
Single person households 3,159
Persons per household 4.23
Persons per family 4.49

Household Population, 2008§§

Persons living in households 98,963
Persons living in group quarters 804
Persons per household 3.9

Labor & Employment

Total civilian labor force, 2008§§ 44,200
Unemployment rate, 2008 ....10.3%
Total civilian labor force, 2000* 36,290

Employed persons 16 years and over by occupation, 2007

Managers & professionals ....NA
Service occupations ....NA
Sales & office occupations ....NA
Farming, fishing & forestry ....NA
Construction & maintenance ....NA
Production & transportation ....NA
Self-employed persons 3,340

† see Appendix D for 2000 Decennial Census Data
* US Census Bureau
** 2007 American Community Survey
§ California Department of Finance
§§ California Employment Development Dept

General Information

City of Rialto
150 S Palm Ave
Rialto, CA 92376
909-820-2525

Website ....www.rialtoca.gov
Elevation ....1,205 ft.
Land Area (sq. miles) 21.9
Water Area (sq. miles) 0
Year of Incorporation 1911
Government type ....General law
Sales tax rate 8.75%

Voters & Officials

Registered Voters, October 2008

Total 37,264
Democrats 19,346
Republicans 10,977
Declined to state 5,614

Legislative Districts

US Congressional 43
State Senatorial 32
State Assembly 62

Local Officials, 2009

Mayor ....Grace Vargas
Manager ....Henry Garcia
City Clerk ....Barbara McGee
Attorney ....Jimmy L. Gutierrez
Finance Dir ....June Overholt
Public Works ....Ahmad Ansari
Planning/Dev Dir ....Michael Story
Building ....Chaz Ferguson
Police Chief ....Mark Kling
Emergency/Fire Dir ....Robert Espinosa

Public Safety

Number of officers, 2007 105
Violent crimes, 2007 747
Property crimes, 2007 2,281
Arson, 2007 20

Public Library

Rialto Branch Library
San Bernardino County Library System
251 W First St
Rialto, CA 92376
909-875-0144

Branch Librarian ....Joyce Martell

Library system statistics, FY 2007

Population served 1,177,092
Internet terminals 12
Annual users 45,343

Per capita:

Operating income $14.27
percent from local government 73.3%
Operating expenditure $13.86
Total materials 0.86
Print holdings 0.79
Visits per capita 5.83

Housing & Construction

Housing Units

Total, 2008§ 26,854
Single family units, attached 586
Single family units, detached 19,014
Multiple family units 5,451
Mobile home units 1,803
Occupied 25,426
Vacancy rate 5.3%
Median rent, 2007** $1,070
Median SF home value, 2007** $378,100

New Privately Owned Housing Units Authorized by Building Permit, 2007*

	Units	Construction Cost
Single	49	$12,446,619
Total	230	$25,684,644

Municipal Finance

(For local fiscal year ended in 2006)

Revenues

Total $87,186,349
Taxes 43,994,635
Special benefits assessment 1,370,850
Licenses & permits 483,459
Fines & forfeitures 384,926
Revenues from use of money & property 4,860,158
Intergovernmental 5,200,654
Service charges 25,977,749
Other revenues 4,913,918
Other financing sources 0

Expenditures

Total $71,360,016
General government 7,598,510
Public safety 32,754,572
Transportation 5,749,882
Community development 939,224
Health 10,868,719
Culture & leisure 4,049,154
Other 0

Local School District

(Data from School year 2007-08 except as noted)

Rialto Unified
182 East Walnut Ave
Rialto, CA 92376
(909) 820-7700

Superintendent ....Harold Cebrun
Grade plan K-12
Number of schools 28
Enrollment 29,070
High school graduates, 2006-07 1,386
Dropout rate 5.8%
Pupil/teacher ratio 21.7
Average class size 28.1
Students per computer 5.1
Classrooms with internet 1,126
Avg. Daily Attendance (ADA) 26,898
Cost per ADA $8,241
Avg. Teacher Salary $66,574

California Achievement Tests 6th ed., 2008

(Pct scoring at or above 50th National Percentile Rank)

	Math	Reading	Language
Grade 3	46%	24%	36%
Grade 7	34%	35%	35%

Academic Performance Index, 2008

Number of students tested 21,725
Number of valid scores 20,927
2007 API (base) 669
2008 API (growth) 680

SAT Testing, 2006-07

Enrollment, Grade 12 1,994
Number taking test 634
percent taking test 31.8%
percent with total score 1,500+ 5.40%

Average Scores:

Math	Verbal	Writing	Total
429	423	423	1,275

Federal No Child Left Behind, 2008

(Adequate Yearly Progress standards met)

	Participation Rate	Pct Proficient
ELA	Yes	No
Math	Yes	No

API criteria ....Yes
Graduation rate ....No
\# criteria met/possible 42/32

Other school districts for this city

(see Appendix E for information on these districts)

None

See Introduction for an explanation of all data sources.

Demographics & Socio-Economic Characteristics†

(2007 American Community Survey, except as noted)

Population

1990* 87,425
2007 97,279
Male 47,100
Female 50,179
Jan. 2008 (estimate)§ 103,577
Persons per sq. mi. of land 3,452.6

Race & Hispanic Origin, 2007

Race
White 32,337
Black/African American 26,608
North American Native 0
Asian 17,330
Pacific Islander 64
Other Race 18,304
Two or more races 2,636
Hispanic origin, total 34,876
Mexican 24,433
Puerto Rican 295
Cuban 45
Other Hispanic 10,103

Age & Nativity, 2007

Under 5 years 6,538
18 years and over 73,159
65 years and over 10,109
85 years and over 1,196
Median Age 35.1
Native-born 65,056
Foreign-born 32,223

Educational Attainment, 2007

Population 25 years and over 62,984
Less than 9th grade 12.5%
High school grad or higher 76.9%
Bachelor's degree or higher 23.9%
Graduate degree 7.0%

Income & Poverty, 2007

Per capita income $23,767
Median household income $50,293
Median family income $54,940
Persons in poverty 17.6%
H'holds receiving public assistance 1,679
H'holds receiving social security 7,953

Households, 2007

Total households 33,457
With persons under 18 12,163
With persons over 65 7,416
Family households 22,578
Single person households 9,432
Persons per household 2.89
Persons per family 3.59

Household Population, 2008§§

Persons living in households 101,949
Persons living in group quarters 1,628
Persons per household 2.8

Labor & Employment

Total civilian labor force, 2008§§ 52,500
Unemployment rate, 2008 .... 10.2%
Total civilian labor force, 2000* 46,360

Employed persons 16 years and over by occupation, 2007

Managers & professionals 11,743
Service occupations 10,487
Sales & office occupations 9,975
Farming, fishing & forestry 53
Construction & maintenance 4,785
Production & transportation 5,542
Self-employed persons 3,662

† see Appendix D for 2000 Decennial Census Data
* US Census Bureau
** 2007 American Community Survey
§ California Department of Finance
§§ California Employment Development Dept

General Information

City of Richmond
1401 Marina Way South
Richmond, CA 94804
510-620-6500

Website .... www.ci.richmond.ca.us
Elevation .... 55 ft.
Land Area (sq. miles) 30.0
Water Area (sq. miles) 22.6
Year of Incorporation 1905
Government type .... Chartered
Sales tax rate 9.75%

Voters & Officials

Registered Voters, October 2008

Total 41,681
Democrats 29,392
Republicans 3,356
Declined to state 7,277

Legislative Districts

US Congressional 7
State Senatorial 7, 9
State Assembly 14

Local Officials, 2009

Mayor .... Gayle McLaughlin
Manager .... William Lindsay
City Clerk .... Diane Holmes
Attorney .... Randy Riddle
Finance Dir .... Jim Goins
Public Works .... Yader Bermudez
Community Dev Dir .... Steve Duran
Building .... Richard Mitchell
Police Chief .... Chris Magnus
Fire Chief .... Michael Banks

Public Safety

Number of officers, 2007 161
Violent crimes, 2007 1,220
Property crimes, 2007 5,507
Arson, 2007 45

Public Library

Richmond Public Library
325 Civic Center Plaza
Richmond, CA 94804
510-620-6555

Director .... Monique Le Conge

Library statistics, FY 2007

Population served 103,828
Internet terminals 114
Annual users 248,606

Per capita:

Operating income $52.93
percent from local government 95.3%
Operating expenditure $52.93
Total materials 2.14
Print holdings 1.99
Visits per capita 4.34

Housing & Construction

Housing Units

Total, 2008§ 38,258
Single family units, attached 2,931
Single family units, detached 21,694
Multiple family units 13,512
Mobile home units 121
Occupied 36,751
Vacancy rate 3.9%
Median rent, 2007** $1,012
Median SF home value, 2007** $484,000

New Privately Owned Housing Units Authorized by Building Permit, 2007*

	Units	Construction Cost
Single	115	$24,729,225
Total	282	$40,087,827

Municipal Finance

(For local fiscal year ended in 2006)

Revenues

Total $177,832,886
Taxes 98,975,791
Special benefits assessment 0
Licenses & permits 2,973,538
Fines & forfeitures 697,038
Revenues from use of money & property 3,698,962
Intergovernmental 48,568,270
Service charges 16,998,177
Other revenues 5,921,110
Other financing sources 0

Expenditures

Total $159,663,543
General government 15,543,265
Public safety 60,924,857
Transportation 34,082,121
Community development 39,513,911
Health 1,468,030
Culture & leisure 7,481,913
Other 0

Local School District

(Data from School year 2007-08 except as noted)

West Contra Costa Unified
1108 Bissell Ave
Richmond, CA 94801
(510) 231-1101

Superintendent .... Bruce Harter
Grade plan K-12
Number of schools 65
Enrollment 30,830
High school graduates, 2006-07 1,622
Dropout rate 9.3%
Pupil/teacher ratio 19.7
Average class size 24.8
Students per computer 6.4
Classrooms with internet 1,508
Avg. Daily Attendance (ADA) 28,599
Cost per ADA $9,365
Avg. Teacher Salary $56,030

California Achievement Tests 6th ed., 2008

(Pct scoring at or above 50th National Percentile Rank)

	Math	Reading	Language
Grade 3	47%	27%	38%
Grade 7	36%	33%	31%

Academic Performance Index, 2008

Number of students tested 22,407
Number of valid scores 20,863
2007 API (base) 674
2008 API (growth) 682

SAT Testing, 2006-07

Enrollment, Grade 12 1,839
Number taking test 853
percent taking test 46.4%
percent with total score 1,500+ 13.90%

Average Scores:

Math	Verbal	Writing	Total
462	455	456	1,373

Federal No Child Left Behind, 2008

(Adequate Yearly Progress standards met)

	Participation Rate	Pct Proficient
ELA	Yes	No
Math	Yes	No

API criteria .... Yes
Graduation rate .... No
criteria met/possible 42/34

Other school districts for this city

(see Appendix E for information on these districts)

None

See Introduction for an explanation of all data sources.

Demographics & Socio-Economic Characteristics

(2000 Decennial Census, except as noted)

Population

1990* 27,725
2000 24,927
Male 12,441
Female 12,486
Jan. 2008 (estimate)§ 28,038
Persons per sq. mi. of land 1,328.8

Race & Hispanic Origin, 2000

Race
White 20,446
Black/African American 879
North American Native 270
Asian 967
Pacific Islander 144
Other Race 1,229
Two or more races 992
Hispanic origin, total 3,001
Mexican 2,288
Puerto Rican 107
Cuban 19
Other Hispanic 587

Age & Nativity, 2000

Under 5 years 1,845
18 years and over 17,676
65 years and over 2,823
85 years and over 254
Median Age 35.5
Native-born 23,444
Foreign-born 1,751

Educational Attainment, 2000

Population 25 years and over 15,702
Less than 9th grade 3.7%
High school grad or higher 87.4%
Bachelor's degree or higher 24.4%
Graduate degree 8.5%

Income & Poverty, 1999

Per capita income $21,312
Median household income $44,971
Median family income $52,725
Persons in poverty 12.2%
H'holds receiving public assistance 496
H'holds receiving social security 2,051

Households, 2000

Total households 9,826
With persons under 18 3,713
With persons over 65 2,058
Family households 6,689
Single person households 2,708
Persons per household 2.51
Persons per family 3.06

Household Population, 2008§§

Persons living in households 27,772
Persons living in group quarters 266
Persons per household 2.6

Labor & Employment

Total civilian labor force, 2008§§ 15,800
Unemployment rate, 2008 .... 5.5%
Total civilian labor force, 2000 11,341

Employed persons 16 years and over by occupation, 2000

Managers & professionals 4,300
Service occupations 1,844
Sales & office occupations 2,387
Farming, fishing & forestry 12
Construction & maintenance 1,091
Production & transportation 935
Self-employed persons 733

* US Census Bureau
** 2000 Decennial Census
§ California Department of Finance
§§ California Employment Development Dept

General Information

City of Ridgecrest
100 W California Ave
Ridgecrest, CA 93555
760-499-5000

Website .... www.ci.ridgecrest.ca.us
Elevation .... 2,289 ft.
Land Area (sq. miles) 21.1
Water Area (sq. miles) 0.3
Year of Incorporation 1963
Government type .... General law
Sales tax rate 8.25%

Voters & Officials

Registered Voters, October 2008

Total 13,878
Democrats 3,477
Republicans 7,080
Declined to state 2,763

Legislative Districts

US Congressional 22
State Senatorial 18
State Assembly 32

Local Officials, 2009

Mayor .... Steven P. Morgan
Manager .... Michael Avery
City Clerk .... Rita Gable
Attorney .... Wayne K. Lemieux
Treasurer .... Tess Sloan (Int)
Public Works .... Dennis Speer
Planning/Dev Dir .... Jim McRea
Building .... Gary Parsons
Police Chief .... Ronald Strand
Fire/Emergency Mgmt .... (County)

Public Safety

Number of officers, 2007 35
Violent crimes, 2007 152
Property crimes, 2007 621
Arson, 2007 4

Public Library

Ridgecrest Branch Library
Kern County Library System
131 E Las Flores
Ridgecrest, CA 93555
760-384-5870

Branch Librarian .... Marsha Lloyd

Library system statistics, FY 2007

Population served 801,648
Internet terminals 237
Annual users 337,030

Per capita:

Operating income $12.11
percent from local government 90.4%
Operating expenditure $12.11
Total materials 1.37
Print holdings 1.29
Visits per capita 2.09

Housing & Construction

Housing Units

Total, 2008§ 11,830
Single family units, attached 414
Single family units, detached 7,900
Multiple family units 2,480
Mobile home units 1,036
Occupied 10,826
Vacancy rate 8.5%
Median rent, 2000** $500
Median SF home value, 2000** $72,400

New Privately Owned Housing Units Authorized by Building Permit, 2007*

	Units	Construction Cost
Single	48	$6,339,453
Total	128	$14,072,188

Municipal Finance

(For local fiscal year ended in 2006)

Revenues

Total $17,893,271
Taxes 7,526,630
Special benefits assessment 143,887
Licenses & permits 467,766
Fines & forfeitures 32,184
Revenues from use of money & property 880,400
Intergovernmental 1,711,666
Service charges 5,747,731
Other revenues 1,383,007
Other financing sources 0

Expenditures

Total $17,504,541
General government 3,974,379
Public safety 5,829,081
Transportation 4,197,724
Community development 882,027
Health 810,930
Culture & leisure 1,810,400
Other 0

Local School District

(Data from School year 2007-08 except as noted)

Sierra Sands Unified
113 Felspar
Ridgecrest, CA 93555
(760) 375-3363

Superintendent .... Joanna Rummer
Grade plan K-12
Number of schools 11
Enrollment 5,516
High school graduates, 2006-07 387
Dropout rate 1.7%
Pupil/teacher ratio 20.3
Average class size 24.0
Students per computer 3.9
Classrooms with internet 291
Avg. Daily Attendance (ADA) 5,330
Cost per ADA $8,742
Avg. Teacher Salary $56,299

California Achievement Tests 6th ed., 2008

(Pct scoring at or above 50th National Percentile Rank)

	Math	Reading	Language
Grade 3	59%	45%	48%
Grade 7	49%	52%	48%

Academic Performance Index, 2008

Number of students tested 4,120
Number of valid scores 3,769
2007 API (base) 753
2008 API (growth) 768

SAT Testing, 2006-07

Enrollment, Grade 12 442
Number taking test 104
percent taking test 23.5%
percent with total score 1,500+ 16.30%

Average Scores:

Math	Verbal	Writing	Total
556	538	531	1,625

Federal No Child Left Behind, 2008

(Adequate Yearly Progress standards met)

	Participation Rate	Pct Proficient
ELA	Yes	No
Math	Yes	No

API criteria .... Yes
Graduation rate .... Yes
criteria met/possible 30/26

Other school districts for this city

(see Appendix E for information on these districts)

None

See Introduction for an explanation of all data sources.

Demographics & Socio-Economic Characteristics

(2000 Decennial Census, except as noted)

Population

1990* ... 3,012
2000 ... 3,174
Male ... 1,576
Female ... 1,598
Jan. 2008 (estimate)§ ... 3,284
Persons per sq. mi. of land ... 1,728.4

Race & Hispanic Origin, 2000

Race
White ... 2,718
Black/African American ... 5
North American Native ... 123
Asian ... 12
Pacific Islander ... 1
Other Race ... 182
Two or more races ... 133
Hispanic origin, total ... 343
Mexican ... 287
Puerto Rican ... 4
Cuban ... 4
Other Hispanic ... 48

Age & Nativity, 2000

Under 5 years ... 220
18 years and over ... 2,277
65 years and over ... 433
85 years and over ... 37
Median Age ... 35.8
Native-born ... 2,926
Foreign-born ... 247

Educational Attainment, 2000

Population 25 years and over ... 2,006
Less than 9th grade ... 7.0%
High school grad or higher ... 77.2%
Bachelor's degree or higher ... 6.0%
Graduate degree ... 2.1%

Income & Poverty, 1999

Per capita income ... $12,569
Median household income ... $29,254
Median family income ... $36,464
Persons in poverty ... 23.1%
H'holds receiving public assistance ... 78
H'holds receiving social security ... 431

Households, 2000

Total households ... 1,221
With persons under 18 ... 464
With persons over 65 ... 314
Family households ... 830
Single person households ... 305
Persons per household ... 2.59
Persons per family ... 3.08

Household Population, 2008§§

Persons living in households ... 3,274
Persons living in group quarters ... 10
Persons per household ... 2.6

Labor & Employment

Total civilian labor force, 2008§§ ... 1,400
Unemployment rate, 2008 ... 11.0%
Total civilian labor force, 2000 ... 1,378

Employed persons 16 years and over by occupation, 2000

Managers & professionals ... 156
Service occupations ... 211
Sales & office occupations ... 312
Farming, fishing & forestry ... 85
Construction & maintenance ... 149
Production & transportation ... 287
Self-employed persons ... 114

* US Census Bureau
** 2000 Decennial Census
§ California Department of Finance
§§ California Employment Development Dept

General Information

City of Rio Dell
675 Wildwood Ave
Rio Dell, CA 95562
707-764-3532

Website ... www.riodellcity.com
Elevation ... 126 ft.
Land Area (sq. miles) ... 1.9
Water Area (sq. miles) ... 0.1
Year of Incorporation ... 1965
Government type ... General law
Sales tax rate ... 8.25%

Voters & Officials

Registered Voters, October 2008

Total ... 1,587
Democrats ... 607
Republicans ... 584
Declined to state ... 290

Legislative Districts

US Congressional ... 1
State Senatorial ... 2
State Assembly ... 1

Local Officials, 2009

Mayor ... Julie Woodall
Manager ... Nancy Flemming
City Clerk ... Karen Dunham
Attorney ... David Martinek
Finance Dir ... Stephanie Beauchaine
Public Works ... James Hale
Planning/Dev Dir ... NA
Building ... NA
Police Chief ... Graham Hill
Emergency/Fire Dir ... Shane Wilson

Public Safety

Number of officers, 2007 ... 7
Violent crimes, 2007 ... 9
Property crimes, 2007 ... 65
Arson, 2007 ... 1

Public Library

Rio Dell Library
Humboldt County Library System
715 Wildwood Ave
Rio Dell, CA 95562
707-764-3333

Branch Librarian ... Jeanine Lancaster

Library system statistics, FY 2007

Population served ... 131,959
Internet terminals ... 46
Annual users ... 20,083

Per capita:

Operating income ... $22.91
percent from local government ... 90.6%
Operating expenditure ... $18.80
Total materials ... 2.54
Print holdings ... 2.38
Visits per capita ... 4.15

Housing & Construction

Housing Units

Total, 2008§ ... 1,504
Single family units, attached ... 26
Single family units, detached ... 1,047
Multiple family units ... 187
Mobile home units ... 244
Occupied ... 1,280
Vacancy rate ... 14.9%
Median rent, 2000** ... $491
Median SF home value, 2000** ... $95,800

New Privately Owned Housing Units Authorized by Building Permit, 2007*

	Units	Construction Cost
Single	5	$609,463
Total	5	$609,463

Municipal Finance

(For local fiscal year ended in 2006)

Revenues

Total ... $8,298,979
Taxes ... 600,586
Special benefits assessment ... 0
Licenses & permits ... 44,782
Fines & forfeitures ... 0
Revenues from use of money & property ... 47,401
Intergovernmental ... 6,422,553
Service charges ... 1,182,797
Other revenues ... 860
Other financing sources ... 0

Expenditures

Total ... $2,180,237
General government ... 581,013
Public safety ... 423,838
Transportation ... 134,646
Community development ... 0
Health ... 455,974
Culture & leisure ... 0
Other ... 0

Local School District

(Data from School year 2007-08 except as noted)

Fortuna Union High
379 12th St
Fortuna, CA 95540
(707) 725-4461

Superintendent ... Gordon Dexter
Grade plan ... 9-12
Number of schools ... 4
Enrollment ... 1,232
High school graduates, 2006-07 ... 218
Dropout rate ... 2.6%
Pupil/teacher ratio ... 21.4
Average class size ... 23.8
Students per computer ... 2.8
Classrooms with internet ... 81
Avg. Daily Attendance (ADA) ... 1,119
Cost per ADA ... $8,720
Avg. Teacher Salary ... $57,839

California Achievement Tests 6th ed., 2008

(Pct scoring at or above 50th National Percentile Rank)

	Math	Reading	Language
Grade 3	NA	NA	NA
Grade 7	NA	NA	NA

Academic Performance Index, 2008

Number of students tested ... 871
Number of valid scores ... 837
2007 API (base) ... 674
2008 API (growth) ... 699

SAT Testing, 2006-07

Enrollment, Grade 12 ... 264
Number taking test ... 67
percent taking test ... 25.4%
percent with total score 1,500+ ... 13.60%

Average Scores:

Math	Verbal	Writing	Total
528	513	506	1,547

Federal No Child Left Behind, 2008

(Adequate Yearly Progress standards met)

	Participation Rate	Pct Proficient
ELA	Yes	Yes
Math	No	Yes

API criteria ... Yes
Graduation rate ... Yes
\# criteria met/possible ... 14/13

Other school districts for this city

(see Appendix E for information on these districts)

Rio Dell Elem

See Introduction for an explanation of all data sources.

Demographics & Socio-Economic Characteristics

(2000 Decennial Census, except as noted)

Population

1990* 3,316
2000 4,571
Male 2,232
Female 2,339
Jan. 2008 (estimate)§ 8,071
Persons per sq. mi. of land 1,186.9

Race & Hispanic Origin, 2000

Race
White 4,038
Black/African American 54
North American Native 42
Asian 73
Pacific Islander 1
Other Race 187
Two or more races 176
Hispanic origin, total 522
Mexican 385
Puerto Rican 14
Cuban 5
Other Hispanic 118

Age & Nativity, 2000

Under 5 years 299
18 years and over 3,430
65 years and over 901
85 years and over 81
Median Age 40.7
Native-born 4,244
Foreign-born 373

Educational Attainment, 2000

Population 25 years and over 3,219
Less than 9th grade 3.8%
High school grad or higher 84.0%
Bachelor's degree or higher 16.6%
Graduate degree 5.7%

Income & Poverty, 1999

Per capita income $24,627
Median household income $44,534
Median family income $52,007
Persons in poverty 10.1%
H'holds receiving public assistance 52
H'holds receiving social security 679

Households, 2000

Total households 1,881
With persons under 18 601
With persons over 65 661
Family households 1,286
Single person households 496
Persons per household 2.43
Persons per family 2.92

Household Population, 2008§§

Persons living in households 8,071
Persons living in group quarters 0
Persons per household 2.3

Labor & Employment

Total civilian labor force, 2008§§ 2,400
Unemployment rate, 2008 .... 5.0%
Total civilian labor force, 2000 2,031

Employed persons 16 years and over by occupation, 2000

Managers & professionals 583
Service occupations 262
Sales & office occupations 555
Farming, fishing & forestry 17
Construction & maintenance 287
Production & transportation 237
Self-employed persons 192

* US Census Bureau
** 2000 Decennial Census
§ California Department of Finance
§§ California Employment Development Dept

General Information

City of Rio Vista
One Main St
Rio Vista, CA 94571
707-374-6451

Website .... www.rio-vista-ca.com
Elevation .... 22 ft.
Land Area (sq. miles) 6.8
Water Area (sq. miles) 0.4
Year of Incorporation 1894
Government type .... General law
Sales tax rate 8.38%

Voters & Officials

Registered Voters, October 2008

Total 4,527
Democrats 2,025
Republicans 1,608
Declined to state 708

Legislative Districts

US Congressional 3
State Senatorial 2
State Assembly 8

Local Officials, 2009

Mayor .... Jan Vick
Manager .... Hector De La Rosa
City Clerk .... Carolyn Parkinson (Int)
Attorney .... Kara Ueda
Finance Dir .... Michelle Mingay (Actg)
Public Works .... Kirt Hunter (Int)
Community Dev Dir .... Tom Bland
Building .... NA
Police Chief .... William Bowen
Emergency/Fire Dir .... Tom Myers (Int)

Public Safety

Number of officers, 2007 14
Violent crimes, 2007 .... NA
Property crimes, 2007 118
Arson, 2007 0

Public Library

Rio Vista Library
Solano County Library System
44 S Second St
Rio Vista, CA 94571
707-374-2664

Branch Librarian .... Susan Reeve

Library system statistics, FY 2007

Population served 371,000
Internet terminals 248
Annual users 562,512

Per capita:

Operating income $54.42
percent from local government 94.0%
Operating expenditure $47.19
Total materials 1.88
Print holdings 1.57
Visits per capita 5.20

Housing & Construction

Housing Units

Total, 2008§ 3,667
Single family units, attached 34
Single family units, detached 3,248
Multiple family units 274
Mobile home units 111
Occupied 3,502
Vacancy rate 4.5%
Median rent, 2000** $706
Median SF home value, 2000** $162,400

New Privately Owned Housing Units Authorized by Building Permit, 2007*

	Units	Construction Cost
Single	170	$37,048,615
Total	170	$37,048,615

Municipal Finance

(For local fiscal year ended in 2006)

Revenues

Total $20,208,815
Taxes 2,844,614
Special benefits assessment 0
Licenses & permits 766,594
Fines & forfeitures 39,217
Revenues from use of money & property 914,134
Intergovernmental 936,666
Service charges 14,210,405
Other revenues 497,185
Other financing sources 0

Expenditures

Total $31,883,984
General government 1,255,990
Public safety 3,532,781
Transportation 1,259,404
Community development 1,276,256
Health 22,469,350
Culture & leisure 947,742
Other 0

Local School District

(Data from School year 2007-08 except as noted)

River Delta Joint Unified
445 Montezuma St
Rio Vista, CA 94571
(707) 374-1700

Superintendent .... Richard Hennes
Grade plan K-12
Number of schools 12
Enrollment 2,213
High school graduates, 2006-07 138
Dropout rate 3.5%
Pupil/teacher ratio 17.9
Average class size 22.1
Students per computer 3.5
Classrooms with internet 274
Avg. Daily Attendance (ADA) 2,053
Cost per ADA $9,801
Avg. Teacher Salary $52,353

California Achievement Tests 6th ed., 2008

(Pct scoring at or above 50th National Percentile Rank)

	Math	Reading	Language
Grade 3	46%	37%	44%
Grade 7	56%	49%	43%

Academic Performance Index, 2008

Number of students tested 1,601
Number of valid scores 1,474
2007 API (base) 698
2008 API (growth) 718

SAT Testing, 2006-07

Enrollment, Grade 12 144
Number taking test 58
percent taking test 40.3%
percent with total score 1,500+ 21.50%

Average Scores:

Math	Verbal	Writing	Total
506	498	506	1,510

Federal No Child Left Behind, 2008

(Adequate Yearly Progress standards met)

	Participation Rate	Pct Proficient
ELA	Yes	No
Math	Yes	Yes

API criteria .... Yes
Graduation rate .... Yes
\# criteria met/possible 26/23

Other school districts for this city

(see Appendix E for information on these districts)

None

See Introduction for an explanation of all data sources.

Demographics & Socio-Economic Characteristics

(2000 Decennial Census, except as noted)

Population

1990* 7,455
2000 10,146
Male 4,911
Female 5,235
Jan. 2008 (estimate)§ 14,915
Persons per sq. mi. of land 3,637.8

Race & Hispanic Origin, 2000

Race
White 8,575
Black/African American 35
North American Native 62
Asian 153
Pacific Islander 28
Other Race 893
Two or more races 400
Hispanic origin, total 1,843
Mexican 1,525
Puerto Rican 43
Cuban 5
Other Hispanic 270

Age & Nativity, 2000

Under 5 years 707
18 years and over 6,901
65 years and over 1,028
85 years and over 203
Median Age 34.2
Native-born 9,437
Foreign-born 697

Educational Attainment, 2000

Population 25 years and over 6,157
Less than 9th grade 6.6%
High school grad or higher 82.2%
Bachelor's degree or higher 20.6%
Graduate degree 5.0%

Income & Poverty, 1999

Per capita income $20,978
Median household income $56,979
Median family income $62,592
Persons in poverty 6.1%
H'holds receiving public assistance 127
H'holds receiving social security 798

Households, 2000

Total households 3,368
With persons under 18 1,625
With persons over 65 662
Family households 2,681
Single person households 570
Persons per household 2.98
Persons per family 3.37

Household Population, 2008§§

Persons living in households 14,804
Persons living in group quarters 111
Persons per household 3.0

Labor & Employment

Total civilian labor force, 2008§§ 5,900
Unemployment rate, 2008 .... 6.1%
Total civilian labor force, 2000 4,889

Employed persons 16 years and over by occupation, 2000

Managers & professionals 1,507
Service occupations 675
Sales & office occupations 1,267
Farming, fishing & forestry 67
Construction & maintenance 497
Production & transportation 581
Self-employed persons 292

* US Census Bureau
** 2000 Decennial Census
§ California Department of Finance
§§ California Employment Development Dept

General Information

City of Ripon
259 N Wilma Ave
Ripon, CA 95366
209-599-2108

Website .... www.cityofripon.org
Elevation .... 62 ft.
Land Area (sq. miles) 4.1
Water Area (sq. miles) 0.1
Year of Incorporation 1945
Government type .... General law
Sales tax rate 8.75%

Voters & Officials

Registered Voters, October 2008

Total 7,390
Democrats 1,928
Republicans 4,138
Declined to state 1,028

Legislative Districts

US Congressional 11
State Senatorial 14
State Assembly 26

Local Officials, 2009

Mayor .... Chuck Winn
Manager .... Everett Compton
City Clerk .... Lynette Van Laar
Attorney .... Thomas Terpstra
Finance Dir .... Lynette Van Laar
Public Works .... Ted Johnston
Planning/Dev Dir .... Ken Zuidervaart
Building .... Ted Johnston
Police Chief .... Richard Bull
Emergency/Fire Dir .... Dennis Bitters

Public Safety

Number of officers, 2007 24
Violent crimes, 2007 36
Property crimes, 2007 383
Arson, 2007 .... NA

Public Library

Ripon Library
Stockton-San Joaquin County Public Library
333 W Main St
Ripon, CA 95366
209-937-8221

Branch Librarian .... Melinda Kopp

Library system statistics, FY 2007

Population served 619,292
Internet terminals 125
Annual users 255,083

Per capita:

Operating income $21.59
percent from local government 96.0%
Operating expenditure $19.98
Total materials 1.65
Print holdings 1.52
Visits per capita 2.20

Housing & Construction

Housing Units

Total, 2008§ 4,987
Single family units, attached 192
Single family units, detached 4,218
Multiple family units 566
Mobile home units 11
Occupied 4,874
Vacancy rate 2.3%
Median rent, 2000** $643
Median SF home value, 2000** $166,500

New Privately Owned Housing Units Authorized by Building Permit, 2007*

	Units	Construction Cost
Single	88	$20,803,126
Total	123	$23,948,747

Municipal Finance

(For local fiscal year ended in 2006)

Revenues

Total $16,916,784
Taxes 8,012,526
Special benefits assessment 339,928
Licenses & permits 875,086
Fines & forfeitures 0
Revenues from use of money & property 754,654
Intergovernmental 573,712
Service charges 5,480,413
Other revenues 880,465
Other financing sources 0

Expenditures

Total $22,673,588
General government 5,033,643
Public safety 4,232,390
Transportation 1,614,026
Community development 1,711,125
Health 938,507
Culture & leisure 3,474,371
Other 0

Local School District

(Data from School year 2007-08 except as noted)

Ripon Unified
304 North Acacia Ave
Ripon, CA 95366
(209) 599-2131

Superintendent .... Louise Nan
Grade plan K-12
Number of schools 7
Enrollment 2,992
High school graduates, 2006-07 191
Dropout rate 3.5%
Pupil/teacher ratio 21.2
Average class size 24.7
Students per computer 4.3
Classrooms with internet 161
Avg. Daily Attendance (ADA) 2,939
Cost per ADA $7,214
Avg. Teacher Salary $61,632

California Achievement Tests 6th ed., 2008

(Pct scoring at or above 50th National Percentile Rank)

	Math	Reading	Language
Grade 3	68%	50%	62%
Grade 7	73%	72%	67%

Academic Performance Index, 2008

Number of students tested 2,364
Number of valid scores 2,252
2007 API (base) 798
2008 API (growth) 803

SAT Testing, 2006-07

Enrollment, Grade 12 216
Number taking test 90
percent taking test 41.7%
percent with total score 1,500+ 19.90%

Average Scores:

Math	Verbal	Writing	Total
505	492	496	1,493

Federal No Child Left Behind, 2008

(Adequate Yearly Progress standards met)

	Participation Rate	Pct Proficient
ELA	Yes	No
Math	Yes	No

API criteria .... Yes
Graduation rate .... Yes
\# criteria met/possible 26/24

Other school districts for this city

(see Appendix E for information on these districts)

None

See Introduction for an explanation of all data sources.

Demographics & Socio-Economic Characteristics

(2000 Decennial Census, except as noted)

Population

1990* . . . 8,547
2000 . . . 15,826
Male . . . 7,810
Female . . . 8,016
Jan. 2008 (estimate)§ . . . 21,757
Persons per sq. mi. of land . . . 7,018.4

Race & Hispanic Origin, 2000

Race
White . . . 10,579
Black/African American . . . 242
North American Native . . . 227
Asian . . . 208
Pacific Islander . . . 20
Other Race . . . 3,803
Two or more races . . . 747
Hispanic origin, total . . . 7,266
Mexican . . . 6,334
Puerto Rican . . . 72
Cuban . . . 8
Other Hispanic . . . 852

Age & Nativity, 2000

Under 5 years . . . 1,445
18 years and over . . . 10,458
65 years and over . . . 1,147
85 years and over . . . 104
Median Age . . . 29.6
Native-born . . . 12,260
Foreign-born . . . 3,597

Educational Attainment, 2000

Population 25 years and over . . . 8,999
Less than 9th grade . . . 18.6%
High school grad or higher . . . 64.9%
Bachelor's degree or higher . . . 11.6%
Graduate degree . . . 2.0%

Income & Poverty, 1999

Per capita income . . . $14,972
Median household income . . . $44,668
Median family income . . . $47,411
Persons in poverty . . . 12.3%
H'holds receiving public assistance . . . 202
H'holds receiving social security . . . 979

Households, 2000

Total households . . . 4,544
With persons under 18 . . . 2,528
With persons over 65 . . . 804
Family households . . . 3,821
Single person households . . . 539
Persons per household . . . 3.45
Persons per family . . . 3.73

Household Population, 2008§§

Persons living in households . . . 21,622
Persons living in group quarters . . . 135
Persons per household . . . 3.5

Labor & Employment

Total civilian labor force, 2008§§ . . . 8,500
Unemployment rate, 2008 . . . 16.4%
Total civilian labor force, 2000 . . . 7,198

Employed persons 16 years and over by occupation, 2000

Managers & professionals . . . 1,528
Service occupations . . . 881
Sales & office occupations . . . 1,336
Farming, fishing & forestry . . . 270
Construction & maintenance . . . 707
Production & transportation . . . 1,243
Self-employed persons . . . 427

* US Census Bureau
** 2000 Decennial Census
§ California Department of Finance
§§ California Employment Development Dept

General Information

City of Riverbank
6707 Third St
Riverbank, CA 95367
209-869-7101

Website . . . www.riverbank.org
Elevation . . . 133 ft.
Land Area (sq. miles) . . . 3.1
Water Area (sq. miles) . . . 0.1
Year of Incorporation . . . 1922
Government type . . . General law
Sales tax rate . . . 8.38%

Voters & Officials

Registered Voters, October 2008

Total . . . 8,942
Democrats . . . 3,819
Republicans . . . 3,216
Declined to state . . . 1,534

Legislative Districts

US Congressional . . . 19
State Senatorial . . . 14
State Assembly . . . 25

Local Officials, 2009

Mayor . . . David I White
Manager . . . Richard Holmer
City Clerk . . . Linda Abid-Cummings
Attorney . . . Tom Hallinan
Finance Dir . . . Marisela Hernandez
Public Works . . . David Melilli
Planning/Dev Dir . . . J.D. Hightower
Building . . . NA
Police Chief . . . Bill Pooley
Emergency/Fire Dir . . . Steve Mayotte

Public Safety

Number of officers, 2007 . . . 19
Violent crimes, 2007 . . . 64
Property crimes, 2007 . . . 837
Arson, 2007 . . . NA

Public Library

Riverbank Library
Stanislaus County Free Library
3442 Santa Fe Ave
Riverbank, CA 95367
209-869-7008

Branch Librarian . . . Laurie Futrell

Library system statistics, FY 2007

Population served . . . 521,497
Internet terminals . . . 128
Annual users . . . 256,298

Per capita:

Operating income . . . $20.76
percent from local government . . . 91.0%
Operating expenditure . . . $20.19
Total materials . . . 1.66
Print holdings . . . 1.56
Visits per capita . . . NA

Housing & Construction

Housing Units

Total, 2008§ . . . 6,447
Single family units, attached . . . 187
Single family units, detached . . . 5,605
Multiple family units . . . 366
Mobile home units . . . 289
Occupied . . . 6,237
Vacancy rate . . . 3.3%
Median rent, 2000** . . . $680
Median SF home value, 2000** . . . $118,100

New Privately Owned Housing Units Authorized by Building Permit, 2007*

	Units	Construction Cost
Single	129	$19,388,095
Total	129	$19,388,095

Municipal Finance

(For local fiscal year ended in 2006)

Revenues

Total . . . $18,459,325
Taxes . . . 8,862,208
Special benefits assessment . . . 0
Licenses & permits . . . 425,332
Fines & forfeitures . . . 169,522
Revenues from use of money & property . . . 888,239
Intergovernmental . . . 1,793,126
Service charges . . . 4,767,665
Other revenues . . . 1,553,233
Other financing sources . . . 0

Expenditures

Total . . . $19,122,862
General government . . . 1,491,470
Public safety . . . 2,950,983
Transportation . . . 8,776,240
Community development . . . 625,175
Health . . . 1,604,481
Culture & leisure . . . 2,281,979
Other . . . 0

Local School District

(Data from School year 2007-08 except as noted)

Riverbank Unified
6715 Seventh St
Riverbank, CA 95367
(209) 869-2538

Superintendent . . . Ken Geisick
Grade plan . . . K-12
Number of schools . . . 7
Enrollment . . . 2,903
High school graduates, 2006-07 . . . 127
Dropout rate . . . 3.8%
Pupil/teacher ratio . . . 20.1
Average class size . . . 25.2
Students per computer . . . 4.3
Classrooms with internet . . . 149
Avg. Daily Attendance (ADA) . . . 2,634
Cost per ADA . . . $9,158
Avg. Teacher Salary . . . $63,158

California Achievement Tests 6th ed., 2008

(Pct scoring at or above 50th National Percentile Rank)

	Math	Reading	Language
Grade 3	49%	29%	31%
Grade 7	44%	36%	32%

Academic Performance Index, 2008

Number of students tested . . . 2,116
Number of valid scores . . . 1,983
2007 API (base) . . . 682
2008 API (growth) . . . 686

SAT Testing, 2006-07

Enrollment, Grade 12 . . . 173
Number taking test . . . 36
percent taking test . . . 20.8%
percent with total score 1,500+ . . . 7.50%

Average Scores:

Math	Verbal	Writing	Total
490	458	444	1,392

Federal No Child Left Behind, 2008

(Adequate Yearly Progress standards met)

	Participation Rate	Pct Proficient
ELA	Yes	No
Math	Yes	No

API criteria . . . Yes
Graduation rate . . . Yes
\# criteria met/possible . . . 26/19

Other school districts for this city

(see Appendix E for information on these districts)

None

See Introduction for an explanation of all data sources.

Demographics & Socio-Economic Characteristics†

(2007 American Community Survey, except as noted)

Population

1990*	226,505
2007	316,154
Male	157,541
Female	158,613
Jan. 2008 (estimate)§	296,842
Persons per sq. mi. of land	3,800.8

Race & Hispanic Origin, 2007

Race	
White	192,183
Black/African American	18,215
North American Native	2,338
Asian	19,202
Pacific Islander	342
Other Race	66,977
Two or more races	16,897
Hispanic origin, total	154,691
Mexican	135,901
Puerto Rican	3,057
Cuban	1,132
Other Hispanic	14,601

Age & Nativity, 2007

Under 5 years	25,089
18 years and over	226,977
65 years and over	24,365
85 years and over	3,569
Median Age	28.8
Native-born	239,804
Foreign-born	76,350

Educational Attainment, 2007

Population 25 years and over	182,338
Less than 9th grade	11.8%
High school grad or higher	77.8%
Bachelor's degree or higher	20.0%
Graduate degree	7.5%

Income & Poverty, 2007

Per capita income	$22,001
Median household income	$55,999
Median family income	$61,938
Persons in poverty	12.2%
H'holds receiving public assistance	1,975
H'holds receiving social security	17,594

Households, 2007

Total households	91,878
With persons under 18	40,959
With persons over 65	16,457
Family households	66,608
Single person households	16,853
Persons per household	3.34
Persons per family	3.91

Household Population, 2008§§

Persons living in households	287,341
Persons living in group quarters	9,501
Persons per household	3.1

Labor & Employment

Total civilian labor force, 2008§§	161,500
Unemployment rate, 2008	8.7%
Total civilian labor force, 2000*	116,008

Employed persons 16 years and over by occupation, 2007

Managers & professionals	42,580
Service occupations	25,123
Sales & office occupations	34,898
Farming, fishing & forestry	172
Construction & maintenance	16,915
Production & transportation	24,175
Self-employed persons	12,091

† see Appendix D for 2000 Decennial Census Data
* US Census Bureau
** 2007 American Community Survey
§ California Department of Finance
§§ California Employment Development Dept

General Information

City of Riverside
3900 Main St
Riverside, CA 92522
951-826-5311

Website	www.riversideca.gov
Elevation	858 ft.
Land Area (sq. miles)	78.1
Water Area (sq. miles)	0.3
Year of Incorporation	1883
Government type	Chartered
Sales tax rate	8.75%

Voters & Officials

Registered Voters, October 2008

Total	117,728
Democrats	47,866
Republicans	42,745
Declined to state	21,253

Legislative Districts

US Congressional	44
State Senatorial	31
State Assembly	63, 64, 66

Local Officials, 2009

Mayor	Ron Loveridge
Manager	Brad Hudson
City Clerk	Colleen Nicol
Attorney	Greg Priamos
Finance Dir	Paul Sundeen
Public Works	Siobhan Foster
Planning/Dev Dir	Scott Barber
Building	NA
Police Chief	Russ Leach
Emergency/Fire Dir.	Tedd Laycock

Public Safety

Number of officers, 2007	402
Violent crimes, 2007	1,893
Property crimes, 2007	11,154
Arson, 2007	103

Public Library

Riverside Public Library
3581 Mission Inn Ave
Riverside, CA 92501
951-826-5213

Director	Barbara Custen

Library statistics, FY 2007

Population served	291,398
Internet terminals	373
Annual users	265,248

Per capita:

Operating income	$35.64
percent from local government	90.6%
Operating expenditure	$32.29
Total materials	1.82
Print holdings	1.67
Visits per capita	2.25

Housing & Construction

Housing Units

Total, 2008§	98,441
Single family units, attached	4,144
Single family units, detached	61,595
Multiple family units	30,225
Mobile home units	2,477
Occupied	93,973
Vacancy rate	4.5%
Median rent, 2007**	$1,085
Median SF home value, 2007**	$423,400

New Privately Owned Housing Units Authorized by Building Permit, 2007*

	Units	Construction Cost
Single	342	$88,770,574
Total	934	$147,102,643

Municipal Finance

(For local fiscal year ended in 2006)

Revenues

Total	$759,464,083
Taxes	163,798,348
Special benefits assessment	3,976,076
Licenses & permits	3,595,368
Fines & forfeitures	1,908,047
Revenues from use of money & property	21,232,238
Intergovernmental	50,686,206
Service charges	359,395,148
Other revenues	29,163,404
Other financing sources	125,709,248

Expenditures

Total	$630,592,019
General government	101,247,922
Public safety	115,375,076
Transportation	62,838,038
Community development	18,595,531
Health	32,580,825
Culture & leisure	34,702,238
Other	0

Local School District

(Data from School year 2007-08 except as noted)

Riverside Unified
PO Box 2800
Riverside, CA 92516
(951) 788-7135

Superintendent	Gladys Walker
Grade plan	K-12
Number of schools	48
Enrollment	43,560
High school graduates, 2006-07	2,683
Dropout rate	3.2%
Pupil/teacher ratio	24.7
Average class size	27.3
Students per computer	5.9
Classrooms with internet	1,904
Avg. Daily Attendance (ADA)	42,109
Cost per ADA	$7,832
Avg. Teacher Salary	$69,084

California Achievement Tests 6th ed., 2008

(Pct scoring at or above 50th National Percentile Rank)

	Math	Reading	Language
Grade 3	50%	35%	44%
Grade 7	51%	48%	45%

Academic Performance Index, 2008

Number of students tested	33,388
Number of valid scores	31,033
2007 API (base)	737
2008 API (growth)	748

SAT Testing, 2006-07

Enrollment, Grade 12	2,779
Number taking test	1,170
percent taking test	42.1%
percent with total score 1,500+	16.20%

Average Scores:

Math	Verbal	Writing	Total
483	471	475	1,429

Federal No Child Left Behind, 2008

(Adequate Yearly Progress standards met)

	Participation Rate	Pct Proficient
ELA	Yes	No
Math	Yes	No

API criteria	Yes
Graduation rate	Yes
# criteria met/possible	46/44

Other school districts for this city

(see Appendix E for information on these districts)

Alvord Unified, Jurupa Unified, Moreno Valley Unified

See Introduction for an explanation of all data sources.

Demographics & Socio-Economic Characteristics

(2000 Decennial Census, except as noted)

Population

1990* . . . 19,033
2000 . . . 36,330
Male . . . 17,760
Female . . . 18,570
Jan. 2008 (estimate)§ . . . 53,843
Persons per sq. mi. of land . . . 3,323.6

Race & Hispanic Origin, 2000

Race
White . . . 32,086
Black/African American . . . 330
North American Native . . . 291
Asian . . . 1,510
Pacific Islander . . . 70
Other Race . . . 701
Two or more races . . . 1,342
Hispanic origin, total . . . 2,874
Mexican . . . 1,855
Puerto Rican . . . 108
Cuban . . . 41
Other Hispanic . . . 870

Age & Nativity, 2000

Under 5 years . . . 2,873
18 years and over . . . 25,436
65 years and over . . . 3,136
85 years and over . . . 242
Median Age . . . 34.5
Native-born . . . 34,652
Foreign-born . . . 1,911

Educational Attainment, 2000

Population 25 years and over . . . 23,029
Less than 9th grade . . . 1.2%
High school grad or higher . . . 94.4%
Bachelor's degree or higher . . . 36.1%
Graduate degree . . . 10.1%

Income & Poverty, 1999

Per capita income . . . $26,910
Median household income . . . $64,737
Median family income . . . $72,245
Persons in poverty . . . 4.5%
H'holds receiving public assistance . . . 272
H'holds receiving social security . . . 2,624

Households, 2000

Total households . . . 13,258
With persons under 18 . . . 5,942
With persons over 65 . . . 2,279
Family households . . . 10,016
Single person households . . . 2,478
Persons per household . . . 2.74
Persons per family . . . 3.15

Household Population, 2008§§

Persons living in households . . . 53,465
Persons living in group quarters . . . 378
Persons per household . . . 2.6

Labor & Employment

Total civilian labor force, 2008§§ . . . 26,900
Unemployment rate, 2008 . . . 4.5%
Total civilian labor force, 2000 . . . 19,002

Employed persons 16 years and over by occupation, 2000

Managers & professionals . . . 8,090
Service occupations . . . 1,992
Sales & office occupations . . . 5,749
Farming, fishing & forestry . . . 0
Construction & maintenance . . . 1,336
Production & transportation . . . 1,319
Self-employed persons . . . 1,345

* US Census Bureau
** 2000 Decennial Census
§ California Department of Finance
§§ California Employment Development Dept

General Information

City of Rocklin
3970 Rocklin Rd
Rocklin, CA 95677
916-625-5000

Website . . . www.rocklin.ca.us
Elevation . . . 248 ft.
Land Area (sq. miles) . . . 16.2
Water Area (sq. miles) . . . 0
Year of Incorporation . . . 1893
Government type . . . General law
Sales tax rate . . . 8.25%

Voters & Officials

Registered Voters, October 2008

Total . . . 30,751
Democrats . . . 8,587
Republicans . . . 15,522
Declined to state . . . 5,677

Legislative Districts

US Congressional . . . 4
State Senatorial . . . 4
State Assembly . . . 4

Local Officials, 2009

Mayor . . . Peter Hill
City Manager . . . Carlos Urrutia
City Clerk . . . Barbara Ivanusich
Attorney . . . Russell Hildebrand
Finance Dir . . . Kim Sarkovich
Public Works . . . Kent Foster
Community Dev Dir . . . Terry Richardson
Building . . . Pete Guisasola
Police Chief . . . Mark Siemens
Emergency/Fire Dir . . . Bill Mikesell

Public Safety

Number of officers, 2007 . . . 55
Violent crimes, 2007 . . . 101
Property crimes, 2007 . . . 1,096
Arson, 2007 . . . 14

Public Library

Rocklin Library
Placer County Library System
5460 Fifth St
Rocklin, CA 95677
916-624-3133

Branch Librarian . . . Mary George

Library system statistics, FY 2007

Population served . . . 180,819
Internet terminals . . . 56
Annual users . . . 48,341

Per capita:

Operating income . . . $24.99
percent from local government . . . 85.7%
Operating expenditure . . . $24.01
Total materials . . . 1.96
Print holdings . . . 1.74
Visits per capita . . . 3.30

Housing & Construction

Housing Units

Total, 2008§ . . . 21,036
Single family units, attached . . . 990
Single family units, detached . . . 14,865
Multiple family units . . . 4,741
Mobile home units . . . 440
Occupied . . . 20,253
Vacancy rate . . . 3.7%
Median rent, 2000** . . . $900
Median SF home value, 2000** . . . $213,100

New Privately Owned Housing Units Authorized by Building Permit, 2007*

	Units	Construction Cost
Single	251	$87,032,931
Total	251	$87,032,931

Municipal Finance

(For local fiscal year ended in 2006)

Revenues

Total . . . $56,435,896
Taxes . . . 27,261,751
Special benefits assessment . . . 4,648,965
Licenses & permits . . . 2,073,824
Fines & forfeitures . . . 231,792
Revenues from use of money & property . . . 2,176,057
Intergovernmental . . . 5,172,187
Service charges . . . 5,893,582
Other revenues . . . 8,977,738
Other financing sources . . . 0

Expenditures

Total . . . $60,196,138
General government . . . 10,763,774
Public safety . . . 18,522,305
Transportation . . . 3,630,008
Community development . . . 14,306,432
Health . . . 0
Culture & leisure . . . 12,973,619
Other . . . 0

Local School District

(Data from School year 2007-08 except as noted)

Rocklin Unified
2615 Sierra Meadows Dr
Rocklin, CA 95677
(916) 624-2428

Superintendent . . . Kevin Brown
Grade plan . . . K-12
Number of schools . . . 18
Enrollment . . . 10,617
High school graduates, 2006-07 . . . 610
Dropout rate . . . 2.1%
Pupil/teacher ratio . . . 20.9
Average class size . . . 27.6
Students per computer . . . 3.6
Classrooms with internet . . . 556
Avg. Daily Attendance (ADA) . . . 9,979
Cost per ADA . . . $7,028
Avg. Teacher Salary . . . $58,438

California Achievement Tests 6th ed., 2008

(Pct scoring at or above 50th National Percentile Rank)

	Math	Reading	Language
Grade 3	74%	62%	65%
Grade 7	76%	76%	72%

Academic Performance Index, 2008

Number of students tested . . . 8,024
Number of valid scores . . . 7,665
2007 API (base) . . . 844
2008 API (growth) . . . 856

SAT Testing, 2006-07

Enrollment, Grade 12 . . . 668
Number taking test . . . 321
percent taking test . . . 48.1%
percent with total score 1,500+ . . . 30.70%

Average Scores:

Math	Verbal	Writing	Total
545	517	510	1,572

Federal No Child Left Behind, 2008

(Adequate Yearly Progress standards met)

	Participation Rate	Pct Proficient
ELA	Yes	Yes
Math	Yes	Yes

API criteria . . . Yes
Graduation rate . . . Yes
\# criteria met/possible . . . 38/38

Other school districts for this city

(see Appendix E for information on these districts)

None

Demographics & Socio-Economic Characteristics

(2000 Decennial Census, except as noted)

Population

1990* . . . 36,326
2000 . . . 42,236
Male . . . 20,474
Female . . . 21,762
Jan. 2008 (estimate)§ . . . 43,062
Persons per sq. mi. of land . . . 6,728.4

Race & Hispanic Origin, 2000

Race
White . . . 33,907
Black/African American . . . 833
North American Native . . . 329
Asian . . . 2,356
Pacific Islander . . . 177
Other Race . . . 2,417
Two or more races . . . 2,217
Hispanic origin, total . . . 5,731
Mexican . . . 4,009
Puerto Rican . . . 190
Cuban . . . 41
Other Hispanic . . . 1,491

Age & Nativity, 2000

Under 5 years . . . 2,656
18 years and over . . . 31,562
65 years and over . . . 3,416
85 years and over . . . 447
Median Age . . . 31.5
Native-born . . . 37,180
Foreign-born . . . 5,208

Educational Attainment, 2000

Population 25 years and over . . . 25,518
Less than 9th grade . . . 3.9%
High school grad or higher . . . 88.0%
Bachelor's degree or higher . . . 24.7%
Graduate degree . . . 6.7%

Income & Poverty, 1999

Per capita income . . . $23,035
Median household income . . . $51,942
Median family income . . . $61,420
Persons in poverty . . . 7.8%
H'holds receiving public assistance . . . 366
H'holds receiving social security . . . 3,025

Households, 2000

Total households . . . 15,503
With persons under 18 . . . 5,891
With persons over 65 . . . 2,663
Family households . . . 9,799
Single person households . . . 3,727
Persons per household . . . 2.65
Persons per family . . . 3.20

Household Population, 2008§§

Persons living in households . . . 41,961
Persons living in group quarters . . . 1,101
Persons per household . . . 2.6

Labor & Employment

Total civilian labor force, 2008§§ . . . 25,700
Unemployment rate, 2008 . . . 5.6%
Total civilian labor force, 2000 . . . 23,547

Employed persons 16 years and over by occupation, 2000

Managers & professionals . . . 6,935
Service occupations . . . 3,490
Sales & office occupations . . . 7,342
Farming, fishing & forestry . . . 12
Construction & maintenance . . . 2,289
Production & transportation . . . 2,549
Self-employed persons . . . 1,380

* US Census Bureau
** 2000 Decennial Census
§ California Department of Finance
§§ California Employment Development Dept

General Information

City of Rohnert Park
6750 Commerce Blvd
Rohnert Park, CA 94928
707-588-2200

Website . . . www.rpcity.org
Elevation . . . 100 ft.
Land Area (sq. miles) . . . 6.4
Water Area (sq. miles) . . . 0
Year of Incorporation . . . 1962
Government type . . . General law
Sales tax rate . . . 9.00%

Voters & Officials

Registered Voters, October 2008

Total . . . 19,192
Democrats . . . 9,716
Republicans . . . 4,447
Declined to state . . . 4,039

Legislative Districts

US Congressional . . . 6
State Senatorial . . . 3
State Assembly . . . 6

Local Officials, 2009

Mayor . . . Amie L. Breeze
City Manager . . . Daniel Schwarz (Int)
City Clerk . . . Judy Hauff
Attorney . . . Michelle Marchetta Kenyon
Admin Svcs Dir . . . Sandra M. Lipitz
Public Works . . . Darrin W. Jenkins
Community Dev Dir . . . Ron Bendorff
Building . . . Peter Bruck
Police Chief . . . Brian Masterson
Director of Public Safety . . Brian Masterson

Public Safety

Number of officers, 2007 . . . 74
Violent crimes, 2007 . . . 238
Property crimes, 2007 . . . 953
Arson, 2007 . . . 12

Public Library

Rohnert Park-Cotati Regional Library
Sonoma County Library System
6250 Lynne Conde Way
Rohnert Park, CA 95428
707-584-9121

Branch Librarian . . . Kathy Dennison

Library system statistics, FY 2007

Population served . . . 481,785
Internet terminals . . . 140
Annual users . . . 299,464

Per capita:

Operating income . . . $32.97
percent from local government . . . 87.7%
Operating expenditure . . . $30.18
Total materials . . . 1.60
Print holdings . . . 1.49
Visits per capita . . . 5.11

Housing & Construction

Housing Units

Total, 2008§ . . . 16,544
Single family units, attached . . . 1,701
Single family units, detached . . . 7,660
Multiple family units . . . 5,770
Mobile home units . . . 1,413
Occupied . . . 16,225
Vacancy rate . . . 1.9%
Median rent, 2000** . . . $903
Median SF home value, 2000** . . . $237,300

New Privately Owned Housing Units Authorized by Building Permit, 2007*

	Units	Construction Cost
Single	0	$0
Total	24	$3,160,303

Municipal Finance

(For local fiscal year ended in 2006)

Revenues

Total . . . $51,541,401
Taxes . . . 16,600,847
Special benefits assessment . . . 452,569
Licenses & permits . . . 330,292
Fines & forfeitures . . . 252,100
Revenues from use of money & property . . . 2,653,133
Intergovernmental . . . 2,004,563
Service charges . . . 25,162,367
Other revenues . . . 3,262,530
Other financing sources . . . 823,000

Expenditures

Total . . . $64,789,977
General government . . . 6,378,717
Public safety . . . 17,750,291
Transportation . . . 1,553,145
Community development . . . 2,682,786
Health . . . 23,559,863
Culture & leisure . . . 4,748,468
Other . . . 0

Local School District

(Data from School year 2007-08 except as noted)

Cotati-Rohnert Park Unified
5860 Labath Ave
Rohnert Park, CA 94928
(707) 792-4722

Superintendent . . . Barbara Vrankovich
Grade plan . . . K-12
Number of schools . . . 15
Enrollment . . . 6,655
High school graduates, 2006-07 . . . 477
Dropout rate . . . 3.7%
Pupil/teacher ratio . . . 21.9
Average class size . . . 26.1
Students per computer . . . 4.9
Classrooms with internet . . . 319
Avg. Daily Attendance (ADA) . . . 6,439
Cost per ADA . . . $8,498
Avg. Teacher Salary . . . $60,779

California Achievement Tests 6th ed., 2008

(Pct scoring at or above 50th National Percentile Rank)

	Math	Reading	Language
Grade 3	58%	43%	55%
Grade 7	50%	53%	52%

Academic Performance Index, 2008

Number of students tested . . . 5,067
Number of valid scores . . . 4,875
2007 API (base) . . . 743
2008 API (growth) . . . 750

SAT Testing, 2006-07

Enrollment, Grade 12 . . . 562
Number taking test . . . 141
percent taking test . . . 25.1%
percent with total score 1,500+ . . . 14.40%

Average Scores:

Math	Verbal	Writing	Total
529	504	505	1,538

Federal No Child Left Behind, 2008

(Adequate Yearly Progress standards met)

	Participation Rate	Pct Proficient
ELA	Yes	No
Math	Yes	Yes

API criteria . . . Yes
Graduation rate . . . Yes
\# criteria met/possible . . . 34/31

Other school districts for this city

(see Appendix E for information on these districts)

None

See Introduction for an explanation of all data sources.

Demographics & Socio-Economic Characteristics

(2000 Decennial Census, except as noted)

Population

1990* . . . 1,871
2000 . . . 1,871
Male . . . 917
Female . . . 954
Jan. 2008 (estimate)§ . . . 1,967
Persons per sq. mi. of land . . . 634.5

Race & Hispanic Origin, 2000

Race
White . . . 1,493
Black/African American . . . 38
North American Native . . . 0
Asian . . . 262
Pacific Islander . . . 9
Other Race . . . 22
Two or more races . . . 47
Hispanic origin, total . . . 85
Mexican . . . 37
Puerto Rican . . . 1
Cuban . . . 4
Other Hispanic . . . 43

Age & Nativity, 2000

Under 5 years . . . 69
18 years and over . . . 1,386
65 years and over . . . 413
85 years and over . . . 26
Median Age . . . 47.7
Native-born . . . 1,549
Foreign-born . . . 322

Educational Attainment, 2000

Population 25 years and over . . . 1,334
Less than 9th grade . . . 2.4%
High school grad or higher . . . 96.8%
Bachelor's degree or higher . . . 65.1%
Graduate degree . . . 32.5%

Income & Poverty, 1999

Per capita income . . . $111,031
Median household income . . . $200,001
Median family income . . . $200,001
Persons in poverty . . . 1.3%
H'holds receiving public assistance . . . 0
H'holds receiving social security . . . 242

Households, 2000

Total households . . . 645
With persons under 18 . . . 230
With persons over 65 . . . 269
Family households . . . 554
Single person households . . . 80
Persons per household . . . 2.90
Persons per family . . . 3.11

Household Population, 2008§§

Persons living in households . . . 1,967
Persons living in group quarters . . . 0
Persons per household . . . 3.0

Labor & Employment

Total civilian labor force, 2008§§ . . . 900
Unemployment rate, 2008 . . . 0.7%
Total civilian labor force, 2000 . . . 790

Employed persons 16 years and over by occupation, 2000

Managers & professionals . . . 576
Service occupations . . . 39
Sales & office occupations . . . 132
Farming, fishing & forestry . . . 0
Construction & maintenance . . . 29
Production & transportation . . . 8
Self-employed persons . . . 120

* US Census Bureau
** 2000 Decennial Census
§ California Department of Finance
§§ California Employment Development Dept

General Information

City of Rolling Hills
2 Portuguese Bend Rd
Rolling Hills, CA 90274
310-377-1521

Website . . . www.palosverdes.com/rh
Elevation . . . NA
Land Area (sq. miles) . . . 3.1
Water Area (sq. miles) . . . 0
Year of Incorporation . . . 1957
Government type . . . General law
Sales tax rate . . . 9.25%

Voters & Officials

Registered Voters, October 2008

Total . . . 1,434
Democrats . . . 281
Republicans . . . 881
Declined to state . . . 230

Legislative Districts

US Congressional . . . 46
State Senatorial . . . 25
State Assembly . . . 54

Local Officials, 2009

Mayor . . . Thomas F. Heinsheimer
Manager . . . Anton Dahlerbruch
City Clerk . . . Anton Dahlerbruch
Attorney . . . Michael Jenkins
Finance Dir . . . James Walker
Public Works . . . NA
Planning/Dev Dir . . . Yolanta Schwartz
Building . . . NA
Police Chief . . . (County)
Fire/Emergency Mgmt . . . (County)

Public Safety

Number of officers, 2007 . . . NA
Violent crimes, 2007 . . . 0
Property crimes, 2007 . . . 9
Arson, 2007 . . . 0

Public Library

Peninsula Center Library
Palos Verdes Library District
701 Silver Spur Rd
Rolling Hills Estates, CA 90274
310-377-9584

Director . . . Katherine Gould

Library system statistics, FY 2007

Population served . . . 67,286
Internet terminals . . . 34
Annual users . . . 53,850

Per capita:

Operating income . . . $92.15
percent from local government . . . 84.1%
Operating expenditure . . . $85.75
Total materials . . . 3.52
Print holdings . . . 3.09
Visits per capita . . . 9.36

Housing & Construction

Housing Units

Total, 2008§ . . . 696
Single family units, attached . . . 7
Single family units, detached . . . 689
Multiple family units . . . 0
Mobile home units . . . 0
Occupied . . . 655
Vacancy rate . . . 5.9%
Median rent, 2000** . . . $2,001
Median SF home value, 2000** . . $1,000,001

New Privately Owned Housing Units Authorized by Building Permit, 2007*

	Units	Construction Cost
Single	NA	NA
Total	NA	NA

Municipal Finance

(For local fiscal year ended in 2006)

Revenues

Total . . . $2,450,193
Taxes . . . 922,551
Special benefits assessment . . . 1,450
Licenses & permits . . . 373,700
Fines & forfeitures . . . 12,166
Revenues from use of money & property . . . 255,621
Intergovernmental . . . 152,553
Service charges . . . 732,152
Other revenues . . . 0
Other financing sources . . . 0

Expenditures

Total . . . $2,185,453
General government . . . 645,504
Public safety . . . 427,993
Transportation . . . 117,721
Community development . . . 343,797
Health . . . 626,281
Culture & leisure . . . 18,078
Other . . . 0

Local School District

(Data from School year 2007-08 except as noted)

Palos Verdes Peninsula Unified
3801 Via la Selva
Palos Verdes Estates, CA 90274
(310) 378-9966

Superintendent . . . Walker Williams
Grade plan . . . K-12
Number of schools . . . 17
Enrollment . . . 12,000
High school graduates, 2006-07 . . . 1,034
Dropout rate . . . 0.1%
Pupil/teacher ratio . . . 22.4
Average class size . . . 25.9
Students per computer . . . 4.5
Classrooms with internet . . . 602
Avg. Daily Attendance (ADA) . . . 11,751
Cost per ADA . . . $8,162
Avg. Teacher Salary . . . $67,734

California Achievement Tests 6th ed., 2008

(Pct scoring at or above 50th National Percentile Rank)

	Math	Reading	Language
Grade 3	89%	75%	81%
Grade 7	85%	80%	79%

Academic Performance Index, 2008

Number of students tested . . . 9,415
Number of valid scores . . . 9,216
2007 API (base) . . . 899
2008 API (growth) . . . 904

SAT Testing, 2006-07

Enrollment, Grade 12 . . . 1,046
Number taking test . . . 905
percent taking test . . . 86.5%
percent with total score 1,500+ . . . 66.40%

Average Scores:

Math	Verbal	Writing	Total
600	556	568	1,724

Federal No Child Left Behind, 2008

(Adequate Yearly Progress standards met)

	Participation Rate	Pct Proficient
ELA	Yes	Yes
Math	Yes	Yes

API criteria . . . Yes
Graduation rate . . . Yes
\# criteria met/possible . . . 38/38

Other school districts for this city

(see Appendix E for information on these districts)

None

See Introduction for an explanation of all data sources.

Demographics & Socio-Economic Characteristics

(2000 Decennial Census, except as noted)

Population

1990* . . . 7,789
2000 . . . 7,676
Male . . . 3,727
Female . . . 3,949
Jan. 2008 (estimate)§ . . . 8,185
Persons per sq. mi. of land . . . 2,273.6

Race & Hispanic Origin, 2000

Race
White . . . 5,673
Black/African American . . . 89
North American Native . . . 25
Asian . . . 1,557
Pacific Islander . . . 6
Other Race . . . 76
Two or more races . . . 250
Hispanic origin, total . . . 366
Mexican . . . 203
Puerto Rican . . . 10
Cuban . . . 18
Other Hispanic . . . 135

Age & Nativity, 2000

Under 5 years . . . 385
18 years and over . . . 5,809
65 years and over . . . 1,453
85 years and over . . . 72
Median Age . . . 44.9
Native-born . . . 6,211
Foreign-born . . . 1,458

Educational Attainment, 2000

Population 25 years and over . . . 5,287
Less than 9th grade . . . 0.5%
High school grad or higher . . . 96.9%
Bachelor's degree or higher . . . 60.8%
Graduate degree . . . 28.5%

Income & Poverty, 1999

Per capita income . . . $51,849
Median household income . . . $109,010
Median family income . . . $119,974
Persons in poverty . . . 1.7%
H'holds receiving public assistance . . . 8
H'holds receiving social security . . . 879

Households, 2000

Total households . . . 2,806
With persons under 18 . . . 998
With persons over 65 . . . 976
Family households . . . 2,334
Single person households . . . 420
Persons per household . . . 2.73
Persons per family . . . 3.02

Household Population, 2008§§

Persons living in households . . . 8,173
Persons living in group quarters . . . 12
Persons per household . . . 2.8

Labor & Employment

Total civilian labor force, 2008§§ . . . 4,100
Unemployment rate, 2008 . . . 1.9%
Total civilian labor force, 2000 . . . 3,559

Employed persons 16 years and over by occupation, 2000

Managers & professionals . . . 2,242
Service occupations . . . 198
Sales & office occupations . . . 760
Farming, fishing & forestry . . . 0
Construction & maintenance . . . 98
Production & transportation . . . 185
Self-employed persons . . . 492

* US Census Bureau
** 2000 Decennial Census
§ California Department of Finance
§§ California Employment Development Dept

General Information

City of Rolling Hills Estates
4045 Palos Verdes Dr N
Rolling Hills Estates, CA 90274
310-377-1577

Website . . . ci.rolling-hills-estates.ca.us
Elevation . . . 400 ft.
Land Area (sq. miles) . . . 3.6
Water Area (sq. miles) . . . 0
Year of Incorporation . . . 1957
Government type . . . General law
Sales tax rate . . . 9.25%

Voters & Officials

Registered Voters, October 2008

Total . . . 5,612
Democrats . . . 1,600
Republicans . . . 2,957
Declined to state . . . 869

Legislative Districts

US Congressional . . . 46
State Senatorial . . . 25
State Assembly . . . 54

Local Officials, 2009

Mayor . . . Judy Mitchell
Manager . . . Douglas Prichard
City Clerk . . . Hope Nolan (Dep)
Attorney . . . Kristin Pelletier
Finance Dir . . . Mike Whitehead
Public Works . . . Sam Wise
Planning/Dev Dir . . . David Wahba
Building . . . NA
Police Chief . . . (County)
Fire/Emergency Mgmt . . . (County)

Public Safety

Number of officers, 2007 . . . NA
Violent crimes, 2007 . . . 18
Property crimes, 2007 . . . 183
Arson, 2007 . . . 1

Public Library

Peninsula Center Library
Palos Verdes Library District
701 Silver Spur Rd
Rolling Hills Estates, CA 90274
310-377-9584

Director . . . Katherine Gould

Library system statistics, FY 2007

Population served . . . 67,286
Internet terminals . . . 34
Annual users . . . 53,850

Per capita:

Operating income . . . $92.15
percent from local government . . . 84.1%
Operating expenditure . . . $85.75
Total materials . . . 3.52
Print holdings . . . 3.09
Visits per capita . . . 9.36

Housing & Construction

Housing Units

Total, 2008§ . . . 2,964
Single family units, attached . . . 565
Single family units, detached . . . 2,306
Multiple family units . . . 89
Mobile home units . . . 4
Occupied . . . 2,889
Vacancy rate . . . 2.5%
Median rent, 2000** . . . $2,001
Median SF home value, 2000** . . . $637,800

New Privately Owned Housing Units Authorized by Building Permit, 2007*

	Units	Construction Cost
Single	NA	NA
Total	NA	NA

Municipal Finance

(For local fiscal year ended in 2006)

Revenues

Total . . . $7,790,812
Taxes . . . 4,753,837
Special benefits assessment . . . 0
Licenses & permits . . . 1,012,309
Fines & forfeitures . . . 104,315
Revenues from use of money & property . . . 216,136
Intergovernmental . . . 440,709
Service charges . . . 1,114,081
Other revenues . . . 149,425
Other financing sources . . . 0

Expenditures

Total . . . $8,227,408
General government . . . 1,633,738
Public safety . . . 1,742,616
Transportation . . . 1,178,084
Community development . . . 1,380,114
Health . . . 33,480
Culture & leisure . . . 2,259,376
Other . . . 0

Local School District

(Data from School year 2007-08 except as noted)

Palos Verdes Peninsula Unified
3801 Via la Selva
Palos Verdes Estates, CA 90274
(310) 378-9966

Superintendent . . . Walker Williams
Grade plan . . . K-12
Number of schools . . . 17
Enrollment . . . 12,000
High school graduates, 2006-07 . . . 1,034
Dropout rate . . . 0.1%
Pupil/teacher ratio . . . 22.4
Average class size . . . 25.9
Students per computer . . . 4.5
Classrooms with internet . . . 602
Avg. Daily Attendance (ADA) . . . 11,751
Cost per ADA . . . $8,162
Avg. Teacher Salary . . . $67,734

California Achievement Tests 6th ed., 2008

(Pct scoring at or above 50th National Percentile Rank)

	Math	Reading	Language
Grade 3	89%	75%	81%
Grade 7	85%	80%	79%

Academic Performance Index, 2008

Number of students tested . . . 9,415
Number of valid scores . . . 9,216
2007 API (base) . . . 899
2008 API (growth) . . . 904

SAT Testing, 2006-07

Enrollment, Grade 12 . . . 1,046
Number taking test . . . 905
percent taking test . . . 86.5%
percent with total score 1,500+ . . . 66.40%

Average Scores:

Math	Verbal	Writing	Total
600	556	568	1,724

Federal No Child Left Behind, 2008

(Adequate Yearly Progress standards met)

	Participation Rate	Pct Proficient
ELA	Yes	Yes
Math	Yes	Yes

API criteria . . . Yes
Graduation rate . . . Yes
criteria met/possible . . . 38/38

Other school districts for this city

(see Appendix E for information on these districts)

None

See Introduction for an explanation of all data sources.

Demographics & Socio-Economic Characteristics

(2000 Decennial Census, except as noted)

Population

1990* . . . 51,638
2000 . . . 53,505
Male . . . 26,264
Female . . . 27,241
Jan. 2008 (estimate)§ . . . 57,422
Persons per sq. mi. of land . . . 11,259.2

Race & Hispanic Origin, 2000

Race
White . . . 14,217
Black/African American . . . 363
North American Native . . . 456
Asian . . . 26,090
Pacific Islander . . . 34
Other Race . . . 10,535
Two or more races . . . 1,810
Hispanic origin, total . . . 22,097
Mexican . . . 17,853
Puerto Rican . . . 124
Cuban . . . 193
Other Hispanic . . . 3,927

Age & Nativity, 2000

Under 5 years . . . 4,017
18 years and over . . . 38,776
65 years and over . . . 5,685
85 years and over . . . 631
Median Age . . . 32.3
Native-born . . . 23,256
Foreign-born . . . 30,024

Educational Attainment, 2000

Population 25 years and over . . . 32,879
Less than 9th grade . . . 29.7%
High school grad or higher . . . 53.2%
Bachelor's degree or higher . . . 12.9%
Graduate degree . . . 2.9%

Income & Poverty, 1999

Per capita income . . . $12,146
Median household income . . . $36,181
Median family income . . . $36,552
Persons in poverty . . . 22.5%
H'holds receiving public assistance . . . 1,516
H'holds receiving social security . . . 2,905

Households, 2000

Total households . . . 13,913
With persons under 18 . . . 7,122
With persons over 65 . . . 4,098
Family households . . . 11,628
Single person households . . . 1,759
Persons per household . . . 3.80
Persons per family . . . 4.11

Household Population, 2008§§

Persons living in households . . . 56,810
Persons living in group quarters . . . 612
Persons per household . . . 4.0

Labor & Employment

Total civilian labor force, 2008§§ . . . 25,400
Unemployment rate, 2008 . . . 6.6%
Total civilian labor force, 2000 . . . 21,881

Employed persons 16 years and over by occupation, 2000

Managers & professionals . . . 4,515
Service occupations . . . 3,683
Sales & office occupations . . . 5,583
Farming, fishing & forestry . . . 26
Construction & maintenance . . . 1,431
Production & transportation . . . 5,012
Self-employed persons . . . 1,278

* US Census Bureau
** 2000 Decennial Census
§ California Department of Finance
§§ California Employment Development Dept

General Information

City of Rosemead
8838 E Valley Blvd
PO Box 399
Rosemead, CA 91770
626-569-2100

Website . . . www.cityofrosemead.org
Elevation . . . 322 ft.
Land Area (sq. miles) . . . 5.1
Water Area (sq. miles) . . . 0
Year of Incorporation . . . 1959
Government type . . . General law
Sales tax rate . . . 9.25%

Voters & Officials

Registered Voters, October 2008

Total . . . 18,929
Democrats . . . 8,826
Republicans . . . 3,624
Declined to state . . . 5,588

Legislative Districts

US Congressional . . . 32
State Senatorial . . . 24
State Assembly . . . 49

Local Officials, 2009

Mayor . . . John Tran
City Manager . . . Oliver Chi
City Clerk . . . Gloria Molleda
Attorney . . . Bonifacio Bonny Garcia
Finance Dir . . . Steve Brisco
Public Works . . . NA
Planning Dir . . . (vacant)
Building . . . Jim Donovan
Police Chief . . . Richard Shaw
Fire/Emergency Mgmt . . . (County)

Public Safety

Number of officers, 2007 . . . NA
Violent crimes, 2007 . . . 252
Property crimes, 2007 . . . 1,393
Arson, 2007 . . . 3

Public Library

Rosemead Library
Los Angeles County Public Library System
8800 Valley Blvd
Rosemead, CA 91770
626-573-5220

Branch Librarian . . . Desiree Lee

Library system statistics, FY 2007

Population served . . . 3,673,313
Internet terminals . . . 749
Annual users . . . 3,748,771

Per capita:

Operating income . . . $30.06
percent from local government . . . 93.6%
Operating expenditure . . . $28.36
Total materials . . . 2.22
Print holdings . . . 1.97
Visits per capita . . . 3.25

Housing & Construction

Housing Units

Total, 2008§ . . . 14,702
Single family units, attached . . . 2,030
Single family units, detached . . . 9,996
Multiple family units . . . 2,272
Mobile home units . . . 404
Occupied . . . 14,259
Vacancy rate . . . 3.0%
Median rent, 2000** . . . $722
Median SF home value, 2000** . . . $182,200

New Privately Owned Housing Units Authorized by Building Permit, 2007*

	Units	Construction Cost
Single	63	$14,707,900
Total	79	$16,674,086

Municipal Finance

(For local fiscal year ended in 2006)

Revenues

Total . . . $23,745,174
Taxes . . . 12,756,017
Special benefits assessment . . . 631,654
Licenses & permits . . . 1,466,133
Fines & forfeitures . . . 807,939
Revenues from use of money & property . . . 987,086
Intergovernmental . . . 4,678,945
Service charges . . . 705,086
Other revenues . . . 1,712,314
Other financing sources . . . 0

Expenditures

Total . . . $21,223,244
General government . . . 2,463,902
Public safety . . . 6,825,619
Transportation . . . 3,357,846
Community development . . . 4,121,663
Health . . . 53,059
Culture & leisure . . . 4,401,155
Other . . . 0

Local School District

(Data from School year 2007-08 except as noted)

El Monte Union High
3537 Johnson Ave
El Monte, CA 91731
(626) 444-9005

Superintendent . . . Kathy Furnald
Grade plan . . . 9-12
Number of schools . . . 7
Enrollment . . . 10,614
High school graduates, 2006-07 . . . 1,665
Dropout rate . . . 1.8%
Pupil/teacher ratio . . . 23.4
Average class size . . . 27.3
Students per computer . . . 2.8
Classrooms with internet . . . 529
Avg. Daily Attendance (ADA) . . . 10,804
Cost per ADA . . . $8,087
Avg. Teacher Salary . . . $68,066

California Achievement Tests 6th ed., 2008

(Pct scoring at or above 50th National Percentile Rank)

	Math	Reading	Language
Grade 3	NA	NA	NA
Grade 7	NA	NA	NA

Academic Performance Index, 2008

Number of students tested . . . 7,727
Number of valid scores . . . 7,301
2007 API (base) . . . 648
2008 API (growth) . . . 670

SAT Testing, 2006-07

Enrollment, Grade 12 . . . 2,388
Number taking test . . . 700
percent taking test . . . 29.3%
percent with total score 1,500+ . . . 9.70%

Average Scores:

Math	Verbal	Writing	Total
492	450	447	1,389

Federal No Child Left Behind, 2008

(Adequate Yearly Progress standards met)

	Participation Rate	Pct Proficient
ELA	Yes	No
Math	Yes	No

API criteria . . . Yes
Graduation rate . . . Yes
criteria met/possible . . . 27/24

Other school districts for this city

(see Appendix E for information on these districts)

Garvey Elem, Rosemead Elem

See Introduction for an explanation of all data sources.

Demographics & Socio-Economic Characteristics†

(2007 American Community Survey, except as noted)

Population

1990*	44,685
2007	114,958
Male	55,749
Female	59,209
Jan. 2008 (estimate)§	109,154
Persons per sq. mi. of land	3,578.8

Race & Hispanic Origin, 2007

Race	
White	94,580
Black/African American	2,771
North American Native	490
Asian	8,033
Pacific Islander	48
Other Race	4,823
Two or more races	4,213
Hispanic origin, total	16,933
Mexican	10,198
Puerto Rican	975
Cuban	336
Other Hispanic	5,424

Age & Nativity, 2007

Under 5 years	8,478
18 years and over	87,795
65 years and over	15,013
85 years and over	2,470
Median Age	34.8
Native-born	101,865
Foreign-born	13,093

Educational Attainment, 2007

Population 25 years and over	78,664
Less than 9th grade	3.1%
High school grad or higher	92.5%
Bachelor's degree or higher	36.3%
Graduate degree	10.5%

Income & Poverty, 2007

Per capita income	$33,373
Median household income	$68,273
Median family income	$84,863
Persons in poverty	6.0%
H'holds receiving public assistance	795
H'holds receiving social security	11,403

Households, 2007

Total households	43,733
With persons under 18	16,462
With persons over 65	10,289
Family households	29,163
Single person households	11,727
Persons per household	2.60
Persons per family	3.13

Household Population, 2008§§

Persons living in households	108,100
Persons living in group quarters	1,054
Persons per household	2.5

Labor & Employment

Total civilian labor force, 2008§§	55,400
Unemployment rate, 2008	6.6%
Total civilian labor force, 2000*	38,804

Employed persons 16 years and over by occupation, 2007

Managers & professionals	22,345
Service occupations	7,946
Sales & office occupations	18,346
Farming, fishing & forestry	156
Construction & maintenance	4,165
Production & transportation	4,414
Self-employed persons	3,772

† see Appendix D for 2000 Decennial Census Data
* US Census Bureau
** 2007 American Community Survey
§ California Department of Finance
§§ California Employment Development Dept

General Information

City of Roseville
311 Vernon Street
Roseville, CA 95678
530-774-5200

Website	www.roseville.ca.us
Elevation	160 ft.
Land Area (sq. miles)	30.5
Water Area (sq. miles)	0
Year of Incorporation	1909
Government type	Chartered
Sales tax rate	8.25%

Voters & Officials

Registered Voters, October 2008

Total	62,852
Democrats	19,412
Republicans	30,138
Declined to state	11,483

Legislative Districts

US Congressional	4
State Senatorial	1
State Assembly	4, 5

Local Officials, 2009

Mayor	Gina Garbolino
Manager	W. Craig Robinson
City Clerk	Sonia Orozco
Attorney	Brita McNay
Finance Dir	Russ Branson
Public Works	Rob Jensen
Planning/Dev Dir	Paul Richardson
Building	Gene Paolini
Police Chief	Michael Blair
Fire Chief	Ken Wagner

Public Safety

Number of officers, 2007	128
Violent crimes, 2007	387
Property crimes, 2007	3,960
Arson, 2007	9

Public Library

Roseville Public Library
225 Taylor St
Roseville, CA 95678
916-774-5221

Director	Dianne Bish

Library statistics, FY 2007

Population served	106,266
Internet terminals	658
Annual users	909,745

Per capita:

Operating income	$35.37
percent from local government	90.6%
Operating expenditure	$32.03
Total materials	1.45
Print holdings	1.31
Visits per capita	2.18

Housing & Construction

Housing Units

Total, 2008§	45,230
Single family units, attached	1,082
Single family units, detached	33,427
Multiple family units	10,178
Mobile home units	543
Occupied	43,612
Vacancy rate	3.6%
Median rent, 2007**	$1,083
Median SF home value, 2007**	$447,100

New Privately Owned Housing Units Authorized by Building Permit, 2007*

	Units	Construction Cost
Single	1,050	$233,672,844
Total	1,153	$243,717,894

Municipal Finance

(For local fiscal year ended in 2006)

Revenues

Total	$479,967,871
Taxes	86,383,284
Special benefits assessment	4,392,791
Licenses & permits	2,020,467
Fines & forfeitures	1,345,751
Revenues from use of money & property	17,964,840
Intergovernmental	11,424,806
Service charges	191,620,438
Other revenues	162,575,729
Other financing sources	2,239,765

Expenditures

Total	$548,172,518
General government	32,398,046
Public safety	46,048,164
Transportation	98,912,009
Community development	26,854,721
Health	49,493,894
Culture & leisure	27,413,425
Other	0

Local School District

(Data from School year 2007-08 except as noted)

Roseville Joint Union High
1750 Cirby Way
Roseville, CA 95661
(916) 786-2051

Superintendent	Tony Monetti
Grade plan	9-12
Number of schools	6
Enrollment	9,056
High school graduates, 2006-07	1,739
Dropout rate	1.8%
Pupil/teacher ratio	22.0
Average class size	26.7
Students per computer	4.3
Classrooms with internet	417
Avg. Daily Attendance (ADA)	8,694
Cost per ADA	$7,803
Avg. Teacher Salary	$67,749

California Achievement Tests 6th ed., 2008

(Pct scoring at or above 50th National Percentile Rank)

	Math	Reading	Language
Grade 3	NA	NA	NA
Grade 7	NA	NA	NA

Academic Performance Index, 2008

Number of students tested	6,830
Number of valid scores	6,594
2007 API (base)	764
2008 API (growth)	786

SAT Testing, 2006-07

Enrollment, Grade 12	2,089
Number taking test	896
percent taking test	42.9%
percent with total score 1,500+	25.70%

Average Scores:

Math	Verbal	Writing	Total
538	517	516	1,571

Federal No Child Left Behind, 2008

(Adequate Yearly Progress standards met)

	Participation Rate	Pct Proficient
ELA	Yes	No
Math	Yes	No

API criteria	Yes
Graduation rate	Yes
# criteria met/possible	30/28

Other school districts for this city

(see Appendix E for information on these districts)

Roseville City Elem, Dry Creek Joint Elem, Eureka Union Elem

See Introduction for an explanation of all data sources.

Demographics & Socio-Economic Characteristics

(2000 Decennial Census, except as noted)

Population

1990* . . . 2,123
2000 . . . 2,329
Male . . . 1,134
Female . . . 1,195
Jan. 2008 (estimate)§ . . . 2,393
Persons per sq. mi. of land . . . 1,495.6

Race & Hispanic Origin, 2000

Race
White . . . 2,238
Black/African American . . . 3
North American Native . . . 2
Asian . . . 33
Pacific Islander . . . 4
Other Race . . . 9
Two or more races . . . 40
Hispanic origin, total . . . 54
Mexican . . . 26
Puerto Rican . . . 0
Cuban . . . 0
Other Hispanic . . . 28

Age & Nativity, 2000

Under 5 years . . . 169
18 years and over . . . 1,626
65 years and over . . . 288
85 years and over . . . 24
Median Age . . . 42.5
Native-born . . . 2,145
Foreign-born . . . 165

Educational Attainment, 2000

Population 25 years and over . . . 1,527
Less than 9th grade . . . 2.9%
High school grad or higher . . . 91.9%
Bachelor's degree or higher . . . 74.0%
Graduate degree . . . 36.5%

Income & Poverty, 1999

Per capita income . . . $51,150
Median household income . . . $102,015
Median family income . . . $102,593
Persons in poverty . . . 8.4%
H'holds receiving public assistance . . . 0
H'holds receiving social security . . . 157

Households, 2000

Total households . . . 761
With persons under 18 . . . 349
With persons over 65 . . . 200
Family households . . . 626
Single person households . . . 97
Persons per household . . . 2.94
Persons per family . . . 3.21

Household Population, 2008§§

Persons living in households . . . 2,299
Persons living in group quarters . . . 94
Persons per household . . . 3.0

Labor & Employment

Total civilian labor force, 2008§§ . . . NA
Unemployment rate, 2008 . . . NA
Total civilian labor force, 2000 . . . 928

Employed persons 16 years and over by occupation, 2000

Managers & professionals . . . 649
Service occupations . . . 40
Sales & office occupations . . . 186
Farming, fishing & forestry . . . 0
Construction & maintenance . . . 25
Production & transportation . . . 20
Self-employed persons . . . 185

* US Census Bureau
** 2000 Decennial Census
§ California Department of Finance
§§ California Employment Development Dept

General Information

Town of Ross
PO Box 320
Ross, CA 94957
415-453-1453

Website . . . www.townofross.org
Elevation . . . 23 ft.
Land Area (sq. miles) . . . 1.6
Water Area (sq. miles) . . . 0
Year of Incorporation . . . 1908
Government type . . . General law
Sales tax rate . . . 9.00%

Voters & Officials

Registered Voters, October 2008

Total . . . 1,704
Democrats . . . 744
Republicans . . . 550
Declined to state . . . 363

Legislative Districts

US Congressional . . . 6
State Senatorial . . . 3
State Assembly . . . 6

Local Officials, 2009

Mayor . . . William R. Cahill
Manager . . . Gary Broad
City Clerk . . . NA
Attorney . . . Hadden Roth
Finance Dir . . . NA
Public Works . . . Mel Jarjoura
Planning/Dev Dir . . . Gary Broad
Building . . . Mel Jarjoura
Police Chief . . . James Reis
Fire Chief . . . Tom Vallee

Public Safety

Number of officers, 2007 . . . 8
Violent crimes, 2007 . . . 0
Property crimes, 2007 . . . 20
Arson, 2007 . . . NA

Public Library

Served by County Library

Library system statistics, FY 2007

Population served . . . NA
Internet terminals . . . NA
Annual users . . . NA

Per capita:

Operating income . . . NA
percent from local government . . . NA
Operating expenditure . . . NA
Total materials . . . NA
Print holdings . . . NA
Visits per capita . . . NA

Housing & Construction

Housing Units

Total, 2008§ . . . 819
Single family units, attached . . . 0
Single family units, detached . . . 799
Multiple family units . . . 12
Mobile home units . . . 8
Occupied . . . 775
Vacancy rate . . . 5.4%
Median rent, 2000** . . . $2,001
Median SF home value, 2000** . . $1,000,001

New Privately Owned Housing Units Authorized by Building Permit, 2007*

	Units	Construction Cost
Single	0	$0
Total	0	$0

Municipal Finance

(For local fiscal year ended in 2006)

Revenues

Total . . . $5,323,057
Taxes . . . 3,427,626
Special benefits assessment . . . 100,000
Licenses & permits . . . 761,458
Fines & forfeitures . . . 35,524
Revenues from use of money & property . . . 388,693
Intergovernmental . . . 243,376
Service charges . . . 198,235
Other revenues . . . 168,145
Other financing sources . . . 0

Expenditures

Total . . . $4,972,327
General government . . . 661,609
Public safety . . . 3,026,388
Transportation . . . 611,851
Community development . . . 672,479
Health . . . 0
Culture & leisure . . . 0
Other . . . 0

Local School District

(Data from School year 2007-08 except as noted)

Tamalpais Union High
PO Box 605
Larkspur, CA 94977
(415) 945-3720

Superintendent . . . Laurie Kimbrel
Grade plan . . . 9-12
Number of schools . . . 5
Enrollment . . . 3,889
High school graduates, 2006-07 . . . 959
Dropout rate . . . 0.8%
Pupil/teacher ratio . . . 17.4
Average class size . . . 24.4
Students per computer . . . 2.6
Classrooms with internet . . . 232
Avg. Daily Attendance (ADA) . . . 3,715
Cost per ADA . . . $13,492
Avg. Teacher Salary . . . $81,923

California Achievement Tests 6th ed., 2008

(Pct scoring at or above 50th National Percentile Rank)

	Math	Reading	Language
Grade 3	NA	NA	NA
Grade 7	NA	NA	NA

Academic Performance Index, 2008

Number of students tested . . . 2,800
Number of valid scores . . . 2,766
2007 API (base) . . . 848
2008 API (growth) . . . 855

SAT Testing, 2006-07

Enrollment, Grade 12 . . . 997
Number taking test . . . 730
percent taking test . . . 73.2%
percent with total score 1,500+ . . . 58.30%

Average Scores:

Math	Verbal	Writing	Total
574	574	574	1,722

Federal No Child Left Behind, 2008

(Adequate Yearly Progress standards met)

	Participation Rate	Pct Proficient
ELA	Yes	Yes
Math	Yes	Yes

API criteria . . . Yes
Graduation rate . . . Yes
criteria met/possible . . . 10/10

Other school districts for this city

(see Appendix E for information on these districts)

Ross Elem

See Introduction for an explanation of all data sources.

Demographics & Socio-Economic Characteristics†

(2007 American Community Survey, except as noted)

Population

1990* 369,365
2007 451,404
  Male 219,274
  Female 232,130
Jan. 2008 (estimate)§ 475,743
  Persons per sq. mi. of land 4,894.5

Race & Hispanic Origin, 2007

Race
  White 225,330
  Black/African American 62,406
  North American Native 4,451
  Asian 83,891
  Pacific Islander 5,971
  Other Race 44,123
  Two or more races 25,232
Hispanic origin, total 110,669
  Mexican 92,615
  Puerto Rican 3,422
  Cuban 199
  Other Hispanic 14,433

Age & Nativity, 2007

Under 5 years 32,602
18 years and over 339,374
65 years and over 49,067
85 years and over 7,206
  Median Age 33.6
Native-born 346,299
Foreign-born 105,105

Educational Attainment, 2007

Population 25 years and over 292,350
Less than 9th grade 10.9%
High school grad or higher 80.7%
Bachelor's degree or higher 28.9%
Graduate degree 10.1%

Income & Poverty, 2007

Per capita income $25,536
Median household income $49,849
Median family income $55,762
Persons in poverty 14.3%
H'holds receiving public assistance 9,004
H'holds receiving social security 38,065

Households, 2007

Total households 170,358
  With persons under 18 57,643
  With persons over 65 35,327
  Family households 99,561
  Single person households 54,626
Persons per household 2.60
Persons per family 3.37

Household Population, 2008§§

Persons living in households 466,851
Persons living in group quarters 8,892
Persons per household 2.6

Labor & Employment

Total civilian labor force, 2008§§ 217,500
  Unemployment rate, 2008 .... 8.5%
Total civilian labor force, 2000* 184,330

Employed persons 16 years and over by occupation, 2007

  Managers & professionals 76,995
  Service occupations 39,284
  Sales & office occupations 56,114
  Farming, fishing & forestry 687
  Construction & maintenance 17,294
  Production & transportation 18,769
  Self-employed persons 14,042

† see Appendix D for 2000 Decennial Census Data
* US Census Bureau
** 2007 American Community Survey
§ California Department of Finance
§§ California Employment Development Dept

General Information

City of Sacramento
915 I Street
1st Floor
Sacramento, CA 95814
916-808-7200

Website .... www.cityofsacramento.org
Elevation .... 25 ft.
Land Area (sq. miles) 97.2
Water Area (sq. miles) 2.1
Year of Incorporation 1850
Government type .... Chartered
Sales tax rate 8.75%

Voters & Officials

Registered Voters, October 2008

Total 216,220
  Democrats 118,144
  Republicans 44,463
  Declined to state 43,266

Legislative Districts

US Congressional 5
State Senatorial 6
State Assembly 5, 9, 10

Local Officials, 2009

Mayor .... Kevin Johnson
Manager .... Ray Kerridge
City Clerk .... Shirley Concolino
Attorney .... Ilene Teichert
Finance Dir .... Leyne Milstein
Public Works .... NA
Planning/Dev Dir .... NA
Building .... NA
Police Chief .... Rick Braziel
Fire Chief .... Joe Cherry

Public Safety

Number of officers, 2007 712
Violent crimes, 2007 5,128
Property crimes, 2007 24,399
Arson, 2007 281

Public Library

Sacramento Central Library
Sacramento Public Library System
828 I St
Sacramento, CA 95814
916-264-2770

Director .... Anne Marie Gold

Library system statistics, FY 2007

Population served 1,335,969
Internet terminals 49
  Annual users 27,435

Per capita:

Operating income $25.83
  percent from local government 91.0%
Operating expenditure $23.08
Total materials 1.57
Print holdings 1.45
Visits per capita 1.18

Housing & Construction

Housing Units

Total, 2008§ 192,371
  Single family units, attached 12,959
  Single family units, detached 113,418
  Multiple family units 62,308
  Mobile home units 3,686
  Occupied 181,538
  Vacancy rate 5.6%
Median rent, 2007** $923
Median SF home value, 2007** $354,200

New Privately Owned Housing Units Authorized by Building Permit, 2007*

	Units	Construction Cost
Single	1,337	$229,913,184
Total	1,973	$303,875,391

Municipal Finance

(For local fiscal year ended in 2006)

Revenues

Total $1,100,606,000
Taxes 311,809,000
Special benefits assessment 21,616,000
Licenses & permits 15,953,000
Fines & forfeitures 8,724,000
Revenues from use of
  money & property 21,103,000
Intergovernmental 104,834,000
Service charges 288,677,000
Other revenues 60,677,000
Other financing sources 267,213,000

Expenditures

Total $923,235,000
General government 122,892,000
Public safety 270,860,000
Transportation 152,065,000
Community development 38,214,000
Health 94,275,000
Culture & leisure 122,015,000
Other 0

Local School District

(Data from School year 2007-08 except as noted)

Sacramento City Unified
PO Box 246870
Sacramento, CA 95824
(916) 643-9000

Superintendent .... Susan Miller
Grade plan K-12
Number of schools 90
Enrollment 48,446
High school graduates, 2006-07 2,406
Dropout rate 5.9%
Pupil/teacher ratio 20.2
Average class size 24.1
Students per computer 3.8
Classrooms with internet 2,440
Avg. Daily Attendance (ADA) 44,024
  Cost per ADA $8,929
Avg. Teacher Salary $60,464

California Achievement Tests 6th ed., 2008

(Pct scoring at or above 50th National Percentile Rank)

	Math	Reading	Language
Grade 3	53%	30%	40%
Grade 7	52%	45%	44%

Academic Performance Index, 2008

Number of students tested 34,999
Number of valid scores 32,019
2007 API (base) 719
2008 API (growth) 734

SAT Testing, 2006-07

Enrollment, Grade 12 3,111
Number taking test 1,149
  percent taking test 36.9%
  percent with total score 1,500+ 12.70%

Average Scores:

Math	Verbal	Writing	Total
478	458	455	1,391

Federal No Child Left Behind, 2008

(Adequate Yearly Progress standards met)

	Participation Rate	Pct Proficient
ELA	Yes	No
Math	Yes	Yes

API criteria .... Yes
Graduation rate .... Yes
criteria met/possible 46/44

Other school districts for this city

(see Appendix E for information on these districts)

Elk Grove Unified, Natomas Unified, Robla Elem, San Juan Unified, Twin Rivers Unified

See Introduction for an explanation of all data sources.

Demographics & Socio-Economic Characteristics

(2000 Decennial Census, except as noted)

Population

1990* . . . 4,990
2000 . . . 5,950
  Male . . . 2,733
  Female . . . 3,217
Jan. 2008 (estimate)§ . . . 5,924
  Persons per sq. mi. of land . . . 1,260.4

Race & Hispanic Origin, 2000

Race
  White . . . 4,900
  Black/African American . . . 26
  North American Native . . . 27
  Asian . . . 42
  Pacific Islander . . . 10
  Other Race . . . 786
  Two or more races . . . 159
Hispanic origin, total . . . 1,691
  Mexican . . . 1,494
  Puerto Rican . . . 14
  Cuban . . . 5
  Other Hispanic . . . 178

Age & Nativity, 2000

Under 5 years . . . 359
18 years and over . . . 4,456
65 years and over . . . 1,028
85 years and over . . . 221
  Median Age . . . 39.9
Native-born . . . 4,823
Foreign-born . . . 1,128

Educational Attainment, 2000

Population 25 years and over . . . 4,032
Less than 9th grade . . . 8.5%
High school grad or higher . . . 81.5%
Bachelor's degree or higher . . . 39.9%
Graduate degree . . . 11.1%

Income & Poverty, 1999

Per capita income . . . $31,971
Median household income . . . $58,902
Median family income . . . $68,831
Persons in poverty . . . 6.3%
H'holds receiving public assistance . . . 30
H'holds receiving social security . . . 726

Households, 2000

Total households . . . 2,380
  With persons under 18 . . . 777
  With persons over 65 . . . 757
  Family households . . . 1,482
  Single person households . . . 752
Persons per household . . . 2.48
Persons per family . . . 3.19

Household Population, 2008§§

Persons living in households . . . 5,872
Persons living in group quarters . . . 52
Persons per household . . . 2.4

Labor & Employment

Total civilian labor force, 2008§§ . . . 3,600
  Unemployment rate, 2008 . . . 5.1%
Total civilian labor force, 2000 . . . 2,922

Employed persons 16 years and over by occupation, 2000

  Managers & professionals . . . 1,010
  Service occupations . . . 525
  Sales & office occupations . . . 636
  Farming, fishing & forestry . . . 89
  Construction & maintenance . . . 170
  Production & transportation . . . 367
  Self-employed persons . . . 408

* US Census Bureau
** 2000 Decennial Census
§ California Department of Finance
§§ California Employment Development Dept

General Information

City of St. Helena
1480 Main St
St. Helena, CA 94574
707-967-2792

Website . . . www.sthelenacity.com
Elevation . . . 257 ft.
Land Area (sq. miles) . . . 4.7
Water Area (sq. miles) . . . 0
Year of Incorporation . . . 1876
Government type . . . General law
Sales tax rate . . . 8.75%

Voters & Officials

Registered Voters, October 2008

Total . . . 3,353
  Democrats . . . 1,598
  Republicans . . . 958
  Declined to state . . . 668

Legislative Districts

US Congressional . . . 1
State Senatorial . . . 2
State Assembly . . . 7

Local Officials, 2009

Mayor . . . Del Britton
Manager . . . Bert Johansson
City Clerk . . . Delia Guijosa
Attorney . . . Amy Valukevich
Finance Dir . . . Karen Scalabrini
Public Works . . . John Ferons (Int)
Planning/Dev Dir . . . Carol Poole
Building . . . Leo DePaula
Police Chief . . . Monty Castillo
Emergency/Fire Dir . . . Kevin Twohey

Public Safety

Number of officers, 2007 . . . 13
Violent crimes, 2007 . . . 8
Property crimes, 2007 . . . 89
Arson, 2007 . . . 1

Public Library

St. Helena Public Library
1492 Library Ln
St. Helena, CA 94574
707-963-5244

Director . . . Jennifer Baker

Library statistics, FY 2007

Population served . . . 5,993
Internet terminals . . . 23
  Annual users . . . 30,972

Per capita:

Operating income . . . $167.59
  percent from local government . . . 87.0%
Operating expenditure . . . $167.59
Total materials . . . 15.04
Print holdings . . . 11.42
Visits per capita . . . 24.06

Housing & Construction

Housing Units

Total, 2008§ . . . 2,745
  Single family units, attached . . . 215
  Single family units, detached . . . 1,691
  Multiple family units . . . 694
  Mobile home units . . . 145
  Occupied . . . 2,414
  Vacancy rate . . . 12.1%
Median rent, 2000** . . . $826
Median SF home value, 2000** . . . $453,600

New Privately Owned Housing Units Authorized by Building Permit, 2007*

	Units	Construction Cost
Single	5	$1,214,275
Total	5	$1,214,275

Municipal Finance

(For local fiscal year ended in 2006)

Revenues

Total . . . $30,137,975
Taxes . . . 6,952,945
Special benefits assessment . . . 3,154
Licenses & permits . . . 179,509
Fines & forfeitures . . . 90,075
Revenues from use of
  money & property . . . 720,417
Intergovernmental . . . 4,657,664
Service charges . . . 4,301,486
Other revenues . . . 1,822,444
Other financing sources . . . 11,410,281

Expenditures

Total . . . $20,103,072
General government . . . 1,800,194
Public safety . . . 3,814,086
Transportation . . . 3,081,546
Community development . . . 1,342,936
Health . . . 2,477,381
Culture & leisure . . . 1,719,582
Other . . . 0

Local School District

(Data from School year 2007-08 except as noted)

St. Helena Unified
465 Main St
St. Helena, CA 94574
(707) 967-2708

Superintendent . . . Allan Gordon
Grade plan . . . K-12
Number of schools . . . 4
Enrollment . . . 1,376
High school graduates, 2006-07 . . . 0
Dropout rate . . . 6.0%
Pupil/teacher ratio . . . 15.5
Average class size . . . 22.0
Students per computer . . . 2.8
Classrooms with internet . . . 90
Avg. Daily Attendance (ADA) . . . 1,464
  Cost per ADA . . . $13,978
Avg. Teacher Salary . . . $78,289

California Achievement Tests 6th ed., 2008

(Pct scoring at or above 50th National Percentile Rank)

	Math	Reading	Language
Grade 3	67%	51%	47%
Grade 7	50%	48%	57%

Academic Performance Index, 2008

Number of students tested . . . 1,052
Number of valid scores . . . 968
2007 API (base) . . . 778
2008 API (growth) . . . 777

SAT Testing, 2006-07

Enrollment, Grade 12 . . . 125
Number taking test . . . 60
  percent taking test . . . 48.0%
  percent with total score 1,500+ . . . 28.80%

Average Scores:

Math	Verbal	Writing	Total
534	517	526	1,577

Federal No Child Left Behind, 2008

(Adequate Yearly Progress standards met)

	Participation Rate	Pct Proficient
ELA	Yes	No
Math	Yes	Yes

API criteria . . . Yes
Graduation rate . . . No
\# criteria met/possible . . . 26/24

Other school districts for this city

(see Appendix E for information on these districts)

None

See Introduction for an explanation of all data sources.

Demographics & Socio-Economic Characteristics†

(2007 American Community Survey, except as noted)

Population

1990* . . . 108,777
2007 . . . 140,499
Male . . . 71,175
Female . . . 69,324
Jan. 2008 (estimate)§ . . . 150,898
Persons per sq. mi. of land . . . 7,942.0

Race & Hispanic Origin, 2007

Race
White . . . 72,331
Black/African American . . . 2,893
North American Native . . . 511
Asian . . . 8,728
Pacific Islander . . . 88
Other Race . . . 53,484
Two or more races . . . 2,464
Hispanic origin, total . . . 102,311
Mexican . . . 96,997
Puerto Rican . . . 331
Cuban . . . 62
Other Hispanic . . . 4,921

Age & Nativity, 2007

Under 5 years . . . 14,988
18 years and over . . . 95,278
65 years and over . . . 11,650
85 years and over . . . 937
Median Age . . . 28.6
Native-born . . . 87,010
Foreign-born . . . 53,489

Educational Attainment, 2007

Population 25 years and over . . . 79,848
Less than 9th grade . . . 29.4%
High school grad or higher . . . 56.0%
Bachelor's degree or higher . . . 11.8%
Graduate degree . . . 3.7%

Income & Poverty, 2007

Per capita income . . . $18,824
Median household income . . . $52,560
Median family income . . . $52,175
Persons in poverty . . . 15.7%
H'holds receiving public assistance . . . 1,796
H'holds receiving social security . . . 8,539

Households, 2007

Total households . . . 39,657
With persons under 18 . . . 20,202
With persons over 65 . . . 7,798
Family households . . . 29,612
Single person households . . . 7,728
Persons per household . . . 3.51
Persons per family . . . 3.99

Household Population, 2008§§

Persons living in households . . . 148,446
Persons living in group quarters . . . 2,452
Persons per household . . . 3.6

Labor & Employment

Total civilian labor force, 2008§§ . . . 73,700
Unemployment rate, 2008 . . . 12.0%
Total civilian labor force, 2000* . . . 62,418

Employed persons 16 years and over by occupation, 2007

Managers & professionals . . . 13,444
Service occupations . . . 10,134
Sales & office occupations . . . 13,356
Farming, fishing & forestry . . . 12,334
Construction & maintenance . . . 6,052
Production & transportation . . . 7,679
Self-employed persons . . . 2,852

† see Appendix D for 2000 Decennial Census Data
* US Census Bureau
** 2007 American Community Survey
§ California Department of Finance
§§ California Employment Development Dept

General Information

City of Salinas
200 Lincoln Ave
Salinas, CA 93901
831-758-7201

Website . . . www.ci.salinas.ca.us
Elevation . . . 53 ft.
Land Area (sq. miles) . . . 19.0
Water Area (sq. miles) . . . 0
Year of Incorporation . . . 1874
Government type . . . Chartered
Sales tax rate . . . 8.75%

Voters & Officials

Registered Voters, October 2008

Total . . . 45,452
Democrats . . . 25,519
Republicans . . . 10,570
Declined to state . . . 8,031

Legislative Districts

US Congressional . . . 17
State Senatorial . . . 12
State Assembly . . . 28

Local Officials, 2009

Mayor . . . Dennis Donohue
Manager . . . Artie Fields
City Clerk . . . Ann Camel
Attorney . . . Vanessa Vallarta
Finance Dir . . . Tom Kever
Public Works . . . Robert Russell
Community Dev Dir . . . Robert Russell
Building . . . NA
Police Chief . . . Dan Ortega
Emergency/Fire Dir . . . (vacant)

Public Safety

Number of officers, 2007 . . . 174
Violent crimes, 2007 . . . 1,154
Property crimes, 2007 . . . 6,878
Arson, 2007 . . . 37

Public Library

Steinbeck Library
Salinas Public Library System
350 Lincoln Ave
Salinas, CA 93901
831-758-7311

Director . . . Elizabeth Martinez

Library system statistics, FY 2007

Population served . . . 149,539
Internet terminals . . . 4
Annual users . . . 8,313

Per capita:

Operating income . . . $25.70
percent from local government . . . 93.7%
Operating expenditure . . . $23.24
Total materials . . . 1.54
Print holdings . . . 1.43
Visits per capita . . . 1.32

Housing & Construction

Housing Units

Total, 2008§ . . . 42,268
Single family units, attached . . . 3,594
Single family units, detached . . . 22,848
Multiple family units . . . 14,540
Mobile home units . . . 1,286
Occupied . . . 40,816
Vacancy rate . . . 3.4%
Median rent, 2007** . . . $960
Median SF home value, 2007** . . . $596,200

New Privately Owned Housing Units Authorized by Building Permit, 2007*

	Units	Construction Cost
Single	72	$18,000,686
Total	244	$44,334,664

Municipal Finance

(For local fiscal year ended in 2006)

Revenues

Total . . . $107,915,076
Taxes . . . 66,037,888
Special benefits assessment . . . 994,060
Licenses & permits . . . 1,533,005
Fines & forfeitures . . . 913,142
Revenues from use of money & property . . . 2,231,379
Intergovernmental . . . 19,229,877
Service charges . . . 13,207,987
Other revenues . . . 1,827,913
Other financing sources . . . 1,939,825

Expenditures

Total . . . $108,831,345
General government . . . 6,148,600
Public safety . . . 53,088,458
Transportation . . . 20,050,407
Community development . . . 8,615,280
Health . . . 9,755,889
Culture & leisure . . . 11,164,424
Other . . . 0

Local School District

(Data from School year 2007-08 except as noted)

Salinas Union High
431 West Alisal St
Salinas, CA 93901
(831) 796-7000

Superintendent . . . Roger Anton
Grade plan . . . 7-12
Number of schools . . . 10
Enrollment . . . 13,572
High school graduates, 2006-07 . . . 1,490
Dropout rate . . . 2.6%
Pupil/teacher ratio . . . 24.7
Average class size . . . 26.7
Students per computer . . . 6.6
Classrooms with internet . . . 579
Avg. Daily Attendance (ADA) . . . 13,601
Cost per ADA . . . $7,903
Avg. Teacher Salary . . . $66,801

California Achievement Tests 6th ed., 2008

(Pct scoring at or above 50th National Percentile Rank)

	Math	Reading	Language
Grade 3	NA	NA	NA
Grade 7	38%	34%	34%

Academic Performance Index, 2008

Number of students tested . . . 11,062
Number of valid scores . . . 10,147
2007 API (base) . . . 653
2008 API (growth) . . . 677

SAT Testing, 2006-07

Enrollment, Grade 12 . . . 2,132
Number taking test . . . 668
percent taking test . . . 31.3%
percent with total score 1,500+ . . . 9.10%

Average Scores:

Math	Verbal	Writing	Total
455	449	447	1,351

Federal No Child Left Behind, 2008

(Adequate Yearly Progress standards met)

	Participation Rate	Pct Proficient
ELA	No	No
Math	Yes	No

API criteria . . . Yes
Graduation rate . . . Yes
\# criteria met/possible . . . 34/29

Other school districts for this city

(see Appendix E for information on these districts)

Complete list in Appendix E

See Introduction for an explanation of all data sources.

Demographics & Socio-Economic Characteristics

(2000 Decennial Census, except as noted)

Population

1990* 11,743
2000 12,378
Male 5,836
Female 6,542
Jan. 2008 (estimate)§ 12,601
Persons per sq. mi. of land 4,667.0

Race & Hispanic Origin, 2000

Race
White 11,341
Black/African American 130
North American Native 50
Asian 361
Pacific Islander 15
Other Race 118
Two or more races 363
Hispanic origin, total 513
Mexican 209
Puerto Rican 16
Cuban 29
Other Hispanic 259

Age & Nativity, 2000

Under 5 years 725
18 years and over 9,679
65 years and over 1,402
85 years and over 184
Median Age 41.3
Native-born 11,404
Foreign-born 1,117

Educational Attainment, 2000

Population 25 years and over 9,238
Less than 9th grade 1.1%
High school grad or higher 96.9%
Bachelor's degree or higher 59.0%
Graduate degree 21.9%

Income & Poverty, 1999

Per capita income $41,977
Median household income $71,488
Median family income $86,528
Persons in poverty 5.1%
H'holds receiving public assistance 57
H'holds receiving social security 1,051

Households, 2000

Total households 5,267
With persons under 18 1,651
With persons over 65 1,005
Family households 3,191
Single person households 1,511
Persons per household 2.30
Persons per family 2.84

Household Population, 2008§§

Persons living in households 12,340
Persons living in group quarters 261
Persons per household 2.3

Labor & Employment

Total civilian labor force, 2008§§ 7,800
Unemployment rate, 2008 .... 5.6%
Total civilian labor force, 2000 7,517

Employed persons 16 years and over by occupation, 2000

Managers & professionals 4,236
Service occupations 700
Sales & office occupations 1,605
Farming, fishing & forestry 31
Construction & maintenance 413
Production & transportation 258
Self-employed persons 1,622

* US Census Bureau
** 2000 Decennial Census
§ California Department of Finance
§§ California Employment Development Dept

General Information

Town of San Anselmo
525 San Anselmo Ave
San Anselmo, CA 94960
415-258-4600

Website .... www.townofsananselmo.org
Elevation .... 45 ft.
Land Area (sq. miles) 2.7
Water Area (sq. miles) 0
Year of Incorporation 1907
Government type .... General law
Sales tax rate 9.00%

Voters & Officials

Registered Voters, October 2008

Total 8,505
Democrats 5,246
Republicans 1,084
Declined to state 1,763

Legislative Districts

US Congressional 6
State Senatorial 3
State Assembly 6

Local Officials, 2009

Mayor .... Peter Breen
Manager .... Debra Stutsman
City Clerk .... Barbara Chambers
Attorney .... Robert Epstein
Finance Dir .... Janet Pendoley
Public Works .... (vacant)
Planning Dir .... Lisa Wight
Building .... Keith Angerman
Police Chief .... Charles Maynard
Fire Chief .... Roger Meagor

Public Safety

Number of officers, 2007 18
Violent crimes, 2007 26
Property crimes, 2007 281
Arson, 2007 2

Public Library

San Anselmo Public Library
110 Tunstead Ave
San Anselmo, CA 94960
415-258-4656

Director .... Sara Loyster

Library statistics, FY 2007

Population served 12,518
Internet terminals 9
Annual users 10,268

Per capita:

Operating income $35.17
percent from local government 56.0%
Operating expenditure $35.17
Total materials 4.81
Print holdings 3.79
Visits per capita 1.75

Housing & Construction

Housing Units

Total, 2008§ 5,445
Single family units, attached 187
Single family units, detached 3,997
Multiple family units 1,243
Mobile home units 18
Occupied 5,304
Vacancy rate 2.6%
Median rent, 2000** $1,074
Median SF home value, 2000** $507,300

New Privately Owned Housing Units Authorized by Building Permit, 2007*

	Units	Construction Cost
Single	10	$11,535,800
Total	18	$12,765,800

Municipal Finance

(For local fiscal year ended in 2006)

Revenues

Total $16,023,402
Taxes 9,904,980
Special benefits assessment 0
Licenses & permits 627,441
Fines & forfeitures 229,708
Revenues from use of money & property 359,906
Intergovernmental 1,666,329
Service charges 2,286,187
Other revenues 948,851
Other financing sources 0

Expenditures

Total $16,471,152
General government 2,430,024
Public safety 8,235,136
Transportation 1,862,422
Community development 1,626,831
Health 0
Culture & leisure 2,316,739
Other 0

Local School District

(Data from School year 2007-08 except as noted)

Tamalpais Union High
PO Box 605
Larkspur, CA 94977
(415) 945-3720

Superintendent .... Laurie Kimbrel
Grade plan 9-12
Number of schools 5
Enrollment 3,889
High school graduates, 2006-07 959
Dropout rate 0.8%
Pupil/teacher ratio 17.4
Average class size 24.4
Students per computer 2.6
Classrooms with internet 232
Avg. Daily Attendance (ADA) 3,715
Cost per ADA $13,492
Avg. Teacher Salary $81,923

California Achievement Tests 6th ed., 2008

(Pct scoring at or above 50th National Percentile Rank)

	Math	Reading	Language
Grade 3	NA	NA	NA
Grade 7	NA	NA	NA

Academic Performance Index, 2008

Number of students tested 2,800
Number of valid scores 2,766
2007 API (base) 848
2008 API (growth) 855

SAT Testing, 2006-07

Enrollment, Grade 12 997
Number taking test 730
percent taking test 73.2%
percent with total score 1,500+ 58.30%

Average Scores:

Math	Verbal	Writing	Total
574	574	574	1,722

Federal No Child Left Behind, 2008

(Adequate Yearly Progress standards met)

	Participation Rate	Pct Proficient
ELA	Yes	Yes
Math	Yes	Yes

API criteria .... Yes
Graduation rate .... Yes
criteria met/possible 10/10

Other school districts for this city

(see Appendix E for information on these districts)

Ross Valley Elem

See Introduction for an explanation of all data sources.

Demographics & Socio-Economic Characteristics†

(2007 American Community Survey, except as noted)

Population

1990* . . . 164,164
2007 . . . 203,691
Male . . . 102,760
Female . . . 100,931
Jan. 2008 (estimate)§ . . . 205,493
Persons per sq. mi. of land . . . 3,494.8

Race & Hispanic Origin, 2007

Race
White . . . 84,491
Black/African American . . . 33,136
North American Native . . . 2,259
Asian . . . 9,425
Pacific Islander . . . 535
Other Race . . . 67,292
Two or more races . . . 6,553
Hispanic origin, total . . . 116,500
Mexican . . . 102,359
Puerto Rican . . . 1,825
Cuban . . . 0
Other Hispanic . . . 12,316

Age & Nativity, 2007

Under 5 years . . . 21,047
18 years and over . . . 137,596
65 years and over . . . 13,951
85 years and over . . . 1,771
Median Age . . . 27.9
Native-born . . . 157,133
Foreign-born . . . 46,558

Educational Attainment, 2007

Population 25 years and over . . . 113,024
Less than 9th grade . . . 13.8%
High school grad or higher . . . 69.2%
Bachelor's degree or higher . . . 11.8%
Graduate degree . . . 3.7%

Income & Poverty, 2007

Per capita income . . . $15,976
Median household income . . . $41,744
Median family income . . . $44,855
Persons in poverty . . . 22.5%
H'holds receiving public assistance . . . 3,658
H'holds receiving social security . . . 11,975

Households, 2007

Total households . . . 60,579
With persons under 18 . . . 29,483
With persons over 65 . . . 10,667
Family households . . . 43,291
Single person households . . . 13,215
Persons per household . . . 3.24
Persons per family . . . 3.86

Household Population, 2008§§

Persons living in households . . . 198,562
Persons living in group quarters . . . 6,931
Persons per household . . . 3.4

Labor & Employment

Total civilian labor force, 2008§§ . . . 84,900
Unemployment rate, 2008 . . . 10.9%
Total civilian labor force, 2000* . . . 70,280

Employed persons 16 years and over by occupation, 2007

Managers & professionals . . . 18,887
Service occupations . . . 14,356
Sales & office occupations . . . 21,477
Farming, fishing & forestry . . . 0
Construction & maintenance . . . 9,382
Production & transportation . . . 14,969
Self-employed persons . . . 3,816

† see Appendix D for 2000 Decennial Census Data
* US Census Bureau
** 2007 American Community Survey
§ California Department of Finance
§§ California Employment Development Dept

General Information

City of San Bernardino
300 North D St
PO Box 1318
San Bernardino, CA 92418
909-384-5211

Website . . . www.sbcity.org
Elevation . . . 1,049 ft.
Land Area (sq. miles) . . . 58.8
Water Area (sq. miles) . . . 0.4
Year of Incorporation . . . 1869
Government type . . . Chartered
Sales tax rate . . . 9.00%

Voters & Officials

Registered Voters, October 2008

Total . . . 76,060
Democrats . . . 36,980
Republicans . . . 24,065
Declined to state . . . 11,839

Legislative Districts

US Congressional . . . 41
State Senatorial . . . 31, 32
State Assembly . . . 59, 62, 63

Local Officials, 2009

Mayor . . . Patrick Morris
Manager . . . Mark Weinberg (Int)
City Clerk . . . Rachel Clark
Attorney . . . James Penman
Finance Dir . . . Barbara Pachon
Public Works . . . Ken Fischer
Planning/Dev Dir . . . Valerie Ross
Building . . . NA
Police Chief . . . Michael Billdt
Emergency/Fire Dir . . . Michael Conrad

Public Safety

Number of officers, 2007 . . . 330
Violent crimes, 2007 . . . 2,150
Property crimes, 2007 . . . 10,090
Arson, 2007 . . . 81

Public Library

Norman Feldheym Library
San Bernardino Public Library System
555 W Sixth St
San Bernardino, CA 92410
909-381-8201

Director . . . Ophelia Georgiev Roop

Library system statistics, FY 2007

Population served . . . 205,010
Internet terminals . . . 459
Annual users . . . 574,764

Per capita:

Operating income . . . $15.41
percent from local government . . . 85.0%
Operating expenditure . . . $13.99
Total materials . . . 1.21
Print holdings . . . 1.14
Visits per capita . . . 2.87

Housing & Construction

Housing Units

Total, 2008§ . . . 66,606
Single family units, attached . . . 2,729
Single family units, detached . . . 39,273
Multiple family units . . . 20,119
Mobile home units . . . 4,485
Occupied . . . 59,253
Vacancy rate . . . 11.0%
Median rent, 2007** . . . $872
Median SF home value, 2007** . . . $327,000

New Privately Owned Housing Units Authorized by Building Permit, 2007*

	Units	Construction Cost
Single	159	$22,162,576
Total	249	$26,121,261

Municipal Finance

(For local fiscal year ended in 2006)

Revenues

Total . . . $292,383,133
Taxes . . . 100,444,547
Special benefits assessment . . . 531,000
Licenses & permits . . . 10,987,900
Fines & forfeitures . . . 2,698,102
Revenues from use of money & property . . . 2,701,846
Intergovernmental . . . 22,610,917
Service charges . . . 93,633,395
Other revenues . . . 5,706,460
Other financing sources . . . 53,068,966

Expenditures

Total . . . $296,588,711
General government . . . 72,392,053
Public safety . . . 88,491,096
Transportation . . . 18,858,925
Community development . . . 12,120,002
Health . . . 48,562,196
Culture & leisure . . . 10,016,843
Other . . . 0

Local School District

(Data from School year 2007-08 except as noted)

San Bernardino City Unified
777 North F St
San Bernardino, CA 92410
(909) 381-1100

Superintendent . . . Arturo Delgado
Grade plan . . . K-12
Number of schools . . . 70
Enrollment . . . 56,727
High school graduates, 2006-07 . . . 2,198
Dropout rate . . . 8.3%
Pupil/teacher ratio . . . 21.9
Average class size . . . 26.8
Students per computer . . . 4.0
Classrooms with internet . . . 2,351
Avg. Daily Attendance (ADA) . . . 51,623
Cost per ADA . . . $9,872
Avg. Teacher Salary . . . $67,331

California Achievement Tests 6th ed., 2008

(Pct scoring at or above 50th National Percentile Rank)

	Math	Reading	Language
Grade 3	40%	21%	29%
Grade 7	34%	30%	28%

Academic Performance Index, 2008

Number of students tested . . . 41,283
Number of valid scores . . . 37,234
2007 API (base) . . . 643
2008 API (growth) . . . 656

SAT Testing, 2006-07

Enrollment, Grade 12 . . . 2,200
Number taking test . . . 946
percent taking test . . . 43.0%
percent with total score 1,500+ . . . 9.60%

Average Scores:

Math	Verbal	Writing	Total
441	432	431	1,304

Federal No Child Left Behind, 2008

(Adequate Yearly Progress standards met)

	Participation Rate	Pct Proficient
ELA	Yes	No
Math	Yes	No

API criteria . . . Yes
Graduation rate . . . Yes
criteria met/possible . . . 44/32

Other school districts for this city

(see Appendix E for information on these districts)

Redlands Unified, Colton Joint Unified

See Introduction for an explanation of all data sources.

Demographics & Socio-Economic Characteristics

(2000 Decennial Census, except as noted)

Population

1990* 38,961
2000 40,165
Male 19,822
Female 20,343
Jan. 2008 (estimate)§ 43,444
Persons per sq. mi. of land 7,898.9

Race & Hispanic Origin, 2000

Race
White 23,156
Black/African American 807
North American Native 189
Asian 7,506
Pacific Islander 1,156
Other Race 4,346
Two or more races 3,005
Hispanic origin, total 9,686
Mexican 5,050
Puerto Rican 302
Cuban 64
Other Hispanic 4,270

Age & Nativity, 2000

Under 5 years 2,440
18 years and over 30,936
65 years and over 4,512
85 years and over 479
Median Age 36.3
Native-born 27,143
Foreign-born 13,021

Educational Attainment, 2000

Population 25 years and over 27,680
Less than 9th grade 5.8%
High school grad or higher 84.5%
Bachelor's degree or higher 26.2%
Graduate degree 7.7%

Income & Poverty, 1999

Per capita income $26,360
Median household income $62,081
Median family income $70,251
Persons in poverty 4.4%
H'holds receiving public assistance 216
H'holds receiving social security 3,159

Households, 2000

Total households 14,677
With persons under 18 5,097
With persons over 65 3,248
Family households 9,917
Single person households 3,749
Persons per household 2.72
Persons per family 3.29

Household Population, 2008§§

Persons living in households 43,208
Persons living in group quarters 236
Persons per household 2.8

Labor & Employment

Total civilian labor force, 2008§§ 22,600
Unemployment rate, 2008 .... 4.1%
Total civilian labor force, 2000 21,964

Employed persons 16 years and over by occupation, 2000

Managers & professionals 6,887
Service occupations 3,373
Sales & office occupations 6,902
Farming, fishing & forestry 27
Construction & maintenance 2,002
Production & transportation 2,173
Self-employed persons 1,341

* US Census Bureau
** 2000 Decennial Census
§ California Department of Finance
§§ California Employment Development Dept

General Information

City of San Bruno
567 El Camino Real
San Bruno, CA 94066
650-616-7058

Website .... sanbruno.ca.gov
Elevation .... 16 ft.
Land Area (sq. miles) 5.5
Water Area (sq. miles) 0
Year of Incorporation 1914
Government type .... General law
Sales tax rate 9.25%

Voters & Officials

Registered Voters, October 2008

Total 21,209
Democrats 11,889
Republicans 3,604
Declined to state 4,879

Legislative Districts

US Congressional 12
State Senatorial 8
State Assembly 19

Local Officials, 2009

Mayor .... Larry Franzella
Manager .... Connie Jackson
City Clerk .... Carol Bonner
Attorney .... Pamela Thompson
Finance Dir .... Jim O'Leary
Public Works .... NA
Planning/Dev Dir .... Aaron Akinin
Building .... NA
Police Chief .... Neil Telford
Emergency/Fire Dir .... Dennis Haag

Public Safety

Number of officers, 2007 45
Violent crimes, 2007 108
Property crimes, 2007 822
Arson, 2007 2

Public Library

San Bruno Public Library
701 Angus Ave W
San Bruno, CA 94066
650-616-7078

Director .... John Alita (Int)

Library statistics, FY 2007

Population served 42,145
Internet terminals 588
Annual users 1,622,210

Per capita:

Operating income $46.45
percent from local government 90.5%
Operating expenditure $37.38
Total materials 2.79
Print holdings 2.25
Visits per capita 4.59

Housing & Construction

Housing Units

Total, 2008§ 15,917
Single family units, attached 566
Single family units, detached 9,155
Multiple family units 6,174
Mobile home units 22
Occupied 15,696
Vacancy rate 1.4%
Median rent, 2000** $1,162
Median SF home value, 2000** $385,100

New Privately Owned Housing Units Authorized by Building Permit, 2007*

	Units	Construction Cost
Single	73	$28,623,322
Total	73	$28,623,322

Municipal Finance

(For local fiscal year ended in 2006)

Revenues

Total $69,173,075
Taxes 19,783,905
Special benefits assessment 903,953
Licenses & permits 2,553,702
Fines & forfeitures 731,407
Revenues from use of money & property 2,143,689
Intergovernmental 4,483,479
Service charges 30,490,089
Other revenues 6,853,553
Other financing sources 1,229,298

Expenditures

Total $63,197,518
General government 10,550,864
Public safety 16,913,625
Transportation 4,930,745
Community development 1,810,829
Health 7,323,760
Culture & leisure 6,041,261
Other 0

Local School District

(Data from School year 2007-08 except as noted)

San Mateo Union High
650 North Delaware St
San Mateo, CA 94401
(650) 558-2299

Superintendent .... David Miller
Grade plan 9-12
Number of schools 7
Enrollment 8,626
High school graduates, 2006-07 1,833
Dropout rate 1.3%
Pupil/teacher ratio 21.3
Average class size 26.9
Students per computer 4.0
Classrooms with internet 425
Avg. Daily Attendance (ADA) 8,291
Cost per ADA $9,930
Avg. Teacher Salary $74,785

California Achievement Tests 6th ed., 2008

(Pct scoring at or above 50th National Percentile Rank)

	Math	Reading	Language
Grade 3	NA	NA	NA
Grade 7	NA	NA	NA

Academic Performance Index, 2008

Number of students tested 6,229
Number of valid scores 6,003
2007 API (base) 774
2008 API (growth) 781

SAT Testing, 2006-07

Enrollment, Grade 12 2,145
Number taking test 1,188
percent taking test 55.4%
percent with total score 1,500+ 37.60%

Average Scores:

Math	Verbal	Writing	Total
572	534	536	1,642

Federal No Child Left Behind, 2008

(Adequate Yearly Progress standards met)

	Participation Rate	Pct Proficient
ELA	Yes	No
Math	Yes	No

API criteria .... Yes
Graduation rate .... Yes
\# criteria met/possible 32/30

Other school districts for this city

(see Appendix E for information on these districts)

Pacifica Elem, San Bruno Park Elem, South San Francisco Unified

See Introduction for an explanation of all data sources.

Demographics & Socio-Economic Characteristics

(2000 Decennial Census, except as noted)

Population

1990* . . . 26,167
2000 . . . 27,718
Male . . . 13,326
Female . . . 14,392
Jan. 2008 (estimate)§ . . . 28,857
Persons per sq. mi. of land . . . 4,891.0

Race & Hispanic Origin, 2000

Race
White . . . 23,434
Black/African American . . . 209
North American Native . . . 53
Asian . . . 2,182
Pacific Islander . . . 110
Other Race . . . 664
Two or more races . . . 1,066
Hispanic origin, total . . . 2,133
Mexican . . . 1,003
Puerto Rican . . . 89
Cuban . . . 32
Other Hispanic . . . 1,009

Age & Nativity, 2000

Under 5 years . . . 1,951
18 years and over . . . 21,595
65 years and over . . . 3,976
85 years and over . . . 614
Median Age . . . 39.9
Native-born . . . 23,365
Foreign-born . . . 4,332

Educational Attainment, 2000

Population 25 years and over . . . 20,393
Less than 9th grade . . . 1.1%
High school grad or higher . . . 94.6%
Bachelor's degree or higher . . . 49.8%
Graduate degree . . . 19.9%

Income & Poverty, 1999

Per capita income . . . $46,628
Median household income . . . $88,460
Median family income . . . $103,971
Persons in poverty . . . 2.7%
H'holds receiving public assistance . . . 121
H'holds receiving social security . . . 2,774

Households, 2000

Total households . . . 11,455
With persons under 18 . . . 3,551
With persons over 65 . . . 2,791
Family households . . . 7,608
Single person households . . . 2,949
Persons per household . . . 2.40
Persons per family . . . 2.93

Household Population, 2008§§

Persons living in households . . . 28,674
Persons living in group quarters . . . 183
Persons per household . . . 2.4

Labor & Employment

Total civilian labor force, 2008§§ . . . 15,800
Unemployment rate, 2008 . . . 3.2%
Total civilian labor force, 2000 . . . 15,440

Employed persons 16 years and over by occupation, 2000

Managers & professionals . . . 8,486
Service occupations . . . 1,219
Sales & office occupations . . . 3,914
Farming, fishing & forestry . . . 0
Construction & maintenance . . . 828
Production & transportation . . . 681
Self-employed persons . . . 1,436

* US Census Bureau
** 2000 Decennial Census
§ California Department of Finance
§§ California Employment Development Dept

General Information

City of San Carlos
600 Elm St
San Carlos, CA 94070
650-802-4100

Website . . . www.cityofsancarlos.org
Elevation . . . 40 ft.
Land Area (sq. miles) . . . 5.9
Water Area (sq. miles) . . . 0
Year of Incorporation . . . 1925
Government type . . . General law
Sales tax rate . . . 9.25%

Voters & Officials

Registered Voters, October 2008

Total . . . 19,525
Democrats . . . 9,301
Republicans . . . 5,322
Declined to state . . . 4,216

Legislative Districts

US Congressional . . . 12
State Senatorial . . . 11
State Assembly . . . 21

Local Officials, 2009

Mayor . . . Robert J. Grassilli
Manager . . . Mark D. Weiss
City Clerk . . . Christine D. Boland
Attorney . . . Gregory J. Rubens
Admin Svcs Dir . . . Jeff D. Maltbie
Public Works . . . Robert Weil
Community Dev Dir . . . Al D. Savay
Building . . . Christopher Valley
Police Chief . . . Gregory D. Rothaus
Fire Chief . . . Doug D. Fry

Public Safety

Number of officers, 2007 . . . 28
Violent crimes, 2007 . . . 35
Property crimes, 2007 . . . 451
Arson, 2007 . . . 8

Public Library

San Carlos Library
San Mateo County Library System
610 Elm St
San Carlos, CA 94070
650-591-0341

Branch Librarian . . . Chet Mulawka

Library system statistics, FY 2007

Population served . . . 278,388
Internet terminals . . . 26
Annual users . . . 49,920

Per capita:

Operating income . . . $90.21
percent from local government . . . 63.5%
Operating expenditure . . . $60.41
Total materials . . . 2.65
Print holdings . . . 2.16
Visits per capita . . . 5.44

Housing & Construction

Housing Units

Total, 2008§ . . . 11,960
Single family units, attached . . . 609
Single family units, detached . . . 8,285
Multiple family units . . . 3,050
Mobile home units . . . 16
Occupied . . . 11,794
Vacancy rate . . . 1.4%
Median rent, 2000** . . . $1,181
Median SF home value, 2000** . . . $626,400

New Privately Owned Housing Units Authorized by Building Permit, 2007*

	Units	Construction Cost
Single	24	$10,919,364
Total	42	$14,899,364

Municipal Finance

(For local fiscal year ended in 2006)

Revenues

Total . . . $40,874,189
Taxes . . . 16,340,610
Special benefits assessment . . . 420,566
Licenses & permits . . . 1,068,699
Fines & forfeitures . . . 241,987
Revenues from use of money & property . . . 928,814
Intergovernmental . . . 4,351,563
Service charges . . . 8,440,366
Other revenues . . . 966,584
Other financing sources . . . 8,115,000

Expenditures

Total . . . $41,319,380
General government . . . 5,409,202
Public safety . . . 12,678,658
Transportation . . . 2,685,060
Community development . . . 1,662,509
Health . . . 4,213,956
Culture & leisure . . . 14,669,995
Other . . . 0

Local School District

(Data from School year 2007-08 except as noted)

Sequoia Union High
480 James Ave
Redwood City, CA 94062
(650) 369-1411

Superintendent . . . Patrick Gemma
Grade plan . . . 9-12
Number of schools . . . 6
Enrollment . . . 8,510
High school graduates, 2006-07 . . . 1,546
Dropout rate . . . 3.2%
Pupil/teacher ratio . . . 19.7
Average class size . . . 26.4
Students per computer . . . 3.0
Classrooms with internet . . . 402
Avg. Daily Attendance (ADA) . . . 7,811
Cost per ADA . . . $11,470
Avg. Teacher Salary . . . $76,194

California Achievement Tests 6th ed., 2008

(Pct scoring at or above 50th National Percentile Rank)

	Math	Reading	Language
Grade 3	NA	NA	NA
Grade 7	NA	NA	NA

Academic Performance Index, 2008

Number of students tested . . . 5,874
Number of valid scores . . . 5,525
2007 API (base) . . . 753
2008 API (growth) . . . 753

SAT Testing, 2006-07

Enrollment, Grade 12 . . . 2,000
Number taking test . . . 945
percent taking test . . . 47.3%
percent with total score 1,500+ . . . 29.10%

Average Scores:

Math	Verbal	Writing	Total
546	530	530	1,606

Federal No Child Left Behind, 2008

(Adequate Yearly Progress standards met)

	Participation Rate	Pct Proficient
ELA	Yes	No
Math	Yes	No

API criteria . . . Yes
Graduation rate . . . Yes
criteria met/possible . . . 28/25

Other school districts for this city

(see Appendix E for information on these districts)

San Carlos Elem

See Introduction for an explanation of all data sources.

Demographics & Socio-Economic Characteristics

(2000 Decennial Census, except as noted)

Population

1990* ... 41,100
2000 ... 49,936
Male ... 25,264
Female ... 24,672
Jan. 2008 (estimate)§ ... 67,892
Persons per sq. mi. of land ... 3,857.5

Race & Hispanic Origin, 2000

Race
White ... 43,905
Black/African American ... 385
North American Native ... 307
Asian ... 1,317
Pacific Islander ... 69
Other Race ... 2,552
Two or more races ... 1,401
Hispanic origin, total ... 7,933
Mexican ... 6,317
Puerto Rican ... 132
Cuban ... 58
Other Hispanic ... 1,426

Age & Nativity, 2000

Under 5 years ... 3,223
18 years and over ... 37,903
65 years and over ... 6,534
85 years and over ... 696
Median Age ... 38.0
Native-born ... 43,132
Foreign-born ... 6,729

Educational Attainment, 2000

Population 25 years and over ... 34,599
Less than 9th grade ... 3.5%
High school grad or higher ... 90.7%
Bachelor's degree or higher ... 36.1%
Graduate degree ... 11.4%

Income & Poverty, 1999

Per capita income ... $34,169
Median household income ... $63,507
Median family income ... $76,261
Persons in poverty ... 7.5%
H'holds receiving public assistance ... 233
H'holds receiving social security ... 4,659

Households, 2000

Total households ... 19,395
With persons under 18 ... 6,343
With persons over 65 ... 4,536
Family households ... 13,015
Single person households ... 4,541
Persons per household ... 2.56
Persons per family ... 3.05

Household Population, 2008§§

Persons living in households ... 67,600
Persons living in group quarters ... 292
Persons per household ... 2.7

Labor & Employment

Total civilian labor force, 2008§§ ... 30,000
Unemployment rate, 2008 ... 4.2%
Total civilian labor force, 2000 ... 25,641

Employed persons 16 years and over by occupation, 2000

Managers & professionals ... 10,076
Service occupations ... 3,340
Sales & office occupations ... 7,188
Farming, fishing & forestry ... 37
Construction & maintenance ... 2,091
Production & transportation ... 1,922
Self-employed persons ... 3,238

* US Census Bureau
** 2000 Decennial Census
§ California Department of Finance
§§ California Employment Development Dept

General Information

City of San Clemente
100 Avenida Presidio
San Clemente, CA 92672
949-361-8301

Website ... www.san-clemente.org
Elevation ... 200 ft.
Land Area (sq. miles) ... 17.6
Water Area (sq. miles) ... 0.7
Year of Incorporation ... 1928
Government type ... General law
Sales tax rate ... 8.75%

Voters & Officials

Registered Voters, October 2008

Total ... 41,271
Democrats ... 9,919
Republicans ... 21,167
Declined to state ... 8,226

Legislative Districts

US Congressional ... 44
State Senatorial ... 38
State Assembly ... 73

Local Officials, 2009

Mayor ... Lori Donchak
Manager ... George Scarborough
City Clerk ... Joanne Baade
Attorney ... Jeffrey Oderman
Finance Dir ... NA
Public Works ... Bill Cameron
Planning/Dev Dir ... Jim Pechous
Building ... Mike Jorgensen
Police Chief ... Paul D'Auria
Emergency/Fire Dir ... (County)

Public Safety

Number of officers, 2007 ... NA
Violent crimes, 2007 ... 83
Property crimes, 2007 ... 779
Arson, 2007 ... 12

Public Library

San Clemente Branch Library
Orange County Public Library System
242 Avenida Del Mar
San Clemente, CA 92672
949-492-3493

Branch Librarian ... Maureen Gebelein

Library system statistics, FY 2007

Population served ... 1,532,758
Internet terminals ... 505
Annual users ... 680,874

Per capita:

Operating income ... $24.71
percent from local government ... 90.0%
Operating expenditure ... $24.18
Total materials ... 1.93
Print holdings ... 1.84
Visits per capita ... 4.02

Housing & Construction

Housing Units

Total, 2008§ ... 27,131
Single family units, attached ... 2,669
Single family units, detached ... 15,488
Multiple family units ... 8,572
Mobile home units ... 402
Occupied ... 25,477
Vacancy rate ... 6.1%
Median rent, 2000** ... $916
Median SF home value, 2000** ... $372,400

New Privately Owned Housing Units Authorized by Building Permit, 2007*

	Units	Construction Cost
Single	149	$65,204,429
Total	149	$65,204,429

Municipal Finance

(For local fiscal year ended in 2006)

Revenues

Total ... $90,670,896
Taxes ... 34,119,921
Special benefits assessment ... 665,762
Licenses & permits ... 2,034,886
Fines & forfeitures ... 1,223,715
Revenues from use of money & property ... 4,773,740
Intergovernmental ... 7,522,531
Service charges ... 32,636,881
Other revenues ... 7,693,460
Other financing sources ... 0

Expenditures

Total ... $82,580,403
General government ... 7,383,575
Public safety ... 16,213,645
Transportation ... 11,559,705
Community development ... 8,556,354
Health ... 14,478,871
Culture & leisure ... 12,502,187
Other ... 0

Local School District

(Data from School year 2007-08 except as noted)

Capistrano Unified
33122 Valle Rd
San Juan Capistrano, CA 92675
(949) 234-9200

Superintendent ... A. Carter
Grade plan ... K-12
Number of schools ... 61
Enrollment ... 52,390
High school graduates, 2006-07 ... 3,205
Dropout rate ... 0.5%
Pupil/teacher ratio ... 23.4
Average class size ... 28.7
Students per computer ... 4.8
Classrooms with internet ... 2,308
Avg. Daily Attendance (ADA) ... 50,036
Cost per ADA ... $7,694
Avg. Teacher Salary ... $75,390

California Achievement Tests 6th ed., 2008

(Pct scoring at or above 50th National Percentile Rank)

	Math	Reading	Language
Grade 3	71%	56%	63%
Grade 7	73%	71%	68%

Academic Performance Index, 2008

Number of students tested ... 39,589
Number of valid scores ... 38,275
2007 API (base) ... 826
2008 API (growth) ... 837

SAT Testing, 2006-07

Enrollment, Grade 12 ... 3,414
Number taking test ... 1,770
percent taking test ... 51.9%
percent with total score 1,500+ ... 34.90%

Average Scores:

Math	Verbal	Writing	Total
552	541	537	1,630

Federal No Child Left Behind, 2008

(Adequate Yearly Progress standards met)

	Participation Rate	Pct Proficient
ELA	Yes	No
Math	Yes	Yes

API criteria ... Yes
Graduation rate ... Yes
criteria met/possible ... 42/41

Other school districts for this city

(see Appendix E for information on these districts)

None

See Introduction for an explanation of all data sources.

Demographics & Socio-Economic Characteristics†

(2007 American Community Survey, except as noted)

Population

1990* ... 1,110,549
2007 ... 1,276,740
Male ... 649,237
Female ... 627,503
Jan. 2008 (estimate)§ ... 1,336,865
Persons per sq. mi. of land ... 4,122.3

Race & Hispanic Origin, 2007

Race
White ... 859,649
Black/African American ... 85,159
North American Native ... 6,526
Asian ... 189,625
Pacific Islander ... 3,931
Other Race ... 83,637
Two or more races ... 48,213
Hispanic origin, total ... 350,190
Mexican ... 316,177
Puerto Rican ... 4,470
Cuban ... 841
Other Hispanic ... 28,702

Age & Nativity, 2007

Under 5 years ... 91,350
18 years and over ... 985,646
65 years and over ... 131,540
85 years and over ... 18,978
Median Age ... 33.1
Native-born ... 953,963
Foreign-born ... 322,777

Educational Attainment, 2007

Population 25 years and over ... 819,987
Less than 9th grade ... 6.8%
High school grad or higher ... 86.3%
Bachelor's degree or higher ... 40.4%
Graduate degree ... 15.5%

Income & Poverty, 2007

Per capita income ... $31,924
Median household income ... $61,863
Median family income ... $72,980
Persons in poverty ... 12.1%
H'holds receiving public assistance ... 9,004
H'holds receiving social security ... 96,335

Households, 2007

Total households ... 468,469
With persons under 18 ... 144,740
With persons over 65 ... 93,655
Family households ... 273,262
Single person households ... 140,732
Persons per household ... 2.60
Persons per family ... 3.32

Household Population, 2008§§

Persons living in households ... 1,293,528
Persons living in group quarters ... 43,337
Persons per household ... 2.7

Labor & Employment

Total civilian labor force, 2008§§ ... 699,200
Unemployment rate, 2008 ... 6.0%
Total civilian labor force, 2000* ... 593,740

Employed persons 16 years and over by occupation, 2007

Managers & professionals ... 274,596
Service occupations ... 102,786
Sales & office occupations ... 146,064
Farming, fishing & forestry ... 753
Construction & maintenance ... 40,379
Production & transportation ... 44,941
Self-employed persons ... 48,873

† see Appendix D for 2000 Decennial Census Data
* US Census Bureau
** 2007 American Community Survey
§ California Department of Finance
§§ California Employment Development Dept

General Information

City of San Diego
202 C St
San Diego, CA 92101
619-236-5555

Website ... www.sandiego.gov
Elevation ... 42 ft.
Land Area (sq. miles) ... 324.3
Water Area (sq. miles) ... 47.7
Year of Incorporation ... 1850
Government type ... Chartered
Sales tax rate ... 8.75%

Voters & Officials

Registered Voters, October 2008

Total ... 654,817
Democrats ... 267,636
Republicans ... 195,205
Declined to state ... 164,000

Legislative Districts

US Congressional ... 49-53
State Senatorial ... 36, 38-40
State Assembly ... 74-79

Local Officials, 2009

Mayor ... Jerry Sanders
Manager ... NA
City Clerk ... Elizabeth Maland
Attorney ... Dan Goldsmith
Finance Dir ... Mary Lewis
Public Works ... David Jarrell
Planning/Dev Dir ... William Anderson
Building ... Kelly Broughton
Police Chief ... William Lansdowne
Emergency/Fire Dir ... Tracy Jarman

Public Safety

Number of officers, 2007 ... 1,924
Violent crimes, 2007 ... 6,332
Property crimes, 2007 ... 44,167
Arson, 2007 ... 200

Public Library

San Diego Central Library
San Diego Public Library System
820 E St
San Diego, CA 92101
619-236-5830

Director ... Anna Tatar

Library system statistics, FY 2007

Population served ... 1,316,837
Internet terminals ... 403
Annual users ... 16,476,655

Per capita:

Operating income ... $32.86
percent from local government ... 90.0%
Operating expenditure ... $30.86
Total materials ... 3.92
Print holdings ... 3.65
Visits per capita ... 3.77

Housing & Construction

Housing Units

Total, 2008§ ... 505,422
Single family units, attached ... 45,882
Single family units, detached ... 229,267
Multiple family units ... 223,932
Mobile home units ... 6,341
Occupied ... 485,061
Vacancy rate ... 4.0%
Median rent, 2007** ... $1,209
Median SF home value, 2007** ... $558,100

New Privately Owned Housing Units Authorized by Building Permit, 2007*

	Units	Construction Cost
Single	748	$146,759,338
Total	3,760	$490,083,338

Municipal Finance

(For local fiscal year ended in 2006)

Revenues

Total ... NA
Taxes ... NA
Special benefits assessment ... NA
Licenses & permits ... NA
Fines & forfeitures ... NA
Revenues from use of money & property ... NA
Intergovernmental ... NA
Service charges ... NA
Other revenues ... NA
Other financing sources ... NA

Expenditures

Total ... NA
General government ... NA
Public safety ... NA
Transportation ... NA
Community development ... NA
Health ... NA
Culture & leisure ... NA
Other ... NA

Local School District

(Data from School year 2007-08 except as noted)

San Diego City Unified
4100 Normal St
San Diego, CA 92103
(619) 725-8000

Superintendent ... Terry Grier
Grade plan ... K-12
Number of schools ... 215
Enrollment ... 131,577
High school graduates, 2006-07 ... 6,335
Dropout rate ... 4.5%
Pupil/teacher ratio ... 18.8
Average class size ... 22.0
Students per computer ... 3.4
Classrooms with internet ... 7,307
Avg. Daily Attendance (ADA) ... 113,165
Cost per ADA ... $10,426
Avg. Teacher Salary ... $63,424

California Achievement Tests 6th ed., 2008

(Pct scoring at or above 50th National Percentile Rank)

	Math	Reading	Language
Grade 3	59%	39%	47%
Grade 7	54%	49%	47%

Academic Performance Index, 2008

Number of students tested ... 87,031
Number of valid scores ... 82,160
2007 API (base) ... 734
2008 API (growth) ... 748

SAT Testing, 2006-07

Enrollment, Grade 12 ... 8,039
Number taking test ... 3,887
percent taking test ... 48.4%
percent with total score 1,500+ ... 21.20%

Average Scores:

Math	Verbal	Writing	Total
496	484	478	1,458

Federal No Child Left Behind, 2008

(Adequate Yearly Progress standards met)

	Participation Rate	Pct Proficient
ELA	Yes	No
Math	Yes	No

API criteria ... Yes
Graduation rate ... No
\# criteria met/possible ... 46/42

Other school districts for this city

(see Appendix E for information on these districts)

South Bay Union Elem, Chula Vista Elem, Poway Unified

See Introduction for an explanation of all data sources.

Demographics & Socio-Economic Characteristics

(2000 Decennial Census, except as noted)

Population

1990* 32,397
2000 34,980
Male 16,783
Female 18,197
Jan. 2008 (estimate)§ 36,874
Persons per sq. mi. of land 2,379.0

Race & Hispanic Origin, 2000

Race
White 26,116
Black/African American 1,156
North American Native 243
Asian 3,286
Pacific Islander 73
Other Race 2,569
Two or more races 1,537
Hispanic origin, total 8,163
Mexican 6,029
Puerto Rican 190
Cuban 208
Other Hispanic 1,736

Age & Nativity, 2000

Under 5 years 2,051
18 years and over 26,046
65 years and over 4,159
85 years and over 605
Median Age 37.3
Native-born 29,647
Foreign-born 5,417

Educational Attainment, 2000

Population 25 years and over 23,056
Less than 9th grade 3.7%
High school grad or higher 87.3%
Bachelor's degree or higher 28.4%
Graduate degree 9.2%

Income & Poverty, 1999

Per capita income $28,321
Median household income $62,885
Median family income $72,124
Persons in poverty 6.2%
H'holds receiving public assistance 327
H'holds receiving social security 2,773

Households, 2000

Total households 12,163
With persons under 18 4,750
With persons over 65 2,765
Family households 8,985
Single person households 2,558
Persons per household 2.78
Persons per family 3.23

Household Population, 2008§§

Persons living in households 35,665
Persons living in group quarters 1,209
Persons per household 2.9

Labor & Employment

Total civilian labor force, 2008§§ 20,600
Unemployment rate, 2008 .... 4.3%
Total civilian labor force, 2000 18,017

Employed persons 16 years and over by occupation, 2000

Managers & professionals 7,193
Service occupations 2,090
Sales & office occupations 5,076
Farming, fishing & forestry 27
Construction & maintenance 1,140
Production & transportation 1,516
Self-employed persons 1,427

* US Census Bureau
** 2000 Decennial Census
§ California Department of Finance
§§ California Employment Development Dept

General Information

City of San Dimas
245 E Bonita Ave
San Dimas, CA 91773
909-394-6200

Website .... www.cityofsandimas.com
Elevation .... 952 ft.
Land Area (sq. miles) 15.5
Water Area (sq. miles) 0.1
Year of Incorporation 1960
Government type .... General law
Sales tax rate 9.25%

Voters & Officials

Registered Voters, October 2008

Total 19,966
Democrats 6,884
Republicans 8,906
Declined to state 3,361

Legislative Districts

US Congressional 26
State Senatorial 29
State Assembly 59, 60

Local Officials, 2009

Mayor .... Curtis Morris
Manager .... Blaine Michaelis
City Clerk .... Ina Rios
Attorney .... J. Kenneth Brown
Finance Dir .... Blaine Michaels
Public Works .... Krishna Patel
Development Svcs Dir .... Dan Coleman
Building .... NA
Police Chief .... NA
Fire/Emergency Mgmt .... NA

Public Safety

Number of officers, 2007 .... NA
Violent crimes, 2007 82
Property crimes, 2007 898
Arson, 2007 9

Public Library

San Dimas Library
Los Angeles County Public Library System
145 N Walnut Ave
San Dimas, CA 91773
909-599-6738

Branch Librarian .... Debbie Yasher

Library system statistics, FY 2007

Population served 3,673,313
Internet terminals 749
Annual users 3,748,771

Per capita:

Operating income $30.06
percent from local government 93.6%
Operating expenditure $28.36
Total materials 2.22
Print holdings 1.97
Visits per capita 3.25

Housing & Construction

Housing Units

Total, 2008§ 12,600
Single family units, attached 2,100
Single family units, detached 7,582
Multiple family units 1,975
Mobile home units 943
Occupied 12,258
Vacancy rate 2.7%
Median rent, 2000** $876
Median SF home value, 2000** $232,400

New Privately Owned Housing Units Authorized by Building Permit, 2007*

	Units	Construction Cost
Single	5	$2,698,177
Total	5	$2,698,177

Municipal Finance

(For local fiscal year ended in 2006)

Revenues

Total $24,029,184
Taxes 15,377,312
Special benefits assessment 682,109
Licenses & permits 531,474
Fines & forfeitures 523,462
Revenues from use of money & property 1,853,023
Intergovernmental 2,666,285
Service charges 2,386,449
Other revenues 9,070
Other financing sources 0

Expenditures

Total $19,734,015
General government 4,594,220
Public safety 6,006,111
Transportation 3,434,530
Community development 2,028,780
Health 56,130
Culture & leisure 3,614,244
Other 0

Local School District

(Data from School year 2007-08 except as noted)

Bonita Unified
115 West Allen Ave
San Dimas, CA 91773
(909) 971-8200

Superintendent .... Gary Rapkin
Grade plan K-12
Number of schools 14
Enrollment 10,100
High school graduates, 2006-07 806
Dropout rate 1.2%
Pupil/teacher ratio 23.8
Average class size 27.4
Students per computer 4.8
Classrooms with internet 485
Avg. Daily Attendance (ADA) 9,920
Cost per ADA $7,796
Avg. Teacher Salary $69,444

California Achievement Tests 6th ed., 2008

(Pct scoring at or above 50th National Percentile Rank)

	Math	Reading	Language
Grade 3	68%	53%	59%
Grade 7	63%	61%	60%

Academic Performance Index, 2008

Number of students tested 7,820
Number of valid scores 7,483
2007 API (base) 799
2008 API (growth) 818

SAT Testing, 2006-07

Enrollment, Grade 12 914
Number taking test 388
percent taking test 42.5%
percent with total score 1,500+ 20.80%

Average Scores:

Math	Verbal	Writing	Total
504	502	501	1,507

Federal No Child Left Behind, 2008

(Adequate Yearly Progress standards met)

	Participation Rate	Pct Proficient
ELA	Yes	No
Math	Yes	No

API criteria .... Yes
Graduation rate .... Yes
criteria met/possible 38/36

Other school districts for this city

(see Appendix E for information on these districts)

None

Demographics & Socio-Economic Characteristics

(2000 Decennial Census, except as noted)

Population

1990* 22,580
2000 23,564
Male 11,881
Female 11,683
Jan. 2008 (estimate)§ 25,230
Persons per sq. mi. of land 10,512.5

Race & Hispanic Origin, 2000

Race
White 10,076
Black/African American 231
North American Native 399
Asian 264
Pacific Islander 26
Other Race 11,629
Two or more races 939
Hispanic origin, total 21,038
Mexican 18,504
Puerto Rican 57
Cuban 25
Other Hispanic 2,452

Age & Nativity, 2000

Under 5 years 2,255
18 years and over 15,455
65 years and over 1,660
85 years and over 167
Median Age 27.3
Native-born 13,309
Foreign-born 10,225

Educational Attainment, 2000

Population 25 years and over 12,932
Less than 9th grade 33.3%
High school grad or higher 41.9%
Bachelor's degree or higher 5.4%
Graduate degree 1.9%

Income & Poverty, 1999

Per capita income $11,485
Median household income $39,909
Median family income $40,138
Persons in poverty 18.9%
H'holds receiving public assistance 370
H'holds receiving social security 1,199

Households, 2000

Total households 5,774
With persons under 18 3,493
With persons over 65 1,273
Family households 4,834
Single person households 717
Persons per household 4.07
Persons per family 4.33

Household Population, 2008§§

Persons living in households 25,184
Persons living in group quarters 46
Persons per household 4.3

Labor & Employment

Total civilian labor force, 2008§§ 10,600
Unemployment rate, 2008 .... 7.3%
Total civilian labor force, 2000 9,184

Employed persons 16 years and over by occupation, 2000

Managers & professionals 1,401
Service occupations 1,625
Sales & office occupations 2,043
Farming, fishing & forestry 29
Construction & maintenance 1,146
Production & transportation 2,209
Self-employed persons 527

* US Census Bureau
** 2000 Decennial Census
§ California Department of Finance
§§ California Employment Development Dept

General Information

City of San Fernando
117 Macneil St
San Fernando, CA 91340
818-898-1200

Website .... www.ci.san-fernando.ca.us
Elevation .... 1,061 ft.
Land Area (sq. miles) 2.4
Water Area (sq. miles) 0
Year of Incorporation 1911
Government type .... General law
Sales tax rate 9.25%

Voters & Officials

Registered Voters, October 2008

Total 7,742
Democrats 4,964
Republicans 1,071
Declined to state 1,429

Legislative Districts

US Congressional 28
State Senatorial 20
State Assembly 39

Local Officials, 2009

Mayor .... Steven Veres
Manager .... Jose Pulido
City Clerk .... Elena G. Chavez
Attorney .... Michael Estrada
Finance Dir .... Lorena Quijano
Public Works .... Ron Ruiz
Planning/Dev Dir .... Paul Deibel
Building .... Francisco Villalva
Police Chief .... Robert Ordelheide
Fire/Emergency Mgmt .... NA

Public Safety

Number of officers, 2007 35
Violent crimes, 2007 .... NA
Property crimes, 2007 .... NA
Arson, 2007 .... NA

Public Library

San Fernando Library
Los Angeles County Public Library System
217 N Maclay Ave
San Fernando, CA 91340
818-365-6928

Branch Librarian .... Kathy Coakley

Library system statistics, FY 2007

Population served 3,673,313
Internet terminals 749
Annual users 3,748,771

Per capita:

Operating income $30.06
percent from local government 93.6%
Operating expenditure $28.36
Total materials 2.22
Print holdings 1.97
Visits per capita 3.25

Housing & Construction

Housing Units

Total, 2008§ 6,061
Single family units, attached 671
Single family units, detached 4,044
Multiple family units 1,273
Mobile home units 73
Occupied 5,901
Vacancy rate 2.6%
Median rent, 2000** $665
Median SF home value, 2000** $144,400

New Privately Owned Housing Units Authorized by Building Permit, 2007*

	Units	Construction Cost
Single	12	$1,556,845
Total	49	$8,556,843

Municipal Finance

(For local fiscal year ended in 2006)

Revenues

Total $28,671,006
Taxes 12,959,354
Special benefits assessment 329,521
Licenses & permits 272,739
Fines & forfeitures 1,022,754
Revenues from use of money & property 652,827
Intergovernmental 1,818,587
Service charges 9,382,280
Other revenues 2,232,944
Other financing sources 0

Expenditures

Total $26,462,894
General government 6,828,175
Public safety 8,857,938
Transportation 1,569,081
Community development 1,382,299
Health 2,868,534
Culture & leisure 2,072,688
Other 0

Local School District

(Data from School year 2007-08 except as noted)

Los Angeles Unified
333 South Beaudry Ave
Los Angeles, CA 90017
(213) 241-1000

Superintendent .... Ramon Cortines
Grade plan PK-12
Number of schools 827
Enrollment 693,680
High school graduates, 2006-07 28,545
Dropout rate 7.8%
Pupil/teacher ratio 19.8
Average class size 24.9
Students per computer 3.7
Classrooms with internet 31,112
Avg. Daily Attendance (ADA) 653,672
Cost per ADA $10,053
Avg. Teacher Salary $63,391

California Achievement Tests 6th ed., 2008

(Pct scoring at or above 50th National Percentile Rank)

	Math	Reading	Language
Grade 3	49%	27%	39%
Grade 7	37%	33%	33%

Academic Performance Index, 2008

Number of students tested 495,046
Number of valid scores 471,641
2007 API (base) 662
2008 API (growth) 683

SAT Testing, 2006-07

Enrollment, Grade 12 32,370
Number taking test 15,447
percent taking test 47.7%
percent with total score 1,500+ 12.50%

Average Scores:

Math	Verbal	Writing	Total
443	438	441	1,322

Federal No Child Left Behind, 2008

(Adequate Yearly Progress standards met)

	Participation Rate	Pct Proficient
ELA	Yes	No
Math	Yes	No

API criteria .... Yes
Graduation rate .... Yes
\# criteria met/possible 46/38

Other school districts for this city

(see Appendix E for information on these districts)

None

See Introduction for an explanation of all data sources.

Demographics & Socio-Economic Characteristics†

(2007 American Community Survey, except as noted)

Population

1990* 723,959
2007 764,976
Male 389,132
Female 375,844
Jan. 2008 (estimate)§ 824,525
Persons per sq. mi. of land 17,655.8

Race & Hispanic Origin, 2007

Race
White 419,636
Black/African American 51,103
North American Native 2,843
Asian 240,532
Pacific Islander 2,956
Other Race 25,987
Two or more races 21,919
Hispanic origin, total 106,914
Mexican 52,741
Puerto Rican 4,863
Cuban 1,242
Other Hispanic 48,068

Age & Nativity, 2007

Under 5 years 40,147
18 years and over 655,258
65 years and over 110,880
85 years and over 18,649
Median Age 40.0
Native-born 494,904
Foreign-born 270,072

Educational Attainment, 2007

Population 25 years and over 596,067
Less than 9th grade 9.1%
High school grad or higher 84.9%
Bachelor's degree or higher 49.9%
Graduate degree 19.2%

Income & Poverty, 2007

Per capita income $45,410
Median household income $68,023
Median family income $82,320
Persons in poverty 10.5%
H'holds receiving public assistance . . . 6,158
H'holds receiving social security 67,614

Households, 2007

Total households 321,947
With persons under 18 61,780
With persons over 65 75,763
Family households 141,384
Single person households 138,437
Persons per household 2.33
Persons per family 3.35

Household Population, 2008§§

Persons living in households 803,419
Persons living in group quarters 21,106
Persons per household 2.3

Labor & Employment

Total civilian labor force, 2008§§ . . . 450,400
Unemployment rate, 2008 . . . . 5.3%
Total civilian labor force, 2000* 448,432

Employed persons 16 years and over by occupation, 2007

Managers & professionals 212,067
Service occupations 71,855
Sales & office occupations 99,011
Farming, fishing & forestry 0
Construction & maintenance 21,085
Production & transportation 24,684
Self-employed persons 41,933

† see Appendix D for 2000 Decennial Census Data
* US Census Bureau
** 2007 American Community Survey
§ California Department of Finance
§§ California Employment Development Dept

General Information

City of San Francisco
1 Dr Carlton B. Goodlett
City Hall
San Francisco, CA 94102
415-554-4950

Website . . . . www.sfgov.org
Elevation . . . . 63 ft.
Land Area (sq. miles) 46.7
Water Area (sq. miles) 185.2
Year of Incorporation 1850
Government type . . . . Chartered
Sales tax rate 9.50%

Voters & Officials

Registered Voters, October 2008

Total 477,356
Democrats 269,664
Republicans 45,157
Declined to state 140,102

Legislative Districts

US Congressional 8, 12
State Senatorial 3, 8
State Assembly 12, 13

Local Officials, 2009

Mayor . . . . Gavin Newsom
Manager . . . . Edwin Lee
City Clerk . . . . Edwin Lee
Attorney . . . . Dennis Herrera
Finance Dir . . . . Jose Cisneros
Public Works . . . . Ed Reiskin
Planning/Dev Dir . . . . John Rahaim
Building . . . . Vivian Day (Actg)
Police Chief . . . . Heather J. Fong
Fire Chief . . . . Joanne Hayes-White

Public Safety

Number of officers, 2007 2,337
Violent crimes, 2007 6,414
Property crimes, 2007 34,456
Arson, 2007 232

Public Library

San Francisco Main Library
San Francisco Public Library System
100 Larkin St
San Francisco, CA 94102
415-557-4400

City Librarian . . . . Luis Herrera

Library system statistics, FY 2007

Population served 808,844
Internet terminals 910
Annual users 2,109,135

Per capita:

Operating income $89.45
percent from local government 95.1%
Operating expenditure $83.09
Total materials 4.04
Print holdings 3.74
Visits per capita 7.85

Housing & Construction

Housing Units

Total, 2008§ 361,777
Single family units, attached 48,700
Single family units, detached 63,046
Multiple family units 249,471
Mobile home units 560
Occupied 344,792
Vacancy rate 4.7%
Median rent, 2007** $1,192
Median SF home value, 2007** $830,700

New Privately Owned Housing Units Authorized by Building Permit, 2007*

	Units	Construction Cost
Single	55	$11,482,079
Total	2,475	$304,387,984

Municipal Finance

(For local fiscal year ended in 2006)

Revenues

Total $6,863,549,839
Taxes 1,990,465,376
Special benefits assessment 0
Licenses & permits 34,247,705
Fines & forfeitures 15,221,561
Revenues from use of money & property 136,738,901
Intergovernmental 1,200,034,960
Service charges 1,940,404,496
Other revenues 217,199,740
Other financing sources 1,329,237,100

Expenditures

Total $6,441,882,716
General government 822,855,960
Public safety 875,826,723
Transportation 1,945,217,250
Community development 179,262,410
Health 1,806,630,811
Culture & leisure 259,403,410
Other 0

Local School District

(Data from School year 2007-08 except as noted)

San Francisco Unified
555 Franklin St
San Francisco, CA 94102
(415) 241-6000

Superintendent . . . . Carlos Garcia
Grade plan PK-12
Number of schools 112
Enrollment 55,069
High school graduates, 2006-07 3,773
Dropout rate 4.9%
Pupil/teacher ratio 17.7
Average class size 21.4
Students per computer 4.2
Classrooms with internet 2,938
Avg. Daily Attendance (ADA) 49,101
Cost per ADA $8,913
Avg. Teacher Salary $59,448

California Achievement Tests 6th ed., 2008

(Pct scoring at or above 50th National Percentile Rank)

	Math	Reading	Language
Grade 3	62%	37%	50%
Grade 7	59%	47%	49%

Academic Performance Index, 2008

Number of students tested 39,442
Number of valid scores 37,219
2007 API (base) 764
2008 API (growth) 771

SAT Testing, 2006-07

Enrollment, Grade 12 3,799
Number taking test 2,759
percent taking test 72.6%
percent with total score 1,500+ . . . 32.30%

Average Scores:

Math	Verbal	Writing	Total
528	476	474	1,478

Federal No Child Left Behind, 2008

(Adequate Yearly Progress standards met)

	Participation Rate	Pct Proficient
ELA	Yes	No
Math	Yes	No

API criteria . . . . Yes
Graduation rate . . . . Yes
\# criteria met/possible 46/38

Other school districts for this city

(see Appendix E for information on these districts)

None

See Introduction for an explanation of all data sources.

Demographics & Socio-Economic Characteristics

(2000 Decennial Census, except as noted)

Population

1990* ... 37,120
2000 ... 39,804
Male ... 19,091
Female ... 20,713
Jan. 2008 (estimate)§ ... 42,762
Persons per sq. mi. of land ... 10,429.8

Race & Hispanic Origin, 2000

Race
White ... 13,294
Black/African American ... 420
North American Native ... 331
Asian ... 19,470
Pacific Islander ... 39
Other Race ... 4,921
Two or more races ... 1,329
Hispanic origin, total ... 12,223
Mexican ... 9,559
Puerto Rican ... 123
Cuban ... 139
Other Hispanic ... 2,402

Age & Nativity, 2000

Under 5 years ... 2,653
18 years and over ... 30,449
65 years and over ... 5,352
85 years and over ... 920
Median Age ... 35.6
Native-born ... 18,647
Foreign-born ... 20,659

Educational Attainment, 2000

Population 25 years and over ... 26,962
Less than 9th grade ... 17.1%
High school grad or higher ... 69.2%
Bachelor's degree or higher ... 24.6%
Graduate degree ... 7.5%

Income & Poverty, 1999

Per capita income ... $16,807
Median household income ... $41,791
Median family income ... $45,287
Persons in poverty ... 15.4%
H'holds receiving public assistance ... 817
H'holds receiving social security ... 2,440

Households, 2000

Total households ... 12,587
With persons under 18 ... 5,092
With persons over 65 ... 3,464
Family households ... 9,567
Single person households ... 2,290
Persons per household ... 3.10
Persons per family ... 3.52

Household Population, 2008§§

Persons living in households ... 42,007
Persons living in group quarters ... 755
Persons per household ... 3.3

Labor & Employment

Total civilian labor force, 2008§§ ... 21,000
Unemployment rate, 2008 ... 6.1%
Total civilian labor force, 2000 ... 18,028

Employed persons 16 years and over by occupation, 2000

Managers & professionals ... 5,729
Service occupations ... 2,720
Sales & office occupations ... 5,016
Farming, fishing & forestry ... 8
Construction & maintenance ... 940
Production & transportation ... 2,424
Self-employed persons ... 1,260

* US Census Bureau
** 2000 Decennial Census
§ California Department of Finance
§§ California Employment Development Dept

General Information

City of San Gabriel
425 S Mission Dr
San Gabriel, CA 91776
626-308-2800

Website ... www.sangabrielcity.com
Elevation ... 430 ft.
Land Area (sq. miles) ... 4.1
Water Area (sq. miles) ... 0
Year of Incorporation ... 1913
Government type ... General law
Sales tax rate ... 9.25%

Voters & Officials

Registered Voters, October 2008

Total ... 15,120
Democrats ... 6,459
Republicans ... 3,838
Declined to state ... 4,314

Legislative Districts

US Congressional ... 29
State Senatorial ... 21
State Assembly ... 49

Local Officials, 2009

Mayor ... Harry L. Baldwin
Manager ... P. Michael Paules
City Clerk ... Nina Castruita (Dep)
Attorney ... Robert Kress
Finance Dir ... Thomas Marston
Public Works ... Robert Bustos
Planning/Dev Dir ... Steven A. Preston
Building ... Evan Zeisel
Police Chief ... David Lawton
Emergency/Fire Dir ... Joseph Nestor

Public Safety

Number of officers, 2007 ... 55
Violent crimes, 2007 ... 195
Property crimes, 2007 ... 770
Arson, 2007 ... 9

Public Library

San Gabriel Library
Los Angeles County Public Library System
500 S Del Mar Ave
San Gabriel, CA 91776
626-287-0761

Branch Librarian ... Julie Sorensen

Library system statistics, FY 2007

Population served ... 3,673,313
Internet terminals ... 749
Annual users ... 3,748,771

Per capita:

Operating income ... $30.06
percent from local government ... 93.6%
Operating expenditure ... $28.36
Total materials ... 2.22
Print holdings ... 1.97
Visits per capita ... 3.25

Housing & Construction

Housing Units

Total, 2008§ ... 13,251
Single family units, attached ... 1,223
Single family units, detached ... 7,117
Multiple family units ... 4,867
Mobile home units ... 44
Occupied ... 12,920
Vacancy rate ... 2.5%
Median rent, 2000** ... $759
Median SF home value, 2000** ... $232,600

New Privately Owned Housing Units Authorized by Building Permit, 2007*

	Units	Construction Cost
Single	17	$5,011,498
Total	44	$13,657,548

Municipal Finance

(For local fiscal year ended in 2006)

Revenues

Total ... $31,012,514
Taxes ... 19,027,347
Special benefits assessment ... 42,040
Licenses & permits ... 1,279,600
Fines & forfeitures ... 935,568
Revenues from use of money & property ... 1,142,161
Intergovernmental ... 3,139,246
Service charges ... 4,205,849
Other revenues ... 1,240,703
Other financing sources ... 0

Expenditures

Total ... $27,586,982
General government ... 4,499,505
Public safety ... 14,361,509
Transportation ... 4,014,651
Community development ... 1,978,346
Health ... 46,037
Culture & leisure ... 2,686,934
Other ... 0

Local School District

(Data from School year 2007-08 except as noted)

San Gabriel Unified
408 Junipero Serra Dr
San Gabriel, CA 91776
(626) 451-5400

Superintendent ... Susan Parks
Grade plan ... K-12
Number of schools ... 9
Enrollment ... 6,228
High school graduates, 2006-07 ... 505
Dropout rate ... 10.5%
Pupil/teacher ratio ... 20.7
Average class size ... 25.8
Students per computer ... 4.7
Classrooms with internet ... 278
Avg. Daily Attendance (ADA) ... 5,565
Cost per ADA ... $7,987
Avg. Teacher Salary ... $63,168

California Achievement Tests 6th ed., 2008

(Pct scoring at or above 50th National Percentile Rank)

	Math	Reading	Language
Grade 3	64%	43%	55%
Grade 7	63%	56%	55%

Academic Performance Index, 2008

Number of students tested ... 4,348
Number of valid scores ... 4,089
2007 API (base) ... 790
2008 API (growth) ... 812

SAT Testing, 2006-07

Enrollment, Grade 12 ... 546
Number taking test ... 243
percent taking test ... 44.5%
percent with total score 1,500+ ... 25.50%

Average Scores:

Math	Verbal	Writing	Total
539	503	502	1,544

Federal No Child Left Behind, 2008

(Adequate Yearly Progress standards met)

	Participation Rate	Pct Proficient
ELA	Yes	No
Math	Yes	No

API criteria ... Yes
Graduation rate ... Yes
\# criteria met/possible ... 30/28

Other school districts for this city

(see Appendix E for information on these districts)

Temple City Unified, Alhambra Unified, Garvey Elem

See Introduction for an explanation of all data sources.

Demographics & Socio-Economic Characteristics

(2000 Decennial Census, except as noted)

Population

1990* 16,210
2000 23,779
Male 11,512
Female 12,267
Jan. 2008 (estimate)§ 35,672
Persons per sq. mi. of land 1,432.6

Race & Hispanic Origin, 2000

Race
White 16,488
Black/African American 630
North American Native 556
Asian 267
Pacific Islander 38
Other Race 4,641
Two or more races 1,159
Hispanic origin, total 9,583
Mexican 7,945
Puerto Rican 135
Cuban 33
Other Hispanic 1,470

Age & Nativity, 2000

Under 5 years 1,982
18 years and over 16,328
65 years and over 4,092
85 years and over 418
Median Age 33.7
Native-born 19,718
Foreign-born 4,205

Educational Attainment, 2000

Population 25 years and over 14,582
Less than 9th grade 14.1%
High school grad or higher 68.6%
Bachelor's degree or higher 8.8%
Graduate degree 3.3%

Income & Poverty, 1999

Per capita income $13,265
Median household income $30,627
Median family income $34,717
Persons in poverty 20.2%
H'holds receiving public assistance 556
H'holds receiving social security 3,325

Households, 2000

Total households 8,314
With persons under 18 3,324
With persons over 65 2,917
Family households 5,837
Single person households 2,108
Persons per household 2.84
Persons per family 3.41

Household Population, 2008§§

Persons living in households 35,482
Persons living in group quarters 190
Persons per household 2.9

Labor & Employment

Total civilian labor force, 2008§§ 12,200
Unemployment rate, 2008 . . . . . 13.2%
Total civilian labor force, 2000 8,603

Employed persons 16 years and over by occupation, 2000

Managers & professionals 1,714
Service occupations 1,669
Sales & office occupations 1,711
Farming, fishing & forestry 196
Construction & maintenance 973
Production & transportation 1,343
Self-employed persons 740

* US Census Bureau
** 2000 Decennial Census
§ California Department of Finance
§§ California Employment Development Dept

General Information

City of San Jacinto
595 S. San Jacinto Ave
San Jacinto, CA 92583
951-654-7337

Website . . . . . www.ci.san-jacinto.ca.us
Elevation . . . . . 1,567 ft.
Land Area (sq. miles) 24.9
Water Area (sq. miles) 0.4
Year of Incorporation 1888
Government type . . . . . General law
Sales tax rate 8.75%

Voters & Officials

Registered Voters, October 2008

Total 14,084
Democrats 5,330
Republicans 5,753
Declined to state 2,348

Legislative Districts

US Congressional 41
State Senatorial 37
State Assembly 65

Local Officials, 2009

Mayor . . . . . Dale Stubblefield
Manager . . . . . Barry McClellan
City Clerk . . . . . Dorothy Chouinard
Attorney . . . . . Jeff Ballinger
Finance Dir . . . . Connie Rogers-Elmore (Int)
Public Works . . . . . Mike Emberton
Planning Dir . . . . . Asher Hartel
Building . . . . . Joe Lancaster
Police Chief . . . . . William Tyler
Fire Chief . . . . . Robert Michael

Public Safety

Number of officers, 2007 . . . . . NA
Violent crimes, 2007 158
Property crimes, 2007 1,215
Arson, 2007 4

Public Library

San Jacinto Branch Library
Riverside County Library Service
500 Idyllwild Dr
San Jacinto, CA 92583
909-654-8635

Branch Librarian . . . . . Teri Pilate

Library system statistics, FY 2007

Population served 1,047,996
Internet terminals 37
Annual users 69,346

Per capita:

Operating income $19.38
percent from local government 49.8%
Operating expenditure $20.45
Total materials 1.43
Print holdings 1.30
Visits per capita 4.06

Housing & Construction

Housing Units

Total, 2008§ 14,015
Single family units, attached 596
Single family units, detached 9,527
Multiple family units 1,231
Mobile home units 2,661
Occupied 12,288
Vacancy rate 12.3%
Median rent, 2000** $513
Median SF home value, 2000** $96,900

New Privately Owned Housing Units Authorized by Building Permit, 2007*

	Units	Construction Cost
Single	276	$48,195,748
Total	358	$53,791,596

Municipal Finance

(For local fiscal year ended in 2006)

Revenues

Total $40,840,852
Taxes 13,473,140
Special benefits assessment 6,212,052
Licenses & permits 5,022,396
Fines & forfeitures 83,350
Revenues from use of money & property 1,568,849
Intergovernmental 3,404,579
Service charges 7,660,680
Other revenues 3,415,806
Other financing sources 0

Expenditures

Total $25,482,237
General government 1,662,593
Public safety 11,312,664
Transportation 1,237,133
Community development 5,719,330
Health 1,941,206
Culture & leisure 825,179
Other 0

Local School District

(Data from School year 2007-08 except as noted)

San Jacinto Unified
2045 South San Jacinto Ave
San Jacinto, CA 92583
(951) 929-7700

Superintendent . . . . . Shari Fox
Grade plan K-12
Number of schools 13
Enrollment 9,591
High school graduates, 2006-07 403
Dropout rate 7.1%
Pupil/teacher ratio 21.5
Average class size 26.3
Students per computer 5.3
Classrooms with internet 413
Avg. Daily Attendance (ADA) 8,702
Cost per ADA $8,299
Avg. Teacher Salary $64,101

California Achievement Tests 6th ed., 2008

(Pct scoring at or above 50th National Percentile Rank)

	Math	Reading	Language
Grade 3	44%	26%	38%
Grade 7	37%	37%	32%

Academic Performance Index, 2008

Number of students tested 6,842
Number of valid scores 6,061
2007 API (base) 671
2008 API (growth) 693

SAT Testing, 2006-07

Enrollment, Grade 12 566
Number taking test 109
percent taking test 19.3%
percent with total score 1,500+ 4.40%

Average Scores:

Math	Verbal	Writing	Total
442	447	441	1,330

Federal No Child Left Behind, 2008

(Adequate Yearly Progress standards met)

	Participation Rate	Pct Proficient
ELA	Yes	No
Math	Yes	No

API criteria . . . . . Yes
Graduation rate . . . . . No
criteria met/possible 34/25

Other school districts for this city

(see Appendix E for information on these districts)

None

See Introduction for an explanation of all data sources.

Demographics & Socio-Economic Characteristics

(2000 Decennial Census, except as noted)

Population

1990* . . . 2,311
2000 . . . 3,270
Male . . . 1,739
Female . . . 1,531
Jan. 2008 (estimate)§ . . . 4,062
Persons per sq. mi. of land . . . 4,062.0

Race & Hispanic Origin, 2000

Race
White . . . 1,159
Black/African American . . . 7
North American Native . . . 51
Asian . . . 118
Pacific Islander . . . 0
Other Race . . . 1,757
Two or more races . . . 178
Hispanic origin, total . . . 3,008
Mexican . . . 2,722
Puerto Rican . . . 4
Cuban . . . 0
Other Hispanic . . . 282

Age & Nativity, 2000

Under 5 years . . . 386
18 years and over . . . 1,922
65 years and over . . . 131
85 years and over . . . 4
Median Age . . . 22.1
Native-born . . . 1,420
Foreign-born . . . 1,881

Educational Attainment, 2000

Population 25 years and over . . . 1,507
Less than 9th grade . . . 60.5%
High school grad or higher . . . 20.6%
Bachelor's degree or higher . . . 2.9%
Graduate degree . . . 0.8%

Income & Poverty, 1999

Per capita income . . . $6,607
Median household income . . . $24,934
Median family income . . . $25,441
Persons in poverty . . . 34.8%
H'holds receiving public assistance . . . 87
H'holds receiving social security . . . 99

Households, 2000

Total households . . . 702
With persons under 18 . . . 527
With persons over 65 . . . 107
Family households . . . 637
Single person households . . . 47
Persons per household . . . 4.66
Persons per family . . . 4.79

Household Population, 2008§§

Persons living in households . . . 4,062
Persons living in group quarters . . . 0
Persons per household . . . 4.7

Labor & Employment

Total civilian labor force, 2008§§ . . . 1,500
Unemployment rate, 2008 . . . 25.8%
Total civilian labor force, 2000 . . . 1,175

Employed persons 16 years and over by occupation, 2000

Managers & professionals . . . 56
Service occupations . . . 77
Sales & office occupations . . . 81
Farming, fishing & forestry . . . 363
Construction & maintenance . . . 53
Production & transportation . . . 213
Self-employed persons . . . 24

* US Census Bureau
** 2000 Decennial Census
§ California Department of Finance
§§ California Employment Development Dept

General Information

City of San Joaquin
PO Box 758
San Joaquin, CA 93660
559-693-4311

Website . . . www.cityofsanjoaquin.org
Elevation . . . 170 ft.
Land Area (sq. miles) . . . 1.0
Water Area (sq. miles) . . . 0
Year of Incorporation . . . 1920
Government type . . . General law
Sales tax rate . . . 8.98%

Voters & Officials

Registered Voters, October 2008

Total . . . 576
Democrats . . . 347
Republicans . . . 120
Declined to state . . . 65

Legislative Districts

US Congressional . . . 20
State Senatorial . . . 16
State Assembly . . . 31

Local Officials, 2009

Mayor . . . Amarpreet Dhaliwal
Manager . . . Cruz Ramos
City Clerk . . . Diana Brooks
Attorney . . . Hilda Montoy
Finance Dir . . . Vacant
Public Works . . . Leo Cantu
Planning/Dev Dir . . . Lupe Estrada
Building . . . Stan Bulla
Police Chief . . . (County)
Fire/Emergency Mgmt . . . Cal Fire

Public Safety

Number of officers, 2007 . . . NA
Violent crimes, 2007 . . . NA
Property crimes, 2007 . . . NA
Arson, 2007 . . . NA

Public Library

San Joaquin Branch Library
Fresno County Public Library System
8781 Main St
San Joaquin, CA 93660
559-693-2171

Branch Librarian . . . Beth Goering

Library system statistics, FY 2007

Population served . . . 889,019
Internet terminals . . . 277
Annual users . . . 861,240

Per capita:

Operating income . . . $23.69
percent from local government . . . 89.3%
Operating expenditure . . . $23.37
Total materials . . . 2.89
Print holdings . . . 2.69
Visits per capita . . . NA

Housing & Construction

Housing Units

Total, 2008§ . . . 895
Single family units, attached . . . 80
Single family units, detached . . . 531
Multiple family units . . . 224
Mobile home units . . . 60
Occupied . . . 857
Vacancy rate . . . 4.2%
Median rent, 2000** . . . $354
Median SF home value, 2000** . . . $82,900

New Privately Owned Housing Units Authorized by Building Permit, 2007*

	Units	Construction Cost
Single	5	$1,300,000
Total	51	$9,700,000

Municipal Finance

(For local fiscal year ended in 2006)

Revenues

Total . . . $2,275,596
Taxes . . . 768,966
Special benefits assessment . . . 12,797
Licenses & permits . . . 130,718
Fines & forfeitures . . . 19,944
Revenues from use of money & property . . . 97,808
Intergovernmental . . . 240,707
Service charges . . . 987,262
Other revenues . . . 17,394
Other financing sources . . . 0

Expenditures

Total . . . $1,630,877
General government . . . 346,825
Public safety . . . 211,575
Transportation . . . 187,260
Community development . . . 0
Health . . . 505,126
Culture & leisure . . . 77,449
Other . . . 0

Local School District

(Data from School year 2007-08 except as noted)

Golden Plains Unified
PO Box 937
San Joaquin, CA 93660
(559) 693-1115

Superintendent . . . Marie Banuelos
Grade plan . . . K-12
Number of schools . . . 7
Enrollment . . . 1,854
High school graduates, 2006-07 . . . 89
Dropout rate . . . 6.5%
Pupil/teacher ratio . . . 20.4
Average class size . . . 24.4
Students per computer . . . 3.0
Classrooms with internet . . . 120
Avg. Daily Attendance (ADA) . . . 1,847
Cost per ADA . . . $9,028
Avg. Teacher Salary . . . $56,497

California Achievement Tests 6th ed., 2008

(Pct scoring at or above 50th National Percentile Rank)

	Math	Reading	Language
Grade 3	42%	24%	32%
Grade 7	52%	36%	32%

Academic Performance Index, 2008

Number of students tested . . . 1,405
Number of valid scores . . . 1,339
2007 API (base) . . . 644
2008 API (growth) . . . 656

SAT Testing, 2006-07

Enrollment, Grade 12 . . . 115
Number taking test . . . 39
percent taking test . . . 33.9%
percent with total score 1,500+ . . . 1.70%

Average Scores:

Math	Verbal	Writing	Total
425	384	391	1,200

Federal No Child Left Behind, 2008

(Adequate Yearly Progress standards met)

	Participation Rate	Pct Proficient
ELA	Yes	No
Math	Yes	Yes

API criteria . . . Yes
Graduation rate . . . Yes
\# criteria met/possible . . . 18/14

Other school districts for this city

(see Appendix E for information on these districts)

None

See Introduction for an explanation of all data sources.

Demographics & Socio-Economic Characteristics†

(2007 American Community Survey, except as noted)

Population

1990* 782,248
2007 922,389
Male 474,261
Female 448,128
Jan. 2008 (estimate)§ 989,496
Persons per sq. mi. of land 5,657.5

Race & Hispanic Origin, 2007

Race
White 471,129
Black/African American 28,054
North American Native 5,565
Asian 276,681
Pacific Islander 4,466
Other Race 104,503
Two or more races 31,991
Hispanic origin, total 301,259
Mexican 261,832
Puerto Rican 4,474
Cuban 1,504
Other Hispanic 33,449

Age & Nativity, 2007

Under 5 years 68,331
18 years and over 696,645
65 years and over 88,167
85 years and over 9,579
Median Age 35.7
Native-born 554,827
Foreign-born 367,562

Educational Attainment, 2007

Population 25 years and over 611,985
Less than 9th grade 11.3%
High school grad or higher 80.5%
Bachelor's degree or higher 34.7%
Graduate degree 12.6%

Income & Poverty, 2007

Per capita income $33,265
Median household income $76,963
Median family income $86,822
Persons in poverty 9.9%
H'holds receiving public assistance 8,150
H'holds receiving social security 53,838

Households, 2007

Total households 290,680
With persons under 18 117,526
With persons over 65 57,655
Family households 210,191
Single person households 64,212
Persons per household 3.14
Persons per family 3.66

Household Population, 2008§§

Persons living in households 977,529
Persons living in group quarters 11,967
Persons per household 3.2

Labor & Employment

Total civilian labor force, 2008§§ 460,100
Unemployment rate, 2008 ....6.7%
Total civilian labor force, 2000* 456,442

Employed persons 16 years and over by occupation, 2007

Managers & professionals 184,898
Service occupations 72,345
Sales & office occupations 102,928
Farming, fishing & forestry 702
Construction & maintenance 46,048
Production & transportation 47,669
Self-employed persons 33,477

† see Appendix D for 2000 Decennial Census Data
* US Census Bureau
** 2007 American Community Survey
§ California Department of Finance
§§ California Employment Development Dept

General Information

City of San Jose
200 E Santa Clara St
San Jose, CA 95113
408-535-3500

Website ....www.sanjoseca.gov
Elevation ....87 ft.
Land Area (sq. miles) 174.9
Water Area (sq. miles) 3.3
Year of Incorporation 1850
Government type ....Chartered
Sales tax rate 9.25%

Voters & Officials

Registered Voters, October 2008

Total 389,819
Democrats 185,646
Republicans 89,875
Declined to state 100,319

Legislative Districts

US Congressional 14-16
State Senatorial 10, 11, 13, 1
State Assembly 20-24, 27, 28

Local Officials, 2009

Mayor ....Chuck Reed
Manager ....Debra Figone
City Clerk ....Lee Price
Attorney ....Richard Doyle
Finance Dir ....Scott Johnson
Public Works ....Katy Allen
Planning/Dev Dir ....Joseph Horwedel
Building ....Joseph Horwedel
Police Chief ....Robert Davis
Emergency/Fire Dir ....Darryl Von Raesfeld

Public Safety

Number of officers, 2007 1,396
Violent crimes, 2007 3,759
Property crimes, 2007 24,062
Arson, 2007 339

Public Library

San Jose Main Library
San Jose Public Library System
150 E San Fernando St
San Jose, CA 95112
408-808-2000

Director ....Jane Light

Library system statistics, FY 2007

Population served 973,672
Internet terminals 6
Annual users ....NA

Per capita:

Operating income $40.08
percent from local government 94.8%
Operating expenditure $35.35
Total materials 2.18
Print holdings 1.75
Visits per capita 5.66

Housing & Construction

Housing Units

Total, 2008§ 307,613
Single family units, attached 28,227
Single family units, detached 167,873
Multiple family units 100,485
Mobile home units 11,028
Occupied 301,892
Vacancy rate 1.9%
Median rent, 2007** $1,249
Median SF home value, 2007** $687,600

New Privately Owned Housing Units Authorized by Building Permit, 2007*

	Units	Construction Cost
Single	325	$49,290,421
Total	1,942	$238,967,574

Municipal Finance

(For local fiscal year ended in 2006)

Revenues

Total $1,464,667,404
Taxes 574,831,587
Special benefits assessment 6,253,268
Licenses & permits 34,323,432
Fines & forfeitures 14,497,309
Revenues from use of money & property 85,715,833
Intergovernmental 103,777,221
Service charges 408,070,752
Other revenues 106,704,002
Other financing sources 130,494,000

Expenditures

Total $1,436,085,662
General government 155,412,637
Public safety 354,742,965
Transportation 296,755,006
Community development 149,344,061
Health 236,361,687
Culture & leisure 217,295,606
Other 0

Local School District

(Data from School year 2007-08 except as noted)

San Jose Unified
855 Lenzen Ave
San Jose, CA 95126
(408) 535-6000

Superintendent ....Don Iglesias
Grade plan K-12
Number of schools 52
Enrollment 31,230
High school graduates, 2006-07 1,843
Dropout rate 2.9%
Pupil/teacher ratio 20.5
Average class size 22.4
Students per computer 2.3
Classrooms with internet 1,464
Avg. Daily Attendance (ADA) 29,849
Cost per ADA $9,504
Avg. Teacher Salary $69,723

California Achievement Tests 6th ed., 2008

(Pct scoring at or above 50th National Percentile Rank)

	Math	Reading	Language
Grade 3	59%	42%	51%
Grade 7	55%	54%	53%

Academic Performance Index, 2008

Number of students tested 23,244
Number of valid scores 22,131
2007 API (base) 758
2008 API (growth) 770

SAT Testing, 2006-07

Enrollment, Grade 12 2,276
Number taking test 956
percent taking test 42.0%
percent with total score 1,500+ 25.40%

Average Scores:

Math	Verbal	Writing	Total
545	523	522	1,590

Federal No Child Left Behind, 2008

(Adequate Yearly Progress standards met)

	Participation Rate	Pct Proficient
ELA	Yes	No
Math	Yes	No

API criteria ....Yes
Graduation rate ....Yes
\# criteria met/possible 46/42

Other school districts for this city

(see Appendix E for information on these districts)

Complete list in Appendix E

See Introduction for an explanation of all data sources.

Demographics & Socio-Economic Characteristics

(2000 Decennial Census, except as noted)

Population

1990* . . . 1,570
2000 . . . 1,549
Male . . . 767
Female . . . 782
Jan. 2008 (estimate)§ . . . 1,874
Persons per sq. mi. of land . . . 2,677.1

Race & Hispanic Origin, 2000

Race
White . . . 965
Black/African American . . . 21
North American Native . . . 19
Asian . . . 41
Pacific Islander . . . 8
Other Race . . . 391
Two or more races . . . 104
Hispanic origin, total . . . 733
Mexican . . . 644
Puerto Rican . . . 4
Cuban . . . 0
Other Hispanic . . . 85

Age & Nativity, 2000

Under 5 years . . . 116
18 years and over . . . 1,117
65 years and over . . . 169
85 years and over . . . 12
Median Age . . . 35.9
Native-born . . . 1,231
Foreign-born . . . 200

Educational Attainment, 2000

Population 25 years and over . . . 927
Less than 9th grade . . . 10.0%
High school grad or higher . . . 75.6%
Bachelor's degree or higher . . . 12.8%
Graduate degree . . . 4.7%

Income & Poverty, 1999

Per capita income . . . $19,882
Median household income . . . $43,355
Median family income . . . $47,656
Persons in poverty . . . 14.3%
H'holds receiving public assistance . . . 33
H'holds receiving social security . . . 145

Households, 2000

Total households . . . 567
With persons under 18 . . . 218
With persons over 65 . . . 126
Family households . . . 389
Single person households . . . 134
Persons per household . . . 2.73
Persons per family . . . 3.24

Household Population, 2008§§

Persons living in households . . . 1,874
Persons living in group quarters . . . 0
Persons per household . . . 2.8

Labor & Employment

Total civilian labor force, 2008§§ . . . 700
Unemployment rate, 2008 . . . 10.5%
Total civilian labor force, 2000 . . . 701

Employed persons 16 years and over by occupation, 2000

Managers & professionals . . . 154
Service occupations . . . 119
Sales & office occupations . . . 168
Farming, fishing & forestry . . . 24
Construction & maintenance . . . 81
Production & transportation . . . 104
Self-employed persons . . . 60

* US Census Bureau
** 2000 Decennial Census
§ California Department of Finance
§§ California Employment Development Dept

General Information

City of San Juan Bautista
311 Second St
PO Box 1420
San Juan Bautista, CA 95045
831-623-4661

Website . . . www.san-juan-bautista.ca.us
Elevation . . . NA
Land Area (sq. miles) . . . 0.7
Water Area (sq. miles) . . . 0
Year of Incorporation . . . 1896
Government type . . . General law
Sales tax rate . . . 9.00%

Voters & Officials

Registered Voters, October 2008

Total . . . 923
Democrats . . . 468
Republicans . . . 229
Declined to state . . . 175

Legislative Districts

US Congressional . . . 17
State Senatorial . . . 12
State Assembly . . . 28

Local Officials, 2009

Mayor . . . Rick Edge
Manager . . . Stephen Julian
City Clerk . . . Linda McIntyre
Attorney . . . George Thacher
Finance Dir . . . Colleen Johnson
Public Works . . . NA
Planning/Dev Dir . . . NA
Building . . . NA
Police Chief . . . NA
Emergency/Fire Dir . . . Scott Freels

Public Safety

Number of officers, 2007 . . . NA
Violent crimes, 2007 . . . NA
Property crimes, 2007 . . . NA
Arson, 2007 . . . NA

Public Library

San Juan Bautista City Library
801 Second St
San Juan Bautista, CA 95045
831-623-4687

Director . . . Dee Dee Hanania

Library statistics, FY 2007

Population served . . . 1,825
Internet terminals . . . 90
Annual users . . . 203,080

Per capita:

Operating income . . . $50.42
percent from local government . . . 98.9%
Operating expenditure . . . $50.42
Total materials . . . 5.96
Print holdings . . . 5.44
Visits per capita . . . 6.54

Housing & Construction

Housing Units

Total, 2008§ . . . 731
Single family units, attached . . . 82
Single family units, detached . . . 459
Multiple family units . . . 173
Mobile home units . . . 17
Occupied . . . 674
Vacancy rate . . . 7.8%
Median rent, 2000** . . . $806
Median SF home value, 2000** . . . $265,100

New Privately Owned Housing Units Authorized by Building Permit, 2007*

	Units	Construction Cost
Single	3	$594,000
Total	3	$594,000

Municipal Finance

(For local fiscal year ended in 2006)

Revenues

Total . . . $2,906,647
Taxes . . . 953,501
Special benefits assessment . . . 93,936
Licenses & permits . . . 3,674
Fines & forfeitures . . . 461
Revenues from use of money & property . . . 82,922
Intergovernmental . . . 255,028
Service charges . . . 925,542
Other revenues . . . 591,583
Other financing sources . . . 0

Expenditures

Total . . . $2,485,091
General government . . . 1,099,622
Public safety . . . 373,689
Transportation . . . 77,940
Community development . . . 148,573
Health . . . 434,748
Culture & leisure . . . 76,816
Other . . . 0

Local School District

(Data from School year 2007-08 except as noted)

Aromas-San Juan Unified
2300 San Juan Hwy
San Juan Bautista, CA 95045
(831) 623-4500

Superintendent . . . Jacquelyn Munoz
Grade plan . . . K-12
Number of schools . . . 3
Enrollment . . . 1,296
High school graduates, 2006-07 . . . 76
Dropout rate . . . 1.0%
Pupil/teacher ratio . . . 21.5
Average class size . . . 28.7
Students per computer . . . 3.7
Classrooms with internet . . . 73
Avg. Daily Attendance (ADA) . . . 1,212
Cost per ADA . . . $8,988
Avg. Teacher Salary . . . $63,607

California Achievement Tests 6th ed., 2008

(Pct scoring at or above 50th National Percentile Rank)

	Math	Reading	Language
Grade 3	31%	21%	36%
Grade 7	47%	41%	49%

Academic Performance Index, 2008

Number of students tested . . . 980
Number of valid scores . . . 907
2007 API (base) . . . 697
2008 API (growth) . . . 684

SAT Testing, 2006-07

Enrollment, Grade 12 . . . 86
Number taking test . . . 37
percent taking test . . . 43.0%
percent with total score 1,500+ . . . 22.10%

Average Scores:

Math	Verbal	Writing	Total
504	513	505	1,522

Federal No Child Left Behind, 2008

(Adequate Yearly Progress standards met)

	Participation Rate	Pct Proficient
ELA	Yes	No
Math	Yes	No

API criteria . . . Yes
Graduation rate . . . Yes
\# criteria met/possible . . . 22/15

Other school districts for this city

(see Appendix E for information on these districts)

None

See Introduction for an explanation of all data sources.

Demographics & Socio-Economic Characteristics

(2000 Decennial Census, except as noted)

Population

1990* 26,183
2000 33,826
Male 16,648
Female 17,178
Jan. 2008 (estimate)§ 36,782
Persons per sq. mi. of land 2,590.3

Race & Hispanic Origin, 2000

Race
White 26,543
Black/African American 265
North American Native 363
Asian 651
Pacific Islander 38
Other Race 4,806
Two or more races 1,160
Hispanic origin, total 11,206
Mexican 9,668
Puerto Rican 73
Cuban 43
Other Hispanic 1,422

Age & Nativity, 2000

Under 5 years 2,420
18 years and over 24,326
65 years and over 4,415
85 years and over 659
Median Age 36.4
Native-born 25,915
Foreign-born 8,030

Educational Attainment, 2000

Population 25 years and over 21,758
Less than 9th grade 10.2%
High school grad or higher 81.6%
Bachelor's degree or higher 30.7%
Graduate degree 11.9%

Income & Poverty, 1999

Per capita income $29,926
Median household income $62,392
Median family income $69,481
Persons in poverty 10.5%
H'holds receiving public assistance 154
H'holds receiving social security 2,869

Households, 2000

Total households 10,930
With persons under 18 4,357
With persons over 65 3,045
Family households 8,196
Single person households 2,152
Persons per household 3.06
Persons per family 3.45

Household Population, 2008§§

Persons living in households 36,324
Persons living in group quarters 458
Persons per household 3.2

Labor & Employment

Total civilian labor force, 2008§§ 18,100
Unemployment rate, 2008 .... 4.6%
Total civilian labor force, 2000 15,458

Employed persons 16 years and over by occupation, 2000

Managers & professionals 5,215
Service occupations 2,455
Sales & office occupations 4,410
Farming, fishing & forestry 97
Construction & maintenance 1,279
Production & transportation 1,359
Self-employed persons 1,754

* US Census Bureau
** 2000 Decennial Census
§ California Department of Finance
§§ California Employment Development Dept

General Information

City of San Juan Capistrano
32400 Paseo Adelanto
San Juan Capistrano, CA 92675
949-493-1171

Website .... www.sanjuancapistrano.org
Elevation .... NA
Land Area (sq. miles) 14.2
Water Area (sq. miles) 0.1
Year of Incorporation 1961
Government type .... General law
Sales tax rate 8.75%

Voters & Officials

Registered Voters, October 2008

Total 19,448
Democrats 5,154
Republicans 9,926
Declined to state 3,519

Legislative Districts

US Congressional 44, 48
State Senatorial 38
State Assembly 73

Local Officials, 2009

Mayor .... Mark Nielsen
City Manager .... Dave Adams
City Clerk .... Meg Monahan
Attorney .... Omar Sandoval
Finance Dir .... Cynthia Russell
Public Works .... Nasser Abbaszadeh
Community Dev Dir .... Steven Apple
Building .... Steven Apple
Police Chief .... Dan Dwyer
Fire/Emergency Mgmt .... NA

Public Safety

Number of officers, 2007 .... NA
Violent crimes, 2007 67
Property crimes, 2007 490
Arson, 2007 9

Public Library

San Juan Capistrano Regional Library
Orange County Public Library System
31495 El Camino Real
San Juan Capistrano, CA 92675
949-493-1752

Branch Librarian .... Teri Garza

Library system statistics, FY 2007

Population served 1,532,758
Internet terminals 505
Annual users 680,874

Per capita:

Operating income $24.71
percent from local government 90.0%
Operating expenditure $24.18
Total materials 1.93
Print holdings 1.84
Visits per capita 4.02

Housing & Construction

Housing Units

Total, 2008§ 11,877
Single family units, attached 2,395
Single family units, detached 6,154
Multiple family units 1,809
Mobile home units 1,519
Occupied 11,468
Vacancy rate 3.4%
Median rent, 2000** $1,006
Median SF home value, 2000** $337,800

New Privately Owned Housing Units Authorized by Building Permit, 2007*

	Units	Construction Cost
Single	89	$31,260,651
Total	89	$31,260,651

Municipal Finance

(For local fiscal year ended in 2006)

Revenues

Total $53,804,366
Taxes 18,157,349
Special benefits assessment 98,202
Licenses & permits 1,970,216
Fines & forfeitures 919,623
Revenues from use of money & property 2,373,970
Intergovernmental 8,044,760
Service charges 20,865,998
Other revenues 1,374,248
Other financing sources 0

Expenditures

Total $55,319,775
General government 3,258,614
Public safety 6,734,707
Transportation 8,047,066
Community development 4,325,747
Health 3,362,995
Culture & leisure 7,445,994
Other 0

Local School District

(Data from School year 2007-08 except as noted)

Capistrano Unified
33122 Valle Rd
San Juan Capistrano, CA 92675
(949) 234-9200

Superintendent .... A. Carter
Grade plan K-12
Number of schools 61
Enrollment 52,390
High school graduates, 2006-07 3,205
Dropout rate 0.5%
Pupil/teacher ratio 23.4
Average class size 28.7
Students per computer 4.8
Classrooms with internet 2,308
Avg. Daily Attendance (ADA) 50,036
Cost per ADA $7,694
Avg. Teacher Salary $75,390

California Achievement Tests 6th ed., 2008

(Pct scoring at or above 50th National Percentile Rank)

	Math	Reading	Language
Grade 3	71%	56%	63%
Grade 7	73%	71%	68%

Academic Performance Index, 2008

Number of students tested 39,589
Number of valid scores 38,275
2007 API (base) 826
2008 API (growth) 837

SAT Testing, 2006-07

Enrollment, Grade 12 3,414
Number taking test 1,770
percent taking test 51.9%
percent with total score 1,500+ 34.90%

Average Scores:

Math	Verbal	Writing	Total
552	541	537	1,630

Federal No Child Left Behind, 2008

(Adequate Yearly Progress standards met)

	Participation Rate	Pct Proficient
ELA	Yes	No
Math	Yes	Yes

API criteria .... Yes
Graduation rate .... Yes
\# criteria met/possible 42/41

Other school districts for this city

(see Appendix E for information on these districts)

None

See Introduction for an explanation of all data sources.

Demographics & Socio-Economic Characteristics†

(2007 American Community Survey, except as noted)

Population

1990* 68,223
2007 96,186
Male 47,621
Female 48,565
Jan. 2008 (estimate)§ 81,851
Persons per sq. mi. of land 6,248.2

Race & Hispanic Origin, 2007

Race
White 48,418
Black/African American 12,393
North American Native 634
Asian 27,220
Pacific Islander 212
Other Race 4,251
Two or more races 3,058
Hispanic origin, total 24,285
Mexican 16,748
Puerto Rican 2,034
Cuban 0
Other Hispanic 5,503

Age & Nativity, 2007

Under 5 years 5,844
18 years and over 73,696
65 years and over 11,389
85 years and over 1,516
Median Age 36.7
Native-born 59,784
Foreign-born 36,402

Educational Attainment, 2007

Population 25 years and over........65,636
Less than 9th grade.....................6.7%
High school grad or higher 84.6%
Bachelor's degree or higher 26.2%
Graduate degree.........................5.6%

Income & Poverty, 2007

Per capita income....................$28,807
Median household income...........$63,173
Median family income $75,866
Persons in poverty.....................11.7%
H'holds receiving public assistance 856
H'holds receiving social security 8,084

Households, 2007

Total households 33,280
With persons under 18 10,708
With persons over 65 8,385
Family households....................20,615
Single person households...........10,294
Persons per household 2.89
Persons per family........................3.71

Household Population, 2008§§

Persons living in households.........81,024
Persons living in group quarters...........827
Persons per household 2.6

Labor & Employment

Total civilian labor force, 2008§§ 42,000
Unemployment rate, 2008 ....6.1%
Total civilian labor force, 2000* 39,906

Employed persons 16 years and over by occupation, 2007

Managers & professionals 14,098
Service occupations....................6,449
Sales & office occupations 14,343
Farming, fishing & forestry...............0
Construction & maintenance 6,346
Production & transportation 7,665
Self-employed persons.................2,573

† see Appendix D for 2000 Decennial Census Data
* US Census Bureau
** 2007 American Community Survey
§ California Department of Finance
§§ California Employment Development Dept

General Information

City of San Leandro
835 E 14th St
San Leandro, CA 94577
510-577-3200

Website ....www.ci.san-leandro.ca.us
Elevation ....45 ft.
Land Area (sq. miles) 13.1
Water Area (sq. miles).....................2.4
Year of Incorporation 1872
Government type....................Chartered
Sales tax rate............................9.75%

Voters & Officials

Registered Voters, October 2008

Total 41,927
Democrats..............................25,129
Republicans 6,451
Declined to state 8,739

Legislative Districts

US Congressional 13
State Senatorial..............................10
State Assembly 18

Local Officials, 2009

Mayor.....................Anthony B. Santos
City Manager ....Stephen Hollister
City Clerk ....Marian Handa
Attorney ....Jayne Williams
Finance Dir................Perry Carter (Int)
Public Works ....Mike Bakaldin
Community Dev Dir ....Luke Sims
Building.....................William Schock
Police Chief.....................Ian Willis (Int)
Fire Chief......................Sheldon Gilbert

Public Safety

Number of officers, 2007 91
Violent crimes, 2007.........................547
Property crimes, 2007......................3,978
Arson, 2007....................................15

Public Library

Main Library
San Leandro Public Library System
300 Estudillo Ave
San Leandro, CA 94577
510-577-3970

Director.........................David Bohne

Library system statistics, FY 2007

Population served 81,466
Internet terminals 48
Annual users 53,302

Per capita:

Operating income $62.65
percent from local government.... 98.5%
Operating expenditure..................$61.81
Total materials 3.89
Print holdings.............................3.63
Visits per capita 3.50

Housing & Construction

Housing Units

Total, 2008§............................31,904
Single family units, attached.......2,028
Single family units, detached 19,467
Multiple family units 9,505
Mobile home units 904
Occupied................................31,200
Vacancy rate 2.2%
Median rent, 2007** $1,057
Median SF home value, 2007** $597,400

New Privately Owned Housing Units Authorized by Building Permit, 2007*

	Units	Construction Cost
Single	19	$4,251,474
Total	32	$6,205,821

Municipal Finance

(For local fiscal year ended in 2006)

Revenues

Total.......................$106,064,292
Taxes 63,367,797
Special benefits assessment 732,863
Licenses & permits 2,129,478
Fines & forfeitures.................837,602
Revenues from use of money & property 2,970,234
Intergovernmental..............9,604,529
Service charges................21,235,081
Other revenues..................5,186,708
Other financing sources.....................0

Expenditures

Total.......................$108,468,799
General government 13,354,123
Public safety 42,336,945
Transportation.................16,446,419
Community development 7,048,028
Health 8,206,248
Culture & leisure 21,077,036
Other 0

Local School District

(Data from School year 2007-08 except as noted)

San Leandro Unified
14735 Juniper St
San Leandro, CA 94579
(510) 667-3500

Superintendent.............Christine Lim
Grade plan..............................K-12
Number of schools.........................12
Enrollment 8,719
High school graduates, 2006-07.........517
Dropout rate................................4.7%
Pupil/teacher ratio.........................20.2
Average class size.........................26.7
Students per computer 5.9
Classrooms with internet..................397
Avg. Daily Attendance (ADA).........8,474
Cost per ADA...........................$8,135
Avg. Teacher Salary...................$71,154

California Achievement Tests 6th ed., 2008

(Pct scoring at or above 50th National Percentile Rank)

	Math	Reading	Language
Grade 3	49%	28%	41%
Grade 7	39%	37%	38%

Academic Performance Index, 2008

Number of students tested...........6,590
Number of valid scores...............6,189
2007 API (base) 710
2008 API (growth)..........................711

SAT Testing, 2006-07

Enrollment, Grade 12 638
Number taking test 317
percent taking test........................49.7%
percent with total score 1,500+....16.10%

Average Scores:

Math	Verbal	Writing	Total
470	450	447	1,367

Federal No Child Left Behind, 2008

(Adequate Yearly Progress standards met)

	Participation Rate	Pct Proficient
ELA	Yes	No
Math	Yes	No

API criteria ....Yes
Graduation rate ....No
\# criteria met/possible...................40/31

Other school districts for this city

(see Appendix E for information on these districts)

San Lorenzo Unified

See Introduction for an explanation of all data sources.

Demographics & Socio-Economic Characteristics

(2000 Decennial Census, except as noted)

Population

1990* ... 41,958
2000 ... 44,174
Male ... 22,705
Female ... 21,469
Jan. 2008 (estimate)§ ... 44,697
Persons per sq. mi. of land ... 4,177.3

Race & Hispanic Origin, 2000

Race
White ... 37,155
Black/African American ... 644
North American Native ... 287
Asian ... 2,331
Pacific Islander ... 58
Other Race ... 2,130
Two or more races ... 1,569
Hispanic origin, total ... 5,147
Mexican ... 3,877
Puerto Rican ... 118
Cuban ... 64
Other Hispanic ... 1,088

Age & Nativity, 2000

Under 5 years ... 1,513
18 years and over ... 37,911
65 years and over ... 5,330
85 years and over ... 929
Median Age ... 26.2
Native-born ... 39,934
Foreign-born ... 4,214

Educational Attainment, 2000

Population 25 years and over ... 23,220
Less than 9th grade ... 3.5%
High school grad or higher ... 91.1%
Bachelor's degree or higher ... 40.9%
Graduate degree ... 15.3%

Income & Poverty, 1999

Per capita income ... $20,386
Median household income ... $31,926
Median family income ... $56,319
Persons in poverty ... 25.8%
H'holds receiving public assistance ... 243
H'holds receiving social security ... 3,913

Households, 2000

Total households ... 18,639
With persons under 18 ... 3,482
With persons over 65 ... 3,636
Family households ... 7,696
Single person households ... 6,094
Persons per household ... 2.27
Persons per family ... 2.86

Household Population, 2008§§

Persons living in households ... 42,835
Persons living in group quarters ... 1,862
Persons per household ... 2.2

Labor & Employment

Total civilian labor force, 2008§§ ... 27,800
Unemployment rate, 2008 ... 6.3%
Total civilian labor force, 2000 ... 23,817

Employed persons 16 years and over by occupation, 2000

Managers & professionals ... 8,595
Service occupations ... 4,354
Sales & office occupations ... 6,315
Farming, fishing & forestry ... 191
Construction & maintenance ... 1,203
Production & transportation ... 1,399
Self-employed persons ... 1,911

* US Census Bureau
** 2000 Decennial Census
§ California Department of Finance
§§ California Employment Development Dept

General Information

City of San Luis Obispo
990 Palm St
San Luis Obispo, CA 93401
805-781-7100

Website ... www.slocity.org
Elevation ... 234 ft.
Land Area (sq. miles) ... 10.7
Water Area (sq. miles) ... 0.2
Year of Incorporation ... 1856
Government type ... Chartered
Sales tax rate ... 8.75%

Voters & Officials

Registered Voters, October 2008

Total ... 29,619
Democrats ... 12,633
Republicans ... 8,670
Declined to state ... 6,535

Legislative Districts

US Congressional ... 23
State Senatorial ... 15
State Assembly ... 33

Local Officials, 2009

Mayor ... Dave Romero
Manager ... Ken Hampian
City Clerk ... Audrey Hooper
Attorney ... Jonathan P. Lowell
Finance Dir ... Bill Statler
Public Works ... Jay Walter
Planning/Dev Dir ... John Mandeville
Building ... Tim Girvin
Police Chief ... Deborah Linden
Emergency/Fire Dir ... John Callahan

Public Safety

Number of officers, 2007 ... 62
Violent crimes, 2007 ... 168
Property crimes, 2007 ... 1,846
Arson, 2007 ... NA

Public Library

San Luis Obispo Library
San Luis Obispo City-County Library System
995 Palm St
San Luis Obispo, CA 93401
805-781-5991

Director ... Brian Reynolds

Library system statistics, FY 2007

Population served ... 235,386
Internet terminals ... 3
Annual users ... 10,554

Per capita:

Operating income ... $33.17
percent from local government ... 90.2%
Operating expenditure ... $30.54
Total materials ... 1.72
Print holdings ... 1.46
Visits per capita ... 5.51

Housing & Construction

Housing Units

Total, 2008§ ... 20,222
Single family units, attached ... 1,311
Single family units, detached ... 9,418
Multiple family units ... 7,991
Mobile home units ... 1,502
Occupied ... 19,524
Vacancy rate ... 3.5%
Median rent, 2000** ... $724
Median SF home value, 2000** ... $278,800

New Privately Owned Housing Units Authorized by Building Permit, 2007*

	Units	Construction Cost
Single	48	$9,113,236
Total	73	$12,439,511

Municipal Finance

(For local fiscal year ended in 2006)

Revenues

Total ... $96,518,900
Taxes ... 38,282,800
Special benefits assessment ... 0
Licenses & permits ... 54,500
Fines & forfeitures ... 213,900
Revenues from use of money & property ... 1,292,600
Intergovernmental ... 7,944,400
Service charges ... 30,696,700
Other revenues ... 1,571,700
Other financing sources ... 16,462,300

Expenditures

Total ... $86,785,400
General government ... 11,774,528
Public safety ... 20,002,623
Transportation ... 20,893,700
Community development ... 4,909,300
Health ... 10,043,400
Culture & leisure ... 7,666,849
Other ... 0

Local School District

(Data from School year 2007-08 except as noted)

San Luis Coastal Unified
1500 Lizzie St
San Luis Obispo, CA 93401
(805) 549-1200

Superintendent ... Edward Valentine
Grade plan ... K-12
Number of schools ... 16
Enrollment ... 7,145
High school graduates, 2006-07 ... 570
Dropout rate ... 1.1%
Pupil/teacher ratio ... 23.8
Average class size ... 23.6
Students per computer ... 3.2
Classrooms with internet ... 452
Avg. Daily Attendance (ADA) ... 6,805
Cost per ADA ... $9,535
Avg. Teacher Salary ... $69,299

California Achievement Tests 6th ed., 2008

(Pct scoring at or above 50th National Percentile Rank)

	Math	Reading	Language
Grade 3	70%	64%	66%
Grade 7	71%	64%	64%

Academic Performance Index, 2008

Number of students tested ... 5,349
Number of valid scores ... 5,111
2007 API (base) ... 820
2008 API (growth) ... 824

SAT Testing, 2006-07

Enrollment, Grade 12 ... 593
Number taking test ... 253
percent taking test ... 42.7%
percent with total score 1,500+ ... 30.70%

Average Scores:

Math	Verbal	Writing	Total
556	554	542	1,652

Federal No Child Left Behind, 2008

(Adequate Yearly Progress standards met)

	Participation Rate	Pct Proficient
ELA	Yes	No
Math	Yes	No

API criteria ... Yes
Graduation rate ... Yes
criteria met/possible ... 30/27

Other school districts for this city

(see Appendix E for information on these districts)

None

See Introduction for an explanation of all data sources.

Demographics & Socio-Economic Characteristics†

(2007 American Community Survey, except as noted)

Population

1990* . . . 38,974
2007 . . . 75,217
Male . . . 37,510
Female . . . 37,707
Jan. 2008 (estimate)§ . . . 82,743
Persons per sq. mi. of land . . . 3,476.6

Race & Hispanic Origin, 2007

Race
White . . . 57,045
Black/African American . . . 2,138
North American Native . . . 370
Asian . . . 3,769
Pacific Islander . . . 369
Other Race . . . 9,757
Two or more races . . . 1,769
Hispanic origin, total . . . 31,985
Mexican . . . NA
Puerto Rican . . . NA
Cuban . . . NA
Other Hispanic . . . NA

Age & Nativity, 2007

Under 5 years . . . 8,406
18 years and over . . . 52,243
65 years and over . . . 6,320
85 years and over . . . 771
Median Age . . . 30.2
Native-born . . . 56,453
Foreign-born . . . 18,764

Educational Attainment, 2007

Population 25 years and over . . . 42,953
Less than 9th grade . . . 14.0%
High school grad or higher . . . 78.0%
Bachelor's degree or higher . . . 26.4%
Graduate degree . . . 9.5%

Income & Poverty, 2007

Per capita income . . . $25,422
Median household income . . . $60,786
Median family income . . . $68,164
Persons in poverty . . . 14.5%
H'holds receiving public assistance . . . 366
H'holds receiving social security . . . 5,059

Households, 2007

Total households . . . 24,259
With persons under 18 . . . 11,050
With persons over 65 . . . 4,529
Family households . . . 17,592
Single person households . . . 4,972
Persons per household . . . 3.10
Persons per family . . . 3.58

Household Population, 2008§§

Persons living in households . . . 82,054
Persons living in group quarters . . . 689
Persons per household . . . 3.1

Labor & Employment

Total civilian labor force, 2008§§ . . . 31,100
Unemployment rate, 2008 . . . 6.0%
Total civilian labor force, 2000* . . . 25,956

Employed persons 16 years and over by occupation, 2007

Managers & professionals . . . 12,069
Service occupations . . . 6,383
Sales & office occupations . . . 7,855
Farming, fishing & forestry . . . 201
Construction & maintenance . . . 2,867
Production & transportation . . . 4,170
Self-employed persons . . . 1,957

† see Appendix D for 2000 Decennial Census Data
* US Census Bureau
** 2007 American Community Survey
§ California Department of Finance
§§ California Employment Development Dept

General Information

City of San Marcos
1 Civic Center Dr
San Marcos, CA 92069
760-744-1050

Website . . . www.san-marcos.net
Elevation . . . 579
Land Area (sq. miles) . . . 23.8
Water Area (sq. miles) . . . 0.1
Year of Incorporation . . . 1963
Government type . . . Chartered
Sales tax rate . . . 8.75%

Voters & Officials

Registered Voters, October 2008

Total . . . 35,232
Democrats . . . 10,686
Republicans . . . 14,677
Declined to state . . . 8,290

Legislative Districts

US Congressional . . . 50
State Senatorial . . . 38
State Assembly . . . 74

Local Officials, 2009

Mayor . . . Jim Desmond
Manager . . . Paul Malone
City Clerk . . . Susie Vasquez
Attorney . . . Helen Holmes Peak
Finance Dir . . . Liliane Serio
Public Works . . . Richard Cook
Planning/Dev Dir . . . Jerry Backoff
Building . . . Carl Blaisdell
Police Chief . . . (County)
Fire Chief . . . Todd Newman

Public Safety

Number of officers, 2007 . . . NA
Violent crimes, 2007 . . . 287
Property crimes, 2007 . . . 1,669
Arson, 2007 . . . NA

Public Library

San Marcos Library
San Diego County Library System
2 Civic Center Dr
San Marcos, CA 92069
760-891-3000

Branch Librarian . . . Ann Terrell

Library system statistics, FY 2007

Population served . . . 1,049,868
Internet terminals . . . 394
Annual users . . . NA

Per capita:

Operating income . . . $33.43
percent from local government . . . 80.6%
Operating expenditure . . . $31.30
Total materials . . . 1.54
Print holdings . . . 1.32
Visits per capita . . . 6.31

Housing & Construction

Housing Units

Total, 2008§ . . . 27,630
Single family units, attached . . . 1,083
Single family units, detached . . . 14,170
Multiple family units . . . 8,717
Mobile home units . . . 3,660
Occupied . . . 26,532
Vacancy rate . . . 4.0%
Median rent, 2007** . . . $1,138
Median SF home value, 2007** . . . $519,500

New Privately Owned Housing Units Authorized by Building Permit, 2007*

	Units	Construction Cost
Single	220	$78,190,248
Total	273	$88,621,818

Municipal Finance

(For local fiscal year ended in 2006)

Revenues

Total . . . $88,907,088
Taxes . . . 43,660,775
Special benefits assessment . . . 6,869,795
Licenses & permits . . . 2,216,954
Fines & forfeitures . . . 169,261
Revenues from use of money & property . . . 6,318,746
Intergovernmental . . . 10,783,933
Service charges . . . 13,374,234
Other revenues . . . 5,056,484
Other financing sources . . . 456,906

Expenditures

Total . . . $103,025,822
General government . . . 9,217,494
Public safety . . . 27,838,459
Transportation . . . 45,231,956
Community development . . . 6,946,260
Health . . . 0
Culture & leisure . . . 12,600,306
Other . . . 1,170,952

Local School District

(Data from School year 2007-08 except as noted)

San Marcos Unified
255 Pico Ave, Ste 250
San Marcos, CA 92069
(760) 752-1299

Superintendent . . . Kevin Holt
Grade plan . . . K-12
Number of schools . . . 18
Enrollment . . . 17,380
High school graduates, 2006-07 . . . 844
Dropout rate . . . 2.7%
Pupil/teacher ratio . . . 23.2
Average class size . . . 25.6
Students per computer . . . 5.3
Classrooms with internet . . . 1,260
Avg. Daily Attendance (ADA) . . . 16,811
Cost per ADA . . . $7,672
Avg. Teacher Salary . . . $65,977

California Achievement Tests 6th ed., 2008

(Pct scoring at or above 50th National Percentile Rank)

	Math	Reading	Language
Grade 3	64%	44%	52%
Grade 7	62%	56%	55%

Academic Performance Index, 2008

Number of students tested . . . 13,008
Number of valid scores . . . 12,253
2007 API (base) . . . 786
2008 API (growth) . . . 810

SAT Testing, 2006-07

Enrollment, Grade 12 . . . 1,004
Number taking test . . . 342
percent taking test . . . 34.1%
percent with total score 1,500+ . . . 16.20%

Average Scores:

Math	Verbal	Writing	Total
505	496	498	1,499

Federal No Child Left Behind, 2008

(Adequate Yearly Progress standards met)

	Participation Rate	Pct Proficient
ELA	Yes	Yes
Math	Yes	Yes

API criteria . . . Yes
Graduation rate . . . Yes
criteria met/possible . . . 38/38

Other school districts for this city

(see Appendix E for information on these districts)

None

See Introduction for an explanation of all data sources.

Demographics & Socio-Economic Characteristics

(2000 Decennial Census, except as noted)

Population

1990* 12,959
2000 12,945
Male 6,240
Female 6,705
Jan. 2008 (estimate)§ 13,455
Persons per sq. mi. of land 3,540.8

Race & Hispanic Origin, 2000

Race
White 6,177
Black/African American 33
North American Native 6
Asian 6,286
Pacific Islander 10
Other Race 135
Two or more races 298
Hispanic origin, total 571
Mexican 393
Puerto Rican 11
Cuban 16
Other Hispanic 151

Age & Nativity, 2000

Under 5 years 637
18 years and over 9,520
65 years and over 2,099
85 years and over 235
Median Age 42.7
Native-born 8,149
Foreign-born 4,824

Educational Attainment, 2000

Population 25 years and over 8,737
Less than 9th grade 2.1%
High school grad or higher 95.4%
Bachelor's degree or higher 69.7%
Graduate degree 33.0%

Income & Poverty, 1999

Per capita income $59,150
Median household income $117,267
Median family income $125,708
Persons in poverty 5.0%
H'holds receiving public assistance 21
H'holds receiving social security 1,165

Households, 2000

Total households 4,266
With persons under 18 1,859
With persons over 65 1,419
Family households 3,674
Single person households 514
Persons per household 3.03
Persons per family 3.29

Household Population, 2008§§

Persons living in households 13,448
Persons living in group quarters 7
Persons per household 3.1

Labor & Employment

Total civilian labor force, 2008§§ 6,400
Unemployment rate, 2008 .... 3.3%
Total civilian labor force, 2000 5,500

Employed persons 16 years and over by occupation, 2000

Managers & professionals 3,503
Service occupations 200
Sales & office occupations 1,396
Farming, fishing & forestry 0
Construction & maintenance 45
Production & transportation 156
Self-employed persons 745

* US Census Bureau
** 2000 Decennial Census
§ California Department of Finance
§§ California Employment Development Dept

General Information

City of San Marino
2200 Huntington Dr
San Marino, CA 91108
626-300-0700

Website .... www.cityofsanmarino.org
Elevation .... 566 ft.
Land Area (sq. miles) 3.8
Water Area (sq. miles) 0
Year of Incorporation 1913
Government type .... General law
Sales tax rate 9.25%

Voters & Officials

Registered Voters, October 2008

Total 8,520
Democrats 1,956
Republicans 3,992
Declined to state 2,362

Legislative Districts

US Congressional 26
State Senatorial 22
State Assembly 49

Local Officials, 2009

Mayor .... Robert Twist
Manager .... Matt Ballantyne
City Clerk .... Carol Robb
Attorney .... Steve Dorsey
Finance Dir .... Lisa Bailey
Public Works .... Cindy Collins
Planning/Dev Dir .... David Saldana
Building .... David Saldana
Police Chief .... John T. Schaefer
Emergency/Fire Dir .... John Penido

Public Safety

Number of officers, 2007 25
Violent crimes, 2007 16
Property crimes, 2007 267
Arson, 2007 0

Public Library

Crowell Public Library
1890 Huntington Dr
San Marino, CA 91108
626-300-0777

Director .... Carolyn Crain

Library statistics, FY 2007

Population served 13,507
Internet terminals 127
Annual users 293,641

Per capita:

Operating income $62.56
percent from local government 91.1%
Operating expenditure $60.44
Total materials 7.63
Print holdings 7.24
Visits per capita 6.18

Housing & Construction

Housing Units

Total, 2008§ 4,453
Single family units, attached 19
Single family units, detached 4,417
Multiple family units 17
Mobile home units 0
Occupied 4,282
Vacancy rate 3.8%
Median rent, 2000** $2,001
Median SF home value, 2000** $690,800

New Privately Owned Housing Units Authorized by Building Permit, 2007*

	Units	Construction Cost
Single	2	$726,712
Total	2	$726,712

Municipal Finance

(For local fiscal year ended in 2006)

Revenues

Total $19,864,682
Taxes 12,193,700
Special benefits assessment 2,150,771
Licenses & permits 686,521
Fines & forfeitures 98,340
Revenues from use of money & property 882,743
Intergovernmental 1,117,397
Service charges 2,115,894
Other revenues 619,316
Other financing sources 0

Expenditures

Total $19,371,843
General government 3,423,218
Public safety 8,757,153
Transportation 1,652,424
Community development 721,602
Health 0
Culture & leisure 4,817,446
Other 0

Local School District

(Data from School year 2007-08 except as noted)

San Marino Unified
1665 West Dr
San Marino, CA 91108
(626) 299-7000

Superintendent .... Gary Woods
Grade plan K-12
Number of schools 4
Enrollment 3,199
High school graduates, 2006-07 315
Dropout rate 0.2%
Pupil/teacher ratio 20.1
Average class size 22.8
Students per computer 3.0
Classrooms with internet 169
Avg. Daily Attendance (ADA) 3,156
Cost per ADA $9,178
Avg. Teacher Salary $68,690

California Achievement Tests 6th ed., 2008

(Pct scoring at or above 50th National Percentile Rank)

	Math	Reading	Language
Grade 3	98%	80%	87%
Grade 7	91%	89%	88%

Academic Performance Index, 2008

Number of students tested 2,560
Number of valid scores 2,510
2007 API (base) 938
2008 API (growth) 944

SAT Testing, 2006-07

Enrollment, Grade 12 317
Number taking test 311
percent taking test 98.1%
percent with total score 1,500+ 83.90%

Average Scores:

Math	Verbal	Writing	Total
645	582	594	1,821

Federal No Child Left Behind, 2008

(Adequate Yearly Progress standards met)

	Participation Rate	Pct Proficient
ELA	Yes	Yes
Math	Yes	Yes

API criteria .... Yes
Graduation rate .... Yes
\# criteria met/possible 24/24

Other school districts for this city

(see Appendix E for information on these districts)

None

See Introduction for an explanation of all data sources.

Demographics & Socio-Economic Characteristics†

(2007 American Community Survey, except as noted)

Population

1990*	85,486
2007	91,461
Male	42,826
Female	48,635
Jan. 2008 (estimate)§	95,776
Persons per sq. mi. of land	7,850.5

Race & Hispanic Origin, 2007

Race	
White	59,878
Black/African American	2,346
North American Native	273
Asian	20,731
Pacific Islander	705
Other Race	3,796
Two or more races	3,732
Hispanic origin, total	17,687
Mexican	7,658
Puerto Rican	257
Cuban	218
Other Hispanic	9,554

Age & Nativity, 2007

Under 5 years	5,840
18 years and over	72,667
65 years and over	14,519
85 years and over	3,571
Median Age	40.4
Native-born	59,290
Foreign-born	32,171

Educational Attainment, 2007

Population 25 years and over	66,889
Less than 9th grade	5.0%
High school grad or higher	89.9%
Bachelor's degree or higher	41.9%
Graduate degree	13.0%

Income & Poverty, 2007

Per capita income	$43,591
Median household income	$80,820
Median family income	$98,750
Persons in poverty	3.8%
H'holds receiving public assistance	286
H'holds receiving social security	9,876

Households, 2007

Total households	35,607
With persons under 18	10,144
With persons over 65	9,268
Family households	21,422
Single person households	11,896
Persons per household	2.52
Persons per family	3.32

Household Population, 2008§§

Persons living in households	94,460
Persons living in group quarters	1,316
Persons per household	2.5

Labor & Employment

Total civilian labor force, 2008§§	50,800
Unemployment rate, 2008	3.7%
Total civilian labor force, 2000*	49,650

Employed persons 16 years and over by occupation, 2007

Managers & professionals	21,317
Service occupations	8,209
Sales & office occupations	13,469
Farming, fishing & forestry	62
Construction & maintenance	2,843
Production & transportation	2,935
Self-employed persons	5,588

† see Appendix D for 2000 Decennial Census Data
* US Census Bureau
** 2007 American Community Survey
§ California Department of Finance
§§ California Employment Development Dept

General Information

City of San Mateo
330 W 20th Ave
San Mateo, CA 94403
650-522-7000

Website	www.cityofsanmateo.org
Elevation	28 ft.
Land Area (sq. miles)	12.2
Water Area (sq. miles)	3.7
Year of Incorporation	1894
Government type	Chartered
Sales tax rate	9.25%

Voters & Officials

Registered Voters, October 2008

Total	51,616
Democrats	26,380
Republicans	11,438
Declined to state	11,887

Legislative Districts

US Congressional	12
State Senatorial	8
State Assembly	19

Local Officials, 2009

Mayor	Brandt Grotte
Manager	Susan M. Loftus
City Clerk	Norma Gomez
Attorney	Shawn Mason
Finance Dir	Hossein Golestan
Public Works	Larry Patterson
Planning/Dev Dir	Robert Beyer
Building	Stephen Lau
Police Chief	Susan E. Manheimer
Emergency/Fire Dir.	Daniel T. Belville

Public Safety

Number of officers, 2007	114
Violent crimes, 2007	306
Property crimes, 2007	2,073
Arson, 2007	20

Public Library

San Mateo Public Library
San Mateo Public Library System
55 W 3rd Ave
San Mateo, CA 94402
650-522-7802

City Librarian	Ben Ocon

Library system statistics, FY 2007

Population served	99,217
Internet terminals	297
Annual users	714,984

Per capita:

Operating income	$60.76
percent from local government	90.6%
Operating expenditure	$50.79
Total materials	3.42
Print holdings	3.14
Visits per capita	8.10

Housing & Construction

Housing Units

Total, 2008§	39,168
Single family units, attached	3,493
Single family units, detached	17,736
Multiple family units	17,894
Mobile home units	45
Occupied	38,481
Vacancy rate	1.8%
Median rent, 2007**	$1,414
Median SF home value, 2007**	$821,400

New Privately Owned Housing Units Authorized by Building Permit, 2007*

	Units	Construction Cost
Single	11	$4,930,627
Total	11	$4,930,627

Municipal Finance

(For local fiscal year ended in 2006)

Revenues

Total	$131,037,323
Taxes	66,230,013
Special benefits assessment	0
Licenses & permits	3,030,226
Fines & forfeitures	2,074,584
Revenues from use of money & property	3,954,615
Intergovernmental	16,057,692
Service charges	31,726,089
Other revenues	7,964,104
Other financing sources	0

Expenditures

Total	$147,501,325
General government	7,694,688
Public safety	44,045,118
Transportation	10,691,129
Community development	7,045,817
Health	31,706,335
Culture & leisure	46,318,238
Other	0

Local School District

(Data from School year 2007-08 except as noted)

San Mateo Union High
650 North Delaware St
San Mateo, CA 94401
(650) 558-2299

Superintendent	David Miller
Grade plan	9-12
Number of schools	7
Enrollment	8,626
High school graduates, 2006-07	1,833
Dropout rate	1.3%
Pupil/teacher ratio	21.3
Average class size	26.9
Students per computer	4.0
Classrooms with internet	425
Avg. Daily Attendance (ADA)	8,291
Cost per ADA	$9,930
Avg. Teacher Salary	$74,785

California Achievement Tests 6th ed., 2008

(Pct scoring at or above 50th National Percentile Rank)

	Math	Reading	Language
Grade 3	NA	NA	NA
Grade 7	NA	NA	NA

Academic Performance Index, 2008

Number of students tested	6,229
Number of valid scores	6,003
2007 API (base)	774
2008 API (growth)	781

SAT Testing, 2006-07

Enrollment, Grade 12	2,145
Number taking test	1,188
percent taking test	55.4%
percent with total score 1,500+	37.60%

Average Scores:

Math	Verbal	Writing	Total
572	534	536	1,642

Federal No Child Left Behind, 2008

(Adequate Yearly Progress standards met)

	Participation Rate	Pct Proficient
ELA	Yes	No
Math	Yes	No

API criteria	Yes
Graduation rate	Yes
# criteria met/possible	32/30

Other school districts for this city

(see Appendix E for information on these districts)

San Mateo-Foster City Elem

See Introduction for an explanation of all data sources.

Demographics & Socio-Economic Characteristics

(2000 Decennial Census, except as noted)

Population

1990* ... 25,158
2000 ... 30,215
Male ... 14,839
Female ... 15,376
Jan. 2008 (estimate)§ ... 31,190
Persons per sq. mi. of land ... 11,996.2

Race & Hispanic Origin, 2000

Race
White ... 9,555
Black/African American ... 5,539
North American Native ... 271
Asian ... 4,945
Pacific Islander ... 154
Other Race ... 7,688
Two or more races ... 2,063
Hispanic origin, total ... 13,490
Mexican ... 9,567
Puerto Rican ... 166
Cuban ... 17
Other Hispanic ... 3,740

Age & Nativity, 2000

Under 5 years ... 2,738
18 years and over ... 20,635
65 years and over ... 2,621
85 years and over ... 412
Median Age ... 29.5
Native-born ... 17,790
Foreign-born ... 12,331

Educational Attainment, 2000

Population 25 years and over ... 17,347
Less than 9th grade ... 20.7%
High school grad or higher ... 62.4%
Bachelor's degree or higher ... 10.4%
Graduate degree ... 2.4%

Income & Poverty, 1999

Per capita income ... $14,303
Median household income ... $37,184
Median family income ... $42,042
Persons in poverty ... 17.6%
H'holds receiving public assistance ... 742
H'holds receiving social security ... 1,845

Households, 2000

Total households ... 9,051
With persons under 18 ... 4,567
With persons over 65 ... 1,878
Family households ... 6,490
Single person households ... 2,034
Persons per household ... 3.29
Persons per family ... 3.87

Household Population, 2008§§

Persons living in households ... 30,725
Persons living in group quarters ... 465
Persons per household ... 3.2

Labor & Employment

Total civilian labor force, 2008§§ ... 13,700
Unemployment rate, 2008 ... 12.8%
Total civilian labor force, 2000 ... 11,939

Employed persons 16 years and over by occupation, 2000

Managers & professionals ... 2,183
Service occupations ... 2,531
Sales & office occupations ... 2,789
Farming, fishing & forestry ... 71
Construction & maintenance ... 1,493
Production & transportation ... 1,751
Self-employed persons ... 574

* US Census Bureau
** 2000 Decennial Census
§ California Department of Finance
§§ California Employment Development Dept

General Information

City of San Pablo
One Alvarado Square
San Pablo, CA 94806
510-215-3000

Website ... www.ci.san-pablo.ca.us
Elevation ... 45 ft.
Land Area (sq. miles) ... 2.6
Water Area (sq. miles) ... 0
Year of Incorporation ... 1948
Government type ... General law
Sales tax rate ... 9.25%

Voters & Officials

Registered Voters, October 2008

Total ... 8,053
Democrats ... 5,412
Republicans ... 710
Declined to state ... 1,592

Legislative Districts

US Congressional ... 7
State Senatorial ... 9
State Assembly ... 14

Local Officials, 2009

Mayor ... Leonard McNeil
Manager ... Brock Arner
City Clerk ... Ted Denney
Attorney ... Brian Libow
Finance Dir ... Bradley J. Ward
Public Works ... Adele Ho
Comm Svcs Dir ... Kelsey D. Worthy
Building ... Kelsey D. Worthy
Police Chief ... Joe Aita
Fire/Emergency Mgmt ... (County)

Public Safety

Number of officers, 2007 ... 56
Violent crimes, 2007 ... 314
Property crimes, 2007 ... 1,693
Arson, 2007 ... 5

Public Library

San Pablo Library
Contra Costa County Library System
2300 El Portal Dr, librAddr2
San Pablo, CA 94806
510-374-3998

Branch Librarian ... Lauga Martinengo

Library system statistics, FY 2007

Population served ... 938,513
Internet terminals ... 324
Annual users ... 670,618

Per capita:

Operating income ... $27.05
percent from local government ... 82.0%
Operating expenditure ... $27.82
Total materials ... 1.57
Print holdings ... 1.41
Visits per capita ... 3.65

Housing & Construction

Housing Units

Total, 2008§ ... 9,802
Single family units, attached ... 852
Single family units, detached ... 4,243
Multiple family units ... 3,899
Mobile home units ... 808
Occupied ... 9,499
Vacancy rate ... 3.1%
Median rent, 2000** ... $687
Median SF home value, 2000** ... $146,100

New Privately Owned Housing Units Authorized by Building Permit, 2007*

	Units	Construction Cost
Single	49	$8,098,783
Total	49	$8,098,783

Municipal Finance

(For local fiscal year ended in 2006)

Revenues

Total ... $27,358,043
Taxes ... 16,731,146
Special benefits assessment ... 1,180,405
Licenses & permits ... 680,681
Fines & forfeitures ... 449,540
Revenues from use of money & property ... 588,874
Intergovernmental ... 2,073,495
Service charges ... 732,407
Other revenues ... 4,921,495
Other financing sources ... 0

Expenditures

Total ... $24,460,093
General government ... 2,016,584
Public safety ... 17,458,253
Transportation ... 2,262,379
Community development ... 1,643,011
Health ... 0
Culture & leisure ... 1,079,866
Other ... 0

Local School District

(Data from School year 2007-08 except as noted)

West Contra Costa Unified
1108 Bissell Ave
Richmond, CA 94801
(510) 231-1101

Superintendent ... Bruce Harter
Grade plan ... K-12
Number of schools ... 65
Enrollment ... 30,830
High school graduates, 2006-07 ... 1,622
Dropout rate ... 9.3%
Pupil/teacher ratio ... 19.7
Average class size ... 24.8
Students per computer ... 6.4
Classrooms with internet ... 1,508
Avg. Daily Attendance (ADA) ... 28,599
Cost per ADA ... $9,365
Avg. Teacher Salary ... $56,030

California Achievement Tests 6th ed., 2008

(Pct scoring at or above 50th National Percentile Rank)

	Math	Reading	Language
Grade 3	47%	27%	38%
Grade 7	36%	33%	31%

Academic Performance Index, 2008

Number of students tested ... 22,407
Number of valid scores ... 20,863
2007 API (base) ... 674
2008 API (growth) ... 682

SAT Testing, 2006-07

Enrollment, Grade 12 ... 1,839
Number taking test ... 853
percent taking test ... 46.4%
percent with total score 1,500+ ... 13.90%

Average Scores:

Math	Verbal	Writing	Total
462	455	456	1,373

Federal No Child Left Behind, 2008

(Adequate Yearly Progress standards met)

	Participation Rate	Pct Proficient
ELA	Yes	No
Math	Yes	No

API criteria ... Yes
Graduation rate ... No
\# criteria met/possible ... 42/34

Other school districts for this city

(see Appendix E for information on these districts)

None

See Introduction for an explanation of all data sources.

Demographics & Socio-Economic Characteristics

(2000 Decennial Census, except as noted)

Population

1990* 48,404
2000 56,063
Male 27,777
Female 28,286
Jan. 2008 (estimate)§ 58,235
Persons per sq. mi. of land 3,508.1

Race & Hispanic Origin, 2000

Race
White 42,472
Black/African American 1,257
North American Native 312
Asian 3,133
Pacific Islander 95
Other Race 6,256
Two or more races 2,538
Hispanic origin, total 13,070
Mexican 6,007
Puerto Rican 139
Cuban 67
Other Hispanic 6,857

Age & Nativity, 2000

Under 5 years 3,271
18 years and over 45,126
65 years and over 8,055
85 years and over 1,419
Median Age 38.5
Native-born 40,386
Foreign-born 15,746

Educational Attainment, 2000

Population 25 years and over 40,684
Less than 9th grade 8.8%
High school grad or higher 84.7%
Bachelor's degree or higher 43.6%
Graduate degree 16.9%

Income & Poverty, 1999

Per capita income $35,762
Median household income $60,994
Median family income $74,398
Persons in poverty 10.0%
H'holds receiving public assistance 551
H'holds receiving social security 5,247

Households, 2000

Total households 22,371
With persons under 18 6,242
With persons over 65 5,453
Family households 12,776
Single person households 7,187
Persons per household 2.42
Persons per family 2.99

Household Population, 2008§§

Persons living in households 56,165
Persons living in group quarters 2,070
Persons per household 2.4

Labor & Employment

Total civilian labor force, 2008§§ 31,200
Unemployment rate, 2008 .... 5.4%
Total civilian labor force, 2000 30,190

Employed persons 16 years and over by occupation, 2000

Managers & professionals 13,102
Service occupations 4,842
Sales & office occupations 7,319
Farming, fishing & forestry 15
Construction & maintenance 2,068
Production & transportation 1,730
Self-employed persons 4,343

* US Census Bureau
** 2000 Decennial Census
§ California Department of Finance
§§ California Employment Development Dept

General Information

City of San Rafael
PO Box 151560
San Rafael, CA 94915
415-485-3070

Website .... www.cityofsanrafael.org
Elevation .... 34 ft.
Land Area (sq. miles) 16.6
Water Area (sq. miles) 5.8
Year of Incorporation 1874
Government type .... Chartered
Sales tax rate 9.50%

Voters & Officials

Registered Voters, October 2008

Total 29,928
Democrats 16,440
Republicans 5,989
Declined to state 6,342

Legislative Districts

US Congressional 6
State Senatorial 3
State Assembly 6

Local Officials, 2009

Mayor .... Albert Boro
Manager .... Ken Nordhoff
City Clerk .... Esther C. Beirne
Attorney .... Robert F. Epstein
Finance Dir .... Cindy Mosser
Public Works .... (vacant)
Planning/Dev Dir .... Robert Brown
Building .... Robert Brown
Police Chief .... Mathew Odetto
Fire Chief .... Christopher R. Gray

Public Safety

Number of officers, 2007 73
Violent crimes, 2007 280
Property crimes, 2007 1,763
Arson, 2007 17

Public Library

San Rafael Public Library
1100 E St
San Rafael, CA 94901
415-485-3319

Director .... David Dodd

Library statistics, FY 2007

Population served 58,047
Internet terminals 52
Annual users 46,000

Per capita:

Operating income $44.47
percent from local government 80.7%
Operating expenditure $35.86
Total materials 2.50
Print holdings 2.16
Visits per capita 1.31

Housing & Construction

Housing Units

Total, 2008§ 23,636
Single family units, attached 2,006
Single family units, detached 10,661
Multiple family units 10,480
Mobile home units 489
Occupied 23,042
Vacancy rate 2.5%
Median rent, 2000** $1,040
Median SF home value, 2000** $477,100

New Privately Owned Housing Units Authorized by Building Permit, 2007*

	Units	Construction Cost
Single	4	$4,717,775
Total	4	$4,717,775

Municipal Finance

(For local fiscal year ended in 2006)

Revenues

Total $69,513,841
Taxes 41,031,317
Special benefits assessment 3,978,543
Licenses & permits 1,175,031
Fines & forfeitures 622,495
Revenues from use of money & property 969,668
Intergovernmental 4,065,937
Service charges 16,023,655
Other revenues 1,647,195
Other financing sources 0

Expenditures

Total $69,700,696
General government 6,730,299
Public safety 36,206,330
Transportation 10,190,297
Community development 5,263,485
Health 0
Culture & leisure 11,310,285
Other 0

Local School District

(Data from School year 2007-08 except as noted)

San Rafael City High
310 Nova Albion Way
San Rafael, CA 94903
(415) 492-3233

Superintendent .... Michael Watenpaugh
Grade plan 9-12
Number of schools 4
Enrollment 2,186
High school graduates, 2006-07 431
Dropout rate 1.8%
Pupil/teacher ratio 19.8
Average class size 20.8
Students per computer 3.4
Classrooms with internet 124
Avg. Daily Attendance (ADA) 2,153
Cost per ADA $10,969
Avg. Teacher Salary $71,627

California Achievement Tests 6th ed., 2008

(Pct scoring at or above 50th National Percentile Rank)

	Math	Reading	Language
Grade 3	NA	NA	NA
Grade 7	NA	NA	NA

Academic Performance Index, 2008

Number of students tested 1,653
Number of valid scores 1,541
2007 API (base) 729
2008 API (growth) 738

SAT Testing, 2006-07

Enrollment, Grade 12 480
Number taking test 289
percent taking test 60.2%
percent with total score 1,500+ 40.80%

Average Scores:

Math	Verbal	Writing	Total
551	544	542	1,637

Federal No Child Left Behind, 2008

(Adequate Yearly Progress standards met)

	Participation Rate	Pct Proficient
ELA	Yes	No
Math	Yes	No

API criteria .... Yes
Graduation rate .... Yes
\# criteria met/possible 22/17

Other school districts for this city

(see Appendix E for information on these districts)

Dixie Elem, San Rafael City Elem

See Introduction for an explanation of all data sources.

Demographics & Socio-Economic Characteristics
(2000 Decennial Census, except as noted)

Population
1990* 35,303
2000 44,722
Male 22,058
Female 22,664
Jan. 2008 (estimate)§ 59,002
Persons per sq. mi. of land 5,086.4

Race & Hispanic Origin, 2000
Race
White 34,354
Black/African American 862
North American Native 160
Asian 6,680
Pacific Islander 95
Other Race 968
Two or more races 1,603
Hispanic origin, total 3,238
Mexican 1,844
Puerto Rican 155
Cuban 69
Other Hispanic 1,170

Age & Nativity, 2000
Under 5 years 3,329
18 years and over 32,961
65 years and over 2,709
85 years and over 310
Median Age 36.5
Native-born 37,169
Foreign-born 7,308

Educational Attainment, 2000
Population 25 years and over 30,297
Less than 9th grade 1.0%
High school grad or higher 96.5%
Bachelor's degree or higher 52.7%
Graduate degree 16.8%

Income & Poverty, 1999
Per capita income $42,336
Median household income $95,856
Median family income $106,321
Persons in poverty 2.0%
H'holds receiving public assistance 111
H'holds receiving social security 2,050

Households, 2000
Total households 16,944
With persons under 18 6,650
With persons over 65 1,994
Family households 12,143
Single person households 3,575
Persons per household 2.63
Persons per family 3.12

Household Population, 2008§§
Persons living in households 58,917
Persons living in group quarters 85
Persons per household 2.6

Labor & Employment
Total civilian labor force, 2008§§ 29,100
Unemployment rate, 2008 .... 2.5%
Total civilian labor force, 2000 26,226

Employed persons 16 years and over by occupation, 2000
Managers & professionals 14,115
Service occupations 1,549
Sales & office occupations 7,893
Farming, fishing & forestry 0
Construction & maintenance 1,167
Production & transportation 1,037
Self-employed persons 1,927

* US Census Bureau
** 2000 Decennial Census
§ California Department of Finance
§§ California Employment Development Dept

General Information
City of San Ramon
2222 Camino Ramon
San Ramon, CA 94583
925-973-2500

Website .... sanramon.ca.gov
Elevation .... NA
Land Area (sq. miles) 11.6
Water Area (sq. miles) 0
Year of Incorporation 1983
Government type .... Chartered
Sales tax rate 9.25%

Voters & Officials
Registered Voters, October 2008
Total 33,919
Democrats 13,295
Republicans 11,332
Declined to state 8,117

Legislative Districts
US Congressional 11
State Senatorial 7
State Assembly 15

Local Officials, 2009
Mayor .... H. Abram Wilson
Manager .... Herb Moniz
City Clerk .... Patricia Edwards
Attorney .... Byron D. Athan
Finance Dir .... Greg Rogers
Public Works .... Karen McNamara
Planning Dir .... Phil Wong
Building .... Reggie Meigs
Police Chief .... Scott Holder
Emergency/Fire Dir .... Richard Price

Public Safety
Number of officers, 2007 56
Violent crimes, 2007 54
Property crimes, 2007 1,052
Arson, 2007 3

Public Library
San Ramon Branch Library
Contra Costa County Library System
100 Montgomery St
San Ramon, CA 94583
925-973-2850

Branch Librarian .... Anna Koch

Library system statistics, FY 2007
Population served 938,513
Internet terminals 324
Annual users 670,618

Per capita:
Operating income $27.05
percent from local government 82.0%
Operating expenditure $27.82
Total materials 1.57
Print holdings 1.41
Visits per capita 3.65

Housing & Construction
Housing Units
Total, 2008§ 23,559
Single family units, attached 2,563
Single family units, detached 14,656
Multiple family units 6,329
Mobile home units 11
Occupied 22,745
Vacancy rate 3.5%
Median rent, 2000** $1,388
Median SF home value, 2000** $428,700

New Privately Owned Housing Units Authorized by Building Permit, 2007*

	Units	Construction Cost
Single	76	$40,564,939
Total	76	$40,564,939

Municipal Finance
(For local fiscal year ended in 2006)

Revenues
Total $41,878,734
Taxes 26,070,328
Special benefits assessment 2,991,110
Licenses & permits 1,102,218
Fines & forfeitures 947,403
Revenues from use of money & property 1,465,730
Intergovernmental 3,084,879
Service charges 6,203,499
Other revenues 13,567
Other financing sources 0

Expenditures
Total $49,085,446
General government 10,487,800
Public safety 10,814,389
Transportation 2,728,914
Community development 11,127,496
Health 147,433
Culture & leisure 13,779,414
Other 0

Local School District
(Data from School year 2007-08 except as noted)
San Ramon Valley Unified
699 Old Orchard Dr
Danville, CA 94526
(925) 552-5500

Superintendent .... Steven Enoch
Grade plan K-12
Number of schools 34
Enrollment 25,959
High school graduates, 2006-07 1,818
Dropout rate 0.6%
Pupil/teacher ratio 21.3
Average class size 26.5
Students per computer 4.3
Classrooms with internet 1,361
Avg. Daily Attendance (ADA) 25,488
Cost per ADA $7,914
Avg. Teacher Salary $64,878

California Achievement Tests 6th ed., 2008
(Pct scoring at or above 50th National Percentile Rank)

	Math	Reading	Language
Grade 3	87%	72%	78%
Grade 7	85%	81%	80%

Academic Performance Index, 2008
Number of students tested 20,092
Number of valid scores 19,436
2007 API (base) 893
2008 API (growth) 904

SAT Testing, 2006-07
Enrollment, Grade 12 1,905
Number taking test 1,273
percent taking test 66.8%
percent with total score 1,500+ ... 50.80%

Average Scores:

Math	Verbal	Writing	Total
582	556	555	1,693

Federal No Child Left Behind, 2008
(Adequate Yearly Progress standards met)

	Participation Rate	Pct Proficient
ELA	Yes	Yes
Math	Yes	Yes

API criteria .... Yes
Graduation rate .... Yes
criteria met/possible 38/38

Other school districts for this city
(see Appendix E for information on these districts)
None

See Introduction for an explanation of all data sources.

Demographics & Socio-Economic Characteristics

(2000 Decennial Census, except as noted)

Population

- 1990* ... 192
- 2000 ... 261
  - Male ... 157
  - Female ... 104
- Jan. 2008 (estimate)§ ... 298
  - Persons per sq. mi. of land ... 496.7

Race & Hispanic Origin, 2000

- Race
  - White ... 186
  - Black/African American ... 13
  - North American Native ... 8
  - Asian ... 4
  - Pacific Islander ... 0
  - Other Race ... 38
  - Two or more races ... 12
- Hispanic origin, total ... 72
  - Mexican ... 50
  - Puerto Rican ... 1
  - Cuban ... 1
  - Other Hispanic ... 20

Age & Nativity, 2000

- Under 5 years ... 11
- 18 years and over ... 219
- 65 years and over ... 13
- 85 years and over ... 1
  - Median Age ... 37.7
- Native-born ... 152
- Foreign-born ... 52

Educational Attainment, 2000

- Population 25 years and over ... 115
- Less than 9th grade ... 14.8%
- High school grad or higher ... 67.0%
- Bachelor's degree or higher ... 13.0%
- Graduate degree ... 3.5%

Income & Poverty, 1999

- Per capita income ... $15,455
- Median household income ... $34,375
- Median family income ... $37,500
- Persons in poverty ... 21.8%
- H'holds receiving public assistance ... 0
- H'holds receiving social security ... 19

Households, 2000

- Total households ... 80
  - With persons under 18 ... 20
  - With persons over 65 ... 10
  - Family households ... 33
  - Single person households ... 33
- Persons per household ... 2.46
- Persons per family ... 3.42

Household Population, 2008§§

- Persons living in households ... 234
- Persons living in group quarters ... 64
- Persons per household ... 2.4

Labor & Employment

- Total civilian labor force, 2008§§ ... 200
  - Unemployment rate, 2008 ... 3.1%
- Total civilian labor force, 2000 ... 136

Employed persons 16 years and over by occupation, 2000

- Managers & professionals ... 15
- Service occupations ... 54
- Sales & office occupations ... 34
- Farming, fishing & forestry ... 3
- Construction & maintenance ... 19
- Production & transportation ... 7
- Self-employed persons ... 17

* US Census Bureau
** 2000 Decennial Census
§ California Department of Finance
§§ California Employment Development Dept

General Information

City of Sand City
No 1 Sylvan Park
Sand City, CA 93955
831-394-3054

- Website ... www.sandcity.org
- Elevation ... NA
- Land Area (sq. miles) ... 0.6
- Water Area (sq. miles) ... 2.4
- Year of Incorporation ... 1960
- Government type ... Chartered
- Sales tax rate ... 8.75%

Voters & Officials

Registered Voters, October 2008

- Total ... 130
  - Democrats ... 50
  - Republicans ... 31
  - Declined to state ... 34

Legislative Districts

- US Congressional ... 17
- State Senatorial ... 15
- State Assembly ... 27

Local Officials, 2009

- Mayor ... David K. Pendergrass
- Manager ... Steve Matarazzo
- City Clerk ... Steve Matarazzo
- Attorney ... James Heisinger
- Finance Dir ... Kelly Morgan
- Public Works ... NA
- Planning/Dev Dir ... Steve Matarazzo
- Building ... NA
- Police Chief ... J. Michael Klein
- Fire/Emergency Mgmt ... NA

Public Safety

- Number of officers, 2007 ... 9
- Violent crimes, 2007 ... 8
- Property crimes, 2007 ... 128
- Arson, 2007 ... 0

Public Library

Served by Seaside City Library

Library system statistics, FY 2007

- Population served ... NA
- Internet terminals ... NA
  - Annual users ... NA

Per capita:

- Operating income ... NA
  - percent from local government ... NA
- Operating expenditure ... NA
- Total materials ... NA
- Print holdings ... NA
- Visits per capita ... NA

Housing & Construction

Housing Units

- Total, 2008§ ... 138
  - Single family units, attached ... 7
  - Single family units, detached ... 58
  - Multiple family units ... 68
  - Mobile home units ... 5
  - Occupied ... 96
  - Vacancy rate ... 30.4%
- Median rent, 2000** ... $775
- Median SF home value, 2000** ... $275,000

New Privately Owned Housing Units Authorized by Building Permit, 2007*

	Units	Construction Cost
Single	0	$0
Total	0	$0

Municipal Finance

(For local fiscal year ended in 2006)

Revenues

- Total ... $5,605,462
- Taxes ... 4,909,482
- Special benefits assessment ... 0
- Licenses & permits ... 107,440
- Fines & forfeitures ... 24,199
- Revenues from use of money & property ... 238,570
- Intergovernmental ... 158,775
- Service charges ... 62,232
- Other revenues ... 16,090
- Other financing sources ... 88,674

Expenditures

- Total ... $4,044,248
- General government ... 1,031,872
- Public safety ... 1,905,916
- Transportation ... 630,625
- Community development ... 417,257
- Health ... 0
- Culture & leisure ... 58,578
- Other ... 0

Local School District

(Data from School year 2007-08 except as noted)

Monterey Peninsula Unified
PO Box 1031
Monterey, CA 93942
(831) 645-1200

- Superintendent ... Marilyn Shepherd
- Grade plan ... K-12
- Number of schools ... 22
- Enrollment ... 11,613
- High school graduates, 2006-07 ... 590
- Dropout rate ... 2.0%
- Pupil/teacher ratio ... 20.5
- Average class size ... 24.3
- Students per computer ... 8.5
- Classrooms with internet ... 518
- Avg. Daily Attendance (ADA) ... 10,537
  - Cost per ADA ... $8,271
- Avg. Teacher Salary ... $57,857

California Achievement Tests 6th ed., 2008

(Pct scoring at or above 50th National Percentile Rank)

	Math	Reading	Language
Grade 3	56%	35%	43%
Grade 7	49%	44%	43%

Academic Performance Index, 2008

- Number of students tested ... 8,210
- Number of valid scores ... 7,687
- 2007 API (base) ... 716
- 2008 API (growth) ... 728

SAT Testing, 2006-07

- Enrollment, Grade 12 ... 682
- Number taking test ... 262
  - percent taking test ... 38.4%
  - percent with total score 1,500+ ... 15.10%

Average Scores:

Math	Verbal	Writing	Total
504	487	481	1,472

Federal No Child Left Behind, 2008

(Adequate Yearly Progress standards met)

	Participation Rate	Pct Proficient
ELA	Yes	No
Math	Yes	No

- API criteria ... Yes
- Graduation rate ... Yes
- # criteria met/possible ... 42/36

Other school districts for this city

(see Appendix E for information on these districts)

None

See Introduction for an explanation of all data sources.

Demographics & Socio-Economic Characteristics

(2000 Decennial Census, except as noted)

Population

1990* 16,839
2000 18,931
Male 9,495
Female 9,436
Jan. 2008 (estimate)§ 25,404
Persons per sq. mi. of land 5,405.1

Race & Hispanic Origin, 2000

Race
White 9,376
Black/African American 80
North American Native 228
Asian 371
Pacific Islander 16
Other Race 8,170
Two or more races 690
Hispanic origin, total 15,319
Mexican 13,418
Puerto Rican 35
Cuban 3
Other Hispanic 1,863

Age & Nativity, 2000

Under 5 years 1,719
18 years and over 12,474
65 years and over 1,909
85 years and over 257
Median Age 28.1
Native-born 12,956
Foreign-born 5,985

Educational Attainment, 2000

Population 25 years and over 10,230
Less than 9th grade 32.7%
High school grad or higher 51.1%
Bachelor's degree or higher 8.2%
Graduate degree 2.6%

Income & Poverty, 1999

Per capita income $11,625
Median household income $32,072
Median family income $33,219
Persons in poverty 23.4%
H'holds receiving public assistance 498
H'holds receiving social security 1,385

Households, 2000

Total households 5,220
With persons under 18 2,857
With persons over 65 1,340
Family households 4,308
Single person households 748
Persons per household 3.60
Persons per family 3.91

Household Population, 2008§§

Persons living in households 25,264
Persons living in group quarters 140
Persons per household 3.7

Labor & Employment

Total civilian labor force, 2008§§ 10,200
Unemployment rate, 2008 .... 16.5%
Total civilian labor force, 2000 8,043

Employed persons 16 years and over by occupation, 2000

Managers & professionals 1,177
Service occupations 1,062
Sales & office occupations 1,448
Farming, fishing & forestry 933
Construction & maintenance 512
Production & transportation 1,444
Self-employed persons 219

* US Census Bureau
** 2000 Decennial Census
§ California Department of Finance
§§ California Employment Development Dept

General Information

City of Sanger
1700 7th St
Sanger, CA 93657
559-876-6300

Website .... www.ci.sanger.ca.us
Elevation .... 363 ft.
Land Area (sq. miles) 4.7
Water Area (sq. miles) 0
Year of Incorporation 1911
Government type .... General law
Sales tax rate 9.73%

Voters & Officials

Registered Voters, October 2008

Total 8,474
Democrats 4,299
Republicans 2,836
Declined to state 876

Legislative Districts

US Congressional 20
State Senatorial 16
State Assembly 31

Local Officials, 2009

Mayor .... Jose R. Villarrea
Manager .... Jim Drinkhouse
City Clerk .... Barbara Mergan
Attorney .... David Weiland
Finance Dir .... Carlos Sanchez
Public Works .... John White
Planning/Dev Dir .... Tim Chapa
Building .... Tim Chapa
Police Chief .... Thomas Klose
Emergency/Fire Dir .... Clyde Clinton

Public Safety

Number of officers, 2007 27
Violent crimes, 2007 91
Property crimes, 2007 697
Arson, 2007 .... NA

Public Library

Sanger Branch Library
Fresno County Public Library System
1812 Seventh St
Sanger, CA 93657
559-875-2435

Branch Librarian .... Barbara Light

Library system statistics, FY 2007

Population served 889,019
Internet terminals 277
Annual users 861,240

Per capita:

Operating income $23.69
percent from local government 89.3%
Operating expenditure $23.37
Total materials 2.89
Print holdings 2.69
Visits per capita .... NA

Housing & Construction

Housing Units

Total, 2008§ 7,177
Single family units, attached 194
Single family units, detached 5,478
Multiple family units 1,342
Mobile home units 163
Occupied 6,865
Vacancy rate 4.4%
Median rent, 2000** $543
Median SF home value, 2000** $92,200

New Privately Owned Housing Units Authorized by Building Permit, 2007*

	Units	Construction Cost
Single	72	$10,390,524
Total	72	$10,390,524

Municipal Finance

(For local fiscal year ended in 2006)

Revenues

Total $21,702,191
Taxes 6,938,357
Special benefits assessment 133,633
Licenses & permits 1,509,887
Fines & forfeitures 102,018
Revenues from use of money & property 459,639
Intergovernmental 2,321,278
Service charges 9,774,881
Other revenues 462,498
Other financing sources 0

Expenditures

Total $23,896,849
General government 676,681
Public safety 7,538,430
Transportation 2,323,801
Community development 1,209,905
Health 6,030,080
Culture & leisure 1,642,608
Other 0

Local School District

(Data from School year 2007-08 except as noted)

Sanger Unified
1905 Seventh St
Sanger, CA 93657
(559) 875-6521

Superintendent .... Marcus Johnson
Grade plan K-12
Number of schools 19
Enrollment 10,129
High school graduates, 2006-07 516
Dropout rate 2.2%
Pupil/teacher ratio 19.4
Average class size 24.4
Students per computer 4.7
Classrooms with internet 450
Avg. Daily Attendance (ADA) 8,982
Cost per ADA $8,253
Avg. Teacher Salary $57,613

California Achievement Tests 6th ed., 2008

(Pct scoring at or above 50th National Percentile Rank)

	Math	Reading	Language
Grade 3	60%	39%	50%
Grade 7	54%	48%	49%

Academic Performance Index, 2008

Number of students tested 7,873
Number of valid scores 7,240
2007 API (base) 754
2008 API (growth) 779

SAT Testing, 2006-07

Enrollment, Grade 12 638
Number taking test 129
percent taking test 20.2%
percent with total score 1,500+ 4.90%

Average Scores:

Math	Verbal	Writing	Total
452	448	438	1,338

Federal No Child Left Behind, 2008

(Adequate Yearly Progress standards met)

	Participation Rate	Pct Proficient
ELA	Yes	No
Math	Yes	Yes

API criteria .... Yes
Graduation rate .... Yes
\# criteria met/possible 34/33

Other school districts for this city

(see Appendix E for information on these districts)

None

See Introduction for an explanation of all data sources.

Demographics & Socio-Economic Characteristics†

(2007 American Community Survey, except as noted)

Population

1990*	293,742
2007	327,780
Male	173,381
Female	154,399
Jan. 2008 (estimate)§	353,184
Persons per sq. mi. of land	13,032.6

Race & Hispanic Origin, 2007

Race	
White	137,413
Black/African American	3,446
North American Native	741
Asian	30,417
Pacific Islander	1,407
Other Race	149,417
Two or more races	4,939
Hispanic origin, total	260,838
Mexican	243,026
Puerto Rican	434
Cuban	851
Other Hispanic	16,527

Age & Nativity, 2007

Under 5 years	32,407
18 years and over	225,351
65 years and over	19,727
85 years and over	2,804
Median Age	28.6
Native-born	160,866
Foreign-born	166,914

Educational Attainment, 2007

Population 25 years and over	187,040
Less than 9th grade	33.7%
High school grad or higher	48.0%
Bachelor's degree or higher	11.9%
Graduate degree	4.1%

Income & Poverty, 2007

Per capita income	$16,663
Median household income	$53,661
Median family income	$52,062
Persons in poverty	17.1%
H'holds receiving public assistance	2,686
H'holds receiving social security	12,836

Households, 2007

Total households	74,972
With persons under 18	39,464
With persons over 65	13,655
Family households	58,074
Single person households	11,676
Persons per household	4.30
Persons per family	4.62

Household Population, 2008§§

Persons living in households	347,537
Persons living in group quarters	5,647
Persons per household	4.7

Labor & Employment

Total civilian labor force, 2008§§	162,000
Unemployment rate, 2008	8.5%
Total civilian labor force, 2000*	138,567

Employed persons 16 years and over by occupation, 2007

Managers & professionals	24,100
Service occupations	36,636
Sales & office occupations	33,403
Farming, fishing & forestry	1,532
Construction & maintenance	20,353
Production & transportation	38,204
Self-employed persons	7,898

† see Appendix D for 2000 Decennial Census Data
* US Census Bureau
** 2007 American Community Survey
§ California Department of Finance
§§ California Employment Development Dept

General Information

City of Santa Ana
20 Civic Center Plaza
Santa Ana, CA 92701
714-647-5400

Website	www.ci.santa-ana.ca.us
Elevation	110 ft.
Land Area (sq. miles)	27.1
Water Area (sq. miles)	0.3
Year of Incorporation	1886
Government type	Chartered
Sales tax rate	8.75%

Voters & Officials

Registered Voters, October 2008

Total	103,290
Democrats	50,371
Republicans	30,929
Declined to state	18,702

Legislative Districts

US Congressional	46-48
State Senatorial	33-35
State Assembly	69

Local Officials, 2009

Mayor	Miguel Pulido
Manager	David Ream
City Clerk	Patricia Healy
Attorney	Joseph Fletcher
Finance Dir	Francisco Gutierrez
Public Works	James Ross
Planning/Dev Dir	Jay Trevino
Building	NA
Police Chief	Paul Walters
Fire Chief	Marc Martin

Public Safety

Number of officers, 2007	363
Violent crimes, 2007	1,947
Property crimes, 2007	7,797
Arson, 2007	120

Public Library

Santa Ana Public Library
Santa Ana Public Library System
26 Civic Center Plaza
Santa Ana, CA 92701
714-647-5250

Director	Robert Richard

Library system statistics, FY 2007

Population served	353,428
Internet terminals	57
Annual users	388,501

Per capita:

Operating income	$15.23
percent from local government	93.9%
Operating expenditure	$9.45
Total materials	0.84
Print holdings	0.79
Visits per capita	5.29

Housing & Construction

Housing Units

Total, 2008§	75,462
Single family units, attached	6,702
Single family units, detached	33,750
Multiple family units	31,101
Mobile home units	3,909
Occupied	73,856
Vacancy rate	2.1%
Median rent, 2007**	$1,172
Median SF home value, 2007**	$553,200

New Privately Owned Housing Units Authorized by Building Permit, 2007*

	Units	Construction Cost
Single	99	$19,101,795
Total	99	$19,101,795

Municipal Finance

(For local fiscal year ended in 2006)

Revenues

Total	$370,801,301
Taxes	154,215,372
Special benefits assessment	0
Licenses & permits	3,926,214
Fines & forfeitures	7,256,968
Revenues from use of money & property	22,144,597
Intergovernmental	82,495,268
Service charges	89,819,097
Other revenues	10,943,785
Other financing sources	0

Expenditures

Total	$348,178,931
General government	14,244,595
Public safety	160,774,395
Transportation	36,790,212
Community development	56,457,450
Health	18,318,481
Culture & leisure	25,115,210
Other	0

Local School District

(Data from School year 2007-08 except as noted)

Santa Ana Unified
1601 East Chestnut Ave
Santa Ana, CA 92701
(714) 558-5501

Superintendent	Jane Russo
Grade plan	K-12
Number of schools	59
Enrollment	57,061
High school graduates, 2006-07	2,258
Dropout rate	1.9%
Pupil/teacher ratio	22.0
Average class size	28.7
Students per computer	4.6
Classrooms with internet	2,686
Avg. Daily Attendance (ADA)	54,239
Cost per ADA	$8,944
Avg. Teacher Salary	$76,279

California Achievement Tests 6th ed., 2008

(Pct scoring at or above 50th National Percentile Rank)

	Math	Reading	Language
Grade 3	48%	21%	34%
Grade 7	38%	34%	34%

Academic Performance Index, 2008

Number of students tested	41,501
Number of valid scores	40,362
2007 API (base)	668
2008 API (growth)	685

SAT Testing, 2006-07

Enrollment, Grade 12	3,109
Number taking test	932
percent taking test	30.0%
percent with total score 1,500+	8.70%

Average Scores:

Math	Verbal	Writing	Total
459	446	442	1,347

Federal No Child Left Behind, 2008

(Adequate Yearly Progress standards met)

	Participation Rate	Pct Proficient
ELA	Yes	No
Math	Yes	No

API criteria	Yes
Graduation rate	Yes
# criteria met/possible	34/28

Other school districts for this city

(see Appendix E for information on these districts)

Garden Grove Unified, Orange Unified, Tustin Unified

See Introduction for an explanation of all data sources.

Demographics & Socio-Economic Characteristics†

(2007 American Community Survey, except as noted)

Population

1990* . . . 85,571
2007 . . . 89,959
Male . . . 45,704
Female . . . 44,255
Jan. 2008 (estimate)§ . . . 90,305
Persons per sq. mi. of land . . . 4,752.9

Race & Hispanic Origin, 2007

Race
White . . . 69,036
Black/African American . . . 1,476
North American Native . . . 257
Asian . . . 3,537
Pacific Islander . . . 58
Other Race . . . 12,835
Two or more races . . . 2,760
Hispanic origin, total . . . 32,657
Mexican . . . NA
Puerto Rican . . . NA
Cuban . . . NA
Other Hispanic . . . NA

Age & Nativity, 2007

Under 5 years . . . 5,508
18 years and over . . . 73,150
65 years and over . . . 12,245
85 years and over . . . 1,892
Median Age . . . 36.6
Native-born . . . 67,880
Foreign-born . . . 22,079

Educational Attainment, 2007

Population 25 years and over . . . 60,945
Less than 9th grade . . . 10.7%
High school grad or higher . . . 82.8%
Bachelor's degree or higher . . . 39.6%
Graduate degree . . . 14.4%

Income & Poverty, 2007

Per capita income . . . $31,907
Median household income . . . $57,547
Median family income . . . $70,596
Persons in poverty . . . 13.9%
H'holds receiving public assistance . . . 771
H'holds receiving social security . . . 8,455

Households, 2007

Total households . . . 35,679
With persons under 18 . . . 9,202
With persons over 65 . . . 9,118
Family households . . . 18,278
Single person households . . . 11,119
Persons per household . . . 2.44
Persons per family . . . 3.11

Household Population, 2008§§

Persons living in households . . . 88,443
Persons living in group quarters . . . 1,862
Persons per household . . . 2.4

Labor & Employment

Total civilian labor force, 2008§§ . . . 56,100
Unemployment rate, 2008 . . . 3.8%
Total civilian labor force, 2000* . . . 50,705

Employed persons 16 years and over by occupation, 2007

Managers & professionals . . . 21,840
Service occupations . . . 9,029
Sales & office occupations . . . 10,024
Farming, fishing & forestry . . . 421
Construction & maintenance . . . 3,193
Production & transportation . . . 2,730
Self-employed persons . . . 4,361

† see Appendix D for 2000 Decennial Census Data
* US Census Bureau
** 2007 American Community Survey
§ California Department of Finance
§§ California Employment Development Dept

General Information

City of Santa Barbara
735 Anacapa St
PO Box 1990
Santa Barbara, CA 93102
805-564-5309

Website . . . www.santabarbaraca.gov
Elevation . . . 42 ft.
Land Area (sq. miles) . . . 19.0
Water Area (sq. miles) . . . 22.4
Year of Incorporation . . . 1850
Government type . . . Chartered
Sales tax rate . . . 8.75%

Voters & Officials

Registered Voters, October 2008

Total . . . 48,510
Democrats . . . 25,504
Republicans . . . 10,463
Declined to state . . . 9,936

Legislative Districts

US Congressional . . . 23
State Senatorial . . . 19
State Assembly . . . 35

Local Officials, 2009

Mayor . . . Marty Blum
City Admin . . . James L. Armstrong
City Clerk . . . Cynthia M. Rodriguez
Attorney . . . Stephen P. Wiley
Finance Dir . . . Robert Peirson
Public Works . . . Christine Andersen
Planning/Dev Dir . . . Paul Casey
Building . . . NA
Police Chief . . . Camerino Sanchez
Fire Chief . . . Ron Prince

Public Safety

Number of officers, 2007 . . . 132
Violent crimes, 2007 . . . 445
Property crimes, 2007 . . . 2,277
Arson, 2007 . . . NA

Public Library

Main Branch
Santa Barbara Public Library
40 E Anapamu St
Santa Barbara, CA 93101
805-962-7653

Director . . . Irene Macias

Library system statistics, FY 2007

Population served . . . 233,434
Internet terminals . . . 86
Annual users . . . 66,000

Per capita:

Operating income . . . $25.05
percent from local government . . . 84.4%
Operating expenditure . . . $27.43
Total materials . . . 1.73
Print holdings . . . 1.48
Visits per capita . . . 12.44

Housing & Construction

Housing Units

Total, 2008§ . . . 37,675
Single family units, attached . . . 2,914
Single family units, detached . . . 17,269
Multiple family units . . . 16,974
Mobile home units . . . 518
Occupied . . . 36,231
Vacancy rate . . . 3.8%
Median rent, 2007** . . . $1,310
Median SF home value, 2007** . . $1,000,001

New Privately Owned Housing Units Authorized by Building Permit, 2007*

	Units	Construction Cost
Single	32	$13,589,719
Total	92	$23,570,710

Municipal Finance

(For local fiscal year ended in 2006)

Revenues

Total . . . $222,577,050
Taxes . . . 71,338,665
Special benefits assessment . . . 0
Licenses & permits . . . 3,216,598
Fines & forfeitures . . . 3,316,411
Revenues from use of money & property . . . 4,519,386
Intergovernmental . . . 25,169,761
Service charges . . . 111,942,573
Other revenues . . . 3,073,656
Other financing sources . . . 0

Expenditures

Total . . . $192,697,373
General government . . . 12,958,638
Public safety . . . 49,369,726
Transportation . . . 51,885,281
Community development . . . 12,452,318
Health . . . 16,750,360
Culture & leisure . . . 24,065,935
Other . . . 0

Local School District

(Data from School year 2007-08 except as noted)
‡combined elementary and high school data

Santa Barbara High
720 Santa Barbara St
Santa Barbara, CA 93101
(805) 963-4331

Superintendent . . . J. Sarvis
Grade plan . . . 6-12
Number of schools . . . 13
Enrollment . . . 10,196
High school graduates, 2006-07 . . . 1,468
Dropout rate . . . 2.8%
Pupil/teacher ratio . . . 26.0
Average class size . . . 26.7
Students per computer . . . 4.9
Classrooms with internet . . . 453
Avg. Daily Attendance (ADA)‡ . . . 14,151
Cost per ADA‡ . . . $8,313
Avg. Teacher Salary‡ . . . $64,731

California Achievement Tests 6th ed., 2008

(Pct scoring at or above 50th National Percentile Rank)

	Math	Reading	Language
Grade 3	NA	NA	NA
Grade 7	62%	60%	60%

Academic Performance Index, 2008

Number of students tested . . . 8,121
Number of valid scores . . . 7,830
2007 API (base) . . . 753
2008 API (growth) . . . 771

SAT Testing, 2006-07

Enrollment, Grade 12 . . . 1,738
Number taking test . . . 836
percent taking test . . . 48.1%
percent with total score 1,500+ . . . 32.40%

Average Scores:

Math	Verbal	Writing	Total
560	547	537	1,644

Federal No Child Left Behind, 2008

(Adequate Yearly Progress standards met)

	Participation Rate	Pct Proficient
ELA	Yes	No
Math	Yes	No

API criteria . . . Yes
Graduation rate . . . Yes
criteria met/possible . . . 34/28

Other school districts for this city

(see Appendix E for information on these districts)
Complete list in Appendix E

See Introduction for an explanation of all data sources.

Demographics & Socio-Economic Characteristics†

(2007 American Community Survey, except as noted)

Population

1990* 93,613
2007 105,591
Male 52,131
Female 53,460
Jan. 2008 (estimate)§ 115,503
Persons per sq. mi. of land 6,277.3

Race & Hispanic Origin, 2007

Race
White 47,738
Black/African American 1,928
North American Native 441
Asian 42,541
Pacific Islander 1,340
Other Race 8,149
Two or more races 3,454
Hispanic origin, total 18,105
Mexican 13,510
Puerto Rican 174
Cuban 600
Other Hispanic 3,821

Age & Nativity, 2007

Under 5 years 9,597
18 years and over 82,674
65 years and over 10,735
85 years and over 1,312
Median Age 34.3
Native-born 61,901
Foreign-born 43,690

Educational Attainment, 2007

Population 25 years and over 71,490
Less than 9th grade 4.7%
High school grad or higher 89.1%
Bachelor's degree or higher 49.5%
Graduate degree 20.1%

Income & Poverty, 2007

Per capita income $35,814
Median household income $75,687
Median family income $98,977
Persons in poverty 12.3%
H'holds receiving public assistance 570
H'holds receiving social security 6,535

Households, 2007

Total households 39,069
With persons under 18 14,358
With persons over 65 6,987
Family households 23,254
Single person households 12,879
Persons per household 2.61
Persons per family 3.38

Household Population, 2008§§

Persons living in households 112,716
Persons living in group quarters 2,787
Persons per household 2.6

Labor & Employment

Total civilian labor force, 2008§§ 56,800
Unemployment rate, 2008 .... 5.5%
Total civilian labor force, 2000* 57,472

Employed persons 16 years and over by occupation, 2007

Managers & professionals 28,694
Service occupations 6,642
Sales & office occupations 11,719
Farming, fishing & forestry 0
Construction & maintenance 2,427
Production & transportation 3,125
Self-employed persons 2,776

† see Appendix D for 2000 Decennial Census Data
* US Census Bureau
** 2007 American Community Survey
§ California Department of Finance
§§ California Employment Development Dept

General Information

City of Santa Clara
1500 Warburton Ave
Santa Clara, CA 95050
408-615-2200

Website .... www.ci.santa-clara.ca.us
Elevation .... 88 ft.
Land Area (sq. miles) 18.4
Water Area (sq. miles) 0
Year of Incorporation 1852
Government type .... Chartered
Sales tax rate 9.25%

Voters & Officials

Registered Voters, October 2008

Total 46,570
Democrats 22,210
Republicans 10,369
Declined to state 12,188

Legislative Districts

US Congressional 15
State Senatorial 13
State Assembly 22, 24

Local Officials, 2009

Mayor .... Patricia M. Mahan
Manager .... Jennifer Sparacino
City Clerk .... Rod Diridon Jr
Attorney .... Helene Leichter
Finance Dir .... Mary Ann Parrot
Public Works .... Rajeev Batra
Planning/Dev Dir .... Kevin Riley
Building .... Kevin Riley
Police Chief .... Stephen D. Lodge
Emergency/Fire Dir .... Phil Kleinheinz

Public Safety

Number of officers, 2007 137
Violent crimes, 2007 231
Property crimes, 2007 3,430
Arson, 2007 13

Public Library

Santa Clara City/Central Park Library
Santa Clara City Library System
2635 Homestead Rd
Santa Clara, CA 95051
408-615-2930

City Librarian .... Karen Saunders

Library system statistics, FY 2007

Population served 114,238
Internet terminals 181
Annual users 368,395

Per capita:

Operating income $63.94
percent from local government 90.8%
Operating expenditure $56.49
Total materials 3.55
Print holdings 3.14
Visits per capita 7.22

Housing & Construction

Housing Units

Total, 2008§ 44,275
Single family units, attached 3,759
Single family units, detached 18,617
Multiple family units 21,790
Mobile home units 109
Occupied 43,042
Vacancy rate 2.8%
Median rent, 2007** $1,318
Median SF home value, 2007** $686,400

New Privately Owned Housing Units Authorized by Building Permit, 2007*

	Units	Construction Cost
Single	85	$19,257,950
Total	90	$20,148,211

Municipal Finance

(For local fiscal year ended in 2006)

Revenues

Total $393,550,380
Taxes 74,776,800
Special benefits assessment 0
Licenses & permits 2,575,029
Fines & forfeitures 1,302,437
Revenues from use of money & property 12,260,681
Intergovernmental 21,471,042
Service charges 269,553,085
Other revenues 11,611,306
Other financing sources 0

Expenditures

Total $468,143,810
General government 34,464,728
Public safety 67,267,428
Transportation 20,477,915
Community development 7,166,374
Health 27,316,717
Culture & leisure 26,727,587
Other 0

Local School District

(Data from School year 2007-08 except as noted)

Santa Clara Unified
PO Box 397
Santa Clara, CA 95052
(408) 423-2000

Superintendent .... Steve Stavis
Grade plan K-12
Number of schools 24
Enrollment 14,343
High school graduates, 2006-07 806
Dropout rate 3.0%
Pupil/teacher ratio 20.9
Average class size 26.1
Students per computer 3.8
Classrooms with internet 704
Avg. Daily Attendance (ADA) 14,007
Cost per ADA $8,593
Avg. Teacher Salary $70,925

California Achievement Tests 6th ed., 2008

(Pct scoring at or above 50th National Percentile Rank)

	Math	Reading	Language
Grade 3	62%	43%	54%
Grade 7	54%	50%	50%

Academic Performance Index, 2008

Number of students tested 10,678
Number of valid scores 9,866
2007 API (base) 753
2008 API (growth) 765

SAT Testing, 2006-07

Enrollment, Grade 12 1,014
Number taking test 381
percent taking test 37.6%
percent with total score 1,500+ 17.30%

Average Scores:

Math	Verbal	Writing	Total
515	487	481	1,483

Federal No Child Left Behind, 2008

(Adequate Yearly Progress standards met)

	Participation Rate	Pct Proficient
ELA	Yes	No
Math	Yes	No

API criteria .... Yes
Graduation rate .... Yes
\# criteria met/possible 42/39

Other school districts for this city

(see Appendix E for information on these districts)

Cupertino Union Elem

See Introduction for an explanation of all data sources.

Demographics & Socio-Economic Characteristics†

(2007 American Community Survey, except as noted)

Population

1990* 110,642
2007 177,740
Male 90,584
Female 87,156
Jan. 2008 (estimate)§ 177,045
Persons per sq. mi. of land 3,703.9

Race & Hispanic Origin, 2007

Race
White 113,396
Black/African American 4,715
North American Native 879
Asian 11,192
Pacific Islander 565
Other Race 33,575
Two or more races 13,418
Hispanic origin, total 57,655
Mexican 38,708
Puerto Rican 254
Cuban 769
Other Hispanic 17,924

Age & Nativity, 2007

Under 5 years 12,143
18 years and over 127,989
65 years and over 14,435
85 years and over 1,502
Median Age 35.4
Native-born 140,926
Foreign-born 36,814

Educational Attainment, 2007

Population 25 years and over 110,920
Less than 9th grade 5.0%
High school grad or higher 88.0%
Bachelor's degree or higher 31.0%
Graduate degree 9.3%

Income & Poverty, 2007

Per capita income $31,531
Median household income $79,004
Median family income $91,450
Persons in poverty 8.9%
H'holds receiving public assistance 592
H'holds receiving social security 12,042

Households, 2007

Total households 58,761
With persons under 18 24,004
With persons over 65 11,153
Family households 40,413
Single person households 14,658
Persons per household 2.99
Persons per family 3.54

Household Population, 2008§§

Persons living in households 175,652
Persons living in group quarters 1,393
Persons per household 3.1

Labor & Employment

Total civilian labor force, 2008§§ 91,800
Unemployment rate, 2008 .... 4.5%
Total civilian labor force, 2000* 79,149

Employed persons 16 years and over by occupation, 2007

Managers & professionals 35,447
Service occupations 14,850
Sales & office occupations 24,315
Farming, fishing & forestry 301
Construction & maintenance 7,302
Production & transportation 8,848
Self-employed persons 6,976

† see Appendix D for 2000 Decennial Census Data
* US Census Bureau
** 2007 American Community Survey
§ California Department of Finance
§§ California Employment Development Dept

General Information

City of Santa Clarita
23920 Valencia Blvd
Suite 300
Santa Clarita, CA 91355
661-259-2489

Website .... www.santa-clarita.com
Elevation .... NA
Land Area (sq. miles) 47.8
Water Area (sq. miles) 0
Year of Incorporation 1987
Government type .... General Law
Sales tax rate 9.25%

Voters & Officials

Registered Voters, October 2008

Total 88,487
Democrats 30,301
Republicans 38,570
Declined to state 15,843

Legislative Districts

US Congressional 25
State Senatorial 17, 19
State Assembly 38

Local Officials, 2009

Mayor .... Frank Ferry
Manager .... Ken Pulskamp
City Clerk .... Sharon Dawson
Attorney .... Carl Newton
Finance Dir .... Darren Hernandez
Public Works .... Robert Newman
Planning/Dev Dir .... Paul Brotzman
Building .... Ruben Barrera
Sheriff .... Anthony La Berge
Emergency/Fire Dir .... Michael Freeman

Public Safety

Number of officers, 2007 .... NA
Violent crimes, 2007 372
Property crimes, 2007 3,782
Arson, 2007 26

Public Library

Served by Canyon Country, Newhall and Valencia branches of County Library system

Library system statistics, FY 2007

Population served .... NA
Internet terminals .... NA
Annual users .... NA

Per capita:

Operating income .... NA
percent from local government .... NA
Operating expenditure .... NA
Total materials .... NA
Print holdings .... NA
Visits per capita .... NA

Housing & Construction

Housing Units

Total, 2008§ 58,714
Single family units, attached 6,937
Single family units, detached 36,160
Multiple family units 13,377
Mobile home units 2,240
Occupied 56,856
Vacancy rate 3.2%
Median rent, 2007** $1,411
Median SF home value, 2007** $548,500

New Privately Owned Housing Units Authorized by Building Permit, 2007*

	Units	Construction Cost
Single	198	$64,793,915
Total	222	$70,151,226

Municipal Finance

(For local fiscal year ended in 2006)

Revenues

Total $198,845,064
Taxes 112,510,161
Special benefits assessment 10,683,208
Licenses & permits 5,009,505
Fines & forfeitures 1,904,273
Revenues from use of money & property 2,842,178
Intergovernmental 25,760,245
Service charges 14,273,173
Other revenues 8,162,321
Other financing sources 17,700,000

Expenditures

Total $153,286,201
General government 43,575,737
Public safety 15,375,472
Transportation 66,935,566
Community development 16,273,389
Health 1,285,240
Culture & leisure 9,840,797
Other 0

Local School District

(Data from School year 2007-08 except as noted)

William S. Hart Union High
21515 Centre Pointe Pkwy
Santa Clarita, CA 91350
(661) 259-0033

Superintendent .... Jaime Castellanos
Grade plan 7-12
Number of schools 19
Enrollment 25,243
High school graduates, 2006-07 3,510
Dropout rate 3.5%
Pupil/teacher ratio 24.3
Average class size 28.3
Students per computer 5.3
Classrooms with internet 991
Avg. Daily Attendance (ADA) 23,093
Cost per ADA $7,645
Avg. Teacher Salary $66,436

California Achievement Tests 6th ed., 2008

(Pct scoring at or above 50th National Percentile Rank)

	Math	Reading	Language
Grade 3	NA	NA	NA
Grade 7	69%	65%	62%

Academic Performance Index, 2008

Number of students tested 18,822
Number of valid scores 18,271
2007 API (base) 791
2008 API (growth) 804

SAT Testing, 2006-07

Enrollment, Grade 12 3,850
Number taking test 1,437
percent taking test 37.3%
percent with total score 1,500+ 23.90%

Average Scores:

Math	Verbal	Writing	Total
547	521	526	1,594

Federal No Child Left Behind, 2008

(Adequate Yearly Progress standards met)

	Participation Rate	Pct Proficient
ELA	Yes	No
Math	Yes	No

API criteria .... Yes
Graduation rate .... Yes
criteria met/possible 38/36

Other school districts for this city

(see Appendix E for information on these districts)

Newhall Elem, Saugus Union Elem, Sulphur Springs Union Elem

See Introduction for an explanation of all data sources.

Demographics & Socio-Economic Characteristics

(2000 Decennial Census, except as noted)

Population

1990*	49,040
2000	54,593
Male	27,180
Female	27,413
Jan. 2008 (estimate)[§]	58,125
Persons per sq. mi. of land	4,650.0

Race & Hispanic Origin, 2000

Race	
White	42,984
Black/African American	945
North American Native	469
Asian	2,677
Pacific Islander	72
Other Race	4,990
Two or more races	2,456
Hispanic origin, total	9,491
Mexican	7,184
Puerto Rican	170
Cuban	77
Other Hispanic	2,060

Age & Nativity, 2000

Under 5 years	2,664
18 years and over	45,130
65 years and over	4,663
85 years and over	703
Median Age	31.7
Native-born	46,139
Foreign-born	8,225

Educational Attainment, 2000

Population 25 years and over	33,896
Less than 9th grade	5.5%
High school grad or higher	89.1%
Bachelor's degree or higher	44.4%
Graduate degree	17.5%

Income & Poverty, 1999

Per capita income	$25,758
Median household income	$50,605
Median family income	$62,231
Persons in poverty	15.3%
H'holds receiving public assistance	550
H'holds receiving social security	3,746

Households, 2000

Total households	20,442
With persons under 18	5,513
With persons over 65	3,433
Family households	10,401
Single person households	5,986
Persons per household	2.44
Persons per family	2.98

Household Population, 2008[§§]

Persons living in households	52,581
Persons living in group quarters	5,544
Persons per household	2.4

Labor & Employment

Total civilian labor force, 2008[§§]	32,500
Unemployment rate, 2008	6.1%
Total civilian labor force, 2000	31,578

Employed persons 16 years and over by occupation, 2000

Managers & professionals	13,381
Service occupations	4,782
Sales & office occupations	6,983
Farming, fishing & forestry	250
Construction & maintenance	2,257
Production & transportation	1,991
Self-employed persons	3,605

* US Census Bureau
** 2000 Decennial Census
§ California Department of Finance
§§ California Employment Development Dept

General Information

City of Santa Cruz
809 Center St
Santa Cruz, CA 95060
831-420-5030

Website	www.ci.santa-cruz.ca.us
Elevation	20 ft.
Land Area (sq. miles)	12.5
Water Area (sq. miles)	3.1
Year of Incorporation	1866
Government type	Chartered
Sales tax rate	9.50%

Voters & Officials

Registered Voters, October 2008

Total	37,909
Democrats	23,071
Republicans	3,783
Declined to state	7,346

Legislative Districts

US Congressional	17
State Senatorial	11
State Assembly	27

Local Officials, 2009

Mayor	Cynthia Mathews
Manager	Richard Wilson
City Clerk	Lorrie Brewer
Attorney	John Barisone
Finance Dir	Jack Dilles
Public Works	Mark Dettle
Planning Dir	Juliana Rebagliati (Actg)
Building	John Ancic (Int)
Police Chief	Howard Skerry
Fire Chief	Ron Oliver

Public Safety

Number of officers, 2007	85
Violent crimes, 2007	481
Property crimes, 2007	2,432
Arson, 2007	33

Public Library

Central Branch Library
Santa Cruz Libraries
224 Church St
Santa Cruz, CA 95060
831-420-5700

Director	Anne Turner

Library system statistics, FY 2007

Population served	205,669
Internet terminals	24
Annual users	23,239

Per capita:

Operating income	$59.06
percent from local government	95.9%
Operating expenditure	$58.55
Total materials	2.52
Print holdings	2.13
Visits per capita	NA

Housing & Construction

Housing Units

Total, 2008[§]	23,379
Single family units, attached	2,082
Single family units, detached	12,386
Multiple family units	8,470
Mobile home units	441
Occupied	22,069
Vacancy rate	5.6%
Median rent, 2000**	$941
Median SF home value, 2000**	$411,900

New Privately Owned Housing Units Authorized by Building Permit, 2007*

	Units	Construction Cost
Single	60	$19,650,605
Total	417	$97,508,103

Municipal Finance

(For local fiscal year ended in 2006)

Revenues

Total	$138,848,736
Taxes	41,233,964
Special benefits assessment	0
Licenses & permits	615,449
Fines & forfeitures	1,979,060
Revenues from use of money & property	6,519,265
Intergovernmental	6,170,887
Service charges	60,371,019
Other revenues	2,059,364
Other financing sources	19,899,728

Expenditures

Total	$121,877,608
General government	6,849,870
Public safety	29,396,662
Transportation	6,476,392
Community development	4,585,556
Health	38,680,333
Culture & leisure	15,857,251
Other	1,435,266

Local School District

(Data from School year 2007-08 except as noted)
‡combined elementary and high school data

Santa Cruz City High
405 Old San Jose Rd
Soquel, CA 95073
(831) 429-3410

Superintendent	Alan Pagano
Grade plan	K-12
Number of schools	9
Enrollment	4,847
High school graduates, 2006-07	905
Dropout rate	1.2%
Pupil/teacher ratio	22.9
Average class size	24.4
Students per computer	3.7
Classrooms with internet	244
Avg. Daily Attendance (ADA)[‡]	6,438
Cost per ADA[‡]	$9,723
Avg. Teacher Salary[‡]	$60,324

California Achievement Tests 6th ed., 2008

(Pct scoring at or above 50th National Percentile Rank)

	Math	Reading	Language
Grade 3	NA	NA	NA
Grade 7	65%	68%	64%

Academic Performance Index, 2008

Number of students tested	3,635
Number of valid scores	3,485
2007 API (base)	745
2008 API (growth)	753

SAT Testing, 2006-07

Enrollment, Grade 12	997
Number taking test	404
percent taking test	40.5%
percent with total score 1,500+	29.30%

Average Scores:

Math	Verbal	Writing	Total
557	547	540	1,644

Federal No Child Left Behind, 2008

(Adequate Yearly Progress standards met)

	Participation Rate	Pct Proficient
ELA	No	No
Math	No	No

API criteria	Yes
Graduation rate	Yes
# criteria met/possible	26/16

Other school districts for this city

(see Appendix E for information on these districts)

Complete list in Appendix E

See Introduction for an explanation of all data sources.

Demographics & Socio-Economic Characteristics

(2000 Decennial Census, except as noted)

Population

1990* . . . 15,520
2000 . . . 17,438
Male . . . 8,724
Female . . . 8,714
Jan. 2008 (estimate)§ . . . 17,790
Persons per sq. mi. of land . . . 2,021.6

Race & Hispanic Origin, 2000

Race
White . . . 8,932
Black/African American . . . 679
North American Native . . . 250
Asian . . . 688
Pacific Islander . . . 35
Other Race . . . 6,102
Two or more races . . . 752
Hispanic origin, total . . . 12,447
Mexican . . . 10,059
Puerto Rican . . . 112
Cuban . . . 122
Other Hispanic . . . 2,154

Age & Nativity, 2000

Under 5 years . . . 1,269
18 years and over . . . 12,371
65 years and over . . . 2,234
85 years and over . . . 126
Median Age . . . 33.1
Native-born . . . 13,205
Foreign-born . . . 4,629

Educational Attainment, 2000

Population 25 years and over . . . 10,903
Less than 9th grade . . . 15.8%
High school grad or higher . . . 62.9%
Bachelor's degree or higher . . . 9.2%
Graduate degree . . . 2.3%

Income & Poverty, 1999

Per capita income . . . $14,547
Median household income . . . $44,540
Median family income . . . $49,867
Persons in poverty . . . 12.1%
H'holds receiving public assistance . . . 266
H'holds receiving social security . . . 1,568

Households, 2000

Total households . . . 4,834
With persons under 18 . . . 2,294
With persons over 65 . . . 1,688
Family households . . . 3,779
Single person households . . . 886
Persons per household . . . 3.35
Persons per family . . . 3.82

Household Population, 2008§§

Persons living in households . . . 17,572
Persons living in group quarters . . . 218
Persons per household . . . 3.5

Labor & Employment

Total civilian labor force, 2008§§ . . . 8,000
Unemployment rate, 2008 . . . 6.2%
Total civilian labor force, 2000 . . . 6,931

Employed persons 16 years and over by occupation, 2000

Managers & professionals . . . 1,477
Service occupations . . . 831
Sales & office occupations . . . 1,940
Farming, fishing & forestry . . . 20
Construction & maintenance . . . 536
Production & transportation . . . 1,653
Self-employed persons . . . 314

* US Census Bureau
** 2000 Decennial Census
§ California Department of Finance
§§ California Employment Development Dept

General Information

City of Santa Fe Springs
11710 Telegraph Rd
Santa Fe Springs, CA 90670
562-868-0511

Website . . . www.santafesprings.org
Elevation . . . 130 ft.
Land Area (sq. miles) . . . 8.8
Water Area (sq. miles) . . . 0.1
Year of Incorporation . . . 1957
Government type . . . General law
Sales tax rate . . . 9.25%

Voters & Officials

Registered Voters, October 2008

Total . . . 8,528
Democrats . . . 5,112
Republicans . . . 1,827
Declined to state . . . 1,318

Legislative Districts

US Congressional . . . 38
State Senatorial . . . 30
State Assembly . . . 56

Local Officials, 2009

Mayor . . . Luis M. Gonzalez
Manager . . . Frederick W. Latham
City Clerk . . . Barbara E. Earl
Attorney . . . Steven Skolnik
Finance Dir . . . Jose Gomez
Public Works . . . Donald Jensen
Planning/Dev Dir . . . Paul R. Ashworth
Building . . . NA
Police Chief . . . David Singer
Emergency/Fire Dir . . . Alex Rodriguez

Public Safety

Number of officers, 2007 . . . NA
Violent crimes, 2007 . . . 137
Property crimes, 2007 . . . 1,515
Arson, 2007 . . . NA

Public Library

Santa Fe Springs City Library
Santa Fe Springs City Library System
11700 E Telegraph Rd
Santa Fe Springs, CA 90670
562-868-7738

Director . . . Hilary Keith

Library system statistics, FY 2007

Population served . . . 17,849
Internet terminals . . . 18
Annual users . . . 104,940

Per capita:

Operating income . . . $102.59
percent from local government . . . 90.1%
Operating expenditure . . . $96.74
Total materials . . . 5.68
Print holdings . . . 5.11
Visits per capita . . . 3.07

Housing & Construction

Housing Units

Total, 2008§ . . . 5,107
Single family units, attached . . . 286
Single family units, detached . . . 3,101
Multiple family units . . . 1,593
Mobile home units . . . 127
Occupied . . . 5,004
Vacancy rate . . . 2.0%
Median rent, 2000** . . . $747
Median SF home value, 2000** . . . $169,400

New Privately Owned Housing Units Authorized by Building Permit, 2007*

	Units	Construction Cost
Single	0	$0
Total	66	$5,808,000

Municipal Finance

(For local fiscal year ended in 2006)

Revenues

Total . . . $55,292,018
Taxes . . . 33,072,458
Special benefits assessment . . . 275,847
Licenses & permits . . . 1,876,755
Fines & forfeitures . . . 694,752
Revenues from use of money & property . . . 2,331,068
Intergovernmental . . . 2,702,727
Service charges . . . 12,588,837
Other revenues . . . 1,666,884
Other financing sources . . . 82,690

Expenditures

Total . . . $56,242,532
General government . . . 6,147,437
Public safety . . . 24,381,457
Transportation . . . 3,578,224
Community development . . . 2,698,425
Health . . . 4,300,692
Culture & leisure . . . 8,389,797
Other . . . 0

Local School District

(Data from School year 2007-08 except as noted)

Whittier Union High
9401 South Painter Ave
Whittier, CA 90605
(562) 698-8121

Superintendent . . . Sandra Thorstenson
Grade plan . . . 9-12
Number of schools . . . 7
Enrollment . . . 13,854
High school graduates, 2006-07 . . . 2,523
Dropout rate . . . 2.0%
Pupil/teacher ratio . . . 24.9
Average class size . . . 28.1
Students per computer . . . 4.5
Classrooms with internet . . . 503
Avg. Daily Attendance (ADA) . . . 13,239
Cost per ADA . . . $8,911
Avg. Teacher Salary . . . $71,206

California Achievement Tests 6th ed., 2008

(Pct scoring at or above 50th National Percentile Rank)

	Math	Reading	Language
Grade 3	NA	NA	NA
Grade 7	NA	NA	NA

Academic Performance Index, 2008

Number of students tested . . . 9,803
Number of valid scores . . . 9,357
2007 API (base) . . . 703
2008 API (growth) . . . 728

SAT Testing, 2006-07

Enrollment, Grade 12 . . . 3,426
Number taking test . . . 1,034
percent taking test . . . 30.2%
percent with total score 1,500+ . . . 8.80%

Average Scores:

Math	Verbal	Writing	Total
467	451	447	1,365

Federal No Child Left Behind, 2008

(Adequate Yearly Progress standards met)

	Participation Rate	Pct Proficient
ELA	Yes	No
Math	Yes	No

API criteria . . . Yes
Graduation rate . . . Yes
\# criteria met/possible . . . 26/24

Other school districts for this city

(see Appendix E for information on these districts)

Little Lake City Elem, Los Nietos Elem

See Introduction for an explanation of all data sources.

Demographics & Socio-Economic Characteristics†

(2007 American Community Survey, except as noted)

Population

1990* 61,284
2007 86,160
Male 42,391
Female 43,769
Jan. 2008 (estimate)§ 91,110
Persons per sq. mi. of land 4,720.7

Race & Hispanic Origin, 2007

Race
White 64,188
Black/African American 886
North American Native 291
Asian 3,527
Pacific Islander 151
Other Race 14,009
Two or more races 3,108
Hispanic origin, total 58,829
Mexican .... NA
Puerto Rican .... NA
Cuban .... NA
Other Hispanic .... NA

Age & Nativity, 2007

Under 5 years 9,925
18 years and over 57,728
65 years and over 8,755
85 years and over 1,083
Median Age 28.8
Native-born 58,589
Foreign-born 27,571

Educational Attainment, 2007

Population 25 years and over 48,633
Less than 9th grade 26.6%
High school grad or higher 62.8%
Bachelor's degree or higher 11.9%
Graduate degree 3.8%

Income & Poverty, 2007

Per capita income $18,157
Median household income $47,215
Median family income $48,275
Persons in poverty 13.4%
H'holds receiving public assistance ... 1,098
H'holds receiving social security 6,265

Households, 2007

Total households 25,346
With persons under 18 12,981
With persons over 65 5,742
Family households 18,923
Single person households 5,160
Persons per household 3.36
Persons per family 3.86

Household Population, 2008§§

Persons living in households 88,912
Persons living in group quarters 2,198
Persons per household 3.3

Labor & Employment

Total civilian labor force, 2008§§ 39,500
Unemployment rate, 2008 .... 8.6%
Total civilian labor force, 2000* 33,536

Employed persons 16 years and over by occupation, 2007

Managers & professionals 7,355
Service occupations 6,799
Sales & office occupations 7,063
Farming, fishing & forestry 7,873
Construction & maintenance 3,203
Production & transportation 4,039
Self-employed persons 2,280

† see Appendix D for 2000 Decennial Census Data
* US Census Bureau
** 2007 American Community Survey
§ California Department of Finance
§§ California Employment Development Dept

General Information

City of Santa Maria
110 E Cook St
Room 1
Santa Maria, CA 93454
805-925-0951

Website .... www.ci.santa-maria.ca.us
Elevation .... 216 ft.
Land Area (sq. miles) 19.3
Water Area (sq. miles) 0.4
Year of Incorporation 1905
Government type .... Chartered
Sales tax rate 8.75%

Voters & Officials

Registered Voters, October 2008

Total 27,685
Democrats 11,466
Republicans 10,050
Declined to state 4,961

Legislative Districts

US Congressional 23
State Senatorial 15
State Assembly 33

Local Officials, 2009

Mayor .... Larry Lavagnino
Manager .... Tim Ness
City Clerk .... Patti Rodriguez
Attorney .... Gil Trujillo
Finance Dir .... Lynda Snodgrass
Public Works .... David Whitehead
Planning/Dev Dir .... Peggy Woods (Actg)
Building .... NA
Police Chief .... Danny Macagni
Emergency/Fire Dir .... Frank Ortiz

Public Safety

Number of officers, 2007 101
Violent crimes, 2007 604
Property crimes, 2007 2,616
Arson, 2007 12

Public Library

Main Branch
Santa Maria Public Library
421 S McLelland
Santa Maria, CA 93454
805-925-0994

City Librarian .... Jack Buchanan (Int)

Library system statistics, FY 2007

Population served 118,839
Internet terminals 141
Annual users 273,093

Per capita:

Operating income $21.45
percent from local government 82.1%
Operating expenditure $17.72
Total materials 2.35
Print holdings 2.06
Visits per capita 14.96

Housing & Construction

Housing Units

Total, 2008§ 27,387
Single family units, attached 1,655
Single family units, detached 17,098
Multiple family units 7,053
Mobile home units 1,581
Occupied 26,602
Vacancy rate 2.9%
Median rent, 2007** $962
Median SF home value, 2007** $410,600

New Privately Owned Housing Units Authorized by Building Permit, 2007*

	Units	Construction Cost
Single	146	$26,149,595
Total	317	$48,106,175

Municipal Finance

(For local fiscal year ended in 2006)

Revenues

Total $131,896,674
Taxes 52,405,675
Special benefits assessment 1,812,387
Licenses & permits 2,431,692
Fines & forfeitures 443,758
Revenues from use of money & property 4,449,351
Intergovernmental 12,284,396
Service charges 53,510,581
Other revenues 4,558,834
Other financing sources 0

Expenditures

Total $111,077,342
General government 7,834,733
Public safety 26,479,914
Transportation 17,399,282
Community development 4,008,222
Health 18,186,430
Culture & leisure 11,248,624
Other 0

Local School District

(Data from School year 2007-08 except as noted)

Santa Maria Joint Union High
2560 Skyway Dr
Santa Maria, CA 93455
(805) 922-4573

Superintendent .... Jeffery Hearn
Grade plan 9-12
Number of schools 4
Enrollment 7,746
High school graduates, 2006-07 1,248
Dropout rate 3.2%
Pupil/teacher ratio 24.8
Average class size 26.5
Students per computer 1.9
Classrooms with internet 317
Avg. Daily Attendance (ADA) 7,514
Cost per ADA $7,864
Avg. Teacher Salary $70,761

California Achievement Tests 6th ed., 2008

(Pct scoring at or above 50th National Percentile Rank)

	Math	Reading	Language
Grade 3	NA	NA	NA
Grade 7	NA	NA	NA

Academic Performance Index, 2008

Number of students tested 5,688
Number of valid scores 5,378
2007 API (base) 680
2008 API (growth) 692

SAT Testing, 2006-07

Enrollment, Grade 12 1,657
Number taking test 366
percent taking test 22.1%
percent with total score 1,500+ 8.60%

Average Scores:

Math	Verbal	Writing	Total
495	465	464	1,424

Federal No Child Left Behind, 2008

(Adequate Yearly Progress standards met)

	Participation Rate	Pct Proficient
ELA	Yes	No
Math	No	No

API criteria .... Yes
Graduation rate .... Yes
\# criteria met/possible 26/21

Other school districts for this city

(see Appendix E for information on these districts)

Blochman Union Elem, Orcutt Union Elem, Santa Maria-Bonita

See Introduction for an explanation of all data sources.

Demographics & Socio-Economic Characteristics†

(2007 American Community Survey, except as noted)

Population

1990* 86,905
2007 86,857
Male 43,206
Female 43,651
Jan. 2008 (estimate)§ 91,439
Persons per sq. mi. of land 11,016.7

Race & Hispanic Origin, 2007

Race
White 67,989
Black/African American 1,747
North American Native 193
Asian 9,814
Pacific Islander 86
Other Race 4,610
Two or more races 2,418
Hispanic origin, total 9,493
Mexican 6,433
Puerto Rican 0
Cuban 469
Other Hispanic 2,591

Age & Nativity, 2007

Under 5 years 4,586
18 years and over 74,068
65 years and over 9,951
85 years and over 1,682
Median Age 39.6
Native-born 67,904
Foreign-born 18,953

Educational Attainment, 2007

Population 25 years and over 67,704
Less than 9th grade 1.4%
High school grad or higher 95.5%
Bachelor's degree or higher 65.6%
Graduate degree 28.0%

Income & Poverty, 2007

Per capita income $61,959
Median household income $71,796
Median family income $100,657
Persons in poverty 9.0%
H'holds receiving public assistance 725
H'holds receiving social security 8,490

Households, 2007

Total households 45,843
With persons under 18 7,858
With persons over 65 8,189
Family households 17,662
Single person households 23,463
Persons per household 1.88
Persons per family 2.83

Household Population, 2008§§

Persons living in households 88,833
Persons living in group quarters 2,606
Persons per household 1.9

Labor & Employment

Total civilian labor force, 2008§§ 58,500
Unemployment rate, 2008 .... 6.2%
Total civilian labor force, 2000* 50,815

Employed persons 16 years and over by occupation, 2007

Managers & professionals 32,798
Service occupations 4,383
Sales & office occupations 11,426
Farming, fishing & forestry 0
Construction & maintenance 1,365
Production & transportation 1,193
Self-employed persons 8,514

† see Appendix D for 2000 Decennial Census Data
* US Census Bureau
** 2007 American Community Survey
§ California Department of Finance
§§ California Employment Development Dept

General Information

City of Santa Monica
1685 Main St
Santa Monica, CA 90407
310-458-8211

Website .... www.smgov.net
Elevation .... 101 ft.
Land Area (sq. miles) 8.3
Water Area (sq. miles) 7.6
Year of Incorporation 1886
Government type .... Chartered
Sales tax rate 9.25%

Voters & Officials

Registered Voters, October 2008

Total 61,027
Democrats 33,390
Republicans 10,273
Declined to state 14,345

Legislative Districts

US Congressional 30
State Senatorial 23
State Assembly 41

Local Officials, 2009

Mayor .... Ken Genser
Manager .... Lamont Ewell
City Clerk .... Maria Stewart
Attorney .... Marsha Jones Moutrie
Finance Dir .... Carol Swindell
Public Works .... NA
Planning/Dev Dir .... NA
Building .... NA
Police Chief .... Timothy Jackman
Emergency/Fire Dir .... James Hone

Public Safety

Number of officers, 2007 209
Violent crimes, 2007 596
Property crimes, 2007 3,108
Arson, 2007 13

Public Library

Santa Monica Public Library
Santa Monica Public Library System
601 Santa Monica Blvd
Santa Monica, CA 90401
310-458-8600

City Librarian .... Greg Mullen

Library system statistics, FY 2007

Population served 91,124
Internet terminals 9
Annual users 12,673

Per capita:

Operating income $106.79
percent from local government 94.1%
Operating expenditure $106.79
Total materials 4.66
Print holdings 4.18
Visits per capita 3.74

Housing & Construction

Housing Units

Total, 2008§ 49,740
Single family units, attached 1,931
Single family units, detached 9,346
Multiple family units 38,174
Mobile home units 289
Occupied 46,242
Vacancy rate 7.0%
Median rent, 2007** $1,354
Median SF home value, 2007** $987,900

New Privately Owned Housing Units Authorized by Building Permit, 2007*

	Units	Construction Cost
Single	46	$24,171,660
Total	633	$103,205,597

Municipal Finance

(For local fiscal year ended in 2006)

Revenues

Total $367,122,854
Taxes 186,679,883
Special benefits assessment 918,807
Licenses & permits 20,301,339
Fines & forfeitures 12,951,878
Revenues from use of money & property 16,296,982
Intergovernmental 22,822,197
Service charges 91,833,062
Other revenues 15,318,706
Other financing sources 0

Expenditures

Total $382,284,508
General government 25,420,783
Public safety 93,733,920
Transportation 78,626,332
Community development 46,837,409
Health 64,304,514
Culture & leisure 60,548,374
Other 0

Local School District

(Data from School year 2007-08 except as noted)

Santa Monica-Malibu Unified
1651 16th St
Santa Monica, CA 90404
(310) 450-8338

Superintendent .... Tim Cuneo
Grade plan K-12
Number of schools 17
Enrollment 11,688
High school graduates, 2006-07 848
Dropout rate 2.9%
Pupil/teacher ratio 20.1
Average class size 25.4
Students per computer 3.5
Classrooms with internet 596
Avg. Daily Attendance (ADA) 11,424
Cost per ADA $9,835
Avg. Teacher Salary $67,843

California Achievement Tests 6th ed., 2008

(Pct scoring at or above 50th National Percentile Rank)

	Math	Reading	Language
Grade 3	76%	59%	69%
Grade 7	69%	69%	68%

Academic Performance Index, 2008

Number of students tested 8,897
Number of valid scores 8,505
2007 API (base) 819
2008 API (growth) 832

SAT Testing, 2006-07

Enrollment, Grade 12 954
Number taking test 632
percent taking test 66.3%
percent with total score 1,500+ 44.00%

Average Scores:

Math	Verbal	Writing	Total
556	542	544	1,642

Federal No Child Left Behind, 2008

(Adequate Yearly Progress standards met)

	Participation Rate	Pct Proficient
ELA	No	Yes
Math	Yes	Yes

API criteria .... Yes
Graduation rate .... Yes
\# criteria met/possible 34/33

Other school districts for this city

(see Appendix E for information on these districts)

Los Angeles Unified

See Introduction for an explanation of all data sources.

Demographics & Socio-Economic Characteristics

(2000 Decennial Census, except as noted)

Population

1990* . . . 25,062
2000 . . . 28,598
Male . . . 14,562
Female . . . 14,036
Jan. 2008 (estimate)§ . . . 29,539
Persons per sq. mi. of land . . . 6,421.5

Race & Hispanic Origin, 2000

Race
White . . . 15,795
Black/African American . . . 118
North American Native . . . 404
Asian . . . 200
Pacific Islander . . . 54
Other Race . . . 10,688
Two or more races . . . 1,339
Hispanic origin, total . . . 20,360
Mexican . . . 18,069
Puerto Rican . . . 30
Cuban . . . 15
Other Hispanic . . . 2,246

Age & Nativity, 2000

Under 5 years . . . 2,529
18 years and over . . . 19,608
65 years and over . . . 3,048
85 years and over . . . 415
Median Age . . . 29.6
Native-born . . . 20,193
Foreign-born . . . 8,438

Educational Attainment, 2000

Population 25 years and over . . . 16,544
Less than 9th grade . . . 25.5%
High school grad or higher . . . 57.8%
Bachelor's degree or higher . . . 8.6%
Graduate degree . . . 3.2%

Income & Poverty, 1999

Per capita income . . . $15,736
Median household income . . . $41,651
Median family income . . . $45,419
Persons in poverty . . . 14.5%
H'holds receiving public assistance . . . 391
H'holds receiving social security . . . 2,412

Households, 2000

Total households . . . 8,136
With persons under 18 . . . 4,104
With persons over 65 . . . 2,201
Family households . . . 6,433
Single person households . . . 1,396
Persons per household . . . 3.49
Persons per family . . . 3.86

Household Population, 2008§§

Persons living in households . . . 29,296
Persons living in group quarters . . . 243
Persons per household . . . 3.5

Labor & Employment

Total civilian labor force, 2008§§ . . . 14,600
Unemployment rate, 2008 . . . 10.6%
Total civilian labor force, 2000 . . . 12,186

Employed persons 16 years and over by occupation, 2000

Managers & professionals . . . 2,036
Service occupations . . . 1,628
Sales & office occupations . . . 3,098
Farming, fishing & forestry . . . 1,291
Construction & maintenance . . . 1,253
Production & transportation . . . 1,907
Self-employed persons . . . 681

* US Census Bureau
** 2000 Decennial Census
§ California Department of Finance
§§ California Employment Development Dept

General Information

City of Santa Paula
PO Box 569
Santa Paula, CA 93061
805-525-4478

Website . . . www.ci.santa-paula.ca.us
Elevation . . . 274 ft.
Land Area (sq. miles) . . . 4.6
Water Area (sq. miles) . . . 0
Year of Incorporation . . . 1902
Government type . . . General law
Sales tax rate . . . 8.25%

Voters & Officials

Registered Voters, October 2008

Total . . . 11,372
Democrats . . . 6,310
Republicans . . . 2,821
Declined to state . . . 1,769

Legislative Districts

US Congressional . . . 24
State Senatorial . . . 17
State Assembly . . . 37

Local Officials, 2009

Mayor . . . Ralph J. Fernandez
Manager . . . Wally Bobkiewicz
City Clerk . . . Judy Rice
Attorney . . . Karl H. Berger
Finance Dir . . . John Quinn
Public Works . . . Cliff Finley
Planning/Dev Dir . . . Janna Minsk
Building . . . Richard Araiza
Police Chief . . . Stephen MacKinnon
Fire Chief . . . Richard Araiza

Public Safety

Number of officers, 2007 . . . 34
Violent crimes, 2007 . . . 99
Property crimes, 2007 . . . 717
Arson, 2007 . . . 0

Public Library

Blanchard Community Library
Blanchard-Santa Paula Public Library Dist
119 N Eighth St
Santa Paula, CA 93060
805-525-3615

Director . . . Daniel Robles

Library system statistics, FY 2007

Population served . . . 29,182
Internet terminals . . . 10
Annual users . . . 54,020

Per capita:

Operating income . . . $25.56
percent from local government . . . 85.5%
Operating expenditure . . . $23.67
Total materials . . . 2.79
Print holdings . . . 2.69
Visits per capita . . . 15.01

Housing & Construction

Housing Units

Total, 2008§ . . . 8,576
Single family units, attached . . . 767
Single family units, detached . . . 5,060
Multiple family units . . . 1,962
Mobile home units . . . 787
Occupied . . . 8,366
Vacancy rate . . . 2.5%
Median rent, 2000** . . . $689
Median SF home value, 2000** . . . $179,800

New Privately Owned Housing Units Authorized by Building Permit, 2007*

	Units	Construction Cost
Single	33	$8,613,632
Total	40	$9,663,040

Municipal Finance

(For local fiscal year ended in 2006)

Revenues

Total . . . $28,976,668
Taxes . . . 7,672,450
Special benefits assessment . . . 837,727
Licenses & permits . . . 607,196
Fines & forfeitures . . . 129,236
Revenues from use of money & property . . . 1,273,106
Intergovernmental . . . 4,422,481
Service charges . . . 13,310,367
Other revenues . . . 724,105
Other financing sources . . . 0

Expenditures

Total . . . $21,846,649
General government . . . 1,764,143
Public safety . . . 6,835,716
Transportation . . . 2,927,225
Community development . . . 1,439,507
Health . . . 3,058,977
Culture & leisure . . . 885,344
Other . . . 0

Local School District

(Data from School year 2007-08 except as noted)

Santa Paula Union High
500 East Santa Barbara St
Santa Paula, CA 93060
(805) 525-0988

Superintendent . . . David Gomez
Grade plan . . . 9-12
Number of schools . . . 2
Enrollment . . . 1,698
High school graduates, 2006-07 . . . 298
Dropout rate . . . 1.7%
Pupil/teacher ratio . . . 23.8
Average class size . . . 28.3
Students per computer . . . 3.5
Classrooms with internet . . . 76
Avg. Daily Attendance (ADA) . . . 1,678
Cost per ADA . . . $7,885
Avg. Teacher Salary . . . NA

California Achievement Tests 6th ed., 2008

(Pct scoring at or above 50th National Percentile Rank)

	Math	Reading	Language
Grade 3	NA	NA	NA
Grade 7	NA	NA	NA

Academic Performance Index, 2008

Number of students tested . . . 1,201
Number of valid scores . . . 1,090
2007 API (base) . . . 666
2008 API (growth) . . . 676

SAT Testing, 2006-07

Enrollment, Grade 12 . . . 385
Number taking test . . . 105
percent taking test . . . 27.3%
percent with total score 1,500+ . . . 6.00%

Average Scores:

Math	Verbal	Writing	Total
434	440	443	1,317

Federal No Child Left Behind, 2008

(Adequate Yearly Progress standards met)

	Participation Rate	Pct Proficient
ELA	Yes	Yes
Math	Yes	Yes

API criteria . . . Yes
Graduation rate . . . Yes
criteria met/possible . . . 18/18

Other school districts for this city

(see Appendix E for information on these districts)

Briggs Elem, Mupu Elem, Santa Clara Elem, Santa Paula Elem

See Introduction for an explanation of all data sources.

Demographics & Socio-Economic Characteristics†

(2007 American Community Survey, except as noted)

Population

1990* . . . 113,313
2007 . . . 147,516
Male . . . 73,440
Female . . . 74,076
Jan. 2008 (estimate)§ . . . 159,981
Persons per sq. mi. of land . . . 3,989.6

Race & Hispanic Origin, 2007

Race
White . . . 108,978
Black/African American . . . 2,300
North American Native . . . 1,358
Asian . . . 7,944
Pacific Islander . . . 70
Other Race . . . 19,155
Two or more races . . . 7,711
Hispanic origin, total . . . 33,792
Mexican . . . 30,422
Puerto Rican . . . 891
Cuban . . . 0
Other Hispanic . . . 2,479

Age & Nativity, 2007

Under 5 years . . . 8,531
18 years and over . . . 115,288
65 years and over . . . 20,413
85 years and over . . . 3,714
Median Age . . . 39.0
Native-born . . . 119,207
Foreign-born . . . 28,309

Educational Attainment, 2007

Population 25 years and over . . . 99,087
Less than 9th grade . . . 8.6%
High school grad or higher . . . 84.4%
Bachelor's degree or higher . . . 27.6%
Graduate degree . . . 9.1%

Income & Poverty, 2007

Per capita income . . . $30,207
Median household income . . . $56,966
Median family income . . . $66,031
Persons in poverty . . . 12.7%
H'holds receiving public assistance . . . 584
H'holds receiving social security . . . 15,813

Households, 2007

Total households . . . 58,550
With persons under 18 . . . 18,640
With persons over 65 . . . 14,701
Family households . . . 35,793
Single person households . . . 17,549
Persons per household . . . 2.48
Persons per family . . . 3.07

Household Population, 2008§§

Persons living in households . . . 156,247
Persons living in group quarters . . . 3,734
Persons per household . . . 2.5

Labor & Employment

Total civilian labor force, 2008§§ . . . 83,700
Unemployment rate, 2008 . . . 5.7%
Total civilian labor force, 2000* . . . 75,826

Employed persons 16 years and over by occupation, 2007

Managers & professionals . . . 23,150
Service occupations . . . 13,495
Sales & office occupations . . . 18,660
Farming, fishing & forestry . . . 128
Construction & maintenance . . . 7,970
Production & transportation . . . 9,001
Self-employed persons . . . 8,061

† see Appendix D for 2000 Decennial Census Data
* US Census Bureau
** 2007 American Community Survey
§ California Department of Finance
§§ California Employment Development Dept

General Information

City of Santa Rosa
100 Santa Rosa Ave
Santa Rosa, CA 95404
707-543-3010

Website . . . www.ci.santa-rosa.ca.us
Elevation . . . 167 ft.
Land Area (sq. miles) . . . 40.1
Water Area (sq. miles) . . . 0.2
Year of Incorporation . . . 1868
Government type . . . Chartered
Sales tax rate . . . 9.25%

Voters & Officials

Registered Voters, October 2008

Total . . . 78,443
Democrats . . . 41,264
Republicans . . . 18,629
Declined to state . . . 14,977

Legislative Districts

US Congressional . . . 6
State Senatorial . . . 2
State Assembly . . . 7

Local Officials, 2009

Mayor . . . Susan Gorin
Manager . . . Jeff Kolin
City Clerk . . . Susan Stoneman
Attorney . . . Caroline Fowler
Finance Dir . . . David Heath
Public Works . . . NA
Planning/Dev Dir . . . Chuck Regalia
Building . . . NA
Police Chief . . . Thomas Simms
Fire Chief . . . Bruce Varner

Public Safety

Number of officers, 2007 . . . 171
Violent crimes, 2007 . . . 771
Property crimes, 2007 . . . 3,732
Arson, 2007 . . . 21

Public Library

Central Library
Sonoma County Library System
Third Street & E Street
Santa Rosa, CA 95404
707-545-0831

Branch Librarian . . . Virginia McLaren

Library system statistics, FY 2007

Population served . . . 481,785
Internet terminals . . . 140
Annual users . . . 299,464

Per capita:

Operating income . . . $32.97
percent from local government . . . 87.7%
Operating expenditure . . . $30.18
Total materials . . . 1.60
Print holdings . . . 1.49
Visits per capita . . . 5.11

Housing & Construction

Housing Units

Total, 2008§ . . . 64,238
Single family units, attached . . . 6,022
Single family units, detached . . . 38,423
Multiple family units . . . 17,079
Mobile home units . . . 2,714
Occupied . . . 62,524
Vacancy rate . . . 2.7%
Median rent, 2007** . . . $1,163
Median SF home value, 2007** . . . $557,800

New Privately Owned Housing Units Authorized by Building Permit, 2007*

	Units	Construction Cost
Single	368	$71,868,442
Total	840	$134,734,607

Municipal Finance

(For local fiscal year ended in 2006)

Revenues

Total . . . $274,240,872
Taxes . . . 97,971,378
Special benefits assessment . . . 0
Licenses & permits . . . 3,119,238
Fines & forfeitures . . . 1,912,045
Revenues from use of money & property . . . 9,322,927
Intergovernmental . . . 15,834,431
Service charges . . . 124,455,358
Other revenues . . . 20,216,495
Other financing sources . . . 1,409,000

Expenditures

Total . . . $265,514,120
General government . . . 22,513,601
Public safety . . . 75,950,046
Transportation . . . 34,740,933
Community development . . . 13,385,799
Health . . . 68,101,431
Culture & leisure . . . 17,988,801
Other . . . 0

Local School District

(Data from School year 2007-08 except as noted)
‡combined elementary and high school data

City of Santa Rosa High
211 Ridgway Ave
Santa Rosa, CA 95401
(707) 528-5181

Superintendent . . . Sharon Liddell
Grade plan . . . 7-12
Number of schools . . . 19
Enrollment . . . 11,962
High school graduates, 2006-07 . . . 1,691
Dropout rate . . . 3.0%
Pupil/teacher ratio . . . 20.2
Average class size . . . 23.3
Students per computer . . . 4.6
Classrooms with internet . . . 608
Avg. Daily Attendance (ADA)‡ . . . 15,295
Cost per ADA‡ . . . $8,574
Avg. Teacher Salary‡ . . . $68,056

California Achievement Tests 6th ed., 2008

(Pct scoring at or above 50th National Percentile Rank)

	Math	Reading	Language
Grade 3	NA	NA	NA
Grade 7	55%	52%	50%

Academic Performance Index, 2008

Number of students tested . . . NA
Number of valid scores . . . NA
2007 API (base) . . . NA
2008 API (growth) . . . NA

SAT Testing, 2006-07

Enrollment, Grade 12 . . . 2,212
Number taking test . . . 738
percent taking test . . . 33.4%
percent with total score 1,500+ . . . 22.80%

Average Scores:

Math	Verbal	Writing	Total
552	544	544	1,640

Federal No Child Left Behind, 2008

(Adequate Yearly Progress standards met)

	Participation Rate	Pct Proficient
ELA	NA	NA
Math	NA	NA

API criteria . . . NA
Graduation rate . . . NA
criteria met/possible . . . NA/NA

Other school districts for this city

(see Appendix E for information on these districts)
Complete list in Appendix E

See Introduction for an explanation of all data sources.

Demographics & Socio-Economic Characteristics

(2000 Decennial Census, except as noted)

Population

1990* 52,902
2000 52,975
Male 25,559
Female 27,416
Jan. 2008 (estimate)§ 56,068
Persons per sq. mi. of land 3,482.5

Race & Hispanic Origin, 2000

Race
White 45,929
Black/African American 783
North American Native 429
Asian 1,350
Pacific Islander 216
Other Race 2,134
Two or more races 2,134
Hispanic origin, total 6,016
Mexican 4,337
Puerto Rican 210
Cuban 51
Other Hispanic 1,418

Age & Nativity, 2000

Under 5 years 3,561
18 years and over 38,011
65 years and over 4,718
85 years and over 433
Median Age 34.8
Native-born 49,572
Foreign-born 3,518

Educational Attainment, 2000

Population 25 years and over 33,609
Less than 9th grade 2.8%
High school grad or higher 88.4%
Bachelor's degree or higher 17.0%
Graduate degree 5.0%

Income & Poverty, 1999

Per capita income $21,311
Median household income $53,624
Median family income $57,874
Persons in poverty 5.3%
H'holds receiving public assistance 539
H'holds receiving social security 3,876

Households, 2000

Total households 18,470
With persons under 18 8,211
With persons over 65 3,459
Family households 14,018
Single person households 3,358
Persons per household 2.81
Persons per family 3.19

Household Population, 2008§§

Persons living in households 55,025
Persons living in group quarters 1,043
Persons per household 2.9

Labor & Employment

Total civilian labor force, 2008§§ 33,100
Unemployment rate, 2008 . . . . . 5.0%
Total civilian labor force, 2000 27,552

Employed persons 16 years and over by occupation, 2000

Managers & professionals 8,256
Service occupations 3,819
Sales & office occupations 8,484
Farming, fishing & forestry 19
Construction & maintenance 3,191
Production & transportation 2,531
Self-employed persons 2,014

* US Census Bureau
** 2000 Decennial Census
§ California Department of Finance
§§ California Employment Development Dept

General Information

City of Santee
10601 Magnolia Ave
Santee, CA 92071
619-258-4100

Website . . . . . www.ci.santee.ca.us
Elevation . . . . . 369 ft.
Land Area (sq. miles) 16.1
Water Area (sq. miles) 0.2
Year of Incorporation 1980
Government type . . . . . General law
Sales tax rate 8.75%

Voters & Officials

Registered Voters, October 2008

Total 29,635
Democrats 8,529
Republicans 13,481
Declined to state 6,164

Legislative Districts

US Congressional 52
State Senatorial 36
State Assembly 77

Local Officials, 2009

Mayor . . . . . Randy Voepel
Manager . . . . . Keith Till
City Clerk . . . . . Patsy Bell (Int)
Attorney . . . . . Shawn Hagerty
Finance Dir . . . . . Tim McDermott
Public Works . . . . . NA
Community Dev Dir . . . . . Jim O'Grady (Int)
Building . . . . . NA
Police Chief . . . . . Patricia Duke
Emergency/Fire Dir . . . . . Mike Rottenberg

Public Safety

Number of officers, 2007 . . . . . NA
Violent crimes, 2007 147
Property crimes, 2007 1,140
Arson, 2007 5

Public Library

Santee Library
San Diego County Library System
9225 Carlton Hills Blvd #17
Santee, CA 92071
619-448-1866

Branch Librarian . . . . . Melanie Boerner

Library system statistics, FY 2007

Population served 1,049,868
Internet terminals 394
Annual users . . . . . NA

Per capita:

Operating income $33.43
percent from local government 80.6%
Operating expenditure $31.30
Total materials 1.54
Print holdings 1.32
Visits per capita 6.31

Housing & Construction

Housing Units

Total, 2008§ 19,528
Single family units, attached 1,975
Single family units, detached 10,827
Multiple family units 4,223
Mobile home units 2,503
Occupied 19,151
Vacancy rate 1.9%
Median rent, 2000** $833
Median SF home value, 2000** $187,700

New Privately Owned Housing Units Authorized by Building Permit, 2007*

	Units	Construction Cost
Single	248	$48,544,628
Total	248	$48,544,628

Municipal Finance

(For local fiscal year ended in 2006)

Revenues

Total $38,382,025
Taxes 23,925,783
Special benefits assessment 3,679,770
Licenses & permits 936,612
Fines & forfeitures 442,986
Revenues from use of money & property 1,120,063
Intergovernmental 6,740,022
Service charges 786,088
Other revenues 750,701
Other financing sources 0

Expenditures

Total $42,148,788
General government 5,607,167
Public safety 19,447,791
Transportation 11,626,746
Community development 3,717,834
Health 89,884
Culture & leisure 1,659,366
Other 0

Local School District

(Data from School year 2007-08 except as noted)

Grossmont Union High
PO Box 1043
La Mesa, CA 91944
(619) 644-8000

Superintendent . . . . . Robert Collins
Grade plan PK-12
Number of schools 19
Enrollment 24,195
High school graduates, 2006-07 4,597
Dropout rate 3.3%
Pupil/teacher ratio 24.2
Average class size 25.8
Students per computer 3.3
Classrooms with internet 1,450
Avg. Daily Attendance (ADA) 19,436
Cost per ADA $8,940
Avg. Teacher Salary $68,475

California Achievement Tests 6th ed., 2008

(Pct scoring at or above 50th National Percentile Rank)

	Math	Reading	Language
Grade 3	NA	NA	NA
Grade 7	NA	NA	NA

Academic Performance Index, 2008

Number of students tested 14,311
Number of valid scores 13,392
2007 API (base) 704
2008 API (growth) 713

SAT Testing, 2006-07

Enrollment, Grade 12 5,999
Number taking test 1,875
percent taking test 31.3%
percent with total score 1,500+ 15.30%

Average Scores:

Math	Verbal	Writing	Total
513	495	494	1,502

Federal No Child Left Behind, 2008

(Adequate Yearly Progress standards met)

	Participation Rate	Pct Proficient
ELA	Yes	No
Math	Yes	No

API criteria . . . . . Yes
Graduation rate . . . . . Yes
criteria met/possible 34/31

Other school districts for this city

(see Appendix E for information on these districts)

Santee Elem

See Introduction for an explanation of all data sources.

Demographics & Socio-Economic Characteristics

(2000 Decennial Census, except as noted)

Population

1990* 28,061
2000 29,843
Male 14,659
Female 15,184
Jan. 2008 (estimate)§ 31,592
Persons per sq. mi. of land 2,610.9

Race & Hispanic Origin, 2000

Race
White 20,111
Black/African American 115
North American Native 46
Asian 8,679
Pacific Islander 25
Other Race 171
Two or more races 696
Hispanic origin, total 936
Mexican 543
Puerto Rican 14
Cuban 15
Other Hispanic 364

Age & Nativity, 2000

Under 5 years 1,597
18 years and over 22,079
65 years and over 4,859
85 years and over 456
Median Age 43.2
Native-born 22,199
Foreign-born 7,656

Educational Attainment, 2000

Population 25 years and over 20,952
Less than 9th grade 1.0%
High school grad or higher 96.5%
Bachelor's degree or higher 68.2%
Graduate degree 33.6%

Income & Poverty, 1999

Per capita income $65,400
Median household income $139,895
Median family income $155,246
Persons in poverty 2.8%
H'holds receiving public assistance 76
H'holds receiving social security 2,793

Households, 2000

Total households 10,450
With persons under 18 4,199
With persons over 65 3,182
Family households 8,602
Single person households 1,490
Persons per household 2.83
Persons per family 3.13

Household Population, 2008§§

Persons living in households 31,231
Persons living in group quarters 361
Persons per household 2.9

Labor & Employment

Total civilian labor force, 2008§§ 13,600
Unemployment rate, 2008 . . . . . 3.0%
Total civilian labor force, 2000 13,587

Employed persons 16 years and over by occupation, 2000

Managers & professionals 9,670
Service occupations 493
Sales & office occupations 2,493
Farming, fishing & forestry 0
Construction & maintenance 297
Production & transportation 391
Self-employed persons 1,523

* US Census Bureau
** 2000 Decennial Census
§ California Department of Finance
§§ California Employment Development Dept

General Information

City of Saratoga
13777 Fruitvale Ave
Saratoga, CA 95070
408-868-1200

Website . . . . . www.saratoga.ca.us
Elevation . . . . . 455 ft.
Land Area (sq. miles) 12.1
Water Area (sq. miles) 0
Year of Incorporation 1956
Government type . . . . . General law
Sales tax rate 9.25%

Voters & Officials

Registered Voters, October 2008

Total 20,016
Democrats 6,857
Republicans 7,150
Declined to state 5,553

Legislative Districts

US Congressional 14
State Senatorial 15
State Assembly 24

Local Officials, 2009

Mayor . . . . . Chuck Page
City Manager . . . . . Dave Anderson
City Clerk . . . . . Ann Sullivan
Attorney . . . . . Richard Taylor
Finance Dir . . . . . Mary Furey
Public Works . . . . . John Cherbone
Community Dev Dir . . . . . John Livingstone
Building . . . . . Brad Lind
Police Chief . . . . . (County)
Fire/Emergency Mgmt . . . . . Ken Waldvogel

Public Safety

Number of officers, 2007 . . . . . NA
Violent crimes, 2007 29
Property crimes, 2007 300
Arson, 2007 5

Public Library

Saratoga Community Library
Santa Clara County Library System
13650 Saratoga Ave
Saratoga, CA 95070
408-867-6126

Branch Librarian Barbara Morrow Williams

Library system statistics, FY 2007

Population served 419,141
Internet terminals 133
Annual users 650,000

Per capita:

Operating income $77.89
percent from local government 85.7%
Operating expenditure $66.37
Total materials 4.01
Print holdings 3.27
Visits per capita 6.16

Housing & Construction

Housing Units

Total, 2008§ 11,093
Single family units, attached 560
Single family units, detached 9,728
Multiple family units 798
Mobile home units 7
Occupied 10,886
Vacancy rate 1.9%
Median rent, 2000** $1,689
Median SF home value, 2000** $1,000,001

New Privately Owned Housing Units Authorized by Building Permit, 2007*

	Units	Construction Cost
Single	25	$27,724,880
Total	25	$27,724,880

Municipal Finance

(For local fiscal year ended in 2006)

Revenues

Total $19,536,026
Taxes 9,988,845
Special benefits assessment 348,804
Licenses & permits 1,573,600
Fines & forfeitures 259,256
Revenues from use of money & property 928,233
Intergovernmental 3,525,440
Service charges 2,579,375
Other revenues 332,473
Other financing sources 0

Expenditures

Total $17,296,230
General government 3,416,816
Public safety 3,552,974
Transportation 4,268,236
Community development 2,292,095
Health 462,264
Culture & leisure 3,303,845
Other 0

Local School District

(Data from School year 2007-08 except as noted)

Los Gatos-Saratoga Joint Union High
17421 Farley Road West
Los Gatos, CA 95030
(408) 354-2520

Superintendent . . . . . Cary Matsuoka
Grade plan 9-12
Number of schools 2
Enrollment 3,164
High school graduates, 2006-07 729
Dropout rate 0.3%
Pupil/teacher ratio 21.5
Average class size 25.5
Students per computer 2.5
Classrooms with internet 168
Avg. Daily Attendance (ADA) 3,100
Cost per ADA $10,706
Avg. Teacher Salary $88,151

California Achievement Tests 6th ed., 2008

(Pct scoring at or above 50th National Percentile Rank)

	Math	Reading	Language
Grade 3	NA	NA	NA
Grade 7	NA	NA	NA

Academic Performance Index, 2008

Number of students tested 2,298
Number of valid scores 2,269
2007 API (base) 872
2008 API (growth) 879

SAT Testing, 2006-07

Enrollment, Grade 12 753
Number taking test 578
percent taking test 76.8%
percent with total score 1,500+ 70.50%

Average Scores:

Math	Verbal	Writing	Total
641	607	614	1,862

Federal No Child Left Behind, 2008

(Adequate Yearly Progress standards met)

	Participation Rate	Pct Proficient
ELA	No	Yes
Math	Yes	Yes

API criteria . . . . . Yes
Graduation rate . . . . . Yes
criteria met/possible 14/13

Other school districts for this city

(see Appendix E for information on these districts)

Complete list in Appendix E

See Introduction for an explanation of all data sources.

Demographics & Socio-Economic Characteristics

(2000 Decennial Census, except as noted)

Population

1990* . . . 7,152
2000 . . . 7,330
Male . . . 3,541
Female . . . 3,789
Jan. 2008 (estimate)§ . . . 7,503
Persons per sq. mi. of land . . . 3,948.9

Race & Hispanic Origin, 2000

Race
White . . . 6,718
Black/African American . . . 48
North American Native . . . 21
Asian . . . 306
Pacific Islander . . . 18
Other Race . . . 52
Two or more races . . . 167
Hispanic origin, total . . . 244
Mexican . . . 95
Puerto Rican . . . 17
Cuban . . . 10
Other Hispanic . . . 122

Age & Nativity, 2000

Under 5 years . . . 222
18 years and over . . . 6,786
65 years and over . . . 898
85 years and over . . . 76
Median Age . . . 45.4
Native-born . . . 6,174
Foreign-born . . . 1,151

Educational Attainment, 2000

Population 25 years and over . . . 6,686
Less than 9th grade . . . 0.3%
High school grad or higher . . . 98.0%
Bachelor's degree or higher . . . 69.9%
Graduate degree . . . 29.0%

Income & Poverty, 1999

Per capita income . . . $81,040
Median household income . . . $87,469
Median family income . . . $123,467
Persons in poverty . . . 5.1%
H'holds receiving public assistance . . . 18
H'holds receiving social security . . . 718

Households, 2000

Total households . . . 4,254
With persons under 18 . . . 393
With persons over 65 . . . 715
Family households . . . 1,663
Single person households . . . 1,945
Persons per household . . . 1.72
Persons per family . . . 2.34

Household Population, 2008§§

Persons living in households . . . 7,491
Persons living in group quarters . . . 12
Persons per household . . . 1.7

Labor & Employment

Total civilian labor force, 2008§§ . . . 5,400
Unemployment rate, 2008 . . . 3.2%
Total civilian labor force, 2000 . . . 5,294

Employed persons 16 years and over by occupation, 2000

Managers & professionals . . . 3,470
Service occupations . . . 385
Sales & office occupations . . . 1,085
Farming, fishing & forestry . . . 10
Construction & maintenance . . . 161
Production & transportation . . . 72
Self-employed persons . . . 1,136

* US Census Bureau
** 2000 Decennial Census
§ California Department of Finance
§§ California Employment Development Dept

General Information

City of Sausalito
420 Litho St
Sausalito, CA 94965
415-289-4100

Website . . . www.ci.sausalito.ca.us
Elevation . . . 14 ft.
Land Area (sq. miles) . . . 1.9
Water Area (sq. miles) . . . 0.3
Year of Incorporation . . . 1893
Government type . . . General law
Sales tax rate . . . 9.00%

Voters & Officials

Registered Voters, October 2008

Total . . . 5,482
Democrats . . . 2,875
Republicans . . . 911
Declined to state . . . 1,485

Legislative Districts

US Congressional . . . 6
State Senatorial . . . 3
State Assembly . . . 6

Local Officials, 2009

Mayor . . . Jonathan Leone
Manager . . . Adam W. Politzer
City Clerk . . . Debbie Pagliaro
Attorney . . . Mary Wagner
Finance Dir . . . Charles Francis (Int)
Public Works . . . Jonathon Goldman
Planning/Dev Dir . . . Jeremy Graves
Building . . . Kenneth Henry
Police Chief . . . Scott Paulin
Fire Chief . . . Jim Irving

Public Safety

Number of officers, 2007 . . . 18
Violent crimes, 2007 . . . 5
Property crimes, 2007 . . . 173
Arson, 2007 . . . 0

Public Library

Sausalito Public Library
420 Litho St
Sausalito, CA 94965
415-289-4121

Director . . . Mary Richardson

Library statistics, FY 2007

Population served . . . 7,454
Internet terminals . . . 41
Annual users . . . 49,354

Per capita:

Operating income . . . $79.59
percent from local government . . . 91.6%
Operating expenditure . . . $79.20
Total materials . . . 10.06
Print holdings . . . 8.33
Visits per capita . . . 1.99

Housing & Construction

Housing Units

Total, 2008§ . . . 4,567
Single family units, attached . . . 427
Single family units, detached . . . 1,743
Multiple family units . . . 2,173
Mobile home units . . . 224
Occupied . . . 4,308
Vacancy rate . . . 5.7%
Median rent, 2000** . . . $1,660
Median SF home value, 2000** . . . $786,200

New Privately Owned Housing Units Authorized by Building Permit, 2007*

	Units	Construction Cost
Single	2	$1,855,000
Total	4	$3,255,000

Municipal Finance

(For local fiscal year ended in 2006)

Revenues

Total . . . $16,377,847
Taxes . . . 9,179,230
Special benefits assessment . . . 104,177
Licenses & permits . . . 248,521
Fines & forfeitures . . . 415,643
Revenues from use of money & property . . . 1,276,730
Intergovernmental . . . 641,526
Service charges . . . 4,265,063
Other revenues . . . 246,957
Other financing sources . . . 0

Expenditures

Total . . . $14,871,329
General government . . . 4,021,920
Public safety . . . 5,679,369
Transportation . . . 1,904,248
Community development . . . 820,015
Health . . . 1,188,839
Culture & leisure . . . 1,256,938
Other . . . 0

Local School District

(Data from School year 2007-08 except as noted)

Tamalpais Union High
PO Box 605
Larkspur, CA 94977
(415) 945-3720

Superintendent . . . Laurie Kimbrel
Grade plan . . . 9-12
Number of schools . . . 5
Enrollment . . . 3,889
High school graduates, 2006-07 . . . 959
Dropout rate . . . 0.8%
Pupil/teacher ratio . . . 17.4
Average class size . . . 24.4
Students per computer . . . 2.6
Classrooms with internet . . . 232
Avg. Daily Attendance (ADA) . . . 3,715
Cost per ADA . . . $13,492
Avg. Teacher Salary . . . $81,923

California Achievement Tests 6th ed., 2008

(Pct scoring at or above 50th National Percentile Rank)

	Math	Reading	Language
Grade 3	NA	NA	NA
Grade 7	NA	NA	NA

Academic Performance Index, 2008

Number of students tested . . . 2,800
Number of valid scores . . . 2,766
2007 API (base) . . . 848
2008 API (growth) . . . 855

SAT Testing, 2006-07

Enrollment, Grade 12 . . . 997
Number taking test . . . 730
percent taking test . . . 73.2%
percent with total score 1,500+ . . . 58.30%

Average Scores:

Math	Verbal	Writing	Total
574	574	574	1,722

Federal No Child Left Behind, 2008

(Adequate Yearly Progress standards met)

	Participation Rate	Pct Proficient
ELA	Yes	Yes
Math	Yes	Yes

API criteria . . . Yes
Graduation rate . . . Yes
criteria met/possible . . . 10/10

Other school districts for this city

(see Appendix E for information on these districts)

Sausalito Elem

See Introduction for an explanation of all data sources.

Demographics & Socio-Economic Characteristics

(2000 Decennial Census, except as noted)

Population

1990* . . . 8,615
2000 . . . 11,385
Male . . . 5,544
Female . . . 5,841
Jan. 2008 (estimate)§ . . . 11,697
Persons per sq. mi. of land . . . 2,542.8

Race & Hispanic Origin, 2000

Race
White . . . 10,090
Black/African American . . . 55
North American Native . . . 46
Asian . . . 526
Pacific Islander . . . 21
Other Race . . . 245
Two or more races . . . 402
Hispanic origin, total . . . 729
Mexican . . . 476
Puerto Rican . . . 27
Cuban . . . 4
Other Hispanic . . . 222

Age & Nativity, 2000

Under 5 years . . . 774
18 years and over . . . 8,446
65 years and over . . . 1,573
85 years and over . . . 408
Median Age . . . 38.3
Native-born . . . 10,312
Foreign-born . . . 1,206

Educational Attainment, 2000

Population 25 years and over . . . 7,702
Less than 9th grade . . . 1.3%
High school grad or higher . . . 94.8%
Bachelor's degree or higher . . . 40.9%
Graduate degree . . . 13.1%

Income & Poverty, 1999

Per capita income . . . $35,684
Median household income . . . $72,449
Median family income . . . $88,573
Persons in poverty . . . 2.4%
H'holds receiving public assistance . . . 49
H'holds receiving social security . . . 1,083

Households, 2000

Total households . . . 4,273
With persons under 18 . . . 1,627
With persons over 65 . . . 1,028
Family households . . . 2,968
Single person households . . . 1,001
Persons per household . . . 2.56
Persons per family . . . 3.05

Household Population, 2008§§

Persons living in households . . . 11,245
Persons living in group quarters . . . 452
Persons per household . . . 2.5

Labor & Employment

Total civilian labor force, 2008§§ . . . 6,100
Unemployment rate, 2008 . . . 3.2%
Total civilian labor force, 2000 . . . 5,690

Employed persons 16 years and over by occupation, 2000

Managers & professionals . . . 2,949
Service occupations . . . 554
Sales & office occupations . . . 1,378
Farming, fishing & forestry . . . 29
Construction & maintenance . . . 352
Production & transportation . . . 279
Self-employed persons . . . 532

* US Census Bureau
** 2000 Decennial Census
§ California Department of Finance
§§ California Employment Development Dept

General Information

City of Scotts Valley
One Civic Center Dr
Scotts Valley, CA 95066
831-440-5600

Website . . . www.scottsvalley.org
Elevation . . . 570 ft.
Land Area (sq. miles) . . . 4.6
Water Area (sq. miles) . . . 0
Year of Incorporation . . . 1966
Government type . . . General law
Sales tax rate . . . 9.25%

Voters & Officials

Registered Voters, October 2008

Total . . . 7,372
Democrats . . . 3,134
Republicans . . . 2,435
Declined to state . . . 1,215

Legislative Districts

US Congressional . . . 14
State Senatorial . . . 15
State Assembly . . . 27

Local Officials, 2009

Mayor . . . Randy Johnson
City Manager . . . Steve Ando
City Clerk . . . Tracy Ferrara
Attorney . . . Kirsten Powell
Finance Dir . . . Steve Ando
Public Works . . . Ken Anderson
Community Dev Dir . . Susan Westman (Int)
Building . . . NA
Police Chief . . . John Weiss
Emergency/Fire Dir . . . Mike McMurry

Public Safety

Number of officers, 2007 . . . 19
Violent crimes, 2007 . . . 11
Property crimes, 2007 . . . 269
Arson, 2007 . . . 3

Public Library

Scotts Valley Branch Library
Santa Cruz Libraries
230D Mount Hermon Rd
Scotts Valley, CA 95066
831-420-5369

Branch Librarian . . . Gale Farthing

Library system statistics, FY 2007

Population served . . . 205,669
Internet terminals . . . 24
Annual users . . . 23,239

Per capita:

Operating income . . . $59.06
percent from local government . . . 95.9%
Operating expenditure . . . $58.55
Total materials . . . 2.52
Print holdings . . . 2.13
Visits per capita . . . NA

Housing & Construction

Housing Units

Total, 2008§ . . . 4,646
Single family units, attached . . . 415
Single family units, detached . . . 2,512
Multiple family units . . . 914
Mobile home units . . . 805
Occupied . . . 4,488
Vacancy rate . . . 3.4%
Median rent, 2000** . . . $1,177
Median SF home value, 2000** . . . $447,900

New Privately Owned Housing Units Authorized by Building Permit, 2007*

	Units	Construction Cost
Single	2	$1,200,000
Total	2	$1,200,000

Municipal Finance

(For local fiscal year ended in 2006)

Revenues

Total . . . $12,867,198
Taxes . . . 6,356,674
Special benefits assessment . . . 49,519
Licenses & permits . . . 297,907
Fines & forfeitures . . . 85,427
Revenues from use of money & property . . . 584,661
Intergovernmental . . . 1,870,789
Service charges . . . 3,050,724
Other revenues . . . 571,497
Other financing sources . . . 0

Expenditures

Total . . . $11,722,647
General government . . . 2,168,172
Public safety . . . 3,750,705
Transportation . . . 1,563,218
Community development . . . 951,614
Health . . . 1,886,432
Culture & leisure . . . 1,402,506
Other . . . 0

Local School District

(Data from School year 2007-08 except as noted)

Scotts Valley Unified
4444 Scotts Valley Dr, Suite 5B
Scotts Valley, CA 95066
(831) 438-1820

Superintendent . . . Susan Silver
Grade plan . . . K-11
Number of schools . . . 4
Enrollment . . . 2,645
High school graduates, 2006-07 . . . 188
Dropout rate . . . 1.3%
Pupil/teacher ratio . . . 21.8
Average class size . . . 26.2
Students per computer . . . 3.0
Classrooms with internet . . . 129
Avg. Daily Attendance (ADA) . . . 2,548
Cost per ADA . . . $7,450
Avg. Teacher Salary . . . $55,586

California Achievement Tests 6th ed., 2008

(Pct scoring at or above 50th National Percentile Rank)

	Math	Reading	Language
Grade 3	84%	75%	72%
Grade 7	80%	78%	71%

Academic Performance Index, 2008

Number of students tested . . . 2,001
Number of valid scores . . . 1,930
2007 API (base) . . . 829
2008 API (growth) . . . 846

SAT Testing, 2006-07

Enrollment, Grade 12 . . . 203
Number taking test . . . 118
percent taking test . . . 58.1%
percent with total score 1,500+ . . . 40.90%

Average Scores:

Math	Verbal	Writing	Total
553	537	528	1,618

Federal No Child Left Behind, 2008

(Adequate Yearly Progress standards met)

	Participation Rate	Pct Proficient
ELA	No	Yes
Math	No	Yes

API criteria . . . Yes
Graduation rate . . . Yes
\# criteria met/possible . . . 19/17

Other school districts for this city

(see Appendix E for information on these districts)

None

Demographics & Socio-Economic Characteristics
(2000 Decennial Census, except as noted)

Population
1990* 25,098
2000 24,157
Male 10,612
Female 13,545
Jan. 2008 (estimate)§ 25,986
Persons per sq. mi. of land 2,259.7

Race & Hispanic Origin, 2000
Race
White 21,477
Black/African American 347
North American Native 73
Asian 1,386
Pacific Islander 43
Other Race 309
Two or more races 522
Hispanic origin, total 1,554
Mexican 1,032
Puerto Rican 58
Cuban 85
Other Hispanic 379

Age & Nativity, 2000
Under 5 years 776
18 years and over 20,940
65 years and over 9,068
85 years and over 1,840
Median Age 54.1
Native-born 21,471
Foreign-born 2,812

Educational Attainment, 2000
Population 25 years and over 19,997
Less than 9th grade 2.3%
High school grad or higher 90.5%
Bachelor's degree or higher 37.9%
Graduate degree 14.3%

Income & Poverty, 1999
Per capita income $34,589
Median household income $42,079
Median family income $72,071
Persons in poverty 5.5%
H'holds receiving public assistance 173
H'holds receiving social security 6,844

Households, 2000
Total households 13,048
With persons under 18 1,901
With persons over 65 7,066
Family households 5,884
Single person households 6,367
Persons per household 1.83
Persons per family 2.65

Household Population, 2008§§
Persons living in households 25,723
Persons living in group quarters 263
Persons per household 1.9

Labor & Employment
Total civilian labor force, 2008§§ 11,600
Unemployment rate, 2008 .... 3.8%
Total civilian labor force, 2000 9,922

Employed persons 16 years and over by occupation, 2000
Managers & professionals 5,056
Service occupations 1,117
Sales & office occupations 2,538
Farming, fishing & forestry 10
Construction & maintenance 361
Production & transportation 496
Self-employed persons 837

* US Census Bureau
** 2000 Decennial Census
§ California Department of Finance
§§ California Employment Development Dept

General Information
City of Seal Beach
211 - 8th Street
Seal Beach, CA 90740
562-431-2527

Website .... www.ci.seal-beach.ca.us
Elevation .... 10 ft.
Land Area (sq. miles) 11.5
Water Area (sq. miles) 1.7
Year of Incorporation 1915
Government type .... Chartered
Sales tax rate 8.75%

Voters & Officials
Registered Voters, October 2008
Total 20,114
Democrats 7,282
Republicans 9,065
Declined to state 3,111

Legislative Districts
US Congressional 46
State Senatorial 35
State Assembly 67

Local Officials, 2009
Mayor .... Gordon Shanks
Manager .... David N. Carmany
City Clerk .... Linda Devine
Attorney .... Quinn M. Barrow
Admin Svcs Dir .... Robbeyn Bird
Public Works .... Vince Mastrosimone
Development Svcs Dir .... Lee Whittenberg
Building .... Darik Doggett
Police Chief .... Jeffrey Kirkpatrick
Fire Services .... (County)

Public Safety
Number of officers, 2007 30
Violent crimes, 2007 37
Property crimes, 2007 406
Arson, 2007 3

Public Library
Mary Wilson Branch Library
Orange County Public Library System
12700 Montecito Rd
Seal Beach, CA 90740
562-430-1048

Branch Librarian .... NA

Library system statistics, FY 2007
Population served 1,532,758
Internet terminals 505
Annual users 680,874

Per capita:
Operating income $24.71
percent from local government 90.0%
Operating expenditure $24.18
Total materials 1.93
Print holdings 1.84
Visits per capita 4.02

Housing & Construction
Housing Units
Total, 2008§ 14,537
Single family units, attached 2,121
Single family units, detached 4,699
Multiple family units 7,554
Mobile home units 163
Occupied 13,439
Vacancy rate 7.6%
Median rent, 2000** $1,036
Median SF home value, 2000** $363,500

New Privately Owned Housing Units Authorized by Building Permit, 2007*

	Units	Construction Cost
Single	23	$7,296,700
Total	23	$7,296,700

Municipal Finance
(For local fiscal year ended in 2006)

Revenues
Total $34,997,159
Taxes 17,767,288
Special benefits assessment 291,023
Licenses & permits 890,161
Fines & forfeitures 872,151
Revenues from use of money & property 1,517,377
Intergovernmental 3,653,843
Service charges 9,736,018
Other revenues 269,298
Other financing sources 0

Expenditures
Total $30,850,144
General government 3,627,559
Public safety 11,408,406
Transportation 9,420,882
Community development 939,057
Health 1,549,097
Culture & leisure 825,565
Other 0

Local School District
(Data from School year 2007-08 except as noted)
Los Alamitos Unified
10293 Bloomfield St
Los Alamitos, CA 90720
(562) 799-4700

Superintendent .... Gregory Franklin
Grade plan PK-12
Number of schools 10
Enrollment 9,372
High school graduates, 2006-07 734
Dropout rate 0.6%
Pupil/teacher ratio 23.3
Average class size 27.9
Students per computer 5.3
Classrooms with internet 407
Avg. Daily Attendance (ADA) 9,283
Cost per ADA $7,266
Avg. Teacher Salary $76,063

California Achievement Tests 6th ed., 2008
(Pct scoring at or above 50th National Percentile Rank)

	Math	Reading	Language
Grade 3	82%	61%	72%
Grade 7	74%	80%	79%

Academic Performance Index, 2008
Number of students tested 7,384
Number of valid scores 7,153
2007 API (base) 871
2008 API (growth) 881

SAT Testing, 2006-07
Enrollment, Grade 12 794
Number taking test 509
percent taking test 64.1%
percent with total score 1,500+ 40.40%

Average Scores:

Math	Verbal	Writing	Total
544	524	529	1,597

Federal No Child Left Behind, 2008
(Adequate Yearly Progress standards met)

	Participation Rate	Pct Proficient
ELA	Yes	Yes
Math	Yes	Yes

API criteria .... Yes
Graduation rate .... Yes
criteria met/possible 38/38

Other school districts for this city
(see Appendix E for information on these districts)
None

See Introduction for an explanation of all data sources.

Demographics & Socio-Economic Characteristics

(2000 Decennial Census, except as noted)

Population

1990* . . . 38,901
2000 . . . 31,696
Male . . . 16,136
Female . . . 15,560
Jan. 2008 (estimate)§ . . . 34,194
Persons per sq. mi. of land . . . 3,885.7

Race & Hispanic Origin, 2000

Race
White . . . 15,599
Black/African American . . . 3,997
North American Native . . . 331
Asian . . . 3,197
Pacific Islander . . . 410
Other Race . . . 5,834
Two or more races . . . 2,328
Hispanic origin, total . . . 10,929
Mexican . . . 8,353
Puerto Rican . . . 281
Cuban . . . 17
Other Hispanic . . . 2,278

Age & Nativity, 2000

Under 5 years . . . 3,059
18 years and over . . . 22,121
65 years and over . . . 2,684
85 years and over . . . 200
Median Age . . . 29.5
Native-born . . . 21,865
Foreign-born . . . 9,921

Educational Attainment, 2000

Population 25 years and over . . . 18,831
Less than 9th grade . . . 14.8%
High school grad or higher . . . 70.1%
Bachelor's degree or higher . . . 17.5%
Graduate degree . . . 5.3%

Income & Poverty, 1999

Per capita income . . . $15,183
Median household income . . . $41,393
Median family income . . . $43,259
Persons in poverty . . . 12.0%
H'holds receiving public assistance . . . 467
H'holds receiving social security . . . 2,082

Households, 2000

Total households . . . 9,833
With persons under 18 . . . 4,721
With persons over 65 . . . 2,023
Family households . . . 7,399
Single person households . . . 1,780
Persons per household . . . 3.21
Persons per family . . . 3.59

Household Population, 2008§§

Persons living in households . . . 31,576
Persons living in group quarters . . . 2,618
Persons per household . . . 3.2

Labor & Employment

Total civilian labor force, 2008§§ . . . 16,400
Unemployment rate, 2008 . . . 4.9%
Total civilian labor force, 2000 . . . 13,524

Employed persons 16 years and over by occupation, 2000

Managers & professionals . . . 2,610
Service occupations . . . 4,418
Sales & office occupations . . . 3,040
Farming, fishing & forestry . . . 309
Construction & maintenance . . . 1,159
Production & transportation . . . 1,286
Self-employed persons . . . 1,132

* US Census Bureau
** 2000 Decennial Census
§ California Department of Finance
§§ California Employment Development Dept

General Information

City of Seaside
440 Harcourt Ave
Seaside, CA 93955
831-899-6700

Website . . . www.ci.seaside.ca.us
Elevation . . . 20 ft.
Land Area (sq. miles) . . . 8.8
Water Area (sq. miles) . . . 0.1
Year of Incorporation . . . 1954
Government type . . . General law
Sales tax rate . . . 9.25%

Voters & Officials

Registered Voters, October 2008

Total . . . 11,094
Democrats . . . 6,102
Republicans . . . 2,256
Declined to state . . . 2,314

Legislative Districts

US Congressional . . . 17
State Senatorial . . . 15
State Assembly . . . 27

Local Officials, 2009

Mayor . . . Ralph Rubio
Manager . . . Ray Corpuz
City Clerk . . . Joyce E. Newsome
Attorney . . . Don Freeman
Finance Dir . . . Daphne H. Hodgson (Dep)
Public Works . . . Diana Ingersoll (Dep)
Planning/Dev Dir . . . Diana Ingersoll (Dep)
Building . . . Diana Ingersoll
Police Chief . . . Steve Cercone
Emergency/Fire Dir . . . Gerard Wombacher

Public Safety

Number of officers, 2007 . . . 43
Violent crimes, 2007 . . . 218
Property crimes, 2007 . . . 712
Arson, 2007 . . . NA

Public Library

Seaside Branch Library
Monterey County Free Libraries
550 Harcourt Ave
Seaside, CA 93955
831-899-2055

Branch Librarian . . . Jayanti Addleman (Int)

Library system statistics, FY 2007

Population served . . . 226,803
Internet terminals . . . 160
Annual users . . . 229,676

Per capita:

Operating income . . . $29.19
percent from local government . . . 91.7%
Operating expenditure . . . $27.42
Total materials . . . 1.92
Print holdings . . . 1.81
Visits per capita . . . 3.65

Housing & Construction

Housing Units

Total, 2008§ . . . 11,257
Single family units, attached . . . 2,339
Single family units, detached . . . 6,296
Multiple family units . . . 2,190
Mobile home units . . . 432
Occupied . . . 9,943
Vacancy rate . . . 11.7%
Median rent, 2000** . . . $810
Median SF home value, 2000** . . . $237,700

New Privately Owned Housing Units Authorized by Building Permit, 2007*

	Units	Construction Cost
Single	6	$1,878,456
Total	6	$1,878,456

Municipal Finance

(For local fiscal year ended in 2006)

Revenues

Total . . . $21,554,237
Taxes . . . 15,809,847
Special benefits assessment . . . 60,257
Licenses & permits . . . 397,837
Fines & forfeitures . . . 238,560
Revenues from use of money & property . . . 785,787
Intergovernmental . . . 1,690,521
Service charges . . . 1,170,698
Other revenues . . . 857,563
Other financing sources . . . 543,167

Expenditures

Total . . . $21,113,091
General government . . . 1,836,798
Public safety . . . 11,701,640
Transportation . . . 3,598,080
Community development . . . 987,386
Health . . . 0
Culture & leisure . . . 1,471,619
Other . . . 975,530

Local School District

(Data from School year 2007-08 except as noted)

Monterey Peninsula Unified
PO Box 1031
Monterey, CA 93942
(831) 645-1200

Superintendent . . . Marilyn Shepherd
Grade plan . . . K-12
Number of schools . . . 22
Enrollment . . . 11,613
High school graduates, 2006-07 . . . 590
Dropout rate . . . 2.0%
Pupil/teacher ratio . . . 20.5
Average class size . . . 24.3
Students per computer . . . 8.5
Classrooms with internet . . . 518
Avg. Daily Attendance (ADA) . . . 10,537
Cost per ADA . . . $8,271
Avg. Teacher Salary . . . $57,857

California Achievement Tests 6th ed., 2008

(Pct scoring at or above 50th National Percentile Rank)

	Math	Reading	Language
Grade 3	56%	35%	43%
Grade 7	49%	44%	43%

Academic Performance Index, 2008

Number of students tested . . . 8,210
Number of valid scores . . . 7,687
2007 API (base) . . . 716
2008 API (growth) . . . 728

SAT Testing, 2006-07

Enrollment, Grade 12 . . . 682
Number taking test . . . 262
percent taking test . . . 38.4%
percent with total score 1,500+ . . . 15.10%

Average Scores:

Math	Verbal	Writing	Total
504	487	481	1,472

Federal No Child Left Behind, 2008

(Adequate Yearly Progress standards met)

	Participation Rate	Pct Proficient
ELA	Yes	No
Math	Yes	No

API criteria . . . Yes
Graduation rate . . . Yes
\# criteria met/possible . . . 42/36

Other school districts for this city

(see Appendix E for information on these districts)

None

See Introduction for an explanation of all data sources.

Demographics & Socio-Economic Characteristics

(2000 Decennial Census, except as noted)

Population

1990* 7,004
2000 7,774
Male 3,481
Female 4,293
Jan. 2008 (estimate)§ 7,714
Persons per sq. mi. of land 4,060.0

Race & Hispanic Origin, 2000

Race
White 6,985
Black/African American 51
North American Native 61
Asian 118
Pacific Islander 8
Other Race 300
Two or more races 251
Hispanic origin, total 720
Mexican 582
Puerto Rican 20
Cuban 6
Other Hispanic 112

Age & Nativity, 2000

Under 5 years 340
18 years and over 5,938
65 years and over 1,279
85 years and over 267
Median Age 41.5
Native-born 7,523
Foreign-born 509

Educational Attainment, 2000

Population 25 years and over 5,578
Less than 9th grade 5.3%
High school grad or higher 88.4%
Bachelor's degree or higher 35.5%
Graduate degree 12.8%

Income & Poverty, 1999

Per capita income $22,881
Median household income $46,436
Median family income $55,792
Persons in poverty 6.9%
H'holds receiving public assistance 68
H'holds receiving social security 909

Households, 2000

Total households 3,250
With persons under 18 1,099
With persons over 65 855
Family households 1,952
Single person households 1,033
Persons per household 2.33
Persons per family 2.95

Household Population, 2008§§

Persons living in households 7,503
Persons living in group quarters 211
Persons per household 2.3

Labor & Employment

Total civilian labor force, 2008§§ 4,400
Unemployment rate, 2008 .... 3.3%
Total civilian labor force, 2000 4,056

Employed persons 16 years and over by occupation, 2000

Managers & professionals 1,666
Service occupations 528
Sales & office occupations 885
Farming, fishing & forestry 31
Construction & maintenance 484
Production & transportation 362
Self-employed persons 641

* US Census Bureau
** 2000 Decennial Census
§ California Department of Finance
§§ California Employment Development Dept

General Information

City of Sebastopol
7120 Bodega Ave
Sebastopol, CA 95472
707-823-1153

Website .... www.ci.sebastopol.ca.us
Elevation .... 78 ft.
Land Area (sq. miles) 1.9
Water Area (sq. miles) 0
Year of Incorporation 1902
Government type .... General law
Sales tax rate 9.25%

Voters & Officials

Registered Voters, October 2008

Total 4,722
Democrats 2,865
Republicans 639
Declined to state 830

Legislative Districts

US Congressional 6
State Senatorial 2
State Assembly 1

Local Officials, 2009

Mayor .... Sarah Glade Gurney
City Manager .... Jack Griffin
City Clerk .... Mary Gourley
Attorney .... Larry McLaughlin
Admin Svcs Dir .... Ron Puccinelli
Public Works .... Richard Emig
Planning/Dev Dir .... Kenyon Webster
Building .... Glenn Schainblatt
Police Chief .... Jeffrey Weaver
Emergency/Fire Dir. .... John Zanzi

Public Safety

Number of officers, 2007 15
Violent crimes, 2007 7
Property crimes, 2007 193
Arson, 2007 3

Public Library

Sebastopol Regional Library
Sonoma County Library System
7140 Bodega Ave
Sebastopol, CA 95472
707-823-7691

Branch Librarian .... Arlene Kallen

Library system statistics, FY 2007

Population served 481,785
Internet terminals 140
Annual users 299,464

Per capita:

Operating income $32.97
percent from local government 87.7%
Operating expenditure $30.18
Total materials 1.60
Print holdings 1.49
Visits per capita 5.11

Housing & Construction

Housing Units

Total, 2008§ 3,380
Single family units, attached 257
Single family units, detached 2,029
Multiple family units 1,032
Mobile home units 62
Occupied 3,309
Vacancy rate 2.1%
Median rent, 2000** $801
Median SF home value, 2000** $291,500

New Privately Owned Housing Units Authorized by Building Permit, 2007*

	Units	Construction Cost
Single	23	$3,636,120
Total	23	$3,636,120

Municipal Finance

(For local fiscal year ended in 2006)

Revenues

Total $11,594,656
Taxes 4,863,969
Special benefits assessment 0
Licenses & permits 305,841
Fines & forfeitures 74,181
Revenues from use of money & property 187,377
Intergovernmental 585,667
Service charges 3,800,895
Other revenues 1,776,726
Other financing sources 0

Expenditures

Total $9,883,696
General government 900,499
Public safety 3,308,444
Transportation 1,201,380
Community development 890,176
Health 2,205,818
Culture & leisure 343,272
Other 0

Local School District

(Data from School year 2007-08 except as noted)

West Sonoma County Union High
462 Johnson St
Sebastopol, CA 95472
(707) 824-6403

Superintendent .... Keller McDonald
Grade plan 7-12
Number of schools 5
Enrollment 2,435
High school graduates, 2006-07 565
Dropout rate 2.1%
Pupil/teacher ratio 20.5
Average class size 24.8
Students per computer 3.7
Classrooms with internet 116
Avg. Daily Attendance (ADA) 2,255
Cost per ADA $9,468
Avg. Teacher Salary $62,527

California Achievement Tests 6th ed., 2008

(Pct scoring at or above 50th National Percentile Rank)

	Math	Reading	Language
Grade 3	NA	NA	NA
Grade 7	NA	NA	NA

Academic Performance Index, 2008

Number of students tested 1,657
Number of valid scores 1,608
2007 API (base) 766
2008 API (growth) 774

SAT Testing, 2006-07

Enrollment, Grade 12 643
Number taking test 252
percent taking test 39.2%
percent with total score 1,500+ 27.20%

Average Scores:

Math	Verbal	Writing	Total
545	546	536	1,627

Federal No Child Left Behind, 2008

(Adequate Yearly Progress standards met)

	Participation Rate	Pct Proficient
ELA	Yes	Yes
Math	Yes	Yes

API criteria .... Yes
Graduation rate .... Yes
\# criteria met/possible 14/14

Other school districts for this city

(see Appendix E for information on these districts)

Complete list in Appendix E

See Introduction for an explanation of all data sources.

Demographics & Socio-Economic Characteristics

(2000 Decennial Census, except as noted)

Population

1990* 14,757
2000 19,444
Male 9,744
Female 9,700
Jan. 2008 (estimate)§ 23,286
Persons per sq. mi. of land 5,415.3

Race & Hispanic Origin, 2000

Race
White 8,536
Black/African American 146
North American Native 304
Asian 619
Pacific Islander 6
Other Race 8,962
Two or more races 871
Hispanic origin, total 13,952
Mexican 11,953
Puerto Rican 41
Cuban 16
Other Hispanic 1,942

Age & Nativity, 2000

Under 5 years 1,805
18 years and over 13,017
65 years and over 2,006
85 years and over 270
Median Age 28.4
Native-born 14,655
Foreign-born 4,695

Educational Attainment, 2000

Population 25 years and over 10,739
Less than 9th grade 24.8%
High school grad or higher 57.9%
Bachelor's degree or higher 8.0%
Graduate degree 1.8%

Income & Poverty, 1999

Per capita income $12,834
Median household income $34,713
Median family income $36,510
Persons in poverty 22.4%
H'holds receiving public assistance 435
H'holds receiving social security 1,468

Households, 2000

Total households 5,596
With persons under 18 2,946
With persons over 65 1,412
Family households 4,541
Single person households 876
Persons per household 3.45
Persons per family 3.76

Household Population, 2008§§

Persons living in households 23,156
Persons living in group quarters 130
Persons per household 3.5

Labor & Employment

Total civilian labor force, 2008§§ 10,600
Unemployment rate, 2008 .... 13.4%
Total civilian labor force, 2000 8,331

Employed persons 16 years and over by occupation, 2000

Managers & professionals 1,384
Service occupations 1,056
Sales & office occupations 1,818
Farming, fishing & forestry 851
Construction & maintenance 530
Production & transportation 1,451
Self-employed persons 312

* US Census Bureau
** 2000 Decennial Census
§ California Department of Finance
§§ California Employment Development Dept

General Information

City of Selma
1710 Tucker St
Selma, CA 93662
559-891-2200

Website .... www.cityofselma.com
Elevation .... 308 ft.
Land Area (sq. miles) 4.3
Water Area (sq. miles) 0
Year of Incorporation 1893
Government type .... General law
Sales tax rate 9.48%

Voters & Officials

Registered Voters, October 2008

Total 7,863
Democrats 3,758
Republicans 2,936
Declined to state 772

Legislative Districts

US Congressional 20
State Senatorial 16
State Assembly 31

Local Officials, 2009

Mayor .... Dennis Lujan
Manager .... D.B. Heusser
City Clerk .... Melanie Carter
Attorney .... Neal Costanzo
Finance Dir .... Roberta Araki
Public Works .... Robert Weaver
Planning/Dev Dir .... Michael Gaston
Building .... NA
Police Chief .... Tom Whiteside
Emergency/Fire Dir .... Jeff Kestly

Public Safety

Number of officers, 2007 35
Violent crimes, 2007 89
Property crimes, 2007 1,065
Arson, 2007 .... NA

Public Library

Selma Branch Library
Fresno County Public Library System
2200 Selma St
Selma, CA 93662
559-896-3393

Branch Librarian .... Susan Hill

Library system statistics, FY 2007

Population served 889,019
Internet terminals 277
Annual users 861,240

Per capita:

Operating income $23.69
percent from local government 89.3%
Operating expenditure $23.37
Total materials 2.89
Print holdings 2.69
Visits per capita .... NA

Housing & Construction

Housing Units

Total, 2008§ 6,820
Single family units, attached 148
Single family units, detached 5,103
Multiple family units 1,143
Mobile home units 426
Occupied 6,564
Vacancy rate 3.8%
Median rent, 2000** $520
Median SF home value, 2000** $97,000

New Privately Owned Housing Units Authorized by Building Permit, 2007*

	Units	Construction Cost
Single	41	$5,310,221
Total	41	$5,310,221

Municipal Finance

(For local fiscal year ended in 2006)

Revenues

Total $15,825,191
Taxes 9,281,867
Special benefits assessment 132,270
Licenses & permits 424,814
Fines & forfeitures 71,308
Revenues from use of money & property 363,672
Intergovernmental 2,001,474
Service charges 3,138,216
Other revenues 411,570
Other financing sources 0

Expenditures

Total $15,410,274
General government 1,798,105
Public safety 7,013,032
Transportation 2,359,772
Community development 1,622,105
Health 787,614
Culture & leisure 1,829,646
Other 0

Local School District

(Data from School year 2007-08 except as noted)

Selma Unified
3036 Thompson Ave
Selma, CA 93662
(559) 898-6500

Superintendent .... Mark Sutton
Grade plan K-12
Number of schools 12
Enrollment 6,480
High school graduates, 2006-07 287
Dropout rate 2.6%
Pupil/teacher ratio 21.3
Average class size 26.4
Students per computer 5.6
Classrooms with internet 367
Avg. Daily Attendance (ADA) 6,309
Cost per ADA $8,352
Avg. Teacher Salary $64,631

California Achievement Tests 6th ed., 2008

(Pct scoring at or above 50th National Percentile Rank)

	Math	Reading	Language
Grade 3	50%	32%	41%
Grade 7	42%	42%	38%

Academic Performance Index, 2008

Number of students tested 4,819
Number of valid scores 4,574
2007 API (base) 727
2008 API (growth) 739

SAT Testing, 2006-07

Enrollment, Grade 12 376
Number taking test 94
percent taking test 25.0%
percent with total score 1,500+ 6.40%

Average Scores:

Math	Verbal	Writing	Total
469	449	452	1,370

Federal No Child Left Behind, 2008

(Adequate Yearly Progress standards met)

	Participation Rate	Pct Proficient
ELA	Yes	No
Math	Yes	No

API criteria .... Yes
Graduation rate .... Yes
\# criteria met/possible 30/28

Other school districts for this city

(see Appendix E for information on these districts)

None

See Introduction for an explanation of all data sources.

Demographics & Socio-Economic Characteristics

(2000 Decennial Census, except as noted)

Population

1990* ... 8,409
2000 ... 12,736
Male ... 6,501
Female ... 6,235
Jan. 2008 (estimate)§ ... 15,609
Persons per sq. mi. of land ... 867.2

Race & Hispanic Origin, 2000

Race
White ... 5,670
Black/African American ... 204
North American Native ... 159
Asian ... 40
Pacific Islander ... 18
Other Race ... 6,159
Two or more races ... 486
Hispanic origin, total ... 8,667
Mexican ... 7,169
Puerto Rican ... 26
Cuban ... 2
Other Hispanic ... 1,470

Age & Nativity, 2000

Under 5 years ... 1,303
18 years and over ... 8,069
65 years and over ... 1,028
85 years and over ... 156
Median Age ... 26.1
Native-born ... 9,187
Foreign-born ... 3,570

Educational Attainment, 2000

Population 25 years and over ... 6,594
Less than 9th grade ... 32.4%
High school grad or higher ... 47.3%
Bachelor's degree or higher ... 5.6%
Graduate degree ... 2.2%

Income & Poverty, 1999

Per capita income ... $10,961
Median household income ... $29,515
Median family income ... $31,457
Persons in poverty ... 27.7%
H'holds receiving public assistance ... 404
H'holds receiving social security ... 873

Households, 2000

Total households ... 3,293
With persons under 18 ... 1,919
With persons over 65 ... 698
Family households ... 2,760
Single person households ... 439
Persons per household ... 3.67
Persons per family ... 3.98

Household Population, 2008§§

Persons living in households ... 14,968
Persons living in group quarters ... 641
Persons per household ... 3.8

Labor & Employment

Total civilian labor force, 2008§§ ... 5,900
Unemployment rate, 2008 ... 17.6%
Total civilian labor force, 2000 ... 4,355

Employed persons 16 years and over by occupation, 2000

Managers & professionals ... 563
Service occupations ... 439
Sales & office occupations ... 726
Farming, fishing & forestry ... 588
Construction & maintenance ... 330
Production & transportation ... 792
Self-employed persons ... 187

* US Census Bureau
** 2000 Decennial Census
§ California Department of Finance
§§ California Employment Development Dept

General Information

City of Shafter
336 Pacific Ave
Shafter, CA 93263
661-746-5001

Website ... www.shafter.com
Elevation ... 345 ft.
Land Area (sq. miles) ... 18.0
Water Area (sq. miles) ... 0
Year of Incorporation ... 1938
Government type ... Chartered
Sales tax rate ... 8.25%

Voters & Officials

Registered Voters, October 2008

Total ... 4,488
Democrats ... 2,184
Republicans ... 1,651
Declined to state ... 532

Legislative Districts

US Congressional ... 20
State Senatorial ... 16
State Assembly ... 30

Local Officials, 2009

Mayor ... Cathy L Prout
Manager ... John D Guinn
City Clerk ... Christine Wilson
Attorney ... Best, Best & Kreiger
Finance Dir ... Jo Barrick
Public Works ... Mike James
Community Dev Dir ... Jake Sweeny
Building ... Dennis Fiddler
Police Chief ... Charlie Fivecoat
Fire/Emergency Mgmt ... (County)

Public Safety

Number of officers, 2007 ... 20
Violent crimes, 2007 ... 68
Property crimes, 2007 ... 610
Arson, 2007 ... 32

Public Library

Shafter Branch Library
Kern County Library System
236 James St
Shafter, CA 93263
661-746-2156

Branch Librarian ... Judy Knox

Library system statistics, FY 2007

Population served ... 801,648
Internet terminals ... 237
Annual users ... 337,030

Per capita:

Operating income ... $12.11
percent from local government ... 90.4%
Operating expenditure ... $12.11
Total materials ... 1.37
Print holdings ... 1.29
Visits per capita ... 2.09

Housing & Construction

Housing Units

Total, 2008§ ... 4,345
Single family units, attached ... 177
Single family units, detached ... 3,395
Multiple family units ... 564
Mobile home units ... 209
Occupied ... 3,948
Vacancy rate ... 9.1%
Median rent, 2000** ... $437
Median SF home value, 2000** ... $78,900

New Privately Owned Housing Units Authorized by Building Permit, 2007*

	Units	Construction Cost
Single	101	$13,409,508
Total	101	$13,409,508

Municipal Finance

(For local fiscal year ended in 2006)

Revenues

Total ... $29,600,242
Taxes ... 5,270,591
Special benefits assessment ... 109,998
Licenses & permits ... 9,640
Fines & forfeitures ... 102,172
Revenues from use of money & property ... 3,001,999
Intergovernmental ... 4,799,200
Service charges ... 15,632,175
Other revenues ... 674,467
Other financing sources ... 0

Expenditures

Total ... $25,498,353
General government ... 1,412,414
Public safety ... 13,264,350
Transportation ... 4,203,914
Community development ... 2,411,478
Health ... 1,941,660
Culture & leisure ... 638,362
Other ... 0

Local School District

(Data from School year 2007-08 except as noted)

Kern Union High
5801 Sundale Ave
Bakersfield, CA 93309
(661) 827-3100

Superintendent ... Donald Carter
Grade plan ... 9-12
Number of schools ... 22
Enrollment ... 37,341
High school graduates, 2006-07 ... 6,321
Dropout rate ... 5.3%
Pupil/teacher ratio ... 23.3
Average class size ... 26.2
Students per computer ... 4.2
Classrooms with internet ... 1,524
Avg. Daily Attendance (ADA) ... 37,540
Cost per ADA ... $8,547
Avg. Teacher Salary ... $63,074

California Achievement Tests 6th ed., 2008

(Pct scoring at or above 50th National Percentile Rank)

	Math	Reading	Language
Grade 3	NA	NA	NA
Grade 7	NA	NA	NA

Academic Performance Index, 2008

Number of students tested ... 26,804
Number of valid scores ... 24,540
2007 API (base) ... 654
2008 API (growth) ... 661

SAT Testing, 2006-07

Enrollment, Grade 12 ... 8,277
Number taking test ... 2,144
percent taking test ... 25.9%
percent with total score 1,500+ ... 9.90%

Average Scores:

Math	Verbal	Writing	Total
488	471	464	1,423

Federal No Child Left Behind, 2008

(Adequate Yearly Progress standards met)

	Participation Rate	Pct Proficient
ELA	Yes	No
Math	Yes	No

API criteria ... Yes
Graduation rate ... No
\# criteria met/possible ... 34/29

Other school districts for this city

(see Appendix E for information on these districts)

Maple Elem, Richland-Lerdo Elem

See Introduction for an explanation of all data sources.

Demographics & Socio-Economic Characteristics

(2000 Decennial Census, except as noted)

Population

1990* .... NA
2000 9,008
Male 4,454
Female 4,554
Jan. 2008 (estimate)§ 10,279
Persons per sq. mi. of land 943.0

Race & Hispanic Origin, 2000

Race
White 7,911
Black/African American 65
North American Native 399
Asian 32
Pacific Islander 8
Other Race 180
Two or more races 413
Hispanic origin, total 557
Mexican 403
Puerto Rican 18
Cuban 3
Other Hispanic 133

Age & Nativity, 2000

Under 5 years 615
18 years and over 6,417
65 years and over 1,184
85 years and over 138
Median Age 36.5
Native-born 8,807
Foreign-born 220

Educational Attainment, 2000

Population 25 years and over 5,689
Less than 9th grade 4.4%
High school grad or higher 76.1%
Bachelor's degree or higher 6.8%
Graduate degree 1.3%

Income & Poverty, 1999

Per capita income $13,678
Median household income $26,275
Median family income $33,010
Persons in poverty 20.0%
H'holds receiving public assistance 341
H'holds receiving social security 1,121

Households, 2000

Total households 3,391
With persons under 18 1,320
With persons over 65 885
Family households 2,377
Single person households 803
Persons per household 2.64
Persons per family 3.09

Household Population, 2008§§

Persons living in households 10,227
Persons living in group quarters 52
Persons per household 2.6

Labor & Employment

Total civilian labor force, 2008§§ 4,400
Unemployment rate, 2008 .... 13.2%
Total civilian labor force, 2000 3,812

Employed persons 16 years and over by occupation, 2000

Managers & professionals 682
Service occupations 716
Sales & office occupations 926
Farming, fishing & forestry 36
Construction & maintenance 484
Production & transportation 530
Self-employed persons 340

* US Census Bureau
** 2000 Decennial Census
§ California Department of Finance
§§ California Employment Development Dept

General Information

City of Shasta Lake
1650 Stanton Dr
PO Box 777
Shasta Lake, CA 96019
530-275-7400

Website .... www.ci.shasta-lake.ca.us
Elevation .... NA
Land Area (sq. miles) 10.9
Water Area (sq. miles) 0
Year of Incorporation 1993
Government type .... General law
Sales tax rate 8.25%

Voters & Officials

Registered Voters, October 2008

Total 5,001
Democrats 1,701
Republicans 2,023
Declined to state 1,016

Legislative Districts

US Congressional 2
State Senatorial 4
State Assembly 2

Local Officials, 2009

Mayor .... Gracious Palmer
Manager .... Carol Martin
City Clerk .... Toni Coates
Attorney .... John Kenny
Finance Dir .... John Deckett
Public Works .... Jim Grabow
Development Svcs Dir .... Carla Thompson
Building .... NA
Police Chief .... NA
Fire/Emergency Mgmt .... NA

Public Safety

Number of officers, 2007 .... NA
Violent crimes, 2007 .... NA
Property crimes, 2007 .... NA
Arson, 2007 .... NA

Public Library

Shasta Lake City Library
Shasta Dam Blvd
Shasta Lake, CA 96019
530-275-7474

City Librarian .... NA

Library statistics, FY 2007

Population served .... NA
Internet terminals .... NA
Annual users .... NA

Per capita:

Operating income .... NA
percent from local government .... NA
Operating expenditure .... NA
Total materials .... NA
Print holdings .... NA
Visits per capita .... NA

Housing & Construction

Housing Units

Total, 2008§ 4,273
Single family units, attached 27
Single family units, detached 3,400
Multiple family units 361
Mobile home units 485
Occupied 3,887
Vacancy rate 9.0%
Median rent, 2000** $560
Median SF home value, 2000** $91,100

New Privately Owned Housing Units Authorized by Building Permit, 2007*

	Units	Construction Cost
Single	30	$5,851,777
Total	30	$5,851,777

Municipal Finance

(For local fiscal year ended in 2006)

Revenues

Total $38,194,208
Taxes 2,536,086
Special benefits assessment 0
Licenses & permits 126,075
Fines & forfeitures 112,491
Revenues from use of money & property 1,287,529
Intergovernmental 6,253,877
Service charges 22,485,161
Other revenues 392,989
Other financing sources 5,000,000

Expenditures

Total $25,188,672
General government 2,363,941
Public safety 2,346,718
Transportation 2,670,215
Community development 1,997,298
Health 1,667,776
Culture & leisure 275,646
Other 0

Local School District

(Data from School year 2007-08 except as noted)

Gateway Unified
4411 Mountain Lakes Blvd
Redding, CA 96003
(530) 245-7900

Superintendent .... John Strohmayer
Grade plan K-12
Number of schools 12
Enrollment 3,264
High school graduates, 2006-07 237
Dropout rate 2.4%
Pupil/teacher ratio 18.6
Average class size 22.2
Students per computer 4.5
Classrooms with internet 190
Avg. Daily Attendance (ADA) 2,695
Cost per ADA $9,341
Avg. Teacher Salary $56,556

California Achievement Tests 6th ed., 2008

(Pct scoring at or above 50th National Percentile Rank)

	Math	Reading	Language
Grade 3	56%	45%	50%
Grade 7	50%	52%	48%

Academic Performance Index, 2008

Number of students tested 2,118
Number of valid scores 1,853
2007 API (base) 731
2008 API (growth) 753

SAT Testing, 2006-07

Enrollment, Grade 12 305
Number taking test 54
percent taking test 17.7%
percent with total score 1,500+ 6.60%

Average Scores:

Math	Verbal	Writing	Total
486	478	458	1,422

Federal No Child Left Behind, 2008

(Adequate Yearly Progress standards met)

	Participation Rate	Pct Proficient
ELA	Yes	Yes
Math	Yes	Yes

API criteria .... Yes
Graduation rate .... Yes
\# criteria met/possible 26/26

Other school districts for this city

(see Appendix E for information on these districts)

None

See Introduction for an explanation of all data sources.

Demographics & Socio-Economic Characteristics

(2000 Decennial Census, except as noted)

Population

1990* 10,762
2000 10,578
Male 4,996
Female 5,582
Jan. 2008 (estimate)§ 11,116
Persons per sq. mi. of land 3,705.3

Race & Hispanic Origin, 2000

Race
White 9,077
Black/African American 121
North American Native 37
Asian 592
Pacific Islander 11
Other Race 319
Two or more races 421
Hispanic origin, total 1,054
Mexican 710
Puerto Rican 13
Cuban 39
Other Hispanic 292

Age & Nativity, 2000

Under 5 years 556
18 years and over 8,579
65 years and over 1,665
85 years and over 209
Median Age 42.6
Native-born 9,463
Foreign-born 1,115

Educational Attainment, 2000

Population 25 years and over 8,094
Less than 9th grade 0.8%
High school grad or higher 94.5%
Bachelor's degree or higher 49.7%
Graduate degree 21.6%

Income & Poverty, 1999

Per capita income $41,104
Median household income $65,900
Median family income $79,588
Persons in poverty 3.7%
H'holds receiving public assistance 27
H'holds receiving social security 1,067

Households, 2000

Total households 4,756
With persons under 18 1,181
With persons over 65 1,178
Family households 2,740
Single person households 1,666
Persons per household 2.20
Persons per family 2.87

Household Population, 2008§§

Persons living in households 10,989
Persons living in group quarters 127
Persons per household 2.3

Labor & Employment

Total civilian labor force, 2008§§ 7,100
Unemployment rate, 2008 .... 2.1%
Total civilian labor force, 2000 6,108

Employed persons 16 years and over by occupation, 2000

Managers & professionals 3,409
Service occupations 490
Sales & office occupations 1,501
Farming, fishing & forestry 10
Construction & maintenance 293
Production & transportation 259
Self-employed persons 710

* US Census Bureau
** 2000 Decennial Census
§ California Department of Finance
§§ California Employment Development Dept

General Information

City of Sierra Madre
232 W Sierra Madre Blvd
Sierra Madre, CA 91024
626-355-7135

Website .... cityofsierramadre.com
Elevation .... 840 ft.
Land Area (sq. miles) 3.0
Water Area (sq. miles) 0
Year of Incorporation 1907
Government type .... General law
Sales tax rate 9.25%

Voters & Officials

Registered Voters, October 2008

Total 7,781
Democrats 2,920
Republicans 3,083
Declined to state 1,391

Legislative Districts

US Congressional 26
State Senatorial 29
State Assembly 59

Local Officials, 2009

Mayor .... Kurt Zimmerman
Manager .... Elaine Aguilar
City Clerk .... Nancy Shollenberger
Attorney .... Sandi Levin
Finance Dir .... Karen Schnaider
Public Works .... Bruce Inman
Planning/Dev Dir .... Danny Castro
Building .... Richard Temple
Police Chief .... Marilyn Diaz
Emergency/Fire Dir .... Steve Heydorff

Public Safety

Number of officers, 2007 15
Violent crimes, 2007 23
Property crimes, 2007 170
Arson, 2007 0

Public Library

Sierra Madre Public Library
440 W Sierra Madre Blvd
Sierra Madre, CA 91024
626-355-7186

Director .... Toni G. Buckner

Library statistics, FY 2007

Population served 11,039
Internet terminals 6
Annual users 9,000

Per capita:

Operating income $67.31
percent from local government 90.4%
Operating expenditure $67.31
Total materials 6.77
Print holdings 5.66
Visits per capita 4.55

Housing & Construction

Housing Units

Total, 2008§ 5,000
Single family units, attached 215
Single family units, detached 3,415
Multiple family units 1,343
Mobile home units 27
Occupied 4,831
Vacancy rate 3.4%
Median rent, 2000** $836
Median SF home value, 2000** $370,500

New Privately Owned Housing Units Authorized by Building Permit, 2007*

	Units	Construction Cost
Single	19	$3,327,359
Total	19	$3,327,359

Municipal Finance

(For local fiscal year ended in 2006)

Revenues

Total $10,788,785
Taxes 4,763,514
Special benefits assessment 8,219
Licenses & permits 90,765
Fines & forfeitures 63,517
Revenues from use of money & property 76,819
Intergovernmental 1,848,065
Service charges 3,800,185
Other revenues 137,701
Other financing sources 0

Expenditures

Total $9,676,881
General government 783,980
Public safety 2,321,703
Transportation 22,231
Community development 2,796,134
Health 0
Culture & leisure 962,681
Other 162,661

Local School District

(Data from School year 2007-08 except as noted)

Pasadena Unified
351 South Hudson Ave
Pasadena, CA 91101
(626) 795-6981

Superintendent .... Edwin Diaz
Grade plan K-12
Number of schools 33
Enrollment 20,905
High school graduates, 2006-07 1,058
Dropout rate 4.1%
Pupil/teacher ratio 20.7
Average class size 25.6
Students per computer 5.3
Classrooms with internet 1,219
Avg. Daily Attendance (ADA) 20,132
Cost per ADA $9,704
Avg. Teacher Salary $61,180

California Achievement Tests 6th ed., 2008

(Pct scoring at or above 50th National Percentile Rank)

	Math	Reading	Language
Grade 3	54%	33%	45%
Grade 7	44%	40%	39%

Academic Performance Index, 2008

Number of students tested 15,095
Number of valid scores 14,162
2007 API (base) 707
2008 API (growth) 720

SAT Testing, 2006-07

Enrollment, Grade 12 1,315
Number taking test 553
percent taking test 42.1%
percent with total score 1,500+ 11.20%

Average Scores:

Math	Verbal	Writing	Total
451	442	440	1,333

Federal No Child Left Behind, 2008

(Adequate Yearly Progress standards met)

	Participation Rate	Pct Proficient
ELA	Yes	No
Math	Yes	No

API criteria .... Yes
Graduation rate .... Yes
\# criteria met/possible 38/35

Other school districts for this city

(see Appendix E for information on these districts)

None

See Introduction for an explanation of all data sources.

Demographics & Socio-Economic Characteristics

(2000 Decennial Census, except as noted)

Population

1990* . . . 8,371
2000 . . . 9,333
Male . . . 4,599
Female . . . 4,734
Jan. 2008 (estimate)§ . . . 11,402
Persons per sq. mi. of land . . . 5,182.7

Race & Hispanic Origin, 2000

Race
White . . . 4,245
Black/African American . . . 1,212
North American Native . . . 55
Asian . . . 1,539
Pacific Islander . . . 194
Other Race . . . 1,510
Two or more races . . . 578
Hispanic origin, total . . . 2,707
Mexican . . . 1,967
Puerto Rican . . . 46
Cuban . . . 13
Other Hispanic . . . 681

Age & Nativity, 2000

Under 5 years . . . 766
18 years and over . . . 6,873
65 years and over . . . 671
85 years and over . . . 52
Median Age . . . 33.4
Native-born . . . 6,582
Foreign-born . . . 2,691

Educational Attainment, 2000

Population 25 years and over . . . 6,090
Less than 9th grade . . . 9.8%
High school grad or higher . . . 79.0%
Bachelor's degree or higher . . . 24.6%
Graduate degree . . . 8.5%

Income & Poverty, 1999

Per capita income . . . $24,399
Median household income . . . $48,938
Median family income . . . $46,439
Persons in poverty . . . 17.0%
H'holds receiving public assistance . . . 231
H'holds receiving social security . . . 592

Households, 2000

Total households . . . 3,621
With persons under 18 . . . 1,254
With persons over 65 . . . 514
Family households . . . 2,095
Single person households . . . 1,108
Persons per household . . . 2.56
Persons per family . . . 3.34

Household Population, 2008§§

Persons living in households . . . 11,348
Persons living in group quarters . . . 54
Persons per household . . . 2.7

Labor & Employment

Total civilian labor force, 2008§§ . . . 5,800
Unemployment rate, 2008 . . . 5.6%
Total civilian labor force, 2000 . . . 5,052

Employed persons 16 years and over by occupation, 2000

Managers & professionals . . . 1,746
Service occupations . . . 639
Sales & office occupations . . . 1,326
Farming, fishing & forestry . . . 0
Construction & maintenance . . . 375
Production & transportation . . . 657
Self-employed persons . . . 444

* US Census Bureau
** 2000 Decennial Census
§ California Department of Finance
§§ California Employment Development Dept

General Information

City of Signal Hill
2175 Cherry Ave
Signal Hill, CA 90755
562-989-7300

Website . . . www.cityofsignalhill.org
Elevation . . . 100 ft.
Land Area (sq. miles) . . . 2.2
Water Area (sq. miles) . . . 0
Year of Incorporation . . . 1924
Government type . . . Chartered
Sales tax rate . . . 9.25%

Voters & Officials

Registered Voters, October 2008

Total . . . 5,425
Democrats . . . 2,717
Republicans . . . 1,423
Declined to state . . . 1,060

Legislative Districts

US Congressional . . . 37
State Senatorial . . . 27
State Assembly . . . 54

Local Officials, 2009

Mayor . . . Ellen Ward
Manager . . . Ken Farfsing
City Clerk . . . Kathleen Pacheco
Attorney . . . David Aleshire
Finance Dir . . . Maida Alcantara
Public Works . . . Barbara Munoz
Planning/Dev Dir . . . Gary Jones
Building . . . Donn Showers
Police Chief . . . Tom Sonoff
Emergency/Fire Dir . . . Michael Freeman

Public Safety

Number of officers, 2007 . . . 32
Violent crimes, 2007 . . . 60
Property crimes, 2007 . . . 455
Arson, 2007 . . . 1

Public Library

Signal Hill Public Library
Cerritos Public Library System
1770 E Hill St
Signal Hill, CA 90755
562-989-7324

City Librarian . . . Carole Molloy

Library system statistics, FY 2007

Population served . . . 54,943
Internet terminals . . . 155
Annual users . . . 312,644

Per capita:

Operating income . . . $101.11
percent from local government . . . 98.8%
Operating expenditure . . . $92.04
Total materials . . . 4.38
Print holdings . . . 4.06
Visits per capita . . . 19.86

Housing & Construction

Housing Units

Total, 2008§ . . . 4,432
Single family units, attached . . . 488
Single family units, detached . . . 1,444
Multiple family units . . . 2,492
Mobile home units . . . 8
Occupied . . . 4,228
Vacancy rate . . . 4.6%
Median rent, 2000** . . . $725
Median SF home value, 2000** . . . $202,600

New Privately Owned Housing Units Authorized by Building Permit, 2007*

	Units	Construction Cost
Single	12	$4,702,050
Total	12	$4,702,050

Municipal Finance

(For local fiscal year ended in 2006)

Revenues

Total . . . $24,764,119
Taxes . . . 15,887,368
Special benefits assessment . . . 39,691
Licenses & permits . . . 311,197
Fines & forfeitures . . . 356,199
Revenues from use of money & property . . . 1,068,713
Intergovernmental . . . 1,371,042
Service charges . . . 4,773,040
Other revenues . . . 956,869
Other financing sources . . . 0

Expenditures

Total . . . $21,772,028
General government . . . 2,217,057
Public safety . . . 7,137,544
Transportation . . . 2,316,828
Community development . . . 1,991,048
Health . . . 613,713
Culture & leisure . . . 2,517,915
Other . . . 0

Local School District

(Data from School year 2007-08 except as noted)

Long Beach Unified
1515 Hughes Way
Long Beach, CA 90810
(562) 997-8000

Superintendent . . . Christopher Steinhauser
Grade plan . . . K-12
Number of schools . . . 93
Enrollment . . . 88,186
High school graduates, 2006-07 . . . 4,706
Dropout rate . . . 5.1%
Pupil/teacher ratio . . . 20.9
Average class size . . . 27.3
Students per computer . . . 4.9
Classrooms with internet . . . 4,149
Avg. Daily Attendance (ADA) . . . 87,009
Cost per ADA . . . $8,964
Avg. Teacher Salary . . . $70,071

California Achievement Tests 6th ed., 2008

(Pct scoring at or above 50th National Percentile Rank)

	Math	Reading	Language
Grade 3	60%	34%	41%
Grade 7	47%	43%	41%

Academic Performance Index, 2008

Number of students tested . . . 67,372
Number of valid scores . . . 64,269
2007 API (base) . . . 729
2008 API (growth) . . . 744

SAT Testing, 2006-07

Enrollment, Grade 12 . . . 6,154
Number taking test . . . 2,120
percent taking test . . . 34.5%
percent with total score 1,500+ . . . 14.30%

Average Scores:

Math	Verbal	Writing	Total
496	478	476	1,450

Federal No Child Left Behind, 2008

(Adequate Yearly Progress standards met)

	Participation Rate	Pct Proficient
ELA	Yes	No
Math	Yes	No

API criteria . . . Yes
Graduation rate . . . Yes
\# criteria met/possible . . . 46/43

Other school districts for this city

(see Appendix E for information on these districts)

None

See Introduction for an explanation of all data sources.

Demographics & Socio-Economic Characteristics†

(2007 American Community Survey, except as noted)

Population

1990*	100,217
2007	127,053
Male	63,679
Female	63,374
Jan. 2008 (estimate)§	125,657
Persons per sq. mi. of land	3,205.5

Race & Hispanic Origin, 2007

Race	
White	92,009
Black/African American	2,047
North American Native	607
Asian	8,678
Pacific Islander	0
Other Race	20,359
Two or more races	3,353
Hispanic origin, total	29,852
Mexican	22,380
Puerto Rican	570
Cuban	1,167
Other Hispanic	5,735

Age & Nativity, 2007

Under 5 years	8,441
18 years and over	93,395
65 years and over	11,331
85 years and over	1,867
Median Age	35.9
Native-born	102,193
Foreign-born	24,860

Educational Attainment, 2007

Population 25 years and over	81,576
Less than 9th grade	4.4%
High school grad or higher	90.2%
Bachelor's degree or higher	31.3%
Graduate degree	8.9%

Income & Poverty, 2007

Per capita income	$33,814
Median household income	$88,406
Median family income	$91,658
Persons in poverty	5.2%
H'holds receiving public assistance	98
H'holds receiving social security	7,415

Households, 2007

Total households	39,466
With persons under 18	17,293
With persons over 65	7,785
Family households	31,064
Single person households	6,456
Persons per household	3.21
Persons per family	3.52

Household Population, 2008§§

Persons living in households	124,857
Persons living in group quarters	800
Persons per household	3.1

Labor & Employment

Total civilian labor force, 2008§§	70,200
Unemployment rate, 2008	5.2%
Total civilian labor force, 2000*	59,510

Employed persons 16 years and over by occupation, 2007

Managers & professionals	26,659
Service occupations	9,627
Sales & office occupations	21,229
Farming, fishing & forestry	210
Construction & maintenance	5,368
Production & transportation	5,638
Self-employed persons	7,763

† see Appendix D for 2000 Decennial Census Data
* US Census Bureau
** 2007 American Community Survey
§ California Department of Finance
§§ California Employment Development Dept

General Information

City of Simi Valley
2929 Tapo Canyon Rd
Simi Valley, CA 93063
805-583-6700

Website	www.simivalley.org
Elevation	820 ft.
Land Area (sq. miles)	39.2
Water Area (sq. miles)	0.3
Year of Incorporation	1969
Government type	General law
Sales tax rate	8.25%

Voters & Officials

Registered Voters, October 2008

Total	69,698
Democrats	21,863
Republicans	32,266
Declined to state	12,450

Legislative Districts

US Congressional	24
State Senatorial	19
State Assembly	37, 38

Local Officials, 2009

Mayor	Paul Miller
City Manager	Mike Sedell
City Clerk	Mike Sedell
Attorney	(vacant)
Admin Svcs Dir	Jim Purtee
Public Works	Ron Fuchiwaki
Environmental Svcs Dir	Peter Lyons
Building	Amal Sinha
Police Chief	Mike Lewis
Fire/Emergency Mgmt	(County)

Public Safety

Number of officers, 2007	125
Violent crimes, 2007	181
Property crimes, 2007	2,383
Arson, 2007	9

Public Library

Simi Valley Library
Ventura County Library System
2969 Tapo Canyon Rd
Simi Valley, CA 93063
805-526-1735

Branch Librarian	Dale Redfield

Library system statistics, FY 2007

Population served	439,444
Internet terminals	188
Annual users	216,575

Per capita:

Operating income	$25.05
percent from local government	86.2%
Operating expenditure	$25.02
Total materials	1.81
Print holdings	1.70
Visits per capita	NA

Housing & Construction

Housing Units

Total, 2008§	41,890
Single family units, attached	3,147
Single family units, detached	30,646
Multiple family units	7,205
Mobile home units	892
Occupied	40,933
Vacancy rate	2.3%
Median rent, 2007**	$1,603
Median SF home value, 2007**	$638,600

New Privately Owned Housing Units Authorized by Building Permit, 2007*

	Units	Construction Cost
Single	132	$32,636,782
Total	189	$41,225,048

Municipal Finance

(For local fiscal year ended in 2006)

Revenues

Total	$101,475,582
Taxes	53,188,594
Special benefits assessment	0
Licenses & permits	4,489,743
Fines & forfeitures	678,799
Revenues from use of money & property	3,978,208
Intergovernmental	10,582,100
Service charges	22,049,693
Other revenues	6,508,445
Other financing sources	0

Expenditures

Total	$110,798,809
General government	13,442,374
Public safety	27,654,260
Transportation	20,293,583
Community development	34,355,169
Health	13,219,205
Culture & leisure	1,742,487
Other	91,731

Local School District

(Data from School year 2007-08 except as noted)

Simi Valley Unified
875 East Cochran
Simi Valley, CA 93065
(805) 520-6500

Superintendent	Kathryn Scroggin
Grade plan	K-12
Number of schools	29
Enrollment	21,137
High school graduates, 2006-07	1,370
Dropout rate	2.9%
Pupil/teacher ratio	22.6
Average class size	26.7
Students per computer	4.9
Classrooms with internet	1,002
Avg. Daily Attendance (ADA)	20,295
Cost per ADA	$7,719
Avg. Teacher Salary	$64,940

California Achievement Tests 6th ed., 2008

(Pct scoring at or above 50th National Percentile Rank)

	Math	Reading	Language
Grade 3	67%	50%	57%
Grade 7	66%	62%	60%

Academic Performance Index, 2008

Number of students tested	16,093
Number of valid scores	15,562
2007 API (base)	802
2008 API (growth)	808

SAT Testing, 2006-07

Enrollment, Grade 12	1,790
Number taking test	543
percent taking test	30.3%
percent with total score 1,500+	19.60%

Average Scores:

Math	Verbal	Writing	Total
543	529	523	1,595

Federal No Child Left Behind, 2008

(Adequate Yearly Progress standards met)

	Participation Rate	Pct Proficient
ELA	Yes	No
Math	Yes	Yes

API criteria	Yes
Graduation rate	Yes
# criteria met/possible	40/38

Other school districts for this city

(see Appendix E for information on these districts)

None

See Introduction for an explanation of all data sources.

Demographics & Socio-Economic Characteristics

(2000 Decennial Census, except as noted)

Population

1990* . . . 12,962
2000 . . . 12,979
Male . . . 6,395
Female . . . 6,584
Jan. 2008 (estimate)§ . . . 13,500
Persons per sq. mi. of land . . . 3,857.1

Race & Hispanic Origin, 2000

Race
White . . . 11,293
Black/African American . . . 65
North American Native . . . 54
Asian . . . 449
Pacific Islander . . . 18
Other Race . . . 725
Two or more races . . . 375
Hispanic origin, total . . . 1,922
Mexican . . . 1,600
Puerto Rican . . . 22
Cuban . . . 17
Other Hispanic . . . 283

Age & Nativity, 2000

Under 5 years . . . 594
18 years and over . . . 10,654
65 years and over . . . 2,239
85 years and over . . . 265
Median Age . . . 41.6
Native-born . . . 10,994
Foreign-born . . . 1,893

Educational Attainment, 2000

Population 25 years and over . . . 9,772
Less than 9th grade . . . 4.1%
High school grad or higher . . . 92.1%
Bachelor's degree or higher . . . 58.2%
Graduate degree . . . 25.6%

Income & Poverty, 1999

Per capita income . . . $48,547
Median household income . . . $71,774
Median family income . . . $96,652
Persons in poverty . . . 6.6%
H'holds receiving public assistance . . . 27
H'holds receiving social security . . . 1,581

Households, 2000

Total households . . . 5,754
With persons under 18 . . . 1,299
With persons over 65 . . . 1,589
Family households . . . 3,280
Single person households . . . 1,814
Persons per household . . . 2.25
Persons per family . . . 2.83

Household Population, 2008§§

Persons living in households . . . 13,466
Persons living in group quarters . . . 34
Persons per household . . . 2.3

Labor & Employment

Total civilian labor force, 2008§§ . . . 8,500
Unemployment rate, 2008 . . . 3.6%
Total civilian labor force, 2000 . . . 7,158

Employed persons 16 years and over by occupation, 2000

Managers & professionals . . . 3,823
Service occupations . . . 942
Sales & office occupations . . . 1,652
Farming, fishing & forestry . . . 0
Construction & maintenance . . . 298
Production & transportation . . . 187
Self-employed persons . . . 1,176

* US Census Bureau
** 2000 Decennial Census
§ California Department of Finance
§§ California Employment Development Dept

General Information

City of Solana Beach
635 S Highway 101
Solana Beach, CA 92075
858-720-2400

Website . . . www.ci.solana-beach.ca.us
Elevation . . . NA
Land Area (sq. miles) . . . 3.5
Water Area (sq. miles) . . . 0.1
Year of Incorporation . . . 1986
Government type . . . General Law
Sales tax rate . . . 8.75%

Voters & Officials

Registered Voters, October 2008

Total . . . 8,352
Democrats . . . 2,791
Republicans . . . 3,301
Declined to state . . . 1,942

Legislative Districts

US Congressional . . . 50
State Senatorial . . . 38
State Assembly . . . 74

Local Officials, 2009

Mayor . . . Mike Nichols
Manager . . . David Ott
City Clerk . . . Angela Ivey
Attorney . . . Johanna N Canlas
Finance Dir . . . Dennis Coleman
Public Works . . . Mo Sammak
Planning/Dev Dir . . . Tina Christiansen
Building . . . NA
Police Chief . . . NA
Emergency/Fire Dir . . . David Ott

Public Safety

Number of officers, 2007 . . . NA
Violent crimes, 2007 . . . 26
Property crimes, 2007 . . . 271
Arson, 2007 . . . 2

Public Library

Solana Beach Library
San Diego County Library System
157 Stevens Ave
Solana Beach, CA 92075
858-755-7859

Branch Librarian . . . Judith Gregg

Library system statistics, FY 2007

Population served . . . 1,049,868
Internet terminals . . . 394
Annual users . . . NA

Per capita:

Operating income . . . $33.43
percent from local government . . . 80.6%
Operating expenditure . . . $31.30
Total materials . . . 1.54
Print holdings . . . 1.32
Visits per capita . . . 6.31

Housing & Construction

Housing Units

Total, 2008§ . . . 6,572
Single family units, attached . . . 1,265
Single family units, detached . . . 3,020
Multiple family units . . . 2,248
Mobile home units . . . 39
Occupied . . . 5,859
Vacancy rate . . . 10.9%
Median rent, 2000** . . . $1,112
Median SF home value, 2000** . . . $474,500

New Privately Owned Housing Units Authorized by Building Permit, 2007*

	Units	Construction Cost
Single	11	$3,939,425
Total	11	$3,939,425

Municipal Finance

(For local fiscal year ended in 2006)

Revenues

Total . . . $23,210,177
Taxes . . . 10,298,145
Special benefits assessment . . . 1,235,026
Licenses & permits . . . 335,433
Fines & forfeitures . . . 381,016
Revenues from use of money & property . . . 895,908
Intergovernmental . . . 2,114,630
Service charges . . . 4,849,858
Other revenues . . . 3,100,161
Other financing sources . . . 0

Expenditures

Total . . . $17,753,769
General government . . . 2,955,950
Public safety . . . 6,401,373
Transportation . . . 2,870,048
Community development . . . 1,814,387
Health . . . 2,910,811
Culture & leisure . . . 801,200
Other . . . 0

Local School District

(Data from School year 2007-08 except as noted)

San Dieguito Union High
710 Encinitas Blvd
Encinitas, CA 92024
(760) 753-6491

Superintendent . . . Ken Noah
Grade plan . . . 7-12
Number of schools . . . 10
Enrollment . . . 12,482
High school graduates, 2006-07 . . . 1,874
Dropout rate . . . 1.4%
Pupil/teacher ratio . . . 25.4
Average class size . . . 30.5
Students per computer . . . 3.5
Classrooms with internet . . . 613
Avg. Daily Attendance (ADA) . . . 12,349
Cost per ADA . . . $8,092
Avg. Teacher Salary . . . $75,620

California Achievement Tests 6th ed., 2008

(Pct scoring at or above 50th National Percentile Rank)

	Math	Reading	Language
Grade 3	NA	NA	NA
Grade 7	83%	79%	78%

Academic Performance Index, 2008

Number of students tested . . . 10,153
Number of valid scores . . . 9,873
2007 API (base) . . . 853
2008 API (growth) . . . 855

SAT Testing, 2006-07

Enrollment, Grade 12 . . . 2,038
Number taking test . . . 1,532
percent taking test . . . 75.2%
percent with total score 1,500+ . . . 57.90%

Average Scores:

Math	Verbal	Writing	Total
590	555	560	1,705

Federal No Child Left Behind, 2008

(Adequate Yearly Progress standards met)

	Participation Rate	Pct Proficient
ELA	Yes	Yes
Math	Yes	Yes

API criteria . . . Yes
Graduation rate . . . Yes
criteria met/possible . . . 30/30

Other school districts for this city

(see Appendix E for information on these districts)

Solana Beach Elem

See Introduction for an explanation of all data sources.

Demographics & Socio-Economic Characteristics

(2000 Decennial Census, except as noted)

Population

1990* . . . 7,146
2000 . . . 11,263
Male . . . 5,847
Female . . . 5,416
Jan. 2008 (estimate)§ . . . 27,905
Persons per sq. mi. of land . . . 6,644.0

Race & Hispanic Origin, 2000

Race
White . . . 3,593
Black/African American . . . 129
North American Native . . . 195
Asian . . . 265
Pacific Islander . . . 9
Other Race . . . 6,596
Two or more races . . . 476
Hispanic origin, total . . . 9,779
Mexican . . . 8,798
Puerto Rican . . . 24
Cuban . . . 3
Other Hispanic . . . 954

Age & Nativity, 2000

Under 5 years . . . 1,182
18 years and over . . . 7,129
65 years and over . . . 670
85 years and over . . . 73
Median Age . . . 25.2
Native-born . . . 6,412
Foreign-born . . . 4,871

Educational Attainment, 2000

Population 25 years and over . . . 5,713
Less than 9th grade . . . 46.5%
High school grad or higher . . . 39.2%
Bachelor's degree or higher . . . 4.1%
Graduate degree . . . 1.8%

Income & Poverty, 1999

Per capita income . . . $11,442
Median household income . . . $42,602
Median family income . . . $41,188
Persons in poverty . . . 18.3%
H'holds receiving public assistance . . . 103
H'holds receiving social security . . . 546

Households, 2000

Total households . . . 2,472
With persons under 18 . . . 1,712
With persons over 65 . . . 468
Family households . . . 2,241
Single person households . . . 178
Persons per household . . . 4.54
Persons per family . . . 4.58

Household Population, 2008§§

Persons living in households . . . 16,743
Persons living in group quarters . . . 11,162
Persons per household . . . 4.5

Labor & Employment

Total civilian labor force, 2008§§ . . . 5,700
Unemployment rate, 2008 . . . 10.9%
Total civilian labor force, 2000 . . . 4,697

Employed persons 16 years and over by occupation, 2000

Managers & professionals . . . 454
Service occupations . . . 512
Sales & office occupations . . . 555
Farming, fishing & forestry . . . 1,665
Construction & maintenance . . . 300
Production & transportation . . . 702
Self-employed persons . . . 83

* US Census Bureau
** 2000 Decennial Census
§ California Department of Finance
§§ California Employment Development Dept

General Information

City of Soledad
248 Main St
PO Box 156
Soledad, CA 93960
831-223-5000

Website . . . www.cityofsoledad.com
Elevation . . . NA
Land Area (sq. miles) . . . 4.2
Water Area (sq. miles) . . . 0
Year of Incorporation . . . 1921
Government type . . . General law
Sales tax rate . . . 8.25%

Voters & Officials

Registered Voters, October 2008

Total . . . 4,100
Democrats . . . 2,598
Republicans . . . 680
Declined to state . . . 720

Legislative Districts

US Congressional . . . 17
State Senatorial . . . 12
State Assembly . . . 28

Local Officials, 2009

Mayor . . . Richard V. Ortiz
City Manager . . . Adela P. Gonzalez
City Clerk . . . Adela P. Gonzalez
Attorney . . . Michael F. Rodriquez
Finance Dir . . . Uma Chokkalingam (Int)
Public Works . . . Clifton Price
Community Dev Dir . . . Steven McHarris
Building . . . Doug Rick
Police Chief . . . Richard Cox
Fire Chief . . . Richard Foster

Public Safety

Number of officers, 2007 . . . 22
Violent crimes, 2007 . . . NA
Property crimes, 2007 . . . 459
Arson, 2007 . . . 3

Public Library

Soledad Branch Library
Monterey County Free Libraries
401 Gabilan Dr
Soledad, CA 93960
831-678-2430

Branch Librarian . . . Angie Lopez

Library system statistics, FY 2007

Population served . . . 226,803
Internet terminals . . . 160
Annual users . . . 229,676

Per capita:

Operating income . . . $29.19
percent from local government . . . 91.7%
Operating expenditure . . . $27.42
Total materials . . . 1.92
Print holdings . . . 1.81
Visits per capita . . . 3.65

Housing & Construction

Housing Units

Total, 2008§ . . . 3,810
Single family units, attached . . . 214
Single family units, detached . . . 2,834
Multiple family units . . . 639
Mobile home units . . . 123
Occupied . . . 3,718
Vacancy rate . . . 2.4%
Median rent, 2000** . . . $623
Median SF home value, 2000** . . . $153,800

New Privately Owned Housing Units Authorized by Building Permit, 2007*

	Units	Construction Cost
Single	22	$4,906,918
Total	297	$36,507,836

Municipal Finance

(For local fiscal year ended in 2006)

Revenues

Total . . . $13,019,724
Taxes . . . 4,519,432
Special benefits assessment . . . 1,022,382
Licenses & permits . . . 421,675
Fines & forfeitures . . . 57,841
Revenues from use of money & property . . . 619,764
Intergovernmental . . . 1,004,899
Service charges . . . 5,300,803
Other revenues . . . 72,928
Other financing sources . . . 0

Expenditures

Total . . . $15,248,230
General government . . . 2,877,678
Public safety . . . 2,673,173
Transportation . . . 3,374,560
Community development . . . 1,330,562
Health . . . 3,500,120
Culture & leisure . . . 384,622
Other . . . 0

Local School District

(Data from School year 2007-08 except as noted)

Soledad Unified
PO Box 186
Soledad, CA 93960
(831) 678-3987

Superintendent . . . Jorge Guzman
Grade plan . . . K-12
Number of schools . . . 9
Enrollment . . . 4,315
High school graduates, 2006-07 . . . 187
Dropout rate . . . 3.9%
Pupil/teacher ratio . . . 22.7
Average class size . . . 27.3
Students per computer . . . 3.5
Classrooms with internet . . . 237
Avg. Daily Attendance (ADA) . . . 4,190
Cost per ADA . . . $7,720
Avg. Teacher Salary . . . $60,405

California Achievement Tests 6th ed., 2008

(Pct scoring at or above 50th National Percentile Rank)

	Math	Reading	Language
Grade 3	40%	21%	33%
Grade 7	33%	29%	29%

Academic Performance Index, 2008

Number of students tested . . . 3,334
Number of valid scores . . . 3,105
2007 API (base) . . . 629
2008 API (growth) . . . 656

SAT Testing, 2006-07

Enrollment, Grade 12 . . . 279
Number taking test . . . 96
percent taking test . . . 34.4%
percent with total score 1,500+ . . . 4.70%

Average Scores:

Math	Verbal	Writing	Total
402	409	412	1,223

Federal No Child Left Behind, 2008

(Adequate Yearly Progress standards met)

	Participation Rate	Pct Proficient
ELA	Yes	No
Math	Yes	No

API criteria . . . Yes
Graduation rate . . . Yes
criteria met/possible . . . 22/12

Other school districts for this city

(see Appendix E for information on these districts)

Mission Union Elem

See Introduction for an explanation of all data sources.

Demographics & Socio-Economic Characteristics

(2000 Decennial Census, except as noted)

Population

1990* 4,741
2000 5,332
Male 2,522
Female 2,810
Jan. 2008 (estimate)§ 5,555
Persons per sq. mi. of land 2,222.0

Race & Hispanic Origin, 2000

Race
White 4,705
Black/African American 23
North American Native 35
Asian 56
Pacific Islander 2
Other Race 294
Two or more races 217
Hispanic origin, total 1,059
Mexican 919
Puerto Rican 6
Cuban 8
Other Hispanic 126

Age & Nativity, 2000

Under 5 years 267
18 years and over 4,162
65 years and over 1,221
85 years and over 257
Median Age 43.2
Native-born 4,492
Foreign-born 923

Educational Attainment, 2000

Population 25 years and over 3,948
Less than 9th grade 7.2%
High school grad or higher 84.3%
Bachelor's degree or higher 29.1%
Graduate degree 10.8%

Income & Poverty, 1999

Per capita income $25,363
Median household income $45,799
Median family income $57,703
Persons in poverty 6.6%
H'holds receiving public assistance 33
H'holds receiving social security 773

Households, 2000

Total households 2,185
With persons under 18 625
With persons over 65 754
Family households 1,415
Single person households 659
Persons per household 2.37
Persons per family 2.96

Household Population, 2008§§

Persons living in households 5,395
Persons living in group quarters 160
Persons per household 2.3

Labor & Employment

Total civilian labor force, 2008§§ 3,100
Unemployment rate, 2008 .... 1.5%
Total civilian labor force, 2000 2,705

Employed persons 16 years and over by occupation, 2000

Managers & professionals 794
Service occupations 694
Sales & office occupations 734
Farming, fishing & forestry 40
Construction & maintenance 195
Production & transportation 196
Self-employed persons 357

* US Census Bureau
** 2000 Decennial Census
§ California Department of Finance
§§ California Employment Development Dept

General Information

City of Solvang
1644 Oak St
Solvang, CA 93463
805-688-5575

Website .... www.cityofsolvang.com
Elevation .... NA
Land Area (sq. miles) 2.5
Water Area (sq. miles) 0
Year of Incorporation 1985
Government type .... Charter City
Sales tax rate 8.75%

Voters & Officials

Registered Voters, October 2008

Total 3,166
Democrats 963
Republicans 1,580
Declined to state 502

Legislative Districts

US Congressional 24
State Senatorial 19
State Assembly 35

Local Officials, 2009

Mayor .... Linda Jackson
Manager .... Brad Vidro
City Clerk .... Mary Ellen Rio
Attorney .... Roy Hanley
Finance Dir .... Dana Waite
Public Works .... Tully Clifford
Planning/Dev Dir .... Shelley Stahl
Building .... NA
Police Chief .... Phil Willis
Fire Chief .... (County)

Public Safety

Number of officers, 2007 .... NA
Violent crimes, 2007 12
Property crimes, 2007 78
Arson, 2007 0

Public Library

Solvang Library
Santa Barbara Public Library
1745 Mission Dr
Solvang, CA 93463
805-688-4214

Branch Librarian .... Carey McKinnon

Library system statistics, FY 2007

Population served 233,434
Internet terminals 86
Annual users 66,000

Per capita:

Operating income $25.05
percent from local government 84.4%
Operating expenditure $27.43
Total materials 1.73
Print holdings 1.48
Visits per capita 12.44

Housing & Construction

Housing Units

Total, 2008§ 2,347
Single family units, attached 153
Single family units, detached 1,351
Multiple family units 624
Mobile home units 219
Occupied 2,302
Vacancy rate 1.9%
Median rent, 2000** $855
Median SF home value, 2000** $372,800

New Privately Owned Housing Units Authorized by Building Permit, 2007*

	Units	Construction Cost
Single	NA	NA
Total	NA	NA

Municipal Finance

(For local fiscal year ended in 2006)

Revenues

Total $15,122,189
Taxes 5,920,302
Special benefits assessment 167,782
Licenses & permits 79,323
Fines & forfeitures 24,933
Revenues from use of money & property 634,298
Intergovernmental 902,993
Service charges 6,461,001
Other revenues 931,557
Other financing sources 0

Expenditures

Total $12,098,392
General government 1,486,733
Public safety 1,724,656
Transportation 1,738,847
Community development 904,343
Health 1,532,001
Culture & leisure 1,008,055
Other 0

Local School District

(Data from School year 2007-08 except as noted)

Santa Ynez Valley Union High
PO Box 398
Santa Ynez, CA 93460
(805) 688-6487

Superintendent .... Paul Turnbull
Grade plan 9-12
Number of schools 2
Enrollment 1,130
High school graduates, 2006-07 257
Dropout rate 1.3%
Pupil/teacher ratio 23.1
Average class size 24.3
Students per computer 2.4
Classrooms with internet 73
Avg. Daily Attendance (ADA) 1,069
Cost per ADA $10,952
Avg. Teacher Salary $69,469

California Achievement Tests 6th ed., 2008

(Pct scoring at or above 50th National Percentile Rank)

	Math	Reading	Language
Grade 3	NA	NA	NA
Grade 7	NA	NA	NA

Academic Performance Index, 2008

Number of students tested 819
Number of valid scores 793
2007 API (base) 795
2008 API (growth) 787

SAT Testing, 2006-07

Enrollment, Grade 12 279
Number taking test 136
percent taking test 48.8%
percent with total score 1,500+ 32.30%

Average Scores:

Math	Verbal	Writing	Total
537	539	526	1,602

Federal No Child Left Behind, 2008

(Adequate Yearly Progress standards met)

	Participation Rate	Pct Proficient
ELA	No	Yes
Math	Yes	Yes

API criteria .... Yes
Graduation rate .... Yes
\# criteria met/possible 20/19

Other school districts for this city

(see Appendix E for information on these districts)

Ballard Elem, Solvang Elem

See Introduction for an explanation of all data sources.

Demographics & Socio-Economic Characteristics

(2000 Decennial Census, except as noted)

Population

1990*	8,121
2000	9,128
Male	4,100
Female	5,028
Jan. 2008 (estimate)§	9,943
Persons per sq. mi. of land	3,682.6

Race & Hispanic Origin, 2000

Race	
White	8,562
Black/African American	33
North American Native	31
Asian	155
Pacific Islander	5
Other Race	147
Two or more races	195
Hispanic origin, total	625
Mexican	421
Puerto Rican	21
Cuban	3
Other Hispanic	180

Age & Nativity, 2000

Under 5 years	450
18 years and over	7,434
65 years and over	2,213
85 years and over	446
Median Age	46.8
Native-born	8,159
Foreign-born	719

Educational Attainment, 2000

Population 25 years and over	6,921
Less than 9th grade	2.4%
High school grad or higher	91.7%
Bachelor's degree or higher	38.8%
Graduate degree	12.6%

Income & Poverty, 1999

Per capita income	$32,387
Median household income	$50,505
Median family income	$65,600
Persons in poverty	3.6%
H'holds receiving public assistance	65
H'holds receiving social security	1,687

Households, 2000

Total households	4,373
With persons under 18	989
With persons over 65	1,676
Family households	2,362
Single person households	1,716
Persons per household	2.07
Persons per family	2.77

Household Population, 2008§§

Persons living in households	9,852
Persons living in group quarters	91
Persons per household	2.0

Labor & Employment

Total civilian labor force, 2008§§	4,900
Unemployment rate, 2008	4.1%
Total civilian labor force, 2000	4,454

Employed persons 16 years and over by occupation, 2000

Managers & professionals	1,995
Service occupations	568
Sales & office occupations	1,155
Farming, fishing & forestry	13
Construction & maintenance	331
Production & transportation	255
Self-employed persons	599

* US Census Bureau
** 2000 Decennial Census
§ California Department of Finance
§§ California Employment Development Dept

General Information

City of Sonoma
No 1, The Plaza
Sonoma, CA 95476
707-938-3681

Website	www.sonomacity.org
Elevation	84 ft.
Land Area (sq. miles)	2.7
Water Area (sq. miles)	0
Year of Incorporation	1883
Government type	General law
Sales tax rate	9.00%

Voters & Officials

Registered Voters, October 2008

Total	6,600
Democrats	3,503
Republicans	1,584
Declined to state	1,230

Legislative Districts

US Congressional	1
State Senatorial	2
State Assembly	6

Local Officials, 2009

Mayor	Ken Brown
Manager	Linda Kelly
City Clerk	Gay Rainsbarger
Attorney	Tom Curry
Finance Dir	Carol Giovanatto
Public Works	Milenka Bates
Planning/Dev Dir	David Goodison
Building	Wayne Wirick
Police Chief	Bret Sackett
Fire Chief	Phil Garcia

Public Safety

Number of officers, 2007	NA
Violent crimes, 2007	33
Property crimes, 2007	252
Arson, 2007	4

Public Library

Sonoma Valley Regional Library
Sonoma County Library System
755 W Napa St
Sonoma, CA 95476
707-996-5217

Branch Librarian	Stephan Buffy

Library system statistics, FY 2007

Population served	481,785
Internet terminals	140
Annual users	299,464

Per capita:

Operating income	$32.97
percent from local government	87.7%
Operating expenditure	$30.18
Total materials	1.60
Print holdings	1.49
Visits per capita	5.11

Housing & Construction

Housing Units

Total, 2008§	5,218
Single family units, attached	752
Single family units, detached	2,957
Multiple family units	1,072
Mobile home units	437
Occupied	4,890
Vacancy rate	6.3%
Median rent, 2000**	$959
Median SF home value, 2000**	$342,900

New Privately Owned Housing Units Authorized by Building Permit, 2007*

	Units	Construction Cost
Single	33	$7,304,385
Total	33	$7,304,385

Municipal Finance

(For local fiscal year ended in 2006)

Revenues

Total	$19,673,779
Taxes	7,306,325
Special benefits assessment	57,337
Licenses & permits	21,236
Fines & forfeitures	55,357
Revenues from use of money & property	589,073
Intergovernmental	1,345,783
Service charges	7,309,782
Other revenues	2,988,886
Other financing sources	0

Expenditures

Total	$16,998,741
General government	2,587,771
Public safety	7,457,980
Transportation	1,297,790
Community development	1,100,149
Health	516,020
Culture & leisure	476,360
Other	0

Local School District

(Data from School year 2007-08 except as noted)

Sonoma Valley Unified
17850 Railroad Ave
Sonoma, CA 95476
(707) 935-6000

Superintendent	Pamela Martens
Grade plan	K-12
Number of schools	13
Enrollment	4,797
High school graduates, 2006-07	290
Dropout rate	2.2%
Pupil/teacher ratio	19.7
Average class size	24.1
Students per computer	5.2
Classrooms with internet	242
Avg. Daily Attendance (ADA)	4,330
Cost per ADA	$8,455
Avg. Teacher Salary	$58,442

California Achievement Tests 6th ed., 2008

(Pct scoring at or above 50th National Percentile Rank)

	Math	Reading	Language
Grade 3	48%	36%	39%
Grade 7	47%	48%	46%

Academic Performance Index, 2008

Number of students tested	3,333
Number of valid scores	3,178
2007 API (base)	732
2008 API (growth)	728

SAT Testing, 2006-07

Enrollment, Grade 12	330
Number taking test	117
percent taking test	35.5%
percent with total score 1,500+	23.60%

Average Scores:

Math	Verbal	Writing	Total
543	535	540	1,618

Federal No Child Left Behind, 2008

(Adequate Yearly Progress standards met)

	Participation Rate	Pct Proficient
ELA	Yes	No
Math	Yes	No

API criteria	Yes
Graduation rate	Yes
# criteria met/possible	26/18

Other school districts for this city

(see Appendix E for information on these districts)

None

See Introduction for an explanation of all data sources.

Demographics & Socio-Economic Characteristics

(2000 Decennial Census, except as noted)

Population

1990* . . . 4,153
2000 . . . 4,423
Male . . . 2,003
Female . . . 2,420
Jan. 2008 (estimate)§ . . . 4,698
Persons per sq. mi. of land . . . 1,566.0

Race & Hispanic Origin, 2000

Race
White . . . 4,041
Black/African American . . . 30
North American Native . . . 66
Asian . . . 54
Pacific Islander . . . 6
Other Race . . . 88
Two or more races . . . 138
Hispanic origin, total . . . 372
Mexican . . . 249
Puerto Rican . . . 15
Cuban . . . 0
Other Hispanic . . . 108

Age & Nativity, 2000

Under 5 years . . . 265
18 years and over . . . 3,522
65 years and over . . . 901
85 years and over . . . 203
Median Age . . . 41.1
Native-born . . . 4,269
Foreign-born . . . 124

Educational Attainment, 2000

Population 25 years and over . . . 2,963
Less than 9th grade . . . 6.5%
High school grad or higher . . . 86.1%
Bachelor's degree or higher . . . 16.2%
Graduate degree . . . 6.8%

Income & Poverty, 1999

Per capita income . . . $19,248
Median household income . . . $28,858
Median family income . . . $39,722
Persons in poverty . . . 16.0%
H'holds receiving public assistance . . . 85
H'holds receiving social security . . . 615

Households, 2000

Total households . . . 2,051
With persons under 18 . . . 543
With persons over 65 . . . 572
Family households . . . 1,045
Single person households . . . 827
Persons per household . . . 2.06
Persons per family . . . 2.75

Household Population, 2008§§

Persons living in households . . . 4,499
Persons living in group quarters . . . 199
Persons per household . . . 2.0

Labor & Employment

Total civilian labor force, 2008§§ . . . 2,480
Unemployment rate, 2008 . . . 8.1%
Total civilian labor force, 2000 . . . 2,062

Employed persons 16 years and over by occupation, 2000

Managers & professionals . . . 583
Service occupations . . . 434
Sales & office occupations . . . 406
Farming, fishing & forestry . . . 8
Construction & maintenance . . . 252
Production & transportation . . . 216
Self-employed persons . . . 183

* US Census Bureau
** 2000 Decennial Census
§ California Department of Finance
§§ California Employment Development Dept

General Information

City of Sonora
94 N Washington St
Sonora, CA 95370
209-532-4541

Website . . . www.sonoraca.com
Elevation . . . NA
Land Area (sq. miles) . . . 3.0
Water Area (sq. miles) . . . 0
Year of Incorporation . . . 1851
Government type . . . General law
Sales tax rate . . . 8.75%

Voters & Officials

Registered Voters, October 2008

Total . . . 2,719
Democrats . . . 1,061
Republicans . . . 980
Declined to state . . . 542

Legislative Districts

US Congressional . . . 19
State Senatorial . . . 14
State Assembly . . . 25

Local Officials, 2009

Mayor . . . Ron Stearn
Manager . . . Greg Applegate
City Clerk . . . Marijane Cassinetto
Attorney . . . R. Matranga
Finance Dir . . . Karen Stark
Public Works . . . Ed Wyllie
Planning/Dev Dir . . . Ed Wyllie
Building . . . Ed Wyllie
Police Chief . . . Mark Stinson
Emergency/Fire Dir . . . Mike Barrows

Public Safety

Number of officers, 2007 . . . 17
Violent crimes, 2007 . . . 15
Property crimes, 2007 . . . 399
Arson, 2007 . . . 1

Public Library

Main Branch
Tuolumne County Library System
480 Greenley Rd
Sonora, CA 95370
209-533-5945

Director Lib Svcs . . . Constance Corcoran

Library system statistics, FY 2007

Population served . . . 57,223
Internet terminals . . . 22
Annual users . . . 21,300

Per capita:

Operating income . . . $18.20
percent from local government . . . 86.5%
Operating expenditure . . . $20.58
Total materials . . . 1.50
Print holdings . . . 1.39
Visits per capita . . . 6.45

Housing & Construction

Housing Units

Total, 2008§ . . . 2,411
Single family units, attached . . . 86
Single family units, detached . . . 1,441
Multiple family units . . . 850
Mobile home units . . . 34
Occupied . . . 2,251
Vacancy rate . . . 6.6%
Median rent, 2000** . . . $481
Median SF home value, 2000** . . . $136,400

New Privately Owned Housing Units Authorized by Building Permit, 2007*

	Units	Construction Cost
Single	3	$651,215
Total	3	$651,215

Municipal Finance

(For local fiscal year ended in 2006)

Revenues

Total . . . $8,060,375
Taxes . . . 3,796,513
Special benefits assessment . . . 89,810
Licenses & permits . . . 172,292
Fines & forfeitures . . . 128,364
Revenues from use of money & property . . . 384,899
Intergovernmental . . . 2,968,522
Service charges . . . 103,669
Other revenues . . . 335,216
Other financing sources . . . 81,090

Expenditures

Total . . . $6,500,228
General government . . . 765,065
Public safety . . . 3,903,725
Transportation . . . 962,967
Community development . . . 666,306
Health . . . 41,308
Culture & leisure . . . 160,857
Other . . . 0

Local School District

(Data from School year 2007-08 except as noted)

Sonora Union High
251 South Barretta St
Sonora, CA 95370
(209) 533-8510

Superintendent . . . Michael McCoy
Grade plan . . . 9-12
Number of schools . . . 4
Enrollment . . . 1,540
High school graduates, 2006-07 . . . 390
Dropout rate . . . 2.4%
Pupil/teacher ratio . . . 23.5
Average class size . . . 26.2
Students per computer . . . 2.8
Classrooms with internet . . . 77
Avg. Daily Attendance (ADA) . . . 1,419
Cost per ADA . . . $9,617
Avg. Teacher Salary . . . $64,518

California Achievement Tests 6th ed., 2008

(Pct scoring at or above 50th National Percentile Rank)

	Math	Reading	Language
Grade 3	NA	NA	NA
Grade 7	NA	NA	NA

Academic Performance Index, 2008

Number of students tested . . . 1,099
Number of valid scores . . . 1,052
2007 API (base) . . . 729
2008 API (growth) . . . 739

SAT Testing, 2006-07

Enrollment, Grade 12 . . . 421
Number taking test . . . 104
percent taking test . . . 24.7%
percent with total score 1,500+ . . . 16.40%

Average Scores:

Math	Verbal	Writing	Total
529	546	536	1,611

Federal No Child Left Behind, 2008

(Adequate Yearly Progress standards met)

	Participation Rate	Pct Proficient
ELA	Yes	Yes
Math	Yes	Yes

API criteria . . . Yes
Graduation rate . . . Yes
criteria met/possible . . . 14/14

Other school districts for this city

(see Appendix E for information on these districts)

Belleview Elem, Curtis Creek Elem, Sonora Elem

See Introduction for an explanation of all data sources.

Demographics & Socio-Economic Characteristics

(2000 Decennial Census, except as noted)

Population

1990* 20,850
2000 21,144
Male 10,856
Female 10,288
Jan. 2008 (estimate)§ 22,391
Persons per sq. mi. of land 7,721.0

Race & Hispanic Origin, 2000

Race
White 8,586
Black/African American 80
North American Native 332
Asian 1,783
Pacific Islander 39
Other Race 9,300
Two or more races 1,024
Hispanic origin, total 18,190
Mexican 15,687
Puerto Rican 45
Cuban 32
Other Hispanic 2,426

Age & Nativity, 2000

Under 5 years 2,017
18 years and over 14,057
65 years and over 1,518
85 years and over 119
Median Age 26.9
Native-born 10,074
Foreign-born 10,861

Educational Attainment, 2000

Population 25 years and over 11,137
Less than 9th grade 39.3%
High school grad or higher 35.6%
Bachelor's degree or higher 3.1%
Graduate degree 1.0%

Income & Poverty, 1999

Per capita income $10,130
Median household income $34,656
Median family income $34,349
Persons in poverty 18.7%
H'holds receiving public assistance 476
H'holds receiving social security 1,028

Households, 2000

Total households 4,620
With persons under 18 2,931
With persons over 65 1,133
Family households 4,088
Single person households 371
Persons per household 4.57
Persons per family 4.61

Household Population, 2008§§

Persons living in households 22,373
Persons living in group quarters 18
Persons per household 4.8

Labor & Employment

Total civilian labor force, 2008§§ 9,500
Unemployment rate, 2008 .... 9.1%
Total civilian labor force, 2000 8,220

Employed persons 16 years and over by occupation, 2000

Managers & professionals 849
Service occupations 992
Sales & office occupations 1,678
Farming, fishing & forestry 47
Construction & maintenance 704
Production & transportation 3,132
Self-employed persons 337

* US Census Bureau
** 2000 Decennial Census
§ California Department of Finance
§§ California Employment Development Dept

General Information

City of South El Monte
1415 Santa Anita Ave
South El Monte, CA 91733
626-579-6540

Website .... www.ci.south-el-monte.ca.us
Elevation .... 244 ft.
Land Area (sq. miles) 2.9
Water Area (sq. miles) 0
Year of Incorporation 1958
Government type .... General law
Sales tax rate 9.25%

Voters & Officials

Registered Voters, October 2008

Total 6,422
Democrats 3,906
Republicans 952
Declined to state 1,353

Legislative Districts

US Congressional 32
State Senatorial 30
State Assembly 49

Local Officials, 2009

Mayor .... Blanca Figueroa
Manager .... Anthony R. Ybarra
City Clerk .... Vida Barone (Int)
Attorney .... Quinn Barrow
Finance Dir .... Ira Peterson
Public Works .... Patrick Lang
Community Dev Dir .... Manuel A. Mancha
Building .... NA
Police Captain .... Richard Shaw
Fire Chief .... (County)

Public Safety

Number of officers, 2007 .... NA
Violent crimes, 2007 144
Property crimes, 2007 641
Arson, 2007 4

Public Library

South El Monte Library
Los Angeles County Public Library System
1430 N Central Ave
South El Monte, CA 91733
626-443-4158

Branch Librarian .... Roberta Marquez

Library system statistics, FY 2007

Population served 3,673,313
Internet terminals 749
Annual users 3,748,771

Per capita:

Operating income $30.06
percent from local government 93.6%
Operating expenditure $28.36
Total materials 2.22
Print holdings 1.97
Visits per capita 3.25

Housing & Construction

Housing Units

Total, 2008§ 4,774
Single family units, attached 458
Single family units, detached 2,984
Multiple family units 828
Mobile home units 504
Occupied 4,669
Vacancy rate 2.2%
Median rent, 2000** $684
Median SF home value, 2000** $157,100

New Privately Owned Housing Units Authorized by Building Permit, 2007*

	Units	Construction Cost
Single	5	$870,829
Total	5	$870,829

Municipal Finance

(For local fiscal year ended in 2006)

Revenues

Total $11,483,179
Taxes 8,559,545
Special benefits assessment 0
Licenses & permits 455,909
Fines & forfeitures 234,564
Revenues from use of money & property 254,016
Intergovernmental 1,689,211
Service charges 132,225
Other revenues 157,709
Other financing sources 0

Expenditures

Total $12,305,530
General government 3,036,983
Public safety 3,033,610
Transportation 2,883,595
Community development 1,348,970
Health 0
Culture & leisure 2,002,372
Other 0

Local School District

(Data from School year 2007-08 except as noted)

El Monte Union High
3537 Johnson Ave
El Monte, CA 91731
(626) 444-9005

Superintendent .... Kathy Furnald
Grade plan 9-12
Number of schools 7
Enrollment 10,614
High school graduates, 2006-07 1,665
Dropout rate 1.8%
Pupil/teacher ratio 23.4
Average class size 27.3
Students per computer 2.8
Classrooms with internet 529
Avg. Daily Attendance (ADA) 10,804
Cost per ADA $8,087
Avg. Teacher Salary $68,066

California Achievement Tests 6th ed., 2008

(Pct scoring at or above 50th National Percentile Rank)

	Math	Reading	Language
Grade 3	NA	NA	NA
Grade 7	NA	NA	NA

Academic Performance Index, 2008

Number of students tested 7,727
Number of valid scores 7,301
2007 API (base) 648
2008 API (growth) 670

SAT Testing, 2006-07

Enrollment, Grade 12 2,388
Number taking test 700
percent taking test 29.3%
percent with total score 1,500+ 9.70%

Average Scores:

Math	Verbal	Writing	Total
492	450	447	1,389

Federal No Child Left Behind, 2008

(Adequate Yearly Progress standards met)

	Participation Rate	Pct Proficient
ELA	Yes	No
Math	Yes	No

API criteria .... Yes
Graduation rate .... Yes
\# criteria met/possible 27/24

Other school districts for this city

(see Appendix E for information on these districts)

El Monte Elem, Mountain View Elem, Valle Lindo Elem

See Introduction for an explanation of all data sources.

Demographics & Socio-Economic Characteristics†

(2007 American Community Survey, except as noted)

Population

1990* ... 86,284
2007 ... 104,031
Male ... 52,074
Female ... 51,957
Jan. 2008 (estimate)§ ... 102,816
Persons per sq. mi. of land ... 13,894.1

Race & Hispanic Origin, 2007

Race
White ... 57,459
Black/African American ... 301
North American Native ... 652
Asian ... 479
Pacific Islander ... 0
Other Race ... 44,443
Two or more races ... 697
Hispanic origin, total ... NA
Mexican ... 86,978
Puerto Rican ... 118
Cuban ... 946
Other Hispanic ... 13,072

Age & Nativity, 2007

Under 5 years ... 8,744
18 years and over ... 71,154
65 years and over ... 6,330
85 years and over ... 812
Median Age ... 27.7
Native-born ... 53,926
Foreign-born ... 50,105

Educational Attainment, 2007

Population 25 years and over ... 56,891
Less than 9th grade ... 38.8%
High school grad or higher ... 45.9%
Bachelor's degree or higher ... 5.9%
Graduate degree ... 1.8%

Income & Poverty, 2007

Per capita income ... $13,282
Median household income ... $41,196
Median family income ... $42,621
Persons in poverty ... 16.1%
H'holds receiving public assistance ... 1,229
H'holds receiving social security ... 4,379

Households, 2007

Total households ... 24,361
With persons under 18 ... 15,034
With persons over 65 ... 4,579
Family households ... 22,424
Single person households ... 1,725
Persons per household ... 4.27
Persons per family ... 4.49

Household Population, 2008§§

Persons living in households ... 102,675
Persons living in group quarters ... 141
Persons per household ... 4.3

Labor & Employment

Total civilian labor force, 2008§§ ... 41,700
Unemployment rate, 2008 ... 9.7%
Total civilian labor force, 2000* ... 35,782

Employed persons 16 years and over by occupation, 2007

Managers & professionals ... 5,259
Service occupations ... 9,755
Sales & office occupations ... 13,875
Farming, fishing & forestry ... 211
Construction & maintenance ... 3,851
Production & transportation ... 9,186
Self-employed persons ... 1,232

† see Appendix D for 2000 Decennial Census Data
* US Census Bureau
** 2007 American Community Survey
§ California Department of Finance
§§ California Employment Development Dept

General Information

City of South Gate
8650 California Ave
South Gate, CA 90280
323-563-9500

Website ... www.cityofsouthgate.org
Elevation ... 111 ft.
Land Area (sq. miles) ... 7.4
Water Area (sq. miles) ... 0.1
Year of Incorporation ... 1923
Government type ... General law
Sales tax rate ... 10.25%

Voters & Officials

Registered Voters, October 2008

Total ... 30,931
Democrats ... 19,937
Republicans ... 4,288
Declined to state ... 5,464

Legislative Districts

US Congressional ... 39
State Senatorial ... 27, 30
State Assembly ... 50

Local Officials, 2009

Mayor ... Gil Hurtado
Manager ... Ronald Bates
City Clerk ... Carmen Avalos
Attorney ... Raul F. Salinas
Finance Dir ... Rudy Navarro
Public Works ... Robert Dickey
Planning/Dev Dir ... NA
Building ... NA
Police Chief ... Vincent Avila
Fire/Emergency Mgmt ... (County)

Public Safety

Number of officers, 2007 ... 91
Violent crimes, 2007 ... 577
Property crimes, 2007 ... 2,921
Arson, 2007 ... 23

Public Library

Leland R. Weaver Library
Los Angeles County Public Library System
4035 Tweedy Blvd
South Gate, CA 90280
323-567-8853

Library Manager ... Eileen McAllen Tokar

Library system statistics, FY 2007

Population served ... 3,673,313
Internet terminals ... 749
Annual users ... 3,748,771

Per capita:

Operating income ... $30.06
percent from local government ... 93.6%
Operating expenditure ... $28.36
Total materials ... 2.22
Print holdings ... 1.97
Visits per capita ... 3.25

Housing & Construction

Housing Units

Total, 2008§ ... 24,708
Single family units, attached ... 3,294
Single family units, detached ... 12,543
Multiple family units ... 8,582
Mobile home units ... 289
Occupied ... 23,633
Vacancy rate ... 4.4%
Median rent, 2007** ... $952
Median SF home value, 2007** ... $469,200

New Privately Owned Housing Units Authorized by Building Permit, 2007*

	Units	Construction Cost
Single	65	$7,955,352
Total	65	$7,955,352

Municipal Finance

(For local fiscal year ended in 2006)

Revenues

Total ... $79,104,108
Taxes ... 24,265,019
Special benefits assessment ... 2,063,016
Licenses & permits ... 1,479,765
Fines & forfeitures ... 3,117,063
Revenues from use of money & property ... 3,518,689
Intergovernmental ... 13,796,399
Service charges ... 17,734,582
Other revenues ... 11,704,575
Other financing sources ... 1,425,000

Expenditures

Total ... $68,580,754
General government ... 10,234,902
Public safety ... 20,280,908
Transportation ... 9,577,739
Community development ... 11,541,466
Health ... 3,570,190
Culture & leisure ... 3,958,297
Other ... 280,031

Local School District

(Data from School year 2007-08 except as noted)

Los Angeles Unified
333 South Beaudry Ave
Los Angeles, CA 90017
(213) 241-1000

Superintendent ... Ramon Cortines
Grade plan ... PK-12
Number of schools ... 827
Enrollment ... 693,680
High school graduates, 2006-07 ... 28,545
Dropout rate ... 7.8%
Pupil/teacher ratio ... 19.8
Average class size ... 24.9
Students per computer ... 3.7
Classrooms with internet ... 31,112
Avg. Daily Attendance (ADA) ... 653,672
Cost per ADA ... $10,053
Avg. Teacher Salary ... $63,391

California Achievement Tests 6th ed., 2008

(Pct scoring at or above 50th National Percentile Rank)

	Math	Reading	Language
Grade 3	49%	27%	39%
Grade 7	37%	33%	33%

Academic Performance Index, 2008

Number of students tested ... 495,046
Number of valid scores ... 471,641
2007 API (base) ... 662
2008 API (growth) ... 683

SAT Testing, 2006-07

Enrollment, Grade 12 ... 32,370
Number taking test ... 15,447
percent taking test ... 47.7%
percent with total score 1,500+ ... 12.50%

Average Scores:

Math	Verbal	Writing	Total
443	438	441	1,322

Federal No Child Left Behind, 2008

(Adequate Yearly Progress standards met)

	Participation Rate	Pct Proficient
ELA	Yes	No
Math	Yes	No

API criteria ... Yes
Graduation rate ... Yes
criteria met/possible ... 46/38

Other school districts for this city

(see Appendix E for information on these districts)

Paramount Unified

See Introduction for an explanation of all data sources.

Demographics & Socio-Economic Characteristics

(2000 Decennial Census, except as noted)

Population

1990* 21,586
2000 23,609
Male 12,203
Female 11,406
Jan. 2008 (estimate)§ 23,725
Persons per sq. mi. of land 2,349.0

Race & Hispanic Origin, 2000

Race
White 17,878
Black/African American 178
North American Native 228
Asian 1,419
Pacific Islander 40
Other Race 2,946
Two or more races 920
Hispanic origin, total 6,294
Mexican 5,216
Puerto Rican 70
Cuban 26
Other Hispanic 982

Age & Nativity, 2000

Under 5 years 1,564
18 years and over 17,669
65 years and over 2,023
85 years and over 163
Median Age 33.4
Native-born 18,406
Foreign-born 5,314

Educational Attainment, 2000

Population 25 years and over 15,011
Less than 9th grade 7.8%
High school grad or higher 80.8%
Bachelor's degree or higher 18.6%
Graduate degree 4.8%

Income & Poverty, 1999

Per capita income $18,452
Median household income $34,707
Median family income $40,572
Persons in poverty 12.4%
H'holds receiving public assistance 387
H'holds receiving social security 1,919

Households, 2000

Total households 9,410
With persons under 18 3,164
With persons over 65 1,579
Family households 5,389
Single person households 2,741
Persons per household 2.50
Persons per family 3.15

Household Population, 2008§§

Persons living in households 23,597
Persons living in group quarters 128
Persons per household 2.4

Labor & Employment

Total civilian labor force, 2008§§ 15,400
Unemployment rate, 2008 .... 9.5%
Total civilian labor force, 2000 12,909

Employed persons 16 years and over by occupation, 2000

Managers & professionals 2,691
Service occupations 4,502
Sales & office occupations 2,745
Farming, fishing & forestry 121
Construction & maintenance 1,014
Production & transportation 880
Self-employed persons 985

* US Census Bureau
** 2000 Decennial Census
§ California Department of Finance
§§ California Employment Development Dept

General Information

City of South Lake Tahoe
1901 Airport Rd
South Lake Tahoe, CA 96150
530-542-6000

Website .... www.cityofslt.us
Elevation .... 6,260 ft.
Land Area (sq. miles) 10.1
Water Area (sq. miles) 6.4
Year of Incorporation 1965
Government type .... General law
Sales tax rate 8.75%

Voters & Officials

Registered Voters, October 2008

Total 9,792
Democrats 3,979
Republicans 2,311
Declined to state 2,672

Legislative Districts

US Congressional 4
State Senatorial 1
State Assembly 4

Local Officials, 2009

Mayor .... Jerry Birdwell
Manager .... David Jinkens
City Clerk .... Susan Alessi
Attorney .... Catherine DiCamillo
Finance Dir .... Christine Vuletich
Public Works .... John Greenhut
Planning/Dev Dir .... Teri Jamin
Building .... Ron Ticknor
Police Chief .... Terry Daniels
Fire Chief .... Lorenzo Gigliotti

Public Safety

Number of officers, 2007 35
Violent crimes, 2007 163
Property crimes, 2007 603
Arson, 2007 1

Public Library

South Lake Tahoe Library
El Dorado County Library
1000 Rufus Allen Blvd
South Lake Tahoe, CA 96150
530-573-3185

Branch Librarian .... Sally Neitling

Library system statistics, FY 2007

Population served 178,674
Internet terminals 39
Annual users 71,838

Per capita:

Operating income $16.42
percent from local government 85.4%
Operating expenditure $16.31
Total materials 2.07
Print holdings 1.94
Visits per capita 1.38

Housing & Construction

Housing Units

Total, 2008§ 14,355
Single family units, attached 361
Single family units, detached 9,063
Multiple family units 4,263
Mobile home units 668
Occupied 9,645
Vacancy rate 32.8%
Median rent, 2000** $642
Median SF home value, 2000** $157,800

New Privately Owned Housing Units Authorized by Building Permit, 2007*

	Units	Construction Cost
Single	52	$12,728,971
Total	52	$12,728,971

Municipal Finance

(For local fiscal year ended in 2006)

Revenues

Total $36,462,792
Taxes 24,156,006
Special benefits assessment 0
Licenses & permits 996,372
Fines & forfeitures 393,326
Revenues from use of money & property 821,312
Intergovernmental 4,949,884
Service charges 5,024,677
Other revenues 121,215
Other financing sources 0

Expenditures

Total $38,572,465
General government 9,269,064
Public safety 13,679,092
Transportation 6,800,662
Community development 5,703,029
Health 0
Culture & leisure 3,120,618
Other 0

Local School District

(Data from School year 2007-08 except as noted)

Lake Tahoe Unified
1021 Al Tahoe Blvd
South Lake Tahoe, CA 96150
(530) 541-2850

Superintendent .... James Tarwater
Grade plan K-12
Number of schools 8
Enrollment 4,182
High school graduates, 2006-07 342
Dropout rate 5.0%
Pupil/teacher ratio 19.8
Average class size 24.8
Students per computer 2.7
Classrooms with internet 231
Avg. Daily Attendance (ADA) 3,925
Cost per ADA $9,281
Avg. Teacher Salary $65,239

California Achievement Tests 6th ed., 2008

(Pct scoring at or above 50th National Percentile Rank)

	Math	Reading	Language
Grade 3	48%	35%	41%
Grade 7	62%	57%	51%

Academic Performance Index, 2008

Number of students tested 3,040
Number of valid scores 2,883
2007 API (base) 736
2008 API (growth) 741

SAT Testing, 2006-07

Enrollment, Grade 12 388
Number taking test 118
percent taking test 30.4%
percent with total score 1,500+ 18.30%

Average Scores:

Math	Verbal	Writing	Total
524	514	516	1,554

Federal No Child Left Behind, 2008

(Adequate Yearly Progress standards met)

	Participation Rate	Pct Proficient
ELA	Yes	No
Math	Yes	No

API criteria .... Yes
Graduation rate .... Yes
criteria met/possible 26/19

Other school districts for this city

(see Appendix E for information on these districts)

None

See Introduction for an explanation of all data sources.

Demographics & Socio-Economic Characteristics

(2000 Decennial Census, except as noted)

Population

1990* 23,936
2000 24,292
Male 11,272
Female 13,020
Jan. 2008 (estimate)§ 25,792
Persons per sq. mi. of land 7,585.9

Race & Hispanic Origin, 2000

Race
White 14,653
Black/African American 738
North American Native 83
Asian 6,456
Pacific Islander 20
Other Race 1,257
Two or more races 1,085
Hispanic origin, total 3,903
Mexican 2,697
Puerto Rican 57
Cuban 87
Other Hispanic 1,062

Age & Nativity, 2000

Under 5 years 1,162
18 years and over 18,804
65 years and over 2,772
85 years and over 357
Median Age 37.4
Native-born 18,377
Foreign-born 5,926

Educational Attainment, 2000

Population 25 years and over 17,064
Less than 9th grade 1.8%
High school grad or higher 93.6%
Bachelor's degree or higher 56.1%
Graduate degree 25.0%

Income & Poverty, 1999

Per capita income $32,620
Median household income $55,728
Median family income $72,039
Persons in poverty 6.0%
H'holds receiving public assistance 159
H'holds receiving social security 2,008

Households, 2000

Total households 10,477
With persons under 18 3,241
With persons over 65 2,000
Family households 6,003
Single person households 3,661
Persons per household 2.30
Persons per family 3.05

Household Population, 2008§§

Persons living in households 25,605
Persons living in group quarters 187
Persons per household 2.4

Labor & Employment

Total civilian labor force, 2008§§ 15,700
Unemployment rate, 2008 . . . . 3.7%
Total civilian labor force, 2000 13,466

Employed persons 16 years and over by occupation, 2000

Managers & professionals 7,709
Service occupations 1,049
Sales & office occupations 3,250
Farming, fishing & forestry 9
Construction & maintenance 315
Production & transportation 623
Self-employed persons 1,443

* US Census Bureau
** 2000 Decennial Census
§ California Department of Finance
§§ California Employment Development Dept

General Information

City of South Pasadena
1414 Mission St
South Pasadena, CA 91030
626-403-7230

Website . . . . www.ci.south-pasadena.ca.us
Elevation . . . . 660 ft.
Land Area (sq. miles) 3.4
Water Area (sq. miles) 0
Year of Incorporation 1888
Government type . . . . General law
Sales tax rate 9.25%

Voters & Officials

Registered Voters, October 2008

Total 15,441
Democrats 7,072
Republicans 4,199
Declined to state 3,551

Legislative Districts

US Congressional 29
State Senatorial 22
State Assembly 44

Local Officials, 2009

Mayor . . . . David Sifuentes
Manager . . . . Lillian Myers
City Clerk . . . . Sally Kilby
Attorney . . . . Richard Adams II
Finance Dir . . . . Chu Thai
Public Works . . . . Matthew Sweeney
Planning/Dev Dir . . . . David Watkins
Building . . . . David Watkins
Police Chief . . . . Daniel Watson
Fire Chief . . . . Jerry Wallace

Public Safety

Number of officers, 2007 36
Violent crimes, 2007 36
Property crimes, 2007 436
Arson, 2007 4

Public Library

South Pasadena Public Library
1100 Oxley St
South Pasadena, CA 91030
626-403-7330

City Librarian . . . . Steve Fjeldsted

Library statistics, FY 2007

Population served 25,824
Internet terminals 8
Annual users 30,047

Per capita:

Operating income $60.18
percent from local government 91.4%
Operating expenditure $54.70
Total materials 5.50
Print holdings 5.02
Visits per capita 10.12

Housing & Construction

Housing Units

Total, 2008§ 11,001
Single family units, attached 646
Single family units, detached 5,101
Multiple family units 5,240
Mobile home units 14
Occupied 10,623
Vacancy rate 3.4%
Median rent, 2000** $833
Median SF home value, 2000** $383,600

New Privately Owned Housing Units Authorized by Building Permit, 2007*

	Units	Construction Cost
Single	7	$1,909,360
Total	26	$3,884,360

Municipal Finance

(For local fiscal year ended in 2006)

Revenues

Total $29,236,918
Taxes 12,958,480
Special benefits assessment 1,300,567
Licenses & permits 823,059
Fines & forfeitures 603,086
Revenues from use of money & property 874,865
Intergovernmental 4,478,038
Service charges 7,385,654
Other revenues 813,169
Other financing sources 0

Expenditures

Total $31,056,092
General government 3,664,665
Public safety 10,239,819
Transportation 5,244,416
Community development 982,838
Health 526,014
Culture & leisure 2,582,865
Other 0

Local School District

(Data from School year 2007-08 except as noted)

South Pasadena Unified
1020 El Centro St
South Pasadena, CA 91030
(626) 441-5810

Superintendent . . . . Brian Bristol
Grade plan K-12
Number of schools 5
Enrollment 4,258
High school graduates, 2006-07 365
Dropout rate 0.8%
Pupil/teacher ratio 23.0
Average class size 27.5
Students per computer 7.2
Classrooms with internet 198
Avg. Daily Attendance (ADA) 4,210
Cost per ADA $7,530
Avg. Teacher Salary $73,096

California Achievement Tests 6th ed., 2008

(Pct scoring at or above 50th National Percentile Rank)

	Math	Reading	Language
Grade 3	88%	72%	81%
Grade 7	83%	78%	77%

Academic Performance Index, 2008

Number of students tested 3,354
Number of valid scores 3,219
2007 API (base) 879
2008 API (growth) 891

SAT Testing, 2006-07

Enrollment, Grade 12 395
Number taking test 307
percent taking test 77.7%
percent with total score 1,500+ 59.50%

Average Scores:

Math	Verbal	Writing	Total
597	550	550	1,697

Federal No Child Left Behind, 2008

(Adequate Yearly Progress standards met)

	Participation Rate	Pct Proficient
ELA	No	Yes
Math	Yes	Yes

API criteria . . . . Yes
Graduation rate . . . . Yes
\# criteria met/possible 30/29

Other school districts for this city

(see Appendix E for information on these districts)

None

See Introduction for an explanation of all data sources.

Demographics & Socio-Economic Characteristics

(2000 Decennial Census, except as noted)

Population

1990* . . . 54,312
2000 . . . 60,552
Male . . . 30,009
Female . . . 30,543
Jan. 2008 (estimate)§ . . . 63,744
Persons per sq. mi. of land . . . 7,082.7

Race & Hispanic Origin, 2000

Race
White . . . 26,671
Black/African American . . . 1,707
North American Native . . . 362
Asian . . . 17,510
Pacific Islander . . . 944
Other Race . . . 9,091
Two or more races . . . 4,267
Hispanic origin, total . . . 19,282
Mexican . . . 11,086
Puerto Rican . . . 504
Cuban . . . 75
Other Hispanic . . . 7,617

Age & Nativity, 2000

Under 5 years . . . 3,914
18 years and over . . . 45,886
65 years and over . . . 7,632
85 years and over . . . 713
Median Age . . . 35.7
Native-born . . . 36,988
Foreign-born . . . 23,739

Educational Attainment, 2000

Population 25 years and over . . . 40,422
Less than 9th grade . . . 9.4%
High school grad or higher . . . 79.8%
Bachelor's degree or higher . . . 25.2%
Graduate degree . . . 5.9%

Income & Poverty, 1999

Per capita income . . . $23,562
Median household income . . . $61,764
Median family income . . . $66,598
Persons in poverty . . . 5.2%
H'holds receiving public assistance . . . 394
H'holds receiving social security . . . 5,349

Households, 2000

Total households . . . 19,677
With persons under 18 . . . 7,877
With persons over 65 . . . 5,586
Family households . . . 14,650
Single person households . . . 3,923
Persons per household . . . 3.05
Persons per family . . . 3.51

Household Population, 2008§§

Persons living in households . . . 63,301
Persons living in group quarters . . . 443
Persons per household . . . 3.1

Labor & Employment

Total civilian labor force, 2008§§ . . . 32,100
Unemployment rate, 2008 . . . 5.9%
Total civilian labor force, 2000 . . . 30,981

Employed persons 16 years and over by occupation, 2000

Managers & professionals . . . 8,973
Service occupations . . . 4,321
Sales & office occupations . . . 9,546
Farming, fishing & forestry . . . 121
Construction & maintenance . . . 2,879
Production & transportation . . . 3,956
Self-employed persons . . . 1,639

* US Census Bureau
** 2000 Decennial Census
§ California Department of Finance
§§ California Employment Development Dept

General Information

City of South San Francisco
400 Grand Ave
PO Box 711
South San Francisco, CA 94080
650-877-8518

Website . . . www.ssf.net
Elevation . . . 19 ft.
Land Area (sq. miles) . . . 9.0
Water Area (sq. miles) . . . 20.7
Year of Incorporation . . . 1908
Government type . . . General law
Sales tax rate . . . 9.25%

Voters & Officials

Registered Voters, October 2008

Total . . . 30,363
Democrats . . . 17,561
Republicans . . . 4,435
Declined to state . . . 7,339

Legislative Districts

US Congressional . . . 12
State Senatorial . . . 8
State Assembly . . . 19

Local Officials, 2009

Mayor . . . Karyl Matsumoto
Manager . . . Barry M. Nagel
City Clerk . . . Krista J. Martinelli-Larson
Attorney . . . Steve Mattas
Finance Dir . . . Jim Steele
Public Works . . . Terry White
Planning/Dev Dir . . . Susy Kalkin
Building . . . Jim Kirkman
Police Chief . . . Mark Raffaelli
Emergency/Fire Dir . . . Phil White

Public Safety

Number of officers, 2007 . . . 75
Violent crimes, 2007 . . . 177
Property crimes, 2007 . . . 1,567
Arson, 2007 . . . 26

Public Library

Main Library
South San Francisco Public Library System
840 W Orange Ave
South San Francisco, CA 94080
650-829-3860

Director . . . Valerie Sommer

Library system statistics, FY 2007

Population served . . . 62,614
Internet terminals . . . 65
Annual users . . . 98,182

Per capita:

Operating income . . . $72.82
percent from local government . . . 76.8%
Operating expenditure . . . $74.32
Total materials . . . 3.35
Print holdings . . . 2.93
Visits per capita . . . 5.39

Housing & Construction

Housing Units

Total, 2008§ . . . 20,826
Single family units, attached . . . 2,551
Single family units, detached . . . 12,020
Multiple family units . . . 5,846
Mobile home units . . . 409
Occupied . . . 20,487
Vacancy rate . . . 1.6%
Median rent, 2000** . . . $1,057
Median SF home value, 2000** . . . $352,900

New Privately Owned Housing Units Authorized by Building Permit, 2007*

	Units	Construction Cost
Single	12	$4,165,286
Total	111	$27,865,286

Municipal Finance

(For local fiscal year ended in 2006)

Revenues

Total . . . $90,956,755
Taxes . . . 41,414,696
Special benefits assessment . . . 0
Licenses & permits . . . 3,577,738
Fines & forfeitures . . . 889,085
Revenues from use of money & property . . . 3,974,259
Intergovernmental . . . 7,131,784
Service charges . . . 29,426,496
Other revenues . . . 4,542,697
Other financing sources . . . 0

Expenditures

Total . . . $81,922,935
General government . . . 7,244,814
Public safety . . . 32,672,991
Transportation . . . 13,123,095
Community development . . . 4,943,689
Health . . . 12,800,745
Culture & leisure . . . 11,137,601
Other . . . 0

Local School District

(Data from School year 2007-08 except as noted)

South San Francisco Unified
398 B St
South San Francisco, CA 94080
(650) 877-8700

Superintendent . . . Barbara Olds
Grade plan . . . K-12
Number of schools . . . 15
Enrollment . . . 9,416
High school graduates, 2006-07 . . . 619
Dropout rate . . . 1.7%
Pupil/teacher ratio . . . 21.8
Average class size . . . 26.6
Students per computer . . . 4.4
Classrooms with internet . . . 495
Avg. Daily Attendance (ADA) . . . 9,189
Cost per ADA . . . $6,959
Avg. Teacher Salary . . . $58,590

California Achievement Tests 6th ed., 2008

(Pct scoring at or above 50th National Percentile Rank)

	Math	Reading	Language
Grade 3	64%	35%	47%
Grade 7	51%	42%	47%

Academic Performance Index, 2008

Number of students tested . . . 7,143
Number of valid scores . . . 6,779
2007 API (base) . . . 745
2008 API (growth) . . . 757

SAT Testing, 2006-07

Enrollment, Grade 12 . . . 682
Number taking test . . . 284
percent taking test . . . 41.6%
percent with total score 1,500+ . . . 15.50%

Average Scores:

Math	Verbal	Writing	Total
512	471	471	1,454

Federal No Child Left Behind, 2008

(Adequate Yearly Progress standards met)

	Participation Rate	Pct Proficient
ELA	Yes	No
Math	Yes	No

API criteria . . . Yes
Graduation rate . . . Yes
\# criteria met/possible . . . 42/39

Other school districts for this city

(see Appendix E for information on these districts)

None

See Introduction for an explanation of all data sources.

Demographics & Socio-Economic Characteristics

(2000 Decennial Census, except as noted)

Population

1990* ... 30,491
2000 ... 37,403
Male ... 18,920
Female ... 18,483
Jan. 2008 (estimate)§ ... 39,276
Persons per sq. mi. of land ... 12,669.7

Race & Hispanic Origin, 2000

Race
White ... 18,541
Black/African American ... 848
North American Native ... 397
Asian ... 5,780
Pacific Islander ... 344
Other Race ... 9,616
Two or more races ... 1,877
Hispanic origin, total ... 18,285
Mexican ... 15,496
Puerto Rican ... 180
Cuban ... 56
Other Hispanic ... 2,553

Age & Nativity, 2000

Under 5 years ... 3,487
18 years and over ... 26,026
65 years and over ... 3,581
85 years and over ... 597
Median Age ... 30.0
Native-born ... 21,691
Foreign-born ... 15,243

Educational Attainment, 2000

Population 25 years and over ... 22,001
Less than 9th grade ... 18.3%
High school grad or higher ... 62.7%
Bachelor's degree or higher ... 11.9%
Graduate degree ... 2.8%

Income & Poverty, 1999

Per capita income ... $14,197
Median household income ... $39,127
Median family income ... $40,162
Persons in poverty ... 17.4%
H'holds receiving public assistance ... 625
H'holds receiving social security ... 2,230

Households, 2000

Total households ... 10,767
With persons under 18 ... 5,085
With persons over 65 ... 2,532
Family households ... 7,804
Single person households ... 2,316
Persons per household ... 3.43
Persons per family ... 3.93

Household Population, 2008§§

Persons living in households ... 38,758
Persons living in group quarters ... 518
Persons per household ... 3.6

Labor & Employment

Total civilian labor force, 2008§§ ... 18,700
Unemployment rate, 2008 ... 8.6%
Total civilian labor force, 2000 ... 15,960

Employed persons 16 years and over by occupation, 2000

Managers & professionals ... 2,884
Service occupations ... 2,417
Sales & office occupations ... 4,017
Farming, fishing & forestry ... 21
Construction & maintenance ... 1,707
Production & transportation ... 3,649
Self-employed persons ... 649

* US Census Bureau
** 2000 Decennial Census
§ California Department of Finance
§§ California Employment Development Dept

General Information

City of Stanton
7800 Katella Ave
Stanton, CA 90680
714-379-9222

Website ... www.ci.stanton.ca.us
Elevation ... 60 ft.
Land Area (sq. miles) ... 3.1
Water Area (sq. miles) ... 0
Year of Incorporation ... 1956
Government type ... General law
Sales tax rate ... 8.75%

Voters & Officials

Registered Voters, October 2008

Total ... 15,021
Democrats ... 6,080
Republicans ... 5,297
Declined to state ... 2,961

Legislative Districts

US Congressional ... 40
State Senatorial ... 34
State Assembly ... 67, 68

Local Officials, 2009

Mayor ... Al Ethans
Manager ... Carol Jacobs
City Clerk ... Brenda Green
Attorney ... Ralph D. Hanson
Finance Dir ... Carol Jacobs
Public Works ... Sean Crumby
Community Dev Dir ... Omar Dadabhoy
Building ... Lance Miller
Police Chief ... Jeff Passalaqua
Fire/Emergency Mgmt ... (County)

Public Safety

Number of officers, 2007 ... NA
Violent crimes, 2007 ... 169
Property crimes, 2007 ... 738
Arson, 2007 ... 16

Public Library

Stanton Branch Library
Orange County Public Library System
7850 Katella Ave
Stanton, CA 90680
714-898-3302

Branch Librarian ... Ros Wilkes

Library system statistics, FY 2007

Population served ... 1,532,758
Internet terminals ... 505
Annual users ... 680,874

Per capita:

Operating income ... $24.71
percent from local government ... 90.0%
Operating expenditure ... $24.18
Total materials ... 1.93
Print holdings ... 1.84
Visits per capita ... 4.02

Housing & Construction

Housing Units

Total, 2008§ ... 11,161
Single family units, attached ... 1,873
Single family units, detached ... 3,029
Multiple family units ... 4,997
Mobile home units ... 1,262
Occupied ... 10,914
Vacancy rate ... 2.2%
Median rent, 2000** ... $793
Median SF home value, 2000** ... $164,000

New Privately Owned Housing Units Authorized by Building Permit, 2007*

	Units	Construction Cost
Single	39	$6,292,021
Total	39	$6,292,021

Municipal Finance

(For local fiscal year ended in 2006)

Revenues

Total ... $22,423,605
Taxes ... 11,425,733
Special benefits assessment ... 846,577
Licenses & permits ... 311,377
Fines & forfeitures ... 392,039
Revenues from use of money & property ... 2,527,852
Intergovernmental ... 2,763,700
Service charges ... 875,220
Other revenues ... 3,281,107
Other financing sources ... 0

Expenditures

Total ... $16,886,736
General government ... 1,475,294
Public safety ... 10,516,560
Transportation ... 2,632,011
Community development ... 646,261
Health ... 573,744
Culture & leisure ... 1,042,866
Other ... 0

Local School District

(Data from School year 2007-08 except as noted)

Garden Grove Unified
10331 Stanford Ave
Garden Grove, CA 92840
(714) 663-6000

Superintendent ... Laura Schwalm
Grade plan ... K-12
Number of schools ... 67
Enrollment ... 48,669
High school graduates, 2006-07 ... 2,803
Dropout rate ... 1.2%
Pupil/teacher ratio ... 23.1
Average class size ... 26.9
Students per computer ... 5.2
Classrooms with internet ... 2,130
Avg. Daily Attendance (ADA) ... 47,531
Cost per ADA ... $8,420
Avg. Teacher Salary ... $77,535

California Achievement Tests 6th ed., 2008

(Pct scoring at or above 50th National Percentile Rank)

	Math	Reading	Language
Grade 3	59%	31%	44%
Grade 7	58%	52%	52%

Academic Performance Index, 2008

Number of students tested ... 37,558
Number of valid scores ... 35,426
2007 API (base) ... 767
2008 API (growth) ... 778

SAT Testing, 2006-07

Enrollment, Grade 12 ... 3,163
Number taking test ... 1,156
percent taking test ... 36.6%
percent with total score 1,500+ ... 16.50%

Average Scores:

Math	Verbal	Writing	Total
521	480	480	1,481

Federal No Child Left Behind, 2008

(Adequate Yearly Progress standards met)

	Participation Rate	Pct Proficient
ELA	Yes	No
Math	Yes	No

API criteria ... Yes
Graduation rate ... Yes
\# criteria met/possible ... 42/40

Other school districts for this city

(see Appendix E for information on these districts)

Anaheim Union High, Magnolia Elem, Savanna Elem

See Introduction for an explanation of all data sources.

Demographics & Socio-Economic Characteristics†

(2007 American Community Survey, except as noted)

Population

1990* 210,943
2007 295,070
Male 145,846
Female 149,224
Jan. 2008 (estimate)§ 289,927
Persons per sq. mi. of land 5,300.3

Race & Hispanic Origin, 2007

Race
White 125,419
Black/African American 36,058
North American Native 2,278
Asian 63,296
Pacific Islander 1,223
Other Race 52,027
Two or more races 14,769
Hispanic origin, total 108,019
Mexican 98,732
Puerto Rican 1,448
Cuban 0
Other Hispanic 7,839

Age & Nativity, 2007

Under 5 years 25,057
18 years and over 206,566
65 years and over 30,220
85 years and over 5,409
Median Age 30.2
Native-born 208,463
Foreign-born 86,607

Educational Attainment, 2007

Population 25 years and over 174,657
Less than 9th grade 13.6%
High school grad or higher 72.6%
Bachelor's degree or higher 16.6%
Graduate degree 4.7%

Income & Poverty, 2007

Per capita income $20,567
Median household income $48,132
Median family income $51,632
Persons in poverty 17.6%
H'holds receiving public assistance 4,783
H'holds receiving social security 21,793

Households, 2007

Total households 89,609
With persons under 18 42,337
With persons over 65 19,241
Family households 66,394
Single person households 17,514
Persons per household 3.20
Persons per family 3.66

Household Population, 2008§§

Persons living in households 285,367
Persons living in group quarters 4,560
Persons per household 3.1

Labor & Employment

Total civilian labor force, 2008§§ 123,900
Unemployment rate, 2008 . . . . 12.7%
Total civilian labor force, 2000* 101,758

Employed persons 16 years and over by occupation, 2007

Managers & professionals 29,944
Service occupations 18,305
Sales & office occupations 27,975
Farming, fishing & forestry 7,149
Construction & maintenance 11,902
Production & transportation 20,552
Self-employed persons 8,345

† see Appendix D for 2000 Decennial Census Data
* US Census Bureau
** 2007 American Community Survey
§ California Department of Finance
§§ California Employment Development Dept

General Information

City of Stockton
425 N El Dorado St
Stockton, CA 95202
209-937-8212

Website . . . . www.stocktongov.com
Elevation . . . . 13 ft.
Land Area (sq. miles) 54.7
Water Area (sq. miles) 1.2
Year of Incorporation 1850
Government type . . . . Chartered
Sales tax rate 9.00%

Voters & Officials

Registered Voters, October 2008

Total 108,577
Democrats 54,038
Republicans 36,733
Declined to state 14,340

Legislative Districts

US Congressional 11, 18
State Senatorial 5
State Assembly 10, 15, 17, 26

Local Officials, 2009

Mayor . . . . Ann Johnston
Manager . . . . J. Gordon Palmer Jr
City Clerk . . . . Katherine Gong Meissner
Attorney . . . . Ren Nosky
Finance Dir . . . . Mark Moses
Public Works . . . . Bob Murdock (Int)
Planning/Dev Dir . . . . Mike Niblock
Building . . . . Christine Tien
Police Chief . . . . Blair Ulring (Actg)
Emergency/Fire Dir . . . . Ron Hittle

Public Safety

Number of officers, 2007 387
Violent crimes, 2007 4,216
Property crimes, 2007 18,677
Arson, 2007 47

Public Library

Cesar Chavez Central Library
Stockton-San Joaquin County Public Library
605 N El Dorado St
Stockton, CA 95202
209-937-8221

Director . . . . Natalie Rencher

Library system statistics, FY 2007

Population served 619,292
Internet terminals 125
Annual users 255,083

Per capita:

Operating income $21.59
percent from local government 96.0%
Operating expenditure $19.98
Total materials 1.65
Print holdings 1.52
Visits per capita 2.20

Housing & Construction

Housing Units

Total, 2008§ 96,553
Single family units, attached 6,592
Single family units, detached 62,729
Multiple family units 25,944
Mobile home units 1,288
Occupied 92,450
Vacancy rate 4.3%
Median rent, 2007** $869
Median SF home value, 2007** $364,700

New Privately Owned Housing Units Authorized by Building Permit, 2007*

	Units	Construction Cost
Single	617	$151,269,018
Total	706	$162,156,000

Municipal Finance

(For local fiscal year ended in 2006)

Revenues

Total $430,203,885
Taxes 169,248,446
Special benefits assessment 0
Licenses & permits 8,960,478
Fines & forfeitures 3,930,694
Revenues from use of money & property 12,607,371
Intergovernmental 84,643,504
Service charges 133,239,433
Other revenues 3,169,029
Other financing sources 14,404,930

Expenditures

Total $330,466,035
General government 38,483,072
Public safety 151,679,495
Transportation 16,689,299
Community development 23,284,343
Health 36,994,053
Culture & leisure 39,682,055
Other 0

Local School District

(Data from School year 2007-08 except as noted)

Stockton Unified
701 North Madison St
Stockton, CA 95202
(209) 933-7000

Superintendent . . . . Anthony Amato
Grade plan K-12
Number of schools 61
Enrollment 38,408
High school graduates, 2006-07 1,311
Dropout rate 14.6%
Pupil/teacher ratio 21.8
Average class size 23.6
Students per computer 5.7
Classrooms with internet 1,978
Avg. Daily Attendance (ADA) 35,229
Cost per ADA $9,526
Avg. Teacher Salary $58,262

California Achievement Tests 6th ed., 2008

(Pct scoring at or above 50th National Percentile Rank)

	Math	Reading	Language
Grade 3	42%	20%	32%
Grade 7	40%	32%	33%

Academic Performance Index, 2008

Number of students tested 28,507
Number of valid scores 26,421
2007 API (base) 645
2008 API (growth) 654

SAT Testing, 2006-07

Enrollment, Grade 12 2,220
Number taking test 459
percent taking test 20.7%
percent with total score 1,500+ 4.20%

Average Scores:

Math	Verbal	Writing	Total
447	416	419	1,282

Federal No Child Left Behind, 2008

(Adequate Yearly Progress standards met)

	Participation Rate	Pct Proficient
ELA	Yes	No
Math	Yes	No

API criteria . . . . Yes
Graduation rate . . . . No
\# criteria met/possible 46/34

Other school districts for this city

(see Appendix E for information on these districts)

Lodi Unified, Manteca Unified, Lincoln Unified

See Introduction for an explanation of all data sources.

Demographics & Socio-Economic Characteristics

(2000 Decennial Census, except as noted)

Population

1990* 22,686
2000 26,118
Male 12,931
Female 13,187
Jan. 2008 (estimate)§ 28,193
Persons per sq. mi. of land 7,048.3

Race & Hispanic Origin, 2000

Race
White 11,606
Black/African American 5,044
North American Native 189
Asian 4,621
Pacific Islander 268
Other Race 2,225
Two or more races 2,165
Hispanic origin, total 4,652
Mexican 3,042
Puerto Rican 246
Cuban 28
Other Hispanic 1,336

Age & Nativity, 2000

Under 5 years 2,008
18 years and over 17,619
65 years and over 1,489
85 years and over 143
Median Age 31.7
Native-born 20,884
Foreign-born 5,166

Educational Attainment, 2000

Population 25 years and over 15,187
Less than 9th grade 6.2%
High school grad or higher 85.6%
Bachelor's degree or higher 17.3%
Graduate degree 3.8%

Income & Poverty, 1999

Per capita income $20,386
Median household income $60,848
Median family income $63,616
Persons in poverty 6.4%
H'holds receiving public assistance 304
H'holds receiving social security 1,228

Households, 2000

Total households 7,987
With persons under 18 4,276
With persons over 65 1,109
Family households 6,447
Single person households 1,139
Persons per household 3.26
Persons per family 3.59

Household Population, 2008§§

Persons living in households 28,099
Persons living in group quarters 94
Persons per household 3.2

Labor & Employment

Total civilian labor force, 2008§§ 14,900
Unemployment rate, 2008 . . . . 7.1%
Total civilian labor force, 2000 12,740

Employed persons 16 years and over by occupation, 2000

Managers & professionals 3,111
Service occupations 2,009
Sales & office occupations 3,602
Farming, fishing & forestry 20
Construction & maintenance 1,472
Production & transportation 1,729
Self-employed persons 570

* US Census Bureau
** 2000 Decennial Census
§ California Department of Finance
§§ California Employment Development Dept

General Information

City of Suisun City
701 Civic Center Blvd
Suisun City, CA 94585
707-421-7300

Website . . . . www.suisun.com
Elevation . . . . NA
Land Area (sq. miles) 4.0
Water Area (sq. miles) 0
Year of Incorporation 1868
Government type . . . . General law
Sales tax rate 8.38%

Voters & Officials

Registered Voters, October 2008

Total 11,926
Democrats 6,594
Republicans 2,408
Declined to state 2,517

Legislative Districts

US Congressional 10
State Senatorial 5
State Assembly 8

Local Officials, 2009

Mayor . . . . Pete Sanchez
Manager . . . . Suzanne Bragdon
City Clerk . . . . Linda Hobson
Attorney . . . . Meyers, Nave, Riback
Finance Dir . . . . Mark Joseph
Public Works . . . . Fernando Bravo
Planning/Dev Dir . . . . Hearther McCollister
Building . . . . Daniel Kasperson
Police Chief . . . . Ed Dadisho
Fire Chief . . . . Mike O'Brien

Public Safety

Number of officers, 2007 23
Violent crimes, 2007 144
Property crimes, 2007 733
Arson, 2007 6

Public Library

Suisun City Library
Solano County Library System
333 Sunset Ave, librAddr2
Suisun City, CA 94585
707-421-6937

Branch Librarian . . . . Suzanne Olawski

Library system statistics, FY 2007

Population served 371,000
Internet terminals 248
Annual users 562,512

Per capita:

Operating income $54.42
percent from local government 94.0%
Operating expenditure $47.19
Total materials 1.88
Print holdings 1.57
Visits per capita 5.20

Housing & Construction

Housing Units

Total, 2008§ 9,054
Single family units, attached 189
Single family units, detached 7,706
Multiple family units 1,093
Mobile home units 66
Occupied 8,877
Vacancy rate 2.0%
Median rent, 2000** $870
Median SF home value, 2000** $160,700

New Privately Owned Housing Units Authorized by Building Permit, 2007*

	Units	Construction Cost
Single	60	$13,249,544
Total	68	$14,607,725

Municipal Finance

(For local fiscal year ended in 2006)

Revenues

Total $18,277,732
Taxes 5,450,476
Special benefits assessment 1,162,365
Licenses & permits 1,369,584
Fines & forfeitures 169,831
Revenues from use of money & property 905,313
Intergovernmental 4,700,579
Service charges 1,948,919
Other revenues 2,570,665
Other financing sources 0

Expenditures

Total $16,381,149
General government 1,586,960
Public safety 4,884,295
Transportation 3,867,287
Community development 4,123,659
Health 0
Culture & leisure 1,918,948
Other 0

Local School District

(Data from School year 2007-08 except as noted)

Fairfield-Suisun Unified
2490 Hilborn Rd
Fairfield, CA 94534
(707) 399-5000

Superintendent . . . . Jacki Cottingim
Grade plan K-12
Number of schools 31
Enrollment 22,774
High school graduates, 2006-07 1,306
Dropout rate 5.0%
Pupil/teacher ratio 20.8
Average class size 26.8
Students per computer 4.5
Classrooms with internet 1,128
Avg. Daily Attendance (ADA) 21,946
Cost per ADA $7,610
Avg. Teacher Salary $61,992

California Achievement Tests 6th ed., 2008

(Pct scoring at or above 50th National Percentile Rank)

	Math	Reading	Language
Grade 3	53%	35%	45%
Grade 7	52%	48%	48%

Academic Performance Index, 2008

Number of students tested 17,275
Number of valid scores 16,630
2007 API (base) 714
2008 API (growth) 724

SAT Testing, 2006-07

Enrollment, Grade 12 1,755
Number taking test 603
percent taking test 34.4%
percent with total score 1,500+ 14.80%

Average Scores:

Math	Verbal	Writing	Total
491	474	469	1,434

Federal No Child Left Behind, 2008

(Adequate Yearly Progress standards met)

	Participation Rate	Pct Proficient
ELA	Yes	No
Math	Yes	No

API criteria . . . . Yes
Graduation rate . . . . Yes
\# criteria met/possible 46/38

Other school districts for this city

(see Appendix E for information on these districts)

None

See Introduction for an explanation of all data sources.

Demographics & Socio-Economic Characteristics†

(2007 American Community Survey, except as noted)

Population

1990* . . . 117,229
2007 . . . 135,548
Male . . . 71,720
Female . . . 63,828
Jan. 2008 (estimate)§ . . . 137,538
Persons per sq. mi. of land . . . 6,280.3

Race & Hispanic Origin, 2007

Race
White . . . 62,117
Black/African American . . . 3,692
North American Native . . . 488
Asian . . . 53,895
Pacific Islander . . . 211
Other Race . . . 9,399
Two or more races . . . 5,746
Hispanic origin, total . . . 18,735
Mexican . . . 14,148
Puerto Rican . . . 407
Cuban . . . 64
Other Hispanic . . . 4,116

Age & Nativity, 2007

Under 5 years . . . 11,053
18 years and over . . . 106,969
65 years and over . . . 13,538
85 years and over . . . 1,381
Median Age . . . 36.7
Native-born . . . 76,470
Foreign-born . . . 59,078

Educational Attainment, 2007

Population 25 years and over . . . 96,307
Less than 9th grade . . . 4.2%
High school grad or higher . . . 90.7%
Bachelor's degree or higher . . . 58.3%
Graduate degree . . . 27.0%

Income & Poverty, 2007

Per capita income . . . $42,696
Median household income . . . $87,417
Median family income . . . $104,439
Persons in poverty . . . 5.0%
H'holds receiving public assistance . . . 328
H'holds receiving social security . . . 8,783

Households, 2007

Total households . . . 51,319
With persons under 18 . . . 16,589
With persons over 65 . . . 9,349
Family households . . . 32,005
Single person households . . . 15,278
Persons per household . . . 2.63
Persons per family . . . 3.30

Household Population, 2008§§

Persons living in households . . . 136,663
Persons living in group quarters . . . 875
Persons per household . . . 2.5

Labor & Employment

Total civilian labor force, 2008§§ . . . 75,700
Unemployment rate, 2008 . . . 5.1%
Total civilian labor force, 2000* . . . 75,227

Employed persons 16 years and over by occupation, 2007

Managers & professionals . . . 42,603
Service occupations . . . 9,916
Sales & office occupations . . . 13,783
Farming, fishing & forestry . . . 144
Construction & maintenance . . . 3,766
Production & transportation . . . 4,350
Self-employed persons . . . 3,804

† see Appendix D for 2000 Decennial Census Data
* US Census Bureau
** 2007 American Community Survey
§ California Department of Finance
§§ California Employment Development Dept

General Information

City of Sunnyvale
456 W Olive Ave
PO Box 3707
Sunnyvale, CA 94086
408-730-7500

Website . . . www.sunnyvale.ca.gov
Elevation . . . 130 ft.
Land Area (sq. miles) . . . 21.9
Water Area (sq. miles) . . . 0.7
Year of Incorporation . . . 1912
Government type . . . Chartered
Sales tax rate . . . 9.25%

Voters & Officials

Registered Voters, October 2008

Total . . . 56,393
Democrats . . . 25,661
Republicans . . . 12,808
Declined to state . . . 16,040

Legislative Districts

US Congressional . . . 14
State Senatorial . . . 13
State Assembly . . . 22

Local Officials, 2009

Mayor . . . Anthony Spitaleri
Manager . . . Gary Luebbers
City Clerk . . . Katherine Chappelear (Int)
Attorney . . . David Kahn
Finance Dir . . . Mary Bradley
Public Works . . . Marvin Rose
Community Dev Dir . . . Hanson Hom
Building . . . Marvin Rose
Police Chief . . . Don Johnson
Emergency/Fire Dir . . . Don Johnson

Public Safety

Number of officers, 2007 . . . 223
Violent crimes, 2007 . . . 154
Property crimes, 2007 . . . 2,629
Arson, 2007 . . . 16

Public Library

Sunnyvale Public Library
665 W Olive Ave
Sunnyvale, CA 94086
408-730-7314

Director . . . Deborah Barrow

Library statistics, FY 2007

Population served . . . 135,721
Internet terminals . . . 39
Annual users . . . 297,191

Per capita:

Operating income . . . $50.82
percent from local government . . . 94.8%
Operating expenditure . . . $48.17
Total materials . . . 2.38
Print holdings . . . 1.95
Visits per capita . . . 5.67

Housing & Construction

Housing Units

Total, 2008§ . . . 55,394
Single family units, attached . . . 5,176
Single family units, detached . . . 21,241
Multiple family units . . . 24,881
Mobile home units . . . 4,096
Occupied . . . 54,144
Vacancy rate . . . 2.3%
Median rent, 2007** . . . $1,378
Median SF home value, 2007** . . . $742,400

New Privately Owned Housing Units Authorized by Building Permit, 2007*

	Units	Construction Cost
Single	317	$56,053,369
Total	317	$56,053,369

Municipal Finance

(For local fiscal year ended in 2006)

Revenues

Total . . . $222,301,939
Taxes . . . 80,454,410
Special benefits assessment . . . 62,881
Licenses & permits . . . 5,779,621
Fines & forfeitures . . . 582,449
Revenues from use of money & property . . . 6,631,800
Intergovernmental . . . 22,397,155
Service charges . . . 103,428,028
Other revenues . . . 2,965,595
Other financing sources . . . 0

Expenditures

Total . . . $226,610,039
General government . . . 15,846,979
Public safety . . . 63,204,150
Transportation . . . 14,367,706
Community development . . . 25,283,850
Health . . . 63,940,004
Culture & leisure . . . 25,535,150
Other . . . 0

Local School District

(Data from School year 2007-08 except as noted)

Fremont Union High
PO Box F
Sunnyvale, CA 94087
(408) 522-2200

Superintendent . . . Polly Bove
Grade plan . . . 9-12
Number of schools . . . 6
Enrollment . . . 10,333
High school graduates, 2006-07 . . . 2,224
Dropout rate . . . 1.0%
Pupil/teacher ratio . . . 23.9
Average class size . . . 28.7
Students per computer . . . 3.6
Classrooms with internet . . . 416
Avg. Daily Attendance (ADA) . . . 10,314
Cost per ADA . . . $8,843
Avg. Teacher Salary . . . $72,288

California Achievement Tests 6th ed., 2008

(Pct scoring at or above 50th National Percentile Rank)

	Math	Reading	Language
Grade 3	NA	NA	NA
Grade 7	NA	NA	NA

Academic Performance Index, 2008

Number of students tested . . . 7,579
Number of valid scores . . . 7,305
2007 API (base) . . . 840
2008 API (growth) . . . 857

SAT Testing, 2006-07

Enrollment, Grade 12 . . . 2,423
Number taking test . . . 1,756
percent taking test . . . 72.5%
percent with total score 1,500+ . . . 59.10%

Average Scores:

Math	Verbal	Writing	Total
638	574	578	1,790

Federal No Child Left Behind, 2008

(Adequate Yearly Progress standards met)

	Participation Rate	Pct Proficient
ELA	No	Yes
Math	Yes	Yes

API criteria . . . Yes
Graduation rate . . . Yes
criteria met/possible . . . 30/29

Other school districts for this city

(see Appendix E for information on these districts)

Sunnyvale Elem

See Introduction for an explanation of all data sources.

Demographics & Socio-Economic Characteristics

(2000 Decennial Census, except as noted)

Population

1990* . . . 7,279
2000 . . . 13,541
Male . . . 9,001
Female . . . 4,540
Jan. 2008 (estimate)§ . . . 17,570
Persons per sq. mi. of land . . . 2,978.0

Race & Hispanic Origin, 2000

Race
White . . . 10,295
Black/African American . . . 1,692
North American Native . . . 431
Asian . . . 155
Pacific Islander . . . 120
Other Race . . . 469
Two or more races . . . 379
Hispanic origin, total . . . 2,109
Mexican . . . 1,869
Puerto Rican . . . 26
Cuban . . . 2
Other Hispanic . . . 212

Age & Nativity, 2000

Under 5 years . . . 698
18 years and over . . . 10,839
65 years and over . . . 1,049
85 years and over . . . 161
Median Age . . . 32.1
Native-born . . . 13,401
Foreign-born . . . 173

Educational Attainment, 2000

Population 25 years and over . . . 9,058
Less than 9th grade . . . 4.5%
High school grad or higher . . . 80.1%
Bachelor's degree or higher . . . 11.1%
Graduate degree . . . 3.1%

Income & Poverty, 1999

Per capita income . . . $13,238
Median household income . . . $35,675
Median family income . . . $45,216
Persons in poverty . . . 9.1%
H'holds receiving public assistance . . . 236
H'holds receiving social security . . . 795

Households, 2000

Total households . . . 3,516
With persons under 18 . . . 1,409
With persons over 65 . . . 723
Family households . . . 2,250
Single person households . . . 1,053
Persons per household . . . 2.49
Persons per family . . . 3.10

Household Population, 2008§§

Persons living in households . . . 8,971
Persons living in group quarters . . . 8,599
Persons per household . . . 2.4

Labor & Employment

Total civilian labor force, 2008§§ . . . 4,840
Unemployment rate, 2008 . . . 9.1%
Total civilian labor force, 2000 . . . 4,144

Employed persons 16 years and over by occupation, 2000

Managers & professionals . . . 1,191
Service occupations . . . 1,219
Sales & office occupations . . . 772
Farming, fishing & forestry . . . 62
Construction & maintenance . . . 285
Production & transportation . . . 240
Self-employed persons . . . 326

* US Census Bureau
** 2000 Decennial Census
§ California Department of Finance
§§ California Employment Development Dept

General Information

City of Susanville
66 N Lassen St
Susanville, CA 96130
530-257-1000

Website . . . www.cityofsusanville.org
Elevation . . . 4,258 ft.
Land Area (sq. miles) . . . 5.9
Water Area (sq. miles) . . . 0
Year of Incorporation . . . 1900
Government type . . . General law
Sales tax rate . . . 8.25%

Voters & Officials

Registered Voters, October 2008

Total . . . 4,696
Democrats . . . 1,406
Republicans . . . 2,100
Declined to state . . . 934

Legislative Districts

US Congressional . . . 4
State Senatorial . . . 1
State Assembly . . . 3

Local Officials, 2009

Mayor . . . Kurt Bonham
Administrator . . . Rob Hill
City Clerk . . . Debra Magginetti
Attorney . . . Peter Talia
Finance Dir . . . Robert Porfiri
Public Works . . . Craig Platt
Planning/Dev Dir . . . Bill Nebeker
Building . . . NA
Police Chief . . . Jeff Atkinson
Emergency/Fire Dir . . . Stuart A. Ratner

Public Safety

Number of officers, 2007 . . . 16
Violent crimes, 2007 . . . 68
Property crimes, 2007 . . . 380
Arson, 2007 . . . 2

Public Library

Lassen Library District
1618 Main St
Susanville, CA 96130
530-257-8113

Director . . . John Flaherty

Library statistics, FY 2007

Population served . . . 36,375
Internet terminals . . . 11
Annual users . . . 9,292

Per capita:

Operating income . . . $5.10
percent from local government . . . 63.6%
Operating expenditure . . . $5.02
Total materials . . . 1.24
Print holdings . . . 1.13
Visits per capita . . . 1.28

Housing & Construction

Housing Units

Total, 2008§ . . . 4,197
Single family units, attached . . . 131
Single family units, detached . . . 3,008
Multiple family units . . . 848
Mobile home units . . . 210
Occupied . . . 3,802
Vacancy rate . . . 9.4%
Median rent, 2000** . . . $568
Median SF home value, 2000** . . . $103,800

New Privately Owned Housing Units Authorized by Building Permit, 2007*

	Units	Construction Cost
Single	19	$3,519,396
Total	19	$3,519,396

Municipal Finance

(For local fiscal year ended in 2006)

Revenues

Total . . . $14,885,927
Taxes . . . 4,733,560
Special benefits assessment . . . 287,161
Licenses & permits . . . 179,505
Fines & forfeitures . . . 42,719
Revenues from use of money & property . . . 149,056
Intergovernmental . . . 2,118,329
Service charges . . . 7,192,497
Other revenues . . . 183,100
Other financing sources . . . 0

Expenditures

Total . . . $14,254,167
General government . . . 1,793,846
Public safety . . . 3,451,995
Transportation . . . 730,115
Community development . . . 1,048,656
Health . . . 0
Culture & leisure . . . 828,873
Other . . . 40,197

Local School District

(Data from School year 2007-08 except as noted)

Lassen Union High
55 South Weatherlow St
Susanville, CA 96130
(530) 251-1198

Superintendent . . . Rebekah Barakos-Cartwright
Grade plan . . . 9-12
Number of schools . . . 5
Enrollment . . . 1,150
High school graduates, 2006-07 . . . 237
Dropout rate . . . 3.9%
Pupil/teacher ratio . . . 25.2
Average class size . . . 22.1
Students per computer . . . 2.4
Classrooms with internet . . . 69
Avg. Daily Attendance (ADA) . . . 995
Cost per ADA . . . $10,276
Avg. Teacher Salary . . . $56,956

California Achievement Tests 6th ed., 2008

(Pct scoring at or above 50th National Percentile Rank)

	Math	Reading	Language
Grade 3	NA	NA	NA
Grade 7	NA	NA	NA

Academic Performance Index, 2008

Number of students tested . . . 812
Number of valid scores . . . 749
2007 API (base) . . . 701
2008 API (growth) . . . 731

SAT Testing, 2006-07

Enrollment, Grade 12 . . . 265
Number taking test . . . 99
percent taking test . . . 37.4%
percent with total score 1,500+ . . . 16.60%

Average Scores:

Math	Verbal	Writing	Total
508	500	474	1,482

Federal No Child Left Behind, 2008

(Adequate Yearly Progress standards met)

	Participation Rate	Pct Proficient
ELA	Yes	Yes
Math	Yes	Yes

API criteria . . . Yes
Graduation rate . . . Yes
\# criteria met/possible . . . 14/14

Other school districts for this city

(see Appendix E for information on these districts)

Johnstonville Elem, Ravendale-Termo Elem, Richmond Elem, Susanville Elem

See Introduction for an explanation of all data sources.

Demographics & Socio-Economic Characteristics

(2000 Decennial Census, except as noted)

Population

1990* . . . 1,835
2000 . . . 2,303
Male . . . 1,047
Female . . . 1,256
Jan. 2008 (estimate)§ . . . 2,902
Persons per sq. mi. of land . . . 1,707.1

Race & Hispanic Origin, 2000

Race
White . . . 2,106
Black/African American . . . 5
North American Native . . . 30
Asian . . . 24
Pacific Islander . . . 7
Other Race . . . 49
Two or more races . . . 82
Hispanic origin, total . . . 134
Mexican . . . 80
Puerto Rican . . . 3
Cuban . . . 1
Other Hispanic . . . 50

Age & Nativity, 2000

Under 5 years . . . 103
18 years and over . . . 1,768
65 years and over . . . 517
85 years and over . . . 80
Median Age . . . 45.3
Native-born . . . 2,236
Foreign-born . . . 106

Educational Attainment, 2000

Population 25 years and over . . . 1,648
Less than 9th grade . . . 3.0%
High school grad or higher . . . 90.5%
Bachelor's degree or higher . . . 28.3%
Graduate degree . . . 11.2%

Income & Poverty, 1999

Per capita income . . . $23,100
Median household income . . . $47,000
Median family income . . . $55,795
Persons in poverty . . . 7.9%
H'holds receiving public assistance . . . 23
H'holds receiving social security . . . 392

Households, 2000

Total households . . . 1,025
With persons under 18 . . . 302
With persons over 65 . . . 384
Family households . . . 658
Single person households . . . 329
Persons per household . . . 2.25
Persons per family . . . 2.79

Household Population, 2008§§

Persons living in households . . . 2,901
Persons living in group quarters . . . 1
Persons per household . . . 2.1

Labor & Employment

Total civilian labor force, 2008§§ . . . 1,500
Unemployment rate, 2008 . . . 9.4%
Total civilian labor force, 2000 . . . 1,169

Employed persons 16 years and over by occupation, 2000

Managers & professionals . . . 372
Service occupations . . . 275
Sales & office occupations . . . 296
Farming, fishing & forestry . . . 0
Construction & maintenance . . . 63
Production & transportation . . . 101
Self-employed persons . . . 110

* US Census Bureau
** 2000 Decennial Census
§ California Department of Finance
§§ California Employment Development Dept

General Information

City of Sutter Creek
18 Main St
Sutter Creek, CA 95685
209-267-5647

Website . . . www.ci.sutter-creek.ca.us
Elevation . . . 1,198 ft.
Land Area (sq. miles) . . . 1.7
Water Area (sq. miles) . . . 0
Year of Incorporation . . . 1913
Government type . . . General law
Sales tax rate . . . 8.75%

Voters & Officials

Registered Voters, October 2008

Total . . . 1,669
Democrats . . . 666
Republicans . . . 672
Declined to state . . . 244

Legislative Districts

US Congressional . . . 3
State Senatorial . . . 1
State Assembly . . . 10

Local Officials, 2009

Mayor . . . Gary Wooten
Manager . . . J. Robert Duke
City Clerk . . . Judy Allen
Attorney . . . J. Dennis Crabb
Finance Dir . . . Jeff Gardner
Public Works . . . George Christner
Planning/Dev Dir . . . Sean Rabe
Building . . . Jeff Kelly
Police Chief . . . J. Robert Duke
Fire Services . . . Butch Martin

Public Safety

Number of officers, 2007 . . . 8
Violent crimes, 2007 . . . 16
Property crimes, 2007 . . . 102
Arson, 2007 . . . 0

Public Library

Sutter Creek Branch
Amador County Library System
35 Main St
Sutter Creek, CA 95685
209-267-5489

Branch Librarian . . . Brad Barrow

Library system statistics, FY 2007

Population served . . . 38,435
Internet terminals . . . 18
Annual users . . . 74,880

Per capita:

Operating income . . . $24.71
percent from local government . . . 94.0%
Operating expenditure . . . $20.44
Total materials . . . 2.18
Print holdings . . . 1.97
Visits per capita . . . 2.04

Housing & Construction

Housing Units

Total, 2008§ . . . 1,467
Single family units, attached . . . 111
Single family units, detached . . . 829
Multiple family units . . . 445
Mobile home units . . . 82
Occupied . . . 1,359
Vacancy rate . . . 7.4%
Median rent, 2000** . . . $714
Median SF home value, 2000** . . . $169,700

New Privately Owned Housing Units Authorized by Building Permit, 2007*

	Units	Construction Cost
Single	7	$913,881
Total	7	$913,881

Municipal Finance

(For local fiscal year ended in 2006)

Revenues

Total . . . $3,479,676
Taxes . . . 1,315,513
Special benefits assessment . . . 31,207
Licenses & permits . . . 79,101
Fines & forfeitures . . . 14,986
Revenues from use of money & property . . . 76,992
Intergovernmental . . . 542,841
Service charges . . . 1,417,336
Other revenues . . . 1,700
Other financing sources . . . 0

Expenditures

Total . . . $3,429,435
General government . . . 261,773
Public safety . . . 1,085,744
Transportation . . . 469,504
Community development . . . 364,302
Health . . . 1,011,407
Culture & leisure . . . 236,705
Other . . . 0

Local School District

(Data from School year 2007-08 except as noted)

Amador County Unified
217 Rex Ave
Jackson, CA 95642
(209) 223-1750

Superintendent . . . Dick Glock
Grade plan . . . K-12
Number of schools . . . 12
Enrollment . . . 4,362
High school graduates, 2006-07 . . . 373
Dropout rate . . . 3.8%
Pupil/teacher ratio . . . 22.8
Average class size . . . 23.3
Students per computer . . . 3.9
Classrooms with internet . . . 308
Avg. Daily Attendance (ADA) . . . 4,219
Cost per ADA . . . $6,964
Avg. Teacher Salary . . . $60,591

California Achievement Tests 6th ed., 2008

(Pct scoring at or above 50th National Percentile Rank)

	Math	Reading	Language
Grade 3	59%	52%	54%
Grade 7	54%	60%	55%

Academic Performance Index, 2008

Number of students tested . . . 3,491
Number of valid scores . . . 3,322
2007 API (base) . . . 751
2008 API (growth) . . . 769

SAT Testing, 2006-07

Enrollment, Grade 12 . . . 442
Number taking test . . . 103
percent taking test . . . 23.3%
percent with total score 1,500+ . . . 13.60%

Average Scores:

Math	Verbal	Writing	Total
519	520	516	1,555

Federal No Child Left Behind, 2008

(Adequate Yearly Progress standards met)

	Participation Rate	Pct Proficient
ELA	Yes	No
Math	Yes	No

API criteria . . . Yes
Graduation rate . . . Yes
\# criteria met/possible . . . 26/22

Other school districts for this city

(see Appendix E for information on these districts)

None

See Introduction for an explanation of all data sources.

Demographics & Socio-Economic Characteristics

(2000 Decennial Census, except as noted)

Population

1990* 5,902
2000 6,400
Male 3,331
Female 3,069
Jan. 2008 (estimate)§ 9,228
Persons per sq. mi. of land 611.1

Race & Hispanic Origin, 2000

Race
White 5,322
Black/African American 126
North American Native 54
Asian 81
Pacific Islander 28
Other Race 665
Two or more races 124
Hispanic origin, total 995
Mexican 655
Puerto Rican 11
Cuban 2
Other Hispanic 327

Age & Nativity, 2000

Under 5 years 436
18 years and over 4,761
65 years and over 822
85 years and over 86
Median Age 34.3
Native-born 7,377
Foreign-born 528

Educational Attainment, 2000

Population 25 years and over 5,231
Less than 9th grade 6.0%
High school grad or higher 72.3%
Bachelor's degree or higher 8.8%
Graduate degree 2.4%

Income & Poverty, 1999

Per capita income $17,564
Median household income $33,861
Median family income $42,468
Persons in poverty 16.0%
H'holds receiving public assistance 163
H'holds receiving social security 667

Households, 2000

Total households 2,233
With persons under 18 833
With persons over 65 587
Family households 1,566
Single person households 556
Persons per household 2.62
Persons per family 3.09

Household Population, 2008§§

Persons living in households 6,170
Persons living in group quarters 3,058
Persons per household 2.7

Labor & Employment

Total civilian labor force, 2008§§ 3,500
Unemployment rate, 2008 .... 9.5%
Total civilian labor force, 2000 2,571

Employed persons 16 years and over by occupation, 2000

Managers & professionals 521
Service occupations 469
Sales & office occupations 525
Farming, fishing & forestry 44
Construction & maintenance 398
Production & transportation 315
Self-employed persons 130

* US Census Bureau
** 2000 Decennial Census
§ California Department of Finance
§§ California Employment Development Dept

General Information

City of Taft
209 E Kern St
Taft, CA 93268
661-763-1222

Website .... www.cityoftaft.org
Elevation .... 984 ft.
Land Area (sq. miles) 15.1
Water Area (sq. miles) 0
Year of Incorporation 1910
Government type .... General law
Sales tax rate 8.25%

Voters & Officials

Registered Voters, October 2008

Total 3,003
Democrats 771
Republicans 1,664
Declined to state 444

Legislative Districts

US Congressional 22
State Senatorial 18
State Assembly 32

Local Officials, 2009

Mayor .... Dave Noerr
Manager .... Robert L. Gorson Jr
City Clerk .... Louise Hudgens
Attorney .... Katherine Gibson
Finance Dir .... Teresa Statler
Public Works .... Craig Jones
Redevelopment Dir .... Paul Gorte
Building .... NA
Police Chief .... Kenneth D. McMinn
Emergency/Fire Dir .... (County)

Public Safety

Number of officers, 2007 13
Violent crimes, 2007 38
Property crimes, 2007 404
Arson, 2007 7

Public Library

Taft Branch Library
Kern County Library System
27 Emmons Park Dr
Taft, CA 93268
661-763-3294

Branch Librarian .... Catherine Edgecomb

Library system statistics, FY 2007

Population served 801,648
Internet terminals 237
Annual users 337,030

Per capita:

Operating income $12.11
percent from local government 90.4%
Operating expenditure $12.11
Total materials 1.37
Print holdings 1.29
Visits per capita 2.09

Housing & Construction

Housing Units

Total, 2008§ 2,534
Single family units, attached 52
Single family units, detached 1,843
Multiple family units 539
Mobile home units 100
Occupied 2,284
Vacancy rate 9.9%
Median rent, 2000** $456
Median SF home value, 2000** $86,000

New Privately Owned Housing Units Authorized by Building Permit, 2007*

	Units	Construction Cost
Single	2	$325,933
Total	4	$434,693

Municipal Finance

(For local fiscal year ended in 2006)

Revenues

Total .... NA
Taxes .... NA
Special benefits assessment .... NA
Licenses & permits .... NA
Fines & forfeitures .... NA
Revenues from use of money & property .... NA
Intergovernmental .... NA
Service charges .... NA
Other revenues .... NA
Other financing sources .... NA

Expenditures

Total .... NA
General government .... NA
Public safety .... NA
Transportation .... NA
Community development .... NA
Health .... NA
Culture & leisure .... NA
Other .... NA

Local School District

(Data from School year 2007-08 except as noted)

Taft Union High
701 7th St
Taft, CA 93268
(661) 763-2330

Superintendent .... Mark Richardson
Grade plan 9-12
Number of schools 3
Enrollment 1,108
High school graduates, 2006-07 187
Dropout rate 2.6%
Pupil/teacher ratio 14.2
Average class size 17.5
Students per computer 1.4
Classrooms with internet 54
Avg. Daily Attendance (ADA) 1,066
Cost per ADA $20,578
Avg. Teacher Salary $73,403

California Achievement Tests 6th ed., 2008

(Pct scoring at or above 50th National Percentile Rank)

	Math	Reading	Language
Grade 3	NA	NA	NA
Grade 7	NA	NA	NA

Academic Performance Index, 2008

Number of students tested 789
Number of valid scores 723
2007 API (base) 627
2008 API (growth) 676

SAT Testing, 2006-07

Enrollment, Grade 12 202
Number taking test 42
percent taking test 20.8%
percent with total score 1,500+ 5.50%

Average Scores:

Math	Verbal	Writing	Total
469	459	454	1,382

Federal No Child Left Behind, 2008

(Adequate Yearly Progress standards met)

	Participation Rate	Pct Proficient
ELA	Yes	Yes
Math	Yes	Yes

API criteria .... Yes
Graduation rate .... Yes
\# criteria met/possible 22/22

Other school districts for this city

(see Appendix E for information on these districts)

Taft City Elem

See Introduction for an explanation of all data sources.

Demographics & Socio-Economic Characteristics

(2000 Decennial Census, except as noted)

Population

1990* . . . 5,791
2000 . . . 10,957
Male . . . 7,584
Female . . . 3,373
Jan. 2008 (estimate)§ . . . 13,089
Persons per sq. mi. of land . . . 1,363.4

Race & Hispanic Origin, 2000

Race
White . . . 6,264
Black/African American . . . 1,512
North American Native . . . 148
Asian . . . 81
Pacific Islander . . . 17
Other Race . . . 2,610
Two or more races . . . 325
Hispanic origin, total . . . 3,583
Mexican . . . 3,347
Puerto Rican . . . 17
Cuban . . . 0
Other Hispanic . . . 219

Age & Nativity, 2000

Under 5 years . . . 481
18 years and over . . . 8,931
65 years and over . . . 1,029
85 years and over . . . 94
Median Age . . . 33.2
Native-born . . . 10,117
Foreign-born . . . 760

Educational Attainment, 2000

Population 25 years and over . . . 7,504
Less than 9th grade . . . 9.6%
High school grad or higher . . . 71.9%
Bachelor's degree or higher . . . 6.4%
Graduate degree . . . 1.8%

Income & Poverty, 1999

Per capita income . . . $18,220
Median household income . . . $29,208
Median family income . . . $40,030
Persons in poverty . . . 12.0%
H'holds receiving public assistance . . . 159
H'holds receiving social security . . . 833

Households, 2000

Total households . . . 2,533
With persons under 18 . . . 980
With persons over 65 . . . 758
Family households . . . 1,710
Single person households . . . 730
Persons per household . . . 2.59
Persons per family . . . 3.19

Household Population, 2008§§

Persons living in households . . . 8,328
Persons living in group quarters . . . 4,761
Persons per household . . . 2.7

Labor & Employment

Total civilian labor force, 2008§§ . . . 3,400
Unemployment rate, 2008 . . . 6.5%
Total civilian labor force, 2000 . . . 2,448

Employed persons 16 years and over by occupation, 2000

Managers & professionals . . . 544
Service occupations . . . 580
Sales & office occupations . . . 557
Farming, fishing & forestry . . . 53
Construction & maintenance . . . 215
Production & transportation . . . 303
Self-employed persons . . . 234

* US Census Bureau
** 2000 Decennial Census
§ California Department of Finance
§§ California Employment Development Dept

General Information

City of Tehachapi
115 S Robinson St
Tehachapi, CA 93561
661-822-2200

Website . . . www.tehachapicityhall.com
Elevation . . . 3,973 ft.
Land Area (sq. miles) . . . 9.6
Water Area (sq. miles) . . . 0
Year of Incorporation . . . 1909
Government type . . . General law
Sales tax rate . . . 8.25%

Voters & Officials

Registered Voters, October 2008

Total . . . 3,837
Democrats . . . 1,111
Republicans . . . 1,833
Declined to state . . . 696

Legislative Districts

US Congressional . . . 22
State Senatorial . . . 18
State Assembly . . . 32

Local Officials, 2009

Mayor . . . Linda Vernon
Manager . . . Greg Garrett
City Clerk . . . Julie Drimakis
Attorney . . . Thomas Schroeter
Finance Dir . . . Hannah Chung
Public Works . . . Dennis Wahlstrom
Planning/Dev Dir . . . David James
Building . . . NA
Police Chief . . . Jeff Kermode
Fire/Emergency Mgmt . . . NA

Public Safety

Number of officers, 2007 . . . NA
Violent crimes, 2007 . . . NA
Property crimes, 2007 . . . NA
Arson, 2007 . . . NA

Public Library

Tehachapi Branch Library
Kern County Library System
1001 W Tehachapi Blvd, librAddr2
Tehachapi, CA 93561
661-822-4938

Branch Librarian . . . Kristine Duke

Library system statistics, FY 2007

Population served . . . 801,648
Internet terminals . . . 237
Annual users . . . 337,030

Per capita:

Operating income . . . $12.11
percent from local government . . . 90.4%
Operating expenditure . . . $12.11
Total materials . . . 1.37
Print holdings . . . 1.29
Visits per capita . . . 2.09

Housing & Construction

Housing Units

Total, 2008§ . . . 3,583
Single family units, attached . . . 150
Single family units, detached . . . 2,400
Multiple family units . . . 686
Mobile home units . . . 347
Occupied . . . 3,116
Vacancy rate . . . 13.0%
Median rent, 2000** . . . $477
Median SF home value, 2000** . . . $90,000

New Privately Owned Housing Units Authorized by Building Permit, 2007*

	Units	Construction Cost
Single	NA	NA
Total	NA	NA

Municipal Finance

(For local fiscal year ended in 2006)

Revenues

Total . . . $11,130,696
Taxes . . . 3,779,085
Special benefits assessment . . . 0
Licenses & permits . . . 114,137
Fines & forfeitures . . . 99,538
Revenues from use of money & property . . . 171,637
Intergovernmental . . . 1,483,820
Service charges . . . 5,470,079
Other revenues . . . 12,400
Other financing sources . . . 0

Expenditures

Total . . . $9,985,337
General government . . . 951,969
Public safety . . . 2,385,831
Transportation . . . 991,626
Community development . . . 2,174,746
Health . . . 2,091,787
Culture & leisure . . . 200
Other . . . 0

Local School District

(Data from School year 2007-08 except as noted)

Tehachapi Unified
400 South Snyder
Tehachapi, CA 93561
(661) 822-2100

Superintendent . . . Richard Swanson
Grade plan . . . K-12
Number of schools . . . 6
Enrollment . . . 4,927
High school graduates, 2006-07 . . . 3
Dropout rate . . . 0.7%
Pupil/teacher ratio . . . 22.9
Average class size . . . 26.4
Students per computer . . . 4.5
Classrooms with internet . . . 224
Avg. Daily Attendance (ADA) . . . 4,671
Cost per ADA . . . $7,624
Avg. Teacher Salary . . . $62,480

California Achievement Tests 6th ed., 2008

(Pct scoring at or above 50th National Percentile Rank)

	Math	Reading	Language
Grade 3	55%	46%	61%
Grade 7	57%	55%	49%

Academic Performance Index, 2008

Number of students tested . . . 3,720
Number of valid scores . . . 3,604
2007 API (base) . . . 758
2008 API (growth) . . . 765

SAT Testing, 2006-07

Enrollment, Grade 12 . . . 390
Number taking test . . . 90
percent taking test . . . 23.1%
percent with total score 1,500+ . . . 13.30%

Average Scores:

Math	Verbal	Writing	Total
508	525	506	1,539

Federal No Child Left Behind, 2008

(Adequate Yearly Progress standards met)

	Participation Rate	Pct Proficient
ELA	Yes	No
Math	Yes	No

API criteria . . . Yes
Graduation rate . . . Met on Appeal
\# criteria met/possible . . . 26/22

Other school districts for this city

(see Appendix E for information on these districts)

None

See Introduction for an explanation of all data sources.

Demographics & Socio-Economic Characteristics

(2000 Decennial Census, except as noted)

Population

1990* 401
2000 432
Male 218
Female 214
Jan. 2008 (estimate)§ 429
Persons per sq. mi. of land 536.3

Race & Hispanic Origin, 2000

Race
White 342
Black/African American 3
North American Native 15
Asian 0
Pacific Islander 3
Other Race 53
Two or more races 16
Hispanic origin, total 85
Mexican 82
Puerto Rican 0
Cuban 0
Other Hispanic 3

Age & Nativity, 2000

Under 5 years 23
18 years and over 335
65 years and over 90
85 years and over 6
Median Age 41.3
Native-born 388
Foreign-born 46

Educational Attainment, 2000

Population 25 years and over 269
Less than 9th grade 13.0%
High school grad or higher 66.9%
Bachelor's degree or higher 8.2%
Graduate degree 0.0%

Income & Poverty, 1999

Per capita income $13,044
Median household income $27,500
Median family income $35,125
Persons in poverty 16.7%
H'holds receiving public assistance 5
H'holds receiving social security 64

Households, 2000

Total households 179
With persons under 18 57
With persons over 65 67
Family households 125
Single person households 46
Persons per household 2.41
Persons per family 2.86

Household Population, 2008§§

Persons living in households 429
Persons living in group quarters 0
Persons per household 2.3

Labor & Employment

Total civilian labor force, 2008§§ 170
Unemployment rate, 2008 ....8.2%
Total civilian labor force, 2000 155

Employed persons 16 years and over by occupation, 2000

Managers & professionals 19
Service occupations 35
Sales & office occupations 41
Farming, fishing & forestry 3
Construction & maintenance 13
Production & transportation 30
Self-employed persons 10

* US Census Bureau
** 2000 Decennial Census
§ California Department of Finance
§§ California Employment Development Dept

General Information

City of Tehama
250 Cavalier Ave
PO Box 70
Tehama, CA 96090
530-384-1501

Website ....NA
Elevation ....NA
Land Area (sq. miles) 0.8
Water Area (sq. miles) 0
Year of Incorporation 1906
Government type ....General law
Sales tax rate 8.25%

Voters & Officials

Registered Voters, October 2008

Total 243
Democrats 81
Republicans 97
Declined to state 48

Legislative Districts

US Congressional 2
State Senatorial 4
State Assembly 2

Local Officials, 2009

Mayor ....Robert Mitchell
Manager/Admin ....Carolyn Steffan
City Clerk ....Carolyn Steffan
Attorney ....Gregory Einhorn
Finance Dir ....Carolyn Steffan
Public Works ....Carolyn Steffan
Planning/Dev Dir ....Carolyn Steffan
Building ....Carolyn Steffan
Police Chief ....(County)
Emergency/Fire Dir ....Carolyn Steffan

Public Safety

Number of officers, 2007 ....NA
Violent crimes, 2007 ....NA
Property crimes, 2007 ....NA
Arson, 2007 ....NA

Public Library

Main Branch
Tehama County Library System
645 Madison St
Red Bluff, CA 96080
530-527-0604

Library system statistics, FY 2007

Population served 61,774
Internet terminals 21
Annual users 15,734

Per capita:

Operating income $9.05
percent from local government 89.6%
Operating expenditure $8.17
Total materials 1.93
Print holdings 1.86
Visits per capita 1.33

Housing & Construction

Housing Units

Total, 2008§ 201
Single family units, attached 4
Single family units, detached 172
Multiple family units 10
Mobile home units 15
Occupied 184
Vacancy rate 8.5%
Median rent, 2000** $483
Median SF home value, 2000** $91,100

New Privately Owned Housing Units Authorized by Building Permit, 2007*

	Units	Construction Cost
Single	NA	NA
Total	NA	NA

Municipal Finance

(For local fiscal year ended in 2006)

Revenues

Total $1,851,479
Taxes 73,494
Special benefits assessment 15,626
Licenses & permits 0
Fines & forfeitures 398
Revenues from use of money & property 14,375
Intergovernmental 1,320,913
Service charges 59,127
Other revenues 367,546
Other financing sources 0

Expenditures

Total $1,611,381
General government 27,472
Public safety 5,081
Transportation 370,464
Community development 906,116
Health 0
Culture & leisure 0
Other 0

Local School District

(Data from School year 2007-08 except as noted)

Los Molinos Unified
7851 Highway 99-E
Los Molinos, CA 96055
(530) 384-7826

Superintendent ....Dave Pilger
Grade plan K-12
Number of schools 5
Enrollment 581
High school graduates, 2006-07 37
Dropout rate 1.0%
Pupil/teacher ratio 17.7
Average class size 20.2
Students per computer 3.3
Classrooms with internet 43
Avg. Daily Attendance (ADA) 549
Cost per ADA $9,966
Avg. Teacher Salary $53,842

California Achievement Tests 6th ed., 2008

(Pct scoring at or above 50th National Percentile Rank)

	Math	Reading	Language
Grade 3	57%	43%	61%
Grade 7	47%	47%	40%

Academic Performance Index, 2008

Number of students tested 438
Number of valid scores 399
2007 API (base) 766
2008 API (growth) 771

SAT Testing, 2006-07

Enrollment, Grade 12 43
Number taking test 3
percent taking test 7.0%
percent with total score 1,500+ ....NA

Average Scores:

Math	Verbal	Writing	Total
NA	NA	NA	NA

Federal No Child Left Behind, 2008

(Adequate Yearly Progress standards met)

	Participation Rate	Pct Proficient
ELA	Yes	Yes
Math	Yes	Yes

API criteria ....Yes
Graduation rate ....Yes
criteria met/possible 22/22

Other school districts for this city

(see Appendix E for information on these districts)

None

See Introduction for an explanation of all data sources.

Demographics & Socio-Economic Characteristics†

(2007 American Community Survey, except as noted)

Population

1990* . . . 27,099
2007 . . . 93,743
Male . . . 45,942
Female . . . 47,801
Jan. 2008 (estimate)§ . . . 101,057
Persons per sq. mi. of land . . . 3,842.5

Race & Hispanic Origin, 2007

Race
White . . . 68,288
Black/African American . . . 2,133
North American Native . . . 1,039
Asian . . . 8,674
Pacific Islander . . . 354
Other Race . . . 10,170
Two or more races . . . 3,085
Hispanic origin, total . . . 19,803
Mexican . . . NA
Puerto Rican . . . NA
Cuban . . . NA
Other Hispanic . . . NA

Age & Nativity, 2007

Under 5 years . . . 7,667
18 years and over . . . 65,006
65 years and over . . . 6,860
85 years and over . . . 867
Median Age . . . 31.1
Native-born . . . 79,087
Foreign-born . . . 14,656

Educational Attainment, 2007

Population 25 years and over . . . 55,577
Less than 9th grade . . . 3.3%
High school grad or higher . . . 91.3%
Bachelor's degree or higher . . . 28.6%
Graduate degree . . . 9.5%

Income & Poverty, 2007

Per capita income . . . $27,345
Median household income . . . $71,975
Median family income . . . $78,852
Persons in poverty . . . 7.8%
H'holds receiving public assistance . . . 68
H'holds receiving social security . . . 5,154

Households, 2007

Total households . . . 29,943
With persons under 18 . . . 15,445
With persons over 65 . . . 4,963
Family households . . . 23,628
Single person households . . . 5,234
Persons per household . . . 3.13
Persons per family . . . 3.56

Household Population, 2008§§

Persons living in households . . . 101,035
Persons living in group quarters . . . 22
Persons per household . . . 3.2

Labor & Employment

Total civilian labor force, 2008§§ . . . 37,400
Unemployment rate, 2008 . . . 5.8%
Total civilian labor force, 2000* . . . 26,438

Employed persons 16 years and over by occupation, 2007

Managers & professionals . . . 15,988
Service occupations . . . 8,977
Sales & office occupations . . . 12,528
Farming, fishing & forestry . . . 0
Construction & maintenance . . . 2,613
Production & transportation . . . 4,047
Self-employed persons . . . 3,215

† see Appendix D for 2000 Decennial Census Data
* US Census Bureau
** 2007 American Community Survey
§ California Department of Finance
§§ California Employment Development Dept

General Information

City of Temecula
43200 Business Park Dr
PO Box 9033
Temecula, CA 92589
951-694-6444

Website . . . www.cityoftemecula.org
Elevation . . . 1,300
Land Area (sq. miles) . . . 26.3
Water Area (sq. miles) . . . 0
Year of Incorporation . . . 1989
Government type . . . General Law
Sales tax rate . . . 8.75%

Voters & Officials

Registered Voters, October 2008

Total . . . 41,995
Democrats . . . 10,815
Republicans . . . 21,059
Declined to state . . . 8,316

Legislative Districts

US Congressional . . . 49
State Senatorial . . . 36
State Assembly . . . 64, 66

Local Officials, 2009

Mayor . . . Maryann Edwards
Manager . . . Shawn Nelson
City Clerk . . . Susan Jones
Attorney . . . Peter Thorson
Finance Dir . . . Genie Roberts
Public Works . . . Greg Butler
Planning/Dev Dir . . . Bob Johnson
Building . . . Rich Johnston
Police Chief . . . Jerry Williams
Emergency/Fire Dir . . . Glenn Patterson

Public Safety

Number of officers, 2007 . . . NA
Violent crimes, 2007 . . . 207
Property crimes, 2007 . . . 2,654
Arson, 2007 . . . 6

Public Library

Grace Mellman Community Library
Riverside County Library Service
41000 County Center
Temecula, CA 92591
951-600-6262

Branch Librarian . . . Emily Gerstbacher

Library system statistics, FY 2007

Population served . . . 1,047,996
Internet terminals . . . 37
Annual users . . . 69,346

Per capita:

Operating income . . . $19.38
percent from local government . . . 49.8%
Operating expenditure . . . $20.45
Total materials . . . 1.43
Print holdings . . . 1.30
Visits per capita . . . 4.06

Housing & Construction

Housing Units

Total, 2008§ . . . 32,453
Single family units, attached . . . 511
Single family units, detached . . . 25,976
Multiple family units . . . 5,645
Mobile home units . . . 321
Occupied . . . 31,135
Vacancy rate . . . 4.1%
Median rent, 2007** . . . $1,308
Median SF home value, 2007** . . . $468,000

New Privately Owned Housing Units Authorized by Building Permit, 2007*

	Units	Construction Cost
Single	668	$155,478,796
Total	905	$181,794,596

Municipal Finance

(For local fiscal year ended in 2006)

Revenues

Total . . . $89,130,649
Taxes . . . 57,908,541
Special benefits assessment . . . 922,004
Licenses & permits . . . 5,995,723
Fines & forfeitures . . . 1,348,667
Revenues from use of money & property . . . 2,082,000
Intergovernmental . . . 8,473,687
Service charges . . . 1,770,840
Other revenues . . . 10,629,187
Other financing sources . . . 0

Expenditures

Total . . . $90,897,968
General government . . . 10,918,756
Public safety . . . 19,999,168
Transportation . . . 21,225,573
Community development . . . 7,952,151
Health . . . 0
Culture & leisure . . . 30,802,320
Other . . . 0

Local School District

(Data from School year 2007-08 except as noted)

Temecula Valley Unified
31350 Rancho Vista Rd
Temecula, CA 92592
(951) 676-2661

Superintendent . . . Carol Leighty
Grade plan . . . K-12
Number of schools . . . 31
Enrollment . . . 29,435
High school graduates, 2006-07 . . . 1,724
Dropout rate . . . 2.1%
Pupil/teacher ratio . . . 21.5
Average class size . . . 27.0
Students per computer . . . 5.5
Classrooms with internet . . . 1,684
Avg. Daily Attendance (ADA) . . . 27,629
Cost per ADA . . . $7,662
Avg. Teacher Salary . . . $71,718

California Achievement Tests 6th ed., 2008

(Pct scoring at or above 50th National Percentile Rank)

	Math	Reading	Language
Grade 3	72%	57%	67%
Grade 7	71%	68%	66%

Academic Performance Index, 2008

Number of students tested . . . 22,251
Number of valid scores . . . 20,865
2007 API (base) . . . 822
2008 API (growth) . . . 836

SAT Testing, 2006-07

Enrollment, Grade 12 . . . 2,032
Number taking test . . . 906
percent taking test . . . 44.6%
percent with total score 1,500+ . . . 22.60%

Average Scores:

Math	Verbal	Writing	Total
517	509	500	1,526

Federal No Child Left Behind, 2008

(Adequate Yearly Progress standards met)

	Participation Rate	Pct Proficient
ELA	Yes	Yes
Math	Yes	Yes

API criteria . . . Yes
Graduation rate . . . Yes
\# criteria met/possible . . . 46/46

Other school districts for this city

(see Appendix E for information on these districts)

None

See Introduction for an explanation of all data sources.

Demographics & Socio-Economic Characteristics

(2000 Decennial Census, except as noted)

Population

1990* . . . 31,100
2000 . . . 33,377
Male . . . 15,879
Female . . . 17,498
Jan. 2008 (estimate)§ . . . 35,683
Persons per sq. mi. of land . . . 8,920.8

Race & Hispanic Origin, 2000

Race
White . . . 16,266
Black/African American . . . 307
North American Native . . . 148
Asian . . . 12,980
Pacific Islander . . . 19
Other Race . . . 2,496
Two or more races . . . 1,161
Hispanic origin, total . . . 6,836
Mexican . . . 5,032
Puerto Rican . . . 68
Cuban . . . 154
Other Hispanic . . . 1,582

Age & Nativity, 2000

Under 5 years . . . 1,891
18 years and over . . . 25,381
65 years and over . . . 4,658
85 years and over . . . 686
Median Age . . . 38.6
Native-born . . . 20,451
Foreign-born . . . 12,845

Educational Attainment, 2000

Population 25 years and over . . . 22,330
Less than 9th grade . . . 7.4%
High school grad or higher . . . 83.5%
Bachelor's degree or higher . . . 28.5%
Graduate degree . . . 8.9%

Income & Poverty, 1999

Per capita income . . . $20,267
Median household income . . . $48,722
Median family income . . . $54,455
Persons in poverty . . . 9.2%
H'holds receiving public assistance . . . 384
H'holds receiving social security . . . 2,524

Households, 2000

Total households . . . 11,338
With persons under 18 . . . 4,546
With persons over 65 . . . 3,175
Family households . . . 8,661
Single person households . . . 2,238
Persons per household . . . 2.90
Persons per family . . . 3.33

Household Population, 2008§§

Persons living in households . . . 35,172
Persons living in group quarters . . . 511
Persons per household . . . 3.0

Labor & Employment

Total civilian labor force, 2008§§ . . . 18,600
Unemployment rate, 2008 . . . 4.8%
Total civilian labor force, 2000 . . . 15,889

Employed persons 16 years and over by occupation, 2000

Managers & professionals . . . 5,717
Service occupations . . . 1,858
Sales & office occupations . . . 4,827
Farming, fishing & forestry . . . 15
Construction & maintenance . . . 1,186
Production & transportation . . . 1,499
Self-employed persons . . . 1,528

* US Census Bureau
** 2000 Decennial Census
§ California Department of Finance
§§ California Employment Development Dept

General Information

City of Temple City
9701 Las Tunas Dr
Temple City, CA 91780
626-285-2171

Website . . . www.templecity.us
Elevation . . . 400 ft.
Land Area (sq. miles) . . . 4.0
Water Area (sq. miles) . . . 0
Year of Incorporation . . . 1960
Government type . . . Chartered
Sales tax rate . . . 9.25%

Voters & Officials

Registered Voters, October 2008

Total . . . 16,590
Democrats . . . 6,001
Republicans . . . 5,297
Declined to state . . . 4,729

Legislative Districts

US Congressional . . . 29
State Senatorial . . . 21
State Assembly . . . 44

Local Officials, 2009

Mayor . . . Cathe Wilson
Manager . . . Charles Martin
City Clerk . . . Mary Flandrick
Attorney . . . Charles Martin
Finance Dir . . . Monica Molina
Public Works . . . Chuck Erickson
Planning/Dev Dir . . . Joe Lambert
Building . . . NA
Police Chief . . . NA
Fire/Emergency Mgmt . . . NA

Public Safety

Number of officers, 2007 . . . NA
Violent crimes, 2007 . . . 85
Property crimes, 2007 . . . 697
Arson, 2007 . . . 4

Public Library

Temple City Library
Los Angeles County Public Library System
5939 Golden West Ave
Temple City, CA 91780
626-285-2136

Branch Librarian . . . Joseph Zagami

Library system statistics, FY 2007

Population served . . . 3,673,313
Internet terminals . . . 749
Annual users . . . 3,748,771

Per capita:

Operating income . . . $30.06
percent from local government . . . 93.6%
Operating expenditure . . . $28.36
Total materials . . . 2.22
Print holdings . . . 1.97
Visits per capita . . . 3.25

Housing & Construction

Housing Units

Total, 2008§ . . . 11,921
Single family units, attached . . . 802
Single family units, detached . . . 9,657
Multiple family units . . . 1,404
Mobile home units . . . 58
Occupied . . . 11,578
Vacancy rate . . . 2.9%
Median rent, 2000** . . . $800
Median SF home value, 2000** . . . $234,800

New Privately Owned Housing Units Authorized by Building Permit, 2007*

	Units	Construction Cost
Single	23	$5,359,335
Total	212	$10,931,013

Municipal Finance

(For local fiscal year ended in 2006)

Revenues

Total . . . $14,779,419
Taxes . . . 8,360,130
Special benefits assessment . . . 929,267
Licenses & permits . . . 880,720
Fines & forfeitures . . . 409,291
Revenues from use of money & property . . . 1,144,480
Intergovernmental . . . 1,823,699
Service charges . . . 964,995
Other revenues . . . 266,837
Other financing sources . . . 0

Expenditures

Total . . . $10,866,283
General government . . . 2,201,351
Public safety . . . 4,081,521
Transportation . . . 2,080,481
Community development . . . 764,174
Health . . . 11,708
Culture & leisure . . . 1,727,048
Other . . . 0

Local School District

(Data from School year 2007-08 except as noted)

Temple City Unified
9700 Las Tunas Dr
Temple City, CA 91780
(626) 548-5000

Superintendent . . . Chelsea Kang-Smith
Grade plan . . . K-12
Number of schools . . . 8
Enrollment . . . 5,588
High school graduates, 2006-07 . . . 540
Dropout rate . . . 1.5%
Pupil/teacher ratio . . . 22.0
Average class size . . . 26.1
Students per computer . . . 4.0
Classrooms with internet . . . 248
Avg. Daily Attendance (ADA) . . . 5,577
Cost per ADA . . . $7,522
Avg. Teacher Salary . . . $68,150

California Achievement Tests 6th ed., 2008

(Pct scoring at or above 50th National Percentile Rank)

	Math	Reading	Language
Grade 3	75%	57%	65%
Grade 7	80%	69%	70%

Academic Performance Index, 2008

Number of students tested . . . 4,475
Number of valid scores . . . 4,219
2007 API (base) . . . 841
2008 API (growth) . . . 853

SAT Testing, 2006-07

Enrollment, Grade 12 . . . 582
Number taking test . . . 358
percent taking test . . . 61.5%
percent with total score 1,500+ . . . 39.70%

Average Scores:

Math	Verbal	Writing	Total
587	526	522	1,635

Federal No Child Left Behind, 2008

(Adequate Yearly Progress standards met)

	Participation Rate	Pct Proficient
ELA	Yes	Yes
Math	Yes	Yes

API criteria . . . Yes
Graduation rate . . . Yes
criteria met/possible . . . 30/30

Other school districts for this city

(see Appendix E for information on these districts)

Arcadia Unified, El Monte Elem

See Introduction for an explanation of all data sources.

Demographics & Socio-Economic Characteristics†

(2007 American Community Survey, except as noted)

Population

1990* . . . 104,352
2007 . . . 128,519
Male . . . 62,193
Female . . . 66,326
Jan. 2008 (estimate)§ . . . 128,650
Persons per sq. mi. of land . . . 2,343.4

Race & Hispanic Origin, 2007

Race
White . . . 106,818
Black/African American . . . 1,276
North American Native . . . 389
Asian . . . 10,015
Pacific Islander . . . 130
Other Race . . . 6,892
Two or more races . . . 2,999
Hispanic origin, total . . . 15,030
Mexican . . . 9,595
Puerto Rican . . . 177
Cuban . . . 148
Other Hispanic . . . 5,110

Age & Nativity, 2007

Under 5 years . . . 8,744
18 years and over . . . 96,126
65 years and over . . . 16,018
85 years and over . . . 1,710
Median Age . . . 39.8
Native-born . . . 109,020
Foreign-born . . . 19,499

Educational Attainment, 2007

Population 25 years and over . . . 84,672
Less than 9th grade . . . 2.7%
High school grad or higher . . . 94.4%
Bachelor's degree or higher . . . 50.0%
Graduate degree . . . 19.9%

Income & Poverty, 2007

Per capita income . . . $42,423
Median household income . . . $89,953
Median family income . . . $99,870
Persons in poverty . . . 4.2%
H'holds receiving public assistance . . . 387
H'holds receiving social security . . . 11,396

Households, 2007

Total households . . . 44,598
With persons under 18 . . . 16,819
With persons over 65 . . . 10,744
Family households . . . 34,088
Single person households . . . 8,580
Persons per household . . . 2.85
Persons per family . . . 3.24

Household Population, 2008§§

Persons living in households . . . 126,699
Persons living in group quarters . . . 1,951
Persons per household . . . 2.8

Labor & Employment

Total civilian labor force, 2008§§ . . . 71,800
Unemployment rate, 2008 . . . 4.9%
Total civilian labor force, 2000* . . . 61,387

Employed persons 16 years and over by occupation, 2007

Managers & professionals . . . 30,411
Service occupations . . . 7,048
Sales & office occupations . . . 18,085
Farming, fishing & forestry . . . 172
Construction & maintenance . . . 3,734
Production & transportation . . . 3,195
Self-employed persons . . . 7,575

† see Appendix D for 2000 Decennial Census Data
* US Census Bureau
** 2007 American Community Survey
§ California Department of Finance
§§ California Employment Development Dept

General Information

City of Thousand Oaks
2100 Thousand Oaks Blvd
Thousand Oaks, CA 91362
805-449-2100

Website . . . www.toaks.org
Elevation . . . 800 ft.
Land Area (sq. miles) . . . 54.9
Water Area (sq. miles) . . . 0.2
Year of Incorporation . . . 1964
Government type . . . General law
Sales tax rate . . . 8.25%

Voters & Officials

Registered Voters, October 2008

Total . . . 78,103
Democrats . . . 25,562
Republicans . . . 34,185
Declined to state . . . 14,979

Legislative Districts

US Congressional . . . 24
State Senatorial . . . 19
State Assembly . . . 37

Local Officials, 2009

Mayor . . . Thomas P. Glancy
Manager . . . Scott Mitnick
City Clerk . . . Linda D. Lawrence
Attorney . . . Amy Albano
Finance Dir . . . John Adams (Int)
Public Works . . . Mark Watkins
Planning/Dev Dir . . . John Prescott
Building . . . Hueners David
Police Chief . . . Jeff Matson
Emergency/Fire Dir . . . Bob Roper

Public Safety

Number of officers, 2007 . . . NA
Violent crimes, 2007 . . . 146
Property crimes, 2007 . . . 1,942
Arson, 2007 . . . 14

Public Library

Thousand Oaks Library
Thousand Oaks Library System
1401 E Janss Rd
Thousand Oaks, CA 91362
805-449-2660

Director . . . Stephen Brogden

Library system statistics, FY 2007

Population served . . . 127,739
Internet terminals . . . 60
Annual users . . . 294,830

Per capita:

Operating income . . . $38.30
percent from local government . . . 93.0%
Operating expenditure . . . $64.65
Total materials . . . 3.84
Print holdings . . . 3.40
Visits per capita . . . 5.11

Housing & Construction

Housing Units

Total, 2008§ . . . 47,075
Single family units, attached . . . 5,256
Single family units, detached . . . 31,353
Multiple family units . . . 9,394
Mobile home units . . . 1,072
Occupied . . . 45,798
Vacancy rate . . . 2.7%
Median rent, 2007** . . . $1,629
Median SF home value, 2007** . . . $722,500

New Privately Owned Housing Units Authorized by Building Permit, 2007*

	Units	Construction Cost
Single	71	$27,250,658
Total	79	$28,143,218

Municipal Finance

(For local fiscal year ended in 2006)

Revenues

Total . . . $141,602,445
Taxes . . . 63,740,092
Special benefits assessment . . . 4,246,902
Licenses & permits . . . 4,449,842
Fines & forfeitures . . . 1,199,812
Revenues from use of money & property . . . 6,587,788
Intergovernmental . . . 7,514,283
Service charges . . . 50,964,395
Other revenues . . . 2,899,331
Other financing sources . . . 0

Expenditures

Total . . . $129,802,173
General government . . . 17,946,516
Public safety . . . 22,732,365
Transportation . . . 22,343,423
Community development . . . 12,044,899
Health . . . 19,082,359
Culture & leisure . . . 21,993,678
Other . . . 0

Local School District

(Data from School year 2007-08 except as noted)

Conejo Valley Unified
1400 East Janss Rd
Thousand Oaks, CA 91362
(805) 497-9511

Superintendent . . . Mario Contini
Grade plan . . . K-12
Number of schools . . . 29
Enrollment . . . 21,209
High school graduates, 2006-07 . . . 1,742
Dropout rate . . . 2.1%
Pupil/teacher ratio . . . 21.3
Average class size . . . 27.1
Students per computer . . . 3.7
Classrooms with internet . . . 992
Avg. Daily Attendance (ADA) . . . 21,562
Cost per ADA . . . $7,709
Avg. Teacher Salary . . . $67,528

California Achievement Tests 6th ed., 2008

(Pct scoring at or above 50th National Percentile Rank)

	Math	Reading	Language
Grade 3	78%	62%	69%
Grade 7	78%	75%	71%

Academic Performance Index, 2008

Number of students tested . . . 17,069
Number of valid scores . . . 15,598
2007 API (base) . . . 853
2008 API (growth) . . . 860

SAT Testing, 2006-07

Enrollment, Grade 12 . . . 1,723
Number taking test . . . 1,019
percent taking test . . . 59.1%
percent with total score 1,500+ . . . 44.10%

Average Scores:

Math	Verbal	Writing	Total
579	555	558	1,692

Federal No Child Left Behind, 2008

(Adequate Yearly Progress standards met)

	Participation Rate	Pct Proficient
ELA	Yes	Yes
Math	Yes	Yes

API criteria . . . Yes
Graduation rate . . . Yes
criteria met/possible . . . 40/40

Other school districts for this city

(see Appendix E for information on these districts)

None

See Introduction for an explanation of all data sources.

Demographics & Socio-Economic Characteristics

(2000 Decennial Census, except as noted)

Population

1990* 7,532
2000 8,666
Male 4,064
Female 4,602
Jan. 2008 (estimate)§ 8,917
Persons per sq. mi. of land 1,981.6

Race & Hispanic Origin, 2000

Race
White 7,879
Black/African American 75
North American Native 19
Asian 383
Pacific Islander 10
Other Race 65
Two or more races 235
Hispanic origin, total 317
Mexican 110
Puerto Rican 14
Cuban 19
Other Hispanic 174

Age & Nativity, 2000

Under 5 years 520
18 years and over 6,767
65 years and over 1,434
85 years and over 158
Median Age 45.4
Native-born 7,123
Foreign-born 1,624

Educational Attainment, 2000

Population 25 years and over 6,582
Less than 9th grade 0.7%
High school grad or higher 98.6%
Bachelor's degree or higher 69.6%
Graduate degree 33.7%

Income & Poverty, 1999

Per capita income $85,966
Median household income $106,611
Median family income $149,041
Persons in poverty 3.3%
H'holds receiving public assistance 7
H'holds receiving social security 993

Households, 2000

Total households 3,712
With persons under 18 1,060
With persons over 65 1,017
Family households 2,408
Single person households 1,026
Persons per household 2.31
Persons per family 2.82

Household Population, 2008§§

Persons living in households 8,811
Persons living in group quarters 106
Persons per household 2.3

Labor & Employment

Total civilian labor force, 2008§§ .... NA
Unemployment rate, 2008 .... NA
Total civilian labor force, 2000 4,360

Employed persons 16 years and over by occupation, 2000

Managers & professionals 2,846
Service occupations 307
Sales & office occupations 932
Farming, fishing & forestry 0
Construction & maintenance 77
Production & transportation 132
Self-employed persons 910

* US Census Bureau
** 2000 Decennial Census
§ California Department of Finance
§§ California Employment Development Dept

General Information

Town of Tiburon
1505 Tiburon Blvd
Tiburon, CA 94920
415-435-7373

Website .... www.ci.tiburon.ca.us
Elevation .... 90 ft.
Land Area (sq. miles) 4.5
Water Area (sq. miles) 8.7
Year of Incorporation 1964
Government type .... General law
Sales tax rate 9.00%

Voters & Officials

Registered Voters, October 2008

Total 6,053
Democrats 2,805
Republicans 1,627
Declined to state 1,450

Legislative Districts

US Congressional 6
State Senatorial 3
State Assembly 6

Local Officials, 2009

Mayor .... Alice Fredericks
Manager .... Margaret A. Curran
City Clerk .... Diane Crane Iacopi
Attorney .... Ann Danforth
Finance Dir .... Heidi Bigall
Public Works .... Nicholas Nguyen
Planning/Dev Dir .... Scott Anderson
Building .... Dean Bloomquist
Police Chief .... Michael Cronin
Emergency/Fire Dir .... Rich Pearce

Public Safety

Number of officers, 2007 13
Violent crimes, 2007 6
Property crimes, 2007 129
Arson, 2007 0

Public Library

Belvedere-Tiburon Library
1501 Tiburon Blvd
Tiburon, CA 94920
415-789-2665

Director .... Deborah Mazzolini

Library statistics, FY 2007

Population served 11,031
Internet terminals 20
Annual users 34,682

Per capita:

Operating income $143.66
percent from local government 81.0%
Operating expenditure $136.94
Total materials 7.15
Print holdings 5.65
Visits per capita .... NA

Housing & Construction

Housing Units

Total, 2008§ 3,963
Single family units, attached 237
Single family units, detached 2,422
Multiple family units 1,304
Mobile home units 0
Occupied 3,778
Vacancy rate 4.7%
Median rent, 2000** $1,557
Median SF home value, 2000** .. $1,000,001

New Privately Owned Housing Units Authorized by Building Permit, 2007*

	Units	Construction Cost
Single	6	$6,565,052
Total	6	$6,565,052

Municipal Finance

(For local fiscal year ended in 2006)

Revenues

Total $10,147,565
Taxes 3,931,154
Special benefits assessment 1,420,819
Licenses & permits 1,089,236
Fines & forfeitures 284,213
Revenues from use of money & property 710,192
Intergovernmental 767,299
Service charges 1,551,601
Other revenues 393,051
Other financing sources 0

Expenditures

Total $8,308,713
General government 1,909,550
Public safety 2,698,006
Transportation 2,407,170
Community development 968,938
Health 0
Culture & leisure 325,049
Other 0

Local School District

(Data from School year 2007-08 except as noted)

Tamalpais Union High
PO Box 605
Larkspur, CA 94977
(415) 945-3720

Superintendent .... Laurie Kimbrel
Grade plan 9-12
Number of schools 5
Enrollment 3,889
High school graduates, 2006-07 959
Dropout rate 0.8%
Pupil/teacher ratio 17.4
Average class size 24.4
Students per computer 2.6
Classrooms with internet 232
Avg. Daily Attendance (ADA) 3,715
Cost per ADA $13,492
Avg. Teacher Salary $81,923

California Achievement Tests 6th ed., 2008

(Pct scoring at or above 50th National Percentile Rank)

	Math	Reading	Language
Grade 3	NA	NA	NA
Grade 7	NA	NA	NA

Academic Performance Index, 2008

Number of students tested 2,800
Number of valid scores 2,766
2007 API (base) 848
2008 API (growth) 855

SAT Testing, 2006-07

Enrollment, Grade 12 997
Number taking test 730
percent taking test 73.2%
percent with total score 1,500+ ... 58.30%

Average Scores:

Math	Verbal	Writing	Total
574	574	574	1,722

Federal No Child Left Behind, 2008

(Adequate Yearly Progress standards met)

	Participation Rate	Pct Proficient
ELA	Yes	Yes
Math	Yes	Yes

API criteria .... Yes
Graduation rate .... Yes
criteria met/possible 10/10

Other school districts for this city

(see Appendix E for information on these districts)

Reed Union Elem

See Introduction for an explanation of all data sources.

Demographics & Socio-Economic Characteristics†

(2007 American Community Survey, except as noted)

Population

1990* . . . 133,107
2007 . . . 143,628
Male . . . 69,053
Female . . . 74,575
Jan. 2008 (estimate)§ . . . 148,965
Persons per sq. mi. of land . . . 7,266.6

Race & Hispanic Origin, 2007

Race
White . . . 77,555
Black/African American . . . 3,707
North American Native . . . 131
Asian . . . 42,170
Pacific Islander . . . 705
Other Race . . . 12,070
Two or more races . . . 7,290
Hispanic origin, total . . . 22,994
Mexican . . . 13,901
Puerto Rican . . . 357
Cuban . . . 1,220
Other Hispanic . . . 7,516

Age & Nativity, 2007

Under 5 years . . . 8,359
18 years and over . . . 111,532
65 years and over . . . 21,891
85 years and over . . . 3,076
Median Age . . . 41.3
Native-born . . . 100,489
Foreign-born . . . 43,139

Educational Attainment, 2007

Population 25 years and over . . . 100,658
Less than 9th grade . . . 2.9%
High school grad or higher . . . 91.7%
Bachelor's degree or higher . . . 39.8%
Graduate degree . . . 14.5%

Income & Poverty, 2007

Per capita income . . . $34,621
Median household income . . . $70,834
Median family income . . . $84,771
Persons in poverty . . . 4.5%
H'holds receiving public assistance . . . 685
H'holds receiving social security . . . 14,337

Households, 2007

Total households . . . 54,934
With persons under 18 . . . 18,754
With persons over 65 . . . 15,267
Family households . . . 37,082
Single person households . . . 15,022
Persons per household . . . 2.59
Persons per family . . . 3.20

Household Population, 2008§§

Persons living in households . . . 147,716
Persons living in group quarters . . . 1,249
Persons per household . . . 2.6

Labor & Employment

Total civilian labor force, 2008§§ . . . 82,100
Unemployment rate, 2008 . . . 3.7%
Total civilian labor force, 2000* . . . 70,314

Employed persons 16 years and over by occupation, 2007

Managers & professionals . . . 35,614
Service occupations . . . 7,800
Sales & office occupations . . . 19,956
Farming, fishing & forestry . . . 0
Construction & maintenance . . . 3,432
Production & transportation . . . 5,278
Self-employed persons . . . 7,770

† see Appendix D for 2000 Decennial Census Data
* US Census Bureau
** 2007 American Community Survey
§ California Department of Finance
§§ California Employment Development Dept

General Information

City of Torrance
3031 Torrance Blvd
Torrance, CA 90503
310-618-5880

Website . . . www.tornet.com
Elevation . . . 84 ft.
Land Area (sq. miles) . . . 20.5
Water Area (sq. miles) . . . 0
Year of Incorporation . . . 1921
Government type . . . Chartered
Sales tax rate . . . 9.25%

Voters & Officials

Registered Voters, October 2008

Total . . . 77,572
Democrats . . . 28,766
Republicans . . . 29,646
Declined to state . . . 16,054

Legislative Districts

US Congressional . . . 36
State Senatorial . . . 28
State Assembly . . . 53

Local Officials, 2009

Mayor . . . Frank Scotto
Manager . . . LeRoy J. Jackson
City Clerk . . . Sue Herbers
Attorney . . . John Fellows III
Finance Dir . . . Eric Tsao
Public Works . . . Robert Beste
Planning/Dev Dir . . . Jeff Gibson
Building . . . Jeff Gibson
Police Chief . . . John Neu
Emergency/Fire Dir. . . . Willie Racowschi

Public Safety

Number of officers, 2007 . . . 234
Violent crimes, 2007 . . . 343
Property crimes, 2007 . . . 3,187
Arson, 2007 . . . 16

Public Library

Katy Geissert Civic Center Library
Torrance Public Library System
3301 Torrance Blvd
Torrance, CA 90503
310-618-5950

City Librarian . . . Paula Weiner

Library system statistics, FY 2007

Population served . . . 148,558
Internet terminals . . . 75
Annual users . . . 61,000

Per capita:

Operating income . . . $47.03
percent from local government . . . 96.1%
Operating expenditure . . . $45.20
Total materials . . . 4.07
Print holdings . . . 3.67
Visits per capita . . . 5.22

Housing & Construction

Housing Units

Total, 2008§ . . . 57,743
Single family units, attached . . . 3,693
Single family units, detached . . . 30,704
Multiple family units . . . 22,163
Mobile home units . . . 1,183
Occupied . . . 56,275
Vacancy rate . . . 2.5%
Median rent, 2007** . . . $1,303
Median SF home value, 2007** . . . $675,100

New Privately Owned Housing Units Authorized by Building Permit, 2007*

	Units	Construction Cost
Single	81	$16,467,588
Total	163	$29,382,072

Municipal Finance

(For local fiscal year ended in 2006)

Revenues

Total . . . $240,560,794
Taxes . . . 133,685,918
Special benefits assessment . . . 1,182,141
Licenses & permits . . . 2,960,695
Fines & forfeitures . . . 2,138,723
Revenues from use of money & property . . . 9,577,553
Intergovernmental . . . 20,208,790
Service charges . . . 61,369,723
Other revenues . . . 9,437,251
Other financing sources . . . 0

Expenditures

Total . . . $235,024,672
General government . . . 21,834,076
Public safety . . . 87,280,107
Transportation . . . 39,738,065
Community development . . . 22,566,170
Health . . . 15,229,768
Culture & leisure . . . 23,566,431
Other . . . 0

Local School District

(Data from School year 2007-08 except as noted)

Torrance Unified
2335 Plaza del Amo
Torrance, CA 90509
(310) 972-6500

Superintendent . . . George Mannon
Grade plan . . . K-12
Number of schools . . . 31
Enrollment . . . 24,972
High school graduates, 2006-07 . . . 2,124
Dropout rate . . . 0.6%
Pupil/teacher ratio . . . 22.6
Average class size . . . 25.1
Students per computer . . . 6.1
Classrooms with internet . . . 1,252
Avg. Daily Attendance (ADA) . . . 24,588
Cost per ADA . . . $7,611
Avg. Teacher Salary . . . $61,745

California Achievement Tests 6th ed., 2008

(Pct scoring at or above 50th National Percentile Rank)

	Math	Reading	Language
Grade 3	76%	53%	66%
Grade 7	73%	64%	64%

Academic Performance Index, 2008

Number of students tested . . . 19,340
Number of valid scores . . . 18,611
2007 API (base) . . . 820
2008 API (growth) . . . 831

SAT Testing, 2006-07

Enrollment, Grade 12 . . . 2,245
Number taking test . . . 1,299
percent taking test . . . 57.9%
percent with total score 1,500+ . . . 32.80%

Average Scores:

Math	Verbal	Writing	Total
550	505	505	1,560

Federal No Child Left Behind, 2008

(Adequate Yearly Progress standards met)

	Participation Rate	Pct Proficient
ELA	Yes	Yes
Math	Yes	Yes

API criteria . . . Yes
Graduation rate . . . Yes
criteria met/possible . . . 46/46

Other school districts for this city

(see Appendix E for information on these districts)

None

See Introduction for an explanation of all data sources.

Demographics & Socio-Economic Characteristics†

(2007 American Community Survey, except as noted)

Population

1990* . . . 33,558
2007 . . . 82,383
Male . . . 40,546
Female . . . 41,837
Jan. 2008 (estimate)§ . . . 81,548
Persons per sq. mi. of land . . . 3,883.2

Race & Hispanic Origin, 2007

Race
White . . . 38,295
Black/African American . . . 7,169
North American Native . . . 694
Asian . . . 10,918
Pacific Islander . . . 163
Other Race . . . 19,657
Two or more races . . . 5,487
Hispanic origin, total . . . 33,056
Mexican . . . 25,634
Puerto Rican . . . 503
Cuban . . . 774
Other Hispanic . . . 6,145

Age & Nativity, 2007

Under 5 years . . . 7,601
18 years and over . . . 56,825
65 years and over . . . 4,516
85 years and over . . . 89
Median Age . . . 29.5
Native-born . . . 61,510
Foreign-born . . . 20,873

Educational Attainment, 2007

Population 25 years and over . . . 48,003
Less than 9th grade . . . 6.1%
High school grad or higher . . . 86.9%
Bachelor's degree or higher . . . 19.3%
Graduate degree . . . 2.5%

Income & Poverty, 2007

Per capita income . . . $26,432
Median household income . . . $76,075
Median family income . . . $86,033
Persons in poverty . . . 6.6%
H'holds receiving public assistance . . . 646
H'holds receiving social security . . . 4,045

Households, 2007

Total households . . . 24,483
With persons under 18 . . . 13,386
With persons over 65 . . . 3,455
Family households . . . 19,682
Single person households . . . 3,758
Persons per household . . . 3.36
Persons per family . . . 3.70

Household Population, 2008§§

Persons living in households . . . 81,203
Persons living in group quarters . . . 345
Persons per household . . . 3.3

Labor & Employment

Total civilian labor force, 2008§§ . . . 33,300
Unemployment rate, 2008 . . . 6.4%
Total civilian labor force, 2000* . . . 27,073

Employed persons 16 years and over by occupation, 2007

Managers & professionals . . . 11,295
Service occupations . . . 6,965
Sales & office occupations . . . 12,051
Farming, fishing & forestry . . . 157
Construction & maintenance . . . 2,956
Production & transportation . . . 6,137
Self-employed persons . . . 2,082

† see Appendix D for 2000 Decennial Census Data
* US Census Bureau
** 2007 American Community Survey
§ California Department of Finance
§§ California Employment Development Dept

General Information

City of Tracy
333 Civic Center Plaza
Tracy, CA 95376
209-831-6000

Website . . . www.ci.tracy.ca.us
Elevation . . . 48 ft.
Land Area (sq. miles) . . . 21.0
Water Area (sq. miles) . . . 0
Year of Incorporation . . . 1910
Government type . . . General law
Sales tax rate . . . 8.75%

Voters & Officials

Registered Voters, October 2008

Total . . . 30,702
Democrats . . . 13,658
Republicans . . . 10,312
Declined to state . . . 5,565

Legislative Districts

US Congressional . . . 11
State Senatorial . . . 5
State Assembly . . . 17

Local Officials, 2009

Mayor . . . Brent H. Ives
Manager . . . Leon Churchill Jr
City Clerk . . . Sandra Edwards
Attorney . . . Daniel Sodergren
Finance & Admin Svcs . . . Zane Johnston
Public Works . . . Kevin Tobeck
Development Dir. . . . Andrew Malik
Building . . . Kevin Jorgensen
Police Chief . . . Janet Thiessen
Emergency/Fire Dir. . . . Chris Bosch

Public Safety

Number of officers, 2007 . . . 87
Violent crimes, 2007 . . . 136
Property crimes, 2007 . . . 2,538
Arson, 2007 . . . 24

Public Library

Tracy Library
Stockton-San Joaquin County Public Library
20 E Eaton Ave
Tracy, CA 95376
209-937-8221

Branch Librarian . . . Kathleen Buffleben

Library system statistics, FY 2007

Population served . . . 619,292
Internet terminals . . . 125
Annual users . . . 255,083

Per capita:

Operating income . . . $21.59
percent from local government . . . 96.0%
Operating expenditure . . . $19.98
Total materials . . . 1.65
Print holdings . . . 1.52
Visits per capita . . . 2.20

Housing & Construction

Housing Units

Total, 2008§ . . . 25,478
Single family units, attached . . . 1,027
Single family units, detached . . . 20,934
Multiple family units . . . 3,041
Mobile home units . . . 476
Occupied . . . 24,820
Vacancy rate . . . 2.6%
Median rent, 2007** . . . $1,493
Median SF home value, 2007** . . . $543,200

New Privately Owned Housing Units Authorized by Building Permit, 2007*

	Units	Construction Cost
Single	27	$4,030,929
Total	29	$4,290,357

Municipal Finance

(For local fiscal year ended in 2006)

Revenues

Total . . . $160,219,154
Taxes . . . 43,594,798
Special benefits assessment . . . 2,414,130
Licenses & permits . . . 1,662,767
Fines & forfeitures . . . 290,367
Revenues from use of money & property . . . 6,590,838
Intergovernmental . . . 11,852,638
Service charges . . . 43,430,272
Other revenues . . . 1,623,344
Other financing sources . . . 48,760,000

Expenditures

Total . . . $118,167,376
General government . . . 19,818,143
Public safety . . . 32,105,486
Transportation . . . 9,988,632
Community development . . . 9,916,987
Health . . . 23,185,414
Culture & leisure . . . 12,973,603
Other . . . 0

Local School District

(Data from School year 2007-08 except as noted)

Tracy Joint Unified
1975 West Lowell Ave
Tracy, CA 95376
(209) 830-3200

Superintendent . . . James Franco
Grade plan . . . PK-12
Number of schools . . . 24
Enrollment . . . 17,333
High school graduates, 2006-07 . . . 1,127
Dropout rate . . . 4.1%
Pupil/teacher ratio . . . 20.7
Average class size . . . 26.0
Students per computer . . . 5.6
Classrooms with internet . . . 770
Avg. Daily Attendance (ADA) . . . 15,863
Cost per ADA . . . $7,398
Avg. Teacher Salary . . . $60,577

California Achievement Tests 6th ed., 2008

(Pct scoring at or above 50th National Percentile Rank)

	Math	Reading	Language
Grade 3	47%	33%	40%
Grade 7	47%	51%	47%

Academic Performance Index, 2008

Number of students tested . . . 12,664
Number of valid scores . . . 11,908
2007 API (base) . . . 711
2008 API (growth) . . . 722

SAT Testing, 2006-07

Enrollment, Grade 12 . . . 1,336
Number taking test . . . 448
percent taking test . . . 33.5%
percent with total score 1,500+ . . . 14.30%

Average Scores:

Math	Verbal	Writing	Total
493	478	478	1,449

Federal No Child Left Behind, 2008

(Adequate Yearly Progress standards met)

	Participation Rate	Pct Proficient
ELA	Yes	No
Math	Yes	No

API criteria . . . Yes
Graduation rate . . . Yes
criteria met/possible . . . 42/33

Other school districts for this city

(see Appendix E for information on these districts)

Banta Elem, Jefferson Elem, Lammersville Elem, New Jerusalem Elem

See Introduction for an explanation of all data sources.

Demographics & Socio-Economic Characteristics

(2000 Decennial Census, except as noted)

Population

1990* . . . 362
2000 . . . 311
Male . . . 154
Female . . . 157
Jan. 2008 (estimate)§ . . . 314
Persons per sq. mi. of land . . . 628.0

Race & Hispanic Origin, 2000

Race
White . . . 295
Black/African American . . . 5
North American Native . . . 1
Asian . . . 2
Pacific Islander . . . 1
Other Race . . . 1
Two or more races . . . 6
Hispanic origin, total . . . 7
Mexican . . . 3
Puerto Rican . . . 1
Cuban . . . 1
Other Hispanic . . . 2

Age & Nativity, 2000

Under 5 years . . . 8
18 years and over . . . 276
65 years and over . . . 62
85 years and over . . . 8
Median Age . . . 50.2
Native-born . . . 314
Foreign-born . . . 17

Educational Attainment, 2000

Population 25 years and over . . . 263
Less than 9th grade . . . 1.5%
High school grad or higher . . . 88.2%
Bachelor's degree or higher . . . 50.6%
Graduate degree . . . 17.9%

Income & Poverty, 1999

Per capita income . . . $28,050
Median household income . . . $40,000
Median family income . . . $50,357
Persons in poverty . . . 9.3%
H'holds receiving public assistance . . . 0
H'holds receiving social security . . . 38

Households, 2000

Total households . . . 168
With persons under 18 . . . 21
With persons over 65 . . . 50
Family households . . . 73
Single person households . . . 68
Persons per household . . . 1.85
Persons per family . . . 2.51

Household Population, 2008§§

Persons living in households . . . 314
Persons living in group quarters . . . 0
Persons per household . . . 1.8

Labor & Employment

Total civilian labor force, 2008§§ . . . 200
Unemployment rate, 2008 . . . 5.5%
Total civilian labor force, 2000 . . . 179

Employed persons 16 years and over by occupation, 2000

Managers & professionals . . . 91
Service occupations . . . 24
Sales & office occupations . . . 24
Farming, fishing & forestry . . . 0
Construction & maintenance . . . 7
Production & transportation . . . 21
Self-employed persons . . . 32

* US Census Bureau
** 2000 Decennial Census
§ California Department of Finance
§§ California Employment Development Dept

General Information

City of Trinidad
409 Trinity St
PO Box 390
Trinidad, CA 95570
707-677-0223

Website . . . www.trinidad.ca.gov
Elevation . . . NA
Land Area (sq. miles) . . . 0.5
Water Area (sq. miles) . . . 0.2
Year of Incorporation . . . 1870
Government type . . . General law
Sales tax rate . . . 9.00%

Voters & Officials

Registered Voters, October 2008

Total . . . 280
Democrats . . . 154
Republicans . . . 51
Declined to state . . . 52

Legislative Districts

US Congressional . . . 1
State Senatorial . . . 2
State Assembly . . . 1

Local Officials, 2009

Mayor . . . Chi-Wei Lin
City Manager . . . Steve Albright
City Clerk . . . Gabriel Adams
Attorney . . . Paul Hagen
Finance Dir . . . NA
Public Works . . . Bryan Buckman
City Planner . . . Trever Parker
Building . . . NA
Police Chief . . . Ken Thrailkill
Emergency/Fire Dir. . . . Tom Marquette

Public Safety

Number of officers, 2007 . . . 2
Violent crimes, 2007 . . . 0
Property crimes, 2007 . . . 35
Arson, 2007 . . . 0

Public Library

Trinidad Branch Library
Humboldt County Library System
300 Trinity St, librAddr2
Trinidad, CA 95570
707-677-0227

Branch Librarian . . . Kenzie Mullen

Library system statistics, FY 2007

Population served . . . 131,959
Internet terminals . . . 46
Annual users . . . 20,083

Per capita:

Operating income . . . $22.91
percent from local government . . . 90.6%
Operating expenditure . . . $18.80
Total materials . . . 2.54
Print holdings . . . 2.38
Visits per capita . . . 4.15

Housing & Construction

Housing Units

Total, 2008§ . . . 233
Single family units, attached . . . 8
Single family units, detached . . . 183
Multiple family units . . . 11
Mobile home units . . . 31
Occupied . . . 172
Vacancy rate . . . 26.2%
Median rent, 2000** . . . $830
Median SF home value, 2000** . . . $321,200

New Privately Owned Housing Units Authorized by Building Permit, 2007*

	Units	Construction Cost
Single	0	$0
Total	0	$0

Municipal Finance

(For local fiscal year ended in 2006)

Revenues

Total . . . $1,099,288
Taxes . . . 375,902
Special benefits assessment . . . 0
Licenses & permits . . . 9,719
Fines & forfeitures . . . 4,124
Revenues from use of money & property . . . 87,363
Intergovernmental . . . 367,477
Service charges . . . 234,142
Other revenues . . . 20,561
Other financing sources . . . 0

Expenditures

Total . . . $866,417
General government . . . 68,489
Public safety . . . 237,079
Transportation . . . 115,431
Community development . . . 38,894
Health . . . 137,225
Culture & leisure . . . 83,241
Other . . . 0

Local School District

(Data from School year 2007-08 except as noted)

Northern Humboldt Union High
2755 McKinleyville Ave
McKinleyville, CA 95519
(707) 839-6470

Superintendent . . . Kenny Richards
Grade plan . . . 9-12
Number of schools . . . 7
Enrollment . . . 1,775
High school graduates, 2006-07 . . . 402
Dropout rate . . . 2.7%
Pupil/teacher ratio . . . 20.1
Average class size . . . 23.9
Students per computer . . . 2.7
Classrooms with internet . . . 115
Avg. Daily Attendance (ADA) . . . 1,613
Cost per ADA . . . $9,767
Avg. Teacher Salary . . . $59,111

California Achievement Tests 6th ed., 2008

(Pct scoring at or above 50th National Percentile Rank)

	Math	Reading	Language
Grade 3	NA	NA	NA
Grade 7	NA	NA	NA

Academic Performance Index, 2008

Number of students tested . . . 1,265
Number of valid scores . . . 1,211
2007 API (base) . . . 735
2008 API (growth) . . . 765

SAT Testing, 2006-07

Enrollment, Grade 12 . . . 480
Number taking test . . . 162
percent taking test . . . 33.8%
percent with total score 1,500+ . . . 24.60%

Average Scores:

Math	Verbal	Writing	Total
553	560	546	1,659

Federal No Child Left Behind, 2008

(Adequate Yearly Progress standards met)

	Participation Rate	Pct Proficient
ELA	Yes	Yes
Math	Yes	Yes

API criteria . . . Yes
Graduation rate . . . Yes
criteria met/possible . . . 14/14

Other school districts for this city

(see Appendix E for information on these districts)

Big Lagoon Union Elem, Trinidad Union Elem

See Introduction for an explanation of all data sources.

Demographics & Socio-Economic Characteristics

(2000 Decennial Census, except as noted)

Population

1990* .....NA
2000 13,864
Male 7,328
Female 6,536
Jan. 2008 (estimate)§ 16,165
Persons per sq. mi. of land 497.4

Race & Hispanic Origin, 2000

Race
White 12,254
Black/African American 34
North American Native 82
Asian 120
Pacific Islander 24
Other Race 1,050
Two or more races 300
Hispanic origin, total 1,773
Mexican 1,506
Puerto Rican 23
Cuban 10
Other Hispanic 234

Age & Nativity, 2000

Under 5 years 875
18 years and over 10,167
65 years and over 765
85 years and over 53
Median Age 35.3
Native-born 12,719
Foreign-born 1,248

Educational Attainment, 2000

Population 25 years and over 9,248
Less than 9th grade 3.1%
High school grad or higher 89.9%
Bachelor's degree or higher 33.0%
Graduate degree 8.4%

Income & Poverty, 1999

Per capita income $26,786
Median household income $58,848
Median family income $62,746
Persons in poverty 4.6%
H'holds receiving public assistance 115
H'holds receiving social security 650

Households, 2000

Total households 5,149
With persons under 18 1,990
With persons over 65 551
Family households 3,561
Single person households 961
Persons per household 2.68
Persons per family 3.09

Household Population, 2008§§

Persons living in households 16,124
Persons living in group quarters 41
Persons per household 2.6

Labor & Employment

Total civilian labor force, 2008§§ 9,840
Unemployment rate, 2008 .....5.4%
Total civilian labor force, 2000 8,435

Employed persons 16 years and over by occupation, 2000

Managers & professionals 2,597
Service occupations 1,559
Sales & office occupations 2,006
Farming, fishing & forestry 43
Construction & maintenance 1,305
Production & transportation 600
Self-employed persons 1,284

* US Census Bureau
** 2000 Decennial Census
§ California Department of Finance
§§ California Employment Development Dept

General Information

Town of Truckee
10183 Truckee Airport Rd
Truckee, CA 96161
530-582-7700

Website .....www.townoftruckee.com
Elevation .....5,995 ft.
Land Area (sq. miles) 32.5
Water Area (sq. miles) 1.3
Year of Incorporation 1993
Government type .....Charter
Sales tax rate 8.88%

Voters & Officials

Registered Voters, October 2008

Total 8,796
Democrats 3,441
Republicans 2,422
Declined to state 2,355

Legislative Districts

US Congressional 4
State Senatorial 1
State Assembly 3

Local Officials, 2009

Mayor .....Mark Brown
Manager .....Tony Lashbrook
City Clerk .....Judy Price
Attorney .....J. Dennis Crabb
Admin Svcs Dir .....Kim Szczurek
Public Works .....Daniel Wilkins
Planning/Dev Dir .....John McLaughlin
Building .....John McLaughlin
Police Chief .....Scott Berry
Emergency/Fire Dir .....Mike Terwilliger

Public Safety

Number of officers, 2007 24
Violent crimes, 2007 59
Property crimes, 2007 312
Arson, 2007 7

Public Library

Truckee Library
Nevada County Library System
10031 Levon Ave
Truckee, CA 96161
530-582-7846

Branch Librarian .....Lauri Ferguson

Library system statistics, FY 2007

Population served 99,766
Internet terminals 41
Annual users 46,411

Per capita:

Operating income $24.65
percent from local government 89.7%
Operating expenditure $24.33
Total materials 2.13
Print holdings 1.85
Visits per capita 4.86

Housing & Construction

Housing Units

Total, 2008§ 11,930
Single family units, attached 330
Single family units, detached 9,814
Multiple family units 1,488
Mobile home units 298
Occupied 6,296
Vacancy rate 47.2%
Median rent, 2000** $893
Median SF home value, 2000** $247,800

New Privately Owned Housing Units Authorized by Building Permit, 2007*

	Units	Construction Cost
Single	133	$41,419,453
Total	189	$50,125,237

Municipal Finance

(For local fiscal year ended in 2006)

Revenues

Total $29,489,949
Taxes 18,023,536
Special benefits assessment 818,348
Licenses & permits 974,505
Fines & forfeitures 459,328
Revenues from use of money & property 1,522,161
Intergovernmental 3,224,760
Service charges 3,360,660
Other revenues 1,106,651
Other financing sources 0

Expenditures

Total $27,083,459
General government 7,865,760
Public safety 4,660,649
Transportation 9,179,159
Community development 3,525,888
Health 1,584,201
Culture & leisure 267,802
Other 0

Local School District

(Data from School year 2007-08 except as noted)

Tahoe-Truckee Unified
11839 Donner Pass Rd
Truckee, CA 96161
(530) 582-2500

Superintendent .....Stephen Jennings
Grade plan K-12
Number of schools 11
Enrollment 4,090
High school graduates, 2006-07 277
Dropout rate 1.5%
Pupil/teacher ratio 17.1
Average class size 21.2
Students per computer 3.3
Classrooms with internet 247
Avg. Daily Attendance (ADA) 3,854
Cost per ADA $10,963
Avg. Teacher Salary $61,839

California Achievement Tests 6th ed., 2008

(Pct scoring at or above 50th National Percentile Rank)

	Math	Reading	Language
Grade 3	62%	57%	56%
Grade 7	71%	69%	62%

Academic Performance Index, 2008

Number of students tested 2,942
Number of valid scores 2,757
2007 API (base) 792
2008 API (growth) 792

SAT Testing, 2006-07

Enrollment, Grade 12 329
Number taking test 157
percent taking test 47.7%
percent with total score 1,500+ 25.50%

Average Scores:

Math	Verbal	Writing	Total
522	491	495	1,508

Federal No Child Left Behind, 2008

(Adequate Yearly Progress standards met)

	Participation Rate	Pct Proficient
ELA	No	No
Math	Yes	No

API criteria .....Yes
Graduation rate .....Yes
\# criteria met/possible 26/20

Other school districts for this city

(see Appendix E for information on these districts)

None

See Introduction for an explanation of all data sources.

Demographics & Socio-Economic Characteristics

(2000 Decennial Census, except as noted)

Population

1990* . . . 33,249
2000 . . . 43,994
Male . . . 21,364
Female . . . 22,630
Jan. 2008 (estimate)§ . . . 57,375
Persons per sq. mi. of land . . . 3,456.3

Race & Hispanic Origin, 2000

Race
White . . . 24,804
Black/African American . . . 2,209
North American Native . . . 616
Asian . . . 890
Pacific Islander . . . 54
Other Race . . . 12,798
Two or more races . . . 2,623
Hispanic origin, total . . . 20,058
Mexican . . . 17,006
Puerto Rican . . . 122
Cuban . . . 14
Other Hispanic . . . 2,916

Age & Nativity, 2000

Under 5 years . . . 4,230
18 years and over . . . 28,781
65 years and over . . . 4,119
85 years and over . . . 485
Median Age . . . 28.5
Native-born . . . 36,166
Foreign-born . . . 7,749

Educational Attainment, 2000

Population 25 years and over . . . 24,546
Less than 9th grade . . . 18.8%
High school grad or higher . . . 65.0%
Bachelor's degree or higher . . . 8.2%
Graduate degree . . . 2.6%

Income & Poverty, 1999

Per capita income . . . $13,655
Median household income . . . $33,637
Median family income . . . $36,935
Persons in poverty . . . 20.4%
H'holds receiving public assistance . . . 1,299
H'holds receiving social security . . . 3,263

Households, 2000

Total households . . . 13,543
With persons under 18 . . . 6,999
With persons over 65 . . . 2,938
Family households . . . 10,758
Single person households . . . 2,255
Persons per household . . . 3.22
Persons per family . . . 3.57

Household Population, 2008§§

Persons living in households . . . 56,928
Persons living in group quarters . . . 447
Persons per household . . . 3.3

Labor & Employment

Total civilian labor force, 2008§§ . . . 23,500
Unemployment rate, 2008 . . . 9.2%
Total civilian labor force, 2000 . . . 17,791

Employed persons 16 years and over by occupation, 2000

Managers & professionals . . . 3,285
Service occupations . . . 2,745
Sales & office occupations . . . 4,359
Farming, fishing & forestry . . . 935
Construction & maintenance . . . 1,661
Production & transportation . . . 2,897
Self-employed persons . . . 1,122

* US Census Bureau
** 2000 Decennial Census
§ California Department of Finance
§§ California Employment Development Dept

General Information

City of Tulare
411 E Kern
Tulare, CA 93274
559-684-4200

Website . . . www.ci.tulare.ca.us
Elevation . . . 288 ft.
Land Area (sq. miles) . . . 16.6
Water Area (sq. miles) . . . 0.1
Year of Incorporation . . . 1888
Government type . . . Chartered
Sales tax rate . . . 9.25%

Voters & Officials

Registered Voters, October 2008

Total . . . 19,502
Democrats . . . 7,514
Republicans . . . 8,195
Declined to state . . . 3,143

Legislative Districts

US Congressional . . . 21
State Senatorial . . . 18
State Assembly . . . 34

Local Officials, 2009

Mayor . . . Craig Vejvoda
Manager . . . Darrel L. Pyle
City Clerk . . . Darrel L. Pyle
Attorney . . . Steve Kabot
Finance Dir . . . Darlene Thompson
Public Works . . . Lew Nelson
Planning & Bldg Dir . . . Mark Kielty
Building . . . Ken Ramage
Police Chief . . . Roger Hill
Emergency/Fire Dir . . . Michael Threlkeld

Public Safety

Number of officers, 2007 . . . 68
Violent crimes, 2007 . . . 432
Property crimes, 2007 . . . NA
Arson, 2007 . . . 100

Public Library

Tulare Public Library
113 North F St
Tulare, CA 93274
559-685-2341

Director . . . Michael Stowell

Library statistics, FY 2007

Population served . . . 55,935
Internet terminals . . . 8
Annual users . . . 23,874

Per capita:

Operating income . . . $14.91
percent from local government . . . 91.8%
Operating expenditure . . . $13.37
Total materials . . . 2.17
Print holdings . . . 2.04
Visits per capita . . . 3.78

Housing & Construction

Housing Units

Total, 2008§ . . . 18,219
Single family units, attached . . . 511
Single family units, detached . . . 14,025
Multiple family units . . . 2,907
Mobile home units . . . 776
Occupied . . . 17,312
Vacancy rate . . . 5.0%
Median rent, 2000** . . . $541
Median SF home value, 2000** . . . $94,700

New Privately Owned Housing Units Authorized by Building Permit, 2007*

	Units	Construction Cost
Single	573	$76,851,703
Total	578	$77,259,973

Municipal Finance

(For local fiscal year ended in 2006)

Revenues

Total . . . $68,325,547
Taxes . . . 27,629,021
Special benefits assessment . . . 157,925
Licenses & permits . . . 1,505,099
Fines & forfeitures . . . 128,401
Revenues from use of money & property . . . 1,637,121
Intergovernmental . . . 5,327,503
Service charges . . . 27,625,319
Other revenues . . . 4,315,158
Other financing sources . . . 0

Expenditures

Total . . . $53,866,543
General government . . . 3,890,011
Public safety . . . 14,252,191
Transportation . . . 9,622,377
Community development . . . 2,858,295
Health . . . 16,162,600
Culture & leisure . . . 3,237,891
Other . . . 82,483

Local School District

(Data from School year 2007-08 except as noted)

Tulare Joint Union High
426 North Blackstone
Tulare, CA 93274
(559) 688-2021

Superintendent . . . Howard Berger
Grade plan . . . 9-12
Number of schools . . . 6
Enrollment . . . 4,923
High school graduates, 2006-07 . . . 939
Dropout rate . . . 4.5%
Pupil/teacher ratio . . . 23.7
Average class size . . . 27.6
Students per computer . . . 3.5
Classrooms with internet . . . 182
Avg. Daily Attendance (ADA) . . . 4,546
Cost per ADA . . . $7,952
Avg. Teacher Salary . . . $64,863

California Achievement Tests 6th ed., 2008

(Pct scoring at or above 50th National Percentile Rank)

	Math	Reading	Language
Grade 3	NA	NA	NA
Grade 7	NA	NA	NA

Academic Performance Index, 2008

Number of students tested . . . 3,703
Number of valid scores . . . 3,344
2007 API (base) . . . 679
2008 API (growth) . . . 697

SAT Testing, 2006-07

Enrollment, Grade 12 . . . 1,118
Number taking test . . . 268
percent taking test . . . 24.0%
percent with total score 1,500+ . . . 8.10%

Average Scores:

Math	Verbal	Writing	Total
478	461	461	1,400

Federal No Child Left Behind, 2008

(Adequate Yearly Progress standards met)

	Participation Rate	Pct Proficient
ELA	Yes	No
Math	Yes	Yes

API criteria . . . Yes
Graduation rate . . . No
\# criteria met/possible . . . 22/20

Other school districts for this city

(see Appendix E for information on these districts)

Complete list in Appendix E

See Introduction for an explanation of all data sources.

Demographics & Socio-Economic Characteristics

(2000 Decennial Census, except as noted)

Population

1990* 1,010
2000 1,020
Male 509
Female 511
Jan. 2008 (estimate)§ 970
Persons per sq. mi. of land 2,425.0

Race & Hispanic Origin, 2000

Race
White 732
Black/African American 11
North American Native 13
Asian 3
Pacific Islander 0
Other Race 172
Two or more races 89
Hispanic origin, total 462
Mexican 398
Puerto Rican 5
Cuban 1
Other Hispanic 58

Age & Nativity, 2000

Under 5 years 104
18 years and over 655
65 years and over 119
85 years and over 12
Median Age 30.2
Native-born 687
Foreign-born 322

Educational Attainment, 2000

Population 25 years and over 562
Less than 9th grade 26.9%
High school grad or higher 55.0%
Bachelor's degree or higher 6.9%
Graduate degree 0.5%

Income & Poverty, 1999

Per capita income $10,244
Median household income $23,750
Median family income $27,750
Persons in poverty 34.0%
H'holds receiving public assistance 30
H'holds receiving social security 81

Households, 2000

Total households 358
With persons under 18 160
With persons over 65 85
Family households 256
Single person households 90
Persons per household 2.85
Persons per family 3.48

Household Population, 2008§§

Persons living in households 970
Persons living in group quarters 0
Persons per household 2.7

Labor & Employment

Total civilian labor force, 2008§§ . . . . . NA
Unemployment rate, 2008 . . . . . NA
Total civilian labor force, 2000 426

Employed persons 16 years and over by occupation, 2000

Managers & professionals 57
Service occupations 56
Sales & office occupations 65
Farming, fishing & forestry 87
Construction & maintenance 25
Production & transportation 64
Self-employed persons 20

* US Census Bureau
** 2000 Decennial Census
§ California Department of Finance
§§ California Employment Development Dept

General Information

City of Tulelake
City Hall
PO Box 847
Tulelake, CA 96134
530-667-5522

Website . . . . . NA
Elevation . . . . . NA
Land Area (sq. miles) 0.4
Water Area (sq. miles) 0
Year of Incorporation 1937
Government type . . . . . General law
Sales tax rate 8.25%

Voters & Officials

Registered Voters, October 2008

Total 295
Democrats 72
Republicans 153
Declined to state 61

Legislative Districts

US Congressional 2
State Senatorial 4
State Assembly 2

Local Officials, 2009

Mayor . . . . . Jennifer Cooney
Manager/Admin . . . . . NA
City Clerk . . . . . Joe Cordonier
Attorney . . . . . John Kenny
Finance Dir . . . . . Elona Bunch
Public Works . . . . . Henry Ebinger
Planning/Dev Dir . . . . . NA
Building . . . . . Will Baley
Police Chief . . . . . Tony Ross
Emergency/Fire Dir . . . . . Steve Scott

Public Safety

Number of officers, 2007 3
Violent crimes, 2007 1
Property crimes, 2007 10
Arson, 2007 2

Public Library

Tulelake Branch Library
Siskiyou County Free Library System
451 Main Street
Tulelake, CA 96134
530-667-2291

Branch Librarian . . . . . Margaret McAuliffe

Library system statistics, FY 2007

Population served 45,953
Internet terminals 31
Annual users 48,766

Per capita:

Operating income $20.36
percent from local government 90.2%
Operating expenditure $20.12
Total materials 4.06
Print holdings 3.88
Visits per capita . . . . . NA

Housing & Construction

Housing Units

Total, 2008§ 461
Single family units, attached 2
Single family units, detached 316
Multiple family units 63
Mobile home units 80
Occupied 360
Vacancy rate 21.9%
Median rent, 2000** $412
Median SF home value, 2000** $42,700

New Privately Owned Housing Units Authorized by Building Permit, 2007*

	Units	Construction Cost
Single	0	$0
Total	0	$0

Municipal Finance

(For local fiscal year ended in 2006)

Revenues

Total . . . . . NA
Taxes . . . . . NA
Special benefits assessment . . . . . NA
Licenses & permits . . . . . NA
Fines & forfeitures . . . . . NA
Revenues from use of money & property . . . . . NA
Intergovernmental . . . . . NA
Service charges . . . . . NA
Other revenues . . . . . NA
Other financing sources . . . . . NA

Expenditures

Total . . . . . NA
General government . . . . . NA
Public safety . . . . . NA
Transportation . . . . . NA
Community development . . . . . NA
Health . . . . . NA
Culture & leisure . . . . . NA
Other . . . . . NA

Local School District

(Data from School year 2007-08 except as noted)

Tulelake Basin Joint Unified
PO Box 640
Tulelake, CA 96134
(530) 667-2295

Superintendent . . . . . Patricia Reeder
Grade plan K-12
Number of schools 5
Enrollment 543
High school graduates, 2006-07 33
Dropout rate 2.5%
Pupil/teacher ratio 15.9
Average class size 17.5
Students per computer 1.8
Classrooms with internet 50
Avg. Daily Attendance (ADA) 547
Cost per ADA $11,550
Avg. Teacher Salary $66,065

California Achievement Tests 6th ed., 2008

(Pct scoring at or above 50th National Percentile Rank)

	Math	Reading	Language
Grade 3	54%	46%	43%
Grade 7	58%	56%	54%

Academic Performance Index, 2008

Number of students tested 415
Number of valid scores 389
2007 API (base) 724
2008 API (growth) 716

SAT Testing, 2006-07

Enrollment, Grade 12 36
Number taking test 18
percent taking test 50.0%
percent with total score 1,500+ 13.90%

Average Scores:

Math	Verbal	Writing	Total
482	431	441	1,354

Federal No Child Left Behind, 2008

(Adequate Yearly Progress standards met)

	Participation Rate	Pct Proficient
ELA	Yes	No
Math	Yes	No

API criteria . . . . . Yes
Graduation rate . . . . . No
\# criteria met/possible 22/18

Other school districts for this city

(see Appendix E for information on these districts)

None

See Introduction for an explanation of all data sources.

Demographics & Socio-Economic Characteristics†

(2007 American Community Survey, except as noted)

Population

1990* . . . 42,198
2007 . . . 69,330
Male . . . 33,266
Female . . . 36,064
Jan. 2008 (estimate)§ . . . 70,158
Persons per sq. mi. of land . . . 5,275.0

Race & Hispanic Origin, 2007

Race
White . . . 50,769
Black/African American . . . 2,114
North American Native . . . 686
Asian . . . 3,781
Pacific Islander . . . 204
Other Race . . . 10,221
Two or more races . . . 1,555
Hispanic origin, total . . . 19,091
Mexican . . . NA
Puerto Rican . . . NA
Cuban . . . NA
Other Hispanic . . . NA

Age & Nativity, 2007

Under 5 years . . . 3,872
18 years and over . . . 50,462
65 years and over . . . 6,104
85 years and over . . . 998
Median Age . . . 30.3
Native-born . . . 54,720
Foreign-born . . . 14,610

Educational Attainment, 2007

Population 25 years and over . . . 40,562
Less than 9th grade . . . 6.5%
High school grad or higher . . . 83.2%
Bachelor's degree or higher . . . 22.7%
Graduate degree . . . 6.1%

Income & Poverty, 2007

Per capita income . . . $21,971
Median household income . . . $48,077
Median family income . . . $56,725
Persons in poverty . . . 10.0%
H'holds receiving public assistance . . . 1,176
H'holds receiving social security . . . 5,716

Households, 2007

Total households . . . 22,933
With persons under 18 . . . 10,170
With persons over 65 . . . 4,532
Family households . . . 16,206
Single person households . . . 5,151
Persons per household . . . 3.02
Persons per family . . . 3.57

Household Population, 2008§§

Persons living in households . . . 67,790
Persons living in group quarters . . . 2,368
Persons per household . . . 2.9

Labor & Employment

Total civilian labor force, 2008§§ . . . 28,900
Unemployment rate, 2008 . . . 8.4%
Total civilian labor force, 2000* . . . 24,552

Employed persons 16 years and over by occupation, 2007

Managers & professionals . . . 9,198
Service occupations . . . 5,749
Sales & office occupations . . . 9,216
Farming, fishing & forestry . . . 378
Construction & maintenance . . . 2,436
Production & transportation . . . 5,030
Self-employed persons . . . 2,444

† see Appendix D for 2000 Decennial Census Data
* US Census Bureau
** 2007 American Community Survey
§ California Department of Finance
§§ California Employment Development Dept

General Information

City of Turlock
156 S Broadway
Turlock, CA 95380
209-668-5540

Website . . . www.cityofturlock.org
Elevation . . . 101 ft.
Land Area (sq. miles) . . . 13.3
Water Area (sq. miles) . . . 0
Year of Incorporation . . . 1908
Government type . . . General law
Sales tax rate . . . 8.38%

Voters & Officials

Registered Voters, October 2008

Total . . . 31,402
Democrats . . . 12,243
Republicans . . . 12,688
Declined to state . . . 5,216

Legislative Districts

US Congressional . . . 19
State Senatorial . . . 12
State Assembly . . . 26

Local Officials, 2009

Mayor . . . John S. Lazar
Manager . . . Gary Hampton
City Clerk . . . Rhonda Greenlee
Attorney . . . Phaedra Norton
Finance Dir . . . Sheila Cumberland
Public Works . . . Mike Pitcock
Planning/Dev Dir . . . Debra Whitmore
Building . . . Mark Ellis
Police Chief . . . Gary Hampton
Emergency/Fire Dir . . . Mark Langley

Public Safety

Number of officers, 2007 . . . 68
Violent crimes, 2007 . . . 499
Property crimes, 2007 . . . 3,583
Arson, 2007 . . . NA

Public Library

Turlock Library
Stanislaus County Free Library
550 Minaret Ave
Turlock, CA 95380
209-664-8100

Branch Librarian . . . Diane Barlett

Library system statistics, FY 2007

Population served . . . 521,497
Internet terminals . . . 128
Annual users . . . 256,298

Per capita:

Operating income . . . $20.76
percent from local government . . . 91.0%
Operating expenditure . . . $20.19
Total materials . . . 1.66
Print holdings . . . 1.56
Visits per capita . . . NA

Housing & Construction

Housing Units

Total, 2008§ . . . 23,993
Single family units, attached . . . 961
Single family units, detached . . . 16,614
Multiple family units . . . 5,814
Mobile home units . . . 604
Occupied . . . 23,130
Vacancy rate . . . 3.6%
Median rent, 2007** . . . $888
Median SF home value, 2007** . . . $363,400

New Privately Owned Housing Units Authorized by Building Permit, 2007*

	Units	Construction Cost
Single	152	$23,835,782
Total	365	$43,050,328

Municipal Finance

(For local fiscal year ended in 2006)

Revenues

Total . . . $84,021,780
Taxes . . . 32,308,547
Special benefits assessment . . . 1,662,869
Licenses & permits . . . 103,623
Fines & forfeitures . . . 477,217
Revenues from use of money & property . . . 2,593,054
Intergovernmental . . . 9,804,935
Service charges . . . 34,429,399
Other revenues . . . 1,881,336
Other financing sources . . . 760,800

Expenditures

Total . . . $72,903,685
General government . . . 4,338,202
Public safety . . . 19,138,570
Transportation . . . 11,313,986
Community development . . . 6,152,039
Health . . . 22,854,371
Culture & leisure . . . 4,099,217
Other . . . 0

Local School District

(Data from School year 2007-08 except as noted)

Turlock Unified
PO Box 819013
Turlock, CA 95381
(209) 667-0633

Superintendent . . . Sonny Da Marto
Grade plan . . . K-12
Number of schools . . . 16
Enrollment . . . 13,890
High school graduates, 2006-07 . . . 974
Dropout rate . . . 4.3%
Pupil/teacher ratio . . . 21.6
Average class size . . . 25.7
Students per computer . . . 5.0
Classrooms with internet . . . 634
Avg. Daily Attendance (ADA) . . . 13,215
Cost per ADA . . . $8,002
Avg. Teacher Salary . . . $70,993

California Achievement Tests 6th ed., 2008

(Pct scoring at or above 50th National Percentile Rank)

	Math	Reading	Language
Grade 3	50%	32%	42%
Grade 7	50%	49%	46%

Academic Performance Index, 2008

Number of students tested . . . 10,476
Number of valid scores . . . 9,790
2007 API (base) . . . 723
2008 API (growth) . . . 732

SAT Testing, 2006-07

Enrollment, Grade 12 . . . 1,113
Number taking test . . . 282
percent taking test . . . 25.3%
percent with total score 1,500+ . . . 11.50%

Average Scores:

Math	Verbal	Writing	Total
506	497	497	1,500

Federal No Child Left Behind, 2008

(Adequate Yearly Progress standards met)

	Participation Rate	Pct Proficient
ELA	Yes	No
Math	Yes	No

API criteria . . . Yes
Graduation rate . . . Yes
\# criteria met/possible . . . 34/28

Other school districts for this city

(see Appendix E for information on these districts)

None

See Introduction for an explanation of all data sources.

Demographics & Socio-Economic Characteristics†

(2007 American Community Survey, except as noted)

Population

1990* ... 50,689
2007 ... 63,524
Male ... 31,027
Female ... 32,497
Jan. 2008 (estimate)§ ... 74,218
Persons per sq. mi. of land ... 6,510.4

Race & Hispanic Origin, 2007

Race
White ... 38,647
Black/African American ... 829
North American Native ... 844
Asian ... 12,040
Pacific Islander ... 0
Other Race ... 9,969
Two or more races ... 1,195
Hispanic origin, total ... 24,446
Mexican ... 20,157
Puerto Rican ... 162
Cuban ... 0
Other Hispanic ... 4,127

Age & Nativity, 2007

Under 5 years ... 5,500
18 years and over ... 47,429
65 years and over ... 6,501
85 years and over ... 288
Median Age ... 35.4
Native-born ... 40,606
Foreign-born ... 22,918

Educational Attainment, 2007

Population 25 years and over ... 41,861
Less than 9th grade ... 7.6%
High school grad or higher ... 84.8%
Bachelor's degree or higher ... 40.2%
Graduate degree ... 12.0%

Income & Poverty, 2007

Per capita income ... $32,906
Median household income ... $63,301
Median family income ... $70,110
Persons in poverty ... 5.7%
H'holds receiving public assistance ... 212
H'holds receiving social security ... 4,295

Households, 2007

Total households ... 22,435
With persons under 18 ... 8,366
With persons over 65 ... 4,435
Family households ... 15,516
Single person households ... 5,698
Persons per household ... 2.83
Persons per family ... 3.34

Household Population, 2008§§

Persons living in households ... 73,800
Persons living in group quarters ... 418
Persons per household ... 2.9

Labor & Employment

Total civilian labor force, 2008§§ ... 42,800
Unemployment rate, 2008 ... 5.2%
Total civilian labor force, 2000* ... 36,646

Employed persons 16 years and over by occupation, 2007

Managers & professionals ... 15,315
Service occupations ... 4,341
Sales & office occupations ... 10,067
Farming, fishing & forestry ... 0
Construction & maintenance ... 1,875
Production & transportation ... 2,097
Self-employed persons ... 3,044

† see Appendix D for 2000 Decennial Census Data
* US Census Bureau
** 2007 American Community Survey
§ California Department of Finance
§§ California Employment Development Dept

General Information

City of Tustin
300 Centennial Way
Tustin, CA 92780
714-573-3000

Website ... www.tustinca.org
Elevation ... 130 ft.
Land Area (sq. miles) ... 11.4
Water Area (sq. miles) ... 0
Year of Incorporation ... 1927
Government type ... General law
Sales tax rate ... 8.75%

Voters & Officials

Registered Voters, October 2008

Total ... 34,729
Democrats ... 11,061
Republicans ... 14,541
Declined to state ... 7,728

Legislative Districts

US Congressional ... 48
State Senatorial ... 33
State Assembly ... 70, 71

Local Officials, 2009

Mayor ... Jerry Amante
Manager ... William A. Huston
City Clerk ... Pamela Stoker
Attorney ... Douglas C. Holland
Finance Dir ... Pam Arends-King
Public Works ... Tim Serlet
Planning/Dev Dir ... Elizabeth Binsack
Building ... Henry Huang
Police Chief ... Scott Jordan
Fire/Emergency Mgmt ... NA

Public Safety

Number of officers, 2007 ... 94
Violent crimes, 2007 ... 137
Property crimes, 2007 ... 1,575
Arson, 2007 ... 19

Public Library

Tustin Branch Library
Orange County Public Library System
345 E Main St
Tustin, CA 92780
714-544-7725

Branch Librarian ... Sharon Nicola

Library system statistics, FY 2007

Population served ... 1,532,758
Internet terminals ... 505
Annual users ... 680,874

Per capita:

Operating income ... $24.71
percent from local government ... 90.0%
Operating expenditure ... $24.18
Total materials ... 1.93
Print holdings ... 1.84
Visits per capita ... 4.02

Housing & Construction

Housing Units

Total, 2008§ ... 25,994
Single family units, attached ... 4,133
Single family units, detached ... 8,888
Multiple family units ... 12,065
Mobile home units ... 908
Occupied ... 25,290
Vacancy rate ... 2.7%
Median rent, 2007** ... $1,362
Median SF home value, 2007** ... $615,500

New Privately Owned Housing Units Authorized by Building Permit, 2007*

	Units	Construction Cost
Single	354	$75,028,779
Total	424	$80,127,024

Municipal Finance

(For local fiscal year ended in 2006)

Revenues

Total ... $75,984,170
Taxes ... 39,994,721
Special benefits assessment ... 1,360,230
Licenses & permits ... 2,124,569
Fines & forfeitures ... 784,967
Revenues from use of money & property ... 2,719,606
Intergovernmental ... 4,046,335
Service charges ... 18,542,723
Other revenues ... 6,411,019
Other financing sources ... 0

Expenditures

Total ... $78,133,572
General government ... 5,368,933
Public safety ... 24,824,314
Transportation ... 23,832,410
Community development ... 11,718,553
Health ... 0
Culture & leisure ... 4,353,997
Other ... 0

Local School District

(Data from School year 2007-08 except as noted)

Tustin Unified
300 South C St
Tustin, CA 92780
(714) 730-7301

Superintendent ... Richard Bray
Grade plan ... K-12
Number of schools ... 28
Enrollment ... 20,909
High school graduates, 2006-07 ... 1,135
Dropout rate ... 1.1%
Pupil/teacher ratio ... 23.6
Average class size ... 28.3
Students per computer ... 5.1
Classrooms with internet ... 929
Avg. Daily Attendance (ADA) ... 20,462
Cost per ADA ... $7,474
Avg. Teacher Salary ... $69,708

California Achievement Tests 6th ed., 2008

(Pct scoring at or above 50th National Percentile Rank)

	Math	Reading	Language
Grade 3	70%	50%	60%
Grade 7	64%	64%	61%

Academic Performance Index, 2008

Number of students tested ... 16,143
Number of valid scores ... 15,272
2007 API (base) ... 815
2008 API (growth) ... 827

SAT Testing, 2006-07

Enrollment, Grade 12 ... 1,301
Number taking test ... 593
percent taking test ... 45.6%
percent with total score 1,500+ ... 27.60%

Average Scores:

Math	Verbal	Writing	Total
543	523	523	1,589

Federal No Child Left Behind, 2008

(Adequate Yearly Progress standards met)

	Participation Rate	Pct Proficient
ELA	Yes	Yes
Math	Yes	Yes

API criteria ... Yes
Graduation rate ... Yes
\# criteria met/possible ... 38/38

Other school districts for this city

(see Appendix E for information on these districts)

Santa Ana Unified

See Introduction for an explanation of all data sources.

Demographics & Socio-Economic Characteristics

(2000 Decennial Census, except as noted)

Population

1990*	11,821
2000	14,764
Male	7,449
Female	7,315
Jan. 2008 (estimate)§	27,966
Persons per sq. mi. of land	510.3

Race & Hispanic Origin, 2000

Race	
White	10,485
Black/African American	1,381
North American Native	215
Asian	563
Pacific Islander	260
Other Race	921
Two or more races	939
Hispanic origin, total	2,202
Mexican	1,512
Puerto Rican	143
Cuban	35
Other Hispanic	512

Age & Nativity, 2000

Under 5 years	1,442
18 years and over	10,163
65 years and over	1,273
85 years and over	120
Median Age	26.9
Native-born	13,782
Foreign-born	872

Educational Attainment, 2000

Population 25 years and over	7,677
Less than 9th grade	4.0%
High school grad or higher	82.0%
Bachelor's degree or higher	13.3%
Graduate degree	4.8%

Income & Poverty, 1999

Per capita income	$14,613
Median household income	$31,178
Median family income	$32,251
Persons in poverty	16.5%
H'holds receiving public assistance	354
H'holds receiving social security	1,284

Households, 2000

Total households	5,653
With persons under 18	2,407
With persons over 65	956
Family households	3,856
Single person households	1,421
Persons per household	2.60
Persons per family	3.12

Household Population, 2008§§

Persons living in households	20,283
Persons living in group quarters	7,683
Persons per household	2.7

Labor & Employment

Total civilian labor force, 2008§§	6,200
Unemployment rate, 2008	9.2%
Total civilian labor force, 2000	5,073

Employed persons 16 years and over by occupation, 2000

Managers & professionals	1,321
Service occupations	1,134
Sales & office occupations	1,309
Farming, fishing & forestry	0
Construction & maintenance	414
Production & transportation	410
Self-employed persons	373

* US Census Bureau
** 2000 Decennial Census
§ California Department of Finance
§§ California Employment Development Dept

General Information

City of Twentynine Palms
6136 Adobe Rd
Twentynine Palms, CA 92277
760-367-6799

Website	www.ci.twentynine-palms.ca.us
Elevation	NA
Land Area (sq. miles)	54.8
Water Area (sq. miles)	0
Year of Incorporation	1987
Government type	General Law
Sales tax rate	8.75%

Voters & Officials

Registered Voters, October 2008

Total	6,250
Democrats	1,768
Republicans	2,677
Declined to state	1,483

Legislative Districts

US Congressional	41
State Senatorial	18
State Assembly	65

Local Officials, 2009

Mayor	Joel Klink
Manager	Michael Tree
City Clerk	Char Sherwood
Attorney	Patrick Munoz
Finance Dir	Ron Peck
Public Works	Jose Nieves
Planning/Dev Dir	Charles LaClaire
Building	Jerry Arrasmith
Police Chief	Donnie Miller
Emergency/Fire Dir	Jim Thompson

Public Safety

Number of officers, 2007	NA
Violent crimes, 2007	96
Property crimes, 2007	493
Arson, 2007	9

Public Library

Twentynine Palms Branch Library
San Bernardino County Library System
6078 Adobe Rd
Twentynine Palms, CA 92277
760-367-9519

Branch Librarian . . . . Linda Muller

Library system statistics, FY 2007

Population served	1,177,092
Internet terminals	12
Annual users	45,343

Per capita:

Operating income	$14.27
percent from local government	73.3%
Operating expenditure	$13.86
Total materials	0.86
Print holdings	0.79
Visits per capita	5.83

Housing & Construction

Housing Units

Total, 2008§	9,185
Single family units, attached	1,303
Single family units, detached	5,139
Multiple family units	2,194
Mobile home units	549
Occupied	7,446
Vacancy rate	18.9%
Median rent, 2000**	$470
Median SF home value, 2000**	$75,400

New Privately Owned Housing Units Authorized by Building Permit, 2007*

	Units	Construction Cost
Single	99	$9,949,197
Total	125	$11,108,347

Municipal Finance

(For local fiscal year ended in 2006)

Revenues

Total	$10,496,797
Taxes	6,368,968
Special benefits assessment	22,839
Licenses & permits	565,738
Fines & forfeitures	37,904
Revenues from use of money & property	325,896
Intergovernmental	2,350,697
Service charges	379,771
Other revenues	243,440
Other financing sources	201,544

Expenditures

Total	$8,657,300
General government	1,029,783
Public safety	2,431,439
Transportation	1,974,358
Community development	789,018
Health	82,001
Culture & leisure	2,350,701
Other	0

Local School District

(Data from School year 2007-08 except as noted)

Morongo Unified
PO Box 1209
Twentynine Palms, CA 92277
(760) 367-9191

Superintendent	James Majchrzak
Grade plan	K-12
Number of schools	18
Enrollment	9,631
High school graduates, 2006-07	491
Dropout rate	4.0%
Pupil/teacher ratio	20.1
Average class size	22.7
Students per computer	4.0
Classrooms with internet	481
Avg. Daily Attendance (ADA)	9,009
Cost per ADA	$8,507
Avg. Teacher Salary	$62,656

California Achievement Tests 6th ed., 2008

(Pct scoring at or above 50th National Percentile Rank)

	Math	Reading	Language
Grade 3	52%	38%	48%
Grade 7	54%	51%	46%

Academic Performance Index, 2008

Number of students tested	7,280
Number of valid scores	6,492
2007 API (base)	728
2008 API (growth)	741

SAT Testing, 2006-07

Enrollment, Grade 12	641
Number taking test	126
percent taking test	19.7%
percent with total score 1,500+	10.80%

Average Scores:

Math	Verbal	Writing	Total
528	504	506	1,538

Federal No Child Left Behind, 2008

(Adequate Yearly Progress standards met)

	Participation Rate	Pct Proficient
ELA	Yes	No
Math	Yes	No

API criteria	Yes
Graduation rate	Yes
# criteria met/possible	32/28

Other school districts for this city

(see Appendix E for information on these districts)

None

See Introduction for an explanation of all data sources.

Demographics & Socio-Economic Characteristics

(2000 Decennial Census, except as noted)

Population

1990*	14,599
2000	15,497
Male	7,416
Female	8,081
Jan. 2008 (estimate)§	15,758
Persons per sq. mi. of land	3,352.8

Race & Hispanic Origin, 2000

Race	
White	12,325
Black/African American	148
North American Native	587
Asian	261
Pacific Islander	15
Other Race	1,499
Two or more races	662
Hispanic origin, total	2,993
Mexican	2,556
Puerto Rican	23
Cuban	15
Other Hispanic	399

Age & Nativity, 2000

Under 5 years	1,078
18 years and over	11,383
65 years and over	2,209
85 years and over	416
Median Age	35.0
Native-born	13,543
Foreign-born	1,570

Educational Attainment, 2000

Population 25 years and over	9,591
Less than 9th grade	9.1%
High school grad or higher	78.0%
Bachelor's degree or higher	16.1%
Graduate degree	5.9%

Income & Poverty, 1999

Per capita income	$17,601
Median household income	$32,707
Median family income	$39,524
Persons in poverty	16.9%
H'holds receiving public assistance	413
H'holds receiving social security	1,724

Households, 2000

Total households	5,985
With persons under 18	2,179
With persons over 65	1,608
Family households	3,654
Single person households	1,927
Persons per household	2.47
Persons per family	3.12

Household Population, 2008§§

Persons living in households	15,024
Persons living in group quarters	734
Persons per household	2.4

Labor & Employment

Total civilian labor force, 2008§§	7,490
Unemployment rate, 2008	7.0%
Total civilian labor force, 2000	7,097

Employed persons 16 years and over by occupation, 2000

Managers & professionals	1,911
Service occupations	1,127
Sales & office occupations	1,932
Farming, fishing & forestry	161
Construction & maintenance	542
Production & transportation	899
Self-employed persons	554

* US Census Bureau
** 2000 Decennial Census
§ California Department of Finance
§§ California Employment Development Dept

General Information

City of Ukiah
300 Seminary Ave
Ukiah, CA 95482
707-463-6200

Website	www.cityofukiah.com
Elevation	639 ft.
Land Area (sq. miles)	4.7
Water Area (sq. miles)	0
Year of Incorporation	1876
Government type	General law
Sales tax rate	8.75%

Voters & Officials

Registered Voters, October 2008

Total	7,801
Democrats	3,733
Republicans	1,996
Declined to state	1,576

Legislative Districts

US Congressional	1
State Senatorial	2
State Assembly	1

Local Officials, 2009

Mayor	Philip E. Baldwin
Manager	Jane A. Chambers
City Clerk	Linda C. Brown
Attorney	David Rapport
Finance Dir	Gordon Elton
Public Works	NA
Planning/Dev Dir	NA
Building	NA
Police Chief	Chris Dewey
Emergency/Fire Dir	Chris Dewey

Public Safety

Number of officers, 2007	28
Violent crimes, 2007	134
Property crimes, 2007	474
Arson, 2007	4

Public Library

Ukiah Branch Library
Marin County Free Library System
105 N Main St
Ukiah, CA 95482
707-463-4490

County Library Dir ..... Melanie Lightbody

Library system statistics, FY 2007

Population served	90,291
Internet terminals	20
Annual users	37,258

Per capita:

Operating income	$18.48
percent from local government	58.6%
Operating expenditure	$19.03
Total materials	2.07
Print holdings	1.94
Visits per capita	NA

Housing & Construction

Housing Units

Total, 2008§	6,399
Single family units, attached	379
Single family units, detached	3,548
Multiple family units	2,010
Mobile home units	462
Occupied	6,240
Vacancy rate	2.5%
Median rent, 2000**	$599
Median SF home value, 2000**	$146,900

New Privately Owned Housing Units Authorized by Building Permit, 2007*

	Units	Construction Cost
Single	4	$813,627
Total	6	$1,125,102

Municipal Finance

(For local fiscal year ended in 2006)

Revenues

Total	$127,740,360
Taxes	8,662,778
Special benefits assessment	0
Licenses & permits	153,096
Fines & forfeitures	70,851
Revenues from use of money & property	3,060,586
Intergovernmental	1,884,827
Service charges	24,798,038
Other revenues	-304,816
Other financing sources	89,415,000

Expenditures

Total	$51,270,132
General government	1,034,969
Public safety	7,493,574
Transportation	3,504,097
Community development	925,504
Health	10,913,322
Culture & leisure	3,642,647
Other	0

Local School District

(Data from School year 2007-08 except as noted)

Ukiah Unified
925 North State St
Ukiah, CA 95482
(707) 463-5211

Superintendent	Lois Nash
Grade plan	K-12
Number of schools	16
Enrollment	6,425
High school graduates, 2006-07	442
Dropout rate	3.8%
Pupil/teacher ratio	20.2
Average class size	24.4
Students per computer	3.6
Classrooms with internet	318
Avg. Daily Attendance (ADA)	5,397
Cost per ADA	$9,198
Avg. Teacher Salary	$58,250

California Achievement Tests 6th ed., 2008

(Pct scoring at or above 50th National Percentile Rank)

	Math	Reading	Language
Grade 3	40%	24%	32%
Grade 7	48%	50%	46%

Academic Performance Index, 2008

Number of students tested	4,309
Number of valid scores	4,068
2007 API (base)	688
2008 API (growth)	696

SAT Testing, 2006-07

Enrollment, Grade 12	515
Number taking test	140
percent taking test	27.2%
percent with total score 1,500+	17.10%

Average Scores:

Math	Verbal	Writing	Total
538	516	505	1,559

Federal No Child Left Behind, 2008

(Adequate Yearly Progress standards met)

	Participation Rate	Pct Proficient
ELA	Yes	No
Math	Yes	No

API criteria	Yes
Graduation rate	Yes
# criteria met/possible	30/21

Other school districts for this city

(see Appendix E for information on these districts)

None

See Introduction for an explanation of all data sources.

Demographics & Socio-Economic Characteristics†

(2007 American Community Survey, except as noted)

Population

1990* ... 53,762
2007 ... 73,212
Male ... 37,879
Female ... 35,333
Jan. 2008 (estimate)§ ... 73,402
Persons per sq. mi. of land ... 3,803.2

Race & Hispanic Origin, 2007

Race
White ... 23,914
Black/African American ... 4,587
North American Native ... 74
Asian ... 34,020
Pacific Islander ... 470
Other Race ... 8,148
Two or more races ... 1,999
Hispanic origin, total ... 15,376
Mexican ... NA
Puerto Rican ... NA
Cuban ... NA
Other Hispanic ... NA

Age & Nativity, 2007

Under 5 years ... 5,422
18 years and over ... 54,465
65 years and over ... 8,659
85 years and over ... 2,524
Median Age ... 37.9
Native-born ... 40,152
Foreign-born ... 33,060

Educational Attainment, 2007

Population 25 years and over ... 48,384
Less than 9th grade ... 9.3%
High school grad or higher ... 83.6%
Bachelor's degree or higher ... 36.6%
Graduate degree ... 9.0%

Income & Poverty, 2007

Per capita income ... $28,461
Median household income ... $87,891
Median family income ... $87,307
Persons in poverty ... 7.9%
H'holds receiving public assistance ... 652
H'holds receiving social security ... 3,899

Households, 2007

Total households ... 19,291
With persons under 18 ... 9,602
With persons over 65 ... 3,707
Family households ... 16,683
Single person households ... 1,840
Persons per household ... 3.62
Persons per family ... 3.75

Household Population, 2008§§

Persons living in households ... 73,060
Persons living in group quarters ... 342
Persons per household ... 3.6

Labor & Employment

Total civilian labor force, 2008§§ ... 34,700
Unemployment rate, 2008 ... 5.8%
Total civilian labor force, 2000* ... 32,949

Employed persons 16 years and over by occupation, 2007

Managers & professionals ... 11,429
Service occupations ... 5,361
Sales & office occupations ... 8,222
Farming, fishing & forestry ... 0
Construction & maintenance ... 2,891
Production & transportation ... 4,988
Self-employed persons ... 1,722

† see Appendix D for 2000 Decennial Census Data
* US Census Bureau
** 2007 American Community Survey
§ California Department of Finance
§§ California Employment Development Dept

General Information

City of Union City
34009 Alvarado-Niles Rd
Union City, CA 94587
510-471-3232

Website ... www.ci.union-city.ca.us
Elevation ... 10 ft.
Land Area (sq. miles) ... 19.3
Water Area (sq. miles) ... 0
Year of Incorporation ... 1959
Government type ... General law
Sales tax rate ... 9.75%

Voters & Officials

Registered Voters, October 2008

Total ... 41,758
Democrats ... 17,544
Republicans ... 14,279
Declined to state ... 8,357

Legislative Districts

US Congressional ... 13
State Senatorial ... 10
State Assembly ... 20

Local Officials, 2009

Mayor ... Mark Green
Manager ... Larry Cheeves
City Clerk ... Renee Elliott
Attorney ... Mike Riback
Admin Svcs Dir ... Richard Digre
Public Works ... Mintze Cheng
Planning/Dev Dir ... Carmela Campbell
Building ... Kevin Reese
Police Chief ... Greg Stewart
Fire Chief ... Carlos Rodriguez

Public Safety

Number of officers, 2007 ... 80
Violent crimes, 2007 ... 449
Property crimes, 2007 ... 2,022
Arson, 2007 ... 22

Public Library

Union City Library
Alameda County Library System
34007 Alvarado-Niles Rd
Union City, CA 94587
510-745-1464

Branch Librarian ... Mira Geroy

Library system statistics, FY 2007

Population served ... 527,926
Internet terminals ... 193
Annual users ... 358,689

Per capita:

Operating income ... $41.07
percent from local government ... 94.7%
Operating expenditure ... $36.47
Total materials ... 2.21
Print holdings ... 1.91
Visits per capita ... 4.32

Housing & Construction

Housing Units

Total, 2008§ ... 20,483
Single family units, attached ... 2,381
Single family units, detached ... 12,926
Multiple family units ... 4,249
Mobile home units ... 927
Occupied ... 20,227
Vacancy rate ... 1.3%
Median rent, 2007** ... $1,293
Median SF home value, 2007** ... $639,900

New Privately Owned Housing Units Authorized by Building Permit, 2007*

	Units	Construction Cost
Single	177	$47,165,421
Total	569	$93,933,007

Municipal Finance

(For local fiscal year ended in 2006)

Revenues

Total ... $64,433,825
Taxes ... 38,540,839
Special benefits assessment ... 6,724,123
Licenses & permits ... 1,962,413
Fines & forfeitures ... 769,533
Revenues from use of money & property ... 1,343,671
Intergovernmental ... 5,437,064
Service charges ... 9,178,994
Other revenues ... 477,188
Other financing sources ... 0

Expenditures

Total ... $63,073,516
General government ... 6,878,269
Public safety ... 28,805,717
Transportation ... 8,805,225
Community development ... 2,823,483
Health ... 410,586
Culture & leisure ... 15,350,236
Other ... 0

Local School District

(Data from School year 2007-08 except as noted)

New Haven Unified
34200 Alvarado-Niles Rd
Union City, CA 94587
(510) 471-1100

Superintendent ... Karen McVeigh
Grade plan ... K-12
Number of schools ... 15
Enrollment ... 13,004
High school graduates, 2006-07 ... 832
Dropout rate ... 2.9%
Pupil/teacher ratio ... 20.6
Average class size ... 26.9
Students per computer ... 2.7
Classrooms with internet ... 635
Avg. Daily Attendance (ADA) ... 12,776
Cost per ADA ... $8,202
Avg. Teacher Salary ... $77,092

California Achievement Tests 6th ed., 2008

(Pct scoring at or above 50th National Percentile Rank)

	Math	Reading	Language
Grade 3	62%	35%	43%
Grade 7	49%	47%	48%

Academic Performance Index, 2008

Number of students tested ... 9,913
Number of valid scores ... 9,352
2007 API (base) ... 754
2008 API (growth) ... 768

SAT Testing, 2006-07

Enrollment, Grade 12 ... 1,100
Number taking test ... 481
percent taking test ... 43.7%
percent with total score 1,500+ ... 18.90%

Average Scores:

Math	Verbal	Writing	Total
512	475	478	1,465

Federal No Child Left Behind, 2008

(Adequate Yearly Progress standards met)

	Participation Rate	Pct Proficient
ELA	Yes	No
Math	Yes	No

API criteria ... Yes
Graduation rate ... Yes
criteria met/possible ... 42/40

Other school districts for this city

(see Appendix E for information on these districts)

None

See Introduction for an explanation of all data sources.

Demographics & Socio-Economic Characteristics†

(2007 American Community Survey, except as noted)

Population
1990* 63,374
2007 78,260
Male 38,223
Female 40,037
Jan. 2008 (estimate)§ 75,137
Persons per sq. mi. of land 4,976.0

Race & Hispanic Origin, 2007
Race
White 46,124
Black/African American 4,987
North American Native 177
Asian 7,797
Pacific Islander 120
Other Race 12,900
Two or more races 6,155
Hispanic origin, total 27,044
Mexican 20,188
Puerto Rican 272
Cuban 338
Other Hispanic 6,246

Age & Nativity, 2007
Under 5 years 6,049
18 years and over 57,996
65 years and over 8,026
85 years and over 1,265
Median Age 33.3
Native-born 63,738
Foreign-born 14,522

Educational Attainment, 2007
Population 25 years and over 50,223
Less than 9th grade 3.8%
High school grad or higher 89.3%
Bachelor's degree or higher 29.5%
Graduate degree 9.4%

Income & Poverty, 2007
Per capita income $28,659
Median household income $63,519
Median family income $74,199
Persons in poverty 6.5%
H'holds receiving public assistance 344
H'holds receiving social security 5,863

Households, 2007
Total households 26,918
With persons under 18 10,528
With persons over 65 5,845
Family households 19,074
Single person households 5,711
Persons per household 2.91
Persons per family 3.47

Household Population, 2008§§
Persons living in households 74,552
Persons living in group quarters 585
Persons per household 2.9

Labor & Employment
Total civilian labor force, 2008§§ 41,400
Unemployment rate, 2008 .... 5.4%
Total civilian labor force, 2000* 34,012

Employed persons 16 years and over by occupation, 2007
Managers & professionals 13,975
Service occupations 6,358
Sales & office occupations 12,267
Farming, fishing & forestry 0
Construction & maintenance 3,030
Production & transportation 3,617
Self-employed persons 3,079

† see Appendix D for 2000 Decennial Census Data
* US Census Bureau
** 2007 American Community Survey
§ California Department of Finance
§§ California Employment Development Dept

General Information

City of Upland
460 N Euclid Ave
Upland, CA 91786
909-931-4100

Website .... www.ci.upland.ca.us
Elevation .... 1,245 ft.
Land Area (sq. miles) 15.1
Water Area (sq. miles) 0
Year of Incorporation 1906
Government type .... General law
Sales tax rate 8.75%

Voters & Officials

Registered Voters, October 2008
Total 53,171
Democrats 32,965
Republicans 8,270
Declined to state 10,215

Legislative Districts
US Congressional 26
State Senatorial 31
State Assembly 63

Local Officials, 2009
Mayor .... John Pomierski
Manager .... Robb Quincy
City Clerk .... Stephanie Mendenhall
Attorney .... William P. Curley III
Finance Dir .... Stephen Dunn
Public Works .... NA
Planning/Dev Dir .... NA
Building .... NA
Police Chief .... Steve Adams
Emergency/Fire Dir .... Michael Antonucci

Public Safety

Number of officers, 2007 79
Violent crimes, 2007 291
Property crimes, 2007 2,731
Arson, 2007 8

Public Library

Upland Public Library
450 N Euclid Ave
Upland, CA 91786
909-931-4200

Director .... Kathryn Bloomberg-Rissman

Library statistics, FY 2007
Population served 75,169
Internet terminals 11
Annual users 19,982

Per capita:
Operating income $25.05
percent from local government 90.9%
Operating expenditure $22.00
Total materials 1.93
Print holdings 1.67
Visits per capita 2.73

Housing & Construction

Housing Units
Total, 2008§ 26,628
Single family units, attached 1,770
Single family units, detached 15,300
Multiple family units 8,713
Mobile home units 845
Occupied 25,669
Vacancy rate 3.6%
Median rent, 2007** $1,122
Median SF home value, 2007** $575,500

New Privately Owned Housing Units Authorized by Building Permit, 2007*

	Units	Construction Cost
Single	86	$18,818,670
Total	86	$18,818,670

Municipal Finance

(For local fiscal year ended in 2006)

Revenues
Total $81,428,245
Taxes 26,830,035
Special benefits assessment 559,942
Licenses & permits 2,191,481
Fines & forfeitures 1,236,448
Revenues from use of money & property 1,838,562
Intergovernmental 6,610,618
Service charges 30,544,617
Other revenues 11,616,542
Other financing sources 0

Expenditures
Total $81,050,284
General government 4,738,016
Public safety 22,783,177
Transportation 20,137,282
Community development 3,664,047
Health 15,531,418
Culture & leisure 4,228,593
Other 0

Local School District

(Data from School year 2007-08 except as noted)
Upland Unified
390 North Euclid Ave
Upland, CA 91786
(909) 985-1864

Superintendent .... Gary Rutherford
Grade plan K-12
Number of schools 15
Enrollment 14,232
High school graduates, 2006-07 989
Dropout rate 14.0%
Pupil/teacher ratio 21.7
Average class size 26.5
Students per computer 4.6
Classrooms with internet 526
Avg. Daily Attendance (ADA) 11,772
Cost per ADA $7,448
Avg. Teacher Salary $71,473

California Achievement Tests 6th ed., 2008
(Pct scoring at or above 50th National Percentile Rank)

	Math	Reading	Language
Grade 3	62%	48%	57%
Grade 7	60%	54%	52%

Academic Performance Index, 2008
Number of students tested 9,595
Number of valid scores 8,967
2007 API (base) 785
2008 API (growth) 788

SAT Testing, 2006-07
Enrollment, Grade 12 1,139
Number taking test 347
percent taking test 30.5%
percent with total score 1,500+ 16.20%

Average Scores:

Math	Verbal	Writing	Total
534	499	496	1,529

Federal No Child Left Behind, 2008
(Adequate Yearly Progress standards met)

	Participation Rate	Pct Proficient
ELA	Yes	No
Math	Yes	No

API criteria .... Yes
Graduation rate .... Yes
\# criteria met/possible 38/36

Other school districts for this city
(see Appendix E for information on these districts)
None

See Introduction for an explanation of all data sources.

Demographics & Socio-Economic Characteristics†

(2007 American Community Survey, except as noted)

Population

1990* . . . 71,479
2007 . . . 93,795
Male . . . 50,775
Female . . . 43,020
Jan. 2008 (estimate)§ . . . 96,905
Persons per sq. mi. of land . . . 3,575.8

Race & Hispanic Origin, 2007

Race
White . . . 65,685
Black/African American . . . 10,016
North American Native . . . 471
Asian . . . 5,884
Pacific Islander . . . 1,095
Other Race . . . 6,623
Two or more races . . . 4,021
Hispanic origin, total . . . 15,984
Mexican . . . NA
Puerto Rican . . . NA
Cuban . . . NA
Other Hispanic . . . NA

Age & Nativity, 2007

Under 5 years . . . 4,398
18 years and over . . . 70,718
65 years and over . . . 9,241
85 years and over . . . 1,039
Median Age . . . 36.8
Native-born . . . 85,602
Foreign-born . . . 8,193

Educational Attainment, 2007

Population 25 years and over . . . 61,785
Less than 9th grade . . . 4.7%
High school grad or higher . . . 85.9%
Bachelor's degree or higher . . . 18.6%
Graduate degree . . . 6.0%

Income & Poverty, 2007

Per capita income . . . $27,700
Median household income . . . $68,704
Median family income . . . $79,865
Persons in poverty . . . 6.1%
H'holds receiving public assistance . . . 837
H'holds receiving social security . . . 7,842

Households, 2007

Total households . . . 30,262
With persons under 18 . . . 12,204
With persons over 65 . . . 6,800
Family households . . . 20,817
Single person households . . . 8,075
Persons per household . . . 2.76
Persons per family . . . 3.36

Household Population, 2008§§

Persons living in households . . . 87,444
Persons living in group quarters . . . 9,461
Persons per household . . . 2.7

Labor & Employment

Total civilian labor force, 2008§§ . . . 45,800
Unemployment rate, 2008 . . . 5.1%
Total civilian labor force, 2000* . . . 39,347

Employed persons 16 years and over by occupation, 2007

Managers & professionals . . . 12,000
Service occupations . . . 8,103
Sales & office occupations . . . 11,540
Farming, fishing & forestry . . . 0
Construction & maintenance . . . 4,195
Production & transportation . . . 4,048
Self-employed persons . . . 1,724

† see Appendix D for 2000 Decennial Census Data
* US Census Bureau
** 2007 American Community Survey
§ California Department of Finance
§§ California Employment Development Dept

General Information

City of Vacaville
650 Merchant St
Vacaville, CA 95688
707-449-5100

Website . . . www.cityofvacaville.com
Elevation . . . 179 ft.
Land Area (sq. miles) . . . 27.1
Water Area (sq. miles) . . . 0
Year of Incorporation . . . 1892
Government type . . . General law
Sales tax rate . . . 8.38%

Voters & Officials

Registered Voters, October 2008

Total . . . 58
Democrats . . . 18
Republicans . . . 24
Declined to state . . . 12

Legislative Districts

US Congressional . . . 7
State Senatorial . . . 5
State Assembly . . . 8

Local Officials, 2009

Mayor . . . Len Augustine
City Manager . . . Laura Kuhn (Int)
City Clerk . . . Michelle Thornbrugh
Attorney . . . Jerry Hobrecht
Finance Dir . . . Ken Campo
Public Works . . . Rod Moresco
Planning/Dev Dir . . . Scott Sexton
Building . . . Jay Salazar
Police Chief . . . Richard Word
Emergency/Fire Dir . . . Brian Preciado

Public Safety

Number of officers, 2007 . . . 111
Violent crimes, 2007 . . . 263
Property crimes, 2007 . . . 2,036
Arson, 2007 . . . 37

Public Library

Vacaville Public Library-Cultural Center
Solano County Library System
1020 Ulatis Dr
Vacaville, CA 95687
707-449-6290

Branch Librarian . . . Jan Stevens

Library system statistics, FY 2007

Population served . . . 371,000
Internet terminals . . . 248
Annual users . . . 562,512

Per capita:

Operating income . . . $54.42
percent from local government . . . 94.0%
Operating expenditure . . . $47.19
Total materials . . . 1.88
Print holdings . . . 1.57
Visits per capita . . . 5.20

Housing & Construction

Housing Units

Total, 2008§ . . . 32,552
Single family units, attached . . . 1,040
Single family units, detached . . . 22,719
Multiple family units . . . 7,485
Mobile home units . . . 1,308
Occupied . . . 31,883
Vacancy rate . . . 2.1%
Median rent, 2007** . . . $1,131
Median SF home value, 2007** . . . $461,800

New Privately Owned Housing Units Authorized by Building Permit, 2007*

	Units	Construction Cost
Single	291	$80,744,587
Total	351	$83,889,254

Municipal Finance

(For local fiscal year ended in 2006)

Revenues

Total . . . $175,621,585
Taxes . . . 52,105,893
Special benefits assessment . . . 0
Licenses & permits . . . 774,956
Fines & forfeitures . . . 460,180
Revenues from use of money & property . . . 6,482,720
Intergovernmental . . . 10,928,314
Service charges . . . 59,391,216
Other revenues . . . 43,403,306
Other financing sources . . . 2,075,000

Expenditures

Total . . . $144,514,991
General government . . . 11,094,489
Public safety . . . 38,552,333
Transportation . . . 27,001,552
Community development . . . 29,250,549
Health . . . 16,319,361
Culture & leisure . . . 10,884,222
Other . . . 0

Local School District

(Data from School year 2007-08 except as noted)

Vacaville Unified
751 School St
Vacaville, CA 95688
(707) 453-6117

Superintendent . . . John Aycock
Grade plan . . . K-12
Number of schools . . . 17
Enrollment . . . 13,183
High school graduates, 2006-07 . . . 990
Dropout rate . . . 4.2%
Pupil/teacher ratio . . . 19.8
Average class size . . . 24.1
Students per computer . . . 4.7
Classrooms with internet . . . 755
Avg. Daily Attendance (ADA) . . . 11,823
Cost per ADA . . . $7,632
Avg. Teacher Salary . . . $59,202

California Achievement Tests 6th ed., 2008

(Pct scoring at or above 50th National Percentile Rank)

	Math	Reading	Language
Grade 3	59%	44%	56%
Grade 7	57%	55%	49%

Academic Performance Index, 2008

Number of students tested . . . 10,026
Number of valid scores . . . 9,472
2007 API (base) . . . 760
2008 API (growth) . . . 765

SAT Testing, 2006-07

Enrollment, Grade 12 . . . 961
Number taking test . . . 352
percent taking test . . . 36.6%
percent with total score 1,500+ . . . 18.70%

Average Scores:

Math	Verbal	Writing	Total
521	502	491	1,514

Federal No Child Left Behind, 2008

(Adequate Yearly Progress standards met)

	Participation Rate	Pct Proficient
ELA	Yes	No
Math	Yes	No

API criteria . . . Yes
Graduation rate . . . Yes
criteria met/possible . . . 42/38

Other school districts for this city

(see Appendix E for information on these districts)

Travis Unified

See Introduction for an explanation of all data sources.

Demographics & Socio-Economic Characteristics†

(2007 American Community Survey, except as noted)

Population

1990* . . . 109,199
2007 . . . 106,608
Male . . . 50,404
Female . . . 56,204
Jan. 2008 (estimate)§ . . . 121,097
Persons per sq. mi. of land . . . 4,009.8

Race & Hispanic Origin, 2007

Race
White . . . 38,225
Black/African American . . . 22,485
North American Native . . . 1,455
Asian . . . 26,335
Pacific Islander . . . 1,487
Other Race . . . 10,067
Two or more races . . . 6,554
Hispanic origin, total . . . 20,728
Mexican . . . 13,651
Puerto Rican . . . 1,133
Cuban . . . 64
Other Hispanic . . . 5,880

Age & Nativity, 2007

Under 5 years . . . 7,062
18 years and over . . . 83,141
65 years and over . . . 13,665
85 years and over . . . 1,644
Median Age . . . 39.2
Native-born . . . 78,723
Foreign-born . . . 27,885

Educational Attainment, 2007

Population 25 years and over . . . 70,574
Less than 9th grade . . . 8.6%
High school grad or higher . . . 82.7%
Bachelor's degree or higher . . . 25.1%
Graduate degree . . . 5.8%

Income & Poverty, 2007

Per capita income . . . $27,498
Median household income . . . $60,935
Median family income . . . $70,665
Persons in poverty . . . 11.8%
H'holds receiving public assistance . . . 1,307
H'holds receiving social security . . . 9,696

Households, 2007

Total households . . . 36,650
With persons under 18 . . . 13,343
With persons over 65 . . . 8,907
Family households . . . 25,038
Single person households . . . 9,872
Persons per household . . . 2.88
Persons per family . . . 3.55

Household Population, 2008§§

Persons living in households . . . 118,835
Persons living in group quarters . . . 2,262
Persons per household . . . 2.8

Labor & Employment

Total civilian labor force, 2008§§ . . . 64,700
Unemployment rate, 2008 . . . 8.6%
Total civilian labor force, 2000* . . . 55,661

Employed persons 16 years and over by occupation, 2007

Managers & professionals . . . 15,464
Service occupations . . . 9,035
Sales & office occupations . . . 13,112
Farming, fishing & forestry . . . 230
Construction & maintenance . . . 6,306
Production & transportation . . . 5,190
Self-employed persons . . . 2,768

† see Appendix D for 2000 Decennial Census Data
* US Census Bureau
** 2007 American Community Survey
§ California Department of Finance
§§ California Employment Development Dept

General Information

City of Vallejo
555 Santa Clara St
PO Box 3068
Vallejo, CA 94590
707-648-4527

Website . . . www.ci.vallejo.ca.us
Elevation . . . 50 ft.
Land Area (sq. miles) . . . 30.2
Water Area (sq. miles) . . . 18.6
Year of Incorporation . . . 1868
Government type . . . Chartered
Sales tax rate . . . 8.38%

Voters & Officials

Registered Voters, October 2008

Total . . . 38,127
Democrats . . . 16,361
Republicans . . . 13,170
Declined to state . . . 6,944

Legislative Districts

US Congressional . . . 7
State Senatorial . . . 2
State Assembly . . . 7

Local Officials, 2009

Mayor . . . Osby Davis
Manager . . . Joseph M. Tanner
City Clerk . . . Mary Ellsworth
Attorney . . . Fred Soley
Finance Dir . . . Robert Stout
Public Works . . . Gary Leach
Planning/Dev Dir . . . Bob Adams
Building . . . Gary West
Police Chief . . . Robert Nichelini
Emergency/Fire Dir . . . Russell Sherman

Public Safety

Number of officers, 2007 . . . 145
Violent crimes, 2007 . . . 1,089
Property crimes, 2007 . . . 6,063
Arson, 2007 . . . 96

Public Library

John F. Kennedy Library
Solano County Library System
505 Santa Clara St
Vallejo, CA 94590
707-553-5568

Branch Librarian . . . Linda Matchette

Library system statistics, FY 2007

Population served . . . 371,000
Internet terminals . . . 248
Annual users . . . 562,512

Per capita:

Operating income . . . $54.42
percent from local government . . . 94.0%
Operating expenditure . . . $47.19
Total materials . . . 1.88
Print holdings . . . 1.57
Visits per capita . . . 5.20

Housing & Construction

Housing Units

Total, 2008§ . . . 43,840
Single family units, attached . . . 1,792
Single family units, detached . . . 30,580
Multiple family units . . . 10,122
Mobile home units . . . 1,346
Occupied . . . 42,120
Vacancy rate . . . 3.9%
Median rent, 2007** . . . $1,102
Median SF home value, 2007** . . . $445,000

New Privately Owned Housing Units Authorized by Building Permit, 2007*

	Units	Construction Cost
Single	70	$19,056,822
Total	118	$31,053,723

Municipal Finance

(For local fiscal year ended in 2006)

Revenues

Total . . . $195,097,892
Taxes . . . 68,966,408
Special benefits assessment . . . 2,901,339
Licenses & permits . . . 2,246,020
Fines & forfeitures . . . 1,719,935
Revenues from use of money & property . . . 5,674,956
Intergovernmental . . . 44,918,746
Service charges . . . 64,331,016
Other revenues . . . 4,339,472
Other financing sources . . . 0

Expenditures

Total . . . $194,693,494
General government . . . 13,999,210
Public safety . . . 63,218,250
Transportation . . . 34,696,832
Community development . . . 46,347,950
Health . . . 2,334,372
Culture & leisure . . . 2,552,346
Other . . . 0

Local School District

(Data from School year 2007-08 except as noted)

Vallejo City Unified
665 Walnut Ave
Vallejo, CA 94592
(707) 556-8921

Superintendent . . . Mary Bull
Grade plan . . . K-12
Number of schools . . . 29
Enrollment . . . 17,408
High school graduates, 2006-07 . . . 901
Dropout rate . . . 10.7%
Pupil/teacher ratio . . . 20.7
Average class size . . . 25.7
Students per computer . . . 4.6
Classrooms with internet . . . 740
Avg. Daily Attendance (ADA) . . . 15,603
Cost per ADA . . . $8,796
Avg. Teacher Salary . . . $57,604

California Achievement Tests 6th ed., 2008

(Pct scoring at or above 50th National Percentile Rank)

	Math	Reading	Language
Grade 3	42%	28%	35%
Grade 7	39%	42%	40%

Academic Performance Index, 2008

Number of students tested . . . 12,372
Number of valid scores . . . 10,603
2007 API (base) . . . 671
2008 API (growth) . . . 684

SAT Testing, 2006-07

Enrollment, Grade 12 . . . 959
Number taking test . . . 387
percent taking test . . . 40.4%
percent with total score 1,500+ . . . 12.60%

Average Scores:

Math	Verbal	Writing	Total
466	457	455	1,378

Federal No Child Left Behind, 2008

(Adequate Yearly Progress standards met)

	Participation Rate	Pct Proficient
ELA	No	No
Math	No	No

API criteria . . . Yes
Graduation rate . . . No
criteria met/possible . . . 42/31

Other school districts for this city

(see Appendix E for information on these districts)

None

See Introduction for an explanation of all data sources.

Demographics & Socio-Economic Characteristics†

(2007 American Community Survey, except as noted)

Population

1990* . . . 92,575
2007 . . . 105,673
Male . . . 52,125
Female . . . 53,548
Jan. 2008 (estimate)§ . . . 108,261
Persons per sq. mi. of land . . . 5,130.9

Race & Hispanic Origin, 2007

Race
White . . . 71,333
Black/African American . . . 1,340
North American Native . . . 1,341
Asian . . . 2,482
Pacific Islander . . . 879
Other Race . . . 22,195
Two or more races . . . 6,103
Hispanic origin, total . . . 35,843
Mexican . . . NA
Puerto Rican . . . NA
Cuban . . . NA
Other Hispanic . . . NA

Age & Nativity, 2007

Under 5 years . . . 7,533
18 years and over . . . 78,172
65 years and over . . . 12,401
85 years and over . . . 2,247
Median Age . . . 37.2
Native-born . . . 88,366
Foreign-born . . . 17,307

Educational Attainment, 2007

Population 25 years and over . . . 70,218
Less than 9th grade . . . 6.1%
High school grad or higher . . . 86.1%
Bachelor's degree or higher . . . 28.0%
Graduate degree . . . 11.3%

Income & Poverty, 2007

Per capita income . . . $29,578
Median household income . . . $64,769
Median family income . . . $74,997
Persons in poverty . . . 9.1%
H'holds receiving public assistance . . . 306
H'holds receiving social security . . . 9,459

Households, 2007

Total households . . . 40,089
With persons under 18 . . . 13,499
With persons over 65 . . . 9,681
Family households . . . 26,034
Single person households . . . 11,452
Persons per household . . . 2.62
Persons per family . . . 3.26

Household Population, 2008§§

Persons living in households . . . 105,508
Persons living in group quarters . . . 2,753
Persons per household . . . 2.6

Labor & Employment

Total civilian labor force, 2008§§ . . . 61,600
Unemployment rate, 2008 . . . 5.7%
Total civilian labor force, 2000* . . . 52,404

Employed persons 16 years and over by occupation, 2007

Managers & professionals . . . 17,903
Service occupations . . . 8,849
Sales & office occupations . . . 15,535
Farming, fishing & forestry . . . 227
Construction & maintenance . . . 4,597
Production & transportation . . . 5,820
Self-employed persons . . . 4,830

† see Appendix D for 2000 Decennial Census Data
* US Census Bureau
** 2007 American Community Survey
§ California Department of Finance
§§ California Employment Development Dept

General Information

City of Ventura
501 Poli St
PO Box 99
Ventura, CA 93002
805-654-7800

Website . . . www.cityofventura.net
Elevation . . . 50 ft.
Land Area (sq. miles) . . . 21.1
Water Area (sq. miles) . . . 11.6
Year of Incorporation . . . 1866
Government type . . . Chartered
Sales tax rate . . . 8.25%

Voters & Officials

Registered Voters, October 2008

Total . . . 65,578
Democrats . . . 29,319
Republicans . . . 21,957
Declined to state . . . 11,127

Legislative Districts

US Congressional . . . 23
State Senatorial . . . 19
State Assembly . . . 35

Local Officials, 2009

Mayor . . . Christy Weir
Manager . . . Rick Cole
City Clerk . . . Mabi Covarrubias Plisky
Attorney . . . Ariel Pierre Calonne
Finance Dir . . . Jay Panzica
Public Works . . . Ron Calkins
Planning/Dev Dir . . . Nelson Hernandez
Building . . . Andrew Stuffler
Police Chief . . . Pat Miller
Emergency/Fire Dir . . . Mike Lavery

Public Safety

Number of officers, 2007 . . . 134
Violent crimes, 2007 . . . 368
Property crimes, 2007 . . . 3,827
Arson, 2007 . . . 27

Public Library

Avenue Library
Ventura County Library System
606 N Ventura Ave
Ventura, CA 93001
805-643-6393

Director . . . Jackie Griffin

Library system statistics, FY 2007

Population served . . . 439,444
Internet terminals . . . 188
Annual users . . . 216,575

Per capita:

Operating income . . . $25.05
percent from local government . . . 86.2%
Operating expenditure . . . $25.02
Total materials . . . 1.81
Print holdings . . . 1.70
Visits per capita . . . NA

Housing & Construction

Housing Units

Total, 2008§ . . . 42,407
Single family units, attached . . . 3,430
Single family units, detached . . . 23,548
Multiple family units . . . 12,806
Mobile home units . . . 2,623
Occupied . . . 41,044
Vacancy rate . . . 3.2%
Median rent, 2007** . . . $1,319
Median SF home value, 2007** . . . $604,400

New Privately Owned Housing Units Authorized by Building Permit, 2007*

	Units	Construction Cost
Single	150	$41,048,610
Total	405	$86,942,650

Municipal Finance

(For local fiscal year ended in 2006)

Revenues

Total . . . $124,686,602
Taxes . . . 62,775,815
Special benefits assessment . . . 1,716,558
Licenses & permits . . . 1,793,230
Fines & forfeitures . . . 1,802,109
Revenues from use of money & property . . . 6,283,693
Intergovernmental . . . 6,158,099
Service charges . . . 42,466,075
Other revenues . . . 1,691,023
Other financing sources . . . 0

Expenditures

Total . . . $137,858,460
General government . . . 24,837,956
Public safety . . . 47,339,957
Transportation . . . 20,166,524
Community development . . . 5,665,146
Health . . . 10,174,828
Culture & leisure . . . 15,632,176
Other . . . 0

Local School District

(Data from School year 2007-08 except as noted)

Ventura Unified
255 West Stanley Ave, Suite 100
Ventura, CA 93001
(805) 641-5000

Superintendent . . . Trudy Arriaga
Grade plan . . . K-12
Number of schools . . . 31
Enrollment . . . 17,321
High school graduates, 2006-07 . . . 1,151
Dropout rate . . . 1.7%
Pupil/teacher ratio . . . 23.5
Average class size . . . 27.1
Students per computer . . . 4.1
Classrooms with internet . . . 851
Avg. Daily Attendance (ADA) . . . 16,857
Cost per ADA . . . $7,945
Avg. Teacher Salary . . . $63,863

California Achievement Tests 6th ed., 2008

(Pct scoring at or above 50th National Percentile Rank)

	Math	Reading	Language
Grade 3	65%	45%	50%
Grade 7	64%	63%	60%

Academic Performance Index, 2008

Number of students tested . . . 13,329
Number of valid scores . . . 12,728
2007 API (base) . . . 786
2008 API (growth) . . . 789

SAT Testing, 2006-07

Enrollment, Grade 12 . . . 1,387
Number taking test . . . 487
percent taking test . . . 35.1%
percent with total score 1,500+ . . . 22.20%

Average Scores:

Math	Verbal	Writing	Total
531	531	522	1,584

Federal No Child Left Behind, 2008

(Adequate Yearly Progress standards met)

	Participation Rate	Pct Proficient
ELA	Yes	No
Math	Yes	Yes

API criteria . . . Yes
Graduation rate . . . Yes
criteria met/possible . . . 42/40

Other school districts for this city

(see Appendix E for information on these districts)

None

See Introduction for an explanation of all data sources.

Demographics & Socio-Economic Characteristics

(2000 Decennial Census, except as noted)

Population

1990* 152
2000 91
Male 43
Female 48
Jan. 2008 (estimate)§ 95
Persons per sq. mi. of land 19.0

Race & Hispanic Origin, 2000

Race
White 43
Black/African American 0
North American Native 0
Asian 1
Pacific Islander 0
Other Race 43
Two or more races 4
Hispanic origin, total 81
Mexican 79
Puerto Rican 0
Cuban 0
Other Hispanic 2

Age & Nativity, 2000

Under 5 years 8
18 years and over 57
65 years and over 6
85 years and over 0
Median Age 28.8
Native-born 85
Foreign-born 9

Educational Attainment, 2000

Population 25 years and over 44
Less than 9th grade 0.0%
High school grad or higher 59.1%
Bachelor's degree or higher 18.2%
Graduate degree 6.8%

Income & Poverty, 1999

Per capita income $17,812
Median household income $60,000
Median family income $63,750
Persons in poverty 0.0%
H'holds receiving public assistance 0
H'holds receiving social security 2

Households, 2000

Total households 25
With persons under 18 15
With persons over 65 3
Family households 23
Single person households 2
Persons per household 3.64
Persons per family 3.78

Household Population, 2008§§

Persons living in households 95
Persons living in group quarters 0
Persons per household 3.8

Labor & Employment

Total civilian labor force, 2008§§ .... NA
Unemployment rate, 2008 .... NA
Total civilian labor force, 2000 38

Employed persons 16 years and over by occupation, 2000

Managers & professionals 2
Service occupations 14
Sales & office occupations 12
Farming, fishing & forestry 0
Construction & maintenance 8
Production & transportation 2
Self-employed persons 0

* US Census Bureau
** 2000 Decennial Census
§ California Department of Finance
§§ California Employment Development Dept

General Information

City of Vernon
4305 Santa Fe Ave
Vernon, CA 90058
323-583-8811

Website .... www.cityofvernon.org
Elevation .... NA
Land Area (sq. miles) 5.0
Water Area (sq. miles) 0.2
Year of Incorporation 1905
Government type .... Chartered
Sales tax rate 9.25%

Voters & Officials

Registered Voters, October 2008

Total 58
Democrats 18
Republicans 24
Declined to state 12

Legislative Districts

US Congressional 34
State Senatorial 22
State Assembly 46

Local Officials, 2009

Mayor .... Leonis Malburg
Administrator .... Eric Fresch
City Clerk .... Manuela Giron
Attorney .... Jeff Harrison
Finance Dir .... Rory Burnett
Public Works .... Kevin Wilson
Comm Svcs Dir .... Kevin Wilson
Building .... Kevin Wilson
Police Chief .... Steve Towles
Fire Chief .... Mark C. Whitworth

Public Safety

Number of officers, 2007 51
Violent crimes, 2007 46
Property crimes, 2007 448
Arson, 2007 2

Public Library

Vernon Public Library
4305 Santa Fe Ave
Vernon, CA 90058
323-583-8811

City Clerk .... Nelly Giron

Library statistics, FY 2007

Population served 95
Internet terminals 0
Annual users .... NA

Per capita:

Operating income $0.00
percent from local government .... NA
Operating expenditure $0.00
Total materials .... NA
Print holdings 0.00
Visits per capita 0.00

Housing & Construction

Housing Units

Total, 2008§ 26
Single family units, attached 0
Single family units, detached 19
Multiple family units 7
Mobile home units 0
Occupied 25
Vacancy rate 3.9%
Median rent, 2000** $289
Median SF home value, 2000** $225,000

New Privately Owned Housing Units Authorized by Building Permit, 2007*

	Units	Construction Cost
Single	0	$0
Total	0	$0

Municipal Finance

(For local fiscal year ended in 2006)

Revenues

Total $211,314,975
Taxes 15,663,405
Special benefits assessment 0
Licenses & permits 1,102,871
Fines & forfeitures 208,860
Revenues from use of money & property 5,829,142
Intergovernmental 3,735,636
Service charges 184,760,505
Other revenues 14,556
Other financing sources 0

Expenditures

Total $254,321,172
General government 27,712,664
Public safety 21,350,803
Transportation 2,974,711
Community development 12,050,057
Health 2,110,477
Culture & leisure 12,625
Other 0

Local School District

(Data from School year 2007-08 except as noted)

Los Angeles Unified
333 South Beaudry Ave
Los Angeles, CA 90017
(213) 241-1000

Superintendent .... Ramon Cortines
Grade plan PK-12
Number of schools 827
Enrollment 693,680
High school graduates, 2006-07 28,545
Dropout rate 7.8%
Pupil/teacher ratio 19.8
Average class size 24.9
Students per computer 3.7
Classrooms with internet 31,112
Avg. Daily Attendance (ADA) 653,672
Cost per ADA $10,053
Avg. Teacher Salary $63,391

California Achievement Tests 6th ed., 2008

(Pct scoring at or above 50th National Percentile Rank)

	Math	Reading	Language
Grade 3	49%	27%	39%
Grade 7	37%	33%	33%

Academic Performance Index, 2008

Number of students tested 495,046
Number of valid scores 471,641
2007 API (base) 662
2008 API (growth) 683

SAT Testing, 2006-07

Enrollment, Grade 12 32,370
Number taking test 15,447
percent taking test 47.7%
percent with total score 1,500+ 12.50%

Average Scores:

Math	Verbal	Writing	Total
443	438	441	1,322

Federal No Child Left Behind, 2008

(Adequate Yearly Progress standards met)

	Participation Rate	Pct Proficient
ELA	Yes	No
Math	Yes	No

API criteria .... Yes
Graduation rate .... Yes
\# criteria met/possible 46/38

Other school districts for this city

(see Appendix E for information on these districts)

None

See Introduction for an explanation of all data sources.

Demographics & Socio-Economic Characteristics†

(2007 American Community Survey, except as noted)

Population

1990* . . . 40,674
2007 . . . 97,534
Male . . . 49,723
Female . . . 47,811
Jan. 2008 (estimate)§ . . . 107,408
Persons per sq. mi. of land . . . 1,475.4

Race & Hispanic Origin, 2007

Race
White . . . 62,840
Black/African American . . . 14,763
North American Native . . . 1,474
Asian . . . 3,103
Pacific Islander . . . 138
Other Race . . . 10,656
Two or more races . . . 4,560
Hispanic origin, total . . . 43,070
Mexican . . . 36,832
Puerto Rican . . . 1,042
Cuban . . . 130
Other Hispanic . . . 5,066

Age & Nativity, 2007

Under 5 years . . . 8,723
18 years and over . . . 64,500
65 years and over . . . 7,259
85 years and over . . . 1,080
Median Age . . . 28.1
Native-born . . . 80,489
Foreign-born . . . 17,045

Educational Attainment, 2007

Population 25 years and over . . . 53,427
Less than 9th grade . . . 8.3%
High school grad or higher . . . 77.0%
Bachelor's degree or higher . . . 12.7%
Graduate degree . . . 3.7%

Income & Poverty, 2007

Per capita income . . . $16,790
Median household income . . . $48,162
Median family income . . . $50,320
Persons in poverty . . . 16.0%
H'holds receiving public assistance . . . 1,384
H'holds receiving social security . . . 6,377

Households, 2007

Total households . . . 27,376
With persons under 18 . . . 14,850
With persons over 65 . . . 4,895
Family households . . . 21,572
Single person households . . . 4,745
Persons per household . . . 3.38
Persons per family . . . 3.74

Household Population, 2008§§

Persons living in households . . . 102,637
Persons living in group quarters . . . 4,771
Persons per household . . . 3.2

Labor & Employment

Total civilian labor force, 2008§§ . . . 30,300
Unemployment rate, 2008 . . . 9.7%
Total civilian labor force, 2000* . . . 24,853

Employed persons 16 years and over by occupation, 2007

Managers & professionals . . . 8,801
Service occupations . . . 6,838
Sales & office occupations . . . 8,025
Farming, fishing & forestry . . . 0
Construction & maintenance . . . 5,269
Production & transportation . . . 3,374
Self-employed persons . . . 2,139

† see Appendix D for 2000 Decennial Census Data
* US Census Bureau
** 2007 American Community Survey
§ California Department of Finance
§§ California Employment Development Dept

General Information

City of Victorville
14343 Civic Dr
Victorville, CA 92392
760-955-5000

Website . . . www.ci.victorville.ca.us
Elevation . . . 2,715 ft.
Land Area (sq. miles) . . . 72.8
Water Area (sq. miles) . . . 0.5
Year of Incorporation . . . 1962
Government type . . . General law
Sales tax rate . . . 8.75%

Voters & Officials

Registered Voters, October 2008

Total . . . 38,127
Democrats . . . 16,361
Republicans . . . 13,170
Declined to state . . . 6,944

Legislative Districts

US Congressional . . . 25
State Senatorial . . . 17
State Assembly . . . 36

Local Officials, 2009

Mayor . . . Rudy Cabriales
Manager . . . James L. Cox
City Clerk . . . Carolee Bates
Attorney . . . Andre de Bortnowsky
Finance Dir . . . John G. Sullivan
Public Works . . . Amer Jakhner
Planning/Dev Dir . . . Bill Webb
Building . . . Bill Webb
Police Chief . . . Mark Taylor
Fire Chief . . . Sid Hultquist

Public Safety

Number of officers, 2007 . . . NA
Violent crimes, 2007 . . . 660
Property crimes, 2007 . . . 4,039
Arson, 2007 . . . 16

Public Library

Victorville Public Library
(Previously a branch of County Library)
15011 Circle Dr
Victorville, CA 92395
760-245-4222

Director . . . Karen Everett

Library system statistics, FY 2007

Population served . . . 102,538
Internet terminals . . . 14
Annual users . . . NA

Per capita:

Operating income . . . $12.44
percent from local government . . . 93.9%
Operating expenditure . . . $0.00
Total materials . . . NA
Print holdings . . . 0.01
Visits per capita . . . 0.00

Housing & Construction

Housing Units

Total, 2008§ . . . 34,876
Single family units, attached . . . 389
Single family units, detached . . . 27,767
Multiple family units . . . 4,929
Mobile home units . . . 1,791
Occupied . . . 32,186
Vacancy rate . . . 7.7%
Median rent, 2007** . . . $941
Median SF home value, 2007** . . . $306,900

New Privately Owned Housing Units Authorized by Building Permit, 2007*

	Units	Construction Cost
Single	1,090	$229,104,165
Total	1,549	$258,374,698

Municipal Finance

(For local fiscal year ended in 2006)

Revenues

Total . . . $103,556,643
Taxes . . . 46,045,536
Special benefits assessment . . . 1,841,297
Licenses & permits . . . 5,981,597
Fines & forfeitures . . . 805,676
Revenues from use of money & property . . . 2,680,572
Intergovernmental . . . 9,548,230
Service charges . . . 35,790,806
Other revenues . . . 862,929
Other financing sources . . . 0

Expenditures

Total . . . $96,957,445
General government . . . 26,177,005
Public safety . . . 16,431,566
Transportation . . . 8,831,723
Community development . . . 13,114,713
Health . . . 9,762,110
Culture & leisure . . . 6,995,225
Other . . . 0

Local School District

(Data from School year 2007-08 except as noted)

Victor Valley Union High
16350 Mojave Dr
Victorville, CA 92395
(760) 955-3201

Superintendent . . . Julian Weaver
Grade plan . . . 7-12
Number of schools . . . 12
Enrollment . . . 13,671
High school graduates, 2006-07 . . . 1,459
Dropout rate . . . 16.3%
Pupil/teacher ratio . . . 24.1
Average class size . . . 30.2
Students per computer . . . 5.0
Classrooms with internet . . . 566
Avg. Daily Attendance (ADA) . . . 10,395
Cost per ADA . . . $7,840
Avg. Teacher Salary . . . $60,749

California Achievement Tests 6th ed., 2008

(Pct scoring at or above 50th National Percentile Rank)

	Math	Reading	Language
Grade 3	NA	NA	NA
Grade 7	42%	40%	37%

Academic Performance Index, 2008

Number of students tested . . . 8,599
Number of valid scores . . . 7,799
2007 API (base) . . . 669
2008 API (growth) . . . 669

SAT Testing, 2006-07

Enrollment, Grade 12 . . . 1,663
Number taking test . . . 386
percent taking test . . . 23.2%
percent with total score 1,500+ . . . 6.50%

Average Scores:

Math	Verbal	Writing	Total
452	450	450	1,352

Federal No Child Left Behind, 2008

(Adequate Yearly Progress standards met)

	Participation Rate	Pct Proficient
ELA	Yes	No
Math	No	No

API criteria . . . Yes
Graduation rate . . . No
\# criteria met/possible . . . 30/21

Other school districts for this city

(see Appendix E for information on these districts)

Hesperia Unified, Snowline Joint Unified, Victor Elem

See Introduction for an explanation of all data sources.

Demographics & Socio-Economic Characteristics

(2000 Decennial Census, except as noted)

Population

1990* . . . 6,299
2000 . . . 5,999
Male . . . 3,018
Female . . . 2,981
Jan. 2008 (estimate)§ . . . 6,259
Persons per sq. mi. of land . . . 2,980.5

Race & Hispanic Origin, 2000

Race
White . . . 4,943
Black/African American . . . 48
North American Native . . . 26
Asian . . . 775
Pacific Islander . . . 2
Other Race . . . 56
Two or more races . . . 149
Hispanic origin, total . . . 354
Mexican . . . 237
Puerto Rican . . . 10
Cuban . . . 11
Other Hispanic . . . 96

Age & Nativity, 2000

Under 5 years . . . 238
18 years and over . . . 4,520
65 years and over . . . 888
85 years and over . . . 58
Median Age . . . 43.6
Native-born . . . 5,268
Foreign-born . . . 822

Educational Attainment, 2000

Population 25 years and over . . . 4,184
Less than 9th grade . . . 1.1%
High school grad or higher . . . 95.4%
Bachelor's degree or higher . . . 57.3%
Graduate degree . . . 25.2%

Income & Poverty, 1999

Per capita income . . . $53,130
Median household income . . . $116,203
Median family income . . . $124,852
Persons in poverty . . . 2.6%
H'holds receiving public assistance . . . 49
H'holds receiving social security . . . 550

Households, 2000

Total households . . . 1,950
With persons under 18 . . . 739
With persons over 65 . . . 612
Family households . . . 1,764
Single person households . . . 154
Persons per household . . . 3.07
Persons per family . . . 3.22

Household Population, 2008§§

Persons living in households . . . 6,238
Persons living in group quarters . . . 21
Persons per household . . . 3.2

Labor & Employment

Total civilian labor force, 2008§§ . . . 3,500
Unemployment rate, 2008 . . . 2.6%
Total civilian labor force, 2000 . . . 3,016

Employed persons 16 years and over by occupation, 2000

Managers & professionals . . . 1,600
Service occupations . . . 139
Sales & office occupations . . . 976
Farming, fishing & forestry . . . 0
Construction & maintenance . . . 119
Production & transportation . . . 107
Self-employed persons . . . 467

* US Census Bureau
** 2000 Decennial Census
§ California Department of Finance
§§ California Employment Development Dept

General Information

City of Villa Park
17855 Santiago Blvd
Villa Park, CA 92861
714-998-1500

Website . . . www.villapark.org
Elevation . . . 310 ft.
Land Area (sq. miles) . . . 2.1
Water Area (sq. miles) . . . 0
Year of Incorporation . . . 1962
Government type . . . General law
Sales tax rate . . . 8.75%

Voters & Officials

Registered Voters, October 2008

Total . . . 4,529
Democrats . . . 777
Republicans . . . 3,012
Declined to state . . . 635

Legislative Districts

US Congressional . . . 40
State Senatorial . . . 33
State Assembly . . . 60

Local Officials, 2009

Mayor . . . James Rheins
Interim City Manager . . . Don Powell
City Clerk . . . Jarad Hildenbrand (Actg)
Attorney . . . Todd Litfin
Finance Dir . . . Michelle Danaher
Public Works . . . Mike Knowles
Planning/Dev Dir . . . Jason Carson
Building . . . Bill Tarin
Police Chief . . . Tom Gallivan
Batallion Fire Chief . . . Michael Moore

Public Safety

Number of officers, 2007 . . . NA
Violent crimes, 2007 . . . 4
Property crimes, 2007 . . . 115
Arson, 2007 . . . 0

Public Library

Villa Park Branch Library
Orange County Public Library System
17865 Santiago Blvd
Villa Park, CA 92861
714-998-0861

Branch Librarian . . . Joyce Hensley

Library system statistics, FY 2007

Population served . . . 1,532,758
Internet terminals . . . 505
Annual users . . . 680,874

Per capita:

Operating income . . . $24.71
percent from local government . . . 90.0%
Operating expenditure . . . $24.18
Total materials . . . 1.93
Print holdings . . . 1.84
Visits per capita . . . 4.02

Housing & Construction

Housing Units

Total, 2008§ . . . 2,021
Single family units, attached . . . 18
Single family units, detached . . . 1,992
Multiple family units . . . 6
Mobile home units . . . 5
Occupied . . . 1,963
Vacancy rate . . . 2.9%
Median rent, 2000** . . . $850
Median SF home value, 2000** . . . $596,500

New Privately Owned Housing Units Authorized by Building Permit, 2007*

	Units	Construction Cost
Single	3	$2,202,200
Total	3	$2,202,200

Municipal Finance

(For local fiscal year ended in 2006)

Revenues

Total . . . $3,174,797
Taxes . . . 1,809,106
Special benefits assessment . . . 0
Licenses & permits . . . 229,457
Fines & forfeitures . . . 53,062
Revenues from use of money & property . . . 65,335
Intergovernmental . . . 904,857
Service charges . . . 31,089
Other revenues . . . 81,891
Other financing sources . . . 0

Expenditures

Total . . . $3,213,612
General government . . . 517,575
Public safety . . . 1,113,883
Transportation . . . 973,134
Community development . . . 354,576
Health . . . 195,351
Culture & leisure . . . 59,093
Other . . . 0

Local School District

(Data from School year 2007-08 except as noted)

Orange Unified
PO Box 11022
Orange, CA 92867
(714) 628-4000

Superintendent . . . Renae Dreier
Grade plan . . . K-12
Number of schools . . . 43
Enrollment . . . 30,127
High school graduates, 2006-07 . . . 1,959
Dropout rate . . . 1.5%
Pupil/teacher ratio . . . 22.1
Average class size . . . 27.2
Students per computer . . . 5.1
Classrooms with internet . . . 1,383
Avg. Daily Attendance (ADA) . . . 28,411
Cost per ADA . . . $7,954
Avg. Teacher Salary . . . $70,298

California Achievement Tests 6th ed., 2008

(Pct scoring at or above 50th National Percentile Rank)

	Math	Reading	Language
Grade 3	61%	43%	52%
Grade 7	57%	58%	55%

Academic Performance Index, 2008

Number of students tested . . . 22,272
Number of valid scores . . . 21,079
2007 API (base) . . . 783
2008 API (growth) . . . 787

SAT Testing, 2006-07

Enrollment, Grade 12 . . . 2,286
Number taking test . . . 971
percent taking test . . . 42.5%
percent with total score 1,500+ . . . 24.60%

Average Scores:

Math	Verbal	Writing	Total
535	515	519	1,569

Federal No Child Left Behind, 2008

(Adequate Yearly Progress standards met)

	Participation Rate	Pct Proficient
ELA	Yes	No
Math	Yes	No

API criteria . . . Yes
Graduation rate . . . Yes
\# criteria met/possible . . . 42/38

Other school districts for this city

(see Appendix E for information on these districts)

None

See Introduction for an explanation of all data sources.

Demographics & Socio-Economic Characteristics†

(2007 American Community Survey, except as noted)

Population

1990* 75,636
2007 115,899
Male 56,692
Female 59,207
Jan. 2008 (estimate)§ 120,958
Persons per sq. mi. of land 4,229.3

Race & Hispanic Origin, 2007

Race
White 94,496
Black/African American 2,363
North American Native 1,396
Asian 5,114
Pacific Islander 0
Other Race 8,251
Two or more races 4,279
Hispanic origin, total 45,353
Mexican . . . . . NA
Puerto Rican . . . . . NA
Cuban . . . . . NA
Other Hispanic . . . . . NA

Age & Nativity, 2007

Under 5 years 12,198
18 years and over 80,323
65 years and over 11,549
85 years and over 2,175
Median Age 30.2
Native-born 102,533
Foreign-born 13,366

Educational Attainment, 2007

Population 25 years and over 69,766
Less than 9th grade 7.3%
High school grad or higher 80.7%
Bachelor's degree or higher 19.7%
Graduate degree 6.0%

Income & Poverty, 2007

Per capita income $23,281
Median household income $50,170
Median family income $56,845
Persons in poverty 17.9%
H'holds receiving public assistance . . . 1,161
H'holds receiving social security 8,870

Households, 2007

Total households 37,374
With persons under 18 15,912
With persons over 65 7,687
Family households 26,096
Single person households 9,485
Persons per household 3.03
Persons per family 3.68

Household Population, 2008§§

Persons living in households 119,336
Persons living in group quarters 1,622
Persons per household 3.0

Labor & Employment

Total civilian labor force, 2008§§ 55,100
Unemployment rate, 2008 . . . . . 6.6%
Total civilian labor force, 2000* 41,899

Employed persons 16 years and over by occupation, 2007

Managers & professionals 14,469
Service occupations 8,648
Sales & office occupations 11,452
Farming, fishing & forestry 1,514
Construction & maintenance 5,190
Production & transportation 5,080
Self-employed persons 3,452

† see Appendix D for 2000 Decennial Census Data
* US Census Bureau
** 2007 American Community Survey
§ California Department of Finance
§§ California Employment Development Dept

General Information

City of Visalia
707 W Acequia St
PO Box 5078
Visalia, CA 93278
559-713-4300

Website . . . . . www.ci.visalia.ca.us
Elevation . . . . . 331 ft.
Land Area (sq. miles) 28.6
Water Area (sq. miles) 0
Year of Incorporation 1874
Government type . . . . . Chartered
Sales tax rate 9.00%

Voters & Officials

Registered Voters, October 2008

Total 51,718
Democrats 16,505
Republicans 25,410
Declined to state 8,033

Legislative Districts

US Congressional 21
State Senatorial 18
State Assembly 34

Local Officials, 2009

Mayor . . . . . Jesus J. Gamboa
City Manager . . . . . Steve Salomon
City Clerk . . . . . Steve Salomon
Attorney . . . . . Alex Peltzer
Admin Svcs Dir . . . . . Eric Frost
Public Works . . . . . Andrew Benelli
Comm Dev Dir . . . . . Mike Olmos
Building . . . . . Dennis Lehman
Police Chief . . . . . Bob Carden
Fire Chief . . . . . Mark Nelson Glass (Actg)

Public Safety

Number of officers, 2007 128
Violent crimes, 2007 667
Property crimes, 2007 5,204
Arson, 2007 19

Public Library

Visalia Branch Library
Tulare County Free Library System
200 W Oak St
Visalia, CA 93291
559-733-6954

County Librarian . . . . . Brian Lewis

Library system statistics, FY 2007

Population served 321,604
Internet terminals 83
Annual users 86,301

Per capita:

Operating income $10.97
percent from local government 86.0%
Operating expenditure $8.74
Total materials 1.08
Print holdings 1.05
Visits per capita 0.96

Housing & Construction

Housing Units

Total, 2008§ 42,434
Single family units, attached 1,572
Single family units, detached 32,092
Multiple family units 7,300
Mobile home units 1,470
Occupied 40,111
Vacancy rate 5.5%
Median rent, 2007** $863
Median SF home value, 2007** $260,600

New Privately Owned Housing Units Authorized by Building Permit, 2007*

	Units	Construction Cost
Single	927	$194,353,168
Total	1,195	$219,866,325

Municipal Finance

(For local fiscal year ended in 2006)

Revenues

Total $139,227,649
Taxes 65,700,636
Special benefits assessment 71,788
Licenses & permits 2,476,398
Fines & forfeitures 1,042,547
Revenues from use of money & property 5,532,873
Intergovernmental 17,435,688
Service charges 40,586,369
Other revenues 6,381,350
Other financing sources 0

Expenditures

Total $117,153,216
General government 13,143,015
Public safety 30,189,524
Transportation 29,348,431
Community development 16,039,303
Health 21,931,257
Culture & leisure 6,501,686
Other 0

Local School District

(Data from School year 2007-08 except as noted)

Visalia Unified
5000 West Cypress Ave
Visalia, CA 93277
(559) 730-7300

Superintendent . . . . . Stan Carrizosa
Grade plan K-12
Number of schools 36
Enrollment 26,722
High school graduates, 2006-07 1,514
Dropout rate 3.8%
Pupil/teacher ratio 23.4
Average class size 26.7
Students per computer 4.3
Classrooms with internet 1,225
Avg. Daily Attendance (ADA) 25,735
Cost per ADA $7,481
Avg. Teacher Salary $64,230

California Achievement Tests 6th ed., 2008

(Pct scoring at or above 50th National Percentile Rank)

	Math	Reading	Language
Grade 3	46%	33%	42%
Grade 7	51%	51%	46%

Academic Performance Index, 2008

Number of students tested 20,446
Number of valid scores 19,099
2007 API (base) 716
2008 API (growth) 735

SAT Testing, 2006-07

Enrollment, Grade 12 1,955
Number taking test 482
percent taking test 24.7%
percent with total score 1,500+ . . . 10.90%

Average Scores:

Math	Verbal	Writing	Total
497	489	480	1,466

Federal No Child Left Behind, 2008

(Adequate Yearly Progress standards met)

	Participation Rate	Pct Proficient
ELA	Yes	No
Math	Yes	No

API criteria . . . . . Yes
Graduation rate . . . . . No
\# criteria met/possible 42/37

Other school districts for this city

(see Appendix E for information on these districts)

Outside Creek Elem, Stone Corral Elem, Liberty Elem

See Introduction for an explanation of all data sources.

Demographics & Socio-Economic Characteristics†

(2007 American Community Survey, except as noted)

Population

1990* 71,872
2007 97,977
Male 51,118
Female 46,859
Jan. 2008 (estimate)§ 95,770
Persons per sq. mi. of land 5,121.4

Race & Hispanic Origin, 2007

Race
White 62,149
Black/African American 3,980
North American Native 237
Asian 3,468
Pacific Islander 299
Other Race 22,966
Two or more races 4,878
Hispanic origin, total 46,055
Mexican 43,604
Puerto Rican 330
Cuban 162
Other Hispanic 1,959

Age & Nativity, 2007

Under 5 years 7,954
18 years and over 72,148
65 years and over 9,689
85 years and over 1,330
Median Age 31.5
Native-born 69,323
Foreign-born 28,654

Educational Attainment, 2007

Population 25 years and over 58,965
Less than 9th grade 12.7%
High school grad or higher 75.2%
Bachelor's degree or higher 17.1%
Graduate degree 5.6%

Income & Poverty, 2007

Per capita income $21,536
Median household income $52,406
Median family income $54,409
Persons in poverty 14.1%
H'holds receiving public assistance 372
H'holds receiving social security 6,557

Households, 2007

Total households 29,806
With persons under 18 11,480
With persons over 65 6,153
Family households 22,803
Single person households 5,659
Persons per household 3.18
Persons per family 3.57

Household Population, 2008§§

Persons living in households 93,504
Persons living in group quarters 2,266
Persons per household 3.1

Labor & Employment

Total civilian labor force, 2008§§ 48,800
Unemployment rate, 2008 .... 6.7%
Total civilian labor force, 2000* 41,170

Employed persons 16 years and over by occupation, 2007

Managers & professionals 12,159
Service occupations 9,006
Sales & office occupations 9,688
Farming, fishing & forestry 71
Construction & maintenance 5,747
Production & transportation 8,658
Self-employed persons 3,032

† see Appendix D for 2000 Decennial Census Data
* US Census Bureau
** 2007 American Community Survey
§ California Department of Finance
§§ California Employment Development Dept

General Information

City of Vista
600 Eucalyptus Ave
Vista, CA 92084
760-726-1340

Website .... www.cityofvista.com
Elevation .... 331 ft.
Land Area (sq. miles) 18.7
Water Area (sq. miles) 0
Year of Incorporation 1963
Government type .... Charter City
Sales tax rate 9.25%

Voters & Officials

Registered Voters, October 2008

Total 33,315
Democrats 10,444
Republicans 13,568
Declined to state 7,601

Legislative Districts

US Congressional 49
State Senatorial 38
State Assembly 74

Local Officials, 2009

Mayor .... Morris B. Vance
Manager .... Rita Geldert
City Clerk .... Marci Kilian
Attorney .... Darold Pieper
Finance Dir .... Thomas Gardner
Public Works .... Mauro Garcia
Planning/Dev Dir .... John Conley
Building .... Rick Snider
Police Chief .... (County)
Emergency/Fire Dir .... Gary Fisher

Public Safety

Number of officers, 2007 .... NA
Violent crimes, 2007 526
Property crimes, 2007 2,149
Arson, 2007 6

Public Library

Vista Library
San Diego County Library System
700 Eucalyptus Ave
Vista, CA 92084
760-643-5113

Branch Librarian .... Alice Rigg

Library system statistics, FY 2007

Population served 1,049,868
Internet terminals 394
Annual users .... NA

Per capita:

Operating income $33.43
percent from local government 80.6%
Operating expenditure $31.30
Total materials 1.54
Print holdings 1.32
Visits per capita 6.31

Housing & Construction

Housing Units

Total, 2008§ 31,144
Single family units, attached 2,029
Single family units, detached 15,540
Multiple family units 11,446
Mobile home units 2,129
Occupied 30,165
Vacancy rate 3.1%
Median rent, 2007** $1,174
Median SF home value, 2007** $507,700

New Privately Owned Housing Units Authorized by Building Permit, 2007*

	Units	Construction Cost
Single	63	$17,118,161
Total	69	$18,127,664

Municipal Finance

(For local fiscal year ended in 2006)

Revenues

Total $81,552,509
Taxes 38,570,861
Special benefits assessment 1,350,890
Licenses & permits 890,131
Fines & forfeitures 1,915,175
Revenues from use of money & property 3,754,832
Intergovernmental 7,900,644
Service charges 26,784,677
Other revenues 385,299
Other financing sources 0

Expenditures

Total $78,652,327
General government 7,535,816
Public safety 32,533,336
Transportation 6,301,155
Community development 7,925,797
Health 14,214,742
Culture & leisure 10,141,481
Other 0

Local School District

(Data from School year 2007-08 except as noted)

Vista Unified
1234 Arcadia Ave
Vista, CA 92084
(760) 726-2170

Superintendent .... Joyce Bales
Grade plan K-12
Number of schools 33
Enrollment 27,002
High school graduates, 2006-07 1,947
Dropout rate 18.2%
Pupil/teacher ratio 21.6
Average class size 25.2
Students per computer 3.9
Classrooms with internet 1,486
Avg. Daily Attendance (ADA) 22,986
Cost per ADA $8,338
Avg. Teacher Salary $63,443

California Achievement Tests 6th ed., 2008

(Pct scoring at or above 50th National Percentile Rank)

	Math	Reading	Language
Grade 3	58%	35%	43%
Grade 7	57%	55%	50%

Academic Performance Index, 2008

Number of students tested 17,712
Number of valid scores 16,704
2007 API (base) 746
2008 API (growth) 762

SAT Testing, 2006-07

Enrollment, Grade 12 3,648
Number taking test 556
percent taking test 15.2%
percent with total score 1,500+ 8.20%

Average Scores:

Math	Verbal	Writing	Total
517	507	506	1,530

Federal No Child Left Behind, 2008

(Adequate Yearly Progress standards met)

	Participation Rate	Pct Proficient
ELA	Yes	No
Math	Yes	No

API criteria .... Yes
Graduation rate .... Yes
\# criteria met/possible 42/38

Other school districts for this city

(see Appendix E for information on these districts)

None

See Introduction for an explanation of all data sources.

Demographics & Socio-Economic Characteristics
(2000 Decennial Census, except as noted)

Population
1990* . . . 29,105
2000 . . . 30,004
Male . . . 14,748
Female . . . 15,256
Jan. 2008 (estimate)§ . . . 32,299
Persons per sq. mi. of land . . . 3,588.8

Race & Hispanic Origin, 2000
Race
White . . . 8,513
Black/African American . . . 1,259
North American Native . . . 72
Asian . . . 16,728
Pacific Islander . . . 24
Other Race . . . 2,296
Two or more races . . . 1,112
Hispanic origin, total . . . 5,803
Mexican . . . 4,413
Puerto Rican . . . 101
Cuban . . . 96
Other Hispanic . . . 1,193

Age & Nativity, 2000
Under 5 years . . . 1,466
18 years and over . . . 21,675
65 years and over . . . 2,085
85 years and over . . . 161
Median Age . . . 37.2
Native-born . . . 16,130
Foreign-born . . . 13,874

Educational Attainment, 2000
Population 25 years and over . . . 18,699
Less than 9th grade . . . 5.3%
High school grad or higher . . . 88.8%
Bachelor's degree or higher . . . 41.9%
Graduate degree . . . 12.5%

Income & Poverty, 1999
Per capita income . . . $25,196
Median household income . . . $81,015
Median family income . . . $82,977
Persons in poverty . . . 6.5%
H'holds receiving public assistance . . . 239
H'holds receiving social security . . . 1,042

Households, 2000
Total households . . . 8,260
With persons under 18 . . . 4,567
With persons over 65 . . . 1,532
Family households . . . 7,580
Single person households . . . 477
Persons per household . . . 3.63
Persons per family . . . 3.74

Household Population, 2008§§
Persons living in households . . . 32,259
Persons living in group quarters . . . 40
Persons per household . . . 3.8

Labor & Employment
Total civilian labor force, 2008§§ . . . 17,000
Unemployment rate, 2008 . . . 3.6%
Total civilian labor force, 2000 . . . 14,552

Employed persons 16 years and over by occupation, 2000
Managers & professionals . . . 6,720
Service occupations . . . 1,142
Sales & office occupations . . . 4,295
Farming, fishing & forestry . . . 0
Construction & maintenance . . . 675
Production & transportation . . . 1,177
Self-employed persons . . . 1,008

* US Census Bureau
** 2000 Decennial Census
§ California Department of Finance
§§ California Employment Development Dept

General Information
City of Walnut
21201 La Puente Rd
PO Box 682
Walnut, CA 91789
909-595-7543

Website . . . www.ci.walnut.ca.us
Elevation . . . 569 ft.
Land Area (sq. miles) . . . 9.0
Water Area (sq. miles) . . . 0
Year of Incorporation . . . 1959
Government type . . . General law
Sales tax rate . . . 9.25%

Voters & Officials

Registered Voters, October 2008
Total . . . 16,785
Democrats . . . 5,687
Republicans . . . 5,177
Declined to state . . . 5,356

Legislative Districts
US Congressional . . . 26
State Senatorial . . . 29
State Assembly . . . 60

Local Officials, 2009
Mayor . . . Mary Su
Manager . . . Robert Wishner
City Clerk . . . Teresa DeDios
Attorney . . . Michael Montgomery
Finance Dir . . . Christine Londo
Public Works . . . NA
Planning/Dev Dir . . . Daniel Fox
Building . . . NA
Police Chief . . . NA
Fire/Emergency Mgmt . . . NA

Public Safety
Number of officers, 2007 . . . NA
Violent crimes, 2007 . . . 56
Property crimes, 2007 . . . 550
Arson, 2007 . . . 5

Public Library
Walnut Library
Los Angeles County Public Library System
21155 La Puente Rd
Walnut, CA 91789
909-595-0757

Branch Librarian . . . Jenny Cheng

Library system statistics, FY 2007
Population served . . . 3,673,313
Internet terminals . . . 749
Annual users . . . 3,748,771

Per capita:
Operating income . . . $30.06
percent from local government . . . 93.6%
Operating expenditure . . . $28.36
Total materials . . . 2.22
Print holdings . . . 1.97
Visits per capita . . . 3.25

Housing & Construction

Housing Units
Total, 2008§ . . . 8,624
Single family units, attached . . . 119
Single family units, detached . . . 8,159
Multiple family units . . . 346
Mobile home units . . . 0
Occupied . . . 8,486
Vacancy rate . . . 1.6%
Median rent, 2000** . . . $1,223
Median SF home value, 2000** . . . $279,700

New Privately Owned Housing Units Authorized by Building Permit, 2007*

	Units	Construction Cost
Single	9	$3,545,532
Total	9	$3,545,532

Municipal Finance
(For local fiscal year ended in 2006)

Revenues
Total . . . $17,479,446
Taxes . . . 8,942,164
Special benefits assessment . . . 1,726,214
Licenses & permits . . . 311,763
Fines & forfeitures . . . 261,156
Revenues from use of money & property . . . 1,031,659
Intergovernmental . . . 2,187,064
Service charges . . . 2,191,193
Other revenues . . . 828,233
Other financing sources . . . 0

Expenditures
Total . . . $17,761,169
General government . . . 2,235,418
Public safety . . . 2,922,965
Transportation . . . 7,691,202
Community development . . . 1,122,043
Health . . . 179,862
Culture & leisure . . . 3,609,679
Other . . . 0

Local School District
(Data from School year 2007-08 except as noted)
Walnut Valley Unified
880 South Lemon Ave
Walnut, CA 91789
(909) 595-1261

Superintendent . . . Cynthia Simms
Grade plan . . . K-12
Number of schools . . . 15
Enrollment . . . 15,316
High school graduates, 2006-07 . . . 1,527
Dropout rate . . . 1.8%
Pupil/teacher ratio . . . 23.2
Average class size . . . 28.5
Students per computer . . . 5.1
Classrooms with internet . . . 738
Avg. Daily Attendance (ADA) . . . 15,162
Cost per ADA . . . $7,443
Avg. Teacher Salary . . . $71,372

California Achievement Tests 6th ed., 2008
(Pct scoring at or above 50th National Percentile Rank)

	Math	Reading	Language
Grade 3	82%	60%	71%
Grade 7	81%	74%	75%

Academic Performance Index, 2008
Number of students tested . . . 12,371
Number of valid scores . . . 12,061
2007 API (base) . . . 869
2008 API (growth) . . . 876

SAT Testing, 2006-07
Enrollment, Grade 12 . . . 1,552
Number taking test . . . 1,192
percent taking test . . . 76.8%
percent with total score 1,500+ . . . 52.20%

Average Scores:

Math	Verbal	Writing	Total
593	528	529	1,650

Federal No Child Left Behind, 2008
(Adequate Yearly Progress standards met)

	Participation Rate	Pct Proficient
ELA	Yes	No
Math	Yes	Yes

API criteria . . . Yes
Graduation rate . . . Yes
criteria met/possible . . . 38/37

Other school districts for this city
(see Appendix E for information on these districts)
Rowland Unified

See Introduction for an explanation of all data sources.

Demographics & Socio-Economic Characteristics

(2000 Decennial Census, except as noted)

Population

1990* 60,569
2000 64,296
Male 29,683
Female 34,613
Jan. 2008 (estimate)§ 65,306
Persons per sq. mi. of land 3,281.7

Race & Hispanic Origin, 2000

Race
White 53,937
Black/African American 688
North American Native 210
Asian 6,017
Pacific Islander 94
Other Race 1,263
Two or more races 2,087
Hispanic origin, total 3,851
Mexican 2,099
Puerto Rican 137
Cuban 63
Other Hispanic 1,552

Age & Nativity, 2000

Under 5 years 2,854
18 years and over 52,987
65 years and over 16,281
85 years and over 3,185
Median Age 45.1
Native-born 52,836
Foreign-born 11,747

Educational Attainment, 2000

Population 25 years and over 49,986
Less than 9th grade 1.8%
High school grad or higher 95.0%
Bachelor's degree or higher 54.0%
Graduate degree 20.5%

Income & Poverty, 1999

Per capita income $39,875
Median household income $63,238
Median family income $83,794
Persons in poverty 3.7%
H'holds receiving public assistance 223
H'holds receiving social security 11,271

Households, 2000

Total households 30,301
With persons under 18 6,649
With persons over 65 11,551
Family households 16,551
Single person households 11,509
Persons per household 2.09
Persons per family 2.78

Household Population, 2008§§

Persons living in households 64,155
Persons living in group quarters 1,151
Persons per household 2.1

Labor & Employment

Total civilian labor force, 2008§§ 34,900
Unemployment rate, 2008 . . . . . 4.1%
Total civilian labor force, 2000 31,522

Employed persons 16 years and over by occupation, 2000

Managers & professionals 16,878
Service occupations 2,748
Sales & office occupations 8,393
Farming, fishing & forestry 17
Construction & maintenance 1,257
Production & transportation 1,093
Self-employed persons 3,204

* US Census Bureau
** 2000 Decennial Census
§ California Department of Finance
§§ California Employment Development Dept

General Information

City of Walnut Creek
1666 N Main St
Walnut Creek, CA 94596
925-943-5800

Website . . . . . www.walnut-creek.org
Elevation . . . . . 135 ft.
Land Area (sq. miles) 19.9
Water Area (sq. miles) 0
Year of Incorporation 1914
Government type . . . . . General law
Sales tax rate 9.25%

Voters & Officials

Registered Voters, October 2008

Total 42,824
Democrats 19,111
Republicans 14,194
Declined to state 7,960

Legislative Districts

US Congressional 10
State Senatorial 7
State Assembly 15

Local Officials, 2009

Mayor . . . . . Gary Skrel
Manager . . . . . Gary Pokorny
City Clerk . . . . . Patrice Olds
Attorney . . . . . Paul Valle-Riestra
Finance Dir . . . . . Lorie Tinfow
Public Works . . . . . Heather Ballenger
Community Dev Dir . . . . . Sandra Meyer (Int)
Building . . . . . Robert Woods
Police Chief . . . . . NA
Fire/Emergency Mgmt . . . . . NA

Public Safety

Number of officers, 2007 70
Violent crimes, 2007 90
Property crimes, 2007 2,586
Arson, 2007 . . . . . NA

Public Library

Walnut Creek Park Place Library
Contra Costa County Library System
1395 Civic Drive
Walnut Creek, CA 94596
925-646-6773

Branch Librarian . . . . . Cindy Brittain

Library system statistics, FY 2007

Population served 938,513
Internet terminals 324
Annual users 670,618

Per capita:

Operating income $27.05
percent from local government 82.0%
Operating expenditure $27.82
Total materials 1.57
Print holdings 1.41
Visits per capita 3.65

Housing & Construction

Housing Units

Total, 2008§ 32,343
Single family units, attached 4,857
Single family units, detached 12,257
Multiple family units 15,181
Mobile home units 48
Occupied 31,187
Vacancy rate 3.6%
Median rent, 2000** $1,024
Median SF home value, 2000** $391,200

New Privately Owned Housing Units Authorized by Building Permit, 2007*

	Units	Construction Cost
Single	17	$7,832,594
Total	57	$14,792,594

Municipal Finance

(For local fiscal year ended in 2006)

Revenues

Total $72,358,807
Taxes 43,694,882
Special benefits assessment 1,244,056
Licenses & permits 1,418,601
Fines & forfeitures 1,923,960
Revenues from use of money & property 3,916,935
Intergovernmental 3,089,536
Service charges 15,348,917
Other revenues 1,721,920
Other financing sources 0

Expenditures

Total $69,476,103
General government 15,709,581
Public safety 20,077,039
Transportation 7,330,163
Community development 5,922,464
Health 0
Culture & leisure 20,436,856
Other 0

Local School District

(Data from School year 2007-08 except as noted)

Mt. Diablo Unified
1936 Carlotta Dr
Concord, CA 94519
(925) 682-8000

Superintendent . . . . . Richard Nicholl
Grade plan K-12
Number of schools 55
Enrollment 35,355
High school graduates, 2006-07 2,153
Dropout rate 6.0%
Pupil/teacher ratio 20.4
Average class size 26.4
Students per computer 5.2
Classrooms with internet 1,777
Avg. Daily Attendance (ADA) 33,956
Cost per ADA $8,368
Avg. Teacher Salary $60,714

California Achievement Tests 6th ed., 2008

(Pct scoring at or above 50th National Percentile Rank)

	Math	Reading	Language
Grade 3	60%	45%	55%
Grade 7	53%	53%	51%

Academic Performance Index, 2008

Number of students tested 26,357
Number of valid scores 25,920
2007 API (base) 747
2008 API (growth) 755

SAT Testing, 2006-07

Enrollment, Grade 12 2,734
Number taking test 1,063
percent taking test 38.9%
percent with total score 1,500+ 22.80%

Average Scores:

Math	Verbal	Writing	Total
543	521	518	1,582

Federal No Child Left Behind, 2008

(Adequate Yearly Progress standards met)

	Participation Rate	Pct Proficient
ELA	Yes	No
Math	Yes	No

API criteria . . . . . Yes
Graduation rate . . . . . Yes
\# criteria met/possible 46/36

Other school districts for this city

(see Appendix E for information on these districts)

Walnut Creek Elem

See Introduction for an explanation of all data sources.

Demographics & Socio-Economic Characteristics

(2000 Decennial Census, except as noted)

Population

1990* . . . 12,412
2000 . . . 21,263
Male . . . 13,764
Female . . . 7,499
Jan. 2008 (estimate)§ . . . 24,999
Persons per sq. mi. of land . . . 3,289.3

Race & Hispanic Origin, 2000

Race
White . . . 7,366
Black/African American . . . 2,183
North American Native . . . 217
Asian . . . 143
Pacific Islander . . . 32
Other Race . . . 10,730
Two or more races . . . 592
Hispanic origin, total . . . 14,187
Mexican . . . 12,538
Puerto Rican . . . 111
Cuban . . . 2
Other Hispanic . . . 1,536

Age & Nativity, 2000

Under 5 years . . . 1,604
18 years and over . . . 15,427
65 years and over . . . 1,149
85 years and over . . . 112
Median Age . . . 29.3
Native-born . . . 16,315
Foreign-born . . . 4,962

Educational Attainment, 2000

Population 25 years and over . . . 12,376
Less than 9th grade . . . 24.9%
High school grad or higher . . . 54.1%
Bachelor's degree or higher . . . 4.2%
Graduate degree . . . 1.1%

Income & Poverty, 1999

Per capita income . . . $14,228
Median household income . . . $28,997
Median family income . . . $30,506
Persons in poverty . . . 19.4%
H'holds receiving public assistance . . . 434
H'holds receiving social security . . . 926

Households, 2000

Total households . . . 3,971
With persons under 18 . . . 2,462
With persons over 65 . . . 827
Family households . . . 3,403
Single person households . . . 462
Persons per household . . . 3.79
Persons per family . . . 4.07

Household Population, 2008§§

Persons living in households . . . 18,702
Persons living in group quarters . . . 6,297
Persons per household . . . 3.9

Labor & Employment

Total civilian labor force, 2008§§ . . . 8,000
Unemployment rate, 2008 . . . 18.3%
Total civilian labor force, 2000 . . . 5,967

Employed persons 16 years and over by occupation, 2000

Managers & professionals . . . 723
Service occupations . . . 755
Sales & office occupations . . . 1,012
Farming, fishing & forestry . . . 930
Construction & maintenance . . . 399
Production & transportation . . . 841
Self-employed persons . . . 269

* US Census Bureau
** 2000 Decennial Census
§ California Department of Finance
§§ California Employment Development Dept

General Information

City of Wasco
746 8th St
PO Box 190
Wasco, CA 93280
661-758-7200

Website . . . www.ci.wasco.ca.us
Elevation . . . 333 ft.
Land Area (sq. miles) . . . 7.6
Water Area (sq. miles) . . . 0
Year of Incorporation . . . 1945
Government type . . . General law
Sales tax rate . . . 8.25%

Voters & Officials

Registered Voters, October 2008

Total . . . 5,332
Democrats . . . 2,885
Republicans . . . 1,580
Declined to state . . . 726

Legislative Districts

US Congressional . . . 20
State Senatorial . . . 16
State Assembly . . . 30

Local Officials, 2009

Mayor . . . Fred West Jr
Manager . . . Ron Mittag
City Clerk . . . Vickie Hight
Attorney . . . Bonificio Garcia
Finance Dir . . . Jim Zervis
Public Works . . . Dan Allen
Planning/Dev Dir . . . John Heiser
Building . . . NA
Police Chief . . . NA
Fire/Emergency Mgmt . . . NA

Public Safety

Number of officers, 2007 . . . NA
Violent crimes, 2007 . . . NA
Property crimes, 2007 . . . NA
Arson, 2007 . . . NA

Public Library

Wasco Branch Library
Kern County Library System
1102 Seventh St
Wasco, CA 93280
661-758-2114

Branch Librarian . . . Linda Anderson

Library system statistics, FY 2007

Population served . . . 801,648
Internet terminals . . . 237
Annual users . . . 337,030

Per capita:

Operating income . . . $12.11
percent from local government . . . 90.4%
Operating expenditure . . . $12.11
Total materials . . . 1.37
Print holdings . . . 1.29
Visits per capita . . . 2.09

Housing & Construction

Housing Units

Total, 2008§ . . . 5,123
Single family units, attached . . . 361
Single family units, detached . . . 3,797
Multiple family units . . . 831
Mobile home units . . . 134
Occupied . . . 4,781
Vacancy rate . . . 6.7%
Median rent, 2000** . . . $406
Median SF home value, 2000** . . . $81,700

New Privately Owned Housing Units Authorized by Building Permit, 2007*

	Units	Construction Cost
Single	82	$7,247,660
Total	84	$7,360,050

Municipal Finance

(For local fiscal year ended in 2006)

Revenues

Total . . . $14,085,553
Taxes . . . 3,611,311
Special benefits assessment . . . 0
Licenses & permits . . . 566,380
Fines & forfeitures . . . 66,631
Revenues from use of money & property . . . 341,151
Intergovernmental . . . 3,433,446
Service charges . . . 5,933,964
Other revenues . . . 132,670
Other financing sources . . . 0

Expenditures

Total . . . $12,049,535
General government . . . 1,166,452
Public safety . . . 2,492,586
Transportation . . . 2,215,123
Community development . . . 926,576
Health . . . 3,070,539
Culture & leisure . . . 48,789
Other . . . 0

Local School District

(Data from School year 2007-08 except as noted)

Wasco Union High
2100 Seventh St
Wasco, CA 93280
(661) 758-8447

Superintendent . . . Elizabeth McCray
Grade plan . . . 9-12
Number of schools . . . 2
Enrollment . . . 1,765
High school graduates, 2006-07 . . . 243
Dropout rate . . . 3.9%
Pupil/teacher ratio . . . 23.5
Average class size . . . 25.9
Students per computer . . . 5.2
Classrooms with internet . . . 76
Avg. Daily Attendance (ADA) . . . 1,709
Cost per ADA . . . $8,797
Avg. Teacher Salary . . . $60,350

California Achievement Tests 6th ed., 2008

(Pct scoring at or above 50th National Percentile Rank)

	Math	Reading	Language
Grade 3	NA	NA	NA
Grade 7	NA	NA	NA

Academic Performance Index, 2008

Number of students tested . . . 1,250
Number of valid scores . . . 1,183
2007 API (base) . . . 602
2008 API (growth) . . . 612

SAT Testing, 2006-07

Enrollment, Grade 12 . . . 363
Number taking test . . . 75
percent taking test . . . 20.7%
percent with total score 1,500+ . . . 4.10%

Average Scores:

Math	Verbal	Writing	Total
428	414	422	1,264

Federal No Child Left Behind, 2008

(Adequate Yearly Progress standards met)

	Participation Rate	Pct Proficient
ELA	Yes	No
Math	Yes	No

API criteria . . . Yes
Graduation rate . . . Yes
criteria met/possible . . . 18/12

Other school districts for this city

(see Appendix E for information on these districts)

Semitropic Elem, Wasco Union Elem

See Introduction for an explanation of all data sources.

Demographics & Socio-Economic Characteristics

(2000 Decennial Census, except as noted)

Population

1990* . . . 4,771
2000 . . . 6,924
Male . . . 3,486
Female . . . 3,438
Jan. 2008 (estimate)§ . . . 8,763
Persons per sq. mi. of land . . . 5,476.9

Race & Hispanic Origin, 2000

Race
White . . . 5,002
Black/African American . . . 33
North American Native . . . 106
Asian . . . 52
Pacific Islander . . . 11
Other Race . . . 1,384
Two or more races . . . 336
Hispanic origin, total . . . 2,454
Mexican . . . 2,117
Puerto Rican . . . 17
Cuban . . . 2
Other Hispanic . . . 318

Age & Nativity, 2000

Under 5 years . . . 574
18 years and over . . . 4,401
65 years and over . . . 492
85 years and over . . . 59
Median Age . . . 28.5
Native-born . . . 5,702
Foreign-born . . . 1,094

Educational Attainment, 2000

Population 25 years and over . . . 3,719
Less than 9th grade . . . 15.0%
High school grad or higher . . . 67.7%
Bachelor's degree or higher . . . 9.7%
Graduate degree . . . 1.5%

Income & Poverty, 1999

Per capita income . . . $13,933
Median household income . . . $39,286
Median family income . . . $41,698
Persons in poverty . . . 12.0%
H'holds receiving public assistance . . . 143
H'holds receiving social security . . . 423

Households, 2000

Total households . . . 1,990
With persons under 18 . . . 1,155
With persons over 65 . . . 354
Family households . . . 1,681
Single person households . . . 226
Persons per household . . . 3.47
Persons per family . . . 3.71

Household Population, 2008§§

Persons living in households . . . 8,746
Persons living in group quarters . . . 17
Persons per household . . . 3.5

Labor & Employment

Total civilian labor force, 2008§§ . . . 3,600
Unemployment rate, 2008 . . . 10.3%
Total civilian labor force, 2000 . . . 2,991

Employed persons 16 years and over by occupation, 2000

Managers & professionals . . . 589
Service occupations . . . 378
Sales & office occupations . . . 543
Farming, fishing & forestry . . . 210
Construction & maintenance . . . 325
Production & transportation . . . 624
Self-employed persons . . . 177

* US Census Bureau
** 2000 Decennial Census
§ California Department of Finance
§§ California Employment Development Dept

General Information

City of Waterford
312 E Street
Waterford, CA 95386
209-874-2328

Website . . . www.cityofwaterford.org
Elevation . . . NA
Land Area (sq. miles) . . . 1.6
Water Area (sq. miles) . . . 0
Year of Incorporation . . . 1969
Government type . . . General law
Sales tax rate . . . 8.38%

Voters & Officials

Registered Voters, October 2008

Total . . . 3,247
Democrats . . . 1,158
Republicans . . . 1,290
Declined to state . . . 632

Legislative Districts

US Congressional . . . 19
State Senatorial . . . 14
State Assembly . . . 25

Local Officials, 2009

Mayor . . . Charle Goeken
Manager . . . Charles Deschenes
City Clerk . . . Lori Martin
Attorney . . . Corbett J. Browning
Finance Dir . . . (vacant)
Public Works . . . Matt Erickson
Planning/Dev Dir . . . Robert Borchard
Building . . . Bruce Stewart
Police Chief . . . Darin Gharat
Emergency/Fire Dir . . . Jim Weigend

Public Safety

Number of officers, 2007 . . . NA
Violent crimes, 2007 . . . 40
Property crimes, 2007 . . . 272
Arson, 2007 . . . 1

Public Library

Waterford Library
Stanislaus County Free Library
324 E St
Waterford, CA 95386
209-874-2191

Branch Librarian . . . Vanessa Czopek

Library system statistics, FY 2007

Population served . . . 521,497
Internet terminals . . . 128
Annual users . . . 256,298

Per capita:

Operating income . . . $20.76
percent from local government . . . 91.0%
Operating expenditure . . . $20.19
Total materials . . . 1.66
Print holdings . . . 1.56
Visits per capita . . . NA

Housing & Construction

Housing Units

Total, 2008§ . . . 2,623
Single family units, attached . . . 64
Single family units, detached . . . 2,181
Multiple family units . . . 349
Mobile home units . . . 29
Occupied . . . 2,510
Vacancy rate . . . 4.3%
Median rent, 2000** . . . $554
Median SF home value, 2000** . . . $100,800

New Privately Owned Housing Units Authorized by Building Permit, 2007*

	Units	Construction Cost
Single	20	$3,573,209
Total	20	$3,573,209

Municipal Finance

(For local fiscal year ended in 2006)

Revenues

Total . . . $8,832,594
Taxes . . . 2,412,408
Special benefits assessment . . . 78,365
Licenses & permits . . . 81,120
Fines & forfeitures . . . 61,454
Revenues from use of money & property . . . 111,570
Intergovernmental . . . 723,056
Service charges . . . 1,707,680
Other revenues . . . 3,656,941
Other financing sources . . . 0

Expenditures

Total . . . $6,073,570
General government . . . 1,397,438
Public safety . . . 1,241,554
Transportation . . . 454,764
Community development . . . 1,734,483
Health . . . 567,929
Culture & leisure . . . 555,652
Other . . . 0

Local School District

(Data from School year 2007-08 except as noted)

Waterford Unified
219 North Reinway
Waterford, CA 95386
(209) 874-1809

Superintendent . . . Howard Cohen
Grade plan . . . K-12
Number of schools . . . 5
Enrollment . . . 3,791
High school graduates, 2006-07 . . . 297
Dropout rate . . . 8.2%
Pupil/teacher ratio . . . 20.3
Average class size . . . 18.9
Students per computer . . . 3.4
Classrooms with internet . . . 731
Avg. Daily Attendance (ADA) . . . 1,944
Cost per ADA . . . $8,427
Avg. Teacher Salary . . . $62,758

California Achievement Tests 6th ed., 2008

(Pct scoring at or above 50th National Percentile Rank)

	Math	Reading	Language
Grade 3	44%	35%	47%
Grade 7	31%	38%	36%

Academic Performance Index, 2008

Number of students tested . . . 1,466
Number of valid scores . . . 1,365
2007 API (base) . . . 731
2008 API (growth) . . . 770

SAT Testing, 2006-07

Enrollment, Grade 12 . . . 309
Number taking test . . . 57
percent taking test . . . 18.5%
percent with total score 1,500+ . . . 6.50%

Average Scores:

Math	Verbal	Writing	Total
476	478	463	1,417

Federal No Child Left Behind, 2008

(Adequate Yearly Progress standards met)

	Participation Rate	Pct Proficient
ELA	Yes	Yes
Math	Yes	Yes

API criteria . . . Yes
Graduation rate . . . Yes
\# criteria met/possible . . . 26/26

Other school districts for this city

(see Appendix E for information on these districts)

None

See Introduction for an explanation of all data sources.

Demographics & Socio-Economic Characteristics

(2000 Decennial Census, except as noted)

Population

1990* . . . 31,099
2000 . . . 44,265
Male . . . 22,240
Female . . . 22,025
Jan. 2008 (estimate)§ . . . 51,703
Persons per sq. mi. of land . . . 8,078.6

Race & Hispanic Origin, 2000

Race
White . . . 19,036
Black/African American . . . 334
North American Native . . . 768
Asian . . . 1,455
Pacific Islander . . . 53
Other Race . . . 20,328
Two or more races . . . 2,291
Hispanic origin, total . . . 33,254
Mexican . . . 29,953
Puerto Rican . . . 39
Cuban . . . 25
Other Hispanic . . . 3,237

Age & Nativity, 2000

Under 5 years . . . 4,100
18 years and over . . . 29,228
65 years and over . . . 3,802
85 years and over . . . 576
Median Age . . . 27.4
Native-born . . . 24,819
Foreign-born . . . 19,656

Educational Attainment, 2000

Population 25 years and over . . . 24,045
Less than 9th grade . . . 36.4%
High school grad or higher . . . 49.1%
Bachelor's degree or higher . . . 8.7%
Graduate degree . . . 2.7%

Income & Poverty, 1999

Per capita income . . . $13,205
Median household income . . . $37,617
Median family income . . . $40,293
Persons in poverty . . . 18.9%
H'holds receiving public assistance . . . 659
H'holds receiving social security . . . 3,118

Households, 2000

Total households . . . 11,381
With persons under 18 . . . 6,248
With persons over 65 . . . 2,724
Family households . . . 8,865
Single person households . . . 2,005
Persons per household . . . 3.84
Persons per family . . . 4.26

Household Population, 2008§§

Persons living in households . . . 51,150
Persons living in group quarters . . . 553
Persons per household . . . 3.7

Labor & Employment

Total civilian labor force, 2008§§ . . . 22,200
Unemployment rate, 2008 . . . 16.0%
Total civilian labor force, 2000 . . . 19,739

Employed persons 16 years and over by occupation, 2000

Managers & professionals . . . 2,899
Service occupations . . . 3,093
Sales & office occupations . . . 3,438
Farming, fishing & forestry . . . 2,940
Construction & maintenance . . . 1,707
Production & transportation . . . 3,208
Self-employed persons . . . 928

* US Census Bureau
** 2000 Decennial Census
§ California Department of Finance
§§ California Employment Development Dept

General Information

City of Watsonville
PO Box 50,000
Watsonville, CA 95077
831-768-3040

Website . . . www.ci.watsonville.ca.us
Elevation . . . 29 ft.
Land Area (sq. miles) . . . 6.4
Water Area (sq. miles) . . . 0.1
Year of Incorporation . . . 1868
Government type . . . Chartered
Sales tax rate . . . 9.25%

Voters & Officials

Registered Voters, October 2008

Total . . . 14,492
Democrats . . . 9,334
Republicans . . . 2,104
Declined to state . . . 1,910

Legislative Districts

US Congressional . . . 17
State Senatorial . . . 15
State Assembly . . . 28

Local Officials, 2009

Mayor . . . Antonio Rivas
Manager . . . Carlos Palacios
City Clerk . . . Beatriz Vazquez Flores
Attorney . . . Alan Smith
Finance Dir . . . Marc Pimentel
Public Works . . . David Koch
Planning/Dev Dir . . . Marcela Tavantzis
Building . . . NA
Police Chief . . . Terry Medina
Emergency/Fire Dir . . . Mark Bisbee

Public Safety

Number of officers, 2007 . . . 60
Violent crimes, 2007 . . . 397
Property crimes, 2007 . . . 2,276
Arson, 2007 . . . 11

Public Library

Main Library
Watsonville Public Library System
310 Union St
Watsonville, CA 95076
831-768-3400

Director . . . Carol Heitzig

Library system statistics, FY 2007

Population served . . . 58,456
Internet terminals . . . 48
Annual users . . . 68,297

Per capita:

Operating income . . . $57.59
percent from local government . . . 88.8%
Operating expenditure . . . $41.08
Total materials . . . 2.16
Print holdings . . . 1.96
Visits per capita . . . 6.93

Housing & Construction

Housing Units

Total, 2008§ . . . 14,066
Single family units, attached . . . 1,819
Single family units, detached . . . 7,294
Multiple family units . . . 4,053
Mobile home units . . . 900
Occupied . . . 13,689
Vacancy rate . . . 2.7%
Median rent, 2000** . . . $742
Median SF home value, 2000** . . . $224,700

New Privately Owned Housing Units Authorized by Building Permit, 2007*

	Units	Construction Cost
Single	123	$21,597,789
Total	232	$30,713,710

Municipal Finance

(For local fiscal year ended in 2006)

Revenues

Total . . . $82,737,142
Taxes . . . 26,406,618
Special benefits assessment . . . 515,004
Licenses & permits . . . 1,098,815
Fines & forfeitures . . . 564,169
Revenues from use of money & property . . . 3,304,698
Intergovernmental . . . 17,769,761
Service charges . . . 32,345,898
Other revenues . . . 732,179
Other financing sources . . . 0

Expenditures

Total . . . $103,572,913
General government . . . 13,188,926
Public safety . . . 20,601,846
Transportation . . . 11,810,136
Community development . . . 10,771,685
Health . . . 18,936,775
Culture & leisure . . . 20,667,848
Other . . . 0

Local School District

(Data from School year 2007-08 except as noted)

Pajaro Valley Unified
294 Green Valley Rd
Watsonville, CA 95076
(831) 786-2100

Superintendent . . . Dorma Baker
Grade plan . . . K-12
Number of schools . . . 33
Enrollment . . . 19,420
High school graduates, 2006-07 . . . 941
Dropout rate . . . 5.7%
Pupil/teacher ratio . . . 22.3
Average class size . . . 25.5
Students per computer . . . 6.0
Classrooms with internet . . . 1,273
Avg. Daily Attendance (ADA) . . . 18,514
Cost per ADA . . . $9,503
Avg. Teacher Salary . . . $54,717

California Achievement Tests 6th ed., 2008

(Pct scoring at or above 50th National Percentile Rank)

	Math	Reading	Language
Grade 3	44%	23%	32%
Grade 7	41%	39%	38%

Academic Performance Index, 2008

Number of students tested . . . 14,509
Number of valid scores . . . 13,646
2007 API (base) . . . 667
2008 API (growth) . . . 678

SAT Testing, 2006-07

Enrollment, Grade 12 . . . 1,323
Number taking test . . . 417
percent taking test . . . 31.5%
percent with total score 1,500+ . . . 12.40%

Average Scores:

Math	Verbal	Writing	Total
486	467	470	1,423

Federal No Child Left Behind, 2008

(Adequate Yearly Progress standards met)

	Participation Rate	Pct Proficient
ELA	Yes	No
Math	Yes	No

API criteria . . . Yes
Graduation rate . . . Yes
criteria met/possible . . . 33/25

Other school districts for this city

(see Appendix E for information on these districts)

None

See Introduction for an explanation of all data sources.

Demographics & Socio-Economic Characteristics

(2000 Decennial Census, except as noted)

Population

1990* . . . 3,062
2000 . . . 2,978
Male . . . 1,449
Female . . . 1,529
Jan. 2008 (estimate)§ . . . 3,030
Persons per sq. mi. of land . . . 618.4

Race & Hispanic Origin, 2000

Race
White . . . 2,182
Black/African American . . . 276
North American Native . . . 58
Asian . . . 136
Pacific Islander . . . 14
Other Race . . . 164
Two or more races . . . 148
Hispanic origin, total . . . 380
Mexican . . . 330
Puerto Rican . . . 9
Cuban . . . 2
Other Hispanic . . . 39

Age & Nativity, 2000

Under 5 years . . . 210
18 years and over . . . 2,215
65 years and over . . . 513
85 years and over . . . 97
Median Age . . . 35.3
Native-born . . . 2,675
Foreign-born . . . 295

Educational Attainment, 2000

Population 25 years and over . . . 1,744
Less than 9th grade . . . 9.6%
High school grad or higher . . . 73.7%
Bachelor's degree or higher . . . 7.3%
Graduate degree . . . 2.1%

Income & Poverty, 1999

Per capita income . . . $12,434
Median household income . . . $23,333
Median family income . . . $32,197
Persons in poverty . . . 22.8%
H'holds receiving public assistance . . . 117
H'holds receiving social security . . . 466

Households, 2000

Total households . . . 1,184
With persons under 18 . . . 407
With persons over 65 . . . 359
Family households . . . 747
Single person households . . . 342
Persons per household . . . 2.41
Persons per family . . . 2.98

Household Population, 2008§§

Persons living in households . . . 2,861
Persons living in group quarters . . . 169
Persons per household . . . 2.3

Labor & Employment

Total civilian labor force, 2008§§ . . . 1,250
Unemployment rate, 2008 . . . 19.6%
Total civilian labor force, 2000 . . . 1,220

Employed persons 16 years and over by occupation, 2000

Managers & professionals . . . 222
Service occupations . . . 250
Sales & office occupations . . . 246
Farming, fishing & forestry . . . 29
Construction & maintenance . . . 68
Production & transportation . . . 179
Self-employed persons . . . 92

* US Census Bureau
** 2000 Decennial Census
§ California Department of Finance
§§ California Employment Development Dept

General Information

City of Weed
550 Main St
PO Box 470
Weed, CA 96094
530-938-5020

Website . . . www.ci.weed.ca.us
Elevation . . . 3,466 ft.
Land Area (sq. miles) . . . 4.9
Water Area (sq. miles) . . . 0
Year of Incorporation . . . 1961
Government type . . . General law
Sales tax rate . . . 8.25%

Voters & Officials

Registered Voters, October 2008

Total . . . 1,395
Democrats . . . 691
Republicans . . . 339
Declined to state . . . 279

Legislative Districts

US Congressional . . . 2
State Senatorial . . . 4
State Assembly . . . 2

Local Officials, 2009

Mayor . . . Chuck Sutton
Administrator . . . Earl Wilson
City Clerk . . . Deborah Salvestrin
Attorney . . . Robert Winston
Finance Dir . . . M. Kelly McKinnis
Public Works . . . Craig Sharp
Planning/Comm Dev . . . NA
Building . . . NA
Police Chief . . . Martin Nicholas
Emergency/Fire Dir . . . Darin Quigley

Public Safety

Number of officers, 2007 . . . 10
Violent crimes, 2007 . . . 22
Property crimes, 2007 . . . 127
Arson, 2007 . . . 0

Public Library

Weed Branch Library
Siskiyou County Free Library System
780 S Davis St
Weed, CA 96094
530-938-4769

Branch Librarian . . . Shelley Green

Library system statistics, FY 2007

Population served . . . 45,953
Internet terminals . . . 31
Annual users . . . 48,766

Per capita:

Operating income . . . $20.36
percent from local government . . . 90.2%
Operating expenditure . . . $20.12
Total materials . . . 4.06
Print holdings . . . 3.88
Visits per capita . . . NA

Housing & Construction

Housing Units

Total, 2008§ . . . 1,368
Single family units, attached . . . 19
Single family units, detached . . . 901
Multiple family units . . . 387
Mobile home units . . . 61
Occupied . . . 1,253
Vacancy rate . . . 8.4%
Median rent, 2000** . . . $401
Median SF home value, 2000** . . . $72,300

New Privately Owned Housing Units Authorized by Building Permit, 2007*

	Units	Construction Cost
Single	NA	NA
Total	NA	NA

Municipal Finance

(For local fiscal year ended in 2006)

Revenues

Total . . . $6,228,399
Taxes . . . 1,629,818
Special benefits assessment . . . 0
Licenses & permits . . . 15,504
Fines & forfeitures . . . 22,979
Revenues from use of money & property . . . 77,474
Intergovernmental . . . 2,239,296
Service charges . . . 1,117,555
Other revenues . . . 1,125,773
Other financing sources . . . 0

Expenditures

Total . . . $6,123,952
General government . . . 407,305
Public safety . . . 1,685,561
Transportation . . . 710,587
Community development . . . 2,267,595
Health . . . 783,432
Culture & leisure . . . 0
Other . . . 0

Local School District

(Data from School year 2007-08 except as noted)

Siskiyou Union High
624 Everitt Memorial Hwy
Mt. Shasta, CA 96067
(530) 926-3006

Superintendent . . . Michael Matheson
Grade plan . . . 9-12
Number of schools . . . 8
Enrollment . . . 1,029
High school graduates, 2006-07 . . . 170
Dropout rate . . . 5.8%
Pupil/teacher ratio . . . 17.1
Average class size . . . 17.7
Students per computer . . . 2.4
Classrooms with internet . . . 72
Avg. Daily Attendance (ADA) . . . 679
Cost per ADA . . . $11,519
Avg. Teacher Salary . . . $52,824

California Achievement Tests 6th ed., 2008

(Pct scoring at or above 50th National Percentile Rank)

	Math	Reading	Language
Grade 3	NA	NA	NA
Grade 7	NA	NA	NA

Academic Performance Index, 2008

Number of students tested . . . 564
Number of valid scores . . . 542
2007 API (base) . . . 758
2008 API (growth) . . . 753

SAT Testing, 2006-07

Enrollment, Grade 12 . . . 203
Number taking test . . . 69
percent taking test . . . 34.0%
percent with total score 1,500+ . . . 15.80%

Average Scores:

Math	Verbal	Writing	Total
496	486	497	1,479

Federal No Child Left Behind, 2008

(Adequate Yearly Progress standards met)

	Participation Rate	Pct Proficient
ELA	Yes	Yes
Math	Yes	Yes

API criteria . . . Yes
Graduation rate . . . Yes
\# criteria met/possible . . . 14/14

Other school districts for this city

(see Appendix E for information on these districts)

Butteville Union Elem, Weed Union Elem

See Introduction for an explanation of all data sources.

Demographics & Socio-Economic Characteristics†

(2007 American Community Survey, except as noted)

Population

1990* 96,086
2007 103,154
Male 48,470
Female 54,684
Jan. 2008 (estimate)§ 112,666
Persons per sq. mi. of land 6,997.9

Race & Hispanic Origin, 2007

Race
White 37,534
Black/African American 3,317
North American Native 120
Asian 25,335
Pacific Islander 71
Other Race 33,671
Two or more races 3,106
Hispanic origin, total 54,645
Mexican 44,295
Puerto Rican 507
Cuban 365
Other Hispanic 9,478

Age & Nativity, 2007

Under 5 years 7,405
18 years and over 77,055
65 years and over 12,297
85 years and over 1,353
Median Age 36.1
Native-born 65,989
Foreign-born 37,165

Educational Attainment, 2007

Population 25 years and over 66,625
Less than 9th grade 8.0%
High school grad or higher 81.5%
Bachelor's degree or higher 23.3%
Graduate degree 6.8%

Income & Poverty, 2007

Per capita income $25,192
Median household income $69,484
Median family income $76,243
Persons in poverty 10.4%
H'holds receiving public assistance 957
H'holds receiving social security 8,249

Households, 2007

Total households 31,163
With persons under 18 13,129
With persons over 65 8,784
Family households 23,401
Single person households 6,074
Persons per household 3.27
Persons per family 3.78

Household Population, 2008§§

Persons living in households 111,858
Persons living in group quarters 808
Persons per household 3.5

Labor & Employment

Total civilian labor force, 2008§§ 56,300
Unemployment rate, 2008 .... 6.6%
Total civilian labor force, 2000* 48,358

Employed persons 16 years and over by occupation, 2007

Managers & professionals 16,180
Service occupations 9,324
Sales & office occupations 14,254
Farming, fishing & forestry 0
Construction & maintenance 4,148
Production & transportation 6,076
Self-employed persons 2,964

† see Appendix D for 2000 Decennial Census Data
* US Census Bureau
** 2007 American Community Survey
§ California Department of Finance
§§ California Employment Development Dept

General Information

City of West Covina
1444 W Garvey Ave S
West Covina, CA 91790
626-939-8400

Website .... www.westcovina.org
Elevation .... 362 ft.
Land Area (sq. miles) 16.1
Water Area (sq. miles) 0
Year of Incorporation 1923
Government type .... General law
Sales tax rate 9.25%

Voters & Officials

Registered Voters, October 2008

Total 47,923
Democrats 22,787
Republicans 13,550
Declined to state 9,745

Legislative Districts

US Congressional 32
State Senatorial 24
State Assembly 57

Local Officials, 2009

Mayor .... Roger Hernandez
Manager .... Andrew Pasmant
City Clerk .... Laurie Carrico
Attorney .... Arnold Alvarez-Glasman
Finance Dir .... Thomas Bachman
Public Works .... Shannon Yauchzee
Community Dev Dir .... Christopher Chung
Building .... NA
Police Chief .... Frank Wills
Fire Chief .... Paul Segalla

Public Safety

Number of officers, 2007 113
Violent crimes, 2007 392
Property crimes, 2007 3,865
Arson, 2007 4

Public Library

West Covina Branch
Los Angeles County Public Library System
1601 W Covina Pkwy
West Covina, CA 91790
626-962-3541

Branch Librarian .... Beth Wilson

Library system statistics, FY 2007

Population served 3,673,313
Internet terminals 749
Annual users 3,748,771

Per capita:

Operating income $30.06
percent from local government 93.6%
Operating expenditure $28.36
Total materials 2.22
Print holdings 1.97
Visits per capita 3.25

Housing & Construction

Housing Units

Total, 2008§ 32,816
Single family units, attached 2,812
Single family units, detached 21,361
Multiple family units 8,295
Mobile home units 348
Occupied 32,155
Vacancy rate 2.0%
Median rent, 2007** $1,231
Median SF home value, 2007** $557,500

New Privately Owned Housing Units Authorized by Building Permit, 2007*

	Units	Construction Cost
Single	38	$11,795,525
Total	38	$11,795,525

Municipal Finance

(For local fiscal year ended in 2006)

Revenues

Total $71,370,045
Taxes 38,098,708
Special benefits assessment 4,655,145
Licenses & permits 1,532,442
Fines & forfeitures 1,236,649
Revenues from use of money & property 5,675,291
Intergovernmental 13,631,856
Service charges 5,886,791
Other revenues 653,163
Other financing sources 0

Expenditures

Total $77,410,641
General government 10,756,055
Public safety 41,916,346
Transportation 11,306,456
Community development 2,302,439
Health 816,634
Culture & leisure 10,312,711
Other 0

Local School District

(Data from School year 2007-08 except as noted)

West Covina Unified
1717 West Merced Ave
West Covina, CA 91790
(626) 939-4600

Superintendent .... Liliam Castillo
Grade plan K-12
Number of schools 14
Enrollment 13,167
High school graduates, 2006-07 575
Dropout rate 1.6%
Pupil/teacher ratio 21.8
Average class size 25.4
Students per computer 3.0
Classrooms with internet 3,404
Avg. Daily Attendance (ADA) 8,884
Cost per ADA $7,490
Avg. Teacher Salary $65,384

California Achievement Tests 6th ed., 2008

(Pct scoring at or above 50th National Percentile Rank)

	Math	Reading	Language
Grade 3	62%	37%	50%
Grade 7	58%	54%	54%

Academic Performance Index, 2008

Number of students tested 8,083
Number of valid scores 7,548
2007 API (base) 760
2008 API (growth) 773

SAT Testing, 2006-07

Enrollment, Grade 12 780
Number taking test 249
percent taking test 31.9%
percent with total score 1,500+ 9.50%

Average Scores:

Math	Verbal	Writing	Total
463	456	449	1,368

Federal No Child Left Behind, 2008

(Adequate Yearly Progress standards met)

	Participation Rate	Pct Proficient
ELA	Yes	No
Math	Yes	No

API criteria .... Yes
Graduation rate .... Yes
\# criteria met/possible 38/36

Other school districts for this city

(see Appendix E for information on these districts)

Covina-Valley Unified, Rowland Unified

See Introduction for an explanation of all data sources.

Demographics & Socio-Economic Characteristics

(2000 Decennial Census, except as noted)

Population

1990* ... 36,118
2000 ... 35,716
Male ... 19,732
Female ... 15,984
Jan. 2008 (estimate)§ ... 37,563
Persons per sq. mi. of land ... 19,770.0

Race & Hispanic Origin, 2000

Race
White ... 30,868
Black/African American ... 1,104
North American Native ... 129
Asian ... 1,350
Pacific Islander ... 41
Other Race ... 1,026
Two or more races ... 1,198
Hispanic origin, total ... 3,142
Mexican ... 1,532
Puerto Rican ... 190
Cuban ... 129
Other Hispanic ... 1,291

Age & Nativity, 2000

Under 5 years ... 588
18 years and over ... 33,682
65 years and over ... 6,088
85 years and over ... 915
Median Age ... 39.4
Native-born ... 22,907
Foreign-born ... 12,809

Educational Attainment, 2000

Population 25 years and over ... 31,725
Less than 9th grade ... 3.2%
High school grad or higher ... 91.1%
Bachelor's degree or higher ... 46.8%
Graduate degree ... 15.7%

Income & Poverty, 1999

Per capita income ... $38,302
Median household income ... $38,914
Median family income ... $41,463
Persons in poverty ... 11.4%
H'holds receiving public assistance ... 602
H'holds receiving social security ... 3,725

Households, 2000

Total households ... 23,120
With persons under 18 ... 1,479
With persons over 65 ... 4,853
Family households ... 5,211
Single person households ... 13,990
Persons per household ... 1.53
Persons per family ... 2.50

Household Population, 2008§§

Persons living in households ... 37,327
Persons living in group quarters ... 236
Persons per household ... 1.6

Labor & Employment

Total civilian labor force, 2008§§ ... 27,500
Unemployment rate, 2008 ... 6.3%
Total civilian labor force, 2000 ... 23,680

Employed persons 16 years and over by occupation, 2000

Managers & professionals ... 11,950
Service occupations ... 2,870
Sales & office occupations ... 5,746
Farming, fishing & forestry ... 0
Construction & maintenance ... 570
Production & transportation ... 948
Self-employed persons ... 2,991

* US Census Bureau
** 2000 Decennial Census
§ California Department of Finance
§§ California Employment Development Dept

General Information

City of West Hollywood
8300 Santa Monica Blvd
West Hollywood, CA 90069
323-848-6400

Website ... www.weho.org
Elevation ... 287 ft.
Land Area (sq. miles) ... 1.9
Water Area (sq. miles) ... 0
Year of Incorporation ... 1984
Government type ... General law
Sales tax rate ... 9.25%

Voters & Officials

Registered Voters, October 2008

Total ... 24,121
Democrats ... 14,935
Republicans ... 2,537
Declined to state ... 5,509

Legislative Districts

US Congressional ... 30
State Senatorial ... 23
State Assembly ... 42

Local Officials, 2009

Mayor ... Jeffrey Prang
Manager ... Paul Arevalo
City Clerk ... Thomas R. West
Attorney ... Jenkins & Hogin
Finance Dir ... Anil Gandhy
Public Works ... NA
Planning/Dev Dir ... Susan Healy-Keene
Building ... NA
Police Chief ... Buddy Goldman
Fire/Emergency Mgmt ... NA

Public Safety

Number of officers, 2007 ... NA
Violent crimes, 2007 ... 338
Property crimes, 2007 ... 1,430
Arson, 2007 ... 7

Public Library

West Hollywood Library
Los Angeles County Public Library System
715 N San Vicente Blvd
West Hollywood, CA 90069
310-652-5340

Branch Librarian ... Laura Frakes

Library system statistics, FY 2007

Population served ... 3,673,313
Internet terminals ... 749
Annual users ... 3,748,771

Per capita:

Operating income ... $30.06
percent from local government ... 93.6%
Operating expenditure ... $28.36
Total materials ... 2.22
Print holdings ... 1.97
Visits per capita ... 3.25

Housing & Construction

Housing Units

Total, 2008§ ... 24,499
Single family units, attached ... 679
Single family units, detached ... 1,796
Multiple family units ... 22,024
Mobile home units ... 0
Occupied ... 23,497
Vacancy rate ... 4.1%
Median rent, 2000** ... $773
Median SF home value, 2000** ... $406,400

New Privately Owned Housing Units Authorized by Building Permit, 2007*

	Units	Construction Cost
Single	2	$570,598
Total	109	$23,970,522

Municipal Finance

(For local fiscal year ended in 2006)

Revenues

Total ... $76,753,164
Taxes ... 39,550,129
Special benefits assessment ... 1,491,587
Licenses & permits ... 2,417,070
Fines & forfeitures ... 2,301,871
Revenues from use of money & property ... 2,129,855
Intergovernmental ... 4,241,086
Service charges ... 20,223,659
Other revenues ... 4,397,907
Other financing sources ... 0

Expenditures

Total ... $63,275,784
General government ... 12,608,635
Public safety ... 12,920,806
Transportation ... 16,395,008
Community development ... 10,607,993
Health ... 7,479,839
Culture & leisure ... 3,263,503
Other ... 0

Local School District

(Data from School year 2007-08 except as noted)

Los Angeles Unified
333 South Beaudry Ave
Los Angeles, CA 90017
(213) 241-1000

Superintendent ... Ramon Cortines
Grade plan ... PK-12
Number of schools ... 827
Enrollment ... 693,680
High school graduates, 2006-07 ... 28,545
Dropout rate ... 7.8%
Pupil/teacher ratio ... 19.8
Average class size ... 24.9
Students per computer ... 3.7
Classrooms with internet ... 31,112
Avg. Daily Attendance (ADA) ... 653,672
Cost per ADA ... $10,053
Avg. Teacher Salary ... $63,391

California Achievement Tests 6th ed., 2008

(Pct scoring at or above 50th National Percentile Rank)

	Math	Reading	Language
Grade 3	49%	27%	39%
Grade 7	37%	33%	33%

Academic Performance Index, 2008

Number of students tested ... 495,046
Number of valid scores ... 471,641
2007 API (base) ... 662
2008 API (growth) ... 683

SAT Testing, 2006-07

Enrollment, Grade 12 ... 32,370
Number taking test ... 15,447
percent taking test ... 47.7%
percent with total score 1,500+ ... 12.50%

Average Scores:

Math	Verbal	Writing	Total
443	438	441	1,322

Federal No Child Left Behind, 2008

(Adequate Yearly Progress standards met)

	Participation Rate	Pct Proficient
ELA	Yes	No
Math	Yes	No

API criteria ... Yes
Graduation rate ... Yes
\# criteria met/possible ... 46/38

Other school districts for this city

(see Appendix E for information on these districts)

None

See Introduction for an explanation of all data sources.

Demographics & Socio-Economic Characteristics

(2000 Decennial Census, except as noted)

Population

1990* 28,898
2000 31,615
Male 15,612
Female 16,003
Jan. 2008 (estimate)§ 47,068
Persons per sq. mi. of land 2,252.1

Race & Hispanic Origin, 2000

Race
White 20,548
Black/African American 811
North American Native 555
Asian 2,282
Pacific Islander 184
Other Race 5,056
Two or more races 2,179
Hispanic origin, total 9,470
Mexican 8,071
Puerto Rican 110
Cuban 20
Other Hispanic 1,269

Age & Nativity, 2000

Under 5 years 2,431
18 years and over 22,185
65 years and over 4,007
85 years and over 383
Median Age 34.0
Native-born 23,682
Foreign-born 7,922

Educational Attainment, 2000

Population 25 years and over 19,201
Less than 9th grade 14.2%
High school grad or higher 69.9%
Bachelor's degree or higher 9.8%
Graduate degree 2.7%

Income & Poverty, 1999

Per capita income $15,245
Median household income $31,718
Median family income $36,371
Persons in poverty 22.1%
H'holds receiving public assistance . . . 1,247
H'holds receiving social security 3,024

Households, 2000

Total households 11,404
With persons under 18 4,458
With persons over 65 3,001
Family households 7,600
Single person households 3,092
Persons per household 2.75
Persons per family 3.39

Household Population, 2008§§

Persons living in households 46,862
Persons living in group quarters 206
Persons per household 2.7

Labor & Employment

Total civilian labor force, 2008§§ 16,400
Unemployment rate, 2008 . . . . . 11.6%
Total civilian labor force, 2000 13,146

Employed persons 16 years and over by occupation, 2000

Managers & professionals 2,470
Service occupations 2,341
Sales & office occupations 3,511
Farming, fishing & forestry 144
Construction & maintenance 1,500
Production & transportation 1,927
Self-employed persons 936

* US Census Bureau
** 2000 Decennial Census
§ California Department of Finance
§§ California Employment Development Dept

General Information

City of West Sacramento
1110 W Capitol Ave
West Sacramento, CA 95691
916-617-4500

Website . . . . www.cityofwestsacramento.org
Elevation . . . . . 18 ft.
Land Area (sq. miles) 20.9
Water Area (sq. miles) 1.9
Year of Incorporation 1987
Government type . . . . . General Law
Sales tax rate 8.75%

Voters & Officials

Registered Voters, October 2008

Total 23,111
Democrats 10,818
Republicans 6,057
Declined to state 4,802

Legislative Districts

US Congressional 1
State Senatorial 5
State Assembly 8

Local Officials, 2009

Mayor . . . . . Chrisopher Cabaldon
Manager . . . . . Toby Ross
City Clerk . . . . . Kryss Rankin
Attorney . . . . . Robert Murphy
Finance Dir . . . . . Evelyne Hayden
Public Works . . . . . Steve Patek
Planning/Dev Dir . . . . . Steve Patek
Building . . . . . Steve Patek
Police Chief . . . . . Dan Drummond
Fire Chief . . . . . Al Terrell

Public Safety

Number of officers, 2007 71
Violent crimes, 2007 371
Property crimes, 2007 1,386
Arson, 2007 21

Public Library

A.F. Turner Branch Library
Yolo County Library System
1212 Merkley Ave
West Sacramento, CA 95691
916-375-6465

Branch Librarian . . . . . Dale Gilliard

Library system statistics, FY 2007

Population served 139,923
Internet terminals 43
Annual users 276,902

Per capita:

Operating income $33.44
percent from local government 89.8%
Operating expenditure $27.76
Total materials 2.68
Print holdings 2.44
Visits per capita 4.51

Housing & Construction

Housing Units

Total, 2008§ 18,254
Single family units, attached 879
Single family units, detached 11,615
Multiple family units 4,183
Mobile home units 1,577
Occupied 17,158
Vacancy rate 6.0%
Median rent, 2000** $525
Median SF home value, 2000** $113,000

New Privately Owned Housing Units Authorized by Building Permit, 2007*

	Units	Construction Cost
Single	291	$52,026,703
Total	461	$63,913,774

Municipal Finance

(For local fiscal year ended in 2006)

Revenues

Total $118,376,159
Taxes 47,388,455
Special benefits assessment 1,992,292
Licenses & permits 1,169,184
Fines & forfeitures 110,197
Revenues from use of money & property 4,693,984
Intergovernmental 4,440,684
Service charges 33,316,470
Other revenues 25,264,893
Other financing sources 0

Expenditures

Total $104,821,690
General government 9,452,231
Public safety 25,890,987
Transportation 28,407,612
Community development 10,369,501
Health 11,939,618
Culture & leisure 5,659,552
Other 0

Local School District

(Data from School year 2007-08 except as noted)

Washington Unified
930 Westacre Rd
West Sacramento, CA 95691
(916) 375-7600

Superintendent . . . . . Steven Lawrence
Grade plan K-12
Number of schools 13
Enrollment 7,237
High school graduates, 2006-07 303
Dropout rate 6.1%
Pupil/teacher ratio 20.4
Average class size 25.8
Students per computer 6.0
Classrooms with internet 350
Avg. Daily Attendance (ADA) 6,820
Cost per ADA $8,125
Avg. Teacher Salary $55,251

California Achievement Tests 6th ed., 2008

(Pct scoring at or above 50th National Percentile Rank)

	Math	Reading	Language
Grade 3	50%	33%	39%
Grade 7	45%	39%	38%

Academic Performance Index, 2008

Number of students tested 5,417
Number of valid scores 4,964
2007 API (base) 700
2008 API (growth) 713

SAT Testing, 2006-07

Enrollment, Grade 12 384
Number taking test 104
percent taking test 27.1%
percent with total score 1,500+ 7.80%

Average Scores:

Math	Verbal	Writing	Total
477	438	445	1,360

Federal No Child Left Behind, 2008

(Adequate Yearly Progress standards met)

	Participation Rate	Pct Proficient
ELA	Yes	No
Math	Yes	No

API criteria . . . . . Yes
Graduation rate . . . . . Yes
criteria met/possible 40/34

Other school districts for this city

(see Appendix E for information on these districts)

None

See Introduction for an explanation of all data sources.

Demographics & Socio-Economic Characteristics

(2000 Decennial Census, except as noted)

Population

1990* 7,455
2000 8,368
Male 4,025
Female 4,343
Jan. 2008 (estimate)§ 8,867
Persons per sq. mi. of land 1,705.2

Race & Hispanic Origin, 2000

Race
White 7,506
Black/African American 69
North American Native 11
Asian 509
Pacific Islander 6
Other Race 85
Two or more races 182
Hispanic origin, total 386
Mexican 187
Puerto Rican 23
Cuban 21
Other Hispanic 155

Age & Nativity, 2000

Under 5 years 380
18 years and over 6,378
65 years and over 1,451
85 years and over 114
Median Age 44.6
Native-born 7,501
Foreign-born 1,162

Educational Attainment, 2000

Population 25 years and over 6,327
Less than 9th grade 1.1%
High school grad or higher 95.3%
Bachelor's degree or higher 51.4%
Graduate degree 22.5%

Income & Poverty, 1999

Per capita income $49,596
Median household income $94,571
Median family income $109,310
Persons in poverty 2.5%
H'holds receiving public assistance 21
H'holds receiving social security 1,035

Households, 2000

Total households 3,270
With persons under 18 1,095
With persons over 65 1,005
Family households 2,492
Single person households 631
Persons per household 2.56
Persons per family 2.93

Household Population, 2008§§

Persons living in households 8,858
Persons living in group quarters 9
Persons per household 2.7

Labor & Employment

Total civilian labor force, 2008§§ 5,000
Unemployment rate, 2008 . . . . . 3.7%
Total civilian labor force, 2000 4,317

Employed persons 16 years and over by occupation, 2000

Managers & professionals 2,409
Service occupations 406
Sales & office occupations 1,099
Farming, fishing & forestry 0
Construction & maintenance 134
Production & transportation 93
Self-employed persons 605

* US Census Bureau
** 2000 Decennial Census
§ California Department of Finance
§§ California Employment Development Dept

General Information

City of Westlake Village
31200 Oak Crest Dr
Westlake Village, CA 91361
818-706-1613

Website . . . . . www.wlv.org
Elevation . . . . . NA
Land Area (sq. miles) 5.2
Water Area (sq. miles) 0.5
Year of Incorporation 1981
Government type . . . . . General law
Sales tax rate 9.25%

Voters & Officials

Registered Voters, October 2008

Total 5,861
Democrats 1,939
Republicans 2,588
Declined to state 1,098

Legislative Districts

US Congressional 30
State Senatorial 23
State Assembly 41

Local Officials, 2009

Mayor . . . . . Robert Slavin
City Manager . . . . . Raymond Taylor
City Clerk . . . . . Beth Schott
Attorney . . . . . Terence Boga
Finance Dir . . . . . Bob Biery
Public Works . . . . . (County)
Planning/Dev Dir . . . . . Robert Theobald
Building . . . . . (County)
Police Chief . . . . . Tom Martin
Emergency/Fire Dir . . . . . Reggie Lee

Public Safety

Number of officers, 2007 . . . . . NA
Violent crimes, 2007 13
Property crimes, 2007 168
Arson, 2007 1

Public Library

Westlake Village Library
Los Angeles County Public Library System
31220 W Oak Crest Dr
Westlake Village, CA 91361
818-865-9230

Branch Librarian . . . . . Mark Totten

Library system statistics, FY 2007

Population served 3,673,313
Internet terminals 749
Annual users 3,748,771

Per capita:

Operating income $30.06
percent from local government 93.6%
Operating expenditure $28.36
Total materials 2.22
Print holdings 1.97
Visits per capita 3.25

Housing & Construction

Housing Units

Total, 2008§ 3,384
Single family units, attached 608
Single family units, detached 2,242
Multiple family units 359
Mobile home units 175
Occupied 3,306
Vacancy rate 2.3%
Median rent, 2000** $1,582
Median SF home value, 2000** $433,800

New Privately Owned Housing Units Authorized by Building Permit, 2007*

	Units	Construction Cost
Single	NA	NA
Total	NA	NA

Municipal Finance

(For local fiscal year ended in 2006)

Revenues

Total $11,992,631
Taxes 6,440,042
Special benefits assessment 814,244
Licenses & permits 1,493,954
Fines & forfeitures 89,761
Revenues from use of money & property 773,573
Intergovernmental 1,088,254
Service charges 1,217,706
Other revenues 75,097
Other financing sources 0

Expenditures

Total $10,480,090
General government 2,541,371
Public safety 1,915,387
Transportation 3,984,454
Community development 1,156,489
Health 157,503
Culture & leisure 724,886
Other 0

Local School District

(Data from School year 2007-08 except as noted)

Las Virgenes Unified
4111 North Las Virgenes Rd
Calabasas, CA 91302
(818) 880-4000

Superintendent . . . . . Donald Zimring
Grade plan K-12
Number of schools 15
Enrollment 11,803
High school graduates, 2006-07 1,004
Dropout rate 1.4%
Pupil/teacher ratio 25.0
Average class size 28.8
Students per computer 6.1
Classrooms with internet 515
Avg. Daily Attendance (ADA) 11,596
Cost per ADA $8,255
Avg. Teacher Salary $66,468

California Achievement Tests 6th ed., 2008

(Pct scoring at or above 50th National Percentile Rank)

	Math	Reading	Language
Grade 3	82%	67%	75%
Grade 7	80%	75%	75%

Academic Performance Index, 2008

Number of students tested 9,240
Number of valid scores 9,058
2007 API (base) 872
2008 API (growth) 876

SAT Testing, 2006-07

Enrollment, Grade 12 1,069
Number taking test 746
percent taking test 69.8%
percent with total score 1,500+ 54.20%

Average Scores:

Math	Verbal	Writing	Total
578	549	570	1,697

Federal No Child Left Behind, 2008

(Adequate Yearly Progress standards met)

	Participation Rate	Pct Proficient
ELA	Yes	Yes
Math	Yes	Yes

API criteria . . . . . Yes
Graduation rate . . . . . Yes
\# criteria met/possible 34/34

Other school districts for this city

(see Appendix E for information on these districts)

None

See Introduction for an explanation of all data sources.

Demographics & Socio-Economic Characteristics†

(2007 American Community Survey, except as noted)

Population

1990* ... 78,118
2007 ... 91,994
Male ... 45,751
Female ... 46,243
Jan. 2008 (estimate)§ ... 93,027
Persons per sq. mi. of land ... 9,210.6

Race & Hispanic Origin, 2007

Race
White ... 38,555
Black/African American ... 1,817
North American Native ... 169
Asian ... 47,463
Pacific Islander ... 0
Other Race ... 2,784
Two or more races ... 1,206
Hispanic origin, total ... 17,453
Mexican ... NA
Puerto Rican ... NA
Cuban ... NA
Other Hispanic ... NA

Age & Nativity, 2007

Under 5 years ... 5,524
18 years and over ... 70,288
65 years and over ... 14,689
85 years and over ... 1,536
Median Age ... 39.2
Native-born ... 46,524
Foreign-born ... 45,470

Educational Attainment, 2007

Population 25 years and over ... 64,020
Less than 9th grade ... 14.2%
High school grad or higher ... 73.4%
Bachelor's degree or higher ... 21.4%
Graduate degree ... 4.8%

Income & Poverty, 2007

Per capita income ... $23,424
Median household income ... $52,477
Median family income ... $58,295
Persons in poverty ... 8.8%
H'holds receiving public assistance ... 846
H'holds receiving social security ... 8,120

Households, 2007

Total households ... 27,454
With persons under 18 ... 10,946
With persons over 65 ... 9,144
Family households ... 21,230
Single person households ... 4,837
Persons per household ... 3.34
Persons per family ... 3.85

Household Population, 2008§§

Persons living in households ... 92,475
Persons living in group quarters ... 552
Persons per household ... 3.4

Labor & Employment

Total civilian labor force, 2008§§ ... 47,100
Unemployment rate, 2008 ... 5.9%
Total civilian labor force, 2000* ... 40,301

Employed persons 16 years and over by occupation, 2007

Managers & professionals ... 11,608
Service occupations ... 8,283
Sales & office occupations ... 10,490
Farming, fishing & forestry ... 0
Construction & maintenance ... 4,448
Production & transportation ... 7,260
Self-employed persons ... 3,269

† see Appendix D for 2000 Decennial Census Data
* US Census Bureau
** 2007 American Community Survey
§ California Department of Finance
§§ California Employment Development Dept

General Information

City of Westminster
8200 Westminster Blvd
Westminster, CA 92683
714-898-3311

Website ... www.ci.westminster.ca.us
Elevation ... 30 ft.
Land Area (sq. miles) ... 10.1
Water Area (sq. miles) ... 0
Year of Incorporation ... 1957
Government type ... General law
Sales tax rate ... 8.75%

Voters & Officials

Registered Voters, October 2008

Total ... 47,697
Democrats ... 14,999
Republicans ... 20,402
Declined to state ... 10,317

Legislative Districts

US Congressional ... 40, 46
State Senatorial ... 34, 35
State Assembly ... 67, 68

Local Officials, 2009

Mayor ... Margie L. Rice
Manager ... Ramon Silver
City Clerk ... Marian Contreras
Attorney ... Richard Jones
Finance Dir ... Paul Espinoza
Public Works ... Marwan Youssef
Planning/Dev Dir ... Doug McIsaac
Building ... NA
Police Chief ... Andrew Hall
Emergency/Fire Dir ... Charles Prather

Public Safety

Number of officers, 2007 ... 98
Violent crimes, 2007 ... 355
Property crimes, 2007 ... 2,657
Arson, 2007 ... 25

Public Library

Westminster Branch Library
Orange County Public Library System
8180 13th St
Westminster, CA 92683
714-893-5057

Branch Librarian ... Mary Hutton

Library system statistics, FY 2007

Population served ... 1,532,758
Internet terminals ... 505
Annual users ... 680,874

Per capita:

Operating income ... $24.71
percent from local government ... 90.0%
Operating expenditure ... $24.18
Total materials ... 1.93
Print holdings ... 1.84
Visits per capita ... 4.02

Housing & Construction

Housing Units

Total, 2008§ ... 27,419
Single family units, attached ... 2,553
Single family units, detached ... 14,895
Multiple family units ... 6,903
Mobile home units ... 3,068
Occupied ... 26,876
Vacancy rate ... 2.0%
Median rent, 2007** ... $1,247
Median SF home value, 2007** ... $589,200

New Privately Owned Housing Units Authorized by Building Permit, 2007*

	Units	Construction Cost
Single	17	$3,151,000
Total	174	$24,262,192

Municipal Finance

(For local fiscal year ended in 2006)

Revenues

Total ... $62,782,054
Taxes ... 35,392,784
Special benefits assessment ... 1,105,076
Licenses & permits ... 602,460
Fines & forfeitures ... 1,115,973
Revenues from use of money & property ... 1,725,738
Intergovernmental ... 6,225,409
Service charges ... 16,311,673
Other revenues ... 302,941
Other financing sources ... 0

Expenditures

Total ... $67,348,673
General government ... 1,134,049
Public safety ... 32,071,082
Transportation ... 6,303,393
Community development ... 6,108,384
Health ... 0
Culture & leisure ... 11,491,002
Other ... 0

Local School District

(Data from School year 2007-08 except as noted)

Huntington Beach Union High
5832 Bolsa Ave
Huntington Beach, CA 92649
(714) 903-7000

Superintendent ... Van Riley
Grade plan ... 9-12
Number of schools ... 9
Enrollment ... 16,052
High school graduates, 2006-07 ... 3,154
Dropout rate ... 1.3%
Pupil/teacher ratio ... 25.4
Average class size ... 23.4
Students per computer ... 3.8
Classrooms with internet ... 611
Avg. Daily Attendance (ADA) ... 15,841
Cost per ADA ... $8,287
Avg. Teacher Salary ... $76,735

California Achievement Tests 6th ed., 2008

(Pct scoring at or above 50th National Percentile Rank)

	Math	Reading	Language
Grade 3	NA	NA	NA
Grade 7	NA	NA	NA

Academic Performance Index, 2008

Number of students tested ... 11,830
Number of valid scores ... 11,519
2007 API (base) ... 763
2008 API (growth) ... 795

SAT Testing, 2006-07

Enrollment, Grade 12 ... 3,647
Number taking test ... 1,435
percent taking test ... 39.4%
percent with total score 1,500+ ... 25.50%

Average Scores:

Math	Verbal	Writing	Total
561	527	525	1,613

Federal No Child Left Behind, 2008

(Adequate Yearly Progress standards met)

	Participation Rate	Pct Proficient
ELA	No	No
Math	Yes	No

API criteria ... Yes
Graduation rate ... Yes
\# criteria met/possible ... 34/31

Other school districts for this city

(see Appendix E for information on these districts)

Ocean View Elem, Westminster Elem, Garden Grove Unified

See Introduction for an explanation of all data sources.

Demographics & Socio-Economic Characteristics

(2000 Decennial Census, except as noted)

Population

1990* 1,380
2000 2,131
Male 1,035
Female 1,096
Jan. 2008 (estimate)§ 2,406
Persons per sq. mi. of land 6,015.0

Race & Hispanic Origin, 2000

Race
White 1,188
Black/African American 22
North American Native 15
Asian 7
Pacific Islander 1
Other Race 840
Two or more races 58
Hispanic origin, total 1,752
Mexican 1,588
Puerto Rican 3
Cuban 2
Other Hispanic 159

Age & Nativity, 2000

Under 5 years 196
18 years and over 1,369
65 years and over 204
85 years and over 16
Median Age 28.9
Native-born 1,337
Foreign-born 823

Educational Attainment, 2000

Population 25 years and over 1,152
Less than 9th grade 37.0%
High school grad or higher 40.4%
Bachelor's degree or higher 4.3%
Graduate degree 1.5%

Income & Poverty, 1999

Per capita income $8,941
Median household income $23,365
Median family income $26,667
Persons in poverty 27.6%
H'holds receiving public assistance 64
H'holds receiving social security 183

Households, 2000

Total households 625
With persons under 18 345
With persons over 65 161
Family households 502
Single person households 106
Persons per household 3.41
Persons per family 3.87

Household Population, 2008§§

Persons living in households 2,406
Persons living in group quarters 0
Persons per household 3.4

Labor & Employment

Total civilian labor force, 2008§§ 1,300
Unemployment rate, 2008 . . . . 32.1%
Total civilian labor force, 2000 837

Employed persons 16 years and over by occupation, 2000

Managers & professionals 89
Service occupations 159
Sales & office occupations 133
Farming, fishing & forestry 133
Construction & maintenance 68
Production & transportation 98
Self-employed persons 29

* US Census Bureau
** 2000 Decennial Census
§ California Department of Finance
§§ California Employment Development Dept

General Information

City of Westmorland
355 S Center St
PO Box 699
Westmorland, CA 92281
760-344-3411

Website . . . . www.cityofwestmorland.net
Elevation . . . . 159 ft.
Land Area (sq. miles) 0.4
Water Area (sq. miles) 0
Year of Incorporation 1934
Government type . . . . General law
Sales tax rate 8.75%

Voters & Officials

Registered Voters, October 2008

Total 741
Democrats 413
Republicans 188
Declined to state 110

Legislative Districts

US Congressional 51
State Senatorial 40
State Assembly 80

Local Officials, 2009

Mayor . . . . Henry Graham
Manager/Admin . . . . (vacant)
City Clerk . . . . Sally Traylor
Attorney . . . . Mitch Driskill
Treasurer . . . . Anne Graham
Public Works . . . . Joe Diaz
Planning/Dev Dir . . . . Joel Hamby
Building . . . . Joel Hamby
Police Chief . . . . Fred Beltran
Fire Chief . . . . Sergio Cruz

Public Safety

Number of officers, 2007 5
Violent crimes, 2007 3
Property crimes, 2007 21
Arson, 2007 0

Public Library

Westmorland Branch Library
Imperial County Library System
200 South C St
Westmorland, CA 92281
NA

Branch Librarian . . . . Evie Ford

Library system statistics, FY 2007

Population served 55,503
Internet terminals 27
Annual users 21,222

Per capita:

Operating income $14.19
percent from local government 83.9%
Operating expenditure $12.85
Total materials 1.05
Print holdings 0.96
Visits per capita 0.80

Housing & Construction

Housing Units

Total, 2008§ 756
Single family units, attached 16
Single family units, detached 443
Multiple family units 257
Mobile home units 40
Occupied 710
Vacancy rate 6.1%
Median rent, 2000** $423
Median SF home value, 2000** $84,000

New Privately Owned Housing Units Authorized by Building Permit, 2007*

	Units	Construction Cost
Single	4	$457,565
Total	4	$457,565

Municipal Finance

(For local fiscal year ended in 2006)

Revenues

Total $3,238,885
Taxes 485,015
Special benefits assessment 467,896
Licenses & permits 27,705
Fines & forfeitures 7,529
Revenues from use of money & property 25,808
Intergovernmental 876,141
Service charges 825,240
Other revenues 523,551
Other financing sources 0

Expenditures

Total $2,754,334
General government 190,598
Public safety 445,187
Transportation 47,053
Community development 856,741
Health 436,592
Culture & leisure 48,095
Other 0

Local School District

(Data from School year 2007-08 except as noted)

Brawley Union High
480 North Imperial Ave
Brawley, CA 92227
(760) 312-5819

Superintendent . . . . Antonio Munguia
Grade plan 9-12
Number of schools 3
Enrollment 1,981
High school graduates, 2006-07 352
Dropout rate 2.9%
Pupil/teacher ratio 23.9
Average class size 27.1
Students per computer 4.0
Classrooms with internet 101
Avg. Daily Attendance (ADA) 1,817
Cost per ADA $8,779
Avg. Teacher Salary $73,148

California Achievement Tests 6th ed., 2008

(Pct scoring at or above 50th National Percentile Rank)

	Math	Reading	Language
Grade 3	NA	NA	NA
Grade 7	NA	NA	NA

Academic Performance Index, 2008

Number of students tested 1,430
Number of valid scores 1,369
2007 API (base) 661
2008 API (growth) 682

SAT Testing, 2006-07

Enrollment, Grade 12 466
Number taking test 135
percent taking test 29.0%
percent with total score 1,500+ 8.40%

Average Scores:

Math	Verbal	Writing	Total
460	453	449	1,362

Federal No Child Left Behind, 2008

(Adequate Yearly Progress standards met)

	Participation Rate	Pct Proficient
ELA	Yes	Yes
Math	Yes	Yes

API criteria . . . . Yes
Graduation rate . . . . Yes
criteria met/possible 18/18

Other school districts for this city

(see Appendix E for information on these districts)

Westmorland Union Elem

Demographics & Socio-Economic Characteristics

(2000 Decennial Census, except as noted)

Population

1990* . . . 1,631
2000 . . . 2,275
Male . . . 1,101
Female . . . 1,174
Jan. 2008 (estimate)§ . . . 3,510
Persons per sq. mi. of land . . . 4,387.5

Race & Hispanic Origin, 2000

Race
White . . . 1,698
Black/African American . . . 26
North American Native . . . 33
Asian . . . 118
Pacific Islander . . . 3
Other Race . . . 252
Two or more races . . . 145
Hispanic origin, total . . . 483
Mexican . . . 430
Puerto Rican . . . 3
Cuban . . . 0
Other Hispanic . . . 50

Age & Nativity, 2000

Under 5 years . . . 174
18 years and over . . . 1,526
65 years and over . . . 287
85 years and over . . . 18
Median Age . . . 31.7
Native-born . . . 2,020
Foreign-born . . . 260

Educational Attainment, 2000

Population 25 years and over . . . 1,338
Less than 9th grade . . . 12.9%
High school grad or higher . . . 76.9%
Bachelor's degree or higher . . . 11.4%
Graduate degree . . . 3.5%

Income & Poverty, 1999

Per capita income . . . $14,889
Median household income . . . $34,861
Median family income . . . $39,375
Persons in poverty . . . 19.7%
H'holds receiving public assistance . . . 59
H'holds receiving social security . . . 258

Households, 2000

Total households . . . 785
With persons under 18 . . . 355
With persons over 65 . . . 217
Family households . . . 584
Single person households . . . 169
Persons per household . . . 2.90
Persons per family . . . 3.37

Household Population, 2008§§

Persons living in households . . . 3,510
Persons living in group quarters . . . 0
Persons per household . . . 3.0

Labor & Employment

Total civilian labor force, 2008§§ . . . 1,200
Unemployment rate, 2008 . . . 11.7%
Total civilian labor force, 2000 . . . 997

Employed persons 16 years and over by occupation, 2000

Managers & professionals . . . 202
Service occupations . . . 156
Sales & office occupations . . . 213
Farming, fishing & forestry . . . 40
Construction & maintenance . . . 110
Production & transportation . . . 166
Self-employed persons . . . 63

* US Census Bureau
** 2000 Decennial Census
§ California Department of Finance
§§ California Employment Development Dept

General Information

City of Wheatland
313 Main St
PO Box 395
Wheatland, CA 95692
530-633-2761

Website . . . www.wheatland.ca.gov
Elevation . . . 87 ft.
Land Area (sq. miles) . . . 0.8
Water Area (sq. miles) . . . 0
Year of Incorporation . . . 1874
Government type . . . General law
Sales tax rate . . . 8.25%

Voters & Officials

Registered Voters, October 2008

Total . . . 1,716
Democrats . . . 504
Republicans . . . 808
Declined to state . . . 324

Legislative Districts

US Congressional . . . 2
State Senatorial . . . 4
State Assembly . . . 3

Local Officials, 2009

Mayor . . . Enita Elphick
Manager . . . Stephen Wright
City Clerk . . . Lisa J. Thomason
Attorney . . . Richard Shanahan
Admin Svcs Dir . . . Rex Milller
Public Works . . . Larry Panteloglow Sr
Community Dev Dir . . . Raney Mgmt
Building . . . Todd Cunningham
Police Chief . . . Mike McCrary
Emergency/Fire Dir . . . Bob Verburg

Public Safety

Number of officers, 2007 . . . 6
Violent crimes, 2007 . . . 5
Property crimes, 2007 . . . 87
Arson, 2007 . . . 0

Public Library

Served by County Library

Library system statistics, FY 2007

Population served . . . NA
Internet terminals . . . NA
Annual users . . . NA

Per capita:

Operating income . . . NA
percent from local government . . . NA
Operating expenditure . . . NA
Total materials . . . NA
Print holdings . . . NA
Visits per capita . . . NA

Housing & Construction

Housing Units

Total, 2008§ . . . 1,216
Single family units, attached . . . 37
Single family units, detached . . . 930
Multiple family units . . . 210
Mobile home units . . . 39
Occupied . . . 1,169
Vacancy rate . . . 3.9%
Median rent, 2000** . . . $474
Median SF home value, 2000** . . . $107,000

New Privately Owned Housing Units Authorized by Building Permit, 2007*

	Units	Construction Cost
Single	5	$653,225
Total	5	$653,225

Municipal Finance

(For local fiscal year ended in 2006)

Revenues

Total . . . $4,599,632
Taxes . . . 780,591
Special benefits assessment . . . 71,239
Licenses & permits . . . 34,860
Fines & forfeitures . . . 11,107
Revenues from use of money & property . . . 138,557
Intergovernmental . . . 304,909
Service charges . . . 2,504,939
Other revenues . . . 137,245
Other financing sources . . . 616,185

Expenditures

Total . . . $3,752,232
General government . . . 242,347
Public safety . . . 675,781
Transportation . . . 175,959
Community development . . . 665,294
Health . . . 1,145,200
Culture & leisure . . . 323,393
Other . . . 0

Local School District

(Data from School year 2007-08 except as noted)

Wheatland Union High
1010 Wheatland Rd
Wheatland, CA 95692
(530) 633-3100

Superintendent . . . Wayne Gadberry
Grade plan . . . 9-12
Number of schools . . . 2
Enrollment . . . 792
High school graduates, 2006-07 . . . 144
Dropout rate . . . 2.6%
Pupil/teacher ratio . . . 18.5
Average class size . . . 22.8
Students per computer . . . 3.1
Classrooms with internet . . . 70
Avg. Daily Attendance (ADA) . . . 675
Cost per ADA . . . $8,708
Avg. Teacher Salary . . . NA

California Achievement Tests 6th ed., 2008

(Pct scoring at or above 50th National Percentile Rank)

	Math	Reading	Language
Grade 3	NA	NA	NA
Grade 7	NA	NA	NA

Academic Performance Index, 2008

Number of students tested . . . 577
Number of valid scores . . . 532
2007 API (base) . . . 719
2008 API (growth) . . . 730

SAT Testing, 2006-07

Enrollment, Grade 12 . . . 177
Number taking test . . . 48
percent taking test . . . 27.1%
percent with total score 1,500+ . . . 7.90%

Average Scores:

Math	Verbal	Writing	Total
480	460	456	1,396

Federal No Child Left Behind, 2008

(Adequate Yearly Progress standards met)

	Participation Rate	Pct Proficient
ELA	Yes	Yes
Math	Yes	Yes

API criteria . . . Yes
Graduation rate . . . Yes
\# criteria met/possible . . . 14/14

Other school districts for this city

(see Appendix E for information on these districts)

Wheatland Elem

See Introduction for an explanation of all data sources.

Demographics & Socio-Economic Characteristics†

(2007 American Community Survey, except as noted)

Population

1990*	77,671
2007	82,755
Male	40,756
Female	41,999
Jan. 2008 (estimate)§	86,945
Persons per sq. mi. of land	5,955.1

Race & Hispanic Origin, 2007

Race	
White	47,558
Black/African American	826
North American Native	1,196
Asian	2,219
Pacific Islander	224
Other Race	28,957
Two or more races	1,775
Hispanic origin, total	53,526
Mexican	46,435
Puerto Rican	835
Cuban	64
Other Hispanic	6,192

Age & Nativity, 2007

Under 5 years	7,050
18 years and over	59,695
65 years and over	9,141
85 years and over	1,034
Median Age	33.9
Native-born	66,748
Foreign-born	16,007

Educational Attainment, 2007

Population 25 years and over	51,333
Less than 9th grade	8.6%
High school grad or higher	81.0%
Bachelor's degree or higher	21.9%
Graduate degree	7.2%

Income & Poverty, 2007

Per capita income	$27,319
Median household income	$62,210
Median family income	$70,318
Persons in poverty	6.4%
H'holds receiving public assistance	805
H'holds receiving social security	6,681

Households, 2007

Total households	27,099
With persons under 18	10,886
With persons over 65	6,704
Family households	19,148
Single person households	6,646
Persons per household	3.02
Persons per family	3.65

Household Population, 2008§§

Persons living in households	85,355
Persons living in group quarters	1,590
Persons per household	3.0

Labor & Employment

Total civilian labor force, 2008§§	44,600
Unemployment rate, 2008	5.3%
Total civilian labor force, 2000*	38,785

Employed persons 16 years and over by occupation, 2007

Managers & professionals	14,313
Service occupations	3,995
Sales & office occupations	10,293
Farming, fishing & forestry	139
Construction & maintenance	5,232
Production & transportation	3,963
Self-employed persons	2,678

† see Appendix D for 2000 Decennial Census Data
* US Census Bureau
** 2007 American Community Survey
§ California Department of Finance
§§ California Employment Development Dept

General Information

City of Whittier
13230 Penn St
Whittier, CA 90602
562-945-8200

Website	www.cityofwhittier.org
Elevation	365 ft.
Land Area (sq. miles)	14.6
Water Area (sq. miles)	0
Year of Incorporation	1898
Government type	Council-Mgr
Sales tax rate	9.25%

Voters & Officials

Registered Voters, October 2008

Total	42,460
Democrats	18,660
Republicans	15,635
Declined to state	6,545

Legislative Districts

US Congressional	32, 38-39, 42
State Senatorial	30
State Assembly	56, 58, 60

Local Officials, 2009

Mayor	Joe Vinatieri
City Manager	Stephen W. Helvey
City Clerk	Kathryn A. Marshall
Attorney	Richard D. Jones
Finance Dir	Rod Hill
Public Works	David Pelser
Community Dev Dir	Jeff Collier
Building	Jeff Collier
Police Chief	David Singer
Fire/Emergency Mgmt	NA

Public Safety

Number of officers, 2007	128
Violent crimes, 2007	340
Property crimes, 2007	2,328
Arson, 2007	NA

Public Library

Whittier Public Library
Whittier Public Library System
7344 S Washington Ave
Whittier, CA 90602
562-464-3450

Director	Paymaneh Maghsoudi

Library system statistics, FY 2007

Population served	87,190
Internet terminals	31
Annual users	64,728

Per capita:

Operating income	$40.38
percent from local government	84.8%
Operating expenditure	$34.25
Total materials	2.35
Print holdings	2.10
Visits per capita	5.45

Housing & Construction

Housing Units

Total, 2008§	29,014
Single family units, attached	1,480
Single family units, detached	19,088
Multiple family units	8,232
Mobile home units	214
Occupied	28,307
Vacancy rate	2.4%
Median rent, 2007**	$984
Median SF home value, 2007**	$614,300

New Privately Owned Housing Units Authorized by Building Permit, 2007*

	Units	Construction Cost
Single	4	$1,204,730
Total	4	$1,204,730

Municipal Finance

(For local fiscal year ended in 2006)

Revenues

Total	$63,942,106
Taxes	32,918,764
Special benefits assessment	43,593
Licenses & permits	875,842
Fines & forfeitures	1,065,718
Revenues from use of money & property	4,631,971
Intergovernmental	7,699,644
Service charges	16,460,537
Other revenues	246,037
Other financing sources	0

Expenditures

Total	$60,040,863
General government	8,182,813
Public safety	25,238,175
Transportation	10,829,708
Community development	1,961,080
Health	0
Culture & leisure	13,829,087
Other	0

Local School District

(Data from School year 2007-08 except as noted)

Whittier Union High
9401 South Painter Ave
Whittier, CA 90605
(562) 698-8121

Superintendent	Sandra Thorstenson
Grade plan	9-12
Number of schools	7
Enrollment	13,854
High school graduates, 2006-07	2,523
Dropout rate	2.0%
Pupil/teacher ratio	24.9
Average class size	28.1
Students per computer	4.5
Classrooms with internet	503
Avg. Daily Attendance (ADA)	13,239
Cost per ADA	$8,911
Avg. Teacher Salary	$71,206

California Achievement Tests 6th ed., 2008

(Pct scoring at or above 50th National Percentile Rank)

	Math	Reading	Language
Grade 3	NA	NA	NA
Grade 7	NA	NA	NA

Academic Performance Index, 2008

Number of students tested	9,803
Number of valid scores	9,357
2007 API (base)	703
2008 API (growth)	728

SAT Testing, 2006-07

Enrollment, Grade 12	3,426
Number taking test	1,034
percent taking test	30.2%
percent with total score 1,500+	8.80%

Average Scores:

Math	Verbal	Writing	Total
467	451	447	1,365

Federal No Child Left Behind, 2008

(Adequate Yearly Progress standards met)

	Participation Rate	Pct Proficient
ELA	Yes	No
Math	Yes	No

API criteria	Yes
Graduation rate	Yes
# criteria met/possible	26/24

Other school districts for this city

(see Appendix E for information on these districts)

Complete list in Appendix E

See Introduction for an explanation of all data sources.

Demographics & Socio-Economic Characteristics

(2000 Decennial Census, except as noted)

Population

1990* .... NA
2000 .... NA
Male .... NA
Female .... NA
Jan. 2008 (estimate)§ .... NA
Persons per sq. mi. of land .... NA

Race & Hispanic Origin, 2000

Race
White .... NA
Black/African American .... NA
North American Native .... NA
Asian .... NA
Pacific Islander .... NA
Other Race .... NA
Two or more races .... NA
Hispanic origin, total .... NA
Mexican .... NA
Puerto Rican .... NA
Cuban .... NA
Other Hispanic .... NA

Age & Nativity, 2000

Under 5 years .... NA
18 years and over .... NA
65 years and over .... NA
85 years and over .... NA
Median Age .... NA
Native-born .... NA
Foreign-born .... NA

Educational Attainment, 2000

Population 25 years and over .... NA
Less than 9th grade .... NA
High school grad or higher .... NA
Bachelor's degree or higher .... NA
Graduate degree .... NA

Income & Poverty, 1999

Per capita income .... NA
Median household income .... NA
Median family income .... NA
Persons in poverty .... NA
H'holds receiving public assistance .... NA
H'holds receiving social security .... NA

Households, 2000

Total households .... NA
With persons under 18 .... NA
With persons over 65 .... NA
Family households .... NA
Single person households .... NA
Persons per household .... NA
Persons per family .... NA

Household Population, 2008§§

Persons living in households .... NA
Persons living in group quarters .... NA
Persons per household .... NA

Labor & Employment

Total civilian labor force, 2008§§ 8,100
Unemployment rate, 2008 .... 7.1%
Total civilian labor force, 2000 .... NA

Employed persons 16 years and over by occupation, 2000

Managers & professionals .... NA
Service occupations .... NA
Sales & office occupations .... NA
Farming, fishing & forestry .... NA
Construction & maintenance .... NA
Production & transportation .... NA
Self-employed persons .... NA

* US Census Bureau
** 2000 Decennial Census
§ California Department of Finance
§§ California Employment Development Dept

General Information

City of Wildomar
23873 Clinton Keith Rd
Suite 111
Wildomar, CA 92595
951-677-7751

Website .... www.cityofwildomar.org
Elevation .... NA
Land Area (sq. miles) .... NA
Water Area (sq. miles) .... NA
Year of Incorporation 2008
Government type .... NA
Sales tax rate 8.75%

Voters & Officials

Registered Voters, October 2008

Total 13,393
Democrats 3,746
Republicans 6,390
Declined to state 2,530

Legislative Districts

US Congressional .... NA
State Senatorial .... NA
State Assembly .... NA

Local Officials, 2009

Mayor .... Scott Farnam
City Manager .... John Danielson
City Clerk .... Sheryll Schroeder
Attorney .... Julie Biggs
Finance Dir .... Gary Nordquist
Public Works .... Mike Kashiwagi
Planning Dir .... Gary Wayne
Building .... Jeff Thomas
Police Chief .... Joseph Cleary
Fire/Emergency Mgmt .... Steve Beach

Public Safety

Number of officers, 2007 .... NA
Violent crimes, 2007 .... NA
Property crimes, 2007 .... NA
Arson, 2007 .... NA

Public Library

Mission Trail Community Library
Riverside County Library Service
34303 Mission Trail
Wildomar, CA 92595
951-471-3855

Library Manager .... Jennie Jackson

Library system statistics, FY 2007

Population served 1,047,996
Internet terminals 37
Annual users 69,346

Per capita:

Operating income $19.38
percent from local government 49.8%
Operating expenditure $20.45
Total materials 1.43
Print holdings 1.30
Visits per capita 4.06

Housing & Construction

Housing Units

Total, 2008§ .... NA
Single family units, attached .... NA
Single family units, detached .... NA
Multiple family units .... NA
Mobile home units .... NA
Occupied .... NA
Vacancy rate .... NA
Median rent, 2000** .... NA
Median SF home value, 2000** .... NA

New Privately Owned Housing Units Authorized by Building Permit, 2007*

	Units	Construction Cost
Single	NA	NA
Total	NA	NA

Municipal Finance

(For local fiscal year ended in 2006)

Revenues

Total .... NA
Taxes .... NA
Special benefits assessment .... NA
Licenses & permits .... NA
Fines & forfeitures .... NA
Revenues from use of money & property .... NA
Intergovernmental .... NA
Service charges .... NA
Other revenues .... NA
Other financing sources .... NA

Expenditures

Total .... NA
General government .... NA
Public safety .... NA
Transportation .... NA
Community development .... NA
Health .... NA
Culture & leisure .... NA
Other .... NA

Local School District

(Data from School year 2007-08 except as noted)

Lake Elsinore Unified
545 Chaney St
Lake Elsinore, CA 92530
(951) 253-7000

Superintendent .... Frank Passarella
Grade plan K-12
Number of schools 26
Enrollment 22,109
High school graduates, 2006-07 1,211
Dropout rate 2.1%
Pupil/teacher ratio 22.2
Average class size 27.7
Students per computer 5.2
Classrooms with internet 1,221
Avg. Daily Attendance (ADA) 21,229
Cost per ADA $8,008
Avg. Teacher Salary $68,317

California Achievement Tests 6th ed., 2008

(Pct scoring at or above 50th National Percentile Rank)

	Math	Reading	Language
Grade 3	61%	39%	50%
Grade 7	50%	47%	43%

Academic Performance Index, 2008

Number of students tested 16,937
Number of valid scores 14,554
2007 API (base) 729
2008 API (growth) 775

SAT Testing, 2006-07

Enrollment, Grade 12 1,425
Number taking test 360
percent taking test 25.3%
percent with total score 1,500+ 9.80%

Average Scores:

Math	Verbal	Writing	Total
485	480	471	1,436

Federal No Child Left Behind, 2008

(Adequate Yearly Progress standards met)

	Participation Rate	Pct Proficient
ELA	Yes	Yes
Math	Yes	Yes

API criteria .... Yes
Graduation rate .... Yes
criteria met/possible 38/38

Other school districts for this city

(see Appendix E for information on these districts)

None

See Introduction for an explanation of all data sources.

Demographics & Socio-Economic Characteristics

(2000 Decennial Census, except as noted)

Population

1990* . . . 2,297
2000 . . . 3,670
Male . . . 1,896
Female . . . 1,774
Jan. 2008 (estimate)§ . . . 5,310
Persons per sq. mi. of land . . . 983.3

Race & Hispanic Origin, 2000

Race
White . . . 1,668
Black/African American . . . 18
North American Native . . . 42
Asian . . . 42
Pacific Islander . . . 0
Other Race . . . 1,670
Two or more races . . . 230
Hispanic origin, total . . . 2,613
Mexican . . . 2,365
Puerto Rican . . . 1
Cuban . . . 0
Other Hispanic . . . 247

Age & Nativity, 2000

Under 5 years . . . 327
18 years and over . . . 2,402
65 years and over . . . 339
85 years and over . . . 67
Median Age . . . 26.6
Native-born . . . 1,848
Foreign-born . . . 1,819

Educational Attainment, 2000

Population 25 years and over . . . 1,907
Less than 9th grade . . . 43.7%
High school grad or higher . . . 43.2%
Bachelor's degree or higher . . . 5.4%
Graduate degree . . . 1.3%

Income & Poverty, 1999

Per capita income . . . $11,010
Median household income . . . $32,042
Median family income . . . $36,389
Persons in poverty . . . 18.7%
H'holds receiving public assistance . . . 45
H'holds receiving social security . . . 225

Households, 2000

Total households . . . 924
With persons under 18 . . . 514
With persons over 65 . . . 201
Family households . . . 746
Single person households . . . 156
Persons per household . . . 3.70
Persons per family . . . 4.18

Household Population, 2008§§

Persons living in households . . . 5,060
Persons living in group quarters . . . 250
Persons per household . . . 3.7

Labor & Employment

Total civilian labor force, 2008§§ . . . 1,830
Unemployment rate, 2008 . . . 20.5%
Total civilian labor force, 2000 . . . 1,376

Employed persons 16 years and over by occupation, 2000

Managers & professionals . . . 164
Service occupations . . . 262
Sales & office occupations . . . 178
Farming, fishing & forestry . . . 255
Construction & maintenance . . . 107
Production & transportation . . . 191
Self-employed persons . . . 68

* US Census Bureau
** 2000 Decennial Census
§ California Department of Finance
§§ California Employment Development Dept

General Information

City of Williams
810 E St
PO Box 310
Williams, CA 95987
530-473-5389

Website . . . www.cityofwilliams.net
Elevation . . . 801 ft.
Land Area (sq. miles) . . . 5.4
Water Area (sq. miles) . . . 0
Year of Incorporation . . . 1920
Government type . . . General law
Sales tax rate . . . 8.75%

Voters & Officials

Registered Voters, October 2008

Total . . . 1,125
Democrats . . . 463
Republicans . . . 396
Declined to state . . . 241

Legislative Districts

US Congressional . . . 2
State Senatorial . . . 4
State Assembly . . . 2

Local Officials, 2009

Mayor . . . Patricia Ash
City Administrator . . . James Manning
City Clerk . . . Rene Miles
Attorney . . . Ann Siprelle
Finance Dir . . . Patricia Cervantes
Public Works . . . Wes Goforth
City Planner . . . James Manning
Building . . . Debbie Rich
Police Chief . . . James Saso
Emergency/Fire Dir . . . Jeff Gilbert

Public Safety

Number of officers, 2007 . . . 10
Violent crimes, 2007 . . . 17
Property crimes, 2007 . . . 99
Arson, 2007 . . . NA

Public Library

Williams Branch
Colusa County Free Library
901 E St
Williams, CA 95987
530-473-5955

Branch Librarian . . . Dixie Armfield

Library system statistics, FY 2007

Population served . . . 21,951
Internet terminals . . . 28
Annual users . . . 11,172

Per capita:

Operating income . . . $29.05
percent from local government . . . 76.6%
Operating expenditure . . . $29.05
Total materials . . . 4.60
Print holdings . . . 4.18
Visits per capita . . . 1.32

Housing & Construction

Housing Units

Total, 2008§ . . . 1,421
Single family units, attached . . . 33
Single family units, detached . . . 1,058
Multiple family units . . . 263
Mobile home units . . . 67
Occupied . . . 1,356
Vacancy rate . . . 4.6%
Median rent, 2000** . . . $559
Median SF home value, 2000** . . . $96,200

New Privately Owned Housing Units Authorized by Building Permit, 2007*

	Units	Construction Cost
Single	6	$1,557,622
Total	6	$1,557,622

Municipal Finance

(For local fiscal year ended in 2006)

Revenues

Total . . . $5,375,901
Taxes . . . 2,637,405
Special benefits assessment . . . 41,526
Licenses & permits . . . 133,845
Fines & forfeitures . . . 60,296
Revenues from use of money & property . . . 113,740
Intergovernmental . . . 370,663
Service charges . . . 1,839,196
Other revenues . . . 179,230
Other financing sources . . . 0

Expenditures

Total . . . $3,799,421
General government . . . 768,921
Public safety . . . 1,005,003
Transportation . . . 280,667
Community development . . . 307,257
Health . . . 969,715
Culture & leisure . . . 164,641
Other . . . 0

Local School District

(Data from School year 2007-08 except as noted)

Williams Unified
PO Box 7
Williams, CA 95987
(530) 473-2550

Superintendent . . . Judith Rossi
Grade plan . . . K-12
Number of schools . . . 4
Enrollment . . . 1,193
High school graduates, 2006-07 . . . 70
Dropout rate . . . 7.6%
Pupil/teacher ratio . . . 17.2
Average class size . . . 19.7
Students per computer . . . 3.3
Classrooms with internet . . . 67
Avg. Daily Attendance (ADA) . . . 1,172
Cost per ADA . . . $8,295
Avg. Teacher Salary . . . $56,245

California Achievement Tests 6th ed., 2008

(Pct scoring at or above 50th National Percentile Rank)

	Math	Reading	Language
Grade 3	58%	35%	41%
Grade 7	46%	29%	37%

Academic Performance Index, 2008

Number of students tested . . . 889
Number of valid scores . . . 833
2007 API (base) . . . 694
2008 API (growth) . . . 702

SAT Testing, 2006-07

Enrollment, Grade 12 . . . 84
Number taking test . . . 26
percent taking test . . . 31.0%
percent with total score 1,500+ . . . 3.60%

Average Scores:

Math	Verbal	Writing	Total
429	381	395	1,205

Federal No Child Left Behind, 2008

(Adequate Yearly Progress standards met)

	Participation Rate	Pct Proficient
ELA	Yes	No
Math	Yes	Yes

API criteria . . . Yes
Graduation rate . . . No
\# criteria met/possible . . . 18/13

Other school districts for this city

(see Appendix E for information on these districts)

None

See Introduction for an explanation of all data sources.

Demographics & Socio-Economic Characteristics

(2000 Decennial Census, except as noted)

Population

1990* 5,027
2000 5,073
Male 2,413
Female 2,660
Jan. 2008 (estimate)§ 5,032
Persons per sq. mi. of land 1,797.1

Race & Hispanic Origin, 2000

Race
White 4,247
Black/African American 32
North American Native 179
Asian 59
Pacific Islander 2
Other Race 359
Two or more races 195
Hispanic origin, total 745
Mexican 633
Puerto Rican 7
Cuban 4
Other Hispanic 101

Age & Nativity, 2000

Under 5 years 373
18 years and over 3,594
65 years and over 709
85 years and over 118
Median Age 35.8
Native-born 4,942
Foreign-born 263

Educational Attainment, 2000

Population 25 years and over 3,311
Less than 9th grade 5.9%
High school grad or higher 75.4%
Bachelor's degree or higher 13.0%
Graduate degree 5.5%

Income & Poverty, 1999

Per capita income $16,642
Median household income $26,283
Median family income $36,193
Persons in poverty 14.4%
H'holds receiving public assistance 163
H'holds receiving social security 584

Households, 2000

Total households 1,935
With persons under 18 772
With persons over 65 519
Family households 1,230
Single person households 585
Persons per household 2.56
Persons per family 3.15

Household Population, 2008§§

Persons living in households 4,906
Persons living in group quarters 126
Persons per household 2.5

Labor & Employment

Total civilian labor force, 2008§§ 2,550
Unemployment rate, 2008 .... 6.6%
Total civilian labor force, 2000 2,411

Employed persons 16 years and over by occupation, 2000

Managers & professionals 464
Service occupations 484
Sales & office occupations 568
Farming, fishing & forestry 69
Construction & maintenance 274
Production & transportation 385
Self-employed persons 257

* US Census Bureau
** 2000 Decennial Census
§ California Department of Finance
§§ California Employment Development Dept

General Information

City of Willits
111 E Commercial St
Willits, CA 95490
707-459-4601

Website .... www.willitscity.com
Elevation .... 1,364 ft.
Land Area (sq. miles) 2.8
Water Area (sq. miles) 0
Year of Incorporation 1888
Government type .... General law
Sales tax rate 8.75%

Voters & Officials

Registered Voters, October 2008

Total 2,539
Democrats 1,202
Republicans 566
Declined to state 550

Legislative Districts

US Congressional 1
State Senatorial 2
State Assembly 1

Local Officials, 2009

Mayor .... Larry Stranske
Manager .... Paul Cayler
City Clerk .... Marilyn Harden
Attorney .... James Lance
Finance Dir .... Joanne Cavallari
Public Works .... Dave Madrigal
Planning/Dev Dir .... Alan Falleri
Building .... NA
Police Chief .... Gerry Gonzalez
Emergency/Fire Dir .... Shane Burke

Public Safety

Number of officers, 2007 11
Violent crimes, 2007 45
Property crimes, 2007 92
Arson, 2007 .... NA

Public Library

Willits Branch Library
Marin County Free Library System
390 E Commercial St
Willits, CA 95490
707-459-5908

Branch Librarian .... Donna Kern

Library system statistics, FY 2007

Population served 90,291
Internet terminals 20
Annual users 37,258

Per capita:

Operating income $18.48
percent from local government 58.6%
Operating expenditure $19.03
Total materials 2.07
Print holdings 1.94
Visits per capita .... NA

Housing & Construction

Housing Units

Total, 2008§ 2,045
Single family units, attached 84
Single family units, detached 1,196
Multiple family units 614
Mobile home units 151
Occupied 1,967
Vacancy rate 3.8%
Median rent, 2000** $552
Median SF home value, 2000** $129,000

New Privately Owned Housing Units Authorized by Building Permit, 2007*

	Units	Construction Cost
Single	20	$5,023,350
Total	30	$5,762,742

Municipal Finance

(For local fiscal year ended in 2006)

Revenues

Total $8,653,408
Taxes 3,032,944
Special benefits assessment 0
Licenses & permits 50,022
Fines & forfeitures 43,638
Revenues from use of money & property 26,725
Intergovernmental 966,911
Service charges 4,425,107
Other revenues 108,061
Other financing sources 0

Expenditures

Total $8,436,766
General government 1,058,617
Public safety 2,164,687
Transportation 1,540,996
Community development 719,922
Health 1,336,336
Culture & leisure 155,903
Other 0

Local School District

(Data from School year 2007-08 except as noted)

Willits Unified
120 Pearl St
Willits, CA 95490
(707) 459-5314

Superintendent .... Debra Kubin
Grade plan K-12
Number of schools 11
Enrollment 2,133
High school graduates, 2006-07 151
Dropout rate 3.5%
Pupil/teacher ratio 17.9
Average class size 18.6
Students per computer 5.5
Classrooms with internet 146
Avg. Daily Attendance (ADA) 1,703
Cost per ADA $9,878
Avg. Teacher Salary $55,130

California Achievement Tests 6th ed., 2008

(Pct scoring at or above 50th National Percentile Rank)

	Math	Reading	Language
Grade 3	50%	50%	45%
Grade 7	35%	36%	39%

Academic Performance Index, 2008

Number of students tested 1,377
Number of valid scores 1,310
2007 API (base) 706
2008 API (growth) 707

SAT Testing, 2006-07

Enrollment, Grade 12 183
Number taking test 46
percent taking test 25.1%
percent with total score 1,500+ 15.30%

Average Scores:

Math	Verbal	Writing	Total
558	551	523	1,632

Federal No Child Left Behind, 2008

(Adequate Yearly Progress standards met)

	Participation Rate	Pct Proficient
ELA	Yes	No
Math	Yes	No

API criteria .... Yes
Graduation rate .... Yes
\# criteria met/possible 26/21

Other school districts for this city

(see Appendix E for information on these districts)

None

See Introduction for an explanation of all data sources.

Demographics & Socio-Economic Characteristics

(2000 Decennial Census, except as noted)

Population

1990* 5,988
2000 6,220
Male 3,080
Female 3,140
Jan. 2008 (estimate)§ 6,502
Persons per sq. mi. of land 2,242.1

Race & Hispanic Origin, 2000

Race
White 4,308
Black/African American 55
North American Native 140
Asian 641
Pacific Islander 15
Other Race 765
Two or more races 296
Hispanic origin, total 1,446
Mexican 1,240
Puerto Rican 2
Cuban 0
Other Hispanic 204

Age & Nativity, 2000

Under 5 years 462
18 years and over 4,186
65 years and over 770
85 years and over 125
Median Age 31.0
Native-born 5,085
Foreign-born 1,114

Educational Attainment, 2000

Population 25 years and over 3,595
Less than 9th grade 17.3%
High school grad or higher 70.8%
Bachelor's degree or higher 9.0%
Graduate degree 2.3%

Income & Poverty, 1999

Per capita income $12,523
Median household income $27,466
Median family income $35,856
Persons in poverty 23.8%
H'holds receiving public assistance 238
H'holds receiving social security 577

Households, 2000

Total households 2,134
With persons under 18 888
With persons over 65 538
Family households 1,513
Single person households 528
Persons per household 2.83
Persons per family 3.40

Household Population, 2008§§

Persons living in households 6,321
Persons living in group quarters 181
Persons per household 2.9

Labor & Employment

Total civilian labor force, 2008§§ 2,910
Unemployment rate, 2008 .... 8.3%
Total civilian labor force, 2000 2,742

Employed persons 16 years and over by occupation, 2000

Managers & professionals 528
Service occupations 594
Sales & office occupations 627
Farming, fishing & forestry 203
Construction & maintenance 211
Production & transportation 384
Self-employed persons 265

* US Census Bureau
** 2000 Decennial Census
§ California Department of Finance
§§ California Employment Development Dept

General Information

City of Willows
201 N Lassen Street
Willows, CA 95988
530-934-7041

Website .... www.cityofwillows.org
Elevation .... 135 ft.
Land Area (sq. miles) 2.9
Water Area (sq. miles) 0
Year of Incorporation 1886
Government type .... General law
Sales tax rate 8.25%

Voters & Officials

Registered Voters, October 2008

Total 2,582
Democrats 886
Republicans 1,092
Declined to state 477

Legislative Districts

US Congressional 2
State Senatorial 4
State Assembly 2

Local Officials, 2009

Mayor .... Peter Towne
Manager .... Steve Holsinger
City Clerk .... Natalie Butler
Attorney .... Leonard Krup
Finance Dir .... Tim Sailsbery
Public Works .... Greg Tyhurst
Planning Dir .... Pacific Muni Consultants
Building .... Clay Dawley
Police Chief .... William Spears
Emergency/Fire Dir .... Wayne Peabody

Public Safety

Number of officers, 2007 11
Violent crimes, 2007 31
Property crimes, 2007 239
Arson, 2007 0

Public Library

Willows Public Library
Willows Public Library System
201 N Lassen St
Willows, CA 95988
530-934-5156

Director .... Cha Yang (Int)

Library system statistics, FY 2007

Population served 14,098
Internet terminals 8
Annual users 5,031

Per capita:

Operating income $21.22
percent from local government 83.1%
Operating expenditure $21.04
Total materials 5.06
Print holdings 4.70
Visits per capita 2.19

Housing & Construction

Housing Units

Total, 2008§ 2,430
Single family units, attached 54
Single family units, detached 1,601
Multiple family units 768
Mobile home units 7
Occupied 2,191
Vacancy rate 9.8%
Median rent, 2000** $429
Median SF home value, 2000** $92,200

New Privately Owned Housing Units Authorized by Building Permit, 2007*

	Units	Construction Cost
Single	3	$508,964
Total	3	$508,964

Municipal Finance

(For local fiscal year ended in 2006)

Revenues

Total $8,970,482
Taxes 2,510,322
Special benefits assessment 0
Licenses & permits 74,366
Fines & forfeitures 25,225
Revenues from use of money & property 131,809
Intergovernmental 811,788
Service charges 1,324,420
Other revenues 71,963
Other financing sources 4,020,589

Expenditures

Total $9,461,569
General government 480,975
Public safety 1,559,768
Transportation 423,781
Community development 331,189
Health 6,116,998
Culture & leisure 544,660
Other 0

Local School District

(Data from School year 2007-08 except as noted)

Willows Unified
823 West Laurel St
Willows, CA 95988
(530) 934-6600

Superintendent .... Steven Olmos
Grade plan K-12
Number of schools 7
Enrollment 1,783
High school graduates, 2006-07 96
Dropout rate 5.3%
Pupil/teacher ratio 21.4
Average class size 23.2
Students per computer 3.9
Classrooms with internet 103
Avg. Daily Attendance (ADA) 1,691
Cost per ADA $7,852
Avg. Teacher Salary $74,112

California Achievement Tests 6th ed., 2008

(Pct scoring at or above 50th National Percentile Rank)

	Math	Reading	Language
Grade 3	59%	43%	56%
Grade 7	48%	50%	48%

Academic Performance Index, 2008

Number of students tested 1,304
Number of valid scores 1,222
2007 API (base) 750
2008 API (growth) 749

SAT Testing, 2006-07

Enrollment, Grade 12 116
Number taking test 32
percent taking test 27.6%
percent with total score 1,500+ 12.90%

Average Scores:

Math	Verbal	Writing	Total
495	484	485	1,464

Federal No Child Left Behind, 2008

(Adequate Yearly Progress standards met)

	Participation Rate	Pct Proficient
ELA	Yes	No
Math	Yes	No

API criteria .... Yes
Graduation rate .... Yes
criteria met/possible 22/20

Other school districts for this city

(see Appendix E for information on these districts)

None

See Introduction for an explanation of all data sources.

Demographics & Socio-Economic Characteristics

(2000 Decennial Census, except as noted)

Population

1990* .... NA
2000 22,744
Male 11,164
Female 11,580
Jan. 2008 (estimate)§ 26,564
Persons per sq. mi. of land 3,964.8

Race & Hispanic Origin, 2000

Race
White 17,968
Black/African American 178
North American Native 336
Asian 521
Pacific Islander 32
Other Race 2,825
Two or more races 884
Hispanic origin, total 5,364
Mexican 4,541
Puerto Rican 62
Cuban 29
Other Hispanic 732

Age & Nativity, 2000

Under 5 years 1,818
18 years and over 15,737
65 years and over 2,534
85 years and over 291
Median Age 35.2
Native-born 19,672
Foreign-born 3,284

Educational Attainment, 2000

Population 25 years and over 14,576
Less than 9th grade 7.1%
High school grad or higher 83.8%
Bachelor's degree or higher 24.7%
Graduate degree 7.4%

Income & Poverty, 1999

Per capita income $24,336
Median household income $63,252
Median family income $67,992
Persons in poverty 5.2%
H'holds receiving public assistance 173
H'holds receiving social security 2,006

Households, 2000

Total households 7,589
With persons under 18 3,506
With persons over 65 1,822
Family households 5,778
Single person households 1,415
Persons per household 2.98
Persons per family 3.40

Household Population, 2008§§

Persons living in households 26,473
Persons living in group quarters 91
Persons per household 2.9

Labor & Employment

Total civilian labor force, 2008§§ 12,700
Unemployment rate, 2008 .... 4.6%
Total civilian labor force, 2000 11,597

Employed persons 16 years and over by occupation, 2000

Managers & professionals 3,661
Service occupations 1,590
Sales & office occupations 2,987
Farming, fishing & forestry 264
Construction & maintenance 1,315
Production & transportation 1,380
Self-employed persons 1,028

* US Census Bureau
** 2000 Decennial Census
§ California Department of Finance
§§ California Employment Development Dept

General Information

Town of Windsor
9291 Old Redwood Hwy
PO Box 100
Windsor, CA 95492
707-838-1000

Website .... www.townofwindsor.com
Elevation .... NA
Land Area (sq. miles) 6.7
Water Area (sq. miles) 0
Year of Incorporation 1992
Government type .... General Law
Sales tax rate 9.00%

Voters & Officials

Registered Voters, October 2008

Total 13,026
Democrats 6,206
Republicans 3,844
Declined to state 2,429

Legislative Districts

US Congressional 1
State Senatorial 2
State Assembly 1

Local Officials, 2009

Mayor .... Robin Goble
Manager .... J. Matthew Mullan
City Clerk .... Maria De la O
Attorney .... Richard R. Rudnansky
Finance Dir .... Jim McAdler
Public Works .... Richard Burtt
Planning/Dev Dir .... Peter Chamberlin
Building .... Steve Pantazes
Police Chief .... Steve Freitas
Emergency/Fire Dir .... Ron Collier

Public Safety

Number of officers, 2007 .... NA
Violent crimes, 2007 87
Property crimes, 2007 329
Arson, 2007 3

Public Library

Windsor Regional Library
Sonoma County Library System
9291 Old Redwood Hwy #100
Windsor, CA 95492
707-838-1020

Branch Librarian .... Bill Coolidge

Library system statistics, FY 2007

Population served 481,785
Internet terminals 140
Annual users 299,464

Per capita:

Operating income $32.97
percent from local government 87.7%
Operating expenditure $30.18
Total materials 1.60
Print holdings 1.49
Visits per capita 5.11

Housing & Construction

Housing Units

Total, 2008§ 9,265
Single family units, attached 461
Single family units, detached 7,242
Multiple family units 740
Mobile home units 822
Occupied 9,098
Vacancy rate 1.8%
Median rent, 2000** $889
Median SF home value, 2000** $268,200

New Privately Owned Housing Units Authorized by Building Permit, 2007*

	Units	Construction Cost
Single	42	$10,918,569
Total	44	$11,281,744

Municipal Finance

(For local fiscal year ended in 2006)

Revenues

Total $26,182,440
Taxes 13,506,032
Special benefits assessment 4,487,574
Licenses & permits 1,241,630
Fines & forfeitures 53,992
Revenues from use of money & property 1,244,157
Intergovernmental 1,235,364
Service charges 820,473
Other revenues 3,593,218
Other financing sources 0

Expenditures

Total $25,759,241
General government 1,231,302
Public safety 6,095,504
Transportation 12,929,289
Community development 4,799,798
Health 0
Culture & leisure 703,348
Other 0

Local School District

(Data from School year 2007-08 except as noted)

Windsor Unified
9291 Old Redwood Hwy, Bldg 500
Windsor, CA 95492
(707) 837-7701

Superintendent .... Steve Herrington
Grade plan K-12
Number of schools 8
Enrollment 5,344
High school graduates, 2006-07 278
Dropout rate 6.3%
Pupil/teacher ratio 21.2
Average class size 25.5
Students per computer 5.5
Classrooms with internet 250
Avg. Daily Attendance (ADA) 5,215
Cost per ADA $7,592
Avg. Teacher Salary $58,962

California Achievement Tests 6th ed., 2008

(Pct scoring at or above 50th National Percentile Rank)

	Math	Reading	Language
Grade 3	61%	48%	52%
Grade 7	64%	63%	60%

Academic Performance Index, 2008

Number of students tested 4,033
Number of valid scores 3,927
2007 API (base) 734
2008 API (growth) 747

SAT Testing, 2006-07

Enrollment, Grade 12 338
Number taking test 115
percent taking test 34.0%
percent with total score 1,500+ 19.20%

Average Scores:

Math	Verbal	Writing	Total
519	523	515	1,557

Federal No Child Left Behind, 2008

(Adequate Yearly Progress standards met)

	Participation Rate	Pct Proficient
ELA	Yes	No
Math	Yes	Yes

API criteria .... Yes
Graduation rate .... No
\# criteria met/possible 26/22

Other school districts for this city

(see Appendix E for information on these districts)

Healdsburg Unified

See Introduction for an explanation of all data sources.

Demographics & Socio-Economic Characteristics

(2000 Decennial Census, except as noted)

Population

1990* 4,639
2000 6,125
Male 3,109
Female 3,016
Jan. 2008 (estimate)§ 7,052
Persons per sq. mi. of land 2,518.6

Race & Hispanic Origin, 2000

Race
White 4,276
Black/African American 41
North American Native 54
Asian 61
Pacific Islander 17
Other Race 1,382
Two or more races 294
Hispanic origin, total 2,720
Mexican 2,268
Puerto Rican 14
Cuban 4
Other Hispanic 434

Age & Nativity, 2000

Under 5 years 479
18 years and over 4,084
65 years and over 477
85 years and over 55
Median Age 31.1
Native-born 4,634
Foreign-born 1,479

Educational Attainment, 2000

Population 25 years and over 3,553
Less than 9th grade 16.9%
High school grad or higher 72.2%
Bachelor's degree or higher 18.1%
Graduate degree 6.1%

Income & Poverty, 1999

Per capita income $17,133
Median household income $48,678
Median family income $55,183
Persons in poverty 5.0%
H'holds receiving public assistance 25
H'holds receiving social security 375

Households, 2000

Total households 1,907
With persons under 18 1,018
With persons over 65 350
Family households 1,547
Single person households 276
Persons per household 3.21
Persons per family 3.56

Household Population, 2008§§

Persons living in households 7,046
Persons living in group quarters 6
Persons per household 3.2

Labor & Employment

Total civilian labor force, 2008§§ 3,500
Unemployment rate, 2008 .... 7.0%
Total civilian labor force, 2000 2,927

Employed persons 16 years and over by occupation, 2000

Managers & professionals 733
Service occupations 391
Sales & office occupations 597
Farming, fishing & forestry 245
Construction & maintenance 303
Production & transportation 459
Self-employed persons 198

* US Census Bureau
** 2000 Decennial Census
§ California Department of Finance
§§ California Employment Development Dept

General Information

City of Winters
318 First St
Winters, CA 95694
530-795-4910

Website .... www.cityofwinters.org
Elevation .... 135 ft.
Land Area (sq. miles) 2.8
Water Area (sq. miles) 0
Year of Incorporation 1898
Government type .... General law
Sales tax rate 8.25%

Voters & Officials

Registered Voters, October 2008

Total 3,412
Democrats 1,539
Republicans 1,007
Declined to state 701

Legislative Districts

US Congressional 1
State Senatorial 5
State Assembly 8

Local Officials, 2009

Mayor .... Michael Martin
Manager .... John Donlevy
City Clerk .... Nanci Mills
Attorney .... John Wallace
Finance Dir .... Shelly Gunby
Public Works .... Eric Lucero
Planning/Dev Dir .... Nellie Dyer
Building .... Gene Ashdown
Police Chief .... Bruce Muramoto
Emergency/Fire Dir .... Scott Dozier

Public Safety

Number of officers, 2007 11
Violent crimes, 2007 13
Property crimes, 2007 227
Arson, 2007 0

Public Library

Winters Branch Library
Yolo County Library System
201 First St
Winters, CA 95694
530-795-4955

Branch Librarian .... Karla Knabke

Library system statistics, FY 2007

Population served 139,923
Internet terminals 43
Annual users 276,902

Per capita:

Operating income $33.44
percent from local government 89.8%
Operating expenditure $27.76
Total materials 2.68
Print holdings 2.44
Visits per capita 4.51

Housing & Construction

Housing Units

Total, 2008§ 2,269
Single family units, attached 106
Single family units, detached 1,802
Multiple family units 283
Mobile home units 78
Occupied 2,214
Vacancy rate 2.4%
Median rent, 2000** $692
Median SF home value, 2000** $148,600

New Privately Owned Housing Units Authorized by Building Permit, 2007*

	Units	Construction Cost
Single	0	$0
Total	0	$0

Municipal Finance

(For local fiscal year ended in 2006)

Revenues

Total $6,331,118
Taxes 2,763,795
Special benefits assessment 186,341
Licenses & permits 176,360
Fines & forfeitures 7,047
Revenues from use of money & property 445,068
Intergovernmental 1,135,604
Service charges 1,574,835
Other revenues 42,068
Other financing sources 0

Expenditures

Total $6,420,673
General government 320,813
Public safety 1,934,946
Transportation 1,055,714
Community development 726,392
Health 800,386
Culture & leisure 925,840
Other 0

Local School District

(Data from School year 2007-08 except as noted)

Winters Joint Unified
909 West Grant Ave
Winters, CA 95694
(530) 795-6100

Superintendent .... Pat Lewis
Grade plan K-12
Number of schools 5
Enrollment 1,739
High school graduates, 2006-07 155
Dropout rate 2.2%
Pupil/teacher ratio 18.2
Average class size 22.4
Students per computer 3.7
Classrooms with internet 101
Avg. Daily Attendance (ADA) 1,690
Cost per ADA $8,229
Avg. Teacher Salary $57,414

California Achievement Tests 6th ed., 2008

(Pct scoring at or above 50th National Percentile Rank)

	Math	Reading	Language
Grade 3	39%	37%	35%
Grade 7	44%	52%	43%

Academic Performance Index, 2008

Number of students tested 1,359
Number of valid scores 1,292
2007 API (base) 721
2008 API (growth) 737

SAT Testing, 2006-07

Enrollment, Grade 12 169
Number taking test 56
percent taking test 33.1%
percent with total score 1,500+ 15.40%

Average Scores:

Math	Verbal	Writing	Total
516	517	506	1,539

Federal No Child Left Behind, 2008

(Adequate Yearly Progress standards met)

	Participation Rate	Pct Proficient
ELA	Yes	No
Math	Yes	No

API criteria .... Yes
Graduation rate .... Yes
\# criteria met/possible 26/21

Other school districts for this city

(see Appendix E for information on these districts)

None

See Introduction for an explanation of all data sources.

Demographics & Socio-Economic Characteristics

(2000 Decennial Census, except as noted)

Population

1990* . . . 5,678
2000 . . . 6,651
Male . . . 3,425
Female . . . 3,226
Jan. 2008 (estimate)§ . . . 7,489
Persons per sq. mi. of land . . . 3,744.5

Race & Hispanic Origin, 2000

Race
White . . . 3,130
Black/African American . . . 22
North American Native . . . 72
Asian . . . 60
Pacific Islander . . . 3
Other Race . . . 3,047
Two or more races . . . 317
Hispanic origin, total . . . 5,575
Mexican . . . 5,052
Puerto Rican . . . 3
Cuban . . . 2
Other Hispanic . . . 518

Age & Nativity, 2000

Under 5 years . . . 662
18 years and over . . . 4,138
65 years and over . . . 500
85 years and over . . . 55
Median Age . . . 25.3
Native-born . . . 3,802
Foreign-born . . . 2,821

Educational Attainment, 2000

Population 25 years and over . . . 3,282
Less than 9th grade . . . 45.2%
High school grad or higher . . . 39.4%
Bachelor's degree or higher . . . 3.9%
Graduate degree . . . 1.0%

Income & Poverty, 1999

Per capita income . . . $8,842
Median household income . . . $23,653
Median family income . . . $23,880
Persons in poverty . . . 36.2%
H'holds receiving public assistance . . . 229
H'holds receiving social security . . . 423

Households, 2000

Total households . . . 1,777
With persons under 18 . . . 1,064
With persons over 65 . . . 371
Family households . . . 1,496
Single person households . . . 230
Persons per household . . . 3.74
Persons per family . . . 4.02

Household Population, 2008§§

Persons living in households . . . 7,480
Persons living in group quarters . . . 9
Persons per household . . . 3.8

Labor & Employment

Total civilian labor force, 2008§§ . . . 3,200
Unemployment rate, 2008 . . . 13.7%
Total civilian labor force, 2000 . . . 2,444

Employed persons 16 years and over by occupation, 2000

Managers & professionals . . . 288
Service occupations . . . 296
Sales & office occupations . . . 354
Farming, fishing & forestry . . . 572
Construction & maintenance . . . 175
Production & transportation . . . 366
Self-employed persons . . . 163

* US Census Bureau
** 2000 Decennial Census
§ California Department of Finance
§§ California Employment Development Dept

General Information

City of Woodlake
350 N Valencia Blvd
Woodlake, CA 93286
559-564-8055

Website . . . www.cityofwoodlake.com
Elevation . . . 430 ft.
Land Area (sq. miles) . . . 2.0
Water Area (sq. miles) . . . 0.5
Year of Incorporation . . . 1941
Government type . . . Chartered
Sales tax rate . . . 8.75%

Voters & Officials

Registered Voters, October 2008

Total . . . 1,710
Democrats . . . 925
Republicans . . . 424
Declined to state . . . 310

Legislative Districts

US Congressional . . . 21
State Senatorial . . . 16
State Assembly . . . 34

Local Officials, 2009

Mayor . . . Raul Gonzales Jr
Manager . . . William Lewis
City Clerk . . . Ruth Gonzalez
Attorney . . . Tom Watson
Finance Dir . . . William Lewis
Public Works . . . Ruben De Leon
Planning/Dev Dir . . . Greg Collins
Building . . . Ruben De Leon
Police Chief . . . John Zapalac
Emergency/Fire Dir . . . Joe Perez

Public Safety

Number of officers, 2007 . . . 14
Violent crimes, 2007 . . . 37
Property crimes, 2007 . . . 224
Arson, 2007 . . . 7

Public Library

Woodlake Library
Tulare County Free Library System
400 W Whitney
Woodlake, CA 93286
559-564-4824

Branch Librarian . . . Rita Pena

Library system statistics, FY 2007

Population served . . . 321,604
Internet terminals . . . 83
Annual users . . . 86,301

Per capita:

Operating income . . . $10.97
percent from local government . . . 86.0%
Operating expenditure . . . $8.74
Total materials . . . 1.08
Print holdings . . . 1.05
Visits per capita . . . 0.96

Housing & Construction

Housing Units

Total, 2008§ . . . 2,064
Single family units, attached . . . 126
Single family units, detached . . . 1,369
Multiple family units . . . 509
Mobile home units . . . 60
Occupied . . . 1,957
Vacancy rate . . . 5.2%
Median rent, 2000** . . . $375
Median SF home value, 2000** . . . $81,800

New Privately Owned Housing Units Authorized by Building Permit, 2007*

	Units	Construction Cost
Single	22	$4,033,897
Total	65	$7,408,016

Municipal Finance

(For local fiscal year ended in 2006)

Revenues

Total . . . $5,148,586
Taxes . . . 1,559,663
Special benefits assessment . . . 24,407
Licenses & permits . . . 58,362
Fines & forfeitures . . . 22,109
Revenues from use of money & property . . . 105,826
Intergovernmental . . . 1,105,694
Service charges . . . 2,245,997
Other revenues . . . 26,528
Other financing sources . . . 0

Expenditures

Total . . . $4,743,305
General government . . . 184,054
Public safety . . . 1,748,454
Transportation . . . 462,429
Community development . . . 938,195
Health . . . 943,631
Culture & leisure . . . 81,443
Other . . . 0

Local School District

(Data from School year 2007-08 except as noted)

Woodlake Union High
300 West Whitney Ave
Woodlake, CA 93286
(559) 564-8081

Superintendent . . . Tim Hire
Grade plan . . . 9-12
Number of schools . . . 3
Enrollment . . . 867
High school graduates, 2006-07 . . . 143
Dropout rate . . . 4.2%
Pupil/teacher ratio . . . 23.9
Average class size . . . 25.8
Students per computer . . . 2.8
Classrooms with internet . . . 37
Avg. Daily Attendance (ADA) . . . 810
Cost per ADA . . . $8,618
Avg. Teacher Salary . . . $53,725

California Achievement Tests 6th ed., 2008

(Pct scoring at or above 50th National Percentile Rank)

	Math	Reading	Language
Grade 3	NA	NA	NA
Grade 7	NA	NA	NA

Academic Performance Index, 2008

Number of students tested . . . 658
Number of valid scores . . . 623
2007 API (base) . . . 595
2008 API (growth) . . . 600

SAT Testing, 2006-07

Enrollment, Grade 12 . . . 183
Number taking test . . . 55
percent taking test . . . 30.1%
percent with total score 1,500+ . . . 3.30%

Average Scores:

Math	Verbal	Writing	Total
420	413	404	1,237

Federal No Child Left Behind, 2008

(Adequate Yearly Progress standards met)

	Participation Rate	Pct Proficient
ELA	Yes	Yes
Math	Yes	No

API criteria . . . Yes
Graduation rate . . . Yes
\# criteria met/possible . . . 18/16

Other school districts for this city

(see Appendix E for information on these districts)

Woodlake Union Elem

See Introduction for an explanation of all data sources.

Demographics & Socio-Economic Characteristics

(2000 Decennial Census, except as noted)

Population

1990* 39,802
2000 49,151
Male 24,099
Female 25,052
Jan. 2008 (estimate)§ 55,867
Persons per sq. mi. of land 5,424.0

Race & Hispanic Origin, 2000

Race
White 32,851
Black/African American 631
North American Native 718
Asian 1,851
Pacific Islander 136
Other Race 10,566
Two or more races 2,398
Hispanic origin, total 19,084
Mexican 16,642
Puerto Rican 126
Cuban 40
Other Hispanic 2,276

Age & Nativity, 2000

Under 5 years 3,958
18 years and over 34,532
65 years and over 5,166
85 years and over 811
Median Age 32.4
Native-born 39,581
Foreign-born 9,551

Educational Attainment, 2000

Population 25 years and over 29,924
Less than 9th grade 12.9%
High school grad or higher 73.0%
Bachelor's degree or higher 18.0%
Graduate degree 5.7%

Income & Poverty, 1999

Per capita income $18,042
Median household income $44,449
Median family income $48,689
Persons in poverty 11.8%
H'holds receiving public assistance 833
H'holds receiving social security 4,034

Households, 2000

Total households 16,751
With persons under 18 7,406
With persons over 65 3,534
Family households 12,285
Single person households 3,521
Persons per household 2.89
Persons per family 3.37

Household Population, 2008§§

Persons living in households 54,489
Persons living in group quarters 1,378
Persons per household 2.9

Labor & Employment

Total civilian labor force, 2008§§ 29,000
Unemployment rate, 2008 .... 8.7%
Total civilian labor force, 2000 23,365

Employed persons 16 years and over by occupation, 2000

Managers & professionals 5,908
Service occupations 3,413
Sales & office occupations 6,064
Farming, fishing & forestry 665
Construction & maintenance 2,109
Production & transportation 3,523
Self-employed persons 1,353

* US Census Bureau
** 2000 Decennial Census
§ California Department of Finance
§§ California Employment Development Dept

General Information

City of Woodland
300 First St
Woodland, CA 95695
530-661-5850

Website .... www.cityofwoodland.org
Elevation .... 65 ft.
Land Area (sq. miles) 10.3
Water Area (sq. miles) 0
Year of Incorporation 1871
Government type .... General law
Sales tax rate 8.75%

Voters & Officials

Registered Voters, October 2008

Total 26,238
Democrats 11,671
Republicans 8,458
Declined to state 4,869

Legislative Districts

US Congressional 1-2
State Senatorial 5
State Assembly 8

Local Officials, 2009

Mayor .... Marlin "Skip" Davies
City Manager .... Mark Deven
City Clerk .... Sue Vannucci
Attorney .... Andrew Morris
Finance Dir .... Amber D'Amato
Public Works .... Greg Meyer
Community Dev Dir ..... Barry Munowitch
Building .... Paul Siegel
Police Chief .... Carey Sullivan
Fire Chief .... Tod Reddish

Public Safety

Number of officers, 2007 65
Violent crimes, 2007 154
Property crimes, 2007 1,807
Arson, 2007 28

Public Library

Woodland Public Library
250 First St
Woodland, CA 95695
530-661-5984

Director .... Carol Beckham (Int)

Library statistics, FY 2007

Population served 54,060
Internet terminals 14
Annual users 22,774

Per capita:

Operating income $33.81
percent from local government 83.8%
Operating expenditure $31.99
Total materials 1.73
Print holdings 1.57
Visits per capita 4.04

Housing & Construction

Housing Units

Total, 2008§ 19,451
Single family units, attached 1,313
Single family units, detached 12,239
Multiple family units 5,218
Mobile home units 681
Occupied 19,031
Vacancy rate 2.2%
Median rent, 2000** $655
Median SF home value, 2000** $153,100

New Privately Owned Housing Units Authorized by Building Permit, 2007*

	Units	Construction Cost
Single	343	$64,106,976
Total	357	$65,493,196

Municipal Finance

(For local fiscal year ended in 2006)

Revenues

Total $120,444,889
Taxes 40,472,238
Special benefits assessment 892,856
Licenses & permits 10,979,526
Fines & forfeitures 355,807
Revenues from use of money & property 2,669,708
Intergovernmental 4,946,035
Service charges 14,038,748
Other revenues 6,836,608
Other financing sources 39,253,363

Expenditures

Total $112,418,331
General government 15,369,107
Public safety 22,496,875
Transportation 32,038,001
Community development 10,365,896
Health 10,688,499
Culture & leisure 17,856,606
Other 0

Local School District

(Data from School year 2007-08 except as noted)

Woodland Joint Unified
435 Sixth St
Woodland, CA 95695
(530) 662-0201

Superintendent .... Carmela Franco
Grade plan K-12
Number of schools 19
Enrollment 10,657
High school graduates, 2006-07 608
Dropout rate 2.7%
Pupil/teacher ratio 20.0
Average class size 24.5
Students per computer 5.0
Classrooms with internet 848
Avg. Daily Attendance (ADA) 10,361
Cost per ADA $8,162
Avg. Teacher Salary .... NA

California Achievement Tests 6th ed., 2008

(Pct scoring at or above 50th National Percentile Rank)

	Math	Reading	Language
Grade 3	51%	33%	45%
Grade 7	50%	46%	43%

Academic Performance Index, 2008

Number of students tested 8,081
Number of valid scores 7,740
2007 API (base) 709
2008 API (growth) 714

SAT Testing, 2006-07

Enrollment, Grade 12 836
Number taking test 281
percent taking test 33.6%
percent with total score 1,500+ ... 13.90%

Average Scores:

Math	Verbal	Writing	Total
482	476	474	1,432

Federal No Child Left Behind, 2008

(Adequate Yearly Progress standards met)

	Participation Rate	Pct Proficient
ELA	Yes	No
Math	Yes	No

API criteria .... Yes
Graduation rate .... Yes
\# criteria met/possible 30/25

Other school districts for this city

(see Appendix E for information on these districts)

None

See Introduction for an explanation of all data sources.

Demographics & Socio-Economic Characteristics

(2000 Decennial Census, except as noted)

Population

1990* . . . 5,035
2000 . . . 5,352
Male . . . 2,654
Female . . . 2,698
Jan. 2008 (estimate)§ . . . 5,625
Persons per sq. mi. of land . . . 476.7

Race & Hispanic Origin, 2000

Race
White . . . 4,828
Black/African American . . . 20
North American Native . . . 8
Asian . . . 267
Pacific Islander . . . 6
Other Race . . . 70
Two or more races . . . 153
Hispanic origin, total . . . 232
Mexican . . . 156
Puerto Rican . . . 4
Cuban . . . 1
Other Hispanic . . . 71

Age & Nativity, 2000

Under 5 years . . . 325
18 years and over . . . 4,100
65 years and over . . . 855
85 years and over . . . 74
Median Age . . . 44.4
Native-born . . . 4,589
Foreign-born . . . 664

Educational Attainment, 2000

Population 25 years and over . . . 3,845
Less than 9th grade . . . 0.6%
High school grad or higher . . . 97.1%
Bachelor's degree or higher . . . 67.1%
Graduate degree . . . 36.5%

Income & Poverty, 1999

Per capita income . . . $104,667
Median household income . . . $171,126
Median family income . . . $196,505
Persons in poverty . . . 2.8%
H'holds receiving public assistance . . . 0
H'holds receiving social security . . . 533

Households, 2000

Total households . . . 1,949
With persons under 18 . . . 665
With persons over 65 . . . 584
Family households . . . 1,516
Single person households . . . 309
Persons per household . . . 2.74
Persons per family . . . 2.98

Household Population, 2008§§

Persons living in households . . . 5,619
Persons living in group quarters . . . 6
Persons per household . . . 2.8

Labor & Employment

Total civilian labor force, 2008§§ . . . NA
Unemployment rate, 2008 . . . NA
Total civilian labor force, 2000 . . . 2,479

Employed persons 16 years and over by occupation, 2000

Managers & professionals . . . 1,689
Service occupations . . . 191
Sales & office occupations . . . 423
Farming, fishing & forestry . . . 6
Construction & maintenance . . . 84
Production & transportation . . . 57
Self-employed persons . . . 410

* US Census Bureau
** 2000 Decennial Census
§ California Department of Finance
§§ California Employment Development Dept

General Information

Town of Woodside
PO Box 620005
Woodside, CA 94062
650-851-6790

Website . . . www.woodsidetown.org
Elevation . . . 382 ft.
Land Area (sq. miles) . . . 11.8
Water Area (sq. miles) . . . 0
Year of Incorporation . . . 1956
Government type . . . General law
Sales tax rate . . . 9.25%

Voters & Officials

Registered Voters, October 2008

Total . . . 4,088
Democrats . . . 1,534
Republicans . . . 1,534
Declined to state . . . 868

Legislative Districts

US Congressional . . . 14
State Senatorial . . . 8
State Assembly . . . 21

Local Officials, 2009

Mayor . . . Peter Mason
Manager . . . Susan George
City Clerk . . . Janet Koelsch
Attorney . . . Jean Savaree
Finance Dir . . . NA
Public Works . . . Paul Nagengast
Planning/Dev Dir . . . Jackie Young
Building . . . Curtis Clark
Police Chief . . . NA
Emergency/Fire Dir . . . Armando Muela

Public Safety

Number of officers, 2007 . . . NA
Violent crimes, 2007 . . . NA
Property crimes, 2007 . . . NA
Arson, 2007 . . . NA

Public Library

Woodside Library
San Mateo County Library System
3140 Woodside Rd
Woodside, CA 94062
650-851-0147

Branch Librarian . . . Susan Goetz

Library system statistics, FY 2007

Population served . . . 278,388
Internet terminals . . . 26
Annual users . . . 49,920

Per capita:

Operating income . . . $90.21
percent from local government . . . 63.5%
Operating expenditure . . . $60.41
Total materials . . . 2.65
Print holdings . . . 2.16
Visits per capita . . . 5.44

Housing & Construction

Housing Units

Total, 2008§ . . . 2,095
Single family units, attached . . . 28
Single family units, detached . . . 2,033
Multiple family units . . . 33
Mobile home units . . . 1
Occupied . . . 2,026
Vacancy rate . . . 3.3%
Median rent, 2000** . . . $1,557
Median SF home value, 2000** . . . $1,000,001

New Privately Owned Housing Units Authorized by Building Permit, 2007*

	Units	Construction Cost
Single	11	$14,041,400
Total	11	$14,041,400

Municipal Finance

(For local fiscal year ended in 2006)

Revenues

Total . . . $8,758,254
Taxes . . . 4,303,417
Special benefits assessment . . . 0
Licenses & permits . . . 409,793
Fines & forfeitures . . . 22,632
Revenues from use of money & property . . . 282,353
Intergovernmental . . . 659,397
Service charges . . . 1,106,864
Other revenues . . . 1,973,798
Other financing sources . . . 0

Expenditures

Total . . . $6,401,743
General government . . . 1,145,640
Public safety . . . 715,476
Transportation . . . 1,527,055
Community development . . . 1,650,220
Health . . . 220,881
Culture & leisure . . . 1,142,471
Other . . . 0

Local School District

(Data from School year 2007-08 except as noted)

Sequoia Union High
480 James Ave
Redwood City, CA 94062
(650) 369-1411

Superintendent . . . Patrick Gemma
Grade plan . . . 9-12
Number of schools . . . 6
Enrollment . . . 8,510
High school graduates, 2006-07 . . . 1,546
Dropout rate . . . 3.2%
Pupil/teacher ratio . . . 19.7
Average class size . . . 26.4
Students per computer . . . 3.0
Classrooms with internet . . . 402
Avg. Daily Attendance (ADA) . . . 7,811
Cost per ADA . . . $11,470
Avg. Teacher Salary . . . $76,194

California Achievement Tests 6th ed., 2008

(Pct scoring at or above 50th National Percentile Rank)

	Math	Reading	Language
Grade 3	NA	NA	NA
Grade 7	NA	NA	NA

Academic Performance Index, 2008

Number of students tested . . . 5,874
Number of valid scores . . . 5,525
2007 API (base) . . . 753
2008 API (growth) . . . 753

SAT Testing, 2006-07

Enrollment, Grade 12 . . . 2,000
Number taking test . . . 945
percent taking test . . . 47.3%
percent with total score 1,500+ . . . 29.10%

Average Scores:

Math	Verbal	Writing	Total
546	530	530	1,606

Federal No Child Left Behind, 2008

(Adequate Yearly Progress standards met)

	Participation Rate	Pct Proficient
ELA	Yes	No
Math	Yes	No

API criteria . . . Yes
Graduation rate . . . Yes
\# criteria met/possible . . . 28/25

Other school districts for this city

(see Appendix E for information on these districts)

Woodside Elem

See Introduction for an explanation of all data sources.

Demographics & Socio-Economic Characteristics†

(2007 American Community Survey, except as noted)

Population

1990* . . . 52,422
2007 . . . 57,550
Male . . . 29,248
Female . . . 28,302
Jan. 2008 (estimate)§ . . . 68,312
Persons per sq. mi. of land . . . 3,521.2

Race & Hispanic Origin, 2007

Race
White . . . 44,176
Black/African American . . . 867
North American Native . . . 845
Asian . . . 8,144
Pacific Islander . . . 64
Other Race . . . 1,424
Two or more races . . . 2,030
Hispanic origin, total . . . 6,763
Mexican . . . NA
Puerto Rican . . . NA
Cuban . . . NA
Other Hispanic . . . NA

Age & Nativity, 2007

Under 5 years . . . 3,063
18 years and over . . . 43,666
65 years and over . . . 6,167
85 years and over . . . 323
Median Age . . . 41.6
Native-born . . . 49,176
Foreign-born . . . 8,374

Educational Attainment, 2007

Population 25 years and over . . . 37,782
Less than 9th grade . . . 0.5%
High school grad or higher . . . 96.3%
Bachelor's degree or higher . . . 46.1%
Graduate degree . . . 15.5%

Income & Poverty, 2007

Per capita income . . . $47,087
Median household income . . . $109,681
Median family income . . . $122,373
Persons in poverty . . . 1.8%
H'holds receiving public assistance . . . 112
H'holds receiving social security . . . 4,324

Households, 2007

Total households . . . 19,174
With persons under 18 . . . 7,322
With persons over 65 . . . 4,287
Family households . . . 15,908
Single person households . . . 2,892
Persons per household . . . 3.00
Persons per family . . . 3.32

Household Population, 2008§§

Persons living in households . . . 68,177
Persons living in group quarters . . . 135
Persons per household . . . 3.2

Labor & Employment

Total civilian labor force, 2008§§ . . . 36,400
Unemployment rate, 2008 . . . 3.5%
Total civilian labor force, 2000* . . . 31,092

Employed persons 16 years and over by occupation, 2007

Managers & professionals . . . 15,975
Service occupations . . . 2,285
Sales & office occupations . . . 11,146
Farming, fishing & forestry . . . 0
Construction & maintenance . . . 1,395
Production & transportation . . . 1,459
Self-employed persons . . . 3,004

† see Appendix D for 2000 Decennial Census Data
* US Census Bureau
** 2007 American Community Survey
§ California Department of Finance
§§ California Employment Development Dept

General Information

City of Yorba Linda
4845 Casa Loma Ave
Yorba Linda, CA 92886
714-961-7100

Website . . . www.ci.yorba-linda.ca.us
Elevation . . . 397 ft.
Land Area (sq. miles) . . . 19.4
Water Area (sq. miles) . . . 0.5
Year of Incorporation . . . 1967
Government type . . . General law
Sales tax rate . . . 8.75%

Voters & Officials

Registered Voters, October 2008

Total . . . 43,010
Democrats . . . 9,704
Republicans . . . 24,880
Declined to state . . . 7,034

Legislative Districts

US Congressional . . . 42
State Senatorial . . . 29
State Assembly . . . 60, 72

Local Officials, 2009

Mayor . . . Mark Schwing
Manager . . . William Kelly (Int)
City Clerk . . . Kathie Mendoza
Attorney . . . Sonia Rubio Carvalho
Finance Dir . . . Susan Hartman
Public Works . . . Mark Stowell
Planning/Dev Dir . . . Steve Harris
Building . . . Bob Silva
Police Chief . . . Billy Hutchison
Emergency/Fire Dir . . . (County)

Public Safety

Number of officers, 2007 . . . NA
Violent crimes, 2007 . . . 44
Property crimes, 2007 . . . 1,031
Arson, 2007 . . . 9

Public Library

Yorba Linda Public Library
18181 Imperial Hwy
Yorba Linda, CA 92886
714-777-2873

Branch Director . . . Melinda Steep (Actg)

Library statistics, FY 2007

Population served . . . 67,904
Internet terminals . . . 20
Annual users . . . 68,798

Per capita:

Operating income . . . $64.45
percent from local government . . . 89.2%
Operating expenditure . . . $64.45
Total materials . . . 2.20
Print holdings . . . 1.96
Visits per capita . . . 4.26

Housing & Construction

Housing Units

Total, 2008§ . . . 21,893
Single family units, attached . . . 2,395
Single family units, detached . . . 17,205
Multiple family units . . . 1,982
Mobile home units . . . 311
Occupied . . . 21,540
Vacancy rate . . . 1.6%
Median rent, 2007** . . . $1,355
Median SF home value, 2007** . . . $837,300

New Privately Owned Housing Units Authorized by Building Permit, 2007*

	Units	Construction Cost
Single	126	$84,507,347
Total	130	$85,524,163

Municipal Finance

(For local fiscal year ended in 2006)

Revenues

Total . . . $53,843,834
Taxes . . . 25,334,844
Special benefits assessment . . . 5,634,868
Licenses & permits . . . 2,810,053
Fines & forfeitures . . . 414,386
Revenues from use of money & property . . . 2,029,610
Intergovernmental . . . 3,143,966
Service charges . . . 14,203,776
Other revenues . . . 272,331
Other financing sources . . . 0

Expenditures

Total . . . $48,761,823
General government . . . 3,968,196
Public safety . . . 10,245,818
Transportation . . . 8,565,196
Community development . . . 4,624,834
Health . . . 4,448,639
Culture & leisure . . . 16,909,140
Other . . . 0

Local School District

(Data from School year 2007-08 except as noted)

Placentia-Yorba Linda Unified
1301 East Orangethorpe Ave
Placentia, CA 92870
(714) 996-2550

Superintendent . . . Dennis Smith
Grade plan . . . K-12
Number of schools . . . 32
Enrollment . . . 26,243
High school graduates, 2006-07 . . . 1,865
Dropout rate . . . 1.1%
Pupil/teacher ratio . . . 23.9
Average class size . . . 26.6
Students per computer . . . 4.4
Classrooms with internet . . . 1,176
Avg. Daily Attendance (ADA) . . . 25,745
Cost per ADA . . . $7,949
Avg. Teacher Salary . . . $75,643

California Achievement Tests 6th ed., 2008

(Pct scoring at or above 50th National Percentile Rank)

	Math	Reading	Language
Grade 3	68%	47%	57%
Grade 7	69%	64%	63%

Academic Performance Index, 2008

Number of students tested . . . 20,317
Number of valid scores . . . 19,531
2007 API (base) . . . 816
2008 API (growth) . . . 822

SAT Testing, 2006-07

Enrollment, Grade 12 . . . 1,939
Number taking test . . . 999
percent taking test . . . 51.5%
percent with total score 1,500+ . . . 33.40%

Average Scores:

Math	Verbal	Writing	Total
561	526	525	1,612

Federal No Child Left Behind, 2008

(Adequate Yearly Progress standards met)

	Participation Rate	Pct Proficient
ELA	Yes	No
Math	Yes	No

API criteria . . . Yes
Graduation rate . . . Yes
criteria met/possible . . . 38/36

Other school districts for this city

(see Appendix E for information on these districts)

None

See Introduction for an explanation of all data sources.

Demographics & Socio-Economic Characteristics

(2000 Decennial Census, except as noted)

Population

1990* . . . 3,259
2000 . . . 2,916
Male . . . 1,627
Female . . . 1,289
Jan. 2008 (estimate)§ . . . 3,263
Persons per sq. mi. of land . . . 2,039.4

Race & Hispanic Origin, 2000

Race
White . . . 2,687
Black/African American . . . 32
North American Native . . . 17
Asian . . . 40
Pacific Islander . . . 2
Other Race . . . 82
Two or more races . . . 56
Hispanic origin, total . . . 281
Mexican . . . 242
Puerto Rican . . . 6
Cuban . . . 0
Other Hispanic . . . 33

Age & Nativity, 2000

Under 5 years . . . 79
18 years and over . . . 2,591
65 years and over . . . 1,314
85 years and over . . . 223
Median Age . . . 60.4
Native-born . . . 2,672
Foreign-born . . . 244

Educational Attainment, 2000

Population 25 years and over . . . 2,516
Less than 9th grade . . . 5.2%
High school grad or higher . . . 82.5%
Bachelor's degree or higher . . . 30.6%
Graduate degree . . . 10.1%

Income & Poverty, 1999

Per capita income . . . $30,721
Median household income . . . $46,944
Median family income . . . $56,250
Persons in poverty . . . 5.3%
H'holds receiving public assistance . . . 12
H'holds receiving social security . . . 401

Households, 2000

Total households . . . 1,048
With persons under 18 . . . 195
With persons over 65 . . . 388
Family households . . . 553
Single person households . . . 417
Persons per household . . . 1.95
Persons per family . . . 2.59

Household Population, 2008§§

Persons living in households . . . 2,112
Persons living in group quarters . . . 1,151
Persons per household . . . 1.9

Labor & Employment

Total civilian labor force, 2008§§ . . . 1,300
Unemployment rate, 2008 . . . 3.2%
Total civilian labor force, 2000 . . . 1,018

Employed persons 16 years and over by occupation, 2000

Managers & professionals . . . 446
Service occupations . . . 205
Sales & office occupations . . . 213
Farming, fishing & forestry . . . 41
Construction & maintenance . . . 30
Production & transportation . . . 56
Self-employed persons . . . 161

* US Census Bureau
** 2000 Decennial Census
§ California Department of Finance
§§ California Employment Development Dept

General Information

Town of Yountville
6550 Yount St
Yountville, CA 94599
707-944-8851

Website . . . www.townofyountville.com
Elevation . . . 97 ft.
Land Area (sq. miles) . . . 1.6
Water Area (sq. miles) . . . 0
Year of Incorporation . . . 1965
Government type . . . General law
Sales tax rate . . . 8.75%

Voters & Officials

Registered Voters, October 2008

Total . . . 2,201
Democrats . . . 1,071
Republicans . . . 623
Declined to state . . . 387

Legislative Districts

US Congressional . . . 1
State Senatorial . . . 2
State Assembly . . . 7

Local Officials, 2009

Mayor . . . Cynthia Saucerman
Town Manager . . . Steve Rogers
City Clerk . . . Michelle Price
Attorney . . . Amy Valukevich
Finance Dir . . . (vacant)
Public Works . . . Myke Praul
Planning/Dev Dir . . . Bob Tiernan
Building . . . NA
Police Chief . . . NA
Fire/Emergency Mgmt . . . NA

Public Safety

Number of officers, 2007 . . . NA
Violent crimes, 2007 . . . 5
Property crimes, 2007 . . . 58
Arson, 2007 . . . 0

Public Library

Yountville Library
Napa City/County Library
6548 Yount St
Yountville, CA 94599
707-944-1888

County Library Dir . . . Daris Kreimeier

Library system statistics, FY 2007

Population served . . . 129,976
Internet terminals . . . 58
Annual users . . . NA

Per capita:

Operating income . . . $50.32
percent from local government . . . 88.9%
Operating expenditure . . . $45.25
Total materials . . . 1.58
Print holdings . . . 1.37
Visits per capita . . . 3.16

Housing & Construction

Housing Units

Total, 2008§ . . . 1,195
Single family units, attached . . . 172
Single family units, detached . . . 637
Multiple family units . . . 78
Mobile home units . . . 308
Occupied . . . 1,101
Vacancy rate . . . 7.9%
Median rent, 2000** . . . $966
Median SF home value, 2000** . . . $318,800

New Privately Owned Housing Units Authorized by Building Permit, 2007*

	Units	Construction Cost
Single	4	$1,977,809
Total	4	$1,977,809

Municipal Finance

(For local fiscal year ended in 2006)

Revenues

Total . . . $6,956,307
Taxes . . . 4,415,358
Special benefits assessment . . . 0
Licenses & permits . . . 58,916
Fines & forfeitures . . . 16,179
Revenues from use of money & property . . . 309,206
Intergovernmental . . . 637,784
Service charges . . . 1,485,475
Other revenues . . . 33,389
Other financing sources . . . 0

Expenditures

Total . . . $8,802,277
General government . . . 846,022
Public safety . . . 918,101
Transportation . . . 1,738,972
Community development . . . 613,589
Health . . . 846,817
Culture & leisure . . . 2,049,606
Other . . . 0

Local School District

(Data from School year 2007-08 except as noted)

Napa Valley Unified
2425 Jefferson St
Napa, CA 94558
(707) 253-3715

Superintendent . . . John Glaser
Grade plan . . . K-12
Number of schools . . . 37
Enrollment . . . 17,552
High school graduates, 2006-07 . . . 1,092
Dropout rate . . . 3.6%
Pupil/teacher ratio . . . 19.1
Average class size . . . 24.6
Students per computer . . . 4.2
Classrooms with internet . . . 844
Avg. Daily Attendance (ADA) . . . 14,837
Cost per ADA . . . $8,130
Avg. Teacher Salary . . . $66,178

California Achievement Tests 6th ed., 2008

(Pct scoring at or above 50th National Percentile Rank)

	Math	Reading	Language
Grade 3	56%	41%	50%
Grade 7	56%	50%	51%

Academic Performance Index, 2008

Number of students tested . . . 13,136
Number of valid scores . . . 12,469
2007 API (base) . . . 755
2008 API (growth) . . . 765

SAT Testing, 2006-07

Enrollment, Grade 12 . . . 1,328
Number taking test . . . 406
percent taking test . . . 30.6%
percent with total score 1,500+ . . . 18.70%

Average Scores:

Math	Verbal	Writing	Total
538	521	515	1,574

Federal No Child Left Behind, 2008

(Adequate Yearly Progress standards met)

	Participation Rate	Pct Proficient
ELA	Yes	No
Math	Yes	No

API criteria . . . Yes
Graduation rate . . . Yes
criteria met/possible . . . 42/39

Other school districts for this city

(see Appendix E for information on these districts)

None

See Introduction for an explanation of all data sources.

Demographics & Socio-Economic Characteristics

(2000 Decennial Census, except as noted)

Population

1990* 6,948
2000 7,290
Male 3,418
Female 3,872
Jan. 2008 (estimate)§ 7,441
Persons per sq. mi. of land 744.1

Race & Hispanic Origin, 2000

Race
White 6,310
Black/African American 35
North American Native 440
Asian 133
Pacific Islander 5
Other Race 124
Two or more races 243
Hispanic origin, total 392
Mexican 283
Puerto Rican 14
Cuban 7
Other Hispanic 88

Age & Nativity, 2000

Under 5 years 404
18 years and over 5,432
65 years and over 1,413
85 years and over 211
Median Age 40.6
Native-born 7,113
Foreign-born 329

Educational Attainment, 2000

Population 25 years and over 4,968
Less than 9th grade 5.4%
High school grad or higher 82.9%
Bachelor's degree or higher 18.6%
Graduate degree 5.7%

Income & Poverty, 1999

Per capita income $16,664
Median household income $27,398
Median family income $37,448
Persons in poverty 21.0%
H'holds receiving public assistance 220
H'holds receiving social security 1,191

Households, 2000

Total households 3,114
With persons under 18 993
With persons over 65 1,007
Family households 1,882
Single person households 1,084
Persons per household 2.27
Persons per family 2.92

Household Population, 2008§§

Persons living in households 7,221
Persons living in group quarters 220
Persons per household 2.2

Labor & Employment

Total civilian labor force, 2008§§ 3,260
Unemployment rate, 2008 . . . . . 8.5%
Total civilian labor force, 2000 3,205

Employed persons 16 years and over by occupation, 2000

Managers & professionals 947
Service occupations 661
Sales & office occupations 853
Farming, fishing & forestry 41
Construction & maintenance 162
Production & transportation 286
Self-employed persons 394

* US Census Bureau
** 2000 Decennial Census
§ California Department of Finance
§§ California Employment Development Dept

General Information

City of Yreka
701 Fourth St
Yreka, CA 96097
530-841-2386

Email . . . . . casson@ci.yreka.ca.us
Elevation . . . . . 2,625 ft.
Land Area (sq. miles) 10.0
Water Area (sq. miles) 0.1
Year of Incorporation 1857
Government type . . . . . General law
Sales tax rate 8.25%

Voters & Officials

Registered Voters, October 2008

Total 4,329
Democrats 1,493
Republicans 1,867
Declined to state 769

Legislative Districts

US Congressional 2
State Senatorial 4
State Assembly 2

Local Officials, 2009

Mayor . . . . . Tom Amaral
Manager . . . . . Brian Meek
City Clerk . . . . . Elizabeth Casson
Attorney . . . . . Mary Frances McHugh
Finance Dir . . . . . Rhetta Hogan
Public Works . . . . . Steve Neill
Planning/Dev Dir . . . . . Pam Hayden
Building . . . . . Mark Schmitt
Police Chief . . . . . Brian Bowles
Fire Chief . . . . . Joe Sutter (Vol)

Public Safety

Number of officers, 2007 16
Violent crimes, 2007 54
Property crimes, 2007 297
Arson, 2007 2

Public Library

Main Branch
Siskiyou County Free Library System
719 Fourth St
Yreka, CA 96097
530-842-4175

County Librarian . . . . . Betsy Emry

Library system statistics, FY 2007

Population served 45,953
Internet terminals 31
Annual users 48,766

Per capita:

Operating income $20.36
percent from local government 90.2%
Operating expenditure $20.12
Total materials 4.06
Print holdings 3.88
Visits per capita . . . . . NA

Housing & Construction

Housing Units

Total, 2008§ 3,561
Single family units, attached 140
Single family units, detached 2,242
Multiple family units 927
Mobile home units 252
Occupied 3,358
Vacancy rate 5.7%
Median rent, 2000** $465
Median SF home value, 2000** $96,600

New Privately Owned Housing Units Authorized by Building Permit, 2007*

	Units	Construction Cost
Single	14	$2,467,734
Total	14	$2,467,734

Municipal Finance

(For local fiscal year ended in 2006)

Revenues

Total $10,530,902
Taxes 4,259,362
Special benefits assessment . . . . . -1
Licenses & permits 167,566
Fines & forfeitures 80,397
Revenues from use of money & property 519,716
Intergovernmental 1,213,542
Service charges 3,853,999
Other revenues 436,321
Other financing sources 0

Expenditures

Total $9,446,808
General government 1,073,978
Public safety 2,345,723
Transportation 523,606
Community development 735,242
Health 2,144,206
Culture & leisure 1,079,541
Other 0

Local School District

(Data from School year 2007-08 except as noted)

Yreka Union High
431 Knapp St
Yreka, CA 96097
(530) 842-2521

Superintendent . . . . . Mark Greenfield
Grade plan 9-12
Number of schools 3
Enrollment 796
High school graduates, 2006-07 148
Dropout rate 2.3%
Pupil/teacher ratio 19.6
Average class size 23.0
Students per computer 1.8
Classrooms with internet 74
Avg. Daily Attendance (ADA) 772
Cost per ADA $9,573
Avg. Teacher Salary $58,927

California Achievement Tests 6th ed., 2008

(Pct scoring at or above 50th National Percentile Rank)

	Math	Reading	Language
Grade 3	NA	NA	NA
Grade 7	NA	NA	NA

Academic Performance Index, 2008

Number of students tested 584
Number of valid scores 562
2007 API (base) 719
2008 API (growth) 748

SAT Testing, 2006-07

Enrollment, Grade 12 176
Number taking test 47
percent taking test 26.7%
percent with total score 1,500+ 17.10%

Average Scores:

Math	Verbal	Writing	Total
541	512	498	1,551

Federal No Child Left Behind, 2008

(Adequate Yearly Progress standards met)

	Participation Rate	Pct Proficient
ELA	No	Yes
Math	Yes	Yes

API criteria . . . . . Yes
Graduation rate . . . . . Yes
criteria met/possible 14/13

Other school districts for this city

(see Appendix E for information on these districts)

Yreka Union Elem

See Introduction for an explanation of all data sources.

Demographics & Socio-Economic Characteristics

(2000 Decennial Census, except as noted)

Population

1990* . . . 27,437
2000 . . . 36,758
Male . . . 17,960
Female . . . 18,798
Jan. 2008 (estimate)§ . . . 63,338
Persons per sq. mi. of land . . . 6,738.1

Race & Hispanic Origin, 2000

Race
White . . . 24,611
Black/African American . . . 1,035
North American Native . . . 643
Asian . . . 3,284
Pacific Islander . . . 107
Other Race . . . 5,281
Two or more races . . . 1,797
Hispanic origin, total . . . 9,029
Mexican . . . 7,678
Puerto Rican . . . 131
Cuban . . . 7
Other Hispanic . . . 1,213

Age & Nativity, 2000

Under 5 years . . . 2,981
18 years and over . . . 26,101
65 years and over . . . 4,488
85 years and over . . . 712
Median Age . . . 31.8
Native-born . . . 29,452
Foreign-born . . . 7,134

Educational Attainment, 2000

Population 25 years and over . . . 22,202
Less than 9th grade . . . 12.8%
High school grad or higher . . . 72.6%
Bachelor's degree or higher . . . 14.4%
Graduate degree . . . 4.4%

Income & Poverty, 1999

Per capita income . . . $15,928
Median household income . . . $32,858
Median family income . . . $39,381
Persons in poverty . . . 17.5%
H'holds receiving public assistance . . . 892
H'holds receiving social security . . . 3,263

Households, 2000

Total households . . . 13,290
With persons under 18 . . . 5,375
With persons over 65 . . . 3,014
Family households . . . 8,947
Single person households . . . 3,524
Persons per household . . . 2.70
Persons per family . . . 3.28

Household Population, 2008§§

Persons living in households . . . 62,382
Persons living in group quarters . . . 956
Persons per household . . . 2.9

Labor & Employment

Total civilian labor force, 2008§§ . . . 19,600
Unemployment rate, 2008 . . . 13.7%
Total civilian labor force, 2000 . . . 16,344

Employed persons 16 years and over by occupation, 2000

Managers & professionals . . . 3,788
Service occupations . . . 2,369
Sales & office occupations . . . 3,716
Farming, fishing & forestry . . . 559
Construction & maintenance . . . 1,578
Production & transportation . . . 2,164
Self-employed persons . . . 1,016

* US Census Bureau
** 2000 Decennial Census
§ California Department of Finance
§§ California Employment Development Dept

General Information

City of Yuba City
1201 Civic Center Blvd
Yuba City, CA 95993
530-822-4601

Website . . . www.yubacity.net
Elevation . . . 70 ft.
Land Area (sq. miles) . . . 9.4
Water Area (sq. miles) . . . 0.1
Year of Incorporation . . . 1908
Government type . . . General law
Sales tax rate . . . 8.25%

Voters & Officials

Registered Voters, October 2008

Total . . . 27,014
Democrats . . . 9,546
Republicans . . . 11,992
Declined to state . . . 4,352

Legislative Districts

US Congressional . . . 2
State Senatorial . . . 4
State Assembly . . . 2

Local Officials, 2009

Mayor . . . Leslie McBride
City Manager . . . Steven R Jepsen
City Clerk . . . Terrel Locke
Attorney . . . Tim Hayes
Finance Dir . . . Robin Bertagna
Public Works . . . George Musallam
Community Dev Dir . . . Aaron Busch
Building . . . Aaron Busch
Police Chief . . . Rob Landon
Fire Chief . . . Marc Boomgaarden

Public Safety

Number of officers, 2007 . . . 67
Violent crimes, 2007 . . . 245
Property crimes, 2007 . . . 1,913
Arson, 2007 . . . 10

Public Library

Main Branch
Sutter County Library System
750 Forbes Ave
Yuba City, CA 95991
530-822-7137

Director . . . Nancy Aabery

Library system statistics, FY 2007

Population served . . . 93,919
Internet terminals . . . 53
Annual users . . . 112,000

Per capita:

Operating income . . . $13.36
percent from local government . . . 64.0%
Operating expenditure . . . $13.36
Total materials . . . 1.51
Print holdings . . . 1.47
Visits per capita . . . 10.49

Housing & Construction

Housing Units

Total, 2008§ . . . 22,427
Single family units, attached . . . 851
Single family units, detached . . . 15,163
Multiple family units . . . 5,459
Mobile home units . . . 954
Occupied . . . 21,501
Vacancy rate . . . 4.1%
Median rent, 2000** . . . $496
Median SF home value, 2000** . . . $115,700

New Privately Owned Housing Units Authorized by Building Permit, 2007*

	Units	Construction Cost
Single	158	$33,971,796
Total	182	$35,436,276

Municipal Finance

(For local fiscal year ended in 2006)

Revenues

Total . . . $88,508,547
Taxes . . . 24,550,639
Special benefits assessment . . . 1,039,995
Licenses & permits . . . 2,137,748
Fines & forfeitures . . . 455,367
Revenues from use of money & property . . . 5,308,100
Intergovernmental . . . 3,805,969
Service charges . . . 25,286,715
Other revenues . . . 299,014
Other financing sources . . . 25,625,000

Expenditures

Total . . . $74,774,144
General government . . . 4,312,593
Public safety . . . 19,465,783
Transportation . . . 1,284,689
Community development . . . 10,700,287
Health . . . 10,007,232
Culture & leisure . . . 3,398,695
Other . . . 0

Local School District

(Data from School year 2007-08 except as noted)

Yuba City Unified
750 Palora Ave
Yuba City, CA 95991
(530) 822-5200

Superintendent . . . Nancy Aaberg
Grade plan . . . K-12
Number of schools . . . 21
Enrollment . . . 13,210
High school graduates, 2006-07 . . . 739
Dropout rate . . . 3.7%
Pupil/teacher ratio . . . 19.7
Average class size . . . 23.2
Students per computer . . . 4.4
Classrooms with internet . . . 689
Avg. Daily Attendance (ADA) . . . 12,246
Cost per ADA . . . $7,753
Avg. Teacher Salary . . . $56,235

California Achievement Tests 6th ed., 2008

(Pct scoring at or above 50th National Percentile Rank)

	Math	Reading	Language
Grade 3	59%	41%	49%
Grade 7	54%	49%	46%

Academic Performance Index, 2008

Number of students tested . . . 9,691
Number of valid scores . . . 8,943
2007 API (base) . . . 750
2008 API (growth) . . . 758

SAT Testing, 2006-07

Enrollment, Grade 12 . . . 867
Number taking test . . . 235
percent taking test . . . 27.1%
percent with total score 1,500+ . . . 13.50%

Average Scores:

Math	Verbal	Writing	Total
525	492	488	1,505

Federal No Child Left Behind, 2008

(Adequate Yearly Progress standards met)

	Participation Rate	Pct Proficient
ELA	Yes	No
Math	Yes	No

API criteria . . . Yes
Graduation rate . . . Yes
\# criteria met/possible . . . 42/39

Other school districts for this city

(see Appendix E for information on these districts)

Franklin Elem

See Introduction for an explanation of all data sources.

Demographics & Socio-Economic Characteristics

(2000 Decennial Census, except as noted)

Population

1990* . . . 32,824
2000 . . . 41,207
Male . . . 19,910
Female . . . 21,297
Jan. 2008 (estimate)§ . . . 52,063
Persons per sq. mi. of land . . . 1,872.8

Race & Hispanic Origin, 2000

Race
White . . . 35,113
Black/African American . . . 369
North American Native . . . 445
Asian . . . 486
Pacific Islander . . . 55
Other Race . . . 3,314
Two or more races . . . 1,425
Hispanic origin, total . . . 7,561
Mexican . . . 6,206
Puerto Rican . . . 93
Cuban . . . 56
Other Hispanic . . . 1,206

Age & Nativity, 2000

Under 5 years . . . 2,693
18 years and over . . . 29,445
65 years and over . . . 6,375
85 years and over . . . 1,067
Median Age . . . 36.8
Native-born . . . 37,914
Foreign-born . . . 3,385

Educational Attainment, 2000

Population 25 years and over . . . 26,261
Less than 9th grade . . . 4.8%
High school grad or higher . . . 80.9%
Bachelor's degree or higher . . . 14.3%
Graduate degree . . . 5.4%

Income & Poverty, 1999

Per capita income . . . $18,949
Median household income . . . $39,144
Median family income . . . $48,683
Persons in poverty . . . 11.1%
H'holds receiving public assistance . . . 739
H'holds receiving social security . . . 4,865

Households, 2000

Total households . . . 15,193
With persons under 18 . . . 5,903
With persons over 65 . . . 4,527
Family households . . . 10,679
Single person households . . . 3,838
Persons per household . . . 2.67
Persons per family . . . 3.21

Household Population, 2008§§

Persons living in households . . . 51,491
Persons living in group quarters . . . 572
Persons per household . . . 2.8

Labor & Employment

Total civilian labor force, 2008§§ . . . 22,500
Unemployment rate, 2008 . . . 6.3%
Total civilian labor force, 2000 . . . 18,447

Employed persons 16 years and over by occupation, 2000

Managers & professionals . . . 5,096
Service occupations . . . 3,015
Sales & office occupations . . . 4,437
Farming, fishing & forestry . . . 91
Construction & maintenance . . . 2,289
Production & transportation . . . 2,336
Self-employed persons . . . 1,468

* US Census Bureau
** 2000 Decennial Census
§ California Department of Finance
§§ California Employment Development Dept

General Information

City of Yucaipa
34272 Yucaipa Blvd
Yucaipa, CA 92399
909-797-2489

Website . . . www.yucaipa.org
Elevation . . . 2,000 ft.
Land Area (sq. miles) . . . 27.8
Water Area (sq. miles) . . . 0
Year of Incorporation . . . 1989
Government type . . . General Law
Sales tax rate . . . 8.75%

Voters & Officials

Registered Voters, October 2008

Total . . . 26,611
Democrats . . . 7,803
Republicans . . . 13,411
Declined to state . . . 4,072

Legislative Districts

US Congressional . . . 41
State Senatorial . . . 31
State Assembly . . . 63, 65

Local Officials, 2009

Mayor . . . Dick Riddell
Manager . . . Ray Casey
City Clerk . . . Jennifer Shankland
Attorney . . . Michael Estrada
Finance Dir . . . Greg Franklin
Public Works . . . Bill Hensley
Planning/Dev Dir . . . John McMains
Building . . . NA
Police Chief . . . Bart Gray
Emergency/Fire Dir . . . Steve Shaw

Public Safety

Number of officers, 2007 . . . NA
Violent crimes, 2007 . . . 52
Property crimes, 2007 . . . 914
Arson, 2007 . . . 3

Public Library

Yucaipa Branch Library
San Bernardino County Library System
12040 Fifth St
Yucaipa, CA 92399
909-790-3146

Branch Librarian . . . Mike Houston

Library system statistics, FY 2007

Population served . . . 1,177,092
Internet terminals . . . 12
Annual users . . . 45,343

Per capita:

Operating income . . . $14.27
percent from local government . . . 73.3%
Operating expenditure . . . $13.86
Total materials . . . 0.86
Print holdings . . . 0.79
Visits per capita . . . 5.83

Housing & Construction

Housing Units

Total, 2008§ . . . 19,416
Single family units, attached . . . 394
Single family units, detached . . . 13,159
Multiple family units . . . 1,636
Mobile home units . . . 4,227
Occupied . . . 18,307
Vacancy rate . . . 5.7%
Median rent, 2000** . . . $610
Median SF home value, 2000** . . . $140,000

New Privately Owned Housing Units Authorized by Building Permit, 2007*

	Units	Construction Cost
Single	103	$16,083,129
Total	103	$16,083,129

Municipal Finance

(For local fiscal year ended in 2006)

Revenues

Total . . . $30,219,442
Taxes . . . 18,328,434
Special benefits assessment . . . 2,823,085
Licenses & permits . . . 1,550,670
Fines & forfeitures . . . 225,057
Revenues from use of money & property . . . 1,705,845
Intergovernmental . . . 2,695,058
Service charges . . . 1,752,163
Other revenues . . . 1,139,130
Other financing sources . . . 0

Expenditures

Total . . . $22,620,378
General government . . . 2,816,071
Public safety . . . 6,889,265
Transportation . . . 5,690,783
Community development . . . 4,257,479
Health . . . 59,666
Culture & leisure . . . 2,907,114
Other . . . 0

Local School District

(Data from School year 2007-08 except as noted)

Yucaipa-Calimesa Joint Unified
12797 Third St
Yucaipa, CA 92399
(909) 797-0174

Superintendent . . . Sherry Kendrick
Grade plan . . . K-12
Number of schools . . . 15
Enrollment . . . 10,023
High school graduates, 2006-07 . . . 615
Dropout rate . . . 5.6%
Pupil/teacher ratio . . . 23.7
Average class size . . . 28.7
Students per computer . . . 5.0
Classrooms with internet . . . 439
Avg. Daily Attendance (ADA) . . . 9,545
Cost per ADA . . . $7,594
Avg. Teacher Salary . . . $70,909

California Achievement Tests 6th ed., 2008

(Pct scoring at or above 50th National Percentile Rank)

	Math	Reading	Language
Grade 3	61%	42%	47%
Grade 7	56%	54%	48%

Academic Performance Index, 2008

Number of students tested . . . 7,633
Number of valid scores . . . 7,117
2007 API (base) . . . 750
2008 API (growth) . . . 763

SAT Testing, 2006-07

Enrollment, Grade 12 . . . 749
Number taking test . . . 263
percent taking test . . . 35.1%
percent with total score 1,500+ . . . 14.20%

Average Scores:

Math	Verbal	Writing	Total
475	480	479	1,434

Federal No Child Left Behind, 2008

(Adequate Yearly Progress standards met)

	Participation Rate	Pct Proficient
ELA	Yes	No
Math	Yes	No

API criteria . . . Yes
Graduation rate . . . Yes
criteria met/possible . . . 28/25

Other school districts for this city

(see Appendix E for information on these districts)

None

See Introduction for an explanation of all data sources.

Demographics & Socio-Economic Characteristics

(2000 Decennial Census, except as noted)

Population

1990* ... NA
2000 ... 16,865
Male ... 8,021
Female ... 8,844
Jan. 2008 (estimate)§ ... 21,268
Persons per sq. mi. of land ... 531.7

Race & Hispanic Origin, 2000

Race
White ... 14,716
Black/African American ... 379
North American Native ... 227
Asian ... 218
Pacific Islander ... 51
Other Race ... 772
Two or more races ... 502
Hispanic origin, total ... 1,922
Mexican ... 1,484
Puerto Rican ... 74
Cuban ... 13
Other Hispanic ... 351

Age & Nativity, 2000

Under 5 years ... 989
18 years and over ... 12,630
65 years and over ... 3,849
85 years and over ... 592
Median Age ... 41.6
Native-born ... 15,937
Foreign-born ... 873

Educational Attainment, 2000

Population 25 years and over ... 11,477
Less than 9th grade ... 3.0%
High school grad or higher ... 81.9%
Bachelor's degree or higher ... 12.9%
Graduate degree ... 3.8%

Income & Poverty, 1999

Per capita income ... $16,020
Median household income ... $30,420
Median family income ... $36,650
Persons in poverty ... 19.3%
H'holds receiving public assistance ... 475
H'holds receiving social security ... 2,919

Households, 2000

Total households ... 6,949
With persons under 18 ... 2,157
With persons over 65 ... 2,664
Family households ... 4,487
Single person households ... 2,084
Persons per household ... 2.38
Persons per family ... 2.94

Household Population, 2008§§

Persons living in households ... 20,957
Persons living in group quarters ... 311
Persons per household ... 2.5

Labor & Employment

Total civilian labor force, 2008§§ ... 7,600
Unemployment rate, 2008 ... 8.0%
Total civilian labor force, 2000 ... 6,223

Employed persons 16 years and over by occupation, 2000

Managers & professionals ... 1,621
Service occupations ... 1,153
Sales & office occupations ... 1,512
Farming, fishing & forestry ... 0
Construction & maintenance ... 973
Production & transportation ... 443
Self-employed persons ... 692

* US Census Bureau
** 2000 Decennial Census
§ California Department of Finance
§§ California Employment Development Dept

General Information

Town of Yucca Valley
57090 Twentynine Palms Hwy
Yucca Valley, CA 92284
760-369-7207

Website ... www.yucca-valley.org
Elevation ... NA
Land Area (sq. miles) ... 40.0
Water Area (sq. miles) ... 0
Year of Incorporation ... 1991
Government type ... General Law
Sales tax rate ... 8.75%

Voters & Officials

Registered Voters, October 2008

Total ... 10,247
Democrats ... 3,016
Republicans ... 4,833
Declined to state ... 1,839

Legislative Districts

US Congressional ... 41
State Senatorial ... 31
State Assembly ... 65

Local Officials, 2009

Mayor ... Frank Lukino
Manager ... Andy Takata
City Clerk ... Jamie Anderson
Attorney ... Naomi Silvergleid
Finance Dir ... Curtis Yakimow
Public Works ... Art de Rosa
Planning/Comm Dev ... NA
Building ... NA
Police Chief ... (County)
Fire/Emergency Mgmt ... (County)

Public Safety

Number of officers, 2007 ... NA
Violent crimes, 2007 ... 74
Property crimes, 2007 ... 563
Arson, 2007 ... 8

Public Library

Yucca Valley Branch Library
San Bernardino County Library System
57098 Twentynine Palms Hwy
Yucca Valley, CA 92284
760-228-5455

Branch Librarian ... Peggy Bryant

Library system statistics, FY 2007

Population served ... 1,177,092
Internet terminals ... 12
Annual users ... 45,343

Per capita:

Operating income ... $14.27
percent from local government ... 73.3%
Operating expenditure ... $13.86
Total materials ... 0.86
Print holdings ... 0.79
Visits per capita ... 5.83

Housing & Construction

Housing Units

Total, 2008§ ... 9,574
Single family units, attached ... 140
Single family units, detached ... 7,662
Multiple family units ... 1,065
Mobile home units ... 707
Occupied ... 8,366
Vacancy rate ... 12.6%
Median rent, 2000** ... $518
Median SF home value, 2000** ... $83,200

New Privately Owned Housing Units Authorized by Building Permit, 2007*

	Units	Construction Cost
Single	87	$10,639,841
Total	99	$11,432,877

Municipal Finance

(For local fiscal year ended in 2006)

Revenues

Total ... $12,162,860
Taxes ... 7,443,752
Special benefits assessment ... 0
Licenses & permits ... 26,274
Fines & forfeitures ... 59,842
Revenues from use of money & property ... 348,701
Intergovernmental ... 2,925,925
Service charges ... 1,024,233
Other revenues ... 213,805
Other financing sources ... 120,328

Expenditures

Total ... $11,256,962
General government ... 1,799,515
Public safety ... 3,665,605
Transportation ... 2,844,692
Community development ... 1,555,023
Health ... 0
Culture & leisure ... 1,392,127
Other ... 0

Local School District

(Data from School year 2007-08 except as noted)

Morongo Unified
PO Box 1209
Twentynine Palms, CA 92277
(760) 367-9191

Superintendent ... James Majchrzak
Grade plan ... K-12
Number of schools ... 18
Enrollment ... 9,631
High school graduates, 2006-07 ... 491
Dropout rate ... 4.0%
Pupil/teacher ratio ... 20.1
Average class size ... 22.7
Students per computer ... 4.0
Classrooms with internet ... 481
Avg. Daily Attendance (ADA) ... 9,009
Cost per ADA ... $8,507
Avg. Teacher Salary ... $62,656

California Achievement Tests 6th ed., 2008

(Pct scoring at or above 50th National Percentile Rank)

	Math	Reading	Language
Grade 3	52%	38%	48%
Grade 7	54%	51%	46%

Academic Performance Index, 2008

Number of students tested ... 7,280
Number of valid scores ... 6,492
2007 API (base) ... 728
2008 API (growth) ... 741

SAT Testing, 2006-07

Enrollment, Grade 12 ... 641
Number taking test ... 126
percent taking test ... 19.7%
percent with total score 1,500+ ... 10.80%

Average Scores:

Math	Verbal	Writing	Total
528	504	506	1,538

Federal No Child Left Behind, 2008

(Adequate Yearly Progress standards met)

	Participation Rate	Pct Proficient
ELA	Yes	No
Math	Yes	No

API criteria ... Yes
Graduation rate ... Yes
\# criteria met/possible ... 32/28

Other school districts for this city

(see Appendix E for information on these districts)

None

See Introduction for an explanation of all data sources.

California

Cities, Towns & Counties

2009

Demographics & Socio-Economic Characteristics[†]

(2007 American Community Survey, except as noted)

Population

1990* ... 1,279,182
2007 ... 1,464,202
Male ... 724,095
Female ... 740,107
Jan. 2008 (estimate)[§] ... 1,543,000
Living in unincorporated area ... 9.1%
2020 (projected)* ... 1,663,481

Race & Hispanic Origin, 2007

Race
White ... 704,408
Black/African American ... 189,722
North American Native ... 5,887
Asian ... 362,798
Pacific Islander ... 10,794
Other Race ... 133,357
Two or more races ... 57,236
Hispanic origin, total ... 312,752
Mexican ... 231,887
Puerto Rican ... 12,091
Cuban ... 1,852
Other Hispanic ... 66,922

Age & Nativity, 2007

Under 5 years ... 99,673
18 years and over ... 1,120,056
65 years and over ... 156,860
85 years and over ... 23,325
Median Age ... 36.9
Native-born ... 1,014,797
Foreign-born ... 449,405

Educational Attainment, 2007

Population 25 years and over ... 981,165
Less than 9th grade ... 7.5%
High school grad or higher ... 85.7%
Bachelor's degree or higher ... 40.3%
Graduate degree ... 15.9%

Income & Poverty, 2007

Per capita income ... $33,400
Median household income ... $68,740
Median family income ... $83,769
Persons in poverty ... 11.0%
H'holds receiving public assistance ... 15,231
H'holds receiving social security ... 106,671

Households, 2007

Total households ... 519,809
With persons under 18 ... 181,135
With persons over 65 ... 104,629
Family households ... 330,873
Single person households ... 147,943
Persons per household ... 2.74
Persons per family ... 3.41

Labor & Employment

Total civilian labor force, 2008[§§] ... 766,500
Unemployment rate ... 6.2%
Total civilian labor force, 2000* ... 733,194

Employed persons 16 years and over by occupation, 2007

Managers & professionals ... 306,627
Service occupations ... 101,754
Sales & office occupations ... 173,618
Farming, fishing & forestry ... 748
Construction & maintenance ... 59,785
Production & transportation ... 66,111
Self-employed persons ... 56,731

† see Appendix D for 2000 Decennial Census Data
* US Census Bureau
** 2007 American Community Survey
§ California Department of Finance
§§ California Employment Development Dept

General Information

1221 Oak St #536
Oakland, CA 94612
510-272-6984

Website ... www.acgov.org
Incorporated ... March 25, 1853
Form of Government ... Charter
Land Area (sq. miles) ... 737.6
Water Area (sq. miles) ... 83.6
Persons per sq. mi. of land, 2008 ... 2,091.9
Sales tax rate ... 8.75%

Voters & Gov't Officials

Registered Voters, October 2008

Total ... 803,009
Democrats ... 462,445
Republicans ... 121,853
Declined to state ... 181,752
Unincorporated area ... 71,691
Democrats ... 39,398
Republicans ... 15,156
Declined to state ... 14,101

Legislative Districts

US Congressional ... 9, 10-11, 13
State Senatorial ... 9, 10
State Assembly ... 14-16, 18, 20

County Officials, 2009

Administrator ... Susan S. Muranishi
County Clerk ... Patrick O'Connell
District Attorney ... Thomas Orloff
Auditor-Controller ... Patrick O'Connell
Tax Assessor ... Ron Thomsen
Treasurer/Tax Coll ... Donald White
Comm Dev Dir ... Chris Bazar
Public Works ... Daniel Woldesenbet
Building ... NA
Sheriff ... Gregory Ahern
Fire Chief ... Sheldon Gilbert
Elections Official ... Dave Macdonald
County supervisors
District 1 ... Scott Haggerty
District 2 ... Gail Steele
District 3 ... Alice Lai-Bitker
District 4 ... Nate Miley
District 5 ... Keith Carson

Public Safety

County Sheriff's office, 2007

Number of officers ... 967
Violent crimes ... 683
Property crimes ... 2,864
Arson ... 33

Housing & Construction

Housing Units

Total, January 2008[§] ... 570,619
Single family units, attached ... 39,742
Single family units, detached ... 303,613
Multiple family units ... 219,609
Mobile home units ... 7,655
Occupied units ... 553,501
Vacancy rate ... 3.0%
Median rent, 2007** ... $1,110
Median SF home value, 2007** ... $651,800

New Privately Owned Housing Units Authorized by Building Permit, 2007*

	Units	Construction Cost
Single	1,315	$419,240,508
Total	3,138	$724,659,182

Property Taxation, FY 2008

Total assessed value ... $193,743,077,525
Total tax levied ... $308,966,582
Delinquency rate ... 3.510%

County Finance, FY 2007

Revenues

Total ... $2,002,680,697
Taxes ... 530,810,273
Special benefits assessment ... 0
Licenses, permits & franchises ... 7,120,875
Fines, forfeitures & penalties ... 11,356,470
Use of money & property ... 56,054,942
Intergovernmental ... 1,045,652,660
Service charges ... 252,355,641
Miscellaneous revenues ... 65,408,786
Other financing sources ... 11,713,214

Expenditures

Total ... $1,840,512,393
General ... 169,587,273
Public protection ... 559,545,578
Public ways & facilities ... 29,172,285
Health ... 439,825,771
Sanitation ... 0
Public assistance ... 543,431,550
Education ... 18,919,307
Recreation & culture ... 545,562
Debt service ... 79,485,067

County Schools

Alameda County Office of Education
313 West Winton Ave
Hayward, CA 94544
(510) 887-0152

Superintendent ... Sheila Jordan

County-wide School Totals

(2007-08 except where noted)

Number of districts ... 16
Number of schools ... 386
Enrollment ... 202,749
High school graduates, 2006-07 ... 12,692
Pupil/teacher ratio ... 18.4
Average class size ... 13.4
Students per computer ... 4.9
Cost per ADA ... $9,094
Avg teacher salary ... $67,691

California Achievement Tests 6th ed., 2008

(Pct scoring at or above 50th National Percentile Rank)

	Math	Reading	Language
Grade 3	NA	NA	NA
Grade 7	NA	NA	NA

Academic Performance Index, 2008

Number of students tested ... 145,815
2007 API (base) ... 502
2008 API (growth) ... 497

SAT Testing, 2006-07

Enrollment, Grade 12 ... 15,794
percent taking test ... 48.8%
percent with total score 1,500+ ... 25.9%

Average Scores:

Math	Verbal	Writing	Total
532	502	502	1,536

County Library

Alameda County Library
2450 Stevenson Blvd
Fremont, CA 94538
510-745-1400

Librarian ... Jean Hofacket

Library statistics, FY 2007

Population served ... 527,926
Internet terminals ... 193
Annual users ... 358,689

Per capita:

Operating income ... $41.07
percent from local government ... 94.7%
Operating expenditure ... $36.47
Total materials ... 2.21
Print holdings ... 1.91
Visits ... 4.32

See Introduction for an explanation of all data sources.

Demographics & Socio-Economic Characteristics

(2000 U.S. Census, except as noted)

Population

1990* . . . 1,113
2000 . . . 1,208
  Male . . . 635
  Female . . . 573
Jan. 2008 (estimate)§ . . . 1,222
  Living in unincorporated area . . . 100%
2020 (projected)* . . . 1,453

Race & Hispanic Origin, 2000

Race
  White . . . 890
  Black/African American . . . 7
  North American Native . . . 228
  Asian . . . 4
  Pacific Islander . . . 1
  Other Race . . . 17
  Two or more races . . . 61
Hispanic origin, total . . . 94
  Mexican . . . 75
  Puerto Rican . . . 8
  Cuban . . . NA
  Other Hispanic . . . 11

Age & Nativity, 2000

Under 5 years . . . 61
18 years and over . . . 932
65 years and over . . . 120
85 years and over . . . 13
  Median Age . . . 39.3
Native-born . . . 1,169
Foreign-born . . . 39

Educational Attainment, 2000

Population 25 years and over . . . 797
Less than 9th grade . . . 2.6%
High school grad or higher . . . 88.3%
Bachelor's degree or higher . . . 28.2%
Graduate degree . . . 8.4%

Income & Poverty, 1999

Per capita income . . . $24,431
Median household income . . . $41,875
Median family income . . . $50,250
Persons in poverty . . . 19.2%
H'holds receiving public assistance . . . 26
H'holds receiving social security . . . 107

Households, 2000

Total households . . . 483
  With persons under 18 . . . 151
  With persons over 65 . . . 86
  Family households . . . 295
  Single person households . . . 134
Persons per household . . . 2.50
Persons per family . . . 2.96

Labor & Employment

Total civilian labor force, 2008§§ . . . 500
  Unemployment rate . . . 10.3%
Total civilian labor force, 2000 . . . 683

Employed persons 16 years and over by occupation, 2000

  Managers & professionals . . . 167
  Service occupations . . . 168
  Sales & office occupations . . . 156
  Farming, fishing & forestry . . . 18
  Construction & maintenance . . . 62
  Production & transportation . . . 57
Self-employed persons . . . 39

* US Census Bureau
** 2000 Decennial Census
§ California Department of Finance
§§ California Employment Development Dept

General Information

County Admin Bldg
PO Box 158
Markleeville, CA 96120
530-694-2281

Website . . . www.alpinecountyca.gov
Incorporated . . . March 16, 1864
Form of Government . . . General law
Land Area (sq. miles) . . . 738.6
Water Area (sq. miles) . . . 4.6
Persons per sq. mi. of land, 2008 . . . 1.7
Sales tax rate . . . 7.25%

Voters & Gov't Officials

Registered Voters, October 2008

Total . . . 816
  Democrats . . . 306
  Republicans . . . 280
  Declined to state . . . 177
Unincorporated area . . . 816
  Democrats . . . 306
  Republicans . . . 280
  Declined to state . . . 177

Legislative Districts

US Congressional . . . 3
State Senatorial . . . 1
State Assembly . . . 4

County Officials, 2009

Chief Admin Officer . . . Pamela Knorr
County Clerk . . . Barbara Howard
District Attorney . . . Will Richmond
Finance Dir . . . Randi Makley
Tax Assessor . . . David Peets
Tax Collector . . . Carol McElroy
Planning/Dev Dir . . . Brian Peters
Public Works . . . Dennis Cardoza
Building Dept Dir . . . NA
Sheriff . . . John Crawford
Fire/Emerg Mgmt Dir . . . NA
Elections Official . . . Barbara Howard
County supervisors
  District 1 . . . Donald Jardine
  District 2 . . . Henry Veatch
  District 3 . . . Phillip Bennett
  District 4 . . . Terry Woodrow
  District 5 . . . Tom Sweeney

Public Safety

County Sheriff's office, 2007

Number of officers . . . 15
Violent crimes . . . 15
Property crimes . . . 74
Arson . . . 0

Housing & Construction

Housing Units

Total, January 2008§ . . . 1,748
  Single family units, attached . . . 51
  Single family units, detached . . . 1,014
  Multiple family units . . . 621
  Mobile home units . . . 62
  Occupied units . . . 556
  Vacancy rate . . . 68.2%
Median rent, 2000** . . . $659
Median SF home value, 2000** . . . $184,200

New Privately Owned Housing Units Authorized by Building Permit, 2007*

	Units	Construction Cost
Single	15	$10,727,981
Total	35	$17,649,523

Property Taxation, FY 2008

Total assessed value . . . $722,578,160
Total tax levied . . . $4,471,493
Delinquency rate . . . 3.000%

County Finance, FY 2007

Revenues

Total . . . $14,567,327
Taxes . . . 5,450,820
Special benefits assessment . . . 0
Licenses, permits & franchises . . . 366,793
Fines, forfeitures & penalties . . . 146,781
Use of money & property . . . 542,414
Intergovernmental . . . 6,720,166
Service charges . . . 1,198,603
Miscellaneous revenues . . . 141,750
Other financing sources . . . 0

Expenditures

Total . . . $15,807,990
General . . . 5,005,185
Public protection . . . 4,460,033
Public ways & facilities . . . 2,112,156
Health . . . 1,690,557
Sanitation . . . 6,713
Public assistance . . . 1,339,948
Education . . . 508,813
Recreation & culture . . . 617,014
Debt service . . . 67,571

County Schools

Alpine County Office of Education
43 Hawkside Dr
Markleeville, CA 96120
(530) 694-2230

Superintendent . . . James Parsons

County-wide School Totals

(2007-08 except where noted)

Number of districts . . . 1
Number of schools . . . 1
Enrollment . . . 1
High school graduates, 2006-07 . . . 0
Pupil/teacher ratio . . . 0.5
Average class size . . . 10.0
Students per computer . . . 0.3
Cost per ADA . . . $26,425
Avg teacher salary . . . NA

California Achievement Tests 6th ed., 2008

(Pct scoring at or above 50th National Percentile Rank)

	Math	Reading	Language
Grade 3	NA	NA	NA
Grade 7	NA	NA	NA

Academic Performance Index, 2008

Number of students tested . . . 2
2007 API (base) . . . NA
2008 API (growth) . . . NA

SAT Testing, 2006-07

Enrollment, Grade 12 . . . 3
  percent taking test . . . 66.7%
  percent with total score 1,500+ . . . NA

Average Scores:

Math	Verbal	Writing	Total
NA	NA	NA	NA

County Library

Alpine County Library
PO Box 187
Markleeville, CA 96120
530-694-2120

Librarian . . . Bessie Platten

Library statistics, FY 2007

Population served . . . 1,261
Internet terminals . . . 5
  Annual users . . . 4,113

Per capita:

Operating income . . . $262.03
  percent from local government . . . 94.1%
Operating expenditure . . . $246.53
Total materials . . . 16.83
Print holdings . . . 14.74
Visits . . . 12.61

See Introduction for an explanation of all data sources.

Demographics & Socio-Economic Characteristics

(2000 U.S. Census, except as noted)

Population

1990* . . . 30,039
2000 . . . 35,100
Male . . . 19,328
Female . . . 15,772
Jan. 2008 (estimate)§ . . . 37,943
Living in unincorporated area . . . 58.2%
2020 (projected)* . . . 47,593

Race & Hispanic Origin, 2000

Race
White . . . 30,113
Black/African American . . . 1,359
North American Native . . . 626
Asian . . . 350
Pacific Islander . . . 36
Other Race . . . 1,769
Two or more races . . . 847
Hispanic origin, total . . . 3,126
Mexican . . . 2,347
Puerto Rican . . . 60
Cuban . . . 20
Other Hispanic . . . 699

Age & Nativity, 2000

Under 5 years . . . 1,478
18 years and over . . . 27,877
65 years and over . . . 6,329
85 years and over . . . 645
Median Age . . . 42.7
Native-born . . . 33,920
Foreign-born . . . 1,180

Educational Attainment, 2000

Population 25 years and over . . . 25,549
Less than 9th grade . . . 3.9%
High school grad or higher . . . 84.0%
Bachelor's degree or higher . . . 16.6%
Graduate degree . . . 6.0%

Income & Poverty, 1999

Per capita income . . . $22,412
Median household income . . . $42,280
Median family income . . . $51,226
Persons in poverty . . . 8.0%
H'holds receiving public assistance . . . 298
H'holds receiving social security . . . 4,802

Households, 2000

Total households . . . 12,759
With persons under 18 . . . 3,691
With persons over 65 . . . 4,312
Family households . . . 9,069
Single person households . . . 3,055
Persons per household . . . 2.39
Persons per family . . . 2.81

Labor & Employment

Total civilian labor force, 2008§§ . . . 18,080
Unemployment rate . . . 7.7%
Total civilian labor force, 2000 . . . 14,230

Employed persons 16 years and over by occupation, 2000

Managers & professionals . . . 4,089
Service occupations . . . 3,039
Sales & office occupations . . . 3,254
Farming, fishing & forestry . . . 203
Construction & maintenance . . . 1,520
Production & transportation . . . 1,505
Self-employed persons . . . 1,958

* US Census Bureau
** 2000 Decennial Census
§ California Department of Finance
§§ California Employment Development Dept

General Information

810 Court St
Jackson, CA 95642
209-223-6470

Website . . . www.co.amador.ca.us
Incorporated . . . May 11, 1854
Form of Government . . . General law
Land Area (sq. miles) . . . 593.0
Water Area (sq. miles) . . . 11.7
Persons per sq. mi. of land, 2008 . . . 64.0
Sales tax rate . . . 7.25%

Voters & Gov't Officials

Registered Voters, October 2008

Total . . . 21,462
Democrats . . . 7,501
Republicans . . . 9,727
Declined to state . . . 3,148
Unincorporated area . . . 14,469
Democrats . . . 4,997
Republicans . . . 6,610
Declined to state . . . 2,139

Legislative Districts

US Congressional . . . 3
State Senatorial . . . 1
State Assembly . . . 10

County Officials, 2009

Manager/Admin . . . Terri Daly
Clerk-Recorder . . . Sheldon Johnson
District Attorney . . . Todd Riebe
Finance Dir . . . Joe Lowe
Tax Assessor . . . Jim Rooney
Tax Collector . . . Michael Ryan
Planning Dir. . . . Susan Grijalva
Public Works . . . Kristin Bengyel (Int)
Building . . . NA
Sheriff . . . Martin A. Ryan
Fire Chief . . . Jim McCart
Elections Official . . . NA
County supervisors
District 1 . . . John Plasse
District 2 . . . Richard Forster
District 3 . . . Ted Novelli
District 4 . . . Louis D. Boitano
District 5 . . . Brian Oneto

Public Safety

County Sheriff's office, 2007

Number of officers . . . 45
Violent crimes . . . 104
Property crimes . . . 457
Arson . . . 0

Housing & Construction

Housing Units

Total, January 2008§ . . . 17,345
Single family units, attached . . . 409
Single family units, detached . . . 14,078
Multiple family units . . . 1,262
Mobile home units . . . 1,596
Occupied units . . . 14,964
Vacancy rate . . . 13.7%
Median rent, 2000** . . . $685
Median SF home value, 2000** . . . $153,600

New Privately Owned Housing Units Authorized by Building Permit, 2007*

	Units	Construction Cost
Single	159	$29,169,731
Total	159	$29,169,731

Property Taxation, FY 2008

Total assessed value . . . $4,580,089,518
Total tax levied . . . $14,911,804
Delinquency rate . . . 2.260%

County Finance, FY 2007

Revenues

Total . . . $62,508,713
Taxes . . . 21,230,237
Special benefits assessment . . . 0
Licenses, permits & franchises . . . 2,308,112
Fines, forfeitures & penalties . . . 2,542,632
Use of money & property . . . 1,345,091
Intergovernmental . . . 29,087,415
Service charges . . . 4,975,782
Miscellaneous revenues . . . 1,019,444
Other financing sources . . . 0

Expenditures

Total . . . $67,567,224
General . . . 17,050,813
Public protection . . . 24,896,687
Public ways & facilities . . . 9,183,901
Health . . . 6,927,330
Sanitation . . . 0
Public assistance . . . 7,576,670
Education . . . 970,769
Recreation & culture . . . 353,664
Debt service . . . 607,390

County Schools

Amador County Office of Education
217 Rex Ave
Jackson, CA 95642
(209) 257-5353

Superintendent . . . Dick Glock

County-wide School Totals

(2007-08 except where noted)

Number of districts . . . 6
Number of schools . . . 62
Enrollment . . . 22,077
High school graduates, 2006-07 . . . 1,878
Pupil/teacher ratio . . . 6.6
Average class size . . . 7.9
Students per computer . . . 2.6
Cost per ADA . . . $6,964
Avg teacher salary . . . $60,591

California Achievement Tests 6th ed., 2008

(Pct scoring at or above 50th National Percentile Rank)

	Math	Reading	Language
Grade 3	NA	NA	NA
Grade 7	16%	22%	16%

Academic Performance Index, 2008

Number of students tested . . . 17,580
2007 API (base) . . . 520
2008 API (growth) . . . 508

SAT Testing, 2006-07

Enrollment, Grade 12 . . . 537
percent taking test . . . 19.2%
percent with total score 1,500+ . . . 11.2%

Average Scores:

Math	Verbal	Writing	Total
519	520	516	1,555

County Library

Amador County Library
530 Sutter St
Jackson, CA 95642
209-223-6400

Librarian . . . Laura Einstadter

Library statistics, FY 2007

Population served . . . 38,435
Internet terminals . . . 18
Annual users . . . 74,880

Per capita:

Operating income . . . $24.71
percent from local government . . . 94.0%
Operating expenditure . . . $20.44
Total materials . . . 2.18
Print holdings . . . 1.97
Visits . . . 2.04

See Introduction for an explanation of all data sources.

Demographics & Socio-Economic Characteristics†

(2007 American Community Survey, except as noted)

Population

1990* . . . 182,120
2007 . . . 218,779
Male . . . 107,503
Female . . . 111,276
Jan. 2008 (estimate)§ . . . 220,407
Living in unincorporated area . . . 38.3%
2020 (projected)* . . . 281,442

Race & Hispanic Origin, 2007

Race
White . . . 181,005
Black/African American . . . 3,312
North American Native . . . 3,096
Asian . . . 8,771
Pacific Islander . . . 455
Other Race . . . 11,536
Two or more races . . . 10,604
Hispanic origin, total . . . 27,388
Mexican . . . 23,851
Puerto Rican . . . 505
Cuban . . . 93
Other Hispanic . . . 2,939

Age & Nativity, 2007

Under 5 years . . . 12,030
18 years and over . . . 172,943
65 years and over . . . 32,174
85 years and over . . . 5,689
Median Age . . . 34.9
Native-born . . . 199,755
Foreign-born . . . 19,024

Educational Attainment, 2007

Population 25 years and over . . . 138,556
Less than 9th grade . . . 6.1%
High school grad or higher . . . 83.3%
Bachelor's degree or higher . . . 23.9%
Graduate degree . . . 7.3%

Income & Poverty, 2007

Per capita income . . . $21,865
Median household income . . . $39,529
Median family income . . . $49,202
Persons in poverty . . . 16.8%
H'holds receiving public assistance . . . 5,113
H'holds receiving social security . . . 27,946

Households, 2007

Total households . . . 85,845
With persons under 18 . . . 27,168
With persons over 65 . . . 22,690
Family households . . . 53,003
Single person households . . . 23,675
Persons per household . . . 2.50
Persons per family . . . 3.02

Labor & Employment

Total civilian labor force, 2008§§ . . . 104,300
Unemployment rate . . . 8.4%
Total civilian labor force, 2000* . . . 90,897

Employed persons 16 years and over by occupation, 2007

Managers & professionals . . . 30,144
Service occupations . . . 19,548
Sales & office occupations . . . 22,737
Farming, fishing & forestry . . . 2,088
Construction & maintenance . . . 8,858
Production & transportation . . . 9,688
Self-employed persons . . . 9,518

† see Appendix D for 2000 Decennial Census Data
* US Census Bureau
** 2007 American Community Survey
§ California Department of Finance
§§ California Employment Development Dept

General Information

25 County Center Dr
Oroville, CA 95965
530-538-7631

Website . . . www.buttecounty.net
Incorporated . . . February 18, 1850
Form of Government . . . Charter
Land Area (sq. miles) . . . 1,639.5
Water Area (sq. miles) . . . 37.6
Persons per sq. mi. of land, 2008 . . . 134.4
Sales tax rate . . . 7.25%

Voters & Gov't Officials

Registered Voters, October 2008

Total . . . 122,841
Democrats . . . 44,808
Republicans . . . 47,506
Declined to state . . . 22,901
Unincorporated area . . . 48,877
Democrats . . . 15,976
Republicans . . . 21,640
Declined to state . . . 8,402

Legislative Districts

US Congressional . . . 2, 4
State Senatorial . . . 4
State Assembly . . . 2, 3

County Officials, 2009

Manager/Admin . . . Gregory Iturria
County Clerk . . . Candace Grubbs
District Attorney . . . Mike Ramsey
Auditor-Controller . . . Dave Houser
Tax Assessor . . . Ken Reimers
Tax Collector . . . Linda Barnes
Planning/Comm Dev . . . NA
Public Works . . . Mike Crump
Building . . . NA
Sheriff . . . Perry Reniff
Fire Chief . . . Henri Brachais
Elections Official . . . Candace Grubbs
County supervisors
District 1 . . . Bill Connelly
District 2 . . . Jane Dolan
District 3 . . . Maureen Kirk
District 4 . . . Steve Lambert
District 5 . . . Kim Yamaguchi

Public Safety

County Sheriff's office, 2007

Number of officers . . . 112
Violent crimes . . . 217
Property crimes . . . 1,502
Arson . . . 50

Housing & Construction

Housing Units

Total, January 2008§ . . . 95,692
Single family units, attached . . . 2,436
Single family units, detached . . . 58,749
Multiple family units . . . 18,660
Mobile home units . . . 15,847
Occupied units . . . 89,506
Vacancy rate . . . 6.5%
Median rent, 2007** . . . $818
Median SF home value, 2007** . . . $288,100

New Privately Owned Housing Units Authorized by Building Permit, 2007*

	Units	Construction Cost
Single	804	$114,269,587
Total	985	$130,063,130

Property Taxation, FY 2008

Total assessed value . . . $18,044,023,347
Total tax levied . . . $22,403,675
Delinquency rate . . . 3.210%

County Finance, FY 2007

Revenues

Total . . . $327,768,069
Taxes . . . 51,264,393
Special benefits assessment . . . 0
Licenses, permits & franchises . . . 4,250,362
Fines, forfeitures & penalties . . . 5,067,815
Use of money & property . . . 3,318,287
Intergovernmental . . . 235,235,849
Service charges . . . 18,759,722
Miscellaneous revenues . . . 9,628,537
Other financing sources . . . 24,014

Expenditures

Total . . . $329,161,170
General . . . 21,118,379
Public protection . . . 94,723,316
Public ways & facilities . . . 15,523,067
Health . . . 60,602,741
Sanitation . . . 0
Public assistance . . . 127,402,839
Education . . . 2,961,358
Recreation & culture . . . 442,585
Debt service . . . 6,386,885

County Schools

Butte County Office of Education
1859 Bird St
Oroville, CA 95965
(530) 532-5761

Superintendent . . . Don McNelis

County-wide School Totals

(2007-08 except where noted)

Number of districts . . . 10
Number of schools . . . 84
Enrollment . . . 29,809
High school graduates, 2006-07 . . . 2,149
Pupil/teacher ratio . . . 17.6
Average class size . . . 12.0
Students per computer . . . 3.6
Cost per ADA . . . $8,456
Avg teacher salary . . . $61,099

California Achievement Tests 6th ed., 2008

(Pct scoring at or above 50th National Percentile Rank)

	Math	Reading	Language
Grade 3	22%	26%	43%
Grade 7	35%	45%	45%

Academic Performance Index, 2008

Number of students tested . . . 21,627
2007 API (base) . . . 641
2008 API (growth) . . . 634

SAT Testing, 2006-07

Enrollment, Grade 12 . . . 2,712
percent taking test . . . 24.7%
percent with total score 1,500+ . . . 13.5%

Average Scores:

Math	Verbal	Writing	Total
524	506	493	1,523

County Library

Butte County Library
1820 Mitchell Ave
Oroville, CA 95966
530-538-7642

Librarian . . . Derek Wolfgram

Library statistics, FY 2007

Population served . . . 218,069
Internet terminals . . . 47
Annual users . . . 90,296

Per capita:

Operating income . . . $12.21
percent from local government . . . 84.5%
Operating expenditure . . . $12.71
Total materials . . . 1.41
Print holdings . . . 1.33
Visits . . . 3.01

See Introduction for an explanation of all data sources.

Demographics & Socio-Economic Characteristics

(2000 U.S. Census, except as noted)

Population

1990* 31,998
2000 40,554
Male 20,122
Female 20,432
Jan. 2008 (estimate)§ 46,127
Living in unincorporated area 92.2%
2020 (projected)* 56,318

Race & Hispanic Origin, 2000

Race
White 36,982
Black/African American 304
North American Native 705
Asian 345
Pacific Islander 38
Other Race 839
Two or more races 1,341
Hispanic origin, total 2,765
Mexican 1,916
Puerto Rican 106
Cuban 41
Other Hispanic 702

Age & Nativity, 2000

Under 5 years 1,791
18 years and over 31,306
65 years and over 7,373
85 years and over 649
Median Age 44.6
Native-born 39,335
Foreign-born 1,219

Educational Attainment, 2000

Population 25 years and over 29,201
Less than 9th grade 2.9%
High school grad or higher 85.7%
Bachelor's degree or higher 17.1%
Graduate degree 5.6%

Income & Poverty, 1999

Per capita income $21,420
Median household income $41,022
Median family income $47,379
Persons in poverty 11.6%
H'holds receiving public assistance 605
H'holds receiving social security 6,044

Households, 2000

Total households 16,469
With persons under 18 4,928
With persons over 65 5,181
Family households 11,747
Single person households 3,831
Persons per household 2.44
Persons per family 2.85

Labor & Employment

Total civilian labor force, 2008§§ 20,940
Unemployment rate 8.7%
Total civilian labor force, 2000 17,555

Employed persons 16 years and over by occupation, 2000

Managers & professionals 5,035
Service occupations 2,949
Sales & office occupations 3,879
Farming, fishing & forestry 116
Construction & maintenance 2,356
Production & transportation 1,867
Self-employed persons 2,645

* US Census Bureau
** 2000 Decennial Census
§ California Department of Finance
§§ California Employment Development Dept

General Information

891 Mountain Ranch Rd
San Andreas, CA 95249
209-754-6303

Website .... www.co.calaveras.ca.us
Incorporated .... February 18, 1850
Form of Government .... General law
Land Area (sq. miles) 1,020.0
Water Area (sq. miles) 16.8
Persons per sq. mi. of land, 2008 ...... 45.2
Sales tax rate 7.25%

Voters & Gov't Officials

Registered Voters, October 2008

Total 28,388
Democrats 9,632
Republicans 12,309
Declined to state 4,698
Unincorporated area 26,064
Democrats 8,832
Republicans 11,297
Declined to state 4,331

Legislative Districts

US Congressional 3
State Senatorial 1
State Assembly 25

County Officials, 2009

Manager/Admin .... Robert Lawton
County Clerk .... Karen Varni
District Attorney .... Jeffrey Tuttle
Finance Dir .... Linda S. Churches
Tax Assessor .... Grant Metzger
Tax Collector .... Lynette Norfolk
Planning Dir .... Bob Sellman
Public Works .... (vacant)
Building Dept Dir ...... Stephanie Moreno
Sheriff .... Dennis Downum
Emergency Svcs Dir. .... Clay Hawkins
Elections Official .... Karen Varni
County supervisors
District 1 .... Gary Tofanelli
District 2 .... Steve Wilensky
District 3 .... Merita Callaway
District 4 .... Thomas Tryon
District 5 .... Russell Thomas

Public Safety

County Sheriff's office, 2007

Number of officers 64
Violent crimes 48
Property crimes 633
Arson 3

Housing & Construction

Housing Units

Total, January 2008§ 27,803
Single family units, attached 573
Single family units, detached 23,548
Multiple family units 886
Mobile home units 2,796
Occupied units 19,973
Vacancy rate 28.2%
Median rent, 2000** $599
Median SF home value, 2000** $156,900

New Privately Owned Housing Units Authorized by Building Permit, 2007*

	Units	Construction Cost
Single	262	$69,617,406
Total	277	$71,725,621

Property Taxation, FY 2008

Total assessed value $7,088,529,934
Total tax levied $13,635,338
Delinquency rate 3.650%

County Finance, FY 2007

Revenues

Total $66,543,880
Taxes 21,939,229
Special benefits assessment 0
Licenses, permits & franchises ... 4,280,248
Fines, forfeitures & penalties 2,317,820
Use of money & property 1,328,506
Intergovernmental 29,348,378
Service charges 5,682,426
Miscellaneous revenues 1,639,713
Other financing sources 7,560

Expenditures

Total $65,033,218
General 11,947,754
Public protection 20,535,656
Public ways & facilities 9,271,644
Health 7,747,177
Sanitation 0
Public assistance 13,183,408
Education 832,170
Recreation & culture 682,007
Debt service 833,402

County Schools

Calaveras County Office of Education
PO Box 760
Angels Camp, CA 95221
(209) 736-4662

Superintendent .... John Brophy

County-wide School Totals

(2007-08 except where noted)

Number of districts 3
Number of schools 11
Enrollment 2,256
High school graduates, 2006-07 301
Pupil/teacher ratio 16.5
Average class size 8.5
Students per computer 3.1
Cost per ADA $8,630
Avg teacher salary $60,231

California Achievement Tests 6th ed., 2008

(Pct scoring at or above 50th National Percentile Rank)

	Math	Reading	Language
Grade 3	36%	40%	36%
Grade 7	31%	47%	42%

Academic Performance Index, 2008

Number of students tested 1,737
2007 API (base) 619
2008 API (growth) 619

SAT Testing, 2006-07

Enrollment, Grade 12 562
percent taking test 26.5%
percent with total score 1,500+ 14.1%

Average Scores:

Math	Verbal	Writing	Total
515	513	508	1,536

County Library

Calaveras County Library
1299 Gold Hunter Rd
San Andreas, CA 95249
209-754-6700

Librarian .... Maurie Hoekstra

Library statistics, FY 2007

Population served 46,028
Internet terminals 20
Annual users 25,550

Per capita:

Operating income $13.72
percent from local government 87.3%
Operating expenditure $13.72
Total materials 2.28
Print holdings 2.02
Visits 1.61

See Introduction for an explanation of all data sources.

Demographics & Socio-Economic Characteristics

(2000 U.S. Census, except as noted)

Population

1990* . . . 16,275
2000 . . . 18,804
Male . . . 9,559
Female . . . 9,245
Jan. 2008 (estimate)§ . . . 21,910
Living in unincorporated area . . . 49.6%
2020 (projected)* . . . 29,588

Race & Hispanic Origin, 2000

Race
White . . . 12,090
Black/African American . . . 103
North American Native . . . 439
Asian . . . 228
Pacific Islander . . . 74
Other Race . . . 5,017
Two or more races . . . 853
Hispanic origin, total . . . 8,752
Mexican . . . 7,771
Puerto Rican . . . 14
Cuban . . . 2
Other Hispanic . . . 965

Age & Nativity, 2000

Under 5 years . . . 1,517
18 years and over . . . 12,867
65 years and over . . . 2,135
85 years and over . . . 253
Median Age . . . 31.5
Native-born . . . 13,623
Foreign-born . . . 5,181

Educational Attainment, 2000

Population 25 years and over . . . 10,912
Less than 9th grade . . . 23.1%
High school grad or higher . . . 64.0%
Bachelor's degree or higher . . . 10.6%
Graduate degree . . . 2.8%

Income & Poverty, 1999

Per capita income . . . $14,730
Median household income . . . $35,062
Median family income . . . $40,138
Persons in poverty . . . 15.8%
H'holds receiving public assistance . . . 277
H'holds receiving social security . . . 1,733

Households, 2000

Total households . . . 6,097
With persons under 18 . . . 2,759
With persons over 65 . . . 1,517
Family households . . . 4,576
Single person households . . . 1,308
Persons per household . . . 3.01
Persons per family . . . 3.51

Labor & Employment

Total civilian labor force, 2008§§ . . . 10,570
Unemployment rate . . . 14.0%
Total civilian labor force, 2000 . . . 8,105

Employed persons 16 years and over by occupation, 2000

Managers & professionals . . . 1,658
Service occupations . . . 1,302
Sales & office occupations . . . 1,499
Farming, fishing & forestry . . . 1,069
Construction & maintenance . . . 695
Production & transportation . . . 1,014
Self-employed persons . . . 830

* US Census Bureau
** 2000 Decennial Census
§ California Department of Finance
§§ California Employment Development Dept

General Information

546 Jay St
Colusa, CA 95932
530-458-0500

Website . . . www.colusacountyclerk.com
Incorporated . . . February 18, 1850
Form of Government . . . General law
Land Area (sq. miles) . . . 1,150.7
Water Area (sq. miles) . . . 5.5
Persons per sq. mi. of land, 2008 . . . 19.0
Sales tax rate . . . 7.25%

Voters & Gov't Officials

Registered Voters, October 2008

Total . . . 7,866
Democrats . . . 2,825
Republicans . . . 3,625
Declined to state . . . 1,231
Unincorporated area . . . 4,442
Democrats . . . 1,504
Republicans . . . 2,178
Declined to state . . . 664

Legislative Districts

US Congressional . . . 2
State Senatorial . . . 4
State Assembly . . . 2

County Officials, 2009

Manager/Admin . . . NA
County Clerk . . . Kathleen Moran
District Attorney . . . John Poyner
Auditor-Controller . . . Peggy Scroggins
Tax Assessor . . . Wayne Zoller
Tax Collector . . . Dan Charter
Planning/Dev Dir . . . Stephen Hackney
Public Works . . . Loren Clifton
Building Dept Dir . . . Stephen Hackney
Sheriff-Coroner . . . Scott Marshall
Emergy Mgmt Dir . . . Scott Marshall
Elections Official . . . Kathleen Moran
County supervisors
District 1 . . . Kim Vann
District 2 . . . Thomas Indrieri
District 3 . . . Mark Marshall
District 4 . . . Gary Evans
District 5 . . . Denise Carter

Public Safety

County Sheriff's office, 2007

Number of officers . . . 31
Violent crimes . . . 34
Property crimes . . . 310
Arson . . . 0

Housing & Construction

Housing Units

Total, January 2008§ . . . 7,763
Single family units, attached . . . 229
Single family units, detached . . . 5,804
Multiple family units . . . 881
Mobile home units . . . 849
Occupied units . . . 7,002
Vacancy rate . . . 9.8%
Median rent, 2000** . . . $494
Median SF home value, 2000** . . . $107,500

New Privately Owned Housing Units Authorized by Building Permit, 2007*

	Units	Construction Cost
Single	25	$9,901,200
Total	105	$16,690,716

Property Taxation, FY 2008

Total assessed value . . . $2,550,981,557
Total tax levied . . . $6,826,376
Delinquency rate . . . 3.465%

County Finance, FY 2007

Revenues

Total . . . $39,396,684
Taxes . . . 10,376,115
Special benefits assessment . . . 0
Licenses, permits & franchises . . . 1,473,452
Fines, forfeitures & penalties . . . 1,570,326
Use of money & property . . . 667,690
Intergovernmental . . . 21,287,815
Service charges . . . 2,784,592
Miscellaneous revenues . . . 1,194,038
Other financing sources . . . 41,141

Expenditures

Total . . . $39,595,258
General . . . 4,237,533
Public protection . . . 13,524,015
Public ways & facilities . . . 6,740,619
Health . . . 6,236,874
Sanitation . . . 0
Public assistance . . . 7,227,189
Education . . . 878,856
Recreation & culture . . . 40,710
Debt service . . . 709,462

County Schools

Colusa County Office of Education
146 Seventh St
Colusa, CA 95932
(530) 458-0350

Superintendent . . . Kay Spurgeon

County-wide School Totals

(2007-08 except where noted)

Number of districts . . . 3
Number of schools . . . 13
Enrollment . . . 2,729
High school graduates, 2006-07 . . . 162
Pupil/teacher ratio . . . 6.2
Average class size . . . 15.9
Students per computer . . . 2.2
Cost per ADA . . . $8,360
Avg teacher salary . . . $57,225

California Achievement Tests 6th ed., 2008

(Pct scoring at or above 50th National Percentile Rank)

	Math	Reading	Language
Grade 3	NA	NA	NA
Grade 7	0%	0%	0%

Academic Performance Index, 2008

Number of students tested . . . 2,057
2007 API (base) . . . 577
2008 API (growth) . . . 482

SAT Testing, 2006-07

Enrollment, Grade 12 . . . 323
percent taking test . . . 30.0%
percent with total score 1,500+ . . . 9.6%

Average Scores:

Math	Verbal	Writing	Total
467	451	454	1,372

County Library

Colusa County Free Library
738 Market St
Colusa, CA 95932
530-458-7671

Librarian . . . Ellen Brow

Library statistics, FY 2007

Population served . . . 21,951
Internet terminals . . . 28
Annual users . . . 11,172

Per capita:

Operating income . . . $29.05
percent from local government . . . 76.6%
Operating expenditure . . . $29.05
Total materials . . . 4.60
Print holdings . . . 4.18
Visits . . . 1.32

See Introduction for an explanation of all data sources.

Demographics & Socio-Economic Characteristics†

(2007 American Community Survey, except as noted)

Population

1990* . . . 803,732
2007 . . . 1,019,640
Male . . . 500,710
Female . . . 518,930
Jan. 2008 (estimate)§ . . . 1,051,674
Living in unincorporated area . . . 16.5%
2020 (projected)* . . . 1,237,544

Race & Hispanic Origin, 2007

Race
White . . . 612,689
Black/African American . . . 93,122
North American Native . . . 4,191
Asian . . . 137,533
Pacific Islander . . . 3,741
Other Race . . . 124,580
Two or more races . . . 43,784
Hispanic origin, total . . . 228,114
Mexican . . . 160,755
Puerto Rican . . . 6,061
Cuban . . . 1,438
Other Hispanic . . . 59,860

Age & Nativity, 2007

Under 5 years . . . 66,113
18 years and over . . . 768,698
65 years and over . . . 120,461
85 years and over . . . 17,053
Median Age . . . 37.9
Native-born . . . 778,999
Foreign-born . . . 240,641

Educational Attainment, 2007

Population 25 years and over . . . 674,084
Less than 9th grade . . . 6.1%
High school grad or higher . . . 87.9%
Bachelor's degree or higher . . . 37.1%
Graduate degree . . . 13.4%

Income & Poverty, 2007

Per capita income . . . $37,036
Median household income . . . $76,436
Median family income . . . $86,709
Persons in poverty . . . 8.9%
H'holds receiving public assistance . . . 7,441
H'holds receiving social security . . . 89,824

Households, 2007

Total households . . . 366,428
With persons under 18 . . . 137,304
With persons over 65 . . . 84,191
Family households . . . 259,301
Single person households . . . 85,155
Persons per household . . . 2.76
Persons per family . . . 3.28

Labor & Employment

Total civilian labor force, 2008§§ . . . 529,200
Unemployment rate . . . 6.2%
Total civilian labor force, 2000* . . . 474,037

Employed persons 16 years and over by occupation, 2007

Managers & professionals . . . 193,552
Service occupations . . . 80,103
Sales & office occupations . . . 135,381
Farming, fishing & forestry . . . 513
Construction & maintenance . . . 43,471
Production & transportation . . . 36,847
Self-employed persons . . . 44,232

† see Appendix D for 2000 Decennial Census Data
* US Census Bureau
** 2007 American Community Survey
§ California Department of Finance
§§ California Employment Development Dept

General Information

651 Pine St
Room 106
Martinez, CA 94553
925-335-1900

Website . . . www.co.contra-costa.ca.us
Incorporated . . . February 18, 1850
Form of Government . . . General law
Land Area (sq. miles) . . . 719.9
Water Area (sq. miles) . . . 82.2
Persons per sq. mi. of land, 2008 . . . 1,460.9
Sales tax rate . . . 8.25%

Voters & Gov't Officials

Registered Voters, October 2008

Total . . . 527,145
Democrats . . . 263,853
Republicans . . . 140,864
Declined to state . . . 101,413
Unincorporated area . . . 84,764
Democrats . . . 40,106
Republicans . . . 25,426
Declined to state . . . 15,652

Legislative Districts

US Congressional . . . 7, 10-11
State Senatorial . . . 7, 9
State Assembly . . . 11, 14, 15

County Officials, 2009

Administrator . . . David J. Twa
Clerk-Recorder . . . Stephen Weir
District Attorney . . . Robert Kochly
Auditor-Controller . . . Stephen Ybarra
Tax Assessor . . . Gus Kramer
Treasurer/Tax Coll . . . William Pollacek
Comm Dev Dir . . . Catherine Kutsuris
Public Works . . . Julia Bueren
Building Inspection Dir . . . Jason Crapo
Sheriff . . . Warren Rupf
Fire Chief . . . Keith Richter
Elections Official . . . Candy Lopez
County supervisors
District 1 . . . John Gioia
District 2 . . . Gayle B. Uilkema
District 3 . . . Mary N. Piepho
District 4 . . . Susan Bonilla
District 5 . . . Federal Glover

Public Safety

County Sheriff's office, 2007

Number of officers . . . 674
Violent crimes . . . 666
Property crimes . . . 3,503
Arson . . . 35

Housing & Construction

Housing Units

Total, January 2008§ . . . 397,499
Single family units, attached . . . 32,057
Single family units, detached . . . 264,592
Multiple family units . . . 93,227
Mobile home units . . . 7,623
Occupied units . . . 385,733
Vacancy rate . . . 3.0%
Median rent, 2007** . . . $1,212
Median SF home value, 2007** . . . $622,200

New Privately Owned Housing Units Authorized by Building Permit, 2007*

	Units	Construction Cost
Single	2,753	$817,802,452
Total	3,700	$916,086,248

Property Taxation, FY 2008

Total assessed value . . . $157,920,334,029
Total tax levied . . . $205,375,072
Delinquency rate . . . 4.109%

County Finance, FY 2007

Revenues

Total . . . $1,380,770,704
Taxes . . . 323,704,532
Special benefits assessment . . . 0
Licenses, permits & franchises . . . 37,035,679
Fines, forfeitures & penalties . . . 18,278,266
Use of money & property . . . 31,716,146
Intergovernmental . . . 670,865,093
Service charges . . . 247,994,026
Miscellaneous revenues . . . 27,132,234
Other financing sources . . . 24,044,728

Expenditures

Total . . . $1,310,288,576
General . . . 147,080,953
Public protection . . . 378,496,945
Public ways & facilities . . . 126,731,928
Health . . . 181,999,690
Sanitation . . . 0
Public assistance . . . 390,858,668
Education . . . 25,697,241
Recreation & culture . . . 0
Debt service . . . 59,423,151

County Schools

Contra Costa County Office of Education
77 Santa Barbara Rd
Pleasant Hill, CA 94523
(925) 942-3388

Superintendent . . . Joseph Ovick

County-wide School Totals

(2007-08 except where noted)

Number of districts . . . 29
Number of schools . . . 817
Enrollment . . . 493,926
High school graduates, 2006-07 . . . 32,273
Pupil/teacher ratio . . . 10.7
Average class size . . . 14.6
Students per computer . . . 2.2
Cost per ADA . . . $8,280
Avg teacher salary . . . $61,574

California Achievement Tests 6th ed., 2008

(Pct scoring at or above 50th National Percentile Rank)

	Math	Reading	Language
Grade 3	27%	9%	18%
Grade 7	14%	22%	19%

Academic Performance Index, 2008

Number of students tested . . . 367,049
2007 API (base) . . . 597
2008 API (growth) . . . 602

SAT Testing, 2006-07

Enrollment, Grade 12 . . . 12,502
percent taking test . . . 44.3%
percent with total score 1,500+ . . . 26.4%

Average Scores:

Math	Verbal	Writing	Total
540	522	521	1,583

County Library

Contra Costa County Library
1750 Oak Park Blvd
Pleasant Hill, CA 94523
925-646-6423

Librarian . . . Anne Cain

Library statistics, FY 2007

Population served . . . 938,513
Internet terminals . . . 324
Annual users . . . 670,618

Per capita:

Operating income . . . $27.05
percent from local government . . . 82.0%
Operating expenditure . . . $27.82
Total materials . . . 1.57
Print holdings . . . 1.41
Visits . . . 3.65

See Introduction for an explanation of all data sources.

Del Norte County

Demographics & Socio-Economic Characteristics

(2000 U.S. Census, except as noted)

Population

1990* . . . 23,460
2000 . . . 27,507
Male . . . 15,186
Female . . . 12,321
Jan. 2008 (estimate)§ . . . 29,419
Living in unincorporated area . . . 73.9%
2020 (projected)* . . . 36,077

Race & Hispanic Origin, 2000

Race
White . . . 21,693
Black/African American . . . 1,184
North American Native . . . 1,770
Asian . . . 637
Pacific Islander . . . 23
Other Race . . . 1,079
Two or more races . . . 1,121
Hispanic origin, total . . . 3,829
Mexican . . . 3,344
Puerto Rican . . . 53
Cuban . . . 3
Other Hispanic . . . 429

Age & Nativity, 2000

Under 5 years . . . 1,525
18 years and over . . . 20,611
65 years and over . . . 3,448
85 years and over . . . 375
Median Age . . . 36.4
Native-born . . . 25,928
Foreign-born . . . 1,579

Educational Attainment, 2000

Population 25 years and over . . . 18,459
Less than 9th grade . . . 6.7%
High school grad or higher . . . 71.6%
Bachelor's degree or higher . . . 11.0%
Graduate degree . . . 3.0%

Income & Poverty, 1999

Per capita income . . . $14,573
Median household income . . . $29,642
Median family income . . . $36,056
Persons in poverty . . . 17.3%
H'holds receiving public assistance . . . 813
H'holds receiving social security . . . 3,006

Households, 2000

Total households . . . 9,170
With persons under 18 . . . 3,422
With persons over 65 . . . 2,459
Family households . . . 6,293
Single person households . . . 2,322
Persons per household . . . 2.58
Persons per family . . . 3.08

Labor & Employment

Total civilian labor force, 2008§§ . . . 11,530
Unemployment rate . . . 8.8%
Total civilian labor force, 2000 . . . 10,029

Employed persons 16 years and over by occupation, 2000

Managers & professionals . . . 2,176
Service occupations . . . 2,825
Sales & office occupations . . . 1,947
Farming, fishing & forestry . . . 381
Construction & maintenance . . . 784
Production & transportation . . . 846
Self-employed persons . . . 890

* US Census Bureau
** 2000 Decennial Census
§ California Department of Finance
§§ California Employment Development Dept

General Information

981 H St
Suite 200
Crescent City, CA 95531
707-464-7204

Website . . . www.co.del-norte.ca.us
Incorporated . . . March 2, 1857
Form of Government . . . General law
Land Area (sq. miles) . . . 1,007.8
Water Area (sq. miles) . . . 221.9
Persons per sq. mi. of land, 2008 . . . 29.2
Sales tax rate . . . 7.25%

Voters & Gov't Officials

Registered Voters, October 2008

Total . . . 12,681
Democrats . . . 4,782
Republicans . . . 4,789
Declined to state . . . 2,366
Unincorporated area . . . 10,984
Democrats . . . 4,079
Republicans . . . 4,284
Declined to state . . . 1,991

Legislative Districts

US Congressional . . . 1
State Senatorial . . . 4
State Assembly . . . 1

County Officials, 2009

Admin/Manager . . . Jeannine Galatioto
County Clerk . . . Vicki Frazier
District Attorney . . . Michael Riese
Auditor-Controller . . . Christie Babich
Tax Assessor . . . E. Louise Wilson
Tax Collector . . . Dawn Langston
Planning/Dev Dir . . . Ernie Perry
Public Works . . . Ernie Perry
Building Dept Dir . . . Ernie Perry
Sheriff . . . Dean Wilson
Fire/Emerg Mgmt Dir . . . NA
Elections Official . . . Vicki Frazier
County supervisors
District 1 . . . Leslie McNamer
District 2 . . . Martha McClure
District 3 . . . Michael Sullivan
District 4 . . . Gerry Hemmingsen
District 5 . . . David Finigan

Public Safety

County Sheriff's office, 2007

Number of officers . . . 32
Violent crimes . . . 57
Property crimes . . . 225
Arson . . . 3

Housing & Construction

Housing Units

Total, January 2008§ . . . 11,100
Single family units, attached . . . 188
Single family units, detached . . . 6,570
Multiple family units . . . 1,383
Mobile home units . . . 2,959
Occupied units . . . 9,752
Vacancy rate . . . 12.1%
Median rent, 2000** . . . $519
Median SF home value, 2000** . . . $121,100

New Privately Owned Housing Units Authorized by Building Permit, 2007*

	Units	Construction Cost
Single	76	$14,898,556
Total	76	$14,898,556

Property Taxation, FY 2008

Total assessed value . . . $1,647,011,562
Total tax levied . . . $2,970,337
Delinquency rate . . . 3.340%

County Finance, FY 2007

Revenues

Total . . . $53,951,625
Taxes . . . 7,425,198
Special benefits assessment . . . 0
Licenses, permits & franchises . . . 989,341
Fines, forfeitures & penalties . . . 2,659,436
Use of money & property . . . 688,682
Intergovernmental . . . 37,439,973
Service charges . . . 3,875,762
Miscellaneous revenues . . . 873,233
Other financing sources . . . 0

Expenditures

Total . . . $53,415,861
General . . . 6,456,703
Public protection . . . 15,834,602
Public ways & facilities . . . 3,159,145
Health . . . 7,794,752
Sanitation . . . 0
Public assistance . . . 18,735,662
Education . . . 66,720
Recreation & culture . . . 306,202
Debt service . . . 1,062,075

County Schools

Del Norte County Office of Education
301 West Washington Blvd
Crescent City, CA 95531
(707) 464-0200

Superintendent . . . Janice Moorehouse

County-wide School Totals

(2007-08 except where noted)

Number of districts . . . 2
Number of schools . . . 20
Enrollment . . . 4,522
High school graduates, 2006-07 . . . 280
Pupil/teacher ratio . . . 16.3
Average class size . . . 10.8
Students per computer . . . 1.4
Cost per ADA . . . $9,640
Avg teacher salary . . . $60,042

California Achievement Tests 6th ed., 2008

(Pct scoring at or above 50th National Percentile Rank)

	Math	Reading	Language
Grade 3	NA	NA	NA
Grade 7	26%	29%	24%

Academic Performance Index, 2008

Number of students tested . . . 3,313
2007 API (base) . . . 568
2008 API (growth) . . . 574

SAT Testing, 2006-07

Enrollment, Grade 12 . . . 458
percent taking test . . . 21.8%
percent with total score 1,500+ . . . 8.3%

Average Scores:

Math	Verbal	Writing	Total
497	469	463	1,429

County Library

Del Norte County Library District
190 Price Mall
Crescent City, CA 95531
707-464-9793

Librarian . . . Kelly Nolan

Library statistics, FY 2007

Population served . . . 29,341
Internet terminals . . . 4
Annual users . . . 19,968

Per capita:

Operating income . . . $7.33
percent from local government . . . 71.3%
Operating expenditure . . . $7.82
Total materials . . . 1.62
Print holdings . . . 1.53
Visits . . . 3.79

See Introduction for an explanation of all data sources.

Demographics & Socio-Economic Characteristics†
(2007 American Community Survey, except as noted)

Population
1990* ... 125,995
2007 ... 175,689
  Male ... 87,203
  Female ... 88,486
Jan. 2008 (estimate)§ ... 179,722
  Living in unincorporated area ... 81.1%
2020 (projected)* ... 221,140

Race & Hispanic Origin, 2007
Race
  White ... 153,815
  Black/African American ... 828
  North American Native ... 1,936
  Asian ... 8,483
  Pacific Islander ... 49
  Other Race ... 6,597
  Two or more races ... 3,981
Hispanic origin, total ... 20,056
  Mexican ... 15,125
  Puerto Rican ... 139
  Cuban ... 180
  Other Hispanic ... 4,612

Age & Nativity, 2007
Under 5 years ... 9,827
18 years and over ... 137,389
65 years and over ... 19,894
85 years and over ... 2,649
  Median Age ... 40.2
Native-born ... 162,023
Foreign-born ... 13,666

Educational Attainment, 2007
Population 25 years and over ... 120,034
Less than 9th grade ... 2.4%
High school grad or higher ... 92.5%
Bachelor's degree or higher ... 31.0%
Graduate degree ... 9.3%

Income & Poverty, 2007
Per capita income ... $33,095
Median household income ... $64,188
Median family income ... $79,116
Persons in poverty ... 9.0%
H'holds receiving public assistance ... 2,047
H'holds receiving social security ... 17,450

Households, 2007
Total households ... 67,506
  With persons under 18 ... 22,568
  With persons over 65 ... 14,040
  Family households ... 46,763
  Single person households ... 14,969
Persons per household ... 2.59
Persons per family ... 3.05

Labor & Employment
Total civilian labor force, 2008§§ ... 92,400
  Unemployment rate ... 6.9%
Total civilian labor force, 2000* ... 78,027
Employed persons 16 years and over by occupation, 2007
  Managers & professionals ... 33,011
  Service occupations ... 18,709
  Sales & office occupations ... 22,642
  Farming, fishing & forestry ... 80
  Construction & maintenance ... 8,070
  Production & transportation ... 7,496
Self-employed persons ... 9,602

† see Appendix D for 2000 Decennial Census Data
* US Census Bureau
** 2007 American Community Survey
§ California Department of Finance
§§ California Employment Development Dept

General Information
330 Fair Lane
Placerville, CA 95667
530-621-5530

Website ... www.co.el-dorado.ca.us
Incorporated ... February 18, 1850
Form of Government ... Charter
Land Area (sq. miles) ... 1,710.8
Water Area (sq. miles) ... 77.2
Persons per sq. mi. of land, 2008 ... 105.1
Sales tax rate ... 7.25%

Voters & Gov't Officials
Registered Voters, October 2008
Total ... 111,325
  Democrats ... 34,592
  Republicans ... 49,997
  Declined to state ... 20,714
Unincorporated area ... 96,070
  Democrats ... 28,626
  Republicans ... 45,611
  Declined to state ... 16,979

Legislative Districts
US Congressional ... 4
State Senatorial ... 1
State Assembly ... 4, 10

County Officials, 2009
Manager/Admin ... Gayle Hamlin
Clerk-Recorder ... William Schultz
District Attorney ... Vern Pierson
Finance Dir ... Joe Harn
Tax Assessor ... Tim Holcomb
Tax Collector ... Cherie Raffety
Development Svcs Dir ... Roger Trout
Public Works ... Jim Wari (Int)
Building Dept Dir ... Roger Trout
Sheriff ... Jeff Neves
Fire/Emerg Mgmt Dir ... NA
Elections Official ... William Schultz
County supervisors
  District 1 ... John Knight
  District 2 ... Ray Nutting
  District 3 ... Jack Sweeney
  District 4 ... Ron Briggs
  District 5 ... Norma Santiago

Public Safety
County Sheriff's office, 2007
Number of officers ... 196
Violent crimes ... 236
Property crimes ... 2,034
Arson ... 20

Housing & Construction
Housing Units
Total, January 2008§ ... 83,275
  Single family units, attached ... 1,833
  Single family units, detached ... 67,596
  Multiple family units ... 9,469
  Mobile home units ... 4,377
  Occupied units ... 69,251
  Vacancy rate ... 16.8%
Median rent, 2007** ... $965
Median SF home value, 2007** ... $506,500

New Privately Owned Housing Units Authorized by Building Permit, 2007*

	Units	Construction Cost
Single	604	$215,801,698
Total	604	$215,801,698

Property Taxation, FY 2008
Total assessed value ... $26,968,207,448
Total tax levied ... $62,947,250
Delinquency rate ... 3.490%

County Finance, FY 2007
Revenues
Total ... $293,255,465
Taxes ... 92,724,939
Special benefits assessment ... 0
Licenses, permits & franchises ... 46,584,456
Fines, forfeitures & penalties ... 4,594,223
Use of money & property ... 9,602,868
Intergovernmental ... 107,703,889
Service charges ... 27,737,945
Miscellaneous revenues ... 3,393,840
Other financing sources ... 2,515

Expenditures
Total ... $273,191,327
General ... 41,762,747
Public protection ... 102,500,714
Public ways & facilities ... 48,882,876
Health ... 33,050,252
Sanitation ... 0
Public assistance ... 40,376,678
Education ... 3,249,073
Recreation & culture ... 1,071,555
Debt service ... 2,297,432

County Schools
El Dorado County Office of Education
6767 Green Valley Rd
Placerville, CA 95667
(530) 622-7130
Superintendent ... Vicki Barber

County-wide School Totals
(2007-08 except where noted)
Number of districts ... 7
Number of schools ... 38
Enrollment ... 16,355
High school graduates, 2006-07 ... 1,946
Pupil/teacher ratio ... 12.6
Average class size ... 13.0
Students per computer ... 4.1
Cost per ADA ... $7,978
Avg teacher salary ... $62,393

California Achievement Tests 6th ed., 2008
(Pct scoring at or above 50th National Percentile Rank)

	Math	Reading	Language
Grade 3	53%	61%	72%
Grade 7	45%	51%	42%

Academic Performance Index, 2008
Number of students tested ... 11,514
2007 API (base) ... 611
2008 API (growth) ... 615

SAT Testing, 2006-07
Enrollment, Grade 12 ... 2,438
  percent taking test ... 34.7%
  percent with total score 1,500+ ... 23.0%
Average Scores:

Math	Verbal	Writing	Total
552	529	520	1,601

County Library
El Dorado County Library
345 Fair Lane
Placerville, CA 95667
530-621-5540
Librarian ... Jeanne Amos

Library statistics, FY 2007
Population served ... 178,674
Internet terminals ... 39
  Annual users ... 71,838
Per capita:
Operating income ... $16.42
  percent from local government ... 85.4%
Operating expenditure ... $16.31
Total materials ... 2.07
Print holdings ... 1.94
Visits ... 1.38

See Introduction for an explanation of all data sources.

Demographics & Socio-Economic Characteristics†

(2007 American Community Survey, except as noted)

Population

1990* 667,490
2007 899,348
Male 453,150
Female 446,198
Jan. 2008 (estimate)§ 931,098
Living in unincorporated area 18.7%
2020 (projected)* 1,201,792

Race & Hispanic Origin, 2007

Race
White 561,002
Black/African American 44,318
North American Native 9,845
Asian 78,557
Pacific Islander 1,317
Other Race 172,723
Two or more races 31,586
Hispanic origin, total 433,427
Mexican 403,534
Puerto Rican 1,596
Cuban 435
Other Hispanic 27,862

Age & Nativity, 2007

Under 5 years 78,852
18 years and over 630,500
65 years and over 87,161
85 years and over 14,014
Median Age 30.2
Native-born 703,029
Foreign-born 196,319

Educational Attainment, 2007

Population 25 years and over 526,070
Less than 9th grade 16.3%
High school grad or higher 73.0%
Bachelor's degree or higher 18.6%
Graduate degree 5.8%

Income & Poverty, 2007

Per capita income $20,589
Median household income $47,298
Median family income $53,132
Persons in poverty 20.0%
H'holds receiving public assistance 19,211
H'holds receiving social security 64,720

Households, 2007

Total households 280,493
With persons under 18 124,547
With persons over 65 60,763
Family households 203,322
Single person households 61,494
Persons per household 3.15
Persons per family 3.72

Labor & Employment

Total civilian labor force, 2008§§ 435,200
Unemployment rate 10.6%
Total civilian labor force, 2000* 341,640

Employed persons 16 years and over by occupation, 2007

Managers & professionals 106,321
Service occupations 66,994
Sales & office occupations 95,833
Farming, fishing & forestry 29,940
Construction & maintenance 34,085
Production & transportation 46,302
Self-employed persons 26,551

† see Appendix D for 2000 Decennial Census Data
* US Census Bureau
** 2007 American Community Survey
§ California Department of Finance
§§ California Employment Development Dept

General Information

2281 Tulare St
Room 304
Fresno, CA 93721
559-488-1710

Website .... www.co.fresno.ca.us
Incorporated .... April 19, 1856
Form of Government .... Charter
Land Area (sq. miles) 5,962.7
Water Area (sq. miles) 54.7
Persons per sq. mi. of land, 2008 .... 156.2
Sales tax rate 7.98%

Voters & Gov't Officials

Registered Voters, October 2008

Total 382,827
Democrats 153,434
Republicans 163,453
Declined to state 42,911
Unincorporated area 79,784
Democrats 27,498
Republicans 39,793
Declined to state 7,998

Legislative Districts

US Congressional 18-21
State Senatorial 14, 16
State Assembly 29-31

County Officials, 2009

Manager/Admin .... John Navarrette
County Clerk .... Victor Salazar
District Attorney .... Elizabeth Egan
Finance Dir .... Vicki Crow
Tax Assessor .... Robert Werner
Tax Collector .... Vicki Crow
Planning/Dev Dir .... Bernard Jimenez
Public Works .... Alan Weaver
Building Dept Dir .... Bernard Jimenez
Sheriff .... Margaret Mims
Fire/Emerg Mgmt Dir .... NA
Elections Official .... Victor Salazar
County supervisors
District 1 .... Phil Larson
District 2 .... Susan Anderson
District 3 .... Henry Perea
District 4 .... Judy Case
District 5 .... Debbie Poochigian

Public Safety

County Sheriff's office, 2007

Number of officers 487
Violent crimes 618
Property crimes 6,497
Arson .... NA

Housing & Construction

Housing Units

Total, January 2008§ 308,403
Single family units, attached 10,169
Single family units, detached 206,494
Multiple family units 77,745
Mobile home units 13,995
Occupied units 288,552
Vacancy rate 6.4%
Median rent, 2007** $789
Median SF home value, 2007** $296,300

New Privately Owned Housing Units Authorized by Building Permit, 2007*

	Units	Construction Cost
Single	3,645	$622,971,816
Total	4,855	$725,928,287

Property Taxation, FY 2008

Total assessed value $61,749,354,583
Total tax levied $87,862,914
Delinquency rate 2.394%

County Finance, FY 2007

Revenues

Total $1,141,272,138
Taxes 222,301,500
Special benefits assessment 0
Licenses, permits & franchises 9,307,456
Fines, forfeitures & penalties 13,092,834
Use of money & property 15,317,484
Intergovernmental 767,137,405
Service charges 106,571,097
Miscellaneous revenues 5,035,266
Other financing sources 2,509,096

Expenditures

Total $1,143,991,031
General 61,102,432
Public protection 313,203,908
Public ways & facilities 52,618,787
Health 163,891,116
Sanitation 0
Public assistance 490,541,542
Education 29,116,651
Recreation & culture 3,331,118
Debt service 30,185,477

County Schools

Fresno County Office of Education
1111 Van Ness Ave
Fresno, CA 93721
(559) 265-3000

Superintendent .... Larry Powell

County-wide School Totals

(2007-08 except where noted)

Number of districts 28
Number of schools 439
Enrollment 276,874
High school graduates, 2006-07 13,454
Pupil/teacher ratio 10.3
Average class size 13.8
Students per computer 2.2
Cost per ADA $8,643
Avg teacher salary $61,407

California Achievement Tests 6th ed., 2008

(Pct scoring at or above 50th National Percentile Rank)

	Math	Reading	Language
Grade 3	NA	NA	NA
Grade 7	10%	8%	6%

Academic Performance Index, 2008

Number of students tested 201,440
2007 API (base) 534
2008 API (growth) 598

SAT Testing, 2006-07

Enrollment, Grade 12 12,255
percent taking test 30.9%
percent with total score 1,500+ 10.6%

Average Scores:

Math	Verbal	Writing	Total
478	459	456	1,393

County Library

Fresno County Public Library
2420 Mariposa St
Fresno, CA 93721
559-488-3185

Librarian .... Karen Bosch Cobb

Library statistics, FY 2007

Population served 889,019
Internet terminals 277
Annual users 861,240

Per capita:

Operating income $23.69
percent from local government 89.3%
Operating expenditure $23.37
Total materials 2.89
Print holdings 2.69
Visits .... NA

See Introduction for an explanation of all data sources.

Demographics & Socio-Economic Characteristics

(2000 U.S. Census, except as noted)

Population

1990* . . . 24,798
2000 . . . 26,453
Male . . . 13,373
Female . . . 13,080
Jan. 2008 (estimate)§ . . . 29,195
Living in unincorporated area . . . 52.5%
2020 (projected)* . . . 37,959

Race & Hispanic Origin, 2000

Race
White . . . 18,988
Black/African American . . . 155
North American Native . . . 552
Asian . . . 893
Pacific Islander . . . 35
Other Race . . . 4,810
Two or more races . . . 1,020
Hispanic origin, total . . . 7,840
Mexican . . . 6,973
Puerto Rican . . . 39
Cuban . . . 4
Other Hispanic . . . 824

Age & Nativity, 2000

Under 5 years . . . 1,992
18 years and over . . . 18,312
65 years and over . . . 3,431
85 years and over . . . 434
Median Age . . . 33.7
Native-born . . . 21,734
Foreign-born . . . 4,719

Educational Attainment, 2000

Population 25 years and over . . . 16,099
Less than 9th grade . . . 16.0%
High school grad or higher . . . 68.5%
Bachelor's degree or higher . . . 10.7%
Graduate degree . . . 2.9%

Income & Poverty, 1999

Per capita income . . . $14,069
Median household income . . . $32,107
Median family income . . . $37,023
Persons in poverty . . . 17.9%
H'holds receiving public assistance . . . 626
H'holds receiving social security . . . 2,647

Households, 2000

Total households . . . 9,172
With persons under 18 . . . 3,802
With persons over 65 . . . 2,473
Family households . . . 6,733
Single person households . . . 2,022
Persons per household . . . 2.84
Persons per family . . . 3.33

Labor & Employment

Total civilian labor force, 2008§§ . . . 12,330
Unemployment rate . . . 10.5%
Total civilian labor force, 2000 . . . 11,580

Employed persons 16 years and over by occupation, 2000

Managers & professionals . . . 2,566
Service occupations . . . 1,853
Sales & office occupations . . . 2,301
Farming, fishing & forestry . . . 1,276
Construction & maintenance . . . 884
Production & transportation . . . 1,647
Self-employed persons . . . 1,394

* US Census Bureau
** 2000 Decennial Census
§ California Department of Finance
§§ California Employment Development Dept

General Information

526 W Sycamore St
PO Box 931
Willows, CA 95988
530-934-6400

Website . . . www.countyofglenn.net
Incorporated . . . March 11, 1891
Form of Government . . . General law
Land Area (sq. miles) . . . 1,314.8
Water Area (sq. miles) . . . 12.4
Persons per sq. mi. of land, 2008 . . . 22.2
Sales tax rate . . . 7.25%

Voters & Gov't Officials

Registered Voters, October 2008

Total . . . 12,421
Democrats . . . 4,047
Republicans . . . 5,705
Declined to state . . . 2,103
Unincorporated area . . . 6,991
Democrats . . . 2,199
Republicans . . . 3,399
Declined to state . . . 1,074

Legislative Districts

US Congressional . . . 2
State Senatorial . . . 4
State Assembly . . . 2

County Officials, 2009

Administrator . . . David Shoemaker
Clerk-Recorder . . . Sheryl Thur
District Attorney . . . Robert Holzapfel
Auditor-Controller . . . Don Santoro
Tax Assessor . . . Sheryl Thur
Treasurer/Tax Coll . . . Don Santoro
Planning Dir . . . David Shoemaker (Int)
Public Works . . . David Shoemaker (Int)
Building Dept Dir . . David Shoemaker (Int)
Sheriff . . . Larry Jones
Fire/Emerg Mgmt Dir . . . NA
Elections Official . . . Sheryl Thur
County supervisors
District 1 . . . John Viegas
District 2 . . . Tracey Quarne
District 3 . . . Steve Soeth
District 4 . . . Michael Murray
District 5 . . . Leigh McDaniel

Public Safety

County Sheriff's office, 2007

Number of officers . . . 29
Violent crimes . . . 9
Property crimes . . . 133
Arson . . . 1

Housing & Construction

Housing Units

Total, January 2008§ . . . 10,804
Single family units, attached . . . 222
Single family units, detached . . . 7,543
Multiple family units . . . 1,487
Mobile home units . . . 1,552
Occupied units . . . 9,936
Vacancy rate . . . 8.0%
Median rent, 2000** . . . $458
Median SF home value, 2000** . . . $94,900

New Privately Owned Housing Units Authorized by Building Permit, 2007*

	Units	Construction Cost
Single	116	$21,495,946
Total	116	$21,495,946

Property Taxation, FY 2008

Total assessed value . . . $2,419,895,080
Total tax levied . . . $5,052,523
Delinquency rate . . . 2.660%

County Finance, FY 2007

Revenues

Total . . . $61,111,428
Taxes . . . 9,255,435
Special benefits assessment . . . 0
Licenses, permits & franchises . . . 1,075,777
Fines, forfeitures & penalties . . . 1,871,336
Use of money & property . . . 862,732
Intergovernmental . . . 42,141,141
Service charges . . . 4,753,172
Miscellaneous revenues . . . 447,947
Other financing sources . . . 10,960

Expenditures

Total . . . $61,901,393
General . . . 5,315,121
Public protection . . . 18,092,024
Public ways & facilities . . . 4,657,858
Health . . . 12,155,597
Sanitation . . . 0
Public assistance . . . 20,881,735
Education . . . 363,369
Recreation & culture . . . 0
Debt service . . . 435,689

County Schools

Glenn County Office of Education
311 South Villa Ave
Willows, CA 95988
(530) 934-6575

Superintendent . . . Arturo Barrera

County-wide School Totals

(2007-08 except where noted)

Number of districts . . . 6
Number of schools . . . 21
Enrollment . . . 4,804
High school graduates, 2006-07 . . . 263
Pupil/teacher ratio . . . 10.7
Average class size . . . 9.2
Students per computer . . . 1.6
Cost per ADA . . . $8,387
Avg teacher salary . . . $60,915

California Achievement Tests 6th ed., 2008

(Pct scoring at or above 50th National Percentile Rank)

	Math	Reading	Language
Grade 3	NA	NA	NA
Grade 7	38%	29%	5%

Academic Performance Index, 2008

Number of students tested . . . 3,529
2007 API (base) . . . 646
2008 API (growth) . . . 660

SAT Testing, 2006-07

Enrollment, Grade 12 . . . 429
percent taking test . . . 21.2%
percent with total score 1,500+ . . . 9.1%

Average Scores:

Math	Verbal	Writing	Total
490	475	470	1,435

County Library

Served by Orland City Library and Willows City Library

Library statistics, FY 2007

Population served . . . NA
Internet terminals . . . NA
Annual users . . . NA

Per capita:

Operating income . . . NA
percent from local government . . . NA
Operating expenditure . . . NA
Total materials . . . NA
Print holdings . . . NA
Visits . . . NA

See Introduction for an explanation of all data sources.

Demographics & Socio-Economic Characteristics†

(2007 American Community Survey, except as noted)

Population

1990* ... 119,118
2007 ... 128,864
Male ... 64,265
Female ... 64,599
Jan. 2008 (estimate)§ ... 132,821
Living in unincorporated area ... 53.9%
2020 (projected)* ... 142,167

Race & Hispanic Origin, 2007

Race
White ... 105,676
Black/African American ... 1,482
North American Native ... 6,238
Asian ... 2,652
Pacific Islander ... 353
Other Race ... 5,103
Two or more races ... 7,360
Hispanic origin, total ... 10,497
Mexican ... 7,370
Puerto Rican ... 375
Cuban ... 0
Other Hispanic ... 2,752

Age & Nativity, 2007

Under 5 years ... 7,275
18 years and over ... 103,106
65 years and over ... 16,022
85 years and over ... 2,770
Median Age ... 35.3
Native-born ... 122,010
Foreign-born ... 6,854

Educational Attainment, 2007

Population 25 years and over ... 85,890
Less than 9th grade ... 4.3%
High school grad or higher ... 88.9%
Bachelor's degree or higher ... 26.7%
Graduate degree ... 8.2%

Income & Poverty, 2007

Per capita income ... $22,886
Median household income ... $36,870
Median family income ... $48,254
Persons in poverty ... 16.7%
H'holds receiving public assistance ... 1,716
H'holds receiving social security ... 13,557

Households, 2007

Total households ... 51,902
With persons under 18 ... 14,165
With persons over 65 ... 11,666
Family households ... 29,793
Single person households ... 17,083
Persons per household ... 2.38
Persons per family ... 3.00

Labor & Employment

Total civilian labor force, 2008§§ ... 61,000
Unemployment rate ... 7.2%
Total civilian labor force, 2000* ... 60,635

Employed persons 16 years and over by occupation, 2007

Managers & professionals ... 16,786
Service occupations ... 12,184
Sales & office occupations ... 14,272
Farming, fishing & forestry ... 1,791
Construction & maintenance ... 6,386
Production & transportation ... 5,367
Self-employed persons ... 8,814

† see Appendix D for 2000 Decennial Census Data
* US Census Bureau
** 2007 American Community Survey
§ California Department of Finance
§§ California Employment Development Dept

General Information

825 5th St
Eureka, CA 95501
707-445-7266

Website ... www.co.humboldt.ca.us
Incorporated ... May 12, 1853
Form of Government ... General law
Land Area (sq. miles) ... 3,572.5
Water Area (sq. miles) ... 479.7
Persons per sq. mi. of land, 2008 ... 37.2
Sales tax rate ... 7.25%

Voters & Gov't Officials

Registered Voters, October 2008

Total ... 79,140
Democrats ... 34,098
Republicans ... 21,715
Declined to state ... 16,816
Unincorporated area ... 43,156
Democrats ... 18,449
Republicans ... 12,569
Declined to state ... 8,655

Legislative Districts

US Congressional ... 1
State Senatorial ... 2
State Assembly ... 1

County Officials, 2009

Admin Officer ... Loretta Nickolaus
Clerk-Recorder ... Carolyn Crnich
District Attorney ... Paul Gallegos
Auditor-Controller ... Michael Giacone
Assessor ... Linda Hill
Treasurer/Tax Coll ... Stephen A. Strawn
Comm Dev Dir ... Kirk Girard
Public Works ... Tom Mattson
Building ... Steven Taylor
Sheriff ... Gary Philp
Emerg Mgmt Dir ... Gary Philip
Elections Official ... Carolyn Crnich
County supervisors
District 1 ... Jimmy Smith
District 2 ... Cliff Clendenen
District 3 ... Mark Lovelace
District 4 ... Bonnie Neely
District 5 ... Jill Geist

Public Safety

County Sheriff's office, 2007

Number of officers ... 164
Violent crimes ... 136
Property crimes ... 894
Arson ... 4

Housing & Construction

Housing Units

Total, January 2008§ ... 59,370
Single family units, attached ... 1,610
Single family units, detached ... 40,843
Multiple family units ... 10,740
Mobile home units ... 6,177
Occupied units ... 54,389
Vacancy rate ... 8.4%
Median rent, 2007** ... $796
Median SF home value, 2007** ... $321,000

New Privately Owned Housing Units Authorized by Building Permit, 2007*

	Units	Construction Cost
Single	302	$30,957,672
Total	397	$37,248,299

Property Taxation, FY 2008

Total assessed value ... $9,994,853,377
Total tax levied ... $20,118,147
Delinquency rate ... 2.670%

County Finance, FY 2007

Revenues

Total ... $219,418,043
Taxes ... 41,336,302
Special benefits assessment ... 0
Licenses, permits & franchises ... 3,095,953
Fines, forfeitures & penalties ... 2,965,856
Use of money & property ... 1,222,606
Intergovernmental ... 151,028,040
Service charges ... 14,095,136
Miscellaneous revenues ... 5,674,150
Other financing sources ... 0

Expenditures

Total ... $211,538,572
General ... 18,144,258
Public protection ... 55,449,071
Public ways & facilities ... 12,337,720
Health ... 54,877,222
Sanitation ... 0
Public assistance ... 65,064,157
Education ... 2,896,426
Recreation & culture ... 771,667
Debt service ... 1,998,051

County Schools

Humboldt County Office of Education
901 Myrtle Ave
Eureka, CA 95501
(707) 445-7000

Superintendent ... Garry Eagles

County-wide School Totals

(2007-08 except where noted)

Number of districts ... 22
Number of schools ... 77
Enrollment ... 18,008
High school graduates, 2006-07 ... 2,119
Pupil/teacher ratio ... 12.3
Average class size ... 16.3
Students per computer ... 4.4
Cost per ADA ... $9,285
Avg teacher salary ... $56,492

California Achievement Tests 6th ed., 2008

(Pct scoring at or above 50th National Percentile Rank)

	Math	Reading	Language
Grade 3	NA	NA	NA
Grade 7	6%	13%	6%

Academic Performance Index, 2008

Number of students tested ... 12,791
2007 API (base) ... 442
2008 API (growth) ... 516

SAT Testing, 2006-07

Enrollment, Grade 12 ... 1,700
percent taking test ... 25.1%
percent with total score 1,500+ ... 15.8%

Average Scores:

Math	Verbal	Writing	Total
537	537	524	1,598

County Library

Humboldt County Library
1313 Third St
Eureka, CA 95501
707-269-1900

Librarian ... Victor Zazueta (Int)

Library statistics, FY 2007

Population served ... 131,959
Internet terminals ... 46
Annual users ... 20,083

Per capita:

Operating income ... $22.91
percent from local government ... 90.6%
Operating expenditure ... $18.80
Total materials ... 2.54
Print holdings ... 2.38
Visits ... 4.15

See Introduction for an explanation of all data sources.

Demographics & Socio-Economic Characteristics†

(2007 American Community Survey, except as noted)

Population

1990* 109,303
2007 161,867
Male 83,514
Female 78,353
Jan. 2008 (estimate)§ 176,158
Living in unincorporated area 21.7%
2020 (projected)* 239,149

Race & Hispanic Origin, 2007

Race
White 120,389
Black/African American 5,209
North American Native 2,641
Asian 3,025
Pacific Islander 85
Other Race 26,181
Two or more races 4,337
Hispanic origin, total 123,318
Mexican 120,168
Puerto Rican 118
Cuban 0
Other Hispanic 3,032

Age & Nativity, 2007

Under 5 years 15,147
18 years and over 114,470
65 years and over 16,725
85 years and over 2,143
Median Age 30.4
Native-born 115,034
Foreign-born 46,833

Educational Attainment, 2007

Population 25 years and over 93,249
Less than 9th grade 20.3%
High school grad or higher 62.1%
Bachelor's degree or higher 10.6%
Graduate degree 3.2%

Income & Poverty, 2007

Per capita income $14,996
Median household income $31,912
Median family income $39,639
Persons in poverty 21.6%
H'holds receiving public assistance ... 5,283
H'holds receiving social security 13,695

Households, 2007

Total households 46,312
With persons under 18 22,733
With persons over 65 11,986
Family households 36,705
Single person households 8,809
Persons per household 3.25
Persons per family 3.72

Labor & Employment

Total civilian labor force, 2008§§ 73,500
Unemployment rate 22.9%
Total civilian labor force, 2000* 50,467

Employed persons 16 years and over by occupation, 2007

Managers & professionals 13,696
Service occupations 11,885
Sales & office occupations 14,438
Farming, fishing & forestry 2,939
Construction & maintenance 4,369
Production & transportation 6,596
Self-employed persons 3,932

† see Appendix D for 2000 Decennial Census Data
* US Census Bureau
** 2007 American Community Survey
§ California Department of Finance
§§ California Employment Development Dept

General Information

940 Main St
El Centro, CA 92243
760-482-4220

Website .... www.co.imperial.ca.us
Incorporated .... August 15, 1907
Form of Government .... General law
Land Area (sq. miles) 4,174.7
Water Area (sq. miles) 307.0
Persons per sq. mi. of land, 2008 ...... 42.2
Sales tax rate 7.75%

Voters & Gov't Officials

Registered Voters, October 2008

Total 58,150
Democrats 30,564
Republicans 16,249
Declined to state 9,484
Unincorporated area 10,988
Democrats 4,848
Republicans 3,933
Declined to state 1,734

Legislative Districts

US Congressional 51
State Senatorial 40
State Assembly 80

County Officials, 2009

Manager/Admin .... Ralph Cordova Jr
County Clerk .... Sylvia Burmudez
District Attorney .... Gilbert Otero
Finance Dir .... Doug Newland
Tax Assessor .... Roy Buckner
Tax Collector .... Karen Vogel
Planning/Dev Dir .... Jurg Heuberger
Public Works .... William Brunet
Building .... Jurg Heuberger
Sheriff .... Raymond Loera
Fire Chief .... Fred Nippons
Elections Official .... Dolores Provencio
County supervisors
District 1 .... Victor Carrillo
District 2 .... Jack Terrazas
District 3 .... Michael Kelley
District 4 .... Gary Wyatt
District 5 .... Wally Leimgruber

Public Safety

County Sheriff's office, 2007

Number of officers 177
Violent crimes 106
Property crimes 945
Arson 6

Housing & Construction

Housing Units

Total, January 2008§ 55,599
Single family units, attached 2,124
Single family units, detached 34,235
Multiple family units 11,385
Mobile home units 7,855
Occupied units 49,484
Vacancy rate 11.0%
Median rent, 2007** $615
Median SF home value, 2007** $247,000

New Privately Owned Housing Units Authorized by Building Permit, 2007*

	Units	Construction Cost
Single	648	$96,909,036
Total	969	$120,179,501

Property Taxation, FY 2008

Total assessed value $10,233,444,219
Total tax levied $15,573,556
Delinquency rate 11.400%

County Finance, FY 2007

Revenues

Total $239,828,531
Taxes 40,408,384
Special benefits assessment 0
Licenses, permits & franchises ... 4,398,839
Fines, forfeitures & penalties 6,714,443
Use of money & property 2,613,459
Intergovernmental 161,049,898
Service charges 20,614,884
Miscellaneous revenues 2,982,303
Other financing sources 264,298

Expenditures

Total $229,615,051
General 18,846,847
Public protection 67,604,880
Public ways & facilities 11,007,348
Health 38,994,729
Sanitation 0
Public assistance 84,567,407
Education 1,219,582
Recreation & culture 476,478
Debt service 6,897,780

County Schools

Imperial County Office of Education
1398 Sperber Rd
El Centro, CA 92243
(760) 312-6464

Superintendent .... John Anderson

County-wide School Totals

(2007-08 except where noted)

Number of districts 15
Number of schools 60
Enrollment 36,120
High school graduates, 2006-07 2,391
Pupil/teacher ratio 17.1
Average class size 20.2
Students per computer 3.0
Cost per ADA $8,225
Avg teacher salary $64,054

California Achievement Tests 6th ed., 2008

(Pct scoring at or above 50th National Percentile Rank)

	Math	Reading	Language
Grade 3	NA	NA	NA
Grade 7	9%	12%	12%

Academic Performance Index, 2008

Number of students tested 27,734
2007 API (base) 461
2008 API (growth) 476

SAT Testing, 2006-07

Enrollment, Grade 12 2,529
percent taking test 29.2%
percent with total score 1,500+ 7.5%

Average Scores:

Math	Verbal	Writing	Total
458	450	441	1,349

County Library

Imperial County Library
1331 S Clark
El Centro, CA 92243
760-339-6460

Librarian .... Connie Barrington

Library statistics, FY 2007

Population served 55,503
Internet terminals 27
Annual users 21,222

Per capita:

Operating income $14.19
percent from local government 83.9%
Operating expenditure $12.85
Total materials 1.05
Print holdings 0.96
Visits 0.80

See Introduction for an explanation of all data sources.

Demographics & Socio-Economic Characteristics

(2000 U.S. Census, except as noted)

Population

1990* . . . 18,281
2000 . . . 17,945
Male . . . 8,761
Female . . . 9,184
Jan. 2008 (estimate)§ . . . 18,152
Living in unincorporated area . . . 80.4%
2020 (projected)* . . . 20,495

Race & Hispanic Origin, 2000

Race
White . . . 14,367
Black/African American . . . 29
North American Native . . . 1,802
Asian . . . 163
Pacific Islander . . . 15
Other Race . . . 825
Two or more races . . . 744
Hispanic origin, total . . . 2,257
Mexican . . . 1,945
Puerto Rican . . . 17
Cuban . . . 11
Other Hispanic . . . 284

Age & Nativity, 2000

Under 5 years . . . 961
18 years and over . . . 13,569
65 years and over . . . 3,429
85 years and over . . . 415
Median Age . . . 42.8
Native-born . . . 16,578
Foreign-born . . . 1,367

Educational Attainment, 2000

Population 25 years and over . . . 12,566
Less than 9th grade . . . 4.3%
High school grad or higher . . . 82.3%
Bachelor's degree or higher . . . 17.1%
Graduate degree . . . 6.6%

Income & Poverty, 1999

Per capita income . . . $19,639
Median household income . . . $35,006
Median family income . . . $44,970
Persons in poverty . . . 12.5%
H'holds receiving public assistance . . . 290
H'holds receiving social security . . . 2,584

Households, 2000

Total households . . . 7,703
With persons under 18 . . . 2,331
With persons over 65 . . . 2,421
Family households . . . 4,937
Single person households . . . 2,416
Persons per household . . . 2.31
Persons per family . . . 2.88

Labor & Employment

Total civilian labor force, 2008§§ . . . 9,190
Unemployment rate . . . 6.7%
Total civilian labor force, 2000 . . . 8,510

Employed persons 16 years and over by occupation, 2000

Managers & professionals . . . 2,212
Service occupations . . . 1,865
Sales & office occupations . . . 1,994
Farming, fishing & forestry . . . 117
Construction & maintenance . . . 957
Production & transportation . . . 862
Self-employed persons . . . 718

* US Census Bureau
** 2000 Decennial Census
§ California Department of Finance
§§ California Employment Development Dept

General Information

PO Drawer N
168 N Edwards St
Independence, CA 93526
760-878-0366

Website . . . www.countyofinyo.org
Incorporated . . . March 22, 1866
Form of Government . . . General law
Land Area (sq. miles) . . . 10,203.1
Water Area (sq. miles) . . . 23.9
Persons per sq. mi. of land, 2008 . . . 1.8
Sales tax rate . . . 7.75%

Voters & Gov't Officials

Registered Voters, October 2008

Total . . . 10,258
Democrats . . . 3,406
Republicans . . . 4,581
Declined to state . . . 1,747
Unincorporated area . . . 8,570
Democrats . . . 2,817
Republicans . . . 3,895
Declined to state . . . 1,408

Legislative Districts

US Congressional . . . 25
State Senatorial . . . 18
State Assembly . . . 34

County Officials, 2009

Manager/Admin . . . Kevin Carunchio
County Clerk . . . Mary Roper
District Attorney . . . Art Maillet
Auditor/Controller . . . Leslie Chapman
Tax Assessor . . . Tom Lanshaw
Treasurer/Tax Coll . . . Alisha McMurtrie
Economic Dev Dir . . . Kevin Carunchio
Public Works . . . Bernard Pedersen
Building Dept Dir . . . Bernard Pedersen
Sheriff . . . Bill Lutze
Fire/Emerg Mgmt Dir . . . NA
Elections Official . . . Mary Roper
County supervisors
District 1 . . . Linda Arcularius
District 2 . . . Susan Cash
District 3 . . . Beverly Brown
District 4 . . . Marty Fortney
District 5 . . . Richard Cervantes

Public Safety

County Sheriff's office, 2007

Number of officers . . . 51
Violent crimes . . . 104
Property crimes . . . 132
Arson . . . 2

Housing & Construction

Housing Units

Total, January 2008§ . . . 9,277
Single family units, attached . . . 215
Single family units, detached . . . 5,536
Multiple family units . . . 887
Mobile home units . . . 2,639
Occupied units . . . 7,903
Vacancy rate . . . 14.8%
Median rent, 2000** . . . $516
Median SF home value, 2000** . . . $161,300

New Privately Owned Housing Units Authorized by Building Permit, 2007*

	Units	Construction Cost
Single	13	$3,290,935
Total	25	$3,689,330

Property Taxation, FY 2008

Total assessed value . . . $3,500,152,254
Total tax levied . . . $10,450,050
Delinquency rate . . . 1.300%

County Finance, FY 2007

Revenues

Total . . . $55,045,332
Taxes . . . 14,859,304
Special benefits assessment . . . 0
Licenses, permits & franchises . . . 471,946
Fines, forfeitures & penalties . . . 1,735,822
Use of money & property . . . 2,188,834
Intergovernmental . . . 31,414,605
Service charges . . . 4,274,923
Miscellaneous revenues . . . 82,827
Other financing sources . . . 17,071

Expenditures

Total . . . $52,554,321
General . . . 9,263,650
Public protection . . . 20,887,631
Public ways & facilities . . . 4,180,200
Health . . . 8,482,380
Sanitation . . . 24,659
Public assistance . . . 6,303,072
Education . . . 765,454
Recreation & culture . . . 1,686,304
Debt service . . . 960,971

County Schools

Inyo County Office of Education
PO Drawer G
Independence, CA 93526
(760) 878-2426

Superintendent . . . Terence McAteer

County-wide School Totals

(2007-08 except where noted)

Number of districts . . . 3
Number of schools . . . 10
Enrollment . . . 2,084
High school graduates, 2006-07 . . . 194
Pupil/teacher ratio . . . 6.0
Average class size . . . 4.7
Students per computer . . . 1.1
Cost per ADA . . . $10,597
Avg teacher salary . . . $60,079

California Achievement Tests 6th ed., 2008

(Pct scoring at or above 50th National Percentile Rank)

	Math	Reading	Language
Grade 3	NA	NA	NA
Grade 7	NA	NA	NA

Academic Performance Index, 2008

Number of students tested . . . 1,564
2007 API (base) . . . 403
2008 API (growth) . . . 480

SAT Testing, 2006-07

Enrollment, Grade 12 . . . 264
percent taking test . . . 41.3%
percent with total score 1,500+ . . . 21.6%

Average Scores:

Math	Verbal	Writing	Total
516	516	492	1,524

County Library

Inyo County Free Library
PO Drawer K
Independence, CA 93526
760-878-0262

Librarian . . . Kevin Carunchio

Library statistics, FY 2007

Population served . . . 18,383
Internet terminals . . . 10
Annual users . . . 20,730

Per capita:

Operating income . . . $36.81
percent from local government . . . 97.1%
Operating expenditure . . . $36.81
Total materials . . . 5.76
Print holdings . . . 5.43
Visits . . . NA

See Introduction for an explanation of all data sources.

Demographics & Socio-Economic Characteristics†

(2007 American Community Survey, except as noted)

Population

1990* ... 543,477
2007 ... 790,710
Male ... 409,510
Female ... 381,200
Jan. 2008 (estimate)§ ... 817,517
Living in unincorporated area ... 36.5%
2020 (projected)* ... 1,086,113

Race & Hispanic Origin, 2007

Race
White ... 483,273
Black/African American ... 46,146
North American Native ... 8,323
Asian ... 30,519
Pacific Islander ... 1,038
Other Race ... 195,821
Two or more races ... 25,590
Hispanic origin, total ... 365,836
Mexican ... 333,745
Puerto Rican ... 2,950
Cuban ... 517
Other Hispanic ... 28,624

Age & Nativity, 2007

Under 5 years ... 70,418
18 years and over ... 553,690
65 years and over ... 69,562
85 years and over ... 8,316
Median Age ... 29.8
Native-born ... 627,960
Foreign-born ... 162,750

Educational Attainment, 2007

Population 25 years and over ... 465,482
Less than 9th grade ... 15.7%
High school grad or higher ... 70.1%
Bachelor's degree or higher ... 14.1%
Graduate degree ... 4.9%

Income & Poverty, 2007

Per capita income ... $19,921
Median household income ... $47,105
Median family income ... $50,707
Persons in poverty ... 18.1%
H'holds receiving public assistance ... 12,117
H'holds receiving social security ... 59,325

Households, 2007

Total households ... 239,662
With persons under 18 ... 116,648
With persons over 65 ... 48,568
Family households ... 181,544
Single person households ... 47,436
Persons per household ... 3.13
Persons per family ... 3.58

Labor & Employment

Total civilian labor force, 2008§§ ... 363,700
Unemployment rate ... 9.8%
Total civilian labor force, 2000* ... 264,158

Employed persons 16 years and over by occupation, 2007

Managers & professionals ... 79,429
Service occupations ... 60,657
Sales & office occupations ... 68,896
Farming, fishing & forestry ... 21,595
Construction & maintenance ... 40,195
Production & transportation ... 38,296
Self-employed persons ... 20,178

† see Appendix D for 2000 Decennial Census Data
* US Census Bureau
** 2007 American Community Survey
§ California Department of Finance
§§ California Employment Development Dept

General Information

1115 Truxtun Ave
Bakersfield, CA 93301
661-868-3140

Website ... www.co.kern.ca.us
Incorporated ... April 2, 1866
Form of Government ... General law
Land Area (sq. miles) ... 8,141.0
Water Area (sq. miles) ... 20.5
Persons per sq. mi. of land, 2008 ... 100.4
Sales tax rate ... 7.25%

Voters & Gov't Officials

Registered Voters, October 2008

Total ... 311,137
Democrats ... 112,084
Republicans ... 140,043
Declined to state ... 47,873
Unincorporated area ... 119,792
Democrats ... 39,396
Republicans ... 57,373
Declined to state ... 18,092

Legislative Districts

US Congressional ... 20, 22
State Senatorial ... 16, 18
State Assembly ... 30, 32, 34

County Officials, 2009

Admin Officer ... Elisa D. Ladd (Int)
County Clerk ... Ann Barnett
District Attorney ... Ed Jagels
Auditor-Controller ... Ann Barnett
Tax Assessor ... Jim Fitch
Tax Collector ... Jackie Denny
Comm & Econ Dev Dir ... Barry Jung
Public Works ... NA
Building Dept Dir ... Charles Lackey
Sheriff ... Donny Youngblood
Fire Chief ... Dennis Thompson
Elections Official ... Ann Barnett
County supervisors
District 1 ... Jon McQuiston
District 2 ... Don Maben
District 3 ... Mike Maggard
District 4 ... Ray Watson
District 5 ... Michael J. Rubio

Public Safety

County Sheriff's office, 2007

Number of officers ... 476
Violent crimes ... 1,918
Property crimes ... 11,001
Arson ... 286

Housing & Construction

Housing Units

Total, January 2008§ ... 276,602
Single family units, attached ... 8,550
Single family units, detached ... 193,696
Multiple family units ... 48,165
Mobile home units ... 26,191
Occupied units ... 249,380
Vacancy rate ... 9.8%
Median rent, 2007** ... $758
Median SF home value, 2007** ... $256,800

New Privately Owned Housing Units Authorized by Building Permit, 2007*

	Units	Construction Cost
Single	3,318	$462,847,124
Total	4,202	$525,296,922

Property Taxation, FY 2008

Total assessed value ... $79,198,986,938
Total tax levied ... $216,584,819
Delinquency rate ... 3.480%

County Finance, FY 2007

Revenues

Total ... $1,170,495,350
Taxes ... 336,365,116
Special benefits assessment ... 0
Licenses, permits & franchises ... 15,051,930
Fines, forfeitures & penalties ... 23,212,634
Use of money & property ... 31,119,325
Intergovernmental ... 641,276,870
Service charges ... 110,652,900
Miscellaneous revenues ... 12,537,284
Other financing sources ... 279,291

Expenditures

Total ... $1,065,031,239
General ... 73,602,709
Public protection ... 395,125,121
Public ways & facilities ... 41,974,123
Health ... 127,346,147
Sanitation ... 0
Public assistance ... 365,291,491
Education ... 9,877,997
Recreation & culture ... 13,353,502
Debt service ... 38,460,149

County Schools

Kern County Office of Education
1300 17th St, City Centre
Bakersfield, CA 93301
(661) 636-4000

Superintendent ... Larry Reider

County-wide School Totals

(2007-08 except where noted)

Number of districts ... 35
Number of schools ... 270
Enrollment ... 238,362
High school graduates, 2006-07 ... 21,244
Pupil/teacher ratio ... 14.0
Average class size ... 11.8
Students per computer ... 4.3
Cost per ADA ... $8,411
Avg teacher salary ... $59,912

California Achievement Tests 6th ed., 2008

(Pct scoring at or above 50th National Percentile Rank)

	Math	Reading	Language
Grade 3	28%	26%	30%
Grade 7	27%	29%	27%

Academic Performance Index, 2008

Number of students tested ... 176,628
2007 API (base) ... 702
2008 API (growth) ... 693

SAT Testing, 2006-07

Enrollment, Grade 12 ... 12,087
percent taking test ... 23.7%
percent with total score 1,500+ ... 9.0%

Average Scores:

Math	Verbal	Writing	Total
486	469	463	1,418

County Library

Kern County Library
701 Truxtun Ave
Bakersfield, CA 93301
661-868-0700

Librarian ... Diane Duquette

Library statistics, FY 2007

Population served ... 801,648
Internet terminals ... 237
Annual users ... 337,030

Per capita:

Operating income ... $12.11
percent from local government ... 90.4%
Operating expenditure ... $12.11
Total materials ... 1.37
Print holdings ... 1.29
Visits ... 2.09

See Introduction for an explanation of all data sources.

Demographics & Socio-Economic Characteristics†

(2007 American Community Survey, except as noted)

Population

1990* . . . 101,469
2007 . . . 148,875
Male . . . 86,400
Female . . . 62,475
Jan. 2008 (estimate)§ . . . 154,434
Living in unincorporated area . . . 22.9%
2020 (projected)* . . . 205,707

Race & Hispanic Origin, 2007

Race
White . . . 97,124
Black/African American . . . 11,882
North American Native . . . 1,704
Asian . . . 5,383
Pacific Islander . . . 145
Other Race . . . 28,119
Two or more races . . . 4,518
Hispanic origin, total . . . 71,812
Mexican . . . 66,170
Puerto Rican . . . 1,287
Cuban . . . 151
Other Hispanic . . . 4,204

Age & Nativity, 2007

Under 5 years . . . 12,437
18 years and over . . . 108,863
65 years and over . . . 10,611
85 years and over . . . 1,159
Median Age . . . 29.5
Native-born . . . 119,472
Foreign-born . . . 29,403

Educational Attainment, 2007

Population 25 years and over . . . 88,446
Less than 9th grade . . . 16.0%
High school grad or higher . . . 72.1%
Bachelor's degree or higher . . . 12.8%
Graduate degree . . . 3.9%

Income & Poverty, 2007

Per capita income . . . $17,228
Median household income . . . $46,756
Median family income . . . $51,906
Persons in poverty . . . 15.1%
H'holds receiving public assistance . . . 2,795
H'holds receiving social security . . . 8,158

Households, 2007

Total households . . . 39,014
With persons under 18 . . . 19,915
With persons over 65 . . . 7,884
Family households . . . 30,501
Single person households . . . 6,998
Persons per household . . . 3.30
Persons per family . . . 3.72

Labor & Employment

Total civilian labor force, 2008§§ . . . 59,000
Unemployment rate . . . 10.7%
Total civilian labor force, 2000* . . . 45,717

Employed persons 16 years and over by occupation, 2007

Managers & professionals . . . 13,421
Service occupations . . . 8,297
Sales & office occupations . . . 9,643
Farming, fishing & forestry . . . 6,197
Construction & maintenance . . . 4,666
Production & transportation . . . 7,437
Self-employed persons . . . 3,036

† see Appendix D for 2000 Decennial Census Data
* US Census Bureau
** 2007 American Community Survey
§ California Department of Finance
§§ California Employment Development Dept

General Information

1400 W Lacey Blvd
Hanford, CA 93230
559-582-3211

Website . . . www.countyofkings.com
Incorporated . . . March 22, 1893
Form of Government . . . General law
Land Area (sq. miles) . . . 1,391.0
Water Area (sq. miles) . . . 0.5
Persons per sq. mi. of land, 2008 . . . 111.0
Sales tax rate . . . 7.25%

Voters & Gov't Officials

Registered Voters, October 2008

Total . . . 49,658
Democrats . . . 18,626
Republicans . . . 22,685
Declined to state . . . 6,585
Unincorporated area . . . 11,919
Democrats . . . 4,121
Republicans . . . 5,921
Declined to state . . . 1,467

Legislative Districts

US Congressional . . . 20
State Senatorial . . . 16
State Assembly . . . 30

County Officials, 2009

Administrator . . . Larry Spikes
Clerk-Recorder . . . Ken Baird
District Attorney . . . Ron Calhoun
Auditor-Controller . . . Doil T. O'Steen
Tax Assessor . . . Ken Baird
Treasurer/Tax Coll . . . Doil T. O'Steen
Planning Dir . . . Bill Zumwalt
Public Works . . . Harry Verheul
Building Dept Dir . . . Bill Zumwalt
Sheriff . . . Chris Jordan
Fire Chief . . . Jim Kilner
Elections Official . . . Ken Baird
County supervisors
District 1 . . . Joe Neves
District 2 . . . Richard Valle
District 3 . . . Tony Oliveira
District 4 . . . Tony Barba
District 5 . . . Richard Fagundes

Public Safety

County Sheriff's office, 2007

Number of officers . . . 81
Violent crimes . . . 113
Property crimes . . . 460
Arson . . . NA

Housing & Construction

Housing Units

Total, January 2008§ . . . 42,161
Single family units, attached . . . 2,737
Single family units, detached . . . 29,696
Multiple family units . . . 7,476
Mobile home units . . . 2,252
Occupied units . . . 39,767
Vacancy rate . . . 5.7%
Median rent, 2007** . . . $716
Median SF home value, 2007** . . . $240,700

New Privately Owned Housing Units Authorized by Building Permit, 2007*

	Units	Construction Cost
Single	472	$75,292,920
Total	497	$77,097,595

Property Taxation, FY 2008

Total assessed value . . . $7,853,008,491
Total tax levied . . . $19,048,417
Delinquency rate . . . 3.400%

County Finance, FY 2007

Revenues

Total . . . $174,045,503
Taxes . . . 38,603,060
Special benefits assessment . . . 0
Licenses, permits & franchises . . . 1,473,184
Fines, forfeitures & penalties . . . 1,104,630
Use of money & property . . . 3,421,438
Intergovernmental . . . 112,130,232
Service charges . . . 10,465,263
Miscellaneous revenues . . . 6,831,734
Other financing sources . . . 15,962

Expenditures

Total . . . $169,144,073
General . . . 15,318,231
Public protection . . . 58,948,678
Public ways & facilities . . . 5,475,403
Health . . . 25,131,464
Sanitation . . . 0
Public assistance . . . 60,048,553
Education . . . 1,747,361
Recreation & culture . . . 1,559,113
Debt service . . . 915,270

County Schools

Kings County Office of Education
1144 West Lacey Blvd
Hanford, CA 93230
(559) 584-1441

Superintendent . . . John Stankovich

County-wide School Totals

(2007-08 except where noted)

Number of districts . . . 14
Number of schools . . . 60
Enrollment . . . 26,601
High school graduates, 2006-07 . . . 1,217
Pupil/teacher ratio . . . 11.2
Average class size . . . 14.9
Students per computer . . . 2.3
Cost per ADA . . . $8,334
Avg teacher salary . . . $59,464

California Achievement Tests 6th ed., 2008

(Pct scoring at or above 50th National Percentile Rank)

	Math	Reading	Language
Grade 3	NA	NA	NA
Grade 7	NA	NA	NA

Academic Performance Index, 2008

Number of students tested . . . 20,113
2007 API (base) . . . 429
2008 API (growth) . . . 496

SAT Testing, 2006-07

Enrollment, Grade 12 . . . 1,748
percent taking test . . . 24.3%
percent with total score 1,500+ . . . 7.7%

Average Scores:

Math	Verbal	Writing	Total
466	456	446	1,368

County Library

Kings County Library
401 N Douty St
Hanford, CA 93230
559-582-0261

Librarian . . . Eleanor Louise Hodges

Library statistics, FY 2007

Population served . . . 151,381
Internet terminals . . . 59
Annual users . . . 42,581

Per capita:

Operating income . . . $11.91
percent from local government . . . 86.5%
Operating expenditure . . . $11.91
Total materials . . . 1.20
Print holdings . . . 1.17
Visits . . . NA

See Introduction for an explanation of all data sources.

Demographics & Socio-Economic Characteristics†

(2007 American Community Survey, except as noted)

Population

1990* 50,631
2007 64,664
Male 32,081
Female 32,583
Jan. 2008 (estimate)§ 64,059
Living in unincorporated area 69.9%
2020 (projected)* 77,912

Race & Hispanic Origin, 2007

Race
White 56,968
Black/African American 1,177
North American Native 1,910
Asian 660
Pacific Islander 0
Other Race 1,593
Two or more races 2,356
Hispanic origin, total 9,911
Mexican .... NA
Puerto Rican .... NA
Cuban .... NA
Other Hispanic .... NA

Age & Nativity, 2007

Under 5 years 4,206
18 years and over 50,570
65 years and over 11,168
85 years and over 1,046
Median Age 42.1
Native-born 60,896
Foreign-born 3,768

Educational Attainment, 2007

Population 25 years and over 46,582
Less than 9th grade 3.5%
High school grad or higher 87.9%
Bachelor's degree or higher 15.3%
Graduate degree 4.7%

Income & Poverty, 2007

Per capita income $22,057
Median household income $40,946
Median family income $51,994
Persons in poverty 15.5%
H'holds receiving public assistance 1,357
H'holds receiving social security 7,714

Households, 2007

Total households 23,326
With persons under 18 7,024
With persons over 65 7,001
Family households 15,680
Single person households 5,915
Persons per household 2.74
Persons per family 3.23

Labor & Employment

Total civilian labor force, 2008§§ 24,620
Unemployment rate 10.8%
Total civilian labor force, 2000* 23,025

Employed persons 16 years and over by occupation, 2007

Managers & professionals .... NA
Service occupations .... NA
Sales & office occupations .... NA
Farming, fishing & forestry .... NA
Construction & maintenance .... NA
Production & transportation .... NA
Self-employed persons 3,181

† see Appendix D for 2000 Decennial Census Data
* US Census Bureau
** 2007 American Community Survey
§ California Department of Finance
§§ California Employment Development Dept

General Information

255 North Forbes St
Lakeport, CA 95453
707-263-2311

Website .... www.co.lake.ca.us
Incorporated .... May 20, 1861
Form of Government .... General law
Land Area (sq. miles) 1,258.0
Water Area (sq. miles) 71.5
Persons per sq. mi. of land, 2008 .... 50.9
Sales tax rate 7.25%

Voters & Gov't Officials

Registered Voters, October 2008

Total 35,154
Democrats 15,292
Republicans 10,545
Declined to state 7,335
Unincorporated area 25,893
Democrats 10,852
Republicans 8,229
Declined to state 5,356

Legislative Districts

US Congressional 1
State Senatorial 2
State Assembly 1

County Officials, 2009

Administrator .... Kelly Cox
County Clerk .... Pam Cochrane
District Attorney .... Jon Hopkins
Auditor-Controller .... Pam Cochrane
Tax Assessor .... Douglas Wacker
Treasurer/Tax Coll .... Sandra Kacharos
Comm Dev Dir .... Rick Coel
Public Works .... Brent Siemer
Building Dept Dir .... Rick Coel
Sheriff .... Rod Mitchell
Emerg Mgmt Coord .... Jerry Wilson
Elections Official .... Diane C. Fridley
County supervisors
District 1 .... Ed Robey
District 2 .... Jeff Smith
District 3 .... Denise Rushing
District 4 .... Anthony Farrington
District 5 .... Rob Brown

Public Safety

County Sheriff's office, 2007

Number of officers 57
Violent crimes 147
Property crimes 754
Arson 18

Housing & Construction

Housing Units

Total, January 2008§ 35,348
Single family units, attached 863
Single family units, detached 22,129
Multiple family units 2,031
Mobile home units 10,325
Occupied units 26,042
Vacancy rate 26.3%
Median rent, 2007** $875
Median SF home value, 2007** $301,800

New Privately Owned Housing Units Authorized by Building Permit, 2007*

	Units	Construction Cost
Single	335	$57,644,290
Total	405	$64,219,540

Property Taxation, FY 2008

Total assessed value $6,678,012,687
Total tax levied $15,199,819
Delinquency rate 5.087%

County Finance, FY 2007

Revenues

Total $112,912,122
Taxes 28,890,186
Special benefits assessment 0
Licenses, permits & franchises 2,103,719
Fines, forfeitures & penalties 1,663,947
Use of money & property 2,695,082
Intergovernmental 65,329,991
Service charges 10,315,841
Miscellaneous revenues 1,901,546
Other financing sources 11,810

Expenditures

Total $108,704,855
General 13,923,556
Public protection 33,698,849
Public ways & facilities 7,903,467
Health 17,257,104
Sanitation 0
Public assistance 32,201,268
Education 1,398,553
Recreation & culture 2,322,058
Debt service 0

County Schools

Lake County Office of Education
1152 South Main St
Lakeport, CA 95453
(707) 262-4100

Superintendent .... David Geck

County-wide School Totals

(2007-08 except where noted)

Number of districts 3
Number of schools 20
Enrollment 4,873
High school graduates, 2006-07 307
Pupil/teacher ratio 18.8
Average class size 15.1
Students per computer 0.9
Cost per ADA $9,030
Avg teacher salary $52,271

California Achievement Tests 6th ed., 2008

(Pct scoring at or above 50th National Percentile Rank)

	Math	Reading	Language
Grade 3	NA	NA	NA
Grade 7	NA	NA	NA

Academic Performance Index, 2008

Number of students tested 3,751
2007 API (base) 480
2008 API (growth) 466

SAT Testing, 2006-07

Enrollment, Grade 12 754
percent taking test 22.9%
percent with total score 1,500+ 11.1%

Average Scores:

Math	Verbal	Writing	Total
500	497	488	1,485

County Library

Lake County Library
1425 N High St
Lakeport, CA 95453
707-263-8816

Librarian .... Kathleen Jansen

Library statistics, FY 2007

Population served 64,276
Internet terminals 24
Annual users 20,128

Per capita:

Operating income $20.31
percent from local government 53.0%
Operating expenditure $18.27
Total materials 2.08
Print holdings 1.98
Visits 3.73

Lassen County

Demographics & Socio-Economic Characteristics

(2000 U.S. Census, except as noted)

Population

1990*	27,598
2000	33,828
Male	21,241
Female	12,587
Jan. 2008 (estimate)§	35,757
Living in unincorporated area	50.9%
2020 (projected)*	42,394

Race & Hispanic Origin, 2000

Race	
White	27,336
Black/African American	2,992
North American Native	1,104
Asian	249
Pacific Islander	146
Other Race	1,092
Two or more races	909
Hispanic origin, total	4,681
Mexican	4,101
Puerto Rican	63
Cuban	17
Other Hispanic	500

Age & Nativity, 2000

Under 5 years	1,679
18 years and over	26,439
65 years and over	3,054
85 years and over	291
Median Age	34.6
Native-born	33,039
Foreign-born	789

Educational Attainment, 2000

Population 25 years and over	22,963
Less than 9th grade	4.2%
High school grad or higher	79.6%
Bachelor's degree or higher	10.7%
Graduate degree	3.0%

Income & Poverty, 1999

Per capita income	$14,749
Median household income	$36,310
Median family income	$43,398
Persons in poverty	10.3%
H'holds receiving public assistance	626
H'holds receiving social security	2,645

Households, 2000

Total households	9,625
With persons under 18	3,734
With persons over 65	2,186
Family households	6,777
Single person households	2,354
Persons per household	2.59
Persons per family	3.08

Labor & Employment

Total civilian labor force, 2008§§	13,100
Unemployment rate	9.5%
Total civilian labor force, 2000	11,218

Employed persons 16 years and over by occupation, 2000

Managers & professionals	3,044
Service occupations	2,852
Sales & office occupations	2,099
Farming, fishing & forestry	234
Construction & maintenance	1,021
Production & transportation	911
Self-employed persons	1,006

* US Census Bureau
** 2000 Decennial Census
§ California Department of Finance
§§ California Employment Development Dept

General Information

221 S Roop St
Suite 4
Susanville, CA 96130
530-251-8333

Website	www.lassencounty.org
Incorporated	April 1, 1864
Form of Government	General law
Land Area (sq. miles)	4,557.3
Water Area (sq. miles)	163.1
Persons per sq. mi. of land, 2008	7.8
Sales tax rate	7.25%

Voters & Gov't Officials

Registered Voters, October 2008

Total	14,097
Democrats	4,040
Republicans	6,714
Declined to state	2,557
Unincorporated area	9,401
Democrats	2,634
Republicans	4,614
Declined to state	1,623

Legislative Districts

US Congressional	4
State Senatorial	1
State Assembly	3

County Officials, 2009

Manager/Admin	John Ketelsen
County Clerk	Julie Bustamante
District Attorney	Robert Burns
Auditor-Controller	Karen Fouch
Tax Assessor	Kenneth Bunch
Tax Collector	Richard Egan
Comm Dev Dir.	Conrad Montgomery
Public Works	Larry Millar
Building Dept Dir	(vacant)
Sheriff	Steve Warren
Fire Chief	Brad Lutts
Elections Official	Julie Bustamante
County supervisors	
District 1	Robert Pyle
District 2	Jim Chapman
District 3	Lloyd Keefer
District 4	Brian Dahle
District 5	Jack Hanson

Public Safety

County Sheriff's office, 2007

Number of officers	69
Violent crimes	36
Property crimes	117
Arson	3

Housing & Construction

Housing Units

Total, January 2008§	13,067
Single family units, attached	352
Single family units, detached	8,989
Multiple family units	1,039
Mobile home units	2,687
Occupied units	10,546
Vacancy rate	19.3%
Median rent, 2000**	$561
Median SF home value, 2000**	$106,700

New Privately Owned Housing Units Authorized by Building Permit, 2007*

	Units	Construction Cost
Single	59	$11,794,229
Total	59	$11,794,229

Property Taxation, FY 2008

Total assessed value	$2,093,803,485
Total tax levied	$4,208,825
Delinquency rate	4.200%

County Finance, FY 2007

Revenues

Total	$58,390,531
Taxes	8,690,510
Special benefits assessment	0
Licenses, permits & franchises	596,808
Fines, forfeitures & penalties	1,666,170
Use of money & property	2,140,440
Intergovernmental	36,415,299
Service charges	7,624,084
Miscellaneous revenues	1,257,220
Other financing sources	0

Expenditures

Total	$56,717,348
General	8,014,366
Public protection	18,059,275
Public ways & facilities	7,738,679
Health	7,602,656
Sanitation	0
Public assistance	14,491,996
Education	85,001
Recreation & culture	109,536
Debt service	615,839

County Schools

Lassen County Office of Education
472-013 Johnstonville Rd North
Susanville, CA 96130
(530) 257-2197

Superintendent	Jud Jensen

County-wide School Totals

(2007-08 except where noted)

Number of districts	6
Number of schools	17
Enrollment	2,987
High school graduates, 2006-07	242
Pupil/teacher ratio	4.5
Average class size	3.6
Students per computer	4.8
Cost per ADA	$9,248
Avg teacher salary	$56,079

California Achievement Tests 6th ed., 2008

(Pct scoring at or above 50th National Percentile Rank)

	Math	Reading	Language
Grade 3	NA	NA	NA
Grade 7	NA	NA	NA

Academic Performance Index, 2008

Number of students tested	2,221
2007 API (base)	567
2008 API (growth)	494

SAT Testing, 2006-07

Enrollment, Grade 12	476
percent taking test	25.4%
percent with total score 1,500+	11.8%

Average Scores:

Math	Verbal	Writing	Total
502	499	474	1,475

County Library

Lassen Library District
1618 Main St
Susanville, CA 96130
530-251-8127

Librarian	John Flaherty

Library statistics, FY 2007

Population served	36,375
Internet terminals	11
Annual users	9,292

Per capita:

Operating income	$5.10
percent from local government	63.6%
Operating expenditure	$5.02
Total materials	1.24
Print holdings	1.13
Visits	1.28

See Introduction for an explanation of all data sources.

Demographics & Socio-Economic Characteristics[†]

(2007 American Community Survey, except as noted)

Population

1990*	8,863,164
2007	9,878,554
Male	4,893,177
Female	4,985,377
Jan. 2008 (estimate)[§]	10,363,850
Living in unincorporated area	10.5%
2020 (projected)*	11,214,237

Race & Hispanic Origin, 2007

Race	
White	4,931,877
Black/African American	872,098
North American Native	45,714
Asian	1,291,178
Pacific Islander	24,783
Other Race	2,421,369
Two or more races	291,535
Hispanic origin, total	4,677,411
Mexican	3,587,906
Puerto Rican	40,428
Cuban	40,250
Other Hispanic	1,008,827

Age & Nativity, 2007

Under 5 years	711,253
18 years and over	7,296,004
65 years and over	1,029,610
85 years and over	135,714
Median Age	34.5
Native-born	6,300,078
Foreign-born	3,578,476

Educational Attainment, 2007

Population 25 years and over	6,262,307
Less than 9th grade	14.0%
High school grad or higher	75.2%
Bachelor's degree or higher	28.3%
Graduate degree	9.6%

Income & Poverty, 2007

Per capita income	$26,539
Median household income	$53,573
Median family income	$60,264
Persons in poverty	14.7%
H'holds receiving public assistance	102,832
H'holds receiving social security	685,282

Households, 2007

Total households	3,181,903
With persons under 18	1,233,235
With persons over 65	711,540
Family households	2,141,488
Single person households	833,467
Persons per household	3.05
Persons per family	3.75

Labor & Employment

Total civilian labor force, 2008[§§]	4,972,000
Unemployment rate	7.5%
Total civilian labor force, 2000*	4,307,762

Employed persons 16 years and over by occupation, 2007

Managers & professionals	1,535,929
Service occupations	805,314
Sales & office occupations	1,194,854
Farming, fishing & forestry	8,548
Construction & maintenance	400,402
Production & transportation	621,396
Self-employed persons	445,016

† see Appendix D for 2000 Decennial Census Data
* US Census Bureau
** 2007 American Community Survey
§ California Department of Finance
§§ California Employment Development Dept

General Information

500 W Temple St
Room 358
Los Angeles, CA 90012
213-974-1311

Website	lacounty.gov
Incorporated	February 18, 1850
Form of Government	Charter
Land Area (sq. miles)	4,060.9
Water Area (sq. miles)	691.5
Persons per sq. mi. of land, 2008	2,552.1
Sales tax rate	8.25%

Voters & Gov't Officials

Registered Voters, October 2008

Total	4,298,440
Democrats	2,226,641
Republicans	1,034,213
Declined to state	859,076
Unincorporated area	447,146
Democrats	231,287
Republicans	114,886
Declined to state	83,271

Legislative Districts

US Congressional	22, 25-39, 42, 46
State Senatorial	17, 19-30, 32
State Assembly	36-61

County Officials, 2009

Chief Exec Officer	William T Fujioka
Clerk-Recorder	Dean C Logan
District Attorney	Steve Cooley
Auditor-Controller	Wendy Watanabe
Assessor	Rick Auerbach
Treasurer/Tax Coll	Mark J Saladino
Executive Director	Corde Carrillo (Actg)
Public Works	Gail Farber
Building	Gail Farber
Sheriff	Lee Baca
Fire Chief	Michael Freeman
Elections Official	Dean C. Logan
County supervisors	
District 1	Gloria Molina
District 2	Mark Ridley-Thomas
District 3	Zev Yaroslavsky
District 4	Don Knabe
District 5	Michael Antonovich

Public Safety

County Sheriff's office, 2007

Number of officers	9,278
Violent crimes	7,784
Property crimes	20,516
Arson	455

Housing & Construction

Housing Units

Total, January 2008[§]	3,403,480
Single family units, attached	244,606
Single family units, detached	1,642,973
Multiple family units	1,459,215
Mobile home units	56,686
Occupied units	3,260,434
Vacancy rate	4.2%
Median rent, 2007**	$1,036
Median SF home value, 2007**	$589,100

New Privately Owned Housing Units Authorized by Building Permit, 2007*

	Units	Construction Cost
Single	7,102	$1,904,209,768
Total	19,244	$3,788,533,866

Property Taxation, FY 2008

Total assessed value	$1,010,019,713,739
Total tax levied	$2,441,016,559
Delinquency rate	3.710%

County Finance, FY 2007

Revenues

Total	$13,925,667,211
Taxes	3,872,159,785
Special benefits assessment	6,296,769
Licenses, permits & franchises	52,125,614
Fines, forfeitures & penalties	310,917,375
Use of money & property	345,484,190
Intergovernmental	7,470,457,091
Service charges	1,637,282,736
Miscellaneous revenues	219,104,416
Other financing sources	2,859,968

Expenditures

Total	$12,356,375,298
General	802,556,120
Public protection	4,045,859,470
Public ways & facilities	237,752,173
Health	2,210,165,564
Sanitation	0
Public assistance	4,428,537,007
Education	99,518,564
Recreation & culture	222,317,901
Debt service	309,668,499

County Schools

Los Angeles County Office of Education
9300 Imperial Hwy
Downey, CA 90242
(562) 922-6111

Superintendent	Darline Robles

County-wide School Totals

(2007-08 except where noted)

Number of districts	128
Number of schools	12,908
Enrollment	10,829,016
High school graduates, 2006-07	490,193
Pupil/teacher ratio	12.9
Average class size	17.0
Students per computer	3.4
Cost per ADA	$9,041
Avg teacher salary	$65,500

California Achievement Tests 6th ed., 2008

(Pct scoring at or above 50th National Percentile Rank)

	Math	Reading	Language
Grade 3	28%	13%	19%
Grade 7	6%	4%	4%

Academic Performance Index, 2008

Number of students tested	7,813,428
2007 API (base)	639
2008 API (growth)	643

SAT Testing, 2006-07

Enrollment, Grade 12	106,820
percent taking test	41.3%
percent with total score 1,500+	16.8%

Average Scores:

Math	Verbal	Writing	Total
492	472	474	1,438

County Library

Los Angeles County Public Library
630 W Fifth St
Los Angeles, CA 90071
562-940-8462

Librarian	Margaret Donnellan Todd

Library statistics, FY 2007

Population served	4,018,080
Internet terminals	2,269
Annual users	4,995,278

Per capita:

Operating income	$30.36
percent from local government	91.9%
Operating expenditure	$30.36
Total materials	1.68
Print holdings	1.56
Visits	3.98

See Introduction for an explanation of all data sources.

Madera County

Demographics & Socio-Economic Characteristics†

(2007 American Community Survey, except as noted)

Population

- 1990* ... 88,090
- 2007 ... 146,513
  - Male ... 70,971
  - Female ... 75,542
- Jan. 2008 (estimate)§ ... 150,887
  - Living in unincorporated area ... 50.0%
- 2020 (projected)* ... 212,874

Race & Hispanic Origin, 2007

- Race
  - White ... 115,553
  - Black/African American ... 5,799
  - North American Native ... 2,572
  - Asian ... 2,859
  - Pacific Islander ... 215
  - Other Race ... 15,086
  - Two or more races ... 4,429
- Hispanic origin, total ... 73,536
  - Mexican ... 67,665
  - Puerto Rican ... 1,739
  - Cuban ... 148
  - Other Hispanic ... 3,984

Age & Nativity, 2007

- Under 5 years ... 11,702
- 18 years and over ... 105,433
- 65 years and over ... 14,865
- 85 years and over ... 2,156
  - Median Age ... 31.9
- Native-born ... 114,139
- Foreign-born ... 32,374

Educational Attainment, 2007

- Population 25 years and over ... 90,012
- Less than 9th grade ... 18.6%
- High school grad or higher ... 67.6%
- Bachelor's degree or higher ... 13.5%
- Graduate degree ... 5.1%

Income & Poverty, 2007

- Per capita income ... $19,822
- Median household income ... $44,975
- Median family income ... $50,727
- Persons in poverty ... 14.5%
- H'holds receiving public assistance ... 883
- H'holds receiving social security ... 11,613

Households, 2007

- Total households ... 43,355
  - With persons under 18 ... 19,528
  - With persons over 65 ... 10,348
  - Family households ... 33,618
  - Single person households ... 8,112
- Persons per household ... 3.17
- Persons per family ... 3.59

Labor & Employment

- Total civilian labor force, 2008§§ ... 66,300
  - Unemployment rate ... 9.4%
- Total civilian labor force, 2000* ... 48,600

Employed persons 16 years and over by occupation, 2007

- Managers & professionals ... 13,587
- Service occupations ... 8,087
- Sales & office occupations ... 13,840
- Farming, fishing & forestry ... 8,663
- Construction & maintenance ... 5,463
- Production & transportation ... 8,067
- Self-employed persons ... 5,405

† see Appendix D for 2000 Decennial Census Data
* US Census Bureau
** 2007 American Community Survey
§ California Department of Finance
§§ California Employment Development Dept

General Information

200 West Fourth St
Madera, CA 93637
559-675-7703

- Website ... www.madera-county.com
- Incorporated ... March 11, 1893
- Form of Government ... General law
- Land Area (sq. miles) ... 2,135.9
- Water Area (sq. miles) ... 17.5
- Persons per sq. mi. of land, 2008 ... 70.6
- Sales tax rate ... 7.25%

Voters & Gov't Officials

Registered Voters, October 2008

- Total ... 54,003
  - Democrats ... 19,033
  - Republicans ... 25,002
  - Declined to state ... 8,048
- Unincorporated area ... 34,745
  - Democrats ... 10,752
  - Republicans ... 17,633
  - Declined to state ... 5,060

Legislative Districts

- US Congressional ... 18-19
- State Senatorial ... 12, 14
- State Assembly ... 25, 29

County Officials, 2009

- Manager/Admin ... Stell Manfredi
- Clerk-Recorder ... Rebecca Martinez
- District Attorney ... Michael Keitz
- Finance Dir ... Jim Boyajian (Actg)
- Tax Assessor ... Thomas Kidwell
- Tax Collector ... Tracy K. Desmond
- Planning/Dev Dir ... Rayburn Beach
- Public Works ... Dave Herb
- Building ... NA
- Sheriff ... John Anderson
- Fire Chief ... (CalFire)
- Elections Official ... Rebecca Martinez
- County supervisors
  - District 1 ... Frank Bigelow
  - District 2 ... Vern Moss
  - District 3 ... Ronn Dominici
  - District 4 ... Max Rodriguez
  - District 5 ... Tom Wheeler

Public Safety

County Sheriff's office, 2007

- Number of officers ... 76
- Violent crimes ... 310
- Property crimes ... 1,282
- Arson ... 2

Housing & Construction

Housing Units

- Total, January 2008§ ... 49,372
  - Single family units, attached ... 1,336
  - Single family units, detached ... 38,773
  - Multiple family units ... 5,523
  - Mobile home units ... 3,740
  - Occupied units ... 44,353
  - Vacancy rate ... 10.2%
- Median rent, 2007** ... $759
- Median SF home value, 2007** ... $332,200

New Privately Owned Housing Units Authorized by Building Permit, 2007*

	Units	Construction Cost
Single	486	$91,804,425
Total	509	$93,626,492

Property Taxation, FY 2008

- Total assessed value ... $11,498,382,317
- Total tax levied ... $17,090,950
- Delinquency rate ... 9.121%

County Finance, FY 2007

Revenues

- Total ... $166,939,660
- Taxes ... 44,355,863
- Special benefits assessment ... 0
- Licenses, permits & franchises ... 3,891,241
- Fines, forfeitures & penalties ... 2,375,653
- Use of money & property ... 3,901,095
- Intergovernmental ... 97,741,088
- Service charges ... 11,775,544
- Miscellaneous revenues ... 2,319,579
- Other financing sources ... 28,295

Expenditures

- Total ... $184,825,916
- General ... 41,595,112
- Public protection ... 53,184,575
- Public ways & facilities ... 12,897,433
- Health ... 23,204,233
- Sanitation ... 1,080,520
- Public assistance ... 49,272,770
- Education ... 1,670,600
- Recreation & culture ... 0
- Debt service ... 1,920,673

County Schools

Madera County Office of Education
28123 Avenue 14
Madera, CA 93638
(559) 673-6051

- Superintendent ... Sally Frazier

County-wide School Totals

(2007-08 except where noted)

- Number of districts ... 6
- Number of schools ... 51
- Enrollment ... 24,928
- High school graduates, 2006-07 ... 1,203
- Pupil/teacher ratio ... 11.3
- Average class size ... 13.2
- Students per computer ... 2.7
- Cost per ADA ... $8,104
- Avg teacher salary ... $59,009

California Achievement Tests 6th ed., 2008

(Pct scoring at or above 50th National Percentile Rank)

	Math	Reading	Language
Grade 3	NA	NA	NA
Grade 7	6%	12%	6%

Academic Performance Index, 2008

- Number of students tested ... 18,460
- 2007 API (base) ... 481
- 2008 API (growth) ... 495

SAT Testing, 2006-07

- Enrollment, Grade 12 ... 2,013
  - percent taking test ... 17.8%
  - percent with total score 1,500+ ... 6.8%

Average Scores:

Math	Verbal	Writing	Total
493	480	472	1,445

County Library

Madera County Library
121 N G St
Madera, CA 93637
559-675-7871

- Librarian ... Linda Sitterding

Library statistics, FY 2007

- Population served ... 148,721
- Internet terminals ... 26
  - Annual users ... 43,295

Per capita:

- Operating income ... $10.35
  - percent from local government ... 95.5%
- Operating expenditure ... $9.22
- Total materials ... 1.88
- Print holdings ... 1.79
- Visits ... 1.97

See Introduction for an explanation of all data sources.

Demographics & Socio-Economic Characteristics†

(2007 American Community Survey, except as noted)

Population

1990* . . . 230,096
2007 . . . 248,096
Male . . . 123,316
Female . . . 124,780
Jan. 2008 (estimate)§ . . . 257,406
Living in unincorporated area . . . 27.1%
2020 (projected)* . . . 260,305

Race & Hispanic Origin, 2007

Race
White . . . 202,905
Black/African American . . . 7,865
North American Native . . . 953
Asian . . . 14,131
Pacific Islander . . . 465
Other Race . . . 15,313
Two or more races . . . 6,464
Hispanic origin, total . . . 33,956
Mexican . . . 15,944
Puerto Rican . . . 680
Cuban . . . 453
Other Hispanic . . . 16,879

Age & Nativity, 2007

Under 5 years . . . 13,877
18 years and over . . . 199,640
65 years and over . . . 38,639
85 years and over . . . 5,208
Median Age . . . 44.2
Native-born . . . 202,853
Foreign-born . . . 45,243

Educational Attainment, 2007

Population 25 years and over . . . 181,645
Less than 9th grade . . . 4.5%
High school grad or higher . . . 91.0%
Bachelor's degree or higher . . . 52.1%
Graduate degree . . . 21.8%

Income & Poverty, 2007

Per capita income . . . $50,554
Median household income . . . $83,870
Median family income . . . $104,830
Persons in poverty . . . 6.4%
H'holds receiving public assistance . . . 1,279
H'holds receiving social security . . . 27,061

Households, 2007

Total households . . . 99,627
With persons under 18 . . . 28,780
With persons over 65 . . . 26,742
Family households . . . 61,736
Single person households . . . 30,866
Persons per household . . . 2.39
Persons per family . . . 2.97

Labor & Employment

Total civilian labor force, 2008§§ . . . 137,200
Unemployment rate . . . 4.6%
Total civilian labor force, 2000* . . . 132,805

Employed persons 16 years and over by occupation, 2007

Managers & professionals . . . 62,319
Service occupations . . . 19,296
Sales & office occupations . . . 32,184
Farming, fishing & forestry . . . 339
Construction & maintenance . . . 9,887
Production & transportation . . . 4,557
Self-employed persons . . . 22,976

† see Appendix D for 2000 Decennial Census Data
* US Census Bureau
** 2007 American Community Survey
§ California Department of Finance
§§ California Employment Development Dept

General Information

3501 Civic Center Dr
San Rafael, CA 94903
415-499-6358

Website . . . www.co.marin.ca.us
Incorporated . . . February 18, 1850
Form of Government . . . General law
Land Area (sq. miles) . . . 519.8
Water Area (sq. miles) . . . 308.4
Persons per sq. mi. of land, 2008 . . . 495.2
Sales tax rate . . . 7.75%

Voters & Gov't Officials

Registered Voters, October 2008

Total . . . 155,640
Democrats . . . 84,605
Republicans . . . 31,220
Declined to state . . . 33,431
Unincorporated area . . . 43,263
Democrats . . . 23,843
Republicans . . . 8,330
Declined to state . . . 9,174

Legislative Districts

US Congressional . . . 6
State Senatorial . . . 3
State Assembly . . . 6

County Officials, 2009

Administrator . . . Matthew Hymel
County Clerk . . . Michael Smith
District Attorney . . . Edward Berberian
Auditor-Controller . . . Bryon Karow
Assessor . . . Joan Thayer
Treasurer/Tax Coll . . . Michael Smith
Comm Dev Exec Admin . . Brian Crawford
Public Works . . . Farhad Mansourian
Building Inspector . . . William Kelley (Dep)
Sheriff . . . Robert Doyle
Fire Chief . . . Ken Massucco
Elections Official . . . Elaine Ginnold
County supervisors
District 1 . . . Susan Adams
District 2 . . . Harold Brown Jr
District 3 . . . Charles McGlashan
District 4 . . . Steve Kinsey
District 5 . . . Judy Arnold

Public Safety

County Sheriff's office, 2007

Number of officers . . . 209
Violent crimes . . . 130
Property crimes . . . 822
Arson . . . NA

Housing & Construction

Housing Units

Total, January 2008§ . . . 108,538
Single family units, attached . . . 8,624
Single family units, detached . . . 65,793
Multiple family units . . . 31,990
Mobile home units . . . 2,131
Occupied units . . . 104,113
Vacancy rate . . . 4.1%
Median rent, 2007** . . . $1,418
Median SF home value, 2007** . . . $918,700

New Privately Owned Housing Units Authorized by Building Permit, 2007*

	Units	Construction Cost
Single	268	$114,462,532
Total	430	$132,318,756

Property Taxation, FY 2008

Total assessed value . . . $52,554,005,358
Total tax levied . . . $99,215,446
Delinquency rate . . . 1.780%

County Finance, FY 2007

Revenues

Total . . . $397,271,521
Taxes . . . 156,584,629
Special benefits assessment . . . 1,703,132
Licenses, permits & franchises . . . 6,646,100
Fines, forfeitures & penalties . . . 7,462,239
Use of money & property . . . 7,683,306
Intergovernmental . . . 174,244,653
Service charges . . . 37,457,359
Miscellaneous revenues . . . 5,490,103
Other financing sources . . . 0

Expenditures

Total . . . $389,448,430
General . . . 91,604,218
Public protection . . . 119,181,368
Public ways & facilities . . . 10,425,133
Health . . . 79,841,957
Sanitation . . . 0
Public assistance . . . 56,116,249
Education . . . 11,471,373
Recreation & culture . . . 8,892,347
Debt service . . . 11,915,785

County Schools

Marin County Office of Education
PO Box 4925
San Rafael, CA 94913
(415) 472-4110

Superintendent . . . Mary Jane Burke

County-wide School Totals

(2007-08 except where noted)

Number of districts . . . 23
Number of schools . . . 105
Enrollment . . . 58,190
High school graduates, 2006-07 . . . 9,675
Pupil/teacher ratio . . . 12.1
Average class size . . . 8.7
Students per computer . . . 2.6
Cost per ADA . . . $10,515
Avg teacher salary . . . $67,415

California Achievement Tests 6th ed., 2008

(Pct scoring at or above 50th National Percentile Rank)

	Math	Reading	Language
Grade 3	NA	NA	NA
Grade 7	30%	25%	29%

Academic Performance Index, 2008

Number of students tested . . . 42,276
2007 API (base) . . . 577
2008 API (growth) . . . 478

SAT Testing, 2006-07

Enrollment, Grade 12 . . . 2,254
percent taking test . . . 61.6%
percent with total score 1,500+ . . . 44.8%

Average Scores:

Math	Verbal	Writing	Total
560	556	555	1,671

County Library

Marin County Free Library
3501 Civic Center Dr
San Rafael, CA 94903
415-499-3220

Librarian . . . Carol Starr

Library statistics, FY 2007

Population served . . . 140,989
Internet terminals . . . 95
Annual users . . . 198,739

Per capita:

Operating income . . . $77.23
percent from local government . . . 90.0%
Operating expenditure . . . $77.23
Total materials . . . 3.56
Print holdings . . . 3.12
Visits . . . 7.73

Mariposa County

Demographics & Socio-Economic Characteristics

(2000 U.S. Census, except as noted)

Population

1990* . . . 14,302
2000 . . . 17,130
Male . . . 8,762
Female . . . 8,368
Jan. 2008 (estimate)§ . . . 18,406
Living in unincorporated area . . . 100%
2020 (projected)* . . . 21,743

Race & Hispanic Origin, 2000

Race
White . . . 15,234
Black/African American . . . 114
North American Native . . . 602
Asian . . . 122
Pacific Islander . . . 22
Other Race . . . 457
Two or more races . . . 579
Hispanic origin, total . . . 1,329
Mexican . . . 978
Puerto Rican . . . 47
Cuban . . . 35
Other Hispanic . . . 269

Age & Nativity, 2000

Under 5 years . . . 754
18 years and over . . . 13,427
65 years and over . . . 2,940
85 years and over . . . 279
Median Age . . . 42.9
Native-born . . . 16,655
Foreign-born . . . 475

Educational Attainment, 2000

Population 25 years and over . . . 12,196
Less than 9th grade . . . 3.7%
High school grad or higher . . . 85.1%
Bachelor's degree or higher . . . 20.2%
Graduate degree . . . 5.9%

Income & Poverty, 1999

Per capita income . . . $18,190
Median household income . . . $34,626
Median family income . . . $42,655
Persons in poverty . . . 14.5%
H'holds receiving public assistance . . . 328
H'holds receiving social security . . . 2,475

Households, 2000

Total households . . . 6,613
With persons under 18 . . . 1,878
With persons over 65 . . . 2,087
Family households . . . 4,490
Single person households . . . 1,755
Persons per household . . . 2.37
Persons per family . . . 2.86

Labor & Employment

Total civilian labor force, 2008§§ . . . 9,490
Unemployment rate . . . 7.5%
Total civilian labor force, 2000 . . . 7,958

Employed persons 16 years and over by occupation, 2000

Managers & professionals . . . 1,960
Service occupations . . . 1,493
Sales & office occupations . . . 1,715
Farming, fishing & forestry . . . 27
Construction & maintenance . . . 817
Production & transportation . . . 821
Self-employed persons . . . 950

* US Census Bureau
** 2000 Decennial Census
§ California Department of Finance
§§ California Employment Development Dept

General Information

PO Box 784
Mariposa, CA 95338
209-966-3222

Website . . . www.mariposacounty.org
Incorporated . . . February 18, 1850
Form of Government . . . General law
Land Area (sq. miles) . . . 1,451.1
Water Area (sq. miles) . . . 11.7
Persons per sq. mi. of land, 2008 . . . 12.7
Sales tax rate . . . 7.75%

Voters & Gov't Officials

Registered Voters, October 2008

Total . . . 11,693
Democrats . . . 3,767
Republicans . . . 5,287
Declined to state . . . 1,898
Unincorporated area . . . 11,693
Democrats . . . 3,767
Republicans . . . 5,287
Declined to state . . . 1,898

Legislative Districts

US Congressional . . . 19
State Senatorial . . . 14
State Assembly . . . 25

County Officials, 2009

Manager/Admin . . . Rick Benson
County Clerk . . . Keith M. Williams
District Attorney . . . Robert Brown
Finance Dir . . . Chris Ebie
Tax Assessor . . . Becky Crafts
Tax Collector . . . Keith M. Williams
Planning/Dev Dir . . . Kris Schenk
Public Works . . . Dana Hertfelder
Building Dept Dir . . . Fred Lustenberger
Sheriff . . . Brian Muller
Fire Chief . . . Jim Wilson
Elections Official . . . Keith M. Williams
County supervisors
District 1 . . . Brad Aborn
District 2 . . . Lyle Turpin
District 3 . . . Janet Bibby
District 4 . . . Kevin Cann
District 5 . . . Jim Allen

Public Safety

County Sheriff's office, 2007

Number of officers . . . 60
Violent crimes . . . 31
Property crimes . . . 306
Arson . . . 0

Housing & Construction

Housing Units

Total, January 2008§ . . . 10,347
Single family units, attached . . . 648
Single family units, detached . . . 6,336
Multiple family units . . . 597
Mobile home units . . . 2,766
Occupied units . . . 7,754
Vacancy rate . . . 25.1%
Median rent, 2000** . . . $502
Median SF home value, 2000** . . . $141,900

New Privately Owned Housing Units Authorized by Building Permit, 2007*

	Units	Construction Cost
Single	100	$23,417,409
Total	102	$23,626,049

Property Taxation, FY 2008

Total assessed value . . . $1,955,091,620
Total tax levied . . . $5,070,187
Delinquency rate . . . 3.270%

County Finance, FY 2007

Revenues

Total . . . $45,257,260
Taxes . . . 17,999,461
Special benefits assessment . . . 0
Licenses, permits & franchises . . . 703,455
Fines, forfeitures & penalties . . . 515,683
Use of money & property . . . 445,986
Intergovernmental . . . 22,391,924
Service charges . . . 2,776,752
Miscellaneous revenues . . . 423,999
Other financing sources . . . 0

Expenditures

Total . . . $43,908,275
General . . . 8,020,428
Public protection . . . 15,643,918
Public ways & facilities . . . 4,880,879
Health . . . 4,997,148
Sanitation . . . 0
Public assistance . . . 8,663,275
Education . . . 699,908
Recreation & culture . . . 698,096
Debt service . . . 304,623

County Schools

Mariposa County Office of Education
PO Box 8
Mariposa, CA 95338
(209) 742-0250
Superintendent . . . Randy Panietz

County-wide School Totals

(2007-08 except where noted)

Number of districts . . . 1
Number of schools . . . 3
Enrollment . . . 58
High school graduates, 2006-07 . . . 5
Pupil/teacher ratio . . . 5.2
Average class size . . . 14.3
Students per computer . . . 3.6
Cost per ADA . . . $9,766
Avg teacher salary . . . $57,531

California Achievement Tests 6th ed., 2008

(Pct scoring at or above 50th National Percentile Rank)

	Math	Reading	Language
Grade 3	NA	NA	NA
Grade 7	NA	NA	NA

Academic Performance Index, 2008

Number of students tested . . . 32
2007 API (base) . . . 672
2008 API (growth) . . . 741

SAT Testing, 2006-07

Enrollment, Grade 12 . . . 215
percent taking test . . . 25.1%
percent with total score 1,500+ . . . 14.0%

Average Scores:

Math	Verbal	Writing	Total
515	520	505	1,540

County Library

Mariposa County Library
PO Box 106
Mariposa, CA 95338
209-966-2140
Librarian . . . Janet Chase-Williams (Int)

Library statistics, FY 2007

Population served . . . 18,254
Internet terminals . . . 31
Annual users . . . 17,024

Per capita:

Operating income . . . $22.87
percent from local government . . . 89.8%
Operating expenditure . . . $22.82
Total materials . . . 3.72
Print holdings . . . 3.08
Visits . . . 7.26

See Introduction for an explanation of all data sources.

Demographics & Socio-Economic Characteristics†

(2007 American Community Survey, except as noted)

Population

1990*	80,345
2007	86,273
Male	43,383
Female	42,890
Jan. 2008 (estimate)§	90,163
Living in unincorporated area	68.8%
2020 (projected)*	102,017

Race & Hispanic Origin, 2007

Race	
White	75,480
Black/African American	318
North American Native	4,075
Asian	811
Pacific Islander	0
Other Race	2,858
Two or more races	2,731
Hispanic origin, total	17,335
Mexican	16,137
Puerto Rican	212
Cuban	119
Other Hispanic	867

Age & Nativity, 2007

Under 5 years	5,489
18 years and over	66,758
65 years and over	12,469
85 years and over	1,582
Median Age	41.2
Native-born	76,597
Foreign-born	9,676

Educational Attainment, 2007

Population 25 years and over	59,394
Less than 9th grade	9.6%
High school grad or higher	79.4%
Bachelor's degree or higher	23.7%
Graduate degree	9.0%

Income & Poverty, 2007

Per capita income	$22,040
Median household income	$42,941
Median family income	$53,862
Persons in poverty	14.9%
H'holds receiving public assistance	448
H'holds receiving social security	10,572

Households, 2007

Total households	33,482
With persons under 18	9,598
With persons over 65	8,958
Family households	22,674
Single person households	8,935
Persons per household	2.53
Persons per family	3.00

Labor & Employment

Total civilian labor force, 2008§§	43,900
Unemployment rate	6.9%
Total civilian labor force, 2000*	41,592

Employed persons 16 years and over by occupation, 2007

Managers & professionals	12,136
Service occupations	6,820
Sales & office occupations	9,334
Farming, fishing & forestry	1,157
Construction & maintenance	5,715
Production & transportation	3,811
Self-employed persons	6,671

† see Appendix D for 2000 Decennial Census Data
* US Census Bureau
** 2007 American Community Survey
§ California Department of Finance
§§ California Employment Development Dept

General Information

501 Low Gap Road
Room 1010
Ukiah, CA 95482
707-463-4441

Website	www.co.mendocino.ca.us
Incorporated	February 18, 1850
Form of Government	General law
Land Area (sq. miles)	3,509.0
Water Area (sq. miles)	369.2
Persons per sq. mi. of land, 2008	25.7
Sales tax rate	7.25%

Voters & Gov't Officials

Registered Voters, October 2008

Total	50,721
Democrats	24,114
Republicans	11,677
Declined to state	10,519
Unincorporated area	36,629
Democrats	17,204
Republicans	8,441
Declined to state	7,604

Legislative Districts

US Congressional	1
State Senatorial	2
State Assembly	1

County Officials, 2009

Chief Exec Officer	Tom Mitchell
Clerk-Recorder	Sue Ranochak
District Attorney	Meredith Lintott
Auditor-Controller	Meredith Ford
Assessor	Sue Ranochak
Treasurer/Tax Coll	Shari Schapmire
Planning Dir	Nash Gonzalez
Public Works	Howard Dashiell
Building Svcs Dir	Nash Gonzalez
Sheriff-Coroner	Thomas Allman
Fire Chief	(CalFire)
Elections Official	Sue Ranochak
County supervisors	
District 1	Carre Brown
District 2	John McCowen
District 3	John Pinches
District 4	Kendall Smith
District 5	J. David Colfax

Public Safety

County Sheriff's office, 2007

Number of officers	127
Violent crimes	319
Property crimes	716
Arson	13

Housing & Construction

Housing Units

Total, January 2008§	39,563
Single family units, attached	1,163
Single family units, detached	27,958
Multiple family units	4,984
Mobile home units	5,458
Occupied units	35,598
Vacancy rate	10.0%
Median rent, 2007**	$854
Median SF home value, 2007**	$469,000

New Privately Owned Housing Units Authorized by Building Permit, 2007*

	Units	Construction Cost
Single	220	$33,806,618
Total	232	$34,857,485

Property Taxation, FY 2008

Total assessed value	$9,309,745,987
Total tax levied	$27,044,904
Delinquency rate	3.616%

County Finance, FY 2007

Revenues

Total	$173,702,009
Taxes	47,317,884
Special benefits assessment	0
Licenses, permits & franchises	3,215,383
Fines, forfeitures & penalties	3,472,188
Use of money & property	2,451,124
Intergovernmental	102,680,848
Service charges	12,651,189
Miscellaneous revenues	1,878,045
Other financing sources	35,348

Expenditures

Total	$171,279,117
General	16,181,840
Public protection	42,296,928
Public ways & facilities	12,446,355
Health	27,920,381
Sanitation	0
Public assistance	52,268,910
Education	1,765,490
Recreation & culture	322,874
Debt service	18,076,339

County Schools

Mendocino County Office of Education
2240 Old River Rd
Ukiah, CA 95482
(707) 467-5000

Superintendent	Paul Tichinin

County-wide School Totals

(2007-08 except where noted)

Number of districts	6
Number of schools	43
Enrollment	11,200
High school graduates, 2006-07	763
Pupil/teacher ratio	9.0
Average class size	14.4
Students per computer	1.9
Cost per ADA	$10,385
Avg teacher salary	$54,891

California Achievement Tests 6th ed., 2008

(Pct scoring at or above 50th National Percentile Rank)

	Math	Reading	Language
Grade 3	NA	NA	NA
Grade 7	0%	0%	4%

Academic Performance Index, 2008

Number of students tested	7,610
2007 API (base)	462
2008 API (growth)	482

SAT Testing, 2006-07

Enrollment, Grade 12	1,092
percent taking test	31.4%
percent with total score 1,500+	17.6%

Average Scores:

Math	Verbal	Writing	Total
526	520	511	1,557

County Library

Mendocino County Library
105 N Main St
Ukiah, CA 95482
707-463-4491

Librarian	Melanie Lightbody

Library statistics, FY 2007

Population served	90,291
Internet terminals	20
Annual users	37,258

Per capita:

Operating income	$18.48
percent from local government	58.6%
Operating expenditure	$19.03
Total materials	2.07
Print holdings	1.94
Visits	NA

See Introduction for an explanation of all data sources.

Demographics & Socio-Economic Characteristics†

(2007 American Community Survey, except as noted)

Population

1990* . . . 178,403
2007 . . . 245,514
Male . . . 124,013
Female . . . 121,501
Jan. 2008 (estimate)§ . . . 255,250
Living in unincorporated area . . . 34.1%
2020 (projected)* . . . 348,690

Race & Hispanic Origin, 2007

Race
White . . . 137,583
Black/African American . . . 9,136
North American Native . . . 1,982
Asian . . . 15,975
Pacific Islander . . . 654
Other Race . . . 72,414
Two or more races . . . 7,770
Hispanic origin, total . . . 128,742
Mexican . . . 121,174
Puerto Rican . . . 658
Cuban . . . 76
Other Hispanic . . . 6,834

Age & Nativity, 2007

Under 5 years . . . 21,848
18 years and over . . . 167,978
65 years and over . . . 23,170
85 years and over . . . 3,135
Median Age . . . 28.9
Native-born . . . 184,363
Foreign-born . . . 61,151

Educational Attainment, 2007

Population 25 years and over . . . 139,312
Less than 9th grade . . . 21.0%
High school grad or higher . . . 66.5%
Bachelor's degree or higher . . . 12.4%
Graduate degree . . . 4.1%

Income & Poverty, 2007

Per capita income . . . $19,012
Median household income . . . $44,410
Median family income . . . $46,800
Persons in poverty . . . 19.4%
H'holds receiving public assistance . . . 5,912
H'holds receiving social security . . . 18,007

Households, 2007

Total households . . . 73,482
With persons under 18 . . . 38,447
With persons over 65 . . . 15,144
Family households . . . 58,200
Single person households . . . 12,716
Persons per household . . . 3.31
Persons per family . . . 3.67

Labor & Employment

Total civilian labor force, 2008§§ . . . 103,400
Unemployment rate . . . 12.7%
Total civilian labor force, 2000* . . . 86,663

Employed persons 16 years and over by occupation, 2007

Managers & professionals . . . 23,511
Service occupations . . . 15,255
Sales & office occupations . . . 20,131
Farming, fishing & forestry . . . 7,801
Construction & maintenance . . . 10,677
Production & transportation . . . 18,496
Self-employed persons . . . 6,973

† see Appendix D for 2000 Decennial Census Data
* US Census Bureau
** 2007 American Community Survey
§ California Department of Finance
§§ California Employment Development Dept

General Information

2222 M St
Merced, CA 95340
209-385-7366

Website . . . www.co.merced.ca.us
Incorporated . . . April 19, 1855
Form of Government . . . General law
Land Area (sq. miles) . . . 1,928.7
Water Area (sq. miles) . . . 43.2
Persons per sq. mi. of land, 2008 . . . 132.3
Sales tax rate . . . 7.25%

Voters & Gov't Officials

Registered Voters, October 2008

Total . . . 97,179
Democrats . . . 44,704
Republicans . . . 35,955
Declined to state . . . 13,430
Unincorporated area . . . 33,927
Democrats . . . 14,232
Republicans . . . 14,115
Declined to state . . . 4,521

Legislative Districts

US Congressional . . . 18
State Senatorial . . . 12
State Assembly . . . 17

County Officials, 2009

Admin/Manager . . . Demitrios Tatum
County Clerk . . . Lisa Cardella-Presto
District Attorney . . . Larry Morse
Finance Dir . . . Lisa Cardello-Presto
Tax Assessor . . . Kent Christenson
Tax Collector . . . Karen Adams
Planning/Dev Dir . . . Robert Lewis
Public Works . . . Paul Fillebrown
Building Dept Dir . . . Richard Graves
Sheriff . . . Mark Pazin
Fire Chief . . . Mikel Martin
Elections Official . . . Lisa Cardella-Presto
County supervisors
District 1 . . . John Pedrozo
District 2 . . . Hubert Walsh
District 3 . . . Michael Nelson
District 4 . . . Deidre Kelsey
District 5 . . . Jerry O'Banion

Public Safety

County Sheriff's office, 2007

Number of officers . . . 199
Violent crimes . . . 451
Property crimes . . . 2,240
Arson . . . 17

Housing & Construction

Housing Units

Total, January 2008§ . . . 84,631
Single family units, attached . . . 2,551
Single family units, detached . . . 62,684
Multiple family units . . . 13,655
Mobile home units . . . 5,741
Occupied units . . . 78,952
Vacancy rate . . . 6.7%
Median rent, 2007** . . . $770
Median SF home value, 2007** . . . $323,700

New Privately Owned Housing Units Authorized by Building Permit, 2007*

	Units	Construction Cost
Single	780	$136,907,670
Total	794	$138,508,048

Property Taxation, FY 2008

Total assessed value . . . $20,357,037,135
Total tax levied . . . $48,184,322
Delinquency rate . . . 6.250%

County Finance, FY 2007

Revenues

Total . . . $374,748,261
Taxes . . . 85,313,888
Special benefits assessment . . . 0
Licenses, permits & franchises . . . 4,624,002
Fines, forfeitures & penalties . . . 11,128,453
Use of money & property . . . 10,740,278
Intergovernmental . . . 224,566,149
Service charges . . . 28,206,040
Miscellaneous revenues . . . 4,671,577
Other financing sources . . . 5,370,306

Expenditures

Total . . . $346,829,247
General . . . 43,176,218
Public protection . . . 94,603,393
Public ways & facilities . . . 14,480,209
Health . . . 43,344,499
Sanitation . . . 0
Public assistance . . . 137,496,810
Education . . . 2,615,480
Recreation & culture . . . 2,133,662
Debt service . . . 8,978,976

County Schools

Merced County Office of Education
632 West 13th St
Merced, CA 95341
(209) 381-6600
Superintendent . . . Lee Andersen

County-wide School Totals

(2007-08 except where noted)

Number of districts . . . 13
Number of schools . . . 92
Enrollment . . . 68,923
High school graduates, 2006-07 . . . 6,714
Pupil/teacher ratio . . . 14.7
Average class size . . . 17.2
Students per computer . . . 3.0
Cost per ADA . . . $8,067
Avg teacher salary . . . $63,817

California Achievement Tests 6th ed., 2008

(Pct scoring at or above 50th National Percentile Rank)

	Math	Reading	Language
Grade 3	NA	NA	NA
Grade 7	15%	24%	16%

Academic Performance Index, 2008

Number of students tested . . . 51,536
2007 API (base) . . . 458
2008 API (growth) . . . 487

SAT Testing, 2006-07

Enrollment, Grade 12 . . . 3,945
percent taking test . . . 24.5%
percent with total score 1,500+ . . . 7.7%

Average Scores:

Math	Verbal	Writing	Total
475	455	461	1,391

County Library

Merced County Library
2100 O St
Merced, CA 95340
209-385-7484
Librarian . . . Charlene Renteria

Library statistics, FY 2007

Population served . . . 251,510
Internet terminals . . . 91
Annual users . . . 124,530

Per capita:

Operating income . . . $8.99
percent from local government . . . 91.3%
Operating expenditure . . . $8.99
Total materials . . . 1.61
Print holdings . . . 1.60
Visits . . . 1.75

See Introduction for an explanation of all data sources.

Demographics & Socio-Economic Characteristics

(2000 U.S. Census, except as noted)

Population

1990* . . . 9,678
2000 . . . 9,449
Male . . . 4,780
Female . . . 4,669
Jan. 2008 (estimate)§ . . . 9,702
Living in unincorporated area . . . 71.1%
2020 (projected)* . . . 13,134

Race & Hispanic Origin, 2000

Race
White . . . 8,120
Black/African American . . . 65
North American Native . . . 398
Asian . . . 58
Pacific Islander . . . 7
Other Race . . . 538
Two or more races . . . 263
Hispanic origin, total . . . 1,088
Mexican . . . 898
Puerto Rican . . . 13
Cuban . . . NA
Other Hispanic . . . 177

Age & Nativity, 2000

Under 5 years . . . 528
18 years and over . . . 7,026
65 years and over . . . 1,663
85 years and over . . . 163
Median Age . . . 41.8
Native-born . . . 8,893
Foreign-born . . . 556

Educational Attainment, 2000

Population 25 years and over . . . 6,464
Less than 9th grade . . . 7.4%
High school grad or higher . . . 77.1%
Bachelor's degree or higher . . . 12.4%
Graduate degree . . . 3.6%

Income & Poverty, 1999

Per capita income . . . $17,285
Median household income . . . $27,522
Median family income . . . $35,978
Persons in poverty . . . 20.8%
H'holds receiving public assistance . . . 302
H'holds receiving social security . . . 1,264

Households, 2000

Total households . . . 3,784
With persons under 18 . . . 1,211
With persons over 65 . . . 1,168
Family households . . . 2,551
Single person households . . . 1,064
Persons per household . . . 2.39
Persons per family . . . 2.91

Labor & Employment

Total civilian labor force, 2008§§ . . . 3,990
Unemployment rate . . . 9.7%
Total civilian labor force, 2000 . . . 4,128

Employed persons 16 years and over by occupation, 2000

Managers & professionals . . . 1,086
Service occupations . . . 767
Sales & office occupations . . . 817
Farming, fishing & forestry . . . 267
Construction & maintenance . . . 308
Production & transportation . . . 390
Self-employed persons . . . 570

* US Census Bureau
** 2000 Decennial Census
§ California Department of Finance
§§ California Employment Development Dept

General Information

114 East North St
Alturas, CA 96101
530-233-6426

Website . . . www.modoccounty.us
Incorporated . . . February 17, 1874
Form of Government . . . General law
Land Area (sq. miles) . . . 3,944.1
Water Area (sq. miles) . . . 259.3
Persons per sq. mi. of land, 2008 . . . 2.5
Sales tax rate . . . 7.25%

Voters & Gov't Officials

Registered Voters, October 2008

Total . . . 5,507
Democrats . . . 1,601
Republicans . . . 2,745
Declined to state . . . 902
Unincorporated area . . . 3,871
Democrats . . . 1,028
Republicans . . . 2,044
Declined to state . . . 623

Legislative Districts

US Congressional . . . 4
State Senatorial . . . 1
State Assembly . . . 2

County Officials, 2009

Administrator . . . Mark Charlton
Clerk-Recorder . . . Alice Marrs (Int)
District Attorney . . . Gary Wolverton
Auditor-Controller . . . Alice Marrs (Int)
Tax Assessor . . . Sheri Budmark
Treasurer/Tax Coll . . . Cheryl Knoch
Planning/Comm Dev . . . Kim Hunter
Public Works . . . Rick Rudometkin
Building . . . NA
Sheriff . . . Mark Gentry
Fire/Emerg Mgmt Dir . . . NA
Elections Official . . . Alice Marrs (Int)
County supervisors
District 1 . . . Dan Macsay
District 2 . . . Jeff Bullock
District 3 . . . Patricia Cantrall
District 4 . . . Shorty Crabtree
District 5 . . . Dave Bradshaw

Public Safety

County Sheriff's office, 2007

Number of officers . . . 22
Violent crimes . . . 19
Property crimes . . . 104
Arson . . . 1

Housing & Construction

Housing Units

Total, January 2008§ . . . 5,166
Single family units, attached . . . 88
Single family units, detached . . . 3,506
Multiple family units . . . 256
Mobile home units . . . 1,316
Occupied units . . . 4,058
Vacancy rate . . . 21.4%
Median rent, 2000** . . . $429
Median SF home value, 2000** . . . $69,100

New Privately Owned Housing Units Authorized by Building Permit, 2007*

	Units	Construction Cost
Single	18	$2,046,239
Total	18	$2,046,239

Property Taxation, FY 2008

Total assessed value . . . $989,507,502
Total tax levied . . . $2,735,250
Delinquency rate . . . 4.140%

County Finance, FY 2007

Revenues

Total . . . $24,817,645
Taxes . . . 4,033,104
Special benefits assessment . . . 393,832
Licenses, permits & franchises . . . 205,160
Fines, forfeitures & penalties . . . 256,617
Use of money & property . . . 252,237
Intergovernmental . . . 18,447,213
Service charges . . . 1,158,182
Miscellaneous revenues . . . 71,300
Other financing sources . . . 0

Expenditures

Total . . . $25,584,449
General . . . 3,075,426
Public protection . . . 6,024,738
Public ways & facilities . . . 5,823,205
Health . . . 4,601,883
Sanitation . . . 0
Public assistance . . . 5,217,377
Education . . . 516,824
Recreation & culture . . . 231,251
Debt service . . . 93,745

County Schools

Modoc County Office of Education
139 Henderson St
Alturas, CA 96101
(530) 233-7101

Superintendent . . . Gary Jones

County-wide School Totals

(2007-08 except where noted)

Number of districts . . . 3
Number of schools . . . 19
Enrollment . . . 2,041
High school graduates, 2006-07 . . . 172
Pupil/teacher ratio . . . 4.8
Average class size . . . 18.6
Students per computer . . . 1.1
Cost per ADA . . . $10,523
Avg teacher salary . . . $55,562

California Achievement Tests 6th ed., 2008

(Pct scoring at or above 50th National Percentile Rank)

	Math	Reading	Language
Grade 3	NA	NA	NA
Grade 7	NA	NA	NA

Academic Performance Index, 2008

Number of students tested . . . 1,193
2007 API (base) . . . 499
2008 API (growth) . . . 572

SAT Testing, 2006-07

Enrollment, Grade 12 . . . 210
percent taking test . . . 22.9%
percent with total score 1,500+ . . . 11.9%

Average Scores:

Math	Verbal	Writing	Total
494	484	471	1,449

County Library

Modoc County Library
212 W Third St
Alturas, CA 96101
530-233-6326

Librarian . . . Cheryl Baker

Library statistics, FY 2007

Population served . . . 9,721
Internet terminals . . . 15
Annual users . . . 7,191

Per capita:

Operating income . . . $35.81
percent from local government . . . 92.8%
Operating expenditure . . . $39.34
Total materials . . . 7.28
Print holdings . . . 6.89
Visits . . . NA

See Introduction for an explanation of all data sources.

Demographics & Socio-Economic Characteristics

(2000 U.S. Census, except as noted)

Population

1990* . . . 9,956
2000 . . . 12,853
Male . . . 7,059
Female . . . 5,794
Jan. 2008 (estimate)§ . . . 13,759
Living in unincorporated area . . . 46.1%
2020 (projected)* . . . 18,080

Race & Hispanic Origin, 2000

Race
White . . . 10,818
Black/African American . . . 61
North American Native . . . 309
Asian . . . 143
Pacific Islander . . . 11
Other Race . . . 1,222
Two or more races . . . 289
Hispanic origin, total . . . 2,274
Mexican . . . 1,892
Puerto Rican . . . 73
Cuban . . . 7
Other Hispanic . . . 302

Age & Nativity, 2000

Under 5 years . . . 727
18 years and over . . . 9,900
65 years and over . . . 976
85 years and over . . . 60
Median Age . . . 36.0
Native-born . . . 11,255
Foreign-born . . . 1,598

Educational Attainment, 2000

Population 25 years and over . . . 8,674
Less than 9th grade . . . 4.8%
High school grad or higher . . . 87.9%
Bachelor's degree or higher . . . 28.9%
Graduate degree . . . 9.9%

Income & Poverty, 1999

Per capita income . . . $23,422
Median household income . . . $44,992
Median family income . . . $50,487
Persons in poverty . . . 11.3%
H'holds receiving public assistance . . . 127
H'holds receiving social security . . . 826

Households, 2000

Total households . . . 5,137
With persons under 18 . . . 1,587
With persons over 65 . . . 714
Family households . . . 3,145
Single person households . . . 1,366
Persons per household . . . 2.43
Persons per family . . . 2.98

Labor & Employment

Total civilian labor force, 2008§§ . . . 8,670
Unemployment rate . . . 6.0%
Total civilian labor force, 2000 . . . 7,593

Employed persons 16 years and over by occupation, 2000

Managers & professionals . . . 2,529
Service occupations . . . 1,646
Sales & office occupations . . . 1,550
Farming, fishing & forestry . . . 22
Construction & maintenance . . . 929
Production & transportation . . . 477
Self-employed persons . . . 908

* US Census Bureau
** 2000 Decennial Census
§ California Department of Finance
§§ California Employment Development Dept

General Information

County Administration
PO Box 696
Bridgeport, CA 93517
760-932-5440

Website . . . www.monocounty.ca.gov
Incorporated . . . April 24, 1861
Form of Government . . . General law
Land Area (sq. miles) . . . 3,044.4
Water Area (sq. miles) . . . 87.4
Persons per sq. mi. of land, 2008 . . . 4.5
Sales tax rate . . . 7.25%

Voters & Gov't Officials

Registered Voters, October 2008

Total . . . 6,722
Democrats . . . 2,197
Republicans . . . 2,502
Declined to state . . . 1,661
Unincorporated area . . . 3,315
Democrats . . . 1,036
Republicans . . . 1,446
Declined to state . . . 687

Legislative Districts

US Congressional . . . 25
State Senatorial . . . 1
State Assembly . . . 25

County Officials, 2009

Manager/Admin . . . David Wilbrecht
County Clerk . . . Lynda Roberts
District Attorney . . . George Booth
Finance Dir . . . Brian Muir
Tax Assessor . . . Jody Henning
Tax Collector . . . Brian Muir
Planning/Dev Dir . . . Scott Burns
Public Works . . . Evan Nikirk
Building . . . NA
Sheriff . . . Richard Scholl
Fire Chief . . . Mark Mikulicich
Elections Official . . . Lynda Roberts
County supervisors
District 1 . . . Tom Farnetti
District 2 . . . Duane Hazard
District 3 . . . Vikki Magee-Bauer
District 4 . . . Bill Reid
District 5 . . . Byng Hunt

Public Safety

County Sheriff's office, 2007

Number of officers . . . 26
Violent crimes . . . 14
Property crimes . . . 93
Arson . . . 0

Housing & Construction

Housing Units

Total, January 2008§ . . . 13,691
Single family units, attached . . . 1,259
Single family units, detached . . . 5,251
Multiple family units . . . 6,102
Mobile home units . . . 1,079
Occupied units . . . 6,069
Vacancy rate . . . 55.7%
Median rent, 2000** . . . $682
Median SF home value, 2000** . . . $236,300

New Privately Owned Housing Units Authorized by Building Permit, 2007*

	Units	Construction Cost
Single	73	$25,433,577
Total	84	$27,706,575

Property Taxation, FY 2008

Total assessed value . . . $5,366,959,795
Total tax levied . . . $16,053,630
Delinquency rate . . . 3.000%

County Finance, FY 2007

Revenues

Total . . . $44,674,063
Taxes . . . 20,730,368
Special benefits assessment . . . 0
Licenses, permits & franchises . . . 387,468
Fines, forfeitures & penalties . . . 722,882
Use of money & property . . . 1,312,805
Intergovernmental . . . 15,886,643
Service charges . . . 4,610,129
Miscellaneous revenues . . . 1,023,768
Other financing sources . . . 0

Expenditures

Total . . . $40,225,091
General . . . 10,467,728
Public protection . . . 12,088,773
Public ways & facilities . . . 4,639,708
Health . . . 8,744,439
Sanitation . . . 0
Public assistance . . . 2,999,521
Education . . . 27,328
Recreation & culture . . . 787,465
Debt service . . . 470,129

County Schools

Mono County Office of Education
PO Box 477
Bridgeport, CA 93517
(760) 932-7311

Superintendent . . . Catherine Hiatt

County-wide School Totals

(2007-08 except where noted)

Number of districts . . . 2
Number of schools . . . 11
Enrollment . . . 1,433
High school graduates, 2006-07 . . . 86
Pupil/teacher ratio . . . 18.5
Average class size . . . 9.1
Students per computer . . . 3.5
Cost per ADA . . . $12,387
Avg teacher salary . . . $56,438

California Achievement Tests 6th ed., 2008

(Pct scoring at or above 50th National Percentile Rank)

	Math	Reading	Language
Grade 3	NA	NA	NA
Grade 7	NA	NA	NA

Academic Performance Index, 2008

Number of students tested . . . 930
2007 API (base) . . . 518
2008 API (growth) . . . 483

SAT Testing, 2006-07

Enrollment, Grade 12 . . . 175
percent taking test . . . 24.6%
percent with total score 1,500+ . . . 13.7%

Average Scores:

Math	Verbal	Writing	Total
502	524	531	1,557

County Library

Mono County Free Library
400 Sierra Park Rd
Mammoth Lakes, CA 93546
760-934-4777

Librarian . . . Bill Michael

Library statistics, FY 2007

Population served . . . 13,985
Internet terminals . . . 51
Annual users . . . 46,068

Per capita:

Operating income . . . $52.81
percent from local government . . . 88.8%
Operating expenditure . . . $52.81
Total materials . . . 8.54
Print holdings . . . 7.73
Visits . . . 9.11

See Introduction for an explanation of all data sources.

Demographics & Socio-Economic Characteristics†

(2007 American Community Survey, except as noted)

Population

1990* . . . 355,660
2007 . . . 407,637
Male . . . 211,619
Female . . . 196,018
Jan. 2008 (estimate)§ . . . 428,549
Living in unincorporated area . . . 25.1%
2020 (projected)* . . . 476,642

Race & Hispanic Origin, 2007

Race
White . . . 251,084
Black/African American . . . 13,123
North American Native . . . 1,699
Asian . . . 25,008
Pacific Islander . . . 1,802
Other Race . . . 101,695
Two or more races . . . 13,226
Hispanic origin, total . . . 212,688
Mexican . . . 197,644
Puerto Rican . . . 1,323
Cuban . . . 523
Other Hispanic . . . 13,198

Age & Nativity, 2007

Under 5 years . . . 34,861
18 years and over . . . 296,141
65 years and over . . . 40,794
85 years and over . . . 4,755
Median Age . . . 32.1
Native-born . . . 282,067
Foreign-born . . . 125,570

Educational Attainment, 2007

Population 25 years and over . . . 250,543
Less than 9th grade . . . 19.8%
High school grad or higher . . . 69.5%
Bachelor's degree or higher . . . 23.6%
Graduate degree . . . 9.0%

Income & Poverty, 2007

Per capita income . . . $25,158
Median household income . . . $57,056
Median family income . . . $62,396
Persons in poverty . . . 11.6%
H'holds receiving public assistance . . . 3,430
H'holds receiving social security . . . 31,002

Households, 2007

Total households . . . 126,010
With persons under 18 . . . 50,811
With persons over 65 . . . 29,047
Family households . . . 88,367
Single person households . . . 28,517
Persons per household . . . 3.09
Persons per family . . . 3.65

Labor & Employment

Total civilian labor force, 2008§§ . . . 214,500
Unemployment rate . . . 8.5%
Total civilian labor force, 2000* . . . 179,645

Employed persons 16 years and over by occupation, 2007

Managers & professionals . . . 50,796
Service occupations . . . 33,720
Sales & office occupations . . . 39,896
Farming, fishing & forestry . . . 22,975
Construction & maintenance . . . 16,892
Production & transportation . . . 18,270
Self-employed persons . . . 16,380

† see Appendix D for 2000 Decennial Census Data
* US Census Bureau
** 2007 American Community Survey
§ California Department of Finance
§§ California Employment Development Dept

General Information

168 W Alisal St
County Courthouse
Salinas, CA 93901
831-755-5115

Website . . . www.co.monterey.ca.us
Incorporated . . . February 18, 1850
Form of Government . . . General law
Land Area (sq. miles) . . . 3,322.0
Water Area (sq. miles) . . . 449.1
Persons per sq. mi. of land, 2008 . . . 129.0
Sales tax rate . . . 7.25%

Voters & Gov't Officials

Registered Voters, October 2008

Total . . . 158,391
Democrats . . . 79,803
Republicans . . . 43,265
Declined to state . . . 29,641
Unincorporated area . . . 52,990
Democrats . . . 22,773
Republicans . . . 18,629
Declined to state . . . 9,539

Legislative Districts

US Congressional . . . 17
State Senatorial . . . 12, 15
State Assembly . . . 27, 28

County Officials, 2009

Manager/Admin . . . Lew Bauman
Clerk-Recorder . . . Stephen Vagnini
District Attorney . . . Dean Flippo
Auditor-Controller . . . Micheal Miller
Tax Assessor . . . Stephen Vagnini
Treasurer/Tax Coll . . . Louis G. Solton
Planning/Dev Dir . . . Mike Novo
Public Works . . . Yazdan Emrani
Building Dept Dir . . . Tim McCormick
Sheriff . . . Mike Kanalakis
Emerg Mgmt Dir . . . Paul Ireland
Elections Official . . . Linda Tulett
County supervisors
District 1 . . . Fernando Armenta
District 2 . . . Louis Calgagno
District 3 . . . Simone Salinas
District 4 . . . Jane Parker
District 5 . . . Dave Potter

Public Safety

County Sheriff's office, 2007

Number of officers . . . 317
Violent crimes . . . 219
Property crimes . . . 1,952
Arson . . . 14

Housing & Construction

Housing Units

Total, January 2008§ . . . 140,296
Single family units, attached . . . 12,587
Single family units, detached . . . 86,242
Multiple family units . . . 35,467
Mobile home units . . . 6,000
Occupied units . . . 129,271
Vacancy rate . . . 7.9%
Median rent, 2007** . . . $1,061
Median SF home value, 2007** . . . $658,700

New Privately Owned Housing Units Authorized by Building Permit, 2007*

	Units	Construction Cost
Single	563	$200,226,946
Total	1,107	$270,456,608

Property Taxation, FY 2008

Total assessed value . . . $51,579,833,274
Total tax levied . . . $80,336,213
Delinquency rate . . . 3.000%

County Finance, FY 2007

Revenues

Total . . . $630,454,750
Taxes . . . 150,690,107
Special benefits assessment . . . 0
Licenses, permits & franchises . . . 20,353,228
Fines, forfeitures & penalties . . . 10,930,024
Use of money & property . . . 12,150,410
Intergovernmental . . . 301,434,402
Service charges . . . 65,097,811
Miscellaneous revenues . . . 10,504,979
Other financing sources . . . 53,641,932

Expenditures

Total . . . $579,058,997
General . . . 75,379,238
Public protection . . . 164,596,453
Public ways & facilities . . . 69,770,833
Health . . . 110,243,043
Sanitation . . . 143,209
Public assistance . . . 136,347,974
Education . . . 6,810,931
Recreation & culture . . . 7,041,525
Debt service . . . 8,725,791

County Schools

Monterey County Office of Education
PO Box 80851
Salinas, CA 93912
(831) 755-0301

Superintendent . . . Nancy Kotowski

County-wide School Totals

(2007-08 except where noted)

Number of districts . . . 23
Number of schools . . . 210
Enrollment . . . 116,797
High school graduates, 2006-07 . . . 6,214
Pupil/teacher ratio . . . 7.8
Average class size . . . 11.2
Students per computer . . . 3.5
Cost per ADA . . . $8,502
Avg teacher salary . . . $63,147

California Achievement Tests 6th ed., 2008

(Pct scoring at or above 50th National Percentile Rank)

	Math	Reading	Language
Grade 3	17%	25%	33%
Grade 7	48%	59%	65%

Academic Performance Index, 2008

Number of students tested . . . 84,648
2007 API (base) . . . 476
2008 API (growth) . . . 576

SAT Testing, 2006-07

Enrollment, Grade 12 . . . 4,695
percent taking test . . . 31.8%
percent with total score 1,500+ . . . 10.8%

Average Scores:

Math	Verbal	Writing	Total
470	462	460	1,392

County Library

Montery County Free Library
26 Central Ave
Salinas, CA 93901
831-755-5838

Librarian . . . Robert McElroy

Library statistics, FY 2007

Population served . . . 226,803
Internet terminals . . . 160
Annual users . . . 229,676

Per capita:

Operating income . . . $29.19
percent from local government . . . 91.7%
Operating expenditure . . . $27.42
Total materials . . . 1.92
Print holdings . . . 1.81
Visits . . . 3.65

See Introduction for an explanation of all data sources.

Napa County

Demographics & Socio-Economic Characteristics†

(2007 American Community Survey, except as noted)

Population

1990* . . . 110,765
2007 . . . 132,565
Male . . . 67,641
Female . . . 64,924
Jan. 2008 (estimate)§ . . . 136,704
Living in unincorporated area . . . 21.1%
2020 (projected)* . . . 165,786

Race & Hispanic Origin, 2007

Race
White . . . 111,200
Black/African American . . . 2,512
North American Native . . . 1,185
Asian . . . 7,771
Pacific Islander . . . 534
Other Race . . . 6,004
Two or more races . . . 3,359
Hispanic origin, total . . . 39,089
Mexican . . . 35,413
Puerto Rican . . . 8
Cuban . . . 26
Other Hispanic . . . 3,642

Age & Nativity, 2007

Under 5 years . . . 7,999
18 years and over . . . 102,746
65 years and over . . . 19,642
85 years and over . . . 3,942
Median Age . . . 39.2
Native-born . . . 101,083
Foreign-born . . . 31,482

Educational Attainment, 2007

Population 25 years and over . . . 88,811
Less than 9th grade . . . 12.2%
High school grad or higher . . . 80.4%
Bachelor's degree or higher . . . 26.3%
Graduate degree . . . 8.5%

Income & Poverty, 2007

Per capita income . . . $32,555
Median household income . . . $62,081
Median family income . . . $73,963
Persons in poverty . . . 9.6%
H'holds receiving public assistance . . . 601
H'holds receiving social security . . . 14,830

Households, 2007

Total households . . . 49,069
With persons under 18 . . . 14,290
With persons over 65 . . . 14,169
Family households . . . 30,794
Single person households . . . 13,752
Persons per household . . . 2.57
Persons per family . . . 3.22

Labor & Employment

Total civilian labor force, 2008§§ . . . 76,300
Unemployment rate . . . 5.1%
Total civilian labor force, 2000* . . . 61,120

Employed persons 16 years and over by occupation, 2007

Managers & professionals . . . 21,214
Service occupations . . . 13,404
Sales & office occupations . . . 14,034
Farming, fishing & forestry . . . 3,219
Construction & maintenance . . . 6,996
Production & transportation . . . 6,792
Self-employed persons . . . 7,259

† see Appendix D for 2000 Decennial Census Data
* US Census Bureau
** 2007 American Community Survey
§ California Department of Finance
§§ California Employment Development Dept

General Information

1195 3rd St
Room 310
Napa, CA 94559
707-253-4421

Website . . . www.co.napa.ca.us
Incorporated . . . February 18, 1850
Form of Government . . . General law
Land Area (sq. miles) . . . 753.7
Water Area (sq. miles) . . . 34.5
Persons per sq. mi. of land, 2008 . . . 181.4
Sales tax rate . . . 7.75%

Voters & Gov't Officials

Registered Voters, October 2008

Total . . . 71,517
Democrats . . . 34,073
Republicans . . . 20,464
Declined to state . . . 13,465
Unincorporated area . . . 16,688
Democrats . . . 6,739
Republicans . . . 5,909
Declined to state . . . 3,139

Legislative Districts

US Congressional . . . 1
State Senatorial . . . 2
State Assembly . . . 7

County Officials, 2009

Manager/Admin . . . Nancy Watt
County Clerk . . . John Tuteur
District Attorney . . . Gary Lieberstein
Finance Dir . . . Pam Kindig
Tax Assessor . . . John Tuteur
Treasurer/Tax Coll . . . Tamie Frasier
Planning/Dev Dir . . . Hillary Gitelman
Public Works . . . Robert Peterson
Building . . . NA
Sheriff . . . Doug Koford
Fire Chief . . . Ernie Loveless
Elections Official . . . John Tuteur
County supervisors
District 1 . . . Brad Wagenknecht
District 2 . . . Mark Luce
District 3 . . . Diane Dillon
District 4 . . . Bill Dodd
District 5 . . . Keith Caldwell

Public Safety

County Sheriff's office, 2007

Number of officers . . . 93
Violent crimes . . . 79
Property crimes . . . 562
Arson . . . 6

Housing & Construction

Housing Units

Total, January 2008§ . . . 53,950
Single family units, attached . . . 3,585
Single family units, detached . . . 36,246
Multiple family units . . . 10,138
Mobile home units . . . 3,981
Occupied units . . . 50,588
Vacancy rate . . . 6.2%
Median rent, 2007** . . . $1,152
Median SF home value, 2007** . . . $643,400

New Privately Owned Housing Units Authorized by Building Permit, 2007*

	Units	Construction Cost
Single	272	$117,319,354
Total	330	$125,300,942

Property Taxation, FY 2008

Total assessed value . . . $25,455,033,891
Total tax levied . . . $50,169,049
Delinquency rate . . . 2.280%

County Finance, FY 2007

Revenues

Total . . . $207,713,127
Taxes . . . 78,833,070
Special benefits assessment . . . 0
Licenses, permits & franchises . . . 7,747,594
Fines, forfeitures & penalties . . . 4,544,369
Use of money & property . . . 3,755,298
Intergovernmental . . . 82,935,347
Service charges . . . 25,513,002
Miscellaneous revenues . . . 3,370,601
Other financing sources . . . 1,013,846

Expenditures

Total . . . $201,686,404
General . . . 41,068,087
Public protection . . . 83,109,979
Public ways & facilities . . . 7,610,172
Health . . . 35,587,342
Sanitation . . . 0
Public assistance . . . 29,719,465
Education . . . 350,201
Recreation & culture . . . 220,599
Debt service . . . 4,020,559

County Schools

Napa County Office of Education
2121 Imola Ave
Napa, CA 94559
(707) 253-6810
Superintendent . . . Barbara Nemko

County-wide School Totals

(2007-08 except where noted)

Number of districts . . . 6
Number of schools . . . 123
Enrollment . . . 55,062
High school graduates, 2006-07 . . . 3,363
Pupil/teacher ratio . . . 17.7
Average class size . . . 16.2
Students per computer . . . 4.2
Cost per ADA . . . $8,850
Avg teacher salary . . . $67,891

California Achievement Tests 6th ed., 2008

(Pct scoring at or above 50th National Percentile Rank)

	Math	Reading	Language
Grade 3	NA	NA	NA
Grade 7	NA	NA	NA

Academic Performance Index, 2008

Number of students tested . . . 41,279
2007 API (base) . . . 418
2008 API (growth) . . . 509

SAT Testing, 2006-07

Enrollment, Grade 12 . . . 1,611
percent taking test . . . 30.2%
percent with total score 1,500+ . . . 18.1%

Average Scores:

Math	Verbal	Writing	Total
538	519	515	1,572

County Library

Napa City-County Library
580 Coombs St
Napa, CA 94559
707-253-4241

Librarian . . . Janet McCoy

Library statistics, FY 2007

Population served . . . 129,976
Internet terminals . . . 58
Annual users . . . NA

Per capita:

Operating income . . . $50.32
percent from local government . . . 88.9%
Operating expenditure . . . $45.25
Total materials . . . 1.58
Print holdings . . . 1.37
Visits . . . 3.16

See Introduction for an explanation of all data sources.

Demographics & Socio-Economic Characteristics†

(2007 American Community Survey, except as noted)

Population

1990* 78,510
2007 97,027
Male 48,567
Female 48,460
Jan. 2008 (estimate)§ 99,186
Living in unincorporated area 67.6%
2020 (projected)* 114,451

Race & Hispanic Origin, 2007

Race
White 90,604
Black/African American 394
North American Native 2,145
Asian 1,344
Pacific Islander 55
Other Race 628
Two or more races 1,857
Hispanic origin, total 7,310
Mexican . . . . NA
Puerto Rican . . . . NA
Cuban . . . . NA
Other Hispanic . . . . NA

Age & Nativity, 2007

Under 5 years 3,942
18 years and over 79,487
65 years and over 17,483
85 years and over 2,218
Median Age 45.2
Native-born 91,718
Foreign-born 5,309

Educational Attainment, 2007

Population 25 years and over 72,177
Less than 9th grade 1.1%
High school grad or higher 92.9%
Bachelor's degree or higher 31.5%
Graduate degree 9.3%

Income & Poverty, 2007

Per capita income $29,511
Median household income $59,150
Median family income $63,845
Persons in poverty 9.4%
H'holds receiving public assistance 1,156
H'holds receiving social security 13,379

Households, 2007

Total households 39,708
With persons under 18 12,071
With persons over 65 11,469
Family households 27,823
Single person households 7,597
Persons per household 2.42
Persons per family 2.67

Labor & Employment

Total civilian labor force, 2008§§ 51,100
Unemployment rate 6.6%
Total civilian labor force, 2000* 43,624

Employed persons 16 years and over by occupation, 2007

Managers & professionals 15,303
Service occupations 9,023
Sales & office occupations 13,527
Farming, fishing & forestry 0
Construction & maintenance 7,016
Production & transportation 3,785
Self-employed persons 9,620

† see Appendix D for 2000 Decennial Census Data
* US Census Bureau
** 2007 American Community Survey
§ California Department of Finance
§§ California Employment Development Dept

General Information

950 Maidu Ave
Nevada City, CA 95959
530-265-7040

Website . . . . www.mynevadacounty.com
Incorporated . . . . April 25, 1851
Form of Government . . . . General law
Land Area (sq. miles) 957.6
Water Area (sq. miles) 16.9
Persons per sq. mi. of land, 2008 . . . . 103.6
Sales tax rate 7.38%

Voters & Gov't Officials

Registered Voters, October 2008

Total 63,769
Democrats 21,716
Republicans 25,992
Declined to state 12,327
Unincorporated area 45,998
Democrats 14,721
Republicans 20,549
Declined to state 8,150

Legislative Districts

US Congressional 4
State Senatorial 1, 4
State Assembly 3

County Officials, 2009

Manager/Admin . . . . Rick Haffey
County Clerk . . . . Gregory J. Diaz
District Attorney . . . . Clifford Newell
Auditor-Controller . . . . Marcia Salter
Tax Assessor . . . . Dale Flippin
Treasurer/Tax Coll . . . . Marcia Salter
Planning/Comm Dev . . . . Jory Stewart
Public Works . . . . Michael Hill-Weld
Building . . . . NA
Sheriff . . . . Keith Royal
Fire/Emerg Mgmt Dir . . . . NA
Elections Official . . . . Gregory J. Diaz
County supervisors
District 1 . . . . Nate Beason
District 2 . . . . Ed Scofield
District 3 . . . . John Spencer
District 4 . . . . Hank Weston
District 5 . . . . Ted Owens

Public Safety

County Sheriff's office, 2007

Number of officers 71
Violent crimes 132
Property crimes 597
Arson 1

Housing & Construction

Housing Units

Total, January 2008§ 50,364
Single family units, attached 964
Single family units, detached 41,027
Multiple family units 4,498
Mobile home units 3,875
Occupied units 41,658
Vacancy rate 17.3%
Median rent, 2007** $1,077
Median SF home value, 2007** $477,900

New Privately Owned Housing Units Authorized by Building Permit, 2007*

	Units	Construction Cost
Single	389	$93,759,648
Total	449	$103,129,354

Property Taxation, FY 2008

Total assessed value $15,973,938,406
Total tax levied $23,201,834
Delinquency rate 2.710%

County Finance, FY 2007

Revenues

Total $120,246,163
Taxes 38,453,202
Special benefits assessment 0
Licenses, permits & franchises 2,680,314
Fines, forfeitures & penalties 2,667,363
Use of money & property 1,952,942
Intergovernmental 59,681,424
Service charges 12,045,587
Miscellaneous revenues 2,764,787
Other financing sources 544

Expenditures

Total $115,421,710
General 9,934,809
Public protection 47,787,730
Public ways & facilities 11,077,800
Health 17,659,392
Sanitation 0
Public assistance 24,504,508
Education 2,522,122
Recreation & culture 0
Debt service 1,935,349

County Schools

Nevada County Office of Education
112 Nevada City Hwy
Nevada City, CA 95959
(530) 478-6400

Superintendent . . . . Holly Hermansen

County-wide School Totals

(2007-08 except where noted)

Number of districts 10
Number of schools 65
Enrollment 17,117
High school graduates, 2006-07 2,092
Pupil/teacher ratio 22.3
Average class size 13.3
Students per computer 7.0
Cost per ADA $8,444
Avg teacher salary $63,975

California Achievement Tests 6th ed., 2008

(Pct scoring at or above 50th National Percentile Rank)

	Math	Reading	Language
Grade 3	46%	54%	50%
Grade 7	58%	71%	56%

Academic Performance Index, 2008

Number of students tested 11,900
2007 API (base) 537
2008 API (growth) 736

SAT Testing, 2006-07

Enrollment, Grade 12 2,083
percent taking test 17.4%
percent with total score 1,500+ 11.3%

Average Scores:

Math	Verbal	Writing	Total
550	538	528	1,616

County Library

Nevada County Library
980 Helling Way
Nevada City, CA 95959
530-265-7050

Librarian . . . . Mary Ann Trygg

Library statistics, FY 2007

Population served 99,766
Internet terminals 41
Annual users 46,411

Per capita:

Operating income $24.65
percent from local government 89.7%
Operating expenditure $24.33
Total materials 2.13
Print holdings 1.85
Visits 4.86

See Introduction for an explanation of all data sources.

Orange County

Demographics & Socio-Economic Characteristics†

(2007 American Community Survey, except as noted)

Population

1990* ... 2,410,556
2007 ... 2,997,033
Male ... 1,499,209
Female ... 1,497,824
Jan. 2008 (estimate)§ ... 3,121,251
Living in unincorporated area ... 3.9%
2020 (projected)* ... 3,520,265

Race & Hispanic Origin, 2007

Race
White ... 1,844,932
Black/African American ... 52,818
North American Native ... 14,749
Asian ... 483,004
Pacific Islander ... 8,959
Other Race ... 520,535
Two or more races ... 72,036
Hispanic origin, total ... 998,032
Mexican ... 863,139
Puerto Rican ... 10,188
Cuban ... 10,299
Other Hispanic ... 114,406

Age & Nativity, 2007

Under 5 years ... 210,667
18 years and over ... 2,230,800
65 years and over ... 331,780
85 years and over ... 42,982
Median Age ... 35.9
Native-born ... 2,086,946
Foreign-born ... 910,087

Educational Attainment, 2007

Population 25 years and over ... 1,936,090
Less than 9th grade ... 9.7%
High school grad or higher ... 82.6%
Bachelor's degree or higher ... 35.4%
Graduate degree ... 12.4%

Income & Poverty, 2007

Per capita income ... $33,794
Median household income ... $73,263
Median family income ... $83,015
Persons in poverty ... 8.9%
H'holds receiving public assistance ... 16,802
H'holds receiving social security ... 222,580

Households, 2007

Total households ... 976,713
With persons under 18 ... 373,176
With persons over 65 ... 228,513
Family households ... 689,605
Single person households ... 221,841
Persons per household ... 3.03
Persons per family ... 3.56

Labor & Employment

Total civilian labor force, 2008§§ ... 1,638,600
Unemployment rate ... 5.3%
Total civilian labor force, 2000* ... 1,409,897

Employed persons 16 years and over by occupation, 2007

Managers & professionals ... 571,282
Service occupations ... 222,362
Sales & office occupations ... 402,456
Farming, fishing & forestry ... 4,557
Construction & maintenance ... 114,798
Production & transportation ... 154,940
Self-employed persons ... 120,734

† see Appendix D for 2000 Decennial Census Data
* US Census Bureau
** 2007 American Community Survey
§ California Department of Finance
§§ California Employment Development Dept

General Information

10 Civic Center Plaza
Santa Ana, CA 92701
714-834-2311

Website ... www.ocrecorder.com
Incorporated ... March 11, 1889
Form of Government ... General law
Land Area (sq. miles) ... 789.4
Water Area (sq. miles) ... 158.6
Persons per sq. mi. of land, 2008 ... 3,954.0
Sales tax rate ... 7.75%

Voters & Gov't Officials

Registered Voters, October 2008

Total ... 1,607,989
Democrats ... 511,641
Republicans ... 713,986
Declined to state ... 319,293
Unincorporated area ... 73,245
Democrats ... 18,799
Republicans ... 38,864
Declined to state ... 13,041

Legislative Districts

US Congressional ... 40, 42, 44, 46-48
State Senatorial ... 29, 33-35, 38
State Assembly ... 56, 60, 67-73

County Officials, 2009

Exec Officer ... Tom Mauk
County Clerk ... Tom Daly
District Attorney ... Tony Rackauckas
Finance Dir ... David Sundstrom
Tax Assessor ... Webster Guillory
Tax Collector ... Chris Street
Planning/Comm Dev ... NA
Public Works ... Alisa Drakokaiois
Building ... NA
Sheriff ... Michael Carona
Fire/Emerg Mgmt Dir ... NA
Elections Official ... NA
County supervisors
District 1 ... Janet Nguyen
District 2 ... John Moorlach
District 3 ... Bill Campbell
District 4 ... Chris Norby
District 5 ... Pat Bates

Public Safety

County Sheriff's office, 2007

Number of officers ... 1,753
Violent crimes ... 178
Property crimes ... 1,481
Arson ... 25

Housing & Construction

Housing Units

Total, January 2008§ ... 1,030,289
Single family units, attached ... 128,489
Single family units, detached ... 519,755
Multiple family units ... 349,947
Mobile home units ... 32,098
Occupied units ... 995,989
Vacancy rate ... 3.3%
Median rent, 2007** ... $1,372
Median SF home value, 2007** ... $670,600

New Privately Owned Housing Units Authorized by Building Permit, 2007*

	Units	Construction Cost
Single	2,279	$728,503,750
Total	7,372	$1,386,097,639

Property Taxation, FY 2008

Total assessed value ... $410,016,640,580
Total tax levied ... $264,470,010
Delinquency rate ... 2.597%

County Finance, FY 2007

Revenues

Total ... $3,284,262,678
Taxes ... 540,219,400
Special benefits assessment ... 137,587
Licenses, permits & franchises ... 22,232,964
Fines, forfeitures & penalties ... 119,669,003
Use of money & property ... 125,219,272
Intergovernmental ... 1,567,537,146
Service charges ... 370,650,348
Miscellaneous revenues ... 312,586,104
Other financing sources ... 211,880,464

Expenditures

Total ... $3,070,017,986
General ... 533,273,593
Public protection ... 1,017,978,597
Public ways & facilities ... 48,617,692
Health ... 501,916,950
Sanitation ... 0
Public assistance ... 676,839,420
Education ... 35,026,904
Recreation & culture ... 18,235,245
Debt service ... 238,129,585

County Schools

Orange County Department of Education
PO Box 9050
Costa Mesa, CA 92628
(714) 966-4000

Superintendent ... William Habermehl

County-wide School Totals

(2007-08 except where noted)

Number of districts ... 57
Number of schools ... 1,644
Enrollment ... 1,467,972
High school graduates, 2006-07 ... 107,944
Pupil/teacher ratio ... 18.2
Average class size ... 21.2
Students per computer ... 6.1
Cost per ADA ... $8,224
Avg teacher salary ... $75,014

California Achievement Tests 6th ed., 2008

(Pct scoring at or above 50th National Percentile Rank)

	Math	Reading	Language
Grade 3	54%	46%	61%
Grade 7	29%	37%	32%

Academic Performance Index, 2008

Number of students tested ... 1,115,889
2007 API (base) ... 602
2008 API (growth) ... 624

SAT Testing, 2006-07

Enrollment, Grade 12 ... 35,546
percent taking test ... 43.8%
percent with total score 1,500+ ... 26.4%

Average Scores:

Math	Verbal	Writing	Total
549	520	521	1,590

County Library

Orange County Public Library
1501 E St Andrew Pl
Santa Ana, CA 92705
714-566-3000

Librarian ... John Adams

Library statistics, FY 2007

Population served ... 1,532,758
Internet terminals ... 505
Annual users ... 680,874

Per capita:

Operating income ... $24.71
percent from local government ... 90.0%
Operating expenditure ... $24.18
Total materials ... 1.93
Print holdings ... 1.84
Visits ... 4.02

See Introduction for an explanation of all data sources.

Demographics & Socio-Economic Characteristics†

(2007 American Community Survey, except as noted)

Population

1990* . . . 172,796
2007 . . . 332,920
Male . . . 163,673
Female . . . 169,247
Jan. 2008 (estimate)§ . . . 333,401
Living in unincorporated area . . . 32.7%
2020 (projected)* . . . 428,535

Race & Hispanic Origin, 2007

Race
White . . . 284,060
Black/African American . . . 4,828
North American Native . . . 2,272
Asian . . . 18,598
Pacific Islander . . . 240
Other Race . . . 12,454
Two or more races . . . 10,468
Hispanic origin, total . . . 38,808
Mexican . . . 26,933
Puerto Rican . . . 1,224
Cuban . . . 393
Other Hispanic . . . 10,258

Age & Nativity, 2007

Under 5 years . . . 20,063
18 years and over . . . 259,194
65 years and over . . . 49,083
85 years and over . . . 6,631
Median Age . . . 37.6
Native-born . . . 297,463
Foreign-born . . . 35,457

Educational Attainment, 2007

Population 25 years and over . . . 228,575
Less than 9th grade . . . 3.2%
High school grad or higher . . . 92.6%
Bachelor's degree or higher . . . 34.3%
Graduate degree . . . 10.5%

Income & Poverty, 2007

Per capita income . . . $34,467
Median household income . . . $69,076
Median family income . . . $82,641
Persons in poverty . . . 6.1%
H'holds receiving public assistance . . . 1,813
H'holds receiving social security . . . 36,202

Households, 2007

Total households . . . 126,847
With persons under 18 . . . 45,784
With persons over 65 . . . 34,007
Family households . . . 88,545
Single person households . . . 30,850
Persons per household . . . 2.58
Persons per family . . . 3.04

Labor & Employment

Total civilian labor force, 2008§§ . . . 176,200
Unemployment rate . . . 6.5%
Total civilian labor force, 2000* . . . 123,619

Employed persons 16 years and over by occupation, 2007

Managers & professionals . . . 65,595
Service occupations . . . 24,374
Sales & office occupations . . . 48,834
Farming, fishing & forestry . . . 347
Construction & maintenance . . . 16,197
Production & transportation . . . 12,110
Self-employed persons . . . 14,525

† see Appendix D for 2000 Decennial Census Data
* US Census Bureau
** 2007 American Community Survey
§ California Department of Finance
§§ California Employment Development Dept

General Information

175 Fulweiler Ave
Auburn, CA 95603
530-889-4000

Website . . . www.placer.ca.gov
Incorporated . . . April 25, 1851
Form of Government . . . Charter
Land Area (sq. miles) . . . 1,404.4
Water Area (sq. miles) . . . 98.4
Persons per sq. mi. of land, 2008 . . . 237.4
Sales tax rate . . . 7.25%

Voters & Gov't Officials

Registered Voters, October 2008

Total . . . 198,963
Democrats . . . 59,076
Republicans . . . 96,965
Declined to state . . . 36,317
Unincorporated area . . . 68,514
Democrats . . . 19,651
Republicans . . . 33,420
Declined to state . . . 12,746

Legislative Districts

US Congressional . . . 4
State Senatorial . . . 1, 4
State Assembly . . . 3-5

County Officials, 2009

Chief Exec Officer . . . Thomas Miller
Clerk-Recorder . . . Jim McCauley
District Attorney . . . Brad Fenocchio
Auditor-Controller . . . Katherine Martinis
Tax Assessor . . . Kristen Spears
Treasurer/Tax Coll . . . J. Windeshausen
Comm Dev Dir . . . Michael Johnson
Public Works . . . Ken Grehm
Building Dept Dir . . . Bob Martino
Sheriff . . . Ed Bonner
Fire/Emerg Mgmt Dir . . . NA
Elections Official . . . Jim McCauley
County supervisors
District 1 . . . F.C. Rockholm
District 2 . . . Robert Weygandt
District 3 . . . Jim Holmes
District 4 . . . Kirk Uhler
District 5 . . . Jennifer Montgomery

Public Safety

County Sheriff's office, 2007

Number of officers . . . 259
Violent crimes . . . 255
Property crimes . . . 1,997
Arson . . . 19

Housing & Construction

Housing Units

Total, January 2008§ . . . 147,408
Single family units, attached . . . 4,738
Single family units, detached . . . 114,893
Multiple family units . . . 23,032
Mobile home units . . . 4,745
Occupied units . . . 131,707
Vacancy rate . . . 10.7%
Median rent, 2007** . . . $1,094
Median SF home value, 2007** . . . $483,700

New Privately Owned Housing Units Authorized by Building Permit, 2007*

	Units	Construction Cost
Single	2,188	$574,889,338
Total	2,412	$607,342,921

Property Taxation, FY 2008

Total assessed value . . . $57,654,914,123
Total tax levied . . . $106,660,017
Delinquency rate . . . 2.650%

County Finance, FY 2007

Revenues

Total . . . $476,321,059
Taxes . . . 174,423,721
Special benefits assessment . . . 22,644
Licenses, permits & franchises . . . 9,522,231
Fines, forfeitures & penalties . . . 9,673,550
Use of money & property . . . 18,770,747
Intergovernmental . . . 199,407,278
Service charges . . . 60,131,042
Miscellaneous revenues . . . 2,711,175
Other financing sources . . . 281,657

Expenditures

Total . . . $433,792,266
General . . . 84,770,008
Public protection . . . 151,060,122
Public ways & facilities . . . 47,513,856
Health . . . 48,716,579
Sanitation . . . 0
Public assistance . . . 89,786,546
Education . . . 5,285,311
Recreation & culture . . . 4,275,037
Debt service . . . 2,384,807

County Schools

Placer County Office of Education
360 Nevada St
Auburn, CA 95603
(530) 889-8020

Superintendent . . . Gayle Garbolino-Mojica

County-wide School Totals

(2007-08 except where noted)

Number of districts . . . 15
Number of schools . . . 118
Enrollment . . . 72,470
High school graduates, 2006-07 . . . 6,575
Pupil/teacher ratio . . . 8.1
Average class size . . . 9.9
Students per computer . . . 4.9
Cost per ADA . . . $7,612
Avg teacher salary . . . $62,473

California Achievement Tests 6th ed., 2008

(Pct scoring at or above 50th National Percentile Rank)

	Math	Reading	Language
Grade 3	24%	23%	18%
Grade 7	36%	42%	29%

Academic Performance Index, 2008

Number of students tested . . . 53,064
2007 API (base) . . . 558
2008 API (growth) . . . 626

SAT Testing, 2006-07

Enrollment, Grade 12 . . . 4,984
percent taking test . . . 37.6%
percent with total score 1,500+ . . . 23.2%

Average Scores:

Math	Verbal	Writing	Total
540	520	516	1,576

County Library

Auburn-Placer County Library
350 Nevada St
Auburn, CA 95603
530-886-4500

Librarian . . . Mark Parker

Library statistics, FY 2007

Population served . . . 180,819
Internet terminals . . . 56
Annual users . . . 48,341

Per capita:

Operating income . . . $24.99
percent from local government . . . 85.7%
Operating expenditure . . . $24.01
Total materials . . . 1.96
Print holdings . . . 1.74
Visits . . . 3.30

See Introduction for an explanation of all data sources.

Demographics & Socio-Economic Characteristics

(2000 U.S. Census, except as noted)

Population

1990* . . . 19,739
2000 . . . 20,824
Male . . . 10,403
Female . . . 10,421
Jan. 2008 (estimate)§ . . . 20,917
Living in unincorporated area . . . 90.2%
2020 (projected)* . . . 22,934

Race & Hispanic Origin, 2000

Race
White . . . 19,113
Black/African American . . . 130
North American Native . . . 530
Asian . . . 110
Pacific Islander . . . 20
Other Race . . . 377
Two or more races . . . 544
Hispanic origin, total . . . 1,177
Mexican . . . 871
Puerto Rican . . . 24
Cuban . . . 12
Other Hispanic . . . 270

Age & Nativity, 2000

Under 5 years . . . 929
18 years and over . . . 16,097
65 years and over . . . 3,725
85 years and over . . . 342
Median Age . . . 44.2
Native-born . . . 20,298
Foreign-born . . . 526

Educational Attainment, 2000

Population 25 years and over . . . 14,786
Less than 9th grade . . . 2.9%
High school grad or higher . . . 88.0%
Bachelor's degree or higher . . . 17.5%
Graduate degree . . . 5.8%

Income & Poverty, 1999

Per capita income . . . $19,391
Median household income . . . $36,351
Median family income . . . $46,119
Persons in poverty . . . 12.9%
H'holds receiving public assistance . . . 369
H'holds receiving social security . . . 2,995

Households, 2000

Total households . . . 9,000
With persons under 18 . . . 2,564
With persons over 65 . . . 2,545
Family households . . . 6,051
Single person households . . . 2,478
Persons per household . . . 2.29
Persons per family . . . 2.77

Labor & Employment

Total civilian labor force, 2008§§ . . . 10,000
Unemployment rate . . . 10.6%
Total civilian labor force, 2000 . . . 9,413

Employed persons 16 years and over by occupation, 2000

Managers & professionals . . . 2,555
Service occupations . . . 1,676
Sales & office occupations . . . 1,931
Farming, fishing & forestry . . . 167
Construction & maintenance . . . 1,038
Production & transportation . . . 1,153
Self-employed persons . . . 1,096

* US Census Bureau
** 2000 Decennial Census
§ California Department of Finance
§§ California Employment Development Dept

General Information

520 Main St
Room 309
Quincy, CA 95971
530-283-6315

Website . . . www.countyofplumas.com
Incorporated . . . March 18, 1854
Form of Government . . . General law
Land Area (sq. miles) . . . 2,553.7
Water Area (sq. miles) . . . 59.8
Persons per sq. mi. of land, 2008 . . . 8.2
Sales tax rate . . . 7.25%

Voters & Gov't Officials

Registered Voters, October 2008

Total . . . 13,744
Democrats . . . 4,621
Republicans . . . 5,886
Declined to state . . . 2,493
Unincorporated area . . . 12,525
Democrats . . . 4,164
Republicans . . . 5,508
Declined to state . . . 2,191

Legislative Districts

US Congressional . . . 4
State Senatorial . . . 1
State Assembly . . . 3

County Officials, 2009

Manager/Admin . . . Jack Ingstad
County Clerk . . . Kathy Williams
District Attorney . . . Jeff Cunan
Auditor-Controller . . . Shawn Montgomery
Tax Assessor . . . Charles Leonhardt
Tax Collector . . . Susie Bryant-Grant
Planning/Dev Dir . . . Randy Wilson
Public Works . . . Bob Perreault
Building . . . NA
Sheriff . . . Terry Bergstrand
Fire Chief . . . Andy Anderson
Elections Official . . . Kathy Williams
County supervisors
District 1 . . . Terry Swofford
District 2 . . . Robert Meacher
District 3 . . . Sharon Thrall
District 4 . . . Lori Simpson
District 5 . . . Ole Olsen

Public Safety

County Sheriff's office, 2007

Number of officers . . . 38
Violent crimes . . . NA
Property crimes . . . 405
Arson . . . NA

Housing & Construction

Housing Units

Total, January 2008§ . . . 15,457
Single family units, attached . . . 447
Single family units, detached . . . 11,912
Multiple family units . . . 771
Mobile home units . . . 2,327
Occupied units . . . 10,368
Vacancy rate . . . 32.9%
Median rent, 2000** . . . $525
Median SF home value, 2000** . . . $137,900

New Privately Owned Housing Units Authorized by Building Permit, 2007*

	Units	Construction Cost
Single	154	$26,528,302
Total	154	$26,528,302

Property Taxation, FY 2008

Total assessed value . . . $3,959,166,127
Total tax levied . . . $8,692,471
Delinquency rate . . . 3.000%

County Finance, FY 2007

Revenues

Total . . . $54,429,732
Taxes . . . 14,349,648
Special benefits assessment . . . 0
Licenses, permits & franchises . . . 2,172,107
Fines, forfeitures & penalties . . . 957,605
Use of money & property . . . 1,462,668
Intergovernmental . . . 28,600,404
Service charges . . . 5,863,472
Miscellaneous revenues . . . 977,021
Other financing sources . . . 36,807

Expenditures

Total . . . $56,454,476
General . . . 11,068,148
Public protection . . . 15,716,344
Public ways & facilities . . . 8,175,481
Health . . . 9,591,507
Sanitation . . . 0
Public assistance . . . 9,211,684
Education . . . 781,829
Recreation & culture . . . 562,419
Debt service . . . 1,347,064

County Schools

Plumas County Office of Education
50 Church St, Suite B
Quincy, CA 95971
(530) 283-6500

Superintendent . . . Glenn Harris

County-wide School Totals

(2007-08 except where noted)

Number of districts . . . 2
Number of schools . . . 15
Enrollment . . . 2,641
High school graduates, 2006-07 . . . 223
Pupil/teacher ratio . . . 3.9
Average class size . . . 0.0
Students per computer . . . 1.4
Cost per ADA . . . $10,173
Avg teacher salary . . . $58,155

California Achievement Tests 6th ed., 2008

(Pct scoring at or above 50th National Percentile Rank)

	Math	Reading	Language
Grade 3	NA	NA	NA
Grade 7	NA	NA	NA

Academic Performance Index, 2008

Number of students tested . . . 1,786
2007 API (base) . . . 499
2008 API (growth) . . . 585

SAT Testing, 2006-07

Enrollment, Grade 12 . . . 233
percent taking test . . . 31.3%
percent with total score 1,500+ . . . 13.7%

Average Scores:

Math	Verbal	Writing	Total
488	500	484	1,472

County Library

Plumas County Library
445 Jackson St
Quincy, CA 95971
530-283-6310

Librarian . . . Margaret Miles

Library statistics, FY 2007

Population served . . . 24,613
Internet terminals . . . 18
Annual users . . . 19,223

Per capita:

Operating income . . . $27.64
percent from local government . . . 81.9%
Operating expenditure . . . $27.64
Total materials . . . 3.15
Print holdings . . . 3.07
Visits . . . NA

See Introduction for an explanation of all data sources.

Demographics & Socio-Economic Characteristics†

(2007 American Community Survey, except as noted)

Population

1990* 1,170,413
2007 2,073,571
Male 1,036,644
Female 1,036,927
Jan. 2008 (estimate)§ 2,088,322
Living in unincorporated area 26.6%
2020 (projected)* 2,904,848

Race & Hispanic Origin, 2007

Race
White 1,314,662
Black/African American 126,648
North American Native 18,792
Asian 108,755
Pacific Islander 6,021
Other Race 422,541
Two or more races 76,152
Hispanic origin, total 896,116
Mexican 791,337
Puerto Rican 11,830
Cuban 5,525
Other Hispanic 87,424

Age & Nativity, 2007

Under 5 years 165,240
18 years and over 1,490,860
65 years and over 233,079
85 years and over 27,783
Median Age 31.4
Native-born 1,602,561
Foreign-born 471,010

Educational Attainment, 2007

Population 25 years and over 1,271,662
Less than 9th grade 9.8%
High school grad or higher 79.6%
Bachelor's degree or higher 20.1%
Graduate degree 6.8%

Income & Poverty, 2007

Per capita income $24,885
Median household income $58,145
Median family income $64,572
Persons in poverty 11.7%
H'holds receiving public assistance .. 14,917
H'holds receiving social security ... 173,233

Households, 2007

Total households 649,863
With persons under 18 286,419
With persons over 65 161,274
Family households 478,614
Single person households 130,862
Persons per household 3.14
Persons per family 3.66

Labor & Employment

Total civilian labor force, 2008§§ ... 918,800
Unemployment rate 8.6%
Total civilian labor force, 2000* 651,952

Employed persons 16 years and over by occupation, 2007

Managers & professionals 256,293
Service occupations 167,843
Sales & office occupations 244,551
Farming, fishing & forestry 7,601
Construction & maintenance 109,457
Production & transportation 116,383
Self-employed persons 78,903

† see Appendix D for 2000 Decennial Census Data
* US Census Bureau
** 2007 American Community Survey
§ California Department of Finance
§§ California Employment Development Dept

General Information

4080 Lemon St
Riverside, CA 92501
951-955-1000

Website .... www.countyofriverside.us
Incorporated .... March 11, 1893
Form of Government .... General law
Land Area (sq. miles) 7,207.4
Water Area (sq. miles) 95.8
Persons per sq. mi. of land, 2008 .... 289.7
Sales tax rate 7.75%

Voters & Gov't Officials

Registered Voters, October 2008

Total 837,389
Democrats 307,593
Republicans 350,885
Declined to state 143,589
Unincorporated area 218,463
Democrats 75,993
Republicans 95,543
Declined to state 37,489

Legislative Districts

US Congressional 41, 44-45, 49
State Senatorial 31, 36, 37, 40
State Assembly 63-66, 71, 80

County Officials, 2009

Manager/Admin .... Bill Luna
County Clerk .... Larry Ward
District Attorney .... Rod Pacheo
Auditor-Controller .... Robert Byrd
Tax Assessor .... Larry Ward
Tax Collector .... Don Kent
Planning/Comm Dev .... NA
Public Works .... NA
Building .... NA
Sheriff .... Stanley Sniff
Fire Chief .... John Hawkins
Elections Official .... Barbara Dunmore
County supervisors
District 1 .... Robert Buster
District 2 .... John Tavaglione
District 3 .... Jeff Stone
District 4 .... Roy Wilson
District 5 .... Marion Ashley

Public Safety

County Sheriff's office, 2007

Number of officers 1,965
Violent crimes 2,243
Property crimes 14,935
Arson 61

Housing & Construction

Housing Units

Total, January 2008§ 773,331
Single family units, attached 46,960
Single family units, detached 512,205
Multiple family units 127,740
Mobile home units 86,426
Occupied units 671,036
Vacancy rate 13.2%
Median rent, 2007** $1,066
Median SF home value, 2007** $406,300

New Privately Owned Housing Units Authorized by Building Permit, 2007*

	Units	Construction Cost
Single	9,717	$2,180,372,317
Total	12,334	$2,411,025,433

Property Taxation, FY 2008

Total assessed value $237,388,487,198
Total tax levied $295,114,987
Delinquency rate 2.500%

County Finance, FY 2007

Revenues

Total $2,631,785,124
Taxes 588,760,551
Special benefits assessment 0
Licenses, permits & franchises .. 68,864,992
Fines, forfeitures & penalties 79,640,195
Use of money & property 89,500,920
Intergovernmental 1,390,278,852
Service charges 378,872,690
Miscellaneous revenues 34,321,717
Other financing sources 1,306,179

Expenditures

Total $2,441,031,651
General 250,487,746
Public protection 926,776,477
Public ways & facilities 141,184,903
Health 341,496,264
Sanitation 0
Public assistance 699,149,630
Education 14,822,535
Recreation & culture 196,969
Debt service 66,917,127

County Schools

Riverside County Office of Education
PO Box 868
Riverside, CA 92502
(951) 826-6530
Superintendent .... Kenneth Young

County-wide School Totals

(2007-08 except where noted)
Number of districts 35
Number of schools 853
Enrollment 780,848
High school graduates, 2006-07 41,666
Pupil/teacher ratio 18.5
Average class size 18.8
Students per computer 6.7
Cost per ADA $7,913
Avg teacher salary $69,010

California Achievement Tests 6th ed., 2008

(Pct scoring at or above 50th National Percentile Rank)

	Math	Reading	Language
Grade 3	NA	NA	NA
Grade 7	10%	7%	6%

Academic Performance Index, 2008

Number of students tested 593,238
2007 API (base) 517
2008 API (growth) 553

SAT Testing, 2006-07

Enrollment, Grade 12 27,730
percent taking test 30.4%
percent with total score 1,500+ 11.2%

Average Scores:

Math	Verbal	Writing	Total
481	470	467	1,418

County Library

Riverside County Library Service
4080 Lemon St
Riverside, CA 92501
951-955-1114
Librarian .... Nancy Johnson

Library statistics, FY 2007

Population served 1,047,996
Internet terminals 37
Annual users 69,346

Per capita:

Operating income $19.38
percent from local government 49.8%
Operating expenditure $20.45
Total materials 1.43
Print holdings 1.30
Visits 4.06

See Introduction for an explanation of all data sources.

Sacramento County

Demographics & Socio-Economic Characteristics†

(2007 American Community Survey, except as noted)

Population

1990* 1,041,219
2007 1,386,667
Male 680,517
Female 706,150
Jan. 2008 (estimate)§ 1,424,415
Living in unincorporated area 39.6%
2020 (projected)* 1,622,306

Race & Hispanic Origin, 2007

Race
White 856,942
Black/African American 140,486
North American Native 10,349
Asian 188,317
Pacific Islander 11,111
Other Race 118,503
Two or more races 60,959
Hispanic origin, total 272,182
Mexican 214,352
Puerto Rican 7,083
Cuban 1,080
Other Hispanic 49,667

Age & Nativity, 2007

Under 5 years 103,197
18 years and over 1,023,807
65 years and over 153,693
85 years and over 21,255
Median Age 34.3
Native-born 1,117,496
Foreign-born 269,171

Educational Attainment, 2007

Population 25 years and over 890,850
Less than 9th grade 7.3%
High school grad or higher 85.1%
Bachelor's degree or higher 27.0%
Graduate degree 8.6%

Income & Poverty, 2007

Per capita income $26,817
Median household income $56,987
Median family income $64,520
Persons in poverty 12.1%
H'holds receiving public assistance 22,226
H'holds receiving social security 117,627

Households, 2007

Total households 503,357
With persons under 18 185,756
With persons over 65 107,409
Family households 331,677
Single person households 133,723
Persons per household 2.70
Persons per family 3.30

Labor & Employment

Total civilian labor force, 2008§§ 690,400
Unemployment rate 7.2%
Total civilian labor force, 2000* 584,886

Employed persons 16 years and over by occupation, 2007

Managers & professionals 232,215
Service occupations 114,401
Sales & office occupations 179,289
Farming, fishing & forestry 1,576
Construction & maintenance 61,233
Production & transportation 54,652
Self-employed persons 44,843

† see Appendix D for 2000 Decennial Census Data
* US Census Bureau
** 2007 American Community Survey
§ California Department of Finance
§§ California Employment Development Dept

General Information

700 H St
Room 2450
Sacramento, CA 95814
916-874-5411

Website .... www.saccounty.net
Incorporated .... February 18, 1850
Form of Government .... Charter
Land Area (sq. miles) 965.7
Water Area (sq. miles) 29.8
Persons per sq. mi. of land, 2008 .... 1,475.0
Sales tax rate 7.75%

Voters & Gov't Officials

Registered Voters, October 2008

Total 684,588
Democrats 305,682
Republicans 216,239
Declined to state 132,299
Unincorporated area 277,235
Democrats 113,117
Republicans 100,287
Declined to state 51,779

Legislative Districts

US Congressional 3-5, 10
State Senatorial 1, 5, 6
State Assembly 4-5, 9-10, 15

County Officials, 2009

Manager/Admin .... Terry Schutten
County Clerk .... NA
District Attorney .... Jan Scully
Finance Dir .... Dave Irish
Tax Assessor .... Ken Steiger
Tax Collector .... Dave Irish
Planning/Comm Dev .... NA
Public Works .... Paul Hahn
Building .... NA
Sheriff .... John McGinness
Fire/Emerg Mgmt Dir .... NA
Elections Official .... NA
County supervisors
District 1 .... Roger Dickinson
District 2 .... Jimmie R. Yee
District 3 .... Susan Peters
District 4 .... Roberta MacGlashan
District 5 .... Don Nottoli

Public Safety

County Sheriff's office, 2007

Number of officers 1,419
Violent crimes 3,231
Property crimes 14,912
Arson 111

Housing & Construction

Housing Units

Total, January 2008§ 551,219
Single family units, attached 34,360
Single family units, detached 354,371
Multiple family units 146,707
Mobile home units 15,781
Occupied units 527,592
Vacancy rate 4.3%
Median rent, 2007** $936
Median SF home value, 2007** $370,600

New Privately Owned Housing Units Authorized by Building Permit, 2007*

	Units	Construction Cost
Single	3,410	$678,043,423
Total	4,112	$760,008,964

Property Taxation, FY 2008

Total assessed value $133,720,620,425
Total tax levied $243,718,027
Delinquency rate 3.700%

County Finance, FY 2007

Revenues

Total $2,326,881,351
Taxes 546,784,980
Special benefits assessment 348,528
Licenses, permits & franchises 38,426,457
Fines, forfeitures & penalties 25,558,218
Use of money & property 64,032,531
Intergovernmental 1,380,869,481
Service charges 188,460,926
Miscellaneous revenues 78,661,780
Other financing sources 3,738,450

Expenditures

Total $2,308,628,438
General 159,812,898
Public protection 684,522,931
Public ways & facilities 96,323,184
Health 616,441,316
Sanitation 0
Public assistance 620,603,981
Education 20,179,340
Recreation & culture 18,642,794
Debt service 92,101,994

County Schools

Sacramento County Office of Education
PO Box 269003
Sacramento, CA 95826
(916) 228-2500

Superintendent .... David Gordon

County-wide School Totals

(2007-08 except where noted)

Number of districts 19
Number of schools 567
Enrollment 362,786
High school graduates, 2006-07 22,103
Pupil/teacher ratio 12.3
Average class size 14.6
Students per computer 2.0
Cost per ADA $8,396
Avg teacher salary $63,314

California Achievement Tests 6th ed., 2008

(Pct scoring at or above 50th National Percentile Rank)

	Math	Reading	Language
Grade 3	NA	NA	NA
Grade 7	6%	8%	5%

Academic Performance Index, 2008

Number of students tested 268,219
2007 API (base) 420
2008 API (growth) 481

SAT Testing, 2006-07

Enrollment, Grade 12 16,886
percent taking test 33.9%
percent with total score 1,500+ 15.5%

Average Scores:

Math	Verbal	Writing	Total
505	487	483	1,475

County Library

Sacramento Public Library
828 I St
Sacramento, CA 95814
916-264-2770

Librarian .... Ann Marie Gold

Library statistics, FY 2007

Population served 1,335,969
Internet terminals 49
Annual users 27,435

Per capita:

Operating income $25.83
percent from local government 91.0%
Operating expenditure $23.08
Total materials 1.57
Print holdings 1.45
Visits 1.18

See Introduction for an explanation of all data sources.

Demographics & Socio-Economic Characteristics

(2000 U.S. Census, except as noted)

Population

1990* . . . 36,697
2000 . . . 53,234
Male . . . 26,941
Female . . . 26,293
Jan. 2008 (estimate)§ . . . 57,784
Living in unincorporated area . . . 32.6%
2020 (projected)* . . . 83,792

Race & Hispanic Origin, 2000

Race
White . . . 34,695
Black/African American . . . 573
North American Native . . . 616
Asian . . . 1,277
Pacific Islander . . . 99
Other Race . . . 13,237
Two or more races . . . 2,737
Hispanic origin, total . . . 25,516
Mexican . . . 21,908
Puerto Rican . . . 157
Cuban . . . 34
Other Hispanic . . . 3,417

Age & Nativity, 2000

Under 5 years . . . 4,705
18 years and over . . . 36,091
65 years and over . . . 4,315
85 years and over . . . 463
Median Age . . . 31.4
Native-born . . . 43,208
Foreign-born . . . 10,026

Educational Attainment, 2000

Population 25 years and over . . . 31,401
Less than 9th grade . . . 13.2%
High school grad or higher . . . 74.9%
Bachelor's degree or higher . . . 17.1%
Graduate degree . . . 5.1%

Income & Poverty, 1999

Per capita income . . . $20,932
Median household income . . . $57,469
Median family income . . . $60,665
Persons in poverty . . . 9.8%
H'holds receiving public assistance . . . 643
H'holds receiving social security . . . 3,292

Households, 2000

Total households . . . 15,885
With persons under 18 . . . 8,144
With persons over 65 . . . 3,049
Family households . . . 12,893
Single person households . . . 2,245
Persons per household . . . 3.32
Persons per family . . . 3.64

Labor & Employment

Total civilian labor force, 2008§§ . . . 25,300
Unemployment rate . . . 9.6%
Total civilian labor force, 2000 . . . 25,343

Employed persons 16 years and over by occupation, 2000

Managers & professionals . . . 7,152
Service occupations . . . 3,484
Sales & office occupations . . . 5,930
Farming, fishing & forestry . . . 1,119
Construction & maintenance . . . 2,834
Production & transportation . . . 3,144
Self-employed persons . . . 1,803

* US Census Bureau
** 2000 Decennial Census
§ California Department of Finance
§§ California Employment Development Dept

General Information

481 Fourth St
Hollister, CA 95023
831-636-4000

Website . . . www.san-benito.ca.us
Incorporated . . . February 12, 1874
Form of Government . . . General law
Land Area (sq. miles) . . . 1,389.1
Water Area (sq. miles) . . . 1.7
Persons per sq. mi. of land, 2008 . . . 41.6
Sales tax rate . . . 8.25%

Voters & Gov't Officials

Registered Voters, October 2008

Total . . . 25,355
Democrats . . . 11,764
Republicans . . . 7,971
Declined to state . . . 4,635
Unincorporated area . . . 10,166
Democrats . . . 3,917
Republicans . . . 4,162
Declined to state . . . 1,712

Legislative Districts

US Congressional . . . 17
State Senatorial . . . 12
State Assembly . . . 28

County Officials, 2009

Manager/Admin . . . Susan Thompson
County Clerk . . . Joe Paul Gonzalez
District Attorney . . . Candice Hooper-Mancino
Auditor-Controller . . . Joe Paul Gonzalez
Tax Assessor . . . Tom Slavich
Tax Collector . . . Mary Lou Andrade
Planning/Dev Dir . . . Arthur E. Henriques
Public Works . . . Janelle Cox (Actg)
Building Dept Dir . . . NA
Sheriff . . . Curtis Hill
Fire Chief . . . Curt Itson
Elections Official . . . Joe Paul Gonzalez
County supervisors
District 1 . . . Marjorie Barrios
District 2 . . . Anthony Botelho
District 3 . . . Pat Loe
District 4 . . . Reb Monaco
District 5 . . . Jaime De La Cruz

Public Safety

County Sheriff's office, 2007

Number of officers . . . 32
Violent crimes . . . 57
Property crimes . . . 327
Arson . . . 9

Housing & Construction

Housing Units

Total, January 2008§ . . . 17,769
Single family units, attached . . . 1,034
Single family units, detached . . . 13,798
Multiple family units . . . 2,058
Mobile home units . . . 879
Occupied units . . . 17,102
Vacancy rate . . . 3.8%
Median rent, 2000** . . . $765
Median SF home value, 2000** . . . $284,000

New Privately Owned Housing Units Authorized by Building Permit, 2007*

	Units	Construction Cost
Single	32	$11,757,693
Total	32	$11,757,693

Property Taxation, FY 2008

Total assessed value . . . $6,743,893,879
Total tax levied . . . $10,197,871
Delinquency rate . . . 3.000%

County Finance, FY 2007

Revenues

Total . . . $68,074,434
Taxes . . . 15,463,497
Special benefits assessment . . . 404,214
Licenses, permits & franchises . . . 1,057,156
Fines, forfeitures & penalties . . . 1,340,116
Use of money & property . . . 2,277,889
Intergovernmental . . . 40,908,754
Service charges . . . 6,619,906
Miscellaneous revenues . . . 0
Other financing sources . . . 2,902

Expenditures

Total . . . $65,490,860
General . . . 9,008,760
Public protection . . . 21,382,064
Public ways & facilities . . . 9,501,091
Health . . . 7,602,262
Sanitation . . . 0
Public assistance . . . 16,870,660
Education . . . 690,935
Recreation & culture . . . 199,923
Debt service . . . 235,165

County Schools

San Benito County Office of Education
460 Fifth St
Hollister, CA 95023
(831) 637-5393

Superintendent . . . Tim Foley

County-wide School Totals

(2007-08 except where noted)

Number of districts . . . 8
Number of schools . . . 20
Enrollment . . . 11,275
High school graduates, 2006-07 . . . 646
Pupil/teacher ratio . . . 16.7
Average class size . . . 10.6
Students per computer . . . 3.3
Cost per ADA . . . $8,360
Avg teacher salary . . . $65,334

California Achievement Tests 6th ed., 2008

(Pct scoring at or above 50th National Percentile Rank)

	Math	Reading	Language
Grade 3	NA	NA	NA
Grade 7	21%	21%	7%

Academic Performance Index, 2008

Number of students tested . . . 8,541
2007 API (base) . . . 469
2008 API (growth) . . . 474

SAT Testing, 2006-07

Enrollment, Grade 12 . . . 770
percent taking test . . . 31.8%
percent with total score 1,500+ . . . 14.9%

Average Scores:

Math	Verbal	Writing	Total
501	488	479	1,468

County Library

San Benito County Free Library
470 Fifth St
Hollister, CA 95023
831-636-4107

Librarian . . . Nora Conte

Library statistics, FY 2007

Population served . . . 55,978
Internet terminals . . . 49
Annual users . . . 105,480

Per capita:

Operating income . . . $10.82
percent from local government . . . 83.3%
Operating expenditure . . . $10.77
Total materials . . . 1.61
Print holdings . . . 1.52
Visits . . . 11.07

See Introduction for an explanation of all data sources.

Demographics & Socio-Economic Characteristics†

(2007 American Community Survey, except as noted)

Population

1990* . . . 1,418,380
2007 . . . 2,007,800
Male . . . 1,005,119
Female . . . 1,002,681
Jan. 2008 (estimate)§ . . . 2,055,766
Living in unincorporated area . . . 14.5%
2020 (projected)* . . . 2,581,371

Race & Hispanic Origin, 2007

Race
White . . . 1,142,600
Black/African American . . . 177,042
North American Native . . . 20,103
Asian . . . 118,658
Pacific Islander . . . 5,399
Other Race . . . 456,373
Two or more races . . . 87,625
Hispanic origin, total . . . 938,798
Mexican . . . 805,321
Puerto Rican . . . 12,647
Cuban . . . 5,356
Other Hispanic . . . 115,474

Age & Nativity, 2007

Under 5 years . . . 165,085
18 years and over . . . 1,410,383
65 years and over . . . 165,549
85 years and over . . . 18,719
Median Age . . . 30.2
Native-born . . . 1,566,828
Foreign-born . . . 440,972

Educational Attainment, 2007

Population 25 years and over . . . 1,182,325
Less than 9th grade . . . 10.2%
High school grad or higher . . . 77.3%
Bachelor's degree or higher . . . 18.1%
Graduate degree . . . 6.3%

Income & Poverty, 2007

Per capita income . . . $21,608
Median household income . . . $56,428
Median family income . . . $61,702
Persons in poverty . . . 11.8%
H'holds receiving public assistance . . 20,754
H'holds receiving social security . . . 132,419

Households, 2007

Total households . . . 592,449
With persons under 18 . . . 277,876
With persons over 65 . . . 116,760
Family households . . . 451,365
Single person households . . . 112,680
Persons per household . . . 3.31
Persons per family . . . 3.80

Labor & Employment

Total civilian labor force, 2008§§ . . . 876,300
Unemployment rate . . . 8.0%
Total civilian labor force, 2000* . . . 721,185

Employed persons 16 years and over by occupation, 2007

Managers & professionals . . . 237,778
Service occupations . . . 145,540
Sales & office occupations . . . 239,580
Farming, fishing & forestry . . . 1,933
Construction & maintenance . . . 104,450
Production & transportation . . . 133,828
Self-employed persons . . . 61,056

† see Appendix D for 2000 Decennial Census Data
* US Census Bureau
** 2007 American Community Survey
§ California Department of Finance
§§ California Employment Development Dept

General Information

385 N Arrowhead Ave
San Bernardino, CA 92415
909-387-2020

Website . . . www.sbcounty.gov
Incorporated . . . April 26, 1853
Form of Government . . . Charter
Land Area (sq. miles) . . . 20,052.5
Water Area (sq. miles) . . . 52.8
Persons per sq. mi. of land, 2008 . . . 102.5
Sales tax rate . . . 7.75%

Voters & Gov't Officials

Registered Voters, October 2008

Total . . . 829,756
Democrats . . . 331,097
Republicans . . . 320,077
Declined to state . . . 143,301
Unincorporated area . . . 124,308
Democrats . . . 41,825
Republicans . . . 54,264
Declined to state . . . 21,558

Legislative Districts

US Congressional . . . 25-26, 41-43
State Senatorial . . . 17-18, 29, 31-32
State Assembly . . . 32, 34, 36, 59-63

County Officials, 2009

Admin Officer . . . Mark H. Uffer
Clerk . . . Larry Walker
District Attorney . . . Mike Ramos
Finance Dir . . . Dean Arabatzis
Assessor . . . Harlow Cameron
Treasurer/Tax Coll . . . Dick Larsen
Comm Dev . . . Mitch Slagerman
Public Works . . . Vana Olson
Land Use Dir . . . Julie Rynerson Rock
Sheriff . . . Gary Penrod
Fire Chief . . . Pat Dennen
Elections Official . . . Kari Verjil
County supervisors
District 1 . . . Brad Mitzelfelt
District 2 . . . Paul Biane
District 3 . . . Neil Derry
District 4 . . . Gary Ovitt
District 5 . . . Josie Gonzales

Public Safety

County Sheriff's office, 2007

Number of officers . . . 1,783
Violent crimes . . . 1,286
Property crimes . . . 6,569
Arson . . . 114

Housing & Construction

Housing Units

Total, January 2008§ . . . 685,642
Single family units, attached . . . 28,459
Single family units, detached . . . 483,447
Multiple family units . . . 129,035
Mobile home units . . . 44,701
Occupied units . . . 606,005
Vacancy rate . . . 11.6%
Median rent, 2007** . . . $1,029
Median SF home value, 2007** . . . $387,000

New Privately Owned Housing Units Authorized by Building Permit, 2007*

	Units	Construction Cost
Single	6,302	$1,211,200,704
Total	7,752	$1,323,199,636

Property Taxation, FY 2008

Total assessed value . . . $176,135,269,285
Total tax levied . . . $199,566,283
Delinquency rate . . . 5.610%

County Finance, FY 2007

Revenues

Total . . . $2,373,605,058
Taxes . . . 471,260,438
Special benefits assessment . . . 3,228,458
Licenses, permits & franchises . . 25,010,339
Fines, forfeitures & penalties . . . 25,759,213
Use of money & property . . . 57,696,741
Intergovernmental . . . 1,422,940,833
Service charges . . . 308,272,452
Miscellaneous revenues . . . 47,697,161
Other financing sources . . . 1,762,423

Expenditures

Total . . . $2,140,180,658
General . . . 194,857,226
Public protection . . . 689,589,696
Public ways & facilities . . . 83,263,113
Health . . . 281,125,780
Sanitation . . . 0
Public assistance . . . 780,879,392
Education . . . 18,301,543
Recreation & culture . . . 19,616,282
Debt service . . . 72,547,626

County Schools

San Bernardino County Office of Education
601 North E St
San Bernardino, CA 92410
(909) 888-3228

Superintendent . . . Gary Thomas

County-wide School Totals

(2007-08 except where noted)

Number of districts . . . 37
Number of schools . . . 798
Enrollment . . . 705,250
High school graduates, 2006-07 . . . 45,846
Pupil/teacher ratio . . . 11.4
Average class size . . . 12.9
Students per computer . . . 3.3
Cost per ADA . . . $8,073
Avg teacher salary . . . $67,210

California Achievement Tests 6th ed., 2008

(Pct scoring at or above 50th National Percentile Rank)

	Math	Reading	Language
Grade 3	11%	4%	7%
Grade 7	8%	10%	6%

Academic Performance Index, 2008

Number of students tested . . . 526,637
2007 API (base) . . . 530
2008 API (growth) . . . 484

SAT Testing, 2006-07

Enrollment, Grade 12 . . . 28,660
percent taking test . . . 29.7%
percent with total score 1,500+ . . . 10.9%

Average Scores:

Math	Verbal	Writing	Total
479	467	465	1,411

County Library

San Bernardino County Library
104 W Fourth St
San Bernardino, CA 92415
909-387-5720

Librarian . . . Ed Kieczykowski

Library statistics, FY 2007

Population served . . . 1,177,092
Internet terminals . . . 12
Annual users . . . 45,343

Per capita:

Operating income . . . $14.27
percent from local government . . . 73.3%
Operating expenditure . . . $13.86
Total materials . . . 0.86
Print holdings . . . 0.79
Visits . . . 5.83

See Introduction for an explanation of all data sources.

Demographics & Socio-Economic Characteristics†

(2007 American Community Survey, except as noted)

Population

1990* . . . 2,498,016
2007 . . . 2,974,859
Male . . . 1,493,808
Female . . . 1,481,051
Jan. 2008 (estimate)§ . . . 3,146,274
Living in unincorporated area . . . 15.6%
2020 (projected)* . . . 3,550,714

Race & Hispanic Origin, 2007

Race
White . . . 2,083,989
Black/African American . . . 149,870
North American Native . . . 20,028
Asian . . . 307,032
Pacific Islander . . . 12,671
Other Race . . . 284,386
Two or more races . . . 116,883
Hispanic origin, total . . . 901,369
Mexican . . . 816,788
Puerto Rican . . . 14,334
Cuban . . . 3,158
Other Hispanic . . . 67,089

Age & Nativity, 2007

Under 5 years . . . 221,458
18 years and over . . . 2,233,454
65 years and over . . . 330,720
85 years and over . . . 47,709
Median Age . . . 34.2
Native-born . . . 2,300,775
Foreign-born . . . 674,084

Educational Attainment, 2007

Population 25 years and over . . . 1,887,786
Less than 9th grade . . . 7.1%
High school grad or higher . . . 85.2%
Bachelor's degree or higher . . . 33.5%
Graduate degree . . . 12.2%

Income & Poverty, 2007

Per capita income . . . $30,080
Median household income . . . $61,794
Median family income . . . $71,823
Persons in poverty . . . 11.1%
H'holds receiving public assistance . . 23,406
H'holds receiving social security . . . 241,074

Households, 2007

Total households . . . 1,045,265
With persons under 18 . . . 365,871
With persons over 65 . . . 230,646
Family households . . . 684,440
Single person households . . . 270,818
Persons per household . . . 2.74
Persons per family . . . 3.36

Labor & Employment

Total civilian labor force, 2008§§ . 1,566,200
Unemployment rate . . . 6.0%
Total civilian labor force, 2000* . . . 1,319,517

Employed persons 16 years and over by occupation, 2007

Managers & professionals . . . 543,364
Service occupations . . . 235,711
Sales & office occupations . . . 348,873
Farming, fishing & forestry . . . 4,726
Construction & maintenance . . . 118,257
Production & transportation . . . 119,123
Self-employed persons . . . 122,559

† see Appendix D for 2000 Decennial Census Data
* US Census Bureau
** 2007 American Community Survey
§ California Department of Finance
§§ California Employment Development Dept

General Information

1600 Pacific Hwy
San Diego, CA 92101
619-531-5880

Website . . . www.sdcounty.ca.gov
Incorporated . . . February 18, 1850
Form of Government . . . Charter
Land Area (sq. miles) . . . 4,199.9
Water Area (sq. miles) . . . 325.6
Persons per sq. mi. of land, 2008 . . . 749.1
Sales tax rate . . . 7.75%

Voters & Gov't Officials

Registered Voters, October 2008

Total . . . 1,488,157
Democrats . . . 539,560
Republicans . . . 539,939
Declined to state . . . 343,928
Unincorporated area . . . 241,035
Democrats . . . 67,017
Republicans . . . 115,950
Declined to state . . . 47,306

Legislative Districts

US Congressional . . . 49-53
State Senatorial . . . 36, 38-40
State Assembly . . . 66, 73-79

County Officials, 2009

Manager/Admin . . . Walt Ekard
County Clerk . . . David Butler (Actg)
District Attorney . . . Bonnie Dumanis
Finance Dir . . . Donald Steuer
Tax Assessor . . . David Butler (Actg)
Tax Collector . . . Dan McAllister
Planning/Dev Dir . . . Eric Gibson
Public Works . . . John Snyder
Building Dept Dir . . . Eric Gibson
Sheriff . . . Bill Kolender
Fire/Emerg Mgmt Dir . . . NA
Elections Official . . . Deborah Seiler
County supervisors
District 1 . . . Greg Cox
District 2 . . . Dianne Jacob
District 3 . . . Pam Slater-Price
District 4 . . . Ron Roberts
District 5 . . . Bill Horn

Public Safety

County Sheriff's office, 2007

Number of officers . . . 2,191
Violent crimes . . . 1,699
Property crimes . . . 7,564
Arson . . . 58

Housing & Construction

Housing Units

Total, January 2008§ . . . 1,138,857
Single family units, attached . . . 98,809
Single family units, detached . . . 582,188
Multiple family units . . . 409,978
Mobile home units . . . 47,882
Occupied units . . . 1,088,700
Vacancy rate . . . 4.4%
Median rent, 2007** . . . $1,168
Median SF home value, 2007** . . . $556,500

New Privately Owned Housing Units Authorized by Building Permit, 2007*

	Units	Construction Cost
Single	3,422	$955,600,811
Total	7,435	$1,430,827,853

Property Taxation, FY 2008

Total assessed value . . . $386,925,410,225
Total tax levied . . . $538,210,653
Delinquency rate . . . 2.800%

County Finance, FY 2007

Revenues

Total . . . $3,388,359,745
Taxes . . . 869,282,662
Special benefits assessment . . . 0
Licenses, permits & franchises . . 36,676,850
Fines, forfeitures & penalties . . . 56,100,053
Use of money & property . . . 107,846,832
Intergovernmental . . . 1,912,242,533
Service charges . . . 377,706,059
Miscellaneous revenues . . . 26,582,826
Other financing sources . . . 1,594,930

Expenditures

Total . . . $3,202,058,532
General . . . 412,464,190
Public protection . . . 1,002,413,250
Public ways & facilities . . . 102,449,032
Health . . . 510,196,574
Sanitation . . . 9,572,958
Public assistance . . . 932,944,583
Education . . . 28,513,862
Recreation & culture . . . 20,523,984
Debt service . . . 182,980,099

County Schools

San Diego County Office of Education
6401 Linda Vista Rd
San Diego, CA 92111
(858) 292-3500

Superintendent . . . Randolph Ward

County-wide School Totals

(2007-08 except where noted)

Number of districts . . . 35
Number of schools . . . 818
Enrollment . . . 683,786
High school graduates, 2006-07 . . . 60,599
Pupil/teacher ratio . . . 17.1
Average class size . . . 15.8
Students per computer . . . 3.2
Cost per ADA . . . $8,940
Avg teacher salary . . . $66,735

California Achievement Tests 6th ed., 2008

(Pct scoring at or above 50th National Percentile Rank)

	Math	Reading	Language
Grade 3	43%	35%	43%
Grade 7	19%	17%	18%

Academic Performance Index, 2008

Number of students tested . . . 483,270
2007 API (base) . . . 568
2008 API (growth) . . . 592

SAT Testing, 2006-07

Enrollment, Grade 12 . . . 38,359
percent taking test . . . 38.3%
percent with total score 1,500+ . . . 19.5%

Average Scores:

Math	Verbal	Writing	Total
517	501	497	1,515

County Library

San Diego County Library
5555 Overland Ave
San Diego, CA 92123
858-694-2415

Librarian . . . Jose Aponte

Library statistics, FY 2007

Population served . . . 1,049,868
Internet terminals . . . 394
Annual users . . . NA

Per capita:

Operating income . . . $33.43
percent from local government . . . 80.6%
Operating expenditure . . . $31.30
Total materials . . . 1.54
Print holdings . . . 1.32
Visits . . . 6.31

See Introduction for an explanation of all data sources.

Demographics & Socio-Economic Characteristics†

(2007 American Community Survey, except as noted)

Population

1990* . . . 723,959
2007 . . . 764,976
Male . . . 389,132
Female . . . 375,844
Jan. 2008 (estimate)§ . . . 824,525
Living in unincorporated area . . . 0%
2020 (projected)* . . . 844,466

Race & Hispanic Origin, 2007

Race
White . . . 419,636
Black/African American . . . 51,103
North American Native . . . 2,843
Asian . . . 240,532
Pacific Islander . . . 2,956
Other Race . . . 25,987
Two or more races . . . 21,919
Hispanic origin, total . . . 106,914
Mexican . . . 52,741
Puerto Rican . . . 4,863
Cuban . . . 1,242
Other Hispanic . . . 48,068

Age & Nativity, 2007

Under 5 years . . . 40,147
18 years and over . . . 655,258
65 years and over . . . 110,880
85 years and over . . . 18,649
Median Age . . . 40.0
Native-born . . . 494,904
Foreign-born . . . 270,072

Educational Attainment, 2007

Population 25 years and over . . . 596,067
Less than 9th grade . . . 9.1%
High school grad or higher . . . 84.9%
Bachelor's degree or higher . . . 49.9%
Graduate degree . . . 19.2%

Income & Poverty, 2007

Per capita income . . . $45,410
Median household income . . . $68,023
Median family income . . . $82,320
Persons in poverty . . . 10.5%
H'holds receiving public assistance . . . 6,158
H'holds receiving social security . . . 67,614

Households, 2007

Total households . . . 321,947
With persons under 18 . . . 61,780
With persons over 65 . . . 75,763
Family households . . . 141,384
Single person households . . . 138,437
Persons per household . . . 2.33
Persons per family . . . 3.35

Labor & Employment

Total civilian labor force, 2008§§ . . . 450,400
Unemployment rate . . . 5.3%
Total civilian labor force, 2000* . . . 448,432

Employed persons 16 years and over by occupation, 2007

Managers & professionals . . . 212,067
Service occupations . . . 71,855
Sales & office occupations . . . 99,011
Farming, fishing & forestry . . . 0
Construction & maintenance . . . 21,085
Production & transportation . . . 24,684
Self-employed persons . . . 41,933

† see Appendix D for 2000 Decennial Census Data
* US Census Bureau
** 2007 American Community Survey
§ California Department of Finance
§§ California Employment Development Dept

General Information

1 Dr Carlton B Goodlett Pl
San Francisco, CA 94102
415-554-4000

Website . . . www.sfgov.org
Incorporated . . . February 18, 1850
Form of Government . . . Charter
Land Area (sq. miles) . . . 46.7
Water Area (sq. miles) . . . 185.2
Persons per sq. mi. of land, 2008 . . . 17,655.8
Sales tax rate . . . 8.50%

Voters & Gov't Officials

Registered Voters, October 2008

Total . . . 477,356
Democrats . . . 269,664
Republicans . . . 45,157
Declined to state . . . 140,102
Unincorporated area . . . NA
Democrats . . . NA
Republicans . . . NA
Declined to state . . . NA

Legislative Districts

US Congressional . . . 8, 12
State Senatorial . . . 3, 8
State Assembly . . . 12, 13

County Officials, 2009

Manager/Admin . . . Edwin Lee
County Clerk . . . Edwin Lee
District Attorney . . . Kamala Harris
Finance Dir . . . Ben Rosenfeld
Tax Assessor . . . Phil Ting
Tax Collector . . . Jose Cisneros
Planning Dir . . . John Rahaim
Public Works . . . Ed Riedskin
Building Dept Dir . . . Dan Lowrey
Sheriff . . . Mike Hennessey
Fire Chief . . . Joanna Hayes-White
Elections Official . . . John Arntz
County supervisors
District 1 . . . Eric Mar
District 2 . . . Micheala Alioto-Pier
District 3 . . . David Chiu
District 4 . . . Carmen Chu
District 5 . . . Ross Mirkarimi

Public Safety

County Sheriff's office, 2007

Number of officers . . . 831
Violent crimes . . . 6,414
Property crimes . . . 34,456
Arson . . . 232

Housing & Construction

Housing Units

Total, January 2008§ . . . 361,777
Single family units, attached . . . 48,700
Single family units, detached . . . 63,046
Multiple family units . . . 249,471
Mobile home units . . . 560
Occupied units . . . 344,792
Vacancy rate . . . 4.7%
Median rent, 2007** . . . $1,192
Median SF home value, 2007** . . . $830,700

New Privately Owned Housing Units Authorized by Building Permit, 2007*

	Units	Construction Cost
Single	55	$11,482,079
Total	2,475	$304,387,984

Property Taxation, FY 2008

Total assessed value . . . $130,004,478,543
Total tax levied . . . $907,655,021
Delinquency rate . . . 6.400%

County Finance, FY 2007

Revenues

Total . . . $6,120,131,863
Taxes . . . 2,155,648,101
Special benefits assessment . . . 0
Licenses, permits & franchises . . . 60,520,171
Fines, forfeitures & penalties . . . 12,165,167
Use of money & property . . . 180,308,668
Intergovernmental . . . 1,242,454,639
Service charges . . . 2,029,982,542
Miscellaneous revenues . . . 204,215,201
Other financing sources . . . 234,837,374

Expenditures

Total . . . $6,906,519,986
General . . . 1,538,057,132
Public protection . . . 1,111,772,394
Public ways & facilities . . . 1,015,313,402
Health . . . 1,205,280,594
Sanitation . . . 112,502,964
Public assistance . . . 573,608,894
Education . . . 67,006,227
Recreation & culture . . . 210,726,016
Debt service . . . 834,197,768

County Schools

San Francisco County Office of Education
555 Franklin St
San Francisco, CA 94102
(415) 241-6000

Superintendent . . . Carlos Garcia

County-wide School Totals

(2007-08 except where noted)

Number of districts . . . 2
Number of schools . . . 116
Enrollment . . . 55,749
High school graduates, 2006-07 . . . 3,791
Pupil/teacher ratio . . . 9.5
Average class size . . . 7.8
Students per computer . . . 1.8
Cost per ADA . . . $8,913
Avg teacher salary . . . $59,448

California Achievement Tests 6th ed., 2008

(Pct scoring at or above 50th National Percentile Rank)

	Math	Reading	Language
Grade 3	NA	NA	NA
Grade 7	12%	9%	3%

Academic Performance Index, 2008

Number of students tested . . . 39,941
2007 API (base) . . . 401
2008 API (growth) . . . 427

SAT Testing, 2006-07

Enrollment, Grade 12 . . . 3,874
percent taking test . . . 71.2%
percent with total score 1,500+ . . . 31.6%

Average Scores:

Math	Verbal	Writing	Total
528	476	474	1,478

County Library

San Francisco Public Library
100 Larkin St
San Francisco, CA 94102
415-557-4400

Librarian . . . Luis Herrera

Library statistics, FY 2007

Population served . . . 808,844
Internet terminals . . . 910
Annual users . . . 2,109,135

Per capita:

Operating income . . . $89.45
percent from local government . . . 95.1%
Operating expenditure . . . $83.09
Total materials . . . 4.04
Print holdings . . . 3.74
Visits . . . 7.85

See Introduction for an explanation of all data sources.

Demographics & Socio-Economic Characteristics†

(2007 American Community Survey, except as noted)

Population

1990* ... 480,628
2007 ... 670,990
Male ... 335,808
Female ... 335,182
Jan. 2008 (estimate)§ ... 685,660
Living in unincorporated area ... 21.1%
2020 (projected)* ... 965,094

Race & Hispanic Origin, 2007

Race
White ... 368,643
Black/African American ... 51,058
North American Native ... 5,226
Asian ... 91,638
Pacific Islander ... 3,396
Other Race ... 116,817
Two or more races ... 34,212
Hispanic origin, total ... 244,129
Mexican ... 215,697
Puerto Rican ... 3,057
Cuban ... 1,169
Other Hispanic ... 24,206

Age & Nativity, 2007

Under 5 years ... 55,619
18 years and over ... 475,667
65 years and over ... 66,547
85 years and over ... 9,453
Median Age ... 31.8
Native-born ... 507,827
Foreign-born ... 163,163

Educational Attainment, 2007

Population 25 years and over ... 404,764
Less than 9th grade ... 11.0%
High school grad or higher ... 76.6%
Bachelor's degree or higher ... 16.8%
Graduate degree ... 4.3%

Income & Poverty, 2007

Per capita income ... $22,559
Median household income ... $52,470
Median family income ... $58,837
Persons in poverty ... 14.1%
H'holds receiving public assistance ... 7,767
H'holds receiving social security ... 50,292

Households, 2007

Total households ... 207,370
With persons under 18 ... 94,450
With persons over 65 ... 44,510
Family households ... 156,276
Single person households ... 39,868
Persons per household ... 3.13
Persons per family ... 3.59

Labor & Employment

Total civilian labor force, 2008§§ ... 297,200
Unemployment rate ... 10.4%
Total civilian labor force, 2000* ... 244,277

Employed persons 16 years and over by occupation, 2007

Managers & professionals ... 74,351
Service occupations ... 44,857
Sales & office occupations ... 69,302
Farming, fishing & forestry ... 11,946
Construction & maintenance ... 29,940
Production & transportation ... 45,660
Self-employed persons ... 20,336

† see Appendix D for 2000 Decennial Census Data
* US Census Bureau
** 2007 American Community Survey
§ California Department of Finance
§§ California Employment Development Dept

General Information

222 E Weber Ave #707
Stockton, CA 95202
209-468-3203

Website ... www.sjgov.org
Incorporated ... February 18, 1850
Form of Government ... General law
Land Area (sq. miles) ... 1,399.3
Water Area (sq. miles) ... 27.0
Persons per sq. mi. of land, 2008 ... 490.0
Sales tax rate ... 7.75%

Voters & Gov't Officials

Registered Voters, October 2008

Total ... 268,476
Democrats ... 115,571
Republicans ... 105,544
Declined to state ... 37,579
Unincorporated area ... 58,732
Democrats ... 22,400
Republicans ... 26,734
Declined to state ... 7,389

Legislative Districts

US Congressional ... 11, 18
State Senatorial ... 5, 14
State Assembly ... 10, 15, 17, 26

County Officials, 2009

Administrator ... Manuel Lopez
Clerk-Recorder ... Ken Blakemore
District Attorney ... James Willett
Auditor-Controller ... Adrian Van Houten
Tax Assessor ... Ken Blakemore
Treasurer/Tax Coll ... Shabbir Khan
Comm Dev Dir ... Kerry Sullivan
Public Works ... Tom Flinn
Building ... NA
Sheriff ... Stephen Moore
Emerg Mgmt Dir ... Ron Baldwin
Elections Official ... Austin Erdman
County supervisors
District 1 ... Carlos Villapudua
District 2 ... Larry Ruhstaller
District 3 ... Steve Bestolarides
District 4 ... Ken Vogel
District 5 ... Leroy Ornellas

Public Safety

County Sheriff's office, 2007

Number of officers ... 296
Violent crimes ... 1,081
Property crimes ... 5,269
Arson ... 26

Housing & Construction

Housing Units

Total, January 2008§ ... 227,339
Single family units, attached ... 11,689
Single family units, detached ... 164,378
Multiple family units ... 41,541
Mobile home units ... 9,731
Occupied units ... 218,390
Vacancy rate ... 3.9%
Median rent, 2007** ... $902
Median SF home value, 2007** ... $399,500

New Privately Owned Housing Units Authorized by Building Permit, 2007*

	Units	Construction Cost
Single	2,201	$499,205,918
Total	2,426	$525,714,286

Property Taxation, FY 2008

Total assessed value ... $64,083,543,308
Total tax levied ... $133,420,665
Delinquency rate ... 5.943%

County Finance, FY 2007

Revenues

Total ... $872,503,457
Taxes ... 237,725,299
Special benefits assessment ... 0
Licenses, permits & franchises ... 7,563,754
Fines, forfeitures & penalties ... 11,459,902
Use of money & property ... 13,531,835
Intergovernmental ... 509,154,761
Service charges ... 79,855,829
Miscellaneous revenues ... 13,212,077
Other financing sources ... 0

Expenditures

Total ... $791,148,909
General ... 64,661,545
Public protection ... 238,099,750
Public ways & facilities ... 43,894,269
Health ... 105,979,063
Sanitation ... 53,971
Public assistance ... 318,262,425
Education ... 6,185,022
Recreation & culture ... 4,840,156
Debt service ... 9,172,708

County Schools

San Joaquin County Office of Education
PO Box 213030
Stockton, CA 95213
(209) 468-4800
Superintendent ... Fredrick Wentworth

County-wide School Totals

(2007-08 except where noted)

Number of districts ... 15
Number of schools ... 319
Enrollment ... 211,948
High school graduates, 2006-07 ... 10,747
Pupil/teacher ratio ... 16.9
Average class size ... 19.9
Students per computer ... 2.5
Cost per ADA ... $8,246
Avg teacher salary ... $59,936

California Achievement Tests 6th ed., 2008

(Pct scoring at or above 50th National Percentile Rank)

	Math	Reading	Language
Grade 3	NA	NA	NA
Grade 7	3%	5%	3%

Academic Performance Index, 2008

Number of students tested ... 156,824
2007 API (base) ... 506
2008 API (growth) ... 454

SAT Testing, 2006-07

Enrollment, Grade 12 ... 9,734
percent taking test ... 24.8%
percent with total score 1,500+ ... 9.3%

Average Scores:

Math	Verbal	Writing	Total
487	467	464	1,418

County Library

Stockton-San Joaquin County Public Libr
605 N El Dorado St
Stockton, CA 95202
209-937-8362
Librarian ... Natalie Rencher

Library statistics, FY 2007

Population served ... 619,292
Internet terminals ... 125
Annual users ... 255,083

Per capita:

Operating income ... $21.59
percent from local government ... 96.0%
Operating expenditure ... $19.98
Total materials ... 1.65
Print holdings ... 1.52
Visits ... 2.20

See Introduction for an explanation of all data sources.

Demographics & Socio-Economic Characteristics†

(2007 American Community Survey, except as noted)

Population

1990* . . . 217,162
2007 . . . 262,436
Male . . . 135,700
Female . . . 126,736
Jan. 2008 (estimate)§ . . . 269,337
Living in unincorporated area . . . 43.3%
2020 (projected)* . . . 293,540

Race & Hispanic Origin, 2007

Race
White . . . 219,936
Black/African American . . . 5,322
North American Native . . . 2,271
Asian . . . 7,716
Pacific Islander . . . 331
Other Race . . . 18,513
Two or more races . . . 8,347
Hispanic origin, total . . . 49,364
Mexican . . . 40,314
Puerto Rican . . . 643
Cuban . . . 104
Other Hispanic . . . 8,303

Age & Nativity, 2007

Under 5 years . . . 13,331
18 years and over . . . 213,152
65 years and over . . . 37,782
85 years and over . . . 6,238
Median Age . . . 37.4
Native-born . . . 238,114
Foreign-born . . . 24,322

Educational Attainment, 2007

Population 25 years and over . . . 171,755
Less than 9th grade . . . 4.5%
High school grad or higher . . . 87.9%
Bachelor's degree or higher . . . 29.9%
Graduate degree . . . 11.5%

Income & Poverty, 2007

Per capita income . . . $29,829
Median household income . . . $56,952
Median family income . . . $72,090
Persons in poverty . . . 11.8%
H'holds receiving public assistance . . . 1,600
H'holds receiving social security . . . 27,660

Households, 2007

Total households . . . 104,382
With persons under 18 . . . 28,778
With persons over 65 . . . 24,929
Family households . . . 64,251
Single person households . . . 25,357
Persons per household . . . 2.33
Persons per family . . . 2.82

Labor & Employment

Total civilian labor force, 2008§§ . . . 138,100
Unemployment rate . . . 5.7%
Total civilian labor force, 2000* . . . 116,580

Employed persons 16 years and over by occupation, 2007

Managers & professionals . . . 46,461
Service occupations . . . 23,695
Sales & office occupations . . . 31,869
Farming, fishing & forestry . . . 1,109
Construction & maintenance . . . 10,582
Production & transportation . . . 8,204
Self-employed persons . . . 14,561

† see Appendix D for 2000 Decennial Census Data
* US Census Bureau
** 2007 American Community Survey
§ California Department of Finance
§§ California Employment Development Dept

General Information

1055 Monterey St
Room 430
San Luis Obispo, CA 93408
805-781-5000

Website . . . www.slocounty.ca.gov
Incorporated . . . February 18, 1850
Form of Government . . . General law
Land Area (sq. miles) . . . 3,304.3
Water Area (sq. miles) . . . 311.2
Persons per sq. mi. of land, 2008 . . . 81.5
Sales tax rate . . . 7.25%

Voters & Gov't Officials

Registered Voters, October 2008

Total . . . 161,256
Democrats . . . 57,855
Republicans . . . 64,541
Declined to state . . . 30,005
Unincorporated area . . . 67,953
Democrats . . . 23,150
Republicans . . . 29,015
Declined to state . . . 12,043

Legislative Districts

US Congressional . . . 22-23
State Senatorial . . . 15
State Assembly . . . 33

County Officials, 2009

Manager/Admin . . . David Edge
County Clerk . . . Julie Rodewald
District Attorney . . . Gerald Shea
Finance Dir . . . Gere Sibbach
Tax Assessor . . . Tom Bordonaro
Tax Collector . . . Frank Freitas
Planning & Bldg Dir . . . Vic Holanda
Public Works . . . Paavo Ogren
Building Dept Dir . . . Vic Holanda
Sheriff . . . Patrick Hedges
Fire Chief . . . Matt Jenkins
Elections Official . . . Julie Rodewald
County supervisors
District 1 . . . Frank Mecham
District 2 . . . Bruce Gibson
District 3 . . . Adam Hill
District 4 . . . K. H. Achadjian
District 5 . . . James Patterson

Public Safety

County Sheriff's office, 2007

Number of officers . . . 162
Violent crimes . . . 239
Property crimes . . . 1,356
Arson . . . 7

Housing & Construction

Housing Units

Total, January 2008§ . . . 116,171
Single family units, attached . . . 6,815
Single family units, detached . . . 76,414
Multiple family units . . . 20,822
Mobile home units . . . 12,120
Occupied units . . . 105,391
Vacancy rate . . . 9.3%
Median rent, 2007** . . . $1,071
Median SF home value, 2007** . . . $578,900

New Privately Owned Housing Units Authorized by Building Permit, 2007*

	Units	Construction Cost
Single	919	$175,345,559
Total	1,266	$212,960,198

Property Taxation, FY 2008

Total assessed value . . . $40,943,990,098
Total tax levied . . . $100,695,998
Delinquency rate . . . 2.290%

County Finance, FY 2007

Revenues

Total . . . $400,167,066
Taxes . . . 140,660,026
Special benefits assessment . . . 0
Licenses, permits & franchises . . . 7,339,348
Fines, forfeitures & penalties . . . 7,918,423
Use of money & property . . . 8,127,618
Intergovernmental . . . 182,757,288
Service charges . . . 39,677,906
Miscellaneous revenues . . . 12,109,829
Other financing sources . . . 284,215

Expenditures

Total . . . $381,503,018
General . . . 51,857,798
Public protection . . . 115,109,932
Public ways & facilities . . . 32,725,398
Health . . . 63,516,953
Sanitation . . . 509,868
Public assistance . . . 92,820,116
Education . . . 8,846,013
Recreation & culture . . . 6,361,618
Debt service . . . 9,755,322

County Schools

San Luis Obispo County Office of Education
3350 Education Dr
San Luis Obispo, CA 93405
(805) 543-7732

Superintendent . . . Julian Crocker

County-wide School Totals

(2007-08 except where noted)

Number of districts . . . 8
Number of schools . . . 111
Enrollment . . . 59,460
High school graduates, 2006-07 . . . 4,506
Pupil/teacher ratio . . . 13.2
Average class size . . . 17.1
Students per computer . . . 2.2
Cost per ADA . . . $8,279
Avg teacher salary . . . $62,685

California Achievement Tests 6th ed., 2008

(Pct scoring at or above 50th National Percentile Rank)

	Math	Reading	Language
Grade 3	NA	NA	NA
Grade 7	0%	5%	0%

Academic Performance Index, 2008

Number of students tested . . . 45,171
2007 API (base) . . . 486
2008 API (growth) . . . 534

SAT Testing, 2006-07

Enrollment, Grade 12 . . . 3,130
percent taking test . . . 31.7%
percent with total score 1,500+ . . . 20.8%

Average Scores:

Math	Verbal	Writing	Total
539	535	526	1,600

County Library

San Luis Obispo City-County Library
PO Box 8107
San Luis Obispo, CA 93403
805-781-5784

Librarian . . . Brian Reynolds

Library statistics, FY 2007

Population served . . . 235,386
Internet terminals . . . 3
Annual users . . . 10,554

Per capita:

Operating income . . . $33.17
percent from local government . . . 90.2%
Operating expenditure . . . $30.54
Total materials . . . 1.72
Print holdings . . . 1.46
Visits . . . 5.51

See Introduction for an explanation of all data sources.

Demographics & Socio-Economic Characteristics†

(2007 American Community Survey, except as noted)

Population

1990* . . . 649,623
2007 . . . 706,984
Male . . . 350,717
Female . . . 356,267
Jan. 2008 (estimate)§ . . . 739,469
Living in unincorporated area . . . 8.9%
2020 (projected)* . . . 761,455

Race & Hispanic Origin, 2007

Race
White . . . 432,261
Black/African American . . . 21,160
North American Native . . . 2,047
Asian . . . 169,880
Pacific Islander . . . 9,583
Other Race . . . 45,629
Two or more races . . . 26,424
Hispanic origin, total . . . 162,508
Mexican . . . 102,706
Puerto Rican . . . 3,206
Cuban . . . 1,773
Other Hispanic . . . 54,823

Age & Nativity, 2007

Under 5 years . . . 47,154
18 years and over . . . 549,407
65 years and over . . . 92,701
85 years and over . . . 15,557
Median Age . . . 40.1
Native-born . . . 467,338
Foreign-born . . . 239,646

Educational Attainment, 2007

Population 25 years and over . . . 490,398
Less than 9th grade . . . 6.2%
High school grad or higher . . . 88.8%
Bachelor's degree or higher . . . 43.5%
Graduate degree . . . 16.2%

Income & Poverty, 2007

Per capita income . . . $43,239
Median household income . . . $83,109
Median family income . . . $97,137
Persons in poverty . . . 5.9%
H'holds receiving public assistance . . . 2,264
H'holds receiving social security . . . 63,643

Households, 2007

Total households . . . 251,357
With persons under 18 . . . 87,007
With persons over 65 . . . 63,458
Family households . . . 171,351
Single person households . . . 64,503
Persons per household . . . 2.77
Persons per family . . . 3.36

Labor & Employment

Total civilian labor force, 2008§§ . . . 384,400
Unemployment rate . . . 4.7%
Total civilian labor force, 2000* . . . 373,831

Employed persons 16 years and over by occupation, 2007

Managers & professionals . . . 149,085
Service occupations . . . 65,609
Sales & office occupations . . . 97,374
Farming, fishing & forestry . . . 1,536
Construction & maintenance . . . 25,491
Production & transportation . . . 25,826
Self-employed persons . . . 38,255

† see Appendix D for 2000 Decennial Census Data
* US Census Bureau
** 2007 American Community Survey
§ California Department of Finance
§§ California Employment Development Dept

General Information

400 County Center
Redwood City, CA 94063
650-363-4000

Website . . . www.co.sanmateo.ca.us
Incorporated . . . April 19, 1856
Form of Government . . . Charter
Land Area (sq. miles) . . . 449.1
Water Area (sq. miles) . . . 291.9
Persons per sq. mi. of land, 2008 . . . 1,646.6
Sales tax rate . . . 8.25%

Voters & Gov't Officials

Registered Voters, October 2008

Total . . . 389,718
Democrats . . . 199,569
Republicans . . . 83,411
Declined to state . . . 92,126
Unincorporated area . . . 35,609
Democrats . . . 18,125
Republicans . . . 7,790
Declined to state . . . 8,036

Legislative Districts

US Congressional . . . 12, 14
State Senatorial . . . 8, 11
State Assembly . . . 12, 19, 21

County Officials, 2009

Manager . . . David S. Boesch
Clerk-Recorder . . . Warren Slocum
District Attorney . . . James Fox
Controller . . . Tom Huening
Assessor . . . Warren Slocum
Treasurer/Tax Coll . . . Lee Buffington
Comm Dev Dir . . . Duane Bay
Public Works . . . Jim Porter
Building . . . Lisa Grote
Sheriff . . . Greg Munks
Fire/Emerg Mgmt Dir . . . NA
Elections Official . . . Warren Slocum
County supervisors
District 1 . . . Mark Church
District 2 . . . Carole Groom
District 3 . . . Richard Gordon
District 4 . . . Rose Jacobs-Gibson
District 5 . . . Adrienne Tissier

Public Safety

County Sheriff's office, 2007

Number of officers . . . 433
Violent crimes . . . 238
Property crimes . . . 1,598
Arson . . . 4

Housing & Construction

Housing Units

Total, January 2008§ . . . 268,301
Single family units, attached . . . 22,937
Single family units, detached . . . 153,583
Multiple family units . . . 88,182
Mobile home units . . . 3,599
Occupied units . . . 263,252
Vacancy rate . . . 1.9%
Median rent, 2007** . . . $1,445
Median SF home value, 2007** . . . $843,100

New Privately Owned Housing Units Authorized by Building Permit, 2007*

	Units	Construction Cost
Single	664	$318,352,576
Total	817	$352,557,839

Property Taxation, FY 2008

Total assessed value . . . $132,938,103,700
Total tax levied . . . $194,580,936
Delinquency rate . . . 1.914%

County Finance, FY 2007

Revenues

Total . . . $937,904,280
Taxes . . . 267,476,074
Special benefits assessment . . . 0
Licenses, permits & franchises . . . 14,139,468
Fines, forfeitures & penalties . . . 10,574,045
Use of money & property . . . 33,221,840
Intergovernmental . . . 450,971,505
Service charges . . . 124,427,572
Miscellaneous revenues . . . 26,532,196
Other financing sources . . . 1,768

Expenditures

Total . . . $827,651,517
General . . . 103,816,931
Public protection . . . 288,808,542
Public ways & facilities . . . 19,669,259
Health . . . 177,009,554
Sanitation . . . 7,794,258
Public assistance . . . 200,428,873
Education . . . 138,344
Recreation & culture . . . 8,582,490
Debt service . . . 21,403,266

County Schools

San Mateo County Office of Education
101 Twin Dolphin Dr
Redwood City, CA 94065
(650) 802-5550

Superintendent . . . Jean Holbrook

County-wide School Totals

(2007-08 except where noted)

Number of districts . . . 40
Number of schools . . . 286
Enrollment . . . 220,071
High school graduates, 2006-07 . . . 29,549
Pupil/teacher ratio . . . 5.7
Average class size . . . 11.9
Students per computer . . . 3.2
Cost per ADA . . . $9,194
Avg teacher salary . . . $66,904

California Achievement Tests 6th ed., 2008

(Pct scoring at or above 50th National Percentile Rank)

	Math	Reading	Language
Grade 3	NA	NA	NA
Grade 7	NA	NA	NA

Academic Performance Index, 2008

Number of students tested . . . 158,100
2007 API (base) . . . 572
2008 API (growth) . . . 624

SAT Testing, 2006-07

Enrollment, Grade 12 . . . 6,613
percent taking test . . . 47.7%
percent with total score 1,500+ . . . 27.7%

Average Scores:

Math	Verbal	Writing	Total
545	515	516	1,576

County Library

San Mateo County Library
125 Lessingia Ct
San Mateo, CA 94402
650-312-5258

Librarian . . . Victoria Johnson

Library statistics, FY 2007

Population served . . . 278,388
Internet terminals . . . 26
Annual users . . . 49,920

Per capita:

Operating income . . . $90.21
percent from local government . . . 63.5%
Operating expenditure . . . $60.41
Total materials . . . 2.65
Print holdings . . . 2.16
Visits . . . 5.44

See Introduction for an explanation of all data sources.

Demographics & Socio-Economic Characteristics†

(2007 American Community Survey, except as noted)

Population

1990* . . . 369,608
2007 . . . 404,197
  Male . . . 202,595
  Female . . . 201,602
Jan. 2008 (estimate)§ . . . 428,655
  Living in unincorporated area . . . 33.3%
2020 (projected)* . . . 459,498

Race & Hispanic Origin, 2007

Race
  White . . . 300,202
  Black/African American . . . 6,124
  North American Native . . . 3,194
  Asian . . . 19,744
  Pacific Islander . . . 705
  Other Race . . . 60,261
  Two or more races . . . 13,967
Hispanic origin, total . . . 156,500
  Mexican . . . 143,168
  Puerto Rican . . . 1,618
  Cuban . . . 200
  Other Hispanic . . . 11,514

Age & Nativity, 2007

Under 5 years . . . 28,897
18 years and over . . . 307,898
65 years and over . . . 51,933
85 years and over . . . 6,617
  Median Age . . . 33.9
Native-born . . . 314,057
Foreign-born . . . 90,140

Educational Attainment, 2007

Population 25 years and over . . . 249,149
Less than 9th grade . . . 11.6%
High school grad or higher . . . 81.3%
Bachelor's degree or higher . . . 30.1%
Graduate degree . . . 11.5%

Income & Poverty, 2007

Per capita income . . . $29,523
Median household income . . . $58,401
Median family income . . . $68,711
Persons in poverty . . . 11.9%
H'holds receiving public assistance . . . 3,508
H'holds receiving social security . . . 36,726

Households, 2007

Total households . . . 142,465
  With persons under 18 . . . 49,687
  With persons over 65 . . . 36,123
  Family households . . . 89,390
  Single person households . . . 37,779
Persons per household . . . 2.70
Persons per family . . . 3.30

Labor & Employment

Total civilian labor force, 2008§§ . . . 221,200
  Unemployment rate . . . 5.4%
Total civilian labor force, 2000* . . . 193,720

Employed persons 16 years and over by occupation, 2007

  Managers & professionals . . . 69,945
  Service occupations . . . 36,643
  Sales & office occupations . . . 42,881
  Farming, fishing & forestry . . . 9,846
  Construction & maintenance . . . 15,318
  Production & transportation . . . 14,721
Self-employed persons . . . 16,268

† see Appendix D for 2000 Decennial Census Data
* US Census Bureau
** 2007 American Community Survey
§ California Department of Finance
§§ California Employment Development Dept

General Information

105 E Anapamu St
Santa Barbara, CA 93101
805-681-4200

Website . . . www.countyofsb.org
Incorporated . . . Februray 18, 1850
Form of Government . . . General law
Land Area (sq. miles) . . . 2,737.0
Water Area (sq. miles) . . . 1,052.1
Persons per sq. mi. of land, 2008 . . . 156.6
Sales tax rate . . . 7.75%

Voters & Gov't Officials

Registered Voters, October 2008

Total . . . 204,440
  Democrats . . . 88,293
  Republicans . . . 67,106
  Declined to state . . . 39,293
Unincorporated area . . . 81,710
  Democrats . . . 31,770
  Republicans . . . 30,531
  Declined to state . . . 15,645

Legislative Districts

US Congressional . . . 23-24
State Senatorial . . . 15, 19
State Assembly . . . 33, 35

County Officials, 2009

Exec Officer . . . Michael F. Brown
Clerk-Recorder . . . Joseph Holland
District Attorney . . . Christie Stanley
Finance Dir . . . Robert Geis
Assessor . . . Joseph Holland
Tax Collector . . . Bernice James
Planning/Dev Dir . . . John Baker
Public Works . . . Scott McGolpin
Building . . . NA
Sheriff . . . Bill Brown
Fire Chief . . . John Scherrei
Elections Official . . . Joseph Holland
County supervisors
  District 1 . . . Salud Carbajal
  District 2 . . . Janet Wolf
  District 3 . . . Brooks Firestone
  District 4 . . . Joni Gray
  District 5 . . . Joseph Centeno

Public Safety

County Sheriff's office, 2007

Number of officers . . . 309
Violent crimes . . . 193
Property crimes . . . 1,602
Arson . . . 6

Housing & Construction

Housing Units

Total, January 2008§ . . . 154,452
  Single family units, attached . . . 11,602
  Single family units, detached . . . 90,185
  Multiple family units . . . 43,921
  Mobile home units . . . 8,744
  Occupied units . . . 147,855
  Vacancy rate . . . 4.3%
Median rent, 2007** . . . $1,205
Median SF home value, 2007** . . . $641,800

New Privately Owned Housing Units Authorized by Building Permit, 2007*

	Units	Construction Cost
Single	470	$148,455,189
Total	711	$181,698,266

Property Taxation, FY 2008

Total assessed value . . . $58,263,332,909
Total tax levied . . . $114,439,733
Delinquency rate . . . 2.100%

County Finance, FY 2007

Revenues

Total . . . $656,463,906
Taxes . . . 181,873,732
Special benefits assessment . . . 0
Licenses, permits & franchises . . . 15,018,343
Fines, forfeitures & penalties . . . 11,192,886
Use of money & property . . . 9,624,901
Intergovernmental . . . 288,506,876
Service charges . . . 137,359,647
Miscellaneous revenues . . . 8,980,231
Other financing sources . . . 3,668,340

Expenditures

Total . . . $643,662,675
General . . . 74,804,885
Public protection . . . 247,092,716
Public ways & facilities . . . 27,425,037
Health . . . 148,234,476
Sanitation . . . 0
Public assistance . . . 123,252,678
Education . . . 2,894,283
Recreation & culture . . . 9,495,962
Debt service . . . 10,462,638

County Schools

Santa Barbara County Office of Education
PO Box 6307
Santa Barbara, CA 93160
(805) 964-4711

Superintendent . . . William Cirone

County-wide School Totals

(2007-08 except where noted)

Number of districts . . . 22
Number of schools . . . 130
Enrollment . . . 83,655
High school graduates, 2006-07 . . . 6,731
Pupil/teacher ratio . . . 10.1
Average class size . . . 8.1
Students per computer . . . 2.8
Cost per ADA . . . $8,562
Avg teacher salary . . . $67,397

California Achievement Tests 6th ed., 2008

(Pct scoring at or above 50th National Percentile Rank)

	Math	Reading	Language
Grade 3	NA	NA	NA
Grade 7	6%	20%	0%

Academic Performance Index, 2008

Number of students tested . . . 62,910
2007 API (base) . . . 454
2008 API (growth) . . . 466

SAT Testing, 2006-07

Enrollment, Grade 12 . . . 4,828
  percent taking test . . . 33.6%
  percent with total score 1,500+ . . . 19.1%

Average Scores:

Math	Verbal	Writing	Total
532	517	510	1,559

County Library

Served by municipal libraries of Lompoc, Santa Barbara and Santa Maria

Library statistics, FY 2007

Population served . . . NA
Internet terminals . . . NA
  Annual users . . . NA

Per capita:

Operating income . . . NA
  percent from local government . . . NA
Operating expenditure . . . NA
Total materials . . . NA
Print holdings . . . NA
Visits . . . NA

See Introduction for an explanation of all data sources.

Demographics & Socio-Economic Characteristics†

(2007 American Community Survey, except as noted)

Population

1990* 1,497,577
2007 1,748,976
Male 894,417
Female 854,559
Jan. 2008 (estimate)§ 1,837,075
Living in unincorporated area 5.4%
2020 (projected)* 1,992,805

Race & Hispanic Origin, 2007

Race
White 934,827
Black/African American 44,510
North American Native 8,068
Asian 531,488
Pacific Islander 6,717
Other Race 164,291
Two or more races 59,075
Hispanic origin, total 449,133
Mexican 383,697
Puerto Rican 7,707
Cuban 3,319
Other Hispanic 54,410

Age & Nativity, 2007

Under 5 years 127,012
18 years and over 1,329,654
65 years and over 186,747
85 years and over 22,120
Median Age 36.6
Native-born 1,093,641
Foreign-born 655,335

Educational Attainment, 2007

Population 25 years and over 1,171,071
Less than 9th grade 8.1%
High school grad or higher 85.4%
Bachelor's degree or higher 44.5%
Graduate degree 19.3%

Income & Poverty, 2007

Per capita income $39,237
Median household income $84,360
Median family income $99,972
Persons in poverty 8.3%
H'holds receiving public assistance 12,077
H'holds receiving social security 117,088

Households, 2007

Total households 582,172
With persons under 18 220,698
With persons over 65 123,210
Family households 406,327
Single person households 142,739
Persons per household 2.94
Persons per family 3.51

Labor & Employment

Total civilian labor force, 2008§§ 879,900
Unemployment rate 6.0%
Total civilian labor force, 2000* 878,106

Employed persons 16 years and over by occupation, 2007

Managers & professionals 417,396
Service occupations 118,270
Sales & office occupations 181,570
Farming, fishing & forestry 2,136
Construction & maintenance 67,715
Production & transportation 71,678
Self-employed persons 60,648

† see Appendix D for 2000 Decennial Census Data
* US Census Bureau
** 2007 American Community Survey
§ California Department of Finance
§§ California Employment Development Dept

General Information

70 W Hedding St
San Jose, CA 95110
408-299-5001

Website .... www.santaclaracounty.org
Incorporated .... February 18, 1850
Form of Government .... Charter
Land Area (sq. miles) 1,290.7
Water Area (sq. miles) 13.3
Persons per sq. mi. of land, 2008 .... 1,423.3
Sales tax rate 8.25%

Voters & Gov't Officials

Registered Voters, October 2008

Total 788,821
Democrats 366,590
Republicans 190,680
Declined to state 204,495
Unincorporated area 47,407
Democrats 22,379
Republicans 13,202
Declined to state 10,180

Legislative Districts

US Congressional 11, 14-16
State Senatorial 10, 11, 13, 15
State Assembly 20-24, 27-28

County Officials, 2009

Manager/Admin .... Peter Kutras
County Clerk .... Gary Graves (Actg)
District Attorney .... Dolores Carr
Finance Dir .... John Guthrie
Tax Assessor .... Larry Stone
Tax Collector .... Martha Williams
Planning/Dev Dir .... Val Alexeeff
Public Works .... Larry Jenkins
Building .... NA
Sheriff .... Laurie Smith
Fire Chief .... Ken Waldvogel
Elections Official .... Jesse Durazo
County supervisors
District 1 .... Don Gage
District 2 .... George Shirakawa
District 3 .... Dave Cortese
District 4 .... Ken Yeager
District 5 .... Liz Kniss

Public Safety

County Sheriff's office, 2007

Number of officers 517
Violent crimes 321
Property crimes 1,757
Arson 5

Housing & Construction

Housing Units

Total, January 2008§ 622,779
Single family units, attached 55,834
Single family units, detached 336,196
Multiple family units 211,083
Mobile home units 19,666
Occupied units 608,652
Vacancy rate 2.3%
Median rent, 2007** $1,324
Median SF home value, 2007** $758,100

New Privately Owned Housing Units Authorized by Building Permit, 2007*

	Units	Construction Cost
Single	1,923	$615,572,493
Total	4,162	$997,999,372

Property Taxation, FY 2008

Total assessed value $284,970,470,989
Total tax levied $472,462,911
Delinquency rate 2.366%

County Finance, FY 2007

Revenues

Total $2,406,284,242
Taxes 650,696,469
Special benefits assessment 5,925,132
Licenses, permits & franchises 25,041,890
Fines, forfeitures & penalties 51,791,553
Use of money & property 52,464,321
Intergovernmental 1,298,960,848
Service charges 189,909,736
Miscellaneous revenues 25,218,284
Other financing sources 4,982,471

Expenditures

Total $2,242,414,100
General 340,862,894
Public protection 656,108,312
Public ways & facilities 89,256,587
Health 389,299,366
Sanitation 1,306,035
Public assistance 602,577,057
Education 30,704,832
Recreation & culture 33,580,279
Debt service 98,718,738

County Schools

Santa Clara County Office of Education
1290 Ridder Park Dr
San Jose, CA 95131
(408) 453-6500

Superintendent .... Charles Weis

County-wide School Totals

(2007-08 except where noted)

Number of districts 39
Number of schools 418
Enrollment 290,855
High school graduates, 2006-07 21,959
Pupil/teacher ratio 12.0
Average class size 16.2
Students per computer 3.2
Cost per ADA $8,787
Avg teacher salary $70,596

California Achievement Tests 6th ed., 2008

(Pct scoring at or above 50th National Percentile Rank)

	Math	Reading	Language
Grade 3	95%	80%	85%
Grade 7	5%	10%	3%

Academic Performance Index, 2008

Number of students tested 215,539
2007 API (base) 591
2008 API (growth) 648

SAT Testing, 2006-07

Enrollment, Grade 12 18,971
percent taking test 48.0%
percent with total score 1,500+ 31.1%

Average Scores:

Math	Verbal	Writing	Total
572	534	533	1,639

County Library

Santa Clara County Library
14600 Winchester Blvd
Los Gatos, CA 95032
408-293-2326

Librarian .... Melinda Cervantes

Library statistics, FY 2007

Population served 419,141
Internet terminals 133
Annual users 650,000

Per capita:

Operating income $77.89
percent from local government 85.7%
Operating expenditure $66.37
Total materials 4.01
Print holdings 3.27
Visits 6.16

See Introduction for an explanation of all data sources.

Demographics & Socio-Economic Characteristics†

(2007 American Community Survey, except as noted)

Population

1990* . . . 229,734
2007 . . . 251,747
Male . . . 125,629
Female . . . 126,118
Jan. 2008 (estimate)§ . . . 266,519
Living in unincorporated area . . . 50.6%
2020 (projected)* . . . 287,480

Race & Hispanic Origin, 2007

Race
White . . . 213,808
Black/African American . . . 1,640
North American Native . . . 1,765
Asian . . . 9,962
Pacific Islander . . . 294
Other Race . . . 13,616
Two or more races . . . 10,662
Hispanic origin, total . . . 72,453
Mexican . . . 66,589
Puerto Rican . . . 512
Cuban . . . 82
Other Hispanic . . . 5,270

Age & Nativity, 2007

Under 5 years . . . 16,149
18 years and over . . . 197,516
65 years and over . . . 26,323
85 years and over . . . 3,753
Median Age . . . 37.1
Native-born . . . 206,169
Foreign-born . . . 45,578

Educational Attainment, 2007

Population 25 years and over . . . 164,548
Less than 9th grade . . . 10.4%
High school grad or higher . . . 82.9%
Bachelor's degree or higher . . . 39.9%
Graduate degree . . . 14.5%

Income & Poverty, 2007

Per capita income . . . $33,759
Median household income . . . $63,778
Median family income . . . $80,045
Persons in poverty . . . 10.1%
H'holds receiving public assistance . . . 1,107
H'holds receiving social security . . . 21,831

Households, 2007

Total households . . . 93,690
With persons under 18 . . . 28,407
With persons over 65 . . . 19,333
Family households . . . 56,253
Single person households . . . 25,880
Persons per household . . . 2.60
Persons per family . . . 3.18

Labor & Employment

Total civilian labor force, 2008§§ . . . 148,400
Unemployment rate . . . 7.3%
Total civilian labor force, 2000* . . . 137,722

Employed persons 16 years and over by occupation, 2007

Managers & professionals . . . 52,563
Service occupations . . . 23,223
Sales & office occupations . . . 27,475
Farming, fishing & forestry . . . 5,639
Construction & maintenance . . . 11,092
Production & transportation . . . 10,420
Self-employed persons . . . 16,596

† see Appendix D for 2000 Decennial Census Data
* US Census Bureau
** 2007 American Community Survey
§ California Department of Finance
§§ California Employment Development Dept

General Information

701 Ocean St
Room 520
Santa Cruz, CA 95060
831-454-2000

Website . . . www.co.santa-cruz.ca.us
Incorporated . . . February 18, 1850
Form of Government . . . General law
Land Area (sq. miles) . . . 445.2
Water Area (sq. miles) . . . 161.9
Persons per sq. mi. of land, 2008 . . . 598.7
Sales tax rate . . . 8.00%

Voters & Gov't Officials

Registered Voters, October 2008

Total . . . 148,364
Democrats . . . 81,484
Republicans . . . 27,348
Declined to state . . . 25,933
Unincorporated area . . . 82,356
Democrats . . . 42,552
Republicans . . . 17,830
Declined to state . . . 14,368

Legislative Districts

US Congressional . . . 14, 17
State Senatorial . . . 11, 15
State Assembly . . . 27-28

County Officials, 2009

Manager/Admin . . . Susan Mauriello
County Clerk . . . Gail Pellerin
District Attorney . . . Bob Lee
Auditor-Controller . . . Mary Jo Walker
Tax Assessor . . . Gary Hazelton
Tax Collector . . . Fred Keeley
Planning/Dev Dir . . . Tom Burns
Public Works . . . Tom Bolich
Building . . . NA
Sheriff . . . Steve Robbins
Fire Chief . . . John Ferreira
Elections Official . . . Gail Pellerin
County supervisors
District 1 . . . John Leopold
District 2 . . . Ellen Pirie
District 3 . . . Neal Coonerty
District 4 . . . Tony Campos
District 5 . . . Mark Stone

Public Safety

County Sheriff's office, 2007

Number of officers . . . 137
Violent crimes . . . 256
Property crimes . . . 2,396
Arson . . . 29

Housing & Construction

Housing Units

Total, January 2008§ . . . 104,479
Single family units, attached . . . 9,213
Single family units, detached . . . 65,650
Multiple family units . . . 22,361
Mobile home units . . . 7,255
Occupied units . . . 96,311
Vacancy rate . . . 7.8%
Median rent, 2007** . . . $1,159
Median SF home value, 2007** . . . $756,800

New Privately Owned Housing Units Authorized by Building Permit, 2007*

	Units	Construction Cost
Single	321	$79,581,237
Total	842	$174,595,291

Property Taxation, FY 2008

Total assessed value . . . $33,343,349,993
Total tax levied . . . $43,479,178
Delinquency rate . . . 2.567%

County Finance, FY 2007

Revenues

Total . . . $380,471,181
Taxes . . . 87,571,371
Special benefits assessment . . . 0
Licenses, permits & franchises . . . 10,237,493
Fines, forfeitures & penalties . . . 8,809,140
Use of money & property . . . 6,179,081
Intergovernmental . . . 213,196,986
Service charges . . . 49,055,759
Miscellaneous revenues . . . 5,420,851
Other financing sources . . . 500

Expenditures

Total . . . $378,588,604
General . . . 38,476,642
Public protection . . . 105,088,767
Public ways & facilities . . . 14,365,493
Health . . . 104,543,009
Sanitation . . . 0
Public assistance . . . 98,011,420
Education . . . 4,710,522
Recreation & culture . . . 6,592,494
Debt service . . . 6,800,257

County Schools

Santa Cruz County Office of Education
400 Encinal Street
Santa Cruz, CA 95060
(831) 466-5600

Superintendent . . . Michael Watkins

County-wide School Totals

(2007-08 except where noted)

Number of districts . . . 10
Number of schools . . . 77
Enrollment . . . 39,162
High school graduates, 2006-07 . . . 3,175
Pupil/teacher ratio . . . 15.7
Average class size . . . 20.2
Students per computer . . . 3.2
Cost per ADA . . . $9,189
Avg teacher salary . . . $56,686

California Achievement Tests 6th ed., 2008

(Pct scoring at or above 50th National Percentile Rank)

	Math	Reading	Language
Grade 3	NA	NA	NA
Grade 7	5%	15%	5%

Academic Performance Index, 2008

Number of students tested . . . 28,795
2007 API (base) . . . 564
2008 API (growth) . . . 556

SAT Testing, 2006-07

Enrollment, Grade 12 . . . 3,206
percent taking test . . . 35.6%
percent with total score 1,500+ . . . 21.6%

Average Scores:

Math	Verbal	Writing	Total
530	521	516	1,567

County Library

Santa Cruz City-County Public Library
1543 Pacific Ave
Santa Cruz, CA 95060
831-420-5600

Librarian . . . Anne Turner

Library statistics, FY 2007

Population served . . . 205,669
Internet terminals . . . 24
Annual users . . . 23,239

Per capita:

Operating income . . . $59.06
percent from local government . . . 95.9%
Operating expenditure . . . $58.55
Total materials . . . 2.52
Print holdings . . . 2.13
Visits . . . NA

See Introduction for an explanation of all data sources.

Demographics & Socio-Economic Characteristics†

(2007 American Community Survey, except as noted)

Population

1990* ... 147,036
2007 ... 179,427
Male ... 88,521
Female ... 90,906
Jan. 2008 (estimate)§ ... 182,236
Living in unincorporated area ... 38.9%
2020 (projected)* ... 224,386

Race & Hispanic Origin, 2007

Race
White ... 160,197
Black/African American ... 1,541
North American Native ... 4,292
Asian ... 4,548
Pacific Islander ... 0
Other Race ... 3,610
Two or more races ... 5,239
Hispanic origin, total ... 13,805
Mexican ... NA
Puerto Rican ... NA
Cuban ... NA
Other Hispanic ... NA

Age & Nativity, 2007

Under 5 years ... 10,944
18 years and over ... 138,764
65 years and over ... 26,903
85 years and over ... 3,975
Median Age ... 37.9
Native-born ... 172,065
Foreign-born ... 7,362

Educational Attainment, 2007

Population 25 years and over ... 120,038
Less than 9th grade ... 2.3%
High school grad or higher ... 88.3%
Bachelor's degree or higher ... 18.8%
Graduate degree ... 6.5%

Income & Poverty, 2007

Per capita income ... $23,452
Median household income ... $41,901
Median family income ... $54,275
Persons in poverty ... 12.8%
H'holds receiving public assistance ... 1,820
H'holds receiving social security ... 23,460

Households, 2007

Total households ... 69,474
With persons under 18 ... 22,518
With persons over 65 ... 18,706
Family households ... 46,002
Single person households ... 20,514
Persons per household ... 2.55
Persons per family ... 3.12

Labor & Employment

Total civilian labor force, 2008§§ ... 83,700
Unemployment rate ... 10.1%
Total civilian labor force, 2000* ... 72,131

Employed persons 16 years and over by occupation, 2007

Managers & professionals ... 23,757
Service occupations ... 16,838
Sales & office occupations ... 23,198
Farming, fishing & forestry ... 193
Construction & maintenance ... 7,790
Production & transportation ... 7,526
Self-employed persons ... 8,598

† see Appendix D for 2000 Decennial Census Data
* US Census Bureau
** 2007 American Community Survey
§ California Department of Finance
§§ California Employment Development Dept

General Information

1450 Court St
Suite 1
Redding, CA 96001
530-245-6600

Website ... www.co.shasta.ca.us
Incorporated ... February 18, 1850
Form of Government ... General law
Land Area (sq. miles) ... 3,785.2
Water Area (sq. miles) ... 62.2
Persons per sq. mi. of land, 2008 ... 48.1
Sales tax rate ... 7.25%

Voters & Gov't Officials

Registered Voters, October 2008

Total ... 96,804
Democrats ... 28,894
Republicans ... 46,256
Declined to state ... 17,425
Unincorporated area ... 40,449
Democrats ... 11,780
Republicans ... 19,940
Declined to state ... 6,907

Legislative Districts

US Congressional ... 2
State Senatorial ... 4
State Assembly ... 2

County Officials, 2009

Manager/Admin ... Lawrence Lees
County Clerk ... Cathy Darling
District Attorney ... Jerry Benito
Finance Dir ... Connie Regnell
Tax Assessor ... Leslie Morgan
Tax Collector ... Lori Scott
Planning/Comm Dev ... NA
Public Works ... Pat Minturn
Building ... NA
Sheriff ... Tom Bosenko
Fire/Emerg Mgmt Dir ... NA
Elections Official ... Cathy Darling
County supervisors
District 1 ... David Kehoe
District 2 ... Leonard Moty
District 3 ... Glenn Hawes
District 4 ... Linda Hartman
District 5 ... Les Baugh

Public Safety

County Sheriff's office, 2007

Number of officers ... 147
Violent crimes ... 349
Property crimes ... 968
Arson ... 20

Housing & Construction

Housing Units

Total, January 2008§ ... 77,118
Single family units, attached ... 1,525
Single family units, detached ... 52,672
Multiple family units ... 11,559
Mobile home units ... 11,362
Occupied units ... 71,107
Vacancy rate ... 7.8%
Median rent, 2007** ... $788
Median SF home value, 2007** ... $255,500

New Privately Owned Housing Units Authorized by Building Permit, 2007*

	Units	Construction Cost
Single	545	$100,036,886
Total	712	$111,888,860

Property Taxation, FY 2008

Total assessed value ... $15,627,392,486
Total tax levied ... $21,775,328
Delinquency rate ... 4.735%

County Finance, FY 2007

Revenues

Total ... $254,522,330
Taxes ... 45,824,331
Special benefits assessment ... 2,029
Licenses, permits & franchises ... 3,857,687
Fines, forfeitures & penalties ... 4,688,316
Use of money & property ... 5,357,067
Intergovernmental ... 171,854,983
Service charges ... 18,348,665
Miscellaneous revenues ... 4,241,864
Other financing sources ... 66,117

Expenditures

Total ... $252,043,169
General ... 18,237,358
Public protection ... 75,137,082
Public ways & facilities ... 18,038,098
Health ... 49,416,792
Sanitation ... 0
Public assistance ... 84,857,103
Education ... 1,758,579
Recreation & culture ... 203,536
Debt service ... 4,394,621

County Schools

Shasta County Office of Education
1644 Magnolia Ave
Redding, CA 96001
(530) 225-0200

Superintendent ... Tom Armelino

County-wide School Totals

(2007-08 except where noted)

Number of districts ... 14
Number of schools ... 90
Enrollment ... 28,534
High school graduates, 2006-07 ... 2,117
Pupil/teacher ratio ... 11.7
Average class size ... 14.7
Students per computer ... 4.9
Cost per ADA ... $8,933
Avg teacher salary ... $57,751

California Achievement Tests 6th ed., 2008

(Pct scoring at or above 50th National Percentile Rank)

	Math	Reading	Language
Grade 3	NA	NA	NA
Grade 7	3%	6%	3%

Academic Performance Index, 2008

Number of students tested ... 20,186
2007 API (base) ... 460
2008 API (growth) ... 498

SAT Testing, 2006-07

Enrollment, Grade 12 ... 2,493
percent taking test ... 19.6%
percent with total score 1,500+ ... 12.5%

Average Scores:

Math	Verbal	Writing	Total
539	529	519	1,587

County Library

Shasta County Library
1855 Shasta St
Redding, CA 96001
530-225-5769

Librarian ... Kim Ingram (Int)

Library statistics, FY 2007

Population served ... 181,401
Internet terminals ... 8
Annual users ... 15,226

Per capita:

Operating income ... $9.89
percent from local government ... 96.3%
Operating expenditure ... $12.63
Total materials ... 1.23
Print holdings ... 1.12
Visits ... NA

See Introduction for an explanation of all data sources.

Demographics & Socio-Economic Characteristics

(2000 U.S. Census, except as noted)

Population

1990* . . . 3,318
2000 . . . 3,555
Male . . . 1,795
Female . . . 1,760
Jan. 2008 (estimate)§ . . . 3,380
Living in unincorporated area . . . 74.8%
2020 (projected)* . . . 3,508

Race & Hispanic Origin, 2000

Race
White . . . 3,348
Black/African American . . . 7
North American Native . . . 67
Asian . . . 6
Pacific Islander . . . 3
Other Race . . . 37
Two or more races . . . 87
Hispanic origin, total . . . 213
Mexican . . . 142
Puerto Rican . . . 5
Cuban . . . 4
Other Hispanic . . . 62

Age & Nativity, 2000

Under 5 years . . . 147
18 years and over . . . 2,725
65 years and over . . . 629
85 years and over . . . 84
Median Age . . . 43.7
Native-born . . . 3,448
Foreign-born . . . 107

Educational Attainment, 2000

Population 25 years and over . . . 2,540
Less than 9th grade . . . 4.8%
High school grad or higher . . . 85.2%
Bachelor's degree or higher . . . 17.2%
Graduate degree . . . 5.8%

Income & Poverty, 1999

Per capita income . . . $18,815
Median household income . . . $35,827
Median family income . . . $42,756
Persons in poverty . . . 11.2%
H'holds receiving public assistance . . . 55
H'holds receiving social security . . . 489

Households, 2000

Total households . . . 1,520
With persons under 18 . . . 448
With persons over 65 . . . 442
Family households . . . 986
Single person households . . . 441
Persons per household . . . 2.32
Persons per family . . . 2.83

Labor & Employment

Total civilian labor force, 2008§§ . . . 1,640
Unemployment rate . . . 10.5%
Total civilian labor force, 2000 . . . 1,672

Employed persons 16 years and over by occupation, 2000

Managers & professionals . . . 526
Service occupations . . . 315
Sales & office occupations . . . 262
Farming, fishing & forestry . . . 18
Construction & maintenance . . . 210
Production & transportation . . . 184
Self-employed persons . . . 133

* US Census Bureau
** 2000 Decennial Census
§ California Department of Finance
§§ California Employment Development Dept

General Information

PO Box D
Downieville, CA 95936
530-289-3295

Website . . . www.sierracounty.ws
Incorporated . . . April 16, 1852
Form of Government . . . General law
Land Area (sq. miles) . . . 953.4
Water Area (sq. miles) . . . 8.6
Persons per sq. mi. of land, 2008 . . . 3.5
Sales tax rate . . . 7.25%

Voters & Gov't Officials

Registered Voters, October 2008

Total . . . 2,321
Democrats . . . 724
Republicans . . . 994
Declined to state . . . 426
Unincorporated area . . . 1,855
Democrats . . . 555
Republicans . . . 813
Declined to state . . . 343

Legislative Districts

US Congressional . . . 4
State Senatorial . . . 1
State Assembly . . . 3

County Officials, 2009

Manager/Admin . . . NA
County Clerk . . . Heather Foster
District Attorney . . . Larry Allen
Auditor-Controller . . . Van Maddox
Tax Assessor . . . Richard Nourse
Treasurer/Tax Coll . . . Stephanie Levings
Comm Dev Dir . . . Tim Beals
Public Works . . . Tim Beals
Building Dept Dir . . . Tim Beals
Sheriff . . . John Evans
Fire/Emerg Mgmt Dir . . . NA
Elections Official . . . Heather Foster
County supervisors
District 1 . . . Lee Adams
District 2 . . . Peter Huebner
District 3 . . . Bill Nunes
District 4 . . . Dave Goicoechea
District 5 . . . Patricia Whitley

Public Safety

County Sheriff's office, 2007

Number of officers . . . 11
Violent crimes . . . 15
Property crimes . . . 69
Arson . . . 0

Housing & Construction

Housing Units

Total, January 2008§ . . . 2,289
Single family units, attached . . . 49
Single family units, detached . . . 1,898
Multiple family units . . . 110
Mobile home units . . . 232
Occupied units . . . 1,585
Vacancy rate . . . 30.8%
Median rent, 2000** . . . $513
Median SF home value, 2000** . . . $128,600

New Privately Owned Housing Units Authorized by Building Permit, 2007*

	Units	Construction Cost
Single	14	$4,574,433
Total	14	$4,574,433

Property Taxation, FY 2008

Total assessed value . . . $559,515,393
Total tax levied . . . $3,016,313
Delinquency rate . . . 1.500%

County Finance, FY 2007

Revenues

Total . . . $17,035,921
Taxes . . . 3,907,978
Special benefits assessment . . . 0
Licenses, permits & franchises . . . 191,645
Fines, forfeitures & penalties . . . 448,066
Use of money & property . . . 233,282
Intergovernmental . . . 10,823,777
Service charges . . . 959,549
Miscellaneous revenues . . . 244,068
Other financing sources . . . 0

Expenditures

Total . . . $17,107,930
General . . . 2,881,872
Public protection . . . 5,223,538
Public ways & facilities . . . 3,495,353
Health . . . 2,472,633
Sanitation . . . 0
Public assistance . . . 2,545,679
Education . . . 39,061
Recreation & culture . . . 144,613
Debt service . . . 305,181

County Schools

Sierra County Office of Education
PO Box 157
Sierraville, CA 96126
(530) 994-1044

Superintendent . . . Stan Hardeman

County-wide School Totals

(2007-08 except where noted)

Number of districts . . . 2
Number of schools . . . 8
Enrollment . . . 497
High school graduates, 2006-07 . . . 47
Pupil/teacher ratio . . . 1.1
Average class size . . . 4.0
Students per computer . . . 0.3
Cost per ADA . . . $13,272
Avg teacher salary . . . $49,608

California Achievement Tests 6th ed., 2008

(Pct scoring at or above 50th National Percentile Rank)

	Math	Reading	Language
Grade 3			
Grade 7			

Academic Performance Index, 2008

Number of students tested . . . 364
2007 API (base) . . . NA
2008 API (growth) . . . NA

SAT Testing, 2006-07

Enrollment, Grade 12 . . . 56
percent taking test . . . 53.6%
percent with total score 1,500+ . . . 17.9%

Average Scores:

Math	Verbal	Writing	Total
494	482	480	1,456

County Library

Served by Plumas County Library

Library statistics, FY 2007

Population served . . . NA
Internet terminals . . . NA
Annual users . . . NA

Per capita:

Operating income . . . NA
percent from local government . . . NA
Operating expenditure . . . NA
Total materials . . . NA
Print holdings . . . NA
Visits . . . NA

See Introduction for an explanation of all data sources.

Demographics & Socio-Economic Characteristics

(2000 U.S. Census, except as noted)

Population

1990* 43,531
2000 44,301
Male 21,752
Female 22,549
Jan. 2008 (estimate)§ 45,971
Living in unincorporated area 55.1%
2020 (projected)* 51,283

Race & Hispanic Origin, 2000

Race
White 38,573
Black/African American 580
North American Native 1,726
Asian 526
Pacific Islander 57
Other Race 1,224
Two or more races 1,615
Hispanic origin, total 3,354
Mexican 2,657
Puerto Rican 89
Cuban 24
Other Hispanic 584

Age & Nativity, 2000

Under 5 years 2,260
18 years and over 33,681
65 years and over 8,040
85 years and over 894
Median Age 43.0
Native-born 41,919
Foreign-born 2,382

Educational Attainment, 2000

Population 25 years and over 30,682
Less than 9th grade 5.0%
High school grad or higher 83.8%
Bachelor's degree or higher 17.7%
Graduate degree 5.9%

Income & Poverty, 1999

Per capita income $17,570
Median household income $29,530
Median family income $36,890
Persons in poverty 18.3%
H'holds receiving public assistance 997
H'holds receiving social security 6,796

Households, 2000

Total households 18,556
With persons under 18 5,629
With persons over 65 5,760
Family households 12,231
Single person households 5,310
Persons per household 2.35
Persons per family 2.87

Labor & Employment

Total civilian labor force, 2008§§ 19,470
Unemployment rate 10.2%
Total civilian labor force, 2000 19,094

Employed persons 16 years and over by occupation, 2000

Managers & professionals 5,316
Service occupations 3,361
Sales & office occupations 4,205
Farming, fishing & forestry 792
Construction & maintenance 1,566
Production & transportation 2,029
Self-employed persons 2,701

* US Census Bureau
** 2000 Decennial Census
§ California Department of Finance
§§ California Employment Development Dept

General Information

PO Box 750
Yreka, CA 96097
530-842-8005

Website .... www.co.siskiyou.ca.us
Incorporated .... March 22, 1852
Form of Government .... General law
Land Area (sq. miles) 6,286.8
Water Area (sq. miles) 60.7
Persons per sq. mi. of land, 2008 .... 7.3
Sales tax rate 7.25%

Voters & Gov't Officials

Registered Voters, October 2008

Total 26,643
Democrats 9,435
Republicans 10,959
Declined to state 4,782
Unincorporated area 15,513
Democrats 5,089
Republicans 6,919
Declined to state 2,640

Legislative Districts

US Congressional 2
State Senatorial 4
State Assembly 2

County Officials, 2009

Manager/Admin .... Brian McDermott
County Clerk .... Colleen Setzer
District Attorney .... J. Kirk Andrus
Auditor-Controller .... Leanna Dancer
Tax Assessor .... Mike Mallory
Tax Collector .... Wayne Hammar
Comm Dev Dir. .... Terry Barber
Public Works .... Brian McDermott
Building Dept Dir .... Mike Crawford
Sheriff .... Rick Riggins
Fire Protection Svcs. .... (CalFire)
Elections Official .... Colleen Setzer
County supervisors
District 1 .... Jim Cook
District 2 .... Ed Valenzuela
District 3 .... Michael Kobseff
District 4 .... Grace Bennett
District 5 .... Marcia Armstrong

Public Safety

County Sheriff's office, 2007

Number of officers 99
Violent crimes 50
Property crimes 217
Arson 9

Housing & Construction

Housing Units

Total, January 2008§ 24,044
Single family units, attached 499
Single family units, detached 16,781
Multiple family units 2,631
Mobile home units 4,133
Occupied units 20,311
Vacancy rate 15.5%
Median rent, 2000** $471
Median SF home value, 2000** $100,300

New Privately Owned Housing Units Authorized by Building Permit, 2007*

	Units	Construction Cost
Single	144	$28,467,020
Total	148	$28,903,520

Property Taxation, FY 2008

Total assessed value $4,023,729,679
Total tax levied $8,877,683
Delinquency rate 3.100%

County Finance, FY 2007

Revenues

Total $88,817,575
Taxes 15,938,509
Special benefits assessment 0
Licenses, permits & franchises ... 1,164,834
Fines, forfeitures & penalties 2,425,568
Use of money & property 1,690,870
Intergovernmental 60,665,144
Service charges 5,470,652
Miscellaneous revenues 1,065,291
Other financing sources 15,600

Expenditures

Total $84,578,909
General 8,616,824
Public protection 27,670,923
Public ways & facilities 11,546,991
Health 17,739,615
Sanitation 0
Public assistance 17,716,672
Education 1,003,826
Recreation & culture 100,022
Debt service 184,036

County Schools

Siskiyou County Office of Education
609 South Gold St
Yreka, CA 96097
(530) 842-8400

Superintendent .... Kermith Walters

County-wide School Totals

(2007-08 except where noted)

Number of districts 20
Number of schools 74
Enrollment 8,275
High school graduates, 2006-07 690
Pupil/teacher ratio 6.7
Average class size 7.9
Students per computer 1.6
Cost per ADA $10,463
Avg teacher salary $52,407

California Achievement Tests 6th ed., 2008

(Pct scoring at or above 50th National Percentile Rank)

	Math	Reading	Language
Grade 3	NA	NA	NA
Grade 7	NA	NA	NA

Academic Performance Index, 2008

Number of students tested 5,830
2007 API (base) .... NA
2008 API (growth) .... NA

SAT Testing, 2006-07

Enrollment, Grade 12 507
percent taking test 25.8%
percent with total score 1,500+ 13.0%

Average Scores:

Math	Verbal	Writing	Total
512	491	492	1,495

County Library

Siskiyou County Free Library
719 Fourth St
Yreka, CA 96097
530-841-4175

Librarian .... Betsy Emry

Library statistics, FY 2007

Population served 45,953
Internet terminals 31
Annual users 48,766

Per capita:

Operating income $20.36
percent from local government 90.2%
Operating expenditure $20.12
Total materials 4.06
Print holdings 3.88
Visits .... NA

See Introduction for an explanation of all data sources.

Demographics & Socio-Economic Characteristics†

(2007 American Community Survey, except as noted)

Population

1990* . . . 340,421
2007 . . . 408,599
Male . . . 205,290
Female . . . 203,309
Jan. 2008 (estimate)§ . . . 426,757
Living in unincorporated area . . . 4.7%
2020 (projected)* . . . 503,248

Race & Hispanic Origin, 2007

Race
White . . . 218,618
Black/African American . . . 61,788
North American Native . . . 3,059
Asian . . . 55,964
Pacific Islander . . . 3,292
Other Race . . . 43,033
Two or more races . . . 22,845
Hispanic origin, total . . . 89,728
Mexican . . . 66,563
Puerto Rican . . . 2,662
Cuban . . . 378
Other Hispanic . . . 20,125

Age & Nativity, 2007

Under 5 years . . . 28,039
18 years and over . . . 303,848
65 years and over . . . 44,325
85 years and over . . . 5,264
Median Age . . . 36.0
Native-born . . . 329,736
Foreign-born . . . 78,863

Educational Attainment, 2007

Population 25 years and over . . . 262,992
Less than 9th grade . . . 6.9%
High school grad or higher . . . 84.6%
Bachelor's degree or higher . . . 22.4%
Graduate degree . . . 6.2%

Income & Poverty, 2007

Per capita income . . . $27,620
Median household income . . . $66,880
Median family income . . . $75,338
Persons in poverty . . . 9.6%
H'holds receiving public assistance . . . 4,328
H'holds receiving social security . . . 32,897

Households, 2007

Total households . . . 135,338
With persons under 18 . . . 53,953
With persons over 65 . . . 30,345
Family households . . . 97,471
Single person households . . . 30,860
Persons per household . . . 2.93
Persons per family . . . 3.45

Labor & Employment

Total civilian labor force, 2008§§ . . . 213,500
Unemployment rate . . . 6.9%
Total civilian labor force, 2000* . . . 183,595

Employed persons 16 years and over by occupation, 2007

Managers & professionals . . . 59,727
Service occupations . . . 32,166
Sales & office occupations . . . 49,231
Farming, fishing & forestry . . . 1,822
Construction & maintenance . . . 21,007
Production & transportation . . . 19,414
Self-employed persons . . . 9,776

† see Appendix D for 2000 Decennial Census Data
* US Census Bureau
** 2007 American Community Survey
§ California Department of Finance
§§ California Employment Development Dept

General Information

675 Texas St
Suite 6500
Fairfield, CA 94533
707-784-6100

Website . . . www.solanocounty.com
Incorporated . . . February 18, 1850
Form of Government . . . General law
Land Area (sq. miles) . . . 829.2
Water Area (sq. miles) . . . 77.5
Persons per sq. mi. of land, 2008 . . . 514.7
Sales tax rate . . . 7.38%

Voters & Gov't Officials

Registered Voters, October 2008

Total . . . 190,477
Democrats . . . 96,621
Republicans . . . 49,663
Declined to state . . . 37,303
Unincorporated area . . . 10,323
Democrats . . . 3,879
Republicans . . . 4,207
Declined to state . . . 1,814

Legislative Districts

US Congressional . . . 3, 7, 10
State Senatorial . . . 2, 5
State Assembly . . . 7, 8

County Officials, 2009

Admin/Manager . . . Michael D. Johnson
County Clerk . . . Charles Lomeli
District Attorney . . . David Paulson
Finance Dir . . . Simona Padilla-Scholtens
Tax Assessor . . . Marc Tonnesen
Tax Collector . . . Charles Lomeli
Resource Mgmt Dir . . . David Clich
Public Works . . . Paul Wiese
Building . . . NA
Sheriff . . . Gary Stanton
Emerg Mgmt Dir . . . Robert Powell
Elections Official . . . Ira Rosenthal
County supervisors
District 1 . . . Barbara Kondylis
District 2 . . . Linda Seifert
District 3 . . . James Spering
District 4 . . . John Vasquez
District 5 . . . Mike Reagan

Public Safety

County Sheriff's office, 2007

Number of officers . . . 118
Violent crimes . . . 186
Property crimes . . . 518
Arson . . . 23

Housing & Construction

Housing Units

Total, January 2008§ . . . 152,041
Single family units, attached . . . 7,291
Single family units, detached . . . 108,624
Multiple family units . . . 31,450
Mobile home units . . . 4,676
Occupied units . . . 146,191
Vacancy rate . . . 3.8%
Median rent, 2007** . . . $1,118
Median SF home value, 2007** . . . $479,500

New Privately Owned Housing Units Authorized by Building Permit, 2007*

	Units	Construction Cost
Single	866	$206,650,911
Total	1,019	$226,056,315

Property Taxation, FY 2008

Total assessed value . . . $46,415,656,374
Total tax levied . . . $83,561,943
Delinquency rate . . . 4.718%

County Finance, FY 2007

Revenues

Total . . . $558,562,195
Taxes . . . 130,904,822
Special benefits assessment . . . 0
Licenses, permits & franchises . . . 13,466,724
Fines, forfeitures & penalties . . . 13,866,108
Use of money & property . . . 14,538,106
Intergovernmental . . . 305,714,353
Service charges . . . 72,548,405
Miscellaneous revenues . . . 3,812,383
Other financing sources . . . 3,711,294

Expenditures

Total . . . $532,099,874
General . . . 47,490,670
Public protection . . . 173,794,812
Public ways & facilities . . . 16,385,561
Health . . . 99,091,797
Sanitation . . . 0
Public assistance . . . 145,851,408
Education . . . 21,073,671
Recreation & culture . . . 1,373,441
Debt service . . . 27,038,514

County Schools

Solano County Office of Education
5100 Business Center Dr
Fairfield, CA 94534
(707) 399-4400

Superintendent . . . Dee Alarc

County-wide School Totals

(2007-08 except where noted)

Number of districts . . . 8
Number of schools . . . 137
Enrollment . . . 91,041
High school graduates, 2006-07 . . . 5,530
Pupil/teacher ratio . . . 7.8
Average class size . . . 7.0
Students per computer . . . 2.7
Cost per ADA . . . $7,940
Avg teacher salary . . . $60,799

California Achievement Tests 6th ed., 2008

(Pct scoring at or above 50th National Percentile Rank)

	Math	Reading	Language
Grade 3	NA	NA	NA
Grade 7	NA	NA	NA

Academic Performance Index, 2008

Number of students tested . . . 68,324
2007 API (base) . . . 592
2008 API (growth) . . . 627

SAT Testing, 2006-07

Enrollment, Grade 12 . . . 4,931
percent taking test . . . 36.9%
percent with total score 1,500+ . . . 16.9%

Average Scores:

Math	Verbal	Writing	Total
501	485	479	1,465

County Library

Solano County Library
1150 Kentucky St
Fairfield, CA 94533
707-421-6510

Librarian . . . Ann Cousineau

Library statistics, FY 2007

Population served . . . 371,000
Internet terminals . . . 248
Annual users . . . 562,512

Per capita:

Operating income . . . $54.42
percent from local government . . . 94.0%
Operating expenditure . . . $47.19
Total materials . . . 1.88
Print holdings . . . 1.57
Visits . . . 5.20

See Introduction for an explanation of all data sources.

Demographics & Socio-Economic Characteristics†

(2007 American Community Survey, except as noted)

Population

1990* ... 388,222
2007 ... 464,435
Male ... 230,409
Female ... 234,026
Jan. 2008 (estimate)§ ... 484,470
Living in unincorporated area ... 31.4%
2020 (projected)* ... 546,151

Race & Hispanic Origin, 2007

Race
White ... 364,288
Black/African American ... 5,562
North American Native ... 5,446
Asian ... 16,857
Pacific Islander ... 868
Other Race ... 53,829
Two or more races ... 17,585
Hispanic origin, total ... 104,862
Mexican ... 91,098
Puerto Rican ... 2,020
Cuban ... 745
Other Hispanic ... 10,999

Age & Nativity, 2007

Under 5 years ... 28,278
18 years and over ... 361,472
65 years and over ... 59,860
85 years and over ... 10,278
Median Age ... 39.8
Native-born ... 385,761
Foreign-born ... 78,674

Educational Attainment, 2007

Population 25 years and over ... 314,808
Less than 9th grade ... 7.4%
High school grad or higher ... 86.2%
Bachelor's degree or higher ... 30.7%
Graduate degree ... 10.5%

Income & Poverty, 2007

Per capita income ... $32,397
Median household income ... $62,399
Median family income ... $75,106
Persons in poverty ... 8.9%
H'holds receiving public assistance ... 2,233
H'holds receiving social security ... 46,351

Households, 2007

Total households ... 178,505
With persons under 18 ... 55,792
With persons over 65 ... 42,704
Family households ... 113,622
Single person households ... 50,262
Persons per household ... 2.54
Persons per family ... 3.14

Labor & Employment

Total civilian labor force, 2008§§ ... 263,400
Unemployment rate ... 5.7%
Total civilian labor force, 2000* ... 239,445

Employed persons 16 years and over by occupation, 2007

Managers & professionals ... 78,351
Service occupations ... 44,322
Sales & office occupations ... 56,253
Farming, fishing & forestry ... 5,469
Construction & maintenance ... 23,885
Production & transportation ... 24,543
Self-employed persons ... 26,975

† see Appendix D for 2000 Decennial Census Data
* US Census Bureau
** 2007 American Community Survey
§ California Department of Finance
§§ California Employment Development Dept

General Information

575 Administration Dr #100A
Santa Rosa, CA 95403
707-565-2431

Website ... www.sonoma-county.org
Incorporated ... February 18, 1850
Form of Government ... General law
Land Area (sq. miles) ... 1,575.9
Water Area (sq. miles) ... 192.3
Persons per sq. mi. of land, 2008 ... 307.4
Sales tax rate ... 7.75%

Voters & Gov't Officials

Registered Voters, October 2008

Total ... 248,122
Democrats ... 129,942
Republicans ... 58,570
Declined to state ... 47,071
Unincorporated area ... 81,625
Democrats ... 42,745
Republicans ... 19,312
Declined to state ... 14,897

Legislative Districts

US Congressional ... 1, 6
State Senatorial ... 2-3
State Assembly ... 1, 6-7

County Officials, 2009

Manager/Admin ... Bob Deis
Clerk-Recorder ... Janice Atkinson
District Attorney ... Stephan Passalacqua
Finance Dir ... Rod Dole
Assessor ... Janice Atkinson
Tax Collector ... Rod Dole
Comm Dev Dir ... Kathleen Kane
Public Works ... Phillip M. Demery
Building ... NA
Sheriff ... Bill Cogbill
Fire Protection Svcs ... Vern A. Losh
Elections Official ... Janice Atkinson
County supervisors
District 1 ... Valerie Brown
District 2 ... Mike Kerns
District 3 ... Shirlee Zane
District 4 ... Paul Kelley
District 5 ... Efren Carrillo

Public Safety

County Sheriff's office, 2007

Number of officers ... 534
Violent crimes ... 524
Property crimes ... 1,726
Arson ... 22

Housing & Construction

Housing Units

Total, January 2008§ ... 197,907
Single family units, attached ... 14,842
Single family units, detached ... 134,808
Multiple family units ... 36,820
Mobile home units ... 11,437
Occupied units ... 186,568
Vacancy rate ... 5.7%
Median rent, 2007** ... $1,171
Median SF home value, 2007** ... $613,900

New Privately Owned Housing Units Authorized by Building Permit, 2007*

	Units	Construction Cost
Single	910	$222,047,804
Total	1,431	$291,960,658

Property Taxation, FY 2008

Total assessed value ... $67,478,927,005
Total tax levied ... $151,207,516
Delinquency rate ... 2.900%

County Finance, FY 2007

Revenues

Total ... $664,663,652
Taxes ... 206,173,837
Special benefits assessment ... 0
Licenses, permits & franchises ... 17,477,406
Fines, forfeitures & penalties ... 11,294,784
Use of money & property ... 21,045,493
Intergovernmental ... 341,803,888
Service charges ... 54,655,912
Miscellaneous revenues ... 12,140,999
Other financing sources ... 0

Expenditures

Total ... $689,262,375
General ... 104,939,542
Public protection ... 241,337,852
Public ways & facilities ... 45,984,105
Health ... 118,036,815
Sanitation ... 0
Public assistance ... 134,579,037
Education ... 1,006,730
Recreation & culture ... 12,905,370
Debt service ... 30,472,924

County Schools

Sonoma County Office of Education
5340 Skylane Blvd
Santa Rosa, CA 95403
(707) 524-2600

Superintendent ... Carl Wong

County-wide School Totals

(2007-08 except where noted)

Number of districts ... 33
Number of schools ... 181
Enrollment ... 77,588
High school graduates, 2006-07 ... 5,115
Pupil/teacher ratio ... 11.2
Average class size ... 7.7
Students per computer ... 3.4
Cost per ADA ... $8,574
Avg teacher salary ... $62,197

California Achievement Tests 6th ed., 2008

(Pct scoring at or above 50th National Percentile Rank)

	Math	Reading	Language
Grade 3	NA	NA	NA
Grade 7	4%	8%	12%

Academic Performance Index, 2008

Number of students tested ... 37,264
2007 API (base) ... 480
2008 API (growth) ... 487

SAT Testing, 2006-07

Enrollment, Grade 12 ... 5,586
percent taking test ... 33.5%
percent with total score 1,500+ ... 21.8%

Average Scores:

Math	Verbal	Writing	Total
541	532	532	1,605

County Library

Sonoma County Library
Third And E Streets
Santa Rosa, CA 95404
707-545-0831

Librarian ... Sandy Cooper

Library statistics, FY 2007

Population served ... 481,785
Internet terminals ... 140
Annual users ... 299,464

Per capita:

Operating income ... $32.97
percent from local government ... 87.7%
Operating expenditure ... $30.18
Total materials ... 1.60
Print holdings ... 1.49
Visits ... 5.11

See Introduction for an explanation of all data sources.

Demographics & Socio-Economic Characteristics†

(2007 American Community Survey, except as noted)

Population

1990*	370,522
2007	511,263
Male	252,956
Female	258,307
Jan. 2008 (estimate)§	525,903
Living in unincorporated area	21.9%
2020 (projected)*	699,144

Race & Hispanic Origin, 2007

Race	
White	358,148
Black/African American	14,453
North American Native	4,105
Asian	26,190
Pacific Islander	2,454
Other Race	86,594
Two or more races	19,319
Hispanic origin, total	199,543
Mexican	185,802
Puerto Rican	2,511
Cuban	607
Other Hispanic	10,623

Age & Nativity, 2007

Under 5 years	41,166
18 years and over	364,315
65 years and over	52,568
85 years and over	6,833
Median Age	31.6
Native-born	410,412
Foreign-born	100,851

Educational Attainment, 2007

Population 25 years and over	309,855
Less than 9th grade	12.7%
High school grad or higher	75.8%
Bachelor's degree or higher	16.4%
Graduate degree	4.7%

Income & Poverty, 2007

Per capita income	$21,267
Median household income	$50,616
Median family income	$57,511
Persons in poverty	13.5%
H'holds receiving public assistance	6,236
H'holds receiving social security	43,064

Households, 2007

Total households	157,262
With persons under 18	68,613
With persons over 65	34,885
Family households	116,259
Single person households	32,160
Persons per household	3.19
Persons per family	3.71

Labor & Employment

Total civilian labor force, 2008§§	235,000
Unemployment rate	11.1%
Total civilian labor force, 2000*	197,320

Employed persons 16 years and over by occupation, 2007

Managers & professionals	56,659
Service occupations	33,642
Sales & office occupations	54,809
Farming, fishing & forestry	6,630
Construction & maintenance	25,061
Production & transportation	34,022
Self-employed persons	15,263

† see Appendix D for 2000 Decennial Census Data
* US Census Bureau
** 2007 American Community Survey
§ California Department of Finance
§§ California Employment Development Dept

General Information

1010 Tenth St
Suite 6800
Modesto, CA 95354
209-525-6333

Website	www.co.stanislaus.ca.us
Incorporated	April 1, 1854
Form of Government	General law
Land Area (sq. miles)	1,493.8
Water Area (sq. miles)	20.9
Persons per sq. mi. of land, 2008	352.1
Sales tax rate	7.38%

Voters & Gov't Officials

Registered Voters, October 2008

Total	230,046
Democrats	95,928
Republicans	88,346
Declined to state	36,046
Unincorporated area	47,359
Democrats	18,302
Republicans	20,424
Declined to state	6,716

Legislative Districts

US Congressional	18-19
State Senatorial	12, 14
State Assembly	17, 25, 26

County Officials, 2009

Exec Officer	Rick Robinson
County Clerk	Lee Lundrigan
District Attorney	Birgit Fladager
Auditor-Controller	Larry Haugh
Tax Assessor	Doug Harms
Treasurer/Tax Coll	Gordon Ford
Planning/Comm Dev	Kirk Ford
Public Works	Matt Machado
Building Dept Dir	Kirk Ford
Sheriff	Adam Christianson
Fire Warden	Gary Hinshaw
Elections Official	Lee Lundrigan
County supervisors	
District 1	William O'Brien
District 2	Vito Chiesa
District 3	Jeff Grover
District 4	Dick Monteith
District 5	Jim DeMartini

Public Safety

County Sheriff's office, 2007

Number of officers	233
Violent crimes	779
Property crimes	3,826
Arson	253

Housing & Construction

Housing Units

Total, January 2008§	176,622
Single family units, attached	7,753
Single family units, detached	131,959
Multiple family units	27,579
Mobile home units	9,331
Occupied units	170,036
Vacancy rate	3.7%
Median rent, 2007**	$914
Median SF home value, 2007**	$358,500

New Privately Owned Housing Units Authorized by Building Permit, 2007*

	Units	Construction Cost
Single	1,352	$257,963,932
Total	1,865	$306,406,459

Property Taxation, FY 2008

Total assessed value	$42,782,371,241
Total tax levied	$47,776,722
Delinquency rate	6.590%

County Finance, FY 2007

Revenues

Total	$666,564,850
Taxes	149,450,018
Special benefits assessment	0
Licenses, permits & franchises	5,634,967
Fines, forfeitures & penalties	13,331,741
Use of money & property	22,451,807
Intergovernmental	400,590,079
Service charges	65,552,936
Miscellaneous revenues	7,123,262
Other financing sources	336,164

Expenditures

Total	$633,652,108
General	61,413,729
Public protection	174,944,287
Public ways & facilities	19,766,450
Health	110,398,450
Sanitation	0
Public assistance	221,028,009
Education	10,270,675
Recreation & culture	8,430,190
Debt service	27,400,318

County Schools

Stanislaus County Office of Education
1100 H St
Modesto, CA 95354
(209) 238-1700

Superintendent . . . . Tom Changnon

County-wide School Totals

(2007-08 except where noted)

Number of districts	20
Number of schools	186
Enrollment	117,681
High school graduates, 2006-07	6,471
Pupil/teacher ratio	19.8
Average class size	18.0
Students per computer	5.4
Cost per ADA	$8,129
Avg teacher salary	$70,181

California Achievement Tests 6th ed., 2008

(Pct scoring at or above 50th National Percentile Rank)

	Math	Reading	Language
Grade 3	0%	0%	0%
Grade 7	10%	9%	9%

Academic Performance Index, 2008

Number of students tested	85,794
2007 API (base)	471
2008 API (growth)	508

SAT Testing, 2006-07

Enrollment, Grade 12	7,654
percent taking test	20.2%
percent with total score 1,500+	9.8%

Average Scores:

Math	Verbal	Writing	Total
507	498	494	1,499

County Library

Stanislaus County Free Library
1500 I St
Modesto, CA 95354
209-558-7800

Librarian . . . . Vanesa Czopek

Library statistics, FY 2007

Population served	521,497
Internet terminals	128
Annual users	256,298

Per capita:

Operating income	$20.76
percent from local government	91.0%
Operating expenditure	$20.19
Total materials	1.66
Print holdings	1.56
Visits	NA

See Introduction for an explanation of all data sources.

Demographics & Socio-Economic Characteristics†

(2007 American Community Survey, except as noted)

Population

1990* 64,415
2007 92,040
Male 45,562
Female 46,478
Jan. 2008 (estimate)§ 95,878
Living in unincorporated area 25.0%
2020 (projected)* 141,159

Race & Hispanic Origin, 2007

Race
White 61,497
Black/African American 1,421
North American Native 1,308
Asian 11,102
Pacific Islander 376
Other Race 10,826
Two or more races 5,510
Hispanic origin, total 24,985
Mexican .... NA
Puerto Rican .... NA
Cuban .... NA
Other Hispanic .... NA

Age & Nativity, 2007

Under 5 years 7,169
18 years and over 67,377
65 years and over 11,335
85 years and over 1,337
Median Age 33.3
Native-born 72,863
Foreign-born 19,177

Educational Attainment, 2007

Population 25 years and over 57,817
Less than 9th grade 10.8%
High school grad or higher 78.7%
Bachelor's degree or higher 17.2%
Graduate degree 6.3%

Income & Poverty, 2007

Per capita income $22,625
Median household income $51,382
Median family income $57,300
Persons in poverty 9.9%
H'holds receiving public assistance ... 1,280
H'holds receiving social security 9,165

Households, 2007

Total households 31,214
With persons under 18 14,018
With persons over 65 7,687
Family households 23,709
Single person households 6,485
Persons per household 2.93
Persons per family 3.42

Labor & Employment

Total civilian labor force, 2008§§ 42,000
Unemployment rate 12.3%
Total civilian labor force, 2000* 35,107

Employed persons 16 years and over by occupation, 2007

Managers & professionals 11,649
Service occupations 5,652
Sales & office occupations 8,601
Farming, fishing & forestry 1,647
Construction & maintenance 6,361
Production & transportation 5,400
Self-employed persons 3,056

† see Appendix D for 2000 Decennial Census Data
* US Census Bureau
** 2007 American Community Survey
§ California Department of Finance
§§ California Employment Development Dept

General Information

1160 Civic Center Blvd
Suite A
Yuba City, CA 95993
530-822-7100

Website .... www.suttercounty.org
Incorporated .... February 18, 1850
Form of Government .... General law
Land Area (sq. miles) 602.5
Water Area (sq. miles) 6.0
Persons per sq. mi. of land, 2008 ..... 159.1
Sales tax rate 7.25%

Voters & Gov't Officials

Registered Voters, October 2008

Total 41,604
Democrats 14,086
Republicans 19,523
Declined to state 6,341
Unincorporated area 11,782
Democrats 3,257
Republicans 6,608
Declined to state 1,513

Legislative Districts

US Congressional 2
State Senatorial 4
State Assembly 2

County Officials, 2009

Manager/Admin .... Larry T. Combs
County Clerk .... Donna M. Johnston
District Attorney .... Carl Adams
Finance Dir .... Robert Stark
Tax Assessor .... Mike Strong
Tax Collector .... Jim Stevens
Planning/Dev Dir .... Larry Bagley
Public Works .... Douglas Gault
Building .... NA
Sheriff .... Jim Denney
Fire Chief .... John DeBeaux
Elections Official .... Donna M. Johnston
County supervisors
District 1 .... Larry Montna
District 2 .... Stanley Cleveland Jr
District 3 .... Larry Munger
District 4 .... Jim Whiteaker
District 5 .... James Gallagher

Public Safety

County Sheriff's office, 2007

Number of officers 100
Violent crimes 124
Property crimes 938
Arson 12

Housing & Construction

Housing Units

Total, January 2008§ 33,491
Single family units, attached 1,203
Single family units, detached 24,657
Multiple family units 5,918
Mobile home units 1,713
Occupied units 31,988
Vacancy rate 4.5%
Median rent, 2007** $819
Median SF home value, 2007** $292,700

New Privately Owned Housing Units Authorized by Building Permit, 2007*

	Units	Construction Cost
Single	245	$58,233,937
Total	269	$59,698,417

Property Taxation, FY 2008

Total assessed value $8,557,086,219
Total tax levied $14,190,857
Delinquency rate 3.050%

County Finance, FY 2007

Revenues

Total $130,726,410
Taxes 29,546,157
Special benefits assessment 0
Licenses, permits & franchises ... 2,744,399
Fines, forfeitures & penalties 2,702,900
Use of money & property 2,430,462
Intergovernmental 84,122,580
Service charges 7,106,783
Miscellaneous revenues 2,055,809
Other financing sources 17,320

Expenditures

Total $118,564,246
General 21,441,849
Public protection 28,456,914
Public ways & facilities 5,826,628
Health 32,504,099
Sanitation 0
Public assistance 27,818,915
Education 1,432,022
Recreation & culture 711,944
Debt service 371,875

County Schools

Sutter County Office of Education
970 Klamath Ln
Yuba City, CA 95993
(530) 822-2900

Superintendent .... Jeff Holland

County-wide School Totals

(2007-08 except where noted)

Number of districts 5
Number of schools 33
Enrollment 16,391
High school graduates, 2006-07 892
Pupil/teacher ratio 11.4
Average class size 13.7
Students per computer 4.4
Cost per ADA $7,777
Avg teacher salary $56,509

California Achievement Tests 6th ed., 2008

(Pct scoring at or above 50th National Percentile Rank)

	Math	Reading	Language
Grade 3	NA	NA	NA
Grade 7	11%	11%	6%

Academic Performance Index, 2008

Number of students tested 11,788
2007 API (base) 573
2008 API (growth) 544

SAT Testing, 2006-07

Enrollment, Grade 12 1,500
percent taking test 23.4%
percent with total score 1,500+ 11.1%

Average Scores:

Math	Verbal	Writing	Total
518	488	483	1,489

County Library

Sutter County Library
750 Forbes Ave
Yuba City, CA 95991
530-822-7137

Librarian .... Roxanna Parker

Library statistics, FY 2007

Population served 93,919
Internet terminals 53
Annual users 112,000

Per capita:

Operating income $13.36
percent from local government 64.0%
Operating expenditure $13.36
Total materials 1.51
Print holdings 1.47
Visits 10.49

See Introduction for an explanation of all data sources.

Tehama County

Demographics & Socio-Economic Characteristics

(2000 U.S. Census, except as noted)

Population

1990* . . . 49,625
2000 . . . 56,039
Male . . . 27,692
Female . . . 28,347
Jan. 2008 (estimate)§ . . . 62,419
Living in unincorporated area . . . 65.6%
2020 (projected)* . . . 79,484

Race & Hispanic Origin, 2000

Race
White . . . 47,518
Black/African American . . . 318
North American Native . . . 1,178
Asian . . . 440
Pacific Islander . . . 55
Other Race . . . 4,631
Two or more races . . . 1,899
Hispanic origin, total . . . 8,871
Mexican . . . 7,429
Puerto Rican . . . 109
Cuban . . . 28
Other Hispanic . . . 1,305

Age & Nativity, 2000

Under 5 years . . . 3,534
18 years and over . . . 40,665
65 years and over . . . 8,923
85 years and over . . . 981
Median Age . . . 37.8
Native-born . . . 51,615
Foreign-born . . . 4,424

Educational Attainment, 2000

Population 25 years and over . . . 36,261
Less than 9th grade . . . 8.2%
High school grad or higher . . . 75.7%
Bachelor's degree or higher . . . 11.3%
Graduate degree . . . 2.9%

Income & Poverty, 1999

Per capita income . . . $15,793
Median household income . . . $31,206
Median family income . . . $37,277
Persons in poverty . . . 17.0%
H'holds receiving public assistance . . . 1,401
H'holds receiving social security . . . 7,508

Households, 2000

Total households . . . 21,013
With persons under 18 . . . 7,675
With persons over 65 . . . 6,325
Family households . . . 14,897
Single person households . . . 5,045
Persons per household . . . 2.62
Persons per family . . . 3.08

Labor & Employment

Total civilian labor force, 2008§§ . . . 25,700
Unemployment rate . . . 9.1%
Total civilian labor force, 2000 . . . 23,288

Employed persons 16 years and over by occupation, 2000

Managers & professionals . . . 5,320
Service occupations . . . 3,941
Sales & office occupations . . . 4,763
Farming, fishing & forestry . . . 909
Construction & maintenance . . . 1,950
Production & transportation . . . 4,135
Self-employed persons . . . 2,582

* US Census Bureau
** 2000 Decennial Census
§ California Department of Finance
§§ California Employment Development Dept

General Information

PO Box 250
Red Bluff, CA 96080
530-527-4655

Website . . . www.co.tehama.ca.us
Incorporated . . . April 9, 1856
Form of Government . . . Charter
Land Area (sq. miles) . . . 2,951.0
Water Area (sq. miles) . . . 11.3
Persons per sq. mi. of land, 2008 . . . 21.2
Sales tax rate . . . 7.25%

Voters & Gov't Officials

Registered Voters, October 2008

Total . . . 31,259
Democrats . . . 10,289
Republicans . . . 13,974
Declined to state . . . 5,101
Unincorporated area . . . 22,419
Democrats . . . 6,985
Republicans . . . 10,649
Declined to state . . . 3,485

Legislative Districts

US Congressional . . . 2
State Senatorial . . . 4
State Assembly . . . 2

County Officials, 2009

Admin/Manager . . . Williams Goodwin
County Clerk . . . Beverly Ross
District Attorney . . . Gregg Cohen
Finance Dir . . . LeRoy Anderson
Assessor . . . Mark Columbo
Tax Collector . . . Dana Hollmer
Planning Dir . . . George Robson
Public Works . . . Gary Antone
Building . . . John Stover
Sheriff . . . Clay Parker
Fire Chief . . . Gary Durden
Elections Official . . . Beverly Ross
County supervisors
District 1 . . . Greg Avilla
District 2 . . . George Russell
District 3 . . . Charles Willard
District 4 . . . Robert Williams
District 5 . . . Ron Warner

Public Safety

County Sheriff's office, 2007

Number of officers . . . 72
Violent crimes . . . 192
Property crimes . . . 416
Arson . . . 20

Housing & Construction

Housing Units

Total, January 2008§ . . . 27,308
Single family units, attached . . . 522
Single family units, detached . . . 16,614
Multiple family units . . . 3,110
Mobile home units . . . 7,062
Occupied units . . . 24,343
Vacancy rate . . . 10.9%
Median rent, 2000** . . . $486
Median SF home value, 2000** . . . $103,000

New Privately Owned Housing Units Authorized by Building Permit, 2007*

	Units	Construction Cost
Single	225	$35,260,613
Total	247	$37,063,345

Property Taxation, FY 2008

Total assessed value . . . $4,843,005,196
Total tax levied . . . $12,298,597
Delinquency rate . . . 4.280%

County Finance, FY 2007

Revenues

Total . . . $96,776,867
Taxes . . . 21,978,124
Special benefits assessment . . . 0
Licenses, permits & franchises . . . 2,220,665
Fines, forfeitures & penalties . . . 1,603,475
Use of money & property . . . 1,976,744
Intergovernmental . . . 59,411,746
Service charges . . . 8,444,939
Miscellaneous revenues . . . 1,112,989
Other financing sources . . . 28,185

Expenditures

Total . . . $95,574,753
General . . . 11,802,977
Public protection . . . 27,352,885
Public ways & facilities . . . 7,849,964
Health . . . 13,567,306
Sanitation . . . 12,605
Public assistance . . . 32,622,235
Education . . . 663,257
Recreation & culture . . . 260,402
Debt service . . . 1,443,122

County Schools

Tehama County Office of Education
PO Box 689
Red Bluff, CA 96080
(530) 527-5811

Superintendent . . . Larry Champion

County-wide School Totals

(2007-08 except where noted)

Number of districts . . . 11
Number of schools . . . 35
Enrollment . . . 9,157
High school graduates, 2006-07 . . . 666
Pupil/teacher ratio . . . 11.3
Average class size . . . 18.2
Students per computer . . . 2.1
Cost per ADA . . . $8,677
Avg teacher salary . . . $57,277

California Achievement Tests 6th ed., 2008

(Pct scoring at or above 50th National Percentile Rank)

	Math	Reading	Language
Grade 3	NA	NA	NA
Grade 7	NA	NA	NA

Academic Performance Index, 2008

Number of students tested . . . 6,838
2007 API (base) . . . 797
2008 API (growth) . . . 804

SAT Testing, 2006-07

Enrollment, Grade 12 . . . 860
percent taking test . . . 15.5%
percent with total score 1,500+ . . . 7.9%

Average Scores:

Math	Verbal	Writing	Total
523	501	491	1,515

County Library

Tehama County Library
645 Madison St
Red Bluff, CA 96080
530-527-0604

Librarian . . . Caryn Brown

Library statistics, FY 2007

Population served . . . 61,774
Internet terminals . . . 21
Annual users . . . 15,734

Per capita:

Operating income . . . $9.05
percent from local government . . . 89.6%
Operating expenditure . . . $8.17
Total materials . . . 1.93
Print holdings . . . 1.86
Visits . . . 1.33

See Introduction for an explanation of all data sources.

Demographics & Socio-Economic Characteristics

(2000 U.S. Census, except as noted)

Population

1990* . . . 13,063
2000 . . . 13,022
Male . . . 6,644
Female . . . 6,378
Jan. 2008 (estimate)§ . . . 13,966
Living in unincorporated area . . . 100%
2020 (projected)* . . . 18,236

Race & Hispanic Origin, 2000

Race
White . . . 11,573
Black/African American . . . 58
North American Native . . . 631
Asian . . . 61
Pacific Islander . . . 15
Other Race . . . 114
Two or more races . . . 570
Hispanic origin, total . . . 517
Mexican . . . 346
Puerto Rican . . . 26
Cuban . . . 2
Other Hispanic . . . 143

Age & Nativity, 2000

Under 5 years . . . 552
18 years and over . . . 10,048
65 years and over . . . 2,241
85 years and over . . . 174
Median Age . . . 44.6
Native-born . . . 12,816
Foreign-born . . . 206

Educational Attainment, 2000

Population 25 years and over . . . 9,433
Less than 9th grade . . . 3.4%
High school grad or higher . . . 81.0%
Bachelor's degree or higher . . . 15.5%
Graduate degree . . . 4.9%

Income & Poverty, 1999

Per capita income . . . $16,868
Median household income . . . $27,711
Median family income . . . $34,343
Persons in poverty . . . 18.2%
H'holds receiving public assistance . . . 281
H'holds receiving social security . . . 1,974

Households, 2000

Total households . . . 5,587
With persons under 18 . . . 1,571
With persons over 65 . . . 1,641
Family households . . . 3,625
Single person households . . . 1,648
Persons per household . . . 2.29
Persons per family . . . 2.80

Labor & Employment

Total civilian labor force, 2008§§ . . . 5,080
Unemployment rate . . . 12.4%
Total civilian labor force, 2000 . . . 5,263

Employed persons 16 years and over by occupation, 2000

Managers & professionals . . . 1,281
Service occupations . . . 967
Sales & office occupations . . . 1,032
Farming, fishing & forestry . . . 129
Construction & maintenance . . . 490
Production & transportation . . . 630
Self-employed persons . . . 725

* US Census Bureau
** 2000 Decennial Census
§ California Department of Finance
§§ California Employment Development Dept

General Information

11 Court St
PO Box 1613
Weaverville, CA 96093
530-623-1217

Website . . . www.trinitycounty.org
Incorporated . . . February 18, 1850
Form of Government . . . General law
Land Area (sq. miles) . . . 3,178.6
Water Area (sq. miles) . . . 28.9
Persons per sq. mi. of land, 2008 . . . 4.4
Sales tax rate . . . 7.25%

Voters & Gov't Officials

Registered Voters, October 2008

Total . . . 8,397
Democrats . . . 3,065
Republicans . . . 3,104
Declined to state . . . 1,547
Unincorporated area . . . 8,397
Democrats . . . 3,065
Republicans . . . 3,104
Declined to state . . . 1,547

Legislative Districts

US Congressional . . . 2
State Senatorial . . . 4
State Assembly . . . 1

County Officials, 2009

Manager/Admin . . . Dero Forslund
County Clerk . . . Deanna Bradford
District Attorney . . . Mike Harper
Finance Dir . . . David Nelson
Tax Assessor . . . Deanna Bradford
Tax Collector . . . (vacant)
Planning/Dev Dir . . . (vacant)
Public Works . . . Carl Bonomini
Building Dept Dir . . . Carl Bonomini
Sheriff . . . Lorrac Craig
Emerg Mgmt Dir . . . Eric Palmer
Elections Official . . . Deanna Bradford
County supervisors
District 1 . . . Judy Pflueger
District 2 . . . Judy Morris
District 3 . . . Roger Jaegel
District 4 . . . Howard Freeman
District 5 . . . Wendy Reiss

Public Safety

County Sheriff's office, 2007

Number of officers . . . 20
Violent crimes . . . 21
Property crimes . . . 112
Arson . . . 0

Housing & Construction

Housing Units

Total, January 2008§ . . . 8,482
Single family units, attached . . . 112
Single family units, detached . . . 5,613
Multiple family units . . . 252
Mobile home units . . . 2,505
Occupied units . . . 5,938
Vacancy rate . . . 30.0%
Median rent, 2000** . . . $487
Median SF home value, 2000** . . . $112,000

New Privately Owned Housing Units Authorized by Building Permit, 2007*

	Units	Construction Cost
Single	49	$9,437,941
Total	49	$9,437,941

Property Taxation, FY 2008

Total assessed value . . . $1,073,682,276
Total tax levied . . . $3,184,963
Delinquency rate . . . 3.700%

County Finance, FY 2007

Revenues

Total . . . $41,516,562
Taxes . . . 6,584,407
Special benefits assessment . . . 0
Licenses, permits & franchises . . . 623,842
Fines, forfeitures & penalties . . . 196,705
Use of money & property . . . 587,451
Intergovernmental . . . 29,620,579
Service charges . . . 2,356,931
Miscellaneous revenues . . . 1,545,847
Other financing sources . . . 800

Expenditures

Total . . . $40,076,543
General . . . 6,085,231
Public protection . . . 11,375,697
Public ways & facilities . . . 8,428,930
Health . . . 6,234,653
Sanitation . . . 0
Public assistance . . . 6,024,803
Education . . . 277,648
Recreation & culture . . . 0
Debt service . . . 1,649,581

County Schools

Trinity County Office of Education
PO Box 1256
Weaverville, CA 96093
(530) 623-2861

Superintendent . . . James French

County-wide School Totals

(2007-08 except where noted)

Number of districts . . . 2
Number of schools . . . 3
Enrollment . . . 55
High school graduates, 2006-07 . . . 2
Pupil/teacher ratio . . . 4.8
Average class size . . . 12.4
Students per computer . . . 1.5
Cost per ADA . . . $12,639
Avg teacher salary . . . $53,197

California Achievement Tests 6th ed., 2008

(Pct scoring at or above 50th National Percentile Rank)

	Math	Reading	Language
Grade 3	NA	NA	NA
Grade 7	NA	NA	NA

Academic Performance Index, 2008

Number of students tested . . . 41
2007 API (base) . . . 500
2008 API (growth) . . . 636

SAT Testing, 2006-07

Enrollment, Grade 12 . . . 171
percent taking test . . . 30.4%
percent with total score 1,500+ . . . 13.5%

Average Scores:

Math	Verbal	Writing	Total
508	482	464	1,454

County Library

Trinity County Free Library
PO Box 1226
Weaverville, CA 96093
530-623-1373

Librarian . . . Oresta Esquibel

Library statistics, FY 2007

Population served . . . 14,171
Internet terminals . . . 12
Annual users . . . 4,969

Per capita:

Operating income . . . $21.14
percent from local government . . . 88.9%
Operating expenditure . . . $21.33
Total materials . . . 4.23
Print holdings . . . 4.12
Visits . . . 2.15

See Introduction for an explanation of all data sources.

Demographics & Socio-Economic Characteristics†

(2007 American Community Survey, except as noted)

Population

1990* . . . 311,921
2007 . . . 421,553
Male . . . 211,994
Female . . . 209,559
Jan. 2008 (estimate)§ . . . 435,254
Living in unincorporated area . . . 33.1%
2020 (projected)* . . . 599,117

Race & Hispanic Origin, 2007

Race
White . . . 328,134
Black/African American . . . 7,086
North American Native . . . 4,735
Asian . . . 14,138
Pacific Islander . . . 329
Other Race . . . 56,337
Two or more races . . . 10,794
Hispanic origin, total . . . 239,066
Mexican . . . 229,930
Puerto Rican . . . 755
Cuban . . . 67
Other Hispanic . . . 8,314

Age & Nativity, 2007

Under 5 years . . . 40,080
18 years and over . . . 287,055
65 years and over . . . 39,918
85 years and over . . . 6,048
Median Age . . . 29.2
Native-born . . . 322,358
Foreign-born . . . 99,195

Educational Attainment, 2007

Population 25 years and over . . . 240,493
Less than 9th grade . . . 20.1%
High school grad or higher . . . 65.8%
Bachelor's degree or higher . . . 12.7%
Graduate degree . . . 4.1%

Income & Poverty, 2007

Per capita income . . . $17,349
Median household income . . . $40,595
Median family income . . . $42,674
Persons in poverty . . . 23.7%
H'holds receiving public assistance . . . 7,941
H'holds receiving social security . . . 30,746

Households, 2007

Total households . . . 122,613
With persons under 18 . . . 59,319
With persons over 65 . . . 26,499
Family households . . . 93,782
Single person households . . . 23,540
Persons per household . . . 3.38
Persons per family . . . 3.87

Labor & Employment

Total civilian labor force, 2008§§ . . . 201,700
Unemployment rate . . . 10.8%
Total civilian labor force, 2000* . . . 153,687

Employed persons 16 years and over by occupation, 2007

Managers & professionals . . . 36,548
Service occupations . . . 28,604
Sales & office occupations . . . 33,167
Farming, fishing & forestry . . . 25,934
Construction & maintenance . . . 15,789
Production & transportation . . . 22,034
Self-employed persons . . . 11,249

† see Appendix D for 2000 Decennial Census Data
* US Census Bureau
** 2007 American Community Survey
§ California Department of Finance
§§ California Employment Development Dept

General Information

County Civic Center
2800 W Burrel Ave
Visalia, CA 93291
559-733-6531

Website . . . www.co.tulare.ca.us
Incorporated . . . April 20, 1852
Form of Government . . . General law
Land Area (sq. miles) . . . 4,824.0
Water Area (sq. miles) . . . 15.1
Persons per sq. mi. of land, 2008 . . . 90.2
Sales tax rate . . . 8.0%

Voters & Gov't Officials

Registered Voters, October 2008

Total . . . 146,415
Democrats . . . 51,855
Republicans . . . 66,785
Declined to state . . . 22,527
Unincorporated area . . . 42,272
Democrats . . . 14,505
Republicans . . . 20,302
Declined to state . . . 5,975

Legislative Districts

US Congressional . . . 21
State Senatorial . . . 16, 18
State Assembly . . . 29-31, 34

County Officials, 2009

Administrator . . . Jean Rousseau
County Clerk . . . Greg Hardcastle
District Attorney . . . Phillip Cline
Finance Dir . . . Rita Woodard
Tax Assessor . . . Greg Hardcastle
Tax Collector . . . Rita Woodard
Planning/Dev Dir . . . William Hayter
Public Works . . . Henry Hash
Code Enforcement Dir . . . Bruce Kendell
Sheriff . . . Bill Wittman
Fire Chief . . . Steve Sunderland
Elections Official . . . Hiley Wallis
County supervisors
District 1 . . . Allen Ishida
District 2 . . . Pete Vander Poel
District 3 . . . Phillip Cox
District 4 . . . J. Steven Worthley
District 5 . . . Mike Ennis

Public Safety

County Sheriff's office, 2007

Number of officers . . . 450
Violent crimes . . . 488
Property crimes . . . NA
Arson . . . NA

Housing & Construction

Housing Units

Total, January 2008§ . . . 139,359
Single family units, attached . . . 4,915
Single family units, detached . . . 104,229
Multiple family units . . . 18,653
Mobile home units . . . 11,562
Occupied units . . . 128,936
Vacancy rate . . . 7.5%
Median rent, 2007** . . . $697
Median SF home value, 2007** . . . $235,100

New Privately Owned Housing Units Authorized by Building Permit, 2007*

	Units	Construction Cost
Single	2,254	$406,516,604
Total	2,689	$447,231,142

Property Taxation, FY 2008

Total assessed value . . . $26,375,709,124
Total tax levied . . . $54,942,343
Delinquency rate . . . 4.319%

County Finance, FY 2007

Revenues

Total . . . $600,973,615
Taxes . . . 104,820,353
Special benefits assessment . . . 0
Licenses, permits & franchises . . . 9,060,129
Fines, forfeitures & penalties . . . 7,030,370
Use of money & property . . . 4,057,091
Intergovernmental . . . 388,877,842
Service charges . . . 64,410,008
Miscellaneous revenues . . . 16,908,890
Other financing sources . . . 1,468,157

Expenditures

Total . . . $589,454,537
General . . . 28,374,820
Public protection . . . 169,114,909
Public ways & facilities . . . 28,915,504
Health . . . 121,395,233
Sanitation . . . 0
Public assistance . . . 222,394,092
Education . . . 3,976,000
Recreation & culture . . . 1,861,144
Debt service . . . 13,422,835

County Schools

Tulare County Office of Education
PO Box 5091
Visalia, CA 93278
(559) 733-6300

Superintendent . . . Jim Vidak

County-wide School Totals

(2007-08 except where noted)

Number of districts . . . 26
Number of schools . . . 145
Enrollment . . . 81,691
High school graduates, 2006-07 . . . 4,512
Pupil/teacher ratio . . . 14.4
Average class size . . . 15.6
Students per computer . . . 3.8
Cost per ADA . . . $7,921
Avg teacher salary . . . $63,269

California Achievement Tests 6th ed., 2008

(Pct scoring at or above 50th National Percentile Rank)

	Math	Reading	Language
Grade 3	NA	NA	NA
Grade 7	24%	30%	0%

Academic Performance Index, 2008

Number of students tested . . . 61,561
2007 API (base) . . . 557
2008 API (growth) . . . 558

SAT Testing, 2006-07

Enrollment, Grade 12 . . . 6,194
percent taking test . . . 22.5%
percent with total score 1,500+ . . . 8.1%

Average Scores:

Math	Verbal	Writing	Total
482	467	465	1,414

County Library

Tulare County Free Library
200 W Oak Ave
Visalia, CA 93291
559-733-6954

Librarian . . . Brian Lewis

Library statistics, FY 2007

Population served . . . 321,604
Internet terminals . . . 83
Annual users . . . 86,301

Per capita:

Operating income . . . $10.97
percent from local government . . . 86.0%
Operating expenditure . . . $8.74
Total materials . . . 1.08
Print holdings . . . 1.05
Visits . . . 0.96

See Introduction for an explanation of all data sources.

Demographics & Socio-Economic Characteristics

(2000 U.S. Census, except as noted)

Population

1990* 48,456
2000 54,501
Male 28,738
Female 25,763
Jan. 2008 (estimate)§ 56,799
Living in unincorporated area 91.7%
2020 (projected)* 64,161

Race & Hispanic Origin, 2000

Race
White 48,750
Black/African American 1,146
North American Native 992
Asian 395
Pacific Islander 91
Other Race 1,577
Two or more races 1,550
Hispanic origin, total 4,445
Mexican 3,394
Puerto Rican 101
Cuban 31
Other Hispanic 919

Age & Nativity, 2000

Under 5 years 2,466
18 years and over 43,201
65 years and over 10,067
85 years and over 967
Median Age 42.9
Native-born 52,777
Foreign-born 1,724

Educational Attainment, 2000

Population 25 years and over 38,977
Less than 9th grade 3.2%
High school grad or higher 84.3%
Bachelor's degree or higher 16.1%
Graduate degree 6.0%

Income & Poverty, 1999

Per capita income $21,015
Median household income $38,725
Median family income $44,327
Persons in poverty 10.4%
H'holds receiving public assistance 898
H'holds receiving social security 8,081

Households, 2000

Total households 21,004
With persons under 18 6,071
With persons over 65 6,917
Family households 14,249
Single person households 5,453
Persons per household 2.36
Persons per family 2.82

Labor & Employment

Total civilian labor force, 2008§§ 26,550
Unemployment rate 7.9%
Total civilian labor force, 2000 22,113

Employed persons 16 years and over by occupation, 2000

Managers & professionals 6,059
Service occupations 4,363
Sales & office occupations 5,035
Farming, fishing & forestry 182
Construction & maintenance 2,470
Production & transportation 2,310
Self-employed persons 2,967

* US Census Bureau
** 2000 Decennial Census
§ California Department of Finance
§§ California Employment Development Dept

General Information

2 S Green St
Sonora, CA 95370
209-533-5511

Website ....www.tuolumnecounty.ca.gov
Incorporated ....February 18, 1850
Form of Government ....General law
Land Area (sq. miles) 2,235.4
Water Area (sq. miles) 38.9
Persons per sq. mi. of land, 2008 ....25.4
Sales tax rate 7.25%

Voters & Gov't Officials

Registered Voters, October 2008

Total 33,640
Democrats 11,863
Republicans 14,457
Declined to state 5,554
Unincorporated area 30,921
Democrats 10,802
Republicans 13,477
Declined to state 5,012

Legislative Districts

US Congressional 19
State Senatorial 14
State Assembly 25

County Officials, 2009

Manager/Admin ....Craig L. Pedro
County Clerk ....Deborah Russell
District Attorney ....Donald Segerstrom Jr
Finance Dir ....Frank D. Hodges
Tax Assessor ....Ken Caetano
Tax Collector ....Frank D. Hodges
Planning/Dev Dir ....Beverly Shane
Public Works ....Peter Rei
Building Dept Dir ....Beverly Shane
Sheriff ....Jim Mele
Fire Chief ....Craig L. Pedro
Elections Official ....Deborah Russell
County supervisors
District 1 ....Liz Bass
District 2 ....Paolo Maffei
District 3 ....Teri Murrison
District 4 ....John Gray
District 5 ....Richard Pland

Public Safety

County Sheriff's office, 2007

Number of officers 60
Violent crimes 108
Property crimes 875
Arson 7

Housing & Construction

Housing Units

Total, January 2008§ 30,521
Single family units, attached 662
Single family units, detached 23,328
Multiple family units 2,292
Mobile home units 4,239
Occupied units 22,634
Vacancy rate 25.8%
Median rent, 2000** $611
Median SF home value, 2000** $149,800

New Privately Owned Housing Units Authorized by Building Permit, 2007*

	Units	Construction Cost
Single	146	$46,716,737
Total	149	$47,274,064

Property Taxation, FY 2008

Total assessed value $6,319,640,283
Total tax levied $18,791,301
Delinquency rate 4.700%

County Finance, FY 2007

Revenues

Total $105,153,750
Taxes 30,414,445
Special benefits assessment 227,424
Licenses, permits & franchises 2,353,455
Fines, forfeitures & penalties 1,924,056
Use of money & property 738,854
Intergovernmental 45,467,121
Service charges 16,556,948
Miscellaneous revenues 901,217
Other financing sources 6,570,230

Expenditures

Total $96,128,869
General 22,922,119
Public protection 31,410,399
Public ways & facilities 7,901,417
Health 10,795,764
Sanitation 2,702,086
Public assistance 17,812,750
Education 1,354,704
Recreation & culture 1,229,630
Debt service 0

County Schools

Tuolumne County Superintendent of Schools
175 South Fairview Ln
Sonora, CA 95370
(209) 536-2000

Superintendent ....Joseph Silva

County-wide School Totals

(2007-08 except where noted)

Number of districts 5
Number of schools 16
Enrollment 3,195
High school graduates, 2006-07 392
Pupil/teacher ratio 7.1
Average class size 6.1
Students per computer 2.2
Cost per ADA $9,359
Avg teacher salary $61,513

California Achievement Tests 6th ed., 2008

(Pct scoring at or above 50th National Percentile Rank)

	Math	Reading	Language
Grade 3	NA	NA	NA
Grade 7	NA	NA	NA

Academic Performance Index, 2008

Number of students tested 2,341
2007 API (base) 526
2008 API (growth) 618

SAT Testing, 2006-07

Enrollment, Grade 12 636
percent taking test 27.2%
percent with total score 1,500+ 15.4%

Average Scores:

Math	Verbal	Writing	Total
506	530	519	1,555

County Library

Tuolumne County Free Library
480 Greenley Rd
Sonora, CA 95370
209-533-5507

Librarian ....Constance Corcoran

Library statistics, FY 2007

Population served 57,223
Internet terminals 22
Annual users 21,300

Per capita:

Operating income $18.20
percent from local government 86.5%
Operating expenditure $20.58
Total materials 1.50
Print holdings 1.39
Visits 6.45

See Introduction for an explanation of all data sources.

Demographics & Socio-Economic Characteristics†

(2007 American Community Survey, except as noted)

Population

1990* 669,016
2007 798,364
Male 399,889
Female 398,475
Jan. 2008 (estimate)§ 831,587
Living in unincorporated area 11.6%
2020 (projected)* 956,392

Race & Hispanic Origin, 2007

Race
White 536,830
Black/African American 14,744
North American Native 6,555
Asian 52,428
Pacific Islander 1,895
Other Race 157,946
Two or more races 27,966
Hispanic origin, total 296,745
Mexican 268,762
Puerto Rican 2,992
Cuban 1,584
Other Hispanic 23,407

Age & Nativity, 2007

Under 5 years 57,845
18 years and over 589,284
65 years and over 89,154
85 years and over 12,659
Median Age 35.6
Native-born 613,157
Foreign-born 185,207

Educational Attainment, 2007

Population 25 years and over 506,769
Less than 9th grade 10.0%
High school grad or higher 82.2%
Bachelor's degree or higher 31.3%
Graduate degree 11.4%

Income & Poverty, 2007

Per capita income $31,013
Median household income $73,250
Median family income $80,793
Persons in poverty 8.5%
H'holds receiving public assistance . . . 4,876
H'holds receiving social security 62,870

Households, 2007

Total households 255,668
With persons under 18 102,525
With persons over 65 62,929
Family households 190,216
Single person households 53,597
Persons per household 3.09
Persons per family 3.58

Labor & Employment

Total civilian labor force, 2008§§ . . . 432,500
Unemployment rate 6.3%
Total civilian labor force, 2000* 367,453

Employed persons 16 years and over by occupation, 2007

Managers & professionals 136,374
Service occupations 59,555
Sales & office occupations 103,745
Farming, fishing & forestry 11,983
Construction & maintenance 33,117
Production & transportation 39,693
Self-employed persons 37,214

† see Appendix D for 2000 Decennial Census Data
* US Census Bureau
** 2007 American Community Survey
§ California Department of Finance
§§ California Employment Development Dept

General Information

800 S Victoria Ave
Ventura, CA 93009
805-654-5000

Website . . . . . www.countyofventura.org
Incorporated . . . . . March 22, 1872
Form of Government . . . . . General law
Land Area (sq. miles) 1,845.3
Water Area (sq. miles) 362.9
Persons per sq. mi. of land, 2008 . . . . . 450.7
Sales tax rate 7.25%

Voters & Gov't Officials

Registered Voters, October 2008

Total 425,968
Democrats 170,429
Republicans 160,279
Declined to state 76,436
Unincorporated area 54,412
Democrats 21,261
Republicans 20,813
Declined to state 9,663

Legislative Districts

US Congressional 23-24
State Senatorial 17, 19, 23
State Assembly 35, 37-38, 41

County Officials, 2009

Exec Officer . . . . . Marty Robinson
Clerk-Recorder . . . . . (vacant)
District Attorney . . . . . Gregory Totten
Auditor-Controller . . . . . Christine Cohen
Tax Assessor . . . . . Daniel Goodwin
Treasurer/Tax Coll . . . . Lawrence Matheney
Planning Dir . . . . . Kim Rodriguez
Public Works . . . . . Jeff Pratt
Building . . . . . Jim MacDonald
Sheriff . . . . . Bob Brooks
Fire Chief . . . . . Bob Roper
Elections Official . . . . . (vacant)
County supervisors
District 1 . . . . . Steve Bennett
District 2 . . . . . Linda Parks
District 3 . . . . . Kathy Long
District 4 . . . . . Peter Foy
District 5 . . . . . John Zaragoza

Public Safety

County Sheriff's office, 2007

Number of officers 748
Violent crimes 184
Property crimes 1,303
Arson 19

Housing & Construction

Housing Units

Total, January 2008§ 276,320
Single family units, attached 28,131
Single family units, detached 176,979
Multiple family units 58,879
Mobile home units 12,331
Occupied units 266,885
Vacancy rate 3.4%
Median rent, 2007** $1,326
Median SF home value, 2007** $641,300

New Privately Owned Housing Units Authorized by Building Permit, 2007*

	Units	Construction Cost
Single	862	$235,615,386
Total	1,595	$330,609,741

Property Taxation, FY 2008

Total assessed value $103,943,537,873
Total tax levied $179,882,104
Delinquency rate 2.910%

County Finance, FY 2007

Revenues

Total $933,871,347
Taxes 273,985,241
Special benefits assessment 0
Licenses, permits & franchises . . . 17,053,811
Fines, forfeitures & penalties 14,849,481
Use of money & property 13,421,098
Intergovernmental 443,608,761
Service charges 147,325,916
Miscellaneous revenues 14,730,345
Other financing sources 8,896,694

Expenditures

Total $875,627,702
General 85,518,270
Public protection 387,316,682
Public ways & facilities 42,315,438
Health 119,059,177
Sanitation 0
Public assistance 187,098,261
Education 11,068,531
Recreation & culture 0
Debt service 43,251,343

County Schools

Ventura County Office of Education
5189 Verdugo Way
Camarillo, CA 93012
(805) 383-1900

Superintendent . . . . . Stanley Mantooth

County-wide School Totals

(2007-08 except where noted)

Number of districts 19
Number of schools 216
Enrollment 165,716
High school graduates, 2006-07 13,953
Pupil/teacher ratio 15.3
Average class size 15.0
Students per computer 4.6
Cost per ADA $7,999
Avg teacher salary $66,126

California Achievement Tests 6th ed., 2008

(Pct scoring at or above 50th National Percentile Rank)

	Math	Reading	Language
Grade 3	NA	NA	NA
Grade 7	9%	17%	8%

Academic Performance Index, 2008

Number of students tested 123,656
2007 API (base) 631
2008 API (growth) 528

SAT Testing, 2006-07

Enrollment, Grade 12 11,013
percent taking test 34.6%
percent with total score 1,500+ 21.3%

Average Scores:

Math	Verbal	Writing	Total
540	523	523	1,586

County Library

Ventura County Library Services
646 County Square Dr
Ventura, CA 93003
805-477-7331

Librarian . . . . . Jackie Griffin

Library statistics, FY 2007

Population served 439,444
Internet terminals 188
Annual users 216,575

Per capita:

Operating income $25.05
percent from local government 86.2%
Operating expenditure $25.02
Total materials 1.81
Print holdings 1.70
Visits . . . . . NA

See Introduction for an explanation of all data sources.

Demographics & Socio-Economic Characteristics†

(2007 American Community Survey, except as noted)

Population

1990*	141,092
2007	195,844
Male	96,508
Female	99,336
Jan. 2008 (estimate)§	199,066
Living in unincorporated area	11.7%
2020 (projected)*	245,052

Race & Hispanic Origin, 2007

Race	
White	138,378
Black/African American	4,904
North American Native	2,424
Asian	24,524
Pacific Islander	517
Other Race	17,746
Two or more races	7,351
Hispanic origin, total	54,767
Mexican	45,652
Puerto Rican	992
Cuban	129
Other Hispanic	7,994

Age & Nativity, 2007

Under 5 years	12,279
18 years and over	151,126
65 years and over	18,031
85 years and over	2,780
Median Age	30.1
Native-born	152,907
Foreign-born	42,937

Educational Attainment, 2007

Population 25 years and over	115,094
Less than 9th grade	8.8%
High school grad or higher	84.3%
Bachelor's degree or higher	40.7%
Graduate degree	20.2%

Income & Poverty, 2007

Per capita income	$28,185
Median household income	$59,384
Median family income	$74,220
Persons in poverty	14.7%
H'holds receiving public assistance	1,412
H'holds receiving social security	13,699

Households, 2007

Total households	68,506
With persons under 18	22,830
With persons over 65	12,655
Family households	41,464
Single person households	18,383
Persons per household	2.77
Persons per family	3.43

Labor & Employment

Total civilian labor force, 2008§§	99,500
Unemployment rate	7.4%
Total civilian labor force, 2000*	82,547

Employed persons 16 years and over by occupation, 2007

Managers & professionals	42,081
Service occupations	14,328
Sales & office occupations	18,512
Farming, fishing & forestry	2,870
Construction & maintenance	8,146
Production & transportation	8,599
Self-employed persons	6,147

† see Appendix D for 2000 Decennial Census Data
* US Census Bureau
** 2007 American Community Survey
§ California Department of Finance
§§ California Employment Development Dept

General Information

625 Court St
Woodland, CA 95695
530-666-8150

Website	www.yolocounty.org
Incorporated	February 18, 1850
Form of Government	General law
Land Area (sq. miles)	1,013.3
Water Area (sq. miles)	9.6
Persons per sq. mi. of land, 2008	196.5
Sales tax rate	7.25%

Voters & Gov't Officials

Registered Voters, October 2008

Total	106,295
Democrats	51,402
Republicans	26,373
Declined to state	23,003
Unincorporated area	12,538
Democrats	5,176
Republicans	4,288
Declined to state	2,500

Legislative Districts

US Congressional	1-2
State Senatorial	5
State Assembly	2, 8

County Officials, 2009

Administrator	Sharon Jensen
County Clerk	Freddie Oakley
District Attorney	Jeff Reisig
Auditor-Controller	Howard Newens
Tax Assessor	Joel Butler
Treasurer/Tax Coll	Howard Newens
Economic Dev Mgr	Wes Ervin
Public Works	John Bencomo
Building	NA
Sheriff	Ed Prieto
Office of Emerg Svcs	Bill Martin
Elections Official	Freddie Oakley
County supervisors	
District 1	Michael McGowan
District 2	Helen Thomson
District 3	Matt Rexroad
District 4	Jim Provenza
District 5	Duane Chamberlain

Public Safety

County Sheriff's office, 2007

Number of officers	87
Violent crimes	30
Property crimes	389
Arson	10

Housing & Construction

Housing Units

Total, January 2008§	73,138
Single family units, attached	5,019
Single family units, detached	42,189
Multiple family units	22,213
Mobile home units	3,717
Occupied units	70,575
Vacancy rate	3.5%
Median rent, 2007**	$976
Median SF home value, 2007**	$444,100

New Privately Owned Housing Units Authorized by Building Permit, 2007*

	Units	Construction Cost
Single	722	$137,592,869
Total	922	$153,750,841

Property Taxation, FY 2008

Total assessed value	$20,115,181,068
Total tax levied	$19,407,148
Delinquency rate	2.360%

County Finance, FY 2007

Revenues

Total	$241,423,148
Taxes	44,708,049
Special benefits assessment	684,600
Licenses, permits & franchises	5,490,603
Fines, forfeitures & penalties	7,447,884
Use of money & property	4,873,293
Intergovernmental	147,583,933
Service charges	17,105,696
Miscellaneous revenues	2,867,802
Other financing sources	10,661,288

Expenditures

Total	$245,891,935
General	44,555,430
Public protection	66,251,388
Public ways & facilities	10,136,131
Health	44,531,440
Sanitation	0
Public assistance	73,045,735
Education	4,298,391
Recreation & culture	1,384,649
Debt service	1,688,771

County Schools

Yolo County Office of Education
1280 Santa Anita Ct, Suite 100
Woodland, CA 95776
(530) 668-6700

Superintendent	Jorge Ayala

County-wide School Totals

(2007-08 except where noted)

Number of districts	5
Number of schools	58
Enrollment	28,444
High school graduates, 2006-07	1,751
Pupil/teacher ratio	13.3
Average class size	15.6
Students per computer	1.2
Cost per ADA	$8,216
Avg teacher salary	$59,044

California Achievement Tests 6th ed., 2008

(Pct scoring at or above 50th National Percentile Rank)

	Math	Reading	Language
Grade 3	NA	NA	NA
Grade 7	NA	NA	NA

Academic Performance Index, 2008

Number of students tested	21,476
2007 API (base)	384
2008 API (growth)	464

SAT Testing, 2006-07

Enrollment, Grade 12	2,268
percent taking test	43.0%
percent with total score 1,500+	26.9%

Average Scores:

Math	Verbal	Writing	Total
549	536	531	1,616

County Library

Yolo County Library
226 Buckeye St
Woodland, CA 95695
530-666-8005

Librarian	Katy Curl

Library statistics, FY 2007

Population served	139,923
Internet terminals	43
Annual users	276,902

Per capita:

Operating income	$33.44
percent from local government	89.8%
Operating expenditure	$27.76
Total materials	2.68
Print holdings	2.44
Visits	4.51

See Introduction for an explanation of all data sources.

Demographics & Socio-Economic Characteristics†

(2007 American Community Survey, except as noted)

Population

1990* . . . 58,228
2007 . . . 72,098
Male . . . 36,350
Female . . . 35,748
Jan. 2008 (estimate)§ . . . 71,929
Living in unincorporated area . . . 77.4%
2020 (projected)* . . . 109,216

Race & Hispanic Origin, 2007

Race
White . . . 50,567
Black/African American . . . 1,359
North American Native . . . 1,928
Asian . . . 5,338
Pacific Islander . . . 199
Other Race . . . 8,084
Two or more races . . . 4,623
Hispanic origin, total . . . 16,245
Mexican . . . NA
Puerto Rican . . . NA
Cuban . . . NA
Other Hispanic . . . NA

Age & Nativity, 2007

Under 5 years . . . 6,684
18 years and over . . . 51,197
65 years and over . . . 6,128
85 years and over . . . 866
Median Age . . . 29.6
Native-born . . . 64,214
Foreign-born . . . 7,884

Educational Attainment, 2007

Population 25 years and over . . . 41,969
Less than 9th grade . . . 8.3%
High school grad or higher . . . 80.3%
Bachelor's degree or higher . . . 10.7%
Graduate degree . . . 3.1%

Income & Poverty, 2007

Per capita income . . . $19,707
Median household income . . . $42,712
Median family income . . . $49,174
Persons in poverty . . . 21.2%
H'holds receiving public assistance . . . 2,570
H'holds receiving social security . . . 6,275

Households, 2007

Total households . . . 24,236
With persons under 18 . . . 11,201
With persons over 65 . . . 4,667
Family households . . . 17,466
Single person households . . . 5,205
Persons per household . . . 2.93
Persons per family . . . 3.30

Labor & Employment

Total civilian labor force, 2008§§ . . . 28,100
Unemployment rate . . . 12.0%
Total civilian labor force, 2000* . . . 22,810

Employed persons 16 years and over by occupation, 2007

Managers & professionals . . . 7,494
Service occupations . . . 4,573
Sales & office occupations . . . 7,296
Farming, fishing & forestry . . . 412
Construction & maintenance . . . 4,373
Production & transportation . . . 4,786
Self-employed persons . . . 1,934

† see Appendix D for 2000 Decennial Census Data
* US Census Bureau
** 2007 American Community Survey
§ California Department of Finance
§§ California Employment Development Dept

General Information

915 8th St
Suite 121
Marysville, CA 95901
530-749-7575

Website . . . www.co.yuba.ca.us
Incorporated . . . February 18, 1850
Form of Government . . . General law
Land Area (sq. miles) . . . 630.7
Water Area (sq. miles) . . . 13.0
Persons per sq. mi. of land, 2008 . . . 114.0
Sales tax rate . . . 7.25%

Voters & Gov't Officials

Registered Voters, October 2008

Total . . . 29,771
Democrats . . . 10,313
Republicans . . . 12,072
Declined to state . . . 5,764
Unincorporated area . . . 22,895
Democrats . . . 7,800
Republicans . . . 9,263
Declined to state . . . 4,533

Legislative Districts

US Congressional . . . 2
State Senatorial . . . 4
State Assembly . . . 3

County Officials, 2009

Manager/Admin . . . Robert Bendorf
County Clerk . . . Terry Hansen
District Attorney . . . Pat McGrath
Auditor-Controller . . . Dean Sellers
Assessor . . . David Brown
Tax Collector . . . James Kennedy
Planning Dir. . . . Kevin Mallen
Public Works . . . Mike Lee
Chief Building Official . . . Martin Griffin
Sheriff . . . Steve Durfor
Fire Chief . . . Aaron Ward
Elections Official . . . Terry Hansen
County supervisors
District 1 . . . NA
District 2 . . . John Nicoletti
District 3 . . . Mary Jane Griego
District 4 . . . Roger Abe
District 5 . . . Hal Stocker

Public Safety

County Sheriff's office, 2007

Number of officers . . . 137
Violent crimes . . . 222
Property crimes . . . 1,138
Arson . . . 20

Housing & Construction

Housing Units

Total, January 2008§ . . . 27,672
Single family units, attached . . . 1,291
Single family units, detached . . . 18,563
Multiple family units . . . 3,880
Mobile home units . . . 3,938
Occupied units . . . 24,310
Vacancy rate . . . 12.1%
Median rent, 2007** . . . $695
Median SF home value, 2007** . . . $284,100

New Privately Owned Housing Units Authorized by Building Permit, 2007*

	Units	Construction Cost
Single	683	$104,117,973
Total	759	$109,945,874

Property Taxation, FY 2008

Total assessed value . . . $5,590,057,975
Total tax levied . . . $14,227,069
Delinquency rate . . . 5.190%

County Finance, FY 2007

Revenues

Total . . . $126,219,099
Taxes . . . 27,276,491
Special benefits assessment . . . 0
Licenses, permits & franchises . . . 3,609,753
Fines, forfeitures & penalties . . . 2,479,401
Use of money & property . . . 2,812,548
Intergovernmental . . . 67,490,772
Service charges . . . 12,157,495
Miscellaneous revenues . . . 9,909,293
Other financing sources . . . 9,004

Expenditures

Total . . . $123,571,543
General . . . 12,086,654
Public protection . . . 42,100,501
Public ways & facilities . . . 13,224,450
Health . . . 6,924,386
Sanitation . . . 0
Public assistance . . . 48,208,834
Education . . . 729,747
Recreation & culture . . . 0
Debt service . . . 296,971

County Schools

Yuba County Office of Education
935 14th St
Marysville, CA 95901
(530) 749-4900
Superintendent . . . Richard Teagarden

County-wide School Totals

(2007-08 except where noted)

Number of districts . . . 5
Number of schools . . . 39
Enrollment . . . 13,907
High school graduates, 2006-07 . . . 742
Pupil/teacher ratio . . . 14.5
Average class size . . . 7.9
Students per computer . . . 5.0
Cost per ADA . . . $8,655
Avg teacher salary . . . $60,053

California Achievement Tests 6th ed., 2008

(Pct scoring at or above 50th National Percentile Rank)

	Math	Reading	Language
Grade 3	NA	NA	NA
Grade 7	15%	30%	22%

Academic Performance Index, 2008

Number of students tested . . . 10,228
2007 API (base) . . . 519
2008 API (growth) . . . 509

SAT Testing, 2006-07

Enrollment, Grade 12 . . . 1,121
percent taking test . . . 18.2%
percent with total score 1,500+ . . . 5.4%

Average Scores:

Math	Verbal	Writing	Total
482	455	444	1,381

County Library

Yuba County Library
303 Second St
Marysville, CA 95901
530-749-7380
Librarian . . . Loren McRory

Library statistics, FY 2007

Population served . . . 70,745
Internet terminals . . . 27
Annual users . . . 25,000

Per capita:

Operating income . . . $13.04
percent from local government . . . 96.2%
Operating expenditure . . . $13.04
Total materials . . . 2.09
Print holdings . . . 1.94
Visits . . . 2.90

See Introduction for an explanation of all data sources.

California

Cities, Towns & Counties

2009

Note to the reader:

These pages are extracted from the 2009 edition of the *Almanac of the 50 States*, also published by Information Publications. Please refer to that volume for similar information on each of the 50 States, the District of Columbia, and the United States in general (ISBN: 978-0-929960-52-4, paper; 978-0-929960-53-1, hardcover).

California 1

State Summary

Capital city . . . . Sacramento
Governor . . . . Arnold Schwarzenegger

Office of the Governor
State Capitol
Sacramento, CA 95814
(916) 445-2841

Admitted as a state 1850
Area (square miles) 163,696
Population, 2008 (estimate) 36,756,666
Largest city . . . . Los Angeles
Population, 2007 3,834,340
Personal income per capita, 2007 (in current dollars) $41,571
Gross domestic product, 2007 ($ mil) . . $1,812,968

Leading industries by payroll, 2006

Professional/Scientific/Technical, Manufacturing, Health care/Social assistance

Leading agricultural commodities by receipts, 2007

Dairy products, Greenhouse/nursery, Grapes, Lettuce, Almonds

Geography & Environment

Total area (square miles) 163,696
land 155,959
water 7,736
Highest point . . . . Mt. Whitney
elevation (feet) 14,494
Lowest point . . . . Death Valley
elevation (feet) . . . . -282
General coastline (miles) 840
Tidal shoreline (miles) 3,427
Capital city . . . . Sacramento
Population 2000 407,018
Population 2007 460,242
Largest city . . . . Los Angeles
Population 2000 3,694,820
Population 2007 3,834,340

Number of cities with over 100,000 population

1990 43
2000 56
2007 62

State park and recreation areas, 2006

Area (x 1,000 acres) 1,560
Number of visitors (x 1,000) 79,782
Revenues ($1,000) 88,330
percent of operating expenditures 18.9%

National Park Service Areas, 2007

Total area (x 1,000 acres) 105.0
Federal land 101.7
Nonfederal land 3.3
Recreation visits (x 1,000) 2,741.1

National forest system land, 2008

Acres 20,802,641

Demographics & Population Characteristics

Population

1980 23,667,902
1990 29,760,021
2000 33,871,650
2007 36,553,215
Male 18,277,795
Female 18,275,420
Living in group quarters, 2007 862,406
percent of total 2.4%
2008 (estimate) 36,756,666
persons per square mile of land 235.7
2020 (projected) 42,206,743
2030 (projected) 46,444,861

Population of Core-Based Statistical Areas (formerly Metropolitan Areas), x 1,000

	CBSA	Non-CBSA
1990	29,540	218
2000	33,628	243
2007	36,295	259

Change in population, 2000-2008

Number 2,885,016
percent 8.5%
Natural increase (births minus deaths) . . 2,549,081
Net internal migration . . . . -1,378,706
Net international migration 1,825,697

Persons by age, 2007

Under 5 years 2,660,386
5 to 17 years 6,723,538
18 years and over 27,169,291
65 years and over 4,003,593
85 years and over 584,500
Median age 34.7

Race, 2007

One Race
White 28,081,544
Black or African American 2,450,444
Asian 4,544,182
American Indian/Alaska Native 423,238
Hawaiian Native/Pacific Islander 152,675
Two or more races 901,132

Persons of Asian origin, 2007

Total Asian 4,511,407
Asian Indian 479,871
Chinese 1,160,433
Filipino 1,155,543
Japanese 289,362
Korean 422,414
Vietnamese 547,070

Persons of Hispanic origin, 2007

Total Hispanic or Latino 13,220,888
Mexican 10,966,462
Puerto Rican 164,460
Cuban 83,764

2 California

Marital status, 2007

Population 15 years & over	28,831,162
Never married	9,966,272
Married	13,880,741
Separated	708,072
Widowed	1,539,382
Divorced	2,736,695

Language spoken at home, 2007

Population 5 years and older	33,891,325
English only	19,449,674
Spanish	9,664,383
French	130,730
German	139,587
Chinese	932,784

Households & families, 2007

Households	12,200,672
with persons under 18 years	4,657,557
with persons over 65 years	2,766,411
persons per household	2.93
Families	8,330,684
persons per family	3.53
Married couples	6,065,746
Unmarried couples	734,861
Same-sex	104,723
Male couple	57,662
Female couple	47,061
Female householder, no husband present	1,563,486
One-person households	3,030,693
Grandparents living with grandkids	964,937
Financially responsible for children	275,987
Not financially responsible	688,950

Nativity, 2007

Number of residents born in state	19,239,727
percent of population	52.6%

Immigration & naturalization, 2007

Legal permanent residents admitted	228,941
Persons naturalized	181,684
Non-immigrant admissions	6,253,111

Vital Statistics and Health

Marriages

2005	228,762
2006	225,341
2007	225,832

Divorces

2005	NA
2006	NA
2007	NA

Physicians, 2006

Total	95,676
rate per 100,000 persons	262

Health care expenditures, 2004

Total expenditures ($ mil)	$166,236
per capita	$4,638

Births, 2006

Total	562,440
Birth rate (per 1,000)	15.4
Teen birth rate (per 1,000)	39.9
White, non-Hispanic	158,426
Black, non-Hispanic	32,056
Hispanic	293,322
Asian/Pacific Islander	70,812
American Indian/Alaska Native	3,428
Low birth weight (2,500g or less)	6.8%
Cesarian births	31.3%
Preterm births	10.7%
To unmarried mothers	37.6%
2007 (provisional)	566,388

Deaths, 2005

All causes	237,037
rate per 100,000	713.0
Heart disease	64,916
rate per 100,000	196.3
Malignant neoplasms	54,732
rate per 100,000	167.0
Cerebrovascular disease	15,585
rate per 100,000	47.4
Chronic lower respiratory disease	13,188
rate per 100,000	40.9
Diabetes	7,697
rate per 100,000	23.5
2006 (preliminary)	237,069
rate per 100,000	700.2
2007 (provisional)	237,059

Infant deaths

2004	2,811
rate per 1,000	5.2
2005	2,930
rate per 1,000	5.34

HIV and AIDS, 2006

HIV (non-AIDS) cases	6,581
estimated living with HIV	NA
AIDS cases	3,960
estimated living with AIDS	61,555

Abortions, 2005

Total performed in state	NA
rate per 1,000 women age 15-44	NA
% obtained by out-of-state residents	NA

Health risks for adults, 2007

Cigarette smokers	14.3%
Binge drinkers	16.9%
Overweight (BMI > 25)	59.0%
Obese (BMI > 30)	23.3%
No exercise	23.1%
Recommended level of exercise	50.2%
Eat 5 fruit & vegetable servings per day	28.9%

Disability status of population, 2007

5 to 15 years	4.5%
16 to 64 years	10.2%
65 years and over	40.6%

California 3

Education

Educational attainment, 2007

Population over 25 years 23,331,762
Less than 9th grade. 10.6%
High school graduate or more 80.2%
College graduate or more. 29.5%
Graduate or professional degree. 10.5%

Public school enrollment, 2006-07

Total. 6,406,821
Pre-kindergarten through grade 8. . .4,405,450
Grades 9 through 12 1,993,972

Graduates and dropouts, 2005-06

Graduation rate 69.9%
Dropout rate. 3.7%

SAT scores, 2008

Average critical reading score. 499
Average writing score 498
Average math score 515
Percent of graduates taking test 48%

Public school teachers, 2008-09 (estimate)

Total (x 1,000) 303.2
Elementary 215.4
Secondary 87.8
Average salary $66,986

State receipts & expenditures for public schools, 2008-09 (estimate)

Total receipts ($ mil). $83,147
Revenue receipts $73,073
Total expenditures ($ mil) $78,757
for public day schools $59,871
per capita $1,629
per pupil $9,921

NAEP proficiency scores, 2007

	Reading		Math	
	Basic	Proficient	Basic	Proficient
Grade 4	53.2%	22.9%	69.6%	29.7%
Grade 8	62.3%	21.5%	59.1%	23.9%

Higher education enrollment, fall 2006

Total. 2,434,774
Full-time men 552,589
Full-time women. 687,488
Part-time men 523,741
Part-time women. 670,956

Minority enrollment in institutions of higher education, 2006

Black, non-Hispanic 187,898
Hispanic 654,999
Asian/Pacific Islander 459,765
American Indian/Alaska Native. 22,334

Institutions of higher education, 2006-07

Total. 412
Public. 147
Private 265

Earned degrees conferred, 2005-06

Associate's. 92,737
Bachelor's 151,021
Master's 56,029
First-professional. 8,721
Doctor's. 6,675

Public Libraries, FY 2006

Number of libraries. 179
Number of outlets 1,162
Annual visits per capita .4.1
Circulation per capita. 5.3
Print holdings per capita 2.0

State & local financial support for higher education, FY 2007

Full-time equivalent enrollment (x 1,000) . . 1,686.8
Appropriations per FTE. $7,083

Social Insurance & Welfare Programs

Social Security benefits & beneficiaries, 2007

Beneficiaries (x 1,000) 4,505
Retired & dependents. 3,229
Survivors. 564
Disabled & dependents. 711
Annual benefit payments ($ mil) $50,790
Retired & dependents. $34,700
Survivors. $8,220
Disabled & dependents. $7,870
Median monthly benefit
Retired & dependents. $1,041.50
Disabled & dependents. $920.50
Widowed. $1,035.50

Medicare, 2007

Enrollment (x 1,000). 4,369
Payment per enrollee $8,332

Medicaid, 2005

Beneficiaries (x 1,000). 10,509
Payments ($ mil) $28,638

State Children's Health Insurance Program, 2007

Enrollment (x 1,000). 1,538.4
Expenditures ($ mil). $980.7

Federal and state public aid

State unemployment insurance, 2007
Recipients, first payments (x 1,000) 1,018
Total payments ($ mil) $5,157
Average weekly benefit $298
Temporary Assistance for Needy Families, 2007
Recipients (x 1,000). 13,927.7
Families (x 1,000) 5,663.9
Supplemental Security Income, 2007
Recipients (x 1,000). 1,226.7
Payments ($ mil) $8,300.4
Supplemental Nutritional Asst. Program, 2007
Avg monthly participants (x 1,000) 2,048.2
Total benefits ($ mil). $2,569.8

4 California

Persons without health insurance, 2007
Number (x 1,000) 6,613
percent 18.2%
Number of children (x 1,000) 1,013
percent of children 10.8%

Type of health insurance coverage, 2007
Some coverage 81.8%
Private 62.6%
Government 26.5%
Medicaid 16.0%
Medicare 11.3%

Housing & Construction

Housing units
Total 2006 (estimate) 13,174,862
Total 2007 (estimate) 13,308,346
Single-family home 7,755,251
Multifamily dwelling 5,009,795
Mobile home or trailer 527,759
Seasonal or recreational use, 2007 302,572
Owner-occupied, 2007 7,076,972
Median home value $532,300
Homeowner vacancy rate 2.3%
Renter-occupied, 2007 5,123,700
Median rent $1,078
Rental vacancy rate 6.1%
Home ownership rate, 2006 .... 60.2%
Home ownership rate, 2007 .... 58.3%

New privately-owned housing units
Number authorized, 2007 (x 1,000) 110.1
Value ($ mil) $21,335.3
Started 2005 (x 1,000, estimate) 165.0
Started 2006 (x 1,000, estimate) 154.2

Existing home sales
2006 (x 1,000) 459.9
2007 (x 1,000) 355.0

Government & Elections

State officials 2009
Governor .... Arnold Schwarzenegger
Republican, term expires 1/11
Lieutenant Governor .... John Garamendi
Secretary of State .... Debra Bowen
Attorney General .... Jerry Brown
Chief Justice .... Ronald George

Governorship
Minimum age 18
Length of term .... 4 years
Consecutive terms permitted 2
Who succeeds .... Lieutenant Governor

State government employment, 2007
Full-time equivalent employees 387,168
Payroll ($ mil) $2,118.8

Local government employment, 2007
Full-time equivalent employees 1,448,284
Payroll ($ mil) $7,388.1

State legislature
Name .... Legislature
Upper chamber .... Senate
Number of members 40
Length of term .... 4 years
Party in majority, 2009 .... Democratic
Lower chamber .... Assembly
Number of members 80
Length of term .... 2 years
Party in majority, 2009 .... Democratic

Federal representation, 2009 (111th Congress)
Senator .... Barbara Boxer
Party .... Democratic
Year term expires 2011
Senator .... Dianne Feinstein
Party .... Democratic
Year term expires 2013
Representatives, total 53
Democrats 34
Republicans 19

Presidential election, 2008
Total popular vote 13,561,900
Barack Obama 8,274,473
John McCain 5,011,781
Total electoral votes 55

Votes cast for US Senators
2004
Total vote (x 1,000) 12,053
Leading party .... Democratic
Percent for leading party 57.7%
2006
Total vote (x 1,000) 8,541
Leading party .... Democratic
Percent for leading party 59.4%

Votes cast for US Representatives
2004
Total vote (x 1,000) 11,624
Democratic 6,224
Republican 5,031
Leading party .... Democratic
Percent for leading party 53.5%
2006
Total vote (x 1,000) 8,296
Democratic 4,720
Republican 3,314
Leading party .... Democratic
Percent for leading party 56.9%

Voters in November 2006 election (estimate)
Total 10,103,659
Male 4,806,091
Female 5,297,568
White 8,335,875
Black 608,009
Hispanic 868,190
Asian 882,153

California 5

Local governments by type, 2007

Total 4,344
- County 57
- Municipal 478
- Township 0
- School District 2,765
- Special District 1,044

Women holding public office, 2009

US Congress 21
Statewide elected office 1
State legislature 33

Black public officials, 2002

Total 234
- US and state legislatures 10
- City/county/regional offices 78
- Judicial/law enforcement 76
- Education/school boards 70

Hispanic public officials, 2007

Total 1,090
- State executives & legislators 35
- City/county/regional offices 391
- Judicial/law enforcement 45
- Education/school boards 619

Governmental Finance

State government revenues, 2007

Total revenue (x $1,000) $299,948,562
- per capita $8,205.81

General revenue (x $1,000) $189,543,916
- *per capita, total* $5,185.42
  - Intergovernmental 1,364.85
  - Taxes 3,138.90
    - Sales taxes 1,106.16
    - General sales tax 893.74
    - Selective sales taxes 212.41
    - Individual income tax 1,458.65
    - Corporate income tax 305.25
  - License fees 205.23
  - Current charges 379.67
  - Miscellaneous 302.00

State government expenditure, 2007

Total expenditure (x $1,000) $233,578,021
- per capita $6,390.08

General expenditure (x $1,000) $198,541,221
- *per capita, total* *$5,431.57*
  - Education 1,991.75
  - Public welfare 1,540.40
  - Health 314.47
  - Hospitals 170.86
  - Highways 249.57
  - Police protection 39.69
  - Corrections 221.41
  - Natural resources 133.07
  - Parks & recreation 12.63
  - Governmental administration 230.23
  - Interest on general debt 146.64

State debt & cash, 2007 ($ per capita)

Debt $3,137.94
Cash/security holdings $15,844.61

Federal government grants to state & local government, 2007 (x $1,000)

Total $57,636,140

by Federal agency
- Defense 435,597
- Education 4,451,854
- Energy 239,057
- Environmental Protection Agency 282,201
- Health & Human Services 36,070,063
- Homeland Security 153,382
- Housing & Urban Development 4,020,415
- Justice 340,342
- Labor 1,018,793
- Transportation 6,113,863

Crime & Law Enforcement

Crime, 2007 (rates per 100,000 residents)

Property crimes 1,108,660
- Burglary 237,025
- Larceny 652,243
- Motor vehicle theft 219,392
- Property crime rate 3,033.0

Violent crimes 191,025
- Murder 2,260
- Forcible rape 9,013
- Robbery 70,542
- Aggravated assault 109,210
- Violent crime rate 522.6

Hate crimes 1,789

Child abuse and neglect cases, 2006

Number of reports 225,911
Children subject of investigation 427,122
Number of child victims 89,500

Law enforcement agencies, 2007

Total agencies 459
Total employees 120,976
- Officers 78,516
- Civilians 42,460

Prisoners, probation, and parole, 2007

Total prisoners, 12/31/2007 174,282
- percent change from 2006 . . . . -0.7%
- in private facilities 2.9%
- in local jails 1.6%

Sentenced to more than one year 172,856
- rate per 100,000 residents 471
  - Male 880
  - Female 62

Adults on probation 353,969
Adults on parole 123,764

Prisoner demographics, June 30, 2005 (rate per 100,000 residents)

White 460
Black 2,992
Hispanic 782

6 California

Arrests, 2007
Total.......1,540,894
Persons under 18 years of age........ 233,558

Persons under sentence of death, 1/1/08
Total....... 667
White....... 251
Black....... 239
Hispanic....... 143

Fraud and identity theft, 2007
Fraud complaints.......61,409
rate per 100,000 residents.......168.0
Identity theft complaints....... 43,892
rate per 100,000 residents.......120.1

State's highest court
Name.......Supreme Court
Number of members....... 7
Length of term....... 12 years
Intermediate appeals court?.......yes

Labor & Income

Civilian labor force, 2007 (x 1,000)
Total....... 18,207
Men.......10,134
Women.......8,073
Persons 16-19 years....... 773
White.......14,143
Black.......1,068
Hispanic.......6,196

Civilian labor force as a percent of civilian non-institutional population, 2007
Total....... 65.6%
Men....... 74.3%
Women....... 57.2%
Persons 16-19 years....... 36.1%
White....... 66.2%
Black....... 60.9%
Hispanic....... 69.1%

Employment, 2007 (x 1,000)
Total.......17,234
Men.......9,580
Women.......7,654
Persons 16-19 years....... 634
White.......13,418
Black....... 965
Hispanic.......5,799

Unemployment rate, 2007
Total....... 5.3%
Men....... 5.5%
Women....... 5.2%
Persons 16-19 years....... 18.0%
White....... 5.1%
Black....... 9.6%
Hispanic....... 6.4%

Hourly wages, 2007
Mean hourly wage.......$22.11
Median hourly wage.......$16.91

Average annual and weekly wages, 2007
Average annual wages....... $50,538
increase from 2006....... 4.5%
Average weekly wage....... $972

Experienced civilian labor force by private industry, 2007
Total.......13,216,728
Natural resources & mining....... 410,959
Construction.......887,963
Manufacturing.......1,452,100
Trade, transportation & utilities... 2,886,309
Information....... 470,846
Finance....... 899,933
Professional & business.......2,258,149
Education & health.......1,628,413
Leisure & hospitality.......1,552,111
Other....... 718,009

Experienced civilian labor force by occupation, May 2007
Management....... 839,270
Business & financial....... 762,020
Legal.......111,780
Sales.......1,582,930
Office & admin. support.......2,718,950
Computers & math....... 394,840
Architecture & engineering....... 334,030
Arts & entertainment....... 281,520
Education....... 979,040
Social services....... 190,470
Health care practitioner & technical.... 634,760
Health care support....... 331,290
Maintenance & repair....... 508,820
Construction....... 794,020
Transportation & moving.......1,013,430
Production....... 960,440
Farming, fishing & forestry.......189,510

Income and poverty, 2007
Median household income....... $59,948
Median family income....... $67,484
Personal income, per capita (current $)... $41,571
in constant (2000) dollars....... $35,352
Disposable income (current $)....... $35,588
in constant (2000) dollars....... $30,264
Persons below poverty level....... 12.4%

Labor unions, 2007
Members of unions (x 1,000).......2,474
percent of employed....... 16.7%
Represented by unions (x 1,000)....... 2,650
percent of employed....... 17.8%

Federal individual income tax returns, 2006
Returns filed.......15,987,519
Adjusted gross income ($1,000)... $1,035,151,862
Total tax liability ($1,000).......$145,391,006
Charitable contributions (x 1,000)....... 5,257.2
Total amount ($1,000).......$24,359,073

California 7

Economy, Business, Industry & Agriculture

Bankruptcy cases filed, FY 2007..........62,951
Business 3,113
Non-business....................... 59,838
Patents awarded, 2008 22,122
Trademarks awarded, 2008..............19,318

Business firm ownership, 2002

Women-owned...................... 870,496
Sales ($ mil) $137,692
Black-owned.........................112,815
Sales ($ mil) $9,741
Hispanic-owned......................427,678
Sales ($ mil) $57,186
Asian-owned 371,530
Sales ($ mil) $125,757
Amer. Indian/Alaska Native-owned 40,541
Sales ($ mil) $4,387
Hawaiian/Pacific Islander-owned 7,074
Sales ($ mil) $1,230

Gross domestic product, 2007 ($ mil)

Total gross domestic product $1,812,968
Agriculture, forestry, fishing and hunting 28,255
Mining............................ 14,326
Utilities 31,841
Construction 69,743
Manufacturing, durable goods....... 102,707
Manufacturing, non-durable goods 76,315
Wholesale trade................... 104,096
Retail trade....................... 125,744
Transportation & warehousing 41,957
Information 112,554
Finance & insurance............... 120,546
Real estate, rental & leasing 301,209
Professional and technical services... 159,087
Educational services................ 14,658
Health care and social assistance..... 108,831
Accommodation/food services.........49,623
Other services, except government 41,135
Government....................... 205,163

Establishments, payroll, employees & receipts, by major industry group, 2006

Total.............................. 878,128
Annual payroll ($1,000).........$633,801,812
Paid employees 13,834,264

Forestry, fishing & agriculture.............2,010
Annual payroll ($1,000)............ $749,354
Paid employees 23,820

Mining................................. 873
Annual payroll ($1,000)...........$1,623,663
Paid employees 21,285
Receipts, 2002 ($1,000) $7,293,240

Utilities 1,120
Annual payroll ($1,000)...........$5,148,729
Paid employees 59,815
Receipts, 2002 ($1,000) ....NA

Construction...........................77,785
Annual payroll ($1,000)......... $43,808,271
Paid employees 958,436
Receipts, 2002 ($1,000) $150,527,556

Manufacturing....................... 44,474
Annual payroll ($1,000)..........$75,714,222
Paid employees 1,449,769
Receipts, 2002 ($1,000) $378,661,414

Wholesale trade........................59,935
Annual payroll ($1,000)......... $50,038,361
Paid employees 825,742
Receipts, 2002 ($1,000) $655,954,708

Retail trade......................... 113,307
Annual payroll ($1,000)..........$45,771,768
Paid employees 1,700,802
Receipts, 2002 ($1,000) $359,120,365

Transportation & warehousing.......... 20,776
Annual payroll ($1,000)..........$19,288,573
Paid employees 453,208
Receipts, 2002 ($1,000) $45,507,276

Information.......................... 20,954
Annual payroll ($1,000)......... $42,196,998
Paid employees 525,756
Receipts, 2002 ($1,000) ....NA

Finance & insurance................... 53,985
Annual payroll ($1,000)..........$59,106,693
Paid employees 733,723
Receipts, 2002 ($1,000) ....NA

Professional, scientific & technical.......112,691
Annual payroll ($1,000)..........$83,745,958
Paid employees 1,224,939
Receipts, 2002 ($1,000) $145,236,098

Education 10,752
Annual payroll ($1,000)..........$10,079,488
Paid employees 317,408
Receipts, 2002 ($1,000) $4,270,794

Health care & social assistance.......... 95,048
Annual payroll ($1,000)..........$67,945,691
Paid employees 1,556,748
Receipts, 2002 ($1,000) $136,397,384

Arts and entertainment 19,434
Annual payroll ($1,000)..........$12,168,275
Paid employees 302,529
Receipts, 2002 ($1,000) $26,292,138

Real estate............................51,094
Annual payroll ($1,000)..........$14,565,494
Paid employees 327,928
Receipts, 2002 ($1,000) $54,377,915

Accommodation & food service.......... 72,849
Annual payroll ($1,000)......... $21,243,809
Paid employees 1,321,880
Receipts, 2002 ($1,000) $55,559,669

8 California

Exports, 2007
Value of exported goods ($ mil) $134,152
Manufactured $97,035
Non-manufactured..................$14,029

Foreign direct investment in US affiliates, 2005
Property, plants & equipment ($ mil) ... $93,733
Employment (x 1,000).................. 542.6

Agriculture, 2007
Number of farms...................... 75,000
Farm acreage (x 1,000) 26,200
Acres per farm 349
Farm marketings and income ($ mil)
Total..............................$36,574.9
Crops $25,839.9
Livestock.........................$10,734.9
Net farm income $12,746.8

Principal agricultural commodities, in order by marketing receipts, 2007
Dairy products, Greenhouse/nursery, Grapes, Lettuce, Almonds

Federal economic activity in state
Expenditures, 2007 ($ mil)
Total............................ $260,422
Per capita $7,124.46
Defense $47,433
Non-defense...................... $212,989
Defense department, 2006 ($ mil)
Payroll...........................$15,270
Contract awards $32,126
Grants $350
Homeland security grants ($1,000)
2007............................ $242,245
2008............................ $272,563

FDIC-insured financial institutions, 2007
Number of institutions................... 312
Assets ($ billion) $452.4
Number of offices.......................7,122
Deposits ($ billion)..................$751.0

Communication, Energy & Transportation

Communication
Households with internet access, 2007 .... 66.1%
using broadband 56.4%
using dialup 9.4%
High-speed internet providers, 12/2007...... 84
Total high-speed internet lines.......17,158,292
Residential 9,843,965
Business.........................7,314,327
Cable modem....................3,603,105
DSL 4,780,051
Wireless phone customers, 12/2007 ... 32,247,015

FCC-licensed stations (as of January 1, 2009)
TV stations 108
FM radio stations........................ 363
AM radio stations 185

Energy
Energy consumption, 2006
Total (trillion Btu)..................8,420.4
Per capita (million Btu) 232.3
By source of production (trillion Btu)
Coal 67.0
Natural gas 2,331.0
Petroleum..........................3,915.5
Nuclear electric power 333.5
Hydroelectric power...................476.6
By end-use sector (trillion Btu)
Residential 1,552.3
Commercial 1,583.3
Industrial 1,941.8
Transportation 3,343.0
Energy spending, 2006 ($ mil) $115,990
per capita $3,200
price per million Btu $19.30
Electric energy, 2006
Primary source of electricity............. Gas
Net generation (billion kWh) 216.8
percent from renewable sources...... 33.2%
Net summer capability (million kW) 63.2
Retail sales (billion kWh) 263.0
per capita (MWh) 7.3
price per kWh .... 12.82¢
Natural gas utilities, 2006
Customers (x 1,000) 10,763
Sales (trillion Btu)...................... 740
Revenues ($ mil) $7,900
Nuclear power plants, 2008 4
CO_2 emitted, 2005 (mil. metric tons) 395.5

Transportation, 2007
Public road & street mileage 171,154
Urban............................. 87,709
Rural 83,445
Interstate............................2,461
Vehicle miles of travel (millions) 328,312
per capita 9,025
Total motor vehicle registrations......33,935,386
Automobiles.....................20,037,727
Trucks 13,839,571
Motorcycles 767,319
Licensed drivers 23,467,452
19 years & under 945,539
Deaths from motor vehicle accidents 3,974
involving alcohol.......................35%
driver with blood alcohol level over .08 ...29%
Gasoline consumed (x 1,000 gallons) ... 15,697,794
per capita 431.5

Commuting Statistics, 2007
Average commute time (min) 27.3
Drove to work alone 73.2%
Carpooled........................... 11.9%
Public transit 5.1%
Walk to work 2.8%
Work from home...................... 4.8%

Alameda County
Alameda
Albany
Berkeley
Dublin
Emeryville
Fremont
Hayward
Livermore
Newark
Oakland
Piedmont
Pleasanton
San Leandro
Union City

Alpine County
(Unincorporated)

Amador County
Amador City
Ione
Jackson
Plymouth
Sutter Creek

Butte County
Biggs
Chico
Gridley
Oroville
Paradise

Calaveras County
Angels Camp

Colusa County
Colusa
Williams

Contra Costa County
Antioch
Brentwood
Clayton
Concord
Danville
El Cerrito
Hercules
Lafayette
Martinez
Moraga
Oakley
Orinda
Pinole
Pittsburg
Pleasant Hill
Richmond
San Pablo
San Ramon
Walnut Creek

Del Norte County
Crescent City

El Dorado County
Placerville
South Lake Tahoe

Fresno County
Clovis
Coalinga
Firebaugh
Fowler
Fresno
Huron
Kerman
Kingsburg
Mendota
Orange Cove
Parlier
Reedley
San Joaquin
Sanger
Selma

Glenn County
Orland
Willows

Humboldt County
Arcata
Blue Lake
Eureka
Ferndale
Fortuna
Rio Dell
Trinidad

Imperial County
Brawley
Calexico
Calipatria
El Centro
Holtville
Imperial
Westmorland

Inyo County
Bishop

Kern County
Arvin
Bakersfield
California City
Delano
Maricopa
Mc Farland
Ridgecrest
Shafter
Taft
Tehachapi
Wasco

Kings County
Avenal
Corcoran
Hanford
Lemoore

Lake County
Clearlake
Lakeport

Lassen County
Susanville

Los Angeles County
Agoura Hills
Alhambra
Arcadia
Artesia
Avalon
Azusa
Baldwin Park
Bell
Bell Gardens
Bellflower
Beverly Hills
Bradbury
Burbank
Calabasas
Carson
Cerritos
Claremont
Commerce
Compton
Covina
Cudahy
Culver City
Diamond Bar
Downey
Duarte
El Monte
El Segundo
Gardena
Glendale
Glendora
Hawaiian Gardens
Hawthorne
Hermosa Beach
Hidden Hills
Huntington Park
Industry
Inglewood
Irwindale
La Canada Flintridge
La Habra Heights
La Mirada
La Puente
La Verne
Lakewood
Lancaster
Lawndale

Los Angeles County *(cont.)*
Lomita
Long Beach
Los Angeles
Lynwood
Malibu
Manhattan Beach
Maywood
Monrovia
Montebello
Monterey Park
Norwalk
Palmdale
Palos Verdes Estates
Paramount
Pasadena
Pico Rivera
Pomona
Rancho Palos Verdes
Redondo Beach
Rolling Hills
Rolling Hills Estates
Rosemead
San Dimas
San Fernando
San Gabriel
San Marino
Santa Clarita
Santa Fe Springs
Santa Monica
Sierra Madre
Signal Hill
South El Monte
South Gate
South Pasadena
Temple City
Torrance
Vernon
Walnut
West Covina
West Hollywood
Westlake Village
Whittier

Madera County
Chowchilla
Madera

Marin County
Belvedere
Corte Madera
Fairfax
Larkspur
Mill Valley
Novato
Ross
San Anselmo
San Rafael
Sausalito
Tiburon

Mariposa County
(Unincorporated)

Mendocino County
Fort Bragg
Point Arena
Ukiah
Willits

Merced County
Atwater
Dos Palos
Gustine
Livingston
Los Banos
Merced

Modoc County
Alturas

Mono County
Mammoth Lakes

Monterey County
Carmel-by-the-Sea
Del Rey Oaks
Gonzales
Greenfield
King City
Marina
Monterey
Pacific Grove
Salinas
Sand City
Seaside
Soledad

Napa County
American Canyon
Calistoga
Napa
St. Helena
Yountville

Nevada County
Grass Valley
Nevada City
Truckee

Orange County
Aliso Viejo
Anaheim
Brea
Buena Park
Costa Mesa
Cypress
Dana Point
Fountain Valley
Fullerton
Garden Grove
Huntington Beach
Irvine
La Habra
La Palma
Laguna Beach
Laguna Hills
Laguna Niguel
Laguna Woods
Lake Forest
Los Alamitos
Mission Viejo
Newport Beach
Orange
Placentia
Rancho Santa Margarita
San Clemente
San Juan Capistrano
Santa Ana
Seal Beach
Stanton
Tustin
Villa Park
Westminster
Yorba Linda

Placer County
Auburn
Colfax
Lincoln
Loomis
Rocklin
Roseville

Plumas County
Portola

Riverside County
Banning
Beaumont
Blythe
Calimesa
Canyon Lake
Cathedral City
Coachella
Corona
Desert Hot Springs
Hemet
Indian Wells
Indio
La Quinta
Lake Elsinore
Menifee
Moreno Valley
Murrieta
Norco
Palm Desert
Palm Springs
Perris
Rancho Mirage
Riverside
San Jacinto
Temecula
Wildomar

Sacramento County
Citrus Heights
Elk Grove
Folsom
Galt
Isleton
Rancho Cordova
Sacramento

San Benito County
Hollister
San Juan Bautista

San Bernardino County
Adelanto
Apple Valley
Barstow
Big Bear Lake
Chino
Chino Hills
Colton
Fontana
Grand Terrace
Hesperia
Highland
Loma Linda
Montclair
Needles
Ontario
Rancho Cucamonga
Redlands
Rialto
San Bernardino
Twentynine Palms
Upland
Victorville
Yucaipa
Yucca Valley

San Diego County
Carlsbad
Chula Vista
Coronado
Del Mar
El Cajon
Encinitas
Escondido
Imperial Beach
La Mesa
Lemon Grove
National City
Oceanside
Poway
San Diego
San Marcos
Santee
Solana Beach
Vista

San Francisco County
San Francisco

San Joaquin County
Escalon
Lathrop
Lodi
Manteca
Ripon
Stockton
Tracy

San Luis Obispo County
Arroyo Grande
Atascadero
Grover Beach
Morro Bay
Paso Robles
Pismo Beach
San Luis Obispo

San Mateo County
Atherton
Belmont
Brisbane
Burlingame
Colma
Daly City
East Palo Alto
Foster City
Half Moon Bay
Hillsborough
Menlo Park
Millbrae
Pacifica
Portola Valley
Redwood City
San Bruno
San Carlos
San Mateo
South San Francisco
Woodside

Santa Barbara County
Buellton
Carpinteria
Goleta
Guadalupe
Lompoc
Santa Barbara
Santa Maria
Solvang

Santa Clara County
Campbell
Cupertino
Gilroy
Los Altos
Los Altos Hills
Los Gatos
Milpitas
Monte Sereno
Morgan Hill
Mountain View
Palo Alto
San Jose
Santa Clara
Saratoga
Sunnyvale

Santa Cruz County
Capitola
Santa Cruz
Scotts Valley
Watsonville

Shasta County
Anderson
Redding
Shasta Lake

Sierra County
Loyalton

Siskiyou County
Dorris
Dunsmuir
Etna
Fort Jones
Montague
Mount Shasta
Tulelake
Weed
Yreka

Solano County
Benicia
Dixon
Fairfield
Rio Vista
Suisun City
Vacaville
Vallejo

Sonoma County
Cloverdale
Cotati
Healdsburg
Petaluma
Rohnert Park
Santa Rosa
Sebastopol
Sonoma
Windsor

Stanislaus County
Ceres
Hughson
Modesto
Newman
Oakdale
Patterson
Riverbank
Turlock
Waterford

Sutter County
Live Oak
Yuba City

Tehama County
Corning
Red Bluff
Tehama

Trinity County
(Unincorporated)

Tulare County
Dinuba
Exeter
Farmersville
Lindsay
Porterville
Tulare
Visalia
Woodlake

Tuolumne County
Sonora

Ventura County
Camarillo
Fillmore
Moorpark
Ojai
Oxnard
Port Hueneme
Santa Paula
Simi Valley
Thousand Oaks
Ventura

Yolo County
Davis
West Sacramento
Winters
Woodland

Yuba County
Marysville
Wheatland

Note: The 2007 American Community Survey (ACS) collected one-year demographic estimates for cities and counties with populations of at least 65,000 — in California's case, 40 out of 58 counties. For those counties, ACS data is included in the profiles in order to provide the most current data. However, to allow direct comparisons, data from the 2000 Decennial Census for those counties is presented here.

Alameda County

Item	Value
Population	
Total	1,443,741
Male	709,300
Female	734,441
Race & Hispanic Origin	
Race	
White	704,334
Black/African American	215,598
North American Native	9,146
Asian	295,218
Pacific Islander	9,142
Other Race	129,079
Two or more races	81,224
Hispanic origin, total	273,910
Mexican	193,011
Puerto Rican	10,186
Cuban	1,935
Other Hispanic	68,778
Age & Nativity	
Under 5 years	98,378
18 years and over	1,089,169
65 years and over	147,591
85 years and over	18,823
Median Age	34.5
Native-born	1,051,085
Foreign-born	392,656
Educational Attainment	
Population 25 years and over	953,716
0-8 yrs of school	8.0%
High School grad or higher	82.4%
Bachelor's degree or higher	34.9%
Graduate degree	13.7%
Income & Poverty, 1999	
Per capita income	$26,680
Median household income	$55,946
Median family income	$65,857
Persons in poverty	156,804
H'holds receiving public assistance	22,240
H'holds receiving social security	102,397
Households	
Total households	523,366
With persons under 18	190,790
With persons over 65	107,144
Family households	339,096
Single person households	136,066
Persons per household	2.71
Persons per family	3.31
Employed persons 16 years and over by occupation	
Managers & professionals	293,312
Service occupations	82,773
Sales & office occupations	182,205
Farming, fishing & forestry	1,065
Construction & maintenance	51,816
Production & transportation	81,662
Self-employed persons	49,197
Housing	
Median val. single fam. home	$303,100
Median rent	$852

Butte County

Item	Value
Population	
Total	203,171
Male	99,546
Female	103,625
Race & Hispanic Origin	
Race	
White	171,728
Black/African American	2,816
North American Native	3,866
Asian	6,752
Pacific Islander	296
Other Race	9,790
Two or more races	7,923
Hispanic origin, total	21,339
Mexican	17,134
Puerto Rican	391
Cuban	127
Other Hispanic	3,687
Age & Nativity	
Under 5 years	11,637
18 years and over	154,404
65 years and over	32,056
85 years and over	4,219
Median Age	35.8
Native-born	187,503
Foreign-born	15,668
Educational Attainment	
Population 25 years and over	126,736
0-8 yrs of school	5.9%
High School grad or higher	82.3%
Bachelor's degree or higher	21.8%
Graduate degree	7.0%
Income & Poverty, 1999	
Per capita income	$17,517
Median household income	$31,924
Median family income	$41,010
Persons in poverty	39,148
H'holds receiving public assistance	5,174
H'holds receiving social security	24,953
Households	
Total households	79,566
With persons under 18	24,810
With persons over 65	22,122
Family households	49,386
Single person households	21,636
Persons per household	2.48
Persons per family	3.02
Employed persons 16 years and over by occupation	
Managers & professionals	26,100
Service occupations	15,411
Sales & office occupations	21,968
Farming, fishing & forestry	1,654
Construction & maintenance	7,690
Production & transportation	9,580
Self-employed persons	9,245
Housing	
Median val. single fam. home	$129,800
Median rent	$563

Contra Costa County

Item	Value
Population	
Total	948,816
Male	463,270
Female	485,546
Race & Hispanic Origin	
Race	
White	621,490
Black/African American	88,813
North American Native	5,830
Asian	103,993
Pacific Islander	3,466
Other Race	76,510
Two or more races	48,714
Hispanic origin, total	167,776
Mexican	112,245
Puerto Rican	4,957
Cuban	1,167
Other Hispanic	49,407
Age & Nativity	
Under 5 years	66,128
18 years and over	697,022
65 years and over	107,272
85 years and over	13,371
Median Age	36.4
Native-born	768,328
Foreign-born	180,488
Educational Attainment	
Population 25 years and over	625,641
0-8 yrs of school	5.2%
High School grad or higher	86.9%
Bachelor's degree or higher	35.0%
Graduate degree	12.2%
Income & Poverty, 1999	
Per capita income	$30,615
Median household income	$63,675
Median family income	$73,039
Persons in poverty	71,575
H'holds receiving public assistance	9,745
H'holds receiving social security	77,906
Households	
Total households	344,129
With persons under 18	133,372
With persons over 65	76,255
Family households	242,233
Single person households	78,759
Persons per household	2.72
Persons per family	3.23
Employed persons 16 years and over by occupation	
Managers & professionals	185,100
Service occupations	60,299
Sales & office occupations	126,183
Farming, fishing & forestry	937
Construction & maintenance	40,341
Production & transportation	38,497
Self-employed persons	38,535
Housing	
Median val. single fam. home	$267,800
Median rent	$898

Note: The 2007 American Community Survey (ACS) collected one-year demographic estimates for cities and counties with populations of at least 65,000 — in California's case, 40 out of 58 counties. For those counties, ACS data is included in the profiles in order to provide the most current data. However, to allow direct comparisons, data from the 2000 Decennial Census for those counties is presented here.

El Dorado County

Population

Total	156,299
Male	77,963
Female	78,336

Race & Hispanic Origin

Race	
White	140,209
Black/African American	813
North American Native	1,566
Asian	3,328
Pacific Islander	209
Other Race	5,547
Two or more races	4,627
Hispanic origin, total	14,566
Mexican	10,871
Puerto Rican	340
Cuban	104
Other Hispanic	3,251

Age & Nativity

Under 5 years	8,946
18 years and over	115,507
65 years and over	19,334
85 years and over	1,768
Median Age	39.4
Native-born	145,116
Foreign-born	11,183

Educational Attainment

Population 25 years and over	105,034
0-8 yrs of school	2.8%
High School grad or higher	89.1%
Bachelor's degree or higher	26.5%
Graduate degree	8.4%

Income & Poverty, 1999

Per capita income	$25,560
Median household income	$51,484
Median family income	$60,250
Persons in poverty	11,079
H'holds receiving public assistance	1,626
H'holds receiving social security	15,305

Households

Total households	58,939
With persons under 18	21,684
With persons over 65	13,544
Family households	43,029
Single person households	11,859
Persons per household	2.63
Persons per family	3.04

Employed persons 16 years and over by occupation

Managers & professionals	27,508
Service occupations	14,064
Sales & office occupations	18,535
Farming, fishing & forestry	461
Construction & maintenance	7,642
Production & transportation	5,611
Self-employed persons	8,697

Housing

Median val. single fam. home	$194,400
Median rent	$702

Fresno County

Population

Total	799,407
Male	400,476
Female	398,931

Race & Hispanic Origin

Race	
White	434,045
Black/African American	42,337
North American Native	12,790
Asian	64,362
Pacific Islander	1,000
Other Race	207,061
Two or more races	37,812
Hispanic origin, total	351,636
Mexican	302,120
Puerto Rican	1,711
Cuban	441
Other Hispanic	47,364

Age & Nativity

Under 5 years	67,827
18 years and over	542,982
65 years and over	79,209
85 years and over	9,707
Median Age	29.9
Native-born	630,690
Foreign-born	168,717

Educational Attainment

Population 25 years and over	455,540
0-8 yrs of school	18.3%
High School grad or higher	67.5%
Bachelor's degree or higher	17.5%
Graduate degree	5.5%

Income & Poverty, 1999

Per capita income	$15,495
Median household income	$34,725
Median family income	$38,455
Persons in poverty	179,085
H'holds receiving public assistance	21,581
H'holds receiving social security	59,845

Households

Total households	252,940
With persons under 18	115,871
With persons over 65	56,331
Family households	186,736
Single person households	52,100
Persons per household	3.09
Persons per family	3.59

Employed persons 16 years and over by occupation

Managers & professionals	88,796
Service occupations	48,665
Sales & office occupations	78,299
Farming, fishing & forestry	19,780
Construction & maintenance	25,698
Production & transportation	40,068
Self-employed persons	22,345

Housing

Median val. single fam. home	$104,900
Median rent	$534

Humboldt County

Population

Total	126,518
Male	62,532
Female	63,986

Race & Hispanic Origin

Race	
White	107,179
Black/African American	1,111
North American Native	7,241
Asian	2,091
Pacific Islander	241
Other Race	3,099
Two or more races	5,556
Hispanic origin, total	8,210
Mexican	6,107
Puerto Rican	225
Cuban	114
Other Hispanic	1,764

Age & Nativity

Under 5 years	7,125
18 years and over	97,105
65 years and over	15,776
85 years and over	2,002
Median Age	36.3
Native-born	120,769
Foreign-born	5,749

Educational Attainment

Population 25 years and over	81,501
0-8 yrs of school	4.0%
High School grad or higher	84.9%
Bachelor's degree or higher	23.0%
Graduate degree	7.4%

Income & Poverty, 1999

Per capita income	$17,203
Median household income	$31,226
Median family income	$39,370
Persons in poverty	24,059
H'holds receiving public assistance	3,139
H'holds receiving social security	13,480

Households

Total households	51,238
With persons under 18	16,094
With persons over 65	11,327
Family households	30,645
Single person households	14,826
Persons per household	2.39
Persons per family	2.95

Employed persons 16 years and over by occupation

Managers & professionals	17,470
Service occupations	10,859
Sales & office occupations	13,780
Farming, fishing & forestry	1,466
Construction & maintenance	4,856
Production & transportation	6,995
Self-employed persons	7,157

Housing

Median val. single fam. home	$133,500
Median rent	$537

Note: The 2007 American Community Survey (ACS) collected one-year demographic estimates for cities and counties with populations of at least 65,000 — in California's case, 40 out of 58 counties. For those counties, ACS data is included in the profiles in order to provide the most current data. However, to allow direct comparisons, data from the 2000 Decennial Census for those counties is presented here.

Imperial County

Population

Total	142,361
Male	74,330
Female	68,031

Race & Hispanic Origin

Race	
White	70,290
Black/African American	5,624
North American Native	2,666
Asian	2,836
Pacific Islander	119
Other Race	55,634
Two or more races	5,192
Hispanic origin, total	102,817
Mexican	92,696
Puerto Rican	280
Cuban	78
Other Hispanic	9,763

Age & Nativity

Under 5 years	10,902
18 years and over	97,615
65 years and over	14,305
85 years and over	1,213
Median Age	31.0
Native-born	96,578
Foreign-born	45,783

Educational Attainment

Population 25 years and over	83,632
0-8 yrs of school	23.8%
High School grad or higher	59.0%
Bachelor's degree or higher	10.3%
Graduate degree	3.7%

Income & Poverty, 1999

Per capita income	$13,239
Median household income	$31,870
Median family income	$35,226
Persons in poverty	29,681
H'holds receiving public assistance	4,049
H'holds receiving social security	11,387

Households

Total households	39,384
With persons under 18	21,036
With persons over 65	10,491
Family households	31,465
Single person households	6,724
Persons per household	3.33
Persons per family	3.77

Employed persons 16 years and over by occupation

Managers & professionals	10,907
Service occupations	8,676
Sales & office occupations	11,302
Farming, fishing & forestry	4,113
Construction & maintenance	3,948
Production & transportation	5,146
Self-employed persons	3,027

Housing

Median val. single fam. home	$100,000
Median rent	$504

Kern County

Population

Total	661,645
Male	339,382
Female	322,263

Race & Hispanic Origin

Race	
White	407,581
Black/African American	39,798
North American Native	9,999
Asian	22,268
Pacific Islander	972
Other Race	153,610
Two or more races	27,417
Hispanic origin, total	254,036
Mexican	210,828
Puerto Rican	2,811
Cuban	469
Other Hispanic	39,928

Age & Nativity

Under 5 years	55,707
18 years and over	450,266
65 years and over	62,054
85 years and over	6,457
Median Age	30.6
Native-born	549,701
Foreign-born	111,944

Educational Attainment

Population 25 years and over	383,667
0-8 yrs of school	15.0%
High School grad or higher	68.5%
Bachelor's degree or higher	13.5%
Graduate degree	4.5%

Income & Poverty, 1999

Per capita income	$15,760
Median household income	$35,446
Median family income	$39,403
Persons in poverty	130,949
H'holds receiving public assistance	15,572
H'holds receiving social security	51,830

Households

Total households	208,652
With persons under 18	97,731
With persons over 65	44,993
Family households	156,401
Single person households	42,379
Persons per household	3.03
Persons per family	3.50

Employed persons 16 years and over by occupation

Managers & professionals	62,700
Service occupations	40,983
Sales & office occupations	56,117
Farming, fishing & forestry	15,517
Construction & maintenance	25,660
Production & transportation	31,484
Self-employed persons	18,074

Housing

Median val. single fam. home	$93,300
Median rent	$518

Kings County

Population

Total	129,461
Male	74,332
Female	55,129

Race & Hispanic Origin

Race	
White	69,492
Black/African American	10,747
North American Native	2,178
Asian	3,980
Pacific Islander	250
Other Race	36,611
Two or more races	6,203
Hispanic origin, total	56,461
Mexican	49,943
Puerto Rican	376
Cuban	73
Other Hispanic	6,069

Age & Nativity

Under 5 years	10,437
18 years and over	91,933
65 years and over	9,557
85 years and over	1,089
Median Age	30.2
Native-born	108,704
Foreign-born	20,757

Educational Attainment

Population 25 years and over	77,095
0-8 yrs of school	15.7%
High School grad or higher	68.8%
Bachelor's degree or higher	10.4%
Graduate degree	2.7%

Income & Poverty, 1999

Per capita income	$15,848
Median household income	$35,749
Median family income	$38,111
Persons in poverty	21,307
H'holds receiving public assistance	2,613
H'holds receiving social security	7,562

Households

Total households	34,418
With persons under 18	17,552
With persons over 65	6,722
Family households	26,989
Single person households	5,843
Persons per household	3.18
Persons per family	3.56

Employed persons 16 years and over by occupation

Managers & professionals	10,228
Service occupations	7,777
Sales & office occupations	9,014
Farming, fishing & forestry	3,711
Construction & maintenance	3,378
Production & transportation	5,403
Self-employed persons	2,757

Housing

Median val. single fam. home	$97,600
Median rent	$533

Note: The 2007 American Community Survey (ACS) collected one-year demographic estimates for cities and counties with populations of at least 65,000 — in California's case, 40 out of 58 counties. For those counties, ACS data is included in the profiles in order to provide the most current data. However, to allow direct comparisons, data from the 2000 Decennial Census for those counties is presented here.

Lake County

Population

Total	58,309
Male	28,796
Female	29,513

Race & Hispanic Origin

Race	
White	50,289
Black/African American	1,233
North American Native	1,772
Asian	482
Pacific Islander	93
Other Race	2,398
Two or more races	2,042
Hispanic origin, total	6,639
Mexican	5,226
Puerto Rican	146
Cuban	32
Other Hispanic	1,235

Age & Nativity

Under 5 years	3,074
18 years and over	44,247
65 years and over	11,359
85 years and over	1,182
Median Age	42.7
Native-born	54,487
Foreign-born	3,822

Educational Attainment

Population 25 years and over	40,717
0-8 yrs of school	6.3%
High School grad or higher	77.3%
Bachelor's degree or higher	12.1%
Graduate degree	4.5%

Income & Poverty, 1999

Per capita income	$16,825
Median household income	$29,627
Median family income	$35,818
Persons in poverty	10,081
H'holds receiving public assistance	1,988
H'holds receiving social security	9,672

Households

Total households	23,974
With persons under 18	7,198
With persons over 65	8,122
Family households	15,370
Single person households	6,954
Persons per household	2.39
Persons per family	2.92

Employed persons 16 years and over by occupation

Managers & professionals	5,576
Service occupations	4,429
Sales & office occupations	4,836
Farming, fishing & forestry	520
Construction & maintenance	2,825
Production & transportation	2,317
Self-employed persons	2,641

Housing

Median val. single fam. home	$122,600
Median rent	$567

Los Angeles County

Population

Total	9,519,338
Male	4,704,105
Female	4,815,233

Race & Hispanic Origin

Race	
White	4,637,062
Black/African American	930,957
North American Native	76,988
Asian	1,137,500
Pacific Islander	27,053
Other Race	2,239,997
Two or more races	469,781
Hispanic origin, total	4,242,213
Mexican	3,041,974
Puerto Rican	37,862
Cuban	38,664
Other Hispanic	1,123,713

Age & Nativity

Under 5 years	737,631
18 years and over	6,851,362
65 years and over	926,673
85 years and over	109,147
Median Age	32.0
Native-born	6,069,894
Foreign-born	3,449,444

Educational Attainment

Population 25 years and over	5,882,948
0-8 yrs of school	16.2%
High School grad or higher	69.9%
Bachelor's degree or higher	24.9%
Graduate degree	8.8%

Income & Poverty, 1999

Per capita income	$20,683
Median household income	$42,189
Median family income	$46,452
Persons in poverty	1,674,599
H'holds receiving public assistance	199,328
H'holds receiving social security	618,121

Households

Total households	3,133,774
With persons under 18	1,293,674
With persons over 65	674,787
Family households	2,136,977
Single person households	771,854
Persons per household	2.98
Persons per family	3.61

Employed persons 16 years and over by occupation

Managers & professionals	1,355,973
Service occupations	580,809
Sales & office occupations	1,090,059
Farming, fishing & forestry	6,650
Construction & maintenance	306,450
Production & transportation	613,474
Self-employed persons	341,295

Housing

Median val. single fam. home	$209,300
Median rent	$704

Madera County

Population

Total	123,109
Male	58,911
Female	64,198

Race & Hispanic Origin

Race	
White	76,612
Black/African American	5,072
North American Native	3,212
Asian	1,566
Pacific Islander	210
Other Race	29,979
Two or more races	6,458
Hispanic origin, total	54,515
Mexican	46,989
Puerto Rican	392
Cuban	169
Other Hispanic	6,965

Age & Nativity

Under 5 years	9,443
18 years and over	86,642
65 years and over	13,596
85 years and over	1,388
Median Age	32.7
Native-born	98,356
Foreign-born	24,753

Educational Attainment

Population 25 years and over	74,830
0-8 yrs of school	18.4%
High School grad or higher	65.4%
Bachelor's degree or higher	12.0%
Graduate degree	3.8%

Income & Poverty, 1999

Per capita income	$14,682
Median household income	$36,286
Median family income	$39,226
Persons in poverty	24,514
H'holds receiving public assistance	2,909
H'holds receiving social security	10,511

Households

Total households	36,155
With persons under 18	16,333
With persons over 65	9,464
Family households	28,610
Single person households	5,975
Persons per household	3.18
Persons per family	3.52

Employed persons 16 years and over by occupation

Managers & professionals	10,403
Service occupations	7,095
Sales & office occupations	9,898
Farming, fishing & forestry	4,084
Construction & maintenance	4,284
Production & transportation	6,402
Self-employed persons	4,030

Housing

Median val. single fam. home	$118,800
Median rent	$562

Note: The 2007 American Community Survey (ACS) collected one-year demographic estimates for cities and counties with populations of at least 65,000 — in California's case, 40 out of 58 counties. For those counties, ACS data is included in the profiles in order to provide the most current data. However, to allow direct comparisons, data from the 2000 Decennial Census for those counties is presented here.

Marin County

Population	
Total	247,289
Male	122,552
Female	124,737
Race & Hispanic Origin	
Race	
White	207,800
Black/African American	7,142
North American Native	1,061
Asian	11,203
Pacific Islander	388
Other Race	11,116
Two or more races	8,579
Hispanic origin, total	27,351
Mexican	14,202
Puerto Rican	539
Cuban	293
Other Hispanic	12,317
Age & Nativity	
Under 5 years	13,396
18 years and over	197,104
65 years and over	33,432
85 years and over	4,581
Median Age	41.3
Native-born	206,129
Foreign-born	41,160
Educational Attainment	
Population 25 years and over	183,694
0-8 yrs of school	3.5%
High School grad or higher	91.2%
Bachelor's degree or higher	51.3%
Graduate degree	20.5%
Income & Poverty, 1999	
Per capita income	$44,962
Median household income	$71,306
Median family income	$88,934
Persons in poverty	15,601
H'holds receiving public assistance	1,457
H'holds receiving social security	23,674
Households	
Total households	100,650
With persons under 18	29,130
With persons over 65	23,614
Family households	60,679
Single person households	30,041
Persons per household	2.34
Persons per family	2.90
Employed persons 16 years and over by occupation	
Managers & professionals	67,674
Service occupations	15,446
Sales & office occupations	31,867
Farming, fishing & forestry	374
Construction & maintenance	7,706
Production & transportation	5,788
Self-employed persons	22,420
Housing	
Median val. single fam. home	$514,600
Median rent	$1,162

Mendocino County

Population	
Total	86,265
Male	42,900
Female	43,365
Race & Hispanic Origin	
Race	
White	69,671
Black/African American	536
North American Native	4,103
Asian	1,038
Pacific Islander	126
Other Race	7,427
Two or more races	3,364
Hispanic origin, total	14,213
Mexican	12,233
Puerto Rican	126
Cuban	68
Other Hispanic	1,786
Age & Nativity	
Under 5 years	5,138
18 years and over	64,226
65 years and over	11,709
85 years and over	1,483
Median Age	38.9
Native-born	77,432
Foreign-born	8,833
Educational Attainment	
Population 25 years and over	56,886
0-8 yrs of school	6.7%
High School grad or higher	80.8%
Bachelor's degree or higher	20.2%
Graduate degree	8.0%
Income & Poverty, 1999	
Per capita income	$19,443
Median household income	$35,996
Median family income	$42,168
Persons in poverty	13,505
H'holds receiving public assistance	1,982
H'holds receiving social security	9,580
Households	
Total households	33,266
With persons under 18	11,658
With persons over 65	8,445
Family households	21,864
Single person households	8,983
Persons per household	2.53
Persons per family	3.04
Employed persons 16 years and over by occupation	
Managers & professionals	11,430
Service occupations	7,512
Sales & office occupations	8,876
Farming, fishing & forestry	1,550
Construction & maintenance	4,221
Production & transportation	4,986
Self-employed persons	5,772
Housing	
Median val. single fam. home	$170,200
Median rent	$600

Merced County

Population	
Total	210,554
Male	104,931
Female	105,623
Race & Hispanic Origin	
Race	
White	118,350
Black/African American	8,064
North American Native	2,510
Asian	14,321
Pacific Islander	396
Other Race	55,013
Two or more races	11,900
Hispanic origin, total	95,466
Mexican	82,701
Puerto Rican	595
Cuban	105
Other Hispanic	12,065
Age & Nativity	
Under 5 years	18,693
18 years and over	137,870
65 years and over	20,004
85 years and over	2,099
Median Age	29.0
Native-born	158,370
Foreign-born	52,184
Educational Attainment	
Population 25 years and over	116,725
0-8 yrs of school	21.6%
High School grad or higher	63.8%
Bachelor's degree or higher	11.0%
Graduate degree	3.4%
Income & Poverty, 1999	
Per capita income	$14,257
Median household income	$35,532
Median family income	$38,009
Persons in poverty	45,059
H'holds receiving public assistance	5,799
H'holds receiving social security	15,364
Households	
Total households	63,815
With persons under 18	31,919
With persons over 65	14,393
Family households	49,760
Single person households	11,318
Persons per household	3.25
Persons per family	3.69
Employed persons 16 years and over by occupation	
Managers & professionals	19,285
Service occupations	11,876
Sales & office occupations	16,560
Farming, fishing & forestry	6,529
Construction & maintenance	7,946
Production & transportation	13,125
Self-employed persons	5,778
Housing	
Median val. single fam. home	$111,100
Median rent	$518

Note: The 2007 American Community Survey (ACS) collected one-year demographic estimates for cities and counties with populations of at least 65,000 — in California's case, 40 out of 58 counties. For those counties, ACS data is included in the profiles in order to provide the most current data. However, to allow direct comparisons, data from the 2000 Decennial Census for those counties is presented here.

Monterey County

Population	
Total	401,762
Male	207,941
Female	193,821
Race & Hispanic Origin	
Race	
White	224,682
Black/African American	15,050
North American Native	4,202
Asian	24,245
Pacific Islander	1,789
Other Race	111,782
Two or more races	20,012
Hispanic origin, total	187,969
Mexican	162,318
Puerto Rican	1,698
Cuban	299
Other Hispanic	23,654
Age & Nativity	
Under 5 years	31,248
18 years and over	287,712
65 years and over	40,299
85 years and over	4,699
Median Age	31.7
Native-born	285,203
Foreign-born	116,559
Educational Attainment	
Population 25 years and over	244,128
0-8 yrs of school	18.9%
High School grad or higher	68.4%
Bachelor's degree or higher	22.5%
Graduate degree	8.7%
Income & Poverty, 1999	
Per capita income	$20,165
Median household income	$48,305
Median family income	$51,169
Persons in poverty	51,692
H'holds receiving public assistance	4,793
H'holds receiving social security	29,772
Households	
Total households	121,236
With persons under 18	52,697
With persons over 65	28,994
Family households	87,931
Single person households	25,748
Persons per household	3.14
Persons per family	3.65
Employed persons 16 years and over by occupation	
Managers & professionals	47,818
Service occupations	27,601
Sales & office occupations	38,069
Farming, fishing & forestry	18,333
Construction & maintenance	13,947
Production & transportation	18,219
Self-employed persons	14,747
Housing	
Median val. single fam. home	$265,800
Median rent	$776

Napa County

Population	
Total	124,279
Male	62,016
Female	62,263
Race & Hispanic Origin	
Race	
White	99,396
Black/African American	1,645
North American Native	1,045
Asian	3,694
Pacific Islander	289
Other Race	13,604
Two or more races	4,606
Hispanic origin, total	29,416
Mexican	25,226
Puerto Rican	324
Cuban	110
Other Hispanic	3,756
Age & Nativity	
Under 5 years	7,563
18 years and over	94,281
65 years and over	19,086
85 years and over	2,926
Median Age	38.3
Native-born	101,792
Foreign-born	22,487
Educational Attainment	
Population 25 years and over	83,938
0-8 yrs of school	9.6%
High School grad or higher	80.4%
Bachelor's degree or higher	26.4%
Graduate degree	9.4%
Income & Poverty, 1999	
Per capita income	$26,395
Median household income	$51,738
Median family income	$61,410
Persons in poverty	9,913
H'holds receiving public assistance	1,149
H'holds receiving social security	13,020
Households	
Total households	45,402
With persons under 18	15,606
With persons over 65	12,652
Family households	30,694
Single person households	11,733
Persons per household	2.62
Persons per family	3.16
Employed persons 16 years and over by occupation	
Managers & professionals	20,258
Service occupations	10,540
Sales & office occupations	13,785
Farming, fishing & forestry	1,775
Construction & maintenance	5,467
Production & transportation	6,676
Self-employed persons	6,302
Housing	
Median val. single fam. home	$251,300
Median rent	$818

Nevada County

Population	
Total	92,033
Male	45,617
Female	46,416
Race & Hispanic Origin	
Race	
White	85,948
Black/African American	259
North American Native	814
Asian	715
Pacific Islander	81
Other Race	1,782
Two or more races	2,434
Hispanic origin, total	5,201
Mexican	3,753
Puerto Rican	163
Cuban	73
Other Hispanic	1,212
Age & Nativity	
Under 5 years	4,306
18 years and over	70,756
65 years and over	16,049
85 years and over	1,756
Median Age	43.1
Native-born	87,968
Foreign-born	4,065
Educational Attainment	
Population 25 years and over	65,148
0-8 yrs of school	1.8%
High School grad or higher	90.3%
Bachelor's degree or higher	26.1%
Graduate degree	8.8%
Income & Poverty, 1999	
Per capita income	$24,007
Median household income	$45,864
Median family income	$52,697
Persons in poverty	7,332
H'holds receiving public assistance	909
H'holds receiving social security	12,158
Households	
Total households	36,894
With persons under 18	11,538
With persons over 65	10,986
Family households	25,930
Single person households	8,429
Persons per household	2.47
Persons per family	2.88
Employed persons 16 years and over by occupation	
Managers & professionals	14,240
Service occupations	6,811
Sales & office occupations	11,148
Farming, fishing & forestry	284
Construction & maintenance	5,112
Production & transportation	3,958
Self-employed persons	7,046
Housing	
Median val. single fam. home	$205,700
Median rent	$746

Note: The 2007 American Community Survey (ACS) collected one-year demographic estimates for cities and counties with populations of at least 65,000 — in California's case, 40 out of 58 counties. For those counties, ACS data is included in the profiles in order to provide the most current data. However, to allow direct comparisons, data from the 2000 Decennial Census for those counties is presented here.

	Orange County	Placer County	Riverside County
Population			
Total	2,846,289	248,399	1,545,387
Male	1,416,045	121,892	769,384
Female	1,430,244	126,507	776,003
Race & Hispanic Origin			
Race			
White	1,844,652	220,053	1,013,478
Black/African American	47,649	2,031	96,421
North American Native	19,906	2,199	18,168
Asian	386,785	7,317	56,954
Pacific Islander	8,938	386	3,902
Other Race	421,208	8,432	288,868
Two or more races	117,151	7,981	67,596
Hispanic origin, total	875,579	24,019	559,575
Mexican	712,496	17,699	463,465
Puerto Rican	8,877	702	7,388
Cuban	6,703	238	3,228
Other Hispanic	147,503	5,380	85,494
Age & Nativity			
Under 5 years	216,014	15,924	121,629
18 years and over	2,077,870	182,641	1,076,696
65 years and over	280,763	32,560	195,964
85 years and over	34,094	3,690	21,084
Median Age	33.3	38.0	33.1
Native-born	1,996,390	230,837	1,251,675
Foreign-born	849,899	17,562	293,712
Educational Attainment			
Population 25 years and over	1,813,456	165,894	936,024
0-8 yrs of school	10.5%	3.1%	10.6%
High School grad or higher	79.5%	90.5%	75.0%
Bachelor's degree or higher	30.8%	30.3%	16.6%
Graduate degree	10.4%	9.5%	5.9%
Income & Poverty, 1999			
Per capita income	$25,826	$27,963	$18,689
Median household income	$58,820	$57,535	$42,887
Median family income	$64,611	$65,858	$48,409
Persons in poverty	289,475	14,272	214,084
H'holds receiving public assistance	25,319	2,211	21,877
H'holds receiving social security	189,440	24,336	146,251
Households			
Total households	935,287	93,382	506,218
With persons under 18	378,343	35,225	218,742
With persons over 65	199,741	22,133	137,243
Family households	667,917	67,742	372,386
Single person households	197,650	19,860	104,557
Persons per household	3.00	2.63	2.98
Persons per family	3.48	3.06	3.47
Employed persons 16 years and over by occupation			
Managers & professionals	509,542	47,106	167,739
Service occupations	177,001	15,664	105,446
Sales & office occupations	383,888	33,174	163,095
Farming, fishing & forestry	4,067	609	9,499
Construction & maintenance	97,456	11,795	70,974
Production & transportation	166,884	10,299	86,103
Self-employed persons	109,071	12,079	50,874
Housing			
Median val. single fam. home	$270,000	$213,900	$146,500
Median rent	$923	$780	$660

Note: The 2007 American Community Survey (ACS) collected one-year demographic estimates for cities and counties with populations of at least 65,000 — in California's case, 40 out of 58 counties. For those counties, ACS data is included in the profiles in order to provide the most current data. However, to allow direct comparisons, data from the 2000 Decennial Census for those counties is presented here.

Sacramento County

Population	
Total	1,223,499
Male	598,815
Female	624,684
Race & Hispanic Origin	
Race	
White	783,240
Black/African American	121,804
North American Native	13,359
Asian	134,899
Pacific Islander	7,264
Other Race	91,541
Two or more races	71,392
Hispanic origin, total	195,890
Mexican	150,909
Puerto Rican	5,746
Cuban	1,238
Other Hispanic	37,997
Age & Nativity	
Under 5 years	88,922
18 years and over	885,897
65 years and over	135,875
85 years and over	15,517
Median Age	33.8
Native-born	1,026,304
Foreign-born	197,195
Educational Attainment	
Population 25 years and over	772,488
0-8 yrs of school	6.7%
High School grad or higher	83.3%
Bachelor's degree or higher	24.8%
Graduate degree	8.1%
Income & Poverty, 1999	
Per capita income	$21,142
Median household income	$43,816
Median family income	$50,717
Persons in poverty	169,784
H'holds receiving public assistance	29,896
H'holds receiving social security	101,678
Households	
Total households	453,602
With persons under 18	169,353
With persons over 65	96,579
Family households	297,596
Single person households	120,985
Persons per household	2.64
Persons per family	3.24
Employed persons 16 years and over by occupation	
Managers & professionals	198,004
Service occupations	79,285
Sales & office occupations	163,268
Farming, fishing & forestry	2,205
Construction & maintenance	47,691
Production & transportation	55,472
Self-employed persons	37,643
Housing	
Median val. single fam. home	$144,200
Median rent	$659

San Bernardino County

Population	
Total	1,709,434
Male	853,024
Female	856,410
Race & Hispanic Origin	
Race	
White	1,006,960
Black/African American	155,348
North American Native	19,915
Asian	80,217
Pacific Islander	5,110
Other Race	355,843
Two or more races	86,041
Hispanic origin, total	669,387
Mexican	532,186
Puerto Rican	9,927
Cuban	4,201
Other Hispanic	123,073
Age & Nativity	
Under 5 years	143,076
18 years and over	1,157,387
65 years and over	146,459
85 years and over	15,250
Median Age	30.3
Native-born	1,390,787
Foreign-born	318,647
Educational Attainment	
Population 25 years and over	983,273
0-8 yrs of school	10.4%
High School grad or higher	74.2%
Bachelor's degree or higher	15.9%
Graduate degree	5.5%
Income & Poverty, 1999	
Per capita income	$16,856
Median household income	$42,066
Median family income	$46,574
Persons in poverty	263,412
H'holds receiving public assistance	34,211
H'holds receiving social security	116,733
Households	
Total households	528,594
With persons under 18	258,158
With persons over 65	106,110
Family households	404,327
Single person households	97,482
Persons per household	3.15
Persons per family	3.58
Employed persons 16 years and over by occupation	
Managers & professionals	186,096
Service occupations	104,728
Sales & office occupations	180,447
Farming, fishing & forestry	3,040
Construction & maintenance	74,519
Production & transportation	112,442
Self-employed persons	46,468
Housing	
Median val. single fam. home	$131,500
Median rent	$648

San Diego County

Population	
Total	2,813,833
Male	1,415,097
Female	1,398,736
Race & Hispanic Origin	
Race	
White	1,871,839
Black/African American	161,480
North American Native	24,337
Asian	249,802
Pacific Islander	13,561
Other Race	360,847
Two or more races	131,967
Hispanic origin, total	750,965
Mexican	628,460
Puerto Rican	14,937
Cuban	3,883
Other Hispanic	103,685
Age & Nativity	
Under 5 years	198,621
18 years and over	2,090,172
65 years and over	313,750
85 years and over	36,407
Median Age	33.2
Native-born	2,207,579
Foreign-born	606,254
Educational Attainment	
Population 25 years and over	1,773,327
0-8 yrs of school	7.9%
High School grad or higher	82.6%
Bachelor's degree or higher	29.5%
Graduate degree	10.9%
Income & Poverty, 1999	
Per capita income	$22,926
Median household income	$47,067
Median family income	$53,438
Persons in poverty	338,399
H'holds receiving public assistance	35,533
H'holds receiving social security	224,466
Households	
Total households	994,677
With persons under 18	369,833
With persons over 65	222,153
Family households	663,170
Single person households	240,756
Persons per household	2.73
Persons per family	3.29
Employed persons 16 years and over by occupation	
Managers & professionals	467,386
Service occupations	199,384
Sales & office occupations	337,603
Farming, fishing & forestry	6,502
Construction & maintenance	107,450
Production & transportation	122,933
Self-employed persons	107,894
Housing	
Median val. single fam. home	$227,200
Median rent	$761

Note: The 2007 American Community Survey (ACS) collected one-year demographic estimates for cities and counties with populations of at least 65,000 — in California's case, 40 out of 58 counties. For those counties, ACS data is included in the profiles in order to provide the most current data. However, to allow direct comparisons, data from the 2000 Decennial Census for those counties is presented here.

San Francisco County

Population

Total 776,733
Male 394,828
Female 381,905

Race & Hispanic Origin

Race
White 385,728
Black/African American 60,515
North American Native 3,458
Asian 239,565
Pacific Islander 3,844
Other Race 50,368
Two or more races 33,255
Hispanic origin, total 109,504
Mexican 48,935
Puerto Rican 3,758
Cuban 1,632
Other Hispanic 55,179

Age & Nativity

Under 5 years 31,633
18 years and over 663,931
65 years and over 106,111
85 years and over 14,227
Median Age 36.5
Native-born 491,192
Foreign-born 285,541

Educational Attainment

Population 25 years and over 595,805
0-8 yrs of school 10.5%
High School grad or higher 81.2%
Bachelor's degree or higher 45.0%
Graduate degree 16.4%

Income & Poverty, 1999

Per capita income $34,556
Median household income $55,221
Median family income $63,545
Persons in poverty 86,585
H'holds receiving public assistance 12,942
H'holds receiving social security 69,250

Households

Total households 329,700
With persons under 18 63,867
With persons over 65 78,716
Family households 145,186
Single person households 127,376
Persons per household 2.30
Persons per family 3.22

Employed persons 16 years and over by occupation

Managers & professionals 206,804
Service occupations 61,364
Sales & office occupations 109,316
Farming, fishing & forestry 462
Construction & maintenance 17,990
Production & transportation 31,887
Self-employed persons 37,140

Housing

Median val. single fam. home $396,400
Median rent $928

San Joaquin County

Population

Total 563,598
Male 281,627
Female 281,971

Race & Hispanic Origin

Race
White 327,607
Black/African American 37,689
North American Native 6,377
Asian 64,283
Pacific Islander 1,955
Other Race 91,613
Two or more races 34,074
Hispanic origin, total 172,073
Mexican 144,220
Puerto Rican 2,770
Cuban 385
Other Hispanic 24,698

Age & Nativity

Under 5 years 44,960
18 years and over 389,029
65 years and over 59,799
85 years and over 7,507
Median Age 31.9
Native-born 453,786
Foreign-born 109,812

Educational Attainment

Population 25 years and over 333,572
0-8 yrs of school 13.3%
High School grad or higher 71.2%
Bachelor's degree or higher 14.5%
Graduate degree 4.4%

Income & Poverty, 1999

Per capita income $17,365
Median household income $41,282
Median family income $46,919
Persons in poverty 97,105
H'holds receiving public assistance 13,073
H'holds receiving social security 44,736

Households

Total households 181,629
With persons under 18 82,308
With persons over 65 42,161
Family households 134,708
Single person households 37,650
Persons per household 3.00
Persons per family 3.48

Employed persons 16 years and over by occupation

Managers & professionals 59,397
Service occupations 31,921
Sales & office occupations 59,341
Farming, fishing & forestry 9,044
Construction & maintenance 22,439
Production & transportation 36,858
Self-employed persons 14,254

Housing

Median val. single fam. home $142,400
Median rent $617

San Luis Obispo County

Population

Total 246,681
Male 126,704
Female 119,977

Race & Hispanic Origin

Race
White 208,699
Black/African American 5,002
North American Native 2,335
Asian 6,568
Pacific Islander 286
Other Race 15,312
Two or more races 8,479
Hispanic origin, total 40,196
Mexican 32,390
Puerto Rican 595
Cuban 220
Other Hispanic 6,991

Age & Nativity

Under 5 years 12,358
18 years and over 193,268
65 years and over 35,685
85 years and over 4,176
Median Age 37.3
Native-born 224,665
Foreign-born 22,016

Educational Attainment

Population 25 years and over 159,196
0-8 yrs of school 4.9%
High School grad or higher 85.6%
Bachelor's degree or higher 26.7%
Graduate degree 9.3%

Income & Poverty, 1999

Per capita income $21,864
Median household income $42,428
Median family income $52,447
Persons in poverty 29,775
H'holds receiving public assistance 2,157
H'holds receiving social security 27,091

Households

Total households 92,739
With persons under 18 28,305
With persons over 65 24,828
Family households 58,654
Single person households 24,081
Persons per household 2.49
Persons per family 3.01

Employed persons 16 years and over by occupation

Managers & professionals 37,581
Service occupations 20,573
Sales & office occupations 27,793
Farming, fishing & forestry 2,281
Construction & maintenance 10,732
Production & transportation 10,709
Self-employed persons 13,679

Housing

Median val. single fam. home $230,000
Median rent $719

Note: The 2007 American Community Survey (ACS) collected one-year demographic estimates for cities and counties with populations of at least 65,000 — in California's case, 40 out of 58 counties. For those counties, ACS data is included in the profiles in order to provide the most current data. However, to allow direct comparisons, data from the 2000 Decennial Census for those counties is presented here.

San Mateo County

Population	
Total	707,161
Male	349,651
Female	357,510
Race & Hispanic Origin	
Race	
White	420,683
Black/African American	24,840
North American Native	3,140
Asian	141,684
Pacific Islander	9,403
Other Race	71,910
Two or more races	35,501
Hispanic origin, total	154,708
Mexican	92,939
Puerto Rican	3,236
Cuban	953
Other Hispanic	57,580
Age & Nativity	
Under 5 years	45,374
18 years and over	545,061
65 years and over	88,085
85 years and over	11,343
Median Age	36.8
Native-born	479,043
Foreign-born	228,118
Educational Attainment	
Population 25 years and over	490,285
0-8 yrs of school	7.2%
High School grad or higher	85.3%
Bachelor's degree or higher	39.0%
Graduate degree	14.6%
Income & Poverty, 1999	
Per capita income	$36,045
Median household income	$70,819
Median family income	$80,737
Persons in poverty	40,692
H'holds receiving public assistance	4,041
H'holds receiving social security	59,575
Households	
Total households	254,103
With persons under 18	87,234
With persons over 65	62,327
Family households	171,249
Single person households	62,626
Persons per household	2.74
Persons per family	3.29
Employed persons 16 years and over by occupation	
Managers & professionals	154,419
Service occupations	48,869
Sales & office occupations	98,865
Farming, fishing & forestry	1,157
Construction & maintenance	27,227
Production & transportation	31,103
Self-employed persons	29,864
Housing	
Median val. single fam. home	$469,200
Median rent	$1,144

Santa Barbara County

Population	
Total	399,347
Male	199,763
Female	199,584
Race & Hispanic Origin	
Race	
White	290,418
Black/African American	9,195
North American Native	4,784
Asian	16,344
Pacific Islander	700
Other Race	60,683
Two or more races	17,223
Hispanic origin, total	136,668
Mexican	117,326
Puerto Rican	1,070
Cuban	366
Other Hispanic	17,906
Age & Nativity	
Under 5 years	26,008
18 years and over	299,845
65 years and over	50,765
85 years and over	6,896
Median Age	33.4
Native-born	314,521
Foreign-born	84,826
Educational Attainment	
Population 25 years and over	246,729
0-8 yrs of school	10.9%
High School grad or higher	79.2%
Bachelor's degree or higher	29.4%
Graduate degree	11.4%
Income & Poverty, 1999	
Per capita income	$23,059
Median household income	$46,677
Median family income	$54,042
Persons in poverty	55,086
H'holds receiving public assistance	4,178
H'holds receiving social security	36,586
Households	
Total households	136,622
With persons under 18	48,691
With persons over 65	35,085
Family households	89,555
Single person households	33,210
Persons per household	2.80
Persons per family	3.33
Employed persons 16 years and over by occupation	
Managers & professionals	63,893
Service occupations	30,865
Sales & office occupations	45,775
Farming, fishing & forestry	8,818
Construction & maintenance	13,940
Production & transportation	17,425
Self-employed persons	19,361
Housing	
Median val. single fam. home	$293,000
Median rent	$830

Santa Clara County

Population	
Total	1,682,585
Male	852,974
Female	829,611
Race & Hispanic Origin	
Race	
White	905,660
Black/African American	47,182
North American Native	11,350
Asian	430,095
Pacific Islander	5,773
Other Race	204,088
Two or more races	78,437
Hispanic origin, total	403,401
Mexican	323,489
Puerto Rican	6,396
Cuban	1,852
Other Hispanic	71,664
Age & Nativity	
Under 5 years	119,418
18 years and over	1,266,183
65 years and over	160,527
85 years and over	17,987
Median Age	34.0
Native-born	1,109,455
Foreign-born	573,130
Educational Attainment	
Population 25 years and over	1,113,058
0-8 yrs of school	8.0%
High School grad or higher	83.4%
Bachelor's degree or higher	40.5%
Graduate degree	16.4%
Income & Poverty, 1999	
Per capita income	$32,795
Median household income	$74,335
Median family income	$81,717
Persons in poverty	124,470
H'holds receiving public assistance	15,306
H'holds receiving social security	102,897
Households	
Total households	565,863
With persons under 18	218,176
With persons over 65	113,316
Family households	395,561
Single person households	121,109
Persons per household	2.92
Persons per family	3.41
Employed persons 16 years and over by occupation	
Managers & professionals	409,371
Service occupations	88,797
Sales & office occupations	191,719
Farming, fishing & forestry	3,494
Construction & maintenance	55,616
Production & transportation	94,915
Self-employed persons	52,302
Housing	
Median val. single fam. home	$446,400
Median rent	$1,185

Note: The 2007 American Community Survey (ACS) collected one-year demographic estimates for cities and counties with populations of at least 65,000 — in California's case, 40 out of 58 counties. For those counties, ACS data is included in the profiles in order to provide the most current data. However, to allow direct comparisons, data from the 2000 Decennial Census for those counties is presented here.

Santa Cruz County

Population

Total 255,602
Male 127,579
Female 128,023

Race & Hispanic Origin

Race
White 191,931
Black/African American 2,477
North American Native 2,461
Asian 8,789
Pacific Islander 382
Other Race 38,391
Two or more races 11,171
Hispanic origin, total 68,486
Mexican 58,290
Puerto Rican 572
Cuban 232
Other Hispanic 9,392

Age & Nativity

Under 5 years 15,544
18 years and over 194,861
65 years and over 25,487
85 years and over 3,845
Median Age 35.0
Native-born 209,100
Foreign-born 46,502

Educational Attainment

Population 25 years and over 164,999
0-8 yrs of school 9.7%
High School grad or higher 83.2%
Bachelor's degree or higher 34.2%
Graduate degree 12.5%

Income & Poverty, 1999

Per capita income $26,396
Median household income $53,998
Median family income $61,941
Persons in poverty 29,383
H'holds receiving public assistance . . . 2,495
H'holds receiving social security 19,469

Households

Total households 91,139
With persons under 18 31,665
With persons over 65 18,173
Family households 57,132
Single person households 22,905
Persons per household 2.71
Persons per family 3.25

Employed persons 16 years and over by occupation

Managers & professionals 52,088
Service occupations 19,187
Sales & office occupations 30,256
Farming, fishing & forestry 4,802
Construction & maintenance 11,489
Production & transportation 11,558
Self-employed persons 14,990

Housing

Median val. single fam. home $377,500
Median rent $924

Shasta County

Population

Total 163,256
Male 79,572
Female 83,684

Race & Hispanic Origin

Race
White 145,826
Black/African American 1,225
North American Native 4,528
Asian 3,048
Pacific Islander 178
Other Race 2,790
Two or more races 5,661
Hispanic origin, total 8,998
Mexican 6,582
Puerto Rican 277
Cuban 64
Other Hispanic 2,075

Age & Nativity

Under 5 years 9,643
18 years and over 120,582
65 years and over 24,861
85 years and over 2,875
Median Age 38.9
Native-born 156,768
Foreign-born 6,488

Educational Attainment

Population 25 years and over 107,272
0-8 yrs of school 4.2%
High School grad or higher 83.3%
Bachelor's degree or higher 16.6%
Graduate degree 5.3%

Income & Poverty, 1999

Per capita income $17,738
Median household income $34,335
Median family income $40,491
Persons in poverty 24,556
H'holds receiving public assistance . . . 4,404
H'holds receiving social security 20,375

Households

Total households 63,426
With persons under 18 22,220
With persons over 65 17,345
Family households 44,002
Single person households 15,650
Persons per household 2.52
Persons per family 2.98

Employed persons 16 years and over by occupation

Managers & professionals 20,039
Service occupations 12,893
Sales & office occupations 17,766
Farming, fishing & forestry 579
Construction & maintenance 6,450
Production & transportation 8,101
Self-employed persons 6,739

Housing

Median val. single fam. home $120,800
Median rent $563

Solano County

Population

Total 394,542
Male 198,694
Female 195,848

Race & Hispanic Origin

Race
White 222,387
Black/African American 58,827
North American Native 3,110
Asian 50,299
Pacific Islander 3,078
Other Race 31,612
Two or more races 25,229
Hispanic origin, total 69,598
Mexican 49,095
Puerto Rican 2,801
Cuban 447
Other Hispanic 17,255

Age & Nativity

Under 5 years 28,784
18 years and over 282,690
65 years and over 37,426
85 years and over 3,915
Median Age 33.9
Native-born 328,046
Foreign-born 66,496

Educational Attainment

Population 25 years and over 246,488
0-8 yrs of school 6.2%
High School grad or higher 83.8%
Bachelor's degree or higher 21.4%
Graduate degree 6.3%

Income & Poverty, 1999

Per capita income $21,731
Median household income $54,099
Median family income $60,597
Persons in poverty 31,344
H'holds receiving public assistance . . . 5,083
H'holds receiving social security 27,252

Households

Total households 130,403
With persons under 18 58,196
With persons over 65 26,293
Family households 97,375
Single person households 25,525
Persons per household 2.90
Persons per family 3.33

Employed persons 16 years and over by occupation

Managers & professionals 53,326
Service occupations 28,231
Sales & office occupations 48,318
Farming, fishing & forestry 1,099
Construction & maintenance 18,896
Production & transportation 22,485
Self-employed persons 10,366

Housing

Median val. single fam. home $178,300
Median rent $797

Note: The 2007 American Community Survey (ACS) collected one-year demographic estimates for cities and counties with populations of at least 65,000 — in California's case, 40 out of 58 counties. For those counties, ACS data is included in the profiles in order to provide the most current data. However, to allow direct comparisons, data from the 2000 Decennial Census for those counties is presented here.

Sonoma County

Sonoma County	
Population	
Total	458,614
Male	225,804
Female	232,810
Race & Hispanic Origin	
Race	
White	374,209
Black/African American	6,522
North American Native	5,389
Asian	14,098
Pacific Islander	934
Other Race	38,717
Two or more races	18,745
Hispanic origin, total	79,511
Mexican	63,879
Puerto Rican	1,391
Cuban	359
Other Hispanic	13,882
Age & Nativity	
Under 5 years	27,597
18 years and over	346,461
65 years and over	57,977
85 years and over	8,254
Median Age	37.5
Native-born	392,888
Foreign-born	65,726
Educational Attainment	
Population 25 years and over	306,564
0-8 yrs of school	6.7%
High School grad or higher	84.9%
Bachelor's degree or higher	28.5%
Graduate degree	9.7%
Income & Poverty, 1999	
Per capita income	$25,724
Median household income	$53,076
Median family income	$61,921
Persons in poverty	36,349
H'holds receiving public assistance	3,990
H'holds receiving social security	44,073
Households	
Total households	172,403
With persons under 18	59,796
With persons over 65	41,314
Family households	112,397
Single person households	44,340
Persons per household	2.60
Persons per family	3.12
Employed persons 16 years and over by occupation	
Managers & professionals	80,333
Service occupations	34,646
Sales & office occupations	60,935
Farming, fishing & forestry	3,744
Construction & maintenance	23,442
Production & transportation	26,127
Self-employed persons	26,882
Housing	
Median val. single fam. home	$273,200
Median rent	$864

Stanislaus County

Stanislaus County	
Population	
Total	446,997
Male	219,912
Female	227,085
Race & Hispanic Origin	
Race	
White	309,901
Black/African American	11,521
North American Native	5,676
Asian	18,848
Pacific Islander	1,529
Other Race	75,187
Two or more races	24,335
Hispanic origin, total	141,871
Mexican	119,252
Puerto Rican	1,947
Cuban	290
Other Hispanic	20,382
Age & Nativity	
Under 5 years	35,582
18 years and over	307,775
65 years and over	46,697
85 years and over	5,819
Median Age	31.7
Native-born	365,382
Foreign-born	81,615
Educational Attainment	
Population 25 years and over	264,578
0-8 yrs of school	13.7%
High School grad or higher	70.4%
Bachelor's degree or higher	14.1%
Graduate degree	4.4%
Income & Poverty, 1999	
Per capita income	$16,913
Median household income	$40,101
Median family income	$44,703
Persons in poverty	70,406
H'holds receiving public assistance	9,151
H'holds receiving social security	36,506
Households	
Total households	145,146
With persons under 18	66,426
With persons over 65	32,662
Family households	109,517
Single person households	28,211
Persons per household	3.03
Persons per family	3.47
Employed persons 16 years and over by occupation	
Managers & professionals	46,182
Service occupations	26,856
Sales & office occupations	44,706
Farming, fishing & forestry	6,226
Construction & maintenance	19,877
Production & transportation	30,481
Self-employed persons	14,197
Housing	
Median val. single fam. home	$125,300
Median rent	$611

Sutter County

Sutter County	
Population	
Total	78,930
Male	39,061
Female	39,869
Race & Hispanic Origin	
Race	
White	53,291
Black/African American	1,509
North American Native	1,225
Asian	8,884
Pacific Islander	161
Other Race	10,232
Two or more races	3,628
Hispanic origin, total	17,529
Mexican	15,138
Puerto Rican	193
Cuban	33
Other Hispanic	2,165
Age & Nativity	
Under 5 years	5,728
18 years and over	56,061
65 years and over	9,755
85 years and over	1,170
Median Age	34.1
Native-born	63,702
Foreign-born	15,228
Educational Attainment	
Population 25 years and over	49,071
0-8 yrs of school	12.7%
High School grad or higher	73.0%
Bachelor's degree or higher	15.3%
Graduate degree	4.4%
Income & Poverty, 1999	
Per capita income	$17,428
Median household income	$38,375
Median family income	$44,330
Persons in poverty	12,031
H'holds receiving public assistance	1,383
H'holds receiving social security	7,204
Households	
Total households	27,033
With persons under 18	11,334
With persons over 65	6,677
Family households	19,946
Single person households	5,732
Persons per household	2.87
Persons per family	3.35
Employed persons 16 years and over by occupation	
Managers & professionals	8,825
Service occupations	4,585
Sales & office occupations	7,575
Farming, fishing & forestry	1,791
Construction & maintenance	3,412
Production & transportation	4,792
Self-employed persons	2,846
Housing	
Median val. single fam. home	$120,700
Median rent	$506

Note: The 2007 American Community Survey (ACS) collected one-year demographic estimates for cities and counties with populations of at least 65,000 — in California's case, 40 out of 58 counties. For those counties, ACS data is included in the profiles in order to provide the most current data. However, to allow direct comparisons, data from the 2000 Decennial Census for those counties is presented here.

Tulare County

Population

Total	368,021
Male	184,010
Female	184,011

Race & Hispanic Origin

Race	
White	213,751
Black/African American	5,852
North American Native	5,737
Asian	12,018
Pacific Islander	408
Other Race	113,317
Two or more races	16,938
Hispanic origin, total	186,846
Mexican	163,401
Puerto Rican	902
Cuban	144
Other Hispanic	22,399

Age & Nativity

Under 5 years	32,826
18 years and over	243,769
65 years and over	35,917
85 years and over	4,337
Median Age	29.2
Native-born	284,897
Foreign-born	83,124

Educational Attainment

Population 25 years and over	204,888
0-8 yrs of school	23.0%
High School grad or higher	61.7%
Bachelor's degree or higher	11.5%
Graduate degree	3.7%

Income & Poverty, 1999

Per capita income	$14,006
Median household income	$33,983
Median family income	$36,297
Persons in poverty	86,572
H'holds receiving public assistance	9,525
H'holds receiving social security	27,866

Households

Total households	110,385
With persons under 18	55,169
With persons over 65	25,222
Family households	87,061
Single person households	18,913
Persons per household	3.28
Persons per family	3.67

Employed persons 16 years and over by occupation

Managers & professionals	33,892
Service occupations	21,708
Sales & office occupations	30,447
Farming, fishing & forestry	17,643
Construction & maintenance	11,296
Production & transportation	19,108
Self-employed persons	11,174

Housing

Median val. single fam. home	$97,800
Median rent	$516

Ventura County

Population

Total	753,197
Male	375,988
Female	377,209

Race & Hispanic Origin

Race	
White	526,721
Black/African American	14,664
North American Native	7,106
Asian	40,284
Pacific Islander	1,671
Other Race	133,178
Two or more races	29,573
Hispanic origin, total	251,734
Mexican	211,925
Puerto Rican	2,286
Cuban	1,043
Other Hispanic	36,480

Age & Nativity

Under 5 years	56,231
18 years and over	538,953
65 years and over	76,804
85 years and over	9,289
Median Age	34.2
Native-born	597,284
Foreign-born	155,913

Educational Attainment

Population 25 years and over	471,756
0-8 yrs of school	10.4%
High School grad or higher	80.1%
Bachelor's degree or higher	26.9%
Graduate degree	9.5%

Income & Poverty, 1999

Per capita income	$24,600
Median household income	$59,666
Median family income	$65,285
Persons in poverty	68,540
H'holds receiving public assistance	7,046
H'holds receiving social security	56,552

Households

Total households	243,234
With persons under 18	106,140
With persons over 65	54,516
Family households	182,959
Single person households	45,931
Persons per household	3.04
Persons per family	3.46

Employed persons 16 years and over by occupation

Managers & professionals	127,157
Service occupations	46,762
Sales & office occupations	95,006
Farming, fishing & forestry	10,869
Construction & maintenance	28,589
Production & transportation	39,955
Self-employed persons	31,536

Housing

Median val. single fam. home	$248,700
Median rent	$892

Yolo County

Population

Total	168,660
Male	82,451
Female	86,209

Race & Hispanic Origin

Race	
White	114,129
Black/African American	3,425
North American Native	1,953
Asian	16,614
Pacific Islander	507
Other Race	23,214
Two or more races	8,818
Hispanic origin, total	43,707
Mexican	36,699
Puerto Rican	452
Cuban	136
Other Hispanic	6,420

Age & Nativity

Under 5 years	10,964
18 years and over	126,181
65 years and over	15,782
85 years and over	1,973
Median Age	29.5
Native-born	134,489
Foreign-born	34,171

Educational Attainment

Population 25 years and over	95,423
0-8 yrs of school	10.0%
High School grad or higher	79.8%
Bachelor's degree or higher	34.1%
Graduate degree	16.0%

Income & Poverty, 1999

Per capita income	$19,365
Median household income	$40,769
Median family income	$51,623
Persons in poverty	29,787
H'holds receiving public assistance	2,617
H'holds receiving social security	11,760

Households

Total households	59,375
With persons under 18	21,673
With persons over 65	11,202
Family households	37,468
Single person households	13,829
Persons per household	2.71
Persons per family	3.25

Employed persons 16 years and over by occupation

Managers & professionals	31,725
Service occupations	10,860
Sales & office occupations	18,226
Farming, fishing & forestry	1,979
Construction & maintenance	5,479
Production & transportation	8,379
Self-employed persons	5,251

Housing

Median val. single fam. home	$169,800
Median rent	$687

Note: The 2007 American Community Survey (ACS) collected one-year demographic estimates for cities and counties with populations of at least 65,000 — in California's case, 40 out of 58 counties. For those counties, ACS data is included in the profiles in order to provide the most current data. However, to allow direct comparisons, data from the 2000 Decennial Census for those counties is presented here.

Yuba County

Population

Total	60,219
Male	30,346
Female	29,873

Race & Hispanic Origin

Race	
White	42,537
Black/African American	1,904
North American Native	1,569
Asian	4,519
Pacific Islander	123
Other Race	5,989
Two or more races	3,578
Hispanic origin, total	10,449
Mexican	8,587
Puerto Rican	221
Cuban	43
Other Hispanic	1,598

Age & Nativity

Under 5 years	4,960
18 years and over	41,529
65 years and over	6,410
85 years and over	610
Median Age	31.4
Native-born	52,288
Foreign-born	7,931

Educational Attainment

Population 25 years and over	35,218
0-8 yrs of school	12.4%
High School grad or higher	71.8%
Bachelor's degree or higher	10.3%
Graduate degree	3.5%

Income & Poverty, 1999

Per capita income	$14,124
Median household income	$30,460
Median family income	$34,103
Persons in poverty	12,205
H'holds receiving public assistance	1,956
H'holds receiving social security	5,333

Households

Total households	20,535
With persons under 18	8,767
With persons over 65	4,705
Family households	14,801
Single person households	4,456
Persons per household	2.87
Persons per family	3.34

Employed persons 16 years and over by occupation

Managers & professionals	4,655
Service occupations	3,757
Sales & office occupations	4,994
Farming, fishing & forestry	936
Construction & maintenance	2,523
Production & transportation	3,358
Self-employed persons	1,940

Housing

Median val. single fam. home	$89,700
Median rent	$488

Note: The 2007 American Community Survey (ACS) collected one-year demographic estimates for cities and counties with populations of at least 65,000 — in California's case, 118 out of 480 municipalities. For those municipalities, ACS data is included in the profiles in order to provide the most current data. However, to allow direct comparisons, data from the 2000 Decennial Census for those municipalities is presented here.

Alameda

Population

Total	72,259
Male	34,689
Female	37,570

Race & Hispanic Origin

Race	
White	41,148
Black/African American	4,488
North American Native	484
Asian	18,894
Pacific Islander	434
Other Race	2,380
Two or more races	4,431
Hispanic origin, total	6,725
Mexican	3,858
Puerto Rican	413
Cuban	139
Other Hispanic	2,315

Age & Nativity

Under 5 years	4,057
18 years and over	56,725
65 years and over	9,605
85 years and over	1,324
Median Age	38.3
Native-born	53,429
Foreign-born	18,830

Educational Attainment

Population 25 years and over	51,952
0-8 yrs of school	4.0%
High School grad or higher	88.4%
Bachelor's degree or higher	42.2%
Graduate degree	15.0%

Income & Poverty, 1999

Per capita income	$30,982
Median household income	$56,285
Median family income	$68,625
Persons in poverty	5,887
H'holds receiving public assistance	921
H'holds receiving social security	6,417

Households

Total households	30,226
With persons under 18	9,075
With persons over 65	6,868
Family households	17,858
Single person households	9,747
Persons per household	2.35
Persons per family	3.04

Employed persons 16 years and over by occupation

Managers & professionals	17,975
Service occupations	4,345
Sales & office occupations	9,766
Farming, fishing & forestry	59
Construction & maintenance	2,114
Production & transportation	3,032
Self-employed persons	3,157

Housing

Median val. single fam. home	$345,000
Median rent	$899

Alhambra

Population

Total	85,804
Male	40,418
Female	45,386

Race & Hispanic Origin

Race	
White	25,758
Black/African American	1,437
North American Native	614
Asian	40,520
Pacific Islander	86
Other Race	13,947
Two or more races	3,442
Hispanic origin, total	30,453
Mexican	22,857
Puerto Rican	330
Cuban	427
Other Hispanic	6,839

Age & Nativity

Under 5 years	5,350
18 years and over	66,631
65 years and over	11,316
85 years and over	1,750
Median Age	35.0
Native-born	42,329
Foreign-born	43,632

Educational Attainment

Population 25 years and over	58,579
0-8 yrs of school	14.7%
High School grad or higher	73.0%
Bachelor's degree or higher	27.5%
Graduate degree	8.4%

Income & Poverty, 1999

Per capita income	$17,350
Median household income	$39,213
Median family income	$43,245
Persons in poverty	12,057
H'holds receiving public assistance	1,750
H'holds receiving social security	5,921

Households

Total households	29,111
With persons under 18	10,839
With persons over 65	7,775
Family households	20,669
Single person households	6,562
Persons per household	2.88
Persons per family	3.41

Employed persons 16 years and over by occupation

Managers & professionals	13,772
Service occupations	5,250
Sales & office occupations	11,301
Farming, fishing & forestry	9
Construction & maintenance	2,194
Production & transportation	4,895
Self-employed persons	2,347

Housing

Median val. single fam. home	$210,400
Median rent	$721

Anaheim

Population

Total	328,014
Male	164,058
Female	163,956

Race & Hispanic Origin

Race	
White	179,627
Black/African American	8,735
North American Native	3,041
Asian	39,311
Pacific Islander	1,393
Other Race	79,427
Two or more races	16,480
Hispanic origin, total	153,374
Mexican	126,017
Puerto Rican	1,306
Cuban	897
Other Hispanic	25,154

Age & Nativity

Under 5 years	30,206
18 years and over	229,050
65 years and over	26,773
85 years and over	3,213
Median Age	30.3
Native-born	203,381
Foreign-born	123,976

Educational Attainment

Population 25 years and over	194,374
0-8 yrs of school	16.1%
High School grad or higher	69.3%
Bachelor's degree or higher	19.6%
Graduate degree	5.9%

Income & Poverty, 1999

Per capita income	$18,266
Median household income	$47,122
Median family income	$49,969
Persons in poverty	45,615
H'holds receiving public assistance	3,532
H'holds receiving social security	18,143

Households

Total households	96,969
With persons under 18	46,217
With persons over 65	18,669
Family households	73,502
Single person households	17,540
Persons per household	3.34
Persons per family	3.75

Employed persons 16 years and over by occupation

Managers & professionals	39,296
Service occupations	22,252
Sales & office occupations	40,443
Farming, fishing & forestry	418
Construction & maintenance	13,502
Production & transportation	26,914
Self-employed persons	8,607

Housing

Median val. single fam. home	$213,800
Median rent	$818

Note: The 2007 American Community Survey (ACS) collected one-year demographic estimates for cities and counties with populations of at least 65,000 — in California's case, 118 out of 480 municipalities. For those municipalities, ACS data is included in the profiles in order to provide the most current data. However, to allow direct comparisons, data from the 2000 Decennial Census for those municipalities is presented here.

Antioch

Population

Total . . . 90,532
Male . . . 44,331
Female . . . 46,201

Race & Hispanic Origin

Race
White . . . 59,148
Black/African American . . . 8,824
North American Native . . . 843
Asian . . . 6,697
Pacific Islander . . . 360
Other Race . . . 8,352
Two or more races . . . 6,308
Hispanic origin, total . . . 20,024
Mexican . . . 13,619
Puerto Rican . . . 792
Cuban . . . 120
Other Hispanic . . . 5,493

Age & Nativity

Under 5 years . . . 7,820
18 years and over . . . 61,314
65 years and over . . . 6,708
85 years and over . . . 735
Median Age . . . 32.3
Native-born . . . 78,800
Foreign-born . . . 12,014

Educational Attainment

Population 25 years and over . . . 54,041
0-8 yrs of school . . . 4.5%
High School grad or higher . . . 85.7%
Bachelor's degree or higher . . . 18.2%
Graduate degree . . . 4.6%

Income & Poverty, 1999

Per capita income . . . $22,152
Median household income . . . $60,359
Median family income . . . $64,723
Persons in poverty . . . 7,683
H'holds receiving public assistance . . . 1,227
H'holds receiving social security . . . 5,254

Households

Total households . . . 29,338
With persons under 18 . . . 14,877
With persons over 65 . . . 4,901
Family households . . . 23,173
Single person households . . . 4,666
Persons per household . . . 3.07
Persons per family . . . 3.42

Employed persons 16 years and over by occupation

Managers & professionals . . . 12,116
Service occupations . . . 6,280
Sales & office occupations . . . 12,962
Farming, fishing & forestry . . . 73
Construction & maintenance . . . 5,473
Production & transportation . . . 4,694
Self-employed persons . . . 2,376

Housing

Median val. single fam. home . . . $196,600
Median rent . . . $786

Apple Valley

Population

Total . . . 54,239
Male . . . 26,251
Female . . . 27,988

Race & Hispanic Origin

Race
White . . . 41,449
Black/African American . . . 4,277
North American Native . . . 530
Asian . . . 1,198
Pacific Islander . . . 123
Other Race . . . 4,296
Two or more races . . . 2,366
Hispanic origin, total . . . 10,067
Mexican . . . 7,488
Puerto Rican . . . 293
Cuban . . . 86
Other Hispanic . . . 2,200

Age & Nativity

Under 5 years . . . 3,875
18 years and over . . . 37,124
65 years and over . . . 7,445
85 years and over . . . 601
Median Age . . . 35.4
Native-born . . . 50,035
Foreign-born . . . 4,140

Educational Attainment

Population 25 years and over . . . 32,892
0-8 yrs of school . . . 4.1%
High School grad or higher . . . 82.4%
Bachelor's degree or higher . . . 16.4%
Graduate degree . . . 6.6%

Income & Poverty, 1999

Per capita income . . . $17,830
Median household income . . . $40,421
Median family income . . . $45,070
Persons in poverty . . . 9,296
H'holds receiving public assistance . . . 1,379
H'holds receiving social security . . . 6,028

Households

Total households . . . 18,557
With persons under 18 . . . 8,049
With persons over 65 . . . 5,160
Family households . . . 14,358
Single person households . . . 3,349
Persons per household . . . 2.90
Persons per family . . . 3.27

Employed persons 16 years and over by occupation

Managers & professionals . . . 6,143
Service occupations . . . 3,061
Sales & office occupations . . . 5,269
Farming, fishing & forestry . . . 44
Construction & maintenance . . . 2,472
Production & transportation . . . 2,769
Self-employed persons . . . 2,176

Housing

Median val. single fam. home . . . $112,700
Median rent . . . $573

Bakersfield

Population

Total . . . 247,057
Male . . . 120,105
Female . . . 126,952

Race & Hispanic Origin

Race
White . . . 152,849
Black/African American . . . 22,641
North American Native . . . 3,454
Asian . . . 10,708
Pacific Islander . . . 298
Other Race . . . 46,151
Two or more races . . . 10,956
Hispanic origin, total . . . 80,170
Mexican . . . 64,700
Puerto Rican . . . 921
Cuban . . . 189
Other Hispanic . . . 14,360

Age & Nativity

Under 5 years . . . 21,736
18 years and over . . . 166,374
65 years and over . . . 21,681
85 years and over . . . 2,687
Median Age . . . 30.1
Native-born . . . 213,754
Foreign-born . . . 33,631

Educational Attainment

Population 25 years and over . . . 142,060
0-8 yrs of school . . . 10.0%
High School grad or higher . . . 75.9%
Bachelor's degree or higher . . . 19.3%
Graduate degree . . . 6.4%

Income & Poverty, 1999

Per capita income . . . $17,678
Median household income . . . $39,982
Median family income . . . $45,556
Persons in poverty . . . 43,781
H'holds receiving public assistance . . . 5,613
H'holds receiving social security . . . 17,987

Households

Total households . . . 83,441
With persons under 18 . . . 38,815
With persons over 65 . . . 15,483
Family households . . . 60,959
Single person households . . . 17,962
Persons per household . . . 2.92
Persons per family . . . 3.41

Employed persons 16 years and over by occupation

Managers & professionals . . . 32,626
Service occupations . . . 17,912
Sales & office occupations . . . 26,729
Farming, fishing & forestry . . . 3,024
Construction & maintenance . . . 9,887
Production & transportation . . . 11,823
Self-employed persons . . . 7,507

Housing

Median val. single fam. home . . . $106,500
Median rent . . . $564

Note: The 2007 American Community Survey (ACS) collected one-year demographic estimates for cities and counties with populations of at least 65,000 — in California's case, 118 out of 480 municipalities. For those municipalities, ACS data is included in the profiles in order to provide the most current data. However, to allow direct comparisons, data from the 2000 Decennial Census for those municipalities is presented here.

Baldwin Park

Population

Total	75,837
Male	37,911
Female	37,926

Race & Hispanic Origin

Race	
White	30,472
Black/African American	1,219
North American Native	1,096
Asian	8,826
Pacific Islander	112
Other Race	30,718
Two or more races	3,394
Hispanic origin, total	59,660
Mexican	49,046
Puerto Rican	278
Cuban	211
Other Hispanic	10,125

Age & Nativity

Under 5 years	7,324
18 years and over	49,360
65 years and over	4,666
85 years and over	438
Median Age	26.9
Native-born	41,111
Foreign-born	34,642

Educational Attainment

Population 25 years and over	40,417
0-8 yrs of school	30.6%
High School grad or higher	47.5%
Bachelor's degree or higher	9.0%
Graduate degree	1.6%

Income & Poverty, 1999

Per capita income	$11,562
Median household income	$41,629
Median family income	$41,256
Persons in poverty	13,541
H'holds receiving public assistance	1,587
H'holds receiving social security	3,289

Households

Total households	16,961
With persons under 18	11,157
With persons over 65	3,478
Family households	15,069
Single person households	1,379
Persons per household	4.44
Persons per family	4.53

Employed persons 16 years and over by occupation

Managers & professionals	3,936
Service occupations	4,740
Sales & office occupations	6,899
Farming, fishing & forestry	69
Construction & maintenance	2,804
Production & transportation	7,705
Self-employed persons	1,468

Housing

Median val. single fam. home	$146,400
Median rent	$724

Bellflower

Population

Total	72,878
Male	35,520
Female	37,358

Race & Hispanic Origin

Race	
White	33,593
Black/African American	9,540
North American Native	667
Asian	7,062
Pacific Islander	511
Other Race	17,766
Two or more races	3,739
Hispanic origin, total	31,503
Mexican	24,433
Puerto Rican	485
Cuban	223
Other Hispanic	6,362

Age & Nativity

Under 5 years	6,943
18 years and over	49,665
65 years and over	6,145
85 years and over	734
Median Age	29.7
Native-born	52,150
Foreign-born	20,679

Educational Attainment

Population 25 years and over	42,270
0-8 yrs of school	12.3%
High School grad or higher	70.8%
Bachelor's degree or higher	12.9%
Graduate degree	3.1%

Income & Poverty, 1999

Per capita income	$15,982
Median household income	$39,362
Median family income	$42,822
Persons in poverty	11,385
H'holds receiving public assistance	1,546
H'holds receiving social security	4,657

Households

Total households	23,367
With persons under 18	11,325
With persons over 65	4,594
Family households	17,117
Single person households	4,921
Persons per household	3.09
Persons per family	3.59

Employed persons 16 years and over by occupation

Managers & professionals	7,160
Service occupations	4,605
Sales & office occupations	9,174
Farming, fishing & forestry	21
Construction & maintenance	3,024
Production & transportation	5,338
Self-employed persons	1,757

Housing

Median val. single fam. home	$179,800
Median rent	$704

Berkeley

Population

Total	102,743
Male	50,456
Female	52,287

Race & Hispanic Origin

Race	
White	60,797
Black/African American	14,007
North American Native	467
Asian	16,837
Pacific Islander	146
Other Race	4,764
Two or more races	5,725
Hispanic origin, total	10,001
Mexican	6,448
Puerto Rican	379
Cuban	213
Other Hispanic	2,961

Age & Nativity

Under 5 years	4,109
18 years and over	88,230
65 years and over	10,484
85 years and over	1,522
Median Age	32.5
Native-born	81,820
Foreign-born	20,923

Educational Attainment

Population 25 years and over	66,133
0-8 yrs of school	3.4%
High School grad or higher	92.2%
Bachelor's degree or higher	64.3%
Graduate degree	34.3%

Income & Poverty, 1999

Per capita income	$30,477
Median household income	$44,485
Median family income	$70,434
Persons in poverty	19,495
H'holds receiving public assistance	1,034
H'holds receiving social security	8,139

Households

Total households	44,955
With persons under 18	8,884
With persons over 65	7,977
Family households	18,646
Single person households	17,139
Persons per household	2.16
Persons per family	2.84

Employed persons 16 years and over by occupation

Managers & professionals	34,282
Service occupations	5,366
Sales & office occupations	11,326
Farming, fishing & forestry	70
Construction & maintenance	2,023
Production & transportation	2,765
Self-employed persons	6,611

Housing

Median val. single fam. home	$380,200
Median rent	$740

Note: The 2007 American Community Survey (ACS) collected one-year demographic estimates for cities and counties with populations of at least 65,000 — in California's case, 118 out of 480 municipalities. For those municipalities, ACS data is included in the profiles in order to provide the most current data. However, to allow direct comparisons, data from the 2000 Decennial Census for those municipalities is presented here.

Buena Park

Population	
Total	78,282
Male	38,800
Female	39,482
Race & Hispanic Origin	
Race	
White	41,479
Black/African American	3,000
North American Native	750
Asian	16,490
Pacific Islander	397
Other Race	11,893
Two or more races	4,273
Hispanic origin, total	26,221
Mexican	20,893
Puerto Rican	420
Cuban	294
Other Hispanic	4,614
Age & Nativity	
Under 5 years	6,306
18 years and over	55,261
65 years and over	7,305
85 years and over	639
Median Age	32.0
Native-born	52,521
Foreign-born	25,837
Educational Attainment	
Population 25 years and over	48,066
0-8 yrs of school	11.2%
High School grad or higher	75.8%
Bachelor's degree or higher	19.7%
Graduate degree	5.1%
Income & Poverty, 1999	
Per capita income	$18,031
Median household income	$50,336
Median family income	$52,327
Persons in poverty	8,754
H'holds receiving public assistance	852
H'holds receiving social security	4,900
Households	
Total households	23,332
With persons under 18	11,334
With persons over 65	5,162
Family households	18,733
Single person households	3,361
Persons per household	3.32
Persons per family	3.64
Employed persons 16 years and over by occupation	
Managers & professionals	10,017
Service occupations	4,688
Sales & office occupations	10,644
Farming, fishing & forestry	57
Construction & maintenance	3,247
Production & transportation	5,885
Self-employed persons	2,052
Housing	
Median val. single fam. home	$199,400
Median rent	$841

Burbank

Population	
Total	100,316
Male	48,635
Female	51,681
Race & Hispanic Origin	
Race	
White	72,409
Black/African American	2,066
North American Native	549
Asian	9,181
Pacific Islander	142
Other Race	9,908
Two or more races	6,061
Hispanic origin, total	24,953
Mexican	14,216
Puerto Rican	506
Cuban	1,082
Other Hispanic	9,149
Age & Nativity	
Under 5 years	5,759
18 years and over	77,979
65 years and over	12,859
85 years and over	1,858
Median Age	36.4
Native-born	69,104
Foreign-born	31,212
Educational Attainment	
Population 25 years and over	70,523
0-8 yrs of school	7.5%
High School grad or higher	83.1%
Bachelor's degree or higher	29.0%
Graduate degree	8.4%
Income & Poverty, 1999	
Per capita income	$25,713
Median household income	$47,467
Median family income	$56,767
Persons in poverty	10,484
H'holds receiving public assistance	1,586
H'holds receiving social security	8,648
Households	
Total households	41,608
With persons under 18	12,801
With persons over 65	9,691
Family households	24,362
Single person households	13,977
Persons per household	2.39
Persons per family	3.14
Employed persons 16 years and over by occupation	
Managers & professionals	20,302
Service occupations	5,768
Sales & office occupations	15,163
Farming, fishing & forestry	56
Construction & maintenance	3,252
Production & transportation	4,858
Self-employed persons	4,761
Housing	
Median val. single fam. home	$256,400
Median rent	$778

Carlsbad

Population	
Total	78,247
Male	38,291
Female	39,956
Race & Hispanic Origin	
Race	
White	67,723
Black/African American	753
North American Native	329
Asian	3,315
Pacific Islander	155
Other Race	3,636
Two or more races	2,336
Hispanic origin, total	9,170
Mexican	7,107
Puerto Rican	213
Cuban	120
Other Hispanic	1,730
Age & Nativity	
Under 5 years	5,028
18 years and over	60,007
65 years and over	10,980
85 years and over	1,130
Median Age	38.9
Native-born	68,068
Foreign-born	9,930
Educational Attainment	
Population 25 years and over	54,655
0-8 yrs of school	2.8%
High School grad or higher	93.1%
Bachelor's degree or higher	45.7%
Graduate degree	16.4%
Income & Poverty, 1999	
Per capita income	$34,863
Median household income	$65,145
Median family income	$77,151
Persons in poverty	4,576
H'holds receiving public assistance	408
H'holds receiving social security	7,593
Households	
Total households	31,521
With persons under 18	10,183
With persons over 65	7,369
Family households	20,894
Single person households	7,830
Persons per household	2.46
Persons per family	2.96
Employed persons 16 years and over by occupation	
Managers & professionals	19,079
Service occupations	4,544
Sales & office occupations	10,830
Farming, fishing & forestry	101
Construction & maintenance	2,157
Production & transportation	2,052
Self-employed persons	4,983
Housing	
Median val. single fam. home	$330,100
Median rent	$989

Note: The 2007 American Community Survey (ACS) collected one-year demographic estimates for cities and counties with populations of at least 65,000 — in California's case, 118 out of 480 municipalities. For those municipalities, ACS data is included in the profiles in order to provide the most current data. However, to allow direct comparisons, data from the 2000 Decennial Census for those municipalities is presented here.

Carson

Population

Total	89,730
Male	43,315
Female	46,415

Race & Hispanic Origin

Race	
White	23,049
Black/African American	22,804
North American Native	505
Asian	19,987
Pacific Islander	2,680
Other Race	16,137
Two or more races	4,568
Hispanic origin, total	31,332
Mexican	25,275
Puerto Rican	571
Cuban	226
Other Hispanic	5,260

Age & Nativity

Under 5 years	6,192
18 years and over	64,245
65 years and over	9,561
85 years and over	773
Median Age	33.7
Native-born	60,117
Foreign-born	29,432

Educational Attainment

Population 25 years and over	55,241
0-8 yrs of school	13.9%
High School grad or higher	70.6%
Bachelor's degree or higher	18.1%
Graduate degree	4.3%

Income & Poverty, 1999

Per capita income	$17,107
Median household income	$52,284
Median family income	$54,886
Persons in poverty	8,216
H'holds receiving public assistance	1,343
H'holds receiving social security	6,094

Households

Total households	24,648
With persons under 18	12,070
With persons over 65	6,966
Family households	20,243
Single person households	3,506
Persons per household	3.59
Persons per family	3.92

Employed persons 16 years and over by occupation

Managers & professionals	9,980
Service occupations	5,374
Sales & office occupations	11,574
Farming, fishing & forestry	68
Construction & maintenance	2,854
Production & transportation	7,450
Self-employed persons	1,840

Housing

Median val. single fam. home	$183,200
Median rent	$754

Chico

Population

Total	59,954
Male	29,422
Female	30,532

Race & Hispanic Origin

Race	
White	49,377
Black/African American	1,215
North American Native	782
Asian	2,524
Pacific Islander	115
Other Race	3,390
Two or more races	2,551
Hispanic origin, total	7,351
Mexican	5,915
Puerto Rican	140
Cuban	34
Other Hispanic	1,262

Age & Nativity

Under 5 years	3,602
18 years and over	47,281
65 years and over	5,932
85 years and over	1,180
Median Age	25.9
Native-born	54,120
Foreign-born	5,324

Educational Attainment

Population 25 years and over	31,072
0-8 yrs of school	5.0%
High School grad or higher	87.3%
Bachelor's degree or higher	33.6%
Graduate degree	10.5%

Income & Poverty, 1999

Per capita income	$16,970
Median household income	$29,359
Median family income	$43,077
Persons in poverty	15,121
H'holds receiving public assistance	1,224
H'holds receiving social security	4,509

Households

Total households	23,476
With persons under 18	6,789
With persons over 65	3,856
Family households	11,641
Single person households	6,874
Persons per household	2.42
Persons per family	3.03

Employed persons 16 years and over by occupation

Managers & professionals	9,703
Service occupations	5,359
Sales & office occupations	7,837
Farming, fishing & forestry	345
Construction & maintenance	1,735
Production & transportation	2,484
Self-employed persons	2,077

Housing

Median val. single fam. home	$141,600
Median rent	$594

Chino

Population

Total	67,168
Male	37,223
Female	29,945

Race & Hispanic Origin

Race	
White	37,412
Black/African American	5,250
North American Native	628
Asian	3,308
Pacific Islander	139
Other Race	17,169
Two or more races	3,262
Hispanic origin, total	31,830
Mexican	26,232
Puerto Rican	247
Cuban	237
Other Hispanic	5,114

Age & Nativity

Under 5 years	4,809
18 years and over	48,040
65 years and over	3,933
85 years and over	376
Median Age	30.9
Native-born	53,777
Foreign-born	13,823

Educational Attainment

Population 25 years and over	40,039
0-8 yrs of school	11.2%
High School grad or higher	70.7%
Bachelor's degree or higher	13.0%
Graduate degree	3.3%

Income & Poverty, 1999

Per capita income	$17,574
Median household income	$55,401
Median family income	$59,638
Persons in poverty	4,976
H'holds receiving public assistance	644
H'holds receiving social security	3,098

Households

Total households	17,304
With persons under 18	9,284
With persons over 65	2,997
Family households	14,102
Single person households	2,432
Persons per household	3.43
Persons per family	3.77

Employed persons 16 years and over by occupation

Managers & professionals	7,702
Service occupations	3,649
Sales & office occupations	7,920
Farming, fishing & forestry	230
Construction & maintenance	2,528
Production & transportation	4,952
Self-employed persons	1,702

Housing

Median val. single fam. home	$173,600
Median rent	$769

Note: The 2007 American Community Survey (ACS) collected one-year demographic estimates for cities and counties with populations of at least 65,000 — in California's case, 118 out of 480 municipalities. For those municipalities, ACS data is included in the profiles in order to provide the most current data. However, to allow direct comparisons, data from the 2000 Decennial Census for those municipalities is presented here.

Chino Hills

Population	
Total	66,787
Male	33,207
Female	33,580

Race & Hispanic Origin	
Race	
White	37,656
Black/African American	3,697
North American Native	375
Asian	14,744
Pacific Islander	85
Other Race	7,062
Two or more races	3,168
Hispanic origin, total	17,151
Mexican	12,923
Puerto Rican	305
Cuban	308
Other Hispanic	3,615

Age & Nativity	
Under 5 years	5,836
18 years and over	44,841
65 years and over	2,828
85 years and over	189
Median Age	32.3
Native-born	51,593
Foreign-born	15,123

Educational Attainment	
Population 25 years and over	40,032
0-8 yrs of school	3.7%
High School grad or higher	89.9%
Bachelor's degree or higher	37.6%
Graduate degree	10.6%

Income & Poverty, 1999	
Per capita income	$26,182
Median household income	$78,374
Median family income	$81,794
Persons in poverty	3,419
H'holds receiving public assistance	206
H'holds receiving social security	1,902

Households	
Total households	20,039
With persons under 18	11,426
With persons over 65	2,166
Family households	17,075
Single person households	2,170
Persons per household	3.33
Persons per family	3.61

Employed persons 16 years and over by occupation	
Managers & professionals	14,540
Service occupations	3,275
Sales & office occupations	9,544
Farming, fishing & forestry	45
Construction & maintenance	2,075
Production & transportation	2,856
Self-employed persons	2,459

Housing	
Median val. single fam. home	$242,600
Median rent	$1,035

Chula Vista

Population	
Total	173,556
Male	84,237
Female	89,319

Race & Hispanic Origin	
Race	
White	95,553
Black/African American	8,022
North American Native	1,352
Asian	19,063
Pacific Islander	1,013
Other Race	38,404
Two or more races	10,149
Hispanic origin, total	86,073
Mexican	74,867
Puerto Rican	1,421
Cuban	306
Other Hispanic	9,479

Age & Nativity	
Under 5 years	13,565
18 years and over	123,692
65 years and over	19,119
85 years and over	1,856
Median Age	33.0
Native-born	124,018
Foreign-born	49,842

Educational Attainment	
Population 25 years and over	107,496
0-8 yrs of school	9.8%
High School grad or higher	78.5%
Bachelor's degree or higher	22.2%
Graduate degree	7.2%

Income & Poverty, 1999	
Per capita income	$18,556
Median household income	$44,861
Median family income	$50,136
Persons in poverty	18,357
H'holds receiving public assistance	2,216
H'holds receiving social security	13,890

Households	
Total households	57,705
With persons under 18	26,136
With persons over 65	14,133
Family households	43,549
Single person households	11,239
Persons per household	2.99
Persons per family	3.44

Employed persons 16 years and over by occupation	
Managers & professionals	23,505
Service occupations	12,025
Sales & office occupations	21,233
Farming, fishing & forestry	136
Construction & maintenance	6,879
Production & transportation	7,417
Self-employed persons	4,424

Housing	
Median val. single fam. home	$197,000
Median rent	$707

Citrus Heights

Population	
Total	85,071
Male	41,155
Female	43,916

Race & Hispanic Origin	
Race	
White	72,001
Black/African American	2,442
North American Native	860
Asian	2,423
Pacific Islander	288
Other Race	3,032
Two or more races	4,025
Hispanic origin, total	8,539
Mexican	5,882
Puerto Rican	349
Cuban	67
Other Hispanic	2,241

Age & Nativity	
Under 5 years	5,786
18 years and over	63,611
65 years and over	11,014
85 years and over	1,370
Median Age	34.9
Native-born	77,401
Foreign-born	7,829

Educational Attainment	
Population 25 years and over	55,087
0-8 yrs of school	2.8%
High School grad or higher	88.5%
Bachelor's degree or higher	18.2%
Graduate degree	5.3%

Income & Poverty, 1999	
Per capita income	$20,744
Median household income	$43,859
Median family income	$51,207
Persons in poverty	6,942
H'holds receiving public assistance	1,323
H'holds receiving social security	8,715

Households	
Total households	33,478
With persons under 18	11,515
With persons over 65	7,768
Family households	21,647
Single person households	9,006
Persons per household	2.52
Persons per family	3.06

Employed persons 16 years and over by occupation	
Managers & professionals	12,137
Service occupations	6,095
Sales & office occupations	14,022
Farming, fishing & forestry	31
Construction & maintenance	5,343
Production & transportation	4,256
Self-employed persons	3,013

Housing	
Median val. single fam. home	$137,300
Median rent	$728

Note: The 2007 American Community Survey (ACS) collected one-year demographic estimates for cities and counties with populations of at least 65,000 — in California's case, 118 out of 480 municipalities. For those municipalities, ACS data is included in the profiles in order to provide the most current data. However, to allow direct comparisons, data from the 2000 Decennial Census for those municipalities is presented here.

Clovis

Population

Total	68,468
Male	32,868
Female	35,600

Race & Hispanic Origin

Race	
White	51,914
Black/African American	1,302
North American Native	1,025
Asian	4,441
Pacific Islander	108
Other Race	6,502
Two or more races	3,176
Hispanic origin, total	13,876
Mexican	11,442
Puerto Rican	155
Cuban	39
Other Hispanic	2,240

Age & Nativity

Under 5 years	5,204
18 years and over	47,471
65 years and over	6,406
85 years and over	875
Median Age	32.8
Native-born	62,734
Foreign-born	5,463

Educational Attainment

Population 25 years and over	41,135
0-8 yrs of school	5.1%
High School grad or higher	85.0%
Bachelor's degree or higher	23.1%
Graduate degree	6.0%

Income & Poverty, 1999

Per capita income	$18,690
Median household income	$42,283
Median family income	$50,859
Persons in poverty	7,160
H'holds receiving public assistance	1,020
H'holds receiving social security	5,195

Households

Total households	24,347
With persons under 18	10,900
With persons over 65	4,617
Family households	17,665
Single person households	5,420
Persons per household	2.79
Persons per family	3.29

Employed persons 16 years and over by occupation

Managers & professionals	11,068
Service occupations	4,583
Sales & office occupations	9,320
Farming, fishing & forestry	392
Construction & maintenance	2,974
Production & transportation	3,149
Self-employed persons	2,336

Housing

Median val. single fam. home	$125,200
Median rent	$580

Compton

Population

Total	93,493
Male	45,857
Female	47,636

Race & Hispanic Origin

Race	
White	15,625
Black/African American	37,690
North American Native	656
Asian	237
Pacific Islander	985
Other Race	34,911
Two or more races	3,389
Hispanic origin, total	53,143
Mexican	43,839
Puerto Rican	161
Cuban	68
Other Hispanic	9,075

Age & Nativity

Under 5 years	9,736
18 years and over	57,500
65 years and over	6,437
85 years and over	441
Median Age	25.0
Native-born	63,945
Foreign-born	29,281

Educational Attainment

Population 25 years and over	46,604
0-8 yrs of school	30.1%
High School grad or higher	48.0%
Bachelor's degree or higher	5.9%
Graduate degree	1.8%

Income & Poverty, 1999

Per capita income	$10,389
Median household income	$31,819
Median family income	$33,021
Persons in poverty	25,771
H'holds receiving public assistance	3,329
H'holds receiving social security	5,198

Households

Total households	22,327
With persons under 18	13,888
With persons over 65	5,006
Family households	18,613
Single person households	2,952
Persons per household	4.16
Persons per family	4.45

Employed persons 16 years and over by occupation

Managers & professionals	4,068
Service occupations	4,864
Sales & office occupations	6,810
Farming, fishing & forestry	84
Construction & maintenance	2,507
Production & transportation	8,786
Self-employed persons	1,036

Housing

Median val. single fam. home	$136,200
Median rent	$597

Concord

Population

Total	121,780
Male	60,147
Female	61,633

Race & Hispanic Origin

Race	
White	86,114
Black/African American	3,706
North American Native	929
Asian	11,438
Pacific Islander	612
Other Race	11,752
Two or more races	7,229
Hispanic origin, total	26,560
Mexican	17,446
Puerto Rican	666
Cuban	179
Other Hispanic	8,269

Age & Nativity

Under 5 years	8,625
18 years and over	90,937
65 years and over	13,066
85 years and over	1,538
Median Age	35.1
Native-born	93,232
Foreign-born	28,478

Educational Attainment

Population 25 years and over	80,130
0-8 yrs of school	6.8%
High School grad or higher	84.7%
Bachelor's degree or higher	25.9%
Graduate degree	7.2%

Income & Poverty, 1999

Per capita income	$24,727
Median household income	$55,597
Median family income	$62,093
Persons in poverty	9,151
H'holds receiving public assistance	1,410
H'holds receiving social security	9,472

Households

Total households	44,020
With persons under 18	16,602
With persons over 65	9,115
Family households	30,322
Single person households	10,228
Persons per household	2.74
Persons per family	3.22

Employed persons 16 years and over by occupation

Managers & professionals	20,275
Service occupations	10,599
Sales & office occupations	16,667
Farming, fishing & forestry	51
Construction & maintenance	6,490
Production & transportation	5,573
Self-employed persons	4,557

Housing

Median val. single fam. home	$233,700
Median rent	$880

Note: The 2007 American Community Survey (ACS) collected one-year demographic estimates for cities and counties with populations of at least 65,000 — in California's case, 118 out of 480 municipalities. For those municipalities, ACS data is included in the profiles in order to provide the most current data. However, to allow direct comparisons, data from the 2000 Decennial Census for those municipalities is presented here.

Corona

Population

Total	124,966
Male	61,849
Female	63,117

Race & Hispanic Origin

Race	
White	77,514
Black/African American	8,031
North American Native	1,086
Asian	9,425
Pacific Islander	387
Other Race	21,894
Two or more races	6,629
Hispanic origin, total	44,569
Mexican	36,212
Puerto Rican	603
Cuban	446
Other Hispanic	7,308

Age & Nativity

Under 5 years	12,249
18 years and over	83,233
65 years and over	7,289
85 years and over	812
Median Age	29.9
Native-born	98,230
Foreign-born	26,705

Educational Attainment

Population 25 years and over	72,375
0-8 yrs of school	8.7%
High School grad or higher	80.6%
Bachelor's degree or higher	22.0%
Graduate degree	6.5%

Income & Poverty, 1999

Per capita income	$21,001
Median household income	$59,615
Median family income	$63,505
Persons in poverty	10,244
H'holds receiving public assistance	914
H'holds receiving social security	5,570

Households

Total households	37,839
With persons under 18	20,347
With persons over 65	5,257
Family households	30,391
Single person households	5,466
Persons per household	3.29
Persons per family	3.64

Employed persons 16 years and over by occupation

Managers & professionals	18,771
Service occupations	7,285
Sales & office occupations	16,927
Farming, fishing & forestry	148
Construction & maintenance	5,328
Production & transportation	8,817
Self-employed persons	3,944

Housing

Median val. single fam. home	$194,400
Median rent	$812

Costa Mesa

Population

Total	108,724
Male	55,694
Female	53,030

Race & Hispanic Origin

Race	
White	75,542
Black/African American	1,520
North American Native	845
Asian	7,501
Pacific Islander	656
Other Race	18,018
Two or more races	4,642
Hispanic origin, total	34,523
Mexican	26,133
Puerto Rican	311
Cuban	174
Other Hispanic	7,905

Age & Nativity

Under 5 years	7,735
18 years and over	83,452
65 years and over	9,182
85 years and over	1,075
Median Age	32.0
Native-born	77,063
Foreign-born	31,722

Educational Attainment

Population 25 years and over	71,622
0-8 yrs of school	11.6%
High School grad or higher	79.1%
Bachelor's degree or higher	29.1%
Graduate degree	8.3%

Income & Poverty, 1999

Per capita income	$23,342
Median household income	$50,732
Median family income	$55,456
Persons in poverty	13,393
H'holds receiving public assistance	904
H'holds receiving social security	6,756

Households

Total households	39,206
With persons under 18	12,549
With persons over 65	6,671
Family households	22,766
Single person households	11,006
Persons per household	2.69
Persons per family	3.34

Employed persons 16 years and over by occupation

Managers & professionals	20,361
Service occupations	9,591
Sales & office occupations	16,917
Farming, fishing & forestry	172
Construction & maintenance	4,351
Production & transportation	5,289
Self-employed persons	5,790

Housing

Median val. single fam. home	$273,100
Median rent	$956

Daly City

Population

Total	103,621
Male	50,971
Female	52,650

Race & Hispanic Origin

Race	
White	26,836
Black/African American	4,720
North American Native	456
Asian	52,522
Pacific Islander	940
Other Race	11,735
Two or more races	6,412
Hispanic origin, total	23,072
Mexican	8,651
Puerto Rican	662
Cuban	116
Other Hispanic	13,643

Age & Nativity

Under 5 years	6,246
18 years and over	80,343
65 years and over	12,486
85 years and over	1,262
Median Age	35.4
Native-born	49,336
Foreign-born	54,213

Educational Attainment

Population 25 years and over	69,660
0-8 yrs of school	9.0%
High School grad or higher	82.0%
Bachelor's degree or higher	29.1%
Graduate degree	6.5%

Income & Poverty, 1999

Per capita income	$21,900
Median household income	$62,310
Median family income	$68,365
Persons in poverty	7,265
H'holds receiving public assistance	873
H'holds receiving social security	7,702

Households

Total households	30,775
With persons under 18	12,538
With persons over 65	8,872
Family households	23,089
Single person households	5,558
Persons per household	3.34
Persons per family	3.78

Employed persons 16 years and over by occupation

Managers & professionals	14,983
Service occupations	8,609
Sales & office occupations	17,687
Farming, fishing & forestry	134
Construction & maintenance	3,546
Production & transportation	5,926
Self-employed persons	2,503

Housing

Median val. single fam. home	$335,000
Median rent	$1,074

Note: The 2007 American Community Survey (ACS) collected one-year demographic estimates for cities and counties with populations of at least 65,000 — in California's case, 118 out of 480 municipalities. For those municipalities, ACS data is included in the profiles in order to provide the most current data. However, to allow direct comparisons, data from the 2000 Decennial Census for those municipalities is presented here.

Downey

Population

Total	107,323
Male	52,176
Female	55,147

Race & Hispanic Origin

Race	
White	57,395
Black/African American	4,028
North American Native	929
Asian	8,308
Pacific Islander	236
Other Race	31,180
Two or more races	5,247
Hispanic origin, total	62,089
Mexican	43,241
Puerto Rican	661
Cuban	2,100
Other Hispanic	16,087

Age & Nativity

Under 5 years	8,606
18 years and over	75,966
65 years and over	11,829
85 years and over	1,422
Median Age	31.6
Native-born	69,398
Foreign-born	37,925

Educational Attainment

Population 25 years and over	65,773
0-8 yrs of school	12.7%
High School grad or higher	72.3%
Bachelor's degree or higher	17.3%
Graduate degree	5.4%

Income & Poverty, 1999

Per capita income	$18,197
Median household income	$45,667
Median family income	$50,017
Persons in poverty	11,714
H'holds receiving public assistance	1,387
H'holds receiving social security	8,086

Households

Total households	33,989
With persons under 18	15,733
With persons over 65	8,482
Family households	25,997
Single person households	6,479
Persons per household	3.11
Persons per family	3.55

Employed persons 16 years and over by occupation

Managers & professionals	12,678
Service occupations	5,458
Sales & office occupations	14,692
Farming, fishing & forestry	22
Construction & maintenance	3,879
Production & transportation	7,379
Self-employed persons	3,680

Housing

Median val. single fam. home	$209,700
Median rent	$731

El Cajon

Population

Total	94,869
Male	46,279
Female	48,590

Race & Hispanic Origin

Race	
White	70,206
Black/African American	5,090
North American Native	941
Asian	2,643
Pacific Islander	352
Other Race	9,950
Two or more races	5,687
Hispanic origin, total	21,313
Mexican	17,271
Puerto Rican	565
Cuban	88
Other Hispanic	3,389

Age & Nativity

Under 5 years	7,752
18 years and over	68,438
65 years and over	10,749
85 years and over	1,467
Median Age	31.9
Native-born	78,236
Foreign-born	16,583

Educational Attainment

Population 25 years and over	57,867
0-8 yrs of school	7.3%
High School grad or higher	79.2%
Bachelor's degree or higher	14.5%
Graduate degree	4.7%

Income & Poverty, 1999

Per capita income	$16,698
Median household income	$35,566
Median family income	$40,045
Persons in poverty	15,469
H'holds receiving public assistance	2,388
H'holds receiving social security	7,755

Households

Total households	34,199
With persons under 18	13,774
With persons over 65	7,162
Family households	23,163
Single person households	8,247
Persons per household	2.70
Persons per family	3.21

Employed persons 16 years and over by occupation

Managers & professionals	10,237
Service occupations	7,228
Sales & office occupations	13,071
Farming, fishing & forestry	51
Construction & maintenance	5,117
Production & transportation	4,633
Self-employed persons	2,868

Housing

Median val. single fam. home	$190,200
Median rent	$671

El Monte

Population

Total	115,965
Male	58,584
Female	57,381

Race & Hispanic Origin

Race	
White	41,360
Black/African American	889
North American Native	1,596
Asian	21,465
Pacific Islander	140
Other Race	45,544
Two or more races	4,971
Hispanic origin, total	83,945
Mexican	69,880
Puerto Rican	283
Cuban	431
Other Hispanic	13,351

Age & Nativity

Under 5 years	11,553
18 years and over	76,460
65 years and over	8,018
85 years and over	852
Median Age	27.1
Native-born	56,660
Foreign-born	59,589

Educational Attainment

Population 25 years and over	62,422
0-8 yrs of school	33.3%
High School grad or higher	44.2%
Bachelor's degree or higher	7.1%
Graduate degree	2.0%

Income & Poverty, 1999

Per capita income	$10,316
Median household income	$32,439
Median family income	$32,402
Persons in poverty	29,939
H'holds receiving public assistance	3,291
H'holds receiving social security	4,589

Households

Total households	27,034
With persons under 18	16,604
With persons over 65	5,774
Family households	22,995
Single person households	2,945
Persons per household	4.24
Persons per family	4.43

Employed persons 16 years and over by occupation

Managers & professionals	6,267
Service occupations	6,562
Sales & office occupations	9,163
Farming, fishing & forestry	257
Construction & maintenance	4,597
Production & transportation	13,736
Self-employed persons	1,970

Housing

Median val. single fam. home	$158,100
Median rent	$672

Note: The 2007 American Community Survey (ACS) collected one-year demographic estimates for cities and counties with populations of at least 65,000 — in California's case, 118 out of 480 municipalities. For those municipalities, ACS data is included in the profiles in order to provide the most current data. However, to allow direct comparisons, data from the 2000 Decennial Census for those municipalities is presented here.

Elk Grove

Item	Value
Population	
Total	59,984
Male	29,268
Female	30,716
Race & Hispanic Origin	
Race	
White	35,464
Black/African American	5,110
North American Native	562
Asian	10,553
Pacific Islander	355
Other Race	3,865
Two or more races	4,075
Hispanic origin, total	8,398
Mexican	6,300
Puerto Rican	236
Cuban	56
Other Hispanic	1,806
Age & Nativity	
Under 5 years	4,720
18 years and over	40,221
65 years and over	4,049
85 years and over	452
Median Age	32.0
Native-born	50,412
Foreign-born	9,843
Educational Attainment	
Population 25 years and over	35,569
0-8 yrs of school	5.3%
High School grad or higher	86.7%
Bachelor's degree or higher	24.1%
Graduate degree	6.3%
Income & Poverty, 1999	
Per capita income	$20,916
Median household income	$60,661
Median family income	$64,069
Persons in poverty	3,073
H'holds receiving public assistance	735
H'holds receiving social security	3,026
Households	
Total households	18,526
With persons under 18	9,917
With persons over 65	2,806
Family households	15,366
Single person households	2,383
Persons per household	3.22
Persons per family	3.51
Employed persons 16 years and over by occupation	
Managers & professionals	10,657
Service occupations	3,542
Sales & office occupations	9,052
Farming, fishing & forestry	95
Construction & maintenance	2,468
Production & transportation	3,089
Self-employed persons	1,672
Housing	
Median val. single fam. home	$151,400
Median rent	$800

Escondido

Item	Value
Population	
Total	133,559
Male	66,233
Female	67,326
Race & Hispanic Origin	
Race	
White	90,578
Black/African American	3,009
North American Native	1,646
Asian	5,957
Pacific Islander	311
Other Race	25,636
Two or more races	6,422
Hispanic origin, total	51,693
Mexican	44,726
Puerto Rican	647
Cuban	118
Other Hispanic	6,202
Age & Nativity	
Under 5 years	11,712
18 years and over	93,872
65 years and over	14,720
85 years and over	2,409
Median Age	31.2
Native-born	99,523
Foreign-born	34,005
Educational Attainment	
Population 25 years and over	79,691
0-8 yrs of school	14.1%
High School grad or higher	72.6%
Bachelor's degree or higher	20.1%
Graduate degree	6.6%
Income & Poverty, 1999	
Per capita income	$18,241
Median household income	$42,567
Median family income	$48,456
Persons in poverty	17,759
H'holds receiving public assistance	1,705
H'holds receiving social security	11,175
Households	
Total households	43,817
With persons under 18	18,667
With persons over 65	10,353
Family households	31,162
Single person households	9,801
Persons per household	3.01
Persons per family	3.50
Employed persons 16 years and over by occupation	
Managers & professionals	16,050
Service occupations	10,760
Sales & office occupations	14,888
Farming, fishing & forestry	837
Construction & maintenance	6,681
Production & transportation	8,210
Self-employed persons	5,071
Housing	
Median val. single fam. home	$192,600
Median rent	$746

Fairfield

Item	Value
Population	
Total	96,178
Male	47,882
Female	48,296
Race & Hispanic Origin	
Race	
White	54,063
Black/African American	14,446
North American Native	744
Asian	10,471
Pacific Islander	899
Other Race	8,431
Two or more races	7,124
Hispanic origin, total	18,050
Mexican	12,894
Puerto Rican	850
Cuban	116
Other Hispanic	4,190
Age & Nativity	
Under 5 years	8,163
18 years and over	67,519
65 years and over	8,634
85 years and over	833
Median Age	31.1
Native-born	80,521
Foreign-born	15,647
Educational Attainment	
Population 25 years and over	56,512
0-8 yrs of school	5.8%
High School grad or higher	85.0%
Bachelor's degree or higher	20.4%
Graduate degree	6.1%
Income & Poverty, 1999	
Per capita income	$20,617
Median household income	$51,151
Median family income	$55,503
Persons in poverty	8,496
H'holds receiving public assistance	1,326
H'holds receiving social security	6,073
Households	
Total households	30,870
With persons under 18	14,788
With persons over 65	5,731
Family households	24,018
Single person households	5,251
Persons per household	2.98
Persons per family	3.33
Employed persons 16 years and over by occupation	
Managers & professionals	11,468
Service occupations	6,676
Sales & office occupations	11,179
Farming, fishing & forestry	160
Construction & maintenance	4,268
Production & transportation	5,435
Self-employed persons	1,997
Housing	
Median val. single fam. home	$174,700
Median rent	$778

Note: The 2007 American Community Survey (ACS) collected one-year demographic estimates for cities and counties with populations of at least 65,000 — in California's case, 118 out of 480 municipalities. For those municipalities, ACS data is included in the profiles in order to provide the most current data. However, to allow direct comparisons, data from the 2000 Decennial Census for those municipalities is presented here.

Folsom

Population

Total	51,884
Male	28,658
Female	23,226

Race & Hispanic Origin

Race	
White	40,415
Black/African American	3,109
North American Native	302
Asian	3,731
Pacific Islander	100
Other Race	2,446
Two or more races	1,781
Hispanic origin, total	4,914
Mexican	3,727
Puerto Rican	167
Cuban	50
Other Hispanic	970

Age & Nativity

Under 5 years	3,591
18 years and over	39,327
65 years and over	4,569
85 years and over	558
Median Age	35.9
Native-born	47,335
Foreign-born	4,577

Educational Attainment

Population 25 years and over	36,010
0-8 yrs of school	2.2%
High School grad or higher	88.9%
Bachelor's degree or higher	37.6%
Graduate degree	11.9%

Income & Poverty, 1999

Per capita income	$30,210
Median household income	$73,175
Median family income	$82,448
Persons in poverty	3,541
H'holds receiving public assistance	335
H'holds receiving social security	3,068

Households

Total households	17,196
With persons under 18	7,019
With persons over 65	3,186
Family households	12,527
Single person households	3,754
Persons per household	2.61
Persons per family	3.08

Employed persons 16 years and over by occupation

Managers & professionals	12,167
Service occupations	2,555
Sales & office occupations	6,179
Farming, fishing & forestry	171
Construction & maintenance	1,147
Production & transportation	1,246
Self-employed persons	1,780

Housing

Median val. single fam. home	$228,700
Median rent	$939

Fontana

Population

Total	128,929
Male	63,982
Female	64,947

Race & Hispanic Origin

Race	
White	58,006
Black/African American	15,255
North American Native	1,450
Asian	5,618
Pacific Islander	427
Other Race	41,185
Two or more races	6,988
Hispanic origin, total	74,424
Mexican	59,386
Puerto Rican	855
Cuban	315
Other Hispanic	13,868

Age & Nativity

Under 5 years	13,313
18 years and over	80,135
65 years and over	6,113
85 years and over	618
Median Age	26.2
Native-born	93,684
Foreign-born	34,490

Educational Attainment

Population 25 years and over	66,706
0-8 yrs of school	16.1%
High School grad or higher	65.4%
Bachelor's degree or higher	10.3%
Graduate degree	3.0%

Income & Poverty, 1999

Per capita income	$14,208
Median household income	$45,782
Median family income	$46,957
Persons in poverty	18,676
H'holds receiving public assistance	2,325
H'holds receiving social security	4,783

Households

Total households	34,014
With persons under 18	21,725
With persons over 65	4,590
Family households	29,022
Single person households	3,708
Persons per household	3.78
Persons per family	4.02

Employed persons 16 years and over by occupation

Managers & professionals	9,875
Service occupations	6,866
Sales & office occupations	13,500
Farming, fishing & forestry	155
Construction & maintenance	5,590
Production & transportation	11,466
Self-employed persons	2,216

Housing

Median val. single fam. home	$130,400
Median rent	$636

Fremont

Population

Total	203,413
Male	102,273
Female	101,140

Race & Hispanic Origin

Race	
White	96,968
Black/African American	6,310
North American Native	1,048
Asian	75,165
Pacific Islander	819
Other Race	11,230
Two or more races	11,873
Hispanic origin, total	27,409
Mexican	18,848
Puerto Rican	1,233
Cuban	172
Other Hispanic	7,156

Age & Nativity

Under 5 years	15,137
18 years and over	150,961
65 years and over	16,967
85 years and over	1,640
Median Age	34.5
Native-born	127,919
Foreign-born	75,494

Educational Attainment

Population 25 years and over	136,242
0-8 yrs of school	5.1%
High School grad or higher	88.4%
Bachelor's degree or higher	43.2%
Graduate degree	16.7%

Income & Poverty, 1999

Per capita income	$31,411
Median household income	$76,579
Median family income	$82,199
Persons in poverty	10,915
H'holds receiving public assistance	1,725
H'holds receiving social security	10,783

Households

Total households	68,237
With persons under 18	29,700
With persons over 65	11,912
Family households	52,228
Single person households	11,287
Persons per household	2.96
Persons per family	3.34

Employed persons 16 years and over by occupation

Managers & professionals	50,862
Service occupations	7,981
Sales & office occupations	25,234
Farming, fishing & forestry	108
Construction & maintenance	6,412
Production & transportation	11,590
Self-employed persons	5,145

Housing

Median val. single fam. home	$363,400
Median rent	$1,196

Note: The 2007 American Community Survey (ACS) collected one-year demographic estimates for cities and counties with populations of at least 65,000 — in California's case, 118 out of 480 municipalities. For those municipalities, ACS data is included in the profiles in order to provide the most current data. However, to allow direct comparisons, data from the 2000 Decennial Census for those municipalities is presented here.

Fresno

Item	Value
Population	
Total	427,652
Male	210,107
Female	217,545
Race & Hispanic Origin	
Race	
White	214,556
Black/African American	35,763
North American Native	6,763
Asian	48,028
Pacific Islander	583
Other Race	99,898
Two or more races	22,061
Hispanic origin, total	170,520
Mexican	144,772
Puerto Rican	1,105
Cuban	288
Other Hispanic	24,355
Age & Nativity	
Under 5 years	38,996
18 years and over	286,861
65 years and over	39,574
85 years and over	5,211
Median Age	28.5
Native-born	340,287
Foreign-born	86,937
Educational Attainment	
Population 25 years and over	236,704
0-8 yrs of school	16.3%
High School grad or higher	69.1%
Bachelor's degree or higher	19.0%
Graduate degree	6.1%
Income & Poverty, 1999	
Per capita income	$15,010
Median household income	$32,236
Median family income	$35,892
Persons in poverty	109,703
H'holds receiving public assistance	14,960
H'holds receiving social security	30,088
Households	
Total households	140,079
With persons under 18	62,700
With persons over 65	28,660
Family households	97,923
Single person households	32,646
Persons per household	2.99
Persons per family	3.57
Employed persons 16 years and over by occupation	
Managers & professionals	48,632
Service occupations	27,820
Sales & office occupations	45,348
Farming, fishing & forestry	4,479
Construction & maintenance	12,857
Production & transportation	20,640
Self-employed persons	10,946
Housing	
Median val. single fam. home	$97,300
Median rent	$538

Fullerton

Item	Value
Population	
Total	126,003
Male	62,276
Female	63,727
Race & Hispanic Origin	
Race	
White	77,977
Black/African American	2,861
North American Native	865
Asian	20,259
Pacific Islander	296
Other Race	18,666
Two or more races	5,079
Hispanic origin, total	38,014
Mexican	31,252
Puerto Rican	422
Cuban	349
Other Hispanic	5,991
Age & Nativity	
Under 5 years	8,772
18 years and over	94,320
65 years and over	14,274
85 years and over	1,739
Median Age	32.9
Native-born	89,815
Foreign-born	36,431
Educational Attainment	
Population 25 years and over	80,010
0-8 yrs of school	8.8%
High School grad or higher	81.8%
Bachelor's degree or higher	31.3%
Graduate degree	10.8%
Income & Poverty, 1999	
Per capita income	$23,370
Median household income	$50,269
Median family income	$57,345
Persons in poverty	14,116
H'holds receiving public assistance	1,238
H'holds receiving social security	9,405
Households	
Total households	43,609
With persons under 18	15,847
With persons over 65	9,772
Family households	29,625
Single person households	10,229
Persons per household	2.83
Persons per family	3.37
Employed persons 16 years and over by occupation	
Managers & professionals	21,958
Service occupations	7,553
Sales & office occupations	17,521
Farming, fishing & forestry	98
Construction & maintenance	4,046
Production & transportation	8,156
Self-employed persons	4,504
Housing	
Median val. single fam. home	$241,900
Median rent	$820

Garden Grove

Item	Value
Population	
Total	165,196
Male	82,688
Female	82,508
Race & Hispanic Origin	
Race	
White	77,443
Black/African American	2,168
North American Native	1,260
Asian	51,078
Pacific Islander	1,081
Other Race	25,362
Two or more races	6,804
Hispanic origin, total	53,608
Mexican	43,576
Puerto Rican	578
Cuban	360
Other Hispanic	9,094
Age & Nativity	
Under 5 years	13,109
18 years and over	118,178
65 years and over	15,765
85 years and over	1,538
Median Age	32.3
Native-born	94,359
Foreign-born	71,351
Educational Attainment	
Population 25 years and over	103,456
0-8 yrs of school	15.9%
High School grad or higher	67.8%
Bachelor's degree or higher	15.0%
Graduate degree	4.0%
Income & Poverty, 1999	
Per capita income	$16,209
Median household income	$47,754
Median family income	$49,697
Persons in poverty	22,779
H'holds receiving public assistance	2,715
H'holds receiving social security	9,212
Households	
Total households	45,791
With persons under 18	22,169
With persons over 65	11,063
Family households	36,460
Single person households	6,977
Persons per household	3.56
Persons per family	3.90
Employed persons 16 years and over by occupation	
Managers & professionals	17,354
Service occupations	10,873
Sales & office occupations	18,359
Farming, fishing & forestry	211
Construction & maintenance	7,225
Production & transportation	15,334
Self-employed persons	4,682
Housing	
Median val. single fam. home	$199,700
Median rent	$827

Note: The 2007 American Community Survey (ACS) collected one-year demographic estimates for cities and counties with populations of at least 65,000 — in California's case, 118 out of 480 municipalities. For those municipalities, ACS data is included in the profiles in order to provide the most current data. However, to allow direct comparisons, data from the 2000 Decennial Census for those municipalities is presented here.

Glendale

Population
Total 194,973
Male 93,074
Female 101,899

Race & Hispanic Origin
Race
White 123,960
Black/African American 2,468
North American Native 629
Asian 31,424
Pacific Islander 163
Other Race 16,715
Two or more races 19,614
Hispanic origin, total 38,452
Mexican 20,810
Puerto Rican 624
Cuban 1,838
Other Hispanic 15,180

Age & Nativity
Under 5 years 11,088
18 years and over 151,347
65 years and over 27,114
85 years and over 3,799
Median Age 37.5
Native-born 88,928
Foreign-born 106,119

Educational Attainment
Population 25 years and over 135,054
0-8 yrs of school 11.3%
High School grad or higher 79.0%
Bachelor's degree or higher 32.1%
Graduate degree 11.2%

Income & Poverty, 1999
Per capita income $22,227
Median household income $41,805
Median family income $47,633
Persons in poverty 29,927
H'holds receiving public assistance . . . 6,085
H'holds receiving social security 14,347

Households
Total households 71,805
With persons under 18 25,393
With persons over 65 19,265
Family households 49,636
Single person households 18,440
Persons per household 2.68
Persons per family 3.27

Employed persons 16 years and over by occupation
Managers & professionals 34,475
Service occupations 10,463
Sales & office occupations 25,832
Farming, fishing & forestry 118
Construction & maintenance 5,459
Production & transportation 8,766
Self-employed persons 9,033

Housing
Median val. single fam. home $325,700
Median rent $758

Hawthorne

Population
Total 84,112
Male 40,448
Female 43,664

Race & Hispanic Origin
Race
White 24,618
Black/African American 27,775
North American Native 629
Asian 5,660
Pacific Islander 721
Other Race 20,320
Two or more races 4,389
Hispanic origin, total 37,227
Mexican 22,385
Puerto Rican 687
Cuban 954
Other Hispanic 13,201

Age & Nativity
Under 5 years 8,469
18 years and over 57,485
65 years and over 5,164
85 years and over 492
Median Age 28.7
Native-born 56,031
Foreign-born 27,932

Educational Attainment
Population 25 years and over 48,336
0-8 yrs of school 15.0%
High School grad or higher 66.8%
Bachelor's degree or higher 12.7%
Graduate degree 4.1%

Income & Poverty, 1999
Per capita income $15,022
Median household income $31,887
Median family income $35,149
Persons in poverty 16,870
H'holds receiving public assistance . . . 2,332
H'holds receiving social security 3,798

Households
Total households 28,536
With persons under 18 13,853
With persons over 65 3,894
Family households 19,775
Single person households 6,996
Persons per household 2.93
Persons per family 3.50

Employed persons 16 years and over by occupation
Managers & professionals 7,632
Service occupations 6,366
Sales & office occupations 10,812
Farming, fishing & forestry 51
Construction & maintenance 2,474
Production & transportation 5,468
Self-employed persons 1,530

Housing
Median val. single fam. home $183,700
Median rent $636

Hayward

Population
Total 140,030
Male 69,490
Female 70,540

Race & Hispanic Origin
Race
White 60,146
Black/African American 15,374
North American Native 1,177
Asian 26,579
Pacific Islander 2,679
Other Race 23,539
Two or more races 10,536
Hispanic origin, total 47,850
Mexican 34,035
Puerto Rican 2,177
Cuban 213
Other Hispanic 11,425

Age & Nativity
Under 5 years 11,011
18 years and over 102,531
65 years and over 14,227
85 years and over 1,746
Median Age 31.9
Native-born 91,276
Foreign-born 48,619

Educational Attainment
Population 25 years and over 87,792
0-8 yrs of school 11.3%
High School grad or higher 75.1%
Bachelor's degree or higher 19.9%
Graduate degree 5.4%

Income & Poverty, 1999
Per capita income $19,695
Median household income $51,177
Median family income $54,712
Persons in poverty 13,805
H'holds receiving public assistance . . . 1,910
H'holds receiving social security 9,870

Households
Total households 44,804
With persons under 18 19,045
With persons over 65 9,934
Family households 31,931
Single person households 9,369
Persons per household 3.08
Persons per family 3.58

Employed persons 16 years and over by occupation
Managers & professionals 16,881
Service occupations 8,524
Sales & office occupations 19,001
Farming, fishing & forestry 136
Construction & maintenance 6,912
Production & transportation 11,816
Self-employed persons 2,938

Housing
Median val. single fam. home $237,300
Median rent $921

Note: The 2007 American Community Survey (ACS) collected one-year demographic estimates for cities and counties with populations of at least 65,000 — in California's case, 118 out of 480 municipalities. For those municipalities, ACS data is included in the profiles in order to provide the most current data. However, to allow direct comparisons, data from the 2000 Decennial Census for those municipalities is presented here.

Hemet

Population	
Total	58,812
Male	26,941
Female	31,871
Race & Hispanic Origin	
Race	
White	47,335
Black/African American	1,527
North American Native	708
Asian	872
Pacific Islander	79
Other Race	6,225
Two or more races	2,066
Hispanic origin, total	13,585
Mexican	10,963
Puerto Rican	272
Cuban	68
Other Hispanic	2,282
Age & Nativity	
Under 5 years	3,843
18 years and over	45,543
65 years and over	19,447
85 years and over	3,494
Median Age	44.6
Native-born	51,993
Foreign-born	6,777
Educational Attainment	
Population 25 years and over	41,594
0-8 yrs of school	8.6%
High School grad or higher	73.5%
Bachelor's degree or higher	10.8%
Graduate degree	3.7%
Income & Poverty, 1999	
Per capita income	$16,226
Median household income	$26,839
Median family income	$33,579
Persons in poverty	9,374
H'holds receiving public assistance	1,211
H'holds receiving social security	12,985
Households	
Total households	25,252
With persons under 18	6,402
With persons over 65	12,758
Family households	15,187
Single person households	8,694
Persons per household	2.26
Persons per family	2.90
Employed persons 16 years and over by occupation	
Managers & professionals	3,848
Service occupations	3,587
Sales & office occupations	4,516
Farming, fishing & forestry	231
Construction & maintenance	2,035
Production & transportation	2,741
Self-employed persons	1,332
Housing	
Median val. single fam. home	$93,700
Median rent	$563

Hesperia

Population	
Total	62,582
Male	30,865
Female	31,717
Race & Hispanic Origin	
Race	
White	46,485
Black/African American	2,522
North American Native	796
Asian	670
Pacific Islander	122
Other Race	9,051
Two or more races	2,936
Hispanic origin, total	18,400
Mexican	14,184
Puerto Rican	345
Cuban	189
Other Hispanic	3,682
Age & Nativity	
Under 5 years	4,937
18 years and over	42,086
65 years and over	6,888
85 years and over	637
Median Age	32.0
Native-born	56,465
Foreign-born	6,113
Educational Attainment	
Population 25 years and over	36,550
0-8 yrs of school	8.7%
High School grad or higher	72.6%
Bachelor's degree or higher	8.0%
Graduate degree	2.6%
Income & Poverty, 1999	
Per capita income	$15,487
Median household income	$40,201
Median family income	$43,004
Persons in poverty	8,762
H'holds receiving public assistance	1,586
H'holds receiving social security	5,854
Households	
Total households	19,966
With persons under 18	9,616
With persons over 65	4,920
Family households	15,775
Single person households	3,296
Persons per household	3.12
Persons per family	3.47
Employed persons 16 years and over by occupation	
Managers & professionals	4,707
Service occupations	3,434
Sales & office occupations	5,900
Farming, fishing & forestry	37
Construction & maintenance	3,792
Production & transportation	4,663
Self-employed persons	1,609
Housing	
Median val. single fam. home	$95,900
Median rent	$625

Huntington Beach

Population	
Total	189,594
Male	95,004
Female	94,590
Race & Hispanic Origin	
Race	
White	150,194
Black/African American	1,527
North American Native	1,224
Asian	17,709
Pacific Islander	456
Other Race	11,019
Two or more races	7,465
Hispanic origin, total	27,798
Mexican	20,894
Puerto Rican	629
Cuban	485
Other Hispanic	5,790
Age & Nativity	
Under 5 years	11,728
18 years and over	147,411
65 years and over	19,656
85 years and over	1,953
Median Age	36.0
Native-born	157,785
Foreign-born	32,155
Educational Attainment	
Population 25 years and over	131,982
0-8 yrs of school	3.8%
High School grad or higher	89.6%
Bachelor's degree or higher	36.0%
Graduate degree	12.2%
Income & Poverty, 1999	
Per capita income	$31,964
Median household income	$64,824
Median family income	$74,378
Persons in poverty	12,442
H'holds receiving public assistance	1,480
H'holds receiving social security	14,425
Households	
Total households	73,657
With persons under 18	23,137
With persons over 65	14,304
Family households	47,716
Single person households	17,912
Persons per household	2.56
Persons per family	3.08
Employed persons 16 years and over by occupation	
Managers & professionals	45,285
Service occupations	11,407
Sales & office occupations	30,827
Farming, fishing & forestry	90
Construction & maintenance	7,207
Production & transportation	8,050
Self-employed persons	8,959
Housing	
Median val. single fam. home	$311,800
Median rent	$985

Note: The 2007 American Community Survey (ACS) collected one-year demographic estimates for cities and counties with populations of at least 65,000 — in California's case, 118 out of 480 municipalities. For those municipalities, ACS data is included in the profiles in order to provide the most current data. However, to allow direct comparisons, data from the 2000 Decennial Census for those municipalities is presented here.

Indio

Population

Total	49,116
Male	24,710
Female	24,406

Race & Hispanic Origin

Race	
White	23,903
Black/African American	1,361
North American Native	510
Asian	742
Pacific Islander	49
Other Race	20,638
Two or more races	1,913
Hispanic origin, total	37,028
Mexican	32,985
Puerto Rican	93
Cuban	31
Other Hispanic	3,919

Age & Nativity

Under 5 years	5,100
18 years and over	31,798
65 years and over	4,450
85 years and over	380
Median Age	27.3
Native-born	32,837
Foreign-born	16,322

Educational Attainment

Population 25 years and over	26,303
0-8 yrs of school	23.8%
High School grad or higher	55.7%
Bachelor's degree or higher	8.6%
Graduate degree	3.2%

Income & Poverty, 1999

Per capita income	$13,525
Median household income	$34,624
Median family income	$35,564
Persons in poverty	10,419
H'holds receiving public assistance	891
H'holds receiving social security	3,314

Households

Total households	13,871
With persons under 18	7,615
With persons over 65	3,157
Family households	11,073
Single person households	2,213
Persons per household	3.48
Persons per family	3.88

Employed persons 16 years and over by occupation

Managers & professionals	3,064
Service occupations	5,226
Sales & office occupations	4,043
Farming, fishing & forestry	832
Construction & maintenance	2,760
Production & transportation	1,876
Self-employed persons	1,074

Housing

Median val. single fam. home	$99,000
Median rent	$579

Inglewood

Population

Total	112,580
Male	53,423
Female	59,157

Race & Hispanic Origin

Race	
White	21,505
Black/African American	53,060
North American Native	773
Asian	1,280
Pacific Islander	410
Other Race	30,823
Two or more races	4,729
Hispanic origin, total	51,829
Mexican	37,272
Puerto Rican	454
Cuban	426
Other Hispanic	13,677

Age & Nativity

Under 5 years	10,257
18 years and over	76,143
65 years and over	7,978
85 years and over	879
Median Age	29.6
Native-born	79,280
Foreign-born	33,202

Educational Attainment

Population 25 years and over	64,589
0-8 yrs of school	18.7%
High School grad or higher	63.7%
Bachelor's degree or higher	13.3%
Graduate degree	4.8%

Income & Poverty, 1999

Per capita income	$14,776
Median household income	$34,269
Median family income	$36,541
Persons in poverty	25,007
H'holds receiving public assistance	3,140
H'holds receiving social security	6,399

Households

Total households	36,805
With persons under 18	17,897
With persons over 65	6,142
Family households	25,851
Single person households	9,329
Persons per household	3.02
Persons per family	3.63

Employed persons 16 years and over by occupation

Managers & professionals	10,425
Service occupations	8,707
Sales & office occupations	13,027
Farming, fishing & forestry	84
Construction & maintenance	3,216
Production & transportation	6,916
Self-employed persons	2,585

Housing

Median val. single fam. home	$175,000
Median rent	$673

Irvine

Population

Total	143,072
Male	69,235
Female	73,837

Race & Hispanic Origin

Race	
White	87,354
Black/African American	2,068
North American Native	257
Asian	42,672
Pacific Islander	194
Other Race	3,627
Two or more races	6,900
Hispanic origin, total	10,539
Mexican	6,409
Puerto Rican	351
Cuban	319
Other Hispanic	3,460

Age & Nativity

Under 5 years	7,997
18 years and over	109,517
65 years and over	10,302
85 years and over	1,104
Median Age	33.1
Native-born	97,157
Foreign-born	45,877

Educational Attainment

Population 25 years and over	88,960
0-8 yrs of school	1.8%
High School grad or higher	95.3%
Bachelor's degree or higher	58.4%
Graduate degree	24.2%

Income & Poverty, 1999

Per capita income	$32,196
Median household income	$72,057
Median family income	$85,624
Persons in poverty	12,379
H'holds receiving public assistance	531
H'holds receiving social security	6,860

Households

Total households	51,199
With persons under 18	19,207
With persons over 65	7,764
Family households	34,380
Single person households	11,650
Persons per household	2.66
Persons per family	3.17

Employed persons 16 years and over by occupation

Managers & professionals	42,523
Service occupations	5,565
Sales & office occupations	20,696
Farming, fishing & forestry	44
Construction & maintenance	1,738
Production & transportation	3,141
Self-employed persons	6,548

Housing

Median val. single fam. home	$316,800
Median rent	$1,272

Note: The 2007 American Community Survey (ACS) collected one-year demographic estimates for cities and counties with populations of at least 65,000 — in California's case, 118 out of 480 municipalities. For those municipalities, ACS data is included in the profiles in order to provide the most current data. However, to allow direct comparisons, data from the 2000 Decennial Census for those municipalities is presented here.

Lake Forest

Population

Total . . . 58,707
Male . . . 28,863
Female . . . 29,844

Race & Hispanic Origin

Race
White . . . 44,629
Black/African American . . . 1,073
North American Native . . . 295
Asian . . . 5,693
Pacific Islander . . . 120
Other Race . . . 4,408
Two or more races . . . 2,489
Hispanic origin, total . . . 10,913
Mexican . . . 7,789
Puerto Rican . . . 208
Cuban . . . 148
Other Hispanic . . . 2,768

Age & Nativity

Under 5 years . . . 4,143
18 years and over . . . 42,884
65 years and over . . . 5,051
85 years and over . . . 1,033
Median Age . . . 35.1
Native-born . . . 46,383
Foreign-born . . . 12,423

Educational Attainment

Population 25 years and over . . . 38,060
0-8 yrs of school . . . 5.3%
High School grad or higher . . . 88.7%
Bachelor's degree or higher . . . 33.9%
Graduate degree . . . 9.8%

Income & Poverty, 1999

Per capita income . . . $28,583
Median household income . . . $67,967
Median family income . . . $75,121
Persons in poverty . . . 3,093
H'holds receiving public assistance . . . 227
H'holds receiving social security . . . 3,169

Households

Total households . . . 20,008
With persons under 18 . . . 8,382
With persons over 65 . . . 3,306
Family households . . . 14,741
Single person households . . . 3,881
Persons per household . . . 2.89
Persons per family . . . 3.31

Employed persons 16 years and over by occupation

Managers & professionals . . . 12,920
Service occupations . . . 3,709
Sales & office occupations . . . 10,359
Farming, fishing & forestry . . . 26
Construction & maintenance . . . 1,859
Production & transportation . . . 2,409
Self-employed persons . . . 2,462

Housing

Median val. single fam. home . . . $278,000
Median rent . . . $1,085

Lakewood

Population

Total . . . 79,345
Male . . . 38,421
Female . . . 40,924

Race & Hispanic Origin

Race
White . . . 49,724
Black/African American . . . 5,825
North American Native . . . 473
Asian . . . 10,716
Pacific Islander . . . 489
Other Race . . . 8,012
Two or more races . . . 4,106
Hispanic origin, total . . . 18,071
Mexican . . . 13,506
Puerto Rican . . . 466
Cuban . . . 311
Other Hispanic . . . 3,788

Age & Nativity

Under 5 years . . . 5,619
18 years and over . . . 57,487
65 years and over . . . 9,414
85 years and over . . . 828
Median Age . . . 35.3
Native-born . . . 64,287
Foreign-born . . . 15,125

Educational Attainment

Population 25 years and over . . . 51,138
0-8 yrs of school . . . 5.4%
High School grad or higher . . . 85.1%
Bachelor's degree or higher . . . 20.7%
Graduate degree . . . 5.1%

Income & Poverty, 1999

Per capita income . . . $22,095
Median household income . . . $58,214
Median family income . . . $63,342
Persons in poverty . . . 5,820
H'holds receiving public assistance . . . 859
H'holds receiving social security . . . 6,768

Households

Total households . . . 26,853
With persons under 18 . . . 11,502
With persons over 65 . . . 6,903
Family households . . . 20,550
Single person households . . . 4,950
Persons per household . . . 2.95
Persons per family . . . 3.37

Employed persons 16 years and over by occupation

Managers & professionals . . . 12,718
Service occupations . . . 4,832
Sales & office occupations . . . 11,190
Farming, fishing & forestry . . . 0
Construction & maintenance . . . 3,765
Production & transportation . . . 4,846
Self-employed persons . . . 2,193

Housing

Median val. single fam. home . . . $202,800
Median rent . . . $886

Lancaster

Population

Total . . . 118,718
Male . . . 60,257
Female . . . 58,461

Race & Hispanic Origin

Race
White . . . 74,573
Black/African American . . . 19,009
North American Native . . . 1,213
Asian . . . 4,523
Pacific Islander . . . 278
Other Race . . . 13,190
Two or more races . . . 5,932
Hispanic origin, total . . . 28,644
Mexican . . . 20,120
Puerto Rican . . . 718
Cuban . . . 263
Other Hispanic . . . 7,543

Age & Nativity

Under 5 years . . . 9,544
18 years and over . . . 80,329
65 years and over . . . 10,201
85 years and over . . . 1,173
Median Age . . . 31.1
Native-born . . . 103,307
Foreign-born . . . 15,476

Educational Attainment

Population 25 years and over . . . 69,282
0-8 yrs of school . . . 6.0%
High School grad or higher . . . 78.3%
Bachelor's degree or higher . . . 15.8%
Graduate degree . . . 5.6%

Income & Poverty, 1999

Per capita income . . . $16,935
Median household income . . . $41,127
Median family income . . . $44,681
Persons in poverty . . . 18,239
H'holds receiving public assistance . . . 3,531
H'holds receiving social security . . . 8,131

Households

Total households . . . 38,224
With persons under 18 . . . 18,004
With persons over 65 . . . 7,232
Family households . . . 27,684
Single person households . . . 8,437
Persons per household . . . 2.92
Persons per family . . . 3.41

Employed persons 16 years and over by occupation

Managers & professionals . . . 13,948
Service occupations . . . 7,517
Sales & office occupations . . . 11,297
Farming, fishing & forestry . . . 63
Construction & maintenance . . . 4,965
Production & transportation . . . 5,388
Self-employed persons . . . 2,482

Housing

Median val. single fam. home . . . $103,700
Median rent . . . $643

Note: The 2007 American Community Survey (ACS) collected one-year demographic estimates for cities and counties with populations of at least 65,000 — in California's case, 118 out of 480 municipalities. For those municipalities, ACS data is included in the profiles in order to provide the most current data. However, to allow direct comparisons, data from the 2000 Decennial Census for those municipalities is presented here.

Livermore

Population

Total . . . 73,345
Male . . . 36,664
Female . . . 36,681

Race & Hispanic Origin

Race
White . . . 60,070
Black/African American . . . 1,148
North American Native . . . 444
Asian . . . 4,251
Pacific Islander . . . 208
Other Race . . . 3,915
Two or more races . . . 3,309
Hispanic origin, total . . . 10,541
Mexican . . . 7,573
Puerto Rican . . . 386
Cuban . . . 63
Other Hispanic . . . 2,519

Age & Nativity

Under 5 years . . . 5,650
18 years and over . . . 52,705
65 years and over . . . 5,516
85 years and over . . . 562
Median Age . . . 35.0
Native-born . . . 64,484
Foreign-born . . . 8,952

Educational Attainment

Population 25 years and over . . . 47,453
0-8 yrs of school . . . 3.8%
High School grad or higher . . . 89.6%
Bachelor's degree or higher . . . 31.6%
Graduate degree . . . 11.5%

Income & Poverty, 1999

Per capita income . . . $31,062
Median household income . . . $75,322
Median family income . . . $82,421
Persons in poverty . . . 3,891
H'holds receiving public assistance . . . 552
H'holds receiving social security . . . 4,109

Households

Total households . . . 26,123
With persons under 18 . . . 11,197
With persons over 65 . . . 3,982
Family households . . . 19,512
Single person households . . . 4,915
Persons per household . . . 2.80
Persons per family . . . 3.20

Employed persons 16 years and over by occupation

Managers & professionals . . . 16,094
Service occupations . . . 4,792
Sales & office occupations . . . 10,007
Farming, fishing & forestry . . . 45
Construction & maintenance . . . 3,981
Production & transportation . . . 3,606
Self-employed persons . . . 2,453

Housing

Median val. single fam. home . . . $314,600
Median rent . . . $1,035

Long Beach

Population

Total . . . 461,522
Male . . . 226,718
Female . . . 234,804

Race & Hispanic Origin

Race
White . . . 208,410
Black/African American . . . 68,618
North American Native . . . 3,881
Asian . . . 55,591
Pacific Islander . . . 5,605
Other Race . . . 95,107
Two or more races . . . 24,310
Hispanic origin, total . . . 165,092
Mexican . . . 127,129
Puerto Rican . . . 2,339
Cuban . . . 1,067
Other Hispanic . . . 34,557

Age & Nativity

Under 5 years . . . 38,587
18 years and over . . . 326,883
65 years and over . . . 41,902
85 years and over . . . 5,621
Median Age . . . 30.8
Native-born . . . 329,213
Foreign-born . . . 132,168

Educational Attainment

Population 25 years and over . . . 277,410
0-8 yrs of school . . . 14.2%
High School grad or higher . . . 72.7%
Bachelor's degree or higher . . . 23.9%
Graduate degree . . . 8.2%

Income & Poverty, 1999

Per capita income . . . $19,040
Median household income . . . $37,270
Median family income . . . $40,002
Persons in poverty . . . 103,434
H'holds receiving public assistance . . 14,433
H'holds receiving social security . . . 28,974

Households

Total households . . . 163,088
With persons under 18 . . . 63,346
With persons over 65 . . . 29,901
Family households . . . 99,663
Single person households . . . 48,207
Persons per household . . . 2.77
Persons per family . . . 3.55

Employed persons 16 years and over by occupation

Managers & professionals . . . 65,060
Service occupations . . . 30,019
Sales & office occupations . . . 51,516
Farming, fishing & forestry . . . 276
Construction & maintenance . . . 14,649
Production & transportation . . . 27,967
Self-employed persons . . . 12,304

Housing

Median val. single fam. home . . . $210,000
Median rent . . . $639

Los Angeles

Population

Total . . . 3,694,820
Male . . . 1,841,805
Female . . . 1,853,015

Race & Hispanic Origin

Race
White . . . 1,734,036
Black/African American . . . 415,195
North American Native . . . 29,412
Asian . . . 369,254
Pacific Islander . . . 5,915
Other Race . . . 949,720
Two or more races . . . 191,288
Hispanic origin, total . . . 1,719,073
Mexican . . . 1,091,686
Puerto Rican . . . 13,427
Cuban . . . 12,431
Other Hispanic . . . 601,529

Age & Nativity

Under 5 years . . . 285,976
18 years and over . . . 2,713,509
65 years and over . . . 357,129
85 years and over . . . 44,189
Median Age . . . 31.6
Native-born . . . 2,182,114
Foreign-born . . . 1,512,720

Educational Attainment

Population 25 years and over . . . 2,308,887
0-8 yrs of school . . . 19.0%
High School grad or higher . . . 66.6%
Bachelor's degree or higher . . . 25.5%
Graduate degree . . . 9.1%

Income & Poverty, 1999

Per capita income . . . $20,671
Median household income . . . $36,687
Median family income . . . $39,942
Persons in poverty . . . 801,050
H'holds receiving public assistance . . 88,017
H'holds receiving social security . . . 234,939

Households

Total households . . . 1,275,412
With persons under 18 . . . 478,946
With persons over 65 . . . 262,689
Family households . . . 798,719
Single person households . . . 363,457
Persons per household . . . 2.83
Persons per family . . . 3.56

Employed persons 16 years and over by occupation

Managers & professionals . . . 524,440
Service occupations . . . 245,498
Sales & office occupations . . . 409,696
Farming, fishing & forestry . . . 2,511
Construction & maintenance . . . 117,561
Production & transportation . . . 232,368
Self-employed persons . . . 153,551

Housing

Median val. single fam. home . . . $221,600
Median rent . . . $672

Note: The 2007 American Community Survey (ACS) collected one-year demographic estimates for cities and counties with populations of at least 65,000 — in California's case, 118 out of 480 municipalities. For those municipalities, ACS data is included in the profiles in order to provide the most current data. However, to allow direct comparisons, data from the 2000 Decennial Census for those municipalities is presented here.

Lynwood

Item	Value
Population	
Total	69,845
Male	35,702
Female	34,143
Race & Hispanic Origin	
Race	
White	23,481
Black/African American	9,451
North American Native	839
Asian	533
Pacific Islander	269
Other Race	32,225
Two or more races	3,047
Hispanic origin, total	57,503
Mexican	46,491
Puerto Rican	173
Cuban	94
Other Hispanic	10,745
Age & Nativity	
Under 5 years	7,401
18 years and over	43,276
65 years and over	2,931
85 years and over	344
Median Age	24.4
Native-born	39,424
Foreign-born	30,475
Educational Attainment	
Population 25 years and over	34,029
0-8 yrs of school	37.1%
High School grad or higher	38.5%
Bachelor's degree or higher	4.5%
Graduate degree	1.8%
Income & Poverty, 1999	
Per capita income	$9,542
Median household income	$35,888
Median family income	$35,808
Persons in poverty	15,850
H'holds receiving public assistance	1,790
H'holds receiving social security	1,776
Households	
Total households	14,395
With persons under 18	10,447
With persons over 65	2,070
Family households	12,943
Single person households	1,109
Persons per household	4.70
Persons per family	4.76
Employed persons 16 years and over by occupation	
Managers & professionals	2,630
Service occupations	3,219
Sales & office occupations	5,451
Farming, fishing & forestry	85
Construction & maintenance	2,236
Production & transportation	7,377
Self-employed persons	1,130
Housing	
Median val. single fam. home	$146,700
Median rent	$629

Merced

Item	Value
Population	
Total	63,893
Male	31,226
Female	32,667
Race & Hispanic Origin	
Race	
White	33,481
Black/African American	4,044
North American Native	818
Asian	7,267
Pacific Islander	133
Other Race	14,813
Two or more races	3,337
Hispanic origin, total	26,425
Mexican	22,616
Puerto Rican	200
Cuban	44
Other Hispanic	3,565
Age & Nativity	
Under 5 years	5,860
18 years and over	41,732
65 years and over	6,021
85 years and over	798
Median Age	27.8
Native-born	49,839
Foreign-born	14,152
Educational Attainment	
Population 25 years and over	34,422
0-8 yrs of school	18.1%
High School grad or higher	68.5%
Bachelor's degree or higher	13.6%
Graduate degree	4.8%
Income & Poverty, 1999	
Per capita income	$13,115
Median household income	$30,429
Median family income	$32,470
Persons in poverty	17,489
H'holds receiving public assistance	2,675
H'holds receiving social security	4,783
Households	
Total households	20,435
With persons under 18	9,652
With persons over 65	4,387
Family households	14,632
Single person households	4,626
Persons per household	3.06
Persons per family	3.62
Employed persons 16 years and over by occupation	
Managers & professionals	6,093
Service occupations	4,041
Sales & office occupations	5,552
Farming, fishing & forestry	981
Construction & maintenance	2,148
Production & transportation	3,452
Self-employed persons	1,402
Housing	
Median val. single fam. home	$106,400
Median rent	$509

Milpitas

Item	Value
Population	
Total	62,698
Male	32,960
Female	29,738
Race & Hispanic Origin	
Race	
White	19,353
Black/African American	2,295
North American Native	388
Asian	32,482
Pacific Islander	393
Other Race	4,687
Two or more races	3,100
Hispanic origin, total	10,417
Mexican	8,132
Puerto Rican	221
Cuban	53
Other Hispanic	2,011
Age & Nativity	
Under 5 years	4,484
18 years and over	47,261
65 years and over	4,411
85 years and over	293
Median Age	33.4
Native-born	33,068
Foreign-born	29,646
Educational Attainment	
Population 25 years and over	41,089
0-8 yrs of school	36.5%
High School grad or higher	7.9%
Bachelor's degree or higher	83.2%
Graduate degree	12.2%
Income & Poverty, 1999	
Per capita income	$27,823
Median household income	$84,429
Median family income	$84,827
Persons in poverty	2,983
H'holds receiving public assistance	437
H'holds receiving social security	2,466
Households	
Total households	17,132
With persons under 18	8,315
With persons over 65	3,277
Family households	14,002
Single person households	1,970
Persons per household	3.47
Persons per family	3.72
Employed persons 16 years and over by occupation	
Managers & professionals	13,781
Service occupations	2,527
Sales & office occupations	7,031
Farming, fishing & forestry	130
Construction & maintenance	1,849
Production & transportation	4,984
Self-employed persons	1,278
Housing	
Median val. single fam. home	$372,900
Median rent	$1,279

Note: The 2007 American Community Survey (ACS) collected one-year demographic estimates for cities and counties with populations of at least 65,000 — in California's case, 118 out of 480 municipalities. For those municipalities, ACS data is included in the profiles in order to provide the most current data. However, to allow direct comparisons, data from the 2000 Decennial Census for those municipalities is presented here.

Mission Viejo

Population

Total . . . 93,102
Male . . . 45,525
Female . . . 47,577

Race & Hispanic Origin

Race
White . . . 77,418
Black/African American . . . 1,067
North American Native . . . 348
Asian . . . 7,199
Pacific Islander . . . 174
Other Race . . . 3,553
Two or more races . . . 3,343
Hispanic origin, total . . . 11,266
Mexican . . . 7,400
Puerto Rican . . . 301
Cuban . . . 245
Other Hispanic . . . 3,320

Age & Nativity

Under 5 years . . . 6,428
18 years and over . . . 67,829
65 years and over . . . 10,139
85 years and over . . . 1,345
Median Age . . . 37.5
Native-born . . . 77,489
Foreign-born . . . 15,291

Educational Attainment

Population 25 years and over . . . 61,480
0-8 yrs of school . . . 2.0%
High School grad or higher . . . 93.8%
Bachelor's degree or higher . . . 41.2%
Graduate degree . . . 12.9%

Income & Poverty, 1999

Per capita income . . . $33,302
Median household income . . . $78,248
Median family income . . . $86,902
Persons in poverty . . . 3,480
H'holds receiving public assistance . . . 371
H'holds receiving social security . . . 6,717

Households

Total households . . . 32,449
With persons under 18 . . . 13,568
With persons over 65 . . . 6,665
Family households . . . 25,204
Single person households . . . 5,599
Persons per household . . . 2.84
Persons per family . . . 3.22

Employed persons 16 years and over by occupation

Managers & professionals . . . 21,903
Service occupations . . . 4,822
Sales & office occupations . . . 14,688
Farming, fishing & forestry . . . 18
Construction & maintenance . . . 2,398
Production & transportation . . . 3,029
Self-employed persons . . . 4,051

Housing

Median val. single fam. home . . . $293,300
Median rent . . . $1,145

Modesto

Population

Total . . . 188,856
Male . . . 91,572
Female . . . 97,284

Race & Hispanic Origin

Race
White . . . 131,414
Black/African American . . . 7,499
North American Native . . . 2,335
Asian . . . 11,388
Pacific Islander . . . 951
Other Race . . . 24,066
Two or more races . . . 11,203
Hispanic origin, total . . . 48,310
Mexican . . . 38,819
Puerto Rican . . . 1,049
Cuban . . . 153
Other Hispanic . . . 8,289

Age & Nativity

Under 5 years . . . 14,335
18 years and over . . . 132,071
65 years and over . . . 20,962
85 years and over . . . 2,796
Median Age . . . 32.7
Native-born . . . 159,595
Foreign-born . . . 29,865

Educational Attainment

Population 25 years and over . . . 114,658
0-8 yrs of school . . . 10.1%
High School grad or higher . . . 75.0%
Bachelor's degree or higher . . . 16.5%
Graduate degree . . . 5.3%

Income & Poverty, 1999

Per capita income . . . $17,797
Median household income . . . $40,394
Median family income . . . $45,681
Persons in poverty . . . 29,363
H'holds receiving public assistance . . . 4,046
H'holds receiving social security . . . 16,184

Households

Total households . . . 64,959
With persons under 18 . . . 27,845
With persons over 65 . . . 14,547
Family households . . . 46,642
Single person households . . . 14,633
Persons per household . . . 2.86
Persons per family . . . 3.36

Employed persons 16 years and over by occupation

Managers & professionals . . . 21,760
Service occupations . . . 12,206
Sales & office occupations . . . 21,200
Farming, fishing & forestry . . . 973
Construction & maintenance . . . 8,079
Production & transportation . . . 12,349
Self-employed persons . . . 5,702

Housing

Median val. single fam. home . . . $126,000
Median rent . . . $639

Moreno Valley

Population

Total . . . 142,381
Male . . . 69,645
Female . . . 72,736

Race & Hispanic Origin

Race
White . . . 66,689
Black/African American . . . 28,310
North American Native . . . 1,343
Asian . . . 8,427
Pacific Islander . . . 733
Other Race . . . 28,584
Two or more races . . . 8,295
Hispanic origin, total . . . 54,689
Mexican . . . 43,485
Puerto Rican . . . 1,177
Cuban . . . 417
Other Hispanic . . . 9,610

Age & Nativity

Under 5 years . . . 12,519
18 years and over . . . 89,969
65 years and over . . . 7,809
85 years and over . . . 510
Median Age . . . 27.1
Native-born . . . 114,063
Foreign-born . . . 28,485

Educational Attainment

Population 25 years and over . . . 74,976
0-8 yrs of school . . . 10.8%
High School grad or higher . . . 74.5%
Bachelor's degree or higher . . . 14.0%
Graduate degree . . . 4.6%

Income & Poverty, 1999

Per capita income . . . $14,983
Median household income . . . $47,387
Median family income . . . $48,965
Persons in poverty . . . 20,141
H'holds receiving public assistance . . . 2,641
H'holds receiving social security . . . 6,454

Households

Total households . . . 39,225
With persons under 18 . . . 23,674
With persons over 65 . . . 5,864
Family households . . . 33,363
Single person households . . . 4,314
Persons per household . . . 3.61
Persons per family . . . 3.86

Employed persons 16 years and over by occupation

Managers & professionals . . . 14,206
Service occupations . . . 8,408
Sales & office occupations . . . 17,328
Farming, fishing & forestry . . . 205
Construction & maintenance . . . 6,377
Production & transportation . . . 9,905
Self-employed persons . . . 3,430

Housing

Median val. single fam. home . . . $118,900
Median rent . . . $743

Note: The 2007 American Community Survey (ACS) collected one-year demographic estimates for cities and counties with populations of at least 65,000 — in California's case, 118 out of 480 municipalities. For those municipalities, ACS data is included in the profiles in order to provide the most current data. However, to allow direct comparisons, data from the 2000 Decennial Census for those municipalities is presented here.

Mountain View

Population	
Total	70,708
Male	36,523
Female	34,185
Race & Hispanic Origin	
Race	
White	45,090
Black/African American	1,789
North American Native	273
Asian	14,613
Pacific Islander	182
Other Race	5,884
Two or more races	2,877
Hispanic origin, total	12,911
Mexican	9,243
Puerto Rican	282
Cuban	88
Other Hispanic	3,298
Age & Nativity	
Under 5 years	4,270
18 years and over	58,012
65 years and over	7,416
85 years and over	899
Median Age	34.6
Native-born	45,806
Foreign-born	24,661
Educational Attainment	
Population 25 years and over	52,353
0-8 yrs of school	5.3%
High School grad or higher	89.0%
Bachelor's degree or higher	55.3%
Graduate degree	25.5%
Income & Poverty, 1999	
Per capita income	$39,693
Median household income	$69,362
Median family income	$80,379
Persons in poverty	4,749
H'holds receiving public assistance	441
H'holds receiving social security	4,760
Households	
Total households	31,242
With persons under 18	7,396
With persons over 65	5,344
Family households	15,909
Single person households	11,133
Persons per household	2.25
Persons per family	2.97
Employed persons 16 years and over by occupation	
Managers & professionals	25,711
Service occupations	3,846
Sales & office occupations	7,376
Farming, fishing & forestry	109
Construction & maintenance	1,698
Production & transportation	2,386
Self-employed persons	2,580
Housing	
Median val. single fam. home	$546,900
Median rent	$1,222

Murrieta

Population	
Total	44,282
Male	21,704
Female	22,578
Race & Hispanic Origin	
Race	
White	36,152
Black/African American	1,500
North American Native	293
Asian	1,775
Pacific Islander	98
Other Race	2,553
Two or more races	1,911
Hispanic origin, total	7,739
Mexican	5,790
Puerto Rican	252
Cuban	128
Other Hispanic	1,569
Age & Nativity	
Under 5 years	3,338
18 years and over	29,363
65 years and over	5,063
85 years and over	343
Median Age	34.4
Native-born	40,521
Foreign-born	3,829
Educational Attainment	
Population 25 years and over	26,664
0-8 yrs of school	2.7%
High School grad or higher	90.0%
Bachelor's degree or higher	23.0%
Graduate degree	7.4%
Income & Poverty, 1999	
Per capita income	$23,290
Median household income	$60,911
Median family income	$65,904
Persons in poverty	1,915
H'holds receiving public assistance	172
H'holds receiving social security	3,488
Households	
Total households	14,320
With persons under 18	7,222
With persons over 65	3,421
Family households	11,706
Single person households	2,072
Persons per household	3.08
Persons per family	3.42
Employed persons 16 years and over by occupation	
Managers & professionals	6,529
Service occupations	2,700
Sales & office occupations	5,692
Farming, fishing & forestry	33
Construction & maintenance	1,907
Production & transportation	1,989
Self-employed persons	1,861
Housing	
Median val. single fam. home	$190,700
Median rent	$842

Napa

Population	
Total	72,585
Male	35,635
Female	36,950
Race & Hispanic Origin	
Race	
White	58,302
Black/African American	381
North American Native	657
Asian	1,241
Pacific Islander	117
Other Race	9,181
Two or more races	2,706
Hispanic origin, total	19,475
Mexican	16,889
Puerto Rican	177
Cuban	52
Other Hispanic	2,357
Age & Nativity	
Under 5 years	4,906
18 years and over	53,915
65 years and over	10,037
85 years and over	1,675
Median Age	36.1
Native-born	58,708
Foreign-born	14,073
Educational Attainment	
Population 25 years and over	48,000
0-8 yrs of school	11.1%
High School grad or higher	79.2%
Bachelor's degree or higher	23.3%
Graduate degree	8.3%
Income & Poverty, 1999	
Per capita income	$23,642
Median household income	$49,154
Median family income	$58,788
Persons in poverty	6,398
H'holds receiving public assistance	751
H'holds receiving social security	7,382
Households	
Total households	26,978
With persons under 18	9,671
With persons over 65	7,099
Family households	17,940
Single person households	7,229
Persons per household	2.64
Persons per family	3.20
Employed persons 16 years and over by occupation	
Managers & professionals	11,258
Service occupations	6,386
Sales & office occupations	8,250
Farming, fishing & forestry	1,006
Construction & maintenance	3,294
Production & transportation	4,184
Self-employed persons	3,018
Housing	
Median val. single fam. home	$238,300
Median rent	$819

Note: The 2007 American Community Survey (ACS) collected one-year demographic estimates for cities and counties with populations of at least 65,000 — in California's case, 118 out of 480 municipalities. For those municipalities, ACS data is included in the profiles in order to provide the most current data. However, to allow direct comparisons, data from the 2000 Decennial Census for those municipalities is presented here.

Newport Beach

Population

Total ... 70,032
Male ... 34,638
Female ... 35,394

Race & Hispanic Origin

Race
White ... 64,583
Black/African American ... 371
North American Native ... 179
Asian ... 2,804
Pacific Islander ... 83
Other Race ... 792
Two or more races ... 1,220
Hispanic origin, total ... 3,301
Mexican ... 2,016
Puerto Rican ... 120
Cuban ... 108
Other Hispanic ... 1,057

Age & Nativity

Under 5 years ... 2,832
18 years and over ... 59,018
65 years and over ... 12,295
85 years and over ... 1,483
Median Age ... 41.6
Native-born ... 62,517
Foreign-born ... 7,505

Educational Attainment

Population 25 years and over ... 54,755
0-8 yrs of school ... 0.7%
High School grad or higher ... 96.7%
Bachelor's degree or higher ... 58.5%
Graduate degree ... 21.4%

Income & Poverty, 1999

Per capita income ... $63,015
Median household income ... $83,455
Median family income ... $111,166
Persons in poverty ... 3,075
H'holds receiving public assistance ... 291
H'holds receiving social security ... 8,285

Households

Total households ... 33,071
With persons under 18 ... 6,271
With persons over 65 ... 8,556
Family households ... 16,979
Single person households ... 11,666
Persons per household ... 2.09
Persons per family ... 2.71

Employed persons 16 years and over by occupation

Managers & professionals ... 22,070
Service occupations ... 2,806
Sales & office occupations ... 11,143
Farming, fishing & forestry ... 29
Construction & maintenance ... 1,032
Production & transportation ... 1,236
Self-employed persons ... 5,018

Housing

Median val. single fam. home ... $708,200
Median rent ... $1,257

Norwalk

Population

Total ... 103,298
Male ... 51,109
Female ... 52,189

Race & Hispanic Origin

Race
White ... 46,303
Black/African American ... 4,774
North American Native ... 1,201
Asian ... 11,924
Pacific Islander ... 404
Other Race ... 33,829
Two or more races ... 4,863
Hispanic origin, total ... 64,965
Mexican ... 52,652
Puerto Rican ... 480
Cuban ... 332
Other Hispanic ... 11,501

Age & Nativity

Under 5 years ... 8,935
18 years and over ... 70,117
65 years and over ... 9,312
85 years and over ... 794
Median Age ... 29.7
Native-born ... 65,642
Foreign-born ... 37,581

Educational Attainment

Population 25 years and over ... 59,257
0-8 yrs of school ... 18.5%
High School grad or higher ... 63.0%
Bachelor's degree or higher ... 10.6%
Graduate degree ... 2.5%

Income & Poverty, 1999

Per capita income ... $14,022
Median household income ... $46,047
Median family income ... $47,524
Persons in poverty ... 12,058
H'holds receiving public assistance ... 1,658
H'holds receiving social security ... 6,029

Households

Total households ... 26,887
With persons under 18 ... 14,828
With persons over 65 ... 6,578
Family households ... 22,522
Single person households ... 3,416
Persons per household ... 3.79
Persons per family ... 4.08

Employed persons 16 years and over by occupation

Managers & professionals ... 8,267
Service occupations ... 5,871
Sales & office occupations ... 11,753
Farming, fishing & forestry ... 36
Construction & maintenance ... 4,193
Production & transportation ... 9,111
Self-employed persons ... 2,145

Housing

Median val. single fam. home ... $161,100
Median rent ... $767

Oakland

Population

Total ... 399,484
Male ... 192,757
Female ... 206,727

Race & Hispanic Origin

Race
White ... 125,013
Black/African American ... 142,460
North American Native ... 2,655
Asian ... 60,851
Pacific Islander ... 2,002
Other Race ... 46,592
Two or more races ... 19,911
Hispanic origin, total ... 87,467
Mexican ... 65,094
Puerto Rican ... 2,325
Cuban ... 581
Other Hispanic ... 19,467

Age & Nativity

Under 5 years ... 28,292
18 years and over ... 299,725
65 years and over ... 41,788
85 years and over ... 5,981
Median Age ... 33.3
Native-born ... 293,361
Foreign-born ... 106,116

Educational Attainment

Population 25 years and over ... 261,402
0-8 yrs of school ... 13.3%
High School grad or higher ... 73.9%
Bachelor's degree or higher ... 30.9%
Graduate degree ... 12.9%

Income & Poverty, 1999

Per capita income ... $21,936
Median household income ... $40,055
Median family income ... $44,384
Persons in poverty ... 76,489
H'holds receiving public assistance ... 11,930
H'holds receiving social security ... 29,624

Households

Total households ... 150,790
With persons under 18 ... 50,511
With persons over 65 ... 31,587
Family households ... 86,347
Single person households ... 48,952
Persons per household ... 2.60
Persons per family ... 3.38

Employed persons 16 years and over by occupation

Managers & professionals ... 68,465
Service occupations ... 27,570
Sales & office occupations ... 43,913
Farming, fishing & forestry ... 338
Construction & maintenance ... 12,885
Production & transportation ... 21,572
Self-employed persons ... 14,362

Housing

Median val. single fam. home ... $235,500
Median rent ... $696

Note: The 2007 American Community Survey (ACS) collected one-year demographic estimates for cities and counties with populations of at least 65,000 — in California's case, 118 out of 480 municipalities. For those municipalities, ACS data is included in the profiles in order to provide the most current data. However, to allow direct comparisons, data from the 2000 Decennial Census for those municipalities is presented here.

Oceanside

Item	Value
Population	
Total	161,029
Male	79,719
Female	81,310
Race & Hispanic Origin	
Race	
White	106,866
Black/African American	10,189
North American Native	1,370
Asian	8,896
Pacific Islander	2,042
Other Race	23,342
Two or more races	8,324
Hispanic origin, total	48,691
Mexican	40,729
Puerto Rican	1,306
Cuban	206
Other Hispanic	6,450
Age & Nativity	
Under 5 years	12,194
18 years and over	116,573
65 years and over	21,859
85 years and over	2,177
Median Age	33.3
Native-born	127,940
Foreign-born	32,965
Educational Attainment	
Population 25 years and over	100,688
0-8 yrs of school	9.6%
High School grad or higher	80.8%
Bachelor's degree or higher	22.2%
Graduate degree	7.3%
Income & Poverty, 1999	
Per capita income	$20,329
Median household income	$46,301
Median family income	$52,232
Persons in poverty	18,492
H'holds receiving public assistance	1,657
H'holds receiving social security	15,812
Households	
Total households	56,488
With persons under 18	21,790
With persons over 65	15,479
Family households	39,285
Single person households	12,834
Persons per household	2.83
Persons per family	3.33
Employed persons 16 years and over by occupation	
Managers & professionals	21,439
Service occupations	11,653
Sales & office occupations	18,745
Farming, fishing & forestry	678
Construction & maintenance	6,195
Production & transportation	9,353
Self-employed persons	5,691
Housing	
Median val. single fam. home	$195,800
Median rent	$818

Ontario

Item	Value
Population	
Total	158,007
Male	79,225
Female	78,782
Race & Hispanic Origin	
Race	
White	75,575
Black/African American	11,864
North American Native	1,682
Asian	6,125
Pacific Islander	587
Other Race	53,807
Two or more races	8,367
Hispanic origin, total	94,610
Mexican	77,476
Puerto Rican	717
Cuban	401
Other Hispanic	16,016
Age & Nativity	
Under 5 years	15,338
18 years and over	103,703
65 years and over	9,322
85 years and over	1,048
Median Age	27.6
Native-born	108,550
Foreign-born	48,789
Educational Attainment	
Population 25 years and over	85,671
0-8 yrs of school	19.8%
High School grad or higher	62.5%
Bachelor's degree or higher	10.5%
Graduate degree	2.7%
Income & Poverty, 1999	
Per capita income	$14,244
Median household income	$42,452
Median family income	$44,031
Persons in poverty	24,133
H'holds receiving public assistance	2,632
H'holds receiving social security	7,524
Households	
Total households	43,525
With persons under 18	24,321
With persons over 65	6,947
Family households	34,699
Single person households	6,583
Persons per household	3.60
Persons per family	3.96
Employed persons 16 years and over by occupation	
Managers & professionals	12,927
Service occupations	9,456
Sales & office occupations	16,874
Farming, fishing & forestry	943
Construction & maintenance	7,218
Production & transportation	14,999
Self-employed persons	3,261
Housing	
Median val. single fam. home	$140,000
Median rent	$720

Orange

Item	Value
Population	
Total	128,821
Male	64,665
Female	64,156
Race & Hispanic Origin	
Race	
White	90,822
Black/African American	2,056
North American Native	1,010
Asian	12,000
Pacific Islander	296
Other Race	17,804
Two or more races	4,833
Hispanic origin, total	41,434
Mexican	34,329
Puerto Rican	338
Cuban	272
Other Hispanic	6,495
Age & Nativity	
Under 5 years	9,533
18 years and over	94,480
65 years and over	12,409
85 years and over	1,381
Median Age	33.2
Native-born	96,141
Foreign-born	32,297
Educational Attainment	
Population 25 years and over	82,138
0-8 yrs of school	9.7%
High School grad or higher	80.4%
Bachelor's degree or higher	28.0%
Graduate degree	9.5%
Income & Poverty, 1999	
Per capita income	$24,294
Median household income	$58,994
Median family income	$64,573
Persons in poverty	12,404
H'holds receiving public assistance	1,057
H'holds receiving social security	8,211
Households	
Total households	40,930
With persons under 18	16,711
With persons over 65	8,568
Family households	30,168
Single person households	7,964
Persons per household	3.02
Persons per family	3.43
Employed persons 16 years and over by occupation	
Managers & professionals	22,816
Service occupations	8,416
Sales & office occupations	18,290
Farming, fishing & forestry	129
Construction & maintenance	4,998
Production & transportation	6,971
Self-employed persons	5,360
Housing	
Median val. single fam. home	$256,600
Median rent	$884

Note: The 2007 American Community Survey (ACS) collected one-year demographic estimates for cities and counties with populations of at least 65,000 — in California's case, 118 out of 480 municipalities. For those municipalities, ACS data is included in the profiles in order to provide the most current data. However, to allow direct comparisons, data from the 2000 Decennial Census for those municipalities is presented here.

Oxnard

Population	
Total	170,358
Male	87,090
Female	83,268
Race & Hispanic Origin	
Race	
White	71,688
Black/African American	6,446
North American Native	2,143
Asian	12,581
Pacific Islander	698
Other Race	68,753
Two or more races	8,049
Hispanic origin, total	112,807
Mexican	101,264
Puerto Rican	529
Cuban	125
Other Hispanic	10,889
Age & Nativity	
Under 5 years	15,213
18 years and over	116,242
65 years and over	13,830
85 years and over	1,264
Median Age	28.9
Native-born	107,693
Foreign-born	62,902
Educational Attainment	
Population 25 years and over	96,399
0-8 yrs of school	25.4%
High School grad or higher	59.5%
Bachelor's degree or higher	13.7%
Graduate degree	4.6%
Income & Poverty, 1999	
Per capita income	$15,288
Median household income	$48,603
Median family income	$49,150
Persons in poverty	25,505
H'holds receiving public assistance	2,249
H'holds receiving social security	9,932
Households	
Total households	43,576
With persons under 18	23,271
With persons over 65	9,893
Family households	34,959
Single person households	6,351
Persons per household	3.85
Persons per family	4.16
Employed persons 16 years and over by occupation	
Managers & professionals	15,233
Service occupations	10,597
Sales & office occupations	17,555
Farming, fishing & forestry	6,879
Construction & maintenance	6,327
Production & transportation	13,804
Self-employed persons	3,853
Housing	
Median val. single fam. home	$189,400
Median rent	$780

Palmdale

Population	
Total	116,670
Male	57,338
Female	59,332
Race & Hispanic Origin	
Race	
White	63,905
Black/African American	16,913
North American Native	1,198
Asian	4,468
Pacific Islander	224
Other Race	23,858
Two or more races	6,104
Hispanic origin, total	43,991
Mexican	30,117
Puerto Rican	858
Cuban	586
Other Hispanic	12,430
Age & Nativity	
Under 5 years	10,808
18 years and over	72,352
65 years and over	6,520
85 years and over	489
Median Age	28.2
Native-born	93,499
Foreign-born	23,074
Educational Attainment	
Population 25 years and over	63,006
0-8 yrs of school	9.6%
High School grad or higher	74.0%
Bachelor's degree or higher	13.3%
Graduate degree	3.8%
Income & Poverty, 1999	
Per capita income	$16,384
Median household income	$46,941
Median family income	$49,293
Persons in poverty	18,272
H'holds receiving public assistance	2,814
H'holds receiving social security	5,650
Households	
Total households	34,285
With persons under 18	20,303
With persons over 65	5,043
Family households	28,105
Single person households	4,762
Persons per household	3.40
Persons per family	3.72
Employed persons 16 years and over by occupation	
Managers & professionals	12,263
Service occupations	6,992
Sales & office occupations	11,999
Farming, fishing & forestry	60
Construction & maintenance	5,261
Production & transportation	6,899
Self-employed persons	2,713
Housing	
Median val. single fam. home	$116,400
Median rent	$630

Pasadena

Population	
Total	133,936
Male	65,495
Female	68,441
Race & Hispanic Origin	
Race	
White	71,469
Black/African American	19,319
North American Native	952
Asian	13,399
Pacific Islander	132
Other Race	21,444
Two or more races	7,221
Hispanic origin, total	44,734
Mexican	32,276
Puerto Rican	429
Cuban	504
Other Hispanic	11,525
Age & Nativity	
Under 5 years	9,202
18 years and over	102,980
65 years and over	16,222
85 years and over	2,561
Median Age	34.5
Native-born	90,594
Foreign-born	43,277
Educational Attainment	
Population 25 years and over	90,934
0-8 yrs of school	11.3%
High School grad or higher	79.5%
Bachelor's degree or higher	41.3%
Graduate degree	17.8%
Income & Poverty, 1999	
Per capita income	$28,186
Median household income	$46,012
Median family income	$53,639
Persons in poverty	20,909
H'holds receiving public assistance	2,709
H'holds receiving social security	10,406
Households	
Total households	51,844
With persons under 18	15,709
With persons over 65	11,602
Family households	29,858
Single person households	17,460
Persons per household	2.52
Persons per family	3.30
Employed persons 16 years and over by occupation	
Managers & professionals	30,264
Service occupations	9,914
Sales & office occupations	14,700
Farming, fishing & forestry	53
Construction & maintenance	3,243
Production & transportation	4,930
Self-employed persons	6,041
Housing	
Median val. single fam. home	$286,400
Median rent	$746

Note: The 2007 American Community Survey (ACS) collected one-year demographic estimates for cities and counties with populations of at least 65,000 — in California's case, 118 out of 480 municipalities. For those municipalities, ACS data is included in the profiles in order to provide the most current data. However, to allow direct comparisons, data from the 2000 Decennial Census for those municipalities is presented here.

Pleasanton

Population

Total	63,654
Male	31,270
Female	32,384

Race & Hispanic Origin

Race	
White	51,203
Black/African American	876
North American Native	210
Asian	7,444
Pacific Islander	85
Other Race	1,495
Two or more races	2,341
Hispanic origin, total	5,011
Mexican	3,218
Puerto Rican	179
Cuban	76
Other Hispanic	1,538

Age & Nativity

Under 5 years	4,359
18 years and over	45,702
65 years and over	4,838
85 years and over	555
Median Age	36.9
Native-born	54,512
Foreign-born	9,057

Educational Attainment

Population 25 years and over	42,370
0-8 yrs of school	1.4%
High School grad or higher	94.2%
Bachelor's degree or higher	47.3%
Graduate degree	15.8%

Income & Poverty, 1999

Per capita income	$41,623
Median household income	$90,859
Median family income	$102,796
Persons in poverty	1,619
H'holds receiving public assistance	254
H'holds receiving social security	3,461

Households

Total households	23,311
With persons under 18	9,906
With persons over 65	3,451
Family households	17,395
Single person households	4,496
Persons per household	2.72
Persons per family	3.15

Employed persons 16 years and over by occupation

Managers & professionals	17,543
Service occupations	2,912
Sales & office occupations	9,611
Farming, fishing & forestry	15
Construction & maintenance	1,585
Production & transportation	1,942
Self-employed persons	2,008

Housing

Median val. single fam. home	$435,300
Median rent	$1,219

Pomona

Population

Total	149,473
Male	75,630
Female	73,843

Race & Hispanic Origin

Race	
White	62,419
Black/African American	14,398
North American Native	1,883
Asian	10,762
Pacific Islander	311
Other Race	52,213
Two or more races	7,487
Hispanic origin, total	96,370
Mexican	79,757
Puerto Rican	602
Cuban	370
Other Hispanic	15,641

Age & Nativity

Under 5 years	14,125
18 years and over	97,731
65 years and over	9,551
85 years and over	1,171
Median Age	26.5
Native-born	94,751
Foreign-born	54,893

Educational Attainment

Population 25 years and over	78,809
0-8 yrs of school	25.8%
High School grad or higher	54.9%
Bachelor's degree or higher	12.8%
Graduate degree	3.8%

Income & Poverty, 1999

Per capita income	$13,336
Median household income	$40,021
Median family income	$40,852
Persons in poverty	31,149
H'holds receiving public assistance	3,090
H'holds receiving social security	6,902

Households

Total households	37,855
With persons under 18	21,416
With persons over 65	6,939
Family households	29,798
Single person households	5,846
Persons per household	3.82
Persons per family	4.22

Employed persons 16 years and over by occupation

Managers & professionals	11,872
Service occupations	9,197
Sales & office occupations	13,142
Farming, fishing & forestry	232
Construction & maintenance	6,086
Production & transportation	12,983
Self-employed persons	2,980

Housing

Median val. single fam. home	$137,700
Median rent	$644

Rancho Cucamonga

Population

Total	127,743
Male	63,895
Female	63,848

Race & Hispanic Origin

Race	
White	84,987
Black/African American	10,059
North American Native	855
Asian	7,656
Pacific Islander	341
Other Race	16,931
Two or more races	6,914
Hispanic origin, total	35,491
Mexican	26,537
Puerto Rican	841
Cuban	457
Other Hispanic	7,656

Age & Nativity

Under 5 years	8,900
18 years and over	89,598
65 years and over	7,788
85 years and over	690
Median Age	32.2
Native-born	110,517
Foreign-born	17,644

Educational Attainment

Population 25 years and over	77,297
0-8 yrs of school	4.4%
High School grad or higher	86.0%
Bachelor's degree or higher	23.3%
Graduate degree	7.3%

Income & Poverty, 1999

Per capita income	$23,702
Median household income	$60,931
Median family income	$66,446
Persons in poverty	8,955
H'holds receiving public assistance	1,006
H'holds receiving social security	6,104

Households

Total households	40,863
With persons under 18	19,941
With persons over 65	5,846
Family households	31,827
Single person households	6,861
Persons per household	3.04
Persons per family	3.44

Employed persons 16 years and over by occupation

Managers & professionals	22,080
Service occupations	8,164
Sales & office occupations	18,918
Farming, fishing & forestry	117
Construction & maintenance	5,248
Production & transportation	7,423
Self-employed persons	4,363

Housing

Median val. single fam. home	$182,200
Median rent	$872

Note: The 2007 American Community Survey (ACS) collected one-year demographic estimates for cities and counties with populations of at least 65,000 — in California's case, 118 out of 480 municipalities. For those municipalities, ACS data is included in the profiles in order to provide the most current data. However, to allow direct comparisons, data from the 2000 Decennial Census for those municipalities is presented here.

Redding

Population

Total	80,865
Male	38,750
Female	42,115

Race & Hispanic Origin

Race	
White	71,727
Black/African American	851
North American Native	1,802
Asian	2,386
Pacific Islander	94
Other Race	1,324
Two or more races	2,681
Hispanic origin, total	4,393
Mexican	3,141
Puerto Rican	161
Cuban	35
Other Hispanic	1,056

Age & Nativity

Under 5 years	5,331
18 years and over	59,750
65 years and over	12,569
85 years and over	1,722
Median Age	36.7
Native-born	77,089
Foreign-born	4,109

Educational Attainment

Population 25 years and over	52,101
0-8 yrs of school	4.3%
High School grad or higher	85.2%
Bachelor's degree or higher	19.4%
Graduate degree	6.1%

Income & Poverty, 1999

Per capita income	$18,207
Median household income	$34,194
Median family income	$41,164
Persons in poverty	12,307
H'holds receiving public assistance	2,333
H'holds receiving social security	9,860

Households

Total households	32,103
With persons under 18	11,156
With persons over 65	8,650
Family households	20,994
Single person households	8,865
Persons per household	2.44
Persons per family	2.97

Employed persons 16 years and over by occupation

Managers & professionals	10,750
Service occupations	6,869
Sales & office occupations	9,798
Farming, fishing & forestry	111
Construction & maintenance	2,672
Production & transportation	3,547
Self-employed persons	3,023

Housing

Median val. single fam. home	$121,600
Median rent	$576

Redlands

Population

Total	63,591
Male	30,024
Female	33,567

Race & Hispanic Origin

Race	
White	46,858
Black/African American	2,739
North American Native	597
Asian	3,257
Pacific Islander	146
Other Race	7,204
Two or more races	2,790
Hispanic origin, total	15,304
Mexican	12,196
Puerto Rican	285
Cuban	120
Other Hispanic	2,703

Age & Nativity

Under 5 years	3,964
18 years and over	46,940
65 years and over	7,981
85 years and over	1,259
Median Age	35.1
Native-born	55,515
Foreign-born	8,157

Educational Attainment

Population 25 years and over	40,274
0-8 yrs of school	4.9%
High School grad or higher	86.6%
Bachelor's degree or higher	35.2%
Graduate degree	16.4%

Income & Poverty, 1999

Per capita income	$24,237
Median household income	$48,155
Median family income	$56,254
Persons in poverty	6,492
H'holds receiving public assistance	1,086
H'holds receiving social security	5,676

Households

Total households	23,593
With persons under 18	8,704
With persons over 65	5,505
Family households	16,027
Single person households	6,143
Persons per household	2.61
Persons per family	3.18

Employed persons 16 years and over by occupation

Managers & professionals	13,719
Service occupations	4,290
Sales & office occupations	7,167
Farming, fishing & forestry	26
Construction & maintenance	2,097
Production & transportation	2,643
Self-employed persons	2,105

Housing

Median val. single fam. home	$159,300
Median rent	$689

Redondo Beach

Population

Total	63,261
Male	31,870
Female	31,391

Race & Hispanic Origin

Race	
White	49,735
Black/African American	1,592
North American Native	295
Asian	5,756
Pacific Islander	224
Other Race	2,762
Two or more races	2,897
Hispanic origin, total	8,524
Mexican	5,158
Puerto Rican	305
Cuban	295
Other Hispanic	2,766

Age & Nativity

Under 5 years	3,634
18 years and over	51,371
65 years and over	5,366
85 years and over	517
Median Age	36.7
Native-born	52,523
Foreign-born	10,738

Educational Attainment

Population 25 years and over	47,851
0-8 yrs of school	2.2%
High School grad or higher	92.5%
Bachelor's degree or higher	48.0%
Graduate degree	17.4%

Income & Poverty, 1999

Per capita income	$38,305
Median household income	$69,173
Median family income	$80,543
Persons in poverty	3,719
H'holds receiving public assistance	523
H'holds receiving social security	4,276

Households

Total households	28,566
With persons under 18	7,212
With persons over 65	4,239
Family households	15,242
Single person households	9,452
Persons per household	2.21
Persons per family	2.87

Employed persons 16 years and over by occupation

Managers & professionals	20,249
Service occupations	3,827
Sales & office occupations	10,092
Farming, fishing & forestry	19
Construction & maintenance	2,054
Production & transportation	1,865
Self-employed persons	3,658

Housing

Median val. single fam. home	$353,300
Median rent	$995

Note: The 2007 American Community Survey (ACS) collected one-year demographic estimates for cities and counties with populations of at least 65,000 — in California's case, 118 out of 480 municipalities. For those municipalities, ACS data is included in the profiles in order to provide the most current data. However, to allow direct comparisons, data from the 2000 Decennial Census for those municipalities is presented here.

Redwood City

Population	
Total	75,402
Male	37,930
Female	37,472
Race & Hispanic Origin	
Race	
White	52,008
Black/African American	1,916
North American Native	384
Asian	6,715
Pacific Islander	663
Other Race	10,535
Two or more races	3,181
Hispanic origin, total	23,557
Mexican	16,450
Puerto Rican	264
Cuban	157
Other Hispanic	6,686
Age & Nativity	
Under 5 years	5,679
18 years and over	57,911
65 years and over	7,691
85 years and over	1,117
Median Age	34.8
Native-born	52,776
Foreign-born	22,671
Educational Attainment	
Population 25 years and over	51,677
0-8 yrs of school	8.7%
High School grad or higher	82.9%
Bachelor's degree or higher	35.7%
Graduate degree	14.0%
Income & Poverty, 1999	
Per capita income	$34,042
Median household income	$66,748
Median family income	$73,798
Persons in poverty	4,418
H'holds receiving public assistance	530
H'holds receiving social security	5,456
Households	
Total households	28,060
With persons under 18	9,518
With persons over 65	5,529
Family households	17,902
Single person households	7,618
Persons per household	2.62
Persons per family	3.20
Employed persons 16 years and over by occupation	
Managers & professionals	16,972
Service occupations	6,022
Sales & office occupations	9,623
Farming, fishing & forestry	113
Construction & maintenance	3,711
Production & transportation	3,659
Self-employed persons	3,616
Housing	
Median val. single fam. home	$517,800
Median rent	$1,105

Rialto

Population	
Total	91,873
Male	44,913
Female	46,960
Race & Hispanic Origin	
Race	
White	36,168
Black/African American	20,464
North American Native	965
Asian	2,271
Pacific Islander	392
Other Race	26,824
Two or more races	4,789
Hispanic origin, total	47,050
Mexican	37,589
Puerto Rican	677
Cuban	258
Other Hispanic	8,526
Age & Nativity	
Under 5 years	8,688
18 years and over	57,247
65 years and over	5,912
85 years and over	534
Median Age	26.4
Native-born	71,272
Foreign-born	20,439
Educational Attainment	
Population 25 years and over	47,766
0-8 yrs of school	14.7%
High School grad or higher	66.5%
Bachelor's degree or higher	8.7%
Graduate degree	2.3%
Income & Poverty, 1999	
Per capita income	$13,375
Median household income	$41,254
Median family income	$42,638
Persons in poverty	15,778
H'holds receiving public assistance	2,142
H'holds receiving social security	5,020
Households	
Total households	24,659
With persons under 18	14,910
With persons over 65	4,478
Family households	20,523
Single person households	3,299
Persons per household	3.69
Persons per family	4.01
Employed persons 16 years and over by occupation	
Managers & professionals	6,569
Service occupations	5,241
Sales & office occupations	9,261
Farming, fishing & forestry	65
Construction & maintenance	3,651
Production & transportation	7,673
Self-employed persons	1,492
Housing	
Median val. single fam. home	$116,900
Median rent	$631

Richmond

Population	
Total	99,216
Male	48,233
Female	50,983
Race & Hispanic Origin	
Race	
White	31,117
Black/African American	35,777
North American Native	639
Asian	12,198
Pacific Islander	498
Other Race	13,754
Two or more races	5,233
Hispanic origin, total	26,319
Mexican	18,396
Puerto Rican	458
Cuban	119
Other Hispanic	7,346
Age & Nativity	
Under 5 years	7,669
18 years and over	71,722
65 years and over	9,806
85 years and over	1,091
Median Age	32.8
Native-born	73,965
Foreign-born	25,751
Educational Attainment	
Population 25 years and over	62,662
0-8 yrs of school	11.2%
High School grad or higher	75.4%
Bachelor's degree or higher	22.4%
Graduate degree	8.3%
Income & Poverty, 1999	
Per capita income	$19,788
Median household income	$44,210
Median family income	$46,659
Persons in poverty	15,873
H'holds receiving public assistance	2,189
H'holds receiving social security	7,512
Households	
Total households	34,625
With persons under 18	13,857
With persons over 65	7,392
Family households	23,042
Single person households	9,083
Persons per household	2.82
Persons per family	3.44
Employed persons 16 years and over by occupation	
Managers & professionals	14,088
Service occupations	7,748
Sales & office occupations	11,296
Farming, fishing & forestry	90
Construction & maintenance	3,857
Production & transportation	5,690
Self-employed persons	2,876
Housing	
Median val. single fam. home	$171,900
Median rent	$764

Note: The 2007 American Community Survey (ACS) collected one-year demographic estimates for cities and counties with populations of at least 65,000 — in California's case, 118 out of 480 municipalities. For those municipalities, ACS data is included in the profiles in order to provide the most current data. However, to allow direct comparisons, data from the 2000 Decennial Census for those municipalities is presented here.

Riverside

Population

Total . . . 255,166
Male . . . 125,705
Female . . . 129,461

Race & Hispanic Origin

Race
White . . . 151,377
Black/African American . . . 18,906
North American Native . . . 2,779
Asian . . . 14,501
Pacific Islander . . . 991
Other Race . . . 53,591
Two or more races . . . 13,021
Hispanic origin, total . . . 97,315
Mexican . . . 79,041
Puerto Rican . . . 1,562
Cuban . . . 608
Other Hispanic . . . 16,104

Age & Nativity

Under 5 years . . . 20,435
18 years and over . . . 178,462
65 years and over . . . 23,054
85 years and over . . . 2,823
Median Age . . . 29.8
Native-born . . . 204,285
Foreign-born . . . 50,808

Educational Attainment

Population 25 years and over . . . 146,189
0-8 yrs of school . . . 10.7%
High School grad or higher . . . 74.9%
Bachelor's degree or higher . . . 19.1%
Graduate degree . . . 7.9%

Income & Poverty, 1999

Per capita income . . . $17,882
Median household income . . . $41,646
Median family income . . . $47,254
Persons in poverty . . . 39,060
H'holds receiving public assistance . . . 4,573
H'holds receiving social security . . . 17,474

Households

Total households . . . 82,005
With persons under 18 . . . 36,466
With persons over 65 . . . 16,382
Family households . . . 58,155
Single person households . . . 17,615
Persons per household . . . 3.02
Persons per family . . . 3.54

Employed persons 16 years and over by occupation

Managers & professionals . . . 32,974
Service occupations . . . 16,546
Sales & office occupations . . . 28,401
Farming, fishing & forestry . . . 405
Construction & maintenance . . . 12,247
Production & transportation . . . 16,232
Self-employed persons . . . 7,119

Housing

Median val. single fam. home . . . $138,500
Median rent . . . $670

Roseville

Population

Total . . . 79,921
Male . . . 38,302
Female . . . 41,619

Race & Hispanic Origin

Race
White . . . 68,756
Black/African American . . . 1,047
North American Native . . . 559
Asian . . . 3,442
Pacific Islander . . . 157
Other Race . . . 3,141
Two or more races . . . 2,819
Hispanic origin, total . . . 9,225
Mexican . . . 6,861
Puerto Rican . . . 283
Cuban . . . 81
Other Hispanic . . . 2,000

Age & Nativity

Under 5 years . . . 5,839
18 years and over . . . 58,537
65 years and over . . . 11,566
85 years and over . . . 1,375
Median Age . . . 36.4
Native-born . . . 72,913
Foreign-born . . . 7,179

Educational Attainment

Population 25 years and over . . . 53,006
0-8 yrs of school . . . 3.4%
High School grad or higher . . . 90.9%
Bachelor's degree or higher . . . 31.4%
Graduate degree . . . 9.8%

Income & Poverty, 1999

Per capita income . . . $27,021
Median household income . . . $57,367
Median family income . . . $65,929
Persons in poverty . . . 3,916
H'holds receiving public assistance . . . 671
H'holds receiving social security . . . 8,343

Households

Total households . . . 30,783
With persons under 18 . . . 11,593
With persons over 65 . . . 7,691
Family households . . . 21,849
Single person households . . . 7,118
Persons per household . . . 2.57
Persons per family . . . 3.03

Employed persons 16 years and over by occupation

Managers & professionals . . . 15,565
Service occupations . . . 4,509
Sales & office occupations . . . 10,894
Farming, fishing & forestry . . . 64
Construction & maintenance . . . 3,131
Production & transportation . . . 3,093
Self-employed persons . . . 2,568

Housing

Median val. single fam. home . . . $194,900
Median rent . . . $809

Sacramento

Population

Total . . . 407,018
Male . . . 197,784
Female . . . 209,234

Race & Hispanic Origin

Race
White . . . 196,549
Black/African American . . . 62,968
North American Native . . . 5,300
Asian . . . 67,635
Pacific Islander . . . 3,861
Other Race . . . 44,627
Two or more races . . . 26,078
Hispanic origin, total . . . 87,974
Mexican . . . 70,758
Puerto Rican . . . 2,053
Cuban . . . 474
Other Hispanic . . . 14,689

Age & Nativity

Under 5 years . . . 29,066
18 years and over . . . 295,728
65 years and over . . . 46,443
85 years and over . . . 6,079
Median Age . . . 32.8
Native-born . . . 324,459
Foreign-born . . . 82,616

Educational Attainment

Population 25 years and over . . . 254,921
0-8 yrs of school . . . 10.5%
High School grad or higher . . . 77.3%
Bachelor's degree or higher . . . 23.9%
Graduate degree . . . 8.4%

Income & Poverty, 1999

Per capita income . . . $18,721
Median household income . . . $37,049
Median family income . . . $42,051
Persons in poverty . . . 79,737
H'holds receiving public assistance . . 13,201
H'holds receiving social security . . . 34,984

Households

Total households . . . 154,581
With persons under 18 . . . 52,798
With persons over 65 . . . 34,169
Family households . . . 91,137
Single person households . . . 49,542
Persons per household . . . 2.57
Persons per family . . . 3.35

Employed persons 16 years and over by occupation

Managers & professionals . . . 61,498
Service occupations . . . 27,432
Sales & office occupations . . . 48,567
Farming, fishing & forestry . . . 634
Construction & maintenance . . . 12,980
Production & transportation . . . 18,676
Self-employed persons . . . 10,236

Housing

Median val. single fam. home . . . $128,800
Median rent . . . $625

Note: The 2007 American Community Survey (ACS) collected one-year demographic estimates for cities and counties with populations of at least 65,000 — in California's case, 118 out of 480 municipalities. For those municipalities, ACS data is included in the profiles in order to provide the most current data. However, to allow direct comparisons, data from the 2000 Decennial Census for those municipalities is presented here.

Salinas

Population

Total . . . 151,060
Male . . . 80,361
Female . . . 70,699

Race & Hispanic Origin

Race
White . . . 68,218
Black/African American . . . 4,943
North American Native . . . 1,903
Asian . . . 9,390
Pacific Islander . . . 407
Other Race . . . 58,466
Two or more races . . . 7,733
Hispanic origin, total . . . 96,880
Mexican . . . 84,815
Puerto Rican . . . 583
Cuban . . . 86
Other Hispanic . . . 11,396

Age & Nativity

Under 5 years . . . 13,988
18 years and over . . . 102,671
65 years and over . . . 10,673
85 years and over . . . 1,321
Median Age . . . 28.5
Native-born . . . 97,708
Foreign-born . . . 53,016

Educational Attainment

Population 25 years and over . . . 84,514
0-8 yrs of school . . . 26.8%
High School grad or higher . . . 56.0%
Bachelor's degree or higher . . . 12.3%
Graduate degree . . . 4.0%

Income & Poverty, 1999

Per capita income . . . $14,495
Median household income . . . $43,720
Median family income . . . $44,667
Persons in poverty . . . 23,676
H'holds receiving public assistance . . . 2,167
H'holds receiving social security . . . 8,177

Households

Total households . . . 38,298
With persons under 18 . . . 20,919
With persons over 65 . . . 7,619
Family households . . . 30,008
Single person households . . . 6,531
Persons per household . . . 3.66
Persons per family . . . 4.07

Employed persons 16 years and over by occupation

Managers & professionals . . . 11,736
Service occupations . . . 8,888
Sales & office occupations . . . 13,191
Farming, fishing & forestry . . . 8,178
Construction & maintenance . . . 5,022
Production & transportation . . . 7,887
Self-employed persons . . . 2,996

Housing

Median val. single fam. home . . . $195,700
Median rent . . . $725

San Bernardino

Population

Total . . . 185,401
Male . . . 91,150
Female . . . 94,251

Race & Hispanic Origin

Race
White . . . 83,849
Black/African American . . . 30,425
North American Native . . . 2,591
Asian . . . 7,772
Pacific Islander . . . 680
Other Race . . . 50,286
Two or more races . . . 9,798
Hispanic origin, total . . . 88,022
Mexican . . . 71,891
Puerto Rican . . . 1,077
Cuban . . . 251
Other Hispanic . . . 14,803

Age & Nativity

Under 5 years . . . 18,177
18 years and over . . . 120,221
65 years and over . . . 15,266
85 years and over . . . 1,770
Median Age . . . 27.6
Native-born . . . 147,140
Foreign-born . . . 38,248

Educational Attainment

Population 25 years and over . . . 99,325
0-8 yrs of school . . . 14.4%
High School grad or higher . . . 64.9%
Bachelor's degree or higher . . . 11.6%
Graduate degree . . . 3.9%

Income & Poverty, 1999

Per capita income . . . $12,925
Median household income . . . $31,140
Median family income . . . $33,357
Persons in poverty . . . 49,691
H'holds receiving public assistance . . . 6,731
H'holds receiving social security . . . 12,317

Households

Total households . . . 56,330
With persons under 18 . . . 28,198
With persons over 65 . . . 11,300
Family households . . . 41,099
Single person households . . . 11,869
Persons per household . . . 3.19
Persons per family . . . 3.72

Employed persons 16 years and over by occupation

Managers & professionals . . . 14,507
Service occupations . . . 12,420
Sales & office occupations . . . 16,659
Farming, fishing & forestry . . . 269
Construction & maintenance . . . 7,126
Production & transportation . . . 11,308
Self-employed persons . . . 3,635

Housing

Median val. single fam. home . . . $98,700
Median rent . . . $563

San Diego

Population

Total . . . 1,223,400
Male . . . 616,884
Female . . . 606,516

Race & Hispanic Origin

Race
White . . . 736,207
Black/African American . . . 96,216
North American Native . . . 7,543
Asian . . . 166,968
Pacific Islander . . . 5,853
Other Race . . . 151,532
Two or more races . . . 59,081
Hispanic origin, total . . . 310,752
Mexican . . . 259,219
Puerto Rican . . . 5,938
Cuban . . . 1,922
Other Hispanic . . . 43,673

Age & Nativity

Under 5 years . . . 82,523
18 years and over . . . 929,492
65 years and over . . . 128,008
85 years and over . . . 14,447
Median Age . . . 32.5
Native-born . . . 909,114
Foreign-born . . . 314,227

Educational Attainment

Population 25 years and over . . . 779,242
0-8 yrs of school . . . 8.2%
High School grad or higher . . . 82.8%
Bachelor's degree or higher . . . 35.0%
Graduate degree . . . 13.4%

Income & Poverty, 1999

Per capita income . . . $23,609
Median household income . . . $45,733
Median family income . . . $53,060
Persons in poverty . . . 172,527
H'holds receiving public assistance . . 17,816
H'holds receiving social security . . . 90,875

Households

Total households . . . 450,691
With persons under 18 . . . 150,318
With persons over 65 . . . 92,545
Family households . . . 271,398
Single person households . . . 126,210
Persons per household . . . 2.61
Persons per family . . . 3.30

Employed persons 16 years and over by occupation

Managers & professionals . . . 233,054
Service occupations . . . 88,462
Sales & office occupations . . . 147,136
Farming, fishing & forestry . . . 1,391
Construction & maintenance . . . 37,174
Production & transportation . . . 50,165
Self-employed persons . . . 43,960

Housing

Median val. single fam. home . . . $233,100
Median rent . . . $763

Note: The 2007 American Community Survey (ACS) collected one-year demographic estimates for cities and counties with populations of at least 65,000 — in California's case, 118 out of 480 municipalities. For those municipalities, ACS data is included in the profiles in order to provide the most current data. However, to allow direct comparisons, data from the 2000 Decennial Census for those municipalities is presented here.

San Francisco

Population

Total	776,733
Male	394,828
Female	381,905

Race & Hispanic Origin

Race	
White	385,728
Black/African American	60,515
North American Native	3,458
Asian	239,565
Pacific Islander	3,844
Other Race	50,368
Two or more races	33,255
Hispanic origin, total	109,504
Mexican	48,935
Puerto Rican	3,758
Cuban	1,632
Other Hispanic	55,179

Age & Nativity

Under 5 years	31,633
18 years and over	663,931
65 years and over	106,111
85 years and over	14,227
Median Age	36.5
Native-born	491,192
Foreign-born	285,541

Educational Attainment

Population 25 years and over	595,805
0-8 yrs of school	10.5%
High School grad or higher	81.2%
Bachelor's degree or higher	45.0%
Graduate degree	16.4%

Income & Poverty, 1999

Per capita income	$34,556
Median household income	$55,221
Median family income	$63,545
Persons in poverty	86,585
H'holds receiving public assistance	12,942
H'holds receiving social security	69,250

Households

Total households	329,700
With persons under 18	63,867
With persons over 65	78,716
Family households	145,186
Single person households	127,376
Persons per household	2.30
Persons per family	3.22

Employed persons 16 years and over by occupation

Managers & professionals	206,804
Service occupations	61,364
Sales & office occupations	109,316
Farming, fishing & forestry	462
Construction & maintenance	17,990
Production & transportation	31,887
Self-employed persons	37,140

Housing

Median val. single fam. home	$396,400
Median rent	$928

San Jose

Population

Total	894,943
Male	454,798
Female	440,145

Race & Hispanic Origin

Race	
White	425,017
Black/African American	31,349
North American Native	6,865
Asian	240,375
Pacific Islander	3,584
Other Race	142,691
Two or more races	45,062
Hispanic origin, total	269,989
Mexican	221,148
Puerto Rican	4,072
Cuban	1,001
Other Hispanic	43,768

Age & Nativity

Under 5 years	68,243
18 years and over	658,819
65 years and over	73,860
85 years and over	7,813
Median Age	32.6
Native-born	564,132
Foreign-born	329,757

Educational Attainment

Population 25 years and over	570,755
0-8 yrs of school	10.8%
High School grad or higher	78.3%
Bachelor's degree or higher	31.6%
Graduate degree	10.7%

Income & Poverty, 1999

Per capita income	$26,697
Median household income	$70,243
Median family income	$74,813
Persons in poverty	77,893
H'holds receiving public assistance	10,329
H'holds receiving social security	46,189

Households

Total households	276,598
With persons under 18	119,063
With persons over 65	52,797
Family households	203,681
Single person households	50,938
Persons per household	3.20
Persons per family	3.62

Employed persons 16 years and over by occupation

Managers & professionals	178,366
Service occupations	53,782
Sales & office occupations	106,472
Farming, fishing & forestry	1,383
Construction & maintenance	34,560
Production & transportation	62,327
Self-employed persons	23,697

Housing

Median val. single fam. home	$394,000
Median rent	$1,123

San Leandro

Population

Total	79,452
Male	38,300
Female	41,152

Race & Hispanic Origin

Race	
White	40,754
Black/African American	7,849
North American Native	609
Asian	18,242
Pacific Islander	683
Other Race	6,737
Two or more races	4,578
Hispanic origin, total	15,939
Mexican	10,719
Puerto Rican	696
Cuban	97
Other Hispanic	4,427

Age & Nativity

Under 5 years	5,032
18 years and over	61,798
65 years and over	12,688
85 years and over	1,747
Median Age	37.7
Native-born	57,558
Foreign-born	21,728

Educational Attainment

Population 25 years and over	55,846
0-8 yrs of school	8.3%
High School grad or higher	80.9%
Bachelor's degree or higher	23.3%
Graduate degree	6.6%

Income & Poverty, 1999

Per capita income	$23,895
Median household income	$51,081
Median family income	$60,266
Persons in poverty	5,037
H'holds receiving public assistance	861
H'holds receiving social security	8,499

Households

Total households	30,642
With persons under 18	9,923
With persons over 65	9,156
Family households	19,817
Single person households	8,745
Persons per household	2.57
Persons per family	3.19

Employed persons 16 years and over by occupation

Managers & professionals	12,393
Service occupations	4,437
Sales & office occupations	11,983
Farming, fishing & forestry	69
Construction & maintenance	3,251
Production & transportation	5,696
Self-employed persons	2,167

Housing

Median val. single fam. home	$235,500
Median rent	$873

Note: The 2007 American Community Survey (ACS) collected one-year demographic estimates for cities and counties with populations of at least 65,000 — in California's case, 118 out of 480 municipalities. For those municipalities, ACS data is included in the profiles in order to provide the most current data. However, to allow direct comparisons, data from the 2000 Decennial Census for those municipalities is presented here.

San Marcos

Population	
Total	54,977
Male	27,271
Female	27,706
Race & Hispanic Origin	
Race	
White	37,051
Black/African American	1,099
North American Native	453
Asian	2,567
Pacific Islander	130
Other Race	11,212
Two or more races	2,465
Hispanic origin, total	20,271
Mexican	17,609
Puerto Rican	258
Cuban	50
Other Hispanic	2,354
Age & Nativity	
Under 5 years	4,821
18 years and over	38,972
65 years and over	6,525
85 years and over	933
Median Age	32.1
Native-born	41,049
Foreign-born	14,111
Educational Attainment	
Population 25 years and over	34,030
0-8 yrs of school	13.1%
High School grad or higher	75.1%
Bachelor's degree or higher	20.0%
Graduate degree	5.8%
Income & Poverty, 1999	
Per capita income	$18,657
Median household income	$45,908
Median family income	$51,292
Persons in poverty	6,592
H'holds receiving public assistance	372
H'holds receiving social security	4,999
Households	
Total households	18,111
With persons under 18	7,628
With persons over 65	4,752
Family households	13,212
Single person households	3,677
Persons per household	3.03
Persons per family	3.46
Employed persons 16 years and over by occupation	
Managers & professionals	7,100
Service occupations	3,873
Sales & office occupations	6,618
Farming, fishing & forestry	388
Construction & maintenance	2,729
Production & transportation	3,795
Self-employed persons	2,022
Housing	
Median val. single fam. home	$206,400
Median rent	$797

San Mateo

Population	
Total	92,482
Male	45,201
Female	47,281
Race & Hispanic Origin	
Race	
White	61,251
Black/African American	2,397
North American Native	447
Asian	13,961
Pacific Islander	1,517
Other Race	8,260
Two or more races	4,649
Hispanic origin, total	18,973
Mexican	10,345
Puerto Rican	369
Cuban	150
Other Hispanic	8,109
Age & Nativity	
Under 5 years	5,631
18 years and over	73,648
65 years and over	13,932
85 years and over	2,344
Median Age	37.5
Native-born	64,508
Foreign-born	27,864
Educational Attainment	
Population 25 years and over	67,134
0-8 yrs of school	6.8%
High School grad or higher	85.9%
Bachelor's degree or higher	38.6%
Graduate degree	13.1%
Income & Poverty, 1999	
Per capita income	$36,176
Median household income	$64,757
Median family income	$76,223
Persons in poverty	5,608
H'holds receiving public assistance	417
H'holds receiving social security	9,653
Households	
Total households	37,338
With persons under 18	10,549
With persons over 65	10,033
Family households	22,310
Single person households	11,785
Persons per household	2.44
Persons per family	3.09
Employed persons 16 years and over by occupation	
Managers & professionals	20,855
Service occupations	6,546
Sales & office occupations	13,457
Farming, fishing & forestry	56
Construction & maintenance	3,569
Production & transportation	3,792
Self-employed persons	4,114
Housing	
Median val. single fam. home	$477,300
Median rent	$1,168

Santa Ana

Population	
Total	337,977
Male	175,219
Female	162,758
Race & Hispanic Origin	
Race	
White	144,425
Black/African American	5,749
North American Native	4,013
Asian	29,778
Pacific Islander	1,160
Other Race	137,360
Two or more races	15,492
Hispanic origin, total	257,097
Mexican	222,719
Puerto Rican	730
Cuban	551
Other Hispanic	33,097
Age & Nativity	
Under 5 years	34,816
18 years and over	222,470
65 years and over	18,565
85 years and over	2,040
Median Age	26.5
Native-born	157,579
Foreign-born	179,933
Educational Attainment	
Population 25 years and over	178,745
0-8 yrs of school	36.3%
High School grad or higher	43.2%
Bachelor's degree or higher	9.2%
Graduate degree	2.8%
Income & Poverty, 1999	
Per capita income	$12,152
Median household income	$43,412
Median family income	$41,050
Persons in poverty	65,268
H'holds receiving public assistance	4,130
H'holds receiving social security	11,656
Households	
Total households	73,002
With persons under 18	44,455
With persons over 65	13,402
Family households	59,784
Single person households	9,295
Persons per household	4.55
Persons per family	4.72
Employed persons 16 years and over by occupation	
Managers & professionals	21,089
Service occupations	27,271
Sales & office occupations	28,594
Farming, fishing & forestry	2,115
Construction & maintenance	14,417
Production & transportation	34,044
Self-employed persons	6,336
Housing	
Median val. single fam. home	$184,500
Median rent	$815

Note: The 2007 American Community Survey (ACS) collected one-year demographic estimates for cities and counties with populations of at least 65,000 — in California's case, 118 out of 480 municipalities. For those municipalities, ACS data is included in the profiles in order to provide the most current data. However, to allow direct comparisons, data from the 2000 Decennial Census for those municipalities is presented here.

Santa Barbara

Population

Total	92,325
Male	45,454
Female	46,871

Race & Hispanic Origin

Race	
White	68,355
Black/African American	1,636
North American Native	990
Asian	2,554
Pacific Islander	126
Other Race	15,110
Two or more races	3,554
Hispanic origin, total	32,330
Mexican	27,529
Puerto Rican	198
Cuban	108
Other Hispanic	4,495

Age & Nativity

Under 5 years	5,194
18 years and over	74,070
65 years and over	12,727
85 years and over	2,474
Median Age	34.6
Native-born	68,864
Foreign-born	23,332

Educational Attainment

Population 25 years and over	61,096
0-8 yrs of school	9.5%
High School grad or higher	81.3%
Bachelor's degree or higher	39.6%
Graduate degree	15.6%

Income & Poverty, 1999

Per capita income	$26,466
Median household income	$47,498
Median family income	$57,880
Persons in poverty	11,846
H'holds receiving public assistance	714
H'holds receiving social security	8,981

Households

Total households	35,605
With persons under 18	9,578
With persons over 65	8,871
Family households	18,954
Single person households	11,706
Persons per household	2.47
Persons per family	3.17

Employed persons 16 years and over by occupation

Managers & professionals	19,521
Service occupations	8,910
Sales & office occupations	12,092
Farming, fishing & forestry	282
Construction & maintenance	3,138
Production & transportation	3,816
Self-employed persons	5,838

Housing

Median val. single fam. home	$479,800
Median rent	$936

Santa Clara

Population

Total	102,361
Male	52,086
Female	50,275

Race & Hispanic Origin

Race	
White	56,903
Black/African American	2,341
North American Native	542
Asian	29,966
Pacific Islander	437
Other Race	7,102
Two or more races	5,070
Hispanic origin, total	16,364
Mexican	11,862
Puerto Rican	343
Cuban	183
Other Hispanic	3,976

Age & Nativity

Under 5 years	6,688
18 years and over	81,966
65 years and over	10,900
85 years and over	1,225
Median Age	33.4
Native-born	66,410
Foreign-born	35,694

Educational Attainment

Population 25 years and over	70,097
0-8 yrs of school	5.8%
High School grad or higher	86.9%
Bachelor's degree or higher	42.4%
Graduate degree	16.6%

Income & Poverty, 1999

Per capita income	$31,755
Median household income	$69,466
Median family income	$77,189
Persons in poverty	7,786
H'holds receiving public assistance	851
H'holds receiving social security	7,021

Households

Total households	38,526
With persons under 18	11,777
With persons over 65	7,758
Family households	24,100
Single person households	9,987
Persons per household	2.58
Persons per family	3.14

Employed persons 16 years and over by occupation

Managers & professionals	28,498
Service occupations	5,142
Sales & office occupations	12,862
Farming, fishing & forestry	94
Construction & maintenance	3,033
Production & transportation	5,899
Self-employed persons	2,612

Housing

Median val. single fam. home	$396,500
Median rent	$1,238

Santa Clarita

Population

Total	151,088
Male	74,764
Female	76,324

Race & Hispanic Origin

Race	
White	120,157
Black/African American	3,122
North American Native	886
Asian	7,923
Pacific Islander	220
Other Race	12,896
Two or more races	5,884
Hispanic origin, total	30,968
Mexican	21,603
Puerto Rican	634
Cuban	704
Other Hispanic	8,027

Age & Nativity

Under 5 years	11,829
18 years and over	105,314
65 years and over	10,725
85 years and over	1,243
Median Age	33.4
Native-born	126,654
Foreign-born	24,727

Educational Attainment

Population 25 years and over	93,648
0-8 yrs of school	4.7%
High School grad or higher	87.6%
Bachelor's degree or higher	29.1%
Graduate degree	8.8%

Income & Poverty, 1999

Per capita income	$26,841
Median household income	$66,717
Median family income	$73,588
Persons in poverty	9,552
H'holds receiving public assistance	1,057
H'holds receiving social security	8,496

Households

Total households	50,787
With persons under 18	23,898
With persons over 65	8,020
Family households	38,222
Single person households	9,482
Persons per household	2.95
Persons per family	3.38

Employed persons 16 years and over by occupation

Managers & professionals	30,829
Service occupations	10,605
Sales & office occupations	21,095
Farming, fishing & forestry	16
Construction & maintenance	6,142
Production & transportation	6,674
Self-employed persons	5,952

Housing

Median val. single fam. home	$229,200
Median rent	$943

Note: The 2007 American Community Survey (ACS) collected one-year demographic estimates for cities and counties with populations of at least 65,000 — in California's case, 118 out of 480 municipalities. For those municipalities, ACS data is included in the profiles in order to provide the most current data. However, to allow direct comparisons, data from the 2000 Decennial Census for those municipalities is presented here.

Santa Maria

Population

Total . . . 77,423
Male . . . 39,312
Female . . . 38,111

Race & Hispanic Origin

Race
White . . . 44,962
Black/African American . . . 1,449
North American Native . . . 1,360
Asian . . . 3,673
Pacific Islander . . . 138
Other Race . . . 21,691
Two or more races . . . 4,150
Hispanic origin, total . . . 46,196
Mexican . . . 40,719
Puerto Rican . . . 235
Cuban . . . 27
Other Hispanic . . . 5,215

Age & Nativity

Under 5 years . . . 7,000
18 years and over . . . 52,953
65 years and over . . . 8,776
85 years and over . . . 1,149
Median Age . . . 29.2
Native-born . . . 52,466
Foreign-born . . . 24,647

Educational Attainment

Population 25 years and over . . . 43,768
0-8 yrs of school . . . 24.0%
High School grad or higher . . . 61.0%
Bachelor's degree or higher . . . 11.0%
Graduate degree . . . 3.3%

Income & Poverty, 1999

Per capita income . . . $13,780
Median household income . . . $36,541
Median family income . . . $39,277
Persons in poverty . . . 14,823
H'holds receiving public assistance . . . 1,391
H'holds receiving social security . . . 6,477

Households

Total households . . . 22,146
With persons under 18 . . . 10,486
With persons over 65 . . . 5,879
Family households . . . 16,654
Single person households . . . 4,434
Persons per household . . . 3.40
Persons per family . . . 3.85

Employed persons 16 years and over by occupation

Managers & professionals . . . 5,442
Service occupations . . . 5,025
Sales & office occupations . . . 7,167
Farming, fishing & forestry . . . 5,735
Construction & maintenance . . . 2,753
Production & transportation . . . 4,534
Self-employed persons . . . 2,063

Housing

Median val. single fam. home . . . $145,600
Median rent . . . $675

Santa Monica

Population

Total . . . 84,084
Male . . . 40,517
Female . . . 43,567

Race & Hispanic Origin

Race
White . . . 65,832
Black/African American . . . 3,176
North American Native . . . 396
Asian . . . 6,100
Pacific Islander . . . 86
Other Race . . . 5,019
Two or more races . . . 3,475
Hispanic origin, total . . . 11,304
Mexican . . . 7,571
Puerto Rican . . . 257
Cuban . . . 238
Other Hispanic . . . 3,238

Age & Nativity

Under 5 years . . . 3,448
18 years and over . . . 71,770
65 years and over . . . 12,078
85 years and over . . . 2,163
Median Age . . . 39.3
Native-born . . . 63,193
Foreign-born . . . 20,891

Educational Attainment

Population 25 years and over . . . 67,176
0-8 yrs of school . . . 3.8%
High School grad or higher . . . 91.0%
Bachelor's degree or higher . . . 54.8%
Graduate degree . . . 23.2%

Income & Poverty, 1999

Per capita income . . . $42,874
Median household income . . . $50,714
Median family income . . . $75,989
Persons in poverty . . . 8,636
H'holds receiving public assistance . . . 1,015
H'holds receiving social security . . . 8,050

Households

Total households . . . 44,497
With persons under 18 . . . 7,488
With persons over 65 . . . 8,878
Family households . . . 16,783
Single person households . . . 22,786
Persons per household . . . 1.83
Persons per family . . . 2.80

Employed persons 16 years and over by occupation

Managers & professionals . . . 28,378
Service occupations . . . 4,430
Sales & office occupations . . . 10,955
Farming, fishing & forestry . . . 0
Construction & maintenance . . . 1,575
Production & transportation . . . 1,721
Self-employed persons . . . 7,038

Housing

Median val. single fam. home . . . $625,900
Median rent . . . $792

Santa Rosa

Population

Total . . . 147,595
Male . . . 72,078
Female . . . 75,517

Race & Hispanic Origin

Race
White . . . 114,527
Black/African American . . . 3,177
North American Native . . . 2,099
Asian . . . 5,675
Pacific Islander . . . 382
Other Race . . . 15,180
Two or more races . . . 6,555
Hispanic origin, total . . . 28,318
Mexican . . . 22,779
Puerto Rican . . . 502
Cuban . . . 111
Other Hispanic . . . 4,926

Age & Nativity

Under 5 years . . . 9,606
18 years and over . . . 111,790
65 years and over . . . 20,576
85 years and over . . . 3,397
Median Age . . . 36.2
Native-born . . . 123,517
Foreign-born . . . 24,015

Educational Attainment

Population 25 years and over . . . 97,503
0-8 yrs of school . . . 7.2%
High School grad or higher . . . 84.2%
Bachelor's degree or higher . . . 27.6%
Graduate degree . . . 9.1%

Income & Poverty, 1999

Per capita income . . . $24,495
Median household income . . . $50,931
Median family income . . . $59,659
Persons in poverty . . . 12,391
H'holds receiving public assistance . . . 1,586
H'holds receiving social security . . . 15,212

Households

Total households . . . 56,036
With persons under 18 . . . 18,848
With persons over 65 . . . 14,558
Family households . . . 35,117
Single person households . . . 15,599
Persons per household . . . 2.57
Persons per family . . . 3.14

Employed persons 16 years and over by occupation

Managers & professionals . . . 24,762
Service occupations . . . 11,565
Sales & office occupations . . . 20,084
Farming, fishing & forestry . . . 647
Construction & maintenance . . . 6,461
Production & transportation . . . 8,994
Self-employed persons . . . 6,991

Housing

Median val. single fam. home . . . $245,000
Median rent . . . $862

Note: The 2007 American Community Survey (ACS) collected one-year demographic estimates for cities and counties with populations of at least 65,000 — in California's case, 118 out of 480 municipalities. For those municipalities, ACS data is included in the profiles in order to provide the most current data. However, to allow direct comparisons, data from the 2000 Decennial Census for those municipalities is presented here.

Simi Valley

Population

Total	111,351
Male	55,098
Female	56,253

Race & Hispanic Origin

Race	
White	90,561
Black/African American	1,401
North American Native	780
Asian	7,052
Pacific Islander	154
Other Race	7,235
Two or more races	4,168
Hispanic origin, total	18,729
Mexican	12,501
Puerto Rican	449
Cuban	302
Other Hispanic	5,477

Age & Nativity

Under 5 years	8,163
18 years and over	79,672
65 years and over	8,504
85 years and over	806
Median Age	34.7
Native-born	94,710
Foreign-born	16,837

Educational Attainment

Population 25 years and over	71,130
0-8 yrs of school	4.1%
High School grad or higher	86.9%
Bachelor's degree or higher	24.9%
Graduate degree	7.1%

Income & Poverty, 1999

Per capita income	$26,586
Median household income	$70,370
Median family income	$75,140
Persons in poverty	6,453
H'holds receiving public assistance	816
H'holds receiving social security	6,557

Households

Total households	36,421
With persons under 18	16,828
With persons over 65	6,213
Family households	28,952
Single person households	5,338
Persons per household	3.04
Persons per family	3.33

Employed persons 16 years and over by occupation

Managers & professionals	21,788
Service occupations	7,051
Sales & office occupations	17,505
Farming, fishing & forestry	98
Construction & maintenance	4,812
Production & transportation	5,747
Self-employed persons	4,776

Housing

Median val. single fam. home	$239,900
Median rent	$1,058

South Gate

Population

Total	96,375
Male	47,767
Female	48,608

Race & Hispanic Origin

Race	
White	40,136
Black/African American	923
North American Native	901
Asian	804
Pacific Islander	114
Other Race	49,112
Two or more races	4,385
Hispanic origin, total	88,669
Mexican	68,181
Puerto Rican	576
Cuban	761
Other Hispanic	19,151

Age & Nativity

Under 5 years	9,692
18 years and over	62,097
65 years and over	5,249
85 years and over	640
Median Age	26.0
Native-born	48,862
Foreign-born	47,556

Educational Attainment

Population 25 years and over	50,032
0-8 yrs of school	36.4%
High School grad or higher	39.9%
Bachelor's degree or higher	4.9%
Graduate degree	1.7%

Income & Poverty, 1999

Per capita income	$10,602
Median household income	$35,695
Median family income	$35,789
Persons in poverty	18,418
H'holds receiving public assistance	1,847
H'holds receiving social security	3,946

Households

Total households	23,213
With persons under 18	15,192
With persons over 65	4,185
Family households	20,063
Single person households	2,414
Persons per household	4.15
Persons per family	4.37

Employed persons 16 years and over by occupation

Managers & professionals	4,831
Service occupations	4,557
Sales & office occupations	8,925
Farming, fishing & forestry	143
Construction & maintenance	3,081
Production & transportation	10,663
Self-employed persons	1,450

Housing

Median val. single fam. home	$161,400
Median rent	$620

Stockton

Population

Total	243,771
Male	118,751
Female	125,020

Race & Hispanic Origin

Race	
White	105,446
Black/African American	27,417
North American Native	2,727
Asian	48,506
Pacific Islander	981
Other Race	42,208
Two or more races	16,486
Hispanic origin, total	79,217
Mexican	66,900
Puerto Rican	1,056
Cuban	175
Other Hispanic	11,086

Age & Nativity

Under 5 years	20,977
18 years and over	164,687
65 years and over	24,975
85 years and over	3,314
Median Age	29.8
Native-born	183,345
Foreign-born	59,369

Educational Attainment

Population 25 years and over	138,343
0-8 yrs of school	16.2%
High School grad or higher	68.2%
Bachelor's degree or higher	15.4%
Graduate degree	4.9%

Income & Poverty, 1999

Per capita income	$15,405
Median household income	$35,453
Median family income	$40,434
Persons in poverty	56,783
H'holds receiving public assistance	8,275
H'holds receiving social security	18,199

Households

Total households	78,556
With persons under 18	36,132
With persons over 65	17,829
Family households	56,186
Single person households	17,972
Persons per household	3.04
Persons per family	3.59

Employed persons 16 years and over by occupation

Managers & professionals	23,659
Service occupations	14,404
Sales & office occupations	24,691
Farming, fishing & forestry	3,658
Construction & maintenance	7,606
Production & transportation	15,147
Self-employed persons	5,085

Housing

Median val. single fam. home	$119,500
Median rent	$581

Note: The 2007 American Community Survey (ACS) collected one-year demographic estimates for cities and counties with populations of at least 65,000 — in California's case, 118 out of 480 municipalities. For those municipalities, ACS data is included in the profiles in order to provide the most current data. However, to allow direct comparisons, data from the 2000 Decennial Census for those municipalities is presented here.

Sunnyvale

Population

Total	131,760
Male	67,783
Female	63,977

Race & Hispanic Origin

Race	
White	70,193
Black/African American	2,927
North American Native	608
Asian	42,524
Pacific Islander	428
Other Race	9,474
Two or more races	5,606
Hispanic origin, total	20,390
Mexican	14,405
Puerto Rican	452
Cuban	129
Other Hispanic	5,404

Age & Nativity

Under 5 years	9,270
18 years and over	104,863
65 years and over	13,957
85 years and over	1,436
Median Age	34.3
Native-born	79,915
Foreign-born	51,990

Educational Attainment

Population 25 years and over	95,278
0-8 yrs of school	4.7%
High School grad or higher	89.4%
Bachelor's degree or higher	50.8%
Graduate degree	21.9%

Income & Poverty, 1999

Per capita income	$36,524
Median household income	$74,409
Median family income	$81,634
Persons in poverty	7,127
H'holds receiving public assistance	949
H'holds receiving social security	9,511

Households

Total households	52,539
With persons under 18	15,743
With persons over 65	9,883
Family households	32,664
Single person households	14,220
Persons per household	2.49
Persons per family	3.06

Employed persons 16 years and over by occupation

Managers & professionals	43,322
Service occupations	6,578
Sales & office occupations	14,110
Farming, fishing & forestry	48
Construction & maintenance	3,142
Production & transportation	5,556
Self-employed persons	3,658

Housing

Median val. single fam. home	$495,200
Median rent	$1,270

Temecula

Population

Total	57,716
Male	28,510
Female	29,206

Race & Hispanic Origin

Race	
White	45,555
Black/African American	1,974
North American Native	497
Asian	2,728
Pacific Islander	174
Other Race	4,276
Two or more races	2,512
Hispanic origin, total	10,974
Mexican	8,440
Puerto Rican	447
Cuban	124
Other Hispanic	1,963

Age & Nativity

Under 5 years	5,115
18 years and over	37,684
65 years and over	4,095
85 years and over	277
Median Age	31.3
Native-born	50,528
Foreign-born	6,897

Educational Attainment

Population 25 years and over	32,843
0-8 yrs of school	3.5%
High School grad or higher	90.1%
Bachelor's degree or higher	25.0%
Graduate degree	7.1%

Income & Poverty, 1999

Per capita income	$21,557
Median household income	$59,516
Median family income	$62,270
Persons in poverty	3,864
H'holds receiving public assistance	309
H'holds receiving social security	2,905

Households

Total households	18,293
With persons under 18	10,084
With persons over 65	2,882
Family households	15,162
Single person households	2,296
Persons per household	3.15
Persons per family	3.45

Employed persons 16 years and over by occupation

Managers & professionals	8,947
Service occupations	3,734
Sales & office occupations	7,251
Farming, fishing & forestry	52
Construction & maintenance	2,184
Production & transportation	3,011
Self-employed persons	2,118

Housing

Median val. single fam. home	$190,100
Median rent	$846

Thousand Oaks

Population

Total	117,005
Male	57,440
Female	59,565

Race & Hispanic Origin

Race	
White	99,563
Black/African American	1,241
North American Native	627
Asian	6,873
Pacific Islander	124
Other Race	5,274
Two or more races	3,303
Hispanic origin, total	15,328
Mexican	10,097
Puerto Rican	324
Cuban	224
Other Hispanic	4,683

Age & Nativity

Under 5 years	7,851
18 years and over	86,617
65 years and over	12,994
85 years and over	1,816
Median Age	37.7
Native-born	98,560
Foreign-born	18,165

Educational Attainment

Population 25 years and over	78,458
0-8 yrs of school	3.4%
High School grad or higher	91.4%
Bachelor's degree or higher	42.2%
Graduate degree	15.6%

Income & Poverty, 1999

Per capita income	$34,314
Median household income	$76,815
Median family income	$86,041
Persons in poverty	5,714
H'holds receiving public assistance	634
H'holds receiving social security	8,978

Households

Total households	41,793
With persons under 18	16,467
With persons over 65	8,938
Family households	31,162
Single person households	8,191
Persons per household	2.75
Persons per family	3.15

Employed persons 16 years and over by occupation

Managers & professionals	28,671
Service occupations	6,783
Sales & office occupations	16,515
Farming, fishing & forestry	87
Construction & maintenance	3,218
Production & transportation	3,777
Self-employed persons	6,519

Housing

Median val. single fam. home	$324,800
Median rent	$1,131

Note: The 2007 American Community Survey (ACS) collected one-year demographic estimates for cities and counties with populations of at least 65,000 — in California's case, 118 out of 480 municipalities. For those municipalities, ACS data is included in the profiles in order to provide the most current data. However, to allow direct comparisons, data from the 2000 Decennial Census for those municipalities is presented here.

Torrance

Item	Value
Population	
Total	137,946
Male	67,087
Female	70,859
Race & Hispanic Origin	
Race	
White	81,605
Black/African American	3,022
North American Native	560
Asian	39,462
Pacific Islander	481
Other Race	6,307
Two or more races	6,509
Hispanic origin, total	17,637
Mexican	10,398
Puerto Rican	549
Cuban	740
Other Hispanic	5,950
Age & Nativity	
Under 5 years	7,834
18 years and over	106,206
65 years and over	19,427
85 years and over	2,217
Median Age	38.7
Native-born	99,859
Foreign-born	38,074
Educational Attainment	
Population 25 years and over	97,014
0-8 yrs of school	3.3%
High School grad or higher	90.6%
Bachelor's degree or higher	36.4%
Graduate degree	11.7%
Income & Poverty, 1999	
Per capita income	$28,144
Median household income	$56,489
Median family income	$67,098
Persons in poverty	8,815
H'holds receiving public assistance	1,084
H'holds receiving social security	13,297
Households	
Total households	54,542
With persons under 18	18,253
With persons over 65	13,709
Family households	36,276
Single person households	15,005
Persons per household	2.51
Persons per family	3.10
Employed persons 16 years and over by occupation	
Managers & professionals	30,905
Service occupations	6,817
Sales & office occupations	20,284
Farming, fishing & forestry	25
Construction & maintenance	4,174
Production & transportation	5,368
Self-employed persons	6,141
Housing	
Median val. single fam. home	$320,700
Median rent	$903

Tracy

Item	Value
Population	
Total	56,929
Male	28,492
Female	28,437
Race & Hispanic Origin	
Race	
White	37,127
Black/African American	3,117
North American Native	518
Asian	4,633
Pacific Islander	315
Other Race	7,445
Two or more races	3,774
Hispanic origin, total	15,765
Mexican	12,420
Puerto Rican	511
Cuban	70
Other Hispanic	2,764
Age & Nativity	
Under 5 years	5,360
18 years and over	37,330
65 years and over	3,637
85 years and over	514
Median Age	30.9
Native-born	47,275
Foreign-born	9,564
Educational Attainment	
Population 25 years and over	33,055
0-8 yrs of school	7.3%
High School grad or higher	81.5%
Bachelor's degree or higher	18.0%
Graduate degree	4.3%
Income & Poverty, 1999	
Per capita income	$21,397
Median household income	$62,794
Median family income	$67,464
Persons in poverty	3,928
H'holds receiving public assistance	510
H'holds receiving social security	2,743
Households	
Total households	17,620
With persons under 18	9,809
With persons over 65	2,593
Family households	14,308
Single person households	2,530
Persons per household	3.21
Persons per family	3.56
Employed persons 16 years and over by occupation	
Managers & professionals	7,825
Service occupations	3,085
Sales & office occupations	7,579
Farming, fishing & forestry	209
Construction & maintenance	2,782
Production & transportation	4,012
Self-employed persons	1,371
Housing	
Median val. single fam. home	$214,200
Median rent	$807

Turlock

Item	Value
Population	
Total	55,810
Male	26,870
Female	28,940
Race & Hispanic Origin	
Race	
White	40,370
Black/African American	798
North American Native	523
Asian	2,518
Pacific Islander	153
Other Race	8,460
Two or more races	2,988
Hispanic origin, total	16,422
Mexican	13,965
Puerto Rican	144
Cuban	41
Other Hispanic	2,272
Age & Nativity	
Under 5 years	4,505
18 years and over	39,154
65 years and over	6,605
85 years and over	1,073
Median Age	30.9
Native-born	43,572
Foreign-born	11,916
Educational Attainment	
Population 25 years and over	32,628
0-8 yrs of school	14.5%
High School grad or higher	70.4%
Bachelor's degree or higher	19.1%
Graduate degree	6.1%
Income & Poverty, 1999	
Per capita income	$16,844
Median household income	$39,050
Median family income	$44,501
Persons in poverty	8,798
H'holds receiving public assistance	1,178
H'holds receiving social security	4,639
Households	
Total households	18,408
With persons under 18	8,043
With persons over 65	4,379
Family households	13,434
Single person households	3,911
Persons per household	2.92
Persons per family	3.42
Employed persons 16 years and over by occupation	
Managers & professionals	6,737
Service occupations	3,342
Sales & office occupations	5,644
Farming, fishing & forestry	781
Construction & maintenance	1,850
Production & transportation	3,930
Self-employed persons	1,839
Housing	
Median val. single fam. home	$128,300
Median rent	$590

Note: The 2007 American Community Survey (ACS) collected one-year demographic estimates for cities and counties with populations of at least 65,000 — in California's case, 118 out of 480 municipalities. For those municipalities, ACS data is included in the profiles in order to provide the most current data. However, to allow direct comparisons, data from the 2000 Decennial Census for those municipalities is presented here.

Tustin

Population

Total	67,504
Male	33,044
Female	34,460

Race & Hispanic Origin

Race	
White	39,639
Black/African American	1,970
North American Native	448
Asian	10,058
Pacific Islander	203
Other Race	12,113
Two or more races	3,073
Hispanic origin, total	23,110
Mexican	17,955
Puerto Rican	214
Cuban	170
Other Hispanic	4,771

Age & Nativity

Under 5 years	5,815
18 years and over	49,382
65 years and over	4,804
85 years and over	483
Median Age	31.8
Native-born	45,030
Foreign-born	22,521

Educational Attainment

Population 25 years and over	42,967
0-8 yrs of school	9.4%
High School grad or higher	79.9%
Bachelor's degree or higher	33.4%
Graduate degree	11.7%

Income & Poverty, 1999

Per capita income	$25,932
Median household income	$55,985
Median family income	$60,092
Persons in poverty	5,689
H'holds receiving public assistance	570
H'holds receiving social security	3,357

Households

Total households	23,831
With persons under 18	9,418
With persons over 65	3,585
Family households	16,055
Single person households	5,734
Persons per household	2.82
Persons per family	3.37

Employed persons 16 years and over by occupation

Managers & professionals	14,124
Service occupations	4,583
Sales & office occupations	10,318
Farming, fishing & forestry	33
Construction & maintenance	1,957
Production & transportation	3,891
Self-employed persons	2,050

Housing

Median val. single fam. home	$273,300
Median rent	$925

Union City

Population

Total	66,869
Male	33,248
Female	33,621

Race & Hispanic Origin

Race	
White	20,198
Black/African American	4,479
North American Native	356
Asian	29,016
Pacific Islander	610
Other Race	7,709
Two or more races	4,501
Hispanic origin, total	16,020
Mexican	11,960
Puerto Rican	510
Cuban	42
Other Hispanic	3,508

Age & Nativity

Under 5 years	4,870
18 years and over	48,307
65 years and over	5,436
85 years and over	569
Median Age	32.8
Native-born	37,442
Foreign-born	29,419

Educational Attainment

Population 25 years and over	42,039
0-8 yrs of school	9.9%
High School grad or higher	80.5%
Bachelor's degree or higher	29.5%
Graduate degree	8.3%

Income & Poverty, 1999

Per capita income	$22,890
Median household income	$71,926
Median family income	$74,910
Persons in poverty	4,340
H'holds receiving public assistance	870
H'holds receiving social security	3,191

Households

Total households	18,642
With persons under 18	9,639
With persons over 65	3,867
Family households	15,700
Single person households	2,100
Persons per household	3.57
Persons per family	3.83

Employed persons 16 years and over by occupation

Managers & professionals	11,170
Service occupations	3,539
Sales & office occupations	8,317
Farming, fishing & forestry	66
Construction & maintenance	2,323
Production & transportation	5,865
Self-employed persons	1,444

Housing

Median val. single fam. home	$312,600
Median rent	$1,094

Upland

Population

Total	68,393
Male	32,872
Female	35,521

Race & Hispanic Origin

Race	
White	45,966
Black/African American	5,164
North American Native	518
Asian	4,969
Pacific Islander	101
Other Race	8,437
Two or more races	3,238
Hispanic origin, total	18,830
Mexican	14,177
Puerto Rican	323
Cuban	260
Other Hispanic	4,070

Age & Nativity

Under 5 years	4,815
18 years and over	49,694
65 years and over	7,358
85 years and over	835
Median Age	34.5
Native-born	57,317
Foreign-born	11,110

Educational Attainment

Population 25 years and over	43,311
0-8 yrs of school	5.4%
High School grad or higher	83.8%
Bachelor's degree or higher	26.7%
Graduate degree	10.3%

Income & Poverty, 1999

Per capita income	$23,343
Median household income	$48,734
Median family income	$57,471
Persons in poverty	8,106
H'holds receiving public assistance	839
H'holds receiving social security	5,399

Households

Total households	24,551
With persons under 18	9,827
With persons over 65	5,175
Family households	17,868
Single person households	5,176
Persons per household	2.76
Persons per family	3.21

Employed persons 16 years and over by occupation

Managers & professionals	11,548
Service occupations	4,344
Sales & office occupations	9,528
Farming, fishing & forestry	72
Construction & maintenance	2,687
Production & transportation	3,898
Self-employed persons	2,921

Housing

Median val. single fam. home	$211,000
Median rent	$710

Note: The 2007 American Community Survey (ACS) collected one-year demographic estimates for cities and counties with populations of at least 65,000 — in California's case, 118 out of 480 municipalities. For those municipalities, ACS data is included in the profiles in order to provide the most current data. However, to allow direct comparisons, data from the 2000 Decennial Census for those municipalities is presented here.

Vacaville

Population

Total 88,625
  Male 48,050
  Female 40,575

Race & Hispanic Origin

Race
  White 63,909
  Black/African American 8,880
  North American Native 856
  Asian 3,706
  Pacific Islander 403
  Other Race 5,970
  Two or more races 4,901
Hispanic origin, total 15,847
  Mexican 11,090
  Puerto Rican 608
  Cuban 146
  Other Hispanic 4,003

Age & Nativity

Under 5 years 5,891
18 years and over 64,704
65 years and over 7,320
85 years and over 695
  Median Age 33.9
Native-born 80,646
Foreign-born 7,998

Educational Attainment

Population 25 years and over 57,088
0-8 yrs of school 5.0%
High School grad or higher 83.9%
Bachelor's degree or higher 19.4%
Graduate degree 6.7%

Income & Poverty, 1999

Per capita income $21,557
Median household income $57,667
Median family income $63,950
Persons in poverty 4,801
H'holds receiving public assistance 868
H'holds receiving social security 5,511

Households

Total households 28,105
  With persons under 18 12,729
  With persons over 65 5,095
  Family households 20,962
  Single person households 5,406
Persons per household 2.83
Persons per family 3.24

Employed persons 16 years and over by occupation

  Managers & professionals 11,699
  Service occupations 5,851
  Sales & office occupations 10,482
  Farming, fishing & forestry 157
  Construction & maintenance 4,489
  Production & transportation 4,931
Self-employed persons 1,993

Housing

Median val. single fam. home $181,300
Median rent $842

Vallejo

Population

Total 116,760
  Male 56,553
  Female 60,207

Race & Hispanic Origin

Race
  White 41,996
  Black/African American 27,655
  North American Native 767
  Asian 28,205
  Pacific Islander 1,276
  Other Race 9,196
  Two or more races 7,665
Hispanic origin, total 18,591
  Mexican 12,253
  Puerto Rican 814
  Cuban 87
  Other Hispanic 5,437

Age & Nativity

Under 5 years 8,399
18 years and over 84,541
65 years and over 13,115
85 years and over 1,616
  Median Age 34.9
Native-born 87,603
Foreign-born 28,748

Educational Attainment

Population 25 years and over 74,155
0-8 yrs of school 7.2%
High School grad or higher 81.7%
Bachelor's degree or higher 21.1%
Graduate degree 4.7%

Income & Poverty, 1999

Per capita income $20,415
Median household income $50,030
Median family income $56,805
Persons in poverty 11,588
H'holds receiving public assistance . . . 1,980
H'holds receiving social security 9,057

Households

Total households 39,601
  With persons under 18 16,771
  With persons over 65 9,384
  Family households 28,245
  Single person households 8,988
Persons per household 2.90
Persons per family 3.43

Employed persons 16 years and over by occupation

  Managers & professionals 15,090
  Service occupations 9,187
  Sales & office occupations 14,794
  Farming, fishing & forestry 115
  Construction & maintenance 5,296
  Production & transportation 6,938
Self-employed persons 2,533

Housing

Median val. single fam. home $166,400
Median rent $781

Ventura

Population

Total 100,916
  Male 49,654
  Female 51,262

Race & Hispanic Origin

Race
  White 79,511
  Black/African American 1,421
  North American Native 1,173
  Asian 3,028
  Pacific Islander 175
  Other Race 11,245
  Two or more races 4,363
Hispanic origin, total 24,573
  Mexican 19,968
  Puerto Rican 294
  Cuban 100
  Other Hispanic 4,211

Age & Nativity

Under 5 years 6,641
18 years and over 75,654
65 years and over 12,931
85 years and over 1,684
  Median Age 36.8
Native-born 87,989
Foreign-born 13,166

Educational Attainment

Population 25 years and over 67,718
0-8 yrs of school 5.7%
High School grad or higher 85.7%
Bachelor's degree or higher 29.2%
Graduate degree 11.3%

Income & Poverty, 1999

Per capita income $25,065
Median household income $52,298
Median family income $60,466
Persons in poverty 8,904
H'holds receiving public assistance . . . 1,044
H'holds receiving social security 9,805

Households

Total households 38,524
  With persons under 18 13,482
  With persons over 65 9,174
  Family households 25,244
  Single person households 10,206
Persons per household 2.56
Persons per family 3.12

Employed persons 16 years and over by occupation

  Managers & professionals 19,534
  Service occupations 6,845
  Sales & office occupations 13,734
  Farming, fishing & forestry 412
  Construction & maintenance 4,307
  Production & transportation 4,959
Self-employed persons 4,978

Housing

Median val. single fam. home $245,400
Median rent $841

Note: The 2007 American Community Survey (ACS) collected one-year demographic estimates for cities and counties with populations of at least 65,000 — in California's case, 118 out of 480 municipalities. For those municipalities, ACS data is included in the profiles in order to provide the most current data. However, to allow direct comparisons, data from the 2000 Decennial Census for those municipalities is presented here.

Victorville

Population

Total	64,029
Male	31,004
Female	33,025

Race & Hispanic Origin

Race	
White	39,091
Black/African American	7,630
North American Native	713
Asian	2,226
Pacific Islander	129
Other Race	10,408
Two or more races	3,832
Hispanic origin, total	21,426
Mexican	16,091
Puerto Rican	623
Cuban	185
Other Hispanic	4,527

Age & Nativity

Under 5 years	5,537
18 years and over	42,112
65 years and over	7,152
85 years and over	614
Median Age	30.7
Native-born	56,579
Foreign-born	7,937

Educational Attainment

Population 25 years and over	36,777
0-8 yrs of school	7.6%
High School grad or higher	76.7%
Bachelor's degree or higher	10.6%
Graduate degree	3.7%

Income & Poverty, 1999

Per capita income	$14,454
Median household income	$36,187
Median family income	$39,988
Persons in poverty	11,885
H'holds receiving public assistance	1,615
H'holds receiving social security	5,835

Households

Total households	20,893
With persons under 18	10,217
With persons over 65	5,143
Family households	15,883
Single person households	4,052
Persons per household	3.03
Persons per family	3.47

Employed persons 16 years and over by occupation

Managers & professionals	5,733
Service occupations	4,224
Sales & office occupations	6,092
Farming, fishing & forestry	56
Construction & maintenance	2,659
Production & transportation	3,621
Self-employed persons	1,539

Housing

Median val. single fam. home	$98,700
Median rent	$584

Visalia

Population

Total	91,565
Male	44,167
Female	47,398

Race & Hispanic Origin

Race	
White	63,654
Black/African American	1,754
North American Native	1,235
Asian	4,683
Pacific Islander	117
Other Race	16,293
Two or more races	3,829
Hispanic origin, total	32,619
Mexican	27,918
Puerto Rican	270
Cuban	72
Other Hispanic	4,359

Age & Nativity

Under 5 years	7,413
18 years and over	62,950
65 years and over	9,966
85 years and over	1,407
Median Age	31.7
Native-born	79,780
Foreign-born	11,733

Educational Attainment

Population 25 years and over	53,916
0-8 yrs of school	11.2%
High School grad or higher	76.4%
Bachelor's degree or higher	18.9%
Graduate degree	6.3%

Income & Poverty, 1999

Per capita income	$18,422
Median household income	$41,349
Median family income	$45,830
Persons in poverty	15,201
H'holds receiving public assistance	2,291
H'holds receiving social security	7,139

Households

Total households	30,883
With persons under 18	13,781
With persons over 65	6,787
Family households	22,901
Single person households	6,392
Persons per household	2.91
Persons per family	3.37

Employed persons 16 years and over by occupation

Managers & professionals	13,100
Service occupations	6,613
Sales & office occupations	10,072
Farming, fishing & forestry	1,188
Construction & maintenance	2,868
Production & transportation	4,560
Self-employed persons	3,110

Housing

Median val. single fam. home	$115,300
Median rent	$578

Vista

Population

Total	89,857
Male	44,891
Female	44,966

Race & Hispanic Origin

Race	
White	57,750
Black/African American	3,814
North American Native	895
Asian	3,323
Pacific Islander	607
Other Race	19,168
Two or more races	4,300
Hispanic origin, total	34,990
Mexican	29,802
Puerto Rican	556
Cuban	71
Other Hispanic	4,561

Age & Nativity

Under 5 years	7,726
18 years and over	63,204
65 years and over	9,006
85 years and over	1,259
Median Age	30.3
Native-born	68,101
Foreign-born	22,030

Educational Attainment

Population 25 years and over	53,004
0-8 yrs of school	13.0%
High School grad or higher	75.9%
Bachelor's degree or higher	19.6%
Graduate degree	6.5%

Income & Poverty, 1999

Per capita income	$18,027
Median household income	$42,594
Median family income	$45,649
Persons in poverty	12,533
H'holds receiving public assistance	902
H'holds receiving social security	6,294

Households

Total households	28,877
With persons under 18	12,750
With persons over 65	6,036
Family households	20,783
Single person households	5,924
Persons per household	3.03
Persons per family	3.48

Employed persons 16 years and over by occupation

Managers & professionals	10,673
Service occupations	6,552
Sales & office occupations	10,534
Farming, fishing & forestry	579
Construction & maintenance	4,236
Production & transportation	5,652
Self-employed persons	3,272

Housing

Median val. single fam. home	$201,600
Median rent	$788

Note: The 2007 American Community Survey (ACS) collected one-year demographic estimates for cities and counties with populations of at least 65,000 — in California's case, 118 out of 480 municipalities. For those municipalities, ACS data is included in the profiles in order to provide the most current data. However, to allow direct comparisons, data from the 2000 Decennial Census for those municipalities is presented here.

West Covina

Population

Total	105,080
Male	51,019
Female	54,061

Race & Hispanic Origin

Race	
White	46,086
Black/African American	6,696
North American Native	823
Asian	23,849
Pacific Islander	226
Other Race	22,295
Two or more races	5,105
Hispanic origin, total	48,051
Mexican	37,206
Puerto Rican	560
Cuban	482
Other Hispanic	9,803

Age & Nativity

Under 5 years	8,013
18 years and over	75,128
65 years and over	10,879
85 years and over	970
Median Age	32.7
Native-born	70,840
Foreign-born	34,053

Educational Attainment

Population 25 years and over	65,008
0-8 yrs of school	8.9%
High School grad or higher	78.2%
Bachelor's degree or higher	21.9%
Graduate degree	5.7%

Income & Poverty, 1999

Per capita income	$19,342
Median household income	$53,002
Median family income	$57,614
Persons in poverty	9,400
H'holds receiving public assistance	1,379
H'holds receiving social security	7,266

Households

Total households	31,411
With persons under 18	15,083
With persons over 65	7,764
Family households	25,261
Single person households	4,660
Persons per household	3.32
Persons per family	3.67

Employed persons 16 years and over by occupation

Managers & professionals	14,269
Service occupations	5,442
Sales & office occupations	14,934
Farming, fishing & forestry	14
Construction & maintenance	3,761
Production & transportation	6,549
Self-employed persons	2,754

Housing

Median val. single fam. home	$190,200
Median rent	$828

Westminster

Population

Total	88,207
Male	44,080
Female	44,127

Race & Hispanic Origin

Race	
White	40,392
Black/African American	871
North American Native	535
Asian	33,629
Pacific Islander	406
Other Race	8,991
Two or more races	3,383
Hispanic origin, total	19,138
Mexican	15,389
Puerto Rican	269
Cuban	208
Other Hispanic	3,272

Age & Nativity

Under 5 years	6,419
18 years and over	65,335
65 years and over	9,843
85 years and over	867
Median Age	34.1
Native-born	50,407
Foreign-born	37,477

Educational Attainment

Population 25 years and over	57,313
0-8 yrs of school	12.8%
High School grad or higher	71.5%
Bachelor's degree or higher	18.1%
Graduate degree	4.8%

Income & Poverty, 1999

Per capita income	$18,218
Median household income	$49,450
Median family income	$52,677
Persons in poverty	11,757
H'holds receiving public assistance	1,851
H'holds receiving social security	5,822

Households

Total households	26,406
With persons under 18	11,416
With persons over 65	7,131
Family households	20,403
Single person households	4,471
Persons per household	3.32
Persons per family	3.71

Employed persons 16 years and over by occupation

Managers & professionals	11,300
Service occupations	5,348
Sales & office occupations	10,558
Farming, fishing & forestry	58
Construction & maintenance	3,291
Production & transportation	7,538
Self-employed persons	2,996

Housing

Median val. single fam. home	$227,300
Median rent	$842

Whittier

Population

Total	83,680
Male	40,687
Female	42,993

Race & Hispanic Origin

Race	
White	52,876
Black/African American	1,019
North American Native	1,105
Asian	2,770
Pacific Islander	126
Other Race	21,588
Two or more races	4,196
Hispanic origin, total	46,765
Mexican	38,565
Puerto Rican	393
Cuban	343
Other Hispanic	7,464

Age & Nativity

Under 5 years	6,533
18 years and over	60,013
65 years and over	10,486
85 years and over	1,406
Median Age	32.8
Native-born	68,537
Foreign-born	15,301

Educational Attainment

Population 25 years and over	51,648
0-8 yrs of school	8.2%
High School grad or higher	78.8%
Bachelor's degree or higher	21.9%
Graduate degree	7.4%

Income & Poverty, 1999

Per capita income	$21,409
Median household income	$49,256
Median family income	$55,726
Persons in poverty	8,549
H'holds receiving public assistance	1,050
H'holds receiving social security	7,325

Households

Total households	28,271
With persons under 18	11,788
With persons over 65	7,275
Family households	20,470
Single person households	6,319
Persons per household	2.88
Persons per family	3.38

Employed persons 16 years and over by occupation

Managers & professionals	12,283
Service occupations	4,412
Sales & office occupations	11,494
Farming, fishing & forestry	5
Construction & maintenance	2,899
Production & transportation	5,377
Self-employed persons	2,222

Housing

Median val. single fam. home	$211,700
Median rent	$723

Note: The 2007 American Community Survey (ACS) collected one-year demographic estimates for cities and counties with populations of at least 65,000 — in California's case, 118 out of 480 municipalities. For those municipalities, ACS data is included in the profiles in order to provide the most current data. However, to allow direct comparisons, data from the 2000 Decennial Census for those municipalities is presented here.

Yorba Linda

Population

Total	58,918
Male	28,943
Female	29,975

Race & Hispanic Origin

Race	
White	48,015
Black/African American	688
North American Native	220
Asian	6,537
Pacific Islander	56
Other Race	1,593
Two or more races	1,809
Hispanic origin, total	6,044
Mexican	4,315
Puerto Rican	135
Cuban	144
Other Hispanic	1,450

Age & Nativity

Under 5 years	3,507
18 years and over	41,655
65 years and over	4,526
85 years and over	374
Median Age	37.4
Native-born	50,467
Foreign-born	8,128

Educational Attainment

Population 25 years and over	37,459
0-8 yrs of school	1.8%
High School grad or higher	93.4%
Bachelor's degree or higher	41.5%
Graduate degree	15.4%

Income & Poverty, 1999

Per capita income	$36,173
Median household income	$89,593
Median family income	$96,132
Persons in poverty	1,756
H'holds receiving public assistance	269
H'holds receiving social security	3,139

Households

Total households	19,252
With persons under 18	9,093
With persons over 65	3,295
Family households	16,096
Single person households	2,387
Persons per household	3.05
Persons per family	3.35

Employed persons 16 years and over by occupation

Managers & professionals	15,050
Service occupations	2,414
Sales & office occupations	9,219
Farming, fishing & forestry	26
Construction & maintenance	1,631
Production & transportation	1,793
Self-employed persons	2,907

Housing

Median val. single fam. home	$346,100
Median rent	$1,191

Complete list of other school districts serving selected municipalities

Anaheim
Anaheim City Elementary, Centralia Elementary, Magnolia Elementary, Orange Unified, Placentia-Yorba Linda Unified, Savanna Elementary

Bakersfield
Bakersfield City Elementary, Beardsley Elementary, Edison Elementary, Fairfax Elementary, Fruitvale Elementary, General Shafter Elementary, Greenfield Union, Lakeside Union Elementary, Norris Elementary, Panama Buena Vista Union Elementary, Richland-Lerdo Elementary, Rio Bravo-Greeley Union Elementary, Rosedale Union Elementary, Standard Elementary, Vineland Elementary

Buena Park
Anaheim Union High, Buena Park Elementary, Centralia Elementary, Cypress Elementary, Savanna Elementary

Fresno
American Union Elementary, Central Unified, Monroe Elementary, Orange Center Elementary, Pacific Union Elementary, Washington Colony Elementary, Washington Union High, West Fresno Elementary, West Park Elementary

Grass Valley
Chicago Park Elementary, Clear Creek Elementary, Grass Valley Elementary, Pleasant Ridge Union Elementary, Union Hill Elementary

Hanford
Delta View Joint Union Elementary, Hanford Elementary, Kings River-Hardwick Union Elementary, Kit Carson Union Elementary, Lakeside Union Elementary, Pioneer Union Elementary

Huntington Beach
Fountain Valley Elementary, Huntington Beach City Elementary, Ocean View Elementary, Westminster Elementary

Los Gatos
Campbell Union Elementary, Lakeside Joint Elementary, Loma Prieta Joint Union Elementary, Los Gatos Union Elementary, Union Elementary

Modesto
Ceres Unified, Empire Union Elementary, Hart-Ransom Union Elementary, Modesto City Elementary, Paradise Elementary, Riverbank Unified, Salida Union Elementary, Shiloh Elementary, Stanislaus Union Elementary, Sylvan Union Elementary

Montague
Big Springs Union Elementary, Bogus Elementary, Delphic Elementary, Little Shasta Elementary, Montague Elementary, Willow Creek Elementary

Petaluma
Cinnabar Elementary, Dunham Elementary, Laguna Joint Elementary, Liberty Elementary, Lincoln Elementary, Old Adobe Union Elementary, Petaluma City Elementary, Two Rock Union Elementary, Union Joint Elementary, Waugh Elementary, Wilmar Union Elementary

Placerville
Gold Oak Union Elementary, Gold Trail Union Elementary, Mother Lode Union Elementary, Placerville Union Elementary

Porterville
Alta Vista Elementary, Burton Elementary, Citrus South Tule Elementary, Hope Elementary, Pleasant View Elementary, Rockford Elementary, Woodville Elementary

Redding
Columbia Elementary, Cottonwood Union Elementary, Enterprise Elementary, Gateway Unified, Grant Elementary, Pacheco Union Elementary, Redding Elementary, Shasta Union Elementary

Salinas
Alisal Union, Graves Elementary, Lagunita Elementary, North Monterey County Unified, Salinas City Elementary, Santa Rita Union Elementary, Washington Union Elementary

San Jose
Alum Rock Union Elementary, Berryessa Union Elementary, Cambrian, Campbell Union Elementary, Campbell Union High, Cupertino Union Elementary, East Side Union High, Evergreen Elementary, Franklin-McKinley Elementary, Luther Burbank Elementary, Moreland Elementary, Mt. Pleasant Elementary, Oak Grove Elementary, Orchard Elementary, Union Elementary

Santa Barbara
Cold Spring Elementary, Goleta Union Elementary, Hope Elementary, Montecito Union Elementary, Santa Barbara Elementary

Santa Cruz
Bonny Doon Union Elementary, Happy Valley Elementary, Live Oak Elementary, Santa Cruz City Elementary, Soquel Union Elementary

Santa Rosa
Bellevue Union Elementary, Bennett Valley Union Elementary, Mark West Union Elementary, Oak Grove Union Elementary, Piner-Olivet Union Elementary, Rincon Valley Union Elementary, Roseland Elementary, Santa Rosa Elementary, Wright Elementary

Saratoga
Campbell Union Elementary, Campbell Union High, Cupertino Union Elementary, Saratoga Union Elementary

Sebastopol
Gravenstein Union Elementary, Oak Grove Union Elementary, Sebastopol Union Elementary, Twin Hills Union Elementary

Tulare
Buena Vista Elementary, Oak Valley Union Elementary, Palo Verde Union Elementary, Sundale Union Elementary, Tulare City Elementary

Whittier
East Whittier City Elementary, Los Nietos Elementary, Lowell Joint Elementary, South Whittier Elementary, Whittier City Elementary

Note on District Reorganizations

In 2008, Grant Joint Union High, Del Past Heights Elementary, North Sacramento Elementary, and Rio Linda Union Elementary were merged into a new district, Twin Rivers Unified. Since the district is too new to have available data, the appendix gives information on the old districts, but gives the contact information for the new one.

ABC Unified

Los Angeles County
16700 Norwalk Blvd
Cerritos, CA 90703
(562) 926-5566

Superint. . . . . Gary Smuts
Grade plan. K-12
Number of schools. 30
Enrollment 20,860
High school graduates, 2006-07. . . . 1,621
Dropout rate. 2
Pupil/teacher ratio. 22.6%
Average class size. 26.8
Students per computer 3.9
Avg. Teacher Salary, ... $72,259
Avg. Daily Attendence (ADA). 20,919
Cost per ADA. $8,129

California Achievement Tests 6th ed., 2008
(Pct scoring at or above 50th National Percentile Rank)

	Math	Reading	Language
Grade 3	62%	42%	54%
Grade 7	60%	55%	55%

Academic Performance Index, 2009
Number of valid scores. 15,478
2007 API (base) 784
2008 API (growth). 795

SAT Testing, 2006-07
Enrollment, Grade 12 1,827
percent taking test. 47.1%
number with total score 1,500+ 571

Average Scores:

Math	Verbal	Writing	Total
589	530	538	1,657

Federal No Child Left Behind, 2008
(Adequate Yearly Progress standards met)

	Participation Rate	Pct Proficient
ELA	Yes	No
Math	Yes	No

API Criteria . . . . Yes
Graduation rate . . . . Yes
criteria met/possible. 42/40

Ackerman Elem

Placer County
13777 Bowman Rd
Auburn, CA 95603
(530) 885-1974

Superint. . . . . Marilyn Gilbert
Grade plan. K-8
Number of schools. 2
Enrollment 448
High school graduates, 2006-07. 0
Dropout rate. 0
Pupil/teacher ratio. 17.9%
Average class size. 22.9
Students per computer 8.1
Avg. Teacher Salary, ... $54,200
Avg. Daily Attendence (ADA). 440
Cost per ADA. $6,726

California Achievement Tests 6th ed., 2008
(Pct scoring at or above 50th National Percentile Rank)

	Math	Reading	Language
Grade 3	64%	57%	57%
Grade 7	68%	66%	64%

Academic Performance Index, 2009
Number of valid scores. 334
2007 API (base) 830
2008 API (growth). 822

SAT Testing, 2006-07
Enrollment, Grade 12 . . . . NA
percent taking test. . . . . NA
number with total score 1,500+ . . . . . . NA

Average Scores:

Math	Verbal	Writing	Total
NA	NA	NA	NA

Federal No Child Left Behind, 2008
(Adequate Yearly Progress standards met)

	Participation Rate	Pct Proficient
ELA	Yes	Yes
Math	Yes	Yes

API Criteria . . . . Yes
Graduation rate . . . . NA
criteria met/possible. 13/13

Adelanto Elem

San Bernardino County
PO Box 70
Adelanto, CA 92301
(760) 246-8691

Superint. . . . . Christopher van Zee
Grade plan. K-6
Number of schools. 12
Enrollment 8,653
High school graduates, 2006-07. 0
Dropout rate. 0
Pupil/teacher ratio. 23.2%
Average class size. 24.1
Students per computer 7.9
Avg. Teacher Salary, ... $56,494
Avg. Daily Attendence (ADA). 8,223
Cost per ADA. $7,344

California Achievement Tests 6th ed., 2008
(Pct scoring at or above 50th National Percentile Rank)

	Math	Reading	Language
Grade 3	43%	27%	37%
Grade 7	37%	34%	32%

Academic Performance Index, 2009
Number of valid scores. 5,712
2007 API (base) 706
2008 API (growth). 734

SAT Testing, 2006-07
Enrollment, Grade 12 . . . . NA
percent taking test. . . . . NA
number with total score 1,500+ . . . . . . NA

Average Scores:

Math	Verbal	Writing	Total
NA	NA	NA	NA

Federal No Child Left Behind, 2008
(Adequate Yearly Progress standards met)

	Participation Rate	Pct Proficient
ELA	Yes	No
Math	Yes	Yes

API Criteria . . . . Yes
Graduation rate . . . . NA
criteria met/possible. 33/32

Alexander Valley Union Elem

Sonoma County
8511 Highway 128
Healdsburg, CA 95448
(707) 433-1375

Superint. . . . . Bob Raines
Grade plan. K-6
Number of schools. 1
Enrollment 120
High school graduates, 2006-07. 0
Dropout rate. . . . . NA
Pupil/teacher ratio. 14.6%
Average class size. 16.5
Students per computer 6.0
Avg. Teacher Salary, ... NA
Avg. Daily Attendence (ADA). 121
Cost per ADA. $13,652

California Achievement Tests 6th ed., 2008
(Pct scoring at or above 50th National Percentile Rank)

	Math	Reading	Language
Grade 3	80%	60%	50%
Grade 7	NA	NA	NA

Academic Performance Index, 2009
Number of valid scores. 79
2007 API (base) 804
2008 API (growth). 806

SAT Testing, 2006-07
Enrollment, Grade 12 . . . . NA
percent taking test. . . . . NA
number with total score 1,500+ . . . . . . NA

Average Scores:

Math	Verbal	Writing	Total
NA	NA	NA	NA

Federal No Child Left Behind, 2008
(Adequate Yearly Progress standards met)

	Participation Rate	Pct Proficient
ELA	Yes	Yes
Math	Yes	Yes

API Criteria . . . . Yes
Graduation rate . . . . NA
criteria met/possible. 5/5

Alhambra Unified

Los Angeles County
1515 West Mission Rd
Alhambra, CA 91803
(626) 943-3000

Superint. . . . . Donna Perez
Grade plan. K-12
Number of schools. 18
Enrollment 18,976
High school graduates, 2006-07. . . . 1,869
Dropout rate. 1.6
Pupil/teacher ratio. 23.7%
Average class size. 29.2
Students per computer 4.2
Avg. Teacher Salary, ... $68,117
Avg. Daily Attendence (ADA). 19,060
Cost per ADA. $8,203

California Achievement Tests 6th ed., 2008
(Pct scoring at or above 50th National Percentile Rank)

	Math	Reading	Language
Grade 3	64%	41%	54%
Grade 7	66%	55%	55%

Academic Performance Index, 2009
Number of valid scores. 14,057
2007 API (base) 768
2008 API (growth). 782

SAT Testing, 2006-07
Enrollment, Grade 12 2,260
percent taking test. 45.1%
number with total score 1,500+ 512

Average Scores:

Math	Verbal	Writing	Total
548	478	478	1,504

Federal No Child Left Behind, 2008
(Adequate Yearly Progress standards met)

	Participation Rate	Pct Proficient
ELA	Yes	No
Math	Yes	No

API Criteria . . . . Yes
Graduation rate . . . . Yes
criteria met/possible. 34/32

Alisal Union

Monterey County
1205 East Market St
Salinas, CA 93905
(831) 753-5700

Superint. . . . . Esperanza Zendejas
Grade plan. K-6
Number of schools. 12
Enrollment 7,508
High school graduates, 2006-07. 0
Dropout rate. . . . . NA
Pupil/teacher ratio. 21.5%
Average class size. 24.3
Students per computer 5.2
Avg. Teacher Salary, ... $63,540
Avg. Daily Attendence (ADA). 7,257
Cost per ADA. $8,438

California Achievement Tests 6th ed., 2008
(Pct scoring at or above 50th National Percentile Rank)

	Math	Reading	Language
Grade 3	36%	17%	28%
Grade 7	NA	NA	NA

Academic Performance Index, 2009
Number of valid scores. 4,731
2007 API (base) 674
2008 API (growth). 688

SAT Testing, 2006-07
Enrollment, Grade 12 . . . . NA
percent taking test. . . . . NA
number with total score 1,500+ . . . . . . NA

Average Scores:

Math	Verbal	Writing	Total
NA	NA	NA	NA

Federal No Child Left Behind, 2008
(Adequate Yearly Progress standards met)

	Participation Rate	Pct Proficient
ELA	Yes	No
Math	Yes	No

API Criteria . . . . Yes
Graduation rate . . . . NA
criteria met/possible. 29/22

Data from school year 2007-08 except where noted
†Combined data for elementary and high schools

Alta Vista Elem

Tulare County
2293 East Crabtree Ave
Porterville, CA 93257
(559) 782-5700

Superint.......Japer Land
Grade plan.......K-8
Number of schools.......2
Enrollment.......485
High school graduates, 2006-07.......0
Dropout rate.......0
Pupil/teacher ratio.......19.8%
Average class size.......20.6
Students per computer.......4.8
Avg. Teacher Salary,.......$55,364
Avg. Daily Attendence (ADA).......472
Cost per ADA.......$8,759

California Achievement Tests 6th ed., 2008
(Pct scoring at or above 50th National Percentile Rank)

	Math	Reading	Language
Grade 3	15%	13%	15%
Grade 7	30%	20%	20%

Academic Performance Index, 2009
Number of valid scores.......303
2007 API (base).......638
2008 API (growth).......650

SAT Testing, 2006-07
Enrollment, Grade 12.......NA
percent taking test.......NA
number with total score 1,500+.......NA

Average Scores:

Math	Verbal	Writing	Total
NA	NA	NA	NA

Federal No Child Left Behind, 2008
(Adequate Yearly Progress standards met)

	Participation Rate	Pct Proficient
ELA	Yes	No
Math	Yes	No

API Criteria.......Yes
Graduation rate.......NA
criteria met/possible.......21/15

Alum Rock Union Elem

Santa Clara County
2930 Gay Ave
San Jose, CA 95127
(408) 928-6800

Superint.......Jose Manzo
Grade plan.......K-8
Number of schools.......28
Enrollment.......13,841
High school graduates, 2006-07.......0
Dropout rate.......0
Pupil/teacher ratio.......18.1%
Average class size.......24.2
Students per computer.......4.7
Avg. Teacher Salary,.......$65,216
Avg. Daily Attendence (ADA).......13,556
Cost per ADA.......$9,148

California Achievement Tests 6th ed., 2008
(Pct scoring at or above 50th National Percentile Rank)

	Math	Reading	Language
Grade 3	46%	20%	33%
Grade 7	40%	33%	31%

Academic Performance Index, 2009
Number of valid scores.......9,057
2007 API (base).......704
2008 API (growth).......707

SAT Testing, 2006-07
Enrollment, Grade 12.......NA
percent taking test.......NA
number with total score 1,500+.......NA

Average Scores:

Math	Verbal	Writing	Total
NA	NA	NA	NA

Federal No Child Left Behind, 2008
(Adequate Yearly Progress standards met)

	Participation Rate	Pct Proficient
ELA	Yes	No
Math	Yes	No

API Criteria.......Yes
Graduation rate.......NA
criteria met/possible.......37/29

Alview-Dairyland Union Elem

Madera County
12861 Avenue 18 1/2
Chowchilla, CA 93610
(559) 665-2394

Superint.......Lori Flanagan
Grade plan.......K-8
Number of schools.......2
Enrollment.......360
High school graduates, 2006-07.......0
Dropout rate.......0
Pupil/teacher ratio.......21.2%
Average class size.......22.1
Students per computer.......4.1
Avg. Teacher Salary,.......$58,085
Avg. Daily Attendence (ADA).......354
Cost per ADA.......$7,620

California Achievement Tests 6th ed., 2008
(Pct scoring at or above 50th National Percentile Rank)

	Math	Reading	Language
Grade 3	67%	31%	36%
Grade 7	50%	63%	55%

Academic Performance Index, 2009
Number of valid scores.......250
2007 API (base).......763
2008 API (growth).......797

SAT Testing, 2006-07
Enrollment, Grade 12.......NA
percent taking test.......NA
number with total score 1,500+.......NA

Average Scores:

Math	Verbal	Writing	Total
NA	NA	NA	NA

Federal No Child Left Behind, 2008
(Adequate Yearly Progress standards met)

	Participation Rate	Pct Proficient
ELA	Yes	Yes
Math	Yes	Yes

API Criteria.......Yes
Graduation rate.......NA
criteria met/possible.......21/21

Alvord Unified

Riverside County
10365 Keller Ave
Riverside, CA 92505
(951) 509-5070

Superint.......Wendel Tucker
Grade plan.......K-12
Number of schools.......22
Enrollment.......19,987
High school graduates, 2006-07.......934
Dropout rate.......2.6
Pupil/teacher ratio.......22.7%
Average class size.......28.3
Students per computer.......5.0
Avg. Teacher Salary,.......$71,234
Avg. Daily Attendence (ADA).......19,368
Cost per ADA.......$7,989

California Achievement Tests 6th ed., 2008
(Pct scoring at or above 50th National Percentile Rank)

	Math	Reading	Language
Grade 3	51%	27%	39%
Grade 7	45%	39%	35%

Academic Performance Index, 2009
Number of valid scores.......14,108
2007 API (base).......693
2008 API (growth).......706

SAT Testing, 2006-07
Enrollment, Grade 12.......896
percent taking test.......41.6%
number with total score 1,500+.......110

Average Scores:

Math	Verbal	Writing	Total
471	457	453	1,381

Federal No Child Left Behind, 2008
(Adequate Yearly Progress standards met)

	Participation Rate	Pct Proficient
ELA	Yes	No
Math	Yes	Yes

API Criteria.......Yes
Graduation rate.......Yes
criteria met/possible.......38/34

American Union Elem

Fresno County
2801 West Adams Ave
Fresno, CA 93706
(559) 268-1213

Superint.......Edward Gonzalez
Grade plan.......K-8
Number of schools.......1
Enrollment.......321
High school graduates, 2006-07.......0
Dropout rate.......0
Pupil/teacher ratio.......14.9%
Average class size.......27.2
Students per computer.......3.6
Avg. Teacher Salary,.......NA
Avg. Daily Attendence (ADA).......319
Cost per ADA.......$9,765

California Achievement Tests 6th ed., 2008
(Pct scoring at or above 50th National Percentile Rank)

	Math	Reading	Language
Grade 3	48%	24%	43%
Grade 7	52%	46%	50%

Academic Performance Index, 2009
Number of valid scores.......239
2007 API (base).......725
2008 API (growth).......753

SAT Testing, 2006-07
Enrollment, Grade 12.......NA
percent taking test.......NA
number with total score 1,500+.......NA

Average Scores:

Math	Verbal	Writing	Total
NA	NA	NA	NA

Federal No Child Left Behind, 2008
(Adequate Yearly Progress standards met)

	Participation Rate	Pct Proficient
ELA	Yes	No
Math	Yes	Yes

API Criteria.......Yes
Graduation rate.......NA
criteria met/possible.......21/19

Anaheim City Elem

Orange County
1001 South East St
Anaheim, CA 92805
(714) 517-7500

Superint.......Jos? Banda
Grade plan.......K-6
Number of schools.......24
Enrollment.......19,332
High school graduates, 2006-07.......0
Dropout rate.......NA
Pupil/teacher ratio.......20.5%
Average class size.......25.1
Students per computer.......4.1
Avg. Teacher Salary,.......$76,230
Avg. Daily Attendence (ADA).......18,895
Cost per ADA.......$8,820

California Achievement Tests 6th ed., 2008
(Pct scoring at or above 50th National Percentile Rank)

	Math	Reading	Language
Grade 3	40%	21%	32%
Grade 7	NA	NA	NA

Academic Performance Index, 2009
Number of valid scores.......12,801
2007 API (base).......694
2008 API (growth).......725

SAT Testing, 2006-07
Enrollment, Grade 12.......NA
percent taking test.......NA
number with total score 1,500+.......NA

Average Scores:

Math	Verbal	Writing	Total
NA	NA	NA	NA

Federal No Child Left Behind, 2008
(Adequate Yearly Progress standards met)

	Participation Rate	Pct Proficient
ELA	Yes	No
Math	Yes	No

API Criteria.......Yes
Graduation rate.......NA
criteria met/possible.......37/32

Data from school year 2007-08 except where noted.
†Combined data for elementary and high schools.

Anaheim Union High

Orange County
PO Box 3520
Anaheim, CA 92803
(714) 999-3511

Superint. . . . . Joseph Farley
Grade plan. 7-12
Number of schools. 22
Enrollment 33,343
High school graduates, 2006-07 3,668
Dropout rate. 1.7
Pupil/teacher ratio. 23.7%
Average class size. 20.2
Students per computer 3.4
Avg. Teacher Salary, ... $79,030
Avg. Daily Attendence (ADA). 33,034
Cost per ADA. $8,336

California Achievement Tests 6th ed., 2008
(Pct scoring at or above 50th National Percentile Rank)

	Math	Reading	Language
Grade 3	NA	NA	NA
Grade 7	49%	43%	43%

Academic Performance Index, 2009
Number of valid scores. 26,586
2007 API (base) 715
2008 API (growth). 729

SAT Testing, 2006-07
Enrollment, Grade 12 4,777
percent taking test. 33.3%
number with total score 1,500+ 717

Average Scores:

Math	Verbal	Writing	Total
519	485	489	1,493

Federal No Child Left Behind, 2008
(Adequate Yearly Progress standards met)

	Participation Rate	Pct Proficient
ELA	Yes	No
Math	Yes	No

API Criteria . . . . Yes
Graduation rate . . . . Yes
criteria met/possible. 42/35

Antelope Elem

Tehama County
22630 Antelope Blvd
Red Bluff, CA 96080
(530) 527-1272

Superint. . . . . Albert Graham
Grade plan. K-8
Number of schools. 3
Enrollment 668
High school graduates, 2006-07 0
Dropout rate. 0
Pupil/teacher ratio. 17.4%
Average class size. 23.2
Students per computer 1.7
Avg. Teacher Salary, ... $54,807
Avg. Daily Attendence (ADA). 639
Cost per ADA. $7,875

California Achievement Tests 6th ed., 2008
(Pct scoring at or above 50th National Percentile Rank)

	Math	Reading	Language
Grade 3	55%	45%	45%
Grade 7	54%	54%	56%

Academic Performance Index, 2009
Number of valid scores. 484
2007 API (base) 804
2008 API (growth). .808

SAT Testing, 2006-07
Enrollment, Grade 12 . . . . NA
percent taking test. . . . . NA
number with total score 1,500+ . . . . NA

Average Scores:

Math	Verbal	Writing	Total
NA	NA	NA	NA

Federal No Child Left Behind, 2008
(Adequate Yearly Progress standards met)

	Participation Rate	Pct Proficient
ELA	Yes	Yes
Math	Yes	Yes

API Criteria . . . . Yes
Graduation rate . . . . NA
criteria met/possible. 13/13

Antioch Unified

Contra Costa County
510 G St
Antioch, CA 94509
(925) 706-4100

Superint. . . . . Deborah Sims
Grade plan. K-12
Number of schools. 26
Enrollment 20,086
High school graduates, 2006-07 1,279
Dropout rate. 8.1
Pupil/teacher ratio. 20.7%
Average class size. 27.5
Students per computer 5.0
Avg. Teacher Salary, ... $61,953
Avg. Daily Attendence (ADA). 18,934
Cost per ADA. $7,448

California Achievement Tests 6th ed., 2008
(Pct scoring at or above 50th National Percentile Rank)

	Math	Reading	Language
Grade 3	47%	30%	39%
Grade 7	44%	41%	40%

Academic Performance Index, 2009
Number of valid scores. 13,987
2007 API (base) 716
2008 API (growth). 712

SAT Testing, 2006-07
Enrollment, Grade 12 1,813
percent taking test. 23.8%
number with total score 1,500+ 174

Average Scores:

Math	Verbal	Writing	Total
492	482	472	1,446

Federal No Child Left Behind, 2008
(Adequate Yearly Progress standards met)

	Participation Rate	Pct Proficient
ELA	Yes	No
Math	Yes	No

API Criteria . . . . Yes
Graduation rate . . . . No
criteria met/possible. 46/39

Arcadia Unified

Los Angeles County
234 Campus Dr
Arcadia, CA 91007
(626) 821-8300

Superint. . . . . Joel Shawn
Grade plan. K-12
Number of schools. 11
Enrollment 9,900
High school graduates, 2006-07 939
Dropout rate. 0.3
Pupil/teacher ratio. 23.0%
Average class size. 27.0
Students per computer 2.4
Avg. Teacher Salary, ... $76,787
Avg. Daily Attendence (ADA). 9,840
Cost per ADA. $7,367

California Achievement Tests 6th ed., 2008
(Pct scoring at or above 50th National Percentile Rank)

	Math	Reading	Language
Grade 3	88%	71%	79%
Grade 7	90%	80%	80%

Academic Performance Index, 2009
Number of valid scores. 7,633
2007 API (base) 894
2008 API (growth). 904

SAT Testing, 2006-07
Enrollment, Grade 12 1,000
percent taking test. 62.2%
number with total score 1,500+ 461

Average Scores:

Math	Verbal	Writing	Total
612	544	554	1,710

Federal No Child Left Behind, 2008
(Adequate Yearly Progress standards met)

	Participation Rate	Pct Proficient
ELA	Yes	Yes
Math	Yes	Yes

API Criteria . . . . Yes
Graduation rate . . . . Yes
criteria met/possible. 34/34

Arcata Elem

Humboldt County
1435 Buttermilk Ln
Arcata, CA 95521
(707) 822-0351

Superint. . . . . Timothy Parisi
Grade plan. K-8
Number of schools. 5
Enrollment 935
High school graduates, 2006-07 0
Dropout rate. 0
Pupil/teacher ratio. 18.9%
Average class size. 23.8
Students per computer 6.4
Avg. Teacher Salary, ... $57,335
Avg. Daily Attendence (ADA). 551
Cost per ADA. $9,156

California Achievement Tests 6th ed., 2008
(Pct scoring at or above 50th National Percentile Rank)

	Math	Reading	Language
Grade 3	72%	56%	49%
Grade 7	71%	80%	77%

Academic Performance Index, 2009
Number of valid scores. 497
2007 API (base) 814
2008 API (growth). .843

SAT Testing, 2006-07
Enrollment, Grade 12 . . . . NA
percent taking test. . . . . NA
number with total score 1,500+ . . . . NA

Average Scores:

Math	Verbal	Writing	Total
NA	NA	NA	NA

Federal No Child Left Behind, 2008
(Adequate Yearly Progress standards met)

	Participation Rate	Pct Proficient
ELA	Yes	No
Math	Yes	Yes

API Criteria . . . . Yes
Graduation rate . . . . NA
criteria met/possible. 17/16

Arena Union Elem

Mendocino County
PO Box 87
Point Arena, CA 95468
(707) 882-2803

Superint. . . . . Mark Iacuaniello
Grade plan. K-8
Number of schools. 2
Enrollment 309
High school graduates, 2006-07 1
Dropout rate. 0
Pupil/teacher ratio. 12.4%
Average class size. 18.5
Students per computer 3.0
Avg. Teacher Salary,† $48,273
Avg. Daily Attendence (ADA)† 364
Cost per ADA† $16,419

California Achievement Tests 6th ed., 2008
(Pct scoring at or above 50th National Percentile Rank)

	Math	Reading	Language
Grade 3	38%	56%	50%
Grade 7	43%	55%	48%

Academic Performance Index, 2009
Number of valid scores. 154
2007 API (base) 729
2008 API (growth). .679

SAT Testing, 2006-07
Enrollment, Grade 12 1
percent taking test. . . . . NA
number with total score 1,500+ . . . . NA

Average Scores:

Math	Verbal	Writing	Total
NA	NA	NA	NA

Federal No Child Left Behind, 2008
(Adequate Yearly Progress standards met)

	Participation Rate	Pct Proficient
ELA	Yes	No
Math	Yes	No

API Criteria . . . . Yes
Graduation rate . . . . NA
criteria met/possible. 19/14

Data from school year 2007-08 except where noted
†Combined data for elementary and high schools

Arvin Union Elem

Kern County
737 Bear Mountain Blvd
Arvin, CA 93203
(661) 854-6500

Superint. . . . . .Jerelle Kavanagh
Grade plan. K-8
Number of schools. .4
Enrollment 3,312
High school graduates, 2006-07. 0
Dropout rate. 0
Pupil/teacher ratio. 20.3%
Average class size. 22.9
Students per computer 2.9
Avg. Teacher Salary, ...$56,065
Avg. Daily Attendence (ADA). 3,267
Cost per ADA. $8,183

California Achievement Tests 6th ed., 2008
(Pct scoring at or above 50th National Percentile Rank)

	Math	Reading	Language
Grade 3	36%	23%	33%
Grade 7	28%	27%	28%

Academic Performance Index, 2009
Number of valid scores. 2,321
2007 API (base) 624
2008 API (growth). 650

SAT Testing, 2006-07
Enrollment, Grade 12 . . . . .NA
percent taking test. . . . . .NA
number with total score 1,500+ . . . . . .NA

Average Scores:

Math	Verbal	Writing	Total
NA	NA	NA	NA

Federal No Child Left Behind, 2008
(Adequate Yearly Progress standards met)

	Participation Rate	Pct Proficient
ELA	Yes	No
Math	Yes	No

API Criteria . . . . .Yes
Graduation rate . . . . .NA
criteria met/possible. 21/11

Atwater Elem

Merced County
1401 Broadway Ave
Atwater, CA 95301
(209) 357-6100

Superint. . . . . Melinda Hennes
Grade plan. K-8
Number of schools. .9
Enrollment 4,652
High school graduates, 2006-07. 0
Dropout rate. 0
Pupil/teacher ratio. 20.6%
Average class size. 24.3
Students per computer 3.6
Avg. Teacher Salary, ...$74,921
Avg. Daily Attendence (ADA). 4,491
Cost per ADA. $7,816

California Achievement Tests 6th ed., 2008
(Pct scoring at or above 50th National Percentile Rank)

	Math	Reading	Language
Grade 3	48%	35%	40%
Grade 7	49%	46%	42%

Academic Performance Index, 2009
Number of valid scores. 3,156
2007 API (base) 735
2008 API (growth). 739

SAT Testing, 2006-07
Enrollment, Grade 12 . . . . .NA
percent taking test. . . . . .NA
number with total score 1,500+ . . . . . .NA

Average Scores:

Math	Verbal	Writing	Total
NA	NA	NA	NA

Federal No Child Left Behind, 2008
(Adequate Yearly Progress standards met)

	Participation Rate	Pct Proficient
ELA	Yes	No
Math	Yes	No

API Criteria . . . . .Yes
Graduation rate . . . . .NA
criteria met/possible. 33/28

Auburn Union Elem

Placer County
255 Epperle Ln
Auburn, CA 95603
(530) 885-7242

Superint. . . . . Michele Schuetz
Grade plan. K-8
Number of schools. .5
Enrollment 2,230
High school graduates, 2006-07. 0
Dropout rate. 0
Pupil/teacher ratio. 20.7%
Average class size. 25.2
Students per computer 5.8
Avg. Teacher Salary, ...$62,160
Avg. Daily Attendence (ADA). 2,182
Cost per ADA. $7,601

California Achievement Tests 6th ed., 2008
(Pct scoring at or above 50th National Percentile Rank)

	Math	Reading	Language
Grade 3	59%	48%	54%
Grade 7	61%	62%	56%

Academic Performance Index, 2009
Number of valid scores. 1,670
2007 API (base) 786
2008 API (growth). 787

SAT Testing, 2006-07
Enrollment, Grade 12 . . . . .NA
percent taking test. . . . . .NA
number with total score 1,500+ . . . . . .NA

Average Scores:

Math	Verbal	Writing	Total
NA	NA	NA	NA

Federal No Child Left Behind, 2008
(Adequate Yearly Progress standards met)

	Participation Rate	Pct Proficient
ELA	Yes	No
Math	Yes	No

API Criteria . . . . .Yes
Graduation rate . . . . .NA
criteria met/possible. 25/21

Azusa Unified

Los Angeles County
PO Box 500
Azusa, CA 91702
(626) 967-6211

Superint. . . . . .Cynthia McGuire
Grade plan. K-12
Number of schools. 18
Enrollment 11,219
High school graduates, 2006-07. 562
Dropout rate. 3.1
Pupil/teacher ratio. 21.0%
Average class size. 26.9
Students per computer 4.1
Avg. Teacher Salary, ...NA
Avg. Daily Attendence (ADA). 11,019
Cost per ADA. $8,264

California Achievement Tests 6th ed., 2008
(Pct scoring at or above 50th National Percentile Rank)

	Math	Reading	Language
Grade 3	45%	23%	34%
Grade 7	36%	33%	31%

Academic Performance Index, 2009
Number of valid scores. 8,229
2007 API (base) 660
2008 API (growth). 672

SAT Testing, 2006-07
Enrollment, Grade 12 591
percent taking test. 30.3%
number with total score 1,500+ 43

Average Scores:

Math	Verbal	Writing	Total
463	436	441	1,340

Federal No Child Left Behind, 2008
(Adequate Yearly Progress standards met)

	Participation Rate	Pct Proficient
ELA	Yes	No
Math	Yes	No

API Criteria . . . . .Yes
Graduation rate . . . . .Yes
criteria met/possible. 34/26

Bakersfield City Elem

Kern County
1300 Baker St
Bakersfield, CA 93305
(661) 631-4600

Superint. . . . . Mike Lingo
Grade plan. K-8
Number of schools. 42
Enrollment 27,080
High school graduates, 2006-07. 0
Dropout rate. 0
Pupil/teacher ratio. 19.6%
Average class size. 23.7
Students per computer 3.7
Avg. Teacher Salary, ...$60,763
Avg. Daily Attendence (ADA). 25,920
Cost per ADA. $9,054

California Achievement Tests 6th ed., 2008
(Pct scoring at or above 50th National Percentile Rank)

	Math	Reading	Language
Grade 3	39%	23%	32%
Grade 7	31%	30%	31%

Academic Performance Index, 2009
Number of valid scores. 18,853
2007 API (base) 654
2008 API (growth). 676

SAT Testing, 2006-07
Enrollment, Grade 12 . . . . .NA
percent taking test. . . . . .NA
number with total score 1,500+ . . . . . .NA

Average Scores:

Math	Verbal	Writing	Total
NA	NA	NA	NA

Federal No Child Left Behind, 2008
(Adequate Yearly Progress standards met)

	Participation Rate	Pct Proficient
ELA	Yes	No
Math	Yes	No

API Criteria . . . . .Yes
Graduation rate . . . . .NA
criteria met/possible. 41/29

Ballard Elem

Santa Barbara County
2425 School St
Solvang, CA 93463
(805) 688-4812

Superint. . . . . .Allan Pelletier
Grade plan. K-6
Number of schools. .1
Enrollment 110
High school graduates, 2006-07. 0
Dropout rate. . . . . .NA
Pupil/teacher ratio. 15.7%
Average class size. 15.7
Students per computer 4.4
Avg. Teacher Salary, ...$70,462
Avg. Daily Attendence (ADA). 106
Cost per ADA. $11,786

California Achievement Tests 6th ed., 2008
(Pct scoring at or above 50th National Percentile Rank)

	Math	Reading	Language
Grade 3	94%	94%	94%
Grade 7	NA	NA	NA

Academic Performance Index, 2009
Number of valid scores. 72
2007 API (base) 900
2008 API (growth). 928

SAT Testing, 2006-07
Enrollment, Grade 12 . . . . .NA
percent taking test. . . . . .NA
number with total score 1,500+ . . . . . .NA

Average Scores:

Math	Verbal	Writing	Total
NA	NA	NA	NA

Federal No Child Left Behind, 2008
(Adequate Yearly Progress standards met)

	Participation Rate	Pct Proficient
ELA	Yes	Yes
Math	Yes	Yes

API Criteria . . . . .Yes
Graduation rate . . . . .NA
criteria met/possible. 5/5

Data from school year 2007-08 except where noted.
†Combined data for elementary and high schools.

Banta Elem
San Joaquin County
22345 South El Rancho Rd
Tracy, CA 95376
(209) 835-0171

Superint	William Draa
Grade plan	K-8
Number of schools	1
Enrollment	296
High school graduates, 2006-07	0
Dropout rate	0
Pupil/teacher ratio	21.1%
Average class size	22.6
Students per computer	2.3
Avg. Teacher Salary,	$57,471
Avg. Daily Attendence (ADA)	285
Cost per ADA	$8,090

California Achievement Tests 6th ed., 2008
(Pct scoring at or above 50th National Percentile Rank)

	Math	Reading	Language
Grade 3	32%	26%	39%
Grade 7	69%	63%	53%

Academic Performance Index, 2009

Number of valid scores	225
2007 API (base)	749
2008 API (growth)	706

SAT Testing, 2006-07

Enrollment, Grade 12	NA
percent taking test	NA
number with total score 1,500+	NA

Average Scores:

Math	Verbal	Writing	Total
NA	NA	NA	NA

Federal No Child Left Behind, 2008
(Adequate Yearly Progress standards met)

	Participation Rate	Pct Proficient
ELA	Yes	No
Math	Yes	No

API Criteria	Yes
Graduation rate	NA
# criteria met/possible	21/16

Bassett Unified
Los Angeles County
904 North Willow Ave
La Puente, CA 91746
(626) 931-3000

Superint	Robert Watanabe
Grade plan	K-12
Number of schools	8
Enrollment	5,231
High school graduates, 2006-07	269
Dropout rate	6.6
Pupil/teacher ratio	22.1%
Average class size	25.0
Students per computer	5.1
Avg. Teacher Salary,	NA
Avg. Daily Attendence (ADA)	5,046
Cost per ADA	$9,116

California Achievement Tests 6th ed., 2008
(Pct scoring at or above 50th National Percentile Rank)

	Math	Reading	Language
Grade 3	49%	29%	40%
Grade 7	52%	41%	39%

Academic Performance Index, 2009

Number of valid scores	3,742
2007 API (base)	702
2008 API (growth)	714

SAT Testing, 2006-07

Enrollment, Grade 12	333
percent taking test	34.2%
number with total score 1,500+	25

Average Scores:

Math	Verbal	Writing	Total
449	417	420	1,286

Federal No Child Left Behind, 2008
(Adequate Yearly Progress standards met)

	Participation Rate	Pct Proficient
ELA	Yes	No
Math	Yes	Yes

API Criteria	Yes
Graduation rate	No
# criteria met/possible	22/19

Bayshore Elem
San Mateo County
1 Martin St
Daly City, CA 94014
(415) 467-5444

Superint	Norman Fobert
Grade plan	K-8
Number of schools	2
Enrollment	445
High school graduates, 2006-07	0
Dropout rate	0
Pupil/teacher ratio	20.2%
Average class size	22.2
Students per computer	9.7
Avg. Teacher Salary,	$61,894
Avg. Daily Attendence (ADA)	433
Cost per ADA	$8,380

California Achievement Tests 6th ed., 2008
(Pct scoring at or above 50th National Percentile Rank)

	Math	Reading	Language
Grade 3	37%	22%	29%
Grade 7	41%	39%	37%

Academic Performance Index, 2009

Number of valid scores	335
2007 API (base)	707
2008 API (growth)	701

SAT Testing, 2006-07

Enrollment, Grade 12	NA
percent taking test	NA
number with total score 1,500+	NA

Average Scores:

Math	Verbal	Writing	Total
NA	NA	NA	NA

Federal No Child Left Behind, 2008
(Adequate Yearly Progress standards met)

	Participation Rate	Pct Proficient
ELA	Yes	No
Math	Yes	No

API Criteria	Yes
Graduation rate	NA
# criteria met/possible	25/19

Beardsley Elem
Kern County
1001 Roberts Ln
Bakersfield, CA 93308
(661) 392-0878

Superint	Richard Stotler
Grade plan	K-8
Number of schools	4
Enrollment	1,765
High school graduates, 2006-07	0
Dropout rate	0
Pupil/teacher ratio	19.4%
Average class size	21.3
Students per computer	2.6
Avg. Teacher Salary,	$52,924
Avg. Daily Attendence (ADA)	1,704
Cost per ADA	$7,921

California Achievement Tests 6th ed., 2008
(Pct scoring at or above 50th National Percentile Rank)

	Math	Reading	Language
Grade 3	54%	35%	51%
Grade 7	39%	36%	29%

Academic Performance Index, 2009

Number of valid scores	1,157
2007 API (base)	705
2008 API (growth)	715

SAT Testing, 2006-07

Enrollment, Grade 12	NA
percent taking test	NA
number with total score 1,500+	NA

Average Scores:

Math	Verbal	Writing	Total
NA	NA	NA	NA

Federal No Child Left Behind, 2008
(Adequate Yearly Progress standards met)

	Participation Rate	Pct Proficient
ELA	Yes	No
Math	Yes	No

API Criteria	Yes
Graduation rate	NA
# criteria met/possible	25/22

Belleview Elem
Tuolumne County
22736 Kuien Mill Rd
Sonora, CA 95370
(209) 586-5510

Superint	John Pendley
Grade plan	K-8
Number of schools	2
Enrollment	160
High school graduates, 2006-07	0
Dropout rate	0
Pupil/teacher ratio	21.3%
Average class size	18.8
Students per computer	2.5
Avg. Teacher Salary,	NA
Avg. Daily Attendence (ADA)	128
Cost per ADA	$10,039

California Achievement Tests 6th ed., 2008
(Pct scoring at or above 50th National Percentile Rank)

	Math	Reading	Language
Grade 3	81%	75%	75%
Grade 7	69%	69%	62%

Academic Performance Index, 2009

Number of valid scores	92
2007 API (base)	786
2008 API (growth)	780

SAT Testing, 2006-07

Enrollment, Grade 12	NA
percent taking test	NA
number with total score 1,500+	NA

Average Scores:

Math	Verbal	Writing	Total
NA	NA	NA	NA

Federal No Child Left Behind, 2008
(Adequate Yearly Progress standards met)

	Participation Rate	Pct Proficient
ELA	Yes	Yes
Math	Yes	Yes

API Criteria	Yes
Graduation rate	NA
# criteria met/possible	7/7

Bellevue Union Elem
Sonoma County
3223 Primrose Ave
Santa Rosa, CA 95407
(707) 542-5197

Superint	Tony Roehrick
Grade plan	K-6
Number of schools	4
Enrollment	1,726
High school graduates, 2006-07	0
Dropout rate	NA
Pupil/teacher ratio	17.7%
Average class size	21.8
Students per computer	4.9
Avg. Teacher Salary,	$57,237
Avg. Daily Attendence (ADA)	1,707
Cost per ADA	$8,889

California Achievement Tests 6th ed., 2008
(Pct scoring at or above 50th National Percentile Rank)

	Math	Reading	Language
Grade 3	44%	22%	33%
Grade 7	NA	NA	NA

Academic Performance Index, 2009

Number of valid scores	1,088
2007 API (base)	677
2008 API (growth)	691

SAT Testing, 2006-07

Enrollment, Grade 12	NA
percent taking test	NA
number with total score 1,500+	NA

Average Scores:

Math	Verbal	Writing	Total
NA	NA	NA	NA

Federal No Child Left Behind, 2008
(Adequate Yearly Progress standards met)

	Participation Rate	Pct Proficient
ELA	Yes	No
Math	Yes	Yes

API Criteria	Yes
Graduation rate	NA
# criteria met/possible	25/20

Data from school year 2007-08 except where noted
†Combined data for elementary and high schools

Bellflower Unified

Los Angeles County
16703 South Clark Ave
Bellflower, CA 90706
(562) 866-9011

Superint	Rick Kemppainen
Grade plan	K-12
Number of schools	15
Enrollment	14,672
High school graduates, 2006-07	953
Dropout rate	3.9
Pupil/teacher ratio	22.1%
Average class size	26.1
Students per computer	4.7
Avg. Teacher Salary,	$65,560
Avg. Daily Attendence (ADA)	14,472
Cost per ADA	$7,782

California Achievement Tests 6th ed., 2008
(Pct scoring at or above 50th National Percentile Rank)

	Math	Reading	Language
Grade 3	63%	38%	48%
Grade 7	49%	42%	45%

Academic Performance Index, 2009

Number of valid scores	10,546
2007 API (base)	739
2008 API (growth)	751

SAT Testing, 2006-07

Enrollment, Grade 12	1,187
percent taking test	27.7%
number with total score 1,500+	105

Average Scores:

Math	Verbal	Writing	Total
472	458	454	1,384

Federal No Child Left Behind, 2008
(Adequate Yearly Progress standards met)

	Participation Rate	Pct Proficient
ELA	Yes	No
Math	Yes	No

API Criteria	Yes
Graduation rate	Yes
# criteria met/possible	42/40

Belmont-Redwood Shores Elem

San Mateo County
2960 Hallmark Dr
Belmont, CA 94002
(650) 637-4800

Superint	Emerita Orta-Camilleri
Grade plan	K-8
Number of schools	6
Enrollment	2,616
High school graduates, 2006-07	0
Dropout rate	0
Pupil/teacher ratio	19.7%
Average class size	25.2
Students per computer	3.7
Avg. Teacher Salary,	$68,226
Avg. Daily Attendence (ADA)	2,484
Cost per ADA	$9,705

California Achievement Tests 6th ed., 2008
(Pct scoring at or above 50th National Percentile Rank)

	Math	Reading	Language
Grade 3	78%	66%	74%
Grade 7	77%	77%	74%

Academic Performance Index, 2009

Number of valid scores	1,841
2007 API (base)	878
2008 API (growth)	889

SAT Testing, 2006-07

Enrollment, Grade 12	NA
percent taking test	NA
number with total score 1,500+	NA

Average Scores:

Math	Verbal	Writing	Total
NA	NA	NA	NA

Federal No Child Left Behind, 2008
(Adequate Yearly Progress standards met)

	Participation Rate	Pct Proficient
ELA	Yes	Yes
Math	Yes	Yes

API Criteria	Yes
Graduation rate	NA
# criteria met/possible	29/29

Bend Elem

Tehama County
22270 Bend Ferry Rd
Red Bluff, CA 96080
(530) 527-4648

Superint	Kathleen Wheeler
Grade plan	K-8
Number of schools	1
Enrollment	83
High school graduates, 2006-07	0
Dropout rate	0
Pupil/teacher ratio	16.6%
Average class size	16.4
Students per computer	3.8
Avg. Teacher Salary,	NA
Avg. Daily Attendence (ADA)	80
Cost per ADA	$9,524

California Achievement Tests 6th ed., 2008
(Pct scoring at or above 50th National Percentile Rank)

	Math	Reading	Language
Grade 3	NA	NA	NA
Grade 7	NA	NA	NA

Academic Performance Index, 2009

Number of valid scores	62
2007 API (base)	698
2008 API (growth)	683

SAT Testing, 2006-07

Enrollment, Grade 12	NA
percent taking test	NA
number with total score 1,500+	NA

Average Scores:

Math	Verbal	Writing	Total
NA	NA	NA	NA

Federal No Child Left Behind, 2008
(Adequate Yearly Progress standards met)

	Participation Rate	Pct Proficient
ELA	Yes	Yes
Math	Yes	Yes

API Criteria	Yes
Graduation rate	NA
# criteria met/possible	5/5

Bennett Valley Union Elem

Sonoma County
2250 Mesquite Dr
Santa Rosa, CA 95405
(707) 542-2201

Superint	Susan Field
Grade plan	K-6
Number of schools	2
Enrollment	951
High school graduates, 2006-07	0
Dropout rate	NA
Pupil/teacher ratio	21.5%
Average class size	22.5
Students per computer	5.0
Avg. Teacher Salary,	$56,160
Avg. Daily Attendence (ADA)	919
Cost per ADA	$7,388

California Achievement Tests 6th ed., 2008
(Pct scoring at or above 50th National Percentile Rank)

	Math	Reading	Language
Grade 3	80%	68%	66%
Grade 7	NA	NA	NA

Academic Performance Index, 2009

Number of valid scores	644
2007 API (base)	869
2008 API (growth)	872

SAT Testing, 2006-07

Enrollment, Grade 12	NA
percent taking test	NA
number with total score 1,500+	NA

Average Scores:

Math	Verbal	Writing	Total
NA	NA	NA	NA

Federal No Child Left Behind, 2008
(Adequate Yearly Progress standards met)

	Participation Rate	Pct Proficient
ELA	Yes	Yes
Math	Yes	Yes

API Criteria	Yes
Graduation rate	NA
# criteria met/possible	17/17

Berryessa Union Elem

Santa Clara County
1376 Piedmont Rd
San Jose, CA 95132
(408) 923-1800

Superint	Marc Liebman
Grade plan	K-8
Number of schools	14
Enrollment	8,297
High school graduates, 2006-07	0
Dropout rate	0
Pupil/teacher ratio	20.9%
Average class size	25.9
Students per computer	6.0
Avg. Teacher Salary,	$66,916
Avg. Daily Attendence (ADA)	8,279
Cost per ADA	$7,335

California Achievement Tests 6th ed., 2008
(Pct scoring at or above 50th National Percentile Rank)

	Math	Reading	Language
Grade 3	69%	43%	57%
Grade 7	65%	59%	57%

Academic Performance Index, 2009

Number of valid scores	6,263
2007 API (base)	796
2008 API (growth)	813

SAT Testing, 2006-07

Enrollment, Grade 12	NA
percent taking test	NA
number with total score 1,500+	NA

Average Scores:

Math	Verbal	Writing	Total
NA	NA	NA	NA

Federal No Child Left Behind, 2008
(Adequate Yearly Progress standards met)

	Participation Rate	Pct Proficient
ELA	Yes	No
Math	Yes	No

API Criteria	Yes
Graduation rate	NA
# criteria met/possible	37/33

Big Lagoon Union Elem

Humboldt County
269 Big Lagoon Park Rd
Trinidad, CA 95570
(707) 677-3688

Superint	Kim Blanc
Grade plan	K-12
Number of schools	2
Enrollment	47
High school graduates, 2006-07	17
Dropout rate	0
Pupil/teacher ratio	14.7%
Average class size	10.4
Students per computer	1.9
Avg. Teacher Salary,	NA
Avg. Daily Attendence (ADA)	43
Cost per ADA	$13,272

California Achievement Tests 6th ed., 2008
(Pct scoring at or above 50th National Percentile Rank)

	Math	Reading	Language
Grade 3	NA	NA	NA
Grade 7	NA	NA	NA

Academic Performance Index, 2009

Number of valid scores	31
2007 API (base)	834
2008 API (growth)	875

SAT Testing, 2006-07

Enrollment, Grade 12	19
percent taking test	79.0%
number with total score 1,500+	12

Average Scores:

Math	Verbal	Writing	Total
551	581	556	1,688

Federal No Child Left Behind, 2008
(Adequate Yearly Progress standards met)

	Participation Rate	Pct Proficient
ELA	Yes	Yes
Math	Yes	Yes

API Criteria	Yes
Graduation rate	Yes
# criteria met/possible	6/6

Data from school year 2007-08 except where noted.
†Combined data for elementary and high schools.

Big Springs Union Elem

Siskiyou County
7405 Highway A-12
Montague, CA 96064
(530) 459-3189

Superint. . . . . Terry Weatherby
Grade plan. K-8
Number of schools. 1
Enrollment 86
High school graduates, 2006-07. 0
Dropout rate. 0
Pupil/teacher ratio. 17.2%
Average class size. 18.0
Students per computer 2.5
Avg. Teacher Salary, ...NA
Avg. Daily Attendence (ADA). 85
Cost per ADA. $12,232

California Achievement Tests 6th ed., 2008
(Pct scoring at or above 50th National Percentile Rank)

	Math	Reading	Language
Grade 3	46%	62%	62%
Grade 7	42%	50%	58%

Academic Performance Index, 2009
Number of valid scores. 58
2007 API (base) 764
2008 API (growth). 749

SAT Testing, 2006-07
Enrollment, Grade 12 . . . . .NA
percent taking test. . . . . .NA
number with total score 1,500+ . . . . . .NA

Average Scores:

Math	Verbal	Writing	Total
NA	NA	NA	NA

Federal No Child Left Behind, 2008
(Adequate Yearly Progress standards met)

	Participation Rate	Pct Proficient
ELA	Yes	Yes
Math	Yes	Yes

API Criteria . . . . .Yes
Graduation rate . . . . .NA
criteria met/possible. 5/5

Bishop Union Elem

Inyo County
800 West Elm St
Bishop, CA 93514
(760) 872-1060

Superint. . . . . Barry Simpson
Grade plan. K-8
Number of schools. 4
Enrollment 1,248
High school graduates, 2006-07. 0
Dropout rate. 0
Pupil/teacher ratio. 19.3%
Average class size. 24.3
Students per computer 5.0
Avg. Teacher Salary, ... $57,951
Avg. Daily Attendence (ADA). 1,201
Cost per ADA. $8,935

California Achievement Tests 6th ed., 2008
(Pct scoring at or above 50th National Percentile Rank)

	Math	Reading	Language
Grade 3	39%	30%	32%
Grade 7	55%	53%	52%

Academic Performance Index, 2009
Number of valid scores. 945
2007 API (base) 744
2008 API (growth). 752

SAT Testing, 2006-07
Enrollment, Grade 12 . . . . .NA
percent taking test. . . . . .NA
number with total score 1,500+ . . . . . .NA

Average Scores:

Math	Verbal	Writing	Total
NA	NA	NA	NA

Federal No Child Left Behind, 2008
(Adequate Yearly Progress standards met)

	Participation Rate	Pct Proficient
ELA	Yes	No
Math	Yes	No

API Criteria . . . . .Yes
Graduation rate . . . . .NA
criteria met/possible. 27/23

Bitterwater-Tully Union Elem

San Benito County
Lonoak Rt, Box 10
King City, CA 93930
(831) 385-5339

Superint. . . . . Kevin Kirschman
Grade plan. K-8
Number of schools. 1
Enrollment 27
High school graduates, 2006-07. 0
Dropout rate. 0
Pupil/teacher ratio. 13.5%
Average class size. 10.0
Students per computer 2.2
Avg. Teacher Salary, ...NA
Avg. Daily Attendence (ADA). 28
Cost per ADA. $12,471

California Achievement Tests 6th ed., 2008
(Pct scoring at or above 50th National Percentile Rank)

	Math	Reading	Language
Grade 3	NA	NA	NA
Grade 7	NA	NA	NA

Academic Performance Index, 2009
Number of valid scores. 23
2007 API (base) 890
2008 API (growth). 828

SAT Testing, 2006-07
Enrollment, Grade 12 . . . . .NA
percent taking test. . . . . .NA
number with total score 1,500+ . . . . . .NA

Average Scores:

Math	Verbal	Writing	Total
NA	NA	NA	NA

Federal No Child Left Behind, 2008
(Adequate Yearly Progress standards met)

	Participation Rate	Pct Proficient
ELA	Yes	Yes
Math	Yes	Yes

API Criteria . . . . .Yes
Graduation rate . . . . .NA
criteria met/possible. 5/5

Blochman Union Elem

Santa Barbara County
4949 Foxen Canyon Rd
Santa Maria, CA 93454
(805) 937-1148

Superint. . . . . Kristin Garrison-Lima
Grade plan. K-8
Number of schools. 2
Enrollment 420
High school graduates, 2006-07. 12
Dropout rate. 3.6
Pupil/teacher ratio. 15.5%
Average class size. 8.0
Students per computer 6.8
Avg. Teacher Salary, ... $48,120
Avg. Daily Attendence (ADA). 105
Cost per ADA. $7,894

California Achievement Tests 6th ed., 2008
(Pct scoring at or above 50th National Percentile Rank)

	Math	Reading	Language
Grade 3	NA	NA	NA
Grade 7	NA	NA	NA

Academic Performance Index, 2009
Number of valid scores. 282
2007 API (base) 743
2008 API (growth). 740

SAT Testing, 2006-07
Enrollment, Grade 12 20
percent taking test. . . . . .NA
number with total score 1,500+ . . . . . .NA

Average Scores:

Math	Verbal	Writing	Total
NA	NA	NA	NA

Federal No Child Left Behind, 2008
(Adequate Yearly Progress standards met)

	Participation Rate	Pct Proficient
ELA	Yes	Yes
Math	Yes	Yes

API Criteria . . . . .Yes
Graduation rate . . . . .No
criteria met/possible. 14/13

Blue Lake Union Elem

Humboldt County
PO Box 268
Blue Lake, CA 95525
(707) 668-5674

Superint. . . . . .Paula Wyant-Kelso
Grade plan. K-8
Number of schools. 1
Enrollment 154
High school graduates, 2006-07. 0
Dropout rate. 0
Pupil/teacher ratio. 17.3%
Average class size. 20.8
Students per computer 3.4
Avg. Teacher Salary, ... $60,818
Avg. Daily Attendence (ADA). 149
Cost per ADA. $10,523

California Achievement Tests 6th ed., 2008
(Pct scoring at or above 50th National Percentile Rank)

	Math	Reading	Language
Grade 3	NA	NA	NA
Grade 7	74%	63%	58%

Academic Performance Index, 2009
Number of valid scores. 107
2007 API (base) 755
2008 API (growth). 789

SAT Testing, 2006-07
Enrollment, Grade 12 . . . . .NA
percent taking test. . . . . .NA
number with total score 1,500+ . . . . . .NA

Average Scores:

Math	Verbal	Writing	Total
NA	NA	NA	NA

Federal No Child Left Behind, 2008
(Adequate Yearly Progress standards met)

	Participation Rate	Pct Proficient
ELA	Yes	Yes
Math	Yes	Yes

API Criteria . . . . .Yes
Graduation rate . . . . .NA
criteria met/possible. 13/13

Bogus Elem

Siskiyou County
13735 Ager-Beswick Rd
Montague, CA 96064
(530) 459-3163

Superint. . . . . Fred Ehmke
Grade plan. K-6
Number of schools. 1
Enrollment 11
High school graduates, 2006-07. 0
Dropout rate. 0
Pupil/teacher ratio. 11.0%
Average class size. 11.0
Students per computer 2.8
Avg. Teacher Salary, ...NA
Avg. Daily Attendence (ADA). 11
Cost per ADA. $16,648

California Achievement Tests 6th ed., 2008
(Pct scoring at or above 50th National Percentile Rank)

	Math	Reading	Language
Grade 3	NA	NA	NA
Grade 7	NA	NA	NA

Academic Performance Index, 2009
Number of valid scores. . . . .
2007 API (base) . . . . .NA
2008 API (growth). . . . . .NA

SAT Testing, 2006-07
Enrollment, Grade 12 . . . . .NA
percent taking test. . . . . .NA
number with total score 1,500+ . . . . . .NA

Average Scores:

Math	Verbal	Writing	Total
NA	NA	NA	NA

Federal No Child Left Behind, 2008
(Adequate Yearly Progress standards met)

	Participation Rate	Pct Proficient
ELA	Yes	Yes
Math	Yes	Yes

API Criteria . . . . .Yes
Graduation rate . . . . .NA
criteria met/possible. 5/5

Data from school year 2007-08 except where noted
†Combined data for elementary and high schools

Bonny Doon Union Elem

Santa Cruz County
1492 Pine Flat Rd
Santa Cruz, CA 95060
(831) 427-2300

Superint. . . . . Gail Levine
Grade plan. K-6
Number of schools. 1
Enrollment 131
High school graduates, 2006-07. 0
Dropout rate. . . . . NA
Pupil/teacher ratio. 16.4%
Average class size. 18.7
Students per computer 6.6
Avg. Teacher Salary, ... NA
Avg. Daily Attendence (ADA). 125
Cost per ADA. $12,592

California Achievement Tests 6th ed., 2008
(Pct scoring at or above 50th National Percentile Rank)

	Math	Reading	Language
Grade 3	58%	50%	67%
Grade 7	NA	NA	NA

Academic Performance Index, 2009
Number of valid scores. 87
2007 API (base) 845
2008 API (growth). 816

SAT Testing, 2006-07
Enrollment, Grade 12 . . . . NA
percent taking test. . . . . NA
number with total score 1,500+ . . . . . . NA

Average Scores:

Math	Verbal	Writing	Total
NA	NA	NA	NA

Federal No Child Left Behind, 2008
(Adequate Yearly Progress standards met)

	Participation Rate	Pct Proficient
ELA	Yes	Yes
Math	Yes	Yes

API Criteria . . . . Yes
Graduation rate . . . . NA
criteria met/possible. 5/5

Brawley Elem

Imperial County
261 D St
Brawley, CA 92227
(760) 344-2330

Superint. Terri Decker
Grade plan. K-8
Number of schools. 5
Enrollment 3,623
High school graduates, 2006-07. 0
Dropout rate. 0
Pupil/teacher ratio. 20.4%
Average class size. 23.2
Students per computer 4.3
Avg. Teacher Salary, ... $68,362
Avg. Daily Attendence (ADA). 3,543
Cost per ADA. $8,161

California Achievement Tests 6th ed., 2008
(Pct scoring at or above 50th National Percentile Rank)

	Math	Reading	Language
Grade 3	51%	31%	43%
Grade 7	45%	42%	42%

Academic Performance Index, 2009
Number of valid scores. 2,634
2007 API (base) 728
2008 API (growth). 745

SAT Testing, 2006-07
Enrollment, Grade 12 . . . . NA
percent taking test. . . . . NA
number with total score 1,500+ . . . . . . NA

Average Scores:

Math	Verbal	Writing	Total
NA	NA	NA	NA

Federal No Child Left Behind, 2008
(Adequate Yearly Progress standards met)

	Participation Rate	Pct Proficient
ELA	Yes	No
Math	Yes	Yes

API Criteria . . . . Yes
Graduation rate . . . . NA
criteria met/possible. 25/22

Brentwood Union Elem

Contra Costa County
255 Guthrie Ln
Brentwood, CA 94513
(925) 513-6300

Superint. Merrill Grant
Grade plan. K-8
Number of schools. 10
Enrollment 8,105
High school graduates, 2006-07. 0
Dropout rate. 0
Pupil/teacher ratio. 20.3%
Average class size. 26.2
Students per computer 4.6
Avg. Teacher Salary, ... $67,153
Avg. Daily Attendence (ADA). 7,919
Cost per ADA. $7,153

California Achievement Tests 6th ed., 2008
(Pct scoring at or above 50th National Percentile Rank)

	Math	Reading	Language
Grade 3	58%	47%	55%
Grade 7	56%	57%	55%

Academic Performance Index, 2009
Number of valid scores. 6,132
2007 API (base) 783
2008 API (growth). 789

SAT Testing, 2006-07
Enrollment, Grade 12 . . . . NA
percent taking test. . . . . NA
number with total score 1,500+ . . . . . . NA

Average Scores:

Math	Verbal	Writing	Total
NA	NA	NA	NA

Federal No Child Left Behind, 2008
(Adequate Yearly Progress standards met)

	Participation Rate	Pct Proficient
ELA	Yes	No
Math	Yes	No

API Criteria . . . . Yes
Graduation rate . . . . NA
criteria met/possible. 37/32

Briggs Elem

Ventura County
12465 Foothill Rd
Santa Paula, CA 93036
(805) 525-7540

Superint. . . . . Mike McLaughlin
Grade plan. K-8
Number of schools. 2
Enrollment 425
High school graduates, 2006-07. 0
Dropout rate. 0
Pupil/teacher ratio. 22.8%
Average class size. 27.3
Students per computer 1.8
Avg. Teacher Salary, ... $57,143
Avg. Daily Attendence (ADA). 416
Cost per ADA. $8,243

California Achievement Tests 6th ed., 2008
(Pct scoring at or above 50th National Percentile Rank)

	Math	Reading	Language
Grade 3	67%	23%	43%
Grade 7	54%	42%	52%

Academic Performance Index, 2009
Number of valid scores. 325
2007 API (base) 691
2008 API (growth). 716

SAT Testing, 2006-07
Enrollment, Grade 12 . . . . NA
percent taking test. . . . . NA
number with total score 1,500+ . . . . . . NA

Average Scores:

Math	Verbal	Writing	Total
NA	NA	NA	NA

Federal No Child Left Behind, 2008
(Adequate Yearly Progress standards met)

	Participation Rate	Pct Proficient
ELA	Yes	No
Math	Yes	No

API Criteria . . . . Yes
Graduation rate . . . . NA
criteria met/possible. 21/17

Brisbane Elem

San Mateo County
1 Solano St
Brisbane, CA 94005
(415) 467-0550

Superint. . . . . Toni Presta
Grade plan. K-8
Number of schools. 3
Enrollment 589
High school graduates, 2006-07. 0
Dropout rate. 0
Pupil/teacher ratio. 15.8%
Average class size. 21.4
Students per computer 4.9
Avg. Teacher Salary, ... $62,431
Avg. Daily Attendence (ADA). 577
Cost per ADA. $9,829

California Achievement Tests 6th ed., 2008
(Pct scoring at or above 50th National Percentile Rank)

	Math	Reading	Language
Grade 3	51%	39%	56%
Grade 7	73%	59%	55%

Academic Performance Index, 2009
Number of valid scores. 446
2007 API (base) 773
2008 API (growth). 792

SAT Testing, 2006-07
Enrollment, Grade 12 . . . . NA
percent taking test. . . . . NA
number with total score 1,500+ . . . . . . NA

Average Scores:

Math	Verbal	Writing	Total
NA	NA	NA	NA

Federal No Child Left Behind, 2008
(Adequate Yearly Progress standards met)

	Participation Rate	Pct Proficient
ELA	Yes	No
Math	Yes	No

API Criteria . . . . Yes
Graduation rate . . . . NA
criteria met/possible. 29/26

Buellton Union Elem

Santa Barbara County
595 Second St
Buellton, CA 93427
(805) 686-2767

Superint. . . . . William Cirone
Grade plan. K-8
Number of schools. 2
Enrollment 665
High school graduates, 2006-07. 0
Dropout rate. 0
Pupil/teacher ratio. 18.4%
Average class size. 19.7
Students per computer 10.9
Avg. Teacher Salary, ... $58,926
Avg. Daily Attendence (ADA). 694
Cost per ADA. $10,356

California Achievement Tests 6th ed., 2008
(Pct scoring at or above 50th National Percentile Rank)

	Math	Reading	Language
Grade 3	64%	51%	57%
Grade 7	70%	67%	60%

Academic Performance Index, 2009
Number of valid scores. 487
2007 API (base) 830
2008 API (growth). 843

SAT Testing, 2006-07
Enrollment, Grade 12 . . . . NA
percent taking test. . . . . NA
number with total score 1,500+ . . . . . . NA

Average Scores:

Math	Verbal	Writing	Total
NA	NA	NA	NA

Federal No Child Left Behind, 2008
(Adequate Yearly Progress standards met)

	Participation Rate	Pct Proficient
ELA	Yes	Yes
Math	Yes	Yes

API Criteria . . . . Yes
Graduation rate . . . . NA
criteria met/possible. 21/21

Data from school year 2007-08 except where noted.
†Combined data for elementary and high schools.

Buena Park Elem

Orange County
6885 Orangethorpe Ave
Buena Park, CA 90620
(714) 522-8412

Superint. . . . . Greg Magnuson
Grade plan. K-8
Number of schools. 7
Enrollment 5,766
High school graduates, 2006-07. 0
Dropout rate. 0
Pupil/teacher ratio. 23.3%
Average class size. 25.0
Students per computer 4.2
Avg. Teacher Salary, ... $73,110
Avg. Daily Attendence (ADA). 5,567
Cost per ADA. $8,240

California Achievement Tests 6th ed., 2008
(Pct scoring at or above 50th National Percentile Rank)

	Math	Reading	Language
Grade 3	59%	35%	48%
Grade 7	48%	45%	46%

Academic Performance Index, 2009
Number of valid scores. 4,043
2007 API (base) 758
2008 API (growth). 769

SAT Testing, 2006-07
Enrollment, Grade 12 . . . . . NA
percent taking test. . . . . NA
number with total score 1,500+ . . . . . NA

Average Scores:

Math	Verbal	Writing	Total
NA	NA	NA	NA

Federal No Child Left Behind, 2008
(Adequate Yearly Progress standards met)

	Participation Rate	Pct Proficient
ELA	Yes	No
Math	Yes	No

API Criteria . . . . . Yes
Graduation rate . . . . . NA
\# criteria met/possible. 37/35

Buena Vista Elem

Tulare County
21660 Road 60
Tulare, CA 93274
(559) 686-2015

Superint. . . . . Carole Mederos
Grade plan. K-8
Number of schools. 1
Enrollment 194
High school graduates, 2006-07. 0
Dropout rate. 0
Pupil/teacher ratio. 19.4%
Average class size. 21.8
Students per computer 10.2
Avg. Teacher Salary, ... $49,460
Avg. Daily Attendence (ADA). 189
Cost per ADA. $7,189

California Achievement Tests 6th ed., 2008
(Pct scoring at or above 50th National Percentile Rank)

	Math	Reading	Language
Grade 3	41%	32%	41%
Grade 7	69%	62%	65%

Academic Performance Index, 2009
Number of valid scores. 147
2007 API (base) 745
2008 API (growth). 780

SAT Testing, 2006-07
Enrollment, Grade 12 . . . . . NA
percent taking test. . . . . NA
number with total score 1,500+ . . . . . NA

Average Scores:

Math	Verbal	Writing	Total
NA	NA	NA	NA

Federal No Child Left Behind, 2008
(Adequate Yearly Progress standards met)

	Participation Rate	Pct Proficient
ELA	Yes	Yes
Math	Yes	Yes

API Criteria . . . . . Yes
Graduation rate . . . . . NA
\# criteria met/possible. 15/15

Burlingame Elem

San Mateo County
1825 Trousdale Dr
Burlingame, CA 94010
(650) 259-3800

Superint. . . . . Dianne Talarico
Grade plan. K-8
Number of schools. 6
Enrollment 2,411
High school graduates, 2006-07. 0
Dropout rate. 0
Pupil/teacher ratio. 19.5%
Average class size. 25.5
Students per computer 3.7
Avg. Teacher Salary, ... $63,121
Avg. Daily Attendence (ADA). 2,357
Cost per ADA. $7,754

California Achievement Tests 6th ed., 2008
(Pct scoring at or above 50th National Percentile Rank)

	Math	Reading	Language
Grade 3	80%	63%	66%
Grade 7	73%	70%	69%

Academic Performance Index, 2009
Number of valid scores. 1,753
2007 API (base) 874
2008 API (growth). 884

SAT Testing, 2006-07
Enrollment, Grade 12 . . . . . NA
percent taking test. . . . . NA
number with total score 1,500+ . . . . . NA

Average Scores:

Math	Verbal	Writing	Total
NA	NA	NA	NA

Federal No Child Left Behind, 2008
(Adequate Yearly Progress standards met)

	Participation Rate	Pct Proficient
ELA	Yes	Yes
Math	Yes	Yes

API Criteria . . . . . Yes
Graduation rate . . . . . NA
\# criteria met/possible. 29/29

Burton Elem

Tulare County
264 North Westwood St
Porterville, CA 93257
(559) 781-8020

Superint. . . . . Gary Mekeel
Grade plan. K-8
Number of schools. 7
Enrollment 3,364
High school graduates, 2006-07. 0
Dropout rate. 0
Pupil/teacher ratio. 19.6%
Average class size. 22.3
Students per computer 5.8
Avg. Teacher Salary, ... $59,518
Avg. Daily Attendence (ADA). 2,882
Cost per ADA. $7,314

California Achievement Tests 6th ed., 2008
(Pct scoring at or above 50th National Percentile Rank)

	Math	Reading	Language
Grade 3	48%	30%	41%
Grade 7	44%	42%	38%

Academic Performance Index, 2009
Number of valid scores. 2,476
2007 API (base) 730
2008 API (growth). 739

SAT Testing, 2006-07
Enrollment, Grade 12 . . . . . NA
percent taking test. . . . . NA
number with total score 1,500+ . . . . . NA

Average Scores:

Math	Verbal	Writing	Total
NA	NA	NA	NA

Federal No Child Left Behind, 2008
(Adequate Yearly Progress standards met)

	Participation Rate	Pct Proficient
ELA	Yes	No
Math	Yes	Yes

API Criteria . . . . . Yes
Graduation rate . . . . . Yes
\# criteria met/possible. 26/22

Butteville Union Elem

Siskiyou County
24512 Edgewood Rd
Edgewood, CA 96094
(530) 938-2255

Superint. . . . . Mike Michelon
Grade plan. K-8
Number of schools. 1
Enrollment 160
High school graduates, 2006-07. 0
Dropout rate. 0
Pupil/teacher ratio. 16.1%
Average class size. 16.6
Students per computer 2.8
Avg. Teacher Salary, ... $41,876
Avg. Daily Attendence (ADA). 153
Cost per ADA. $8,683

California Achievement Tests 6th ed., 2008
(Pct scoring at or above 50th National Percentile Rank)

	Math	Reading	Language
Grade 3	39%	39%	56%
Grade 7	86%	93%	79%

Academic Performance Index, 2009
Number of valid scores. 107
2007 API (base) 810
2008 API (growth). 785

SAT Testing, 2006-07
Enrollment, Grade 12 . . . . . NA
percent taking test. . . . . NA
number with total score 1,500+ . . . . . NA

Average Scores:

Math	Verbal	Writing	Total
NA	NA	NA	NA

Federal No Child Left Behind, 2008
(Adequate Yearly Progress standards met)

	Participation Rate	Pct Proficient
ELA	Yes	Yes
Math	Yes	Yes

API Criteria . . . . . Yes
Graduation rate . . . . . NA
\# criteria met/possible. 11/11

Cabrillo Unified

San Mateo County
498 Kelly Ave
Half Moon Bay, CA 94019
(650) 712-7100

Superint. . . . . Robert Gaskill
Grade plan. K-12
Number of schools. 7
Enrollment 3,363
High school graduates, 2006-07. 239
Dropout rate. 3.8
Pupil/teacher ratio. 21.7%
Average class size. 24.7
Students per computer 4.8
Avg. Teacher Salary, ... $63,222
Avg. Daily Attendence (ADA). 3,427
Cost per ADA. $7,639

California Achievement Tests 6th ed., 2008
(Pct scoring at or above 50th National Percentile Rank)

	Math	Reading	Language
Grade 3	58%	46%	51%
Grade 7	59%	63%	57%

Academic Performance Index, 2009
Number of valid scores. 2,462
2007 API (base) 772
2008 API (growth). 777

SAT Testing, 2006-07
Enrollment, Grade 12 313
percent taking test. 42.8%
number with total score 1,500+ 97

Average Scores:

Math	Verbal	Writing	Total
564	548	550	1,662

Federal No Child Left Behind, 2008
(Adequate Yearly Progress standards met)

	Participation Rate	Pct Proficient
ELA	Yes	No
Math	Yes	No

API Criteria . . . . . Yes
Graduation rate . . . . . Yes
\# criteria met/possible. 26/19

Data from school year 2007-08 except where noted
†Combined data for elementary and high schools

Cambrian

Santa Clara County
4115 Jacksol Dr
San Jose, CA 95124
(408) 377-2103

Superint.................... Thomas Dase
Grade plan.......................... K-8
Number of schools....................... 6
Enrollment 3,075
High school graduates, 2006-07........ 0
Dropout rate.......................... 0
Pupil/teacher ratio............... 21.0%
Average class size.................. 25.1
Students per computer 3.2
Avg. Teacher Salary, ... $70,330
Avg. Daily Attendence (ADA)........ 3,050
Cost per ADA.................. $8,016

California Achievement Tests 6th ed., 2008
(Pct scoring at or above 50th National Percentile Rank)

	Math	Reading	Language
Grade 3	79%	64%	68%
Grade 7	70%	65%	60%

Academic Performance Index, 2009
Number of valid scores.............. 2,273
2007 API (base) 853
2008 API (growth)..................... 861

SAT Testing, 2006-07
Enrollment, Grade 12................. NA
percent taking test.................. NA
number with total score 1,500+ ...... NA

Average Scores:

Math	Verbal	Writing	Total
NA	NA	NA	NA

Federal No Child Left Behind, 2008
(Adequate Yearly Progress standards met)

	Participation Rate	Pct Proficient
ELA	Yes	Yes
Math	Yes	Yes

API Criteria .... Yes
Graduation rate .... NA
criteria met/possible............... 29/29

Campbell Union Elem

Santa Clara County
155 North Third St
Campbell, CA 95008
(408) 364-4200

Superint........... Johanna VanderMolen
Grade plan.......................... K-8
Number of schools...................... 13
Enrollment 7,338
High school graduates, 2006-07........ 0
Dropout rate.......................... 0
Pupil/teacher ratio............... 20.5%
Average class size.................. 25.2
Students per computer 3.5
Avg. Teacher Salary, ... $66,766
Avg. Daily Attendence (ADA)........ 7,264
Cost per ADA.................. $8,473

California Achievement Tests 6th ed., 2008
(Pct scoring at or above 50th National Percentile Rank)

	Math	Reading	Language
Grade 3	61%	45%	54%
Grade 7	56%	52%	50%

Academic Performance Index, 2009
Number of valid scores.............. 5,245
2007 API (base) 776
2008 API (growth)..................... 793

SAT Testing, 2006-07
Enrollment, Grade 12................. NA
percent taking test.................. NA
number with total score 1,500+ ...... NA

Average Scores:

Math	Verbal	Writing	Total
NA	NA	NA	NA

Federal No Child Left Behind, 2008
(Adequate Yearly Progress standards met)

	Participation Rate	Pct Proficient
ELA	Yes	No
Math	Yes	No

API Criteria .... Yes
Graduation rate .... NA
criteria met/possible............... 37/33

Campbell Union High

Santa Clara County
3235 Union Ave
San Jose, CA 95124
(408) 371-0960

Superint.................. Rhonda Farber
Grade plan......................... 9-12
Number of schools....................... 7
Enrollment 7,838
High school graduates, 2006-07.... 1,447
Dropout rate........................ 4.5
Pupil/teacher ratio............... 22.5%
Average class size.................. 25.4
Students per computer 3.8
Avg. Teacher Salary, ... $64,628
Avg. Daily Attendence (ADA)........ 7,486
Cost per ADA.................. $8,580

California Achievement Tests 6th ed., 2008
(Pct scoring at or above 50th National Percentile Rank)

	Math	Reading	Language
Grade 3			
Grade 7			

Academic Performance Index, 2009
Number of valid scores.............. 5,320
2007 API (base) 752
2008 API (growth)..................... 749

SAT Testing, 2006-07
Enrollment, Grade 12............... 1,842
percent taking test............... 43.0%
number with total score 1,500+ 511

Average Scores:

Math	Verbal	Writing	Total
551	530	526	1,607

Federal No Child Left Behind, 2008
(Adequate Yearly Progress standards met)

	Participation Rate	Pct Proficient
ELA	Yes	No
Math	Yes	No

API Criteria .... Yes
Graduation rate .... No
criteria met/possible............... 30/27

Capay Joint Union Elem

Glenn County
7504 Cutting Ave
Orland, CA 95963
(530) 865-1222

Superint.................... Jim Scribner
Grade plan.......................... K-8
Number of schools....................... 1
Enrollment 145
High school graduates, 2006-07........ 0
Dropout rate.......................... 0
Pupil/teacher ratio............... 20.7%
Average class size.................. 20.7
Students per computer 3.8
Avg. Teacher Salary, ... NA
Avg. Daily Attendence (ADA).......... 143
Cost per ADA.................. $6,459

California Achievement Tests 6th ed., 2008
(Pct scoring at or above 50th National Percentile Rank)

	Math	Reading	Language
Grade 3	73%	53%	67%
Grade 7	NA	NA	NA

Academic Performance Index, 2009
Number of valid scores................. 98
2007 API (base) 816
2008 API (growth)..................... 835

SAT Testing, 2006-07
Enrollment, Grade 12................. NA
percent taking test.................. NA
number with total score 1,500+ ...... NA

Average Scores:

Math	Verbal	Writing	Total
NA	NA	NA	NA

Federal No Child Left Behind, 2008
(Adequate Yearly Progress standards met)

	Participation Rate	Pct Proficient
ELA	Yes	Yes
Math	Yes	Yes

API Criteria .... Yes
Graduation rate .... NA
criteria met/possible................. 7/7

Capistrano Unified

Orange County
33122 Valle Rd
San Juan Capistrano, CA 92675
(949) 234-9200

Superint....................... A. Carter
Grade plan......................... K-12
Number of schools...................... 61
Enrollment 52,390
High school graduates, 2006-07.... 3,205
Dropout rate........................ 0.5
Pupil/teacher ratio............... 23.4%
Average class size.................. 28.7
Students per computer 4.8
Avg. Teacher Salary, ... $75,390
Avg. Daily Attendence (ADA)....... 50,036
Cost per ADA.................. $7,694

California Achievement Tests 6th ed., 2008
(Pct scoring at or above 50th National Percentile Rank)

	Math	Reading	Language
Grade 3	71%	56%	63%
Grade 7	73%	71%	68%

Academic Performance Index, 2009
Number of valid scores............. 38,275
2007 API (base) 826
2008 API (growth)..................... 837

SAT Testing, 2006-07
Enrollment, Grade 12............... 3,414
percent taking test............... 51.9%
number with total score 1,500+ 1,193

Average Scores:

Math	Verbal	Writing	Total
552	541	537	1,630

Federal No Child Left Behind, 2008
(Adequate Yearly Progress standards met)

	Participation Rate	Pct Proficient
ELA	Yes	No
Math	Yes	Yes

API Criteria .... Yes
Graduation rate .... Yes
criteria met/possible............... 42/41

Cardiff Elem

San Diego County
1888 Montgomery Ave
Cardiff-by-the-Sea, CA 92007
(760) 632-5890

Superint.................. Tom Pellegrino
Grade plan.......................... K-6
Number of schools....................... 2
Enrollment 724
High school graduates, 2006-07........ 0
Dropout rate......................... NA
Pupil/teacher ratio............... 17.7%
Average class size.................. 20.0
Students per computer 2.9
Avg. Teacher Salary, ... $69,370
Avg. Daily Attendence (ADA).......... 698
Cost per ADA.................. $9,683

California Achievement Tests 6th ed., 2008
(Pct scoring at or above 50th National Percentile Rank)

	Math	Reading	Language
Grade 3	84%	71%	77%
Grade 7	NA	NA	NA

Academic Performance Index, 2009
Number of valid scores................ 476
2007 API (base) 878
2008 API (growth)..................... 894

SAT Testing, 2006-07
Enrollment, Grade 12................. NA
percent taking test.................. NA
number with total score 1,500+ ...... NA

Average Scores:

Math	Verbal	Writing	Total
NA	NA	NA	NA

Federal No Child Left Behind, 2008
(Adequate Yearly Progress standards met)

	Participation Rate	Pct Proficient
ELA	Yes	Yes
Math	Yes	Yes

API Criteria .... Yes
Graduation rate .... NA
criteria met/possible............... 17/17

Data from school year 2007-08 except where noted.
†Combined data for elementary and high schools.

Cascade Union Elem

Shasta County
1645 West Mill St
Anderson, CA 96007
(530) 378-7000

Superint....................Wesley Smith
Grade plan............................K-8
Number of schools.......................7
Enrollment......................1,526
High school graduates, 2006-07........0
Dropout rate..........................0
Pupil/teacher ratio............... 20.6%
Average class size.................. 23.9
Students per computer.............. 2.5
Avg. Teacher Salary, ...$53,914
Avg. Daily Attendence (ADA)........1,425
Cost per ADA..................$9,134

California Achievement Tests 6th ed., 2008
(Pct scoring at or above 50th National Percentile Rank)

	Math	Reading	Language
Grade 3	62%	52%	55%
Grade 7	42%	46%	37%

Academic Performance Index, 2009
Number of valid scores..............1,001
2007 API (base).......................728
2008 API (growth).....................747

SAT Testing, 2006-07
Enrollment, Grade 12..................NA
percent taking test...................NA
number with total score 1,500+ ......NA

Average Scores:

Math	Verbal	Writing	Total
NA	NA	NA	NA

Federal No Child Left Behind, 2008
(Adequate Yearly Progress standards met)

	Participation Rate	Pct Proficient
ELA	Yes	No
Math	Yes	No

API Criteria..........................Yes
Graduation rate.......................NA
criteria met/possible...............25/23

Casmalia Elem

Santa Barbara County
(merged into Orcutt Union Elem)
Soares St and Dyer St
Orcutt, CA 93457
(805) 938-8900

Superint..............Sharon McHolland
Grade plan............................K-8
Number of schools.......................1
Enrollment..........................18
High school graduates, 2006-07........0
Dropout rate..........................0
Pupil/teacher ratio.............. 18.0%
Average class size.................. 0.0
Students per computer.............. 0.7
Avg. Teacher Salary, ...NA
Avg. Daily Attendence (ADA)...........16
Cost per ADA.................$15,081

California Achievement Tests 6th ed., 2008
(Pct scoring at or above 50th National Percentile Rank)

	Math	Reading	Language
Grade 3	NA	NA	NA
Grade 7	NA	NA	NA

Academic Performance Index, 2009
Number of valid scores..................
2007 API (base)........................NA
2008 API (growth)......................NA

SAT Testing, 2006-07
Enrollment, Grade 12..................NA
percent taking test...................NA

Average Scores:

Math	Verbal	Writing	Total
NA	NA	NA	NA

Federal No Child Left Behind, 2008
(Adequate Yearly Progress standards met)

	Participation Rate	Pct Proficient
ELA	Yes	Yes
Math	Yes	Yes

API Criteria..........................Yes
Graduation rate.......................NA
criteria met/possible.................5/5

Central Elem

San Bernardino County
10601 Church St, Ste 112
Rancho Cucamonga, CA 91730
(909) 989-8541

Superint....................Sharon Nagel
Grade plan............................K-8
Number of schools.......................7
Enrollment.......................4,845
High school graduates, 2006-07........0
Dropout rate..........................0
Pupil/teacher ratio............... 23.8%
Average class size.................. 28.1
Students per computer.............. 6.1
Avg. Teacher Salary, ...$68,075
Avg. Daily Attendence (ADA)........4,751
Cost per ADA...................$6,667

California Achievement Tests 6th ed., 2008
(Pct scoring at or above 50th National Percentile Rank)

	Math	Reading	Language
Grade 3	62%	44%	55%
Grade 7	56%	56%	49%

Academic Performance Index, 2009
Number of valid scores..............3,608
2007 API (base).......................795
2008 API (growth).....................803

SAT Testing, 2006-07
Enrollment, Grade 12..................NA
percent taking test...................NA
number with total score 1,500+ ......NA

Average Scores:

Math	Verbal	Writing	Total
NA	NA	NA	NA

Federal No Child Left Behind, 2008
(Adequate Yearly Progress standards met)

	Participation Rate	Pct Proficient
ELA	Yes	No
Math	Yes	No

API Criteria..........................Yes
Graduation rate.......................NA
criteria met/possible...............33/31

Central Unified

Fresno County
4605 North Polk Ave
Fresno, CA 93722
(559) 274-4700

Superint..................Marilou Ryder
Grade plan...........................K-12
Number of schools......................19
Enrollment......................14,180
High school graduates, 2006-07......694
Dropout rate........................ 4.9
Pupil/teacher ratio................21.7%
Average class size.................. 26.9
Students per computer.............. 5.8
Avg. Teacher Salary, ...$57,528
Avg. Daily Attendence (ADA).......13,750
Cost per ADA...................$7,411

California Achievement Tests 6th ed., 2008
(Pct scoring at or above 50th National Percentile Rank)

	Math	Reading	Language
Grade 3	52%	33%	40%
Grade 7	46%	47%	48%

Academic Performance Index, 2009
Number of valid scores..............9,972
2007 API (base).......................704
2008 API (growth).....................716

SAT Testing, 2006-07
Enrollment, Grade 12.................905
percent taking test............... 26.5%
number with total score 1,500+ 46

Average Scores:

Math	Verbal	Writing	Total
451	429	429	1,309

Federal No Child Left Behind, 2008
(Adequate Yearly Progress standards met)

	Participation Rate	Pct Proficient
ELA	No	No
Math	Yes	No

API Criteria..........................Yes
Graduation rate.......................No
criteria met/possible...............38/30

Central Union Elem

Kings County
15783 18th Ave
Lemoore, CA 93245
(559) 924-3405

Superint......................Ron Seaver
Grade plan............................K-8
Number of schools.......................4
Enrollment......................1,941
High school graduates, 2006-07........0
Dropout rate..........................0
Pupil/teacher ratio................17.6%
Average class size.................. 23.1
Students per computer.............. 2.1
Avg. Teacher Salary, ...$73,362
Avg. Daily Attendence (ADA)........1,887
Cost per ADA.................$10,154

California Achievement Tests 6th ed., 2008
(Pct scoring at or above 50th National Percentile Rank)

	Math	Reading	Language
Grade 3	54%	47%	47%
Grade 7	57%	55%	48%

Academic Performance Index, 2009
Number of valid scores..............1,291
2007 API (base).......................798
2008 API (growth).....................808

SAT Testing, 2006-07
Enrollment, Grade 12..................NA
percent taking test...................NA
number with total score 1,500+ ......NA

Average Scores:

Math	Verbal	Writing	Total
NA	NA	NA	NA

Federal No Child Left Behind, 2008
(Adequate Yearly Progress standards met)

	Participation Rate	Pct Proficient
ELA	Yes	No
Math	Yes	No

API Criteria..........................Yes
Graduation rate.......................NA
criteria met/possible...............31/28

Centralia Elem

Orange County
6625 La Palma Ave
Buena Park, CA 90620
(714) 228-3100

Superint................Diane Scheerhorn
Grade plan............................K-6
Number of schools.......................9
Enrollment.......................4,808
High school graduates, 2006-07........0
Dropout rate.........................NA
Pupil/teacher ratio............... 22.9%
Average class size.................. 24.4
Students per computer.............. 7.5
Avg. Teacher Salary, ...$72,624
Avg. Daily Attendence (ADA)........4,635
Cost per ADA...................$8,475

California Achievement Tests 6th ed., 2008
(Pct scoring at or above 50th National Percentile Rank)

	Math	Reading	Language
Grade 3	57%	41%	49%
Grade 7	NA	NA	NA

Academic Performance Index, 2009
Number of valid scores..............3,194
2007 API (base).......................780
2008 API (growth).....................804

SAT Testing, 2006-07
Enrollment, Grade 12..................NA
percent taking test...................NA
number with total score 1,500+ ......NA

Average Scores:

Math	Verbal	Writing	Total
NA	NA	NA	NA

Federal No Child Left Behind, 2008
(Adequate Yearly Progress standards met)

	Participation Rate	Pct Proficient
ELA	Yes	No
Math	Yes	Yes

API Criteria..........................Yes
Graduation rate.......................NA
criteria met/possible...............37/36

Data from school year 2007-08 except where noted
†Combined data for elementary and high schools

Ceres Unified

Stanislaus County
PO Box 307
Modesto, CA 95358
(209) 556-1500

Superint. . . . . Walt Hanline
Grade plan. K-12
Number of schools. 21
Enrollment 12,476
High school graduates, 2006-07. 541
Dropout rate. 4.6
Pupil/teacher ratio. 21.8%
Average class size. 26.9
Students per computer 5.2
Avg. Teacher Salary, ... $68,121
Avg. Daily Attendence (ADA). 11,687
Cost per ADA. $7,408

California Achievement Tests 6th ed., 2008
(Pct scoring at or above 50th National Percentile Rank)

	Math	Reading	Language
Grade 3	53%	30%	37%
Grade 7	48%	46%	41%

Academic Performance Index, 2009
Number of valid scores. 8,609
2007 API (base) 721
2008 API (growth). 737

SAT Testing, 2006-07
Enrollment, Grade 12 689
percent taking test. 14.1%
number with total score 1,500+ 41

Average Scores:

Math	Verbal	Writing	Total
486	475	474	1,435

Federal No Child Left Behind, 2008
(Adequate Yearly Progress standards met)

	Participation Rate	Pct Proficient
ELA	Yes	No
Math	Yes	No

API Criteria . . . . . Yes
Graduation rate . . . . . No
criteria met/possible. 34/28

Charter Oak Unified

Los Angeles County
20240 Cienega Ave
Covina, CA 91723
(626) 966-8331

Superint. . . . . Clint Harwick
Grade plan. K-12
Number of schools. 10
Enrollment 6,501
High school graduates, 2006-07. 498
Dropout rate. 2.1
Pupil/teacher ratio. 23.6%
Average class size. 28.5
Students per computer 5.3
Avg. Teacher Salary, ... $69,456
Avg. Daily Attendence (ADA). 6,395
Cost per ADA. $7,693

California Achievement Tests 6th ed., 2008
(Pct scoring at or above 50th National Percentile Rank)

	Math	Reading	Language
Grade 3	61%	42%	52%
Grade 7	52%	51%	50%

Academic Performance Index, 2009
Number of valid scores. 4,760
2007 API (base) 733
2008 API (growth). 762

SAT Testing, 2006-07
Enrollment, Grade 12 578
percent taking test. 39.6%
number with total score 1,500+ 83

Average Scores:

Math	Verbal	Writing	Total
486	476	476	1,438

Federal No Child Left Behind, 2008
(Adequate Yearly Progress standards met)

	Participation Rate	Pct Proficient
ELA	Yes	No
Math	Yes	No

API Criteria . . . . . Yes
Graduation rate . . . . . Yes
criteria met/possible. 38/36

Chicago Park Elem

Nevada County
15725 Mt Olive Rd
Grass Valley, CA 95945
(530) 346-2153

Superint. . . . . Dan Zeisler
Grade plan. K-8
Number of schools. 1
Enrollment 164
High school graduates, 2006-07. 0
Dropout rate. 0
Pupil/teacher ratio. 20.8%
Average class size. 24.7
Students per computer 4.0
Avg. Teacher Salary, ... $54,416
Avg. Daily Attendence (ADA). 156
Cost per ADA. $7,495

California Achievement Tests 6th ed., 2008
(Pct scoring at or above 50th National Percentile Rank)

	Math	Reading	Language
Grade 3	62%	62%	67%
Grade 7	91%	87%	91%

Academic Performance Index, 2009
Number of valid scores. 134
2007 API (base) 837
2008 API (growth). 841

SAT Testing, 2006-07
Enrollment, Grade 12 . . . . . NA
percent taking test. . . . . NA
number with total score 1,500+ . . . . . NA

Average Scores:

Math	Verbal	Writing	Total
NA	NA	NA	NA

Federal No Child Left Behind, 2008
(Adequate Yearly Progress standards met)

	Participation Rate	Pct Proficient
ELA	Yes	Yes
Math	Yes	Yes

API Criteria . . . . . Yes
Graduation rate . . . . . NA
criteria met/possible. 9/9

Chino Valley Unified

San Bernardino County
5130 Riverside Dr
Chino, CA 91710
(909) 628-1201

Superint. . . . . Edmond Heatley
Grade plan. K-12
Number of schools. 36
Enrollment 33,047
High school graduates, 2006-07. 2,318
Dropout rate. 2.4
Pupil/teacher ratio. 23.3%
Average class size. 27.6
Students per computer 5.4
Avg. Teacher Salary, ... $73,141
Avg. Daily Attendence (ADA). 32,268
Cost per ADA. $7,400

California Achievement Tests 6th ed., 2008
(Pct scoring at or above 50th National Percentile Rank)

	Math	Reading	Language
Grade 3	68%	43%	56%
Grade 7	65%	59%	58%

Academic Performance Index, 2009
Number of valid scores. 25,049
2007 API (base) 782
2008 API (growth). 784

SAT Testing, 2006-07
Enrollment, Grade 12 2,589
percent taking test. 40.9%
number with total score 1,500+ 465

Average Scores:

Math	Verbal	Writing	Total
505	482	479	1,466

Federal No Child Left Behind, 2008
(Adequate Yearly Progress standards met)

	Participation Rate	Pct Proficient
ELA	Yes	No
Math	Yes	No

API Criteria . . . . . Yes
Graduation rate . . . . . Yes
criteria met/possible. 38/35

Chowchilla Elem

Madera County
PO Box 910
Chowchilla, CA 93610
(559) 665-8000

Superint. . . . . Michelle Steagall
Grade plan. K-8
Number of schools. 5
Enrollment 1,929
High school graduates, 2006-07. 0
Dropout rate. 0
Pupil/teacher ratio. 20.2%
Average class size. 23.4
Students per computer 6.0
Avg. Teacher Salary, ... $52,273
Avg. Daily Attendence (ADA). 1,889
Cost per ADA. $7,590

California Achievement Tests 6th ed., 2008
(Pct scoring at or above 50th National Percentile Rank)

	Math	Reading	Language
Grade 3	44%	27%	35%
Grade 7	40%	41%	40%

Academic Performance Index, 2009
Number of valid scores. 1,305
2007 API (base) 680
2008 API (growth). 728

SAT Testing, 2006-07
Enrollment, Grade 12 . . . . . NA
percent taking test. . . . . NA
number with total score 1,500+ . . . . . NA

Average Scores:

Math	Verbal	Writing	Total
NA	NA	NA	NA

Federal No Child Left Behind, 2008
(Adequate Yearly Progress standards met)

	Participation Rate	Pct Proficient
ELA	Yes	No
Math	Yes	Yes

API Criteria . . . . . Yes
Graduation rate . . . . . NA
criteria met/possible. 21/18

Chula Vista Elem

San Diego County
84 East J St
Chula Vista, CA 91910
(619) 425-9600

Superint. . . . . Lowell Billings
Grade plan. K-6
Number of schools. 44
Enrollment 27,264
High school graduates, 2006-07. 0
Dropout rate. 0
Pupil/teacher ratio. 19.3%
Average class size. 21.4
Students per computer 4.3
Avg. Teacher Salary, ... $65,589
Avg. Daily Attendence (ADA). 22,048
Cost per ADA. $8,542

California Achievement Tests 6th ed., 2008
(Pct scoring at or above 50th National Percentile Rank)

	Math	Reading	Language
Grade 3	60%	38%	47%
Grade 7	73%	82%	72%

Academic Performance Index, 2009
Number of valid scores. 15,040
2007 API (base) 791
2008 API (growth). 811

SAT Testing, 2006-07
Enrollment, Grade 12 . . . . . NA
percent taking test. . . . . NA
number with total score 1,500+ . . . . . NA

Average Scores:

Math	Verbal	Writing	Total
NA	NA	NA	NA

Federal No Child Left Behind, 2008
(Adequate Yearly Progress standards met)

	Participation Rate	Pct Proficient
ELA	Yes	Yes
Math	Yes	Yes

API Criteria . . . . . Yes
Graduation rate . . . . . NA
criteria met/possible. 41/41

Data from school year 2007-08 except where noted.
†Combined data for elementary and high schools.

Cienega Union Elem

San Benito County
11936 Cienega Rd
Hollister, CA 95023
(831) 637-3821

Superint. . . . . Nancy MacLean
Grade plan. K-8
Number of schools. 1
Enrollment 24
High school graduates, 2006-07 0
Dropout rate. 0
Pupil/teacher ratio. 26.4%
Average class size. 12.0
Students per computer 1.3
Avg. Teacher Salary, ...NA
Avg. Daily Attendence (ADA). 25
Cost per ADA. $10,842

California Achievement Tests 6th ed., 2008
(Pct scoring at or above 50th National Percentile Rank)

	Math	Reading	Language
Grade 3	NA	NA	NA
Grade 7	NA	NA	NA

Academic Performance Index, 2009
Number of valid scores. 23
2007 API (base) 849
2008 API (growth). 805

SAT Testing, 2006-07
Enrollment, Grade 12 . . . . .NA
percent taking test. . . . . .NA
number with total score 1,500+ . . . . . .NA

Average Scores:

Math	Verbal	Writing	Total
NA	NA	NA	NA

Federal No Child Left Behind, 2008
(Adequate Yearly Progress standards met)

	Participation Rate	Pct Proficient
ELA	Yes	Yes
Math	Yes	Yes

API Criteria . . . . Yes
Graduation rate . . . . .NA
criteria met/possible. 5/5

Cinnabar Elem

Sonoma County
PO Box 750399
Petaluma, CA 94975
(707) 765-4345

Superint. Robert Ecker
Grade plan. K-6
Number of schools. 1
Enrollment 205
High school graduates, 2006-07 0
Dropout rate. . . . . .NA
Pupil/teacher ratio. 15.0%
Average class size. 19.5
Students per computer 3.3
Avg. Teacher Salary, ... $57,403
Avg. Daily Attendence (ADA). 207
Cost per ADA. $9,472

California Achievement Tests 6th ed., 2008
(Pct scoring at or above 50th National Percentile Rank)

	Math	Reading	Language
Grade 3	67%	30%	45%
Grade 7	NA	NA	NA

Academic Performance Index, 2009
Number of valid scores. 136
2007 API (base) 757
2008 API (growth). 724

SAT Testing, 2006-07
Enrollment, Grade 12 . . . . .NA
percent taking test. . . . . .NA
number with total score 1,500+ . . . . . .NA

Average Scores:

Math	Verbal	Writing	Total
NA	NA	NA	NA

Federal No Child Left Behind, 2008
(Adequate Yearly Progress standards met)

	Participation Rate	Pct Proficient
ELA	Yes	No
Math	Yes	No

API Criteria . . . . Yes
Graduation rate . . . . .NA
criteria met/possible. 21/15

Citrus South Tule Elem

Tulare County
31374 Success Valley Dr
Porterville, CA 93257
(559) 784-6333

Superint. . . . . J. Brown
Grade plan. K-6
Number of schools. 1
Enrollment 54
High school graduates, 2006-07 0
Dropout rate. . . . . .NA
Pupil/teacher ratio. 18.0%
Average class size. 18.0
Students per computer 5.4
Avg. Teacher Salary, ... $54,289
Avg. Daily Attendence (ADA). 48
Cost per ADA. $11,471

California Achievement Tests 6th ed., 2008
(Pct scoring at or above 50th National Percentile Rank)

	Math	Reading	Language
Grade 3	NA	NA	NA
Grade 7	NA	NA	NA

Academic Performance Index, 2009
Number of valid scores. 31
2007 API (base) 558
2008 API (growth). 582

SAT Testing, 2006-07
Enrollment, Grade 12 . . . . .NA
percent taking test. . . . . .NA
number with total score 1,500+ . . . . . .NA

Average Scores:

Math	Verbal	Writing	Total
NA	NA	NA	NA

Federal No Child Left Behind, 2008
(Adequate Yearly Progress standards met)

	Participation Rate	Pct Proficient
ELA	Yes	Yes
Math	Yes	Yes

API Criteria . . . . Yes
Graduation rate . . . . .NA
criteria met/possible. 5/5

Clay Joint Elem

Fresno County
12449 South Smith Ave
Kingsburg, CA 93631
(559) 897-4185

Superint. . . . . Bill Mannlein
Grade plan. K-8
Number of schools. 1
Enrollment 221
High school graduates, 2006-07 0
Dropout rate. 0
Pupil/teacher ratio. 20.1%
Average class size. 24.6
Students per computer 3.9
Avg. Teacher Salary, ... $54,377
Avg. Daily Attendence (ADA). 219
Cost per ADA. $6,848

California Achievement Tests 6th ed., 2008
(Pct scoring at or above 50th National Percentile Rank)

	Math	Reading	Language
Grade 3	75%	71%	50%
Grade 7	91%	87%	61%

Academic Performance Index, 2009
Number of valid scores. 173
2007 API (base) 861
2008 API (growth). 863

SAT Testing, 2006-07
Enrollment, Grade 12 . . . . .NA
percent taking test. . . . . .NA
number with total score 1,500+ . . . . . .NA

Average Scores:

Math	Verbal	Writing	Total
NA	NA	NA	NA

Federal No Child Left Behind, 2008
(Adequate Yearly Progress standards met)

	Participation Rate	Pct Proficient
ELA	Yes	Yes
Math	Yes	Yes

API Criteria . . . . Yes
Graduation rate . . . . .NA
criteria met/possible. 13/13

Clear Creek Elem

Nevada County
17700 McCourtney Rd
Grass Valley, CA 95949
(530) 273-3664

Superint. . . . . .Scott Lay
Grade plan. K-8
Number of schools. 1
Enrollment 129
High school graduates, 2006-07 0
Dropout rate. 0
Pupil/teacher ratio. 19.8%
Average class size. 15.5
Students per computer 2.3
Avg. Teacher Salary, ... $53,888
Avg. Daily Attendence (ADA). 124
Cost per ADA. $8,587

California Achievement Tests 6th ed., 2008
(Pct scoring at or above 50th National Percentile Rank)

	Math	Reading	Language
Grade 3	63%	56%	38%
Grade 7	NA	NA	NA

Academic Performance Index, 2009
Number of valid scores. 93
2007 API (base) 820
2008 API (growth). 816

SAT Testing, 2006-07
Enrollment, Grade 12 . . . . .NA
percent taking test. . . . . .NA
number with total score 1,500+ . . . . . .NA

Average Scores:

Math	Verbal	Writing	Total
NA	NA	NA	NA

Federal No Child Left Behind, 2008
(Adequate Yearly Progress standards met)

	Participation Rate	Pct Proficient
ELA	Yes	Yes
Math	Yes	Yes

API Criteria . . . . Yes
Graduation rate . . . . .NA
criteria met/possible. 5/5

Cold Spring Elem

Santa Barbara County
2243 Sycamore Canyon Rd
Santa Barbara, CA 93108
(805) 969-2678

Superint. . . . . Bryan McCabe
Grade plan. K-6
Number of schools. 1
Enrollment 188
High school graduates, 2006-07 0
Dropout rate. . . . . .NA
Pupil/teacher ratio. 11.9%
Average class size. 14.5
Students per computer 1.1
Avg. Teacher Salary, ... $66,261
Avg. Daily Attendence (ADA). 181
Cost per ADA. $15,767

California Achievement Tests 6th ed., 2008
(Pct scoring at or above 50th National Percentile Rank)

	Math	Reading	Language
Grade 3	81%	78%	78%
Grade 7	NA	NA	NA

Academic Performance Index, 2009
Number of valid scores. 133
2007 API (base) 961
2008 API (growth). 950

SAT Testing, 2006-07
Enrollment, Grade 12 . . . . .NA
percent taking test. . . . . .NA
number with total score 1,500+ . . . . . .NA

Average Scores:

Math	Verbal	Writing	Total
NA	NA	NA	NA

Federal No Child Left Behind, 2008
(Adequate Yearly Progress standards met)

	Participation Rate	Pct Proficient
ELA	Yes	Yes
Math	Yes	Yes

API Criteria . . . . Yes
Graduation rate . . . . .NA
criteria met/possible. 9/9

Data from school year 2007-08 except where noted
†Combined data for elementary and high schools

Colfax Elem
Placer County
24825 Ben Taylor Rd
Colfax, CA 95713
(530) 346-2202

Superint........................Jon Ray
Grade plan........................K-8
Number of schools....................2
Enrollment........................374
High school graduates, 2006-07........0
Dropout rate..........................0
Pupil/teacher ratio...............15.5%
Average class size.................21.1
Students per computer...............6.0
Avg. Teacher Salary, ...$57,726
Avg. Daily Attendence (ADA).........370
Cost per ADA..................$9,374

California Achievement Tests 6th ed., 2008
(Pct scoring at or above 50th National Percentile Rank)

	Math	Reading	Language
Grade 3	47%	36%	44%
Grade 7	79%	73%	65%

Academic Performance Index, 2009
Number of valid scores...............279
2007 API (base)......................758
2008 API (growth)....................785

SAT Testing, 2006-07
Enrollment, Grade 12.................NA
percent taking test..................NA
number with total score 1,500+......NA

Average Scores:

Math	Verbal	Writing	Total
NA	NA	NA	NA

Federal No Child Left Behind, 2008
(Adequate Yearly Progress standards met)

	Participation Rate	Pct Proficient
ELA	Yes	Yes
Math	Yes	Yes

API Criteria.........................Yes
Graduation rate......................NA
criteria met/possible..............13/13

Columbia Elem
Shasta County
10140 Old Oregon Trail
Redding, CA 96003
(530) 223-1915

Superint.................Frank Adelman
Grade plan........................K-8
Number of schools....................4
Enrollment......................1,058
High school graduates, 2006-07........0
Dropout rate..........................0
Pupil/teacher ratio..............22.3%
Average class size.................22.4
Students per computer...............4.5
Avg. Teacher Salary, ...$56,235
Avg. Daily Attendence (ADA)........1,020
Cost per ADA..................$7,639

California Achievement Tests 6th ed., 2008
(Pct scoring at or above 50th National Percentile Rank)

	Math	Reading	Language
Grade 3	60%	42%	46%
Grade 7	65%	69%	64%

Academic Performance Index, 2009
Number of valid scores...............761
2007 API (base)......................811
2008 API (growth)....................829

SAT Testing, 2006-07
Enrollment, Grade 12.................NA
percent taking test..................NA
number with total score 1,500+......NA

Average Scores:

Math	Verbal	Writing	Total
NA	NA	NA	NA

Federal No Child Left Behind, 2008
(Adequate Yearly Progress standards met)

	Participation Rate	Pct Proficient
ELA	Yes	Yes
Math	Yes	Yes

API Criteria.........................Yes
Graduation rate......................NA
criteria met/possible..............13/13

Compton Unified
Los Angeles County
501 South Santa Fe Ave
Compton, CA 90221
(310) 639-4321

Superint..................Kaye Burnside
Grade plan........................K-12
Number of schools...................40
Enrollment.....................28,081
High school graduates, 2006-07......722
Dropout rate.......................10.2
Pupil/teacher ratio..............22.9%
Average class size.................27.2
Students per computer...............6.3
Avg. Teacher Salary, ...$61,789
Avg. Daily Attendence (ADA).......26,704
Cost per ADA..................$9,053

California Achievement Tests 6th ed., 2008
(Pct scoring at or above 50th National Percentile Rank)

	Math	Reading	Language
Grade 3	39%	20%	31%
Grade 7	25%	19%	19%

Academic Performance Index, 2009
Number of valid scores............19,873
2007 API (base)......................608
2008 API (growth)....................627

SAT Testing, 2006-07
Enrollment, Grade 12..............1,287
percent taking test...............25.0%
number with total score 1,500+.......25

Average Scores:

Math	Verbal	Writing	Total
389	388	391	1,168

Federal No Child Left Behind, 2008
(Adequate Yearly Progress standards met)

	Participation Rate	Pct Proficient
ELA	No	No
Math	Yes	No

API Criteria.........................Yes
Graduation rate......................No
criteria met/possible..............30/16

Corning Union Elem
Tehama County
1590 South St
Corning, CA 96021
(530) 824-7700

Superint.................Stephen Kelish
Grade plan........................K-8
Number of schools....................6
Enrollment......................1,928
High school graduates, 2006-07........0
Dropout rate..........................0
Pupil/teacher ratio..............20.8%
Average class size.................24.3
Students per computer...............3.0
Avg. Teacher Salary, ...$55,801
Avg. Daily Attendence (ADA)........1,879
Cost per ADA..................$8,163

California Achievement Tests 6th ed., 2008
(Pct scoring at or above 50th National Percentile Rank)

	Math	Reading	Language
Grade 3	47%	32%	40%
Grade 7	43%	48%	38%

Academic Performance Index, 2009
Number of valid scores.............1,380
2007 API (base)......................732
2008 API (growth)....................728

SAT Testing, 2006-07
Enrollment, Grade 12.................NA
percent taking test..................NA
number with total score 1,500+......NA

Average Scores:

Math	Verbal	Writing	Total
NA	NA	NA	NA

Federal No Child Left Behind, 2008
(Adequate Yearly Progress standards met)

	Participation Rate	Pct Proficient
ELA	Yes	No
Math	Yes	No

API Criteria.........................Yes
Graduation rate......................NA
criteria met/possible..............25/20

Cottonwood Union Elem
Shasta County
20512 West First St
Cottonwood, CA 96022
(530) 347-3165

Superint...................Dale Hansen
Grade plan........................K-8
Number of schools....................4
Enrollment......................1,151
High school graduates, 2006-07........0
Dropout rate..........................0
Pupil/teacher ratio..............17.9%
Average class size.................23.6
Students per computer...............3.7
Avg. Teacher Salary, ...$56,278
Avg. Daily Attendence (ADA)........1,102
Cost per ADA..................$8,701

California Achievement Tests 6th ed., 2008
(Pct scoring at or above 50th National Percentile Rank)

	Math	Reading	Language
Grade 3	61%	56%	60%
Grade 7	72%	70%	61%

Academic Performance Index, 2009
Number of valid scores...............838
2007 API (base)......................806
2008 API (growth)....................827

SAT Testing, 2006-07
Enrollment, Grade 12.................NA
percent taking test..................NA
number with total score 1,500+......NA

Average Scores:

Math	Verbal	Writing	Total
NA	NA	NA	NA

Federal No Child Left Behind, 2008
(Adequate Yearly Progress standards met)

	Participation Rate	Pct Proficient
ELA	Yes	Yes
Math	Yes	Yes

API Criteria.........................Yes
Graduation rate......................NA
criteria met/possible..............13/13

Covina-Valley Unified
Los Angeles County
PO Box 269
Covina, CA 91723
(626) 974-7000

Superint...................Louis Pappas
Grade plan........................K-12
Number of schools...................19
Enrollment.....................14,646
High school graduates, 2006-07....1,178
Dropout rate........................1.7
Pupil/teacher ratio..............23.3%
Average class size.................25.5
Students per computer...............4.3
Avg. Teacher Salary, ...$65,572
Avg. Daily Attendence (ADA).......14,219
Cost per ADA..................$7,978

California Achievement Tests 6th ed., 2008
(Pct scoring at or above 50th National Percentile Rank)

	Math	Reading	Language
Grade 3	55%	34%	45%
Grade 7	52%	47%	45%

Academic Performance Index, 2009
Number of valid scores............10,871
2007 API (base)......................731
2008 API (growth)....................747

SAT Testing, 2006-07
Enrollment, Grade 12..............1,306
percent taking test...............38.9%
number with total score 1,500+......184

Average Scores:

Math	Verbal	Writing	Total
487	476	472	1,435

Federal No Child Left Behind, 2008
(Adequate Yearly Progress standards met)

	Participation Rate	Pct Proficient
ELA	Yes	No
Math	Yes	No

API Criteria.........................Yes
Graduation rate......................Yes
criteria met/possible..............38/35

Data from school year 2007-08 except where noted.
†Combined data for elementary and high schools.

Cucamonga Elem
San Bernardino County
8776 Archibald Ave
Rancho Cucamonga, CA 91730
(909) 987-8942

Superint. . . . . Claudia Maidenberg
Grade plan. K-8
Number of schools. 4
Enrollment 2,836
High school graduates, 2006-07. 0
Dropout rate. 0
Pupil/teacher ratio. 22.9%
Average class size. 26.3
Students per computer 5.4
Avg. Teacher Salary, ...$63,650
Avg. Daily Attendence (ADA). 2,739
Cost per ADA. $7,403

California Achievement Tests 6th ed., 2008
(Pct scoring at or above 50th National Percentile Rank)

	Math	Reading	Language
Grade 3	44%	27%	41%
Grade 7	49%	39%	41%

Academic Performance Index, 2009
Number of valid scores. 2,019
2007 API (base) 737
2008 API (growth). 743

SAT Testing, 2006-07
Enrollment, Grade 12 . . . . .NA
percent taking test. . . . . .NA
number with total score 1,500+ . . . . . .NA

Average Scores:

Math	Verbal	Writing	Total
NA	NA	NA	NA

Federal No Child Left Behind, 2008
(Adequate Yearly Progress standards met)

	Participation Rate	Pct Proficient
ELA	Yes	No
Math	Yes	No

API Criteria . . . . .Yes
Graduation rate . . . . .NA
criteria met/possible. 29/27

Cupertino Union Elem
Santa Clara County
10301 Vista Dr
Cupertino, CA 95014
(408) 252-3000

Superint. . . . . .Phil Quon
Grade plan. K-8
Number of schools. 25
Enrollment 17,294
High school graduates, 2006-07. 0
Dropout rate. 0
Pupil/teacher ratio. 21.5%
Average class size. 27.6
Students per computer 3.7
Avg. Teacher Salary, ... $69,165
Avg. Daily Attendence (ADA). 17,148
Cost per ADA. $7,720

California Achievement Tests 6th ed., 2008
(Pct scoring at or above 50th National Percentile Rank)

	Math	Reading	Language
Grade 3	87%	71%	82%
Grade 7	90%	82%	85%

Academic Performance Index, 2009
Number of valid scores. 12,849
2007 API (base) 930
2008 API (growth). 941

SAT Testing, 2006-07
Enrollment, Grade 12 . . . . .NA
percent taking test. . . . . .NA
number with total score 1,500+ . . . . . .NA

Average Scores:

Math	Verbal	Writing	Total
NA	NA	NA	NA

Federal No Child Left Behind, 2008
(Adequate Yearly Progress standards met)

	Participation Rate	Pct Proficient
ELA	Yes	Yes
Math	No	Yes

API Criteria . . . . .Yes
Graduation rate . . . . .NA
criteria met/possible. 37/36

Curtis Creek Elem
Tuolumne County
18755 Standard Rd
Sonora, CA 95370
(209) 533-1083

Superint. . . . . Britta Skavdahl
Grade plan. K-8
Number of schools. 3
Enrollment 627
High school graduates, 2006-07. 0
Dropout rate. 0
Pupil/teacher ratio. 18.7%
Average class size. 22.5
Students per computer 4.1
Avg. Teacher Salary, ... $55,838
Avg. Daily Attendence (ADA). 607
Cost per ADA. $7,998

California Achievement Tests 6th ed., 2008
(Pct scoring at or above 50th National Percentile Rank)

	Math	Reading	Language
Grade 3	65%	39%	45%
Grade 7	63%	61%	53%

Academic Performance Index, 2009
Number of valid scores. 460
2007 API (base) 793
2008 API (growth). 795

SAT Testing, 2006-07
Enrollment, Grade 12 . . . . .NA
percent taking test. . . . . .NA
number with total score 1,500+ . . . . . .NA

Average Scores:

Math	Verbal	Writing	Total
NA	NA	NA	NA

Federal No Child Left Behind, 2008
(Adequate Yearly Progress standards met)

	Participation Rate	Pct Proficient
ELA	Yes	Yes
Math	Yes	Yes

API Criteria . . . . .Yes
Graduation rate . . . . .NA
criteria met/possible. 13/13

Cypress Elem
Orange County
9470 Moody St
Cypress, CA 90630
(714) 220-6900

Superint. . . . . Sheri Loewenstein
Grade plan. K-6
Number of schools. 9
Enrollment 4,101
High school graduates, 2006-07. 0
Dropout rate. . . . . .NA
Pupil/teacher ratio. 19.8%
Average class size. 22.4
Students per computer 4.8
Avg. Teacher Salary, ...$71,229
Avg. Daily Attendence (ADA). 4,019
Cost per ADA. $8,101

California Achievement Tests 6th ed., 2008
(Pct scoring at or above 50th National Percentile Rank)

	Math	Reading	Language
Grade 3	67%	53%	64%
Grade 7	NA	NA	NA

Academic Performance Index, 2009
Number of valid scores. 2,913
2007 API (base) 853
2008 API (growth). 860

SAT Testing, 2006-07
Enrollment, Grade 12 . . . . .NA
percent taking test. . . . . .NA
number with total score 1,500+ . . . . . .NA

Average Scores:

Math	Verbal	Writing	Total
NA	NA	NA	NA

Federal No Child Left Behind, 2008
(Adequate Yearly Progress standards met)

	Participation Rate	Pct Proficient
ELA	Yes	Yes
Math	Yes	Yes

API Criteria . . . . .Yes
Graduation rate . . . . .NA
criteria met/possible. 37/37

Dehesa Elem
San Diego County
4612 Dehesa Rd
El Cajon, CA 92019
(619) 444-2161

Superint. . . . . .Janet Wilson
Grade plan. K-12
Number of schools. 2
Enrollment 843
High school graduates, 2006-07. 57
Dropout rate. 10.9
Pupil/teacher ratio. 18.0%
Average class size. 5.3
Students per computer 11.4
Avg. Teacher Salary, ...NA
Avg. Daily Attendence (ADA). 167
Cost per ADA. $11,876

California Achievement Tests 6th ed., 2008
(Pct scoring at or above 50th National Percentile Rank)

	Math	Reading	Language
Grade 3	39%	39%	56%
Grade 7	NA	NA	NA

Academic Performance Index, 2009
Number of valid scores. 101
2007 API (base) 815
2008 API (growth). 778

SAT Testing, 2006-07
Enrollment, Grade 12 64
percent taking test. 6.3%
number with total score 1,500+ . . . . . .NA

Average Scores:

Math	Verbal	Writing	Total
NA	NA	NA	NA

Federal No Child Left Behind, 2008
(Adequate Yearly Progress standards met)

	Participation Rate	Pct Proficient
ELA	Yes	Yes
Math	Yes	Yes

API Criteria . . . . .Yes
Graduation rate . . . . .NA
criteria met/possible. 9/9

Del Mar Union Elem
San Diego County
225 Ninth St
Del Mar, CA 92014
(858) 755-9301

Superint. . . . . Janet Bernard
Grade plan. K-6
Number of schools. 8
Enrollment 4,057
High school graduates, 2006-07. 0
Dropout rate. . . . . .NA
Pupil/teacher ratio. 16.9%
Average class size. 21.0
Students per computer 4.9
Avg. Teacher Salary, ... $67,389
Avg. Daily Attendence (ADA). 4,050
Cost per ADA. $9,031

California Achievement Tests 6th ed., 2008
(Pct scoring at or above 50th National Percentile Rank)

	Math	Reading	Language
Grade 3	87%	75%	80%
Grade 7	NA	NA	NA

Academic Performance Index, 2009
Number of valid scores. 2,800
2007 API (base) 946
2008 API (growth). 948

SAT Testing, 2006-07
Enrollment, Grade 12 . . . . .NA
percent taking test. . . . . .NA
number with total score 1,500+ . . . . . .NA

Average Scores:

Math	Verbal	Writing	Total
NA	NA	NA	NA

Federal No Child Left Behind, 2008
(Adequate Yearly Progress standards met)

	Participation Rate	Pct Proficient
ELA	Yes	Yes
Math	Yes	Yes

API Criteria . . . . .Yes
Graduation rate . . . . .NA
criteria met/possible. 29/29

Data from school year 2007-08 except where noted
†Combined data for elementary and high schools

Del Paso Heights Elem

Sacramento County
(merged into Twin Rivers Unified)
5115 Dudley Blvd
North Highlands, CA 95660
(916) 566-1786

Superint	Frank Porter
Grade plan	K-6
Number of schools	5
Enrollment	1,737
High school graduates, 2006-07	0
Dropout rate	NA
Pupil/teacher ratio	17.7%
Average class size	20.6
Students per computer	3.4
Avg. Teacher Salary,	NA
Avg. Daily Attendence (ADA)	1,684
Cost per ADA	$10,665

California Achievement Tests 6th ed., 2008
(Pct scoring at or above 50th National Percentile Rank)

	Math	Reading	Language
Grade 3	35%	19%	30%
Grade 7	NA	NA	NA

Academic Performance Index, 2009

Number of valid scores	1,061
2007 API (base)	651
2008 API (growth)	684

SAT Testing, 2006-07

Enrollment, Grade 12	NA
percent taking test	NA
number with total score 1,500+	NA

Average Scores:

Math	Verbal	Writing	Total
NA	NA	NA	NA

Federal No Child Left Behind, 2008
(Adequate Yearly Progress standards met)

	Participation Rate	Pct Proficient
ELA	Yes	No
Math	Yes	Yes

API Criteria	Yes
Graduation rate	NA
# criteria met/possible	29/24

Delano Union Elem

Kern County
1405 12th Ave
Delano, CA 93215
(661) 721-5000

Superint	Ronald Garcia
Grade plan	K-8
Number of schools	11
Enrollment	7,629
High school graduates, 2006-07	0
Dropout rate	0
Pupil/teacher ratio	20.8%
Average class size	25.0
Students per computer	4.0
Avg. Teacher Salary,	$59,709
Avg. Daily Attendence (ADA)	7,440
Cost per ADA	$8,342

California Achievement Tests 6th ed., 2008
(Pct scoring at or above 50th National Percentile Rank)

	Math	Reading	Language
Grade 3	39%	20%	34%
Grade 7	37%	36%	34%

Academic Performance Index, 2009

Number of valid scores	5,468
2007 API (base)	690
2008 API (growth)	707

SAT Testing, 2006-07

Enrollment, Grade 12	NA
percent taking test	NA
number with total score 1,500+	NA

Average Scores:

Math	Verbal	Writing	Total
NA	NA	NA	NA

Federal No Child Left Behind, 2008
(Adequate Yearly Progress standards met)

	Participation Rate	Pct Proficient
ELA	Yes	No
Math	Yes	No

API Criteria	Yes
Graduation rate	NA
# criteria met/possible	29/23

Delphic Elem

Siskiyou County
1420 Delphic Rd
Montague, CA 96064
(530) 842-3653

Superint	Debbie Faulkner
Grade plan	K-8
Number of schools	1
Enrollment	53
High school graduates, 2006-07	0
Dropout rate	0
Pupil/teacher ratio	13.2%
Average class size	17.7
Students per computer	2.3
Avg. Teacher Salary,	NA
Avg. Daily Attendence (ADA)	54
Cost per ADA	$9,429

California Achievement Tests 6th ed., 2008
(Pct scoring at or above 50th National Percentile Rank)

	Math	Reading	Language
Grade 3	50%	42%	42%
Grade 7	NA	NA	NA

Academic Performance Index, 2009

Number of valid scores	39
2007 API (base)	755
2008 API (growth)	736

SAT Testing, 2006-07

Enrollment, Grade 12	NA
percent taking test	NA
number with total score 1,500+	NA

Average Scores:

Math	Verbal	Writing	Total
NA	NA	NA	NA

Federal No Child Left Behind, 2008
(Adequate Yearly Progress standards met)

	Participation Rate	Pct Proficient
ELA	Yes	Yes
Math	Yes	Yes

API Criteria	Yes
Graduation rate	NA
# criteria met/possible	5/5

Delta View Joint Union Elem

Kings County
1201 Lacey Blvd
Hanford, CA 93230
(559) 582-3122

Superint	Anthony Luis
Grade plan	K-8
Number of schools	1
Enrollment	101
High school graduates, 2006-07	0
Dropout rate	0
Pupil/teacher ratio	20.2%
Average class size	20.0
Students per computer	2.9
Avg. Teacher Salary,	$43,718
Avg. Daily Attendence (ADA)	91
Cost per ADA	$8,265

California Achievement Tests 6th ed., 2008
(Pct scoring at or above 50th National Percentile Rank)

	Math	Reading	Language
Grade 3	NA	NA	NA
Grade 7	NA	NA	NA

Academic Performance Index, 2009

Number of valid scores	63
2007 API (base)	652
2008 API (growth)	641

SAT Testing, 2006-07

Enrollment, Grade 12	NA
percent taking test	NA
number with total score 1,500+	NA

Average Scores:

Math	Verbal	Writing	Total
NA	NA	NA	NA

Federal No Child Left Behind, 2008
(Adequate Yearly Progress standards met)

	Participation Rate	Pct Proficient
ELA	Yes	Yes
Math	Yes	No

API Criteria	Yes
Graduation rate	NA
# criteria met/possible	5/4

Desert Sands Unified

Riverside County
47-950 Dune Palms Rd
La Quinta, CA 92253
(760) 777-4200

Superint	Sharon McGehee
Grade plan	K-12
Number of schools	33
Enrollment	28,775
High school graduates, 2006-07	1,630
Dropout rate	4
Pupil/teacher ratio	22.2%
Average class size	28.2
Students per computer	5.6
Avg. Teacher Salary,	$70,970
Avg. Daily Attendence (ADA)	27,315
Cost per ADA	$8,140

California Achievement Tests 6th ed., 2008
(Pct scoring at or above 50th National Percentile Rank)

	Math	Reading	Language
Grade 3	56%	35%	46%
Grade 7	44%	44%	43%

Academic Performance Index, 2009

Number of valid scores	20,761
2007 API (base)	734
2008 API (growth)	752

SAT Testing, 2006-07

Enrollment, Grade 12	2,045
percent taking test	32.3%
number with total score 1,500+	273

Average Scores:

Math	Verbal	Writing	Total
489	480	480	1,449

Federal No Child Left Behind, 2008
(Adequate Yearly Progress standards met)

	Participation Rate	Pct Proficient
ELA	Yes	No
Math	Yes	Yes

API Criteria	Yes
Graduation rate	Yes
# criteria met/possible	38/36

Di Giorgio Elem

Kern County
19405 Buena Vista Blvd
Arvin, CA 93203
(661) 854-2604

Superint	Paul Boatman
Grade plan	K-8
Number of schools	1
Enrollment	201
High school graduates, 2006-07	0
Dropout rate	0
Pupil/teacher ratio	18.3%
Average class size	22.3
Students per computer	3.7
Avg. Teacher Salary,	$53,499
Avg. Daily Attendence (ADA)	197
Cost per ADA	$8,570

California Achievement Tests 6th ed., 2008
(Pct scoring at or above 50th National Percentile Rank)

	Math	Reading	Language
Grade 3	53%	11%	16%
Grade 7	30%	37%	26%

Academic Performance Index, 2009

Number of valid scores	148
2007 API (base)	708
2008 API (growth)	716

SAT Testing, 2006-07

Enrollment, Grade 12	NA
percent taking test	NA
number with total score 1,500+	NA

Average Scores:

Math	Verbal	Writing	Total
NA	NA	NA	NA

Federal No Child Left Behind, 2008
(Adequate Yearly Progress standards met)

	Participation Rate	Pct Proficient
ELA	Yes	No
Math	Yes	Yes

API Criteria	Yes
Graduation rate	NA
# criteria met/possible	17/13

Data from school year 2007-08 except where noted.
†Combined data for elementary and high schools.

Dixie Elem
Marin County
380 Nova Albion Way
San Rafael, CA 94903
(415) 492-3700

Superint. . . . . Thomas Lohwasser
Grade plan. K-8
Number of schools. 4
Enrollment 1,749
High school graduates, 2006-07. 0
Dropout rate. 0
Pupil/teacher ratio. 18.8%
Average class size. 24.4
Students per computer 2.7
Avg. Teacher Salary, ... $70,679
Avg. Daily Attendence (ADA). 1,721
Cost per ADA. $9,780

California Achievement Tests 6th ed., 2008
(Pct scoring at or above 50th National Percentile Rank)

	Math	Reading	Language
Grade 3	79%	71%	71%
Grade 7	75%	70%	75%

Academic Performance Index, 2009
Number of valid scores. 1,373
2007 API (base) 871
2008 API (growth). 876

SAT Testing, 2006-07
Enrollment, Grade 12 . . . . NA
percent taking test. . . . . NA
number with total score 1,500+ . . . . . . NA

Average Scores:

Math	Verbal	Writing	Total
NA	NA	NA	NA

Federal No Child Left Behind, 2008
(Adequate Yearly Progress standards met)

	Participation Rate	Pct Proficient
ELA	Yes	Yes
Math	Yes	No

API Criteria . . . . Yes
Graduation rate . . . . NA
criteria met/possible. 29/28

Dry Creek Joint Elem
Placer County
9707 Cook Riolo Rd
Roseville, CA 95747
(916) 770-8800

Superint. . . . . Mark Geyer
Grade plan. K-8
Number of schools. 9
Enrollment 7,395
High school graduates, 2006-07. 0
Dropout rate. 0
Pupil/teacher ratio. 20.7%
Average class size. 26.5
Students per computer 6.1
Avg. Teacher Salary, ... $60,593
Avg. Daily Attendence (ADA). 7,198
Cost per ADA. $7,002

California Achievement Tests 6th ed., 2008
(Pct scoring at or above 50th National Percentile Rank)

	Math	Reading	Language
Grade 3	76%	63%	69%
Grade 7	66%	64%	60%

Academic Performance Index, 2009
Number of valid scores. 5,678
2007 API (base) 843
2008 API (growth). 849

SAT Testing, 2006-07
Enrollment, Grade 12 . . . . NA
percent taking test. . . . . NA
number with total score 1,500+ . . . . . . NA

Average Scores:

Math	Verbal	Writing	Total
NA	NA	NA	NA

Federal No Child Left Behind, 2008
(Adequate Yearly Progress standards met)

	Participation Rate	Pct Proficient
ELA	Yes	Yes
Math	Yes	Yes

API Criteria . . . . Yes
Graduation rate . . . . NA
criteria met/possible. 37/37

Dunham Elem
Sonoma County
4111 Roblar Rd
Petaluma, CA 94952
(707) 795-5050

Superint. Kim Wilding
Grade plan. K-6
Number of schools. 1
Enrollment 174
High school graduates, 2006-07. 0
Dropout rate. . . . . NA
Pupil/teacher ratio. 18.5%
Average class size. 20.6
Students per computer 11.6
Avg. Teacher Salary, ... NA
Avg. Daily Attendence (ADA). 168
Cost per ADA. $8,159

California Achievement Tests 6th ed., 2008
(Pct scoring at or above 50th National Percentile Rank)

	Math	Reading	Language
Grade 3	52%	46%	42%
Grade 7	NA	NA	NA

Academic Performance Index, 2009
Number of valid scores. 120
2007 API (base) 857
2008 API (growth). 810

SAT Testing, 2006-07
Enrollment, Grade 12 . . . . NA
percent taking test. . . . . NA
number with total score 1,500+ . . . . . . NA

Average Scores:

Math	Verbal	Writing	Total
NA	NA	NA	NA

Federal No Child Left Behind, 2008
(Adequate Yearly Progress standards met)

	Participation Rate	Pct Proficient
ELA	Yes	Yes
Math	Yes	Yes

API Criteria . . . . Yes
Graduation rate . . . . NA
criteria met/possible. 9/9

Dunsmuir Elem
Siskiyou County
4760 Siskiyou Ave
Dunsmuir, CA 96025
(530) 235-4828

Superint. . . . . Mike Michelon
Grade plan. K-8
Number of schools. 2
Enrollment 172
High school graduates, 2006-07. 0
Dropout rate. 0
Pupil/teacher ratio. 15.6%
Average class size. 20.6
Students per computer 2.0
Avg. Teacher Salary, ... $46,347
Avg. Daily Attendence (ADA). 169
Cost per ADA. $11,556

California Achievement Tests 6th ed., 2008
(Pct scoring at or above 50th National Percentile Rank)

	Math	Reading	Language
Grade 3	42%	32%	21%
Grade 7	79%	60%	60%

Academic Performance Index, 2009
Number of valid scores. 130
2007 API (base) 700
2008 API (growth). 733

SAT Testing, 2006-07
Enrollment, Grade 12 . . . . NA
percent taking test. . . . . NA
number with total score 1,500+ . . . . . . NA

Average Scores:

Math	Verbal	Writing	Total
NA	NA	NA	NA

Federal No Child Left Behind, 2008
(Adequate Yearly Progress standards met)

	Participation Rate	Pct Proficient
ELA	Yes	Yes
Math	Yes	Yes

API Criteria . . . . Yes
Graduation rate . . . . NA
criteria met/possible. 13/13

East Side Union High
Santa Clara County
830 North Capitol Ave
San Jose, CA 95133
(408) 347-5000

Superint. . . . . Bob Nunez
Grade plan. 9-12
Number of schools. 21
Enrollment 26,280
High school graduates, 2006-07. . . . 4,525
Dropout rate. 5.1
Pupil/teacher ratio. 22.2%
Average class size. 26.8
Students per computer 2.7
Avg. Teacher Salary, ... $76,370
Avg. Daily Attendence (ADA). 24,720
Cost per ADA. $9,036

California Achievement Tests 6th ed., 2008
(Pct scoring at or above 50th National Percentile Rank)

	Math	Reading	Language
Grade 3			
Grade 7			

Academic Performance Index, 2009
Number of valid scores. 17,285
2007 API (base) 709
2008 API (growth). 720

SAT Testing, 2006-07
Enrollment, Grade 12 6,374
percent taking test. 37.2%
number with total score 1,500+ 1,062

Average Scores:

Math	Verbal	Writing	Total
519	477	476	1,472

Federal No Child Left Behind, 2008
(Adequate Yearly Progress standards met)

	Participation Rate	Pct Proficient
ELA	No	No
Math	No	No

API Criteria . . . . Yes
Graduation rate . . . . No
criteria met/possible. 38/33

East Whittier City Elem
Los Angeles County
14535 East Whittier Blvd
Whittier, CA 90605
(562) 907-5900

Superint. . . . . Joe Gillentine
Grade plan. K-8
Number of schools. 13
Enrollment 8,727
High school graduates, 2006-07. 0
Dropout rate. 0
Pupil/teacher ratio. 19.6%
Average class size. 23.8
Students per computer 5.1
Avg. Teacher Salary, ... $71,414
Avg. Daily Attendence (ADA). 8,674
Cost per ADA. $8,959

California Achievement Tests 6th ed., 2008
(Pct scoring at or above 50th National Percentile Rank)

	Math	Reading	Language
Grade 3	59%	39%	53%
Grade 7	52%	53%	53%

Academic Performance Index, 2009
Number of valid scores. 6,651
2007 API (base) 778
2008 API (growth). 789

SAT Testing, 2006-07
Enrollment, Grade 12 . . . . NA
percent taking test. . . . . NA
number with total score 1,500+ . . . . . . NA

Average Scores:

Math	Verbal	Writing	Total
NA	NA	NA	NA

Federal No Child Left Behind, 2008
(Adequate Yearly Progress standards met)

	Participation Rate	Pct Proficient
ELA	Yes	No
Math	Yes	No

API Criteria . . . . Yes
Graduation rate . . . . NA
criteria met/possible. 29/26

Data from school year 2007-08 except where noted
†Combined data for elementary and high schools

Eastside Union Elem

Los Angeles County
45006 30th St East
Lancaster, CA 93535
(661) 952-1200

Superint. . . . . Roberto Villa
Grade plan. PK-8
Number of schools. 4
Enrollment 3,252
High school graduates, 2006-07. 0
Dropout rate. 0
Pupil/teacher ratio. 21.8%
Average class size. 24.2
Students per computer 7.7
Avg. Teacher Salary, ... $60,497
Avg. Daily Attendence (ADA). 3,150
Cost per ADA. $7,848

California Achievement Tests 6th ed., 2008
(Pct scoring at or above 50th National Percentile Rank)

	Math	Reading	Language
Grade 3	32%	17%	26%
Grade 7	30%	31%	33%

Academic Performance Index, 2009
Number of valid scores. 2,148
2007 API (base) 683
2008 API (growth). 673

SAT Testing, 2006-07
Enrollment, Grade 12 . . . . NA
percent taking test. . . . . NA
number with total score 1,500+ . . . . . . NA

Average Scores:

Math	Verbal	Writing	Total
NA	NA	NA	NA

Federal No Child Left Behind, 2008
(Adequate Yearly Progress standards met)

	Participation Rate	Pct Proficient
ELA	No	No
Math	Yes	No

API Criteria . . . . Yes
Graduation rate . . . . NA
criteria met/possible. 29/16

Edison Elem

Kern County
PO Box 368
Edison, CA 93307
(661) 363-5394

Superint. . . . . Danny Whetton
Grade plan. K-8
Number of schools. 2
Enrollment 1,149
High school graduates, 2006-07. 0
Dropout rate. 0
Pupil/teacher ratio. 19.7%
Average class size. 21.9
Students per computer 3.2
Avg. Teacher Salary, ... $53,316
Avg. Daily Attendence (ADA). 1,113
Cost per ADA. $7,485

California Achievement Tests 6th ed., 2008
(Pct scoring at or above 50th National Percentile Rank)

	Math	Reading	Language
Grade 3	44%	25%	31%
Grade 7	33%	28%	27%

Academic Performance Index, 2009
Number of valid scores. 811
2007 API (base) 664
2008 API (growth). 660

SAT Testing, 2006-07
Enrollment, Grade 12 . . . . NA
percent taking test. . . . . NA
number with total score 1,500+ . . . . . . NA

Average Scores:

Math	Verbal	Writing	Total
NA	NA	NA	NA

Federal No Child Left Behind, 2008
(Adequate Yearly Progress standards met)

	Participation Rate	Pct Proficient
ELA	Yes	No
Math	Yes	No

API Criteria . . . . Yes
Graduation rate . . . . NA
criteria met/possible. 21/13

El Centro Elem

Imperial County
1256 Broadway
El Centro, CA 92243
(760) 352-5712

Superint. . . . . Robert Pletka
Grade plan. K-8
Number of schools. 11
Enrollment 5,744
High school graduates, 2006-07. 0
Dropout rate. 0
Pupil/teacher ratio. 22.1%
Average class size. 26.5
Students per computer 4.4
Avg. Teacher Salary, ... $68,096
Avg. Daily Attendence (ADA). 5,663
Cost per ADA. $8,284

California Achievement Tests 6th ed., 2008
(Pct scoring at or above 50th National Percentile Rank)

	Math	Reading	Language
Grade 3	56%	32%	44%
Grade 7	50%	39%	37%

Academic Performance Index, 2009
Number of valid scores. 4,129
2007 API (base) 727
2008 API (growth). 754

SAT Testing, 2006-07
Enrollment, Grade 12 . . . . NA
percent taking test. . . . . NA
number with total score 1,500+ . . . . . . NA

Average Scores:

Math	Verbal	Writing	Total
NA	NA	NA	NA

Federal No Child Left Behind, 2008
(Adequate Yearly Progress standards met)

	Participation Rate	Pct Proficient
ELA	Yes	No
Math	Yes	Yes

API Criteria . . . . Yes
Graduation rate . . . . NA
criteria met/possible. 29/27

El Monte City Elem

Los Angeles County
3540 North Lexington Ave
El Monte, CA 91731
(626) 453-3700

Superint. . . . . Jeff Seymour
Grade plan. K-8
Number of schools. 18
Enrollment 10,336
High school graduates, 2006-07. 0
Dropout rate. 0
Pupil/teacher ratio. 20.1%
Average class size. 24.0
Students per computer 4.6
Avg. Teacher Salary, ... $71,930
Avg. Daily Attendence (ADA). 10,360
Cost per ADA. $8,789

California Achievement Tests 6th ed., 2008
(Pct scoring at or above 50th National Percentile Rank)

	Math	Reading	Language
Grade 3	49%	27%	40%
Grade 7	49%	44%	43%

Academic Performance Index, 2009
Number of valid scores. 7,508
2007 API (base) 722
2008 API (growth). 743

SAT Testing, 2006-07
Enrollment, Grade 12 . . . . NA
percent taking test. . . . . NA
number with total score 1,500+ . . . . . . NA

Average Scores:

Math	Verbal	Writing	Total
NA	NA	NA	NA

Federal No Child Left Behind, 2008
(Adequate Yearly Progress standards met)

	Participation Rate	Pct Proficient
ELA	Yes	No
Math	Yes	Yes

API Criteria . . . . Yes
Graduation rate . . . . NA
criteria met/possible. 29/26

Elk Grove Unified

Sacramento County
9510 Elk Grove-Florin Rd
Elk Grove, CA 95624
(916) 686-5085

Superint. . . . . Steven Ladd
Grade plan. K-12
Number of schools. 65
Enrollment 62,294
High school graduates, 2006-07. . . . 3,684
Dropout rate. 3.4
Pupil/teacher ratio. 20.9%
Average class size. 26.1
Students per computer 6.2
Avg. Teacher Salary, ... $63,945
Avg. Daily Attendence (ADA). 59,792
Cost per ADA. $7,926

California Achievement Tests 6th ed., 2008
(Pct scoring at or above 50th National Percentile Rank)

	Math	Reading	Language
Grade 3	61%	42%	51%
Grade 7	60%	55%	54%

Academic Performance Index, 2009
Number of valid scores. 44,718
2007 API (base) 764
2008 API (growth). 775

SAT Testing, 2006-07
Enrollment, Grade 12 4,535
percent taking test. 40.1%
number with total score 1,500+ 730

Average Scores:

Math	Verbal	Writing	Total
492	475	470	1,437

Federal No Child Left Behind, 2008
(Adequate Yearly Progress standards met)

	Participation Rate	Pct Proficient
ELA	Yes	No
Math	Yes	No

API Criteria . . . . Yes
Graduation rate . . . . Yes
criteria met/possible. 46/44

Empire Union Elem

Stanislaus County
116 North McClure Rd
Modesto, CA 95357
(209) 521-2800

Superint. . . . . Robert Price
Grade plan. K-8
Number of schools. 7
Enrollment 3,504
High school graduates, 2006-07. 0
Dropout rate. 0
Pupil/teacher ratio. 20.1%
Average class size. 24.7
Students per computer 4.1
Avg. Teacher Salary, ... $65,877
Avg. Daily Attendence (ADA). 3,340
Cost per ADA. $7,920

California Achievement Tests 6th ed., 2008
(Pct scoring at or above 50th National Percentile Rank)

	Math	Reading	Language
Grade 3	58%	40%	53%
Grade 7	46%	57%	51%

Academic Performance Index, 2009
Number of valid scores. 2,406
2007 API (base) 768
2008 API (growth). 773

SAT Testing, 2006-07
Enrollment, Grade 12 . . . . NA
percent taking test. . . . . NA
number with total score 1,500+ . . . . . . NA

Average Scores:

Math	Verbal	Writing	Total
NA	NA	NA	NA

Federal No Child Left Behind, 2008
(Adequate Yearly Progress standards met)

	Participation Rate	Pct Proficient
ELA	Yes	No
Math	Yes	No

API Criteria . . . . Yes
Graduation rate . . . . NA
criteria met/possible. 33/31

Data from school year 2007-08 except where noted.
†Combined data for elementary and high schools.

Encinitas Union Elem
San Diego County
101 South Rancho Santa Fe Rd
Encinitas, CA 92024
(760) 944-4300

Superint. . . . . L. King
Grade plan. K-6
Number of schools. 10
Enrollment 5,728
High school graduates, 2006-07 0
Dropout rate. . . . . NA
Pupil/teacher ratio. 21.1%
Average class size. 21.9
Students per computer 4.0
Avg. Teacher Salary, ... $70,542
Avg. Daily Attendence (ADA). 5,320
Cost per ADA. $8,660

California Achievement Tests 6th ed., 2008
(Pct scoring at or above 50th National Percentile Rank)

	Math	Reading	Language
Grade 3	74%	65%	70%
Grade 7	NA	NA	NA

Academic Performance Index, 2009
Number of valid scores. 3,800
2007 API (base) 881
2008 API (growth). 891

SAT Testing, 2006-07
Enrollment, Grade 12 . . . . NA
percent taking test. . . . . NA
number with total score 1,500+ . . . . . . NA

Average Scores:

Math	Verbal	Writing	Total
NA	NA	NA	NA

Federal No Child Left Behind, 2008
(Adequate Yearly Progress standards met)

	Participation Rate	Pct Proficient
ELA	Yes	No
Math	Yes	Yes

API Criteria . . . . Yes
Graduation rate . . . . NA
criteria met/possible. 29/28

Enterprise Elem
Shasta County
1155 Mistletoe Ln
Redding, CA 96002
(530) 224-4100

Superint. . . . . Brian Winstead
Grade plan. K-8
Number of schools. 8
Enrollment 3,379
High school graduates, 2006-07 0
Dropout rate. 0
Pupil/teacher ratio. 19.7%
Average class size. 24.5
Students per computer 4.7
Avg. Teacher Salary, ... $57,959
Avg. Daily Attendence (ADA). 3,206
Cost per ADA. $8,397

California Achievement Tests 6th ed., 2008
(Pct scoring at or above 50th National Percentile Rank)

	Math	Reading	Language
Grade 3	60%	51%	51%
Grade 7	57%	54%	47%

Academic Performance Index, 2009
Number of valid scores. 2,288
2007 API (base) 781
2008 API (growth). 810

SAT Testing, 2006-07
Enrollment, Grade 12 . . . . NA
percent taking test. . . . . NA
number with total score 1,500+ . . . . . . NA

Average Scores:

Math	Verbal	Writing	Total
NA	NA	NA	NA

Federal No Child Left Behind, 2008
(Adequate Yearly Progress standards met)

	Participation Rate	Pct Proficient
ELA	Yes	No
Math	Yes	Yes

API Criteria . . . . Yes
Graduation rate . . . . NA
criteria met/possible. 37/36

Escondido Union Elem
San Diego County
2310 Aldergrove Ave
Escondido, CA 92029
(760) 432-2400

Superint. . . . . Jennifer Walters
Grade plan. PK-8
Number of schools. 25
Enrollment 19,445
High school graduates, 2006-07 0
Dropout rate. 0
Pupil/teacher ratio. 19.2%
Average class size. 25.7
Students per computer 3.4
Avg. Teacher Salary, ... $63,892
Avg. Daily Attendence (ADA). 18,023
Cost per ADA. $7,692

California Achievement Tests 6th ed., 2008
(Pct scoring at or above 50th National Percentile Rank)

	Math	Reading	Language
Grade 3	47%	30%	36%
Grade 7	48%	45%	43%

Academic Performance Index, 2009
Number of valid scores. 13,618
2007 API (base) 724
2008 API (growth). 734

SAT Testing, 2006-07
Enrollment, Grade 12 . . . . NA
percent taking test. . . . . NA
number with total score 1,500+ . . . . . . NA

Average Scores:

Math	Verbal	Writing	Total
NA	NA	NA	NA

Federal No Child Left Behind, 2008
(Adequate Yearly Progress standards met)

	Participation Rate	Pct Proficient
ELA	Yes	No
Math	Yes	No

API Criteria . . . . Yes
Graduation rate . . . . NA
criteria met/possible. 37/29

Etiwanda Elem
San Bernardino County
6061 East Ave
Etiwanda, CA 91739
(909) 899-2451

Superint. . . . . Shawn Judson
Grade plan. K-8
Number of schools. 16
Enrollment 12,340
High school graduates, 2006-07 0
Dropout rate. 0
Pupil/teacher ratio. 23.7%
Average class size. 28.0
Students per computer 5.0
Avg. Teacher Salary, ... $65,330
Avg. Daily Attendence (ADA). 12,137
Cost per ADA. $6,791

California Achievement Tests 6th ed., 2008
(Pct scoring at or above 50th National Percentile Rank)

	Math	Reading	Language
Grade 3	67%	48%	59%
Grade 7	67%	62%	60%

Academic Performance Index, 2009
Number of valid scores. 9,463
2007 API (base) 815
2008 API (growth). 837

SAT Testing, 2006-07
Enrollment, Grade 12 . . . . NA
percent taking test. . . . . NA
number with total score 1,500+ . . . . . . NA

Average Scores:

Math	Verbal	Writing	Total
NA	NA	NA	NA

Federal No Child Left Behind, 2008
(Adequate Yearly Progress standards met)

	Participation Rate	Pct Proficient
ELA	Yes	Yes
Math	Yes	Yes

API Criteria . . . . Yes
Graduation rate . . . . NA
criteria met/possible. 37/37

Eureka Union Elem
Placer County
5455 Eureka Rd
Granite Bay, CA 95746
(916) 791-4939

Superint. . . . . Tim McCarty
Grade plan. K-8
Number of schools. 9
Enrollment 3,841
High school graduates, 2006-07 0
Dropout rate. 0
Pupil/teacher ratio. 21.4%
Average class size. 25.5
Students per computer 3.4
Avg. Teacher Salary, ... $65,375
Avg. Daily Attendence (ADA). 3,774
Cost per ADA. $7,496

California Achievement Tests 6th ed., 2008
(Pct scoring at or above 50th National Percentile Rank)

	Math	Reading	Language
Grade 3	84%	75%	76%
Grade 7	83%	81%	76%

Academic Performance Index, 2009
Number of valid scores. 3,081
2007 API (base) 883
2008 API (growth). 888

SAT Testing, 2006-07
Enrollment, Grade 12 . . . . NA
percent taking test. . . . . NA
number with total score 1,500+ . . . . . . NA

Average Scores:

Math	Verbal	Writing	Total
NA	NA	NA	NA

Federal No Child Left Behind, 2008
(Adequate Yearly Progress standards met)

	Participation Rate	Pct Proficient
ELA	Yes	Yes
Math	Yes	Yes

API Criteria . . . . Yes
Graduation rate . . . . NA
criteria met/possible. 21/21

Evergreen Elem
Santa Clara County
3188 Quimby Rd
San Jose, CA 95148
(408) 270-6800

Superint. . . . . Clifton Black
Grade plan. K-8
Number of schools. 18
Enrollment 13,317
High school graduates, 2006-07 0
Dropout rate. 0
Pupil/teacher ratio. 21.9%
Average class size. 25.7
Students per computer 3.8
Avg. Teacher Salary, ... $72,849
Avg. Daily Attendence (ADA). 13,244
Cost per ADA. $7,135

California Achievement Tests 6th ed., 2008
(Pct scoring at or above 50th National Percentile Rank)

	Math	Reading	Language
Grade 3	74%	50%	61%
Grade 7	67%	59%	60%

Academic Performance Index, 2009
Number of valid scores. 9,984
2007 API (base) 833
2008 API (growth). 849

SAT Testing, 2006-07
Enrollment, Grade 12 . . . . NA
percent taking test. . . . . NA
number with total score 1,500+ . . . . . . NA

Average Scores:

Math	Verbal	Writing	Total
NA	NA	NA	NA

Federal No Child Left Behind, 2008
(Adequate Yearly Progress standards met)

	Participation Rate	Pct Proficient
ELA	Yes	No
Math	Yes	No

API Criteria . . . . Yes
Graduation rate . . . . NA
criteria met/possible. 41/39

Data from school year 2007-08 except where noted
†Combined data for elementary and high schools

Exeter Union Elem

Tulare County
134 South E St
Exeter, CA 93221
(559) 592-9421

Superint. . . . . Renee Whitson
Grade plan. K-8
Number of schools. 4
Enrollment 2,014
High school graduates, 2006-07 0
Dropout rate 0
Pupil/teacher ratio. 19.9%
Average class size. 25.4
Students per computer 4.0
Avg. Teacher Salary, ... $65,392
Avg. Daily Attendence (ADA). 1,979
Cost per ADA. $7,695

California Achievement Tests 6th ed., 2008
(Pct scoring at or above 50th National Percentile Rank)

	Math	Reading	Language
Grade 3	57%	40%	50%
Grade 7	49%	54%	51%

Academic Performance Index, 2009
Number of valid scores. 1,473
2007 API (base) 751
2008 API (growth). 764

SAT Testing, 2006-07
Enrollment, Grade 12 . . . . .NA
percent taking test. . . . . .NA
number with total score 1,500+ . . . . . .NA

Average Scores:

Math	Verbal	Writing	Total
NA	NA	NA	NA

Federal No Child Left Behind, 2008
(Adequate Yearly Progress standards met)

	Participation Rate	Pct Proficient
ELA	Yes	No
Math	Yes	No

API Criteria . . . . .Yes
Graduation rate . . . . .NA
criteria met/possible. 25/21

Fairfax Elem

Kern County
1500 South Fairfax Rd
Bakersfield, CA 93307
(661) 366-7221

Superint. . . . . Desiree VonFlue
Grade plan. K-8
Number of schools. 3
Enrollment 2,171
High school graduates, 2006-07 0
Dropout rate. 0
Pupil/teacher ratio. 20.3%
Average class size. 25.3
Students per computer 4.3
Avg. Teacher Salary, ... $53,754
Avg. Daily Attendence (ADA). 2,088
Cost per ADA. $7,554

California Achievement Tests 6th ed., 2008
(Pct scoring at or above 50th National Percentile Rank)

	Math	Reading	Language
Grade 3	27%	19%	17%
Grade 7	33%	26%	28%

Academic Performance Index, 2009
Number of valid scores. 1,475
2007 API (base) 608
2008 API (growth). 620

SAT Testing, 2006-07
Enrollment, Grade 12 . . . . .NA
percent taking test. . . . . .NA
number with total score 1,500+ . . . . . .NA

Average Scores:

Math	Verbal	Writing	Total
NA	NA	NA	NA

Federal No Child Left Behind, 2008
(Adequate Yearly Progress standards met)

	Participation Rate	Pct Proficient
ELA	Yes	No
Math	Yes	No

API Criteria . . . . .Yes
Graduation rate . . . . .NA
criteria met/possible. 25/14

Fallbrook Union Elem

San Diego County
321 North Iowa St
Fallbrook, CA 92028
(760) 731-5400

Superint. . . . . Janice Schultz
Grade plan. K-8
Number of schools. .10
Enrollment 5,485
High school graduates, 2006-07 0
Dropout rate. 0
Pupil/teacher ratio. 22.3%
Average class size. 24.3
Students per computer 2.9
Avg. Teacher Salary, ... $70,871
Avg. Daily Attendence (ADA). 5,373
Cost per ADA. $9,133

California Achievement Tests 6th ed., 2008
(Pct scoring at or above 50th National Percentile Rank)

	Math	Reading	Language
Grade 3	55%	37%	42%
Grade 7	56%	58%	55%

Academic Performance Index, 2009
Number of valid scores. 3,867
2007 API (base) 768
2008 API (growth). 776

SAT Testing, 2006-07
Enrollment, Grade 12 . . . . .NA
percent taking test. . . . . .NA
number with total score 1,500+ . . . . . .NA

Average Scores:

Math	Verbal	Writing	Total
NA	NA	NA	NA

Federal No Child Left Behind, 2008
(Adequate Yearly Progress standards met)

	Participation Rate	Pct Proficient
ELA	No	No
Math	No	No

API Criteria . . . . .Yes
Graduation rate . . . . .NA
criteria met/possible. 29/24

Fortuna Union Elem

Humboldt County
843 L St
Fortuna, CA 95540
(707) 725-2293

Superint. .Patti Hafner
Grade plan. K-8
Number of schools. 2
Enrollment 749
High school graduates, 2006-07 0
Dropout rate. 0
Pupil/teacher ratio. 19.8%
Average class size. 24.6
Students per computer 4.9
Avg. Teacher Salary, ... $57,722
Avg. Daily Attendence (ADA). 732
Cost per ADA. $8,132

California Achievement Tests 6th ed., 2008
(Pct scoring at or above 50th National Percentile Rank)

	Math	Reading	Language
Grade 3	50%	37%	38%
Grade 7	56%	68%	63%

Academic Performance Index, 2009
Number of valid scores. 510
2007 API (base) 713
2008 API (growth). 774

SAT Testing, 2006-07
Enrollment, Grade 12 . . . . .NA
percent taking test. . . . . .NA
number with total score 1,500+ . . . . . .NA

Average Scores:

Math	Verbal	Writing	Total
NA	NA	NA	NA

Federal No Child Left Behind, 2008
(Adequate Yearly Progress standards met)

	Participation Rate	Pct Proficient
ELA	Yes	Yes
Math	Yes	Yes

API Criteria . . . . .Yes
Graduation rate . . . . .NA
criteria met/possible. 21/21

Fountain Valley Elem

Orange County
10055 Slater Ave
Fountain Valley, CA 92708
(714) 843-3200

Superint. Marc Ecker
Grade plan. K-8
Number of schools. .11
Enrollment 6,123
High school graduates, 2006-07 0
Dropout rate. 0
Pupil/teacher ratio. 23.2%
Average class size. 28.6
Students per computer 4.8
Avg. Teacher Salary, ... $72,232
Avg. Daily Attendence (ADA). 5,989
Cost per ADA. $7,716

California Achievement Tests 6th ed., 2008
(Pct scoring at or above 50th National Percentile Rank)

	Math	Reading	Language
Grade 3	75%	59%	70%
Grade 7	76%	73%	73%

Academic Performance Index, 2009
Number of valid scores. 4,791
2007 API (base) 864
2008 API (growth). 879

SAT Testing, 2006-07
Enrollment, Grade 12 . . . . .NA
percent taking test. . . . . .NA
number with total score 1,500+ . . . . . .NA

Average Scores:

Math	Verbal	Writing	Total
NA	NA	NA	NA

Federal No Child Left Behind, 2008
(Adequate Yearly Progress standards met)

	Participation Rate	Pct Proficient
ELA	Yes	Yes
Math	Yes	Yes

API Criteria . . . . .Yes
Graduation rate . . . . .NA
criteria met/possible. 29/29

Franklin Elem

Sutter County
332 North Township Rd
Yuba City, CA 95993
(530) 822-5151

Superint. . . . . .Douglas Reeder
Grade plan. K-8
Number of schools. 1
Enrollment 431
High school graduates, 2006-07 0
Dropout rate. 0
Pupil/teacher ratio. 21.8%
Average class size. 25.3
Students per computer 6.7
Avg. Teacher Salary, ...NA
Avg. Daily Attendence (ADA). 412
Cost per ADA. $6,585

California Achievement Tests 6th ed., 2008
(Pct scoring at or above 50th National Percentile Rank)

	Math	Reading	Language
Grade 3	66%	51%	55%
Grade 7	62%	66%	43%

Academic Performance Index, 2009
Number of valid scores. 348
2007 API (base) 811
2008 API (growth). 818

SAT Testing, 2006-07
Enrollment, Grade 12 . . . . .NA
percent taking test. . . . . .NA
number with total score 1,500+ . . . . . .NA

Average Scores:

Math	Verbal	Writing	Total
NA	NA	NA	NA

Federal No Child Left Behind, 2008
(Adequate Yearly Progress standards met)

	Participation Rate	Pct Proficient
ELA	Yes	Yes
Math	Yes	Yes

API Criteria . . . . .Yes
Graduation rate . . . . .NA
criteria met/possible. 13/13

Data from school year 2007-08 except where noted.
†Combined data for elementary and high schools.

Franklin-McKinley Elem
Santa Clara County
645 Wool Creek Dr
San Jose, CA 95112
(408) 283-6000

Superint. . . . . John Porter
Grade plan. K-8
Number of schools. 17
Enrollment 9,957
High school graduates, 2006-07. 0
Dropout rate. 0
Pupil/teacher ratio. 21.6%
Average class size. 24.8
Students per computer 5.2
Avg. Teacher Salary, ... $70,812
Avg. Daily Attendence (ADA). 9,610
Cost per ADA. $8,324

California Achievement Tests 6th ed., 2008
(Pct scoring at or above 50th National Percentile Rank)

	Math	Reading	Language
Grade 3	49%	22%	37%
Grade 7	44%	38%	36%

Academic Performance Index, 2009
Number of valid scores. 6,796
2007 API (base) 711
2008 API (growth). 718

SAT Testing, 2006-07
Enrollment, Grade 12 . . . . NA
percent taking test. . . . . NA
number with total score 1,500+ . . . . . . NA

Average Scores:

Math	Verbal	Writing	Total
NA	NA	NA	NA

Federal No Child Left Behind, 2008
(Adequate Yearly Progress standards met)

	Participation Rate	Pct Proficient
ELA	Yes	No
Math	Yes	No

API Criteria . . . . Yes
Graduation rate . . . . NA
criteria met/possible. 37/29

Freshwater Elem
Humboldt County
75 Greenwood Heights Dr
Eureka, CA 95503
(707) 442-1405

Superint. . . . . Thom McMahon
Grade plan. K-8
Number of schools. 2
Enrollment 317
High school graduates, 2006-07. 0
Dropout rate. 0
Pupil/teacher ratio. 18.1%
Average class size. 22.6
Students per computer 9.3
Avg. Teacher Salary, ... NA
Avg. Daily Attendence (ADA). 306
Cost per ADA. $8,329

California Achievement Tests 6th ed., 2008
(Pct scoring at or above 50th National Percentile Rank)

	Math	Reading	Language
Grade 3	71%	75%	71%
Grade 7	71%	80%	72%

Academic Performance Index, 2009
Number of valid scores. 231
2007 API (base) 855
2008 API (growth). 851

SAT Testing, 2006-07
Enrollment, Grade 12 . . . . NA
percent taking test. . . . . NA
number with total score 1,500+ . . . . . . NA

Average Scores:

Math	Verbal	Writing	Total
NA	NA	NA	NA

Federal No Child Left Behind, 2008
(Adequate Yearly Progress standards met)

	Participation Rate	Pct Proficient
ELA	Yes	Yes
Math	Yes	Yes

API Criteria . . . . Yes
Graduation rate . . . . NA
criteria met/possible. 13/13

Fresno Unified
Fresno County
2309 Tulare St
Fresno, CA 93721
(559) 457-3000

Superint. . . . . Michael Hanson
Grade plan. K-12
Number of schools. 108
Enrollment 76,460
High school graduates, 2006-07. . . . 3,480
Dropout rate. 7.9
Pupil/teacher ratio. 19.5%
Average class size. 25.1
Students per computer 3.9
Avg. Teacher Salary, ... $64,816
Avg. Daily Attendence (ADA). 69,774
Cost per ADA. $9,413

California Achievement Tests 6th ed., 2008
(Pct scoring at or above 50th National Percentile Rank)

	Math	Reading	Language
Grade 3	42%	25%	34%
Grade 7	39%	33%	34%

Academic Performance Index, 2009
Number of valid scores. 49,980
2007 API (base) 670
2008 API (growth). 684

SAT Testing, 2006-07
Enrollment, Grade 12 4,029
percent taking test. 30.3%
number with total score 1,500+ 321

Average Scores:

Math	Verbal	Writing	Total
457	440	436	1,333

Federal No Child Left Behind, 2008
(Adequate Yearly Progress standards met)

	Participation Rate	Pct Proficient
ELA	Yes	No
Math	Yes	No

API Criteria . . . . Yes
Graduation rate . . . . Yes
criteria met/possible. 46/39

Fruitvale Elem
Kern County
7311 Rosedale Hwy
Bakersfield, CA 93308
(661) 589-3830

Superint. . . . . Carl Olsen
Grade plan. K-8
Number of schools. 5
Enrollment 3,151
High school graduates, 2006-07. 0
Dropout rate. 0
Pupil/teacher ratio. 19.7%
Average class size. 22.6
Students per computer 7.2
Avg. Teacher Salary, ... $63,189
Avg. Daily Attendence (ADA). 3,075
Cost per ADA. $7,474

California Achievement Tests 6th ed., 2008
(Pct scoring at or above 50th National Percentile Rank)

	Math	Reading	Language
Grade 3	75%	58%	66%
Grade 7	67%	63%	63%

Academic Performance Index, 2009
Number of valid scores. 2,366
2007 API (base) 832
2008 API (growth). 833

SAT Testing, 2006-07
Enrollment, Grade 12 . . . . NA
percent taking test. . . . . NA
number with total score 1,500+ . . . . . . NA

Average Scores:

Math	Verbal	Writing	Total
NA	NA	NA	NA

Federal No Child Left Behind, 2008
(Adequate Yearly Progress standards met)

	Participation Rate	Pct Proficient
ELA	Yes	No
Math	Yes	Yes

API Criteria . . . . Yes
Graduation rate . . . . NA
criteria met/possible. 25/24

Fullerton Elem
Orange County
1401 West Valencia Dr
Fullerton, CA 92833
(714) 447-7400

Superint. . . . . Mitch Hovey
Grade plan. K-8
Number of schools. 20
Enrollment 13,597
High school graduates, 2006-07. 0
Dropout rate. 0
Pupil/teacher ratio. 23.6%
Average class size. 28.7
Students per computer 2.1
Avg. Teacher Salary, ... $69,772
Avg. Daily Attendence (ADA). 13,470
Cost per ADA. $7,851

California Achievement Tests 6th ed., 2008
(Pct scoring at or above 50th National Percentile Rank)

	Math	Reading	Language
Grade 3	57%	37%	46%
Grade 7	65%	58%	57%

Academic Performance Index, 2009
Number of valid scores. 10,185
2007 API (base) 798
2008 API (growth). 813

SAT Testing, 2006-07
Enrollment, Grade 12 . . . . NA
percent taking test. . . . . NA
number with total score 1,500+ . . . . . . NA

Average Scores:

Math	Verbal	Writing	Total
NA	NA	NA	NA

Federal No Child Left Behind, 2008
(Adequate Yearly Progress standards met)

	Participation Rate	Pct Proficient
ELA	Yes	No
Math	Yes	No

API Criteria . . . . Yes
Graduation rate . . . . NA
criteria met/possible. 37/35

Fullerton Joint Union High
Orange County
1051 West Bastanchury Rd
Fullerton, CA 92833
(714) 870-2800

Superint. . . . . George Giokaris
Grade plan. 9-12
Number of schools. 8
Enrollment 16,321
High school graduates, 2006-07. . . . 2,914
Dropout rate. 2.3
Pupil/teacher ratio. 27.7%
Average class size. 29.9
Students per computer 3.7
Avg. Teacher Salary, ... $82,860
Avg. Daily Attendence (ADA). 15,436
Cost per ADA. $7,977

California Achievement Tests 6th ed., 2008
(Pct scoring at or above 50th National Percentile Rank)

	Math	Reading	Language
Grade 3			
Grade 7			

Academic Performance Index, 2009
Number of valid scores. 10,168
2007 API (base) 775
2008 API (growth). 794

SAT Testing, 2006-07
Enrollment, Grade 12 2,962
percent taking test. 51.6%
number with total score 1,500+ 953

Average Scores:

Math	Verbal	Writing	Total
568	529	536	1,633

Federal No Child Left Behind, 2008
(Adequate Yearly Progress standards met)

	Participation Rate	Pct Proficient
ELA	Yes	No
Math	Yes	No

API Criteria . . . . Yes
Graduation rate . . . . Yes
criteria met/possible. 34/32

Data from school year 2007-08 except where noted
†Combined data for elementary and high schools

Galt Joint Union Elem

Sacramento County
1018 C St Ste 210
Galt, CA 95632
(209) 744-4545

Superint. . . . . Karen Schauer
Grade plan. K-8
Number of schools. 7
Enrollment 4,292
High school graduates, 2006-07. 0
Dropout rate. 0
Pupil/teacher ratio. 18.1%
Average class size. 23.1
Students per computer 4.7
Avg. Teacher Salary, ... $59,956
Avg. Daily Attendence (ADA). 4,186
Cost per ADA. $7,858

California Achievement Tests 6th ed., 2008
(Pct scoring at or above 50th National Percentile Rank)

	Math	Reading	Language
Grade 3	58%	43%	44%
Grade 7	55%	50%	48%

Academic Performance Index, 2009
Number of valid scores. 3,236
2007 API (base) 759
2008 API (growth). 772

SAT Testing, 2006-07
Enrollment, Grade 12 . . . . NA
percent taking test. . . . . NA
number with total score 1,500+ . . . . . . NA

Average Scores:

Math	Verbal	Writing	Total
NA	NA	NA	NA

Federal No Child Left Behind, 2008
(Adequate Yearly Progress standards met)

	Participation Rate	Pct Proficient
ELA	Yes	No
Math	Yes	No

API Criteria . . . . Yes
Graduation rate . . . . NA
criteria met/possible. 25/22

Garden Grove Unified

Orange County
10331 Stanford Ave
Garden Grove, CA 92840
(714) 663-6000

Superint. . . . . Laura Schwalm
Grade plan. K-12
Number of schools. 67
Enrollment 48,669
High school graduates, 2006-07. . . . 2,803
Dropout rate. 1.2
Pupil/teacher ratio. 23.1%
Average class size. 26.9
Students per computer 5.2
Avg. Teacher Salary, ... $77,535
Avg. Daily Attendence (ADA). 47,531
Cost per ADA. $8,420

California Achievement Tests 6th ed., 2008
(Pct scoring at or above 50th National Percentile Rank)

	Math	Reading	Language
Grade 3	59%	31%	44%
Grade 7	58%	52%	52%

Academic Performance Index, 2009
Number of valid scores. 35,426
2007 API (base) 767
2008 API (growth). 778

SAT Testing, 2006-07
Enrollment, Grade 12 3,163
percent taking test. 36.6%
number with total score 1,500+ 523

Average Scores:

Math	Verbal	Writing	Total
521	480	480	1,481

Federal No Child Left Behind, 2008
(Adequate Yearly Progress standards met)

	Participation Rate	Pct Proficient
ELA	Yes	No
Math	Yes	No

API Criteria . . . . Yes
Graduation rate . . . . Yes
criteria met/possible. 42/40

Garfield Elem

Humboldt County
2200 Freshwater Rd
Eureka, CA 95503
(707) 442-5471

Superint. . . . . Barbara McMahon
Grade plan. K-6
Number of schools. 1
Enrollment 60
High school graduates, 2006-07. 0
Dropout rate. . . . . NA
Pupil/teacher ratio. 18.9%
Average class size. 20.0
Students per computer 2.9
Avg. Teacher Salary, ... $43,857
Avg. Daily Attendence (ADA). 58
Cost per ADA. $9,402

California Achievement Tests 6th ed., 2008
(Pct scoring at or above 50th National Percentile Rank)

	Math	Reading	Language
Grade 3	NA	NA	NA
Grade 7	NA	NA	NA

Academic Performance Index, 2009
Number of valid scores. 43
2007 API (base) 923
2008 API (growth). 932

SAT Testing, 2006-07
Enrollment, Grade 12 . . . . NA
percent taking test. . . . . NA
number with total score 1,500+ . . . . . . NA

Average Scores:

Math	Verbal	Writing	Total
NA	NA	NA	NA

Federal No Child Left Behind, 2008
(Adequate Yearly Progress standards met)

	Participation Rate	Pct Proficient
ELA	Yes	Yes
Math	Yes	Yes

API Criteria . . . . Yes
Graduation rate . . . . NA
criteria met/possible. 5/5

Garvey Elem

Los Angeles County
2730 North Del Mar Ave
Rosemead, CA 91770
(626) 307-3444

Superint. . . . . Virginia Peterson
Grade plan. K-8
Number of schools. 12
Enrollment 5,961
High school graduates, 2006-07. 0
Dropout rate. 0
Pupil/teacher ratio. 21.7%
Average class size. 27.0
Students per computer 3.1
Avg. Teacher Salary, ... $67,256
Avg. Daily Attendence (ADA). 5,951
Cost per ADA. $8,670

California Achievement Tests 6th ed., 2008
(Pct scoring at or above 50th National Percentile Rank)

	Math	Reading	Language
Grade 3	66%	31%	49%
Grade 7	65%	50%	49%

Academic Performance Index, 2009
Number of valid scores. 4,483
2007 API (base) 759
2008 API (growth). 786

SAT Testing, 2006-07
Enrollment, Grade 12 . . . . NA
percent taking test. . . . . NA
number with total score 1,500+ . . . . . . NA

Average Scores:

Math	Verbal	Writing	Total
NA	NA	NA	NA

Federal No Child Left Behind, 2008
(Adequate Yearly Progress standards met)

	Participation Rate	Pct Proficient
ELA	Yes	No
Math	Yes	No

API Criteria . . . . Yes
Graduation rate . . . . NA
criteria met/possible. 25/21

Gateway Unified

Shasta County
4411 Mountain Lakes Blvd
Redding, CA 96003
(530) 245-7900

Superint. . . . . John Strohmayer
Grade plan. K-12
Number of schools. 12
Enrollment 3,264
High school graduates, 2006-07. 237
Dropout rate. 2.4
Pupil/teacher ratio. 18.6%
Average class size. 22.2
Students per computer 4.5
Avg. Teacher Salary, ... $56,556
Avg. Daily Attendence (ADA). 2,695
Cost per ADA. $9,341

California Achievement Tests 6th ed., 2008
(Pct scoring at or above 50th National Percentile Rank)

	Math	Reading	Language
Grade 3	56%	45%	50%
Grade 7	50%	52%	48%

Academic Performance Index, 2009
Number of valid scores. 1,853
2007 API (base) 731
2008 API (growth). 753

SAT Testing, 2006-07
Enrollment, Grade 12 305
percent taking test. 17.7%
number with total score 1,500+ 20

Average Scores:

Math	Verbal	Writing	Total
486	478	458	1,422

Federal No Child Left Behind, 2008
(Adequate Yearly Progress standards met)

	Participation Rate	Pct Proficient
ELA	Yes	Yes
Math	Yes	Yes

API Criteria . . . . Yes
Graduation rate . . . . Yes
criteria met/possible. 26/26

General Shafter Elem

Kern County
1825 Shafter Rd
Bakersfield, CA 93313
(661) 837-1931

Superint. . . . . Deborah Rodrigues
Grade plan. K-8
Number of schools. 1
Enrollment 198
High school graduates, 2006-07. 0
Dropout rate. 0
Pupil/teacher ratio. 24.8%
Average class size. 24.8
Students per computer 11.6
Avg. Teacher Salary, ... $52,504
Avg. Daily Attendence (ADA). 194
Cost per ADA. $9,403

California Achievement Tests 6th ed., 2008
(Pct scoring at or above 50th National Percentile Rank)

	Math	Reading	Language
Grade 3	50%	56%	67%
Grade 7	55%	59%	45%

Academic Performance Index, 2009
Number of valid scores. 163
2007 API (base) 742
2008 API (growth). 719

SAT Testing, 2006-07
Enrollment, Grade 12 . . . . NA
percent taking test. . . . . NA
number with total score 1,500+ . . . . . . NA

Average Scores:

Math	Verbal	Writing	Total
NA	NA	NA	NA

Federal No Child Left Behind, 2008
(Adequate Yearly Progress standards met)

	Participation Rate	Pct Proficient
ELA	Yes	Yes
Math	Yes	Yes

API Criteria . . . . Yes
Graduation rate . . . . NA
criteria met/possible. 21/21

Data from school year 2007-08 except where noted.
†Combined data for elementary and high schools.

Gold Oak Union Elem
El Dorado County
3171 Pleasant Valley Rd
Placerville, CA 95667
(530) 626-3150

Superint. . . . . Richard Williams
Grade plan. K-8
Number of schools. 3
Enrollment 692
High school graduates, 2006-07 0
Dropout rate. 0
Pupil/teacher ratio. 19.5%
Average class size. 24.0
Students per computer 2.3
Avg. Teacher Salary, ... $55,869
Avg. Daily Attendence (ADA). 656
Cost per ADA. $7,659

California Achievement Tests 6th ed., 2008
(Pct scoring at or above 50th National Percentile Rank)

	Math	Reading	Language
Grade 3	60%	47%	59%
Grade 7	71%	71%	65%

Academic Performance Index, 2009
Number of valid scores. 541
2007 API (base) 821
2008 API (growth). 819

SAT Testing, 2006-07
Enrollment, Grade 12 . . . . NA
percent taking test. . . . . NA
number with total score 1,500+ . . . . . . NA

Average Scores:

Math	Verbal	Writing	Total
NA	NA	NA	NA

Federal No Child Left Behind, 2008
(Adequate Yearly Progress standards met)

	Participation Rate	Pct Proficient
ELA	Yes	Yes
Math	Yes	Yes

API Criteria . . . . Yes
Graduation rate . . . . NA
criteria met/possible. 13/13

Gold Trail Union Elem
El Dorado County
1575 Old Ranch Rd
Placerville, CA 95667
(530) 626-3194

Superint. . . . . Joe Murchison
Grade plan. K-8
Number of schools. 2
Enrollment 552
High school graduates, 2006-07 0
Dropout rate. 0
Pupil/teacher ratio. 21.1%
Average class size. 26.0
Students per computer 7.5
Avg. Teacher Salary, ... $61,847
Avg. Daily Attendence (ADA). 549
Cost per ADA. $7,741

California Achievement Tests 6th ed., 2008
(Pct scoring at or above 50th National Percentile Rank)

	Math	Reading	Language
Grade 3	79%	75%	69%
Grade 7	79%	79%	71%

Academic Performance Index, 2009
Number of valid scores. 430
2007 API (base) 837
2008 API (growth). 847

SAT Testing, 2006-07
Enrollment, Grade 12 . . . . NA
percent taking test. . . . . NA
number with total score 1,500+ . . . . . . NA

Average Scores:

Math	Verbal	Writing	Total
NA	NA	NA	NA

Federal No Child Left Behind, 2008
(Adequate Yearly Progress standards met)

	Participation Rate	Pct Proficient
ELA	Yes	Yes
Math	Yes	Yes

API Criteria . . . . Yes
Graduation rate . . . . NA
criteria met/possible. 9/9

Golden Feather Union Elem
Butte County
11679 Nelson Bar Rd
Oroville, CA 95965
(530) 533-3833

Superint. Lora Haston
Grade plan. K-8
Number of schools. 3
Enrollment 144
High school graduates, 2006-07 0
Dropout rate. 0
Pupil/teacher ratio. 14.0%
Average class size. 15.8
Students per computer 3.1
Avg. Teacher Salary, ... NA
Avg. Daily Attendence (ADA). 132
Cost per ADA. $13,111

California Achievement Tests 6th ed., 2008
(Pct scoring at or above 50th National Percentile Rank)

	Math	Reading	Language
Grade 3	NA	NA	NA
Grade 7	35%	24%	12%

Academic Performance Index, 2009
Number of valid scores. 93
2007 API (base) 679
2008 API (growth). 691

SAT Testing, 2006-07
Enrollment, Grade 12 . . . . NA
percent taking test. . . . . NA
number with total score 1,500+ . . . . . . NA

Average Scores:

Math	Verbal	Writing	Total
NA	NA	NA	NA

Federal No Child Left Behind, 2008
(Adequate Yearly Progress standards met)

	Participation Rate	Pct Proficient
ELA	Yes	No
Math	Yes	Yes

API Criteria . . . . Yes
Graduation rate . . . . NA
criteria met/possible. 9/8

Golden Valley Unified
Madera County
37479 Avenue 12
Madera, CA 93638
(559) 645-7500

Superint. . . . . Sarah Koligian
Grade plan. K-12
Number of schools. 8
Enrollment 2,033
High school graduates, 2006-07 128
Dropout rate. 2.4
Pupil/teacher ratio. 19.8%
Average class size. 23.9
Students per computer 5.8
Avg. Teacher Salary, ... $56,212
Avg. Daily Attendence (ADA). 1,973
Cost per ADA. $8,363

California Achievement Tests 6th ed., 2008
(Pct scoring at or above 50th National Percentile Rank)

	Math	Reading	Language
Grade 3	68%	54%	59%
Grade 7	59%	69%	61%

Academic Performance Index, 2009
Number of valid scores. 1,448
2007 API (base) 787
2008 API (growth). 804

SAT Testing, 2006-07
Enrollment, Grade 12 140
percent taking test. 37.1%
number with total score 1,500+ 18

Average Scores:

Math	Verbal	Writing	Total
482	474	475	1,431

Federal No Child Left Behind, 2008
(Adequate Yearly Progress standards met)

	Participation Rate	Pct Proficient
ELA	Yes	Yes
Math	Yes	Yes

API Criteria . . . . Yes
Graduation rate . . . . Yes
criteria met/possible. 22/22

Goleta Union Elem
Santa Barbara County
401 North Fairview Ave
Goleta, CA 93117
(805) 681-1200

Superint. . . . . Kathleen Boomer
Grade plan. K-6
Number of schools. 9
Enrollment 3,533
High school graduates, 2006-07 0
Dropout rate. . . . . NA
Pupil/teacher ratio. 18.2%
Average class size. 19.6
Students per computer 2.7
Avg. Teacher Salary, ... $71,146
Avg. Daily Attendence (ADA). 3,443
Cost per ADA. $10,650

California Achievement Tests 6th ed., 2008
(Pct scoring at or above 50th National Percentile Rank)

	Math	Reading	Language
Grade 3	66%	46%	53%
Grade 7	NA	NA	NA

Academic Performance Index, 2009
Number of valid scores. 2,434
2007 API (base) 810
2008 API (growth). 811

SAT Testing, 2006-07
Enrollment, Grade 12 . . . . NA
percent taking test. . . . . NA
number with total score 1,500+ . . . . . . NA

Average Scores:

Math	Verbal	Writing	Total
NA	NA	NA	NA

Federal No Child Left Behind, 2008
(Adequate Yearly Progress standards met)

	Participation Rate	Pct Proficient
ELA	Yes	No
Math	Yes	No

API Criteria . . . . Yes
Graduation rate . . . . NA
criteria met/possible. 29/24

Grant Elem
Shasta County
8835 Swasey Dr
Redding, CA 96001
(530) 243-0561

Superint. John Krinkel
Grade plan. K-8
Number of schools. 1
Enrollment 603
High school graduates, 2006-07 0
Dropout rate. 0
Pupil/teacher ratio. 20.5%
Average class size. 23.1
Students per computer 5.2
Avg. Teacher Salary, ... NA
Avg. Daily Attendence (ADA). 598
Cost per ADA. $8,336

California Achievement Tests 6th ed., 2008
(Pct scoring at or above 50th National Percentile Rank)

	Math	Reading	Language
Grade 3	80%	71%	71%
Grade 7	81%	87%	84%

Academic Performance Index, 2009
Number of valid scores. 442
2007 API (base) 879
2008 API (growth). 891

SAT Testing, 2006-07
Enrollment, Grade 12 . . . . NA
percent taking test. . . . . NA
number with total score 1,500+ . . . . . . NA

Average Scores:

Math	Verbal	Writing	Total
NA	NA	NA	NA

Federal No Child Left Behind, 2008
(Adequate Yearly Progress standards met)

	Participation Rate	Pct Proficient
ELA	Yes	Yes
Math	Yes	Yes

API Criteria . . . . Yes
Graduation rate . . . . NA
criteria met/possible. 9/9

Data from school year 2007-08 except where noted
†Combined data for elementary and high schools

Grant Joint Union High

Sacramento County
(merged into Twin Rivers Unified)
5115 Dudley Blvd
North Highlands, CA 95660
(916) 566-1786

Superint. . . . . Frank Porter
Grade plan. 7-12
Number of schools. 22
Enrollment 14,043
High school graduates, 2006-07. . . . 1,331
Dropout rate. 6.8
Pupil/teacher ratio. 21.8%
Average class size. 24.9
Students per computer 3.2
Avg. Teacher Salary, ... $59,627
Avg. Daily Attendence (ADA). 11,015
Cost per ADA. $10,284

California Achievement Tests 6th ed., 2008
(Pct scoring at or above 50th National Percentile Rank)

	Math	Reading	Language
Grade 3	43%	21%	32%
Grade 7	34%	30%	28%

Academic Performance Index, 2009
Number of valid scores. 8,000
2007 API (base) 647
2008 API (growth). 647

SAT Testing, 2006-07
Enrollment, Grade 12 1,697
percent taking test. 17.5%

Average Scores:

Math	Verbal	Writing	Total
453	434	427	1,314

Federal No Child Left Behind, 2008
(Adequate Yearly Progress standards met)

	Participation Rate	Pct Proficient
ELA	Yes	No
Math	Yes	No

API Criteria . . . . Yes
Graduation rate . . . . Yes
\# criteria met/possible. 38/24

Grass Valley Elem

Nevada County
10840 Gilmore Way
Grass Valley, CA 95945
(530) 273-4483

Superint. . . . . Jon Byerrum
Grade plan. K-8
Number of schools. 6
Enrollment 1,671
High school graduates, 2006-07. 0
Dropout rate. 0
Pupil/teacher ratio. 18.1%
Average class size. 23.9
Students per computer 3.0
Avg. Teacher Salary, ... $62,045
Avg. Daily Attendence (ADA). 1,369
Cost per ADA. $8,705

California Achievement Tests 6th ed., 2008
(Pct scoring at or above 50th National Percentile Rank)

	Math	Reading	Language
Grade 3	59%	51%	51%
Grade 7	64%	60%	57%

Academic Performance Index, 2009
Number of valid scores. 1,259
2007 API (base) 783
2008 API (growth). 774

SAT Testing, 2006-07
Enrollment, Grade 12 . . . . NA
percent taking test. . . . . NA
number with total score 1,500+ . . . . . . NA

Average Scores:

Math	Verbal	Writing	Total
NA	NA	NA	NA

Federal No Child Left Behind, 2008
(Adequate Yearly Progress standards met)

	Participation Rate	Pct Proficient
ELA	Yes	No
Math	Yes	No

API Criteria . . . . Yes
Graduation rate . . . . NA
\# criteria met/possible. 21/19

Gravenstein Union Elem

Sonoma County
3840 Twig Ave
Sebastopol, CA 95472
(707) 823-7008

Superint. . . . . Linda La Marre
Grade plan. K-8
Number of schools. 2
Enrollment 508
High school graduates, 2006-07. 0
Dropout rate. 0
Pupil/teacher ratio. 17.0%
Average class size. 23.2
Students per computer 5.2
Avg. Teacher Salary, ... $50,124
Avg. Daily Attendence (ADA). 484
Cost per ADA. $7,735

California Achievement Tests 6th ed., 2008
(Pct scoring at or above 50th National Percentile Rank)

	Math	Reading	Language
Grade 3	74%	57%	63%
Grade 7	76%	83%	79%

Academic Performance Index, 2009
Number of valid scores. 384
2007 API (base) 846
2008 API (growth). 862

SAT Testing, 2006-07
Enrollment, Grade 12 . . . . NA
percent taking test. . . . . NA
number with total score 1,500+ . . . . . . NA

Average Scores:

Math	Verbal	Writing	Total
NA	NA	NA	NA

Federal No Child Left Behind, 2008
(Adequate Yearly Progress standards met)

	Participation Rate	Pct Proficient
ELA	Yes	Yes
Math	Yes	Yes

API Criteria . . . . Yes
Graduation rate . . . . NA
\# criteria met/possible. 13/13

Graves Elem

Monterey County
15 McFadden Rd
Salinas, CA 93908
(831) 422-6392

Superint. . . . . Rosemarie Grounds
Grade plan. K-8
Number of schools. 1
Enrollment 38
High school graduates, 2006-07. 0
Dropout rate. 0
Pupil/teacher ratio. 19.0%
Average class size. 19.0
Students per computer 2.7
Avg. Teacher Salary, ... NA
Avg. Daily Attendence (ADA). 37
Cost per ADA. $7,757

California Achievement Tests 6th ed., 2008
(Pct scoring at or above 50th National Percentile Rank)

	Math	Reading	Language
Grade 3	NA	NA	NA
Grade 7	NA	NA	NA

Academic Performance Index, 2009
Number of valid scores. 29
2007 API (base) 795
2008 API (growth). 789

SAT Testing, 2006-07
Enrollment, Grade 12 . . . . NA
percent taking test. . . . . NA
number with total score 1,500+ . . . . . . NA

Average Scores:

Math	Verbal	Writing	Total
NA	NA	NA	NA

Federal No Child Left Behind, 2008
(Adequate Yearly Progress standards met)

	Participation Rate	Pct Proficient
ELA	Yes	Yes
Math	Yes	Yes

API Criteria . . . . Yes
Graduation rate . . . . NA
\# criteria met/possible. 5/5

Green Point Elem

Humboldt County
180 Valkensar Ln
Blue Lake, CA 95525
(707) 668-5921

Superint. . . . . Carole Boshears
Grade plan. K-8
Number of schools. 1
Enrollment 12
High school graduates, 2006-07. 0
Dropout rate. 0
Pupil/teacher ratio. 8.0%
Average class size. 6.0
Students per computer 1.7
Avg. Teacher Salary, ... NA
Avg. Daily Attendence (ADA). 13
Cost per ADA. $18,067

California Achievement Tests 6th ed., 2008
(Pct scoring at or above 50th National Percentile Rank)

	Math	Reading	Language
Grade 3	NA	NA	NA
Grade 7	NA	NA	NA

Academic Performance Index, 2009
Number of valid scores. . . . .
2007 API (base) . . . . NA
2008 API (growth). . . . . NA

SAT Testing, 2006-07
Enrollment, Grade 12 . . . . NA
percent taking test. . . . . NA
number with total score 1,500+ . . . . . . NA

Average Scores:

Math	Verbal	Writing	Total
NA	NA	NA	NA

Federal No Child Left Behind, 2008
(Adequate Yearly Progress standards met)

	Participation Rate	Pct Proficient
ELA	Yes	Yes
Math	Yes	Yes

API Criteria . . . . Yes
Graduation rate . . . . NA
\# criteria met/possible. 5/5

Greenfield Union

Kern County
1624 Fairview Rd
Bakersfield, CA 93307
(661) 837-6000

Superint. . . . . Gary Rice
Grade plan. K-8
Number of schools. 11
Enrollment 8,521
High school graduates, 2006-07. 0
Dropout rate. 0
Pupil/teacher ratio. 20.0%
Average class size. 24.3
Students per computer 3.7
Avg. Teacher Salary, ...
Avg. Daily Attendence (ADA). 8,357
Cost per ADA. $7,504

California Achievement Tests 6th ed., 2008
(Pct scoring at or above 50th National Percentile Rank)

	Math	Reading	Language
Grade 3	39%	24%	29%
Grade 7	33%	34%	30%

Academic Performance Index, 2009
Number of valid scores. 5,819
2007 API (base) 713
2008 API (growth). 723

SAT Testing, 2006-07
Enrollment, Grade 12 . . . . NA
percent taking test. . . . . NA
number with total score 1,500+ . . . . . . NA

Average Scores:

Math	Verbal	Writing	Total
NA	NA	NA	NA

Federal No Child Left Behind, 2008
(Adequate Yearly Progress standards met)

	Participation Rate	Pct Proficient
ELA	Yes	No
Math	Yes	No

API Criteria . . . . Yes
Graduation rate . . . . NA
\# criteria met/possible. 33/25

Data from school year 2007-08 except where noted.
†Combined data for elementary and high schools.

Greenfield Union Elem

Monterey County
493 El Camino Real
Greenfield, CA 93927
(831) 674-2840

Superint. . . . . Elida Garza
Grade plan. K-8
Number of schools. 4
Enrollment 2,506
High school graduates, 2006-07. 0
Dropout rate. 0
Pupil/teacher ratio. 20.3%
Average class size. 24.5
Students per computer 8.8
Avg. Teacher Salary, ... $55,041
Avg. Daily Attendence (ADA). 2,503
Cost per ADA. $7,712

California Achievement Tests 6th ed., 2008
(Pct scoring at or above 50th National Percentile Rank)

	Math	Reading	Language
Grade 3	26%	13%	26%
Grade 7	24%	25%	29%

Academic Performance Index, 2009
Number of valid scores. 1,744
2007 API (base) 587
2008 API (growth). 605

SAT Testing, 2006-07
Enrollment, Grade 12 . . . . . NA
percent taking test. . . . . NA
number with total score 1,500+ . . . . . NA

Average Scores:

Math	Verbal	Writing	Total
NA	NA	NA	NA

Federal No Child Left Behind, 2008
(Adequate Yearly Progress standards met)

	Participation Rate	Pct Proficient
ELA	Yes	No
Math	Yes	No

API Criteria . . . . . Yes
Graduation rate . . . . . NA
criteria met/possible. 21/11

Guadalupe Union Elem

Santa Barbara County
PO Box 788
Guadalupe, CA 93434
(805) 343-2114

Superint. . . . . Hugo Lara
Grade plan. K-8
Number of schools. 2
Enrollment 1,088
High school graduates, 2006-07. 0
Dropout rate. 0
Pupil/teacher ratio. 19.1%
Average class size. 22.3
Students per computer 4.4
Avg. Teacher Salary, ... $70,476
Avg. Daily Attendence (ADA). 1,063
Cost per ADA. $8,707

California Achievement Tests 6th ed., 2008
(Pct scoring at or above 50th National Percentile Rank)

	Math	Reading	Language
Grade 3	45%	18%	35%
Grade 7	34%	34%	36%

Academic Performance Index, 2009
Number of valid scores. 762
2007 API (base) 667
2008 API (growth). 696

SAT Testing, 2006-07
Enrollment, Grade 12 . . . . . NA
percent taking test. . . . . NA
number with total score 1,500+ . . . . . NA

Average Scores:

Math	Verbal	Writing	Total
NA	NA	NA	NA

Federal No Child Left Behind, 2008
(Adequate Yearly Progress standards met)

	Participation Rate	Pct Proficient
ELA	Yes	No
Math	Yes	No

API Criteria . . . . . Yes
Graduation rate . . . . . NA
criteria met/possible. 17/9

Hanford Elem

Kings County
PO Box 1067
Hanford, CA 93232
(559) 585-3600

Superint. . . . . Paul Terry
Grade plan. K-8
Number of schools. 11
Enrollment 5,449
High school graduates, 2006-07. 0
Dropout rate. 0
Pupil/teacher ratio. 20.1%
Average class size. 24.3
Students per computer 5.2
Avg. Teacher Salary, ... $57,083
Avg. Daily Attendence (ADA). 5,177
Cost per ADA. $8,273

California Achievement Tests 6th ed., 2008
(Pct scoring at or above 50th National Percentile Rank)

	Math	Reading	Language
Grade 3	42%	28%	36%
Grade 7	47%	41%	39%

Academic Performance Index, 2009
Number of valid scores. 3,829
2007 API (base) 688
2008 API (growth). 710

SAT Testing, 2006-07
Enrollment, Grade 12 . . . . . NA
percent taking test. . . . . NA
number with total score 1,500+ . . . . . NA

Average Scores:

Math	Verbal	Writing	Total
NA	NA	NA	NA

Federal No Child Left Behind, 2008
(Adequate Yearly Progress standards met)

	Participation Rate	Pct Proficient
ELA	Yes	No
Math	Yes	No

API Criteria . . . . . Yes
Graduation rate . . . . . NA
criteria met/possible. 29/21

Happy Valley Elem

Santa Cruz County
3125 Branciforte Dr
Santa Cruz, CA 95065
(831) 429-1456

Superint. . . . . Chris McGriff
Grade plan. K-6
Number of schools. 1
Enrollment 141
High school graduates, 2006-07. 0
Dropout rate. . . . . NA
Pupil/teacher ratio. 19.1%
Average class size. 23.5
Students per computer 1.1
Avg. Teacher Salary, ... $54,729
Avg. Daily Attendence (ADA). 135
Cost per ADA. $9,266

California Achievement Tests 6th ed., 2008
(Pct scoring at or above 50th National Percentile Rank)

	Math	Reading	Language
Grade 3	100%	79%	84%
Grade 7	NA	NA	NA

Academic Performance Index, 2009
Number of valid scores. 103
2007 API (base) 888
2008 API (growth). 904

SAT Testing, 2006-07
Enrollment, Grade 12 . . . . . NA
percent taking test. . . . . NA
number with total score 1,500+ . . . . . NA

Average Scores:

Math	Verbal	Writing	Total
NA	NA	NA	NA

Federal No Child Left Behind, 2008
(Adequate Yearly Progress standards met)

	Participation Rate	Pct Proficient
ELA	Yes	Yes
Math	Yes	Yes

API Criteria . . . . . Yes
Graduation rate . . . . . NA
criteria met/possible. 9/9

Happy Valley Union Elem

Shasta County
16300 Cloverdale Rd
Anderson, CA 96007
(530) 357-2134

Superint. . . . . Lawrence Robins
Grade plan. K-8
Number of schools. 3
Enrollment 604
High school graduates, 2006-07. 0
Dropout rate. 0
Pupil/teacher ratio. 20.1%
Average class size. 23.7
Students per computer 2.7
Avg. Teacher Salary, ... $53,927
Avg. Daily Attendence (ADA). 569
Cost per ADA. $9,209

California Achievement Tests 6th ed., 2008
(Pct scoring at or above 50th National Percentile Rank)

	Math	Reading	Language
Grade 3	43%	29%	41%
Grade 7	62%	54%	49%

Academic Performance Index, 2009
Number of valid scores. 414
2007 API (base) 743
2008 API (growth). 745

SAT Testing, 2006-07
Enrollment, Grade 12 . . . . . NA
percent taking test. . . . . NA
number with total score 1,500+ . . . . . NA

Average Scores:

Math	Verbal	Writing	Total
NA	NA	NA	NA

Federal No Child Left Behind, 2008
(Adequate Yearly Progress standards met)

	Participation Rate	Pct Proficient
ELA	Yes	Yes
Math	Yes	Yes

API Criteria . . . . . Yes
Graduation rate . . . . . NA
criteria met/possible. 13/13

Hart-Ransom Union Elem

Stanislaus County
3920 Shoemake Ave
Modesto, CA 95358
(209) 523-9996

Superint. . . . . Ream Lochry
Grade plan. K-8
Number of schools. 2
Enrollment 1,001
High school graduates, 2006-07. 0
Dropout rate. 0
Pupil/teacher ratio. 22.4%
Average class size. 26.9
Students per computer 7.9
Avg. Teacher Salary, ... $65,266
Avg. Daily Attendence (ADA). 683
Cost per ADA. $7,617

California Achievement Tests 6th ed., 2008
(Pct scoring at or above 50th National Percentile Rank)

	Math	Reading	Language
Grade 3	57%	39%	49%
Grade 7	58%	71%	59%

Academic Performance Index, 2009
Number of valid scores. 731
2007 API (base) 779
2008 API (growth). 785

SAT Testing, 2006-07
Enrollment, Grade 12 . . . . . NA
percent taking test. . . . . NA
number with total score 1,500+ . . . . . NA

Average Scores:

Math	Verbal	Writing	Total
NA	NA	NA	NA

Federal No Child Left Behind, 2008
(Adequate Yearly Progress standards met)

	Participation Rate	Pct Proficient
ELA	Yes	No
Math	Yes	Yes

API Criteria . . . . . Yes
Graduation rate . . . . . NA
criteria met/possible. 21/20

Data from school year 2007-08 except where noted
†Combined data for elementary and high schools

Hawthorne Elem

Los Angeles County
14120 South Hawthorne Blvd
Hawthorne, CA 90250
(310) 676-2276

Superint. . . . . Donald Carrington
Grade plan. K-8
Number of schools. .11
Enrollment 9,180
High school graduates, 2006-07. 81
Dropout rate. 0.4
Pupil/teacher ratio. 22.0%
Average class size. 28.5
Students per computer 4.8
Avg. Teacher Salary, ...$63,075
Avg. Daily Attendence (ADA). 8,350
Cost per ADA. $8,117

California Achievement Tests 6th ed., 2008
(Pct scoring at or above 50th National Percentile Rank)

	Math	Reading	Language
Grade 3	47%	19%	34%
Grade 7	51%	38%	36%

Academic Performance Index, 2009
Number of valid scores. 6,692
2007 API (base) 728
2008 API (growth). 748

SAT Testing, 2006-07
Enrollment, Grade 12 92
percent taking test. 23.9%
number with total score 1,500+ 3

Average Scores:

Math	Verbal	Writing	Total
437	434	415	1,286

Federal No Child Left Behind, 2008
(Adequate Yearly Progress standards met)

	Participation Rate	Pct Proficient
ELA	Yes	No
Math	Yes	No

API Criteria . . . . .Yes
Graduation rate . . . . .Yes
criteria met/possible. 38/34

Healdsburg Unified

Sonoma County
1028 Prince St
Healdsburg, CA 95448
(707) 431-3488

Superint. .Jeff Harding
Grade plan. K-12
Number of schools. 4
Enrollment 2,266
High school graduates, 2006-07. 187
Dropout rate. 4.7
Pupil/teacher ratio. 20.4%
Average class size. 25.6
Students per computer 4.7
Avg. Teacher Salary, ...$58,946
Avg. Daily Attendence (ADA). 2,172
Cost per ADA. $9,053

California Achievement Tests 6th ed., 2008
(Pct scoring at or above 50th National Percentile Rank)

	Math	Reading	Language
Grade 3	41%	23%	31%
Grade 7	47%	43%	41%

Academic Performance Index, 2009
Number of valid scores. 1,660
2007 API (base) 715
2008 API (growth). 730

SAT Testing, 2006-07
Enrollment, Grade 12 260
percent taking test. 36.2%
number with total score 1,500+ 60

Average Scores:

Math	Verbal	Writing	Total
539	514	515	1,568

Federal No Child Left Behind, 2008
(Adequate Yearly Progress standards met)

	Participation Rate	Pct Proficient
ELA	Yes	No
Math	Yes	No

API Criteria . . . . .Yes
Graduation rate . . . . .Yes
criteria met/possible. 26/18

Hermosa Beach City Elem

Los Angeles County
1645 Valley Dr
Hermosa Beach, CA 90254
(310) 937-5877

Superint. . . . . Sharon McClain
Grade plan. K-8
Number of schools. 2
Enrollment 1,130
High school graduates, 2006-07. 0
Dropout rate. 0
Pupil/teacher ratio. 20.3%
Average class size. 23.3
Students per computer 3.8
Avg. Teacher Salary, ...$68,193
Avg. Daily Attendence (ADA). 1,101
Cost per ADA. $8,356

California Achievement Tests 6th ed., 2008
(Pct scoring at or above 50th National Percentile Rank)

	Math	Reading	Language
Grade 3	85%	66%	78%
Grade 7	87%	79%	81%

Academic Performance Index, 2009
Number of valid scores. 815
2007 API (base) 904
2008 API (growth). 909

SAT Testing, 2006-07
Enrollment, Grade 12 . . . . .NA
percent taking test. . . . . .NA
number with total score 1,500+ . . . . . .NA

Average Scores:

Math	Verbal	Writing	Total
NA	NA	NA	NA

Federal No Child Left Behind, 2008
(Adequate Yearly Progress standards met)

	Participation Rate	Pct Proficient
ELA	Yes	Yes
Math	Yes	Yes

API Criteria . . . . .Yes
Graduation rate . . . . .NA
criteria met/possible. 9/9

Hesperia Unified

San Bernardino County
15576 Main St
Hesperia, CA 92345
(760) 244-4411

Superint. . . . . Mark McKinney
Grade plan. K-12
Number of schools. .29
Enrollment 22,481
High school graduates, 2006-07. . . . 1,208
Dropout rate. 4.9
Pupil/teacher ratio. 22.7%
Average class size. 27.0
Students per computer 5.2
Avg. Teacher Salary, ...$59,696
Avg. Daily Attendence (ADA). 20,763
Cost per ADA. $7,578

California Achievement Tests 6th ed., 2008
(Pct scoring at or above 50th National Percentile Rank)

	Math	Reading	Language
Grade 3	47%	30%	39%
Grade 7	43%	42%	40%

Academic Performance Index, 2009
Number of valid scores. 15,965
2007 API (base) 700
2008 API (growth). 715

SAT Testing, 2006-07
Enrollment, Grade 12 1,345
percent taking test. 23.4%
number with total score 1,500+ 123

Average Scores:

Math	Verbal	Writing	Total
482	473	471	1,426

Federal No Child Left Behind, 2008
(Adequate Yearly Progress standards met)

	Participation Rate	Pct Proficient
ELA	Yes	No
Math	Yes	No

API Criteria . . . . .Yes
Graduation rate . . . . .No
criteria met/possible. 34/28

Hillsborough City Elem

San Mateo County
300 El Cerrito Ave
Hillsborough, CA 94010
(650) 342-5193

Superint. . . . . Marilyn Loushin-Miller
Grade plan. K-8
Number of schools. 4
Enrollment 1,451
High school graduates, 2006-07. 0
Dropout rate. 0
Pupil/teacher ratio. 14.4%
Average class size. 20.6
Students per computer 2.4
Avg. Teacher Salary, ...$80,943
Avg. Daily Attendence (ADA). 1,419
Cost per ADA. $13,641

California Achievement Tests 6th ed., 2008
(Pct scoring at or above 50th National Percentile Rank)

	Math	Reading	Language
Grade 3	95%	84%	88%
Grade 7	94%	88%	87%

Academic Performance Index, 2009
Number of valid scores. 1,136
2007 API (base) 957
2008 API (growth). 961

SAT Testing, 2006-07
Enrollment, Grade 12 . . . . .NA
percent taking test. . . . . .NA
number with total score 1,500+ . . . . . .NA

Average Scores:

Math	Verbal	Writing	Total
NA	NA	NA	NA

Federal No Child Left Behind, 2008
(Adequate Yearly Progress standards met)

	Participation Rate	Pct Proficient
ELA	Yes	Yes
Math	Yes	Yes

API Criteria . . . . .Yes
Graduation rate . . . . .NA
criteria met/possible. 17/17

Hollister Elem

San Benito County
2690 Cienega Rd
Hollister, CA 95023
(831) 630-6300

Superint. . . . . Ronald Crates
Grade plan. K-8
Number of schools. 9
Enrollment 5,826
High school graduates, 2006-07. 0
Dropout rate. 0
Pupil/teacher ratio. 19.4%
Average class size. 25.5
Students per computer 8.7
Avg. Teacher Salary, ...$66,464
Avg. Daily Attendence (ADA). 5,687
Cost per ADA. $8,405

California Achievement Tests 6th ed., 2008
(Pct scoring at or above 50th National Percentile Rank)

	Math	Reading	Language
Grade 3	50%	33%	38%
Grade 7	53%	50%	47%

Academic Performance Index, 2009
Number of valid scores. 4,101
2007 API (base) 736
2008 API (growth). 750

SAT Testing, 2006-07
Enrollment, Grade 12 . . . . .NA
percent taking test. . . . . .NA
number with total score 1,500+ . . . . . .NA

Average Scores:

Math	Verbal	Writing	Total
NA	NA	NA	NA

Federal No Child Left Behind, 2008
(Adequate Yearly Progress standards met)

	Participation Rate	Pct Proficient
ELA	Yes	No
Math	Yes	No

API Criteria . . . . .Yes
Graduation rate . . . . .NA
criteria met/possible. 25/21

Data from school year 2007-08 except where noted.
†Combined data for elementary and high schools.

Hope Elem

Santa Barbara County
613 West Teapot Dome Ave
Porterville, CA 93257
(805) 682-2564

Superint. . . . . Gerrie Fausett
Grade plan. K-6
Number of schools. 3
Enrollment 1,165
High school graduates, 2006-07 0
Dropout rate. . . . . .NA
Pupil/teacher ratio. 20.5%
Average class size. 21.5
Students per computer 3.3
Avg. Teacher Salary, ...
Avg. Daily Attendence (ADA). 1,131
Cost per ADA. $8,511

California Achievement Tests 6th ed., 2008
(Pct scoring at or above 50th National Percentile Rank)

	Math	Reading	Language
Grade 3	77%	65%	72%
Grade 7	NA	NA	NA

Academic Performance Index, 2009
Number of valid scores. 883
2007 API (base) 890
2008 API (growth). 893

SAT Testing, 2006-07
Enrollment, Grade 12 . . . . .NA
percent taking test. . . . . .NA
number with total score 1,500+ . . . . . .NA

Average Scores:

Math	Verbal	Writing	Total
NA	NA	NA	NA

Federal No Child Left Behind, 2008
(Adequate Yearly Progress standards met)

	Participation Rate	Pct Proficient
ELA	Yes	Yes
Math	Yes	Yes

API Criteria . . . . Yes
Graduation rate . . . . .NA
criteria met/possible. 21/21

Hope Elem

Tulare County
3970 La Colina Rd
Santa Barbara, CA 93110
(559) 784-1064

Superint. . . . . Deborah McCaskill
Grade plan. K-8
Number of schools. 1
Enrollment 138
High school graduates, 2006-07 0
Dropout rate. 0
Pupil/teacher ratio. 23.0%
Average class size. 23.0
Students per computer 3.6
Avg. Teacher Salary, ...NA
Avg. Daily Attendence (ADA). 140
Cost per ADA. $7,382

California Achievement Tests 6th ed., 2008
(Pct scoring at or above 50th National Percentile Rank)

	Math	Reading	Language
Grade 3	12%	18%	12%
Grade 7	57%	43%	43%

Academic Performance Index, 2009
Number of valid scores. 104
2007 API (base) 695
2008 API (growth). 666

SAT Testing, 2006-07
Enrollment, Grade 12 . . . . .NA
percent taking test. . . . . .NA
number with total score 1,500+ . . . . . .NA

Average Scores:

Math	Verbal	Writing	Total
NA	NA	NA	NA

Federal No Child Left Behind, 2008
(Adequate Yearly Progress standards met)

	Participation Rate	Pct Proficient
ELA	Yes	No
Math	Yes	No

API Criteria . . . . Yes
Graduation rate . . . . .NA
criteria met/possible. 13/10

Hueneme Elem

Ventura County
205 North Ventura Rd
Port Hueneme, CA 93041
(805) 488-3588

Superint. . . . . .Jerry Dannenberg
Grade plan. K-8
Number of schools. 11
Enrollment 8,091
High school graduates, 2006-07 0
Dropout rate. 0
Pupil/teacher ratio. 22.4%
Average class size. 26.9
Students per computer 3.2
Avg. Teacher Salary, ... $73,257
Avg. Daily Attendence (ADA). 7,915
Cost per ADA. $7,991

California Achievement Tests 6th ed., 2008
(Pct scoring at or above 50th National Percentile Rank)

	Math	Reading	Language
Grade 3	45%	24%	33%
Grade 7	43%	40%	40%

Academic Performance Index, 2009
Number of valid scores. 5,798
2007 API (base) 697
2008 API (growth). 704

SAT Testing, 2006-07
Enrollment, Grade 12 . . . . .NA
percent taking test. . . . . .NA
number with total score 1,500+ . . . . . .NA

Average Scores:

Math	Verbal	Writing	Total
NA	NA	NA	NA

Federal No Child Left Behind, 2008
(Adequate Yearly Progress standards met)

	Participation Rate	Pct Proficient
ELA	Yes	No
Math	Yes	No

API Criteria . . . . Yes
Graduation rate . . . . .NA
criteria met/possible. 33/25

Huntington Beach City Elem

Orange County
20451 Craimer Ln
Huntington Beach, CA 92646
(714) 964-8888

Superint. . . . . Roberta DeLuca
Grade plan. K-8
Number of schools. 9
Enrollment 6,566
High school graduates, 2006-07 0
Dropout rate. 0
Pupil/teacher ratio. 25.5%
Average class size. 26.9
Students per computer 0.0
Avg. Teacher Salary, ... $73,754
Avg. Daily Attendence (ADA). 6,388
Cost per ADA. $7,529

California Achievement Tests 6th ed., 2008
(Pct scoring at or above 50th National Percentile Rank)

	Math	Reading	Language
Grade 3	76%	63%	69%
Grade 7	71%	69%	64%

Academic Performance Index, 2009
Number of valid scores. 4,975
2007 API (base) 858
2008 API (growth). 859

SAT Testing, 2006-07
Enrollment, Grade 12 . . . . .NA
percent taking test. . . . . .NA
number with total score 1,500+ . . . . . .NA

Average Scores:

Math	Verbal	Writing	Total
NA	NA	NA	NA

Federal No Child Left Behind, 2008
(Adequate Yearly Progress standards met)

	Participation Rate	Pct Proficient
ELA	Yes	Yes
Math	Yes	Yes

API Criteria . . . . Yes
Graduation rate . . . . .NA
criteria met/possible. 29/29

Island Union Elem

Kings County
7799 21st Ave
Lemoore, CA 93245
(559) 924-6424

Superint. . . . . Robin Jones
Grade plan. K-8
Number of schools. 1
Enrollment 267
High school graduates, 2006-07 0
Dropout rate. 0
Pupil/teacher ratio. 26.7%
Average class size. 26.9
Students per computer 3.7
Avg. Teacher Salary, ...NA
Avg. Daily Attendence (ADA). 256
Cost per ADA. $7,169

California Achievement Tests 6th ed., 2008
(Pct scoring at or above 50th National Percentile Rank)

	Math	Reading	Language
Grade 3	36%	36%	36%
Grade 7	61%	69%	64%

Academic Performance Index, 2009
Number of valid scores. 195
2007 API (base) 761
2008 API (growth). 778

SAT Testing, 2006-07
Enrollment, Grade 12 . . . . .NA
percent taking test. . . . . .NA
number with total score 1,500+ . . . . . .NA

Average Scores:

Math	Verbal	Writing	Total
NA	NA	NA	NA

Federal No Child Left Behind, 2008
(Adequate Yearly Progress standards met)

	Participation Rate	Pct Proficient
ELA	Yes	No
Math	Yes	No

API Criteria . . . . Yes
Graduation rate . . . . .NA
criteria met/possible. 17/15

Jacoby Creek Elem

Humboldt County
1617 Old Arcata Rd
Bayside, CA 95524
(707) 822-4896

Superint. . . . . Eric Grantz
Grade plan. . . . . .NA
Number of schools. 1
Enrollment 395
High school graduates, 2006-07 0
Dropout rate. 0
Pupil/teacher ratio. 19.2%
Average class size. 21.9
Students per computer 7.1
Avg. Teacher Salary, ...NA
Avg. Daily Attendence (ADA). 389
Cost per ADA. $8,351

California Achievement Tests 6th ed., 2008
(Pct scoring at or above 50th National Percentile Rank)

	Math	Reading	Language
Grade 3	83%	73%	85%
Grade 7	89%	78%	73%

Academic Performance Index, 2009
Number of valid scores. 293
2007 API (base) 900
2008 API (growth). 891

SAT Testing, 2006-07
Enrollment, Grade 12 . . . . .NA
percent taking test. . . . . .NA
number with total score 1,500+ . . . . . .NA

Average Scores:

Math	Verbal	Writing	Total
NA	NA	NA	NA

Federal No Child Left Behind, 2008
(Adequate Yearly Progress standards met)

	Participation Rate	Pct Proficient
ELA	Yes	Yes
Math	Yes	Yes

API Criteria . . . . Yes
Graduation rate . . . . .NA
criteria met/possible. 9/9

Data from school year 2007-08 except where noted
†Combined data for elementary and high schools

Jefferson Elem
San Joaquin County
1219 Whispering Wind Dr
Tracy, CA 95377
(209) 836-3388

Superint. . . . . Ed Quinn
Grade plan. K-8
Number of schools. 4
Enrollment 2,435
High school graduates, 2006-07 0
Dropout rate. 0
Pupil/teacher ratio. 21.0%
Average class size. 24.9
Students per computer 5.3
Avg. Teacher Salary, ...
Avg. Daily Attendence (ADA). 2,427
Cost per ADA. $6,727

California Achievement Tests 6th ed., 2008
(Pct scoring at or above 50th National Percentile Rank)

	Math	Reading	Language
Grade 3	66%	48%	62%
Grade 7	58%	54%	53%

Academic Performance Index, 2009
Number of valid scores. 1,820
2007 API (base) 811
2008 API (growth). 813

SAT Testing, 2006-07
Enrollment, Grade 12 . . . . .NA
percent taking test. . . . . .NA
number with total score 1,500+ . . . . . .NA

Average Scores:

Math	Verbal	Writing	Total
NA	NA	NA	NA

Federal No Child Left Behind, 2008
(Adequate Yearly Progress standards met)

	Participation Rate	Pct Proficient
ELA	Yes	Yes
Math	Yes	Yes

API Criteria . . . . .Yes
Graduation rate . . . . .NA
criteria met/possible. 37/37

Jefferson Elem
San Mateo County
101 Lincoln Ave
Daly City, CA 94015
(650) 991-1000

Superint. Matteo Rizzo
Grade plan. K-8
Number of schools. .15
Enrollment 6,288
High school graduates, 2006-07 0
Dropout rate. 20
Pupil/teacher ratio. 21.2%
Average class size. 25.2
Students per computer 4.4
Avg. Teacher Salary, ... $59,013
Avg. Daily Attendence (ADA). 5,810
Cost per ADA. $7,496

California Achievement Tests 6th ed., 2008
(Pct scoring at or above 50th National Percentile Rank)

	Math	Reading	Language
Grade 3	60%	30%	44%
Grade 7	50%	47%	49%

Academic Performance Index, 2009
Number of valid scores. 4,269
2007 API (base) 752
2008 API (growth). 763

SAT Testing, 2006-07
Enrollment, Grade 12 . . . . .NA
percent taking test. . . . . .NA
number with total score 1,500+ . . . . . .NA

Average Scores:

Math	Verbal	Writing	Total
NA	NA	NA	NA

Federal No Child Left Behind, 2008
(Adequate Yearly Progress standards met)

	Participation Rate	Pct Proficient
ELA	Yes	No
Math	Yes	No

API Criteria . . . . .Yes
Graduation rate . . . . .NA
criteria met/possible. 37/31

John Swett Unified
Contra Costa County
400 Parker Ave
Rodeo, CA 94572
(510) 245-4300

Superint. . . . . Mike McLaughlin
Grade plan. K-12
Number of schools. 4
Enrollment 1,745
High school graduates, 2006-07 138
Dropout rate. 5
Pupil/teacher ratio. 18.7%
Average class size. 23.8
Students per computer 5.1
Avg. Teacher Salary, ... $54,594
Avg. Daily Attendence (ADA). 1,666
Cost per ADA. $8,982

California Achievement Tests 6th ed., 2008
(Pct scoring at or above 50th National Percentile Rank)

	Math	Reading	Language
Grade 3	55%	38%	51%
Grade 7	54%	39%	43%

Academic Performance Index, 2009
Number of valid scores. 1,198
2007 API (base) 703
2008 API (growth). 714

SAT Testing, 2006-07
Enrollment, Grade 12 175
percent taking test. 29.7%
number with total score 1,500+ 21

Average Scores:

Math	Verbal	Writing	Total
495	478	471	1,444

Federal No Child Left Behind, 2008
(Adequate Yearly Progress standards met)

	Participation Rate	Pct Proficient
ELA	Yes	No
Math	Yes	No

API Criteria . . . . .Yes
Graduation rate . . . . .Yes
criteria met/possible. 34/31

Johnstonville Elem
Lassen County
704-795 Bangham Ln
Susanville, CA 96130
(530) 257-2471

Superint. . . . . Lou Istrice
Grade plan. K-8
Number of schools. 1
Enrollment 240
High school graduates, 2006-07 0
Dropout rate. 0
Pupil/teacher ratio. 24.0%
Average class size. 24.1
Students per computer 4.0
Avg. Teacher Salary, ... $57,632
Avg. Daily Attendence (ADA). 220
Cost per ADA. $7,332

California Achievement Tests 6th ed., 2008
(Pct scoring at or above 50th National Percentile Rank)

	Math	Reading	Language
Grade 3	71%	52%	52%
Grade 7	57%	71%	52%

Academic Performance Index, 2009
Number of valid scores. 164
2007 API (base) 737
2008 API (growth). 763

SAT Testing, 2006-07
Enrollment, Grade 12 . . . . .NA
percent taking test. . . . . .NA
number with total score 1,500+ . . . . . .NA

Average Scores:

Math	Verbal	Writing	Total
NA	NA	NA	NA

Federal No Child Left Behind, 2008
(Adequate Yearly Progress standards met)

	Participation Rate	Pct Proficient
ELA	Yes	Yes
Math	Yes	Yes

API Criteria . . . . .Yes
Graduation rate . . . . .NA
criteria met/possible. 13/13

Jurupa Unified
Riverside County
4850 Pedley Rd
Riverside, CA 92509
(951) 360-4160

Superint. . . . . Elliott Duchon
Grade plan. K-12
Number of schools. .25
Enrollment 20,657
High school graduates, 2006-07 1,044
Dropout rate. 6
Pupil/teacher ratio. 22.0%
Average class size. 26.8
Students per computer 6.1
Avg. Teacher Salary, ... $73,449
Avg. Daily Attendence (ADA). 20,376
Cost per ADA. $7,774

California Achievement Tests 6th ed., 2008
(Pct scoring at or above 50th National Percentile Rank)

	Math	Reading	Language
Grade 3	52%	30%	41%
Grade 7	44%	39%	36%

Academic Performance Index, 2009
Number of valid scores. 13,968
2007 API (base) 705
2008 API (growth). 718

SAT Testing, 2006-07
Enrollment, Grade 12 1,372
percent taking test. 23.6%
number with total score 1,500+ 70

Average Scores:

Math	Verbal	Writing	Total
454	442	433	1,329

Federal No Child Left Behind, 2008
(Adequate Yearly Progress standards met)

	Participation Rate	Pct Proficient
ELA	Yes	No
Math	Yes	No

API Criteria . . . . .Yes
Graduation rate . . . . .No
criteria met/possible. 34/30

Keppel Union Elem
Los Angeles County
PO Box 186
Pearblossom, CA 93553
(661) 944-2155

Superint. . . . . Linda Wagner
Grade plan. K-8
Number of schools. 6
Enrollment 3,067
High school graduates, 2006-07 0
Dropout rate. 0
Pupil/teacher ratio. 20.2%
Average class size. 25.5
Students per computer 8.2
Avg. Teacher Salary, ... $60,098
Avg. Daily Attendence (ADA). 2,899
Cost per ADA. $8,418

California Achievement Tests 6th ed., 2008
(Pct scoring at or above 50th National Percentile Rank)

	Math	Reading	Language
Grade 3	36%	28%	33%
Grade 7	36%	36%	35%

Academic Performance Index, 2009
Number of valid scores. 2,153
2007 API (base) 656
2008 API (growth). 696

SAT Testing, 2006-07
Enrollment, Grade 12 . . . . .NA
percent taking test. . . . . .NA
number with total score 1,500+ . . . . . .NA

Average Scores:

Math	Verbal	Writing	Total
NA	NA	NA	NA

Federal No Child Left Behind, 2008
(Adequate Yearly Progress standards met)

	Participation Rate	Pct Proficient
ELA	No	No
Math	Yes	No

API Criteria . . . . .Yes
Graduation rate . . . . .NA
criteria met/possible. 29/21

Data from school year 2007-08 except where noted.
†Combined data for elementary and high schools.

King City Union

Monterey County
800 Broadway
King City, CA 93930
(831) 385-1144

Superint . . . . . Tom Michaelson
Grade plan K-8
Number of schools 5
Enrollment 2,455
High school graduates, 2006-07 0
Dropout rate 0
Pupil/teacher ratio 17.5%
Average class size 21.5
Students per computer 3.9
Avg. Teacher Salary, ... $57,003
Avg. Daily Attendence (ADA) 2,171
Cost per ADA $9,027

California Achievement Tests 6th ed., 2008
(Pct scoring at or above 50th National Percentile Rank)

	Math	Reading	Language
Grade 3	37%	25%	37%
Grade 7	43%	39%	45%

Academic Performance Index, 2009
Number of valid scores 1,711
2007 API (base) 668
2008 API (growth) 670

SAT Testing, 2006-07
Enrollment, Grade 12 . . . . . NA
percent taking test . . . . . NA
number with total score 1,500+ . . . . . NA

Average Scores:

Math	Verbal	Writing	Total
NA	NA	NA	NA

Federal No Child Left Behind, 2008
(Adequate Yearly Progress standards met)

	Participation Rate	Pct Proficient
ELA	Yes	No
Math	Yes	No

API Criteria . . . . . Yes
Graduation rate . . . . . NA
criteria met/possible 25/15

Kings River-Hardwick Union Elem

Kings County
10300 Excelsior Ave
Hanford, CA 93230
(559) 584-4475

Superint . . . . . Jean Fetterhoff
Grade plan K-8
Number of schools 1
Enrollment 643
High school graduates, 2006-07 0
Dropout rate 0
Pupil/teacher ratio 20.6%
Average class size 21.4
Students per computer 4.5
Avg. Teacher Salary, ... $58,041
Avg. Daily Attendence (ADA) 627
Cost per ADA $7,582

California Achievement Tests 6th ed., 2008
(Pct scoring at or above 50th National Percentile Rank)

	Math	Reading	Language
Grade 3	64%	44%	49%
Grade 7	69%	74%	69%

Academic Performance Index, 2009
Number of valid scores 450
2007 API (base) 805
2008 API (growth) 810

SAT Testing, 2006-07
Enrollment, Grade 12 . . . . . NA
percent taking test . . . . . NA
number with total score 1,500+ . . . . . NA

Average Scores:

Math	Verbal	Writing	Total
NA	NA	NA	NA

Federal No Child Left Behind, 2008
(Adequate Yearly Progress standards met)

	Participation Rate	Pct Proficient
ELA	Yes	Yes
Math	Yes	Yes

API Criteria . . . . . Yes
Graduation rate . . . . . NA
criteria met/possible 17/17

Kingsburg Joint Union Elem

Fresno County
1310 Stroud Ave
Kingsburg, CA 93631
(559) 897-2331

Superint . . . . . Mark Ford
Grade plan K-8
Number of schools 6
Enrollment 2,250
High school graduates, 2006-07 0
Dropout rate 0
Pupil/teacher ratio 20.6%
Average class size 24.7
Students per computer 9.2
Avg. Teacher Salary, ... $56,863
Avg. Daily Attendence (ADA) 2,237
Cost per ADA $6,988

California Achievement Tests 6th ed., 2008
(Pct scoring at or above 50th National Percentile Rank)

	Math	Reading	Language
Grade 3	53%	39%	56%
Grade 7	60%	57%	50%

Academic Performance Index, 2009
Number of valid scores 1,640
2007 API (base) 773
2008 API (growth) 777

SAT Testing, 2006-07
Enrollment, Grade 12 . . . . . NA
percent taking test . . . . . NA
number with total score 1,500+ . . . . . NA

Average Scores:

Math	Verbal	Writing	Total
NA	NA	NA	NA

Federal No Child Left Behind, 2008
(Adequate Yearly Progress standards met)

	Participation Rate	Pct Proficient
ELA	Yes	No
Math	Yes	No

API Criteria . . . . . Yes
Graduation rate . . . . . NA
criteria met/possible 25/21

Kirkwood Elem

Tehama County
2049 Kirkwood Rd
Corning, CA 96021
(530) 824-7773

Superint . . . . . John Lalaguna
Grade plan K-8
Number of schools 1
Enrollment 64
High school graduates, 2006-07 0
Dropout rate 0
Pupil/teacher ratio 16.0%
Average class size 15.8
Students per computer 4.9
Avg. Teacher Salary, ... NA
Avg. Daily Attendence (ADA) 62
Cost per ADA $7,745

California Achievement Tests 6th ed., 2008
(Pct scoring at or above 50th National Percentile Rank)

	Math	Reading	Language
Grade 3	NA	NA	NA
Grade 7	NA	NA	NA

Academic Performance Index, 2009
Number of valid scores 42
2007 API (base) 766
2008 API (growth) 757

SAT Testing, 2006-07
Enrollment, Grade 12 . . . . . NA
percent taking test . . . . . NA
number with total score 1,500+ . . . . . NA

Average Scores:

Math	Verbal	Writing	Total
NA	NA	NA	NA

Federal No Child Left Behind, 2008
(Adequate Yearly Progress standards met)

	Participation Rate	Pct Proficient
ELA	Yes	Yes
Math	Yes	Yes

API Criteria . . . . . Yes
Graduation rate . . . . . NA
criteria met/possible 5/5

Kit Carson Union Elem

Kings County
9895 Seventh Ave
Hanford, CA 93230
(559) 582-2843

Superint . . . . . John Sousa
Grade plan K-8
Number of schools 2
Enrollment 458
High school graduates, 2006-07 0
Dropout rate 0
Pupil/teacher ratio 19.1%
Average class size 23.7
Students per computer 7.5
Avg. Teacher Salary, ... NA
Avg. Daily Attendence (ADA) 422
Cost per ADA $7,307

California Achievement Tests 6th ed., 2008
(Pct scoring at or above 50th National Percentile Rank)

	Math	Reading	Language
Grade 3	41%	42%	47%
Grade 7	32%	36%	30%

Academic Performance Index, 2009
Number of valid scores 347
2007 API (base) 759
2008 API (growth) 742

SAT Testing, 2006-07
Enrollment, Grade 12 . . . . . NA
percent taking test . . . . . NA
number with total score 1,500+ . . . . . NA

Average Scores:

Math	Verbal	Writing	Total
NA	NA	NA	NA

Federal No Child Left Behind, 2008
(Adequate Yearly Progress standards met)

	Participation Rate	Pct Proficient
ELA	Yes	No
Math	Yes	Yes

API Criteria . . . . . Yes
Graduation rate . . . . . NA
criteria met/possible 21/19

La Habra City Elem

Orange County
PO Box 307
La Habra, CA 90633
(562) 690-2305

Superint . . . . . Richard Hermann
Grade plan K-8
Number of schools 9
Enrollment 5,746
High school graduates, 2006-07 0
Dropout rate 0
Pupil/teacher ratio 22.2%
Average class size 26.1
Students per computer 6.0
Avg. Teacher Salary, ... $77,509
Avg. Daily Attendence (ADA) 5,644
Cost per ADA $8,280

California Achievement Tests 6th ed., 2008
(Pct scoring at or above 50th National Percentile Rank)

	Math	Reading	Language
Grade 3	46%	29%	33%
Grade 7	42%	43%	43%

Academic Performance Index, 2009
Number of valid scores 4,313
2007 API (base) 724
2008 API (growth) 738

SAT Testing, 2006-07
Enrollment, Grade 12 . . . . . NA
percent taking test . . . . . NA
number with total score 1,500+ . . . . . NA

Average Scores:

Math	Verbal	Writing	Total
NA	NA	NA	NA

Federal No Child Left Behind, 2008
(Adequate Yearly Progress standards met)

	Participation Rate	Pct Proficient
ELA	Yes	No
Math	Yes	No

API Criteria . . . . . Yes
Graduation rate . . . . . NA
criteria met/possible 25/20

Data from school year 2007-08 except where noted
†Combined data for elementary and high schools

La Mesa-Spring Valley Elem
San Diego County
4750 Date Ave
La Mesa, CA 91941
(619) 668-5700

Superint.................Brian Marshall
Grade plan...........................K-8
Number of schools.....................23
Enrollment....................13,071
High school graduates, 2006-07........0
Dropout rate..........................0
Pupil/teacher ratio.................18.6%
Average class size...................25.8
Students per computer................3.2
Avg. Teacher Salary,..............$72,222
Avg. Daily Attendence (ADA).......12,712
Cost per ADA..................$8,450

California Achievement Tests 6th ed., 2008
(Pct scoring at or above 50th National Percentile Rank)

	Math	Reading	Language
Grade 3	61%	46%	52%
Grade 7	53%	49%	44%

Academic Performance Index, 2009
Number of valid scores..............9,659
2007 API (base).......................774
2008 API (growth).....................784

SAT Testing, 2006-07
Enrollment, Grade 12.................NA
percent taking test..................NA
number with total score 1,500+......NA

Average Scores:

Math	Verbal	Writing	Total
NA	NA	NA	NA

Federal No Child Left Behind, 2008
(Adequate Yearly Progress standards met)

	Participation Rate	Pct Proficient
ELA	Yes	No
Math	Yes	No

API Criteria..........................Yes
Graduation rate.......................NA
criteria met/possible..............41/38

Lafayette Elem
Contra Costa County
PO Box 1029
Lafayette, CA 94549
(925) 927-3504

Superint......................Fred Brill
Grade plan...........................K-8
Number of schools......................5
Enrollment.....................3,178
High school graduates, 2006-07........0
Dropout rate..........................0
Pupil/teacher ratio.................18.4%
Average class size...................24.4
Students per computer................2.5
Avg. Teacher Salary,..............$64,608
Avg. Daily Attendence (ADA)........3,112
Cost per ADA..................$8,457

California Achievement Tests 6th ed., 2008
(Pct scoring at or above 50th National Percentile Rank)

	Math	Reading	Language
Grade 3	84%	70%	78%
Grade 7	87%	81%	79%

Academic Performance Index, 2009
Number of valid scores..............2,511
2007 API (base).......................914
2008 API (growth).....................919

SAT Testing, 2006-07
Enrollment, Grade 12.................NA
percent taking test..................NA
number with total score 1,500+......NA

Average Scores:

Math	Verbal	Writing	Total
NA	NA	NA	NA

Federal No Child Left Behind, 2008
(Adequate Yearly Progress standards met)

	Participation Rate	Pct Proficient
ELA	Yes	Yes
Math	Yes	Yes

API Criteria..........................Yes
Graduation rate.......................NA
criteria met/possible..............21/21

Laguna Joint Elem
Marin County
2657 Chileno Valley Rd
Petaluma, CA 94952
(707) 762-6051

Superint.....................Luke McCann
Grade plan...........................K-6
Number of schools......................1
Enrollment.........................29
High school graduates, 2006-07........0
Dropout rate.........................NA
Pupil/teacher ratio.................11.6%
Average class size...................15.0
Students per computer................1.9
Avg. Teacher Salary,..............$50,165
Avg. Daily Attendence (ADA)...........28
Cost per ADA..................$9,311

California Achievement Tests 6th ed., 2008
(Pct scoring at or above 50th National Percentile Rank)

	Math	Reading	Language
Grade 3	NA	NA	NA
Grade 7	NA	NA	NA

Academic Performance Index, 2009
Number of valid scores.................18
2007 API (base).......................829
2008 API (growth).....................897

SAT Testing, 2006-07
Enrollment, Grade 12.................NA
percent taking test..................NA
number with total score 1,500+......NA

Average Scores:

Math	Verbal	Writing	Total
NA	NA	NA	NA

Federal No Child Left Behind, 2008
(Adequate Yearly Progress standards met)

	Participation Rate	Pct Proficient
ELA	Yes	Yes
Math	Yes	Yes

API Criteria..........................Yes
Graduation rate.......................NA
criteria met/possible................5/5

Lagunita Elem
Monterey County
975 San Juan Grade Rd
Salinas, CA 93907
(831) 449-2800

Superint..................Marsha Filbin
Grade plan...........................K-8
Number of schools......................1
Enrollment.........................80
High school graduates, 2006-07........0
Dropout rate..........................0
Pupil/teacher ratio.................20.3%
Average class size...................19.8
Students per computer................2.3
Avg. Teacher Salary,.................NA
Avg. Daily Attendence (ADA)...........76
Cost per ADA..................$8,531

California Achievement Tests 6th ed., 2008
(Pct scoring at or above 50th National Percentile Rank)

	Math	Reading	Language
Grade 3	NA	NA	NA
Grade 7	NA	NA	NA

Academic Performance Index, 2009
Number of valid scores.................58
2007 API (base).......................873
2008 API (growth).....................839

SAT Testing, 2006-07
Enrollment, Grade 12.................NA
percent taking test..................NA
number with total score 1,500+......NA

Average Scores:

Math	Verbal	Writing	Total
NA	NA	NA	NA

Federal No Child Left Behind, 2008
(Adequate Yearly Progress standards met)

	Participation Rate	Pct Proficient
ELA	Yes	Yes
Math	Yes	Yes

API Criteria..........................Yes
Graduation rate.......................NA
criteria met/possible................5/5

Lake Elem
Glenn County
4672 County Road N
Orland, CA 95963
(530) 865-1255

Superint...................Grant Sandro
Grade plan...........................K-8
Number of schools......................1
Enrollment........................132
High school graduates, 2006-07........0
Dropout rate..........................0
Pupil/teacher ratio.................20.3%
Average class size...................22.0
Students per computer................4.9
Avg. Teacher Salary,.................NA
Avg. Daily Attendence (ADA)..........128
Cost per ADA..................$6,727

California Achievement Tests 6th ed., 2008
(Pct scoring at or above 50th National Percentile Rank)

	Math	Reading	Language
Grade 3	88%	75%	81%
Grade 7	NA	NA	NA

Academic Performance Index, 2009
Number of valid scores.................85
2007 API (base).......................800
2008 API (growth).....................810

SAT Testing, 2006-07
Enrollment, Grade 12.................NA
percent taking test..................NA
number with total score 1,500+......NA

Average Scores:

Math	Verbal	Writing	Total
NA	NA	NA	NA

Federal No Child Left Behind, 2008
(Adequate Yearly Progress standards met)

	Participation Rate	Pct Proficient
ELA	Yes	Yes
Math	Yes	Yes

API Criteria..........................Yes
Graduation rate.......................NA
criteria met/possible................5/5

Lakeside Joint Elem
Santa Clara County
19621 Black Rd
Los Gatos, CA 95033
(408) 354-2372

Superint...................Bob Chrisman
Grade plan...........................K-6
Number of schools......................1
Enrollment.........................90
High school graduates, 2006-07........0
Dropout rate.........................NA
Pupil/teacher ratio.................15.0%
Average class size...................15.5
Students per computer................2.4
Avg. Teacher Salary,.................NA
Avg. Daily Attendence (ADA)...........87
Cost per ADA.................$13,583

California Achievement Tests 6th ed., 2008
(Pct scoring at or above 50th National Percentile Rank)

	Math	Reading	Language
Grade 3	NA	NA	NA
Grade 7	NA	NA	NA

Academic Performance Index, 2009
Number of valid scores.................58
2007 API (base).......................924
2008 API (growth).....................940

SAT Testing, 2006-07
Enrollment, Grade 12.................NA
percent taking test..................NA
number with total score 1,500+......NA

Average Scores:

Math	Verbal	Writing	Total
NA	NA	NA	NA

Federal No Child Left Behind, 2008
(Adequate Yearly Progress standards met)

	Participation Rate	Pct Proficient
ELA	Yes	Yes
Math	Yes	Yes

API Criteria..........................Yes
Graduation rate.......................NA
criteria met/possible................5/5

Data from school year 2007-08 except where noted.
†Combined data for elementary and high schools.

Lakeside Union Elem
Kern County
14535 Old River Rd
Bakersfield, CA 93311
(661) 836-6658

Superint ... Nick Kouklis
Grade plan ... K-8
Number of schools ... 2
- Enrollment ... 1,355
- High school graduates, 2006-07 ... 0
- Dropout rate ... 0
- Pupil/teacher ratio ... 18.5%
- Average class size ... 22.0
- Students per computer ... 9.7

Avg. Teacher Salary, ...
Avg. Daily Attendence (ADA) ... 1,305
- Cost per ADA ... $7,653

California Achievement Tests 6th ed., 2008
(Pct scoring at or above 50th National Percentile Rank)

	Math	Reading	Language
Grade 3	49%	49%	56%
Grade 7	49%	45%	43%

Academic Performance Index, 2009
Number of valid scores ... 964
2007 API (base) ... 730
2008 API (growth) ... 751

SAT Testing, 2006-07
Enrollment, Grade 12 ... NA
- percent taking test ... NA
- number with total score 1,500+ ... NA

Average Scores:

Math	Verbal	Writing	Total
NA	NA	NA	NA

Federal No Child Left Behind, 2008
(Adequate Yearly Progress standards met)

	Participation Rate	Pct Proficient
ELA	Yes	No
Math	Yes	No

API Criteria ... Yes
Graduation rate ... NA
criteria met/possible ... 21/17

Lakeside Union Elem
Kings County
9100 Jersey Ave
Hanford, CA 93230
(559) 582-2868

Superint ... Dale Ellis
Grade plan ... K-8
Number of schools ... 3
- Enrollment ... 355
- High school graduates, 2006-07 ... 0
- Dropout rate ... 0
- Pupil/teacher ratio ... 18.7%
- Average class size ... 20.5
- Students per computer ... 2.2

Avg. Teacher Salary, ...
Avg. Daily Attendence (ADA) ... 339
- Cost per ADA ... $8,997

California Achievement Tests 6th ed., 2008
(Pct scoring at or above 50th National Percentile Rank)

	Math	Reading	Language
Grade 3	42%	18%	26%
Grade 7	19%	14%	23%

Academic Performance Index, 2009
Number of valid scores ... 228
2007 API (base) ... 684
2008 API (growth) ... 615

SAT Testing, 2006-07
Enrollment, Grade 12 ... NA
- percent taking test ... NA
- number with total score 1,500+ ... NA

Average Scores:

Math	Verbal	Writing	Total
NA	NA	NA	NA

Federal No Child Left Behind, 2008
(Adequate Yearly Progress standards met)

	Participation Rate	Pct Proficient
ELA	Yes	No
Math	Yes	Yes

API Criteria ... No
Graduation rate ... NA
criteria met/possible ... 17/12

Lammersville Elem
San Joaquin County
300 Legacy Dr
Mountain House, CA 95391
(209) 836-7400

Superint ... Dale Hansen
Grade plan ... K-8
Number of schools ... 4
- Enrollment ... 1,491
- High school graduates, 2006-07 ... 0
- Dropout rate ... 0
- Pupil/teacher ratio ... 18.6%
- Average class size ... 21.0
- Students per computer ... 8.0

Avg. Teacher Salary, ... $50,795
Avg. Daily Attendence (ADA) ... 1,504
- Cost per ADA ... $6,602

California Achievement Tests 6th ed., 2008
(Pct scoring at or above 50th National Percentile Rank)

	Math	Reading	Language
Grade 3	71%	45%	65%
Grade 7	62%	59%	61%

Academic Performance Index, 2009
Number of valid scores ... 1,059
2007 API (base) ... 816
2008 API (growth) ... 830

SAT Testing, 2006-07
Enrollment, Grade 12 ... NA
- percent taking test ... NA
- number with total score 1,500+ ... NA

Average Scores:

Math	Verbal	Writing	Total
NA	NA	NA	NA

Federal No Child Left Behind, 2008
(Adequate Yearly Progress standards met)

	Participation Rate	Pct Proficient
ELA	Yes	Yes
Math	Yes	Yes

API Criteria ... Yes
Graduation rate ... NA
criteria met/possible ... 35/35

Lancaster Elem
Los Angeles County
44711 North Cedar Ave
Lancaster, CA 93534
(661) 948-4661

Superint ... Howard Sundberg
Grade plan ... K-8
Number of schools ... 19
- Enrollment ... 15,793
- High school graduates, 2006-07 ... 0
- Dropout rate ... 0
- Pupil/teacher ratio ... 20.3%
- Average class size ... 24.6
- Students per computer ... 9.9

Avg. Teacher Salary, ... $63,265
Avg. Daily Attendence (ADA) ... 14,660
- Cost per ADA ... $8,382

California Achievement Tests 6th ed., 2008
(Pct scoring at or above 50th National Percentile Rank)

	Math	Reading	Language
Grade 3	36%	23%	31%
Grade 7	36%	37%	34%

Academic Performance Index, 2009
Number of valid scores ... 10,668
2007 API (base) ... 678
2008 API (growth) ... 687

SAT Testing, 2006-07
Enrollment, Grade 12 ... NA
- percent taking test ... NA
- number with total score 1,500+ ... NA

Average Scores:

Math	Verbal	Writing	Total
NA	NA	NA	NA

Federal No Child Left Behind, 2008
(Adequate Yearly Progress standards met)

	Participation Rate	Pct Proficient
ELA	No	No
Math	Yes	No

API Criteria ... Yes
Graduation rate ... NA
criteria met/possible ... 37/24

Larkspur
Marin County
230 Doherty Dr
Larkspur, CA 94939
(415) 927-6960

Superint ... Valerie Pitts
Grade plan ... K-8
Number of schools ... 2
- Enrollment ... 1,173
- High school graduates, 2006-07 ... 0
- Dropout rate ... 0
- Pupil/teacher ratio ... 17.6%
- Average class size ... 23.0
- Students per computer ... 2.3

Avg. Teacher Salary, ... $68,314
Avg. Daily Attendence (ADA) ... 1,139
- Cost per ADA ... $10,391

California Achievement Tests 6th ed., 2008
(Pct scoring at or above 50th National Percentile Rank)

	Math	Reading	Language
Grade 3	75%	80%	84%
Grade 7	89%	88%	92%

Academic Performance Index, 2009
Number of valid scores ... 848
2007 API (base) ... 899
2008 API (growth) ... 918

SAT Testing, 2006-07
Enrollment, Grade 12 ... NA
- percent taking test ... NA
- number with total score 1,500+ ... NA

Average Scores:

Math	Verbal	Writing	Total
NA	NA	NA	NA

Federal No Child Left Behind, 2008
(Adequate Yearly Progress standards met)

	Participation Rate	Pct Proficient
ELA	Yes	Yes
Math	Yes	Yes

API Criteria ... Yes
Graduation rate ... NA
criteria met/possible ... 11/11

Las Lomitas Elem
San Mateo County
1011 Altschul Ave
Menlo Park, CA 94025
(650) 854-2880

Superint ... Eric Hartwig
Grade plan ... K-8
Number of schools ... 2
- Enrollment ... 1,136
- High school graduates, 2006-07 ... 0
- Dropout rate ... 0
- Pupil/teacher ratio ... 16.1%
- Average class size ... 21.0
- Students per computer ... 3.0

Avg. Teacher Salary, ... $88,335
Avg. Daily Attendence (ADA) ... 1,110
- Cost per ADA ... $13,650

California Achievement Tests 6th ed., 2008
(Pct scoring at or above 50th National Percentile Rank)

	Math	Reading	Language
Grade 3	82%	73%	79%
Grade 7	92%	90%	91%

Academic Performance Index, 2009
Number of valid scores ... 819
2007 API (base) ... 947
2008 API (growth) ... 957

SAT Testing, 2006-07
Enrollment, Grade 12 ... NA
- percent taking test ... NA
- number with total score 1,500+ ... NA

Average Scores:

Math	Verbal	Writing	Total
NA	NA	NA	NA

Federal No Child Left Behind, 2008
(Adequate Yearly Progress standards met)

	Participation Rate	Pct Proficient
ELA	Yes	Yes
Math	Yes	Yes

API Criteria ... Yes
Graduation rate ... NA
criteria met/possible ... 13/13

Data from school year 2007-08 except where noted
†Combined data for elementary and high schools

Lawndale Elem

Los Angeles County
4161 West 147th St
Lawndale, CA 90260
(310) 973-1300

Superint.................. Joseph Condon
Grade plan.......................... K-12
Number of schools....................... 9
Enrollment....................... 6,240
High school graduates, 2006-07....... 34
Dropout rate......................... 3.2
Pupil/teacher ratio................. 21.2%
Average class size................... 25.3
Students per computer.............. 5.0
Avg. Teacher Salary,............... $71,121
Avg. Daily Attendence (ADA)........ 5,702
Cost per ADA.................... $8,576

California Achievement Tests 6th ed., 2008
(Pct scoring at or above 50th National Percentile Rank)

	Math	Reading	Language
Grade 3	52%	25%	36%
Grade 7	39%	38%	38%

Academic Performance Index, 2009
Number of valid scores.............. 4,273
2007 API (base)...................... 718
2008 API (growth).................... 738

SAT Testing, 2006-07
Enrollment, Grade 12................. 44
percent taking test............... 90.9%
number with total score 1,500+........ 1

Average Scores:

Math	Verbal	Writing	Total
365	373	373	1,111

Federal No Child Left Behind, 2008
(Adequate Yearly Progress standards met)

	Participation Rate	Pct Proficient
ELA	Yes	No
Math	Yes	No

API Criteria.......................... Yes
Graduation rate....................... NA
criteria met/possible.............. 33/30

Lemon Grove

San Diego County
8025 Lincoln St
Lemon Grove, CA 91945
(619) 825-5600

Superint.................. Ernest Anastos
Grade plan........................... K-8
Number of schools....................... 8
Enrollment....................... 4,030
High school graduates, 2006-07........ 0
Dropout rate........................... 0
Pupil/teacher ratio................ 20.3%
Average class size................... 25.5
Students per computer.............. 1.3
Avg. Teacher Salary,............... $66,322
Avg. Daily Attendence (ADA)........ 3,835
Cost per ADA.................... $8,434

California Achievement Tests 6th ed., 2008
(Pct scoring at or above 50th National Percentile Rank)

	Math	Reading	Language
Grade 3	49%	29%	37%
Grade 7	44%	35%	33%

Academic Performance Index, 2009
Number of valid scores.............. 2,783
2007 API (base)...................... 723
2008 API (growth).................... 730

SAT Testing, 2006-07
Enrollment, Grade 12................. NA
percent taking test.................. NA
number with total score 1,500+...... NA

Average Scores:

Math	Verbal	Writing	Total
NA	NA	NA	NA

Federal No Child Left Behind, 2008
(Adequate Yearly Progress standards met)

	Participation Rate	Pct Proficient
ELA	Yes	No
Math	Yes	No

API Criteria.......................... Yes
Graduation rate....................... NA
criteria met/possible.............. 31/28

Lemoore Union Elem

Kings County
1200 West Cinnamon Dr
Lemoore, CA 93245
(559) 924-6800

Superint.................. Richard Rayburn
Grade plan........................... K-8
Number of schools....................... 6
Enrollment....................... 3,320
High school graduates, 2006-07........ 0
Dropout rate........................... 0
Pupil/teacher ratio................ 19.7%
Average class size................... 22.5
Students per computer.............. 2.9
Avg. Teacher Salary,............... $54,314
Avg. Daily Attendence (ADA)........ 3,019
Cost per ADA.................... $7,646

California Achievement Tests 6th ed., 2008
(Pct scoring at or above 50th National Percentile Rank)

	Math	Reading	Language
Grade 3	47%	27%	37%
Grade 7	53%	47%	44%

Academic Performance Index, 2009
Number of valid scores.............. 2,429
2007 API (base)...................... 727
2008 API (growth).................... 739

SAT Testing, 2006-07
Enrollment, Grade 12................. NA
percent taking test.................. NA
number with total score 1,500+...... NA

Average Scores:

Math	Verbal	Writing	Total
NA	NA	NA	NA

Federal No Child Left Behind, 2008
(Adequate Yearly Progress standards met)

	Participation Rate	Pct Proficient
ELA	Yes	No
Math	Yes	No

API Criteria.......................... Yes
Graduation rate....................... NA
criteria met/possible.............. 33/27

Liberty Elem

Sonoma County
11535 Avenue 264
Visalia, CA 93277
(707) 795-4380

Superint.................. Chris Rafanelli
Grade plan........................... K-6
Number of schools....................... 2
Enrollment......................... 635
High school graduates, 2006-07........ 0
Dropout rate......................... 3.1
Pupil/teacher ratio................ 14.3%
Average class size................... 21.7
Students per computer.............. 0.9
Avg. Teacher Salary,....................
Avg. Daily Attendence (ADA).......... 196
Cost per ADA.................... $8,443

California Achievement Tests 6th ed., 2008
(Pct scoring at or above 50th National Percentile Rank)

	Math	Reading	Language
Grade 3	87%	83%	87%
Grade 7	NA	NA	NA

Academic Performance Index, 2009
Number of valid scores................ 139
2007 API (base)...................... 921
2008 API (growth).................... 916

SAT Testing, 2006-07
Enrollment, Grade 12................. NA
percent taking test.................. NA
number with total score 1,500+...... NA

Average Scores:

Math	Verbal	Writing	Total
NA	NA	NA	NA

Federal No Child Left Behind, 2008
(Adequate Yearly Progress standards met)

	Participation Rate	Pct Proficient
ELA	Yes	Yes
Math	Yes	Yes

API Criteria.......................... Yes
Graduation rate....................... NA
criteria met/possible................ 9/9

Liberty Elem

Tulare County
170 Liberty School Rd
Petaluma, CA 94952
(559) 686-1675

Superint....................... Al George
Grade plan........................... K-8
Number of schools....................... 1
Enrollment......................... 262
High school graduates, 2006-07........ 0
Dropout rate........................... 0
Pupil/teacher ratio................ 22.8%
Average class size................... 21.8
Students per computer.............. 9.7
Avg. Teacher Salary,............... $52,404
Avg. Daily Attendence (ADA).......... 258
Cost per ADA.................... $7,424

California Achievement Tests 6th ed., 2008
(Pct scoring at or above 50th National Percentile Rank)

	Math	Reading	Language
Grade 3	50%	48%	48%
Grade 7	48%	48%	57%

Academic Performance Index, 2009
Number of valid scores................ 165
2007 API (base)...................... 735
2008 API (growth).................... 713

SAT Testing, 2006-07
Enrollment, Grade 12................. NA
percent taking test.................. NA
number with total score 1,500+...... NA

Average Scores:

Math	Verbal	Writing	Total
NA	NA	NA	NA

Federal No Child Left Behind, 2008
(Adequate Yearly Progress standards met)

	Participation Rate	Pct Proficient
ELA	Yes	Yes
Math	Yes	No

API Criteria.......................... Yes
Graduation rate....................... NA
criteria met/possible.............. 17/15

Lincoln Elem

Marin County
1300 Hicks Valley Rd
Petaluma, CA 94952
(707) 763-0045

Superint..................... Luke McCann
Grade plan........................... K-6
Number of schools....................... 1
Enrollment........................... 19
High school graduates, 2006-07........ 0
Dropout rate.......................... NA
Pupil/teacher ratio................ 19.0%
Average class size................... 19.0
Students per computer.............. 3.2
Avg. Teacher Salary,............... $57,540
Avg. Daily Attendence (ADA)........... 18
Cost per ADA.................... $9,462

California Achievement Tests 6th ed., 2008
(Pct scoring at or above 50th National Percentile Rank)

	Math	Reading	Language
Grade 3	NA	NA	NA
Grade 7	NA	NA	NA

Academic Performance Index, 2009
Number of valid scores................. 13
2007 API (base)........................ B
2008 API (growth).................... 821

SAT Testing, 2006-07
Enrollment, Grade 12................. NA
percent taking test.................. NA
number with total score 1,500+...... NA

Average Scores:

Math	Verbal	Writing	Total
NA	NA	NA	NA

Federal No Child Left Behind, 2008
(Adequate Yearly Progress standards met)

	Participation Rate	Pct Proficient
ELA	Yes	Yes
Math	Yes	Yes

API Criteria.......................... Yes
Graduation rate....................... NA
criteria met/possible................ 5/5

Data from school year 2007-08 except where noted.
†Combined data for elementary and high schools.

Lincoln Unified

San Joaquin County
2010 West Swain Rd
Stockton, CA 95207
(209) 953-8700

Superint. . . . . .Steve Lowder
Grade plan. K-12
Number of schools. .11
Enrollment 8,572
High school graduates, 2006-07. 496
Dropout rate. 3.3
Pupil/teacher ratio. 20.4%
Average class size. 25.5
Students per computer 3.8
Avg. Teacher Salary, ... $59,669
Avg. Daily Attendence (ADA). 8,252
Cost per ADA. $7,730

California Achievement Tests 6th ed., 2008
(Pct scoring at or above 50th National Percentile Rank)

	Math	Reading	Language
Grade 3	54%	38%	44%
Grade 7	61%	52%	50%

Academic Performance Index, 2009
Number of valid scores. 6,090
2007 API (base) 750
2008 API (growth). 764

SAT Testing, 2006-07
Enrollment, Grade 12 604
percent taking test. 31.3%
number with total score 1,500+ 96

Average Scores:

Math	Verbal	Writing	Total
526	499	499	1,524

Federal No Child Left Behind, 2008
(Adequate Yearly Progress standards met)

	Participation Rate	Pct Proficient
ELA	Yes	No
Math	Yes	Yes

API Criteria . . . . .Yes
Graduation rate . . . . .Yes
criteria met/possible. 38/37

Little Lake City Elem

Los Angeles County
10515 South Pioneer Blvd
Santa Fe Springs, CA 90670
(562) 868-8241

Superint. Phillip Perez
Grade plan. K-8
Number of schools. 9
Enrollment 4,973
High school graduates, 2006-07. 0
Dropout rate. 0
Pupil/teacher ratio. 20.5%
Average class size. 26.1
Students per computer 5.6
Avg. Teacher Salary, ... $65,780
Avg. Daily Attendence (ADA). 4,892
Cost per ADA. $8,101

California Achievement Tests 6th ed., 2008
(Pct scoring at or above 50th National Percentile Rank)

	Math	Reading	Language
Grade 3	50%	27%	41%
Grade 7	45%	43%	41%

Academic Performance Index, 2009
Number of valid scores. 3,765
2007 API (base) 745
2008 API (growth). 774

SAT Testing, 2006-07
Enrollment, Grade 12 . . . . .NA
percent taking test. . . . . .NA
number with total score 1,500+ . . . . . .NA

Average Scores:

Math	Verbal	Writing	Total
NA	NA	NA	NA

Federal No Child Left Behind, 2008
(Adequate Yearly Progress standards met)

	Participation Rate	Pct Proficient
ELA	Yes	No
Math	Yes	Yes

API Criteria . . . . .Yes
Graduation rate . . . . .NA
criteria met/possible. 27/25

Little Shasta Elem

Siskiyou County
8409 Lower Little Shasta Rd
Montague, CA 96064
(530) 459-3269

Superint. . . . . Kathleen Koon
Grade plan. K-6
Number of schools. 1
Enrollment 31
High school graduates, 2006-07. 0
Dropout rate. . . . . .NA
Pupil/teacher ratio. 15.5%
Average class size. 15.5
Students per computer 3.9
Avg. Teacher Salary, ...NA
Avg. Daily Attendence (ADA). 31
Cost per ADA. $8,715

California Achievement Tests 6th ed., 2008
(Pct scoring at or above 50th National Percentile Rank)

	Math	Reading	Language
Grade 3	NA	NA	NA
Grade 7	NA	NA	NA

Academic Performance Index, 2009
Number of valid scores. 25
2007 API (base) 828
2008 API (growth). 747

SAT Testing, 2006-07
Enrollment, Grade 12 . . . . .NA
percent taking test. . . . . .NA
number with total score 1,500+ . . . . . .NA

Average Scores:

Math	Verbal	Writing	Total
NA	NA	NA	NA

Federal No Child Left Behind, 2008
(Adequate Yearly Progress standards met)

	Participation Rate	Pct Proficient
ELA	Yes	Yes
Math	Yes	Yes

API Criteria . . . . .Yes
Graduation rate . . . . .NA
criteria met/possible. 5/5

Live Oak Elem

Santa Cruz County
984-1 Bostwick Ln
Santa Cruz, CA 95062
(831) 475-6333

Superint. . . . . .David Paine
Grade plan. K-12
Number of schools. 7
Enrollment 2,194
High school graduates, 2006-07. 15
Dropout rate. 13.2
Pupil/teacher ratio. 21.7%
Average class size. 24.2
Students per computer 3.7
Avg. Teacher Salary, ... $57,017
Avg. Daily Attendence (ADA). 1,889
Cost per ADA. $8,199

California Achievement Tests 6th ed., 2008
(Pct scoring at or above 50th National Percentile Rank)

	Math	Reading	Language
Grade 3	49%	39%	45%
Grade 7	45%	46%	47%

Academic Performance Index, 2009
Number of valid scores. 1,512
2007 API (base) 729
2008 API (growth). 727

SAT Testing, 2006-07
Enrollment, Grade 12 23
percent taking test. 39.1%
number with total score 1,500+ . . . . . .NA

Average Scores:

Math	Verbal	Writing	Total
NA	NA	NA	NA

Federal No Child Left Behind, 2008
(Adequate Yearly Progress standards met)

	Participation Rate	Pct Proficient
ELA	No	No
Math	Yes	No

API Criteria . . . . .Yes
Graduation rate . . . . .Yes
criteria met/possible. 26/17

Livingston Union Elem

Merced County
922 B St
Livingston, CA 95334
(209) 394-5400

Superint. . . . . Henry Escobar
Grade plan. K-8
Number of schools. 4
Enrollment 2,551
High school graduates, 2006-07. 0
Dropout rate. 0
Pupil/teacher ratio. 19.8%
Average class size. 22.5
Students per computer 2.5
Avg. Teacher Salary, ... $67,961
Avg. Daily Attendence (ADA). 2,557
Cost per ADA. $8,026

California Achievement Tests 6th ed., 2008
(Pct scoring at or above 50th National Percentile Rank)

	Math	Reading	Language
Grade 3	53%	36%	46%
Grade 7	47%	36%	41%

Academic Performance Index, 2009
Number of valid scores. 1,773
2007 API (base) 719
2008 API (growth). 738

SAT Testing, 2006-07
Enrollment, Grade 12 . . . . .NA
percent taking test. . . . . .NA
number with total score 1,500+ . . . . . .NA

Average Scores:

Math	Verbal	Writing	Total
NA	NA	NA	NA

Federal No Child Left Behind, 2008
(Adequate Yearly Progress standards met)

	Participation Rate	Pct Proficient
ELA	Yes	No
Math	Yes	Yes

API Criteria . . . . .Yes
Graduation rate . . . . .NA
criteria met/possible. 29/26

Lodi Unified

San Joaquin County
1305 East Vine St
Lodi, CA 95240
(209) 331-7000

Superint. . . . . Cathy Washer
Grade plan. K-12
Number of schools. .54
Enrollment 31,609
High school graduates, 2006-07. . . . 1,655
Dropout rate. 3.9
Pupil/teacher ratio. 19.7%
Average class size. 24.9
Students per computer 4.4
Avg. Teacher Salary, ... $63,130
Avg. Daily Attendence (ADA). 29,005
Cost per ADA. $8,333

California Achievement Tests 6th ed., 2008
(Pct scoring at or above 50th National Percentile Rank)

	Math	Reading	Language
Grade 3	51%	31%	38%
Grade 7	46%	44%	41%

Academic Performance Index, 2009
Number of valid scores. 21,545
2007 API (base) 708
2008 API (growth). 720

SAT Testing, 2006-07
Enrollment, Grade 12 2,299
percent taking test. 25.6%
number with total score 1,500+ 269

Average Scores:

Math	Verbal	Writing	Total
515	484	481	1,480

Federal No Child Left Behind, 2008
(Adequate Yearly Progress standards met)

	Participation Rate	Pct Proficient
ELA	Yes	No
Math	Yes	No

API Criteria . . . . .Yes
Graduation rate . . . . .Yes
criteria met/possible. 46/39

Data from school year 2007-08 except where noted
†Combined data for elementary and high schools

Loma Prieta Joint Union Elem

Santa Clara County
23800 Summit Rd
Los Gatos, CA 95033
(408) 353-1101

Superint. . . . . Henry Castaniada
Grade plan. K-8
Number of schools. 2
Enrollment 401
High school graduates, 2006-07. 0
Dropout rate. 0
Pupil/teacher ratio. 18.2%
Average class size. 22.6
Students per computer 2.1
Avg. Teacher Salary, ... $70,173
Avg. Daily Attendence (ADA). 388
Cost per ADA. $11,377

California Achievement Tests 6th ed., 2008
(Pct scoring at or above 50th National Percentile Rank)

	Math	Reading	Language
Grade 3	69%	64%	72%
Grade 7	87%	87%	87%

Academic Performance Index, 2009
Number of valid scores. 325
2007 API (base) 909
2008 API (growth). 892

SAT Testing, 2006-07
Enrollment, Grade 12 . . . . .NA
percent taking test. . . . . .NA
number with total score 1,500+ . . . . . .NA

Average Scores:

Math	Verbal	Writing	Total
NA	NA	NA	NA

Federal No Child Left Behind, 2008
(Adequate Yearly Progress standards met)

	Participation Rate	Pct Proficient
ELA	Yes	Yes
Math	Yes	Yes

API Criteria . . . . .Yes
Graduation rate . . . . .NA
criteria met/possible. 9/9

Loomis Union Elem

Placer County
3290 Humphrey Rd
Loomis, CA 95650
(916) 652-1800

Superint. Paul Johnson
Grade plan. K-8
Number of schools. 5
Enrollment 2,123
High school graduates, 2006-07. 0
Dropout rate. 0
Pupil/teacher ratio. 21.8%
Average class size. 26.7
Students per computer 4.1
Avg. Teacher Salary, ... $59,327
Avg. Daily Attendence (ADA). 2,096
Cost per ADA. $6,962

California Achievement Tests 6th ed., 2008
(Pct scoring at or above 50th National Percentile Rank)

	Math	Reading	Language
Grade 3	83%	64%	69%
Grade 7	81%	78%	75%

Academic Performance Index, 2009
Number of valid scores. 1,729
2007 API (base) 874
2008 API (growth). 871

SAT Testing, 2006-07
Enrollment, Grade 12 . . . . .NA
percent taking test. . . . . .NA
number with total score 1,500+ . . . . . .NA

Average Scores:

Math	Verbal	Writing	Total
NA	NA	NA	NA

Federal No Child Left Behind, 2008
(Adequate Yearly Progress standards met)

	Participation Rate	Pct Proficient
ELA	Yes	Yes
Math	Yes	Yes

API Criteria . . . . .Yes
Graduation rate . . . . .NA
criteria met/possible. 17/17

Los Altos Elem

Santa Clara County
201 Covington Rd
Los Altos, CA 94024
(650) 947-1150

Superint. . . . . Tim Justus
Grade plan. K-8
Number of schools. 9
Enrollment 4,270
High school graduates, 2006-07. 0
Dropout rate. 0
Pupil/teacher ratio. 19.3%
Average class size. 22.9
Students per computer 2.8
Avg. Teacher Salary, ... $73,308
Avg. Daily Attendence (ADA). 4,222
Cost per ADA. $9,427

California Achievement Tests 6th ed., 2008
(Pct scoring at or above 50th National Percentile Rank)

	Math	Reading	Language
Grade 3	93%	83%	90%
Grade 7	91%	88%	85%

Academic Performance Index, 2009
Number of valid scores. 3,211
2007 API (base) 954
2008 API (growth). 959

SAT Testing, 2006-07
Enrollment, Grade 12 . . . . .NA
percent taking test. . . . . .NA
number with total score 1,500+ . . . . . .NA

Average Scores:

Math	Verbal	Writing	Total
NA	NA	NA	NA

Federal No Child Left Behind, 2008
(Adequate Yearly Progress standards met)

	Participation Rate	Pct Proficient
ELA	Yes	Yes
Math	Yes	Yes

API Criteria . . . . .Yes
Graduation rate . . . . .NA
criteria met/possible. 25/25

Los Angeles Unified

Los Angeles County
333 South Beaudry Ave
Los Angeles, CA 90017
(213) 241-1000

Superint. . . . . Ramon Cortines
Grade plan. PK-12
Number of schools. 827
Enrollment .693,680
High school graduates, 2006-07. . . 28,545
Dropout rate. 7.8
Pupil/teacher ratio. 19.8%
Average class size. 24.9
Students per computer 3.7
Avg. Teacher Salary, ... $63,391
Avg. Daily Attendence (ADA). 653,672
Cost per ADA. $10,053

California Achievement Tests 6th ed., 2008
(Pct scoring at or above 50th National Percentile Rank)

	Math	Reading	Language
Grade 3	49%	27%	39%
Grade 7	37%	33%	33%

Academic Performance Index, 2009
Number of valid scores. 471,641
2007 API (base) 662
2008 API (growth). 683

SAT Testing, 2006-07
Enrollment, Grade 12 32,370
percent taking test. 47.7%
number with total score 1,500+ 4,049

Average Scores:

Math	Verbal	Writing	Total
443	438	441	1,322

Federal No Child Left Behind, 2008
(Adequate Yearly Progress standards met)

	Participation Rate	Pct Proficient
ELA	Yes	No
Math	Yes	No

API Criteria . . . . .Yes
Graduation rate . . . . .Yes
criteria met/possible. 46/38

Los Gatos Union Elem

Santa Clara County
17010 Roberts Rd
Los Gatos, CA 95032
(408) 335-2000

Superint. J. Whitmore
Grade plan. K-8
Number of schools. 5
Enrollment 2,706
High school graduates, 2006-07. 0
Dropout rate. 0
Pupil/teacher ratio. 19.5%
Average class size. 24.3
Students per computer 3.6
Avg. Teacher Salary, ... $72,397
Avg. Daily Attendence (ADA). 2,644
Cost per ADA. $9,444

California Achievement Tests 6th ed., 2008
(Pct scoring at or above 50th National Percentile Rank)

	Math	Reading	Language
Grade 3	85%	78%	80%
Grade 7	82%	86%	81%

Academic Performance Index, 2009
Number of valid scores. 2,050
2007 API (base) 888
2008 API (growth). 911

SAT Testing, 2006-07
Enrollment, Grade 12 . . . . .NA
percent taking test. . . . . .NA
number with total score 1,500+ . . . . . .NA

Average Scores:

Math	Verbal	Writing	Total
NA	NA	NA	NA

Federal No Child Left Behind, 2008
(Adequate Yearly Progress standards met)

	Participation Rate	Pct Proficient
ELA	Yes	Yes
Math	Yes	Yes

API Criteria . . . . .Yes
Graduation rate . . . . .NA
criteria met/possible. 17/17

Los Nietos

Los Angeles County
8324 South Westman Ave
Whittier, CA 90606
(562) 692-0271

Superint. . . . . Lillian French
Grade plan. K-8
Number of schools. 4
Enrollment 2,124
High school graduates, 2006-07. 0
Dropout rate. 0
Pupil/teacher ratio. 21.2%
Average class size. 22.1
Students per computer 6.1
Avg. Teacher Salary, ... $61,814
Avg. Daily Attendence (ADA). 2,101
Cost per ADA. $8,619

California Achievement Tests 6th ed., 2008
(Pct scoring at or above 50th National Percentile Rank)

	Math	Reading	Language
Grade 3	54%	24%	39%
Grade 7	25%	23%	22%

Academic Performance Index, 2009
Number of valid scores. 1,477
2007 API (base) 687
2008 API (growth). 707

SAT Testing, 2006-07
Enrollment, Grade 12 . . . . .NA
percent taking test. . . . . .NA
number with total score 1,500+ . . . . . .NA

Average Scores:

Math	Verbal	Writing	Total
NA	NA	NA	NA

Federal No Child Left Behind, 2008
(Adequate Yearly Progress standards met)

	Participation Rate	Pct Proficient
ELA	Yes	No
Math	Yes	Yes

API Criteria . . . . .Yes
Graduation rate . . . . .NA
criteria met/possible. 21/17

Data from school year 2007-08 except where noted.
†Combined data for elementary and high schools.

Lowell Joint Elem
Los Angeles County
11019 Valley Home Ave
Whittier, CA 90603
(562) 943-0211

Superint. . . . . Patricia Howell
Grade plan. K-8
Number of schools. 6
Enrollment 3,122
High school graduates, 2006-07. 0
Dropout rate. 0
Pupil/teacher ratio. 24.3%
Average class size. 27.8
Students per computer 7.6
Avg. Teacher Salary, ... $67,115
Avg. Daily Attendence (ADA). 3,036
Cost per ADA. $7,046

California Achievement Tests 6th ed., 2008
(Pct scoring at or above 50th National Percentile Rank)

	Math	Reading	Language
Grade 3	64%	44%	59%
Grade 7	66%	59%	62%

Academic Performance Index, 2009
Number of valid scores. 2,400
2007 API (base) 829
2008 API (growth). 828

SAT Testing, 2006-07
Enrollment, Grade 12 . . . . NA
percent taking test. . . . . NA
number with total score 1,500+ . . . . . . NA

Average Scores:

Math	Verbal	Writing	Total
NA	NA	NA	NA

Federal No Child Left Behind, 2008
(Adequate Yearly Progress standards met)

	Participation Rate	Pct Proficient
ELA	Yes	Yes
Math	Yes	Yes

API Criteria . . . . Yes
Graduation rate . . . . NA
criteria met/possible. 25/25

Luther Burbank Elem
Santa Clara County
4 Wabash Ave
San Jose, CA 95128
(408) 295-2450

Superint. . . . . Richard Rodriguez
Grade plan. K-8
Number of schools. 1
Enrollment 544
High school graduates, 2006-07. 0
Dropout rate. 0
Pupil/teacher ratio. 20.9%
Average class size. 21.7
Students per computer 3.0
Avg. Teacher Salary, ... $64,225
Avg. Daily Attendence (ADA). 519
Cost per ADA. $7,983

California Achievement Tests 6th ed., 2008
(Pct scoring at or above 50th National Percentile Rank)

	Math	Reading	Language
Grade 3	50%	31%	45%
Grade 7	49%	36%	34%

Academic Performance Index, 2009
Number of valid scores. 345
2007 API (base) 729
2008 API (growth). 762

SAT Testing, 2006-07
Enrollment, Grade 12 . . . . NA
percent taking test. . . . . NA
number with total score 1,500+ . . . . . . NA

Average Scores:

Math	Verbal	Writing	Total
NA	NA	NA	NA

Federal No Child Left Behind, 2008
(Adequate Yearly Progress standards met)

	Participation Rate	Pct Proficient
ELA	Yes	Yes
Math	Yes	Yes

API Criteria . . . . Yes
Graduation rate . . . . NA
criteria met/possible. 17/17

Magnolia Elem
Orange County
2705 West Orange Ave
Anaheim, CA 92804
(714) 761-5533

Superint. . . . . Ellen Curtin
Grade plan. K-6
Number of schools. 9
Enrollment 6,341
High school graduates, 2006-07. 0
Dropout rate. . . . . NA
Pupil/teacher ratio. 19.8%
Average class size. 22.4
Students per computer 3.9
Avg. Teacher Salary, ... $72,713
Avg. Daily Attendence (ADA). 6,258
Cost per ADA. $7,994

California Achievement Tests 6th ed., 2008
(Pct scoring at or above 50th National Percentile Rank)

	Math	Reading	Language
Grade 3	50%	31%	41%
Grade 7	NA	NA	NA

Academic Performance Index, 2009
Number of valid scores. 4,177
2007 API (base) 741
2008 API (growth). 771

SAT Testing, 2006-07
Enrollment, Grade 12 . . . . NA
percent taking test. . . . . NA
number with total score 1,500+ . . . . . . NA

Average Scores:

Math	Verbal	Writing	Total
NA	NA	NA	NA

Federal No Child Left Behind, 2008
(Adequate Yearly Progress standards met)

	Participation Rate	Pct Proficient
ELA	Yes	No
Math	Yes	Yes

API Criteria . . . . Yes
Graduation rate . . . . NA
criteria met/possible. 37/36

Magnolia Union Elem
Imperial County
4502 Casey Rd
Brawley, CA 92227
(760) 344-2494

Superint. . . . . Blaine Smith
Grade plan. K-8
Number of schools. 1
Enrollment 114
High school graduates, 2006-07. 0
Dropout rate. 0
Pupil/teacher ratio. 18.2%
Average class size. 19.0
Students per computer 2.3
Avg. Teacher Salary, ... $65,356
Avg. Daily Attendence (ADA). 113
Cost per ADA. $8,099

California Achievement Tests 6th ed., 2008
(Pct scoring at or above 50th National Percentile Rank)

	Math	Reading	Language
Grade 3	17%	25%	8%
Grade 7	76%	76%	76%

Academic Performance Index, 2009
Number of valid scores. 86
2007 API (base) 846
2008 API (growth). 815

SAT Testing, 2006-07
Enrollment, Grade 12 . . . . NA
percent taking test. . . . . NA
number with total score 1,500+ . . . . . . NA

Average Scores:

Math	Verbal	Writing	Total
NA	NA	NA	NA

Federal No Child Left Behind, 2008
(Adequate Yearly Progress standards met)

	Participation Rate	Pct Proficient
ELA	Yes	Yes
Math	Yes	Yes

API Criteria . . . . Yes
Graduation rate . . . . NA
criteria met/possible. 5/5

Manhattan Beach Unified
Los Angeles County
325 South Peck Ave
Manhattan Beach, CA 90266
(310) 318-7345

Superint. . . . . Beverly Rohrer
Grade plan. K-12
Number of schools. 7
Enrollment 6,332
High school graduates, 2006-07. 546
Dropout rate. 2.2
Pupil/teacher ratio. 21.2%
Average class size. 28.2
Students per computer 5.8
Avg. Teacher Salary, ... $65,918
Avg. Daily Attendence (ADA). 6,214
Cost per ADA. $8,020

California Achievement Tests 6th ed., 2008
(Pct scoring at or above 50th National Percentile Rank)

	Math	Reading	Language
Grade 3	91%	81%	84%
Grade 7	91%	86%	85%

Academic Performance Index, 2009
Number of valid scores. 4,587
2007 API (base) 900
2008 API (growth). 909

SAT Testing, 2006-07
Enrollment, Grade 12 557
percent taking test. 79.2%
number with total score 1,500+ 338

Average Scores:

Math	Verbal	Writing	Total
584	560	571	1,715

Federal No Child Left Behind, 2008
(Adequate Yearly Progress standards met)

	Participation Rate	Pct Proficient
ELA	Yes	Yes
Math	Yes	Yes

API Criteria . . . . Yes
Graduation rate . . . . Yes
criteria met/possible. 22/22

Manteca Unified
San Joaquin County
PO Box 32
Manteca, CA 95336
(209) 825-3200

Superint. . . . . Jason Messer
Grade plan. K-12
Number of schools. 28
Enrollment 23,654
High school graduates, 2006-07. . . . 1,290
Dropout rate. 3.3
Pupil/teacher ratio. 21.7%
Average class size. 26.2
Students per computer 5.0
Avg. Teacher Salary, ... $59,600
Avg. Daily Attendence (ADA). 22,902
Cost per ADA. $7,460

California Achievement Tests 6th ed., 2008
(Pct scoring at or above 50th National Percentile Rank)

	Math	Reading	Language
Grade 3	55%	37%	46%
Grade 7	47%	47%	44%

Academic Performance Index, 2009
Number of valid scores. 16,762
2007 API (base) 724
2008 API (growth). 731

SAT Testing, 2006-07
Enrollment, Grade 12 1,597
percent taking test. 30.9%
number with total score 1,500+ 164

Average Scores:

Math	Verbal	Writing	Total
471	468	454	1,393

Federal No Child Left Behind, 2008
(Adequate Yearly Progress standards met)

	Participation Rate	Pct Proficient
ELA	Yes	No
Math	Yes	No

API Criteria . . . . Yes
Graduation rate . . . . Yes
criteria met/possible. 46/41

Data from school year 2007-08 except where noted
†Combined data for elementary and high schools

Manzanita Elem

Butte County
627 East Evans-Reimer Rd
Gridley, CA 95948
(530) 846-5594

Superint.................... Brad Roberts
Grade plan............................K-8
Number of schools.......................1
Enrollment.........................276
High school graduates, 2006-07........0
Dropout rate..........................0
Pupil/teacher ratio...............21.5%
Average class size.................. 24.1
Students per computer 3.1
Avg. Teacher Salary, ...NA
Avg. Daily Attendence (ADA)..........270
Cost per ADA.................. $7,003

California Achievement Tests 6th ed., 2008
(Pct scoring at or above 50th National Percentile Rank)

	Math	Reading	Language
Grade 3	60%	50%	50%
Grade 7	72%	64%	56%

Academic Performance Index, 2009
Number of valid scores................193
2007 API (base)......................797
2008 API (growth)....................830

SAT Testing, 2006-07
Enrollment, Grade 12.................NA
percent taking test..................NA
number with total score 1,500+ ......NA

Average Scores:

Math	Verbal	Writing	Total
NA	NA	NA	NA

Federal No Child Left Behind, 2008
(Adequate Yearly Progress standards met)

	Participation Rate	Pct Proficient
ELA	Yes	Yes
Math	Yes	Yes

API Criteria ....Yes
Graduation rate ....NA
criteria met/possible............... 17/17

Maple Elem

Kern County
29161 Fresno Ave
Shafter, CA 93263
(661) 746-4439

Superint................. Rebecca Devahl
Grade plan............................K-8
Number of schools.......................1
Enrollment.........................272
High school graduates, 2006-07........0
Dropout rate..........................0
Pupil/teacher ratio...............27.2%
Average class size.................. 30.2
Students per computer 4.2
Avg. Teacher Salary, ...$54,977
Avg. Daily Attendence (ADA)..........264
Cost per ADA.................. $6,505

California Achievement Tests 6th ed., 2008
(Pct scoring at or above 50th National Percentile Rank)

	Math	Reading	Language
Grade 3	61%	45%	55%
Grade 7	73%	53%	50%

Academic Performance Index, 2009
Number of valid scores................200
2007 API (base)......................779
2008 API (growth)....................774

SAT Testing, 2006-07
Enrollment, Grade 12.................NA
percent taking test..................NA
number with total score 1,500+ ......NA

Average Scores:

Math	Verbal	Writing	Total
NA	NA	NA	NA

Federal No Child Left Behind, 2008
(Adequate Yearly Progress standards met)

	Participation Rate	Pct Proficient
ELA	Yes	Yes
Math	Yes	Yes

API Criteria ....Yes
Graduation rate ....NA
criteria met/possible............... 17/17

Mark Twain Union Elem

Calaveras County
PO Box 1359
Angels Camp, CA 95222
(209) 736-1855

Superint.............. Kathy Northington
Grade plan............................K-8
Number of schools.......................3
Enrollment.........................813
High school graduates, 2006-07........0
Dropout rate..........................0
Pupil/teacher ratio...............21.8%
Average class size.................. 23.0
Students per computer 3.8
Avg. Teacher Salary, ...$55,985
Avg. Daily Attendence (ADA)..........775
Cost per ADA.................. $7,418

California Achievement Tests 6th ed., 2008
(Pct scoring at or above 50th National Percentile Rank)

	Math	Reading	Language
Grade 3	58%	43%	50%
Grade 7	47%	62%	49%

Academic Performance Index, 2009
Number of valid scores................593
2007 API (base)......................764
2008 API (growth)....................780

SAT Testing, 2006-07
Enrollment, Grade 12.................NA
percent taking test..................NA
number with total score 1,500+ ......NA

Average Scores:

Math	Verbal	Writing	Total
NA	NA	NA	NA

Federal No Child Left Behind, 2008
(Adequate Yearly Progress standards met)

	Participation Rate	Pct Proficient
ELA	Yes	Yes
Math	Yes	No

API Criteria ....Yes
Graduation rate ....NA
criteria met/possible............... 17/16

Mark West Union Elem

Sonoma County
305 Mark West Springs Rd
Santa Rosa, CA 95404
(707) 524-2970

Superint..................... Kay Schultz
Grade plan............................K-6
Number of schools.......................4
Enrollment...................... 1,421
High school graduates, 2006-07........0
Dropout rate..........................0
Pupil/teacher ratio...............19.6%
Average class size.................. 19.8
Students per computer 2.8
Avg. Teacher Salary, ...$62,723
Avg. Daily Attendence (ADA)........ 1,285
Cost per ADA.................. $8,332

California Achievement Tests 6th ed., 2008
(Pct scoring at or above 50th National Percentile Rank)

	Math	Reading	Language
Grade 3	63%	50%	49%
Grade 7	78%	80%	73%

Academic Performance Index, 2009
Number of valid scores................901
2007 API (base)......................827
2008 API (growth)....................815

SAT Testing, 2006-07
Enrollment, Grade 12.................NA
percent taking test..................NA
number with total score 1,500+ ......NA

Average Scores:

Math	Verbal	Writing	Total
NA	NA	NA	NA

Federal No Child Left Behind, 2008
(Adequate Yearly Progress standards met)

	Participation Rate	Pct Proficient
ELA	Yes	Yes
Math	Yes	Yes

API Criteria ....Yes
Graduation rate ....NA
criteria met/possible............... 25/25

McCabe Union Elem

Imperial County
701 West McCabe Rd
El Centro, CA 92243
(760) 352-5443

Superint................. Amanda Brooke
Grade plan............................K-8
Number of schools.......................1
Enrollment...................... 1,065
High school graduates, 2006-07........0
Dropout rate..........................0
Pupil/teacher ratio.............. 22.2%
Average class size.................. 23.6
Students per computer 9.9
Avg. Teacher Salary, ...$57,770
Avg. Daily Attendence (ADA)........ 1,035
Cost per ADA.................. $6,179

California Achievement Tests 6th ed., 2008
(Pct scoring at or above 50th National Percentile Rank)

	Math	Reading	Language
Grade 3	70%	45%	53%
Grade 7	75%	69%	62%

Academic Performance Index, 2009
Number of valid scores................811
2007 API (base)......................822
2008 API (growth)....................843

SAT Testing, 2006-07
Enrollment, Grade 12.................NA
percent taking test..................NA
number with total score 1,500+ ......NA

Average Scores:

Math	Verbal	Writing	Total
NA	NA	NA	NA

Federal No Child Left Behind, 2008
(Adequate Yearly Progress standards met)

	Participation Rate	Pct Proficient
ELA	Yes	Yes
Math	Yes	Yes

API Criteria ....Yes
Graduation rate ....NA
criteria met/possible............... 21/21

McSwain Union Elem

Merced County
926 Scott Rd
Merced, CA 95341
(209) 723-3266

Superint..................... Stan Mollart
Grade plan............................K-8
Number of schools.......................1
Enrollment.........................799
High school graduates, 2006-07........0
Dropout rate..........................0
Pupil/teacher ratio...............21.6%
Average class size.................. 26.1
Students per computer 3.6
Avg. Teacher Salary, ...$65,192
Avg. Daily Attendence (ADA)..........813
Cost per ADA.................. $7,207

California Achievement Tests 6th ed., 2008
(Pct scoring at or above 50th National Percentile Rank)

	Math	Reading	Language
Grade 3	78%	54%	65%
Grade 7	77%	69%	60%

Academic Performance Index, 2009
Number of valid scores................618
2007 API (base)......................832
2008 API (growth)....................852

SAT Testing, 2006-07
Enrollment, Grade 12.................NA
percent taking test..................NA
number with total score 1,500+ ......NA

Average Scores:

Math	Verbal	Writing	Total
NA	NA	NA	NA

Federal No Child Left Behind, 2008
(Adequate Yearly Progress standards met)

	Participation Rate	Pct Proficient
ELA	Yes	Yes
Math	Yes	Yes

API Criteria ....Yes
Graduation rate ....NA
criteria met/possible............... 21/21

Data from school year 2007-08 except where noted.
†Combined data for elementary and high schools.

Meadows Union Elem

Imperial County
2059 Bowker Rd
El Centro, CA 92243
(760) 352-7512

Superint. . . . . Sue Hess
Grade plan. K-8
Number of schools. 1
Enrollment 483
High school graduates, 2006-07 0
Dropout rate. 0
Pupil/teacher ratio. 17.1%
Average class size. 21.0
Students per computer 3.1
Avg. Teacher Salary, ... $64,010
Avg. Daily Attendence (ADA). 491
Cost per ADA. $8,942

California Achievement Tests 6th ed., 2008
(Pct scoring at or above 50th National Percentile Rank)

	Math	Reading	Language
Grade 3	43%	19%	21%
Grade 7	41%	39%	39%

Academic Performance Index, 2009
Number of valid scores. 344
2007 API (base) 696
2008 API (growth). 712

SAT Testing, 2006-07
Enrollment, Grade 12 . . . . NA
percent taking test. . . . . NA
number with total score 1,500+ . . . . . . NA

Average Scores:

Math	Verbal	Writing	Total
NA	NA	NA	NA

Federal No Child Left Behind, 2008
(Adequate Yearly Progress standards met)

	Participation Rate	Pct Proficient
ELA	Yes	No
Math	Yes	No

API Criteria . . . . Yes
Graduation rate . . . . NA
criteria met/possible. 17/15

Menifee Union Elem

Riverside County
30205 Menifee Rd
Menifee, CA 92584
(951) 672-1851

Superint. . . . . Linda Callaway
Grade plan. K-8
Number of schools. 11
Enrollment 9,181
High school graduates, 2006-07 0
Dropout rate. 2.7%
Pupil/teacher ratio. 21.9
Average class size. 24.6
Students per computer 7.7
Avg. Teacher Salary, ... $64,091
Avg. Daily Attendence (ADA). 8,490
Cost per ADA. $7,239

California Achievement Tests 6th ed., 2008
(Pct scoring at or above 50th National Percentile Rank)

	Math	Reading	Language
Grade 3	62%	44%	51%
Grade 7	51%	48%	47%

Academic Performance Index, 2009
Number of valid scores. 6,367
2007 API (base) 772
2008 API (growth). 787

SAT Testing, 2006-07
Enrollment, Grade 12 . . . . NA
percent taking test. . . . . NA
number with total score 1,500+ . . . . . . NA

Average Scores:

Math	Verbal	Writing	Total
NA	NA	NA	NA

Federal No Child Left Behind, 2008
(Adequate Yearly Progress standards met)

	Participation Rate	Pct Proficient
ELA	Yes	No
Math	Yes	Yes

API Criteria . . . . Yes
Graduation rate . . . . NA
criteria met/possible. 37/35

Menlo Park City Elem

San Mateo County
181 Encinal Ave
Atherton, CA 94027
(650) 321-7140

Superint. . . . . Kenneth Ranella
Grade plan. K-8
Number of schools. 4
Enrollment 2,326
High school graduates, 2006-07 0
Dropout rate. 0
Pupil/teacher ratio. 17.2%
Average class size. 22.2
Students per computer 2.8
Avg. Teacher Salary, ... $84,416
Avg. Daily Attendence (ADA). 2,269
Cost per ADA. $11,358

California Achievement Tests 6th ed., 2008
(Pct scoring at or above 50th National Percentile Rank)

	Math	Reading	Language
Grade 3	82%	77%	76%
Grade 7	85%	82%	80%

Academic Performance Index, 2009
Number of valid scores. 1,662
2007 API (base) 911
2008 API (growth). 915

SAT Testing, 2006-07
Enrollment, Grade 12 . . . . NA
percent taking test. . . . . NA
number with total score 1,500+ . . . . . . NA

Average Scores:

Math	Verbal	Writing	Total
NA	NA	NA	NA

Federal No Child Left Behind, 2008
(Adequate Yearly Progress standards met)

	Participation Rate	Pct Proficient
ELA	Yes	Yes
Math	Yes	Yes

API Criteria . . . . Yes
Graduation rate . . . . NA
criteria met/possible. 25/25

Merced City Elem

Merced County
444 West 23rd St
Merced, CA 95340
(209) 385-6600

Superint. . . . . Terry Brace
Grade plan. K-8
Number of schools. 19
Enrollment 10,981
High school graduates, 2006-07 0
Dropout rate. 0
Pupil/teacher ratio. 21.5%
Average class size. 24.7
Students per computer 3.3
Avg. Teacher Salary, ... $70,839
Avg. Daily Attendence (ADA). 10,028
Cost per ADA. $8,192

California Achievement Tests 6th ed., 2008
(Pct scoring at or above 50th National Percentile Rank)

	Math	Reading	Language
Grade 3	51%	34%	45%
Grade 7	44%	42%	36%

Academic Performance Index, 2009
Number of valid scores. 7,823
2007 API (base) 721
2008 API (growth). 729

SAT Testing, 2006-07
Enrollment, Grade 12 . . . . NA
percent taking test. . . . . NA
number with total score 1,500+ . . . . . . NA

Average Scores:

Math	Verbal	Writing	Total
NA	NA	NA	NA

Federal No Child Left Behind, 2008
(Adequate Yearly Progress standards met)

	Participation Rate	Pct Proficient
ELA	No	No
Math	Yes	No

API Criteria . . . . Yes
Graduation rate . . . . NA
criteria met/possible. 33/23

Mill Valley Elem

Marin County
411 Sycamore Ave
Mill Valley, CA 94941
(415) 389-7700

Superint. . . . . Ken Benny
Grade plan. K-8
Number of schools. 6
Enrollment 2,421
High school graduates, 2006-07 0
Dropout rate. 0
Pupil/teacher ratio. 17.3%
Average class size. 21.5
Students per computer 3.8
Avg. Teacher Salary, ... $69,899
Avg. Daily Attendence (ADA). 2,334
Cost per ADA. $11,042

California Achievement Tests 6th ed., 2008
(Pct scoring at or above 50th National Percentile Rank)

	Math	Reading	Language
Grade 3	85%	77%	82%
Grade 7	81%	83%	83%

Academic Performance Index, 2009
Number of valid scores. 1,773
2007 API (base) 916
2008 API (growth). 912

SAT Testing, 2006-07
Enrollment, Grade 12 . . . . NA
percent taking test. . . . . NA
number with total score 1,500+ . . . . . . NA

Average Scores:

Math	Verbal	Writing	Total
NA	NA	NA	NA

Federal No Child Left Behind, 2008
(Adequate Yearly Progress standards met)

	Participation Rate	Pct Proficient
ELA	Yes	Yes
Math	Yes	Yes

API Criteria . . . . Yes
Graduation rate . . . . NA
criteria met/possible. 21/21

Millbrae Elem

San Mateo County
555 Richmond Dr
Millbrae, CA 94030
(650) 697-5693

Superint. . . . . Shirley Martin
Grade plan. K-8
Number of schools. 5
Enrollment 2,124
High school graduates, 2006-07 0
Dropout rate. 0
Pupil/teacher ratio. 20.1%
Average class size. 25.3
Students per computer 4.1
Avg. Teacher Salary, ... $63,062
Avg. Daily Attendence (ADA). 2,082
Cost per ADA. $7,457

California Achievement Tests 6th ed., 2008
(Pct scoring at or above 50th National Percentile Rank)

	Math	Reading	Language
Grade 3	73%	51%	60%
Grade 7	80%	66%	67%

Academic Performance Index, 2009
Number of valid scores. 1,657
2007 API (base) 841
2008 API (growth). 841

SAT Testing, 2006-07
Enrollment, Grade 12 . . . . NA
percent taking test. . . . . NA
number with total score 1,500+ . . . . . . NA

Average Scores:

Math	Verbal	Writing	Total
NA	NA	NA	NA

Federal No Child Left Behind, 2008
(Adequate Yearly Progress standards met)

	Participation Rate	Pct Proficient
ELA	No	No
Math	Yes	No

API Criteria . . . . Yes
Graduation rate . . . . NA
criteria met/possible. 33/30

Data from school year 2007-08 except where noted
†Combined data for elementary and high schools

Mission Union Elem

Monterey County
36825 Foothill Rd
Soledad, CA 93960
(831) 678-3524

Superint....................Jerry Tollefson
Grade plan..........................K-8
Number of schools.......................1
Enrollment..........................102
High school graduates, 2006-07........0
Dropout rate..........................0
Pupil/teacher ratio................19.2%
Average class size.................. 21.1
Students per computer 2.4
Avg. Teacher Salary, ...NA
Avg. Daily Attendence (ADA).........100
Cost per ADA.................. $7,711

California Achievement Tests 6th ed., 2008
(Pct scoring at or above 50th National Percentile Rank)

	Math	Reading	Language
Grade 3	77%	69%	69%
Grade 7	58%	83%	58%

Academic Performance Index, 2009
Number of valid scores.................76
2007 API (base)......................774
2008 API (growth)....................817

SAT Testing, 2006-07
Enrollment, Grade 12.................NA
percent taking test..................NA
number with total score 1,500+ ......NA

Average Scores:

Math	Verbal	Writing	Total
NA	NA	NA	NA

Federal No Child Left Behind, 2008
(Adequate Yearly Progress standards met)

	Participation Rate	Pct Proficient
ELA	Yes	Yes
Math	Yes	Yes

API Criteria ....Yes
Graduation rate ....NA
\# criteria met/possible................. 5/5

Modesto City Elem

Stanislaus County
426 Locust St
Modesto, CA 95351
(209) 576-4011

Superint....................Arturo Flores
Grade plan..........................K-8
Number of schools......................27
Enrollment 16,147
High school graduates, 2006-07........0
Dropout rate..........................0
Pupil/teacher ratio................19.0%
Average class size.................. 24.7
Students per computer 3.9
Avg. Teacher Salary,† $80,360
Avg. Daily Attendence (ADA)† 30,234
Cost per ADA† $8,630

California Achievement Tests 6th ed., 2008
(Pct scoring at or above 50th National Percentile Rank)

	Math	Reading	Language
Grade 3	44%	25%	36%
Grade 7	40%	41%	35%

Academic Performance Index, 2009
Number of valid scores............. 11,047
2007 API (base)......................723
2008 API (growth)....................724

SAT Testing, 2006-07
Enrollment, Grade 12.................NA
percent taking test..................NA
number with total score 1,500+ ......NA

Average Scores:

Math	Verbal	Writing	Total
NA	NA	NA	NA

Federal No Child Left Behind, 2008
(Adequate Yearly Progress standards met)

	Participation Rate	Pct Proficient
ELA	Yes	No
Math	Yes	No

API Criteria ....Yes
Graduation rate ....NA
\# criteria met/possible............... 39/33

Monroe Elem

Fresno County
11842 South Chestnut Ave
Fresno, CA 93725
(559) 834-2895

Superint.................. Shelley Manser
Grade plan..........................K-8
Number of schools.......................1
Enrollment..........................191
High school graduates, 2006-07........0
Dropout rate..........................0
Pupil/teacher ratio................17.0%
Average class size.................. 21.7
Students per computer 8.7
Avg. Teacher Salary, ...$45,029
Avg. Daily Attendence (ADA)..........182
Cost per ADA.................. $8,104

California Achievement Tests 6th ed., 2008
(Pct scoring at or above 50th National Percentile Rank)

	Math	Reading	Language
Grade 3	42%	17%	29%
Grade 7	75%	63%	56%

Academic Performance Index, 2009
Number of valid scores................127
2007 API (base)......................725
2008 API (growth)....................766

SAT Testing, 2006-07
Enrollment, Grade 12.................NA
percent taking test..................NA
number with total score 1,500+ ......NA

Average Scores:

Math	Verbal	Writing	Total
NA	NA	NA	NA

Federal No Child Left Behind, 2008
(Adequate Yearly Progress standards met)

	Participation Rate	Pct Proficient
ELA	Yes	Yes
Math	Yes	Yes

API Criteria ....Yes
Graduation rate ....NA
\# criteria met/possible............... 17/17

Montague Elem

Siskiyou County
PO Box 308
Montague, CA 96064
(530) 459-3001

Superint.................Gilbert Pimentel
Grade plan..........................K-8
Number of schools.......................2
Enrollment..........................137
High school graduates, 2006-07........0
Dropout rate..........................0
Pupil/teacher ratio............... 12.8%
Average class size.................. 14.1
Students per computer 1.7
Avg. Teacher Salary, ...NA
Avg. Daily Attendence (ADA)..........132
Cost per ADA.................. $11,338

California Achievement Tests 6th ed., 2008
(Pct scoring at or above 50th National Percentile Rank)

	Math	Reading	Language
Grade 3	59%	71%	53%
Grade 7	15%	23%	15%

Academic Performance Index, 2009
Number of valid scores................104
2007 API (base)......................698
2008 API (growth)....................718

SAT Testing, 2006-07
Enrollment, Grade 12.................NA
percent taking test..................NA
number with total score 1,500+ ......NA

Average Scores:

Math	Verbal	Writing	Total
NA	NA	NA	NA

Federal No Child Left Behind, 2008
(Adequate Yearly Progress standards met)

	Participation Rate	Pct Proficient
ELA	Yes	No
Math	Yes	Yes

API Criteria ....Yes
Graduation rate ....NA
\# criteria met/possible............... 13/12

Montebello Elem

Santa Clara County
15101 Montebello Rd
Cupertino, CA 95014
(408) 867-3618

Superint................. Barbara Wagner
Grade plan..........................K-6
Number of schools.......................1
Enrollment...........................21
High school graduates, 2006-07........0
Dropout rate.........................NA
Pupil/teacher ratio.................9.1%
Average class size.................. 11.0
Students per computer 1.0
Avg. Teacher Salary, ...NA
Avg. Daily Attendence (ADA)...........21
Cost per ADA.................. $17,830

California Achievement Tests 6th ed., 2008
(Pct scoring at or above 50th National Percentile Rank)

	Math	Reading	Language
Grade 3	NA	NA	NA
Grade 7	NA	NA	NA

Academic Performance Index, 2009
Number of valid scores.................13
2007 API (base)......................782
2008 API (growth)....................787

SAT Testing, 2006-07
Enrollment, Grade 12.................NA
percent taking test..................NA
number with total score 1,500+ ......NA

Average Scores:

Math	Verbal	Writing	Total
NA	NA	NA	NA

Federal No Child Left Behind, 2008
(Adequate Yearly Progress standards met)

	Participation Rate	Pct Proficient
ELA	Yes	Yes
Math	Yes	Yes

API Criteria ....Yes
Graduation rate ....NA
\# criteria met/possible................. 5/5

Montebello Unified

Los Angeles County
123 South Montebello Blvd
Montebello, CA 90640
(323) 887-7900

Superint............... Edward Velasquez
Grade plan.........................K-12
Number of schools......................29
Enrollment 33,493
High school graduates, 2006-07.... 1,721
Dropout rate........................ 3.2
Pupil/teacher ratio................23.7%
Average class size.................. 29.7
Students per computer 6.6
Avg. Teacher Salary, ...$70,515
Avg. Daily Attendence (ADA).......32,764
Cost per ADA.................. $8,211

California Achievement Tests 6th ed., 2008
(Pct scoring at or above 50th National Percentile Rank)

	Math	Reading	Language
Grade 3	47%	24%	38%
Grade 7	39%	31%	32%

Academic Performance Index, 2009
Number of valid scores............. 24,510
2007 API (base)......................668
2008 API (growth)....................679

SAT Testing, 2006-07
Enrollment, Grade 12............... 2,168
percent taking test............... 26.8%
number with total score 1,500+ 144

Average Scores:

Math	Verbal	Writing	Total
461	443	440	1,344

Federal No Child Left Behind, 2008
(Adequate Yearly Progress standards met)

	Participation Rate	Pct Proficient
ELA	Yes	No
Math	Yes	No

API Criteria ....Yes
Graduation rate ....Yes
\# criteria met/possible............... 30/25

Data from school year 2007-08 except where noted.
†Combined data for elementary and high schools.

Montecito Union Elem

Santa Barbara County
385 San Ysidro Rd
Santa Barbara, CA 93108
(805) 969-3249

- Superint: Richard Douglas
- Grade plan: K-6
- Number of schools: 1
  - Enrollment: 415
  - High school graduates, 2006-07: 0
  - Dropout rate: NA
  - Pupil/teacher ratio: 12.6%
  - Average class size: 16.6
  - Students per computer: 1.7
- Avg. Teacher Salary,: $91,035
- Avg. Daily Attendence (ADA): 394
  - Cost per ADA: $18,281

California Achievement Tests 6th ed., 2008
(Pct scoring at or above 50th National Percentile Rank)

	Math	Reading	Language
Grade 3	81%	81%	81%
Grade 7	NA	NA	NA

Academic Performance Index, 2009
- Number of valid scores: 284
- 2007 API (base): 921
- 2008 API (growth): 931

SAT Testing, 2006-07
- Enrollment, Grade 12: NA
  - percent taking test: NA
  - number with total score 1,500+: NA

Average Scores:

Math	Verbal	Writing	Total
NA	NA	NA	NA

Federal No Child Left Behind, 2008
(Adequate Yearly Progress standards met)

	Participation Rate	Pct Proficient
ELA	Yes	Yes
Math	Yes	Yes

- API Criteria: Yes
- Graduation rate: NA
- # criteria met/possible: 9/9

Moraga Elem

Contra Costa County
PO Box 158
Moraga, CA 94556
(925) 376-5943

- Superint: Richard Schafer
- Grade plan: K-8
- Number of schools: 4
  - Enrollment: 1,735
  - High school graduates, 2006-07: 0
  - Dropout rate: 0
  - Pupil/teacher ratio: 20.6%
  - Average class size: 25.9
  - Students per computer: 4.0
- Avg. Teacher Salary,: $61,851
- Avg. Daily Attendence (ADA): 1,699
  - Cost per ADA: $8,751

California Achievement Tests 6th ed., 2008
(Pct scoring at or above 50th National Percentile Rank)

	Math	Reading	Language
Grade 3	93%	87%	90%
Grade 7	93%	89%	85%

Academic Performance Index, 2009
- Number of valid scores: 1,368
- 2007 API (base): 942
- 2008 API (growth): 947

SAT Testing, 2006-07
- Enrollment, Grade 12: NA
  - percent taking test: NA
  - number with total score 1,500+: NA

Average Scores:

Math	Verbal	Writing	Total
NA	NA	NA	NA

Federal No Child Left Behind, 2008
(Adequate Yearly Progress standards met)

	Participation Rate	Pct Proficient
ELA	Yes	Yes
Math	Yes	Yes

- API Criteria: Yes
- Graduation rate: NA
- # criteria met/possible: 17/17

Moreland Elem

Santa Clara County
4711 Campbell Ave
San Jose, CA 95130
(408) 874-2900

- Superint: Glen Ishiwata
- Grade plan: K-8
- Number of schools: 6
  - Enrollment: 3,921
  - High school graduates, 2006-07: 0
  - Dropout rate: 0
  - Pupil/teacher ratio: 20.9%
  - Average class size: 26.4
  - Students per computer: 6.1
- Avg. Teacher Salary,: $68,083
- Avg. Daily Attendence (ADA): 3,807
  - Cost per ADA: $9,245

California Achievement Tests 6th ed., 2008
(Pct scoring at or above 50th National Percentile Rank)

	Math	Reading	Language
Grade 3	71%	56%	65%
Grade 7	69%	62%	62%

Academic Performance Index, 2009
- Number of valid scores: 2,770
- 2007 API (base): 818
- 2008 API (growth): 828

SAT Testing, 2006-07
- Enrollment, Grade 12: NA
  - percent taking test: NA
  - number with total score 1,500+: NA

Average Scores:

Math	Verbal	Writing	Total
NA	NA	NA	NA

Federal No Child Left Behind, 2008
(Adequate Yearly Progress standards met)

	Participation Rate	Pct Proficient
ELA	Yes	No
Math	Yes	No

- API Criteria: Yes
- Graduation rate: NA
- # criteria met/possible: 33/29

Moreno Valley Unified

Riverside County
25634 Alessandro Blvd
Moreno Valley, CA 92553
(951) 571-7500

- Superint: Rowena Lagrosa
- Grade plan: K-12
- Number of schools: 39
  - Enrollment: 37,126
  - High school graduates, 2006-07: 1,833
  - Dropout rate: 7.7
  - Pupil/teacher ratio: 22.3%
  - Average class size: 27.9
  - Students per computer: 4.4
- Avg. Teacher Salary,: $68,655
- Avg. Daily Attendence (ADA): 35,485
  - Cost per ADA: $7,946

California Achievement Tests 6th ed., 2008
(Pct scoring at or above 50th National Percentile Rank)

	Math	Reading	Language
Grade 3	47%	28%	38%
Grade 7	40%	37%	35%

Academic Performance Index, 2009
- Number of valid scores: 26,065
- 2007 API (base): 669
- 2008 API (growth): 686

SAT Testing, 2006-07
- Enrollment, Grade 12: 2,739
  - percent taking test: 22.9%
  - number with total score 1,500+: 167

Average Scores:

Math	Verbal	Writing	Total
455	444	444	1,343

Federal No Child Left Behind, 2008
(Adequate Yearly Progress standards met)

	Participation Rate	Pct Proficient
ELA	Yes	No
Math	Yes	No

- API Criteria: Yes
- Graduation rate: No
- # criteria met/possible: 44/35

Mother Lode Union Elem

El Dorado County
3783 Forni Rd
Placerville, CA 95667
(530) 622-6464

- Superint: Shanda Hahn
- Grade plan: K-8
- Number of schools: 3
  - Enrollment: 1,450
  - High school graduates, 2006-07: 0
  - Dropout rate: 0
  - Pupil/teacher ratio: 20.5%
  - Average class size: 23.6
  - Students per computer: 4.9
- Avg. Teacher Salary,: $55,154
- Avg. Daily Attendence (ADA): 1,415
  - Cost per ADA: $7,786

California Achievement Tests 6th ed., 2008
(Pct scoring at or above 50th National Percentile Rank)

	Math	Reading	Language
Grade 3	67%	56%	64%
Grade 7	78%	75%	71%

Academic Performance Index, 2009
- Number of valid scores: 1,047
- 2007 API (base): 838
- 2008 API (growth): 846

SAT Testing, 2006-07
- Enrollment, Grade 12: NA
  - percent taking test: NA
  - number with total score 1,500+: NA

Average Scores:

Math	Verbal	Writing	Total
NA	NA	NA	NA

Federal No Child Left Behind, 2008
(Adequate Yearly Progress standards met)

	Participation Rate	Pct Proficient
ELA	Yes	Yes
Math	Yes	Yes

- API Criteria: Yes
- Graduation rate: NA
- # criteria met/possible: 23/23

Mountain View Elem

Los Angeles County
3320 Gilman Rd
El Monte, CA 91732
(626) 652-4000

- Superint: Gloria Diaz
- Grade plan: K-8
- Number of schools: 12
  - Enrollment: 8,912
  - High school graduates, 2006-07: 0
  - Dropout rate: 0
  - Pupil/teacher ratio: 20.4%
  - Average class size: 25.0
  - Students per computer: 4.6
- Avg. Teacher Salary,:
- Avg. Daily Attendence (ADA): 8,889
  - Cost per ADA: $9,092

California Achievement Tests 6th ed., 2008
(Pct scoring at or above 50th National Percentile Rank)

	Math	Reading	Language
Grade 3	54%	30%	40%
Grade 7	40%	37%	35%

Academic Performance Index, 2009
- Number of valid scores: 6,351
- 2007 API (base): 695
- 2008 API (growth): 711

SAT Testing, 2006-07
- Enrollment, Grade 12: NA
  - percent taking test: NA
  - number with total score 1,500+: NA

Average Scores:

Math	Verbal	Writing	Total
NA	NA	NA	NA

Federal No Child Left Behind, 2008
(Adequate Yearly Progress standards met)

	Participation Rate	Pct Proficient
ELA	Yes	No
Math	Yes	Yes

- API Criteria: Yes
- Graduation rate: NA
- # criteria met/possible: 25/20

Data from school year 2007-08 except where noted
†Combined data for elementary and high schools

Mountain View Elem

San Bernardino County
2585 South Archibald Ave
Ontario, CA 91761
(909) 947-2992

Superint. . . . . Rick Carr
Grade plan. K-8
Number of schools. 4
Enrollment 2,976
High school graduates, 2006-07 0
Dropout rate. 0
Pupil/teacher ratio. 21.8%
Average class size. 26.2
Students per computer 4.3
Avg. Teacher Salary, ... $74,552
Avg. Daily Attendence (ADA). 2,895
Cost per ADA. $7,226

California Achievement Tests 6th ed., 2008
(Pct scoring at or above 50th National Percentile Rank)

	Math	Reading	Language
Grade 3	60%	39%	53%
Grade 7	47%	46%	48%

Academic Performance Index, 2009
Number of valid scores. 2,184
2007 API (base) 783
2008 API (growth). 799

SAT Testing, 2006-07
Enrollment, Grade 12 . . . . NA
percent taking test. . . . . NA
number with total score 1,500+ . . . . . . NA

Average Scores:

Math	Verbal	Writing	Total
NA	NA	NA	NA

Federal No Child Left Behind, 2008
(Adequate Yearly Progress standards met)

	Participation Rate	Pct Proficient
ELA	No	No
Math	Yes	No

API Criteria . . . . Yes
Graduation rate . . . . NA
criteria met/possible. 29/26

Mountain View Whisman

Santa Clara County
750 A San Pierre Way
Mountain View, CA 94043
(650) 526-3500

Superint. . . . . Maurice Ghysels
Grade plan. K-8
Number of schools. 8
Enrollment 4,406
High school graduates, 2006-07 0
Dropout rate. 0
Pupil/teacher ratio. 20.1%
Average class size. 24.6
Students per computer 4.2
Avg. Teacher Salary, ... $61,094
Avg. Daily Attendence (ADA). 4,309
Cost per ADA. $8,900

California Achievement Tests 6th ed., 2008
(Pct scoring at or above 50th National Percentile Rank)

	Math	Reading	Language
Grade 3	63%	41%	51%
Grade 7	62%	54%	55%

Academic Performance Index, 2009
Number of valid scores. 2,968
2007 API (base) 785
2008 API (growth). 806

SAT Testing, 2006-07
Enrollment, Grade 12 . . . . NA
percent taking test. . . . . NA
number with total score 1,500+ . . . . . . NA

Average Scores:

Math	Verbal	Writing	Total
NA	NA	NA	NA

Federal No Child Left Behind, 2008
(Adequate Yearly Progress standards met)

	Participation Rate	Pct Proficient
ELA	Yes	No
Math	Yes	No

API Criteria . . . . Yes
Graduation rate . . . . NA
criteria met/possible. 37/33

Mt. Diablo Unified

Contra Costa County
1936 Carlotta Dr
Concord, CA 94519
(925) 682-8000

Superint. . . . . Richard Nicholl
Grade plan. K-12
Number of schools. 55
Enrollment 35,355
High school graduates, 2006-07 2,153
Dropout rate. 6
Pupil/teacher ratio. 20.4%
Average class size. 26.4
Students per computer 5.2
Avg. Teacher Salary, ... $60,714
Avg. Daily Attendence (ADA). 33,956
Cost per ADA. $8,368

California Achievement Tests 6th ed., 2008
(Pct scoring at or above 50th National Percentile Rank)

	Math	Reading	Language
Grade 3	60%	45%	55%
Grade 7	53%	53%	51%

Academic Performance Index, 2009
Number of valid scores. 25,920
2007 API (base) 747
2008 API (growth). 755

SAT Testing, 2006-07
Enrollment, Grade 12 2,734
percent taking test. 38.9%
number with total score 1,500+ 622

Average Scores:

Math	Verbal	Writing	Total
543	521	518	1,582

Federal No Child Left Behind, 2008
(Adequate Yearly Progress standards met)

	Participation Rate	Pct Proficient
ELA	Yes	No
Math	Yes	No

API Criteria . . . . Yes
Graduation rate . . . . Yes
criteria met/possible. 46/36

Mt. Pleasant Elem

Santa Clara County
3434 Marten Ave
San Jose, CA 95148
(408) 223-3700

Superint. . . . . George Perez
Grade plan. K-8
Number of schools. 5
Enrollment 2,925
High school graduates, 2006-07 0
Dropout rate. 0
Pupil/teacher ratio. 20.5%
Average class size. 24.7
Students per computer 5.8
Avg. Teacher Salary, ... $62,180
Avg. Daily Attendence (ADA). 2,846
Cost per ADA. $8,449

California Achievement Tests 6th ed., 2008
(Pct scoring at or above 50th National Percentile Rank)

	Math	Reading	Language
Grade 3	45%	26%	37%
Grade 7	46%	41%	37%

Academic Performance Index, 2009
Number of valid scores. 2,094
2007 API (base) 729
2008 API (growth). 734

SAT Testing, 2006-07
Enrollment, Grade 12 . . . . NA
percent taking test. . . . . NA
number with total score 1,500+ . . . . . . NA

Average Scores:

Math	Verbal	Writing	Total
NA	NA	NA	NA

Federal No Child Left Behind, 2008
(Adequate Yearly Progress standards met)

	Participation Rate	Pct Proficient
ELA	Yes	No
Math	Yes	No

API Criteria . . . . Yes
Graduation rate . . . . NA
criteria met/possible. 31/28

Mt. Shasta Union Elem

Siskiyou County
595 East Alma St
Mt. Shasta, CA 96067
(530) 926-6007

Superint. . . . . Gary Lampella
Grade plan. K-8
Number of schools. 3
Enrollment 630
High school graduates, 2006-07 0
Dropout rate. 0
Pupil/teacher ratio. 17.3%
Average class size. 24.3
Students per computer 2.5
Avg. Teacher Salary, ... $56,635
Avg. Daily Attendence (ADA). 582
Cost per ADA. $8,903

California Achievement Tests 6th ed., 2008
(Pct scoring at or above 50th National Percentile Rank)

	Math	Reading	Language
Grade 3	70%	65%	65%
Grade 7	81%	88%	83%

Academic Performance Index, 2009
Number of valid scores. 472
2007 API (base) 849
2008 API (growth). 842

SAT Testing, 2006-07
Enrollment, Grade 12 . . . . NA
percent taking test. . . . . NA
number with total score 1,500+ . . . . . . NA

Average Scores:

Math	Verbal	Writing	Total
NA	NA	NA	NA

Federal No Child Left Behind, 2008
(Adequate Yearly Progress standards met)

	Participation Rate	Pct Proficient
ELA	Yes	Yes
Math	Yes	Yes

API Criteria . . . . Yes
Graduation rate . . . . NA
criteria met/possible. 13/13

Mulberry Elem

Imperial County
1391 East Rutherford Rd
Brawley, CA 92227
(760) 344-8600

Superint. . . . . Danny Eddins
Grade plan. K-8
Number of schools. 1
Enrollment 78
High school graduates, 2006-07 0
Dropout rate. 0
Pupil/teacher ratio. 19.5%
Average class size. 19.5
Students per computer 4.1
Avg. Teacher Salary, ... $44,141
Avg. Daily Attendence (ADA). 73
Cost per ADA. $9,136

California Achievement Tests 6th ed., 2008
(Pct scoring at or above 50th National Percentile Rank)

	Math	Reading	Language
Grade 3	NA	NA	NA
Grade 7	NA	NA	NA

Academic Performance Index, 2009
Number of valid scores. 43
2007 API (base) 845
2008 API (growth). 809

SAT Testing, 2006-07
Enrollment, Grade 12 . . . . NA
percent taking test. . . . . NA
number with total score 1,500+ . . . . . . NA

Average Scores:

Math	Verbal	Writing	Total
NA	NA	NA	NA

Federal No Child Left Behind, 2008
(Adequate Yearly Progress standards met)

	Participation Rate	Pct Proficient
ELA	Yes	Yes
Math	Yes	Yes

API Criteria . . . . Yes
Graduation rate . . . . NA
criteria met/possible. 5/5

Data from school year 2007-08 except where noted.
†Combined data for elementary and high schools.

Mupu Elem
Ventura County
4410 North Ojai Rd
Santa Paula, CA 93060
(805) 525-0422

Superint. . . . . Jeanine Gore
Grade plan. K-8
Number of schools. 1
Enrollment 127
High school graduates, 2006-07. 0
Dropout rate. 0
Pupil/teacher ratio. 18.8%
Average class size. 18.6
Students per computer 6.4
Avg. Teacher Salary, ... $60,020
Avg. Daily Attendence (ADA). 129
Cost per ADA. $7,124

California Achievement Tests 6th ed., 2008
(Pct scoring at or above 50th National Percentile Rank)

	Math	Reading	Language
Grade 3	69%	77%	46%
Grade 7	56%	44%	50%

Academic Performance Index, 2009
Number of valid scores. 95
2007 API (base) 770
2008 API (growth). 788

SAT Testing, 2006-07
Enrollment, Grade 12 . . . . . NA
percent taking test. . . . . NA
number with total score 1,500+ . . . . . NA

Average Scores:

Math	Verbal	Writing	Total
NA	NA	NA	NA

Federal No Child Left Behind, 2008
(Adequate Yearly Progress standards met)

	Participation Rate	Pct Proficient
ELA	Yes	Yes
Math	Yes	Yes

API Criteria . . . . . Yes
Graduation rate . . . . . NA
criteria met/possible. 7/7

Muroc Joint Unified
Kern County
17100 Foothill Ave
North Edwards, CA 93523
(760) 769-4821

Superint. . . . . Rob Challinor
Grade plan. K-12
Number of schools. 7
Enrollment 1,989
High school graduates, 2006-07. 159
Dropout rate. 2
Pupil/teacher ratio. 19.5%
Average class size. 22.0
Students per computer 4.0
Avg. Teacher Salary, ... $59,021
Avg. Daily Attendence (ADA). 1,921
Cost per ADA. $9,660

California Achievement Tests 6th ed., 2008
(Pct scoring at or above 50th National Percentile Rank)

	Math	Reading	Language
Grade 3	69%	50%	58%
Grade 7	63%	65%	59%

Academic Performance Index, 2009
Number of valid scores. 1,386
2007 API (base) 773
2008 API (growth). 796

SAT Testing, 2006-07
Enrollment, Grade 12 157
percent taking test. 35.0%
number with total score 1,500+ 26

Average Scores:

Math	Verbal	Writing	Total
518	498	486	1,502

Federal No Child Left Behind, 2008
(Adequate Yearly Progress standards met)

	Participation Rate	Pct Proficient
ELA	Yes	Yes
Math	Yes	Yes

API Criteria . . . . . Yes
Graduation rate . . . . . Yes
criteria met/possible. 26/26

National Elem
San Diego County
1500 N Ave
National City, CA 91950
(619) 336-7500

Superint. . . . . Dennis Doyle
Grade plan. K-6
Number of schools. 11
Enrollment 5,900
High school graduates, 2006-07. 0
Dropout rate. . . . . NA
Pupil/teacher ratio. 21.8%
Average class size. 22.1
Students per computer 2.6
Avg. Teacher Salary, ... $64,308
Avg. Daily Attendence (ADA). 5,668
Cost per ADA. $8,320

California Achievement Tests 6th ed., 2008
(Pct scoring at or above 50th National Percentile Rank)

	Math	Reading	Language
Grade 3	55%	25%	35%
Grade 7	NA	NA	NA

Academic Performance Index, 2009
Number of valid scores. 3,851
2007 API (base) 745
2008 API (growth). 763

SAT Testing, 2006-07
Enrollment, Grade 12 . . . . . NA
percent taking test. . . . . NA
number with total score 1,500+ . . . . . NA

Average Scores:

Math	Verbal	Writing	Total
NA	NA	NA	NA

Federal No Child Left Behind, 2008
(Adequate Yearly Progress standards met)

	Participation Rate	Pct Proficient
ELA	Yes	Yes
Math	Yes	Yes

API Criteria . . . . . Yes
Graduation rate . . . . . NA
criteria met/possible. 31/31

Natomas Unified
Sacramento County
1901 Arena Blvd
Sacramento, CA 95834
(916) 567-5400

Superint. . . . . Steve Farrar
Grade plan. K-12
Number of schools. 16
Enrollment 11,406
High school graduates, 2006-07. 631
Dropout rate. 4.7
Pupil/teacher ratio. 20.7%
Average class size. 27.1
Students per computer 4.0
Avg. Teacher Salary, ... $58,286
Avg. Daily Attendence (ADA). 9,747
Cost per ADA. $7,621

California Achievement Tests 6th ed., 2008
(Pct scoring at or above 50th National Percentile Rank)

	Math	Reading	Language
Grade 3	54%	36%	43%
Grade 7	47%	49%	47%

Academic Performance Index, 2009
Number of valid scores. 8,000
2007 API (base) 731
2008 API (growth). 727

SAT Testing, 2006-07
Enrollment, Grade 12 671
percent taking test. 38.2%
number with total score 1,500+ 82

Average Scores:

Math	Verbal	Writing	Total
474	460	457	1,391

Federal No Child Left Behind, 2008
(Adequate Yearly Progress standards met)

	Participation Rate	Pct Proficient
ELA	Yes	No
Math	No	No

API Criteria . . . . . Yes
Graduation rate . . . . . Yes
criteria met/possible. 40/36

Nevada City Elem
Nevada County
800 Hoover Ln
Nevada City, CA 95959
(530) 265-1826

Superint. . . . . Roger Steel
Grade plan. K-8
Number of schools. 6
Enrollment 1,286
High school graduates, 2006-07. 0
Dropout rate. 0
Pupil/teacher ratio. 20.4%
Average class size. 22.5
Students per computer 4.7
Avg. Teacher Salary, ... $62,612
Avg. Daily Attendence (ADA). 1,167
Cost per ADA. $8,056

California Achievement Tests 6th ed., 2008
(Pct scoring at or above 50th National Percentile Rank)

	Math	Reading	Language
Grade 3	68%	67%	65%
Grade 7	77%	76%	68%

Academic Performance Index, 2009
Number of valid scores. 1,013
2007 API (base) 842
2008 API (growth). 851

SAT Testing, 2006-07
Enrollment, Grade 12 . . . . . NA
percent taking test. . . . . NA
number with total score 1,500+ . . . . . NA

Average Scores:

Math	Verbal	Writing	Total
NA	NA	NA	NA

Federal No Child Left Behind, 2008
(Adequate Yearly Progress standards met)

	Participation Rate	Pct Proficient
ELA	Yes	Yes
Math	Yes	Yes

API Criteria . . . . . Yes
Graduation rate . . . . . NA
criteria met/possible. 17/17

New Jerusalem Elem
San Joaquin County
31400 South Koster Rd
Tracy, CA 95304
(209) 835-2597

Superint. . . . . David Thoming
Grade plan. K-12
Number of schools. 3
Enrollment 614
High school graduates, 2006-07. 62
Dropout rate. 6.6
Pupil/teacher ratio. 20.8%
Average class size. 26.2
Students per computer 3.2
Avg. Teacher Salary, ... $47,931
Avg. Daily Attendence (ADA). 238
Cost per ADA. $8,062

California Achievement Tests 6th ed., 2008
(Pct scoring at or above 50th National Percentile Rank)

	Math	Reading	Language
Grade 3	46%	46%	54%
Grade 7	50%	54%	44%

Academic Performance Index, 2009
Number of valid scores. 176
2007 API (base) 686
2008 API (growth). 747

SAT Testing, 2006-07
Enrollment, Grade 12 72
percent taking test. 5.6%
number with total score 1,500+ . . . . . NA

Average Scores:

Math	Verbal	Writing	Total
NA	NA	NA	NA

Federal No Child Left Behind, 2008
(Adequate Yearly Progress standards met)

	Participation Rate	Pct Proficient
ELA	Yes	No
Math	Yes	Yes

API Criteria . . . . . Yes
Graduation rate . . . . . Yes
criteria met/possible. 18/17

Data from school year 2007-08 except where noted
†Combined data for elementary and high schools

Newhall Elem
Los Angeles County
25375 Orchard Village Rd, Ste 200, Suite 200
Valencia, CA 91355
(661) 291-4000

Superint.................... Marc Winger
Grade plan........................... K-6
Number of schools..................... 10
Enrollment...................... 7,008
High school graduates, 2006-07........ 0
Dropout rate........................ NA
Pupil/teacher ratio................ 21.2%
Average class size.................. 21.4
Students per computer.............. 4.3
Avg. Teacher Salary,.............. $61,674
Avg. Daily Attendence (ADA)........ 6,893
Cost per ADA................... $7,357

California Achievement Tests 6th ed., 2008
(Pct scoring at or above 50th National Percentile Rank)

	Math	Reading	Language
Grade 3	73%	54%	64%
Grade 7	NA	NA	NA

Academic Performance Index, 2009
Number of valid scores.............. 4,805
2007 API (base)...................... 873
2008 API (growth).................... 882

SAT Testing, 2006-07
Enrollment, Grade 12................. NA
percent taking test.................. NA
number with total score 1,500+...... NA

Average Scores:

Math	Verbal	Writing	Total
NA	NA	NA	NA

Federal No Child Left Behind, 2008
(Adequate Yearly Progress standards met)

	Participation Rate	Pct Proficient
ELA	Yes	Yes
Math	Yes	Yes

API Criteria.......................... Yes
Graduation rate...................... NA
criteria met/possible............... 37/37

Norris Elem
Kern County
6940 Calloway Dr
Bakersfield, CA 93312
(661) 387-7000

Superint............. Wallace McCormick
Grade plan........................... K-8
Number of schools...................... 5
Enrollment...................... 3,872
High school graduates, 2006-07........ 0
Dropout rate.......................... 0
Pupil/teacher ratio............... 22.9%
Average class size.................. 25.6
Students per computer.............. 4.6
Avg. Teacher Salary,.................. NA
Avg. Daily Attendence (ADA)........ 3,376
Cost per ADA................... $6,235

California Achievement Tests 6th ed., 2008
(Pct scoring at or above 50th National Percentile Rank)

	Math	Reading	Language
Grade 3	72%	57%	63%
Grade 7	62%	55%	53%

Academic Performance Index, 2009
Number of valid scores.............. 2,510
2007 API (base)...................... 820
2008 API (growth).................... 814

SAT Testing, 2006-07
Enrollment, Grade 12................. NA
percent taking test.................. NA
number with total score 1,500+...... NA

Average Scores:

Math	Verbal	Writing	Total
NA	NA	NA	NA

Federal No Child Left Behind, 2008
(Adequate Yearly Progress standards met)

	Participation Rate	Pct Proficient
ELA	Yes	Yes
Math	Yes	No

API Criteria.......................... Yes
Graduation rate...................... NA
criteria met/possible............... 29/28

North County Joint Union Elem
San Benito County
500 Spring Grove Rd
Hollister, CA 95023
(831) 637-5574

Superint.................... Evelyn Muro
Grade plan........................... K-8
Number of schools...................... 1
Enrollment........................ 564
High school graduates, 2006-07........ 0
Dropout rate.......................... 0
Pupil/teacher ratio............... 19.7%
Average class size.................. 23.0
Students per computer.............. 8.1
Avg. Teacher Salary,.............. $57,763
Avg. Daily Attendence (ADA).......... 561
Cost per ADA................... $7,547

California Achievement Tests 6th ed., 2008
(Pct scoring at or above 50th National Percentile Rank)

	Math	Reading	Language
Grade 3	70%	43%	51%
Grade 7	70%	55%	51%

Academic Performance Index, 2009
Number of valid scores................ 404
2007 API (base)...................... 792
2008 API (growth).................... 805

SAT Testing, 2006-07
Enrollment, Grade 12................. NA
percent taking test.................. NA
number with total score 1,500+...... NA

Average Scores:

Math	Verbal	Writing	Total
NA	NA	NA	NA

Federal No Child Left Behind, 2008
(Adequate Yearly Progress standards met)

	Participation Rate	Pct Proficient
ELA	Yes	Yes
Math	Yes	Yes

API Criteria.......................... Yes
Graduation rate...................... NA
criteria met/possible............... 21/21

North Monterey County Unified
Monterey County
8142 Moss Landing Rd
Moss Landing, CA 95039
(831) 633-3343

Superint.................... Carolyn Post
Grade plan.......................... K-12
Number of schools...................... 8
Enrollment...................... 4,628
High school graduates, 2006-07...... 376
Dropout rate........................ 2.9
Pupil/teacher ratio................ 21.1%
Average class size.................. 26.0
Students per computer.............. 4.4
Avg. Teacher Salary,.................. NA
Avg. Daily Attendence (ADA)........ 4,418
Cost per ADA................... $8,361

California Achievement Tests 6th ed., 2008
(Pct scoring at or above 50th National Percentile Rank)

	Math	Reading	Language
Grade 3	38%	17%	22%
Grade 7	39%	38%	36%

Academic Performance Index, 2009
Number of valid scores.............. 3,212
2007 API (base)...................... 679
2008 API (growth).................... 683

SAT Testing, 2006-07
Enrollment, Grade 12................. 418
percent taking test................ 33.7%
number with total score 1,500+....... 43

Average Scores:

Math	Verbal	Writing	Total
457	462	439	1,358

Federal No Child Left Behind, 2008
(Adequate Yearly Progress standards met)

	Participation Rate	Pct Proficient
ELA	Yes	No
Math	Yes	No

API Criteria.......................... Yes
Graduation rate...................... Yes
criteria met/possible............... 26/17

North Sacramento Elem
Sacramento County
(merged into Twin Rivers Unified)
5115 Dudley Blvd
North Highlands, CA 95660
(916) 566-1786

Superint.................... Frank Porter
Grade plan........................... K-6
Number of schools..................... 10
Enrollment...................... 5,017
High school graduates, 2006-07........ 0
Dropout rate.......................... 0
Pupil/teacher ratio............... 18.8%
Average class size.................. 21.6
Students per computer.............. 4.3
Avg. Teacher Salary,.............. $60,863
Avg. Daily Attendence (ADA)........ 3,805
Cost per ADA.................. $10,258

California Achievement Tests 6th ed., 2008
(Pct scoring at or above 50th National Percentile Rank)

	Math	Reading	Language
Grade 3	37%	23%	31%
Grade 7	38%	38%	37%

Academic Performance Index, 2009
Number of valid scores.............. 3,165
2007 API (base)...................... 699
2008 API (growth).................... 718

SAT Testing, 2006-07
Enrollment, Grade 12................. NA
percent taking test.................. NA

Average Scores:

Math	Verbal	Writing	Total
NA	NA	NA	NA

Federal No Child Left Behind, 2008
(Adequate Yearly Progress standards met)

	Participation Rate	Pct Proficient
ELA	Yes	No
Math	Yes	No

API Criteria.......................... Yes
Graduation rate...................... NA
criteria met/possible............... 33/26

Nuestro Elem
Sutter County
3934 Broadway Rd
Live Oak, CA 95953
(530) 822-5100

Superint...................... Irwin Karp
Grade plan........................... K-8
Number of schools...................... 2
Enrollment........................ 394
High school graduates, 2006-07........ 0
Dropout rate.......................... 0
Pupil/teacher ratio............... 14.6%
Average class size.................. 21.2
Students per computer.............. 1.3
Avg. Teacher Salary,.................. NA
Avg. Daily Attendence (ADA).......... 128
Cost per ADA................... $7,729

California Achievement Tests 6th ed., 2008
(Pct scoring at or above 50th National Percentile Rank)

	Math	Reading	Language
Grade 3	53%	59%	59%
Grade 7	45%	55%	64%

Academic Performance Index, 2009
Number of valid scores................. 96
2007 API (base)...................... 776
2008 API (growth).................... 753

SAT Testing, 2006-07
Enrollment, Grade 12................. NA
percent taking test.................. NA
number with total score 1,500+...... NA

Average Scores:

Math	Verbal	Writing	Total
NA	NA	NA	NA

Federal No Child Left Behind, 2008
(Adequate Yearly Progress standards met)

	Participation Rate	Pct Proficient
ELA	Yes	Yes
Math	Yes	Yes

API Criteria.......................... Yes
Graduation rate...................... NA
criteria met/possible................. 7/7

Data from school year 2007-08 except where noted.
†Combined data for elementary and high schools.

Oak Grove Elem
Santa Clara County
6578 Santa Teresa Blvd
San Jose, CA 95119
(408) 227-8300

Superint. . . . . Manny Barbara
Grade plan. K-8
Number of schools. 20
Enrollment 11,874
High school graduates, 2006-07. 0
Dropout rate. 0
Pupil/teacher ratio. 21.9%
Average class size. 25.3
Students per computer 5.9
Avg. Teacher Salary, ... $66,854
Avg. Daily Attendence (ADA). 11,691
Cost per ADA. $7,977

California Achievement Tests 6th ed., 2008
(Pct scoring at or above 50th National Percentile Rank)

	Math	Reading	Language
Grade 3	63%	40%	52%
Grade 7	59%	51%	49%

Academic Performance Index, 2009
Number of valid scores. 8,672
2007 API (base) 774
2008 API (growth). 788

SAT Testing, 2006-07
Enrollment, Grade 12 . . . . NA
percent taking test. . . . . NA
number with total score 1,500+ . . . . . . NA

Average Scores:

Math	Verbal	Writing	Total
NA	NA	NA	NA

Federal No Child Left Behind, 2008
(Adequate Yearly Progress standards met)

	Participation Rate	Pct Proficient
ELA	Yes	No
Math	Yes	No

API Criteria . . . . Yes
Graduation rate . . . . NA
\# criteria met/possible. 37/35

Oak Grove Union Elem
Sonoma County
5299 Hall Rd
Santa Rosa, CA 95401
(707) 545-0171

Superint. . . . . Noel Buehler
Grade plan. K-8
Number of schools. 2
Enrollment 722
High school graduates, 2006-07. 0
Dropout rate. 0
Pupil/teacher ratio. 20.2%
Average class size. 27.2
Students per computer 5.7
Avg. Teacher Salary, ... $55,358
Avg. Daily Attendence (ADA). 714
Cost per ADA. $7,819

California Achievement Tests 6th ed., 2008
(Pct scoring at or above 50th National Percentile Rank)

	Math	Reading	Language
Grade 3	91%	84%	70%
Grade 7	68%	70%	68%

Academic Performance Index, 2009
Number of valid scores. 593
2007 API (base) 809
2008 API (growth). 822

SAT Testing, 2006-07
Enrollment, Grade 12 . . . . NA
percent taking test. . . . . NA
number with total score 1,500+ . . . . . . NA

Average Scores:

Math	Verbal	Writing	Total
NA	NA	NA	NA

Federal No Child Left Behind, 2008
(Adequate Yearly Progress standards met)

	Participation Rate	Pct Proficient
ELA	Yes	Yes
Math	Yes	Yes

API Criteria . . . . Yes
Graduation rate . . . . NA
\# criteria met/possible. 17/17

Oak Valley Union Elem
Tulare County
24500 Road 68
Tulare, CA 93274
(559) 688-2908

Superint. . . . . Kerry Beauchaine
Grade plan. K-8
Number of schools. 1
Enrollment 461
High school graduates, 2006-07. 0
Dropout rate. 0
Pupil/teacher ratio. 23.0%
Average class size. 24.2
Students per computer 5.8
Avg. Teacher Salary, ... $58,130
Avg. Daily Attendence (ADA). 452
Cost per ADA. $6,603

California Achievement Tests 6th ed., 2008
(Pct scoring at or above 50th National Percentile Rank)

	Math	Reading	Language
Grade 3	44%	33%	44%
Grade 7	51%	49%	51%

Academic Performance Index, 2009
Number of valid scores. 323
2007 API (base) 766
2008 API (growth). 767

SAT Testing, 2006-07
Enrollment, Grade 12 . . . . NA
percent taking test. . . . . NA
number with total score 1,500+ . . . . . . NA

Average Scores:

Math	Verbal	Writing	Total
NA	NA	NA	NA

Federal No Child Left Behind, 2008
(Adequate Yearly Progress standards met)

	Participation Rate	Pct Proficient
ELA	Yes	No
Math	Yes	Yes

API Criteria . . . . Yes
Graduation rate . . . . NA
\# criteria met/possible. 21/20

Oakley Union Elem
Contra Costa County
91 Mercedes Ln
Oakley, CA 94561
(925) 625-0700

Superint. . . . . Richard Rogers
Grade plan. K-8
Number of schools. 7
Enrollment 4,637
High school graduates, 2006-07. 0
Dropout rate. 0
Pupil/teacher ratio. 19.7%
Average class size. 25.6
Students per computer 5.7
Avg. Teacher Salary, ... $61,570
Avg. Daily Attendence (ADA). 4,562
Cost per ADA. $7,405

California Achievement Tests 6th ed., 2008
(Pct scoring at or above 50th National Percentile Rank)

	Math	Reading	Language
Grade 3	46%	34%	41%
Grade 7	49%	55%	54%

Academic Performance Index, 2009
Number of valid scores. 3,488
2007 API (base) 749
2008 API (growth). 739

SAT Testing, 2006-07
Enrollment, Grade 12 . . . . NA
percent taking test. . . . . NA
number with total score 1,500+ . . . . . . NA

Average Scores:

Math	Verbal	Writing	Total
NA	NA	NA	NA

Federal No Child Left Behind, 2008
(Adequate Yearly Progress standards met)

	Participation Rate	Pct Proficient
ELA	Yes	No
Math	Yes	No

API Criteria . . . . Yes
Graduation rate . . . . NA
\# criteria met/possible. 33/24

Ocean View Elem
Orange County
4200 Olds Rd
Oxnard, CA 93033
(714) 847-2551

Superint. . . . . Alan Rasmussen
Grade plan. K-8
Number of schools. 15
Enrollment 9,412
High school graduates, 2006-07. 0
Dropout rate. 0
Pupil/teacher ratio. 22.8%
Average class size. 26.9
Students per computer 3.9
Avg. Teacher Salary, ...
Avg. Daily Attendence (ADA). 9,215
Cost per ADA. $8,185

California Achievement Tests 6th ed., 2008
(Pct scoring at or above 50th National Percentile Rank)

	Math	Reading	Language
Grade 3	69%	49%	60%
Grade 7	68%	62%	58%

Academic Performance Index, 2009
Number of valid scores. 6,943
2007 API (base) 831
2008 API (growth). 845

SAT Testing, 2006-07
Enrollment, Grade 12 . . . . NA
percent taking test. . . . . NA
number with total score 1,500+ . . . . . . NA

Average Scores:

Math	Verbal	Writing	Total
NA	NA	NA	NA

Federal No Child Left Behind, 2008
(Adequate Yearly Progress standards met)

	Participation Rate	Pct Proficient
ELA	Yes	No
Math	Yes	No

API Criteria . . . . Yes
Graduation rate . . . . NA
\# criteria met/possible. 33/31

Ocean View Elem
Ventura County
17200 Pinehurst Ln
Huntington Beach, CA 92647
(805) 488-4441

Superint. . . . . Nancy Carroll
Grade plan. K-8
Number of schools. 4
Enrollment 2,476
High school graduates, 2006-07. 0
Dropout rate. 0
Pupil/teacher ratio. 19.3%
Average class size. 26.3
Students per computer 7.2
Avg. Teacher Salary, ... $63,185
Avg. Daily Attendence (ADA). 2,480
Cost per ADA. $8,764

California Achievement Tests 6th ed., 2008
(Pct scoring at or above 50th National Percentile Rank)

	Math	Reading	Language
Grade 3	54%	27%	36%
Grade 7	49%	37%	40%

Academic Performance Index, 2009
Number of valid scores. 1,702
2007 API (base) 706
2008 API (growth). 716

SAT Testing, 2006-07
Enrollment, Grade 12 . . . . NA
percent taking test. . . . . NA
number with total score 1,500+ . . . . . . NA

Average Scores:

Math	Verbal	Writing	Total
NA	NA	NA	NA

Federal No Child Left Behind, 2008
(Adequate Yearly Progress standards met)

	Participation Rate	Pct Proficient
ELA	Yes	No
Math	Yes	No

API Criteria . . . . Yes
Graduation rate . . . . NA
\# criteria met/possible. 25/19

Data from school year 2007-08 except where noted
†Combined data for elementary and high schools

Old Adobe Union Elem

Sonoma County
845 Crinella Dr
Petaluma, CA 94954
(707) 765-4322

Superint. . . . . Diane Zimmerman
Grade plan. K-6
Number of schools. 5
Enrollment 1,832
High school graduates, 2006-07 0
Dropout rate. . . . . NA
Pupil/teacher ratio. 21.6%
Average class size. 21.6
Students per computer 4.0
Avg. Teacher Salary, ... $63,768
Avg. Daily Attendence (ADA). 1,801
Cost per ADA. $8,192

California Achievement Tests 6th ed., 2008
(Pct scoring at or above 50th National Percentile Rank)

	Math	Reading	Language
Grade 3	58%	47%	52%
Grade 7	NA	NA	NA

Academic Performance Index, 2009
Number of valid scores. 1,242
2007 API (base) 802
2008 API (growth). 805

SAT Testing, 2006-07
Enrollment, Grade 12 . . . . .NA
percent taking test. . . . . .NA
number with total score 1,500+ . . . . . .NA

Average Scores:

Math	Verbal	Writing	Total
NA	NA	NA	NA

Federal No Child Left Behind, 2008
(Adequate Yearly Progress standards met)

	Participation Rate	Pct Proficient
ELA	Yes	No
Math	Yes	Yes

API Criteria . . . . .Yes
Graduation rate . . . . .NA
criteria met/possible. 25/22

Ontario-Montclair Elem

San Bernardino County
950 West D St
Ontario, CA 91762
(909) 459-2500

Superint. Virgil Barnes
Grade plan. K-8
Number of schools. .33
Enrollment 23,307
High school graduates, 2006-07 0
Dropout rate. 0
Pupil/teacher ratio. 20.9%
Average class size. 25.6
Students per computer 6.2
Avg. Teacher Salary, ... $66,530
Avg. Daily Attendence (ADA). 23,213
Cost per ADA. $8,177

California Achievement Tests 6th ed., 2008
(Pct scoring at or above 50th National Percentile Rank)

	Math	Reading	Language
Grade 3	38%	22%	33%
Grade 7	39%	32%	32%

Academic Performance Index, 2009
Number of valid scores. 16,888
2007 API (base) 680
2008 API (growth). 699

SAT Testing, 2006-07
Enrollment, Grade 12 . . . . .NA
percent taking test. . . . . .NA
number with total score 1,500+ . . . . . .NA

Average Scores:

Math	Verbal	Writing	Total
NA	NA	NA	NA

Federal No Child Left Behind, 2008
(Adequate Yearly Progress standards met)

	Participation Rate	Pct Proficient
ELA	Yes	No
Math	Yes	No

API Criteria . . . . .Yes
Graduation rate . . . . .NA
criteria met/possible. 37/30

Orange Center

Fresno County
3530 South Cherry Ave
Fresno, CA 93706
(559) 237-0437

Superint. . . . . John Stahl
Grade plan. K-8
Number of schools. 1
Enrollment 348
High school graduates, 2006-07 0
Dropout rate. 0
Pupil/teacher ratio. 21.1%
Average class size. 21.8
Students per computer 3.9
Avg. Teacher Salary, ... $52,849
Avg. Daily Attendence (ADA). 324
Cost per ADA. $9,940

California Achievement Tests 6th ed., 2008
(Pct scoring at or above 50th National Percentile Rank)

	Math	Reading	Language
Grade 3	50%	24%	32%
Grade 7	33%	15%	15%

Academic Performance Index, 2009
Number of valid scores. 219
2007 API (base) 639
2008 API (growth). 661

SAT Testing, 2006-07
Enrollment, Grade 12 . . . . .NA
percent taking test. . . . . .NA
number with total score 1,500+ . . . . . .NA

Average Scores:

Math	Verbal	Writing	Total
NA	NA	NA	NA

Federal No Child Left Behind, 2008
(Adequate Yearly Progress standards met)

	Participation Rate	Pct Proficient
ELA	Yes	Yes
Math	Yes	Yes

API Criteria . . . . .Yes
Graduation rate . . . . .NA
criteria met/possible. 17/17

Orange Unified

Orange County
PO Box 11022
Orange, CA 92867
(714) 628-4000

Superint. . . . . Renae Dreier
Grade plan. K-12
Number of schools. .43
Enrollment 30,127
High school graduates, 2006-07. . . . 1,959
Dropout rate. 1.5
Pupil/teacher ratio. 22.1%
Average class size. 27.2
Students per computer 5.1
Avg. Teacher Salary, ... $70,298
Avg. Daily Attendence (ADA). 28,411
Cost per ADA. $7,954

California Achievement Tests 6th ed., 2008
(Pct scoring at or above 50th National Percentile Rank)

	Math	Reading	Language
Grade 3	61%	43%	52%
Grade 7	57%	58%	55%

Academic Performance Index, 2009
Number of valid scores. 21,079
2007 API (base) 783
2008 API (growth). 787

SAT Testing, 2006-07
Enrollment, Grade 12 2,286
percent taking test. 42.5%
number with total score 1,500+ 563

Average Scores:

Math	Verbal	Writing	Total
535	515	519	1,569

Federal No Child Left Behind, 2008
(Adequate Yearly Progress standards met)

	Participation Rate	Pct Proficient
ELA	Yes	No
Math	Yes	No

API Criteria . . . . .Yes
Graduation rate . . . . .Yes
criteria met/possible. 42/38

Orchard Elem

Santa Clara County
921 Fox Ln
San Jose, CA 95131
(408) 944-0397

Superint. . . . . .Joseph Amelio
Grade plan. K-8
Number of schools. 1
Enrollment 828
High school graduates, 2006-07 0
Dropout rate. 0
Pupil/teacher ratio. 20.2%
Average class size. 24.8
Students per computer 3.3
Avg. Teacher Salary, ... $68,735
Avg. Daily Attendence (ADA). 819
Cost per ADA. $8,278

California Achievement Tests 6th ed., 2008
(Pct scoring at or above 50th National Percentile Rank)

	Math	Reading	Language
Grade 3	59%	32%	51%
Grade 7	42%	38%	44%

Academic Performance Index, 2009
Number of valid scores. 579
2007 API (base) 738
2008 API (growth). 728

SAT Testing, 2006-07
Enrollment, Grade 12 . . . . .NA
percent taking test. . . . . .NA
number with total score 1,500+ . . . . . .NA

Average Scores:

Math	Verbal	Writing	Total
NA	NA	NA	NA

Federal No Child Left Behind, 2008
(Adequate Yearly Progress standards met)

	Participation Rate	Pct Proficient
ELA	Yes	No
Math	Yes	No

API Criteria . . . . .Yes
Graduation rate . . . . .NA
criteria met/possible. 21/17

Orcutt Union Elem

Santa Barbara County
Soares St and Dyer St
Orcutt, CA 93457
(805) 938-8900

Superint. . . . . .Sharon McHolland
Grade plan. K-8
Number of schools. 8
Enrollment 4,607
High school graduates, 2006-07 0
Dropout rate. 0
Pupil/teacher ratio. 21.5%
Average class size. 24.3
Students per computer 5.3
Avg. Teacher Salary, ... $66,729
Avg. Daily Attendence (ADA). 4,500
Cost per ADA. $7,579

California Achievement Tests 6th ed., 2008
(Pct scoring at or above 50th National Percentile Rank)

	Math	Reading	Language
Grade 3	68%	60%	61%
Grade 7	66%	60%	58%

Academic Performance Index, 2009
Number of valid scores. 3,557
2007 API (base) 824
2008 API (growth). 824

SAT Testing, 2006-07
Enrollment, Grade 12 . . . . .NA
percent taking test. . . . . .NA
number with total score 1,500+ . . . . . .NA

Average Scores:

Math	Verbal	Writing	Total
NA	NA	NA	NA

Federal No Child Left Behind, 2008
(Adequate Yearly Progress standards met)

	Participation Rate	Pct Proficient
ELA	Yes	No
Math	Yes	Yes

API Criteria . . . . .Yes
Graduation rate . . . . .NA
criteria met/possible. 25/24

Data from school year 2007-08 except where noted.
†Combined data for elementary and high schools.

Orinda Union Elem

Contra Costa County
8 Altarinda Rd
Orinda, CA 94563
(925) 254-4901

Superint. Joe Jaconette
Grade plan. K-8
Number of schools. 5
Enrollment 2,446
High school graduates, 2006-07. 0
Dropout rate. 0
Pupil/teacher ratio. 17.3%
Average class size. 23.0
Students per computer 2.8
Avg. Teacher Salary, ... $63,932
Avg. Daily Attendence (ADA). 2,395
Cost per ADA. $10,005

California Achievement Tests 6th ed., 2008
(Pct scoring at or above 50th National Percentile Rank)

	Math	Reading	Language
Grade 3	89%	81%	87%
Grade 7	94%	90%	88%

Academic Performance Index, 2009
Number of valid scores. 1,892
2007 API (base) 948
2008 API (growth). 955

SAT Testing, 2006-07
Enrollment, Grade 12 . . . . .NA
percent taking test. . . . . .NA
number with total score 1,500+ . . . . . .NA

Average Scores:

Math	Verbal	Writing	Total
NA	NA	NA	NA

Federal No Child Left Behind, 2008
(Adequate Yearly Progress standards met)

	Participation Rate	Pct Proficient
ELA	Yes	Yes
Math	Yes	Yes

API Criteria . . . . .Yes
Graduation rate . . . . .NA
criteria met/possible. 17/17

Oroville Elem

Butte County
2795 Yard St
Oroville, CA 95966
(530) 532-3000

Superint. . . . . .Penny Chennell-Carter
Grade plan. K-8
Number of schools. 8
Enrollment 2,832
High school graduates, 2006-07. 0
Dropout rate. 0
Pupil/teacher ratio. 19.9%
Average class size. 23.0
Students per computer 3.6
Avg. Teacher Salary, ... $69,561
Avg. Daily Attendence (ADA). 2,664
Cost per ADA. $8,988

California Achievement Tests 6th ed., 2008
(Pct scoring at or above 50th National Percentile Rank)

	Math	Reading	Language
Grade 3	51%	32%	33%
Grade 7	45%	46%	36%

Academic Performance Index, 2009
Number of valid scores. 2,039
2007 API (base) 725
2008 API (growth). 732

SAT Testing, 2006-07
Enrollment, Grade 12 . . . . .NA
percent taking test. . . . . .NA
number with total score 1,500+ . . . . . .NA

Average Scores:

Math	Verbal	Writing	Total
NA	NA	NA	NA

Federal No Child Left Behind, 2008
(Adequate Yearly Progress standards met)

	Participation Rate	Pct Proficient
ELA	Yes	No
Math	Yes	No

API Criteria . . . . .Yes
Graduation rate . . . . .NA
criteria met/possible. 37/26

Outside Creek Elem

Tulare County
26452 Road 164
Visalia, CA 93292
(559) 747-0710

Superint. . . . . .Elaine Brainard
Grade plan. K-8
Number of schools. 1
Enrollment 127
High school graduates, 2006-07. 0
Dropout rate. 0
Pupil/teacher ratio. 25.4%
Average class size. 27.8
Students per computer 4.2
Avg. Teacher Salary, ...NA
Avg. Daily Attendence (ADA). 127
Cost per ADA. $6,745

California Achievement Tests 6th ed., 2008
(Pct scoring at or above 50th National Percentile Rank)

	Math	Reading	Language
Grade 3	27%	36%	18%
Grade 7	46%	31%	31%

Academic Performance Index, 2009
Number of valid scores. 84
2007 API (base) 732
2008 API (growth). 722

SAT Testing, 2006-07
Enrollment, Grade 12 . . . . .NA
percent taking test. . . . . .NA
number with total score 1,500+ . . . . . .NA

Average Scores:

Math	Verbal	Writing	Total
NA	NA	NA	NA

Federal No Child Left Behind, 2008
(Adequate Yearly Progress standards met)

	Participation Rate	Pct Proficient
ELA	Yes	Yes
Math	Yes	Yes

API Criteria . . . . .Yes
Graduation rate . . . . .NA
criteria met/possible. 9/9

Oxnard Elem

Ventura County
1051 South A St
Oxnard, CA 93030
(805) 487-3918

Superint. . . . . .Richard Miller
Grade plan. K-8
Number of schools. .21
Enrollment 15,281
High school graduates, 2006-07. 0
Dropout rate. 0
Pupil/teacher ratio. 22.5%
Average class size. 25.7
Students per computer 4.9
Avg. Teacher Salary, ...$68,596
Avg. Daily Attendence (ADA). 14,858
Cost per ADA. $8,339

California Achievement Tests 6th ed., 2008
(Pct scoring at or above 50th National Percentile Rank)

	Math	Reading	Language
Grade 3	45%	24%	32%
Grade 7	40%	34%	33%

Academic Performance Index, 2009
Number of valid scores. 11,016
2007 API (base) 688
2008 API (growth). 701

SAT Testing, 2006-07
Enrollment, Grade 12 . . . . .NA
percent taking test. . . . . .NA
number with total score 1,500+ . . . . . .NA

Average Scores:

Math	Verbal	Writing	Total
NA	NA	NA	NA

Federal No Child Left Behind, 2008
(Adequate Yearly Progress standards met)

	Participation Rate	Pct Proficient
ELA	Yes	No
Math	Yes	No

API Criteria . . . . .Yes
Graduation rate . . . . .NA
criteria met/possible. 37/31

Pacheco Union Elem

Shasta County
20981 Dersch Rd
Anderson, CA 96007
(530) 365-3335

Superint. . . . . Deidra Hoffman
Grade plan. K-8
Number of schools. 3
Enrollment 684
High school graduates, 2006-07. 0
Dropout rate. 0
Pupil/teacher ratio. 20.3%
Average class size. 21.7
Students per computer 3.2
Avg. Teacher Salary, ... $55,331
Avg. Daily Attendence (ADA). 666
Cost per ADA. $8,781

California Achievement Tests 6th ed., 2008
(Pct scoring at or above 50th National Percentile Rank)

	Math	Reading	Language
Grade 3	58%	45%	55%
Grade 7	63%	57%	53%

Academic Performance Index, 2009
Number of valid scores. 496
2007 API (base) 746
2008 API (growth). 784

SAT Testing, 2006-07
Enrollment, Grade 12 . . . . .NA
percent taking test. . . . . .NA
number with total score 1,500+ . . . . . .NA

Average Scores:

Math	Verbal	Writing	Total
NA	NA	NA	NA

Federal No Child Left Behind, 2008
(Adequate Yearly Progress standards met)

	Participation Rate	Pct Proficient
ELA	Yes	Yes
Math	Yes	Yes

API Criteria . . . . .Yes
Graduation rate . . . . .NA
criteria met/possible. 13/13

Pacific Union Elem

Humboldt County
2065 East Bowles Ave
Fresno, CA 93725
(707) 822-4619

Superint. . . . . John McGuire
Grade plan. K-8
Number of schools. 2
Enrollment 512
High school graduates, 2006-07. 0
Dropout rate. 0
Pupil/teacher ratio. 17.6%
Average class size. 22.5
Students per computer 3.0
Avg. Teacher Salary, ... $59,070
Avg. Daily Attendence (ADA). 457
Cost per ADA. $7,973

California Achievement Tests 6th ed., 2008
(Pct scoring at or above 50th National Percentile Rank)

	Math	Reading	Language
Grade 3	52%	48%	46%
Grade 7	82%	78%	72%

Academic Performance Index, 2009
Number of valid scores. 380
2007 API (base) 788
2008 API (growth). 793

SAT Testing, 2006-07
Enrollment, Grade 12 . . . . .NA
percent taking test. . . . . .NA
number with total score 1,500+ . . . . . .NA

Average Scores:

Math	Verbal	Writing	Total
NA	NA	NA	NA

Federal No Child Left Behind, 2008
(Adequate Yearly Progress standards met)

	Participation Rate	Pct Proficient
ELA	Yes	No
Math	Yes	No

API Criteria . . . . .Yes
Graduation rate . . . . .NA
criteria met/possible. 17/15

Data from school year 2007-08 except where noted
†Combined data for elementary and high schools

Pacific Union Elem

Fresno County
3001 Janes Rd
Arcata, CA 95521
(559) 834-2533

Superint. . . . . .Warren Jennings
Grade plan. K-8
Number of schools. 1
Enrollment 383
High school graduates, 2006-07. 0
Dropout rate. 0
Pupil/teacher ratio. 17.4%
Average class size. 22.1
Students per computer 4.7
Avg. Teacher Salary, ...
Avg. Daily Attendence (ADA). 378
Cost per ADA. $8,159

California Achievement Tests 6th ed., 2008
(Pct scoring at or above 50th National Percentile Rank)

	Math	Reading	Language
Grade 3	60%	33%	40%
Grade 7	41%	46%	32%

Academic Performance Index, 2009
Number of valid scores. 275
2007 API (base) 730
2008 API (growth). 741

SAT Testing, 2006-07
Enrollment, Grade 12 . . . . .NA
percent taking test. . . . . .NA
number with total score 1,500+ . . . . . .NA

Average Scores:

Math	Verbal	Writing	Total
NA	NA	NA	NA

Federal No Child Left Behind, 2008
(Adequate Yearly Progress standards met)

	Participation Rate	Pct Proficient
ELA	Yes	No
Math	Yes	Yes

API Criteria . . . . .Yes
Graduation rate . . . . .NA
criteria met/possible. 21/20

Pacifica Elem

San Mateo County
375 Reina del Mar Ave
Pacifica, CA 94044
(650) 738-6600

Superint. . . . . James Lianides
Grade plan. K-8
Number of schools. 7
Enrollment 3,100
High school graduates, 2006-07. 0
Dropout rate. 0
Pupil/teacher ratio. 21.0%
Average class size. 23.8
Students per computer 6.4
Avg. Teacher Salary, ... $55,854
Avg. Daily Attendence (ADA). 2,996
Cost per ADA. $7,648

California Achievement Tests 6th ed., 2008
(Pct scoring at or above 50th National Percentile Rank)

	Math	Reading	Language
Grade 3	68%	49%	60%
Grade 7	64%	63%	58%

Academic Performance Index, 2009
Number of valid scores. 2,316
2007 API (base) 809
2008 API (growth). 823

SAT Testing, 2006-07
Enrollment, Grade 12 . . . . .NA
percent taking test. . . . . .NA
number with total score 1,500+ . . . . . .NA

Average Scores:

Math	Verbal	Writing	Total
NA	NA	NA	NA

Federal No Child Left Behind, 2008
(Adequate Yearly Progress standards met)

	Participation Rate	Pct Proficient
ELA	Yes	No
Math	No	No

API Criteria . . . . .Yes
Graduation rate . . . . .NA
criteria met/possible. 37/34

Palm Springs Unified

Riverside County
980 East Tahquitz Canyon Way
Palm Springs, CA 92262
(760) 416-6000

Superint. . . . . .Lorri McCune
Grade plan. K-12
Number of schools. .25
Enrollment 24,400
High school graduates, 2006-07. . . . 1,146
Dropout rate. 5.8
Pupil/teacher ratio. 21.9%
Average class size. 28.3
Students per computer 5.9
Avg. Teacher Salary, ...$66,086
Avg. Daily Attendence (ADA). 22,873
Cost per ADA. $8,379

California Achievement Tests 6th ed., 2008
(Pct scoring at or above 50th National Percentile Rank)

	Math	Reading	Language
Grade 3	44%	28%	36%
Grade 7	37%	35%	32%

Academic Performance Index, 2009
Number of valid scores. 17,207
2007 API (base) 673
2008 API (growth). 700

SAT Testing, 2006-07
Enrollment, Grade 12 1,704
percent taking test. 25.7%
number with total score 1,500+ 151

Average Scores:

Math	Verbal	Writing	Total
469	468	454	1,391

Federal No Child Left Behind, 2008
(Adequate Yearly Progress standards met)

	Participation Rate	Pct Proficient
ELA	Yes	No
Math	Yes	No

API Criteria . . . . .Yes
Graduation rate . . . . No
criteria met/possible. 38/31

Palmdale Elem

Los Angeles County
39139 10th Street East
Palmdale, CA 93550
(661) 947-7191

Superint. . . . . Roger Gallizzi
Grade plan. K-8
Number of schools. .28
Enrollment 22,193
High school graduates, 2006-07. 0
Dropout rate. 0
Pupil/teacher ratio. 24.0%
Average class size. 27.3
Students per computer 5.5
Avg. Teacher Salary, ...$58,772
Avg. Daily Attendence (ADA). 21,248
Cost per ADA. $7,341

California Achievement Tests 6th ed., 2008
(Pct scoring at or above 50th National Percentile Rank)

	Math	Reading	Language
Grade 3	41%	25%	34%
Grade 7	38%	36%	34%

Academic Performance Index, 2009
Number of valid scores. 15,211
2007 API (base) 683
2008 API (growth). 700

SAT Testing, 2006-07
Enrollment, Grade 12 . . . . .NA
percent taking test. . . . . .NA
number with total score 1,500+ . . . . . .NA

Average Scores:

Math	Verbal	Writing	Total
NA	NA	NA	NA

Federal No Child Left Behind, 2008
(Adequate Yearly Progress standards met)

	Participation Rate	Pct Proficient
ELA	Yes	No
Math	Yes	No

API Criteria . . . . .Yes
Graduation rate . . . . .NA
criteria met/possible. 37/26

Palo Verde Union Elem

Tulare County
9637 Avenue 196
Tulare, CA 93274
(559) 688-0648

Superint. . . . . .John Manning
Grade plan. K-8
Number of schools. 1
Enrollment 560
High school graduates, 2006-07. 0
Dropout rate. 0
Pupil/teacher ratio. 23.3%
Average class size. 24.0
Students per computer 4.7
Avg. Teacher Salary, ...$59,678
Avg. Daily Attendence (ADA). 559
Cost per ADA. $6,905

California Achievement Tests 6th ed., 2008
(Pct scoring at or above 50th National Percentile Rank)

	Math	Reading	Language
Grade 3	52%	48%	52%
Grade 7	56%	47%	42%

Academic Performance Index, 2009
Number of valid scores. 381
2007 API (base) 766
2008 API (growth). 741

SAT Testing, 2006-07
Enrollment, Grade 12 . . . . .NA
percent taking test. . . . . .NA
number with total score 1,500+ . . . . . .NA

Average Scores:

Math	Verbal	Writing	Total
NA	NA	NA	NA

Federal No Child Left Behind, 2008
(Adequate Yearly Progress standards met)

	Participation Rate	Pct Proficient
ELA	Yes	No
Math	Yes	Yes

API Criteria . . . . .Yes
Graduation rate . . . . .NA
criteria met/possible. 21/20

Panama Buena Vista Union Elem

Kern County
4200 Ashe Rd
Bakersfield, CA 93313
(661) 831-8331

Superint. Kip Hearron
Grade plan. K-8
Number of schools. .22
Enrollment 16,561
High school graduates, 2006-07. 0
Dropout rate. 0
Pupil/teacher ratio. 20.5%
Average class size. 24.0
Students per computer 4.8
Avg. Teacher Salary, ...$61,738
Avg. Daily Attendence (ADA). 15,770
Cost per ADA. $7,781

California Achievement Tests 6th ed., 2008
(Pct scoring at or above 50th National Percentile Rank)

	Math	Reading	Language
Grade 3	54%	38%	49%
Grade 7	48%	48%	46%

Academic Performance Index, 2009
Number of valid scores. 12,146
2007 API (base) 759
2008 API (growth). 763

SAT Testing, 2006-07
Enrollment, Grade 12 . . . . .NA
percent taking test. . . . . .NA
number with total score 1,500+ . . . . . .NA

Average Scores:

Math	Verbal	Writing	Total
NA	NA	NA	NA

Federal No Child Left Behind, 2008
(Adequate Yearly Progress standards met)

	Participation Rate	Pct Proficient
ELA	Yes	No
Math	Yes	No

API Criteria . . . . .Yes
Graduation rate . . . . .NA
criteria met/possible. 37/32

Data from school year 2007-08 except where noted.
†Combined data for elementary and high schools.

Paradise Elem

Stanislaus County
3361 California Ave
Modesto, CA 95358
(209) 524-0184

Superint	Douglas Fraser
Grade plan	K-8
Number of schools	2
Enrollment	182
High school graduates, 2006-07	0
Dropout rate	0
Pupil/teacher ratio	20.2%
Average class size	20.0
Students per computer	3.1
Avg. Teacher Salary,	NA
Avg. Daily Attendence (ADA)	171
Cost per ADA	$8,014

California Achievement Tests 6th ed., 2008
(Pct scoring at or above 50th National Percentile Rank)

	Math	Reading	Language
Grade 3	NA	NA	NA
Grade 7	NA	NA	NA

Academic Performance Index, 2009

Number of valid scores	133
2007 API (base)	808
2008 API (growth)	755

SAT Testing, 2006-07

Enrollment, Grade 12	NA
percent taking test	NA
number with total score 1,500+	NA

Average Scores:

Math	Verbal	Writing	Total
NA	NA	NA	NA

Federal No Child Left Behind, 2008
(Adequate Yearly Progress standards met)

	Participation Rate	Pct Proficient
ELA	Yes	Yes
Math	Yes	Yes

API Criteria	Yes
Graduation rate	NA
# criteria met/possible	17/17

Paramount Unified

Los Angeles County
15110 California Ave
Paramount, CA 90723
(562) 602-6000

Superint	David Verdugo
Grade plan	K-12
Number of schools	20
Enrollment	15,952
High school graduates, 2006-07	654
Dropout rate	7.3
Pupil/teacher ratio	21.4%
Average class size	26.7
Students per computer	3.3
Avg. Teacher Salary,	$67,411
Avg. Daily Attendence (ADA)	15,974
Cost per ADA	$8,338

California Achievement Tests 6th ed., 2008
(Pct scoring at or above 50th National Percentile Rank)

	Math	Reading	Language
Grade 3	45%	22%	38%
Grade 7	35%	37%	35%

Academic Performance Index, 2009

Number of valid scores	11,584
2007 API (base)	686
2008 API (growth)	705

SAT Testing, 2006-07

Enrollment, Grade 12	1,019
percent taking test	23.4%
number with total score 1,500+	38

Average Scores:

Math	Verbal	Writing	Total
445	413	414	1,272

Federal No Child Left Behind, 2008
(Adequate Yearly Progress standards met)

	Participation Rate	Pct Proficient
ELA	Yes	No
Math	Yes	No

API Criteria	Yes
Graduation rate	No
# criteria met/possible	30/24

Peninsula Union Elem

Humboldt County
PO Box 175
Samoa, CA 95564
(707) 443-2731

Superint	Mary Beth Wolford
Grade plan	NA
Number of schools	1
Enrollment	35
High school graduates, 2006-07	0
Dropout rate	0
Pupil/teacher ratio	10.0%
Average class size	10.5
Students per computer	2.9
Avg. Teacher Salary,	$42,734
Avg. Daily Attendence (ADA)	30
Cost per ADA	$17,461

California Achievement Tests 6th ed., 2008
(Pct scoring at or above 50th National Percentile Rank)

	Math	Reading	Language
Grade 3	NA	NA	NA
Grade 7	NA	NA	NA

Academic Performance Index, 2009

Number of valid scores	21
2007 API (base)	615
2008 API (growth)	603

SAT Testing, 2006-07

Enrollment, Grade 12	NA
percent taking test	NA
number with total score 1,500+	NA

Average Scores:

Math	Verbal	Writing	Total
NA	NA	NA	NA

Federal No Child Left Behind, 2008
(Adequate Yearly Progress standards met)

	Participation Rate	Pct Proficient
ELA	Yes	Yes
Math	Yes	Yes

API Criteria	No
Graduation rate	NA
# criteria met/possible	5/4

Perris Elem

Riverside County
143 East First St
Perris, CA 92570
(951) 657-3118

Superint	Edward Agundez
Grade plan	K-6
Number of schools	8
Enrollment	5,670
High school graduates, 2006-07	0
Dropout rate	NA
Pupil/teacher ratio	19.2%
Average class size	21.6
Students per computer	7.5
Avg. Teacher Salary,	$63,827
Avg. Daily Attendence (ADA)	5,448
Cost per ADA	$8,741

California Achievement Tests 6th ed., 2008
(Pct scoring at or above 50th National Percentile Rank)

	Math	Reading	Language
Grade 3	34%	16%	27%
Grade 7	NA	NA	NA

Academic Performance Index, 2009

Number of valid scores	3,569
2007 API (base)	676
2008 API (growth)	698

SAT Testing, 2006-07

Enrollment, Grade 12	NA
percent taking test	NA
number with total score 1,500+	NA

Average Scores:

Math	Verbal	Writing	Total
NA	NA	NA	NA

Federal No Child Left Behind, 2008
(Adequate Yearly Progress standards met)

	Participation Rate	Pct Proficient
ELA	Yes	No
Math	Yes	No

API Criteria	Yes
Graduation rate	NA
# criteria met/possible	29/22

Perris High

Riverside County
155 East Fourth St
Perris, CA 92570
(951) 943-6369

Superint	Jonathan Greenberg
Grade plan	7-12
Number of schools	8
Enrollment	9,764
High school graduates, 2006-07	1,323
Dropout rate	4.8
Pupil/teacher ratio	24.5%
Average class size	28.4
Students per computer	6.9
Avg. Teacher Salary,	$67,839
Avg. Daily Attendence (ADA)	8,911
Cost per ADA	$8,412

California Achievement Tests 6th ed., 2008
(Pct scoring at or above 50th National Percentile Rank)

	Math	Reading	Language
Grade 3	NA	NA	NA
Grade 7	31%	27%	26%

Academic Performance Index, 2009

Number of valid scores	7,119
2007 API (base)	657
2008 API (growth)	675

SAT Testing, 2006-07

Enrollment, Grade 12	1,619
percent taking test	23.5%
number with total score 1,500+	129

Average Scores:

Math	Verbal	Writing	Total
474	460	455	1,389

Federal No Child Left Behind, 2008
(Adequate Yearly Progress standards met)

	Participation Rate	Pct Proficient
ELA	Yes	No
Math	Yes	No

API Criteria	Yes
Graduation rate	No
# criteria met/possible	30/18

Petaluma City Elem

Sonoma County
200 Douglas St
Petaluma, CA 94952
(707) 778-4795

Superint	Greta Viguie
Grade plan	K-6
Number of schools	8
Enrollment	2,271
High school graduates, 2006-07	0
Dropout rate	0
Pupil/teacher ratio	17.5%
Average class size	20.3
Students per computer	5.3
Avg. Teacher Salary,†	$62,191
Avg. Daily Attendence (ADA)†	7,594
Cost per ADA†	$8,755

California Achievement Tests 6th ed., 2008
(Pct scoring at or above 50th National Percentile Rank)

	Math	Reading	Language
Grade 3	61%	45%	54%
Grade 7	NA	NA	NA

Academic Performance Index, 2009

Number of valid scores	NA
2007 API (base)	NA
2008 API (growth)	NA

SAT Testing, 2006-07

Enrollment, Grade 12	NA
percent taking test	NA
number with total score 1,500+	NA

Average Scores:

Math	Verbal	Writing	Total
NA	NA	NA	NA

Federal No Child Left Behind, 2008
(Adequate Yearly Progress standards met)

	Participation Rate	Pct Proficient
ELA	NA	NA
Math	NA	NA

API Criteria	NA
Graduation rate	NA
# criteria met/possible	NA/NA

Data from school year 2007-08 except where noted
†Combined data for elementary and high schools

Piner-Olivet Union Elem

Sonoma County
3450 Coffey Ln
Santa Rosa, CA 95403
(707) 522-3000

Superint. . . . . .Marion Guillen
Grade plan. K-8
Number of schools. 6
Enrollment 1,683
High school graduates, 2006-07 0
Dropout rate 2.4
Pupil/teacher ratio. 20.8%
Average class size. 21.8
Students per computer 6.7
Avg. Teacher Salary, ... $66,916
Avg. Daily Attendence (ADA). 1,343
Cost per ADA. $7,968

California Achievement Tests 6th ed., 2008
(Pct scoring at or above 50th National Percentile Rank)

	Math	Reading	Language
Grade 3	53%	41%	48%
Grade 7	73%	71%	58%

Academic Performance Index, 2009
Number of valid scores. 911
2007 API (base) 792
2008 API (growth). 790

SAT Testing, 2006-07
Enrollment, Grade 12 . . . . .NA
percent taking test. . . . . .NA
number with total score 1,500+ . . . . . .NA

Average Scores:

Math	Verbal	Writing	Total
NA	NA	NA	NA

Federal No Child Left Behind, 2008
(Adequate Yearly Progress standards met)

	Participation Rate	Pct Proficient
ELA	Yes	Yes
Math	Yes	Yes

API Criteria . . . . .Yes
Graduation rate . . . . .NA
criteria met/possible. 21/21

Pioneer Union Elem

Kings County
1888 North Mustang Dr
Hanford, CA 93230
(559) 585-8400

Superint. . . . . Diane Cox
Grade plan. K-8
Number of schools. 2
Enrollment 1,589
High school graduates, 2006-07 0
Dropout rate 0
Pupil/teacher ratio. 21.6%
Average class size. 24.3
Students per computer 4.1
Avg. Teacher Salary, ... $59,586
Avg. Daily Attendence (ADA). 1,541
Cost per ADA. $7,036

California Achievement Tests 6th ed., 2008
(Pct scoring at or above 50th National Percentile Rank)

	Math	Reading	Language
Grade 3	70%	54%	58%
Grade 7	63%	64%	61%

Academic Performance Index, 2009
Number of valid scores. 1,203
2007 API (base) 809
2008 API (growth). 815

SAT Testing, 2006-07
Enrollment, Grade 12 . . . . .NA
percent taking test. . . . . .NA
number with total score 1,500+ . . . . . .NA

Average Scores:

Math	Verbal	Writing	Total
NA	NA	NA	NA

Federal No Child Left Behind, 2008
(Adequate Yearly Progress standards met)

	Participation Rate	Pct Proficient
ELA	Yes	No
Math	Yes	Yes

API Criteria . . . . .Yes
Graduation rate . . . . .NA
criteria met/possible. 25/24

Placentia-Yorba Linda Unified

Orange County
1301 East Orangethorpe Ave
Placentia, CA 92870
(714) 996-2550

Superint. . . . . Dennis Smith
Grade plan. K-12
Number of schools. .32
Enrollment 26,243
High school graduates, 2006-07 1,865
Dropout rate 1.1
Pupil/teacher ratio. 23.9%
Average class size. 26.6
Students per computer 4.4
Avg. Teacher Salary, ... $75,643
Avg. Daily Attendence (ADA). 25,745
Cost per ADA. $7,949

California Achievement Tests 6th ed., 2008
(Pct scoring at or above 50th National Percentile Rank)

	Math	Reading	Language
Grade 3	68%	47%	57%
Grade 7	69%	64%	63%

Academic Performance Index, 2009
Number of valid scores. 19,531
2007 API (base) 816
2008 API (growth). 822

SAT Testing, 2006-07
Enrollment, Grade 12 1,939
percent taking test. 51.5%
number with total score 1,500+ 647

Average Scores:

Math	Verbal	Writing	Total
561	526	525	1,612

Federal No Child Left Behind, 2008
(Adequate Yearly Progress standards met)

	Participation Rate	Pct Proficient
ELA	Yes	No
Math	Yes	No

API Criteria . . . . .Yes
Graduation rate . . . . .Yes
criteria met/possible. 38/36

Placerville Union Elem

El Dorado County
1032 Thompson Way
Placerville, CA 95667
(530) 622-7216

Superint. . . . . .Nancy Lynch
Grade plan. K-8
Number of schools. 4
Enrollment 1,140
High school graduates, 2006-07 0
Dropout rate 0
Pupil/teacher ratio. 19.1%
Average class size. 22.7
Students per computer 3.9
Avg. Teacher Salary, ... $59,835
Avg. Daily Attendence (ADA). 1,105
Cost per ADA. $8,618

California Achievement Tests 6th ed., 2008
(Pct scoring at or above 50th National Percentile Rank)

	Math	Reading	Language
Grade 3	69%	58%	66%
Grade 7	54%	57%	52%

Academic Performance Index, 2009
Number of valid scores. 762
2007 API (base) 800
2008 API (growth). 821

SAT Testing, 2006-07
Enrollment, Grade 12 . . . . .NA
percent taking test. . . . . .NA
number with total score 1,500+ . . . . . .NA

Average Scores:

Math	Verbal	Writing	Total
NA	NA	NA	NA

Federal No Child Left Behind, 2008
(Adequate Yearly Progress standards met)

	Participation Rate	Pct Proficient
ELA	Yes	No
Math	Yes	Yes

API Criteria . . . . .Yes
Graduation rate . . . . .NA
criteria met/possible. 21/20

Plainsburg Union Elem

Merced County
3708 South Plainsburg Rd
Merced, CA 95341
(209) 389-4707

Superint. . . . . Vernon Snodderly
Grade plan. K-8
Number of schools. 1
Enrollment 103
High school graduates, 2006-07 0
Dropout rate 0
Pupil/teacher ratio. 20.6%
Average class size. 22.8
Students per computer 2.6
Avg. Teacher Salary, ... $42,136
Avg. Daily Attendence (ADA). 102
Cost per ADA. $7,009

California Achievement Tests 6th ed., 2008
(Pct scoring at or above 50th National Percentile Rank)

	Math	Reading	Language
Grade 3	25%	50%	67%
Grade 7	NA	NA	NA

Academic Performance Index, 2009
Number of valid scores. 67
2007 API (base) 830
2008 API (growth). 792

SAT Testing, 2006-07
Enrollment, Grade 12 . . . . .NA
percent taking test. . . . . .NA
number with total score 1,500+ . . . . . .NA

Average Scores:

Math	Verbal	Writing	Total
NA	NA	NA	NA

Federal No Child Left Behind, 2008
(Adequate Yearly Progress standards met)

	Participation Rate	Pct Proficient
ELA	Yes	Yes
Math	Yes	Yes

API Criteria . . . . .Yes
Graduation rate . . . . .NA
criteria met/possible. 5/5

Plaza Elem

Glenn County
7322 County Road 24
Orland, CA 95963
(530) 865-1250

Superint. . . . . .Grant Sandro
Grade plan. K-8
Number of schools. 1
Enrollment 138
High school graduates, 2006-07 0
Dropout rate 0
Pupil/teacher ratio. 23.0%
Average class size. 24.4
Students per computer 4.2
Avg. Teacher Salary, ...NA
Avg. Daily Attendence (ADA). 134
Cost per ADA. $6,699

California Achievement Tests 6th ed., 2008
(Pct scoring at or above 50th National Percentile Rank)

	Math	Reading	Language
Grade 3	81%	56%	69%
Grade 7	67%	60%	60%

Academic Performance Index, 2009
Number of valid scores. 103
2007 API (base) 835
2008 API (growth). 838

SAT Testing, 2006-07
Enrollment, Grade 12 . . . . .NA
percent taking test. . . . . .NA
number with total score 1,500+ . . . . . .NA

Average Scores:

Math	Verbal	Writing	Total
NA	NA	NA	NA

Federal No Child Left Behind, 2008
(Adequate Yearly Progress standards met)

	Participation Rate	Pct Proficient
ELA	Yes	Yes
Math	Yes	Yes

API Criteria . . . . .Yes
Graduation rate . . . . .NA
criteria met/possible. 9/9

Data from school year 2007-08 except where noted.
†Combined data for elementary and high schools.

Pleasant Ridge Union Elem

Nevada County
22580 Kingston Ln
Grass Valley, CA 95949
(530) 268-2800

Superint. . . . . James Meshwert
Grade plan. K-8
Number of schools. .5
Enrollment 1,785
High school graduates, 2006-07 0
Dropout rate. 0
Pupil/teacher ratio. 20.5%
Average class size. 24.0
Students per computer 4.3
Avg. Teacher Salary, ... $69,638
Avg. Daily Attendence (ADA). 1,719
Cost per ADA. $7,566

California Achievement Tests 6th ed., 2008
(Pct scoring at or above 50th National Percentile Rank)

	Math	Reading	Language
Grade 3	76%	54%	63%
Grade 7	76%	76%	71%

Academic Performance Index, 2009
Number of valid scores. 1,466
2007 API (base) 847
2008 API (growth). 844

SAT Testing, 2006-07
Enrollment, Grade 12 . . . . .NA
percent taking test. . . . . .NA
number with total score 1,500+ . . . . . .NA

Average Scores:

Math	Verbal	Writing	Total
NA	NA	NA	NA

Federal No Child Left Behind, 2008
(Adequate Yearly Progress standards met)

	Participation Rate	Pct Proficient
ELA	Yes	No
Math	No	No

API Criteria . . . . .Yes
Graduation rate . . . . .NA
criteria met/possible. 17/14

Pleasant Valley Elem

Ventura County
600 Temple Ave
Camarillo, CA 93010
(805) 482-2763

Superint. Luis Villegas
Grade plan. K-8
Number of schools. 15
Enrollment 7,151
High school graduates, 2006-07 0
Dropout rate. 0
Pupil/teacher ratio. 20.0%
Average class size. 26.3
Students per computer 3.8
Avg. Teacher Salary, ...
Avg. Daily Attendence (ADA). 6,422
Cost per ADA. $7,754

California Achievement Tests 6th ed., 2008
(Pct scoring at or above 50th National Percentile Rank)

	Math	Reading	Language
Grade 3	73%	56%	65%
Grade 7	68%	63%	60%

Academic Performance Index, 2009
Number of valid scores. 4,991
2007 API (base) 846
2008 API (growth). 850

SAT Testing, 2006-07
Enrollment, Grade 12 . . . . .NA
percent taking test. . . . . .NA
number with total score 1,500+ . . . . . .NA

Average Scores:

Math	Verbal	Writing	Total
NA	NA	NA	NA

Federal No Child Left Behind, 2008
(Adequate Yearly Progress standards met)

	Participation Rate	Pct Proficient
ELA	Yes	Yes
Math	Yes	Yes

API Criteria . . . . .Yes
Graduation rate . . . . .NA
criteria met/possible. 37/37

Pleasant View Elem

Tulare County
14004 Road 184
Porterville, CA 93257
(559) 784-6769

Superint. . . . . Collin Bromley
Grade plan. K-8
Number of schools. .3
Enrollment 547
High school graduates, 2006-07 0
Dropout rate. 0
Pupil/teacher ratio. 17.6%
Average class size. 21.1
Students per computer 5.1
Avg. Teacher Salary, ... $55,231
Avg. Daily Attendence (ADA). 545
Cost per ADA. $8,044

California Achievement Tests 6th ed., 2008
(Pct scoring at or above 50th National Percentile Rank)

	Math	Reading	Language
Grade 3	48%	24%	44%
Grade 7	58%	48%	50%

Academic Performance Index, 2009
Number of valid scores. 378
2007 API (base) 679
2008 API (growth). 711

SAT Testing, 2006-07
Enrollment, Grade 12 . . . . .NA
percent taking test. . . . . .NA
number with total score 1,500+ . . . . . .NA

Average Scores:

Math	Verbal	Writing	Total
NA	NA	NA	NA

Federal No Child Left Behind, 2008
(Adequate Yearly Progress standards met)

	Participation Rate	Pct Proficient
ELA	Yes	No
Math	Yes	Yes

API Criteria . . . . .Yes
Graduation rate . . . . .NA
criteria met/possible. 17/14

Plumas Lake Elem

Yuba County
2743 Plumas School Rd
Olivehurst, CA 95961
(530) 743-4428

Superint. . . . . Paul Carras
Grade plan. K-12
Number of schools. .4
Enrollment 1,056
High school graduates, 2006-07 2
Dropout rate. 10
Pupil/teacher ratio. 18.8%
Average class size. 20.8
Students per computer 6.0
Avg. Teacher Salary, ...
Avg. Daily Attendence (ADA). 1,005
Cost per ADA. $8,045

California Achievement Tests 6th ed., 2008
(Pct scoring at or above 50th National Percentile Rank)

	Math	Reading	Language
Grade 3	63%	49%	58%
Grade 7	52%	52%	48%

Academic Performance Index, 2009
Number of valid scores. 706
2007 API (base) 737
2008 API (growth). 759

SAT Testing, 2006-07
Enrollment, Grade 12 8
percent taking test. . . . . .NA
number with total score 1,500+ . . . . . .NA

Average Scores:

Math	Verbal	Writing	Total
NA	NA	NA	NA

Federal No Child Left Behind, 2008
(Adequate Yearly Progress standards met)

	Participation Rate	Pct Proficient
ELA	Yes	No
Math	Yes	Yes

API Criteria . . . . .Yes
Graduation rate . . . . .No
criteria met/possible. 22/19

Pomona Unified

Los Angeles County
PO Box 2900
Pomona, CA 91769
(909) 397-4800

Superint. . . . Thelma Melendez de Santa Ana
Grade plan. K-12
Number of schools. 44
Enrollment 30,779
High school graduates, 2006-07 1,443
Dropout rate. 6.2
Pupil/teacher ratio. 20.8%
Average class size. 25.5
Students per computer 2.4
Avg. Teacher Salary, ... $68,768
Avg. Daily Attendence (ADA). 29,821
Cost per ADA. $9,168

California Achievement Tests 6th ed., 2008
(Pct scoring at or above 50th National Percentile Rank)

	Math	Reading	Language
Grade 3	43%	24%	37%
Grade 7	39%	34%	34%

Academic Performance Index, 2009
Number of valid scores. 22,089
2007 API (base) 694
2008 API (growth). 705

SAT Testing, 2006-07
Enrollment, Grade 12 1,607
percent taking test. 42.1%
number with total score 1,500+ 207

Average Scores:

Math	Verbal	Writing	Total
465	450	448	1,363

Federal No Child Left Behind, 2008
(Adequate Yearly Progress standards met)

	Participation Rate	Pct Proficient
ELA	Yes	No
Math	Yes	No

API Criteria . . . . .Yes
Graduation rate . . . . .No
criteria met/possible. 38/32

Portola Valley Elem

San Mateo County
4575 Alpine Rd
Portola Valley, CA 94028
(650) 851-1777

Superint. . . . . .Anne Campbell
Grade plan. K-8
Number of schools. .2
Enrollment 706
High school graduates, 2006-07 0
Dropout rate. 0
Pupil/teacher ratio. 15.0%
Average class size. 17.6
Students per computer 1.7
Avg. Teacher Salary, ... $88,388
Avg. Daily Attendence (ADA). 682
Cost per ADA. $16,418

California Achievement Tests 6th ed., 2008
(Pct scoring at or above 50th National Percentile Rank)

	Math	Reading	Language
Grade 3	90%	81%	80%
Grade 7	89%	89%	85%

Academic Performance Index, 2009
Number of valid scores. 529
2007 API (base) 944
2008 API (growth). 954

SAT Testing, 2006-07
Enrollment, Grade 12 . . . . .NA
percent taking test. . . . . .NA
number with total score 1,500+ . . . . . .NA

Average Scores:

Math	Verbal	Writing	Total
NA	NA	NA	NA

Federal No Child Left Behind, 2008
(Adequate Yearly Progress standards met)

	Participation Rate	Pct Proficient
ELA	Yes	Yes
Math	Yes	Yes

API Criteria . . . . .Yes
Graduation rate . . . . .NA
criteria met/possible. 9/9

Data from school year 2007-08 except where noted
†Combined data for elementary and high schools

Poway Unified
San Diego County
13626 Twin Peaks Rd
Poway, CA 92064
(858) 748-0010

Superint....Donald Phillips
Grade plan....K-12
Number of schools....34
Enrollment....33,283
High school graduates, 2006-07....2,522
Dropout rate....0.9
Pupil/teacher ratio....22.8%
Average class size....27.2
Students per computer....5.1
Avg. Teacher Salary,....$69,827
Avg. Daily Attendence (ADA)....32,638
Cost per ADA....$7,954

California Achievement Tests 6th ed., 2008
(Pct scoring at or above 50th National Percentile Rank)

	Math	Reading	Language
Grade 3	83%	67%	74%
Grade 7	82%	77%	76%

Academic Performance Index, 2009
Number of valid scores....24,648
2007 API (base)....864
2008 API (growth)....872

SAT Testing, 2006-07
Enrollment, Grade 12....2,845
percent taking test....62.4%
number with total score 1,500+....1,223

Average Scores:

Math	Verbal	Writing	Total
569	541	538	1,648

Federal No Child Left Behind, 2008
(Adequate Yearly Progress standards met)

	Participation Rate	Pct Proficient
ELA	Yes	Yes
Math	Yes	Yes

API Criteria....Yes
Graduation rate....Yes
criteria met/possible....42/42

Ravendale-Termo Elem
Lassen County
PO Box 99
Termo, CA 96132
(530) 234-2010

Superint....Robert Pace
Grade plan....K-8
Number of schools....1
Enrollment....11
High school graduates, 2006-07....0
Dropout rate....0
Pupil/teacher ratio....7.9%
Average class size....10.0
Students per computer....0.9
Avg. Teacher Salary,....NA
Avg. Daily Attendence (ADA)....9
Cost per ADA....$30,819

California Achievement Tests 6th ed., 2008
(Pct scoring at or above 50th National Percentile Rank)

	Math	Reading	Language
Grade 3	NA	NA	NA
Grade 7	NA	NA	NA

Academic Performance Index, 2009
Number of valid scores....
2007 API (base)....NA
2008 API (growth)....NA

SAT Testing, 2006-07
Enrollment, Grade 12....NA
percent taking test....NA
number with total score 1,500+....NA

Average Scores:

Math	Verbal	Writing	Total
NA	NA	NA	NA

Federal No Child Left Behind, 2008
(Adequate Yearly Progress standards met)

	Participation Rate	Pct Proficient
ELA	Yes	Yes
Math	Yes	Yes

API Criteria....Yes
Graduation rate....NA
criteria met/possible....5/5

Ravenswood City Elem
San Mateo County
2120 Euclid Ave
East Palo Alto, CA 94303
(650) 329-2800

Superint....Maria De La Vega
Grade plan....K-12
Number of schools....11
Enrollment....4,936
High school graduates, 2006-07....38
Dropout rate....2
Pupil/teacher ratio....22.7%
Average class size....23.1
Students per computer....4.5
Avg. Teacher Salary,....$58,926
Avg. Daily Attendence (ADA)....2,678
Cost per ADA....$13,011

California Achievement Tests 6th ed., 2008
(Pct scoring at or above 50th National Percentile Rank)

	Math	Reading	Language
Grade 3	28%	12%	22%
Grade 7	21%	21%	20%

Academic Performance Index, 2009
Number of valid scores....2,560
2007 API (base)....631
2008 API (growth)....636

SAT Testing, 2006-07
Enrollment, Grade 12....57
percent taking test....54.4%
number with total score 1,500+....-

Average Scores:

Math	Verbal	Writing	Total
334	348	348	1,030

Federal No Child Left Behind, 2008
(Adequate Yearly Progress standards met)

	Participation Rate	Pct Proficient
ELA	Yes	No
Math	Yes	No

API Criteria....Yes
Graduation rate....NA
criteria met/possible....29/15

Red Bluff Union Elem
Tehama County
1755 Airport Blvd, Admin Bldg
Red Bluff, CA 96080
(530) 527-7200

Superint....Charles Allen
Grade plan....K-8
Number of schools....6
Enrollment....2,173
High school graduates, 2006-07....0
Dropout rate....0
Pupil/teacher ratio....19.2%
Average class size....21.6
Students per computer....6.0
Avg. Teacher Salary,....$56,553
Avg. Daily Attendence (ADA)....2,124
Cost per ADA....$7,937

California Achievement Tests 6th ed., 2008
(Pct scoring at or above 50th National Percentile Rank)

	Math	Reading	Language
Grade 3	54%	37%	45%
Grade 7	61%	55%	50%

Academic Performance Index, 2009
Number of valid scores....1,540
2007 API (base)....761
2008 API (growth)....768

SAT Testing, 2006-07
Enrollment, Grade 12....NA
percent taking test....NA
number with total score 1,500+....NA

Average Scores:

Math	Verbal	Writing	Total
NA	NA	NA	NA

Federal No Child Left Behind, 2008
(Adequate Yearly Progress standards met)

	Participation Rate	Pct Proficient
ELA	Yes	No
Math	Yes	No

API Criteria....Yes
Graduation rate....NA
criteria met/possible....25/21

Redding Elem
Shasta County
PO Box 992418
Redding, CA 96099
(530) 225-0011

Superint....Diane Kempley
Grade plan....K-12
Number of schools....11
Enrollment....3,623
High school graduates, 2006-07....11
Dropout rate....4.9
Pupil/teacher ratio....20.4%
Average class size....26.0
Students per computer....1.7
Avg. Teacher Salary,....$60,642
Avg. Daily Attendence (ADA)....3,198
Cost per ADA....$8,677

California Achievement Tests 6th ed., 2008
(Pct scoring at or above 50th National Percentile Rank)

	Math	Reading	Language
Grade 3	57%	48%	53%
Grade 7	56%	66%	59%

Academic Performance Index, 2009
Number of valid scores....2,461
2007 API (base)....768
2008 API (growth)....776

SAT Testing, 2006-07
Enrollment, Grade 12....13
percent taking test....7.7%
number with total score 1,500+....NA

Average Scores:

Math	Verbal	Writing	Total
NA	NA	NA	NA

Federal No Child Left Behind, 2008
(Adequate Yearly Progress standards met)

	Participation Rate	Pct Proficient
ELA	Yes	No
Math	Yes	No

API Criteria....Yes
Graduation rate....No
criteria met/possible....22/19

Redlands Unified
San Bernardino County
PO Box 3008
Redlands, CA 92374
(909) 307-5300

Superint....Lori Rhodes
Grade plan....K-12
Number of schools....23
Enrollment....21,482
High school graduates, 2006-07....1,528
Dropout rate....3.4
Pupil/teacher ratio....21.9%
Average class size....26.4
Students per computer....4.7
Avg. Teacher Salary,....$71,787
Avg. Daily Attendence (ADA)....20,556
Cost per ADA....$7,835

California Achievement Tests 6th ed., 2008
(Pct scoring at or above 50th National Percentile Rank)

	Math	Reading	Language
Grade 3	63%	47%	53%
Grade 7	58%	53%	52%

Academic Performance Index, 2009
Number of valid scores....15,340
2007 API (base)....774
2008 API (growth)....779

SAT Testing, 2006-07
Enrollment, Grade 12....1,794
percent taking test....36.2%
number with total score 1,500+....346

Average Scores:

Math	Verbal	Writing	Total
520	501	506	1,527

Federal No Child Left Behind, 2008
(Adequate Yearly Progress standards met)

	Participation Rate	Pct Proficient
ELA	Yes	No
Math	Yes	Yes

API Criteria....Yes
Graduation rate....Yes
criteria met/possible....42/40

Data from school year 2007-08 except where noted.
†Combined data for elementary and high schools.

Redwood City Elem

San Mateo County
750 Bradford St
Redwood City, CA 94063
(650) 423-2200

Superint. . . . . Jan Christensen
Grade plan. K-8
Number of schools. .17
Enrollment 8,644
High school graduates, 2006-07. 0
Dropout rate. 0
Pupil/teacher ratio. 17.7%
Average class size. 23.0
Students per computer 3.1
Avg. Teacher Salary, ... $67,668
Avg. Daily Attendence (ADA). 7,824
Cost per ADA. $9,814

California Achievement Tests 6th ed., 2008
(Pct scoring at or above 50th National Percentile Rank)

	Math	Reading	Language
Grade 3	58%	34%	45%
Grade 7	50%	43%	44%

Academic Performance Index, 2009
Number of valid scores. 5,793
2007 API (base) 765
2008 API (growth). 764

SAT Testing, 2006-07
Enrollment, Grade 12 . . . . .NA
percent taking test. . . . . .NA
number with total score 1,500+ . . . . . .NA

Average Scores:

Math	Verbal	Writing	Total
NA	NA	NA	NA

Federal No Child Left Behind, 2008
(Adequate Yearly Progress standards met)

	Participation Rate	Pct Proficient
ELA	Yes	No
Math	Yes	No

API Criteria . . . . .Yes
Graduation rate . . . . .NA
criteria met/possible. 37/31

Reed Union Elem

Marin County
277-A Karen Way
Tiburon, CA 94920
(415) 381-1112

Superint. . . . . .Christine Carter
Grade plan. K-8
Number of schools. 3
Enrollment 1,104
High school graduates, 2006-07. 0
Dropout rate. 0
Pupil/teacher ratio. 14.7%
Average class size. 21.5
Students per computer 1.2
Avg. Teacher Salary, ... $75,666
Avg. Daily Attendence (ADA). 1,065
Cost per ADA. $13,648

California Achievement Tests 6th ed., 2008
(Pct scoring at or above 50th National Percentile Rank)

	Math	Reading	Language
Grade 3	87%	85%	85%
Grade 7	91%	83%	78%

Academic Performance Index, 2009
Number of valid scores. 816
2007 API (base) 931
2008 API (growth). 941

SAT Testing, 2006-07
Enrollment, Grade 12 . . . . .NA
percent taking test. . . . . .NA
number with total score 1,500+ . . . . . .NA

Average Scores:

Math	Verbal	Writing	Total
NA	NA	NA	NA

Federal No Child Left Behind, 2008
(Adequate Yearly Progress standards met)

	Participation Rate	Pct Proficient
ELA	Yes	Yes
Math	Yes	Yes

API Criteria . . . . .Yes
Graduation rate . . . . .NA
criteria met/possible. 9/9

Reeds Creek Elem

Tehama County
18335 Johnson Rd
Red Bluff, CA 96080
(530) 527-6006

Superint. .Jack Hansen
Grade plan. K-8
Number of schools. 1
Enrollment 156
High school graduates, 2006-07. 0
Dropout rate. 0
Pupil/teacher ratio. 22.3%
Average class size. 21.6
Students per computer 3.0
Avg. Teacher Salary, ...NA
Avg. Daily Attendence (ADA). 145
Cost per ADA. $7,243

California Achievement Tests 6th ed., 2008
(Pct scoring at or above 50th National Percentile Rank)

	Math	Reading	Language
Grade 3	68%	58%	58%
Grade 7	42%	42%	38%

Academic Performance Index, 2009
Number of valid scores. 112
2007 API (base) 808
2008 API (growth). 754

SAT Testing, 2006-07
Enrollment, Grade 12 . . . . .NA
percent taking test. . . . . .NA
number with total score 1,500+ . . . . . .NA

Average Scores:

Math	Verbal	Writing	Total
NA	NA	NA	NA

Federal No Child Left Behind, 2008
(Adequate Yearly Progress standards met)

	Participation Rate	Pct Proficient
ELA	Yes	Yes
Math	Yes	Yes

API Criteria . . . . .Yes
Graduation rate . . . . .NA
criteria met/possible. 11/11

Richfield Elem

Tehama County
23875 River Rd
Corning, CA 96021
(530) 824-3354

Superint. . . . . .Todd Brose
Grade plan. K-8
Number of schools. 1
Enrollment 234
High school graduates, 2006-07. 0
Dropout rate. 0
Pupil/teacher ratio. 21.1%
Average class size. 23.2
Students per computer 3.7
Avg. Teacher Salary, ... $53,174
Avg. Daily Attendence (ADA). 230
Cost per ADA. $7,421

California Achievement Tests 6th ed., 2008
(Pct scoring at or above 50th National Percentile Rank)

	Math	Reading	Language
Grade 3	80%	92%	88%
Grade 7	93%	85%	81%

Academic Performance Index, 2009
Number of valid scores. 179
2007 API (base) 866
2008 API (growth). 848

SAT Testing, 2006-07
Enrollment, Grade 12 . . . . .NA
percent taking test. . . . . .NA
number with total score 1,500+ . . . . . .NA

Average Scores:

Math	Verbal	Writing	Total
NA	NA	NA	NA

Federal No Child Left Behind, 2008
(Adequate Yearly Progress standards met)

	Participation Rate	Pct Proficient
ELA	Yes	Yes
Math	Yes	Yes

API Criteria . . . . .Yes
Graduation rate . . . . .NA
criteria met/possible. 17/17

Richland Union Elem

Kern County
331 Shafter Ave
Shafter, CA 93263
(661) 746-8600

Superint. . . . . Kenneth Bergevin
Grade plan. K-8
Number of schools. 4
Enrollment 3,031
High school graduates, 2006-07. 0
Dropout rate. 0
Pupil/teacher ratio. 19.2%
Average class size. 22.8
Students per computer 4.0
Avg. Teacher Salary, ... $64,799
Avg. Daily Attendence (ADA). 2,941
Cost per ADA. $8,559

California Achievement Tests 6th ed., 2008
(Pct scoring at or above 50th National Percentile Rank)

	Math	Reading	Language
Grade 3	45%	23%	29%
Grade 7	34%	24%	23%

Academic Performance Index, 2009
Number of valid scores. 2,087
2007 API (base) 654
2008 API (growth). 660

SAT Testing, 2006-07
Enrollment, Grade 12 . . . . .NA
percent taking test. . . . . .NA
number with total score 1,500+ . . . . . .NA

Average Scores:

Math	Verbal	Writing	Total
NA	NA	NA	NA

Federal No Child Left Behind, 2008
(Adequate Yearly Progress standards met)

	Participation Rate	Pct Proficient
ELA	Yes	No
Math	Yes	No

API Criteria . . . . .Yes
Graduation rate . . . . .NA
criteria met/possible. 25/14

Richmond Elem

Lassen County
700-585 Richmond Rd, East
Susanville, CA 96130
(530) 257-2338

Superint. . . . . Cynthia Nellums
Grade plan. K-8
Number of schools. 1
Enrollment 227
High school graduates, 2006-07. 0
Dropout rate. 0
Pupil/teacher ratio. 22.7%
Average class size. 22.7
Students per computer 4.3
Avg. Teacher Salary, ...NA
Avg. Daily Attendence (ADA). 223
Cost per ADA. $6,427

California Achievement Tests 6th ed., 2008
(Pct scoring at or above 50th National Percentile Rank)

	Math	Reading	Language
Grade 3	71%	74%	74%
Grade 7	78%	70%	70%

Academic Performance Index, 2009
Number of valid scores. 183
2007 API (base) 826
2008 API (growth). 835

SAT Testing, 2006-07
Enrollment, Grade 12 . . . . .NA
percent taking test. . . . . .NA
number with total score 1,500+ . . . . . .NA

Average Scores:

Math	Verbal	Writing	Total
NA	NA	NA	NA

Federal No Child Left Behind, 2008
(Adequate Yearly Progress standards met)

	Participation Rate	Pct Proficient
ELA	Yes	Yes
Math	Yes	Yes

API Criteria . . . . .Yes
Graduation rate . . . . .NA
criteria met/possible. 9/9

Data from school year 2007-08 except where noted
†Combined data for elementary and high schools

Rincon Valley Union Elem

Sonoma County
1000 Yulupa Ave
Santa Rosa, CA 95405
(707) 542-7375

Superint. . . . Diane Moresi
Grade plan. . . . K-6
Number of schools. . . . 9
Enrollment 2,965
High school graduates, 2006-07. . . . 0
Dropout rate. . . . 0
Pupil/teacher ratio. . . . 17.8%
Average class size. . . . 21.2
Students per computer 3.9
Avg. Teacher Salary, ... $59,871
Avg. Daily Attendence (ADA). . . . 2,748
Cost per ADA. . . . $8,313

California Achievement Tests 6th ed., 2008
(Pct scoring at or above 50th National Percentile Rank)

	Math	Reading	Language
Grade 3	74%	58%	63%
Grade 7	70%	67%	66%

Academic Performance Index, 2009
Number of valid scores. . . . 1,907
2007 API (base) 868
2008 API (growth). . . . 872

SAT Testing, 2006-07
Enrollment, Grade 12 . . . . NA
percent taking test. . . . NA
number with total score 1,500+ . . . . NA

Average Scores:

Math	Verbal	Writing	Total
NA	NA	NA	NA

Federal No Child Left Behind, 2008
(Adequate Yearly Progress standards met)

	Participation Rate	Pct Proficient
ELA	Yes	Yes
Math	Yes	Yes

API Criteria . . . . Yes
Graduation rate . . . . NA
criteria met/possible. . . . 29/29

Rio Bravo-Greeley Union Elem

Kern County
6521 Enos Ln
Bakersfield, CA 93314
(661) 589-2696

Superint. . . . Ernie Unruh
Grade plan. . . . K-8
Number of schools. . . . 2
Enrollment 902
High school graduates, 2006-07. . . . 0
Dropout rate. . . . 0
Pupil/teacher ratio. . . . 19.6%
Average class size. . . . 24.7
Students per computer 5.2
Avg. Teacher Salary, ... $58,742
Avg. Daily Attendence (ADA). . . . 880
Cost per ADA. . . . $7,146

California Achievement Tests 6th ed., 2008
(Pct scoring at or above 50th National Percentile Rank)

	Math	Reading	Language
Grade 3	66%	43%	55%
Grade 7	57%	52%	47%

Academic Performance Index, 2009
Number of valid scores. . . . 707
2007 API (base) 768
2008 API (growth). . . . 765

SAT Testing, 2006-07
Enrollment, Grade 12 . . . . NA
percent taking test. . . . NA
number with total score 1,500+ . . . . NA

Average Scores:

Math	Verbal	Writing	Total
NA	NA	NA	NA

Federal No Child Left Behind, 2008
(Adequate Yearly Progress standards met)

	Participation Rate	Pct Proficient
ELA	Yes	No
Math	Yes	No

API Criteria . . . . Yes
Graduation rate . . . . NA
criteria met/possible. . . . 21/17

Rio Dell Elem

Humboldt County
95 Center St
Rio Dell, CA 95562
(707) 764-5694

Superint. . . . Mary Varner
Grade plan. . . . K-8
Number of schools. . . . 2
Enrollment 286
High school graduates, 2006-07. . . . 0
Dropout rate. . . . 0
Pupil/teacher ratio. . . . 16.1%
Average class size. . . . 23.0
Students per computer 2.4
Avg. Teacher Salary, ... $52,736
Avg. Daily Attendence (ADA). . . . 277
Cost per ADA. . . . $9,621

California Achievement Tests 6th ed., 2008
(Pct scoring at or above 50th National Percentile Rank)

	Math	Reading	Language
Grade 3	62%	54%	43%
Grade 7	79%	83%	54%

Academic Performance Index, 2009
Number of valid scores. . . . 195
2007 API (base) 741
2008 API (growth). . . . 746

SAT Testing, 2006-07
Enrollment, Grade 12 . . . . NA
percent taking test. . . . NA
number with total score 1,500+ . . . . NA

Average Scores:

Math	Verbal	Writing	Total
NA	NA	NA	NA

Federal No Child Left Behind, 2008
(Adequate Yearly Progress standards met)

	Participation Rate	Pct Proficient
ELA	Yes	Yes
Math	Yes	Yes

API Criteria . . . . Yes
Graduation rate . . . . NA
criteria met/possible. . . . 15/15

Rio Elem

Ventura County
2500 East Vineyard Ave
Oxnard, CA 93036
(805) 485-3111

Superint. . . . Sherianne Cotterell
Grade plan. . . . K-8
Number of schools. . . . 8
Enrollment 4,150
High school graduates, 2006-07. . . . 0
Dropout rate. . . . 0
Pupil/teacher ratio. . . . 22.7%
Average class size. . . . 26.2
Students per computer 4.8
Avg. Teacher Salary, ... $55,209
Avg. Daily Attendence (ADA). . . . 4,102
Cost per ADA. . . . $7,713

California Achievement Tests 6th ed., 2008
(Pct scoring at or above 50th National Percentile Rank)

	Math	Reading	Language
Grade 3	39%	19%	28%
Grade 7	39%	29%	26%

Academic Performance Index, 2009
Number of valid scores. . . . 2,994
2007 API (base) 676
2008 API (growth). . . . 688

SAT Testing, 2006-07
Enrollment, Grade 12 . . . . NA
percent taking test. . . . NA
number with total score 1,500+ . . . . NA

Average Scores:

Math	Verbal	Writing	Total
NA	NA	NA	NA

Federal No Child Left Behind, 2008
(Adequate Yearly Progress standards met)

	Participation Rate	Pct Proficient
ELA	Yes	No
Math	Yes	No

API Criteria . . . . Yes
Graduation rate . . . . NA
criteria met/possible. . . . 29/20

Rio Linda Union Elem

Sacramento County
(merged into Twin Rivers Unified)
5115 Dudley Blvd
North Highlands, CA 95660
(916) 566-1786

Superint. . . . Frank Porter
Grade plan. . . . K-12
Number of schools. . . . 24
Enrollment 10,460
High school graduates, 2006-07. . . . 31
Dropout rate. . . . 1.4
Pupil/teacher ratio. . . . 20.3%
Average class size. . . . 21.8
Students per computer 3.5
Avg. Teacher Salary, ... $59,857
Avg. Daily Attendence (ADA). . . . 9,684
Cost per ADA. . . . $8,897

California Achievement Tests 6th ed., 2008
(Pct scoring at or above 50th National Percentile Rank)

	Math	Reading	Language
Grade 3	52%	33%	41%
Grade 7	79%	74%	70%

Academic Performance Index, 2009
Number of valid scores. . . . 6,695
2007 API (base) 743
2008 API (growth). . . . 763

SAT Testing, 2006-07
Enrollment, Grade 12 35
percent taking test. . . . NA

Average Scores:

Math	Verbal	Writing	Total
NA	NA	NA	NA

Federal No Child Left Behind, 2008
(Adequate Yearly Progress standards met)

	Participation Rate	Pct Proficient
ELA	Yes	No
Math	Yes	No

API Criteria . . . . Yes
Graduation rate . . . . Yes
criteria met/possible. . . . 38/36

Riverbank Unified

Stanislaus County
6715 Seventh St
Riverbank, CA 95367
(209) 869-2538

Superint. . . . Ken Geisick
Grade plan. . . . K-12
Number of schools. . . . 7
Enrollment 2,903
High school graduates, 2006-07. . . . 127
Dropout rate. . . . 3.8
Pupil/teacher ratio. . . . 20.1%
Average class size. . . . 25.2
Students per computer 4.3
Avg. Teacher Salary, ... $63,158
Avg. Daily Attendence (ADA). . . . 2,634
Cost per ADA. . . . $9,158

California Achievement Tests 6th ed., 2008
(Pct scoring at or above 50th National Percentile Rank)

	Math	Reading	Language
Grade 3	49%	29%	31%
Grade 7	44%	36%	32%

Academic Performance Index, 2009
Number of valid scores. . . . 1,983
2007 API (base) 682
2008 API (growth). . . . 686

SAT Testing, 2006-07
Enrollment, Grade 12 173
percent taking test. . . . 20.8%
number with total score 1,500+ 13

Average Scores:

Math	Verbal	Writing	Total
490	458	444	1,392

Federal No Child Left Behind, 2008
(Adequate Yearly Progress standards met)

	Participation Rate	Pct Proficient
ELA	Yes	No
Math	Yes	No

API Criteria . . . . Yes
Graduation rate . . . . Yes
criteria met/possible. . . . 26/19

Data from school year 2007-08 except where noted.
†Combined data for elementary and high schools.

Robla Elem

Sacramento County
5248 Rose St
Sacramento, CA 95838
(916) 991-1728

Superint. . . . . Ralph Friend
Grade plan. K-6
Number of schools. 6
Enrollment 1,980
High school graduates, 2006-07. 0
Dropout rate. . . . . NA
Pupil/teacher ratio. 17.7%
Average class size. 22.3
Students per computer 4.1
Avg. Teacher Salary, ... $66,248
Avg. Daily Attendence (ADA). 1,928
Cost per ADA. $9,341

California Achievement Tests 6th ed., 2008
(Pct scoring at or above 50th National Percentile Rank)

	Math	Reading	Language
Grade 3	52%	24%	30%
Grade 7	NA	NA	NA

Academic Performance Index, 2009
Number of valid scores. 1,282
2007 API (base) 719
2008 API (growth). 724

SAT Testing, 2006-07
Enrollment, Grade 12 . . . . . NA
percent taking test. . . . . NA
number with total score 1,500+ . . . . . NA

Average Scores:

Math	Verbal	Writing	Total
NA	NA	NA	NA

Federal No Child Left Behind, 2008
(Adequate Yearly Progress standards met)

	Participation Rate	Pct Proficient
ELA	Yes	No
Math	Yes	No

API Criteria . . . . . Yes
Graduation rate . . . . . NA
criteria met/possible. 33/26

Rockford Elem

Tulare County
14983 Road 208
Porterville, CA 93257
(559) 784-5406

Superint. . . . . Andrew Schultz
Grade plan. K-8
Number of schools. 1
Enrollment 364
High school graduates, 2006-07. 0
Dropout rate. 0
Pupil/teacher ratio. 19.5%
Average class size. 21.7
Students per computer 4.2
Avg. Teacher Salary, ... $52,273
Avg. Daily Attendence (ADA). 348
Cost per ADA. $6,717

California Achievement Tests 6th ed., 2008
(Pct scoring at or above 50th National Percentile Rank)

	Math	Reading	Language
Grade 3	46%	34%	46%
Grade 7	76%	61%	68%

Academic Performance Index, 2009
Number of valid scores. 260
2007 API (base) 788
2008 API (growth). 804

SAT Testing, 2006-07
Enrollment, Grade 12 . . . . . NA
percent taking test. . . . . NA
number with total score 1,500+ . . . . . NA

Average Scores:

Math	Verbal	Writing	Total
NA	NA	NA	NA

Federal No Child Left Behind, 2008
(Adequate Yearly Progress standards met)

	Participation Rate	Pct Proficient
ELA	Yes	Yes
Math	Yes	Yes

API Criteria . . . . . Yes
Graduation rate . . . . . NA
criteria met/possible. 17/17

Rohnerville Elem

Humboldt County
3850 Rohnerville Rd
Fortuna, CA 95540
(707) 725-7823

Superint. . . . . Rob Williams
Grade plan. K-8
Number of schools. 2
Enrollment 666
High school graduates, 2006-07. 0
Dropout rate. 0
Pupil/teacher ratio. 17.0%
Average class size. 22.2
Students per computer 5.7
Avg. Teacher Salary, ... NA
Avg. Daily Attendence (ADA). 657
Cost per ADA. $7,670

California Achievement Tests 6th ed., 2008
(Pct scoring at or above 50th National Percentile Rank)

	Math	Reading	Language
Grade 3	71%	55%	62%
Grade 7	55%	68%	55%

Academic Performance Index, 2009
Number of valid scores. 469
2007 API (base) 790
2008 API (growth). 797

SAT Testing, 2006-07
Enrollment, Grade 12 . . . . . NA
percent taking test. . . . . NA
number with total score 1,500+ . . . . . NA

Average Scores:

Math	Verbal	Writing	Total
NA	NA	NA	NA

Federal No Child Left Behind, 2008
(Adequate Yearly Progress standards met)

	Participation Rate	Pct Proficient
ELA	Yes	Yes
Math	Yes	Yes

API Criteria . . . . . Yes
Graduation rate . . . . . NA
criteria met/possible. 13/13

Rosedale Union Elem

Kern County
2553 Old Farm Rd
Bakersfield, CA 93312
(661) 588-6000

Superint. . . . . Jamie Henderson
Grade plan. K-8
Number of schools. 9
Enrollment 5,381
High school graduates, 2006-07. 0
Dropout rate. 0
Pupil/teacher ratio. 20.8%
Average class size. 24.2
Students per computer 5.8
Avg. Teacher Salary, ... $57,538
Avg. Daily Attendence (ADA). 5,141
Cost per ADA. $6,774

California Achievement Tests 6th ed., 2008
(Pct scoring at or above 50th National Percentile Rank)

	Math	Reading	Language
Grade 3	62%	45%	57%
Grade 7	54%	52%	50%

Academic Performance Index, 2009
Number of valid scores. 4,005
2007 API (base) 768
2008 API (growth). 778

SAT Testing, 2006-07
Enrollment, Grade 12 . . . . . NA
percent taking test. . . . . NA
number with total score 1,500+ . . . . . NA

Average Scores:

Math	Verbal	Writing	Total
NA	NA	NA	NA

Federal No Child Left Behind, 2008
(Adequate Yearly Progress standards met)

	Participation Rate	Pct Proficient
ELA	Yes	No
Math	Yes	No

API Criteria . . . . . Yes
Graduation rate . . . . . NA
criteria met/possible. 35/31

Roseland Elem

Sonoma County
1934 Biwana Dr
Santa Rosa, CA 95407
(707) 545-0102

Superint. . . . . Gail Ahlas
Grade plan. K-6
Number of schools. 3
Enrollment 1,996
High school graduates, 2006-07. 0
Dropout rate. 0.9
Pupil/teacher ratio. 20.7%
Average class size. 24.0
Students per computer 4.5
Avg. Teacher Salary, ... $52,682
Avg. Daily Attendence (ADA). 1,440
Cost per ADA. $10,507

California Achievement Tests 6th ed., 2008
(Pct scoring at or above 50th National Percentile Rank)

	Math	Reading	Language
Grade 3	48%	21%	35%
Grade 7	54%	36%	46%

Academic Performance Index, 2009
Number of valid scores. 921
2007 API (base) 693
2008 API (growth). 727

SAT Testing, 2006-07
Enrollment, Grade 12 . . . . . NA
percent taking test. . . . . NA
number with total score 1,500+ . . . . . NA

Average Scores:

Math	Verbal	Writing	Total
NA	NA	NA	NA

Federal No Child Left Behind, 2008
(Adequate Yearly Progress standards met)

	Participation Rate	Pct Proficient
ELA	Yes	No
Math	Yes	Yes

API Criteria . . . . . Yes
Graduation rate . . . . . NA
criteria met/possible. 17/13

Rosemead Elem

Los Angeles County
3907 Rosemead Blvd
Rosemead, CA 91770
(626) 312-2900

Superint. . . . . Amy Enomoto-Perez
Grade plan. K-8
Number of schools. 5
Enrollment 3,121
High school graduates, 2006-07. 0
Dropout rate. 0
Pupil/teacher ratio. 22.8%
Average class size. 26.8
Students per computer 3.4
Avg. Teacher Salary, ... $68,598
Avg. Daily Attendence (ADA). 3,067
Cost per ADA. $8,039

California Achievement Tests 6th ed., 2008
(Pct scoring at or above 50th National Percentile Rank)

	Math	Reading	Language
Grade 3	71%	38%	46%
Grade 7	71%	59%	58%

Academic Performance Index, 2009
Number of valid scores. 2,354
2007 API (base) 797
2008 API (growth). 821

SAT Testing, 2006-07
Enrollment, Grade 12 . . . . . NA
percent taking test. . . . . NA
number with total score 1,500+ . . . . . NA

Average Scores:

Math	Verbal	Writing	Total
NA	NA	NA	NA

Federal No Child Left Behind, 2008
(Adequate Yearly Progress standards met)

	Participation Rate	Pct Proficient
ELA	Yes	No
Math	Yes	No

API Criteria . . . . . Yes
Graduation rate . . . . . NA
criteria met/possible. 25/23

Data from school year 2007-08 except where noted
†Combined data for elementary and high schools

Roseville City Elem
Placer County
1050 Main St
Roseville, CA 95678
(916) 771-1600

Superint. . . . . .Richard Pierucci
Grade plan. K-8
Number of schools. 16
Enrollment 8,697
High school graduates, 2006-07. 0
Dropout rate. 0
Pupil/teacher ratio. 20.1%
Average class size. 26.4
Students per computer 6.0
Avg. Teacher Salary, ...$65,867
Avg. Daily Attendence (ADA). 8,522
Cost per ADA. $7,003

California Achievement Tests 6th ed., 2008
(Pct scoring at or above 50th National Percentile Rank)

	Math	Reading	Language
Grade 3	73%	60%	62%
Grade 7	67%	67%	65%

Academic Performance Index, 2009
Number of valid scores. 6,373
2007 API (base) 835
2008 API (growth). 846

SAT Testing, 2006-07
Enrollment, Grade 12 . . . . .NA
percent taking test. . . . . .NA
number with total score 1,500+ . . . . . .NA

Average Scores:

Math	Verbal	Writing	Total
NA	NA	NA	NA

Federal No Child Left Behind, 2008
(Adequate Yearly Progress standards met)

	Participation Rate	Pct Proficient
ELA	Yes	Yes
Math	Yes	Yes

API Criteria . . . . .Yes
Graduation rate . . . . .NA
criteria met/possible. 37/37

Ross Elem
Marin County
PO Box 1058
Ross, CA 94957
(415) 457-2705

Superint. . . . . Tammy Murphy
Grade plan. K-8
Number of schools. 1
Enrollment 374
High school graduates, 2006-07. 0
Dropout rate. 0
Pupil/teacher ratio. 12.7%
Average class size. 20.1
Students per computer 2.1
Avg. Teacher Salary, ...$64,654
Avg. Daily Attendence (ADA). 362
Cost per ADA. $14,843

California Achievement Tests 6th ed., 2008
(Pct scoring at or above 50th National Percentile Rank)

	Math	Reading	Language
Grade 3	82%	82%	84%
Grade 7	87%	87%	83%

Academic Performance Index, 2009
Number of valid scores. 305
2007 API (base) 931
2008 API (growth). 922

SAT Testing, 2006-07
Enrollment, Grade 12 . . . . .NA
percent taking test. . . . . .NA
number with total score 1,500+ . . . . . .NA

Average Scores:

Math	Verbal	Writing	Total
NA	NA	NA	NA

Federal No Child Left Behind, 2008
(Adequate Yearly Progress standards met)

	Participation Rate	Pct Proficient
ELA	Yes	Yes
Math	Yes	Yes

API Criteria . . . . .Yes
Graduation rate . . . . .NA
criteria met/possible. 9/9

Ross Valley Elem
Marin County
110 Shaw Dr
San Anselmo, CA 94960
(415) 454-2162

Superint. . . . . Bryce Sumnick
Grade plan. K-8
Number of schools. 4
Enrollment 1,862
High school graduates, 2006-07. 0
Dropout rate. 0
Pupil/teacher ratio. 19.6%
Average class size. 24.1
Students per computer 4.5
Avg. Teacher Salary, ...$62,345
Avg. Daily Attendence (ADA). 1,819
Cost per ADA. $9,154

California Achievement Tests 6th ed., 2008
(Pct scoring at or above 50th National Percentile Rank)

	Math	Reading	Language
Grade 3	79%	81%	80%
Grade 7	78%	81%	81%

Academic Performance Index, 2009
Number of valid scores. 1,359
2007 API (base) 889
2008 API (growth). 884

SAT Testing, 2006-07
Enrollment, Grade 12 . . . . .NA
percent taking test. . . . . .NA
number with total score 1,500+ . . . . . .NA

Average Scores:

Math	Verbal	Writing	Total
NA	NA	NA	NA

Federal No Child Left Behind, 2008
(Adequate Yearly Progress standards met)

	Participation Rate	Pct Proficient
ELA	Yes	Yes
Math	Yes	Yes

API Criteria . . . . .Yes
Graduation rate . . . . .NA
criteria met/possible. 17/17

Rowland Unified
Los Angeles County
1830 Nogales St
Rowland Heights, CA 91748
(626) 965-2541

Superint. . . . . .Maria Ott
Grade plan. K-12
Number of schools. .23
Enrollment 16,920
High school graduates, 2006-07. 921
Dropout rate. 1.1
Pupil/teacher ratio. 21.1%
Average class size. 26.1
Students per computer 5.1
Avg. Teacher Salary, ...$66,866
Avg. Daily Attendence (ADA). 16,893
Cost per ADA. $8,256

California Achievement Tests 6th ed., 2008
(Pct scoring at or above 50th National Percentile Rank)

	Math	Reading	Language
Grade 3	59%	33%	44%
Grade 7	54%	49%	45%

Academic Performance Index, 2009
Number of valid scores. 12,143
2007 API (base) 757
2008 API (growth). 764

SAT Testing, 2006-07
Enrollment, Grade 12 1,310
percent taking test. 33.1%
number with total score 1,500+ 223

Average Scores:

Math	Verbal	Writing	Total
538	489	483	1,510

Federal No Child Left Behind, 2008
(Adequate Yearly Progress standards met)

	Participation Rate	Pct Proficient
ELA	Yes	No
Math	Yes	No

API Criteria . . . . .Yes
Graduation rate . . . . .Yes
criteria met/possible. 38/36

Saddleback Unified
Orange County
25631 Peter A Hartman Way
Mission Viejo, CA 92691
(949) 586-1234

Superint. . . . . .Steven Fish
Grade plan. K-12
Number of schools. .37
Enrollment 33,558
High school graduates, 2006-07. . . . 2,390
Dropout rate. 1.2
Pupil/teacher ratio. 23.6%
Average class size. 28.6
Students per computer 4.3
Avg. Teacher Salary, ...$77,293
Avg. Daily Attendence (ADA). 33,062
Cost per ADA. $7,562

California Achievement Tests 6th ed., 2008
(Pct scoring at or above 50th National Percentile Rank)

	Math	Reading	Language
Grade 3	73%	58%	66%
Grade 7	72%	71%	68%

Academic Performance Index, 2009
Number of valid scores. 22,315
2007 API (base) 837
2008 API (growth). 847

SAT Testing, 2006-07
Enrollment, Grade 12 2,741
percent taking test. 47.9%
number with total score 1,500+ 897

Average Scores:

Math	Verbal	Writing	Total
565	537	535	1,637

Federal No Child Left Behind, 2008
(Adequate Yearly Progress standards met)

	Participation Rate	Pct Proficient
ELA	Yes	No
Math	Yes	Yes

API Criteria . . . . .Yes
Graduation rate . . . . .Yes
criteria met/possible. 38/37

Salida Union Elem
Stanislaus County
4801 Sisk Rd
Salida, CA 95368
(209) 545-0339

Superint. . . . . Doug Baughn
Grade plan. K-8
Number of schools. 5
Enrollment 3,135
High school graduates, 2006-07. 0
Dropout rate. 0
Pupil/teacher ratio. 21.2%
Average class size. 26.4
Students per computer 4.5
Avg. Teacher Salary, ...$68,331
Avg. Daily Attendence (ADA). 3,272
Cost per ADA. $7,674

California Achievement Tests 6th ed., 2008
(Pct scoring at or above 50th National Percentile Rank)

	Math	Reading	Language
Grade 3	58%	43%	51%
Grade 7	49%	48%	45%

Academic Performance Index, 2009
Number of valid scores. 2,308
2007 API (base) 761
2008 API (growth). 767

SAT Testing, 2006-07
Enrollment, Grade 12 . . . . .NA
percent taking test. . . . . .NA
number with total score 1,500+ . . . . . .NA

Average Scores:

Math	Verbal	Writing	Total
NA	NA	NA	NA

Federal No Child Left Behind, 2008
(Adequate Yearly Progress standards met)

	Participation Rate	Pct Proficient
ELA	Yes	No
Math	Yes	No

API Criteria . . . . .Yes
Graduation rate . . . . .NA
criteria met/possible. 29/26

Data from school year 2007-08 except where noted.
†Combined data for elementary and high schools.

Salinas City Elem

Monterey County
840 South Main St
Salinas, CA 93901
(831) 753-5600

Superint	Donna Vaughan
Grade plan	K-6
Number of schools	12
Enrollment	7,744
High school graduates, 2006-07	0
Dropout rate	NA
Pupil/teacher ratio	20.8%
Average class size	22.5
Students per computer	5.8
Avg. Teacher Salary,	$62,126
Avg. Daily Attendence (ADA)	7,466
Cost per ADA	$8,084

California Achievement Tests 6th ed., 2008
(Pct scoring at or above 50th National Percentile Rank)

	Math	Reading	Language
Grade 3	43%	23%	34%
Grade 7	NA	NA	NA

Academic Performance Index, 2009

Number of valid scores	4,964
2007 API (base)	688
2008 API (growth)	712

SAT Testing, 2006-07

Enrollment, Grade 12	NA
percent taking test	NA
number with total score 1,500+	NA

Average Scores:

Math	Verbal	Writing	Total
NA	NA	NA	NA

Federal No Child Left Behind, 2008
(Adequate Yearly Progress standards met)

	Participation Rate	Pct Proficient
ELA	Yes	No
Math	Yes	No

API Criteria	Yes
Graduation rate	NA
# criteria met/possible	33/27

San Bruno Park Elem

San Mateo County
500 Acacia Ave
San Bruno, CA 94066
(650) 624-3100

Superint	David Hutt
Grade plan	K-8
Number of schools	8
Enrollment	2,625
High school graduates, 2006-07	0
Dropout rate	0
Pupil/teacher ratio	22.3%
Average class size	25.1
Students per computer	3.9
Avg. Teacher Salary,	$59,179
Avg. Daily Attendence (ADA)	2,555
Cost per ADA	$7,504

California Achievement Tests 6th ed., 2008
(Pct scoring at or above 50th National Percentile Rank)

	Math	Reading	Language
Grade 3	58%	46%	51%
Grade 7	56%	45%	43%

Academic Performance Index, 2009

Number of valid scores	1,894
2007 API (base)	776
2008 API (growth)	779

SAT Testing, 2006-07

Enrollment, Grade 12	NA
percent taking test	NA
number with total score 1,500+	NA

Average Scores:

Math	Verbal	Writing	Total
NA	NA	NA	NA

Federal No Child Left Behind, 2008
(Adequate Yearly Progress standards met)

	Participation Rate	Pct Proficient
ELA	Yes	No
Math	Yes	No

API Criteria	Yes
Graduation rate	NA
# criteria met/possible	37/34

San Carlos Elem

San Mateo County
826 Chestnut St
San Carlos, CA 94070
(650) 508-7333

Superint	Steven Mitrovich
Grade plan	K-8
Number of schools	7
Enrollment	2,877
High school graduates, 2006-07	0
Dropout rate	0
Pupil/teacher ratio	20.2%
Average class size	25.4
Students per computer	3.5
Avg. Teacher Salary,	$64,790
Avg. Daily Attendence (ADA)	2,577
Cost per ADA	$8,429

California Achievement Tests 6th ed., 2008
(Pct scoring at or above 50th National Percentile Rank)

	Math	Reading	Language
Grade 3	78%	68%	70%
Grade 7	85%	77%	75%

Academic Performance Index, 2009

Number of valid scores	1,971
2007 API (base)	873
2008 API (growth)	882

SAT Testing, 2006-07

Enrollment, Grade 12	NA
percent taking test	NA
number with total score 1,500+	NA

Average Scores:

Math	Verbal	Writing	Total
NA	NA	NA	NA

Federal No Child Left Behind, 2008
(Adequate Yearly Progress standards met)

	Participation Rate	Pct Proficient
ELA	Yes	Yes
Math	Yes	Yes

API Criteria	Yes
Graduation rate	NA
# criteria met/possible	25/25

San Juan Unified

Sacramento County
PO Box 477
Carmichael, CA 95609
(916) 971-7700

Superint	Pat Jaurequi
Grade plan	K-12
Number of schools	77
Enrollment	47,400
High school graduates, 2006-07	3,761
Dropout rate	8
Pupil/teacher ratio	21.2%
Average class size	22.6
Students per computer	3.1
Avg. Teacher Salary,	$69,097
Avg. Daily Attendence (ADA)	42,550
Cost per ADA	$8,163

California Achievement Tests 6th ed., 2008
(Pct scoring at or above 50th National Percentile Rank)

	Math	Reading	Language
Grade 3	63%	49%	55%
Grade 7	61%	58%	55%

Academic Performance Index, 2009

Number of valid scores	31,698
2007 API (base)	767
2008 API (growth)	777

SAT Testing, 2006-07

Enrollment, Grade 12	4,509
percent taking test	32.0%
number with total score 1,500+	908

Average Scores:

Math	Verbal	Writing	Total
545	531	526	1,602

Federal No Child Left Behind, 2008
(Adequate Yearly Progress standards met)

	Participation Rate	Pct Proficient
ELA	Yes	No
Math	Yes	No

API Criteria	Yes
Graduation rate	No
# criteria met/possible	46/42

San Lorenzo Unified

Alameda County
15510 Usher St
San Lorenzo, CA 94580
(510) 317-4600

Superint	Dennis Byas
Grade plan	K-12
Number of schools	18
Enrollment	11,821
High school graduates, 2006-07	744
Dropout rate	2.5
Pupil/teacher ratio	20.1%
Average class size	25.0
Students per computer	2.8
Avg. Teacher Salary,	$65,027
Avg. Daily Attendence (ADA)	10,818
Cost per ADA	$8,435

California Achievement Tests 6th ed., 2008
(Pct scoring at or above 50th National Percentile Rank)

	Math	Reading	Language
Grade 3	48%	27%	39%
Grade 7	42%	34%	33%

Academic Performance Index, 2009

Number of valid scores	8,076
2007 API (base)	700
2008 API (growth)	703

SAT Testing, 2006-07

Enrollment, Grade 12	940
percent taking test	36.3%
number with total score 1,500+	134

Average Scores:

Math	Verbal	Writing	Total
491	457	454	1,402

Federal No Child Left Behind, 2008
(Adequate Yearly Progress standards met)

	Participation Rate	Pct Proficient
ELA	Yes	No
Math	Yes	No

API Criteria	Yes
Graduation rate	Yes
# criteria met/possible	42/37

San Mateo-Foster City Elem

San Mateo County
1170 Chess Dr
Foster City, CA 94404
(650) 312-7700

Superint	Pendery Clark
Grade plan	K-8
Number of schools	21
Enrollment	10,079
High school graduates, 2006-07	0
Dropout rate	0
Pupil/teacher ratio	19.4%
Average class size	23.9
Students per computer	3.8
Avg. Teacher Salary,	$62,536
Avg. Daily Attendence (ADA)	9,892
Cost per ADA	$8,433

California Achievement Tests 6th ed., 2008
(Pct scoring at or above 50th National Percentile Rank)

	Math	Reading	Language
Grade 3	68%	46%	55%
Grade 7	64%	63%	61%

Academic Performance Index, 2009

Number of valid scores	7,200
2007 API (base)	815
2008 API (growth)	826

SAT Testing, 2006-07

Enrollment, Grade 12	NA
percent taking test	NA
number with total score 1,500+	NA

Average Scores:

Math	Verbal	Writing	Total
NA	NA	NA	NA

Federal No Child Left Behind, 2008
(Adequate Yearly Progress standards met)

	Participation Rate	Pct Proficient
ELA	Yes	No
Math	Yes	No

API Criteria	Yes
Graduation rate	NA
# criteria met/possible	41/33

Data from school year 2007-08 except where noted
†Combined data for elementary and high schools

San Pasqual Union Elem

San Diego County
15305 Rockwood Rd
Escondido, CA 92027
(760) 745-4931

Superint....................Frank Gomez
Grade plan..........................K-8
Number of schools......................1
Enrollment.........................595
High school graduates, 2006-07........0
Dropout rate...........................0
Pupil/teacher ratio.............. 20.9%
Average class size.................. 20.9
Students per computer.............. 1.7
Avg. Teacher Salary, ...$55,309
Avg. Daily Attendence (ADA)..........581
Cost per ADA.................. $7,798

California Achievement Tests 6th ed., 2008
(Pct scoring at or above 50th National Percentile Rank)

	Math	Reading	Language
Grade 3	72%	57%	65%
Grade 7	77%	81%	66%

Academic Performance Index, 2009
Number of valid scores................454
2007 API (base).......................859
2008 API (growth).....................861

SAT Testing, 2006-07
Enrollment, Grade 12..................NA
percent taking test..................NA
number with total score 1,500+ ......NA

Average Scores:

Math	Verbal	Writing	Total
NA	NA	NA	NA

Federal No Child Left Behind, 2008
(Adequate Yearly Progress standards met)

	Participation Rate	Pct Proficient
ELA	Yes	Yes
Math	Yes	Yes

API Criteria ....Yes
Graduation rate ....NA
criteria met/possible...............21/21

San Rafael City Elem

Marin County
310 Nova Albion Way
San Rafael, CA 94903
(415) 492-3233

Superint............Michael Watenpaugh
Grade plan..........................K-8
Number of schools......................8
Enrollment.......................3,599
High school graduates, 2006-07........0
Dropout rate...........................0
Pupil/teacher ratio...............19.0%
Average class size.................. 22.1
Students per computer.............. 3.7
Avg. Teacher Salary, ...$59,805
Avg. Daily Attendence (ADA)........ 3,617
Cost per ADA.................. $8,656

California Achievement Tests 6th ed., 2008
(Pct scoring at or above 50th National Percentile Rank)

	Math	Reading	Language
Grade 3	55%	44%	50%
Grade 7	43%	45%	44%

Academic Performance Index, 2009
Number of valid scores..............2,483
2007 API (base).......................789
2008 API (growth).....................780

SAT Testing, 2006-07
Enrollment, Grade 12..................NA
percent taking test..................NA
number with total score 1,500+ ......NA

Average Scores:

Math	Verbal	Writing	Total
NA	NA	NA	NA

Federal No Child Left Behind, 2008
(Adequate Yearly Progress standards met)

	Participation Rate	Pct Proficient
ELA	Yes	No
Math	Yes	Yes

API Criteria ....Yes
Graduation rate ....NA
criteria met/possible...............29/25

Santa Ana Unified

Orange County
1601 East Chestnut Ave
Santa Ana, CA 92701
(714) 558-5501

Superint.....................Jane Russo
Grade plan.........................K-12
Number of schools.....................59
Enrollment......................57,061
High school graduates, 2006-07.... 2,258
Dropout rate......................... 1.9
Pupil/teacher ratio.............. 22.0%
Average class size.................. 28.7
Students per computer.............. 4.6
Avg. Teacher Salary, ...$76,279
Avg. Daily Attendence (ADA).......54,239
Cost per ADA....................$8,944

California Achievement Tests 6th ed., 2008
(Pct scoring at or above 50th National Percentile Rank)

	Math	Reading	Language
Grade 3	48%	21%	34%
Grade 7	38%	34%	34%

Academic Performance Index, 2009
Number of valid scores.............40,362
2007 API (base).......................668
2008 API (growth).....................685

SAT Testing, 2006-07
Enrollment, Grade 12............... 3,109
percent taking test.............. 30.0%
number with total score 1,500+ 269

Average Scores:

Math	Verbal	Writing	Total
459	446	442	1,347

Federal No Child Left Behind, 2008
(Adequate Yearly Progress standards met)

	Participation Rate	Pct Proficient
ELA	Yes	No
Math	Yes	No

API Criteria ....Yes
Graduation rate ....Yes
criteria met/possible...............34/28

Santa Barbara Elem

Santa Barbara County
720 Santa Barbara St
Santa Barbara, CA 93101
(805) 963-4338

Superint.......................J. Sarvis
Grade plan..........................K-6
Number of schools.....................13
Enrollment.......................5,640
High school graduates, 2006-07........0
Dropout rate...........................0
Pupil/teacher ratio.............. 20.2%
Average class size.................. 20.5
Students per computer.............. 5.0
Avg. Teacher Salary, ...
Avg. Daily Attendence (ADA).............
Cost per ADA.........................

California Achievement Tests 6th ed., 2008
(Pct scoring at or above 50th National Percentile Rank)

	Math	Reading	Language
Grade 3	52%	35%	45%
Grade 7	NA	NA	NA

Academic Performance Index, 2009
Number of valid scores.............. 3,211
2007 API (base).......................759
2008 API (growth).....................759

SAT Testing, 2006-07
Enrollment, Grade 12..................NA
percent taking test..................NA
number with total score 1,500+ ......NA

Average Scores:

Math	Verbal	Writing	Total
NA	NA	NA	NA

Federal No Child Left Behind, 2008
(Adequate Yearly Progress standards met)

	Participation Rate	Pct Proficient
ELA	Yes	No
Math	Yes	No

API Criteria ....Yes
Graduation rate ....NA
criteria met/possible...............25/19

Santa Clara Elem

Ventura County
20030 East Telegraph Rd
Santa Paula, CA 93060
(805) 525-4573

Superint...................Kari Skidmore
Grade plan..........................K-6
Number of schools......................1
Enrollment..........................53
High school graduates, 2006-07........0
Dropout rate..........................NA
Pupil/teacher ratio...............17.7%
Average class size.................. 18.5
Students per computer.............. 3.8
Avg. Teacher Salary, ...$54,652
Avg. Daily Attendence (ADA)...........51
Cost per ADA.................. $9,194

California Achievement Tests 6th ed., 2008
(Pct scoring at or above 50th National Percentile Rank)

	Math	Reading	Language
Grade 3	NA	NA	NA
Grade 7	NA	NA	NA

Academic Performance Index, 2009
Number of valid scores.................37
2007 API (base).......................939
2008 API (growth).....................949

SAT Testing, 2006-07
Enrollment, Grade 12..................NA
percent taking test..................NA
number with total score 1,500+ ......NA

Average Scores:

Math	Verbal	Writing	Total
NA	NA	NA	NA

Federal No Child Left Behind, 2008
(Adequate Yearly Progress standards met)

	Participation Rate	Pct Proficient
ELA	Yes	Yes
Math	Yes	Yes

API Criteria ....Yes
Graduation rate ....NA
criteria met/possible................. 5/5

Santa Cruz City Elem

Santa Cruz County
405 Old San Jose Rd
Soquel, CA 95073
(831) 429-3410

Superint.................... Alan Pagano
Grade plan..........................K-6
Number of schools......................5
Enrollment.......................2,136
High school graduates, 2006-07........0
Dropout rate..........................NA
Pupil/teacher ratio...............17.4%
Average class size.................. 20.5
Students per computer.............. 5.0
Avg. Teacher Salary,†.............$60,324
Avg. Daily Attendence (ADA)†....... 6,438
Cost per ADA†.................. $9,723

California Achievement Tests 6th ed., 2008
(Pct scoring at or above 50th National Percentile Rank)

	Math	Reading	Language
Grade 3	61%	48%	57%
Grade 7	NA	NA	NA

Academic Performance Index, 2009
Number of valid scores.............. 1,265
2007 API (base).......................817
2008 API (growth).....................812

SAT Testing, 2006-07
Enrollment, Grade 12..................NA
percent taking test..................NA
number with total score 1,500+ ......NA

Average Scores:

Math	Verbal	Writing	Total
NA	NA	NA	NA

Federal No Child Left Behind, 2008
(Adequate Yearly Progress standards met)

	Participation Rate	Pct Proficient
ELA	No	No
Math	No	Yes

API Criteria ....Yes
Graduation rate ....NA
criteria met/possible...............25/22

Data from school year 2007-08 except where noted.
†Combined data for elementary and high schools.

Santa Maria-Bonita

Santa Barbara County
708 South Miller St
Santa Maria, CA 93454
(805) 928-1783

Superint. . . . . David Francis
Grade plan. K-8
Number of schools. 19
Enrollment 13,142
High school graduates, 2006-07. 0
Dropout rate. 0
Pupil/teacher ratio. 20.9%
Average class size. 24.9
Students per computer 3.9
Avg. Teacher Salary, ... $69,351
Avg. Daily Attendence (ADA). 12,785
Cost per ADA. $8,334

California Achievement Tests 6th ed., 2008
(Pct scoring at or above 50th National Percentile Rank)

	Math	Reading	Language
Grade 3	40%	20%	28%
Grade 7	47%	37%	36%

Academic Performance Index, 2009
Number of valid scores. 9,510
2007 API (base) 701
2008 API (growth). 708

SAT Testing, 2006-07
Enrollment, Grade 12 . . . . . NA
percent taking test. . . . . NA
number with total score 1,500+ . . . . . NA

Average Scores:

Math	Verbal	Writing	Total
NA	NA	NA	NA

Federal No Child Left Behind, 2008
(Adequate Yearly Progress standards met)

	Participation Rate	Pct Proficient
ELA	Yes	No
Math	Yes	No

API Criteria . . . . . Yes
Graduation rate . . . . . NA
criteria met/possible. 33/27

Santa Rita Union Elem

Monterey County
57 Russell Rd
Salinas, CA 93906
(831) 443-7200

Superint. . . . . James Fontana
Grade plan. K-8
Number of schools. 5
Enrollment 3,017
High school graduates, 2006-07. 0
Dropout rate. 0
Pupil/teacher ratio. 24.1%
Average class size. 28.9
Students per computer 7.0
Avg. Teacher Salary, ... $61,876
Avg. Daily Attendence (ADA). 2,893
Cost per ADA. $6,988

California Achievement Tests 6th ed., 2008
(Pct scoring at or above 50th National Percentile Rank)

	Math	Reading	Language
Grade 3	58%	34%	42%
Grade 7	49%	50%	44%

Academic Performance Index, 2009
Number of valid scores. 2,108
2007 API (base) 732
2008 API (growth). 742

SAT Testing, 2006-07
Enrollment, Grade 12 . . . . . NA
percent taking test. . . . . NA
number with total score 1,500+ . . . . . NA

Average Scores:

Math	Verbal	Writing	Total
NA	NA	NA	NA

Federal No Child Left Behind, 2008
(Adequate Yearly Progress standards met)

	Participation Rate	Pct Proficient
ELA	Yes	No
Math	Yes	No

API Criteria . . . . . Yes
Graduation rate . . . . . NA
criteria met/possible. 29/25

Santa Rosa Elem

Sonoma County
211 Ridgway Ave
Santa Rosa, CA 95401
(707) 528-5352

Superint. . . . . Sharon Liddell
Grade plan. PK-8
Number of schools. 14
Enrollment 4,732
High school graduates, 2006-07. 0
Dropout rate. 0
Pupil/teacher ratio. 17.2%
Average class size. 21.2
Students per computer 4.6
Avg. Teacher Salary,† $68,056
Avg. Daily Attendence (ADA)† 15,295
Cost per ADA† $8,574

California Achievement Tests 6th ed., 2008
(Pct scoring at or above 50th National Percentile Rank)

	Math	Reading	Language
Grade 3	53%	40%	48%
Grade 7	41%	59%	45%

Academic Performance Index, 2009
Number of valid scores. . . . . NA
2007 API (base) . . . . . NA
2008 API (growth). . . . . NA

SAT Testing, 2006-07
Enrollment, Grade 12 . . . . . NA
percent taking test. . . . . NA
number with total score 1,500+ . . . . . NA

Average Scores:

Math	Verbal	Writing	Total
NA	NA	NA	NA

Federal No Child Left Behind, 2008
(Adequate Yearly Progress standards met)

	Participation Rate	Pct Proficient
ELA	NA	NA
Math	NA	NA

API Criteria . . . . . NA
Graduation rate . . . . . NA
criteria met/possible. . . . . NA/NA

Santee Elem

San Diego County
9625 Cuyamaca St
Santee, CA 92071
(619) 258-2300

Superint. . . . . Lisbeth Johnson
Grade plan. K-8
Number of schools. 11
Enrollment 6,173
High school graduates, 2006-07. 0
Dropout rate. 0
Pupil/teacher ratio. 20.2%
Average class size. 25.0
Students per computer 4.8
Avg. Teacher Salary, ... $71,823
Avg. Daily Attendence (ADA). 6,433
Cost per ADA. $7,888

California Achievement Tests 6th ed., 2008
(Pct scoring at or above 50th National Percentile Rank)

	Math	Reading	Language
Grade 3	74%	58%	65%
Grade 7	66%	64%	58%

Academic Performance Index, 2009
Number of valid scores. 4,673
2007 API (base) 828
2008 API (growth). 840

SAT Testing, 2006-07
Enrollment, Grade 12 . . . . . NA
percent taking test. . . . . NA
number with total score 1,500+ . . . . . NA

Average Scores:

Math	Verbal	Writing	Total
NA	NA	NA	NA

Federal No Child Left Behind, 2008
(Adequate Yearly Progress standards met)

	Participation Rate	Pct Proficient
ELA	Yes	No
Math	Yes	No

API Criteria . . . . . Yes
Graduation rate . . . . . NA
criteria met/possible. 31/29

Saratoga Union Elem

Santa Clara County
20460 Forrest Hills Dr
Saratoga, CA 95070
(408) 867-3424

Superint. . . . . Lane Weiss
Grade plan. K-8
Number of schools. 4
Enrollment 2,317
High school graduates, 2006-07. 0
Dropout rate. 0
Pupil/teacher ratio. 19.9%
Average class size. 23.9
Students per computer 3.4
Avg. Teacher Salary, ... $72,337
Avg. Daily Attendence (ADA). 2,274
Cost per ADA. $9,649

California Achievement Tests 6th ed., 2008
(Pct scoring at or above 50th National Percentile Rank)

	Math	Reading	Language
Grade 3	84%	74%	81%
Grade 7	93%	93%	92%

Academic Performance Index, 2009
Number of valid scores. 1,912
2007 API (base) 953
2008 API (growth). 957

SAT Testing, 2006-07
Enrollment, Grade 12 . . . . . NA
percent taking test. . . . . NA
number with total score 1,500+ . . . . . NA

Average Scores:

Math	Verbal	Writing	Total
NA	NA	NA	NA

Federal No Child Left Behind, 2008
(Adequate Yearly Progress standards met)

	Participation Rate	Pct Proficient
ELA	Yes	Yes
Math	Yes	Yes

API Criteria . . . . . Yes
Graduation rate . . . . . NA
criteria met/possible. 21/21

Saugus Union Elem

Los Angeles County
24930 Avenue Stanford
Santa Clarita, CA 91355
(661) 294-5300

Superint. . . . . Judy Fish
Grade plan. K-6
Number of schools. 15
Enrollment 10,507
High school graduates, 2006-07. 0
Dropout rate. . . . . NA
Pupil/teacher ratio. 21.3%
Average class size. 22.5
Students per computer 5.3
Avg. Teacher Salary, ... $69,555
Avg. Daily Attendence (ADA). 10,350
Cost per ADA. $7,769

California Achievement Tests 6th ed., 2008
(Pct scoring at or above 50th National Percentile Rank)

	Math	Reading	Language
Grade 3	72%	55%	63%
Grade 7	NA	NA	NA

Academic Performance Index, 2009
Number of valid scores. 7,447
2007 API (base) 848
2008 API (growth). 852

SAT Testing, 2006-07
Enrollment, Grade 12 . . . . . NA
percent taking test. . . . . NA
number with total score 1,500+ . . . . . NA

Average Scores:

Math	Verbal	Writing	Total
NA	NA	NA	NA

Federal No Child Left Behind, 2008
(Adequate Yearly Progress standards met)

	Participation Rate	Pct Proficient
ELA	Yes	Yes
Math	Yes	Yes

API Criteria . . . . . Yes
Graduation rate . . . . . NA
criteria met/possible. 37/37

Data from school year 2007-08 except where noted
†Combined data for elementary and high schools

Sausalito Marin City

Marin County
630 Nevada St
Sausalito, CA 94965
(415) 332-3190

Superint. . . . . Debra Bradley
Grade plan. K-8
Number of schools. 3
Enrollment 266
High school graduates, 2006-07. 0
Dropout rate. 0
Pupil/teacher ratio. 11.6%
Average class size. 14.0
Students per computer 2.8
Avg. Teacher Salary, ... $79,310
Avg. Daily Attendence (ADA). 147
Cost per ADA. $32,517

California Achievement Tests 6th ed., 2008
(Pct scoring at or above 50th National Percentile Rank)

	Math	Reading	Language
Grade 3	29%	25%	13%
Grade 7	40%	27%	40%

Academic Performance Index, 2009
Number of valid scores. 98
2007 API (base) 727
2008 API (growth). 706

SAT Testing, 2006-07
Enrollment, Grade 12 . . . . NA
percent taking test. . . . . NA
number with total score 1,500+ . . . . . . NA

Average Scores:

Math	Verbal	Writing	Total
NA	NA	NA	NA

Federal No Child Left Behind, 2008
(Adequate Yearly Progress standards met)

	Participation Rate	Pct Proficient
ELA	Yes	Yes
Math	Yes	Yes

API Criteria . . . . Yes
Graduation rate . . . . NA
criteria met/possible. 9/9

Savanna Elem

Orange County
1330 South Knott Ave
Anaheim, CA 92804
(714) 236-3800

Superint. . . . . Sue Johnson
Grade plan. K-6
Number of schools. 4
Enrollment 2,388
High school graduates, 2006-07. 0
Dropout rate. . . . . NA
Pupil/teacher ratio. 23.1%
Average class size. 24.8
Students per computer 5.0
Avg. Teacher Salary, ... $78,430
Avg. Daily Attendence (ADA). 2,346
Cost per ADA. $8,225

California Achievement Tests 6th ed., 2008
(Pct scoring at or above 50th National Percentile Rank)

	Math	Reading	Language
Grade 3	54%	32%	39%
Grade 7	NA	NA	NA

Academic Performance Index, 2009
Number of valid scores. 1,611
2007 API (base) 764
2008 API (growth). 763

SAT Testing, 2006-07
Enrollment, Grade 12 . . . . NA
percent taking test. . . . . NA
number with total score 1,500+ . . . . . . NA

Average Scores:

Math	Verbal	Writing	Total
NA	NA	NA	NA

Federal No Child Left Behind, 2008
(Adequate Yearly Progress standards met)

	Participation Rate	Pct Proficient
ELA	Yes	No
Math	Yes	No

API Criteria . . . . Yes
Graduation rate . . . . NA
criteria met/possible. 29/26

Sebastopol Union Elem

Sonoma County
7611 Huntley St
Sebastopol, CA 95472
(707) 829-4570

Superint. . . . . David Wheeler
Grade plan. K-8
Number of schools. 4
Enrollment 1,173
High school graduates, 2006-07. 0
Dropout rate. 0
Pupil/teacher ratio. 18.3%
Average class size. 24.1
Students per computer 9.0
Avg. Teacher Salary, ... $62,798
Avg. Daily Attendence (ADA). 888
Cost per ADA. $8,145

California Achievement Tests 6th ed., 2008
(Pct scoring at or above 50th National Percentile Rank)

	Math	Reading	Language
Grade 3	61%	58%	54%
Grade 7	66%	60%	63%

Academic Performance Index, 2009
Number of valid scores. 723
2007 API (base) 778
2008 API (growth). 775

SAT Testing, 2006-07
Enrollment, Grade 12 . . . . NA
percent taking test. . . . . NA
number with total score 1,500+ . . . . . . NA

Average Scores:

Math	Verbal	Writing	Total
NA	NA	NA	NA

Federal No Child Left Behind, 2008
(Adequate Yearly Progress standards met)

	Participation Rate	Pct Proficient
ELA	Yes	No
Math	No	No

API Criteria . . . . Yes
Graduation rate . . . . NA
criteria met/possible. 21/17

Semitropic Elem

Kern County
25300 Highway 46
Wasco, CA 93280
(661) 758-6412

Superint. . . . . Bryan Caples
Grade plan. K-8
Number of schools. 1
Enrollment 241
High school graduates, 2006-07. 0
Dropout rate. 0
Pupil/teacher ratio. 27.1%
Average class size. 27.0
Students per computer 9.6
Avg. Teacher Salary, ... $46,653
Avg. Daily Attendence (ADA). 263
Cost per ADA. $7,703

California Achievement Tests 6th ed., 2008
(Pct scoring at or above 50th National Percentile Rank)

	Math	Reading	Language
Grade 3	35%	25%	40%
Grade 7	63%	48%	41%

Academic Performance Index, 2009
Number of valid scores. 183
2007 API (base) 616
2008 API (growth). 642

SAT Testing, 2006-07
Enrollment, Grade 12 . . . . NA
percent taking test. . . . . NA
number with total score 1,500+ . . . . . . NA

Average Scores:

Math	Verbal	Writing	Total
NA	NA	NA	NA

Federal No Child Left Behind, 2008
(Adequate Yearly Progress standards met)

	Participation Rate	Pct Proficient
ELA	Yes	No
Math	Yes	No

API Criteria . . . . Yes
Graduation rate . . . . NA
criteria met/possible. 17/10

Shasta Union Elem

Shasta County
PO Box 1125
Shasta, CA 96087
(530) 243-1110

Superint. . . . . Diane Kempley
Grade plan. K-8
Number of schools. 1
Enrollment 141
High school graduates, 2006-07. 0
Dropout rate. . . . . NA
Pupil/teacher ratio. 20.1%
Average class size. 20.1
Students per computer 3.1
Avg. Teacher Salary, ... $51,173
Avg. Daily Attendence (ADA). 136
Cost per ADA. $9,987

California Achievement Tests 6th ed., 2008
(Pct scoring at or above 50th National Percentile Rank)

	Math	Reading	Language
Grade 3	68%	47%	47%
Grade 7	NA	NA	NA

Academic Performance Index, 2009
Number of valid scores. 90
2007 API (base) 736
2008 API (growth). 755

SAT Testing, 2006-07
Enrollment, Grade 12 . . . . NA
percent taking test. . . . . NA
number with total score 1,500+ . . . . . . NA

Average Scores:

Math	Verbal	Writing	Total
NA	NA	NA	NA

Federal No Child Left Behind, 2008
(Adequate Yearly Progress standards met)

	Participation Rate	Pct Proficient
ELA	Yes	Yes
Math	Yes	Yes

API Criteria . . . . Yes
Graduation rate . . . . NA
criteria met/possible. 5/5

Shiloh Elem

Stanislaus County
6633 Paradise Rd
Modesto, CA 95358
(209) 522-2261

Superint. . . . . Seth Ehrler
Grade plan. K-8
Number of schools. 1
Enrollment 133
High school graduates, 2006-07. 0
Dropout rate. 0
Pupil/teacher ratio. 22.2%
Average class size. 22.2
Students per computer 1.9
Avg. Teacher Salary, ... $55,935
Avg. Daily Attendence (ADA). 126
Cost per ADA. $8,556

California Achievement Tests 6th ed., 2008
(Pct scoring at or above 50th National Percentile Rank)

	Math	Reading	Language
Grade 3	35%	29%	29%
Grade 7	53%	47%	33%

Academic Performance Index, 2009
Number of valid scores. 89
2007 API (base) 750
2008 API (growth). 751

SAT Testing, 2006-07
Enrollment, Grade 12 . . . . NA
percent taking test. . . . . NA
number with total score 1,500+ . . . . . . NA

Average Scores:

Math	Verbal	Writing	Total
NA	NA	NA	NA

Federal No Child Left Behind, 2008
(Adequate Yearly Progress standards met)

	Participation Rate	Pct Proficient
ELA	Yes	Yes
Math	Yes	Yes

API Criteria . . . . Yes
Graduation rate . . . . NA
criteria met/possible. 5/5

Data from school year 2007-08 except where noted.
†Combined data for elementary and high schools.

Snowline Joint Unified
San Bernardino County
PO Box 296000
Phelan, CA 92329
(760) 868-5817

Superint. . . . . Arthur Golden
Grade plan. K-12
Number of schools. 12
Enrollment 9,158
High school graduates, 2006-07. 590
Dropout rate. 1.5
Pupil/teacher ratio. 23.5%
Average class size. 28.1
Students per computer 5.0
Avg. Teacher Salary, ... $66,273
Avg. Daily Attendence (ADA). 8,748
Cost per ADA. $7,407

California Achievement Tests 6th ed., 2008
(Pct scoring at or above 50th National Percentile Rank)

	Math	Reading	Language
Grade 3	56%	44%	52%
Grade 7	52%	53%	50%

Academic Performance Index, 2009
Number of valid scores. 6,416
2007 API (base) 778
2008 API (growth). 779

SAT Testing, 2006-07
Enrollment, Grade 12 664
percent taking test. 28.2%
number with total score 1,500+ 108

Average Scores:

Math	Verbal	Writing	Total
505	509	509	1,523

Federal No Child Left Behind, 2008
(Adequate Yearly Progress standards met)

	Participation Rate	Pct Proficient
ELA	Yes	No
Math	Yes	No

API Criteria . . . . . Yes
Graduation rate . . . . . Yes
criteria met/possible. 34/32

Solana Beach Elem
San Diego County
309 North Rios Ave
Solana Beach, CA 92075
(858) 794-7100

Superint. . . . . Leslie Fausset
Grade plan. K-6
Number of schools. 6
Enrollment 2,744
High school graduates, 2006-07. 0
Dropout rate. . . . . NA
Pupil/teacher ratio. 16.6%
Average class size. 19.2
Students per computer 2.9
Avg. Teacher Salary, ... $70,572
Avg. Daily Attendence (ADA). 2,728
Cost per ADA. $11,027

California Achievement Tests 6th ed., 2008
(Pct scoring at or above 50th National Percentile Rank)

	Math	Reading	Language
Grade 3	84%	73%	80%
Grade 7	NA	NA	NA

Academic Performance Index, 2009
Number of valid scores. 1,908
2007 API (base) 923
2008 API (growth). 931

SAT Testing, 2006-07
Enrollment, Grade 12 . . . . . NA
percent taking test. . . . . NA
number with total score 1,500+ . . . . . NA

Average Scores:

Math	Verbal	Writing	Total
NA	NA	NA	NA

Federal No Child Left Behind, 2008
(Adequate Yearly Progress standards met)

	Participation Rate	Pct Proficient
ELA	Yes	Yes
Math	Yes	Yes

API Criteria . . . . . Yes
Graduation rate . . . . . NA
criteria met/possible. 29/29

Solvang Elem
Santa Barbara County
565 Atterdag Rd
Solvang, CA 93463
(805) 688-4810

Superint. . . . . Chris Whitmore
Grade plan. K-8
Number of schools. 1
Enrollment 590
High school graduates, 2006-07. 0
Dropout rate. 0
Pupil/teacher ratio. 20.8%
Average class size. 20.7
Students per computer 5.7
Avg. Teacher Salary, ... $59,325
Avg. Daily Attendence (ADA). 561
Cost per ADA. $6,854

California Achievement Tests 6th ed., 2008
(Pct scoring at or above 50th National Percentile Rank)

	Math	Reading	Language
Grade 3	77%	58%	56%
Grade 7	78%	74%	72%

Academic Performance Index, 2009
Number of valid scores. 432
2007 API (base) 843
2008 API (growth). 868

SAT Testing, 2006-07
Enrollment, Grade 12 . . . . . NA
percent taking test. . . . . NA
number with total score 1,500+ . . . . . NA

Average Scores:

Math	Verbal	Writing	Total
NA	NA	NA	NA

Federal No Child Left Behind, 2008
(Adequate Yearly Progress standards met)

	Participation Rate	Pct Proficient
ELA	Yes	Yes
Math	Yes	Yes

API Criteria . . . . . Yes
Graduation rate . . . . . NA
criteria met/possible. 21/21

Sonora Elem
Tuolumne County
830 Greenley Rd
Sonora, CA 95370
(209) 532-5491

Superint. . . . . Marguerite Bulkin
Grade plan. K-8
Number of schools. 2
Enrollment 787
High school graduates, 2006-07. 0
Dropout rate. 0
Pupil/teacher ratio. 16.6%
Average class size. 17.2
Students per computer 17.1
Avg. Teacher Salary, ... $60,581
Avg. Daily Attendence (ADA). 747
Cost per ADA. $8,246

California Achievement Tests 6th ed., 2008
(Pct scoring at or above 50th National Percentile Rank)

	Math	Reading	Language
Grade 3	68%	56%	53%
Grade 7	54%	58%	49%

Academic Performance Index, 2009
Number of valid scores. 563
2007 API (base) 766
2008 API (growth). 796

SAT Testing, 2006-07
Enrollment, Grade 12 . . . . . NA
percent taking test. . . . . NA
number with total score 1,500+ . . . . . NA

Average Scores:

Math	Verbal	Writing	Total
NA	NA	NA	NA

Federal No Child Left Behind, 2008
(Adequate Yearly Progress standards met)

	Participation Rate	Pct Proficient
ELA	Yes	Yes
Math	Yes	Yes

API Criteria . . . . . Yes
Graduation rate . . . . . NA
criteria met/possible. 13/13

Soquel Union Elem
Santa Cruz County
620 Monterey Ave
Capitola, CA 95010
(831) 464-5630

Superint. . . . . Kathleen Howard
Grade plan. K-8
Number of schools. 4
Enrollment 1,680
High school graduates, 2006-07. 0
Dropout rate. 0
Pupil/teacher ratio. 19.6%
Average class size. 24.6
Students per computer 4.1
Avg. Teacher Salary, ... $60,976
Avg. Daily Attendence (ADA). 1,629
Cost per ADA. $8,230

California Achievement Tests 6th ed., 2008
(Pct scoring at or above 50th National Percentile Rank)

	Math	Reading	Language
Grade 3	70%	59%	66%
Grade 7	61%	63%	58%

Academic Performance Index, 2009
Number of valid scores. 1,272
2007 API (base) 808
2008 API (growth). 825

SAT Testing, 2006-07
Enrollment, Grade 12 . . . . . NA
percent taking test. . . . . NA
number with total score 1,500+ . . . . . NA

Average Scores:

Math	Verbal	Writing	Total
NA	NA	NA	NA

Federal No Child Left Behind, 2008
(Adequate Yearly Progress standards met)

	Participation Rate	Pct Proficient
ELA	Yes	No
Math	No	No

API Criteria . . . . . Yes
Graduation rate . . . . . NA
criteria met/possible. 25/20

South Bay Union Elem
Humboldt County
6077 Loma Ave
Eureka, CA 95503
(707) 476-8549

Superint. . . . . Marie Twibell
Grade plan. K-12
Number of schools. 3
Enrollment 564
High school graduates, 2006-07. 18
Dropout rate. 18
Pupil/teacher ratio. 18.4%
Average class size. 9.4
Students per computer 3.4
Avg. Teacher Salary, ...
Avg. Daily Attendence (ADA). 364
Cost per ADA. $10,221

California Achievement Tests 6th ed., 2008
(Pct scoring at or above 50th National Percentile Rank)

	Math	Reading	Language
Grade 3	39%	34%	39%
Grade 7	NA	NA	NA

Academic Performance Index, 2009
Number of valid scores. 247
2007 API (base) 728
2008 API (growth). 731

SAT Testing, 2006-07
Enrollment, Grade 12 15
percent taking test. . . . . NA
number with total score 1,500+ . . . . . NA

Average Scores:

Math	Verbal	Writing	Total
NA	NA	NA	NA

Federal No Child Left Behind, 2008
(Adequate Yearly Progress standards met)

	Participation Rate	Pct Proficient
ELA	Yes	Yes
Math	Yes	No

API Criteria . . . . . Yes
Graduation rate . . . . . NA
criteria met/possible. 13/12

Data from school year 2007-08 except where noted
†Combined data for elementary and high schools

South Bay Union Elem
San Diego County
601 Elm Ave
Imperial Beach, CA 91932
(619) 628-1600

Superint. .Carol Parish
Grade plan. K-6
Number of schools. .12
Enrollment 8,147
High school graduates, 2006-07. 0
Dropout rate. . . . . .NA
Pupil/teacher ratio. 20.5%
Average class size. 22.4
Students per computer 6.5
Avg. Teacher Salary, ...$68,960
Avg. Daily Attendence (ADA). 7,722
Cost per ADA. $9,398

California Achievement Tests 6th ed., 2008
(Pct scoring at or above 50th National Percentile Rank)

	Math	Reading	Language
Grade 3	46%	23%	34%
Grade 7	NA	NA	NA

Academic Performance Index, 2009
Number of valid scores. 5,381
2007 API (base) 710
2008 API (growth). 732

SAT Testing, 2006-07
Enrollment, Grade 12 . . . . .NA
percent taking test. . . . . .NA
number with total score 1,500+ . . . . . .NA

Average Scores:

Math	Verbal	Writing	Total
NA	NA	NA	NA

Federal No Child Left Behind, 2008
(Adequate Yearly Progress standards met)

	Participation Rate	Pct Proficient
ELA	Yes	No
Math	Yes	Yes

API Criteria . . . . .Yes
Graduation rate . . . . .NA
criteria met/possible. 33/30

South San Francisco Unified
San Mateo County
398 B St
South San Francisco, CA 94080
(650) 877-8700

Superint. Barbara Olds
Grade plan. K-12
Number of schools. .15
Enrollment 9,416
High school graduates, 2006-07. 619
Dropout rate. 1.7
Pupil/teacher ratio. 21.8%
Average class size. 26.6
Students per computer 4.4
Avg. Teacher Salary, ...$58,590
Avg. Daily Attendence (ADA). 9,189
Cost per ADA. $6,959

California Achievement Tests 6th ed., 2008
(Pct scoring at or above 50th National Percentile Rank)

	Math	Reading	Language
Grade 3	64%	35%	47%
Grade 7	51%	42%	47%

Academic Performance Index, 2009
Number of valid scores. 6,779
2007 API (base) 745
2008 API (growth). 757

SAT Testing, 2006-07
Enrollment, Grade 12 682
percent taking test. 41.6%
number with total score 1,500+ 106

Average Scores:

Math	Verbal	Writing	Total
512	471	471	1,454

Federal No Child Left Behind, 2008
(Adequate Yearly Progress standards met)

	Participation Rate	Pct Proficient
ELA	Yes	No
Math	Yes	No

API Criteria . . . . .Yes
Graduation rate . . . . .Yes
criteria met/possible. 42/39

South Whittier Elem
Los Angeles County
PO Box 3037
Whittier, CA 90605
(562) 944-6231

Superint. . . . . .Erich Kwek
Grade plan. K-8
Number of schools. .8
Enrollment 4,111
High school graduates, 2006-07. 0
Dropout rate. 0
Pupil/teacher ratio. 23.8%
Average class size. 27.0
Students per computer 15.9
Avg. Teacher Salary, ...$76,788
Avg. Daily Attendence (ADA). 3,874
Cost per ADA. $8,752

California Achievement Tests 6th ed., 2008
(Pct scoring at or above 50th National Percentile Rank)

	Math	Reading	Language
Grade 3	49%	24%	37%
Grade 7	42%	34%	32%

Academic Performance Index, 2009
Number of valid scores. 2,831
2007 API (base) 694
2008 API (growth). 714

SAT Testing, 2006-07
Enrollment, Grade 12 . . . . .NA
percent taking test. . . . . .NA
number with total score 1,500+ . . . . . .NA

Average Scores:

Math	Verbal	Writing	Total
NA	NA	NA	NA

Federal No Child Left Behind, 2008
(Adequate Yearly Progress standards met)

	Participation Rate	Pct Proficient
ELA	Yes	No
Math	Yes	Yes

API Criteria . . . . .Yes
Graduation rate . . . . .NA
criteria met/possible. 25/20

Southside Elem
San Benito County
4991 Southside Rd
Hollister, CA 95023
(831) 637-4439

Superint. Eric Johnson
Grade plan. K-8
Number of schools. .1
Enrollment 234
High school graduates, 2006-07. 0
Dropout rate. 0
Pupil/teacher ratio. 19.7%
Average class size. 22.3
Students per computer 2.9
Avg. Teacher Salary, ...NA
Avg. Daily Attendence (ADA). 220
Cost per ADA. $6,970

California Achievement Tests 6th ed., 2008
(Pct scoring at or above 50th National Percentile Rank)

	Math	Reading	Language
Grade 3	88%	76%	64%
Grade 7	73%	64%	64%

Academic Performance Index, 2009
Number of valid scores. 168
2007 API (base) 867
2008 API (growth). 865

SAT Testing, 2006-07
Enrollment, Grade 12 . . . . .NA
percent taking test. . . . . .NA
number with total score 1,500+ . . . . . .NA

Average Scores:

Math	Verbal	Writing	Total
NA	NA	NA	NA

Federal No Child Left Behind, 2008
(Adequate Yearly Progress standards met)

	Participation Rate	Pct Proficient
ELA	Yes	Yes
Math	Yes	Yes

API Criteria . . . . .Yes
Graduation rate . . . . .NA
criteria met/possible. 13/13

Standard Elem
Kern County
1200 North Chester Ave
Bakersfield, CA 93308
(661) 392-2110

Superint. . . . . .Kevin Silberberg
Grade plan. K-8
Number of schools. .4
Enrollment 2,944
High school graduates, 2006-07. 0
Dropout rate. 0
Pupil/teacher ratio. 21.0%
Average class size. 23.9
Students per computer 4.9
Avg. Teacher Salary, ...$60,280
Avg. Daily Attendence (ADA). 2,790
Cost per ADA. $7,459

California Achievement Tests 6th ed., 2008
(Pct scoring at or above 50th National Percentile Rank)

	Math	Reading	Language
Grade 3	46%	33%	36%
Grade 7	37%	37%	36%

Academic Performance Index, 2009
Number of valid scores. 2,027
2007 API (base) 687
2008 API (growth). 695

SAT Testing, 2006-07
Enrollment, Grade 12 . . . . .NA
percent taking test. . . . . .NA
number with total score 1,500+ . . . . . .NA

Average Scores:

Math	Verbal	Writing	Total
NA	NA	NA	NA

Federal No Child Left Behind, 2008
(Adequate Yearly Progress standards met)

	Participation Rate	Pct Proficient
ELA	Yes	No
Math	Yes	No

API Criteria . . . . .Yes
Graduation rate . . . . .NA
criteria met/possible. 25/16

Stanislaus Union Elem
Stanislaus County
3601 Carver Rd
Modesto, CA 95356
(209) 529-9546

Superint. . . . . Wayne Brown
Grade plan. K-8
Number of schools. .7
Enrollment 3,224
High school graduates, 2006-07. 0
Dropout rate. 0
Pupil/teacher ratio. 20.5%
Average class size. 24.7
Students per computer 4.6
Avg. Teacher Salary, ...$69,248
Avg. Daily Attendence (ADA). 3,113
Cost per ADA. $8,525

California Achievement Tests 6th ed., 2008
(Pct scoring at or above 50th National Percentile Rank)

	Math	Reading	Language
Grade 3	53%	38%	47%
Grade 7	46%	41%	41%

Academic Performance Index, 2009
Number of valid scores. 2,265
2007 API (base) 745
2008 API (growth). 743

SAT Testing, 2006-07
Enrollment, Grade 12 . . . . .NA
percent taking test. . . . . .NA
number with total score 1,500+ . . . . . .NA

Average Scores:

Math	Verbal	Writing	Total
NA	NA	NA	NA

Federal No Child Left Behind, 2008
(Adequate Yearly Progress standards met)

	Participation Rate	Pct Proficient
ELA	Yes	No
Math	Yes	No

API Criteria . . . . .Yes
Graduation rate . . . . .NA
criteria met/possible. 33/23

Data from school year 2007-08 except where noted.
†Combined data for elementary and high schools.

Stone Corral Elem
Tulare County
15590 Avenue 383
Visalia, CA 93292
(559) 528-4455

Superint. . . . . . Robert Aguilar
Grade plan. K-8
Number of schools. 1
Enrollment 136
High school graduates, 2006-07. 0
Dropout rate. 0
Pupil/teacher ratio. 18.1%
Average class size. 17.0
Students per computer 5.4
Avg. Teacher Salary, ... NA
Avg. Daily Attendence (ADA). 125
Cost per ADA. $10,725

California Achievement Tests 6th ed., 2008
(Pct scoring at or above 50th National Percentile Rank)

	Math	Reading	Language
Grade 3	10%	0%	5%
Grade 7	NA	NA	NA

Academic Performance Index, 2009
Number of valid scores. 88
2007 API (base) 583
2008 API (growth). 570

SAT Testing, 2006-07
Enrollment, Grade 12 . . . . . . NA
percent taking test. . . . . . NA
number with total score 1,500+ . . . . . . NA

Average Scores:

Math	Verbal	Writing	Total
NA	NA	NA	NA

Federal No Child Left Behind, 2008
(Adequate Yearly Progress standards met)

	Participation Rate	Pct Proficient
ELA	Yes	No
Math	Yes	No

API Criteria . . . . . . No
Graduation rate . . . . . . NA
criteria met/possible. 5/2

Sulphur Springs Union Elem
Los Angeles County
27000 Weyerhaeuser Way
Canyon Country, CA 91351
(661) 252-5131

Superint. . . . . . Robert Nolet
Grade plan. K-6
Number of schools. 8
Enrollment 5,789
High school graduates, 2006-07. 0
Dropout rate. . . . . . NA
Pupil/teacher ratio. 22.4%
Average class size. 22.9
Students per computer 5.5
Avg. Teacher Salary, ... $66,826
Avg. Daily Attendence (ADA). 5,750
Cost per ADA. $7,983

California Achievement Tests 6th ed., 2008
(Pct scoring at or above 50th National Percentile Rank)

	Math	Reading	Language
Grade 3	57%	43%	53%
Grade 7	NA	NA	NA

Academic Performance Index, 2009
Number of valid scores. 3,891
2007 API (base) 813
2008 API (growth). 815

SAT Testing, 2006-07
Enrollment, Grade 12 . . . . . . NA
percent taking test. . . . . . NA
number with total score 1,500+ . . . . . . NA

Average Scores:

Math	Verbal	Writing	Total
NA	NA	NA	NA

Federal No Child Left Behind, 2008
(Adequate Yearly Progress standards met)

	Participation Rate	Pct Proficient
ELA	Yes	No
Math	Yes	No

API Criteria . . . . . . Yes
Graduation rate . . . . . . NA
criteria met/possible. 37/34

Sundale Union Elem
Tulare County
13990 Avenue 240
Tulare, CA 93274
(559) 688-7451

Superint. . . . . . Terri Rufert
Grade plan. K-8
Number of schools. 1
Enrollment 693
High school graduates, 2006-07. 0
Dropout rate. 0
Pupil/teacher ratio. 20.4%
Average class size. 22.4
Students per computer 2.7
Avg. Teacher Salary, ... $56,543
Avg. Daily Attendence (ADA). 682
Cost per ADA. $7,749

California Achievement Tests 6th ed., 2008
(Pct scoring at or above 50th National Percentile Rank)

	Math	Reading	Language
Grade 3	80%	66%	60%
Grade 7	46%	42%	39%

Academic Performance Index, 2009
Number of valid scores. 464
2007 API (base) 770
2008 API (growth). 793

SAT Testing, 2006-07
Enrollment, Grade 12 . . . . . . NA
percent taking test. . . . . . NA
number with total score 1,500+ . . . . . . NA

Average Scores:

Math	Verbal	Writing	Total
NA	NA	NA	NA

Federal No Child Left Behind, 2008
(Adequate Yearly Progress standards met)

	Participation Rate	Pct Proficient
ELA	Yes	No
Math	Yes	Yes

API Criteria . . . . . . Yes
Graduation rate . . . . . . NA
criteria met/possible. 21/20

Sunnyvale
Santa Clara County
PO Box 3217
Sunnyvale, CA 94088
(408) 522-8200

Superint. . . . . . Joseph Rudnicki
Grade plan. K-8
Number of schools. 11
Enrollment 6,027
High school graduates, 2006-07. 0
Dropout rate. 0
Pupil/teacher ratio. 19.1%
Average class size. 25.9
Students per computer 4.5
Avg. Teacher Salary, ... $65,833
Avg. Daily Attendence (ADA). 5,943
Cost per ADA. $9,105

California Achievement Tests 6th ed., 2008
(Pct scoring at or above 50th National Percentile Rank)

	Math	Reading	Language
Grade 3	62%	42%	52%
Grade 7	63%	56%	54%

Academic Performance Index, 2009
Number of valid scores. 4,241
2007 API (base) 776
2008 API (growth). 786

SAT Testing, 2006-07
Enrollment, Grade 12 . . . . . . NA
percent taking test. . . . . . NA
number with total score 1,500+ . . . . . . NA

Average Scores:

Math	Verbal	Writing	Total
NA	NA	NA	NA

Federal No Child Left Behind, 2008
(Adequate Yearly Progress standards met)

	Participation Rate	Pct Proficient
ELA	Yes	No
Math	Yes	No

API Criteria . . . . . . Yes
Graduation rate . . . . . . NA
criteria met/possible. 37/31

Susanville Elem
Lassen County
109 South Gilman St
Susanville, CA 96130
(530) 257-8200

Superint. . . . . . Gary McIntire
Grade plan. K-8
Number of schools. 5
Enrollment 1,221
High school graduates, 2006-07. 0
Dropout rate. 0
Pupil/teacher ratio. 19.1%
Average class size. 22.8
Students per computer 6.1
Avg. Teacher Salary, ... $54,940
Avg. Daily Attendence (ADA). 1,162
Cost per ADA. $7,876

California Achievement Tests 6th ed., 2008
(Pct scoring at or above 50th National Percentile Rank)

	Math	Reading	Language
Grade 3	53%	50%	49%
Grade 7	49%	45%	40%

Academic Performance Index, 2009
Number of valid scores. 873
2007 API (base) 740
2008 API (growth). 739

SAT Testing, 2006-07
Enrollment, Grade 12 . . . . . . NA
percent taking test. . . . . . NA
number with total score 1,500+ . . . . . . NA

Average Scores:

Math	Verbal	Writing	Total
NA	NA	NA	NA

Federal No Child Left Behind, 2008
(Adequate Yearly Progress standards met)

	Participation Rate	Pct Proficient
ELA	Yes	No
Math	Yes	No

API Criteria . . . . . . Yes
Graduation rate . . . . . . NA
criteria met/possible. 17/15

Sylvan Union Elem
Stanislaus County
605 Sylvan Ave
Modesto, CA 95350
(209) 574-5000

Superint. . . . . . John Halverson
Grade plan. K-8
Number of schools. 13
Enrollment 8,217
High school graduates, 2006-07. 0
Dropout rate. 0
Pupil/teacher ratio. 19.5%
Average class size. 25.9
Students per computer 5.0
Avg. Teacher Salary, ... $63,594
Avg. Daily Attendence (ADA). 7,963
Cost per ADA. $7,390

California Achievement Tests 6th ed., 2008
(Pct scoring at or above 50th National Percentile Rank)

	Math	Reading	Language
Grade 3	60%	47%	54%
Grade 7	59%	56%	49%

Academic Performance Index, 2009
Number of valid scores. 6,031
2007 API (base) 801
2008 API (growth). 807

SAT Testing, 2006-07
Enrollment, Grade 12 . . . . . . NA
percent taking test. . . . . . NA
number with total score 1,500+ . . . . . . NA

Average Scores:

Math	Verbal	Writing	Total
NA	NA	NA	NA

Federal No Child Left Behind, 2008
(Adequate Yearly Progress standards met)

	Participation Rate	Pct Proficient
ELA	Yes	Yes
Math	Yes	No

API Criteria . . . . . . Yes
Graduation rate . . . . . . NA
criteria met/possible. 37/36

Data from school year 2007-08 except where noted
†Combined data for elementary and high schools

Taft City

Kern County
820 Sixth St
Taft, CA 93268
(661) 763-1521

Superint. . . . . Mike Brusa
Grade plan. K-8
Number of schools. 7
Enrollment 2,117
High school graduates, 2006-07. 0
Dropout rate. 0
Pupil/teacher ratio. 18.4%
Average class size. 20.6
Students per computer 7.8
Avg. Teacher Salary, ... $51,585
Avg. Daily Attendence (ADA). 2,007
Cost per ADA. $8,074

California Achievement Tests 6th ed., 2008
(Pct scoring at or above 50th National Percentile Rank)

	Math	Reading	Language
Grade 3	49%	37%	40%
Grade 7	36%	43%	35%

Academic Performance Index, 2009
Number of valid scores. 1,496
2007 API (base) 667
2008 API (growth). 670

SAT Testing, 2006-07
Enrollment, Grade 12 . . . . NA
percent taking test. . . . . NA
number with total score 1,500+ . . . . . . NA

Average Scores:

Math	Verbal	Writing	Total
NA	NA	NA	NA

Federal No Child Left Behind, 2008
(Adequate Yearly Progress standards met)

	Participation Rate	Pct Proficient
ELA	Yes	No
Math	Yes	No

API Criteria . . . . Yes
Graduation rate . . . . NA
\# criteria met/possible. 25/14

Temple City Unified

Los Angeles County
9700 Las Tunas Dr
Temple City, CA 91780
(626) 548-5000

Superint. . . . . Chelsea Kang-Smith
Grade plan. K-12
Number of schools. 8
Enrollment 5,588
High school graduates, 2006-07. 540
Dropout rate. 1.5
Pupil/teacher ratio. 22.0%
Average class size. 26.1
Students per computer 4.0
Avg. Teacher Salary, ... $68,150
Avg. Daily Attendence (ADA). 5,577
Cost per ADA. $7,522

California Achievement Tests 6th ed., 2008
(Pct scoring at or above 50th National Percentile Rank)

	Math	Reading	Language
Grade 3	75%	57%	65%
Grade 7	80%	69%	70%

Academic Performance Index, 2009
Number of valid scores. 4,219
2007 API (base) 841
2008 API (growth). 853

SAT Testing, 2006-07
Enrollment, Grade 12 582
percent taking test. 61.5%
number with total score 1,500+ 231

Average Scores:

Math	Verbal	Writing	Total
587	526	522	1,635

Federal No Child Left Behind, 2008
(Adequate Yearly Progress standards met)

	Participation Rate	Pct Proficient
ELA	Yes	Yes
Math	Yes	Yes

API Criteria . . . . Yes
Graduation rate . . . . Yes
\# criteria met/possible. 30/30

Thermalito Union Elem

Butte County
400 Grand Ave
Oroville, CA 95965
(530) 538-2900

Superint. . . . . Gregory Kampf
Grade plan. K-8
Number of schools. 6
Enrollment 1,445
High school graduates, 2006-07. 0
Dropout rate. 0
Pupil/teacher ratio. 17.5%
Average class size. 22.7
Students per computer 3.1
Avg. Teacher Salary, ... $64,100
Avg. Daily Attendence (ADA). 1,389
Cost per ADA. $9,649

California Achievement Tests 6th ed., 2008
(Pct scoring at or above 50th National Percentile Rank)

	Math	Reading	Language
Grade 3	44%	29%	38%
Grade 7	33%	30%	25%

Academic Performance Index, 2009
Number of valid scores. 1,038
2007 API (base) 696
2008 API (growth). 689

SAT Testing, 2006-07
Enrollment, Grade 12 . . . . NA
percent taking test. . . . . NA
number with total score 1,500+ . . . . . . NA

Average Scores:

Math	Verbal	Writing	Total
NA	NA	NA	NA

Federal No Child Left Behind, 2008
(Adequate Yearly Progress standards met)

	Participation Rate	Pct Proficient
ELA	Yes	No
Math	Yes	No

API Criteria . . . . Yes
Graduation rate . . . . NA
\# criteria met/possible. 27/16

Travis Unified

Solano County
2751 De Ronde Dr
Fairfield, CA 94533
(707) 437-4604

Superint. . . . . Kate Wren Gavlak
Grade plan. K-12
Number of schools. 10
Enrollment 5,315
High school graduates, 2006-07. 335
Dropout rate. 1.2
Pupil/teacher ratio. 19.5%
Average class size. 25.6
Students per computer 5.4
Avg. Teacher Salary, ... $66,933
Avg. Daily Attendence (ADA). 5,185
Cost per ADA. $8,188

California Achievement Tests 6th ed., 2008
(Pct scoring at or above 50th National Percentile Rank)

	Math	Reading	Language
Grade 3	68%	51%	58%
Grade 7	71%	68%	65%

Academic Performance Index, 2009
Number of valid scores. 3,862
2007 API (base) 806
2008 API (growth). 816

SAT Testing, 2006-07
Enrollment, Grade 12 356
percent taking test. 41.6%
number with total score 1,500+ 72

Average Scores:

Math	Verbal	Writing	Total
498	486	484	1,468

Federal No Child Left Behind, 2008
(Adequate Yearly Progress standards met)

	Participation Rate	Pct Proficient
ELA	Yes	No
Math	Yes	Yes

API Criteria . . . . Yes
Graduation rate . . . . Yes
\# criteria met/possible. 38/37

Trinidad Union Elem

Humboldt County
PO Box 3030
Trinidad, CA 95570
(707) 677-3631

Superint. . . . . Geoffrey Proust
Grade plan. K-8
Number of schools. 1
Enrollment 147
High school graduates, 2006-07. 0
Dropout rate. 0
Pupil/teacher ratio. 15.8%
Average class size. 18.5
Students per computer 4.1
Avg. Teacher Salary, ... NA
Avg. Daily Attendence (ADA). 137
Cost per ADA. $8,663

California Achievement Tests 6th ed., 2008
(Pct scoring at or above 50th National Percentile Rank)

	Math	Reading	Language
Grade 3	65%	43%	57%
Grade 7	73%	53%	60%

Academic Performance Index, 2009
Number of valid scores. 95
2007 API (base) 829
2008 API (growth). 820

SAT Testing, 2006-07
Enrollment, Grade 12 . . . . NA
percent taking test. . . . . NA
number with total score 1,500+ . . . . . . NA

Average Scores:

Math	Verbal	Writing	Total
NA	NA	NA	NA

Federal No Child Left Behind, 2008
(Adequate Yearly Progress standards met)

	Participation Rate	Pct Proficient
ELA	Yes	Yes
Math	Yes	Yes

API Criteria . . . . Yes
Graduation rate . . . . NA
\# criteria met/possible. 9/9

Tulare City Elem

Tulare County
600 North Cherry Ave
Tulare, CA 93274
(559) 685-7200

Superint. . . . . John Beck
Grade plan. K-8
Number of schools. 16
Enrollment 8,750
High school graduates, 2006-07. 0
Dropout rate. 0
Pupil/teacher ratio. 20.0%
Average class size. 25.2
Students per computer 5.6
Avg. Teacher Salary, ... $67,410
Avg. Daily Attendence (ADA). 8,529
Cost per ADA. $7,374

California Achievement Tests 6th ed., 2008
(Pct scoring at or above 50th National Percentile Rank)

	Math	Reading	Language
Grade 3	52%	32%	41%
Grade 7	50%	44%	41%

Academic Performance Index, 2009
Number of valid scores. 6,311
2007 API (base) 738
2008 API (growth). 745

SAT Testing, 2006-07
Enrollment, Grade 12 . . . . NA
percent taking test. . . . . NA
number with total score 1,500+ . . . . . . NA

Average Scores:

Math	Verbal	Writing	Total
NA	NA	NA	NA

Federal No Child Left Behind, 2008
(Adequate Yearly Progress standards met)

	Participation Rate	Pct Proficient
ELA	Yes	No
Math	Yes	No

API Criteria . . . . Yes
Graduation rate . . . . NA
\# criteria met/possible. 33/28

Data from school year 2007-08 except where noted.
†Combined data for elementary and high schools.

Tustin Unified

Orange County
300 South C St
Tustin, CA 92780
(714) 730-7301

Superint. . . . . Richard Bray
Grade plan. K-12
Number of schools. 28
Enrollment 20,909
High school graduates, 2006-07. . . . 1,135
Dropout rate. 1.1
Pupil/teacher ratio. 23.6%
Average class size. 28.3
Students per computer 5.1
Avg. Teacher Salary, ... $69,708
Avg. Daily Attendence (ADA). 20,462
Cost per ADA. $7,474

California Achievement Tests 6th ed., 2008
(Pct scoring at or above 50th National Percentile Rank)

	Math	Reading	Language
Grade 3	70%	50%	60%
Grade 7	64%	64%	61%

Academic Performance Index, 2009
Number of valid scores. 15,272
2007 API (base) 815
2008 API (growth). 827

SAT Testing, 2006-07
Enrollment, Grade 12 1,301
percent taking test. 45.6%
number with total score 1,500+ 359

Average Scores:

Math	Verbal	Writing	Total
543	523	523	1,589

Federal No Child Left Behind, 2008
(Adequate Yearly Progress standards met)

	Participation Rate	Pct Proficient
ELA	Yes	Yes
Math	Yes	Yes

API Criteria . . . . . Yes
Graduation rate . . . . . Yes
criteria met/possible. 38/38

Twin Hills Union Elem

Sonoma County
700 Water Trough Rd
Sebastopol, CA 95472
(707) 823-0871

Superint. . . . . Les Crawford
Grade plan. K-12
Number of schools. 4
Enrollment 908
High school graduates, 2006-07. 35
Dropout rate. 0
Pupil/teacher ratio. 18.3%
Average class size. 17.2
Students per computer 6.5
Avg. Teacher Salary, ... $54,092
Avg. Daily Attendence (ADA). 519
Cost per ADA. $8,454

California Achievement Tests 6th ed., 2008
(Pct scoring at or above 50th National Percentile Rank)

	Math	Reading	Language
Grade 3	65%	63%	56%
Grade 7	68%	77%	77%

Academic Performance Index, 2009
Number of valid scores. 659
2007 API (base) 807
2008 API (growth). 816

SAT Testing, 2006-07
Enrollment, Grade 12 23
percent taking test. 8.7%
number with total score 1,500+ . . . . . NA

Average Scores:

Math	Verbal	Writing	Total
NA	NA	NA	NA

Federal No Child Left Behind, 2008
(Adequate Yearly Progress standards met)

	Participation Rate	Pct Proficient
ELA	Yes	Yes
Math	Yes	Yes

API Criteria . . . . . Yes
Graduation rate . . . . . Yes
criteria met/possible. 10/10

Twin Ridges Elem

Nevada County
PO Box 529
North San Juan, CA 95960
(530) 265-9052

Superint. . . . . Joan Little
Grade plan. K-12
Number of schools. 13
Enrollment 326
High school graduates, 2006-07. 103
Dropout rate. 3.5
Pupil/teacher ratio. 14.8%
Average class size. 13.6
Students per computer 4.0
Avg. Teacher Salary, ... NA
Avg. Daily Attendence (ADA). 81
Cost per ADA. $19,758

California Achievement Tests 6th ed., 2008
(Pct scoring at or above 50th National Percentile Rank)

	Math	Reading	Language
Grade 3	68%	61%	58%
Grade 7	39%	45%	50%

Academic Performance Index, 2009
Number of valid scores. 217
2007 API (base) 745
2008 API (growth). 753

SAT Testing, 2006-07
Enrollment, Grade 12 102
percent taking test. 19.6%
number with total score 1,500+ 9

Average Scores:

Math	Verbal	Writing	Total
490	521	500	1,511

Federal No Child Left Behind, 2008
(Adequate Yearly Progress standards met)

	Participation Rate	Pct Proficient
ELA	Yes	Yes
Math	Yes	No

API Criteria . . . . . Yes
Graduation rate . . . . . Yes
criteria met/possible. 14/13

Two Rock Union

Sonoma County
5001 Spring Hill Rd
Petaluma, CA 94952
(707) 762-6617

Superint. . . . . Michael Simpson
Grade plan. K-6
Number of schools. 1
Enrollment 152
High school graduates, 2006-07. 0
Dropout rate. . . . . NA
Pupil/teacher ratio. 13.3%
Average class size. 15.2
Students per computer 1.8
Avg. Teacher Salary, ... $55,821
Avg. Daily Attendence (ADA). 155
Cost per ADA. $10,885

California Achievement Tests 6th ed., 2008
(Pct scoring at or above 50th National Percentile Rank)

	Math	Reading	Language
Grade 3	65%	41%	71%
Grade 7	NA	NA	NA

Academic Performance Index, 2009
Number of valid scores. 106
2007 API (base) 874
2008 API (growth). 877

SAT Testing, 2006-07
Enrollment, Grade 12 . . . . . NA
percent taking test. . . . . NA
number with total score 1,500+ . . . . . NA

Average Scores:

Math	Verbal	Writing	Total
NA	NA	NA	NA

Federal No Child Left Behind, 2008
(Adequate Yearly Progress standards met)

	Participation Rate	Pct Proficient
ELA	Yes	Yes
Math	Yes	Yes

API Criteria . . . . . Yes
Graduation rate . . . . . NA
criteria met/possible. 13/13

Union Elem

Santa Clara County
5175 Union Ave
San Jose, CA 95124
(408) 377-8010

Superint. . . . . Jacqueline Horejs
Grade plan. K-8
Number of schools. 8
Enrollment 4,510
High school graduates, 2006-07. 0
Dropout rate. 0
Pupil/teacher ratio. 21.0%
Average class size. 25.3
Students per computer 4.1
Avg. Teacher Salary, ... $68,580
Avg. Daily Attendence (ADA). 4,417
Cost per ADA. $7,753

California Achievement Tests 6th ed., 2008
(Pct scoring at or above 50th National Percentile Rank)

	Math	Reading	Language
Grade 3	79%	64%	70%
Grade 7	74%	69%	67%

Academic Performance Index, 2009
Number of valid scores. 3,403
2007 API (base) 850
2008 API (growth). 869

SAT Testing, 2006-07
Enrollment, Grade 12 . . . . . NA
percent taking test. . . . . NA
number with total score 1,500+ . . . . . NA

Average Scores:

Math	Verbal	Writing	Total
NA	NA	NA	NA

Federal No Child Left Behind, 2008
(Adequate Yearly Progress standards met)

	Participation Rate	Pct Proficient
ELA	Yes	Yes
Math	Yes	Yes

API Criteria . . . . . Yes
Graduation rate . . . . . NA
criteria met/possible. 29/29

Union Hill Elem

Nevada County
10879 Bartlett Dr
Grass Valley, CA 95945
(530) 273-0647

Superint. . . . . Rod Fivelstad
Grade plan. PK-8
Number of schools. 3
Enrollment 814
High school graduates, 2006-07. 0
Dropout rate. 0
Pupil/teacher ratio. 19.7%
Average class size. 24.6
Students per computer 3.2
Avg. Teacher Salary, ... $61,461
Avg. Daily Attendence (ADA). 715
Cost per ADA. $7,645

California Achievement Tests 6th ed., 2008
(Pct scoring at or above 50th National Percentile Rank)

	Math	Reading	Language
Grade 3	79%	68%	66%
Grade 7	85%	75%	64%

Academic Performance Index, 2009
Number of valid scores. 619
2007 API (base) 845
2008 API (growth). 848

SAT Testing, 2006-07
Enrollment, Grade 12 . . . . . NA
percent taking test. . . . . NA
number with total score 1,500+ . . . . . NA

Average Scores:

Math	Verbal	Writing	Total
NA	NA	NA	NA

Federal No Child Left Behind, 2008
(Adequate Yearly Progress standards met)

	Participation Rate	Pct Proficient
ELA	Yes	Yes
Math	Yes	Yes

API Criteria . . . . . Yes
Graduation rate . . . . . NA
criteria met/possible. 9/9

Data from school year 2007-08 except where noted
†Combined data for elementary and high schools

Union Joint Elem
Marin County
5300 Red Hill Rd
Petaluma, CA 94952
(707) 762-2047

Superint. . . . . Luke McCann
Grade plan. K-6
Number of schools. 1
Enrollment 9
High school graduates, 2006-07. 0
Dropout rate. . . . . .NA
Pupil/teacher ratio. 9.0%
Average class size. 9.0
Students per computer 1.3
Avg. Teacher Salary, ...$43,025
Avg. Daily Attendence (ADA). 8
Cost per ADA. $20,540

California Achievement Tests 6th ed., 2008
(Pct scoring at or above 50th National Percentile Rank)

	Math	Reading	Language
Grade 3	NA	NA	NA
Grade 7	NA	NA	NA

Academic Performance Index, 2009
Number of valid scores. . . . .
2007 API (base) . . . . .NA
2008 API (growth). . . . . .NA

SAT Testing, 2006-07
Enrollment, Grade 12 . . . . .NA
percent taking test. . . . . .NA
number with total score 1,500+ . . . . . .NA

Average Scores:

Math	Verbal	Writing	Total
NA	NA	NA	NA

Federal No Child Left Behind, 2008
(Adequate Yearly Progress standards met)

	Participation Rate	Pct Proficient
ELA	Yes	Yes
Math	Yes	Yes

API Criteria . . . . .Yes
Graduation rate . . . . .NA
criteria met/possible. 5/5

Val Verde Unified
Riverside County
975 West Morgan St
Perris, CA 92571
(951) 940-6100

Superint. C. Workman
Grade plan. K-12
Number of schools. .21
Enrollment 19,547
High school graduates, 2006-07. 752
Dropout rate. 6
Pupil/teacher ratio. 22.9%
Average class size. 26.9
Students per computer 7.6
Avg. Teacher Salary, ...$66,104
Avg. Daily Attendence (ADA). 18,915
Cost per ADA. $7,461

California Achievement Tests 6th ed., 2008
(Pct scoring at or above 50th National Percentile Rank)

	Math	Reading	Language
Grade 3	52%	28%	40%
Grade 7	42%	36%	37%

Academic Performance Index, 2009
Number of valid scores. 13,187
2007 API (base) 712
2008 API (growth). 738

SAT Testing, 2006-07
Enrollment, Grade 12 1,118
percent taking test. 22.9%
number with total score 1,500+ 51

Average Scores:

Math	Verbal	Writing	Total
438	425	422	1,285

Federal No Child Left Behind, 2008
(Adequate Yearly Progress standards met)

	Participation Rate	Pct Proficient
ELA	Yes	No
Math	Yes	Yes

API Criteria . . . . .Yes
Graduation rate . . . . No
criteria met/possible. 38/36

Valle Lindo Elem
Los Angeles County
1431 North Central Ave
South El Monte, CA 91733
(626) 580-0610

Superint. . . . . .Mary Labrucherie
Grade plan. K-8
Number of schools. 2
Enrollment 1,176
High school graduates, 2006-07. 0
Dropout rate. 0
Pupil/teacher ratio. 21.4%
Average class size. 22.8
Students per computer 4.1
Avg. Teacher Salary, ...$65,150
Avg. Daily Attendence (ADA). 1,242
Cost per ADA. $7,322

California Achievement Tests 6th ed., 2008
(Pct scoring at or above 50th National Percentile Rank)

	Math	Reading	Language
Grade 3	54%	32%	46%
Grade 7	53%	42%	48%

Academic Performance Index, 2009
Number of valid scores. 887
2007 API (base) 751
2008 API (growth). 766

SAT Testing, 2006-07
Enrollment, Grade 12 . . . . .NA
percent taking test. . . . . .NA
number with total score 1,500+ . . . . . .NA

Average Scores:

Math	Verbal	Writing	Total
NA	NA	NA	NA

Federal No Child Left Behind, 2008
(Adequate Yearly Progress standards met)

	Participation Rate	Pct Proficient
ELA	Yes	No
Math	Yes	Yes

API Criteria . . . . .Yes
Graduation rate . . . . .NA
criteria met/possible. 17/16

Victor Elem
San Bernardino County
15579 Eighth St
Victorville, CA 92395
(760) 245-1691

Superint. .Ralph Baker
Grade plan. K-6
Number of schools. .18
Enrollment 11,982
High school graduates, 2006-07. 0
Dropout rate. . . . . .NA
Pupil/teacher ratio. 23.9%
Average class size. 27.4
Students per computer 4.6
Avg. Teacher Salary, ...$69,071
Avg. Daily Attendence (ADA). 11,398
Cost per ADA. $6,952

California Achievement Tests 6th ed., 2008
(Pct scoring at or above 50th National Percentile Rank)

	Math	Reading	Language
Grade 3	51%	32%	42%
Grade 7	NA	NA	NA

Academic Performance Index, 2009
Number of valid scores. 7,624
2007 API (base) 762
2008 API (growth). 781

SAT Testing, 2006-07
Enrollment, Grade 12 . . . . .NA
percent taking test. . . . . .NA
number with total score 1,500+ . . . . . .NA

Average Scores:

Math	Verbal	Writing	Total
NA	NA	NA	NA

Federal No Child Left Behind, 2008
(Adequate Yearly Progress standards met)

	Participation Rate	Pct Proficient
ELA	Yes	Yes
Math	Yes	Yes

API Criteria . . . . .Yes
Graduation rate . . . . .NA
criteria met/possible. 35/35

Vineland Elem
Kern County
14713 Weedpatch Hwy
Bakersfield, CA 93307
(661) 845-3713

Superint. . . . . Adolph Wirth
Grade plan. K-8
Number of schools. 2
Enrollment 872
High school graduates, 2006-07. 0
Dropout rate. 0
Pupil/teacher ratio. 16.5%
Average class size. 21.9
Students per computer 2.7
Avg. Teacher Salary, ...$56,494
Avg. Daily Attendence (ADA). 833
Cost per ADA. $9,969

California Achievement Tests 6th ed., 2008
(Pct scoring at or above 50th National Percentile Rank)

	Math	Reading	Language
Grade 3	33%	22%	26%
Grade 7	34%	24%	21%

Academic Performance Index, 2009
Number of valid scores. 589
2007 API (base) 640
2008 API (growth). 642

SAT Testing, 2006-07
Enrollment, Grade 12 . . . . .NA
percent taking test. . . . . .NA
number with total score 1,500+ . . . . . .NA

Average Scores:

Math	Verbal	Writing	Total
NA	NA	NA	NA

Federal No Child Left Behind, 2008
(Adequate Yearly Progress standards met)

	Participation Rate	Pct Proficient
ELA	Yes	No
Math	Yes	No

API Criteria . . . . .Yes
Graduation rate . . . . .NA
criteria met/possible. 17/9

Vista Unified
San Diego County
1234 Arcadia Ave
Vista, CA 92084
(760) 726-2170

Superint. . . . . .Joyce Bales
Grade plan. K-12
Number of schools. .33
Enrollment 27,002
High school graduates, 2006-07. . . . 1,947
Dropout rate. 18.2
Pupil/teacher ratio. 21.6%
Average class size. 25.2
Students per computer 3.9
Avg. Teacher Salary, ...$63,443
Avg. Daily Attendence (ADA). 22,986
Cost per ADA. $8,338

California Achievement Tests 6th ed., 2008
(Pct scoring at or above 50th National Percentile Rank)

	Math	Reading	Language
Grade 3	58%	35%	43%
Grade 7	57%	55%	50%

Academic Performance Index, 2009
Number of valid scores. 16,704
2007 API (base) 746
2008 API (growth). 762

SAT Testing, 2006-07
Enrollment, Grade 12 3,648
percent taking test. 15.2%
number with total score 1,500+ 298

Average Scores:

Math	Verbal	Writing	Total
517	507	506	1,530

Federal No Child Left Behind, 2008
(Adequate Yearly Progress standards met)

	Participation Rate	Pct Proficient
ELA	Yes	No
Math	Yes	No

API Criteria . . . . .Yes
Graduation rate . . . . .Yes
criteria met/possible. 42/38

Data from school year 2007-08 except where noted.
†Combined data for elementary and high schools.

Walnut Creek Elem
Contra Costa County
960 Ygnacio Valley Rd
Walnut Creek, CA 94597
(925) 944-6850

Superint. Patricia Wool
Grade plan. K-8
Number of schools. 6
Enrollment 3,125
High school graduates, 2006-07 0
Dropout rate 0
Pupil/teacher ratio 19.1%
Average class size 22.8
Students per computer 3.4
Avg. Teacher Salary, $64,576
Avg. Daily Attendence (ADA) 3,090
Cost per ADA $7,897

California Achievement Tests 6th ed., 2008
(Pct scoring at or above 50th National Percentile Rank)

	Math	Reading	Language
Grade 3	84%	72%	77%
Grade 7	84%	81%	82%

Academic Performance Index, 2009
Number of valid scores 2,430
2007 API (base) 899
2008 API (growth) 903

SAT Testing, 2006-07
Enrollment, Grade 12 NA
percent taking test NA
number with total score 1,500+ NA

Average Scores:

Math	Verbal	Writing	Total
NA	NA	NA	NA

Federal No Child Left Behind, 2008
(Adequate Yearly Progress standards met)

	Participation Rate	Pct Proficient
ELA	Yes	Yes
Math	Yes	Yes

API Criteria Yes
Graduation rate NA
criteria met/possible 29/29

Wasco Union Elem
Kern County
639 Broadway St
Wasco, CA 93280
(661) 758-7100

Superint. Gary Bray
Grade plan. K-8
Number of schools. 5
Enrollment 3,174
High school graduates, 2006-07 0
Dropout rate 0
Pupil/teacher ratio 19.9%
Average class size 23.6
Students per computer 5.5
Avg. Teacher Salary, $58,175
Avg. Daily Attendence (ADA) 3,089
Cost per ADA $8,536

California Achievement Tests 6th ed., 2008
(Pct scoring at or above 50th National Percentile Rank)

	Math	Reading	Language
Grade 3	34%	19%	30%
Grade 7	39%	32%	30%

Academic Performance Index, 2009
Number of valid scores 2,232
2007 API (base) 660
2008 API (growth) 661

SAT Testing, 2006-07
Enrollment, Grade 12 NA
percent taking test NA
number with total score 1,500+ NA

Average Scores:

Math	Verbal	Writing	Total
NA	NA	NA	NA

Federal No Child Left Behind, 2008
(Adequate Yearly Progress standards met)

	Participation Rate	Pct Proficient
ELA	Yes	No
Math	Yes	No

API Criteria Yes
Graduation rate NA
criteria met/possible 25/14

Washington Colony Elem
Fresno County
130 East Lincoln Ave
Fresno, CA 93706
(559) 233-0706

Superint. Dale Drew
Grade plan. K-8
Number of schools. 1
Enrollment 428
High school graduates, 2006-07 0
Dropout rate 0
Pupil/teacher ratio 16.5%
Average class size 20.0
Students per computer 3.6
Avg. Teacher Salary, NA
Avg. Daily Attendence (ADA) 422
Cost per ADA $8,283

California Achievement Tests 6th ed., 2008
(Pct scoring at or above 50th National Percentile Rank)

	Math	Reading	Language
Grade 3	20%	22%	31%
Grade 7	45%	35%	35%

Academic Performance Index, 2009
Number of valid scores 296
2007 API (base) 686
2008 API (growth) 692

SAT Testing, 2006-07
Enrollment, Grade 12 NA
percent taking test NA
number with total score 1,500+ NA

Average Scores:

Math	Verbal	Writing	Total
NA	NA	NA	NA

Federal No Child Left Behind, 2008
(Adequate Yearly Progress standards met)

	Participation Rate	Pct Proficient
ELA	No	No
Math	Yes	No

API Criteria Yes
Graduation rate NA
criteria met/possible 21/12

Washington Union Elem
Monterey County
43 San Benancio Rd
Salinas, CA 93908
(831) 484-2166

Superint. Dee Baker
Grade plan. K-8
Number of schools. 3
Enrollment 959
High school graduates, 2006-07 0
Dropout rate 0
Pupil/teacher ratio 21.6%
Average class size 25.6
Students per computer 4.3
Avg. Teacher Salary, $57,325
Avg. Daily Attendence (ADA) 933
Cost per ADA $6,992

California Achievement Tests 6th ed., 2008
(Pct scoring at or above 50th National Percentile Rank)

	Math	Reading	Language
Grade 3	81%	68%	78%
Grade 7	76%	76%	70%

Academic Performance Index, 2009
Number of valid scores 741
2007 API (base) 890
2008 API (growth) 882

SAT Testing, 2006-07
Enrollment, Grade 12 NA
percent taking test NA
number with total score 1,500+ NA

Average Scores:

Math	Verbal	Writing	Total
NA	NA	NA	NA

Federal No Child Left Behind, 2008
(Adequate Yearly Progress standards met)

	Participation Rate	Pct Proficient
ELA	Yes	Yes
Math	Yes	Yes

API Criteria Yes
Graduation rate NA
criteria met/possible 9/9

Washington Union High
Fresno County
6041 South Elm Ave
Fresno, CA 93706
(559) 485-8805

Superint. John Pestorich
Grade plan. 9-12
Number of schools. 3
Enrollment 1,251
High school graduates, 2006-07 195
Dropout rate 3.1
Pupil/teacher ratio 21.9%
Average class size 23.5
Students per computer 4.2
Avg. Teacher Salary, $50,673
Avg. Daily Attendence (ADA) 1,204
Cost per ADA $9,293

California Achievement Tests 6th ed., 2008
(Pct scoring at or above 50th National Percentile Rank)

	Math	Reading	Language
Grade 3			
Grade 7			

Academic Performance Index, 2009
Number of valid scores 740
2007 API (base) 593
2008 API (growth) 614

SAT Testing, 2006-07
Enrollment, Grade 12 267
percent taking test 15.0%
number with total score 1,500+ 3

Average Scores:

Math	Verbal	Writing	Total
381	373	384	1,138

Federal No Child Left Behind, 2008
(Adequate Yearly Progress standards met)

	Participation Rate	Pct Proficient
ELA	Yes	No
Math	Yes	Yes

API Criteria Yes
Graduation rate Yes
criteria met/possible 18/17

Waugh Elem
Sonoma County
1851 Hartman Ln
Petaluma, CA 94954
(707) 765-3331

Superint. Scott Mahoney
Grade plan. K-6
Number of schools. 2
Enrollment 899
High school graduates, 2006-07 0
Dropout rate NA
Pupil/teacher ratio 19.9%
Average class size 20.5
Students per computer 7.2
Avg. Teacher Salary, $66,584
Avg. Daily Attendence (ADA) 882
Cost per ADA $7,996

California Achievement Tests 6th ed., 2008
(Pct scoring at or above 50th National Percentile Rank)

	Math	Reading	Language
Grade 3	82%	67%	71%
Grade 7	NA	NA	NA

Academic Performance Index, 2009
Number of valid scores 617
2007 API (base) 893
2008 API (growth) 898

SAT Testing, 2006-07
Enrollment, Grade 12 NA
percent taking test NA
number with total score 1,500+ NA

Average Scores:

Math	Verbal	Writing	Total
NA	NA	NA	NA

Federal No Child Left Behind, 2008
(Adequate Yearly Progress standards met)

	Participation Rate	Pct Proficient
ELA	Yes	Yes
Math	Yes	Yes

API Criteria Yes
Graduation rate NA
criteria met/possible 17/17

Data from school year 2007-08 except where noted
†Combined data for elementary and high schools

Weaver Union Elem

Merced County
3076 East Childs Ave
Merced, CA 95340
(209) 723-7606

Superint. . . . . Steven Becker
Grade plan. K-8
Number of schools. 3
Enrollment 2,323
High school graduates, 2006-07. 0
Dropout rate. 0
Pupil/teacher ratio. 18.6%
Average class size. 22.2
Students per computer 8.3
Avg. Teacher Salary, ... $59,808
Avg. Daily Attendence (ADA). 2,225
Cost per ADA. $7,593

California Achievement Tests 6th ed., 2008
(Pct scoring at or above 50th National Percentile Rank)

	Math	Reading	Language
Grade 3	49%	36%	50%
Grade 7	41%	41%	40%

Academic Performance Index, 2009
Number of valid scores. 1,515
2007 API (base) 706
2008 API (growth). 749

SAT Testing, 2006-07
Enrollment, Grade 12 . . . . .NA
percent taking test. . . . . .NA
number with total score 1,500+ . . . . . .NA

Average Scores:

Math	Verbal	Writing	Total
NA	NA	NA	NA

Federal No Child Left Behind, 2008
(Adequate Yearly Progress standards met)

	Participation Rate	Pct Proficient
ELA	Yes	No
Math	Yes	Yes

API Criteria . . . . .Yes
Graduation rate . . . . .NA
criteria met/possible. 31/30

Weed Union Elem

Siskiyou County
595 East Alma St
Mount Shasta, CA 96067
(530) 938-4797

Superint. . . . . Gary Lampella
Grade plan. K-8
Number of schools. 2
Enrollment 350
High school graduates, 2006-07. 0
Dropout rate. 0
Pupil/teacher ratio. 17.1%
Average class size. 21.0
Students per computer 2.7
Avg. Teacher Salary, ... $52,964
Avg. Daily Attendence (ADA). 316
Cost per ADA. $9,212

California Achievement Tests 6th ed., 2008
(Pct scoring at or above 50th National Percentile Rank)

	Math	Reading	Language
Grade 3	56%	38%	42%
Grade 7	53%	40%	36%

Academic Performance Index, 2009
Number of valid scores. 248
2007 API (base) 737
2008 API (growth). 733

SAT Testing, 2006-07
Enrollment, Grade 12 . . . . .NA
percent taking test. . . . . .NA
number with total score 1,500+ . . . . . .NA

Average Scores:

Math	Verbal	Writing	Total
NA	NA	NA	NA

Federal No Child Left Behind, 2008
(Adequate Yearly Progress standards met)

	Participation Rate	Pct Proficient
ELA	Yes	Yes
Math	Yes	No

API Criteria . . . . .Yes
Graduation rate . . . . .NA
criteria met/possible. 13/12

West Fresno Elem

Fresno County
2888 South Ivy St
Fresno, CA 93706
(559) 495-5608

Superint. . . . . Dolphas Trotter
Grade plan. K-12
Number of schools. 3
Enrollment 1,207
High school graduates, 2006-07. 23
Dropout rate. 18.4
Pupil/teacher ratio. 19.2%
Average class size. 20.8
Students per computer 2.2
Avg. Teacher Salary, ... $50,726
Avg. Daily Attendence (ADA). 875
Cost per ADA. $10,071

California Achievement Tests 6th ed., 2008
(Pct scoring at or above 50th National Percentile Rank)

	Math	Reading	Language
Grade 3	31%	11%	16%
Grade 7	26%	22%	15%

Academic Performance Index, 2009
Number of valid scores. 532
2007 API (base) 571
2008 API (growth). 632

SAT Testing, 2006-07
Enrollment, Grade 12 20
percent taking test. . . . . .NA
number with total score 1,500+ . . . . . .NA

Average Scores:

Math	Verbal	Writing	Total
NA	NA	NA	NA

Federal No Child Left Behind, 2008
(Adequate Yearly Progress standards met)

	Participation Rate	Pct Proficient
ELA	Yes	No
Math	Yes	Yes

API Criteria . . . . .Yes
Graduation rate . . . . .NA
criteria met/possible. 25/20

West Park Elem

Fresno County
2695 South Valentine Ave
Fresno, CA 93706
(559) 233-6501

Superint. . . . . .Ralph Vigil
Grade plan. K-12
Number of schools. 2
Enrollment 687
High school graduates, 2006-07. 31
Dropout rate. 13.2
Pupil/teacher ratio. 17.4%
Average class size. 22.4
Students per computer 5.1
Avg. Teacher Salary, ...NA
Avg. Daily Attendence (ADA). 317
Cost per ADA. $11,389

California Achievement Tests 6th ed., 2008
(Pct scoring at or above 50th National Percentile Rank)

	Math	Reading	Language
Grade 3	37%	21%	34%
Grade 7	23%	27%	25%

Academic Performance Index, 2009
Number of valid scores. 183
2007 API (base) 671
2008 API (growth). 680

SAT Testing, 2006-07
Enrollment, Grade 12 49
percent taking test. . . . . .NA
number with total score 1,500+ . . . . . .NA

Average Scores:

Math	Verbal	Writing	Total
NA	NA	NA	NA

Federal No Child Left Behind, 2008
(Adequate Yearly Progress standards met)

	Participation Rate	Pct Proficient
ELA	Yes	No
Math	Yes	No

API Criteria . . . . .Yes
Graduation rate . . . . .NA
criteria met/possible. 17/12

West Side Union Elem

Sonoma County
1201 Felta Rd
Healdsburg, CA 95448
(707) 433-3923

Superint. . . . . Rhonda Bellmer
Grade plan. K-6
Number of schools. 1
Enrollment 163
High school graduates, 2006-07. 0
Dropout rate. . . . . .NA
Pupil/teacher ratio. 20.4%
Average class size. 23.1
Students per computer 3.0
Avg. Teacher Salary, ...NA
Avg. Daily Attendence (ADA). 155
Cost per ADA. $8,347

California Achievement Tests 6th ed., 2008
(Pct scoring at or above 50th National Percentile Rank)

	Math	Reading	Language
Grade 3	52%	39%	57%
Grade 7	NA	NA	NA

Academic Performance Index, 2009
Number of valid scores. 112
2007 API (base) 781
2008 API (growth). 802

SAT Testing, 2006-07
Enrollment, Grade 12 . . . . .NA
percent taking test. . . . . .NA
number with total score 1,500+ . . . . . .NA

Average Scores:

Math	Verbal	Writing	Total
NA	NA	NA	NA

Federal No Child Left Behind, 2008
(Adequate Yearly Progress standards met)

	Participation Rate	Pct Proficient
ELA	Yes	Yes
Math	Yes	Yes

API Criteria . . . . .Yes
Graduation rate . . . . .NA
criteria met/possible. 9/9

Westminster Elem

Orange County
14121 Cedarwood Ave
Westminster, CA 92683
(714) 894-7311

Superint. . . . . .Sharon Nordheim
Grade plan. K-8
Number of schools. .15
Enrollment 9,930
High school graduates, 2006-07. 0
Dropout rate. 0
Pupil/teacher ratio. 21.4%
Average class size. 25.7
Students per computer 3.3
Avg. Teacher Salary, ... $69,323
Avg. Daily Attendence (ADA). 9,842
Cost per ADA. $8,180

California Achievement Tests 6th ed., 2008
(Pct scoring at or above 50th National Percentile Rank)

	Math	Reading	Language
Grade 3	59%	35%	43%
Grade 7	60%	52%	50%

Academic Performance Index, 2009
Number of valid scores. 7,217
2007 API (base) 769
2008 API (growth). 782

SAT Testing, 2006-07
Enrollment, Grade 12 . . . . .NA
percent taking test. . . . . .NA
number with total score 1,500+ . . . . . .NA

Average Scores:

Math	Verbal	Writing	Total
NA	NA	NA	NA

Federal No Child Left Behind, 2008
(Adequate Yearly Progress standards met)

	Participation Rate	Pct Proficient
ELA	Yes	No
Math	Yes	No

API Criteria . . . . .Yes
Graduation rate . . . . .NA
criteria met/possible. 33/28

Data from school year 2007-08 except where noted.
†Combined data for elementary and high schools.

Westmorland Union Elem

Imperial County
PO Box 88
Westmorland, CA 92281
(760) 344-4364

Superint.................... Linda Morse
Grade plan............................K-8
Number of schools.......................1
Enrollment............................387
High school graduates, 2006-07........0
Dropout rate...........................0
Pupil/teacher ratio................13.6%
Average class size.................. 19.4
Students per computer 2.4
Avg. Teacher Salary, ... $57,594
Avg. Daily Attendence (ADA)..........374
Cost per ADA.................. $10,195

California Achievement Tests 6th ed., 2008
(Pct scoring at or above 50th National Percentile Rank)

	Math	Reading	Language
Grade 3	40%	19%	26%
Grade 7	41%	53%	39%

Academic Performance Index, 2009
Number of valid scores................279
2007 API (base).......................709
2008 API (growth).....................728

SAT Testing, 2006-07
Enrollment, Grade 12.................NA
percent taking test..................NA
number with total score 1,500+ ......NA

Average Scores:

Math	Verbal	Writing	Total
NA	NA	NA	NA

Federal No Child Left Behind, 2008
(Adequate Yearly Progress standards met)

	Participation Rate	Pct Proficient
ELA	Yes	No
Math	Yes	Yes

API Criteria ....Yes
Graduation rate ....NA
criteria met/possible............... 17/16

Westside Union Elem

Los Angeles County
41914 50th St West
Quartz Hill, CA 93536
(661) 722-0716

Superint...................Regina Rossall
Grade plan............................K-8
Number of schools......................11
Enrollment....................... 9,115
High school graduates, 2006-07........0
Dropout rate...........................0
Pupil/teacher ratio............... 25.9%
Average class size.................. 26.1
Students per computer 7.0
Avg. Teacher Salary, ... $63,706
Avg. Daily Attendence (ADA)........ 8,747
Cost per ADA.................. $6,657

California Achievement Tests 6th ed., 2008
(Pct scoring at or above 50th National Percentile Rank)

	Math	Reading	Language
Grade 3	60%	43%	49%
Grade 7	57%	59%	58%

Academic Performance Index, 2009
Number of valid scores.............. 6,705
2007 API (base).......................781
2008 API (growth).....................792

SAT Testing, 2006-07
Enrollment, Grade 12.................NA
percent taking test..................NA
number with total score 1,500+ ......NA

Average Scores:

Math	Verbal	Writing	Total
NA	NA	NA	NA

Federal No Child Left Behind, 2008
(Adequate Yearly Progress standards met)

	Participation Rate	Pct Proficient
ELA	Yes	No
Math	Yes	No

API Criteria ....Yes
Graduation rate ....NA
criteria met/possible............... 37/32

Wheatland Elem

Yuba County
PO Box 818
Wheatland, CA 95692
(530) 633-3130

Superint...................Debra Pearson
Grade plan...........................K-12
Number of schools.......................4
Enrollment....................... 1,458
High school graduates, 2006-07........2
Dropout rate...................... 19.2
Pupil/teacher ratio............... 20.0%
Average class size.................. 22.2
Students per computer 1.8
Avg. Teacher Salary, ... $70,545
Avg. Daily Attendence (ADA)........ 1,233
Cost per ADA.................. $11,576

California Achievement Tests 6th ed., 2008
(Pct scoring at or above 50th National Percentile Rank)

	Math	Reading	Language
Grade 3	66%	49%	53%
Grade 7	66%	62%	55%

Academic Performance Index, 2009
Number of valid scores................937
2007 API (base).......................799
2008 API (growth).....................795

SAT Testing, 2006-07
Enrollment, Grade 12....................7
percent taking test..................NA
number with total score 1,500+ ......NA

Average Scores:

Math	Verbal	Writing	Total
NA	NA	NA	NA

Federal No Child Left Behind, 2008
(Adequate Yearly Progress standards met)

	Participation Rate	Pct Proficient
ELA	Yes	Yes
Math	Yes	Yes

API Criteria ....Yes
Graduation rate ....No
criteria met/possible............... 20/19

Whittier City Elem

Los Angeles County
7211 South Whittier Ave
Whittier, CA 90602
(562) 789-3000

Superint.................... Ron Carruth
Grade plan............................K-8
Number of schools......................12
Enrollment....................... 6,735
High school graduates, 2006-07........0
Dropout rate...........................0
Pupil/teacher ratio................21.0%
Average class size.................. 26.0
Students per computer 4.1
Avg. Teacher Salary, ... $66,418
Avg. Daily Attendence (ADA)........ 6,580
Cost per ADA.................. $8,517

California Achievement Tests 6th ed., 2008
(Pct scoring at or above 50th National Percentile Rank)

	Math	Reading	Language
Grade 3	47%	27%	41%
Grade 7	45%	44%	41%

Academic Performance Index, 2009
Number of valid scores.............. 4,917
2007 API (base).......................722
2008 API (growth).....................748

SAT Testing, 2006-07
Enrollment, Grade 12.................NA
percent taking test..................NA
number with total score 1,500+ ......NA

Average Scores:

Math	Verbal	Writing	Total
NA	NA	NA	NA

Federal No Child Left Behind, 2008
(Adequate Yearly Progress standards met)

	Participation Rate	Pct Proficient
ELA	Yes	No
Math	Yes	No

API Criteria ....Yes
Graduation rate ....NA
criteria met/possible............... 25/22

Willow Creek Elem

Siskiyou County
5321 York Rd
Montague, CA 96064
(530) 459-3313

Superint................... Ron Ferrando
Grade plan............................K-8
Number of schools.......................1
Enrollment.............................47
High school graduates, 2006-07........0
Dropout rate...........................0
Pupil/teacher ratio................18.1%
Average class size.................. 24.0
Students per computer 2.6
Avg. Teacher Salary, ...NA
Avg. Daily Attendence (ADA)...........44
Cost per ADA.................. $12,623

California Achievement Tests 6th ed., 2008
(Pct scoring at or above 50th National Percentile Rank)

	Math	Reading	Language
Grade 3	NA	NA	NA
Grade 7	NA	NA	NA

Academic Performance Index, 2009
Number of valid scores.................31
2007 API (base).......................748
2008 API (growth).....................689

SAT Testing, 2006-07
Enrollment, Grade 12.................NA
percent taking test..................NA
number with total score 1,500+ ......NA

Average Scores:

Math	Verbal	Writing	Total
NA	NA	NA	NA

Federal No Child Left Behind, 2008
(Adequate Yearly Progress standards met)

	Participation Rate	Pct Proficient
ELA	Yes	Yes
Math	Yes	Yes

API Criteria ....Yes
Graduation rate ....NA
criteria met/possible................. 5/5

Wilmar Union Elem

Sonoma County
3775 Bodega Ave
Petaluma, CA 94952
(707) 765-4340

Superint.....................Eric Hoppes
Grade plan............................K-6
Number of schools.......................1
Enrollment............................224
High school graduates, 2006-07........0
Dropout rate..........................NA
Pupil/teacher ratio................18.7%
Average class size.................. 14.1
Students per computer 3.4
Avg. Teacher Salary, ... $54,197
Avg. Daily Attendence (ADA)..........225
Cost per ADA.................. $7,906

California Achievement Tests 6th ed., 2008
(Pct scoring at or above 50th National Percentile Rank)

	Math	Reading	Language
Grade 3	53%	61%	64%
Grade 7	NA	NA	NA

Academic Performance Index, 2009
Number of valid scores................147
2007 API (base).......................790
2008 API (growth).....................850

SAT Testing, 2006-07
Enrollment, Grade 12.................NA
percent taking test..................NA
number with total score 1,500+ ......NA

Average Scores:

Math	Verbal	Writing	Total
NA	NA	NA	NA

Federal No Child Left Behind, 2008
(Adequate Yearly Progress standards met)

	Participation Rate	Pct Proficient
ELA	Yes	Yes
Math	Yes	Yes

API Criteria ....Yes
Graduation rate ....NA
criteria met/possible................. 9/9

Data from school year 2007-08 except where noted
†Combined data for elementary and high schools

Wilsona Elem

Los Angeles County
18050 East Avenue O
Palmdale, CA 93591
(661) 264-1111

Superint. . . . . David Andreasen
Grade plan. K-8
Number of schools. 4
Enrollment 1,871
High school graduates, 2006-07. 0
Dropout rate. 0
Pupil/teacher ratio. 21.5%
Average class size. 25.3
Students per computer 6.0
Avg. Teacher Salary, ... NA
Avg. Daily Attendence (ADA). 1,852
Cost per ADA. $9,380

California Achievement Tests 6th ed., 2008
(Pct scoring at or above 50th National Percentile Rank)

	Math	Reading	Language
Grade 3	51%	29%	37%
Grade 7	38%	32%	24%

Academic Performance Index, 2009
Number of valid scores. 1,298
2007 API (base) 709
2008 API (growth). 714

SAT Testing, 2006-07
Enrollment, Grade 12 . . . . NA
percent taking test. . . . . NA
number with total score 1,500+ . . . . . . NA

Average Scores:

Math	Verbal	Writing	Total
NA	NA	NA	NA

Federal No Child Left Behind, 2008
(Adequate Yearly Progress standards met)

	Participation Rate	Pct Proficient
ELA	Yes	No
Math	Yes	No

API Criteria . . . . Yes
Graduation rate . . . . NA
criteria met/possible. 29/20

Wiseburn Elem

Los Angeles County
13530 Aviation Blvd
Hawthorne, CA 90250
(310) 643-3025

Superint. . . . . Tom Johnstone
Grade plan. K-8
Number of schools. 4
Enrollment 2,196
High school graduates, 2006-07. 0
Dropout rate. 0
Pupil/teacher ratio. 21.6%
Average class size. 26.3
Students per computer 3.7
Avg. Teacher Salary, ... $67,358
Avg. Daily Attendence (ADA). 2,159
Cost per ADA. $7,703

California Achievement Tests 6th ed., 2008
(Pct scoring at or above 50th National Percentile Rank)

	Math	Reading	Language
Grade 3	66%	50%	61%
Grade 7	56%	55%	55%

Academic Performance Index, 2009
Number of valid scores. 1,647
2007 API (base) 792
2008 API (growth). 808

SAT Testing, 2006-07
Enrollment, Grade 12 . . . . NA
percent taking test. . . . . NA
number with total score 1,500+ . . . . . . NA

Average Scores:

Math	Verbal	Writing	Total
NA	NA	NA	NA

Federal No Child Left Behind, 2008
(Adequate Yearly Progress standards met)

	Participation Rate	Pct Proficient
ELA	No	Yes
Math	No	Yes

API Criteria . . . . Yes
Graduation rate . . . . NA
criteria met/possible. 29/27

Woodlake Union Elem

Tulare County
300 West Whitney Ave
Woodlake, CA 93286
(559) 564-8081

Superint. . . . . Tim Hire
Grade plan. K-8
Number of schools. 3
Enrollment 1,528
High school graduates, 2006-07. 0
Dropout rate. 0
Pupil/teacher ratio. 20.4%
Average class size. 24.0
Students per computer 3.5
Avg. Teacher Salary, ... $60,459
Avg. Daily Attendence (ADA). 1,513
Cost per ADA. $9,036

California Achievement Tests 6th ed., 2008
(Pct scoring at or above 50th National Percentile Rank)

	Math	Reading	Language
Grade 3	40%	21%	36%
Grade 7	40%	30%	32%

Academic Performance Index, 2009
Number of valid scores. 1,169
2007 API (base) 662
2008 API (growth). 687

SAT Testing, 2006-07
Enrollment, Grade 12 . . . . NA
percent taking test. . . . . NA
number with total score 1,500+ . . . . . . NA

Average Scores:

Math	Verbal	Writing	Total
NA	NA	NA	NA

Federal No Child Left Behind, 2008
(Adequate Yearly Progress standards met)

	Participation Rate	Pct Proficient
ELA	Yes	No
Math	Yes	No

API Criteria . . . . Yes
Graduation rate . . . . NA
criteria met/possible. 21/13

Woodside Elem

San Mateo County
3195 Woodside Rd
Woodside, CA 94062
(650) 851-1571

Superint. . . . . Diana Abbati
Grade plan. K-8
Number of schools. 1
Enrollment 465
High school graduates, 2006-07. 0
Dropout rate. 0
Pupil/teacher ratio. 13.0%
Average class size. 18.1
Students per computer 3.2
Avg. Teacher Salary, ... $86,512
Avg. Daily Attendence (ADA). 439
Cost per ADA. $16,930

California Achievement Tests 6th ed., 2008
(Pct scoring at or above 50th National Percentile Rank)

	Math	Reading	Language
Grade 3	90%	84%	76%
Grade 7	90%	90%	88%

Academic Performance Index, 2009
Number of valid scores. 361
2007 API (base) 939
2008 API (growth). 956

SAT Testing, 2006-07
Enrollment, Grade 12 . . . . NA
percent taking test. . . . . NA
number with total score 1,500+ . . . . . . NA

Average Scores:

Math	Verbal	Writing	Total
NA	NA	NA	NA

Federal No Child Left Behind, 2008
(Adequate Yearly Progress standards met)

	Participation Rate	Pct Proficient
ELA	Yes	Yes
Math	Yes	Yes

API Criteria . . . . Yes
Graduation rate . . . . NA
criteria met/possible. 9/9

Woodville Elem

Tulare County
16563 Road 168
Porterville, CA 93257
(559) 686-9712

Superint. . . . . Clifford Turk
Grade plan. K-8
Number of schools. 1
Enrollment 605
High school graduates, 2006-07. 0
Dropout rate. 0
Pupil/teacher ratio. 14.1%
Average class size. 18.5
Students per computer 5.0
Avg. Teacher Salary, ...
Avg. Daily Attendence (ADA). 589
Cost per ADA. $8,891

California Achievement Tests 6th ed., 2008
(Pct scoring at or above 50th National Percentile Rank)

	Math	Reading	Language
Grade 3	59%	23%	55%
Grade 7	32%	28%	30%

Academic Performance Index, 2009
Number of valid scores. 426
2007 API (base) 721
2008 API (growth). 727

SAT Testing, 2006-07
Enrollment, Grade 12 . . . . NA
percent taking test. . . . . NA
number with total score 1,500+ . . . . . . NA

Average Scores:

Math	Verbal	Writing	Total
NA	NA	NA	NA

Federal No Child Left Behind, 2008
(Adequate Yearly Progress standards met)

	Participation Rate	Pct Proficient
ELA	Yes	Yes
Math	Yes	Yes

API Criteria . . . . Yes
Graduation rate . . . . NA
criteria met/possible. 17/17

Wright Elem

Sonoma County
4385 Price Ave
Santa Rosa, CA 95407
(707) 542-0550

Superint. . . . . Casey D'Angelo
Grade plan. K-6
Number of schools. 3
Enrollment 1,435
High school graduates, 2006-07. 0
Dropout rate. . . . . NA
Pupil/teacher ratio. 18.8%
Average class size. 20.7
Students per computer 9.0
Avg. Teacher Salary, ... $59,048
Avg. Daily Attendence (ADA). 1,427
Cost per ADA. $8,060

California Achievement Tests 6th ed., 2008
(Pct scoring at or above 50th National Percentile Rank)

	Math	Reading	Language
Grade 3	64%	37%	44%
Grade 7	NA	NA	NA

Academic Performance Index, 2009
Number of valid scores. 899
2007 API (base) 798
2008 API (growth). 821

SAT Testing, 2006-07
Enrollment, Grade 12 . . . . NA
percent taking test. . . . . NA
number with total score 1,500+ . . . . . . NA

Average Scores:

Math	Verbal	Writing	Total
NA	NA	NA	NA

Federal No Child Left Behind, 2008
(Adequate Yearly Progress standards met)

	Participation Rate	Pct Proficient
ELA	Yes	Yes
Math	Yes	No

API Criteria . . . . Yes
Graduation rate . . . . NA
criteria met/possible. 25/24

Data from school year 2007-08 except where noted.
†Combined data for elementary and high schools.

Yreka Union Elem

Siskiyou County
309 Jackson St
Yreka, CA 96097
(530) 842-1168

Superint. . . . . Vanston Shaw
Grade plan. K-8
Number of schools. 5
Enrollment 1,034
High school graduates, 2006-07. 0
Dropout rate. 0
Pupil/teacher ratio. 19.4%
Average class size. 24.6
Students per computer 6.3
Avg. Teacher Salary, ... $51,082
Avg. Daily Attendence (ADA). 952
Cost per ADA. $8,095

California Achievement Tests 6th ed., 2008
(Pct scoring at or above 50th National Percentile Rank)

	Math	Reading	Language
Grade 3	60%	50%	42%
Grade 7	55%	56%	41%

Academic Performance Index, 2009
Number of valid scores. 726
2007 API (base) 764
2008 API (growth). 779

SAT Testing, 2006-07
Enrollment, Grade 12 . . . . .NA
percent taking test. . . . . .NA
number with total score 1,500+ . . . . . .NA

Average Scores:

Math	Verbal	Writing	Total
NA	NA	NA	NA

Federal No Child Left Behind, 2008
(Adequate Yearly Progress standards met)

	Participation Rate	Pct Proficient
ELA	Yes	Yes
Math	Yes	Yes

API Criteria . . . . .Yes
Graduation rate . . . . .NA
criteria met/possible. 13/13

Data from school year 2007-08 except where noted
†Combined data for elementary and high schools

Population, January 2008 (estimate)

	County	Population	Percent in Unincorp. Area
1.	Los Angeles	10,363,850	10.5%
2.	San Diego	3,146,274	15.6
3.	Orange	3,121,251	3.9
4.	Riverside	2,088,322	26.6
5.	San Bernardino	2,055,766	14.5
6.	Santa Clara	1,837,075	5.4
7.	Alameda	1,543,000	9.1
8.	Sacramento	1,424,415	39.6
9.	Contra Costa	1,051,674	16.5
10.	Fresno	931,098	18.7
11.	Ventura	831,587	11.6
12.	San Francisco	824,525	0.0
13.	Kern	817,517	36.5
14.	San Mateo	739,469	8.9
15.	San Joaquin	685,660	21.1
16.	Stanislaus	525,903	21.9
17.	Sonoma	484,470	31.4
18.	Tulare	435,254	33.1
19.	Santa Barbara	428,655	33.3
20.	Monterey	428,549	25.1
21.	Solano	426,757	4.7
22.	Placer	333,401	32.7
23.	San Luis Obispo	269,337	43.3
24.	Santa Cruz	266,519	50.6
25.	Marin	257,406	27.1
26.	Merced	255,250	34.1
27.	Butte	220,407	38.3
28.	Yolo	199,066	11.7
29.	Shasta	182,236	38.9
30.	El Dorado	179,722	81.1
31.	Imperial	176,158	21.7
32.	Kings	154,434	22.9
33.	Madera	150,887	50.0
34.	Napa	136,704	21.1
35.	Humboldt	132,821	53.9
36.	Nevada	99,186	67.6
37.	Sutter	95,878	25.0
38.	Mendocino	90,163	68.8
39.	Yuba	71,929	77.4
40.	Lake	64,059	69.9
41.	Tehama	62,419	65.6
42.	San Benito	57,784	32.6
43.	Tuolumne	56,799	91.7
44.	Calaveras	46,127	92.2
45.	Siskiyou	45,971	55.1
46.	Amador	37,943	58.2
47.	Lassen	35,757	50.9
48.	Del Norte	29,419	73.9
49.	Glenn	29,195	52.5
50.	Colusa	21,910	49.6
51.	Plumas	20,917	90.2
52.	Mariposa	18,406	100.0
53.	Inyo	18,152	80.4
54.	Trinity	13,966	100.0
55.	Mono	13,759	46.1
56.	Modoc	9,702	71.1
57.	Sierra	3,380	74.8
58.	Alpine	1,222	100.0

Population 2000

	County	Population
1.	Los Angeles	9,519,338
2.	Orange	2,846,289
3.	San Diego	2,813,833
4.	San Bernardino	1,709,434
5.	Santa Clara	1,682,585
6.	Riverside	1,545,387
7.	Alameda	1,443,741
8.	Sacramento	1,223,499
9.	Contra Costa	948,816
10.	Fresno	799,407
11.	San Francisco	776,733
12.	Ventura	753,197
13.	San Mateo	707,161
14.	Kern	661,645
15.	San Joaquin	563,598
16.	Sonoma	458,614
17.	Stanislaus	446,997
18.	Monterey	401,762
19.	Santa Barbara	399,347
20.	Solano	394,542
21.	Tulare	368,021
22.	Santa Cruz	255,602
23.	Placer	248,399
24.	Marin	247,289
25.	San Luis Obispo	246,681
26.	Merced	210,554
27.	Butte	203,171
28.	Yolo	168,660
29.	Shasta	163,256
30.	El Dorado	156,299
31.	Imperial	142,361
32.	Kings	129,461
33.	Humboldt	126,518
34.	Napa	124,279
35.	Madera	123,109
36.	Nevada	92,033
37.	Mendocino	86,265
38.	Sutter	78,930
39.	Yuba	60,219
40.	Lake	58,309
41.	Tehama	56,039
42.	Tuolumne	54,501
43.	San Benito	53,234
44.	Siskiyou	44,301
45.	Calaveras	40,554
46.	Amador	35,100
47.	Lassen	33,828
48.	Del Norte	27,507
49.	Glenn	26,453
50.	Plumas	20,824
51.	Colusa	18,804
52.	Inyo	17,945
53.	Mariposa	17,130
54.	Trinity	13,022
55.	Mono	12,853
56.	Modoc	9,449
57.	Sierra	3,555
58.	Alpine	1,208

Land Area (square miles)

1.	San Bernardino	20,052.5
2.	Inyo	10,203.1
3.	Kern	8,141.0
4.	Riverside	7,207.4
5.	Siskiyou	6,286.8
6.	Fresno	5,962.7
7.	Tulare	4,824.0
8.	Lassen	4,557.3
9.	San Diego	4,199.9
10.	Imperial	4,174.7
11.	Los Angeles	4,060.9
12.	Modoc	3,944.1
13.	Shasta	3,785.2
14.	Humboldt	3,572.5
15.	Mendocino	3,509.0
16.	Monterey	3,322.0
17.	San Luis Obispo	3,304.3
18.	Trinity	3,178.6
19.	Mono	3,044.4
20.	Tehama	2,951.0
21.	Santa Barbara	2,737.0
22.	Plumas	2,553.7
23.	Tuolumne	2,235.4
24.	Madera	2,135.9
25.	Merced	1,928.7
26.	Ventura	1,845.3
27.	El Dorado	1,710.8
28.	Butte	1,639.5
29.	Sonoma	1,575.9
30.	Stanislaus	1,493.8
31.	Mariposa	1,451.1
32.	Placer	1,404.4
33.	San Joaquin	1,399.3
34.	Kings	1,391.0
35.	San Benito	1,389.1
36.	Glenn	1,314.8
37.	Santa Clara	1,290.7
38.	Lake	1,258.0
39.	Colusa	1,150.7
40.	Calaveras	1,020.0
41.	Yolo	1,013.3
42.	Del Norte	1,007.8
43.	Sacramento	965.7
44.	Nevada	957.6
45.	Sierra	953.4
46.	Solano	829.2
47.	Orange	789.4
48.	Napa	753.7
49.	Alpine	738.6
50.	Alameda	737.6
51.	Contra Costa	719.9
52.	Yuba	630.7
53.	Sutter	602.5
54.	Amador	593.0
55.	Marin	519.8
56.	San Mateo	449.1
57.	Santa Cruz	445.2
58.	San Francisco	46.7

Persons per Square Mile, January 2008

1.	San Francisco	17,655.7
2.	Orange	3,953.9
3.	Los Angeles	2,552.1
4.	Alameda	2,091.9
5.	San Mateo	1,646.5
6.	Sacramento	1,475.0
7.	Contra Costa	1,460.8
8.	Santa Clara	1,423.3
9.	San Diego	749.1
10.	Santa Cruz	598.6
11.	Solano	514.6
12.	Marin	495.2
13.	San Joaquin	490.0
14.	Ventura	450.6
15.	Stanislaus	352.0
16.	Sonoma	307.4
17.	Riverside	289.7
18.	Placer	237.3
19.	Yolo	196.4
20.	Napa	181.3
21.	Sutter	159.1
22.	Santa Barbara	156.6
23.	Fresno	156.1
24.	Butte	134.4
25.	Merced	132.3
26.	Monterey	129.0
27.	Yuba	114.0
28.	Kings	111.0
29.	El Dorado	105.0
30.	Nevada	103.5
31.	San Bernardino	102.5
32.	Kern	100.4
33.	Tulare	90.2
34.	San Luis Obispo	81.5
35.	Madera	70.6
36.	Amador	63.9
37.	Lake	50.9
38.	Shasta	48.1
39.	Calaveras	45.2
40.	Imperial	42.1
41.	San Benito	41.5
42.	Humboldt	37.1
43.	Del Norte	29.1
44.	Mendocino	25.6
45.	Tuolumne	25.4
46.	Glenn	22.2
47.	Tehama	21.1
48.	Colusa	19.0
49.	Mariposa	12.6
50.	Plumas	8.1
51.	Lassen	7.8
52.	Siskiyou	7.3
53.	Mono	4.5
54.	Trinity	4.3
55.	Sierra	3.5
56.	Modoc	2.4
57.	Inyo	1.7
58.	Alpine	1.6

Unemployment Rate 2008

1.	Imperial	22.9%
2.	Colusa	14.0
3.	Merced	12.7
4.	Trinity	12.4
5.	Sutter	12.3
6.	Yuba	12.0
7.	Stanislaus	11.1
8.	Lake	10.8
9.	Tulare	10.8
10.	Kings	10.7
11.	Fresno	10.6
12.	Plumas	10.6
13.	Glenn	10.5
14.	Sierra	10.5
15.	San Joaquin	10.4
16.	Alpine	10.3
17.	Siskiyou	10.2
18.	Shasta	10.1
19.	Kern	9.8
20.	Modoc	9.7
21.	San Benito	9.6
22.	Lassen	9.5
23.	Madera	9.4
24.	Tehama	9.1
25.	Del Norte	8.8
26.	Calaveras	8.7
27.	Riverside	8.6
28.	Monterey	8.5
29.	Butte	8.4
30.	San Bernardino	8.0
31.	Tuolumne	7.9
32.	Amador	7.7
33.	Los Angeles	7.5
34.	Mariposa	7.5
35.	Yolo	7.4
36.	Santa Cruz	7.3
37.	Humboldt	7.2
38.	Sacramento	7.2
39.	El Dorado	6.9
40.	Mendocino	6.9
41.	Solano	6.9
42.	Inyo	6.7
43.	Nevada	6.6
44.	Placer	6.5
45.	Ventura	6.3
46.	Alameda	6.2
47.	Contra Costa	6.2
48.	Mono	6.0
49.	San Diego	6.0
50.	Santa Clara	6.0
51.	San Luis Obispo	5.7
52.	Sonoma	5.7
53.	Santa Barbara	5.4
54.	Orange	5.3
55.	San Francisco	5.3
56.	Napa	5.1
57.	San Mateo	4.7
58.	Marin	4.6

Income per Capita 1999

1.	Marin	$44,962
2.	San Mateo	36,045
3.	San Francisco	34,556
4.	Santa Clara	32,795
5.	Contra Costa	30,615
6.	Placer	27,963
7.	Alameda	26,680
8.	Santa Cruz	26,396
9.	Napa	26,395
10.	Orange	25,826
11.	Sonoma	25,724
12.	El Dorado	25,560
13.	Ventura	24,600
14.	Alpine	24,431
15.	Nevada	24,007
16.	Mono	23,422
17.	Santa Barbara	23,059
18.	San Diego	22,926
19.	Amador	22,412
20.	San Luis Obispo	21,864
21.	Solano	21,731
22.	Calaveras	21,420
23.	Sacramento	21,142
24.	Tuolumne	21,015
25.	San Benito	20,932
26.	Los Angeles	20,683
27.	Monterey	20,165
28.	Inyo	19,639
29.	Mendocino	19,443
30.	Plumas	19,391
31.	Yolo	19,365
32.	Sierra	18,815
33.	Riverside	18,689
34.	Mariposa	18,190
35.	Shasta	17,738
36.	Siskiyou	17,570
37.	Butte	17,517
38.	Sutter	17,428
39.	San Joaquin	17,365
40.	Modoc	17,285
41.	Humboldt	17,203
42.	Stanislaus	16,913
43.	Trinity	16,868
44.	San Bernardino	16,856
45.	Lake	16,825
46.	Kings	15,848
47.	Tehama	15,793
48.	Kern	15,760
49.	Fresno	15,495
50.	Lassen	14,749
51.	Colusa	14,730
52.	Madera	14,682
53.	Del Norte	14,573
54.	Merced	14,257
55.	Yuba	14,124
56.	Glenn	14,069
57.	Tulare	14,006
58.	Imperial	13,239

Population, January 2008 (estimate)

Rank	City	Population
1.	Los Angeles	4,045,873
2.	San Diego	1,336,865
3.	San Jose	989,496
4.	San Francisco	824,525
5.	Long Beach	492,642
6.	Fresno	486,171
7.	Sacramento	475,743
8.	Oakland	420,183
9.	Santa Ana	353,184
10.	Anaheim	346,823
11.	Bakersfield	328,692
12.	Riverside	296,842
13.	Stockton	289,927
14.	Chula Vista	231,305
15.	Fremont	213,512
16.	Modesto	209,936
17.	Irvine	209,806
18.	Glendale	207,157
19.	San Bernardino	205,493
20.	Huntington Beach	201,993
21.	Oxnard	194,905
22.	Fontana	188,498
23.	Moreno Valley	183,860
24.	Oceanside	178,806
25.	Santa Clarita	177,045
26.	Rancho Cucamonga	174,308
27.	Ontario	173,690
28.	Garden Grove	173,067
29.	Pomona	163,405
30.	Santa Rosa	159,981
31.	Salinas	150,898
32.	Hayward	149,205
33.	Torrance	148,965
34.	Pasadena	148,126
35.	Palmdale	147,897
36.	Corona	147,428
37.	Lancaster	145,243
38.	Escondido	143,389
39.	Orange	140,849
40.	Elk Grove	139,542
41.	Sunnyvale	137,538
42.	Fullerton	137,437
43.	Thousand Oaks	128,650
44.	El Monte	126,053
45.	Simi Valley	125,657
46.	Concord	123,776
47.	Vallejo	121,097
48.	Visalia	120,958
49.	Inglewood	118,878
50.	Santa Clara	115,503
51.	Costa Mesa	113,955
52.	Downey	113,379
53.	West Covina	112,666
54.	Norwalk	109,695
55.	Roseville	109,154
56.	Ventura	108,261
57.	Burbank	108,029
58.	Victorville	107,408
59.	Fairfield	106,753
60.	Berkeley	106,697
61.	Daly City	106,361
62.	Carlsbad	103,811
63.	Richmond	103,577
64.	South Gate	102,816
65.	Temecula	101,057
66.	Antioch	100,361
67.	Murrieta	100,173
68.	Rialto	99,767
69.	Compton	99,242
70.	Mission Viejo	98,572
71.	Carson	97,960
72.	El Cajon	97,934
73.	Vacaville	96,905
74.	San Mateo	95,776
75.	Vista	95,770
76.	Clovis	94,289
77.	Westminster	93,027
78.	Santa Monica	91,439
79.	Santa Maria	91,110
80.	Redding	90,491
81.	Santa Barbara	90,305
82.	Hawthorne	90,014
83.	Alhambra	89,259
84.	Hesperia	87,820
85.	Citrus Heights	87,321
86.	Chico	86,949
87.	Whittier	86,945
88.	Newport Beach	84,554
89.	Livermore	83,604
90.	Lakewood	83,486
91.	Buena Park	82,768
92.	San Marcos	82,743
93.	Chino	82,670
94.	San Leandro	81,851
95.	Tracy	81,548
96.	Indio	81,512
97.	Baldwin Park	81,281
98.	Merced	80,608
99.	Chino Hills	78,957
100.	Lake Forest	78,317
101.	Redwood City	77,269
102.	Bellflower	77,110
103.	Napa	77,106
104.	Alameda	75,823
105.	Upland	75,137
106.	Tustin	74,218
107.	Hemet	74,185
108.	Mountain View	73,932
109.	Union City	73,402
110.	Lynwood	73,147
111.	Folsom	72,590
112.	Redlands	71,807
113.	Turlock	70,158
114.	Apple Valley	70,092
115.	Milpitas	69,419
116.	Pleasanton	69,388
117.	Yorba Linda	68,312
118.	San Clemente	67,892
119.	Redondo Beach	67,488
120.	Laguna Niguel	66,877
121.	Pico Rivera	66,867
122.	Manteca	66,451
123.	Davis	65,814
124.	Montebello	65,668
125.	Camarillo	65,453
126.	Walnut Creek	65,306
127.	Huntington Park	64,747
128.	Monterey Park	64,434
129.	Encinitas	63,864
130.	South San Francisco	63,744
131.	Pittsburg	63,652
132.	Palo Alto	63,367
133.	Lodi	63,362
134.	Yuba City	63,338
135.	La Habra	62,635
136.	Gardena	61,781
137.	National City	61,194
138.	Rancho Cordova	60,975
139.	Diamond Bar	60,360
140.	San Ramon	59,002
141.	San Rafael	58,235
142.	Santa Cruz	58,125
143.	Paramount	57,969
144.	Fountain Valley	57,925
145.	Rosemead	57,422
146.	Petaluma	57,418
147.	Tulare	57,375
148.	Madera	56,710
149.	La Mesa	56,666
150.	Arcadia	56,491
151.	Santee	56,068
152.	Woodland	55,867
153.	Cupertino	55,551
154.	Cerritos	54,870
155.	Delano	53,855
156.	Rocklin	53,843
157.	Perris	53,605
158.	Novato	52,737
159.	Highland	52,503
160.	Cathedral City	52,465
161.	Glendora	52,362
162.	Yucaipa	52,063
163.	Hanford	51,965
164.	Colton	51,918
165.	Placentia	51,727

See Introduction for an explanation of all data sources.

Population, January 2008 (estimate, *con't*)

Rank	City	Population
166.	Watsonville	51,703
167.	Porterville	51,638
168.	Gilroy	51,173
169.	Poway	51,103
170.	Palm Desert	50,907
171.	Brentwood	50,614
172.	La Mirada	50,092
173.	Lake Elsinore	49,807
174.	Rancho Santa Margarita	49,764
175.	Covina	49,552
176.	Cypress	49,541
177.	Azusa	48,743
178.	Palm Springs	47,251
179.	West Sacramento	47,068
180.	Dublin	46,934
181.	Bell Gardens	46,766
182.	Aliso Viejo	45,249
183.	San Luis Obispo	44,697
184.	Newark	43,872
185.	San Bruno	43,444
186.	El Centro	43,316
187.	La Puente	43,256
188.	Rohnert Park	43,062
189.	Rancho Palos Verdes	42,964
190.	La Quinta	42,958
191.	Lompoc	42,957
192.	Ceres	42,813
193.	San Gabriel	42,762
194.	Danville	42,629
195.	Culver City	40,694
196.	Coachella	40,517
197.	Campbell	40,161
198.	Brea	40,081
199.	Lincoln	39,758
200.	Pacifica	39,616
201.	Monrovia	39,327
202.	Stanton	39,276
203.	Morgan Hill	39,218
204.	Bell	38,762
205.	Calexico	38,733
206.	West Hollywood	37,563
207.	Claremont	37,242
208.	Hollister	37,051
209.	Montclair	37,017
210.	Dana Point	36,982
211.	San Dimas	36,874
212.	Moorpark	36,814
213.	San Juan Capistrano	36,782
214.	Manhattan Beach	36,505
215.	Martinez	36,144
216.	Los Banos	36,052
217.	Beverly Hills	35,983
218.	Temple City	35,683
219.	San Jacinto	35,672
220.	Seaside	34,194
221.	La Verne	34,046
222.	Lawndale	33,540
223.	Laguna Hills	33,421
224.	Pleasant Hill	33,377
225.	Oakley	33,210
226.	East Palo Alto	32,897
227.	Walnut	32,299
228.	Saratoga	31,592
229.	Menlo Park	31,490
230.	Beaumont	31,477
231.	San Pablo	31,190
232.	Goleta	30,400
233.	Foster City	30,308
234.	Los Gatos	30,296
235.	Maywood	29,971
236.	Paso Robles	29,934
237.	Santa Paula	29,539
238.	Monterey	29,322
239.	Burlingame	28,867
240.	San Carlos	28,857
241.	Atascadero	28,590
242.	Banning	28,348
243.	Los Altos	28,291
244.	Imperial Beach	28,200
245.	Suisun City	28,193
246.	Adelanto	28,181
247.	Ridgecrest	28,038
248.	Benicia	27,978
249.	Twentynine Palms	27,966
250.	Soledad	27,905
251.	Atwater	27,571
252.	Norco	27,255
253.	Windsor	26,564
254.	Brawley	26,513
255.	Paradise	26,368
256.	Eureka	26,157
257.	Belmont	26,078
258.	Desert Hot Springs	26,068
259.	Corcoran	26,047
260.	Seal Beach	25,986
261.	Cudahy	25,879
262.	South Pasadena	25,792
263.	Lemon Grove	25,611
264.	Reedley	25,587
265.	Sanger	25,404
266.	San Fernando	25,230
267.	Laguna Beach	25,131
268.	Wasco	24,999
269.	Lemoore	24,502
270.	Hercules	24,324
271.	Lafayette	23,962
272.	Barstow	23,952
273.	Galt	23,913
274.	Calabasas	23,725
275.	South Lake Tahoe	23,725
276.	Agoura Hills	23,337
277.	El Cerrito	23,320
278.	Selma	23,286
279.	Coronado	23,101
280.	Duarte	22,953
281.	Loma Linda	22,632
282.	South El Monte	22,391
283.	Port Hueneme	22,202
284.	Riverbank	21,757
285.	Blythe	21,695
286.	Millbrae	21,387
287.	La Canada Flintridge	21,276
288.	Yucca Valley	21,268
289.	Patterson	21,229
290.	Lomita	21,056
291.	Dinuba	20,993
292.	Hermosa Beach	19,527
293.	Oakdale	19,337
294.	Pinole	19,193
295.	Marina	19,171
296.	Coalinga	19,064
297.	Chowchilla	18,780
298.	Laguna Woods	18,442
299.	Santa Fe Springs	17,790
300.	Dixon	17,577
301.	Susanville	17,570
302.	Arcata	17,558
303.	Artesia	17,552
304.	Orinda	17,542
305.	Lathrop	17,429
306.	Greenfield	17,316
307.	Rancho Mirage	17,057
308.	Arroyo Grande	17,036
309.	El Segundo	17,002
310.	Albany	16,877
311.	Avenal	16,609
312.	Arvin	16,517
313.	American Canyon	16,293
314.	La Palma	16,176
315.	Truckee	16,165
316.	Moraga	16,138
317.	Hawaiian Gardens	15,900
318.	Ukiah	15,758
319.	Fillmore	15,641
320.	Shafter	15,609
321.	Pacific Grove	15,472
322.	Ripon	14,915
323.	Oroville	14,490
324.	California City	14,365
325.	Carpinteria	14,271
326.	Clearlake	14,247
327.	Palos Verdes Estates	14,046
328.	Mill Valley	13,925
329.	Kerman	13,880
330.	Red Bluff	13,828

See Introduction for an explanation of all data sources.

Population, January 2008 (estimate, *con't*)

Rank	City	Population
331.	Livingston	13,795
332.	Malibu	13,700
333.	Commerce	13,536
334.	Solana Beach	13,500
335.	San Marino	13,455
336.	McFarland	13,390
337.	Parlier	13,326
338.	Auburn	13,273
339.	Grover Beach	13,213
340.	Tehachapi	13,089
341.	Half Moon Bay	13,046
342.	Grass Valley	12,929
343.	Imperial	12,752
344.	Marysville	12,719
345.	San Anselmo	12,601
346.	Grand Terrace	12,543
347.	Larkspur	12,204
348.	Los Alamitos	12,191
349.	King City	11,852
350.	Healdsburg	11,706
351.	Scotts Valley	11,697
352.	Lindsay	11,546
353.	Signal Hill	11,402
354.	Fortuna	11,374
355.	Hillsborough	11,272
356.	Kingsburg	11,259
357.	Sierra Madre	11,116
358.	Piedmont	11,100
359.	Canyon Lake	11,051
360.	Clayton	10,784
361.	Orange Cove	10,775
362.	Exeter	10,656
363.	Newman	10,586
364.	Anderson	10,579
365.	Morro Bay	10,548
366.	Farmersville	10,524
367.	Shasta Lake	10,279
368.	Placerville	10,271
369.	Capitola	10,015
370.	Sonoma	9,943
371.	Mendota	9,788
372.	Emeryville	9,727
373.	Corte Madera	9,512
374.	Taft	9,228
375.	Tiburon	8,917
376.	Westlake Village	8,867
377.	Los Altos Hills	8,837
378.	Gonzales	8,803
379.	Waterford	8,763
380.	Pismo Beach	8,603
381.	Cloverdale	8,577
382.	Live Oak	8,539
383.	Rolling Hills Estates	8,185
384.	Ojai	8,156
385.	Rio Vista	8,071
386.	Calipatria	7,774
387.	Sebastopol	7,714
388.	Crescent City	7,683
389.	Huron	7,554
390.	Calimesa	7,536
391.	Cotati	7,532
392.	Sausalito	7,503
393.	Woodlake	7,489
394.	Atherton	7,475
395.	Yreka	7,441
396.	Ione	7,416
397.	Mammoth Lakes	7,413
398.	Fairfax	7,412
399.	Orland	7,353
400.	Corning	7,226
401.	Escalon	7,131
402.	Winters	7,052
403.	Fort Bragg	6,890
404.	Firebaugh	6,812
405.	Loomis	6,624
406.	Guadalupe	6,541
407.	Willows	6,502
408.	Holtville	6,467
409.	Gridley	6,403
410.	Villa Park	6,259
411.	Big Bear Lake	6,256
412.	Hughson	6,187
413.	La Habra Heights	6,140
414.	St. Helena	5,924
415.	Needles	5,807
416.	Colusa	5,727
417.	Woodside	5,625
418.	Fowler	5,573
419.	Solvang	5,555
420.	Williams	5,310
421.	Calistoga	5,302
422.	Gustine	5,199
423.	Lakeport	5,045
424.	Willits	5,032
425.	Indian Wells	5,025
426.	Dos Palos	5,024
427.	Buellton	4,700
428.	Sonora	4,698
429.	Portola Valley	4,639
430.	Del Mar	4,580
431.	Jackson	4,319
432.	San Joaquin	4,062
433.	Carmel-by-the-Sea	4,049
434.	Brisbane	3,861
435.	Mount Shasta	3,602
436.	Angels Camp	3,593
437.	Monte Sereno	3,579
438.	Bishop	3,551
439.	Avalon	3,532
440.	Wheatland	3,510
441.	Rio Dell	3,284
442.	Yountville	3,263
443.	Nevada City	3,074
444.	Weed	3,030
445.	Sutter Creek	2,902
446.	Alturas	2,804
447.	Westmorland	2,406
448.	Ross	2,393
449.	Belvedere	2,161
450.	Portola	2,051
451.	Hidden Hills	2,016
452.	Rolling Hills	1,967
453.	San Juan Bautista	1,874
454.	Colfax	1,855
455.	Dunsmuir	1,831
456.	Biggs	1,776
457.	Irwindale	1,724
458.	Del Rey Oaks	1,627
459.	Colma	1,613
460.	Montague	1,496
461.	Ferndale	1,428
462.	Blue Lake	1,166
463.	Maricopa	1,132
464.	Plymouth	1,033
465.	Tulelake	970
466.	Bradbury	948
467.	Dorris	864
468.	Loyalton	851
469.	Isleton	817
470.	Industry	798
471.	Etna	751
472.	Fort Jones	657
473.	Point Arena	493
474.	Tehama	429
475.	Trinidad	314
476.	Sand City	298
477.	Amador City	208
478.	Vernon	95
479.	Menifee	NA
480.	Wildomar	NA

See Introduction for an explanation of all data sources.

Population, 2000

Rank	City	Population
1.	Los Angeles	3,694,820
2.	San Diego	1,223,400
3.	San Jose	894,943
4.	San Francisco	776,733
5.	Long Beach	461,522
6.	Fresno	427,652
7.	Sacramento	407,018
8.	Oakland	399,484
9.	Santa Ana	337,977
10.	Anaheim	328,014
11.	Riverside	255,166
12.	Bakersfield	247,057
13.	Stockton	243,771
14.	Fremont	203,413
15.	Glendale	194,973
16.	Huntington Beach	189,594
17.	Modesto	188,856
18.	San Bernardino	185,401
19.	Chula Vista	173,556
20.	Oxnard	170,358
21.	Garden Grove	165,196
22.	Oceanside	161,029
23.	Ontario	158,007
24.	Santa Clarita	151,088
25.	Salinas	151,060
26.	Pomona	149,473
27.	Santa Rosa	147,595
28.	Irvine	143,072
29.	Moreno Valley	142,381
30.	Hayward	140,030
31.	Torrance	137,946
32.	Pasadena	133,936
33.	Escondido	133,559
34.	Sunnyvale	131,760
35.	Fontana	128,929
36.	Orange	128,821
37.	Rancho Cucamonga	127,743
38.	Fullerton	126,003
39.	Corona	124,966
40.	Concord	121,780
41.	Lancaster	118,718
42.	Thousand Oaks	117,005
43.	Vallejo	116,760
44.	Palmdale	116,670
45.	El Monte	115,965
46.	Inglewood	112,580
47.	Simi Valley	111,351
48.	Costa Mesa	108,724
49.	Downey	107,323
50.	West Covina	105,080
51.	Daly City	103,621
52.	Norwalk	103,298
53.	Berkeley	102,743
54.	Santa Clara	102,361
55.	Ventura	100,916
56.	Burbank	100,316
57.	Richmond	99,216
58.	South Gate	96,375
59.	Fairfield	96,178
60.	El Cajon	94,869
61.	Compton	93,493
62.	Mission Viejo	93,102
63.	San Mateo	92,482
64.	Santa Barbara	92,325
65.	Rialto	91,873
66.	Visalia	91,565
67.	Antioch	90,532
68.	Vista	89,857
69.	Carson	89,730
70.	Vacaville	88,625
71.	Westminster	88,207
72.	Alhambra	85,804
73.	Citrus Heights	85,071
74.	Hawthorne	84,112
75.	Santa Monica	84,084
76.	Whittier	83,680
77.	Redding	80,865
78.	Roseville	79,921
79.	San Leandro	79,452
80.	Lakewood	79,345
81.	Buena Park	78,282
82.	Carlsbad	78,247
83.	Santa Maria	77,423
84.	Baldwin Park	75,837
85.	Redwood City	75,402
86.	Livermore	73,345
87.	Bellflower	72,878
88.	Napa	72,585
89.	Alameda	72,259
90.	Mountain View	70,708
91.	Newport Beach	70,032
92.	Lynwood	69,845
93.	Clovis	68,468
94.	Upland	68,393
95.	Tustin	67,504
96.	Chino	67,168
97.	Union City	66,869
98.	Chino Hills	66,787
99.	Walnut Creek	64,296
100.	Victorville	64,029
101.	Merced	63,893
102.	Pleasanton	63,654
103.	Redlands	63,591
104.	Pico Rivera	63,428
105.	Redondo Beach	63,261
106.	Milpitas	62,698
107.	Hesperia	62,582
108.	Montebello	62,150
109.	Laguna Niguel	61,891
110.	Huntington Park	61,348
111.	South San Francisco	60,552
112.	Davis	60,308
113.	Monterey Park	60,051
114.	Elk Grove	59,984
115.	Chico	59,954
116.	La Habra	58,974
117.	Yorba Linda	58,918
118.	Hemet	58,812
119.	Lake Forest	58,707
120.	Palo Alto	58,598
121.	Encinitas	58,014
122.	Gardena	57,746
123.	Temecula	57,716
124.	Camarillo	57,077
125.	Lodi	56,999
126.	Tracy	56,929
127.	Pittsburg	56,769
128.	Diamond Bar	56,287
129.	San Rafael	56,063
130.	Turlock	55,810
131.	Paramount	55,266
132.	Goleta	55,204
133.	Rancho Cordova	55,060
134.	Fountain Valley	54,978
135.	San Marcos	54,977
136.	La Mesa	54,749
137.	Santa Cruz	54,593
138.	Petaluma	54,548
139.	National City	54,260
140.	Apple Valley	54,239
141.	Rosemead	53,505
142.	Arcadia	53,054
143.	Santee	52,975
144.	Folsom	51,884
145.	Cerritos	51,488
146.	Cupertino	50,546
147.	San Clemente	49,936
148.	Glendora	49,415
149.	Manteca	49,258
150.	Woodland	49,151
151.	Indio	49,116
152.	Poway	48,044
153.	Colton	47,662
154.	Novato	47,630
155.	Rancho Santa Margarita	47,214
156.	Covina	46,837
157.	La Mirada	46,783
158.	Placentia	46,488
159.	Cypress	46,229
160.	San Ramon	44,722
161.	Azusa	44,712
162.	Highland	44,605
163.	Murrieta	44,282
164.	Watsonville	44,265
165.	San Luis Obispo	44,174

See Introduction for an explanation of all data sources.

Population, 2000 (*con't*)

Rank	City	Population
166.	Bell Gardens	44,054
167.	Tulare	43,994
168.	Madera	43,207
169.	Palm Springs	42,807
170.	Cathedral City	42,647
171.	Newark	42,471
172.	Rohnert Park	42,236
173.	Danville	41,715
174.	Hanford	41,686
175.	Gilroy	41,464
176.	Yucaipa	41,207
177.	Palm Desert	41,155
178.	Rancho Palos Verdes	41,145
179.	Lompoc	41,103
180.	La Puente	41,063
181.	Aliso Viejo	40,166
182.	San Bruno	40,165
183.	San Gabriel	39,804
184.	Porterville	39,615
185.	Delano	38,824
186.	Culver City	38,816
187.	Pacifica	38,390
188.	Campbell	38,138
189.	El Centro	37,835
190.	Stanton	37,403
191.	Monrovia	36,929
192.	Yuba City	36,758
193.	Bell	36,664
194.	Rocklin	36,330
195.	Perris	36,189
196.	Martinez	35,866
197.	West Hollywood	35,716
198.	Brea	35,410
199.	Dana Point	35,110
200.	San Dimas	34,980
201.	Ceres	34,609
202.	Hollister	34,413
203.	Claremont	33,998
204.	Manhattan Beach	33,852
205.	San Juan Capistrano	33,826
206.	Beverly Hills	33,784
207.	Morgan Hill	33,556
208.	Temple City	33,377
209.	Montclair	33,049
210.	Pleasant Hill	32,837
211.	Lawndale	31,711
212.	Seaside	31,696
213.	La Verne	31,638
214.	West Sacramento	31,615
215.	Moorpark	31,415
216.	Laguna Hills	31,178
217.	Menlo Park	30,785
218.	San Pablo	30,215
219.	Walnut	30,004
220.	Dublin	29,973
221.	Saratoga	29,843
222.	Monterey	29,674
223.	East Palo Alto	29,506
224.	Lake Elsinore	28,928
225.	Foster City	28,803
226.	Santa Paula	28,598
227.	Los Gatos	28,592
228.	Burlingame	28,158
229.	Maywood	28,083
230.	San Carlos	27,718
231.	Los Altos	27,693
232.	Calexico	27,109
233.	Imperial Beach	26,992
234.	Benicia	26,865
235.	Atascadero	26,411
236.	Paradise	26,408
237.	Eureka	26,128
238.	Suisun City	26,118
239.	Los Banos	25,869
240.	Oakley	25,619
241.	Belmont	25,123
242.	Marina	25,101
243.	Ridgecrest	24,927
244.	Lemon Grove	24,918
245.	Paso Robles	24,297
246.	South Pasadena	24,292
247.	Cudahy	24,208
248.	Norco	24,157
249.	Seal Beach	24,157
250.	Coronado	24,100
251.	Lafayette	23,908
252.	San Jacinto	23,779
253.	Laguna Beach	23,727
254.	La Quinta	23,694
255.	South Lake Tahoe	23,609
256.	San Fernando	23,564
257.	Banning	23,562
258.	Brentwood	23,302
259.	El Cerrito	23,171
260.	Atwater	23,113
261.	Windsor	22,744
262.	Coachella	22,724
263.	Brawley	22,052
264.	Port Hueneme	21,845
265.	Duarte	21,486
266.	Wasco	21,263
267.	South El Monte	21,144
268.	Barstow	21,119
269.	Reedley	20,756
270.	Millbrae	20,718
271.	Agoura Hills	20,537
272.	La Canada Flintridge	20,318
273.	Lomita	20,046
274.	Calabasas	20,033
275.	Lemoore	19,712
276.	Hercules	19,488
277.	Galt	19,472
278.	Selma	19,444
279.	Pinole	19,039
280.	Sanger	18,931
281.	Loma Linda	18,681
282.	Hermosa Beach	18,566
283.	Adelanto	18,130
284.	Orinda	17,599
285.	Santa Fe Springs	17,438
286.	Yucca Valley	16,865
287.	Dinuba	16,844
288.	Arcata	16,651
289.	Desert Hot Springs	16,582
290.	Laguna Woods	16,507
291.	Albany	16,444
292.	Artesia	16,380
293.	Moraga	16,290
294.	Dixon	16,103
295.	El Segundo	16,033
296.	Arroyo Grande	15,851
297.	Riverbank	15,826
298.	Pacific Grove	15,522
299.	Oakdale	15,503
300.	Ukiah	15,497
301.	La Palma	15,408
302.	Hawaiian Gardens	14,779
303.	Twentynine Palms	14,764
304.	Avenal	14,674
305.	Corcoran	14,458
306.	Carpinteria	14,194
307.	Truckee	13,864
308.	Fillmore	13,643
309.	Mill Valley	13,600
310.	Susanville	13,541
311.	Palos Verdes Estates	13,340
312.	Rancho Mirage	13,249
313.	Red Bluff	13,147
314.	Clearlake	13,142
315.	Grover Beach	13,067
316.	Oroville	13,004
317.	Solana Beach	12,979
318.	Arvin	12,956
319.	San Marino	12,945
320.	Shafter	12,736
321.	Greenfield	12,583
322.	Malibu	12,575
323.	Commerce	12,568
324.	Auburn	12,462
325.	San Anselmo	12,378
326.	Marysville	12,268
327.	Blythe	12,155
328.	Larkspur	12,014
329.	Half Moon Bay	11,842
330.	Coalinga	11,668

See Introduction for an explanation of all data sources.

Population, 2000 (*con't*)

Rank	Municipality	Population
331.	Grand Terrace	11,626
332.	Patterson	11,606
333.	Los Alamitos	11,536
334.	Scotts Valley	11,385
335.	Beaumont	11,384
336.	Soledad	11,263
337.	Lincoln	11,205
338.	Parlier	11,145
339.	Chowchilla	11,127
340.	King City	11,094
341.	Tehachapi	10,957
342.	Piedmont	10,952
343.	Grass Valley	10,922
344.	Hillsborough	10,825
345.	Clayton	10,762
346.	Healdsburg	10,722
347.	Sierra Madre	10,578
348.	Fortuna	10,497
349.	Livingston	10,473
350.	Lathrop	10,445
351.	Morro Bay	10,350
352.	Lindsay	10,297
353.	Ripon	10,146
354.	Capitola	10,033
355.	Canyon Lake	9,952
356.	American Canyon	9,774
357.	McFarland	9,618
358.	Placerville	9,610
359.	Signal Hill	9,333
360.	Kingsburg	9,199
361.	Exeter	9,168
362.	Sonoma	9,128
363.	Corte Madera	9,100
364.	Anderson	9,022
365.	Shasta Lake	9,008
366.	Farmersville	8,737
367.	Tiburon	8,666
368.	Kerman	8,551
369.	Pismo Beach	8,551
370.	California City	8,385
371.	Westlake Village	8,368
372.	Los Altos Hills	7,902
373.	Mendota	7,890
374.	Ojai	7,862
375.	Sebastopol	7,774
376.	Orange Cove	7,722
377.	Rolling Hills Estates	7,676
378.	Imperial	7,560
379.	Gonzales	7,525
380.	Sausalito	7,330
381.	Fairfax	7,319
382.	Yreka	7,290
383.	Calipatria	7,289
384.	Atherton	7,194
385.	Calimesa	7,139
386.	Ione	7,129
387.	Mammoth Lakes	7,093
388.	Newman	7,093
389.	Fort Bragg	7,026
390.	Waterford	6,924
391.	Emeryville	6,882
392.	Cloverdale	6,831
393.	Corning	6,741
394.	Woodlake	6,651
395.	Cotati	6,471
396.	Taft	6,400
397.	Huron	6,306
398.	Orland	6,281
399.	Loomis	6,260
400.	Live Oak	6,229
401.	Willows	6,220
402.	Winters	6,125
403.	Villa Park	5,999
404.	Escalon	5,963
405.	St. Helena	5,950
406.	Firebaugh	5,743
407.	La Habra Heights	5,712
408.	Guadalupe	5,659
409.	Holtville	5,612
410.	Big Bear Lake	5,438
411.	Colusa	5,402
412.	Gridley	5,382
413.	Woodside	5,352
414.	Solvang	5,332
415.	Calistoga	5,190
416.	Willits	5,073
417.	Needles	4,830
418.	Lakeport	4,820
419.	Gustine	4,698
420.	Dos Palos	4,581
421.	Rio Vista	4,571
422.	Portola Valley	4,462
423.	Sonora	4,423
424.	Del Mar	4,389
425.	Carmel-by-the-Sea	4,081
426.	Crescent City	4,006
427.	Jackson	3,989
428.	Hughson	3,980
429.	Fowler	3,979
430.	Buellton	3,828
431.	Indian Wells	3,816
432.	Williams	3,670
433.	Mount Shasta	3,621
434.	Brisbane	3,597
435.	Bishop	3,575
436.	Monte Sereno	3,483
437.	San Joaquin	3,270
438.	Rio Dell	3,174
439.	Avalon	3,127
440.	Angels Camp	3,004
441.	Nevada City	3,001
442.	Weed	2,978
443.	Yountville	2,916
444.	Alturas	2,892
445.	Ross	2,329
446.	Sutter Creek	2,303
447.	Wheatland	2,275
448.	Portola	2,227
449.	Westmorland	2,131
450.	Belvedere	2,125
451.	Dunsmuir	1,923
452.	Hidden Hills	1,875
453.	Rolling Hills	1,871
454.	Biggs	1,793
455.	Del Rey Oaks	1,650
456.	San Juan Bautista	1,549
457.	Colfax	1,496
458.	Montague	1,456
459.	Irwindale	1,446
460.	Ferndale	1,382
461.	Colma	1,191
462.	Blue Lake	1,135
463.	Maricopa	1,111
464.	Tulelake	1,020
465.	Plymouth	980
466.	Dorris	886
467.	Loyalton	862
468.	Bradbury	855
469.	Isleton	828
470.	Etna	781
471.	Industry	777
472.	Fort Jones	660
473.	Point Arena	474
474.	Tehama	432
475.	Trinidad	311
476.	Sand City	261
477.	Amador City	196
478.	Vernon	91
479.	Menifee	NA
480.	Wildomar	NA

See Introduction for an explanation of all data sources.

Persons per Square Mile, 2008 (estimate)

Rank	City	Persons per Sq. Mile
1.	Maywood	24,975.8
2.	Cudahy	23,526.4
3.	Huntington Park	21,582.3
4.	West Hollywood	19,770.0
5.	Bell Gardens	18,706.4
6.	San Francisco	17,655.8
7.	Lawndale	16,770.0
8.	Hawaiian Gardens	15,900.0
9.	Bell	15,504.8
10.	Lynwood	14,928.0
11.	Hawthorne	14,756.4
12.	Daly City	13,994.9
13.	Hermosa Beach	13,947.9
14.	South Gate	13,894.1
15.	East Palo Alto	13,158.8
16.	El Monte	13,130.5
17.	Inglewood	13,063.5
18.	Santa Ana	13,032.6
19.	Stanton	12,669.7
20.	Bellflower	12,641.0
21.	La Puente	12,358.9
22.	Paramount	12,333.8
23.	Baldwin Park	12,131.5
24.	San Pablo	11,996.2
25.	Alhambra	11,744.6
26.	Norwalk	11,308.8
27.	Rosemead	11,259.2
28.	Lomita	11,082.1
29.	Santa Monica	11,016.7
30.	Artesia	10,970.0
31.	Redondo Beach	10,712.4
32.	Gardena	10,651.9
33.	San Fernando	10,512.5
34.	San Gabriel	10,429.8
35.	Greenfield	10,185.9
36.	Berkeley	10,161.6
37.	Albany	9,927.6
38.	Compton	9,825.9
39.	Long Beach	9,774.6
40.	Garden Grove	9,614.8
41.	Manhattan Beach	9,360.3
42.	Westminster	9,210.6
43.	Elk Grove	9,180.4
44.	Downey	9,143.5
45.	La Palma	8,986.7
46.	Temple City	8,920.8
47.	Lakewood	8,881.5
48.	Los Angeles	8,624.8
49.	La Habra	8,580.1
50.	Monterey Park	8,478.2
51.	Parlier	8,328.8
52.	National City	8,269.5
53.	Emeryville	8,105.8
54.	Watsonville	8,078.6
55.	Pico Rivera	8,056.3
56.	Montebello	8,008.3
57.	Culver City	7,979.2
58.	Foster City	7,975.8
59.	Salinas	7,942.0
60.	San Bruno	7,898.9
61.	San Mateo	7,850.5
62.	Placentia	7,837.4
63.	Buena Park	7,808.3
64.	South El Monte	7,721.0
65.	Oxnard	7,703.8
66.	Huntington Beach	7,651.3
67.	South Pasadena	7,585.9
68.	Newman	7,561.4
69.	Cypress	7,506.2
70.	Oakland	7,489.9
71.	Patterson	7,320.3
72.	Costa Mesa	7,304.8
73.	Torrance	7,266.6
74.	Montclair	7,258.2
75.	Orange Cove	7,183.3
76.	Campbell	7,171.6
77.	Pomona	7,166.9
78.	Anaheim	7,092.5
79.	South San Francisco	7,082.7
80.	Covina	7,078.9
81.	Suisun City	7,048.3
82.	Alameda	7,020.6
83.	Riverbank	7,018.4
84.	West Covina	6,997.9
85.	Glendale	6,769.8
86.	Lemon Grove	6,739.7
87.	Yuba City	6,738.1
88.	Rohnert Park	6,728.4
89.	Burlingame	6,713.3
90.	El Cajon	6,707.8
91.	Millbrae	6,683.4
92.	Soledad	6,644.0
93.	Imperial Beach	6,558.1
94.	Piedmont	6,529.4
95.	Tustin	6,510.4
96.	Fountain Valley	6,508.4
97.	El Cerrito	6,477.8
98.	La Mirada	6,422.1
99.	Santa Paula	6,421.5
100.	Pasadena	6,412.4
101.	Cerritos	6,380.2
102.	McFarland	6,376.2
103.	Beverly Hills	6,312.8
104.	Kerman	6,309.1
105.	Gonzales	6,287.9
106.	Sunnyvale	6,280.3
107.	Santa Clara	6,277.3
108.	Davis	6,268.0
109.	Lake Forest	6,265.4
110.	Capitola	6,259.4
111.	San Leandro	6,248.2
112.	Calexico	6,247.3
113.	Burbank	6,244.5
114.	Ceres	6,204.8
115.	Fullerton	6,190.9
116.	Dinuba	6,174.4
117.	Mountain View	6,110.1
118.	Citrus Heights	6,106.4
119.	La Mesa	6,093.1
120.	Orange	6,019.2
121.	Westmorland	6,015.0
122.	Whittier	5,955.1
123.	Holtville	5,879.1
124.	Modesto	5,864.1
125.	Reedley	5,815.2
126.	Huron	5,810.8
127.	Belmont	5,795.1
128.	Laguna Woods	5,763.1
129.	Grover Beach	5,744.8
130.	Newport Beach	5,713.1
131.	San Jose	5,657.5
132.	Hughson	5,624.5
133.	Hollister	5,613.8
134.	Dana Point	5,603.3
135.	Fillmore	5,586.1
136.	Farmersville	5,538.9
137.	Clovis	5,514.0
138.	Waterford	5,476.9
139.	Azusa	5,476.7
140.	Woodland	5,424.0
141.	Selma	5,415.3
142.	Sanger	5,405.1
143.	Pacific Grove	5,335.2
144.	Delano	5,332.2
145.	Laguna Hills	5,304.9
146.	Stockton	5,300.3
147.	Carpinteria	5,285.6
148.	Turlock	5,275.0
149.	Mission Viejo	5,271.2
150.	Fontana	5,221.6
151.	Carson	5,210.6
152.	Lodi	5,193.6
153.	Signal Hill	5,182.7
154.	Mendota	5,151.6
155.	Arcadia	5,135.5
156.	Ventura	5,130.9
157.	Vista	5,121.4
158.	Atwater	5,105.7
159.	Milpitas	5,104.3
160.	Cupertino	5,096.4
161.	San Ramon	5,086.4
162.	Port Hueneme	5,045.9
163.	Upland	4,976.0
164.	Kingsburg	4,895.2
165.	Sacramento	4,894.5

See Introduction for an explanation of all data sources.

Persons per Square Mile, 2008 (estimate, *con't*)

Rank	City	Persons/Sq Mi
166.	San Carlos	4,891.0
167.	Exeter	4,843.6
168.	Lindsay	4,810.8
169.	Santa Barbara	4,752.9
170.	Chula Vista	4,730.2
171.	Santa Maria	4,720.7
172.	Pleasant Hill	4,701.0
173.	Guadalupe	4,672.1
174.	San Anselmo	4,667.0
175.	Rancho Cucamonga	4,660.6
176.	Fresno	4,656.8
177.	Santa Cruz	4,650.0
178.	Madera	4,610.6
179.	Brawley	4,571.2
180.	Rialto	4,555.6
181.	Laguna Niguel	4,549.5
182.	Irvine	4,541.3
183.	El Centro	4,512.1
184.	Los Banos	4,506.5
185.	Live Oak	4,494.2
186.	Aliso Viejo	4,436.2
187.	Los Altos	4,420.5
188.	Oceanside	4,404.1
189.	Wheatland	4,387.5
190.	Brentwood	4,363.3
191.	Napa	4,356.3
192.	Belvedere	4,322.0
193.	Crescent City	4,268.3
194.	Visalia	4,229.3
195.	Corona	4,200.2
196.	Manteca	4,179.3
197.	San Luis Obispo	4,177.3
198.	Petaluma	4,160.7
199.	San Diego	4,122.3
200.	Concord	4,112.2
201.	La Verne	4,101.9
202.	Pittsburg	4,080.3
203.	Diamond Bar	4,078.4
204.	Corcoran	4,069.8
205.	San Joaquin	4,062.0
206.	Sebastopol	4,060.0
207.	Galt	4,053.1
208.	Merced	4,050.7
209.	Rancho Santa Margarita	4,045.9
210.	Vallejo	4,009.8
211.	Gridley	4,001.9
212.	Santa Rosa	3,989.6
213.	American Canyon	3,973.9
214.	Hanford	3,966.8
215.	Windsor	3,964.8
216.	Cotati	3,964.2
217.	Redwood City	3,962.5
218.	Escondido	3,950.1
219.	Sausalito	3,948.9
220.	Livingston	3,941.4
221.	Larkspur	3,936.8
222.	Chino	3,918.0
223.	Seaside	3,885.7
224.	Tracy	3,883.2
225.	Oakdale	3,867.4
226.	Highland	3,860.5
227.	San Clemente	3,857.5
228.	Solana Beach	3,857.1
229.	Temecula	3,842.5
230.	Brea	3,817.2
231.	Union City	3,803.2
232.	Riverside	3,800.8
233.	Woodlake	3,744.5
234.	Hercules	3,742.2
235.	Antioch	3,730.9
236.	Dublin	3,724.9
237.	Sierra Madre	3,705.3
238.	Santa Clarita	3,703.9
239.	Lompoc	3,703.2
240.	Pinole	3,691.0
241.	Porterville	3,688.4
242.	Sonoma	3,682.6
243.	Carmel-by-the-Sea	3,680.9
244.	Ripon	3,637.8
245.	Marysville	3,634.0
246.	Moreno Valley	3,591.0
247.	Walnut	3,588.8
248.	Grand Terrace	3,583.7
249.	Roseville	3,578.8
250.	Vacaville	3,575.8
251.	Escalon	3,565.5
252.	Biggs	3,552.0
253.	San Marino	3,540.8
254.	Fairfax	3,529.5
255.	Murrieta	3,527.2
256.	Yorba Linda	3,521.2
257.	San Rafael	3,508.1
258.	Livermore	3,498.1
259.	San Bernardino	3,494.8
260.	Monterey	3,490.7
261.	Ontario	3,487.8
262.	Santee	3,482.5
263.	San Marcos	3,476.6
264.	Camarillo	3,463.1
265.	Tulare	3,456.3
266.	Richmond	3,452.6
267.	Arvin	3,441.0
268.	Colton	3,438.3
269.	Cloverdale	3,430.8
270.	Duarte	3,425.8
271.	Colusa	3,368.8
272.	Hayward	3,368.1
273.	Ukiah	3,352.8
274.	Morgan Hill	3,352.0
275.	Dos Palos	3,349.3
276.	Folsom	3,345.2
277.	Encinitas	3,343.7
278.	Rocklin	3,323.6
279.	Wasco	3,289.3
280.	Walnut Creek	3,281.7
281.	Imperial	3,269.7
282.	Del Rey Oaks	3,254.0
283.	Gustine	3,249.4
284.	Coalinga	3,231.2
285.	Gilroy	3,218.4
286.	Simi Valley	3,205.5
287.	King City	3,203.2
288.	Pleasanton	3,197.6
289.	Grass Valley	3,153.4
290.	Pacifica	3,144.1
291.	Chico	3,139.0
292.	Rancho Palos Verdes	3,136.1
293.	Newark	3,133.7
294.	Menlo Park	3,117.8
295.	Loma Linda	3,100.3
296.	El Segundo	3,091.3
297.	Healdsburg	3,080.5
298.	Indio	3,052.9
299.	Los Alamitos	3,047.8
300.	Coronado	3,000.1
301.	Arroyo Grande	2,988.8
302.	Villa Park	2,980.5
303.	Susanville	2,978.0
304.	Corte Madera	2,972.5
305.	Mill Valley	2,962.8
306.	Orland	2,941.2
307.	Martinez	2,938.5
308.	Buellton	2,937.5
309.	Palos Verdes Estates	2,926.3
310.	Bakersfield	2,906.2
311.	Hemet	2,897.9
312.	Lemoore	2,882.6
313.	Monrovia	2,870.6
314.	Laguna Beach	2,855.8
315.	Agoura Hills	2,846.0
316.	Claremont	2,842.9
317.	Loyalton	2,836.7
318.	Fairfield	2,831.6
319.	Los Gatos	2,831.4
320.	Fowler	2,786.5
321.	Fremont	2,783.7
322.	Carlsbad	2,775.7
323.	Clayton	2,765.1
324.	Canyon Lake	2,762.8
325.	Eureka	2,753.4
326.	Glendora	2,741.5
327.	Cathedral City	2,732.6
328.	Rancho Cordova	2,710.0
329.	Del Mar	2,694.1
330.	Oakley	2,678.2

See Introduction for an explanation of all data sources.

Persons per Square Mile, 2008 (estimate, *con't*)

Rank	City	Persons/Sq Mi
331.	San Juan Bautista	2,677.1
332.	Palo Alto	2,673.7
333.	Dixon	2,663.2
334.	Chowchilla	2,645.1
335.	Saratoga	2,610.9
336.	San Juan Capistrano	2,590.3
337.	Fort Bragg	2,551.9
338.	Scotts Valley	2,542.8
339.	Winters	2,518.6
340.	Corning	2,491.7
341.	La Canada Flintridge	2,445.5
342.	Firebaugh	2,432.9
343.	Tulelake	2,425.0
344.	Pismo Beach	2,389.7
345.	San Dimas	2,379.0
346.	Fortuna	2,369.6
347.	Danville	2,355.2
348.	South Lake Tahoe	2,349.0
349.	Thousand Oaks	2,343.4
350.	Rolling Hills Estates	2,273.6
351.	Seal Beach	2,259.7
352.	West Sacramento	2,252.1
353.	Willows	2,242.1
354.	Monte Sereno	2,236.9
355.	Solvang	2,222.0
356.	Marina	2,203.6
357.	Lincoln	2,172.6
358.	Benicia	2,168.8
359.	Calipatria	2,101.1
360.	Palm Desert	2,086.4
361.	Commerce	2,050.9
362.	Isleton	2,042.5
363.	Yountville	2,039.4
364.	Calistoga	2,039.2
365.	Morro Bay	2,028.5
366.	Redlands	2,022.7
367.	Santa Fe Springs	2,021.6
368.	Half Moon Bay	2,007.1
369.	Tiburon	1,981.6
370.	Bishop	1,972.8
371.	Coachella	1,947.9
372.	Blue Lake	1,943.3
373.	Moorpark	1,937.6
374.	Norco	1,933.0
375.	Arcata	1,908.5
376.	Novato	1,903.9
377.	Yucaipa	1,872.8
378.	Red Bluff	1,868.6
379.	Lakeport	1,868.5
380.	Ojai	1,853.6
381.	Hillsborough	1,818.1
382.	Calabasas	1,811.1
383.	Willits	1,797.1
384.	Auburn	1,793.6
385.	Placerville	1,770.9
386.	Chino Hills	1,762.4
387.	Moraga	1,735.3
388.	Paso Robles	1,730.3
389.	Rio Dell	1,728.4
390.	Perris	1,707.2
391.	Sutter Creek	1,707.1
392.	Westlake Village	1,705.2
393.	Anderson	1,653.0
394.	Ione	1,577.9
395.	Lafayette	1,576.4
396.	Sonora	1,566.0
397.	Redding	1,549.5
398.	Lancaster	1,545.1
399.	Atherton	1,525.5
400.	Ross	1,495.6
401.	Victorville	1,475.4
402.	Lake Elsinore	1,473.6
403.	Nevada City	1,463.8
404.	Paradise	1,448.8
405.	San Jacinto	1,432.6
406.	Ferndale	1,428.0
407.	Colfax	1,426.9
408.	Palmdale	1,408.5
409.	Clearlake	1,396.8
410.	Orinda	1,392.2
411.	Tehachapi	1,363.4
412.	La Quinta	1,350.9
413.	Ridgecrest	1,328.8
414.	Hesperia	1,304.9
415.	Poway	1,303.6
416.	Alturas	1,274.5
417.	Avalon	1,261.4
418.	St. Helena	1,260.4
419.	Dorris	1,234.3
420.	Jackson	1,234.0
421.	Banning	1,227.2
422.	Angels Camp	1,197.7
423.	Rio Vista	1,186.9
424.	Hidden Hills	1,185.9
425.	Oroville	1,178.0
426.	Brisbane	1,170.0
427.	Beaumont	1,157.2
428.	Goleta	1,155.9
429.	Plymouth	1,147.8
430.	Desert Hot Springs	1,118.8
431.	Fort Jones	1,095.0
432.	Atascadero	1,070.8
433.	Lathrop	1,062.7
434.	Los Altos Hills	1,027.6
435.	Dunsmuir	1,017.2
436.	Big Bear Lake	993.0
437.	La Habra Heights	990.3
438.	Williams	983.3
439.	Mount Shasta	973.5
440.	Apple Valley	956.2
441.	Shasta Lake	943.0
442.	Etna	938.8
443.	Portola	932.3
444.	Loomis	907.4
445.	Blythe	896.5
446.	Avenal	869.6
447.	Shafter	867.2
448.	Colma	848.9
449.	Montague	831.1
450.	Maricopa	754.7
451.	Yreka	744.1
452.	Barstow	712.9
453.	Rancho Mirage	701.9
454.	Amador City	693.3
455.	Malibu	688.4
456.	Rolling Hills	634.5
457.	Trinidad	628.0
458.	Weed	618.4
459.	Taft	611.1
460.	Tehama	536.3
461.	Yucca Valley	531.7
462.	Adelanto	526.7
463.	Twentynine Palms	510.3
464.	Portola Valley	504.2
465.	Palm Springs	501.6
466.	Bradbury	498.9
467.	Truckee	497.4
468.	Sand City	496.7
469.	Calimesa	483.1
470.	Woodside	476.7
471.	Indian Wells	380.7
472.	Point Arena	352.1
473.	Mammoth Lakes	298.9
474.	Needles	194.9
475.	Irwindale	185.4
476.	California City	70.6
477.	Industry	68.2
478.	Vernon	19.0
479.	Menifee	NA
480.	Wildomar	NA

See Introduction for an explanation of all data sources.

Unemployment Rate 2008

Rank	City	Rate
1.	Westmorland	32.1%
2.	Mendota	29.1
3.	Arvin	26.6
4.	Huron	26.4
5.	Delano	25.9
6.	San Joaquin	25.8
7.	Calexico	25.5
8.	Brawley	25.1
9.	Parlier	24.6
10.	Calipatria	23.5
11.	Orange Cove	22.7
12.	Live Oak	22.6
13.	El Centro	21.6
14.	Reedley	21.0
15.	McFarland	20.7
16.	Holtville	20.6
17.	Williams	20.5
18.	Weed	19.6
19.	Avenal	19.3
20.	Firebaugh	18.7
21.	Gridley	18.6
22.	Wasco	18.3
23.	Shafter	17.6
24.	Dos Palos	16.9
25.	Sanger	16.5
26.	Riverbank	16.4
27.	Gonzales	16.0
28.	Watsonville	16.0
29.	Newman	15.9
30.	Dinuba	15.8
31.	Imperial Beach	15.7
32.	Patterson	15.3
33.	Clearlake	15.2
34.	King City	14.4
35.	Livingston	14.4
36.	Ceres	14.0
37.	Coachella	13.9
38.	Commerce	13.7
39.	Farmersville	13.7
40.	Woodlake	13.7
41.	Yuba City	13.7
42.	Alturas	13.6
43.	Perris	13.6
44.	Hughson	13.5
45.	Kerman	13.5
46.	Madera	13.4
47.	Selma	13.4
48.	Los Banos	13.3
49.	Loyalton	13.2
50.	San Jacinto	13.2
51.	Shasta Lake	13.2
52.	Compton	13.1
53.	Greenfield	13.0
54.	Lindsay	13.0
55.	Atwater	12.9
56.	San Pablo	12.8%
57.	Stockton	12.7
58.	Industry	12.6
59.	Merced	12.5
60.	Dunsmuir	12.3
61.	Anderson	12.2
62.	Bell Gardens	12.2
63.	Coalinga	12.2
64.	Adelanto	12.1
65.	Lynwood	12.1
66.	Lincoln	12.0
67.	Salinas	12.0
68.	National City	11.9
69.	Fowler	11.8
70.	Desert Hot Springs	11.7
71.	Wheatland	11.7
72.	East Palo Alto	11.6
73.	Oroville	11.6
74.	West Sacramento	11.6
75.	Huntington Park	11.4
76.	Galt	11.1
77.	Maywood	11.1
78.	Paramount	11.1
79.	Rio Dell	11.0
80.	Crescent City	10.9
81.	Hemet	10.9
82.	Maricopa	10.9
83.	San Bernardino	10.9
84.	Soledad	10.9
85.	Hollister	10.8
86.	Corcoran	10.7
87.	Lancaster	10.7
88.	Chowchilla	10.6
89.	Corning	10.6
90.	Cudahy	10.6
91.	Santa Paula	10.6
92.	Beaumont	10.5
93.	Biggs	10.5
94.	Red Bluff	10.5
95.	San Juan Bautista	10.5
96.	Hesperia	10.4
97.	Marysville	10.4
98.	Placerville	10.4
99.	Blythe	10.3
100.	Rialto	10.3
101.	Waterford	10.3
102.	Highland	10.2
103.	Nevada City	10.2
104.	Richmond	10.2
105.	Bell	10.1
106.	Orland	10.1
107.	Moreno Valley	10.0
108.	Pittsburg	10.0
109.	Angels Camp	9.9
110.	Banning	9.9
111.	Barstow	9.9%
112.	Fresno	9.9
113.	Hawthorne	9.9
114.	Porterville	9.9
115.	Imperial	9.8
116.	Lompoc	9.8
117.	Oakdale	9.8
118.	Lakeport	9.7
119.	Portola	9.7
120.	South Gate	9.7
121.	Victorville	9.7
122.	Modesto	9.6
123.	Baldwin Park	9.5
124.	Inglewood	9.5
125.	Moraga	9.5
126.	Oakland	9.5
127.	South Lake Tahoe	9.5
128.	Taft	9.5
129.	Colusa	9.4
130.	El Monte	9.4
131.	Palmdale	9.4
132.	Sutter Creek	9.4
133.	Hanford	9.3
134.	Indio	9.3
135.	Escalon	9.2
136.	Tulare	9.2
137.	Twentynine Palms	9.2
138.	Calimesa	9.1
139.	Fillmore	9.1
140.	Gilroy	9.1
141.	South El Monte	9.1
142.	Susanville	9.1
143.	Manteca	9.0
144.	Colfax	8.9
145.	La Puente	8.9
146.	Lemoore	8.9
147.	Apple Valley	8.8
148.	Redding	8.8
149.	Colton	8.7
150.	Oxnard	8.7
151.	Riverside	8.7
152.	Woodland	8.7
153.	Santa Maria	8.6
154.	Stanton	8.6
155.	Vallejo	8.6
156.	American Canyon	8.5
157.	Ontario	8.5
158.	Sacramento	8.5
159.	Santa Ana	8.5
160.	Yreka	8.5
161.	Cathedral City	8.4
162.	Montebello	8.4
163.	Ojai	8.4
164.	Pomona	8.4
165.	Turlock	8.4

See Introduction for an explanation of all data sources.

Unemployment Rate 2008 (*con't*)

Rank	City	Rate
166.	El Cajon	8.3%
167.	Fontana	8.3
168.	Lake Elsinore	8.3
169.	Long Beach	8.3
170.	Los Angeles	8.3
171.	Rancho Cordova	8.3
172.	Willows	8.3
173.	Azusa	8.2
174.	Tehama	8.2
175.	Fort Bragg	8.1
176.	Sonora	8.1
177.	Cloverdale	8.0
178.	Hawaiian Gardens	8.0
179.	Norwalk	8.0
180.	Yucca Valley	8.0
181.	Chico	7.8
182.	Kingsburg	7.8
183.	Lodi	7.8
184.	Morgan Hill	7.8
185.	Brisbane	7.7
186.	Eureka	7.7
187.	Isleton	7.7
188.	Bellflower	7.6
189.	California City	7.6
190.	Carson	7.6
191.	Fairfield	7.6
192.	Montclair	7.6
193.	Arcata	7.5
194.	Irwindale	7.5
195.	Lawndale	7.5
196.	Lemon Grove	7.5
197.	Rancho Mirage	7.5
198.	San Fernando	7.3
199.	Fairfax	7.2
200.	Lathrop	7.2
201.	Chino	7.1
202.	Suisun City	7.1
203.	Wildomar	7.1
204.	Antioch	7.0
205.	Chula Vista	7.0
206.	Gardena	7.0
207.	Guadalupe	7.0
208.	Gustine	7.0
209.	Pico Rivera	7.0
210.	Ukiah	7.0
211.	Winters	7.0
212.	Hayward	6.9
213.	Norco	6.9
214.	Port Hueneme	6.9
215.	Anaheim	6.8
216.	Bakersfield	6.8
217.	Exeter	6.8
218.	Jackson	6.8
219.	Paso Robles	6.8
220.	Concord	6.7
221.	Laguna Woods	6.7%
222.	San Jose	6.7
223.	Vista	6.7
224.	Buena Park	6.6
225.	Garden Grove	6.6
226.	Monrovia	6.6
227.	Palm Springs	6.6
228.	Rosemead	6.6
229.	Roseville	6.6
230.	Visalia	6.6
231.	West Covina	6.6
232.	Willits	6.6
233.	Glendale	6.5
234.	Paradise	6.5
235.	Tehachapi	6.5
236.	Alhambra	6.4
237.	Healdsburg	6.4
238.	Tracy	6.4
239.	Corona	6.3
240.	San Luis Obispo	6.3
241.	West Hollywood	6.3
242.	Yucaipa	6.3
243.	Blue Lake	6.2
244.	Escondido	6.2
245.	Milpitas	6.2
246.	Santa Fe Springs	6.2
247.	Santa Monica	6.2
248.	Burbank	6.1
249.	Ripon	6.1
250.	San Gabriel	6.1
251.	San Leandro	6.1
252.	Santa Cruz	6.1
253.	Bishop	6.0
254.	Downey	6.0
255.	La Habra	6.0
256.	San Diego	6.0
257.	San Marcos	6.0
258.	Berkeley	5.9
259.	Daly City	5.9
260.	Fullerton	5.9
261.	Grass Valley	5.9
262.	Moorpark	5.9
263.	Mount Shasta	5.9
264.	South San Francisco	5.9
265.	Westminster	5.9
266.	Elk Grove	5.8
267.	Fortuna	5.8
268.	Half Moon Bay	5.8
269.	Redlands	5.8
270.	Temecula	5.8
271.	Union City	5.8
272.	Big Bear Lake	5.7
273.	Cotati	5.7
274.	Ione	5.7
275.	Needles	5.7
276.	Newark	5.7%
277.	Oceanside	5.7
278.	Pasadena	5.7
279.	Santa Rosa	5.7
280.	Ventura	5.7
281.	Clovis	5.6
282.	Cypress	5.6
283.	Mammoth Lakes	5.6
284.	Monterey Park	5.6
285.	Murrieta	5.6
286.	Rohnert Park	5.6
287.	San Anselmo	5.6
288.	Signal Hill	5.6
289.	Brentwood	5.5
290.	El Cerrito	5.5
291.	Pacifica	5.5
292.	Ridgecrest	5.5
293.	Santa Clara	5.5
294.	Trinidad	5.5
295.	Auburn	5.4
296.	Dixon	5.4
297.	Grover Beach	5.4
298.	La Palma	5.4
299.	Novato	5.4
300.	San Rafael	5.4
301.	Truckee	5.4
302.	Upland	5.4
303.	Diamond Bar	5.3
304.	Napa	5.3
305.	San Francisco	5.3
306.	Whittier	5.3
307.	Beverly Hills	5.2
308.	Covina	5.2
309.	Petaluma	5.2
310.	Simi Valley	5.2
311.	Tustin	5.2
312.	Artesia	5.1
313.	Campbell	5.1
314.	Culver City	5.1
315.	Lomita	5.1
316.	Rancho Cucamonga	5.1
317.	St. Helena	5.1
318.	Sunnyvale	5.1
319.	Vacaville	5.1
320.	Arroyo Grande	5.0
321.	Citrus Heights	5.0
322.	La Mesa	5.0
323.	Marina	5.0
324.	Palm Desert	5.0
325.	Pleasant Hill	5.0
326.	Rio Vista	5.0
327.	Santee	5.0
328.	Duarte	4.9
329.	Martinez	4.9
330.	Pismo Beach	4.9

See Introduction for an explanation of all data sources.

Unemployment Rate 2008 (*con't*)

Rank	City	Rate
331.	Seaside	4.9%
332.	Thousand Oaks	4.9
333.	Canyon Lake	4.8
334.	Lakewood	4.8
335.	Loma Linda	4.8
336.	Orange	4.8
337.	Temple City	4.8
338.	Costa Mesa	4.7
339.	Davis	4.7
340.	Placentia	4.7
341.	Redwood City	4.7
342.	Atascadero	4.6
343.	San Juan Capistrano	4.6
344.	Windsor	4.6
345.	Camarillo	4.5
346.	Emeryville	4.5
347.	La Mirada	4.5
348.	Rocklin	4.5
349.	Santa Clarita	4.5
350.	Amador City	4.4
351.	Fountain Valley	4.4
352.	Fremont	4.4
353.	La Quinta	4.4
354.	Laguna Hills	4.4
355.	Oakley	4.4
356.	Benicia	4.3
357.	Grand Terrace	4.3
358.	Huntington Beach	4.3
359.	La Verne	4.3
360.	Mountain View	4.3
361.	San Dimas	4.3
362.	Alameda	4.2
363.	Arcadia	4.2
364.	Encinitas	4.2
365.	San Clemente	4.2
366.	Belmont	4.1
367.	Hercules	4.1
368.	Laguna Niguel	4.1
369.	Loomis	4.1
370.	San Bruno	4.1
371.	Sonoma	4.1
372.	Walnut Creek	4.1
373.	Cerritos	4.0
374.	Livermore	4.0
375.	Calistoga	3.9
376.	Carlsbad	3.9
377.	Chino Hills	3.9
378.	Claremont	3.9
379.	Irvine	3.9
380.	Los Gatos	3.9
381.	Pinole	3.9%
382.	Redondo Beach	3.9
383.	Coronado	3.8
384.	Cupertino	3.8
385.	Dana Point	3.8
386.	Glendora	3.8
387.	Laguna Beach	3.8
388.	Menlo Park	3.8
389.	Mission Viejo	3.8
390.	Monterey	3.8
391.	Santa Barbara	3.8
392.	Seal Beach	3.8
393.	Dublin	3.7
394.	Morro Bay	3.7
395.	San Mateo	3.7
396.	South Pasadena	3.7
397.	Torrance	3.7
398.	Westlake Village	3.7
399.	Brea	3.6
400.	Capitola	3.6
401.	Lake Forest	3.6
402.	Solana Beach	3.6
403.	Walnut	3.6
404.	Foster City	3.5
405.	Poway	3.5
406.	Yorba Linda	3.5
407.	Bradbury	3.4
408.	Burlingame	3.4
409.	El Segundo	3.4
410.	Agoura Hills	3.3
411.	Newport Beach	3.3
412.	Rancho Santa Margarita	3.3
413.	San Marino	3.3
414.	Sebastopol	3.3
415.	Avalon	3.2
416.	Calabasas	3.2
417.	Danville	3.2
418.	Folsom	3.2
419.	Larkspur	3.2
420.	Palo Alto	3.2
421.	San Carlos	3.2
422.	Sausalito	3.2
423.	Scotts Valley	3.2
424.	Yountville	3.2
425.	Hermosa Beach	3.1
426.	Mill Valley	3.1
427.	Pleasanton	3.1
428.	Sand City	3.1
429.	Los Altos	3.0
430.	Pacific Grove	3.0
431.	Piedmont	3.0%
432.	Saratoga	3.0
433.	Atherton	2.9
434.	Corte Madera	2.9
435.	Del Mar	2.9
436.	Indian Wells	2.9
437.	Buellton	2.8
438.	Aliso Viejo	2.7
439.	La Canada Flintridge	2.7
440.	La Habra Heights	2.7
441.	Los Alamitos	2.7
442.	Goleta	2.6
443.	Malibu	2.6
444.	Manhattan Beach	2.6
445.	Millbrae	2.6
446.	Plymouth	2.6
447.	Villa Park	2.6
448.	Rancho Palos Verdes	2.5
449.	San Ramon	2.5
450.	Albany	2.4
451.	Carpinteria	2.4
452.	Point Arena	2.4
453.	Lafayette	2.2
454.	Orinda	2.1
455.	Sierra Madre	2.1
456.	Del Rey Oaks	2.0
457.	Rolling Hills Estates	1.9
458.	Hidden Hills	1.8
459.	Hillsborough	1.8
460.	Ferndale	1.6
461.	Carmel-by-the-Sea	1.5
462.	Palos Verdes Estates	1.5
463.	Solvang	1.5
464.	Clayton	1.3
465.	Rolling Hills	0.7
466.	Belvedere	NA
467.	Colma	NA
468.	Dorris	NA
469.	Etna	NA
470.	Fort Jones	NA
471.	Los Altos Hills	NA
472.	Menifee	NA
473.	Montague	NA
474.	Monte Sereno	NA
475.	Portola Valley	NA
476.	Ross	NA
477.	Tiburon	NA
478.	Tulelake	NA
479.	Vernon	NA
480.	Woodside	NA

See Introduction for an explanation of all data sources.

Federal Representatives, 111th Congress

U.S. Senate

Barbara Boxer, Democratic (term expires 2011)

Dianne Feinstein, Democratic (term expires 2013)

U.S. House of Representatives

District	Representative	Party
1	Mike Thompson	Democratic
2	Wally Herger	Republican
3	Daniel E. Lungren	Republican
4	Tom McClintock	Republican
5	Doris O. Matsui	Democratic
6	Lynn C. Woolsey	Democratic
7	George Miller	Democratic
8	Nancy Pelosi	Democratic
9	Barbara Lee	Democratic
10	Ellen O. Tauscher	Democratic
11	Jerry McNerney	Democratic
12	Jackie Speier	Democratic
13	Fortney Pete Stark	Democratic
14	Anna G. Eshoo	Democratic
15	Michael M. Honda	Democratic
16	Zoe Lofgren	Democratic
17	Sam Farr	Democratic
18	Dennis A. Cardoza	Democratic
19	George Radanovich	Republican
20	Jim Costa	Democratic
21	Devin Nunes	Republican
22	Kevin McCarthy	Republican
23	Lois Capps	Democratic
24	Elton Gallegly	Republican
25	Howard P. ``Buck" McKeon	Republican
26	David Dreier	Republican
27	Brad Sherman	Democratic
28	Howard L. Berman	Democratic
29	Adam B. Schiff	Democratic
30	Henry A. Waxman	Democratic
31	Xavier Becerra	Democratic
32	(vacant)	NA
33	Diane E. Watson	Democratic
34	Lucille Roybal-Allard	Democratic
35	Maxine Waters	Democratic
36	Jane Harman	Democratic
37	Laura Richardson	Democratic
38	Grace F. Napolitano	Democratic
39	Linda T. Sánchez	Democratic
40	Edward R. Royce	Republican
41	Jerry Lewis	Republican
42	Gary G. Miller	Republican
43	Joe Baca	Democratic
44	Ken Calvert	Republican
45	Mary Bono Mack	Republican
46	Dana Rohrabacher	Republican
47	Loretta Sanchez	Democratic
48	John Campbell	Republican
49	Darrell E. Issa	Republican
50	Brian P. Bilbray	Republican
51	Bob Filner	Democratic
52	Duncan Hunter	Republican
53	Susan A. Davis	Democratic

California State Legislators, 2009

California State Senate

District	Senator	Party	District	Senator	Party
1	Dave Cox	Republican	21	Carol Liu	Democratic
2	Patrica Wiggins	Democratic	22	Gilbert Cedillo	Democratic
3	Mark Leno	Democratic	23	Fran Pavley	Democratic
4	Sam Aanestad	Republican	24	Gloria Romero	Democratic
5	Lois Wolk	Democratic	25	Rod Wright	Democratic
6	Darrell Steinberg	Democratic	26	(vacant)	NA
7	Mark DeSaulnier	Democratic	27	Alan Lowenthal	Democratic
8	Leland Yee	Democratic	28	Jenny Oropeza	Democratic
9	Loni Hancock	Democratic	29	Bob Huff	Republican
10	Ellen Corbett	Democratic	30	Ron Calderon	Democratic
11	S. Joseph Simitian	Democratic	31	Bob Dutton	Republican
12	Jeff Denham	Republican	32	Gloria Negrete McLeod	Democratic
13	Elaine Alquist	Democratic	33	Mimi Walters	Republican
14	Dave Cogdill	Republican	34	Lou Correa	Democratic
15	Abel Maldonado	Republican	35	Tom Harman	Republican
16	Dean Florez	Democratic	36	Dennis Hollingsworth	Republican
17	George Runner	Republican	37	John J. Benoit	Republican
18	Roy Ashburn	Republican	38	Mark Wyland	Republican
19	Tony Strickland	Republican	39	Christine Kehoe	Democratic
20	Alex Padilla	Democratic	40	Denise Moreno Ducheny	Democratic

California State Legislators, 2009 *(con't)*

California State Assembly

District	Representative	Party	District	Representative	Party
1	Wesley Chesbro	Democratic	41	Julia Brownley	Democratic
2	Jim Nielsen	Republican	42	Mike Feuer	Democratic
3	Dan Logue	Republican	43	Paul Krekorian	Democratic
4	Ted Gaines	Republican	44	Anthony J. Portantino	Democratic
5	Roger Niello	Republican	45	Kevin de Leon	Democratic
6	Jared Huffman	Democratic	46	John A. Pérez	Democratic
7	Noreen Evans	Democratic	47	Karen Bass	Democratic
8	Mariko Yamada	Democratic	48	Mike Davis	Democratic
9	Dave Jones	Democratic	49	Mike Eng	Democratic
10	Alyson Huber	Democratic	50	Hector De La Torre	Democratic
11	Tom Torlakson	Democratic	51	Curren D. Price Jr	Democratic
12	Fiona Ma	Democratic	52	Isadore III Hall	Democratic
13	Tom Ammiano	Democratic	53	Ted W. Lieu	Democratic
14	Nancy Skinner	Democratic	54	Bonnie Lowenthal	Democratic
15	Joan Buchanan	Democratic	55	Warren T. Furutani	Democratic
16	Sandre R. Swanson	Democratic	56	Tony Mendoza	Democratic
17	Cathleen Galgiani	Democratic	57	Edward P. Hernandez	Democratic
18	Mary Hayashi	Democratic	58	Charles M. Calderon	Democratic
19	Jerry Hill	Democratic	59	Anthony Adams	Republican
20	Alberto Torrico	Democratic	60	Curt Hagman	Republican
21	Ira Ruskin	Democratic	61	Norma J. Torres	Democratic
22	Paul Fong	Democratic	62	Wilmer Amina Carter	Democratic
23	Joe Coto	Democratic	63	Bill Emmerson	Republican
24	Jim Jr. Beall	Democratic	64	Brian Nestande	Republican
25	Tom Berryhill	Republican	65	Paul Cook	Republican
26	Bill Berryhill	Republican	66	Kevin Jeffries	Republican
27	William W. Monning	Democratic	67	Jim Silva	Republican
28	Anna M. Caballero	Democratic	68	Van Tran	Republican
29	Michael N. Villines	Republican	69	Jose Solorio	Democratic
30	Danny D. Gilmore	Republican	70	Chuck DeVore	Republican
31	Juan Arambula	Democratic	71	Jeff Miller	Republican
32	Jean Fuller	Republican	72	Michael D. Duvall	Republican
33	Sam Blakeslee	Republican	73	Diane L. Harkey	Republican
34	Connie Conway	Republican	74	Martin Garrick	Republican
35	Pedro Nava	Democratic	75	Nathan Fletcher	Republican
36	Steve Knight	Republican	76	Lori Saldaña	Democratic
37	Audra Strickland	Republican	77	Joel Anderson	Republican
38	Cameron Smyth	Republican	78	Marty Block	Democratic
39	Felipe Fuentes	Democratic	79	Mary Salas	Democratic
40	Bob Blumenfield	Democratic	80	V. Manuel Perez	Democratic